W9-BYJ-592

Handbook of Modern Accounting

SIDNEY DAVIDSON, CPA *Editor*

Arthur Young Professor of Accounting
Graduate School of Business
University of Chicago

ROMAN L. WEIL, CPA, CMA *Associate Editor*

Professor of Accounting
Graduate School of Business
University of Chicago

Second Edition

McGRAW-HILL BOOK COMPANY

*New York   St. Louis   San Francisco   Auckland   Bogotá
Düsseldorf   Johannesburg   London   Madrid
Mexico   Montreal   New Delhi   Panama
Paris   São Paulo   Singapore
Sydney   Tokyo   Toronto*

Library of Congress Cataloging in Publication Data
Main entry under title:

Handbook of modern accounting.

Includes index.
1. Accounting—Handbooks, manuals, etc. I. Davidson,
Sidney, date. II. Weil, Roman L.
HF5635.H23   1977   657   76-28291
ISBN 0-07-015451-1

Copyright © 1977, 1970 by McGraw-Hill, Inc. All rights reserved.
Printed in the United States of America. No part of this
publication may be reproduced, stored in a retrieval system,
or transmitted, in any form or by any means, electronic,
mechanical, photocopying, recording, or otherwise, without
the prior written permission of the publisher.

567890   KPKP   7865432109

*The editors for this book were W. Hodson Mogan and Lynne Lackenbach,
the designer was Naomi Auerbach, and the production supervisor
was Teresa F. Leaden. It was set in Baskerville
by University Graphics, Inc.*

Printed and bound by The Kingsport Press.

The *Handbook of Modern Accounting* contains
quotations from publications copyrighted by the
American Institute of Certified Public Accountants,
Inc., the publisher. These passages have been
reprinted by permission of the AICPA.

Contents

Contributors

HECTOR R. ANTON *Partner, Haskins & Sells, and Professor Emeritus of Business Administration, University of California, Berkeley*

WILLIAM H. BEAVER *Professor of Accounting, Stanford University*

NORTON M. BEDFORD *Arthur Young Distinguished Professor of Accountancy and Business Administration, University of Illinois*

LAWRENCE J. BENNINGER *Professor of Accounting, University of Florida*

R. GLEN BERRYMAN *Professor of Accounting, University of Minnesota*

HOMER A. BLACK *Professor and Chairman of Accounting, Florida State University*

DONALD R. BRINKMAN *President, Valuation Systems Corporation*

HORACE R. BROCK *Professor of Accounting, North Texas State University*

R. LEE BRUMMET *Willard J. Graham Professor of Business Administration, University of North Carolina at Chapel Hill*

WALTER R. BUNGE *Management Consultant*

JOSEPH S. BURNS *Partner, Touche Ross & Co.*

E. JAMES BURTON *Assistant Professor, Florida State University*

PHILIP B. CHENOK *Partner, Main Lafrentz & Co.*

JOSEPH M. CONDER *Partner, Coopers & Lybrand*

J. MICHAEL COOK *Partner, Haskins & Sells*

DONALD A. CORBIN *Professor of Accounting and Business Economics, University of Hawaii*

JOSEPH D. COUGHLAN *Partner, Price Waterhouse & Co.*

SIDNEY DAVIDSON *Arthur Young Professor of Accounting, University of Chicago*

GORDON B. DAVIS *Professor of Business Administration, University of Minnesota*

JOEL S. DEMSKI *Professor of Information and Accounting Systems, Stanford University*

NICHOLAS DOPUCH *Professor of Accounting, University of Chicago*

ALLAN R. DREBIN *Professor of Accounting and Information Systems, Northwestern University*

ROBERT K. ELLIOTT *Partner, Peat, Marwick, Mitchell & Co.*

WILLIAM L. FERRARA *Professor of Accounting and Price Waterhouse Faculty Fellow, Pennsylvania State University*

PAUL M. FOSTER *Partner, Coopers & Lybrand*

MARTIN S. GANS *Partner, Touche Ross & Co.*

OSCAR S. GELLEIN *Retired Partner, Haskins & Sells, and Member, Financial Accounting Standards Board*

DAVID O. GREEN   *Professor of Accounting, University of Chicago*

ERNEST L. HICKS   *Partner, Arthur Young & Company*

RAYMOND A. HOFFMAN   *Partner, Price Waterhouse & Co.*

STEPHEN R. HOLSTAD   *Partner, Ernst & Ernst*

RONALD J. HUEFNER   *Associate Professor of Accounting, State University of New York at Buffalo*

ROBERT K. JAEDICKE   *William R. Kimball Professor of Accounting, Stanford University*

LOUIS H. JORDAN   *Professor of Accounting, Fordham University*

ROBERT S. KAPLAN   *Professor of Industrial Administration, Carnegie-Mellon University*

THOMAS F. KELLER   *R. J. Reynolds Industries Professor of Business Administration and Dean of the Graduate School of Business Administration, Duke University*

ROBERT H. KUHN   *Partner, Ernst & Ernst*

JAMES A. LARGAY III   *Associate Professor of Industrial Management, Georgia Institute of Technology*

JOHN LESLIE LIVINGSTONE   *Fuller E. Callaway Professor, Georgia Institute of Technology*

R. K. MAUTZ   *Partner, Ernst & Ernst*

RENE A. MILLER   *Principal, Arthur Young & Company*

JOHN H. MYERS   *Professor of Accounting, Indiana University*

CARL L. NELSON   *George O. May Professor of Financial Accounting, Columbia University*

JAMES S. SCHINDLER   *Professor of Accounting and Management Systems, State University of New York at Buffalo*

ROBERT E. SEILER   *Professor of Accounting, University of Houston*

GORDON SHILLINGLAW   *Professor of Accounting, Columbia University*

SIDNEY I. SIMON   *Professor of Economics, Rutgers University*

MORTON B. SOLOMON   *Partner, Main Lafrentz & Co.*

DAVID SOLOMONS   *Arthur Young Professor of Accounting, University of Pennsylvania*

CLYDE P. STICKNEY   *Associate Professor of Accounting, University of North Carolina at Chapel Hill*

WILLIARD E. STONE   *Chairman, Department of Accounting, University of Florida*

HERBERT F. TAGGART   *Professor Emeritus of Accounting, University of Michigan*

ARTHUR L. THOMAS   *Harmon Whittington Professor of Accounting, Rice University*

LAWRENCE L. VANCE   *Professor of Business Administration, University of California, Berkeley*

WILLIAM J. VATTER   *Professor Emeritus of Business Administration, University of California, Berkeley*

GEORGE C. WATT   *Retired Partner, Price Waterhouse & Co.*

ROMAN L. WEIL   *Professor of Accounting, University of Chicago*

FRANK T. WESTON   *Retired Partner, Arthur Young & Company*

ARTHUR R. WYATT   *Partner, Arthur Andersen & Co.*

Preface

Accounting is an information system—an information system designed to communicate meaningful economic information about a business firm or other entity to interested parties. The communication process involves senders and receivers of the information. This handbook is designed to help both the senders and the receivers of accounting information. The senders—largely accountants—are presented with a vast array of accounting topics and suggested treatments. The receivers—managers, stockholders, and all those seeking to understand the operations and position of a firm—can find a simple but comprehensive explanation of the meaning of accounting terms and of financial statements.

The accounting message frequently summarizes substantial compilations of data; the process of data collection is undergoing vast change as electronic computers and other recording devices are improved. The analysis of accounting data and financial statements is increasingly being carried on by means of sophisticated mathematical and statistical techniques. The title *Handbook of Modern Accounting* was selected to emphasize the decision to incorporate descriptions of the newest concepts and techniques that are reshaping accounting as well as to give full expression to the time-tested theories and procedures of the accounting art. The volume offers a balanced coverage of the new and the old, the emerging and the traditional topics.

The handbook seeks to provide comprehensive and authoritative information on accounting in a conveniently organized and succinctly stated form. Those faced with accounting problems can reach for the volume and find helpful guidance toward answers. The handbook contains a large amount of practical, how-to-do-it forms and information. However, the contributors have not limited themselves to a "cookbook" approach, but have spiced their sections with observations on the philosophic background and likely development of each accounting topic.

There will be occasions, of course, where the reader will wish to know more about a specific subject than is set forth here. Although it is obvious that a complete book could easily be written on any of the subjects dealt with in a chapter, the contributors were held to strict space limitations to keep the handbook to manageable size. To compensate for this, most authors have included a brief bibliography at the end of their chapters so that the reader who is truly interested in a subject will be directed to further sources of authoritative information. Again because of space limitations, the bibliographies are not extensive, but they do list a few books or articles which the author believes will be helpful in acquiring a deeper understanding of the subject.

This handbook is the work of many people. The contributors were selected because of the knowledge they were known to possess of the subjects assigned to them. As a group, they form a good cross section of accounting thought, representing as they do accounting professors, public accounting, and industry. To each of them, we express our deep appreciation.

Much credit for the successful completion of the handbook must be given to Mary Lee Peeler. She was indefatigable in her styling and typing efforts and in dealing with the vast amount of correspondence involved in the preparation of the handbook. She was assisted in these efforts by Raymonde Rousselot and K. Xenophon-Rybowiak. Cherie Worman prepared the index. Mildred Hetherington and Beatrice Carson of McGraw-Hill worked expertly and cooperatively on book production.

To all who participated—chapter authors, editorial assistants, copy editors, proofreaders, and publisher—goes our unstinting appreciation. Without them, this handbook would not have been possible.

Sidney Davidson
Roman L. Weil

Chapter **1**

Accounting Concepts and Principles and Auditing Standards and Opinions

R. K. MAUTZ
Partner, Ernst & Ernst

ACCOUNTING CONCEPTS

Accounting's claim to status as an intellectual discipline depends largely upon its emergence as the primary analytical discipline concerned with providing information about enterprise status and progress. Accounting is analytical in the sense that it takes a great mass of transaction data and, through classification and summarization, reduces that mass of data to a relatively small number of highly significant and interrelated items, which, if properly presented, tell much about the status and progress of the given enterprise. Any type of analytical classification depends upon a few basic concepts supported by a large number of subordinate concepts. Accounting is no exception. Without an understanding of these concepts, one can neither apply accounting effectively nor understand the reports produced by accountants.

To some, accounting appears to be primarily procedural in nature. Emphasis appears to be placed upon record keeping and preparation of financial statements, rather than upon conceptually based analysis. This appearance is deceiving. Recording is preceded by transaction analysis. From the development of a chart of accounts for a given enterprise to preparation of its financial statements, accounting is concerned primarily with analyzing the nature and effect of its transactions. Thus recognition and development of the conceptual foundation of accounting is of first importance to all those concerned with it.

The Nature of Concepts.   Concepts are essential ideas which permit the identification and classification of phenomena or other ideas. Thus we must have a concept of an asset to separate assets from those items which are not assets. In turn, we must have a concept of current assets in order to separate current assets from noncurrent assets. Not until the essential nature of such concepts is known can one recognize the differences and similarities necessary to make the desired separations. Neither can one understand reports which include such classifications unless one is informed as to the meaning of or the essential differences between each of the several classes. Accounting is in large measure a classificatory art, depending for its classifications upon a variety of distinctions and differences which have been found useful to those evaluating the status and progress of business enterprises.

To be complete, a concept must state all that the given class includes and all that it excludes; all that it is, and all that it is not. This is no small task. For example, one may start with a definition of an asset which states simply that an asset is "anything of value owned," a satisfactory concept for simple situations. One who is familiar with business activities finds that certain types of leases give to the lessee such rights to use the property that for some purposes he has the equivalent of ownership. We tend to modify our rudimentary concept of an asset to include such lease arrangements. Other arrangements suggest other modifications of the basic concept until it becomes complex rather than simple. Because so many of the concepts with which accounting deals are both abstract and very complex, they are not easily stated in any complete sense. We find it necessary to use broad, general terms to describe most concepts and rarely meet the requirements of a complete statement.

Expressed concisely, concepts are definitions. Rarely are these complete, although definitions are often extremely useful in conveying one's understanding to another.

Kinds of Concepts.   A more complete understanding of the nature of concepts may be obtained by examining some of their characteristics which provide separation of concepts into different classes. Thus, we have "ideal" and "real" concepts. Ideal concepts are established for the purposes of theoretical discussion and do not necessarily bear any direct relationship to the real world. For example, lawyers use the concept of "the prudent man" in discussing the rights and obligations of parties to certain contracts. Economists use the concept of "an economic man" to describe the assumed action of an individual in certain circumstances. One cannot go to the real world and pick out either a prudent man or an economic man who fits completely the characteristics included in the concept. Nevertheless, these are important concepts for discussion purposes, particularly in working out theoretical explanations of behavior.

Real concepts represent phenomena or ideas in the real world, such as one's concept of an automobile or of a building or of the Supreme Court. Real-world concepts can be tested against actual observable things or actions.

Accounting must deal with both abstract and real-world phenomena, but accounting to date has given very little attention to ideal concepts, finding its chief usefulness in the world of reality. To date accounting has found little use for ideal concepts, although these are likely to become more useful as accountants give more attention to the development of theory.

The distinction between "native" and "borrowed" concepts is also useful to our understanding. Native concepts are those which are indigenous to the field itself. Borrowed concepts are used within the field but are taken from other disciplines. Accounting's concept of retained earnings, for example, is a native concept; that is, it has been developed by accountants for accounting purposes and is not particularly relevant to other fields of interest. The concept of opportunity cost, however, used by cost accountants in discussing decision theory, is largely borrowed from economics. Accounting has a great number of borrowed concepts taken from law, from economics, and from finance. It also has a substantial number of native concepts, some of which are very well developed and some of which are still rudimentary in nature. In this chapter, our concern is primarily with concepts native to the field of accounting.

Another distinction among concepts may be pointed out in terms of the fields of interest within accounting. There are concepts relevant to financial accounting, to managerial accounting, to tax accounting, and to auditing. Certain concepts are relevant to all these fields. Other concepts have a very specialized usefulness. In this chapter, we shall be concerned primarily with concepts of general interest throughout accounting.

The Importance of Changes in Accounting Concepts. As a subject of study, accounting would be much easier to master if its concepts were fixed and established for all time. It would also be a much less interesting field and certainly less useful. Accounting concepts are continually evolving and changing. This is particularly true of its native concepts. Two reasons may be cited for this evolutionary situation. First is that, as a relatively new field, accounting continues to understand its concepts better year by year as it works with them more intensively and thoughtfully. Even our most experienced practitioners and our most advanced theorists have not yet had the opportunity to exhaust the possible applications of all accounting concepts, so that our understanding increases from time to time as new applications are made available to us. This becomes particularly evident when innovative businesspeople devise new transactions or new modifications of old transactions. Often these bring to light aspects of a concept which had not previously been sufficiently explored.

A second reason is that some concepts, particularly abstractions which cannot be tested against real-world phenomena, tend to change as the perceptions, needs, and expectations of those affected by the application of the concepts change. For example, a historical study would establish that the quantity and quality of information included in the published financial statements of corporations have increased significantly in this country over the last thirty years and the trend appears to be continuing. An increased interest in financial data by investors, creditors, financial analysts, and others together with recognition of the securities market as a major means of resource allocation affecting all interests in the economy has greatly influenced our views of what should be disclosed and thereby some important concepts.

This change is both quantitative and qualitative. Not only is a broader range and a larger amount of detail called for, some critics insist that the fundamental basis of financial reporting should be modified. Accounting first developed as a simple record of transactions. The monetary amounts of transactions provided a ready means of quantifying, recording, and accumulating completed transactions. To separate "reality" from speculation, wishful thinking, and outright misstatement, rules were established restricting accounting to completed transactions, and the concepts of historical cost (transaction price) and stewardship reporting became important influences in accounting theory and practice.

More recently, in the face of continuing inflation and dramatic changes in specific price levels over long periods of time, historical cost and stewardship reporting have been criticized as irrelevant to investment decisions and a strong case has been made for some form of current value as a more relevant basis for corporate financial reporting. A number of authoritative bodies have indicated an awareness of this recommended change in emphasis and its effect if implemented. General price-level adjustments, greater disclosure of current values, and changes in the realization concept have been proposed. For the foreseeable future, the most likely prospect appears to be a period of probable experimentation and change. Whatever may be the situation in other disciplines, it appears highly likely that in accounting we will have a continuing study and reevaluation of our essential concepts.

Interrelatedness of Accounting Concepts. Another characteristic of great importance is the interrelationship among concepts. Very few of our native concepts stand by themselves; most of them depend to a considerable extent upon others. The concept of full disclosure is related to the idea of fair presentation. Our idea of fair presentation in turn is based upon concepts of financial position and results of operations. These in turn are influenced by our notions of what constitutes a transaction, what is an asset, and what is a liability. A change in our notion of an asset might have considerable influence upon either or both of our concepts of revenue and expense, which in turn influence the concept of net income. One could carry on with this sort of explication endlessly, but it may be enough to emphasize that many concepts are tightly interrelated one with another, and that as any one of them grows and evolves or is modified, there is likely to be a series of influences on related concepts.

This suggests that any attempt to discuss concepts in an orderly fashion is necessarily difficult. No single concept can be discussed by itself without some attention to those related to it. One scarcely knows where to begin with such a discussion because it is hard to demonstrate that any single concept is so basic to all other concepts that it can be discussed separately from them.

Relationship of Postulates to Concepts. An adequate appreciation of the nature and limitation of our concepts requires that we give some attention to the postulates that lie at their roots. Postulates are assumptions—not arbitrary, deliberate assumptions, but necessary and often unrecognized assumptions which typically reflect our best judgment of the facts of a situation or the trend of events. For example, in recognizing a liability, we assume that the creditor will hold the debtor for payment, and that the debtor will make such payments. These are assumptions. They are assumptions that have been borne out in the past by the facts, and they are supported by legal institutions making them to some extent enforceable. Yet, in a number of cases, creditors have not held debtors to payment and, in even more cases, debtors have been unable to pay. Thus there is an element of assumption in recognizing a liability as a real obligation. Where such an assumption seems invalid, that is, where we have evidence to believe that a liability will not be paid, we would not recognize it as a valid liability. Thus any postulate, any assumption should be observed only if there is no persuasive evidence to the contrary. Where evidence to the contrary does exist, the most reasonable assumption in the circumstances should be made, and we should account accordingly.

Some people object to the term "postulates" and particularly to interpretation of that term as assumptions, on the grounds that accounting should not be based upon assumptions. Although one can be sympathetic with the attitude that we should not make arbitrary or unfounded assumptions, a more realistic approach is to recognize that postulates unavoidably exist in a world of uncertainty. Accounting statements must be prepared and issued before the ultimate consequences of certain actions can be known. Assumptions about the future course of events cannot be avoided under such circumstances.

Difficulty of Establishing Basic Concepts.   Preparing a complete, classified list of accounting concepts would be a most complex and difficult task. It would have to take into account all classifications of concepts, would have to rank them in some appropriate order, and would then have to reveal their interrelationships. To undertake such a task would be far outside the scope of this brief chapter. At the same time, it would be unwise to attempt to list all the basic concepts unless one had prepared a complete list and worked out their interrelationships. For this reason, it should be made clear that the following list is not an attempt to state the basic concepts of accounting. All that is presented is a relatively brief discussion of a number of basic, native, real concepts, plus an attempt to point out some of the variations within these concepts. Throughout this handbook other concepts will be introduced and explained and some of those mentioned in this chapter will be discussed further. Hopefully, the introductory material in this chapter, plus the illustrative explication of a number of basic concepts, will present the reader with a systematic approach that may help him to see the interrelationships among the concepts discussed and with a method of organizing the other concepts discussed in the book into an orderly system.

BASIC CONCEPTS

Five basic concepts will be discussed; for most of these, the discussion will include some description of related concepts. The five basic concepts follow, with a parenthetical indication of some of the major subsidiary concepts which are necessary to an understanding of the basic concepts.

1. Financial condition (asset, liability, shareholders' equity)
2. Results of operations (revenue, expense, loss, net income, matching)
3. Enterprise (corporate entity, consolidated financial statements)
4. Continuity
5. Present fairly (generally accepted accounting principles, consistency, materiality, full disclosure).

Financial Condition.   It is easy to misinterpret the term "financial condition" because many people use it in ordinary conversation referring to their own financial condition. When used by accountants, however, it is a technical term and typically refers to a profit-directed business enterprise. As used by accountants, financial condition refers to the impression or conclusions one might draw from a balanced array of a company's assets and the claims against those assets. In such an array, the assets and the claims against the assets are described in a semistandardized fashion; that is, certain terms and certain classifications are conventionally used. Conventional methods are also used in measuring or evaluating the assets and the claims against those assets. Unless one has an understanding of the classification and measurement conventions applied in presenting such an array, one could easily come to erroneous conclusions about their meaning and significance. Thus, to explain the concept of financial condition properly, one must move on to some explanation of the concept of assets, liabilities, and shareholders' equity, together with the conventional methods of classifying and measuring these items.

Asset.   An asset may be defined as anything of use to future operations of the enterprise, the beneficial interest in which runs to the enterprise.[1] Assets may be monetary or nonmonetary, tangible or intangible, owned or not owned. So long as they can make a contribution to future operations of the company and the company has the right to so use them without additional cost in excess of the anticipated amount of that contribution, they constitute assets and are so treated in accounting.

Accountants tend to dichotomize assets basically between current and noncurrent assets. The technical definition of current assets approved by the Accounting Principles Board of the American Institute of Certified Public Accountants reads as follows:[2]

> For accounting purposes, the term *current assets* is used to designate cash and other assets or resources commonly identified as those which are reasonably expected to be realized in cash or sold or consumed during the normal operating cycle of the business.

Any asset not meeting the terms of this definition is excluded from the current assets classification. Noncurrent assets are typically reported under a variety of headings such as long-term investments, fixed assets, tangible assets, and other assets. Current assets are set off from noncurrent assets because of their importance in a company's current position. Current position is another concept, subsidiary to the overall notion of financial condition, which has to do with a company's ability to meet its immediate maturing obligations in the ordinary course of business with the assets at hand.

Within the classification of current assets, one typically finds the following:

1. Cash, that is, coin, currency, and bank deposits which are readily available for any purpose the company management chooses
2. Marketable securities intended for conversion into cash within the operating cycle
3. Accounts and notes receivable which will be collected within the normal operating cycle of the business[3]
4. Inventories of raw materials, work in process, and finished goods
5. Any prepaid expenses which, if not prepaid, would be a drain upon other resources within the next operating cycle (infrequently, substantial in amount).

Asset Measurement.   The general rule for asset measurement is that assets be valued at transaction price, reduced proportionately for observed and/or estimated consumption of use value. As used in the expression "transaction price," a transaction refers to an arm's-length exchange transaction between independent parties in which the specific company is one of the parties. Typically, such a transaction has a stated price, which provides the basis for recording the asset acquired. If no stated price exists, a price is inferred from such surrounding circumstances as exist. For example, prices in transactions which are equivalent in

---

[1] In reading the following brief descriptions, one should remember the difficulties of adequately expressing in a few words the essence of any complex concept. In the space available a number of shortcomings are unavoidable, some of which will be obvious.

[2] AICPA Committee on Accounting Procedure, *Accounting Research Bulletin No. 43,* chap. 3A.

[3] "The average time intervening between the acquisition of materials or services entering this process and the final cash realization constitutes an *operating cycle,*" *ibid.*

terms of quantity and timing may be used. If no transaction price either exists or can be inferred from surrounding circumstances with any degree of validity, accountants sometimes measure the asset received in the same terms as the asset given up. Thus, transaction prices constitute the basic data of accounting.

When used in operations, assets are consumed either physically or in terms of their total available service. To reflect this, the amount recorded for the asset is reduced accordingly so that, over its useful life, an asset's recorded valuation declines from the original transaction price to the price expected to be received upon its retirement or to zero, as the case may be.

There are significant exceptions to this general rule for measuring assets. If the anticipated recovery from use or sale of an asset falls below the transaction price, accountants generally write down the carrying value of the asset to the anticipated recovery amount. Note that these are write-downs only. Accountants are loath to write up an asset to a higher anticipated recovery value. This is the most apparent application of the doctrine of conservatism, which is fairly common in accounting. Conservatism holds that, given a situation in which exact measurement is not possible, accountants should err on the side of understatement of assets and overstatement of expenses, rather than vice versa. Obviously, such a doctrine can be misused; for example, it may be employed to continually understate assets. The extent to which such understatement does exist is not easily determinable, although some suspect that it is not uncommon.

This rule of reducing the carrying value of an asset because of an anticipated reduced recovery is typically applied to marketable securities and to inventories, although it may be extended to other assets as well. If marketable securities currently held cannot be disposed of at the price paid for them, they are written down to their present market value for financial statement purposes.[4] The same treatment is applied to inventories, but with an important modification. Inventories are not written down to a lower present realization price but are valued in terms of a rule commonly described as "the lower of cost or market." In this expression, the term " market" is not the sales market but the replacement market. Thus, inventories are typically valued for financial statement purposes at the lower of cost or replacement market.

The argument offered in support is that unless an inventory will bring to the company not only an amount equivalent to its cost, but also the anticipated gross profit, it has lost some of its usefulness, and this usefulness should be recognized through a decrease in its carrying value. Any asset which has lost its utility should be written down, goes the argument, and replacement market is a convenient lay method of determining the utility of inventories.

Challenges to the General Rule for Asset Valuation. Although transaction price accounting for assets is well established and generally accepted for accounting purposes, modified, of course, for the valuation of certain assets as described, there are substantial criticisms directed against it. The critics fall into two quite separate groups. One group of critics directs its objections to the fact that transaction prices, once established, are unaffected by general price-level changes and thus transaction price data tend to become obsolete. The second group would not be satisfied with adjustment of transaction price data for general price-level changes; it charges that accounting should use a valuation method that measures assets in terms as close to current economic value as possible.

Continuing inflation in this and in other countries provides a basis for contend-

---

[4]An exception is sometimes made in the case of organizations (insurance companies, pension funds) holding large quantities of securities for long-term investment purposes. Market declines not expected to be permanent may be disclosed but not recorded as write-downs.

ing that transaction price data become obsolete over time. This is particularly true of the prices for long-lived assets, such as land, buildings, and equipment, although to some extent it may also be true for inventories. During a period of rising prices, not only is the carrying value of fixed assets stated in terms of higher-value dollars, but the proportional amount written off to reflect the cost of using the asset during the period is also usually well below the cost of using a similar asset purchased more recently. Thus not only the balance sheet but the calculation of income is influenced. The recommended remedy is that a general price-level index of some kind be applied against the historical transaction prices to obtain an updated transaction price stated in terms of current dollars. A proposal for adoption of this kind of general price-level adjustment has been before the accounting profession for a number of years, as yet without general acceptance.[5]

The severest critics of accounting, however, would not be content with general price-level adjustments. They feel that accounting has made about as much progress as it can based upon historical transaction prices, whether adjusted or not. Their contention is that accounting should now shift its base of measurement for assets to the closest approximation to current value possible. To the extent available, they would use quoted market prices for investments, inventories, and used machinery. Where no quoted price exists, they would use a replacement market or, failing this, an index-number adjustment of historical cost. At the least, it appears that increased disclosures of current-value information may be required and that modification of the conventional realization test is less likely but possible.

Liabilities.   The claims against the assets of a company are typically classified under two headings: liabilities and shareholders' equity. Liabilities are claims against a company, payable in cash, in other assets, or in services, on a fixed or determinable future date. Like assets, liabilities are generally classified as current or noncurrent. Current liabilities are those which will be paid from among the assets listed as current assets. Thus, there is a direct relationship between the current liabilities and the current assets, generally described as expressing the current position of the company. Noncurrent liabilities do not have the same extent of variety as do noncurrent assets. However, a number of peculiarities might be pointed out.

Included within the general liability section may be found items described as deferred credits. The expression "deferred credits" reminds the reader that ultimately some part or all of the item will be credited to income. This is because the deferred credit includes an element of profit. For example, a company may receive an advance payment on a future sale to a customer. The advance payment may be sufficient to cover not only the cost of delivering the product to the customer but a margin of profit also. For this reason the item may be considered a deferred credit to income. Magazine subscriptions collected in advance are often referred to as deferred credits, as are such items as interest income collected in advance, rent collected in advance, and so on.

An unusual item included among liabilities is deferred federal income tax, which in some cases amounts to a very substantial sum. Because of differences in computing taxable income and income for general business reporting purposes, companies may have reported income in a current year not subject to the current rate of federal income tax. However, if the company continues to operate at a profit and if tax rates remain in effect approximately as they currently exist, there is every expectation that sometime in the future the company will have to pay

---

[5]The Financial Accounting Standards Board has issued a proposed Statement of Financial Accounting Standards, "Financial Reporting in Units of General Purchasing Power," which requires inclusion in published financial statements of certain information stated in terms of units of the general purchasing power of the U.S. dollar. See Chapter 32.

taxes, not only on all future income, but also equal in amount to the taxes not paid on the current year's reported income. Under current standards of accounting, it is required that in such a case the company include, as an expense of the current year, tax expense in an amount proportional to its reported income even if not currently taxed. The difference between what must be paid to the government and the amount considered to be an expense of the current year is carried as a deferred credit until such future date as it must be paid as taxes. Many accountants do not agree that deferred federal income taxes constitute a liability item which ought to be recognized as such, but the consensus within accounting has established this as required practice.

Liability measurement follows the general rule of using transaction price, with the exception, however, that if the amount received at inception of the obligation is substantially below the amount that must be paid at its maturity, the difference may be amortized or allocated over the intervening years. Thus, one may have either a premium or a discount on a long-term debt, which gradually will be reduced until at maturity the amount of the debt is stated at the amount that must then be paid.

One of the advantages of long-term debt during an inflationary period is that the debt can be repaid with cheaper dollars (less purchasing power) than those borrowed years before. General price-level adjustment of financial statement data is intended, among other things, to reveal the price-level "gain" from "holding" such debt.

Shareholders' Equity. The second major class of claims against the assets of an enterprise is commonly described as "shareholders' equity," a term one must interpret with care, as noted in a subsequent paragraph. The amount reported in a balance sheet as the shareholders' equity is the arithmetic difference between the total of the enterprise assets and the total of its liabilities. Thus, in a sense, shareholders' equity is a balancing figure. The amount can also be determined in another way as the sum of the original investment by the shareholders plus the amount of undistributed earnings accumulated since the inception of the company. In current practice, the shareholders' equity section of a balance sheet reports these two items separately, the amount paid in on capital stock and the amount of retained earnings. Somewhat different terminology is used if the enterprise is unincorporated.

The purpose of reporting these amounts separately is to give some indication of the extent to which the company is being financed through the retention of past earnings in comparison with the issuance of shares. When a company has paid stock dividends, the distinction between these two categories becomes blurred because amounts of retained earnings equal to the stock dividend are transferred to capital stock. Some accountants argue that the distinction between what was originally invested by shareholders and the accumulated earnings which they have left in the business is not a significant one in any case, and that the two amounts might be combined for reporting purposes with no loss of important information.

In practice, the distinction is maintained and often elaborated by showing such items as discounts and premiums on the issuance of shares, amounts of shareholders' equity arising from transactions in the company's own stock, the results of asset revaluations, and the effect of quasi-reorganizations. Most of these are sufficiently unusual to be encountered only on relatively rare occasions.

To understand the significance of the amount of the shareholders' equity, one must remember that the assets have been recorded in the balance sheet at cost, reduced proportionally for estimated use value of each asset consumed to date, either through operations or otherwise. In contrast, the economic value of the shareholders' interest in a company is actually based upon anticipated earnings, not on the past cost of its assets. Those who are trading in the company's shares on the market take into account, as best they can, the anticipated future success of the company in providing its product or service to its customers at a profit. Thus stock market values are directly influenced by estimates of future events. Balance sheet amounts are not. One must therefore expect to find the balance sheet amount for shareholders' equity to be different than the amount which would be obtained by multiplying the outstanding shares of stock by the quoted price per share on the market. Only if each asset could be priced for accounting purposes at an amount which accurately reflects its future earning power could the shareholders' equity in the balance sheet be said to reflect the worth of the shareholders' interest in the corporation.

Results of Operations.   As generally used, the expression "results of operations" refers primarily to profit-directed enterprises; it will be so used in this chapter. This is a general term suggesting a presentation of those accounting data which together indicate how well an enterprise has succeeded in fulfilling its profit-seeking purpose during a given period of time. The presentation attempts to show what the enterprise has accomplished and what efforts or costs have been expended in obtaining that accomplishment.

Revenue.   Revenue is the measure of the product or service transferred to customers during the period at the price paid or promised to be paid by those customers. Thus it represents the accomplishment of the enterprise. Traditionally, revenue is not measured or reported until accepted by the market. The realization test for revenue is based upon the existence of an arm's-length transaction between the selling enterprise and its customers. Until production has passed this test, that is, until it has been sold, traditional accounting refuses to accept it as realized. It is not enough that other transactions by other companies indicate what the product is worth. Until the company itself has been successful in selling the product, no revenue has been realized, in the ordinary accounting sense of the term.

There are those who criticize the present realization test, pointing out that other tests of equal objectivity might be established. They note that the realization test may place undue emphasis upon the sale, whereas for some companies some other effort such as production or, in some cases, obtaining orders, or just holding an asset while its market value increases, might be equally or more important. This view is consistent with the arguments for pricing assets at economic value rather than transaction price.

Expenses.   The efforts made by a company to obtain revenues are described in accounting terms as expenses, or sometimes as "costs and expenses." Expenses tend to fall into three general groups, of which the first is the cost of goods or services sold to produce the revenues. There typically is a direct relationship between cost of goods sold and revenues obtained from their sale. Second are those costs of selling and administration which, although not as directly related to the sales of the period, can often be clearly associated with them. Finally, there are other costs of doing business which do not necessarily have any direct relationship with specific revenues. These include the payment of federal income and other taxes, charitable contributions, asset expirations due to catastrophes, and the like.

In some cases there is a causal relationship between efforts (expenses) and accomplishments (revenues). Note that this is not a cause-and-effect relationship in the sense that certain causes always bring about certain effects. Rather, expenses are incurred with the intent and often the effect of producing revenue, but there is no absolute assurance that revenue will follow. In the same sense, revenue may be causal of some expenses. If, for example, the company includes a guarantee or service agreement of some kind in its sales agreement, certain "aftercosts" may almost automatically follow the production of revenue. Other items of expense have no such causal relationship; their only connection with revenue is the time relationship, that is, that both occurred within the same accounting period.

Losses.   The term "loss" is used to describe a concept in accounting which is not well defined. Indeed, the term is used in two ways. It is used first to describe the results when the expenses for a period exceed the revenues. A company is said to have "incurred a loss" when its expenses are greater than its realized revenues. The term is also used to describe those efforts which are unsuccessful in producing revenue. If, for example, certain items of merchandise which have been purchased with the expectation of sale are later found to be unmarketable, the cost of these items would be treated as a loss and charged against the revenue of the period although they themselves did not represent a successful effort in obtaining such revenue.

Relationship of Assets and Expenses.   Note the close relationship between expenses and assets. Theorists have pointed out that all expenses are at least momentarily assets; that is, they are first acquired with the intent that they will benefit operations of a company either immediately or in the future. The purpose of acquiring almost all assets is so that they may be used to make a contribution to revenue. As this contribution is made, they pass from an asset stage into an expense stage. Thus there is a continual cycling of assets into expense which, in turn, produces revenue represented by new assets which can then be used for further operations.

Net Income.   Net income is one of the most important concepts in accounting. It is calculated as the difference between realized revenue for a period and those expenses which are directly related to that revenue or which, for some other reason, must be recognized as occurring within the period. The calculation of net income is typically made in a statement of income which commences with revenues and subtracts the various classifications of expense, generally cost of goods sold, then selling and administrative expenses, and finally those other expenses which must be covered by the revenue of the period. All expenses must be covered if net income is to result. Thus, whether asset decreases are successful in producing revenue and therefore are treated as expenses or are unsuccessful and termed "losses," they must be exceeded in total amount by the revenues of the period. Otherwise, a net loss rather than net income is shown as the result of operations for that accounting period.

Matching.   The term "matching" is used to describe the appropriate association of related revenues and expenses. Accounting presentations strive to associate data on an interpretive basis; that is, those items which are related one to another are presented together, those items which are different from one another are separated. The matching of revenue and related expenses is a specific application of this general principle of associating like items. Matching is applied on a total company basis in that all revenues and all expenses for the company are presented together in the income statement for the period, with the final figure showing the net results of operations. Matching may also be applied to specific parts of the company, to divisions, or to groups of transactions, or for whatever other segment it is useful to report the results of operations. In such cases, the reported revenues and expenses may have a more intimate relationship than they do for the company as a whole. Effective matching, whether on a total company basis or on a less than total company basis, is an essential step in presenting the results of operations. Any failure to reveal significant interrelationships between revenues and expenses to that extent does not present the results of operations fairly.

Enterprise.   The concept of an enterprise is another one of the very few central concepts in accounting. The enterprise is the focus of accounting attention. Accounts are kept, transactions are analyzed, and reports are prepared from the point of view of a specific enterprise. As noted earlier, transactions are usually at least two-party propositions, but the accountant's interest is in only one side of such transactions. The accountant is always concerned with a specific enterprise and its participation in transactions, largely ignoring the effects of the transaction upon the other party or parties.

Accounting is flexible enough to adapt itself to almost any kind of unit which has transactions. Occasionally, in the professional literature, much has been made of the idea of an accounting unit. Actually the only requirements for the application of accounting are that the specific unit be identifiable and that it enter into transactions. Given these two conditions, accounting can record the results of those transactions and present useful, interpretive, decision-oriented data.

Accounting may focus itself upon the legal organization or upon some part of the legal organization. For example, accounts may be kept for a corporation or, if the corporation engages in a variety of activities, individual profit centers may be established for which accounts can be kept. A simple illustration would be a chain of stores. Accounts could be kept for each of the several stores so that the results of their operations could be determined individually. In addition, the results of all the stores taken as a whole for the total company could also be accounted for and reported.

Corporate Entity. Accounting can serve sole proprietorships, partnerships, corporations, trusts, and any other form of legal organization. As a matter of fact, most business activity is carried on under the corporate form, and corporation accounting is a major part of the field of accounting. The corporate entity is used in different ways by different companies. Some large companies manage to operate a substantial number of divisions in widely diversified activities under a single corporate organization. Others use different corporate forms for different purposes within what is essentially a single enterprise. In some cases, differing legal requirements among states, tax provisions, or other reasons encourage a company to form a large number of individual legal entities, all of which effectively are parts of the same total company. In such cases, accounting can provide information about them individually or in total, or preferably both.

The corporate form of organization permits companies to own parts of other companies. Thus, a parent company is one which has a controlling interest in another; that is, it owns a majority of the voting shares of a subsidiary corporation. The terms "parent" and "subsidiary" are typically used when one company has a controlling interest in another. In theory, a controlling interest must be something more than exactly 50 percent of the voting stock of the subsidiary. Practically, this is not always necessary. If a company's outstanding stock is widely disseminated so that no stockholder owns a very large proportion of it, a relatively small holding may have effective control. The point has been made frequently that in such conditions management may perpetuate itself almost indefinitely without holding a majority of the outstanding shares.

Orthodox accounting requires that control be defined in terms of something over 50 percent of the outstanding stock. Critics of orthodox accounting on this particular point contend that the existence of control should be measured on some more realistic basis, whatever the proportionate holding may be. When a company holds an important but less than a controlling interest in another company, the second one is referred to as an "affiliate."

Consolidated Financial Statements. State corporation laws require that each corporate entity maintain accounting records and prepare financial statements. If a single economic entity includes more than one legal entity, the financial statements of the legal entities must be "consolidated" into one set to represent the total company. In the preparation of consolidated financial statements, those companies which are controlled by the parent will generally have their accounts consolidated with it. (Important exceptions to this rule include subsidiaries in foreign countries, particularly if exchange or currency restrictions influence profit with-drawals.) Those which are not controlled will not be consolidated. In consolidated financial statements, all transactions between controlled members of the family group are eliminated on the theory that they do not meet the realization test of transactions at arm's length between independent opposing interests. Transactions with uncontrolled companies are considered to be arm's-length transactions out-side the family group and, therefore, a proper basis for recognizing revenue and expense. Thus, consolidated financial statements present the combined financial position and results of operations of a group of companies controlled by a single managerial body with all intracompany relationships and transactions eliminated, so that, in effect, we see the family group as if it were a single enterprise dealing only with the outside world.

Business Acquisition. In a business acquisition, two or more formerly indepen-dent business entities are combined into one. If certain technical requirements are met, the combination is treated as a "pooling of interests"; otherwise it is a purchase. In accounting for a pooling of interests, the accounts of the two companies are added together including their retained earnings. When one company purchases another company, however, the retained earnings of the purchased company cannot be carried forward because of the accepted theory that income must be earned, not purchased. In accounting for a business acquisition treated as a purchase, the shareholders' equity of the acquired company disap-pears; only its assets and liabilities appear in the balance sheet of the purchaser. When the net assets so acquired exactly match the amount paid, the former substitutes for the latter in the purchaser's balance sheet. If the amount paid by the purchaser exceeds the net assets received, the acquiring company is considered to have purchased an intangible asset commonly described as "goodwill."

Price paid by purchaser		$1,000,000
Company acquired:		
Assets	$1,200,000	
Liabilities	400,000	800,000
Goodwill		$ 200,000

Under the theory that the excess payment would be made only if expected future earnings justified it, goodwill is often described as the price paid for excess future earnings and is required to be amortized as an expense against revenues over a period not to exceed forty years.

The Continuity Concept. Oversimplification has distorted the nature of the continuity concept in some discussions. Some say that the continuity, or going-concern, concept means that the enterprise is considered to exist indefinitely into the future. There is just enough truth in this view to make it misleading. Actually, the continuity concept sees the enterprise continuing in its present form, and, with its present purpose, sufficiently far enough into the future so that its assets will be used for the purpose for which they were acquired and the obligations against them will be paid in due course.

This conception of the continuity idea is the foundation for one of the basic postulates of accounting. Properly expressed, that postulate would be stated somewhat as follows: "Unless and until there is evidence to the contrary, an enterprise must be considered as continuing largely in its present form and with its present purposes."

The opening qualification is of prime importance. Unless there is evidence to the contrary, accountants have no alternative except to treat an enterprise as continuing. If they operated on a contrary assumption, they would have to treat every enterprise as if it were about to liquidate. This would have a severe influence upon the valuation of assets, the treatment of liabilities, and all presentations of financial position and results of operations. Actually, experience tells us otherwise. Experience tells us that most enterprises do continue in business. Obviously when there is evidence to the contrary, when the specific enterprise in which the accountant is interested appears to be liquidating or to have no continuing life, he or she should value the assets and present the liabilities on an entirely different basis, one that reflects the more likely possibility. Thus, the continuity concept actually requires that in certain fairly rare cases, the accountant adopt a liquidation point of view rather than a going-concern point of view.

There may be a little confusion in terming a given item both a concept and a postulate, as has been done here with enterprise continuity. In expressing any accounting postulate, one must use accounting terms, each of which represents a concept of greater or lesser importance. We must comprehend the concept of continuity before we can use the term in stating the postulate.

Present Fairly. The expression "present fairly" is used in a short-form auditor's opinion to suggest that the financial statements examined are satisfactory. It is a difficult term to define and one that itself relies upon a substantial number of other quite important concepts. "Present fairly" is generally coupled with another expression, "generally accepted accounting principles"; that is, a set of financial statements either does or does not present fairly in accordance with generally accepted accounting principles. Accountants have been known to argue over whether this means that the financial statements present fairly *and* are in accordance with generally accepted accounting principles, or that they present fairly *on the basis of* generally accepted accounting principles. The distinction is a fine one, but an important one.

Generally Accepted Accounting Principles. Generally accepted accounting principles include a number of conventions and practices which are currently subject to criticism. There are those who contend that certain generally accepted accounting principles do not present fairly, that their application in some circumstances is something less than useful. To such critics, the expression "presents fairly in accordance with generally accepted accounting principles" is merely a defensive term used to protect accountants from attacks on their reports. The majority of accountants, however, feel that the expression "generally accepted accounting principles" describes those practices and procedures which over time have been found to be most useful, and although they are not necessarily the preferred treatment in every case, in combination they do present a satisfactory picture of the status and progress of the enterprise reported upon.

Consistency. One of the primary purposes of accounting is to present reports on a comparable basis. By themselves, individual accounting figures are seldom informative. Coupled with other figures, for example, reports for the same company for prior periods, they become much more useful. If comparisons are to be made, however, it becomes imperative that reports be prepared on a consistent basis, one year with another. Accountants thus place great reliance upon consistency as a required virtue of accounting data. Consistency means that the same transactions have been treated the same way this year and last year so that the financial statements for the current year can be compared with preceding years without erroneous conclusions being drawn from them. If an inconsistency exists between the presentations of successive years, fair presentation demands that this be disclosed.

Materiality. Obviously it is not required that all transactions, however minor, be handled on a consistent basis; only transactions of material significance require such attention. A "material" transaction or event or item is one the knowledge of which might influence the judgment of an informed reader. If an informed reader would not be concerned with the item because it was not of sufficiently consequential nature or amount, the item is regarded as immaterial.

No objective tests of materiality have been established, although there seems to be a general feeling that an item running in excess of 5 to 10 percent of an appropriate base is likely to be considered material in most cases. Thus, if we found consistency in all cases except for treatment of a given item which constituted, say, 15 percent of the net income for the year, most accountants would agree that the assertion "presents fairly in accordance with generally accepted accounting principles applied on a basis consistent with the preceding year" would require mention of the inconsistent treatment.

Full Disclosure.   The term "full disclosure" is a common one in accounting. Although recommendations have been made for substitution of the term "adequate disclosure," the older term is still widely used. It means that the presented information includes everything that an informed reader should know to come to appropriate conclusions, that nothing of substance has been concealed or omitted. Accountants face a dilemma in summarizing information for reporting purposes. If they were to report the total amount of detail available to them, most readers would be overwhelmed. On the other hand, in condensing and classifying the total mass of transaction detail, they must be careful not to bury or hide items or events which would influence the reader's judgment.

Full disclosure relates especially to transactions between an enterprise and those who are in positions of authority within the enterprise. Thus, any transactions between an enterprise and its officers should be disclosed, as should all other transactions which have any unusual bearing upon the company's financial position or results of operations.

In describing financial statements as presenting fairly, the description typically refers to the financial statements "taken as a whole." The idea here is that although there may well be minor inaccuracies within the financial statements, overall they present a satisfactorily realistic expression of the company's progress and status. No one can guarantee that every item in the balance sheet and income statement is accurate or correct. One can be reasonably certain, however, that any errors that may be included are not sufficiently important to mislead those who read the statements. Thus, when each item is read in context with the others, an overall impression is gained of the company's activities and current position which is satisfactorily objective and fully and fairly disclosed.

ACCOUNTING PRINCIPLES

Accounting concepts are implemented through accounting principles which may be described as guides to proper action. Other things being equal, sound concepts lead to right actions. But not everyone who keeps accounts necessarily has an adequate understanding of accounting concepts. Deficiencies or limitations in one's concepts will affect the propriety of one's accounting. Accounting is a method of analysis designed to represent certain aspects of reality as truthfully as possible. We apprehend reality in terms of our concepts. To the extent that all accountants understand the same concepts, they should account for the same transactions in the same way. To aid those who do not have an adequate understanding of concepts to account on a basis comparable to those who do, principles have been established to indicate consensus. Accounting Principles Board Statement No. 4 rightly describes accounting principles in these terms:[6]

> Generally accepted accounting principles incorporate the consensus at a particular time as to which economic resources and obligations should be recorded as assets and liabilities by financial accounting, which changes in assets and liabilities should be recorded, when these changes should be recorded, how the assets and liabilities and

[6]Accounting Principles Board, "Basic Concepts and Accounting Principles Underlying Financial Statements of Business Enterprises," Statement No. 4, AICPA, New York, 1970.

changes in them should be measured, what information should be disclosed and how it should be disclosed and which financial statements should be prepared.

Accounting data have a variety of uses. They are used as a basis for operating and investment decisions within the company, for credit and investment decisions external to the company, for taxation and regulation, and for a variety of other uses. Some users of accounting data are able to control the data they receive; some are not. For example, internal operating and investment decisions are made by members of the company's management who are able to control the accounting department directly and to obtain the information they require prepared on any basis they consider appropriate. Taxation and regulatory bodies have the power to establish rules and regulations to be followed by those subject to their control and to conduct examinations and enforce observance of those rules and regulations. In contrast, decisions to extend credit to the company and to make investments in it are made by people with no direct control over the accounting information they receive. They must use what they get. Creditors of various kinds, shareholders, labor union representatives, economists, financial analysts, planners, and others must rely on the company for accurate and realistic data.

Accounting principles are thus required for two reasons: first, to guide those who prepare financial statements so they know what the consensus is on appropriate accounting for transactions and events; second, to assure some degree of uniformity and comparability in the data received and relied upon by those who have no direct influence over the accumulation and presentation of the accounting data on which they rely. The expression "generally accepted accounting principles" applies almost completely to the guides followed in preparing accounting data for those without influence. Management, regulators, and taxing bodies are well advised to follow the same accounting principles but are quite free to deviate therefrom if they so desire.

Meaning of Generally Accepted Accounting Principles.   The term "generally accepted accounting principles" came into use in the opinions of certified public accountants in the 1930s as a result of cooperative work between a committee of the American Institute of Certified Public Accountants and the New York Stock Exchange and other developments. The words "practices" and "principles" were used interchangeably in the report of that work, which was later published by the Institute in a pamphlet entitled *Audits of Corporate Accounts.* The adoption of "principles" in the standard form of opinion resulted from conferences between the Institute committee and a committee of the Financial Executive Institute. The comments contained in a joint letter from nine national firms of certified public accountants, included in the pamphlet, make it clear that accepted accounting principles at that time were understood to be the five principles enumerated in the pamphlet, which were later adopted by Council and by the membership of the Institute, and *other accounting principles or practices which have substantial authority back of them.*

The report of a special committee on auditing procedure entitled *Extensions of Auditing Procedure,* approved at the 1939 annual meeting, included a revised form of standard short-form report. The report stated: "The major changes recommended [in the form of report] pertain to the description of the scope of the examination, specifically to include reference to the system of internal control." The committee gave brief reasons for such changes. The revised form of report also made changes in the wording of the opinion paragraph, but no explanation was given for these changes, presumably because they were regarded as not major in character. With regard to accounting principles, the revised wording was: " . . . in conformity with generally accepted accounting principles." Thus the word "generally" was added to the previous phrase without indication of the significance, if any, to be drawn from the change.

The word "generally" means in a general manner and the word "general" has a great many meanings. Webster's New Collegiate Dictionary lists eight meanings, of which the fifth seems most suitable to the use in accountants' reports: "5. Pertaining to many persons, cases, or occasions; prevalent." A synonym for general is "universal," but it is certain that that meaning could not have been attributed in 1939 without completely disregarding the facts. In the light of the circumstances at that time, it is probable that the addition of the word "generally" was intended to add something to the responsibility of CPAs for determining the accounting practices in use by a client really have substantial authority back of them. This responsibility has been inherent in the wording used in the opinion paragraphs of the standard forms of reports since 1934. It is obvious that the mere existence of a practice in one or a few instances does not automatically constitute substantial authoritative support; it may well demonstrate the reverse conclusion. The judgment and knowledge required in meeting this responsibility was dealt with in *Generally Accepted Auditing Standards,* first issued in 1947 by the AIA (later the AICPA) and reissued with no change in substance in 1954, as follows:

> The determination of whether "generally accepted accounting principles" have been adhered to requires the exercise of judgment on the part of the independent certified public accountant, as well as knowledge as to what principles have found general acceptance even though certain of these in manner of application may have received only limited usage. An accounting principle may be found to have only limited usage but still have general acceptance—for example, the sinking-fund principle of depreciation accounting. Moreover, as in all other matters with which the auditor is concerned, materiality is the essence of this standard. The fact that one concern capitalizes certain minor, relatively short-lived items of plant equipment and then depreciates the amount so capitalized, whereas another concern charges off such items forthwith upon purchase or installation, does not operate against recognizing both alike as complying with the depreciation requirement of generally accepted principles of accounting.
>
> In addition to this matter of an accounting principle's being generally accepted even if not generally followed, it is necessary also to bear in mind that there may be a considerable diversity of practices between different concerns in the application of an accounting principle. Whether with regard to provision for depreciation or provision for losses on receivables or any other matter where there will be general agreement as to the end to be achieved, there may be a considerable lack of similarity in the detailed processes by which those principles are effectuated.
>
> Thus, while one concern may follow an accounting procedure distinctly peculiar to itself, this in no way disqualifies it from being accorded a recognition of following "generally accepted accounting principles," if the broad principle which that procedure seeks to implement is, in fact, a generally accepted one. It is thus important not to regard the matter of "generally accepted accounting principles" from a rigidity of viewpoint that could not possibly comport with the wide variety of operating conditions which will be encountered in business resulting in an equally wide variety of detailed accounting processes.

The Uniformity-Flexibility Issue. A continuing question in establishing accounting principles is the extent to which such propositions should be stated as detailed prescriptions or only as general guides. Proponents of flexibility argue that the great variety in business situations and circumstances is such that strict uniform rules would result in only superficial uniformity, that detailed prescriptions applied to substantively different transactions and events supply no true comparability. On the other hand, there are those who can point to serious abuses of the flexibility now permitted in accounting. For example, practices first developed to meet a given set of circumstances have been extended to other circumstances for which they were never originally intended. A study entitled *Effect of Circumstances on the Application of Accounting Principles* published in 1972[7] notes that "Flexibility in

[7]R. K. Mautz, *Effect of Circumstances on the Application of Accounting Principles,* Financial Executives Research Foundation, New York, 1972.

accounting and reporting has been availed of by some for purposes other than those related to obtaining the fairest possible corporate financial reporting," and "Disciplinary elements in the corporate financial reporting process have not been as effective in curbing the misuse of present provisions for flexibility as some desire." The same report further notes: "Comparability and uniformity are not equivalent terms. Uniformity stresses application of the same or similar methods of accounting or reporting to all apparently similar transactions, conditions, or events. Comparability is dependent upon presentations responsive to the substance of the transactions, conditions, and events to be reported and the circumstances in which these occur."

Thus those charged with the responsibility of establishing accounting principles which others are expected to follow must continually be alert to the necessity of steering a fine line between excessively detailed and rigid requirements which may fail to reflect reality in unusual situations and guides stated in such general terms that they lend themselves to misinterpretation and abuse.

Establishment of Accounting Principles.   A variety of efforts to state the principles underlying corporate financial reporting have been made by individuals and committees with and without special commissions from organized bodies. In *The Search for Accounting Principles,*[8] Reed K. Storey points out that the earliest principles formally established by the American Institute of Certified Public Accountants (at that time the American Institute of Accountants) evolved out of correspondence between committees of the American Institute of Certified Public Accountants and the New York Stock Exchange in 1932. The American Institute of Certified Public Accountants established a committee for the purpose of pronouncing on important accounting problems in 1939. During the twenty-year period of its existence, that Committee on Accounting Procedure issued 51 *Accounting Research Bulletins* on a variety of topics. The Committee on Accounting Procedure was replaced by the Accounting Principles Board and an Accounting Research Division, both as units of the American Institute of Certified Public Accountants, in 1959. The Accounting Research Division was intended to provide special research resources in an attempt to strengthen the procedure for establishing authoritative principles. Membership on the Accounting Principles Board varied from 18 to 21 at different times during its life and included representatives of the major public accounting firms, smaller firms, and geographic areas of the country as well as representatives from industry and academia.

The Financial Accounting Standards Board.   Dissatisfaction with the progress made by the Accounting Principles Board in establishing accounting principles resulted in its termination and replacement by the Financial Accounting Standards Board, which was formally established in 1972. A special study by a "blue ribbon committee" recommended establishment of a Financial Accounting Foundation consisting essentially of nine trustees, including the President of the American Institute of Certified Public Accountants serving in an *ex officio* capacity, four certified public accountants in public practice, two financial executives, one financial analyst, and one accounting educator. The Board of Trustees appoints the members of the Financial Accounting Standards Board, undertakes to provide the financial resources to support the work of the Financial Accounting Standards Board, and reviews the Board's activities from time to time to determine whether changes in procedure are desirable.

The Financial Accounting Standards Board is a seven-member Board, four of whom are certified public accountants drawn from public practice. The remaining three members need not, but may, be certified public accountants and must be persons who are well versed in the problems of financial reporting. Members of the Board serve full time and must sever all connections with any other organiza-

[8]Reed K. Storey, *The Search for Accounting Principles,* AICPA, New York, 1964.

tions that might pose a conflict of interests. Except for some initial terms intended to put the membership of the Board on a continually rotating basis, terms are for five years with the possibility of reappointment. A Financial Accounting Standards Advisory Council of not less then 20 persons serving one-year terms to provide advice to the Financial Accounting Standards Board on request is also appointed by the Board of Trustees. Thus far the Council has met quarterly under the chairmanship of the Chairman of the Financial Accounting Standards Board.

The Financial Accounting Standards Board has the authority not only to issue standards but also to issue interpretations of Opinions of the Accounting Principles Board and Accounting Research Bulletins of the Committee on Accounting Procedure. Members of the American Institute of Certified Public Accountants are required by that organization's rules of conduct to accept statements by the Financial Accounting Standards Board as authoritative.

Public Sector Establishment of Accounting Principles.   The Financial Accounting Standards Board organization, like that of the Accounting Principles Board and the Committee on Accounting Procedure before it, is an effort to retain the authority for formulating and establishing accounting principles in the private sector. Some accounting principles, however, are issued within the public sector. The Securities and Exchange Commission (SEC) has authority to establish the accounting principles required in filings to be made with it. In general, the Securities and Exchange Commission has relied upon the accounting profession for the development of accounting principles, but on occasion has differed with the promulgations of the accounting profession and has issued requirements of its own. Recently the Securities and Exchange Commission expressed its approval of the procedures and organization of the Financial Accounting Standards Board and indicated its desire to rely upon statements from that Board whenever possible.[9]

In 1971, the Congress of the United States established a five-member Cost Accounting Standards Board with the Comptroller General of the United States as chairman. The function of this Board is to promulgate cost accounting standards to be followed by contractors and government agencies alike in the negotiation, administration, and settlement of negotiated defense contracts. Promulgations by the Cost Accounting Standards Board accepted by Congress have the full force and effect of law. Certain regulatory agencies such as the Interstate Commerce Commission, the Civil Aeronautics Board, and others also issue accounting rules and regulations applicable to the companies subject to their control.

A number of organizations with different kinds of authority and different functions are thus active in the general field of accounting principles. The extent to which the work of one of these authorities will overlap or conflict with that of another is yet to be determined. Efforts to establish liaison among the several groups have been made in good faith. Hopefully these will be sufficiently effective that conflicting standards will not appear.

Informal Establishment of Accounting Principles.   In addition to these relatively formal methods of establishing accounting principles and standards, informal methods exist. When an industry or even a company faces a new situation, one that no present principle seems to cover, it must develop the best solution it can. The relatively lengthy procedures required by the duly established authorities may take so long that the company or industry facing the problem cannot wait. In such cases, principles are established on an informal, ad hoc basis by the reporting company or an industry group and if adopted by a number of companies may become "generally accepted" until they are reviewed and either more formally accepted or rejected by the appropriate authoritative body.

Because business is a dynamic rather than a passive type of activity with new

[9]SEC, *Accounting Series Release No. 150,* 1973.

agreements, transactions, and practices developing continually and on a random basis, it seems unlikely that any body or group of bodies can state with final authority all generally accepted accounting principles. On the contrary, we will continually find situations sufficiently different that they appear to justify special principles and we will continually be adding to and refining those principles, practices, and procedures referred to as "generally accepted accounting principles."

AUDITING STANDARDS AND OPINIONS

The Role of Auditing.   In a credit economy such as that in the United States and other economically developed nations, accounting data are one of the bases upon which a company's credit-worthiness is determined. But accounting data are produced by the reporting company, so additional steps are necessary to establish their reliability. Independent auditors are professional experts in the examination of the financial statements and underlying accounting records of corporations and other business organizations. An audit is a professional examination meeting certain standards on the basis of which the auditor expresses an independent professional opinion respecting the fairness of presentation of the financial statements at issue. Because of the flexibility permitted by generally accepted accounting standards and the many judgments and estimates necessary to prepare a set of financial statements, any assertion about financial statements more specific than that they "present fairly" is considered by auditors and their legal advisors to be unwise.

To give what is known as an unqualified opinion, the kind that companies most like to receive, an auditor must make his examination in accordance with generally accepted auditing standards.

Generally Accepted Auditing Standards.   Auditing standards differ from auditing procedures in that "procedures" relate to acts to be performed, whereas "standards" deal with measures of the quality of the performance of those acts and the objectives to be attained by the use of the procedures undertaken. *Auditing standards* as distinct from *auditing procedures* thus concern themselves not only with the auditor's professional qualities but also with the judgment exercised by him in the performance of his examination and in his report.

The generally accepted auditing standards as approved and adopted by the membership of the American Institute of Certified Public Accountants are as follows:

General Standards

1. The examination is to be performed by a person or persons having adequate technical training and proficiency as an auditor.

2. In all matters relating to the assignment an independence in mental attitude is to be maintained by the auditor or auditors.

3. Due professional care is to be exercised in the performance of the examination and the preparation of the report.

Standards of Field Work

1. The work is to be adequately planned and assistants, if any, are to be properly supervised.

2. There is to be a proper study and evaluation of the existing internal control as a basis for reliance thereon and for the determination of the resultant extent of the tests to which auditing procedures are to be restricted.

3. Sufficient competent evidential matter is to be obtained through inspection, observation, inquiries, and confirmations to afford a reasonable basis for an opinion regarding the financial statements under examination.

Standards of Reporting

1. The report shall state whether the financial statements are presented in accordance with generally accepted principles of accounting.

2. The report shall state whether such principles have been consistently observed in the current period in relation to the preceding period.

3. Informative disclosures in the financial statements are to be regarded as reasonably adequate unless otherwise stated in the report.

4. The report shall either contain an expression of opinion regarding the financial statements, taken as a whole, or an assertion to the effect that an opinion cannot be expressed. When an overall opinion cannot be expressed, the reasons therefor should be stated. In all cases where an auditor's name is associated with financial statements the report should contain a clear-cut indication of the character of the auditor's examination, if any, and the degree of responsibility he is taking.

Kinds of Audit Opinions. Upon completion of an examination, an auditor can give an unqualified opinion, a qualified opinion, an adverse opinion, or disclaim an opinion. The standard short-form unqualified opinion recommended by the American Institute of Certified Public Accountants consists of a statement describing the nature of the examination, usually referred to as the scope of the examination, and an expression of the auditor's opinion.

Unqualified Opinion. Wording for the standard short-form report follows:

(Scope)

We have examined the balance sheet of X Company as of (at) December 31, 19XX, and the related statements of income, retained earnings and changes in financial position for the year then ended. Our examination was made in accordance with generally accepted auditing standards and, accordingly, included such tests of the accounting records and such other auditing procedures as we considered necessary in the circumstances.

(Opinion)

In our opinion, the financial statements referred to above present fairly the financial position of X Company as of (at) December 31, 19XX, and the results of its operations and the changes in its financial position for the year then ended, in conformity with generally accepted accounting principles applied on a basis consistent with that of the preceding year.

Typically the report is addressed to the company whose financial statements are being examined or to its stockholders or board of directors.

In some circumstances, a departure from the auditor's standard report is recommended, generally for one or more of the following reasons:

1. The scope of the auditor's examination is affected by conditions that preclude the application of one or more auditing procedures he considers necessary in the circumstances.

2. The auditor's opinion is based in part upon the report of another auditor.

3. The financial statements are affected by a departure from a generally accepted accounting principle.

4. The financial statements are affected by a departure from an accounting principle promulgated by the body designated by the AICPA Council to establish such principles.

5. Accounting principles have not been applied consistently.

6. The financial statements are affected by uncertainties concerning future events, the outcome of which is not susceptible to reasonable estimation at the date of the auditor's report.

7. The auditor wishes to emphasize a matter regarding the financial statements.

Qualified Opinion. Statement on Auditing Standards No. 2, issued in October 1974 by the American Institute of Certified Public Accountants,[10] describes a qualified opinion in the following words:

> A qualified opinion states that, "except for" or "subject to" the effects of the matter to which the qualification relates, the financial statements present fairly financial position, results of operations and changes in financial position in conformity with generally accepted accounting principles consistently applied. Such an opinion is expressed when a lack of sufficient competent evidential matter or restrictions on the scope of the auditor's examination have led him to conclude that he cannot express an unqualified opinion, or when the auditor believes, on the basis of his examination, that
>> *a.* the financial statements contain a departure from generally accepted accounting principles, the effect of which is material,
>> *b.* there has been a material change between periods in accounting principles or in the method of their application, or
>> *c.* there are significant uncertainties affecting the financial statements,
> and he has decided not to express an adverse opinion or to disclaim an opinion.

The statement illustrates a number of qualified opinions which vary with the reason for the qualification but which in every case try to point out why the opinion must be qualified and the importance of that qualification.

Adverse Opinion. An adverse opinion states that the financial statements do not present fairly the financial position, results of operations, or changes in financial position of the reporting company in conformity with generally accepted accounting principles. Statement on Auditing Standards No. 2 requires that an auditor who expresses an adverse opinion should disclose in a separate paragraph of the report all the substantive reasons for that adverse opinion and the principal effects of those reasons on the financial position, results of operations, and changes in financial position to the extent that this can be determined. The opinion paragraph should include a direct reference to the separate paragraph that discloses the reason for the adverse opinion.

Disclaimer of Opinion. A disclaimer of opinion states clearly that the auditor does not express an opinion on the financial statements. The auditor who disclaims an opinion is required to state in a separate paragraph of the report all of the substantive reasons for doing so. In most cases the reason for disclaimer of opinion is that the auditor has not made an examination sufficient to provide a basis for expressing an opinion. A disclaimer of an opinion is not appropriate if an auditor has reason to believe that the financial statements do not present fairly what they purport to represent. Thus the auditor who has any reservations regarding fair presentation in conformity with generally accepted accounting principles or in the consistency of their application should so state in the separate paragraph.

Piecemeal opinions, that is, expressions of opinion by the auditor as to certain identified items in financial statements without an overall opinion on the financial statements taken as a whole, were at one time accepted. Statement on Auditing Standards No. 2 makes it clear that piecemeal opinions are no longer appropriate and that they should not be issued in any situation.

Negative Assurance. A negative assurance is a statement to the effect that "nothing came to our attention which would indicate that these amounts or statements are not fairly presented." Reports containing negative assurances as a result of examinations by internal auditors are not approved by the American Institute of Certified Public Accountants with one exception. Negative assurances are permissible in letters required by security underwriters in which the indepen-

---

[10]AICPA, Auditing Standards Executive Committee, Statements on Auditing Standards No. 2, *Reports on Audited Financial Statements,* AICPA, New York, 1974.

dent auditor reports on limited procedures followed with respect to unaudited financial statements or other financial data pertinent to a registration statement filed with the Securities and Exchange Commission. These are viewed as a special kind of report and the one situation in which a negative assurance would not be misleading. The argument against the use of a negative assurance in an audit report is that the less work one does, the stronger the assurance that can be given. But unless the reader has a very sound and specific understanding of the extent of the auditor's work, the negative assurance is not informative.

Professional Ethics Regarding Accountants' Opinions. It is generally recognized that (1) financial statements are representations by management, (2) the CPA has the responsibility for conducting the examination in accordance with generally accepted auditing standards, and (3) the CPA has the sole responsibility for writing the report stating, among other things, whether the financial statements are presented in accordance with generally accepted principles of accounting (reporting standard number 1).

Further light on the responsibilities of the CPA may be gained by reference to the Restatement of the Code of Professional Ethics adopted by the membership of the American Institute of Certified Public Accountants.[11] The specific rules in that Code are based on the following five broad concepts stated as affirmative Ethical Principles:

> *Independence, integrity, and objectivity.* A certified public accountant should maintain his integrity and objectivity and, when engaged in the practice of public accounting, be independent of those he serves.
>
> *Competence and technical standards.* A certified public accountant should observe the profession's technical standards and strive continually to improve his competence and the quality of his services.
>
> *Responsibilities to clients.* A certified public accountant should be fair and candid with his clients and serve them to the best of his ability, with professional concern for their best interests, consistent with his responsibilities to the public.
>
> *Responsibilities to colleagues.* A certified public accountant should conduct himself in a manner which will promote cooperation and good relations among members of the profession.
>
> *Other responsibilities and practices.* A certified public accountant should conduct himself in a manner which will enhance the stature of the profession and its ability to serve the public.

BIBLIOGRAPHY

Accounting Principles Board: "Basic Concepts and Accounting Principles Underlying Financial Statements of Business Enterprises," Statement No. 4, AICPA, New York, 1970.

American Institute of Certified Public Accountants, Committee on Accounting Procedure: *Accounting Research Bulletin No. 43*, AICPA, New York, 1953, chap. 3A.

American Institute of Certified Public Accountants, Study Group: *Objectives of Financial Statements*, AICPA, New York, 1973.

Grady, Paul: "Inventory of Generally Accepted Accounting Principles for Business Enterprises," Accounting Research Study No. 7, AICPA, New York, 1965.

Mautz, R. K.: *Effect of Circumstances on the Application of Accounting Principles*, Financial Executives Research Foundation, New York, 1972.

Moonitz, Maurice: "The Basic Postulates of Accounting," Accounting Research Study No. 1, AICPA, New York, 1961.

Sprouse, Robert T., and Maurice Moonitz: "A Tentative Set of Broad Accounting Principles for Business Enterprises," Accounting Research Study No. 3, AICPA, New York, 1962.

Storey, Reed K.: *The Search for Accounting Principles*, AICPA, New York, 1964.

---

[11]AICPA, *Code of Professional Ethics*, AICPA, New York, 1973.

Chapter **2**

Financial Statements— Income Statements and Balance Sheets

DONALD A. CORBIN
Professor of Accounting and Business Economics,
University of Hawaii

FINANCIAL STATEMENTS—GENERAL CONSIDERATIONS

Two primary financial statements and a statement linking them together are discussed in this chapter. They are

1. Income statements—statements of the increase or decrease in the owners' equity of an entity arising from profit-seeking operations (as distinct from owner investments or withdrawals) during a given period of time

2. Balance sheets—statements of the assets, liabilities, and owners' equity of an entity at a given date

3. Analyses of retained earnings—statements of the changes in the cumulative and current earnings reinvested in the entity.

The funds statement, whose name was changed to "Statement of Changes in Financial Position" in APB Opinion No. 19, is discussed in Chapter 3 of this handbook. Interim financial statements, on which the APB expressed Opinion No. 28, is discussed in Chapter 5. Earnings forecasts is the topic of Chapter 6 of this handbook.

Objective of Financial Statements. The broad purpose of financial statements is to supply readers with information for making rational economic decisions. The statements include primarily information that can be stated in monetary units, and hence represent only a portion of the total information required for many decisions. To enhance clarity, statements include only selected quantitative items which are usually condensed. It follows that in order to be useful, unbiased, and not misleading, as discussed in Chapter 1, financial statements should fully disclose all significant financial data essential for making rational economic decisions. Full disclosure and lack of bias—which have sometimes been called "fairness"—take on even greater importance in view of the range of estimates and alternative accounting conventions which enter into financial statement preparation.

General-Purpose Financial Statements. The field of accounting has often been divided into two parts: "managerial accounting," which deals with accounting information for use by management in planning, control, and other decision-making activities; and "financial accounting," which deals with accounting information for use by nonmanagerial groups making "outsider" decisions. Reports for management are not considered in this chapter. Rather, the focus is on financial statements for use by persons or entities outside the reporting unit.

In meeting the goal of relevant reporting, several important questions arise because of the several needs of various users. Who should report? To whom should they report? What should they report? It is generally accepted that managements of enterprises are responsible for financial statements. They, or higher authorities such as the board of directors or stockholders, engage public accounting firms to audit their records and render an opinion as to the fairness of the presentation. Even though the public accountant often is, in fact, the preparer of the financial statements, ultimate responsibility rests with management. The statements are theirs. In case of disagreement, management presents the statements; then the auditor decides the extent of any qualifications, disagreements, or denials.

The primary outside users of financial statements are present and prospective stockholders, creditors, employees, financial analysts, customers, and some governmental agencies. These users have both coincident and conflicting needs for various types of financial information. The main types of decisions involved are believed to be investment decisions, evaluation of management, credit decisions, employment terms, and other related economic matters.

In many cases, special financial statements are prepared to meet the special needs of particular users. However, there is also need for a single set of general-purpose statements to meet the varied needs of unknown users. The financial statements presented in annual reports to stockholders and attested to by independent public accountants typify general-purpose financial statements.

Relationship Between Income Statements and Balance Sheets. Accountants generally agree that the income statement is more important than the balance sheet. This has led to a shift from a view held earlier that the income statement was the link between two balance sheets. The current view was expressed in *Accounting Research Bulletin No. 43* as follows:

> The fairest possible presentation of periodic net income, with neither material overstatement nor understatement is important. . . . With the increasing importance of the income statement there has been a tendency to regard the balance sheet as the connecting link between successive income statements; however this concept should not obscure the fact that the balance sheet has significant uses of its own.

Audited Financial Statements. Audits of financial statements by independent public accountants are required by stock exchanges, regulatory bodies such as the Securities and Exchange Commission, many creditors, and others. Audited financial statements are of major importance because they involve an examination of the accounting system and records of a firm according to the generally accepted auditing standards of the accounting profession. This is followed by the auditor's opinion on the fairness of the financial statements. Credibility, within the limitations of auditing standards and accounting principles, is added to managements' reports.

Accompanying audited financial statements is the auditor's "short-form report." In its simplest form it has a "scope" paragraph which states that: "Our examination was made in accordance with generally accepted auditing standards, and accordingly included such tests of the accounting records and such other auditing procedures as we considered necessary in the circumstances." A second paragraph, called the "opinion" paragraph, states in essence that the financial statements present fairly the ending financial position and the results of operations for the period "in conformity with generally accepted accounting principles applied on a basis consistent with that of the preceding year."

Fair presentation in financial statements relates directly to existing accounting principles. A certain degree of looseness arises because accounting principles are not codified. In this connection, the Council of the American Institute of Certified Public Accountants stated in 1964 that generally accepted accounting principles are those which have "substantial authoritative support," and requires disclosure of departures from APB Opinions. With the adoption of a restated Code of Professional Ethics in 1972 by the AICPA, the requirements were made tighter. Rule 203 of that Code specifies that a "member shall not express an opinion that financial statements are presented in conformity with generally accepted accounting principles if such statements contain any departure from an accounting principle promulgated by the body designated by the Council to establish such principles (first the APB and now the FASB). . . . An exception is allowed if the member believes that the statements would be misleading without the departure and in that case the departure and its effects must be disclosed." Instances where CPAs have accepted such departures are virtually nonexistent.

Readers of financial statements benefit in several respects from audited statements. Primarily, they can rely on the fact that the statements have been examined by an independent expert. Independence is enhanced by the strong code of ethics for members of the AICPA. Finally, the auditor renders an opinion as to the fairness of the statements. Although this is not a guarantee of the accuracy or truth of the statements (rather, it is called an "attestation"), within the limitations of testing, estimates, and alternative accounting procedures, readers may put much greater reliance on audited than on unaudited financial statements.

Standards of Reporting.   The standards of reporting summarized in the opinion paragraph of the auditor's report are spelled out more fully in *Statement on Auditing Standards 1—Codification of Auditing Standards and Procedures,* issued in 1973 by the AICPA. Standards of reporting are listed in Sections 400 and 500, as follows:

1. The report shall state whether the financial statements are presented in accordance with *generally accepted principles* of accounting.
2. The report shall state whether such principles have been *consistently* observed in the current period in relation to the preceding period.
3. Informative *disclosures* in the financial statements are to be regarded as reasonably *adequate* unless otherwise stated in the report.
4. The report shall either contain an expression of *opinion* regarding the financial statements, taken as a whole, or an assertion to the effect that an opinion cannot be expressed. When an over-all opinion cannot be expressed, the reasons therefor should be stated.

Key words in each standard of reporting have been italicized. Of major importance is item 3, "adequate disclosure."

In affirming the standard of full disclosure, the Securities and Exchange Commission in *Regulation S-X* calls for additional disclosure of various items beyond those required in APB Opinions and FASB Statements. Examples are the effect on earnings of material amounts of expected pollution control expenditures, and disclosure of compensating balance requirements. (See *Accounting Trends and Techniques* of the AICPA.)

Limitations of Financial Statements.   In using financial statements for making decisions, readers should be aware of an inherent limitation. The statements reflect primarily past history, whereas decisions are concerned with the future. The past is only a guide to the future.

More pertinent to this chapter, preparers of financial statements, if cognizant of the limitations of financial statements, may anticipate user needs. This should lead to clearer and more comprehensive disclosure of the relevant information for a variety of uses.

Some of the serious limitations in financial statements arise because:

1. Estimates are required.
2. Alternative accounting methods are used.
3. Differing asset valuation procedures are used.

4. Some assets and liabilities are omitted entirely.
5. Prices change while assets and liabilities are held.
6. Qualitative information and nonquantifiable facts are omitted.

These will be discussed briefly in turn.

Estimates are required involving both assets and liabilities. This makes both net income and certain balance sheet figures subject to a degree of error. As examples, uncollectible accounts receivable, length of life for depreciable assets and for amortizable intangibles such as patents, and income taxes, subject to interpretation by the Internal Revenue Service and the courts, must all be estimated. Errors or bias on the part of estimators may cause serious distortion in financial statements.

Alternative accounting methods are used both within and among business firms. Although consistency within each firm overcomes some of the difficulties, it does not entirely solve the problems. Several examples follow. Intangibles sometimes are shown as assets, but often are charged immediately to expense. Sometimes a given asset is amortized rapidly, other times slowly. Some firms determine the cost of inventories by the last-in, first-out method; others use the first-in, first-out method; and some use both methods for different classes of inventory. Numerous other accepted alternatives could be listed. These differing methods may give rise to wide variations in net income and valuations.

Differing asset valuation procedures are used within each firm. Although cash and net receivables are shown at approximately current value, many other assets— land as an example—are shown at their cost when acquired several periods ago. Some assets, such as inventories, may be shown at the lower-of-cost-or-market value. Companies having similar assets may thus have differing net incomes and asset valuations if the dates or circumstances of asset acquisition differed significantly. Full disclosure of the relevant current values of assets, where determinable objectively, is often suggested, but under AICPA recommendations this degree of full disclosure has not yet been extended to assets other than cash or receivables.

Some assets and liabilities are omitted entirely. Examples of assets that possibly may be omitted are the discovery values of minerals, gas, or oil, the accretion value of animals and timber, and company-developed goodwill. Examples of liabilities omitted are executive compensation contracts of various types.

The main reason for omission of these items has to do with the difficulty of estimating the figures. Accountants require objectively determined accounts in financial statements. Nevertheless, the omitted information is relevant for many types of decisions.

Prices change while assets and liabilities are held, which may cause several complications. Chief among these during inflationary periods are the following:

1. Historical cost figures may be significantly below current replacement costs.
2. As the general price level changes, the dollar becomes a nonuniform measuring unit.
3. Gains or losses from holding nonmonetary assets occur but are not reported.
4. Gains or losses from being a debtor or creditor take place as the value of the dollar changes, but are not reported.
5. A mismatching takes place when certain out-of-date expenses (such as depreciation of old assets) are deducted from relatively current sales revenues.

The net result during inflationary periods seems to be the reporting of lower than current costs on balance sheets. The effect on net income is unpredictable, depending upon whether or not unreported holding and debtor gains offset "overstated" operating income.

Qualitative information and nonquantifiable facts are omitted from financial statements. Examples of these important items are the value of the organizational structure, superior managerial ability, certain contracts, and the backlog of orders. Although good reasons often exist for omission of these factors, such as the subjective nature of the estimates, this information may be the most important of all for making certain types of decisions.

General Recommendations for Preparation of Financial Statements. In meeting the broad goal of communicating useful information for decision making, certain recommended practices will implement the general standards of reporting. Some of these relate to proper communication; others arise in response to the limitations of financial statements discussed directly above.

Several general recommendations for preparation of financial statements are given below:

1. *Heading.* The heading of each financial statement should clearly state the exact name of the company, the appropriate title of the statement, and the date or period of the statement. The state of incorporation is desirable information but is not customarily given. If the financial statements are consolidated, the title should so indicate.

2. *Terminology.* The wording used in financial statements should be descriptive and clear. Although the reader is expected to be reasonably informed regarding financial and business terms, legalistic or overly technical terms are to be avoided. Criticism of both complexity and words with more than one meaning led the AICPA Committee on Terminology to recommend in 1961 in *Accounting Terminology Bulletin No. 1* that qualifying adjectives be used to prevent misinterpretation. Criticism has yet to be stilled; therefore, preparers should lean toward simplicity and clarity.

3. *Classification.* The classification in financial statements should be designed primarily to facilitate the needs of readers. Related items should be grouped, and valuation accounts added or deducted directly from the items which they modify. The classifications should be clearly delineated and subtotals be labeled. Classifications should not overlap.

4. *Conciseness.* Conciseness leads to clarity. In addition to clear wording in titles, summarization and condensation add clarity. Immaterial items should be grouped or combined with related items. However, the philosopher A. N. Whitehead's admonition should be borne in mind, "seek simplicity, but distrust it." The needs of skilled analysts and others should be met by disclosing appropriate details of summarized information in separate schedules.

5. *Comparative statements.* Comparative statements are desirable and generally in use. The AICPA Committee on Terminology stated in its 1961 *Bulletin No. 1,* among other things, that:

> The presentation of comparative financial statements in annual and other reports enhances the usefulness of such reports and brings out more clearly the nature and trends of current changes affecting the enterprise. Such presentation emphasizes the fact that statements for a series of periods are far more significant than those for a single period and that the accounts for one period are but an installment of what is essentially a continuous history.
>
> In any one year it is ordinarily desirable that the balance sheet, the income statement, and the surplus statement be given for one or more preceding years as well as the current year.

The SEC in 1974 required that annual reports contain financial statements for two years covered by the accountant's opinion as well as a summary of operations for the last five years together with management's analysis of the summary.

6. *Correctness.* Financial statements should be mathematically correct. They should also be appropriate to their expected uses.

7. *Rounding.* Rounding adds clarity. The AICPA, in its annual survey of accounting practices, *Accounting Trends and Techniques,* finds that almost all companies omit cents, that many round to the nearest thousand dollars, and that a few round even further.

8. *Uniformity and consistency.* Uniformity in terminology, classifications, and accounting principles is desirable to the extent feasible. Uniformity should also be followed consistently within and among both firms and accounting periods. However, when uniformity or consistency conflicts with full disclosure or proper presentation, appropriately disclosed changes should be made.

In this connection, *A Statement of Basic Accounting Theory,* issued by the American Accounting Association in 1966, says:

> Where various alternative methods of measuring an economic activity exist, it is important that the best available one be used uniformly within a firm, by different firms, and, to the extent practicable, by different industries. This uniformity refers to consistent classification and terminology as well as consistent measurement, and it requires precise meanings. This guideline is required in order to meet a basic need of managers, investors, and creditors to compare results and financial conditions of different segments of firms, different firms, and different industries. . . . The guideline of uniformity of practice should not exclude the choice of the best method available. . . . The standard of relevance and the guideline of appropriateness to intended use may be so crucial in a given setting that a departure from uniformity of practice (with full disclosure) may be justified. . . . Uniformity should never be the justification for inappropriate information.

9. *Objectivity.* Objectivity has two aspects: verifiability and freedom from bias. The latter is sometimes referred to as "fairness." Financial data meet the verifiability test when two or more qualified persons would arrive at the same figure when examining the data. To be free from bias, figures should be determined impartially and in a manner free from external influences. These aspects of objectively reporting financial data are especially important because users of accounting information often have opposing interests.

10. *Timeliness.* Financial statements should be prepared in time to meet the needs of the intended users.

11. *Consolidation.* Consolidation of independent corporate entities is generally required when they are controlled sufficiently to act as one economic entity.

ARB No. 51, "Consolidated Financial Statements," states:

> There is a presumption that consolidated statements are more meaningful than separate statements and that they are usually necessary for a fair presentation when one of the companies in the group directly or indirectly has a controlling financial interest in the other companies. . . .

See Chapter 34 of this handbook for further discussion of consolidated reports.

12. *Full disclosure.* Full disclosure of all material, relevant financial data useful in making decisions regarding investment, managerial ability, credit, and the like, is of primary importance in preparing general-purpose financial statements. Because of the unknown uses, both known and assumed informational needs should be met. Significant relationships appropriate to the expected uses should be clearly revealed. The needs of financial experts also should be provided for. Several specific disclosure recommendations follow:

    a. Sufficient nonquantitative information for proper interpretation of the financial data should be given.

    b. Pertinent details of condensed data should be provided for technical experts.

    c. When differing accounting methods are available, the one chosen should be disclosed. (See APB Opinion No. 22, "Disclosure of Accounting Policies.")

    d. The bases of asset valuations should be disclosed.

    e. Consideration should be given to disclosing significant variations from current valuations.

    f. Changes in accounting principles, methods, or classifications, and the effects thereof, should be disclosed.

Reporting Periods.   The most common period covered in financial statements is the calendar year. *Accounting Trends and Techniques* reports that about two-thirds of the survey companies use the calendar year ending in December. (At the managerial level, monthly income statements and balance sheets are the most common; but with the adoption of electronic data processing and real-time systems, daily summary reports are expected to become more common. Because some tenuous estimates are required, even annual reports must be viewed as estimates.) Interim reports are discussed in Chapter 5, and in APB Opinion No. 28, "Interim Financial Reporting."

In line with the concepts of uniformity and consistency, many accountants recommend regular periods made up of 52 7-day weeks, 28 days to the month, or 12 30-day months. Additionally, seasonal variations may be properly accounted for when uniform periods are used.

Another highly recommended variation is the natural business year. According to *Accounting Trends and Techniques:*

> The natural business year is the period of 12 consecutive months which ends when a business's activities have reached the lowest point in its annual cycle. New businesses generally recognize the advantages of the natural business year and have adopted it in large numbers. For years, the accounting and legal professions, printers, the SEC, and others interested in various aspects of the year-end bottleneck have been advocating the use of the natural business year.

Reporting Supplementary Information.   Several limitations of financial statements have been discussed above. Primarily because financial statements are condensed, permit alternative procedures, and use technical terms sometimes lacking precise meaning, the principle of full disclosure was invoked in the general recommendations above. Full disclosure is implemented by the presentation of supplementary information.

Various methods of reporting supplementary information, arranged in the approximate descending order of greatest disclosure, can be classified as follows:

1. Parenthetical statements
2. Showing information short
3. Disclosure in the auditor's short-form report
4. Footnotes
5. Detail schedules
6. Additional statements
7. Financial summaries, highlights, charts, and letters of presidents or chairmen of boards of directors to stockholders
8. Poststatement disclosures.

These are discussed in turn below. Quotations are taken from Hendriksen's *Accounting Theory.*

1. Parenthetical statements permit showing qualitative information, valuation bases and accounting methods, legal rights and restrictions, additional details of an item, and reference to additional information shown elsewhere. "The most significant information should be presented in the body of a financial statement rather than in footnotes or supplementary schedules. . . . Parenthetical notes, however, must not be long or they will detract from the main data summarized in the statement."

2. Showing information short involves showing titles in the body of financial statements either without a monetary figure, or by showing a monetary figure indented or "short" so that it does not become a part of the monetary subtotals or totals in the statement. This permits disclosure of indeterminate or unconventional financial information. An example would be showing short an upward revaluation in both the asset and equity sections of a balance sheet.

3. Disclosure in the auditor's short-form report takes place when deviations from generally accepted accounting principles or their inconsistent applications have occurred. These and other requirements for disclosure in the auditor's report are discussed fully in the AICPA *Statement on Auditing Standards 1*.

4. The objective of *footnotes* should be to disclose information that cannot be presented adequately in the body of the statement without detracting from the clarity of the statement. Footnotes should not be used as a substitute for proper classification or valuation and description in the statements, nor should they contradict the information in the statements.

> The main disadvantages of footnotes are: (1) they tend to be difficult to read and understand without considerable study and thus they may be overlooked; (2) the textual descriptions are more difficult to use in decision-making than the summarizations of quantitative data in the statements; and (3) because of the increasing complexity of business enterprises, there is a danger of an overuse of footnotes rather than proper development of principles to incorporate new relationships and events in the statements themselves.
>
> The most common types of footnotes can be classified as follows: (1) explanations of techniques or changes in the methods; (2) explanations of rights of creditors to specific assets or priorities of rights; (3) disclosure of contingent assets or contingent liabilities; (4) disclosure of restrictions to dividend payments; (5) descriptions of transactions affecting capital stock and rights of equityholders; and (6) descriptions of executory contracts.

Since the adoption of APB Opinion No. 22, "Disclosure of Accounting Policies," the first footnote in most financial statements is a description of accounting policies being followed.

5. Detailed schedules expand items summarized in the regular financial statements. *Accounting Trends and Techniques* lists the following examples of supplementary schedules covered by auditors' reports:

Long-term indebtedness
Stock options and leases
Inventory composition
Fixed assets, depreciation
Capital stock
Other capital items
Investments—securities, subsidiaries, affiliates
Taxes
Accounts and notes receivable
Various other balance sheet items
Various income and operating items.

6. Additional statements represent those other than the customary income statement and balance sheet. Examples in practice are the individual parent company, domestic subsidiaries and foreign subsidiaries statements when the group has been consolidated; statements of affiliated companies not consolidated; employee benefits statements; and divisional statements.

7. Financial summaries, highlights, charts, and letters of presidents or chairpersons of boards of directors to stockholders are usually found in annual reports. *Accounting Trends and Techniques* lists the following typical types of supplementary information, presented in a variety of forms:

Sales
Net income (earnings)
Distribution of sales
Distribution of income dollar
Sales by product, division, or department
Working capital

Cash flow
Capital structure
Dividends
Employment costs
Depreciation
Plant additions and retirements
Stock ownership
Research and development.

8. Poststatement disclosures are discussed in the next section.

Poststatement Disclosures. Poststatement disclosure is required for certain events which occur subsequent to the balance sheet date. These subsequent events are such that disclosure is needed for proper interpretation of the financial statements. Disclosure is usually given either in the auditor's report or by annotation of the statements.

In Chapter 11 of *SAP No. 33,* this type of disclosure is described as follows:

> Subsequent events . . . are those which have no direct effect on the financial statements of the prior year but their effects may be such that disclosure is advisable. . . . Examples of this type of transaction or event are the sale of a capital stock issue, or large bond issue with restrictive covenants, purchases of businesses, or serious damage from fire, flood, or other casualty.

Subsequent events are described more fully in Section 560 of the AICPA *Statement on Auditing Standards 1.*

INCOME STATEMENTS

Income statements are designed to reveal the results of all profit-seeking operations during a given period of time. In practice, this straightforward goal is not always achieved in a uniform or consistent manner. A variety of formats, titles, and concepts of income are in use. Clear-cut definitions of income or income statements seldom are found in accounting literature or in the pronouncements of accounting associations.

In 1955, the Committe on Terminology of the AICPA reported in *Accounting Terminology Bulletin No. 2* that" . . . the lack of uniformity found in practice is unfortunate and confusing. . . ." It set out " . . . to promote uniformity of usage . . ." but its own definitions were imprecise. Its major recommendation regarding the income statement was that qualifying adjectives should always be used with the word "income."

A great step forward in the area of disclosure was taken in December 1966 by the AICPA in Accounting Principles Board Opinion No. 9, "Reporting the Results of Operations." Although no clear-cut definition of net income was given (and a flaw may exist because the opinion calls for inclusion of *some* corrections of prior periods in the current income computation), the Board did recommend uniform and consistent disclosure of several important items that were handled in a variety of manners in the past. This was strengthened in 1973 in APB Opinion No. 30, "Reporting the Results of Operations", where the Board set forth specific criteria for items to be included within the *extraordinary* classification.

Objectives of Income Statements. The broad purpose of financial statements was given in the preceding section as supplying readers with relevant information for making rational economic decisions. Primary among these decisions are evaluations of investment worth, of management success, and of credit/worthiness. The income statement is generally believed to be the most important financial statement for these purposes.

These purposes of income statements should be borne in mind when they are prepared, so as to maximize their utility. Both the amount of and trends in periodic net income are important. Proper assignment of revenues and expenses to a given period of time is paramount.

Concepts of Business Income. Income, no matter how defined, usually is at best an estimate. Because of the continuing life of most firms, periodic expired costs must be estimated for the use of inventories, plant, equipment, patents, and the like. Additionally, estimates of bad debts, income taxes, and certain liabilities must be made. When prices fall, estimates of market value are also required in determining holding losses. Thus, the exact amount of net income is seldom known unless a venture has been terminated. Errors in estimates may be discovered in later periods, of course; when they are material, a decision must be made whether or not to go back and correct each affected income statement. The alternative is to force the correction into the current or future income statements.

AICPA Approach—Revenues Less Expenses. Under generally accepted accounting principles, net income equals revenues less expired costs or expenses. Revenue, expense, and income are defined by the AICPA Committee on Terminology in *Bulletins Nos. 2* and *4,* respectively, as follows:

> *Revenue* results from the sale of goods and the rendering of services and is measured by the charge made to customers, clients, or tenants for goods and services furnished to them. It also includes gains from the sale or exchange of assets (other than stock in trade), interest and dividends earned on investments, and other increases in the owners' equity except those arising from capital contributions and capital adjustments.
>
> *Expense* in its broadest sense includes all expired costs which are deductible from revenues. In income statements, distinctions are often made between various types of expired costs by captions or titles including such terms as cost, expense, or loss, e.g., cost of goods or services sold, operating expenses, selling and administrative expenses, and loss on sale of property. These distinctions seem generally useful, and indicate that the narrower use of the term expense refers to such items as operating, selling or administrative expenses, interest, and taxes.
>
> The revenue for a period less the cost of goods sold, other expenses, and losses will give the *net results* of business operations for the period.

The realization principle, discussed in Chapter 1 of this handbook, is important in income determination. Potential revenues, income, and gains which have not been realized by sale, rendering of service, or accrual are omitted from net income because of uncertainty as to the amount earned. Holding gains, appraisal increments, and the like are excluded as being subjective and unconservative. The net income calculation under generally accepted accounting principles is limited to realized, objectively determined transactions.

Although the realization principle is initially conservative, it opens the door wide for management of earnings and smoothing of income through choosing the period for realization of appreciation. Hidden reserves are the interim result when unrealized values have risen.

Balance Sheet Approach—Maintenance of Capital. The concept of net income based on revenues less expenses is imprecise because the dollar amounts to be used are not specified. Another approach to net income determination, the balance sheet approach, brings two conflicting major concepts of income into sharp focus. Because of the double-entry relationship between the income statement and two balance sheets, the net income of a period is the increase in the net assets exclusive of owner investments or withdrawals. (Under historical cost accounting this is also equal to revenues minus expenses, since it is when assets and liabilities change that revenues and expenses come into being.) The values assigned to assets determine the size of the two net asset figures and hence of net income. Since there are two major approaches to assigning figures to assets, two major concepts of income arise. They are:

1. Maintenance of *original* invested monetary capital concept. (Assets are valued at original cost, amortized cost, or at the lower-of-cost-or-market value. Net income equals all realized revenues less all expired *historical* costs and expenses.)

2. Maintenance of *current* invested capital concept. (Assets are valued at current costs or net realizable values. Net income equals all earned revenues less all expired *current* costs and expenses.)

Variations of each concept exist, but at the present time only the first is generally accepted.

All-Inclusive, Current Operating Performance, and Modified All-Inclusive Types of Income Statements. Further variations in the determination of net income exist under the generally accepted maintenance of original cost of invested capital approach. These occur because of disagreement over how to handle extraordinary or nonrecurring items and how to handle corrections of prior periods. Theoretically, for a given period all revenues and gains less all expired costs, expenses, and losses (whether operating or nonoperating, ordinary or extraordinary) would be included in the determination of net income; and all material corrections of prior periods would be excluded. If all items were exactly valued, the result would be *the* net income of the current period.

The theoretically correct determination of periodic net income is not generally accepted. Prior to 1967, the "current operating performance" and the "all-inclusive" (clean surplus) types of income statement were in use; subsequently the AICPA, in APB Opinion No. 9, recommended a "modified all-inclusive" type of statement. These three are briefly summarized by quotations from APB Opinion No. 9 as follows:

1. Under one viewpoint, designated *current operating performance*, the principal emphasis is upon the ordinary, normal recurring operations of the entity during the current period. If extraordinary or prior period transactions have occurred, their inclusion might impair the significance of net income to such an extent that misleading inferences might be drawn from the amount so designated.

2. Under the other viewpoint, designated *all inclusive*, net income is presumed to include all transactions affecting the net increase or decrease in proprietorship equity during the current period, except dividend distributions and transactions of a capital nature. . . . Extraordinary items and prior period adjustments are part of the earnings history of an entity and omission of such items from periodic statements of income increases the possibility that these items will be overlooked in a review of operating results for a period of years. They also stress the dangers of possible manipulation of annual earnings figures if such items may be omitted from the determination of net income. . . .

3. [Paragraph 27 *("modified all-inclusive"* type)]: The Board has considered various methods of reporting the effects of extraordinary events and transactions and of prior period adjustments which are recorded in the accounts during a particular accounting period. The Board has concluded that net income should reflect all items of profit and loss recognized during the period with the sole exception of the prior period adjustments described below. *Extraordinary* items should, however, be segregated from the results of ordinary operations and shown separately in the income statement, with disclosure of the nature and amounts thereof.

General Recommendations for Preparation of Income Statements. Several general recommendations follow. Each has a topical heading, followed by a short description.

1. *Heading.* In addition to the name of the company and the name of the statement, a clear indication of the period of time should be given.

2. *Terminology.* Titles and wording should be clear and concise. Precise, uniform meanings should be used consistently.

3. *Classification.* In order to facilitate the needs of readers, classification should reveal the major sources of revenue and the main types of expense.

4. *Comparison.* In line with the recommendation in Chapter 2A of *ARB No. 43,* income statements "should be given for one or more preceding years as well as for the current year."

5. *Summarization.* Condensation adds simplicity and clarity. However, if material, disclosure should be made of revenues; of cost of goods sold, selling expenses, administrative expenses and federal income taxes; of extraordinary gains or losses and gains on bond retirements; and results of discontinued operations.

6. *Disclosure.* Recommendations for further disclosure, and elucidation of certain items in item 5, follow:

    a. Disclosure of extraordinary items should be made at the bottom of the income statement below a subtotal labeled "income before extraordinary items"; the figure should be net of applicable taxes. Gains on debt retirements should be included among extraordinary items. Paragraphs 20, 21, and 22 of APB Opinion No. 9, as modified by paragraphs 19–24 of APB Opinion No. 30 describe the treatment of extraordinary items in detail.

    b. Disclosure of *income tax expense* should be based on the reported income under "income tax allocation," rather than the actual amount currently payable, according to APB Opinion No. 11, "Accounting for Income Taxes." (Dissenters argue reasonably that income tax allocation is not required when postponement of taxes appears indefinite) Accounting for income taxes in special areas such as subsidiaries, joint ventures, savings and loan, and insurance companies calls for special disclosures described in APB Opinions Nos. 23 and 24.

    c. *Earnings per share* of common stock should be disclosed in the income statement. The following quotations are from APB Opinion No. 15:

        12. The Board believes that the significance attached by investors and others to earnings per share data . . . requires that such data be presented prominently in the financial statements. The Board has therefore concluded that earnings per share or net loss per share data should be shown on the face of the income statement.

In the case of corporations with complex capital structures, the Board said:

        15. Corporations with [complex] corporate structure . . . should present two types of earnings per share data (dual presentation) with equal prominence on the face of the income statement. . . . these two presentations are referred to as "primary earnings per share" and "fully diluted earnings per share." . . .

Additional requirements and computational guidelines are given in Chapter 30 of this handbook.

    d. Disclosure requirements for the pension portion of fringe benefits were extended in 1966 by APB Opinion No. 8, "Accounting for the Cost of Pension Plans." The opinion calls for disclosure in the financial statements (or notes thereto) of "pension costs of the period" and details of the plan.

    e. APB Opinion No. 12 requires that "depreciation expense for the period" and "a general description of the method or methods used in computing depreciation with respect to major classes of depreciable assets" be presented.

    f. Disclosure in the income statement (or in notes to the financial statements) is desirable for:
        (1) The method of determining cost of goods sold
        (2) Any changes in accounting principles or methods, and the effect thereof on net income. (See APB Opinion No. 20, "Accounting Changes.")

    g. Disclosure requirements of the effects on operations of a "pooling" are given in paragraphs 63–65 of APB Opinion No. 16, and for a "purchase" in paragraphs 95–96.

h. APB Opinion No. 18, "Equity Method for Investments in Stock," calls for extensive disclosures, including market values and details of assets, liabilities, and results of operations.

i. Extraordinary item treatment in the current income statement for gain or loss on the early extinguishment of debt is required by FASB Statement No. 4.

j. Disclosure of the nature of nonmonetary transactions and any resultant losses and certain gains is required in APB Opinion No. 29.

k. APB Opinion No. 30 calls for the disclosure as a separate component of income from continuing operations transactions that are not to be classified as extraordinary because they do not meet both of the tests of being "unusual in nature" as well as "infrequent in occurrence."

l. The disclosure of lease details in the statements of lessees, originally required in APB Opinion No. 5, was expanded in APB Opinion No. 31, and now also includes the total rental expense. Recommended, but not required, is disclosure of the present value of the total lease committment.

m. An increasing trend is product-line reporting of revenues, and sometimes income or contribution margins, in annual reports. This is required by the SEC in Form 10K.

n. Disclosure of the total R&D costs charged to expense is required by paragraph 13 of FASB Statement No. 2.

o. Recently, suggestions have been made that financial forecasts be included in annual reports to stockholders.

7. *Exclusions.* The following should not be included in the computation of net income for a given period:

a. Common stockholder (owner) transactions

b. "Gains or losses" on the sale of treasury stock

c. Retained earnings appropriations

d. Corrections of prior periods (but see APB Opinion No. 9, par. 23).

Title of Income Statement. "Income" is the key word in the title of the statement since the major purpose is to determine the *net income* of an entity for a given period of time. The wordings "income statement," "statement of income," and "consolidated income statement" are popular. Use of the word "profit" instead of "income" is becoming rare. The alternative word "earnings" is acceptable but is not as common. Popular usages may be found in the current *Accounting Trends and Techniques* of the AICPA.

The income statement and analysis of retained earnings statement are often combined into one statement. A popular title is "combined statement of income and retained earnings."

Format of Income Statement. Income statement format falls into two general types: "single-step," and "multiple-step." In the single-step form, the total of all expenses is deducted from the total of all revenues to arrive at net income. In the multiple-step form, items are related so as to reveal gross margin, operating net income, nonoperating items, and the like. Variations in format are sometimes required for disclosure of extraordinary items, distributions of net income among different classes of stock, and other special items.

An interesting new format which has not yet been adopted in outsider reporting is the "contribution approach." Basically, costs and expenses are divided into fixed and variable components. The latter are first deducted from revenues to arrive at the contribution toward fixed costs and net income. Fixed costs are then deducted to arrive at net income.

Single-Step Form. The single-step income statement has the advantage of simplicity. It appears to have become the most popular format for large corporations. Some believe that it is more realistic than the multiple-step form because it does not show any item labeled as income until all expenses have been deducted. Possibly misleading or confusing classifications are thereby avoided. A simplified single-step income statement for a firm not having extraordinary revenue or expense items might have the following classifications:

```
Revenue:
  Net sales  ...........................................  $xx
  Other revenue  ......................................   xx     $xx
Costs and expenses:
  Cost of goods sold (including depreciation of $xx)  .........  $xx
  Selling expenses (including depreciation of $xx)  ...........   xx
  Administrative expenses (including depreciation of $xx)  ....   xx
  Interest expense  ......................................   xx
  Other expenses  .......................................   xx
  Federal income taxes  .................................   xx     $xx
Net income  ...................................................  $xx
```

If extraordinary or nonrecurring items occurred during the period, the final wording "net income" would be changed to "net income before extraordinary items," and the bottom of the statement would be expanded as follows:

```
Net income before extraordinary items  .....................  $xx
Add or deduct extraordinary items (net of related income tax of
  $xx)  .................................................   xx
Net income  ...............................................  $xx
```

In line with APB Opinion No. 15, per-share data would also appear at the bottom of the statement.

With the above degree of detail, a reader is able to determine the net income for the year, both before and after income taxes and before and after extraordinary items for the period, simply by rearranging the items.

If a firm disposes of a segment of a business during the period (or has a formal plan for disposing of the segment), APB Opinion No. 30 requires that the results of the operations of the segment and the gain or loss on its disposition be shown separately as a component of income before extraordinary items. If there are discontinued operations, the income statement would show:

```
Income for continuing operations  .......................  $xx
Discontinued operations:
  Loss from operations of discontinued Division X (less
    applicable income taxes)  ........................  $xx
  Loss in disposing of Division X (less applicable income
    taxes)  ..........................................   xx    xx
  Net income  .........................................  $xx
```

If there are extraordinary items, the last line shown above would be titled "Income before extraordinary items," and the extraordinary items would then be listed.

Multiple-Step Form.   The multiple-step income statement, although possibly confusing to some readers, may be more informative than the single-step form because of the grouping of items. In order to avoid confusion, qualifying adjectives should be used with each type of income. An example of the multiple-step income statement classifications for a company *not* having any extraordinary or other items follows:

```
Sales  ......................................................  $xx
Less returns, allowances, and discounts  .........................   xx
Net sales  ..................................................  $xx
Less cost of goods sold  .......................................   xx
Gross margin (profit) on sales  .................................  $xx
```

Less operating expenses:
Selling expenses .... $xx
General and administrative expenses .... xx $xx
Net operating income .... $xx
Add or deduct other (nonoperating) revenue and expense xx
Net income before income taxes xx
Less federal income tax .... $xx
Net income xx

Appropriate disclosure of desired details should be made in the statement, in footnotes, or in accompanying schedules. Extraordinary items, per-share data, and depreciation are examples. Detail schedules of cost of goods sold and possibly costs of manufacturing will be useful in some cases.

Contribution-Margin Form.   Although most appropriate for management uses, the contribution-margin format, given sufficient detail, presents additional useful information. The breakdown of costs and expenses into their fixed and variable components gives insight regarding control and volume fluctuations. In summarized form, the classifications under the contribution approach are as follows:

Net sales .... $xx
Less variable costs and expenses:
Variable costs of goods sold .... $xx
Variable selling and administrative expenses xx   xx
Contribution margin .... $xx
Less fixed costs and expenses:
Fixed costs of goods sold .... $xx
Fixed selling and administrative expenses xx   xx
Net income before income taxes .... $xx

Illustrative Income Statements.   Two illustrative income statements are given below. Exhibit 1 is a single-step form, modified by the extraordinary items and

EXHIBIT 1   Modified Single-Step Income Statement

ILLUSTRATIVE CO. A
Income Statement
Years Ended December 31, 19X2 and 19X1
(Dollars in Thousands)

	19X2	19X1
Revenues:		
Net sales...	$84,580	$75,650
Other income.....................................	80	100
	$84,660	$75,750
Costs and expenses:		
Cost of goods sold...............................	$60,000	$55,600
Selling expenses.................................	2,000	1,700
General and administrative expenses..............	3,000	2,900
Interest expense.................................	180	190
Income tax.......................................	9,350	7,370
	$74,530	$67,760
Income before extraordinary items................	$10,130	$ 7,990
Extraordinary gains (losses) net of applicable income tax reduction of $1,880,000 in 19X2 and zero in 19X1........	(2,040)	(1,280)
Net income.......................................	$ 8,090	$ 6,710
Per share of common stock:		
Income before extraordinary items................	$1.73	$1.37
Extraordinary items, net of tax..................	(.34)	(.22)
Net income.......................................	$1.39	$1.15

Notes: . . . .

per-share calculations; Exhibit 2 is a multiple-step form with the same data. Both are adapted from APB Opinion No. 9 exhibits. Parenthetical statements and footnotes have been omitted, but would be appropriate for additional details regarding sales deductions, cost of goods sold, total depreciation, expenses, and extraordinary items.

EXHIBIT 2   Multiple-Step Income Statement

ILLUSTRATIVE CO. B
Income Statement
Years Ended December 31, 19X2 and 19X1
(Dollars in Thousands)

	19X2	*19X1*
Net sales..	$84,580	$75,650
Cost of goods sold...	60,000	55,600
Gross margin...	$24,580	$20,050
Operating expenses:		
Selling expenses...	$ 2,000	$ 1,700
General and administrative expenses.........................	3,000	2,900
Total operating expenses...................................	$ 5,000	$ 4,600
Operating income..	$19,580	$15,450
Nonoperating income.......................................	80	100
Subtotal...	$19,660	$15,550
Nonoperating deductions (interest)...........................	180	190
Income before income taxes and extraordinary items...........	$19,480	$15,360
Income taxes..	9,350	7,370
Income before extraordinary items..........................	$10,130	$ 7,990
Extraordinary gains (losses) net of applicable income tax reduction of $1,880,000 in 19X2 and zero in 19X1...........................	(2,040)	(1,280)
Net income...	$ 8,090	$ 6,710
Per share of common stock:		
Income before extraordinary items...........................	$1.73	$1.37
Extraordinary items net of tax...............................	(.34)	(.22)
Net income...	$1.39	$1.15
Notes:		

Operating Revenues.   The first section in the illustrative income statements is called "operating revenue." "Net sales," "sales," and "net sales and operating revenue" are the most common titles reported in *Accounting Trends and Techniques*.

Deductions from sales in arriving at net sales are sales returns and allowances, sales discounts, and adjustments for estimated uncollectibles. The latter two are sometimes classified as expenses, but theoretically each represents sales or parts of selling prices not collected; hence they qualify as sales deduction items.

Operating revenues represent the services rendered to customers for the regular, most significant activities of a company. Nonoperating revenues from minor or sideline activities are frequently shown separately. If material, sales by major classifications should be disclosed.

It is no longer considered proper to start an income statement with the gross profit figure; the details of net sales and cost of sales are to be disclosed.

Two special recommendations in APB Opinion No. 10, "Omnibus Opinion—1966," relate to operating revenues:

1. In paragraph 3, as amended by APB Opinion No. 18, the Board recommends that if a subsidiary is not consolidated, the investment in the subsidiary should be adjusted under the "equity method" *for the group's share of earnings*—the earnings to be presented as a separate item on the income statement.

2. In paragraph 12, the Board "concludes that, in the absence of the circum-

stances referred to above [that the collection of the sale price is not reasonably assured], the *installment method of recognizing revenue is not acceptable.*"

Cost of Goods Sold. In a multistep income statement, cost of goods sold is deducted from net sales to arrive at gross margin (profit) on sales. Typically, no details on components or method of calculation are given other than that sometimes the amount of depreciation included is indicated. Ideally, material amounts of depreciation related to cost of goods sold, to selling expenses, and to administrative expenses would be distinguished; frequently in practice total depreciation is shown as a separate item and excluded from the cost of goods sold (and selling expense and administrative expense as well). This distorts gross margin and makes meaningful use of this statistic difficult.

Although not required under generally accepted accounting principles, many readers prefer additional disclosure of items classified on the basis of their nature (sometimes called "object of expenditure") rather than by function. Chief among these are depletion, materials, and labor costs (including taxes and other fringe benefits). Alternatively, these could be revealed in the manufacturing statement. (In "governmental accounting" as described in Chapter 45, expenditures are classified by both function and object, as well as by various other classifications.)

According to *ARB No. 43,* Chapter 4, paragraph 14, substantial losses due to *market declines in inventories* should be disclosed *separately* from cost of goods sold.

Operating Expenses. Operating expenses are those regular, normal expenses associated with earning operating revenues. Operating expenses, other than cost of goods sold, should be separated into selling expenses and administrative expenses. The title "general and administrative expenses" is common for the latter.

Selling expenses include those directly related to the sale and delivery of goods or services.

General and administrative expenses are the remaining operating expenses of the entire business other than selling expenses.

Proper and consistent allocation of operating expenses to the above classifications should provide useful information for most readers. Sometimes it may be desirable to give details of these expenses in separate schedules, but this is not common for large companies. The SEC, for example, requires the following disclosure (in addition to cost of goods sold) in the income statement or in supplementary schedules: maintenance and repairs, amortization, taxes, management and service contract fees, rents, royalties, and income taxes.

Financing expenses, such as interest on seasonal inventory loans, are sometimes included in operating expenses. However, financing expenses usually appear as nonoperating items. In the single-step income statement, *interest expense* appears as a separate item.

Nonoperating Income and Expense. Nonoperating items may be distinguished from both operating and extraordinary items. They represent sideline or minor operations, although they may be regular or typical. They tend to recur, and hence are not extraordinary.

Nonoperating revenue is commonly called "nonoperating income" because the revenues often have no direct expenses associated with them; or they are shown "net" after deduction of related expenses. Examples of nonoperating or "other income" items are

Dividends earned
Interest earned
Rent earned
Commissions earned
Royalties earned
Fees earned

Gains from foreign exchange fluctuations

Gains on sales of securities

Gains on sale of miscellaneous operating assets

Earnings (under the equity method) from unconsolidated subsidiaries

Nonoperating expenses are often called "other expenses." Examples are

Interest expense

Losses from foreign exchange fluctuations

Losses from sales of securities

Losses from sales of miscellaneous operating assets (except inventories)

Share of loss on unconsolidated domestic subsidiaries

Loss on firm purchase commitments.

In many statements, *interest expense* (plus or minus any related amortization of discount or premium) would appear on a separate line because of its significance.

Income Taxes.   Income taxes in income statements are seldom equal to the amount on the tax return. Under interperiod tax allocation, the figure is based on the amount reported as "income before income taxes and extraordinary items" (except for "permanent" differences between reported and taxable income) at applicable rates, and may differ considerably from the tax return figure. If extraordinary gains or losses also occur, they are reported separately, after adjustment for any related tax effects of the extraordinary items.

The recommendation for income tax allocation is made in APB Opinion No. 11, "Accounting for Income Taxes," and the method of income statement disclosure is spelled out in paragraphs 60 and 61 of that Opinion. (See Chapter 36, and APB Opinions Nos. 23 and 24.)

The *investment tax credit* received because of purchases of certain assets reduces the actual income taxes owed. Although the Accounting Principles Board recommended in Opinion No. 4, "Accounting for the Investment Credit," that the tax credit be spread over the life of the property acquired, *Accounting Trends and Techniques* reports that the overwhelming majority of large firms reduce the income tax of the year in which the credit was received.

Income tax treatment may be summarized as follows:

1. Income taxes should be separately disclosed.

2. Income taxes should be reasonably related to reported income, under the method of interperiod income tax allocation.

3. The tax effects of extraordinary gains or losses should be associated with the extraordinary items and fully disclosed.

4. Material differences between legal and effective tax rates should be disclosed, usually in a footnote.

Extraordinary Items.   Paragraph 17 of APB Opinion No. 9 states that " . . . extraordinary items should . . . be segregated from the results of ordinary operations and shown separately in the income statement, with disclosure of the nature and amounts thereof. . . ."

Examples of extraordinary items were given as

1. The sale or abandonment of a plant or a significant segment of the business

2. The sale of an investment not acquired for resale

3. The write-off of goodwill due to unusual events or developments within the period

4. The condemnation or expropriation of properties

5. A major devaluation of a foreign currency.

APB Opinion No. 9 was amended in 1973 by APB Opinion No. 30, which defined the extraordinary classification very narrowly in order to curtail its use; it also calls for special reporting of discontinued operations of a segment of a business.

Other AICPA Recommendations.   Most of the AICPA recommendations regarding income statements and individual revenue and expense items have already been referred to in this section. They have come from *Accounting Research Bulletins, Accounting Terminology Bulletins,* and Accounting Principles Board Opinions.

One important recommendation which has not been discussed is found in APB Opinions Nos. 10, 16, and 18. It concerns restatement of financial statements because of a "pooling of interest." In essence, in order to prevent misleading changes (increases) in earnings and earnings per share due simply to mergers and poolings, income statements of prior years, when presented for comparative purposes, are to be restated *on a combined basis.* The goal is to eliminate earnings changes due solely to the combination rather than due to changes in operating results.

AAA Recommendations—Historical-Cost and Current-Cost Statements. Major recommendations for improving income statements were made in 1966 by an American Accounting Association committee. In *A Statement of Basic Accounting Theory* the committee recommended showing income calculations in a single statement under *both* the maintenance of historical-cost and the maintenance of current-cost concepts. The latter would reveal, in addition to the customary results of operations, gains and losses from holding assets which change considerably in value and gains and losses from being a debtor or creditor when price levels change.

The reasons for the AAA recommendations are found in Chapter 3 of the statement, entitled "Accounting Information for External Users." Pertinent quotations follow:

> Accounting information is the chief means of reducing the uncertainty under which external users act as well as a primary means of reporting on stewardship. . . . Most decisions based on accounting information involve some kind of predictions. Common examples include forecasts of future earnings, of probable payment of debt, and of likely managerial effectiveness. . . . Evidence of dissatisfaction with extant accounting practices abounds. A principal criticism relates to the deficiencies of historical cost as a basis of predicting future earnings, solvency, or overall managerial effectiveness. We find historical-cost information relevant but not adequate for all purposes. We accordingly recommend that current-cost information as well as historical-cost information should be reported. Detailed suggestions for implementing this recommendation through multi-column statements are set out in the Appendices.

In Appendix B of the AAA Statement, an illustration of the income statement of a hypothetical company is given for a year during which the general price level rose 4 percent and fixed assets rose 10 percent. The statement is in multiple-step format, distinguishes between fixed and variable items, and reveals holding gains (net of taxes) and debtor gains. A summary version of the illustration is shown in Exhibit 3.

Although the AAA recommendations have not been adopted in practice, a great deal of additional useful information is found in the recommended statement. In particular, it reveals that the results of operations were much less favorable than when conventionally reported if relevant current costs were taken into account. The recommendation is also in line with the one of the AICPA in Chapter 9 of *ARB No. 43,* that supplementary schedules be used to explain the results of changing prices. This recommendation also has *not* been adopted in practice.

Statements of Changes in Stockholders' Equity Accounts. No set of financial statements is complete without full disclosure of the changes in each item making up the total of the owners' investment in the company. Explanation of the changes in retained earnings is predominant, but important changes in capital stock or other capital items sometimes occur. In this connection, paragraph 10 of APB Opinion No. 12 states:

EXHIBIT 3   AAA Recommended Income Statement

XYZ COMPANY
Income Statement
Year Ended December 31, 19X6
(Dollars in Thousands)

	Historical Cost		Current Cost	
Sales (net)...................................		$20,000		$20,000
Cost of goods sold				
(details of depreciation, inventories and fixed costs were given)................................		11,360		11,841
Gross margin................................		$ 8,640		$ 8,159
Operating expenses:				
Selling—variable...........................	$2,000		$2,000	
Selling—fixed (depreciation disclosed)..........	2,000		2,042	
	$4,000		$4,042	
Administrative—variable....................	$ 500		$ 500	
Administrative—fixed (depreciation disclosed)...	3,000		3,028	
	$3,500	7,500	$3,528	7,570
Net operating income.........................		$ 1,140		$ 589
Nonoperating expense—net....................		100		140
Net income before income taxes.................		$ 1,040		$ 449
Federal income taxes applicable.................		510		257
Net income (transaction basis)..................		$ 530		$ 192
Holding gains (net of income taxes of $398(000))...				202
Purchasing power gain on net debt..............				187
Net income...................................				$ 581

When both financial position and results of operations are presented, disclosure of changes in the separate accounts comprising stockholders' equity (in addition to retained earnings) and of the changes in the number of shares of equity securities . . . is required to make the financial statements sufficiently informative. Disclosure of such changes may take the form of separate statements or may be made in the basic financial statements or notes thereto.

The most popular combination of financial statements reported in *Accounting Trends and Techniques* is a balance sheet and a single statement of income and retained earnings. Quite common are separate statements to explain changes in retained earnings. Changes in other capital items are shown either in the owners' equity section of the balance sheet or in the footnotes.

Retained Earnings Statements.   The retained earnings analysis is basic because it connects the income statement with the beginning and ending balance sheet figures of retained earnings. In a corporation having no changes in stockholder equity items except from operations, the analysis of retained earnings would simply be

Retained earnings:	
At beginning of period	$xxx
Add: Net income for period	xx
At end of period	$xxx

The analysis of retained earnings may be disclosed in several manners: (1) in the owners' equity section of the balance sheet, (2) in a separate retained earnings statement, or (3) in a combined statement of income and retained earnings.

More commonly, dividends are declared during the year, resulting in the following analysis:

ANALYSIS OF RETAINED EARNINGS

Retained earnings at beginning of period .... $xxx
Add: Net income for the period xxx

$xxx
Less: Dividends on common stock .... ˙xxx
Retained earnings at end of period .... $xxx

Additional complexities sometimes are found in analyses of retained earnings because of stock dividends, appropriations of retained earnings, and corrections of prior years. The following retained earnings statement illustrates most of the possible classifications of changes in retained earnings:

ABC COMPANY
Retained Earnings Statement
Year 19X3

Balance of retained earnings, Jan. 1, 19X3..................................... $xxx
Add: Correction of prior year—refund of 19X1 income tax................ $xxx
Less: Correction of prior year—loss on claim for damages in 19X2.......... xxx   xxx
Adjusted balance, Jan. 1, 19X3.. $xxx
Add: Net income, year 19X3... $xxx
    Transfer back from retained earnings appropriated for contingencies... xxx   xxx

$xxx
Less: Preferred stock dividend—$6 per share............................ $xxx
    Dividend in shares of common stock.............................. xxx
    Appropriated for bond retirement................................ xxx   xxx
Balance of retained earnings, Dec. 31, 19X3............................... $xxx

---

Corrections of prior periods are shown as adjustments of the opening balance of retained earnings. This is in line with the recommendations in APB Opinion No. 9. However, the Accounting Principles Board has a restrictive definition of "prior period adjustments," making them "rare in modern financial accounting." In theory, *all* material prior period adjustments would be excluded from income so as to get a correct determination of the results of operations for the current period. The board's definition of prior period adjustments permits determinations of current period net income to be affected by some prior period adjustments, presumably so as to prohibit managerial errors or manipulations from hiding revenues or expenses which might never appear in any income statement.

Combined Statement of Income and Retained Earnings. The combined statement was originally recommended so as to reveal on the same page operating, nonoperating, extraordinary items, and corrections of prior periods. All were fully disclosed regardless of whether or not they appeared properly in the income or retained earnings section of the statement. Disclosure alone, however, does not solve the problem because the final net income figure still has to be determined and so labeled.

Two disadvantages of the combined statement are that (1) it may become lengthy and complicated, and (2) the net income figure may not be readily found.

Chapters 2B and 8 of *ARB No. 43*, on the topics of income and earned surplus, were superseded upon issue of APB Opinion No. 9 in 1966, in which no stand was taken by the AICPA regarding separate or combined income and retained earnings statements. Both are illustrated without preference in that Opinion.

The combined income and retained earnings statement continues with the analysis of retained earnings immediately following the determination of net income. This is illustrated below by expanding Exhibit 1 as follows:

ILLUSTRATIVE CO. A
Combined Statement of Income and Retained Earnings
Years Ended December 31, 19X1, and December 31, 19X2
(Dollars in Thousands)

	19X2	19X1
	.	.
	.	.
(Details of net income as shown in Exhibit 1).........	.	.
	.	.
	.	.
Net income.....................................	$ 8,090	$ 6,710
Retained earnings at beginning of year:		
As previously reported..........................	$28,840	$25,110
Adjustments (Note 2)...........................	(3,160)	(1,760)
As restated...................................	$25,680	$23,350
	$33,770	$30,060
Cash dividends on common stock—$0.75 per share.....	4,380	4,380
Retained earnings at end of year...................	$29,390	$25,680
Per share of common stock:		
Income before extraordinary items................	$1.73	$1.37
Extraordinary items, net of tax...................	(.34)	(.22)
Net income.....................................	$1.39	$1.15

Note 2.   The balance of retained earnings at Dec. 31, 19X1, has been restated from amounts previously reported to reflect a retroactive charge of $3,160,000 for additional income taxes settled in 19X2. Of this amount, $1,400,000 ($0.24 per share) is applicable to 19X1 and has been reflected as an increase in tax expense for that year; the balance (applicable to years prior to 19X1) is being charged to retained earnings at Jan. 1, 19X1.

Owners' Equity Statements.   Except in the case of sole proprietorships or partnerships, separate statements of changes in capital stock or other capital items are not common. Most companies make such disclosures as they consider adequate in the stockholders' equity section of the balance sheet and in the notes relative thereto.

The most common changes are changes in capital accounts of owners, common stock, preferred stock, excess of issue price above par or stated value of stock, and treasury stock. Occasionally, donated or revaluation capital changes occur.

No special format is required, but disclosure of number of shares as well as legal details and dollar amounts should be made. The analyses simply show beginning figures, additions, reductions, and ending balances.

BALANCE SHEETS

Objectives and Meaning of Balance Sheets.   The broad purpose of financial statements is to supply readers with information for making rational economic decisions. It is generally agreed that the income statement is the most important statement for making decisions regarding investment, credit, management evaluation, and the like. However, as stated in *ARB No. 43*, " . . . the balance sheet has significant uses of its own. . . ." The information regarding assets, liabilities, and other items found in balance sheets is a useful complement to that in income statements.

The auditor's short-form report expresses an opinion that the balance sheet presents fairly the financial position of a company in conformity with generally accepted accounting principles. It is incorrect to conclude from this, however, that a balance sheet is a statement of financial position in the sense of showing the value of a business. The modifying phrase "in conformity with generally accepted accounting principles" limits the meaning of "financial position." This should be clearly seen by reading the definition of the balance sheet given in Kohler's *A Dictionary for Accountants:* "balance sheet: A statement of financial position of any economic unit, disclosing as at a given moment of time its assets, at cost, depreciated cost, or other indicated value, its liabilities, and the equity of owners. . . ." Thus, the meaning of what is a fair presentation of financial position must be considered within the context of how assets and liabilities are determined under generally accepted accounting principles.

In discussing possible confusion in the minds of readers regarding the meaning and terminology of balance sheets, the AICPA Committee on Terminology stated, in *Accounting Terminology Bulletin No. 1,* "Review and Résumé (1953)": "The failure of accountants to emphasize and explain their conventional uses of these and other terms has given rise to criticism of accounting statements. . . ." They go on to say that "a balance sheet is historically a summary of balances prepared from books of account. . . . Moreover such a summary may fall short of being an adequate statement of assets and liabilities." This led the Committee to the following restrictive definition of the balance sheet: "A tabular statement or summary of balances (debit and credit) carried forward after an actual or constructive closing of books of account kept according to principles of accounting." This definition is more restrictive than Kohler's, in that it does not even require that the debits or credits be assets or liabilities.

The Committee on Terminology then goes on to criticize Bouvier's *Law Dictionary* definition of the balance sheet which characterizes it as a statement of "true values." Herein lies the confusion. Although accountants and users of balance sheets often think of them as being fair presentations of assets and liabilities, they may in fact represent out-of-date costs or omit significant items of value.

The Committee on Terminology concludes its discussion of the balance sheet on the hopeful note that with the development and wider understanding of accounting principles, the "balancing" and "financial position" aspects will be reconciled: "A balance sheet . . . may indeed be the statement of assets and liabilities."

In meeting the needs of users, many contemporary accountants are not satisfied with balance sheets which are simply listings of debits and credits from the accounts (whether the items are assets and liabilities or not), and would insist that a balance sheet be constructed as an up-to-date statement of the actual assets, liabilities, and owners' equity of an entity on a given date. The objective in preparing the balance sheet then becomes one of choosing, within generally accepted accounting principles, those items and accounts which will give readers relevant information for making rational economic decisions. When generally accepted accounting principles put severe limitations on the utility of the figures, full disclosure of alternative, more useful information is called for.

Concepts of the Balance Sheet. The preceding section on the objectives of balance sheets has implicitly revealed two main concepts of financial position: (1) the historical-cost concept, and (2) the current-cost concept. Under the first, assets are essentially based on original cost less estimated depreciation or amortization; whereas under the second, assets are based upon their current replacement costs or net realization values. The first approach is generally accepted; the second is rarely used in practice, except by investment companies.

As discussed in Chapter 1, the historical-cost concept is modified in practice by the lower-of-cost-or-market rule for investments and inventories, but upward revaluations are proscribed. The "cost" and "realization" principles not only adhere to the principle of conservatism; they follow the maxim: "Anticipate no gains; provide for all losses." The historical-cost approach, as modified, also is believed to result in objective figures free from personal, subjective bias.

The current-cost concept, on the other hand, gains adherents when inflation becomes significant. Conservative cost figures tend to be out of date and to lose relevance for decision making. Current, rather than historical, costs become especially important for credit and management evaluation purposes. The problems then faced by current-cost advocates are those of making unbiased, objective valuations for all major assets. These determinations should be at least as valid as the ones under the lower-of-cost-or-market rule for inventories.

At best, determination of financial position, just like the determination of net income, is an estimate. In addition to the problems of changing prices, estimates of uncollectible receivables, estimates of depreciation, estimates of amortization, estimates of liabilities and contingencies, together with the omission of self-generated goodwill, patents, and similar values make balance sheets less than absolute. The total value of a business can rarely be determined objectively. At present, preparers use the historical-cost approach, but current costs should be disclosed in some manner when considered particularly relevant for readers of balance sheets.

General Recommendations for Preparation of Balance Sheets. Several general recommendations pertinent to balance sheets are given. Each has a topical heading, followed by a short discussion.

1. *Heading.* In addition to the name of the company and the name of the statement, the exact day of the balance sheet should be given. The state of incorporation, though not mandatory, may provide useful information.

2. *Terminology.* Titles and wording should be clear and concise. Precise, uniform meanings should be used consistently. Modern AICPA recommendations should be followed, including deletion of the word "reserve" in the title of contra-assets and liabilities, use of the word "value" only if preceded by a qualifying adjective and deletion of all uses of the word "surplus."

3. *Classification.* In order to facilitate the needs of readers, classification should reveal the major types of assets and liabilities. Valuation accounts should be related directly to the items they modify. Offsets, with the rare exception of tax anticipation notes, are not permitted.

4. *Comparison.* As with income statements, balance sheets should be given for one or more preceding years as well as for the current year.

5. *Summarization.* Condensation adds to simplicity and clarity. Immaterial items may be combined with related items. Significant details may be revealed in separate schedules or notes.

6. *Disclosure.* Disclosure of both qualitative and quantitative information for proper interpretation and determination of financial position is desirable. Disclosure should be made of the following specific items:

   a. Methods of valuation of assets and liabilities
   b. Market value when significantly above cost (requirement by AICPA only for securities)
   c. Changes in accounting principles, methods, or classifications, and the effects thereof, as described in APB Opinion No. 20
   d. Changes in depreciating assets and related accumulated depreciation; and a general description of depreciation method, by major classifications
   e. Liquidation preferences of preferred stock
   f. Changes in the details of stockholders' equity items, number of shares, etc., as described in APB Opinion No. 15
   g. A combination by the "pooling of interests" method, as described in great detail in APB Opinion No. 16

   h. The method and period of amortization of Intangibles, called for in APB Opinion No. 17, paragraph 30

   i. The details of material investments in common stock of unconsolidated subsidiaries, as described in paragraph 20 of APB Opinion No. 18 on the "equity method"

   j. The premium or discount on debt, as illustrated in the appendix to APB Opinion No. 21

   k. Accounting policies (see examples in APB Opinion No. 22)

   l. Possible income taxes in special areas, as described in paragraphs 14, 18, 24, and 29 of APB Opinion No. 23

   m. The details of stock option plans, referred to in paragraph 19 of APB Opinion No. 25

   n. Minimum rental commitments and additional lease disclosures, required in paragraphs 9 and 10 of APB Opinion No. 31.

   7. *Exclusions.* The following should *not* be included in balance sheets:

   a. Assets, even those known to exist, if dollar amounts cannot be determined fairly and objectively. ("Cost" is the main criterion used by the AICPA for meeting the objectivity test.) Such assets may be described in the footnotes.

   b. Liabilities that are contingent.

   c. A special hybrid section for "reserves," "allowances," or "deferred credits." These are either liability or owners' equity items.

Title of the Balance Sheet. "Balance" is the main idea expressed in modern statements, and the title "balance sheet" is the most common. Conceptually, this permits neutrality regarding the valuation problem. A significant number, but a minority, of large firms use the title "statement of financial position." A similar alternative is "statement of financial condition." The word "consolidated" is used in the above titles when pertinent.

Format of Balance Sheets. Regardless of difficulties with the conceptual meaning of balance sheets, they are invariably presented as statements of assets, liabilities, and owners' equity on a given day. The basic format is

$$\text{Assets} = \text{liabilities} + \text{stockholders' equity}$$

Although some accountants view the basic format as "assets equal equities," the distinction between debtor equities and ownership equities appears sufficiently great to warrant separate liabilities and stockholders' equity designations. A variation involves: Investment in assets (details given) equals sources of assets (details of both creditor and owner sources given). It is also conceptually sound and may be desirable to view preferred stockholders' equity as a distinct and separate classification, but this is not commonly done.

Assets and liabilities are typically further subdivided so as to set out the current portion of each. This is both customary and in line with the AICPA recommendation in *ARB No. 43,* Chapter 3, titled "Working Capital." Here current items are described in essence as those which will be received (or paid) in one year or one operating cycle, whichever is longer. (Recent suggestions that current items be classified under an "operations" definition of working capital have not yet been adopted in practice.)

As will be shown in the next section, assets and liabilities, in addition to the current classification, are subdivided further in practice. Here they will be referred to as "long-life" assets and "long-term" liabilities. The word "fixed" is another term often used to describe long-term items.

Two conventional or customary forms of balance sheets are the *account form* and the *report form.* Under the *account form,* assets are shown on the left and liabilities and stockholders' equity on the right, as follows:

ACCOUNT FORM OF BALANCE SHEET

Current assets	$ xx	Current liabilities	$ xx
Long-life assets	xx	Long-term liabilities	xx
		Stockholders' equity	xx
	$xxx		$xxx

Under the *report form,* assets appear on top, followed below by liabilities and owners' equity, as follows:

REPORT FORM OF BALANCE SHEET

Current assets	$xxx
Long-life assets	xxx
Total assets	$xxx
Current liabilities	$xxx
Long-term liabilities	xxx
Stockholders' equity	xxx
Total liabilities and stockholders' equity	$xxx

In practice, the overwhelming majority of firms use the account form of balance sheet.

Variations of the report form are in use. An uncommon but useful one emphasizes the net assets by deducting total liabilities from total assets to arrive at the stockholders' equity. The format is as follows:

Assets:		
Current	$xxx	
Long-life	xxx	$xxx
Less: Liabilities:		
Current	$xxx	
Long-term	xxx	xxx
Stockholders' equity		$xxx

Another common format for balance sheets, also a variation of the report form, is called the "financial position form." In this form, working capital and net assets are derived in multiple steps, somewhat as follows:

FINANCIAL POSITION FORM OF BALANCE SHEET

Current assets	$xxx
Less: Current liabilities	xxx
Net working capital	$xxx
Long-life assets	xxx
Subtotal	$xxx
Less: Long-term liabilities	xxx
Stockholders' equity (or net assets)	$xxx

Several variations on this same theme are possible. Some involve not only rearrangement of items but also the use of simplified lay language as an aid to comprehension.

Classifications in Balance Sheets.   Regardless of format, further classifications of assets and liabilities are required. The major details of both current and long-term items involve information which is useful to outsiders in making a variety of decisions. No uniformity has been arrived at in practice, and the AICPA committees have chosen to leave form flexible.

The classifications listed below are simply taken from customary practice. Variations in the number of classifications and the order are common. Further details are discussed following the list. Possible classifications in balance sheets are as follows:

MAJOR BALANCE SHEETS CLASSIFICATIONS

Assets	*Liabilities*
Current assets	Current liabilities
Investments (long-term)	Long-term liabilities
Property, plants, and equipment	
Other (noncurrent) assets	*Stockholders' equity*
	Capital stock
	Other contributed capital
	Retained earnings:
	Appropriated
	Unappropriated
	Treasury stock (contra)

Although the *sequence of items* above (and in the current classifications detailed below) is usually said to be "in the order of liquidity," it has become relatively fixed by custom. Rarely would the order be changed because of shifts in liquidity, such as inventories in short supply being more liquid than slow-moving receivables. Instead, the sequence usually remains the normal, expected order of liquidity in the operating cycle.

The classification sequence above is applicable to a merchandising or industrial firm. Different classification and sequences are found in other industries, where the most important items may appear first. Railroads and public utilities, for example, may show plant and equipment first among assets and stockholders' equity and/or long-term debt first on the other side. Banks also usually show contributed capital first.

Selected details of the major balance sheet classifications are listed below.

Major subdivisions of *current assets* are
  Cash
  Marketable securities (short-term investments)
  Receivables and advances (net of allowances)
  Inventories
  Prepaid items
  Other current items.

Major subdivisions of *investments* (long-term) are
  Investments in subsidiary companies not consolidated
  Advances to subsidiary companies and affiliates
  Properties not related to regular operations
  Investments in stocks and bonds of other companies
  Sinking funds and other earmarked funds
  Cash surrender value of life insurance.

Major subdivisions of *property, plants, and equipment* are
  Land
  Land improvements
  Buildings
  Construction in progress
  Machinery and equipment
  Patterns, dies, etc.
  Small tools
  Furniture and fixtures
  Automotive equipment
  Leaseholds and improvements
  Natural resources
  Containers

[Accumulated depreciation, amortization, and depletion related to the above (except land) are contra to each, respectively.]

Major subdivisions of *other (noncurrent)* assets are
  Intangible assets (long-term rights bestowing value on owner)
  Deferred charges (long-term prepaid costs)
  Deposits and long-term receivables (net of premium or discount).
    (Each of these sometimes appears as a separate classification in the balance sheet, depending on the types and materiality of the items.)

The main types of *intangible assets* are
  Patents
  Copyrights
  Trademarks
  Trade names
  Secret processes
  Leaseholds
  Licenses
  Franchises
  Corporate organization costs
  Stock promotion costs
  Goodwill.

The main types of *deferred charges* are
  Long-term prepayments
  Advertising
  Start-up costs
  Rent
  Plant rearrangement costs
  Employee welfare costs
  Deferred income taxes.

Major subdivisions of *current liabilities* are
  Accounts payable—trade
  Notes payable
  Accrued liabilities (wages, interest, taxes, rent, etc.)
  Dividends payable
  Income taxes payable—estimated
  Advances by customers (precollections)
  Current portion of long-term debt
  Other current liabilities (pensions and other employee benefits, affiliates, deposits, officers, guarantees, loss on purchase commitments, if current, etc.).

Major subdivisions of *long-term liabilities* are
  Bonds payable (plus premium; less discount)
  Mortgages payable
  Contracts payable
  Notes payable (long-term)
  Pensions and other employee benefits payable
  Future income taxes payable (deferred)
  Deposits (long-term)
  Other.

Note: No deferred credit or reserves classification is included. The items are preferably shown either as liabilities or retained earnings.

Major classifications of *capital stock* are
  Preferred stocks (including senior classified common stocks), par value
  Common stock, par or stated value
  Capital stock subscribed.

Major classifications of *other contributed capital* are
  Excess (received, paid-in, contributed) over par or stated value
  Excess of earnings capitalized over par or stated value
  Capital from treasury stock transactions
  Capital resulting from reorganizations
  Capital resulting from consolidation
  Donated capital.
Capital resulting from revaluation of assets
Major classifications of *appropriated retained earnings* (sometimes called
    "reserves") are
  Appropriations for:
  Contingencies (losses from fire, flood, etc.; lawsuits; lower prices; etc.)
  Sinking or retirement funds
  Plant expansion
  Working capital expansion
  Asset replacement at higher prices.
Minority interest in capital stock and retained earnings of a consolidated subsidiary may be shown as a part of stockholders' equity or of liabilities. It frequently is presented, however, as a separate, unclassified item between liabilities and stockholders' equity.

Illustrative Balance Sheets.   Illustrative balance sheets are given below as follows:
  Exhibit 4. Condensed Account Form
  Exhibit 5. Condensed Report Form (A − L = SE type)
  Exhibit 6. Condensed Financial Position Form
  Exhibit 7. Detailed Account Form
  Exhibit 8. Condensed, Simplified Balance Sheet (details in schedules).

In Exhibits 4 to 6, the same figures are used to illustrate the account form and report form. The format is the typical condensed, comparative one used by many large corporations.

Exhibit 7, which is not comparative or condensed, gives many details which might be found in the balance sheet of a small company issuing a statement for general purposes.

Exhibit 8 is an adaptation of an actual large company which used a high degree of condensation and simplification. Details (which are omitted here) were given for the sophisticated reader in schedules on separate pages. Of particular note was the stockholders' equity, consisting of a single figure. When presented in account form, it appears even more simplified.

Footnotes and schedules required for the proper degree of disclosure have been omitted from the exhibits for brevity.

The exhibits are simply illustrative and are not be be viewed as models to fit all cases. Alternatives and improvements are considered below.

Balance Sheet Items: Standards of Presentation.   A discussion of terminology and the standards of statement presentation distilled from generally accepted auditing standards and accounting principles is given below briefly for each of the main items appearing in balance sheets.

Cash as a single word is an appropriate title for all cash items available for immediate withdrawal. The term "cash on hand and in banks" appears to be dying out. Time deposits, if material, should be segregated, as should cash in closed banks, cash advances, foreign banks balances subject to exchange restriction, etc. Requirements to maintain significant minimum bank balances should be disclosed. Net bank overdrafts should be shown as a liability.

Although no valuation problem exists for cash in a given balance sheet, comparisons of cash over time become misleading to the extent that the value of the dollar

EXHIBIT 4   Condensed Account Form

ILLUSTRATIVE CO. C
(A Delaware Corporation)
Consolidated Balance Sheet
December 31, 19X2 and 19X1
(Dollars in Thousands)

Assets

	December 31 19X2	December 31 19X1
Current Assets:		
Cash....................................	$ 25,000	$ 24,000
Marketable securities—at cost (market value of $40,000 in 19X2, $32,000 in 19X1).........	20,000	15,000
Receivables (less allowance for uncollectible $3,000 in 19X2; $2,500 in 19X1)..........	150,000	145,000
Inventories—at cost under first-in, first-out method...........	180,000	170,000
Prepayments...............	15,000	16,000
Total current assets...............	$390,000	$370,000
Investments—at cost...............	18,000	20,000
Property, plant, and equipment—at cost less accumulated depreciation of $20,000 in 19X2, $15,000 in 19X1...............	430,000	435,000
Patents—at cost less $1,000 amortization.........	12,000	—
Total assets...................	$850,000	$825,000

Liabilities and Stockholders' Equity

	December 31 19X2	December 31 19X1
Current Liabilities:		
Accounts payable—trade.........	$160,000	$170,000
Notes payable.........	80,000	90,000
Accrued liabilities.........	30,000	30,000
Income taxes payable.........	40,000	35,000
Total current liabilities.........	$310,000	$325,000
Long-term Liabilities:		
9% Bonds payable—at par (due in 19X9).........	200,000	200,000
Total liabilities.........	$510,000	$525,000
Stockholders' Equity:		
Common stock (no par value; 100,000 shares authorized and outstanding).........	$100,000	$100,000
Retained earnings.........	240,000	200,000
Total stockholders' equity.........	$340,000	$300,000
Total liabilities and stockholders' equity.........	$850,000	$825,000

2-31

EXHIBIT 5   Condensed Report Form (A − L = SE Type)

ILLUSTRATIVE CO. D
Balance Sheet
December 31, 19X2 and 19X1
(Dollars in Thousands)

	December 31, 19X2	December 31, 19X1
Current Assets:		
Cash...	$ 25,000	$ 24,000
Marketable securities—at cost (market value $40,000 in 19X2, $32,000 in 19X1)......................................	20,000	15,000
Receivables (less allowance for uncollectibles $3,000 in 19X2; $2,500 in 19X1)..	150,000	145,000
Inventories—at cost under first-in, first-out method........	180,000	170,000
Prepayments...	15,000	16,000
Total current assets................................	$390,000	$370,000
Investments—at cost...................................	18,000	20,000
Property, plant, and equipment—at cost less accumulated depreciation of $20,000 in 19X2; $15,000 in 19X1...............	430,000	435,000
Patents—at cost less $1,000 amortization...................	12,000	—
Total assets.......................................	$850,000	$825,000
Less Liabilities		
Current Liabilities:		
Accounts payable—trade..............................	$160,000	$170,000
Notes payable.......................................	80,000	90,000
Accrued liabilities...................................	30,000	30,000
Income taxes payable—estimated......................	40,000	35,000
Total current liabilities............................	$310,000	$325,000
9% Bonds payable—at par (due in 19X9)	200,000	200,000
Total liabilities....................................	$510,000	$525,000
Stockholders' Equity (net assets).......................	$340,000	$300,000
Sources of Stockholders' Equity:		
Common stock (no par value: 100,000 shares authorized and outstanding)..	$100,000	$100,000
Retained earnings.....................................	240,000	200,000
Total stockholders' equity...........................	$340,000	$300,000

has changed. (Since this same caution applies to all comparative figures in balance sheets, it will not be repeated below.)

Marketable securities represent currently marketable investments which the company intends to convert to cash within a relatively short period of time. Material amounts of particular types, such as U.S. government securities, are often separately stated. The basis of valuation should be given, such as "cost" or "cost, which approximates market," or "lower-of-cost-or-market value." When the market value exceeds cost significantly, *ARB No. 43,* Chapter 3, calls for disclosure of the current market value at the balance sheet date. Securities of affiliates, subsidiaries, and other long-term items, even if negotiable, should be excluded. Reacquired ("treasury") securities should be shown as deductions from the related debt or owners' equity. Material amounts of pledged securities should be disclosed.

Receivables should be carried at the net amount expected to be collected. The amount of the estimated uncollectibles should be disclosed; this is not to be called a "reserve." Only current receivables should be included in the current assets category; trade accounts should be distinguished from material amounts of notes receivable and other current receivables. Examples of the latter are the current portion of receivables from stockholders, officers, and employees; installment accounts; advances (including debit balances in accounts payable); insurance and

EXHIBIT 6   Condensed Financial Position Form

ILLUSTRATIVE CO. E
Statement of Financial Position
For Years Ended December 31
(Dollars in Thousands)

	19X2	19X1
Current assets:		
Cash...	$ 25,000	$ 24,000
Marketable securities—at cost (market value $40,000 in 19X2, $32,000 in 19X1)...	20,000	15,000
Receivables (less allowance for uncollectibles, $3,000 in 19X2; $2,500 in 19X1)..	150,000	145,000
Inventories—at cost under first-in, first-out method.............	180,000	170,000
Prepayments..	15,000	16,000
Total current assets....................................	$390,000	$370,000
Less: Current liabilities:		
Accounts payable trade.......................................	$160,000	170,000
Notes payable...	80,000	90,000
Accrued liabilities..	30,000	30,000
Income taxes..	40,000	35,000
Total current liabilities................................	$310,000	$325,000
Net working capital...	$ 80,000	$ 45,000
Investments—at cost..	18,000	20,000
Property, plant, and equipment—at cost less accumulated depreciation $20,000 in 19X2; $15,000 in 19X1.......................	430,000	435,000
Patents—at cost less $1,000 amortization........................	12,000	—
Total assets less current liabilities.......................	$540,000	$500,000
Less: 9% Bonds payable—at par (due in 19X9)	200,000	200,000
Net assets...	$340,000	$300,000
Source of net assets (stockholders' equity):		
Common stock (no par value; 100,000 shares authorized and outstanding)...	$100,000	$100,000
Retained earnings...	240,000	200,000
Total...	$340,000	$300,000

tax claims; affiliates; stock subscriptions; accrued interest; and dividends declared. In line with the no-offsetting rule, credit balances in accounts receivable, if material, should be shown as liabilities. Contingent liabilities arising from discounting notes receivable or from selling accounts receivable on a recourse basis should be disclosed, preferably by footnote. Disclosure is also called for of receivables pledged as collateral for loans or credit. Accounting Principles Board Opinion No. 6 calls for unearned discounts included in receivables to be deducted from the receivables.

Unbilled costs, less related advances on account of progress payments, of long-term contractors are often classified separately if material amounts will be receivable in the future.

Inventories are usually carried at the lower-of-cost-or-market value. If material, the individual amounts of materials and supplies, work in process, finished goods, and consigned merchandise should be shown separately. Because prices often exceed cost by significant amounts and because inventory carrying values under the last-in, first-out method of costing becomes badly out of date, acute disclosure problems arise. At present, parenthetical statements or footnotes are recommended to disclose: (1) the basis of pricing (valuation of) the inventory, (2) the method of determining cost (LIFO, FIFO, average, or other), and (3) any inconsistency, and the effect thereof, caused by a change in the method of determining the inventory value. Needed for complete disclosure, but not required by the AICPA

EXHIBIT 7   Detailed Account Form

ILLUSTRATIVE CO. F
(A Nevada Corporation)
Balance Sheet
For Year Ended December 31, 19X0

(000 omitted)

Assets

Current assets:

Cash			$xxx
Marketable securities (market value $2 million)—at cost			xxx
Receivables:			
Trade accounts	$xxx		
Notes and interest	xxx		
Officers and stockholders	xxx		
Dividends	xxx		
	$xxx		
Less: Estimated uncollectibles	xxx		xxx

Inventories (at cost under lifo method adopted in 1959; current market value estimated to be $4 million):

Materials and supplies	$xxx		
Work in process	xxx		
Finished goods	xxx		xxx
Prepaid items:			
Rent	$xxx		
Insurance	xxx		
Property taxes	xxx		xxx
Other current items			xxx
Total current assets			$xxx

Investments:

Affiliates—at cost plus share of earnings	$xxx		
Bond retirement fund—at cost	xxx		
Real estate (market value $500,000)	xxx		xxx

Plant and equipment:

Land			$xxx
Buildings	$xxx		
Less: Accumulated depreciation	xxx		xxx

Other assets:

Deferred costs	$xxx		
Patents—at cost, less $2 million amortization	xxx		
Goodwill (fully amortized)	xxx		xxx
Total assets			$xxx

Liabilities and Stockholders' Equity

Current liabilities:

Accounts payable—trade			$xxx
Notes payable (including interest $25)			xxx
Payable to affiliates			xxx
Wages and commissions			xxx
Payroll taxes			xxx
Dividends			xxx
Income taxes			xxx
Estimated guarantee liability			xxx
Current portion of long-term debt (see below)			xxx
Advances by customers			xxx
Total current liabilities			$xxx

Long-term liabilities:

8% bonds payable (face value $5,000, less discount)			$xxx
9% mortgages payable			xxx
Contracts payable			$xxx
			xxx
Less: Current portion (see above)			xxx
Total long-term liabilities			xxx

Stockholders' equity:

8 % Preferred stock (cumulative; par value $100; liquidation preference $100; 10,000 shares authorized and outstanding) ... xxx

Common stock equity:

No par common stock (authorized 50,000, issued 42,000; held in treasury 2,000 shares)			$xxx
Excess preferred issue price above par			xxx
Capital from donated land			xxx
Retained earnings:			
Appropriated for contingencies	$xxx		
Appropriated for bond retirement	xxx		
Unappropriated	xxx		xxx
			$xxx
Less: Treasury stock (2,000 shares of common at cost)			xxx
Total common stock equity			$xxx
Total liabilities and stockholders' equity			$xxx

2-34

EXHIBIT 8   Condensed, Simplified Balance Sheet (Schedules Omitted)

ILLUSTRATIVE CO. G
Balance Sheet
December 31, 19X2 and 19X1
(Dollars in Millions)

Assets	December 31 19X2	19X1
Current assets:		
Cash and securities (Sch. 1).......................................	$ 60	$ 50
Receivables (Sch. 2)...	310	305
Inventories (Sch. 3)...	200	185
Prepayments..	10	10
Total current assets..	$580	$550
Property and equipment (Sch. 4)....................................	300	270
Other assets (Sch. 5)...	20	20
Totals..	$900	$840

Liabilities and Shareholders' Investment		
Current liabilities:		
Accounts payable and accrued liabilities............................	$130	$120
Federal income taxes..	80	80
Notes payable and long-term debt due within one year.................	10	5
Total current liabilities.......................................	$220	$205
Long-term debt, due after one year (Sch. 6).........................	100	100
Total liabilities...	$320	$305
Shareholders' investment—21 million common shares, outstanding Dec. 31, 19X2 (Sch. 7)...	580	535
Totals..	$900	$840

at present, are also disclosure of (1) current appreciated market value of the inventory, and (2) date of adoption of the LIFO method, if used. (Disclosure of market value would be consistent with the requirement for temporary investments, and no more difficult in most cases than value determinations under the lower-of-cost-or-market rule.) Pledged inventories and significant purchase commitments should also be disclosed.

Prepaid expenses is the customary title frequently, but inappropriately, used for prepayments for such items as insurance, taxes, and rent. They are items that will expire within one operating cycle or one year, whichever is longer. Other examples are prepaid advertising, employee welfare, and royalties. These prepayments are not current assets in the sense that they will be converted to cash; rather, they represent items which if not prepaid would have required utilization of current assets during the operating cycle. Long-term prepayments are usually called "deferred charges" and are classified as noncurrent. Items like prepaid fire insurance, if material, may be classified partly as current and partly as noncurrent. "Prepaid interest" is a misnomer; attempts to prepay interest merely result in lowering the amount borrowed. Prepayments are usually relatively small in amount, so they may be combined for statement purposes and carried at net amortized cost.

Other current assets represent current deposits, advances, and items which do not conveniently fit into the preceding classifications.

Investments is the title commonly used to represent investments, marketable or not, that a company plans to hold for long-term purposes. The basis of valuation should be stated. Although minor deviations from cost are usually ignored, a serious or permanent decline in value calls for recognition. Although not required by the AICPA, material increases in market value may be disclosed parenthetically.

In valuing nonconsolidated subsidiary investments, APB Opinion No. 18 calls for adjustments of cost for the parent's share of subsidiaries' earnings under the "equity method." Material amounts of differing types of investments also should be disclosed. Reacquired treasury securities are not assets. Material amounts of pledged investments should be disclosed.

Property, plant, and equipment is supplanting the title "fixed assets" for operating long-life assets. Nonoperating fixed assets appear as investments. Disclosure requirements for depreciating assets were increased in APB Opinion No. 12 as follows:

> The following disclosures should be made in the financial statements or notes thereto:
> a. Depreciation expense for the period,
> b. Balances of major classes of depreciable assets, by nature or function, at the balance-sheet date,
> c. Accumulated depreciation, either by major classes of depreciable assets or in total, at the balance-sheet date, and
> d. A general description of the method or methods used in computing depreciation with respect to major classes of depreciable assets.

The *basis of valuation* for plant assets also should be disclosed. This is almost always cost, but during a rapid inflationary period some firms have revalued property and equipment to reflect higher prices. This practice was proscribed by APB Opinion No. 6 in 1965, amending *ARB No. 43,* Chapter 9B, "Depreciation on Appreciation," as follows:

> The Board is of the opinion that property, plant and equipment should not be written up by an entity to reflect appraisal, market or current values which are above cost to the entity. . . . This statement may not apply to foreign operations under unusual conditions such as serious inflation or currency devaluation. . . . Whenever appreciation has been recorded on the books, income should be charged with depreciation computed on the written up amounts.

A dissent reads:

> Mr. Davidson agrees with the statement that at the present time "property, plant and equipment should not be written up" to reflect current costs, but only because he feels that current measurement techniques are inadequate for such restatement. When adequate measurement methods are developed, he believes that both the reporting of operations in the income statement and the valuation of plant in the balance sheet would be improved through the use of current rather than acquisition costs. In the meanwhile, strong efforts should be made to develop the techniques for measuring current costs.

Appraised or "discovery" values of natural resources are rarely shown in practice. The American Accounting Association's recommendation of showing both historical- and current-cost balance sheets is illustrated in the next section.

Two additional requirements are that fixed assets fully depreciated but still in use and liens against fixed assets should be fully disclosed.

Two recommendations are violated in the condensed balance sheets of some large companies when land, buildings, and equipment items first are added together and then the total accumulated depreciation is deducted. Land does not depreciate, and accumulated depreciation should be related to the individual classifications. A possible improvement for a single balance sheet is illustrated as follows:

Plant and equipment:

	Cost	Accumulated depreciation	Book value
Land	$ 100,000		$100,000
Buildings	800,000	$ 500,000	300,000
Machinery	700,000	500,000	200,000
Automobiles	200,000	100,000	100,000
Totals	$1,800,000	$1,100,000	$700,000

Other assets, intangibles, and deferred charges should be segregated by type if material in amount. The basis of valuation should be disclosed, and ideally amounts and methods of accumulated amortization. When values of such items as goodwill or promotion costs are uncertain, full disclosure explaining the nature and basis of the figures should be made. For many years discount on bonds payable was often improperly shown as an asset. Paragraph 16 of APB Opinion No. 21 now requires that such a discount be deducted from the liabilities to which it relates.

Deferred research and development costs do not appear as assets since paragraph 12 of FASB Statement No. 2 requires that all R&D costs be charged to expense as incurred.

Current liabilities should be distinguished from long-term liabilities on a basis parallel to the one used to distinguish current assets from fixed assets. Customary classification and the approximate order of current liabilities are given above. To reduce detail, related items may be grouped; however, nontrade accounts and notes payable should be distinguished from trade payables, as should material amounts of payables to officers, stockholders, or affiliates. Credit balances in accounts receivable may be combined with accounts payable, whereas significant net bank overdrafts should be reported separately. The current portion of notes and other long-term borrowing should be classified as current liabilities. Any assets pledged as security against current liabilities should be noted. Contingent liabilities are usually disclosed by footnote. The only offset of assets against liabilities permitted is government securities specifically designated for payment of taxes, as described in APB Opinion No. 10.

Under existing Accounting Principles Board recommendations, the *federal income taxes payable* appearing in current liabilities is composed of (1) the estimated current liability and (2) a current "deferred credit." The confusing state of affairs arose from conclusions in paragraph 34 of APB Opinion No. 11, "Accounting for Income Taxes," which called for "comprehensive interperiod income tax alloca-tion" (even if the tax is not reasonably expected ever to be paid); and in paragraph 57 which stated that "deferred credits relating to timing differences represent the cumulative recognition given to their tax effects and as such do not represent . . . payables in the usual sense. They should be classified in two categories—one for the net current amount and the other for the net noncurrent amount."

A dissent by three members of the board reads in part:

> Messrs. Biegler, Davidson and Queenan further believe that to require classification of deferred taxes as a current asset or current liability, in the circumstances explained in paragraph 57, would contribute to a lack of understanding of working capital, because of the commingling of contingent items with items which are expected to be realized or discharged during the normal operating cycle of a business.

Long-term liabilities reflect amounts to be paid after one year or one operating cycle, whichever is longer. Each type of liability, if material, should be separately described: bonds, mortgages, pensions, contracts, deposits, income taxes, notes, guarantees, employee benefits, etc. An alternative title for long-term items, "fixed liabilities," seems to be dying out. The description of each long-term liability preferably should include the interest rate, maturity date, pledged assets, call dates and amounts if callable, sinking fund requirements, and divided or other major restrictive covenants. Treasury bonds should be deducted from the liability for bonds payable; and premiums or discounts should be treated as liability valuation accounts. Current portions of long-term liabilities should be classified as current liabilities.

Four long-term liability items cause special difficulties in practice: deferred income taxes, deferred investment credits, long-term lease obligations, and esti-mated pensions payable. These are discussed in special chapters in this handbook, and are therefore only mentioned here.

In valuing long-term liabilities, APB Opinion No. 21, "Interest on Receivables and Payables," requires the imputation of a realistic interest rate to most long-term payables not specifically bearing interest or bearing an interest rate lower than the prevailing rate. The discount resulting from this imputation as well as "regular" bond discount should be deducted from the liabilities to which they relate.

Indeterminate-term liabilities has recently been suggested as the title for a new classification of liabilities. It follows logically from the belief that all items on the right-hand side of the balance sheet are either liabilities or owners' equity. Therefore items like *deferred income taxes* which have no certain due date or amount, would be classified as indeterminate. Although *minority interest in consolidated subsidiaries* is often considered similar in practice, under the entity theory of consolidation, it would appear as a part of owners' equity.

Stockholders' equity consists of the preferred equity and the common or residual equity. Because preferred stock is senior to the common, it should be clearly separated from the residual equity. The most important information regarding the common stockholders' equity, other than its total, is (1) the stock's legal description and (in some states) the amount of legal capital and (2) the amount of earnings retained in the business. Important information in the legal description includes: dividend and liquidation preferences; dividend arrearages; par or stated value; number of shares authorized, issued, held in treasury, outstanding, and reserved for special purposes; and dividend or other restrictions. The total amount of retained earnings and cost of treasury stock could be included with this information.

See Exhibit 7, "Detailed Account Form," for a complicated balance sheet which contains all the major classifications of stockholders' equity.

See Exhibit 8, "Condensed, Simplified Balance Sheet," for an illustration which contains only a single total of all the stockholders' equity items, relegating all except the legal description to notes and schedules. Much confusion can be avoided simply by giving only the dollar total for the stock equity and by stating the legal description and the amount of retained earnings in parenthetical or footnote form. Any further accounting details, such as "excess of issue price above par" or "donated capital," would be explained in a schedule, if desired. Although this suggestion is not yet common, it meets all disclosure and legal requirements. It is also in line with the trend toward simplification of the owners' equity section of balance sheets.

Regarding terminology for stockholders' equity, the total "capital," unless qualified, is not recommended because it has several meanings. The title "capital surplus" has been proscribed by the AICPA. Use of the word "reserve" to describe appropriations of retained earnings is still permitted although frowned on.

Special disclosure requirements affecting both preferred and common stock were instituted by the Accounting Principles Board in 1966 and 1967 as follows:

> Accordingly, the Board recommends that . . . the liquidation preference of the stock be disclosed in the equity section of the balance sheet in the aggregate either parenthetically or "in short," rather than on a per share basis or by disclosure in notes ["Liquidation Preference of Preferred Stock," APB Opinion No. 10, par. 10].

> Disclosure of changes in the separate accounts comprising stockholders' equity . . . and of the changes in the number of shares . . . is required. . . . Disclosure of such changes may take the form of separate statements or may be made in the basic financial statements or notes thereto ["Capital Changes," APB Opinion No. 12, pars. 9 and 10].

AAA Recommendations. Major recommendations for improving balance sheets made in 1966 in *A Statement of Basic Accounting Theory* recommended the presentation of current costs as well as conventional historical costs in a single statement of financial position. The inclusion of current-cost information was designed to give timely figures for a variety of predictive and decision-making purposes. Justifications for the recommendations are found in Chapter 3, entitled "Accounting Information for External Users." Pertinent quotations follow:

Accounting does not now fulfill all the requirements that are made of it. . . . A substantial part of the criticism of accounting is concerned with the limitations of historical transaction-based data to serve a significant number of desired uses. . . . Current values . . . possess a high degree of relevance for many uses. . . . The Committee recommends that both kinds of information be presented in a multi-valued report, in which the two kinds of information appear in adjacent columns. . . . Means of expressing accounting information on a current basis which meet the standards of verifiability, freedom from bias, and quantifiability are suggested in Appendix A of this statement.

Additional Disclosure in Balance Sheets. Methods and requirements of making additional disclosure in balance sheets were discussed in the first section of this chapter under the topics "Reporting Supplementary Information," and "Poststatement Disclosures."

BIBLIOGRAPHY

American Accounting Association: *Accounting and Reporting Standards for Corporate Financial Statements*, New York, 1957.
————: *A Statement of Basic Accounting Theory*, Homewood, Ill., 1966.
American Institute of Certified Public Accountants: *Accounting Trends and Techniques*, New York, annually.
————: *Accounting Research Bulletin No. 43* and *Nos. 44 to 51*, New York, 1953–1958.
————: *Statement on Auditing Standards 1, Codification of Auditing Standards and Procedures*, New York, 1973.
————: *Opinions of the Accounting Principles Board*, New York, 1952 to 1973.
Corbin, Donald A.: *Accounting and Economic Decisions*, Dodd, Mead & Company, New York, 1964.
Davidson, Sidney, J. S. Schindler, and Roman L. Weil: *Fundamentals of Accounting*, 5th ed., Dryden Press, Hinsdale, Ill., 1975.
Financial Accounting Standards Board: Statement of Financial Accounting Standards, Stamford, Conn., 1973–present.
Foulke, Roy A.: *Practical Financial Statement Analysis*, 6th ed., McGraw-Hill Book Company, New York, 1968.
Hendriksen, Elson S.: *Accounting Theory*, rev. ed., Richard D. Irwin, Homewood, Ill., 1970.
Kennedy, Ralph D., and Stewart Y. McMullen: *Financial Statements: Form, Analysis, and Interpretation*, 6th ed., Richard D. Irwin, Homewood, Ill., 1973.
Stettler, Howard F.: *Systems Based Independent Audits*, 2nd ed., Prentice-Hall, Englewood Cliffs, N.J., 1974. (See "Statement Presentation" section of individual chapters.)

Chapter **3**

Financial Statements— Statements of Changes in Financial Position and Statement of Cash Flows

HECTOR R. ANTON

Partner, Haskins & Sells, and Professor Emeritus of Business
Administration, University of California, Berkeley

ROBERT K. JAEDICKE

William R. Kimball Professor of Accounting, Stanford University

INTRODUCTION

The concept of income flow is a familiar one in accounting. Accountants think of income as a flow because it is associated with a certain time period—a month, a quarter, a year. Although income is not easy to measure, it is, nevertheless, a concept well understood by accountants, defined to be a function of revenues and expenses for a certain time period. As a flow concept, it measures the changes in the net assets of the firm (net worth) which are a result of operations (furnishing goods and services).

Now consider the concept of funds flow. Flow concepts other than income are potentially useful and therefore important. For example, it may be as important for some purposes to know how the working capital of the firm changed as to know how the net assets of the firm changed as a result of operations. Likewise, a decision maker may be interested in the causes of the changes in the cash account, or the total current assets or, for that matter, any item on the comparative balance sheets. To explain these types of changes, flow concepts other than income are needed, and these concepts are usually thought of as *funds flows*.

However, a problem arises at this point. The term "funds" is ambiguous since it can take on several different meanings. Probably the most common usage is to define funds as being equal to working capital (current assets less current liabilities). Used in this way, the statement of sources and uses of funds is the same as a statement of sources and uses of working capital and the purpose of the statement is to explain the changes in working capital. However, funds are sometimes thought of as cash, current assets, or even total assets. Used in those ways, the concept of funds flow is the same as cash flow, current asset flow, or total resources, respectively, and the purpose of the statement is to explain the changes in cash, current assets, or total resources, respectively.

POSITIONS OF AUTHORITATIVE AGENCIES ON FUNDS STATEMENTS AND CASH FLOWS

The Securities and Exchange Commission (SEC) in October 1970 adopted Article 11A of Regulation S-X, the *Statement of Source and Application of Funds,* effective for filings after December 31, 1970. The relevant part of Article 11A follows:[1]

> *Statement of Source and Application of Funds.* The statement of source and application of funds shall summarize the sources from which funds or working capital have been obtained and their disposition. (See Rule 3-01, "Financial Statements may be filed in such form and order, and may use such generally accepted terminology, as will best indicate their significance and character in the light of the provisions applicable thereto.")
>
> Material changes in the components of the net funds or working capital shall be shown in the statement or in a supporting tabulation.

[1]Securities and Exchange Commission, *Regulation S-X*, Washington, D.C., 1970, Rules 11A-02.

As a minimum, the following shall be reported:
(a) Sources of funds:
 (1) Current operations (showing separately net income or loss and the addition and deduction of specific items which did not require the expenditure or receipt of funds; e.g., depreciation and amortization, deferred income taxes, undistributed earnings or losses of unconsolidated persons, etc.)
 (2) Sale of noncurrent assets (identifying separately such items as investments, fixed assets, intangibles, etc.)
 (3) Issuance of debt securities or other long-term debt
 (4) Issuance or sale of capital stock
(b) Disposition of funds:
 (1) Purchase of noncurrent assets (identifying separately such items as investments, fixed assets, intangibles, etc.)
 (2) Redemption or repayment of debt securities or other long-term debt
 (3) Redemption or purchase of capital stock
 (4) Dividends
(c) Increase (decrease) in net funds or working capital.

In March 1973, the SEC issued Accounting Series Release (ASR) No. 142, *Reporting Cash Flows and Other Related Data.* ASR No. 142 deals with certain funds statement data and will be discussed later.

The Accounting Principles Board (APB) has issued two Opinions on the subject, APB Opinion No. 3, *The Statement of Source and Application of Funds* (1968), and APB Opinion No. 19, *Reporting Changes in Financial Position* (1971). APB Opinion No. 19 supersedes APB Opinion No. 3. In addition, three Interpretations of APB Opinion No. 19 have been issued:

1. *Number of Funds Statements Required* (February 1972);
2. *Funds Statements for Mutuals and Co-ops* (February 1972); and
3. *Funds Statements of Mutual Funds and Real Estate Companies* (June 1972).

Statement on Auditing Procedures No. 50, *Reporting on the Statement of Changes in Financial Position* (1971) required "coverage of the funds statement in both the scope and opinion paragraph," sets forth a recommended short-form accountants' report, and also gives other auditing and reporting criteria.

Many of the issues relevant to funds statements are touched on in APB Opinion No. 19 and will be developed later in the chapter. At this point note only that in spite of the APB's recommendation that "the Statement" be retitled the "Statement of Changes in Financial Position," that many companies, and indeed the AICPA itself (see, for example, the Interpretation to APB Opinion No. 19 which uses "Funds Statements," and the Industry Guide, *Audits of Investment Companies* which uses "Statement of Changes in Net Assets") continue to use either the generic name or other more descriptive titles such as "Statement of Changes in Working Capital" (Erie Lackawanna), "Statement of Sources of Funds for Construction" (Iowa Power and Light), "Statement of Changes in Net Assets" (Lehman Corp.), "Changes in Net Investment Assets" (Tri-Continental Corporation), and others. As noted, the SEC permits any appropriate title, and its Regulation S-X uses "Statement of Sources and Applications of Funds." Within the published statement, a vast majority of firms use terms such as funds from operations, funds applied, sources of funds, and the like. For internal company purposes (projections, budgets, etc.) and in discussions the generic term "funds statement" continues to be preferred. Also, in spite of the recommendation for an "all-inclusive concept" of funds, the evidence is that companies continue to use all the concepts of funds (cash, cash and short-term investments, working capital, total assets, net assets, total resources, net liquid assets, and the like) and then adjust for "as if" items in order to convert to all financial changes. Accordingly, the traditional terms will continue to be used here as being indicative of the genre.

PREPARATION OF FUNDS (WORKING CAPITAL) STATEMENT

In this chapter, the main emphasis will be on funds defined as working capital and funds defined as cash. With some modifications, working capital is the most common definition of funds in terms of financial reporting, but "cash flow" statements are important for credit evaluation and other analytical purposes.

Before discussing in detail the preparation of a statement of changes in financial position—a statement of funds, or of changes in working capital—consider the general categories of items or transactions which affect working capital (see Exhibit 1). Analysis of Exhibit 1 will show that a transaction which gives rise to a source or a use of working capital will affect one or more accounts in Part 1 of the exhibit, and one or more of the accounts in Part II. The types of such transactions are indicated in Exhibit 1.

EXHIBIT 1   Preparation of Funds (Working Capital) Statement

Transaction types	Effect on noncurrent items (Part II)	Effect on working capital (Part I)
1. Purchase of investments, land, buildings and equipment, or other plant assets	Increases the respective accounts	Decreases working capital
2. Retirement of long-term debt or purchase of treasury stock	Decreases respective liability account or shareholders' equity	Decreases working capital
3. Operations, where revenues are *less* than fund expenses (those expenses requiring the use of working capital)	Decreases retained earnings	Decreases working capital
4. Payment of dividends	Decreases retained earnings	Decreases working capital
5. Operations, where total revenues *exceed* fund expenses	Increases retained earnings	Increases working capital
6. Sale of investments, land, buildings and equipment, and other plant assets	Decreases respective plant asset accounts	Increases working capital
7. Issuance of additional long-term debt and/or capital stock	Increases liability account and/or shareholders' equity accounts	Increases working capital

However, if a transaction occurs where the only accounts affected are entirely within Part I or Part II of Exhibit 2, then working capital in total is not changed and the transaction will not appear on the funds statement. For example, assume that cash is used to pay an account payable. Such a transaction will reduce a current asset and a current liability, therefore changing the composition of working capital, but the total working capital—the difference between current assets and current liabilities—is not affected.

As another example, assume that debt is converted into common stock. In this case, long-term liabilities are reduced and the common stock account increased. Since such a transaction affects only accounts appearing in Part II of Exhibit 2 and has no effect on working capital, it will not appear on the funds (working capital) statement. The fact that such a transaction does not show up on the funds (working capital) statement does not make the transaction unimportant. Quite the contrary, for some purposes the knowledge of a large bond conversion may be highly useful. The reason the transaction does not appear on the funds statement

EXHIBIT 2   Pro Forma Balance Sheet

Part I—Working Capital:

Cash	$ xx	Accounts payable	$ xx
Marketable securities	xx	Wages payable	xx
Accounts receivable	xx	Other short-term liabilities	xx
Inventories	xx		
Prepaid expenses	xx	Total current liabilities	$xxx
Total current assets	$xxx		

Part II—Noncurrent Items:

Investments	$ xx	Bonds payable	$ xx
Buildings & equipment	xx		
Patents & other intangibles	xx	Common stock	xx
Other plant assets	xx	Retained earnings	xx
Total assets	$xxx	Total equities	$xxx

is that it has been excluded by definition. As will be shown in a later section, one powerful way to evaluate a measurement definition is to see if it is so narrow as to exclude the effect of transactions which are considered to be important.

As noted before, APB Opinion No. 19 urged that a broad concept of funds be used so as to disclose all important aspects of a firm's financing and investing activities. Specifically, in paragraph 8 the APB urged that "... acquisitions of property by issuance of securities or in exchange for other property, and conversions of long-term debt or preferred stock to common stock should be appropriately referenced in the Statement," even though these transactions do not affect working capital. Modifications of the funds (working capital) statement to comply with APB Opinion No. 19 will be given later, but first a comprehensive example will be given using a strict definition of funds as working capital.

A Comprehensive Example. The following comprehensive example will be used to illustrate the preparation of a statement of sources and uses of funds (working capital).

The beginning of the year balance sheet for the Oakdale Company is given in Exhibit 3.

The transactions for the year 19X2 are summarized below:

1. Operations for the year include credit sales of $200,000 and cash sales of $100,000. Collection of receivables amounts to $180,000.

2. The appropriate adjustment to the allowance for bad debts is estimated at 1 percent of total sales for the period. During the year $1,400 of delinquent accounts were actually written off to the allowance account.

3. Inventory purchases amounted to $180,000 for the year; $150,000 of the purchases were on account and $30,000 for cash. The cost of goods sold was calculated to be $120,000. Payments on accounts payable were $140,000.

4. Operating expenses paid in cash amounted to $55,000; in addition, $1,500 of the prepaid expenses were written off to operating expenses.

5. The note payable of $30,000 was repaid during the year.

6. Ten-year bonds of $200,000 were issued at the beginning of the year for $196,000 cash proceeds. The coupon rate of interest is 5 percent, payable annually.

7. The $100,000 bonds payable at the beginning of the year were retired by paying $60,000 in cash and converting $40,000 of the bonds to common shares on a dollar-for-dollar basis (8,000 shares at $5 par value).

8. A 10 percent stock dividend (on 6,000 shares) was declared and issued to shareholders of record at the beginning of the year. At the time the market value of the stock was $20.

EXHIBIT 3

OAKDALE COMPANY
Balance Sheet
December 31, 19X1

Assets

Cash..		$ 30,000	
Marketable securities (at cost: market $50,000)..................		20,000	
Accounts receivable...............................	$150,000		
Allowance for bad debts............................	(2,500)	147,500	
Inventory...		35,000	
Prepaid expenses.....................................		5,000	
Total current assets................................			$237,500
Investment in Riverbank, Inc. (at equity).....................		$ 80,000	
Plant assets.......................................	$160,000		
Accumulated depreciation...........................	(55,000)	105,000	185,000
Total assets.......................................			$422,500

Equities

Accounts payable...	$ 70,000	
Notes payable..	30,000	
Dividends payable..	4,000	
Total current liabilities................................		$104,000
Bonds payable...............................		100,000
Deferred income taxes......................................		20,000
Common stock ($5 par value)...............................	$ 30,000	
Retained earnings...	168,500	198,500
Total equities......................................		$422,500

---

9. 1,000 common shares were issued during the year. The cash proceeds were $25 per share. Also during the year, the company acquired 100 shares of its own stock from a retired officer at $20 per share.

10. A patent was acquired at the beginning of the year in exchange for 2,000 shares of common stock which at the time of issue had a market value of $20 per share. The useful life of the patent was estimated to be 10 years and $4,000 was written off as an expense for the year.

11. Plant assets originally costing $10,000 were sold for $1,000 at the beginning of the year. The accumulated depreciation was $7,000.

12. Plant assets were purchased for $50,000 cash.

13. The investment in Riverbank, Inc., is carried at equity. During the year, Riverbank earned profits of $25,000; $10,000 was remitted to the Oakdale Company in the form of a cash dividend. Oakdale owns 100 percent of Riverbank's stock.

14. During the year marketable securities costing $5,000 were sold for $12,000.

15. The Oakdale Company uses straight-line depreciation for reporting purposes and sum-of-the-years'-digits depreciation for tax purposes. The income tax differential is deferred. The estimated straight-line depreciation for the year is $12,000. The sum-of-the-years'-digits depreciation is $18,000. The income taxes paid in cash are $65,000; the income tax reported on the income statement is $68,000.

16. At the end of the year, the Oakdale Company acquired a new plant asset by using a long-term lease (20 years). The annual rentals are $10,000 per year payable at the end of each year. The company decided to capitalize the lease using a 6 percent discount rate which gives a capitalized value of $114,700 (i.e., $10,000 × 11.47).

17. At the end of the year, the Oakdale Company paid cash dividends of $10,000. During the year, the company also paid the dividends payable at January 1, 19X2.

The transactions listed above cover most of the situations which prove to be troublesome in funds flow analysis. Also, the example is comprehensive enough to serve as a basis for the discussion contained in later sections.

The transactions have been posted to T-accounts (see Exhibit 4). The income statement for 19X2, the balance sheet at the end of the year 19X2, and the statement of retained earnings for 19X2 are given in Exhibits 5, 6, and 7.

EXHIBIT 4   Oakdale Company Assets

Cash			
Bal.	30,000	(3)	30,000
(1)	180,000	(3)	140,000
(1)	100,000	(4)	55,000
(6)	196,000	(5)	30,000
(9)	25,000	(7)	60,000
(11)	1,000	(9)	2,000
(13)	10,000	(12)	50,000
(14)	12,000	(15)	65,000
		(17)	14,000
	554,000		446,000
Bal.	108,000		

Inventory			
Bal.	35,000	(3)	120,000
(3)	180,000		
Bal.	95,000		

Plant Assets			
Bal.	160,000	(11)	10,000
(12)	50,000		
Bal.	200,000		

Marketable Securities			
Bal.	20,000	(14)	5,000
Bal.	15,000		

Prepaid Expenses			
Bal.	5,000	(4)	1,500
Bal.	3,500		

Accumulated Depreciation			
(11)	7,000	Bal.	55,000
		(15)	12,000
		Bal.	60,000

Accounts Receivable			
Bal.	150,000	(1)	180,000
(1)	200,000	(2)	1,400
Bal.	168,600		

Investment in Riverbank, Inc.		
Bal.	80,000	
(13)	15,000	
Bal.	95,000	

Patents			
(10)	40,000	(10)	4,000
Bal.	36,000		

Leased Assets	
(16)	114,700

Allowance for Bad Debts			
(2)	1,400	Bal.	2,500
		(2)	3,000
		Bal	4,100

(91)

Accounts Payable			
(3)	140,000	Bal.	70,000
		(3)	150,000
		Bal.	80,000

Deferred Income Taxes		
	Bal.	20,000
	(15)	3,000
	Bal.	23,000

Common Stock		
	Bal.	30,000
	(7)	40,000
	(8)	3,000
	(9)	5,000
	(10)	10,000
	Bal.	88,000

Notes Payable			
(5)	30,000	Bal.	30,000

Bond Discount			
(6)	4,000	(6)	400
Bal.	3,600		

Dividends Payable			
(17)	4,000	Bal.	4,000

Interest Payable		
	(6)	10,000

Retained Earnings			
(8)	12,000	Bal.	168,500
(17)	10,000		
		Bal.	146,500

EXHIBIT 4   *(Continued)*

Bonds Payable				
(7)	60,000	Bal.	100,000	
(7)	40,000	(6)	200,000	
		Bal.	200,000	

Lease Obligations	
	(16) 114,700

Capital Contributed in Excess of Par		
	(8)	9,000
	(9)	20,000
	(10)	30,000
	Bal.	59,000

Treasury Stock	
(9) 2,000	

Sales	
	(1) 300,000

Bad Debt Expense	
(2) 3,000	

Other Operating Expenses	
(4) 55,000	
(4) 1,500	
Bal 56,500	

Cost of Goods Sold	
(3) 120,000	

Profits of Subsidiary	
	(13) 25,000

Gain on Sale of Marketable Securities	
	(14) 7,000

Interest Expense	
(6) 10,000	
(6) 400	
Bal 10,400	

Depreciation Expense	
(15) 12,000	

Income Tax Expense	
(15) 68,000	

Amortization of Patents	
(10) 4,000	

Loss on Sale of Plant Assets	
(11) 2,000	

EXHIBIT 5

OAKDALE COMPANY
Income Statement
For the Year Ending December 31, 19X2

Sales...		$300,000
Expenses:		
Cost of goods sold......................	$120,000	
Bad debt expenses.....................	3,000	
Amortization of patent..................	4,000	
Depreciation expense...................	12,000	
Other operating expenses...............	56,500	195,500
Operating profit before taxes........................		$104,500
Other income:		
Profit of subsidiary.....................	$ 25,000	
Gain on sale of marketable securities......	7,000	32,000
		$136,500
Other expenses:		
Interest expense.......................	$ 10,400	
Loss on sale of plant assets...............	2,000	12,400
Income before taxes.............................		$124,100
Income taxes....................................		68,000
Net income.....................................		$ 56,100

EXHIBIT 6

OAKDALE COMPANY
Balance Sheet
December 31, 19X2
Assets

Cash...	$108,000	
Marketable securities (at cost; market $42,000)......	15,000	
Accounts receivable..................... $168,600		
Allowance for bad debts................. 4,100	164,500	
Inventory.......................................	95,000	
Prepaid expenses...............................	3,500	
Total current assets.......................................		$386,000
Investment in Riverbank, Inc............................		95,000
Plant assets—owned........................... $200,000		
Plant assets—leased........................... 114,700		
	$314,700	
Accumulated depreciation........................	60,000	254,700
Patents.......................................		36,000
Total assets...		$771,700

Equities

Accounts payable...............................	$ 80,000	
Interest payable...............................	10,000	
Total current liabilities............................		90,000
Bonds payable.................................	$200,000	
Less: Bond discount...........................	3,600	
	$196,400	
Lease obligations..............................	114,700	
Total long-term liabilities		311,100
Deferred income taxes..................................		23,000
Common stock.............................	$ 88,000	
Capital contributed in excess of par...............	59,000	
Retained earnings..............................	202,600	
	$349,600	
Less: Treasury stock at cost......................	2,000	347,600
Total equities..		$771,700

EXHIBIT 7

OAKDALE COMPANY
Retained Earnings Statement
For the Year Ending December 31, 19X2

Beginning balance.....................		$168,500
Deduct:		
Stock dividend.............. $12,000		
Cash dividend.............. 10,000	22,000	
	$146,500	
Add: Income for 19X2.................	56,100	
Ending balance.....................	$202,600	

Preparation of Funds Statements from Account Data. In the comprehensive example, it is possible to prepare the statement of sources and uses of funds (working capital) by supplementing the information on the financial statements with the information taken directly from the accounts. This type of detailed information would ordinarily be available to the internal manager. In some circumstances (for example, in unaudited statements) a statement of changes in financial position may not be given. However, an approximate funds statement can usually be prepared from the information contained in comparative balance sheets and an income and retained earnings statement for the year in question. The problems encountered in using this method will be discussed in the next section.

A funds (working capital) statement for the Oakdale Company is given in Exhibit 8. That statement explains the change in working capital, which is calculated as follows:

Current assets 12/31/X1	$237,500	
Current liabilities 12/31/X1	104,000	
Working capital 12/31/X1		$133,500
Current assets 12/31/X2	$386,000	
Current liabilities 12/31/X2	90,000	
Working capital 12/31/X2		296,000
Increase in working capital during 19X2		$162,500

The statement in Exhibit 8 shows that the increase in working capital is largely the result of sources of working capital from operations and from the issuance of bonds whereas the major uses of funds were for retirements of bonds, purchase of fixed assets, and the payment of cash dividends.

Note the similarity of the funds statement to the income statement and the retained earnings statement. The income statement explains the change in retained earnings which results from operations. The retained earnings statement shows the causes of the change in total retained earnings. The funds statement explains the change in another balance sheet category, namely, working capital. All three statements explain changes in financial position that have taken place in various balance sheet accounts or relationships during 19X2.

The statement given in Exhibit 8 was prepared by analyzing each transaction. A detailed discussion follows:

1. Credit sales and cash sales total $300,000 and this is a source of working

EXHIBIT 8

OAKDALE COMPANY
Statement of Sources and Uses of Funds (Working Capital)
For the Year Ending December 31, 19X2

Sources of Funds
From operations:

Sales...		$300,000	
Expenses requiring the use of funds:			
Cost of goods sold..............................	$120,000		
Bad debt expense............................	3,000		
Other operating expenses........................	56,500		
Interest expenses..............................	10,000		
Income taxes..................................	65,000	254,500	
Funds provided by operations.......................................			$ 45,500
Gain on sale of marketable securities			7,000
Proceeds from sale of plant assets....................................			1,000
Proceeds from issuance of bonds.......................................			196,000
Proceeds from issuance of stock.......................................			25,000
Dividends received from Riverbank, Inc..............................			10,000
Total sources of funds..			$284,500
Uses of Funds			
Retirement of bonds for cash..............................		$ 60,000	
Purchase of treasury stock................................		2,000	
Purchase of plant assets for cash...........................		50,000	
Cash dividends..		10,000	
Total uses of funds...			122,000
Excess of sources over uses of funds (increase in working capital)............			$162,500

---

capital shown under "operations." Collections of accounts receivable do not affect the working capital balance; this transaction simply changes the form in which the working capital is held.

2. The adjustment to the allowance for bad debts ($3,000) shows up as a use of funds under operations since it involves the write-down of a current asset (net accounts receivable) with a resulting charge to income. This write-down takes place through increasing a contra current asset account, which has the effect of decreasing total current assets.

The write-off of the delinquent accounts has no effect on working capital since the particular current asset account (accounts receivable) is decreased and a *contra* current asset account (allowance for bad debts) is also reduced. There is no effect on working capital, as shown in Exhibit 9.

EXHIBIT 9   Analysis of Accounts Receivable

	Before write-off	Write-off entry	After write-off
Accounts receivable.......	$170,000	($1,400)	$168,600
Allowance for bad debts...	5,500	($1,400)	4,100
Net accounts receivable....	$164,500		$164,500

3. Inventory purchases, whether for cash or on account, do not affect working capital. A cash purchase changes the form in which current assets are held but has no effect on the total current assets. A credit purchase increases both current assets and current liabilities by the same amount, thereby leaving the difference (working capital) unchanged.

Likewise, a payment on accounts payable has no effect on working capital since current assets and current liabilities are both decreased by the same amount.

The cost of inventory used to service customers does decrease working capital, and this decrease ($120,000) is shown as part of the calculation of funds from operations.

4. The total of other operating expenses represents a use of working capital since $55,000 was a decrease in cash and $1,500 a decrease in prepaid expenses, which are considered by the Oakdale Company to be current assets. Note that if prepaid expenses were considered to be noncurrent assets, the use of funds would have been only the amount paid in cash, $55,000. In that situation, the decrease in prepaid expenses would not have affected the total current assets. This is an illustration of the fact that the funds concept and the concept of current assets are closely related.

5. The repayment of the note, which is a current liability, does not affect working capital since both total current assets and total current liabilities are decreased by $30,000 and the difference between them is not affected.

6. The issuance of bonds results in proceeds to the Oakdale Company of $196,000 and this is the amount by which working capital is increased. The discount of $4,000 does not affect working capital.

The interest payable at the end of the year is $10,000 (i.e., 5% × $200,000) and current liabilities are increased by this amount. Thus, the $10,000 portion of the interest expense represents a use of funds and is shown under the calculation of the source of funds from operations.

The amortization of the discount ($400) represents an adjustment in the interest expense for 19X2 but does not affect working capital. For income determination this adjustment is important since it gives recognition to the fact that the effective interest cost to the Oakdale Company is higher than the 5-percent coupon rate of interest. However, for funds (working capital) analysis, the amortization of $4,000 discount will have no effect until the bonds are repaid at maturity.

7. The retirement of the bonds outstanding at the beginning of the year ($100,000) has a mixed effect. The portion retired for cash ($60,000) results in a decrease in total current assets and is a use of funds (working capital). The portion of the bonds retired through conversion affects fixed liabilities and stockholders' equity but has no effect on working capital. Hence, if the definition of funds as working capital is followed literally, the conversion of bonds to stock of $40,000 would not be included in the statement. However, the APB specifies a concept of funds which is broad enough to include the results of all important financial transactions; accordingly, if the statement is part of its financial report the Oakdale Company should include this transaction in order to comply with APB Opinion No. 19. The effect of the transaction is shown in Exhibit 11 (the statement of changes in financial position) by including $40,000 as a use of funds to retire bonds, and $40,000 as a source of funds from the issuance of common stock. Exhibit 8 uses a literal interpretation of funds as equal to working capital and accordingly the transaction is not included there. The general problem of finding a suitable definition is explored in a later section.

8. The stock dividend has no effect on working capital since the entire effect of the transaction takes place within the stockholders' equity section of the balance sheet. Hence, it is excluded from the statement of sources and uses of funds (working capital).

9. The proceeds from the issuance of stock increase cash and working capital while the acquisition of treasury stock decreases cash and working capital. Hence, the effect of both transactions is included in the statement.

10. The acquisition of the patent was accomplished by issuing common shares rather than paying cash; hence, working capital was not affected. A transaction of this sort could also be highly significant. The problem is similar to that discussed under item 7 above (the conversion of bonds to stock). The transaction could be included by showing $40,000 as a use of funds to acquire patents, and $40,000 as a source of funds from issuance of common stock. If the statement is a part of the company's financial reports, such a transaction should be included to comply with APB Opinion No. 19 (see Exhibit 11). Finding a suitable definition of funds that will lead to automatic inclusion of such a transaction is the problem. In Exhibit 8 a literal definition of working capital flows is followed and, therefore, the transaction is excluded.

The amortization of the patent ($4,000), like depreciation of fixed assets to be discussed later, does not affect working capital and is not shown on the funds statement. The amortization reduces net plant assets and stockholders' equity (through the profit calculation) but has no effect on any working capital component.

11. The proceeds from the sale of plant assets ($1,000) appear as a source of funds. The "loss" on the sale has no effect on working capital.

12. The purchase of plant assets for cash represents a major use of funds in most situations. Unlike the acquisition of assets by issuing stock, a cash purchase results in a decrease in total current assets and working capital.

13. The equity method of accounting for nonconsolidated investments poses an interesting situation. The entire profit of the subsidiary is properly included in the income statement of the Oakdale Company, but only the amount of cash dividends received by the parent company has any effect on working capital. Hence, only the $10,000 in dividends received from Riverbank, Inc., has been included in the funds statement.

14. Current assets, such as marketable securities, which are sold at book value would have no effect on total current assets or working capital. However, where such assets are sold at a profit, the increase in cash is greater than the decrease in the respective current asset account and both total current assets and working capital are affected. The gain, then, is included as a source of funds.

15. As explained earlier, the depreciation of plant assets, while important for income calculation, does not affect funds. The process of depreciation results in a decrease in fixed assets and stockholders' equity (through the income calculation), but it is another example of an expense which does not affect current assets or current liabilities and thus does not require the use of funds.

In those situations where one method of depreciation is used for tax purposes and another method for reporting purposes, the income taxes reported on the income statement will usually not be the same as the income taxes paid or accrued as a current liability. This is a result of the use of the tax deferral method. In this case, the proper amount of income tax to include as a use of funds is the portion paid plus the portion accrued as a current liability (in this example a total of $65,000). The portion deferred, $3,000, will appear on the income statement and will result in an increase in deferred income taxes as well, but it will not affect working capital and thus is excluded from the funds statement.

16. The acquisition of plant assets via a lease technically does not affect working capital. If leases are capitalized, the effect is similar to a case where plant assets are acquired by a direct issuance of bonds. That is, plant assets and long-term liabilities are increased but working capital is not affected. The rental payments which take place subsequent to the capitalization of the lease will represent a *use* of funds since these payments serve to retire the liability and pay the interest on the outstanding balance of the liability. It is interesting to note that while a straight lease does not affect working capital, an ordinary sale-and-leaseback would affect the working capital position. In the sale-and-leaseback situation, a plant asset is sold, giving rise to an increase in cash. This results in a source of working capital to the firm. The acquisition of a major asset by use of a lease which is capitalized is yet another example of an important transaction that should be included in a statement appearing in a financial report prepared in accordance with APB Opinion No. 19 even though working capital is not affected (see Exhibit 11). Following the literal definition of working capital used in preparing Exhibit 8, this is a nonfund transaction and is, therefore, excluded.

17. The dividends paid in cash this year ($10,000) represent a use of funds. The payment of the dividends payable liability decreases both current assets and liabilities but does not affect the difference (working capital). A declaration of new dividends would, like a cash payment of new dividends, represent a use of funds since total current liabilities would be increased and working capital reduced.

Alternative Forms of Presenting Funds Statements.   While Exhibit 8 illustrates a complete and analytical presentation of the funds statement, most published funds statements use a summary version. The income statement will ordinarily detail the same data as the "funds from operations" section of the funds statement, but will add back nonfund charges (such as depreciation) and credits. A summary of funds from operations section may be reconstructed by adjusting the net income by the amount of these nonfund items. Exhibit 10 presents a summary funds statement for the Oakdale Company.

THE STATEMENT OF CHANGES IN FINANCIAL POSITION

Exhibit 11 is prepared in compliance with APB Opinion No. 19 and thus gives effect to transactions 7, 10, and 16. It is presented here for illustrative purposes.

EXHIBIT 10

OAKDALE COMPANY
Summary Statement of Sources and Uses of Funds
For the Year Ending December 31, 19X2

Source of Funds

From Operations:

Net income................................	$ 56,100	
Add: Depreciation.........................	12,000	
Amortization of patent....................	4,000	
Deferred taxes............................	3,000	
Amortization of bond discount.............	400	
Loss on sale of plant assets..............	2,000	$ 77,500
Less: Increased equity in Riverbank, Inc............		15,000
Total funds from operations.......................		$ 62,500
From sale of plant assets.........................		1,000
From issuance of bonds............................		196,000
From issuance of stock............................		25,000
Total sources.................................		$284,500

Uses of Funds

Retirement of bonds......................	$60,000	
Purchase of treasury stock...............	2,000	
Purchase of plant assets.................	50,000	
Cash dividends...........................	10,000	
Total uses...................................		$122,000
Excess of sources over uses of funds................		$162,500

EXHIBIT 11

OAKDALE COMPANY
Statement of Changes in Financial Position
For the Year Ended December 31, 19X2

Source of Funds

From Operations:

Net income	$ 56,100	
Add: Depreciation	12,000	
Amortization of patents	4,000	
Deferred taxes	3,000	
Amortization of bond discount	400	
Loss on sale of plant assets	2,000	
		$ 77,500
Less: Increased equity in Riverbank, Inc.		15,000
Total funds from operations		$ 62,500
From sale of plant assets	1,000	
From issuance of common stock	105,000	
From issuance of lease obligations	114,700	
From issuance of bonds	196,000	
Total sources		$479,200

Uses of Funds

Retirement of bonds	$100,000	
Purchase of patents	40,000	
Purchase of long-term leases	114,700	
Purchase of plant assets	50,000	
Acquisition of treasury stock	2,000	
Cash dividends paid	10,000	
Total uses		316,700
Net increase in working capital		$162,500

APB Opinion No. 19 calls for disclosure of net changes in each element of working capital. Accordingly, a schedule of changes in working capital would be required. That schedule is given as Exhibit 13.

PREPARATION TECHNIQUES

In the comprehensive example given in the preceding section, the funds statement was prepared by analyzing each transaction and working directly from the detailed information in the accounts. It is possible to prepare a funds statement from comparative balance sheets, a statement of income and retained earnings, and some realistic assumptions. Obviously, such a statement may differ from one prepared from a detailed knowledge of all transactions. However, in most cases the differences will not be significant enough to affect the usefulness of the statement.

Funds Statements Prepared from Comparative Statements. The first step in this procedure is to isolate the changes that have taken place as reflected by the beginning and ending balance sheets. This is done in Exhibit 12 for the Oakdale Company.

Exhibit 12 shows that working capital has increased by $162,500 and that this increase resulted from current assets increasing by $148,500 and current liabilities decreasing by $14,000. A statement of working capital changes should be prepared which would show the changes in each working capital account. Such a statement is useful because it reflects the changes in the *composition* of working capital. This statement is illustrated in Exhibit 13.

The statement of working capital changes in Exhibit 13 shows which working

EXHIBIT 12

OAKDALE COMPANY
Analysis of Balance Sheet Changes

	12/31/X1	12/31/X2	Increase or (decrease)
Current assets.............................	$237,500	$386,000	$148,500
Current liabilities..........................	104,000	90,000	(14,000)
Working capital............................	$133,500	$296,000	$162,500
Investment in Riverbank, Inc.................	80,000	95,000	15,000
Plant assets—owned.......................	160,000	200,000	40,000
Accumulated depreciation....................	(55,000)	(60,000)	(5,000)
Plant assets—leased.......................	—	114,700	114,700
Patent......................................	—	36,000	36,000
	$318,500	$681,700	$363,200
Bonds payable.............................	$100,000	$200,000	$100,000
Bond discount..............................	—	(3,600)	(3,600)
Lease obligations...........................	—	114,700	114,700
Deferred income taxes.......................	20,000	23,000	3,000
	$120,000	$334,100	$214,100
Total net assets............................	$198,500	$347,600	$149,100
Common stock.............................	$ 30,000	$ 88,000	$ 58,000
Excess of contributed capital over par..........	—	59,000	59,000
Retained earnings...........................	168,500	202,600	34,100
	$198,500	$349,600	$151,100
Less: Treasury stock........................	—	(2,000)	(2,000)
Total shareholders' equity...................	$198,500	$347,600	$149,100

EXHIBIT 13

OAKDALE COMPANY
Statement of Working Capital Changes
For the Year Ending December 31, 19X2

Increases in Working Capital

Increase in cash........................	$78,000	
Increase in net accounts receivable.........	17,000	
Increase in inventories...................	60,000	
Decrease in notes payable................	30,000	
Decrease in dividends payable............	4,000	
		$189,000

Decreases in Working Capital

Decrease in marketable securities...........	$ 5,000	
Decrease in prepaid expenses..............	1,500	
Increase in accounts payable..............	10,000	
Increase in interest payable...............	10,000	
		$ 26,500
Increase in working capital........................		$162,500

---

capital items were affected. The question now is: What caused the aggregate increase of $162,500? This can be answered by analyzing the balance sheet changes calculated in Exhibit 12 and preparing a statement of sources and uses of funds (working capital). The income statement (Exhibit 5) and the retained earnings statement (Exhibit 7) will also be used. It is assumed that no other information is available. The more detail that is given in the financial statements, the closer the funds statement prepared from analyzing balance sheet changes will be to the funds statement prepared from analyzing the detailed transaction data in the accounts. The balance sheet changes are now analyzed in detail.

1. The net increase in the investment in Riverbank, Inc., was $15,000. Yet the profit of the subsidiary reported on the income statement is $25,000. Since the equity method is used in accounting for this investment, it is reasonable to assume that $10,000 of the profit was received in the form of a cash dividend and that this is the source of funds.

2. The Plant Assets—Owned account increased by $40,000 and the Accumulated Depreciation account increased by $5,000. The income statement shows depreciation expense of $12,000 and a loss on the sale of plant assets of $2,000. Using this information, the following T-accounts can be reconstructed.

Plant Assets—Owned				Accumulated Depreciation	
Beginning balance from balance sheet	160,000			Beginning balance from balance sheet	55,000
				Depreciation added as	
(3)	49,000	(2) 9,000	(1) 7,000	per income statement	12,000
Ending balance from balance sheet	200,000			Ending balance from balance sheet	60,000

After using this information, it is apparent that transaction (1), the $7,000 debit in the Accumulated Depreciation account, is needed to make the account balance and it is reasonable to assume that it is associated with the sale of assets. This being so, the credit to the Plant Asset account as a result of the sale (2) would be at least $2,000 greater, or $9,000, to account for the loss. Since the proceeds from the sale are unknown, it is not possible to determine the exact credit to the Plant Asset account. However, (3) using the depreciation write-off plus the loss as the basis for the credit to the Plant Asset account, a debit of $49,000 is needed to make this account balance. This amount, $49,000, is the *net* purchases of plant assets. That is, this amount is the total purchases less the proceeds of any sales. If either the total purchases or the proceeds from sales of assets were known, the uses of funds for purchases and the sources of funds from sales of plant assets could be completely determined. Without this information, an amount of $49,000 is reported as the use of funds for the purchase (net) of plant assets.

3. The increase in the Patent account is $36,000. However, the income statement indicates amortization of $4,000 (a nonfund expense). Hence, it would be assumed that there was a use of funds of $40,000 to acquire a patent. The detailed transaction data reveal that the patent was acquired for shares. However, with only the information available in the financial statements, there would be no way to know that this had happened.

4. The Plant Assets—Leased account increased by $114,700, and so did the long-term liability. Hence, it would be reasonable to assume that the assets were leased outright rather than being leased through a sale-and-leaseback transaction. The increase in the asset and liability account would not be included in the funds (working capital) statement under the strict definition.

5. The Bonds Payable Account increased by $100,000 while the Bond Discount account increased by $3,600. However, it is apparent that $400 of bond discount was amortized since the current liability for interest payable increased by $10,000 while the interest expense shown on the income statement was $10,400. Hence, $96,000 (i.e., $100,000 increase in bonds payable less $4,000 increase in bond discount) would be shown as the net source of funds (working capital) from the issuance of bonds. From the comparative statement data, there is no way of knowing that the net proceeds from issuance were really $196,000 with a $100,000 retirement.

6. Deferred income taxes increased by $3,000, so it would be assumed that the income tax shown on the income statement which actually required a use of funds was $65,000 (i.e., $68,000 less $3,000 increase in deferred income taxes).

7. Common Stock increased by $58,000 and the Excess of Contributed Capital over Par account increased by $59,000. However, the retained earnings statement (Exhibit 7) shows a stock dividend of $12,000. Hence, the source of funds from the issuance of shares would be estimated at $105,000 (i.e., $59,000 plus $58,000 less $12,000 stock dividend). The fact that some of the shares were issued for a patent (see item 3) and some were issued in connection with the bond conversion (see item 5) would not be apparent from the information contained in the comparative statements.

8. The Retained Earnings account increased by $34,100. The retained earnings statement (Exhibit 7) shows a stock dividend of $12,000, which is taken care of by the adjustment to Capital Stock and the related Excess account (see item 7). The $10,000 cash dividend would be shown on the statement as a use of funds.

9. The income after taxes is shown as $56,100. This must be adjusted to eliminate the nonfund items, as summarized below.

Income per income statement		$56,100
Add: Expenses not requiring the use of funds (working capital):		
Amortization of patent (Item 3)	$ 4,000	
Depreciation expense (Item 2)	12,000	
Interest expense (Item 5)	400	
Loss on sale of assets (Item 2)	2,000	
Deferred income taxes (Item 6)	3,000	21,400
		$77,500
Deduct:		
Income from subsidiary; (dividends received shown separately—Item 1)	$25,000	
Gain on sale of marketable securities to be shown separately as source of funds	7,000	32,000
Source of funds from operations		$45,500

10. The increase in the Treasury Stock account would be assumed to be a use of funds to acquire Oakdale Company's own common stock.

The statement of funds (working capital) can now be prepared. (The number in parentheses indicates the item number in which the explanation appears.) This statement is shown in column 1 of Exhibit 14, with the statement prepared directly from the account information (see Exhibit 8) shown in column 2. The differences between the two statements are analyzed below.

EXHIBIT 14

OAKDALE COMPANY
Statement of Source and Uses of Funds (Working Capital)
For the Year Ending December 31, 19X2

	(1) As prepared from comparative statement information	(2) As prepared from information in accounts (see Exhibit 8)	Differences (column 1 less column 2)
Sources			
From operations................	$ 45,500 (9)	$ 45,500	$ —
From sale of plant assets.........	— (2)	1,000	(1,000)
From sale of marketable securities	7,000 (9)	7,000	—
From issuance of bonds..........	96,000 (5)	196,000	(100,000)
From issuance of stock..........	105,000 (7)	25,000	80,000
From Riverbank, Inc., dividends..	10,000 (1)	10,000	—
	$263,500	$284,500	$(21,000)
Uses			
Retirement of bonds............	—	$ 60,000	$(60,000)
Purchase of treasury stock.......	$ 2,000 (10)	2,000	—
Purchase of plant assets.........	49,000 (2)	50,000	(1,000)
Cash dividend..................	10,000 (8)	10,000	—
Purchase of patent.............	40,000 (3)	—	40,000
	$101,000	$122,000	$(21,000)
Increase in working capital........	$162,500	$162,500	$ —

As can be seen from Exhibit 14, both statements explain the change in working capital of $162,500, but in slightly different ways. The statement prepared from comparative statement information (column 1) shows both sources and uses of funds as $21,000 less than the statement prepared from account data (column 2). In the statement prepared from account data, the proceeds from the sale of plant assets of $1,000 is known and is shown as a source. In the statement prepared from published data, this amount could not be isolated and, as a result, purchases of plant assets are shown as a use of funds at a net of $49,000.

The account data reveals that $40,000 of common stock was used to acquire a patent, and $40,000 was used for bond conversion. These facts are not apparent from the comparative statement data; hence, there (column 1 statement) the source of funds from the sale of stock is $80,000 greater than in the account statement. As a result, the patent shows up as a use of funds in the statement prepared from published data, while this is not true of the other statement. Also, $40,000 of the $100,000 difference in the proceeds from the sale of bonds between the two statements results from the fact that the retirement of bonds through conversion to stock does not show up in the comparative statement data. The other $60,000 of the $100,000 difference regarding the proceeds from the sale of bonds is accounted for by the $60,000 cash retirement of bonds, which does not show up in the comparative statement data.

A T-Account Work Sheet.   Several different work-sheet methods are available to aid in the preparation of funds statements. These methods provide a systematic way of handling the data in complex problems. Two of the many methods will be explained here. The first, a T-account method, is discussed below.[2] Another work-sheet method using reversing and reclassification entries is discussed in the next section.[3] The example just given is used as a basis for the discussion of both methods. Hence, the statement that results will be the same as shown in column 1 of Exhibit 14.

Exhibit 15 shows the T-account work sheet. A T-account is used for each of the accounts shown in the statement of balance sheet changes, Exhibit 12. Only the increases and decreases in the respective accounts are shown, and they are identified as debits or credits. Working Capital is debited with the increase in working capital, and all other asset, contra-liability, and contra-capital accounts are debited for increases and credited for decreases. For example, Plant Assets increased by $40,000, so this is recorded as a debit.

The liability, capital, and contra-asset accounts are credited for increases and debited for decreases. For example, bonds payable increased by $100,000, so this amount is recorded as a credit. All of the initial entries of the increases and decreases are numbered (1). Obviously, the debits and credits will be equal since the total *net* credit balances of all the noncurrent accounts must equal the debit balance in the Working Capital account. All of the initial entries are then ruled with a double underscore.

The next step is to record, in a straightforward manner, the individual transactions which gave rise to these initial balances. The individual transactions will be inferred from the comparative statement data in this example since it is assumed that the statement of funds is not being prepared from a detailed knowledge of each transaction that took place during the period. Any time an inferred transaction affects a current asset or liability account, the debit or credit will be to the Working Capital account. For example, the retained earnings statement reveals that cash dividends of $10,000 were paid. Hence, working capital is credited for $10,000 to reflect the use of working capital, and retained earnings is debited for $10,000 (see item 3).

The advantage of this procedure is that the entries can be made in a straightforward manner and the confusion of reversing entries can be avoided. Also, this method provides a partial check on the procedure in that the entries *below* the double underscore should add algebraically to the net debit or credit shown above the double underscore, and the individual items entered in the Working Capital account should completely explain the increase or decrease in working capital for the period. The statement of funds (working capital) can then be prepared from the detail in the Working Capital account. In Exhibit 15, the items entered below

---

[2]See William J. Vatter, "Direct Method for the Preparation of Funds Statements," *Journal of Accountancy,* vol. 21, pp. 479–491, June 1946. A work-sheet approach for the direct method was first illustrated in Roy B. Kester, *Advanced Accounting,* The Ronald Press Company, New York, 1946, pp. 660–675. A more modern treatment of this direct method is contained in chap. 19 of Sidney Davidson, James S. Schindler, and Roman L. Weil, *Fundamentals of Accounting,* 5th ed., The Dryden Press, Hinsdale, Ill., 1975.

[3]For a complete discussion of this method see Glenn L. Johnson and James A. Gentry, Jr., *Finney and Miller's Principles of Accounting—Intermediate,* 7th ed., Prentice-Hall, Englewood Cliffs, N.J., 1974, chap. 25; and Walter B. Meigs, A. N. Mosich, Charles E. Johnson, and Thomas F. Keller, *Intermediate Accounting,* McGraw-Hill Book Company, 3rd ed., New York, 1974, chap. 25.

EXHIBIT 15   The T-Account Work Sheet

Working Capital

(1)	162,500		
(5)	105,000	(3)	10,000
(8)	96,000	(11)	40,000
(9)	10,000	(16)	49,000
(13)	7,000	(17)	2,000
(18)	45,500		

Working Capital— Operations

(2)	56,100	(9)	25,000
(7)	400	(13)	7,000
(10)	4,000	(18)	45,500
(12)	3,000		
(14)	12,000		
(15)	2,000		

Patent

(1)	36,000		
(11)	40,000	(10)	4,000

Common Stock

		(1)	58,000
		(4)	3,000
		(5)	55,000

Treasury Stock

(1)	2,000	
(17)	2,000	

Investment in Riverbank, Inc.

(1)	15,000	
(9)	15,000	

Plant Assets—Leased

(1)	114,700	
(6)	114,700	

Bonds Payable

		(1)	100,000
		(8)	100,000

Lease Obligations

		(1)	114,700
		(6)	114,700

Excess of Capital Contributed over Par

		(1)	59,000
		(4)	9,000
		(5)	50,000

Plant Assets—Owned

(1)	40,000		
(16)	49,000	(15)	9,000

Accumulated Depreciation

		(1)	5,000
(15)	7,000	(14)	12,000

Bond Discount

(1)	3,600		
(8)	4,000	(7)	400

Deferred Income Taxes

		(1)	3,000
		(12)	3,000

Retained Earnings

		(1)	34,100
(3)	10,000		
(4)	12,000	(2)	56,100

the first double underscore in the Working Capital account are the same as those appearing in the funds statement given in column 1 of Exhibit 14.

Each numbered item in Exhibit 15 is explained below:

1. Enter the initial increases and decreases in each account.

2. Transfer the income, $56,100 for 19X2, from Retained Earnings to Working Capital—Operations to facilitate detailed analysis.

3. Record the $10,000 cash dividend (a use of funds—working capital).

4. Record the stock dividend, $12,000.

5. Record the proceeds from the sale of common stock (a source of funds), $105,000.

6. Record the capitalization of the lease.

7. Record the bond discount written off during 19X2.

8. Record the proceeds of the sale of bonds (a source of funds).

9. Record the profit of the subsidiary (show the $10,000 received in the form of dividends as a source of funds).

10. Record the amortization of the patent.

11. Record the acquisition of the patent (a use of funds).

12. Record the deferred income taxes.

13. Record the profit on the sale of current assets—marketable securities (a source of funds).

14. Record the depreciation for 19X2.

15. Record the sale of plant assets.

16. Record the purchase of plant assets (a use of funds).

17. Record the purchase of treasury stock (a use of funds).

18. Transfer funds provided by operations from the account Working Capital—Operations to the Working Capital account.

A Work Sheet Using Reversing and Reclassification Entries. An alternative to the T-account method illustrated above is a work-sheet method which uses reversing and reclassification entries. A work sheet prepared by using this method is illustrated in Exhibit 16. The beginning and ending balance sheets are entered in the first two columns and the debit and credit changes are determined and entered in columns 3 and 4. The changes which have taken place in the current assets and current liabilities are transferred to working capital (columns 9 and 10), and this information is the basis for the statement of changes in working capital as given in Exhibit 13.

The necessary reversing and reclassification entries are given in columns 5 and 6, and each entry is explained as follows:

1. Transfer net income from Retained Earnings to sources of funds from operations to facilitate detailed analysis.

2. Reclassify cash dividends paid as a use of funds.

3. Reverse the effect of the stock dividend, which does not require the use of funds.

4. Reverse the capitalization of leases, which is a nonfund item.

5. Reverse the entry for bond discount and for the portion written off to income since both are nonfund items.

6. Reverse the increase in investment in Riverbank, Inc., which is a nonfund item and reclassify the cash dividends received from Riverbank, Inc., as a separate source of funds.

7. Reverse the amortization of the patent.

8. Reverse the deferred income taxes charged against income.

9. Reclassify the profit on the sale of current assets (marketable securities) as a separate source of funds.

10. Reverse the entry for depreciation expense, which is a nonfund item.

11. Reverse the entry for the sale of plant assets, which is nonfund.

After the entries described above are made, the amounts in the "changes" columns are added to the amounts in columns 5 and 6 for all of the noncurrent accounts, and the balances, if any, are carried to columns 7 and 8 as either sources or uses of funds. The information in the funds columns furnishes the basis for the statement of funds as given in column 1 of Exhibit 14.

USES OF FUNDS ANALYSIS

Authoritative accounting bodies, including the SEC and the APB, have considered the funds statement important enough to require its inclusion in financial reports. In the second section of this chapter the relevant portions of these requirements—the SEC's Article 11A of Regulation S-X and the AICPA's APB Opinion No. 19—were discussed. APB Opinion No. 3, although superseded by APB Opinion No. 19, also contains useful information in the potential uses of funds statements, and the distinction between information regarding the flow of funds and information regarding net income. The latter problem has caused some confusion and will be discussed in a later section. The present section discusses the broad uses of funds analysis.

EXHIBIT 16

OAKDALE COMPANY
Funds Statement Worksheet—Using Reversing and Reclassification Entries
For the Year Ending December 31, 19X2

	Balance sheet		Changes		Reversing and reclassification entries		Funds		Working capital	
	12/31/X1	12/31/X2	Debit	Credit	(Dr)	(Cr)	Uses	Sources	Increases	Decreases
Cash	30,000	108,000	78,000						78,000	
Marketable securities	20,000	15,000		5,000						5,000
Accounts receivable	150,000	168,600	18,600						17,000	
Allowance for bad debts	(2,500)	(4,100)		1,600					{	
Inventory	35,000	95,000	60,000						60,000	
Prepaid expenses	5,000	3,500		1,500						1,500
Total current assets	237,500	386,000								
Accounts payable	70,000	80,000		10,000						10,000
Notes payable	30,000	—	30,000						30,000	
Dividends payable	4,000	—	4,000						4,000	
Interest payable	—	10,000		10,000						10,000
Total current liabilities	104,000	90,000								
Working capital	133,500	296,000	190,600	28,100						
Investment in Riverbank, Inc.	80,000	95,000	15,000		(11) 9,000	(6) 15,000	—	—		
Plant assets—owned	160,000	200,000	40,000		(10) 12,000	(11) 7,000	49,000			
Accumulated depreciation	(55,000)	(60,000)		5,000						
Plant assets—leased	—	114,700	114,700			(4) 114,700	—	—		
Patent	—	36,000	36,000		(7) 4,000		40,000			
	318,500	681,700								
Bonds payable	100,000	200,000		100,000	(5) 4,000			96,000		
Bond discount	—	(3,600)	3,600			(5) 3,600				
Lease obligations	—	114,700		114,700	(4) 114,700		—	—		
Deferred income taxes	20,000	23,000		3,000	(8) 3,000					
	120,000	334,100								
Total net assets	198,500	347,600								

Common stock................	30,000	88,000	(3)	58,000	(3)	3,000							105,000	
Excess of contributed capital over par........	—	59,000	(3)	59,000	(3)	9,000	(2)	10,000			—		—	
Retained earnings........	168,500	202,600	(1)	34,100	(1)	56,100	(3)	12,000						
Less: Treasury stock......	198,500	349,600									2,000		45,500	
	—	(2,000)		2,000										
Total shareholders' equity	198,500	347,600		401,900										
				401,900										
Sources of funds from operations.............			(6)(9)		(11)	2,000								
					(1)	56,100							7,000	
					(5)	400								
					(6)	4,000							10,000	
					(8)	3,000								
					(10)	12,000								
Dividends paid............			(2)	10,000		25,000	(11)	2,000			10,000			
Profit on sale of marketable securities...........					(9)	7,000								
Dividends received from Riverbank, Inc.........					(9)	7,000								
					(6)	10,000								
						256,800								
						256,800								
Total sources and uses of funds.................									101,000		263,500		189,000	26,500
									162,500					162,500
Increase in funds........									263,500		263,500		189,000	189,000

Flow of funds analysis has become an increasingly useful technique. At the macroeconomic level, data has been provided, and the technique has been used by the Department of Commerce in its "National Income and Product Accounts," by the Federal Reserve System in its "Flow-of-Funds National Accounts," by the Council of Economic Advisers and the President in "The Sources and Uses of Corporate Funds" section of *The Economic Report(s) of the President*, and by private researchers and analysts. These have become important tools for economic analysis. Accountants, of course, have long used funds statements for both internal and external use. With the release of APB Opinions No. 3 and 19, however, the use of funds statements in published financial statements was greatly accelerated. As noted by the APB: "Information about the sources from which a company obtains funds and the uses to which such funds are put may be useful for a variety of purposes affecting both operating and investment decisions."

The Funds Statement as an Operating Statement. Some of the more detailed financial questions that may be answered by reference to the funds statement are listed in *Accounting Research Study No. 2:*[4]

1. Where did the profits go?
2. Why were dividends not larger?
3. How was it possible to distribute dividends in excess of current earnings or in the presence of a net loss for the period?
4. Why are the net current assets down although the net income is up?
5. How is it that the net current assets are up even though there was a net loss for the period?
6. Why must money be borrowed to finance purchases of new plant and equipment when the required amount is exceeded by the "cash flow"—(the sum of the net income and depreciation)?
7. How was the expansion in plant and equipment financed?
8. What happened to the proceeds of the sale of plant and equipment resulting from a contraction of operations?
9. How was the retirement of debt accomplished?
10. What became of the assets derived from an increase in outstanding capital stock?
11. What became of the proceeds of the bond issue?
12. How was the increase in working capital financed?

All published funds statements are historical in nature. They may be periodic for a single year, comparative for two or three years, or trendential (summaries for many years). Each type is found in published reports. The type of questions raised by Mason may be answered by reference to single-period or short-run comparative funds statements. Recourse to the longer-run statements, such as a 10- or 20-year summary, will divulge policy and financing patterns on such things as dividend payments (perhaps as a percentage of net income or even related to "funds from operations"), financing of capital expenditures, use of and management of bonded debt, and financing from internal earnings policy. While a single year's statement may give an indication of how such items were treated in the current period, it cannot possibly divulge patterns. For these, the long-run comparative summaries are imperative.

A common use of published funds statements is to help show the relationship of working capital changes to net income (see questions 1, 3, 4, 5). Here the real issue is the understanding that net income is not synonymous with funds (working capital) in the short run, that funds from operations are almost always larger than net income, and that available working capital can be determined only from the entire funds statement and not from a single item. The "funds from operations" section of the statement does serve to explain why some firms may continue to operate in the short run even while suffering losses. The complete statement may

[4]Perry Mason, "Cash Flow Analysis and the Funds Statement," *ARS No. 2*, AICPA, New York, 1961, pp. 49–50.

well explain why some firms go out of business or get into financial difficulties in spite of continued good profits.

Another useful analysis, but one which is as yet limited to internal management, is the ability to measure divisional financial effectiveness. Divisional working capital statements may help corporate management to assess divisional financial management in short-run versus long-run financing, borrowing effectiveness, prudent working capital position, and the like, in addition to determining divisional internal fund generation capabilities. Until divisional reporting becomes more widespread, this type of analysis will be limited to management.

Fund Analyses for Planning and Decision Making.   Historical funds statements are extremely useful in determining past practices and thus obtaining information for current and future decisions. However, as with all historical data, a funds statement must be reinterpreted for its new uses. Companies frequently prepare statements on a projected basis. The projected statements are relatively easy to construct. Sales forecasts are generally made and well known, and costs-to-volume relationships aid in determining not only the expected costs but also the required facilities. These, in turn, aid in the determination of depreciation allowances (and indirectly the magnitude of expected cash outlays for taxes). Funds from operations result from this process. Established patterns for dividend payments, present capital (bond and preferred stock) services, expected asset and bond retirements, and expected working capital requirements may all be projected. The result is a projected working capital funds statement for either single or multiple periods. Financing deficiencies and obligations can then be readily determined; the required financing may be planned or, if that is not feasible, alternative operating plans may have to be developed.

It is possible, further, to run sensitivity tests by varying the major financing premises (sales, cost/volume, plant expenditures, bonds, etc.). Often the life of the long-term debt is crucial. These effects can be estimated by projecting funds statements for the expected period of the loan and observing the results. For example, a 10-year bond issue may prove disastrous if it has to be repaid at the 10-year maturity, but it may be an excellent means of financing a plant expansion if the maturity is longer, say, 20 years. In this way funds analysis serves to point out not only the required financing but also its timing and duration.

Weaknesses of the Working Capital Concept of Funds.   Although the working capital concept of funds had been by far the most used in published financial reports, its use has not been recommended by the APB. In both APB Opinion No. 3 and APB Opinion No. 19, the Board was clearly concerned about working capital being too restrictive a concept. In APB Opinion No. 3, Paragraph 9, the Board said ". . . a concept broader than working capital should be used which can be characterized or defined as 'all financial resources,' so that the statement will include the financial aspects of all significant transactions, e.g. 'non-fund' transactions such as the acquisitions of property through the issue of securities." In APB Opinion No. 19, Paragraph 8, the Board urged the use of a broad concept taking into account all changes in financial position, and recommended the title *Statement of Changes in Financial Position.*

The rationale for the use of working capital, however, is extremely good. First, it clearly differentiates between short- and long-term items. Long-term financing is specifically portrayed in the statement. Long-term items requiring financing in the current period are likewise clearly featured. Working capital requirements, in toto, are shown as residual. This is in keeping with the long-accepted practice of differentiating between current and long-term items. Second, business society is clearly a credit society. For this reason receivables and payables are considered constructive receipts and payments; that is, it is understood that they shall be settled in the short run with short-run funds.

The remaining item, inventory, is not so easy to rationalize. Inventory needs a transformation before it becomes a money asset. Nevertheless, the long-established practice is to include it as a working capital item. Where changes in inventories are significant, however, the relegation of this item to a mere line in a supporting schedule (see Exhibit 13) is a serious shortcoming. Some critics maintain that the working capital concept is too broad—that not only are inventories significant, but also short-run financing is important. These critics maintain that if significant changes occur in either receivables or current payables, the changes should be reflected in the funds statement.

Another weakness of the working capital concept (discussed earlier) has to do with so-called nonfund exchanges such as plant assets acquired directly in exchange for either stock or bonds. Significant transactions of this sort can hardly be ignored. Further, conversions of bonds into stock are similarly nonfund transactions. The omission of such important financial flows poses a real limitation on the working capital concept of funds. Of course, it is possible to treat these items as if two working capital flows had taken place. For example, in the direct exchange of assets for long-term debt, one may assume that there was an inflow of funds from the incurrence of the debt and a concurrent outflow of funds for the asset acquisition.

These weaknesses lend support to other concepts of funds, which will be discussed in the next sections.

PREPARATION OF FUNDS STATEMENTS USING DEFINITIONS OF FUNDS OTHER THAN WORKING CAPITAL

In the preceding sections the primary emphasis has been on the preparation of funds statements, given a definition of funds as working capital. Now the effect on the funds statement of using concepts other than working capital will be developed. In a sense, funds may be defined as any positive asset or net asset classification. For practical purposes, however, the following comprise all the viable alternative concepts of funds: (1) total current assets, (2) total money (quick) assets, (3) net money (quick) assets, (4) total assets, and (5) cash and its equivalent. All five can be modified to comply with APB Opinion No. 19. (See, for example, the earlier adjustment of Exhibit 8 resulting in Exhibit 11.) The first four will be discussed in this section, while the fifth will be discussed in the next section.

The question may be raised as to why so many concepts exist, and furthermore why they are used. The answer is that statements prepared under each of these concepts emphasize different aspects and are therefore more relevant for alternative presentations and analyses. These will be discussed more fully after the effects of the various concepts have been developed. Once again, the data presented in the Oakdale Company example will be used for illustrative purposes. Exhibit 17 shows the funds statements resulting from the use of alternative concepts 1 through 4.

The first three alternative concepts of funds are related to the working capital concept in that they all pertain to items ordinarily classified as current. The working capital concept is most closely related to the first alternative, funds as current assets. Since working capital has been defined as current assets less current liabilities, the primary adjustment to elicit a funds statement based on a current asset definition of funds is to exclude the current liabilities from the funds concept. Therefore, changes affecting current liabilities result in funds flows. These will be explained in detail below.

The second alternative concept, funds defined as total money or quick assets, excludes inventories and prepaid expenses from the fund definition. Otherwise it is identical to alternative 1, funds defined as total current assets. Changes affecting

EXHIBIT 17

OAKDALE COMPANY
Statement of Source and Uses of Funds
For the Year Ending December 31, 19X2

Statement: Concept of Funds	Exhibit 8, working capital	Alternative definitions			
		(1) Total current assets	(2) Total money (quick) assets	(3) Net money (quick) assets	(4) Total assets
Sources of funds from operations:					
(1) Sales.....................	$300,000	$300,000	$300,000	$300,000	$300,000
Less: Expenses requiring the use of funds:					
(2) Cost of goods sold..........	$120,000	$120,000	$120,000	$120,000	$120,000
(3) Bad debt expense...........	3,000	3,000	3,000	3,000	3,000
(4) Operating expenses.........	56,500	56,500	55,000	55,000	56,500
(5) Interest expense............	10,000	10,000	10,000	10,000	10.000
(6) Income taxes..............	65,000	65,000	65,000	65,000	65,000
(7) Patent expense.............	—	—	—	—	4,000
(8) Depreciation expense.......	—	—	—	—	12,000
(9) Total expenses requiring funds	$254,500	$254,500	$253,000	$253,000	$270,500
(10) Funds provided by operations	$ 45,500	$ 45,500	$ 47,000	$ 47,000	$ 29,500
(11) From sale of marketable securities at profit..............	7,000	7,000	7,000	7,000	7,000
(12) From sale of plant assets.....	1,000	1,000	1,000	1,000	(2,000)
(13) Proceeds from issuance of bonds....................	196,000	196,000	196,000	196,000	196,000
(14) Proceeds from issuance of stock.....................	25,000	25,000	25,000	25,000	65,000
(15) Dividends received from Riverbank, Inc.................	10,000	10,000	10,000	10,000	25,000
(16) From lease liability.........	—	—	—	—	114,700
(17) From increase in accounts payable......................	—	10,000	10,000	—	10,000
(18) From increase in interest payable........	—	10,000	10,000	—	10,000
(19) Total sources of funds.......	$284,500	$304,500	$306,000	$286,000	$455,200
Uses of funds:					
(20) Retirement of bonds for cash.	$ 60,000	$ 60,000	$ 60,000	$ 60,000	$ 60,000
(21) Purchase of treasury stock....	2,000	2,000	2,000	2,000	2,000
(22) Purchase of plant assets for cash.......................	50,000	50,000	50,000	50,000	—
(23) Cash dividends paid........	10,000	10,000	10,000	10,000	10,000
(24) Payment of notes payable....	—	30,000	30,000	—	30,000
(25) Payment of dividend payable.	—	4,000	4,000	—	4,000
(26) Increase in inventory........	—	—	60,000	60,000	—
(27) Total uses.................	$122,000	$156,000	$216,000	$182,000	$106,000
(28) Excess of sources over uses of funds....................	$162,500	$148,500	$ 90,000	$104,000	$349,200

these items are considered to result in funds flows rather than simply causing internal changes within the funds concept. The impact of inventory changes will be reported in the funds statement as well as the impact of financing through current liabilities. The third alternative assumes that current liabilities are constructive payments and are included in the definition of funds. The relationship to the working capital concept is simply that inventories (and prepaid expenses) are excluded from the definition. This enables the analyst to focus attention on inventories in the statement.

The fourth alternative defines funds as total assets. Any transaction affecting an asset account results in a funds flow; conversely, changes within the asset group do not. For this reason, some accountants abandon a strict interpretation and include all changes in the funds statement. This would be equivalent to combining Exhibit 8 and Exhibit 13 in one statement, the statement of changes in working capital.

Funds Defined as Total Current Assets.   (See Exhibit 17, alternative 1.) As noted above, the major *change* relative to the working capital concept is caused by the exclusion of current liabilities from the funds concept. The result is to focus attention on these items in the funds statement in addition to those shown on Exhibit 8; these items are noted as (17), (18), (24), and (25). The first two show increases in funds (current assets) supplied by current accounts, $10,000, and interest payable, $10,000; the latter two indicate the use of funds (current assets) to pay notes payable, $30,000, and dividends, $4,000. The effect of these short-term financing changes is clearly indicated in the statement instead of being buried in the working capital schedule (Exhibit 13). The reconciliation noted in Exhibit 18, of course, now relates only to changes within the current asset section: increments in cash, accounts receivable and inventories, and decreases in marketable securities and prepaid items.

Funds Defined as Total Money (Quick) Assets.   (See Exhibit 17, alternative 2.) Here prepaid expenses and inventories, in addition to items (17), (18), (24), and (25), are excluded from the funds concept. The effect of the prepaid expense item is ordinarily minor. It is, therefore, often ignored (left in the funds definition) by arbitrarily defining it as a quick asset. Analysis of the prepaid item then becomes unnecessary. Here the effect shows up in item (4), operating expenses. The portion of expenses recognized by writing off prepaid expenses of $1,500 is eliminated from expenses requiring the use of funds since under the present definition prepaid expenses are not funds. The inventory category is more important. This concept enables the statement to show inventory effects clearly. It is indicated in Exhibit 17 by item (26), a use of funds to finance the increase in inventories, $60,000.

The previous items (17, 18, 24, and 25) relating to current liabilities are treated as in alternative 1. Here, too, as liabilities they are not part of the assets definition of funds.

The reconciliation (Exhibit 18) now is for the money assets only: cash (item 33), and accounts receivable (item 34) have increased by $78,000 and $17,000, respectively, and marketable securities (item 46) have decreased by $5,000, resulting in a net increase in money assets of $90,000 (item 50) which, of course, must be the same as the net increase in funds (Exhibit 17, item 28).

Funds Defined as Net Money (Quick) Assets.   (See Exhibit 17, alternative 3.) Alternative 3 is related to alternative 2, differing only in that current liabilities are excluded from alternative 2 (total money assets), but included in alternative 3 (net money assets). Or, we may reconcile the present alternative (alternative 3) with the main definition of funds—working capital (Exhibit 8). The distinction between these is simply the exclusion of inventories and prepaid items from the funds definition of net money assets. Analysis of Exhibit 17 will indicate that alternative 3, when compared with Exhibit 8 (working capital), shows only a change in item 4,

EXHIBIT 18

OAKDALE COMPANY
Reconciliation Schedules
To Accompany the Sources and Use of Funds Statement
For the Year Ending December 31, 19X2

	Exhibit 8, working capital	Alternative definitions			
		(1) Total current assets	(2) Total money (quick) assets	(3) Net money (quick) assets	(4) Total assets
Reconciliations:					
(30) Fund accounts, beginning balances.................	$133,500	$237,500	$197,500	$ 93,500	$422,500
(31) Fund accounts, ending balances..................	296,000	386,000	287,500	197,500	771,700
(32) Increments...............	$162,500	$148,500	$ 90,000	$104,000	$349,200
Detailed reconciliations:					
Increases:					
(33) Increase in cash...........	$ 78,000	$ 78,000	$ 78,000	$ 78,000	$ 78,000
(34) Increase in accounts receivable	17,000	17,000	17,000	17,000	17,000
(35) Increase in inventories.......	60,000	60,000	—	—	60,000
(36) Decrease in notes payable....	30,000	—	—	30,000	—
(37) Decrease in dividends payable	4,000	—	—	4,000	—
(38) Increase in investment in Riverbank, Inc................	....	....	....	....	15,000
(39) Increase in patents (net).....	....	....	....	....	36,000
Increase in plant assets:					
(40) Leased.....................	....	....	....	....	114,700
(41) Purchased.................	....	....	....	....	50,000
(42) Less depreciation...........	....	....	....	....	(12,000)
(43) Less sale.................	....	....	....	....	(3,000)
(44) Total increases.............	$189,000	$155,000	$ 95,000	$129,000	$355,700
Decreases:					
(45) Increase in interest payable...	$ 10,000	—	—	$ 10,000	—
(46) Decrease in marketable securities.....................	5,000	$ 5,000	$ 5,000	5,000	$ 5,000
(47) Decrease in prepaid expenses..	1,500	1,500	—	—	1,500
(48) Increase in accounts payable..	10,000	—	—	10,000	—
(49) Total decreases.............	$ 26,500	$ 6,500	$ 5,000	$ 25,000	$ 6,500
(50) Net increase in fund items....	$162,500	$148,500	$ 90,000	$104,000	$349,200

of $1,500 ($55,000 versus $56,500) due to prepaid expenses and a change in item 26, increase in inventory of $60,000.

Thus alternative 3, the net money asset concept of funds, has all the advantages of the main (working capital) concept, but in addition focuses attention on inventory movements, an extremely important business indicator.

Funds Defined as Total Assets. (See Exhibit 17, alternative 4.) This is the most radical departure since it includes in the concept of funds not only some or all current assets, but *all* assets. (Note that all liabilities are excluded.) As a result, all transactions exchanging assets for other assets are, by definition, nonfund transactions; that is, no flows of funds occur. Details of asset changes are found only in the reconciliation schedules (see Exhibit 18).

A detailed study of alternative 4 of Exhibit 17 will show some unique features. Items (7) and (8), for example, indicate that expenses which cause a decrease in fixed assets are funds expenses and cause a flow of funds. Further, it is possible to recognize changes in the equity of subsidiaries; item (15) now recognizes not only the cash $10,000 received from the Riverbank, Inc., subsidiary but also the $15,000 equity increment as a source of funds. Also the increase in the lease liability, which results in an increment of a plant asset, is recognized as a funds source (item 16). The definition of funds as total assets, however, results in other peculiarities: the sale of plant assets for $1,000 (item 12) is simply a nonfund exchange; however, the loss on this transaction results in a net decrease in assets of $2,000 ($10,000 cost less $7,000 accumulated depreciation less $1,000 cash received) and is so illustrated. Also the purchase of plant assets for cash (item 22) is simply an exchange within the asset (funds) classification and is ignored.

Since this is a total asset concept, items (17), (18), (24), and (25) are treated as in alternatives 1 and 2; that is, the short-term payables are explicitly recognized, and short-term financing is reported in the funds statement. Inventories are assets, and therefore they are part of the funds. Transactions affecting inventories (for example, inventory changes) are reflected only in the reconciliation schedule (Exhibit 18, item 35).

While there is a broader scope to this variant of the statement, the relegation of the analysis of plant asset changes to the supporting schedule has caused abandonment of strict adherence to the rules. The resulting statement is actually prepared using a concept of funds that incorporates "all balance sheet changes." Additional adjustments are made to reflect the exchange of common stock for bonds ($40,000), and are included in the funds statement. The decreases in marketable securities ($5,000) and prepaid expenses ($1,500) would be shown as additional sources of funds, and the increases in cash ($78,000), accounts receivable ($17,000), inventories ($60,000), investments in Riverbank, Inc. ($15,000), patents ($36,000), leased plant assets ($114,700), and owned plant assets ($35,000) would be shown as uses of funds. Exhibit 19 shows the resulting statement, which is a self-balancing variant of the statement of changes in financial position.

Summary of Advantages and Disadvantages of Each Variant. Earlier the uses of funds analysis with funds defined as working capital were discussed as well as some of the limitations of that concept. This section has been devoted to exploring other definitions of funds and to preparing statements under these alternative concepts. Each concept illustrated has its advocate, and for good reason—each concept has its advantages as well as disadvantages. In general, they all try to provide the same kind of information; but the information is subject to judgmental modification in the short run. In the long run, statements prepared using each concept will move closer to a common one.

In the short run, the advantages will accrue for special and relevant conditions. Where inventories form a significant portion of working capital, the strategy for their acquisition and financing may dictate the use of the net money asset concept (alternative 3). Conversely, where the magnitude or type of financing by short-term creditors is important, either the total current asset (alternative 1) or the total money asset (alternative 2) definition is warranted.

Funds statements prepared under these four concepts are useful for financial planning, and are especially important where internal financing is involved. Where internal financing questions are less significant, the total asset definition of funds may be more relevant. There attention is drawn to those forces shaping all asset changes and, as illustrated above, may be extended to an analysis of all balance sheet changes. Also, the problem of exchanges (nonfund transactions) is minimized. The statement, then, is extremely useful in the analysis of past operations.

EXHIBIT 19

OAKDALE COMPANY
Statement of Changes in Financial Position
For the Year Ending December 31, 19X2

Sources of Funds

From operations (see Exhibit 17, alternative 4)............	$ 29,500
From sale of marketable securities..................	12,000
From decrease in prepaid expenses..................	1,500
From issuance of bonds	196,000
From issuance of stock	105,000
Dividends and equity from Riverbank, Inc...........	25,000
From lease liability...............................	114,700
From increase in accounts payable..................	10,000
From increase in interest payable..................	10,000
Total sources....................................	$503,700

Uses of Funds

Retirement of bonds.............................	$100,000
Purchase of treasury stock........................	2,000
Purchase of plant assets (net).....................	35,000
Loss on sale of plant assets.......................	2,000
Acquisition of patents............................	36,000
Acquisition of leased assets.......................	114,700
Increase in equity in Riverbank, Inc...............	15,000
Cash dividends paid..............................	14,000
Payment of notes payable........................	30,000
Increase in cash.................................	78,000
Increase in accounts receivable....................	17,000
Increase in inventories...........................	60,000
Total uses....................................	$503,700

CASH FLOW ANALYSIS

Cash flow statements and analysis have become so important that more extended coverage is required. In essence, cash flow statements are funds statements prepared on the basis of funds defined as cash or cash equivalent. Cash flow analysis has, however, been extended to certain uses that are more or less foreign to prior usage. Essentially these center around the use of the "funds from operations" figure as an operational benchmark. These uses and their limitations will be discussed later, but first the preparation of cash flow statements will be illustrated. Again, the data from the Oakdale Company example will be used for illustrative purposes.

Cash Flow Statements Prepared from Account Data. A cash flow statement prepared from the account data of the example is shown as statement A of Exhibit 20 (see column 3). The data are the same as those used to prepare Exhibits 8 and 17. Comparisons with these may be made. For convenience, Exhibit 8, source and uses of funds (working capital), is reproduced in column 1 of Exhibit 20.

Significant changes are to be noted in the "funds from operations" section. Since this section is now on a cash basis, noncash transactions are eliminated.

1. Sales (item 1) is adjusted for the effects of uncollected accounts receivable of $20,000, resulting in cash collections on sales of $280,000 ($300,000 less $20,000). The amount may be calculated directly as cash sales, $100,000, plus collections of receivables, $180,000. Some accountants prefer to show the entire sales amount of $300,000 in this section and to show the increase in accounts receivable as a use of cash in order to be able to reconcile with the income statement. However, this flies in the face of the facts and is not recommended.

2. Cost of goods sold is similarly treated as an outlay of funds to the extent that

EXHIBIT 20

OAKDALE COMPANY
Cash Flow Statements
For the Year Ending December 31, 19X2

Statement: Fund Definition	(1) Exhibit 8, working capital	(2) Exhibit 14, working capital	(3) A Cash	(4) B Cash
Basis	Accounts	Compara- tive state- ments	Accounts	Compara- tive state- ments
Source of funds from operations:				
(1) Sales..........................	$300,000	$300,000	$280,000	$280,000
Less: Expenses requiring the use of funds:				
(2) Cost of goods sold..............	$120,000	$120,000	$110,000	$110,000
(3) Bad debt expense...............	3,000	3,000	—	—
(4) Operating expenses..............	56,500	56,500	55,000	55,000
(5) Interest expense................	10,000	10,000	—	—
(6) Income taxes...................	65,000	65,000	65,000	65,000
(7) Total expenses requiring funds....	$254,500	$254,500	$230,000	$230,000
(8) Funds from operations...........	$ 45,500	$ 45,500	$ 50,000	$ 50,000
(9) Funds from sale of marketable securities at a profit.............	7,000	7,000	7,000	7,000
(10) From sale of plant assets........	1,000	—	1,000	—
(11) From issuance of bonds..........	196,000	96,000	196,000	96,000
(12) From issuance of stock..........	25,000	105,000	25,000	105,000
(13) Dividend received from River-bank, Inc.....................	10,000	10,000	10,000	10,000
(14) Total sources..................	$284,500	$263,500	$289,000	$268,000
Use of Funds:				
(15) Retirement of bonds............	$ 60,000	—	$ 60,000	—
(16) Purchase of treasury stock.......	2,000	$ 2,000	2,000	$ 2,000
(17) Purchase of plant assets.........	50,000	49,000	50,000	49,000
(18) Cash dividends paid.............	10,000	10,000	14,000	14,000
(19) Purchase of patent..............	—	40,000	—	40,000
(20) Repayment of notes payable.....	—	—	30,000	30,000
(21) Increase in inventories...........	—	—	—	60,000
(22) Total uses of funds..............	$122,000	$101,000	$216,000	$195,000
(23) Excess of sources over uses of funds	$162,500	$162,500	$ 73,000	$ 73,000
Reconciliations: *Increases:*				
(24) Increase in cash................	$ 78,000	$ 78,000	$ 78,000	$ 78,000
(25) Increase in accounts receivable...	17,000	17,000	—	—
(26) Increase in inventories..........	60,000	60,000	—	—
(27) Decrease in notes payable........	30,000	30,000	—	—
(28) Decrease in dividend payable.....	4,000	4,000	—	—
(29) Total increases.................	$189,000	$189,000	$ 78,000	$ 78,000
Decreases:				
(30) Increase in interest payable......	$ 10,000	$ 10,000	—	—
(31) Increase in accounts payable.....	10,000	10,000	—	—
(32) Decrease in marketable securities.	5,000	5,000	$ 5,000	$ 5,000
(33) Decrease in prepaid expenses.....	1,500	1,500	—	—
(34) Total decreases.................	$ 26,500	$ 26,500	$ 5,000	$ 5,000
(35) Net increase in fund items.......	$162,500	$162,500	$ 73,000	$ 73,000

cash has been paid to suppliers. Item 2 shows $110,000, which is composed of the cash purchases of $30,000 and payments to creditors of $140,000, or a total of $170,000, less the amount paid to creditors for the increased inventories ($60,-000), which are shown separately since they have not yet been sold. The $110,000 figure may also be calculated by deducting the $10,000 increase in accounts payable (representing unpaid purchases) from the cost of goods sold ($120,000 − $10,000 = $110,000).

3. Bad debt expense is entirely eliminated since it represents a noncash expense.

4. Operating expenses are shown at $55,000, the cash outlay. The noncash expense with the corresponding credit to prepaid expenses is ignored since there is no cash flow.

5. The interest expense is nonfund. No cash was credited since the total interest incurred (see the income statement) is still payable according to the interest payable account in the balance sheet.

6. The income tax charge was paid for, according to the T-accounts. The $68,000 shown on the income statement is accounted for by cash payment of $65,000 and the credit to deferred taxes of $3,000. The latter, of course, has caused no cash flow.

The net funds from operations (item 8) then results in $50,000. This indicates that total inflows from operations have been sufficient to cover the outflows. It must be remembered that inventories have increased by $60,000; some accountants may prefer to include this item in the operations section, in which case the deficiency would be $10,000. The remaining sources of funds (items 9 to 13) remain unchanged from Exhibit 8, since the T-accounts clearly indicated these as resulting in cash inflows.

Similarly, items 15, 16, and 17 are reported at amounts identical to those on the funds (working capital) statement since these resulted in cash outflows. Item (18), however, is increased to $14,000; this represents cash dividends paid of $10,000 (as before) plus $4,000 paid on prior years' dividends payable. These two items could have been shown separately, but since both were cash payments they have been combined.

The repayment of the note payable in cash (item 20) represents a cash flow and is so reported. The increase in inventories (item 21) has been discussed above; it has resulted in cash payments to creditors.

The reconciliation now consists simply of noting the increase in cash, $78,000, less the decrease in marketable securities, $5,000, resulting in a net increase of $73,000 (item 35), which is the same as the excess of sources over uses in the cash flow statement (item 23).

Cash Flow Statements Prepared from Comparative Statements. As discussed previously, funds statements may be prepared by analysis of comparative balance sheets and the income and retained earnings statements. The resulting funds and cash flow statements are shown in Exhibit 20, columns 2 (working capital) and 4B (cash flow statement). Column 2 is reproduced from Exhibit 14. The source of funds from operations is the same for the cash flow statement (column 4B) as for the cash flow statement (column 3A), since all the cash transactions may be determined from the comparative data given in published financial statements. This analysis has been given before, but a quick explanation may be useful.

1. Sales, $300,000 less the gross increase in accounts receivable of $20,000 ($17,000 net change plus $3,000 bad debt expense reported in the income statement).

2. Cost of goods sold, $120,000 less the $10,000 increase in accounts payable.

3. Operating expenses, $56,500 less $1,500 decrease in prepaid expenses.

4. Income taxes, $68,000 less deferred income taxes increase of $3,000.

The analysis of the remaining sources of funds is exactly the same as that given earlier in the presentation of Exhibit 14. It should be noted that these items are identical in Exhibit 20 for both the statement based on working capital (column 2) and the cash flow statement (column 4). The reason for this is that in the working capital analysis the working capital item assumed to have increased was cash. The same holds true for the uses of funds for retirement of bonds, purchase of treasury stock, purchase of fixed assets, and purchase of patents.

The three remaining differences between the funds statement (working capital) and the cash flow statement prepared from comparative data are items (18), (20), and (21) in Exhibit 20. In item (18), the cash dividends paid are determined from the dividends charged in the income statement plus the decrease in the dividends payable. It is unreasonable to assume anything other than a cash payment for these. The decrease in the note payable is also assumed to be a repayment. Item (21), the increase in inventories, has been covered before. Since the increase in accounts payable was cleared out against cost of goods sold, the increase in inventories must be assumed to have been entirely from a cash payment.

This concludes the analysis of the preparation of cash flow statements. Study of the two cash flow statements indicates that a reasonably accurate cash flow statement can be prepared from the data in published financial statements. The chief difficulties (as in the working capital example of Exhibit 14) arise from the inability to determine the exact flows when both capital asset acquisitions and retirements have taken place, when bond issues and retirements have taken place, and when stock has been exchanged for assets or bonds have been converted into stock. With more adequate disclosure increasingly being offered in published statements, even these difficulties may be minimized.

Comparison Between Funds (Working Capital) and Funds (Cash). The basic difference between these two concepts, of course, is the narrower definition of funds given by the cash concept. In turn this means a greater amount of detail to be included in the cash flow statement. Proponents maintain that in the last analysis the only tenable definition of funds is cash. Of course, in the long run the two concepts give essentially the same results. In the short run, the periodic cash flow statements will show more detail about the effect of receivables, current payables, and inventories. Also, the cash flow statement can more easily be articulated with cash planning. On the other hand, the cash definition may be too narrow. Although cash is the final medium of exchange, businesses operate in a credit economy. Undue focus on cash may well hide more meaningful flows. Constructive receipts and payments instead of actual payoff may signify the forming of important transactions. If cash flows are too rigidly specified, manipulation of significant items may take place in the short run. Many of the arguments for accrual accounting as opposed to cash accounting apply here, although in a different context.

The cash flow statement can readily be converted into a statement of changes in financial position by including on an "as if" basis those significant transactions that did not require a cash flow. Accordingly, the exchange of stocks for bonds retired, the acquisition of a patent through the issuance of stock, and the acquisition of leased plant assets through a noncancelable lease would be explicitly recognized. The impact of those three transactions on the cash flow statement (column 3 of Exhibit 20) would be to increase the source of funds by $194,700: (1) an $80,000 increase from issuance of stock (item 12) which is increased from $25,000 to $105,000; and (2) a $114,700 increase from incurring a long-term lease obligation. Concurrently, use of funds would be increased (1) $40,000 by the acquisition of patents (item 19), (2) $40,000 by retirement of bonds (item 15 which is increased from $60,000 to $100,000), and (3) $114,700 from the acquisition of leased plant assets.

Cash Flow per Share.   In security analysis the term "cash flow" has come to be a substitute for the generic term "funds from operations." It is often defined as "net income plus depreciation and other nonfund charges." As anyone who has read this section can readily observe, this item, although a very important one in the funds statement, is only part of the total picture. It is only one aspect of the entire financing analysis; it reflects only the basis for an analysis of internal financing and, at that, is still only relative to the requirement for funds (uses). Nonetheless, its use has been extended to the place where "cash flow per share," or "cash earnings per share," are frequently calculated and publicized by analysts. As noted, this does not represent *cash* flow or earnings per share. It represents *funds* (usually working capital as presented in published statements) *from operations* per share. Second, the relationship of this item to a share of stock is ambiguous if not misleading.

What has led to this usage? First is the rather widespread discontent with the figure for reported earnings, a discontent which is discussed elsewhere in this handbook. This has led to the search for a better measure of profitability or economic health. The cash earnings per share has been, apparently, an easy out. For example:

> Union economists said profits reported by corporations are no longer an accurate measure of economic health.
>
> The Union economists figured that while profits after taxes dropped from 5 percent of national production in 1958 to 4.5 percent in 1961, this was more than offset by a rise in cash-flow from 8.2 percent to 9.2 percent in the same period.[5]
>
> And lastly—*and possibly more important*—is the fact that much of the profit margin squeeze is artificial, because one of the most rapidly increasing cost-items is depreciation charged off against newly created facilities.[6]

Clearly these quotations (taken from among hundreds of similar ones) show a marked confusion on the nature of profits. Perhaps a reorientation of the income statement is required. The attempt to return to a profitability measure of "earnings before depreciation" is a throwback to cash accounting from accrual accounting, but at that only a partial one; all other accrual items remain. The main emphasis is clearly on the depreciation adjustment, but it may be worth noting that all other problems dealing with earnings per share continue since *income* is included in the numerator and the denominator remains unaffected by the switch to cash flow per share.

If depreciation is ignored and not deducted as an expense for the profitability measure, it implies that capital recovery is irrelevant. This may be true for the very short run, or for longer periods for a highly labor-intensive production economy. No modern business, of course, can survive without continually replenishing its productive capacity. Depreciation and other amortizations must be charged as current expenses against current income if income is to continue to be viewed as an improvement in economic position. In our increasingly automated economy, depreciation allowances will increase over time as the economy becomes even more capital-intensive. Cash flows thus have a built-in growth factor. We may hope that this will result in greater profits, but that is an overall efficiency factor not measured by the (inverse) effect of depreciation alone, as Mason states:[7] "In no sense can the amount of cash flow or cash income be considered as a substitute for or an improvement upon the net income, properly determined, as an indication of the results of operations."

[5]Cited in William A. Paton, "The Cash Flow Illusion," *The Accounting Review,* vol. 38, p. 243, April 1963.

[6]Ward Gates, "A Sound Approach to 1960 Third Quarter Reports," *The Magazine of Wall Street and Business Analyst,* Nov. 19, 1960, p. 224.

[7]*ARS No. 2, op. cit.,*-p. 42.

Both the APB and the SEC have recommended against the practices of comparing "cash flow" with income and disclosing "cash flow" per share. Paragraph 15 of APB Opinion No. 19 states:[8]

> The amount of working capital or cash provided from operations is not a substitute for or an improvement upon properly determined net income as a measure of results of operations and the consequent effect on financial position. Terms referring to "cash" should not be used to describe amounts provided from operations unless all non-cash items have been appropriately adjusted. The adjusted amount should be described accurately, in conformity with the nature of the adjustments, e.g., "Cash provided from operations for the period" or "Working capital provided from operations for the period" as appropriate. The Board strongly recommends that isolated statistics of working capital or cash provided from operations, especially per-share amounts, not be presented in annual reports to shareholders. If any per-share data relating to flow of working capital or cash are presented, they should as a minimum include amounts for inflow from operations, inflow from other sources, and total outflow, and each per-share amount should be clearly identified with the corresponding total amount shown in the Statement.

The SEC has been even stronger. In ASR No. 142, *Reporting Cash Flow and Other Related Data* (released in 1973), the Commission states:[9] ". . . it is not clear that the simple omission of depreciation and other non-cash charges deducted in the computation of net income provides an appropriate alternative measure of performance for any industry either in theory or in practice." Further, "While presentation of 'funds generated from operations' is useful, these data should be considered in the framework of a source and application of funds which reflects management's decisions as to the use of these funds and the external sources of capital used. . . . Therefore, presentation of one part [only] of a funds statement should be avoided." The Commission continues, "Many of the problems outlined above are accentuated when 'cash flow' data is presented on a per share basis. Most importantly, such a presentation emphasizes the implication that cash flow is more meaningful than net income as a measure of performance, particularly when a per share figure is included in the 'Financial Highlights' section of a report." The Commission concludes, "Such presentations run a high risk of materially misleading investors and companies are urged to avoid this type of disclosures. . . . Accordingly, per share data other than that relating to net income, net assets, and dividends should be avoided in reporting financial results."

BIBLIOGRAPHY

Accounting Principles Board Opinion No. 3: "The Statement of Source and Application of Funds," AICPA, New York, 1963.

Accounting Principles Board Opinion No. 19: "Reporting Changes in Financial Position," AICPA, New York, 1971.

Anton, Hector R.: *Accounting for the Flow of Funds,* Houghton Mifflin Company, Boston, 1962 (bibliography included).

Davidson, Sidney, James S. Schindler, and Roman L. Weil: *Fundamentals of Accounting,* 5th ed., The Dryden Press, Hinsdale, Ill., 1975.

Goodman, Hortense, and Leonard Lorensen: *Illustrations of the Statement of Changes in Financial Position,* AICPA, New York, 1974.

Jaedicke, Robert K., and Robert T. Sprouse: *Accounting Flows: Income, Funds and Cash,* Prentice-Hall, Englewood Cliffs, N.J., 1965, chaps. 5 and 6 (reference list at the end of chap. 6).

[8]APB Opinion No. 19, AICPA, New York, 1971, par. 15.
[9]Securities and Exchange Commission, Accounting Series Release No. 142, "Reporting Cash Flow and Other Related Data," Washington, D.C., 1973.

Johnson, Glenn L., and James A. Gentry, Jr.: *Finney and Miller's Principles of Accounting Intermediate*, Prentice-Hall, Englewood Cliffs, N.J., 1974, chap. 25.

Mason, Perry: "Cash Flow Analysis and the Funds Statement," *Accounting Research Study No. 2*, AICPA, New York, 1961 (bibliography included).

Meigs, Walter B., A. N. Mosich, Charles E. Johnson, and Thomas F. Keller: *Intermediate Accounting*, McGraw-Hill Book Company, 3rd ed., New York, 1974, chap. 25.

National Association of Accountants: *Research Study No. 38, Cash Flow Analysis for Managerial Control*, New York, 1961.

Securities and Exchange Commission: *Accounting Series Release No. 142*, "Reporting Cash Flow and Other Related Data," Washington, D.C., 1973.

————: *Regulation S-X*, Article 11A, "Statement of Source and Application of Funds," Washington, D.C., 1970.

Vatter, William J.: "Direct Method for the Preparation of Funds Statements," *Journal of Accountancy*, vol. 21, pp. 479–491, June 1946.

Chapter **4**

Financial Statement Analysis

WILLIAM H. BEAVER
Professor of Accounting, Stanford University

The purpose of financial statement analysis is to make predictions about a firm in the context of some decision setting. Traditionally, the focus has been upon the decisions of creditors and common stockholders, but other groups such as management, labor unions, and regulatory agencies are increasingly concerned with the same sort of predictions. The analysis of financial statements may constitute only a part of a much more comprehensive inquiry, often involving a study of the economy, the industry, and supplementary data about the firm including an appraisal of the quality of management. This chapter is concerned only with financial statement analysis, and is divided into two main sections: (1) the methods of financial statement analysis, and (2) the uses of financial statement analysis.

METHODS OF FINANCIAL STATEMENT ANALYSIS

The primary method is ratio analysis—the comparison of relationships by placing the data in ratio form. Financial ratio analysis involves three types of comparisons: (1) comparisons of items within a single year's financial statements, (2) comparisons over time, and (3) comparisons among firms.

Single-Year Comparisons.   Ratio analysis of a single year's set of financial statements can be further divided into five categories: profitability ratios, capital structure ratios, liquid asset ratios, turnover ratios, and funds flow ratios. The ratios included in each category are computed in Exhibit 2 for a hypothetical XYZ Company whose financial statements are shown in Exhibit 1. For the ratios

EXHIBIT 1

XYZ COMPANY
Balance Sheet
December 31, 19X1

Assets		*Equities*	
Current assets:			
Cash	$ 175,000	Current liabilities	$ 2,000,000
Marketable securities	325,000	Long-term debt	2,000,000
Accounts receivable	1,500,000	Stockholders' equity .	6,000,000
		(600,000 shares issued	
Inventories	2,500,000	and outstanding)	
Total current assets	$4,500,000		
Property, plant, and equipment			
(net of accumulated			
depreciation)	5,500,000		
Total assets	$10,000,000	Total equities	$10,000,000

XYZ COMPANY
Income Statement
For the Year Ended December 31, 19X1

Sales (net)	$25,000,000
Less: Cost of goods sold	15,000,000
Gross margin	$10,000,000
Less: Selling and administrative expenses	7,400,000
Operating Income	$ 2,600,000
Less: Interest	100,000
Federal income taxes	1,000,000
Net income	$ 1,500,000
Dividends to common stockholders	$ 1,000,000

Additional data: Market price of common stock as of 12/31/X1 was $40 per share. Depreciation deducted in determining above net income figure is $1,400,000.

denoted by an asterisk in Exhibit 2, the average of the beginning and ending balances is most often used. For computational convenience, the ending balance was assumed to be equal to the average balance. Even when the average balance during the year is used in the denominator, results may be somewhat misleading. Davidson, Schindler, and Weil give the following example:[1]

> Sophisticated analysts recognize, however, that when companies use a fiscal year different from the calendar year this averaging of beginning and ending balances may be misleading. Consider, for example, the all capital earnings rate of Sears, Roebuck and Company whose fiscal year ends on January 31. Sears chooses a January 31 closing date at least in part because inventories are at a low level and are therefore easy to count—Christmas merchandise has been sold and Easter merchandise has not yet all been received. Furthermore, by January 31 most Christmas purchases have been paid for, so receivables are not unusually large. Thus, at January 31 the amount of total assets is lower than at many other times during the year. Consequently, the denominator of the all capital earnings rate, total assets, for Sears is more likely to represent the *smallest* rather than the *average* amount of total assets on hand during the year. The all capital earnings rate for Sears and other companies that choose a fiscal year end to coincide with low points in the inventory cycle is likely to be overstated. . . .

Earnings Ratios

ALL CAPITAL EARNINGS RATE (RATE OF RETURN ON ALL CAPITAL).   The numerator of this ratio is defined as reported net income plus interest net of income tax effects.[2] Thus, the numerator is an income figure which is independent of the capital structure of the firm. The denominator may be either the amount of total assets on the balance sheet at year-end or an average of the beginning and ending amounts of total assets. The resulting ratio is income expressed as a percentage of total assets and is often referred to as the return on total capital.

A common modification of this ratio is to define the denominator as total assets minus current liabilities (or equivalently, long-term debt plus stockholders' equity). The reason for this modification is that the numerator is net of implicit interest payments to certain short-term suppliers of capital (for example, trade creditors), and hence it represents the net earnings allocable to the remaining suppliers of capital (long-term creditors, preferred and common stockholders). The denominator should be defined in terms of these suppliers of capital rather than all suppliers of capital.

RATE OF RETURN ON COMMON STOCKHOLDERS' EQUITY.   The numerator is net income. The denominator can be defined either as the year-end figure or as an average of the beginning and ending figures for stockholders' equity.[3]

PAYOUT RATIO.   The numerator is dividends to common stock. The denominator is income to common stock (net income less preferred stock dividends). The ratio is called the "payout ratio" because it indicates what percentage of reported income to common stockholders has been paid out in the form of cash dividends. There is a controversy in the investment literature concerning the importance of the payout ratio. Graham, Dodd, and Cottle, among others, contend that the common stock of high-payout firms will sell at a premium over low-payout firms, other things remaining equal. Miller and Modigliani argue that an effect of the

---

[1]S. Davidson, J. S. Schindler, and R. L. Weil, *Fundamentals of Accounting*, 5th ed., The Dryden Press, Hinsdale, Ill., 1975, pp. 851–852.

[2]In other words, the numerator is $Y + (1 - t)I$, where Y is net income, t is the tax rate, and I is the amount of interest charges.

[3]In the special case of preferred stock in the capital structure, the preferred stock dividends are deducted from the numerator, and the preferred stock account and any additional paid-in capital associated with it is deducted from the denominator.

EXHIBIT 2 XYZ Corporation—Selected Financial Ratios

Usual Name	Components of Computations		Resulting Ratio for XYZ Corporation	
A. Earnings ratios:				
All capital earnings rate	$\dfrac{\text{Net income} + \text{aftertax interest expense}[a]}{\text{Average total assets*}}$	=	$\dfrac{\$1,500,000 + (1 - .40) \times \$100,000}{\$10,000,000}$	
			$= \dfrac{\$1,560,000}{\$10,000,000}$	= 15.6%
Rate of return on stockholders' equity	$\dfrac{\text{Net income less preferred stock dividends}}{\text{Average common stockholders' equity*}}$	=	$\dfrac{\$1,500,000}{\$6,000,000}$	= 25.0%
Payout ratio	$\dfrac{\text{Dividends to common stock}}{\text{Net income less preferred stock dividends}}$	=	$\dfrac{\$1,000,000}{\$1,500,000}$	= 66.7%
Earnings per share	$\dfrac{\text{Net income}}{\text{Average number of shares outstanding}}$	=	$\dfrac{\$1,500,000}{600,000 \text{ shares}}$	= $2.50
Price-earnings ratio	$\dfrac{\text{Market price per share}}{\text{Earnings per share}}$	=	$\dfrac{\$40.00}{\$\ 2.50}$	= 16
B. Capital structure ratios:				
Debt-equity ratio	$\dfrac{\text{Long-term senior securities}}{\text{Long-term senior securities plus stockholders' equity}}$	=	$\dfrac{\$2,000,000}{\$8,000,000}$	= 25%
Times-interest earned	$\dfrac{\text{Net income} + \text{interest expense}[b]}{\text{Interest Expense}}$	=	$\dfrac{\$1,500,000 + \$100,000}{\$100,000}$	= 16
C. Liquid asset ratios:				
Current ratio	$\dfrac{\text{Current assets}}{\text{Current liabilities}}$	=	$\dfrac{\$4,500,000}{\$2,000,000}$	= 2.25
Quick or acid-test ratio	$\dfrac{\text{Quick assets}}{\text{Current liabilities}}$	=	$\dfrac{\$2,000,000}{\$2,000,000}$	= 1
Super quick ratio[c]	$\dfrac{\text{Cash plus marketable securities}}{\text{Current liabilities}}$	=	$\dfrac{\$\ 500,000}{\$2,000,000}$	= .25

D. Turnover ratios:

Average collection period of receivables $= \dfrac{\text{Average accounts receivable*}}{\text{Average daily sales}} = \dfrac{\$1,500,000}{\$25,000,000/360 \text{ days}} = 21.6 \text{ days}$

Profit margin ratio $= \dfrac{\text{Net income}}{\text{Net sales}} = \dfrac{\$1,500,000}{\$25,000,000} = 6.0\%$

Asset turnover $= \dfrac{\text{Net sales}}{\text{Average total assets*}} = \dfrac{\$25,000,000}{\$10,000,000} = 2.5$

Inventory turnover $= \dfrac{\text{Cost of goods sold}}{\text{Average inventory*}} = \dfrac{\$15,000,000}{\$2,500,000} = 6 \text{ times or every 60 days}$

E. Fund statement ratios:

Defensive interval $= \dfrac{\text{Quick assets}}{\text{Daily fund expenditures}^{d}} = \dfrac{\$2,000,000}{\$22,100,000/360 \text{ days}} = 32.6 \text{ days}$

Cash flow to debt ratio $= \dfrac{\text{Funds provided by operations}^{e}}{\text{Total liabilities}} = \dfrac{\$2,900,000}{\$4,000,000} = .725$

[a] Marginal tax rate is 40 percent.
* The average of the beginning and ending balances are most often used. For computational convenience, the ending balance was assumed to be equal to the average balance.
[b] Sometimes income tax expense is added to the numerator. In that case, the interest charges would be covered 26 times.
[c] This ratio has no "usual name." Super quick ratio is probably appropriate.
[d] Daily fund expenditures = all operating expenditures that drain funds plus interest and income taxes = all expenses less depreciation = $15,000,000 + $7,400,000 + $100,000 + $1,000,000 − $1,400,000 = $22,100,000.
[e] Net income plus expenses that do not drain funds (for example, depreciation) = $1,500,000 + $1,400,000 = $2,900,000.

payout ratio is a tax effect resulting from the difference in the tax rate and timing of tax payments for dividends as opposed to capital gains.[4] It is difficult to generalize what the net tax impact would be for the market as a whole, but for individual investors the payout ratio could be quite important in selecting investment securities.

EARNINGS PER SHARE.   If a firm has no convertible securities, stock options, or stock warrants outstanding, the numerator is defined as net income available for common shareholders and the denominator is defined as either the number of shares of common stock outstanding at year-end or, more frequently, the weighted-average number of shares outstanding during that period. Chapter 30 is devoted to an analysis of the problem of calculating earnings per share when the capital structure is more complex.

The earnings per share figure is difficult to interpret. Since most firms retain a portion of earnings (that is, the payout ratio is less than one), the investment represented by each share tends to increase over time. As a result, a change in earnings per share may be caused by a change in the investment base per share or a change in the earning power per dollar of investment or both. Two possible ways to incorporate changes in the investment base into the analysis would be to divide earnings per share by the market price or by the book value per share.[5] Presumably, changes in these ratios isolate changes in the earning power from changes in the investment base. In spite of difficulties of interpretation, earnings per share continues to be the most widely cited measure of earnings power.

PRICE-EARNINGS RATIO.   The price-earnings ratio is price per share divided by earnings per share. Mechanically, it reflects the price currently being paid by the market for each dollar of currently reported earnings per share. However, it is of interest only to the extent that the denominator reflects normal sustainable (that is, expected) earning power associated with the assets. As a result, earnings as reported is usually adjusted for income from discontinued operations and extraordinary items, as well as for any other items not expected to recur.

The resulting ratio is interpreted as the earnings multiplier or capitalization factor applied to earnings to arrive at the current value (that is, price) of the common stock. The price-earnings ratio is a function of the discount rate applied to future expected earnings and of the growth rate in earnings. The meaning of the discount rate is unclear in an uncertain world, but would presumably reflect such factors as the interest rate plus a risk premium. It can also be thought of as the cost of capital, which is the expected return available to investors in other investment opportunities of the same degree of riskiness. Greater risk implies a higher discount rate, and a lower price-earnings ratio. The expected growth in earnings per share is a function of the amount of future asset acquisitions expected to be undertaken by the firm and the expected earnings rate in those acquisitions. In particular, if the expected future earnings rate is equal to the cost of capital, there will be zero growth premium reflected in the price-earnings ratio, and the ratio will equal the reciprocal of the discount rate (that is, the cost of capital). If the expected earnings rate exceeds the cost of capital, the growth premium will be positive, and the price-earnings ratios will exceed the reciprocal of the cost of capital. In such cases, estimates based solely on the price-earnings

---

[4]Benjamin Graham, David L. Dodd, and Sidney Cottle, *Security Analysis*, 4th ed., McGraw-Hill Book Company, New York, 1962, pp. 480–493; Merton Miller and Franco Modigliani, "Dividend Policy, Growth, and the Valuation of Shares," *Journal of Business*, vol. 34, pp. 411–433, October 1961.

[5]In which case, the resulting ratios would be the reciprocal of the price-earnings ratio and the return on equity, respectively.

ratios will underestimate the cost of capital. Empirical evidence indicates that the future growth rates on earnings are difficult to predict.[6]

TREATMENT OF EXTRAORDINARY ITEMS.   A question often arises concerning the inclusion of extraordinary items in the computation of the net income ratios. The AICPA has held that all items both unusual in nature and infrequent in occurrence (except those meeting some very rigid restrictions) must be shown as extraordinary on the income statement.[7] Many of these items in reality constitute adjustments of earnings reported in some prior years; hence they should not be included in the income ratios. Those items which relate to the current year may or may not be included, depending upon the kind of net income concept desired. If a permanent earnings concept is desired, the items should be excluded. If a measure of net income including its transitory components is desired, the items should be included. The latter concept of income may be important for assessing the variability of the income stream over time.

CAPITAL STRUCTURE RATIOS.   There are two common types of relationships that reflect the effect of a firm's financing decisions. The first is leverage, a ratio of long-term senior securities to total capitalization. Long-term senior securities are long-term liabilities, while total capitalization is the sum of long-term senior securities plus stockholders' equity. The second is the times-interest earned ratio, the ratio of income before fixed charges on debt to those fixed charges. Fixed charges on debt are interest currently due plus the implicit interest portion on certain fixed commitments, such as payments under noncancelable leases.[8] The numerator of the times-interest earned ratio is net income plus interest expense. Sometimes income tax expense is added to this amount. It would be more logical, instead, to add only the income tax reduction resulting from the interest deductions (= 40% of $100,000 in the example), but we suspect that this refinement is seldom introduced. The major distinction between the two types of ratios is that the leverage ratios look to the balance sheet, while the times-interest earned calculation looks to the income statement.

One purpose of the capital structure ratios is to provide a measure of solvency, the ability to meet payments on senior securities and other commitments when due. A second purpose of the capital structure ratio is to provide an index of the riskiness of the common stock. As debt is introduced into the capital structure, the return on the common stock becomes more volatile and the stock becomes riskier.

LIQUID ASSET RATIOS.   The capital structure ratios can be thought of as long-run measures of a firm's ability to meet its financial obligations, whereas the liquid asset ratios provide short-run measures of ability to pay its debts by comparing the amount of liquid assets on hand with the short-term obligations (current liabilities). The liquid assets constitute the firm's reservoir of short-run debt-paying power, while current liabilities represent the demands that will be made on the reservoir. Several definitions of liquid assets are used in ratio analysis.

Current assets, in the form of the current ratio (current assets to current liabilities), was the first liquid asset measure to be used, but it has been severely criticized. For example, the inclusion of inventory in current assets may impair its usefulness. It is argued that inventory is not a liquid asset because it must be sold

---

[6]Baruch Lev, *Financial Statement Analysis: A New Approach,* Prentice-Hall, Englewood Cliffs, N.J., 1974, chap. 8.

[7]Accounting Principles Board, Opinion Number 9, "Reporting the Results of Operations," AICPA, New York, 1966, and Opinion No. 30, "Reporting the Results of Operations," AICPA, New York, 1973.

[8]Senior securities can also be defined to include preferred stock, in which case fixed charges would include preferred stock dividends.

before it can be converted into cash or receivables. This factor may be particularly relevant for firms in financial difficulty, who have excessive inventory. If current assets are used as a measure of debt-paying ability, the measure may be misleadingly inflated by including such inventories. This criticism has led to the use of quick assets, which include cash, marketable securities, and receivables, but not inventories. The ratio of quick assets to current liabilities is called the "quick ratio" or the "acid-test ratio."

Cash plus marketable securities is a third measure of liquid assets, although it has not been advocated frequently. It is said to be too conservative a measure in the sense that it implicitly assumes that the short-term cash flow from receivables will be zero, which is very unlikely even when a material portion of the receivables is slow or delinquent.[9]

TURNOVER RATIOS.   Turnover ratios refer to the ratio of a stock (some asset) to a flow (sales or cost of goods sold). The two most popular turnover ratios are receivables and inventory turnover. The numerator of the receivables turnover ratio is average receivables outstanding during the year (usually computed as an average of the beginning and ending balances in accounts receivable). The denominator is average daily net sales, which is computed by dividing annual net sales by 365.[10] The resulting ratio is the number of days of sales in accounts receivable. (Technically, this is not a turnover calculation. To obtain receivables turnover, number of days of sales in accounts receivable must be divided into 365.) This figure will vary according to the credit terms of the industry. Changes in this ratio may signal changes in credit terms, changes in quality of customers to whom credit is extended, or changes in the quality of collection efforts.

The inventory turnover ratio is defined as average inventory divided by cost of goods sold. The resulting ratio is the number of days of "sales" (at cost) in inventory. The inventory turnover will also vary among industries. A change in a firm's ratio over time may be induced by many factors, such as changes in the cost of holding inventories, changes in product mixes, changes in expectations regarding future inventory prices, or changes in production technology.

Perhaps the most comprehensive use of turnover ratios is the Du Pont system for appraising operating performance.[11] The net income to total assets ratio is viewed as a product of two ratios: net income to net sales (the profit margin), and net sales to total assets (capital turnover ratio). The analysis further breaks down the profit margin into various cost elements and the capital turnover ratio into various asset categories. Although the system was designed for evaluation of the firm by management, a similar approach could be adopted by external users.

FUNDS FLOW RATIOS.   There have been several recent suggestions for improvements in traditional ratio analysis. One suggestion is the use of items from the statement of changes in financial position. The major thrust has been twofold: (1) an emphasis on liquid asset flows rather than liquid asset balances, and (2) an emphasis on funds provided by operations (operating revenues that increase funds minus operating expenses that drain funds) rather than upon net income, which includes nonfund items. Sorter and Benston[12] have suggested their interval

---

[9]Both sales and total assets have also been suggested as denominators for the liquid asset measures.

[10]For convenience of computation, net sales is frequently divided by 360 or by 260, the approximate number of working days in a year. As long as the same number is used consistently over time and across firms, it does not make any difference which factor is used.

[11]A. Kline, Jr., and Howard L. Hessler, "The Du Pont Chart System for Appraising Operations Performance," *NACA Bulletin, 1952 Conference Proceedings*.

[12]G. H. Sorter and George Benston, "Appraising the Defensive Position of a Firm: The Interval Measure," *The Accounting Review*, vol. 35, pp. 633–640, October 1960.

measure as a measure of short-term solvency, which compares quick assets to daily fund operating expenditures. Previous research on the prediction of bankruptcy and bond default has indicated that the ratio of funds provided by operations divided by total liabilities is an excellent predictor.

MULTIRATIO ANALYSIS. As early as 1919, the literature suggested that analysis of a single ratio cannot capture all the relevant relationships.[13] In 1926, Wall and Duning suggested the index of credit strength, which was a linear combination of several ratios.[14] However, several questions concerning multivariate analysis were not answered by the originators of the index, and these same questions still remain largely unanswered today. They are: (1) How many ratios are needed for an adequate analysis? (2) Which ratios are to be included in a multiratio analysis? (3) What is the relative importance or weight that should be assigned to each ratio?

Certain multivariate statistical techniques, such as discriminant analysis and regression analysis, offer promise for answering these questions. However, initial investigation of the underlying ratio distributions indicates that they violate many of the assumptions necessary for the multivariate techniques to attain optimal properties (for example, normality, constant variance, serial independence, independence among the predicting variables).[15]

Comparisons over Time. An analysis of a single year's financial statements can often be incomplete. The year being examined may contain large transitory items which make the statements for the year unrepresentative of the past or the future. A time series analysis of several years' financial statements can detect trends that may be helpful in projecting the future position of the firm. A time series analysis can also indicate whether a particular year is unrepresentative. Four techniques used in comparisons over time are (1) comparative analysis, (2) common-size statements, (3) trend percentage analysis, and (4) forecasting techniques.

Comparative Analysis. Comparative analysis examines the financial statements from adjacent fiscal years and compares the statements on an item-by-item basis. The purpose is to determine what events induced the changes and what impact these events are likely to have on the firm in the future. The comparison can be in terms of first differences in the dollar amounts from one period to the next or in terms of percentage changes.

Common-Size Statements. The conventional balance sheet is converted into a common-size balance sheet by dividing each item by total assets and arriving at a percentage figure. The income statement is converted by dividing each item by net sales. The financial statements of different fiscal periods are then compared on an item-by-item basis to detect differences in percentages for a given item between fiscal periods.

Trend Percentage Analysis. A base period is first selected and every financial statement item is assigned an index of 100. Statement items for other years are assigned an index number which is computed by dividing the dollar amount of the item in that year by the dollar amount of the item in the base year. The result is a set of financial statements where each item is measured in terms of its growth or decline relative to the base period. Selection of an atypical base year can impair the usefulness of the approach. One way to avoid this problem would be to define an average of two or three years as the base period.

Forecasting Techniques. Forecasting techniques are methods for using historical

[13]Alexander Wall, "Study of Credit Barometers," *Federal Reserve Bulletin,* March 1919, pp. 229–243.

[14]Alexander Wall and Raymond W. Duning, *Ratio Analysis of Financial Statements,* Harper & Brothers, New York, 1928.

[15]James O. Horrigan, "Some Empirical Bases of Financial Ratio Analysis," *The Accounting Review,* vol. 40, pp. 558–568, July 1965.

data to project the magnitude of financial statement items in the future. Within the scope of this chapter, little can be said except to indicate what techniques are available and to provide a few bibliographic references. The techniques are naive methods, regression analysis, exponential smoothing models, and information theory techniques.[16]

Comparisons Among Firms. Ultimately, financial statement analysis must be concerned with comparisons across firms. An analysis of a single firm is incomplete because the decision maker always has the alternative of investing in or lending funds to other firms. Hence the characteristics of the firm being analyzed must be evaluated relative to the characteristics of other firms.

The use of standard ratios is one approach to interfirm comparisons. A standard ratio is an average ratio for a class of firms. The average is defined as the arithmetic mean or as the median. Since most distributions of ratios are skewed (asymmetrical), the mean and the median can differ considerably. Before the standard ratios are computed, firms may be classified according to industry, asset size, or both. Standard ratios for industries are used because it is felt that the operating characteristics across industries are so different that composite (multi-industry) averages are not useful.[17]

Standard ratios are incorporated into the analysis by comparing the ratios of the firm being analyzed with the standard ratios of the industry and asset size category in which the firm operates. The primary limitation of the use of standard ratios is that they represent only one point on the ratio distribution. When the median is used, the standard ratio represents the 50th percentile. A comparison of a firm's ratio with the standard ratio reveals only whether the ratio is above or below the 50th percentile, it does not answer a more important question: How far above or below the 50th percentile is it? For example, suppose that a firm's current ratio is 2.8 and the standard ratio is 3.6. In what percentile is 2.8? Without any additional knowledge concerning the dispersion of the ratio distribution about the median, it is not possible to answer that question. An even more important question is: How low does the percentile have to be before it is considered dangerous or serious to have a ratio in that percentile? This latter issue will be dealt with in greater detail later.

Accounting Measurement Considerations. The purpose of this section is to discuss some sources of measurement error in the components of the ratios. For example, all capital earnings rate is frequently regarded as the best measure of management performance. Attaching such importance to this ratio has been severely criticized, however, largely because of measurement errors in reported net income and in total assets. The nature of these measurement errors is discussed in the other chapters, but a brief list of them is provided below:[18]

1. Financial statements are not adjusted for changes in the price level.

2. Noncurrent asset balances and depreciation charges are based upon historical cost rather than current replacement cost.

3. Many items are expensed in the period of acquisition that should theoretically be capitalized and expensed in future periods (for example, some research and development and advertising expenditures).

---

[16]Robert G. Brown, *Smoothing, Forecasting and Prediction of Discrete Time Series*, Prentice-Hall, Englewood Cliffs, N.J., 1963; Carl F. Christ, *Econometric Models and Methods*, John Wiley & Sons, New York, 1966; Henri Theil, *Applied Economic Forecasting*, North-Holland Publishing Company, Amsterdam, 1966; and Charles R. Nelson, *Applied Time Series Analysis for Managerial Forecasting*, Holden-Day, San Francisco, 1973.

[17]Industry standard ratios are published periodically by Robert Morris Associates and by Dun & Bradstreet.

[18]For a more thorough discussion of measurement errors, see William J. Vatter, "Does Rate of Return Measure Business Efficiency?" *NAA Bulletin*, January 1959, pp. 33–48.

4. There is a lag between the time a gain or loss occurs and the time it appears in the income statements.

5. Holding gains and losses often are not separated from operating income.

6. Estimates of the future are involved and those estimates may be incorrect (for example, depreciation).

7. Occurrence of extraordinary, nonrecurring items may distort net income for a given period.

8. Tax regulations may inappropriately influence the method of reporting (for example, the tendency to expense rather than capitalize).

These measurement errors make it difficult to compare firms using the same accounting methods. The situation is further complicated by the fact that generally accepted accounting principles permit more than one method of reporting in certain areas. The existence of alternative measurement rules creates a lack of uniformity and constitutes a major problem when analyzing the financial statements of different firms. Seeming differences among firms can emerge solely as a result of the diversity of alternatives employed.

A brief list of some of the alternative measurement rules is provided below:

1. LIFO versus FIFO cost flow assumptions for valuing inventories and cost of goods sold

2. Straight-line versus accelerated methods of depreciation

3. Capitalization versus operating methods of reporting lease obligations

4. Purchase versus pooling treatments for recording business combinations

5. Different treatments of past and prior service costs under pension fund liabilities and expenses.

USES OF FINANCIAL STATEMENT ANALYSIS

One way to view financial statement analysis is to regard the results as signals which require further investigation to determine their causes. According to this view, the purpose of the financial statement analysis is to suggest questions or areas for further investigation rather than to provide answers. An alternative view is to attribute some meaning to the numbers generated by the analysis and to draw inferences from the numbers themselves. If the ultimate purpose of the analysis of financial statements is to facilitate the decisions of external users, then one way to attribute meaning to these numbers is to view them as information that affects predictions of certain parameters. This section will discuss major decision and prediction purposes and the empirical evidence available concerning the role of financial statement data for those purposes.

The two broad purposes of financial statement analysis are (1) solvency determination, and (2) performance evaluation. Solvency determination is the assessment of the probability that a firm will fail (that is, will be unable to meet its financial obligations as they mature). Performance evaluation is the assessment of the probability distribution of return (where return is defined in terms of dividends and capital gains) associated with holding a given security.

Solvency Determination.   Solvency determination was the original purpose for which financial statement analysis was developed. Yet many have criticized its use because of a lack of theory providing an a priori link between the ratios and the probability of failure. Ratio analysis began with the use of a single ratio, the current ratio, but during the 1920s a proliferation of ratios occurred. In many cases, the ratios were generated with little or no justification for their use. Hence the criticism of a lack of theory was a legitimate one.

The a priori link between ratios and the probability of failure has been explored in a classic article by Walter, in which he developed a cash flow model of the firm and demonstrated what elements in that model influence the solvency of the firm.[19] By a slight extension of Walter's analysis, many of the ratios can be shown to be directly related to the probability of failure.[20] Although the cash flow model provided the a priori link, the utility of ratios for solvency determination still had to be tested empirically.

Beaver found that financial ratios are useful in the prediction of failure (bankruptcy and bond default) at least five years prior to failure.[21] Ratios can be used to classify correctly firms as failed or nonfailed to a much greater extent than would be possible through random prediction. The ratios of the failed firms implied higher probability of failure for as much as five years before failure.

Horrigan investigated the ability of ratios to predict bond rating changes and bond ratings on new issues, where bond rating is viewed as a surrogate for the probability of default.[22] He found that the rating changes and new ratings could be correctly predicted to a much greater extent by using ratios than would be possible through random prediction.

Using multiple discriminant analysis, Altman developed a multiratio prediction model, which exhibited excellent discriminatory power in the year before failure but showed marked deterioration in the second through fifth years before failure.[23] Altman compared the multivariate model results on his data with the performance of the cost flow to total debt ratio on the Beaver data. However, such a comparison is difficult to interpret because different definitions of failure were used in the two studies. In a later study, Deakin directly compared their performance on the same set of data and found that the multiratio model produced lower prediction errors.[24] However, even this comparison is clouded by a lack of application to a sample different from those used to derive the discriminant weights. A major task for future research is to explore more fully the use of multiratio models and the issue of the relative predictive ability of different ratios. The latter issue can be meaningfully addressed only in a multivariate context.

Performance Evaluation.   While solvency determination could also be described as analysis of fixed-claim securities, performance evaluation could be described as analysis of common stocks.

There are two major approaches to common stock valuation. The first is a multiperiod, discounted cash flow approach and has its origins in multiperiod valuation under certainty. In a world of uncertainty, its counterpart is the time-state preference model, in which the objects of choice are time-dated state contingent cash flows. Under some simplifying assumptions, the value of common stock can be viewed to be a function of the expected earning power (that is, the cash-flow generating ability) of the current stock of assets, the growth rate in earnings due to future investments, and the rate of discount (that is, the cost of equity capital for securities of that degree of risk). Presumably, one role of financial statement data is

[19]Walter, James E., "Determination of Technical Solvency," *Journal of Business*, vol. 31, pp. 30–43, January 1957.

[20]William H. Beaver, "Financial Ratios as Predictors of Failure," *Empirical Research in Accounting, Selected Studies, 1966,* Supplement to vol. 4, *Journal of Accounting Research,* pp. 71–127; J. W. Wilcox, "A Prediction of Business Failure Using Accounting Data," *Empirical Research in Accounting: Selected Studies, 1973,* Supplement to vol. 11, *Journal of Accounting Research,* pp. 44–62.

[21]Beaver, *op. cit.*

[22]James O. Horrigan, "The Determination of Long-Term Credit Standing with Financial Ratios," *Empirical Research in Accounting, Selected Studies, 1966,* Supplement to vol. 4, *Journal of Accounting Research,* pp. 44–62.

[23]E. I. Altman, "Financial Ratios, Discriminant Analysis and the Prediction of Corporate Bankruptcy," *Journal of Finance,* September 1968, pp. 589–609.

[24]E. B. Deakin, "A Discriminant Analysis of Predictors of Business Failure," *Journal of Accounting Research,* Spring 1972, pp. 167–179.

to provide assessments of future earning power and hence prices. This view is empirically supported by a variety of cross-sectional valuation studies, which attempted to explain interfirm differences in stock prices on the basis of interfirm differences in earnings power and growth in earnings.[25] The contention is also supported by time series studies, which indicate that there is a significant association between unexpected changes in earnings and unexpected changes in stock prices. These studies further indicate that the market is obtaining information about annual earnings via alternative sources (such as interim reports) such that the market price reflects revisions in expectations about earnings starting several months prior to the release of the annual earnings number. In fact, much of the anticipatory price reaction has occurred by the beginning of the announcement month. However, there is still a significant price and volume reaction at the announcement date.[26] These findings have been replicated for quarterly earnings as well.[27] In short, the findings are consistent with a market that considers earnings to be important information and, as a result, seeks out and relies upon a broad information set in attempting to form up-to-date assessments of earnings.

A related issue is the choice of an appropriate earnings forecasting model, which in turn depends upon the nature of the stochastic process generating the earnings series. Empirical evidence indicates that placing almost exclusive weight upon the most recently observed earnings (for example, earnings per share or net income to stockholders' equity) will lead to better forecasts of earnings one period ahead than forecasts based on a weighted average of past earnings over several periods. In other words, the simple, naive forecast that next year's earnings will be equal to this year's earnings is a better forecast than forecasts based on past averages. However, the evidence also indicates that an even better forecasting model would be this year's earnings plus a drift (that is, the average change in earnings over the past several periods).

Based upon this and other evidence, Ball and Watts have concluded that the earnings process is well approximated by a submartingale process.[28] However,

[25]M. Miller and F. Modigliani, "Some Estimates of Cost of Capital for the Electric Utility Industry, 1954–57," *American Economic Review,* June 1966, pp. 333–396; R. Litzenberger and C. Rao, "Estimates of the Marginal Rate of Time Preferences and Average Risk Aversion of Investors in Electric Utility Shares," *Bell Journal of Economics and Management Science,* Spring 1971, pp. 265–277; and J. McDonald, "Required Return on Public Utility Equities: A National and Regional Analysis, 1958–1969," *Bell Journal of Economics and Management Science,* Autumn 1971, pp. 503–514.

[26]Ray Ball and Philip Brown, "An Empirical Evaluation of Accounting Income Numbers," *Journal of Accounting Research,* vol. 6, pp. 159–178, Autumn 1968; William H. Beaver, "The Information Content of Annual Earnings Announcements," *Empirical Research in Accounting, Selected Studies, 1968,* Supplement to vol. 6, *Journal of Accounting Research,* pp. 67–92; George Benston, "Published Corporate Accounting Data and Stock Prices," *Empirical Research in Accounting: Selected Studies, 1967,* Supplement to vol. 5, *Journal of Accounting Research,* pp. 1–54.

[27]P. Brown and J. Kennelly, "The Informational Content of Quarterly Earnings: An Extension and Some Further Evidence," *Journal of Business,* July 1972, pp. 403–415; and Robert May, "The Influence of Quarterly Earnings Announcement on Investor Decisions as Reflected in Common Stock Price Changes," *Empirical Research in Accounting: Selected Studies, 1971,* Supplement to vol. 9, *Journal of Accounting Research,* pp. 119–163.

[28]Ball, R. and R. Watts, "Some Time Series Properties of Accounting Income," *Journal of Finance,* June 1972, pp. 663–682. A martingale process is one where the expected value of the next element in the series is equal to the observed value of the most recent element. For example, if earnings were described by a martingale process, the expected value of earnings in 19X2 would be the earnings in 19X1. This assumes that the expected change in earnings is zero. If earnings is basically described by this martingale-type process but the expected value of the change is greater than zero, then the process is known as a submartingale.

Beaver has suggested an alternative model, a moving average of a mean reverting process, which explains deflated earnings (for example, net income to stockholders' equity) better than a submartingale process.[29] The implication is that for forecasting several periods ahead an unbiased forecast is obtained by positing a gradual reversion to long-run average earnings. Recent work on stock price elasticity with respect to earnings indicates that the market also acts as if it views earnings to be more closely described by such a process. However, considerably more research is needed. In particular, a theoretically developed model of the earnings process must be provided.

The second major approach to common stock valuation is the two-parameter model of portfolio theory and capital asset pricing. Unlike the model discussed above, this approach provides explicit measures of risk and specifies how the expected performance (that is, the expected value of the return) should vary across firms as a function of risk. The role of financial statement data in this framework would be to provide information that would affect assessments of expected return and risk. Empirical research has indicated that several accounting-defined risk variables (such as payout, leverage, and earnings volatility) exhibit significant association with a market-defined measure of systematic risk (that is, beta).[30]

Hence, security prices behave as if the market views financial statement data as providing information regarding both permanent earnings power as well as risk. Two major questions to be answered by future research concerns the existence of alternative information that may be correlated with financial statement data and the nature of the mechanism by which information becomes reflected in security prices.

Market Efficiency.   The evidence discussed above suggests there is a significant association between financial statement data and security prices. A related question is the issue of market efficiency, which is concerned with the speed with which the data become reflected in prices and whether or not the data are "properly" reflected in prices. Empirical evidence indicates that information, once it has been published, becomes reflected in prices virtually instantaneously. In fact, in many cases, prices act as if the information were known prior to its publication. The second aspect, "proper" reaction, often concerns the ability of the market to see through differences in reported numbers induced by differences in accounting methods. This research has taken two forms. The first examines the stock price performance of firms that have changed methods of accounting to see if the change had any effect on price.[31] The evidence indicates that there is essentially no effect on stock price, even though in most cases the effect of the change was to report higher earnings than would have been reported if no change had taken place. The second form of research is to see if firms that use different methods sell for different prices, *ceteris paribus*. For example, with respect to different depreciation methods, security prices are set as if the market recognizes that different depreciation methods were used to compute the earnings of firms.[32] Needless to

[29]W. Beaver, "The Time Series Behavior of Earnings," *Empirical Research in Accounting: Selected Studies, 1970, Supplement to vol. 8, Journal of Accounting Research*, pp. 62–99.

[30]W. Beaver, P. Kettler, and M. Scholes, "The Association Between Market Determined and Accounting Determined Risk Measures," *Accounting Review*, October 1970, pp. 654–682.

[31]T. R. Archibald, "Stock Market Reaction to Depreciation Switch-Back," *Accounting Review*, January 1972, pp. 22–30; R. Kaplan and R. Roll, "Investor Evaluation of Accounting Information: Some Empirical Evidence," *Journal of Business*, April 1972, pp. 225–257; and R. Ball, "Changes in Accounting Techniques and Stock Prices," *Empirical Research in Accounting: Selected Studies, 1972, Supplement to vol. 10, Journal of Accounting Research*, pp. 1–38.

[32]W. Beaver and R. Dukes, "Interperiod Tax Allocation and Delta Depreciation Methods: Some Empirical Results," *Accounting Review*, July 1973, pp. 549–559.

say, the issue of market efficiency has important implications for accounting decisions to be made by management, auditors, and policy making agents such as the SEC or the FASB.[33]

Concluding Remarks. Across a variety of prediction-decision contexts, the evidence indicates that financial statement data appear to have information content. However, the importance of this finding remains difficult to assess until we have more knowledge of competing information sources and the comparative costs of these alternatives. Also the social aspects of financial statement information make evaluation an extremely difficult question.[34]

BIBLIOGRAPHY

Bernstein, Leopold A.: *Financial Statement Analysis: Theory, Application and Interpretation,* Richard D. Irwin, Homewood, Ill., 1974.

Foulke, Roy A.: *Practical Financial Statement Analysis,* 6th ed., McGraw-Hill Book Company, New York, 1968.

Graham, Benjamin, David L. Dodd, and Sidney Cottle: *Security Analysis,* 4th ed., McGraw-Hill Book Company, New York, 1962.

Horrigan, James O.: "A Short History of Financial Ratio Analysis," *The Accounting Review,* vol. 43, pp. 284–294, April 1968.

Kennedy, Ralph D., and Stewart Y. McMullen: *Financial Statements: Form, Analysis and Interpretation,* 6th ed., Richard D. Irwin, Homewood, Ill., 1973.

Lev, Baruch: *Financial Statement Analysis: A New Approach,* Prentice-Hall, Englewood Cliffs, N.J., 1974.

Myer, John N.: *Financial Statement Analysis,* 3rd ed., Prentice-Hall, Englewood Cliffs, N.J., 1968.

[33]W. Beaver, "What Should be the Objectives of the FASB?" *Journal of Accountancy,* August 1973, pp. 49–56.

[34]J. Demski, "Choice Among Financial Reporting Alternatives," *Accounting Review,* April 1974, pp. 221–232.

Chapter **5**

Interim Reports

DAVID O. GREEN
Professor of Accounting, University of Chicago

INTRODUCTION

After decades of benign neglect, almost everyone connected with accounting seems interested in the topic of interim reports. The decade of the 1970s has seen such indications of interest as Opinion No. 28 of the Accounting Principles Board, comment by the Financial Accounting Standards Board (FASB), problems on the Uniform CPA Examination, new reporting requirements promulgated by the Securities and Exchange Commission (SEC), and, as of this writing, a mandate by the SEC to increase the involvement of the public accounting profession with interim reports. Further, the topic has been the subject of a National Association of Accountants' research study[1] and the basis for what has become a large body of empirical research in accounting. By interim reports, we mean accounting statements which cover a time period of less than a year, i.e., a month, a quarter (3 calendar months or 12 or 13 elapsed weeks), or some multiple of one of these.

Benign neglect is, of course, what the topic deserves *if* interim reporting poses no unique accounting problems, and there would be none if each and every calendar quarter within a year were pretty much alike, that is, with similar amounts of revenue and expense, etc. When the firm is faced with some sort of recurring seasonal variation in sales or costs, *the* conceptual problem arises: Should each short period be treated as a mini-fiscal period with the employment of the usual annual procedures, or should it be considered in some other way, that is, as an aid to the reader in predicting the forthcoming annual outcome?[2]

The sudden surge of interest defies explanation (although we attempt one below) since it is fair to say that most major U.S. publicly held corporations have prepared interim reports for at least several decades. These reports have been distributed to shareholders, the press, and others interested in their content. They have been prepared throughout most of this period largely at the insistence of the New York Stock Exchange which had, early-on, determined minimal requirements for content which were imposed in the Exchange's listing agreement. By and large, the bulk of such reports have been quarterly.

PURPOSE AND LIMITATIONS OF INTERIM REPORTS

Why Have Interim Reports?   It seems logical to suppose that interim reports are published because the time between annual reports is too long. Indeed, this was the position of Elijah Watt Sells in an early and eloquent plea for quarterly reports.[3] Sells argued that quarterly reports would "do much to enlighten the public"; he thought they would be a help in achieving "stable markets for negotiable securities." Sells envisioned quarterly balance sheets certified by public accountants and he reported his view that CPAs "generally are advocates of the quarterly report idea." Subsequent events lead one to believe that most of Sells' predictions and beliefs were in error. The involvement of the profession with interim reports has been minimal,[4] although this is in the process of change. Few published

---

[1]James W. Edwards, *et al.*, *Interim Financial Reporting*, National Association of Accountants, New York, 1972.

[2]For a good review article on this point, see W. J. Bollom and J. J. Weygandt, "An Examination of Some Interim Reporting Theories for a Seasonal Business," *The Accounting Review*, January 1972, pp. 75–84.

[3]Elijah Watt Sells, "Periodical Statement of Corporations Open to Severe Criticism— Quarterly Certified Accountings Inspire Faith Among Investors," *The American Banker*, July 11, 1914, pp. 2278–2279.

[4]When the Securities Exchange Act of 1934 was under consideration by Congress, the American Institute of Accountants submitted a memorandum which, in part, questioned the proposal that quarterly reports be certified. See John L. Carey, "The Origins of Modern Financial Reporting," *Journal of Accountancy*, September 1969, p. 45.

interim reports have been certified (with the general exception of parts of years included in a prospectus), and subsequent articles have been cautionary on the proposition of enlightenment. Blough,[5] for example, wrote: "Accountants know the limitations of quarterly, or other very short-term financial statements, but persons to whom the reports are addressed cannot be depended upon to treat them with adequate caution."

The Special Limitations of Short-Term Financial Statements.   As Hatfield[6] once observed, "accountants are asked to perform [a] hopeless task," to take an economic continuum and to chop "it up into arbitrary and meaningless lengths called a year. . . ." Here, of course, Hatfield alludes to the measurement problems inherent with all transactions which originate in one accounting period and terminate in some future accounting period. As the reporting period is shortened from a year to a quarter, it is obvious that the number of incomplete transactions increases. Thus interim reporting shares most if not all of the problems of annual accountings. In addition, it has a few of its own. By "special problems" we mean the attribution of particular revenues, expenses, or losses to a specific calendar quarter, given no problem at all with their attribution to that particular year.

The special problems of interim reports seem to divide into three categories:

1. Unusual or irregular events of the time period
2. The use of accounting measurement methods for the interim report which differ from those used in the annual report
3. Seasonal variations.

These special problems exist only if we expect interim reports to articulate in some special way with each other and with the subsequent annual report, or if we except them to be comparable year to year.

An alternative classification is suggested by Shillinglaw;[7] his factors which "reduce the correlation between the interim statements and the annual statements" are grouped into five categories: (a) seasonal, (b) random, (c) scheduled, (d) cyclical, and (e) nonrecurring. Since, as he observes, cyclical and nonrecurring fluctuations pose no problems unique to interim reporting, only three remain, and these three correspond fairly well with the three listed above.

Articulation and Prediction.   We speculate that the surge of interest in interim reports acknowledged at the outset stems from the realization that at least two views obtain about the principal purpose of an interim report. According to APB Opinion No. 28:

> Some view each interim period as a basic accounting period and conclude that the results of operations for each interim period should be determined in essentially the same manner as if the interim period were an annual accounting period. Under this view deferrals, accruals, and estimations at the end of each interim period are determined by following essentially the same principles and judgments that apply to annual periods.
> Others view each interim period primarily as being an integral part of the annual period. Under this view deferrals, accruals, and estimations at the end of each interim period are affected by judgments made at the interim date as to results of operations for the balance of the annual period. Thus, an expense item that might be considered as falling wholly within an annual accounting period (no fiscal year-end accrual or deferral) could be allocated among interim periods based on estimated time, sales volume, productive activity, or some other basis.

[5]Carmen G. Blough, "Some of the Dangers Inherent in Quarterly Financial Statements," *Journal of Accountancy,* February 1953, p. 221.
[6]Henry R. Hatfield, "An Historical Defense of Bookkeeping," in W. T. Baxter and Sidney Davidson (eds.), *Studies in Accounting Theory,* Sweet and Maxwell Limited, London, 1962, p. 11.
[7]Gordon Shillinglaw, "Concepts Underlying Interim Financial Statements," *The Accounting Review,* vol. 36, p. 222, April 1961.

The APB did conclude " . . . that each interim period should be viewed primarily as an integral part of an annual period" (Paragraph 9). This means that "certain accounting principles and practices followed for annual reporting purposes may require modification at interim reporting dates so that the reported results for the interim period may better relate to the results of operations for the annual periods." APB Opinion No. 28 was effective for fiscal years beginning January 1, 1974. As of this writing, no published paper has appeared which has analyzed the Opinion's impact on interim accounting reports. One CPA problem (May 1973 Theory, Question 7) effectively illustrates the articulation-prediction-integral part approach to the processing of accounting data. The entire problem (and its unofficial answer) is interesting and relevant, and it goes as follows:

Part a. The unaudited quarterly statements of income issued by many corporations to their stockholders are usually prepared on the same basis as annual statements, the statement for each quarter reflecting the transactions of that quarter.

REQUIRED:

1. Why do problems arise in using such quarterly statements to predict the income (before extraordinary items) for the year? Explain.

2. Discuss the ways in which quarterly income can be affected by the behavior of the costs recorded in a Repairs and Maintenance of Factory Machinery account.

3. Do such quarterly statements give management opportunities to manipulate the results of operations for a quarter? If so, explain or give an example.

Part b. The controller of Navar Corporation wants to issue to stockholders quarterly income statements that will be predictive of expected annual results. He proposes to allocate all fixed costs for the year among quarters in proportion to the number of units expected to be sold in each quarter, stating that the annual income can then be predicted through use of the following equation:

$$\frac{\text{Annual}}{\text{income}} = \frac{\text{Quarterly}}{\text{income}} \times \frac{100\%}{\text{Per cent of unit sales}}$$
applicable to quarter

Navar expects the following activity for the year (in thousands of dollars):

	Units	Average Per Unit	Total (000 omitted)
Sales revenue:			
First quarter	500,000	$2.00	$1,000
Second quarter	100,000	1.50	150
Third quarter	200,000	2.00	400
Fourth quarter	200,000	2.00	400
	1,000,000		1,950
Costs to be incurred:			
Variable:			
Manufacturing		$ .70	700
Selling and administrative		.25	250
		$ .95	950
Fixed:			
Manufacturing			380
Selling and administrative			220
			600
Income before income taxes			$ 400

Required (ignore income taxes):

1. Assuming that Navar's activitie; do not vary from expectations, will the controller's plan achieve his objective? If not, how can it be modified to do so? Explain and give illustrative computations.

2. How should the effect of variations of actual activity from expected activity be treated in Navar's quarterly income statements?

3. What assumption has the controller made in regard to inventories? Discuss.

Answer 7

a. 1. If a corporation's activity could be expected to be the same in all quarters, there would be no problems in using quarterly statements to predict annual results, providing one recognized that the normal activities of any corporation could be disrupted by unforeseen events such as strikes, fires, floods, actions of governmental authorities, and unusual changes in demand for goods or supply of raw materials. Most businesses, however, can be expected to have variations in activity among quarters. Any user of the financial statements who is not also a member of management would probably have great difficulty in making accurate predictions.

A basic cause of fluctuating quarterly activity is seasonality. Sales often show a seasonal pattern. Expenses also may show a seasonal pattern, but the pattern for any expense may differ from the patterns for sales or for the other expenses. Production, expressed in physical units, may show still another pattern. The more product lines a business has, the greater the number of varying seasonal patterns that may be present.

2. Repairs and Maintenance of Factory Machinery is an example of an item which may show substantial variations which are not proportionate to either sales or production. In fact, it would not be unusual for many repair and maintenance projects to be performed during the time when production is lowest, thus causing high unit costs (high costs divided by few units) for the quarter. The effect on income would be spread between the quarter of incurrence and later quarters depending on inventory levels and costing methods. Use of predetermined overhead rates would have the same effect (if variances were allocated between inventories and cost of goods sold) or else would confine the effect of the high costs to the current quarter (if variances were included in cost of goods sold). Low costs in periods of high production would result in low unit costs, the effects of which would be spread among quarters as described above.

3. Such quarterly statements do give management opportunities to manipulate the results of operations for a quarter—for instance, through the timing of expenses. Management can defer some expenses in an attempt to make the results of earlier quarters look very profitable, thus delaying discovery of conditions which could reflect on management's performance. On the other hand, management can incur heavy expenses in the earlier quarters in an attempt to show a favorable trend in the later quarters. For example, the time at which maintenance work is undertaken is somewhat discretionary.

b. 1. The controller cannot achieve his objective without modification of his proposal. The basic flaw in his plan arises from allocation of fixed costs in proportion to units sold even though the average sales price per unit varies from time to time. The controller's plan would produce the results . . . following . . . (in thousands of dollars).

	First	Second	Third	Fourth	Total
			Quarter		
Sales	$1,000	$150	$400	$400	$1,950
Variable costs ($.95 per unit)	475	95	190	190	950
Contribution margin	525	55	210	210	1,000
Fixed costs (50%, 10%, 20%, 20%)	300	60	120	120	600
Income (loss) before income taxes	$ 225	$ (5)	$ 90	$ 90	$ 400

In no instance will application of the controller's equation to interim income result in a predicted annual income of $400. Furthermore, the predicted amounts vary significantly as shown below.

Prediction Based on	Predicted Annual Income
First quarter [$225 = 50%]	$450
Second quarter [$(5) = 10%]	(50)
Third quarter [$90 = 20%]	450
First and second quarters [$220 = 60%]	366.7
First, second, and third quarters [$310 = 80%]	387.5

Neither can the controller achieve his objective through allocation of fixed costs in proportion to sales revenue.

Allocation of fixed costs in proportion to contribution margin (sales revenue less variable costs per unit) will achieve the objective as shown in the following schedule.

| | Quarter | | | | |
	First	Second	Third	Fourth	Total
Contribution margin	$525	$55	$210	$210	$1,000
Fixed costs (52.5%, 5.5%, 21%, 21%)	315	33	126	126	600
Income before income taxes	$210	$ 22	$ 84	$ 84	$ 400

Prediction Based on	Predicted Annual Income
First quarter [$210 = 52.5%]	$400
Second quarter [$22 = 5.5%]	400
Third quarter [$84 = 21%]	400
First and second quarters [$232 = 58%]	400
First, second, and third quarters [$316 = 79%]	400

For the statements to serve their intended purpose, the relationship of quarterly activity to total expected activity will have to be disclosed.

2. Variations of actual activity from expectations can be included in income for the quarter in which they occur, provided their effect on income is not material.

Variations having a material effect should be handled through allocation to all quarters. Restatement of quarters preceding the most recent quarter would be the most logical presentation. Alternatively, the entire adjustment could be assigned to the latest quarter; if so, only the combined income of all elapsed quarters (rather than the results of each elapsed quarter) could be used to predict annual income.

3. The controller appears to assume that inventories will be stable in both number of units and in total dollar amount. Such could be the case if, for instance, there are stable inventories costed by the LIFO method or if there are no year-end inventories. If the assumption is not valid, the controller's plan will have to be modified.

Notice the practice employed in the solution; it has been called the seasonalized assignment of fixed costs.[8] In this illustration contribution is not invariant and

[8]David Green, Jr., "Towards a Theory of Interim Reports," *Journal of Accounting Research,* vol. 2, p. 46, Spring 1964. See also Harry D. Moskowitz, "Improving Interim Reports of Seasonal Businesses by Allocation of Fixed Costs," *The New York CPA,* February, 1967.

therefore the seasonalized assignment is based on expected contribution rather than expected sales. APB Opinion No. 28 is not explicit on this point and observable practice has, thus far, lagged the implied recommendation of this unofficial answer. Consider some of the other prospective income statements that could be prepared for the first quarter. The discrete or mini-fiscal income statement would appear as follows:

NAVAR CORPORATION
1st Quarter Income Statement Prepared on a Discrete Basis
(in thousands)

Sales		$1,000
Variable Costs		475
Contribution		$ 525
One-quarter of expected annual fixed manufacturing cost	$95	
One-quarter of expected annual fixed selling and administration cost	55	150
Income Before Income Tax		$ 375

This would be misleading since it attributes to the first quarter 93.75 percent of the expected annual profit.

Perhaps a more ordinary solution would attempt to calculate a predetermined indirect (manufacturing) fixed cost rate. Assume that this would be calculated by dividing the budgeted fixed manufacturing costs of $380,000 by the expected activity of 1 million units—a rate of $0.38 per unit. Then the normal cost of a unit sold would be $0.70 variable plus $0.38 fixed, or $1.08. The income statement that would emerge would appear as follows:

NAVAR CORPORATION
1st Quarter Income Statement Prepared on a Discrete Basis with
an Annualization of Fixed Manufacturing Cost
(in thousands)

Sales		$1,000
Cost of Goods Sold (500,000 × $1.08)		540
Margin		$ 460
Selling and Administrative:		
Variable (500,000 × $.25)	$125	
Fixed (¼ of $220,000)	55	180
Income Before Income Tax		$ 280

This reduction in reported income from $375,000 to $280,000, or $95,000, results from the use of the predetermined indirect cost rate. The discrete income statement reports fixed manufacturing costs of $95,000, whereas annualization charges $190,000 (500,000 units × $0.38) to the first quarter, thereby explaining the difference in reported income of $95,000. The fixed manufacturing cost of $95,000 in the discrete income statement and the difference in income of $95,000 are equal only by coincidence. Notice, then, that the use of a predetermined indirect cost rate tends to operate in the same way as seasonalized fixed cost assignments. Accountants have been reluctant to use similar methods for selling and administrative costs; had there been no such reluctance, then the dilemma of discrete versus integral might never have surfaced since the use of predetermined cost rates is the equivalent of seasonalized cost assignments. For example, if a firm produced in its first quarter entirely for inventory and made no sales, it would expense none of the manufacturing costs incurred—they would all be inventoried.

A question in the May 1975 CPA Exam extends the articulate-predict approach. Although the unofficial answer again seems ahead of practice in some respects, both the question and answer are reproduced below.

The Anderson Manufacturing Company, a California corporation listed on the Pacific Coast Stock Exchange, budgeted activities for 1975 as follows:

	Amount	Units
Net sales	$6,000,000	1,000,000
Cost of goods sold	3,600,000	1,000,000
Gross margin	$2,400,000	
Selling, general, and administrative expenses	1,400,000	
Operating earnings	$1,000,000	
Nonoperating revenues and expenses	—0—	
Earnings before income taxes	$1,000,000	
Estimated income taxes (current and deferred)	550,000	
Net earnings	$ 450,000	
Earnings per share of common stock	$4.50	

Anderson has operated profitably for many years and has experienced a seasonal pattern of sales volume and production similar to the following ones forecasted for 1975. Sales volume is expected to follow a quarterly pattern of 10%, 20%, 35%, 35%, respectively, because of the seasonality of the industry. Also, due to production and storage capacity limitations it is expected that production will follow a pattern of 20%, 25%, 30%, 25%, per quarter, respectively.

At the conclusion of the first quarter of 1975, the controller of Anderson has prepared and issued the following interim report for public release:

	Amount	Units
Net sales	$ 600,000	100,000
Cost of goods sold	360,000	100,000
Gross margin	$ 240,000	
Selling, general, and administrative expenses	275,000	
Operating loss	$ (35,000)	
Loss from warehouse fire	(175,000)	
Loss before income taxes	$(210,000)	
Estimated income taxes	—0—	
Net loss	$(210,000)	
Loss per share of common stock	$(2.10)	

The following additional information is available for the first quarter just completed, but was not included in the public information released:

1. The company uses a standard cost system in which standards are set at currently attainable levels on an annual basis. At the end of the first quarter there was underapplied fixed factory overhead (volume variance) of $50,000 that was treated as an asset at the end of the quarter. Production during the quarter was 200,000 units, of which 100,000 were sold.

2. The selling, general, and administrative expenses were budgeted on a basis of $900,000 fixed expenses for the year plus $0.50 variable expenses per unit of sales.

3. Assume that the warehouse fire loss met the conditions of an extraordinary loss. The warehouse had an undepreciated cost of $320,000; $145,000 was recovered from insurance on the warehouse. No other gains or losses are anticipated this year from similar events or transactions, nor has Anderson had any similar losses in preceding years; thus, the full loss will be deductible as an ordinary loss for income tax purposes.

4. The effective income tax rate, for federal and state taxes combined, is expected to average 55% of earnings before income taxes during 1975. There are no permanent differences between pretax accounting earnings and taxable income.

5. Earnings per share were computed on the basis of 100,000 shares of capital stock outstanding. Anderson has only one class of stock issued, no long-term debt outstanding, and no stock opinion plan.

Required:

a. Without reference to the specific situation described above, what are the standards of disclosure for interim financial data (published interim financial reports) for publicly traded companies? Explain.

b. Identify the weakness in form and content of Anderson's interim report without reference to the additional information.

c. For each of the five items of additional information, indicate the preferable treatment for each item for interim-reporting purposes and explain why that treatment is preferable.

Answer

a. When publicly traded companies report summarized interim financial information to their securityholders at interim dates, the following data should be reported, as a minimum:

- Sales or gross revenues, provision for income taxes, extraordinary items, cumulative effect of a change in accounting principles, and net earnings.
- Primary and fully diluted earnings per share data for each period presented.
- Seasonal revenues, costs or expenses, and contingent items.
- Disposal of a segment of a business and extraordinary, unusual, or infrequently occurring items (including related income tax effects).
- Changes in accounting principles or estimates, including significant changes in estimates or provisions for income taxes.
- Significant changes in financial position.

When summarized interim financial data are regularly reported on a quarterly basis, the foregoing information with respect to the current quarter and the current year-to-date or the last twelve-months-to-date should be furnished together with comparable data for the preceding year. When a separate fourth quarter report or disclosure of the fourth quarter results is not included in the annual report, material year-end adjustments, extraordinary items, and disposals of segments of a business should be disclosed in the annual report in a note to the financial statements.

Management should provide commentary relating to the effects of significant events upon the interim financial results, similar to its commentary in annual reports. Published balance sheet and funds flow data at interim dates are desirable, but disclosure of significant changes in financial position or funds flow should be presented as a minimum.

b. There are two general weaknesses in the form and content of presentation of the first quarter information: (1) some information in the statement needs further explanation and (2) additional financial statements or summarized data should be presented and explained as appropriate in the circumstances. (See discussion presented in a.)

The major weakness in the first quarter report is that it is misleading because the company is expecting a profit for the year, not a loss as normally would be assumed from the published report alone. Both sales and production were equal to the units budgeted for the first quarter, and if actual activity continues as planned for the rest of the year, Anderson will show a profit of $371,250 ($450,000 − [$175,000 (1 − .55)]) for 1975. Thus, Anderson should indicate in the interim report that sales, production, and net income (loss) are in line with expectations, as related to budgeted data and first quarters of prior years.

No other weakness in form and content is evident, except as discussed below in c.

c. 1. The treatment of underapplied fixed factory overhead as an asset in this situation is the preferred method of accounting. The expected year-end result is that actual production will exactly equal budgeted production upon which the standard was based; thus, no volume variance should exist at year end.

2. The manner in which the selling, general, and administrative expenses were handled in the report is the preferred method. These costs are not inventoriable, they cannot be associated directly with the product, and they have been

incurred at expected levels. Thus, they should be expensed as period costs when incurred or be allocated among interim periods based on the estimate of time expired, benefit received, or activity associated with the periods.

3. The warehouse fire loss is an extraordinary item that should be appropriately disclosed in the interim financial report, net of income tax effect. In this situation the $175,000 loss should be reduced by the effective income tax reduction of $96,250. Thus, the loss should reduce net income by $78,750 ($175,000 − $96,250), and the nature of the loss should be appropriately explained in the commentary accompanying the quarterly data.

4. A negative income tax expense (an income tax benefit) should have been included in the interim report. The $35,000 loss from regular operations should have been reduced by $19,250 ($35,000 × 55%), the expected tax reduction to be realized from profitable operations during the remaining three quarters of 1975. The tax effect benefits resulting from losses that arise in the early portion of the year should be recognized only when realization is assured beyond any reasonable doubt. An established seasonal pattern of losses in early interim periods, offset by income in later interim periods, should constitute sufficient evidence that realization is assured beyond reasonable doubt—unless other evidence contradicts this conclusion.

5. Primary and fully diluted earnings per share data for each period presented should be included in the interim report when a company meets the conditions requiring both earnings per share computations. Because Anderson has a simple capital structure, it must show only the primary earnings per share figures. In the situation presented, there should have been a per share amount for the loss, for the extraordinary item, and for the sum of the two.

It is some indication of the rapidity of change in contemporary accounting that some of the answers that would have been acceptable in May 1975 would not be acceptable a year or less later. In particular, the answer to Requirement *a* would be changed as a result of an SEC Release of September 1975. This is discussed in the next section.

INTERIM REPORTS AND THE SECURITIES AND EXCHANGE COMMISSION

Although the Securities Exchange Act of 1934 contained a requirement for "such annual reports . . . and such quarterly reports, as the Commission may prescribe," routine quarterly reports of any data were not required until 1945. During this eleven-year period, the SEC only required the filing of interim report Form 8K when some special event occurred during the year.

In 1945, in anticipation of investors' needs for prompt information as the economy changed over from war activities, the SEC required quarterly reports of sales and unfilled orders and separate acknowledgment of sales attributable to war contracts. In addition, immediate reports were required for terminations of war contracts if the uncompleted portion amounted to 20 percent or more of the registrant's previous fiscal year's sales.

In 1946, the SEC acknowledged a continuing interest in quarterly reports and announced a proposal for quarterly operating information to be supplied to it on Form 8K. The proposal apparently elicited so much adverse comment that the SEC settled for sales reports from companies listed on national securities exchanges indicating quarterly sales. These were to be filed on Form 8K within 45 days of the end of the quarter. With this requirement, the earlier rule on reporting war-related business was rescinded. Toward the end of 1948, the 8K requirement was extended to all companies required to file reports pursuant to Section 15 of the Act.

In 1949, the required data reported on Form 8K was transferred to Form 9K. In 1952, the SEC again proposed that sales data be replaced with a quarterly income statement accompanied by a reconciliation of retained earnings and elicited comment on this proposal. Apparently (the file has not been made available for public inspection) much of the comment received was negative, and in early 1953 the SEC announced that the proposal would be dropped. A few months later, the SEC invited comment on a proposal to discontinue Form 9K; in October of that year, the requirement was rescinded. As a result, there was no longer any SEC requirement for any kind of routine interim report.

In early 1955, the SEC acknowledged that it was considering a new form 9K which would require semiannual reports. The Commission stated that:

> it recognizes that preparing profit and loss statements on a quarterly basis may present problems for some issuers and accordingly the proposed report would not constitute a formal profit and loss statement. . . . [Because] interim earnings figures can frequently be arrived at only by the use of reasonable estimates or on the basis of certain assumptions, the proposal provides that reports of such information would not be subject to liability under Section 18 of the Act.

In mid-1955, the Commission adopted the proposed Form 9K which called for the following nine items to be received within 45 days of the end of the six-month period:

1. Gross sales less discounts, returns, and allowances
2. Operating revenues
3. Total of captions 1 and 2
4. Extraordinary items
5. Net income or loss before taxes on income
6. Provision for taxes on income
7. Net income or loss
8. Special items
9. Earned surplus items.

Specifically exempted from the 9K requirements were:

1. Banks and bank holding companies
2. Investment companies
3. Insurance companies, other than title insurance
4. Public utilities and common carriers which file financial reports with the Federal Power Commission, Federal Communications Commission, or the Interstate Commerce Commission
5. Companies engaged in the seasonal production and seasonal sale of a single-crop agricultural commodity
6. Companies in the promotional or development stage to which paragraph (b) or (c) of Rule 5A–01 of Article 5A of *Regulation S–X* is applicable
7. Foreign issuers other than private issuers domiciled in a North American country or Cuba.

Of these, however, investment companies and certain real estate companies were required to file quarterly reports.

A study group was appointed in late 1967 "to examine the operations of the disclosure provisions of the [Acts] . . . and Commission rules and regulations thereunder." Their report, prepared under the direction of Commissioner Francis M. Wheat, commented on interim reports as follows:[9]

> More and more publicly-held corporations are releasing condensed quarterly financial information. Both the New York and American Stock Exchanges require publication of such information by all listed companies, although the standards which they set for such information are minimal. The Study carefully examined a significant sample of quarterly financial reports and releases provided by the two exchanges. It was readily

[9]Francis M. Wheat, "Disclosure to Investors—A Reappraisal of Federal Administrative Policies under the '33 and '34 Acts," SEC, 1969.

apparent (and acknowledged by representatives of the exchanges) that they varied from extremely useful to extremely poor and uninformative. Conferences were held by the Study with accountants representing both large and small firms throughout the country, with members of a special committee of the Financial Executives Institute, and with the American Society of Corporate Secretaries, regarding the feasibility of condensed quarterly financial reporting. It was the general opinion that such reporting was feasible and that a useful advance in disclosure policy could be achieved by developing standards for such reporting. A special committee of the AICPA greatly assisted the Study in this effort.

The Study proposes that a new form to be designated 10Q be substituted for present Forms 8K and 9K. It would be due 45 days after the close of each fiscal quarter (except that a report of a significant acquisition or disposition of assets would be due 10 days after the execution of a written agreement for such acquisition or disposition). It would consist of two parts. Part I would cover the substance of the present 8K with a number of changes. Part II would consist of condensed, comparative financial information. Part II would not be required for the fourth fiscal quarter. It would not be audited or be subject to the liability provisions of Section 18 of the '34 Act. Quarterly reports to shareholders containing the information required by Part II of Form 10Q could be submitted in lieu of that part of the form.

This proposal for interim reports was accepted and Form 10Q was required from covered companies effective with the year 1970. In late 1974, the SEC issued its *Notice of Proposals to Increase Disclosure of Interim Results by Registrants* (Release No. 33-5549). And a mighty increase in disclosure was proposed, i.e., Comparative Balance Sheets as at the end of the quarter, Comparative Statements of Changes in Financial Position for the year to date, a new narrative analysis of results of operations in addition to less condensed comparative income statements, inclusion of quarterly data in the annual reports, and an increased involvement in the interim reporting procedure by the independent accountant.

The proposed increase in disclosure motivated more than 700 letters of comments; in addition, the Commission held public hearings on the proposals and heard testimony from 14 witnesses. Most of these comments expressed serious concern about the proposals. Nevertheless, the Commission issued *ASR 177* in September 1975 and it became effective for Form 10Q reports covering periods beginning after December 25, 1975. The requirements imposed did not differ importantly from those proposed.

The new rules require [summarized, i.e., less detailed than required by Regulation S-X] income statements for the most recent quarter, the equivalent calendar quarter in the preceding year and year-to-date data for both years. Condensed funds statements are required on a year-to-date basis for the current and prior year. In addition, registrants are permitted to show income statement data and funds statement data for the twelve month period ending at the interim reporting date for both years if they elect to do so. Balance sheets are required as of the end of the most recent quarter and at the same date in the preceding year.

In addition, the new rules require increased pro forma information in the case of business combinations accounted for as purchases, conformity with the principles of accounting measurement set forth in the Accounting Principles Board opinion on interim financial reports and increased disclosure of accounting changes.

In connection with accounting changes, a letter from the registrant's independent public accountant is required to be filed in which the accountant states whether or not the change is to an alternative principle which in his judgment is preferable under the circumstances. . . . [In spite of numerous objections, the] rule has . . . been adopted as proposed.

In addition to financial statements, a new instruction to Form 10Q requires management to provide a narrative analysis of the results of operations. . . . The new instruction requires explanation of the reasons for material changes in the amount of revenue and expense items from one quarter to the next (even though the preceding quarter may not be reported as such in the form 10Q), between the most recent quarter and the equivalent quarter in the preceding year, and between the year-to-date data and comparable data for the prior year. While such explanations are to be presented in narrative form, it is expected that they will include quantitative data in explaining the reasons for changes. In addition to requiring an analysis of operations, the new form includes an instruction which permits the registrant to furnish any additional information which management believes will be of significance to registrants [sic; the word probably was meant to be *investors*]. This same instruction requires the registrant to indicate whether a Form 8K was filed during the quarter reporting either unusual charges or credits to income or a change of auditors.

Under the new rules, Form 10Q must be signed by either the chief financial officer or the chief accounting officer of the corporation. This requirement was included in recognition of the fact that the data in the form were primarily financial, and that it was appropriate to emphasize the responsibility of the chief financial or accounting officer for the representations explicit and implicit in the filing. This signature will not relieve other corporate officers of their responsibilities. . . .

The financial information included in Form 10Q need not be reviewed prior to filing by an independent public accountant. However, certain registrants will be required to include certain data contained in the form 10Q in an unaudited note to financial statements for the year. Such a note must be reviewed by an independent public accountant in accordance with prescribed professional standards in connection with the annual audit. Since review procedures must be applied to quarterly data in connection with the annual audit of such registrants in any event, the additional cost to these registrants of having a review made on a timely basis should be small, particularly if the annual audit is planned with such a review in mind.

The Commission believes that all registrants would find it useful and prudent to have independent public accountants review quarterly financial data on a timely basis during the year prior to the filing of Form 10Q and it encourages registrants to have such a review made. While such a review does not represent an audit and cannot be relied upon to detect all errors and omissions that might be discovered in a full audit of quarterly data, it will bring the reporting, accounting and analytical expertise of independent professional accountants to bear on financial reports included in Form 10Q and therefore should increase the quality and the reliability of the data therein in a cost-effective way.

ASR 177 requires the involvement of the independent accountant with the interim reports of the client, and this is discussed in the following section.

THE PUBLIC ACCOUNTING PROFESSION AND INTERIM REPORTS

Shillinglaw,[10] in what may have been a masterpiece of understatement, pointed out in 1961 that interim reports "have never received the professional attention that has been devoted to annual statements." This certainly was true until the latter part of 1974 when the Big Eight firm of Coopers & Lybrand indicated a willingness, if not a desire, to get involved in their clients' interim reporting process. They proposed "a limited review that would not be equivalent to an audit." Shortly thereafter another Big Eight firm, Arthur Andersen & Co., petitioned the SEC, requesting that it prohibit companies from publishing any reports from CPAs based on "limited reviews" of unaudited quarterly data. One other position taken (Price-Waterhouse) was that the most beneficial CPA involvement in the quarterly reporting process of clients would be to serve as "formally appointed accounting and reporting consultants to the board of directors. . . . "

> Put simply, our role would be to extend the existing skills of the board by providing special accounting and reporting skills not otherwise available. We would help the directors frame (and answer) the questions they ought to ask, and in fact would ask if

[10]Shillinglaw, *op. cit.*

possessed of the necessary accounting background, for example: Are the bases of preparation adequate? Consistent with previous quarters? Have generally accepted accounting principles been applied? Any accounting changes in this quarter? If so, are they handled right and reported appropriately? Are significant new financial developments communicated in the quarterly report? Taken as a whole, is the quarterly report, with its accompanying commentary, an understandable, informative, useful document?

In December 1974, the SEC issued its *Notice of Proposals to Increase Disclosure of Interim Results by Registrants* (Release No. 33-5549) where it considered, in part, the question of increased CPA involvement with quarterly reports. The relevant paragraph reads as follows:

> The Commission also believes that it is useful to investors to have the reporting expertise of independent public accountants drawn upon in the preparation of quarterly reports. In addition, it feels that the involvement of the independent accountant will increase the reliability of such reports even though no audit opinion is issued on the interim financial report. Accordingly, the rules proposed herein encourage this involvement on a timely basis and require an after the fact review of limited interim data at the time of the annual audit by including interim data in the footnotes to the annual financial statements.

Subsequently (April, 1975; Release No. 33-5579), the SEC divulged:

> The proposal which elicited the greatest amount of comment was the proposed amendment to Regulation S-X which would require certain limited quarterly data to be included in a footnote to financial statements for the year. This inclusion would have the effect of involving independent public accountants with quarterly data and it was this effect which was most criticized by commentators.

About this same time (April 15, 1975), the AICPA's Auditing Standards Executive Committee (AudSEC) issued an exposure draft of a proposed statement on auditing standards for *voluntary*, pre-issuance, limited reviews of unaudited interim financial information. This was not enough to satisfy the SEC, and AudSEC was under pressure to prepare a statement that the SEC would find acceptable. Fortunately, the Statement on Auditing Standards No. 10 (SAS No. 10), "Limited Review of Interim Financial Information," issued in December 1975 did satisfy. SAS No. 10 "describes the nature, timing and extent of procedures that the independent certified public accountant should apply to interim information when the accountant has been engaged to make a *limited review* of that information." A limited review differs from an audit; it does not provide a basis for the expression of an opinion because it does not include many of the procedures ordinarily employed in an audit.

SAS No. 10 points out:

> The objective of a limited review of interim financial information is to provide the accountant with a basis for reporting to the board of directors on those matters that he believes should be brought to its attention, based upon applying his objectivity and knowledge of financial reporting practices to significant accounting matters of which he becomes aware through inquiries and analytical procedures.

The procedures for making a limited review consist primarily of inquiries and analyses aimed at the significant accounting aspects of the financial information to be reported. These procedures would include, at least in part, some of the following, which are heavily abbreviated from SAS No. 10: (a) Inquiry about how the accounting system generates interim financial information and about any potential impact a change in the internal control system might have thereon. (b) Analytical review by reference to internal financial statements, trial balances, etc., to discern unusual items if any. This could include comparison of actual results with the budget for the period, with the previous interim period, with the year-ago period, etc. (c) A review of the minutes of meetings of stockholders, the board of directors, and any board subcommittees. (d) A consideration of whether the reportable information conforms to GAAP. (e) Obtaining letters from other accountants who made limited reviews on important segments, subsidiaries, or investees. (f) Extended inquiry of officers and executives responsible for accounting affairs on such issues as conformity, consistency, events subsequent to the statement date, and the like.

According to SAS No. 10, "a limited review of interim financial information is intended to assist members of the board of directors in meeting their responsibilities." SAS No. 10 provides an illustrative letter that might be addressed to the board. Since it summarizes much of the Statement not referred to above, we reproduce it in its entirety.

> We have performed a limited review [describe the data or statements subjected to such review] of ABC Company and consolidated subsidiaries for the three-month and nine-month periods ended September 30, 19X1.
>
> Our limited review was performed in accordance with standards for such reviews promulgated by the American Institute of Certified Public Accountants and, accordingly, consisted principally of obtaining an understanding, by inquiries, of the accounting system for preparation of interim financial information; making an analytical review of pertinent financial data; and making inquiries of and evaluating responses from certain officials of the company who have responsibility for financial and accounting matters. (In addition, at your request we have [describe any other procedures performed].) With regard to the CDE subsidiary whose total assets and revenue constitute 20 percent and 22 percent, respectively, of the related consolidated totals, we read the report of other accountants on their limited review of the interim financial information of such subsidiary.
>
> Because our limited review did not constitute an examination made in accordance with generally accepted auditing standards, we express no opinion on [describe the data or statements subjected to the limited review].
>
> In connection with our limited review and that of the other accountants referred to above, the following (no) matters came to our attention that we believe should be reported to you: [Describe matters that should be brought to the attention of the board of directors.] Had we performed additional procedures or had we made an examination of the [describe the data or statements subjected to the limited review or other procedures] in accordance with generally accepted auditing standards, (other) matters might have come to our attention that would have been reported to you.
>
> This report is solely for the information of the board of directors and management and is not to be quoted in documents setting forth the unaudited interim financial information or in any other document available to the public.

THE FASB AND INTERIM REPORTS

At the time this Handbook goes to press, the FASB has put the topic of interim reports on its emerging problems agenda. As a guess, the FASB will attempt to deal specifically with some of the issues left open by APB Opinion No. 28. As a further guess, the FASB will go into the prediction-articulation problem in greater depth, probably along the lines of the 1975 CPA question and solution which appeared earlier in this chapter.

FASB Statement No. 3 is entitled (and is concerned with) *Reporting Accounting Changes in Interim Financial Statements*, an amendment of APB Opinion No. 28. The statement differentiates changes to LIFO from other accounting changes and also differentiates changes made in the first quarter from those made in other calendar quarters. In brief, for non-LIFO changes:

> If a cumulative effect type accounting change is made during the *first* interim period of an enterprise's fiscal year, the cumulative effect of the change on retained earnings at the *beginning of that fiscal year* shall be included in net income of the first interim period (and in last-twelve-months-to-date financial reports that include that first interim period).
>
> If a cumulative effect type accounting change is made in *other than the first* interim period of an enterprise's fiscal year, *no* cumulative effect of the change shall be included

in net income of the period of change. Instead, financial information for the pre-change interim periods of the fiscal year in which the change is made shall be restated by applying the newly adopted accounting principle to those prechange interim periods. The cumulative effect of the change on retained earnings at the *beginning of that fiscal year* shall be included in restated net income of the first interim period of the fiscal year in which the change is made (and in any year-to-date or last-twelve-months-to-date financial reports that include the first interim period).

Paragraph 11 of this Statement details the necessary disclosure to be made in interim reports. Heavily abbreviated, they are, for the interim period in which the new accounting principle is adopted: (a) explain the nature of and justification for the change, (b) disclose the effect of the change on income of the current period, and (c) disclose the effect of the change on any prior period to which the current period is being compared. Further, "(d) In year-to-date and last-twelve-months-to-date financial reports that include the interim period in which the new accounting principle is adopted, the disclosures specified in . . . (b) . . . and in . . . (c) above shall be made, and (e) in financial reports for a subsequent (post-change) interim period of the fiscal year in which the new accounting principle is adopted, disclosure shall be made of the effect of the change on income. . . ."

For the change to LIFO: If the change is made in the first interim period, the disclosures listed in the preceding paragraph must be made except requirement (c). When this change is made in a period other than the first, the disclosures listed in the preceding paragraph must be made again with the exception of (c); in addition, information for the prechange interim periods of that fiscal year shall be restated. This is exemplified in one of the illustrations of Exhibit 1.

EXHIBIT 1   Illustration of Quarterly Results Reported in Annual Reports

| | Continuing operations* | | | | Total operations | | | |
| | 1974 | | 1973 | | 1974 | | 1973 | |
Quarter	Sales†	Income per share	Sales	Income per share	Sales	Income per share	Sales	Income per share
First	$148.6	$1.10	$135.8	$0.84	$151.6	$0.95	$138.8	$0.78
Second ..	156.6	1.08	138.4	0.88	160.0	1.05	142.0	0.82
Third ...	127.7	0.79	126.8	0.82	130.5	0.73	129.7	0.69
Fourth ..	118.7	0.23	144.3	0.99	120.7	(0.38)	148.0	0.81
Total ...	$551.6	$3.20	$545.3	$3.53	$562.8	$2.35	$558.5	$3.10

*Continuing operations exclude carpet operations and 34 cents per share loss in fourth quarter 1974 on disposal of carpet division.
†Sales are in millions of dollars.
Source: 1974 Annual Report, M. Lowenstein & Sons, Inc.

| | 1974 Net earnings | | | | |
	1st quarter	2nd quarter	3rd quarter	4th quarter	Total
Amounts (thousands)					
Before the restatement	$1,430	$2,500	$2,507	$1,926	$8,363
Effect of the restatement	(164)	(211)	(206)	(183)	(764)
After the restatement	$1,266	$2,289	$2,301	$1,743	$7,599
Per Share					
Before the restatement	$ 0.42	$ 0.74	$ 0.74	$ 0.56	$ 2.45
Effect of the restatement	(0.05)	(0.06)	(0.06)	(0.05)	(0.22)
After the restatement	$ 0.37	$ 0.68	$ 0.68	$ 0.51	$ 2.24

Source: 1974 Annual Report, Lehigh Portland Cement Company.

Statement No. 3 also provides that:

> When a publicly traded company that regularly reports interim information to its securityholders makes an accounting change during the fourth quarter of its fiscal year and does not report the data specified by paragraph 30 of *APB Opinion No. 28* in a separate fourth quarter report or in its annual report to its securityholders, the disclosures about the effect of the accounting change on interim periods that are required by paragraphs 23–26 of APB Opinion No. 28 or by paragraphs 9–13 [which are summarized above] of this Statement, as appropriate, shall be made in a note to the annual financial statements for the fiscal year in which the change is made.

One aspect of interim reporting that has not, as yet, received careful attention is the accounting for the impact of a significant event whose timing is more or less random. As an example consider the following paragraphs taken from *The Wall Street Journal* (August 6, 1975):

> Interlake Inc. said net income from continuing operations for the month of August will be increased by $5 million, or $1.40 a share, because of settlement of a dispute with a supplier of raw material.
> The company refused to give more information. A spokesman said Interlake has an ongoing relationship with the supplier "and it wouldn't be fair to get into details."
> The diversified steel producer previously reported second quarter net profit of $5.5 million, or $1.53 a share, including $1.1 million, or 27 cents a share, from income from discontinued operations.

Another aspect that has gone without serious study is the use of the text portion of the interim report as a vehicle for a company or executive forecast. A good example of this use appears in the second quarter report, June 30, 1974, of Northwest Industries, Inc. The illustrative paragraphs are:

> The results for the second quarter and first six months reinforce our previously expressed view that 1974 will be another record year for your company. Earnings estimates for the year by certain financial institutions, although above last year's earn-

EXHIBIT 2   Decision Diagram—Exemptions Under Rule 3-16(t) of Regulation S-X for SEC Registrants (Courtesy Ernst & Ernst.)

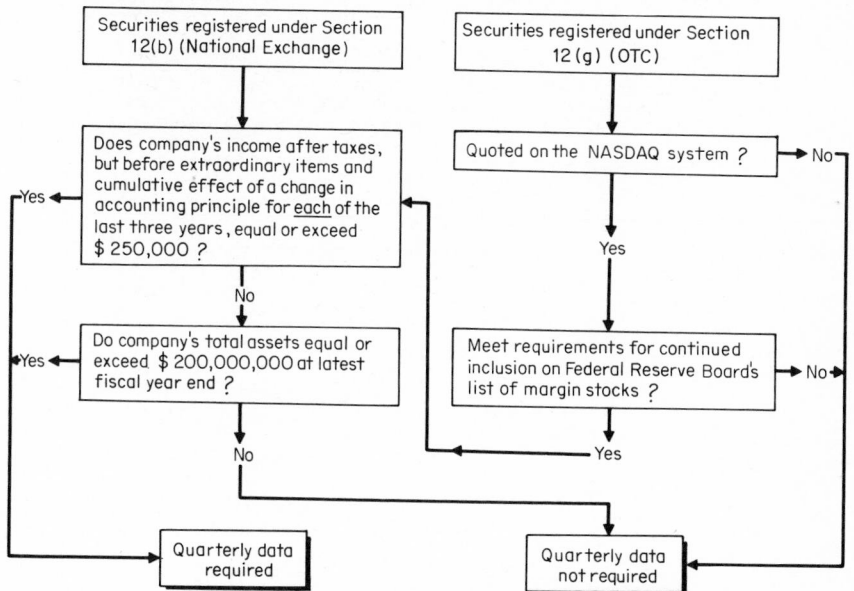

EXHIBIT 3

KENNAMETAL INC. /LATROBE, PA 15650 · PHONE 412-537-3311

August 27, 1975

To the Shareholders of Kennametal Inc.:

Another Record Year

For the third consecutive year, we are pleased to report
record sales and earnings. Net income for the year ended
June 30, 1975, was up 11 percent on a 16 percent increase in sales
and other income.

Final audited results for Kennametal Inc. and subsidiaries
for the last two fiscal years were as follows (in thousands,
except for per share data):

	1975	1974
Net sales and other income	$144,314	$124,326
Net income before taxes	31,247	29,516
Taxes on income	14,430	14,380
Net income - amount	16,817	15,136
Net income - per share	$6.12	$5.48

June Quarter

Strength in domestic mining tool sales and in our foreign
business offset softness experienced in domestic metalworking
sales. The result was an increase of 1.2 percent over revenues
for the June 1974 quarter -- $35.6 million vs. $35.2 million.
After a smaller income tax provision (reflecting a larger investment tax credit), net income for the quarter was $4.2 million
($1.53 per share) as compared with $3.9 million ($1.43 per share)
in the June 1974 quarter. It should be noted, however, that the
June quarter this year contained year-end adjustments of approximately $340,000 net after taxes (12 cents per share) applicable
to the preceding three quarters of this fiscal year.

Proposed Two-for-One Stock Split

Your Board of Directors at its meeting on July 29, voted to
recommend for shareholder approval at the annual meeting to be
held October 21, 1975, an amendment of the Company's articles of
incorporation increasing the authorizied stock from 4 million
shares to 10 million shares, and splitting the outstanding shares
2-for-1, effective November 10, 1975. The Board indicated it

(Cont.)

EXHIBIT 3 *(Continued)*

KENNAMETAL INC.

To the Shareholders of Kennametal Inc. -2-   August 27, 1975

would consider establishing the quarterly dividend rate on the new
shares at 21 cents which would be an increase of 20 percent over
the present dividend. The notice of annual meeting and proxy
statement to be mailed shareholders on September 19 will contain
further details on the above.

<u>Outlook</u>

Although our business held up well through the June quarter,
currently we are feeling the effects of the recession as well as
experiencing seasonal weakness in sales of metalworking tools.
It now appears that this September quarter will be well below a
year ago, but it should be noted that the September quarter last
year set a record for any quarter in the Company's history in both
sales and earnings. Revenues in this quarter last year were $38.0
million and net income was $5.1 million, equal to $1.86 per share,
which included a net of 10 cents per share of nonrecurring income.

Although the current quarter will be down, we expect a
definite improvement in the December quarter. The Company has recently received defense orders for projectile components of $5.1
million, with shipments scheduled over a 13-month period starting
in December 1975.

<u>Dividend</u>

For shareholders of record as of August 12, we enclose a
dividend of 35 cents per share payable today. Total dividends
paid in fiscal 1975 were $1.40, as compared with $1.20 and $ .83
in the preceding two fiscal years.

Sincerely yours,

Alex G. McKenna
President and
Chief Executive Officer

enclosure

ings, were substantially below your management's own outlook. Accordingly, in June we felt it desirable to announce that 1974 earnings are expected to be in excess of $4 a share, assuming full dilution. This compares with the record $3.09 in 1973. Net earnings for 1974 are expected to be above $73 million, compared with $57.1 million last year. As we announced at the annual meeting of stockholders, sales for 1974 should exceed $1 billion for the first time.

If the year continues as we anticipate that it will, this fall we expect to recommend to your board of directors an increase in the common stock dividend from its present annual level of 85 cents a share.

QUARTERLY EARNINGS IN THE ANNUAL REPORT

In his 1966 article, Bows[11] recommended that quarterly earninings be shown in the annual report, "particularly if the company is in a seasonal business." According to Bows, "This gives the shareholder the opportunity of understanding the wide fluctuations which may occur within a year for a particular business, and prepares him for seasonal patterns where the quarterly earnings are normally above or below those of a preceding quarter."

Examples of reporting quarterly earnings in the annual report were then rare, but there were increasing numbers of annual reports with such data over the intervening years. In a random sample of 50 annual reports for 1974, we found 14 companies (28%) which provided such data on a strictly voluntary basis. Exhibit 1 reproduces two of these; the one from Lehigh Portland Cement Company illustrates the procedure for reporting a change to LIFO required by FASB Statement No. 3.

ASR 177, as noted earlier, *requires* certain registrants to include quarterly data in a note to the annual financial statements for years subsequent to 1975. Ernst & Ernst has prepared the decision diagram reproduced in Exhibit 2 to ascertain which registrants are so required.

THE PRELIMINARY ANNUAL REPORT

An increasing number of companies now furnish stockholders and the financial press with so-called preliminary results, probably because it is such a long time between the end of the reporting year and the appearance of the formal annual report. If all reports other than the formal annual report are to be known as interim reports, then this is another interim report, and, in a manner of speaking, it could be considered the fourth interim report of the year even though the emphasis is on the year rather than the fourth quarter. In some instances, it consists of a letter which reports the various comparative details of sales and income. In other instances, abbreviated financial statements appear along with rather extensive textual commentary. See Exhibit 3.

POSTSCRIPT

SAS No. 13, "Reports on a Limited Review of Interim Financial Information," as its name implies, is concerned with the accountant's report that accompanies interim financial information "issued to stockholders and others or in forms filed with regulatory agencies" whether such interim data is presented alone or in a note to audited financial statements. For example, a CPA who has made a limited review as specified in SAS No. 10 may consent to the use of his or her name and the inclusion of the report in a written communication which sets forth the interim

---

[11]Albert J. Bows, "Standards for Consistency in Interim Reports," *Financial Executive,* November 1966, p. 24.

information. If, however, restrictions on the scope of the CPA's review preclude its completion, the CPA should not consent to the use of his or her name. Restrictions on scope may be imposed by the client or they could be caused by such factors as inadequacy of the accounting records or a material weakness in internal control.

SAS No. 13 provides an example of a report; since it differs from the one reproduced on page 5-15, we reproduce it here.

> We have made a limited review, in accordance with standards established by the American Institute of Certified Public Accountants, of (describe the information or statements subjected to such review) of ABC Company and consolidated subsidiaries as of September 30, 19X1, and for the three-month and nine-month periods then ended. Since we did not make an audit, we express no opinion on the (information or statements) referred to above.

Such a report could be addressed to the company, to the board, or to the stockholders. Ordinarily it would bear the date of the completion of limited review. Further, each page of the interim financial information which the report accompanies "should be clearly marked as 'unaudited.'" Incorporation of the work of other accountants is illustrated in a fashion similar to the earlier exhibit here (page 5-15); the phrase "we read the report" was changed to "we were furnished."

Model paragraphs are presented to deal with (1) material adjustments proposed by the accountant, but not effected; (2) information proposed for inclusion by the accountant, but not included; (3) the required exhibit to accompany Form 10-Q; and (4) footnotes in the audited financial statements wherein interim data are reported.

BIBLIOGRAPHY

Accounting Principles Board: "Interim Financial Reporting," Opinion No. 28, AICPA, New York, 1973.

American Institute of Certified Public Accountants: *Statement on Auditing Standards No. 10,* "Limited Review of Interim Financial Information," AICPA, New York, 1975.

Bollom, W. J., and J. J. Weygandt: "An Examination of Some Interim Reporting Theories for a Seasonal Business," *The Accounting Review,* January 1972, pp. 75–84.

Edwards, James W., *et al.: Interim Financial Reporting,* National Association of Accountants, New York, 1972.

Financial Accounting Standards Board: "Reporting Accounting Changes in Interim Financial Statements," Statement No. 3, AICPA, New York, 1974.

Foster, George: "Quarterly Accounting Data: Time Series Properties and Predictive-Ability Results," Graduate School of Business, University of Chicago, 1976.

Green, David, Jr., "Towards a Theory of Interim Reports," *Journal of Accounting Research,* vol. 2, p. 46, Spring 1964.

Shillinglaw, Gordon: "Concepts Underlying Interim Financial Statements," *The Accounting Review,* vol. 36, p. 222, April 1961.

Taylor, Robert G.: "An Examination of the Evolution, Content, Utility and Problems of Published Interim Reports," unpublished Ph.D. dissertation, University of Chicago, 1963.

Wheat, Francis M.: "Disclosure to Investors—A Reappraisal of Federal Administrative Policies under the '33 and '34 Acts," SEC, 1969.

Chapter **6**

Earnings Forecasts

PHILIP B. CHENOK
Partner, Main Lafrentz & Co.

Note: This chapter contains quotations from publications copyright © 1973, 1975 by the American Institute of Certified Public Accountants, Inc., the publisher. These passages are reprinted with the permission of the AICPA.

INTRODUCTION

Management has long been involved in preparing various types of earnings forecasts. Many companies prepare budgets or profit plans for internal planning and control and for considering alternative actions. Some companies have made earnings forecasts available on an informal basis to selected lenders, security analysts, and investors. Earnings forecasts sometimes have been included in offering information for bond issues to finance hospitals, airports, and public facilities.

Nature of Forecasting. Forecasting has been described as follows:[1]

> Forecasts are derived through a combination of judgment and science in which history, plans, reactions, aspirations, constraints, and pressures all play a part. Forecasts are based on management's assumptions of future events, some of which assumptions are explicit, but many of which are implicit. The assumptions, in turn, are based on present circumstances and information currently available, including both internal and external data. Forecasts may be affected favorably or unfavorably by many factors such as revenues, costs, employee relations, taxes, governmental controls, and general economic conditions. Accordingly, there is no assurance that the forecasted results will be achieved.
>
> No one can know the future. Predictions are based on information about the past and present. Of necessity, judgment must be applied to estimate when and how conditions are likely to change. These judgments may subsequently prove to be inaccurate; thus, the accuracy and reliability of a forecast can never be guaranteed. Forecasts by their very nature are subject to error. When a succession of forecasts is made over a period of time, it is inevitable that at some point a particular forecast will turn out to have been significantly inaccurate. Because of this, forecasts may require updating and revision when conditions significantly change.
>
> Forecast information is substantially less subject to objective verification than historical data. Expected results are often not achieved because of unforeseen occurrences. When working with or using forecast information, it is essential to understand the inherent exposure to inaccuracy involved in any forecast.
>
> The difficulty in making a financial forecast can vary significantly from enterprise to enterprise, from industry to industry, and from time to time. Also, a financial forecast can be especially difficult to prepare in the case of a new venture, where no historical record of performance exists upon which to base a forecast.

Recent Proposals. Recently there has been considerable discussion about public disclosure of earnings forecasts on a regular basis.

- The Report of the Study Group on the Objectives of Financial Statements discussed the relationship between the predictive process and the objectives of financial statements and recommended that financial forecasts be provided when they would aid the predictive process.[2]

---

[1]Management Advisory Services Executive Committee, Guideline Series No. 3, "Guidelines for Systems for the Preparation of Financial Forecasts," American Institute of Certified Public Accountants, March 1975, pp. 5 and 6.

[2]"Report of the Study Group on Objectives of Financial Statements," American Institute of Certified Public Accountants, October 1973, pp. 46 and 47.

- The Securities and Exchange Commission (SEC) announced that it would permit forecast information to be included in reports filed with it[3] and has made proposals to implement the filing of such information.[4]
- The Accountants International Study Group recommended "an orderly progress towards the publication of profit forecasts."[5]

Without commenting on the desirability of publishing earnings forecasts or taking a position as to whether forecast information should be made a part of basic financial statements, several divisions of the American Institute of Certified Public Accountants are studying related aspects of earnings forecasts. The Management Advisory Services Division has issued a statement dealing with guidelines for systems to prepare financial forecasts.[6] The Accounting Standards Division has issued a statement of position on the presentation and disclosure of financial forecasts.[7] Finally, the Auditing Standards Division is studying matters related to the CPA's involvement with his client's financial forecast and the appropriate reporting by a CPA on such forecasts.

Why Publish Earnings Forecasts?   The primary reason given for the publication of earnings forecasts relates to investor needs. In the absence of published forecast information, buy-sell decisions are made on the basis of historical information supplemented by forecast information prepared by investment analysts and others external to the enterprise. While these sources provide some helpful information, the best source of information about a company's future prospects is the company itself.[8]

Another reason given for the publication of forecast information is that prompt dissemination will help avoid potential problems for "insiders." It is argued that publication should be made generally and not confined to selected persons "who might thereby attain an unfair advantage."[9]

Attitudes About Published Forecasts.   Each segment of the financial community has expressed its own attitudes toward published forecast information. Management generally objects to required published forecast disclosure. Financial analysts and accountants, on the other hand, seem to feel that published forecast data should be made available.[10]

System Development.   Management is concerned that systems for effective forecast development would cause additional expense since many companies do not presently employ highly sophisticated forecasting techniques. Analysts and accountants are most interested in having systems established, the former because of added credibility and the latter as an aid in the event that forecast information is to be reviewed.

---

[3]Securities Act Release 33-5362, February 2, 1973.
[4]Securities Act Release 33-5581, April 28, 1975.
[5]Accountants International Study Group, "Published Profit Forecasts," December 1974.
[6]Management Advisory Services Executive Committee, Guideline No. 3.
[7]Accounting Standards Division, Statement of Position, "Presentation and Disclosure of Financial Forecasts," American Institute of Certified Public Accountants, August 1975, 9 pp.
[8]Accountants International Study Group, par. 16.
[9]Ibid., par. 18.
[10]The positions attributed to these groups were developed from available literature on the subject, but particularly from the following: "Public Disclosure of Business Forecasts," A. T. Kearney, Inc., 1972 (a research study prepared for Financial Executives Research Foundation); "Disclosure of Corporate Forecasts to the Investor," *The Financial Analysts' Federation*, November 29, 1972; "Statement of the AICPA on Estimates, Forecasts, and Projections of Economic Performance," a testimony given by Wallace E. Olson, Executive Vice President of the AICPA, on December 11, 1972, before the SEC. (These were the views of the AICPA at December 11, 1972, but a final position of the Institute had not yet been reached, as was indicated in Mr. Olson's testimony.)

Presentation and Disclosure.   Concern has also been expressed over the information to be disclosed, and the method and frequency of disclosure. Management believes that disclosures might take away certain competitive advantages and has urged condensation of information to be disclosed. Frequent updating is also of concern because of the cost, particularly if public dissemination is required. Analysts would like to have information as detailed as possible to aid in evaluation. Additionally, requirements for updating would serve to keep analysts aware of changing developments.

Review.   Debate exists over the question of whether forecast information should be reviewed by a third party and, if so, the form of report to be issued. Management objects to review requirements for two primary reasons: (1) added cost, and (2) the possibility of unwarranted credibility being placed on the information since it would be subjected to review. Analysts are not in favor of mandatory review; indeed, they have stated that certification of forecasts is a contradiction in terms, and that quarterly updating requirements would serve as the necessary restraint.

Liability.   The most common reason for opposition to publication of forecast information is the possibility of liability for forecasts which have missed their mark. Costly litigation, diminished credibility, and a general loss of investor confidence could result from material variations between forecasted earnings and actual results. Further, management might be tempted to present too broad a range, causing the information to be of limited usefulness for purposes of analysis.

Forecasting in the United Kingdom.   Experience with forecasting in the United Kingdom has given considerable impetus to developments in the United States. There are a variety of situations in which forecasts are issued, including take-overs, offering of securities to the public and sometimes in circulars to shareholders covering related party transactions, major acquisitions, etc. The offeree in a take-over situation is not required to provide a forecast, but in practice usually does. Most merchant bankers would insert a forecast if the company recommended either for or against the take-over offer. Prospectuses issued by companies listed on the Stock Exchange also usually will contain a forecast.

The City Code on Take-overs and Mergers of 1968 provided, among other things, that an accountant's report, if prepared, had to be made public in connection with a take-over bid. In 1973 the City Code was revised so that any accountant's report must be made public in connection with all offerings of securities to the public.

Presentation of Forecasts.   The information included in the profit forecast is normally highly condensed. Companies ordinarily indicate net profits only, although there are some forecasts which also indicate sales and pretax profits and infrequently sales or profits by department or line of business. Underlying assumptions on which the forecast is based must also be published, but are extremely limited in nature.

Timing of Forecasts.   The profit forecasts may cover any estimate of financial results made in advance of audited financial statements. The City Code does not give any specific maximum forward period for these forecasts, although the trend has been not to exceed an 18-month forward period. In practice, forecasts are made at or very near year-end and even after year-end (but before the audited financial statements are available). The City Code has no provision requiring a forecast to be updated once it has been issued.

Accuracy.   The reliability of profit forecasts since the City Code took effect has been quite high. One study indicated that 81 percent of the 210 bid situations studied came within 10 percent of the eventual outcome.[11] However, it should be

---

[11] Martin E. Zweig, "Clouded Crystal Ball—Even 'Sophisticated' Earnings Projections Often Go Awry," *Barron's*, December 18, 1972, p. 19.

pointed out that approximately 40 percent were issued from the final month of the year through to nine months after the forecast year was complete. Another study revealed that of 173 forecasts, only 35 had missed by 10 percent or more. Upon review only two could not be explained satisfactorily.[12]

Responsibility of Reviewing Accountants. The accountant's report must confine itself to the accounting bases and calculations used. Its wording must not give the impression that the accountant is confirming, guaranteeing, or accepting responsibility for the achievement of the profit forecast. If the reporting accountant has any reason for material reservations about either the accounting bases or the calculations, or their consistency with the stated assumptions, the report should be qualified accordingly.

There appears to be a further unstated responsibility of the accountant: He or she must also review assumptions for reasonableness (as well as for consistency between assumptions and accounting bases and calculations). If assumptions are found to be unrealistic, the accountant must state the facts in the report, or else be disassociated from the report. However, this matter is currently under study.

Legal Liability. The English accountants show a "remarkable lack of apprehension about liability" as it arises in reporting on forecasts.[13] Although the City Code requires that the accountant's report indicate that the profit forecasts are the sole responsibility of the directors, the environment tends to discourage time-consuming and costly litigation:

- Contingency fees for attorneys are not permitted.
- Class action suits are not permitted.
- Third-party litigation against accountants is not an accepted practice.

OBJECTIVES OF FINANCIAL STATEMENTS

The Study Group charged with responsibility for considering the objectives of financial statements devoted considerable attention to the relationship between the predictive process and objectives of financial statements. They concluded that "an objective of financial statements is to provide information useful for the predictive process" and that "financial forecasts should be provided when they will enhance the reliability of users' predictions."[14] The rationale for this conclusion was presented as follows:[15]

> All economic decisions look to the future. Since economic decision-makers cannot know the future, they look to the past and the present. Financial statements that provide information about the past and the present are useful for making predictions on which to base economic decisions. In many instances, however, the past may not be a good indicator of the future. Publication of explicit forecasts of enterprise activities may well fit the objectives of financial statements. The important consideration is not the accuracy of management forecasts themselves, but rather the relative accuracy of users' predictions with and without forecasts in financial statements."

Forecasting Liability. The Study Group had a paper prepared on forecasting liability.[16] The paper examined the common law background and the then-current securities law setting, analyzed relevant cases, and concluded that "On principle it

---

[12]"The Argument for Profit Forecasts . . . and an Expert Who Says They Won't Work," *The Wall Street Journal*, December 11, 1972.

[13]D. R. Carmichael, "Reporting on Forecasts: A U.K. Perspective," *Journal of Accountancy*, January 1973, p. 42.

[14]Report of the Study Group on Objectives of Financial Statements, pp. 46 and 47.

[15]Ibid., p. 65.

[16]David R. Herwitz, "The Risk of Liability for Forecasting," *Objectives of Financial Statements, Volume 2, Selected Papers*, AICPA, pp. 247–273.

would appear that management would not be liable for a forecast merely because it turned out to be wide of the mark, if it were made in good faith and for a proper purpose, if it represented management's actual belief as to the future prospects, and were prepared with reasonable care and skill."[17] However, the paper went on to point out that although "there is little reason to doubt that most managements could and would routinely meet the tests of good faith, proper purpose, and honest belief, . . . carelessness is a fact of life, and hence the real nub of this issue may be the extent of liability when there is a failure of due care in the preparation of the forecast."[18] In this regard concern was expressed over the extent of liability involved:[19]

> It is an open question whether, under general legal principles, negligence in the preparation of a forecast otherwise made in good faith in the normal course of management's reporting function should or would give rise to liability to the entire universe of existing shareholders and prospective investors for losses allegedly resulting therefrom. This question is equally unsettled under the securities law provisions, like Rule 10b-5, which are addressed in general terms to fraud or deception and accordingly would seem to require something akin to intentional or at least knowing misrepresentation, rather than mere negligence, at least in a civil action. Resolution of this question will have to await further clarification by the courts. Section 11 of the Securities Act, dealing with registration of stock for sale to the public, stands on a special footing since the statute appears to expressly require due care and to lay particular onus on anyone cast in the role of an expert, as might be true in the case of a forecast if it were prepared or "certified" by an analyst or, perhaps, an accountant.

THE SECURITIES AND EXCHANGE COMMISSION

On November 1, 1972, the Securities and Exchange Commission announced a reconsideration of its long-standing prohibition against the inclusion of forecast information in information filed with the Commission.[20] Hearings were ordered to gather information relevant to the issue. Testimony was received from 53 witnesses, including representatives of publicly held companies, the securities industry, the academic community, the self-regulatory organizations, and the accounting and legal professions. In addition, letters from over 200 interested parties were received and made part of the public record.[21]

On the basis of the information obtained through the hearings and on the basis of staff recommendations and experience in administering the securities laws, the Commission determined that changes in its policies would be in the public interest. In February 1973, the Commission issued the following public statement:[22]

1. Disclosure of projections in Commission filings should not be required except under the circumstances set forth in paragraphs 7 and 8 below.

2. Issuers who are reporting companies and who meet certain standards relating to their earnings histories and budgeting experience should be permitted to include projections in filings made with the Commission pursuant to the Securities Act and the Exchange Act.

3. Projections disclosed in Commission filings should meet certain standards, for example, the underlying assumptions should be set forth, the projection should be of sales and earnings and expressed as a reasonable definite figure, and the projections should be for a reasonable period of time.

[17]Ibid., p. 247.
[18]Ibid., p. 248.
[19]Ibid., p. 248.
[20]Securities Exchange Act Release 34-9844, November 1, 1972.
[21]Securities Act Release 33-5362.
[22]Ibid.

4. Any issuer who files projection information should be required to update the filed projection on a regular basis and whenever the issuer materially changes its projection.

5. Any issuer who has previously filed projection information should be allowed to stop filing such information if it discloses its decision and the reasons therefor.

6. No statement of verification or certification of the projections by any third party should be permitted in any filing with the Commission at this time.

7. Any issuer who discloses projections outside of filings with the Commission, whether through financial media, financial analysts, or otherwise, should be required to file such projections with the Commission on a special projection form.

8. Any issuer subject to the reporting requirements of the Exchange Act who discloses a projection, whether in a Commission filing or not, should be required to include in its annual report on Form 10-K for the fiscal year during which the projection was made, a statement of the projection made, the circumstances under which it was disclosed, and a comparison of the projection with actual results.

9. The Commission should adopt rules under the securities laws to define the circumstances under which a projection would not be considered to be a misleading statement of a material fact.

10. The Commission should issue a release setting forth certain standards for the preparation and dissemination of projections by management of public companies, financial analysts, and other members of the financial community. The release should highlight the Commission's reservations as to whether anyone who makes a projection with respect to an issuer having a limited history of operations can meet the standards necessary to avoid liability. In addition, the adverse consequences of selective disclosure of material information such as projections should be emphasized.

Specific Proposals.   The Securities and Exchange Commission issued proposals to implement the foregoing policy statement on April 28, 1975.[23] (The proposals were substantially revised in Securities Act Release 33-5699, issued April 23, 1976.) Following is a summary of the 1975 proposals.

Objective.   The proposals are designed to integrate public forecast information (defined as "projections" by the SEC) into the federal securities laws disclosure system. The proposal states that "Management's assessment of a company's future performance is information of significant importance to the investor . . . and that such information should be available . . . on an equitable basis to all investors."

Definition of a "Projection."   A "projection" is defined as a statement made by an issuer regarding material future revenues, sales, net income, or earnings per share of such issuer expressed as a specific amount, range of amounts ($1.80 to $2.20), or percentage variation from a specific amount ($2.20 plus or minus 10 percent or "an increase of 10 percent over last year"), or a confirmation by an issuer of any such statement made by another person.[24]

The definition does not include announcements to the public regarding preliminary results of periods ended but not yet reported, but does include a confirmation that another person's projection is "in the ball park," "attainable," or "on target."

The term "material" is not defined. However, the proposal states that "Any . . . statement relating to the issuer's total future revenues, sales, net income, or earnings per share would be material; a statement relating to the sales or revenues of a subsidiary or of a particular line of business might be material, depending on the facts."

---

[23]Securities Act Release 33-5581.
[24]Ibid.

Under What Circumstances Must Forecast Information Be Filed with the SEC?   The SEC proposal would require with certain exceptions that a report be filed (on Form 8-K) within ten days of a "projection" being furnished to anyone. The exceptions include: private financing; preliminary negotiations with underwriters; business combinations; and, government agencies that have afforded nonpublic treatment to such forecast information.

A report would also be required when there is reason to believe that the information filed no longer has a reasonable basis or, alternatively, if a company determines to cease disclosing (or revising) forecast information. A company also may choose to dissassociate itself from a "projection" made by another person.

Companies that are required to file forecast information must also include in published annual reports and certain registration statements all such information previously filed (or required to be filed) covering the year-end results for the most recent fiscal year. The most recent information would be presented in comparative form with corresponding historical results, with explanations of the reasons for significant variations. Published reports and affected registration statements would also have to include forecast information for at least the first six months for the current fiscal year or for the full fiscal year.

A company may elect to begin disclosing forecast information in the annual report on Form 10-K or in registration statements, provided that the so-called safe harbor requirements are met (see below).

What Information Must Be Filed?   In general the information must relate at a minimum to sales or revenues, net income, and fully diluted earnings per share; be expressed as an exact figure, a reasonable variation from an exact figure or a reasonable range of figures (a 10 percent variation or a range not exceeding 10 percent from the midpoint would be regarded as reasonable); be limited to the current fiscal year and the next fiscal year; be identified as a "projection" and accompanied by a statement which (1) discloses the material underlying assumptions, (2) cautions that there can be no assurance that the forecast will be achieved since its ultimate achievement is dependent upon the occurrence of the specified assumptions, and (3) indicates that the projection has been compiled on the basis of the specified assumptions and is consistent with the accounting principles expected to be used.

Safe Harbor Rules.   To alleviate fears of liability, the Commission proposed certain rules defining circumstances under which forecast information would not be deemed to be "an untrue or misleading statement of a material fact or a manipulative, deceptive, or fraudulent device, contrivance, act or practice" as those terms are used in the various liability provisions of the Securities Acts. It is important to note that the determination as to compliance with the criteria would be based on the facts at the time the forecast information was disclosed and would not be dependent on whether or not the projection was achieved. The Commission emphasized that projections would not necessarily be misleading if they failed to meet the standards of the safe harbor rules. The particular facts and circumstances must be carefully examined in each case.

1. ISSUER CRITERIA.   In general, under the proposed safe harbor rules the issuer must have been subject to the reporting requirements of the Exchange Act for at least three years and have filed all reports required to be filed during the preceding 12 months. In addition, the issuer must have prepared budgets for internal use for its last three fiscal years. The Commission believes that these criteria may provide some assurance that the issuer has had sufficient experience in reporting publicly and in budgeting so that it has a reasonable basis for making public projections.

2. PROJECTION CRITERIA.   The proposed rules set forth criteria which generally relate to the forecast's preparation, form, and manner of disclosure and review.

The forecast information must have been prepared with reasonable care by qualified personnel and carefully reviewed and approved by management at the appropriate levels and must have a reasonable factual basis and represent management's good-faith judgment. Certain of these criteria have generally been considered by courts as requirements concerning the preparation of publicly disclosed projections.

Review.[25]   The proposed rules set forth certain disclosure and reporting standards if the registrant represents that the information has been reviewed by any person other than an officer, director, or employee. A statement would be required disclosing whether or not the reviewer is independent and where a copy of the reviewer's report may be obtained.

Reviewers who are represented to be "independent" must be in fact independent under standards in Regulation S-X (although the reviewers need not be public accountants). To alleviate certain concerns of accountants, the proposal indicates that any certified public accountant or public accountant reviewing or rendering a report on a projection will not be deemed not independent with respect to financial statements of the issuer.

If the reviewer is not represented to be independent, any material relationship between the reviewer and the issuer which exists or is contemplated or which existed at any time during the previous two years would be disclosed, together with the amount of compensation received or to be received as a result of such relationship.

The reviewer's report would have to contain: (1) a statement affirming or denying independence; (2) a statement of the reviewer's qualifications to render the review and report; (3) a statement of the scope of the examination and the methods and procedures followed; (4) a statement that the reviewer is not giving assurance that the projection will be achieved; and (5) a statement that (a) the projection has been compiled on the basis of the assumptions made by the registrant and is consistent with the accounting principles expected to be used by the registrant; (b) the material assumptions underlying the projection are internally consistent and not unreasonable; (c) the methods and procedures employed by the registrant in arriving at the projection are not unreasonable; and (d) such methods and procedures have been applied in a consistent manner.

AICPA EFFORTS

Proposals made by the Institute or in process of development differ in some respects from the proposals made by the SEC.

Financial Forecast.   One major difference in the proposals under consideration relates to the nature of information to be developed and presented. To date, proposals under consideration by the Institute relate to "financial forecasts" rather

---

[25]The Commission indicated in its February 1973 Statement that it would not allow any statement of third-party certification or verification of projection information to be disclosed in filings with the Commission. The Commission noted, however, that it would reconsider this position if generally accepted principles or policies concerning such verification were developed. The 1975 proposal notes that "since 1973 progress has been made toward the development of standards regarding the presentation of projections. Moreover, efforts are being made toward the development of standards for auditor involvement with projections. In light of these developments and the Commission's belief that investors would benefit from a review of projections, the Commission has included the concept of a 'review' in the proposed rules. The Commission believes that if a registrant discloses that its projection has been reviewed, the 'safe harbor' rules should be available only if there has been compliance with the standards set forth in the proposals."

than "feasibility studies," "budgets," "plans," "goals," or "objectives," all of which might be contemplated under the SEC proposals.

A "financial forecast" for an enterprise is defined as an estimate of the most probable financial position, results of operations, and changes in financial position for one or more future periods.[26] In this context "most probable" means that the assumptions have been evaluated by management and that the forecast is based on management's judgment of the most likely set of conditions and its most likely course of action.

GUIDELINES FOR SYSTEMS FOR THE PREPARATION OF FINANCIAL FORECASTS

The guidelines issued by the Management Advisory Services Division are designed to establish broad principles for the preparation of financial forecasts, although as indicated in the document judgment is required to apply them in specific situations. The document also indicates that many different forecasting techniques and methods are available and that the relevance of a particular technique for forecasting for a given enterprise at a given time must be determined largely on a case-by-case basis. Consequently, the guidelines do not address themselves to individual forecasting techniques.[27]

The guidelines are intended to apply to enterprises that prepare financial forecasts on a recurring basis and where updating may be necessary. They would also apply to the preparation of forecasts that are not recurrent or where a formal forecasting system does not exist, if a formal work program and an appropriately constituted forecasting project team are used.

Summary of Guidelines.   Following is a summary of the guidelines as included in the document:[28]

1. *Single Most Probable Result.*   A financial forecasting system should provide a means for management to determine what it considers to be the single most probable forecasted result. In addition, determination of the single most probable result generally should be supplemented by the development of ranges or probabilistic statements.

2. *Accounting Principles Used.*   The financial forecasting system should provide management with the means to prepare financial forecasts using the accounting principles that are expected to be used when the events and transactions envisioned in the forecast occur.

3. *Appropriate Care and Qualified Personnel.*   Financial forecasts should be prepared with appropriate care by qualified personnel.

4. *Best Information Available.*   A financial forecasting system should provide for seeking out the best information, from whatever source, reasonably available at the time.

5. *Reflection of Plans.*   The information used in preparing a financial forecast should reflect the plans of the enterprise.

6. *Reasonable Assumptions Suitably Supported.*   The assumptions used in preparing a financial forecast should be reasonable and appropriate and should be suitably supported.

7. *Relative Effect of Variations.*   The financial forecasting system should provide the means to determine the relative effect of variations in the major underlying assumptions.

[26]Management Advisory Services Executive Committee Guideline No. 3, p. 3.
[27]Ibid., p. 6.
[28]Ibid., p. 7.

8. *Adequate Documentation.*   A financial forecasting system should provide adequate documentation of both the forecast and the forecasting process.

9. *Regular Comparison with Attained Results.*   A financial forecasting system should include the regular comparison of the forecast with attained results.

10. *Adequate Review and Approval.*   The preparation of a financial forecast should include adequate review and approval by management at the appropriate levels.

Commentary.   Detailed comments included in the publication which relate to certain of the concepts in the summary of guidelines are set forth below.[29]

Range and Probabilistic Statements.   The development of ranges, probabilistic statements, or estimates of error as supplements to the single most probable forecasted result is encouraged since such information is useful to underscore the essentially uncertain nature of all forecasts.

Qualified Personnel.   An understanding of the enterprise and industry is essential. Personnel having competence in marketing, operations, finance, research and engineering, and other technical areas as appropriate should participate along with management in the development of the forecast.

Analytical capacity and expertise in the analysis and interpretation of the relevant historical data are also necessary. In appropriate circumstances, expertise in technical forecasting techniques and methodology is required.

Relevant Information.   The acquisition of information ordinarily involves a cost which should be commensurate with the anticipated benefits to be derived from the information. Various sources of information involve different degrees of reliability. The reliability of the basic data should be considered in the forecasting process.

A key consideration in the preparation of a financial forecast is the use of an appropriate level of detail. In certain situations the use of more detail may improve the reliability of a forecast. For example, forecasting sales by product line, instead of in the aggregate, may improve the sales forecast, especially when the products are sold in different markets. However, situations also exist where the use of less detail or a more aggregated approach will improve reliability. For example, forecasting the cost of sales for a manufacturer of thousands of individual items may be done more effectively in groups than by individual item.

Planning and Control.   Plans and budgets are more reliable and credible when developed through the use of effective management planning and control systems. Sound reporting on a timely basis by functional responsibility, together with effective planning and budgeting, is the foundation of a financial forecasting system.

Assumptions.   Assumptions are the essence of forecasting and are the single most important ingredient of a financial forecast. The quality of the underlying assumptions largely determines the reliability of a forecast.

Assumptions vary in their relative potential importance to forecasted results. The attention devoted to the appropriateness of a particular assumption should be commensurate with the likely relative impact of that assumption. Assumptions with great impact should receive more attention and support than those with less impact. Often, assumptions pertaining to sales volumes and revenues have the greatest single impact on the financial forecast for an enterprise.

By nature, a financial forecast always contains a large number of assumptions, some of which may be obvious and explicit but many of which are obscure and implicit. Frequently, the most basic assumptions with enormous potential impact, such as those relating to war or peace conditions, are not addressed explicitly in the

[29]Ibid., pp. 8–14.

preparation of a forecast. However, those assumptions deemed to be most significant at the time of preparation should be made explicit to focus attention on them and to facilitate review by management.

Assumptions should be supported by appropriate evidence. While it is not possible to prove that any given assumption will be borne out by subsequent events, much evidence consisting of data and logical argument or theory is usually developed to support an assumption. Historical data appropriately analyzed will often reveal trends or other likely patterns of behavior. Special scrutiny should be given assumptions that are not consistent with past and current conditions.

Although it is ordinarily not feasible to list exhaustively and otherwise document and support all the assumptions underlying a forecast, nevertheless it is necessary to seek out and explicitly state support for the most crucial or significant assumptions. Despite these precautions, hindsight will often reveal basic assumptions that have been overlooked or that, in the light of later circumstances, received inadequate treatment. Furthermore, the nature of forecasting is such that some assumptions will turn out to be erroneous no matter what effort, analysis, or support may be applied.

In analyzing alternative assumptions, care must be exercised to avoid undue optimism or pessimism and to assess the situation objectively. Relating an assumption to past or present conditions often is a useful approach to check on reasonableness; however, trends are not necessarily reliable indicators of the future. Particular attention should be given to the possibility of changes in conditions, and these must rest mainly on theory and an understanding of the basic causal factors.

Care should be exercised to avoid unrealistic assumptions in situations where any assumption may involve a certain degree of arbitrariness. For example, it may be difficult to predict the precise rate of future inflation, but it is generally more realistic to estimate such a rate than to assume no inflation. Often, the most difficult assumptions to evaluate are those relating to worldwide macroeconomic conditions. In such cases, management is placed in the position of using subjective judgment to a greater degree than in many other cases.

The nature of business enterprise is such that many underlying assumptions are interrelated and certain of their elements may have multiple impacts. For example, a slowdown in economic activity will typically not only result in a slowdown in sales volume, but may also affect prices and the availability and cost of resources.

The conditions assumed in arriving at the sales or revenue forecast should be consistent with those assumed in forecasting the cost of operation. Care should be exercised to ensure that likely costs and revenues have been considered, that sufficient capacity and resources will be available to produce the expected revenues, that capital expenditures have been recognized as appropriate, that provision has been made for applicable taxes, and that the availability of appropriate financing has been considered.

Sensitivity.   In forecasting, an understanding of the relative sensitivity of the results of the assumed conditions permits the allocation of analysis, study, and review to those areas with the most significant impact. Particular attention should be devoted to those items likely to cause large variations in the results.

Knowledge of a particular enterprise or industry frequently permits an initial identification of those key factors upon which the financial success of the business rests. In the absence of such knowledge, additional analysis should be performed to identify the most sensitive elements.

Documentation.   Documentation makes possible management review and approval of a forecast. It facilitates comparison of the forecast with actual financial results, and it provides the discipline necessary for reliable forecasting.

Documentation involves recording the underlying assumptions as well as summarizing the supporting evidence for the assumptions. Documentation should provide the ability to trace forecasted financial results through intermediate calculations back to the basic underlying assumptions.

Adequate documentation makes it possible for persons experienced and qualified in forecasting to reconstruct the forecast. Documentation should cover the system, as well as individual forecasts, and should provide an organized record of both that can be maintained and made available for subsequent use.

Comparison with Attained Results.   The regular comparison with actual results provides a historical measure of forecasting success and may also be useful as an indication of the likely reliability of future forecasts. Regular comparison with actual results and analysis of deviations also provides a basis for making improvements in the forecasting methods and approaches.

The comparison with actual results should not be limited to financial results but should also include comparison of the underlying factors and key assumptions, such as sales volumes, prices, and production rates. Emphasis should be placed on those items sometimes called "leading indicators," such as order rates, backlogs, and changes in capacity that precede attained financial results but that largely determine future results.

Review and Approval.   Adequate review means that the review is conducted in sufficient depth to assure the reviewers that the forecasting process is sound. The reviewer should be satisfied that the forecast and subsequent revisions were prepared in accordance with the guidelines for the preparation of forecasts. Adequate review and approval require formal communication of the forecast, together with its supporting documentation.

Review at intermediate levels of management—including such functions as marketing, operations, engineering, and finance—ensures that the reasonableness of the forecast is evaluated from several vantage points and especially that it is evaluated by those who will be responsible for the subsequent delivery of forecasted results.

PRESENTATION AND DISCLOSURE

Presentation and disclosure of financial forecasts is the subject of a Statement of Position[30] prepared under the auspices of the Institute's Accounting Standards Division. The Statement is designed to provide guidance for those who choose to issue financial forecasts. Specific recommendations are outlined below.

Format.   Financial forecasts preferably should be presented in the format of the historical financial statements[31] expected to be issued but, at a minimum, the presentation should consist of the following information obtained from such a financial forecast:

1. Sales or gross revenues
2. Gross profit
3. Provision for income taxes
4. Net income
5. Results of the disposal of a segment of a business and extraordinary, unusual, or infrequently occurring items
6. Primary and fully diluted earnings per share data for each period presented
7. Significant anticipated changes in financial position.

The statement notes that although "Financial forecasts presented in the format of the historical financial statements would facilitate comparisons, . . . given the

[30]Accounting Standards Division Statement of Position.

[31]The details of each statement may be summarized or condensed, so that only the major items in each are presented. The usual footnotes associated with historical financial statements need not be included as such. Ibid., p. 3.

lack of experience of most enterprises in issuing financial forecasts, there is reason to consider, for the present, recommendations which would not unduly discourage the issuance of financial forecasts and which would permit experimentation in the development of communicative formats."[32]

Accounting Principles.   Financial forecasts should be prepared on a basis consistent with the generally accepted accounting principles expected to be used in the historical financial statements covering the forecast period. This fact, as well as a summary of significant accounting policies, should be disclosed in the forecast. If a forecast is included in a document which contains such a summary, disclosure can be accomplished by cross-referencing.

Expressing the Results.   Financial forecasts should be expressed in specific monetary amounts representing the single most probable forecasted result. The tentative nature of a financial forecast would be emphasized if the single most probable result for key measures (e.g., sales and net income) was supplemented by ranges or probabilistic statements, and the presentation of such information is encouraged.

The Statement includes the following commentary in support of this recommendation:[33]

> While a range informs the user of the probabilistic nature of the forecast, expressing a financial forecast *solely* in terms of ranges could result in the user's attributing an unwarranted degree of reliability to the forecast ranges, because many users might assume (a) that a range represented the spread between the best possible result and the worst possible result, or (b) that the range was based on a scientifically determined interval. Management should be in the best position to determine the single most probable result and this burden should not be placed on outsiders. Also, single point estimates are necessary to aggregate the forecasts of an enterprise's individual operations, as well as to facilitate comparison between the forecast and later historical results.

Assumptions.   Those assumptions should be disclosed which management thinks are most significant to the forecast or are key factors upon which the financial results of the enterprise depend. There ordinarily should be some indication of the basis or rationale for these assumptions. It would also be desirable for the disclosure to include an expression of the relative impact of a variation in the assumption when it would significantly affect the forecasted result.

It is pointed out that frequently certain basic assumptions that have enormous potential impact are considered to be implicit in the forecast (e.g., conditions of peace, absence of natural disasters). A recommendation is made that "Such assumptions need be disclosed only when there is a reasonable possibility that the current conditions will not prevail. In such circumstances, to the extent practicable, the possible impact of a change in the assumptions should be disclosed."[34]

Disclosure of certain important information may not be desirable from the standpoint of the enterprise, particularly when competition or strategies are involved. While all significant assumptions should be disclosed, the Statement takes the position that "they need not be presented in such a manner or in such detail as would adversely affect the competitive position of the enterprise."[35]

The Statement also recommends that (1) assumptions be captioned in a manner which best reflects their nature (e.g., "Summary of Significant Forecast Assumptions"), (2) it be made clear that the assumptions disclosed are not an all-inclusive list of those used in the preparation of the forecast and, (3) that they were based on

---

[32]Ibid., p. 3.
[33]Ibid., p. 4.
[34]Ibid., p. 5.
[35]Ibid., pp. 5 and 6.

circumstances and conditions existing at the time the forecast was prepared.[36] The following language is suggested as an introduction to the summary:[37]

> This financial forecast is based on management's assumptions concerning future events and circumstances. The assumptions disclosed herein are those which management believes are significant to the forecast or are key factors upon which the financial results of the enterprise depend. Some assumptions inevitably will not materialize and unanticipated events and circumstances may occur subsequent to ＿＿＿＿＿＿＿, the date of this forecast. Therefore, the actual results achieved during the forecast period will vary from the forecast and the variations may be material.

Identification of assumptions which, at the time of preparation, appear to be most significant to the forecast or which are key factors upon which the financial results of the business depend requires the careful exercise of good-faith judgment by management, and would include:

1. Assumptions as to which there is a reasonable possibility of the occurrence of a variation that may significantly affect the forecasted results

2. Assumptions about anticipated conditions that are expected to be significantly different from current conditions, which are not otherwise reasonably apparent

3. Other matters deemed important to the forecast or to the interpretation of the forecast.[38]

The following unrelated hypothetical examples of disclosures of assumptions are offered for general guidance.[39]

1. The Company is engaged in several lines of business, two of which are defense-oriented and supplied X percent and Y percent of the Company's sales and gross profit, respectively, in 19X0, as indicated on page ＿＿ of the Annual Report to Stockholders. The Company's other lines of business are diversified.

The sales forecast assumes, among other things, that revenue from the Company's federal defense contracts will continue at the current level and that nondefense sales will increase at the same rate as the anticipated increase in real GNP for 19X1.

If these conditions are not met, results may be significantly affected. For example, a decline of 5 percent from forecasted defense-oriented sales could result in a decline of approximately 8 percent in net income, while a decline of 5 percent from forecasted nondefense sales could result in a decline of approximately 6 percent in net income.

2. The company expects its raw material costs to rise, on an overall basis, commensurate with the rate of inflation. The forecast assumes that any raw material cost increases can be recovered in the form of higher prices.

Labor costs have been forecast using rates provided in the Company's union contract, which does not expire until 19X2.

3. At certain times in the year, the Company is highly dependent on short-term bank borrowing. The Company's forecast of interest expense is based on the seasonal borrowing patterns of prior years for financing inventory and receivables. The Company does not expect to incur any long-term borrowing and anticipates no major changes in the prime rate from its present level of X percent.

4. The provision for income taxes gives no effect to the possibility of an X-percent decrease in the maximum corporate income tax rate, as proposed by the President in a message to Congress.

---

[36] Ibid., p. 6.
[37] Ibid., p. 6.
[38] Ibid., p. 6.
[39] Adapted from ibid., pp. 6 and 7.

5. Manufacture of the Company's major products depends on the availability of relatively small quantities of petroleum by-products. The Company has no guaranteed source for these materials. The forecast assumes continued availability of these raw materials.

6. Earnings per share data have been computed following the same procedures used for historical financial statement purposes, which are in accordance with the provisions of APB Opinion No. 15. In calculations required by the "treasury stock" method, management has assumed, for such purposes, that there will be no significant changes in the price of the Company's stock.

Period to Be Covered.   No fixed period of time is specified. Management should consider its ability to forecast and the needs of the user in determining the period to be covered. Although the degree of uncertainty generally increases with the time span, short-term forecasts may not be meaningful in (1) industries with a lengthy operating cycle, or (2) situations where long-term results are necessary to evaluate the investment consequences involved.

Distinguishing from Historical Financial Statements.   Financial forecasts should be presented separately (or clearly segregated) from the historical financial statements and should be clearly labeled as a "financial forecast" to preclude a reader from confusing a forecast with the historical financial statements.

Applicable historical information, such as prior forecast data and prior historical results, may, however, be presented with any financial forecast in parallel columns. This would facilitate comparison and provide the user with information helpful in evaluating the risks associated with a financial forecast. When such historical information is presented, it should be clearly labeled and distinguished from the forecast information.

Updating Financial Forecasts.   An updated financial forecast should be issued to reflect significant changes in assumptions, actual results, or unanticipated events and circumstances unless (1) the original forecast included a statement that it was not intended to be updated (see below), or (2) issuance of historical financial statements covering the forecast period is imminent.

An updated forecast should be issued if it can be done promptly. The reasons for updating should be described in a note to the updated forecast.

When material changes in a forecast cannot be quantified so as to permit issuance of an updated forecast promptly, appropriate disclosure should be made. Such disclosure would include a description of the circumstances necessitating an updated forecast, and notification that the original forecast should not be used for any purpose and that an updated financial forecast will be issued upon its completion.

If, however, management decides that the current financial forecast should no longer be used for any purpose but it is not appropriate to issue an updated forecast, this decision and the reasons for it should be disclosed.

Forecasts Not Intended to Be Updated.   Financial forecasts may be issued on a "one-time" basis, such as in connection with a search for debt or equity financing, without any intention to issue updated forecasts. In such cases, emphasis should be given to the date of issuance of the forecast and an explicit statement should be made as to the dangers inherent in using forecasts issued some time ago. In addition, management's intention not to update the forecast should be specifically disclosed.

REVIEW OF EARNINGS FORECASTS

The scope and nature of a review of a financial forecast, and indeed whether or not there should be a review at all, are matters of some controversy. At one extreme, some suggest that association with a financial forecast would impair the independence of the reviewer and thus preclude independent auditors from making such reviews. At the other extreme, there is a belief that independence is not affected and that reviews should go so far as to report on the reasonableness of assumptions. Between the two, all manner of alternatives are suggested.

Present Status. At present, certified public accountants are permitted by the Code of Professional Ethics of the AICPA to be associated with earnings forecasts provided that their names are not used "in a manner which may lead to the belief that the member [of the AICPA] . . . vouches for the achievability of the forecast."[40] A certified public accountant's name must not be associated with a forecast unless it discloses the sources of information used and the major assumptions made and the CPA states in the report the scope and character of the study conducted and the degree of responsibility assumed.[41] The Auditing Standards Division of the AICPA has been working to develop standards for a CPA's involvement with forecasts, but many significant issues remain unsettled.

State Regulatory Requirements. Some state regulatory authorities (e.g., California, Michigan, and New Jersey) have established requirements for reporting on certain types of forecasts by CPAs. The California Commissioner of Corporations, for example, has adopted regulations that include requirements that "projections" (forecasts of future results) of operations be included in the prospectus, offering circular or other sales literature to qualify real estate programs. (Similar requirements are included in a statement of policy of the Midwest Securities Commissioners' Association.) The regulations require that "projections" included in such offering documents be the "product of qualified persons or firms" and require the identification of such persons or firms and disclosure of their respective roles in the preparation of the projection.

CPAs in California have frequently assisted their real estate clients in the preparation of projections, and the California State Board of Accountancy has indicated that identification of a CPA in the manner required by the regulations "associates" the CPA with the forecast so that certain reporting requirements apply. The California Society of CPAs has issued guidelines for CPAs associated with projections for real estate programs. The guidelines specify:

Management Involvement. All assumptions included in the projection are those of management, and any association by a CPA with the projection cannot relieve management of that responsibility.

General Considerations. In considering whether to accept the engagement, a CPA may wish to consider the client's general background, financial ability, and organizational structure with respect to the size, type, and duration of the specific project involved.

Assumptions. A CPA should study the assumptions of a projection and the methods and data that management used to develop the assumptions, but the CPA can, at best, conclude only that the study of the assumptions disclosed no reason to question their adequacy and reasonableness.

Compilation. A CPA should be concerned with the accuracy of a projection's compilation (analyses, computations, calculations, reconciliations, and other procedures including internal consistency).

Reporting. "The CPA's report should indicate that the projection was compiled giving effect to the stated assumptions, accounting principles, and methods. If . . . the CPA believes the projection . . . does not contain adequate disclosure of assumptions and accounting principles and methods essential to a reasonable presentation, he should so state in his report."

[40]*Code of Professional Ethics* "Rules of Conduct," Rule 204, American Institute of Certified Public Accountants, March 1, 1973, p. 22.

[41]*Code of Professional Ethics* "Interpretations of Rules of Conduct," 204-1, American Institute of Certified Public Accountants, March 1, 1973, p. 36.

The California Society of CPAs has indicated that their views are subject to modification upon issuance of guidelines by the AICPA.[42]

Current Practice. Most large public accounting firms have developed internal guidelines as to the type of financial forecasts with which they will be associated and the type of assurance they will provide.

Acceptance of Engagement.   Some constraints apply to all financial forecasts with which the firm might be associated in other than a purely advisory role. Examples of common constraints are:

■ The management (or proposed management) of the entity must be in place and be prepared to assume primary responsibility for the forecast and the underlying assumptions.

■ The CPA firm must perform a substantive professional service. Consequently, engagements are not accepted that only involve compiling a forecast and that, therefore, exclude consideration of the reasonableness of underlying assumptions.

■ Other detailed criteria that have the purpose of attempting to exclude highly speculative ventures are also applied.

Some constraints are applied only to forecasts that are expected to have wide public distribution. Forecasts expected to be distributed to a limited number of known and presumed-to-be-knowledgeable users are sometimes exempted. Some CPA firms emphasize certain factors more than others. Examples of factors commonly considered are the following:

■ The entity's operations are of a relatively predictable nature; demand for the entity's product or service is closely related to relatively stable indicators, the entity has good operating control, and does not operate in close proximity to its breakeven point. (This constraint normally excludes merchandising or manufacturing companies and includes entities engaged in relatively noncompetitive activities such as hospitals.)

■ Key elements in the forecast are within the recognized competence of CPAs (tax computations, depreciation, cost analyses, etc.). (This constraint is related to the first. If revenue is relatively predictable, costs are the primary determinant of a profit forecast.)

■ A financial forecast is a key element to investors' decisions because historical financial data are unavailable or of limited relevance.

■ The distribution of the forecast relates to the issuance of a senior security (bonds) or the ownership interest offered has similar characteristics. (One byproduct of this constraint is that a strong element of conservatism is prudent and appropriate.)

The practical result of the constraints applied is that CPAs presently report on financial forecasts in offering documents for tax shelter investments, revenue bonds of municipal authorities such as hospitals, airports, toll bridges, and other public facilities, and private placement of debt.[43]

Scope of Review.   The present practice of CPA firms in publicly reporting on forecasts leads Carmichael to suggest that a CPA's study of a financial forecast should be directed to the following objectives:[44]

1. Was the forecast in all material respects accurately compiled? (Arithmetic and mechanical accuracy)

---

[42]D. R. Carmichael, "Dos and Don'ts of Financial Forecasting—Should the Independent CPA be Involved and If So to What Extent and How?" An outline prepared for presentation at the Second Annual Securities Regulation Institute, January 8–10, 1975, San Diego, California, pp. 5 and 6.

[43]Ibid.

[44]D. R. Carmichael, "Financial Forecasts—The Potential Role of Independent CPAs," *The Journal of Accountancy,* September 1974, pp. 84–86.

2. Was the data used in preparing the forecast internally consistent? (Internal integrity, such as the relationship of sales to productive capacity)
3. Were generally accepted accounting principles followed in presenting future transactions in the forecast and were those principles applied consistently with those expected to be followed in preparing historical statements? (Application of GAAP)
4. Were the significant risks affecting the probability of the forecast being attained adequately disclosed? (Adequacy of disclosure)

Assumptions. One of the key differences among CPA firms that report on forecasts is the form of assurance given on the reasonableness of assumptions. The written expressions of assurance on the reasonableness of assumptions cover the following range:

1. An opinion that the assumptions are reasonable.
2. An opinion that the assumptions are not unreasonable.
3. A denial of an opinion on the reasonableness of assumptions.

A study of the assumptions is included in the scope of the firm's work in any event, and CPA firms would not remain silent if they concluded that significant assumptions were unreasonable, unsupported, or omitted. The decision of how to report on assumptions seems to be based on the convictions of a CPA firm on whether a particular form of reporting will lead users of the forecast to treat uncritically information about which they should be skeptical.[45]

Carmichael has suggested that CPAs not report on reasonableness on the basis that "reasonableness might easily be confused with achievability. CPAs would naturally have to deny an opinion on the achievability of a forecast, and an opinion on reasonableness might be misunderstood to contradict that denial."[46]

Specific Review Procedures. The Accountants International Study Group has published a summary of actual procedures of a number of leading firms of chartered accountants in the United Kingdom. That summary is reproduced as an appendix to this chapter.

BIBLIOGRAPHY

AICPA: *Guidelines for Systems for the Preparation of Financial Forecasts,* prepared by Management Advisory Services Executive Committee (MAS Guideline Series No. 3), March 1975.
AICPA: *Techniques for Forecasting Product Demand* (Management Services Technical Study No. 7), 1968.
California Society of CPAs Committee on Accounting Principles and Auditing Standards: "Guidance for Independent CPAs When Associated with Projections for Real Estate Programs," *The California CPA Quarterly,* September 1974.
Cantor, Jerry: *Pragmatic Forecasting,* American Management Association, New York, 1971.
Chambers, John C., Satinder K. Mullick, and Donald D. Smith: *Executive's Guide to Forecasting,* John Wiley & Sons, New York, 1974.
Corless, John C., and Corine T. Norgaard: "User Responses to CPA Reports on Forecasts," AICPA (Report No. 2), November 1973.
Financial Executives Research Foundation: *Public Disclosure of Business Forecasts* (Part I by A. T. Kearney, Inc., Part II by Sidley & Austin), New York, 1972.
McGrath, Phyllis S., and Francis J. Walsh, Jr.: *Disclosure of Financial Forecasts to Security Analysts and the Public* (Conference Board Report No. 602), 1973.
Prakash, Prem, and Alfred Rappaport: *Public Reporting of Corporate Financial Forecasts* (Proceedings of Conference sponsored by Northwestern University's Center for Advanced Study in Accounting and Management), CCH, Inc., Chicago, 1974.
Wheelwright, Steven C., and Spyros Makridakis: *Forecasting Methods for Management,* John Wiley & Sons, New York, 1973.

[45] D. R. Carmichael, "Dos and Dont's of Financial Forecasting," pp. 7 and 8.
[46] D. R. Carmichael, "Financial Forecasts—The Potential Role of Independent CPAs," p. 86.

APPENDIX: THE PROCESS OF REVIEWING AND REPORTING
ON PROFIT FORECASTS IN THE U.K.[47]

The following is a summary of the actual procedures of a number of leading firms of chartered accountants in the U.K.

Before accepting responsibility for examining the forecasts the accountants should, in terms of the Statement on "Accountants' Reports on Profit Forecasts,"[48] give consideration to the following points:—

(a) The time within which the accountants' report is required—this should not be so severely restricted that it would be plainly impossible for the reporting accountants to obtain sufficient information to enable them properly to exercise their professional judgment for the purpose of reporting.

(b) It should be clearly established that the reporting accountants' instructions and responsibility for reporting under the City Code (where this applies) are confined to the accounting bases and calculations for the profit forecasts, as distinct from the assumptions upon which the directors have based their forecasts.

(c) Since profit forecasts are subject to increasing uncertainty the further forward they reach in time, reporting accountants should not normally undertake to review and report to directors on profit forecasts for more than the current accounting period, and, providing a sufficiently significant part of the current accounting year has elapsed, the next following accounting year. A "sufficiently significant part" would probably be not less than six months.

(d) The reporting accountants should make it clear that they cannot relieve the directors of the responsibility for profit forecasts which are disclosed to and may be relied upon by outsiders.

Additionally, the reporting accountants will wish to establish the following:—

(a) The purpose for which the forecasts have been prepared and the accountants' report is required.

(b) That the directors assume full responsibility for the forecasts under review, and that they will signify such responsibility by formal adoption by the Board and a statement to that effect in any circular.

(c) The identities of the company's merchant bankers and advisers (when not the reporting accountants) reporting in connection with the forecasts.

Finally, a formal letter of instruction from the directors to the accountants should be arranged—

(a) stating the period, nature and purpose of the forecast and the reason the report is required;

(b) asking the reporting accountants to review the accounting bases and calculations;

(c) confirming that the directors assume full responsibility for the forecast and will signify such by formal adoption by the Board; and

(d) confirming that the directors will specify the main assumptions on which the forecast is based.

General Survey

The main matters to which reporting accountants will direct their attention are as follows:—

(a) The nature and background of the company's business. A review will be made of the company's character and recent history, with reference to such matters as the general nature of its activities and its main products, markets, customers, suppliers, divisions, labour force, trend of results, location of subsidiaries, divisions and major branches.

(b) The accounting practices normally followed by the company. The reporting accountants will wish to establish that the practices normally adopted in annual financial statements are acceptable and have been consistently applied in the preparation of interim accounts and profit forecasts.

(c) Areas which may require particular attention. These include—

(i)   Nature and treatment of overheads in relation to stock and work-in-progress, and the treatment of slow-moving or obsolete items.

---

[47]Accountants International Study Group, Appendix 4.

[48]"Accountants Reports on Profit Forecasts," The Council of the Institute of Chartered Accountants in England and Wales in consultation with the Council of the Institute of Chartered Accountants of Scotland, 1969.

(ii)   The bases adopted for recognising profits and for providing for losses in long-term contracts.

(iii)   The accounting treatment of research and development expenditure.

(iv)   The accounting treatment of exceptional and extraordinary items.

(v)   The accounting treatment of taxation and grants.

(vi)   Whether any costing system which may be in operation is reliable.

(vii)   The degree of consistency in the accounting procedures within the group, or among branches.

(d)   The assumptions on which the forecast is based. The reporting accountants will have to satisfy themselves whether or not the forecasts are consistent with the given assumptions, economic, commercial, marketing and financial, which underlie them. A letter from the company specifying the assumptions, as mentioned above, should be obtained. Materiality is an important factor, and a subjective judgement must be made as to whether the supporting evidence and explanations given by the directors show that they have approached the assumptions in a reasonable and responsible manner. Where the reporting accountants are not satisfied with the assumptions, they should qualify their report. Practice Note No. 6 (first issued 30 June 1971 and now contained in the February 1972 issue of the City Code) of the Panel on Take-overs and Mergers gives guidance on the subject of disclosing the assumptions on which a profit forecast is based.

(e)   The procedures followed by the company in preparing forecasts. Regard should be paid to the following:—

(i)   Whether the profit forecasts under review are based on forecasts regularly prepared for the purpose of management, or whether they have been separately and specially prepared for the immediate purpose.

(ii)   Where profit forecasts are regularly prepared for management purposes, the degree of accuracy and reliability and previously achieved, and the frequency and thoroughness with which the estimates are revised and discrepancies investigated.

(iii)   Whether the forecasts under review represent the management's best estimate of results which they reasonably believe can and will be achieved, as distinct from targets which the management has set as desirable.

(iv)   The extent to which forecast results for expired periods are supported by reliable interim accounts.

(v)   The extent to which the forecasts for publication are built up from detailed forecasts in respect of the main divisions or lines of activity, distinguishing between those which show a consistent trend and those of a more volatile nature.

(vi)   How the forecasts take account of any material items, their nature and how they are presented.

(vii)   Whether adequate provision is made for foreseeable losses and contingencies.

(viii)   Whether working capital appears adequate for requirements, as shown by properly prepared cash flow forecasts, and, where short-term finance is required, whether the necessary arrangements have been confirmed.

(ix)   Whether the forecasts have been prepared and presented on acceptable bases consistent with the accounting policies adopted by the company in previous years, and, if not, whether this fact and the effects of any material change of basis are made clear.

(x)   Whether the most recent directors' report, chairman's review, board minutes and press releases show anything likely to affect the forecast.

(xi)   The relationship of fixed and variable costs and the effect on profits of changes in production and sales activity.

(xii)   Whether adjustments for unrealised inter-company profits and for exchange rates have been made in the case of group companies.

Procedures

Generally, verification will be carried out as in a normal audit insofar as detailed calculations and accounting bases are concerned. Such checks will be made as will enable the reporting accountants to express an opinion on the profit figures. A comprehensive file will be built up incorporating copies of the principal statements supporting the forecast and showing the extent of verification work carried out. Where the reporting accountants are not also the auditors, it will be necessary to communicate with the latter, especially where a prospectus is involved because in that case the report will be signed jointly.

If during the course of work it becomes apparent that a qualification to the report is likely to be needed, immediate warning to this effect should be given to the client and advisers.

The examination will be conducted along the lines indicated in the following paragraphs.

Accounting Bases

(a) The reporting accountants will obtain a statement of the accounting bases adopted, adapting for this purpose their own audit questionnaire if necessary.

(b) A written assurance will be obtained from the company that the practices followed in preparing the forecast are consistent with those followed in the previous financial accounts, that all unusual items have been disclosed and that nothing either adverse or favourable has happened since the preparation of the forecasts that would cast doubt on their accuracy.

(c) Where a merger is proposed a statement will be obtained of the bases followed by the other company.

(d) A note will be taken of any bases which—
  (i)   have changed or not been applied consistently, in the period under review;
  (ii) are not normally acceptable; or
  (iii) are found to differ from those of the other party to the merger (where (c) above applies).

(e) The effect of the application of differing accounting bases—
  (i)   on profits; or
  (ii) on net assets
will be calculated: if the results shown in the forecast would be materially altered as a result of this calculation, this fact must be disclosed in the published documents.

Accounting Methods

(a) The following will be obtained:—
  (i)   a manual of accounting procedures;
  (ii) a reconciliation of the last published accounts with the management accounts for the same period; and
  (iii) the supporting working papers for the published and management accounts.

(b) These will be examined, paying particular attention to—
  (i)   the verification and valuation of inventories and provisions for obsolescence and damage;
  (ii) the verification and valuation of contracts and work-in-progress and the method of taking profits and providing for losses;
  (iii) the taking of credit for sales and the computation of the cost of sales;
  (iv) the provision for bad and doubtful debts;
  (v)   the verification and valuation of fixed assets and the computation of depreciation thereon; and
  (vi) the verification of cash in hand and at bank as a starting point for the cash flow forecast.

Forecasting Procedures

(a) Statements will be obtained of the procedures used by the company when preparing normal management forecasts.

(b) If the procedures used by the company for the forecast being examined are different from the normal procedures it will be necessary to enquire whether—
  (i)   statements have been prepared of the variations; and
  (ii) schedules have been prepared showing the effect of the variations on the profit forecast.

The Profit Forecast

(a) The forecast from the company will be obtained in the form in which it will be published.

(b) The assumptions on which the forecast is based will be noted and the reporting accountants will—
  (i)   ensure that they have been stated in the forecast which will be published; and
  (ii) examine any third party reports on which the assumptions are based.

(c) Supporting forecasts from subsidiaries or divisions of a company will be considered individually.
(d) Differences—
   (i)   between recent forecasts and actual;
   (ii) between any earlier forecasts covering the same period as the forecast under review and the current forecast; and
   (iii) between the latest unaudited actual figures and comparable figures for the previous year,
   will be scheduled and explanations obtained for all differences.
(e) A comparison will be made of the following and the realism of the forecasts in terms of the present plant considered as a result of the comparison:—
   (i)   the current volume of production and sales *vis-à-vis* the current profit;
   (ii) the volume of output that will produce a profit;
   (iii) the volume of production and sales *vis-à-vis* the profit target budgeted for the financial year;
   (iv) the effect on profit on volumes of production and sales above and below the planned volume;
   (v)   the productive capacity of the plant.
(f) The adequacy of the margin for contingencies will be considered, having regard to the effect on turnover of labour disputes, etc.
(g) A specific note will be made of factors which cause a forecast to be subject to a high degree of risk (e.g., long-term contracts at fixed prices).
(h) Where consolidated forecasts depend on supporting forecasts from subsidiaries and divisions and these have been examined by other accountants the reporting accountant will—
   (i)   consider whether they have been correctly included in the forecast;
   (ii) check the accuracy of the arithmetic of consolidation; and
   (iii) examine the treatment of inter-group transactions.
(i) The tax computation will be reviewed.
(j) All calculations will be checked.
(k) Letters of representation will be obtained from all subsidiary companies contributing materially to the final forecast.

Cash Flow Forecast

(a) A cash flow statement will be obtained from the company, covering the same period, at least, as the profit forecast.
(b) A source and application of funds statement at the end of the period will also be obtained.
(c) Where a merger is contemplated, the reporting accountants will prepare a cash flow for the new group and consider the adequacy of the working capital.
(d) Previous cash flow forecasts will be compared with subsequent results to ascertain the accuracy of the forecasting methods.
(e) Any material discrepancies will be subjected to enquiry.
(f) If a merger takes place, it is necessary to be satisfied that bank and loan credit facilities will continue.
(g) The reporting accountants will have to ensure that the methods of preparing cash flow forecasts for subsidiaries and divisions are consistent.
(h) They will reconcile cash flow and profits projections and ensure that they are based on similar assumptions.
(i) All calculations will be checked.

Final Points

(a) The final printer's proof of the document in which the profit forecast and the statement of working capital, together with the accountants report, are to be published will be obtained.
(b) The reporting accountants will draft their report to be published in that document.
(c) A detailed report on the profit forecast and the cash flow forecast, not for publication in the document, will usually also be prepared.
(d) All outstanding points will be cleared and the document reviewed to ensure that the statements and figures therein are in accordance with the facts ascertained as a result of the tests made.

Chapter **7**

The Computer and Modern Accounting

GORDON B. DAVIS
Professor of Business Administration, University of Minnesota

The electronic computer does not affect accounting principles because they are independent of processing methods, but the enhanced processing capabilities of the computer have improved the capability of organizations to implement advanced management information systems which were not practical using manual processing methods. Therefore, those involved in the accounting and information system of an organization should understand the capabilities of computers and the changes in data processing potential because of the computer. In organizations using the computer for data processing, the accountant needs to understand computer data processing methods and the organization and processing of computer files because the ability to do analysis, provide meaningful reports, or prepare statements depends, to a great extent, on the existence of appropriate files and processing capabilities. The accountant should also understand quality control for computer processing because the reliance which should be placed on computer-based records is dependent on the quality of files and accuracy of processing. This chapter provides a basic background summary of the computer data processing system and its planning, development, and operation; the chapter describes the organization and management of computer files, processing methods, and control over quality of processing.

ELEMENTS OF A COMPUTER DATA PROCESSING SYSTEM

There are five basic elements in a computer data processing system. These are the hardware, the generalized software, the applications software, the procedures, and the personnel. Each of these will be described briefly.

Hardware. Hardware for computer data processing consists of equipment which can perform the following functions: data preparation; input to the computer; computation, control, and primary storage; secondary (auxiliary) storage; and output from the computer. Equipment which is connected directly to the

EXHIBIT 1   Functions in a Computer System

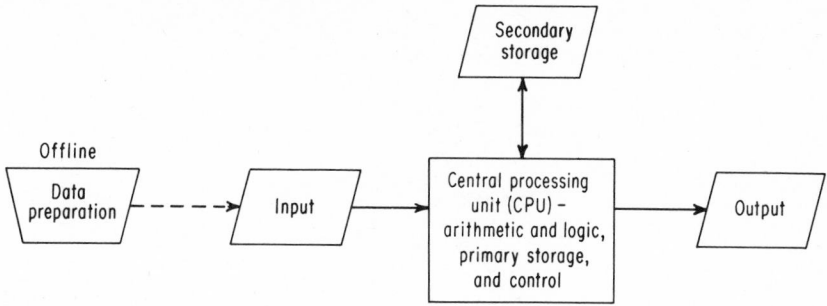

EXHIBIT 2   Medium-Scale Computer System with Both Magnetic Tape and Magnetic Disc Storage (Photo courtesy of IBM.)

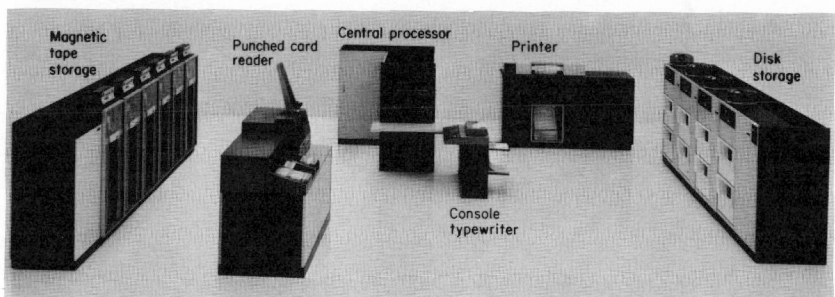

computer is termed "online," whereas equipment which is used separately and is not connected is called "offline." The relationship of these equipment functions is shown in Exhibit 1. A medium-scale computer system is shown in Exhibit 2.

The exact selection of equipment in a computer center will depend on the amount and type of processing being performed and the types of equipment available with the computer system being used. In general, an installation will have one or more pieces of equipment for each of the five equipment functions described earlier. The equipment for each of these functions is summarized in Exhibit 3.

Generalized Software.   Software consists of computer programs and routines (sets of computer instructions) which direct the operation of the computer. Software is as critical to effective use of a computer as hardware. "Software" can refer to generalized routines useful in computer operations or to programs for a specific application (such as payroll). Generalized software provides operating support for individual applications. Generalized software includes computer programs for such tasks as making printouts of machine-readable records, sorting records, organizing and maintaining files, translating of programs written in a symbolic language into machine-language instructions, and scheduling jobs through the computer. It is usually furnished by the manufacturer.

Applications Software.   A complete data processing application usually requires a number of programs. Each of these programs consists of a set of instructions for performing a data processing task. Applications programs are generally written by the user installation but are frequently obtained as prewritten packages from software vendors. Computer manufacturers and independent software vendors

EXHIBIT 3   Type of Equipment for Each Computer Data Processing Function

Function	Type of equipment used
Data preparation	Key-driven card punch Key-driven card verifier Paper tape punch Key-disc encoder Magnetic tape encoder Magnetic ink enscriber Optical character enscriber Data collection devices with keyboard, plastic card sensor, etc., which transcribe onto some machine-readable medium Devices to prepare cards, paper tape, or optical tape as a by-product of another operation Conversion devices such as paper tape to magnetic tape converter and paper tape to punched-card converter
Input	Card reader Magnetic tape unit Paper tape reader Magnetic-ink character reader Optical scanner Console typewriter Online data collection devices
Computation, control, and primary storage	Central processing unit (CPU)
Secondary storage	Storage devices using the following storage media: Magnetic tape Magnetic disc Magnetic drum Magnetic core Semiconductors
Output	Printer Card punch Paper tape punch Console typewriter Visual display (CRT) Graph plotter Audio response unit Computer output microfilm (COM)

can supply application programs for common data processing tasks (payroll, accounts receivable, inventory control, etc.).

Procedures.   The operation of a data processing system requires procedures for obtaining and preparing data, procedures for operating the computer, and procedures for distributing the output from computer processing. These procedures include control steps such as actions to be taken in the event there are errors in the data or there is a malfunctioning of the equipment.

Personnel.   Computer data processing requires specialized skills. Three major jobs are found in data processing installations:

Job Title	*Job Description*
Systems analyst	Study information needs and data processing requirements. Design a data processing application. Prepare specifications and outline of the application. Prepare procedures for use.
Programmer	Prepare computer programs based on specifications prepared by the systems analyst.
Computer operator	Operate the computer.

Of these jobs, the systems analyst requires the broadest background in terms of education and understanding of organizations. The programmer has to have the specialized skill of writing computer instructions. The computer operator requires less training than the other jobs because the operator function involves well-defined tasks which do not require knowledge of the internal workings of either the equipment or the program. A number of other positions may be found, depending on the size and complexity of the installation. Two important additional functions are the librarian and the data administrator. The librarian maintains control over the magnetic tapes, disc packs, card decks, etc. which contain the programs and files for the organization. A data administrator is found in organizations in which files are integrated into a complex data base. The function maintains the data base and is the authority by which access to the data is obtained.

THE INFORMATION SYSTEM MASTER PLAN

A computer-based information processing system is complex and therefore needs an overall plan (often called a master development plan) to guide its construction. The plan describes the information system and how it is to be developed. The plan is normally for three to five years, with more detail for the current year. The master plan, once developed, does not remain constant but is updated as new developments occur.

The master plan has two components—a long-range plan and a short-range plan. When such a plan is presented to management, it provides information by which to assess information system development and evaluate the impact it will have on overall organization planning. The long-range portion provides the general control, and the short-range portion provides a basis for specific accountability as to operational and financial performance.

In general, the master development plan contains four major sections:
1. Organizational goals and objectives
2. Inventory of current capabilities
3. Forecast of developments affecting the plan
4. The specific plan.

Each of these sections of the master development plan is described in more detail.

Organizational Goals and Objectives.   This section of the plan might contain the following parts:
1. Organizational objectives
2. External environment
3. Internal organization constraints such as management philosophy
4. Overall objectives for the information system
5. Overall structure for the information system

Within the context of broad organizational goals and organization-wide plans, there should be goals and objectives for the information system. These can be of two types: general and specific operational goals. The general goals provide guidelines for the direction in which the information system effort should be directed. The operational goals are more specific and should be stated so that performance or nonperformance may be measured.

Current Capabilities.   This section of the plan is a summary of the current status of the computer data processing system. It includes such items as the following:
1. Inventory of
   (a) Equipment
   (b) Generalized software (system software, data management system, etc.)

    (c) Application systems
    (d) Personnel (title, years with firm, etc.)
2. Analysis of
    (a) Expense
    (b) Facilities utilization
3. Status of projects in process
4. Assessment of strengths and weaknesses.

Forecast of Developments Affecting the Plan. The impact of technology developments needs to be part of the long-range plan. It is sometimes difficult to estimate future technology, but most developments are announced one or more years before they become generally available to the user. Also, the broad technological changes can be perceived some years before they are implemented.

The Specific Plan. The plan should include schedules for development of new applications and a schedule of the resource requirements. These requirements can be presented as:

1. A hardware and purchased software schedule
2. Application development schedule
3. Schedule of software maintenance and conversion effect
4. Personnel resources required
5. Financial resources required.

THE DEVELOPMENT OF A COMPUTER DATA PROCESSING APPLICATION

The decisions as to which applications to develop are reflected in the master plan. Once selected for development, every application needs to go through a development process which has been termed an information system development life cycle. The steps or phases in the life cycle for information system development are described differently by different writers,[1] but there is agreement on the basic flow. In order to manage and control the development effort, it is necessary to know what should have been done, what has been done, and what has yet to be accomplished. The phases in the development life cycle provide a basis for this management and control because they define segments of the flow of work which can be identified for managerial purposes and specify the documents to be produced by each phase.

The information system development life cycle consists of three major stages:
1. Definition of the system or application
2. Physical design
3. Implementation.

In other words, there is first the process which defines the requirements for a feasible cost/effective system. The requirements are then translated into a physical system of forms, procedures, programs, etc., by system design, computer programming, and procedure development. The resulting system is tested and put into operation. No system is perfect, so there is always a need for maintenance changes. To complete the cycle, there should be an audit of the system to evaluate how well it performs and how well it meets cost and performance specifications. The three stages of definition, physical design, and implementation can therefore be divided into smaller steps or phases as follows:

[1]See Robert Benjamin, "Control of the Information System Development Cycle," Wiley-Interscience, New York, 1971, p. 29, for a tabular presentation of different categorizations of the information system development life cycle. See also table 1, p. 577, in "Education Related to the Use of Computers in Organizations," *Communications of the ACM,* September 1971.

Phase in Development Cycle	*Comments*
Feasibility assessment	Evaluation of feasibility and cost/benefit of proposed application
Information analysis	Determination of information needed
System design	Design of processing system and preparation of program specifications
Program development	Coding and debugging of computer programs
Procedure development	Design of procedures and writing of user instructions
Conversion	Final test and conversion
Operation and maintenance	Day-to-day operation, modification, and maintenance
Post audit	How well did it turn out?

The eight phases can be organized in terms of the three major stages of information system development:

Stage	*Phase*
Definition	Feasibility assessment
	Information analysis
Physical design	System design
	Program development
	Procedure development
Implementation	Conversion
	Operation and maintenance
	Post audit

Each phase in the development cycle results in documentation. The sum of the documentation for the phases is the documentation of the application. The amount of detailed analysis and documentation in each phase will depend on the type of application. For example, a large, integrated application will require considerable analysis and documentation at each phase; a report requested by a manager will require little analysis and documentation, but all phases of the cycle are still present.

Note that the information system development life cycle does not include the equipment selection and procurement cycle. The reason is that the selection and procurement of equipment (except for some specialized equipment) is generally related to many systems rather than a single application. If an application requires equipment selection, this will generally take place during the physical design development stage.

The following percentages provide a rough idea of the allocation of effort (say, in hours) in the information system development life cycle from inception until the system is operating properly (i.e., excluding operation and maintenance). These percentages will, of course, vary with each project. The ranges shown are indicative of the variations to be expected.

Stage in life cycle	Phase in life cycle	Rough percentage of effort	Range in percentage of effort
Definition	Feasibility assessment	10	5–15
	Information analysis	15	10–20
Physical design	System design	20	10–30
	Program development	25	20–40
	Procedure development	10	5–15
Implementation	Conversion	15	10–20
	Operation and maintenance	(Not applicable)	
	Post audit	5	2–6
		100	

Definition Stage. During the definition stage the project is proposed, a preliminary survey is prepared, and the feasibility assessed. A project may be a system module defined by the master development plan, a major maintenance project, or a project allowed but not scheduled in the master plan.

After the project or problem is proposed, the first step is to define the problem. An analyst is assigned to work with the potential users and prepare a proposal report describing the need, rough benefits, and resources to perform a feasibility assessment. The proposal report is reviewed by the department proposing the project, the information system executive, and the information system planning committee. If the project definition is approved, the feasibility study is begun to assess three types of feasibility: technical feasibility, economic feasibility, and operational feasibility. A feasibility report is prepared including a proposed development plan. If the project is approved, the next phase is information analysis.

One or more analysts work with users to define the information requirements in detail and to define the information flow. The results of the information analysis phase are:

1. Layouts of the outputs (reports, transaction documents, CRT screens, etc.)
2. Layouts of inputs (transaction input forms, CRT screen input, etc.)
3. Data definitions for required data items
4. Specifications regarding items such as a response time, accuracy, frequency of updating, and volume.

These specifications complete the definition of what the system is to do; the next step is to design the physical processing system to produce the defined results.

Physical Design Stage. The design of the processing system is divided into three phases—system design, program development, and procedure development. Upon completion of this stage of the life cycle, the processing system will be ready for implementation.

The physical design stage begins with the system design. This is the design of the processing system that will produce the reports specified in the information analysis. It designs the equipment usage, the files to be maintained, the processing method, the file access method, and flow of processing. The results of the system design phase are:

1. File design layout and specifications
2. System flow charts showing, for example, use of equipment, flow of processing, and processing runs
3. A file-building or file-conversion plan
4. Control flow chart showing controls to be implemented at each stage of processing
5. Backup and security provisions
6. A system test plan
7. A hardware/software selection schedule (if required).

The programming and procedure development phases can proceed concurrently. The programming phase is described later in the chapter. Procedure development involves the preparation of instructions for the following:

1. Users
2. Clerical personnel providing input
3. Control personnel
4. Operating personnel (computer operator, librarian, data administrator, etc.).

The procedure development phase can also include the preparation of training material to be used in implementation.

Implementation Stage. When the programs and procedures are prepared, the conversion phase can begin. Data is collected, files built, and the overall system tested. There are various methods of testing. One is to test the system under simulated conditions; another is to test under actual conditions, operating in parallel with the existing systems and procedures. It is generally considered not good practice to implement a complex system without one of these full system tests.

After all errors and problems that have been detected in the system test are corrected, the system is cut over into actual operation. When it appears to be operating without difficulty, it is turned over to the maintenance group in information processing. Any subsequent errors or minor modifications are handled as application maintenance. This is not a trivial activity—about one-third of the analyst/programmer effort is devoted to maintenance of existing applications. Because of the importance of maintenance, it is necessary that the system be designed and documented for maintainability.

The last phase of the implementation stage is a post audit. This is a review by an audit task force (composed, for example, of a user representative, an internal auditor, and a data processing representative). The audit group reviews the objectives and cost/benefit representations made in behalf of the project and compares these to actual performance and actual cost/value. It also reviews the operational characteristics of the system to determine if they are satisfactory.

TOOLS FOR ANALYSIS AND DESIGN OF COMPUTER PROCESSING APPLICATIONS

There are a number of structured approaches to the task of accumulating data and documenting the design of a data processing application. Almost all of the structured, systematic approaches utilize flow charts, decision tables, and layouts. These are basic tools for analysis and design of processing applications.

Flow Charts. Flow charts can be used to describe a data processing system (often termed a "system flow chart") and also to describe the logic of a computer program (termed a "program flow chart" or "logic flow chart"). Although each person may use whatever flow chart symbols are most meaningful, communication is enhanced if the American National Standard flow chart symbols (also standardized internationally) are used. These are applied to both system and program flow charts (Exhibit 4). It is customary to draw flow charts so that they read from left to right and from top to bottom. If the flow goes in a reverse direction, arrowheads are used. Arrowheads can, of course, be used in normal flow to increase clarity or readability. When it is desirable to identify a symbol for the purpose of referencing it, a notation is placed above the symbol to the left of the vertical bisector or inside the symbol separated by a stripe.

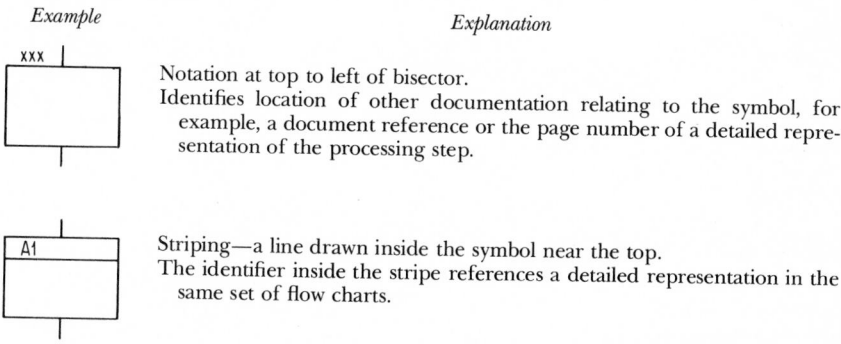

Example   *Explanation*

XXX   Notation at top to left of bisector.
           Identifies location of other documentation relating to the symbol, for example, a document reference or the page number of a detailed representation of the processing step.

A1   Striping—a line drawn inside the symbol near the top.
           The identifier inside the stripe references a detailed representation in the same set of flow charts.

The system flow chart describes both computer and noncomputer processing, identifying major computer runs by a process symbol (Exhibit 5). Each run is documented by one or more program flow charts. A macro program flow chart

EXHIBIT 4 Summary of Major Flow Chart Symbols (Section 5, "Summary of Flowchart Symbols," from ANSI X3.5-1970, *Flowchart Symbols and Their Usage in Information Processing,* p. 15.)

Basic symbols

Input/Output

Process

Flowline

Annotation

Specialized input/output symbols

Punched card

Magnetic tape

Magnetic disk

Punched tape

Document

Manual input

Display

Communication link

Specialized input/output symbols

Online storage

Offline storage

Specialized processing symbols

Decision

Predefined process (subroutine)

Sort

Auxiliary operation

Manual operation

Additional symbols

Connector

Terminal

EXHIBIT 5 Example of System Flow Chart

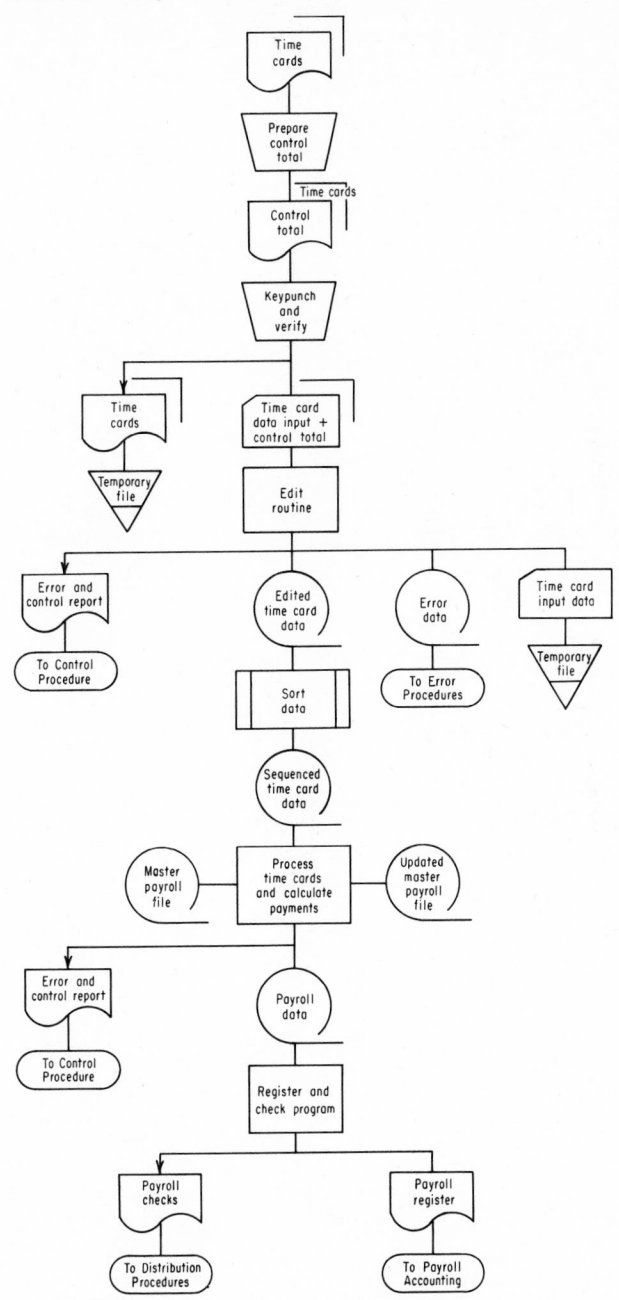

EXHIBIT 6   Use of Macro and Micro Program Flow Charts

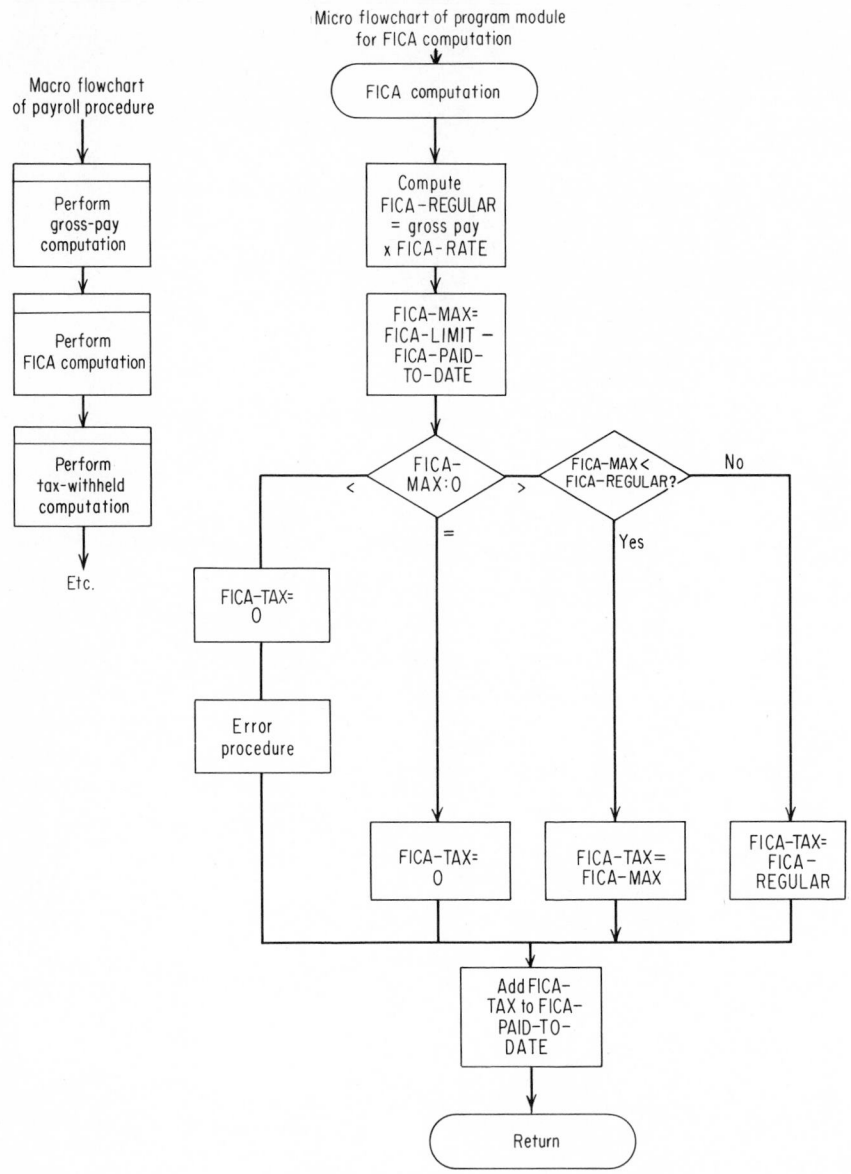

can be used to show the overall flow; a micro program flow chart can document detailed program logic (Exhibit 6). The relationship of different parts (modules) of a program can also be diagrammed by a hierarchy chart similiar in form to an organization chart. Some organizations use a format called HIPO charts to document programs. These consist of a *h*ierarchy chart plus *i*nput, *p*rocess, and *o*utput charts to show the flow of processing.

Decision Tables.   This is another method of describing the logic of a procedure or a computer program. While not as widely used as flow charts, the decision table is useful for describing processing logic for those cases in which there are several sets of conditions which lead to different sets of actions.

The decision table is a tabular form divided into four areas:

Conditions and actions are separated by an "if . . . then . . ." relationship. The table can be read: "*if* a set of conditions exists *then* perform the indicated actions." The stubs describe the conditions or actions and the entries indicate whether or not the element exists; or they may specify other data such as values for the element. The most common approach is a limited entry table with Y used for yes or true as a condition entry and N used for no or false. A dash indicates that either answer is applicable. An X in the action entry specifies that the action is to be taken; a blank indicates that it is not to be taken. Each rule expresses a different set of conditions and actions. A simple decision table given in Exhibit 7 illustrates a table used to document the logic of the credit-granting decision (say for department store credit).

EXHIBIT 7   Example of Decision Table

CREDIT GRANTING TABLE	Rules					
	1	2	3	4	5	6
Conditions						
Held present job more than 1 year	Y	N	Y	N	N	Y
Lived at present residence more than 2 years	–	Y	N	Y	N	Y
Yearly income greater than $ 7,500	Y	Y	N	N	–	N
Actions						
Grant credit	X	X				
Refuse credit			X	X	X	
Refer to credit manager						X

Layouts.   Layouts are used to show the format of input/output records or the placement of data in storage. Preprinted forms are generally used as a convenience. The major layout forms in use are card layout, tape or disc layout, and printer layout. Card and printer layouts are illustrated in Exhibit 8.

EXHIBIT 8   Example of Card Layout and Printer Layout for Design of Input and Output Records

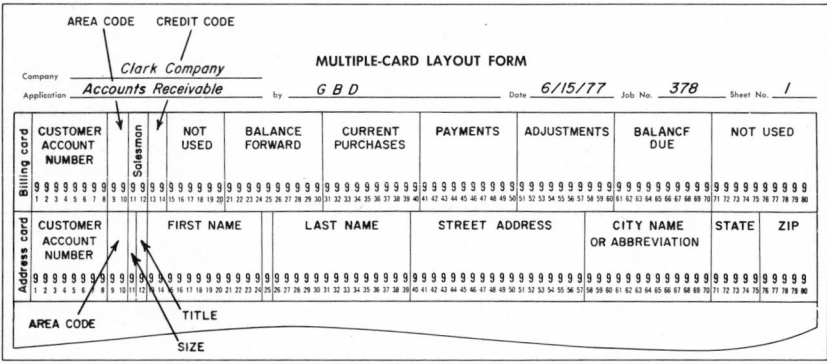

STEPS IN PREPARING A COMPUTER PROGRAM

The computer program development phase of the information system application development life cycle consists of the following general steps:

1. Program planning
2. Coding of computer instructions
3. Compilation (or assembly)
4. Testing and debugging
5. Documentation.

The testing, debugging, and documentation activities are carried out concurrently with the first three activities.

Program Planning.   The system design phase provides general program specifications—the input, processing to be accomplished, and output to be provided. The programmer may be provided with system flow charts and input and output layouts. The purpose of program planning is to define the structure of the computer programs and to describe the logic to be followed by each routine.

The structure of a computer program is generally a set of modules (also called routines or subroutines) which define independent processing tasks within the program. Major modules may be further subdivided into submodules. For example, a simple program to read data cards, perform computations, and produce a listing might have the following modules:

Input module (to read data)

Edit module (to check input data for valid data)

Processing module (to perform computations on valid data)

Error and control module (to provide error messages on bad data and to provide control figures)

Output module (to perform output)

Main routine (to direct use of other modules).

The modular approach simplifies the program structure, allows concurrent writing and testing of individual modules, and simplifies changes and maintenance of programs. A significant program planning activity is the definition of the modular structure. The term structured programming is used to refer to a disciplined approach to modular design. Top down design and development of the modules in a program is generally favored. The top, main directing routine is prepared first; other modules in the hierarchy are coded and tested in order from the highest modules down to the lowest-level modules.

The output from the program planning is a hierarchy chart showing the relationship of the program modules, specifications for each of the modules, and flow charts (where useful). These may be macro program flow charts to show overall logic and micro program flow charts to show detailed logic.

Coding of Computer Instructions. Coding is the writing of the actual computer instructions. Although the computer will accept only instructions written in the absolute or machine language form, the programmer typically codes in a symbolic format more suitable for human use. The symbolic instructions must follow rather rigid rules with respect to format, punctuation, etc. Special coding paper is usually used to assist in following the coding form. The conversion of the symbolic coding to machine language instructions accepted by the computer is done by the assembly or compilation process.

Coding may use a symbolic assembly language which is machine-oriented or a higher-level procedure-oriented language. Most data processing applications are programmed in a procedure-oriented language. Symbolic assembly language coding is used primarily for generalized software and unusual applications requiring attention to machine efficiency.

There are different procedure-oriented languages for different types of problems. The following are the most common:

Type of Problem	Language
Data processing	COBOL (COmmon Business Oriented Language)
	RPG (Report Program Generator)
Mathematical	FORTRAN (FORmula TRANslator)
	BASIC (used primarily in time sharing)
General	PL/I (Programming Language One)

COBOL is the most common data processing language for all except small computers, for which RPG is most used. Exhibit 9 illustrates a simple COBOL program. Note the four divisions of the program: the Identification Division identifies the program, the Environment Division describes the machine environment, the Data Division defines the files and data items in the files, and the Procedure Division describes the processing procedures. A disciplined approach to programming will use coding structures and coding rules that produce clear, easily maintained programs.

EXHIBIT 9   Example of a Simple COBOL Program

```
IDENTIFICATION DIVISION.
PROGRAM-ID. PAYROLL-REPORT.
AUTHOR. GORDON B DAVIS.
REMARKS. SIMPLE COBOL PROGRAM TO READ HOURS-WORKED AND
    RATE-OF-PAY AND TO COMPUTE REGULAR-PAY, OVERTIME-PAY,
    AND GROSS-PAY. OVERTIME-PAY IS ONE-AND-ONE-HALF THE
    REGULAR RATE FOR HOURS OVER 40.
*
ENVIRONMENT DIVISION.
CONFIGURATION SECTION.
SOURCE-COMPUTER. CYBER 74.
OBJECT-COMPUTER. CYBER 74.
INPUT-OUTPUT SECTION.
FILE-CONTROL.
    SELECT PAYROLL-CARD-FILE ASSIGN TO INPUT.
    SELECT PAYROLL-REPORT-FILE ASSIGN TO OUTPUT.
*
DATA DIVISION.
FILE SECTION.
FD  PAYROLL-CARD-FILE LABEL RECORD IS OMITTED
    DATA RECORD IS PAYROLL-CARD.
01  PAYROLL-CARD.
    05  PAYROLL-ID              PICTURE X(5).
    05  HOURS-WORKED            PICTURE 99.
    05  RATE-OF-PAY             PICTURE 9V999.
    05  FILLER                  PICTURE X(69).
FD  PAYROLL-REPORT-FILE LABEL RECORD IS OMITTED
    DATA RECORD IS PRINT-PAY-LINE.
01  PRINT-PAY-LINE.
    05  FILLER                  PICTURE X(10).
    05  PAYROLL-ID              PICTURE X(5).
    05  HOURS-WORKED            PICTURE ZZ99.
    05  RATE-OF-PAY             PICTURE ZZ9.999.
    05  REGULAR-PAY-PRINT       PICTURE $$$$$$9.99.
    05  OVERTIME-PAY-PRINT      PICTURE $$$$$$9.99.
    05  GROSS-PAY-PRINT         PICTURE $$$$$$9.99.
    05  FILLER                  PICTURE X(89).
WORKING-STORAGE SECTION.
77  REGULAR-PAY                 PICTURE S999V99.
77  OVERTIME-PAY                PICTURE S999V99.
77  GROSS-PAY                   PICTURE S999V99.
77  CARDS-FLAG                  PICTURE X(3) VALUE 'YES'.
*
PROCEDURE DIVISION.
MAINLINE-ROUTINE.
    PERFORM INITIALIZATION.
    PERFORM READ-CALCULATE-PRINT UNTIL CARDS-FLAG EQUAL 'NO'.
    PERFORM CLOSING.
    STOP RUN.
INITIALIZATION.
    OPEN INPUT PAYROLL-CARD-FILE OUTPUT PAYROLL-REPORT-FILE.
READ-CALCULATE-PRINT.
    READ PAYROLL-CARD-FILE AT END MOVE 'NO' TO CARDS-FLAG.
    IF CARDS-FLAG EQUAL 'YES'
        PERFORM PAY-PROCESSING.
PAY-PROCESSING.
    IF HOURS-WORKED OF PAYROLL-CARD IS GREATER THAN 40
        PERFORM PAY-CALCULATION-WITH-OVERTIME
    ELSE
        PERFORM PAY-CALCULATION-NO-OVERTIME.
    COMPUTE GROSS-PAY = REGULAR-PAY + OVERTIME-PAY.
    PERFORM WRITE-REPORT-LINE.
PAY-CALCULATION-NO-OVERTIME.
    MULTIPLY HOURS-WORKED OF PAYROLL-CARD BY RATE-OF-PAY OF
        PAYROLL-CARD GIVING REGULAR-PAY ROUNDED.
    COMPUTE OVERTIME-PAY = 0.
PAY-CALCULATION-WITH-OVERTIME.
    MULTIPLY RATE-OF-PAY OF PAYROLL-CARD BY 40 GIVING
        REGULAR-PAY ROUNDED.
    COMPUTE OVERTIME-PAY ROUNDED = (HOURS-WORKED OF PAYROLL-CARD
        - 40) * 1.5 * RATE-OF-PAY OF PAYROLL-CARD.
WRITE-REPORT-LINE.
    MOVE SPACES TO PRINT-PAY-LINE.
    MOVE CORRESPONDING PAYROLL-CARD TO PRINT-PAY-LINE.
    MOVE REGULAR-PAY TO REGULAR-PAY-PRINT.
    MOVE OVERTIME-PAY TO OVERTIME-PAY-PRINT.
    MOVE GROSS-PAY TO GROSS-PAY-PRINT.
    WRITE PRINT-PAY-LINE.
CLOSING.
    CLOSE PAYROLL-CARD-FILE, PAYROLL-REPORT-FILE.
```

Compilation or Assembly.   Assembly is the translation of a program written in symbolic assembly language instructions into machine language instructions. Compilation is the term given to the preparation of a machine language program from a program in a procedure-oriented language. The terms are sometimes used interchangeably although they do have slightly different meanings. A program written in AUTOCODER, SPS, or BAL (names of symbolic assembly languages) is assembled, whereas a program written in FORTRAN, COBOL, BASIC, etc., is compiled. In both cases, the assembly or compilation process is carried out by a computer program (assembler or compiler) furnished by the manufacturer or by an independent software vendor. The result is a machine language program which performs the steps represented by the symbolic coding.

Testing and Debugging.   Application development includes a comprehensive test plan. Testing of programs is a continuous process during program development. As each module of a program is coded, it is desk-checked by the programmer who traces sample transactions through the program module logic. The next checking occurs during translation of the symbolic coding by an assembler or compiler. This process detects language use errors. As each module is completed, it is added to a main line routine and other completed modules and they are tested by running test transactions with the program. The test transactions should use all of the program logic in order to test all program paths. The expected results of processing the transactions are compared with the computer-produced results to detect errors. During development, other programmers may review the program logic and test data in a formal review process called a structured walkthrough. When all modules are completed and tested the application system is tested in operation, frequently being run in parallel with an existing system until all program errors and operating problems can be corrected.

Documentation.   The documentation phase consists of completing parts of the documentation of the program and assembling other documents associated with the program. These are organized as two reports: a run manual and operating instructions. The run manual contains the complete set of documentation for the program. The sections of the run manual are, in general, the following:

Section	*Description of Contents*
Problem definition	A description of the reason why the program was prepared and the program specifications
System description	A general outline of the program and the related environment or application system in which the program operates. The section contains the system flow charts and record layouts.
Program description	The documentation of the program portion of the application. Contains the hierarchy chart, program flow charts, decision tables, program listing, and other descriptions which document the contents of the program
Operating instructions	The instructions required to run the program on the computer
Summary of controls	A summary of the controls built into the program to detect errors.
Acceptance record	A documentation of steps taken to test the program before acceptance, record of approvals, and a record of subsequent changes.

The documentation in the run manual is kept up to date by recording all changes in it. For example, when a change is made in the program, a change record may be placed in the acceptance record section and a reference noted on the appropriate flow chart.

The operating instructions furnished to the computer operator provide all information necessary for the operator. This may consist of the operating instructions section of the run manual.

THE BASIC COMPUTER DATA PROCESSING CYCLE

In the computer data processing literature, *data* is used as a singular noun. This usage varies with the plural form used in accounting. The basic cycle for computer data processing consists of six phases:
1. Data capture
2. Data preparation
3. Input
4. Input editing (data validation)
5. Processing manipulation
6. Output.

The phases in the data processing cycle will be summarized briefly.

Data Capture.   Data capture consists of activities for obtaining data and recording it for subsequent processing steps or other use. Data may be:
1. Recorded in a form that requires preparation before it can be input for computer processing
2. Recorded immediately in a machine-readable form, thereby bypassing part of the data preparation phase
3. Input directly into the computer, eliminating all data preparation and input activities.

Data capture requiring subsequent transcription into machine-readable form consists of written notes and filled-in documents. Examples are manually prepared new employee records, manually recorded hours worked, and handwritten sales orders.

Data capture in machine-readable form involves the preparation of a machine-readable input. Some types of machine-readable input are as follows:

▪ Handwritten numbers to be read by an optical character reader. An example is handwritten recording of meter reading for an electric utility.

▪ Handwritten marks to be read by an optical reader. An example is a machine-scored examination.

▪ Typewritten documents in a machine-readable font prepared at time of data capture. An example is a credit document typed by a credit interviewer directly onto a machine-readable form.

The capturing and direct input of data may use terminals such as a typewriter or cathode ray tube (CRT) visual display unit connected directly via data communications to the computer (online). This direct input eliminates the data preparation and input phases of the processing cycle. Examples are online credit verification, online entry of reservations, and online entry of customer orders.

Data Preparation.   There are four types of data preparation activities to make data ready for computer input:
1. Manual review of data documents and possible correction, addition, or deletion of data.
2. Preparation of processing controls such as assembling data into processing batches and making batch control totals.
3. Transcription to machine-sensible form. The transcription activities may also include verification of the correctness of the transcription and checking the validity of some data items.
4. Conversion from one machine-readable form to a storage medium having faster input characteristics.

The manual review of data prior to processing may be used to add codes or other data as well as to make sure the data is complete, legible, and reasonable.

The documents need to be assembled in batches for control purposes and control totals prepared. Examples of control totals at this point are transaction record counts, totals of financial data fields such as sales, and hash totals of fields such as account numbers. The control total is written on a control document and attached to the batch.

The batches of documents are then transcribed to a machine-readable form. The transcription process may consist of:

- Punching into cards
- Punching into paper tape
- Keying onto disc or tape storage
- Typing onto a document for optical scanning
- Hand writing data onto forms for optical scanning.

Some of these methods of transcription can be checked by a duplicate verification operation; others require proofreading. In the case of keypunches or keydisc units, the equipment can do a validity check on a code containing a check digit. Keydisc units can also make additional checks on the data fields.

Data transcription (or data capture) utilizing an intelligent terminal (essentially a very small computer with a typewriter or CRT input device) may perform some data editing operations because the terminal can be programmed to do logic tests on the data (such as range tests).

The data preparation activities may utilize a direct-entry methodology in which the data preparation device is connected to the computer. The transcription operation (keying of data) transmits the data directly to the computer, where it is edited. This approach eliminates the input phase.

In cases where data capture or data preparation has resulted in machine-readable data on media that is difficult to read or reading is slow, a data preparation phase activity may be the conversion to a more accessible or faster input speed storage. Examples of such conversion to another storage medium are

- Cards to magnetic tape
- Paper tape to magnetic tape
- Documents read by optical character reader and transferred to magnetic tape
- Transfer from keydisc storage to magnetic tape.

Input.   The input phase performs the reading of data and stores it for use in program processing. Input may be direct from a transaction input terminal (such as a typewriter or CRT visual display unit) or may be from input media prepared during the preparation phase. The input editing is generally an integral part of input but will be considered as a separate step because it can be performed separately. If input edit tests are not performed along with input, the input operations should check the control totals developed during the data preparation phase.

Input Editing.   Input editing is the process which examines input data and applies various tests to determine whether or not there are errors. It might properly be termed "data testing" or "data validation." As described earlier, the input editing may be performed in part by a keydisc unit or an intelligent terminal used for data capture or data preparation; however, all data at input should be tested even if prior operations have tested the same data. The tests will be described in more detail later in the chapter. Some major tests are

- Tests of codes using check digits
- Tests of data for reasonableness and within correct range
- Tests for missing fields
- Tests for wrong class (alphabetic characters in numeric field)
- Comparison with file data.

The comparison with file data test can only be performed if the file is available on direct access storage. Control totals are also developed during data editing.

Data which is found to be erroneous by the editing tests is rejected, put into an error file, and sent back to the data originators for correction and reentry. Control totals are adjusted for the rejected items. If there is input editing at an intelligent terminal, errors may be immediately corrected and the corrected input entered. Direct input to the computer also results in an error message to the entry terminal and a rejection of the data until the error is corrected. The data which passes the editing test is presumed to be correct and continues into program processing.

Processing Manipulation.   There are essentially three major processing operations performed on imput data: sequencing, transaction processing, and file updating. Sequencing through sorting may be performed prior to transaction processing or file updating; it may also be performed after program manipulation but prior to output in order to have the output in a convenient sequence. Transaction processing operates with input data to produce a transaction document. For example, a sales order input may be used to produce a sales invoice. File updating may involve additions, corrections, and deletions to the file records as well as updating of fields with transaction data. A transaction may therefore be used both to prepare a transaction document and to update a master file record. For example, a payroll transaction may result both in a paycheck and also in the updating of the master file record for the employee, e.g., updating of wages-to-date, FICA-to-date, etc.

Output.   The output of processing can be a master file or other file to be held for future processing, output files, or direct output to a terminal such as a CRT or typewriter. The output files are generally printed as transaction documents or reports, but other media may be used such as punched card turnaround document and microfilm.

ORGANIZATION AND MANAGEMENT OF COMPUTER FILES

A file is defined as a collection of related records containing data needed for subsequent data processing. Files are created when the need for a collection of records is recognized. This need may come from the processing requirements in preparing a regular report or from the need to facilitate data retrieval in response to inquiries and requests for special analysis. The organization of computer files is an important factor in computer processing methods. File organization is based on the needs of each application plus the characteristics of the file storage devices.

File Storage Devices.   Storage is frequently classified into primary (or internal) storage and secondary (or auxiliary) storage. The active portion of the operating system and programs being executed are in internal storage; files being used and programs not in use but which need to be available are in auxiliary storage. Virtual storage is the use of hardware and software to segment programs in use so that only part of each need be in primary storage at any one time. Other parts of the program are brought in as they become active and are dropped if they become inactive. This method makes it appear to the user as if there were no internal memory constraints on program size.

The most common internal storage is magnetic core or semiconductors; the most common secondary storage uses magnetic disc or magnetic tape. Data is stored on a tape or disc by recording patterns of magnetic polarization on small sections of a ferrite-coated surface. Data is stored in a specific location on the medium; no other data can be stored there without destroying the data already there. However, data can be read without losing the magnetic recording.

Locating data that is stored can be performed serially or directly (also termed randomly). The serial (or sequential) approach to record access on a file is commonly associated with magnetic tape because the tape is read serially starting from the beginning. The first record must pass under the read/write head before the second record can be accessed; the second before the third; etc. In order to access the last record on the file, all previous records must have been read. This is similar to a symphony on a tape cassette. In order to get to the last movement of the symphony all other portions of the symphony must first be played.

In direct access storage, such as disc storage, the storage medium revolves and read/write arms move in and out so that any location is accessed directly by the combination of in or out movement of the arm plus the revolution of the disc. The time to access a record on a disc file consists of the seek time and the rotation time.

1. *Seek time:* The time required to position a movable read/write head over the recording track to be used

2. *Rotation time:* The rotational delay (also termed latency) to move the disc location underneath the read/write head.

It is normal for several arms to move simultaneously so that a set of storage locations (a cylindar) are active at the same time. Note that locations on a magnetic disc can be read serially if this is desired.

Types of Files.   Files are kept for a variety of purposes. Four main types of files are usually identified, as summarized in Exhibit 10. Each record in a file is identified by an identification field. A customer account number, an employee identification number, and a part number are examples of identification items.

EXHIBIT 10   Types of Computer Files

Type	Purpose	Examples
Master file	Relatively permanent records containing statistical, identification, and historical information which is used as a source of reference.	Accounts receivable file
Transaction file	Also called detail file. Collection of records of transactions used to prepare transaction documents and to update a master file.	Sales invoice file Purchases file Material received file
Report file	Records extracted from data in transaction or master files in order to prepare a report.	Report file for taxes withheld Report file for delinquent customer accounts Report file for analysis of employee skills
Sort file	A working file of records to be sequenced. This may be the original or a copy of a transaction file, a master file, or a report file.	

The identification item, used as the basis for sequencing and searching the file, is frequently called the record key. This key can be numeric, such as a social security number, or it can be alphabetic, such as a name. There can be more than one key, and a record may therefore be sequenced on one key in one file and on another key in a second file.

Employee No.	Name	Street Address	City & State	Gross Wages, etc.
984321	Thomas Grant	115 Crowther	New York, N.Y.	115.55

Key for record

A record consists of data items which may themselves be formed from two or more items. This process of subdivision can be continued, the last items being termed elementary items. For example, an item DATE may be formed from three elementary items, MONTH, DAY, and YEAR.

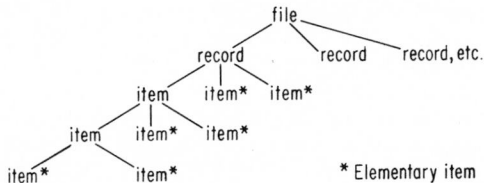

When the item DATE is specified, the entire item is obtained. MONTH will refer only to the MONTH portion of DATE. The relationship of items in a file thus forms a hierarchical or tree form:

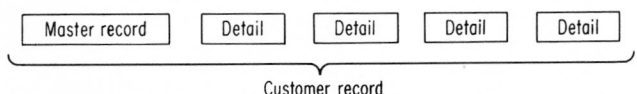

In addition to the data items themselves, records in direct access storage may contain cross-referencing items called pointers. These establish a relationship between the record, or an item in the record, and other records or items.

Some records may be divided into two parts: a master record and detail or trailer records. For example, a customer accounts receivable record may be divided into the master portion containing the name, address, credit rating, etc., and several trailer records each containing the data on an unpaid invoice. The trailer records are often termed detail records or repeating records.

Master record	Detail	Detail	Detail	Detail

Customer record

File Management Activities.   File management refers to all activities relating to the creation, updating, and use of files. These activities can be classed as:
1. File creation
2. File processing and maintenance
3. Selection (retrieval)
4. Extraction.

File creation can refer to the establishing of an entirely new file or to the conversion of an existing file in noncomputer form to a computer file medium. The conversion of existing files is one of the difficult problems of converting to a computer system or from one computer system to another.

File maintenance is the updating of a file to reflect the effects of nonperiodic changes by adding, altering, or deleting data. To maintain a master file, new records are added to the file and obsolete or erroneous records are removed. File processing, on the other hand, is the periodic updating of a master file to reflect the effects of current data (often transaction data) in a detail file.

Selection refers to the retrieval of a record from the file. The retrieval process is straightforward but relatively time consuming with a sequential file organization; it can become complex but requires less time when using direct-access storage organization.

Extraction is the copying of selected records from a file to form a new file for analysis, report preparation, etc. For example, from the file of all employees, the records of employees with more than 20 years of service may be extracted in order to perform an analysis of the characteristics of these employees.

File Organization. The file organization is the method in which the files are organized for retrieval purposes. The major approaches are sequential and direct access organization used in data processing and list organizations used primarily in retrieval applications. The sequential organization means that the records in the file are sequenced in order by a record key such as employee number, customer identification number, social security number, etc. The record with the lowest number key appears in the first location on the file; the record with the next higher numbered key appears next; etc. This organization is very natural for magnetic tape processing but is also used with magnetic disc storage. In the sequential organization, it is not necessary to specify a location address where a record is stored. The records are stored in order, so that as serial processing is performed a record is located when its place in the sequence is found.

The direct organization allows a record to be located without knowing its sequence. Direct access organizations can be implemented in a variety of ways. The two most common are a randomizing procedure and an indexing method. In the randomizing procedure, the record key is manipulated arithmetically to produce a random number which looks like a storage location. This becomes a storage location for that record. If two or more records have the same location using this procedure, one of them is stored in an overflow location and a procedure is established to find the overflow record during processing. The other common direct methodology consists of indexes. An index is established for the file and during processing is searched for the desired record key. When the record key is found in the index, the storage location is indicated. One very common method of organization is indexed sequential in which records are stored sequentially but can also be located directly through indexes.

List organizations are generally fairly complex and are used primarily in retrieval location or applications where it is desirable to know the relationship among records. List organizations use pointers (data fields containing address of other records) to link records together for retrieval purposes or use indexes which identify all records having given attributes.

Data Bases and Data Base Management Systems. Separate applications may utilize separate files having much of the same data. Processing efficiency and improved data control can be achieved by having a common file for all of the applications having common data. Also, lookup and retrieval operations on the data are simplified and improved. However, the common files (termed a data base) require strict control over access to the data and over changes to the data by application programs. This control is achieved by a data administrator responsible for the data and software systems, called data base management systems, to manage all access and updating of the data in the data base.

The data base management system provides data that is requested by an application program and updates data items from data provided by an authorized application program. It in essence removes most of the file access and file update logic from the application program. The data base approach requires direct access files.

Multiple-Computer Access to Files. An organization may choose to have computers and files at several locations but interconnect the computers via data communication so that any computer in the network may access the files at any location. This is termed a distributed network. Another example of multiple access to files are computers which cross company boundaries to access other computers. Airline reservation computers make reservations via data communication directly to connecting airline computers. The networks create a more complex environment but the basic input/input editing/processing manipulation methods apply.

CLASSIFICATION OF PROCESSING METHODS

Data processing literature frequently refers to only two processing methods:
1. Batch processing
2. Online processing.

Batch processing is used to refer to periodic processing of batches of data and online processing refers to immediate processing of individual transactions as they occur. This twofold classification does not take into account the fact that input and input editing may be performed in a different mode than processing manipulation. Also, the type of record access and updating affects the nature of the processing.

A more complete classification of processing methods uses three dimensions: timing of input and input editing, timing of processing manipulation, and the method for accessing and updating file records.

1. *Timing of Input and Input Editing.*   Input of data and input editing may be performed either periodically on batches of transactions or immediately on individual transactions as they occur.

2. *Timing of Processing Manipulation.*   Processing manipulation is performed either periodically on batches of transactions or immediately on individual transactions as they occur.

3. *Method for Accessing and Updating File Records.*   File records may be accessed and updated by (1) reading the file medium serially, updating each record, and rewriting the entire file in the same sequence, or (2) accessing each record directly, updating it, and writing the updated record in the same storage location. This method will be termed inplace updating. Inplace updating requires a direct-access file storage device such as a disc file; the rewriting approach requires a sequenced file and therefore can utilize either serial access storage media such as magnetic tape or a sequenced file on direct-access storage media.

Based on these processing dimensions, data processing applications can be classified into three major types of processing representing five feasible combinations of the above factors. The three major types of processing and related classifications are summarized as follows:

Major type of processing category	Input/editing plus processing categories	Associated file updating method
Periodic serial (batch)	1. Periodic input/editing and periodic serial processing	Serial rewriting
	2. Immediate input/editing and periodic serial processing	Serial rewriting
Periodic direct (batch)	3. Periodic input/editing and periodic direct processing	Inplace
	4. Immediate input/editing and periodic direct processing	Inplace
Immediate (online)	5. Immediate input/editing and immediate processing	Inplace

The three major classifications will now be described in more detail.

Periodic Serial Processing.   Serial processing using batches of input data is the least complex and most common method for data processing applications. The input data is collected into batches and the input, input editing, processing manipulation, and output is performed periodically (say daily, weekly, or monthly). The master file which is used with transaction processing and which is updated with transactions or other data is organized sequentially by a record key (such as employee number). The transactions to be processed (the transaction file) are sorted into the same order as the master file. The master file records are

EXHIBIT 11 Periodic Serial Processing Using Batches of Data

Step 1: Batching of transactions

Transactions are assembled into batches and batch total is prepared.

Step 2: Conversion of transactions to machine–readable form

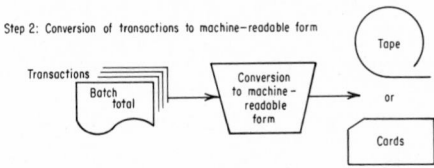

Step 3: Input and input editing

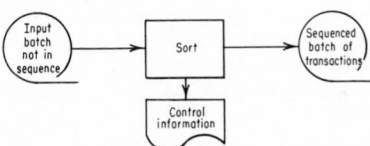

Step 4: Sequencing of transactions

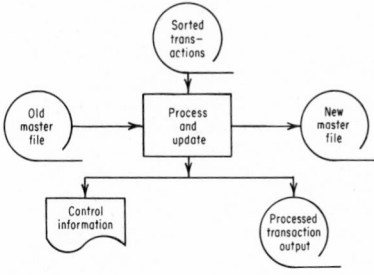

Step 5: Process transactions and update master file

Step 6: Output transaction documents

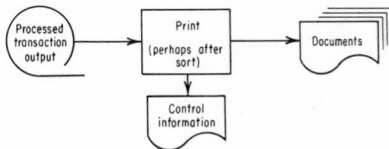

accessed serially. Each record is examined to determine if there is an updating transaction. After updating, the record is written on a new master file (or the record is written without change if there is no updating transaction). The updating process results not only in a new, updated master file but also preserves the old master file which is not altered by the "copy old–alter–write new" sequence. The batch of input transactions is assigned a batch number and all audit trail references are to this batch. A listing of the transactions in each batch is normally prepared for reference purposes. Source documents are usually stored as a batch.

The fact that all processing is performed periodically with serial access to master file records means that the file storage medium can be magnetic tape or punched cards. Disc storage can be organized for serial access (i.e., treated the same as a magnetic tape). The batch serial mode of processing is illustrated in Exhibit 11.

It is possible to have immediate rather than delayed processing of the input. This is often termed direct entry. For example, an application may use terminals through which input data is sent directly to the computer for processing. However, in association with the periodic serial processing method, the only processing that is performed immediately is the input and editing of the data and its collection into batches. All other processing is performed by periodic batch processing runs. In other words, there is immediate data capture by the computer and editing of the input data to detect errors. Error messages are normally sent to the originator of the data so that corrections may be made immediately while the transaction is being prepared and data being entered. The error detection, error reporting, and error correction cycle is therefore substantially reduced.

The direct entry of input data makes the processing control system more complex because there is frequently no feasible method for preparing a batch total prior to input processing. The absence of the input batch means there is no input batch total, filing of documents by batch, and batch input listing. However, a postbatch control can be prepared. As input data is received by the computer and edited for further processing, logical batches are developed which will be the basis for control in subsequent batch processing runs. For example, all transactions of a given type or from a given input station are stored and a control total developed for each logical batch. Listing of batches and batch references are to the logical batch (input device, initiator, type of transaction, etc.) rather than to a batch that was prepared before input occurred. The use of control totals is identical after the formation of the logical batches.

Periodic Direct Processing. In this mode of processing, the input transactions are batched for an input editing run which is part of periodic processing. However, the input batch need not put into sequential order because there is direct access to master file records needed for processing transactions. In contrast to a batch serial mode in which the file is organized and accessed in sequential order and therefore the transactions must be sorted into sequential order before being processed, the batch direct processing approach does not require sorting of transactions into any specific order because the master file records may be accessed without reference to the order of the transactions being processed. As explained previously, records in such a master file are accessed through file indexes or through addressing algorithms.

For control purposes, batch control totals are developed for the input batch. Editing and error feedback are operated in the same way as batch serial processing. Since the data is not in sequential order, any listing of the batch data is not as satisfactory for reference purposes as input data that has been sequenced. For this reason, it may be desirable to sequence transactions before preparing a transaction listing even though sequencing is not required for access.

The batch direct processing is performed in place; that is, each master record

EXHIBIT 12   Periodic Direct Processing

Step 1: Batching of transactions

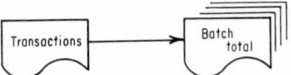

Transactions are assembled into batches and batch total is prepared.

Step 2: Conversion of transactions to machine-readable form

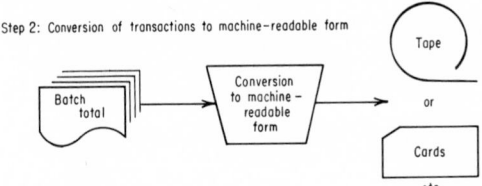

Step 3: Copy master file for backup

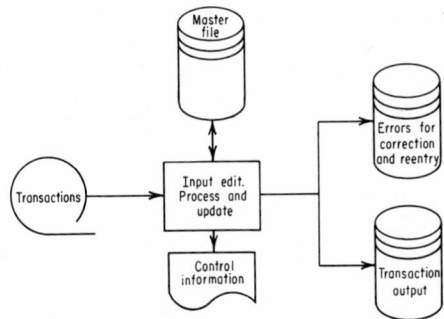

Step 4: Process transactions and update master file

Step 5: Output transaction documents

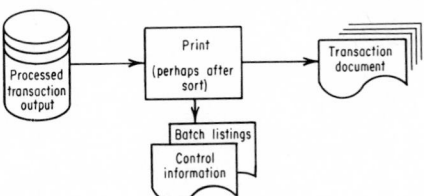

which has to be updated is read, updated, and written back into the same storage location (Exhibit 12). A record which has no transactions for updating purposes is not altered or read. This inplace updating means that after processing has been performed, the old file will no longer exist because it has been altered in place to be the new file. In order to have a backup file for recovery purposes (say in the event of improper updating or destruction of the file by mechanical failure, etc.), it is necessary to copy the file before it is updated. The original is kept as the backup file; the copy is updated.

It is possible to have immediate input and input/editing followed by periodic direct processing of batched transactions. This presents the same problem as the immediate online input and input editing under batch serial processing. However, the existence of a direct-access storage organization means that the immediate online input and input editing can take advantage of a file lookup procedure to examine the master file record associated with each transaction in order to detect any discrepancies between the input data item and the master file record. With this lookup, it is possible to determine whether or not the transaction refers to a valid master record and whether or not it is logically possible for the transaction to apply to the master record. As an example, payment transaction input editing might look up the customer record to see if there is such a customer and if the balance due is reasonable with respect to the payment amount received.

Immediate Processing.   Immediate online processing is the most complex environment for processing (Exhibit 13). In this method of processing a variety of transactions are accepted from remote input terminals. As each transaction is received, the master record against which it is to be processed is read, the transaction is processed, and the record updated and written back into storage. In other words, direct immediate input is followed by immediate processing of the transaction and immediate updating of the master file record. This is also termed online realtime processing.

The online approach has problems such as the fact that two or more transactions which apply to the same record need to be executed sequentially; otherwise updating might be incomplete. If the two transactions, A and B, arrive at the computer at the same time, the first transaction A reads the master record and updates it; transaction B simultaneously reads the record and updates it. When transaction A is complete, the master record with updating from A is written back into its storage location. When transaction B is complete, the master record just updated from B is placed back into storage. The updating performed by transaction A is therefore lost because transaction B was processed without knowledge of transaction A. Such "contention" matters can be handled in online processing, but they illustrate the additional complexity of the online environment.

Since the transactions are being processed online in this method, all the advantages of online input editing are available, including a complete access to the master file for detecting errors related to the master file. The transaction is processed completely online, so any logical errors are immediately detected and the person providing the input is asked for a correction. This process enhances the error detection and error correction cycle over any previous methods. However, the immediate inplace processing causes some problems with respect to audit trail, backup, and recovery. The input transaction can be assembled and sorted into logical batches. Backup and recovery of the file under this method of processing is performed by copying the file at periodic intervals. For example, it might be copied at the beginning of the day before any processing is performed, or in the case of very active files, it may be copied at regular intervals during the day (say, every hour). If there are any problems with the file, the latest copy is used to restore from that point.

The problems of keeping the file records error-free under online processing

EXHIBIT 13   Immediate (Online Realtime) Processing

Step 1: Copy master file for backup

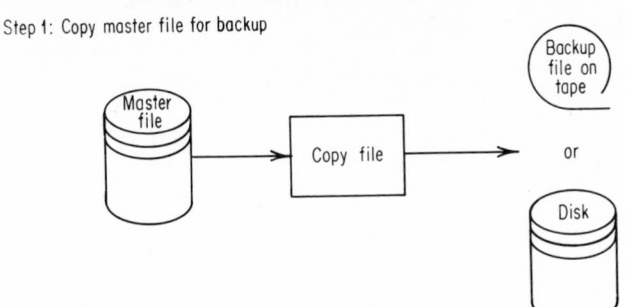

Step 2: Recording, input, editing, logical batching, and terminal output

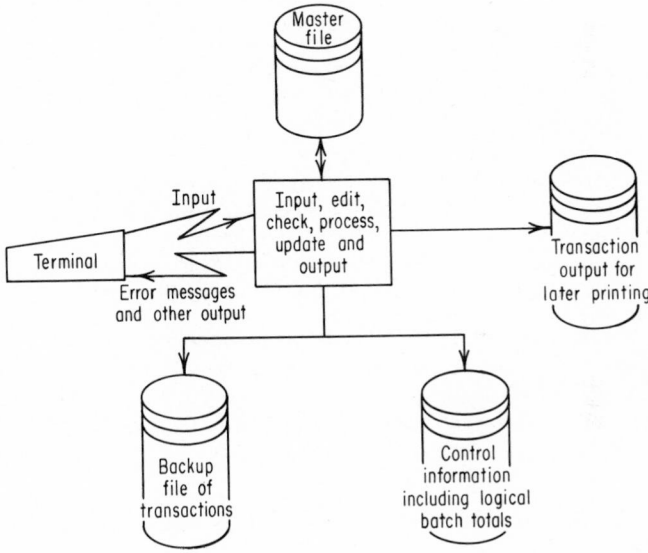

Step 3: Output printed transaction documents

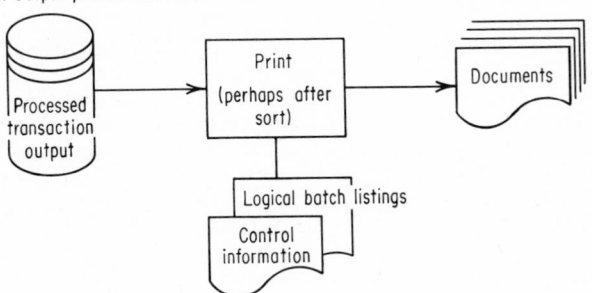

EXHIBIT 14   The Framework of Control in a Computer Data Processing System (Adapted from Gordon B. Davis, *Auditing & EDP*, AICPA, New York, 1968, p. 110.)

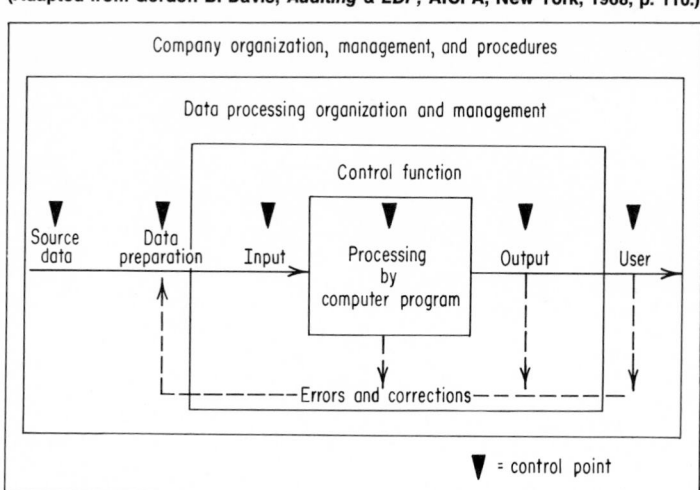

and the audit trail advantages of batch processing have caused some firms to go to a modified form of online processing with online input/editing. The firms essentially do memo processing during the day to produce immediate responses, but in the evening all transactions which have been input during the day are assembled into a batch and are then processed in batch fashion using a copy of the master file that was maintained for this purpose. The processing during the day is therefore up to date in the sense of retrieval from the file, but the file for financial purposes is the one which is processed during the night in a batch processing run. This removes many of the hazards of online processing of the file. If there is a processing or hardware problem during the day, it does not impact the quality of the master file but only the memo file.

CONTROL OVER QUALITY OF COMPUTER PROCESSING

Computer processing is all too often carried out with a higher error rate than is desirable. On the other hand, error control is not without cost, and the manager or user who understands the problems of quality control and its methods is able to evaluate the value of tighter control compared to its cost. With computer processing, there are control problems not found in manual data processing but there are also unique, new control methods because of the capabilities of the computer.

The Organizational Control Framework in a Computer Processing System. There is a hierarchy of control in a computer data processing system. The outer level of control is provided by the company organization management and procedures. Within this framework there operates the organization and management of the data processing activity. A component part of this activity is the control function which monitors the quality of processing. The computer processing operations are not only subject to departmental control activities but the processing programs also contain control features to detect errors. This hierarchy of control is illustrated in Exhibit 14.

Top Management Responsibility.   Top management has the overall responsibility for data processing. This consists of the following:

Responsibility	*Comments*
1. Authorization of major systems additions or changes	Each major addition or change should be presented to management as a proposal to be evaluated in terms of its cost and the benefits to be derived from it.
2. Postimplementation review of actual cost and effectiveness of systems projects	Management should follow up on project proposals and evaluate the reasons for deviations from planned cost, planned schedule, and estimated benefit. The assessment of performance on the postimplementation review (also termed a post audit) will aid in evaluating future systems requests.
3. Review of organization and control practices of the data processing function	Top management has the responsibility for employing competent, adequately trained data processing management personnel and for reviewing the organization and controls which they establish.
4. Monitoring of performance	Management should require a performance plan or standard and the reporting of deviations from this expected level of performance. The plan and variation reporting should cover four types of performance: a. Level of processing activity (transactions, reports, etc.) compared to plan b. Cost of data processing activities compared to planned cost c. Frequency and duration of delays in meeting processing schedules d. Error rates for errors detected at various control points

Data Processing Management Responsibility. In the organization of data processing activity, it is desirable both from an operating standpoint and from a control standpoint to separate the three functions of (1) system design and programming, (2) operations, and (3) control. Some installations also separate system design and programming. Control over the storage media containing data files and programs is increased by the use of a separate file librarian. Control over the data in a database is provided by a data administrator.

Control practices associated with data processing organization and management are as follows:

Standard procedures for application development life cycle
Standard operating procedures
Scheduling and supervision of personnel
Provisions for protection and reconstruction of files and programs
Enforcement of program documentation and program change documentation
Enforcement of requirement for audit trails
Review of operating statistics, error logs, etc.

The application of management principles to computer data processing operations will typically involve the preparation and use of a systems and procedures manual which describes standard operating procedures. The contents of the manual will usually include:

1. Standard programming procedures
2. Standard computer operating procedures
3. Control procedures
4. Organization and personnel.

As with systems and procedures manuals used in other areas of activity, the manual is useful in training, supervision, and evaluation of performance.

The Control Function. The plan of organization and operating procedures should provide for a control function. The control function can be divided into two types: (1) processing control internal to data processing, and (2) independent outside checks. The internal processing control, a function of the data processing department, is concerned with monitoring the accuracy of processing and ensuring that no data is lost or mishandled within the department during processing. For example, if a detail transaction file is processed with the current master file to produce an updated master file, the sum of the transaction file and the related master file records should equal the total of the records on the updated master file. The person charged with the processing control function is responsible for making or reviewing the results of such a comparison. In a small installation, the data processing manager may perform the control activities; in other installations, a control staff will perform this task.

The activities of the control clerk or control group are specified both in the systems and procedures manual and in the description of control activities for each computer application. The control function will include duties such as the following:

1. Logging of input data and recording of control information
2. Recording progress of work through the department
3. Reconciling computer controls with other control information
4. Supervising distribution of output
5. Scrutiny of console logs and control information in accordance with control instructions
6. Liaison with users regarding errors, logging of correction requests, and recording corrections made
7. Scrutiny of error listings and maintenance of error log or error report.

Independent outside checks can take several forms but are basically concerned with an independent check of the functioning of the data processing department. This check may be performed by a user department. If the general ledger is, for instance, maintained on the computer, the accounting department may keep a control total of all debits and credits to be posted by the computer. This control can be compared against the debits and credits from the computer run. Another possibility is an independent quality control evaluation group in a user department where the volume of data to be controlled is large. As an example, one large corporation has a payroll processing control group responsible for evaluating the payroll data produced by the computer.

The Control Points for Computer Processing. Computer data processing requires new controls for detecting and controlling errors but it also provides new methods of control which substitute for human controls. In a manual system, internal control relies upon such factors as human alertness, care, acceptance of responsibility, and division of duties. By concentrating the data processing activity, many controls based on human judgment or division of duties are no longer available. However, the computer program provides an alternative for many manual checks. For example, the lowest-level clerk will normally react when receiving a shipping document on which to insert prices if the item cannot be found on the price list. In a computer operation, a nonmatch such as this must be programmed. Once programmed, however, it will be faithfully executed. In most instances, the computer checks can be more extensive than those performed manually.

The control points at which specific data processing controls are applied to prevent or detect errors are (1) original document preparation, (2) conversion to machine-readable form, (3) computer processing, (4) distribution of output, and (5) users of the output. It is noteworthy that only one of these control points involves machine errors or program errors. This illustrates the fact that data processing controls must include controls over the human errors in source data preparation, conversion, output, and use as well as controls over the operation of the equipment and programs. The system designer should consider the entire set of controls which apply to an application and the organizational and management environment in which they are applied rather than viewing individual controls in isolation. For the purpose of this chapter, these control points will be discussed as control over input and output and programmed control over processing. An additional control problem—the protection of computer records and files—will also be covered. Hardware controls, which protect against undetected equipment malfunctions, are very reliable and normally satisfactory. Therefore, they will not be covered in this chapter.

Control over Input and Output.   Input data is the weakest link in the chain of data processing events. The input data for a program may be in error for one of four general reasons: (1) it may be incorrectly recorded at the point of inception; (2) it may be incorrectly converted to machine-readable form; (3) it may be incorrectly read or otherwise entered into the computer; or (4) it may be lost in handling. Input controls should therefore be established at the point of data creation and conversion to machine-readable form, at the point the data enters the computer, and at points when the data is handled, moved, or transmitted in the organization. As with manual data processing, there should be established procedures for authorization of transactions. The authorization may take the form of signatures or initials on documents from which the input is prepared. If input data may be introduced directly into the computer system without the preparation of documents, there must be alternative means for authorization, such as some form of physical control over access to the input devices or access to the means by which they can be activated.

Before data is used in updating files or other processing, it is usually tested for errors to the extent possible or appropriate in the light of the consequences of input errors. As explained earlier in the chapter, a separate input validation run or input editing run may be used or the checking may be performed at the time of processing. If errors are detected, the erroneous transaction or record found to contain an error is shunted aside rather than stopping the computer to make corrections. It will usually be written on a temporary file to be examined later. There will thus usually be a file of rejects and an error listing indicating the reason for rejection. Items which are rejected by the input editing run should be carefully controlled to make sure they are corrected and reentered at a later run.

Exhibit 15 presents an inventory of methods from which the system designer selects in order to achieve the level of error control required for an application. Each of these methods will be described briefly.

Procedural Controls and Data Review.   Standard clerical practices and well-designed data forms impose procedural controls on the creation of data. For example, if a part number is to be written on a document, boxes may be printed which contain the exact number of spaces required for the part number. Any clerk

EXHIBIT 15   Methods for Input Data Error Control

At point data is created and converted to machine-readable form	At point data is first input to the computer or input to a terminal with checking capabilities	At point data is handled, moved, or transmitted
Procedural controls	File label (internal)	Transmittal controls
Data review	Tests for validity:	Route slip
Verification	—Code	Control total
Check digit	—Character	External file labels
	—Field	
	—Transaction	
	—Combination of fields	
	—Missing data	
	—Check digit	
	—Sequence	
	—Limit or reasonableness test	
	Control total	

writing a part number containing less or more digits than the required number of characters will notice the error. Where direct input devices are used, templates over the keys, identification cards, and other procedural aids help to reduce input errors.

Some installations make a review examination of input data (especially codes which identify part numbers, product, etc.) before conversion to machine-readable form. This checking may be performed in connection with the addition of information or it may be an entirely separate step.

Verification of Conversion to Machine-Readable Form.   When data is punched into cards or keyed onto a keydisc device, the accuracy of the data conversion can be tested by verifying the original keying operation. In the case of punched cards, two separate machines are used, a card punch and a verifier. The data is first punched by a key-punch operator. The punched cards and original data are then given to a verifier operator, who inserts the punched card into the verifier and rekeys the punches using the original source documents. The verifier does not punch but instead compares the data keyed into the verifier with the punches already in the card. If they are the same, the punched card is presumed to be correct. A common indication that this check has been performed is for the verifier to notch over the column containing the difference. Similar verification is used with a keydisc encoder where data is recorded directly on a magnetic disc. The same device is used (at separate times) both to record data and to verify it. The verification process includes the correction of errors.

Verification is a duplicate operation and therefore doubles the cost of data conversion. Various methods are used to reduce the amount of verifying. One method is to verify only part of the data. Some data fields are not critical and an error will not affect further processing. Examples are descriptive fields containing vendor name, part description, etc., which under most circumstances are not critical. The use of prepunched cards, prepunched stubs, and duplication of constant data during key entry may allow verification to be restricted to the variable information added by the data preparation step. A second approach used with statistical data is to verify only if the input error rate is above an acceptable level. Each operator's work is checked on a sample basis. If the operator's error rate is acceptable, no verification is made; if not, there is complete verification. Other control procedures (to be explained) may be substituted for verification such as a check digit on an account number, a batch control total, etc.

Check Digit.   In most applications involving an identification number, the identification number may be verified for accuracy by a check digit. A check digit is determined by performing arithmetic operations on the code number. The arithmetic operations are performed in such a way that the typical errors encountered in transcribing a number will be detected. There are many possible procedures. All involve the use of digit weights and a modulus. For example, a simple check digit procedure might be as follows:

1. Start with a number without the check digit.

2. Multiply each digit by a weight assigned to the digit position. For example, the weights might be 1, 3, 5, 7, and 9.

3. Sum the digits in the resulting products.

4. Divide the sum by the modulus (usually 10 or 11) and keep the remainder as the check digit.

5. Add check digit to number (at end or elsewhere).

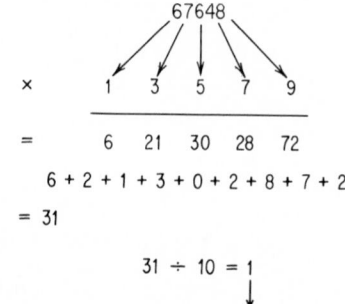

A check digit procedure is not completely error proof but depending on the weights and modulus used, check digits will detect 90 to 100 percent of transposition and transcription errors and about 90 percent of random errors. The check digit does not guard against assignment of an incorrect but valid code, as for example, the assignment of a wrong but valid identification code to a customer.

The checking of the code number for the check digit may be performed either by the input device or it may be programmed into the computer. The use of the check digit as part of the input device has the advantage that an incorrect code is detected before it enters the computer process and a field checked by a check digit does not need to be verified. Example of uses are charge account numbers, employee pay numbers, and bank account numbers.

Internal File Label. A file label is a record at the beginning and also possibly at the end of the file which records identification and control information. File labels are used to ensure that the proper transaction or master file is used and that the entire file has been processed. The label at the beginning is the header label which identifies the file. Typical header label contents are as follows:

Name of file
Creation date
Purge date
Identification number
Reel number (for magnetic tape).

The trailer label is the last record and summarizes record counts, etc., for the file.

Tests for Valid Data. The data, once read by computer, can be subjected to programmed tests to establish that the data is within the limits established for valid data. Some examples of checking which can be done are:

1. VALID CODE. If there is only a limited number of valid codes, say for coding expenses, the code being read may be checked to see if it is one of the valid codes.

2. VALID CHARACTER. If only certain characters are allowed in a data field, the computer can test the field to determine that no invalid characters are used.

3. VALID FIELD SIZE, SIGN, AND COMPOSITION. If a code number should be a specified number of characters in length, the computer may be programmed to test that the field size is as specified. If the sign of a numeric field must always be positive or must always be negative, then a test may be made to ensure that there is not an incorrect sign. If the field should contain only numerics or only alphabetics, then a test may be made to determine that the field does indeed contain a proper composition of characters.

4. VALID TRANSACTION. There is typically a relatively small number of valid transactions which are processed with a particular file. There is a limited number, for example, of trasaction codes which can apply to accounts receivable file updating. As part of input error control, the transaction code can be tested for validity.

5. VALID COMBINATIONS OF FIELD. In addition to each of the individual fields being tested, combinations may be tested for validity. For example, if a salesperson's code may be associated with only a few territory codes, the correspondence can be checked.

6. MISSING DATA TEST. The program may check the data fields to make sure that all data fields necessary to code a transaction have data in them.

7. CHECK DIGIT. The check digit is verified on identification fields having this control feature.

8. SEQUENCE TEST. In batch processing, the data to be processed must be arranged in a sequence which is the same as the sequence of the file. Both the master file and the transaction file may be tested to ensure that they are in a proper sequence, ascending or descending as the case may be. The sequence check can also be used to account for all documents, if these are numbered sequentially.

9. Limit or reasonableness test. This is a basic test for data processing accuracy. Input data should usually fall within certain limits. For example, hours worked should not be less than zero and should not be more than, say, 50 hours. The upper limit may be established from the experience of the particular firm. Input data may be compared against this limit to ensure that no input error has occurred or at least no input error exceeding certain preestablished limits. Examples are the following:

The total amount of a customer order may be compared with the average order amount for the customer. If this order exceeds, say, three times the amount of the average order, then an exception notice may be printed.

A material receipt which exceeds two times the economic order quantity established for the particular item might be subject to question.

A receiving report amount may be compared with the amount requested on the purchase order. If there is more than a small percentage variance, then there is an assumption of an error in the input data.

In a utility billing, consumption is checked against prior periods to detect possible errors or trouble in the customer's installation.

Control Totals. Control totals are a basic method of error control to determine whether or not all items in a batch have been received and processed. The control total procedure requires that a control figure be developed by some previous independent processing and that the current data processing recompute this amount, comparing the resultant total with the previous total. Control totals are normally obtained for batches of data. The batches are kept to a reasonable size so that errors can be easily isolated. For example, the sales slips to be processed by computer are first added on an adding machine to arrive at a control total for the sales in the batch. A control total for payroll might be the number of employees for which checks should be prepared. There are three types of control figures: financial totals, hash totals, and document or record counts.

1. Financial totals. Financial totals are totals such as sales, payroll amounts, inventory dollar amounts, etc., which are normally added together in order to provide financial summaries.

2. Hash totals. Hash totals are totals of data fields which are typically not added. The total has meaning only as a control and is not used in any other way in data processing. To determine that all inventory items are processed, a control total might be developed of the inventory item numbers and this control total would be compared with the sum of the item numbers obtained during the processing run.

3. Document or record count. In many cases, rather than obtaining a financial total or hash total, it may be sufficient merely to obtain a count to ensure that all documents or records have been received and processed.

Control totals prepared prior to computer processing are furnished to computer processing as an input data item. The computer is then programmed to accumulate control totals internally and make a comparison. A message confirming the comparison should be printed out even if the comparison did not disclose an error. These messages are then subject to review by the control staff.

Movement and Handling Controls. Transmittal controls, route slips, control totals, and external file labels are examples of controls over the internal handling and movement of input data. Control totals have already been explained and external file labels are described in connection with file safeguards. The transmittal controls and route slips are discussed in this section.

When records move about through an organization there is always a possibility that they may be lost or otherwise diverted from the proper processing channels. To ensure proper identification of data as it moves through the company, and more especially as it moves through the data processing steps, it is customary to use some form of status identification. As they enter the data processing center, batches of data may be logged on a listing showing the data received. As each batch passes a data processing station, it is registered, recording the fact that the batch has been processed. The batch itself usually carries a route slip which indicates the path of processing it should follow and a record of processing performed.

Output Controls. The distribution of output should be controlled to ensure that only those authorized to receive reports receive them. The output should be reviewed for completeness and agreement with controls and screened for obvious errors. Persons receiving the output are an important error-detection control point, and provisions should be made in application system design for error feedback from recipients of output.

Programmed Control over Processing. The types of program controls which test the computer processing are the limit and reasonableness test, the crossfooting or crosstesting check, and control figures.

As with input data, a control over processing can be exercised by program steps which test the results of processing by comparing them with predetermined limits or by comparison with flexible limits which test the reasonableness of the results. In a payroll application, the net pay can be checked against an upper limit. The upper limit is an amount such that any paycheck exceeding the limit is probably in error. In a billing operation for a relatively homogeneous product, such as steel bars and plates, the weight of the shipment may be divided into the billing order to develop a price per pound. If the price per pound exceeds the average by more than a predetermined percentage, a message will be written for subsequent follow-up to determine if the billing is in error.

It is frequently possible to check computer data processing in a manner similar to the manual method of crossfooting. Individual items are totaled independently and then a crossfooting total developed from the totals. For example, in a payroll application the totals are developed for gross pay, for each of the deduction items, and for net pay. The total for net pay is then obtained independently by taking the total for gross pay and deducting the totals for each of the deduction items. If this crossfooting does not yield identical figures, then there has been some error in the program of processing.

Control figures developed in a manner similar to the input control totals can be used for testing the data processing within the machine. For example, the number of items to be invoiced in a billing run may be used as a control total and compared with the number of items billed on invoices.

Protection of Computer Records and Files. A data processing installation should establish and follow procedures which safeguard the program and data files from loss or accidental destruction. If loss or destruction does occur, advance provisions should have been made for reconstruction of the records. The protection of computer records and files involves physical safeguards, procedural controls, a retention plan, a reconstruction plan, and insurance.

Physical Safeguards. The physical safeguards may be classified as fire and disaster protection, security protection, and off-premises storage. There should be a disaster plan which describes arrangements to be made for disaster recovery, describes what should be done in disaster situations, and defines procedures for recovery using backup facilities, duplicate files, etc. For fire protection, the computer should be housed in a noncombustible environment. There should be storage of vital records in storage cabinets having a class C rating (one hour at 1700°F), separate air conditioning and power controls, carbon dioxide fire extinguishers, etc. Security protection is to safeguard both the hardware installation and the data files. For example, when confidential corporate information is kept in a machine-readable format, it should be subject to the same security precautions which are applied to written records. Off-premises storage is used to provide a further safeguard for essential data processing records. Space can be rented in a secure, fireproof location, or another storage location in the same company can be used.

Procedural Controls. Procedural controls can be used in the management of a computer center in order to minimize the possibility that an operator error will result in the destruction of a data or program file. Some common methods are external labels, magnetic tape file protection rings, and library procedures.

Files should be clearly labeled so that the operator will know the file contents. Punched-card files are usually labeled on the top of the deck by the use of a felt marking pen. File name, identification, and date are commonly written. The first and last cards are also labeled. Magnetic tape reels and disc packs are labeled with a paper label attached to the tape reel or disc pack.

A physical safeguard used to prevent writing on a magnetic tape and destroying information prior to the release date for the tape is a removable plastic or metal ring, the absence of which will prevent writing on the tape.

Library procedures provide a custodian who maintains a storage area for storage of all tapes, discs, program documentation, etc. The librarian checks out the tapes and disc packs needed by each processing run and keeps records on use and condition of storage media.

Retention and Reconstruction Plan. The retention plan of a data processing department provides a means for record or file reconstruction. Source documents are retained at least until the computer file has been proved and balanced with its controls. However, other considerations may require a longer storage period for these documents. Copies of important master files, programs, procedures manuals, forms, etc., should be maintained in secure storage, preferably off-premises.

A retention plan for files updated by serial rewriting (i.e., on magnetic tape) usually uses the son-father-grandfather concept. The files retained under this concept on a Wednesday (assuming daily processing) would be

Wednesday's file	(son)
Tuesday's file	(father)
Monday's file	(grandfather)

If, during processing on Thursday, the Wednesday tape was destroyed, Tuesday's tape would be processed again with Wednesday's transactions to re-create Wednesday's master tape. If no other processing or retention considerations require keeping the tape longer, the old grandfather can be released when a new one is produced.

File processing with inplace updating of records (usually using disc storage), does not automatically produce a duplicate, updated copy of the file. To provide for reconstruction, the disc must be duplicated to provide a reference point and all transactions saved until the next reference file copy is made. The reference copy can be put onto another disc or a magnetic tape.

Insurance and Bonding. Insurance should be part of the protection plan of a data processing installation. The major risk is fire, unless work is performed for others, in which case there should be liability insurance for errors or omissions in doing the work. The ordinary fire insurance policy is limited in its coverage of risks associated with losses connected with data processing. Therefore, many organizations take special data processing insurance coverage.

Although the number of losses arising from the dishonesty of data processing employees is apparently quite small, the amount of each loss has tended to be larger than under manual processing. The risks associated with the concentration of the data processing function in a relatively small number of people suggest that bonding (fidelity insurance) of data processing employees is a desirable practice.

PROCESSING REFERENCE TRAIL FOR COMPUTER APPLICATIONS

A significant consideration in the design of computer processing applications is provision for a processing reference trail. This is a trail of document references, processing references, documentation of processing steps, etc., which allows an investigator to trace data on a source document through processing to its appearance in transaction document outputs or reports or to trace data items on output documents or reports back to the source data or source documents which were processed to produce the result. Although it is termed an "audit trail" and is necessary for auditing, the processing trail is primarily for internal company investigation. To illustrate the processing trail in a periodic or batch processing environment, the references might be as follows:

1. Source documents stored as a batch with a reference number.
2. Transaction or journal listing by batch. Transaction listing may be in the same order as the batch of documents or may be sorted for easier reference use.
3. Batch reference on all processing of input batch.
4. Summary postings to ledgers contain batch reference

When documents are not batched or where no documents are prepared, such as in direct input, the computer should assign reference numbers and prepare logical batches of transactions which are sorted and stored or printed for reference use. For example, various transactions may be input by different operators through an input terminal. The computer maintains a record of the operator, terminal, time, etc., for each transaction. References and control batches are prepared by sorting and printing logical groupings of the transactions. Logical batch might be all transactions of a given type for a day, all transactions by an operator for a day, etc. The logical batch listings form a source reference for the transactions.

In complex processing environments, the intermediate listings and references are often not found. However, the processing trail from source transaction record to output record must still be maintained. This may be done by a combination of document and processing references and processing documentation.

BIBLIOGRAPHY

American Federation of Information Processing Societies, Inc.: *AFIPS System Review Manual on Security*, AFIPS, Montvale, N.J., 1974.

American Institute of Certified Public Accountants: "The Effects of EDP on the Auditor's Study and Evaluation of Internal Control," *Statement on Auditing Standards No. 3*, AICPA, New York, December 1974.

American National Standards Institute, Inc.: *Flowchart Symbols and Their Usage in Information Processing*, ANSI X3.5-1970, New York, 1970.

Auditability Information Catalogue, a catalogue of software aids for audit and control, IBM, GB 21-9883-0, White Plains, N.Y., 1975.

Benjamin, Robert: *Control of the Information System Development Cycle*, Wiley-Interscience, New York, 1971.

Canadian Institute of Chartered Accountants: *Computer Audit Guidelines*, Distributed in the United States by AICPA, New York, 1975.

———: *Computer Control Guidelines*, distributed in the United States by AICPA, New York, 1975.

Davis, Gordon B.: *Auditing & EDP*, AICPA, New York, 1968.

———: *Computer Data Processing*, 2nd ed., McGraw-Hill Book Company, New York, 1973.

———: *Management Information Systems: Conceptual Foundations, Structure, and Development*, McGraw-Hill Book Company, New York, 1974.

Edpacs: a newsletter on EDP audit, control, and security, Automation Training Center, Reston, Va.

Institute of Internal Auditors: "Auditing Computer Centers," *Modern Concepts of Internal Auditing,* IIA, Orlando, Fla., 1974.

———: "Auditing Fast Response Systems," *Modern Concepts of Internal Auditing,* IIA, Orlando, Fla., 1974.

McCracken, Daniel D.: "Revolution in Programming: An Overview," *Datamation,* vol. 19, no. 12, pp. 50–52, December 1973.

Porter, W. Thomas: *EDP Controls and Auditing,* Wadsworth Publishing Company, Belmont, Calif., 1974.

Chapter **8**

Compound Interest—
Concepts and Applications

JAMES A. LARGAY III

Associate Professor of Industrial Management, Georgia Institute of
Technology

ROMAN L. WEIL

Professor of Accounting, University of Chicago

COMPOUND INTEREST

Compound interest refers to *interest on interest* as well as *interest on principal* or to situations where interest is paid periodically during the term of the loan. *Simple interest,* on the other hand, exists when interest applies to the principal only and is paid only once, at maturity of the loan. Compound interest is the basis of most contemporary interest applications. We begin with an illustration of the difference between compound and simple interest.

Let B = the principal amount (amount borrowed or loaned)

i = the interest rate.

	Simple Interest	*Compound Interest*
Amount after 1 period	$B(1 + i)$	$B(1 + i)$
Amount after 2 periods	$B(1 + 2i)$	$B(1 + i)(1 + i)$
Amount after n periods	$B(1 + ni)$	$B(1 + i)^n$

Thus if B = $100, and i = 8 percent, after 5 periods the total amount at simple interest would be $140 [= $100(1.40)], while the amount at compound interest would be $146.93 [= $100(1.46933)]. Simple interest was widely used in the past on many types of loan obligations. With the advent of "truth-in-lending" legislation, however, disclosure of the true effective (compound) rate on loans became required. Thus a two-year loan of $100 with simple interest of 10 percent requires the borrower to make a single payment of $120 at maturity for the loan. Most loans, of course, are paid off in installments, so that the *average* amount borrowed over the two-year period is approximately $50. The true effective rate of interest, then, is close to 20 percent, a fact not disclosed before truth-in-lending.

Amount of $1.   The comparison of simple and compound interest above leads to the first compound interest formula. Specifically, to what amount F will $1 grow at interest rate i, after n periods, with compounding once per period? The general formula is

$$F = (1 + i)^n$$

The $(1 + i)^n$ amount need not be calculated for most interest rates. Tables have been prepared to show the amount of $(1 + i)^n$ for various interest rates and time periods. This amount if referred to as the *amount of $1* or *future value of $1.* An accepted shorthand expression for this is $a_{\overline{n}|i}$ (read "small *a* angle *n* at *i*"). An excerpt from such a table appears in Table 1 in the Appendix to this book. When the principal amount exceeds $1, the *amount of $1* factor is multiplied by the principal amount.

EXAMPLE 1.   To how much will $1,200 grow if placed in a savings account for 4 periods at interest rate 7.5 percent?

$$\begin{aligned} F &= \$1,200(1.075)(1.075)(1.075)(1.075) \\ &= \$1,200(1.075)^4 \\ &= \$1,200(1.33547) \\ &= \$1,602.56 \end{aligned}$$

EXAMPLE 2.   How many periods n are required for our savings account deposit of $1,200 to double? The interest rate is 7.5 percent and F = $2,400.

$$\$2,400 = \$1,200(1.075)^n$$
$$\frac{\$2,400}{\$1,200} = (1.075)^n$$
$$2 = (1.075)^n$$

From a table, we find that $(1.075)^{10} = 2.06103$. Hence, our account will double in slightly less than 10 periods.

EXAMPLE 3.   What must the interest rate on our savings account be if the $1,200 is to triple in 19 periods?

$$\$3,600 = \$1,200(1 + i)^{19}$$
$$\frac{\$3,600}{\$1,200} = (1 + i)^{19}$$
$$3 = (1 + i)^{19}$$

From the table we find that $(1.06)^{19} = 3.02560$. Thus our account will triple in 19 periods if the interest rate is about 6 percent.

Present Value of $1.   Where future value looks *forward*, present value looks *back*. In present value analysis, we determine the value *today* of a sum to be received in the *future*, at discount rate i. Present value calculations are the inverse of future value calculations. Our future value calculation showed that $100 will grow to $146.93 after 5 periods with 8 percent compound interest.

$$\$146.93 = \$100(1.08)(1.08)(1.08)(1.08)(1.08)$$
$$= \$100(1.08)^5$$

Alternatively, $146.93 received 5 periods from now, discounted at 8 percent, has a present value of $100.

$$\$100 = \frac{\$146.93}{(1.08)^5}$$
$$= \$146.93\left(\frac{1}{1.08}\right)^5$$

The $1/(1.08)^5$ is the present value of $1 received after 5 periods, discounted at 8 percent. It is, of course, the inverse of $(1.08)^5$. Tables are usually available showing the present value of $1 received at some time in the future for a variety of discount rates and time periods. An accepted shorthand expression for this is $p_{\overline{n}i}$ (read "small p angle n at i"). See Table 2 of the Appendix.

EXAMPLE 4.   What is the present value (P) of $2,500 to be received 3 periods hence, with a discount rate of .06?

$$P = \$2,500(1.06)^{-1}(1.06)^{-1}(1.06)^{-1}$$
$$= \$2,500(1.06)^{-3}$$
$$= \$2,500(.83962)$$
$$= \$2,099.05$$

Length of the Compounding (Discounting) Period.   Our discussion so far has said nothing about the *length* of the interest period. Usually, however, interest will be quoted on an *annual* basis but compounded more than once per year. Thus if our savings account draws interest at the rate of 6 percent, compounded semiannually, we calculate the future value after five years by compounding for 10 periods with interest of 3 percent per period. If the interest is compounded quarterly, we would use 1.5 percent for 20 periods to get the future value at the end of five years. To illustrate determining annual effective interest rates from rates quoted for shorter periods, consider the often-quoted terms of sale "2/10, n(et)/30." For example, on a $100 gross invoice price, these terms mean that the interest rate during the period of the loan is 2/98, because if the discount is not taken, then a charge of $2 is levied for the use of $98. The $98 is borrowed for 20 (= 30 − 10) days, so the number of compounding periods in a year is 18.25 (= 365/20). The expression for the exact annual rate of interest implied by terms 2/10, n/30 is

$$(1 + 2/98)^{(365/20)} - 1 = 1.020408^{18.25} - 1 = 44.59 \text{ percent}$$

Chapter 13 discusses the implications for cash management of this surprisingly high (at least to some) implied interest rate. (The rate is even higher if the invoice is paid after the 10th day but before the 30th day.)

The limiting case of the compounding period length is *continuous compounding*. The future value formula for continuous compounding of $1 at annual interest rate i for n years is e^{in}, where e is the base of the natural logarithms. Similarly, the present value formula for continuous discounting of $1 received n years in the future at interest rate i is e^{-in}. Continuous compounding and discounting factors are also available in tabular form and need not be calculated each time. Selected values of e^{-x} are shown in Exhibit 1 (i.e., $x = in$).

EXHIBIT 1   Continuous Discount Factors: e^{-x}

x	e^{-x}	x	e^{-x}	x	e^{-x}
.00	1.0000	.30	.7408	2.30	.1003
.01	.9901	.35	.7047	2.40	.0907
.02	.9802	.40	.6703	2.50	.0821
.03	.9704	.45	.6376	2.60	.0743
.04	.9608	.50	.6065	2.70	.0672
.05	.9512	.55	.5770	2.80	.0608
.06	.9417	.60	.5488	2.90	.0550
.07	.9323	.65	.5220	3.00	.0498
.08	.9231	.70	.4966	3.10	.0450
.09	.9139	.75	.4724	3.20	.0408
.10	.9048	.80	.4493	3.40	.0334
.11	.8958	.85	.4274	3.60	.0273
.12	.8869	.90	.4066	3.80	.0224
.13	.8780	.95	.3867	4.00	.0183
.14	.8693	1.00	.3679	4.20	.0150
.15	.8607	1.05	.3499	4.40	.0123
.16	.8521	1.10	.3329	4.60	.0101
.17	.8437	1.15	.3166	4.80	.0082
.18	.8353	1.20	.3012	5.00	.0067
.19	.8270	1.25	.2865	5.50	.0041
.20	.8187	1.30	.2725	6.00	.0025
.21	.8106	1.40	.2466	7.00	.0009
.22	.8025	1.50	.2231	8.00	.0003
.23	.7945	1.60	.2019	9.00	.0001
.24	.7866	1.70	.1827	10.00	.00005
.25	.7788	1.80	.1653		
.26	.7711	1.90	.1496		
.27	.7634	2.00	.1353		
.28	.7558	2.10	.1225		
.29	.7483	2.20	.1108		

A Note on the Equivalence Between Continuous and Discrete Compounding.   In general, the shorter the length of the compounding period, the greater will be the accumulation after n periods for a given annual rate. This is because more "interest on interest" is earned. For example, at 4 percent compounded annually, $1 will grow to $1.04 at the end of one year. If, however, compounding is *quarterly*, then the same dollar will grow to $(1 + .01)^4$ or $1.0406. Under continuous compounding, the $1 will grow by $e^{.04}$ to $1.0408. A *smaller* nominal interest rate is required to cause $1 to grow to a given amount under continuous compounding than is required under discrete compounding. It can be shown that this smaller nominal interest rate is $\ln(1 + i)$ or the *natural logarithm* of $(1 + i)$. This is shown graphically in Exhibit 2, where n is the number of years and B is the principal amount to be compounded.

EXHIBIT 2   Value of an Amount B Compounded at Discrete Interest i per Period or Continuous Interest at ln(1 + i) and i per Period (i = .20)

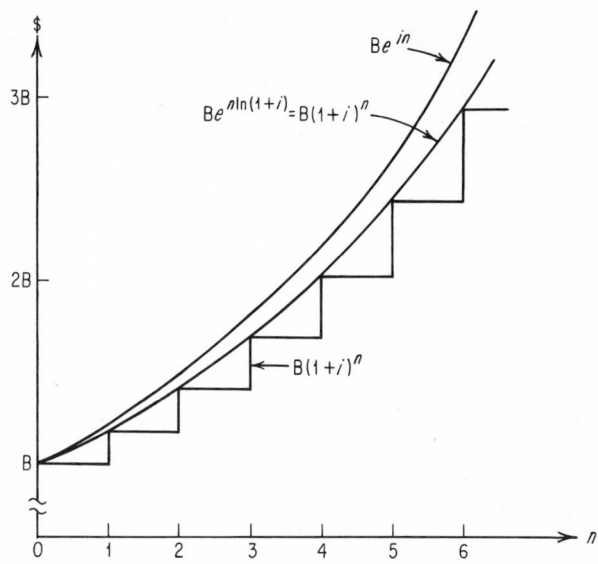

ANNUITIES

An *annuity* is a series of equal payments made at the beginning or end of a series of equal time periods. Bond interest payments, lease payments, and annual payments made to a retired employee under a pension plan are common annuities. An annuity whose payments occur at the *end* of each period is called an *ordinary annuity* or an *annuity in arrears*. Semiannual bond interest payments represent an ordinary annuity because the first interest payment is made *after* the bond has been outstanding for six months. An annuity whose payments occur at *the beginning* of each period is called an *annuity due* or an *annuity in advance*. Rent is usually paid in advance, so a series of rental payments represents an annuity due. An annuity whose payments begin at some time after the end of the first period is called a *deferred annuity*. Prior to retirement age, the annuity payments commencing at retirement represent a deferred annuity. An annuity whose payments continue forever is called a *perpetuity*. The timing of the first payment determines whether a perpetuity is *in arrears* or *in advance*. The British and Canadian governments have, from time to time, issued bonds with no maturity dates. Such bonds are called *consols;* their interest payments represent a *perpetuity in arrears*.

Ordinary Annuities. The formulas for determining the future and present value of ordinary annuities are extensions of the basic compound interest and present value formulas. Consider an ordinary annuity of $1 for 3 periods at 6 percent. The value of the annuity at the end of the third period is calculated as follows:

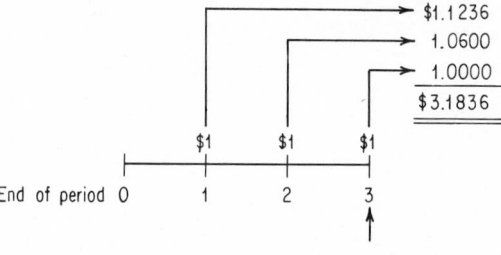

The $1 received at the end of the first period earns interest for 2 periods, so it is worth $1.1236 at the end of period 3. The $1 received at the end of the second period grows to $1.06 by the end of period 3, and the $1 received at the end of period 3 is, of course, worth $1 at the end of period 3. The entire annuity is worth $3.1836 at the end of period 3.

The formula for the future value (F) of the annuity is

$$F = (1 + i)^2 + (1 + i) + 1$$
$$= \$1.1236 + \$1.0600 + \$1.0000$$
$$= \$3.1836$$

which reduces to

$$F = \frac{(1 + i)^3 - 1}{i}$$
$$= \frac{(1.06)^3 - 1}{.06}$$
$$= \frac{1.19102 - 1}{.06}$$
$$= \$3.1836$$

In general, the formula for the future value of an ordinary annuity of $B compounded at rate i for n periods is

$$F = \frac{B\,[(1 + i)^n - 1]}{i}$$

A shorthand expression for $[(1 + i)^n - 1]/i$ is $A_{\overline{n}|i}$.

If we wished to find the *present value* of this ordinary annuity of $1 per period for 3 periods, discounted at 6 percent, we would use the calculations shown here:

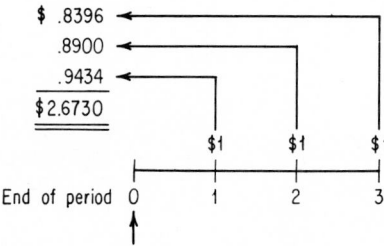

The $1 to be received at the end of period 1 has present value $.9434, the $1 to be received at the end of period 2 has present value $.8900, and the $1 to be received at the end of the third period has present value $.8396. The present value of the annuity is the sum of these individual present values, $2.6730.

The formula for the present value P of the annuity is

$$P = \frac{1}{(1 + i)^3} + \frac{1}{(1 + i)^2} + \frac{1}{(1 + i)}$$
$$= \$.8396 + \$.8900 + \$.9434$$
$$= \$2.6730$$

which reduces to

$$P = \frac{1 - (1 + i)^{-3}}{i}$$
$$= \frac{1 - .83962}{.06}$$
$$= \$2.6730$$

In general, the formula for the present value of an ordinary annuity of $B discounted at i percent for n periods is

$$P = \frac{B\,[1 - (1 + i)^{-n}]}{i}$$

A shorthand expression for $[1 - (1 + i)^{-n}]/i$ is $P_{\overline{n}|i}$.

The values of $A_{\overline{n}|i}$ and $P_{\overline{n}|i}$ have been tabulated for a variety of interest rates and periods, thus simplifying the calculations in annuity problems. Excerpts from such tables appear in the Appendix: $A_{\overline{n}|i}$ in Table 3 and $P_{\overline{n}|i}$ in Table 4.

EXAMPLE 5.[1]   The Roberts Dairy Company switched from delivery trucks with gasoline engines to ones with diesel engines. The diesel trucks cost $2,000 more than the ordinary trucks but $50 per month less to operate. Assume that the operating costs are saved at the end of each month. If Roberts Dairy Company uses a discount rate of 1 percent per month, how long, at a minimum, must the diesel trucks remain in service for the switch to save money in present value terms?

See Table 4 in the Appendix of this book. The present value of an ordinary annuity of $1 per period discounted at 1 percent per period is $40 [= $2,000/50] when the number of annuity periods is between 51 and 52.

Annuities Due.   Recall that the basic difference between an ordinary annuity and an annuity due lies in the timing of the *first payment*. With an ordinary annuity, the first payment is received at the *end* of the first period. With an annuity due, the first payment is received at the *beginning* of the first period. Therefore, if tables for the future value and present value of ordinary annuities are available, it is a simple matter to convert these for use in problems involving *annuities due*. A $1 annuity due for n periods will have a future value equal to the future value of an ordinary annuity for $n + 1$ periods *minus* $1. We can see this by comparing the payments to be made under an annuity due for 3 periods with an ordinary annuity for 4 periods:

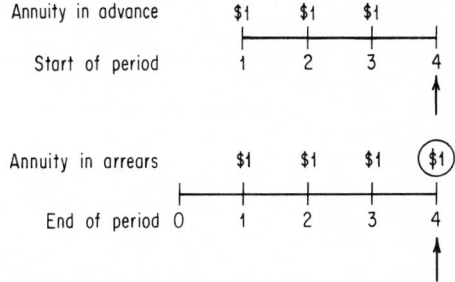

The *circled* $1 is the $1 that must be subtracted from the *4-period* annuity in arrears to get the *3-period* annuity in advance.

Similarly, the present value of an annuity due may be readily determined using the ordinary annuity present value tables. A $1 annuity in advance for n periods has present value equal to the present value of a $1 annuity in arrears for $n - 1$ periods *plus* $1. This can be seen by examining the payments for the present value of an annuity in advance for three periods as shown here:

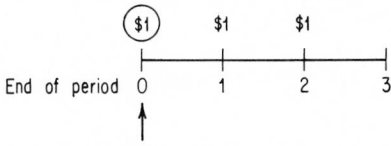

[1]This example is taken from S. Davidson, J. S. Schindler, and R. L. Weil, *Fundamentals of Accounting*, 5th ed., The Dryden Press, Hinsdale, Ill., 1975, p. 405, problem 32.

Notice that except for the first, circled, payment, it looks just like the present value of an ordinary annuity for 2 periods. Therefore, by adding $1 (the circled $1) to the present value of an annuity in arrears for 2 periods we obtain the present value of an annuity due for 3 periods.

EXAMPLE 6.   What is the present value of rents of $350 to be paid monthly, in advance, for one year when the discount rate is 1 percent per month?

The present value will be equal to

$$D = \$350 + \frac{\$350}{1.01} + \frac{\$350}{(1.01)^2} + \cdots + \frac{\$350}{(1.01)^{11}}$$

$$= \$350 \left[1 + \frac{1}{1.01} + \frac{1}{(1.01)^2} + \cdots + \frac{1}{(1.01)^{11}} \right]$$

$$= \$350 + \$350 \frac{[1 - (1.01)^{-11}]}{.01}$$

$$= \$350 + \$350(10.36763)$$

$$= \$3978.67$$

The factor 10.3676 is the present value of an *ordinary annuity* of $1, discounted at 1 percent for 11 periods from the appropriate table, Table 4 of the Appendix.

EXAMPLE 7.   Mr. Mason is 62 years old today. He wishes to invest an amount today and equal amounts on his sixty-third, sixty-fourth, and sixty-fifth birthdays so that starting on his sixty-sixth birthday he can withdraw $5,000 on each birthday for 11 years. His investments will earn 8 percent per year. How much should be invested on the sixty-second through sixty-fifth birthdays?

The timing of the payments is:

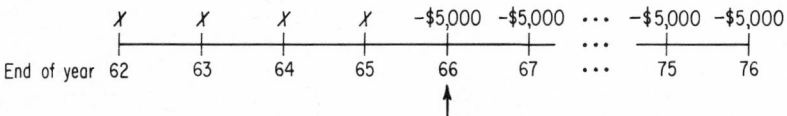

The X's represent the unknown amount of his annual contributions to be made on each of his sixty-second through sixty-fifth birthdays.

For each $1 that Mr. Mason invests on his sixty-second, sixty-third, sixty-fourth, and sixty-fifth birthdays, he will have (see Appendix Table 4) $4.8666 (= $5.86660 − $1) on his sixty-sixth birthday. On his sixty-sixth birthday Mr. Mason needs to have accumulated an amount large enough to fund an 11-year, $5,000 annuity in advance. An 11-year, $1 annuity in advance has present value of $7.71008 (= $6.71008 + $1.) Mr. Mason then needs on his sixty-sixth birthday an accumulation of $5,000 × $7.71008 = $38,550.40. Since each $1 deposited on the sixty-second through sixty-fifth birthdays grows to $4.8666, Mr. Mason must deposit $38,-550.40/$4.8666 = $7,921.42 on each of the sixty-second through sixty-fifth birthdays to accumulate $38,550.40.

Deferred Annuities.   When the first payment of an annuity occurs sometime after the end of the first period, the annuity is *deferred.* The payment schedule for an ordinary annuity of $1 per period for 4 periods, deferred for 2 periods, is:

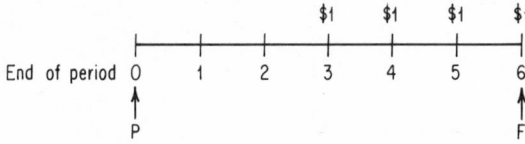

The arrow marked P shows the time for which the present value is calculated; the arrow marked F shows when the future value is calculated. The future value is not affected by the deferral and equals the future value of an ordinary annuity for 4 periods.

There are two ways to calculate the present value of a deferred annuity. The first is to calculate the present value of the annuity and then discount the resulting sum from the period of deferral to the present. The second is somewhat simpler and will be illustrated first. The payment schedule of the 4-period annuity deferred 2 periods is as follows:

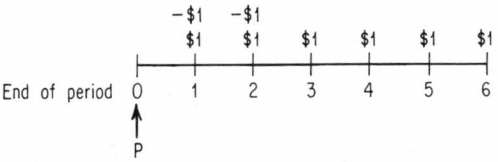

It now reflects the present value of an ordinary annuity for 6 periods *minus* the present value of an ordinary annuity for 2 periods. In general, to calculate the present value of an annuity of n payments deferred for d periods, subtract the present value of an annuity for d periods from the present value of an annuity for $n + d$ periods.

EXAMPLE 8.   What is the present value of Mr. Mason's withdrawals in Example 7? Recall that Mr. Mason is 62 years old, he will receive $5,000 on his sixty-sixth through seventy-sixth birthdays, and his investment earns 8 percent.

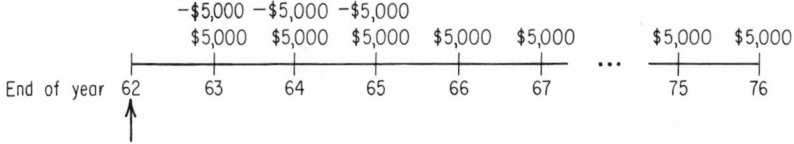

The present value at 8 percent of $5,000 received for 14 years, starting one year hence, is $5,000 × 8.24424 = $41,221.20. The present value at age 62 of the $5,000 he will not receive on birthdays 63 through 65 is −$5,000 × 2.57710 = −$12,885.50. The present value of the actual payments to Mr. Mason is $41,221.20 − $12,885.50 = $28,335.70.

Alternatively, one could discount the present value of an annuity due of $5,000 for 11 periods at 8 percent back to the present. The present value of the 11-period annuity due is $5,000 × (1 + 6.71008) or $38,550.40. Discounting this sum at 8 percent for 4 periods, we have

$$P = \frac{\$38,550.40}{(1.08)^4}$$
$$= \$38,550.40(.73503)$$
$$= \$28,335.70$$

Perpetuities.   A periodic payment to be received forever is called a *perpetuity*. Future values of perpetuities are undefined. If $1 is to be received at the end of every period and the discount rate is i percent, then the present value of the perpetuity is $1/i$. This expression can be derived with algebra or by observing what happens in the expression for the present value of an ordinary annuity of $B per payment as n, the number of payments, approaches infinity:

$$P = \frac{B[1 - (1 + i)^{-n}]}{i}$$

As n approaches infinity, $(1 + i)^{-n}$ approaches zero, so P approaches $B(1/i)$. If the first payment of the perpetuity occurs now, the present value is $B[1 + 1/i]$.

EXAMPLE 9.   The Canadian government offers to pay $30 every six months forever. What is that promise worth if the discount rate is 8 percent compounded semiannually?

Eight percent compounded semiannually is equivalent to 4 percent per six-month period. If the first payment occurs six months from now, the present value is $30/.04 = $750. If the first payment occurs today, the present value is $30 + $750 = $780.

APPLICATIONS IN ACCOUNTING

Compound interest methods have many uses in various kinds of problems in accounting. In the remainder of this chapter, we discuss and illustrate the use of compound interest methods in a representative set of such problems.

Internal Rate of Return or Yield.   We are often interested in the effective interest rate implicit in a stream of cash flows. The yield to maturity of a bond and the internal rate of return on a proposed capital investment are examples. This effective interest rate is referred to as either *yield* or *internal rate of return*. It represents *the interest rate required to make the present value of the cash inflows equal to the present value of the cash outflows.* Alternatively, it is the interest rate which makes the net present value of all the cash flows equal to zero.

EXAMPLE 10.   Investment of $1,000 today will generate four equal payments of $302, one each at the end of the next four years. To solve for the yield, we set up the following equation:

$$0 = -1,000 + \frac{302}{(1 + i)} + \frac{302}{(1 + i)^2} + \frac{302}{(1 + i)^3} + \frac{302}{(1 + i)^4}$$

or

$$1,000 = \frac{302}{1 + i} + \frac{302}{(1 + i)^2} + \frac{302}{(1 + i)^3} + \frac{302}{(1 + i)^4}$$

The internal rate of return, i, must now be computed. In this case, we have an ordinary annuity of $302 for four periods and we wish to determine the interest rate which makes the present value of the annuity equal to $1,000.

$$\$1,000 = \$302 P_{\overline{4}|i}$$
$$\frac{\$1,000}{\$302} = P_{\overline{4}|i}$$
$$3.31126 = P_{\overline{4}|i}$$

By looking in the present value of an ordinary annuity table, we find that $P_{\overline{4}|i} =$ at $i = 8$ percent. Hence the internal rate of return is about 8 percent.

The internal rate of return must usually be estimated using trial-and-error procedures.

EXAMPLE 11.   Find the yield of an investment costing $1,000 which will return $200, $500, and $400 at the end of years 1, 2, and 3, respectively.

$$\$1,000 = \frac{\$200}{1 + i} + \frac{\$500}{(1 + i)^2} + \frac{\$400}{(1 + i)^3}$$

Begin by checking if i is greater than or less than 3 percent. Our investment, evaluated at $i = 3$ percent, has a net present value of

$$\$200(.97087) + \$500(.94260) + \$400(.91514) = \$194.17 + \$471.30 + \$366.06$$
$$= \$1,031.53$$

Now, evaluate the investment at $i = 4$ percent:

$200(.96154) + $500(.92456) + $400(.88900) = $192.31 + $462.28 + $355.60
$$= $1,010.19$$

Now, $i = 4.5$ percent:

$200(.95693) + $500(.91572) + $400(.87629) = $191.39 + $457.86 + $350.52
$$= $999.77$$

The yield is slightly less than 4.5 percent per year.

It is important to recognize that the computed yield reflects the assumption that the periodic cash inflows can be reinvested at the *yield rate*. Consequently, the *realized yield* (ex post) may differ from the *computed yield* (ex ante), depending on the actual interest rate earned by the periodic cash inflows.[2]

Most investments are *conventional* investments. That is, they require an initial outflow followed by a series of net inflows. When a stream of cash flows is characterized by alternating inflows and outflows (i.e., a *nonconventional investment*), *multiple yields* may arise. In other words, such streams of cash flows may have *more than one* interest rate which generates a net present value of zero.

EXAMPLE 12. This example is adapted from one in Harold Bierman, Jr., and Seymour Smidt, *The Capital Budgeting Decision*, 4th ed., The Macmillan Company, New York, 1975, Chapter 3.

Consider an investment with the following cash flows.

Period	0	1	2
Cash Flow	−$72,727	$170,909	−$100,000

The yield of this investment is 10 percent as shown below.

$$0 = -$72,727 + \frac{$170,909}{1.1} - \frac{$100,000}{(1.1)^2}$$
$$= -$72,727 + $170,909(.90909) - $100,000(.82644)$$
$$= -$72,727 + $155,371 - $82,644$$

We now show that the yield is also 25 percent per period.

$$0 = -$72,727 + \frac{$170,909}{1.25} - \frac{$100,000}{(1.25)^2}$$
$$= -$72,727 + $170,909(.8) - $100,000(.64)$$
$$= -$72,727 + $136,727 - $64,000$$

The existence of multiple yields on nonconventional investments has implications for the evaluation of capital expenditures. In short, when multiple yields exist and potential investments are being ranked in terms of yield, it becomes difficult to make accept or reject decisions. Hence, we normally suggest discounting the cash flows with an appropriate discount rate and ranking investments in terms of net present value rather than trying to solve for the yield. Multiple rates of return will not exist, however, when a reinvestment rate is assumed for all cash outflows from an investment. It will always be reasonable to assume a reinvestment rate; therefore, the problem of multiple yields can be avoided.

Valuation of Bonds.   A bond represents a contract in which the lender acquires

[2]For an extensive discussion of this problem and a method of investing in coupon bonds to guarantee a rate of return equal to the originally promised yield under realistic assumptions, see Lawrence Fisher and Roman L. Weil, "Coping with the Risk of Interest Rate Fluctuations: Returns to Bondholders from Naive and Optimal Strategies," *Journal of Business*, vol. 44, no. 4, pp. 408–431, October 1971.

the right to a series of interest payments over the life of the bond and to a payment (usually $1,000) at the bond's maturity. Compound interest methods are essential where bonds are concerned. These methods are used to compute bond values (prices) and yields.

Consider a $1,000 face value bond with semiannual coupons totaling 8 percent per year and with five years until maturity. The cash flows associated with this bond are

$$BP = \frac{\$40}{(1+i)} + \frac{\$40}{(1+i)^2} + \cdots + \frac{\$40}{(1+i)^{10}} + \frac{\$1,000}{(1+i)^{10}}$$

The price of the bond, BP, will be equal to the present value of the interest payments ($40 per six-month period for 10 such periods) plus the present value of the principal payment of $1,000 to be received five years (10 six-month periods) from now. In order to determine the value or price of the bond, we need to know i, the current market rate of interest (or yield) on bonds of similar quality and time to maturity. On the other hand, in order to determine the yield to maturity on this bond (or the rate of return investors require to hold the bond), we need to know BP, the current market price. Once we know either the current market price or the yield to maturity, we can solve for the other variable. The *yield to maturity* is an *internal rate of return.*

If the yield to maturity on this bond is 7 percent, the price would be

$$BP = \frac{\$40}{(1.035)} + \frac{\$40}{(1.035)^2} + \cdots + \frac{\$40}{(1.035)^{10}} + \frac{\$1,000}{(1.035)^{10}}$$

$$= \$40 P_{\overline{10}|.035} + \$1,000 P_{\overline{10}|.035}$$

$$= \$40(8.31661) + \$1,000(.70892)$$

$$= \$1,041.58$$

Bond tables are available which eliminate the necessity to make most tedious bond calculations. Table 6 in the Appendix is an excerpt from a bond table. For 8-percent bonds paying $40 of interest semiannually, Table 6 presents various combinations of yield, price, and time to maturity. (Table 5 shows values for 6-percent semiannual coupon bonds.) Observe that bond prices are usually quoted in percentages of par. The actual price of a $1,000 bond is 10 times the value shown in the table.

If one knows any three of the four important variables—coupon rate, yield, time to maturity, and price, a bond table enables determination of the value of the fourth variable.

Relationship Between Bond Prices and Yields.   The interest payments on a bond are fixed by the contract and normally will not change during the life of the bond. Because the coupon payments are fixed, bond prices are sensitive to changes in market interest rates or yields. Returning to our 8-percent semiannual five-year bond, we observed that if the market yield was 7 percent, the bond would sell for $1,041.58. This is a premium of $41.58 above par, or face, value ($1,000). If market yields increase to 8 percent, the bond price would fall to $1,000.00 and the premium disappears. As interest rates fall, bond prices rise, and vice versa. The reason is that a bond pays a fixed amount of cash. If market yields fall, investors will *pay more* for any given bond because the payments will have a larger present value. If market yields rise, investors will *pay less* for any given bond because the fixed amounts of cash will have a lower present value. For more detail on accounting for bonds, see Chapters 14 and 24.

Capital Expenditure Analysis.   Contemporary firms should employ present value techniques in evaluating proposed capital expenditures. Capital expenditures normally have a life spanning several years. Typically, capital expenditures involve the current investment of funds, in return for cash benefits to be received in the future. Knowledge of the time value of money is basic to adjusting the magnitude of future cash inflows to make them comparable to the investment to be made in the present. Predictions of future cash flows are uncertain; changes in demand, technology, selling prices, costs, and general inflation all create uncertainty in future predictions. Nevertheless, the use of present value techniques allows the explicit introduction of the time value of money (which may itself be uncertain) into the analysis.[3]

The mechanics of capital expenditure analysis are straightforward. The general approach is outlined below.

1. Estimate all cash inflows and outflows during the expected life of the investment.

2. Adjust the cash flows for the effects of income and other taxes. Net cash inflows should be reduced by the income taxes paid on those inflows in each period. Noncash expenses, such as depreciation, which are deductible for tax purposes, generate *tax savings* equal to the amount of the noncash deduction times the relevant tax rate. Special tax provisions such as the investment credit and the tax rules dealing with sale or exchange of property must also be considered.

3. Select a discount rate which reflects the aftertax opportunity cost of money to the firm.

4. Discount all cash flows to the present and select those investments which have a positive net present value (i.e., those for which the present value of the inflows exceeds the present value of the outflows).[4] Reject investments having a net present value less than zero.

To illustrate the approach to present value analysis of capital expenditure proposals, we work through an example.

EXAMPLE 13.   The LW Corporation is contemplating the production of a new product. The equipment necessary for production can be acquired for $100,000. It has an estimated life of 10 years and no salvage value. In addition, it will be eligible for a 10-percent investment credit. The following schedule shows the expected sales volume, selling price, and variable cost per unit of production.

Year	Sales volume	Selling price	Variable cost of production
1	10,000	$5.00	$3.00
2	12,000	5.00	3.10
3	13,000	5.50	3.25
4	15,000	5.75	3.25
5	20,000	6.00	3.30
6	25,000	6.00	3.40
7	20,000	6.10	3.50
8	18,000	6.10	3.50
9	15,000	6.25	3.50
10	15,000	6.30	3.75

Production in each year must be sufficient to meet each year's sales, except that 15,000 units will be produced in year 1 to provide a continuing inventory of 5,000

[3]See, for example, David B. Hertz, "Investment Policies That Pay Off," *Harvard Business Review*, January–February 1968, pp. 96–108.

[4]The existence of mutually exclusive investments and limited availability of investment funds may mean that not all investments having positive net present values can be accepted. For approaches to the problem of *selecting* from a group of acceptable investment projects, see Nicholas Dopuch, Jacob G. Birnberg, and Joel Demski, *Cost Accounting*, 2nd ed., Harcourt Brace Jovanovich, New York, 1974, chap. 6.

units; hence production in year 10 will be only 10,000 units so that at the end of year 10 ending inventory is zero. Inventory will be accounted for using the LIFO cost flow assumption.

The corporation's income tax rate is 40 percent. The corporation's cost of money is 10 percent per year, after taxes. Cash is received at the end of the year when sales are made and expended at the end of the year when costs are incurred. Selling expenses are estimated at $1 per unit sold.

The schedule of cash flows and present value calculations is presented in Exhibit 3. The net present value of the investment is $11,134. This means that, discounted at the firm's cost of money (10 percent), the present value of the inflows from the investment exceeds the present value of the outflows by $11,134. Hence, in the absence of better alternatives (i.e., investments with higher net present values), the investment should be undertaken.

Lease Versus Buy. Corporations often have several options in financing capital acquisitions. One option is the long-term noncancelable lease. Equipment (or other facilities) may be leased as well as purchased. Management must choose between these alternatives for obtaining the services of assets. Proper analysis of the lease-versus-buy decision has been the subject of much controversy and misunderstanding, both in practice and in the financial literature. Probably the most important point to understand is that a noncancelable lease is a form of debt. The lessee makes a commitment to make the lease payments during the term of the lease, even if use of the leased asset is discontinued. For these purposes, we assume either that the term of the lease is the same as the life of the asset or, if the term of the lease is less than the life of the asset, then the asset's salvage value as of the end of the term of the lease is known and can be taken into the discounted cash flow analysis.

To compare outright purchase with a lease, the alternatives should be made as equivalent as possible. Specifically, in evaluating the alternatives, one should separate the investment and financing decisions. Since the form of financing affects interest expense, which in turn affects taxable income and income taxes, identical amounts of borrowing for identical time periods must be incorporated into the alternatives. Only then do the aftertax cash flows become comparable.

In a world with taxes, the timing of the tax deductions plays an important part in determining the net present value of aftertax cash flows. The sooner tax deductions occur, the greater will be the present value of the tax savings. In comparing leasing with buying, we are interested in the timing of the lease payments (which are fully tax deductible as payments are made) in contrast with the depreciation deductions if the asset is bought. But lease payments include an interest expense on borrowed funds. To make buying comparable, we must include equal amounts of borrowing as are implicit in the lease so that the tax shield of the interest payments is comparable under the two alternatives. A complete analysis in which the investment and financing decisions are combined for each alternative is perhaps the simplest approach to a correct decision.[5] To illustrate these points and the methodology, consider the series of examples worked out in Exhibit 4, based on the following assumptions:

1. The cost of debt to the firm is 8 percent per year.

---

[5] In a recent analysis, Miller and Upton show that in competitive markets the kinds of differences we illustrate should not arise. They argue that, on balance, if you believe the leasing and lending markets are competitive, then the cost of doing the kinds of analyses shown in Exhibit 4 exceeds the benefits from finding advantages in one alternative or another. They conclude that taxable firms should always lease and that nontaxable firms should always buy outright. See Merton H. Miller and Charles W. Upton, "Leasing, Buying, and the Cost of Capital Services," *Journal of Finance,* vol. 31, no. 3, June 1976.

EXHIBIT 3 Schedule of Cash Flows and Present Value Calculations

	1	2	3	4	5	6	7	8	9	10
Sales	$ 50,000	$ 60,000	$ 71,500	$ 86,250	$120,000	$150,000	$122,000	$109,800	$ 93,750	$ 94,500
Variable cost of goods sold	30,000	37,200	42,250	48,750	66,000	85,000	70,000	63,000	52,500	52,500*
Selling expenses	10,000	12,000	13,000	15,000	20,000	25,000	20,000	18,000	15,000	15,000
(1) Cash flow from operations	$ 10,000	$ 10,800	$ 16,250	$ 22,500	$ 34,000	$ 40,000	$ 32,000	$ 28,800	$ 26,250	$ 27,000
Depreciation (SL)†	10,000	10,000	10,000	10,000	10,000	10,000	10,000	10,000	10,000	10,000
Taxable income	-0-	800	6,250	12,500	24,000	30,000	22,000	18,800	16,250	17,000
Income tax	-0-	320	2,500	5,000	9,600	12,000	8,800	7,520	6,500	6,800
(2) Cash flow after taxes (1) − (2)	$ 10,000	$ 10,480	$ 13,750	$ 17,500	$ 24,400	$ 28,000	$ 23,200	$ 21,280	$ 19,750	$ 20,200
Inventory adjustment‡	(15,000)									15,000
Net cash flow	(5,000)	10,480	13,750	17,500	24,400	28,000	23,200	21,280	19,750	35,200
Present value factors (10%)	.90909	.82645	.75131	.68301	.62092	.56447	.51316	.46651	.42410	.38554
	($ 4,545)	$ 8,661	$ 10,331	$ 11,953	$ 15,150	$ 15,805	$ 11,905	$ 9,927	$ 8,376	$ 13,571
(3) Total present value of inflows .. $101,134										
Gross investment $100,000										
Less: 10% investment credit ...... (10,000)										
(4) Net investment .... $ 90,000										
Net present value (3) − (4) ...... $ 11,134										

*Cost of goods sold (LIFO) in year 10 consists of 10,000 units produced in year 10 ($37,500) plus cost of 5,000 units produced in year 1 ($15,000) and carried forward as inventory until sold in year 10.

†Depreciation is treated as a period expense in the illustration for simplicity. Given the facts of the illustration, depreciation is a product cost and should be deducted in tax computations in accordance with full absorption costing. This would reduce depreciation claimed on the tax return by $3,333 to $6,667 in Year 1 and increase it by $3,333 to $13,333 in Year 10. This delay in depreciation deductions would result in a decrease of $698 in the net present value of the project as of the beginning of year 1. $698 = (−$3,333 × .90909 × .40) + ($3,333 × .38554 × .40).

‡Adjustment for extra cash expended on production in year 1 (5,000 units × $3.00) and not expended in year 10.

EXHIBIT 4 Lease Versus Buy: Schedule of Cash Flows and Present Value Calculations

		Buy		Lease						Computation of cash flows unrelated to debt (implicit or explicit) except income tax effects of interest, if any			
									Computation of income tax expense				
End of period	Taxable proceeds (1)	Depreciation (2)	Maintenance (3)	Implicit interest payments (4)	Implicit maintenance (5)	Principal repayment (6)	Total tax deduction (7)	Taxable income (8)	Income taxes at 40% (9)	Cash proceeds (10)	Cash deductions (11)	Net cash flow (12)	Present value at 14% (13)
				Case I. Buy; No Borrowing; Straight-Line Depreciation									
1	$32,000	$20,000	$1,718	—	—	—	$21,718	$10,282	$ 4,113	$32,000	$ 5,831	$26,169	$22,955
2	32,000	20,000	1,718	—	—	—	21,718	10,282	4,113	32,000	5,831	26,169	20,136
3	32,000	20,000	1,718	—	—	—	21,718	10,282	4,113	32,000	5,831	26,169	17,663
		$60,000						$30,846	$12,339		$17,493	$78,507	$60,754
									Present value at start of year 1 to acquire asset I				(60,000)
										Net present value of case I			$ 754
				Case II. Buy; Borrow $60,000 at 8%; Straight-Line Depreciation									
1	$32,000	$20,000	$1,718	$4,800	—	—	$26,518	$ 5,482	$ 2,193	$32,000	$3,911	$28,089	$24,639
2	32,000	20,000	1,718	3,321	—	—	25,039	6,961	2,784	32,000	4,502	27,498	21,159
3	32,000	20,000	1,718	1,725	—	—	23,443	8,557	3,423	32,000	5,141	26,859	18,129
		$60,000						$21,000	$8,400		$13,554	$82,446	$63,927
									Present value (using debt rate) at start of year 1 to acquire asset				(60,000)
										Net present value of case II			$ 3,927
				Case III. Lease for $25,000 per Year; Implied Debt Rate Is 8%									
1	$32,000			$1,718	$4,800	$18,482	$25,000	$ 7,000	$ 2,800	$32,000	$ 4,518	$27,482	$24,107
2	32,000			1,718	3,321	19,961	25,000	7,000	2,800	32,000	4,518	27,482	21,147
3	32,000			1,718	1,725	21,557	25,000	7,000	2,800	32,000	4,518	27,482	18,550
						$60,000		$21,000	$ 8,400		$13,554	$82,446	$63,804
									Present value (using debt rate) at start of year 1 to acquire asset				(60,000)[a]
										Net present value of case III			$ 3,804

Case IV. Lease for $24,895 per Year; Implied Debt Rate Is 7¾%

1	$32,000	—	—	$1,718	$18,527	$24,895	$ 7,105	$ 2,842	$ 4,560	$27,440	$24,070
2	32,000	—	—	1,718	19,963	24,895	7,105	2,842	4,560	27,440	21,114
3	32,000	—	—	1,718	21,510	24,895	7,105	2,842	4,560	27,440	18,521
					$60,000		$21,315	$8,526	$13,680	$72,320	$63,705

Present value (using debt rate) at start of year 1 to acquire asset (59,729)b
Net present value of case IV $ 3,976

Case V. Accelerated Lease Payments: $27,631, $24,895, $21,718; Implicit Debt Rate Is 7¾%

1	$32,000	—	—	$1,718	$21,263	$27,631	$ 4,369	$ 1,748	$ 3,466	$28,534	$25,030
2	32,000	—	—	1,718	20,175	24,895	7,105	2,842	4,560	27,440	21,114
3	32,000	—	—	1,718	18,562	21,718	10,282	4,113	5,831	26,169	17,663
					$60,000		$21,646	$ 8,703	$13,857	$82,143	$63,807

Present value at start of year 1 to acquire asset (59,741)c
Net present value of case V $ 4,066

Case VI. Buy; Borrow $60,000 with Accelerated Principal Repayments of $21,263, $20,175, $18,562

1	$32,000	$20,000	$4,800	$1,718	$26,518	$ 5,482	$ 2,193	$ 3,911	$28,089	$24,639
2	32,000	20,000	3,099	1,718	24,817	7,183	2,873	4,591	27,409	21,090
3	32,000	20,000	1,485	1,718	23,203	8,797	3,519	5,237	26,763	18,064
		$60,000				$21,462	$ 8,585	$13,739	$82,261	$63,793

Present value at start of year 1 to acquire asset (60,000)
Net present value of case VI $ 3,798

Case VII. Buy; Borrow $60,000 with Accelerated Principal Repayments as in Case VI; DDB Depreciation

1	$32,000	$40,000	$4,800	$1,718	$46,518	$(14,518)	$(5,807)d	$(4,089)d	$36,089	$31,657
2	32,000	13,333	3,099	1,718	18,150	13,850	5,540	7,258	24,742	19,038
3	32,000	6,667	1,485	1,718	9,870	22,130	8,852	10,570	21,430	14,465
		$60,000				$21,462	$ 8,585	$13,739	$82,261	$65,160

Present value at start of year 1 to acquire asset (60,000)
Net present value of case VII $ 5,160

Footnotes for Exhibit 4 appear on page 8-18.

Footnotes for Exhibit 4:

(1) Given.

(2) From depreciation formulas; straight-line or double-declining balance.

(3) Explicitly stated and paid for with cash at end of year.

(4) Calculated from amortization schedule for $60,000 loan; interest rate is 8 percent for cases II, III, V, VI, and VII, but is 7¾ percent for case IV.

(5) Implicit maintenance fee; assumed equal to amount of explicit maintenance fee when purchased separately.

(6) Implicit principal repayment; lease payment, given, less interest from amortization schedule (column 4) and maintenance (column 5).

(7) Sum of columns (2), (3), and (4) for purchase plans; sum of columns (4), (5), and (6) for lease plans.

(8) Column (1) less column (7).

(9) 40 percent of column (8).

(10) Given; same as column (1).

(11) Sum of columns (3) and (9) for purchase plans; sum of columns (5) and (9) for lease plans. Note that interest expense, although a cash item, is not counted here. Interest expense is part of the borrowing plan. The cash outflows for interest are eliminated in the process of taking the present value of the loan and lease payments. The interest expense, however, does reduce income taxes.

(12) Column (10) less column (11).

(13) Amounts in column (12) multiplied by present value factors at 14 percent; discounting for one year in rows labeled "1," for two years in rows labeled "2," and for three years in rows labeled "3."

[a]Payment to service debt implicit in lease is $23,282 per year in arrears. At 8 percent, the present value of these three payments is $60,000.

[b]Payment to service debt implicit in lease is $23,177 per year in arrears. At 8 percent, the present value of these three payments is $59,729.

[c]Payments to service debt implicit in lease are $25,913 at the end of the first year, $23,177 at the end of the second year, and $20,000 at the end of the third year. At 8 percent, the present value of these payments is $59,741.

[d]Assumes sufficient taxable income from other sources so that loss in year 1 can be used to fully offset other income and save taxes in year 1.

2. The aftertax cost of capital to the firm is 14 percent per year.

3. The investment project under consideration costs $60,000 if purchased.

4. The investment project returns $32,000 per year for three years with the cash revenues, or cash savings, occurring at the end of each year. The project has no salvage value.

5. The acquired asset requires maintenance of $1,718 per year, with the cash outflows occurring at the end of each year. The seller (lessor, depending upon the context) provides the service.

6. Income taxes are 40 percent of taxable income.

Case I.   To introduce the form of analysis, we assume outright purchase, no borrowing, and straight-line depreciation. The analysis is shown in the first panel of Exhibit 4. The net present value of acquiring the asset is $754. That is, the return in excess of the cost of capital to the firm is $754; the project achieves the minimum required rate of return with something to spare. As long as this net present value is greater than zero, the project is worth undertaking.

Case II.   This case is just like the first one except that the purchase price is borrowed at the debt rate, 8 percent, and is repaid in three equal annual installments of $23,282 ($= \$60,000/2.57710$). Since there is borrowing, there is interest expense, lower taxable income, lower taxes, and a higher net present value of $3,927. Note that the analysis separates financing from the investment decision because the debt service payments, both interest and principal repayments, are excluded from the net cash flows of the project. Nevertheless, income taxes are reduced because of the borrowing and we see a higher net present value.

If the results of case I showed a negative net present value, while the results of case II showed a positive net present value (as would occur if the gross revenues from the project were, say, $400 smaller each year), then case II analysis would indicate that the project is worthwhile, while case I would indicate it is not. (This is the phenomenon of "trading on the equity.") The analysis in case I is correct for evaluating outright purchase. Case II, however, is the basis for comparison with leasing, for case II involves borrowing.[6]

Case III. The seller offers to lease the asset for three years on a noncancelable basis with payments of $25,000 each year, in arrears. Maintenance is included in the lease contract. First, we must separate the debt provisions of the lease contract from the maintenance provision. The maintenance provision costs $1,718 per year if purchased separately. We attribute $1,718 of each $25,000 payment to maintenance in ascertaining the $23,282 (= $25,000 − $1,718) of each payment is for debt service. The firm's borrowing rate is 8 percent and the present value at 8 percent of three annual payments in arrears of $23,282 is $60,000 (= 2.57710 × $23,282). The entire $25,000 is deductible for computing taxable income, but $23,282 of that amount is for borrowing. In computing the net present value of the aftertax cash flows from the investment project, we again ignore the cash flows associated with the borrowing as in case II, taking into account only the tax effects related to the deductibility of the lease payments. The net present value in this case is $3,804, which is less than under buy-borrow.

You may wonder why the analysis has to be so complicated. Can't we merely discount the lease payments at 8 percent to get a net present value? If we do that, we are discounting the payments for maintenance at the debt rate, not at the cost of capital. Since the cost of capital, 14 percent, is higher than the debt rate, 8 percent, we would be placing a larger present value on the maintenance payments than they should have. (The analysis can be made even more complicated by assuming that the maintenance payments, while guaranteed under the leasing option, can be discontinued under buy-borrow if the buyer so desires.)

The typical promotion by leasing companies compares cases I and III in an attempt to persuade the "buyer" that leasing is superior to buying. The analyst should be sure to compare cases II and III, rather than cases I and III. Case III implicitly assumes borrowing with its attendant tax deductions for interest payments, so the purchase alternative should also be assumed to include an equal amount of borrowing. In this example, when purchasing is assumed to include the same amount of borrowing as in the lease, purchasing has a higher net present value.

Case IV. The lease payments need not be exactly equal to borrowing at the firm's debt rate plus purchased maintenance. Here we assume that the asset can be leased, including maintenance, for $24,895 per payment for three years. There are two different interpretations of this payment. First, we can assume that the borrowing rate is 8 percent so that the implied maintenance contract costs $1,613 (= $24,895 − $23,282). Or, we can assume that the maintenance contract costs $1,718, the same as when purchased separately, so that the debt service payments are $23,177 (= $24,895 − $1,718). Under this interpretation, the lessor is lending at 7¾ percent per year; the present value of $1 in arrears for three years at 7¾ percent per year is $2.58877 and the present value of $23,177 in arrears for three years at 7¾ percent per year is $60,000 (= 2.58877 × $23,177). Which of these interpretations is correct? The lessor effectively has made a tie-in sale; for the right both to lend *and* to sell the maintenance contract, the lessor offers a combined price lower than if both are purchased separately. Perhaps the transactions costs are less this way and some of the savings are passed along to the lessee.

To separate the two components of the lease contract in a nonarbitrary way is impossible. The outcome of the analysis depends upon whether we assume that the maintenance contract costs the same under both alternatives but with a

---

[6]Note that in cases II–VII additional debt financing is created, either through borrowing or leasing. This addition of debt may cause the cost of additional external financing to rise.

differing debt rate or whether we assume that the borrowing costs are the same under both alternatives with a different cost for the maintenance contract. Reality may, of course, be a combination of these assumptions. The results are nearly the same, whichever choice we make. We find it more reasonable to assume that the maintenance contract costs the same under lease or buy and that the lessor is providing a concession on the loan.[7]

Thus, we assume that the debt service payments are $23,177 per year. Since the firm's borrowing rate is 8 percent in credit markets, the present value of the debt service payments—the implicit cost of the asset—is 2.5771 × $23,177 or $59,729. The lessor's concession in lending, at 7¾ percent rather than 8 percent, translates into a $271 concession in the purchase price. In this case, the net present value of the lease is $3,976 (see column 13) and is preferred to buy-borrow, as shown in case II.

Case V.   Thus far, we have assumed level lease payments. Lessors often offer lease terms where the early lease payments exceed the later ones—an accelerated payment scheme. Lease payments are usually fully deductible for tax purposes when made. The present value of the tax shield, other things being equal, will be larger when the lease payments are accelerated. (After all, the ideal arrangement would be for the acquisition cost to be fully deductible in the first year. This arrangement is equivalent to a 100 percent depreciation rate or to all lease payments being made in the first year. Such arrangements are, of course, not currently allowed for tax reporting.) In this case, accelerated lease terms are offered with an implicit debt rate of 7¾ percent per year when the maintenance contract is assumed to cost $1,718, as in the purchase alternative. The amounts of principal repaid with each payment are shown in column (6).

We cannot conclude that leasing under these terms is preferred to buy-borrow. That is, cases V and II are not comparable because the amounts of borrowing are different. To be sure that leasing is preferred, we must construct a buy-borrow alternative that incorporates the same amount of borrowing as in the accelerated lease scheme; thus, case VI.

Case VI.   Here the borrowing is arranged so that the amount of principal repaid each year is the same as the amount of principal repaid implicit in the accelerated lease. The borrowing rate is still 8 percent in credit markets, so the interest expense is larger than that shown in case V where the implicit rate is 7¾ percent. The net present value is $3,793, which is less than in case V.

Case VII.   Finally, to show the enormous difference tax regulations can make, we assume buy-borrow with accelerated principal repayments, as in cases V and VI, but with accelerated depreciation—double-declining balance. The net present value is 35 percent larger than with straight-line depreciation and all else the same.[8]

Summary.   In evaluating leasing, be sure to separate the financing payments from other payments and to compare the leasing terms offered to buy-borrow where the borrowing is arranged so that equal amounts of funds are borrowed for equal amounts of time as implied in the lease payments.

Compound Interest Depreciation.   Two rationales for compound interest depreciation are as follows. (1) An asset is acquired for its future benefits. Depreciation

---

[7]The mathematical analysis of this problem is given by Katherine Schipper, John R. Twombly, and Roman L. Weil, "Financial Lease Evaluation Under Conditions of Uncertainty: A Comment," *The Accounting Review*, vol. 49, no 4, pp. 796–801, October 1974.

[8]Miller and Upton, *op. cit.*, would argue that in competitive markets where the same depreciation for tax purposes is available to lessors as to lessees, the lease payments will be correspondingly reduced and that the lease alternative would appear as attractive as buy-borrow.

allocates the cost of the asset to the periods of benefits. Compound interest depreciation writes off an amount of cost each year equal to the decline in the present value of the asset's benefits. (2) The *internal rate of return* is the interest rate that equates the present value of a series of cash inflows with the present value of related cash outflows. In capital expenditure analysis, the internal rate of return will be the interest rate that equates the present value of expected cash benefits from the investment with its acquisition cost. Management is often evaluated on the basis of *return on investment* (ROI), the ratio of net income to book value of the investment or investments. If management decides to undertake an investment with an internal rate of return of, say, 20 percent, and the expected cash flows are in fact realized, then a properly computed ROI ratio ought to show 20 percent in each year of the investment's life. Conventional depreciation methods can result in a measurement quite different from the computed (and realized) internal rate of return. Compound interest depreciation is a method of computing depreciation designed to generate a ROI measure consistent with the internal rate of return. The following example contrasts the use of conventional depreciation methods and compound interest depreciation to measure return on investment. Although other bases of "investment" may be used to measure ROI, we use beginning-of-year book value for simplicity.

$$\text{ROI} = \frac{\text{net income of the period}}{\text{investment book value at the beginning of the period}}$$

EXAMPLE 14. The DSW Corporation acquires an asset costing $5,000. It has a five-year life and a salvage value of $200. The net *cash* benefits, including the tax shield of depreciation for tax reporting, generated by the investment over the five years are shown below.

End of Year	Net Cash Benefits (after taxes)
1	$2,450
2	1,980
3	1,460
4	980
5	460

The internal rate of return is 20 percent because

$$\$5,000 = \frac{\$2,450}{1.2} + \frac{\$1,980}{(1.2)^2} + \frac{\$1,460}{(1.2)^3} + \frac{\$980}{(1.2)^4} + \frac{\$460}{(1.2)^5} + \frac{\$200}{(1.2)^5}$$
$$= \$2,450(.83333) + \$1,980(.69444) + \$1,460(.57870)$$
$$+\$980(.48225) + \$460(.40188) + \$200(.40188)$$
$$= \$2,042 + \$1,375 + \$845 + \$473 + \$185 + \$80$$

In Exhibit 5, we have tabulated ROI for this investment as it would be calculated under straight-line, sum-of-the-year's-digits, and compound interest depreciation. Only when ROI is computed on the basis of compound interest depreciation is it equivalent in each period to the investment's internal rate of return. The calculation of compound interest depreciation is shown below.

Beginning of Year	
1	$5,000
2	$3,550 = $1,980(.83333) + $1,460(.69444) + $980(.57870) + $460(.48225) + $200(.48225)
3	$2,280 = $1,460(.8333) + $980(.69444) + $460(.57870) + $200(.57870)
4	$1,276 = $980(.83333) + $460(.69444) + $200(.69444)
5	$ 551 = $460(.83333) + $200(.83333)
6	$ 200 = salvage value

Present Value of Remaining Cash Benefits

Year	Compound Interest Depreciation (Decline in Present Value)
1	$5,000 − $3,550 = $1,450
2	$3,550 − $2,280 = $1,270
3	$2,280 − $1,276 = $1,004
4	$1,276 − $ 551 = $ 725
5	$ 551 − $ 201 = $ 350

EXHIBIT 5   Illustration of Rate of Return Calculation for Five-Year Asset Costing $5,000 with Salvage Value $200

Year (1)	Book value at start of year = cost − accumulated depreciation (2)	Net cash flow (given) (3)	Depreciation charge (calculated) (4)	Income = (3) − (4) (5)	Rate of return = (5)/(2) (6)
		STRAIGHT-LINE METHOD			
1	$5,000	$2,450	$ 960	$1,490	.298
2	4,040	1,980	960	1,020	.252
3	3,080	1,460	960	500	.162
4	2,120	980	960	20	.009
5	1,160	460	960	(500)	−.431
6	200 = salvage value				
		SUM-OF-THE-YEARS'-DIGITS METHOD			
1	$5,000	$2,450	$1,600	$ 850	.170
2	3,400	1,980	1,280	700	.206
3	2,120	1,460	960	500	.236
4	1,160	980	640	340	.293
5	520	460	320	140	.269
6	200 = salvage value				
		COMPOUND INTEREST METHOD (RATE OF RETURN = 20 PERCENT)			
1	$5,000	$2,450	$1,450	$1,000	.200
2	3,550	1,980	1,270	710	.200
3	2,280	1,460	1,004	456	.200
4	1,276	980	725	255	.200
5	551	460	350	110	.200
6	201 = salvage value (rounding error, should be $200)				

As a practical matter, compound interest depreciation may be calculated by "plugging." For example, in year 1, the unamortized investment is $5,000, the 20 percent return is $1,000, and the cash flow is $2,450. Compound interest depreciation is the difference between the cash flow and the 20 percent return on the unamortized investment: $1,450 = $2,450 − .20 × $5,000. Therefore, in Exhibit 5, column (4) = (3) − (6) × (2). Compound interest depreciation writes off an asset's cost in exact "straight-line" proportion to the number of present value dollars of benefits that have been generated by the asset during the period.

Some Approximating Methods. Situations often arise involving compound interest in which it may be desirable to use a shortcut or some method of approximation. For example, one might be concerned with how quickly a given investment will double at various rates of interest. "Doubling periods" are easily approximated with one of the following rules.

Rule of 72. An amount of money invested at i percent per period will double in $72/i$ periods. For example, at 10 percent per period, the rule says that a given sum will double in $72/10 = 7.2$ periods. This is a reasonable approximation, but not nearly as accurate as the *Rule of 69*.

Rule of 69. An amount of money invested at i percent per period will double in $69/i + .35$ periods. This approximation is accurate to one-tenth of a period for interest rates between ¼ and 100 percent per period. For example, at 10 percent per period, the rule says that a given sum will double in $69/10 + .35 = 7.25$ periods. This is quite close to the actual 7.27 periods required for a sum invested at 10 percent per period to double.

Another type of situation in which approximations can be useful is in estimating the effective interest rate implicit in an installment sale contract. In an installment sale contract, the interest and/or carrying charges are added to the price of the merchandise and the total amount is typically paid with a down payment and a series of equal cash payments. An annual simple interest rate is often quoted, multiplied by the amount to be financed and included in the total amount to be repaid. Although truth-in-lending legislation requires disclosure of the effective interest rate, the following formulas can be used either to check the quoted effective rate or to calculate the effective interest rate when truth-in-lending legislation is not applicable. Each of the next three formulas, in one way or another, fails to recognize that (1) there is no such thing as prepaid interest (attempts to repay interest in theory result in reductions in principal), or (2) each payment, in theory, is first charged to accumulated interest and the remainder, if any, is used to reduce principal.

We introduce the following notation to assist in the discussion of several approximating formulas.[9]

> n = the number of payments, excluding the down payment
> m = the number of payments in one year
> i = the annual rate of interest
> R = the payment per payment period
> B = the unpaid balance = cash price − down payment
> $I = Rn − B$ = interest charge (carrying charge).

Merchant's Formula.   This formula reflects the assumption that the periodic payments are applied first against the unpaid principal balance B and then against the interest charge I. The interest rate i is expressed as

$$i = \frac{2mI}{B(n + 1) - I(n - 1)}$$

The Constant Ratio Formula.   This formula reflects the assumption that each payment is to be applied against both the unpaid principal balance and the interest or carrying charge in the same proportion as the original unpaid principal balance and total interest charge imply. The interest rate i is expressed as

$$i = \frac{2mI}{B(n + I)}$$

The Direct Ratio Formula.   This formula expresses the annual interest rate i as

$$i = \frac{6mI}{3B(n + 1) + I(n - 1)}$$

EXAMPLE 15.   An electronic calculator sells for $360. It may be purchased with a down payment of $60 and 10 monthly installments of $35.00 each. Find the rate of interest i using each of the three formulas. In this example, $n = 10$, $m = 12$, $R = \$35$, $B = \$360 - \$60 = \$300$, $I = Rn - B = \$35(10) - \$300 = \$50$.
MERCHANT'S FORMULA:

$$i = \frac{2(12)(50)}{300(11) - 50(9)} = \frac{8}{19} = 42.1 \text{ percent}$$

[9]The discussion of these formulas is based on chap. 6 in Frank Ayres, Jr., *Mathematics of Finance*, Schaum Publishing Company, New York, 1963.

CONSTANT RATIO FORMULA:

$$i = \frac{2(12)(50)}{300(11)} = \frac{4}{11} = 36.4 \text{ percent}$$

DIRECT RATIO FORMULA:

$$i = \frac{6(12)(50)}{3(300)(11) + 50(9)} = \frac{8}{23} = 34.8 \text{ percent}$$

The true interest rate implied in this loan is 2.906 percent per month or 41.02 per year.

Rule of 78.   A third general approximating method is found in the operations of many finance companies. Specifically, finance companies wish to allocate the interest received on installment contracts to the various months of the year. The true allocation is approximated by using the rule of 78. The rule is followed by many finance companies in allocating earnings on *loans* among the months of a year on a sum-of-the-months'-digits basis. The sum of the digits from 1 through 12 is 78, so 12/78 of the year's earnings are allocated to the first month, 11/78 to the second month, and so on. As an example, consider a $1,000 loan which is fully repaid after one year. The total payments amount to $1,078, of which $78 is interest. In month 1, 12/78 ($78) = $12 would be allocated to interest. In month 2, 11/78 ($78) = $11 would be allocated, and so on.

Compound Interest in Risky Situations.   The principles of compound interest are often applied in situations where future outcomes are uncertain. The presence of risk has significant implications for capital expenditure analysis, but a thorough treatment of these issues is beyond the scope of this handbook. We will, however, deal with some topics related to mortality tables, life annuities, and their implications for pension plan accounting.

A *mortality table* tracks the life records of a large representative group of individuals. For life insurance calculations (where the conservative assumption is early death with payments soon) the mortality tables used differ from those used for annuity calculations (where the conservative assumption is a long life with many payments). Covering ages ranging from birth, age 0, up to the 100th birthday, a mortality table shows the number of individuals from the original group remaining alive at each age x (l_x) and the number who died in the year between x and $x + 1$ ($d_x = l_x - l_{x+1}$). It is assumed that the number of individuals attaining age 100 is insignificantly different from zero in most mortality tables (although some annuity tables do not assume death until age 110). From these data, we can write the *probability* that an individual who is alive at age x will live to age $x + n$ as $_np_x = l_{x+n}/l_x$. Similarly, the probability of dying at age x is written $q_x = d_x/l_x$. The probability of dying between age x and age $x + n$ is written $_nq_x = (l_x - l_{x+n})/l_x$.

Mortality tables are generally combined with compound interest tables to construct what are called *commutation tables.*[10] A single commutation table is constructed using a given mortality table and a given interest rate. The terms in commutation tables are called *commutation factors.* These factors provide the following information for a given mortality table/interest rate combination.

D_x = the present value of $1 paid to all individuals of the sample attaining age x. Letting $v^x = (1 + i)^{-x}$, then $D_x = v^x l_x$. (Typically, an annuity-based mortality table is used.)

[10]For more on these matters, see Robert E. Larson and Erwin A. Gaumnitz, *Life Insurance Mathematics,* John Wiley & Sons, New York, and Society of Actuaries, *Monetary Tables Based on the 1958 CSO Mortality Table,* The Society of Actuaries, Chicago, Ill., 1961.

N_x = The present value of \$1 paid to all individuals attaining age x, plus the present value of \$1 paid to all individuals attaining age $x + 1$ plus ...

attaining age 109, or $N_x = \sum\limits_{t=x}^{109} D_{x_t}$ (Typically, an annuity-based mortality table is used.)

C_x = the present value of \$1 paid in year $x + 1$ to all individuals dying at age x ($C_x = v^{x+1}d_x$). (Typically, a life insurance-based mortality table is used.)

M_x = the present value of \$1 paid in year $x + 1$ to all individuals dying at age x plus the present value of \$1 paid in year $x + 2$ to all individuals dying at

age $x + 1$ plus ... dying at year 99, or $M_x = \sum\limits_{t=x}^{99} C_{x_t}$ (Typically, a life insurance-based mortality table is used.)

A *life annuity* is a series of equal payments beginning at some point and continuing for all or part of the life of the *annuitant*. A *pension plan* is a contractual agreement to pay life annuities to retired employees, subject to various provisions regarding benefit levels and vesting.

Commutation tables are used to determine the amount of pension liability accruing each period. As each year passes, additional future pension liabilities are created. The commutation factors D_x and N_x represent the present value of payments of \$1 to be made to each surviving retired employee. Multiplying these factors by expected benefit levels will give the present value of the current period's pension liability which will be discharged in future years, but which is recorded and, perhaps, funded currently.

Similarly, from the point of view of life insurance contracts, the commutation factors C_x and M_x represent the present value of payments of \$1 to be made to those policyholders who die in future years. This enables life insurance companies to compute net premiums (amounts which must be contributed by living policyholders to pay the claims of policyholders who die) as well as the present value of the companies' future liabilities under the terms of existing policies. The premium charged the policyowner is the net premium plus an overhead factor.

BIBLIOGRAPHY

Ayres, Frank, Jr.: *Mathematics of Finance,* Schaum's Outline Series, McGraw-Hill Book Company, New York, 1963.

Bierman, Harold, Jr., and Seymour Smidt: *The Capital Budgeting Decision,* 4th ed., The Macmillan Company, New York, 1975.

Davidson, Sidney, James S. Schindler, Clyde P. Stickney, and Roman L. Weil: *Accounting: The Language of Business,* 2nd ed., Thomas Horton and Daughters, Glen Ridge, N.J., 1975.

Davidson, Sidney, James S. Schindler, and Roman L. Weil: *Fundamentals of Accounting,* 5th ed., The Dryden Press, Hinsdale, Ill., 1975.

Dopuch, Nicholas, Jacob G. Birnberg, and Joel Demski: *Cost Accounting,* 2nd ed., Harcourt Brace Jovanovich, New York, 1974.

Hertz, David B.: "Investment Policies That Pay Off," *Harvard Business Review,* January–February 1968, pp. 96–108.

Hummel, Paul M., and Charles L. Seebeck, Jr.: *Mathematics of Finance,* 3rd ed., McGraw-Hill Book Company, New York, 1971.

Society of Actuaries, *Monetary Tables Based on the 1958 CSO Mortality Table,* The Society of Actuaries, Chicago, Ill., 1961. (Between 50 and 60 volumes published at various dates are currently available.)

Chapter 9

Basic Concepts of Statistics and Hypothesis Testing for Auditing

ROBERT K. ELLIOTT
Partner, Peat, Marwick, Mitchell & Co.

AUDITING AND STATISTICS

Audit Objectives.   All auditors, whether independent public accountants, government auditors, or internal auditors, must reach two important types of conclusions in the course of their audits: (1) whether financial representations are substantially correct and (2) whether systems are operating in accordance with prescribed requirements. The determination of what is a significant error and the acceptable risks of erroneous conclusions may differ according to the purpose of an audit, as may the relative importance of the two types of conclusions. This chapter discusses statistical methods of forming conclusions of these two types from partial (test-basis) examinations.

Because (1) auditors frequently confront enormous masses of data and (2) some level of imprecision can usually be accepted in auditing, nearly all audits are based on partial examinations. The resulting partial (or sample) examination *must* introduce an element of uncertainty into auditors' conclusions, for they must draw inferences from incomplete information. This is true whether or not auditors use statistical sampling procedures.

The uncertainty resulting from partial examination may frustrate the auditor's desire for correct conclusions in two distinct ways:

1. Financial representations may be correct (or a system may be functioning as prescribed), but the auditor may conclude they are incorrect (or that the system is not functioning as prescribed).

2. Financial representations may be substantially in error (or a system may be functioning substantially differently from the prescribed method), but the auditor may conclude they are correct (or that the system is functioning as prescribed).

The auditor who can define what constitutes a substantially wrong conclusion, and what levels of risk (greater than zero) of making the two errors above are acceptable, can then use statistical auditing procedures. In discussing the determination of "substantially erroneous conclusions" and "risk levels" in this chapter, the general objectives of independent public accountants have been most explicitly recognized. If and when these objectives are inappropriate for other types of auditing, the discussion will still be fully applicable if the reader substitutes another determination of substantial error and acceptable risk levels.

Professional Standards.   The use of statistical sampling methods by certified public accountants is governed by *Statement on Auditing Standards No. 1 (SAS 1)* published by the American Institute of Certified Public Accountants (AICPA). All auditors, whether or not certified public accountants, should be familiar with Section 320A, "Relationship of Statistical Sampling to Generally Accepted Auditing Standards," and Section 320B, "Precision and Reliability for Statistical Sampling in Auditing."

This Statement of the AICPA makes clear that statistical sampling is not a fundamentally different audit approach and that its use is permissible rather than mandatory under generally accepted auditing standards.

Substantive Versus Compliance Tests.   Substantive audit tests (as defined in Section 320.70 of *SAS 1*) are those in which the feature of audit interest is the monetary amount of errors that would affect the financial statements being audited, including both unintentional errors and intentional irregularities. By definition, therefore, substantive tests are those concerned with reaching conclusions about whether representations of financial amounts are substantially correct. Therefore, statistical substantive tests should normally use *variables sampling*[1]

---

[1] A "variable" is the quantitative characteristic of a population element, for example, the amount of an account or the number of days it has been outstanding. "Variables sampling" is statistical sampling designed to estimate or test a population quantity (either total or average) based upon the sample.

because the conclusions of variables sampling are stated in monetary-unit terms and can therefore be directly related to financial statement impact.

Compliance tests (as defined in Section 320.50 of *SAS 1*) are those in which the feature of audit interest is the extent of compliance with a prescribed system. By definition, therefore, compliance tests are those concerned with reaching conclusions about whether systems are operating in accordance with prescribed requirements. Therefore, statistical compliance tests normally use *attribute sampling*[2] because the conclusions of attribute sampling are stated in terms of rates of compliance (or noncompliance).

Cautions in Use of Statistical Sampling.   Although the basic concepts in statistical sampling are not difficult to grasp, the application of these concepts may rapidly become complex. Also, the auditor's intuitions in statistical sampling may often prove erroneous. Because of the importance of most audit conclusions and the adverse consequences of erroneous conclusions, it is essential that auditors contemplating the use of statistical sampling techniques be qualified to design and execute valid sampling plans. This chapter is intended as a reference source or refresher in statistical considerations. It should not be used as a self-sufficient guide to statistical auditing for auditors without prior training in statistical auditing.

Statistical sampling is sometimes thought by auditors to reduce the need for, or supplant, judgment in the audit process. That this is not the case is made clear by the following quotation from *SAS 1* (Section 320A.17):

> The competence of evidential matter as referred to in the third standard of field work is solely a matter of auditing judgment that is not comprehended in the statistical design and evaluation of an audit sample. In a strict sense, the statistical evaluation relates only to the probability that items having certain characteristics in terms of monetary amounts, quantities, errors, or other features of interest will be included in the sample—not to the auditor's treatment of such items. Consequently, the use of statistical sampling does not directly affect the auditor's decisions as to the auditing procedures to be performed, the acceptability of the evidential matter obtained with respect to individual items in the sample, or the action which might be taken in the light of the nature and cause of particular errors.

As implied in the preceding quotation, auditors should not confuse their evaluation of the strength of audit evidence with the reliability of the statistical statement about that evidence. For example, assume that the auditor takes quite a large sample, sufficient to give 95 percent reliability that the conclusion is accurate within 1 percent of the true value of the population, but applies a very weak procedure to the sample items selected. The apparent strength of the statistical conclusion should not deceive the auditor into believing that the evidence is stronger than it, in fact, is. The statistical conclusion can be given substantial weight in forming audit conclusions only if the audit procedures performed on each sample item are in fact procedures highly likely to detect those conditions of interest to the auditor. In this regard, the auditor should consider with great care the weight to be given to the evidence received from confirmations from third parties because of the possibility of response errors in such procedures.

IMPORTANT STATISTICAL CONCEPTS

Certain statistical concepts that relate to the design of sampling plans and the interpretation of results must be understood in order to use statistical audit tests. They are discussed below.

[2]An "attribute" is any qualitative characteristic of a population element, for example whether or not a given document was processed in accordance with the prescribed system. "Attribute sampling" is statistical sampling designed to estimate or test a proportion (rate of occurrence) based upon the sample.

Population.   The results of a sample or test cannot be projected beyond the area from which the sample was drawn. The area from which a sample is drawn is known statistically as the *population* (or, sometimes, *universe* or *field*).

The precise definition of the population in light of the test objective is of utmost importance. If statistical sampling is applied to an improperly defined or incomplete population, unsatisfactory audit results may be obtained.

The auditor's ultimate objective in any particular audit test may be to draw a conclusion about the correct balance of a given account. The auditor would therefore like to define the population as all of the components making up the correct balance. Normally, however, there is no convenient way to sample the true components of a balance, and the auditor must be satisfied with sampling the recorded components only. Since the population actually sampled is normally the recorded population elements, the statistical conclusion is valid only as to the recorded population (since unrecorded items had no chance of being included in the sample). Conclusions about the recorded population are useful to the auditor in forming an opinion, but are not always sufficient because the unrecorded population elements may be material. Therefore, in every case, the auditor must perform supplemental tests to determine the completeness of the recorded population. Among the common supplemental tests are evaluation of internal control over recording of transactions; sales, purchases, shipping, receiving, and production cutoffs; cash receipts and disbursements cutoffs; and tests for unrecorded liabilities. Only if these tests do not indicate unrecorded amounts can the auditor be satisfied that the population sampled was reasonably complete. If the tests do disclose significant unrecorded amounts, however, such amounts must be evaluated and considered in conjunction with the statistical results to form an overall conclusion about the account being audited.

Once an item has been selected for sampling, the auditor must audit it in one way or another; every selected item must be followed up to some conclusion.[3] If items not easily located for auditing are ignored, then the population sampled consists only of the easily locatable items, and the statistical conclusion would apply only to that population. Such a conclusion would usually have no audit relevance. Failure to audit all selected items would probably bias the sample result as applied to the entire population. This is particulary true in cases where the unlocated items are missing precisely because they are unusual, troublesome, or, worst of all, fictitious.

The necessity of tracking down all selected items may test the auditor's ingenuity; however, there are usually alternative routes to obtaining evidence about a sample item. If, after exhaustive searching, it becomes obvious that no evidence can be obtained with respect to a given sample item, then the auditor should assume the worst about that item. In the case of an asset, the worst assumption is that the item is worthless. In the case of a liability, the exposure is virtually unlimited, and this makes statistical auditing of liabilities somewhat more difficult. However, it may sometimes be possible (e.g., with certain accounts payable and accrued liabilities) to estimate the maximum exposure on missing sample items by analysis of related evidence. In other cases (e.g., time deposit accounts of a banking institution) it would not normally be possible to estimate the maximum liability for missing sample items; in such cases, statistical variables estimation procèdures may be inappropriate.

Although all selected items must be audited, it does not follow that the originally contemplated audit procedure must be applied to all items. For example, where the audit procedure is confirmation, some accounts will inevitably fail to confirm.

---

[3]There are statistical methods of relaxing this requirement under certain circumstances, but these methods are generally impractical for audit use.

If the auditor can be satisfied as to these nonresponding accounts by means of alternative auditing procedures, the requirement to audit all items can still be met, even though confirmation would have been the preferable procedure. However, the alternative procedures should be complete, not a test within a test. For example, if 100 account balance receivable confirmations are not returned, it would not be adequate to apply alternative tests only to 50 (or even 90) of these accounts, nor to apply alternative procedures to only selected open items within all 100 accounts. All components of the selected items must be audited to some conclusion.

Because every sample item must be audited, *it is not possible to use negative confirmation requests for statistical variables estimation.* There is no way of identifying whether an unreturned confirmation is a nonresponse or an affirmation. With positive confirmations, all nonresponses must be followed up, so there is no danger of inadvertently considering them to be good responses.

Where it is evident in advance that a population contains some items which may not be verifiable by the proposed audit test, it may not be appropriate to use statistical variables estimation procedures to audit that population. If the items that are not verifiable are known in advance, it may be possible to exclude them from the statistically sampled population and audit them by other means, while applying statistical sampling to the remainder of the population. In such cases, the results of the two separate procedures must be combined to reach an overall conclusion on the account being audited.

It is important to define the population so as to be consistent with the audit objective. For example, if the characteristic being tested is internal control over inventory purchases, it would not make sense to define the population as the voucher register, because the voucher register would include many items unrelated to inventory.

The most important point to remember about the population is that statistical conclusions can be related only to the population from which the sample items were selected. The conclusions cannot be extended to items not in the population, nor can they be applied to individual subpopulations within the population being audited.

Sampling Unit.   A population is comprised of *sampling units.* The sampling units consist of the individual elements in the population that will be sampled. They may be elements such as documents, account balances, open items, and entries, each comprising one unit in the sample.

More specifically, the sampling unit is the element in the population whose characteristics are to be measured or determined in order to estimate those characteristics for the population.

In a variables test, the sampling unit may be any element, provided that the sum of all such elements equals the total value to be estimated. For example, the auditor who wishes to verify the total balance of accounts receivable could select any of the following as the sampling unit: branch store (selected branches would then be verified in total), total customer balance (which is a common method when using confirmations), open invoices (which may be more productive if customers are unable to confirm total balances), line items on open invoices (which may be necessary in the case of very complex invoicing procedures), or any other practical element. The designation of the sampling unit for a *variables* test is solely a matter of convenience, economy, and effectiveness, because sampling units at any level of detail (or aggregation), so long as they are mutually exclusive and exhaustive of the population, will result in a valid estimate of the total quantity being audited.

However, the definition of the sampling unit for an *attribute* test must be considered in the light of the test objective. For instance, if the objective of the test is to determine the frequency with which disbursement vouchers occur without the proper authorizing signature, the voucher itself becomes the sampling unit, and the presence or absence of the signature is the characteristic measured. On the other hand, if the objective is to determine that line items on the voucher, of which there may be several, are authorized items, a line item on a voucher becomes the sampling unit, and there may be several sampling units on a single voucher. Thus, it is apparent that the objective of the attribute test determines the sampling unit as well as the characteristic of the sampling unit which is to be measured.

In two-stage sampling, two levels of sampling unit are defined—primary and secondary. For example, in verifying the asset, loan balance, of a finance company, the primary sampling unit may be the branch (a sample of branches is drawn), and the secondary sampling unit may be the individual loan balance (a sample of individual loans within the sampled branches is drawn). When using this "sample-within-a-sample" approach, the mathematics of multistage sampling must be applied. For further information on this approach, see Chapter 10 of *Sampling Techniques* by William G. Cochran.

Sampling Error. Whenever the auditor makes a partial (or sample) examination of a population, there is a risk that the sample is not exactly representative of the entire population. This is true even if 999 out of 1,000 items are examined. The "sampling error" is the difference between the estimate of the population value based upon the sample and an estimate[4] of the population value that would result from applying the same methods to the entire population. *Sampling error* arises only because the examination does not include all population items. In practice, the true value of a population will never be known (otherwise there would be no need for the statistical sample), so the exact sampling error will never be known. However, the unique feature of statistical sampling is that the probable magnitude of sampling error can be calculated and, by adjusting the sample size, can be made to conform with audit objectives. Sampling error also exists in judgmental audit samples, but in such samples it cannot be measured.

The way in which probable sampling error is commonly expressed is the "precision interval." For a hypothetical population, assume that a statistician has computed that 95 percent of all possible sample estimates of a given sample size would be within $10,000 of the true (but unknown) population value. Assume, too, that the statistical estimate of the population total based on one sample of the specified size is $950,000 and that the recorded amount is $1,000,000. The "statistical precision interval" is then $950,000 plus or minus $10,000 at 95 percent reliability. If the true population value were $1,000,000, there is only a 5 percent probability of achieving a statistical estimate as far off as $990,000 or $1,010,000 and a negligible probability of achieving an estimate as far off as $950,000. The auditor is therefore likely to conclude that the true value is not $1,000,000, but is closer to $950,000. In this case, 95 percent is the "reliability" of the estimate, $10,000 is the "precision" of the estimate, $940,000 is the "lower precision limit," $950,000 is the "statistical point estimate," and $960,000 is the "upper precision limit."

Reliability and precision are inversely related; thus, for any given sample size, if the precision limits are made less precise (for example, increased from $10,000 to $15,000) the reliability that the true population value is contained in the precision interval is increased (for example, from 95 percent to 99.7 percent).

Nonsampling Error. When considering the risks of a statistical audit procedure, the auditor must also recognize the possibility, or even likelihood, that the results obtained may be inaccurate because of mistakes made in inspecting or examining the items in the sample. This is referred to as "nonsampling error." Human

---

[4]If there were no nonsampling error (see below for definition), this estimate would be the true value of the population.

fallibility being what it is, mistakes are likely to occur through fatigue, improper understanding of the assignment, ambiguous documents, or otherwise. Should the fact that a voucher was not correct be overlooked by the auditor, the conclusion drawn from the sampling will naturally be wrong. Similarly, incorrect counts would result in an incorrect inventory valuation.

Unfortunately, the risk in nonsampling error is not generally subject to measurement. However, this same risk would exist even if 100 percent of the data in the entire population were examined. Actually, there may be less nonsampling error in a sample than in a complete examination because greater pains can be taken to eliminate many of the possibilities of error when the volume of items to be examined is relatively small.

This point is well understood by statisticians. Roberts[5] says, "A good deal of evidence suggests that non-sampling errors . . . are often more substantial than sampling errors. Since a sample involves a relatively small administrative apparatus as compared with a census [a complete enumeration], it may be possible to reduce the non-sampling errors. . . . One famous example of a sample outperforming a census occurred in the province of Bengal in India, during the late 1930's, when the purpose was to measure the size of the jute harvest. When the true size eventually was ascertained through warehouse records, the census was found to have erred by 20% while the concurrent sample survey came within ½ percent."

The total error inherent in a statistical audit procedure is a composite of the sampling error and the nonsampling error. The probable sampling error can be measured statistically and reduced to a level compatible with the audit objective. Since the nonsampling error cannot be statistically measured and controlled, it is necessary to exercise care to keep it to a minimum so that the audit test produces a valid result. Several precautions are helpful to minimize nonsampling error:

■ Sample objectives and the definition of characteristics to be estimated should be stated very clearly;

■ Auditors doing the detail work should be clearly and thoroughly instructed and should be impressed with the need for careful and complete work; and

■ Detail work should be carefully reviewed.

These precautions should reduce nonsampling error to negligible amounts. The precautions are easier to state, however, than to enforce. Of course, nonsampling error could invalidate any audit work, whether statistical or judgmental; therefore, these same precautions would be applicable to nonstatistical audit work.

Random Sampling. Satisfactory statistical results cannot be achieved unless a random sample is drawn, since only then are the laws of probability, on which statistical mathematics is based, operative. A random sample is one in which each sampling unit has a known, nonzero probability of selection, and each possible sample of a given size has an equal probability of selection. Some examples of random sampling include unrestricted random sampling (all items in the population have an equal probability of selection), stratified random sampling (the population is broken down into mutually exclusive and exhaustive subpopulations called *strata* and unrestricted random sampling is employed in each stratum), and selection with probability proportional to size (all items have a probability of selection directly proportional to their size and all items of the same size have an equal probability of selection). Mere avoidance of personal subjectivity through haphazard choice of items does not provide a random sample.

Systematic sampling (selecting items at equal intervals after a random start) is not random sampling, although in many cases it may be close enough for practical

[5] Harry V. Roberts, *Conversational Statistics*, Hewlett-Packard Company, Cupertino, Calif., 1974, p. 30.

purposes. Before using such a nonrandom technique as a convenient substitute for unrestricted random selection, the auditor should be satisfied that the population is in random order with respect to the characteristic being measured and that the pattern inherent in the systematic sampling interval does not coincide with any pattern in the population.

Selecting the Sample. After a sampling plan has been designed and the sample size has been computed, it becomes necessary to draw the sample. In order that the sample be random, some method of random selection must be devised. This involves selecting random numbers and matching them against the population in such a way that the desired probabilities of selection are achieved.

In principle, it should be easy to select numbers from a random number table, establish some correspondence with the population of audit interest, and draw the items. In practice, however, such manual methods are time consuming, prone to errors, and generally impractical for all but very small samples. Any auditor who must repeatedly draw samples should use some form of computerized selection plan to minimize both the cost and the possibility of errors in sample selection.

Many time-sharing vendors have programs available to select random numbers. In any case, the auditor can enter a random number selection program onto any time-sharing system. Volume VI of the AICPA publication, *An Auditor's Approach to Statistical Sampling,* includes the complete code of a program to select random numbers; this program can easily be entered onto most time-sharing systems.

Many auditors have access to generalized computer audit software that incorporates a random selection feature; such systems can be used effectively where the data to be audited are in machine-readable form.

A third possibility would be for the auditor to program a random selection routine which is used to process auditee data files and select samples. A suitable method of generating random numbers in such programs is the *power residue* method, explained in detail in the publication, *Random Number Generation and Testing,* published by International Business Machines Corporation, Technical Publications Department (document GC20-8011-0).

STATISTICAL SUBSTANTIVE TESTS

Sample Design. In designing a substantive sampling plan, the auditor must consider whether the audit objective is (1) to test the reasonableness of a financial representation (e.g., the auditee's purported receivable balance) or (2) to make an independent estimate of some amount (e.g., an estimate of the FIFO inventory when the books are kept at latest invoice price). In the first case the auditor desires to accept the auditee's representation without adjustment if it is reasonably correct, and to propose an adjustment only if it is probable that there might be a material error in the amount as stated by the auditee. In this case, the auditor should use a *hypothesis-test* approach to the audit, which statistically discriminates between the hypothesis that the amount as represented is correct and the alternative hypothesis that the amount is materially misstated.

On the other hand, when the auditee does not state an amount which purports to be correct (such as when improper accounting principles have been used, or numerous errors are known to exist in the records), the auditor should use a statistical *estimation* approach in order to develop an estimate of the correct account balance. Ordinarily, in such cases the auditor would intend to propose an adjustment to bring the account balance into agreement with the statistical estimate.

The approach chosen for the statistical substantive test—hypothesis test versus estimation—governs the tolerable magnitude of sampling error and the decision rule to be used, once the statistical results are obtained. The choice of hypothesis test versus estimation does not, however, influence other design features (such as the basis and extent of stratification, the method of selecting and auditing sample items, or the method of computing the statistical point estimate and the standard error of that estimate).

This chapter deals principally with audit considerations in determining the tolerable magnitude of sampling error and appropriate decision rules to use. Chapter 10 of this handbook deals with other design considerations, such as stratification, computational methods, and sample size calculations.

Definition of Error in Substantive Test.   Since the feature of audit interest in a substantive test is the monetary amount of errors that would affect the financial statements being audited, a sample item is considered to be in error if it contains a monetary error of any amount. A monetary error would include an item recorded at the wrong amount or entered into the wrong account or entered in the wrong period. Another way of looking at a monetary error is that it is any error that would require an adjustment in the financial statements if the concept of materiality were abolished (i.e., any amount, no matter how small, would be required to be adjusted). When sampling from an account, even small errors must be considered, because their effect must be projected to all the items not selected.

If an auditor found an item misclassified between balance sheet accounts, that would be considered a monetary error. On the other hand, if an auditor found an item misclassified between subsidiary accounts (say, individual accounts receivable) but within the correct general ledger account, that would not ordinarily be considered a monetary error because it would have no effect upon the financial statement balance. However, the auditor should nevertheless consider the effect such an error would have upon the evaluation of internal control.

Valuation Approaches.   The principal source of entries into books of accounts is the recording of bona fide transactions. Although various accrual and valuation entries are made to convert the basic transaction accounting records to financial statements, the accounting records are essentially transaction-based. However, the auditor's report attests not merely to the results of transactions, but also to certain economic facts recognized in the financial statements.

For example, an account receivable resulting from a valid transaction may be a legally enforceable receivable based on a valid transaction, but the customer may be bankrupt and unable to pay; therefore, there may be no economic receivable. The auditor can determine the correct net balance of a given asset account in either of two ways:

1. Estimate the net balance directly; or
2. Estimate the gross balance and the required valuation allowance separately, and then determine the net balance.

To see how these two approaches would be applied in a statistical audit, an illustration of each method is given below for accounts receivable.

Net Valuation Method.   For each account selected, confirm and perform other audit tests related to collectibility and valuation, and for each account selected, estimate the *net realizable value*. From these results, estimate statistically the total net realizable value. (In many cases, of course, it may be difficult to determine a net value for each account, so this method may not be appropriate. It would ordinarily be more practicable for inventory, for example, than for receivables because it is generally possible to obtain the current market value for each item in inventory, whereas it may not be possible to estimate the ultimate realization of each individual receivable.) Although this method will result in a statistically valid conclusion, the differences located in the audit will usually cause the originally determined sample size to be inadequate, thus requiring additional items to be audited to complete the test.

Gross-Less-Allowance Valuation Method.   For each account selected, confirm and establish the legally enforceable obligation, without regard to collectibility. From these results, estimate the total gross receivable balance. Then by other auditing procedures, such as an aging analysis, determine the valuation allowance required to bring the gross balance down to the net realizable value. (This approach will usually be preferable when using statistical methods.)

Although either of the above methods is a valid audit approach, it is important that the statement of statistical objectives identify which is being used. In the first case, the values to be statistically evaluated would be net realizable amounts, while in the second, they would be gross amounts. Therefore, different audit procedures would be required. If auditors on the job misunderstand which method is being used, they may invalidate the test by using the wrong amounts in the statistical evaluation, or by mixing the two methods inadvertently.

100-Percent Stratum.   Most auditors, even in judgment sampling, examine all sampling units that are individually significant. Statistically, there are two good reasons to do this: (1) It reduces the variability of the population to be sampled, thus reducing the sample size and (2) it improves the stability of the standard error of the estimate, thus maintaining the target risk levels of the sampling plan. A useful rule of thumb is to place all sampling units with amounts greater than four or five times the average sampling unit amount into a stratum to be examined 100 percent. (Note that there may be none or very few of such items in many accounting populations.)

Auditors sometimes allocate items to a 100-percent stratum for reasons other than size, for example, items that are old, obsolete, or otherwise attract the auditor's attention. This procedure is perfectly appropriate and statistically valid. The auditor can arbitrarily assign any sampling units to a 100-percent stratum before sampling without introducing statistical bias. However, once the sample has been drawn, it is inappropriate to move items retroactively from the sampled strata to the 100-percent stratum based on sample findings.

Normal Distribution of Sample Estimates.   The mathematical approaches in this chapter are all based upon the use of sampling techniques that result in normally distributed sample estimates with stable estimates of the standard error. Certain sampling methods do not meet these requirements, either because of characteristics of the underlying populations or because they are based upon other mathematical principles. Exhibit 1 summarizes the conditions under which various sampling methods meet these requirements.

EXHIBIT 1   Conditions Under Which Normal Theory Applies to Selected Sampling Methods

Name of sampling method	Conditions under which normal theory applies
Mean-per-unit	Extreme values assigned to 100-percent stratum
Auxiliary information estimators (ratio, difference, linear regression)	Extreme values assigned to 100-percent stratum and error rate in population high enough so there is a reasonably large* expected number of errors in the sample. If few or no errors are expected (or found), normal theory does not apply.
Dollar unit sampling (also referred to as cumulative monetary amounts sampling)	Never. Based on mathematical methods not employing normal theory.

*The question of what constitutes a "reasonably large" number of errors is currently under research, so no definitive answer can be given. Some auditors prefer up to 50 errors, others lesser numbers.

The significance of normal theory is that, if it applies, the auditor can use it to make probability statements and draw statistical inferences. For example, assume that an auditor is sampling from accounts receivable with a true value of $1,000,-000. (Of course the true value would not be known, otherwise there would be no need to sample.) Assume also that the auditor has taken a sample and computed the standard error of estimate[6] to be $20,000. The auditor who uses estimates that are normally distributed knows that estimates from all possible samples of the type and size being taken are normally distributed about the true value. Further, if the sampling procedure produces a stable estimate of the standard error, then the auditor knows that the normal distribution of sample estimates about the true value will have a standard deviation of about $20,000 ("about" because there is also some sampling error in the estimated standard error). If the true standard deviation of sample results is $20,000, then a sampling procedure producing estimates in the range $19,000 to $21,000 would be reasonably stable while one producing estimates in the range $10,000 to $30,000 would be so unstable as to be unusable.

Using the assumed facts in the preceding paragraph, we can plot the distribution of all possible sample results (of the type and size taken by the auditor) as in Figure 1.

FIGURE 1

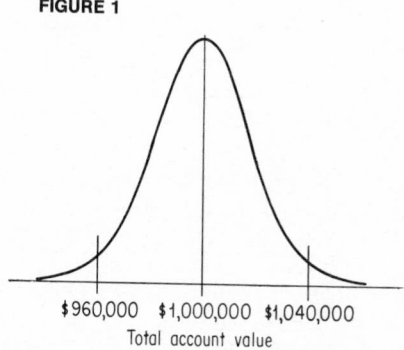

$960,000 $1,000,000 $1,040,000
Total account value

What is the probability, under these conditions, of obtaining a sample estimate of $1,050,000 or greater? In order to find the probability, we must convert these facts into the same units as used in a standard normal table, which we do by computing a Z value.

$$Z = \frac{\$1,050,000 - \$1,000,000}{\$20,000}$$
$$= 2.5$$

The Z value simply expresses the dollar difference as number of standard deviations. We look up 2.5 in a standard normal table (Chapter 10, Exhibit 6) and find that the probability of a sample estimate less than 2.5 standard deviations above the mean ($1,050,000 in this example) is .99379. Conversely, there is only a .00621 probability of a value more than 2.5 standard deviations above the mean

---

[6]In this chapter, the term "standard error of estimate" is used only in the sense of the standard error of the estimated population *total* value, and is the value computed from the sample that is expected to approximate the standard deviation of the distribution of estimates of total value. This is done because auditors typically consider total errors rather than mean errors; the result is more convenient formulas and calculations. The standard error of the estimated total is obtained from the "standard error of the mean" by multiplying by the number of items in the population. Consider the example given in Chapter 10, Exhibit 8. There the mean estimate is $21.17 and the standard error of the mean estimate is $.976. Both of these figures can be converted to estimates of the total population value by multiplying by 100, the number of items in the population. Thus, the estimated population total value is $2,117 (= 100 × $21.17) and the standard error of the estimated total is $97.60 (= 100 × $.976).

($1,050,000 or greater in the example). If we actually obtained an estimate as high as $1,050,000, therefore, we would probably conclude that we were not sampling from a population whose true value was $1,000,000.

Hypothesis Testing.   The purpose of a hypothesis test is to discriminate between two alternative hypotheses:

1. H_0: The account balance as stated (book value) is correct.
2. H_1: The book value is in error by a material amount.

Unless all items comprising the total book value are examined, there is some risk due to sampling error of accepting H_0 as true when in fact H_1 is true. In other words, there is some risk of accepting as correct a balance that is materially in error; this is defined as the β (beta) risk. There is also the possibility of rejecting H_0 as false when it is true, the risk of rejecting a correct balance. This is defined as the α (alpha) risk.

The following table shows the relationship of the α and β risks:

	Book Value	
Audit conclusion	Correct	In error by a material amount
Book value is correct	conclusion correct	β risk
Book value is materially in error	α risk	conclusion correct

To conduct a statistical hypothesis test, it is necessary to specify the amount considered material (M) and the acceptable levels of α and β risks. On the basis of these values, the auditor can compute the target standard error of the estimated total value (SE_T) which must be achieved in the sample to execute the hypothesis test. From that required standard error, the necessary sample size can be estimated using the methods described in Chapter 10.

Required Standard Error of Estimate.   Suppose that the book value (BV) is correct, and thus equal to the true value (TV). Any sample estimate of the total value will result in acceptance of the book value if the estimate lies within $\pm A$ (the acceptance range) of the book value; otherwise the book value will be rejected. The distribution of all possible sample estimates drawn from the population can be illustrated as in Figure 2.

FIGURE 2

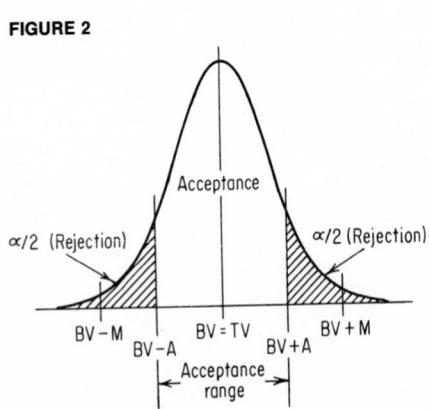

In other words, of all possible samples, a proportion represented by α will yield an estimate of the total value that is outside the predefined acceptance range of $BV \pm A$. This is the α risk.

Because the sample estimates are normally distributed, the α risk, target standard error, and acceptance range can be related as follows (note that Z_x is the number of standard deviations beyond which an area of x is left in the tail, as determined from a standard normal table):

$$A = Z_{\alpha/2} \times SE_T \qquad (1)$$

Now suppose that the book value is in error by exactly a material amount (M). Again the decision rule will be to accept the book value if the sample estimate is within $\pm A$ of the book value and to reject the book value otherwise. The distribution of sample estimates will now be as shown in Figure 3. (Note that Figure 3 shows the situation when $TV = BV - M$; the equivalent situation when $TV = BV + M$ is not illustrated because it is just a mirror image of this figure.) Most samples will result in an estimate that lies in the unshaded portion of the distribution, and will therefore result in the proper rejection of the book value.

FIGURE 3

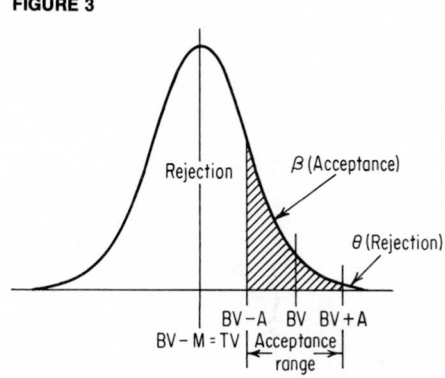

Of all possible samples, a proportion represented by β will yield an estimate that lies within $\pm A$ of the book value, ignoring θ (see below). Each of these samples will give rise to an acceptance of the book value even though it is materially in error. This is the β risk.

There is also the remote possibility of a sample result lying in the extreme tail (θ), and such a result would also lead to the rejection of the book value. However, this possibility is ignored in practice, as θ is negligibly small as long as $\alpha + \beta \leq .60$ (which is typical of most auditing applications).

Again, because the sample estimates are normally distributed, and remembering that θ is negligibly small, the β risk, target standard error, and acceptance range can be related as follows:

$$A = M - Z_\beta \times SE_T \qquad (2)$$

By combining equations (1) and (2), we find that the target standard error for a hypothesis test is as follows:

$$SE_T = \frac{M}{Z_{\alpha/2} + Z_\beta}$$

Recall that M is the dollar amount of a material error. Exhibit 2 provides common Z values to assist in making this calculation.

The auditor must select sufficient sample items to be sure that this target standard error is achieved. When the requirement is met, it is possible to decide whether to accept or reject the book value based on whether the statistically estimated total value lies within the acceptance range or not.

EXHIBIT 2   Z Values for Computing SE_T

α	$Z_{\alpha/2}$	β	Z_β
.05	1.96	.05	1.65
.10	1.65	.10	1.28
.15	1.44	.15	1.04
.20	1.28	.20	.84
.25	1.15	.25	.67
.30	1.04	.30	.52
.35	.94	.35	.39
.40	.84	.40	.25
.45	.76	.45	.13
.50	.67	.50	.00

The accept/reject decision can be shown diagramatically, assuming $\alpha = .05$, and $\beta = .05$, by combining the two previous diagrams, Figures 2 and 3, into Figure 4.

FIGURE 4

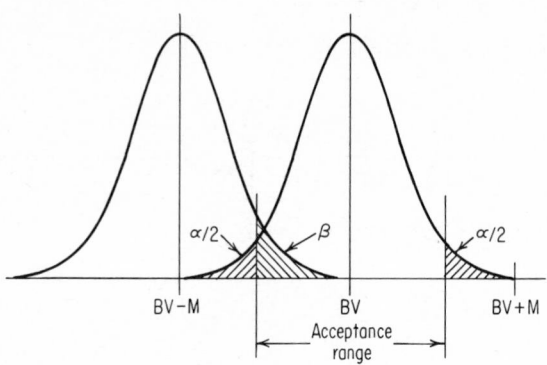

If $\alpha = .05$ and $\beta = .50$, the decision rule would be reflected by the diagram in Figure 5.

FIGURE 5

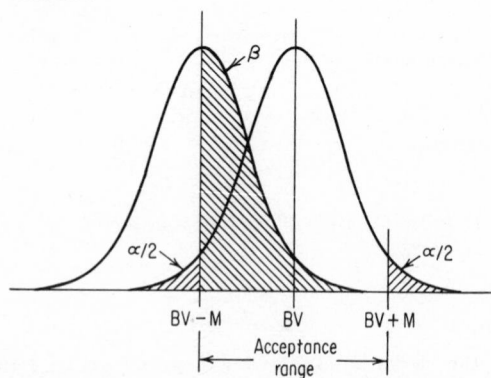

Thus, based on the auditor's specification of M (the amount considered material), α (the risk of rejecting a correct balance), and β (the risk of accepting a balance materially in error), a statistical hypothesis test can be designed. The following sections of this chapter deal with considerations in specifying these values.

The hypothesis test described above is a simple alternative hypothesis test, which considers only two absolute amounts of error: zero and exactly a material amount. In reality, the amount of error in an account balance may vary from zero to infinity. The auditor should be aware of the probabilities of accepting as correct account balances in error by various possible amounts. These probabilities can be calculated for any specified sampling plan, and can be plotted as an "operating characteristic curve." Curves are plotted in Figure 6 for the sampling plans α = .05, β = .05 and α = .05, β = .50—two typical audit sampling plans.

FIGURE 6   Operating characteristics of selected sampling plans.

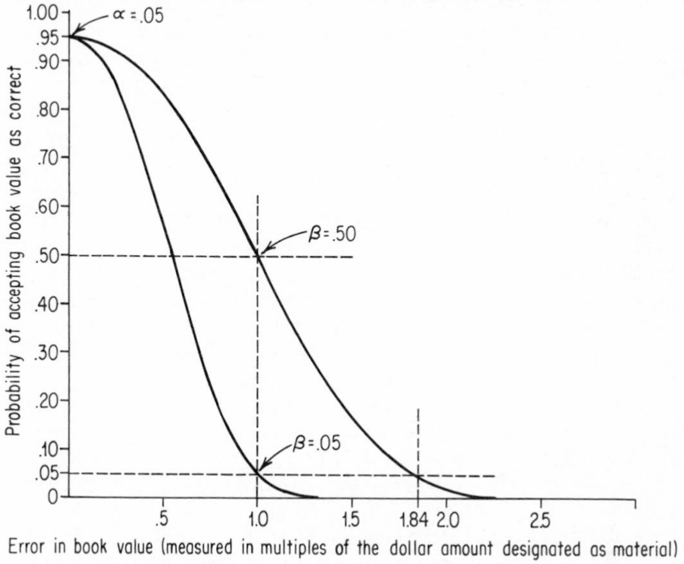

Error in book value (measured in multiples of the dollar amount designated as material)

From inspection of Figure 6, the auditor can determine the probability of accepting book values in error by any amount. A desirable feature of these sampling plans is that the probability of accepting an account balance as correct becomes smaller and smaller as the error in such an account balance becomes larger and larger. For example, even when the auditor uses the sampling plan with α = .05 and β = .50, the probability of accepting the book value as correct is only .05 when the error is 1.84 times the measure of materiality.

Thus it can be seen that even though the auditor specifies acceptance probabilities for only two error levels (zero and M) in designing a hypothesis test, the resulting sampling plan is really a continuous range of acceptance probabilities over a continuous range of error magnitudes.

M: The Measure of Materiality. The amount considered material for the audit test must be specified because that measure defines the alternative hypothesis to be tested:

$$H_0: TV = BV$$
$$H_1: TV = BV \pm M$$

Whenever the auditor draws a conclusion about an entire population after examining only a part of it, the conclusion is subject to sampling error, which occurs solely because the entire population was not examined. With statistical sampling, the probable magnitude of sampling error can be measured and, through adjustment of the sample size, controlled. The concept of materiality is, therefore, important in statistical sampling because it governs the amount of sampling error that can be tolerated in an audit. If, for example, $100,000 is considered material with respect to a set of financial statements, the aggregate sampling error cannot be more than $100,000, for otherwise an error in excess of a material amount could exist in the financial statements with the possibility of not being discovered by the auditor.

This requirement has been recognized in *SAS 1,* Section 320B.27, which states:

> The upper precision limit for errors in an individual substantive test should be established so as to be consistent with the overall audit objective to obtain reasonable assurance that the financial statements taken as a whole are not materially in error.

To perform a statistical variables test, the auditor must therefore specify the measure of materiality for the test. Some auditors may object to the requirement to specify the measure of materiality in advance of performing the test, but it requires no more information than, and is conceptually similar to, evaluating errors after their discovery. The auditor must have some standards for specifying materiality so these standards can be applied in advance to specify a maximum dollar amount of errors which is acceptable. The use of statistical variables sampling necessitates the determination of an amount deemed material.

In general terms, a given fact may be regarded as material if it is significant to a decision maker in the context of the decision to be made. In other words, if the decision maker would reach a different decision if he or she had been aware of the fact in question, then the fact is material. In order to apply this definition to audit decisions about facts, the auditor would have to anticipate what facts would be significant to the user of the audited financial statements. When making judgments, the auditor would have to know: (1) the fact to be considered by the decision maker, (2) who the decision maker is, and (3) the decision process (how the fact is to be used). In practice, the latter two are, at best, dimly known, while the first item may become known only if the auditing procedures are sufficient to discover it.

Materiality has somewhat different meanings in accounting and auditing contexts. There are two aspects to *accounting materiality;* the first is *monetary-error materiality* (i.e., by how much could the financial statements be in error without significantly affecting the user?), and the second is *disclosure materiality* (i.e., would the disclosure or nondisclosure of a certain fact significantly affect the user?). Monetary errors would include errors due to (1) the incorrect quantification of accounting information (whether intentional or unintentional), (2) use of accounting principles not generally accepted, and (3) the incorrect classification of data (by description or date). A disclosure error could occur if a material fact is included in the financial statements but not separately stated, or if a material fact is not included in the financial statements (including the footnotes).

On the other hand, *auditing materiality* is related to the sensitivity of the audit to discovering monetary errors of various magnitudes. If audit procedures are such that a $100,000 error might exist without being discovered, then auditing materiality must be at least $100,000. If, for the same company, the measure of monetary-error accounting materiality were $50,000, the auditing materiality would be too large, for a $50,000 to $100,000 error might exist without being discovered, and this, by the definition of accounting materiality, would clearly be significant. Therefore, auditing materiality must not be greater than monetary-error accounting materiality.

The measure of accounting materiality can also be related to the type of audit opinion. If an auditor knows of a certain error in the financial statements but is willing to issue an unqualified accountants' report, then the error must be deemed immaterial. Conversely, if the auditor qualifies the opinion (or gives an adverse opinion), the error must be deemed material. In this sense, the border of materiality is at the point that the auditor decides to issue a qualified opinion rather than an unqualified opinion.

Often the determination of accounting materiality contemplates such factors as net income (or a normal level of net income for such a company), total assets, equity, and other considerations. In consideration of these factors, the auditor should determine the amount to be considered material with respect to the financial statements taken as a whole.

In contract auditing, the auditor may not be primarily interested in the financial statements taken as a whole, but may be more likely to determine the measure of materiality based on the total contract price and other relevant variables.

Allocating Materiality to Tests.   The measure of auditing materiality selected in accordance with the audit objectives would, of course, be the total materiality for the audit as a whole. When selecting the materiality level for a specific statistical test, a lesser figure should be used; otherwise, there would be no margin for error in any other account. For example, if the auditor decided that the overall measure of auditing materiality for the financial statements as a whole was $100,000 and then tested accounts receivables with an auditing materiality of $100,000, there would be no room for error in any other account. Any error in the other accounts, added to the possible error of $100,000 in accounts receivable, would exceed the amount specified by the auditor as material for the financial statement as a whole.

It is therefore necessary to allocate the overall measure of auditing materiality to the individual statistical audit tests. A method of doing this is described in the paragraphs that follow.

Before allocating the overall measure of statistical materiality to the statistical tests, it is necessary to consider the financial statement amounts that are not audited statistically. In determining the materiality for a specific audit test, the auditor should estimate the total uncertainty in the accounts not audited statistically. The auditor should review the potential problem areas and estimate the probable outside limit of possible error for all these accounts. This total must always be less than the overall measure of auditing materiality, or else the work done will be insufficient to warrant an unqualified opinion.

In determining the estimated limit of error in accounts not audited statistically, the auditor should consider the nature of these accounts. If, for example, they were capital stock, additional paid-in capital, and long-term debt, not much allowance for error would ordinarily need to be assigned because each of these accounts could theoretically be audited to achieve an accurate result. On the other hand, if the accounts not audited statistically included receivables, inventories, or accounts payable, a larger allowance for error would ordinarily be assigned.

Having determined the overall measure of materiality and the estimated limit of error in the accounts not audited statistically, the auditor can allocate the difference to the accounts to be statistically audited. The following formula may be used to determine a proper allocation:

$$\sqrt{\Sigma M_i^2} \leq M_0 - M_{est} \tag{3}$$

where M_i is the materiality of the ith statistically audited account, M_0 is the total measure of auditing materiality available for allocation, and M_{est} is the materiality allocated to all accounts not audited statistically. An example will illustrate the procedure. Assume the following:

Accounts to be audited statistically:
receivables and inventory

M_0: $1,200,000
M_{est}: $ 700,000

In this case, $500,000 is available for allocation to the accounts to be audited statistically ($1,200,000 − $700,000). Then $M_{receivables}$ of $300,000, and $M_{inventory}$ of $400,000 would be a feasible choice because

$$\sqrt{300,000^2 + 400,000^2} = 500,000$$

A whole range of other values would also satisfy this requirement; the allocation is a matter of audit judgment. Note that the sum of all the individual figures ($300,000 for receivables plus $400,000 for inventory plus $700,000 for the nonstatistically audited accounts equals $1,400,000) exceeds the overall measure ($1,200,000) of auditing materiality. This is consistent with the purpose of keeping the probable error within $1,200,000. The reason is that, although accounts receivable could be off by as much as $300,000 statistically, and inventory as much as $400,000, the probability of a $700,000 error in these two accounts is very remote because it would require both accounts to be off by the maximum amount and in the same direction. The formula given in equation (3) adjusts for this to keep the probabilities at a level consistent with audit objectives.

Relation Between Materiality and Sample Size. The sample size in a variables test is most heavily influenced by the ratio of the measure of materiality to the balance of the account being tested. If this ratio is less than 1 percent, the sample size is usually large. Furthermore, if the materiality is halved, the sample size is approximately quadrupled. In order to illustrate the effect upon sample size of varying the measure of materiality for a statistical test, a hypothetical audit case is given below. The same relationship would hold in all cases.

$$\frac{\text{Material Amount}}{\text{Account Balance}} =$$

Materiality Ratio	Approximate Sample Size
4.0%	100 items
2.0	400
1.0	1,600
.4	10,000

The α Risk. The α risk is the probability that the auditor will reject correct financial statement balances. However, there is little likelihood of actually committing such an error. If the tests point to rejection, the auditor will usually investigate further to ascertain and correct the causes. For statistical purposes, therefore, the risk can be considered as the risk that the auditor will unnecessarily be forced to perform follow-up work when an account balance is erroneously rejected. The costs associated with this risk are only those of this unnecessary audit work. There is a theoretical optimum value in each test for α (between 0 and 1) which will minimize total cost, but it is not practicably possible to solve for this value. It is probable that the optimum value is relatively low, say .1 or less. Since sample sizes are substantially larger when α is less than .05, a value in the range .05 to .10 appears most practicable. A reasonable approach would be for the auditor to select an acceptable α risk level and then use it for all statistical tests as a matter of policy.

The β Risk. The β risk is of critical importance to the auditor. When a given audit is complete, the auditor wants to have a great deal of assurance that an unqualified opinion has not been given on materially incorrect financial statements. If the only source of reliance were statistical tests, it is clear that a very low β risk would be required. However, there are other factors in the typical audit.

In carrying out substantive audit tests, the auditor has several sources of reliance for being satisfied that there is no material error condition, or if there is one, that it will be discovered. The auditor must be confident, after considering all sources of reliance, that no material error exists or that any existing material error would come to light. The reliance the auditor places on a statistical test affects the required sample size and is, in turn, influenced by the reliance placed on internal control or on the reliance placed on other (nonstatistical) audit procedures, or both.

The required β risk for a CPA conducting a substantive audit test is discussed in Section 320B.28–.36 of *SAS 1*. The risk that the auditor expresses an unqualified opinion on materially erroneous financial statements (the ultimate risk) is discussed in that section. This risk is expressed as a combination of various other risks—namely that (1) a material error occurs in the financial statements, (2) the internal controls fail to detect and correct the error given that it occurred, (3) the auditor's nonstatistical audit procedures fail to detect the error given that it occurred and was not detected and corrected by the internal controls, and (4) the auditor's statistical audit procedures fail to detect the error given all the foregoing. Because these risks are conditional, they can be multiplied to give the ultimate risk:

$$UR = P(EO) \times P(ICF) \times P(OAPF) \times P(SAPF)$$

where UR = ultimate risk

$P(EO)$ = probability that a material error occurs

$P(ICF)$ = probability that the internal controls fail to detect and correct a material error given that it occurred

$P(OAPF)$ = probability that other audit procedures fail to detect the material error given all the foregoing

$P(SAPF)$ = probability that the statistical audit procedures fail to detect the material error given all the foregoing.

The ultimate risk level desired by the auditor can be set at some reasonable value, and *SAS 1* illustrates a value of .05 (which is used by many auditors). Since $P(EO)$ is difficult to quantify, it is conservatively assumed by many auditors to equal one. Note that $P(SAPF)$ is precisely the β risk as discussed above. Incorporating the above information and solving for β gives

$$\beta = \frac{.05}{P(ICF) \times P(OAPF)} \tag{4}$$

It is clear from this formulation that the auditor must evaluate the strength of internal controls and the other (nonstatistical) audit procedures to determine the β risk to use for a given substantive test.

In evaluating internal controls, the auditor need be concerned only with those specific controls to be relied upon in selecting a β risk. Once reliance is placed upon controls, however, the auditor must test the controls for compliance and effectiveness. Conversely, there is no need for a compliance test when controls are evaluated as nonexistent because, in this case, no reliance will be placed on the controls when selecting a β risk. Furthermore, since the purpose of compliance testing is to permit restriction of other work, it would not be logical to spend more effort on the compliance test than can be saved in the test of financial statement amounts. Before making this decision, the auditor should evaluate which approach will be more efficient. The auditor should remember the purpose of the compliance test and omit it when it is not required or justified.

Even the most effective system of internal control will not prevent deliberate override of the controls by management personnel. Therefore, the auditor must consider the risk of material error through management override of the system of internal control. Although it is impossible to determine with certainty those cases in which management has overriden the internal controls, it should generally be possible to evaluate this risk through consideration of such factors as the type of organization being audited, the susceptibility of the area being examined to misstatement, the requirement for management judgment in determining the amounts in the records, and prior experience in auditing the financial statements of the client. Note that the evaluation is not intended to assess the probability that management *is* overriding the controls, but merely whether the area being examined presents any significant potential for override.

Whenever the risk of override is deemed to be significant, the auditor should limit reliance on internal control, whether or not there is any evidence or reason to believe that management has overriden the controls. Therefore, the auditor should test at a lower β risk, or, more accurately, should not increase the β risk by relying upon internal control.

The other factor the auditor must consider is the nature and effectiveness of other auditing procedures applied in the areas under examination. If the auditor is performing analytic reviews of the ratios and trends or additional detailed audit procedures, or both, reliance on the statistical test is obviously less than it would be in the absence of these other procedures. The auditor can, therefore, use a higher β risk. It is extremely important to note, however, that in increasing the β risk in reliance upon other procedures, the auditor should evaluate carefully any unusual conditions revealed by any of the tests performed. For example, the auditor should not ignore an unusual condition in one test because other tests fail to reveal it. The failure of any single test to reveal a condition of interest is not a positive indication that it does not exist. Unusual circumstances revealed in any test require further investigation regardless of the outcome of other tests.

Other auditing procedures can be classified as to whether they are significantly effective or only moderately effective. A significantly effective additional test would be a test with a relatively high probability of discovering material aggregate error conditions which exist (e.g., most detail tests), while a moderately effective test would have a fair probability of discovering material aggregate errors (e.g., many well-designed analytical tests). For example, assume that the audit test in question were a price test of inventory. The following additional tests would ordinarily be significantly effective: comparison of carrying prices with subsequent sales prices as adjusted to exclude normal gross profit, testing to published price quotations, confirmations with vendors, and detailed appraisals. The following tests would ordinarily be moderately effective: analysis of gross profit ratios by product lines, discussions with knowledgeable and reasonably disinterested persons, and analysis of standard cost system and variances.

In order to calculate the β risk by formula (4), the auditor must quantify $P(ICF)$ and $P(OAPF)$ after evaluating the strength of internal controls and other audit procedures. Research done so far is inadequate to devise accurate methods of quantifying these risks. In the meantime, auditors faced with the necessity of using some β risk have adopted reasonable and conservative guidelines. A scheme used by some auditors is illustrated in Exhibit 3. This scheme is based on the assumption that risks $P(ICF)$ and $P(OAPF)$ decline exponentially from 1 to .1 (a conservative value) as the strength of internal controls and other audit procedures increase to their maximum values. Note that the guidelines illustrated do not recommend a β risk greater than .50, which is consistent with the values illustrated in *SAS 1*.

In order to demonstrate the value of increasing the β risk to the justifiable maximum, some relative sample sizes follow, based on a hypothetical audit case with $\alpha = .05$ (the same sample size *relationship* would hold in all cases):

β risk	Sample Size
.05	340
.10	275
.15	235
.30	160
.50	100

EXHIBIT 3   Illustrative Method of Selection of β Risk

Reliance Assigned to Internal Control
If there is a significant risk that management could override the controls in effect over the area being examined, enter 0.
Otherwise, evaluate the internal controls in effect over the area being examined.

If the Controls Are	Enter
Excellent	4
Good	3
Fair	2
Poor	1
Nonexistent	0

Reliance Assigned to Other Audit Procedures
Evaluate the other audit procedures that might detect material errors of the type being tested for by the statistical test.
For each significantly effective additional test allow 2 points and for each moderately effective additional test allow 1 point. Enter the total (not to exceed 4 points).

Total ═══

If the Total Above Is	Use This β Risk
0	.05
1	.10
2	.15
3	.30
4	.50
5	.50*
6–8	.50**

*In view of these conditions, the auditor may wish to consider increasing the effectiveness of other auditing procedures and omitting the statistical test.
**In view of these conditions, the auditor may wish to consider omitting the statistical test.

Evaluation of Sample Results.   After designing the sampling plan, selecting the sample, and auditing the sample items, the auditor calculates two values from the sample (using the methods discussed in Chapter 10): the estimated total audit value (AV) of the population and the achieved standard error of the estimate (SE_A).

At this point, the auditor has all the information needed to reach a statistical conclusion, namely:

BV = book value of population
AV = statistically estimated total audit value of population
SE_A = achieved standard error of estimate
SE_T = target standard error of estimate
M = measure of materiality for test
α = α risk of test
β = β risk of test
n = sample size.

The decision process is summarized in Exhibit 4.

The first question the auditor must ask is whether the achieved standard error of estimate is less than or equal to the required standard error of estimate. If not, a hypothesis test cannot be completed using the original values for M, α, and β. Although the auditor could relax the requirements on one or more of these values and possibly complete the test at such new value(s), that is not usually desirable, for presumably the original requirements were selected in such a way as to meet certain audit objectives. To loosen the requirements would then be to fail to meet the audit objectives.

If the target standard error of estimate has not been achieved, an additional sample should be selected and audited. The additional sample size required (ignoring the finite population correction factor discussed in Chapter 10) is $n[(SE_A/SE_T)^2 - 1]$. Many auditors add another 10 to 20 percent to this incremental sample to reduce the possibility of failing to meet the target yet again. After the

EXHIBIT 4   Decision Process for Hypothesis Testing

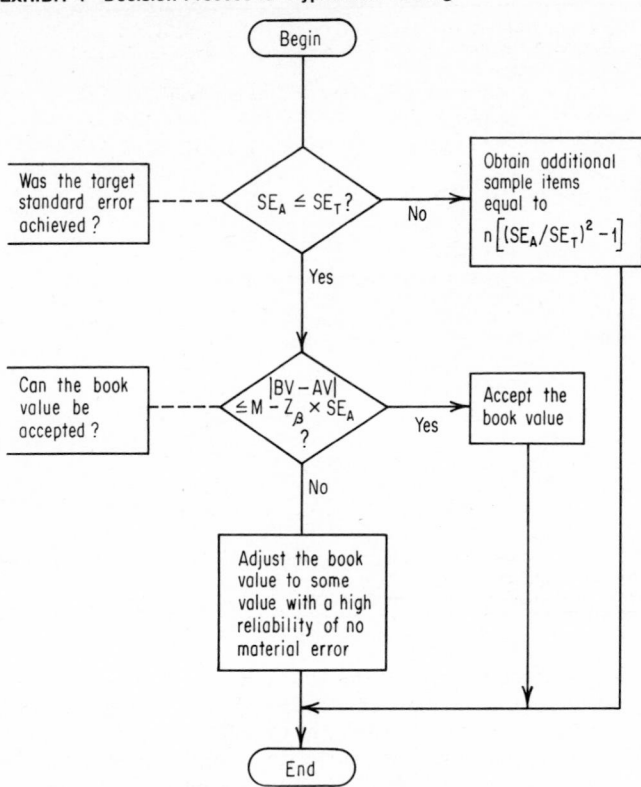

additional sample items are audited, the auditor should recompute the statistically estimated total audit value and the achieved standard error of estimate and begin the decision procedure again.

After the target standard error of estimate has been achieved, the auditor can test to see whether the book value can be accepted. If $SE_A < SE_T$, then either or both of the risk levels can be reduced somewhat (because the sample evidence exceeds the minimum requirements).

If the auditor decides to hold the β risk constant and reduce the α risk, the book value can be accepted if $|BV - AV| \leq M - Z_\beta \times SE_A$. On the other hand, if the auditor decides to hold the α risk constant and reduce the β risk, the book value can be accepted if $|BV - AV| \leq Z_{\alpha/2} \times SE_A$. Either approach is appropriate (because they are both within the original risk levels specified).

If the test for acceptance of the book value is not met, then it must be rejected as possibly being materially in error. However, the auditor does not simply qualify the opinion. Rather the auditor needs to know what amount can be accepted as materially correct and then have the client adjust the books to that amount.

In general, the same sample data used to conduct the hypothesis test can be used to make a dollar-value estimate of an account balance. Given the sample data and the amount specified by the auditor as material, it is possible to calculate the reliability that any specified value of the account balance is materially correct.

The β risk used in the hypothesis test may have been greater than .05 because of reliance upon internal control or other audit procedures. Once the hypothesis test has rejected the account balance, the auditor has an indication that internal controls or other audit procedures relied upon were ineffective. The auditor should therefore adjust the statistical risks so that the risk of the adjusted book value being materially in error is no more than 5 percent.

Therefore the auditor should calculate what value (or range of values) has at least 95 percent reliability of no material error. To achieve at least one point with 95 percent reliability of no material error, the following minimum sample evidence is required:

$$SE_A \leq \frac{M}{1.96}$$

Note that this condition may be more stringent than that required above, and therefore, additional sample evidence may be required in order to achieve at least one point with 95 percent reliability of no material error.

In order to calculate the range into which the book value can be adjusted, we can consider the reliability of no material error if the books are adjusted to the statistically estimated total audit value. The reliability that the estimated total value is materially in error is given by the area in the tails of the normal curve in Figure 7.

FIGURE 7

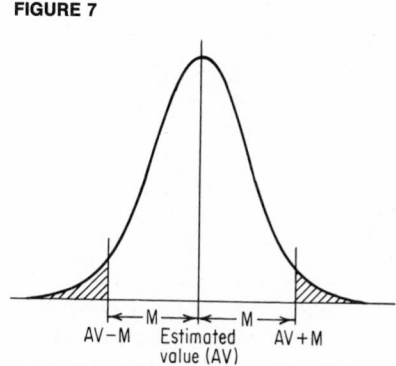

The reliability that the estimated total value is materially in error can be calculated easily:

$$Z = \frac{M}{SE_A}$$

where Z is the number of standard deviations between the estimated total value and the materiality limits. From a standard normal table, the reliability of the true value lying in the tails of the curve can be obtained. For example, suppose that M = \$10,000 and SE_A = \$5,000. Then

$$Z = \frac{\$10,000}{\$\ 5,000} = 2$$

From the normal table, the reliability associated with a normal value of 2 is .0228 (the area in one tail). Hence, the reliability of the estimated total value being in error by a material amount is .0456, as both tails (i.e., materially understated and materially overstated) are considered. Conversely, the estimated total value can be accepted with .9544 reliability of being materially correct. This more than meets the required level of 95 percent.

Because the decision logic above requires the achieved standard error to be at most $M/1.96$ before entering this phase, there is always going to be at least one point that can be accepted with 95 percent reliability of no material error. But can a point very near the estimated total value still be acceptable with at least 95 percent reliability of no material error? In other words, is there a range of values within which any point can be accepted with 95 percent reliability of no material error? Consider Figure 8. It is desired to find the farthest point to which the

FIGURE 8

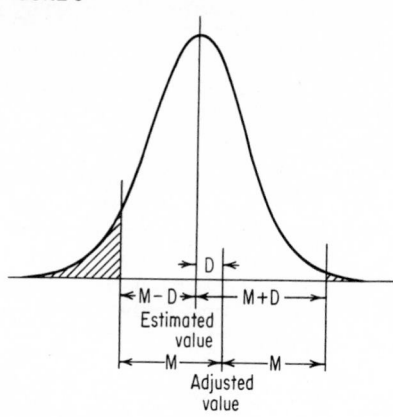

adjusted value can be moved and still have at least 95 percent reliability of no material error. The reliability that the adjusted value is materially overstated is given by the shaded area in the left-hand tail, and the reliability of material understatement is given by the area of the right tail. To have 95 percent reliability of no material error, the total area in the two tails must not exceed .05. This can be written as

$$F\left(\frac{M - D}{SE_A}\right) + F\left(\frac{M + D}{SE_A}\right) \leq .05$$

where $F(X)$ is the area in the tail of the normal curve beyond X standard deviations. To find the adjustment range, this equation must be solved for D. This equation can be solved by trial and error (or the table in Exhibit 5 can be used).

When the decision is to reject the book value and adjust it, the auditor should strive to have the auditee adjust it to the statistically estimated total value, as this is the point with the highest reliability of no material error. However, the auditee may, upon finding that there is a problem, reprocess the accounting data and obtain a new book value. In such a case, if the new book value has at least 95 percent reliability of no material error (i.e., is in the adjustment range) the auditor would be satisfied. Also, the auditee may dispute the auditor's statistical estimate, but be willing to adjust to some other value in the adjustment range. The auditor can accept such an adjustment with at least 95 percent reliability of no material error, which is acceptable, even though some other adjustment might have had even higher reliability of no material error.

Although the decision process above seems formidable at first glance, it can easily be reduced to a simple worksheet, as in Exhibit 5. In order to demonstrate the use of this worksheet, Exhibit 6 is filled in assuming the following data:

$$
\begin{aligned}
BV &= \$10,000,000 \\
AV &= 9,500,000 \\
SE_A &= 98,000 \\
M &= 200,000 \\
\alpha &= .10 \\
\beta &= .35 \\
n &= 300
\end{aligned}
$$

EXHIBIT 5 Statistical Decision Procedure—Hypothesis Testing

Description	Variable		Calculation
Enter known data:			
Book value	BV	①	
Statistically estimated total value	AV	②	
Achieved standard error of estimate	SE_A	③	
Measure of materiality for test	M	④	
Acceptable risk of rejecting correct balance	α	⑤	
Acceptable risk of accepting materially erroneous balance	β	⑥	
Sample size	n	⑦	
STEP 1: Test for adequacy of sample evidence			
Normal value for ⑤ (see Table 1 at right)	$Z_{\alpha/2}$	⑧	
Normal value for ⑥ (see Table 2 at right)	Z_β	⑨	
Calculate	$Z_{\alpha/2} + Z_\beta$	⑩	⑧ + ⑨ = ⑩
Enter ⑩ or 1.96, whichever is larger	SE_T	⑪	
Calculate		⑫	④ ÷ ⑪ = ⑫
If ③ ≤ ⑫ continue to step 2; otherwise calculate additional sample size ⑬, audit additional items and restart evaluation procedure.			
Calculate		⑬	⑦ × [(③ ÷ ⑫)² − 1] = ⑬
STEP 2: Test for acceptance of book value			
Calculate	$Z_\beta \times SE_A$	⑭	③ × ⑨ = ⑭
Maximum estimated error to accept book value	$M - Z_\beta \times SE_A$	⑮	④ − ⑭ = ⑮
Estimated error (absolute value)	$\lvert BV - AV \rvert$	⑯	|① − ②| = ⑯
If ⑯ ≤ ⑮ accept the book value as materially correct; otherwise continue to step 3			Accept/Adjust
STEP 3: Calculation of adjustment range			
Calculate	M/SE_A	⑰	④ ÷ ③ = ⑰
If ⑰ > 2.40, enter ⑰ − 1.65; otherwise enter value from Table 3 at right	D/SE_A	⑱	
Calculate adjustment range	D	⑲	③ × ⑱ = ⑲
Lower limit of adjustment range	$AV - D$	⑳	② − ⑲ = ⑳
Upper limit of adjustment range	$AV + D$	㉑	② + ⑲ = ㉑
Adjust the book value into range ⑳ to ㉑ with 95% reliability of no material error			

Table 1

α	$Z_{\alpha/2}$
.05	1.96
.10	1.65
.15	1.44
.20	1.28
.25	1.15
.30	1.04
.35	.94
.40	.84
.45	.76
.50	.67

For other values, consult standard normal table.

Table 2

β	Z_β
.05	1.65
.10	1.28
.15	1.04
.20	.84
.25	.67
.30	.52
.35	.39
.40	.25
.45	.13
.50	.00

Table 3

M/SE from ⑰	D/SE_A to ⑱
1.96	.00
1.97	.10
1.98	.14
1.99	.18
2.00	.20
2.02	.25
2.04	.29
2.06	.33
2.08	.36
2.10	.39
2.15	.46
2.20	.52
2.25	.58
2.30	.64
2.35	.69
2.40	.75

For intermediate values, interpolate.

EXHIBIT 6 Example of Decision Process

			Value
Enter known data:			
Book value	(1)	BV	10,000,000
Statistically estimated total value	(2)	AV	9,500,000
Achieved standard error of estimate	(3)	SE_A	98,000
Measure of materiality for test	(4)	M	200,000
Acceptable risk of rejecting correct balance	(5)	α	.10
Acceptable risk of accepting materially erroneous balance	(6)	β	.35
Sample size	(7)	n	300
STEP 1: Test for adequacy of sample evidence			
Normal value for (5) see Table 1 at right	(8)	$Z_{\alpha/2}$	1.65
Normal value for (6) see Table 2 at right	(9)	Z_β	.39
Calculate (8) + (9) = (10)		$Z_{\alpha/2} + Z_\beta$	2.04
Enter (10) or 1.96, whichever is larger	(11)		2.04
Calculate (4) ÷ (11) = (12)		SE_T	98,039
If (3) ≤ (12) continue to step 2; otherwise calculate additional sample size (13), audit additional items and restart evaluation procedure.			
Calculate (7) × [((3) ÷ (12))^2 − 1] = (13)			
STEP 2: Test for acceptance of book value			
Calculate (3) × (9) = (14)		$Z_\beta \times SE_A$	38,220
Maximum estimated error to accept book value (4) − (14) = (15)		$M - Z_\beta \times SE_A$	161,780
Estimated error (absolute value) (1) − (2) = (16)		$\lvert BV - AV \rvert$	500,000
If (16) ≤ (15) accept the book value as materially correct; otherwise continue to step 3			Accept / Adjust
STEP 3: Calculation of adjustment range			
Calculate (4) ÷ (3) = (17)		M/SE_A	2.04
If (17) > 2.40, enter (17) − 1.65; otherwise enter value from Table 3 at right	(18)	D/SE_A	.29
Calculate adjustment range (3) × (18) = (19)		D	28,420
Lower limit of adjustment range (2) − (19) = (20)		$AV - D$	9,471,580
Upper limit of adjustment range (2) + (19) = (21)		$AV + D$	9,528,420
Adjust the book value into range (20) to (21) with 95% reliability of no material error			

Table 1

α	$Z_{\alpha/2}$
.05	1.96
.10	1.65
.15	1.44
.20	1.28
.25	1.15
.30	1.04
.35	.94
.40	.84
.45	.76
.50	.67

For other values, consult standard normal table.

Table 2

β	Z_β
.05	1.65
.10	1.28
.15	1.04
.20	.84
.25	.67
.30	.52
.35	.39
.40	.25
.45	.13
.50	.00

Table 3

M/SE_A from (17)	D/SE_A to (18)
1.96	.00
1.97	.10
1.98	.14
1.99	.18
2.00	.20
2.02	.25
2.04	.29
2.06	.33
2.08	.36
2.10	.39
2.15	.46
2.20	.52
2.25	.58
2.30	.64
2.35	.69
2.40	.75

For intermediate values, interpolate.

The audit decision resulting from these data is to adjust the book value somewhere into the range of $9,471,580 to $9,528,420 with 95 percent reliability of no material error.

Audit Conclusion.   After the statistical evaluation has been reached—accept the book value or adjust it—through the analysis in the preceding section, the auditor must not only act on that information, but must also consider whether the sample evidence requires any further action. For example, suppose the auditor found only one small error in the sample and the statistical decision was to accept the book value, but the item in error was fraudulently misstated. Notwithstanding the favorable statistical decision, the auditor would probably rethink the audit objectives and approach in light of the discovered evidence of fraud.

Alternatively, assume that the auditor found evidence of an improper sales cutoff in the sample. Rather than simply adjusting the books to the statistical estimate, the auditor should consider directing audit attention to all the cutoff procedures and adjusting all errors in light of the sample evidence of improper cutoffs.

The important point to remember is that the statistical "decision" arrived at through the methods of this chapter is not the final audit decision, but is merely evidence the auditor must combine with all other known or discovered facts in reaching a sound audit conclusion. The proper use of the statistical information requires professional audit judgment.

Estimation.   The purpose of statistical variables estimation is to estimate some amount of interest to the auditor, such as the total cost of inventory on hand. This method is generally used when the resulting estimate is to be entered onto the books and records as a substitute for a complete enumeration of the components of an account. When this approach is used, a measure of the precision of the estimate is required so the auditor knows whether the resulting amount is sufficiently precise for the purpose.

To design the sampling plan for a statistical estimate, it is necessary to specify the precision and the reliability required. On the basis of these values, the auditor can compute the target standard error of the estimated total value (SE_T) which must be achieved to obtain the required precision. Using the required standard error, the necessary sample size can be computed using the methods in Chapter 10.

Required Standard Error of Estimate.   The relationship between the precision (P), reliability (R), and standard error of estimate (SE_T) can be shown graphically as in Figure 9. In words, of all possible samples, a proportion represented by R will yield an estimate of the total value that is within the predefined precision.

FIGURE 9

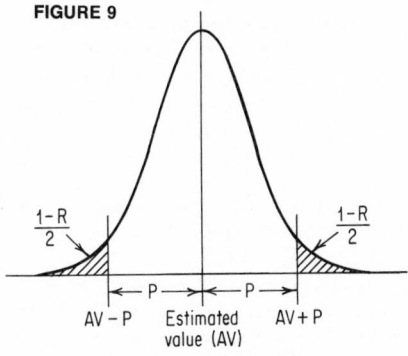

Because the sample estimates are normally distributed, P, R, and SE_T can be related as follows:

$$P = Z_{(1-R)/2} \times SE_T$$

and hence:

$$SE_T = \frac{P}{Z_{(1-R)/2}}$$

Exhibit 7 provides common Z values to assist in making this calculation.

P: The Precision of the Estimate.   The precision of a statistical estimate should be selected by reference to the sampling objective. If the objective is to estimate the total cost of inventory for presentation in financial statements, for example, the considerations of materiality discussed above would apply. In each case, the use of the financial information containing the statistical estimate must be analyzed to determine the upper limit of precision tolerable for the estimation procedure.

The sample size in variables estimation is most heavily influenced by the ratio of the precision to the total amount being sampled. If this ratio is less than 1 percent, the sample size is usually large. Furthermore, if precision is halved, the sample size is approximately quadrupled.

EXHIBIT 7   Z Values for Computing SE_T

$$SE_T = \frac{P}{Z_{(1-R)/2}}$$

R	$Z_{(1-R)/2}$
.99	2.58
.95	1.96
.90	1.65
.85	1.44
.80	1.28

P is dollar amount of precision.

R: The Reliability.   The reliability is the proportion of times, over the long run, that the precision interval computed from the sample will include the true population value.

Section 320B of *SAS 1* illustrates a reliability level of 95 percent in the absence of internal controls. Therefore, many auditors believe that a reliability of 95 percent is appropriate, in conjunction with a precision equal to the amount considered material for an account, for statistical estimation purposes when the amount is to appear in financial statements. Other reliability levels may be appropriate, however, for other statistical estimates, depending on the audit objectives and significance of the information developed.

Evaluation of Sample Results.   After designing the sampling plan, selecting the sample, and auditing the sample items, the auditor calculates two values from the sample (using the methods discussed in Chapter 10): the estimated total audit value (AV) of the population and the achieved standard error of the estimate (SE_A).

The auditor must then ask whether the achieved standard error is less than or equal to the required standard error of estimate. If not, the original precision and reliability requirements cannot be met. In this case, an additional sample should be selected and audited. The additional sample size (ignoring the finite population correction factor) is $n[(SE_A/SE_T)^2 - 1]$, to which many auditors add another 10 to 20 percent to reduce the possibility of failing to meet the target yet again. After the additional items are audited, the auditor should recompute the statistically estimated total audit value and the achieved standard error of estimate.

After the target standard error of estimate has been achieved, the auditor can have the books adjusted to the statistically estimated value. The precision of this estimate can be obtained by use of the following formula:

$$P = Z_{(1-R)/2} \times SE_A$$

For example, if the achieved standard error is $40,000, the auditor can have 95 percent reliability that the statistically estimated total value is within $78,400 of the true value (1.96 × $40,000).

Note that it would *not* be appropriate to make a statistical estimate of a population total and, finding the book value somewhere within the precision interval, accept the book value as materially correct. If this type of decision procedure is to be used, the hypothesis testing approach described above should be employed.

STATISTICAL COMPLIANCE TESTS

The auditor undertakes a compliance test to evaluate the extent of compliance with internal controls. Therefore, statistical compliance tests are normally attribute tests, because the conclusions of attribute tests are stated in terms of rates of compliance (or noncompliance).

Definition of Error in Compliance Test. Since the auditor's interest in a compliance test is the extent of compliance with internal controls, a sample item is considered to be in error if it does not show evidence of compliance with the control(s) being tested. Evidence of noncompliance with controls not being tested is not considered a compliance deviation for purposes of the compliance test. The reason is that the auditor tests compliance only with those controls upon which reliance is placed for the purpose of restricting the extent of substantive tests. Typically, there will be controls that are not to be relied upon, and compliance deviations with respect to these controls would not be considered errors in the compliance test. Although other errors (such as monetary errors) located in a compliance test are not considered errors for purposes of evaluating the compliance test of that specific control, they should nevertheless be evaluated as to their nature and cause, their relationship to other phases of the audit, and their potential effect upon the financial statements.

Statistical Requirements for Compliance Test. The purpose of a compliance test is to provide a reasonable degree of assurance that the internal control procedures are being applied as understood by the auditor. What constitutes a "reasonable degree of assurance" is a matter of auditing judgment. Although statistical sampling provides one means of carrying out compliance testing, it does not eliminate the need for judgment, because the reliability and acceptable upper precision limit on errors are matters of audit judgment. *SAS 1*, paragraphs 320B.17–.24, gives examples of appropriate statistical requirements for use in compliance testing. These are discussed below.

Reliability.   Paragraph 320B.24 illustrates reliability levels of 90 percent and 95 percent for audit compliance tests, although higher levels would also be appropriate.

Upper Precision Limit.   The upper precision limit on compliance deviations represents a critical value established so that the possibility of deviations in excess of that rate would cause the auditor to place less than full reliance on the control being evaluated. Paragraph 320B.22 of *SAS 1* illustrates upper precision limits of 5 percent or 10 percent, depending on factors discussed in paragraphs 320B.19 through .22.

In compliance tests, a relatively high upper precision limit on deviations (e.g., .05 as opposed to .01) is acceptable because an item may have a compliance deviation and yet have no monetary error. A compliance deviation does not necessarily result in a monetary error—it merely means that if a monetary error had occurred in the item, the control procedure would not have detected it. In the typical case, most items would be correct even in the absence of internal control; therefore, a control procedure that was applied to at least 95 percent of all items would, if the control were effective at detecting and correcting errors, reduce the monetary error rate to a negligible percentage.

On the other hand, if the feature of interest in an audit test is monetary errors, the upper precision limit on errors is related to materiality considerations. Since a potential 5 percent error rate for monetary errors might well be unacceptable in transactions being audited, the acceptable upper precision limit on errors in a dual-purpose test (that is, a test with both substantive and compliance objectives) might often be lower than if the test were solely for compliance purposes.

Upper precision limits for compliance tests may be illustrated as follows (illustrations are presented for three specific conditions; however, in practice different values could be chosen for situations that do not exactly meet these conditions):

Reliance on Internal Control	Illustrative Upper Precision Limit
Some reliance, but not a great deal, based upon the auditor's conclusions that substantive work will not be substantially reduced in reliance upon internal control.	10%
Substantial reliance, based upon the auditor's conclusion that substantive work will be substantially reduced in reliance upon internal control (e.g., one-half to two-thirds reduction in substantive work). This is a usual situation when controls are good or excellent.	5%
Very great reliance on internal control, based upon the auditor's conclusion that the inherent limitations on the planned substantive tests are such that an unusually high amount of reliance must be placed upon the internal controls. Such situations, though not rare, would nevertheless be somewhat unusual.	1% (or, rarely, less)

Sample Design.   Attribute tests can be designed after the reliability and upper precision limit on error are established. Based on these, the sample size can be calculated and the sample drawn (see "Selecting the Sample" above), audited, and evaluated. Sample size calculation and evaluation of results are both done through the use of tables too voluminous to reproduce in this handbook. A good set of tables can be found in *Handbook of Sampling for Auditing and Accounting* by Herbert Arkin.

ANNOTATED BIBLIOGRAPHY

American Institute of Certified Public Accountants: *An Auditor's Approach to Statistical Sampling,* six volumes with supplementary sections. These books are programmed instruction texts on statistical sampling, written in easily understandable style. They include formulas, worksheets, and tables for various types of audit sampling.

———: *Statement on Auditing Standards No. 1,* 1973. Sections 320, 320A, and 320B give guidance in the use of statistical sampling in auditing.

Arkin, Herbert: *Handbook of Sampling for Auditing and Accounting,* 2nd ed., McGraw-Hill Book Company, New York, 1974. A basic treatment of statistical audit techniques. Also includes voluminous tables for sample design and evaluation.

Cochran, William G: *Sampling Techniques,* 2nd ed., John Wiley & Sons, New York, 1963. A standard statistical reference, highly mathematical and technical.

Cyert, R. M., and H. Justin Davidson: *Statistical Sampling for Accounting Information,* Prentice-Hall, Englewood Cliffs, N.J., 1962. A medium-difficulty reference, targeted to accounting and auditing problems.

Hansen, M. H., W. M. Hurwitz, and W. G. Madow: *Sample Survey Methods and Theory,* John Wiley & Sons, New York, 1953. A standard statistical reference, highly mathematical and technical.

International Business Machines Corporation: *Random Number Generation and Testing,* Technical Publications Department (document GC20-8011-0). Explains how to program computers to generate random numbers.

Roberts, Harry V.: *Conversational Statistics,* Hewlett-Packard Company, Cupertino, Calif., 1974. An innovative introduction to statistics, stressing understanding, not technique.

Chapter **10**

Statistical Methods
for Auditing and Accounting

ROBERT S. KAPLAN
Professor of Industrial Administration, Carnegie-Mellon University

INTRODUCTION

Accountants frequently confront masses of data from which they would like to draw systematic and logical conclusions. Perhaps the most frequent occurrence of such a confrontation arises when auditing an account such as accounts receivable or inventory which consists of a large number of individual subaccounts. It would be prohibitively expensive for an auditor to verify each item in such an account. Consequently, a representative sample of the entire population is chosen and this sample checked in detail. Based on the findings from this sample, the auditor attempts to draw conclusions about the entire population. Statistical analysis and, in particular, statistical sampling theory provide a scientific method for drawing reliable and valid conclusions about the properties of an entire population when only a properly chosen sample of the population has been studied in detail.

Although statistical sampling is the most useful statistical technique for many accountants (especially auditors), other statistical techniques are also becoming useful in the practice of modern accountants. Foremost among these is multiple regression analysis, which enables one to detect an underlying relationship among a number of simultaneous and interacting variables. At present, regression analysis is used primarily by management accountants within a firm to determine the cost relations which appear to be operating within a cost center or division. Especially important is the ability of regression analysis to approximate the fixed and variable cost components when the firm is operating within its normal range of activity. But regression analysis is becoming increasingly useful for auditors, too, who can use this technique to guide their audit activities to those areas, branches, or divisions whose operations appear to be significantly different from historical relationships or from the operations of comparable units in the same time period.

This chapter surveys both these statistical techniques, sampling theory and regression analysis. Historically, these statistical techniques were difficult to apply because of the long and tedious calculations that had to be performed. Now, however, the widespread use of computers and time-sharing facilities enables accountants to use these techniques without getting bogged down in a mass of detailed hand computations which, by themselves, often introduced a considerable amount of error into the process. We do not devote much space to computational techniques (e.g., how to compute ordinary least-squares estimates of regression coefficients) because an accountant who wishes to use these techniques can use a computer.

A chapter in a handbook is not the place for a first exposure to statistical analysis. I assume that readers of this chapter have already been exposed to an introductory statistics course. Some introductory business statistics books are referenced at the end of the chapter for anyone who wants to sharpen up or review basic statistical concepts. Although I start with elementary material, this serves mainly to define the notation used. I do not expect that this chapter will constitute a self-contained learning experience for those without formal training in statistics.

BASIC STATISTICAL CONCEPTS

Populations and Distributions.   All statistical analysis begins with the basic data to be analyzed. We assume throughout our discussion that we are working with a finite number of items and let N represent the number of items in our population. The population, of course, must be well defined (e.g., the total number of sales invoices, all raw material inventory accounts) so that we can unambiguously decide whether a particular item is included in the population or not. We will typically be interested in quantitative measures associated with each item such as the dollar value of an account receivable or an inventory item. We denote by X_i the amount or value of the ith item in the population, $i = 1, \ldots, N$.

As an illustration which we carry throughout our analysis, consider a hypothetical population of 100 invoices as shown in Exhibit 1.[1] For this example $N = 100$, and $X_1 = 11.87$, $X_2 = 11.18, \ldots, X_{100} = 1.65$.

EXHIBIT 1   Hypothetical Population of 100 Invoices

Invoice number	Invoice value	Invoice number	Invoice value	Invoice number	Invoice value	Invoice number	Invoice value
01	11.87	26	21.06	51	14.54	76	17.94
02	11.18	27	23.38	52	15.12	77	19.93
03	11.32	28	16.32	53	20.57	78	15.98
04	10.16	29	21.54	54	18.36	79	22.50
05	4.15	30	3.65	55	21.27	80	13.98
06	12.35	31	17.69	56	23.57	81	16.36
07	7.89	32	27.14	57	24.40	82	24.27
08	12.74	33	21.60	58	25.08	83	24.52
09	6.86	34	25.30	59	17.48	84	27.20
10	5.08	35	22.34	60	8.95	85	18.77
11	21.18	36	19.88	61	26.89	86	19.33
12	21.90	37	21.84	62	18.59	87	24.05
13	19.98	38	25.00	63	26.68	88	18.27
14	23.23	39	22.28	64	18.70	89	24.40
15	23.60	40	13.18	65	27.58	90	13.69
16	19.04	41	18.85	66	18.86	91	31.01
17	23.33	42	21.04	67	26.96	92	32.08
18	22.06	43	20.56	68	24.45	93	27.63
19	17.84	44	25.38	69	16.76	94	29.41
20	11.74	45	24.20	70	11.90	95	33.68
21	16.64	46	22.26	71	22.04	96	31.96
22	16.63	47	23.85	72	24.62	97	28.36
23	24.25	48	18.50	73	25.78	98	33.41
24	21.76	49	19.97	74	16.01	99	28.40
25	16.01	50	12.52	75	19.28	100	1.65

Total value of 100 invoices: $1,995.34.
Average value of 100 invoices: $19.95.

In some circumstances, an auditor may be interested in a qualitative characteristic of each item in the population, e.g., whether each invoice itemized in Exhibit 1 was properly authorized. In this case, we can let $X_i = 1$ if the ith item has the desired characteristic and $X_i = 0$ if it does not. When auditors examine qualitative characteristics of the population as above, they are interested in estimating the proportion of items that have (or do not have) the desired characteristic. Sampling to estimate proportions is called *attribute sampling*. Sampling to estimate the total value of a population is called *variables sampling*.

One way of displaying the information contained in all the X_i values in a population is to list the value for each item as we did in Exhibit 1. Most populations of interest, however, will contain far too many items for this to be a convenient or even useful practice. The most common alternative to listing all the items in a population is to construct a histogram or frequency diagram to summarize the distribution of values. If the number of possible values that each item can assume is sufficiently small, we would tabulate each possible value and the number of items in the population at this value. For most populations, including the one shown in

[1] This exhibit and subsequent ones derived from it were taken from R. Cyert and J. Davidson, *Statistical Sampling for Accounting Information*, Prentice-Hall, Englewood Cliffs, N.J., 1962.

Exhibit 1, this would not be an interesting way to summarize information because there may be as many different values as there are items in the population. We therefore group the data into a number of somewhat arbitrary ranges and count the number of items whose value falls into each range. Exhibit 2 is a frequency table for the population of invoices shown in Exhibit 1. In this case, because $N = 100$, the number of items in each cell interval equals the percentage of all items in the cell interval. For populations for which N does not equal 100, the numbers tabulated in Exhibit 2 would be divided by N and multiplied by 100 (to yield a percentage between 0 and 100) to compute a relative frequency table. A relative frequency table or distribution for a population displays the percentage of items in the population whose values fall within each cell interval.

EXHIBIT 2   Frequency Table: Invoice Population of Exhibit 1

Cell interval	Number of invoices with values falling in listed interval
$ 0.00– 4.99	3
5.00– 9.99	4
10.00–14.99	13
15.00–19.99	28
20.00–24.99	32
25.00–29.99	15
30.00–34.99	5
Total	100

It is frequently desirable to display this data graphically. Exhibit 3 is a graphic representation of the data in Exhibit 2 and is called a *histogram, bar chart,* or *relative frequency diagram.* Aggregating the basic data into a frequency table or histogram

EXHIBIT 3   Histogram

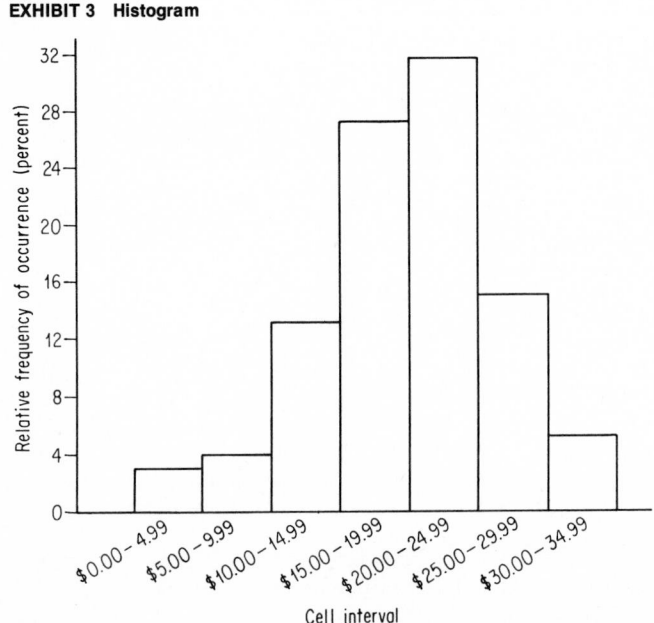

Cell interval

involves some loss of detail, because we lose sight of individual values. Nevertheless, we typically get a much better picture about the distribution of values in the population by aggregating into cell intervals. In fact, we will usually want an even further aggregation of the individual items into perhaps two summary measures that characterize the population:

1. A measure of central tendency; an average or typical value for an item in the population
2. A measure of dispersion or variation of the items in the population; how far away might an invoice be from the measure of central tendency.

We discuss typical measures of central tendency and dispersion in the next two sections.

Measures of Central Tendency

Median. The median of a population is that value for which half the values in the population are above and half are below it. In effect, the median divides the population into two equal sizes. Strictly speaking, a population has a middle item only when it has an odd number of items. For a population with an even number of items, the median can be defined as the average of the two middle numbers. One can check that the 50th and 51st largest values in Exhibit 1 are $20.57 and $21.04, respectively, so that the median for this population would be the average of these two or about $20.80. Although the median of a population is rarely used in statistical inference, it is a valuable summary measure for highly dispersed populations because it is not affected by the particular values assumed by extreme observations. It therefore provides a reasonable representation as to what value a typical item in the population is likely to be near.

Mode. The mode of a population is that value which occurs most frequently. The mode is typically computed on an aggregated frequency table or diagram (Exhibit 2 or 3) rather than the distribution of individual items as shown in Exhibit 1. The modal cell interval for these data is $20.00–$24.99, which contains 32 percent of all the invoices. The mode represents the most typical or the most likely set of values in the population.

Arithmetic Mean. The most common measure of central tendency is the arithmetic mean, sometimes called the *average* or simply the *mean* of the population. The arithmetic mean is computed by summing the values of all the items in the population and dividing by the number of items. Symbolically, letting $\bar{X}$ be the mean of the population,

$$\bar{X} = \frac{\sum_{1}^{N} X_i}{N}$$

For the data in Exhibit 1, $\bar{X} = \$19.95$. If the X_i's are 0–1 variables, as in attribute sampling, $\bar{X}$ would be the fraction of the population which have the attribute being investigated. Although the mean is probably the most useful measure of central tendency in a population, as we shall see, it does have the disadvantage of being strongly influenced by extremely high or extremely low observations. Therefore it may not be representative of the typical or most common item in the population.

Most frequency diagrams or histograms are unimodal; i.e., the height of the curve increases until the mode (highest point) is reached, and decreases for values in excess of the mode. If the histogram or frequency diagram is symmetric, as shown in diagram (a) of Exhibit 4, the median, mode, and mean all occur at the same point. If the distribution is skewed to the left [diagram (b)] the mean, being more influenced by the extreme lower values, is less than the median which, in turn, is less than the mode. If the distribution is skewed to the right [diagram (c)],

EXHIBIT 4   Frequency Distributions

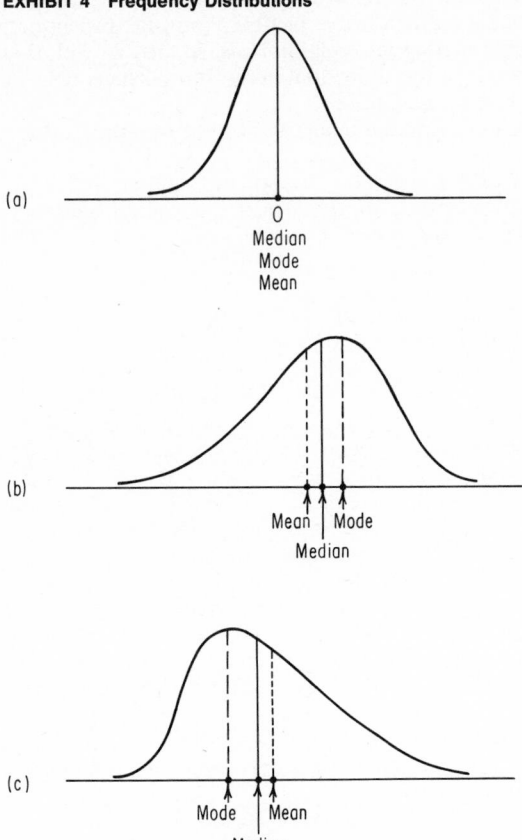

(a)

0
Median
Mode
Mean

(b)

Mean | Mode
Median

(c)

Mode | Mean
Median

the opposite order holds for the three measures of central tendency; the mode is less than the median and the median is less than the mean.

Measures of Dispersion

Range.   The simplest measure of dispersion is the range, the difference between the largest and the smallest item in the population. For example, a weather report will usually report the high and low temperature for the day as a measure of the daily fluctuation in temperature. (Unfortunately, some people average the high and low temperatures of the day and incorrectly report this as the day's "average" temperature.) For the data in Exhibit 1, the largest value is 33.68 (invoice 95) and the smallest value is 1.65 (invoice 100), so the range is 32.03. The range is typically used in quality control applications because of its easy computation. It is not too valuable in sampling studies because it is obviously very sensitive to extreme observations and it is also dependent on sample size. The range statistic will generally increase and certainly never decrease as we increase the sample size.

Interquartile Range.   In order to reduce the dependence of the range statistic on extreme observations and to obtain a statistic that is relatively stable with sample size, a more useful measure is the interval which contains the middle 50 percent of observations. This measure is obtained by identifying Q_{25}, the item value which separates the lowest 25 percent of observations from the upper 75 percent, and

Q_{75}, the item value which separates the upper 25 percent of observations from the lower 75 percent. The interquartile range is then computed as $Q_{75} - Q_{25}$. For the data in Exhibit 1, $Q_{25} = 16.34$ (an average of the 25th smallest invoice, 16.32, and the 26th smallest, 16.23) and $Q_{75} = 24.34$ (an average of 24.27 and 24.40). Therefore the interquartile range is $24.34 - 16.34 = 8.00$. Although this statistic is a useful summary measure of dispersion for long-tailed and/or highly skewed populations, it is not convenient to work with algebraically and hence does not play a central role in statistical sampling or estimation theory.

Average Deviation.   The average or mean deviation is the average of the absolute deviations of each item from the arithmetic mean. Symbolically, it can be written as

$$AD = \frac{\sum |X_i - \bar{X}|}{N}$$

where the vertical bars refer to the absolute value operation; i.e., $|-2| = |+2| = +2$. The deviations are averaged as if they were all positive. The average deviation indicates how far "on average" an item will deviate from the mean. It is an intuitively appealing measure of dispersion but it too is difficult to work with algebraically. The average deviation for the data in Exhibit 1 is $5.11.

Standard Deviation.   The most commonly used measure of dispersion is the standard deviation, σ, of a population. This is defined as

$$\sigma = \left[\frac{\sum\limits_{1}^{N} (X_i - \bar{X})^2}{N} \right]^{1/2}$$

Sometimes, a very similar measure, S, is used to denote the standard deviation of the population, where

$$S = \left[\frac{\sum\limits_{1}^{N} (X_i - \bar{X})^2}{N - 1} \right]^{1/2}$$

The square of the standard deviation, either σ^2 or S^2, is called the variance of the population. The standard deviation, with the square root formula, is more useful than the variance because it is measured in the same units as the individual items in the population and the mean. For computational ease, the above formulas are frequently rewritten in the equivalent form:

$$\sigma = \left[\frac{\sum\limits_{1}^{N} X_i^2}{N} - \frac{\left(\sum\limits_{1}^{N} X_i \right)^2}{N^2} \right]^{1/2}$$

so that the mean and standard deviation can be computed with only one pass through the data. The standard deviation of the data in Exhibit 1 can be calculated as $6.53.

The standard deviation is the easiest measure to work with algebraically and is especially useful when the population is well approximated by a normal or bell-shaped distribution. It is least useful when the population has only a small number of items or when the population is highly skewed, i.e., has a long tail. In these situations, the standard deviation is highly sensitive to values of extreme observations.

Coefficient of Variation.   All of the above measures of dispersion are expressed in the unit of measurement of the individual invoice items, e.g., dollars. In comparing two populations, it is useful to have a measure of dispersion which is independent of the units used to measure the individual items or even the average magnitude of items. The coefficient of variation, $\sigma/\bar{X}$, which is the ratio of the standard deviation to the mean, gives a measure of the degree of variation in the population which is independent of the average magnitude of items or units used to measure these items. For the data in Exhibit 1, this measure is .327, implying an average dispersion of about 33 percent about the mean for individual items.

Skewness.   Skewness refers to the degree of asymmetry or lopsidedness of a distribution. A simple measure of skewness, *Sk*, is a function of the spread between the arithmetic mean and the median,

$$Sk = \frac{3(\bar{X} - \text{median})}{S}$$

where S is the standard deviation previously defined. If the distribution is skewed to the right, the mean is greater than the median, as previously illustrated in Exhibit 4, and the measure will be positive. If the distribution is skewed to the left, the measure will be negative. For the data in Exhibit 1,

$$Sk = \frac{3(19.95 - 20.80)}{6.53} = -.39$$

indicating a slight degree of negative skewness. Examining Exhibit 3, we see that the left-hand tail of the distribution is somewhat longer than the right-hand tail, which confirms this effect.

Many accounting populations are highly skewed. A typical population would have a large number of small-valued items and a relatively few high-valued items accounting for a significant portion of the total dollar value in the population. A population whose skewness measure exceeds 1 would be considered highly skewed.

Another measure of skewness, which is more difficult to compute, is given by G_1, where

$$G_1 = \frac{\displaystyle\sum_i (X_i - \bar{X})^3}{N\sigma^3}$$

G_1 is zero for symmetric distributions; it is positive for distributions skewed to the right.

THE NORMAL DISTRIBUTION

The normal distribution, illustrated in Exhibit 5, is by far the most useful distribution in statistics. The normal distribution is symmetric and is completely characterized by its mean and standard deviation. Although it is possible to express the normal density function (the bell-shaped curve) both mathematically, via an equation, and in tabular form, it is far more convenient to work with the normal distribution function. This function, illustrated and tabulated in Exhibit 6, enables us to compute the probability that an item drawn from a normal distribution with $\bar{X} = 0$ and $\sigma = 1$ will have a value less than or equal to an arbitrary number x. From Exhibit 6, we can see that the probability that an item drawn from a zero-mean, unit-standard-deviation population is less than or equal to 1 is .8413. Although Exhibit 6 tabulates the normal distribution function only for values of x

EXHIBIT 5   Graph of the General Normal Density Function

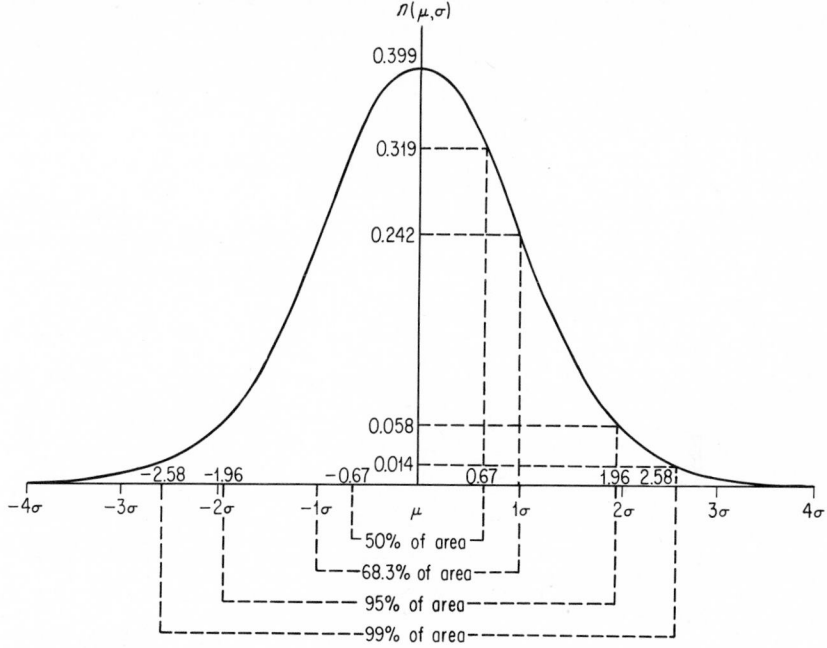

greater than or equal to 0, values for negative values of x can be obtained by exploiting the symmetric properties of the normal distribution; e.g., the probability that X is less than -1 must equal the probability that X is greater than $+1$ or

$$Pr\{X < -1\} = Pr\{X > +1\}$$

But since $Pr\{X \leq +1\} + Pr\{X > +1\} = 1$, we have

$$Pr\{X < -1\} = 1 - Pr\{X \leq +1\} = 1 - .8413 = .1587$$

A similar analysis can be performed for all negative values of x.

It may appear unduly restrictive to have a table for a single normal distribution—the one with mean zero and standard deviation equal to one. Fortunately we can always transform any normal distribution with arbitrary mean and standard deviation into a zero-mean, unit-standard-deviation one. Consider an item, X, drawn from a normal distribution with arbitrary mean $\bar{X}$, and standard deviation, σ. If we are interested in the probability that X is less than or equal to an arbitrary amount, x, we perform the following series of steps:

$$Pr\{X \leq x\} = Pr\{X - \bar{X} \leq x - \bar{X}\} = Pr\left\{\frac{X - \bar{X}}{\sigma} \leq \frac{x - \bar{X}}{\sigma}\right\}$$

The variable $Z = (X - \bar{X})/\sigma$ also has a normal distribution, but it can be shown that the mean of Z is zero and its standard deviation is 1. Therefore the probability that $X \leq x$ can be obtained from the table in Exhibit 6 for the value associated with $(x - \bar{X})/\sigma$.

For example, assume that X comes from a normal distribution with mean 200 and standard deviation 100. The probability that X is less than or equal to 250 is

EXHIBIT 6   The Standardized Normal Distribution Function, F(x)

X	0.00	0.01	0.02	0.03	0.04	0.05	0.06	0.07	0.08	0.09
0.0	0.5000	0.5040	0.5080	0.5120	0.5160	0.5199	0.5239	0.5279	0.5319	0.5359
0.1	0.5398	0.5438	0.5478	0.5517	0.5557	0.5596	0.5636	0.5675	0.5714	0.5753
0.2	0.5793	0.5832	0.5871	0.5910	0.5948	0.5987	0.6026	0.6064	0.6103	0.6141
0.3	0.6179	0 6217	0.6255	0.6293	0.6331	0.6368	0.6406	0.6443	0.6480	0.6517
0.4	0.6554	0.6591	0.6628	0.6664	0.6700	0.6736	0.6772	0.6808	0.6844	0.6879
0.5	0.6915	0.6950	0.6985	0.7019	0.7054	0.7088	0.7123	0.7157	0.7190	0.7224
0.6	0.7257	0.7291	0.7324	0.7357	0.7389	0.7422	0.7454	0.7486	0.7517	0.7549
0.7	0.7580	0.7611	0.7642	0.7673	0.7703	0.7734	0.7764	0.7794	0.7823	0.7852
0.8	0.7881	0.7910	0.7939	0.7967	0.7995	0.8023	0.8051	0.8078	0.8106	0.8133
0.9	0.8159	0.8186	0.8212	0.8238	0.8264	0.8289	0.8315	0.8340	0.8365	0.8389
1.0	0.8413	0.8438	0.8461	0.8485	0.8508	0.8531	0.8554	0.8577	0.8599	0.8621
1.1	0.8643	0.8665	0.8686	0.8708	0.8729	0.8749	0.8770	0.8790	0.8810	0.8830
1.2	0.8849	0.8869	0.8888	0.8907	0.8925	0.8944	0.8962	0.8980	0.8997	0.90147
1.3	0.90320	0.90490	0.90658	0.90824	0.90988	0.91149	0.91309	0.91466	0.91621	0.91774
1.4	0.91924	0.92073	0.92220	0.92364	0.92507	0.92647	0.92785	0.92922	0.93056	0.93189
1.5	0.93319	0.93448	0.93574	0.93699	0.93822	0.93943	0.94062	0.94179	0.94295	0.94408
1.6	0.94520	0.94630	0.94738	0.94845	0.94950	0.95053	0.95154	0.95254	0.95352	0.95449
1.7	0.95543	0.95637	0.95728	0.95818	0.95907	0.95994	0.96080	0.96164	0.96246	0.96327
1.8	0.96407	0.96485	0.96562	0.96638	0.96712	0.96784	0.96856	0.96926	0.96995	0.97062
1.9	0.97128	0.97193	0.97257	0.97320	0.97381	0.97441	0.97500	0.97558	0.97615	0.97670
2.0	0.97725	0.97778	0.97831	0.97882	0.97932	0.97982	0.98030	0.98077	0.98124	0.98169
2.1	0.98214	0.98257	0.98300	0.98341	0.98382	0.98422	0.98461	0.98500	0.98537	0.98574
2.2	0.98610	0.98645	0.98679	0.98713	0.98745	0.98778	0.98809	0.98840	0.98870	0.98899
2.3	0.98928	0.98956	0.98983	$0.9^{2}0097$	$0.9^{2}0358$	$0.9^{2}0613$	$0.9^{2}0863$	$0.9^{2}1106$	$0.9^{2}1344$	$0.9^{2}1576$
2.4	$0.9^{2}1802$	$0.9^{2}2024$	$0.9^{2}2240$	$0.9^{2}2451$	$0.9^{2}2656$	$0.9^{2}2857$	$0.9^{2}3053$	$0.9^{2}3244$	$0.9^{2}3431$	$0.9^{2}3613$
2.5	$0.9^{2}3790$	$0.9^{2}3963$	$0.9^{2}4132$	$0.9^{2}4297$	$0.9^{2}4457$	$0.9^{2}4614$	$0.9^{2}4766$	$0.9^{2}4915$	$0.9^{2}5060$	$0.9^{2}5201$
3.0	$0.9^{2}8650$	$0.9^{2}8694$	$0.9^{2}8736$	$0.9^{2}8777$	$0.9^{2}8817$	$0.9^{2}8856$	$0.9^{2}8893$	$0.9^{2}8930$	$0.9^{2}8965$	$0.9^{2}8999$
3.5	$0.9^{3}7674$	$0.9^{3}7759$	$0.9^{3}7842$	$0.9^{3}7922$	$0.9^{3}7999$	$0.9^{3}8074$	$0.9^{3}8146$	$0.9^{3}8215$	$0.9^{3}8282$	$0.9^{3}8347$
4.0	$0.9^{4}6833$	$0.9^{4}6964$	$0.9^{4}7090$	$0.9^{4}7211$	$0.9^{4}7327$	$0.9^{4}7439$	$0.9^{4}7546$	$0.9^{4}7649$	$0.9^{4}7748$	$0.9^{4}7843$

the probability that a zero-mean unit-standard-deviation normally distributed variable is less than or equal to

$$\frac{(250 - 200)}{100} = .5$$

Therefore, $Pr\{X \leq 250\} = Pr\{Z \leq .5\} = .6915$, where Z is the standard notation for a normally distributed random variable with zero mean and unit standard deviation. For any point, X, from a normal distribution, the standard normal deviate Z [$= (X - \bar{X})/\sigma$] represents the number of standard deviation units the random variable X is above or below the mean.

Using the above analysis, one can verify that for a normal distribution:
68.3% of the area is within 1σ of the mean, $\bar{X}$,
95.5% of the area is within 2σ of $\bar{X}$, and
99.7% of the area is within 3σ of $\bar{X}$.

SIMPLE RANDOM SAMPLING

In order to estimate the mean of an accounting population, the auditor chooses a sample of items. The population mean can be estimated from the mean value of items that were selected in the sample. In simple random sampling, the sample is selected at random from the population as a whole. In order to do valid statistical inference it is vital that each item in the population have a specified probability of being included in the sample. In the simplest case, we assign each item in the population an equal probability of being selected. We accomplish this goal by resorting to a random number table. Many computerized systems have programmed random number generators, but for illustrative purposes we will use a table of 700 random numbers shown in Exhibit 7. These numbers, between 0 and 99999, have been selected and arranged in a random fashion but grouped, for convenience, into rows of 5 and 14 columns. Suppose that we wish to select a random sample of 30 invoices from Exhibit 1. We must first decide how to relate a random number chosen from the table in Exhibit 7 to a particular invoice in Exhibit 1. For this example, such a correspondence is easy. There are exactly 100 invoices in Exhibit 1. Therefore, we can use the first two digits (or the last two or two in the middle, for that matter) of each five-digit number to identify a particular invoice. (We adopt the convention that if the two digits turn out to be 00, we will choose invoice number 100.)

In general we would need to adopt a slightly more complex scheme for identifying random numbers with invoices. For example, if we are dealing with a population of 5,300 invoices we would use the first four digits of each five-digit number from a table as in Exhibit 7 but ignore all numbers we select whose first four digits exceed 5,300. If the population had more than 99,999 invoices, we could group two five-digit numbers to form a ten-digit number and use as many digits as we need to cover the population. The important thing with simple random sampling is that each invoice in the population must have an equal chance of being selected by the random number process.

After establishing the correspondence between random numbers and population items, we select a procedure for choosing a sequence of random numbers from the table. Usually we will go down a column or across a row once a starting number has been selected. A random starting number can be chosen by closing our eyes and pointing to a number on the page with a pencil, e.g., the number in column 5 row 22: 47070. We can then use this number to give us a random start, e.g., the number in row 47, column 7, which is 59744. Starting from this number, we move down successive columns until 30 invoices have been selected as shown in Exhibit 8. If a random number turns up an invoice which has already been selected, we ignore it and choose another number until 30 different invoices have been selected. Once the random sample of 30 invoices has been drawn, we can estimate the mean of the 100 invoices in the population by the average of the sample we have chosen. In this example, we chose a sample whose mean value equalled $21.17. Therefore, we would estimate the average value of all invoices in the population as $21.17. Of course, we know that the true value of the arithmetic mean is $19.95. But for any population we encountered in practice, we would have no way of knowing this $19.95 figure without examining the entire population. The whole idea of sampling is to draw a small random sample and hope that we can come close to estimating the true figure by examining only this much smaller sample.

Distribution of Sample Estimates.   Following the procedure just outlined gives us an estimate of the population mean. This estimate is not very useful, however, unless we have some idea of how close this estimate is to the true mean value.

EXHIBIT 7   Random Numbers

Col.	(1)	(2)	(3)	(4)	(5)	(6)	(7)	(8)	(9)	(10)	(11)	(12)	(13)	(14)
1	10480	15011	01536	02011	81647	91646	69179	14194	62590	36207	20969	99570	91291	90700
2	22368	46573	25595	85393	30995	89198	27982	53402	93965	34095	52666	19174	39615	99505
3	24130	48360	22527	97265	76393	64809	15179	24830	49340	32081	30680	19655	63348	58629
4	42167	93093	06243	61680	07856	16376	39440	53537	71341	57004	00849	74917	97758	16379
5	37570	39975	81837	16656	06121	91782	60468	81305	49684	60672	14110	06927	01263	54613
6	77921	06907	11008	42751	27756	53498	18602	70659	90655	15053	21916	81825	44394	42880
7	99562	72905	56420	69994	98872	31016	71194	18738	44013	48840	63213	21069	10634	12952
8	96301	91977	05463	07972	18876	20922	94595	56869	69014	60045	18425	84903	42508	32307
9	89579	14342	63661	10281	17453	18103	57740	84378	25331	12566	58678	44947	05585	56941
10	85475	36857	43342	53988	53060	59533	38867	62300	08158	17983	16439	11458	18593	64952
11	28918	69578	88231	33276	70997	79936	56865	05859	90106	31595	01547	85590	91610	78188
12	63553	40961	48235	03427	49626	69445	18663	72695	52180	20847	12234	90511	33703	90322
13	09429	93969	52636	92737	88974	33488	36320	17617	30015	08272	84115	27156	30613	74952
14	10365	61129	87529	85689	48237	52267	67689	93394	01511	26358	85104	20285	29975	89868
15	07119	97336	71048	08178	77233	13916	47564	81056	97735	85977	29372	74461	28551	90707
16	51085	12765	51821	51259	77452	16308	60756	92144	49442	53900	70960	63990	75601	40719
17	02368	21382	52404	60268	89368	19885	55322	44819	01188	65255	64835	44919	05944	55157
18	01011	54092	33362	94904	31273	04146	18594	29852	71585	85030	51132	01915	92747	64951
19	52162	53916	46369	58586	23216	14513	83149	98736	23495	64350	94738	17752	35156	35749
20	07056	97628	33787	09998	42698	06691	76988	13602	51851	46104	88916	19509	25625	58104
21	48663	91245	85828	14346	09172	30168	90229	04734	59193	22178	30421	61666	99904	32812
22	54164	58492	22421	74103	47070	25306	76468	26384	58151	06646	21524	15227	96909	44592
23	32639	32363	05597	24200	13363	38005	94342	28728	35806	06912	17012	64161	18296	22851
24	29334	27001	87637	87308	58731	00256	45834	15398	46557	41135	10367	07684	36188	18510
25	02488	33062	28834	07351	19731	92420	60952	61280	50001	67658	32586	86679	50720	94953
26	81525	72295	04839	96423	24878	82651	66566	14778	76797	14780	13300	87074	79666	95725
27	29676	20591	68086	26432	46901	20849	89768	81536	86645	12659	92259	57102	80428	25280
28	00742	57392	39064	66432	84673	40027	32832	61362	98947	96067	64760	64584	96096	98253
29	05366	04213	25669	26422	44407	44048	37937	63904	45766	66134	75470	66520	34693	90449
30	91921	26418	64117	94305	26766	25940	39972	22209	71500	64568	91402	42416	07844	69618
31	00582	04711	87917	77341	42206	35126	74087	99547	81817	42607	43808	76655	62028	76630
32	00725	69884	62797	56170	86324	88072	76222	36086	84637	93161	76038	65855	77919	88006
33	69011	65797	95876	55293	18988	27354	26575	08625	40801	59920	29841	80150	12777	48501
34	25976	57948	29888	88604	67917	48708	18912	82271	65424	69774	33611	54262	85963	03547
35	09763	83473	73577	12908	30883	18317	28290	35797	05998	41688	34952	37888	38917	88050
36	91567	42595	27958	30134	04024	86385	29880	99730	55536	84855	29080	09250	79656	73211
37	17955	56349	90999	49127	20044	59931	06115	20542	18059	02008	73708	83517	36103	42791
38	46503	18584	18845	49618	02304	51038	20655	58727	28168	15475	56942	53389	20562	87338
39	92157	89634	94824	78171	84610	82834	09922	25417	44137	48413	25555	21246	35509	20468
40	14577	62765	35605	81263	39667	47358	56873	56307	61607	49518	89656	20103	77490	18062
41	98427	07523	33362	64270	01638	92477	66969	98420	04880	45585	46565	04102	46880	45709
42	34914	63976	88720	82765	34476	17032	87589	40836	32427	70002	70663	88863	77775	69348
43	70060	28277	39475	46473	23219	53416	94970	25832	69975	94884	19661	72828	00102	66794
44	53976	54914	06990	67245	68350	82948	11398	42878	80287	88267	47363	46634	06541	97809
45	76072	29515	40980	07391	58745	25774	22987	80059	39911	96189	41151	14222	60697	59583
46	90725	52210	83974	29992	65831	38857	50490	83765	55657	14361	31720	57375	56228	41546
47	64364	67412	33339	31926	14883	24413	59744	92351	97473	89286	35931	04110	23726	51900
48	08962	00358	31662	25388	61642	34072	81249	35648	56891	69352	48373	45578	78547	81788
49	95012	68379	93526	70765	10593	04542	76463	54328	02349	17247	28865	14777	62730	92277
50	15664	10493	20492	38391	91132	21999	59516	81652	27195	48223	46751	22923	32261	85653

Naturally, the true mean is unobservable (unless we sample the entire population), so we will never know for sure exactly how close we are to the true mean. The remarkable aspect about statistical inference is that we can use the data in our sample to infer a likely interval within which we expect the true mean to be. The principal vehicle that allows us to make this inference is the *central limit theorem*,

EXHIBIT 8   A Random Sample of 30 Invoices

Random number	Invoice number	Invoice value
59744	59	17.48
81249	81	16.36
76463	76	17.94
59516	59	(already selected)
14194	14	23.23
53402	53	20.57
24830	24	21.76
53537	53	(already selected)
81305	81	(already selected)
70659	70	11.90
18738	18	22.06
56869	56	23.57
84378	84	27.20
62300	62	18.59
05859	05	4.15
72695	72	24.62
17617	17	23.33
93394	93	27.63
81056	81	(already selected)
92144	92	32.08
44819	44	25.38
29852	29	21.54
98736	98	33.41
13602	13	19.98
04734	04	10.16
26384	26	21.06
28728	28	16.32
15398	15	23.60
61280	61	26.89
14778	14	(already selected)
81536	81	(already selected)
61362	61	(already selected)
63904	63	26.68
22209	22	16.63
99547	99	28.40
36086	36	19.88
08625	08	12.74

which states that, for large sample sizes (typically, 50 is a reasonable lower bound), the distribution of sample means tends to be normally distributed, almost independently of the shape of the original population. The fact that sample means from an arbitrary distribution converge to a normal distribution is the reason why the normal distribution plays such a central role in statistical sampling theory.

We can demonstrate the central limit theorem by choosing additional random samples of 30 invoices, i.e., replicating the process that we used to generate Exhibit 8. Exhibit 9 shows the results of choosing 100 random samples of size 30 and computing the mean for each one. The grand mean of all these 100 means is $19.95, which also turns out to be the true value, but there is no guarantee that these two numbers will always be the same. The standard deviation of these 100 means is $1.07. If these sample means were distributed exactly in the form of a normal distribution with mean $19.95 and standard deviation $1.07, we would get a distribution as shown in Exhibit 10. The actual distribution of the 100 sample means is plotted in Exhibit 11. We can see, by inspection, that the actual distribution is approximately the same as the normal distribution. If we had plotted more than 100 samples, the distribution would have converged closer to the normal distribution.

If we accept (as we should) the assertion of the central limit theorem that sample

EXHIBIT 9   Average Invoice Value from 100 Samples of 30 Invoices

Sample number	Sample average	Sample number	Sample average	Sample number	Sample average	Sample number	Sample average
1	$20.22	26	$20.99	51	$20.69	76	$20.49
2	20.19	27	20.85	52	20.66	77	17.54
3	19.59	28	18.60	53	21.54	78	18.96
4	18.96	29	19.83	54	19.72	79	21.50
5	19.08	30	21.98	55	19.06	80	20.66
6	20.01	31	21.67	56	19.89	81	18.84
7	19.76	32	19.32	57	20.30	82	19.49
8	21.83	33	21.79	58	19.37	83	20.95
9	20.49	34	20.60	59	20.75	84	21.34
10	19.14	35	20.12	60	22.42	85	18.99
11	18.08	36	20.30	61	18.63	86	19.98
12	19.11	37	19.01	62	20.02	87	19.70
13	20.72	38	17.48	63	20.33	88	20.21
14	18.86	39	21.07	64	18.87	89	18.29
15	20.60	40	20.83	65	19.65	90	18.95
16	19.89	41	19.06	66	20.11	91	20.02
17	19.13	42	20.54	67	19.29	92	19.72
18	21.68	43	18.88	68	18.78	93	20.63
19	18.76	44	20.19	69	19.93	94	22.80
20	20.09	45	19.64	70	18.59	95	21.71
21	19.73	46	20.77	71	18.66	96	20.32
22	19.43	47	20.69	72	20.26	97	21.49
23	19.73	48	18.14	73	20.09	98	19.11
24	21.52	49	18.02	74	18.59	99	19.85
25	19.61	50	19.24	75	20.76	100	20.99

means converge to a normal distribution, we still need to know to which normal distribution they converge; i.e., what is the mean and standard deviation of the distribution of sample means. The following statements give us the information we need to characterize the distribution of sample means:

Suppose that we have a population of N items with mean $\bar{X}$ and standard

EXHIBIT 10   Normal Distribution of Sample Means

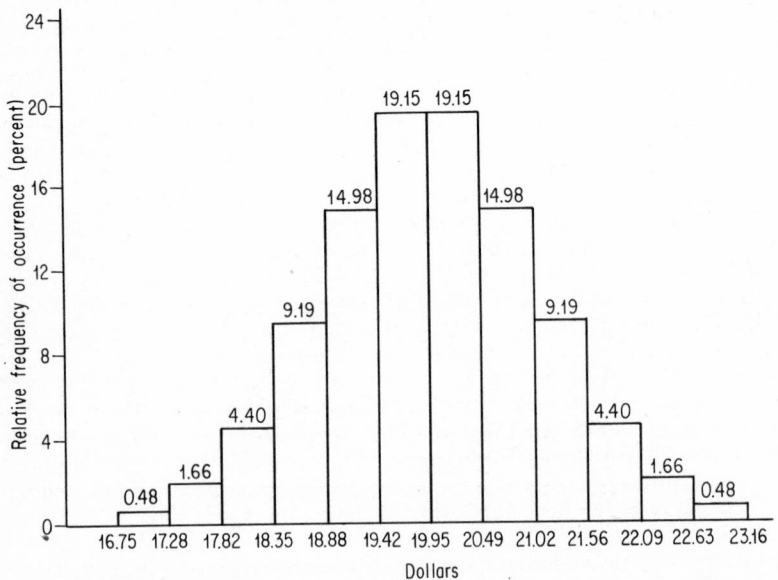

EXHIBIT 11   Actual Distribution of Sample Means

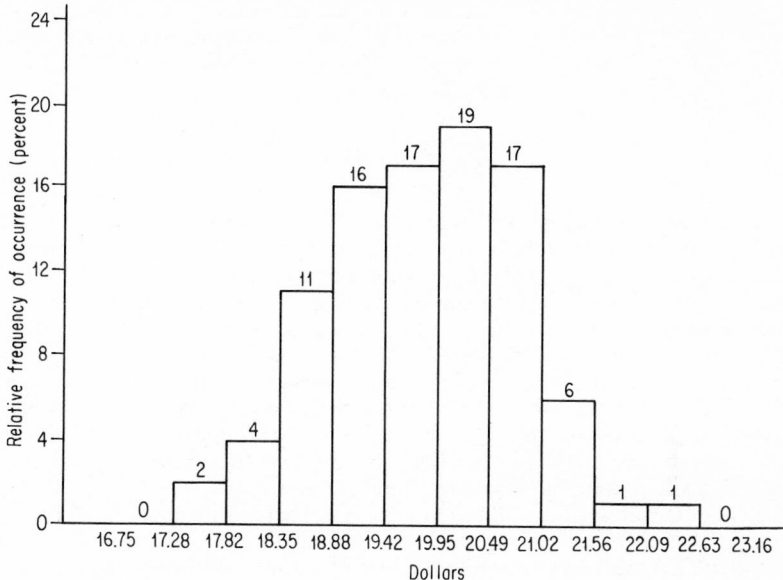

deviation σ. If we take a sample of n items $(n \leq N)$, the sample mean, $\bar{x}$, is normally distributed with mean $\bar{X}$ and standard deviation equal to

$$\sigma_{\bar{x}} = \sqrt{1 - \frac{n}{N}} \; \frac{\sigma}{\sqrt{n}}$$

The first term in the standard deviation formula, $1 - n/N$, is called the finite population correction factor. It is included whenever we sample without replacement as we are doing here (by not allowing the same invoice to enter the population more than once) and indicates that as the sample size n approaches the population size N, there is almost no error in estimating the population mean. The second item, $\sigma/\sqrt{n}$ in the formula is by far the more important one and shows that the uncertainty in estimating the population mean decreases as the sample size increases. The square root of n that appears in the denominator indicates that increasing the sample size by a factor of 4 decreases the standard deviation of the mean estimate by a factor of 2.

In our example we know that the standard deviation, σ, of the population is $6.53. Therefore, if we draw a sample of size 30, the standard error of the mean is given by

$$\sqrt{1 - \frac{30}{100}} \; \frac{6.53}{\sqrt{30}} = .997$$

In practice the standard deviation of the population, σ, will not be known. Fortunately, it can be estimated by the standard deviation of the sample which will be known. If we sample n items and obtain values $x_1, x_2, \ldots, x_n$, we would first compute the sample mean, $\bar{x}$, as

$$\bar{x} = \sum_{i=1}^{n} \frac{x_i}{n}$$

and then compute the sample standard deviation, *s,* as

$$s = \left[\frac{\sum (x_i - \bar{x})^2}{n - 1} \right]^{1/2}$$

or, equivalently, as

$$s = \left(\frac{\sum x_i^2 - n\bar{x}^2}{n - 1} \right)^{1/2}$$

For the random sample drawn in Exhibit 7, we find that $s = 6.39$. We would therefore estimate that the mean estimate of \$21.17 has a standard error of $\sqrt{1 - 30/100}(6.39/\sqrt{30}) = .976$. We expect that in repeated samples of size 30, the average estimated standard error would converge to the true value of .997.

Confidence Intervals.   Now that we have an estimate of the population mean as well as an estimate of the uncertainty in this measure, how can we use this information to infer a range of values within which the true population mean is likely to lie? We use the previously cited result that the sample mean is normally distributed about the true mean $\bar{X}$. Therefore, using the normal distribution and our estimate of the standard deviation, we can construct a confidence interval which will likely contain the true mean value. If we construct confidence intervals within 1σ of the mean, this will contain the true mean value about 68 percent of the time. A 2 σ-wide confidence interval will contain the true value 95.5 percent of the time and a 3σ-wide interval will contain the true value 99.7 percent of the time. Although one may think that it would be fine to construct an interval that will contain the true value such a high percentage of the time, in fact a 3σ confidence interval will be so wide that we will not have restricted the location of the true value very much. In practice a 95-percent confidence interval is typically chosen by using an interval 1.96σ wide.

The width of a confidence interval is usually referred to as the *precision* of the estimate. The percentage figure associated with a given confidence interval (e.g., 95 percent) is called the *reliability* of the estimate. Frequently, people abuse the language when talking about the construction of a confidence interval. They make statements like "the probability is .95 that the true value lies within the confidence interval." Although such a statement may be appropriate for a Bayesian under certain circumstances, it is more accurate to say that "95 percent of the confidence intervals chosen in this manner will contain the true value." For any given confidence interval, the probability is either 0 or 1 that it contains the true value. Since we do not know the true value, we use a procedure such that if a large number of samples of a given size are drawn and a confidence interval 1.96σ wide is constructed as described above, 95 percent of these intervals will include the true population mean. With our numerical example, our 95 percent confidence interval is $\bar{x} \pm 1.96\sigma_{\bar{x}}$ or $21.17 \pm 1.96 \times (.976)$ or $[19.26, 23.08]$. In this case, the 95-percent confidence interval contained the true value. If we repeated the experiment 100 times, about five such intervals would not contain the true mean.

Choosing the Appropriate Sample Size.   In the example discussed so far, we have assumed an arbitrary sample size of 30. The auditor, however, must choose an appropriate sample size so that the sampling procedure yields a conclusion consistent with the objective of the overall audit. Usually, the auditor is concerned with detecting a material error if one exists in the population. Therefore a common procedure is to attempt to construct a confidence interval whose width on either side of the means equals the material amount. Let us denote by A the desired precision or confidence interval width of the sample estimate. Since it is meaningless to think of a confidence interval width or precision without specifying the reliability of the test, the auditor must also specify the desired reliability, too. We continue to assume that the auditor specifies a 95-percent reliability figure.

The auditor therefore wants to choose a sample size, n, such that 1.96 times the standard error of the sample mean $(\sigma_{\bar{x}})$ equals the desired precision figure, A. Mathematically,

$$1.96 \sqrt{1 - \frac{n}{N}} \; \frac{\sigma}{\sqrt{n}} = A$$

Strictly speaking, σ refers to the standard deviation of the distribution of true item values. In practice, however, we may use the standard deviation of the recorded (unaudited) item values in the above equation. Unless large errors are encountered in the sample, the two figures would be quite close to each other. The auditor can thus estimate σ from the list of recorded book values. If such a list is not available, the auditor must estimate σ based on prior judgment, past experience, or even from a preliminary random sample of the account. The above equation is then solved for the sample size n that will yield the desired precision.

If we let $K = 1.96\sigma/A$, we can solve the above equation for n as

$$n = \frac{K^2 N}{K^2 + N}$$

If n is much smaller than N, so that the finite population correction factor can be ignored, we get that

$$n = K^2 = \left(\frac{1.96\sigma}{A}\right)^2$$

In our example of 100 invoices, if we want a 95-percent confidence interval that is ±\$2 wide about the sample mean (a total of \$4 wide, in all), we would first compute K:

$$K = \frac{(1.96)(\sigma)}{2} = .92\sigma$$

and then solve for n.

If we interpret Exhibit 1 as a list of recorded values from which the auditor will select a sample to verify, then we may use the standard deviation of this population, which equals 6.53, as an estimate of the standard deviation of the distribution of true (audited) amounts. In this case we have $K = .92(6.53) = 6.0$ and

$$n = \frac{(6)^2(100)}{(6)^2 + 100} = 26.5$$

Therefore for this population, a sample size of 27 should be adequate to generate a 95-percent confidence interval that is ±\$2 wide. Notice that without the finite population correction factor the required sample size would have been $(6)^2$ or 36.

Depending on the particular items that do get selected and the true (audited) values of these items, the actual confidence interval may be wider or narrower than what was originally intended. For example, in our sample size of 30, the 95-percent confidence interval turned out to be equal to ±1.91. If the ex post confidence interval is wider than the originally desired precision, it may be necessary to choose additional items to sample. To avoid this inconvenience, of having to resample, an auditor may choose to be conservative and increase the indicated sample size by some arbitrary amount, say 10 percent, to be more confident of obtaining the desired precision.

Ex Post Analysis and Statistical Inference.   Once the sample size has been selected, the sample drawn, and the mean and standard error of the mean estimated, we construct a confidence interval based on the desired precision and reliability requirements. If the recorded book value mean falls within the confidence interval, we will conclude that the account is essentially correct, containing no material misstatements. If the confidence interval does not contain the recorded book value mean, we will conclude that the account is materially misstated. At this point, we have the option of using the mean per unit estimate from our sample as the new estimated value for this account. Alternatively, we can choose a larger sample to verify this finding and perhaps get a more precise estimate of the true value of this account.

ADVANCED SAMPLING TECHNIQUES

The simple random sampling approach we have outlined forms the basis of more sophisticated plans, but is rarely adequate by itself for any large-scale application. The principal problem is that the sample sizes required to meet an auditor's materiality objective are prohibitively large when only simple random sampling is used. Whereas our simple example was based on a population of 100 items so that a sample size of between 25 and 30 seemed to be adequate, most interesting auditing populations will contain many thousands of items. With such populations, sample sizes of a thousand or more would not be unusual with simple random sampling. These large sample sizes are caused by two factors: First, accounting populations are likely to be widely dispersed and highly skewed. Therefore the underlying standard deviation, σ, of the population will be large. Second, the auditor's requirement for precision in sampling an account will probably be extremely fine. Although sample surveys in political or social science may be content with confidence intervals whose widths are 5 percent of the value being estimated, auditors may require much more precision in their estimates.

Auditors typically audit balance sheet accounts such as inventory or accounts receivable. As mentioned before, the precision requirement is determined by the materiality percentage. Materiality is usually expressed as a percentage of net income; say 5 to 10 percent of net income. Since many balance sheet accounts are much larger than the income figure, a material error in these accounts must be a lower percentage than the net income percentage. This occurs because any error in these accounts may directly affect the net income figure; e.g., if accounts receivable is three times net income, a 5-percent write-down of accounts receivable is a 15-percent write-down of net income (before taxes). In addition, the overall materiality percentage on net income must be allocated across all balance sheet accounts to ensure that errors of less than a material amount in each account will not build up to produce an overall material error for the entire balance sheet. For these reasons, an auditor could be auditing an account with a precision factor of 1 percent or less. Because the sample size goes up with the square of the inverse of the precision figure, A (recall that for a 95-percent reliability and ignoring the finite population factor, $n = [1.96\sigma/A]^2$), a reduction in A from 5 percent to 1 percent causes the sample size to increase by a factor of 25. Combining this result with the intrinsically high value of σ in accounting populations, we can see that sizes of random samples in realistic problems can become enormous. We now consider two techniques that are useful in reducing these large sample sizes in practice: stratification and auxiliary information estimators.

Stratified Random Sampling. If a population is heterogeneous but can be divided into segments or strata that are relatively homogeneous, we can use stratified sampling techniques to reduce the sample sizes required to achieve a given level of precision and reliability. As an extreme example, consider a population which consists of two categories of items. All items in a category have the same value. If we were to take a simple random sample of items from the entire population we would get an estimate of the mean and some established sampling error. But if we were to group all items into the two categories and take a single sample from each category, we would know the total dollar value of the account with no sampling error at all even though we only drew the two sample items. Although this example is obviously artificial, it does illustrate that if we can stratify the population into groups that are relatively homogeneous, we can sample separately from each group and thereby achieve greater accuracy in our sampling procedure. Accounting populations may not always segregate into natural groupings, but techniques do exist for computing good strata boundaries even in a continuously distributed population.

Assume that the population has been divided into M strata. We will use the following notation:

X_{ij} = value of item i in stratum j $(j = 1, \ldots, M)$

N_j = number of items in stratum j

$\bar{X}_j = \displaystyle\sum_{i=1}^{N_j} X_{ij}/N_j$ = average value of items in stratum j

$S_j = \sqrt{\sum (X_{ij} - \bar{X}_j)^2/N_j}$ = standard deviation of items in stratum j

$N = \displaystyle\sum_{j=1}^{M} N_j$ = total number of items in the population

$W_j = N_j/N$ = proportion of items in stratum j

$\bar{X} = \displaystyle\sum_{j} N_j\bar{X}_j/N$ = average value of all items in the population

Similar notation is used for *sample* values but with lowercase letters substituted for capital letters; e.g., x_{ij} is the value of the ith item sampled in stratum j and n_j is the number of samples taken in stratum j. With this notation, the formula for estimating the population mean, $\hat{\bar{X}}$, is given by

$$\hat{\bar{X}} = \sum_{j=1}^{M} W_j x_j$$

where x_j is the sample mean computed in stratum j. To measure the accuracy of a stratified estimate we must estimate the standard errors of the mean estimate in each stratum and combine these into an overall standard error. The estimated standard error in stratum j, $s_{\bar{x}_j}$ is given by

$$s_{\bar{x}_j} = \frac{s_j}{\sqrt{n_j}} \sqrt{1 - n_j/N_j}$$

where s_j is the estimated standard deviation of stratum j,

$$s_j = \left[\frac{\displaystyle\sum_{i=1}^{n_j} (x_{ij} - \bar{x}_j)^2}{n_j - 1} \right]^{1/2}$$

The factor $\sqrt{1 - n_j/N_j}$ in the formula for $s_{\bar{x}_j}$ is the finite population correction factor in stratum j which can be ignored if the sample size, n_j, in stratum j is a small fraction of the total number of items in stratum j.

The standard error of the overall mean estimate, $s_{\bar{x}}$, is

$$s_{\bar{x}} = \sqrt{\sum_j W_j^2 s_{\bar{x}_j}^2}$$

a weighted sum of the estimated variance in each stratum.

A simple example should help to illustrate the use of stratified random sampling. Suppose that we have a group of invoices which we divide into two strata—a high and a low dollar-value group. The first stratum has 1,000 invoices and we sample 100 of these. The second stratum has 2,000 invoices and we sample 500 of these. These numbers and the sampling statistics are shown in Exhibit 12. The

EXHIBIT 12   Stratified Sample of Invoices

Stratum number (j)	Items in stratum (N_j)	Weight of stratum (W_j)	Items in sample n_j	Mean value of sampled invoices in stratum $\bar{x}_j$	Standard deviation of sampled items in stratum s_j
1	1000	1/3	100	10,000	1000
2	2000	2/3	500	5,000	500

estimate of the population mean is

$$\hat{\bar{X}} = \sum W_j \bar{x}_j = \tfrac{1}{3}(\$10,\!000) + \tfrac{2}{3}(\$5,\!000) = \$6,\!667$$

The standard errors of the mean estimate in each stratum are

$$s_{\bar{x}_1} = \frac{1,\!000}{\sqrt{100}} \sqrt{\frac{1-100}{1,\!000}} = \sqrt{9,\!000}$$

$$s_{\bar{x}_2} = \frac{500}{\sqrt{500}} \sqrt{\frac{1-500}{2,\!000}} = \sqrt{375}$$

Therefore, the standard error for the population mean is

$$s_{\bar{x}} = \sqrt{\sum_j W_j^2 s_{\bar{x}_j}^2} = \sqrt{\tfrac{1}{9}(9,\!000) + \tfrac{4}{9}(375)} = \sqrt{1,\!167}$$

$$= 34$$

It can be shown that a simple random sample of 600 items from the same population would have yielded a standard error close to 100. Thus a simple two-way stratification was able to increase the accuracy of the estimate by a factor of almost 3 in this example.

Sample Size Allocation.   The allocations of sample sizes in the above example (100 to stratum 1 and 500 to stratum 2) was arbitrary. One of the design issues in stratified sampling is how to allocate a given sample size among the various strata. A simple but not optimal method is to use a proportional allocation. In proportional sampling, the proportion of total sampled items allocated to stratum j is equal to the proportion of the number of items in stratum j to the total number of items in the population; e.g.,

$$\frac{n_j}{n} = W_j \quad \text{for} \quad j = 1, \ldots, M$$

In the above example, a proportional allocation would have 200 sample items in stratum 1 and 400 sample items in stratum 2. Note that if we had used this allocation in the example and obtained the same estimates of stratum mean, $\bar{x}_j$ and stratum standard deviation, s_j, the standard errors in each stratum would be

$$s_{x_1} = \sqrt{4{,}500} \text{ and } s_{x_2} = \sqrt{469}$$

and

$$s_{\bar{x}} = \frac{1}{3}\sqrt{4{,}500 + 1{,}876} = 26.6$$

a considerable improvement over the standard error of 34 achieved with the arbitrary (100, 500) allocation. Proportional allocation is useful when either the variability within strata is constant (the S_j's are approximately equal) or else little is known about the variability within each stratum so that one cannot take advantage of prior knowledge of S_j.

If we have prior knowledge about the variability in each stratum, we can compute an optimal allocation of the total sample size to each stratum.

For the optimal allocation, we allocate samples to stratum proportional to the product of the number of items in the stratum and the standard deviation within the stratum.

$$\frac{n_j}{n} = \frac{N_j S_j}{\displaystyle\sum_{k=1}^{M} N_k S_k}$$

Strictly speaking, this allocation is optimal only if there is an equal cost of sampling in each stratum. If there is a cost C_j of sampling each unit in stratum j, then an allocation which has lowest cost for a given precision level or, conversely, has highest precision for a given total sampling cost would allocate proportional to $N_j S_j / \sqrt{C_j}$.

With the optimal allocation, we take a larger sample in a stratum if the stratum itself is larger or has more internal variability than other strata or both. To apply the optimal allocation method to our numerical example, we compute the products $N_j S_j$ for strata 1 and 2, assuming that the population standard deviation in each stratum approximately equals the sample standard deviation

$$N_1 S_1 = N_2 S_2 = 1{,}000{,}000$$

In this case the two product terms are equal, so we would allocate 300 samples to each stratum. Again assuming the same sample results, we estimate the standard errors of the mean estimate in each stratum as

$$s_{\bar{x}_1} = \frac{1{,}000}{\sqrt{300}} \sqrt{1 - \frac{300}{1{,}000}} = \sqrt{2{,}333}$$

$$s_{\bar{x}_2} = \frac{500}{\sqrt{300}} \sqrt{1 - \frac{300}{2{,}000}} = \sqrt{708.3}$$

and the standard error for the population mean is

$$s_{\bar{x}} = \frac{1}{3}\sqrt{2{,}333 + 4(708.3)} = 24$$

The estimated standard error of 24 is below that achieved by proportional allocation (27) and the arbitrary allocation (34).

Total Sample Size Computation. Although we have now given the formulas for the fraction of the total sample size to be allocated to each stratum under both proportional and optimal allocation methods, we still need to compute the total sample size that is required to achieve a given reliability level and precision. With proportional sampling,

$$s_{\bar{x}_j} = \frac{S_j}{\sqrt{n_j}} \sqrt{1 - \frac{n_j}{N_j}} = \frac{S_j}{\sqrt{n W_j}} \sqrt{1 - \frac{n}{N}}$$

and hence,

$$s_{\bar{x}} = \sqrt{\sum W_j^2 s_{x_j}^2} = \frac{\sqrt{1 - n/N}}{\sqrt{n}} \sqrt{\sum W_j S_j^2}$$

With the optimal allocation, substitution yields

$$s_{\bar{x}} = \left[\frac{(\sum W_j S_j)^2}{n} - \frac{\sum W_j S_j^2}{N} \right]^{1/2}$$

If we ignore the effects of the finite population correction factor, which has the conservative effect of increasing the required sample size, we obtain the following simpler results.

Simple random sampling: $s_{\bar{x}}^2 = S^2/n$

Proportional stratified sampling: $s_{\bar{x}}^2 = \sum N_j S_j^2/nN$

Optimal stratified sampling: $s_{\bar{x}}^2 = (\sum N_j S_j)^2/nN^2$.

These formulas give the standard deviation or variance of the mean estimate as a function of known parameters and the total sample size, n. We then solve for the n that gives the desired reliability and precision for the audit test.

Basis of Stratification. One obvious question in this entire development is on what basis are the strata formed for the auditor and how does the auditor know in advance the standard deviation, S_j, in each stratum so that an optimal allocation can be used. We assume that the auditor has a complete list of the recorded book values in the account to be sampled. These book values are the basis upon which strata are formed and the standard deviation of each stratum is estimated. The auditor is, of course, interested in estimating the true dollar value in the account. In the great majority of cases, however, the book values will either equal or be close to the true (audited) values and, hence, they provide an excellent basis for stratification and prior estimation of strata variance.

It is even possible to use the close dependence between book and audited values to compute strata boundaries that result in minimal sample sizes for given precision and reliability. This technique, which should be especially useful for the highly skewed populations frequently encountered by auditors, is described in Section 5A.6 (pp. 128–133) of Cochran [1963]. A related question is how many strata should be used in a stratified sampling plan. Although it is difficult to be definitive on this issue, there is an inherent uncertainty in the sampling process which limits the value of a very large number of strata. One problem is that the estimate of the standard error in each stratum can become highly variable if there are only a few samples allocated to each stratum. Rules of thumb indicate that between 6 and 10 strata are reasonable upper limits. These rules, however, have been developed on populations in which the auxiliary variable, forming the basis of stratification, is not as closely related to the measured variable as the book value is to the audited value in accounting populations. Therefore it is possible that future research may show that more than 10 strata may be useful in the auditing context.

Limitations of Mean Per Unit Estimation. Stratification improves the precision of estimates in auditing but, by itself, may still not provide enough precision to satisfy the auditor's materiality requirements. In addition, a peculiar situation may occasionally develop which would seriously question the validity of the statistical sampling procedure. Recall that with a 95-percent reliability level, 5 percent of the time we will construct a confidence interval which will not contain the true mean value. Thus, 5 percent of the time we will get a sample that, because of sampling variation inherent in the process, will cause us to conclude that an essentially correct population contains material errors. Suppose now that we happen to draw such a sample of book values; i.e., the estimate of the book value mean and the standard deviation of this estimate results in a 95-percent confidence interval that does not contain the overall book value mean. We, of course, will know the book value or recorded mean of all the items in the population, because we assume the auditor has the list of these items before starting the sampling process. In this situation, even if every item that has been selected for audit turns out to be absolutely correct (audited value equals recorded book value for every item sampled), we will construct a confidence interval that does not contain the overall book value mean and, hence, conclude that material errors exist. It would certainly be peculiar to conclude that a population has material misstatements when none of the items audited was in error.

This circumstance arises because of sampling fluctuation in the book values selected for audit. One way to avoid this is always to be sure that the mean book value of items selected for audit equals the overall book value mean. But this is impossible to guarantee when items are selected for audit on a random basis. Another possibility is to keep sampling, past the minimum required sample size, until the sampled book value mean happens to about equal the overall mean. This method, however, may result in much larger sample sizes than are required for the test at given reliability and precision levels. A compromise solution is to sample until at least the confidence interval created by the sample of book values contains the overall mean. This procedure may still require excessive sample sizes. Also, if a few trivial errors turn up in those samples for which the confidence interval just includes the overall mean, the confidence interval based on audited values will not contain the overall mean and the population will be rejected. Those same trivial errors, however, will hardly affect the statistical conclusion of a sample whose book value approximately equals the overall mean.

It seems that a better statistical procedure is needed to eliminate the difficulties that arise because of the whimsical fluctuation in the book value means of the randomly selected sample. Fortunately such a procedure is available when we use ratio, or regression, estimates of the true population mean.

Auxiliary Information Estimators.   We have already mentioned how the auditor can use the list of recorded book values as a basis for stratification. The auditor can also use the information available in the recorded book values of the population in constructing ratio or regression estimators. These estimators are widely used in surveys when extensive information is available on another variable which is correlated with the variable actually being measured by the survey. For example, to estimate consumer spending on leisure, we could use an auxiliary variable of disposable income. This latter figure should be correlated with leisure spending and may be known, in aggregate, for a community from census data. Upon sampling a number of households, we would determine not only the spending figure but also the disposable income for each household. Then the ratio, or regression coefficient, between spending and income is estimated for the households sampled and applied to the mean disposable income of the entire community to arrive at an overall estimate of community leisure spending. This estimate will be more precise than a simple mean per unit estimate, computed from the sampled households, if there is a reasonably high correlation between spending and income. Using an auxiliary variable controls for the sampling variation that would normally occur in the disposable incomes of families that were sampled. A mean per unit estimate of spending would underestimate the true figure if one happened to choose a sample of households whose disposable incomes were below the community average. In the auditing application, mean per unit estimates do not control for the sampling variation in book values of items selected for the sample, as discussed in the previous section.

In applications where auxiliary information estimators are used, the auxiliary information is either a variable which is correlated with the variable being measured (as in the above example) or a rough estimate of the main variable of interest (e.g., an estimate of crop yield on the basis of airplane or photographic surveys). In either case the auxiliary variable is not a perfect surrogate for the variable being estimated. The auditing environment is quite different. The auxiliary variable, the recorded book value of each item in the population, is not just strongly correlated with the main variable, the true (audited) value of each item. In most instances, it is precisely equal to the true value. This condition could lead to greatly reduced sample sizes because the standard error of the estimate is a decreasing function of the correlation between the auxiliary and main variables. Unfortunately, this unique relationship of equality between the two variables can lead to distributional problems in interpreting the standard error of our estimates as we shall subsequently see.

Notation. Assume we have an unstratified population. Let

X_i = recorded dollar value of item i ($i = 1, \ldots, N$)
Y_i = true audited value of item i
$\bar{X} = \Sigma\, X_i/N$ = mean recorded value
$\bar{Y} = \Sigma\, Y_i/N$ = mean true value
$S_x^2 = \Sigma(X_i - \bar{X})^2/(N - 1)$ = population variance of recorded dollar values
$S_y^2 = \Sigma(Y_i - \bar{Y})^2/(N - 1)$ = population variance of true dollar values
$R = \bar{Y}/\bar{X}$ = ratio of true to recorded dollar values
$\rho = \Sigma(Y_i - Y)(X_i - X)/(NS_yS_x)$ = finite population correlation coefficient
$B = \rho S_y/S_x$ = finite population regression coefficient.

As before, sample values are denoted by lowercase versions of the above symbols. The statistical problem is to estimate the true mean value of the population, $\bar{X}$, from our knowledge of $X_1, X_2, \ldots, X_n$, and (x_j, y_j) for $j = 1, \ldots, n$, the items which we have sampled. We also need to obtain an estimate of the standard deviation of our mean dollar value estimate which can be used to construct a confidence interval about the mean estimate.

A Class of Estimators. Almost all auxiliary information estimators of interest are special cases of the general estimator

$$\hat{\bar{Y}} = \bar{y} + z(\bar{X} - \bar{x})$$

where Y is the estimate of the true mean value and z is either a constant or a function of sample values (x_j, y_j). For a mean per unit estimate, the only type considered up to now, simply set $z = 0$. If we set $z = \bar{y}/\bar{x} = r$, the sample estimator of the population ratio, R, we obtain the ratio estimator $(\bar{y}/\bar{x})X$. If we set $z = b$, the sample regression coefficient, where

$$b = \frac{\Sigma\,(x_i - \bar{x})\,(y_i - \bar{y})}{\Sigma\,(x_i - \bar{x})^2}$$

we would obtain the regression estimator. A difference estimator is obtained by setting $z = 1$, which yields

$$\hat{\bar{Y}} = \bar{X} + (\bar{y} - \bar{x})$$

the mean book value adjusted for the difference between sampled audited and book values.

Estimators for which z is computed from sample data, as in ratio and regression estimators, are biased, which implies that the average of sample estimates made from repeated samples from the same population may not converge to the true population parameter. The bias decreases with sample size, however, and has never been reported to be important with the large sample sizes (in excess of 50) typically used in auditing.

With ratio, regression, and difference estimators, a sample in which no errors are found ($y_j = x_j$ for $j = 1, \ldots, n$) will result in a value of z equal to 1. In this case, the estimated true mean value will always equal the recorded mean value $\bar{X}$ (because $z = 1$ and $\bar{y} = \bar{x}$). Thus we will never have the situation which arises with mean per unit estimators in which no errors are found in the sample but the true mean value is estimated as being different from the recorded book value mean. The use of the auxiliary information controls for the sampling variation in book values selected for audit.

Variance of Auxiliary Information Estimators.   The variance of auxiliary information estimators is estimated from the sample as

$$s_{\bar{y}}^2 = \frac{1 - n/N}{n} \left[s_y^2 - 2z\hat{\rho}s_y s_x + z^2 s_x^2 \right]$$

where terms in the square bracket are sample estimates of the corresponding population parameters; e.g., $\hat{\rho}$ = sample correlation coefficient = $\Sigma(x_i - \bar{x})(y_i - \bar{y})/(n-1)s_y s_x$. Results for the particular estimators we have described are presented in Exhibit 13. One can verify that the regression estimator will have the lowest estimated variance of all the auxiliary information estimators. In practice, for low error rate populations in which $y_j = x_j$ for almost all items, there is not much difference in the variance of the ratio, regression, and difference estimators.

EXHIBIT 13   Auxiliary Information Estimators and Their Variances

	$\hat{\bar{Y}} = \bar{y} + z(\bar{X} - \bar{x})$	
Name of estimator	z	$ns_{\bar{y}}^2/(1 - n/N)$
Mean per unit	0	s_y^2
Difference	1	$s_y^2 - 2\hat{\rho}s_y s_x + s_x^2$
Ratio	$r = \bar{y}/\bar{x}$	$s_y^2 - 2r\hat{\rho}s_y s_x + r^2 s_x^2$
Regression	$b = \hat{\rho}s_y/s_x$	$s_y^2(1 - \hat{\rho}^2)$

Note: $\hat{\rho} = \Sigma(y_i - \bar{y})(x_i - \bar{x})/ns_y s_x$.

Once we have chosen a particular auxiliary information estimator, we will estimate the true mean value, $\hat{\bar{Y}}$, and compute the standard deviation of this estimate using the formulas in Exhibit 13. The next step usually assumes that the central limit theorem holds for mean estimates computed using auxiliary information estimators. Therefore, normal distribution theory can be applied to construct confidence intervals about the estimated mean as we did in a previous section, and see whether the recorded mean value is included in such an interval.

Although such a procedure may provide satisfactory results in many circumstances, it is unlikely that the statistical inferences from this procedure will be correct if we are working with a low error rate population. As an extreme case, if no errors are found in the sample, then s_y will equal s_x, $\hat{\rho}$ will equal one, and the standard deviation will be estimated to be zero. If only a few errors are found in the population, the standard errors will be underestimated and confidence intervals will be narrower than they should be. Therefore, instead of 95 percent of the confidence intervals that are $\pm 1.96\sigma_{\bar{y}}$ wide, containing the true mean value, perhaps only 90 percent or 80 percent of the intervals so constructed will contain the true mean value.

Thus, ratio and regression estimators, although avoiding the problem of estimating a true mean value different from the recorded value when no errors are found in the sample, lead to statistical inference problems in low error rate situations. This area is still being explored and investigated. One compromise solution is to use the ratio or regression estimate as the estimate of the true mean but to use the stratified mean per unit standard deviation estimate. This standard deviation estimate is an upper bound on the true standard deviation of the ratio or regression estimate and hence will not produce confidence intervals that are too narrow. The difficulty with this procedure is that we are forced to use a sample size that is larger than is really needed given that we are using a ratio or regression estimate of the mean.

An additional possibility is to use stratified ratio or regression estimates to get the combined advantage of both stratification and auxiliary information estimators. Readers interested in this possibility should consult a text in sampling theory such as Cochran [1963].

HYPOTHESIS TESTING

The discussion in the preceding sections has concentrated on *estimating* the true value of a parameter and developing statistical confidence intervals within which the true value of the parameter is likely to lie. Most of the traditional literature applying statistical sampling to variables estimation in auditing has advocated the use of this estimation approach. Recently, however, authors (see Elliott and Rogers [1972]) have expressed the position that auditors should be more concerned with tests of hypotheses about the parameters of populations rather than estimating these parameters. Although in a certain sense estimation and hypothesis testing can be viewed as being equivalent, the prior specification of the degree of precision or risk may be much easier or more natural for auditors with hypothesis testing than with interval estimation.

Hypothesis testing is most useful when we have some prior feelings about the value of a parameter (such as the mean) of a population. After drawing a random sample of observations from this population we would then wish to test whether this sample is consistent with our prior feelings about the parameter. Typically we test in such a way so that we can conclude either (1) that the sample is inconsistent with our prior feelings so that we reject the hypothesis that the sample could have come from a population with our prespecified value of the parameter; or (2) that the sample is consistent with our prior feelings so that we cannot reject our initial hypothesis about the value of this parameter. This second conclusion is frequently referred to as "accepting our initial hypothesis," but it is more correct to say that "we did not reject it."

To be more specific, let us return to the population of invoices in Exhibit 1 and the random sample of 30 invoices drawn from this population as shown in Exhibit 8. Suppose that we wish to test the hypothesis that these 30 invoices came from a population whose mean equalled $19.95 (the recorded value for the 100 invoices in Exhibit 1). Recall that the sample mean was $21.17 and the sample standard deviation was $6.39. The question we must now ask is: If the true mean of the population were really $19.95, how likely is it that we would draw a random sample of 30 items and find the mean value of the sample to be as high as $21.17, or even higher? In other words, what is the probability that the sample mean could deviate from the true mean by $1.22 just by chance alone. If this probability is sufficiently small, we reject our initial hypothesis (commonly called the *null hypothesis*). If the probability is high enough, we conclude that we cannot reject the null hypothesis.

To test the hypothesis, we use the previously computed standard error of the mean of .976. Thus, the sample mean is $1.22/.976 = 1.25$ standard errors away from the assumed mean. Remembering the implication of the central limit theorem that sample means will be normally distributed, we want to know the probability that a normally distributed random variable could be more than 1.25 standard errors away from its mean. Referring to the normal distribution function tabulated in Exhibit 6, we see that there is a probability of $1 - .8944 = .1056$ of getting such a high observation. Allowing for random fluctuations in both directions (both high and low deviations of at least 1.25σ), we see that there is a probability greater than 1 in 5 of getting a sample mean that is more than 1.25σ from the hypothesized mean. We will likely conclude that this occurence is sufficiently common that we would not wish to reject our initial or null hypothesis. If the sample mean had turned out to be $23.00 with a standard deviation of the mean equal to $1.00, then the sample mean would have been 3.05 standard errors from the assumed mean. The probability of getting such a large deviation by chance alone would be about .002. We would conclude in this case that it was extremely unlikely that the sample came from a population whose mean equalled $19.95 and hence reject the null hypothesis.

Type I and Type II Errors.   Understandably, the question can be raised: What critical value should we select for the probability of getting an observed difference from our null hypothesis by chance, above which we should accept the hypothesis and below which we should reject it? This value is called the *critical probability* or *level of significance,* and is denoted α (alpha). Naturally, the answer to this question is not simple.

Only four possible things can happen when we test a hypothesis. We may be wrong because we:

1. Reject a hypothesis that is really true (a Type I error), or
2. Accept a hypothesis that is false (a Type II error).

Or, we may be right because we:

3. Accept a true hypothesis, or
4. Reject a false hypothesis.

The types of errors, noted as possibilities 1 and 2 above are known either as Type I and Type II errors or as errors of the first kind and errors of the second kind.

Type I Errors.   In a long run of cases in which the hypothesis is in fact *true* (although we do not know it is true, for otherwise there would be no need to test it), we will necessarily either be wrong as in 1 or right as in 3. That is to say, if we make an error it will have to be Type I. Suppose that we adopt 5 percent as the critical probability, accepting the hypothesis when the probability of getting the observed difference by chance exceeds 5 percent and rejecting the hypothesis when this probability proves to be less than 5 percent. This amounts to the decision to accept the hypothesis when the discrepancy of the sample mean is less than 1.96 standard errors and to reject the hypothesis when the discrepancy is more than 1.96 standard errors. Using this value as the critical probability, we would expect to make a Type I error 5 percent of the time. This is because even when the hypothesis is true, 5 percent of all possible sample means still lie farther away than 1.96 standard errors. And whenever by chance we get one of these, and the hypothesis is true, we would make the mistake of rejecting a true hypothesis.

Or, we might choose 1 percent as the critical probability, which would correspond to a discrepancy between hypothesis and sample mean equal to 2.58 standard errors. When the hypothesis is in fact true, only 1 percent of all possible sample means would lie farther away than 2.58 standard errors. We would make a Type I error only when by chance alone we happened to draw one of these. Which is to say, we would now make an error of the first kind only 1 percent of the time.

Type II Errors.   So far we have concerned ourselves only with the first kind of error. But there is also the second kind—the possible error of accepting a false hypothesis. The lower the value we set for the critical probability, in general, the fewer the hypotheses we will reject. But the chances are then increased of accepting more hypotheses which are false. For a fixed sample size we can buy safety in one direction only at the expense of danger in the other.

Unfortunately, it is impossible to predict in general the percentage of times we should expect to commit an error of the second kind on the basis of any particular value adopted for the critical probability. The reason for this is that the chance of accepting a false hypothesis depends also on how far away from the true value the particular hypothesis happens to be. Remember that sample means tend to cluster around the true means of the populations from which they are drawn. If the hypothetical mean is far away from the true mean, it is unlikely that a sample mean will be drawn which appears consistent with the hypothesis. If the hypothetical mean is false but not far from the mark, an error of the second kind is much more likely to be made.

For example, in our population of invoices, if the true mean happened to be $20.50, we would be unlikely to reject the null hypothesis of $19.95 and we would make a Type II error almost all the time. If the true mean were $30, however, we would be correctly rejecting the null hypothesis almost always and, hence, rarely making a Type II error.

In a long run of instances in which hypotheses are actually false, some will be farther from the true mean than others. Therefore, it is impossible to predict in general the probability of accepting false hypotheses. We can appreciate, however, that the chances of accepting false hypotheses are increased as fewer null hypotheses are rejected due to the use of a lower value for the critical probability.

Balancing Type I Against Type II Errors.   In testing hypotheses we thus face two dangers: either rejecting a true hypothesis (Type I error) or not rejecting à false hypothesis (Type II error). The danger of committing a Type I error can be made as low as we wish by reducing the value chosen for the critical probability, α. This can only be done, however, by increasing the probability of committing a Type II error.

In the auditing context, a Type I error corresponds to rejecting perfectly correct financial statements. A Type II error occurs when the auditor accepts financial statements that contain material errors. Although most applications of hypothesis testing are more concerned with making Type I errors rather than Type II errors, we can see that the auditor will be most concerned with making a Type II error. If the auditor makes a Type I error, by rejecting a correct financial statement balance, he will usually investigate further to determine the causes of the errors he found. Thus the costs associated with this risk arise from the unnecessary follow-up work the auditor subsequently performs. The risk of accepting materially incorrect financial statements, however, is of critical importance to the auditor. Therefore, the auditor wishes to set the probability of making a Type II error very low. In fact, being able to control explicitly for Type II errors is the principal reason why hypothesis testing may be preferred to interval estimation by auditors.

So long as a given sample size is assumed, the risk of one type of error can be reduced only by increasing the probability of making the other type of error. By taking a larger sample size, however, we can reduce the probability of making either or both types of errors. As the sample size is increased, the sample mean will tend to become closer to the true mean and the estimate of the standard error of the mean will be reduced. If we hold the probability of making a Type I error constant, an increase in sample size will enable us to reduce the probability of making a Type II error. In summary, the probability of a Type II error decreases as each of the following items increases:

1. The critical probability, α, of a Type I error
2. The difference in parameter values (e.g., mean values) between the null hypothesis and the alternative hypothesis
3. The sample size.

Given prespecified values of the permissible values of making Type I and Type II errors, and the amount considered material (which determines the alternative hypothesis), the auditor can estimate what sample size is required to meet these audit requirements with the population being investigated and the characteristics of the statistical procedure being used.

MULTIPLE REGRESSION ANALYSIS

Introduction. Statistical analysis is frequently used to estimate the relation among a number of simultaneous variables. In the most common application for accountants, regression analysis is used to estimate how costs vary with the level of activity of a process or an entire department. Typically a linear relationship is assumed and the fixed and variable components of costs estimated from historical data. These can then be used for product planning and cost control by predicting the expected level of costs at a variety of output volumes.

Although cost estimation has been the most widespread application of regression analysis for accountants, some accountants are increasingly seeing the value of this technique in financial audits. At a given time, the many similar branches or divisions of a large organization (e.g., branch banks, retail outlets) can be simultaneously compared to determine if the cost or profit performance of any of these units is unusual when compared to the normal performance of the great majority of units. Systematic differences among the units such as size or location can be controlled for in the statistical analysis so that any large deviations from normal performance would be attributable initially to unexplained factors. Units with such unexplained deviations would then become prime candidates for special attention in the audit process.

Simple Regression. Regression analysis starts with a mathematical model which expresses the analyst's beliefs as to how the dependent variable, say cost, varies with the level of one or more independent variables such as measures of output. For example, let Y = monthly overhead cost in a department which produces nothing but widgets and let X_1 be the number of widgets produced in a month. Then we may postulate a linear relation in which

$$Y = \beta_0 + \beta_1 X_1 + \epsilon$$

where β_0 and β_1 are unknown coefficients to be estimated and ϵ is an error term which represents the effects of omitted and transitory random factors that may occur in a month (excessive sickness, variations in worker morale or machine efficiency, etc.). It would be rare for all the observations on output and cost to have an exact linear relationship. The error term, ϵ, attempts to capture the departures from strict linearity.

In the linear relationship, β_0 represents the fixed overhead costs associated with producing widgets and β_1 represents the variable component of overhead costs. That is, if output X_1 goes up by 1 widget, we expect overhead costs to increase by β_1 dollars. The linear relation implies that if X_1 goes up by 100 widgets, expected overhead costs will increase, proportionately, by $100\beta_1$ dollars.

As a simple example consider the data in Exhibit 14, which represent the monthly output of widgets and overhead costs in a 12-month period. The first step in any analysis is to plot the data to see if a linear relationship is a reasonable one to postulate. (See Exhibit 15.) In this case, the data do appear to be scattered about a straight line and we can proceed with the analysis. If the relationship between costs and output appears to be nonlinear, then more complex models would need to be estimated.

A number of heuristic techniques exist for fitting a line to the data, including the time-tested ones of eyeballing and trial and error. Regression analysis provides a way of computing a unique line that minimizes the sum of the squares of the

EXHIBIT 14

Month	No. of widgets produced (X_1)	Overhead cost (Y)
1	9,000	$390,000
2	10,500	410,000
3	13,000	435,000
4	11,000	410,000
5	11,800	431,000
6	15,000	440,000
7	12,000	420,000
8	14,000	434,000
9	16,500	470,000
10	10,000	410,000
11	12,500	430,000
12	14,500	450,000

EXHIBIT 15

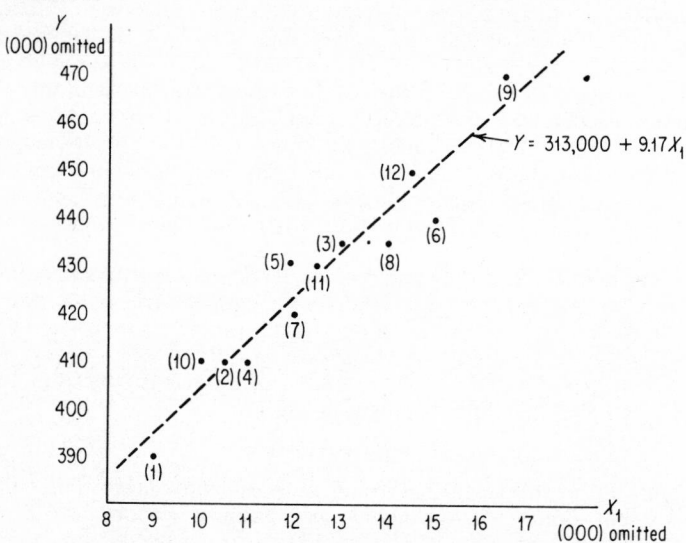

vertical distances (the least-squares criterion) from each observation point to the estimated line. Although this line may be close to ones that would be fitted using less sophisticated procedures, the regression analysis can be easily extended to handle nonlinear functions and also to allow more than one variable to explain the variation in costs. Consider, for example, a department which produced more than one product or which had strong seasonal components in its cost behavior. Regression analysis also provides a measure of the goodness of fit of the assumed linear relationship and enables us to determine statistical confidence limits for the estimated line.

Many texts describe the formulas used to compute regression coefficients and associated statistical measures. In practice, one would always use a prepro-grammed regression routine on a computer to perform the necessary calculations. Therefore, I will not describe the detailed calculations involved but just indicate the results for our numerical example. For the data in Exhibit 14, the least-squares regression line is

$$Y = \$313,000 + \$9.17X_1$$

Thus when X_1 = 10,000 units, departmental overhead costs are estimated at $313,000 + $91,700 = $404,700. When X_1 = 15,000 units, overhead costs are estimated as $450,550. The regression line is drawn on Exhibit 15, and one can see that the estimated line does provide a reasonable fit to the data.

A widely used measure of goodness of fit of the regression line is called the *coefficient of determination*, or R^2. With raw data on only the dependent variable (cost in this case), all we observe, initially, is the variation or variance of this variable about its mean; e.g., $V(Y) = \Sigma(Y_i - Y)^2/(n - 1)$. Without observing any other variables but this one, we would only be able to conclude that this variable—departmental overhead cost—was highly variable over time, ranging from a low of $390,000 in month 1 to a high of $470,000 in month 9. (One can check that the standard deviation of Y is $21,250.) Most of this variation, however, can be explained by the dependence of overhead cost on output and the actual variation of output throughout the year. That is, if there had been less variation in output there would have been less variation in overhead cost. The statistic, R^2, measures how much of the variation in the dependent variable, cost, can be explained by the variation of the independent variable, output. In this case, the linear fit is very good: R^2 = .91, implying that 91 percent of the variation of departmental overhead costs is explained by the regression equation linking cost to output. Therefore, only 9 percent of the variation in departmental costs is nonassignable and due to random, unexplained factors. Such a fit is quite good. One should not always expect that simple linear models will be able to explain complex empirical data so well. Many times we must settle for equations whose R^2 equals 0.5 or less, in which case there is still a considerable amount of scatter of data points about the regression line.

Additional statistics are also available from the regression analysis. It is common to assume that the error term, ϵ, is normally distributed with zero mean and constant variance, regardless of the value of the independent variable X_1. With these assumptions, it is possible to show that the actual values of the dependent variable will be normally distributed about its expected value as estimated from the regression equation. We can then use normal distribution theory to calculate a confidence interval for the predicted level of future overhead costs given an estimate as to what future output will be.

The normality assumption also allows us to construct confidence intervals or test hypotheses about the coefficients of the regression equation. In the above example, the estimated variable overhead coefficient is $9.17 per widget. The standard error of this estimate turns out to be .87. Thus, a confidence interval $\pm 2\sigma$ wide about the estimate would imply that the true value of this coefficient is highly likely to be between $7.43 and $10.91. Alternatively, we frequently want to test whether a given regression coefficient is statistically different from zero. If there is no relation between the dependent and independent variable, the coefficient of the independent variable should be zero. Even if this were the case, sampling fluctuations would cause an estimated coefficient to be different from zero. We would then test whether such an estimate could occur if the true value were zero. A rough rule of thumb in such circumstances is to accept a coefficient as statistically significant if it is at least twice its standard error. In this case the coefficient is more than 10 times its standard error, and we are confident that the relation between overhead cost and output is statistically significant.

Multiple Regression. The discussion so far has assumed that changes in overhead cost are a function of only a single independent variable (output of widgets) and a random error term. In most departments, however, more than one product or type of service is produced, so that it may be difficult to arrive at a single measure of output. Sometimes a measure of input such as direct labor hours, direct labor dollars, or machine hours is used as a proxy variable for output, as in classical flexible budgeting. This technique may not be satisfactory if the different products or services use differing amounts of inputs so that no single measure captures the aggregate level of activity in a department.

Multiple regression analysis enables us to estimate simultaneously the effects on overall departmental costs of all the different activities that are performed in a department. To continue our example, let us consider a department which produces three types of widgets. Let X_i = output of widget type i ($i = 1, 2, 3$) in a period. Exhibit 16 shows, for a 10-month period, the output of widgets and total

EXHIBIT 16 Cost and Output Data for Three Types of Widgets

Month	Widget Type			Total (ΣX_i)	Departmental costs (Y)
	X_1	X_2	X_3		
1	8,000	1,600	2,400	12,000	$450,000
2	7,760	1,720	2,440	11,920	445,000
3	7,080	1,160	2,440	10,680	425,000
4	7,240	1,560	2,320	11,120	430,000
5	7,800	1,520	2,520	11,840	445,000
6	7,440	1,840	2,480	11,760	438,000
7	7,400	1,520	2,320	11,240	434,000
8	7,520	1,680	2,280	11,480	438,000
9	7,280	1,560	2,560	11,400	433,000
10	7,440	1,760	2,320	11,520	437,000

departmental costs for each month. A simple linear regression of departmental costs versus total output in widgets yields the following estimated relationship:

$$Y = \$235,000 + \$17.61 \ \Sigma \ X_i \qquad R^2 = .91$$
$$(1.98)$$

where the standard error of the coefficient of total output appears in parentheses. The fit is quite good and we might normally be satisfied with this estimated relationship. Nevertheless, if we believe that there are significant differences in the variable costs of producing the three types of widgets, we might try to estimate the variable cost of each type of widget separately. Because many accounts are only accumulated on a department-wide basis, we cannot get a finer breakdown that would enable us to estimate the variable cost of each widget type without a statistical analysis. We therefore estimate a relation of the form

$$Y = \beta_0 + \beta_1 X_1 + \beta_2 X_2 + \beta_3 X_3 + \epsilon$$

where β_i is the variable cost of producing widget i, $i = 1, 2, 3$. This equation assumes that the extra cost of producing another widget of type 1 is β_1 and this increase in cost is independent of the level of production of the other widgets (types 2 and 3) as well as the current level of production of widget type 1. If we are not happy with these assumptions, then we may need to estimate a more complex model involving interactions among the widgets or nonlinear costs for each widget separately. (Of course, we are already pushing the limits of our data even with our relatively simple linear model when we estimate four coefficients from only 10 data points.)

When the data in Exhibit 16 are used to estimate the above multiple regression model, we get

$$Y = \$228,727 + \$24.60X_1 + \$6.18X_2 + \$5.99X_3 \qquad R^2 = .99$$
$$(.39) \qquad (.59) \qquad (1.05)$$

We see, from this estimated relation, that widget type 1 apparently costs about four times as much to produce as either widget type 2 or 3. We have also succeeded in explaining almost all the variation in departmental cost over these 10 periods by the variation in production of the three types of widgets. Before performing the statistical analysis, we would know only that departmental cost over these 10 periods had a mean of $437,500 and a standard deviation of $7,560. We might assume that this standard deviation of about 2 percent of the mean is attributable to normal random fluctuations. In fact, however, almost all of the fluctuation in cost is caused by variations in production levels of the three types of widgets. Again, we should not expect to be able to find such an excellent fit when working with actual data.

A possible next step would be to establish a flexible budgeting scheme for the department in which costs are budgeted to fluctuate not on the basis of total output but on the basis of output of the different types of widgets produced in that department, i.e., a flexible budget equation of the form:

$$\text{Budgeted cost} = \$228,700 + \$24.60X_1 + \$6.18X_2 + \$5.99X_3$$

In addition, the standard errors of the regression can be used to construct confidence limits about this regression line to detect when an actual cost is significantly (in a statistical sense) different from the expected level of cost given how much was produced that period.

A Warning.   The above discussion only touches on the basic mechanics of using simple regression techniques for cost analysis. In fact, many subtle problems arise and must be dealt with before one can competently use regression analysis. Issues such as adjusting for inflation when using past cost data, changes in operations or technology over time, and a variety of statistical problems not discussed here frequently arise in applications. Techniques for dealing with these issues do exist but require a considerable amount of sophistication on the part of the user. One of the dangers of having regression routines so widely available on time-shared computers is that regression analysis may be used by individuals not familiar with the pitfalls of this technique, and they may attribute more faith in the relationships uncovered by this technique than may actually be warranted. Conversely, interesting statistical relationships may actually exist in a set of data which do not get discovered because only the most casual analysis is performed. Chapter 3 in Dopuch, Birnberg, and Demski [1974] and references in that chapter provide an interesting discussion of the opportunities and problems that regression analysis holds for accountants. Statistical procedures provide valuable tools for accountants, but misuse of these tools is easy without adequate training and experience.

BIBLIOGRAPHY

Cochran, William G.: *Sampling Techniques*, 2nd ed., John Wiley & Sons, New York, 1963.

Cyert, R. M., and H. Justin Davidson: *Statistical Sampling for Accounting Information*, Prentice-Hall, Englewood Cliffs, N.J., 1962.

Dopuch, Nicholas, Jacob G. Birnberg, and Joel Demski: *Cost Accounting*, 2nd ed., Harcourt Brace Jovanovich, New York, 1974.

Elliott, Robert K., and John R. Rogers: "Relating Statistical Sampling to Audit Objectives," *Journal of Accountancy*, pp. 46–55, July 1972.

Johnston, J.: *Econometric Methods*, 2nd ed., McGraw-Hill Book Company, New York, 1972.

Kaplan, Robert S., "Statistical Sampling in Auditing with Auxiliary Information Estimators," *Journal of Accounting Research*, vol. 11, Autumn 1973.

Neter, John, and James K. Loebbecke, *Behavior of Major Statistical Estimates in Sampling Accounting Populations: An Empirical Study*, AICPA, New York, 1975.

Spurr, William A., and Charles P. Bonini: *Statistical Analysis for Business Decisions*, rev. ed., Richard D. Irwin, Homewood, Ill., 1973.

Chapter **11**

Mathematical Models and Accounting

JOEL S. DEMSKI
Professor of Information and Accounting Systems,
Stanford University

NICHOLAS DOPUCH
Professor of Accounting, University of Chicago

INTRODUCTION

Accountants have long made use of mathematical models in a variety of different contexts. Evidence of this use is abundant, provided that we accept a liberal definition of a mathematical model. Basically, a mathematical model is a descriptive or predictive symbolic representation of some system, object, process, or subject of inquiry.

Based on this definition, we may classify the accountants' financial budget of the firm's operations as a mathematical model. The typical break-even calculation

$$\text{Break-even volume in units} = \frac{\text{fixed costs}}{\text{contribution margin per unit}}$$

can also be viewed as a mathematical model since it implies a particular form of profit function for the firm. That is, a constant contribution margin suggests that the total revenue and total cost curves of the firm have constant slopes over all relevant ranges of output.

The assumption of a linear cost curve has proved to be useful in many types of cost-volume-profit analysis, ranging from simple make-or-buy decisions to complex linear programming problems. This, in turn, has encouraged the use of simple linear regression models in cost estimation and control.

Linear regression estimates of cost functions are generally based on the "least squares" method. This provides an estimate of a total cost—$Y_{est} = a + bx$ (x is some output base)—which has the following property: Given a sample of total cost and output base observations, the sum of the squared differences between the observed cost (Y_0) and its estimate (Y_{est}) is minimized. In terms of symbols, and assuming a sample size of n paired observations, the objective is to minimize

$$\sum_n E^2 = \sum_n (Y_0 - Y_{est})^2 = \sum_n (Y_0 - a - bx)^2$$

The values of a and b which lead to this condition are found by differentiating the equation $\Sigma E^2 = \Sigma(Y_0 - a - bx)^2$ with respect to a and b and setting these partial derivatives equal to 0. (For an elaboration of this technique, see Chapter 10.) The more recent applications of multiple regression in cost analysis represent an extension of the least-squares model to incorporate the relationship between a particular cost and several output variables. This model takes the form:

$$Y_{est} = a + b_1 x_1 + b_2 x_2 + \cdots + b_m x_m$$

The estimates of a, b_1, b_2, . . . , b_m are obtained in the same general manner as in the simple least-squares model.[1]

Mathematical models have also been used in accounting for such problems as the estimate of bad debt allowances,[2] audit planning,[3] cost-volume-profit analysis,[4] and standard cost variance investigation.[5]

[1] A critique of these models is found in G. Benston, "Multiple Regression Analysis of Cost Behavior," *The Accounting Review,* October 1966; and R. E. Jensen, "A Multiple Regression Model for Cost Control—Assumptions and Limitations," *The Accounting Review,* April 1967.

[2] G. Schroderheim, "Using Mathematical Probability to Estimate the Allowance for Doubtful Accounts," *The Accounting Review,* July 1964; and R. M. Cyert, H. J. Davidson, and G. L. Thompson, "Estimation of the Allowance for Doubtful Accounts by Markov Chains," *Management Science,* April 1962.

[3] B. E. Cushing, "A Mathematical Approach to the Analysis and Design of Internal Control Systems," *The Accounting Review,* January 1974; and E. L. Summers, "The Audit Staff Assignment Problem: A Linear Programming Analysis," *The Accounting Review,* July 1972.

These examples illustrate how mathematics may be applied to rather specific kinds of accounting problems. The use of compound interest models in capital budgeting, in the selection of depreciation methods,[6] and in accounting for various liabilities[7] represents more general applications of mathematical analysis in accounting. The same may be said about the use of matrix algebra models[8] and decision theory.[9]

The above are but a few of the many examples which could be cited regarding the application of mathematical models in accounting. An elaboration on these and other uses of mathematics will be found in the appropriate chapters of this handbook.

The number and extent of the applications of mathematics in accounting and other business fields have grown rapidly in the last two decades. Many firms now analyze the traditional problems of asset acquisition and asset utilization with the aid of formal (mathematical) decision models. In particular, a number of firms use inventory and linear programming models to guide their decisions concerning inventory levels and output mixes. The implementation of these formal decision models has implications for the accounting function of providing data for management planning and for the control and evaluation of operating decisions. The nature of these models and their impact on accounting will be discussed in more detail in the remaining sections of this chapter.

THE BASIC INVENTORY MODEL

The problem of inventory management is essentially one of obtaining a proper balance among three types of costs: acquisition costs, storage costs, and stockout costs. Acquisition costs refer to purchase costs plus the costs of processing purchase orders, or, in the event a firm manufactures units for inventory, to costs of manufacturing and setup costs. Storage costs consist of the opportunity cost of capital invested in inventory, the typical warehouse costs, and insurance and taxes on units of inventory held in stock as well as the risk of obsolescence. Stockout costs

---

[4]G. Johnson and S. Simik, "Multiproduct C.V.P. Analysis Under Uncertainty," *Journal of Accounting Research,* Autumn 1971; and R. Manes, "A New Dimension to Break-Even Analysis," *Journal of Accounting Research,* Spring 1966. Also see D. L. Jensen, "The Role of Cost in Pricing Joint Products: A Case of Production in Fixed Proportions," *The Accounting Review,* July 1974; R. S. Kaplan and U. P. Welam, "Overhead Allocation with Imperfect Markets and Nonlinear Technology," *The Accounting Review,* July 1974; and J. S. H. Kornbluth, "Accounting in Multiple Objective Linear Programming," *The Accounting Review,* April 1974.

[5]R. S. Kaplan, "Optimal Investigation Strategies with Imperfect Information," *Journal of Accounting Research,* Spring 1969.

[6]I. Reynolds, "Selecting the Proper Depreciation Policy," *The Accounting Review,* April 1961; also see R. P. Brief and J. Owen, "A Reformulation of the Estimation Problem," *Journal of Accounting Research,* Spring 1973; and Y. Ijiri and R. S. Kaplan, "Sequential Models in Probabilistic Depreciation," *Journal of Accounting Research,* Spring 1970.

[7]Accounting Principles Board Opinion No. 8: "Accounting for the Cost of Pension Plans," *Journal of Accountancy,* January 1967; also see W. G. Frank and J. T. Weygandt, "A Prediction Model for Convertible Debentures," *Journal of Accounting Research,* Spring 1971.

[8]R. S. Kaplan, "Variable and Self-Service Costs in Reciprocal Allocation Models," *The Accounting Review,* October 1973, pp. 738–748; and R. L. Weil, "Reciprocal or Mutual Holdings: Allocating Earnings and Selecting the Accounting Method," *The Accounting Review,* October 1973, pp. 749–758.

[9]J. S. Demski, "Optimal Performance Measurement," *Journal of Accounting Research,* Spring 1972; and G. A. Feltham and J. S. Demski, "The Use of Models in Information Evaluation," *The Accounting Review,* October 1970.

are usually measured by the costs of processing back orders. These costs may, however, include a provision for the loss in goodwill or lost contribution margins stemming from a failure to fill orders on time.

Optimal Order Quantity—No Stockouts. Consider a firm that purchases an inventory item, such as a particular kind of raw material. Over a horizon of length T total usage of this item will be D units. Assume that the firm has established a policy of never permitting a shortage of this item—i.e., stockouts are not allowed. Under these circumstances, the acquisition policy will consist of ordering q units of the item, with separate orders timed to arrive just as the existing inventory becomes depleted. The resultant order cycles during time period T may be diagramed as in Exhibit 1.

EXHIBIT 1

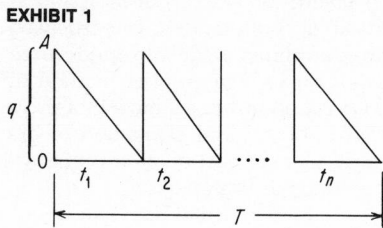

Note that inventory is used at a constant rate from a level of A to 0, at which time a new order q is received. Obviously, assuming a constant usage rate and a constant order size of q ensures that the elapsed time for each cycle, $t_1, t_2, \ldots, t_n$, is equal. In particular, D/q separate order cycles will be experienced, and the elapsed time for each will be $t_1 = t_2 = \cdots = t_n = T/(D/q)$.

The cost of acquiring this material item with such an inventory policy is represented in terms of acquisition and storage costs. The acquisition costs are assumed to consist of a constant amount per unit acquired, which we denote P, and a constant amount per order placed and received, which we denote C_p. Since D units must be acquired, total acquisition cost will be $PD + C_p \cdot$ (number of orders). The storage costs, in turn, are represented by a constant amount per average unit stored. Letting C_s denote this storage cost datum (per average unit stored), total storage cost will be $C_s \cdot$ (average inventory). From Exhibit 1, it is apparent that following this inventory policy will produce an average inventory of $q/2$ units. Also recall that D/q separate orders will be placed and received during the horizon. Admitting to a fixed cost of F, the firm's total inventory related costs over the horizon may now be expressed as follows:

$$TC(q) = F + PD + C_p \frac{D}{q} + C_s \frac{q}{2} \tag{1}$$

As this equation indicates, an optimal inventory policy will depend on the choice of q. We determine a minimum total cost by differentiating the cost function with respect to q and setting this derivative equal to 0. Hence,

$$\frac{dTC}{dq} = -\frac{C_p D}{q^2} + \frac{1}{2}C_s = 0 \tag{2}$$

and

$$q^2 = \frac{C_p D}{C_s/2} = \frac{2C_p D}{C_s}$$

Therefore
$$q^* = \sqrt{\frac{2C_pD}{C_s}}$$

where q^* represents the optimal q.[10]

The result is the familiar EOQ (economic order quantity) formula. Substituting the result of (2) into (1) provides:

$$TC(q^*) = F + PD + \frac{C_pD(C_s)^{1/2}}{(2C_pD)^{1/2}} + \frac{C_s}{2}\left(\frac{2C_pD}{C_s}\right)^{1/2} = F + PD + \frac{(2C_pD)^{1/2}C_s}{2(C_s)^{1/2}} \quad (1a)$$

or
$$TC(q^*) = F + PD + \sqrt{2C_pDC_s}$$

Since we have assumed that the purchase price P is constant, we can easily drop the term PD from our analyses; i.e., the term has no effect on the choice of q^*. Similar comments apply to the fixed cost, F. Thus

$$TC(q^*) = \sqrt{2C_pDC_s} \quad (1b)$$

To give an example, assume that a firm has a total demand for 3,600 units of inventory per year, that its purchase cost per order is \$15, and that its storage costs are \$1.50 per unit per year. The EOQ for this firm would be

$$q^* = \sqrt{\frac{2C_pD}{C_s}} = \sqrt{\frac{2(15)(3,600)}{1.50}} = \sqrt{\frac{108,000}{1.50}}$$
$$= \sqrt{72,000} = 268.33$$
$$\doteq 268 \text{ units}$$

An EOQ of 268 units will require that $3,600/268 \doteq 13.4$ orders be placed. Hence, acquisition cost (exclusive of the PD term) will total $15(13.4) = \$201$. Similarly, an EOQ of 268 units will produce an average inventory of 134 units. Storage cost will therefore total $1.5(134) = \$201$. Total cost of the policy, then, is \$402. That is,

$$TC(q^*) = \sqrt{2C_pDC_s} = \sqrt{2(15)(3,600)(1.5)}$$
$$= \sqrt{\$162,000} = \$402.49$$
$$\doteq \$402$$

Generalizing the Model—The Effect of Stockouts. The EOQ formula may be modified to reflect the more general case in which stockouts are permitted. A single inventory cycle of length t would appear as in Exhibit 2. l represents the inventory level after the order quantity q is received and back orders are filled.

During the time segment t_1 the firm will have an average inventory of $l/2$. Similarly, during the time segment t_2 the firm will be out of stock an average level of $(q - l)/2$. Quite clearly, then, the average inventory over the entire horizon will be $(t_1/t)(l/2)$; and the average stockout over the entire horizon will be $(t_2/t)(q - l)/2$.

[10]Second-order conditions indicate attainment of a minimum:
$$\frac{d^2TC}{dq^2} = \frac{2C_pD}{q^3} > 0$$

Algebraic reduction provides an average inventory of $l^2/2q$ units and an average stockout of $(q - l)^2/2q$ units.[11]

EXHIBIT 2

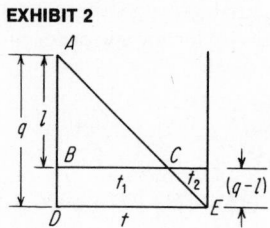

Stockout cost is now represented by a constant amount, denoted C_o, per average unit of stockout. Total stockout cost over the horizon is then $C_o(q - l)^2/2q$. Acquisition and storage cost are represented as before. Collecting terms, we represent the total cost of ordering q units per order and allowing maximum stockouts of $q - l$ in the following manner:

$$TC(q, l) = F + PD + C_p\frac{D}{q} + C_s\frac{l^2}{2q} + C_o\frac{(q - l)^2}{2q} \tag{3}$$

If we differentiate (3) with respect to q and l, and solve for q^{**} and l^*, we obtain:[12]

$$l^* = \sqrt{\frac{2C_pD}{C_s}}\sqrt{\frac{C_o}{C_s + C_o}} \tag{4}$$

and

$$q^{**} = \sqrt{\frac{2C_pD}{C_s}}\sqrt{\frac{C_s + C_o}{C_o}} \tag{5}$$

where q^{**} represents the optimal q and l^* the optimal l. Substituting these results into (3) provides, after suitable manipulation,

$$TC(q^{**}, l^*) = F + PD + \sqrt{2C_pDC_s}\sqrt{\frac{C_o}{C_s + C_o}} \tag{3a}$$

or, dropping the F and PD terms,

---

[11]Note in Exhibit 2 that ABC and ADE are similar triangles. Hence, $t_1/t = l/q$. Therefore,

$$(t_1/t)(l/2) = l^2/2q$$

and

$$(t_2/t)(q - l)/2 = \frac{(t - t_1)}{t}\frac{(q - l)}{2} = \frac{(q - l)^2}{2q}$$

[12]That is,

$$\frac{\partial TC}{\partial q} = \left(-\frac{C_pD}{q^2} - \frac{2l^2C_s}{4q^2} + \frac{2q(2q - 2l)C_o - 2(q - l)^2C_o}{4q^2}\right) = 0$$

and

$$\frac{\partial TC}{\partial l} = \left(\frac{2q2lC_s}{4q^2} + \frac{2q \cdot 2(q - l)(-1)C_o}{4q^2}\right) = 0$$

$$TC(q^{**}, l^*) = \sqrt{2C_pDC_s} \ \sqrt{\frac{C_o}{C_s + C_o}} \tag{3b}$$

To illustrate, use the figures above and assume that stockout costs are \$2.40 per unit per year. The following policies are dictated:

$$l^* = \sqrt{\frac{2C_pD}{C_s}} \ \sqrt{\frac{C_o}{C_s + C_o}}$$

$$= \sqrt{\frac{2(\$15)\,3{,}600}{\$1.50}} \ \sqrt{\frac{\$2.40}{\$1.50 + \$2.40}}$$

$$\doteq 268\,(.784)$$

$$\doteq 210$$

$$q^{**} = \sqrt{\frac{2C_pD}{C_s}} \ \sqrt{\frac{C_s + C_o}{C_o}}$$

$$\doteq 268\,(1.275)$$

$$\doteq 342$$

The optimal policy, then, is to employ an order quantity of $q^{**} = 342$ units and time the orders to arrive when $q^{**} - l^* = 342 - 210 = 132$ back orders are accumulated. D/q or $3{,}600/342 \doteq 10.5$ orders will then be placed and received. Acquisition cost (exclusive of the PD term) will total $15(10.5) \doteq \$158$. Similarly, storage cost will total $1.5(210)^2/2(342) \doteq \$97$ and stockout cost will total $2.4(342 - 210)^2/2(342) \doteq \$61$, or a total cost of \$316, which we can also determine as follows:

$$TC(q^{**}, l^*) = \sqrt{2C_pDC_s} \ \sqrt{\frac{C_o}{C_s + C_o}}$$

$$= \sqrt{2\,(15)\,(3{,}600)\,(1.50)} \ \sqrt{\frac{2.40}{1.50 + 2.40}}$$

$$\doteq 402\,(.784)$$

$$\doteq \$316$$

SENSITIVITY ANALYSIS AND PROBLEMS OF IMPLEMENTING INVENTORY MODELS

Apart from the problem of forecasting both total demand for units of inventory and its rate during each time period t_i, the practical implementation of inventory models has been hampered by difficulties encountered in obtaining reasonable estimates of the three cost factors: C_p (purchase order), C_s (storage), and C_o (stockout). Purchase-order costs tend to be common costs for several types of activities. For example, the cost of processing invoices for payments of orders is usually just one aspect of the controller's or treasurer's function. Similarly, very few firms have purchasing departments which deal only with acquisitions of one class of inventory. Even more difficult problems are encountered in trying to measure storage and stockout costs, particularly the latter. In many cases, it may not be feasible to measure the loss in goodwill caused by the failure to fill an order on time. For example, the customer may or may not take his future business elsewhere. Also, the estimated costs of processing back orders are merely averages of the extra costs incurred in filling late orders since the specific stockout costs will vary from back order to back order.

Storage costs are usually expressed initially as some percentage of the dollar value of inventory held in storage. The primary costs of storage are insurance, taxes, and an imputed cost of capital charge. Insurance and taxes are usually step costs, which means that some estimate must be made of the range of inventory quantities which will be stored before these costs can be estimated. The cost of capital charge is an estimate of the opportunity cost of investing capital in inventory. Thus, the nature of these costs also suggests the possibility of measurement errors.

It should be noted that many of these categories of costs are not recorded in the financial accounts of the firm. Thus, the implementation of inventory models within firms has proceeded with only slight participation by accountants. This is unfortunate since an evaluation of the efficiency of inventory models relies in part on comparisons of actual costs with estimated costs. Significant differences may require changes in the decision rules previously adopted.

Effect of Estimation Errors on Optimal Policies.   The effect of cost estimation errors can be assessed by analyzing how sensitive the inventory model is to changes in the estimated costs. To explore this theme, we shall focus on the simple EOQ model without stockouts. (Extension to the stockout case is straightforward but somewhat cumbersome.)

Suppose, then, that we are interested in assessing the significance of a change in the acquisition cost datum, C_p. Denote the altered value C'_p. From (1b), we know that $TC(q^*) = \sqrt{2C_p DC_s}$. Therefore,

$$T(q^{*\prime}) = \sqrt{2C'_p DC_s}$$

One measure of the significance of changes in C_p is provided by the amount of change in total costs, given that inventory policies are modified in response to a change from C_p to C'_p. Specifically:

$$TC(q^{*\prime}) - TC(q^*) = \sqrt{2C'_p DC_s} - \sqrt{2C_p DC_s}$$

which, upon simplifying, leads to the following result:

$$TC(q^{*\prime}) - TC(q^*) = \sqrt{2DC_s}(\sqrt{C'_p} - \sqrt{C_p}) \tag{6}$$

Note that the procedure reduces to one of calculating the effect of differences between the square roots of C'_p and C_p on the constant term

$$\sqrt{2DC_s}$$

To illustrate, let us use the original EOQ example, where $C_p = \$15$, $C_s = \$1.50$, and $D = 3,600$. If $C'_p = \$20$ (an increase in C_p of \$5, or 33 percent), the change in total costs will equal

$$\sqrt{2(3,600)(1.5)}(\sqrt{20} - \sqrt{15}) \doteq \$103.92(4.47 - 3.87)$$
$$\doteq \$62$$

Similarly, a decrease in C_p of \$5 ($C'_p = \$10$) would change total costs by the amount

$$\$103.92(\sqrt{10} - \sqrt{15}) \doteq \$103.92(\$3.16 - \$3.87)$$
$$\doteq -\$74$$

The effect of changes in the storage cost datum, C_s, can be explored in the same manner. Note, however, that the effect of changes in one cost datum, as illustrated for C_p, can be readily simplified in the manner of (6) only when we hold the other data (D and C_s in the elementary EOQ model) constant. In general, the effects of multiple changes—for example, a change in C_p and C_s of certain magnitudes—must be assessed in a brute force manner. That is, the new costs should be plugged into the original formulas and a new total cost computed.

Further note that this procedure of expressing the change in minimum cost as a function of the cost datum in question provides only a partial answer to the estimation error question. At the planning stage, for example, the question is whether to incur the added expense of developing a more accurate cost estimate. For example, a more accurate measurement of purchase order costs may be obtained if a multiple regression analysis is used to determine the relationship between these costs and several independent variables. However, multiple regression analyses are relatively expensive and should be performed only if the refined measurements will significantly improve the efficiency of the resulting inventory decisions. The central notion, then, is whether a refined cost measurement is warranted. This question can be addressed more directly by comparing the expected inventory cost that will obtain with and without use of a refined cost measurement.

We can illustrate the procedure by extending the C_p datum exploration above. Using the original $C_s = \$1.5$ and $D = 3,600$ units data, suppose that we are uncertain whether C_p is \$10, \$15, or \$20 per order. Each value is regarded as equally likely, and in the absence of additional information, we will use the expected value of C_p—that is,

$$\bar{C}_p = \tfrac{1}{3}(10) + \tfrac{1}{3}(15) + \tfrac{1}{3}(20) = 15$$

This, recall, implies a policy of

$$q^* = \sqrt{\frac{2\,(15)\,(3,600)}{1.5}} \doteq 268 \text{ units}$$

Further, suppose that this $q^* = 268$ policy is implemented but the actual $C_p = 10$. Actual cost, using (1), will be

$$TC(268) = 10\frac{3,600}{268} + 1.5\frac{268}{2} \doteq \$335$$

But, using (1b), the minimum possible cost would have been

$$TC(q^*) = \sqrt{2(10)(3,600)(1.5)} \doteq \$329$$

(which would be achieved with a policy of

$$q^* = \sqrt{\frac{2\,(10)\,(3,600)}{1.5}} \doteq 219 \text{ units})$$

Similarly, if $C_p = 20$ obtains, the actual cost, using the $q^* = 268$ policy, will be

$$TC(268) = 20\frac{3,600}{268} + 1.5\frac{268}{2} \doteq \$469$$

while the minimum possible cost, again using (1b), would be

$$TC(q^*) = \sqrt{2\,(20)\,(3,600)\,(1.5)} \doteq \$465$$

$$\left(\text{with } q^* = \sqrt{\frac{2\,(20)\,(3,600)}{1.5}} \doteq 310\right)$$

Of course, with $C_p = 15$, $q^* = 268$ does in fact produce the minimum possible cost of $\sqrt{2(15)(3,600)(1.5)} = \$402$. Collecting the various figures, now, the expected cost of using the $q^* = 268$ policy is given by

$$\tfrac{1}{3}(335) + \tfrac{1}{3}(402) + \tfrac{1}{3}(469) \doteq \$402^{13}$$

and the expected minimum cost is given by

$$\tfrac{1}{3}(329) + \tfrac{1}{3}(402) + \tfrac{1}{3}(465) \doteq \$399$$

Thus, implementation of the $q^* = 268$ policy is superior to further study of the C_p datum if such study will cost an excess of $\$402 - \$399 = \$3$.[14]

Alternatively, suppose that the C_p parameter is not further analyzed and $q^* = 268$ is implemented. If $C_p = 10$, the opportunity cost of the estimation error is $\$335 - \$329 = \$6$. Similarly, if $C_p = 15$, the opportunity cost is precisely zero, while if $C_p = 20$ obtains it is $\$469 - \$465 = \$4$. Hence, the expected opportunity cost is

$$\tfrac{1}{3}(6) + \tfrac{1}{3}(0) + \tfrac{1}{3}(4) \doteq \$3.$$

Sensitivity Analysis and Inventory Control. These techniques may also be used in the control process to determine whether changes in categories of costs dictate the need to alter the inventory policies adopted by the firm. To illustrate, assume that it is possible to monitor the purchase order costs used in the example above. We saw that if purchase order costs increase to $20 and a new policy is adopted in response to this change, total cost will increase to about $465. Conversely, if the $q^* = 268$ policy is not changed, the firm will experience a total cost of about $469. Hence, altering the policy will result in a savings of $469 - $465 = $4. These figures are not meant to be representative; nevertheless, they do serve to illustrate how a variance in inventory costs may be assessed relative to a firm's inventory policies.

Such procedures can be used only if it is possible to monitor the categories of purchase order, storage, and stockout costs. As mentioned earlier, many of these costs are not recorded in the financial accounts of the firm. The reason given is that these costs are difficult to measure. But certain individual cost items included in these categories of inventory costs are more susceptible to measurement than others. These items should, of course, be monitored if their magnitudes are significant for the inventory policies of firms. Significance, in turn, is defined in terms of the possible improvement in decision quality.

SOME COMPLICATING FACTORS IN INVENTORY ANALYSES

Lead Time and Safety Stocks. "Lead time" is defined as the time interval between the date an order for inventory is placed and the date the order is received. This time interval may be a critical factor for a firm which adopts a policy of zero stockouts. For example, suppose that the *average* demand for inventory is 10 units per day but the actual rate fluctuates between 8 and 12 units per day. If the lead time is 10 days, the consumption of inventory during lead time may range between 80 and 120 units. On the average, the firm will avoid stockouts by placing an order when its inventory level drops to 100 units. At the time of receipt, the expected inventory level will be zero units. However, if the daily usage during lead

---

[13]Note that the expected cost of using the 268 policy is merely the expected value of (1), which simplifies to $\bar{C}_p(D/q) + C_s q/2) = \sqrt{2\bar{C}_p DC_s}$ in this case.

[14]This calculation is an "expected value of information" calculation—where we compare the expected cost, in this case, with and without perfect advance revelation of the event in question. Elaboration of this principle can be found in J. Demski, *Information Analysis,* Addison-Wesley Publishing Company, Reading, Mass., 1972.

time is greater than 10 units, the inventory will be depleted before a new order is received, and back orders will result. The firm can reduce the probability of back orders to zero by placing an order when inventory levels drop to 120 instead of 100 units. The difference between the normal reordering level of 100 units and the conservative level of 120 units is called a "safety stock."

Holding a safety stock can be an expensive policy to adopt. The expectation is that the firm will have to store an extra 20 units of inventory per cycle. If storage costs per unit are high, the firm might be better off adopting a policy of permitting back orders. The decision to hold safety stocks should be based upon the relative costs of stockouts and storage and the probability that the firm will be out of stock during lead time.[15]

Quantity Discounts. In the previous illustrations it was assumed that the price per unit of inventory was constant regardless of the order size. Often suppliers of inventories reduce the quoted price as a function of the order size placed. For example, the price per unit might be $1.00 for order sizes of 0 to 999 units, $0.90 for order sizes of 1,000 to 1,999 units, and $0.80 for order sizes of 2,000 units or more. Note that the purchase cost for 999 units is $999, which is $99 more than the purchase costs of 1,000 units ($0.90 × 1,000). Similarly, total purchase cost at 1,999 units is $199 greater than the cost for 2,000 units ($0.80 × 2,000 = $1,600). The fact that the total cost curves are discontinuous at these price breaks means that the derivations of q^*, q^{**}, and l^* using the calculus will not necessarily lead to optimal inventory policies. Rather, a slightly more elaborate optimization procedure is necessary, but the accounting issues remain essentially the same.

Probabilistic Demand. More complicated analyses are also required if we assume that the demand for inventory can be expressed only as a probability distribution. However, the basic accounting problems of implementation are not altered by different demand assumptions, and we need not extend the discussion to include these more general approaches to inventory analysis. Those who are interested in these models should consult an advanced text on inventory models.[16]

LINEAR PROGRAMMING AND ACCOUNTING

Linear programming probably has had the greatest impact on accounting of any recently developed mathematical model. In a direct sense, linear programming may be viewed as the multiproduct analogue of the accountant's cost-volume-profit analysis or break-even model of the firm.[17]

However, its greatest influence on accounting is of an indirect nature. The implementation of linear programming models within firms offers the accountant a formal basis for analyzing data requirements for planning and controlling the normal operations of a firm.[18]

[15]See A. H. Packer, "Simulation and Adaptive Forecasting as Applied to Inventory Control," *Operations Research,* July-August 1967, for an excellent example of analysis of inventory policies with safety stocks. Also see *NAA Research Report No. 40: Techniques in Inventory Management,* New York, 1960, chap. 4.

[16]Eliezer Naddor, *Inventory Systems,* John Wiley & Sons, New York, 1966.

[17]This relationship is spelled out more clearly in Robert Jaedicke, "Improving B-E Analysis by Linear Programming Techniques," *NAA Bulletin,* March 1961; and A. Charnes, W. W. Cooper, and Y. Ijiri, "Breakeven Budgeting and Programming to Goals," *Journal of Accounting Research,* Spring 1963.

[18]Y. Ijiri, F. Levy, and R. Lyon, "A Linear Programming Model for Budgeting and Financial Planning," *Journal of Accounting Research,* Autumn 1963; A. Rappaport, "Sensitivity Analysis in Decision Making," *The Accounting Review,* July 1967; R. E. Jensen, "Sensitivity Analysis and Integer Linear Programming," *The Accounting Review,* July 1968; N. Dopuch, J. Birnberg, and J. S. Demski, "An extension of Standard Cost Variance Analysis," *The Accounting Review,* July 1967; and J. S. Demski, "An Accounting System Structured on a Linear Programming Model," *The Accounting Review,* October 1967.

A linear programming problem develops whenever a firm uses common facilities to produce two or more different types of output. As a rule, the common facilities constrain the maximum amounts of each output which can be produced. In a single-product firm, it is generally profitable to expand output as long as revenues exceed variable costs. However, in a multiproduct firm, an expansion of the output of *one* product usually introduces an additional cost—the opportunity cost of not being able to produce alternative products.

A Graphic Solution to a Linear Programming Problem. To illustrate, suppose that a firm may produce products X_1 and X_2. Product X_1 has a contribution margin (i.e., revenue minus variable costs) of $3; product X_2's contribution margin is $2. The firm has an available capacity of 500 hours. Each unit of output of X_1 requires 2 hours of capacity and each unit of output of X_2 requires 1 hour of this capacity. Thus, the firm can produce 250 units of X_1, 500 units of X_2, or various linear combinations of X_1 and X_2, provided that $2X_1 + 1X_2 \leq 500$ hours.

This problem is simple enough that it may be solved by comparing relative contribution margins. We note that a unit of X_1 uses 2 hours of the scarce resource and returns $3 in contribution margin. Stated alternatively, X_1 returns $1.50 per hour of capacity used. However, X_2 returns $2 per hour of capacity used; therefore, X_2 is relatively more profitable than X_1. Since all the relationships in the problem are linear, it follows that the firm should produce 500 units of X_2 and no units of X_1 (i.e., every unit of X_1 produced forces the firm to forego two units of X_2; the net effect is a loss of $1 of contribution margin). 500 units of X_2 yields a total contribution margin of $1,000. This is the maximum contribution margin possible, given the statement of the problem.

This problem can also be solved using graphic techniques. Letting the horizontal axis in the graph in Exhibit 3 represent output of X_1 and the vertical the output of X_2, the constraint $2X_1 + X_2 \leq 500$ can be graphed as a straight line joining the X_1 and X_2 coordinates of (250, 0) and (0, 500). Any point on this line represents a combination of X_1 and X_2 which is feasible (i.e., does not violate the constraint of $2X_1 + X_2 \leq 500$). The dashed lines shown in Exhibit 3 represent equal amounts of

EXHIBIT 3

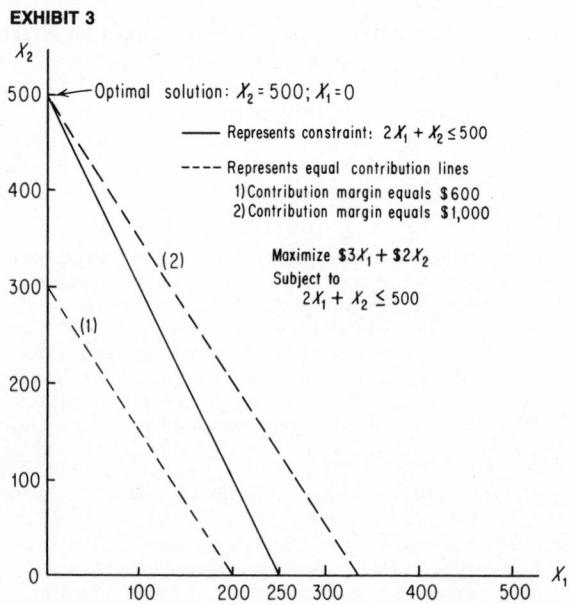

total contribution margin resulting from combinations of outputs of X_1 and X_2. For example, 300 units of X_2 yields the same total contribution margin ($600) as 200 units of X_1. Similarly, 500 units of X_2 yields the same total contribution margin ($1,000) as 333 units of X_1. However, 333 units of X_1 is not feasible since this output would require 666 hours of capacity. Hence, the maximum contribution margin possible is $1,000, achieved by producing 500 units of X_2.

Note that the optimal solution occurs at a point where the total contribution margin line (in this case, cm = $1,000) just touches an extreme point of the feasible region. The feasible region is formed by the triangle with the points moving counterclockwise, (0, 0), (250, 0), (0, 500).

Suppose now that a second constraint is imposed on the problem. For example, assume that the outputs of X_1 and X_2 must pass through a second production department which is constrained as follows: $1.5X_1 + 2X_2 \leq 480$ hours. This constraint implies that the two extremes of either 320 units of X_1 or 240 units of X_2 may be produced in the second department. When this constraint is coupled with the previous one shown in Exhibit 3, the feasible region is modified as shown in Exhibit 4. The output of X_1 is still restricted by the first constraint to a maximum output of 250 units of X_1. The primary effect of the second constraint is to reduce the maximum output of X_2 from 500 to 240 units. This constraint remains binding as we move down it to the right, substituting the output of X_1 for X_2, until we reach the intersection of the two constraints ($X_1 = 208$, $X_2 = 84$), after which the first constraint again becomes binding, as shown in Exhibit 4.

EXHIBIT 4

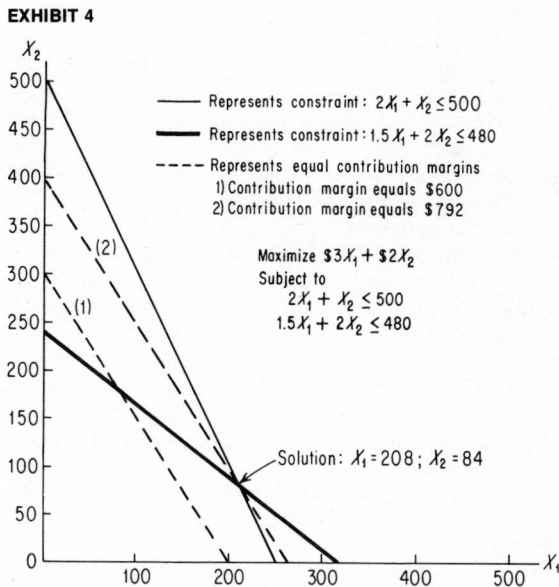

The solution, $X_1 = 208$ and $X_2 = 84$, again occurs where the broken line representing equal contribution margin just touches an extreme point of the feasible region. A contribution margin of $792 is the maximum contribution margin possible with the constraints of $2X_1 + X_2 \leq 500$ and $1.5X_1 + 2X_2 \leq 480$.[19]

[19]This can be checked by comparing the contribution margin yielded at the other extreme points: $X_1 = 250$, $X_2 = 0$; $X_1 = 0$, $X_2 = 240$; and $X_1 = X_2 = 0$.

SENSITIVITY ANALYSIS WITH LINEAR PROGRAMMING

The linear programming solution obtained above relies on estimates of the contribution margins of X_1 and X_2 and their technical coefficients of production. The latter are basically engineering data. However, contribution margins are measured using accounting estimates of product variable costs along with estimates of the revenue per unit of output. These accounting measurements are subject to error, and our concern now is the extent to which we can assess the significance of these errors.

The significance of measurement errors in contribution margins may be assessed in part by analyzing the sensitivity of the solution of the linear programming model to changes in contribution margins. If the solution is sensitive to small changes, it may be profitable to obtain more reliable estimates of variable costs and revenue. The approach here is similar to that described above for inventories. To illustrate, suppose past data indicate that the actual variable costs of product X_2 fluctuate in such a manner that its contribution margin may fall anywhere in the range \$1.00 to \$3.00 (unlikely perhaps, but useful for illustrative purposes).

Referring back to Exhibit 4, we note that if X_2's contribution margin were \$1.00, while X_1's remains at \$3.00, the new optimal solution will become $X_1 = 250$, $X_2 = 0$. Total contribution margin would be \$3(250) + \$2(0) = \$750. However, if X_2's contribution margin were \$3.00, the new optimal solution would be the same as the original one—i.e., $X_1 = 208$, $X_2 = 84$, but with a revised total contribution margin of \$3(208) + \$3(84) = \$876.[20]

These "sensitivity" results can be interpreted as follows. If the accountant knew with certainty that X_2's contribution margin would be \$1.00, the firm would revise its production plan and produce 250 units of X_1, but 0 units of X_2. In contrast, no revision would be necessary were the actual contribution margin of X_2 to increase to \$3.00.

Note, however, that the accountant does not know for sure the future contribution margin of X_2. Instead, he relies on his best estimate, which we assume is \$2.00. Suppose, then, that the original production plan is implemented and actual output is $X_1 = 208$, $X_2 = 84$. Unfortunately, the actual contribution margin of X_2 drops to \$1.00, so that the firm obtains only \$3(208) + \$1.00(84) = \$708$_{(actual)}$. Recall from above that the optimal solution if X_2's contribution margin dropped to \$1.00 was $X_1 = 250$, $X_2 = 0$, yielding a total contribution margin of \$3(250) = \$750.

Hence, the opportunity cost of not knowing in *advance* the actual contribution margin of X_2 is simply \$750 − \$708 = \$42 (i.e., the optimal value of the objective function minus the actual value).

The example could be expanded to consider other possible outcomes for contribution margins along with the prior probabilities of their occurrence. This would permit us to calculate the expected value of perfect information as we did above in the inventory example. However, since the procedures are essentially the same, we will not carry out the analysis.

USING LINEAR ALGEBRA TO SOLVE LINEAR PROGRAMMING PROBLEMS

An Algebraic Solution. The previous problem can be used to illustrate how linear algebra may be used to solve complex linear programming problems. First

[20]For each case, draw new equal contribution margin lines to reflect the revised relationships. Thus, the first change would yield equal contribution margin lines with a slope of −3/1 = −3, whereas the second results in a slope of −3/3 = −1. The original lines have a slope of −3/2.

we must convert the two inequality constraints into equations. This can be done by using two slack variables, S_1 and S_2, to represent the physical units of unused capacity of the two constraints. Thus the problem may be formulated as follows:

Maximize $\qquad\qquad P = \$3X_1 + \$2X_2 + 0S_1 + 0S_2$

subject to $\qquad\qquad 2X_1 + X_2 + S_1 + 0S_2 = 500 \qquad\qquad (7)$

$\qquad\qquad\qquad 1.5X_1 + 2X_2 + 0S_1 + S_2 = 480 \qquad\qquad (8)$

where $\qquad\qquad X_1, X_2, S_1, S_2 \geqslant 0$

The last constraint merely indicates that none of the variables can take on negative values. The contribution margins of S_1 and S_2 are assigned a value of 0 since unused capacity has no effect on total contribution margin.

Because there are only two equations, at most we can solve for two unknowns. (The other two variables must be set equal to zero.) One solution is simply $S_1 = 500$ and $S_2 = 480$ ($X_1 = 0$, $X_2 = 0$). This is merely one of six possible solutions to this problem. Other solutions would consist of values of the respective variables which satisfy the following sets of equations:

$$
\begin{array}{lll}
(X_1,\ S_1) & 2X_1 + S_1 = 500 \\
& 1.5X_1 + 0S_1 = 480 \\
(X_1,\ S_2) & 2X_1 + 0S_2 = 500 \\
& 1.5X_1 + S_2 = 480 \\
(X_2,\ S_1) & X_2 + S_1 = 500 \\
& 2X_2 + 0S_1 = 480 \\
(X_2,\ S_2) & X_2 + 0S_2 = 500 \\
& 2X_2 + S_2 = 480 \\
(X_1,\ X_2) & 2X_1 + X_2 = 500 \\
& 1.5X_1 + 2X_2 = 480
\end{array}
$$

The number of possible solutions is equal to n factorial divided by $[(n - m)$ factorial $\times m$ factorial]; n is the number of variables, 4, and m is the number of equations, 2. All these solutions will result in nonzero values for the variables indicated. These six solutions are called "basic solutions," those in which the number of nonzero variables is equal to the number of equations. However, some of these basic solutions are not "feasible" since they result in negative values being assigned to some of the variables. For example, the solution to the problem:

$$
\begin{aligned}
X_2 + 0S_2 &= 500 \\
2X_2 + S_2 &= 480
\end{aligned}
$$

implies that $X_2 = 500$ and $S_2 = -520$. Such a solution cannot be implemented.

The simplex method in linear programming consists of a set of rules which ensure that comparisons of the profitability of different solutions will be limited to basic feasible solutions.[21] In terms of the graph in Exhibit 4, we note that there are four extreme points in the positive quadrant: (0, 0); (250, 0); (208, 84); and (0, 240). Each of these points represents a basic feasible solution. For example, point (0, 0) is equivalent to the solution: $S_1 = 500$, $S_2 = 480$, and $X_1 = X_2 = 0$. Similarly, (250, 0) represents the solution: $X_1 = 250$, $S_2 = 105$, and $X_2 = S_1 = 0$. The procedures for moving from one basic feasible solution to the next will be illustrated with one change only.

---

[21]We are ignoring the problem of "cycling" which may occur when a nonbasic feasible solution is encountered. This is known as the problem of "degeneracy." For solution techniques in degenerate problems, see G. Hadley, *Linear Programming*, Addison-Wesley Publishing Company, Reading, Mass., 1962, chap. 6.

The first rule is to begin with a basic feasible solution. One basic feasible solution which is obvious is the solution at the origin. That is, we can start with the problem:

$$S_1 + 0S_2 = 500$$
$$0S_1 + S_2 = 480$$

which has the obvious solution $S_1 = 500$, $S_2 = 480$ (and $X_1 = X_2 = 0$). The contribution margin, P, $= \$3(0) + \$2(0) + 0(500) + 0(480) = 0$. P will increase if either X_1 or X_2 is given a positive value. Since X_1 returns \$3 per unit, we shall bring X_1 into the solution.

In order to bring X_1 into the solution, we must drop either S_1 or S_2. If we write out both equations in terms of X_1, we note that

$$2X_1 + X_2 + S_1 + 0S_2 = 500$$
$$2X_1 = 500 - X_2 - S_1 - 0S_2$$
$$X_1 = 250 - \tfrac{1}{2}X_2 - \tfrac{1}{2}S_1 - 0S_2 \qquad (9)$$

which implies that a maximum of 250 units of X_1 can be produced with X_2 and S_1 equal to zero; or

$$1.5X_1 + 2X_2 + 0S_1 + S_2 = 480$$
$$X_1 = 320 - 1.33X_2 - 0S_1 - S_2 \qquad (10)$$

which indicates that a maximum of 320 units of X_1 can be produced with X_2 and S_2 equal to zero. Since the first resource is more binding, we let $S_1 = X_2 = 0$ and $X_1 = 250$ in (9) and substitute (9) in (8), which gives us the following result:

$$1.5(250 - \tfrac{1}{2}X_2 - \tfrac{1}{2}S_1 - 0S_2) + 2X_2 + 0S_1 + S_2 = 480$$
or $$375 - .75X_2 - .75S_1 + 2X_2 + S_2 = 480$$

Therefore $$S_2 = 105 - 1.25X_2 + .75S_1$$
or $$S_2 = 105 \qquad (11)$$
since $$X_2 = S_1 = 0$$

The new contribution margin will be

$$P = \$3(250) + \$2(0) + 0(0) + 0(105) = \$750$$

The next step would be to determine whether X_2 should be brought into the solution and, if so, whether in place of X_1 or S_2. (The former is unlikely.) Equation (9) indicates that for every unit of X_2 produced, X_1 will have to be reduced by one-half unit. Similarly, a unit increase in X_2 will require a reduction in S_2 of 1.25 units [equation (11)]. The effect on P of a positive change in X_2 can be summarized as follows:

$$\$2(1) - [\$3(\tfrac{1}{2}) + 0(\$1.25)] = \$.50$$

This results in a positive change in P, indicating that X_2 should be brought into the solution. To determine whether X_1 or S_2 should be replaced, we first rewrite equations (9) and (11) in terms of X_2. Thus:

$$\tfrac{1}{2}X_2 = 250 - X_1 - \tfrac{1}{2}S_1 - 0S_2$$
$$X_2 = 500 - 2X_1 - S_1 - 0S_2 \qquad (12)$$

and $$1.25X_2 = 105 + .75S_1 - S_2$$
$$X_2 = 84 + .60S_1 - .80S_2 \qquad (13)$$

A comparison of equations (12) and (13) indicates that X_2 must be limited to an output of 84 units, in which case S_2 will equal zero. We may then use (9) and (13) to determine the values of X_1 and X_2 which will satisfy all constraints, leading to the solution

$$S_1 = S_2 = 0$$
$$X_1 = 208$$
and $\qquad\qquad X_2 = 84$

Therefore, $P = \$3(208) + \$2(84) = \$792$, which we know is the optimal solution to this problem.

Simplex Tableaus. The procedures described above are part of the general solution algorithm for linear programming problems known as the simplex method. This solution technique is provided by most computer manufacturers. Thus, users need only be familiar with the reporting format for the outputs of computer codes. Most of these are in the form of "simplex tableaus." The initial and final (optimal) tableaus for our problem are illustrated:

Vectors		x_1	x_2	s_1	s_2		
Contribution margin of each variable		$3	$2	0	0		
Initial tableau Variables in the solution (prices)							
	S_1 (0)	2	1	1	0	500	
	S_2 (0)	1.5	2	0	1	480	
Improvement in P if variable is increased (per unit)		$3	$2	0	0		*Tableau I*
Final tableau							
	X_1 ($3)	1	0	0.80	−0.40	208	
	X_2 ($2)	0	1	−0.60	0.80	84	
Improvement in P if variable is increased (per unit)		0	0	−$1.20	−$0.40		*Tableau II*

The simplex tableaus may be viewed as a series of column vectors which indicate the effect of introducing and eliminating different variables in the solutions to the problem.

In the first tableau, we show the original solution, $S_1 = 500$, $S_2 = 480$. The optimal solution appears in the second tableau.

A Matrix Formulation of the Problem. The final solution consists of the vectors x_1 and x_2 which form the problem:

Maximize $\qquad\qquad \$3X_1 + \$2X_2$
subject to $\qquad\qquad 2X_1 + \ \ X_2 = 500$
$\qquad\qquad\qquad 1.5X_1 + \ 2X_2 = 480$

(i.e., the constraints are now written as equations). Suppose that we define the set of coefficients for X_1 and X_2 as the matrix **B**. Letting **x** be the column vector $\begin{pmatrix} X_1 \\ X_2 \end{pmatrix}$ and **b** the column vector $\begin{pmatrix} 500 \\ 480 \end{pmatrix}$, this problem can be expressed in matrix form as

$$\mathbf{Bx = b}$$

which, when written out, is the following:

$$\begin{bmatrix} 2 & 1 \\ 1.5 & 2 \end{bmatrix} \begin{bmatrix} X_1 \\ X_2 \end{bmatrix} = \begin{bmatrix} 500 \\ 480 \end{bmatrix}$$

In algebra, the expression $ax = b$ can be solved by dividing both sides of the equation by a, the constant. This is the same as multiplying both sides by $1/a = a^{-1}$. Division is not defined in matrix algebra; however, the *inverse* of a matrix performs the same function as a^{-1} in algebra. That is, for the problem above,

$$\mathbf{B^{-1}Bx = B^{-1}b}$$

or
$$\mathbf{Ix = B^{-1}b}$$

and
$$\mathbf{x = B^{-1}b}$$

where $\mathbf{B^{-1}}$ is the inverse of $\mathbf{B}$ and $\mathbf{I}$ is an identity matrix. (An identity matrix is a square matrix which has 1's down the diagonal and 0's elsewhere.)

There are several methods for finding the inverse of a matrix. One method consists of performing what are known as "elementary" row (and column) operations on an identity matrix which are necessary to transform the original matrix into an identity form. For example, $\mathbf{B^{-1}}$ can be determined by performing the same operation on $\begin{bmatrix} 1 & 0 \\ 0 & 1 \end{bmatrix}$ which will change $\begin{bmatrix} 2.0 & 1.0 \\ 1.5 & 2.0 \end{bmatrix}$ to this identity form. To illustrate, we shall write $\mathbf{B}$ and $\mathbf{I}$ as if we were multiplying:

(1)
(2)
$$\begin{bmatrix} 2.0 & 1.0 \\ 1.5 & 2.0 \end{bmatrix} \,\middle\|\, \begin{bmatrix} 1.0 & 0 \\ 0 & 1.0 \end{bmatrix}$$

(a) Divide row (1) by 2 which yields (3) = 1.0, ½ ‖ ½, 0.
(b) Multiply (3) by (-1.5) and add the result to (2). This results in (4) = 0, 1.25 ‖ $-.75$, 1.00.

Combining (3) and (4), we have:

(3)
(4)
$$\begin{bmatrix} 1.0 & \tfrac{1}{2} \\ 0 & 1.25 \end{bmatrix} \,\middle\|\, \begin{bmatrix} \tfrac{1}{2} & 0 \\ -.75 & 1.00 \end{bmatrix}$$

(c) Divide (4) by 1.25, so (6) = 0, 1.0 ‖ $-.60$, .80.
(d) Multiply (6) by $-\frac{1}{2}$ and add the result to (3). This gives (5) = 1.0, 0 ‖ .80 $-.40$.
Combining (5) and (6),

(5)
(6)
$$\begin{bmatrix} 1.0 & 0 \\ 0 & 1.0 \end{bmatrix} \,\middle\|\, \begin{bmatrix} .80 & -.40 \\ -.60 & .80 \end{bmatrix}$$

so that $\begin{bmatrix} .80 & -.40 \\ -.60 & .80 \end{bmatrix}$ should be $\mathbf{B^{-1}}$. We can check the result by determining whether $\mathbf{B^{-1}B = I}$, or whether

$$\begin{bmatrix} .80 & -.40 \\ -.60 & .80 \end{bmatrix} \begin{bmatrix} 2 & 1 \\ 1.5 & 2 \end{bmatrix}$$

$$= \begin{bmatrix} .80(2) - .40(1.5) = 1.0 & .80(1) - .40(2) = 0 \\ -.60(2) + .80(1.5) = 0 & -.60(1) + .80(2) = 1.0 \end{bmatrix}$$

$$= \begin{bmatrix} 1 & 0 \\ 0 & 1 \end{bmatrix}$$

Therefore, since $\mathbf{B^{-1}Bx = B^{-1}b}$, $\mathbf{x = B^{-1}b}$, or

$$\mathbf{x} = \begin{bmatrix} .80 & -.40 \\ -.60 & .80 \end{bmatrix} \begin{bmatrix} 500 \\ 480 \end{bmatrix}$$

or
$$\begin{bmatrix} X_1 \\ X_2 \end{bmatrix} = \begin{bmatrix} .80(500) - .40(480) = 208 \\ -.60(500) + .80(480) = 84 \end{bmatrix}$$

Therefore
$$X_1 = 208$$
$$X_2 = 84$$

which is the result we obtained earlier.

Note that $\mathbf{B}^{-1}$ also appears in the final tableau under the column headings, $\mathbf{s}_1$, $\mathbf{s}_2$. This is not surprising, for $\mathbf{s}_1$ and $\mathbf{s}_2$ originally formed an identity matrix, and the procedures which transformed this matrix to its final form were essentially the row operations needed to transform

$$\begin{array}{cc} \mathbf{x}_1 & \mathbf{x}_2 \end{array}$$
$$\begin{bmatrix} 2 & 1 \\ 1.5 & 2 \end{bmatrix}$$

to an identity form in the final tableau.

ALGEBRAIC TECHNIQUES USED TO ASSESS THE SENSITIVITY OF LINEAR PROGRAMMING SOLUTIONS

Using the Inverse to Assess Changes in Constraints.
The inverse is particularly useful in assessing the effect of changes in either or both of the constraints. For example, suppose that we wish to determine the effect of increasing the constraints from 500 and 480 to 600 and 520, respectively. The new solution is

$$\begin{bmatrix} X_1 \\ X_2 \end{bmatrix} = \begin{bmatrix} .80 & -.40 \\ -.60 & .80 \end{bmatrix} \begin{bmatrix} 600 \\ 520 \end{bmatrix}$$
$$= \begin{bmatrix} .80(600) - .40(520) = 272 \\ -.60(600) + .80(520) = 56 \end{bmatrix}$$

The new contribution margin P will be equal to $\$3(272) + \$2(56) = \$928$. The change in P, $\$928 - \$792 = \$136$, can then be compared to the cost of expanding the capacities to 600 and 520 to determine whether the decision would be profitable.

Note that these increases in capacity will not change the vectors in the optimal solution. That is, the final solution still consists of the vectors $\mathbf{x}_1$, $\mathbf{x}_2$. A change in vectors would have been indicated by a negative value for X_1 or X_2. As an illustration, suppose we consider the effect of increasing the capacity of the first constraint to 700 hours, while the second remains at 480. Using the inverse of $\mathbf{B}$,

$$\begin{bmatrix} X_1 \\ X_2 \end{bmatrix} = \begin{bmatrix} .80 & -.40 \\ -.60 & .80 \end{bmatrix} \begin{bmatrix} 700 \\ 480 \end{bmatrix} = \begin{bmatrix} 368 \\ -.36 \end{bmatrix}$$

This is not a feasible solution since $X_2 = -36$.

Referring to the final tableau, we note that a negative sign appears in the second row in the column $\mathbf{s}_1$. This indicates that a feasible solution will result if S_1 is brought into the solution at a value of $-36/-.60 = 60$ in place of X_2. Assigning S_1 the value of 60 will require a downward adjustment in X_1 of $.80(60) = 48$. (See the coefficient in row 1, column $\mathbf{s}_1$.) Thus the new optimal solution is

$$X_1 = 320$$
$$S_1 = 60$$

The new contribution margin is $\$3(320) = \$960$, which represents an improvement of $\$960 - \$792 = \$168$. This change could be used to evaluate the decision to expand facility 1 to 700 units.

The Role of Shadow Prices.
The figures -1.20 and $-.40$ appearing in the bottom row of the final tableau in the columns $\mathbf{s}_1$ and $\mathbf{s}_2$ represent, respectively, the change in P if S_1 and S_2 are increased. S_1 and S_2 represent the unused capacities of the two constraints. Thus, we may view these figures as the marginal values of having additional units of capacity available. Recall that in the first illustration above, an increase in the capacities of the two facilities from 500 to 600 hours and

480 to 520 hours, respectively, resulted in a new solution of $X_1 = 272$, $X_2 = 56$. The increase in P was \$136. This increase of \$136 can also be accounted for as follows:

$$\Delta P = \$1.20(\Delta \text{ in capacity 1}) + \$0.40(\Delta \text{ in capacity 2})$$

or

$$= \$1.20(100 \text{ hours}) + \$0.40(40 \text{ hours})$$
$$= \$120 + \$16$$
$$= \$136$$

\$1.20 and \$0.40 are called "shadow prices." These shadow prices provide a quick reference to the opportunity costs of not having additional capacity available. They always appear under the columns representing the slack variables. They remain valid as indicators of the marginal value of additional capacity provided the increased capacity would not require a change in the solution basis (as it did in the second illustration when capacity 1 increased to 700 hours).

Shadow prices can also be used internally to charge divisional managers for the use of scarce resources. For example, a unit of X_1 requires 2 hours of capacity 1 and 1.5 hours of capacity 2. Each unit of X_1 returns \$3 in contribution margin. If a divisional manager in charge of X_1 is required to pay \$1.20 for each hour of capacity 1 and \$0.40 for each hour of capacity 2, he will break even on each unit of X_1 produced. That is, \$3 = \$1.20 (2) + \$0.40 (1.5). Similarly, a unit of X_2 would cost the manager \$1.20 (1) + \$0.40 (2) = \$2, which is equal to the contribution margin of X_2.

The use of shadow prices internally is a complex topic which cannot be fully explored here.[22]

Changes in Contribution Margins.   Algebraic techniques also exist for assessing the significance of errors in measuring the contribution margin of the different products. These can be illustrated by the data in the final tableau above.

The solution appearing in the final tableau is optimal because P cannot be improved by the introduction of S_1 or S_2 into the solution. This is indicated by the negative signs preceding the values, \$1.20 and \$0.40. The value, $-\$1.20$, summarizes the effect of reducing X_1 by .80 units and increasing X_2 by .60 units for every unit increase in S_1. A unit of S_1 yields a zero contribution. Therefore, the effect on P if S_1 is increased by one unit is: $0 - (.80 \times \$3 - .60 \times \$2) = -\$1.20$. Similarly, the effect of increasing S_2 is: $0 - (-.40 \times \$3 + .80 \times \$2) = \$1.20 - \$1.60 = -\$0.40$.

Suppose that we wish to assess the effect of an error in measuring the contribution margin of X_1, which we will now denote by C_1. Consider first the effect of a decrease in C_1. The decrease would become significant at the point where either S_1 or S_2 should enter the solution. This will occur when one or both of the values appearing under the s_1 and s_2 columns become positive. A decrease in C_1 will not affect S_2. That is, if C_1 is less than \$3, $0 - (-.40 \times C_1 + .80 \times \$2) = .40 C_1 - \$1.60$, so that decreasing C_1 will result in a figure which must be more negative than $-\$0.40$. However, a sufficient decrease in C_1 will eventually result in the substitution of S_1 for X_1. For example, suppose C_1 drops to \$1.40. The change in P if S_1 were brought into the solution would be: $0 - (.80 \times \$1.40 - .60 \times \$2) = -\$1.12 + \$1.20 = +.08$. The positive value indicates that S_1 should enter the solution. Since it must enter at a positive value, S_1 must replace X_1. The new solution would be $X_2 = 240$, $S_1 = 260$. This is a reasonable effect since a large decrease in C_1 makes X_2 relatively more attractive than X_1. The lower critical value of C_1 can be determined by solving the expression:

---

[22]N. Dopuch and D. Drake, "Accounting Implications of a Mathematical Programming Approach to the Transfer Price Problem," *Journal of Accounting Research*, Spring 1964; and J. M. Samuels, "Opportunity Costing: An Application of Mathematical Programming," *Journal of Accounting Research*, Autumn 1965.

$$0 = (.80 \times C_1 - .60 \times \$2)$$

or
$$\$1.20 = .80C_1$$
$$\$1.50 = C_1$$

If C_1 drops below \$1.50, the original solution is no longer optimal. The technique described here can be used in problems involving large numbers of variables and equations.

The critical maximum value for C_1 can be determined in a similar manner. An increase in C_1 will make X_1 relatively more profitable than X_2, until eventually X_2 will be replaced by S_2. The critical point occurs when

$$0 - (-.40 \times C_1 + .80 \times \$2) = 0$$
$$.40C_1 = \$1.60$$
$$C_1 = \$4$$

Thus, the critical range for C_1 is \$1.50 $\leq C_1 \leq$ \$4.

Applying similar procedures for C_2, we observe that the critical range for C_2 is also \$1.50 $\leq C_2 \leq$ \$4 (a coincidence only). The \$4 upper limit is found by solving the expression

$$0 - (\$.80 \times \$3 - .60C_2) = 0$$

while the lower value is the solution to

$$0 - (-.40 \times \$3 + .80C_2) = 0$$

This result, incidentally, is consistent with our earlier example where we noted that the optimal solution changed when C_2 dropped to \$1.00 ($<$ \$1.50) but remained the same when C_2 increased to \$3.00 (which is less than the upper limit).

Computer codes are available for performing sensitivity analysis on more complex problems and on more complex types of changes in parameter values. As we indicated earlier, sensitivity analysis may be used at the planning stage to assess the value of having improved information about the probability distribution of parameter values. Sensitivity analysis may also be used at the control and evaluation stage, once a particular solution is implemented, to assess the decision significance of variances from anticipated parameter values. The exact procedures for doing so are described elsewhere,[23] so we will not illustrate them here.

LINEAR PROGRAMMING AND INCREMENTAL ANALYSIS

The illustrations in the previous sections are sufficient to indicate how linear programming extends incremental analysis to multiproduct situations. These situations may arise in any one of the traditional cost-volume-profit problems, such as expanding output levels, deciding whether to make or buy products, and processing outputs through additional processes. Programming techniques have also been used to solve constrained capital acquisition problems; however, these applications of programming will not be discussed here.[24]

CONCLUSION

The impact of mathematical models on accounting is still in the development stages. In this chapter, we have surveyed only what seem to be the more common

---

[23]N. Dopuch, J. Birnberg, and J. S. Demski, "An Extension of Standard Cost Variance Analysis," *The Accounting Review*, July 1967; and J. Demski, "An Accounting System Structured on a Linear Programming Model," *The Accounting Review*, October 1967.

[24]See H. M. Weingartner, *Mathematical Programming and the Analysis of Capital Budgeting Problems*, Prentice-Hall, Englewood Cliffs, N.J., 1963.

areas in which mathematical models and accounting overlap. Other mathematical models used by management could also be examined in the same manner as the inventory and linear programming models. For example, we might have considered the information implications of formal models used to guide decisions concerning the replacement of assets, the number of servicing units to maintain (queuing), and the optimal set of interrelated decisions (dynamic programming).

The important point, however, is to recognize that management's use of mathematical models provides accounting with a formal means for assessing the relevance of accounting measurements. A measurement may, that is, be considered relevant in terms of its use in the *implementation* and *control* of management's decision models. Although this idea is not new, the formality of the process is much more apparent in mathematical presentations.

BIBLIOGRAPHY

Corcoran, A. W.: *Mathematical Applications in Accounting,* Harcourt Brace Jovanovich, New York, 1968.

Demski, J. S.: *Information Analysis,* Addison-Wesley Publishing Company, Reading, Mass., 1972.

Dopuch, N., J. Birnberg, and J. Demski: *Cost Accounting: Accounting Data for Management's Decisions,* 2nd ed., Harcourt Brace Jovanovich, New York, 1974.

Horngren, C. T.: *Cost Accounting: A Managerial Emphasis,* 3rd ed., Prentice-Hall, Englewood Cliffs, N.J., 1972.

Wagner, H. M.: *Principles of Operations Research,* Prentice-Hall, Englewood Cliffs, N.J., 1969.

Chapter **12**

Revenue Recognition

ARTHUR L. THOMAS
Harmon Whittington Professor of Accounting, Rice University

Revenue is both one of the main goals of business enterprises and one of the major concepts of accounting. This chapter, which discusses the revenue concept and its reflection in financial statements, is confined to: ·

1. Recognition of revenues on general-purpose financial statements (rather than on internal reports, special reports to creditors, tax returns, and the like).

2. Profit-seeking firms that prepare financial statements in accordance with generally accepted accounting principles (GAAP) (however, the principles discussed are also followed by many not-for-profit and regulated entities).

DEFINITION OF REVENUE

It is convenient to distinguish the concept of revenue from the rules for measuring it. The word "revenue" came into English from the French; the related French word *revenir* essentially means "to come back, to return." The basic notion of revenue is likewise of a *return:* the firm invests resources in its operations, eventually that investment comes back (hopefully, increased by profit). Whatever comes back is the revenue.

Often, this is expressed by saying that a firm's costs reflect its efforts, while its revenues reflect its accomplishments. But what will count as an accomplishment? What should return? The firm's efforts almost always are monetary ones: it pays cash for inputs, or incurs liabilities to pay cash. The parallel rule is that revenue should also be monetary—either cash itself or a right to receive cash (a receivable).

But not all receipts of monetary assets generate revenues, since not all receipts are returns on the firm's efforts to provide goods and services. For example, additional stockholder investment results in an addition to capital, not in revenue, and a loan does not result in revenue, only debt. Instead, firms obtain revenues only by providing goods or services to other entities. Two complications often occur in business practice:

1. Some firms receive the return before they make the effort—they collect in advance. Any company that receives payment for its products or services before providing them fits this description. Until it has done what it has been paid to do, it should report a liability. Once it has extinguished that liability by delivering the product or performing the service, it should report a revenue. Thus, as a rough definition, accountants recognize a revenue whenever a firm exchanges its goods or services for cash, a right to receive cash, or an extinguishment of a liability.

2. The same firm may provide various different goods and services. Some are clearly its customary ones that it is in business to provide; we may call the related revenues "operating" ones. Other, "nonoperating," revenues result from receipts of rent, royalties, interest, and dividends and from incidental sales of used assets (land, buildings, or equipment that are not the firm's regular stock in trade).

Holding Gains (and Losses).   Often the market value of an asset will change during the period that a firm owns it: land bought in the 1930s may now command a price far greater than its cost. Such a difference between an asset's current market value and its cost (as appropriately adjusted for depreciation or depletion in instances other than land) is called a "holding" gain or loss. In their mandatory filings with the SEC, large corporations must report current market values for their inventories, depreciable assets, costs of goods sold, and depreciation expenses via footnote or other supplementary disclosure—see Chapter 46 for details. Nonetheless, in the bodies of their reports accountants do not report holding *gains* until the firm actually sells the related assets.

Holding losses are much more often recognized. When there has been a material, apparently permanent decline in the current market value of an asset held for resale, accountants recognize a loss despite the asset's not yet being sold—a common example is the rule of reporting inventories at the lower of cost or market. The usual rationale for this practice is conservatism. It seems fair to say, however, that this treatment of holding losses is inconsistent with the one given holding gains. Finally, FASB Statement No. 12 requires a complex form of lower-of-cost-or-market revenue recognition for portfolios of current marketable equity securities, under which some recognition of holding gains can occur.

Theoretical Issues. Several other questions concerning both holding gains and losses and revenue recognition generally are reflected in American Accounting Association studies and committee reports and in various AICPA releases. The appropriate timing of revenue recognition is theoretically puzzling. Any firm's revenues are the joint products of all of its activities over its life to date. For example, a manufacturer's current-year revenues result in part from prior-years' product and sales organization development, prior-years' advertising and habituation of customers to buy its products, and so forth. In turn, this year's sales and other activities will profoundly affect future years' revenues. *This makes arbitrary any division of the firm's lifetime revenues into revenues reported for individual years*—for the same reason that assignment of the cost of a joint process to individual joint products is arbitrary.

Many authors have suggested alternatives to GAAP revenue recognition rules—different divisions of the lifetime revenues—that, in effect, recognize holding gains and losses prior to sale on *all* the firm's nonmonetary assets (not just ones held for resale that have declined in value). Readers who are interested in pursuing these matters further may wish to consult Chapter 32 and the works by Hendriksen, Sprouse and Moonitz, Sterling, and Thomas listed in the bibliography of this chapter.

Presentation of Nonoperating Gains and Losses. Firms usually report sales of products and services gross: their revenues equal the full amount of assets received or liabilities extinguished. Costs of assets and services deemed to have been expended to obtain these revenues are then separately reported as expenses. In contrast, firms usually report nonoperating gains and losses net.

EXAMPLE. ABC Company purchased a plot of land for $100,000 in 19X1. On 2/10/X9 it sold this land for $173,000.

CASE 1. ABC Company is a real estate company whose ordinary operations involve dealing in land. Under this assumption, the transaction is an operating one and revenue would be recorded gross, by entries such as the following:

```
Cash  .....................................  173,000
     Land Sales  ..........................          173,000
     To record the sale at its gross amount.

Cost of Land Sold  ........................  100,000
     Land Inventory  ......................          100,000
     To record the cost of the plot of land sold.
```

CASE 2. ABC Company is a manufacturer. Under this assumption, the transaction is a nonoperating one and revenue would be recorded net of the cost of the land:

```
Cash  .....................................  173,000
     Gain on Sale of Land  .................           73,000
     Land  .................................          100,000
     To record the net revenue.
```

Apparently, the main reasons for this difference in treatment are that a firm's nonoperating gains and losses often are of little significance in their own rights or they occur sporadically enough that data about them are of little use for investor predictions and decisions, or both. Accordingly, it is judged appropriate to report the minimum possible amount of detail concerning them.

Some accountants have wished to go further than mere net reporting of nonoperating gains and losses—and have wished to exclude many of them altogether from net income calculations, instead reporting them as direct credits and charges to retained earnings. APB opinions Nos. 9, 20, and 30 prohibit this except in certain rare instances of:

1. "Prior period adjustments":

> . . . material adjustments which (a) can be specifically identified with and directly related to the business activities of particular prior periods, and (b) are not attributable to economic events occurring subsequent to the date of the financial statements for the prior period, and (c) depend primarily on determinations by persons other than management and (d) were not susceptible of reasonable estimation prior to such determination.—APB Opinion No. 9, paragraph 23.

Examples of prior period adjustments include material, nonrecurring adjustments or settlements of income taxes and litigation, and results of renegotiation and utility rate proceedings.

2. Corrections of certain unintentional, material errors that were made in prior years' financial statements:

> . . . mathematical mistakes in the application of accounting principles, or oversight or misuse of facts that existed at the time the financial statements were prepared.—APB Opinion No. 20, paragraph 13.

Gains and losses resulting from such things as changes in depreciation estimates or estimates of collectibility of receivables are explicitly barred from direct credit or charge to retained earnings.

Finally, certain other unusual and infrequent nonoperating gains and losses, called "extraordinary items," are to be reported separately on the income statement, just above the figure for net income:

> Extraordinary items are events and transactions that are distinguished by their unusual nature *and* by the infrequency of their occurrence. Thus, *both* of the following criteria should be met to classify an event or transaction as an extraordinary item:
> a. *Unusual nature*—the underlying event or transaction should possess a high degree of abnormality and be of a type clearly unrelated to, or only incidentally related to, the ordinary and typical activities of the entity, taking into account the environment in which the entity operates. . . .
> b. *Infrequency of occurrence*—the underlying event or transaction should be of a type that would not reasonably be expected to recur in the forseeable future, taking into account the environment in which the entity operates.—APB Opinion No. 30, paragraph 20.

Examples of events that might result in reporting extraordinary items include expropriation or prohibition of a firm's activities by a government, earthquakes, and the like.

Capital from Donations and Treasury Stock.   Two other kinds of receipts remain to be discussed:

1. Occasionally a company will receive a donation of land or buildings as an inducement to conduct its business in a particular locality. Under present accounting rules, such donations are regarded as capital contributions and are not reflected in revenue. Instead, they are directly credited to a special capital account.

2. Occasionally, after a series of transactions in its own treasury stock, a company emerges with more net assets per share than it began with. Once again, the excess is not reflected as revenue but, instead, is directly credited to a special capital account.

In both of these cases it can be argued that the enhancement in asset values resulted from activities far removed from the company's usual efforts and accomplishments and that accordingly their reflection in revenue is inappropriate. With treasury stock transactions it is additionally urged that a company should not seek to profit from transactions with its owners; therefore, reflection in revenue is doubly inappropriate. Counterarguments could be offered to either of these claims, but the point remains that neither kind of asset increase is currently reflected in revenue.

Accounting for Decentralized Operations.   The accountant's concept of revenue pertains mostly to matters discussed in general-purpose published financial statements. But it is natural to extend the use of this concept to certain internal reports for managerial purposes. One such extension occurs when the company has decentralized into separate divisions or branches with a measure of local autonomy or when the company has departmentalized its records. When this happens, management often wishes divisional, branch, or departmental income statements prepared, as discussed in Chapter 44.

To the extent that the subunits' transactions are with outsiders, these reports present no special problems. But when divisions, branches, or departments engage in intracompany transactions, there can be serious problems in defining and calculating subunit revenues. These problems resemble the problems of parent-subsidiary revenues discussed in Chapter 34. The main difficulty with subunit revenues is that the amounts employed are rarely determined by impersonal market forces (as is the case with ordinary revenues). Instead, they are determined by a process of intracompany bargaining and may be arbitrary.

In any case, such subunit revenues should be excluded from general-purpose financial statements. Revenue results from the provision of goods or services to other entities. A company should not recognize revenue from providing goods or services to itself.

Tax Accounting.   Besides preparing financial statements, accountants also prepare tax returns. One would hope to use the same figures for both sets of reports. Unfortunately, though, tax accounting is designed to fulfill purposes that often have little to do with reporting results of enterprise effort, since tax laws serve a variety of other economic and regulatory goals.

Accordingly, there frequently are differences between financial accounting and tax accounting as to when revenues should be recognized, and occasionally there are even differences as to what revenue is. Because of this, for financial accounting purposes, it is best to ignore tax rules when deciding when to recognize revenue.

Summary—Final Definition of Revenue.   The previous discussion leads to the following summary definition of revenue. It should be repeated that this definition is intended only as a description of present practices. A revenue results when an asset (usually cash or a claim to receive cash) is received, or a liability is extinguished, as a result of a company's providing goods or services to another entity. There are two main kinds of revenues:

1. Operating revenues result from the company's providing its main products or services to its customers—those products or services that it is in business to provide. They are reported gross.

2. Nonoperating revenues are incidental gains, such as those which result from sales of noncurrent assets and from retirements of noncurrent liabilities. They are reported net.

The dividing line between operating and nonoperating revenues is not perfectly distinct. There often are difficulties in determining which products or services provided by a company are main ones and which are incidental. In particular, it currently is acceptable to treat minor revenues from rents, royalties, interest, and dividends as either operating or nonoperating.

TIMING AND MEASUREMENT OF REVENUE

Revenue is recognized when three tests are met:

1. The revenue is captured.
2. The revenue is measurable.
3. The revenue is earned.

The Revenue Is Captured. Either the company is certain to retain the related inflows of assets, or the portion that might be lost is small and susceptible to estimate. Ordinarily, amounts resulting from an acquisition of accounts receivable are captured; uncollectibles may be estimated and the amount calculated either used to reduce the amount of revenues recognized or recorded as an expense.

In contrast, holding gains typically are not captured until the related asset is sold; this is one reason why accountants refuse to recognize holding gains as revenues prior to such sale. For example, site land owned by a company may have doubled in market value since it was purchased. But land values fluctuate. The market value may fall again before the company sells the property. Since there is no way to capture the holding gain except by selling the land, the accountant refuses to recognize revenue until the time of sale.

To be captured, the revenue must also be severable. The company must be able to do whatever it will with the related asset inflow. Holding gains on plant assets often violate this requirement. To use the previous example, site land owned by the company may have doubled in market value since it was purchased. But if this is the land upon which the company's plant rests, it is impossible to sell it (unless the company decides to move).

The Revenue Is Measurable. The accountant must have no serious difficulty in valuing the assets received. Cash presents no valuation problem whatever. The problems involved in valuing receivables are manageable:

1. It usually is possible to make estimates of uncollectible accounts receivable.
2. Because of the time period before they are due, noninterest-bearing receivables are not worth quite as much as cash, even when there is no question of their collectibility. With ordinary trade receivables, this difference is not material and the accountant ignores it. APB Opinion No. 21 specifies that material long-lived noninterest-bearing receivables should be discounted.
3. There are various minor problems. For example, any company offering discounts for prompt payment knows that some of its customers will not take their discounts; this also may create a need for estimates.

Accountants are content to make any necessary estimates in measuring revenue; however, there are limits to this tolerance. Some unusual transactions involve exchanges of assets for plant assets, or for the capital stock of another company. If the exchange is for a readily marketable security, it may not be too difficult to measure the amount of asset inflow (and thereby measure the revenue). But sometimes the securities received are not readily marketable. In such cases accountants may find it impossible to value the inflow. If so, they will record the new assets at whatever dollar figure was associated with the assets given up and may refuse to recognize a revenue.

EXAMPLE. ABC Company, a manufacturer, purchased a plot of industrial site land in 19X1 for $100,000. On 2/10/X9 it sold this land.

CASE 1. The land was exchanged for $173,000 cash. There is no problem in valuing the asset inflow. The company would recognize revenue:

Cash	173,000	
Land		100,000
Gain on Sale of Land		73,000
To record the net revenue.		

CASE 2.   The land was exchanged for General Motors Corporation common stock. The stock had a market value of $173,000 at the time of sale. Once again there are no serious problems in valuing the inflow of assets. The company would recognize revenue:

```
Investments  ..............................  173,000
     Land  ..................................          100,000
     Gain on Sale of Land  ...................           73,000
To record the net revenue.
```

CASE 3.   Same as case 2, except that the land was exchanged for DEF Company common stock. DEF Company stock is infrequently traded. Here, reliable valuation of the asset inflow may be impossible. If the accountants believe that they can determine the fair market value of the DEF Company stock, their entry will resemble that in case 2. If they believe they can determine a fair value for the land, they may use that figure instead for recognizing revenue. If *all* such possibilities fail, accountants will not recognize revenue. Accounting Principles Board Opinion No. 29 says (paragraph 26): "If neither the fair value of a nonmonetary asset transferred nor the fair value of a nonmonetary asset received in exchange is determinable within reasonable limits, the recorded amount of the nonmonetary asset transferred from the enterprise may be the only available measure of the transaction." In the example the entry would be:

```
Investments  ..............................  100,000
     Land  ..................................          100,000
To record the exchange of assets.
```

Opinion No. 29 also excludes from revenue recognition exchanges which are largely nominal in nature in that assets of a similar nature are exchanged. Paragraph 21 of the Opinion says:

> If the exchange is not essentially the culmination of an earning process, accounting for an exchange of a nonmonetary asset between an enterprise and another entity should be based on the recorded amount (after reduction, if appropriate, for an indicated impairment of value) of the nonmonetary assets relinquished. The Board believes that the following two types of nonmonetary exchange transactions do not culminate an earning process:
>
> *a.* An exchange of a product or property held for sale in the ordinary course of business for a product or property to be sold in the same line of business to facilitate sales to customers other than the parties to the exchange, and
>
> *b.* An exchange of a productive asset not held for sale in the ordinary course of business for a similar productive asset or an equivalent interest in the same or similar productive asset. . . .

The Revenue Is Earned.   No significant activities remain to be performed for the customer being provided with the related product or service. At the time financial statements are prepared, it often happens that a revenue is captured and measurable but only partly earned. In such cases, the accountant often allocates part of the total revenue to the current period (in proportion to the relative extent to which it has been earned).

EXAMPLE.   On July 1, 19X1, GHI Company acquired a $10,000 note receivable from JKL Company. Principal and interest at 12 percent are due on July 1, 19X3. GHI Company prepares annual financial statements every December 31.

The total revenue for the services that GHI Company is providing to JKL Company will be $10,000 × 12% × 2 = $2,400. This revenue is measurable. Assuming that GHI Company makes suitable estimates of uncollectibles, it is captured, too; it is guaranteed by a firm contract. But, as of 12/31/X1, only one-quarter of the related services has been performed. Only one-quarter of the total revenue has been earned. The accountant allocates one-quarter of the total revenue to the 19X1 income statement:

```
Interest Receivable ................................. 600
    Interest Revenue ..............................     600
To record the accrued revenue.
```

Aftercosts.   Some vendors of products undergo substantial aftercosts for such things as service contracts and warranties. Where aftercosts are significant, it can be argued that only part of the revenue-earning process has been completed at the time of sale and that an allocation of total revenue is necessary.

EXAMPLE.   MNO Company sells a product that requires considerable servicing. The company guarantees servicing for two years after the customer purchases the product. During 19X1 the company's sales of the product totaled $1,000,000. Cost of goods sold was $700,000. 19X1 servicing costs resulting from 19X1 sales were $20,000. The company estimates that over the next two years there will be a total of $80,000 more servicing costs resulting from 19X1 sales.

The company could estimate that the total costs of these sales will be $700,000 + $20,000 + $80,000 = $800,000, and allocate $1,000,000/$800,000 = $1.25 of revenue to every dollar of cost incurred. This would result in its making entries similar to the following for 19X1:

```
Cost of Product Sold  ........................ 700,000
    Finished Product  .......................            700,000
To record the product cost.

Accounts Receivable  ......................... 1,000,000
    Sales ($1.25 × $700,000)  ...............              875,000
    Estimated Service Warranties  ...........              125,000
To record 19X1 sales of product and service
guarantees, with revenue allocated to the two
different activities.

Service Warranties Expense  .................  20,000
    Various  .................................             20,000
To record the 19X1 cost of fulfilling service
guarantees on 19X1 sales.

Estimated Service Warranties  ...............  25,000
    Service Revenues  .......................             25,000
To record 19X1 revenues resulting from fulfilling
service guarantees on 19X1 sales:
$1.25 × $20,000 = $25,000.
```

Suppose that in 19X2 servicing costs resulting from 19X1 sales were $48,000. Then $48,000 × $1.25 = $60,000 of service revenues would be recognized:

```
Service Warranties Expense  .................  48,000
    Various  .................................             48,000
To record the 19X2 cost of fulfilling service guaran-
tees on 19X1 sales.

Estimated Service Warranties  ...............  60,000
    Service Revenues  .......................             60,000
To record 19X2 revenues resulting from fulfilling
service guarantees on 19X1 sales.
```

As is evident from the example, this approach allocates the revenue to both sales and service. Most companies instead prefer to recognize the entire revenue at the time of sale, and recognize any estimated aftercosts as additional expenses of the year of sale. From the standpoint of theory it can be argued that this treatment is not as appropriate as an allocation which would allow all major company activities to generate a normal profit margin. But recognition of all revenue at the time of sale is the method customarily followed.

EXAMPLE.   MNO Company could instead recognize the entire $200,000 profit at the time the product was sold. The 19X1 and 19X2 entries would be:

19X1

Cost of Product Sold	700,000	
Finished Product		700,000
To record the product cost.		

Service Warranties Expense	100,000	
Estimated Service Warranties		100,000
To record the estimated cost of service guarantees on 19X1 sales.		

Accounts Receivable	1,000,000	
Sales		1,000,000
To record 19X1 sales of product and service, with revenues *not* allocated to the two different activities.		

Estimated Service Warranties	20,000	
Various		20,000
To record the 19X1 cost of fulfilling service guarantees on 19X1 sales.		

19X2

Estimated Service Warranties	48,000	
Various		48,000
To record the 19X2 cost of fulfilling service guarantees on 19X1 sales.		

The Spectrum of Revenue Recognition Possibilites.   Accountants recognize revenue at the earliest point at which, in their estimation, it is captured, measurable, and earned. There are three main possible points at which revenue might be recognized:
1. At the time a product or service is produced
2. At the time of sale
3. At the time cash is collected.

These possibilites form a spectrum over time of possible points of revenue recognition. These three possibilites are discussed successively in the three sections that follow.

To assist comparison of these methods, each section begins with a parallel example (of the activities of the imaginary "Simplified Company"). These Simplified Company examples are designed for the reader who desires a quick overview of the revenue recognition possibilites; they omit many complexities. Subsequent examples in each section examine the individual revenue recognition approaches in greater detail.

THE PRODUCTION BASIS

Revenue may be recognized at the time of production of the related product or service. As we saw in an earlier example, this is the essence of what happens when interest revenue is recognized on an accrual basis. In that example, GHI Company provided one-quarter of its total services as a lender in 19X1. So, it accrued one-quarter of the total related interest revenues during 19X1, on a service production basis. Similar accruals are made of revenues relating to rental services and other contractual services that function by the passage of time. In such cases the rate at which revenue is earned is fully determined in advance by the contract, and therefore is both measurable and captured.

Use of the production basis requires that the total revenue be substantially assured (captured) and measurable and that it be possible to estimate the extent to which revenue has been earned. This sometimes will be the case when goods are being manufactured under firm purchase commitments.

EXAMPLE.   On 3/1/X1, Simplified Company obtained a firm contract to manufacture 500,000 units of product for a total contract price of $5,000,000, or $10 a unit. The company is to make delivery in 100,000-unit batches and is entitled to bill 95 percent of the unit selling price upon delivery. The remaining 5 percent is to be retained by the buyer until satisfactory completion of the entire contract. The product costs Simplified Company $6 per unit to manufacture. During 19X1, the company manufactured 370,000 units at a cost of $2,220,000 and delivered 300,000 units. There is much variety in the account titles actually employed by companies following the production basis of revenue recognition; however, appropriate journal entries under the production basis would be:

```
Finished Product—At Cost  .........................  2,220,000
    Work in Process  ..............................              2,220,000
To record the cost of manufacturing 370,000 units of
product @ $6.

Product Expense—Long-Term Contract  .............  2,220,000
    Finished Product—At Cost  ....................              2,220,000
To record product expense on a production basis.
(This entry is similar to a cost of goods sold entry—
370,000 units produced @ $6.)

Finished Product—At Contract Price  ...............  3,700,000
    Revenue on Long-Term Contract  ...............              3,700,000
To record revenue on a production basis—370,000 units
produced @ $10.

Accounts Receivable—Billed  .......................  2,850,000
Accounts Receivable—Retained Percentage  ..........    150,000
    Finished Product—At Contract Price  ...........              3,000,000
To record delivery of 300,000 units @ $10 and billing of
95% of contract price, with a retained percentage of 5%.
```

The two Finished Product accounts and the two Accounts Receivable accounts are assets; Product Expense—Long-Term Contract is an expense account corresponding to the ordinary Cost of Goods Sold account.

In this case use of the production basis involves matching revenues with costs, instead of the (usual) other way around. Reporting revenues at the full contract price (instead of 95 percent of the full contract price) is justified if there appear to be no obstacles to satisfactory completion of the contract.

Long-Term Construction Contracts.   A similar use of the production basis is made with long-term construction contracts where a failure to accrue revenue during the life of the contract could lead to considerable erratic fluctuations in reported revenues from one year to the next.

EXAMPLE.   Simplified Company is a contractor. On 3/1/X1 the company obtained a firm contract to build a building, at a total contract price of $5,000,000. The company is authorized to bill the purchaser for a total of 95 percent of the contract price at various stages during the building's construction; the remaining 5 percent is retained pending satisfactory completion of the contract. Simplified Company estimates that this building will cost $3,000,000 to build. During 19X1 the company's construction costs were $2,220,000 (74 percent of the $3,000,000 total). Bills were submitted for $3,325,000, representing 70 percent completion of the project ($5,000,000 × 70% × 95% = $3,325,000). Appropriate journal entries are shown below. Once again, account titles vary widely in actual practice.

```
Construction in Process—At Cost  .....................  2,220,000
     Various  ........................................          2,220,000
To record the costs of 74% completion of the project.

Construction Expense—Long-Term Contract  ...........  2,220,000
     Construction in Process—At Cost  .................          2,220,000
To record construction expense on a production basis
(similar to a cost of goods sold entry).

Unbilled Construction in Process—At Contract Price  .....  3,700,000
     Revenues on Long-Term Contract  .................          3,700,000
To record revenues on a production basis at 74% completion
($5,000,000 × 74% = $3,700,000).

Accounts Receivable—Billed  .........................  3,325,000
Accounts Receivable—Retained Percentage  ............    175,000
     Unbilled Construction in Process—At Contract Price          3,500,000
To record billing on a 70% completion basis.
```

Construction in Process—at Cost and Unbilled Construction in Process—at Contract Price are both asset accounts. Construction Expense—Long-Term Contract is an expense account corresponding to the ordinary cost of goods sold account.

In the previous illustration, revenue was recorded gross of costs of construction. Often, instead, it is reported net of these costs. (Instead of reporting the revenue from construction activities, the accountant reports the gross margin, after subtracting construction costs.) Using such net recording, the corresponding entries for Simplified Company would be as follows:

```
Construction in Process  ...........................  2,220,000
     Various  ....................................          2,220,000
To record the costs of 74% completion of the project.

Construction in Process  ...........................  1,480,000
     Gross Margin on Long-Term Contracts  ..........          1,480,000
To convert the figure for construction in process to the
amount that eventually will be billed, and to record gross
margin on a production basis.

Accounts Receivable—Billed  .......................  3,325,000
Accounts Receivable—Retained Percentage  ...........    175,000
     Construction in Process  ......................          3,500,000
To record billing on a 70% completion basis.
```

Both the gross and the net approaches to accounting for long-term construction contracts are acceptable. The alternative to use of the production method here would be the "completed contract" method, delaying revenue recognition until the contract was completed.

Occasionally the production basis is also employed by companies manufacturing readily marketable extractive or agricultural products when the market price is known and substantially assured. The production basis is widely employed with cost-plus-fixed-fee contracts; here the net approach is common, with only the fee itself being recognized as revenue.

Some Complications. Certain factors often complicate accounting for long-term construction contracts. The most common form of the production basis for contractors is the "percentage of completion" method. Under this method, the accountant calculates the revenue to be recognized in any period by first estimating the extent to which completion of the contract has been advanced during that period. Then a proportionate share of the total revenue from the contract is allocated to the period concerned. The extent of completion may be estimated in terms of subtasks to be performed by the contractor. Frequently, as in the following example, it is instead estimated in terms of the relationship between estimated total costs of the contract and costs incurred to date.

EXAMPLE. PQR Company is a contractor. On May 15, 19X1, the company signed a contract with STU Company to construct· an office building. PQR Company estimated that costs traceable to this contract would total $7,500,000. The total contract price was $10,000,000, which was intended to cover traceable costs, various untraceable overheads, and PQR Company's profit. STU Company agreed to an escalator clause whereby it would absorb all increases in labor wage rates as additions to the contract price. The contract specified that payments were to be made by STU Company at 20, 40, 60, and 80 percent of completion, with 10 percent retained until final approval of the completed building by STU Company's architect. PQR Company employs the gross form of the percentage of completion method of revenue recognition. The degree of completion of any contract is estimated by comparing total traceable costs incurred to date with the total currently estimated traceable costs of the completed contract. Any costs covered by escalator clauses are excluded from degree of completion calculations. During 19X1 the following events occurred under this contract:

1. The company used materials with a total cost of $2,000,000. Because of an unexpected increase in materials prices, the total cost of materials will be $120,000 higher than originally estimated. There is no indication that material usage will vary from the original estimate.

2. Labor costs were $1,500,000. Total labor costs on this contract are now estimated to be $3,600,000, or $350,000 higher than originally anticipated. Of this difference, $320,000 is due to an increase in labor wage rates, to begin on 1/1/X2. The remaining $30,000 resulted from extra hours being worked during 19X1.

3. The original contract specified that certain parts of the construction were to be subcontracted. Costs of subcontracted activities were originally estimated at $280,000. During 19X1, subcontractors charged $50,000. PQR Company now estimates that subcontracting costs will total only $265,000.

4. Miscellaneous traceable costs totaled $100,100. Estimates of these costs remain unchanged.

5. After construction had begun, PQR Company and STU Company agreed to install special interior partitions costing an additional $300,000. The contract price (exclusive of payments to be made under escalator clauses) was increased to $10,400,000. No expenditures have yet been made relating to these partitions.

6. PQR Company has submitted bills based on 40 percent completion. These bills have· been approved, but payments totaling only $1,872,000 have been received to date.

Calculation of Degree of Completion.   The first step in calculating the degree of completion is to determine the total currently estimated traceable cost of the completed contract, exclusive of costs covered by escalator clauses:

Original estimate of total cost		$7,500,000
Additional costs of materials		120,000
Additional costs of labor	$350,000	
Less: Portion covered by escalator clause	320,000	30,000
Additional costs of special partitions		300,000
Subtotal		$7,950,000
Less: Decrease in estimated subcontracting costs		15,000
Total currently estimated traceable costs of contract		$7,935,000

Next, determine the total traceable costs incurred to date (exclusive of costs covered by escalator clauses, of which there happened to be none in 19X1):

Materials	$2,000,000
Labor	1,500,000
Subcontracting costs	50,000
Miscellaneous costs	100,100
Total incurred to date	$3,650,100

The degree of completion may then be calculated by dividing the total currently estimated cost into the total costs incurred to date:

$$\text{Degree of completion} = \frac{\$3,650,100}{\$7,935,000} = \underline{46\%}$$

Total revenues on this contract (exclusive of payments under escalator clauses) will be $10,400,000. Of these, $10,400,000 × 46% = $4,784,000 should be allocated to 19X1 operations. Bills submitted should total $10,400,000 × 40% × 90% = $3,744,000. The appropriate journal entries are shown below:

Construction in Process—At Cost	3,650,100	
Materials and Supplies		2,000,000
Payrolls		1,500,000
Accounts Payable to Subcontractors		50,000
Various		100,100
To record costs incurred in 19X1.		
Unbilled Construction in Process—At Contract Price	4,784,000	
Revenues on Long-Term Contract		4,784,000
To record revenues on a percentage of completion production basis.		
Construction Expense—Long-Term Contract	3,650,100	
Construction in Process—At Cost		3,650,100
To record construction expense on a production basis (similar to a cost of goods sold entry).		
Accounts Receivable—Billed	3,744,000	
Accounts Receivable—Retained Percentage	416,000	
Unbilled Construction in Process—At Contract Price		4,160,000
To record submission of bills on the basis of 40% completion: $10,400,000 × 40% = $4,160,000.		
Cash	1,872,000	
Accounts Receivable—Billed		1,872,000
To record cash collections from STU Company.		

By-products and Scrap. The accountant's treatment of by-products and scrap sometimes offers an example of an indirect use of the production basis of revenue recognition. From an economic standpoint, by-products and scrap are as valid a part of a manufacurer's total output as any of its other outputs. But the dollar amounts often are minor, and it is hard to determine what by-product outputs cost. This has resulted in there being two main treatments of these assets and the related revenues:

1. Sometimes an asset is recognized, at an amount equal to its selling price less costs to complete and sell. Production costs are relieved by an amount sufficient to accomplish this. The effect is to reduce costs of manufactured inventories and eventually costs of goods sold, and to increase reported net income, by the by-product's or scrap's selling price, whether or not the by-product or scrap has been sold.

2. Sometimes no asset is recognized. Instead, revenues from the sales of by-products and scrap either are reported gross of any costs, or else offset against costs of manufactured inventories.

Both treatments mentioned above are currently acceptable.

THE SALES BASIS

Most revenue recognition occurs at the time that the company's products or services are sold. Indeed, it never would occur to many accountants that they use any other basis of revenue recognition.

EXAMPLE. Simplified Company is a manufacurer. During 19X1 the company manufactured 370,000 units of product and sold 332,500 units. All sales were made on account at a price of $10 per unit. 19X1 collections on these sales totalled $2,850,000. The product cost Simplified Company $6 per unit to manufacture. Appropriate journal entries under the sales basis are as follows:

Finished Goods	2,220,000	
Work in Process		2,220,000
To record the cost of manufacturing 370,000 units of product @ $6.		
Cost of Goods Sold	1,995,000	
Finished Goods		1,995,000
To record product expense on a sales basis: 332,500 units sold @ $6.		
Accounts Receivable	3,325,000	
Sales		3,325,000
To record revenues on a sales basis: 332,500 units sold @ $10.		
Cash	2,850,000	
Accounts Receivable		2,850,000
To record collections on account.		

Although the sales basis is simple and familiar, it leads to certain difficult problems, too. We already have discussed the problem of aftercosts. Other problems arise with sales cutoffs:

1. The exact point at which a sale occurs involves complicated legal questions. Most accountants cut through this problem by expediently treating the point of sale as the point at which delivery is made to the customer (or to a common carrier). So long as some consistent policy is followed from one year to the next, this can be done without serious distortion resulting. However, the details of establishing a good sales cutoff can be quite complicated.

2. Whatever cutoff method is used for sales, a parallel method must be adopted for a cost of goods sold cutoff. Otherwise there will be product expense without any related revenue in some years, and revenues without expenses in other years.

The Realization and Historical-Cost Rules. The rule that revenues should be recognized at the time the company's product or services are sold is often called the realization rule, and it often is asserted that revenues are not realized until the point of sale. The sales basis of revenue recognition has the effect of preserving the magnitudes reported for products (and other nonmonetary assets) at their historical purchase prices until such assets are sold. (With depreciable assets, the magnitude reported is a depreciated historical purchase price.) So, the realization rule is also a historical-cost rule: Nonmonetary assets are to be reported at their historical costs; holding gains are not to be recognized until nonmonetary assets are sold. Of course, as we already have seen, most practicing accountants make two main exceptions to the historical-cost/realization rule:

1. They employ a form of the production basis to interest, rent, and other contractual revenues.

2. They recognize certain holding losses prior to the time of sale (as when they report inventories and marketable equity securities at the lower of cost or market).

Some Complications. The sales basis of revenue recognition often will be more complicated than the previous example would suggest. It is assumed in what follows that the company makes all of its sales on account.

The amount shown on a company's sales invoice does not necessarily equal the amount of revenue that it should recognize at the time of sale. One reason why this is so was indicated when aftercosts were discussed in an earlier section of this chapter. But there are several other reasons why the invoice amount may overstate the revenue.

1. The invoice price may be gross of discounts that the customer is expected to take.

2. Often, a portion of what is furnished customers will be wholly or partly unsatisfactory, resulting in subsequent returns or allowances.

3. Certain accounts receivable may prove to be uncollectible.

Each of these conditions may necessitate adjustment or correction of the amounts recognized as revenue. These revenue adjustments are discussed in detail below. The basic principle involved in all these adjustments is simple: A revenue never should be recognized for an amount greater than what will ultimately be collected from customers. But, as will be seen, in practice this principle is occasionally violated.

Discounts.   There are four main reasons for giving discounts to customers:

1. *Trade discounts.* In many industries it is common for manufacturers to write their invoices at figures equal to list prices—the intended selling prices of products to their final customers. The manufacturer then allows trade discounts off list prices to wholesalers, retailers, and other entities involved in distributing these products. When such trade discounts are employed, revenue always should be recognized for the actual net amount sought by the manufacturer from the entity with which it deals. This net amount is all that the manufacturer expects to collect, so it is all that the related revenues are worth. The amount paid by the final customer is irrelevant, except when the company itself sells to these final customers.

EXAMPLE.   VWX Company is a manufacturer. The company sells to retail dealers, allowing a 40 percent trade discount off list. During 19X1 the company's sales totaled $3,500,000 at list prices.

In this example, revenues should be recognized only for the amount that customers are expected to pay—60 percent of the list price ($3,500,000× 60% = $2,100,000):

```
Accounts Receivable ........................ 2,100,000
     Sales  ...............................              2,100,000
To record sales at the net amount expected to be
received by VWX Company.
```

2. *Employee discounts.* Similarly, many retail establishments allow their employees to make purchases at prices less than the ordinary retail price. When the discount is of minor amount, such sales should also be recorded net. When large discounts are involved, it becomes possible to argue that a form of supplemental employee compensation is present; in such cases actual accounting practice allows the revenue either to be recorded net or to be recorded gross with the discount reported as an expense. If the discount reduces the price below the product's cost, there is much to be said for treating at least part of the discount as an expense.

3. *Cash discounts.* Some companies (mostly retail establishments) allow customers to pay a lesser amount for a cash purchase than they would if they bought on credit, or allow them to pay less if they do not require delivery services. As before, revenue should be recognized equal to the actual amounts received; revenue should be recognized net of cash discounts.

4. *Discounts for prompt payment.* Other companies allow their customers to take a discount if they pay within a set period of time after billing (or after receipt of the goods). The company intends that such discounts be taken by all customers; the discount rate is set high enough to encourage prompt payment. Therefore, in theory, revenue should be recognized net of these discounts. In practice, though, many companies have found it expedient to record such sales at the gross figure. When this gross approach is used, discounts actually taken should be recorded as downward adjustments of this gross revenue figure, rather than as expenses.

EXAMPLE.   YZA Company is a manufacturer. The company allows a 3 percent discount for payment of accounts within 45 days. All sales are on account. During 19X1 the company's sales totaled $2,100,000. Discounts of $51,000 were taken on $1,649,000 payments of accounts totaling $1,700,000 gross. Discounts of $600 lapsed on accounts totaling $20,000 gross, which were paid late. At 12/31/X1, accounts totaling $380,000 gross are still unpaid. The company expects that discounts of $10,500 will be taken on accounts totaling $350,000 gross and that discounts of $900 will lapse on accounts totaling $30,000 gross.

Under the net method, ordinary sales revenue would be recognized at an amount net of the 3 percent discount for prompt payment. There will also be a special revenue, relatively minor in amount, from lapsed sales discounts—the excess over the net price paid by customers who pay late. In theory, this special revenue might be reported separately; in practice, it rarely is. Both versions of the net method are discussed below.

Net Method—in Theory

```
Accounts Receivable .....................................  2,037,000
    Sales  ............................................              2,037,000
To record sales with a gross price of $2,100,000.

Cash  ....................................................  1,669,000
    Accounts Receivable  .............................              1,668,400
    Lapsed Sales Discounts ...........................                    600
To record collections of $1,649,000 + $20,000 = $1,669,000, on
net accounts totaling ($1,700,000 + $20,000) × 97% =
$1,668,400.

Accounts Receivable—Estimated
    Lapsed Sales Discounts .............................        900
    Lapsed Sales Discounts ...........................                    900
Adjusting entry at year-end to correct accounts receivable for
estimated discounts that will not be taken on year-end accounts.
```

Net Method—in Practice. In practice the final $900 accrual entry would almost always be omitted as immaterial; lapsed sales discounts would not be recognized until late payment was actually received. When late payment was received (as in the $600 entry), the credit would usually be either to some miscellaneous revenues account or to Sales.

A similar gap between theory and practice exists under the gross method. In what follows, Sales Discounts is a contra to Sales, not an expense.

Gross Method—in Theory

```
Accounts Receivable  ............................  2,100,000
    Sales  ........................................              2,100,000
To record sales with a gross price of $2,100,000.

Cash  ...........................................  1,669,000
Sales Discounts  ................................     51,600
    Accounts Receivable  .........................              1,720,000
    Lapsed Sales Discounts  ......................                    600
To record cash collections of $1,669,000. The total sales
discount is 3% of the total accounts receivable involved:
$1,720,000 × 3% = $51,600.
```

In theory, an entry similar to the final entry shown for the net method might be made:

```
Sales Discounts  .....................................  10,500
    Accounts Receivable—Estimated Sales Discounts  ......     10,500
To record sales discounts that are estimated will be taken on
accounts totaling $350,000 gross.
```

Gross Method—in Practice. Almost always, the $600 Lapsed Sales Discount would be netted into the Sales Discounts figure, and the final $10,500 accrual omitted (even though the result of this omission is to report Accounts Receivable at an amount $10,500 higher than anticipated collections on account):

```
Accounts Receivable  .............................  2,100,000
     Sales  ......................................           2,100,000
To record sales with a gross price of $2,100,000.

Cash  ..........................................  1,669,000
Sales Discounts ...............................     51,000
     Accounts Receivable  .......................           1,720,000
To record cash collections of $1,669,000.
```

Returns and Allowances. Two possible situations may occur when goods or services prove unsatisfactory and customers are allowed refunds:

1. The customer does not return the goods. In this case the customer is said to receive an allowance.

2. The customer returns goods. Sometimes these goods are taken back into the company's inventory, sometimes not. These are instances of returns.

As with discounts and uncollectibles, if material returns or allowances are anticipated on current-year sales, an estimated adjustment could be made at year-end. However, it is rare for the adjustment involved to be material, and such year-end adjustments for expected returns and allowances are uncommon.

EXAMPLE.   BCD Company is a manufacturer. The company does not provide discounts and does not have uncollectible accounts receivable (except in connection with returns and allowances). All sales are made on account. During 19X1, the company's sales totaled $2,100,000. The related cost of goods sold was $1,400,000. (The company employs a consistent markup of 50 percent over cost.) During 19X1, goods that had sold for $90,000 were returned. Allowances totaling $16,000 were granted to other dissatisfied customers who kept the related goods. Of the goods returned, items that had cost BCD Company $22,500 could be salvaged for resale. Appropriate summary entries are shown below. Account titles employed have not been standardized and vary from company to company. Sales Returns and Sales Allowances are contra-accounts to Sales and are not expenses.

```
Accounts Receivable  .............................  2,100,000
     Sales  ......................................           2,100,000
To record 19X1 sales, before adjustments.

Cost of Goods Sold ..............................  1,400,000
     Finished Goods  ............................           1,400,000
To record 19X1 cost of goods sold, before adjustments.

Sales Allowances  ...............................     16,000
     Accounts Receivable  .......................              16,000
To record actual 19X1 allowances granted, and to cancel
the related sales.

Sales Returns  ..................................     90,000
     Accounts Receivable  .......................              90,000
To record actual 19X1 returns allowed, and to cancel
the related sales.

Returned Goods  .................................     22,500
Loss on Returns  ................................     37,500
     Cost of Goods Sold  ........................              60,000
To record the salvage value of goods returned, and to
cancel the related cost of goods sold. The loss on returns
reflects the damage or other deterioration to these
returned goods.
```

Often this last entry is simplified to the following, especially when the amount of the loss is not material:

```
Returned Goods  .................................    22,500
     Cost of Goods Sold  ........................             22,500
```

Uncollectibles. Adjustments must also be made for uncollectible accounts receivable. Whenever uncollectibles are frequent, it is customary to estimate them in advance. Such estimates may either be in the form of a percentage of the company's credit sales or may be made by an examination of the individual accounts. In theory, the estimate of uncollectibles should lead to a revenue adjustment. However, in practice, estimated uncollectibles often are reported as an expense.

EXAMPLE. EFG Company is a manufacturer. The company's 19X1 sales total $2,100,000, all on account. The company does not offer discounts and has no returns or allowances. It estimates that 2 percent of its sales will prove uncollectible. Appropriate entries would be as follows. "Sales-Uncollectibles" is a contra-account to Sales, not an expense:

```
Accounts Receivable  ...........................  2,100,000
     Sales  ........................................           2,100,000
To record 19X1 sales, before adjustments.

Sales—Uncollectibles  ...........................    42,000
     Accounts Receivable—Estimated Uncollectibles  ..           42,000
To record estimated uncollectibles on 19X1 sales.
Often the debit in this entry would be to an account
called "Bad Debts Expense."
```

Discounts, returns, and allowances are not ordinarily recorded until actually taken by customers; in contrast, it is customary to estimate uncollectibles in advance, ás above. When an actual default by a customer occurs, no revenue adjustment need then be made (or expense be recognized).

During 19X2, $41,000 of EFG Company's 19X1 accounts receivable proved actually uncollectible. The appropriate entry would be:

```
Accounts Receivable—Estimated Uncollectibles  ............  41,000
     Accounts Receivable  ...............................           41,000
To record 19X1 accounts receivable that actually proved
uncollectible in 19X2.
```

The proper treatment of amounts left over in any of the several accounts receivable contra-accounts discussed above is described in Chapter 15.

THE COLLECTION BASIS

The collection basis of revenue recognition involves waiting until cash is actually collected from one's customers before recognizing revenue. The method is widely used by private citizens and by professional men; it has little theoretical merit for companies preparing annual reports unless the assets received for the company's products or services are so hard to value that revenue recognition itself becomes inappropriate. Occasionally, this is true in retailing. An example of recording retail sales on the collection basis is the installment method of revenue recognition whereby revenue is allocated to each installment payment made by an installment purchaser of the company's products. In Opinion No. 10, the Accounting Principles Board specified that the sales method of revenue recognition should be used for such installment sales, except when "there is no reasonable basis for determining the degree of collectibility," and therefore no way to establish allowances for uncollectible accounts. In cases of extreme uncertainty, recognition of any profit at all may be delayed until the entire cost of the product sold is recovered.

EXAMPLE. Simplified Company is a manufacturer. During 19X1 the company manufactured 370,000 units of product and sold 300,000 units. All sales were made on account at a price of $10 per unit. 19X1 collections on these sales totaled $1,000,000. The remaining $2,000,000 is receivable in installments over the next two years. The product costs the company $6 per unit to manufacture. (Most installment sales require the customer to pay finance charges, but for simplicity such charges are omitted from this example; finance charges and other complicating factors are discussed in subsequent examples.) Ordinarily, the sales basis would be appropriate here, with suitable estimates of uncollectible installment accounts. Assuming, though, that there is no reasonable way to make such estimates, the appropriate entries under one form of the installment method might be as shown below. The particular recording approach shown here has been chosen to parallel the Simplified Company examples under the production and sales basis (see the examples at the beginning of those sections).

Installment Method—Gross

Finished Goods	2,220,000	
Work in Process		2,220,000
To record the cost of manufacturing 370,000 units of product @ $6.		
Installment Contracts Receivable	3,000,000	
Deferred Revenues on Installment Sales		3,000,000
A self-balancing memorandum entry to record the total amount owed Simplified Company by installment customers.		
Goods Delivered Under Installment Contracts	1,800,000	
Finished Goods		1,800,000
To record delivery of 300,000 units of product to installment customers, @ $6 per unit.		
Cash	1,000,000	
Installment Contracts Receivable		1,000,000
To record collection of installments for one-third of total 19X1 sales.		
Deferred Revenues on Installment Sales	1,000,000	
Installment Sales		1,000,000
To record revenues equal to cash collection of one-third of total 19X1 sales.		
Cost of Goods Sold	600,000	
Goods Delivered Under Installment Contracts		600,000
To record product expense on a collection basis—one-third of total cost of goods delivered to 19X1 installment customers.		

Goods Delivered Under Installment Contracts is an asset account; Deferred Revenues on Installment Sales is an asset contra-account. In the event that collection was so uncertain that no profit should be recognized until the entire cost of product sold was recovered, the final entry would instead be:

Cost of Goods Sold	1,000,000	
Goods Delivered Under Installment Contracts		1,000,000

All other entries would remain the same. The effect is to record a zero net income for 19X1.

In the previous illustration, revenue was recorded gross of cost of goods sold. Usually, though, it is recorded net of these costs. This exactly parallels the alternative treatment of revenue discussed earlier in accounting for long-term construction contracts. (Instead of reporting the revenue from installment sales, the accountant may report the gross margin, after subtracting cost of goods sold.)

Under such net recording, corresponding entries for Simplified Company might be:

Installment Method—Net

Finished Goods	2,220,000	
Work in Process		2,220,000

To record the cost of manufacturing 370,000 units of product @ $6.

Installment Contracts Receivable	3,000,000	
Installment Sales		3,000,000

To record the total amount of installment sales: 300,000 units of product @ $10. (The apparent recognition of revenue here is canceled in the fourth entry.)

Cost of Installment Sales	1,800,000	
Finished Goods		1,800,000

To record the total product cost of installment sales: 300,000 units of product @ $6. (The apparent recognition of expense is also canceled in the fourth entry.)

Installment Sales	3,000,000	
Cost of Installment Sales		1,800,000
Deferred Gross Margin on Installment Sales		1,200,000

To defer recognition of revenue and expense on installment sales until cash is collected.

Cash	1,000,000	
Installment Contracts Receivable		1,000,000

To record collection of installments for one-third of total 19X1 sales.

Deferred Gross Margin on Installment Sales	400,000	
Gross Margin on Installment Sales		400,000

To record recognition of one-third of total deferred gross profits on 19X1 installment sales. $1,200,000 \times \frac{1}{3} = $400,000.

The account Deferred Gross Margin on Installment Sales is frequently shown on the equities side of the balance sheet. However, conceptually it is better viewed as a contra-account to Installment Contracts Receivable. Since revenues are not recognized until collection, it is logical to report accounts receivable at product cost, which would be the effect of such a contra treatment.

This series of entries can be simplified if the company does not wish to record memorandum information about sales and cost of goods sold. The second, third, and fourth entries may be combined into:

Installment Contracts Receivable	3,000,000	
Finished Goods		1,800,000
Deferred Gross Margin on Installment Sales ...		1,200,000

Any of the methods discussed in this subsection are acceptable.

Some Complications.   Three main complications are apt to develop in accounting for installment sales:

1. Gross profit rates often change somewhat from year to year; this complicates the calculation of cost of goods sold (or of deferred profit recognized) when installment payments are received.

2. Most installment contracts charge interest. Some way must be found to allocate portions of installment payments received to the contract principal, and portions to interest revenue.

3. Defaults and repossessions must be accounted for. (For clarity, the example given below makes the unrealistic assumption of only one default and repossession over a two-year period; in an actual installment sales situation, they would, of course, be much more common.)

EXAMPLE. HIJ Company is a retailer. The company sells its goods on the installment plan and recognizes revenue on the installment sales basis, using the net approach. A 10 percent down payment is collected at the time of purchase. The balance, plus finance charges, is to be paid in 20 equal monthly installments. Finance charges are calculated as a uniform 21 percent of the total amount of installment contracts receivable. The details of the company's 19X1 and 19X2 installment sales are given in Exhibit 1.

EXHIBIT 1

	19X1	19X2
Cost of goods sold on the installment plan	$ 675,000	$ 960,000
Gross margin on installment sales	825,000	1,040,000
Selling price of goods sold on the installment plan	$1,500,000	$2,000,000
Down payment collected (10% of selling price)	150,000	200,000
Balance of selling price	$1,350,000	$1,800,000
Finance charges (21% of total installment contracts receivable)	358,861	478,481
Total installment contracts receivable	$1,708,861	$2,278,481
Collections of 19X1 installment contracts receivable	$ 460,000	$ 970,000
Collections of 19X2 installment contracts receivable	—	620,000

The 19X1 gross margin is $825,000/$1,500,000 = 55 percent of the 19X1 selling price; the 19X2 gross margin is $1,040,000/$2,000,000 = 52 percent of the 19X2 selling price. Finance charges are 21 percent of total installment contracts. For example, in 19X1 they are $1,708,861 × 21% = $358,861. It is acceptable to recognize interest revenue according to several different methods. Most of these involve relatively complicated compound interest calculations. The simplest method is a straight-line one which regards 21 percent of all installment payments collected as pertaining to finance charges. This method is used in this example. Under the straight-line method of recognizing interest revenue, the calculations may be made as shown in Exhibit 2.

EXHIBIT 2

	19X1 contracts		19X2 contracts
	19X1 collections	19X2 collections	19X2 collections
Amount collected	$460,000	$970,000	$620,000
Interest revenue recognized (21%)	96,600	203,700	130,200
Installment sales recognized	$363,400	$766,300	$489,800
Ratio of gross margin to sales	55%	55%	52%
Gross margin recognized	$199,870	$421,465	$254,696

Appropriate journal entries for the company's 19X1 and 19X2 installment sales activities would be as follows:

19X1

Cash (see Exhibit 1)	150,000	
Installment Contracts Receivable—19X1 (see Exhibit 1)	1,708,861	
Finished Goods (see Exhibit 1)		675,000
Gross Margin on Installment Sales		82,500
Deferred 19X1 Profits on Installment Sales		1,101,361
To record 19X1 installment sales and receipts of down payments.		

In this entry, gross margin is recognized on the $150,000 of down payments received: $150,000 × 55% = $82,500. The remaining profits on these contracts are deferred until cash is received:

Gross margin on balance of selling price: $1,350,000 × 55%		$ 742,500
Finance charges		358,861
Deferred 19X1 profits on installment sales		$1,101,361

Cash (see Exhibit 1)	460,000	
Installment Contracts Receivable—19X1		460,000
To record collections of 19X1 contracts in 19X1.		

Deferred 19X1 Profits on Installment Sales	296,470	
Gross Margin on Installment Sales (see Exhibit 2)		199,870
Interest Revenue (see Exhibit 2)		96,600
To recognize revenue on 19X1 contracts on a collection basis.		

19X2

Cash (see Exhibit 1)	200,000	
Installment Contracts Receivable—19X2 (see Exhibit 1)	2,278,481	
Finished Goods (see Exhibit 1)		960,000
Gross Margin on Installment Sales ($200,000 × 52%) ...		104,000
Deferred 19X2 Profits on Installment Sales		1,414,481
To record 19X2 installment sales and receipts of down payments.		

Cash (see Exhibit 1)	970,000	
Installment Contracts Receivable—19X1		970,000
To record collections of 19X1 contracts in 19X2.		

Deferred 19X1 Profits on Installment Sales	625,165	
Gross Margin on Installment Sales (see Exhibit 2)		421,465
Interest Revenue (see Exhibit 2)		203,700
To record revenue on 19X1 contracts on a collection basis.		

Cash (see Exhibit 1)	620,000	
Installment Contracts Receivable—19X2		620,000
To record collection of 19X2 contracts in 19X2.		

Deferred 19X2 Profits on Installment Sales	384,896	
Gross Margin on Installment Sales (see Exhibit 2)		254,696
Interest Revenue (see Exhibit 2)		130,200
To record revenue on 19X2 contracts on a collection basis.		

Defaults. Suppose that in addition to the amounts given above, early in 19X1 a customer made a $15,800 purchase (of goods that had cost HIJ Company $7,110). The customer paid his 10 percent down payment of $1,580. His installment contract was for $18,000. He made five payments of $900, then defaulted. Upon repossession, his goods were worth only $4,000. No further recovery is possible.

Up to the time of default, the entries to record these transactions parallel the entries given earlier:

Cash	1,580	
Installment Contracts Receivable—19X1	18,000	
Finished Goods		7,110
Gross Margin on Installment Sales ($1,580 × 55%)		869
Deferred 19X1 Profits on Installment Sales		11,601
To record the sale and receipt of down payment.		

Cash ($900 × 5)	4,500	
Installment Contracts Receivable—19X1		4,500
Deferred 19X1 Profits on Installment Sales ($11,601 × 5/20).......	2,900*	
Gross Margin on Installment Sales		1,955
Interest Revenue ($4,500 × 21%)		945
To record the five collections.		
*Rounded.		

Upon default, the remaining balances in the installments receivable and deferred profits accounts should be reversed, and the loss on returned goods recorded:

```
Repossessed Goods ...........................................  4,000
Loss on Repossession ........................................    799
Deferred 19X1 Profits on Installment Sales ($11,601 − $2,900)........  8,701
    Installment Contracts Receivable—19X1 ($18,000 − $4,500) ....         13,500
To record the default and repossession.
```

Conditional Sales. With most sales of products, a period of time will elapse between the moment the buyer receives the goods and the time they are paid for. Some sales contracts attempt to protect the seller by retaining title to the goods in the seller until some or all of the price has been paid.

Whenever reasonable estimates of uncollectible accounts can be made, present accounting practice is to ignore technical details of transfer of title and simply record a sale. However, in cases of serious uncertainty, such conditional sales would be recorded on the collection basis.

Sales on approval usually are tentative enough that no sale should be recorded until the purchaser accepts the goods. If such acceptance is accompanied by cash payment, a form of the collection basis would be appropriate. Otherwise, an approach similar to the consignment sales method would be appropriate. This method is discussed next.

Consignment Sales. One other revenue recognition method is widely enough used to merit description. Some manufacturers ship their products to dealers on consignment, retaining ownership until the dealer actually sells them. In such cases there is no sale until the goods have been purchased by the final customers. A special version of the sales basis of revenue recognition has been developed for consignment sales.

EXAMPLE. Simplified Company is a manufacturer. During 19X1, the company manufactured 370,000 units of product and shipped 300,000 units to dealers on consignment. This product sells for $10 per unit and costs the company $6 per unit to manufacture. (There are also dealer commissions and costs of shipping these goods to dealers, but for simplicity such costs are ignored.) During 19X1, dealers reported sales of 285,000 units and remitted a total of $2,500,000. The following journal entries would be appropriate. (Once again, there is little standardization in actual account titles.)

```
Finished Goods ...............................................  2,220,000
    Work in Process .........................................              2,220,000
To record the cost of manufacturing 370,000 units of product @ $6.

Finished Goods on Consignment ...............................  1,800,000
    Finished Goods ..........................................              1,800,000
To record shipment on consignment of 300,000 units @ $6.

Cost of Goods Sold ..........................................  1,710,000
    Finished Goods on Consignment ...........................              1,710,000
To record product expenses on a consignment sales basis: 285,000 units
sold to final customers @ $6.

Accounts Receivable .........................................  2,850,000
    Sales ...................................................              2,850,000
To record sales reported by consignment dealers: 285,000 units sold to
final customers @ $10.

Cash ........................................................  2,500,000
    Accounts Receivable .....................................              2,500,000
To record collections from consignment dealers.
```

Summary—The Various Methods Compared. We can summarize the different revenue recognition methods discussed by observing their similarities:

1. All these methods recognize revenue at some one specific point of time: the time of earning or production (under the production basis), the time of sale (under the sales basis), the time of cash collection (under the collection basis).

2. Over the long run, the total amount of revenue recognized under all of these methods will be the same except where a net approach is employed. Even under a net approach, the total gross margin recognized eventually will be the same under all methods. The differences are only ones of timing—although, of course, such timing differences are very important.

3. All these methods (not just the sales basis) are acceptable under current rules if the circumstances warrant. Also, under any one set of circumstances, current rules usually specify the use of one, and only one, of these methods.

Finally, there are revenue recognition aspects to various technical topics discussed elsewhere in this book and in specialized AICPA and FASB releases. In particular, see Chapters 5, 14, 15, 32, 34–36, 38, and 44, Accounting Research Study No. 11 (extractive industries' reports), the various AICPA Industry Audit Guides, APB Opinions Nos. 7 and 27 (lessors' reports), 9, 20, and 30 (extraordinary items, etc.), 18 (the equity method), 21 (use of the effective interest method in reporting interest revenue), 22 (disclosure of accounting policies), 26 (gains on early extinguishment of debt), 28 (interim reports), 29 (swap and barter transactions), and Statements of Financial Accounting Standards Nos. 4 (extinguishment of debt) and 12 (marketable securities).

BIBLIOGRAPHY

Accounting Principles Board: "Accounting for Leases in Financial Statements of Lessors," Opinion No. 7, AICPA, New York, May 1966.
———: "Reporting the Results of Operations . . . ," Opinion No. 9, AICPA, New York, December 1966.
———: "Omnibus Opinion–1966," Opinion No. 10, AICPA, New York, December 1966.
———: "The Equity Method of Accounting for Investments in Common Stock," Opinion No. 18, AICPA, New York, March 1971.
———: "Accounting Changes," Opinion No. 20, AICPA, New York, July 1971.
———: "Interest on Receivables and Payables," Opinion No. 21, AICPA, New York, August 1971.
———: "Disclosure of Accounting Policies," Opinion No. 22, AICPA, New York, April 1972.
———: "Early Extinguishment of Debt," Opinion No. 26, AICPA, New York, October 1972.
———: "Accounting for Lease Transactions by Manufacturer or Dealer Lessors," Opinion No. 27, AICPA, New York, November 1972.
———: "Interim Financial Reporting," Opinion No. 28, AICPA, New York, May 1973.
———: "Accounting for Nonmonetary Transactions," Opinion No. 29, AICPA, New York, May 1973.
———: "Reporting the Results of Operations . . . ," Opinion No. 30, AICPA, New York, June 1973.
———: "Basic Concepts and Accounting Principles Underlying Financial Statements of Business Enterprises," Statement No. 4, chap. 6 and 7, AICPA, New York, October 1970.
Financial Accounting Standards Board: "Reporting Gains and Losses from Extinguishment of Debt," Statement of Financial Accounting Standards, No. 4, Stamford, Conn., March 1975.
———: "Accounting for Certain Marketable Securities," Statement of Financial Accounting Standards No. 12, Stamford, Conn., December 1975.
Hendriksen, Eldon S.: *Accounting Theory*, rev. ed., Richard D. Irwin, Homewood, Ill., 1970, chaps. 5–7.

Sprouse, Robert T., and Maurice Moonitz: "A Tentative Set of Broad Accounting Principles for Business Enterprises," *Accounting Research Study No. 3,* AICPA, New York, 1962.

Sterling, Robert R.: *Theory of the Measurement of Enterprise Income,* The University Press of Kansas, Lawrence, 1970.

Thomas, Arthur L.: "The Allocation Problem, Part Two," *Studies in Accounting Research No. 9,* American Accounting Association, Sarasota, Fla., 1975.

Chapter **13**

Cash

WILLIARD E. STONE
Professor of Accounting, University of Florida

CASH ITEMS AND REPORTING

A business enterprise is in many ways a living organism, and cash flow is its life stream since few transactions take place that do not begin or end with cash. It is the task of management to assure sufficient cash to meet all needs. Profitable ventures fail because of insufficient cash, but unprofitable ones have been known to continue for long periods if sufficient cash is somehow pumped into the system. Managing and accounting for cash, then, is of the greatest importance to the financial health of the organization. Cash must be carefully monitored through accounting for cash transactions and supplying management with cash reports, cash flow statements, and cash budgets.

Definition of Cash. Cash is any medium of exchange which is immediately negotiable. It must be free of restriction for any business purpose. Prime requirements are general acceptability and availability for instant use in purchasing and payment of debt. Acceptability to a bank for deposit is a common test applied to cash items.

Composition of Cash.· The item "cash" includes coins, paper currency, demand deposits with banks, and timely checks of others, which are orders on banks to supply funds immediately. Other negotiable cash instruments include the following:

A *cashier's check* is a check drawn by a bank and signed by its cashier. A *certified check* is a depositor's check guaranteed by the bank, which certifies on its face that cash has been restricted for immediate payment. A *bank draft* is a cash instrument prepared by one bank instructing another, in which it has deposits (a correspondent bank), to make payment of cash upon demand. A *money order* is a form of check calling for payment upon presentation at a post office (postal money orders) or at an express company (express money orders). *Traveler's checks* are issued by banks or express companies in even dollar amounts. Signed by the purchaser at time of purchase, they must be countersigned to become negotiable. This feature and guaranteed replacement, if lost or fraudulently endorsed, make them a safe currency for travelers.

Letters of credit are authorizations by banks to draw upon them, or upon designated correspondent banks, for funds as needed up to a specified amount. One type, generally used by travelers, requires payment in advance to the issuing bank and is cash to the value of the unused amount. Another type is a formal commitment by a bank to make a loan of funds up to a specified amount within a designated period of time, when and as required by the borrower. The open amount of this type of letter of credit is not cash. It is merely a promise to lend money and is not recognized in accounting records until exercised.

Items which are not counted as cash include postage stamps, IOUs, advances to officers and employees for travel or other purposes, and marketable securities such as United States notes. Postdated checks of customers are included as open accounts receivable until the date the check becomes current. Sometimes checks are returned by the maker's bank as uncollectible because the maker has instructed his or her bank to stop payment or because he or she has insufficient funds in the account to meet the amount of the check (an NSF check). Such checks should be removed from the cash account and carried as open accounts. Often, after contacting the maker, NSF checks may be redeposited and included in cash, if reasonable assurance has been received that they will be honored when presented at the maker's bank.

Amounts in savings accounts are not usually included as cash because they are not intended for operating cash use. Banks may require written notice in advance of withdrawals from such accounts. This restriction, except in times of extreme financial uncertainty, is rarely enforced, however, and if the business has a cash purpose for such funds, they may be designated as cash. Certificates of deposit are issued by banks for amounts of savings (usually in multiples of $100) on which a higher rate of interest is paid in return for the depositor's contracting not to withdraw for a specified period of time. The restriction on withdrawal of these savings removes them from the classification of cash.

Foreign currency on hand and on deposit in foreign banks should be converted to United States dollars at the current rate of exchange and included as cash unless restricted. Some foreign countries have regulations that prohibit the free exchange of their money into that of other countries, and their currency cannot be counted as cash. Others, whose currency is exchangeable, have restrictions on the removal of funds from the country. Either type should be labeled Restricted Deposits in Foreign Banks and not included as cash.

Funds. The term *fund* means a sum restricted for a specific purpose. Funds usually consist of cash but may also include marketable securities. *Change funds* are amounts set aside for the specific purpose of providing coins and currency to cash checks or make change. *Payroll funds* are usually amounts deposited in special bank accounts for paychecks drawn. If employees are paid in cash, however, the payroll fund may be a sum of coins and currency turned over to the paymaster for this purpose. Special bank accounts are also set up as *dividend funds* for dividend payments to stockholders. *Petty cash funds* are established to provide currency for minor business expenditures which are inconvenient to pay by check. At times, petty cash funds consist of coins, currency, undeposited checks cashed from the fund, and paid vouchers for sums expended.

Sinking funds are established for long-term purposes such as repayment of bonds at their maturity date. Typically, the resources of the sinking fund are used to acquire the bonds (or occasionally the preferred stock) of the issue for which the sinking fund was established. Sometimes the sinking fund contains investments in United States bonds or other securities. Other purposes of sinking funds include purchasing new building, payment of pensions to retired employees, repurchase of preferred stock, and contract performance guarantees.

Cash and Funds on the Statement of Financial Position. Cash on hand and on demand deposit in a bank is usually classified under the simple heading of *cash*. Change funds and petty cash funds, when relatively insignificant in amount and for current operating purposes, are usually also included as cash. Although these items may be grouped together for statement purposes, for effective internal control the accounting system should provide separate accounts for each fund and bank account.

Sometimes, under the terms of a loan agreement, *maintenance of a minimum balance* is required in a demand deposit account. If the loan which requires this restriction is a current liability, the minimum balance is included as a current asset under a title such as Cash Restricted by Contract but, in any case, it should not be listed as Cash. Cash restricted for other reasons, such as funds in escrow[1] for the purchase of property, savings account balances for nonoperating purposes, certificates of deposit, and restricted funds of significant size such as sinking funds, are separately designated by descriptive titles and are included as current assets only if they are to become available within one year to pay current debt. Otherwise, they are classified as investments. Cash in closed banks and deposits in foreign banks in countries with currency restrictions are classified as noncurrent, or other, assets.

Bank overdrafts result when checks are issued in an amount greater than the balance in the demand deposit account; they are shown in the current liability

---

[1]Escrow funds are amounts restricted for a specified purpose by parties to an agreement. They are usually placed in the custody of a third party, frequently a trust company, and are released only by the joint instructions of both parties to the contract.

section of the statement of financial position. Overdrafts, if material in amount, should not be offset by positive balances in other bank accounts.

IMPREST PETTY CASH FUND

A sound system of internal control of cash requires that expenditures be made by check. Under this system, it is necessary to have an amount of actual cash available for emergency use or for expenditures so minor in amount that drawing a check is impractical. Although the amount of such a fund is usually not large, it is readily available and the flow through the fund over the year may be a significant amount. Sound accounting is required; this is offered by the imprest sytem. *Imprest* means that a specific amount is established for the fund and placed in the custody of a petty cashier who is accountable for that precise sum, made up of paid petty cash vouchers and remaining cash. The amount selected is determined by the demands on the fund and should usually be sufficient for about one month's needs. Customarily, even amounts such as $50, $100, but usually not exceeding $200, are chosen.

The imprest fund, once established, requires periodic reimbursement. The entry on reimbursement debits the various expense accounts according to the summarized paid petty cash vouchers to that date. The amount of reimbursement (and credit to Cash) is always the total of the summarized petty cash expenditures for the period between reimbursement dates. No entry is made in the petty cash account, which remains at its original amount unless the imprest sum of the fund is increased or decreased.

BANK RECONCILIATION

At regular intervals, usually on a certain day each month, the bank returns the canceled checks and a statement of the depositor's account. If the balance of the bank statement does not agree with the business's Cash account balance, a reconciliation is prepared. The balance shown on the bank statement will rarely correspond to the balance of the Cash in Bank account. The two basic causes of the difference are time lag and errors. In the normal flow of data, some items will have been recorded by either the bank or the firm without having reached the recording point on the other set of records, hence a *time lag* difference. Causes of such differences include: checks outstanding (that is, checks recorded in the check register of the firm, but not yet received by the bank on which they were drawn), deposits made just before the bank statement date which do not appear on the bank statement, and transactions (such as service charges, collections of notes or drafts, and the like) that have not yet been recorded on the firm's books. The other basic difference is caused by errors in record keeping by either the firm or the bank. The process of comparing the bank statement with the books is known as *reconciling* the bank account, and the schedule which is prepared to demonstrate the results of the comparing is called a *bank reconciliation*.

The steps of this process include:

1. Compare canceled checks with bank statement.
2. Sort checks into numerical order.
3. Verify that outstanding items of last reconciliation (checks and deposits) have been received by the bank.
4. Compare canceled checks to cash disbursement entries, noting errors and outstanding checks.
5. Compare deposits on bank statement with cash receipts entries, noting differences.

6. List other items on statement not recorded by the business and items in the business records not on the bank statement.

7. Prepare a bank reconciliation (Exhibit 1).

EXHIBIT 1   Shoreland Realty Co.—Bank Reconciliation December 17, 19X0

Bank			Company		
Balance per bank statement		$2,350.70	Balance per cash account		$2,051.96
Add:			Add:		
Deposit in transit		1,355.20	Note collected (G. Sims)		1,000.00
Check of Shore Bros. deducted			Interest on note		60.00
in error		51.75	Error in Dec. 15 deposit		9.00
Total		$3,757.65	Total		$3,120.96
Less:			Less:		
Outstanding checks			Note collection fee	$ 4.00	
#4321	$627.30		Service charge	11.60	
#4326	111.19		NSF check (Cox Co.)	282.70	
#4350	246.50		Protest fee	2.50	
#4351	52.50	1,037.49	Counter check	100.00	400.80
Adjusted bank balance		$2,720.16	Correct cash balance		$2,720.16

Items on the "bank" side must either be corrected by the bank or will automatically be adjusted when the transaction reaches the bank. They do not require journal entries by the business. The deposit in transit has been sent to the bank too late to be recorded on this statement. A bank error has charged Shoreland Realty Co. with a check drawn by Shore Bros.; this must be corrected by the bank on its records. The outstanding checks have been drawn by Shoreland Realty Co. but have not yet been presented to the bank for payment.

On the "company" side are items commonly found in a bank reconciliation. Notes and interest are frequently collected for a business by the bank because it is convenient and pressures the maker to meet his note when due. The December 15 deposit was understated by $9 because of an error in the total of cash sales. The bank has made a charge of $4 to collect the note and $11.60 for servicing the Shoreland Realty Co. account. A check for $282.70 from Cox Co. was deposited but when presented to Cox Co.'s bank, there were insufficient funds. It was returned to the bank, which deducted the amount and a protest fee (for formal legal protest of the nonpayment) from Shoreland Realty Co.'s account. The counter check was secured at the bank by an officer of the company and cashed for travel funds without notifying the bookkeeper.

Adjusting Entries from Bank Reconciliations. Entries must be made for all differences between the book balance of Cash and the corrected cash balance shown on the reconciliation. "Company" items require journal entries as follows:

```
Cash  ...................................  1,069.00
     Notes Receivable (G. Sims)  ...............         1,000.00
     Interest Revenue  ........................            60.00
     Cash Sales  ..............................             9.00

Bank Charge Expense  ......................    15.60
Accounts Receivable (Cox Co.)  ...............   285.20*
Travel Expense  ...........................   100.00
     Cash  .................................           400.80
```

*Note that Cox Co. is charged for the protest fee.

CONTROL OF CASH

The basic objectives of a system of internal control, listed in order of importance are

1. To promote efficiency in all business operations
2. To assist accuracy and the timely correction of errors
3. To deter fraud and provide for its early detection.

Designing a system of internal control for cash includes establishing a sound business organization, formulating policies, setting up operating procedures for cash transactions, and providing for effective internal audit.

Organization is the designation of clearly defined areas of responsibility and delegation of authority to individuals accountable for each area. *Policies* are overall guides for the control of operations involving business cash. These include establishing maximum and minimum limits for the amount of cash balance, for the method of paying employees by cash or check, for credit terms offered customers, for the rigor of follow-up on collections, requiring daily deposits of total amount of all collections, bonding all employees handling cash, using a voucher system with disbursement by check, and establishing an imprest petty cash fund.

Procedures implement policies by making rules to govern repetitive action. At the heart of the internal control of cash are the procedures set down (usually in an operations manual) to be followed by all who handle cash. These procedures

EXHIBIT 2   Procedural Chart—Cash Receipts Function

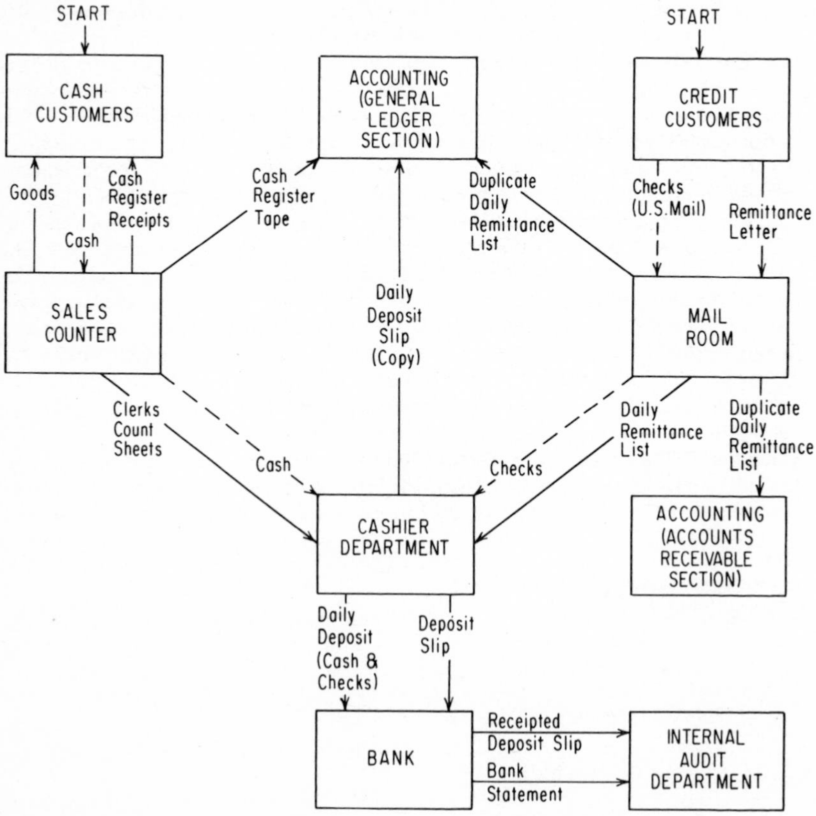

EXHIBIT 3   Procedural Chart—Cash Disbursements Function

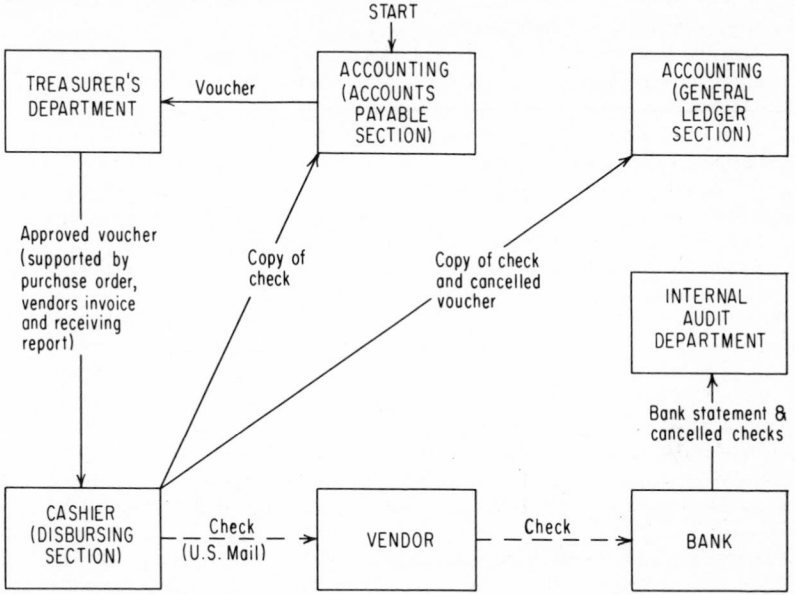

establish an efficient flow of cash, cash documents, and the recording of cash transactions. The *internal audit division,* through surprise examinations, aids in deterring and in the early detection of fraud and errors involving cash. It also makes frequent checks to determine that the system of internal control is adequate as designed and is being followed.

Internal Control Charts. Charting is often used in the design of a system of internal control and in disclosing how it is expected to operate. Auditors also use charts in their examination of the system. Exhibits 2 and 3 chart a system of internal control for cash in a large company. The organization is indicated by the departments and sections, each of which is an area of responsibility with a supervisor accountable for the efficient operation of an assigned portion of the cash function. Cash documents are named and their flow indicated by a solid line. The flow of cash is shown by a dashed line.

Separation of Functions. Although the cash charts presented above are largely self-explanatory, some of the special features are worthy of comment. Note that no employee has responsibility for more than a part of either the cash receipts or the cash disbursements function. No employee who has access to the cash may record cash transactions. Where cash is received and a basic accounting document prepared, special care is taken to maintain good control. For instance, in Exhibit 2, the salesclerk both receives cash from the customer and prepares the cash register tape which is the basis for the accounting entry. The cash register aids in proper recording of the transaction by flashing the amount of the sale for the customer to see and by providing a receipt for the customer. Strict procedural rules for salesclerks further strengthen this control.

1. All clerks have a separate cash drawer, opened only by their own register key (A, B, C, etc.), and all clerks are individually responsible for their own cash.

2. All sales must be recorded on the cash register and the drawer must be closed between sales.

3. Money taken from a customer is placed on the cash register shelf (not in the

cash drawer) and a statement is made to customer, "$1.65 out of $10." After change is counted out to the customer, the $10 bill is placed in the proper compartment and the drawer closed.

4. A cash register receipt must be given to every customer. (Some firms offer an inducement to customers to obtain a receipt, such as stating that a purchase is free if a receipt is not offered or if the receipt contains a red star.)

5. When the cash in a clerk's drawer reaches a certain specified amount, the excess amount is deposited with the supervisor, who issues a receipt.

6. At close of shift, supervisor and clerk prepare a count sheet for money collected by the clerk. With a special key, the supervisor then determines the clerk's register total and determines the cash-over-or-short position.

7. An individual record is maintained of daily cash differences. Excessive amount of overs and shorts are an indication of carelessness or possible fraud.

Mail Receipts.   Another subfunction where both cash and basic recording documents are involved is mail receipt of checks from credit customers. If only checks are received, it is generally sufficient to require that the mail clerk prepare a remittance list showing amount and customer's name. The cashier receives the original with the checks, one duplicate copy is sent to the general ledger department, and a different copy is sent to the accounts receivable department.

Firms should discourage remittances in currency and coins. If, however, currency and coins are received by mail, greater precautions must be taken. One clerk opens mail and calls out the name and amount of cash; a second prepares a listing of the transactions. Cash is deposited immediately in a locked compartment. Clerks working together should be rotated frequently to discourage collusion. A careful analysis of complaints of nondelivery of goods by customers will give warning of trouble.

Document Control.   Automatic cross-checks of one subfunction on another are built into the system wherever possible. Prenumbered documents are an excellent device for this purpose. For instance, in Exhibit 3, the general ledger section maintains a register by check number in which all checks must be accounted for, even voids, and a missing check is investigated immediately. Each check disbursement is posted against its authorizing voucher and a check that cannot be so matched is immediately investigated. Vouchers are heavily canceled or perforated and filed out of the control of the cashier so that they cannot be reused to support disbursements. Note that separate copies of the check are sent to the general ledger section which maintains the control account and to the accounts payable section which has the vendors' subsidiary accounts. Monthly reconciliation of the total of the control account with the total of subsidiary accounts ensures a high degree of accuracy in the recording of cash (and also accounts payable).

In addition to many such automatic cross-checks, the internal audit department makes examinations of all subfunctions to determine that prescribed procedures are being followed and that the system results in efficient operations.

CASH REPORTS

Reports are the chief means by which the accountant communicates to management the data gathered by the accounting system. Cash reports are of particular importance because they inform management about the cash balance and the flow of cash through the business.

Daily Cash Reports.   Exhibit 4 illustrates a daily report of a company with home office and sales branches where daily cash information would be essential to enable the financial officer to control and make the best disposition of funds. Cash reports are designed to satisfy the particular needs of an individual business and will vary

EXHIBIT 4   Marvin Accessories Sales Company, Inc. Daily Cash Report

Date: Thursday, July 22, 19X0

Financial Activities Report (cents omitted)

	Total	Home office	Newtown branch	Oxford branch
Receipts:				
Cash sales..........................	$12,867	$ 6,327	$ 4,620	$1,920
Collections on account..............	43,036	28,655	11,915	2,466
Other...............................	1,767	1,755	12	—
Interbank transfers.................	3,500	3,500	—	—
Total...........................	$61,170	$40,237	$16,547	$4,386
Disbursements:				
Accounts payable...................	$36,691	$20,775	$14,540	$1,376
Payrolls (net)......................	20,100	20,100	—	—
Other...............................	528	400	10	118
Interbank transfers.................	3,500	—	—	3,500
Total...........................	$60,819	$41,275	$14,550	$4,994
Net increase (decrease)................	$ 351	($ 1,038)	$ 1,997	($ 608)

Bank Account Report (cents omitted)

	Total	Home office		Newtown bank	Oxford bank
		Regular a/c	Payroll a/c		
Beginning balance......	$ 66,713	$ 60,320	$ 1,000	$ 2,971	$2,422
Deposits..............	81,270	40,237	20,100	16,547	4,386
Total..............	$147,983	$100,557	$21,100	$19,518	$6,808
Checks drawn..........	80,919	41,275	20,100	14,550	4,994
Closing balance........	$ 67,064	$ 59,282	$ 1,000	$ 4,968	$1,814

widely. A daily cash report for a gasoline service station (Exhibit 5) is more complicated and is a combined report of cash and merchandise sales.

Cash Receipts and Disbursements Reports. Charitable organizations, most of which maintain their records on a cash basis, make use of the cash receipts and disbursements form of report. This statement takes the place of the income statement in reporting the results of operations since a charitable organization is nonprofit-motivated. In Exhibit 6, cents have been omitted for clarity of presentation but retained in the basic records for control purposes. The inclusion of the budgeted figures permits a comparison of actual operating results with preestablished goals and plans for the year.

Statement of Cash Flows. The statement of cash flows discloses cash receipts and cash disbursements for profit-seeking businesses. The form illustrated in Exhibit 7 separates cash flows from operations from the nonoperating flows to permit effective analysis. This statement presents information about the financial management of the company which is not readily available in other financial reports.

The cash flow statement of Tristate Traders, Inc., aided by the inclusion of percentages, might be analyzed by management, creditors, and stockholders as follows: The expansion of facilities during the fiscal year was a major one, as

EXHIBIT 5 Watson's Service Station Daily Report

In Charge: W. Baker, Drawer A
Clerk: R. Paul, Drawer B

Date: August 17, 19X0
Shift: Day X Night __

Register readings	Drawer A		Drawer B		Collections on account
	Cash	Charge	Cash	Charge	
End of shift...........	$2,484.32	$4,750.10	$1,877.60	7,800.56	$5,873.04
Beginning of shift......	2,275.22	4,449.40	1,777.95	7,654.67	5,617.32
To be accounted for..	$ 209.10	$ 300.70	$ 99.65	$ 145.89	$ 255.72

Cash

Cash sales—Drawer A	$209.10	
Cash sales—Drawer B	99.65	$308.75
Rec'd on account		255.72
Other receipts		—
Total receipts		$564.47

Paid Out (Drawer A)

Auto parts	$ 18.20	
Janitorial services	6.00	
Refund on battery	12.50	36.70
To be accounted for		$527.77

Cash Count

Drawer A	$171.33	
Drawer B	99.65	
Checks:		
Holmes .... $ 88.20		
Martin 100.00		
Jones 67.52	255.72	
Deposit in bank	$526.70	
Cash shortage, Drawer A	1.07	$527.77

Sales

Cash sales—Drawer A	$209.10	
Cash sales—Drawer B	99.65	$308.75
Charge sales—Drawer A ...	300.70	
Charge sales—Drawer B ..	145.89	446.59
Total sales		$755.34

Sales Analysis

Regular .... 406 @ .619		$251.31
No-Lead .... 255 @ .639		162.95
Oil .... 28 @ .70		19.60
16 @ 1.00		16.00
Tires		63.70
Accessories		18.75
Washing .... 15 @ 3.00		45.00
Greasing .... 18 @ 5.00		90.00
Tire repairs		6.00
Auto repairs		82.03
Miscellaneous		—
Total sales		$755.34

Pump Readings, gallons

Regular: End	32,571.6
Beginning	32,165.6
Balance	406.0
No-Lead: End	15,925.3
Beginning	15,670.3
Balance	255.0

indicated both by the total amount of funds involved and by the fact that 95 percent of total available funds were used for this purpose. A creditor would applaud the financial management for its major dependence upon funds from stockholders (43 percent) and from company operations (12 percent), and would approve the modest 4 percent return to stockholders as dividends.

Stockholders might be less happy since a greater use of borrowed funds, while increasing the risk of the expansion, might permit favorable trading on equity in the event of successful operations of the new facilities. Stockholders along with management might well be concerned with the magnitude of the expansion, particularly since it required raising 88 percent of cash from nonrecurring sources, and operations provided only 12 percent. The modest 2 percent of total funds used to increase cash on hand is nevertheless important. It more than doubled cash on hand, and a larger balance will be required for the expanded scale of operations. It would be advisable for Tristate Traders, Inc., to forecast their cash flow for the next fiscal year by means of a cash budget.

Cash Budget. The cash budget is a financial plan which forecasts receipts and disbursements of cash, usually for a period of one year into the future. It assists management in securing necessary cash with the best timing and using the most effective method. Short-term requirements can be met by arranging for bank loans, while a chronic shortage of cash may require issuance of capital stock or long-term bonds. It will also aid management in the decision to invest temporary excess cash balances or to retire stock or bonds if there appears to be a long-term excess.

The cash budget is also a means of control when used as a standard against which to measure actual cash receipts and disbursements. When cash transactions significantly deviate from budgeted amounts, an investigation will determine the cause and give management a basis for corrective action. Finally, the cash budget is an excellent document for persuading creditors. Banks are encouraged to make loans if the budget gives evidence that the need is temporary and can be repaid at maturity. Creditors are convinced to extend maturity dates if realistic plans are shown for liquidation of the debt.

The cash budget shows projections by months and quarters. Each month, actual receipts and expenditures are compared with the budget. At the end of each quarter, the next three quarters are reviewed and adjusted for any substantial change in conditions affecting cash and a new fourth-quarter budget is prepared, so that the company continually plans one full year into the future.

Exhibit 8 illustrates the form and detail supplied by the cash budget. The

EXHIBIT 6   Gainesville Charities, Incorporated—Statement of Cash Receipts and Disbursements Year Ending December 31, 19X0

	Operating results, 19X0		Budgeted operations, 19X0		Over (under) budget, 19X0
Balance of cash, Jan. 1, 19X0.		$ 375		$ 375	
Receipts for period:					
Contributions received....	$19,006		$18,500		$506
Allotment from City Council....................	2,500		2,500		—
Proceeds of rummage sale.	366		250		116
Earnings of endowment fund.................	1,704		1,630		74
Total revenue........		23,576		22,880	$696
Amount to be accounted for.		23,951		23,255	$696
Disbursements for period:					
Program expenditures:					
Clothing and medical aid	$ 4,652		$ 4,700		$(48)
Home repair program...	2,506		2,500		6
Preschool program......	3,261		3,200		61
Adult school program...	2,755		2,500		255
Employment bulletin...	2,710	$15,884	2,600	$15,500	110	$384
Administrative expenses:					
Secretarial salary.......	$ 6,800		$ 6,800		—
Stationery and postage..	365		330		$ 35
Office supplies.........	337		250		87
Heat, light, and water...	160		175		(15)
Telephone............	108	7,770	100	7,655	8	115
Total expenditures...		$23,654		$23,155	$499
Balance of cash, Dec. 31, 19X0..................		$ 297		$ 100	$197

EXHIBIT 7   Tristate Traders, Inc.—Statement of Cash Flows, Year Ending June 30, 19X0

			Percentage Analysis
Cash receipts from operations:			
Cash sales............................	$ 85,210		
Collections from customers............	287,655		
Interest and dividends................	826		
Total received from operations...............		$373,691	
Cash disbursements for operations:			
Payments to vendors.................	$132,600		
Wages and salaries...................	96,532		
Selling expenses......................	47,521		
Administrative expenses...............	38,755		
Federal, state and local taxes..........	2,188	317,596	
Cash generated by operations....................		$ 56,095	12 %
Cash receipts from other sources:			
Issuance of common stock.............	$200,000		43 %
Borrowing on long-term notes..........	100,000		21 %
Borrowing on short-term notes........	63,000		13 %
Sale of securities.....................	50,617	413,617	11 %
Cash available for investment, etc................		$469,712	100 %
Nonoperating cash disbursements:			
Dividends............................	$ 18,000		4 %
Purchase of land.....................	30,260		7 %
Purchase of building..................	232,000		50 %
Purchase of equipment................	180,600		37 %
Increase in cash balance...............	8,852		2 %
Total cash disbursements		$469,712	100 %

Cash balance, July 1, 19W9.......	$ 7,632
Increase in cash balance..........	8,852
Cash balance, June 30, 19X0......	$16,484

information is collected with the assistance of various officers of the company and is related to other budgets. Collections from customers, for instance, are calculated by adjusting budgeted sales for the company's collection experience. It might be determined on the basis of past experience, that 30 percent of credit sales (after adjustment for probable uncollectible accounts) are collected in the month of sale, 60 percent in the following month, 8 percent in the third month, and 2 percent later. Payments to vendors are estimated from the purchase budget, allowing for the lag occasioned by vendors' credit terms. Administrative, selling, and research and development expense payments are based on the related budgets. Equipment expenditures are determined by review of projects approved by the board of directors. Debt repayment and interest are estimated on the basis of loan contracts in existence or anticipated.

The amount of cash to be carried as a balance at the end of the month is determined by board of directors' policy. Allco Industries, Inc., has an established policy of maintaining a minimum balance of approximately $10,000. When the balance is expected to be substantially under this amount, as in January, arrangements are made for a short-term loan at the bank. The $11,290 projected balance in February is not sufficiently over the $10,000 maximum to warrant an investment, but the March balance suggests an investment of $20,000 in United States short-term bills.

CASH MANAGEMENT

Cash management has four major functions: determination of minimum cash balances, effective borrowing, advantageous investment of excess cash, and acceleration of cash flow.

The minimum cash balance is established taking into consideration the basic safety cushion needed, minimum bank balance requirements, and the rate of daily cash collections and disbursements. Cash balances should be maintained at the lowest practical minimum because excess cash earns nothing and loses purchasing power in a period of rising prices. The minimum cash balance should be the basic liquidity cushion needed taking into consideration the rate of daily cash collections and disbursements. The average cash balance (size of demand deposit) tentatively determined can be tested against industry standards by use of the ratio of the average cash balance to total operating expenditures for a year. If the company's business is a seasonal one, the desirable cash balance will vary with peaks and valleys of enterprise activities. Such companies will find the ratio of average cash balance for each month to total expenditures for that month a better standard.

Quantitative techniques have been developed to determine the optimal cash balance. Cash management models attempt to measure the optimal cash balance for a given volume of cash transactions by comparing the interest obtainable on short term idle funds with the transactions costs of investing and disinvesting funds. The Baumol model[2] to determine the cost of maintaining cash balances is stated as

$$Z = b\,\frac{T}{C} + i\,\frac{C}{2}$$

where Z = total cost of maintaining cash
T = total expenditures during a given period (one year)

[2]William J. Baumol, "The Transactions Demand for Cash: An Inventory Theoretical Approach," *Quarterly Journal of Economics,* November 1952.

EXHIBIT 8   Allco Industries, Inc.—Cash Budget January 1 to March 31, 19X0

	January	February	March	1st quarter total
Balance, beginning of period........	$ 10,200	$ 9,742	$ 11,290	$ 10,200
Receipts:				
Collections from customers.......	146,500	206,000	247,700	600,200
Cash sales....................	80,000	95,000	82,000	257,000
Investment revenue............	3,500	3,000	4,700	11,200
Total......................	$240,200	$313,742	$345,690	$878,600
Disbursements:				
Payments to vendors...........	$112,200	$122,000	$106,800	$341,000
Administrative expense..........	45,600	46,900	47,200	139,700
Selling expenses...............	86,800	89,500	90,300	266,600
Research and development.......	8,000	8,000	8,000	24,000
Purchase of equipment..........	—	—	16,000	16,000
Equipment installment notes......	5,333	5,333	6,533	17,199
Interest payments..............	675	719	812	2,206
Local taxes...................	1,850	—	—	1,850
Federal income tax.............	—	—	30,500	30,500
Dividends....................	—	10,000	—	10,000
Bank loan repayments..........	—	20,000	10,000	30,000
Total requirements...........	$260,458	$302,452	$316,145	$879,055
Tentative balance..............	$(20,258)	$ 11,290	$ 29,545	$ (455)
Bank loans...................	30,000	—	—	30,000
Investment—U.S. bills.........	—	—	(20,000)	(20,000)
Balance, end of period...........	$ 9,742	$ 11,290	$ 9,545	$ 9,545

C = cash deposited at intervals to meet expenditures (= twice the optimal average cash balance)

b = brokerage fee for each investment or disinvestment

i = annual interest yield obtainable on funds

To determine the optimal cash balance it is necessary to solve for C in the equation that sets the derivative of Z with respect to C equal to zero. Thus:

$$\frac{dZ}{dC} = -b\frac{T}{C^2} + \frac{i}{2} - 0$$

and solving for C,

$$C = \sqrt{\frac{2bT}{i}} \quad \text{(upper limit of cash balance)}$$

$$\frac{C}{2} = \text{(optimal cash balance)}$$

Sastry modified the Baumol model to permit temporary borrowing which permits a smaller average balance. This result is obtained by not requiring a balance sufficiently large that a positive cash position is always maintained as is required by the Baumol model. Sastry's modification of the basic model[3] yields the following optimal solutions:

$$C = \sqrt{\frac{2bT}{i}}\sqrt{\frac{R}{i+R}}$$

$$\frac{C}{2} = \text{(optimal cash balance)}$$

where R is the interest rate for temporary borrowing.

A third model, by Miller and Orr, has been designed to provide a range between an upper limit to the cash balance when funds are invested and a "reorder" or "return-to" point where funds are raised by disinvesting. The lower limit should be determined independently of the upper limit and may be set at zero or at some figure sufficient to meet the bank's requirement for servicing the account. The balance will occasionally rise slightly above the upper limit or fall below the return-to point because of the reaction time necessary for corrective action to be implemented. The Miller-Orr model[4] yields the following optimal solutions:

$$P = \left(\frac{3b\sigma^2}{4i}\right)^{1/3}$$

where P = return-to point

σ^2 = variance of daily net flows of total funds

i = daily interest yield obtainable on excess funds

b = brokerage fee

An average daily balance is approximated by

$$P + \frac{UL}{3}$$

where UL is the upper limit.

[3]A. S. Rama Sastry, "The Effect of Credit on Transactions Demand for Cash," *Journal of Finance,* September 1970.

[4]Merton H. Miller and Daniel Orr, "A Model of the Demand for Money by Firms," *Quarterly Journal of Economics,* August 1966.

The models given above determine a theoretically optimal cash balance. It must be recognized that the average balance in a demand deposit account reimburses the bank for its services. The average balance for optimal bank services charges or the theoretically optimal balance for operations, whichever is higher, should be used as a guideline for management of cash.

Effective borrowing requires knowledge in advance of the amount, timing, and duration of the need. Better terms are often arranged for short-term borrowing if time is available to shop for funds. Forecasting permits lower-interest, longer-term borrowing and avoids the inconvenience of renegotiating loans. Cash above the minimum requirements can be advantageously invested for even short periods of time. United States Treasury bills which mature in 30, 60, or 90 days are available; they offer maximum safety, ready liquidity, and a fair rate of return. Funds which the cash budget indicate can be invested for a longer period of time will earn the higher interest rate offered by longer-term investment in United States and corporate bonds. Effective planning for the investment of excess cash will maximize its earnings.

An improved cash flow, of course, reduces the amount of cash balance required. Receipts may be accelerated by improvements in the billing, collecting, and banking process. Invoices should be mailed the day goods or services are delivered. Offering cash discounts (including an addressed return envelope) and monthly statements showing balance due will accelerate collections. Predesigned letters for follow-up on delinquent accounts and timely recourse to legal pressures, where necessary, will speed collections and reduce bad debt losses. Checks and money collected should be promptly deposited. Some companies have collections returned to post office "lock" boxes accessible to their bank, thus ensuring the least delay in making the deposit. Photostatic advice of such collections is sent by the bank for accounting purposes.

The use of a voucher disbursing system, with unpaid invoices filed according to payment date, assists in making full use of credit terms offered. It is important to take advantage of discounts offered; 2/10, n/30, for instance, is the equivalent of more than 40 percent interest per annum. The computation of this rate is explained in Chapter 8. It is equally important to use the full 30-day credit available if no cash discount is offered. Legal payment takes place when the check is placed in the United States mails. Mailing at the end of day at payment date takes maximum advantage of credit terms.

BIBLIOGRAPHY

Archer, Stephen H., "A Model for the Determination of Firm Cash Balances," *Journal of Financial and Quantitative Analysis,* vol. 1, no. 1, pp. 1–11, March 1966.

Baumol, William J., "The Transactions Demand for Cash: An Inventory Theoretical Approach," *Quarterly Journal of Economics,* November 1952.

Eppen, Gary D., and Eugene F. Fama, "Cash Balance and Simple Dynamic Portfolio Problems with Proportional Costs," *International Economic Review,* vol. 10, no. 2, pp. 119–133, June 1969.

Miller, Merton H., and Daniel Orr, "A Model of the Demand for Money by Firms," *Quarterly Journal of Economics,* August 1966.

Orr, Daniel, *Management and the Demand for Money,* Praeger Publishers, New York, 1971.

Sastry, A. S. Rama, "The Effect of Credit on Transactions Demand for Cash," *Journal of Finance,* September 1970.

Chapter **14**

Marketable Securities and Investments

THOMAS F. KELLER
R. J. Reynolds Industries Professor of Business Administration and
Dean of the Graduate School of Business Administration,
Duke University

GENERAL CONSIDERATIONS

Firms invest resources in securities issued by governments and other firms for essentially two reasons: (1) to satisfy precautionary desires for liquidity and (2) to obtain economic benefits beyond the scope of the investing firm's operating activities. Securities which are held primarily for precautionary reasons are generally considered to be temporary investments and as such are normally reported as current assets by the owning firm. Securities which are held for purposes of gaining economic benefits are normally considered to be long-term investments, more in the nature of plant assets.

This chapter reviews: (1) fundamental investment characteristics of securities; (2) accounting considerations of acquisition, holding, and disposition of securities; (3) essential accounting aspects of special-purpose funds; and (4) problems of disclosure related to marketable securities and investments.

Investment Media. The securities which are available for investment can be broadly classified into three groups: (1) contractual, (2) equity, and (3) hybrid. The characteristics of these three broad types are fairly distinctive; however, there are cases in which the lines of distinction become blurred as the issuing firm attempts to take advantage of its particular strengths or to capitalize on market conditions at specific times.

Contractual Securities. Contractual securities are typified by provisions which specify the time and amount of periodic and final disbursement of cash to the investor. Specific restrictions are frequently placed on the issuing firm for the protection of the investor, with the rights and obligations of the parties to the contract specified. The investor, being interested in a stable dollar return on investment and the return of capital at a future date, attempts to appraise the issuing entity in terms of its short- and long-run financial solvency.

Equity Securities. Equity securities are those which represent residual ownership of the firm. Holders of these securities stand in the ultimate position to reap the rewards of success or to bear the burden of failure. The equity contract contains no specific obligation to pay periodic amounts or to redeem the security. Investors may regain their capital only by finding willing buyers in the marketplace. If the firm's board of directors elects to pay no dividend, there is very little that the investor can do to force payment except in extreme cases. The continuing successful operation of the firm is essential if the investor is to benefit from holding equity securities.

Hybrid Securities.   Securities which have both contractual and equity elements are hybrid securities because they do not meet the criteria of either standard type. Preferred stock is a hybrid security because, although a dividend rate is set by contract and specific provisions are included relative to the investor's rights in the event of nonpayment, there is seldom a maturity date. Convertible securities are hybrid securities because, although they may contain all the features of a bond or preferred stock contract, they also permit the investor to exchange the bond contract for an equity security. It has been argued that the convertible security is in fact two securities: (1) a bond or a preferred stock and (2) a stock option or warrant. The income bond is a third, but extremely rare, type of hybrid security. The income bond differs from a preferred stock in that it has a specific maturity date, but the periodic payments to the holder are dependent on the reported profits of the firm and in some cases the action of the board of directors. A firm, as an investor, must specify its objectives before it chooses the security type form which it will select particular issues.

Investment Objectives and Security Selection.   The objectives to be achieved from the temporary investment of cash and from the expansion of the economic base of the firm are quite different and thus normally dictate different investment policies.

Marketable Securities.   The objective of the firm which is concerned with investing cash held for precautionary or specific purposes is twofold: (1) to increase the return on total resources held, and (2) to maintain the availability of a specific amount of cash for planned or unplanned purposes with a minimum risk of loss. In selecting the security in which idle funds are to be invested, the management must decide whether protection of the number of dollars or the purchasing power of the dollars is most important. Whether consciously or unconsciously made, the decision is most often in favor of number of dollars. In most cases the current return on the investment seems to be a secondary consideration. While there are many issues of common stock which may be readily sold, if the number of shares held is not large in relation to normal trading activity, there is much greater fluctuation in common stock prices than in prices of bond contracts with near-term maturity dates.

Long-Term Investments.   Long-term investments are made with the intention of gaining some degree of influence over the operations of the firm in which the investment is made. The benefits to a firm from holding an investment interest in a competing, supplying, or buying firm can be many and varied; however, the objective is greater profits for the investing firm. Since the benefit desired or expected is derived from the exertion of influence on operations over time as well as the profitability of the firm whose securities are acquired, these investments are seldom made with the intention of selling the securities unless or until the potential for benefit ceases to exist. In view of the fact that the common stockholders usually elect the board of directors, it is natural to expect that most long-term investments will be comprised of shares of common stock. Occasionally the owning firm will lend to the owned firm to avoid interference from outside lenders. The criteria of ready marketability and return on investment through dividends are of only secondary consideration in the selection of securities to be held as long-term investments.

In spite of the different objectives, the accounting procedures for recording transactions in securities, whether held as marketable securities or as long-term investments, are quite similar.

Acquisition Cost.   Securities, like other assets acquired by a firm, are recorded at cost. Cost is generally considered to be the cash or market value of other assets given in exchange for the asset acquired. All outlays incident to the acquisition as well as the outlay for the asset itself are considered to comprise the cost of the asset.

Elements of Cost.   In the case of securities, cost is the market price of the security, brokerage fees, taxes, and other expenditures necessary to complete the transaction. In the event that securities are acquired in exchange for other assets, the accountant must rely on evidence of fair values of the assets exchanged or on an independent appraisal if there are no known market values. Accounting Principles Board Opinion No. 29 says, "Fair value of a nonmonetary asset transferred to or from an enterprise in a nonmonetary transaction should be determined by referring to estimated realizable values in cash transactions of the same or similar assets, quoted market prices, independent appraisals, estimated fair values of assets or services received in exchange or other available evidence."[1]

Basket Purchase.   When more than one type of security is acquired for a single price, the accountant is faced with the problem of allocating the acquisition price among the securities. If the market values of the securities are known, the cost will be prorated on the basis of relative market price at the date of acquisition. If the current price of only one security is known, normally a portion of the cost equal to the market price will be allocated to that security and the remainder will be considered the cost of the other securities. In the event that two or more securities have no market price, the accountant must delay allocation of the cost until a market is established, or he must rely on experts for an independent appraisal of value. These delayed market prices or appraisals are then used to allocate the joint cost among the securities acquired.

The journal entry to record a joint purchase of securities is illustrated for the following example:

XYZ Corporation purchased 1,000 units of a new offering of securities by ABC Company for $110,000. Each unit is comprised of one share of $50 par value 6 percent preferred stock and two shares of $10 par value common stock. The common stock was traded on an organized exchange on the day of purchase at $31 per share. The preferred stock is a new security that has never been traded. Brokerage commissions were paid by the issuing company.

```
Investment in ABC—Common Stock  ..... 62,000
Investment in ABC—Preferred Stock  .... 48,000
    Cash  ...........................        110,000
```

Exchange and Conversions.   Determination of the acquisition cost of securities acquired by an exchange or conversion of securities acquired at an earlier date is a controversial matter. The controversy concerns whether the original cost of the securities exchanged or converted should become the carrying value of the securities acquired in the exchange or whether the market value of the securities acquired by exchange or conversion should be used as the carrying value of the new securities. The question is: Has a gain or loss been realized on the securities being exchanged or converted? If the answer is yes, then the market value should be considered the carrying value of the new securities. If the answer is no, then the new securities take the basis of the securities exchanged.

The common practice seems to be to record the new securities at the cost of those exchanged or converted. The argument cited in support of this position is that, in the case of convertible securities especially, the investor makes only one investment. The gain or loss resulting from changes in market price should not be recognized until the investment position is reduced or eliminated by a transfer, however temporary, into cash. This position also gains support from the tax laws, which permit the deferral of tax on most gains until the investment position is reduced or eliminated by sale.

On the other hand, the advocates of the alternative method argue rather

---

[1]Accounting Principles Board Opinion No. 29, "Accounting for Nonmonetary Transactions," par. 25, AICPA, New York, 1973.

convincingly that the presence of a quoted market value at the date of exchange provides the objective evidence needed by the accountant to enable him to recognize the market value at the date of exchange. They argue further that this is a significant event in which the accounted-for firm has participated, and is not the same as annual recognition of market appreciation or loss on securities held.

Cost Identification. Cost identification of securities, like cost identification of inventories, becomes a problem only if there are two or more purchases of identical items at different prices. The cost of a particular share of stock or bond is important in the determination, at the date of sale, of the realized gain or loss from holding the security.

Specific Identification. It seems simple enough to record the cost of security purchases and to identify the sale of shares by specific certificate number. The problem raised in such cases is that the investor, by careful selection of the shares sold, can influence the reported profit for a certain time period. This same argument against the specific identification method is advanced with regard to inventories. The essential differences between the investment in securities and inventory are (1) the volume of transactions involving securities is normally much less than for the inventory; and (2) the holding period is normally much longer for securities than for inventories, thus providing the opportunity for greater impact on income for each security transaction than for each inventory transaction.

Assumed Flows as an Approximation of Specific Identification. The assumed flows of securities are the same as those discussed with reference to inventories: (1) first-in, first-out; (2) last-in, first-out; and (3) average cost. The most common methods found in practice are the specific identification method and the first-in, first-out method. The apparent reasons for this selection by practicing accountants are that only these two methods are generally in conformity with the tax law and that the volume of transactions is normally small even though the effect on income of a single transaction may be quite large. (Investments in mutual funds held by a custodian may be accounted for with the average cost method.)

Valuation of Securities. The carrying value of investments, both marketable and long-term, has been debated in the profession over the years. The prevailing opinion is that investments in securities, like investments in current assets, should generally be carried at lower of cost or market.

Cost. The acquisition price of an asset represents the resources required to obtain it. Accountants argue that until the asset is disposed of or consumed it should be valued at acquisition price. It is only then that the gain or loss can be objectively determined. Some accountants find this position difficult to support when current market quotations are readily available for the securities held and disposition can be easily accomplished. Some reevaluation of the cost principle has been mandated for marketable securities by FASB Statement No. 12, as discussed below.

Market. The market value of securities held is usually considered to be the current quote less the brokerage and other costs of disposing of the securities. The market price of securities which are being considered for possible acquisition is the market quote plus brokerage and other acquisition costs. Accountants have continually argued that revenue is realized only when there is an exchange between buyer and seller. Procedures which reflect changes in the market price of assets held have generally not been accepted unless the procedures result in the recognition of a diminution of value. For example, *Accounting Research Bulletin No. 43* says of current assets: "Where market value is less than cost by a substantial amount and it is evident that the decline in market value is not due to a mere temporary condition, the amount to be included as a current asset should not exceed the market value."[2] The *Bulletin* also recognized the importance of market price

---

[2]*Accounting Research Bulletin No. 43,* chap. 3A, par. 9, AICPA, New York, 1933.

increases and concluded, "It is important that the amounts at which current assets are stated be supplemented by information which reveals, for temporary investments, their market value. . . ."[3]

In recent years increasing consideration has been given to recognizing changes in the market value of securities. During public hearings held in 1971 on accounting for equity securities which preceded issuance of APB Opinion No. 18, "The Equity Method of Accounting for Investments in Common Stock," a number of alternatives were considered. The question of timing the recognition of income was of primary concern. Does an enterprise have to enter into a transaction in order to recognize revenue, or is revenue earned by a change in the market value of an asset?

This dilemma was never resolved. The APB reasoned, "Reporting of investments in common stock at market value . . . is considered to meet most closely the objective of reporting the economic consequences of holding the investment. However. the market value method is now used only in special circumstances. While the Board believes the market value method provides the best presentation of investments in some situations, it concludes that further study is necessary before the market value method is extended beyond current practice."[4]

Lower of Cost or Market. The lower-of-cost-or-market rule is based on a rather conservative interpretation of the realization principle. The argument supporting the rule is that the market price of an asset reflects the expected earning potential of the asset. If the market price declines, then there must be evidence to support a reduction in expected earning capacity. This loss of earning potential represents an economic loss, which is no less real than if the asset had been physically damaged. To carry the asset at a dollar amount which exceeds this market valuation of future usefulness would be misleading to those relying upon financial statements; therefore, price declines must be recognized by a write-down in the carrying value of the asset. This rationale for write-downs applies both to marketable securities reported as current assets and to securities carried as investments where the equity method (see below) is not used.

In applying the lower-of-cost-or-market valuation basis to marketable securities, it is logical to apply it to each security individually rather than to the securities as a group. Each security is a distinct item; the portfolio does not consist of a homogeneous group, so the usual arguments for basing the valuation on market value of the aggregate group as compared with the cost of the group do not apply. However, for contrary views see Kieso and Weygandt or Welsch, Zlatkovich, and White.[5] FASB Statement No. 12 requires a two-portfolio approach rather than the security-by-security approach. The two dissents by FASB members were based primarily on the implications of using the portfolio, rather than the security-by-security, approach.

Equity. The equity basis of valuation, sometimes referred to as the "economic" basis, requires that securities be recorded initially at acquisition cost and then the carrying value be increased or decreased to reflect the owning company's share of the annual profits or losses of the company whose securities are owned. This valuation method is applicable only to securities which represent a residual claim against assets. All dividends are accounted for as a reduction of the carrying value of the securities. When the equity method is adopted, revenue is recognized in the

---

[3]*Ibid.*

[4]Accounting Principles Board Opinion 18, "The Equity Method of Accounting for Investments in Common Stock," par. 9, AICPA, New York, 1971.

[5]Donald E. Kieso and Jerry J. Weygandt, *Intermediate Accounting,* John Wiley & Sons, New York, 1974, p. 260; Glenn A. Welsch, Charles T. Zlatkovich, and John Arch White, *Intermediate Accounting,* Richard D. Irwin, Homewood, Ill., 1972, p. 239.

period in which profits are reported by the owned company; if the cost method or the lower-of-cost-or-market method is used, revenue is recognized only when dividends are declared.

The equity method of accounting for investments in equity securities was adopted for domestic, nonconsolidated subsidiaries in 1966 as a part of Accounting Principles Board Opinion No. 10. In 1971 a more extensive consideration of the proper method of accounting for equity securities led to an extension of the position adopted in 1966. Specifically, " . . . the Board now extends this conclusion of APB Opinion No. 10 to investments in common stock of all unconsolidated subsidiaries (foreign as well as domestic) in consolidated financial statements."[6]

As was the pattern with APB Opinions, the Board also specified when the equity method was considered appropriate. "The Board concludes that the equity method of accounting for an investment in common stock should also be followed by an investor whose investment in voting stock gives it the ability to exercise significant influence over operating and financial policies of an investee even though the investor holds 50% or less of the voting stock. . . . The Board recognizes that determining the ability of an investor to exercise such influence is not always clear, and applying judgment is necessary to assess the status of each investment. In order to achieve a reasonable degree of uniformity in application, the Board concludes that an investment of 20% or more of the voting stock of an investee should lead to a presumption that in the absence of evidence to the contrary an investor has the ability to exercise significant influence over an investee."[7]

The Board stated that the equity method should be applied as if the investee were included in consolidated financial statements (except when the cumulative share of losses exceeds the investment). It further indicated that the difference between the equity method and consolidated financial statements is limited to the details found in the financial statements. The net income for the period and the stockholders' equity at year-end are the same if a subsidiary is consolidated or accounted for as an unconsolidated subsidiary when the equity method is used. The situation is not sufficient justification for excluding a subsidiary from consolidation if the circumstances would normally require consolidation.

FASB STATEMENT NO. 12

FASB Statement of Financial Accounting Standards No. 12, "Accounting for Certain Marketable Securities," issued in December 1975, changed the accounting principles for marketable equity securities. This section briefly discusses the general principles. Some specific details are discussed throughout the chapter. FASB Statement No. 12 requires that marketable equity securities be carried at the lower of aggregate cost or market.

Applicable Securities.   FASB Statement No. 12 applies only to marketable equity securities, a category that includes ownership shares (common, preferred, and other capital stock) and rights to acquire or dispose of ownership shares at fixed or determinable prices (warrants, rights, put and call options). Securities excluded are treasury shares, preferred stock that must be redeemed by the issuer or is redeemable at the option of the investor, convertible bonds, restricted stock, and investments of marketable securities accounted for under the equity method.

Exempt Industries.   FASB Statement No. 12 does not apply to nonprofit organizations, mutual life insurance companies, and employee benefit plans, but it does apply to mutual savings banks and other profit-seeking mutual enterprises. In ad-

---

[6]APB Opinion No. 18, *op. cit.,* par. 14.
[7]*Ibid.,* par. 17.

dition, companies in industries with specialized industry accounting practices for marketable securities, such as investment companies, broker-dealers, stock life insurance companies, and casualty insurance companies, may continue to follow the specialized accounting practices, which typically involve carrying marketable securities at market and reflecting unrealized gains or losses in the owners' equity section of the balance sheet.

Current vs. Noncurrent Securities.   In comparing cost with market, securities are grouped into two portfolios: securities classified as current assets and securities classified as noncurrent assets. (In unclassified balance sheets, the entire portfolio is considered noncurrent.) The classification of a given security as current or noncurrent may change and the accounting for that change is discussed later. "Cost" of each of these two portfolios is the aggregate acquisition cost, as discussed in the preceding section, of all securities in the portfolio. "Market" is the aggregate market value of all securities in the portfolio. The "lower of cost or market" is the lower of these two aggregates. Thus, a specific security in a portfolio may have a market value below cost, but that security would be shown at cost if other securities in the portfolio have sufficiently high market values that the aggregate market value is greater than aggregate cost.

Effects on Income and Owners' Equity.   When the aggregate market value of either of the two portfolios is below its aggregate cost (or if the securities have been held for more than one accounting period, book value), then an asset contra account, called a valuation allowance, is credited to reduce book value to aggregate market value. The debit is either (1) to a loss account shown in the income statement for the current asset portfolio, or (2) to an owners' equity contra account (unrealized holding losses) for the noncurrent asset portfolio. If, later, the aggregate market value increases above book value, then the valuation allowance is debited and the credit is (1) to income for current assets or (2) to owners' equity for noncurrent assets. In no case, however, is the valuation allowance allowed to have a debit balance; aggregate market increases are recognized only to the extent of previously recognized decreases. The effect of this treatment is to recognize some changes in market value of current assets in income but not to recognize any income effect for changes in market value of noncurrent assets except for the special case considered next.

Permanent Declines in Market Value of the Noncurrent Portfolio. If it is judged that a decline in market value of an individual security in the noncurrent portfolio is "permanent" rather than "temporary," then the current market value of that security becomes the new "cost" basis for that security and a loss is recognized currently on the income statement. Subsequent increases in aggregate market value do not increase the cost basis. Little guidance is available in deciding whether or not a decline should be judged temporary or permanent. In a slightly different context, however, the Staff of the Auditing Standards Division of the AICPA has issued an interpretation on this question. See the *Journal of Accountancy,* April 1975, pages 69–70. The interpretation contains the following sentence: "When the market decline is attributable to specific adverse conditions for a particular security, stocks or bonds, a [permanent] write-down in carrying amount is necessary unless persuasive evidence exists to support the [current] carrying amount." This sentence and the subsequent discussion appear to indicate that only company-specific events will usually lead to the conclusion that the decline is permanent. Cyclical declines in general stock market prices, as occurred between 1968 and 1975, would not of themselves be judged evidence of permanent declines. (The accompanying recession may have adverse company-specific effects which will lead to a judgment of permanency.)

Transfer Between Current and Noncurrent Classification.   The current vs. noncurrent classification of a security may be changed subsequent to its acquisition.

At the time of reclassification, the current market value becomes the new cost basis, if that amount is less than acquisition cost. The total difference between the old and the new cost bases must be reflected in a loss in the income statement for the period of reclassification.

Deferred Income Taxes. Unrealized losses (and later gains, if they occur) are timing differences, as defined in APB Opinion No. 11 and discussed in Chapter 36. Thus the income statement amounts for unrealized holding losses of the period on the current portfolio and the balance sheet amounts of unrealized holding losses on both portfolios should be adjusted for future income tax effects when an offset of the loss with a future taxable gain is assured beyond any reasonable doubt.

INVESTMENTS IN CONTRACTUAL SECURITIES

Investments in contractual securities may be characterized as usually having limited price fluctuation, maximum exposure to purchasing power gains and losses, and constant dollar cash inflow over the contract period. The accounting questions which must be resolved are rather intimately related to these characteristics.

Appraisal of Value. The current price of a security which includes contractual provisions for the payment of stated sums of money at specific dates is a function of the waiting period to maturity and the interest rate required to attract the needed investment. The time to maturity is specified in the contract, and the required interest rate is related to the investors' willingness to invest and the firm's desire for funds.

Structure of Interest Rates. In a normative sense, interest is the payment to the provider of capital for the use of the capital for a specified time period, as rent is payment to the provider of space or other facilities. As there is no such thing as *the* rental rate, so there is no such thing as *the* interest rate. Instead there is a structure of interest rates beginning with the lowest, which is the rate for the use of money for very short periods of time by borrowers who are considered to present an extremely low probability of financial loss to the lender.

The level of interest rates at different times is functionally related to the supply of lendable funds offered by investors and the demand for funds by borrowers. The supply of and demand for funds are influenced in important ways by the level of current economic activity and the expected future level. The expected rate of inflation in the economy is also an extremely important aspect of the decision of both the lender and the borrower. Since, at the present time, substantially all contractual securities provide for the transfer of a specific number of dollars without regard to the purchasing power of those dollars, investors try to protect themselves against the loss in purchasing power by reducing the supply of money placed in contractual investments. Borrowers, to the contrary, find it extremely desirable to be able to buy real goods with dollars of current purchasing power and to repay the loans at a future date with dollars of a lower purchasing power.

The structure of interest rates is further influenced by the length of time elapsing between the time of commitment of money and the date of repayment. The lengthening of the term of the contractual agreement is apparently associated with a feeling of increased risk on the part of the lender and the desire for greater flexibility by the borrower.

Finally, the element of financial risk for each borrower adds further to the multiplicity of interest rates found in the market. The selection of a required rate of return by the investor is a complex matter; nevertheless, it is an important part of the investment decision. Contractual security prices are the result of the clearinghouse function of the market. Market rates of interest for various types of contracts thus emerge. The decision to invest is resolved for a single investor by comparing the required rate of return and degree of acceptable risk with the market rate for comparable risk.

Interest Rates and Bond Prices. Bond contracts embody two distinct obligations: (1) to pay interest periodically, as specified in the contract, until maturity; and (2) to pay the face amount of the bond at maturity. The price of the contract is obtained by discounting each expected receipt (promised payments) at the prevailing market rate of interest and summing them.

For purposes of illustration, assume that ABC purchases one XYZ, 7-percent, 10-year bond for $932.05. The purchase would be recorded as follows:

```
Investment in XYZ Bonds ............... 932.05
    Cash .............................         932.05
```

Serial Bonds. Serial bonds are issued when the borrowing firm needs money for differing lengths of time or in order to meet the demands of investors. They are frequently issued by municipalities because of their particular needs and occasionally by firms in lieu of bonds requiring the accumulation of a sinking fund. Serial bonds can be thought of as a series of individual contracts; however, we frequently view them as one contract because there is normally only one instrument which specifies serial maturity.

The following example will illustrate how a serial contract may be viewed as two separate contracts:

M Company is offering 7-percent bonds in the face amount of $200,000 with interest payable semiannually and maturity being $100,000 at the end of year 9 and $100,000 at the end of year 10. T Company wishes to earn 8 percent before taxes on its investment and accordingly offers $186,875.18 for the bond issue. The offering price (OP_c) is determined as follows:

Nine-year portion	*Ten-year portion*
$PV_f = 100,000\left[\dfrac{1}{(1 + .04)^{18}}\right]$	$= 100,000\left[\dfrac{1}{(1 + .04)^{20}}\right]$
$= \$49,362.81$	$= \$45,638.69$
$PV_r = 3,500\left[\dfrac{1 - 1/(1 + .04)^{18}}{.04}\right]$	$= 3,500\left[\dfrac{1 - 1/(1 + .04)^{20}}{.04}\right]$
$= \$44,307.54$	$= \$47,566.14$
$PV_f + PV_r \qquad \$93,670.35$	$= \qquad \$93,204.83$

$$OP_c = \$93,670.35 + \$93,204.83 = \$186,875.18$$

The purchase of the serial bond, assuming all brokerage and other issue costs were paid by M Company, would be recorded as follows:

```
Investment in M Company Serial Bonds .... 186,875.18
    Cash ..............................          186,875.18
```

Bond Discount or Premium. The difference between the market price of a bond contract and the face amount—the discount or premium—is the result of the difference between the interest rate stated in the contract and the market rate for comparable contracts. The discount or premium is an adjustment of the interest revenue earned over the life of the contract since the bond will be redeemed at face value at maturity, barring financial insolvency of the issuer. The discount or premium is accumulated or amortized over the life of the contract to reflect more accurately the interest earned for each time period during which the bond is owned. In the absence of such procedures, the difference between the acquisition price and the face value will be reported as a gain or loss in the year of maturity, a circumstance which does not reflect the economic activity. There are two methods of accumulating the discount or amortizing the premium: (1) straight-line and (2) effective yield.

Straight-Line Method. The straight-line method of discount accumulation or premium amortization assigns an equal proportion of the discount or premium to each time period. The result is that in the case of a discount, the apparent rate of return on the investment will be greater than the market rate in the early years of the contract and less in the later years. In the case of a premium, the apparent rate of return will be less than the market rate in the early years and greater in the later years. The straight-line method has, as its primary virtue, ease of application. The entry to record the semiannual interest income for the investment in XYZ Company in the earlier illustration would be as follows:

```
Cash  ........................................ 35.00
Investment in XYZ Company Bonds  ............  3.40
     Interest Income  ........................        38.40
To record semiannual interest income on XYZ
Company bonds with the discount accumulated
using the straight-line method.
```

$$\frac{\$1,000 - \$932.05}{20} = \$3.40 \text{ per period}$$

This same entry would be repeated each interest period for 20 periods, or 10 years.

Effective Yield Method. The effective yield method of discount accumulation and premium amortization employs the concept of compound interest calculation used in determining the price of the contractual security. The method produces a return on the investment equal to the market rate of interest prevailing at the date the investment is made. The rate of return is constant over the period from acquisition to maturity. The effective yield method is illustrated for two periods, using the example of the ABC Company investment in XYZ Company bonds:

```
Cash  ........................................ 35.00
Investment in XYZ Company Bonds  ............  2.28
     Interest Revenue  .......................        37.28
To record semiannual interest income on XYZ
Company bonds with the discount accumulated
using the effective yield method.
$932.05 × .04 = $37.28
```

The investment at the beginning of the second interest period is now $934.33 (= $932.05 + $2.28). The entry to record the interest revenue for the second period is

```
Cash  ........................................ 35.00
Investment in XYZ Company Bonds  ............  2.37
     Interest Revenue  .......................        37.37
To record semiannual interest income on XYZ
Company bonds with the discount accumulated
using the effective yield method.
$934.33 × .04 = $37.37
```

Special Problems of Serial Bonds. The discount or premium on serial bonds can be accumulated or amortized for each maturity using either a straight-line or an effective yield method. The effective yield method can be applied to the serial bond as a unit or to each individual component without altering the results. A slight modification of the straight-line method is necessary if each segment cannot be separated. This method, known as the "bonds outstanding" method, is discussed later.

Both the straight-line and the effective yield methods are illustrated for the first interest period of the M Company bonds applied to each segment separately.

Nine-year segment:
1. Straight-line method:

Cash	3,500.00	
Investment in M Company Serial Bonds	351.65	
Interest Revenue		3,851.65
Market Value at Date of Acquisition	$ 93,670.35	
Maturity Amount	100,000.00	
Discount	$ 6,329.65	

Semiannual Accumulation of Discount

$$\left(\frac{\$6,329.65}{18} = \$351.65 \right)$$

2. Effective yield method:

Cash	3,500.00	
Investment in M Company Serial Bonds	246.81	
Interest Revenue		3,746.81
Market Value at Date of Acquisition	$93,670.35	
Effective Semiannual Interest Rate	× .04	
Semiannual Interest Revenue	$ 3,746.81	

Ten-year segment:
1. Straight-line method:

Cash	3,500.00	
Investment in M Company Serial Bonds	339.76	
Interest Revenue		3,839.76
Market Value at Date of Acquisition	$93,204.83	
Maturity Amount	100,000.00	
Discount	$ 6,795.17	

Semiannual Accumulation of Discount

$$\left(\frac{\$6,795.17}{20} = \$339.76 \right)$$

2. Effective yield method:

Cash	3,500.00	
Investment in M Company Serial Bonds	228.19	
Interest Revenue		3,728.19
Market Value at Date of Acquisition	$93,204.83	
Effective Semiannual Interest Rate	.04	
Semiannual Interest Revenue	$ 3,728.19	

The combined discount accumulation for both segments of the serial bond is $691.41 under the straight-line method and $475.00 under the effective yield method. The discount accumulation of each segment, using the effective yield method, will be larger each period as the carrying value of each segment increases, whereas the accumulation using the straight-line method will remain constant for the first 18 periods and then drop to $339.76 per period for the tenth year. It is interesting to note that the effective yield method applied to the investment in serial bonds as a total will yield the same results as if it were applied to individual segments ($186,875.18 × .04 = $7,475.00).

In serial bond investments, a variation of the straight-line method, the bonds outstanding method, is often used. The amortization of bond premium or accumulation of bond discount for a period using this method is determined by computing the percentage relationship of the bonds outstanding during the period (B_i) to the sum of the bonds outstanding during each period of the bond contract. The percentage so computed is the portion of the total premium (B_p) or discount (B_d) which should be amortized or accumulated during the period (B_i).

This relationship can be expressed as follows:

$$\left(\frac{B_i}{\sum\limits_{i=1}^{n} B_i}\right)(B_d) = B_{di}$$

Referring to the example of the M Company, there is $200,000 of bonds outstanding in each of the first nine years and $100,000 in the tenth year. The discount accumulation for the first year is thus $1,506.58, computed as follows:

$$\frac{\$200,000}{\$1,900,000} \times \$13,124.82 = \$1,381.56$$

The complete tabulation of the annual accumulation of the discount is presented below:

Year	Bonds outstanding at maturity value	Fraction of total outstanding	Accumulation of discount	Cash receipts	Interest revenue
1	$ 200,000	2/19	$ 1,381.56	$ 14,000	$ 15,381.56
2	200,000	2/19	1,381.56	14,000	15,381,56
3	200,000	2/19	1,381.56	14,000	15,381.56
4	200,000	2/19	1,381.56	14,000	15,381.56
5	200,000	2/19	1,381.56	14,000	15,381.56
6	200,000	2/19	1,381.56	14,000	15,381.56
7	200,000	2/19	1,381.56	14,000	15,381.56
8	200,000	2/19	1,381.56	14,000	15,381.56
9	200,000	2/19	1,381.56	14,000	15,381.56
10	100,000	1/19	690.78	7,000	7,690.78
	$1,900,000	19/19	$13,124.82	$133,000	$146,124.82

The bonds-outstanding method approximates the discount accumulation obtained under the straight-line method by considering each portion of the serial contract separately. During the first nine years the discount accumulation using the separate calculation, is $1,382.82; it is $679.52 for the tenth year.

Marketable Securities. Frequently the discount or premium on bond investments which are considered temporary will not be accumulated or amortized. The reason given for the failure to handle the discount or premium in the manner suggested is that the holding period is uncertain or will be so short as to make the accumulation or amortization unnecessary.

Sale of Bond Investments Prior to Maturity. Gains or losses frequently result from the sale, prior to maturity, of bond investments. These gains and losses are often attributable to changes in the level of interest rates which, as was discussed earlier, are related to the supply of and demand for money. The gain or loss is the difference between the proceeds derived from the sale of the investment and the carrying value, purchase price plus accumulation of discount or amortization of premium, to the date of sale.

To illustrate the procedure, assume that the XYZ Company bond is sold one year after the date of purchase for $955.00. The discount is accumulated in accordance with the effective yield method, as illustrated earlier. The carrying value is $936.70 (= $932.05 + $2.28 + $2.37). The entry to record the sale and recognize the gain is

```
Cash  ..................................... 955.00
    Investment in XYZ Company Bonds  ....        936.70
    Gain on Sale of Bonds  ...............         18.30
```

This entry assumes that the interest for the two intervening interest periods has been accrued and that the discount has been accumulated correctly. If for any reason the discount had not been accumulated, the investment account would have to be adjusted before the sale could be recorded.

Acquisition or Sale Between Interest Dates.   Interest, being the payment made to investors for the use of their money for specific time periods, is considered an asset separate and apart from the bond contract. The price of a bond is, as previously discussed, the present value of future receipts by the investor. It is the practice in the bond market for bonds to trade at the present value of the future interest and principal receipts less the portion of the next interest receipt earned by the present holder since the date of the most recent interest receipt. The buyer of the bond acquires two assets—a pure bond value and a receivable for the interest earned since the most recent interest date.

Price Determination.   The market value between interest dates of the contractual security is determined using the principles of present value as illustrated in the discussion of acquisition on an interest date. The following example illustrates the method:

Assume that Larson Company 8-percent bonds due in three years and nine months, principal amount $100,000, are being considered for purchase. The market rate of interest is 7 percent. The present value of the bonds four years prior to maturity is

$$PV_{f^4} = \$100,000\left[\frac{1}{(1 + .035)^8}\right] = \$\ 75,941$$

$$PV_{r^4} = \$4,000\left[\frac{1 - 1/(1 + .035)^8}{.035}\right] = \underline{\ \ \ 27,496}$$

Present value four years prior to maturity $103,437
Add: Growth at 7% for three months ($103,437 × .0175) .... <u>1,810</u>
Value of bond and accrued interest at three years nine months: $105,247
Less: Accrued interest for three months: ($100,000 × .020) .... <u>2,000</u>
Value of bond at three years nine months $103,247

The journal entry to record the purchase of the Larson Company bonds is

```
Investment in Larson Company Bonds  ........ 103,247
Accrued Interest Receivable  .................   2,000
     Cash  ...................................          105,247
To record purchase of bonds plus accrued
interest.
```

Interest Accrual.   The interest received on the investments in Larson Company bonds at three years and six months is recorded as follows (using the effective yield method):

```
Cash  ....................................... 4,000
     Investment in Larson Company Bonds  ....        190
     Accrued Interest Receivable  .............      2,000
     Interest Revenue  .......................      1,810
To record collection of semiannual interest.
```

The interest revenue is computed using the investment value at the beginning of the interest period and the market rate of interest at the date of acquisition. Since the bonds were held only three months of the interest period, only one-half of the total revenue for the period is considered earned by the investor—$1,810 (= ¼ × 103,437 × .07). The premium amortization ($190) is the difference between the interest receipt ($2,000) and the interest revenue ($1,810). The other $2,000 cash received is repayment of the accrued interest purchased at the date the bonds were acquired.

Sale Between Interest Dates. The carrying value of a contractual security must be adjusted for the amortization of premium or accumulation of discount before sale if one is to separate price change due to approaching maturity from that due to market forces. If the effective yield method is used, the premium amortization or discount accumulation is allocated on a straight-line basis within the interest period. If the Larson Company bonds are sold two years and eight months before maturity for $102,500 plus accrued interest and if the interest receipt and premium amortization have been recorded using the effective yield method up to the three-year point, the entries to adjust the accounts and record the sale are

```
Accrued Interest Receivable  .................. 2,667
    Investment in Larson Company Bonds ....        271
    Interest Revenue  .......................      2,396
To accrue interest for four months.
```

Carrying value of investment was $102,661 at the beginning of the period.

```
Cash  ...................................... 105,167
    Accrued Interest Receivable .............        2,667
    Investment in Larson Company Bonds ....        102,390
    Gain on Sale of Securities ..............           110
```

The illustrations of interest accrual and sale between interest dates are both presented using the effective yield method. The straight-line method of premium amortization might also be used. The concepts and procedures are the same; the only difference is the periodic amount of the premium amortization and the resulting carrying value of the investment. The final gain on the sale of securities would be different since the carrying value of the securities would be changed.

INVESTMENTS IN EQUITY SECURITIES

Equity securities represent the residual ownership of the assets of the firm. All assets which are not required to satisfy the priority claims of the investors holding preference securities provide the economic basis of the value of equity securities. There are three primary problems in accounting for and reporting the results of transactions related to investments in equity securities: (1) determining and reporting carrying value at date of acquisition and subsequently, (2) measuring and reporting income during the holding period, and (3) measuring and reporting the gain or loss occurring during the holding period, traditionally recognized at the time of disposition.

Determining and Reporting Carrying Value. The problems of determining and reporting the carrying value of equity securities are similar to those for other securities, which have been discussed earlier in this chapter. The most commonly used methods of valuation are the cost-or-market and equity methods, combined with parenthetical or footnote disclosure of market or cost value. Market values are typically reported as the carrying value of equity securities only when the circumstances exist for the application of the lower-of-cost-or-market valuation, as discussed earlier.

The equity investor is frequently in the position of acquiring additional shares of common stock by means other than direct purchase in the market. For example, shares may be received (1) as a pro rata distribution, requiring no payment by the investor from the owned corporation (stock dividend), and (2) by exercise of stock purchase rights which have been acquired as a pro rata distribution, by purchase, or as compensation for services rendered. The determination of acquisition cost in such cases is somewhat more complex than in the case of an outright purchase. These problems are therefore discussed in some detail in this section.

Stock Dividends. Investors occasionally receive shares of common stock as a pro rata distribution from corporations whose common shares they hold as investments. These shares, stock splits and stock dividends, are received without any requirement for the investor to make any payment to the issuing corporation. The investor merely maintains his proportionate interest in the firm. The total equity of the firm whose shares are held, although represented by more shares after the stock dividend or split, does not change as a result of this distribution. The receipt of shares does not increase the assets of the investor or represent income to him. The investor, therefore, needs only to note that the investment is represented by a large number of shares. The carrying value per share is reduced for purposes of determining gains and losses upon the sale of any shares.

Accounting Research Bulletin No. 43 supports the opinion that stock dividends and splits do not constitute income to the investor. The *Bulletin* argues as follows:[8]

> Under conventional accounting concepts, the shareholder has no income solely as a result of the fact that the corporation has income; the increase in his equity through undistributed earnings is no more than potential income to him. It is true that income earned by the corporation may result in an enhancement in the market value of the shares, but until there is a distribution, division, or severance of corporate assets, the shareholder has no income. . . . In the case of a stock dividend or split-up there is no distribution, division, or severance of corporate assets. Moreover, there is nothing resulting therefrom that the shareholder can realize without parting with some of his proportionate interest in the corporation.

With respect to unconsolidated domestic subsidiaries, the Accounting Principles Board has revised its position as to when income should be recognized by a corporate stockholder; however, this change in no way affects the *Bulletin's* conclusion that the receipt of stock dividends and splits does not constitute income to the investor since neither the stock dividend nor the stock split is associated with either the distribution of assets or the earning of income by an unconsolidated domestic subsidiary.

The Internal Revenue Code of 1954, as amended, in general exempts stock dividends and splits from taxation except where the stock distribution is in lieu of cash. The stock distribution reduces the per-share cost of the shares held, as discussed earlier.

Share Purchase Arrangements. The terms "right" and "warrant" are used almost interchangeably in reference to instruments which permit the holder to acquire shares of stock of the issuing firm at a stated price. The instrument specifies the price at which a new share may be purchased, how many shares the holder is entitled to acquire at that price, and the period during which the right to purchase may be exercised. The confusion results because: (1) one form of purchase arrangement (stock right) is normally received by existing shareholders without cost and it conveys to them the privilege of acquiring new shares at a stated price in proportion to the number of shares held at the time of receipt; (2) the other form of instrument (stock warrant) is normally purchased by the investor. The period during which the stock right can be exercised is normally limited to three or four weeks, whereas the period during which the purchased warrant may be exercised is normally quite long and may run for many years. The warrant holder may exercise the warrant (purchase the stipulated number of shares within the specified time period at the stated price) or may sell the warrant, if it is transferable.

The familiar stock option is also a form of a stock warrant, with provisions quite similar to the other forms discussed. It is received in lieu of cash salary by selected

---

[8]*ARB No. 43, op. cit.,* chap. 7B, par. 6.

employees. The exercise period may range up to five years. However, the beginning of the exercise period may be delayed or may be contingent on specific events. The stock option differs from other forms of stock warrants primarily in that it is normally not transferable and is, therefore, seldom held by corporate investors.

Stock Rights. Stock rights are received by existing stockholders in proportion to their holding of common stock—a single right for each share held. The purchase contract specifies the number of rights and the price required for the acquisition of a single new share. The contract also specifies the expiration date of the right. During the interval between issue and expiration, the right may be traded in the market.

The rights received as a distribution represent a portion of the investor's interest in the corporation. The carrying value of the investment must, therefore, be allocated between the rights and the shares held at the time of the distribution on the basis of relative market price. For purposes of illustration, assume that Stelzer Company owns 10,000 shares of Eastern Corporation acquired for $160,000. Stelzer accounts for the investment on the cost basis. On June 1 Stelzer receives 10,000 stock rights. Five rights and $20 are required to acquire one new share from Eastern. The market price of Eastern Corporation stock trading ex-rights was $30 and the market price of a right was $2. (The price of a share including the right was $32.) The carrying value of the 10,000 shares is allocated between the old shares and the rights as follows:

$$\left(\frac{\$2 \times 10,000}{\$32 \times 10,000}\right)(\$160,000) = \$10,000$$

The required journal entry is

Investment in Eastern Corp. Stock Rights	10,000	
Investment in Eastern Corp. Common Stock		10,000
To record portion of the cost allocable to the stock rights.		

When the stock rights are exercised, the cost assigned to the rights plus the cash paid to acquire the new shares is the cost of the new shares. The entry to record the exercise of one-half of the right is

Investment in Eastern Corp. Common Stock	25,000	
Investment in Eastern Corp. Stock Rights		5,000
Cash		20,000
To record acquisition of 1,000 shares of common stock at $20 per share and by exercising 5,000 stock rights.		

If 4,500 of the remaining rights are sold for $2.10 each and the remaining 500 are allowed to lapse, the journal entries to record these facts are as follows:

Cash	9,450	
Investment in Eastern Corp. Stock Rights		4,500
Gain on sale of Stock Rights		4,950
To record sale of 4,500 rights at $2.10 each		
Loss on expiration of Stock Rights	500	
Investment in Eastern Corp. Stock Rights		500
To record the loss suffered by the expiration of stock rights.		

In situations where an investor needs an approximation of the theoretical market value of the stock after a rights offering, an estimate can be made by summing the present market price of the shares which must be held to permit the acquisition of one new share and the cash payment required to acquire one new share, then this total is divided by the number of shares existing after exercise of the right. The difference between the existing price of a share of stock and the theoretical price ex-right is, of course, the theoretical value of the right distributed to present shareholders. This relationship can be expressed as follows

$$\frac{P(m/n) + C}{(m/n) + 1} = P - nR \quad \text{or} \quad P - nR = C + mR$$

where P = market price of a share, rights on (that is, before the issue of the rights)
m = number of rights required to acquire one new share
n = number of rights received for each share held
C = cash payment required to acquire one new share upon exercise of m rights
R = market price of one right

Accounting for Stock Warrants. When stock warrants are acquired by purchase, whether from the issuing company or from stockholders who wish to sell rights received through preemptive provisions, the acquisition is recorded as an investment in stock purchase rights. As an illustration, M Company acquires a warrant for the purchase of 100 shares of R Company common stock at the option of the holder for five years at a price of $30 per share. The cost of the warrant is $1,000. The journal entry to record the purchase is

```
Investment in R Company Warrant ........................ 1,000
    Cash ...............................................        1,000
To record purchase of warrant for 100 shares of R common stock
at $30 a share. The warrant may be exercised any time within five
years.
```

At the time the warrant is exercised, the following entry is made:

```
Investment in R Company Common Stock ................. 4,000
    Investment in R Company Warrant ...................        1,000
    Cash ...............................................        3,000
To record acquisition of 100 shares of R Company common stock
for $30 per share and exercise of warrant purchased for 1,000.
```

The securities acquired by the exercise of stock warrants are accounted for in accordance with the same principles used for securities acquired without benefit of warrants. Acquisition cost must merely be redefined to include the cost assigned to or paid for the warrant.

Measuring and Reporting Income. Timing the recognition of revenue derived from investments in common stock is directly related to the method used to value the asset. When the *cost* method is used, revenue derived from the investment for a period is equal to the claims against the assets of the investee arising from the declaration of dividends during that period. Receipt of assets (cash or physical items) may not occur within the period during which the right to receive the asset arises. There are four dates commonly associated with the declaration and receipt of dividends on common stock: (1) date of declaration, (2) ex-dividend date, (3) date of record, and (4) date of receipt. The dividend obligation becomes a liability of the enterprise on the date declared and attaches to the stock as a definite receivable at that time. A strict application of the principles of accrual accounting would require that the revenue and the receivable be recognized on the date of declaration. On the ex-dividend date, the stock trades without the right to receive the dividend even though the date of record normally occurs three days later. The day of receipt is insignificant in timing the recognition of revenue. In cases where two accounting periods are involved, the dividend revenue should be recognized on the date of declaration and the receivable transferred with the security in the event of sale before the ex-dividend date.

If the *market* method were to be used, the revenue derived from a common stock investment would be the dividend revenue as discussed above plus the change in the market value of the investment during the period under consideration.

In applying the lower-of-cost-or-market valuation basis, losses from declines in aggregate market value of the current asset portfolio are shown in the income statement; subsequent increases in market values of that portfolio are shown as gains.

The equity method is required by APB Opinion No. 18, "The Equity Method of Accounting for Investments in Common Stock," when 20 percent or more of the common stock of the investee is owned. When this method is used, the revenue recognized is the proportionate part of the earnings of the subsidiary recognized for the period under consideration. The distribution of dividends is considered to be a reduction in the investment when the equity method is used. The procedure is to recognize the receivable and reduce the investment account of the investor on the ex-dividend date.

Liquidating Dividends.   Occasionally corporations find themselves in a position of having accumulated large sums of cash for which there appears to be no sufficiently productive use. In such cases, a dividend may be declared and paid which exceeds the profits of the firm for the particular accounting period. The legal interpretation of such distributions is that if the corporation has reinvested earnings which are greater than the dividend, then the distribution constitutes income to the stockholder.

In some cases the dividend received may exceed the earnings reinvested since the stock was acquired by the present holder. The investor may argue that the proper economic interpretation is that the portion of the dividend which exceeds the reinvested earnings is a return *of* capital rather than a return *on* capital. The legal interpretation, however, is that a new investor steps into the shoes of the prior investor with respect to the distinction between dividend income and return of capital. In other words, the law views distributions from the point of view of the corporation and not that of the investor.

If the investor uses the equity method of accounting for this investment, then the economic interpretation with respect to dividends is implemented as a matter of routine. The situation is illustrated as follows: Morgan Company purchased 1,200 of 2,000 shares of Dickens Company for $48,000 five years ago at which time Dickens had retained earnings of $15,000. During the five years since acquisition by Morgan, Dickens has earned a total of $50,000, paid cash dividends of $30,000, and reinvested $20,000. At the end of year 5, Dickens has $35,000 cash which cannot be used profitably in the firm; therefore, the board of directors at the beginning of year 6 declares a cash dividend of $35,000.

The journal entries in summary form to account for this investment are

	Cost method		*Equity method*
Acquisition entry:			
Investment in Dickens Common Stock	48,000		48,000
Cash		48,000	48,000
Summary earnings entry:			
Investment in Dickens Common Stock			30,000
Earnings of Unconsolidated Company			30,000
Summary regular dividend entry:			
Cash	18,000		18,000
Dividend Revenue		18,000	
Investment in Dickens Common Stock			18,000
Special dividend entry:			
Cash	21,000		21,000
Dividend Revenue		21,000	
Investment in Dickens Common Stock			21,000

Either method may be changed to produce the results of the other by changing the special dividend entry as follows:

```
Cash ....................................... 21,000          21,000
    Dividend Revenue .....................    12,000           9,000
    Investment in Dickens Common Stock ....    9,000          12,000
```

If one elects to follow the cost basis of recording, the reported dividend revenue is $39,000 and the carrying value of the investment is $48,000. On the other hand, if the election is to follow the equity method as suggested by the AICPA, the earned revenue is $30,000 (the investor's share of earnings since acquisition) and the carrying value of the investment is $39,000. As demonstrated, the results of either method can be duplicated no matter which of the two methods is adopted for recording purposes. The recording of "liquidating dividends" in accordance with the equity basis changes the cost method so that the results are identical with the equity method.

Under the market method, the receipt of the dividend would be accounted for as under the cost method. In addition, the decline in market value, if any, would be recognized separately as follows:

```
Decline in Value of Investment ...............  xxx
    Investment in Dickens Common Stock ....       xxx
```

The carrying value of the investment would normally not coincide with the carrying value under either of the other methods discussed.

The complete liquidation of an enterprise would, of course, be accounted for by recognizing the difference between the assets received and the carrying value of the investment as a gain or loss on liquidation.

Measuring and Reporting Gain or Loss on Disposition.   If accountants report the carrying value of securities as the current market price, changes in the market price would be recorded as revenue in the period in which the change occurs. In such cases, the gain or loss in the period in which sale or liquidation takes place would be limited to the price change occurring since the most recent revaluation of the holding.

Under presently accepted accounting principles, the gain or loss derived from holding securities is measured by the difference between the carrying value and the net selling price or liquidation proceeds. The carrying value is most often the acquisition cost of the securities as adjusted for market price changes and for subsequent receipt of shares related to prior investments or such adjusted acquisition cost modified by recognition of the investors' share of reported income of the owned company. The reported gain or loss may represent not the price change occurring during the period in which sale or liquidation is accomplished, but rather the total price change during the entire holding period. The total pre-tax revenue derived from a specific investment is not changed by the particular accounting procedures adopted; however, the revenue for any one period may be significantly different, depending upon the accounting method used and the behavior of market prices between acquisition and sale.

APB Opinion No. 18.   The Accounting Principles Board in Opinion No. 18 concludes that the equity method should be used in accounting for investments when the investor has the ability to exercise control over the investee. The Board concluded that a holding of 20 percent or more of the voting stock of the investee leads to a presumption of control in the absence of evidence to the contrary. The Board held conversely that a holding of less than 20 percent was presumed to be inadequate to exercise control.

In this opinion the Board also held that the equity method should be applied so as to achieve results identical with consolidation. The difference between consolidation and the equity method is limited to details. In discussing the application of the equity method, the Board listed the following points:

a.. Intercompany profits and losses should be eliminated until realized by the investor or investee as if the investee company were consolidated. A question arose as to whether 100 percent of the intercompany profit should be eliminated or only the ownership percentage. In an interpretation dated November 1971 the Board recommends that since the equity method is a one-line consolidation that intercompany profits are eliminated only on assets remaining in the accounts of the investee or investor. The Board also recommends that if the transaction is not at "arm's length" then the intercompany profit or loss should be eliminated 100 percent. If the transaction is at "arm's length," then only the investor's interest in the transaction should be eliminated.

b. A difference between the cost of an investment and the amount of the underlying equity in net assets of an investee should be accounted for as if the investee were a consolidated subsidiary. This implies amortization in accordance with Opinion No. 17 if the difference is considered to be goodwill.

c. The investment in common stock should be shown in the balance sheet as a single amount, and the investor's share of earnings or losses of an investee should be shown in the income statement as a single amount except for extraordinary items.

d. The investor's share of extraordinary items and its share of prior period adjustments reported in the financial statements of the investee should be classified in a similar manner unless they are immaterial in relation to the investor.

e. Transactions by investees of a capital nature that affect the investor's share of stockholder's equity of the investee should be accounted for as if the investee were a consolidated subsidiary.

f. Sales of stock of an investee by an investor should be accounted for as gains or losses equal to the difference between the selling price and the carrying amount of the stock sold.

g. If financial statements of investees are not sufficiently timely for an investor to apply the equity method currently, the investor should record its share of the earnings or losses from the most recent available financial statements. Lags in reporting should be consistent from period to period.

h. A loss in value of an investment which is other than a temporary decline should be recognized as are similar losses of other long-term assets. Evidence of a loss might include the inability to recover the carrying value of the investment, inability of the investee to sustain an earnings level that would justify the carrying value, or a decline in quoted market price which appears to be more than temporary.

i. If the carrying value of the investment is reduced to zero due to recognition of the investor's share of the investee's losses, then the investor should discontinue the use of the equity method unless (1) the investor is contingently liable for the investee's obligations or (2) is committed to provide further financial support for the investee. If the investee subsequently reports net income, the investor should resume applying the equity method only after its share of that net income equals the share of net losses not recognized during the period the equity method was suspended.

j. In determining income tax expense, the undistributed earnings of a subsidiary included in consolidated income should be accounted for as a timing difference unless there is evidence to show that the earnings will be remitted in a tax-free liquidation. Income taxes attributable to timing differences in reporting undistributed earnings of a subsidiary should be accounted for in accordance with the concept of comprehensive tax allocation.

k. When the investee has outstanding cumulative preferred stock, an investor should compute its share of earnings after deducting the preferred dividends whether declared or not.

l. When an investor's percentages of ownership falls below that which would justify the use of the equity method, the investor should discontinue accruing its share of the investee's earnings. The investment account should not be adjusted retroactively.

m. When an investor's percentage of ownership increases to a level requiring the use of the equity method, the investor should adopt it. The investment, results of operations, and retained earnings should be adjusted retroactively in a manner consistent with the step-by-step acquisition of a subsidiary.

n. Any difference that exists between the carrying value of the investment and the underlying equity in the net assets of the investee resulting from the step-by-step procedure should be related to specific accounts of the investee if possible; however, if this is not possible, the difference should be considered to be goodwill and amortized over a period not to exceed 40 years.[9]

INVESTMENTS IN HYBRIDS

Securities which are classified as hybrids are those which have some characteristics of both contractual and equity securities. The accounting treatment, therefore, must encompass some aspects of both types of investments.

Preferred Stocks. Preferred stocks have the characteristic of a specified cash receipt in the form of periodic dividends. The sanctions against the issuing firm for nonpayment of dividends are not so strong in most cases as those found in bond contracts. The major difference, however, is found in the fact that most preferred stock contracts do not specify a maturity date. This lack of a maturity date implies that the same periodic dividend will be received indefinitely.

Valuation of a Preferred Stock. The valuation of a preferred stock, therefore, differs from the valuation of a typical bond in that there is only one stream of cash receipts to be discounted; there is no maturity value to discount. The formula for the valuation of a preferred stock can thus be written as

$$PV_r = D\left[\frac{1 - 1/(1 + i)^{\infty}}{i}\right] \Rightarrow D\left[\frac{1}{i}\right]$$

where PV_r = present value of future dividends discounted at the market rate of interest i

D = periodic receipt

The fraction $1/(1 + i)^{\infty}$ goes to zero as the number of periods approaches infinity. For this reason the market value of a preferred stock (or perpetual bond) approximates the periodic receipt divided by the market rate of interest.

Premium or Discount. Preferred stock prices behave quite similarly to bond prices in that as interest rates rise, the prices of the securities decline and as interest rates fall, prices rise. This phenomenon implies that in some instances the prices of preferred stocks are either above or below the face amount or par value of the security. What should be the accounting disposition by the investor of this premium or discount?

Amortization of Premium or Accumulation of Discount. The premium or discount on investments in preferred securities is seldom, if ever, amortized or accumulated. The purpose of premium accumulation or discount amortization is to recognize revenue in the proper period and to value the asset at market if the conditions at date of acquisition prevail throughout the holding period. For this reason, the discount or premium on preferred stock is not accumulated or amortized. The required rate of return will be reflected in the accounts if the periodic dividend is recorded in the proper period. As time passes, there is no charge in the value of the security so long as the market conditions at date of acquisition prevail.

Preferred stocks may be redeemed at the option of the issuer in many cases, but they almost never have a specified maturity. Par value or face value is significant only when the contract provides for dividend payments to the investor expressed as a percentage of par value or in case of liquidation.

Timing Income Receipts. Preferred stock dividends are declared periodically by the board of directors of the issuing corporation. In this sense the periodic

[9]APB Opinion No. 18, *op. cit.,* par. 19.

distribution is more akin to that of common stock than to that of bonds. If the dividend is not declared, it is not paid. In many cases, preferred stock dividends are cumulative, which means that if the dividend is not declared when due, it accumulates and normally must be paid before any distribution can be made to common stock investors. Since preferred stock dividends are not automatically paid, the investor does not accrue the dividend as he does interest. Instead he should record the dividend as he does common stock dividends. The preferred dividend should be recorded as a receivable and the revenue recognized on the declaration date.

Convertible Securities—Bonds and Preferreds.   There is a group of securities broadly referred to as "convertibles." These are basically fixed-income securities (bonds and preferred stocks) with common stock purchase privileges attached. The stock purchase right is normally not detachable from the fixed-income security. The investment characteristics of these securities are such that the investor gets both the advantage of priority of claim, of participation in growth and increased profitability, and the advantage of limited protection against unforeseen disasters which severely hamper future growth prospects.

The value of a convertible security may be determined by computing the value of the fixed-income portion and of the purchase right as separate securities. In effect the investor is making a basket purchase, but determination of the separate values of the two components is complex.

Accounting Procedure.   Historically, acquisitions of convertible securities have been recorded at acquisition price without recognition of the basket purchase features. Any discount or premium was not accumulated or amortized because the deviation from maturity value was more often attributable to fluctuations in common stock prices rather than to a reflection of market adjustment for differences in interest rates. Further, since conversion is the normal expectation, maturity value will probably never be a significant quantity except in those cases in which the price of the common stock has declined to such an extent that conversion is not justified. In such cases the investor receives protection because of the fixed-income provisions so long as the company is financially sound. In some cases convertibles are viewed as merely a stopgap on the way to acquisition of common stock.

In December 1966, the Accounting Principles Board issued Opinion No. 10, "Omnibus Opinion—1966." Among other topics, this Opinion included two paragraphs which deal with accounting problems of the issuers of convertible securities, but its recommendations could have been important to the investor as well. The first paragraph of this section of the Opinion states:[10]

> A portion of the proceeds received for bonds or other debt obligations which are convertible into stock, or which are issued with warrants to purchase stock, is ordinarily attributable to the conversion privilege or to the warrants, a factor that is usually reflected in the stated interest rate. In substance, the acquirer of the debt obligation receives a "call" on the stock. Accordingly, the portion of the proceeds attributable to the conversion feature or the warrants should be accounted for as paid-in capital . . . ; however, as the liability under the debt obligation is not reduced by such attribution, the corresponding charge should be to debt discount.

The implications of the Opinion for the investor would have been that two investment accounts, rather than one, need to be debited when the securities are acquired. The discount or reduced premium on the bond portion of the investment would be accumulated or amortized as in the case of regular bond investments. The following example will serve to illustrate some of the major accounting

---

[10]See Accounting Principles Board Opinion No. 10, "Omnibus Opinion—1966," par. 8, AICPA, New York, 1966.

changes implied by Opinion No. 10 as related to investments in convertible securities. Assume that Northern, Inc., buys for $1,000 a 7-percent convertible bond, $1,000 face value, which matures five years after date of acquisition. The prevailing market rate of interest for nonconvertible securities of a similar risk class is 8 percent at the date of acquisition. Each bond is convertible into 50 shares of common stock, currently selling for $18 per share, at the option of the investor at anytime before maturity. This acquisition would have been recorded as follows, using the ideas expressed in Opinion No. 10.

Investment in Bonds	959.44	
Investment in Conversion Privilege	40.56	
Cash		1,000.00

To record acquisition of 7-percent convertible
bond. The cost is allocated as follows:

Cash 1,000.00
Market value of 7-percent, five-year bond:

$$\text{Principal} - (\$1,000) \left[\frac{1}{(1 + .04)^{10}} \right] = 675.56$$

$$\text{Interest} - (\$35) \left[\frac{1 - 1/(1 + .04)^{10}}{.04} \right] = 283.88 \quad \text{.............} \quad 959.44$$

Market value of conversion privilege 40.56

The subsequent accounting for this investment on the first interest date would be as follows, assuming the use of the effective yield method of discount accumulation:

Cash	35.00	
Investment in Bonds	3.38	
Interest Revenue		38.38

To record interest for six months.

The entry to record the conversion, assuming that conversion takes place immediately after receipt of the interest for the first six months and that we assume conversion should be recorded at the carrying value of the investment rather than market value of the common stock, is as follows:

Investment in Common Stock	1,003.38	
Investment in Bonds		962.82
Investment in Conversion Privilege		40.56

To record conversion of bonds into common stock.

If the conventional method of accounting for convertible securities had been followed, the interest revenue would have been only $35, the carrying value of the investment would have been $1,000; accordingly, the investment cost of the common stock would have been $1,000. The difference of $3.38 in the carrying value of the investment will eventually enter into the income stream when the common stock is sold. The question is: When is the revenue realized and when should it be recognized?

In March 1969 the Accounting Principles Board issued Opinion No. 14 which attempts to distinguish between convertible debt which must be surrendered to convert it into common stock and debt which has detachable warrants entitling the holder to buy a specified number of shares of common stock at a stated price. In this Opinion the Board attached considerable significance to the inseparability of the debt and the conversion option. The Board concluded that when the debt instrument must be surrendered to obtain common stock, no element of common equity had been sold at the time of issuance of the debt. On the other hand, if debt were sold with detachable warrants, there was evidence that equity had been sold at the date of issuance. Throughout this Opinion the Board refers only to the issuer; however, as discussed earlier, since the investor is a party to the transaction under discussion there are implications for the investor as well. Accordingly, if the investment is in convertible debt with detachable warrants, the method illustrated above is appropriate. On the other hand, if the debt must be surrendered to acquire common stock, the investor should record the total investment as an investment in corporate bonds. The impact of this procedure is primarily on the interest revenue recorded during the period that the bonds are held and, to the extent that the discount would have been amortized, on the carrying value of the common stock investment if conversion takes place later.

In this opinion the Board has been accused by some of placing form before substance in the establishment of accounting principles.

Income Bonds. Income bonds are extremely rare instruments of finance in today's world; perhaps the need for income bonds has been supplanted by convertible securities. Income bonds typically have a maturity date and a face value which is paid to the holder at maturity. The unique feature of this instrument is that the periodic receipt, for the use of funds invested, varies depending on the profits of the firm.

Valuation. The problems of valuation of income bonds are found primarily in the estimates of periodic receipts which the investor will receive. If these estimates can be made, then valuation becomes another calculation of the present value of future receipts.

Discount Accumulation and Premium Amortization. Since income bonds generally have definite maturity dates, any discount or premium should be accumulated or amortized. With a definite life, the discount or premium can be accumulated or amortized on the straight-line basis with little difficulty. If the investor makes estimates of future receipts in preparation of making the decision to invest in income bonds, it seems reasonable to argue that these estimates might be used to apply the techniques of the effective yield method as well. The effective yield method would be employed by computing the present value of expected future receipts at the end of each period. The change in the present value of the receipts would be the appropriate amortization or accumulation of premium or discount.

The interest revenue from these bonds could be accrued if a formula were included in the contract specifying how the distribution would be determined. In cases where the distribution of cash is dependent upon the action of the board of directors and is related to common stock dividends, the revenue from these bonds would have to be timed in the same manner as dividends on common stock are timed. The receivable would arise on the date of declaration. The adjustment of the investment would complete the revenue recognition entry.

INVESTMENTS IN SPECIAL-PURPOSE FUNDS

Firms occasionally deposit cash in special-purpose funds as a means of providing cash for desired purposes at specific later points in time or as a means of satisfying specific provisions of contracts between the firm and other parties. The funds required because of specific contract provision are usually administered by trustees who are independent of the firm's management. The voluntary funds created for special purposes at the discretion of management are normally administered by the management of the firm. The cash deposited in either of these types of funds is usually invested in securities so that it will be productive during the holding period. Since in many cases these funds are created to provide specific sums of money at a specified time, the investment medium is usually bonds with maturity dates near the time payment is required. With the obligation to be satisfied stated in dollars, the risk of purchasing power loss present in fixed-dollar securities is not important. On the other hand, the risk of capital loss by large market fluctuation associated with common stock may be extremely important.

Accounting for Funds.   The accounting records related to the activities of any fund depend to some extent on the purpose of the fund and legal considerations related to the fund.

Funds are created, voluntarily or in accordance with contractual provisions, (1) to accumulate resources for the purpose of satisfying specific obligations of the firm, or (2) to accumulate resources for the purpose of satisfying obligations for a separate entity, the fund, but with the firm under contract to make specific periodic deposits in the fund and in some cases being contingently liable for the obligations of the fund. The essential distinction between funds created for these two purposes is that for funds created to satisfy specific obligations of the firm, the obligation rests on the firm whether the fund has adequate resources or not. When the obligation is that of the fund, if the firm has fulfilled its contractual requirements of making periodic deposits, then the liability of the firm has been satisfied regardless of whether the fund accumulated is adequate for its purpose or not, except in those specific cases in which the firm is contingently liable for the obligations of the fund.

When the purpose of the fund is to satisfy obligations of the firm, the fund balance is an asset of the firm, and the revenues and expenses relating to the fund should be included in the determination of periodic net income. The transaction information is for purposes of satisfying accountability requirements. Securities held in such funds are accounted for as though they were being held as temporary or long-term investments. The accounting records should include information about (1) transfer of assets to the fund, (2) investment transactions, especially in company-managed funds, (3) revenues derived from investment operations and expenses of administration, and (4) use of the resources of the fund.

One of the duties of a trustee is to submit periodic reports to the interested parties. The report to the corporation responsible for making payments to the fund includes a report of investment activity, revenues derived from the portfolio and expenses of management. The firm then records these data either in the general ledger accounts or in a subsidiary ledger for which the investment account is the control.

For funds whose purpose it is to satisfy obligations of the fund, the firm's obligation extends merely to the deposit of cash in the fund in accordance with contractual provisions and possible contingent liability. No records are necessary for the firm except those necessary to report the expense—usually limited to the required deposit—associated with the contract between the firm and the outside party. Funds of this latter type are most often created for the benefit of employees through a contract made between the firm and a union, the most common type being a pension fund.

Periodic Deposits.   Funds created by contract, such as a pension fund, for the benefit of employees usually specify how the amount of periodic deposit is determined and at what dates deposits must be made. Deposits are usually related to the payroll of covered employees. Deposits to funds, contractual or voluntary, whose purpose it is to accumulate a specific sum of money for corporate purposes, are frequently specified as to dollar amount and date of deposit. In some cases the contract provides for minimum balances to be accumulated in the fund by stipulated dates. Regardless of whether the periodic deposit is stated in the contract or determined by the firm to meet specified interim levels, the procedure for determining the amount is usually the same.

The deposit may vary each period based on the investment results of the fund, or stated assumptions may be made which permit the calculation of a uniform deposit for each period. The uniform deposit to be made at the beginning of each period can be computed in accordance with the following formula:[11]

$$A_n = R\left[\frac{(1 + i)^n - 1}{i}\right] \quad \text{or} \quad R = A_n\left[\frac{1}{\dfrac{(1 + i)^n - 1}{i}}\right]$$

where A_n = amount desired in the fund at the end of n periods

  R = periodic deposit to be made at the beginning of each period

  i = estimated return, net of management expense, on the assets held by the fund

  n = number of deposits to be made or number of periods until amount needs to be on hand

The use of this formula is illustrated with the following example. X Company is about to issue a $100,000 bond which requires a periodic deposit with a trustee. The trustee is to hold all funds for the benefit of the bondholder. Ten years from the date of issue, the fund is to contain no less than $100,000. The first deposit is to be made at the beginning of the second year after issue of the bond. X Company estimates that the funds can be invested to yield an average of 7 percent and that the management expenses will average approximately 1 percent of the funds held. The company proposes to make nine equal periodic payments at the beginning of each year, starting with year 2. A final payment will be made at the end of the tenth year to bring the cash on deposit to $100,000. If more than $100,000 has been accumulated, the excess will be returned to the firm by the trustee. The uniform periodic deposit can be computed as follows:

$$R = A_n\left[\frac{1}{\dfrac{(1 + i)^n - 1}{i}}\right]$$

$$= \$100,000\left[\frac{1}{\dfrac{(1 + .06)^9 - 1}{.06}}\right]$$

$$= \$100,000\left[\frac{1}{11.4913}\right]$$

$$= \$8,702.24$$

The recording procedures for the first year of operations of the fund, assuming that interest earned is $610 and management expenses are $140, are illustrated below:

Investment in Sinking Fund	8,702.24	
Cash		8,702.24
To record first annual deposit with trustee at the beginning of year 2.		
Sinking Fund Expense	140.00	
Investment in Sinking Fund	470.00	
Sinking Fund Revenue		610.00
To record earnings of the fund and expenses of management for year 2.		

[11]Compound interest tables are published which will permit the immediate evaluation of $[(1 + i)^n - 1]/i$. These tables are titled in various ways, but in essence they provide the user with the amount to which $1 deposited at the beginning of each period for n periods will accumulate, if invested to yield i rate of return. (See the Appendix.)

Assume that after the deposit at the beginning of year 10, the fund balance is $94,000. The interest earned during year 10 is $6,700 and the expenses of management are $900. At the end of year 10, the adjusting deposit is made and the bonds are retired.

```
Sinking Fund Expense ....................................    900.00
Investment in Sinking Fund ...............................  5,800.00
     Sinking Fund Revenue  ................................              6,700.00
To record earnings of the fund and expenses of management for
the tenth year since issuance of the bond or the ninth year of the
fund accumulation.

Investment in Sinking Fund  ..............................    200.00
     Cash .................................................              200.00
To record final deposit in the fund to obtain the required balance.
The net earnings of the fund were inadequate by $200.

Bonds Payable  ...........................................  100,000.00
     Investment in Sinking Fund  ..........................            100,000.00
To record payment of the bond obligation by the trustee.
```

In this illustration, individual transactions involving acquisition, revenue collection, and disposition of securities have been assumed to be recorded by the trustee and no separate records relating to these matters are maintained by the firm.

Cash Surrender Value of Life Insurance.   A firm will occasionally purchase a life insurance policy on the life of a principal officer or owner of the firm with the firm named as beneficiary. The proceeds of the policy are expected to be used to purchase the deceased owner's interest from his estate or to help absorb the extra expense of operating for a short time following the loss of the key executive. The firm has the option of buying either term insurance, which is strictly insurance against loss of life, or permanent insurance, which practically always includes, in addition to the insurance, a savings plan. The accumulated savings in the permanent plan are referred to as the "cash surrender value" of the policy. Permanent insurance policies normally permit the policy owner, in the present case the firm, to borrow an amount equal to the cash surrender value of the policy at the next premium date discounted to the date of the borrowing at the interest rate charged the borrower.

Term Insurance.   Term insurance presents few accounting problems. The cash outlay is made at the beginning of the insurance period. If the insurance period covers parts of more than one accounting period, the expense must be allocated between the accounting periods on the basis of time covered by the insurance policy in each accounting period. If the insurance is acquired from a mutual insurance company, a dividend may be paid at the end of the policy year which reflects the underwriting and investment success of the insurance company during the particular year. If the insurance is acquired from a stock company, there is no dividend or refund at the end of the year, but the premium outlay is normally less.

The accounting problems presented here are: (1) how to record the insurance expense when the policy is purchased from a mutual company and (2) allocation of the net cost between accounting periods when the policy year does not coincide with the business year. The practical solution is to use the insurance company's estimate of the dividend to determine the net cost of the insurance. Any adjustment necessary because the actual dividend was not equal to the estimate can be reflected in the expense of the second period. The amount of the difference is likely to be so small as to be insignificant. The second problem is usually resolved by allocating the net outlay for the insurance coverage on the basis of the time for which coverage is provided in each accounting period.

Permanent Insurance.   Permanent insurance may be purchased from a stock company or a mutual company as in the case of term insurance. The treatment accorded the dividend, where applicable, should be the same as that followed for term insurance. There is the additional problem of accounting for the cash surrender value, which accumulates with most permanent life policies, whether issued by stock or mutual companies.

The cash surrender value is an asset to the firm. At the option of management, the policy may be canceled and an amount of cash equal to the cash surrender value of the policy may be obtained from the insurance company. This asset can also be used as collateral for borrowing from the insurance company. Cash surrender values increase at the end of each policy year.

In many cases both the dividends and the cash surrender values have been treated as reductions of premiums in the year following their accrual. Such a procedure results in insurance expense of the early years which is too high. Most insurance companies provide the buyer with a schedule of guaranteed cash surrender values and an estimate of dividends to be paid on the policy, assuming that the current year's experience is repeated each year. With such data, it seems quite possible to obtain substantially correct figures for each accounting period, with possible small adjustments being made when necessary because of variations in estimated and actual dividend payments.

This approach to the problem of accounting for a permanent plan of insurance purchase from a mutual company is illustrated with the following hypothetical data:

Year	Annual gross premium	Estimated dividend at end of year	Guaranteed cash value increase at end of year
1	$3,000	$420	$ 100
2	3,000	450	700
3	3,000	475	2,500
4	3,000	510	2,550
5	3,000	530	2,600

Assume that the policy year is July 1 to June 30 and that the accounting period ends on December 31. The actual dividend experience is as estimated except for year 4, when the actual dividend paid at the end of year 4 is $525. Selected journal entries for years 19X1, 19X2, 19X4, and 19X5 are as follows:

July 1, 19X1

Prepaid Insurance	3,000	
Cash		3,000

To record payment of annual premium

December 31, 19X1

Insurance Expense	1,240	
Cash Surrender Value	50	
Prepaid Insurance		1,290

To record insurance expense and accrual of CSV for the first six months including estimate of dividend to be received as a reduction of insurance expense.

June 30, 19X2

Dividend Receivable	420	
Insurance Expense	1,240	
Cash Surrender Value	50	
Prepaid Insurance		1,710

To record insurance expense and accrual of CSV for second six months.

July 1, 19X2

Prepaid Insurance	3,000	
Cash		2,580
Dividend Receivable		420

To record payment of second annual premium.

July 1, 19X4

Prepaid Insurance	3,000	
Cash		2,525
Dividend Receivable		475

To record payment of fourth annual premium.

December 31, 19X4

Cash Surrender Value	1,275	
Prepaid Insurance		1,245
Excess of Appreciation over Outlay on Insurance		30

To record increase in cash surrender value and amortization of
prepaid insurance account. Cash surrender value increases by more
than premium expectation.

June 30, 19X5

Dividend Receivable	525	
Cash Surrender Value	1,275	
Prepaid Insurance		1,755
Excess of Appreciation over Outlay on Insurance		45

To record increase in cash surrender value, amortization of
prepaid insurance, and correction of estimated dividend.

July 1, 19X5

Prepaid Insurance	3,000	
Cash		2,475
Dividend Receivable		525

To record payment of fifth annual premium.

The Excess of Appreciation over Outlay on Insurance account is a revenue or other income account and would be closed out each year in the same way as insurance expense.

If the insured should die during the time that the life insurance policy is in effect, the prepaid insurance balance, adjusted for short-term cancellation provisions and the cash surrender value accrued to date of death, would be converted into cash. The difference between the carrying value of these assets and the total cash collected would be credited to an account such as Proceeds from Life Insurance Policy.

FINANCIAL STATEMENT PRESENTATION

The accounting data accumulated relative to investments in securities and special-purpose cash funds must be reported in the three primary financial statements: (1) balance sheet, (2) income statement, and (3) statement of changes in financial position.

Disclosure Requirements of FASB Statement No. 12.   Under the requirements for marketable securities of FASB Statement No. 12, companies not following specialized industry accounting practices must disclose:

1. Aggregate cost and market value of both the current and noncurrent portfolios. If aggregate cost is less than aggregate market value, then the amount to be included in balance sheet totals is cost with market values shown parenthetically on (or in notes to) the balance sheet. If aggregate cost exceeds aggregate market value, then the presentations are reversed, but both are disclosed.

2. Net realized and net unrealized holding gains and losses during each year for which an income statement is presented, with separate disclosure of the amounts affecting income and the amounts affecting only owners' equity.

If specialized industry practices are followed, then the firm must disclose the amounts by which owners' equity has been increased or decreased because of unrealized holding gains or losses for each year for which an income statement is presented. All companies must disclose:

3. Total unrealized gains and losses at the latest balance sheet date segregated between current and noncurrent portfolios, if a classified balance sheet is presented.

4. Significant net realized and unrealized holding gains occurring after the latest balance sheet date occurring prior to the issuance of the statement.

The disclosure requirements are summarized in Exhibit 1, which is taken from a publication by Ernst & Ernst.[12]

EXHIBIT 1   Summary of Disclosure Requirements for Marketable Securities Under FASB Statement No. 12

| | Nonspecialized industries | | | Specialized industries | |
Disclosure	Each balance sheet	Latest balance sheet	Each income statement	Latest balance sheet	Each income statement
1. Aggregate cost and market value, identifying which is the carrying amount	X*			†	
2. Gross unrealized gain (excess of market value over cost)		X*		X	
3. Gross unrealized loss (excess of cost over market value)		X*		X	
4. Significant net realized and net unrealized gain or loss arising after the date of the financial statements but prior to their issuance, applicable to securities owned at the latest balance sheet date		X		X	
5. Change in the valuation allowance included in net income and, separately, the change in the amount included in the equity section of the balance sheet			X	†	
6. Net realized gain or loss included in net income and the basis on which cost was determined in the computation			·X	†	
7. The amount by which equity has been increased or decreased as a result of unrealized gains and losses					X

*Must be segregated between current and noncurrent portfolios when a classified balance sheet is presented.
†Should generally be made in accordance with the requirements of the respective industry audit guides.
SOURCE: Ernst & Ernst, loc. cit.

Balance Sheet. The balance sheet classification and presentation of securities can be subdivided into three parts: (1) marketable securities, (2) investments in affiliated companies, and (3) investments in special-purpose funds. Although many of the problems are common to each category, there are some unique areas of interest which will be viewed individually. There is the underlying assumption in accounting that all assets should be recorded at cost. Under certain conditions, loss of economic potential may be reflected in the accounts and the financial statements; however, increases in economic potential should not be reported until verified by transactions with distinterested parties. There is also the general prohibition against offset reasserted in Accounting Principles Board Opinion No. 10 that:

It is a general principle of accounting that the offsetting of assets and liabilities in the balance sheet is improper except where a right of setoff exists. Accordingly, the offset of cash or other assets against the tax liability or other amounts owing to governmental bodies is not acceptable except . . . when it is clear that a purchase of securities

[12]Ernst & Ernst, "Accounting for Certain Marketable Securities," Retrieval No. 38408, Cleveland, 1976, page 12.

(acceptable for the payment of taxes) is in substance an advance payment of taxes that will be payable in the relatively near future, so that in the special circumstances the purchase is tantamount to the prepayment of taxes.[13]

Marketable Securities.   Accountants generally agree that marketable securities are in fact merely an extension of the cash balance. In many cases the two amounts are combined and reported as cash and marketable securities.

Long-Term Investments.   Long-term investments are generally described as holdings of securities which cannot be readily sold without impairing intercorporate relationships. These investments are typically classified as noncurrent assets; however, if the amount is small relative to other assets in the category, the investments may follow noncurrent assets in a category frequently labeled "other assets."

APB Opinion No. 18 includes disclosure requirements for investments. The required information may be disclosed parenthetically, in notes to financial statements, or in separate statements and schedules. The information which must be disclosed includes:[14]

1. The name of each investee and percentage of ownership of common stock.

2. The accounting policies of the investor with respect to investments in common stock.

3. The difference between the amount at which the investment is carried and the amount of underlying equity in net assets and the accounting treatment of the difference.

4. Where a quoted market price is available, the aggregate value of each identified investment should usually be disclosed.

5. When investments are in the aggregate material, summarized information about the assets, liabilities, and results of operations of the investees should be presented in the notes or separate statements either individually or in groups.

6. Material effect of possible conversions, exercises, or contingent issuances should be disclosed in notes to the financial statements of an investor.

Investments in Special-Purpose Funds.   Investments in special purpose funds are reported along with investments in securities as noncurrent assets or as other assets following the noncurrent asset section. It is important to recognize that the rule pertaining to the offsetting of assets against liabilities applies to special-purpose funds and related obligations of the firm.

Income Statement.   The items to be reported on the income statement in this category can be classified as (1) interest or dividend income, (2) share of earnings of unconsolidated subsidiary or affiliate companies, (3) gains and losses on the sale of investments, and (4) unrealized holding gains and losses on the current asset portfolio of marketable securities. The trend in recent years has been to prepare a single-step income statement instead of the once more popular multistep statement. This means that interest and dividend income is now more often found included among the revenue items before any deductions. In multiple-step statements these items are normally included in a section of nonoperating revenues and expenses.

The requirements for reporting deposits to special-purpose funds, the revenue earned, and the management expenses differ depending on the purposes for which the fund is established. If the fund is established to liquidate a recognized obligation of the firm, the annual deposit to the fund represents the increase in one asset and the decrease of another. No expense is recognized. The revenue earned and expenses of management must be reported in the same way that revenues derived from and expenses associated with security investments are reported. If the deposit is to a fund whose purpose is to pay claims against the

[13]APB Opinion No. 10, *op. cit.,* par. 7.
[14]APB Opinion 18, *op. cit.,* par. 20.

assets of the fund and there is no recognized liability on the part of the firm, then the deposit itself is an expense which must be reported, for example, pension expenses. The revenues and expenses associated with the operation of these independent funds are not a part of the activities of the firm and should not be included in the financial reports of the firm.

Where the equity basis is used, the amount representing the owning firm's share of unconsolidated subsidiary and affiliate profits and losses is normally reported as a separate item of revenue. The Accounting Principles Board in Opinion No. 18 states: "The investor's share of earnings or losses of investees should ordinarily be shown in the income statement as a single amount except for the extraordinary items . . . which should be classified"[15] as such on the investor's income statement. Of course if the investment is carried on the equity basis, there is no dividend income to be reported.

The third item, gains and losses on the sale of investments, is the difference between the selling price and the carrying amount at the date of sale. This amount is shown as a determinant of net income rather than as an extraordinary item. Unrealized holding gains and losses are disclosed as described above.

Statement of Changes in Financial Position.   The definition of funds assumed in this discussion is that of net working capital. The problem of reporting activities related to marketable securities and investments in this statement must be examined in terms of the particular format adopted for the statement itself (see Chapter 3). If we view net income as a source without enumeration of the components, then as far as revenues and expenses are concerned we need only concern ourselves with whether or not to modify the income figure. Of course, all interest and dividend revenue, whether derived from marketable securities or long-term investments, represents an inflow of funds. While the excess of increases in cash surrender value over net insurance premium payments is not an inflow of funds in the normal use of the term, the cash paid for the premium is a use of funds. Similarly, the net revenue earned on cash deposited in a special-purpose fund is not a source of funds in the strict use of the term. The periodic deposit is, of course, a use of funds. In the case of permanent-plan insurance policies and special-purpose funds, if we report the total increase in the noncurrent asset as a use of funds, then the net revenue or expense reported in the income statement need not be eliminated in cases where net income is reported as a source of funds.

When the equity method is used to account for investments in common stock, the owning company's share of the affiliated company's net income is included in net income. This income does not produce working capital for the investor company, except to the extent that the affiliated company distributes dividends. The investor's share of the undistributed earnings of the affiliate appears on the balance sheet as an increase in the nonworking capital item, Investments in Affiliates. That increase in the carrying value of Investments in Affiliates should appear in the operating section of the statement of changes in financial position as a deduction from net income in arriving at funds from operations. If the affiliate suffers a loss, then the investor's portion of the loss which served to reduce the investor's net income must be added to net income in determining funds from operations.

The remaining problem, that of gains and losses resulting from the sale of securities, must be divided into two parts: (1) If the securities are classified as current assets and as such are a part of working capital, a gain or loss on the sale of a security represents an increase or decrease in working capital. (2) On the other hand, gains and losses may not be handled in the same way when they result from the sale of securities held as long-term investments. The total proceeds of the sale

[15]APB Opinion No. 18, *op. cit.,* par. 19.

of long-term investments, not merely the gain, represent an increase in funds. Similarly, a loss does not mean a decrease in funds if the loss results from the sale of securities held as long-term investments. A loss in this case merely means that the proceeds were less than the carrying value by an amount equal to the reported loss. Net income included in the funds statement must therefore be adjusted to eliminate the gains and losses arising from the sale of long-term investments. The proceeds from such sales are included as sources of funds.

Finally, any funds used to expand the holding of securities as long-term investments must be reported as a use of funds. Of course, securities purchased as marketable securities are included in working capital; therefore, cash expended to acquire such securities is not reported in the statement of changes in financial position.

BIBLIOGRAPHY

Beaver, William H.: "Accounting for Marketable Equity Securities," *Journal of Accountancy*, December 1973, pp. 58–64.

———: "Reporting Rules for Marketable Equity Securities," *Journal of Accountancy*, October 1971, pp. 57–61.

Coda, Bernard A., and William J. Morris: "Valuation of Equity Securities," *Journal of Accountancy*, January 1973, pp. 48–54.

Douglas, Patricia P.: "Accounting for Equity Securities," *Journal of Accountancy*, November 1972, pp. 66–70.

Ernst & Ernst, "Accounting for Certain Marketable Securities," Retrieval No. 38408, Cleveland, 1976.

Financial Accounting Standards Board, "Accounting for Certain Marketable Securities," *Statement of Financial Accounting Standards No. 12,* Stamford, Conn., 1975.

Hamre, James C., and Melvin C. O'Connor: "Alternate Methods of Accounting for Long Term Non-Subsidiary Intercorporate Investments in Common Stock," *The Accounting Review*, January 1972, pp. 308–319.

Imdieke, Leroy F., and Jerry J. Weygandt: "Accounting for That Imputed Discount Factor," *Journal of Accountancy*, June 1970, pp. 54–58.

Kieso, Donald E., and Jerry J. Weygandt: *Intermediate Accounting,* John Wiley & Sons, New York, 1974, p. 260.

Loyd, B. M., and Jerry J. Weygandt: "Market Value Information for Non-Subsidiary Investments," *The Accounting Review,* October 1971, pp. 756–764.

McCullers, Levis D.: "An Alternative to APB Opinion No. 14," *Journal of Accounting Research,* Spring 1971, pp. 160–164.

Pacter, Paul: "Applying APB Opinion No. 18—Equity Method," *Journal of Accountancy,* September 1971, pp. 54–62.

Perlow, Morris R.: "Accounting Recognition of Holding Gains and Losses on Marketable Securities," *New York Certified Public* (CPA Journal), February 1969, pp. 95–100.

———: "Several Comments on APB No. 18: The Equity Method of Accounting for Investments in Common Stock," *CPA Journal,* October 1971, pp. 751–73.

———: "Statement on Auditing Procedure No. 51: Long Term Investments," *Journal of Accountancy,* September 1972, pp. 80–82.

Stephens, Matthew J.: "Inseparability and the Valuation of Convertible Bonds," *Journal of Accountancy,* August 1971, pp. 54–62.

Weil, Roman L.: "Reciprocal or Mutual Holdings: Allocating Earnings and Selecting the Accounting Method," *The Accounting Review,* October 1973, pp. 749–758.

Welsch, Glenn A., Charles T. Zlatkovich, and John Arch White: *Intermediate Accounting,* Richard D. Irwin, Homewood, Ill., 1972, p. 239.

Chapter **15**

Receivables

RONALD J. HUEFNER
**Associate Professor of Accounting,
State University of New York at Buffalo**

JAMES S. SCHINDLER
**Professor of Accounting and Management Systems,
State University of New York at Buffalo**

INTRODUCTION

Definition. *Receivables* are claims of various types held by an entity for the future receipt of cash, goods, or services. Most commonly, receivables are claims for the receipt of cash, arising from normal trade or other types of transactions.

Transactions giving rise to receivables, and the descriptive titles commonly employed, are as follows:

1. Sale of goods or services to customers (*trade accounts receivable; trade notes receivable,* if a written promise to pay exists; *installment receivables,* if payments are to be made over several periods of time)

2. Loans made to individuals or other entities (*loans receivable; notes receivable; advances to subsidiaries; advances to employees; officer and employee receivables;* etc.)

3. Leasing property to others (*lease contracts receivable*)

4. Other revenue transactions (*interest receivable; dividends receivable; rent receivable; comissions receivable;* etc.)

5. Deposits of various kinds, to guarantee performance or payment (*deposits receivable; utility deposits; contract retainages;* etc.)

6. Claims in insurance, tax, litigation, and other proceedings (*claims receivable; tax refund receivable; damage claims receivable;* etc.)

7. Subscriptions from investors for the purchase of stock (*stock subscriptions receivable*).

In addition to these fairly general types of transactions, specialized transactions may exist for a particular entity giving rise to differently titled receivable accounts (e.g., *franchise fees receivable* of a franchisor, or *taxes receivable* of a municipality). The accounting, financial reporting, and control of most of these specialized receivables, however, does not differ from the general types listed above.

Significance of Receivables. A substantial majority of the revenue of almost every business entity is derived from the sale of goods and services to customers. Most of these sales for most entities are on credit. Thus, receivables are likely to be a significant asset for very many business entities.

As is the case with most areas of accounting, the important questions concerning receivables center around recognition, measurement, disclosure, and information required for management uses. The chapter is structured around these topics.

ACCOUNTING FOR RECEIVABLES

Trade Accounts Receivable. Trade accounts receivable arise in the course of sales of goods and services to customers. Records of open-account sales provide the evidence underlying these claims; written instruments (such as notes) do not exist for these receivables.

Recognition. The recognition of trade accounts receivable involves the accounting issues of timing (when shall the receivable be recognized?) and measurement (how much shall be initially recorded?).

The timing of recognition is linked to the question of the recognition of revenue. Various bases for the recognition of revenue are discussed in Chapter 12 ("Revenue Recognition"), and thus will not be extensively discussed here. We shall summarize the effect of the different recognition bases on the timing and nature of receivable recognition.

Revenue is most commonly recognized under the *sales (or delivery) basis.* Under this procedure, accounts receivable are recognized at the time of the exchange of goods or services between seller and buyer. This timing corresponds to the creation of a legal claim for payment from the buyer. The recognition of the receivable occurs simultaneously with the recognition of revenue.

Revenue may be recognized under the *production (or percentage of completion) basis*. This method may be appropriate when goods or services are being supplied under a firm contract, such as in the case of long-term construction. Since revenue recognition may occur prior to billing and delivery, no simultaneous claim for payment need be created. The parties to the transaction may, of course, have agreed that payments shall occur at various times during production. Nevertheless, the recognition of revenue gives rise to an entry to an asset account such as "Finished Product—At Contract Price" or "Unbilled Construction in Progress—At Contract Price." Since delivery has not yet occurred, title to the goods involved continues to rest with the seller. Hence the accounts debited are in the nature of inventory accounts rather than receivables. Only when delivery of the finished product occurs (or when percentage-of-completion billings are made pursuant to contractual agreement) is a receivable (i.e., a legal claim for payment) created. Thus, under the production basis for revenue recognition, the recognition of the legal account receivable occurs *after* the recognition of revenue.

A third possibility for the recognition of revenue is the *collection (or cash) basis*. Under this approach, revenue is recognized only when cash is actually collected, either in a single payment or in several payments (installments). This method is appropriate only under the special circumstance when, at the time of sale, collectibility is highly uncertain. Under simple cash-basis accounting, no recognition of accounts receivable ever occurs. The exchange of goods or services, and the resulting claim for payment remain unrecorded until payment occurs. Such accounting most frequently occurs in connection with the sale of services, where the complication of the timing of recognizing an inventory change is not present. Under installment-collection accounting, however, recognition of the receivable occurs at time of sale, with a corresponding credit to inventory and to deferred gross margin. Formal recognition of the sale is necessary so that the inventory decrease can also be recorded. As collections occur, appropriate amounts of revenue or income are recognized. More extensive discussion of installment receivables is presented in a subsequent section. Thus, under the collection basis, the recognition of accounts receivable may occur prior to the recognition of revenue, or may not occur at all.

Measurement of Receivables. Under most circumstances, the *amount* to be recognized is the exchange price between the parties to the transaction. Two factors may complicate the measurement of this exchange price: the availability of discounts, and the intervening length of time between sale and due date of payment.

The problem of discounts centers around those offered for prompt payment. Other types of discounts, such as trade discounts or quantity discounts, are commonly viewed as factors in the determination of the true selling price. Thus, revenues and receivables are recorded net of these amounts. Prompt-payment discounts (commonly called cash discounts), however, are subject to alternative interpretations.

One interpretation (the "gross price method") views the amount before discount as the true selling price, and therefore the amount of the receivable to be recognized. Any discounts subsequently earned by customers are treated as adjustments to gross sales revenue (or as other expense). Since the recognition of the discount occurs at time of payment, the receivable is unaffected. The only exception is at the end of the reporting period, when potential discounts may be considered in the valuation of outstanding accounts. This topic is discussed in the following section.

The alternative interpretation (the "net price method") views the amount net of discount as the correct measure of the selling price and thereby of the receivable. Additional amounts received from customers whose discount period has lapsed are treated as "other revenue," and are normally recorded when received. Again, at the end of the reporting period the valuation of the outstanding receivables may be adjusted to reflect the increase due to lapsed discounts.

The net price method would appear to have greater theoretical support. Revenues and receivables should be recorded at present value—the cash equivalent amount at the time the sale occurs. Certainly, in the case of sales subject to a cash discount, this amount is the net price. Any additional amount received is properly viewed as a financing charge—an amount earned for extending credit—rather than a payment for the goods or services transferred. Moreover, treatment under the net price method is consistent with the treatment of a sale where no cash discount is allowed but a specific interest charge is made for late payment.

A second issue in determining the amount to be recognized involves the intervening length of time between the creation of the receivable and the due date of payment. Ideally, interest should be recognized in determining the amount of the receivable to be recorded (its "present value"). If the terms of payment include specification of interest at a reasonable rate, then the face amount of the receivable should be recorded. If no provision for interest is included in the terms of payment, then the payments ideally should be discounted to a present value, which should be recorded. As a practical matter for trade accounts receivable, the question of interest is usually disregarded unless the due date is quite far removed from the date of sale—say, a year or more. The question of the recognition of interest arises more frequently in the context of notes receivable. Thus, this topic, and the associated Accounting Principles Board Opinion No. 21, will be discussed at length in the "Notes Receivable" section of this chapter.

Valuation.   After the original transaction has been recognized and recorded, the question of valuation of trade accounts receivable arises in connection with their presentation on a statement of financial position (balance sheet). Adjustments to the initially recorded amount may be appropriate to reflect accumulation of interest, or estimated allowances for future discounts, returns, and uncollectible accounts.

If the terms of sale specify interest charges when payment is not made by a given due date, any accumulation of interest should be recognized in arriving at the financial statement figures. Such interest may be considered as an increase in the trade accounts receivable balance or, if material, should be separately classified as interest receivable. Also, if the receivable had initially been recorded at a discounted present value, the accumulation of interest must be recognized in determining the balance at the financial statement date. This procedure will be discussed more fully in the section on "Notes Receivable."

End-of-period valuation for estimated cash discounts depends on the manner of original recording. Under the gross price method, discounts available to customers as of the reporting date may be recognized if the amount is material. An "allowance for outstanding discounts" is created to reduce the receivables balance to an expected realizable value basis (with a corresponding offset to sales revenue). Under the net price method, on the other hand, the receivables balance must be increased by the amount of any discounts which have lapsed. The principle of valuing receivables at expected realizable value also dictates that allowance be made for expected returns, price adjustments, or other allowances against the recorded amount due. An "allowance for expected returns and allowances" would be recognized, with a corresponding offset to sales revenue. Such "allowances" are contra-accounts to the receivable to which they relate.

The major problem in arriving at expected realizable value, however, lies in the determination of the allowance for uncollectible accounts (or "bad debts"). There are two general approaches to the treatment of uncollectible accounts—the "direct write-off" method and the "allowance" method.

The direct write-off method in effect ignores the need to reflect the possibility of uncollectibility in the valuation of accounts receivable. Under this approach, no recognition of uncollectibility occurs until a specific account is determined to be uncollectible, at which point that account is written off. Thus, accounts receivable would be presented at full face value on the balance sheet, and the income statement would reflect only the loss on accounts actually written off during the period. The direct write-off approach lacks sound theoretical support as a means of accounting for uncollectibles. It is likely to produce overvalued asset figures, by presenting the face value rather than the expected realizable value of accounts receivable. Also, this method is inconsistent with the accrual basis of income determination, in that the uncollectability adjustment is not matched with the period in which the revenues originated.

The preferable method of accounting for uncollectibles is the allowance method. Under this approach, an estimate of future uncollectibles is made each period, under one of several possible computational procedures. The estimate may be based on (1) a percentage of credit sales for the period, (2) a percentage of accounts receivable outstanding at the end of the period, (3) different percentages applied to each of several age categories of accounts receivable outstanding at the end of the period, or (4) probability-of-collection analysis of individual accounts or groups of accounts.

If the estimate is based on a percentage of credit sales, the figure being estimated is the provision for uncollectible accounts (the revenue contra, sometimes treated as an expense) for the period. The percentage to be used is normally based on the company's past loss experience. This implicitly assumes that economic conditions and the company's credit and collection policies have not changed over time. If this assumption is not valid, the percentages used may be modified on a subjective basis, although such modification may be difficult to justify to auditors or tax examiners.

If the estimate is based on outstanding accounts receivable (whether determined by percentages or specific analysis), the figure being estimated is the allowance for uncollectible accounts (balance sheet figure). Again, consideration must be given to the assumptions which underlie any relationships based on past experience.

While approaches based on sales and on outstanding accounts receivable are both widely used, the latter would seem to be theoretically preferable. The outstanding accounts approach is based on balances actually outstanding at year-end, and thus uses the latest available data. The percentage-of-sales approach, on the other hand, is based on sales for the entire period, with little if any regard for actual collections. Also, the outstanding accounts approach implicitly corrects past estimates in arriving at the expense for the current year; the percentage-of-sales approach, by focusing on the current-year charge, may permit past misestimates to remain uncorrected.

Disposition.   The normal disposition of trade accounts receivable is via *collection.* Accounts receivable are credited for the amount recorded as a receivable. This amount may differ from the amount received as a result of discounts taken, late charges, returns, and so forth. Such differences are charged or credited to appropriate accounts.

Disposition of accounts receivable balances may also be achieved by *write-off* of uncollectible accounts. If an allowance method is used, the charge is made against the allowance for uncollectible accounts. If a collection is made on an account which has been previously written off, the account should be reestablished in the amount of the collection (and possibly in the entire amount written off, if collection in full can now be expected). The entry to charge the customer's account and reflect the subsequent collection is made so as to show that the customer has attempted to reestablish credit-worthiness by the payment. When the customer's account is recharged, the credit is normally made to the allowance account. If recoveries are unusually large, a separate "other revenue" account (Bad Debts Recovered) may be used.

Finally, receivables may be disposed of by sale to third parties, commonly known as *factoring*. The accounting procedure is the same as in the case of collection, except that disclosure may be required for any contingent liability to the purchaser. This topic is discussed further in later sections.

Notes Receivable. Notes receivable may arise in the course of sales of goods and services to customers (trade notes receivable), or in the course of other transactions, such as loans (to employees, subsidiaries, etc.) or sales of fixed assets. They are evidenced by formal, written instruments, and typically have a longer maturity than accounts receivable.

Under the Uniform Commercial Code, "a negotiable promissory note is an unconditional promise in writing made by one person to another, signed by the maker, engaging to pay on demand, or at a particular time, a sum certain in money to order or to bearer."

Recognition. As in the case of trade accounts receivable, the recognition of notes receivable involves the issues of timing and measurement.

Trade notes receivable may arise directly from a sales transaction, or from the conversion of existing accounts receivable. Nontrade notes may arise from cash loans, nontrade sales, or settlements of indebtedness. In all cases, recognition occurs as of the date of execution of the note.

The amount to be recognized is subject to several factors, as specified by Accounting Principles Board Opinion No. 21. Depending upon the circumstances, a note may be recorded at its face value, or at the fair value of the goods or services exchanged, or at a discounted present value.

APB Opinion No. 21 is applicable in general to receivables which represent a contractual right to receive money on fixed or determinable dates, whether or not a stated provision for interest exists. While such receivables are loosely referred to as "notes," accounts receivable and other forms of receivables may also fall under the definition. The Opinion specifically excludes from its provisions the following six categories of receivables:

1. Receivables arising from transactions with customers in the normal course of business which are due in customary trade terms not exceeding approximately one year

2. Receivables which will not result in future cash collections, but rather will be applied to the purchase price of property, goods, or services (e.g., advance payments for materials)

3. Receivables intended to provide security for one party to an agreement (e.g., retainages on contracts, or security deposits)

4. Receivables arising from the cash lending activities of financial institutions whose primary business is lending money

5. Receivables arising from transactions where interest rates are affected by tax attributes or legal restrictions prescribed by a governmental agency (e.g., income tax settlements, or government-guaranteed obligations)

6. Receivables arising from transactions between parent and subsidiary companies, or between subsidiaries of a common parent

In these cases, the face amount of the note normally serves as the amount to be recognized. In other cases, the "present value" of the note should be used as the basis for recognition.

A note received solely in exchange for cash is presumed to have a present value (at time of issue) equal to the amount of cash exchanged. If, however, other "rights or privileges" are involved in the transaction, these must be recognized. In such a case, the effective rate of interest on the note, which would differ from the stated rate, would be used to determine the present value of the note. The difference between the present value so determined and the cash exchanged would be recorded as a premium or discount. For example, a professional athlete may negotiate a contract which includes a five-year interest-free loan. The present value of this loan should be determined by appropriate discounting, and the resulting premium (cash exchanged less present value) considered as part of the deferred compensation of the athlete over the term of the contract.

In the case of a note received in exchange for property, goods, or services, arising out of a bargained, arms-length transaction, it is generally presumed that the interest rate specified by the parties to the transaction represents fair and adequate compensation for the use of funds. The economic substance of the transaction, however, must be considered as well. Under APB Opinion No. 21, the presumption that the stated interest rate is satisfactory as a basis for recording the transaction should be rejected if (1) no interest rate is specified, (2) the stated interest rate is unreasonably high or low, (3) the face amount of the note is materially different from the market value of the note (at the date of the transaction), or (4) the face amount of the note is materially different from the current cash sales price of the property, goods, or services. In any of these circumstances, it is inappropriate to use the face amount of the note as its present value and hence as the basis for recording the transaction. Rather, the present value of the note should be viewed as either (1) the fair market value of the property, goods, or services exchanged for the note, or (2) the fair market value of the note, whichever is more determinable.

In the case of notes which do not specify a rate of interest, or which specify an unreasonable rate, it is possible that established exchange prices for the property, goods, or services, and also evidence of the note's market value, may both be lacking. In such a circumstance, the present value of the note is to be determined by discounting its future cash flow at an appropriate rate of interest. According to APB Opinion No. 21, in selecting a rate,[1]

> . . . the objective is to approximate the rate which would have resulted if an independent borrower and an independent lender had negotiated a similar transaction under comparable terms and conditions with the option to pay the cash price upon purchase or to give a note for the amount of the purchase which bears the prevailing rates of interest to maturity.

In summary, the amount to be recognized in recording a note receivable may be its face value, or its market value, or the fair value of the property, goods, or services exchanged, or the discounted value of its future cash flows. Whichever of these amounts represents the note's "present value," in light of the facts of the case and the rules of APB Opinion No. 21, serves as the basis for recording the note.

Valuation. Following the initial recognition, the main concern in ongoing valuation of the note centers around the amortization of any premium or discount. In any case where the present value of the note (the amount originally recorded) differs from the face value, a premium or discount is created, which must be amortized over the life of the note.

While straight-line amortization is acceptable, present-value amortization is generally suggested as preferable. Under the latter approach, the note continues to be valued at its present value. For example, assume a company receives a "noninterest-bearing" note with face value of $100,000 and maturity of five years. Assume further that, under the provisions of APB Opinion No. 21, the note is discounted to a present value using an interest rate of 10 percent. This yields a present value (and the amount initially recorded for the note) of $62,092. The resulting discount of $37,908 is to be recognized as interest revenue over the five-

---

[1]Accounting Principles Board Opinion No. 21, "Interest on Receivables and Payables," AICPA, New York, 1971, par. 13.

year period. Straight-line amortization would result in the recognition of $7,581.60 each year. Present-value amortization results in increasing amounts recognized each year, as the present value of the note increases. Each year, 10 percent of the beginning-of-year present value is recognized as revenue, as shown in Exhibit 1.

EXHIBIT 1   Amortization of "Noninterest-Bearing" Note with $100,000 Face Value over Five Years with Interest at 10 Percent

Transaction date	Amortization of discount (and interest revenue)	Note balance (present value)
End of year 0		$ 62,092
1	$ 6,209	68,301
2	6,830	75,131
3	7,513	82,644
4	8,264	90,908
5	9,092 (rounded)	100,000
	$37,908	

In cases where periodic interest payments exist, but the present value of the note differs from its face value (i.e., the discount rate differs from the nominal interest rate), a similar process is used to amortize any premium or discount. For example, suppose that the note in the above illustration bore interest at 3 percent per annum, but again 10 percent was considered an appropriate rate for the determination of present value. The present value of this note (see Tables 2 and 4 in the Appendix) would be as follows:

Face value times present value of $1 for
5 years at 10% ($100,000 × .62092) $62,092
Annual interest payment times present
value of annuity of $1 for 5 years at
10% ($3,000 × 3.79079)   11,372
Present value of note $73,464

The discount of $26,536 would be amortized as shown in Exhibit 2.

EXHIBIT 2   Amortization Schedule for Five-Year Note with Stated Interest at 3 Percent; Effective Interest Is 10 Percent

Transaction date	Interest earned	Interest collected	Amortization of discount	Note balance (present value)
End of year 0				$ 73,464
1	$ 7,346	$ 3,000	$ 4,346	77,810
2	7,781	3,000	4,781	82,591
3	8,259	3,000	5,259	87,850
4	8,785	3,000	5,785	93,635
5	9,365	3,000	6,365	100,000
	$41,536	$15,000	$26,536	

Other aspects of valuation discussed under trade accounts receivable are normally not applicable to notes receivable. For example, an allowance for uncollectibles is typically not determined unless a substantial number of trade notes exist.

Income Tax Aspects.   The requirements of APB Opinion No. 21 may create a timing difference between book income and taxable income, Section 483 of the Internal Revenue Code requires that interest be imputed in certain deferred-payment situations. The rules apply only to sales eligible for capital gain treatment, where the selling price is \$3,000 or more, and payments extend beyond one year. If the note fails to provide for interest of at least 4 percent per year (simple interest), then interest is to be imputed at a rate of 5 percent, compounded semiannually. APB Opinion No. 21, on the other hand, would require use of a rate reflecting borrowing–lending conditions, which would likely be well above 5 percent.

Thus, if the note provides a face interest rate that is less than an appropriate rate, interest for financial reporting purposes might be imputed at, say, 10 percent, while interest for tax purposes would be imputed at 5 percent. This would create timing differences in the recognition of the gain on the transaction and the periodic recognition of interest. The timing difference is a complex one, in that an initial lower book sales revenue or gain is offset by subsequent higher book interest revenue. Initially there would be a deferred tax debit which would be reduced at every interest-recognition date.

A timing difference may also be created if the face interest rate is greater than an appropriate rate. APB Opinion No. 21 would require that the appropriate rate be used, while tax law would require the face rate. Again, a timing difference involving gain and periodic interest would be created. For extensive illustration of the calculation of, and accounting for, deferred taxes under these conditions, see papers by Wharton[2] and Pacter.[3]

Disposition.   Disposition of a note may take the form of collection, write-off, or sale. Collection and write-off are accounted for in the same manner as accounts receivable. Any unamortized premium or discount should be taken into income in the year of disposition.

Sale of a note may occur with or without recourse in the event of nonpayment. A sale without recourse may be accounted for as a collection. The difference between the face value of the note and the proceeds from its sale is often debited to collection expense. A sale with recourse is sometime accounted for by leaving the Notes Receivable account unaffected, and crediting an offsetting account, "Notes Receivable Discounted." When settlement of the note has been completed, both the Notes Receivable and Notes Receivable Discounted balances would be eliminated. If the note is dishonored, the seller's entry for reimbursement of the buyer will eliminate the Notes Receivable Discounted account. The Notes Receivable balance remains. However, in view of the dishonoring of the note, the balance is often reclassified to Accounts Receivable, frequently with a notation that the amount is past due.

Installment Receivables.   An installment sale is characterized by periodic payments over a designated period of time. Such sales occur frequently in retail transactions, as well as in the sale of equipment and land. Typically, the transaction will involve a down payment, with the balance due in equal amounts.

Accounting for Installment Receivables.   In dealing with installment receivables, we may distinguish two methods of revenue recognition: the usual accrual basis, and the installment (i.e., cash collection) basis. Accounting Principles Board Opinion No. 10 states:[4]

> Chapter 1A of ARB No. 43, paragraph 1, states that "Profit is deemed to be realized when a sale in the ordinary course of business is effected, unless the circumstances are such that the collection of the sale price is not reasonably assured." The Board reaffirms

[2]Don Wharton, "Accounting for Interest on Receivables and Payables: Effects of APB Opinion 21," *The Arthur Young Journal,* Spring/Summer 1972, pp. 7–19.
[3]Paul A. Pacter, "A Synopsis of APB Opinion No. 21," *Journal of Accountancy,* vol. 133, no. 3, pp. 57–67, March 1972.
[4]Accounting Principles Board Opinion No. 10, "Omnibus Opinion—1966," AICPA, New York, 1966, par. 12.

this statement; it believes that revenues should ordinarily be accounted for at the time a transaction is completed, with appropriate provision for uncollectible accounts. Accordingly, it concludes that, in the absence of the circumstances referred to above, the installment method of recognizing revenue is not acceptable.

A footnote to this paragraph adds the following:[5]

> The Board recognizes that there are exceptional cases where receivables are collectible over an extended period of time and, because of the terms of the transactions or other conditions, there is no reasonable basis for estimating the degree of collectibility. When such circumstances exist, and as long as they exist, either the installment method or the cost recovery method of accounting may be used.

Thus, under most circumstances, revenue on installment sales will be recognized at the time of sale. The resulting receivables will be treated in the same manner as trade accounts receivable, described above. Installment receivables arising from sales in the normal course of operations are usually classified as current assets, on the ground that the collection period constitues an operating cycle. Installment receivables arising from nonoperating sales (such as the sale of a fixed asset) should be classified as current only to the extent of payments due within one year.

With respect to the treatment of interest charges, usual practice is to record the receivable at selling price, and recognize interest as earned. If the receivable is recorded at gross (selling price plus total finance charges), the unearned charges should be shown as a contra account, analogous to the discount on notes receivable.

Installment sales properly accountable for by the installment method of revenue recognition involve somewhat different accounting. The receivable is recorded at time of sale, inventory is reduced, and gross margin on the transaction is determined. The gross margin (gross profit) is initially recorded as a contra to the receivable or as a deferred credit ("Deferred Gross Profit"), and then is taken into income proportionately as cash is received. The receivable, however, is accounted for in similar fashion as in the case of accrual recognition described above. Further discussion may be found in Chapter 12.

Income Tax Aspects.   In spite of its general nonacceptability for accounting and financial reporting purposes, the installment method is acceptable for tax purposes. Firms regularly making installment sales may elect to recognize gross profit proportionately as cash is received for tax purposes. This same treatment is also made available, under certain conditions, on gains from the installment sale of fixed assets. Since the present value of tax payments is reduced by such an election, it is a sound management policy to elect the use of the installment method for tax purposes in almost all cases.

Use of the installment method for tax purposes and the accrual method for financial reporting purposes creates a timing difference, and thus requires the use of interperiod tax allocation.

Foreign Receivables.   Transactions with foreign customers present the additional problem of currency translation. Chapter 35 presents a comprehensive coverage of this topic. Thus, our coverage here is limited to a brief summary.

Sales to a foreign customer will specify payment either in domestic currency or foreign currency. If domestic currency is specified, the seller faces no different accounting and reporting problems than in the case of sales to domestic customers. If payment is to be in foreign currency, the seller must initially record the receivable by translating the foreign currency into dollars at the appropriate exchange rate. Both "free" and "official" exchange rates may exist; the one which is expected to be applicable to the settlement of the account should be used.

---

[5]*Ibid.,* par. 12, footnote 8.

The exchange rate may change between the time of recording the receivable and the time of collection. On accounts due in foreign currency, this means that a "currency exchange gain or loss" will occur, as the seller receives a greater or lesser amount of domestic currency upon settlement. Normally, the currency exchange gain or loss is recognized at time of collection. However, at the end of the reporting period, outstanding receivables balances (due in foreign currency) should be expressed in terms of the current exchange rate, thereby recognizing any gain or loss at that date.

The seller may hedge against exchange rate fluctuations by simultaneously entering into a currency futures contract. Suppose that on January 10, goods are sold to a foreign customer with payment due in foreign currency in 90 days. The seller could also sell a contract for the future delivery (in 90 days) of the amount of foreign currency involved. The seller would thereby receive the present (January 10) exchange rate (less transaction and interest costs). The seller, after receiving payment 90 days later, would deliver the foreign currency to satisfy the futures contract, and would be unaffected by any change which might have occurred in the exchange rate.

Further considerations involving foreign receivables, including dealings with foreign branches and subsidiaries, may be found in Chapter 35.

Lease Receivables. Brief mention may be given to the receivables arising under the lease transactions of a lessor. More extensive discussion of accounting for leases is found in Chapter 25.

Under the operating method, the lessor recognizes rental revenue as payments accrue. Thus, receivables are recorded only as payments accrue.

Under the financing method, the lease is considered to be in substance a sale. The sales price is measured as the discounted present value of the future lease payments; this is the net amount initially recorded as the receivable. Accounting Principles Board Opinion No. 7 suggests the title "Contracts Receivable for Equipment Rentals" for the receivables account. The receivable may be shown at net (the discounted present value) or, better, at gross rentals receivable, less unearned interest income. The receivable is then accounted for (and interest revenue recognized) by the effective interest (present-value) method, as described above for notes receivable.

Accounting Principles Board Opinion No. 27 specifies the conditions under which a lease made by a manufacturer of, or dealer in, the property leased, should be accounted for as a sale. When these conditions are met, the receivable is recorded at the present value of the lease payments, and accounted for in the same manner as the financing lease.

FINANCIAL REPORTING

Statement Presentation. Presentation of receivables on the statement of financial position is classified according to current and noncurrent categories (discussed below), and according to the major types of receivables which exist. Typical items which, if material in amount, would be separately disclosed on the face of the Statement are

Trade Accounts Receivable
Notes Receivable
Installment Notes and Accounts Receivable
Claims for Income Tax Refunds
Due from Officers and Employees

The specific terms used are likely to vary, as each firm should choose titles which are felt to be most descriptive of the particular types of receivables it holds.

Current versus Noncurrent. Reported receivables are classified as current if collection is reasonably expected within one year, or within the firm's normal operating cycle (if longer than one year).

Use of the normal operating cycle criterion is most common in the case of installment receivables. If a firm is engaged in a business where it is common practice to sell on an installment basis covering more than one year, classification of installment receivables as current assets would be appropriate. However, any significant amounts maturing beyond one year from the date of the statement should be disclosed. Such disclosure might take the following form:

> Installment Notes (including installments of
> $300,000 due after one year) $800,000

Receivables from unconsolidated affiliates may be classified as current if it is the practice of the affiliate to liquidate the accounts periodically, or if there is reasonable assurance that they can be liquidated at an early date. If these conditions are not met, and the receivables are in effect long-term or permanent advances, they should be classified as noncurrent. Receivables from consolidated subsidiaries are eliminated in consolidation.

Allowances. In reporting notes and accounts receivable, the allowance for uncollectible accounts must also be shown. Accounting Principles Board Opinion No. 12 requires that all valuation allowances for losses on receivables be deducted from the assets to which they relate, and be appropriately disclosed. Typical presentation takes the following form:

> Trade Notes and Accounts Receivable (less
> Allowance for Doubtful Accounts of $20,000) $370,000

In addition to the allowance for uncollectible accounts, other allowances reducing the reported valuation of receivables may exist. Accounting Principles Board Opinion No. 6 states that unearned discounts (other than cash or quantity discounts), finance charges, and interest included in the face amount of receivables should be deducted from the assets to which they relate. Presentation might be as follows:

> Installment Notes Receivable (less unearned
> finance charges of $100,000) $620,000

Similarly, Accounting Principles Board Opinion No. 21 requires that the discount (or premium) resulting from the determination of the present value of a receivable be reported as a deduction from (or addition to) to face amount of the receivable. Typical presentation would be (in the case of noncurrent receivables):

> Long-Term Receivables (less unamortized
> discount based on imputed interest rate of
> 9.5%, $1,740,000) $13,360,000

As suggested by the above illustrations, allowances for finance charges, unamortized discount, and the like are most prevalent in the case of longer-term receivables.

Financed Receivables. Various methods of financing may be used in conjunction with receivables, as discussed in a later section of this chapter. Presentation on the statement of financial position depends upon the nature of the financing.

Financing via receivables may be direct (the outright sale of receivables) or indirect (using receivables as security for a loan), with additional possibilities between these two extremes. If receivables are sold, they are eliminated as an asset, and any gain or loss on disposition is recognized. If receivables are merely pledged, they continue to be treated in the normal manner for accounting purposes, with the addition of disclosure of the pledging in financial statements.

When intermediate forms of financing are included, four alternatives for the reporting of financed receivables may be identified:[6]

1. If receivables are sold outright, or assumed without recourse, the buyer assumes the entire risk of collection. These receivables should be eliminated from the statement (since they have in essence been collected).

2. If receivables are sold with a guarantee of repurchase in the event of uncollectibility, the receivables again should be eliminated by virtue of collection. However, a contingent liability (to repurchase) remains, which must be disclosed in a footnote. A typical note would read:

> The Company is contingently liable on approximately $1,500,000 of long-term installment notes sold with recourse.

3. If receivables are assigned with recourse, statement presentation may show gross receivables, less a deduction for the amount assigned, as follows:

Notes Receivable	$450,000	
Less: Notes Receivable		
Discounted	300,000	$150,000

More often, footnote disclosure is used to indicate the existence and amount of the contingent liability.

4. If receivables are pledged as security for indebtedness, the statement should show this fact parenthically, with footnote disclosure of the amount pledged and the details of the indebtedness. For example:

> Receivables in the amount of $7,000,000 have been pledged in connection with the bank loan described in Note 5.

MANAGEMENT OF RECEIVABLES

Credit management is an important element of the overall financial and marketing management of the firm. The essential function of credit management is to trade off the increasing of credit sales against the decreasing of uncollectible account amounts. At one extreme, a company could minimize its uncollectibles by making credit sales only to the most credit-worthy firms, but in so doing, it would restrict the size of its potential market or incur large credit screening costs. At the other extreme, a company could maximize its sales by granting credit to all who request it. In following this course of action, the company would be likely to incur substantial collection costs and uncollectible amounts. An appropriate balance must be achieved between the costs of granting credit and the potential profits foregone by restricting sales.

Efficient credit management benefits the firm in several ways:[7]

> 1. Protection of corporate liquidity. Failure to collect most receivables when due can cause a rapid deterioration in a firm's cash position. Thus, the credit manager must grant credit and achieve collections so as to maintain a regular flow of cash into the firm, thereby minimizing the need for costly short-term financing.
>
> 2. Safeguarding the investment in receivables. According to government data, receivables average about eighteen percent of the total assets of manufacturing firms. The substantial investment becomes one of high risk, with significant potential for loss, if the receivables include many poor-quality accounts. Efficient credit management will reduce the riskiness of this investment by the initial selection of only good quality accounts, and the pursuit of aggressive collection procedures.

---

[6]Albert L. Schaps, "Balance Sheet Treatment of Financed Notes and Accounts Receivable," *The New York Certified Public Accountant,* vol. XXXVI, no. 10, pp. 773–774, October 1966.

[7]The Conference Board, *Managing Trade Receivables,* The Conference Board, Inc., New York, 1972, pp. 4–5.

EXHIBIT 3   Statement of Credit Policy

AMERICAN METAL CLIMAX, INC.

CREDIT POLICY

The Credit Department will have as its dual function the protection of the Company's investment in receivables and the promotion of profitable sales.

The Credit Department will have complete credit responsibility subject to review by Division managers. All accounts shall be classified as to risk and credit approvals will be based on product profitability as related to that risk. Customer's financial condition will be the primary basis for approval. Collateral security may be accepted in marginal cases, but shall not be the predominant basis for approval. Marginal credit risks will be sold as long as such sales are profitable. Within the foregoing context, credit approvals will be liberal.

Temporary terms extensions will be granted to customers in financial straits if such extensions are in the best interests of both companies. Extended selling terms may be established for temporary periods if justified by extraordinary circumstances and approved by both the Sales and Credit Departments. Permanent financing of customers through the medium of extended terms shall not be undertaken.

The Credit Department has all collection responsibility but in unusual circumstances Sales Department assistance may be sought. Collection follow-up will be both strict and uniform for all accounts in accordance will agreed terms.

At all times and in all circumstances, customer contacts will be firm and friendly so as to promote a wholesome respect for the Company and its people.

CREDIT POLICY DEFINITIONS

1. The Credit Department will have as its dual function the protection of the Company's investment in receivables and the promotion of profitable sales.

    Our aim is to spell out clearly the two-edged nature of the credit sword viz. protection and promotion.

2. The Credit Department will have complete credit responsibility subject to review by Division Managers.

    The credit function can best be performed by trained credit personnel subject, of course, to review by competent authority.

3. All accounts shall be classified as to risk and credit approvals will be based on product profitability as related to that risk.

    Risk classifications are prime, good, limited and marginal. The reference to profitability simply means that the greater the profit the greater the risk we can afford to take.

4. Customers' financial condition will be the primary basis for approval.

    If the customers' financial condition is so bad as to preclude open account dealings, credit shall not be extended despite security or guaranties received.

5. Collateral security may be accepted in marginal cases but shall not be the predominant basis for approval.

    Collateral security such as pledged inventory or mortgaged equipment should be accepted only as insurance.

6. Marginal credit risks will be sold as long as such sales are profitable.

    Profits earned on sales to marginal accounts should exceed bad debt losses suffered from sales to such accounts.

7. Within the foregoing context, credit approvals will be liberal.

    Minimal bad debt losses are *not* our aim. Maximum profit is our aim.

---

3. Profit enhancement. Efficient credit management contributes to the firm's profitability by achieving a balance between the costs of extending credit and the gains from expanding sales.

4. Sales assistance. The credit manager complements the efforts of the sales force by assisting in negotiating the financial arrangements of a sale, particularly in cases where special financing is required.

Management Policy.   Credit management involves decisions concerning the extension of credit to customers, protection of the investment in receivables, achievement of timely collections, and maintenance of records. To accomplish these tasks, management establishes credit policies. Such policies involve the duties and responsibilities of the credit manager, general guidelines as to credit terms, collection and write-off procedures, and so forth. Exhibit 3 presents an illustration of a formal statement of credit policy.[8]

[8]*Ibid.,* pp. 35–37.

EXHIBIT 3 *(Continued)*

8. Temporary terms extensions will be granted to customers in financial straits if such extensions are in the best interest of both companies.

   Some terms extensions benefit the seller but not the buyer. It is in our long term interest to make sure that whatever terms extensions we grant are of benefit to both companies.

9. Extended selling terms may be established for temporary periods if justified by extraordinary circumstances and approved by both the Sales and Credit Departments.

   While extended selling terms do not increase sales significantly, it may be necessary to grant such terms to meet competition. The Credit Department through its contact with other credit men, both directly and through credit groups, can determine accurately what terms competitors are giving.

10. Permanent financing of customers through the medium of extended terms shall not be undertaken.

    We are not in the banking business, nor should we take an equity position without the possibility of commensurate reward.

11. The Credit Department has all collection responsibility, but in unusual circumstances Sales Department assistance may be sought.

    Impersonal, consistently applied collection routines are most effective in the preponderance of collections. The credit organization can perform this function well and at the same time leave the salesman free for his primary duty—selling.

12. Collection followup will be both strict and uniform for all accounts in accordance with agreed terms.

    This is to balance our liberal credit approval policy.

13. At all times and in all circumstances, customer contacts will be firm and friendly so as to promote a wholesome respect for the company and its people.

    Sound business practice is widely respected and the Credit Department, through its many contacts with customers can do much to foster that respect.

Decision Analysis. Several components of credit policy are conducive to economic decision analysis, and thus fall within the broad area of management accounting. Numerous studies in this area have appeared in the literature of accounting and related fields. This section will survey some of the findings of this research.

Extending Credit. The decision to extend credit to customers involves consideration of the profit to be gained from the sale against the costs of granting credit (time value of money, collection costs, and risk of loss). Numerous models for this decision have been suggested. One, by Soldofsky,[9] requires that the profit from the sale exceed the sum of (1) the cost not recovered due to uncollectible accounts, (2) the cost of financing, and (3) credit costs (such as investigation, billing, and collection). When expressed quantitatively and simplified, the following model results. Sell if:

$$M - \left(b + Ti + \frac{C}{S}\right) \geqslant 0$$

where M = profit margin expressed as a fraction
 b = probability that a credit sale will become uncollectible
 T = average time that the accounts are outstanding before collection or write-off
 i = interest rate
 C = credit costs per order
 S = order size

It is further suggested that different risk categories be created for credit sales. Some of the above variables (namely b, T, C, and S) may take on different values in different risk classes.

To illustrate, suppose that a company's profit margin is 20 percent, and that a 12 percent interest rate is applicable. For simplicity, assume that no cash discounts are

---

[9] Robert M. Soldofsky, "A Model for Accounts Receivable Management," *Management Accounting,* vol. XLVII, no. 5, pp. 55–58, January 1966.

offered. Four risk classes of customers are established, and the following estimates made:

Risk class	b	T	C	S
1	1%	25/365	$15	$2,000
2	3	35/365	35	1,500
3	6	50/365	60	1,000
4	10	80/365	70	500

Calculating the relationship presented above, we have

Risk class	$M - (b + Ti + C/S) \geqslant 0$
1	$.20 - (.01 + .008 + .008) = +0.174$
2	$.20 - (.03 + .012 + .023) = +0.135$
3	$.20 - (.06 + .016 + .060) = +0.064$
4	$.20 - (.10 + .026 + .140) = -0.066$

The analysis suggests that sales should be made (i.e., credit extended) to risk classes 1, 2, and 3, but that credit should not be granted to customers in risk class 4.

In the decision to extend credit, the amount of potential loss due to uncollectible accounts is typically considered to be the cost of the product sold (often expressed as selling price less profit margin). One author has suggested that the amount should be related to the production-marketing situation faced by the firm.[10] If a strong "seller's market" exists, uncollectible accounts should be viewed in terms of selling price. In an average market, selling price less markup (an approximation of full cost) should be used, and in a strong "buyer's market", out-of-pocket cost should be used. These reflect opportunity costs to the firm. In the seller's market, the firm is producing at capacity, and an uncollectible sale comes at the expense of having made that sale to another customer. In a buyer's market, excess capacity exists, and an uncollectible sale costs only the out-of-pocket costs necessary to produce the product. The average market reflects the normal, long-run situation in which a firm must meet its full costs if it is to survive. Thus, refinements to the credit-granting analysis may be made by incorporating capacity and demand considerations.

Credit Terms. Decisions involving credit terms include the size of cash discounts, the length of the discount period, the length of the total payment period, interest charges on past-due accounts, return and adjustment policies, and special financing arrangements.

The size of cash discounts, for example, should be viewed in terms of the effect on sales and collections. By offering cash discounts, it is hoped that additional sales will be gained. In this context, a discount is essentially a reduction in selling price, and its potential effect may be analyzed in terms of the price elasticity of sales. Secondly, it is hoped that the availability of cash discounts will promote quicker collections. The cost of the discount should be related to the expected reduction in the time the accounts are outstanding. It is often pointed out that, from the buyer's viewpoint, foregoing a discount may be very expensive financing. For example, if payment terms are 2/10, *n*/30, failure to take the discount (and making payment on the 30th day) involves financing at an annual rate of more than 40 percent (see Chapter 8). The same analysis applies to the seller. If offering a 2 percent discount accelerates payment by 20 days, the seller is incurring that same 40+ percent annual rate. Moreover, one author has suggested that the high cost may encourage

---

[10]Charles C. Manger, "A Yardstick for Cost of Investment in Accounts Receivable," *Credit and Financial Management*, vol. 69, no. 6, pp. 24–26, June 1967.

purchasers who do not pay within the discount period to delay their payment well beyond the 30-day "net" period.[11] Thus, the typical cash discount formula, with its single, large increase in payment due, is likely to prove quite costly to both seller (if discounts are taken) and buyer (if discounts are not taken). Moreover, the increase in payment due following the discount period may encourage delay in payment, which is not the behavior the credit manager seeks.

In view of these difficulties with the usual cash discount system, an alternative system is sometimes adopted. Such a system would provide that the invoice price is payable by a specific time (say, 30 days). After that time, an interest charge is made on the past-due balance, in proportion to the length of time overdue. Such a system produces interest costs (to the buyer) and interest revenues (to the seller) that may better represent the cost of financing. Consideration should be given to the possibility that the payment behavior of customers will be affected by stating a price at gross with the possibility of discount compared to stating the price at net with penalty for late payment. Generally, firms selling to other firms adopt the former, while firms selling to individuals adopt the latter (e.g., utility companies, credit card companies).

Whether a discount system or an interest system is employed, consideration must be given to the length of the credit period. In analyzing this decision, it must be recognized that increasing the length of the credit period increases the cost of holding receivables. Funds tied up in receivables are unavailable for other investment uses, and incur an opportunity cost proportionate to the length of time the receivables are outstanding. One author suggests that this decision be analyzed in terms of a "credit-term elasticity," measuring the responsiveness of sales to extension of the credit period. Factors such as the buyer's liquidity position and short-term investment opportunities, and credit terms offered by other sellers, would determine the elasticity.[12] Thus, the behavior of the customer (in terms of likely effect on sales) must be analyzed, and compared to the cost of delaying collections.

Protecting the Investment. One of the important tasks of the credit manager is the protection of the company's investment in trade receivables. Trade receivables are typically unsecured, but in certain cases achieving a security interest in the items sold may be an important means of protection. In the past, security interests usually took the form of conditional sales contracts (retention by the seller of title to the goods, along with right of repossession upon default, until payment is completed) or chattel mortgages (transfer of title to goods to the creditor as security for the debt). With the adoption of the Uniform Commercial Code, these devices have been largely replaced by the financing statement. A financing statement is a legal document which, when filed, creates a public record of the main points of a security agreement executed between a buyer and a seller. Thus, in carrying out a secured commercial transaction, the parties agree in writing as to the terms of the sale, and provide a detailed description of the collateral. The seller, upon delivery of the goods, files a financing statement with the appropriate state authority, so as to obtain a legally recognized interest in the collateral. The use of financing statements provides an easy means for firms to sell on credit while maintaining a clear and virtually unassailable claim on the collateral (which is often the goods themselves) until payment is received.[13]

Another approach to the protection of the investment in trade receivables is

[11]Harlan R. Patterson, "New Life in the Management of Corporate Receivables," *Credit and Financial Management,* vol. 72, no. 2, pp. 15–18, February 1970.

[12]Louis K. Brandt, *Analysis for Financial Management,* Prentice-Hall, Englewood Cliffs, N.J., 1972, pp. 204–206.

[13]*Managing Trade Receivables,* p. 14.

through the purchase of commercial credit insurance. While the firm is expected to bear the normal risks of uncollectible amounts, commercial credit insurance serves to protect against large, abnormal losses, such as the bankruptcy of a major customer. Policy premiums depend upon the amount of coverage, the amount of the deductible provision, the credit ratings of the accounts, and the like. The firm must weigh the cost of the insurance against expected uncollectible amounts (and the effects of a major loss) in deciding which, if any, coverage to acquire.

In addition to protection against large credit losses, credit insurance also may provide an effective collection service, as insurers aid in obtaining payment of delinquent accounts, in the hope of minimizing losses, Finally, credit insurance reduces the risk of expanding sales volume by increasing credit lines available to customers.[14]

Commercial credit insurance applies to losses on business accounts. Thus, it would be acquired by firms such as manufacturers, wholesalers, advertising agencies, and the like, whose customers are other business firms or institutions. This protection is not available for consumer accounts. Only very limited protection from credit losses is available to firms whose customers are individual consumers. For example, credit life insurance protects against credit loss due to the death of the customer, but general loss protection is not generally available.

Analysis and Control.   Analysis is an important task in the ongoing management of trade receivables. Various measures and control procedures exist to assist management in cash planning (by analysis and control of collections), profit planning (by analysis and control of uncollectible account losses), sales planning (by analysis and control of credit granting), and so forth. In any of these areas, performance must be measured, compared with standards, and necessary actions taken where serious deviations from standard exist.

Collections.   Collection results are frequently analyzed in terms of ratios. These attempt to relate collections to sales activity and to the passage of time.

Practice varies as to the exact definition of the terms appearing in the following ratio. It seems most appropriate to define "Trade Receivables" as gross receivables, before deduction of allowances, and to define "Credit Sales" as gross credit sales less sales returns. Alternatively, both receivables and credit sales could be defined net of allowances for discounts, uncollectible accounts, etc.

Days sales outstanding is one such measure. This ratio indicates, as of a given date, the receivables balance in terms of the number of days' sales which it represents. The ratio is

$$\text{Days sales outstanding} = \frac{\text{Trade receivables balance}}{\text{Average daily credit sales}}$$

The resulting figure may be compared to the company's credit terms. If, for example, credit terms are 30 days, the determination of 53 days' sales outstanding would suggest that the company frequently fails to achieve collection within the 30-day period. In analyzing this result, care should be taken to verify that the "average daily credit sales" figure is representative of the period in which the receivables arose.

The *turnover of receivables* ratio is intended to measure the frequency with which receivables are collected. This measure covers a period of time, and thus relates sales to the average amount of receivables outstanding, The usual definition is

$$\text{Turnover} = \frac{\text{Credit sales}}{\text{Average trade receivables}}$$

[14]*Ibid.,* p. 15.

Since the interest is in the analysis of *collections,* and since collections may not parallel sales, it is sometimes suggested that the ratio be stated as

$$\text{Turnover} = \frac{\text{Collections}}{\text{Average trade receivables}}$$

The first form, however, seems to be more widely used.

The inverse of the turnover ratio, multiplied by 365 days, gives the average collection period:

$$\text{Average collection period} = \frac{\text{Average trade receivables}}{\text{Credit sales}} \times 365$$

This ratio presents the same information as the turnover ratio, but may express it in a more understandable way.

Firms offering discounts for prompt payment may wish to determine the frequency with which payment is received during the discount period. One possible measure is the *quality ratio,* defined as

$$\text{Quality ratio} = \frac{\text{Discounts taken}}{\text{Discounts available}}$$

This ratio is most appropriate when all sales offer the same rate of cash discount. When this condition is not met, an alternative measure must be designed.

Uncollectible Accounts.   A major tool in the analysis of potential uncollectibility of accounts is the aging schedule. This schedule presents outstanding accounts according to their date of origination, or according to "current" and various "past-due" categories. Both dollar amounts and percentages may be presented for each category.

This approach may be extended to consider also the age of accounts at time of collection.[15] Derivation of such a distribution makes the aging concept a useful tool in planning cash collections.

Operational Control of Receivables.   When the number of accounts receivable is large, a variety of problems typically emerge as the result of (1) the sheer volume of transactions, (2) the distribution of work loads, and (3) the requirements peculiar to computers and other equipment used for handling the high volume of data. Generally speaking, these problems are most typical of concerns which deal directly with individual consumers, such as utilities, large retailers, credit card companies, gasoline distribution companies, consumer finance companies, and banks. These organizations, as a result of the number and nature of their customers, customarily demand payment not upon presentation of an invoice, as is typical of industrial enterprises, but rather by presentation of a statement showing transactions over a period of time.

The control of large volumes of accounts concerns itself with four principal goals: first, that all sales are recorded; second, that those sales are recorded against the proper accounts; third, that proper statements are presented on a timely basis for each account; and fourth, that collections are credited to the proper accounts.

Symptoms of Control Problems.   System problems in the processing of high volumes of receivables will usually be indicated by certain key symptoms. Among these are (1) delays in preparation and mailing of statements, (2) large inventory shortages, (3) frequent customer complaints concerning incorrect billings, and (4) recurring difficulties in balancing detail to the general ledger.

As volume grows, the first symptoms will generally relate to the distribution of

[15] Haskel Benishay, "Managerial Controls of Accounts Receivable: A Deterministic Approach," *Journal of Accounting Research,* vol. 3, no. 1, pp. 114–132, Spring 1965.

work load. The record-keeping staff will operate at a leisurely pace for most of the month, but at month-end they will not be able to prepare statements in a timely manner without excessive overtime. Further, customers may complain that their statements are inaccurate because of the nonrecognition on the statements of payments made between the statement cutoff and the delivery of the statement.

Cycle Billing. The customary approach to minimizing this problem is the adoption of cycle billing. This is a method of maintaining and billing accounts receivable whereby the accounts are divided into groups, typically on a geographical or alphabetical basis, and each of these groups is billed once a month as of a specified cutoff date. The cycle billing dates are staggered throughout the month to spread the billing load as evenly as possible over all the working days of the period.

When utilized in a manual or machine-posted system, the sales media are sorted daily and filed in applicable customers' account files. Since generally only one cycle is billed on any one day, the customers' account files on any given day contain sales, collection, and adjustment documents supporting an average of a half-month's volume of receivables transactions. The existence of these loose, unproved media at the end of monthly accounting periods poses a major control problem in a cycle billing operation and represents the principal challenge to its success.

There are three distinct types of manual accounts receivable cycle billing control systems in common use. They are the one-control system, the cycle-control system, and the two-control system.

Under the one-control system, the end-of-month balance of accounts receivable is established by adding to the totals of cycles billed during the month a tabulation of the unposted media, which is arrived at through a physical inventory and valuation of the unposted media. The total of the cycles billed plus this physical inventory should agree with the general ledger balance of accounts receivable, which is the control account under this system.

When the cycle-control system is used, the receivables ledger is segregated by individual control accounts for each cycle, which are balanced in total to the general ledger account. The number of controls is often around 20 (one per working day per month) but it may range from just a few up to 100 or more. The objective of the cycle-control system is to establish controls over small segments of the accounts, which will provide for immediate comparisons with the results of the billing of the segments, facilitate the identification of any differences, and allow immediate action to be taken to correct differences. To accomplish this, the daily totals of sales, credits, cash, and other transactions must be broken down by cycles and made available for posting to the individual cycle control records, as well as for posting the totals to the master control account or to the general ledger. As of the cutoff date for a cycle, the totals of the various transactions and the balance of the cycle are determined. These should agree with the taped listing of the statements after their preparation.

The two-control system establishes controls on the totals of transactions in two areas, the billed and the unbilled portions. Again, each type of receivables media (sales, returns, cash, etc.) is sorted daily into its proper billing cycle. Control totals are also developed each day for the groups of cycles which will be billed before the end of the month and those which will not be billed until the following month. The two totals and the grand total are posted to the two detail controls and to the master control. At month-end, the billing trial balance controls for all cycles billed during the month are added to the balance in the unbilled detail control account, and the result should balance to the master control. At the end of the following month, the billed media that originated in the following month are subtracted from the total media actually billed during the later month to establish the amount of prior-month media included; this amount should agree with the balance in the unbilled control at the end of the prior month.

A variation of the two-control system, called the "post-list split of media," establishes the control after billing, using hindsight. Each day's media are date-stamped, but no further control is established until after the media are billed. When the billing of a cycle has been completed, the media are split by type and month of origin. At the end of the month, the sum of the media billed in the current month which originated in the prior month and the media billed in the prior month which originated in that month should agree with last month's total media. Under this system, therefore, a comparison of the control account balance with the general ledger balance for any given month can be made only after the end of the subsequent month.

The major problem under cycle billing is the handling and recording of transfers of amounts between different control accounts. These transfers may be necessary to correct an original misclassification of media either by type of account (regular, budget, installment) or by cycle (missorts). The problem only exists if separate control and general ledger accounts are maintained. Missorts may include errors discovered at the time of billing which affect an unbilled cycle, and errors discovered during billing which affect a cycle already billed.

Under the cycle-control system, all types of correction transfers must be recorded. Under the two-control system, only the adjustments between billed and unbilled controls need recording. No adjustments are necessary under the one-control system, or under the two-control system if a post-list split of media is used.

Account Numbering. As the number of accounts increases, a need for customer account numbers will become apparent. This need will be signaled by a growing frequency in misposted sales and receipts, particularly between individuals with similar names. The assignment of account numbers, by itself, is very simple. The low-order digits can be assigned in the sequence that appears within each ledger control. If desired, the initial assignments can be leapfrogged so that unassigned digits remain available for insertion of new accounts, with retention of both alphabetic and numeric sequence. With a very large volume or where the composition of the accounts turns over rapidly, this dual ordering becomes burdensome and impractical. Higher-order digits are customarily assigned to code the accounts by cycle date, type of account, credit classification, or location. Blocks of numbers may also be assigned for this purpose, but the coding approach is usually more practical if use of computers is contemplated. In any event, the size of the blocks of numbers used should leave very liberal provision for expansion because a reassignment of account numbers can be a very difficult problem. Social security numbers, uniquely assigned by the federal government, make ideal account numbers.

Charge Plates. While the assignment of account numbers is fairly easy, their use presents another major problem: the acquisition of the account number on the sale media. Wherever sales can be initiated at a variety of points and occur frequently, the solution has been the use of charge plates. This circumstance is found in retailing, oil companies, credit card organizations, and even in some large hospitals. The typical charge plate is embossed with the customer's name and account number so that the information may be mechanically inscribed directly on the sale-recording media. Sometimes the address is also shown, but most concerns have found that the frequency with which people move renders such plates obsolete too rapidly. An expiration date is normally shown on those cards that can be used over a wide geographic area, while more localized plates, such as those for department stores, may be valid indefinitely. Since the cards also serve as a credit authorization, most providers also place a limit on the size of a purchase that may be transacted without checking on the total account balance.

The use of account numbers almost always requires the use of charge plates, since the alternatives would allow customers to present wrong numbers and would allow clerks to make transcription errors.

Another variation of the charge plates is a system where a card is issued monthly with an amount shown as a credit limit. As purchases are made, the merchant records the sale on the card as long as unused credit remains. As payments are made, a new card is issued with the available credit indicated. This novel approach avoids having to check account balance and provides a more reliable control against customers exceeding their credit limits.

Automation. At various levels of large receivables volumes, the question of automation should be considered. The considerations are principally economic since manual systems can still be well controlled, given enough people, even though the accounts may number in the hundreds of thousands.

Most small organizations use bookkeeping machines to post their ledgers and subledgers. These machines will enter data in multiple column locations and can be set up to crossfoot appropriate columns. Most of the machines have some limited capability to accumulate control totals in one or more registers. However, the basic bookkeeping machine has no further computational ability.

Control of systems using this type of equipment is generally identical to that of fully manual systems. The design of the cycle billing system remains identical.

The transaction posting should be controlled by the use of "proof columns" which help to assure that the balance brought forward is accurately entered. The registers should be used to total the transactions and to tie the totals to control totals previously established.

Electronic accounting machines provide the next higher level of automation. This equipment is commonly known as "tab" or "punched-card" equipment. Input media must be converted into Hollerith punched cards, commonly referred to as IBM cards. These cards may then be processed by machines that sort, collate, calculate, punch updated cards, and print reports. Extremely high volumes may be handled at relatively low cost.

The conversion of manual media to punched cards provides the principal control problem in these systems. All card inputs must be first keypunched and then verified on a keystroke verifier machine. This duplication of keying operations may be somewhat expensive, but it is essential.

Because sorting is fast and easy with electronic equipment, manual sorts should be avoided, if possible, and all cycles can be posted daily. However, when the return of monthly sales media with statements is required, this capacity still does not eliminate the need for manual sorting. As a result, the electronic systems are more typical of organizations handling high volumes of commercial accounts on a numbered invoice system than of the open charge accounts found in retailing.

The electronic systems are well adapted to processing installment receivables. The accepted policy in these systems is to provide each customer with a book of payment tickets at the time of the loan or purchase. Each ticket may be pre-punched with the customer's account number and payment amount, thereby eliminating the necessity to keypunch. Provision must be made, however, to identify and record any payments made that are not for the prescribed amounts.

Semiautomated systems go a step beyond the posting machines. Equipment of this type is, in effect, an expanded posting machine which posts not only the normal printed characters on each ledger card, but also machine-readable magnetic characters. The magnetically inscribed cards can then be read by other machines which perform calculations, tabulate, sort, and prepare reports.

Another variety of semiautomated systems employs a desk-sized computer. Limited storage capabilities may exist within the machine, but most of the subledger records are maintained in machine-readable form in auxiliary storage devices. The machine can perform fairly complex calculations, prepare reports, and present logic situations for decisions by the operator.

Both varieties use magnetic cards discs, or drums which are machine-readable because they can erase data and inscribe new data, a major advantage over punched cards.

Nevertheless, the initial input data must still be provided manually, and the responsibility for logic and decisions still rests directly with the human equipment operator.

When the expanded versions of posting machines are used, controls are generally the same as with the basic machines since the visually readable ledger cards and control cards are still available.

These media may also be available, although in a slightly different form, with the desk-type computers. With the desk computers there may also be an additional capability that programs the permissible logic paths at specified decision points. Although the decision criteria are not programmed, the sequence of calculations and decisions can be controlled in this manner.

In fully automated systems, the decisions on the treatment of individual transactions are programmed into a computer and performed automatically thereafter. The design and control of such systems for handling receivables are generally the same as the techniques for design and control of other business applications and are therefore outside the scope of this discussion.

Where the account number must be manually transcribed from the sale media to machine-readable input, the generally accepted control is the use of self-checking digits as part of the account number.

A *self-checking digit* is a numeric digit that is a function of the other digits of the account number. One such formula multiplies the first digit by two, the second by one, the third by two, and so forth for each digit in the account number. Then the products obtained are added together and the last digit of this sum becomes the check digit. Other variations of this formula are used as well as completely different formulas.

This calculation can be performed rapidly when the transaction data is introduced into the computer or even, with the proper equipment, at the time it is entered on a key-punch machine.

Descriptive Billings.   Another practice that may become burdensome under high volume is the technique used to report to customers the nature of the purchases included in the current statement. The traditional approach has been to remit to the customer a copy of the sales record which was originally signed by the customer and usually included a description of the purchase. With high volumes, however, the sorting may be performed within a computer and the additional sorting and storage of these media until the statement is prepared may become cumbersome. Banks, with their use of magnetic characters on customer checks, have maintained the practice of returning high volumes of media to customers, but many department stores and credit card companies have turned instead to descriptive billings.

Problems may be encountered with the descriptive billing approach when the descriptions are too vague or misleading. Because such companies generally use computers, the inflexibility attendant to computer systems may further complicate the situation.

Revolving Charge Accounts.   The emergence of revolving charge accounts has further complicated the task of preparing statements. Revolving accounts are those accounts where full payment monthly is not required, but rather only a percentage of the outstanding balance. Unlike installment accounts, the revolving account may be used for small routine purchases as if it were a 30-day open account. The partial payments generally call for 10 to 25 percent of the outstanding balance, with a minimum payment of $10 to $25. Interest is usually charged on balances unpaid within 30 days at a rate of 1 to 2 percent per month.

Basically, the control of these accounts is not much different from that of regular 30-day accounts. However, because interest is usually charged only on the balance unpaid after 30 days, no accurate control can be calculated using the total revolving receivables balance in order to verify the sum of the interest charges on the detail accounts. One customer may pay in full 29 days after receiving his statement but another may pay after 31 days have elapsed. In the first case there is not a charge of 29/30s of a month's finance charge; there is no finance charge at all. On the other hand, the second case is charged for one month, but not for the one day over the month. Therefore, the effective interest yield on the balance in revolving receivables will always be a rate less than the equivalent annual rate that would be indicated if the monthly rate were multiplied by 12. Furthermore, it will fluctuate slightly from month to month according to the particular payment response in each month.

Because of the difficulty in predicting control totals on the interest charges and because considerable working capital may be needed to support this type of receivable, revolving accounts are generally found in larger organizations where the receivables function is automated to some degree. The automation provides greater reliability than does a small system in accurately analyzing the receivables and extending the finance charge on the appropriate balances,

Accounting Systems.   The importance of sales and collections to the success of the firm, and the large number of transactions frequently involved, require that effective accounting systems be maintained for receivables. The system should serve the following objectives:

1. All transactions must be recorded.
2. An account must be established for each customer.
3. Entries to customer accounts must be made promptly and accurately.
4. Periodic statements should be provided to the customer, and appropriate reports provided to management.

The specific details of an accounting system may vary from company to company, depending upon the nature and size of the business, the number of customers, the use of computerized processing, and other factors. Whatever the details, the system will typically include credit histories, customer account records, collection records, and provision for customer statements.

Maintaining Customer Accounts.   The process of transferring information from the sales invoice to the customer account may take various forms. The three major methods are posting via the sales journal, direct posting, and ledgerless bookkeeping.

In posting via the sales journal, invoices are individually posted, usually daily, to the sales journal. Customer accounts are then posted, usually daily, from the sales journal. At the end of the period, customer accounts are balanced to the sales journal and customer statements prepared. This double-posting processing approach is seldom used unless the volume of transactions is small.

Various mechanical devices can be used to streamline this basic posting approach. A device commonly used is the pegboard. Using carbon paper and a pegboard for aligning forms, one writing can be used to post both the sales journal and the customer account. Other mechanical filing and indexing devices can also aid in locating accounts for posting.

When direct posting is employed, invoices are batched, batch totals are computed, and totals are posted to the sales journal. Individual invoices are posted directly to customer accounts and postings are proved to batch totals.

There are a number of variations to this direct posting approach. One type of variation involves the method of posting. Accounts may be posted by hand or by one of the many mechanical or electronic bookkeeping machines. In addition to reducing clerical time, machine approaches improve accuracy, increase control, and produce more attractive statements.

Another variation to the direct-posting approach involves the frequency and size of invoice batching. At one extreme, invoices may be processed daily in small batches of 50 to 100. At the other extreme, invoices may be processed only once a month. Posting in small batches improves control by facilitating the location of posting errors. Posting in large batches improves processing efficiency by decreasing setup operations, such as locating and refiling the customer ledger card.

As the name implies, in a ledgerless bookkeeping system customer ledgers are not maintained. The detailed customer ledger is replaced by a file of unpaid customer invoices. The following processing steps illustrate the principles of ledgerless bookkeeping:

1. Serially numbered invoices are received in batches with control totals.
2. Batch totals are posted to accounts receivable control.
3. Individual invoices in each batch are filed alphabetically by customer name or numerically by customer account number.
4. Remittance advices are received in batches with control totals.
5. Invoices are pulled from the file when cash is to be applied. Fully paid invoices are stamped "paid" or partially paid invoices are stamped "partial payment." Partial payments are entered on the invoices and new balances computed. The "partial payment" invoices are duplicated.
6. Payments on both paid and partially paid invoices are balanced to batch totals. The batch remittance total is posted to accounts receivable control.
7. Paid invoices and copies of partially paid invoices are filed by batch.

With this procedure, the file of unpaid and partially paid invoices constitutes the detailed customer ledger at any time.

When ledgerless bookkeeping is used, a balance-only statement is often prepared at the end of the period.

Statement Formats.   A statement of account is a written record of the amount owed by or owing to a customer as of a specific date. Statements are prepared principally to remind customers that payment is due and to aid customers in their accounting. A third reason—customer and trade practices—reinforces the widespread use of statements.

The detailed information that supports the amount owed or owing shown in the statement varies by type of statement. Principal kinds of statements include unit (or running balance), balance-only, and open-item.

The unit (running balance) statement shows (1) the balance of the customer account at the beginning of the period, (2) charges during the period, (3) credits during the period, and (4) the balance at the end of the period. Each charge and credit transaction is posted separately. The balance after each transaction may not be, but often is, posted.

The unit statement is normally used by businesses selling direct to a final consumer. Typically, the final consumer pays on the basis of the statement, not individual invoices. He may, however, utilize partial payments frequently. Examples of businesses using unit statements are mail-order houses, public utilities, gasoline companies, and department stores.

Department stores use two variations of the unit statement. One variation, "country club" billing, lists balances, charges, and credits. Additional information in support of charges and credits on the statement is supplied by copies of sales tickets and credit memoranda sent with the statement. The second variation, "descriptive" billing, omits copies of sales media. Charges and credits are identified by referencing a department or merchandise classification.

The balance-only statement shows nothing but the balance of the customer account at the end of the period, usually a month, It reminds the customer of the amount owed, but provides the customer little, if any, accounting help. This simple statement format is not widely used.

An open-item statement shows the balance of the customer account at the end of the period supported by a listing of unpaid or open invoices. Open-item statements are usually used by companies selling to other businesses or institutions. Businesses using open-item statements include manufacturers, wholesalers, and jobbers. Typically, the customer pays on the basis of individual invoices where cash discounts are offered. In some cases, the vendor requires customer payment on a specific invoice basis. Partial payments must be infrequent for the open-invoice basis to be practicable.

Financing Receivables.   The management of receivables includes the important task of converting the receivables into cash. In addition to the usual process of collection, conversion to cash may also be accomplished by either of two financing arrangements. The firm may borrow, using its receivables as collateral (commonly called *discounting, accounts receivable financing,* or *commercial financing*), or it may sell its receivables to a third party (known as *factoring*).

Discounting.   Discounting usually signifies a financing arrangement whereby a lender advances funds to a borrower in the form of a loan secured by a pledge of the borrower's open accounts receivable.

Under this arrangement, the firm continues to perform its own credit and collection functions. Interest is charged by the lender on funds advanced, and repayment to the lender occurs when the firm's customers make payments on their account. Such payments are transferred, often in their original form, to the bank or finance company. Customers are normally not notified of the pledge of receivables under discounting arrangements, and so they make payment in normal fashion to the firm. In cases of nonpayment by the customer, the borrowing firm must repay the lender from its other funds (or "replace" the accounts with other previously unpledged accounts).

Accounts receivable financing is typically a continuing arrangement, rather than a one-time transaction. A financing agreement exists between the borrower and lender, perhaps covering a year, or perhaps covering an unspecified time period. The agreement might provide for the assignment of all accounts receivable (perhaps limited to certain categories) as security, in return for which the lender agrees to advance funds up to a specified percentage (e.g., 80 percent) of the accounts pledged. As mentioned above, repayment occurs by transfer of customer remittances to the lender. Upon collection of individual accounts, the lender potentially receives a greater amount than the funds he advanced to the borrower. Some of this difference is consumed by returns, allowances, and discounts on other accounts; additional amounts are consumed by the interest charges on funds advanced. Any remaining difference (known as equity) is either credited against the borrower's account, or returned to the borrower.

The term *discounting* is also used to signify the sale of receivables, with recourse for noncollection from customers. Although the technical details change, the effect of sale with recourse is essentially the same as the secured borrowing described above. The firm retains the risk of loss from nonpayment by its customers, and retains all other credit and collection functions. Discounting (in the sense of sale with recourse) is more frequently encountered with notes receivable than accounts receivable. The following discussion of discounted receivables, while expressed in terms of notes, is equally applicable to accounts receivable.

Although the note is sold by the firm to a third party, the firm remains contingently liable under the recourse agreement. Thus, the accounting treatment of the discounted note must reflect this contingent liability. One alternative is by footnote disclosure. The note receivable is removed from the books when discounted, and disclosure is made in the financial statements of the amount for which the firm is contingently liable should default occur. A second alternative is by use of a contra account ("Notes Receivable Discounted"). Upon sale with recourse, the note receivable remains on the books, and the contra account is credited. Both are presented on the financial statement, indicating that while at present no net asset exists, upon default, the company could reacquire the receivable and acquire an equal liability.

Factoring. Factoring signifies a financing arrangement whereby a third party (a "factor") purchases receivables without recourse for nonpayment. Normally, the customer is notified of the transfer of ownership of the receivable, and the factor assumes all credit and collection functions. In exchange for a commission fee (a small percentage of the face value of the factored accounts), the factor assumes the risk of uncollectible account losses. The selling firm receives the amount of the receivables (less the commission fee) on the account's maturity date (or on the "average due date," where many accounts are involved). If desired, the firm may receive earlier payment, for which an interest charge is made.

Occasionally, factoring is done on a non-notification basis. The selling firm retains the collection function, and its customers are unaware of the transfer of ownership of the receivable. As before, the factor purchases the receivables without recourse, and thus assumes all the risk of uncollectible account losses.

Since factoring involves no contingent liability for nonpayment, the accounting treatments discussed for discounting do not apply. Accounts receivable have been unequivocally liquidated, and converted either into cash or a receivable from the factor. Neither special disclosure nor a contingent liability account is required.

BIBLIOGRAPHY

Benishay, Haskel: "Managerial Controls of Accounts Receivable: A Deterministic Approach," *Journal of Accounting Research,* Spring 1965, pp. 114–132.

Carrithers, Wallace M., and Ernest H, Weinwurm: *Basic Information and Accounting Systems,* Charles E. Merrill, Columbus, Ohio, 1967.

The Conference Board: *Managing Trade Receivables,* The Conference Board, New York, 1972.

Meigs, Walter B., A. N. Mosich, Charles E. Johnson, and Thomas F. Keller: *Intermediate Accounting,* 3rd ed., McGraw-Hill Book Company, New York, 1974.

Pacter, Paul A: "A Synposis of APB Opinion No. 21," *Journal of Accountancy,* March 1972, pp. 57–67.

Randall, Clarence B., and Sally Weimer Burgly: *Systems and Procedures for Business Data Processing,* 2nd ed., South-Western Publishing Company, Cincinnati, Ohio, 1968.

Wharton, Don: "Accounting for Interest on Receivables and Payables: Effects of APB Opinion No. 21," *The Arthur Young Journal,* Spring/Summer 1972, pp. 7–19.

Chapter **16**

Inventories

RAYMOND A. HOFFMAN

JOSEPH D. COUGHLAN
Partners, Price Waterhouse & Co.

The subject of inventories is significant from at least three distinct viewpoints: the physical existence of assets owned, the value of the assets as determined for a particular purpose, and the value as a factor in stating the results (net income or loss) from operating a business during a particular period.

PHYSICAL EXISTENCE OF INVENTORIES

When inventories are viewed as the quantity of goods needed to operate a business efficiently, consideration must be given not only to the expenses and losses incident to owning and caring for the goods, but also to such factors as sales forecasting, production scheduling, optimum purchasing, and the effects of carrying excessive (or inadequate) quantities.

The expenses and losses incident to owning and caring for inventories include:

Earnings from alternative investments of the working capital applied (commonly computed at current interest rates or at the average earning rate of the company)

Personal property taxes

Insurance premiums

Storage expense, which may represent additional rental payments or an allocated portion of maintaining a warehouse or storeroom

Employee compensation payments which are increased because of the handling of excess goods and reduction in efficiency caused by the inconvenience of "working around" the extra bulk

Losses due to deterioration and obsolescence, which are continuing risks inherent in ownership of goods and which tend to be higher with respect to finished goods than to raw materials

Where the excess inventory quantities are a result of a purchasing decision motivated by an anticipated rise in prices, the expenses and losses incident to owning and caring for the goods must be offset against the expected saving from the advance purchases.

Management decisions which take into account such factors as sales forecasting, production scheduling, optimum purchasing, and the effects of carrying excessive (or inadequate) quantities are commonly referred to as an "inventory management system." Any inventory management system seeks to minimize the expenses associated with the maintenance of the goods, and it must recognize the interaction of inventory decisions with other functions in the company. As indicated by the following examples, the management decisions which must be considered involve all facets of the business.

The Marketing Department will normally establish sales forecasts by product or product line and the level of service which will enable the company to maintain its competitive position.

The Operating Department will normally establish the overall production rate in the light of the sales forecast, the plant capacity, and the manpower available, as well as deciding what is to be produced and when and what machines, material, and manpower will be used.

The Financial Department will normally determine whether the working capital can be made available for the carrying out of the plans recommended by those concerned primarily with sales and production.

In larger companies several individuals may be involved in each phase of the operation, whereas in a smaller company the same individual may perform more than one function.

The expenses and losses incident to owning and caring for inventories tend to increase directly with the level of the inventory, whereas the measure of other factors tends to vary inversely with the quantity of goods on hand. Examples of factors which tend to favor higher inventory levels include the following:

Larger inventories of finished goods can be expected to reduce the number of instances when orders cannot be filled promptly, which frequently results in lost sales.

Larger inventories of parts and raw materials can be expected to reduce the number of instances when production must be delayed, which results in operating inefficiencies.

Larger inventories permit increasing the quantities covered by purchase orders and production runs, which results in savings through quantity discounts and lower per-unit expense for machine setups, etc.

These factors are more difficult to measure than those which vary directly with the level of inventory, but they nevertheless are a significant portion of the aggregate of the expenses and losses which are sought to be minimized as the objective of an inventory management system. This objective of an inventory management system is portrayed graphically in Exhibit 1.

EXHIBIT 1   Objective of Inventory Management System

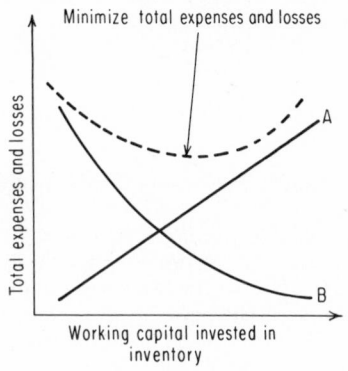

A   Factors which vary directly with level of inventory:

Possible earnings from alternative investments
Personal property taxes
Insurance premiums
Storage expense
Added employee payments
Deterioration and obsolescence

B   Factors which vary inversely with level of inventory:

Lost sales
Production delays
Inefficiency of small purchase orders and short production runs

Classification of Inventory Items to Determine Appropriate Control Measures. Exhibit 2 depicts the commonly accepted *ABC* concept of the classification of goods included in an inventory for the purpose of establishing the appropriate inventory control procedure.

The distribution of annual dollar usage is established by listing the various items in descending order. In a typical manufacturing inventory, it is found that approximately 70 percent of the items carried account for only 5 percent of the annual dollar usage. These items are referred to as the *C* items. Another 15 percent of the items may account for 15 percent of the annual dollar usage; they may be referred to as *B* items. The remaining 15 percent of the items would account for 80 percent of the annual dollar usage and would be referred to as *A* items.

It is necessary to vary the type of control procedures according to the particular characteristics of the items included in the inventory. No single method of inventory control would be appropriate for all items.

Items classified as *A* will justify maximum control measures, such as perpetual inventory records, product identification, and precisely determined reorder quan-

EXHIBIT 2   Typical Distribution of Inventory—Manufacturing Company

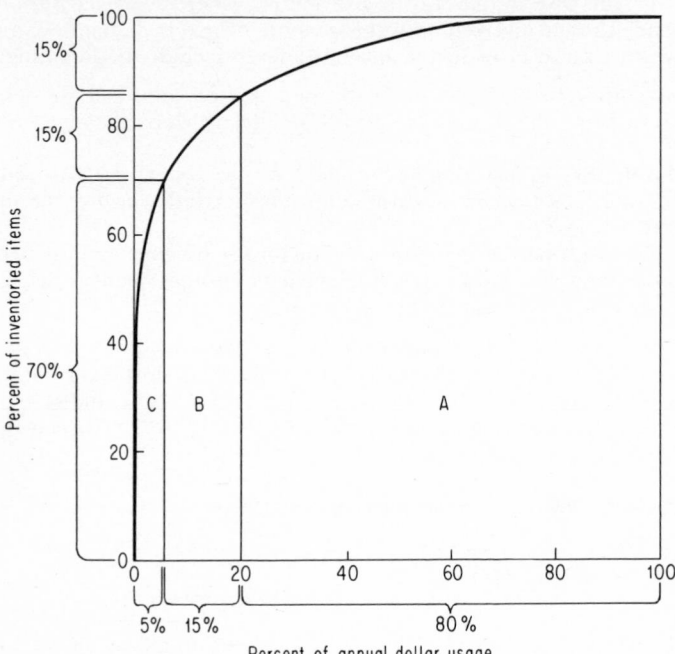

tities. In many cases, the economic order quantity will be established by applying an adaptation of the classical EOQ formula.

The control techniques for the B items will be less sophisticated than for the A items. The updating of perpetual inventory records, if maintained for the B items, may not be as frequent; e.g., such updating may be on a weekly basis whereas the records for the A items may be maintained on a daily basis.

The primary objective in the control of C items may be to minimize the expense involved in maintaining the control. Some minimum procedures for these items

EXHIBIT 3   Economic Order Quantity

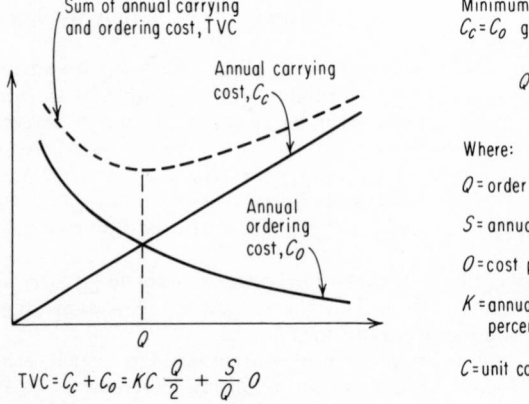

Sum of annual carrying and ordering cost, TVC

Annual carrying cost, C_c

Annual ordering cost, C_o

$$TVC = C_c + C_o = KC\,\frac{Q}{2} + \frac{S}{Q}\,O$$

Minimum TVC occurs where $C_c = C_o$ giving:

$$Q = \sqrt{\frac{2\,SO}{KC}}$$

Where:

Q = order quantity in units

S = annual demand in units

O = cost per order in dollars

K = annual carrying cost as a percentage

C = unit cost in dollars

are, however, essential for any inventory control system. Safety stocks for C items can be relatively high, and in many cases a "2-bin" system can be used to eliminate the necessity of maintaining a perpetual inventory record. Items are used out of one of the bins, and the reorder point is identified when the storeroom must go to the reserve stock in the alternate bin to fill an order. When a new shipment is received in the stock room, the reserve stock bin is filled with a quantity equal to the reorder point, and the excess is placed in the primary storage bin.

Formula for Establishing Economic Order Quantity. The principal factors taken into account in establishing the EOQ for a particular item are reflected in Exhibit 3. The minimum point on the total variable cost curve, TVC, is where the two solid lines intersect or where the annual carrying cost equals the annual ordering cost.

In any particular instance, the basic formula for establishing the economic order quantity must be expanded and modified. For example, Exhibit 4 illustrates a situation in which the material costs vary according to the quantity ordered. In this example, it is assumed that (1) the annual usage is 1,000 units; (2) the ordering cost is $10 per order; and (3) the inventory carrying expenses amount to 15 percent per annum of the working capital tied up in inventory. It is further assumed that for an order under 200 units the cost is $6; this becomes lower as larger quantities are ordered; e.g., the per-unit cost is $5.50 if the order is for between 200 and 500 units.

EXHIBIT 4   Economic Order Quantity Modified

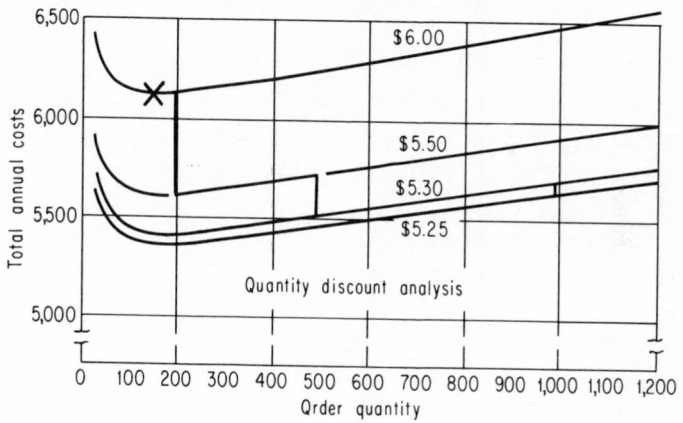

	EOQ	First price break	Second price break	Third price break
Order quantity	150	200	500	1,000
Unit price	$6.00	$5.50	$5.30	$5.25
Annual costs				
Material	$6,000	$5,500	$5,300	$5,250
Ordering	67	50	20	10
Inventory carrying	67	83	199	394
Total........	$6,134	$5,633	$5,519	$5,654
Annual savings	--	$501	$615	$480

Annual usage_____1,000 units
Ordering costs_____$10 per order
Inventory carrying cost_____15%

Exhibit 4 reflects the aggregate annual cost and expense curves for the four unit prices examined. The perpendicular lines on the upper portion of the exhibit show how the analyst moves from one curve to the next at points where a new discount takes effect, such as 200, 500, and 1,000 units. It will be noted that both the per-unit purchase cost and the per-unit expense decrease as order quantities increase, but that the expense of carrying the inventory increases with the order quantity. The annual savings at the three price breaks relative to the economic order quantity levels are $501, $615, and $480, which means that the indicated optimum order quantity is 500 units.

Timing of Orders. After establishing the optimum quantity of goods to be covered by an order, it is essential to determine when orders should be placed. Exhibit 5 reflects the relationship between stock levels, reorder points, order quantities, lead times, and safety stocks. The reorder point R is defined as (1) the

EXHIBIT 5   General Inventory Decisions

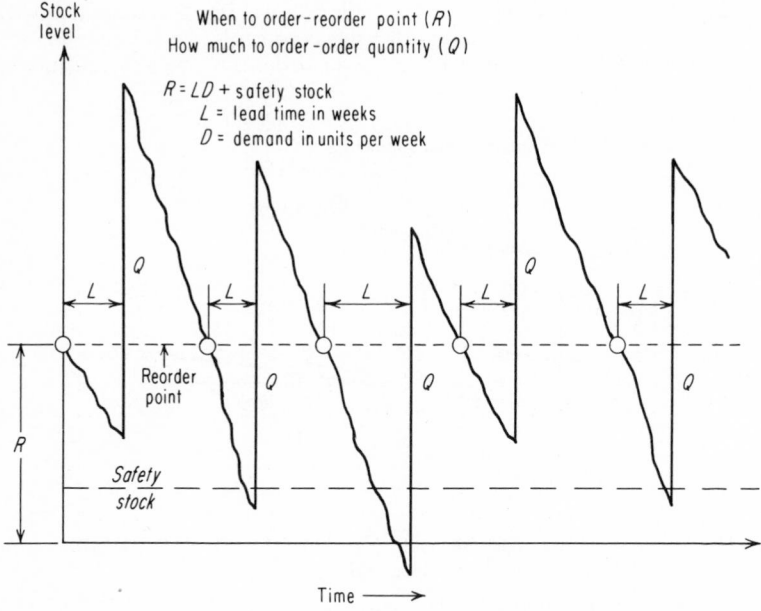

lead time (replenishment time) in days multiplied by the demand per day plus (2) the safety stock. When the stock level reaches the reorder point, action is initiated to issue an order. The lead time L is the elapsed time from the moment the stock level reaches the reorder point until the new order is received. If both the lead time and demand per day were constant, the stock level would reach the safety stock level just as the new order is received. However, both lead times and demand rates represent averages with statistical variations about these averages. If total demand during a lead time period is greater than the average, the stock level will be below that of the total safety stock. The second cycle on the graph shows a case where the demand rate increased above the average and resulted in the stock level being in the safety stock before the new order arrived. The third cycle reflects a stockout situation which came about as a result of an extended lead time.

The size of the safety stock is based on two factors: (1) the likely variability in total demand from the forecast demand during the lead time period, and (2) the acceptable rate of stockouts. If management wants to reduce the number of stockouts, the safety stock must be increased or the variability from forecasted lead time demand must be controlled through improved forecasting of demand and by reducing the number of past-due production or purchase orders.

VALUATION OF INVENTORIES

In accounting literature, the term "valuation" is the one most commonly used in any discussion of inventories. In the majority of instances, however, the amount assigned to a particular inventory for accounting purposes is fundamentally a reflection of cost rather than a determination of value.

There are times when the value of an inventory is of primary significance. For example, where there is to be a forced bulk sale when liquidation of a business is contemplated, the value is the only significant figure. This value will be the amount that a purchaser will pay for all the goods on hand. Value is also significant when a sale of a continuing business is contemplated. For this purpose, the value of the inventory is normally the aggregate of the replacement cost for the individual items on hand which will be useful to the purchaser plus the scrap value of excess quantities and obsolete items.

It may also be necessary to establish the value of an inventory when considering appropriate insurance coverage, the extent to which the inventory will be recognized as collateral for a loan, or the amount upon which property tax assessments are based. In these situations, the amount assigned to the inventory in the course of normal accounting procedures may or may not be the answer. For example, in determining the appropriate base for a property tax, primary consideration must be given to the statutory requirements, local practices, and possibly the equalization factors which are part of the assessor's procedures.

Except for additions and revisions necessitated by recognition of the last-in, first-out (LIFO) method, there have been no substantive changes in the sections pertaining to inventories in the Internal Revenue Code for several decades. The only significant change in the regulations is discussed below under "Tax and Other Influences on Overhead Absorption."

The Internal Revenue Code contains the general requirement that, "Whenever in the opinion of the Secretary or his delegate the use of inventories is necessary in order clearly to determine the income of any taxpayer, inventories shall be taken by such taxpayer. . . ." This section of the law concludes with the requirement that the inventories be taken on the basis which is prescribed by regulations "as conforming as nearly as may be to the best accounting practice in the trade or business and as most clearly reflecting income." The regulations reflect this statutory provision by the conclusions that (1) inventory rules cannot be uniform and (2) an inventory that can be used under the best accounting practice in a balance sheet showing the financial position of the taxpayer can, as a general rule, be regarded as clearly reflecting income.

The federal income tax regulations include only a few general paragraphs to state the meaning of the term "cost." In the case of merchandise on hand at the beginning of the year, cost means the balance sheet valuation of the inventory at the end of the previous year. In the case of merchandise purchased since the beginning of the taxable year, cost means the invoice price less trade or other discounts (except strictly cash discounts approximating a fair interest rate, which may be deducted or not at the option of the taxpayer, provided a consistent course is followed) *plus* transportation or other necessary charges incurred in acquiring possession of the goods. In the case of merchandise produced by the taxpayer since the beginning of the year, the general rule is that cost means the aggregate of[1]

> (1) the cost of raw materials and supplies entering into or consumed in connection with the product, (2) expenditures for direct labor, (3) indirect expenses incident to and necessary for the production of the particular article, including in such indirect expenses a reasonable proportion of management expenses, but not including any cost of selling or return on capital, whether by way of interest or profit.

Use of general language in the income tax regulations is a recognition of the fact that there is no single concept of cost which is appropriate in all businesses.

The Lower of Cost or Market. From the standpoint of modern accounting practice, the concept of value is primarily involved in the principle of stating inventories at the "lower of cost or market." The general rule is that there should be a departure from the cost basis of stating an inventory when the utility of the goods is no longer as great as its cost. The premise is that whether the difference between the cost and the expected utility of the goods is due to physical deterioration, obsolescence, changes in price levels, or other causes, the difference should be recognized as a loss of the period in which the determination of expected utility is made.

As used in the phrase "lower of cost or market," the term "market" means current replacement cost (by purchase or by reproduction, as the case may be) subject to the limitations that (1) market should not exceed the net realizable value, i.e., selling price in the ordinary course of business less reasonably predictable cost of completion and disposal; and (2) market should not be less than the net realizable value reduced by an allowance for an approximately normal profit margin. In the statement on "Inventory Pricing" by the Committee on Accounting Procedures of the American Institute of Certified Public Accountants,[2] this general rule is expanded upon with the following discussion:

> The rule of *cost or market, whichever is lower* is intended to provide a means of measuring the residual usefulness of an inventory expenditure. The term *market* is therefore to be interpreted as indicating utility on the inventory date and may be thought of in terms of the equivalent expenditure which would have to be made in the ordinary course at that date to procure corresponding utility. As a general guide, utility is indicated primarily by the current cost of replacement of the goods as they would be obtained by purchase or reproduction. In applying the rule, however, judgment must always be exercised and no loss should be recognized unless the evidence indicates clearly that a loss has been sustained. There are therefore exceptions to such a standard. Replacement or reproduction prices would not be appropriate as a measure of utility when the estimated sales values, reduced by the costs of completion and disposal, is lower, in which case the realizable value so determined more appropriately measures utility. Furthermore, where the evidence indicates the cost will be recovered with an approximately normal profit upon sale in the ordinary course of business, no loss should be recognized even though replacement or reproduction costs are lower. This might be true, for example, in the case of production under firm sales contracts at fixed prices, or when a reasonable volume of future orders is assured at stable selling prices.

In somewhat similar statements (or proposed statements), national organizations of chartered accountants in the United Kingdom, Canada, and South Africa have all recommended that the term "market value" be discontinued and "net realizable value" be used. These institutes also do not favor the use of "replacement cost" of individual components or the allowance of a normal profit margin (assuring profit in the subsequent period) in determining "net realizable value."

In many instances, the lower-of-cost-or-market rule for stating inventories will

---

[1]Reg. §1.471-3(c).
[2]*Accounting Research Bulletin No. 43*, chap. 4, par. 9.

be applied, as a practical rather than a theoretical matter, in accordance with the federal income tax regulations. The general rule in the regulations is that, under ordinary circumstances and for normal goods in an inventory, cost is to be compared with replacement cost. The regulations also provide, whether cost or the lower-of-cost-or-market inventory method is used, the amount assigned to goods which are "unsalable at normal prices or unusable in the normal way because of damage, imperfections, shop wear, changes of style, odd or broken lots, or other similar causes, including second-hand goods taken in exchange" should not exceed net realizable value.

In applying the rule of lower of cost or market, the scrap value of the items included in the inventory constitutes a *minimum* amount.

The federal income tax regulations state that where an inventory is valued upon the basis of cost or market, whichever is lower, the market value of each article on hand at the inventory date shall be compared with the cost of the article, and the lower shall be taken as the inventory amount for the article. This may be appropriate in those rare cases where specific identification of individual units of inventory is maintained for costing purposes. When one of the more common cost flow assumptions such as first-in, first-out (FIFO) or LIFO is used, there are many instances in practice where the absolute statement in the regulations is not complied with. There is accounting authority for a broader view of the basis for making comparisons between cost and market.

The purpose of reducing inventory to market is to reflect fairly the income of the accounting period. Although probably the most common practice is to compare cost with market separately for each item in an inventory, there are a number of situations in which the comparison of the aggregate cost with the aggregate value is more significant.

Where a single category of end product is being produced, the reduction of the cost of individual items to market value would ordinarily not be justified if the value to the business of the total inventory is in excess of the aggregate cost. This would be particularly true in a case where selling prices are not affected by temporary or relatively small fluctuations in current costs.

When no loss of income is expected to take place as a result of a reduction in cost prices of certain goods because others forming components of the same general category of finished products have a market equally in excess of cost, it is generally held that the components need not be adjusted to market if they are included in the inventory in balanced quantities. If the stock on hand of particular inventory items is excessive in relation to others, clear reflection of income will normally require the direct comparison of cost and value for the excess quantities.

If an item is included in inventory which had been written down to market for purposes of the preceding year's inventory, the comparison should be between the opening inventory value and market at the end of the year. Normally, income should be recognized only from the *disposition* of goods.

In Some Businesses Value May Be an Appropriate Basis for Stating Inventories. Mining companies may inventory gold and silver at current value when there is an effective, viable market. The general rule of modern financial accounting that inventories should not be stated at amounts in excess of cost reflects a practical realization of the uncertainties inherent in doing business in a free competitive economy. Where metals have a fixed monetary value and the sale of the quantities on hand at the end of any particular period at such fixed amounts is practically mechanical, it is appropriate to base the inventory on such value. Any expenditures which will be incurred in the disposition of the inventory should, of course, be taken into account so that the inventory is not stated at an amount in excess of net realizable value. The exception to the general rule sometimes made by mining companies is also justified, at least in part, by the difficulty in establishing the cost for the particular goods in the inventory. The metals may have been extracted from several mines which have been operated over a long period of time with numerous shutdowns. In this situation, the determination of the provision for depreciation which should be appropriately allocated to any particular production may be subject to a wide range of difference in opinion, to say nothing of the difficulty of establishing the appropriate amount of the provision for depletion.

Agriculture is another industry in which value may be an appropriate basis for stating inventories. As a practical matter, many farmers do not maintain adequate records to establish clearly appropriate costs for the products which may be on hand at the end of a year. For federal income tax purposes, this fact is recognized in the permission granted to farmers to report income on a cash receipts and disbursements basis. Where the farm accounting is placed on an accrual basis for financial reporting, since the units are interchangeable and the immediate marketability at established prices is recognized in the normal course of business, value may be accepted as an appropriate basis for stating inventories without the necessity of establishing costs. The "farm-price method" of stating inventories thus provides for a valuation at market price less the estimated direct cost of disposing of the products on hand.

The federal income tax regulations provide that a dealer in securities may use an inventory based upon market values as an alternative to stating his inventories at either cost or the lower of cost or market. The only requirement in the regulations is that the method used for tax purposes be the same as the method regularly used in the dealer's books of account. A dealer in securities is defined in the federal income tax regulations as a merchant of securities (whether an individual, partnership, or corporation) with an established place of business, regularly engaged in the purchase of securities and their resale to customers. It is further provided that if such business is simply a branch of the activities carried on by such person, the securities inventoried at market, or at the lower of cost or market, may include only those held for purposes of resale rather than for investment.

Security dealers are faced with a further complication in that the AICPA Industry Audit Guide, "Audits of Brokers and Dealers in Securities," issued in 1973, concludes that trading and portfolio securities generally should be valued at market in accordance with accounting principles applicable to this industry. Therefore, if either the cost or the lower-of-cost-or-market methods is to be retained for tax purposes, tax normalization should be followed in the adjustments to reflect market values in the published financial statements. Moreover, if the dealer used the LIFO method for tax purposes, an independent accountant would be required to issue a qualified opinion on the dealer's annual financial statements since the requirements of the tax statutes (discussed below) mandate the use of LIFO cost for financial reports if it is to be used on tax returns.

AMOUNTS ASSIGNED TO INVENTORIES TO DETERMINE PERIODIC RESULTS FROM BUSINESS OPERATIONS

If the results of operating a business were determined only at the time of completion of a venture, there would be no need for inventory accounting. Modern business, however, is conducted on a "going-concern" basis. With securities being actively traded on established markets, the relationship between the owners and operators of a business is largely impersonal, and there is a constant change in some portion of the owner group. For these reasons, as well as to make possible some degree of management control, it is accepted (quite aside from the requirements of income tax laws) that the income or loss from operating a business should be determined at least annually. The determination of periodic operating results requires the recognition of inventories.

Treatment of Supplies. The federal income tax regulations recognize the fact that income cannot be fairly stated without giving proper regard to inventories by inclusion of the following paragraph:[3]

> In order to reflect taxable income correctly, inventories at the beginning and end of each taxable year are necessary in every case in which the production, purchase, or sale of merchandise is an income-producing factor. The inventory should include all finished or partly finished goods and, in the case of raw materials and supplies, only those which have been acquired for sale or which will physically become a part of merchandise intended for sale, in which class fall containers, such as kegs, bottles, and cases, whether returnable or not, if title thereto will pass to the purchaser of the product to be sold therein. Merchandise should be included in the inventory only if title thereto is vested in the taxpayer. Accordingly, the seller should include in his inventory goods under contract for sale but not yet segregated and applied to the contract and goods out upon consignment, but should exclude from inventory goods sold (including containers), title to which has passed to the purchaser. A purchaser should include in inventory merchandise purchased (including containers), title to which has passed to him, although such merchandise is in transit or for other reasons has not been reduced to physical possession, but should not include goods ordered for future delivery, transfer of title to which has not yet been effected.

The foregoing quotation from the current federal income tax regulations is more restrictive than the concept of inventory as reflected in modern accounting practice. Modern accounting practice will include supplies which are to be *consumed* in the production of the goods or services to be sold in the ordinary course of the business. Normally the accounting concept of supplies being part of the inventory is accepted in practice for income tax purposes. In recognition of the fact that the income tax law applies to all businesses, regardless of the size of the operation or the sophistication of its accounting records, the regulations include the following paragraph.[4]

> Taxpayers carrying materials and supplies on hand should include in expenses the charges for materials and supplies only in the amount that they are actually consumed and used in operation during the taxable year for which the return is made, provided that the costs of such materials and supplies have not been deducted in determining the net income or loss or taxable income from any previous year. If a taxpayer carries incidental material or supplies on hand for which no record of consumption is kept or of which physical inventories at the beginning and end of the year are not taken, it will be permissible for the taxpayer to include in his expenses and to deduct from gross income the total cost of such supplies and materials as were purchased during the taxable year for which the return is made, provided the taxable income is clearly reflected by this method.

The foregoing statement recognizes that for federal income tax purposes supplies on hand are technically conceived of as being deferred charges rather than inventory. It also recognizes that, as a practical matter, smaller businesses may expense all supplies as purchased, and in the case of the larger businesses certain items, if not material in amount, may be so treated.

Measure of Physical Quantities. Regardless of the concept of cost applied in any particular situation, the computations will be premised on a measure of physical quantities. The importance of an auditor being satisfied as to the physical existence of an inventory was reflected in a report entitled "Extensions of Auditing Procedure," which was issued by a Special Committee on Auditing Procedure of the American Institute of Certified Public Accountants and approved by a vote of the membership of the Institute in 1939. This report concluded that, in addition to making auditing tests and checks of the inventory

[3]Reg. §1.471-1.
[4]Reg. §1.162-3.

accounts and records, the independent certified public accountant should, wherever practical and reasonable, observe the inventory taking. The report also included the following statement:

> In cases where the concern maintains well-kept and controlled perpetual inventory records supported by (1) a complete physical inventory at a date not coincident with the balance sheet date, or (2) physical inventories of individual items taken from time to time so that the quantity of each item on hand is compared with the inventory record for that item at least once in each year, it will be satisfactory to undertake the procedure outlined at any interim date or dates selected by the auditor, his purpose being to satisfy himself as to the credibility of the perpetual inventory records and whether they may be relied upon to support the inventory totals shown on the balance sheet.

In August 1966, the Committee on Auditing Procedure of the AICPA issued Statement No. 36 (Statement on Auditing Standards, No. 1, §331.11–12), which recognized that while the 1939 report had an implied requirement of a complete physical count of all items each year, some companies have developed inventory controls or methods for determining inventories (including statistical sampling) of sufficient reliability to make an annual physical count of each item of inventory unnecessary in certain instances. Even where statistical sampling techniques are used to establish inventory quantities rather than merely to verify the accuracy of perpetual inventory records, the final result is nevertheless premised on a measure of physical quantities.

Assumptions of Movement of Goods. In addition to a difference in the concept of cost in various businesses, there can be a difference in the concept of the assumption applied with respect to identification of the goods on hand. It is only in the most exceptional case that there will be specific identification of the goods. Generally this will be practical and needed for a fair reflection of income only with respect to items of relatively high individual value, such as rare violins, jewels, and valuable paintings. In the operation of a business, identification of particular lots of similar goods is not only impractical but may also distort rather than aid in a fair reflection of income on a going-concern basis. The common practice, therefore, is to reflect in the accounting records average costs, and there is a wide variety of procedures for determining an average. The average may be computed by reference to production or acquisitions during a week, month, or year; or a procedure based upon the theory of a moving average may be developed and appropriately applied in particular cases.

In further recognition of the fact that specifically identified costs are not always the most appropriate, an assumption is commonly made that goods move through the business on a FIFO basis, so that the most recent costs can be applied to the quantities on hand at the inventory date. Since approximately 1940, the LIFO assumption as to the movement of goods has been acceptable for federal income tax purposes, and there has been an increasing proportion of business inventories determined on this basis. The mechanics of determining the cost for an inventory on the LIFO basis are described below in some detail.

Another type of assumption as to the movement of goods is reflected in the retail inventory method, which is commonly used in the retail trade and was developed to meet the practical problems inherent in that industry. Inasmuch as the retail method embraces some of the principles of the lower-of-cost-or-market philosophy and does not involve the detailed questions inherent in establishing a cost for a manufacturing concern, this method is specifically considered in the following section.

Retail Inventory Method. Under the retail inventory method, the total of the retail selling price of the goods on hand at the end of the year in each department is reduced by applying a single percentage based upon the operations of that department during the period. The determination of this percentage adjustment

EXHIBIT 6   Retail Inventory Method

	Computation approximating					
	Lower of cost or market			Cost		
	Selling price	Inventory		Selling price	Inventory	
		Amount	%		Amount	%
Opening inventory........	$ 10,000	$ 6,000	60.00	$ 10,000	$ 6,000	60.00
Purchases..............	100,000	52,000		100,000	52,000	
Incoming freight, etc......	—	2,000		—	2,000	
Additional markups......	1,000	—		1,000	—	
	$111,000	$60,000	54.05			
Markdowns.............	$ 3,000			(3,000)	—	
				$108,000	$60,000	55.56
Sales..................	92,000			$ 92,000		
Discounts.............	1,500			1,500		
Shortages.............	2,500			2,500		
	$ 99,000			$ 96,000		
Closing inventory: At retail..............	$ 12,000			$ 12,000		
Amount approximating: Lower of cost or market (54.05% of $12,000)		$ 6,486				
Cost (55.56% of $12,000)..........					$ 6,667	

to the retail value and the mechanics of the computation are illustrated in Exhibit 6.

In the operation of the retail inventory method, it is important that markdowns be based upon actual reductions in retail sales prices. The required records to be maintained, with respect to each department, are those showing the aggregate cost and initial retail sales price for all purchases, incoming freight where not included in cost, aggregate sales made, markdowns, discounts allowed to employees and others, and additional markups, if any.

Shortages are recognized as inevitable in retail store operations, so that a provision therefore must be made. These shortages can result from errors in the preparation of sales slips as well as from shoplifting. Frequently, a monthly provision will be made for shortages measured by a fixed percentage of sales during the period as reflected by the experience of each department. Inasmuch as the inventory control records are kept in terms of retail selling prices, the amount of shortage is initially measured at that level.

In order that the inventory determined under the retail method will be stated at an amount which will approximate the lower of cost or market, markdowns are not included in the computation of the adjustment percentage. If the LIFO inventory method is used in conjunction with the retail computation, the federal income tax regulations require that retail selling prices be adjusted for markdowns as well as markups in order that the determination will approximate the cost of the goods on hand at the end of the year rather than the lower of cost or market.

Concepts of "Cost" for Manufactured Goods.   Just as there are several concepts of value, there are many concepts of costs. For purposes of establishing selling prices, all amounts expended in the conduct of the business must be recovered in the proceeds of sales in order to make a profit. It is unimportant for this purpose whether expenditures are classified as a cost or an expense. Use of the word "cost" to embrace any and all expenditures can, however, lead to misunderstandings.

Categorizing expenditures is important when the cost of an inventory is being established for the purpose of determining income derived from business operations during a stated period. The basic accounting principle in the measurement of income involves the "matching" of costs and expenses against related revenues. The unabsorbed costs properly chargeable against future sales are carried forward.

Inasmuch as assigning a dollar amount to an inventory reflects a deferment of an expenditure, it is fundamental that an actual expenditure or a commitment resulting in an accrued liability has occurred. From the standpoint of the determination of the cost of an inventory for federal income tax purposes, no amount should be included which does not constitute at least an accrued obligation under the federal income tax rules. For example, the general practice is not to include any portion of a provision for vacation pay not recognized as an accrued liability for tax purposes in determining the cost of goods included in an inventory.

Inclusion of Overhead.   Subject to the adoption of an acceptable practice as to the averaging of costs and a stated assumption as to the flow of goods, generally little difficulty is encountered in determining the appropriate amount to be allocated to an inventory for the cost of materials purchased and expenditures for direct labor. Greater differences of opinion exist with respect to overhead.

Expenditures which do not further a productive activity are not part of overhead includable in cost computations; and the extent to which other expenses are included in any particular instance will depend upon such factors as the complexity of the organization, the attitude and sophistication of the individuals compiling and using the economic data, and the availability of information. Not every business is equipped to analyze its expenditures in the same degree. Further, costs are computed to meet a particular situation, and no one amount can be said to be "correct" to the exclusion of all others.

There are several viewpoints as to the extent to which the expenses relating to production should be included in cost as a matter of principle. The alternatives for inclusion of overhead in production costs may be grouped broadly in four classes:

1. Prime costing, under which no overhead is included.

2. Direct costing, under which expenses which are directly attributable to production and which tend to increase and decrease in proportion to changes in the operating rate are included but no fixed overhead is included.

3. Analytical costing, under which overhead expenses attributable to production are included, except for the portion not taken into account because of the production facilities not being fully utilized.

4. Full absorption costing, under which all overhead expenses attributable to production are included.

Circumstances may make it appropriate and useful to apply procedures falling into any of these four categories in preparing statements and reports for management purposes; and management should understand what procedures have been followed. This is particularly important where the computed costs are utilized in establishing selling prices.

Prime costing has the advantage of simplicity and is applied most frequently where the overhead costs are of little significance. The suitability of this concept of cost for financial statement purposes (in contrast with operating statements prepared for management control purposes) is, however, subject to question. Chapter 4 on "Inventory Pricing" in *Accounting Research Bulletin No. 43* specifically states that "the exclusion of *all* [emphasis supplied] overheads from inventory costs does not constitute an accepted accounting procedure."

Direct costing implies that none of the recurring and continuing overhead expenses are to be included in cost of inventories. The major items are frequently depreciation and plant maintenance. The reasoning is that the expenses were incurred as a consequence of decisions which had nothing to do with any particular units of production; that the expenses would have been incurred whether or not any specific units had been produced; and that corresponding amounts of expense will be incurred in subsequent periods regardless of the quantity of the current production. The practice of not including in overhead certain items considered to be period expenses is a partial application of the direct costing principle. Among the items frequently not included in overhead under this concept are research and development, product guarantees, defective parts and rework, pensions, inventory-taking labor, employee training time, downtime, overtime and shift premiums (where abnormal and incurred to effect shipments rather than to produce the goods in the inventory), and plant rearrangement.

Producers of such items as whiskey, wine, and timber normally carry large inventories for long periods of time without guaranteed or contractually fixed selling prices. Storage and similar continuing expenses are frequently not added to the base cost of the particular goods on hand in this situation.

Analytical costing measures the proportion of the recurring and continuing expenses to be included in the computations of cost by comparing the actual rate of activity with a predetermined norm. Expenses for a particular period are included in cost to the extent that available capacity was actually utilized. The portion of the expenses allocable to the unused capacity is considered to represent a loss. This is an economic loss attributable to the lower than normal level of production during the period, and is not part of the cost of the units actually produced.

Both the direct costing and analytical costing procedures are premised, in part, upon a recognition of the fact that, in addition to variable expenses, overhead includes expenses which are recurring and necessary merely to provide the capacity to carry on production activities. The assumption of a certain level of recurring and continuing expenses is essential to being in a position to carry on any activities. During a particular period, however, production may be all or only a part of the total possible with the available capacity. Judgment is exercised in determining how much of the expenses required to provide the existing capacity to produce should be considered part of the cost of the actual production.

Full absorption costing is most frequently applied in smaller enterprises where detailed analyses of the various expense accounts are not available. It may also be appropriate where a plant is consistently operated at capacity or where the aggregate amount of overhead is relatively small. It shares with prime costing the advantage of simplicity; however, special attention must be given to any elements of overhead attributable to events which are not customarily a part of plant operations, and the full absorption costing concept will not be literally applied where the amount of expense resulting from such events can be identified. Examples of events which could justify special recognition in determining the overhead expenses to be included in cost computations are shortages of materials, receipt of defective materials, labor slowdowns and strikes, and interruptions of production caused by a flood, fire, or other casualty. In a business which does not have a regular program for model or product changes, special recognition might also be given to the effect upon expenses of disruptions caused by such factors as the introduction of a new product, the training of an expanded labor force, and the realignment of facilities incident to equipping a plant to manufacture a different product.

All the authoritative pronouncements on the subject of accounting for inventories uniformly emphasize that greater weight is to be given to consistency than to the use of any particular method.

Illustration of Analytical Costing.   In applying the analytical costing concept, it is necessary first to establish a normal operating rate or practical capacity. Practical capacity is usually determined by starting with a theoretical capacity and allowing for normal interruptions. Capacity may be measured in terms of tons, pounds, yards, labor hours, machine-hours, or any other standard appropriate to the particular operating unit—sometimes a plant, but frequently a department within the plant or other type of "cost center."

The application of this concept may be illustrated on the basis of the following assumptions:

Plant A has a theoretical capacity of 105,000 units per week if operated continuously; however, in determining an annual practical capacity, recognition must be given to the fact that the plant operates on a 5-day week at 8 hours a day. Also, allowances must be made for scheduled holidays, vacation shutdown, and other normal interruptions due to such causes as power failures and shutdowns for repairs. The plant is closed completely for five annual holidays (equivalent to one week of operation) and for two weeks during the vacation period. In this case, a reasonable allowance for breakdowns is 5 percent.

Production Units

Theoretical capacity (105,000 units for 52 weeks)		5,460,000
Reductions to recognize operations:		
On an 8-hour day ($^{16}\!/_{24}$ of 5,460,000)	3,640.000	
On a 5-day week ($^{2}\!/_{7}$ of 1,820,000)	520,000	4,160,000
Capacity on basis of 5-day week at 8 hours per day		1,300,000
Allowances for:		
Scheduled holidays ($^{1}\!/_{52}$ of 1,300,000)	25,000	
Vacation shutdown ($^{2}\!/_{52}$ of 1,300,000)	50,000	75,000
Capacity on basis of scheduled operating time		1,225,000
Allowance for normal interruptions (5%)		61,250
Practical capacity		1,163,750

If 1,100,000 units were produced during the year, the basis on which the fixed overhead would be allocated to production would be 1,100,000/1,163,750, or 94.52 percent. The total of the variable overhead would also be allocated to production. Assuming the inventory consisted of 110,000 units and the FIFO convention is applied, 10 percent of the aggregate fixed overhead allocated to production would be included in the computed cost for the inventory.

Even if the actual production exceeded 1,163,750 units as a result of favorable operating conditions and not as a result of additions to or improvements made in the facilities which would increase the theoretical capacity, only 100 percent of the fixed overhead would be allocated to production. Allocating more than 100 percent would result in including "phantom dollars" in cost rather than actual expenditures.

For purposes of this simple illustration, the rate of activity has been computed on an annual basis; however, depending upon the circumstances, a more significant computation might have been based upon the operations during the last month or final quarter in the year during which the particular articles in the inventory are assumed to have been produced.

Tax and Other Influences on Overhead Absorption.   The foregoing discussion of the problems in allocating overhead to inventory should be considered fundamental in nature. Emphasized is the fact of differing approaches and the need for judgment as well as the validity of various procedures under differing circumstances. More detailed explanations and analyses of major inventory accounting practices, including diversity of procedures, environmental influences, and continuing questions, are clearly presented in the comprehensive, 1973 AICPA Research Study No. 13 entitled "The Accounting Basis of Inventories" by Horace G. Barden.

The Cost Accounting Standards Board exerts considerable influence in the costing of inventories of companies engaged in government contracting through its published Standards applicable to accounting techniques and objectives, record keeping, definitions, and methods of overhead allocation and criteria for allowable costs and expenses. For example, specific Standards cover "Consistency in Estimating, Accumulating and Reporting Costs" (401 and 402), "Allocation of Home Office Expense to Segments" (403), and "Use of Standard Costs of Direct Material and Direct Labor" (407). Since many civilian agencies, as well as the U.S. Department of Defense, have adopted the CASB Standards, many smaller contractors have been forced to change their cost accounting and contract reporting practices.

The International Accounting Standards Committee also drew a number of objections when its 1974 exposure draft on a proposed statement, "Valuation and Presentation of Inventories in the Context of the Historical Cost System," seemed to recommend across-the-board full absorption of production overhead (including depreciation and similar expenses consistently treated as period expenses by several industries).[5]

Actual practice seems reflected in the following general conclusions of Paragraph 3.5 of Statement No. 6 issued in 1973 by the Committee on Management Accounting Practice of the National Association of Accountants:

> (a) Where it is practical and meaningful to do so, expenditures for materials, supplies, labor, and services which are necessary for and indirectly associated with producing the goods should be included in the inventories as part of the inventory amount. In some instances it is neither practical nor meaningful to make allocation to the inventory of charges for depreciation, taxes, and certain other classes of expenditures. However, the judgment as to whether or not a particular class of expenditure is included in the amount of inventories should be applied on a consistent basis.
>
> (b) Many companies adopt what they consider a conservative posture in treating as period expenses certain items which might reasonably be associated with a product amount, if only rather indirectly. The principal reasons for this attitude given by respondents to an NAA research study on allocation of indirect charges are:
> a. Method of allocation would be too arbitrary.
> b. Results would be misleading.
> c. Amounts are often insignificant.
> Out of 1,200 responses which were included in the tabulation, 671 indicated the firms do not allocate all expenditures indirectly related to production (at least on a broad-brush basis) in preparation of their annual financial statements (for the general public). For purposes of management (internal) reporting, 691 companies do not allocate.

In recognition of the complexities in this area and the practical need to rely on consistent industry accounting practices, in 1973 the U.S. Treasury and Internal Revenue Service issued so-called full absorption regulations for manufacturers[6] which most practitioners consider "enlightened." In extending the book/tax conformity objective required for the approval of changes in the accounting methods, the government made mandatory for most manufacturers the inclusion of *direct* production costs (Category I), permitted exclusion of certain indirect costs (Category II) and authorized other indirect expenses (Category III) to be included or excluded depending upon their treatment for financial accounting purposes, provided the treatment was not inconsistent with generally accepted accounting principles. For the few taxpayers who do not have comparable methods of

---

[5]The Institues of Chartered Accountants in the United Kingdom, Canada, and South Africa tend to favor a more inclusive approach in allocating burden to inventories.
[6]Reg. §1.471-11(a).

EXHIBIT 7   Analysis of Indirect Production Costs for Full Absorption Purposes

Description of Cost	Situation A: Taxpayers using comparable methods of accounting for inventory for tax and financial reporting purposes			Situation B: Taxpayers not using comparable methods of accounting for inventory for tax and financial reporting purposes	
	Category 1: Required to be included in inventory cost	Category 2: Not required to be included in inventory cost	Category 3: Required to be treated same as financial statements	Category 1: Required to be included in inventory cost	Category 2: Not required to be included in inventory cost
Repairs and maintenance	X			X	
Utilities	X			X	
Rent	X			X	
Indirect labor and production supervisory wages, including basic compensation, overtime pay, vacation and holiday pay, sick leave [other than payments pursuant to a wage continuation plan under section 105(d)], shift differential, payroll taxes, and contributions to a supplemental unemployment benefit plan	X			X	
Officers' salary related to business activities as a whole		X			X
Officers' salary related to production			X	X	
Pension contributions representing past service cost		X			X
Pension contributions representing current service cost			X		X
Profit-sharing contributions			X		X
Other employee benefit costs, including workmen's compensation expenses, payments under wage continuation plan described in section 105(d), amounts includible in income of an employee under nonqualified pension, profit-sharing, and stock bonus plans, premiums on life and health insurance, and miscellaneous employee benefits			X		X

Indirect materials and supplies		X	
Tools and equipment not capitalized	X	X	X
Costs of quality control and inspection	X	X	X
Marketing, advertising, and distribution expenses	X		
Interest	X		X
Research and experimental expenses	X		X
Losses under section 165	X		X
Depreciation and depletion reported in financial statements		X	
Depreciation and depletion in excess of amount reported in financial statements			
statements	X		X
Income taxes attributable to income received on sale of inventory	X		X
Taxes allowable as a deduction under section 164, excluding state, local, and foreign income taxes, attributable to assets incident to production or manufacturing	X	X	
General and administrative expenses incident to business activities as a whole	X		X
Factory administrative expenses	X	X	X
Costs attributable to strikes, rework labor, scrap, and spoilage	X	X	X
Insurance incident to production	X	X	X

determining inventory for both book and tax purposes, two categories of expenses were mandated: Category I must be included while Category II may be excluded. A liberal, two-year implementation period was established under which the effects on taxable income were spread over ten years after giving effect to a specific "pre-1954 adjustment." Special provisions also applied to significant standard cost variances, LIFO computations, and the practical capacity method discussed earlier in this chapter under "Analytical Costing."

Exhibit 7 illustrates the treatment of typical overhead expenses for manufacturers depending upon their particular tax status under these (almost) full absorption regulations.

LIFO

Reasons for Development of the LIFO Assumption as to the Movement of Goods. The acceptance of conventional accounting procedures which recognize cost, or the lower of cost or market, in stating inventories appears to have been a natural consequence of the thought that the principal financial statement is the balance sheet. In reflecting the financial position of a business, it is logical to determine the shareholders' equity by deducting the total of the liabilities from the valuation of the assets.

The development and acceptance of the LIFO inventory method resulted from increasing emphasis being placed upon the income statement. Under currently accepted accounting concepts, the statement of financial position is conceived of as reflecting amounts for the assets (other than cash, receivables, and sundry assets from which the maximum cash realization is fixed) that merely represent the unabsorbed portion of expenditures incurred in the past but applicable to the future and to be charged against the revenue of some future period. From this viewpoint, it was logical to develop an accounting convention relative to inventories designed to result in a more appropriate charge being made against current sales for the cost of goods sold. The basic principle of LIFO is that current income is better determined by deducting from the sales of the accounting period the cost of replacing the merchandise used in making the sales; in view of the difficulty of computing the cost for each sale, however, the desired end result is approximated by stating the inventory on a LIFO basis.

The physical quantity of goods may remain constant from year to year, but the number of dollars invested in that inventory may increase or decrease solely as a result of changes in prices. So long as a businessman relies upon continuous turnover of inventory to produce income, it is important that the effects of mere changes in prices be distinguished from profits attributable to the sale of merchandise.

If there is on hand at the beginning and end of any year the same physical quantity of goods, but solely as a result of changes in prices the dollar amount attributed to those goods for inventory purposes has increased 10 percent, this 10 percent increase in the dollar amount represents an unrealized inventory profit. This profit cannot be used to pay taxes or wages or dividends but must be retained in the business in order to permit its very continuation by replacing the goods which have been sold. If these unrealized inventory profits continue, the business can be forced to secure additional capital to finance the higher-cost purchases, even though there has been no actual growth.

It is equally significant that a decline in the value of an inventory can, under the FIFO inventory method, depress the operating results; the LIFO method similarly attempts to distinguish this type of charge against income from the normal results of current business operations.

Wherever the quantities in the closing inventory equal or exceed the volume of the opening inventory, the desired result of charging against current income a cost for the goods sold based upon contemporary prices is accomplished within reasonable limits. In the event of a reduction in inventory volume, however, the present-day LIFO method departs from the objective of reflecting current replacement costs and yields to the conventional accounting practice of dealing only with accomplished facts.

From the standpoint of those who put the primary emphasis upon the balance sheet, LIFO is unsatisfactory because the amount assigned to the inventory may have no relationship to current value and may reflect an aggregation of price levels during several unidentified years depending upon the number of "layers" considered as being in the inventory. Similarly, from the standpoint of those who believe that true income can only be stated if all the factors of income, costs, and expenses are expressed in terms of a unit with the same monetary value, LIFO is admittedly deficient where there has been a reduction in the volume of goods on hand at the end of the year.

As the result of taxpayer persistence, in the Revenue Act of 1938, Congress authorized the use of LIFO for specified raw materials used by tanners, and the producers and processors of certain nonferrous metals. The following year Congress expanded the use of LIFO and removed the restrictions as to the industries and classes of inventories to which LIFO could be applied. Under the Revenue Act of 1939, any taxpayer could elect the LIFO method with respect to any of the goods in his inventory.

The present provisions of the Internal Revenue Code do not permit either (1) the "replacement" of inventories and the restoration of previous costs, even where a portion of the inventory has been liquidated as a result of causes entirely beyond the taxpayer's control, or (2) the write-down of inventories to market where market is lower than LIFO costs. A write-down to market is permitted by the regulations for financial reporting purposes only.

Timing the Adoption of LIFO.   The decision as to when LIFO should be adopted depends upon many factors, which will be different in every case. Generally, the principal factors governing the question of "when" include:

1. Rise in prices, since price increases cause paper profits in the inventory.

2. High taxes, since a tax saving (or deferment) is the most tangible benefit from electing LIFO.

3. Normal inventory quantities, since if there is a substantial increase in inventory quantities during years of inflated prices, the equivalent of such increased quantities may remain indefinitely in the LIFO inventory at the high prices.

4. No foreseeable conditions which could cause the liquidation of the inventory during the high-price and high-tax period, since such liquidation would mean that the recognition of income was only temporarily deferred and the income may actually be taxed at a higher rate.

After LIFO is once adopted, it will normally be advantageous, so long as high prices continue, to maintain normal inventory quantities and avoid a liquidation at the end of any year. Inventory liquidations at an interim date are immaterial to the LIFO computations, but the necessity to maintain quantities at each year-end may result in the accounting department of a business temporarily directing the volume of purchases and shipments near the close of the year.

Consequences of Cost Reductions.   If the LIFO method is applied to the aggregate of the elements of the cost of an inventory of manufactured goods and a procedure is developed for substantially reducing production costs, it may be that the cost savings effected through an improvement in production methods are being offset against the price increases attributable to material in the product. This has prompted some companies to limit the application of the LIFO method to the material content of the inventory. Where the LIFO method is applied to manufacturing costs as well as the material content, the volume of inventoriable production costs is commonly measured in terms of direct labor hours or some other unit in order to preserve the benefits of increased efficiency.

There may also be unforeseen consequences of LIFO in the event of product changes. Such changes can result from using a different raw material or the production of items which had previously been purchased, as well as a distinct change in the finished product. As an illustration, members of the wool industry adopted LIFO and subsequently began to substitute artificial fibers for natural wool. Where the inventory volume is measured in terms of yards and LIFO is applied to one particular type of material, such a change in material means the complete liquidation of the original inventory and the inclusion in income of the entire amount previously deferred through election of the LIFO method. With the passage of time, almost every business may expect that new lines will be added and old ones dropped.

In the case of a business anticipating that it may resort to a different type of raw material, it may be helpful to use the dollar-value principle in which the aggregate investment in inventory is considered rather than the quantity of particular items. Where the substituted material has not been the subject of a price increase similar to that of the original material, the dollar-value method does not provide a completely satisfactory solution but is of some benefit.

Conditions to the Use of LIFO for Income Tax Purposes. The two principal conditions to be complied with if LIFO is to be used for federal income tax purposes are (1) the filing of appropriate election forms with the federal income tax return covering the year in which the method is first used and (2) the statutory requirement that no other method be used in determining income for the purpose of annual reports to shareholders, creditors, and other interested parties. Of significance is the fact that the LIFO election need not be made until after the close of the year in which the method is to be used for federal income tax purposes. Although the state income tax laws do not in all cases provide specifically for an exception to the general rule for securing advance approval of changes in accounting methods, the general practice is to follow substantially the same procedure in the state returns as in the federal return.

The requirement in the Internal Revenue Code that no method other than LIFO be used in stating inventories for the purpose of *determining income in annual reports* to shareholders, creditors, and others must be recognized by management and is not a matter of mere detail. Reports to shareholders are frequently prepared before it is necessary to file the federal income tax return and make the final decision as to adoption of the LIFO method for tax purposes. Consequently, it may be necessary to use that method in the annual report going to shareholders even though there is a possibility that the decision will be against the adoption of LIFO for tax purposes.

It is not necessary that the inventory amount as computed for purposes of the financial statements be the same as later used in the tax return. For example, there may be a difference in the classification of the inventory as used in the financial statement computation. The Internal Revenue Code merely requires that no method other than LIFO be used in computing income in financial statements covering a taxable year. The restriction does not apply to interim statements.

Interim Financial Statements and Statements of Product or Departmental Results. Questions naturally arise as to whether, from a practical standpoint, the LIFO principle can be incorporated in a cost accounting system and the commonly used form of statements of product or branch results and of departmental operations. It is reasoned that if the LIFO method results in a better reflection of income, it should be used for all management purposes. In practice, however, LIFO is generally appended to previously used operating statements and cost systems.

In reporting profits of the business as a whole, "ideal" conditions for using LIFO are simple, i.e., when closing inventories equal opening inventories and the goods sold are equivalent to the purchases for each accounting period throughout the year. Since such conditions are rarely, if ever, found in practice, the accounting system must provide for reflecting all possible developments.

If at the end of an interim accounting period the inventory of any LIFO group is below the opening inventory for the year, an estimate must be made of the amount of closing inventory for the year. Assuming that at the interim date no reduction is expected for the year, cost of sales for the interim period should be charged with the cost of goods purchased plus an estimated amount to cover the cost that will be incurred in making good the temporary decrease in inventory. An account should be established (ordinarily shown on the balance sheet among current liabilities) for the difference between the estimated replacement cost and the LIFO inventory cost for the quantities liquidated to the interim date.

The opposite situation is where a reduction is expected in the closing inventory as compared with what was on hand at the beginning of the year. Should a substantial difference exist between LIFO cost and current replacement cost and should the major part of the liquidation occur in one month, the charge to cost of sales for the goods liquidated may be abnormally low (or high) and result in a distortion of monthly profits. In some cases this difference is spread over the months remaining from the time such decrease becomes apparent until the year-end. In other cases cost of sales is charged with amounts computed by reference to current replacement costs and a special credit (or charge) shown as being attributable to the liquidation of a portion of the beginning LIFO inventory.

Estimates of the year-end inventory volume must also be made when there is an increase in inventory at an interim date. If a decrease or at least no substantial increase is expected for the year as a whole, the temporary increase can be priced at the most easily identified acquisition cost. If an increase is expected for the year, such increase will be reflected in the closing inventory at current-year costs. The difference between the actual acquisition costs at the interim date and the cost at which the increased quantity will be included in the closing LIFO inventory (first-purchase costs for the year, last-purchase costs, or average cost) must be taken into cost of sales during some part of the year. If the amount of such difference is large, care should be used not to reflect it in one period so as to distort profits. If it can be predetermined with reasonable accuracy, this type of difference can appropriately be spread over the remainder of the year because the inventory volume at the year-end in excess of the opening inventory is a consequence of the purchasing or production policy followed throughout the year rather than during any particular period.

LIFO Computations Where Quantities Are Determined by Weight or Count. The classification of inventories into groups for LIFO purposes depends primarily upon the character of the goods involved and the complexity of the inventories. Although a LIFO computation wherein quantities are determined directly by weight or count is simple and involves the least amount of clerical effort and expense, the chief disadvantage of this procedure is its limited application in a business that has a variety of raw materials and manufactures many types of goods. If the quantity method were adopted in such a business, there would be numerous LIFO groups, and over a period of years, as quantities increased and decreased, there would be a tendency to restore to income some of the inflationary profit which LIFO was designed to eliminate.

The dollar-value principle of measuring the volume of goods in a LIFO inventory is usually applied except where the inventory as a whole consists of relatively few raw material commodities or products which can be measured and expressed in units of quantity.

When the LIFO method is first adopted, the opening inventory of the year may have to be adjusted. The goods must be reflected in the beginning inventory at *cost* and are considered as having been acquired at the same time. In stating the opening inventory at cost, any write-down to market values with respect to the closing inventory of the preceding year must be restored. Such restorations create additional income or reduce the loss, whichever the case may be, for the preceding year. When the write-down to market is restored, the cost of the goods in the opening inventory will be the cost determined by the method previously used, i.e., the cost determined by reference to specific invoices, by the assumption of FIFO, by the use of an average of the opening inventory and purchases during the year, or by any other procedure consistently followed by the company under the lower-of-cost-or-market rule.

The opening inventory for the first LIFO year is the basic "layer." At the close of the year the quantity on hand is compared with the quantity at the beginning. If there is no increase in quantity, the average cost of the basic layer is applied to the quantity on hand at the end of the year to obtain the inventory amount. If there is an increase in quantity, a current-year's cost must be established. The methods commonly used to establish the current-year's cost are generally described as first-purchase costs, last-purchase costs, or the average cost for the year. Many companies that elect to price quantity increments by reference to the actual cost of goods most recently acquired, or by reference to the actual cost of goods acquired during the taxable year in the order of acquisition, determine an average cost for each month during which acquisitions are made, the aggregate of which equals or exceeds the increase in inventory, and then treat the quantity acquired and average cost as a single "layer" for inventory pricing.

Decreases in quantities are taken from the most recent year's acquisitions.

An illustration of LIFO inventory computations where bushels are the unit for measuring the quantity of goods on hand is set forth in Exhibit 8.

LIFO Computations Where Relative Quantities Are Determined by the Retail Inventory Method.   The procedures for applying the LIFO concept to the determination of amounts to be assigned to retail department store inventories were developed to meet a specific business need. To superimpose the LIFO principle upon the retail method, price fluctuations are adjusted by application of a series of nationwide price indexes to the total dollar value of each departmental inventory.

The LIFO problem peculiar to retailers arises from the fact that because of the nature of the business there is rarely a record of the specific identity of individual inventory items. The retail method consists of accumulating the aggregate retail value of all items in a department at the inventory date and reducing this departmental total by applying an adjustment representing the average gross markup on that department's goods.

The series of inventory price indexes approved by the Treasury Department for federal income tax purposes is based on data furnished by the Bureau of Labor Statistics exclusively for the use of retail stores. Since the tabulations published by the Bureau of Labor Statistics use either January or July, 1941, as 100 percent, department stores electing LIFO as of later dates compute their own accumulative percentage of price change. To aid in these computations, the government statistics show the percentage of price change during each year.

A form of work sheet for the computation of departmental LIFO inventories is illustrated by Exhibit 9. It will be noted that the BLS index is applied to the retail value of the inventory rather than to the cost.

LIFO Computations Where Relative Quantities Are Determined by the Dollar-Value Principle.   The dollar-value principle is that the volume of the goods in annual inventories can be measured in terms of total dollars reflecting cost levels for the inventory items as of a particular year. The appropriate unit of measure for the various items may be yards, tons, gallons, or any combination of these and

EXHIBIT 8 LIFO Computations Where Quantities Are Determined by Weight or Count

				Inventories at end of			
	LIFO base	First year	Second year	Third year	Fourth year	Fifth year
1. Inventory quantities	10,000 bu	12,000 bu	11,000 bu	9,000 bu	10,500 bu	10,000 bu
2. Current-year cost per bushel	$2.00	$2.046	$2.107	$2.090	$2.111	$2.143
Inventory on LIFO basis:						
In bushels, attributable to:						
3. Base year	10,000 bu	10,000 bu	10,000 bu	9,000 bu	9,000 bu	9,000 bu
4. First year		2,000	1,000			
5. Fourth year					1,500	1,000
6. Total	10,000 bu	12,000 bu	11,000 bu	9,000 bu	10,500 bu	10,000 bu
At LIFO cost, attributable to:						
7. Base year (3 × $2.00)	$20,000	$20,000	$20,000	$18,000	$18,000	$18,000
8. First year (4 × $2.046)		4,092	2,046			
9. Fourth year (5 × $2.111) ...					3,167	2,111
10. Total LIFO inventory cost ...	$20,000	$24,092	$22,046	$18,000	$21,167	$20,111
11. Inventory on current cost basis (1 × 2)		24,552	23,177	18,810	22,166	21,430
12. Cumulative inventory effect from use of LIFO method (10 − 11)		$ (460)	$ (1,131)	$ (810)	$ (999)	$ (1,319)

EXHIBIT 9   LIFO Computations Where Relative Quantities Are Determined by the Retail Inventory Method

Department: _____
No.: _____

	LIFO base	First year	Second year	Third year	Fourth year	Fifth year
				Inventories at end of		
Conversion factors:						
1. Percentage change in BLS index during the year		2.30%	3.00%	(0.80)%	1.00%	1.50%
2. Index of price-level change from LIFO base	100.00%	102.30	105.34	104.50	105.55	107.13
3. Percentage of cost to retail value:						
4. As of base year / As of current year	60.00	59.56	59.80	61.00	59.20	60.70
5. Inventory at retail value	$10,000	$12,000	$11,000	$9,000	$10,500	$10,000
6. Inventory at base-year price level (5 ÷ 2)	10,000	11,730	10,442	8,612	9,948	9,334
Inventory on LIFO basis:						
At base-year price level, attributable to:						
7. Base year	$10,000	$10,000	$10,000	$8,612	$8,612	$8,612
8. First year		1,730	442			
9. Fourth year					1,336	722
10. Total	$10,000	$11,730	$10,442	$8,612	$9,948	$9,334
At LIFO cost, attributable to:						
11. Base year (7 × 60.00%)	$ 6,000	$ 6,000	$ 6,000	$5,167	$5,167	$5,167
12. First year (8 × 102.30% × 59.56%)		1,054	269			
13. Fourth year (9 × 105.55% × 59.20%)					835	451
14. Total LIFO inventory cost	$ 6,000	$ 7,054	$ 6,267	$5,167	$6,002	$5,618
15. Inventory on current cost basis (5 × 4)		7,147	6,578	5,490	6,216	6,070
16. Cumulative inventory effect from use of LIFO method (14 − 15)		($ 93)	($ 309)	($ 323)	($ 214)	($ 452)

similar measures, but the common denominator for determining the total volume of goods in the inventories from year to year is dollars.

The term "base-year cost" is the aggregate of the cost (determined as of the beginning of the year for which the LIFO method is first adopted) for all items in the inventory, and the term "base-year unit costs" refers to the individual costs as of that date for the various items. Liquidations and increments for a particular LIFO inventory are reflected only in terms of a net liquidation or increment for the inventory as a whole. Fluctuations will occur in quantities of items within the inventory. New items may be added and discontinued items may be dropped without necessarily effecting a change in the dollar value of the inventory as a whole.

In the case of a manufacturer or processor, the entire inventory which is considered to relate to a "natural business unit" is commonly reflected in a single LIFO computation. Where an enterprise is composed of more than one business unit, a separate inventory must be recognized for each. What constitutes a natural business unit is considered in the following excerpt from the federal income tax regulations:[7]

> Whether an enterprise is composed of more than one natural business unit is a matter of fact to be determined from all the circumstances. The natural business divisions adopted by the taxpayer for internal management purposes, the existence of separate and distinct production facilities and processes, and the maintenance of separate profit and loss records with respect to separate operations are important considerations in determining what is a business unit, unless such divisions, facilities, or accounting records are set up merely because of differences in geographical location. In the case of a manufacturer or processor, a natural business unit ordinarily consists of the entire productive activity of the enterprise within one product line or within two or more related product lines including (to the extent engaged in by the enterprise) the obtaining of materials, the processing of materials, and the selling of manufactured or processed goods. Thus, in the case of a manufacturer or processor, the maintenance and operation of a raw material warehouse does not generally constitute, of itself, a natural business unit. If the taxpayer maintains and operates a supplier unit the production of which is both sold to others and transferred to a different unit of the taxpayer to be used as a component part of another product, the supplier unit will ordinarily constitute a separate and distinct natural business unit. Ordinarily, a processing plant would not in itself be considered a natural business unit if the production of the plant, although saleable at this stage, is not sold to others, but is transferred to another plant of the enterprise, not operated as a separate division, for further processing or incorporation into another product. On the other hand, if the production of a manufacturing or processing plant is transferred to a separate and distinct division of the taxpayer, which constitutes a natural business unit, the supplier unit itself will ordinarily be considered a natural business unit. However, the mere fact that a portion of the production of a manufacturing or processing plant may be sold to others at a certain stage of processing with the remainder of the production being further processed or incorporated into another product will not of itself be determinative that the activities devoted to the production of the portion sold constitute a separate business unit. Where a manufacturer or processor is also engaged in the wholesaling or retailing of goods purchased from others, the wholesaling or retailing operations with respect to such purchased goods shall not be considered a part of any manufacturing or processing unit.

Inventories of wholesalers, retailers, jobbers, and distributors are classified for the purpose of LIFO computations by major lines, types, or classes of goods. Customary business classifications of the particular trade generally provide a satisfactory basis for determining the extent to which items can be combined into a single inventory pool by application of the dollar-value principle. In some cases

[7]Reg. §1.472-8(b)(2)(i).

operations of other than a manufacturer or processor may constitute a single natural business unit.

A wide variety of procedures have been developed for determining an appropriate index to be used in dollar-value LIFO inventory computations. As a general rule, however, a "double-extension method" is used for computing the base-year and current-year cost. Under this method, the quantity of each item in the inventory at the close of the year is extended at both its base-year unit cost and the current-year unit cost. The comparison of the relative volume of the opening and closing inventories, as reflected by the totals of the extensions at the base-year unit costs, indicates whether there has been an increment or liquidation for the year. The relationship between the totals of the extensions of the closing inventory at the current-year unit costs and at the base-year unit costs can be used as the factor to be applied in converting an increment from base-year cost to current-year cost. This conversion factor may be measured by whichever procedure was selected for costing increments, i.e., on the basis of the earliest acquisitions during the year, the most recent acquisitions, or an average for the entire year.

Under the double-extension method, a base-year unit cost must be established for each new item. In many instances it is most practicable to use the earliest actual cost recorded for the item, but a base-year unit cost may be constructed. For an item which was in existence, the base-year unit cost should be the price that would have been paid by the company had the item been used. Where the new item is a product or raw material not in existence in the base year, an amount should be constructed which represents what the cost would have been in the base year had the item been in existence. Frequently the base-year unit cost for a new item is computed by applying to the current-year cost of such item the percentage relationship between the base-year unit cost and current-year unit cost for an item sufficiently similar in physical characteristics to justify an assumption that the changes in unit cost would have been comparable.

With the passage of time, the proportion of the items in an inventory which were not included in the base-year inventory will increase. In recognition of the facts that the base-year unit costs established for LIFO inventory computation purposes can often be utilized for management control purposes and that reasonably current costs are more significant and accurate than reconstructed costs, the double-extension method of applying the dollar-value principle is frequently modified to permit the use of a substitute base year. The updating of the base-year costs does not change the LIFO cost for the inventory, but merely permits the use of the more current and reliable unit costs for purposes of measuring the relative volume of the goods included in the inventories.

Exhibit 10 illustrates LIFO inventory computations where the volume of goods is measured by the dollar-value principle.[8]

Link Chain. In recognition of the reliability and practicality afforded by the comparison of current costs to costs of the immediately preceding year, many companies, especially those with changing products, adopt the "link-chain" method of determining an annual index. The overall change in cost levels is determined by multiplying the last previously determined cumulative index by the most recent annual index, as illustrated in Exhibit 11 using the same assumption as in Exhibit 10. This procedure, which produces slightly different results from the base-year double-extension method, is also used in compiling the BLS indexes for the computation of LIFO inventories by retail stores.

---

[8] For an illustration of the buildup of several LIFO layers, see Davidson, Schindler, and Weil, *Fundamentals of Accounting*, 5th ed., Dryden Press, Hinsdale, Ill., 1975, Chapter 12, Appendix 2.

EXHIBIT 10   LIFO Computations Where Relative Quantities Are Determined by the Dollar-Value Principle

			Inventories at end of			
	LIFO base	First year	Second year	Third year	Fourth year	Fifth year
Conversion factors:						
Inventory extended at:						
1. Current-year unit costs	$100,000	$120,000	$110,000	$90,000	$105,000	$100,000
2. Base-year unit costs	100,000	117,300	104,420	86,120	99,480	93,340
3. Percentage of total base-year cost to total current-year cost (2 ÷ 1)	100.00%	97.75%	94.93%	95.69%	94.74%	93.34%
Inventory on LIFO basis:						
At base-year costs, attributable to:						
4. Base year	$100,000	$100,000	$100,000	$86,120	$86,120	$86,120
5. First year		17,300	4,420			
6. Fourth year					13,360	7,220
7. Total	$100,000	$117,300	$104,420	$86,120	$99,480	$93,340
At LIFO cost, attributable to:						
8. Base Year (4 × 100.00%)	$100,000	$100,000	$100,000	$86,120	$86,120	$86,120
9. First year (5 ÷ 97.75%)		17,698	4,522			
10. Fourth year (6 ÷ 94.74%)					14,102	7,621
11. Total LIFO inventory cost	$100,000	$117,698	$104,522	$86,120	$100,222	$93,741
12. Inventory on current cost basis (line 1)		120,000	110,000	90,000	105,000	100,000
13. Cumulative inventory effect from use of LIFO method (11 − 12)		$ (2,302)	$ (5,478)	$ (3,880)	$ (4,778)	$ (6,259)

EXHIBIT 11 LIFO Computations Where Annual Index Is Determined by the Link-Chain Method

				Inventories at end of		
	LIFO base	First year	Second year	Third year	Fourth year	Fifth year
Conversion factors:						
Inventory extended at:						
1. End of current-year unit costs	$100,000	$120,000	$110,000	$ 90,000	$105,000	$100,000
2. Beginning of current-year unit costs	100,000	117,300	106,832	90,729	103,961	98,520
3. Percentage of total beginning of current-year costs to total end of current-year costs (2 ÷ 1)	100.00%	97.75%	97.12%	100.81%	99.01%	98.52%
4. Cumulative index (previous year's cumulative × current index)	100.00%	97.75%	94.93%	95.70%	94.75%	93.35%
5. Ending inventory at base-year cost (1 × 4)	$100,000	$117,300	$104,423	$ 86,130	$ 99,488	$ 93,350
Inventory on LIFO basis:						
At base-year costs, attributable to:						
6. Base Year	$100,000	$100,000	$100,000	$ 86,130	$ 86,130	$ 86,130
7. First year		17,300	4,423			
8. Fourth year					13,358	7,220
9. Total	$100,000	$117,300	$104,423	$ 86,130	$ 99,488	$ 93,350
At LIFO cost, attributable to:						
10. Base year (6 ÷ 100%)	$100,000	$100,000	$100,000	$ 86,130	$ 86,130	$ 86,130
11. First year (7 ÷ 97.75%)		17,698	4,525			
12. Fourth year (8 ÷ 94.75%)					14,098	7,620
13. Total LIFO inventory cost	$100,000	$117,698	$104,525	$ 86,130	$100,228	$ 93,750
14. Inventory on current cost basis		120,000	110,000	90,000	105,000	100,000
15. Cumulative inventory effect from use of LIFO method (13) − (14)		$ (2,302)	$ (5,475)	$ (3,870)	$ (4,772)	$ (6,250)

Disclosures in Published Financial Statements. In recent years, the Internal Revenue Service has taken an extremely restrictive position in interpreting Section 472 (c) and (e) of the Internal Revenue Code, which prohibits the reporting of income on any basis other than LIFO in reports to shareholders, partners, creditors, etc. In summary, the Service will permit disclosure in financial reports of the effects of LIFO on income, earnings per share, and financial position in accordance with the requirements of Opinion No. 20 of the Accounting Principles Board solely for the year the LIFO method is *adopted*. In all *subsequent* years, the only disclosure permitted is a footnote to the balance sheet indicating the difference between inventories stated at LIFO and current cost (FIFO).

It is interesting to note that the first interpretation issued by the Financial Accounting Standards Board in June 1974 emphasized that a change in the composition of costs included in inventory was governed by the Accounting Change provision of APB Opinion No. 20, while FASB Statement No. 3, issued in December 1974, prescribed the disclosures required in interim and annual financial statements consistent with APB Opinions No. 20 and No. 28 (Interim Financial Reporting) upon the adoption of LIFO. Companies should keep abreast of changing disclosure requirements of the SEC, FASB, Internal Revenue Service, and other regulatory bodies. An inappropriate presentation of the effect of LIFO on income, possibly in a press release or president's letter, might afford a basis for the Internal Revenue Service to terminate a company's LIFO election if the financial statement conformity requirements were considered violated.

BIBLIOGRAPHY

Barden, Horace G.: AICPA Accounting Research Study 13, "The Accounting Basis of Inventories," AICPA, New York, 1973.

Committee on Accounting Procedure: *Accounting Research Bulletin No. 43*, AICPA, New York, 1953, chap. 4, 1953.

Cost Accounting Standards Board, Published and Proposed Standards, Washington, D.C.

Davidson, S., J. S. Schindler, and R. L. Weil: *Fundamentals of Accounting*, 5th ed., Dryden Press, Hinsdale, Ill., 1975.

General Service Administration: The Economic Order Quantity Principle and Applications, Federal Stock No. 7610-543-6765, Washington, D.C., 1966.

Hoffman, R. A., and H. Gunders: *Inventories—Control, Costing and Effect on Income and Taxes*, Ronald Press, New York, 1970.

Institute of Chartered Accountants in England and Wales: Recommendations on Accounting Principles No. 22, "Treatment of Stock-in-trade and Work in Progress in Financial Accounts," London, 1960.

Magee, John F., and David M. Boodman: Production Planning and Inventory Control, 2nd ed., McGraw-Hill Book Company, New York, 1967.

National Association of Accountants, Statement Number 6 on Management Accounting Practices, "Guidelines for Inventory Management," NAA, New York, 1973.

Plosal, G. W., and O. W. Wight: Production and Inventory Control, Prentice-Hall, Englewood Cliffs, N.J., 1967.

Prichard, James W., and Robert H. Eagle: Modern Inventory Management, John Wiley & Sons, New York, 1965.

United States Internal Revenue Code provisions with respect to inventories and related regulations: Code §471 and 472 and Reg. §1.471 and 1.472.

Chapter **17**

Land

MORTON B. SOLOMON
Partner, Main Lafrentz & Co.

INTRODUCTION

Land is a measured area of the surface of the earth which includes the soil, the mineral content beneath the surface, and the space above the surface. Land may be considered for accounting purposes as a variety of rights inherent in its ownership and related to the function which it serves. For example, land may be used:

1. As physical support for a structure, or as a road or other means of passage, involving rights of occupation or easements or rights of way, which rights may be surface, subterranean, or air space;

2. As a source of water, oil and gas, mineral deposits or timber, utilizing diversion, extraction or severance rights;

3. As a medium for the raising or taking of animals or fish, involving rights of grazing and pasture, or hunting and fishing;

4. As a medium for the growth of trees, crops, or shrubs, indicating cultivation and severance rights.

Each of these rights has value; each may be purchased, sold, leased, or licensed. Thus, accounting for land may involve accounting for several rights, each of which may be considered an asset.

Types of Legal Interest.   The legal interest in land rights varies. Where ownership is perpetual and includes all land rights, title is said to be in *fee simple*. An individual may have a *life estate*, granting land usage rights for his or her lifetime. The life estate may include mineral rights, cutting rights or water rights, *etc.* An important variation is the interest of the *remainderman*, who owns a parcel of land subject to either an existing life interest or beneficial interest on the part of another person for a specified term of years.

Limited Interests.   Some situations involve ownership of only a limited interest in land. For example, an *easement* may grant a perpetual right or a right for a limited period to traverse land with a road or a pipeline. Although a limited interest, such as an easement, is not ordinarily characterized as land for accounting purposes (the preference being to use a more descriptive title such as easements), nonetheless, the procedures used in accounting for land also apply to such limited interests in land.

Leases.   An interest in land may be owned through a *lease*. A lease is generally evidenced by a legal document that confers all, or a portion, of the rights to use and enjoyment of land to a person or other entity for a fixed or determinable period of time in consideration of the payment of rent or royalties. A mineral lease allows the lessee to extract the mineral content of the land, usually subject to certain rights retained by the owner of the land.

Liens and Encumbrances.   Land often is purchased subject to a lien or encumbrance in the form of a *mortgage*. A mortgage is generally given to secure an unpaid purchase price or to secure repayment of money advanced as a loan. It represents a security interest which carries with it the right to foreclosure, generally upon nonpayment or nontimely payment of related debt.

BALANCE SHEET PRESENTATION

The purpose for which land is acquired and held determines how it is presented in the balance sheet and what additional disclosures are to be made.

Land as a Part of Property, Plant, and Equipment.   Land, which by conventional criteria has asset status because of its use in productive operations, is generally classified as a part of property, plant, and equipment. Thus land is typically a *plant asset*. However, land held for a future plant site, land held for speculation, or land held as inventory is not so classified.

Land as a Potential Future Plant Site. Land held as a future plant site may be classified either as a long-term investment or among other assets. To the extent practicable in the circumstances, such land should be described as accurately as possible by a caption ("land held for future plant sites").

Land as an Investment. Land has long been a favorite medium for investment. When land is acquired for investment purposes, it should be classified as a long-term investment until the facts of an individual case suggest that it may be classified as a current asset. It may be desirable in certain situations for an entity to disclose in some supplementary fashion the current value of land held as an investment.

Land as Inventory. A significant exception to the general presumption against including land among current assets is the classification of land as inventory by companies whose business includes the sale of land to others. Land is the stock-in-trade of land developers or subdividers; in this case, it should be considered as inventory. Some of the accounting problems peculiar to land developers are considered in a later section, "Retail Land Sales."

Impairment of Economic Usefulness. Regardless of prior classification, if certain land is currently held for sale as a result of adverse factors which evidence impairment of its economic usefulness, such land should be segregated in the balance sheet from other properties held for continuing business advantage. Pending sale, it should be carried forward at recoverable cost if the latter is estimated to be lower than acquisition cost. A current loss provision should be made for that portion of cost deemed to have become "nonrecoverable."

Land Encumbered by a Mortgage. When land encumbered by a mortgage is acquired, the acquirer should record a liability for any unpaid balance of the original debt secured by the mortgage, when the debt covered by the mortgage is assumed by the buyer.

Carying Value. All expenditures made to acquire land and place it in condition for the purpose intended should be considered part of the cost of land. All costs incurred during a holding period between the time of purchase and the time when land is placed in condition for use should be similarly considered part of the cost of land. Thus, the cost of land includes any land option costs; any obligations assumed or payments made to discharge taxes, interest, and other expenses accrued at the time of purchase; obligations or outlays to discharge mortgages and other liens and encumbrances existing at the time of acquisition; finders' fees, attorneys' fees, and title insurance and title search costs; costs of necessary land grading, filling, clearing, or draining; costs of demolition of existing structures (unless the land was acquired with the intent of using such structures); and other costs or expenses necessary to gain access to the land, take possession of the land, and put the land to the use intended.

When land has been acquired for the purpose of supporting a building, all costs incurred up to the point of excavation for the building are generally considered land cost. The cost of excavation for a building is part of the building cost. However, if excavation is undertaken for purposes of contouring land for a golf course or terracing land for farming, such excavation costs would be capitalizable as a component of total land cost.

Appreciation. Valuation at cost (unless reduced to a lower estimated remaining useful cost due to impairment) has long been the rule in financial statement presentation.[1] Accounting Principles Board (APB) Opinion No. 6[2] states in this

---

[1] See Principle C-2 and discussion under the heading "Property Stated on Cost Basis," in Paul Grady, "Inventory of Generally Accepted Accounting Principles for Business Enterprises," *Accounting Research Study No. 7,* AICPA, New York, 1965, pp. 252–253.

[2] Accounting Principles Board, "Status of Accounting Research Bulletins," Opinion No. 6, AICPA, New York, 1965.

connection that " . . . property, plant and equipment should not be written up by an entity to reflect appraisal, market or current values which are above cost to the entity."

Depletion and Amortization.   Costs attributable to land rights that lose value with use (such as the right to extract mineral content) are recognized through systematic charges against income (called *depletion*), but only if there is a practicable basis for measuring or estimating relative periodic utilization of mineral or other content. Although depletion is generally associated with the extraction of mineral resources and severance of timber, there may be cases that justify reflection of depletion for the loss of value of other land rights. For example, the loss of soil fertility (where crop rotation and soil conservation practices were not carried out or when certain natural events have caused abnormal erosion) might give rise to the recognition of depletion.

Costs attributable to land rights that expire with the passage of time are recovered through systematic charges against income called *amortization*. Thus, costs to acquire a lease may be amortized over the term of the lease. Similarly, costs to acquire an easement that expires at the end of a period of time may be amortized over the term of the easement.

Costs attributable to land rights that do not diminish in value either with the passage of time or through use of the land are not amortized or depleted. For example, costs of land purchased to support a structure or a road across the surface ordinarily are not amortized or depleted. Similarly, the *residual value* of land used for mining purposes should remain unamortized even after exhaustion of the mineral or other content for which the land was originally purchased.

Salvage Proceeds.   Proceeds from transactions incidental to preparing land for agricultural or commercial use, such as the sale of timber or crops cleared from the land or the sale of scrap from demolished structures, usually are treated as a reduction of land cost. In theory, the negotiated price reflects such anticipated proceeds.

Income and Costs During a Holding Period.   Often land is acquired as an investment or for a specific future use, which contemplates the passage of time between the purchase date and the later date of sale or placement of the land to a specific use. Since the costs to be incurred during this holding period (such as interest, taxes, or maintenance charges) entered into the decision to acquire the land, these costs logically may be considered a part of the total investment in the land, unless it is likely that a portion of costs so capitalized may not be recoverable; i.e., a prospective future loss on disposition is forseeable. Any incidental income from the land during the holding period (such as income from ground rents or crops) should reduce total land cost. Accounting for interest expense is discussed in more detail in a later section, "Retail Land Sales."

Alternatively, when there is a regularly recurring and material source of income from land during a rather prolonged holding period, both revenue and expense may be reflected currently, particularly if the use of the land is considered an integral part of operations. In that event, the allocation of costs between land and depreciable assets may be necessary.

Land Option Costs.   The cost of an option to acquire land is part of the cost of land. When an option is allowed to expire, expense should be recognized in that period. However, under certain circumstances, if options are obtained on alternative parcels of land, one of which is eventually acquired for the stated purpose, the costs of the expired options as well as the cost of the exercised option may be added to the cost of the parcel of land acquired.

Land Improvements.   The cost of land improvements (such as paving and sidewalks) which deteriorate with use or the passage of time should ordinarily be capitalized and depreciated over their estimated useful lives, as applied to other items or property, plant, and equipment. However, the cost of improvements which do not deteriorate with use or passage of time (such as landscaping) ordinarily are not depreciated. Since these improvements are not depreciated, there is little need to distinguish their cost from the cost of land. Therefore, their cost is often capitalized directly as part of the cost of land.

Soil or Water Conservation Costs.   Costs incurred to protect land from wind or water erosion should be capitalized, since the land is made suitable for the use intended. If, on the other hand, costs are incurred regularly to maintain land in its existing condition and thereby enable its continued use, these costs should be charged to expense currently. An important exception may occur during a "holding period," when even the maintenance costs may be considered as additional costs of land.

Allocation of Cost of "Basket Purchases."   Often the purchase of a parcel of land is an inseparable part of a "basket purchase" of assets or net assets of a going concern. In such cases, the measurement of total cost or consideration is the lump sum paid, plus any liabilities assumed. The basket purchase price should then be allocated among the assets and liabilities acquired, in accordance with APB Opinion No. 16.[3]

The fair market value of each tangible asset purchased is, for the most part, the basis for allocating cost among the various assets. If the basket purchase includes intangible assets, the fair market value of the tangible assets, including land, ordinarily is considered to be their cost, and any residual portion of the total basket purchase cost is then attributed to intangible assets.

The determination of fair market value is a problem which must be solved by reference to all the facts and circumstances in each individual case. Use of a qualified independent appraiser is recommended as the best practice; however, in some cases, appraisals are made by the board of directors. Other methods used to estimate fair market value include:

Recent sales prices for comparable land parcels, which may be used to determine the amount of cost attributable to the land. The remaining portion of the basket purchase price may be deemed to represent the cost of other tangible or intangible assets.

Cost of the land to the predecessor owner, which may indicate fair market value if it is known that such cost represents a recently bargained purchase price.

Replacement cost of other tangible assets which sometimes can be estimated. This replacement cost, reduced by an allowance for depreciation when appropriate (the amount depending upon the age, type of construction, and state of repair of the buildings and improvements), can be attributed to the other tangible assets and the remainder attributed to the land (or possibly, in part, to intangibles).

Assessed value of land for property tax purposes. Usually this is not a reliable indicator of fair market value; however, if the assessed value can be demonstrated to be in constant ratio to the *fair* value, it may assist in determining fair market value.

Future Ability of the Land to Produce Income.   This is sometimes an accepted indicator of fair market value, although its estimation is not subject to exact computations. Probable future income from the land should be considered, however, as a test of the reasonableness of fair market values derived by other means.

Noncash Acquisitions

Exchange of Nonmonetary Assets for Land.   The basic principle expressed in APB Opinion No. 29[4] is that accounting for nonmonetary transactions should be based

---

[3]Accounting Principles Board, "Business Combinations," Opinion No. 16, AICPA, New York, 1970.

[4]Accounting Principles Board, "Accounting for Nonmonetary Transactions," Opinion No. 29, AICPA, New York, 1973.

on the fair values of the assets involved, except for those transactions in which fair value is not determinable or the earnings process is not complete. Thus, an exchange of nonmonetary assets generally should be accounted for at the fair value of the nonmonetary asset surrendered or received, whichever is more clearly evident. Any gain or loss on the exchange should be recognized—except that when "similar" assets are involved, gain will not be recognized currently (unless some cash is received by the party trading in—a rare case). For transactions in which fair value is not determinable, accounting should be based on the recorded amount of the nonmonetary asset relinquished.

Issuance of a corporation's own securities for land is a frequent transaction. In general, the fair market value of the securities issued in exchange is considered to be the cost of the land when there is a reliable and readily ascertainable market value for the securities. This procedure usually is appropriate for companies whose securities are traded actively and in sufficient volume to establish a fair market value. When corporate bonds are issued, the problem of establishing the cost of land acquired is less difficult, since bonds have a specified interest schedule and a contractual settlement price due at a determinable date, which represents a legally enforceable debt obligation ultimately payable in cash. Discounting of both factors at a rate reflecting current interest cost for a firm of this risk gives the valuation of the bonds and, indirectly, that of the land. The par value or stated value of the securities issued is not a reliable indicator of the value of the land purchased in exchange for these securities. If the securities issued have no reliable and readily ascertainable market value, land valuation will have to be determined by the methods described in the previous section on "basket purchases."

Donated Land.   When a parcel of land is acquired by donation (nonreciprocal transfer with nonowner, under provisions of APB Opinion No. 29),[5] the land should be recorded at its fair value at the time the gift becomes effective. Donation of land results in an increase in capital (donated capital or capital contributed in excess of par value) and ordinarily does not result in income.

Land donated subject to continuing restrictions or conditions as to use (such as endowment) may be given asset status at the effective date of the gift, with disclosure of the continuing restrictions clearly indicated. If the unfulfilled conditions preclude reflecting the donated land as an asset until the conditions are met, the contingent nature of the asset and the unfulfilled conditions should be disclosed.

Land Costs Contingent on Future Events.   Sometimes land is purchased for an amount which is dependent on future events; thus, its total cost is uncertain. The extent of this uncertainty determines the accounting treatment. For example, if the purchase contract provides for periodic payments to the seller during his lifetime, the buyer may record the estimated land cost and the related liability based on the present discounted value of the series of annuities payable during the life expectancy for an individual of the age of the seller. Similarly, if land which produces a contractual income (e.g., fixed ground rents for a definite term of years) is acquired in consideration of periodic payments of a percentage of the respective rentals, a basis is provided for measuring the probable cost in terms of the present value of the prospective payments. On the other hand, if the purchase contract provides for payments in the future dependent upon income to be earned from the land which cannot be estimated reasonably, the buyer would not reflect the contingent cost until paid but would disclose the terms of purchase. Future income cannot be considered to be subject to reasonable estimate.[6] Thus

---

[5]*Ibid.*

[6]See cases presented in Edmund F. Ingalls, *Practical Accounting and Auditing Problems,* AICPA, New York, 1966, pp. 1827 and 1829.

there was no entry made at the date of purchase with regard to the contingent payments. Each period thereafter as payments are made, the land account would be debited.

Vested Remainderman Interest in Land. Acquisition of land subject to an intervening life estate may pose special valuation or cost measurement problems. Unless the land is acquired for cash, it will be necessary to determine the present fair market value and then discount that amount by the use of life expectancy tables and an appropriate interest rate. This remainderman interest in land should be classified as an investment or among other assets rather than as property, plant, and equipment. Financial statements should disclose the restricted nature of this asset.

Contribution of Land to a Partnership. Land acquired by a partnership as a part of its capital (i.e., through contribution by one of the partners rather than by outright purchase) raises special problems. For federal income tax purposes, the basis of the land to the partnership usually is the basis to the contributing partner. For financial reporting purposes, however, such land is properly reflected at its fair market value at the date of acquisition.

SALE OF LAND

For many years the accounting practices and principles governing recognition of profit on sales of land were based on the concept expressed in Chapter 1A of *Accounting Research Bulletin (ARB) No. 43:* "Profit is deemed to be realized when a sale in the ordinary course of business is effected, unless the circumstances are such that the collection of the sales price is not reasonably assured."[7] Thus, subject to evaluation of the consideration received in the transaction, profit should be recognized at the time of sale if it could be determined that a bona fide sale had occurred. This concept was reaffirmed in APB Opinion No. 10, which stated: "Revenues should ordinarily be accounted for at the time a transaction is completed with appropriate provision for uncollectible accounts."[8] This opinion provided for revenue recognition on the installment and cost recovery methods only in instances when there was no reasonable basis for estimating the degree of collectibility of the sales price. These concepts served as generally accepted accounting principles for determining the point in time when revenue should be recognized, until the issuance of APB Statement No. 4,[9] which promulgated, in part, more comprehensive principles of revenue recognition. Statement No. 4 defines revenue as "a gross increase in assets or decrease in liabilities . . . that result from those types of profit-directed activities of an enterprise that can change owners' equity. Revenue . . . is derived from three general activities: (a) selling products, (b) rendering services . . . and (c) disposing of resources other than products. . . ." The statement held that realization is the measurement principle upon which revenue recognition is based, and set forth this principle as follows:

> *Realization.* Revenue is generally recognized when both of the following conditions are met (1) the earnings process is complete or virtually complete, and (2) an exchange has taken place.

Inasmuch as these concepts were broad in nature and did not specifically address themselves to the real estate industry, the AICPA issued two industry

[7]Committee on Accounting Procedure, "Restatement and Revision of Accounting Research Bulletins," AICPA, New York, 1953.

[8]Accounting Principles Board, "Omnibus Opinion—1966," Opinion No. 10, AICPA, New York, 1967.

[9]Accounting Principles Board, "Basic Concepts and Accounting Principles Underlying Financial Statements of Business Enterprises," Statement No. 4, AICPA, New York, 1970.

accounting guides: "Accounting for Retail Land Sales"[10] and "Accounting for Profit Recognition on Sales of Real Estate."[11]

The industry accounting guide for profit realization on real estate[12] specifies the two elements that are most important in timing of profit recognition: (1) the extent of the buyer's initial and continuing investment in the property; and (2) the continuing involvement of the seller with the property sold.

General Principles of Profit Recognition on Sale of Real Estate

Timing of Revenue (and Profit) Recognition.   In conventional transactions, revenue can be recognized at the time land is sold providing that two interdependent conditions exist: (1) the amount of revenue is measurable and the collection of the sales price is reasonably assured; and (2) the earnings process is complete or virtually complete and the seller is not involved in significant postsale activities. The installment method or the cost recovery method of accounting must generally be used if collectibility of sales price cannot be reasonably determined. However, the deposit method may also be appropriate if uncertainty as to collectibility exists. Under that method, the date of recognition of the sale is deferred, and no revenue is recognized before the sale is considered to be effective. All cash received before the sale is considered to be effective is accounted for as a deposit on the sales price.

Substance over Form.   Transactions should be carefully analyzed to determine that their economic substance does not differ from their legal form. This is exemplified by transactions that constitute a sale in legal terms but may actually be a construction or service contract, a lease, a joint venture, a deposit, or an option. Under normal circumstances, if a transaction is accounted for as a sale it should: (1) transfer from the seller to the buyer the usual risks and rewards of ownership; and (2) limit the seller's risk to that of a secured creditor.

Sales Must Be Consummated.   If any profit is to be recognized, a sale must be consummated before the end of the accounting period in which it would be reported. This occurs when parties are bound by the contract terms, all considerations are exchanged, and all conditions precedent to closing are performed.

Buyer's Investment.   Because of the uncertainty as to collectibility of receivables that may be present in a sale of real estate, there must be some additional assurance that the sales price will be collected before profit can be recognized. This additional assurance can be obtained by a significant buyer investment (both initial and continuing) which adequately demonstrates a commitment to pay for the property.

Initial Investment.   Factors to be evaluated in determining whether the buyer's initial investment (down payment) is sufficient to indicate a reasonable assurance of collecting the receivable are (1) the relative size of the buyer's down payment compared to the sales value; and (2) the composition of the down payment.

If full profit is to be recognized, the down payment must be equal to the major part of the difference between the usual loan limits of an established lending institution and the sales value of the property. Minimum down payments are set forth in Exhibit A of the industry guide;[13] these range from 5 percent for a single-family house to 25 percent for land which is to be developed after two years and for certain start-up situations. Because property appraisals occasionally differ and specific properties may not fall within the established limits of the industry accounting guide, a sale can also be recognized if the down payment is equal to or

---

[10]Committee on Land Development Companies, "Accounting for Retail Land Sales," Industry Accounting Guide, AICPA, New York, 1973.

[11]Committee on Accounting for Real Estate Transactions, "Accounting for Profit Recognition on Sales of Real Estate," Industry Accounting Guide, AICPA, New York, 1973.

[12]*Ibid.*

[13]*Ibid.*

greater than the amount by which the sales value exceeds 115 percent of (1) the permanent loan or (2) the permanent loan commitment established by an independent lending institution.

To assure collectibility of the receivable, the percentage requirement of the minimum down payment must generally consist of cash or notes supported by irrevocable letters of credit. The buyer may also make payments to third parties to reduce previously existing debt; may pay the seller points or a management fee; or may make other payments that in substance represent a financial investment in the property.

Continuing Investment.   If profit is to be recognized at the time of sale, the buyer must, in addition to making the requisite down payment, be "required to continue to increase his investment [that is, reduce indebtedness] in the property each year."[14] Level annual payments must be made over the customary term of the first mortgage, or over twenty years on a land sale. If this continuing investment on the buyer's part is not met, the seller should recognize a reduced profit. Such reduction is determined by applying an appropriate discount rate to reduce the receivable to its present value of the lowest level of annual payments over the customary term (twenty years for land). In this situation, the buyer's payments must equal the annual level of payments of principal and interest on the maximum first-lien indebtedness available on the property, plus interest at an appropriate rate on the excess of aggregate actual indebtedness.

The initial and continued investment test of the buyer should be applied cumulatively each year. If the above requirements are not met, the installment or cost recovery methods of recognition should be applied.

Receivables Subject to Subordination.   Because of the difficulties in evaluating collectibility of receivables subject to future subordination, profit should be limited to amounts determined under the cost recovery method if the receivable is subject to later subordination. This would not apply to a receivable subordinate to a primary lien on the property existing at the time of sale or to a future loan whose proceeds are used to pay the seller's receivable.

Seller's Continued Involvement.   The second key element determining timing of profit recognition is that of the seller's continued involvement with the property after its sale. This involvement may include the seller's arranging financing; managing, developing, or constructing the property; guaranteeing a return to the buyer; initiating and supporting operations after the property is sold; or participating in a real estate syndication.

Each type of continued seller involvement will have to be separately evaluated (as to substance) to determine appropriate accounting treatment. To the extent that the seller has obligations to perform after the sale, profit should not be recognized until such performance has been accomplished. Additionally, a sales contract should not be accounted for as a sale when the seller retains most of the risks of ownership.

The following summarizes types of seller involvement and the appropriate accounting treatment covered by the industry accounting guide:

1. Seller will participate in future profits without the risk of loss. Full profit can be recognized.

2. Seller is responsible for obtaining or providing permanent financing. Permanent financing must be arranged before the transaction is accounted for as a sale.

3. Seller is to provide management services without compensation (or at less than prevailing rates for the service required). Compensation should be imputed at prevailing rates and their discounted present value deducted from sales price in

---

[14]*Ibid.*

measuring profit at time of sale and recognized over the term of management contract.

4. Seller is obligated to develop property in the future, to construct facilities on the land, or to provide offsite improvements. Where costs of future required work can be reliably estimated, profit should be recognized on a precentage-of-completion basis. In a situation where total cost cannot be estimated, profit should be recognized on the completed-contract method, that is, only when all work is completed.

5. Seller is to initiate or support operations of property for a specific time period, or is to provide for a return on the investment to the buyer. The substance of the transaction should be carefully evaluated to determine if an actual sale has occurred. Accounting treatment should follow the conclusion of this evaluation.

6. A sales contract may, in substance, be a pure financing, leasing, or profit-sharing arrangement rather than a sale. No sale is recognized and payments should be accounted for as funds loaned, rental payments, or transfers required for proper division of profits as the substance of transaction indicates.

Sale-and-Leaseback Transactions. In the absence of exceptional circumstances, sale-and-leaseback transactions should not result in the immediate recognition of income. In Opinion No. 5, the Accounting Principles Board stated:[15]

> The Board is of the opinion that the sale and the leaseback usually cannot be accounted for as independent transactions. Neither the sale price nor the annual rental can be objectively evaluated independently of the other. Consequently, material gains or losses resulting from the sale of properties which are the subject of sale-and-leaseback transactions, together with the related tax effect, should be amortized over the life of the lease as an adjustment of the rental cost. . . .

Sale of Air Rights, Easements, Mineral Interests, or Other Partial Rights to the Land. When a sale is made of one, or a few, of the rights to a parcel of land, the determination of the amount of the gain or loss from the sale depends upon the allocation made of costs attributable to the interest sold. In many cases, a useful and meaningful allocation of costs can be made by obtaining an estimate of the fair market value of the land immediately before and immediately after the partial interest in the land has been sold. The percentage by which the fair market value has declined after the sale is considered to be the percentage of total land costs attributable to the interest sold. Sometimes assessed valuations are used as a basis for allocation.

Distribution of Land to Shareholders. Occasionally, land may be distributed to shareholders as a dividend, particularly in closely held companies. This type of transaction is provided for as a nonreciprocal transfer with owners in APB Opinion No. 29.[16] It should be recorded at the fair value of the asset transferred. Gain or loss (if any) should be recognized on the disposition of that asset.

RETAIL LAND SALES

Land sales companies typically engage in the purchase, development, and resale of land. The land is purchased in one or more large tracts which are subdivided into smaller parcels (lots) on the basis of a master plan. This plan may call for certain offsite improvements and amenities to provide basic recreational and community facilities. The land sales company may complete all development and construction for the entire project. Often, however, the company will complete only certain land improvements (directly or by contract), such as streets and sewers, and then

[15]Accounting Principles Board, "Reporting of Leases in Financial Statements of Lessee," Opinion No. 5, AICPA, New York, 1964.
[16]AICPA, *op. cit.*

sell portions of the tract to other developers or builders for completion. The purchasers of individual lots typically make a small down payment and pay the balance of the land sales contract over a number of years.

The industry accounting guide pertaining to retail land sales[17] applies to retail lot sales on a volume basis, with down payments that are less than those required to evaluate collectibility of casual sales of real estate. The guide specifies accounting under the accrual and installment methods.

Timing of Revenue and Income Recognition. The realization concept, as discussed above under "Sale of Land," and the time when realization occurs determine the accounting period when revenue and expenses should be matched to determine the income or loss of a business activity. Accordingly, costs should be accrued and deferred until the related revenue is recognized to measure periodic income properly. Because of an extended earnings process in land sales, it is difficult to determine the period in which realization is said to occur. Some of the special features of this situation are discussed below.

Accounting Considerations.   A sale transaction involving retail land should not be viewed as giving rise to revenue until conditions indicate that (1) the customer seriously intends to complete the contract; and (2) the company is capable of fulfilling its obligations under the contract so that customers cannot later demand and be entitled to receive refunds for failure to deliver. All of the following three conditions must be satisfied before a contract can be recorded as a sale:

1. The customer has made a down payment and all regularly required subsequent payments until the period during which cancellation with refund is permitted has expired.

2. The aggregate customer payments (including interest) are equal to or greater than 10 percent of the contract sales price.

3. Based upon current circumstances and knowledge, it is apparent that the selling company has the capabilities (currently and prospectively) (a) to provide the land improvements and offsite facilities included in the contract; and (b) to meet any other representations it has made.

Funds collected prior to satisfying all these conditions are recorded as deposits and credited to an account similar to the one usually called Advances from Customers.

Accounting Methods.   The industry accounting guide specifies that the method of accounting (accrual, installment, or cost recovery) for income should in part depend upon the evaluation of collectibility of the receivable resulting from the sale.

The accrual method should be used on a project-by-project basis when there is reasonable evidence that the receivable will be collected and all of the following conditions are met:

1. The properties clearly will be used for residential or recreational purposes when the normal payment period is complete. There must be a reasonable expectation that the land can be developed for its intended purposes.

2. The project's improvements have progressed beyond preliminary stages, and there is evidence that the work will be completed according to plan.

3. The receivable is not subject to subordination to new loans on the property, except for home construction purposes.

4. The company's collection experience on this project indicates with reasonable predictability that the receivable will be collected and that 90 percent of the contracts in force six months after sales are recorded will be collected in full. The "contracts in force" requirement may be measured either in dollars (principal amount) or numbers of contracts, provided that consistency is maintained.

---

[17]AICPA, "Accounting for Retail Land Sales," *op. cit.*

Absence of any of the above conditions requires use of the installment method for recording sales. If, because of existing uncertainties, the sale is recorded on the installment method but these uncertainties are subsequently resolved, thereby fulfilling the above conditions, the accrual method should be adopted. This change should be accounted for as a change in an accounting estimate (without retroactive adjustment of retained earnings), in accordance with Paragraphs 31–33 of APB Opinion No. 20.[18]

Accrual Method. When the above conditions for recording income under the accrual method are met, the following procedures should be applied:

1. Gross sales (the contract price) should be recorded before deducting any discount applicable for valuation of the receivable ("Interest Rate," discussed below) and for revenue to be earned from improvement work to be performed in the future ("Future Performance," discussed below). The portion of the discount price applicable to future improvements should be classified as deferred revenue and recognized as work is performed.

2. A contract recorded as a sale and subsequently cancelled in the same reporting period should be included in and then separately deducted from gross sales or should have other appropriate disclosure.

3. Gross sales should be reduced by those sales that are not expected to be collected due to cancellations in subsequent periods, along with any related discount and deferred revenue to arrive at net sales. A matching debit to an allowance for contract cancellations (a contra to receivables) would be made. When a contract is deemed to be cancelled, the receivable balance should be charged to the allowance for contract cancellations.

4. The computation of cost of sales, such as land and improvement costs incurred and carrying costs, should be based entirely on the net sales thus recorded.

5. On the balance sheet, receivables should be reduced by the unamortized valuation discount and the allowance for contract cancellations.

Delinquency and Cancellation.   In determining when delinquent receivables are presumed to be uncollectible, criteria have been set forth in the industry audit guide. A representative sample of historical data should be selected to determine the company's delinquency experience; such experience should be applied to estimated collection problems encountered in current sales. The industry accounting guide states:[19]

> If receivables in the sample are past due at the end of the period of time selected . . . the receivable should be considered uncollectible and the contracts presumed to be cancelled (for this purpose) if regular payments due are unpaid for the following delinquency periods:

Percent of Contract Price Paid	Delinquency Period
Less than 25%	90 days
25% but less than 50%	120 days
50% and over	150 days

These periods may be extended in certain extenuating circumstances if it can be determined that the purchaser has the ability to complete payment in accordance with the contract and plans to do so.

Interest Rate.   The guide recognizes that contract receivables would have to be discounted to reflect higher interest rates when the stated rate is less than the

---

[18]Accounting Principles Board, "Accounting Changes," Opinion No. 20, AICPA, New York, 1971.

[19]AICPA, "Accounting for Retail Land Sales," *op. cit.*

prevailing rate for an obligation with similar terms, security, and risk. In discussing the initial measure of consideration, the guide states: "Generally the credit ratings of retail land purchasers approximate those of users of retail consumer installment credit provided by commercial banks and established retail organizations." It goes on to conclude that the effective annual yield on the receivable (without a reduction for revenue attributable to future services such as site improvements or deferred income tax) should not be less than the minimum annual rate charged locally by commercial banks and established retail organizations to borrowers financing purchases of customer personal property with installment credit.

Future Performance.   The earnings process may be incomplete at the time the sale is recorded if the seller has an obligation to complete improvements, amenities, and other facilities applicable to lots sold. This causes certain problems in determining the amount of revenue to be recognized upon performance of such obligations. The guide concludes: "The amount of revenue recognized (discounted contract price) at the time a sale is recorded should be based on the stage of completion of the required performance." This stage (percentage) of completion is determined by the ratio of project cost incurred to date to estimated total project costs (including selling costs). Thus, to the extent that the earnings process is complete, total revenue will be recognized; to the extent that there exists an element of future performance, revenue will be deferred and matched against those future expenses.

Installment Method.   The installment method must be applied to those sales that do not qualify for the accrual method under the above-mentioned criteria. The installment method requires application of the following procedures:

1. The entire contract price applicable to the installment sale, without reduction for discounts or cancellations, should be reported as revenue in the year the sale is recorded.

2. The applicable expenses (cost of sales, selling general and administrative, provision for future improvement costs) related to the revenue recorded in 1, above, should be currently charged to income.

3. The difference between 1 and 2, above (gross profit less selling costs directly associated with the project), should be treated as deferred profit and recognized in income as customer payments are received. The unamortized portion of this deferred profit should be shown on the balance sheet as a deduction from contracts receivable.

4. Interest income at the stated contract rate should be recorded as income when payment is received.

5. If both the accrual and installment methods are being used, the portion of receivables and sales applicable to the installment method should be disclosed.

6. If contracts are cancelled, all receivables, liabilities, and deferred profit should be reduced. Recoverable land and improvement costs should be restored, and any remaining costs should be treated as a loss in the period of cancellation.

Deposit Accounting.   Until a contract qualifies as a sale under the accrual method, funds collected (including interest) should be recorded as deposits by crediting an account similar to advances from customers. This is necessitated by the high rate of customer default prevailing in the industry and the inability to predict the likelihood that a customer will fulfill the contract. Project selling costs should be deferred until the sale is recorded, at which time they should be charged to expense. Revenue should not be recognized until the cancellation-with-refund period has expired.

Capitalizable Costs.   All costs (e.g., interest, real estate taxes, and other direct costs) specifically related to inventories of unimproved land or to additional construction necessary to bring such land to a salable condition should be capitalized and carried at a cost not exceeding net realizable value. Interest is capitalized only when it results from (1) "loans for which unimproved land or construction in progress is pledged as collateral; or (2) other loans, if the proceeds are used for improvements or for acquiring unimproved land."

Amenities. Costs of amenities (such as golf courses, club houses, lakes, parks, and utilities) should be evaluated in light of their estimated useful lives, their anticipated return, their effectiveness as selling aids, and expected selling date for the entire project. Unrecoverable costs should be charged to the cost of home sales on a pro rata basis. If these amenities prove to be productive selling aids, their costs can be depreciated over their useful lives or over the period in which lots are projected to be sold, whichever is shorter.

Cost Allocation. Capitalized cost (many of which are joint costs) can be allocated to projects and parcels on any reasonably consistent method that will fairly match such costs with related revenues. The various methods used for this allocation include: (1) area methods (square footage, acres, frontage, or some other measure); (2) value methods (mortgage release prices, estimated selling prices, or appraisals); (3) specific identification methods; or (4) hybrid methods having some element of the other three methods.

Disclosures. The following additional disclosures are required in financial statements of retail land companies:

1. A Statement of Changes in Financial Position, presented for all periods in which earnings information is reported. The statement should be prepared on the basis of sources and uses of cash, rather than changes in working capital.

2. The method of income recognition and the interest rate(s) used for discounting.

3. Receivables, with the following related information: (a) five-year receivable maturities; (b) cancellation policy; (c) method of determining and amount of delinquent accounts; (d) weighted average and range of stated interest rates; (e) amount of contracts not recorded as sales and related receipts.

4. Land and improvement inventories, classified as to; (a) unimproved land, (b) land being improved, (c) fully improved land, and (d) land subject to unrecorded sales contracts. The capitalization policy of costs and the allocation method of amenities and carrying charges should also be disclosed.

5. Estimated costs of future improvements and the method of determining these estimates, five-year debt maturities with weighted average and range of interest rates, liabilities restricted to specific assets, and certain information regarding the composition of the sources (cost) of income.

Valuing Repossessed Properties. When repossessions occur, they are valued either at the lower of (1) original cost, (2) fair value (net realizable value on resale), or (3) the uncollected installment receivable plus refunds, if any, to the defaulting purchasers. When repossession occurs in the same period as the sale, the practice, almost universally, is to value the lot at original cost.

BIBLIOGRAPHY

Bennet, J. W.: "Problems in Land Development Accounting," *Canadian Chartered Accountant,* April 1969.

Cerf, Alan Robert: "Accounting for Retail Land Sales," *The Accounting Review,* vol. 50, no. 3 pp. 451–465, July 1975.

Cole, LeRoy H.: "Accounting Problems of Land Development Companies," *The Arthur Young Journal,* vol. 12, no. 2, October 1964.

Committee on Accounting for Real Estate Transactions: "Accounting for Profit Recognition on Sales of Real Estate," Industry Accounting Guide, AICPA, New York, 1973.

Committee on Land Development Companies: "Accounting for Retail Land Sales," Industry Accounting Guide, AICPA, New York, 1973.

Ingalls, Edmund F.: *Practical Accounting and Auditing Problems,* AICPA, New York, 1966.

Lotharius, Richard D., and Michael Brown: "Accounting for Land Development Costs—A Reappraisal," *The Florida Certified Public Accountant,* May 1965.

McMichael, S. L.: *Real Estate Subdivisions,* Prentice-Hall, Englewood Cliffs, N.J., 1949.

Paton, William A., and William A. Paton, Jr.: *Assets—Accounting and Administration,* Roberts & Roehl, Detroit, 1971.

"Presentation of Practitioners' Views on Accounting for Land Development Companies," *The Chartered Accountant in Australia,* vol. 34, June 1964.

Simons, Harry, and Wilbert E. Karrenbrock: *Intermediate Accounting,* 4th ed., SouthWestern Publishing Company, Cincinnati, 1964.

Chapter **18**

Natural Resources

HORACE R. BROCK
Professor of Accounting, North Texas State University

CHARACTERISTICS OF NATURAL RESOURCE PRODUCERS

Natural Resources Defined. Natural resources, sometimes called "wasting assets," are created primarily by the work of nature. For accounting purposes, the definition is usually sharply limited to "products" that are extracted or removed directly from the earth or sea. Thus, although the surface area of land is in the broad sense a natural resource, it is not normally extracted, removed, or produced, and it is not included in this definition.

Based on the methods employed to extract or remove the product, natural resources may be conveniently classified in three categories. These recovery methods, which largely determine the accounting problems involved, are:

1. Extraction through mining from either open-pit or shaft mines. Most metals, such as copper, iron, lead, silver, and gold, along with minerals such as coal, salt, potash, and limestone, are included in this category. Sand, gravel, clay, stone, and similar products are likewise extracted from mines or quarries.

2. Production through wells drilled below the earth's surface. The principal minerals produced by this means are oil and gas.

3. Harvesting of growing products. Standing timber has historically been considered a wasting asset because until a very few years ago "cut" forests were not replaced with seedlings but were left barren, to be reforested only by nature—if at all. The practices of planting trees as a crop, selective cutting, and reforestation have now become so widespread that the timber industry has many more of the characteristics of agricultural farming than of an extractive industry. For this reason, only a brief description of accounting for standing timber is included at the end of this chapter.

The third category could be further extended to include orchards, fisheries, and similar activities closely related to nature, but these, too, are more akin to farming than to natural resource extraction.

The definition of natural resources emphasizes two factors: (1) the removal or extinguishment of the asset, and (2) replacement of the resource only by action of nature, if at all. Depletion of a natural resource is recognized as the physical quantity of the resource is diminished by production. This may be contrasted with depreciation of assets such as buildings, machinery, and equipment where the asset remains physically intact but the economic service life is diminished by use, passage of time, or obsolescence. Both depreciation and depletion seek to allocate the cost of long-lived assets over the periods of benefit from the asset.

Physical Activities in Natural Resource Industries. Physical activities leading to extraction of natural resources include three significant steps:

1. Finding a potential deposit of the resource and acquiring title to the property. In the early days of mining, these activities were very simple and were popularly referred to as "prospecting" and "staking a claim." Today, the term "geological and geophysical exploration" is more appropriately used to encompass the myriad of sophisticated exploration equipment and techniques such as gravity meters, magnetic meters, seismographs, aerial photography, core drills, and chemical analysis of soil and rocks used in the search for potentially productive ore and mineral deposits. Similarly, purchase or lease contracts necessary to acquire property rights in natural resources have grown complex.

2. "Developing" the property. After a potential deposit has been found, some means must be developed to permit the contents to be extracted. This may require merely the removal of the overlying layers of earth in order to reach the mineral or ore. Frequently, however, underground tunnels or shafts must be constructed to obtain access to the deposit. In still other cases, most notably in producing oil and gas, holes must be drilled deep below the earth's surface to tap and extract the mineral.

The development phase requires large outlays for both depreciable tangible equipment and for "intangible development costs" (usually referred to simply as IDC) that have in themselves no salvage value. Even after production has been attained, additional development costs may be necessary in order to extend the area of production or to gain access to all the resources in the deposit.

3. Extraction of the resource. Once deposits have been found and facilities constructed to remove the product, actual production, which may continue over many years, is begun.

Summary of Basic Accounting Problems.   Most accounting problems peculiar to the extractive industries result from two factors:

1. Large capital outlays are necessary to find and develop natural resource deposits.

2. A high degree of uncertainty or risk is associated with many of these capital investments since the properties to which they apply often prove commercially unproductive. Additionally, there may be a long period between the time that expenditures are made and the time when it is known whether they have resulted in productive assets.

These two factors have combined to produce a rather complicated and inconsistent application of generally accepted accounting principles. The situation is abetted by federal tax laws permitting companies engaged in extractive activities to compute taxable income by methods unacceptable for financial accounting purposes. The number and significance of these special tax situations have been reduced in recent years, but many still remain.

One result of large capital investments, the high degree of uncertainty, and special tax laws has been the development of many unusual contracts and legal arrangements for risk sharing that create unusual accounting problems.

The remainder of this chapter examines some of the principal accounting problems peculiar to companies engaged in extracting natural resources (referred to as "operators"). As suggested by the above discussion, most of these problems relate to capital outlays and may be conveniently examined in the following sequence:

1. Accounting for the acquisition and development of property.

2. Depletion amortization, and depreciation of capitalized costs, and

3. Special property interests.

In addition, brief attention is given to other accounting problems of lesser significance.

ACQUISITION AND DEVELOPMENT OF NATURAL RESOURCES

Matching Costs and Revenues.   Accounting practices in the natural resources industries, as in other businesses, should be based on generally accepted accounting principles, which in turn are founded on an underlying body of assumptions, concepts, postulates, and standards. Of special significance in accounting for activities leading to the finding and developing of wasting assets are the cost principle, the going-concern concept, and the matching principle.

There are many logical arguments supporting the valuation of natural resources at "current value." Similarly, there is strong theoretical support for using current value to account for developed mineral properties. Nevertheless, natural resource properties are almost always recorded at "cost," on the theory that cost is verifiable and, since there is usually no intention to liquidate the business, current values are deemed irrelevant. The major difficulty in implementing the cost principle is in matching acquisition and development costs with the revenues they produce. This process of determining which costs are expired (expenses or losses) and which are unexpired (to be carried forward as assets) is complicated by the uncertainty surrounding most expenditures made in acquiring and developing natural resources and by the difficulty encountered in attempting to associate costs with specific revenues resulting from them. Thus, the fundamental problem is determining when the costs involved should be deducted as expenses or losses in measuring profit.

The Cost Center. In attempting to match acquisition and development costs with revenues generated, it is customary first to assign costs to "cost centers." Similarly, reserves and production are associated with cost centers; therefore costs and revenues from assets are related.

In recent years a great deal of controversy has arisen over the definition of the cost center, especially in the petroleum industry. The two basic concepts are "full costing" and "successful-efforts costing." In actual practice modifications or combinations of the two concepts are used.

The Full Costing Concept. Under a strict interpretation of the full costing concept, the cost center is deemed to be the business enterprise as a whole; that is, *all* costs incurred by a company in seeking to find, acquire, and develop mineral reserves are deemed applicable to whatever resources result from these activities. The cost of the exploration activities that do not prove fruitful are considered to be part of the cost of the productive assets discovered so long as the ratio of successes to failures falls within reasonable bounds. Thus, for normally successful firms all costs incurred in searching for and developing reserves are capitalized. Capitalized costs are deemed to be applicable to all resources owned by the company, and are subsequently amortized on an overall unit-of-production basis as minerals are produced.

The Successful-Efforts Costing Concept. Under successful-efforts costing, only those costs which result directly in discovery or development of mineral deposits (and thus in producing present or future revenues) are capitalized, while costs that do not lead to discovery or development of minerals are charged to current expense. Costs that are capitalized are amortized as the specific minerals to which they apply are produced. The focus under successful-efforts costing is associating as precisely as possible the costs incurred and the revenues, if any, resulting from specific exploration activity. Thus the concept is closely tied to conventional accounting methodology, which holds that only those costs that will yield measurable specific future benefits should be carried forward as assets. (Those who dislike successful-efforts accounting tend to call it "dry-hole accounting.")

Advantages of Each Concept. A number of arguments are given to support the full costing concept:

1. All exploration and development costs are necessary to find and develop whatever reserves result from these activities. There is no way to avoid unsuccessful and nonproductive costs. Without them, present or future reserves would not be obtained.

2. The success of a mineral producing company is measured largely by its ability to discover and develop reserves. Thus, full costing presents fairly the economic facts of the industry.

3. The amortization of costs on an overall basis gives a more meaningful and realistic matching of costs and revenues and, therefore, a more logical measure of income. For example, under successful-efforts costing, a profitable and aggressive company may actually show a loss by charging to expense the unsuccessful efforts

of an active exploration program even though substantial reserves may be added by the company's successful activities. Similarly, a declining company may, under successful-efforts costing, appear to be more successful than it actually is because it has no exploration program to replace the minerals being produced.

4. Full costing reduces the opportunities to manipulate reported profits that are available under successful-efforts costing. For example, under successful-efforts costing, management may postpone decisions to surrender nonproductive acreage that will be charged to income, or it may increase or decrease its drilling and exploration program to substantially influence charges against income. Under full costing all such costs are capitalized, thus eliminating this option on the part of management.

The primary arguments supporting successful-efforts costing may be summarized as follows:

1. The method gives a more direct matching of efforts and accomplishments. Costs that are in themselves nonproductive are not carried forward as assets.

2. The method is more conservative than full costing. Thus the risk of having asset carrying values that exceed the actual value of the reserves involved is reduced.

3. The method gives a better indication of the actual costs of reserves in each individual cost center, enabling management to measure the accomplishments in each mineral venture.

Modifications of the Basic Concepts. Under a strict interpretation of the full cost concept, *all* exploration and development costs are presumed to be incurred to obtain *all* mineral reserves found. Similarly, a strict interpretation of the successful-efforts concept would call for each mine or well to be treated as a cost center. However, there are modifications to the full costing and successful-efforts costing concepts both in the literature of accounting theory and in actual practice.

Many persons supporting full costing believe that because of political and economic problems it is more appropriate to have separate cost centers (areas for which costs are accumulated and matched with related reserves) for countries with similar political and economic attributes. For example, it is often suggested that Canada and the United States be considered as one cost center, while each other country (or area of the world) might be treated as a separate cost center. In other words, a producer might accumulate all its exploration and development costs in the United States and Canada and subsequently amortize this total cost over its mineral reserves in the two countries, while having a similar cost center for all of South America. This procedure is commonly used by those companies endorsing the full cost concept.

Those companies using the successful-efforts concept traditionally use the individual lease as the cost center. The lease has been used as the cost center because it represents the legal unit by which minerals are acquired. Further, the oil producer must maintain cost and revenue records for each lease for federal income tax purposes. Also, revenue records must be accumulated by lease for settlement with the landowner or other royalty owner.

Many mining companies accumulate costs of an entire "range" or field involving two or more mines. Oil and gas producers often combine leases into larger accounting units under "pooling" or "unitization" agreements. Also, in the petroleum industry it is often suggested that the "field," the mineral formation, the "basin," or the deposit be used as the cost center.

Some variation of successful-efforts costing predominates, although a growing number of petroleum companies, especially smaller companies, have adopted full costing.

Efforts to Develop an Authoritative Definition of the Cost Center. For more than a decade, attempts to define authoritatively the cost center for mineral producers have been made. The first major effort was a research project initiated by the

Director of Research of The American Institute of Certified Public Accountants and carried out by Robert E. Field. In the resulting Research Study No. 11, it was suggested that the field is the most appropriate center for accumulating costs and matching them against revenues.

In 1970 a subcommittee of the AICPA's Accounting Principles Board began study of the question, and in 1971 it issued a discussion memorandum on accounting and reporting practices in the petroleum industry. In the discussion memorandum the committee concluded that a producing cost center defined in geological terms is preferable to any other. In the memorandum the committee dismissed the lease or property-acquisition unit, organizational units, full costing, large geological units, and geographical boundaries as appropriate cost center concepts, and tentatively concluded that the field should be selected as the recommended cost center.

At the public hearing on this proposal, proponents of full costing raised strenuous objections to the use of the field as the cost center, and the Committee on Extractive Industries was instructed by the APB to submit new proposals. In 1972 the committee proposed two alternative cost centers—the field and the country. This proposal also was vigorously attacked, primarily on the basis that alternative use of the field or the country as the cost center would produce such widely divergent results that financial statements of companies using different cost centers could not be compared. In 1972 the APB reviewed the topics on its agenda in contemplation of the APB's being replaced by the Financial Accounting Standards Board and concluded that the extractive industries project should be deleted from its agenda. In June 1973, the APB published a summary of the committee's research in accounting for the oil and gas industry, *Accounting and Reporting Practices in the Oil and Gas Industry,* which was designed to provide the FASB with a summary of the committee's research. Clearly the APB did not develop an authoritative statement on the proper cost center, and the FASB placed the topic on its active agenda only in late 1975.

Accounting for Property Rights.   Mining companies customarily acquire ore deposits by outright purchase, resulting in the acquisition of "fee" interests in both land surface and underlying ore deposits. In the petroleum industry, on the other hand, most mineral rights take the form of leaseholds; fee interests are far less frequently acquired. In this chapter the property right to develop and produce the natural resource is called the "working interest," whether a fee interest or a leasehold is involved.

Fee Interests.   The entire purchase price of fee interests, including incidental acquisition costs such as abstracts, attorney's charges, commissions, and stamp taxes, should be capitalized. Ideally, the total purchase price should be allocated between the surface and mineral rights on the basis of relative values. However, it is difficult to measure mineral values in most cases, and the land surface, especially in mountainous mining areas, is often almost worthless. As a result, the purchase price is customarily charged to an Undeveloped Properties account. Then if the property is later developed, the entire cost is treated as being applicable to the natural resource. Where the value of either type of property (surface rights or mineral rights) can be readily ascertained, it is feasible to assign this portion of the purchase price to the property whose value is known and to allocate the remaining cost to the other property element.

Leasehold Interests.   Mineral leases are secured for a primary term, regardless of whether or not mineral production is obtained, and for a secondary term for as "long thereafter as minerals are produced in commercial quantities." A *bonus* is paid at the time of signing the lease. This bonus should be capitalized as cost of the mineral rights and charged to the Undeveloped Properties account. Similarly, miscellaneous acquisition costs such as attorneys' fees and taxes should be capitalized as part of the leasehold cost. *Delay rentals* are paid each year after the first year during the primary term until production is secured or the lease is surrendered. (The lessee may terminate the lease at any time during the primary term by discontinuing rental payments. If development is not begun within the primary term, the lease expires.) Rentals are almost always charged to expense even though a good theoretical argument, based on the "construction period" theory, may be advanced for capitalizing these payments.

When mineral properties are acquired by lease, the lessor retains a *royalty interest*, under which a specified percentage or fractional part (usually one-eighth) of the gross value of all minerals produced will be paid to him. The lessor or royalty owner bears none of the development or production expenses except the production taxes on his share of output. The royalty owner's share of reserves and production are ignored by the operator in accounting entries and computations. More complex contracts involving special property interests in leased mineral rights are examined later in this chapter.

Accounting for Exploration Costs.   Geological and geophysical exploration work to locate potential mineral or ore deposits or to determine whether known deposits are commercially productive may be undertaken either before or after mineral rights are actually acquired. If exploration is carried out prior to acquisition of mineral rights, the operator makes a small payment to the property owner for "rights to explore." Normally the contract gives the operator an option to purchase or lease all or part of the property involved. Sometimes, however, "rights to explore only" contracts, without an option to acquire acreage, may be obtained.

Alternative Procedures.   Generally accepted accounting principles suggest that exploration expenditures eventually leading to production, regardless of whether the exploration is conducted prior to or after property interests have been obtained, should be capitalized as part of the mineral costs. In practice, these costs (as well as intangible development costs) are treated in three ways: (1) all charged as current expense, (2) all capitalized, or (3) a part capitalized and a part charged to expense.

1. Many natural resource producers treat all exploration costs as current expense. A commonly encountered argument for this practice is that most such costs will never result in productive mines or wells. Another justification offered is that the long-run effect on profit will be the same no matter how the costs are treated in the statements. Some accountants suggest that since exploration work is an ongoing, routine activity, the producing mineral company should treat all geological and geophysical expenditures as operating expense. This position was taken in *Accounting Research Study No. 11.*

2. If the full costing concept is followed, *all* exploration and other finding and development costs will be capitalized. As previously observed, this suggestion is based on the reasoning that the entire program of property acquisition, exploration, and development is necessary to obtain whatever reserves may result. Hence all costs apply to these reserves.

3. By far the most common practice is to capitalize those costs leading directly to the acquisition, retention, or development of properties, but to charge to expense (or loss) costs which cannot be traced to specific resource-bearing properties. This procedure is often difficult to apply in practice because of the problem of identifying costs with specific properties. If payments are made to outsiders for performing work on a specific currently owned property, there is no problem. However, several common complications merit special attention.

Cost of Company's Own Staff.   Some companies operate their own exploration departments. The routine operating costs of the company's staff, especially general overhead costs, are extremely difficult to identify with work carried out on specific properties. Since they often have little relation to the amount of work done and remain relatively constant from year to year, these costs are customarily treated as current expenses. However, those costs which can be traced to activities on specific mineral interests should be capitalized.

Exploration on Areas Covered by Shooting Rights.   Another difficult problem is encountered when geological and geophysical surveys are conducted on property where the company has not yet obtained mineral rights, even though it may have options to acquire the property. Frequently in the petroleum industry a "reconnaissance-type" survey is made on a very large area. As a result of the survey one or more "areas of interest" may be indicated, or the survey may show that no potential mineral deposits exist in the area. This situation is usually solved by conforming to the tax rules, which require that the entire cost of the reconnaissance survey be allocated to all areas of interest indicated. If no area of interest is found, the cost is treated as a loss in the year that the project is abandoned. Costs of detailed surveys on areas of interest, along with the allocated general survey costs, are then capitalized as cost of any property obtained. Again, if no property is acquired as a result, the applicable costs are charged off as an abandonment loss.

Although tax rules require that preliminary survey costs be allocated equally to all areas of interest and that all costs applicable to areas of interest be apportioned (usually on the basis of acreage) to any property acquired in that area, many companies allocate both preliminary and detailed survey costs between acreage acquired and that not acquired on some basis such as "shot points," "core tests" or number of acres involved.

Exploration costs are generally accumulated in the accounts as assets until a definite result has been obtained from the project. Then they are capitalized or charged off as a loss, as previously indicated.

Payments for shooting rights only are usually classified as exploration costs and handled accordingly. However, when the shooting rights are coupled with an option to acquire the property, an allocable portion of the cost is almost always treated as capitalized cost of mineral rights obtained, even by those companies that charge all exploration costs to expense.

The federal tax laws governing exploration costs of ore and mineral properties other than oil and gas are rather complicated, but essentially the taxpayer is allowed one of three options (Secs. 615 and 617 of IRC).

1. Capitalize all such expenditures.

2. Take an "unlimited" deduction of all exploration costs located in the United States. (However, when a property reaches production stage or is sold, the amounts so deducted may be "recovered.")

3. Deduct up to $100,000 per year, with a maximum cumulative deduction of $400,000 for the producer. In this case there is no "recovery" when the property becomes productive or is sold.

Test-Well Contributions.   Another practice found primarily in the petroleum industry is to make "test-well contributions." An operator may contribute either leasehold property or cash to another party drilling a nearby test well in return for geological and geophysical information obtained from the well. Cash contributions may be either dry-hole (the contribution is made only if the test well is dry) or bottom-hole (the contribution is made regardless of whether the test well is dry or productive). Acreage contributions are made under bottom-hole contracts, and ordinarily the contributor retains some property interest in the contributed acreage, as described later in this chapter. Dry-hole contributions are charged to expense because they do not add to the value of the donor's property. On the other hand, bottom-hole donations are customarily treated as an expense if the test well is dry; they are capitalized (added to the cost of nearby properties) if the test well is productive, because the existence of a productive well presumably increases the value of surrounding properties. (The recipient normally considers the contribution to be a reduction of his intangible drilling and development costs.)

Development Costs. After geological and geophysical exploration have indicated the probable existence of commercially productive ore or mineral deposits, much development work must be carried out before the reserves in the deposit can actually be produced. The development of mines involves the removal of top layers of earth (strip and pit mining) or the construction of shafts or tunnels into the earth to reach the deposits. Oil and gas reservoirs can be tapped only by the drilling of wells.

Development costs fit into two classifications: tangible equipment and intangible development costs.

Tangible Equipment. Tangible equipment represents equipment and machinery constructed or installed for the production and processing of mineral or ore in the mine or on the mineral property. This category includes such items as ore conveyor systems, ore loading and storage facilities, and processing equipment used in the mine. Pumps, flow lines, treating equipment, and storage tanks are typical examples of tangible equipment used in oil and gas operations.

Costs assigned to tangible equipment should include the associated labor and other installation costs where they can reasonably be identified with the equipment. The accounting records should, of course, contain sufficient classification and detail to provide control over the assets and to enable depreciation and other expenses related to equipment to be identified with specific mineral properties.

Intangible Development Costs. Intangible development costs represent expenditures for items that have in themselves no salvage value and cannot be related to the installation of tangible equipment. For example, the costs of tunnels and shafts, or the removal of top layers of earth in strip mining, are intangible in nature. Similarly, costs incurred in drilling wells in oil and gas fields are intangible drilling and development costs.

Frequently it is difficult to distinguish between geological and geophysical exploration activities and development activities. For example, an oil well may be drilled on a previously undeveloped property. If the well is dry, the costs may be considered as geological and geophysical exploration; if the well is productive, the costs may be treated as development costs. In mining operations often no distinction is made between development costs and exploration costs up to the time that it has been determined that minerals exist in commercially productive quantities. Similarly, it may be difficult, especially in mining activities, to distinguish between development costs and ordinary operating expenses. A cross shaft, may for example, be opened in a mine to reach and remove ores currently being produced, but this shaft also may be used for gaining access to reserves to be produced in the future. Only those expenditures that clearly relate to future production should be treated as development costs, while those relating to current production should be charged to current expense. Many mining companies follow the practice of capitalizing development (or exploration) costs if they are incurred prior to the beginning of production, and treating as an expense all extensions and development costs incurred *after* production has begun. This probably reflects the federal income tax provisions (Sec. 616, IRC) permitting a deduction of all expenditures for intangibles "paid or incurred during the taxable year for the development of a mine or other natural deposit (other than oil or gas wells) if paid or incurred after the existence of ores or minerals in commercially marketable quantities has been disclosed."

There is substantial disagreement over the proper disposition of IDC. As in the case of exploration costs, there are three schools of thought: (1) Charge all such costs to expense; (2) capitalize all IDC; and (3) capitalize costs applicable to productive properties, but expense those relating to nonproductive properties.

Generally accepted accounting principles seem to suggest that the first procedure is not acceptable. There seems little more justification for charging to expense the intangible costs of a productive mining or mineral property than for expensing similar costs incurred in constructing a building. However, this practice is frequently found in the petroleum industry, probably reflecting the federal tax laws that permit oil and gas operators to charge to expense all intangible drilling and development costs as they are incurred. Additionally, it is often argued that the extremely high risk and doubtful value of such investments justifies a conservative treatment.

It is also somewhat difficult to rationalize the idea that development costs on a mine in California that subsequently proves to be worthless and is abandoned contributes substantially to the development of a productive mine in Pennsylvania. As previously noted, however, this procedure is followed by those companies using the full cost concept in the petroleum industry.

The third procedure is the one most commonly used. Theoretically all drilling and development costs incurred in a cost center would be capitalized and amortized over the production from that center. However, in actual practice even those companies that use the lease as the cost center will capitalize only the costs in productive individual wells and will charge as "dry-hole expense" the costs associated with nonproductive wells on the lease. This is obviously inconsistent with the idea that the lease is the cost center.

Abandonments.   When prospective mineral properties are found to be unproductive, further efforts to develop the property are discontinued, and the property is abandoned, under successful-efforts costing all accumulated costs on the abandoned project, including mineral rights costs, capitalized exploration costs, and intangible development costs, should be charged off as a loss, net of any salvage value recovered. Where fee rights in both surface and minerals are owned, the carrying value of the property should be reduced to the fair value of the land. Under the full costing concept no loss is recorded when an individual property is abandoned, since the cost of all properties is included in the cost center.

DEPLETION, AMORTIZATION, AND DEPRECIATION

As previously noted, four types of outlays are incurred in obtaining and developing a mineral deposit:

1. Costs of acquiring the deposit, including the amounts paid for the fee interest or the leasehold bonus and the related miscellaneous acquisition costs
2. Geological and geophysical expenditures
3. Intangible development costs
4. Tangible equipment costs.

The first three of these are considered to be applicable solely to specific reserves of natural resources, and when those reserves are exhausted the costs, except for any salvage value of surface rights, are similarly expired. On the other hand, equipment may be removed and used elsewhere and its useful life does not necessarily coincide with the productive life of the mineral property. Therefore, equipment is not considered to be a part of the mineral resource.

Investment in a natural resource deposit applies equally to each unit of product that will be produced from it; as each unit is extracted from its natural state, costs applicable to it must be removed from the property account and assigned as production costs of the period. This process of assigning natural resource costs to periods of production is referred to as "depletion accounting." Frequently, especially in mining industries, the term "amortization" is used to describe the allocation of intangible development costs (and sometimes exploration costs as well) over production. Since tangible equipment is not considered as part of the minerals' cost, it is not subject to depletion; instead, it is depreciated in the same way as depreciable assets in any other industry.

Depletion and Amortization—Financial Accounting.   Depletion and amortization of costs of natural resources are nearly always computed on the "unit of production" basis for financial accounting purposes. The basic approach is to calculate a rate or cost per unit by dividing the investment in the natural resource by the number of physical units estimated to be contained in the deposit. The rate thus computed is multiplied by the number of units produced during the year, and this total amount is the "depletion" to be removed from the investment, by a credit to the Allowance for Depletion account and a charge to the inventory cost of units severed.

Single Depletion Rate.   Mineral acquisition costs (including capitalized geological and geophysical expenditures) may be combined with intangible development costs to arrive at a single depletion rate; however, many companies compute separate depletion rates for the mineral costs and the intangible development costs.

When a single combined rate is used, the total investment is divided by the estimated reserves recoverable from the entire property unit. This procedure is commonly followed when the cost of the mineral rights is relatively small and when only a short time is required to develop the entire property.

As an illustration, the fee interest in a mineral property has been acquired. Cost assigned to the minerals is $50,000. Intangible development costs of $200,000 incurred on the property have been capitalized. Estimated recoverable reserves from the deposit total 1,000,000 units. The combined depletion rate for mineral costs and IDC is $0.25 per unit (= $250,000/1,000,000 units). During the year, 40,000 units are produced. Depletion recorded for the year is $10,000 (= 40,000 units × $0.25 per unit). Where full costing is employed, a single rate based on total capitalized cost of mineral rights, exploration, and development, and on total reserves of the company, is used.

Multiple Depletion Rates.   The mineral costs apply to total recoverable reserves under the entire property unit, whereas the intangible development costs logically relate only to that portion of the reserves that can be produced as a direct result of the development work completed. If the property is only partially developed, separate depletion rates for the mineral and the intangible costs should be computed; the mineral costs are divided by total reserves contained in the entire property to obtain a depletion rate for that element of cost, while the depletion rate for development costs is calculated by dividing the IDC by only the reserves made recoverable by the partial development.

As an illustration, assume that fee interest in a mineral deposit is acquired at a cost of $50,000. Estimated reserves in the deposit total 1,000,000 units. During the first year of development $200,000 is expended for IDC. It is estimated that as a result of this phase of development a total of 400,000 units can be produced. If depletion is computed separately on mineral rights and on IDC, the rates will be $0.05 (= $50,000/1,000,000 units) and $0.50 (= $200,000/400,000 units), respectively. During the year 40,000 units are produced. Depletion on mineral rights will be $2,000 (= 40,000 units × $0.05 per unit) and on IDC it will be $20,000 (= 40,000 units × $0.05 per unit).

The California Depletion Method.   Another interesting and somewhat controversial approach to the depletion computation, referred to as the "California" system because it is used primarily by oil producers in that state, is sometimes found. The unit rate for mineral costs is determined by dividing the total of such investment by the estimated reserves recoverable from the entire property. The unit rate for IDC is computed by dividing the estimated aggregate development costs, both those already incurred and those expected in the future, by the estimated reserves recoverable from the entire property. The resulting depletion rate for IDC is obviously a rough estimate that is often regarded as unreliable and may need frequent revision as development progresses. However, it does tend to equalize the depletion charge for each unit produced over the entire life of the property, even though there are frequent adjustments in the rate.

For illustration, an oil producer acquires for $15,000 an oil lease on a large block of land. Capitalized geological and geophysical costs total $30,000. An oil deposit estimated to contain 1,500,000 barrels is found, and development is begun. During the first year, intangible drilling and development costs of $100,000 are incurred. It is estimated that an additional $1,100,000 of development costs will be necessary in future years to develop the property completely.

The unit depletion rate for mineral rights is $0.03 per barrel (= $45,000/1,500,000 barrels) and the depletion rate for IDC is $0.80 per barrel (= $1,200,-000/1,500,000 barrels). If during the year 50,000 barrels are produced, the depletion will be $1,500 (= $0.03 per barrel × 50,000 barrels) on mineral rights and $40,000 (= $0.80 per barrel × 50,000 barrels) on IDC.

Omission of Depletion. Some mining companies do not take depletion on mineral costs. This omission is sometimes supported by the argument that depletion accounting is arbitrary because it is based on estimates, often incorrect and subject to revision when there are changes in estimates of the recoverable reserves. Another frequently cited argument is that the value of a natural resource property depends on the resources contained and has no relation to "book value," hence depletion is unnecessary. Obviously, strict adherence to basic accounting concepts and principles, especially the matching principle and cost principle, requires that depletion be recorded. As a very minimum, failure to recognize depletion should be clearly pointed out in the financial statements.

Amortization of IDC. Frequently, published reports of mining companies (both those which do and those which do not record depletion on mineral costs) show "amortization" of intangible development costs, often including exploration costs as well. This amortization is equivalent to depletion of IDC, and is normally computed on the unit of production basis. Some other mining companies record intangible development costs incurred *after* production is secured in a separate account and record amortization of these costs separately, sometimes on a straight-line basis.

Estimates of Reserves. Accuracy of the depletion charge depends on the reliability with which reserves may be estimated. In some cases, especially in coal mines, gravel pits, and some copper mines, it may be possible to estimate the recoverable reserves with a fair degree of accuracy. In other instances—for example, in gold mines and many oil and gas deposits—the estimate is largely informed guesswork, especially where a property has been only partially developed. As better information about the deposit is obtained, changes in estimates must be made.

Modifications in the estimate of recoverable reserves are also caused by improved production techniques and by changes in economic conditions that make formerly marginal deposits become commercially productive. In the late 1960s and early 1970s the increase in world gold prices resulted in the reopening of many gold mines that had been formerly abandoned because they could not be profitably operated at existing prices. Similarly, the escalation of oil and gas prices resulted in drilling of many wells in areas that had previously been "marginal," with a substantial increase in recoverable reserves.

When a change is made in the estimate of recoverable reserves, it is necessary to revise the depletion rate. Usually a new depletion rate per unit is computed by dividing the undepleted book value by the estimated reserves at the beginning of the year. (Estimated reserves at the beginning of the year are the revised estimate at the end of the year plus production during the year.) Ordinarily no adjustment is made to revise depletion taken in prior years. If the corrected estimate would result in a material revision in depletion taken in prior years, a retroactive adjustment of the asset book value and the retained earnings account might be in order, but it is almost never recorded.

To illustrate revision of the estimate of recoverable reserves, assume that a mineral deposit containing an estimated 1,000,000 pounds of a product was acquired several years ago at a total capitalized cost of $500,000. Depletion at the rate of $0.50 per pound was charged on the 232,000 pounds produced prior to the current year—a total charge of $116,000. During the current year 60,000 pounds were produced. At the end of the year a new engineering survey estimates that only 580,000 pounds remain in the deposit.

A new depletion rate of $0.60 per pound is computed by dividing the remaining book value of $384,000 (= $500,000 − $116,000) by the estimated reserves at the beginning of the current year, 640,000 pounds (= 580,000 pounds at the end of the year plus 60,000 pounds produced during the year). Depletion for the current year is thus computed to be $36,000 (= 60,000 pounds × $0.60 per pound).

The Unit of Production.   Ideally the unit in which the product is normally measured should be the unit used in computing depletion. For example, in a coal mine the estimated reserves are measured in tons of coal contained and depletion should be based on tons produced. However, some mining companies use "tons of ore" as the unit for estimating reserves and computing depletion even though the product may be measured in pounds. This may cause widely varying depletion per unit of actual product if the ore removed contains substantially varying percentages of metal or mineral.

Joint Products.   Frequently an ore contains more than one type of product. It may be extremely difficult to estimate the recoverable reserves of each individual product, so that basing the depletion rate on tons of ore may be a practical solution. Traditionally, when more than one product is extracted from a mine, depletion is based on the dominant or main product. This procedure has also been used in the petroleum industry where both oil (measured in barrels) and natural gas (measured in thousands of cubic feet—MCF) are usually produced from the same reservoir. Because of the growing utilization of natural gas produced from predominantly oil-producing wells, some petroleum companies have sought to use a depletion rate based on a measure common to both products, the British thermal unit, a measure of heat content. Each barrel of oil usually contains slightly over six times the number of Btu contained in one MCF of gas, so a factor of 6 is applied to each barrel of oil while a factor of 1 is applied to each MCF of natural gas.

For example, a petroleum lease is developed at a total cost of $390,000 for mineral rights and IDC. On the basis of engineering studies, the lease is estimated to contain reserves of 400,000 barrels of oil and 200,000 MCF of gas. The approximate relative heat content of oil and gas may be computed as:

$$\begin{array}{lll} \text{Oil: } 400,000 \text{ bbl} \times 6 & = 2,400,000 \\ \text{Gas: } 200,000 \text{ MCF} \times 1 & = \underline{200,000} \\ \text{Total relative heat content} & \underline{\underline{2,600,000}} \end{array}$$

Thus, cost assigned to oil is $360,000 (= $^{24}\!/_{26}$ × $390,000) and to gas is $30,000 (= $^{2}\!/_{26}$ × $390,000). Depletion per barrel of oil is thus estimated to be $0.90 (= $360,000/400,000 barrels) and depletion per MCF of gas is estimated to be $0.15 (= $30,000/200,000 MCF).

Disposition of the Depletion Charge.   The periodic depletion is credited to the Allowance for Depletion account, which is, of course, offset against the asset cost accounts on the balance sheet to arrive at the net book value. The depletion charge represents a cost of goods produced and is properly treated in the same way as any other inventory cost. Thus the depletion applicable to units sold is appropriately considered as an element of cost of goods sold, while the portion applicable to goods produced but unsold should be carried as inventory cost in the asset account.

For example, during the year a company produced 80,000 units of mineral, of which 68,000 units were sold and 12,000 were in ending inventory. Depletion has been computed as $6 per unit. Total depletion for the year is thus $480,000 (= 80,000 units × $6 per unit). Of this amount $408,000 (= 68,000 × $6) should be charged to cost of goods sold, while $72,000 (= 12,000 × $6) should be treated as ending inventory.

In practice, many companies treat depletion as a current expense, reporting net income before depletion, then deducting the depletion charge to arrive at a final net income figure. Presumably this procedure is used to emphasize that depletion is strictly an estimate. It is sometimes pointed out that the inventory of product is very small and that relatively little of the depletion charge would be assigned to it, so that failure to assign any part of depletion to the inventory does not result in a material distortion of the financial statements. In the petroleum industry, crude oil inventory is frequently valued at "posted field price" when it is brought to the surface; in this case depletion is logically considered as an expense rather than as an element of inventory cost.

Depletion for Tax Purposes. Procedures used in computing depletion for federal income tax purposes may grossly differ from those used in determining depletion for financial reporting. The amount allowable on the tax return is the higher of (1) depletion based on cost, or (2) percentage depletion.

Cost Depletion. The computation of "cost depletion" for tax purposes may result in a depletion charge vastly different from that computed for financial accounting, even though the same general principles are followed in both cases. Tax depletion is based only on units *sold* (or moved from the property) rather than on units produced. In addition, the depletable "basis" for tax purposes may vary significantly from that for financial accounting. For example, intangible development costs may be capitalized for financial accounting purposes while they are charged to current expense on the tax return. Another major difference is that percentage depletion in a given year may be higher than "cost" depletion and the former amount deducted on the tax return, thus reducing the subsequent basis subject to cost depletion for tax purposes below the basis depletable for financial accounting.

Percentage Depletion. Percentage depletion, often referred to as "statutory" depletion, has virtually no relationship to cost of the property. The producer may deduct as depletion a specified percentage of gross income from each property, regardless of what the unrecovered cost may be. It is thus possible to deduct depletion equal to many times the cost of the property. However, percentage depletion in each year is limited to 50 percent of taxable income from each property in that year.

Almost all metals, minerals, and other natural resources are subject to percentage depletion. The rates specified in the Internal Revenue Code (Sec. 613) vary from 5 to 22 percent of gross income. Selected illustrative rates for some common resources are

Oil and gas	22%
Sulfur, bauxite, asbestos, lead, nickel	22
Granite, limestone, marble, mollusk shells, mica, potash, talc ...	14
Coal, lignite, sodium chloride	10
Gravel, peat, sand, most stone	5

However, the Tax Reduction Act of 1975 severely limited the percentage depletion allowance for oil and gas production, so that it applies only to the first 2,000 barrels of oil (or 12,000,000 cubic feet of gas) produced per day by a company in 1975, and declining to 1,000 barrels of oil (or 6,000,000 cubic feet of gas) per day in 1980. Also, the depletion rate for oil and gas is reduced to 20 percent in 1981, 18 percent in 1982, 16 percent in 1983, and 15 percent in 1984 and subsequent years.

Gross income represents the value for which the product is sold. In the case of gas and oil, this means the sales price, before production and severance taxes, in the immediate vicinity of the well. However, if the producer has leased the mineral property, paying a bonus which has been capitalized as part of the mineral cost, he must reduce gross income by a pro rata portion of the bonus paid, because the bonus is considered as advance royalty on which the lessor has been allowed depletion. Mining gross income includes the value of the extracted ore or mineral, along with the treatment processes considered as mining, and the transportation of the ore or mineral from the point of extraction to the plant or mill where the treatment processes are applied (within 50 miles).

Taxable income is defined as gross income (before the leasehold bonus adjustment) less all production expenses (except depletion), development costs charged to expense, taxes on the property, and an allocated portion of general and administrative overhead expenses.

Percentage depletion is allowed on the value of all product sold even though the depletable investment is zero. Obviously, though, no additional cost depletion can be taken when the investment basis has been depleted to zero. Percentage depletion is clearly not acceptable for financial accounting purposes.

To illustrate tax depletion, assume that an oil company acquired a mineral lease for $30,600. For tax purposes, geological and geophysical costs of $3,400 were capitalized. Total intangible drilling and development costs of $500,000 were incurred on the property, but all these IDC costs were deducted as current expense on the tax return and on the books. Estimated reserves totaled 680,000 barrels. During the first two years 60,000 barrels of oil were sold, and depletion of $3,000, based on cost (= $30,600 + $3,400/680,000 = $.05 per barrel; $.05 × 60,000 = $3,000) was deducted on the tax return.

During the third year 50,000 barrels of oil were produced and sold for $10.20 per barrel, for total sales proceeds of $510,000. Operating expenses on the property, including allocated overhead, were $60,000. Estimated recoverable reserves at the end of the year were 570,000 barrels. Depletion taken on the tax return will be $111,705, computed as follows:

Cost depletion:

$$\text{Depletion per bbl} = \frac{\$31,000}{620,000 \text{ bbl}} = \$.05 \text{ per bbl}$$

$$\text{Depletion for year} = \$.05 \text{ per bbl} \times 50,000 = \$2,500$$

Percentage depletion:

$$\text{Gross income} = \text{sales price} - \text{``pro-rated bonus''}$$
$$= \$510,000 - \left(\frac{\$30,600}{680,000 \text{ bbl}} \times 50,000 \text{ bbl}\right)$$
$$= \$510,000 - \$2,250$$
$$= \$507,750$$
$$\text{Depletion} = 22\% \times \$507,750$$
$$= \$111,705$$

But limited to 50 percent of net income,

$$\text{Depletion} = 50\% \times (\$510,000 - \$60,000)$$
$$= \$225,000$$

Thus depletion for the year would be $111,705, since the limit of 50 percent of net income (taxable income) is greater than the depletion rate multiplied by gross income.

Depreciation. Tangible equipment used in production of natural resources is customarily depreciated on the unit of production basis, very similar to depletion. Depreciation per unit of recoverable reserves is computed by dividing the book value of equipment (less estimated residual salvage) by the estimated recoverable reserves, and this unit rate is applied to units produced during the period.

Often the useful life of an individual asset will be shorter than the productive life of the natural resource deposit. In this case, if the unit of production method is adopted, the estimated reserves used in the computation should be limited to those recoverable during the life of the equipment. Frequently, depreciation is computed on the total of all equipment on the property rather than on individual items.

Other methods (straight-line, sum-of-the-years'-digits, declining-balance, etc.) are also appropriate, and normally will be used for equipment not employed directly in the extraction or treatment of products from an individual property.

Amortization of Undeveloped Properties. As previously pointed out, when mineral rights are acquired by leasehold, the lease contract is for (1) a primary term of a specified number of years, and (2) as long thereafter as minerals are produced in commercial quantities. Since a very large part (in the case of petroleum producers, well over 75 percent) of leases will never become productive and will be "dropped" during their primary terms, there is strong argument for amortizing undeveloped lease costs by periodic charges to profit and loss.

This practice may also be supported on the basis that matching current expenses and revenues requires some provision for anticipating losses from unproductive leases in much the same way as providing for uncollectible accounts receivable.

On the other hand, this procedure is opposed on the grounds that only when a lease is actually abandoned is there a loss or expense. Also, it is often criticized on the basis that it is not "practical" to amortize undeveloped property costs because of the additional accounting records necessary and also because the amortization is not permitted for federal income tax purposes.

A substantial number of oil companies, especially larger producers, do amortize undeveloped leaseholds. Among these companies, two procedures are found:

1. An "allowance" account is maintained at a predetermined percentage (based on past experience) of the total investment in undeveloped properties. Periodic amortization is recorded by charging the Amortization Expense account and crediting the Allowance for Amortization of Undeveloped Properties account for an amount necessary to bring the allowance account to the desired balance. When a property is abandoned or surrendered, its full cost is charged against the allowance account. If a property being amortized by this method becomes productive, its entire original cost is considered depletable.

2. The amortization may be computed for each individual property. The amortization of a property's cost for each period is determined by dividing the total cost of the property by the number of periods in the lease's primary term. An allowance account may be maintained for each lease, or only one overall account may be kept. When a property is surrendered, the allowance account is charged for the amount of amortization previously taken on the lease, and the property's book value (unamortized cost) is charged to an expense account. If a property being amortized by this method becomes productive, only the unamortized costs may be transferred to producing properties to be depleted, or the entire original cost may be considered depletable. In the latter case, any amortization previously taken will be restored by a charge to the allowance for amortization account and a

credit to the amortization expense of the year the lease becomes productive. When full costing is used, amortization of undeveloped properties would not be appropriate.

SPECIAL PROPERTY INTERESTS

Although most mineral property transactions involve simply the acquisition of either fee interests or leasehold working interests, many different types of contracts creating special limited property rights and obligations have been developed, especially in the petroleum industry. These special contracts are usually designed to spread the risk involved in a minerals development program, to secure financial backing, or to take advantage of beneficial tax rulings. The variety of unusual contracts is almost endless; however, only the most commonly encountered and economically important are discussed here.

Farmouts. Frequently the holder of a working interest in a mineral property assigns the interest to another operator but retains an *overriding royalty* (often one-sixteenth of gross production) in the working interest. The lease is developed and operated in the usual manner by the assignee. The overriding royalty holder bears none of the costs of developing or operating the property.

As an illustration, assume that an oil company leases a property, paying a bonus of $28,000, with the landowner retaining the usual one-eighth basic royalty interest. The company does not wish to develop the property, so it "farms out" the working interest to another operator for a consideration of $8,000, retaining an overriding one-sixteenth royalty. The lease is developed by the assignee, and during the year 40,000 barrels of oil are produced. Of the production, 2,500 barrels belong to the overriding royalty holder.

The transaction creates no unusual problems for the operator acquiring the property subject to the overriding royalty. However, the assignee may record the transaction in several different ways.

1. The transaction may be treated as a "sublease," with the full proceeds from assignment, $8,000, being considered as income. The leasehold cost, $28,000, will be assigned to the royalty interest retained and will be depleted over future production. (This method is required for tax purposes.)

2. The proceeds from assignment, $8,000, may be considered as recovery of cost, with the balance of cost, $20,000, being assigned to the overriding royalty.

3. The transaction may be considered as a sale of that portion of mineral rights transferred, and a gain or loss recorded. Cost applicable to the fractional interest retained is assigned to the overriding royalty. In the illustration, the lessee originally possessed $^{14}/_{16}$ of the mineral rights but transfers $^{13}/_{16}$, retaining $^{1}/_{16}$. The transaction would be recorded as follows:

```
Cash ..............................   8,000
Overriding Royalty Interests (asset)  ....   2,000
Loss on Sale .........................  18,000
        Undeveloped Leaseholds ................  28,000
```

Production Payments. A production payment is a "nonoperating" interest in production from a specific mineral property under which the producer agrees to pay a certain amount of money (or a specified number of units of product) to the production payment owner. The payment is made only from a specified fractional share of the operator's gross production "when, if, and as" produced. No part of expenses are borne by the production payment owner. Although production payment contracts originated in the petroleum industry because of favorable tax treatment, they quickly were adopted in financing other types of mineral operations. However, the Tax Reform Act of 1969 effectively eliminated the tax advantages of such transactions, and as a result they have declined in importance. A production payment may be either a "retained" payment or a "carved-out" payment.

Retained Payments.   A retained production payment is created when the operating rights in a property are sold, but the assignor retains a production payment.

For illustration, a company has acquired a mineral property for $20,000. During the current year the working interest is assigned to another operator for $8,000, the assignor retaining a production payment of $30,000 payable out of the first 75 percent of production, when, if, and as produced. During the year the working interest's share of production was 10,000 units of product which was sold for $18,000. Of this amount, $13,500 (= 75% × $18,000) is paid to the production payment owner.

Two different practices may be used by the assignor to record the transfer:

1. Proceeds from the transfer, $8,000 in the illustration, may be considered as a recovery of investment. The excess of cost over proceeds, $12,000, is assigned as cost of the production payment. Any excess of proceeds over cost would be treated as profit from the assignment.

Amounts received from production under the contract, in the example $13,500 in the first year, are treated as revenue, and cost assigned to the payment is amortized or depleted on a pro rata basis. In the above example, $5,400 (= $13,500/$30,000 × $12,000) will be amortized in the first year. (If the receipt of the future payment is highly questionable, all proceeds are treated first as recovery of the cost.)

2. A nominal amount, frequently zero, may be assigned to the production payment. Any difference between the cost of the property and the amount received on assignment is considered to be gain or loss. All proceeds from production are treated as income.

Similarly, the purchaser of the property may treat the transaction in one of several ways, although in any event the cash purchase price will be capitalized.

1. Under the most commonly followed procedure, the net method, the assignee will ignore the production payment in the accounts, except for memorandum entries. Under this procedure, required for tax purposes prior to 1969, reported income may be distorted because, during the years the production payments is being liquidated, the operator will treat as income only that fractional part of revenue which is retained but will deduct all operating expenses. After the production payment has been liquidated, reported net income may sharply increase because then all production will be reported as revenue. Depletion should be based on the operator's net share of reserves and production.

2. As a modification of the above procedure, the operator may capitalize any excess of expenses over reported revenues during the period of production payment liquidation, to be amortized over production after the payment is liquidated.

3. Another modification of the net method is to capitalize during the liquidation period the pro rata portion (75 percent in the illustration) of expenses that relate to the production payment. The capitalized expenses would then be amortized over the minerals produced after payout.

4. Still another procedure is to capitalize as part of the leasehold cost at time of purchase the estimated future "lifting" expenses applicable to the share of production belonging to the payment owner; this amount is also credited to a liability account. Depletion of the leasehold cost is then based on the operator's net share of reserves and production. The estimated liability account is amortized each period on a pro rata basis as the oil payment is liquidated, and the operating expense account is credited for this amortization. This method is feasible only when a producing property is involved in the transfer.

5. The present value of the production payment may be capitalized as part of the leasehold account and credited to an estimated liability account. All proceeds from production are considered as gross income by the operator and payments on the contract will then be considered partly as reduction of the estimated liability and partly as interest expense. Depletion is based on total reserves and production.

"Carved-Out" Production Payments. A carved-out production payment represents merely the sale of a production payment with the operator retaining the mineral working interest. Normally a carved-out payment is from a producing mineral property.

For example, the owner of a producing mineral property conveys for a consideration of $40,000 a production payment of $60,000, to be paid out of 70 percent of the first production belonging to the working interest produced from the property.

The assignor normally reports the cash consideration, $40,000, as deferred income. As payment is made to the production payment holder during the liquidation period, a pro rata portion of the deferred income is recorded as being earned. However, since the proceeds from assignment are taxable income when received, many companies reduce the deferred income by the amount of tax currently payable. A very few companies record the sales proceeds as income when received for financial accounting purposes as well as tax.

The purchaser of the payment debits a Production Payment Receivable account for the purchase price, $40,000. Proceeds received during the liquidation period are credited to income, and the Production Payment account is amortized as proceeds are received. As an alternative, especially where the payment is of doubtful value, the owner might credit all proceeds to the receivable account until full cost is recovered, then report further proceeds as income.

The "ABC" Transaction. One of the most interesting and most important production payment contracts combines elements of both the carved-out and the retained payment. Under this arrangement the owner or lessee, A, of a productive mineral property transfers the working interest, for cash, to a second operator, B. Part of the financing is arranged by A's retaining a production payment which is immediately sold to a third party, C.

In effect, the original property owner A has sold the property for cash and has no accounting problem. Similarly, C, the purchaser of the payment, has merely purchased a carved-out payment. In effect, B has purchased a property subject to a retained production payment. One additional problem is that since a productive property is usually involved, equipment and IDC must be considered. The usual solution is for the purchaser to record the equipment at its fair value, with the balance of capitalized cost being assigned to the mineral interests. Some operators record IDC as a separate asset. Use of the ABC arrangement was sharply curtailed by the Tax Reform Act of 1969.

Net Profits Interests. Another arrangement to finance the sale of mineral properties, frequently found in the petroleum industry, is the "net profits" interest. Under this contract a share of net profit from the property, carefully defined in the contract, is paid to the holder of the right. The net profits interest owner has no personal liability for development or production costs. This type of contract is almost always a retained interest created at the time a mineral property is transferred to another party.

For example, the lessee of an undeveloped mineral property who does not wish to develop the lease transfers the mineral rights to a second operator. As consideration, the transferee agrees to pay to the transferrer an amount equal to one-third of the net profit from the lease, beginning with the first production. Net profit is further defined in the agreement.

An operator who acquires property subject to a retained net profits interest normally does not make accounting entries to record the potential liability under the contract. As payments are made under the contract, they are treated as expenses, or as a reduction of revenue.

The assignor of property subject to a retained net profits interest usually transfers the cost of the lease (less any amounts received at the time of the transfer) to an asset account labeled net profits interest. Amounts received as net profits are recorded as income, and the cost assigned to the profits interest is amortized on the basis of total expected proceeds. Because of the highly uncertain value of the profits interest, many companies consider the first proceeds to be a return of cost assigned to the interest.

"Free-Well" Agreements. A common arrangement in the petroleum industry for sharing costs of exploration work is the free-well agreement, under which the mineral holder assigns an undivided share of the mineral rights to another operator in exchange for the assignee's agreement to drill and equip a well free of cost to the assignor.

For example, an operator acquires a working interest in a mineral property for $40,000. Later the owner enters into an agreement with a second operator under which the latter agrees to drill and equip one well free of cost to the owner. On completion of the well, each operator will have an undivided one-half interest in the property and will share future development costs, operating revenues, and operating expenses equally. The driller completes the well at a cost of $100,000 for IDC and $30,000 for equipment.

If the hole is dry, the assignor makes no entry in the accounting records; the property will usually be abandoned and the entire leasehold cost charged off as a loss. The driller charges the dry-hole cost to expense.

If the well is productive, the assignor of the fractional leasehold interest may follow one of several practices.

1. The usual procedure is to consider that all cost of the mineral property applies to the mineral rights retained. The value of the share of equipment and IDC acquired from the assignment of the leasehold interest is ignored.

2. A proportionate part of the leasehold cost (one-half in this case) may be assigned to the equipment, but IDC will be ignored. In the illustration, $20,000 would be removed from the Leasehold account and charged to the Equipment account.

3. The value (up to the leasehold cost) of the share of equipment acquired is recorded and credited to the Leasehold account. IDC is ignored, and no gain or loss is recognized.

4. A proportionate part of the leasehold cost is removed from the Leasehold account. The share of equipment and IDC acquired are recorded. Gain or loss is recognized. (Some companies use this basic procedure but record only the share of equipment acquired, ignoring IDC.)

The driller of the productive free well also may follow one of several procedures in recording the transactions.

1. The most common procedure, and the one required for federal income tax purposes, is to assign a proportionate part of drilling and equipment costs to the leasehold interest acquired.

2. A proportionate part of equipment costs are assigned to the leasehold interest acquired; all IDC remains in the IDC account.

3. No cost is assigned to the leasehold; all costs of drilling and equipping the property are retained in the IDC and Equipment accounts.

Carried Interests. Frequently the owner of a mineral interest transfers a share of the property to a second operator in return for the latter's agreement to drill, equip, and operate one or more wells on the property. The operator (called the "carrying party") is given the right to recover the carried party's share of the development and production costs out of the carried party's share of production, though the latter has no personal liability for such costs. A wide variety of accounting practices, briefly summarized below, are used by both parties.

Carried Party

1. A common procedure used by the carried party is to make no entry in the accounts until the operator has recouped the carried party's share of costs. After payout, the value of the share of IDC and equipment acquired are capitalized and credited to income.

2. A fractional share of the leasehold cost may be allocated to equipment and IDC when development is completed. No entry is made during the payout period.

3. A fractional part of the leasehold cost is removed, a pro rata portion of the value of IDC and equipment is capitalized, and the difference is treated as profit or loss when development is completed.

4. Pro rata portions of IDC and equipment are capitalized and an offsetting credit is made to a liability account when development is completed. The share of revenue retained by the carrying partner that comes from the carried partner's interest as recovery of cost is credited to income by the carried partner and is charged to the liability account.

Carrying Partner

1. The most common procedure followed by the carrying partner is to capitalize drilling and development costs as they are incurred. No cost, or only a nominal amount, is assigned to the leasehold interest acquired. However, a wide variety of methods of handling revenues and operating expenses may be used:

a. Some companies credit to the IDC and Equipment accounts any amounts recovered from the carried party's share of production.

b. The full cost is left in the Equipment and IDC accounts, with all revenues and expenses being treated as the carrying party's during the payout period.

c. Others treat all revenues and expenses during the payout period as belonging to the carrying party, but amortize the cost of that portion of IDC and equipment that will pass to the carried party.

2. Another procedure sometimes used is for the carrying partner to charge the equipment and IDC accounts with only his share of these items. The costs applicable to the portion of equipment and IDC passing to the carried party is charged to a receivable account. No value is assigned to the leasehold account for the interest obtained. As recovery is made during the payout period, the amount recovered is credited to the receivable account.

Joint Operations. A "joint operating agreement" covering one or more mineral properties is very common in the natural resources industries. Typically, two or more companies jointly acquire operating interests in mineral properties. One of the partners is named the "operator" to develop and produce the property. All operating and development costs are paid by the operator, who in turn bills the partners for their share of costs. The operator charges the usual asset and expense accounts for the share of applicable costs specified in the agreement. On receipt of billing from the operator, the other partners record their shares of assets and expenses and credit a liability account for the amount due the operator.

The major accounting problems for all parties is to make certain that the accounting procedures spelled out in the joint operating agreement are followed, especially that the basis of the operator's charges to nonoperators for such items as equipment, overhead, and supplies are carefully observed.

Pooling and Unitization. In many cases separate mineral properties in an entire field or area are joined together under "pooling" or "unitization" agreements, either on a voluntary basis or because it is required as a conservation measure by the state government. Not only are all working interests combined, but all royalty interests are likewise combined. Each participant in the pool gives up title to individual properties, acquiring instead an undivided interest in all properties involved. The fractional interest acquired is based on the surface area or on the acre-feet of potential reserves contributed by each party.

The major accounting problem in unitization is the treatment of the costs of property contributed and the values of property interests acquired. Although the problem is quite complex, there are two basic approaches.

1. Each participant may be assumed to have disposed of the entire interest in properties contributed to the unit and to have acquired a completely new and different property interest. The entire cost of the property given up (leasehold, IDC, and equipment if the property is developed) is removed, and the fractional interest received in the entire unit's appraised or agreed-on value is recorded. Gain or loss is measured on this basis.

2. Each participant may be assumed to have disposed of only a fractional interest in properties contributed to the unit in exchange for a fractional interest in the properties contributed by other participants. Gain or loss is recognized on this basis.

ACCOUNTING FOR TIMBER RESOURCES

In many ways the accounting problems encountered in the timber industry are identical to those in mining and mineral extraction. The basic problems are: (1) determining which costs are to be capitalized, and (2) computing depletion for the timber cut during the year.

Acquisition and Development of Timber Resources.   In the early decades of this century most Americans considered timber to be an inexhaustible resource. Lumber companies purchased, cut, and milled timber without giving consideration to selective cutting or replanting seedlings. Now, however, lumber companies, paper pulp producers, and other timber users have found it necessary to purchase lands and grow timber for their own use.

As in the case of mineral and ore properties, all acquisition costs relating to the timber should be capitalized. When standing timber and land are purchased, a portion of the purchase price representing the fair value of the surface rights should be charged to the Land account.

Carrying costs of timber being raised, including such items as clearing under-brush, reseeding, fire protection, treatment for insects and disease, and insurance protection, should be capitalized. This is especially appropriate in view of the extremely long period of development that may be required before revenues are generated from the particular tract, the relatively low risk involved in the venture, and the fact that growth of timber increases the value of the property. Even after the cutting has begun, those carrying costs that apply to future production should be capitalized. In actual practice, however, nearly all companies consider these development costs, regardless of whether incurred before or after cutting begins, as current expense.

Other development costs not specifically related to the growing of timber—such as construction of roads, drainage canals, etc.—should logically be capitalized, either as part of the timber cost or in separate accounts to be amortized or depreciated over their useful lives.

Depletion of Timber Costs.   The depletion charge for timber cut during the year is computed on a unit of production basis. The net book value of the timber block at the end of the year is divided by the number of units available for cutting (the units on hand at the end of the year, plus the units cut during the year) in order to arrive at a depletion rate per unit. (Timber units are usually measured in board feet.) The unit rate is then applied to the number of units cut to compute the total depletion for the year. This procedure is followed for both financial accounting and tax purposes. (There is no percentage depletion allowance for timber.)

To illustrate the depletion computation, assume that the remaining book value of a timber block on January 1 was $28,000. During the year additional costs of $2,000 were capitalized and 80,000 board feet were produced from the property. On December 31, estimated remaining standing timber was 520,000 board feet. The depletion rate is thus $0.05 per board foot (= $30,000/600,000 feet), and the depletion charge for the year is $4,000 (= 80,000 feet × $0.05 per foot).

The remaining reserves of timber can be estimated with far greater accuracy than the reserves of most mineral and ore deposits. As a result the depletion charge is more precise and meaningful. It is not unusual for the depletion rate to decrease from year to year because of an increase in estimated "reserves" from the growth of timber.

As previously noted, most timber-producing companies charge to current expense all carrying costs of growing timber, so that blocks which were acquired not as standing forests but as almost-barren lands subsequently planted with seedlings will have little, if any, capitalized depletable cost. This, plus the fact that cutting is normally on a selective basis, with only a part of the standing timber harvested each year, makes many timber operations essentially farming enterprises.

Recording Accretion. Some accountants argue that the increase in value (accretion) resulting from growth of standing timber should be recognized in the accounts each year because the value can be reliably measured and verified. It is argued that the key factor in income production is the growth of the timber, and that this should be reflected in the accounts. Recognition of accretion might be accomplished by a debit to the asset account and a credit to either an income or an unrealized capital (stockholders' equity) account. Accretion is seldom recorded in practice, however, because of adherence to the realization principle in accounting and the uncertainty that the product will ultimately be marketed.

ACCOUNTING RECORDS AND REPORTS

Abandonment of Cost Basis. Cost is almost invariably the basis of accounting for natural resource properties. In cases where property is acquired in exchange for other properties or by issuance of securities, cost is usually measured by the fair market value of the property or securities given up. There are many accountants who believe that a more general use of current market values would make accounting data more meaningful and relevant in any industry, if such values could be determined objectively. There may be special merit in considering this approach in the natural resource industries where current value can be measured with greater confidence.

Recording Discovery Value. Accounting literature is pervaded with frequent references to the use of "discovery value" for wasting assets. No doubt emphasis is placed on this valuation basis because for the years 1913 to 1926 petroleum producers could base depletion on discovery value.

Support for discovery value is based on the argument that when deposits of natural resources are discovered the value is likely to be so great in comparison with recorded cost that the continued use of historical cost results in a gross distortion of the financial statements; thus, the value of the deposit "in place" should be recorded in the accounts, with a corresponding adjustment of the stockholders' equity accounts.

Generally it is suggested that the write-up to discovery value be credited to an Unrealized Capital from Appraisal account, which would be amortized over the productive life of the property by periodic credits to the income account. Depletion would, of course, be based on the appraised value. There are some who argue, however, especially where the company owns only one mineral deposit, that a fresh-start approach should be used, with the appraisal increment credited directly to the capital accounts. Also it has been suggested that the discovery value of reserves might be recognized as income as they are found and all discovery costs charged to expense as incurred.

Asset Write-Downs. It is not uncommon in minerals development programs to capitalize acqustion, exploration, and development costs of a property, only to discover later that, even though the property is productive, the total expected recoverable reserves will be inadequate to recover the investment. In this event the asset account should be written down to the net realizable value of the resources (expected value of production, less estimated production costs). If the surface rights are being carried in the minerals property account, the carrying value should not be reduced below the value of the surface rights.

It is especially important where the full costing concept is being used that the carrying value of properties be limited to the "fair" value of the properties. This should probably be defined as the discounted value of the net future revenues from proved reserves in the cost center. Some companies include in the ceiling on carrying value the cost of undeveloped properties, while other firms exclude undeveloped properties. Obviously, in a cost center in which no production has yet been secured or recoverable reserves yet proved, the above limitation would not be applicable. Instead, it would be proper to retain all costs until such time that a reliable estimate of reserves can be made.

Liquidating Dividends. Accounting literature has emphasized the nature and importance of liquidating dividends in the wasting asset industries. This emphasis results because some states permit companies engaged in wasting asset extraction to pay dividends from "distributable income" computed without a deduction for depletion. Thus, dividends may actually represent the return of invested capital. The major accounting problem where liquidating dividends are paid is to make certain that the financial statements reflect the facts, including a statement as to the amount of capital paid out as dividends in the current year and the accumulated total of such distributions. If no depletion has been deducted, this should be clearly stated in the financial reports or the accompanying notes.

Ledger Accounts. There are few major differences between the general ledger accounts for a producer of natural resources and those of a company in any other industry. Accounts are designed to reflect the different types of property interests (leaseholds, fee interests, overriding royalties, IDC, equipment, etc.) with a proper distinction between producing and nonproducing properties. An asset account of considerable importance is the "incomplete construction" or "asset suspense" account in which exploration and development costs are accumulated until a definite outcome of each project is evident so that the costs can then be transferred to the appropriate asset or loss accounts.

Subsidiary records for assets, revenues, and expenses are of crucial importance in the extractive industries. As previously noted, a record for each mining or minerals property is necessary showing the details of expenditures for mineral rights, exploration, IDC, and equipment on the property so that depletion, depreciation, and amortization can be easily and accurately computed.

Similarly, records must be kept showing production and expenses applicable to each unit. This is essential not only for measuring gross income and taxable income in computing percentage depletion and for managerial control purposes, but also for meeting reporting requirements of various state regulatory agencies.

One of the most interesting records somewhat peculiar to the natural resource industries is the *payout status* record maintained for each property. Most minerals producers establish standards which each new capital project is expected to meet.

For example, the company might invest in no projects that do not promise to return all committed funds within five years. The payout status record simply accumulates for each project the outlays for capital expenditures and expenses, along with revenues earned. Periodically a payout status report is prepared for each property, summarizing the data on the payout record.

Revenues and Expenses. Revenues of natural resource producers are generally recorded on the same basis as those in other types of industries—on realization at the point of sale. However, certain exceptions to the traditional rule are regarded as generally acceptable. When commodities are immediately realizable at quoted market prices with little expense of sale, the production basis of revenue measurement is acceptable. The standard example of this rule is the valuation of precious metals which have a ready market and a relatively fixed market value. Another common illustration of its use is crude oil stored on oil and gas lease sites, which is often valued at "posted field price."

Another exception to the realization test that is often supported, but seldom followed, is recording the accretion in value of standing timber, previously discussed.

The unusual problems of natural resource producers in accounting for operating expenses have already been discussed. The most important of these are the determination of which costs should be capitalized and which charged to expense, and the calculation of the depletion charge. Another interesting problem on which there is a wide divergence of opinion concerns the extent to which overhead costs should be allocated to individual producing properties. All costs of producing the resource, at least in theory, should become an inventory cost. For this reason, most producers allocate to individual properties those overhead costs clearly related to production activities, while such costs as general administrative overhead expense are simply treated as current expense.

Financial Statements. The published financial statements of companies engaged in the extractive industries are very little different from those found in other industries. A great deal of controversy surrounds the information to be included in the supplementary notes, however. Since the most important factor in the financial strength of a natural resource producer is, perhaps, the recoverable reserves owned by the company, many accountants and financial analysts argue that this information must be included in the financial reports if they are to be meaningful. Others point out, however, that inclusion of a statement of recoverable reserves might be misleading. In the first place, the estimate is very likely to be substantially incorrect. Second, the value of a given quantity of reserves may vary considerably, not only because of differences in quality, but also because the necessary expenditures to develop and produce the reserves will be vastly different from one deposit to another. Despite these arguments, increased disclosure of reserve data is now widespread.

Because of the wide variety of applications of accounting principles found in the natural resource industries, it is extremely important that the financial reports state explicitly the practices that have been followed, especially in accounting for exploration, development, and depletion. Unfortunately, annual reports of extractive companies fail to provide all the disclosure that might be desired.

BIBLIOGRAPHY

Accounting Principles Board Committee on the Extractive Industries: "Accounting and Reporting Practices in the Oil and Gas Industry," American Institute of Certified Public Accountants, New York, 1973.

American Petroleum Institute: *Report on Certain Petroleum Industry Accounting Practices,* API, Washington, D.C., 1974.

Bass, Jarman: "Generally Accepted Accounting Principles in the Petroleum Industry: What GAAP?," *Accounting Papers*, University of Tulsa 23rd Conference of Accountants, Tulsa, Okla., 1969.

Bierman, Harold, Roland E. Dukes, and Thomas R. Dyckman: "Financial Reporting in the Petroleum Industry," *Journal of Accountancy*, vol. 138, no. 4, pp. 58–64, October 1974.

Connor, Joseph E.: "Discovery Value—The Oil Industry's Untried Method," *Journal of Accountancy*, vol. 139, no. 5, pp. 54–63, May 1975.

Coutts, W. B.: *Accounting Problems in the Oil and Gas Industry*, Canadian Institute of Chartered Accountants, Toronto, 1963.

Federal Power Commission, Orders Nos. 440 and 440-a (18 CFR Parts 201, 204, 205, Sec. 260.5), November 5, 1971, and January 5, 1972.

Field, Robert E.: *Financial Reporting in the Extractive Industries*, Accounting Research Study No. 11, AICPA, New York, 1969.

Klingstedt, John P.: "Effects of Full Costing in the Petroleum Industry," *Financial Analysts Journal*, vol. 26, no. 5, pp. 52–58, September-October 1970.

————: *Value Accounting in the Petroleum Industry*, Arthur Young and Co., Tulsa, Okla., 1974.

Meyers, John H., *Full Cost vs Successful Efforts in Petroleum Accounting. An Empirical Approach*, published by the author, Bloomington, Ind., 1974.

Porter, Stanley: *Petroleum Accounting Practices*, McGraw-Hill Book Company, New York, 1965.

Smith, C. Aubrey, and Horace R. Brock: *Accounting for Oil and Gas Producers*, Prentice-Hall, New York, 1959.

Sunder, Shyam: "Full Costing and Successful Efforts Costing in the Petroleum Industry," *The Accounting Review*, vol. 51, no. 1, pp. 1–18, January 1976.

Chapter **19**

Buildings and Equipment

JOHN LESLIE LIVINGSTONE
Fuller E. Callaway Professor, Georgia Institute of Technology

CHARACTERISTICS OF BUILDINGS AND EQUIPMENT

Classification of Fixed Assets. Buildings and equipment constitute a subclass of the fixed asset category. Fixed assets consist of long-lived assets not intended for resale in the regular business of the enterprise. Fixed assets are usually classed as either tangible or intangible. Tangible fixed assets are characterized by physical existence; they include land, wasting assets, property improvements, buildings, and equipment. Intangible fixed assets lack physical substance; they include items such as patents, copyrights, organization costs, and goodwill.

Within the class of tangible fixed assets, buildings are normally regarded as construction used to house the activities of people and equipment, and for storage. Buildings are distinguished from construction that does not house operations. For example, roads, railroad tracks, bridges, paving, tunnels, piers, canals, and similar items are usually not regarded as buildings but rather as property improvements.

Equipment comprises industrial and office machinery and tools, transportation equipment (such as automobiles, aircraft, barges, and reusable containers such as barrels and drums), furniture and fixtures, and farm animals.

The distinction between buildings and equipment is not always clear-cut. Items such as elevators, ductwork, power lines and wiring, piping, built-in appliances, sinks and toilets, and other structural fixtures may be classed either with buildings or with equipment.

Nature of Buildings and Equipment. Hendrickson[1] lists the following five distinguishing characteristics of buildings and equipment:

1. These assets are physical goods used for facilitating the output of commodities or to furnish services to the enterprise or its customers in the normal course of business.

2. They all have a finite life, at the termination of which they have to be abandoned, substituted for, or replaced. This life may be a given period of years based on wear and tear in use, or it may be variable according to the level of use and the quality of maintenance.

3. Their value derives from the ability to exclude others in exercising the legal property rights in their use, rather than from enforcement of contractual obligations.

4. They are of nonmonetary nature in that benefits tend to flow from use or sale of their services instead of from their conversion directly into sums of money.

5. Usually the benefits are received over a period greater than a single year or the operating cycle of the enterprise. A few exceptions to this rule occur. For instance some items such as tools may have a useful life shorter than the operating cycle of the entity.

By reason of these characteristics, notably the long-lived nature and repeated use of the services of buildings and equipment, they merit treatment as a separate

[1] Eldon S. Hendrikson, *Accounting Theory*, rev. ed., Richard D. Irwin, Homewood, Ill., 1970, p. 359.

class of assets for accounting purposes. This grouping provides relevant information to users of accounting statements regarding the tangible capital investment of the enterprise.

Importance of Buildings and Equipment. The relation of the investment in buildings and equipment to total assets or revenues naturally varies from one enterprise to another. In general, it may be relatively slight in service industries (such as retailing and insurance) and very substantial in industries such as heavy manufacturing and transportation. For the investor-owned electric utility industry as a whole, net utility plant amounts to more than 90 percent of total assets, and represents more than four years' operating revenues.

U.S. Department of Commerce statistics for a recent year show nongovernment expenditures on new plant and equipment amounting to approximately 10 percent of GNP. Nongovernment fixed investment, excluding residential construction, exceeded 16 percent of GNP. The magnitude of these expenditures, coupled with the obvious observation that virtually all enterprises make use of buildings and equipment, are ample evidence of the economic importance of this class of assets.

PLANNING CAPITAL EXPENDITURES

Long-Range Planning of Capital Expenditures. The results of decisions regarding capital expenditures are generally far-reaching and of significant effect on the success or failure of an enterprise. It may not be possible to dispose of ill-advised capital additions without substantial loss. The incurrence of indebtedness to finance capital expenditures commits future earnings. If sufficiently increased earnings fail to result from capital additions, the ability of the enterprise to service its financial obligations could be seriously impaired and may be economically disastrous. By the same token, failure to engage in desirable capital expenditure programs could deprive an enterprise of valuable opportunities for profitable growth.

Planning Capital Expenditures for Expected Growth. Long-range planning should be related to the present programs and activities of the enterprise. In effect, it provides the bridge between the current situation and longer-term objectives. The integration of short- and long-term goals is necessary to provide for orderly growth in the planned directions. By this means, guideposts can be established to compare actual with intended progress, given a time schedule of planned objectives. Therefore, short-term capital expenditure plans represent the immediate time segment (usually one or two years ahead) of the long-term plan.

Balancing Capital Facilities. Attention should be given to careful balancing of various types of productive capacity at successive stages of the operations and manufacturing processes of the enterprise. This is necessary to avoid facility bottlenecks resulting from unbalanced expansion and the accompanying excess costs and delays. It also protects against uneconomically idle equipment, excessive work in process inventories, and the burden of extra depreciation, insurance, and interest expense.

Well-balanced capital investment is likely to stem from relating capital facilities to anticipated volume of output derived from careful analysis of sales and operating budgets. The productive capacity of each process should be coordinated with the requirements of successive operations, allowing for breakdowns, retooling, spoilage, and other interruptions in production. Capital additions should be planned to maintain or improve the existing balance of facilities.

Evaluation of Projects. An enterprise is likely to have a number of necessary or potentially profitable projects in which to invest funds. The efficiency with which these investment opportunities are analyzed, acted upon, and executed directly influences the future attainment of enterprise objectives such as profitability and maintenance of competitive position. Since the amounts involved are often large and the investments are frequently long-lasting, capital expenditure decisions are one of the most important of all management tasks.

The process of selecting projects is extremely complex. Many important considerations are neither quantifiable nor certain and can only be dealt with by means of intuitive judgment. For example, investment in equipment to reduce air or water pollution may have cost effects amenable to estimation or measurement. However, the benefits are difficult to quantify, as they may consist primarily of avoiding unfavorable publicity and compliance with legal requirements.

While these difficulties must be borne in mind, capital expenditure proposals should be supported by quantitative analysis and compared by means of quantitative criteria as far as reasonably possible. The main methods for these purposes are briefly described below.[2]

Cost of Funds.   In strict theory, enterprises should continue to raise and invest funds to the point where the incremental cost of capital funds required equals the incremental return on investment. However, in practice, there are reasons which usually prevent enterprises from approaching this point. For instance, available management talent may be insufficient to plan and control so rapid a rate of growth; the risk involved in certain investments may deter their acceptance although the expected return equals or exceeds the cost of capital; or certain possible projects may lie outside the area of operation desired by (or permissible under antitrust and other laws to) the enterprise.

Therefore, the cost of funds may not provide a sufficiently strict criterion to distinguish acceptable from unacceptable investment proposals. Project evaluation may employ a minimum acceptable rate of return (or cutoff rate) in excess of the cost of capital, or rate of return may not even be used as one of the project selection criteria.

Payback Period.   This criterion for project evaluation does not employ a rate of return concept. The payback period is the length of time required for cash inflows of an investment project to equal the original cash outlay. For instance, a proposed investment requires a present outlay of $1,000 and has expected cash inflows of $200 at the end of one year and $400 at the end of each succeeding year for the next four years. The payback period will be three years in this case.

Note that this method does not consider the time value of money; that is, it treats all dollars as being equal in value regardless of the time when they are expected to flow in or out. For example, if our illustration were changed to have the first cash inflow consist of $1,000 at the end of three years, the payback period is unaltered although there is postponement of cash inflows of $200 for two years and $400 for one year. In addition, the method ignores investment profitability by neglecting cash flows subsequent to the payback period. As an extreme instance, it shows no discrimination between our original example and one exactly alike except for a cash inflow of $100,000 rather than $400 in the final year. There is little in favor of the payback method except its extreme simplicity and ease in application. However, where liquidity is an overriding factor, its importance is increased. Also, where alternative investment projects are alike or indistinguishable in all other respects, the project with the shortest payback period may be preferred, on the

---

[2]For more comprehensive treatments, readers may consult Harold Bierman, Jr., and Seymour Smidt, *The Capital Budgeting Decision*, 3rd ed., The Macmillan Company, New York, 1971; G. David Quirin, *The Capital Expenditure Decision*, Richard D. Irwin, Homewood, Ill., 1967; and National Association of Accountants, Research Monograph No. 1, *Financial Analysis Techniques for Equipment Replacement Decisions*, NAA, New York, 1965.

grounds of the lesser degree of future uncertainty involved by a faster recovery of invested funds.

If a payback period is used, many accountants would prefer the *discounted* payback period, which is the shortest length of time required for the aggregate *present value* of the future cash flows to equal or exceed the initial cash outlay. The rate of discount normally applied in this case is the firm's cost of capital. While the discounted payback period does recognize the time value of money, it fails to consider inflows occurring after the end of the discounted payback period.

A method that takes into account the cash recovery from a project that is aborted prior to completion of its expected life is the *bailout* or *discounted bailout* period. The bailout period is the length of time during which the initial outlay remains recoverable from cash flows plus the salvage value of the project's assets. The discounted bailout period is the length of time that the initial outlay can still be recovered from discounted cash flows and salvage values.

Accounting Rate of Return.   There are variations in this method, but the most common approach is computation of average net income (= cash flows less depreciation) per year divided by average net book value of the assets over the project life. Alternative rate of return computation methods include use of the first year's cash inflow in place of the average for the numerator, and use of gross rather than net asset book value for the denominator. As an illustration, consider the original example cited under the payback period heading.

Straight-line depreciation for the $1,000 investment over its five-year life is $200 a year, assuming no salvage value. Cash flows after depreciation are zero in year 1 and $200 in each of the next four years, or an average of $\frac{1}{5}$ ($0 + $800) = $160 a year. The average net book value of the assets is $\frac{1}{5}$ ($800 + $600 + $400 + $200 + $0) = $400. The accounting rate of return is 160/400 = 40 percent on net book value, if taxes are ignored.

Since the method treats dollar flows in different periods as equivalent, it ignores the time value of money. For instance, if the $200 cash inflow of year 1 took place in year 5 instead and the $400 cash inflow of the year 5 were switched to year 1, there would be no change in the accounting rate of return. Another limitation of this technique is that results are dependent on the method of depreciation used. Use of accelerated depreciation, rather than straight-line, could materially alter the average earnings and asset book values computed for the project and hence produce a different rate of return. A possible advantage of this method, though, is its consistency with the effect of the project on accounting reports in the future, so that the method of project evaluation before investment takes place is a means of projecting future reported operating results. However, the effect on future accounting reports is not necessarily the best or only criterion for selection of capital expenditure projects.

Internal Rate of Return.   This technique, sometimes referred to as the "investor's method," is based explicitly on the time value of money. In fact, its purpose is to determine a time-adjusted rate of return for any project. This is done by finding a rate of return that, when applied to all cash flows, makes net outflows equal to net inflows.

Again using the previous example, plus a set of present value tables, we find a rate of return at which the present values of cash inflows and outflows are equal.

At a 25 percent rate of return, the discount factors from present value tables and the cash inflows are

Value at end of year 1 of $400 a year for years 2 through 5 = 2.362 × $400 . $ 944.80
Add cash inflow, year 1 ....   200.00
                                                                         $1,144.80
Present value at beginning of year 1 = 0.8 × $1,144.80 .... $ 915.84

Since $915.84 is less than the $1,000 present cash outlay, the internal rate of return on the project is not 25 percent but a lower rate. At 20 percent the results are

Value at end of year 1 of $400 a year for years 2 through 5 = 2.589 × $400 .	$1,035.60
Add cash inflow, year 1	200.00
	$1,235.60
Present value at beginning of year 1 = 0.833 × $1,235.6	$1,029.25

Since $1,029.25 is slightly larger than $1,000, the rate of return is slightly above 20 percent. The precise rate can be found by further trial and error.

This method does take into account both the profitability of the project and the time value of money. However, its drawbacks are as follows:

1. When there are net cash *outflows* in years of project life after the first year, there may be several internal rates of return, all of which are applicable. For instance, a project may have internal rates of return of 20, 30, and 50 percent. In such cases there is no uniquely "correct" rate, or any method of selecting one of the multiple rates as "truly representative" of the project's profitability.

2. The technique assumes reinvestment of all cash inflows at the *same* internal rate of return as that of the project. Where this is not the case, the method is not applicable without modification.

3. If internal rate of return is used to rank a number of projects in order of desirability, the ranking is not reliable unless all projects have both identical initial cash outlays and identical lives.

For these reasons, the internal rate of return method should be used only in circumstances where these limitations are not present.

Present Value Methods. These methods avoid the problem of possible multiple rates of return involved in the internal rate of return method. The approach is to discount future cash flows at a preselected rate, usually the minimum acceptable or cutoff rate of return.

Again using our example, assume a 15 percent cutoff rate of return. At this rate, the present value of the future cash flows is

Value at end of year 1 of $400 a year for years 2 through 5 = 2.855 × $400 .	$1,142
Add cash inflow, year 1	200
	$1,342
Present value at beginning of year 1 = 0.87 × $1,342	$1,168

From this point two alternative techniques may be used. The *net present value* method ranks projects on the excess of the present value over the immediate outlay. In the example above this would be ($1,168 − $1,000) = $168. The greater this excess, the more desirable in general is the project.

The *present value index* method is based on the ratio of the present value of future cash flows to the immediate outlay required. In the example this would be (1,168/1,000) = 1.168. The larger the value of this ratio, or index, the more desirable the project according to the net present value method.

The present value index may give incorrect decisions when projects are mutually exclusive. Correct decisions will result from selecting the projects with positive net present values as between mutually exclusive projects, choose the one with the largest excess present value.[3]

A detailed comparison and evaluation of these two present value methods would far exceed both the space and scope of this chapter. Many complex factors are involved, and the concerned reader is referred to specialized works. Special-

[3]Davidson, Sidney, James S. Schindler, and Roman L. Weil, *Fundamentals of Accounting*, 5th ed., The Dryden Press, Hinsdale, Ill., 1975, chap. 24, p. 767.

ized works should also be consulted for methods and problems not explicitly mentioned above: for example, income tax considerations in capital investment; buy or lease questions; dealing with risk and uncertainty; treatment of complementary, independent, and mutually exclusive projects; the implications of the cost of capital and capital rationing; and estimation of the expected rate of return on reinvested funds.

Control of Capital Expenditures. "Control" in this context does not mean simple downward pressure or minimization of expenditures. Rather it means maintaining a detailed check on all phases of capital expenditure—from inception to completion of each project—to ensure that management plans are executed as nearly as possible. Furthermore, control means coordination of capital expenditure planning with related plans such as cash and operating expense budgets.

Plant and Equipment Budget Procedures. The budgeting process for plant and equipment, while differing from one organization to another, generally includes the following procedures. Periodic requests, typically once a year, are usually made by the head office to the departments and operating units of an enterprise for capital expenditure proposals. Frequently this time table parallels that of the operating budget cycle.

The managers of departments and operating units submit these proposals to the budget director (or the controller or other official performing these functions, according to the organization of the particular enterprise concerned). The budget director reviews the proposals. He and his staff normally make a critical analysis of the information on which the proposals are based. Care is taken to ensure, so far as possible, that predictions such as sales volume and prices, engineering, production, administrative and distribution costs, and working capital requirements are the result of thorough study and realistic estimation. Techniques used for this purpose by the budget director and his staff usually include reference to historical records of similar projects, products, or processes, comparison with available industry information relevant to the respective proposals, and discussion and reexamination with the persons responsible for preparing and submitting the various proposals.

There are many technical aspects of proposals which accountants will not be able to check, especially in cases involving engineering and other specialized areas. However, it can be ensured that these technical aspects have been carefully studied by qualified personnel and are reflected in reliable estimates. A careful review by the budget director's office can be the source of major revisions and improvements of proposals; further, it provides a safeguard against the late discovery of costly errors of estimate in projects to which funds have already been committed. Also, the process of reviewing proposals may suggest alternative courses of action which might be superior to these considered.

Plant and Equipment Budgets. After projects have been reviewed by the budget director and revised where necessary, it is usual for top management to formulate a long-term capital expenditure budget. Examples are shown in Exhibits 1 and 2.

Normally a long-term capital expenditure budget is divided into two classes of items. One class consists of major projects where each one requires a large amount of funds: for instance, buildings, ships, and big items. Capital expenditures of such a nature often involve both construction and outlays extending beyond a single year. It can be seen in Exhibit 1 that all individual designated projects have this characteristic.

The other class of projects covers minor capital expenditures, which may not be planned in detail as far ahead as major projects. These consist of lesser-cost equipment, additions and improvements to buildings, and other smaller items. Items of this type would not usually be considered individually in long-range capital expenditure planning. Normally an aggregate sum is allowed to cover these

EXHIBIT 1   Long-Range Capital Expenditures Budget (Reproduced by permission from Welsch, *Budgeting: Profit Planning and Control)*

The XYZ CORPORATION—Long-Range Plan
Capital Expenditure Budget—Summary by Product and Years
For the period Jan. 1, 19X3, through 19X7
(Expressed in Thousands of Dollars)

Description of projects	Reference for detail	Budgeted Date	Budgeted Amount	Amount authorized to Jan. 1, 19X3	Amount subject to authorization	Amount spent to Jan. 1, 19X3	Unexpended balance of appropriation	Year of expenditure—cash requirements 19X3*	19X4	19X5	19X6	19X7	Subsequent years
Approved projects													
Regular:													
Project A etc.	A-1	19X1	$1,000	$800	$ 200	$700	$100	$150	$ 75	$ 50	$ 25		
Special:													
Project E etc.	E-1	19X2	500	200	300	180	20	220	70	30			
Total approved													
Budgeted projects*													
Regular:													
Project H etc.	H-1	19X3	800		800			100	150	250	200	$ 75	$ 25
Special:													
Project M etc.		19X3	270					50	50	50	60	60	
Undesignated†													
Total budgeted— 19X3													
Total regular													
Total special													
Grand total													
For information only													
Projects under study:													
Project X etc.	X-1	19X4	1,700		1,700				200	350	500	400	250
Total special													
TOTAL—ALL PROJECTS													

* Detailed in 19X3 profit plan.
† To take care of minor capital additions; see annual profit plan for 19X3 departmental appropriations.

Exhibit 2 Long-Term Capital Expenditures Budget (Adapted by permission)

FORM 1

THE BABCOCK & WILCOX COMPANY

DIVISION OR SUBSIDIARY DIAMOND POWER SPECIALTY CORPORATION (CONSOLIDATED)

ESTIMATE OF CAPITAL REQUIREMENTS
FOR THE FIVE-YEAR PERIOD
JANUARY 1, 1941 TO DECEMBER 31, 1945

DATE   JULY 1, 1940

PROJECT DESCRIPTION	DEPARTMENT OR WORKS	ESTIMATED FUTURE CAPITAL REQUIREMENTS			ESTIMATED DATE OF SUBMISSION TO PRESIDENT FOR CONSIDERATION		PERIOD OF ESTIMATED EXPENDITURES													*CAP. ITEMS UNDER 2,500
		REPLACEMENT	NEW CAPACITY	TOTAL	QUARTER	YEAR	1941				1942			1943			1944	1945			
							1ST QUARTER	2ND QUARTER	3RD QUARTER	4TH QUARTER	1ST HALF	2ND HALF	1ST HALF	2ND HALF							
D.P.S.C. (U.S.A.) Mechanical (Incl. Engr.) 1941	Lancaster																				
Factory Addition			275,000	275,000	Fourth	1940	137,500	137,500													
Parking Lot			25,000	25,000	"	"	25,000														
City Utilities			20,000	20,000	"	"	20,000														
500 KVA Sub Station			25,000	25,000	"	"	25,000														
Coupling Machine			15,000	15,000	"	"	15,000														
Heat Treating Facility			35,000	35,000	"	"			35,000				1941			60,800				
20 Ft. Press Brake			34,000	34,000	"	"	14,000						1942			41,100				
Hydraulic Shear			4,500	4,500	"	"		4,500					1943			41,800				
3-Axis Measuring Mach.			21,000	21,000	"	"	21,000						1944			39,400				
36-Gisholt			30,000	30,000	"	"			30,000				1945	Total		14,600				
Precision Indexing Head		3,000		3,000	"	"				3,000						219,700			24,700	
1,100 Sq. Ft. Bsmt. Plant Bldg.			6,000	6,000	"	"	6,000												6,000	
Vertical Checking Fixture			5,000	5,000	"	"	5,000												4,100	
M2G Spot Welder			7,000	7,000	"	"	7,000												1,500	
1A W2G Turret Lathe		39,000		39,000	"	"				39,000									26,300	
#2 Turret Lathe		17,000		17,000	"	"		17,000											22,100	
Tracer Lathe		20,000		20,000	"	"				20,000									13,100	
Calorizing Furnace		17,000		17,000	"	"	17,000												13,700	
1941 Total		93,000	505,500	598,500			287,500	184,000	65,000	62,000									13,900	
1942 Total		194,000	272,500	466,500	Fourth	1941					288,000	238,500							10,600	
1943 Total		89,500	290,000	379,500	"	1942							79,500	300,000						
1944 Total		50,000	170,000	220,000	"	1943									220,000					
1945 Total		80,000	15,000	95,000	"	1944										95,000			73,400	
Total Mechanical		506,500	1,253,000	1,759,500			287,500	184,000	65,000	62,000	288,000	238,500	79,500	300,000	220,000	95,000				
Electronics 1941	Lancaster																			
1942		3,000	370,000	373,000	Fourth	1941					373,000									
1943																				
1944																				
1945																				
Total Electronics		3,000	370,000	373,000							373,000									
Acquisitions 1941 - Process or Pollution Control Japan - Joint Venture			500,000	500,000	First	1941	500,000	500,000	500,000	500,000	750,000	750,000	79,500	300,000	220,000	95,000				
1942 - Electronic Product			350,000	350,000	Fourth	"	350,000													
Total Acquisitions			850,000	850,000			850,000	850,000	500,000	500,000	750,000	750,000	89,000	300,000	67,000	8,000			99,100	
Total D.P.S.C. (U.S.A.)		509,500	4,973,000	5,482,500			287,500	1,034,000	565,000	562,000	1,351,000	988,500	79,500	300,000	220,000	95,000				
D.P.S. LTD. (U.K.)		344,000	344,000	344,000			102,000	34,000			104,000		89,000	300,000	67,000	8,000			120,000	
TOTAL CONSOLIDATED		509,500	5,317,000	5,826,500			389,500	1,068,000	565,000	562,000	1,455,000	988,500	108,500	300,000	287,000	103,000			219,700	

* Items to be capitalized less than $2,500 not included in totals

EXHIBIT 3   Annual Capital Budget (Reproduced by permission from Heckert and Willson, *Business Budgeting and Control*)

THE ALLAN COMPANY
Annual Capital Budget Request—19X3
(In Thousands of Dollars)

Description	Appropriations							Schedule of capital expenditures				
	Prior years	New			19X3	Return on investment (DCF)	Total commitments	19X2 and prior	19X3	19X4	Later years	Total
		1st quarter	2nd quarter	Last half								
Expansion and growth												
Naphthalene plant........				$ 8,650	$ 8,650	22.3	$ 8,650		$ 2,130	$ 3,890	$2,630	$ 8,650
Butadiene recovery system....				3,100	3,100	19.2	3,100		2,200	900		3,100
Hydrogen plant........	$2,600					14.2	2,600	$2,310	290			2,600
Sulfur recovery system.......	1,900					8.7	1,900	1,500	400			1,900
Alkylate plant........			$12,300		12,300	17.6	12,300		6,000	6,300		12,300
Isocracker........		$25,000			25,000	23.8	25,000		6,500	17,300	1,200	25,000
Total expansion........	$4,500	$25,000	$12,300	$11,750	$49,050		$53,550	$3,810	$17,520	$28,390	$3,830	$53,550
Replacements												
Absolutely essential:												
Fitzpatrick grinder........	$ 590						$ 590	$ 400	$ 190			$ 590
Pneumatic tube system....		$ 390			$ 390		390		390			390
"R" plant conveyor....			$ 800		800		800		400	$ 400		800
Rosin crushers........	210						210	190	20			210
"X" air pollution catcher....				$ 1,020	1,020		1,020		300	720		1,020
Other........	20	10	10	30	50		70	15	55			70
Other........	$ 820	$ 400	$ 810	$ 1,050	$ 2,260		$ 3,080	$ 605	$ 1,355	$ 1,120		$ 3,080

	Col1	Col2	Col3	Col4	Col5	%	Col6	Col7	Col8	Col9	Col10	Col11
Competitively necessary:												
"L" quality control lab	$ 300						$ 300	$ 200	$ 100			$ 300
Fine screening plant			$ 670		$ 670		670		240	$ 430		670
Color retention process	20		10	$ 2,300	2,300		2,300	10	870	1,430		2,300
Other				20	50		70		60			70
	$ 320		$ 680	$ 2,320	$ 3,020		$ 3,340	$ 210	$ 1,270	$ 1,860		$ 3,340
Economics basis:												
Urea system		$ 800			$ 800	20.0	$ 800		$ 800			$ 800
Drum dumpers			$ 200		200	16.4	200		200			200
Lift trucks				$ 100	100	12.3	100		100			100
		$ 800	$ 200	$ 100	$ 1,100		$ 1,100		$ 1,100			$ 1,100
Other:												
Roof—North plant	$ 40		$ 70		$ 70		$ 70		70			70
Toledo landscaping		$ 5	10	$ 15	15		15	$ 35	15			15
Miscellaneous	40	5		10	25		65	35	30			65
	$ 40		$ 80	$ 25	$ 110		$ 150	$ 35	$ 115			$ 150
Total replacement	$1,180	$ 1,225	$ 1,770	$ 3,495	$ 6,490		$ 7,670	$ 850	$ 3,840	$ 2,980		$ 7,670
Contingency	$ 300	$ 2,000	$ 700		$ 2,700		$ 3,000	$ 300	$ 1,000	$ 1,700		$ 3,000
Grand total	$5,980	$28,225	$14,770	$15,245	$58,240		$64,220	$4,960	$22,360	$33,070	$3,830	$64,220

expenditures, as in Exhibit 1 where the heading "undesignated" is used for this purpose.

The long-term capital expenditure budget segments expenditures by years. This segmentation is required for coordination with the annual, or short-term, capital expenditure budget. An example of an annual capital budget is shown in Exhibit 3.

Inclusion of a project in the annual capital budget does not necessarily provide automatic authorization to spend funds or incur financial obligations with respect to that project. Controls are generally exercised at three stages: namely, inclusion in the budget, approval of the appropriation of funds, and authorization of

EXHIBIT 4   Appropriation Request (Reproduced by permission from Heckert and Willson, *Business Budgeting and Control)*

Authorization for Capital Expenditure

AFE No. 605

Western division   Los Angeles plant   Date_____6/27/XX_____

This request for authorization of a capital expenditure is made necessary by:

☐ Normal replacement   ☒ Cost reduction
☐ Change in manufacturing method   ☐ New business—product
☐ Change in quality control requirements ☐ Increased volume of business
☐ Change in styling

Title: Automatic Packaging Equipment
Description and Justification:
  Bagomatic to be used in packaging "R" chemical at Smead Avenue warehouse. Cost of container will be reduced by $0.50. Present usage 36,000 per year. See attached study on packaging operation.
                    (Use added sheets if necessary)

Estimated cost		Return on investment	
Materials.....................	$ 800	(Discounted cash flow method)	40.1%
Purchases...................	21,600		
Labor......................	—	Payout period................	2.61 yr
Total.....................	$22,400	Estimated useful life of equipment	6 yr
Contingency 5%..............	1,100	Time to construct.............	—
Total cost.................	$23,500	Salvage value.................	$500

Controller's comments and recommendations:

		Accounting Dept.	
		No.	Amount
Cash flow appears realistic.................. Capital Account		19–790	$23,500
Return is above minimum of 16%			
Approval recommended.......................................			
	Expense		

Approvals and authorization:

	Date		
	Approval	Rejection	Reason for rejection:
Requested by _____	_____	_____	
Approved by _____	_____	_____	
Department head _____	_____	_____	
Executive committee _____	_____	_____	
Board of directors, per____	_____	_____	

expenditures. These controls serve several purposes, one of which is to maintain flexibility in changing the annual capital budget if unforeseen circumstances so require. For this reason, projects may be classified by priority groups, such as essential, profitable, and desirable. In Exhibit 3 it can be seen that there is a category for "expansion and growth" and another category entitled "replacements." The second category is further divided into "absolutely essential," "competitively necessary," "economics basis" (i.e., profitable), and "other." Note that there is also a contingency allowance. This would allow for some variation between budgeted and actual expenditures and, if so desired, the later addition of one or more projects not presently in the budget.

Cash Management.   The annual capital expenditure budget must be coordinated with the cash budget in order to assure compatibility between budgeted capital outlays and availability of funds. Unless these respective budgets are carefully dovetailed, there is danger of being unable to carry out capital expenditures as planned, or of siphoning off cash required for working capital into capital expenditures, thus hampering the ability of the enterprise to meet its current financial obligations.

In order to integrate the cash and capital expenditure budgets fully, the timing of capital expenditures should be explicitly planned by month and by quarter of the year. This detailed breakdown allows short-term cash budgeting to be properly carried out.

Appropriations.   The setting up of an appropriation for a project in the annual capital budget usually signifies management's firm decision to commit funds to that project. Woods[4] states that appropriation provides a means of:

1. Identifying the project specifically so that transactions related to it can be separately recorded

2. Restricting the scope of the project to its approved form

3. Limiting the cost of the project to the budgeted amount, within a given tolerance (commonly plus or minus 10 percent)

4. Recording evidence that the project is consistent with the capital expenditure budget

5. Recording evidence of approval by the proper authority for the commitment of funds to the project.

Exhibit 4 shows an appropriation request form covering a single cost reduction project. Appropriations should be made in advance of any significant expenditures on a project.

Expenditure Authorization.   After the establishment of an appropriation, individual expenditure requests are usually required to authorize the placing of orders or letting of contracts for goods and services required for the project. Expenditure requests must be approved by the designated official. In large enterprises this authority is often delegated according to the amount involved. In one major manufacturing corporation, the following limits are applied.

Management Level	*Maximum Approval Authority*
President	$200,000
Executive vice presidents (3)	100,000
Vice presidents (10)	25,000
General managers	15,000
Directors of engineering, manufacturing, etc.	10,000
General superintendents, regional sales managers, etc.	5,000
Manager, consumer relations	2,000
District managers	500

[4] L. Milton Woods, *Accounting for Capital, Construction, and Maintenance Expenditures,* Prentice-Hall, Englewood Cliffs, N.J., 1967.

Control Reports.   Regular reports should be prepared which compare actual expenditures and commitments with the appropriated amounts. Exhibit 5 is an illustration of this type of report. Not only are such reports useful in the control of capital expenditures, but they also facilitate updating of cash budgets if required.

Even where control of capital expenditures is carefully exercised, some projects may exceed their time or money limits. When it appears likely that a project's expenditures will exceed its appropriation, this should be reported to management as soon as possible. Excess expenditures may signal inefficiency, unpredicted cost increases, or even changes in scope. An early review is desirable, since it may be possible to take action to mitigate or avoid further cost increases if no time is lost. To ensure thorough review, the overexpenditure should be subject to a supplemental appropriation, applying the same requirements for approval as in the case of the original appropriation. The supplemental appropriation should, in turn, be watched carefully for early warning of any further excessive expenditures.

It is more difficult to control time overruns. Nevertheless, significant delays beyond the original time estimate should be reported to management as soon as observed. The presence of delay may be a symptom of errors in project planning or changes in scope. Delay may indicate that increased costs may be incurred, since delay is seldom costless, or that future earnings from the project will not be received in accordance with previous expectations of timing or amount. In any case a thorough review is desirable.

Most companies set up blanket appropriations to cover minor capital expenditures required in the normal course of operations. Normally, an upper limit is set on the amount of any single purchase. It is desirable to exercise careful control over expenditures charged to blanket authorizations, so that temptation to "beat the system" is minimized. Possible temptations include purchase of items over the ceiling limit by means of two or more seemingly separate expenditure requests, and the designation of expenditures related to specific appropriations as pertaining to blanket appropriations (sometimes to avoid showing cost excesses) or vice versa (sometimes to conceal cost savings). There may also be temptation to spend on nonessentials to use up any excess in the blanket appropriation and to avoid possible future reductions in this appropriation.

When it is ascertained that a project is complete, the appropriation is closed. At this point it is desirable to have an inventory taken of the project. For large or complex projects, this requires considerable labor and effort. In the case of so-called "turnkey" contracts, where no detailed listing may be supplied by the contractor the task is even more burdensome. However, the more complicated and extensive the project, the more necessary is the inventory. The inventory provides the evidence for closing the appropriation and forms the basis for the transfers to the fixed asset accounts. Therefore, its accuracy is important. A completion report should be filed.

After closing of the appropriation, it is possible that late charges may arise. Any late charge in excess of a reasonable minimum (possibly $1,000 in the case of larger projects) should require a special appropriation, approved under the same guidelines as supplemental appropriations. The purpose is not simply to penalize lateness. After an appropriation is closed and a project has been inventoried, there is no longer any authority for further expenditures on it. Therefore precautions are required against hidden or unanticipated overexpenditures and possible omissions in the inventory.

Postcompletion Evaluation.   An important part of a sound capital expenditure control system is the postcompletion evaluation or performance audit. The main purposes are (1) to detect areas where action can be taken to improve future performance of the project, and (2) to gain information that will help improve planning and budgeting techniques for future projects.

EXHIBIT 5   Appropriation Status Report (Reproduced by permission from Heckert and Willson, *Business Budget and Control***)**

MONROE MANUFACTURING COMPANY
Appropriation Status Report
As of August 31, 19—

Appropriation No.	Description	Work order No.	Amount appropriated	Actual completion date	Original estimate	Outstanding commitments	Actual expenditures to date	Estimated cost to complete	Indicated total cost	(Over) or under original estimate
24	Ottawa Avenue Plant		$ 750,000							
	Buildings and equipment	241			$670,796.52	$286,672.84	$384,123.68	—	$670,796.52	—
	Site clearance	242			13,552.86		13,552.86	—	13,552.86	—
	Total appropriation 24				$684,349.38	$286,672.81	$397,676.54	—	$684,349.38	—
25	Modifications of Overhead Conveyor	251	35,000							
	Installation Y building				$ 28,353.00	$ 14,533.05	$ 236.39	$13,583.56	$ 28,353.00	($1,655.55)
	Others completed as of 7/31/				2,990.00	—	4,645.55	—	4,645.55	($1,655.55)
	Total appropriation 25				$ 31,343.00	$ 14,533.05	$ 4,881.94	$13,583.56	$ 32,998.55	($1,655.55)
26	Miscellaneous Improvements		183,400							
	Magnesium pilot line	261		7/31	$ 8,910.00	$ 6.50	$ 8,551.48	—	$ 8,551.48	$ 358.52
	Wrapping equipment	262		2/28	16,900.00		14,122.52	—	14,129.02	2,770.98
	Roll mill—design and install—A.C. plant	263			11,680.00	8,944.00	154.00	2,582.00	11,680.00	—
	Intercommunication system and install in Y building	264			24,974.00	4,794.57	20,179.43	—	24,974.00	—
	Move hydraulic press and install in Y building	265		5/31	1,155.50	79.15	926.68	—	1,005.83	149.67
	Design and install air conditioning unit in Y building	266			9,725.00	750.00	8,626.84	348.16	9,725.00	
	Changes and modifications in paint room	267		5/31	30,115.00	29.89	26,664.06	—	26,693.95	3,421.05
	Buggy scales	268			11,275.00	212.20	10,158.39	904.41	11,275.00	
	Tote boxes—A.C. plant	269		7/31	3,597.00	340.57	3,198.86	—	3,539.43	57.57
	Prepare annealing oven for production use	270			7,700.00	1,290.03	6,202.29	207.68	7,700.00	
	Move electric furnaces to A.C. plant	271			3,585.00	2,989.20	—	595.80	3,585.00	—
	Lift truck with oxide batteries and battery charger	272			30,486.00	21,670.19	2,737.83	6,077.98	30,486.00	—
	Purchase and install 100 HP motor in Y building	273		7/31	4,692.00	424.00	3,701.97	—	4,125.97	566.03
	Others completed as of 7/31/				3,701.00		2,482.18	—	2,482.18	1,218.82
	Total appropriation 26				$168,495.50	$ 41,530.30	$107,706.53	$10,716.03	$159,952.86	$8,542.64
29	Aluminum Experimental Unit	291	50,000							
	Construction of unit				$ 50,000.00	$ 5,533.34	$ 15,385.04	$29,081.62	$ 50,000.00	—
	Total appropriation 29				$ 50,000.00	$ 5,533.34	$ 15,385.04	$29,081.62	$ 50,000.00	—
	Grand total		$1,018,400		$934,187.88	$348,269.53	$525,650.05	$53,381.21	$927,300.79	$ 6,887.09

Issued by Accounting Department—Sept. 5, 19—.

EXHIBIT 6 Postevaluation Report (Adapted by permission from Heckert and Willson, *Business Budgeting and Control*)

CAPITAL EXPENDITURE PERFORMANCE REPORT
(Actual versus Justification)

DEPARTMENT Naphthalene TITLE Install Turbogenerator

AUTHORIZATION NO. 12345 DATE APPROVED 6/20/58 AMOUNT $1,200,000 MONTH OPERATION BEGAN April, 1961

REPORT OF STATUS AS OF 12/31/66

ANALYSIS OF DIFFERENCES
BETWEEN ACTUAL AND JUSTIFICATION

(000's omitted)	Original authorization justification to date	Actual to date	Actual over (+) or under (−) justification — Dollars	Actual over (+) or under (−) justification — %	
Expenditures charged to auth. A/C-plant	$ 800	$ 900	$+100	+13	(1)
Expense	350	200	−150	−43	(2)
Investment	50	75	+25	+50	(3)
Total	1,200	1,175	−25	−21	
Other balance sheet charges—inventory, equipment, etc.	100	225	+125	+125	(4)
Total	1,300	1,400	+100	+8	
Net cash income (before F.I.T.):					
For year 1966	400	450	+50	+12	(5)
For all prior years	1,700	1,550	−150	−10	(6)
Total	2,100	2,000	−100	− 5	
Evaluation:					
Cumulative cash position	+800	+600	−200		
Cumulative book income	757	1,065	+308		
Rate of return	19 %	22 %			
Rate of return (approved method)	Original authorization justification life of project				
Rate of return (approved method)	30 %				

(1) Price rise in materials and labor

(2) Lower cost of site clearance

(4) Increase in inventories

(5) Higher sales price

(6) Slower start-up of 9 months accounted for lower income of $125

The scope of postcompletion evaluation procedures varies with individual enterprises and projects. Some firms limit the evaluation to major projects over $1 million in cost. Exhibit 6 shows a specimen evaluation report in brief summary form.

The timing of evaluation is important. It should take place as soon as operating results are no longer significantly affected by start-up problems.

On large projects, such as a new plant, several evaluations are desirable. The initial one might be undertaken during construction, to provide information on progress and revised estimates of cost. A second report should be made on completion of construction, giving an almost-final estimate of construction costs and an updated forecast of output capability. Finally, after the breaking-in period, the actual postcompletion evaluation can be made.

For performance of the postcompletion evaluation, Woods suggests the following steps:

1. A careful physical inspection of the facilities and comparison with the plans and estimates and physical performance data

2. Identification of the specific asset items from the detailed accounting records of work in progress or fixed asset accounts

3. A check of actual operating results regarding income, expense, and working capital with project budget estimates, followed by preparation of revised estimates

4. Comparison of the revised estimates with the budgeted projections and analysis and explanation of any significant differences

5. Submission of a report covering the above-mentioned steps to management.

ACCOUNTING FOR ACQUISITIONS

The Cost Principle. It is generally accepted practice to record and report buildings and equipment at their historical cost. Cost means the amount of the purchase consideration in cash or its equivalent at the time of asset acquisition. Included are all outlays incurred to put the asset into condition and location for use, such as charges for freight and installation.

The cost principle is that assets are to be recorded initially at cost and kept at cost until realization takes place. In the case of fixed assets, depreciation is recognized in the accounts but is based on historical cost. Cost less depreciation is the valuation basis generally adhered to throughout the life of each asset.

Reasons for Use. There are several alternative methods for the valuation of tangible fixed assets. These methods include not only historical cost but also historical cost adjusted for changes in the general price level and/or specific asset reproduction prices. Other bases of valuation are current net resale price (either in a forced or an orderly liquidation) and current cost of replacement of asset services by later-model nonidentical equipment. Thus historical cost is only one of a number of possible bases of tangible fixed asset valuation.

Departures from the cost principle raise serious problems. As the basis of *initial* valuation, cost is a most reasonable choice. Normally asset acquisition results from a market transaction at arm's length by two parties, each presumed to act rationally in his own self-interest. This establishes a strong likelihood that cost is the best measure of value at the time of acquisition.

At subsequent dates, as circumstances have time to change, it can be argued that historical cost and value may no longer be the same. Nevertheless, the cost principle remains the most widely accepted and most often used rule. It has the advantage of being based on an *actual* market transaction, while alternative methods of valuation usually postulate *hypothetical* transactions (such as an imaginary sale or replacement of the asset).

In addition, while historical cost is usually easy to verify by following well-established procedures, the alternative valuation methods incorporate few if any standard procedures and can result in widely varying amounts. It has frequently been said that historical cost is objective, while other valuation methods are subjective in nature.

Variations from Cost. Sometimes it may be evident that, even at the time of acquisition, there is a significant difference between cost and market value. If cost is in excess of market value, this may be the result of defects in judgment, major changes made during construction of plant, excessive delays in completing a building, or other adverse factors. In such cases most authorities agree that recorded cost should not exceed that which would have been incurred under normal circumstances. Hendricksen[5] states:

> Only those costs that would normally be paid for property by reasonably prudent management should be included in prudent costs. This concept has been used by public utility regulators as a method of placing the public interest ahead of the interests of promoters, management, and stockholders. But the prudent cost concept is also applicable to the general valuation of plant and equipment. The costs to be allocated to the services of future periods should not include excessive costs representing costs of inefficiency and other losses incurred in the period of acquisition.

In practice this concept may not be easy to apply since it can be difficult to distinguish between costs that are prudent and costs that are excessive. As a rule the costs agreed to by management at the time of the initial commitment are assumed to be prudent in the absence of evidence to the contrary. Additional costs incurred afterward could be regarded as excessive since evidence is lacking that management would initially have been willing to accept these extra costs.

It is possible for assets to be acquired at a bargain price, perhaps in a distress sale. In this event authorities differ as to whether actual cost should be written up to market value. Since accounting practices tend towards conservatism in ambiguous cases, many (if not most) accountants would not favor writing up in this situation, in conformity with the concept of valuation at the lower-of-cost-or-market price.

"Original" Cost. As used in public utility regulation, this term means the cost of property when first put into public service. Any excess paid over original cost less accumulated depreciation by a subsequent purchaser is not allowed as an expense of operation by most regulatory agencies. This rule attempted to protect consumers from financial manipulation (often by holding companies) in an earlier era. At that time there was temptation for a holding company to reap a profit by selling an asset to a subsidiary at an enhanced price, at the same time inflating the subsidiary's rate base and hence its allowable earnings under regulation.

While there is (or was) merit in this rule for regulatory purposes, it has little application in nonregulated business where earnings are the determinant of asset value, rather than the converse which applies in the regulated sector.

Methods of Acquisition. It is generally accepted that the cost of a fixed asset should include all expenses of transporting the asset to the proper location and placing it in the condition necessary for its intended service. While this broad principle provides the basic accounting guidelines, questions of interpretation arise. The way in which such questions are treated affects not only the initial asset valuation but also the charges to expense in the acquisition period and the amount of depreciation in subsequent periods.

New or Used Assets, Acquired in Completed Form. When an individual asset requir-

[5] Hendriksen, *op. cit.*, p. 364.

ing no further construction is purchased, cost is the aggregate outlay incurred to bring the asset into its intended use. For instance, if a drill press is purchased from a manufacturing firm, f.o.b. its Syracuse plant, for use in a Los Angeles factory, the cost to the acquiring firm is the invoice price, less all cash discounts offered, plus freight from Syracuse to Los Angeles and cartage to the Los Angeles factory, plus costs to install the press and to test and adjust it in order to have it operate according to specifications. Cash discounts available but not taken by the purchaser should, strictly speaking, be treated as an expense rather than as a part of the cost of the asset. In practice this procedure is not always followed.

According to the National Association of Accountants,[6] the costs to be capitalized for equipment include:

1. Original invoice or contract price
2. Freight, drayage and cartage in, import duties, handling and storage charges payable
3. Specific in-transit insurance
4. Sales, use, and other taxes directly related to the purchased equipment
5. Preparation of foundations and other costs of a proper operating site for the equipment
6. Installation costs, including any applicable company overhead on the same basis as it is charged to inventory
7. Charges for testing and preparation for use
8. Reconditioning, if used equipment is purchased.

Equipment used in research and development presents problems of accounting treatment. Where the equipment is of special or single-purpose type, its usefulness may be inherently limited to a specific research or development project. Therefore its ultimate worth may be indeterminate, just as the life, success or failure of the research project may be indeterminate. In these circumstances, there is justification for expensing rather than capitalizing the cost of such equipment. Similarly, research equipment may be subjected to damaging stress, such as testing with corrosive gases or radioactivity, or drastic experimental modification, or "cannibalization" (i.e., assimilation into other pieces of equipment). These possibilities require careful consideration in determining whether specific items of research and development equipment should be given normal capitalization treatment or written off as current research and development expense. In general, the Financial Accounting Standards Board has required by its Statement No. 2 that research and development expenditures should be expensed and not capitalized.[7]

FASB Interpretation No. 4[8] deals with the applicability of FASB Statement No. 2 to business combinations accounted for by the purchase method. It includes the following statement:

> The subsequent accounting by the combined enterprise for the costs allocated to assets[1] to be used in research and development activities shall be determined by reference to Statement No. 2. Paragraph 12 of Statement No. 2 requires that costs identified with research and development activities shall be charged to expense when incurred unless the test of alternative future use in paragraph 11 (a) or 11 (c) is met. That requirement also applies in a business combination accounted for by the purchase method. Accordingly, costs assigned to assets to be used in a particular research and

[6]National Association of Accountants, Statement No. 4 on Management Accounting Practices, "Fixed Asset Accounting: The Capitalization of Costs," 1972, p. 10.

[7]Financial Accounting Standards Board, Statement No. 2.

[8]Financial Accounting Standards Board, "Applicability of FASB Statement No. 2 to Business Combinations Accounted for by the Purchase Method," FASB Interpretation No. 4, February 1975.

development project and that have no alternative future use shall be charged to expense at the date of consummation of the combination. Therefore, the accounting for the cost of an item to be used in research and development activities is the same under paragraphs 11 and 12 of Statement No. 2, whether the item is purchased singly, or as part of a group of assets, or as part of an entire enterprise in a business combination accounted for by the purchase method. (The following is a footnote to this passage: [1]In this regard, paragraph 69 of APB Opinion No. 16 states in part that: "The nature of an asset and not the manner of its acquisition determines an acquirer's subsequent accounting for the cost of that asset.")

A purchase agreement may provide for interest-free installment payments or a series of non-interest-bearing notes covering the purchase consideration. In such a case, the interest charges are implicit and should be ascertained and excluded from the cost recorded for the asset. The amount of the implicit interest may be ascertained by deducting the spot-cash price from the actual price paid. If no spot-cash price can be determined (because the seller may sell only on installment terms), an estimated interest rate can be applied. This procedure is not always followed in practice, however.

Examples of items in addition to the contract price that may be included in the cost of an existing building are:

1. Architects' plans for remodeling
2. Fees and charges of brokers, agents, notaries, attorneys, title companies, inspectors, county clerks, and recorders
3. Initial remodeling, including permanently attached floor coverings and similar items
4. Permits and privileges
5. Payments made to former tenants to cancel leases
6. Property taxes to date of purchase assumed by the purchaser.

The National Association of Accountants[9] states that the following items should not be capitalized:

1. Extraordinary costs associated with construction, such as those due to strike, flood, fire, or other casualty. However, anticipated costs such as rock blasting, piling, or relocating the channel of an underground stream *should* be capitalized.
2. Costs of abandoned construction.
3. Bonus payments to contractors, temporary construction because of shortages of material for permanent construction, and similar costs incurred for the purpose of hastening completion.

Contract Construction.   Fixed assets constructed under contract are usually not entered into the fixed asset records until completion. If, as frequently occurs, the contract calls for advance and partial payments before completion, these payments are normally recorded as advances. By making such payments while construction continues, the payer does not acquire ownership of the fixed assets, but rather has a claim against the contractor. This claim is liquidated by the contractor's delivery of the completed asset. Upon completion, the asset or assets are entered as such in the accounting records.

Self-construction.   When an enterprise constructs its own buildings or equipment, there is no single purchase price or contract amount representing the cost of the new assets. Under these circumstances, problems can arise as to what should be included or excluded in determining asset cost.

One problem relates to the treatment of indirect overhead and its apportionment between the construction activity and the normal production operations. Three alternatives are generally recognized. The first is to assign no indirect

[9]National Association of Accountants, *op. cit.*, p. 11.

overhead to the construction cost of the fixed asset. The reasons given to support this approach are the following:

1. Indirect overhead tends to be fixed in nature and is not increased by irregular construction activity.

2. Work on self-constructed assets tends to be done in slack periods, and absorption of indirect overhead into fixed asset costs results in an arbitrary overstatement of current net income.

3. If normal operations are not curtailed by the construction activity, there is no indication that management would have been willing to incur any greater cost on the construction than the direct charges.

These reasons are based on the assumption that fixed asset self-construction is an irregular rather than a continuing activity.

A second alternative is to assign indirect overhead to construction cost on the same basis as used for the assignment to normal production. The reasons advanced for this approach are the following:

1. It avoids special treatment or exemptions of self-constructed assets from a fair share of overhead costs.

2. It avoids the overcosting of normal production with respect to indirect overhead.

Where firms (such as public utilities and railroads) tend to engage in continuous self-construction, these reasons constitute an appropriate case for full costing.

The third possibility is to allocate indirect overhead to the extent that it would have been assigned to the production that is curtailed because of the construction activity. This proposal is appealing in theory, but it may be difficult to apply since it depends on "what otherwise might have been."

Dyckman[10] suggests that the alternative methods depend on different circumstances. He generally favors the direct cost approach in being reluctant to charge to construction any overhead that does not appear to have resulted directly by reason of the undertaking of construction activity.

On the other hand, Kieso and Weygandt[11] prefer the full costing approach. But these authors add that if the allocated overhead causes construction costs to be in excess of their business usefulness, or in excess of what would be charged by an independent outside contractor, then the excess overhead should be expensed as a period loss rather than capitalized.

Interest During Construction. Whether construction of plant and equipment is contracted out or not, the question of including interest charges in cost arises if the construction period is lengthy and funds are disbursed prior to completion.

One alternative is to charge no interest to construction. It may be argued that interest is not a cost of construction but rather a financial charge. To charge interest to construction may cause the cost of constructed assets to differ according to the method of financing used.

Another alternative is to charge only the interest paid on funds specifically borrowed for the asset construction project. This method is frequently used in practice. It avoids charging interest on funds provided by the owner on the ground that this is an imputed, rather than incurred, cost and leads to unrealized income and valuation of assets in excess of cost. An opposing argument is that no funds are without cost, and that to charge interest on indebtedness but not ownership funds is inconsistent.

---

[10]Thomas R. Dyckman, *Long-Lived Assets,* Wadsworth Publishing Company, Belmont, Calif., 1967.

[11]Kieso, Donald E., and Jerry J. Weygandt, *Intermediate Accounting,* John Wiley & Sons, New York, 1974, p. 438.

The third choice is to charge interest to construction on all funds employed, whether or not separably identifiable. This practice is allowed by Federal Power Commission regulation in the case of electric and gas utility companies. The rate of interest prescribed is the net cost of borrowed funds and a reasonable rate on other funds used. The Interstate Commerce Commission does not allow imputed interest on equity capital, but it is allowed by the Federal Communications Commission. It can strongly be argued that use of such a procedure involves arbitrary allocation decisions, controversial measures of the cost of capital, and possibly the erroneous impression of the level of interest expense to be expected in the future. In practice, sometimes a rate representing the aftertax average embedded cost of capital from all sources, including equity funds, has been used, mainly by electric utility companies. Hendriksen[12] favors this approach on the assumption that the imputed cost of equity funds represents a theoretically logical economic opportunity cost. Dyckman[13] points out that this opportunity cost should be considered in the decision to build or not, but should not be included as part of the asset's cost because the opportunity cost does not in itself enhance the value of the asset. Also, he observes that its inclusion would distort the rate of return on the project. Suelflow[14] points out that capitalized costs for equity funds imply that earnings have increased, but that actually there were no increased earnings as such. Both Suelflow and Kieso and Weygandt note that there is a lack in the uniformity of treatment of capitalized interest during construction by firms in general, and by utilities in particular, which underscores the controversial nature of this item.

Kieso and Weygandt[15] state that the practice of capitalizing interest should be eliminated. As a minimum, if capitalization is permitted, these authors believe that it should be applied consistently by all concerns in the same industry. A recent policy statement by the U.S. Securities and Exchange Commission points out that, except for public utilities, conventional accounting practices have not treated the cost of capital as part of the cost of an asset. Interest on debt is normally regarded as a period expense, while the cost of equity capital normally is reflected neither in asset cost nor in the income statement. In 1974, the Securities and Exchange Commission, in *Accounting Series Release No. 163*, prohibited the capitalization of interest (except in certain industries) unless the company had previously been capitalizing interest on assets of this general kind: "Accordingly, the Commission concludes that companies other than electric, gas, water and telephone utilities and those companies covered by the two exceptions in the authoritative literature described above (see AICPA Guides[16] for "Savings and Loan Associations" and "Retail Land Sales") which had not, as of June 21, 1974, publicly disclosed an accounting policy of capitalizing interest costs shall not follow such a policy in financial statements . . . after June 21, 1974."[17]

On balance, we conclude that accounting opinion is divided on the capitalization of interest on debt, and that it is against the capitalization of the imputed cost of equity funds. The practice of public utility companies in capitalizing interest is therefore not a general rule in other industries, and relies mainly upon the

---

[12]Hendriksen, *op. cit.*, p. 373.

[13]Dyckman, *op. cit.*, p. 32.

[14]Suelflow, James E., *Public Utility Accounting*, Institute of Public Utilities, Michigan State University, 1973, p. 180.

[15]Kieso and Weygandt, *op. cit.*, pp. 436–437.

[16]American Institute of Certified Public Accountants, Industry Audit Guide for "Savings and Loan Associations," 1974; Industry Accounting Guide "Accounting for Retail Land Sales," 1973.

[17]Securities and Exchange Commission, *Accounting Series Release No. 163*, Washington, D.C., November 14, 1974.

concept that a return on funds is virtually assured through the rate-making process in public utility regulation.

As an illustration of the accounting treatment for capitalization of interest, we reproduce below one of the notes to the financial statements for the year ended January 31, 1974 of Sears, Roebuck and Company:

Note 2. Accounting Change

Effective February 1, 1973, the Company adopted the accounting policy of capitalizing the carrying costs, real estate taxes and interest, of construction-in-progress and land held for future use. Under this new policy, all amounts capitalized will be amortized to earnings over the depreciable life of the structure when the property is placed in economic use. The effect of this prospective change was to increase net income for the year ended January 31, 1974, by $14,100,000 (.09 per share).

Some other corporations that have capitalized interest in recent years are American Metal Climax, Inc., R. J. Reynolds Industries, Inc., and Union Camp Corporation.

Donation or Gift.   When assets are obtained by way of gift or donation, the cost principle of valuation cannot be applied. Instead, the fair value of the assets (either the applicable market price or an appraisal in the absence of an available market price) is used. The offsetting credit should be to a proprietorship (paid-in capital) account, separately labeled as "donated capital." This credit should be reduced by an amount equal to any costs incurred in acceptance of the donation, such as legal fees or transportation and installation charges.

It is sometimes argued that donated assets should be excluded from the accounts because no cost was incurred to acquire them. This argument has little support since it results in ignoring values committed to the enterprise and future depreciation charges to operations.

Sometimes gifts are conditional upon performance of certain requirements by the receiver. For instance, local governments may offer a free site and perhaps a building to any firm agreeing to employ a given minimum number of local residents for a certain time period. Regardless of such conditions, the entries should still be made as recommended above. In addition, the accounting records and statements should (usually by means of a note) indicate the contingency and state that clear title has not been obtained.

Other Methods of Acquisition.   Assets may be acquired by means of leasing and through pooling of interests. These methods are dealt with in Chapters 25, "Leases," and 33, "Mergers, Acquisitions, and Pooling of Interests."

Basket Purchases.   This term refers to the acquisition of a group of assets for a single lump-sum price. In the purchaser's accounting records, it is necessary to allocate the cost to the different type of assets acquired. Although accountants are not usually expert in appraising property values, it is an accounting responsibility to see that valuation appraisals made by others seem reasonable and are adequately supported by evidence. This is more easily done before completion of the transaction than after the fact. Therefore, if the accountant knows of a contemplated basket purchase, he should inform management of the importance of careful apportionment of the total cost and request that a sound determination be made.

In the absence of a prior apportionment, the following points should be considered: When current assets are included in the basket purchase, their reasonable value is often not difficult to establish. Inventories of finished goods, work in process, and raw materials can usually be valued at replacement costs. Items sold off may be recorded at the net proceeds of disposal.

Most difficult to appraise are intangibles, such as goodwill, patents, trademarks, and similar items. Frequently, any excess of the total purchase price over the valuation of the tangible assets is assigned as the value of intangible assets.

With respect to buildings and equipment, the joint purchase cost may be allocated in proportion to the relative values of the respective assets. Appraisals made for insurance purposes may be used to determine relative values. However, this information may be incomplete since portions of buildings such as foundations, excavations, and underground conduits are not usually insured against fire and other casualty loss.

Assessed valuations made for property tax purposes may be available. Such information has an objective nature (i.e., third-party impartiality), but it may be neither up to date nor based on diligent investigation. Although it is the most costly method, independent professional appraisal may be required. For major acquisitions its use is probably well advised.

Net book values of the former owner may be ascertainable with little cost or effort. However, their use in apportionment of value in a basket purchase is of dubious worth unless all the assets involved were recently acquired. Book values for older assets are not usually claimed to represent good approximations of relative asset values.

There is a definite necessity for supportability of the results of allocating a lump sum to the different types of assets required. The matter is most significant for income tax purposes, as well as financial reporting purposes. Its importance is underscored by the issue of Opinions No. 16 and 17 of the Accounting Principles Board of the American Institute of Certified Public Accountants. These Opinions set forth criteria for determining the cost of individual assets, while also urging that judgment be used in view of the complexity and imprecise nature of the factors involved. Concerned readers should consult Chapter 33, "Mergers, Acquisitions, and Pooling of Interests."

Methods of Payment. When assets are acquired by means of payment other than cash outlays, direct cost valuation tends to be difficult or impossible. This is especially the case when the method of payment involves the issue of securities or an exchange of assets.

Issue of Securities. Assets may be acquired against the issue of stock or bonds. The par or nominal value of these securities is not a reliable indicator of their worth or of the value of the assets acquired.

Where the securities are actively traded by numerous parties, their current market value is the basis that should be used for asset valuation. When trading is not active or is confined to only a few large holders, it is necessary to estimate the value of the acquired assets, preferably by means of independent appraisal.

Exchange and Trade-in. Where buildings or equipment are acquired in a barter transaction, the market value of the assets given up is usually the most satisfactory basis for valuation. In some cases, as with used automobiles or trucks, such market values may be readily available. Occasionally, there may be more reliable evidence of the value of the new asset being acquired than of the asset being given up, for example, if there are many sales of like-new assets for cash. If so, the current cash price of the new asset would be used for valuation. In general, the goal is to use the most reliable indication of market value available for valuing the new asset.

If there is a cash payment (or receipt) in addition to the trade-in, the amount should be added to (or subtracted from) the market value of the assets given up to determine the valuation of the assets received.

If old equipment is traded in, it is common for the dealer to allow more in trade than the current value of the old asset. This is in lieu of a price concession on the new asset. To avoid overstatement of the cost of the new asset and of current income, the accountant should carefully examine the evidence including, where obtainable, the realistic market values of the old and new assets. If inflation of the trade-in allowance is found, its amount should be deducted from both the cost of the new asset and the amount shown as being received from the disposal of the old asset.

Davidson, Schindler, Stickney, and Weil[18] give the following useful rules for accounting for trade-in transactions:

> The accounting for a trade-in depends upon whether or not the asset received is "similar" to the asset traded in and whether the accounting is for *financial statements* or for *income tax* returns. Assume an old asset cost $5,000, has $3,000 of *accumulated depreciation* (after recording depreciation to the date of the trade-in), and hence has a *book value* of $2,000. The old asset appears to have a market value of $1,500, according to price quotations in used-asset markets. The old asset is traded-in on a new asset with a list price of $10,000. The old asset and $5,500 cash (*boot*) are given for the new asset. The generic entry for the trade-in transaction is:

```
New Asset ............................    A
Accumulated Depreciation (Old Asset) ....  3,000
Adjustment on Exchange of Asset ........   B  or  B
    Old Asset ...........................            5,000
    Cash ................................            5,500
```

(1) The *list-price* method of accounting for trade-ins rests on the assumption that the list price of the new asset closely approximates its market value. The new asset is recorded at its list price (A = $10,000 in the example); B is a *plug* (= $2,500 credit in the example). If B requires a *debit* plug, the Adjustment on Exchange of Asset is a *loss*; if a *credit* plug is required (as in the example), the adjustment is a gain.

(2) Another theoretically sound method of accounting for trade-ins rests on the assumption that the price quotation from used-asset markets gives a more reliable measure of the market value of the old asset than is the list price a reliable measure of the market value of the new asset. This method uses the *fair market value* of the old asset, $1,500 in the example, to determine B (= $2,000 book value − $1,500 assumed proceeds on disposition = $500 debit or loss). The exchange results in a loss if the book value of the old asset exceeds its market value and in a gain if the market value exceeds the book value. The new asset is recorded on the books by plugging for A (= $7,000 in the example).

(3) For income tax reporting, no gain or loss may be recognized on the trade-in. Thus the new asset is recorded on the books by assuming B is zero and plugging for A (= $7,500 in the example). In practice, firms that wish to recognize the loss currently will sell the old asset directly, rather than trading it in, and acquire the new asset entirely for cash.

(4) *Generally accepted accounting principles* (*APB* Opinion No. 29) require a variant of these methods. The basic method is (1) or (2), depending upon whether the list price of the new asset (1) or the quotation of the old asset's market value (2) is the more reliable indication of market value. If, when applying the basic method, a debit entry, or loss, is required for the Adjustment on Exchange of Asset, then the trade-in is recorded as described in (1) or (2) and the full amount of the loss is recognized currently. If, however, a credit entry, or gain, is required for the Adjustment on Exchange of Asset, then the amount of gain recognized currently depends upon whether or not the old asset and the new asset are "similar." If the assets are not similar, then the entire gain is recognized currently. If the assets are similar and cash is not received by the party trading in, then no gain is recognized and the treatment is like that in (3); i.e., B = 0, plug for A. If the assets are similar and cash is received by the party trading in—a rare case—then a portion of the gain is recognized currently. The portion of the gain recognized currently is the fraction *cash received/market value of old asset*. (When the list-price method, (1), is used, the market value of the old asset is assumed to be the list price of the new asset plus the amount of cash received by the party trading in.)

[18]Davidson, Sidney, James S. Schindler, Clyde P. Stickney, and Roman L. Weil, *Accounting: The Language of Business,* 2nd ed., Thomas Horton and Daughters, Inc., Glen Ridge, N.J., 1975.

The results of applying GAAP to the example in case (4) can be summarized as follows:

	Old Asset Compared with New Asset	
More Reliable Information	Similar	Not Similar
New Asset List Price ...... A =	$7,500	A = $10,000
B =	0	B = 2,500 gain
Old Asset Market Price .... A =	$7,000	A = $ 7,000
B =	500 loss	B = 500 loss

Installment Contracts. When assets are acquired by means of installment contracts, title to the property may not pass to the purchaser until payment is completed. Nevertheless, it is generally regarded as proper to record the asset cost at the date of delivery (net of explicit or implicit interest charges) and to recognize the total amount due in payments as a liability.

Accounting Records. It is difficult to exaggerate the importance of maintaining adequate records for effective control and reliable accounting in regard to plant and equipment. The purposes served by these records as given by Woods[19] are as follows:

1. To form the basis for necessary management reports and financial statements

2. To supply the information in sufficient detail for normal internal control procedures, primarily the audit and inventory of tangible fixed assets

3. To provide the required information for preparation of insurance claims for assets that have been damaged or destroyed.

4. To show the location and, to some extent, support the valuation of assets for the purposes of real and personal property tax assessments.

Chart of Accounts. The costs and other details of buildings and equipment should be classified according to a logical property chart of accounts. Exhibit 7 shows an illustrative property chart of accounts which classifies assets by depreciation type and rate, function or use, life, location, cost center, date of acquisition, real and personal property tax group, and amount capitalized.

Uniform charts of accounts, for assets and other items, are prescribed by many regulatory agencies and are recommended for member use by numerous trade associations.

Plant Ledger. The plant ledger contains detailed plant and equipment records and functions as a subsidiary ledger controlled by the general ledger. The plant ledger consists of individual cards for separate assets or asset groups. The property cards described in Exhibit 7 are representative examples. In fully computerized systems, these cards may be replaced with equivalent electronic records on magnetic tapes, discs, drums, or similar devices.

The cards are usually prepared from property acquisition reports. Such reports usually provide for physical control procedures by requiring tagging of assets with a serial number for identification. The serial number is noted on the property card (see Exhibit 7 for an example) for future inventory purposes.

Unit Detail. A separate property card is kept for each unit of property. But how should a "unit" be defined? The property record manual of a major manufacturing company makes the following classifications:

III. CLASSIFICATION OF PLANT ASSETS

For purposes of the property records for purchases after January 1, 19×7, plant assets shall be divided into three classes, with a somewhat different method of handling the records for each class, as follows:

[19]Woods, *op. cit.*

CLASS I. INDIVIDUALLY IDENTIFIABLE UNITS—This class shall include assets which can readily be identified as individual physical units. Most of the productive machinery falls into this class. A separate property record sheet shall be kept for each asset of this class, or, in cases where there are a large number of items of exactly the same type (for example, a group of machine tools of the same type and year of manufacture), a single sheet may be used for the entire group. When assets in this class are sold or discarded, there will be no difficulty in determining from the property record sheets the gross value, accrued depreciation, and residual value of each item.

CLASS II. MAJOR GROUP EQUIPMENT—This class shall include group assets such as lighting systems, water and sewerage systems, plumbing and heating installations, power wiring, shafting, steam piping, yard improvements, etc., the various parts of which cannot readily be identified as separate units. (Landscaping will not be capitalized.) When all or a part of an asset unit in this group is discarded, and adjustment in the plant accounts is required under the rule stated in section IV, paragraph 2-(b), the accounting department shall review the details with plant management, and an estimate shall be made of the cost and accrued depreciation on the portion removed. In order to facilitate the preparation of such estimates, assets in this class shall be broken down, as far as practicable, into groups or sections, either on the basis of the nature of the items involved or on the basis of physical location, and a separate property record sheet shall be set up for each group or section—for example, separate sheets may be set up for plumbing installations in each building, for the shafting and wiring in each major department, etc. Such a breakdown should not be carried beyond the point necessary to make proper adjustment for removals.

CLASS III. MINOR GROUP EQUIPMENT—This class shall include assets which cannot be readily identified except as a relatively small part of a major group. Examples of assets which fall in this class are: office desks and chairs, lockers, bins, etc.; this class should not include any significant items, such as large scales, office machines, etc., which it is possible to identify and put in Class I. For purposes of the property record, items in this class shall be grouped under major headings such as those suggested above; and a single property record sheet shall be maintained for each year's additions in each group, provided that further breakdown may be made by departments or burden centers if desired for purposes of cost or expense allocation.

No attempt shall be made to identify assets in this class which are discarded or to adjust the accounts therefor; the proceeds from any sale of such assets shall be credited to the plant account so that no profit or loss will be shown. As each year's additions in each group become fully depreciated, the entire value thereof shall be credited to the plant account and charged against the reserve, and depreciation thereon shall cease.

The possible degree of detail is almost infinite: a separate record could be kept for each hammer, pencil, or chair, if expense was of no concern. Clearly this is unthinkable, and the question is one of where to draw the line for the ultimate unit.

In some cases, it may be advisable to go within a single asset item. For instance, with expensive trucks or buses, the engine and tires may be segregated, principally because of different expected service lives. The same procedure is followed with aircraft engines. For buildings, the ultimate units may be structural components (such as roof, elevators, flooring, etc.) or materials used (such as plumbing, carpentry, glazing, etc.).

For continuous structures such as railroad tracks, water mains, and power lines, the unit could be each individual stretch by date of installation (or expected replacement or retirement) and location. A more detailed alternative would be each major element in a stretch, such as rails, ties, or ballast.

The choice of ultimate units that are too small and numerous leads to records too cumbersome to be kept up without exorbitant cost and effort. While a reasonable degree of detail is desirable, a balance between practicality and detail must be found.

EXHIBIT 7 Property Chart of Accounts

CODING KEY TO PROPERTY CARDS

CARD POSITION 1

Type of Depreciation—		*Code #*
Old or regular depreciation		1
New or double declining		2

CARD POSITION 2

Rate of Depreciation—		*Code #*
4 year life	25%	1
5 year life	20%	2
25 year life	4%	3
10 year life	10%	4
15 year life	6.7%	5
20 year life	5%	6
33.3 year life	3.3%	7
40 year life	2.5%	8
50 year life	2%	9

CARD POSITIONS 4–8

Property Tag Number
  (Positions 4 and 5 signify year of acquisition.)

CARD POSITIONS 9–10

Assets—Real Property	*Code #* (Class)	*Life* (Yr)	*Code #* (Depr.)
Land	00		
Land improvements	01	10	
Columbus plant—bldgs.	02	50	
Worthington warehouse	03	40	
Viking Engraving	04	50	
Restaurant and canteens	05	33.3	
Century Tank (chrome plating)	06	10	
California plant—bldgs.	07	20	
	08		
Rental property	09	10	4
Shop fixtures—real	10	5	2
Machinery foundations	11	15	5
Heating and ventilating	12	15	5
Electric power and light	13	15	5
Steam, water, and sewer	14	15	5
Elevators and conveyors	15	15	5
Storage tanks	16	15	5
	17	15	5
Automatic sprinklers	18	15	5
Dry rooms and dryers	19	15	5
Deep wells	20	15	5
Boiler house equipment	21	15	5
Water fountains	22	15	5
Pneumatic tubes	23	15	5
Electric transformers	24	15	5

CARD POSITIONS 9–10

Assets—Personal Property	*Code #* (Class)	*Life* (Yr)	*Code #* (Depr.)
Machinery and equipment	50	15	5
Shop fixtures—*personal*	70	5	2
Copper print rolls	72	15	5
Steel rolls—emb.	75	15	5
Paper rolls	76	15	5
Steel plates—emb.	77	15	5
Motor vehicles—trucks	88	4–6	
Motor vehicles—automobile	89	3	
Furniture and fixtures—Columbus	90	10	4
Furniture and fixtures—Worthington	91	10	4
	92		
	93		

EXHIBIT 7 (Cont.)

CARD POSITIONS 9–10

Assets—Personal Property	Code # (Class)	Life (Yr)	Code # (Depr.)
Furniture and fixtures—Atlanta	94	10	4
Furniture and fixtures—Burlingame	95	10	4
Furniture and fixtures—Detroit	96	5	2
Furniture and fixtures—Newark	97	10	4
	98		
Furniture and fixtures—New York	99	10	4

CARD POSITIONS 11–13
Cost Center (Dept. #)   101–999

CARD POSITIONS 14–15
Month of Acquisition   01–12

CARD POSITIONS 16–17
Year of Acquisition   (19)32–present

CARD POSITION 18
Tax Group

Personal property—Columbus	1
Personal property—Worthington	2
Real property—Columbus	3
Personal property—New York	4
Real property—Newark	5
Personal property—Detroit	6
Personal property—Newark	7
Personal property—Atlanta	8
Personal property—Burlingame	9

CARD POSITIONS 19–24
Amount Capitalized

CARD POSITIONS 25–60
Description of Asset

(Reproduced by courtesy of The Borden Company.)

MAINTENANCE AND REPAIRS

Kohler[20] defines *maintenance* as "the keeping of property at a standard of operating condition" and *repair* as "the restoration of a capital asset to its full productive capacity after damage, accident, or prolonged use, without increase in the previously estimated service life or capacity."

While in theory maintenance and repairs do not extend prior estimates of service life or capacity, in practice this principle can be difficult to apply unequivocally. A relatively low level of expenditure on maintenance and repairs may significantly curtail asset service life or capacity, while a relatively large expenditure may accomplish the opposite. Therefore, any estimate of expected service life or capacity assumes a given level of maintenance and repairs. For this reason, a distinction is usually made between ordinary repairs (charged to revenue as an expense) and extraordinary repairs debited to an asset account or to accumulated depreciation.

Capitalization or Expense. Repairs frequently involve replacement of parts of equipment. This factor is a consideration in designating the ultimate property unit for accounting purposes. Where replacement of an entire property unit takes

---

[20]Eric L. Kohler, *A Dictionary for Accountants,* 5th ed., Prentice-Hall, Englewood Cliffs, N.J., 1975,

place, the proper procedure is to record a retirement of the old unit and the capitalization of the new unit. For instance, if the engines of trucks are treated as separate property units distinct from the remaining parts of the trucks, the engines will be written off when replaced. If, however, the entire truck is the property unit, then replacement of engines is normally treated as a repair expense.

An advantage of setting up property units for individual components of single assets is to avoid many of the problems of whether or not to capitalize major repairs. Where individual components constitute more homogeneous groups than do the whole asset units and where the amounts involved justify the expense, it is worthwhile to establish major components as ultimate property units.

In the absence of suitable replacement property units, repairs are usually expensed. Grady[21] states that "Alterations which merely modernize, rather than improve, buildings or equipment are also expensed as incurred, unless the program is so extensive as to warrant reconsideration of the estimated life of the asset."

Accounting Treatment. In addition to the direct expensing of maintenance and repairs, several alternative accounting methods exist. These are as follows:

Budget Allowances. It is sometimes desired to spread the expense of maintenance and repairs evenly over the year (or other operating cycle) rather than have monthly (or other short-period) operating results fluctuate because of varying amounts of maintenance and repair expense. For this purpose a budgetary allowance may be set up. The usual method is to divide the year's budgeted maintenance and repair expense by 12, to charge one-twelfth to operations each month, and to credit a budget (allowance) account. Actual maintenance and repair expenses are then debited to the budget account and the balance is carried forward. Any net balance in the budget allowance account at the end of the year should be treated as an adjustment to operations expenses for the year.

Instead of allowing an equal twelfth for each month, the budget allowance is sometimes set up on the basis of sales, manufacturing volume, direct labor hours or dollars, or some other measure of activity.

Charge to "Reserve." The monthly budget allowance method is sometimes extended beyond individual fiscal periods to encompass estimates maintenance and repairs over the entire life of the asset. Equal annual charges are made to expense, and actual expenditures are charged against the allowance, formerly called a "reserve." The balance in the allowance account is not written off at the end of each year but is carried forward to the following year so long as the asset is in service. The purpose is to equalize annual charges for estimated maintenance and repairs over the life of the asset.

This procedure has been criticized on several grounds. Reliable estimates of future maintenance and repair expenditures are extremely difficult to make. The nature of the credit balance in the allowance is ambiguous. It is not a liability, nor a proprietorship account, nor an asset contra. Paton and Littleton[22] describe this procedure as "a device or policy designed to bring about an artificial smoothing of fluctuations resulting from varying business fortunes over a period of years."

Charge to Accumulated Depreciation. Extraordinary repairs, which increase the service life or capacity of an asset, are sometimes charged to the accumulated depreciation account. The justification offered for this method is that the extension of service life has caused a recovery of part of the accumulated depreciation. Where extraordinary repairs have increased the capacity or productivity of an

---

[21]Paul Grady, "Inventory of Generally Accepted Accounting Principles for Business Enterprises," Accounting Research Study No. 7, AICPA, New York, 1965, p. 156.

[22]W. A. Paton and A. C. Littleton, *An Introduction to Corporate Accounting Standards,* American Accounting Association, Sarasota, Fla., 1940.

asset but have not lengthened its service life, the justification above does not seem to apply.

This method has been criticized on the grounds that it fails to consider that accumulated depreciation may be less than the cost of asset replacement. Also, it allows the cost of parts replaced to remain in the asset account. Continuing extraordinary repairs may extend asset service life by a considerable period, yet the accounts would not reflect the actual cost of the asset if the prices of replaced parts fluctuated over time.

Control of Maintenance. In order to develop sound records and to control maintenance expenditures effectively, careful accounting procedures are required. It is useful to keep a maintenance and repair history record for each major piece of equipment. Exhibit 8 shows a specimen record.

Exhibit 8 Maintenance Record (Reproduced by permission.)

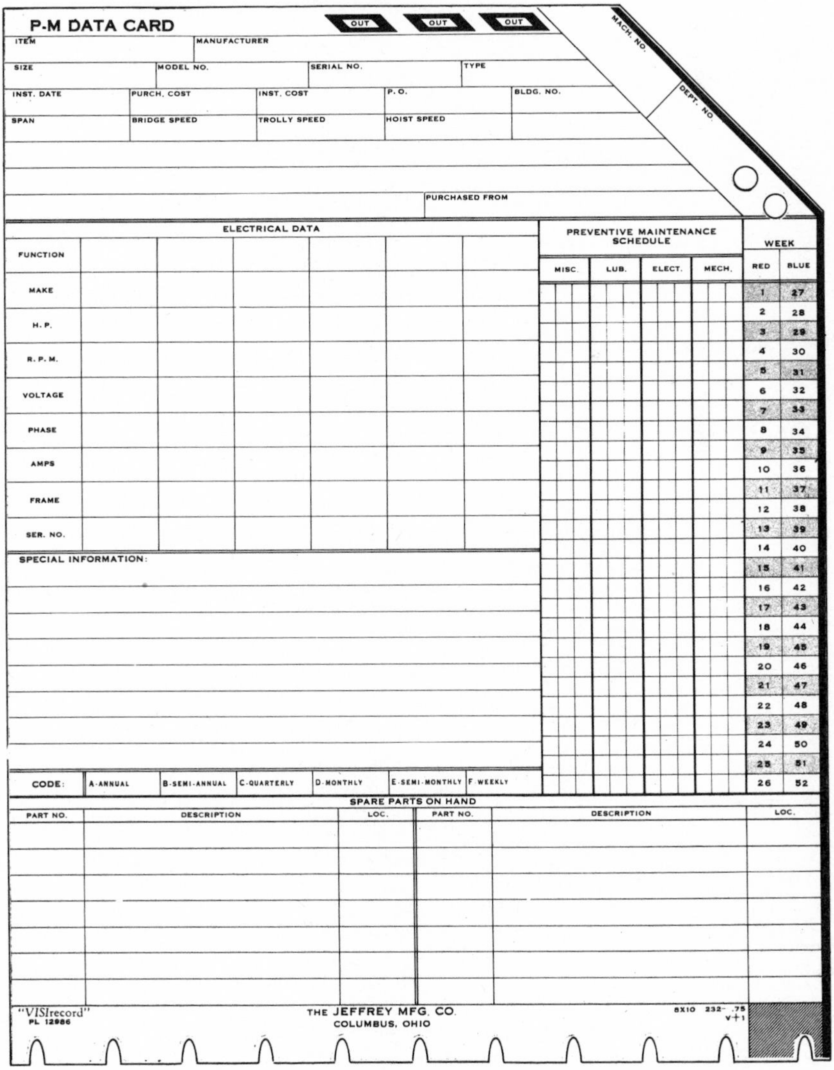

P-M DATA CARD

OUT OUT OUT

MACH. NO.

DEPT. NO.

ITEM	MANUFACTURER		
SIZE	MODEL NO.	SERIAL NO.	TYPE

INST. DATE	PURCH. COST	INST. COST	P. O.	BLDG. NO.
SPAN	BRIDGE SPEED	TROLLY SPEED	HOIST SPEED	

PURCHASED FROM

ELECTRICAL DATA						
FUNCTION						
MAKE						
H. P.						
R. P. M.						
VOLTAGE						
PHASE						
AMPS						
FRAME						
SER. NO.						

SPECIAL INFORMATION:

CODE:	A-ANNUAL	B-SEMI-ANNUAL	C-QUARTERLY	D-MONTHLY	E-SEMI-MONTHLY	F-WEEKLY

PREVENTIVE MAINTENANCE SCHEDULE				WEEK	
MISC.	LUB.	ELECT.	MECH.	RED	BLUE
				1	27
				2	28
				3	29
				4	30
				5	31
				6	32
				7	33
				8	34
				9	35
				10	36
				11	37
				12	38
				13	39
				14	40
				15	41
				16	42
				17	43
				18	44
				19	45
				20	46
				21	47
				22	48
				23	49
				24	50
				25	51
				26	52

SPARE PARTS ON HAND					
PART NO.	DESCRIPTION	LOC.	PART NO.	DESCRIPTION	LOC.

"VISIrecord"
PL 12986

THE JEFFREY MFG. CO.
COLUMBUS, OHIO

8X10 232- .75
V+1

H. BUDGET CONTROL SYSTEM
Work Flow

Responsible Person and Department	Operation
Department 43 Plant maintenance controls Supervisor & budget analyst	1. Prior to the beginning of each fiscal year, department 43 develops a proposed plant maintenance fiscal budget. The forecast dollars are furnished in three (3) major categories as follows: Labor Material and purchased services Supplies and expenses

2. After approval, the budget is distributed into five (5) major categories for each of three (3) departments, 41, 42 and 43 as follows:

	41	*42*	*43*	*Total*
Administration labor	X	X	X	X
Trades labor	X	X	X	X
Materials	X	X	X	X
Purchased services	X	X	X	X
Supplies & expenses	X	X	X	X
Total	X	X	X	X

3. The trades labor, material, and purchased services forecast is further distributed within each department by eight (8) separate work categories, and thirteen (13) separate labor, material, and purchased service accounts.

4. Fiscal labor, material, and purchased service estimates are then developed for each individual job order within each separate work category.

5. The day-to-day and routine job order estimates are routed for signature approval and distributed to maintenance supervision for daily use in charging labor, material, and purchased service, and to accounting for entry of fiscal estimates in the maintenance cost reports. Exceptions are maintenance job orders (M.J.O.'s) which are written on an "as required" basis throughout the year and require individual approval.

6. Each month department 43 submits a monthly budget to department 68 for each of the three maintenance departments (41, 42, 43). This monthly budget is based on the fiscal forecast; but during the year the monthly budgets may be adjusted, depending on the total business trend. However, any change from the fiscal forecast is initiated by department 68.

7. Each month the total actuals for all maintenance expenditures are reported on the overhead summary for all three maintenance departments. The actuals on the overhead summary are from the maintenance cost reports. These actuals are summarized by major category.

8. During the fiscal year, twelve (12) separate budget control charts are utilized by the maintenance manager to compare and control actual monthly costs in relation to budget forecasts.

9. Plant maintenance cost reports—at the present time, the maintenance department receives six (6) data processing reports for the purposes of (1) controlling maintenance

Responsible Person and Department	Operation

expenditures, (2) recording cost information, and (3) forecasting maintenance budgets.

These reports have enabled maintenance administration to develop a high quality in cost control of maintenance expenditures and provide a fast means of collecting cost information of maintenance operations.

(a) *Maintenance cost report no. 1*—monthly—by job order number, account, department by, benefitting department, etc.

Purpose: (1) used monthly to record final job costs on all burden MJO's(1000–3849) Navy requirement on all maintenance and repair of USN facilities.

(2) Used monthly to audit and control actual maintenance expenditures vs. estimated on recurring job orders (1–999).

(3) Used monthly by department 68 to collect data in performance rating of departments 41 and 42.

(b) *Maintenance cost report no. 2*—monthly—by account, benefitting department, department by, job order category, etc.

Purpose: (1) used monthly to develop actual maintenance expenditure information by benefitting departments or divisions as requested by management or department heads.

(2) Used annually to forecast fiscal maintenance expenditures by divisions. (Manufacturing, material, engineering, etc.)

(c) *Maintenance cost report no. 3*—monthly—by department, by account, PE code, job order category, etc.

Purpose: (1) used, as required, to develop maintenance expenditure information by PE codes. (Paved surfaces, roofs, floors, etc.)

(d) *Maintenance cost report no. 4*—monthly—by department, by account, job order category, etc.

Purpose: (1) used monthly to analyze and control maintenance expenditures by job categories.

(2) Used annually to forecast maintenance expenditures by job order categories.

(e) *Maintenance cost report no. 5*—quarterly—by account, PE code, department by, and benefitting department.

Purpose: (1) used to develop semiannual cost reports on actual and estimated maintenance expenditures for class 3 and 4 facilities.

(2) Used to develop other maintenance cost information by PE codes.

(f) *Maintenance cost report no. 6*—monthly—job orders completed during month with cost expenditures.

Purpose: (1) used by department 68 in performance rating of departments 41 and 42.

(2) Used by department 43 for a review of actual vs. estimated costs on completed job orders (1000–9999).

The systems manual of a leading manufacturing corporation covers the following sets of procedures and document flows for plant maintenance:
A. Emergency repair system
B. Minor service order system
C. Preventative maintenance job order system
D. Routine job order system
E. Maintenance job order system
F. Job order system
G. Maintenance service contract system
H. Budget control system
I. Procurement of material system.

Section H, the budget control system reproduced on pages 19-32 to 19-33, serves not only as an illustration of a particular system, but also as a model of part of a carefully written systems manual dealing with maintenance and repair accounting procedures.

ADDITIONS AND IMPROVEMENTS

According to Finney and Miller,[23] an addition is not a simple replacement, but includes new units and extensions, expansions, and enlargements of old units. Additions may comprise entirely separate assets such as a new building, or, for example, extra rooms or wings added to an existing (previously acquired) building, or the installation of two-way radios in a fleet of delivery vehicles.

Improvements or, synonymously, betterments are distinguished from additions. Finney and Miller[24] state that an addition is merely an increase in quantity, whereas an improvement is a substitution with an increase only in quality. Kohler[25] defines a betterment as:

> ... an expenditure having the effect of extending the useful life of an existing fixed asset, increasing its normal rate of output, lowering its operating cost, or otherwise adding to the worth of benefits it can yield. The cost of adapting a fixed asset to a new use is not ordinarily capitalized unless at least one of these tests is met. A betterment is distinguished from an item of *repair* or *maintenance* in that the latter has the effect of keeping the asset in its customary state of operating efficiency without the expectation of added future benefits.

Examples of improvements are substitution of a tile roof for wooden shingles, replacement of pine flooring by hardwood, or the installation of a more powerful motor in a commercial fishing boat. Minor improvements might include the substitution of locking for nonlocking gasoline tank caps on vehicles and the replacement of conventional rearview vehicle mirrors by nonglare mirrors.

In principle, when additions consist of an entirely new unit, the expenditure is of a capital nature and should be charged to an asset account. In the recording of additions which pertain to existing assets and of improvements, it is theoretically correct to charge the new property to an asset account and eliminate the cost of items replaced or removed from the asset accounts.

Minimum Capitalization Amount. In practice, strict observance of capitalization principles would require intolerable attention to detail in regard to minor items, such as the substitution of a 75-watt light bulb in place of a 50-watt bulb.

To avoid this problem, most organizations establish a minimum capitalization amount. Individual expenditures below this minimum are expensed rather than

[23]G. L. Johnson and J. A. Gentry, Jr., *Finney and Miller's Principles of Accounting: Intermediate*, 7th ed., Prentice-Hall, Englewood Cliffs, N.J., 1974, p. 392.
[24]*Ibid.*
[25]Kohler, *op. cit.*

capitalized. The accounting manual of one major Midwestern manufacturing corporation states that no item with a total cost below $250 shall be capitalized.

Leasehold Improvements. Improvements to leased property usually revert to the owner of the property upon termination of the lease, unless the lease agreement specifies otherwise. The cost of improvements made by the lessee should be capitalized in his records with the description of Leasehold Improvements. These assets should be amortized or depreciated over the remaining term of the lease or their expected service life, whichever is shorter. Renewal options in the lease agreement are usually ignored in determining its remaining term, since renewal cannot be predicted with certainty.

Alteration and Rearrangement. Alteration is a term usually applied to the modification of buildings and structures. Included are the cutting of new entry and exit openings, closing old ones, erecting new walls, windows, and partitions, and removing old ones.

Rearrangement refers normally to machinery, involving the removal, shifting, and reinstallation of units, and reconnecting of units in possibly new configurations. Expenditures on alterations and rearrangements should be carefully analyzed in order to determine the amounts that strictly represent improvements. The latter should be capitalized. Sometimes the capitalization treatment used is not a debit to the appropriate fixed asset amount, but rather a debit to an improvement account, to be amortized over the ensuing periods benefiting from the improvements.

It may be difficult to make a clear segregation of improvement expenditures between those to be capitalized and those to be charged to expense. Estimation and judgment may be needed, in which case consideration should be given to the possibility that the new book value, net of accumulated depreciation, may exceed the market cost of a new unit of similar remaining service potential. If this is so, capitalization of improvement expenditures should be limited to an amount that will not cause the new book value to exceed replacement cost.

With respect to reinstallation costs, Finney and Miller[26] state:

> Presumably the cost of one installation will already have been charged to the machinery account. Theoretically, therefore, the cost, or the undepreciated remainder of the cost, of the first installation should be removed from the accounts, and the reinstallation cost should be capitalized by charge to the machinery account.

It may be impracticable to determine original installation costs in the necessary detail, in which case they are often estimated, or ignored if minor.

In the case of building alterations, it may be decided to remove walls between new and old portions of the building or to modify load-bearing structural components. While in principle the asset accounts should be relieved of the old costs, practical considerations often prevent the breaking down of the cost of the building to determine the amount applicable to a relatively minor portion thereof.

In the case of buildings, capitalization for unduly long periods of the costs of successive alteration and remodeling should be avoided. Rented buildings may often be adapted or converted to the different requirements of successive tenants, and it is not reasonable to capitalize all these successive outlays subject to amortization over the life of the structure as a whole. Alterations for an individual tenant should be capitalized in a special account and written off over the term of that particular lease. Although the lease may be renewed or the alterations may have utility for the next tenant, such eventualities cannot be relied upon.

Rebuilding. Alterations of buildings and equipment may be so major that virtually a new building or piece of equipment is the result. The term "rebuilding"

[26]Johnson and Gentry, *op. cit.*, p. 394.

is used in this sense. For example, the rebuilding of a truck engine may involve replacement of all valves, pistons, rings, connecting rods, bearings, cylinder walls, etc., preserving few of the previous components apart from the engine block.

If the rebuilding is very extensive, the transaction may reasonably be treated as a replacement. The book value of the old unit should be closed out, after allowing for parts to be retained in the rebuilt unit. The costs of rebuilding plus the allowance for the retained parts, should be entered in the records as a new unit of property.

A justification for treating the rebuilt unit as a new asset is that its service life after rebuilding is likely to be quite different from the remaining portion of the originally estimated life.

Care should be taken to avoid unwarranted inflation of the book value of the rebuilt asset. Removal costs should not be capitalized, and neither should excessive costs of installation or erection. A rebuilt asset may not be the ideal structure or piece of equipment. Even if the rebuilding expenditure is well justified, the asset may be too large or too small in capacity, or relatively expensive in operation, or less productive than alternative equipment. The rebuilt property should not be carried in the accounts at a cost exceeding the current price of a new unit of equivalent efficiency and capacity, less an allowance reflecting the secondhand nature of the components preserved from the old unit.

Restoration and Rehabilitation.   When buildings or equipment are acquired in a condition requiring expenditures on restoration or rehabilitation, these expenditures should be capitalized. Since it is reasonable to expect that such expenditures, together with any costs of removal and demolition, were considered in arriving at the purchase price they should be charged to the cost of the asset.

On the other hand, restoration or rehabilitation expenditures incurred on assets not recently acquired fall into a different category. The costs of restoring and rehabilitating property that has been owned for a considerable time should generally not be capitalized, except where they clearly can be classified as improvements. In the latter case, capitalization, at least in part, would be required if the old book value of the dilapidated property understates the reasonable cost of the improved property, Such a situation may arise with assets acquired in a serious state of disrepair even if considerable time elapses until rehabilitation occurs.

Accounting Records.   The property ledger cards should include provision for details of additions and improvements. Procedures should be set up to ensure that these records are promptly updated whenever necessitated by addition and improvement expenditures, and that adequate descriptive information is recorded.

Control and Review.   Proposals for additions and improvements should be subject to the same control and review procedures as regular capital expenditure projects. Usually there is no reason not to follow the system of proposal, evaluation, approval, authorization, budgeting, appropriation, and postcompletion audit. Addition and improvement expenditures of relatively smaller amounts may be dealt with under blanket appropriations.

RELOCATION, REPLACEMENT, RETIREMENT, AND DISPOSAL

"Relocation," as the term implies, is simply a change in physical location. "Replacement" involves a substitution of a new asset or a new part for an old asset or an old part. Replacements classified as minor are usually expensed; for instance, new spark plugs for an engine would almost certainly be written off as an expense. Major replacements should be capitalized.

Replacements are distinguished from improvements by the type of substitution made. Substitution in kind, for example, of a new machine identical except in age and condition, is a replacement but not an improvement. Substitution of a superior new machine for an old one is a replacement not in kind, and also an improvement.

Kohler[27] gives as the principal definition of retirement: "The removal of a fixed asset from service, following its sale or the end of its productive life, accompanied by the necessary adjustment of fixed asset and depreciation-reserve accounts."

Elimination of Expired Costs. Paton and Paton[28] point out that replacement is a combination of two distinct transactions: (1) the elimination of the old unit and (2) the acquisition of the new unit.

While the acquisition transaction presents no accounting difficulty, the elimination (or retirement) transaction may not be so easily handled. Where the property record units are such that the old unit is separately identifiable and the book value and accumulated depreciation of the eliminated unit are shown, no problems arise. This is not always possible; however, in the case of discrete, individual items of property such as a building, a ship, a truck, a boiler, and so on, it can be done. But when items are not discrete in nature, as in the case of railroad tracks, power lines, water mains, or other unsegmented, continuous structures, the selection of a property record unit is necessarily arbitrary. This makes it difficult to distinguish between repairs and replacements and, in turn, between proper charges to capital and to revenue.

In order to assure uniformity in accounting under these conditions in regulated industries, regulatory agencies such as the ICC, the FPC, and state public service commissions have prescribed the use of specified retirement units. Generally it is required that replacements involving entire units be capitalized, while replacements of fractional units are to be charged to expense. The prescribed units are usually allowed to be further subdivided into smaller components, but not to be combined or modified so as to result in units larger than those prescribed.

It is sometimes suggested that it is expedient to treat some replacements as a single transaction, rather than two distinct (elimination and acquisition) transactions. This occurs when the cost of a replacement is charged to the depreciation allowance, and no elimination transaction is recognized. Paton and Paton say of this practice:[29]

> Whatever arrangement of entries is employed the practice of charging the cost of the new unit to the allowance for depreciation should be avoided. Even for replacements in kind this treatment is improper. The cost of the property acquired seldom equals that of the asset eliminated; moreover, the depreciation accrued to date on the old asset will almost certainly not equal the expenditures for replacement. The result, accordingly, is misstatement of both plant cost and depreciation allowance. The practice of crediting the amount recovered through salvage or otherwise to the depreciation allowance is also objectionable. Instead there should be a closing out of the cost of plant removed and the accrued depreciation applicable, coupled with clear-cut recognition of removal cost, amount recovered, and retirement loss or gain.

Removal and Reinstallation Costs. As stated previously, removal costs should be capitalized when property is acquired with the intention of modifying it, and, for this purpose, removal of some existing components is necessary. Except in these circumstances, costs of removal, demolition, and the like should generally not be capitalized but should be expensed when incurred. The new unit replacing the old should not have removal charges included in its cost.

[27]Kohler, *op. cit.*
[28]William A. Paton and William A. Paton, Jr., *Assets—Accounting and Administration,* Roberts and Roehl, Inc., Warren, Mich., 1971, p. 252.
[29]*Ibid.,* pp. 252–253.

Where a replacement involves removal and reinstallation of old parts, reinstallation costs should not be capitalized without elimination of the original installation costs. To do otherwise would result in the double counting of both the costs of the original and reinstallation events.

Salvage Recovery.   The proceeds from materials recovered as salvage should be applied to offset the costs chargeable against depreciation allowances. These proceeds may take the form of cash or materials that are reusable by the enterprise. In the latter event, the materials placed in stores should be valued at estimated current cost, with appropriate adjustment for their secondhand condition.

Where salvage is very large, the use of market price valuation may imply indirect recognition of unrealized appreciation.

When retired units are traded in as a part payment on new acquisitions, salvage consists of the allowance made by the vendor. Since the stated amount of the allowance often exceeds actual market value, it may be necessary to substitute an estimate of market value for the stated allowance in order to account properly for the retirement and for the cost of the new asset. See the section on "Exchange and Trade-In" above.

Idle, Reserve, and Standby Capacity.   Sometimes fixed assets are retired from active service but are not disposed of or even removed from their previous locations. If they are retained as standby or reserve capacity, Finney and Miller[30] recommend that no accounting entries be made. However, if their usefulness as operating assets is at an end, these authors suggest that the asset and accumulated depreciation accounts be relieved, that estimated salvage value be recorded in an abandoned property account, and that the estimated loss or gain be recognized.

Extraordinary Obsolescence.   Extraordinary obsolescence may result from sudden style changes, new inventions, or unforeseen cessation of demand. Most accountants would agree to immediate recording of any loss, even though it is unrealized and even though they would be cautious about recognizing unrealized appreciation. Some accountants, influenced perhaps by the practical difficulty of estimating realizable values, would defer recognition of loss until actual disposal or abandonment occurred.

Gains or Losses on Disposal.   When a unit of property is retired, the proper accounting treatment is (1) to complete the recording of depreciation up to the date of retirement, and (2) to relieve the accounts of all amounts pertaining to the retired asset. Whether the retired asset is to be replaced or not has no bearing on these procedures. Likewise the cause of retirement, whatever the reason, is not relevant in this regard. What is essential is to ensure that the retirement is properly recorded so that future accounting statements do not show misleading amounts for fixed assets and for depreciation expense. In addition, proper recording of retirements enables insurance coverage to be adjusted when necessary and also facilitates elimination of retired assets from property tax rolls. The existence of inadequate property records is a severe impediment to the proper treatment of retirements.

To illustrate the recording of a retirement, assume that a machine costing $11,000 has been depreciated at an annual rate of 10 percent for six years, based on an estimated final salvage value of $2,000. In the middle of the seventh year it is sold for $4,000. The entries to be made are

```
(1) Depreciation expense  ...........................................    450
        Accumulated depreciation of equipment  .......................         450
        To record depreciation at 10 percent for 6 months on machine #—,
        costing $11,000 with estimated salvage value of $2,000, sold June 30,
        19×9.
```

[30]Johnson and Gentry, *op. cit.*, p. 400.

```
(2) Cash  ........................................................... 4,000
    Accumulated depreciation of equipment  ........................... 5,850
    Loss on sale of equipment  ....................................... 1,150
        Equipment  ...............................................          11,000
    To record sale of machine #—.
```

If the machine had been sold for $6,000, there would have been a gain of $850 on sale rather than a loss of $1,150.

The example above was based on the procedure of computing depreciation on acquisitions from the date of acquisition until the date of disposal. Sometimes different procedures are employed, such as computing depreciation on every acquisition and disposal for half a year, regardless of the actual dates of acquisition and disposal; or no depreciation may be taken in the year of acquisition, and a full year's depreciation may be taken in the year of disposal, or vice versa. Whichever procedure is adopted, it should be followed consistently.

Gains or losses on disposal of depreciable assets should be treated as income statement items, and, if material in amount, are usually separately disclosed. This treatment is stated in Opinion No. 30 of the Accounting Principles Board of the American Institute of Certified Public Accountants. If the "operations of a segment of a business" are sold, abandoned, spun off, or otherwise disposed of, Opinion No. 30 states that the results of "continuing operations" should be reported separately from "discontinued operations." Also, any gain or loss from disposal of the segment should be reported in conjunction with the related results of discontinued operations and not as an extraordinary item.

Involuntary Conversion and Coinsurance.   Asset services may be lost through fire, casualty, condemnation, or other involuntary events. Gains and losses resulting from involuntary conversion should be treated for accounting purposes no differently than those arising from voluntary disposals.

Federal income tax rules on involuntary conversion specify in most cases that no gain need be recognized at the time of disposal if the owner of the property uses the funds received to replace the involuntarily converted asset.

Property insurance contracts may include a coinsurance clause stipulating that if insurance coverage is below the required minimum, the insured party absorbs a portion of any loss. Since recovery of loss is usually based on fair market value, rather than book value, of the assets lost, insurance settlements may result in either a loss or gain on involuntary conversion due to insured risks.

Tools, Dies, and Other Small Items.   It is not unusual for enterprises to have a significant investment in small assets such as tools, dies, drawings, patterns, jigs, templates, scientific instruments, eating utensils, and bed and table linens. Detailed accounting for these is difficult by virtue of their high mobility, generally short life, and usually low unit cost. Relocations and retirements can seldom be made subject to reliable reporting for record purposes.

Smaller items of relatively high value or relatively long service life may be charged to an appropriate asset account and depreciated at a composite rate sufficiently rapid to allow for the difficulty in maintaining control over them. It is desirable for periodic inventories to be taken so that the records can be verified or adjusted, as the case may be.

Often such items are not capitalized, and the minimum capitalization amount may be set to achieve such a result. However, where the investment in small items is considerable, such a procedure can materially understate reported assets and income.

Frequently, small items are charged to an asset account, and their periodic value and associated depreciation are determined by taking inventory at the close of the fiscal period. Since those on hand can be expected to vary in age and condition, averaging perhaps 50 percent depreciation from their cost, they may be valued at 50 percent of their average cost new.

An alternative practice is to recognize the original expenditures on such items as an asset and, in lieu of depreciation, to charge all subsequent expenditures to expense. If subsequent expenditures represent replacements only, this procedure may be adequate. However, growth and expansion of these expenditures or increases in replacement prices cause this practice to understate assets and income.

Control of the costs of small items may be facilitated by charging them to user departments, if departmental supervision is thereby motiviated to be more cost conscious in respect to these items.

Some degree of physical control may be exercised by charging personnel for items issued to them, and requiring return of those no longer usable before issuing replacements.

Containers.   Concerns that deliver goods in returnable containers such as barrels, drums, carboys, bottles, and metal cylinders, face problems of accounting for this class of equipment.

If container deposits are not billed to customers and nonreturns are considerable, the container costs may be expensed as operating supplies, with the amount being determined by periodic inventories. If carried as fixed assets in these circumstances, the periodic inventory method should be used to determine the asset balance, allowing for depreciation of containers on hand.

Where customers are billed for containers, it may be advisable to keep separate records of balances receivable from customers in cash and balances to be settled by return of containers.

Some containers, even when cash deposits are collected on them, may not be returned because of breakage, negligence, or other causes. In these cases, periodic adjusting entries are required to diminish the asset account for containers (and the deposit liability to customers). Where deposits exceed the cost of the containers, this excess should be credited to income and not to the asset account.

Transfer Reports and Control.   Proper asset control requires authorization and reporting of all relocations, replacements, retirements, and disposals. For this reason well-managed enterprises usually institute and maintain carefully designed procedures to secure adequate control. As an illustration, an excerpt from the property procedure manual of a major manufacturing concern is reproduced below.

IV. PLANT ADDITIONS, REMOVALS, AND TRANSFERS

1. *Authorization Necessary*—No plant assets shall be purchased or removed, and no charges or credits to plant accounts shall be made, unless authorized in advance by the president's office. The procedure for such authorization shall be as follows:

(a) *Authorization for Additions*—Proposals for expenditures for land, building, machinery, and equipment shall be submitted by the Works Manager or Office Manager on the prescribed "Mechanical Equipment Approval" form. When a "Mechanical Equipment Approval" has been approved by the president's office, the Cost Department shall issue a plant order to which all expenditures against the authorization shall be charged; no order covering plant expenditures shall be authoritative unless supported by an approved "Mechanical Equipment Approval." The amount appropriated on any "Mechanical Equipment Approval" shall be available for the specific purpose of that authorization only, and no part thereof may be transferred to any other authorization or used for any other purpose.

(b) *Authorization for Removals*—Proposals for sales or removals of plant assets shall be submitted on the prescribed "Capital Removal Authorization" form. The authorization request shall include information as to the cost and depreciated value of the assets to be removed, the proposed selling price or salvage value, and the gain or loss to be recorded in the accounts as a result of the removal. The approval and procedure for capital removal authorizations shall be the same as described in the preceding paragraph for capital expenditure authorizations.

(c) *Sundry Addition and Removal Authorizations*—In order to reduce the work involved in handling of authorizations for small routine additions or removals, the president's office may issue a "Sundry Authorization" for an amount not exceeding $1,000. These authorizations will not specify any particular work or item.

The Works Manager may assign to a sundry authorization routine additions or removals of items having a gross value of $1,000 or less.

When the total value of the assets added or removed on any sundry authorization approaches the total authorized, a new sundry authorization should be requested, the request being accompanied by a statement of the expenditures or removals applied against the previous sundry authorization.

The purpose of these sundry authorizations is to facilitate the handling of small routine expenditures and emergency needs; it is not intended that they shall be used for all expenditures under the $1,000 limit. Expenditures for additions or improvements (as distinguished from routine replacements) or for wholesale replacements of office equipment, etc., or unusual expenditure of any kind, particularly if over $500 in amount, should be covered by separate authorizations.

An additional reason in favor of a strict system of procedures is that it may be tempting for employees to misappropriate the salvage proceeds from asset disposals. Adequate authorization and reporting requirements for relocations and retirements form part of an efficient internal control system that includes the safeguarding of salvage proceeds.

FINANCIAL STATEMENTS

Balance Sheet Disclosure.   The annual surveys of corporate financial reports made by the American Institute of Certified Public Accountants (*Accounting Trends and Techniques*) show several recent developments regarding the disclosure of property, plant, and equipment.

About 98 percent of the reports stated the basis of valuation of property, plant, and equipment. Of the reports stating a valuation basis, about 97 percent employed cost as the basis. Of the reports stating a valuation basis other than strictly cost, most used bases described as "approximate cost," "substantially at cost," or "principally at cost."

There is a definite trend to replace the word "reserve" in connection with accumulated depreciation. Less than 5 percent of reports presently use the term reserve. The term "accumulated" has gained wider acceptance than any other word, being used by about three-fourths of the reports surveyed.

Description of Buildings and Equipment.   Opinion No. 12 of the Accounting Principles Board of the American Institute of Certified Public Accountants contains this statement:

> . . . the following disclosures should be made in the financial statements or in notes thereto:
> a) Depreciation expense for the period,
> b) Balances of major classes of depreciable assets, by nature or function, at the balance-sheet date,
> c) Accumulated depreciation, either by major classes of depreciable assets or in total, at the balance-sheet date, and
> d) A general description of the method or methods used in computing depreciation with respect to major classes of depreciable assets.

Small Tools, Containers, Dies, etc.   According to a recent issue of *Accounting Trends and Techniques,* items of this nature were separately disclosed in 15 percent of the reports surveyed. Such assets were most commonly shown in the fixed asset section of the balance sheet. However, in some cases they were shown separately or in the current asset section under inventories. Methods of valuation stated were generally inventory value or amortized value.

Liens, Pledges, and Other Encumbrances.   The nature and extent of hypothecated or pledged fixed assets should be shown. The borrowing should be shown as a liability and the amount of any category of fixed assets serving as security should be stated. Retention of protective title by creditors or third parties should also be disclosed. In many cases the description of the liability, for instance "first mortgage bonds," is sufficient disclosure that there is a mortgage lien on all fixed assets and no additional notations of this fact are deemed necessary in the fixed asset section of the balance sheet. However, when the prior claims are unusual or more complex than normal, further disclosure, usually by footnote, is desirable. This may be the case if prior claims restrict the freedom of operation by management, for instance with respect to the declaration of dividends or the financing of asset expansion or replacement.

Revaluation. Assets may be revalued for numerous reasons. The question arises as to whether, and in which circumstances, the cost basis may be departed from in the financial statements. Revaluation has long been a permissible procedure in exceptional circumstances, but it is not a standard procedure in general use. A major issue exists as to whether it should become a standard procedure. For a complete treatment of the controversy, see Chapter 32, "Adjustments for Changing Prices."

When buildings or equipment are stated at appraised amounts instead of cost, the balance sheet should clearly indicate this fact. It is desirable also to indicate the date and basis of the appraisal. Furthermore, it should be disclosed whether the appraisal was made by independent appraisers or by company officers or employees, since the same degree of impartial objectivity may not be attributable to these respective parties.

Fair Value. This term has a special meaning in public utility regulation. It refers to the valuation of the rate base (principally utility plant) on which the investors are entitled to earn a reasonable return. Court decisions have held that the determination of fair value should encompass all relevant factors including the prudent historical costs and costs of reproduction. In practice, fair value has usually turned out to be a weighted average of historical cost and reproduction cost of the rate base. It is therefore not a specific basis of fixed asset valuation that can be applied to financial statements in general. Rather it is a composite of two different valuation bases determined by regulatory agencies for the special purpose of setting permissible rates of return.

Quasi-reorganization. A quasi-reorganization takes place when a corporation, usually in difficult financial circumstances, voluntarily readjusts its paid-in capital without legal action by its creditors and without coming under the supervision of the courts. Normally there is a write-down of overstated asset values which not only exhausts any balance in the Retained Earnings account but also requires a reduction of additional paid-in capital. Thus Retained Earnings is set at zero to provide a fresh starting point from which to record future accumulated earnings on the new basis of accountability.

Despite the effect of obscuring historically significant information through the write-down of asset values and the elimination of a deficit, the procedure is generally accepted because it results in more relevant asset valuation. In addition, a quasi-reorganization allows a corporation to make a fresh start as a profitable concern, freed from the stigma of a large deficit, recurring operating losses, and incapability of declaring cash dividends.

Accounting Research Bulletin No. 43 of the American Institute of Certified Public Accountants includes the following statement referring to quasi-reorganization:

> A write-down of assets below amounts which are likely to be realized thereafter, though it may result in conservatism in the balance sheet at the readjustment date, may also result in overstatement of earnings or of earned surplus when the assets are subsequently realized. Therefore, in general, assets should be carried forward as of the date of readjustment at fair and not unduly conservative amounts, determined with due regard for the accounting to be employed by the company thereafter.

Measurement of Division and "Line of Business" Investment.   There is a noticeable trend toward disclosure of more detail in corporate annual reports. This is particularly the case with diversified or conglomerate corporations, where a clearly voiced demand for information broken down by different product groups or activities is being responded to by greater disclosure.

With respect to the amounts of capital invested in different product groups or activities by a conglomerate company, several accounting problems arise. These include the difficulties of defining meaningful groupings of activities or products for reporting purposes, and methods of allocating (or not allocating) common assets to individual segments. Discussion of such problems is offered in Chapter 44, "Divisional Reports."

BIBLIOGRAPHY

Bierman, Harold, Jr., and Seymour Smidt: *The Capital Budgeting Decision,* 3rd ed., The Macmillan Company, New York, 1971.

Davidson, Sidney, James S. Schindler, Clyde P. Stickney, and Roman L. Weil: *Accounting: The Language of Business,* 2nd ed., Thomas Horton and Daughters, Glen Ridge, N.J,, 1975.

————: *Financial Accounting: An Introduction to Concepts, Methods and Uses,* The Dryden Press, Hinsdale, Ill., 1976.

Davidson, Sidney, James S. Schindler, and Roman L. Weil: *Fundamentals of Accounting,* 5th ed., The Dryden Press, Hinsdale, Ill., 1975.

Dyckman, Thomas R.: *Long-Lived Assets,* Wadsworth Publishing Company, Belmont, Calif., 1967.

Hendriksen, Eldon S.: *Accounting Theory,* rev. ed., Richard D. Irwin, Homewood, Ill., 1970, chap. 12.

Johnson, G. L., and J. A. Gentry, Jr.: *Finney and Miller's Principles of Accounting: Intermediate,* 7th ed., Prentice-Hall, Englewood Cliffs, N.J., 1974.

Kieso, Donald E., and Jerry J. Weygandt: *Intermediate Accounting,* John Wiley & Sons, New York, 1974, chap. 11.

Kohler, Eric L.: *A Dictionary for Accountants,* 5th ed., Prentice-Hall, Englewood Cliffs, N.J., 1975.

National Association of Accountants: Research Monograph No. 1, Financial Analysis Techniques for Equipment Replacement Decisions, NAA, New York, 1965.

————: Statement No. 4 on Management Accounting Practices, "Fixed Asset Accounting: The Capitalization of Costs," NAA, New York, 1972.

Paton, W. A., and A. C. Littleton: *An Introduction to Corporate Accounting Standards,* American Accounting Association, Sarasota, Fla., 1940.

Paton, William A., and William A. Paton, Jr.: *Assets—Accounting and Administration,* Roberts and Roehl, Warren, Mich., 1971.

Quirin, G. David: *The Capital Expenditure Decision,* Richard D. Irwin, Homewood, Ill., 1967.

Suelflow, James E.: *Public Utility Accounting,* Institute of Public Utilities, Michigan State University, East Lansing, Mich., 1973, chap. 8.

Woods, L. Milton: *Accounting for Capital, Construction, and Maintenance Expenditures,* Prentice-Hall, Englewood Cliffs, N.J., 1967.

Chapter **20**

Depreciation

CARL L. NELSON
George O. May Professor of Financial Accounting,
Columbia University

SIGNIFICANCE OF DEPRECIATION ACCOUNTING

On no subject in accounting has there been so much written and so much confusion as on the subject of depreciation. Depreciation is of interest to and has been discussed by economists, engineers, and lawyers, as well as by accountants. To an economist, depreciation is the decrease in market value; to an engineer, depreciation is either the decrease in physical efficiency or the physical deterioration of a building, machinery, or equipment. The legal profession is concerned with depreciation in connection with the rate-setting process for companies operating in regulated industries and in a multitude of other valuation problems.

Definition of Depreciation. Faced with this problem, the Committee on Terminology of the American Institute of Certified Public Accountants[1] concluded that a definition of depreciation as it is used in accounting was necessary. "Depreciation accounting is a system of accounting which aims to distribute the cost or other basic value of tangible capital assets, less salvage (if any), over the estimated useful life of the unit (which may be a group of assets) in a systematic and rational manner. It is a process of allocation, not of valuation."

As an illustration, a tangible capital asset with a cost of $1,000 will be used. The purchase and use of this asset over its useful life to the firm will involve a cost. The total cost will not be known until the disposition of the asset because not until then will the salvage value be known. If at the time of purchase it is estimated to be $50, it is then estimated that the total depreciation cost will be $950. If the useful life is estimated to be nine years, the process of depreciation accounting will allocate a portion of the $950 to each of the nine years. In this illustration, cost is used as a measure of the total depreciation. The use of "alternative basic values" will be discussed later.

Alternatives to Depreciation Accounting. Alternative ways of accounting for the cost are of course possible. One possibility is to treat the $1,000 as a cost of operation of the year in which the asset is purchased. This would be rejected by the accountant on the grounds that years other than the first will receive benefits from the use of the asset and that the accounting process of attempting to match costs with the revenues that result from the costs would not be followed if this method of accounting were used. However, this method is frequently used for expenditures of small amount and is sometimes used for some of the related costs of acquiring a tangible capital asset such as freight-in and installation costs.

Another possible method is to allocate the cost less the salvage value to the year in which the asset is retired. Such "retirement accounting" had widespread use among regulated utilities until 1936. It is now used by some firms in their accounting for hand tools.

A third possibility is replacement accounting. In this case, none of the cost of this asset is allocated to any of the years it is in use. If the asset is replaced with an asset of equal quality, the cost of this new asset is allocated to the year of replacement; if

[1]American Institute of Certified Public Accountants, "Review and Résumé," *Accounting Terminology Bulletin No. 1,* New York, 1953, par. 56.

it is replaced with an asset of higher quality, a portion of the cost of this new asset is allocated to the year of replacement (the cost of acquiring an asset of identical quality) and the remainder is added to the asset. This method of accounting has been widely used in the American railroad industry.

Another possible approach to the problem of accounting for the costs of limited-life physical assets is to take an annual inventory and to assign some "value" to each of the items still on hand. This value could be arrived at by a number of ways based on the physical condition of each asset, its market value, its life, etc. The asset could then be reduced to this amount and the amount of the reduction charged to the costs of the period. This treatment is used by some firms in accounting for tools as a group.

Effect of Depreciation Accounting.   It is impossible to state the effect of depreciation accounting unless it is compared with some other method of accounting for long-lived physical assets. For this purpose it will be compared with retirement accounting.

The result of depreciation accounting is to decrease the book value of the asset to which depreciation accounting applies (building, equipment, etc.). This may be done directly or by setting up an account Accumulated Depreciation (or Allowance for Depreciation or some other title) which is subtracted from the basic asset account on the balance sheet. Offsetting this may be an increase in work-in-process inventory (if the asset is used in the process of producing goods) or in another long-lived physical asset (if the asset is being used in the process of producing such an asset) or in an expense (if the use of the asset benefits current operations). If the asset is used in the process of producing other assets, the change will be reflected in the cost of the asset being produced. In any event, when this other asset is sold or used in the process of producing revenue, an expense will result. The result of the expense is a decrease in net income and in the retained earnings portion of the stockholders' equity. There are no other accounting effects of accounting for depreciation.

It is possible, of course, that management's policies may be different as a result of accounting for depreciation than they would be if there were no such accounting. To the extent that firms determine prices on the basis of accounting costs, the recording of depreciation would tend to result in higher prices. In order for this to be possible, of course, market conditions must permit the higher prices. This process takes place most readily if the firm is a regulated utility and least readily if the firm is operating in a highly competitive market.

If prices are not set in this manner, the lower reported profits resulting from the recording of depreciation may decrease management's willingness to pay higher wages and may lower labor union pressure for wage increases and fringe benefits. Again, the extent to which these possibilities will eventuate will depend on the kind of labor market in which the firm is operating.

Another possibility is that dividends may be decreased. However, there is no clear evidence that dividends are a function of the reported income (as opposed to changes in reported income). In certain cases, depreciation accounting may decrease the amount of dividends which the corporation can legally pay.

Considering all of these possibilities, there is no reason why the depreciation accounting process will necessarily involve a greater flow of funds into the firm or decrease the outflow. Thus, charging depreciation does not provide funds to replace the asset nor does it maintain capital.

Financial literature is replete with statements that depreciation is a source of funds. This, of course, is not true because the source of funds from operating the business is the customer. Producing and selling a product results in an inflow of funds (defined as either cash or working capital) from customers and an outflow of funds to firms and individuals providing materials, merchandise, and other assets or services. There is nothing about depreciation which would affect any of these unless recording depreciation affects the actions of management.

The amount of funds provided by operations can be ascertained by adding the net income to the depreciation for the year (and also adding other nonfund charges to income and subtracting nonfund credits to income). The total of funds provided by operations is not increased as a result of recording depreciation; net income is decreased but depreciation is added and the total funds remain the same as if no depreciation were recorded.

The amount of funds provided by operations is affected by the amount of depreciation deducted on the income tax return in the process of determining taxable income. However, depreciation is deductible on the income tax return regardless of whether and how it is recorded in the books and reported on the financial statements, and there is no reason why the two amounts need to be the same. Thus, accounting depreciation is not a source of funds but income tax depreciation is, however, only in an amount equal to the annual depreciation deduction multiplied by the income tax rate.

If a firm operates at a profit or breaks even, if all the profits are paid in dividends, if no additional noncurrent assets are purchased, and if no noncurrent liabilities are paid, the working capital will increase by the amount of depreciation. The firm will therefore have liquid assets to be used in replacing the asset or for any other use. Depreciation is sometimes said to provide for replacement, but only under these rare conditions will funds be available.

At times, doubt has been cast on the legitimacy of depreciation as an expense. Depreciation has been added to net income and the total has been characterized as a return to the owners. The same amount has been used by security analysts as a substitute for income in evaluating securities. In fact, however, depreciation is no different from any other expense in that it is a cost of operation. Cash (or another asset) has been paid; the asset has a limited life and cannot be used forever. It differs only in that the cash was paid in some previous year rather than in this year and that expense for this year is more of an estimate than other expenses. The existence of alternative depreciation methods also casts some doubt on the reality and meaningfulness of the depreciation allocation.

The reporting of accumulated depreciation on the balance sheet causes some confusion. In past decades, this account was frequently shown among the liabilities and the stockholders' equity under the title Reserve for Depreciation, thus causing some less sophisticated readers to conclude that this was a fund of cash. Subtracting it from the cost of the assets to which it is related and not using the title *Reserve* have presumably eliminated this cause of confusion.

However, deducting accumulated depreciation from the gross asset amount may possibly lead to another misconception, namely, that the net amount of the asset is the market value of the asset. There is nothing in the process of recording depreciation that would produce this result, but the accountant's use of the term "value" may mislead the reader of the balance sheet and also possibly the accountant. The market value of the asset may be above or below the net amount of the asset shown on the balance sheet. The inventory rule of cost or market, whichever is lower, is not generally applied to plant assets. In fact, unanticipated partial obsolescence of plant assets usually goes unrecognized in the accounts. Similarly, substantial increases in the market value of buildings and equipment are not recorded. Accounting Principles Board Opinion No. 6 states: "The Board is of the opinion that property, plant and equipment should not be written up by an entity to reflect appraisal, market or current values which are above cost to the entity." (See, however the qualified assent to paragraph 17 that presages current SEC reporting developments.) Thus, accounting practice follows the precepts of the Terminology Committee presented earlier; the depreciation accounting process deals with an allocation of cost and ignores market values.

USEFUL LIFE OF AN ASSET

The useful life of an asset may come to an end as a result of either physical or economic causes. The use of assets by a firm results in gradual physical deterioration, only some of which can be offset by maintenance; action of the elements and the mere passage of time will have somewhat the same effect. In addition, accidents, earthquakes, and similar disasters may damage the asset beyond economic repair.

Technological development may make it economic to replace the asset even though it is in excellent physical condition. An increase in demand may make more profitable its replacement with a larger unit. A decrease in demand may make its utilization unprofitable. Its use may be barred as a result of legislative or governmental administrative action. Regardless of the cause, all assets are on their way to the rubbish heap.

Accuracy of Estimates. If the life of an asset is limited as a result of physical causes, a forecast of its life should be more accurate than if the life is limited as a result of economic causes. The experience of the firm or of similar firms with assets of the same or similar type should be a relatively reliable indicator of life if the physical condition of the asset results in its retirement. The economic events that will occur in the future are much more difficult to predict. It is not always true that history repeats itself; in the early part of the twentieth century, the steam locomotive was replaced because of physical deterioration; in the decades of the thirties and forties it was replaced by a diesel locomotive as a result of obsolescence.

If the end of an asset's life is the result of physical causes, an estimate of life requires consideration of the maintenance policy. The larger the expenditure on maintenance, the longer should be the lives of the assets in use.

If the firm owns a large number of units of a particular type of fixed asset, an estimation of life by the fitting of statistical curves might be the approach used. These curves are similar to those used by life insurance companies for human mortality. They are based on the fact that even if expected life is 20 years (to take a particular example) some of the units will be retired some years prior to that. By using data for retirements in the early years and fitting a curve to these, an extrapolation process will yield information as to retirement in later years and the average life. This technique has been used primarily in the railroad and public utilities fields.

Class Life ADR System. Many firms use lives designated by the Internal Revenue Service in determining the estimated lives of their own assets in depreciation calculations. Revenue Procedure 72-10, published in 1972 with later modifications, provides lower limits, guideline periods, and upper limits for broad classifications of assets so that one life could be used by a firm if it was operating in only one industry. Guidelines for building, office furniture, and transportation equipment were also published. Exhibit 1 summarizes these asset depreciation ranges (ADR) in years.

SALVAGE VALUE

The salvage value of an asset is the estimated amount that will be received at the time the asset is disposed of, less the cost of removing it or disposing of it. (For income tax purposes, it is the estimated amount that will be received.) It may be, therefore, either positive or negative. The asset may be scrapped or it may be sold or traded in. A common synonym for salvage value is *scrap value,* which may be misleading because the asset may not be scrapped.

Undoubtedly the most commonly used estimate of salvage value is zero. The only general exception is for transportation and dirt-moving equipment. Except for these cases, salvage is usually small. Although the use of a zero salvage value

EXHIBIT 1

	Number of years		
	Lower limit	Guideline period	Upper limit
Transportation equipment			
Aircraft (except aircraft of air transport companies)	5	6	7
Automobiles, taxis	2.5	3	3.5
Buses	7	9	11
General-purpose trucks:			
Light-unloaded weight less than 13,000 pounds	3	4	5
Heavy-unloaded weight 13,000 pounds or more	5	6	7
Railroad cars and locomotives (except if owned by railroad companies)	12	15	18
Tractor units used over-the-road	3	4	5
Trailers and trailer-mounted containers	5	6	7
Vessels, barges, tugs, and similar water transportation equipment .	14.5	18	21.5
Land improvements		20	
Agriculture			
Machinery and equipment	8	10	12
Animals:			
Cattle, breeding or dairy	5.5	7	8.5
Horses, breeding or work	8	10	12
Hogs, breeding	2.5	3	3.5
Sheep and goats, breeding	4	5	6
Farm buildings	20	25	30
Mining	8	10	12
Petroleum and natural gas production			
Drilling of oil and gas wells	5	6	7
Exploration for deposits	11	14	17
Petroleum refining	13	16	19
Marketing of petroleum and products	13	16	19
Contract construction			
Other than marine	4	5	6
Marine	9.5	12	14.5
Manufacture of foods and beverages			
Grain and grain mill products	13.5	17	20.5
Sugar and sugar products	14.5	18	21.5
Vegetable oils and products	14.5	18	21.5
All other food and kindred products	9.5	12	14.5
All food manufacturers—special handling devices	3	4	5
Manufacture of tobacco and tobacco products	12	15	18
Manufacture of textile mill products			
Knitwear and knit products	7	9	11
Other than knitwear	11	14	17
Finishing and dyeing	9.5	12	14.5
Manufacture of apparel	7	9	11
Manufacture of lumber and wood products			
Cutting of timber	5	6	7
Sawing of dimensional stock from logs—permanent sawmills	8	10	12
Sawing of dimensional stock from logs—temporary sawmills	5	6	7
Manufacture of lumber, wood products, and furniture	8	10	12
Manufacture of pulp	13	16	19
Manufacture of paper and paperboard	9.5	12	14.5
Printing and publishing	9	11	13
Manufacture of chemicals	9	11	13
Manufacture of rubber products	11	14	17
Manufacture of rubber products—special tools	3	4	5
Manufacture of plastic products	9	11	13
Manufacture of plastic products—special tools	3	3.5	4
Manufacture of leather	9	11	13
Manufacture of glass products	11	14	17
Manufacture of glass products—special tools	2	2.5	3
Manufacture of cement	16	20	24
Manufacture of other stone and clay products	12	15	18
Manufacture of ferrous metals	14.5	18	21.5

EXHIBIT 1

	Number of years		
	Lower limit	Guideline period	Upper limit
Manufacture of ferrous metals—special tools	5	6.5	8
Manufacture of nonferrous metals	11	14	17
Manufacture of nonferrous metals—special tools	5	6.5	8
Manufacture of fabricated metal products	9.5	12	14.5
Manufacture of fabricated metal products—special tools	2.5	3	3.5
Manufacture of metal-working machinery	9.5	12	14.5
Manufacture of metal-working machinery—special tools	5	6	7
Manufacture of other machines	9.5	12	14.5
Manufacture of other machines—special tools	5	6.5	8
Manufacture of electric equipment	9.5	12	14.5
Manufacture of electric equipment—special tools	4	5	6
Manufacture of electronic products	6.5	8	9.5
Manufacture of motor vehicles	9.5	12	14.5
Manufacture of motor vehicles—special tools	2.5	3	3.5
Manufacture of aerospace products	6.5	8	9.5
Ship and boat building—machinery	9.5	12	14.5
Ship and boat building—dry docks and land improvements	13	16	19
Ship and boat building—special tools	5	6.5	8
Manufacture of locomotives	9	11.5	14
Manufacture of railroad cars	9.5	12	14.5
Manufacture of professional equipment, photographic, optical, watches	9.5	12	14.5
Manufacture of other products	9.5	12	14.5
Railroad machinery and equipment	11	14	17
Railroad structures	24	30	36
Railroad wharves and docks	16	20	24
Motor transport—assets other than buses and trucks	6.5	8	9.5
Water transportation—assets other than vessels, barges, and tugs	16	20	24
Air Transport	6.5	8	9.5
Pipeline transportation	17.5	22	26.5
Telephone—central office buildings	36	45	54
Telephone—central office equipment	16	20	24
Telephone—station equipment	8	10	12
Telephone—distribution plant	28	35	42
Radio and television broadcasting	5	6	7
Telegraph and cable—electric power system	15	19	23
Telegraph and cable—radio and microwave systems	10.5	13	15.5
Telegraph and cable—long-line systems	21	26.5	32
Telegraph and cable—central office control equipment	13	16.5	20
Telegraph and cable—computerized control equipment	8.5	10.5	12.5
Telegraph and cable—satellite ground property	8	10	12
Telegraph and cable—satellite space property	6.5	8	9.5
Telegraph and cable—equipment on customers' premises	8	10	12
Telegraph and cable—support and service equipment	11	13.5	16
Cable television—head-end assets	9	11	13
Cable television—subscriber connection systems	8	10	12
Cable television—program origination assets	7	9	11
Cable television—service and test assets	7	8.5	10
Cable television—microwave systems	7.5	9.5	11.5
Electric utilities—hydraulic production	40	50	60
Electric utilities—nuclear production plants	16	20	24
Electric utilities—nuclear fuel assemblies	4	5	6
Electric utilities—steam production	22.5	28	33.5
Electric utilities—transmission and distribution facilities	24	30	36
Electric utilities—combustion turbine production	16	20	24
Gas utilities—distribution facilities	28	35	42
Manufactured gas production plant	24	30	36
Natural gas production plant	11	14	17
Gas trunk pipelines	17.5	22	26.5
Water utilities	40	50	60
Central steam production and distribution	22.5	28	33.5

EXHIBIT 1 (continued)

	Number of years		
	Lower limit	Guideline period	Upper limit
Industrial steam and electric generation and distribution	22.5	28	33.5
Wholesale and retail trade	8	10	12
Wholesale and retail trade—glassware, silverware, linens	2	2.5	3
Buildings—factories		45	
Buildings—garages		45	
Buildings—machine shops		45	
Loft buildings		50	
Buildings—wholesale or retail trade		60	
Apartment buildings		40	
Dwellings		45	
Office buildings		45	
Storage warehouses		60	
Grain elevators		60	
Bank buildings		50	
Hotel buildings		40	
Theater buildings		40	
Office furniture and fixtures	8	10	12
Information systems	5	6	7
Typewriters, calculators, duplicating equipment	5	6	7
Assets used in provision of personal and professional services	8	10	12
Hotel glassware, silver, linens	2	2.5	3
Recreation industry assets	8	10	12
Theme and amusement parks	10	12.5	15

often tends to overstate the total depreciation over the life of the property, the annual overstatement in depreciation cost is not likely to be material.

The tendency toward use of zero for salvage value is accentuated by Section 167(f) of the Internal Revenue Code, which provides, in effect, that salvage value up to 10 percent of cost may be ignored in depreciation calculations for tax purposes. However, an asset may not be depreciated below reasonable salvage for tax purposes and should not be in financial reporting.

DEPRECIATION METHODS

The last problem to be faced in determining the amount of annual depreciation is a selection of the depreciation method. *Accounting Research Bulletin No. 43,* Chapter 9, states that depreciation accounting involves an allocation which is "systematic and rational."

A method which would not be considered systematic is the annual appraisal method. This would involve management or engineering opinion or some other expert opinion as to the physical and economic efficiency of the asset. From this would be determined the appropriate amount at which the asset should be reported, with the diminution in this amount considered to be the depreciation cost for the period. A systematic allocation would involve the use of a formula and not of judgment.

The most commonly used depreciation methods may be grouped into two main categories: (1) depreciation as a function of use, and (2) depreciation as a function of time.

Depreciation Based on Use.   If depreciation is made a function of use, it is necessary to estimate the life of the asset in terms of the number of hours it is used or its output in units. In many cases, the output is not homogeneous, so no measure of output is possible. For transportation equipment, however, such an estimate can be made, namely, in terms of miles. Where no homogeneous measure of output is available, a measure of use (working hours) is necessary.

The procedure would be as follows:

$$D_t = \frac{(C - S)H_t}{\Sigma H}$$

where D_t = depreciation in period t
C = cost of the asset
S = estimated salvage value of the asset
H_t = number of hours the asset was used in period t
ΣH = estimated total number of hours the asset will be used over its life

The primary justification for the use of this method is that it distributes the cost of the asset in proportion to the benefits it produces. The depreciable asset is purchased for its use; the value of the asset to the firm is based on the firm's ability to use it.

The argument against using this method is that it is more difficult to estimate the life of an asset in terms of use than in terms of years. This is a factual matter, but if reliance is to be placed on published data, there is far more information on life in terms of years. Furthermore, if the life of the asset is ended because of obsolescence rather than because of physical deterioration, the first step must be to estimate life in years before it becomes obsolete, followed by an estimate of the number of hours of use during this period of time. In addition, as will be pointed out later, this method is based on the implicit assumption of a zero interest rate.

Depreciation Based on Time. If depreciation is a function of time, the time value of money (interest methods) may be taken into account, or the time value of money may be ignored. If the time value of money is ignored (as it typically is), the methods can be subdivided into (1) the straight-line method, and (2) accelerated methods, chiefly sum-of-the-years'-digits and declining balance. If the time value of money is recognized, one of the compound interest methods may be appropriate.

STRAIGHT-LINE METHOD

For those methods that allocate depreciation on the basis of time, the straight-line method has been the most widely used. The formula for the annual depreciation under this method is

$$\text{Annual depreciation} = \frac{\text{cost} - \text{estimated salvage value}}{\text{estimated life in years}}$$

The name of this method is derived from the fact that if end-of-the-year asset amounts are plotted, the result will be a straight line with a slope equal to the annual depreciation rate.

To illustrate, if an asset had a cost of $10,000, an estimated salvage value of $2,000, and an estimated life of 10 years, the depreciation per year would be $800. The depreciation rate (depreciation as a percentage of cost) would then be 8 percent. If a zero salvage value is used, the depreciation rate is the reciprocal of the life, 10 percent here.

Advantages of Straight-Line Depreciation. The most frequently cited advantage of this method is its ease of computation and the fact that it is easily understood. These are naïve arguments because certainly the cost of accounting would be less if the asset were charged off at the time of acquisition. Depreciation accounting is relatively costly and can be justified only if more useful results are obtained. If an accounting method results in a relatively high cost, the question must be raised as to whether the added benefits obtained are worth the added cost. Unfortunately, the benefits are not easily measurable. The supposed greater ease of understanding is also subject to question. An individual who understands accounting and, more specifically, depreciation, will have no difficulty understanding the more complex methods. The "ease of understanding" is a delusion; understanding a depreciation method is much more than understanding the arithmetic.

Use of this method ignores the time value of money. If it is proper to do so, the straight-line method is defensible if the use obtained from the asset is roughly equal in each year over its useful life. If use is measured in terms of hours and if there is no variation in use, the results of the straight-line method would be identical to those from the use of the working-hours method.

It has been argued that measuring use in this way is inappropriate. The economic use of the asset involves the use of other assets and services. In the earlier years of the life of the asset, if labor costs are lower and if the quality of the product is higher as a result of a better functioning asset, more economic benefit is being received from the asset's use in the early years. On this basis, therefore, the depreciation cost of the early years should be higher than in the later years.

Repair Costs. Compounding this effect may be the fact that shutdown and repair costs may be higher in the later years of the asset's life. A partial rectification of this is possible by estimating the total amount of repair cost over the life of the asset. Depreciation and repairs are then accounted for as a unit. The annual cost would then be

$$\frac{\text{Cost} - \text{estimated salvage value} + \text{estimated repairs}}{\text{Estimated life in years}}$$

If the cost is $10,000, the estimated salvage value $1,000, the estimated repairs $2,000, and the estimated life five years, the annual cost would be $2,200. This amount would be charged to depreciation and credited to accumulated depreciation each year. As expenditures for repairs are made, charges are made to accumulated depreciation. On the assumption that the estimates are correct and that repair expenditures are as shown, the following schedule will be the annual operating cost and the net amount of the asset:

Year	Depreciation and repairs	Repair expenditure	Net asset at year end
1	$2,200	$ 100	$7,900
2	2,200	200	5,900
3	2,200	300	4,000
4	2,200	1,000	2,800
5	2,200	400	1,000

There still remains the possibility that factors other than repairs may result in a lower economic use being received in the later years of the life of the asset.

The straight-line method is sometimes modified to take into consideration above-normal use of the asset. During World War II and in later emergencies, plants that normally operate one labor shift per day were operated for two or three shifts. The result was more wear and tear than had been originally anticipated and poorer maintenance because of shortage of time for maintenance. The amount of depreciation was therefore adjusted upward by an arbitrary amount.

ACCELERATED METHODS

Sum-of-the-Years'-Digits Method.   Since the revision of the Internal Revenue Code in 1954, two accelerated methods of depreciation have been used widely. One is the sum-of-the-years'-digits, the formula for which is

$$D_t = \frac{n+1-t}{\sum\limits_1^n j}(C - S)$$

where D_t = depreciation in period t
  C = cost of the asset
  S = estimated salvage value of the asset
  n = estimated life of the asset in years
  t = the year of life of the asset (i.e., 1 in the first year, n in the last year)
  $\sum_{1j}^{nj}$ = the sum of the digits from 1 to $n = n(1 + n)/2$

Stated in words, the digits $1, 2, 3, \ldots, n$, with n being the life in years, are added. In the first year, the annual depreciation is determined by multiplying the fraction n over the sum of these digits by the total depreciation over the life of the asset. For an asset with a cost of $1,600, an estimated salvage value of $100, and an estimated life of five years, annual depreciation would be

Year	Fraction of total depreciation	Depreciation amount
1	5/15	$ 500
2	4/15	400
3	3/15	300
4	2/15	200
5	1/15	100
Total	15/15	$1,500

The sum-of-the-years'-digits method can be used for income tax purposes for all new assets with a useful life of at least three years with the exception of nonresidential buildings.

Declining-Balance Method.   Another accelerated method is the declining-balance method. In this method, a fixed rate is applied each year to the net asset balance (i.e., cost minus accumulated depreciation). Since the net asset balance declines each year, the method results in decreasing annual charges for depreciation. There is a variety of methods for determining the rate to be applied to the declining asset amount.

A "pure" declining-balance rate results from the use of the formula:

$$\text{Depreciation rate} = 1 - \sqrt[n]{\frac{\text{salvage value}}{\text{cost}}}$$

with n being the life in years.

Thus, if the cost is $10,000, the life 10 years, and the salvage value $563, the depreciation rate will be 25 percent. The annual depreciation and the amount of the asset at the beginning of each year would be

Year	Asset amount Jan. 1	Depreciation			Asset amount Dec. 31
1	$10,000	25% of $10,000	=	$2,500	$7,500
2	7,500	25% of 7,500	=	1,875	5,625
3	5,625	25% of 5,625	=	1,406	4,219
4	4,219	25% of 4,219	=	1,055	3,164
5	3,164	25% of 3,164	=	791	2,373
6	2,373	25% of 2,373	=	593	1,780
7	1,780	25% of 1,780	=	445	1,335
8	1,335	25% of 1,335	=	334	1,001
9	1,001	25% of 1,001	=	250	751
10	751	25% of 751	=	188	563

Obviously, if the salvage value is zero, the depreciation rate would be 100 percent, which would allocate the entire cost to the year of purchase. The result would not comply with the definition of depreciation accounting. Under this procedure the depreciation rate is very sensitive to small changes in the salvage value; if the salvage value were $283, the depreciation rate would be 30 percent.

Double-Declining-Balance Method. The pure declining-balance method is not widely used in the United States. Instead, a variation of the declining-balance method described in the Internal Revenue Code has come into widespread use; for tax purposes it is limited to new assets. In this approach, the depreciation rate is twice that which would be under the straight-line method if a zero salvage value existed. This rate is applied to the amount of the asset (cost less accumulated depreciation at the beginning of the year). Under most circumstances, the entire depreciation would not be allocated during the life of the asset (i.e., the amount of the asset would exceed the salvage value) so that at a point somewhere near the midpoint of the life of the asset a change is made to the straight-line method. The switch is made when straight-line yields a larger depreciation charge. If salvage value is zero and the life is an odd digit (7, 9, etc.), the year of change will be $n/2 + 1\frac{1}{2}$; if it is even, the year of change will be $n/2 + 2$. If the salvage value is greater than zero, the year of change will be later than this.

As an illustration, if an asset has a cost of $2,000, an estimated life of 10 years, and an estimated salvage value of zero, the depreciation rate would be 20 percent and annual depreciation would be

Year	Asset amount	Depreciation		
1	$2,000	20% of $2,000	=	$400
2	1,600	20% of 1,600	=	320
3	1,280	20% of 1,280	=	256
4	1,024	20% of 1,024	=	205
5	819	20% of 819	=	164
6	655	20% of 655	=	131
7	524	$524\frac{4}{4}$	=	131
8	393	$524\frac{4}{4}$	=	131
9	262	$524\frac{4}{4}$	=	131
10	131	$524\frac{4}{4}$	=	131

A change would be made to the straight-line method in the seventh year because straight-line depreciation on the remaining amount of the asset is then greater than declining-balance depreciation ($105). If the estimated salvage value were

$200, the depreciation would be as above until the seventh year. For this and subsequent years it would be

Year	Asset amount	Depreciation
7	$524	20 % of $524 = $105
8	419	20 % of 419 = 84
9	335	$\dfrac{335 - 200}{2} = 68$
10	267	$\dfrac{335 - 200}{2} = 67$

A change would be made to the straight-line method in the ninth year.

The double-declining-balance method can be used for income tax purposes for all new assets with a useful life of at least three years with the exception of nonresidential buildings. Another variant of the declining-balance method permitted for income tax purposes for used equipment and nonresidential buildings is to use a rate of 150 percent of the straight-line rate. Thus, if used equipment with a cost of $10,000 is purchased and if the estimated life is 10 years, the depreciation for the first year would be $1,500 (= $\frac{1}{10}$ × 150% × $10,000). In the second year depreciation would be $1,275 [= $\frac{1}{10}$ × 150% × ($10,000 − $1,500)]. Subsequent years' depreciation would be based on the net amount of the asset.

Evaluation of Accelerated Methods.   The argument for the use of an accelerated method of depreciation is that the benefits received from the use of the asset are greater in the early years than in the later years. In the later years repair costs are greater, downtime is greater if the asset is a machine, physical output may be reduced, and obsolescence may result in a lower value output from the machine. In addition, the asset is purchased because forecasts of use for the first few years of its life indicate that it is a desirable investment; the future is less certain and contributes less to the economic feasibility of its acquisition. Another advantage is that if the asset is retired earlier than anticipated as a result of unforeseen obsolescence, the loss upon retirement will be less than if straight-line depreciation were used.

Despite these supposed advantages of the accelerated methods, there is no reason to suppose that the economic benefit to be received will decline in the ratio assumed by either the sum-of-the-years'-digits method or any of the declining-balance methods.

For tax accounting purposes, the accelerated methods have a clear advantage over the straight-line method. The larger deductions in the early years mean that at the very least tax payments are postponed for a considerable period. For a stable or growing firm, the postponement may extend to the end of the firm's planning horizon. The two accelerated methods give somewhat comparable results in this regard. The method that gives a tax postponement with the greatest present value depends on the cost of capital of the firm and the service life and salvage value of the asset being depreciated. In general, short service lives, high cost of capital, and high salvage values make declining-balance preferable to sum-of-the-years'-digits.

Taxpayers who use the class life asset depreciation range system may use a combination of double-declining balance and sum-of-the-years'-digits depreciation. If salvage value is zero, the maximum depreciation deduction is obtained by using double-declining balance the first two years and sum-of-the-years'-digits for the remainder of the life. Davidson and Drake estimate that with zero salvage value and customary costs of capital, e.g., 10 to 20 percent, sum-of-the-years'-digits is preferable for assets with service lives of eight years or more.[2]

COMPOUND-INTEREST METHODS

Two compound-interest methods of depreciation that are similar in their effect on income and assets have been described in the literature and have received limited use in the electrical utility industry in the United States.

Sinking-Fund Method. The sinking-fund method is based on the assumption that a fund of assets (which might be invested in securities or in plant) is to be built up and that the amount of this fund should equal the total amount of the depreciation at the end of the useful life of the depreciable asset. Equal annual payments will be made into this fund; the fund will also grow as a result of the earnings on the assets in the fund. The annual depreciation charge is equal to the annual increase in the fund.

To illustrate this method, an asset with a cost of $10,000, life of 10 years, and a salvage value of $200 is used. It is estimated that the assets in the fund will earn 6 percent.

The annual payment necessary to accumulate a fund of $1 at the end of 10 years at 6 percent is .075868 (as read from annuity tables). To accumulate $9,800 would therefore require an annual payment of $743.51. The growth of the fund would be

Year	Annual payment	Earnings of fund (6%)	Increase in fund	Year-end balance of fund
1	$743.51	—	$743.51	$ 743.51
2	743.51	$ 44.61	788.12	1,531.63
3	743.51	91.90	835.41	2,367.04
4	743.51	142.02	885.53	3,252.57
5	743.51	195.15	938.66	4,191.23
6	743.51	251.47	994.98	5,186.21
7	743.51	311.17	1,054.68	6,240.89
8	743.51	374.45	1,117.96	7,358.85
9	743.51	441.53	1,185.04	8,543.89
10	743.51	512.63	1,256.14	9,800.03

The annual depreciation charge would then be the amount shown in the column "Increase in Fund."

The sinking-fund method has a theoretical justification in a regulated industry in which equity must be preserved between investors and customers and between customers of today and customers of the future, but it would appear to have no applicability to nonregulated industries. No depreciation fund ordinarily exists; depreciation accounting is concerned with cost allocation to measure income, not with replacement of the asset.

Annuity Method. The annuity method of depreciation takes the approach that an asset is a bundle of services to be received over the life of the asset and that each

[2]Sidney Davidson and David F. Drake, "Capital Budgeting and the 'Best' Tax Depreciation Method," *Journal of Business,* vol. 34, pp. 442–452, October 1961, and "The 'Best' Tax Depreciation Method—1964," *Journal of Business,* vol. 37, pp. 258–260, July 1964. For results of a similar study applied to more recent tax laws, see Clyde P. Stickney and Jeffrey Wallace, "A Guide to Increasing the Maximum Available Depreciation Deduction Under the ADR System," *Taxation for Accountants,* July 1975, pp. 42–48.

year's depreciation cost must include a portion of the cost of the asset and, in addition, a return on the investment in this asset. It is assumed that the depreciation is to be an equal amount per year.

Using the same facts, the annual depreciation would be calculated by determining the annuity, the present value of which plus the present value of the salvage value would equal $10,000. If X is the annual depreciation, then

$10,000 = X(present value of an annuity of 1 for 10 periods at 6%) + $200 (present value of 1 due 10 periods from now at 6%)
$10,000 = 7.3601 X + $200(.5584)
X = $1,344

The annual charge to operations is then $1,344. Interest Income is credited each year for 6 percent of the net asset at the beginning of the year. The difference between $1,344 and the credit to Interest Income is credited to Accumulated Depreciation. The history of the asset will be

Year	Annual depreciation	Interest income	Increase in accumulated depreciation	Accumulated depreciation	Net asset
0	—	—	—	—	$10,000
1	$1,344	$600	$ 744	$ 744	9,256
2	1,344	555	789	1,533	8,467
3	1,344	508	836	2,369	7,631
4	1,344	458	886	3,255	6,745
5	1,344	405	939	4,194	5,806
6	1,344	348	996	5,190	4,810
7	1,344	289	1,055	6,245	3,755
8	1,344	225	1,119	7,364	2,636
9	1,344	158	1,186	8,550	1,450
10	1,344	87	1,257	9,807	193

The two methods show similar balances in the Accumulated Depreciation account at the end of each year. If the interest income is subtracted from depreciation expense under the annuity method, the net expense under the two methods is the same.

Interest Methods in General.   As was stated earlier, these interest methods have been applied only to regulated industries. However, it is possible to develop an approach to depreciation in general that does include a factor analogous to interest.

Using an asset with a cost of $12,000 and an estimated life of five years, an added estimate is made as to the rate at which the benefits (to be defined later) will be received. It is estimated that the benefits will be larger in the early years and decline in the later years. Although the actual benefits in dollars have not been estimated, the decline in these benefits is estimated to be as follows (the first year's benefits being arbitrarily stated as 100 percent):

Year	Benefits, %
1	100
2	90
3	80
4	65
5	45

The benefits are the increase in cash flows resulting from the use of the asset. Cash inflows may increase as a result of greater output and as a result of the acquisition of a technologically superior asset; other cash outflows, such as insurance, may increase. The cash outflow for income taxes may increase as a result of greater profit. These are the cash flows which might have been estimated as part of the capital budgeting process.

The management of the firm has determined that it is unwilling to make any investment unless it will earn a return of 10 percent. This 10 percent is either the cost of the debt capital and equity capital that is used to finance assets or is the return that management is able to receive from alternative investments.

If management was willing to make investments that would earn a zero rate of return, it would be willing to pay over twice as much for the first year's use of the asset than for the fifth year's use. (Note the relationship of 100 to 45.) Thus if all that was purchased was the first year's use and the fifth year's use and these uses were purchased for $1,450, the use of the joint cost approach would result in a cost allocation of $1,000 to the first year (100/145 of $1,450) and $450 to the fifth year (45/145 of $1,450). This is the same approach as the accountant takes to cost allocation of joint products and to the "basket purchase" problem in the acquisition of the assets of a firm.

Inasmuch as the benefits are received at different points of time, they should be discounted back to the purchase date. Using a rate of 10 percent and denoting the first years' benefits as X, we can state the value of the benefits as

Year	Present value of benefits
1	$.90909 \times (X)$
2	$.82645 \times (.90X)$
3	$.75131 \times (.80X)$
4	$.68301 \times (.65X)$
5	$.62092 \times (.45X)$
	$2.97731 \times X$

Adding these amounts and equating them to the cost of the asset:
$$2.97731X = \$12,000$$
$$X = \$ \ 4,030$$

This amount can be interpreted as the cost of the first year's use in terms of end-of-the-first-year dollars. The cost of the fifth year's dollars would be 45 percent of $4,030, etc. Discounting these amounts back to the time of purchase, the cost of $12,000 would be allocated as follows:

Year	Depreciation
1	$3,664
2	2,998
3	2,423
4	1,789
5	1,126
	$12,000

Comparing this method with methods of depreciation in general use, it could be argued that this provides for a more general approach in that it permits adjustment to any stream of benefits. The straight-line method may be considered to be based upon an assumption of equal benefits; the sum-of-the-years'-digits method upon the assumption of benefits decreasing by a constant amount per period (arithmetic progression); and the declining-balance method upon the assumption of benefits decreasing by a constant percentage per period (geometric progression). In addition, this method recognizes the time value of money; management would not pay the same amount for $1 of benefits to be received in later years as $1 of benefits to be received in early periods. The generally used methods implicitly assume that the appropriate discount rate is zero. This method is an accelerated depreciation method and the approach may be regarded as a defense of accelerated methods.

The above analysis could be supplemented by an additional step. The $12,000 cost is in beginning-of-the-first-year dollars; if the time value of money is recognized, this is equal (at a 10 percent rate) to $13,200 end-of-the-first-year dollars. If the $4,030 end-of-the-first-year dollars is subtracted from $13,200 because the first-year services have been received, the remaining asset becomes $9,170 at the end of the first year. If the decline in the amount of the asset from $12,000 to $9,170 is considered to be the depreciation for the first year and similar calculations are made for the other years, the depreciation over the five-year period will be

Year	Depreciation
1	$2,830
2	2,710
3	2,578
4	2,232
5	1,650

A third approach based upon somewhat similar reasoning would require not only a forecast of the pattern of the benefits but an explicit forecast of the cash flows. Assume that the purchase of the $12,000 asset would increase cash flows as follows:

Year	Cash flows
1	$4,491
2	4,042
3	3,593
4	2,920
5	2,023

These cash flows have a pattern identical to that described above; the cash flows decrease in the pattern of 100, 90, 80, 65, 45. Realization of these cash flows would result in a 15 percent return on the investment of $12,000; the cash flows discounted at the rate of 15 percent are equal to $12,000.

If depreciation is defined as the deduction which will lead to an income equal to 15 percent of the net asset, annual depreciation charges would be calculated as in column (4) of Exhibit 2.

Thus recognition of the time value of money could conceivably lead to three different depreciation schedules. None of these is acceptable today. For some assets, the depreciation in earlier years might be less than in later years. The

EXHIBIT 2   Compound Interest Depreciation Resulting in Equal Annual Return on Asset of 15 Percent

Year	Book value Jan. 1 (1)	15% return (2)^a	Cash inflow (given) (3)	Depreciation charge for year (4)^b	Accumulated depreciation Dec. 31 (5)
1	$12,000	$1,800	$4,491	$ 2,691	$ 2,691
2	9,309	1,396	4,042	2,646	5,337
3	6,663	999	3,593	2,594	7,931
4	4,069	610	2,920	2,310	10,241
5	1,759	264	2,023	1,759	12,000
				$12,000	

^{a}(2) = .15 × (1).
^{b}(4) = (3) − (2).

accounting profession is only gradually becoming willing to use implicit interest rates in the income measurement process. Accounting Principles Board Opinion No. 21 represented a major step forward in this regard.

This general approach is subject to one major conceptual criticism. The cash flows in an industrial corporation are the result of a combination of various types of assets—cash, accounts receivable, inventories, machinery of various types, buildings, and land. To be able to isolate even conceptually the cash flows for each asset (or even class of asset) would require the existence of production and marketing conditions which probably do not exist in practice.

SELECTION OF A DEPRECIATION METHOD

The management of a firm must select a depreciation method for income tax purposes and a depreciation method for general accounting purposes. They need not be the same. In both cases, the selection is subject to constraints. For income tax purposes, the method must be one of those that are approved by the Internal Revenue Code. For general accounting purposes, the method must be one that falls within the area of generally accepted accounting principles. Thus, in general, the choice for both is among the production methods, the straight-line method, the sum-of-the-years'-digits method, and the declining-balance method.

For income tax purposes, if the amounts involved are large enough to be of any importance, the choice will be between the sum-of-the-years'-digits method and the declining-balance method. Both of these result in larger depreciation deductions in the earlier years of the life of the asset and hence leave a larger amount of funds under the control of the management. The criteria for choosing between the two accelerated methods were discussed on page 20–13.

If the same method of depreciation is used for general accounting purposes as for income tax accounting purposes, only one set of depreciation records need be maintained and hence the cost of the accounting process will be lower. Despite this fact many firms elect to use an accelerated depreciation method for income tax accounting purposes and the straight-line method for general accounting purposes.

The straight-line method may be used for general accounting purposes in order to maintain comparability with other firms in the industry which use the straight-line method or to increase the income reported to stockholders and to other outside users of financial statements. It might also be used because management is convinced that its use results in a better measurement of income than does the use of other depreciation methods.

If a different method of depreciation is used for general accounting purposes than for income tax accounting purposes and the difference in the amount of depreciation is material, income tax allocation as described in Chapter 36 is necessary.

SPECIAL DEPRECIATION ACCOUNTING PROBLEMS

Correction of Misestimates of Service Life or Salvage Value. The first step in the depreciation process as described in the previous sections is the estimate of service life and salvage value. All of the previous discussion of depreciation methods assumes that the initial estimates will prove to be correct. The probability of this being true is small.

If the estimate of life is in error (or if the estimate of the salvage value is in error), it is possible that no recognition of this erroneous estimate is made until the asset is retired. If the estimated life is shorter than the actual life, the asset will be used in some years to which no depreciation is allocated. If the estimated life is longer than the actual life, the disposition of the asset will result in the reporting of a loss unless the actual salvage is sufficiently greater than the estimated salvage value to offset the shorter life. If the salvage value is greater than was expected, disposition of the asset may result in a gain.

As an illustration, suppose that an asset cost $10,000, has an estimated life of 10 years, and has an estimated salvage value of zero. If the straight-line method of depreciation is used, the annual depreciation will be $1,000. Now suppose that the asset is retired at the end of 8½ years and the salvage value is $400. Since the accumulated depreciation on the date of retirement is $8,500, there will be a reported loss in the year of retirement of $1,100. This loss will not be an extraordinary item.

On the other hand, suppose that the asset is not retired until the end of the twelfth year and that the actual salvage value is $200. No depreciation would be allocated to the eleventh and twelfth years, and disposal of the asset would result in the reporting of a gain of $200.

However, the incorrect estimate of life might be discovered and recognized prior to the time of retirement. Suppose that at the beginning of the seventh year of the life of the above asset, it is estimated that its life will be only eight years. The remaining cost of the asset amounting to $4,000 (= $10,000 less six years' depreciation at the rate of $1,000 per year) will then be allocated to the last two years of its life. If the double-declining-balance method had been used, a change to the straight-line method would be made in the seventh year. The remaining cost of the asset ($2,621) will then be allocated to the last two years of its life. If the sum-of-the-years'-digits method had been used, the remaining life being two years, the depreciation for the seventh year will be ⅔ of $2,222 or $1,481 and the depreciation for the eighth year will be $741.

If the estimate of life is less than the actual life and no adjustment is made in the annual depreciation, the entire cost of the asset will be charged off before the asset is retired. Under these circumstances, the Accumulated Depreciation account for this asset will have a balance equal to its cost. These amounts should be left in the accounts so that the asset account will show the cost of the assets still in use. In some cases, the Accumulated Depreciation account is debited and the main asset account credited as soon as the total cost is charged to operations, but as a result there is a failure to report the cost of the property in actual use.

Acquisitions and Disposals During the Year.   All of the previous discussion has been based on the assumption that acquisitions and disposals of assets are made at the beginning of each year. If they are not, the following treatments are permissible for income tax purposes:

1. Calculate depreciation on the basis of the portion of the year that the asset is owned.

2. Calculate a half-year's depreciation on all assets acquired or disposed of during the year. This is equivalent to calculating the depreciation on the arithmetic mean (average) of the cost of the assets at the beginning and at the end of the year.

3. Calculate a full year's depreciation on all assets acquired during the first half of the year and on assets disposed of during the second half of the year. The result is that there is no depreciation on the assets disposed of during the first half of the year nor on assets acquired during the second half of the year.

If disposals and acquisitions are of material amount and are not distributed evenly during the year, both the second and third method may distort accounting results. They do, however, simplify procedures.

The half-year assumption is readily handled under the declining-balance and sum-of-the-years'-digits as well as the straight-line method. For example, assume an asset with a cost of $1,500, estimated five-year service life, and zero salvage value. Depreciation under the declining-balance method would be

Year	Depreciation rate	Portion of year	Depreciation charge	Net asset, Dec. 31
1	$\frac{2}{5}$ = .40	.50	$300	$1,200
2	$\frac{2}{5}$ = .40	1.00	480	720
3	$\frac{2}{5}$ = .40	1.00	288	432
4	$\frac{2}{5}$ = .40	1.00	173	259
5	SL = 1.0/1.5	of remaining balance	173	86
6	SL = .5/.5	of remaining balance	86	0

Utilizing the sum-of-the-years'-digits method in the previous example, the depreciation would be

Year	Calculation	Depreciation charge
1	$\frac{1}{2}(\frac{5}{15})$ of 1,500	$250
2	$\frac{1}{2}(\frac{5}{15} + \frac{4}{15})$ of 1,500	450
3	$\frac{1}{2}(\frac{4}{15} + \frac{3}{15})$ of 1,500	350
4	$\frac{1}{2}(\frac{3}{15} + \frac{2}{15})$ of 1,500	250
5	$\frac{1}{2}(\frac{2}{15} + \frac{1}{15})$ of 1,500	150
6	$\frac{1}{2}(\frac{1}{15})$ of 1,500	50

Additions and Renewals. Additional expenditures on an asset may be made over its life. These expenditures may be for additions to the property or renewals of property of such character and size that they are not charged to current operations. In either case, a recalculation of the annual depreciation is necessary.

One approach is to add the amount of these new expenditures to the unamortized cost of the plant and allocate the total over the remaining life of the asset. If a firm owns an asset with a cost of $10,000, an estimated salvage value of zero, and an estimated life of 10 years, and uses the straight-line method of depreciation, the unamortized cost at the beginning of the seventh year is $4,000. If an expenditure of $1,000 is made at the beginning of the seventh year, the total cost to be amortized over the remaining four years is $5,000. The annual depreciation would then be $1,250 per year. If the expenditure of $1,000 is charged to the Asset account, the new depreciation rate would be 11.4 percent ($1,250 divided by $11,000); if it is charged to the Accumulated Depreciation account, the new depreciation rate would be 12.5 percent ($1,250 divided by $10,000).

Another approach is to consider the expenditure as a new cost to be amortized. The result would be additional depreciation of $250 ($1,000 divided by 4). The rate of depreciation on this cost would be 25 percent. The results would be the same regardless of how the calculation was made. It would ordinarily be simpler to take the latter approach, particularly if some method other than the straight-line method were in use.

UNIT AND GROUP METHODS

Depreciation might be calculated on individual assets or on group of assets. The group may be defined as (1) a homogeneous group of assets acquired in a particular year, (2) a homogeneous group of assets whenever purchased, (3) all assets purchased in a particular year, or (4) all assets. If a nonhomogeneous group is used, the depreciation rate will be the weighted arithmetic mean of the depreciation rates, with the weights being the cost of the assets. If the class life ADR system is used, the assets acquired during any one year will be a group (referred to as a *vintage account*) or several vintage accounts may be used, at the option of the taxpayer.

The Unit Method. If the unit method of depreciation is used, it is necessary to determine what the unit should be. A factory building together with all the machinery and equipment installed therein might be considered a unit. At the other extreme, each part of each machine might be considered a depreciable unit. If the depreciation unit is a large one, replacement of parts of it will be considered to be maintenance; if the unit is very small, most of the costs will be treated as replacements. Thus, two firms that are otherwise alike might have different depreciation costs, with the one having a high depreciation cost having correspondingly lower maintenance costs.

The cost of depreciation accounting will obviously be lower if the depreciation unit is large and hence fewer units exist. On the other hand, repair costs might vary considerably from year to year, with a resulting variation in expenses and net income. If the unit is a small one, more expenditures will be capitalized and hence charged off gradually by the depreciation process. Inasmuch as many expenditures are made at the discretion of management, there is greater opportunity for management to control the amount of reported income if the depreciation unit is large.

It is unlikely that the estimated life of the assets will be a correct estimate of the life of each asset; the best that can be expected is that the average life of the assets will be equal to the estimated life. If the assets are depreciated individually, a loss will be shown on the retirement of those assets whose life is less than the estimated life and no depreciation will be allocated to years beyond the estimated life of the asset.

As an illustration, suppose 100 assets, each with a cost of $1,000, are purchased on January 1, 19X0. The estimated life is five years and the estimated salvage value is zero. If the straight-line method of depreciation is used, the depreciation rate will be 20 percent. Actual retirements of units are as follows:

December 31 19X2	10
December 31 19X3	20
December 31 19X4	40
December 31 19X5	20
December 31 19X6	10

If the unit method is used (i.e., depreciation calculated on each asset), depreciation and loss on the retirement of assets will then be as shown in Exhibit 3.

EXHIBIT 3   Depreciation Under Unit Method

Year	Assets in use, Jan. 1		Retirements		Retirement loss	Assets in use, Dec. 31	
	Cost	Depreciation	Cost	Accumulated depreciation		Cost	Accumulated depreciation
19X0	$100,000	$20,000	—	—	—	$100,000	$20,000
19X1	100,000	20,000	—	—	—	100,000	40,000
19X2	100,000	20,000	$10,000	$ 6,000	$4,000	90,000	54,000
19X3	90,000	18,000	20,000	16,000	4,000	70,000	56,000
19X4	70,000	14,000	40,000	40,000	—	30,000	30,000
19X5	30,000	—	20,000	20,000	—	10,000	10,000
19X6	10,000	—	10,000	10,000	—	—	—
Total		$92,000			$8,000		

The Group Method. If the group method is used, no loss is recognized when assets are retired. Instead, the difference between the cost of the asset retired and its salvage value is charged to accumulated depreciation. Based on the data above, the history of the group would be as shown in Exhibit 4.

EXHIBIT 4   Depreciation Under Group Method

Year	Assets in use, Jan. 1		Retirements		Retire-ment loss	Assets in use, Dec. 31	
	Cost	Depre-ciation	Cost	Accumulated depreciation		Cost	Accumulated depreciation
19X0	$100,000	$ 20,000	—	—	—	$100,000	$20,000
19X1	100,000	20,000	—	—	—	100,000	40,000
19X2	100,000	20,000	$10,000	$10,000	—	90,000	50,000
19X3	90,000	18,000	20,000	20,000	—	70,000	48,000
19X4	70,000	14,000	40,000	40,000	—	30,000	22,000
19X5	30,000	6,000	20,000	20,000	—	10,000	8,000
19X6	10,000	2,000	10,000	10,000	—	—	—
Total		$100,000					

In this illustration of the group method, the actual average life was equal to the estimated life. When actual and estimated are not equal, the difference might be noticed during the life of the assets and an adjustment made in the depreciation rate. If it is not noted, there will either be a loss in the final year (if the estimated life is greater than the average life) or no depreciation would be reported in the last years of the lives of the assets (if the average actual life is greater than the estimated life). If groups are not maintained on the basis of the year of acquisition, it is necessary to make periodic studies of experienced lives to permit adjustment of depreciation rates.

The Composite Method. If the group method is used for a nonhomogeneous group of assets, it would be preferable to refer to it as the *composite method*. Use of the composite approach is questionable. If the life estimate of a homogeneous group is correct, the total depreciation over the life of the group will be equal to the total cost. This is not the case with a nonhomogeneous group.

To illustrate, suppose the group is made up of three assets with respective costs and lives as follows:

Cost	Life
$12,000	3
4,000	7
10,000	10
$26,000	20 years

The depreciation rate for the group would be 15 percent (average life of 6⅔ years); the depreciation would be $3,900 for the first three years, $2,100 for the next four years, and $1,500 for the last three years, or a total of $24,600. This is less than of total cost. The only circumstance under which this method would give satisfactory results is if the assets were to be replaced at the end of their estimated lives with similar assets at exactly the same cost. In the above case, over a 40-year (the lowest common denominator of the digits that represent the separate asset lives) period the total depreciation would be equal to the total cost of the assets.

Despite this deficiency, the composite method has great appeal. It simplifies accounting for plant assets because depreciation accruals need not be made for individual assets. Furthermore, the lives published by the Internal Revenue Service are composite lives, and hence their use for income tax purposes is virtually mandatory. The use of guideline lives under the composite method for general accounting purposes as well thus has great advantages.

CURRENT VALUE AS THE DEPRECIATION BASE

It has been assumed up to this point that the basis of depreciation is to be cost. That this assumption is appropriate has been challenged repeatedly, especially in recent years. Some of these challenges are based on concepts of income generally held by accountants; others have challenged these concepts of income.

One frequent proposal has been to calculate depreciation on the replacement cost of the asset. To illustrate, suppose the firm has an asset that cost $10,000 on January 1, 19X0, with an estimated life of five years and a salvage value of zero. The straight-line method of depreciation is used. The replacement cost is determined at the end of each year and the annual depreciation would be 20 percent of this amount.

Year	Replacement cost	Depreciation charge
19X0	$10,500	$ 2,100
19X1	12,000	2,400
19X2	12,400	2,480
19X3	13,200	2,640
19X4	13,300	2,660
		$12,280

A credit to Accumulated Depreciation of $2,000 would be made each year; the difference between the annual depreciation and the $2,000 would be credited to Additional Accumulated Depreciation on Replacement Cost. The nature of this account is ambiguous, although it would probably be viewed as a part of stockholders' equity if the asset were shown at *historical* cost.

A more sophisticated approach would be to adjust the gross asset account to the replacement cost and the Accumulated Depreciation account to the proper percentage of the replacement cost. Thus, at the end of the first year the Accumulated Depreciation account would have a balance equal to 20 percent of the replacement cost; at the end of the third year its balance would be 60 percent of the replacement cost. The net adjustment in assets would be reported as a holding gain. The result, utilizing the data of the previous illustration, would be as shown in Exhibit 5. Thus, no ambiguous additional accumulated depreciation is created. The

EXHIBIT 5   Depreciation Using Current Values

Year	Depreciable asset, Jan. 1			Depreciable asset, Dec. 31 (before depreciation)			Holding gain	Depreciation
	Gross	Accumulated depreciation	Net	Gross	Accumulated depreciation	Net		
19X0	$10,000	—	$10,000	$10,500	—	$10,500	$ 500	$ 2,100
19X1	10,500	$ 2,100	8,400	12,000	$ 2,400	9,600	1,200	2,400
19X2	12,000	4,800	7,200	12,400	4,960	7,440	240	2,480
19X3	12,400	7,440	4,960	13,200	7,920	5,280	320	2,640
19X4	13,200	10,560	2,640	13,300	10,640	2,660	20	2,660
							$2,280	$12,280

holding gain would be reported as a special element in reported income or would be carried directly to a stockholders' equity account, bypassing income entirely. Treating holding gains as an element of reported income is contrary to the conventional accounting criterion of realization before recognizing income.

A variant of this procedure would base the depreciation on the average of beginning-of-the-year and end-of-the-year reproduction cost. This would not change the balance sheet but would result in a change in both the holding gain and the annual depreciation. This is the procedure required by the SEC in *Accounting Series Release No. 190* which calls for certain replacement cost disclosures. See also Chapter 46 and the 1976 article by Vancil and Weil on accounting for depreciable assets.

Year	Holding gain	Depreciation
19X0	$ 450	$ 2,050
19X1	1,050	2,250
19X2	200	2,440
19X3	240	2,560
19X4	10	2,650
	$1,950	$11,950

Because of the problem of determining reproduction costs for individual assets, the use of a price index for classes of equipment has been proposed. Unfortunately, satisfactory specialized price indexes have not yet been developed. In addition, there is the problem of obsolescent assets, for which the use of appraisals would be necessary. Appraised values of such assets are rarely satisfactory.

Another approach to the recognition of price changes involves the use of index numbers of general prices such as the United States Bureau of Labor Statistics Consumer Price Index or the Gross National Product Implicit Price Deflator. Using this approach, income is not measured in traditional dollars but rather in dollars adjusted for general price changes. No holding gain would then be recognized because the stockholders' equity would also be adjusted as general prices changed. (See the discussion of accounting for price changes in Chapter 32.)

BIBLIOGRAPHY

Anton, Hector R.: "Depreciation, Cost Allocation and Investment Decisions," *Accounting Research,* vol. 7, April 1956.

Burt, Oscar R.: "Unified Theory of Depreciation," *Journal of Accounting Research,* vol. 10, pp. 28–57, Spring 1972.

Davidson, Sidney, and David F. Drake: "Capital Budgeting and the 'Best' Tax Depreciation Method," *Journal of Business,* vol. 34, October 1961.

———: "The 'Best' Tax Depreciation Method—1964," *Journal of Business,* vol. 37, July 1964,

Feinschreiber, Robert: "Computing Depreciation Under the Class Life System," *CPA Journal,* vol. 43, pp. 657–862, October 1973.

———: *Tax Depreciation Under the Class Life ADR System,* American Management Association, New York, 1975.

Grant, Eugene L., and Paul T. Norton, Jr.: *Depreciation,* The Ronald Press Company, New York, 1955.

Reynolds, Issac N.: "Selecting the Proper Depreciation Method," *The Accounting Review,* vol. 36, April 1961.

Stickney, Clyde P., and Jeffrey Wallace: "A Guide to Increasing the Maximum Available Depreciation Deduction Under the ADR System," *Taxation for Accountants,* July 1975, pp. 42–48.

Terborgh, George: *Realistic Depreciation Policy,* Machinery and Allied Products Institute, Washington, D.C., 1954.

Thomas, Arthur L.: *Allocation Problem in Financial Accounting,* Studies in Accounting Research No. 3, American Accounting Association, Evanston, Ill., 1969, and Studies in Accounting Research No. 9, American Accounting Association, Sarasota, Fla., 1974.

U.S. Treasury Department: *Depreciation Guidelines and Rules,* Washington, D.C., 1964.

Vancil, Richard F., and Roman L. Weil: "Current Replacement Cost Accounting, Depreciable Assets, and Distributable Income," *Financial Analysts Journal,* July–August 1976, pp. 38–45.

Wright, F. K.: "Towards a General Theory of Depreciation," *Journal of Accounting Research,* vol. 2, Spring 1964.

Chapter **21**

Goodwill

NORTON M. BEDFORD
**Arthur Young Distinguished Professor of Accountancy and
Business Administration, University of Illinois**

E. JAMES BURTON
Assistant Professor, Florida State University

"Accountants, writers on accounting, economists, engineers, and the courts have all tried their hands at defining goodwill, at discussing its nature, and at proposing means of valuing it. The most striking characteristic of this immense amount of writing is the number and variety of disagreements reached."[1] But the existence of such widespread interest and disagreement also directs attention to the importance of the topic. Furthermore, there is always the hope that continuous examination of the concept will lead to a clarification of it. Practically, there is a necessity that goodwill be accounted for in some manner to meet a variety of business and accounting requirements.

NATURE OF GOODWILL

One of the more convincing techniques used by students of accounting to gain intuitive support for an accounting proposition is to relate the proposition to a phenomenon in the physical world. Goodwill has not escaped this analogy. That is, there exists in physiology the phenomenon of synergism, which refers to the cooperative action of discrete agencies such that the total effect is greater than the sum of the two effects taken independently, and some valuation authorities contend that the similar phenomenon in the business world is goodwill. According to this view, goodwill is not an independent asset like cash or merchandise which can be sold or exchanged. Rather it is a special "going-value" valuation account representing the excess of the value of the combined assets of the entity over the sum of their individual values. Although somewhat nebulous in nature, this concept has wide intuitive support, to a large degree, one suspects, because of the widely quoted assertion that "the whole is greater than the sum of its parts." But many serious students of the goodwill concept do contend that the assertion is valid and that goodwill exists independent of all other assets of an entity.

To other accounting authorities, goodwill is merely a valuation of undervalued or unrecorded assets. The notion of undervalued assets includes not only the excess of market value over acquisition cost but also the excess of the value in use over market value. Thus, an asset purchased for $8,000 cash (acquisition cost) may have a replacement value due to changes in prices over time of $10,000 (market value) yet be so useful to the firm that it is worth $15,000 (value in use). While these three distinct values of an asset exist, the latter two are frequently difficult to measure. It is true, of course, that before recognizing goodwill as an asset, there exists a tendency to revalue the recorded assets to market value, but such a process would still leave as goodwill the difference between market value and value in use. In cases where market value is not well defined, the conservative tendency of accounting valuations may result in part of the excess of market value over acquisition cost also being included in goodwill. Thus, the view that goodwill is due in part, at least, to the undervaluation of assets is not without a sound base.

Equally compelling is the belief that goodwill is merely an overall measure of unrecorded assets such as a favorable line of credit, dependable suppliers, a stable work force, and loyal customers. These undervalued or unrecorded assets may arise from advertising and represent a type of deferred advertising cost, from proper business conduct and represent the cost of building a reputation for moral and fair action, or from chance developments and represent a type of unrealized appreciation of recorded assets or such unrecorded assets as a favorable location or a differentiated product. The distinction between undervalued assets and unrecorded assets is merely one of degree. An unrecorded assets is an asset having zero value attached to it, whereas an undervalued asset is one which has a positive

---

[1] John B. Canning, *The Economics of Accountancy*, The Ronald Press Company, New York, 1929, p. 38.

value assigned to it. For both, the goodwill aspect arises from a difference between the accounting value attached to the asset and its economic value. Because of the similar nature of the two types of resources, if one treats their difference as one of degree rather than as a difference in kind, it is appropriate to treat goodwill arising from either type as one kind of goodwill—that arising from the undervaluation of specific known or unknown assets.

Still other accounting authorities combine going value, undervalued recorded assets, and unrecorded assets into one concept of goodwill and refer to it as a master valuation account. This seems to be an expediency necessary because of the accounting inability to identify certain goodwill components and an inability to measure certain other identified elements. The master valuation account is deficient in that measurable identifiable elements could and should be separately disclosed. But the master valuation notion does exist and apparently is now supported on the grounds that the allocation problem is so difficult that at best about all that can be done is to produce one overall general valuation account. Acceptance of the master valuation account concept of goodwill implies that goodwill is a common or joint value which cannot be allocated to individual categories of assets in a meaningful manner. As such it is clearly an accounting concept created because of the measurement difficulty and is recorded as if it had no single distinctive constitutive characteristic.

Measurement Limitations.   There seems to be no measurable way of distinguishing the two broad constitutive concepts of goodwill. That is, there are great measurement limitations to any attempt to distinguish between goodwill as a going-value valuation account and goodwill as the result of undervalued or unrecorded specific assets. In more recent years there have been authoritative pronouncements proposing that an effort be made to assign goodwill from undervalued or unrecorded specific assets to the specific assets even though such a measurement procedure might involve the use of less objective evidence than that traditionally used in valuing assets at acquisition cost. Thus, Accounting Principles Board Opinion No. 16 states that, "A difference between the sum of the assigned costs of the tangible and identifiable intangible assets acquired less liabilities assumed and the cost of the group is evidence of unspecified intangible values."[2]

The implication of this position is that if fair value of the separate resources can be measured accurately, the nature of goodwill should be confined to the value of the unallocable part of the undervalued and unrecorded assets and to the going value of the enterprise. Under this view, goodwill would be the value of the firm as a whole less the sum of the market values of the individual assets.

There might be distinct social advantages in distinguishing and valuing the various types of specific assets included in the concept of goodwill but having no fair market value. Thus, if the goodwill existing because of the commerical morality of a firm could be distinguished and measured effectively, the disclosure of the value of such an unrecorded asset might have a profound effect on commercial morality throughout the country. Similarly, measurement of the goodwill due to a well-qualified labor force would represent a significant contribution to social efforts to measure the value of the human assets of an entity. Despite these social needs, the measurement problems are so difficult that there seems to be no reasonable prospect that an accurate and detailed breakdown of such goodwill can be accomplished in a satisfactory manner.

Because of the measurement problem, goodwill is frequently referred to in the master valuation account sense, which is assumed to provide a measure of the value of the expected excess future earning power of a company over that of

[2]Accounting Principles Board, "Business Combinations," Opinion No. 16, AICPA, New York, 1970.

similar companies. This view is reflected in Canning's observation[3] that "Elementary components of goodwill are interesting to speculate about but only the mass resultant, in any given enterprise, is capable of statistical generalization." Edwards and Bell[4] support this position, stating, "Goodwill reflects expected profitability whether this stems from monopoly position, efficiency, or other factors." In this context goodwill includes both going-value and undervalued assets.

In an overview sense, it is clear that goodwill does not exist as a separate asset; it exists only in combination with other assets. Further, it is restricted to an economic value, since noneconomic social values are not included in its measurement. That it exists is implied by investors who by buying shares of stock in a company purchase a part of the total entity rather than parts of the individual assets owned by the entity. Thus, the typical stockholder asserts that he buys shares of stock of a company not for the individual assets the company has, but for such factors as management competence, anticipated research results, trends in the industry, and the economy as a whole—in other words, for the projected earnings of the firm. To the extent that payment for these qualities exceeds the share of the book value of the individual assets acquired, a payment has been made for something of an intangible nature which belongs to the total entity.

Legal Concepts of Goodwill. According to Simon,[5] legal concepts of goodwill are based on an old English case which held that "goodwill is the probability that customers will return to the old stand." This clearly confines goodwill to customer goodwill and implies that goodwill is a distinct unrecorded asset. Simon credits Judge Cardozo with expanding the goodwill concept to include the tendency for customers to return to the same location or to return to the company because of its name or other reasons regardless of its location. This view also supports the concept that goodwill is a distinct unrecorded asset. Finally, Simon[6] cites several court cases to indicate that the courts include in goodwill "every possible advantage that has been acquired by a firm in carrying on its business." Thus, the emerged legal concept of goodwill refers to advantages in addition to the goodwill of customers. Goodwill of employees, suppliers, and others would be included. Further, such a view could include going value as part of company goodwill.

While the courts have not required excess earning power before recognizing goodwill and have held in the case of a monopoly that excess earning power is not necessarily evidence of goodwill, most of the legal properties of goodwill are of such a nature that excess earning will result. In this indirect way, Morrissey[7] seems to find a common legal and accounting view of goodwill as the "present value of a firm's anticipated 'excess' earnings." The law has trouble, however, in distinguishing between goodwill and other intangibles. As Preinreich noted in an early study:[8]

> The modern law of trademarks . . . has an independent origin, since goodwill as a legal concept has not arisen until much later. . . . Modern advertising campaigns tend to concentrate increasingly upon trademarks at the expense of firm names. Certain brands have thus become household words, although not many consumers know the names of the respective manufacturers. This tendency further increases the transferability of goodwill by attaching it altogether to the product.

[3]Canning, *op. cit.,* p. 39.

[4]Edgar O. Edwards and Philip W. Bell, *The Theory and Measurement of Business Income,* University of California Press, Berkeley, Calif., 1961, p. 37.

[5]Sidney I. Simon, "Court Decisions Concerning Goodwill," *The Accounting Review,* vol. 31, p. 272, April 1956.

[6]*Ibid.*

[7]Leonard Morrissey, "Intangible Costs," in Morton Backer (ed.), *Modern Accounting Theory,* Prentice-Hall, Englewood Cliffs, N.J., 1966, p. 198.

[8]Gabriel A. D. Preinreich, "The Law of Goodwill," *The Accounting Review,* vol. 11, p. 323, December 1936.

The implication is that product goodwill represents the intangible asset "trademark," which exists because of brand loyalty and the like. Such a view confines goodwill to "company goodwill." To the extent that these other intangibles can be separated and valued, more complete disclosure of economic activity results.

Economic Concepts of Goodwill. It seems to be well established in the literature of economics that the economic value of any asset depends upon the future net receipts which the asset will produce. While these receipts to a consumer are receipts of satisfactions, to a business firm the receipts are cash or cash equivalent (more broadly, purchasing power equivalent). Since the future is unknown, different individuals and business entities will have different expectations as to what these future receipts will be. Thus, there is no certainty in any one valuation of an asset. To the contrary, a considerable amount of uncertainty attaches to any valuation. But subject to this variability, the conceptual view of the economic value of any asset is based on the future receipts which the asset will produce. Because individual assets are not used in isolation but as part of an organized entity containing a variety of distinct assets, the economic concept of goodwill is introduced when the future receipts of the organization cannot be assigned as a contribution of a finite list of specific assets. That is, the search to assign a specific cause, in the form of a specific asset, for the expected future receipts requires the introduction of goodwill as an asset.

While different definitions are found, most economic definitions of goodwill can be related back to Edey's conclusion[9] that "Goodwill in the economic sense is another word for organization." This seems to support the "going-value" notion of goodwill, but further discussion reveals that Edey viewed goodwill as a composition of several unrecorded assets. He notes that the value of goodwill

> . . . is derived from the economic benefits that a going concern may enjoy, as compared with a new one, from (a) established relations in all the markets . . . (b) established relations with government departments and other non-commercial bodies . . . (c) the personal relationships. . . . These things cannot be separated from the business and sold as can such assets as plant and machinery.

Actually, any classification of the assets included in such a goodwill concept is an arbitrary classification. It is arbitrary in the nature of the basis selected for breaking down the overall goodwill, and it is arbitrary in the degree of refinement to which the goodwill is broken down. For example, goodwill might be classified according to the various types of feelings various people might have toward a company, to different types of people who have the favorable feeling, to the qualities of the organization which cause the feelings to arise, or to any classification scheme. Then each of these could have a few or a large number of categories into which the goodwill could be divided. Yang,[10] for example, recognized three types of goodwill: customer goodwill, employee goodwill, and creditor goodwill. Other writers have included potential goodwill and suppliers' goodwill as additional categories of items tending to give an enterprise an advantage over its competitors.

Goodwill Factors. To be distinguished from these emotional attachments to an enterprise are such nonemotional factors as goodwill from a favorable location, a monopoly, or a lack of consumer knowledge. Although there are many lists of factors which might contribute to a firm's earning power and hence its goodwill, such things as good labor relations, superior management personnel, excellence of

[9]H. C. Edey, "Business Valuation, Goodwill and the Super-Profit Method," in W. T. Baxter and Sidney Davidson (eds.), *Studies in Accounting Theory,* Richard D. Irwin, Homewood, Ill., 1962, p. 201.

[10]J. M. Yang, *Goodwill and Other Intangibles,* The Ronald Press Company, New York, 1927, pp. 41–56.

location, and favorable supplier relations appear on most such lists. No list is exhaustive, and any list is only indicative of the characteristics of goodwill.

Surplus Value. About the only criterion for selecting a list of items into which goodwill could be separated would be the criterion of information disclosure. Since the concept of information is itself most complex, varying from person to person and from situation to situation, it is not particularly adaptable to a systematic breakdown of goodwill into categories. Because of the indefinite nature of information, most proposals for a breakdown of goodwill are based on intuition rather than systematic logic. Sands, for example, accounts for goodwill as a type of buyers' surplus value resulting from the undervaluation of assets due to the existence of imperfect competition in the economic system. He distinguishes individual goodwill and business goodwill and reconciles them in the following manner:[11]

> The so-called personal goodwill which is attributed to many small businesses, particularly personal service businesses, is another manifestation of the same condition. To the extent that it represents the superior abilities or business connections of an individual as such and not merely of that individual as a representative of a specific business, it is part of the value of the *individual*, not of the business. However, if conditions of imperfect competition make it possible for the individual to be employed for less than he would otherwise get, these conditions constitute intangible value to the business in which he is employed.

This view of goodwill as the result of undervalued human assets may be related back to Marshall's concept of consumer's surplus, which he describes as[12] "The excess of the price which he would be willing to pay rather than go without the thing, over that which he actually does pay. . . ." In all fairness to Marshall, however, it must be noted that he recognized the opportunity for an individual businessman to sell his specialized goods and services above the minimum price at which he would release them. This opportunity was labeled by Marshall as the "opportunity value."[13] It has, of course, an implication of excess earning power.

Accounting Concepts of Goodwill. Accounting concepts of goodwill are directed not so much to the nature of goodwill as to its measurement. That is, accounting concepts are more operational and tend to be confined to a description of the situations where goodwill is presumed to exist. The idea which supports this method of defining goodwill is that verbal descriptions of goodwill are inadequate and that the only way to determine what is meant by goodwill is to observe the way it is measured. This operational concept of goodwill is best explained by an example. Suppose that a company spent a large sum of money on general advertising of the company's name and the question arose as to whether or not goodwill was created. In a constitutive sense, the discussion might start with the nature of goodwill and then reach a conclusion as to whether or not goodwill existed. Depending upon the verbal description of the nature of goodwill, the decision would be made. But if the verbal descriptive did not cover all situations, doubt might still remain as to the proper treatment of a certain part of the advertising expenditure. If, on the other hand, the definition of goodwill was not in terms of a verbal description but in terms of the measurement method used to compute goodwill, ambiguity regarding the precise nature of goodwill would be eliminated. This latter operational approach dominates practical accounting think-

---

[11]J. T. Sands, *Wealth, Income and Intangibles,* University of Toronto Press, Toronto, Canada, 1963, pp. 27–28.

[12]Alfred Marshall, *Principles of Economics,* 8th ed., The Macmillan Company, New York, 1947, p. 124. Edwards and Bell later expanded this concept into the notion of subjective goodwill.

[13]See Edwards and Bell, *op. cit.,* p. 37.

ing about goodwill. This does not mean, however, that no constitutive concept of goodwill underlies the accounting view of goodwill. To the contrary, general criteria do exist, but the precise meaning of these criteria requires a measurement. Broadly, the two constitutive criteria, either of which serves as evidence of the existence of goodwill, which seem to serve as general guides for thinking about accounting goodwill are (1) excess earning power and (2) a payment in excess of an established value of a resource.[14]

Goodwill Sources.   Historically, Preinreich's classic report represents the starting point for most modern-day accounting thinking about goodwill.[15] He cites various references to goodwill as (1) the value of business connections, (2) the value of the probability that present customers will continue to buy, (3) the value of the momentum acquired by a going concern, (4) the value of the reputation of a business concern, (5) the value of the benefits or advantages which attach to a particular business, and (6) the value of the capacity to earn greater than ordinary profits. He concludes that the basic thought underlying all accounting definitions is that commercial goodwill is the present value of the right to receive expected future superprofits. This basic concept pervades much of the accounting literature dealing with the nature of goodwill.

Leonard Spacek reflects accounting thinking about the substance of goodwill in the following terms:[16]

> This goodwill may relate to or arise from countless factors and circumstances such as (1) public acceptance of a company's products, (2) the composition and skills of the management, (3) public relations, or (4) the strength of a research organization.

Morrissey summarizes Spacek's thinking about certain aspects of goodwill as follows:[17]

> 1. Goodwill is not a "producing" asset. It is a cost to the buyer of earnings over and above the cost of the assets required to produce those earnings.
> 2. Amortization accounting for goodwill emphasizes "venture results" rather than "disclosing the earning power of a company's productive facilities." The determination of earning power is masked by amortizing goodwill "against the very earning power we are seeking to measure."
> 3. Carrying goodwill on the balance sheet without amortization is unsatisfactory because the balance sheet should inform the investor of the extent to which his investment is represented by actual producing assets.

Types of Recognized Goodwill.   Because the accounting concept of goodwill is closely related to the way it is measured, an examination of these different measurement processes will reveal different types of recognized goodwill. That is, whatever the factors to which goodwill is related, different types of goodwill are recognized by different measurement processes. The three main types of goodwill which accountants recognize are

1. Partnership goodwill
2. Composite assets goodwill
3. Consolidated goodwill.

Partnership goodwill approaches a measure of individual or personal goodwill, while the other measures are more in accord with the concept of enterprise

---

[14]This goodwill typically arises when consolidated statements are prepared. See *Accounting Research Bulletin No. 51,* pp. 41–51, for a more detailed discussion of this concept.

[15]Gabriel A. D. Preinreich, "Goodwill in Accountancy," *Journal of Accountancy,* vol. 66, pp. 28–50, July 1937.

[16]Leonard Spacek, "The Treatment of Goodwill in the Corporate Balance Sheet," *Journal of Accountancy,* vol. 117, p. 36, February 1964.

[17]Morrissey, *op. cit.,* p. 207.

goodwill. Types 2 and 3 differ in that type 2 represents the excess price paid for a group of assets over the sum of their individual prices whereas type 3 represents the excess of an indirect pricing of both assets and liabilities of an enterprise over the sum of their individual values. In type 2 the goodwill arises from the purchases of assets from one enterprise by another enterprise. Type 3 goodwill arises from the purchase of an ownership equity in a going enterprise and includes both the excess payment for assets and the underpayment for liabilities over their individual market value on the purchase date.

VALUATION OF GOODWILL

It seems to be a well-established principle of accounting that any measure of the value of an asset depends largely on the way the information is to be used. This principle applies to the valuation of goodwill. The valuation of goodwill for purposes of establishing the selling price of a going concern would be different from the valuation for the purpose of explaining how management had used cash resources. Thus, the first criterion to be used in selecting a method for valuing goodwill is to determine how the information is to be used, or, from an accounting point of view, determining the valuation which will be most useful to accounting report readers. That is, the valuation must be relevant to the needs of users.

For public reporting purposes there is also the need for objective valuations to provide reliability or credence to the valuation communicated. That is, the usefulness of a valuation is not unrelated to the degree of confidence that the user has in the valuation method used. As between purported relevant valuations of a subjective nature, the evidence seems to be that the public is better served by the more objective valuation. The reason for this preference appears to rest in the relative nature of investor decisions. That is, investors buy one stock rather than another because relatively one seems better than the other. A precise measure is not essential since a relative measure can be used. Thus, comparability of goodwill valuations among different companies becomes particularly important. Since comparability is established more by objective valuation methods than by subjective ones, a preference for objective valuation methods exists among accountants.

Besides these rather broad guidelines governing the accounting valuation of assets, there is the principle that assets should be valued at acquisition cost. In addition to the objectivity of the acquisition-cost valuation principle, it has the advantage of providing an operation measure of income under the matching concept. By matching cost (effort) against revenue (accomplishment), an income measure results which reveals the overall effectiveness with which management has been able to acquire and use economic resources. While increasing criticism of the matching concept has appeared in accounting literature in recent years, it is still an influential characteristic underlying accounting valuations.

As a result of such accounting valuation characteristics and guidelines, there seems to be general agreement among accountants that for public reporting purposes only purchased goodwill should be recognized in the accounts. The problem is to determine when goodwill is purchased. It is generally held that goodwill created by advertising expenditures, customer service expenditures, and the like, does not represent purchased goodwill. In one sense this is an unusual view because the avowed purpose of these expenditures is to create a favorable customer reaction which will cause customers to "return to the old stand." Thus, in a conceptual sense it appears that certain expenditures to acquire the most basic type of goodwill are not recognized as a purchase of goodwill. Failure to include this goodwill as an asset harkens back to the ultraconservative times of secret reserves and other undervaluation-of-asset methods.

Apparently, it is the measurement problem—the difficulty of assigning an objective valuation to unamortized goodwill—that caused the accounting profession to discard the constitutive concept for an operational concept of goodwill. More precisely, it appears that the inability to amortize in a systematic way the goodwill purchased by advertising and similar expenditures is the cause of the immediate charge-off of any goodwill thus created. In this context, it is inaccurate to say that advertising and similar expenditures do not represent purchased goodwill, because in a constitutive sense they undoubtedly do. More accurately, one should say that such goodwill is immediately amortized and charged off as expense so that no portion of this purchased goodwill ever appears on the balance sheet as an asset. Having no basis for an objectively measurable amortization schedule, accountants have taken a conservative view and amortized immediately as expense most advertising and other goodwill-creation expenditures. A contrary solution for the problem would involve the study of and research in amortization methods. Until that research is completed and accepted, however, it seems appropriate to think of the accounting concept of goodwill as an operational concept having meaning only by studying the way the goodwill is valued.[18]

On the other hand, the admission of a new partner for an equity in excess of the value of resources contributed is considered a partnership purchase of the personal goodwill of the new partner. It is, of course, possible to reconcile this procedure with the concept of a purchase of goodwill by contending that the admission of a new partner implies the creation of a new partnership which has the right to recognize previously unrecognized goodwill. Although the goodwill had not been purchased by the old partners, it is purchased goodwill for the new partnership.

From these considerations emerges the recognition that, by what they do, accountants assume for public reporting purposes that goodwill is purchased only when one of the following conditions prevails:

1. Upon consolidation, a payment for the shares of stock of a subsidiary different from the fair value of the net assets effectively acquired represents the purchase of goodwill (consolidated goodwill).

2. Upon partnership formation or dissolution, an equity grant in a new partnership in excess of the fair value of net assets contributed may be treated as purchased goodwill by the new partnership (partnership goodwill).

3. Upon a bundle purchase of assets representing an operating entity, a payment in excess of the sum of the fair value of the individual assets may occasionally be treated as purchased goodwill (composite assets goodwill).

Consolidated Goodwill. In the case of consolidated goodwill, the purchase concept is extended to imply that a purchase of shares of stock at a price above their book value represents the purchase of goodwill. Consistently, the reverse situation has been held to represent the "purchase" of negative goodwill (badwill). The idea underlying this view of goodwill is that the acquired stock represents a claim to assets so that on consolidation the assets may be substituted for the stock investment. If the price paid for the stock exceeds the book value of the assets substituted, the excess payment is presumed to represent a payment for goodwill. Even if the assets substituted are revalued to their fair market value on the acquisition date to represent their cost to the consolidated entity, there are many reasons why the market price of the stock will not equal the adjusted book value of the assets claimed. The difference presumedly represents the excess earning power of the acquired company and is designated as consolidated goodwill.

---

[18]For additional study of this area see Arthur L. Thomas, *The Allocation Problem in Financial Accounting Theory,* Studies in Accounting Research No. 3 American Accounting Association, Evanston, Ill., 1969, and *The Allocation Problem: Part Two,* Studies in Accounting Research No. 9, American Accounting Association, Sarasota, Fla., 1974.

Measurement of Consolidated Goodwill.   Because of the operational nature of consolidated goodwill, an illustration may best explain its nature. For this purpose, assume that Company H purchased 80 percent of the common stock of Company S for $840,000. Assume also that balance sheets of the two companies immediately after the purchase are as follows:

	Company H	Company S
Current assets	$ 460,000	$ 300,000
Investment in Company S	840,000	
Fixed assets	3,200,000	1,100,000
Total	$4,500,000	$1,400,000
Current liabilities	$ 200,000	$ 100,000
Long-term liabilities	300,000	400,000
Capital stock	3,500,000	800,000
Retained earnings	500,000	100,000
Total	$4,500,000	$1,400,000

From the traditional consolidated point of view, the $840,000 paid for 80 percent of the capital of Company S represents a payment for the assets reflecting the claims of 80 percent of the stock of Company S. That is, of the $1,400,000 of assets of Company S, $900,000 are claimed by the shareholders of Company S, and since Company H owns 80 percent of this, Company H has acquired a claim to assets of Company S having a book value of $720,000. By paying $840,000 for them, Company H has seemingly paid $120,000 for the goodwill attached to these assets. If the balance sheets of the two companies are consolidated into one, the $120,000 of goodwill would be included as one of the resources of the consolidated entity, as follows:

	Consolidated Balance Sheet, Companies H & S
Current assets	$ 760,000
Fixed assets	4,300,000
Goodwill	120,000
Total	$5,180,000
Current liabilities	$ 300,000
Long-term liabilities	700,000
Minority stockholders of Company S (20%)	180,000
Capital stock—Company H	3,500,000
Retained earnings	500,000
Total	$5,180,000

It should be noted that the $120,000 does not represent all the goodwill attached to the combined assets of Company S. At best, it represents only 80 percent of the total goodwill, but it is purchased goodwill whereas the 20 percent unrecognized portion is excluded as an asset because it is not purchased goodwill. According to traditional thinking about consolidated statements, should a determination of the fair value of the individual assets of Company S acquired indicate that $80,000 of the excess payment reflected the excess of 80 percent of the current value of individual assets over their acquisition cost to Company S, this $80,000 should be assigned to the specific assets in the consolidated balance sheet, which would leave a consolidated goodwill of $40,000.

The more modern consolidated point of view is that the $840,000 represents a payment for part of all the assets and liabilities of the subsidiary company. According to this point of view, all the individual assets and liabilities of the subsidiary should be revalued to fair value. Thus, if subsidiary liabilities were overvalued by $10,000 on the books of Company S and the 20 percent of assets not previously considered were undervalued by $20,000, this would reduce consolidated goodwill to $10,000 ($120,000 − $80,000 − 10,000 − 20,000). (If 80 percent were overvalued by $80,000, 20 percent might normally be overvalued by $20,000.) This valuation procedure is specified in APB Opinion No. 16 in the following terms:[19]

> 87. An acquiring corporation should allocate the cost of an acquired company to the assets acquired and liabilities assumed. Allocation should follow the principles described in paragraph 68.
>
> First, all identifiable assets acquired, either individually or by type, and liabilities assumed in a business combination, whether or not shown in the financial statements of the acquired company, should be assigned a portion of the cost of the acquired company, normally equal to their fair values at date of acquisition.
>
> Second, the excess of the cost of the acquired company over the sum of the amounts assigned to identifiable assets acquired less liabilities assumed should be recorded as goodwill. The sum of the market or appraisal values of identifiable assets acquired less liabilities assumed may sometimes exceed the cost of the acquired company. If so, the values otherwise assignable to noncurrent assets acquired (except long-term investments in the marketable securities) should be reduced by a proportionate part of the excess to determine the assigned values. A deferred credit for an excess of assigned value of identifiable assets over cost of an acquired company (sometimes called "negative goodwill") should not be recorded unless those assets are reduced to zero value.

Recognition of Consolidated Goodwill. The preceding discussion of two ways of measuring consolidated goodwill indicates that the meaning of consolidated goodwill requires an understanding of the way it is measured—an operational concept of consolidated goodwill. After careful consideration of the problems involved in measuring consolidated goodwill, Spacek[20] concluded that consolidated goodwill should not be recognized in consolidated statements. Spacek implies that consolidated goodwill should be charged off as soon as acquired in a manner similar to the goodwill acquired by advertising expenditures. Since these charges are ultimately absorbed in retained earnings, the implication is that a similar charge-off of goodwill would also be to retained earnings.

It should be noted that the explicit statement that purchased goodwill exists only to the extent of the excess of purchase price over the appraised fair market value of the assets and liabilities of the company acquired inserts a more subjective feature into accounting valuations than that required in valuing assets and liabilities at cost. The existence of this limited subjective feature of goodwill valuation lends support for Virgil's belief[21] that

> . . . accountants need to place greater emphasis upon the buyer's purposes which, if they materialize in negotiations with the seller, ultimately establish the basis by which the accountant determines whether goodwill has been reacquired in fact and, if so, how it should be treated in measuring and reporting income.

Partnership Goodwill. Partnership goodwill may be recognized as purchased goodwill when a new partner is admitted or an existing partner retires. The justification for recognizing partnership goodwill appears to be that either of the foregoing acts creates a new partnership. The new partnership effectively purchases all resources of the former partnership and receives any resources contributed by the new partner. Should either the former partnership or the new partner have either previously recognized or unrecognized goodwill, the payment by the new partnership for the goodwill would qualify it as purchased goodwill.

---

[19]APB Opinion No. 16, par. 87.
[20]Spacek, *op. cit.,* pp. 39–40.
[21]Robert L. Virgil, Jr., "The Purpose of the Buyer as a Guide in Accounting for Goodwill," *NAA Bulletin,* April 1963, p. 39.

Goodwill from Equity Purchase.   There are two types of actions which partners can take that will enable the accountant for the new partnership to recognize goodwill. Under the first action, the new partner can purchase and the old partners can sell part or all of the equity of an existing partner. If the sales price of old partnership equity sold is above book value, assuming assets and liabilities are valued at fair value on the date of sale, the assumption is that the old partners had previously unrecognized goodwill which should now be recognized as a purchase by the new partnership. To illustrate, if A and B are in partnership and have capitals of $70,000 and $50,000, respectively, a sale of one-third of their combined equity to C for $50,000 would imply a goodwill of $30,000 purchased by the new partnership from the old partners. That is, if C is given a one-third equity in a new partnership for $50,000, the old partners must have contributed an old partnership worth $150,000 to the new partnership. Assuming fair valuation of assets acquired and liabilities assumed, the $30,000 excess of new partnership equities granted ($150,000 − $70,000 − $50,000) would represent a payment for goodwill. It is apparent that the action necessary for this type of goodwill to come into existence is a purchase of the equity of the previous partnership. In many respects, this type of action is very similar to that taken by an acquiring corporation when it acquires the stock of a subsidiary company and pays more than book value for the entities acquired. In fact, the resulting partnership goodwill is somewhat similar in nature to consolidated goodwill. This type of partnership goodwill differs from consolidated goodwill, however, in that all goodwill of the new partnership implied by the change in partnership equities is recognized as goodwill. Although Moonitz[22] and others have advocated similar treatment for corporate consolidated goodwill, a distinction is drawn between such partnership and consolidated goodwill on the reasoning that the purchase by a parent of stock of a subsidiary does not create a new business entity, as does a partnership equity exchange. On the basis of this reasoning, only the goodwill attached to the cost of the shares acquired represents corporate consolidated goodwill.

If the one-third interest were sold to the new partner for $30,000 and assets and liabilities of the former partnership are valued at fair value, it is sometimes contended that the new partner paid $30,000 for a $30,000 equity in the old partnership and also invested his personal goodwill of $15,000. This would result in a total partnership equity for the new partnership of $135,000, of which $90,000 would belong to the old partners and $45,000 to the new partner. Practically, however, this method of valuing goodwill is seldom used.

In the main, this type of goodwill is typically amortized immediately by using an accounting method known as the "bonus" procedure for admitting a new partner. Under this procedure no goodwill is recognized in the accounting records, and the records merely record the change in partnership equities for the new partnership, giving no record of the price for which the equity was sold.

Goodwill from Investment in Partnership.   The second type of action a partner can take that will enable partnership goodwill to be recognized is to invest resources in the partnership. Should he receive in return a partnership equity greater than the tangible resources invested, the assumption is that he must have contributed goodwill. Normally, before this goodwill is recognized, the tangible and other intangible assets of the new partnership are valued at fair market value. This is necessary to avoid recognizing watered partnership equities—equities having no asset values to support them. After revaluation of assets to fair market value, if the equity received by the new partner exceeds his investment, partnership goodwill is recognized. On the contrary, if the new partner invests more than the tangible

[22]Maurice Moonitz, *The Entity Theory of Consolidated Statements,* The Foundation Press, Brooklyn, N.Y., 1951.

equity credit received, the assumption is that the old partners have unrecognized goodwill which should be recognized as partnership goodwill so that the new partner can receive an equity credit equal to his investment. Like the other type of partnership goodwill, there is a tendency to amortize this type of goodwill immediately at the time the new partnership is formed by the use of the bonus procedure.

Because accounting literature typically does not point out that the use of the bonus procedure effectively involves an immediate write-off of goodwill arising when the partnership is formed, it may be appropriate to illustrate this fact. Assume that the partnership of A and B has tangible assets valued at fair market value of $120,000, no liabilities, and capital of $70,000 and $50,000, respectively. If C is admitted to one-third interest in the partnership by investing $70,000, the implication is that A and B have a combined equity of $140,000, including goodwill of $20,000. Under the bonus procedure, however, the goodwill would be charged off to the partners in their income- and loss-sharing ratios, which is assumed in the illustration to be equal. The result would be total assets of $190,000 in the new partnership, in which C would have an equity of $63,333. Thus, C would have given a bonus of $6,667 to A and B; therefore, their capitals in the new partnership would be $73,333 and $53,334, respectively. In numerical terms, the new partnership balance sheets under these three methods are shown in Exhibit 1.

EXHIBIT 1 Various Methods of Recording Entry of New Partners to Partnership

	Goodwill recognized, not amortized	Goodwill recognized, amortized immediately	Bonus procedure used
Tangible assets...............	$190,000	$190,000	$190,000
Goodwill.....................	20,000	—	—
Total assets................	$210,000	$190,000	$190,000
A, Capital....................	$ 80,000	$ 73,333	$ 73,333
B, Capital....................	60,000	53,334	53,334
C, Capital....................	70,000	63,333	63,333
Total equities...............	$210,000	$190,000	$190,000

In summary, assuming all tangible and other intangible assets are valued at fair market value, partnership goodwill which arises at the time a new partner is admitted may be valued according to formulas well described by Sterling[23] as follows:

Definition of symbols:

C = total capital in the old partnership
f = new partner's fractional share of capital of new partnership
I = total assets given up by new partner
G_1 = goodwill brought in by new partner
G_2 = goodwill of old partnership

If the new partner purchased an interest from the old partners:

$$G_2 = \frac{I}{f} - C \quad \text{(if negative, assets are overvalued)}$$

[23]Robert R. Sterling, "Determination of Goodwill and Bonus on the Admission of a Partner," *The Accounting Review,* vol. 37, pp. 766–768, October 1962.

If the new partner invests in the partnership, goodwill is the positive result of one of these two formulas:

$$G_1 = \left(\frac{C}{1-f}\right) - (C+I)$$

$$G_2 = \left(\frac{I}{f}\right) - (C+I)$$

Any partnership goodwill may be amortized immediately by the use of the bonus procedure for recording the admission of a new partner. In a similar manner, goodwill recognized at the time a partner withdraws may be written off by the absorption process into the capital accounts of the remaining partners.

Composite Assets Goodwill.   Occasionally, a firm will purchase not the equity of another firm but only its assets, in total or in part. To the extent that the assets acquired represent an operating economic entity, it is possible for the payment for the combined assets to exceed the sum of the fair market value of the individual assets. Conceptually, this excess payment seems to have characteristics of purchased goodwill and could be recognized as such. The more usual accounting treatment, however, is to treat the purchase as a bundle of tangible assets and apply allocation procedures to apportion the total cost to the individual assets on a reasonable basis. The effect of this procedure, if indeed goodwill is actually included in the purchase, is to classify purchased goodwill as a part of separate assets and not recognize it as a distinct asset. This does not result in an immediate write-off of the goodwill, but, allocated to various assets, any such goodwill would be amortized variously according to the lives of the related assets to which it is assigned.

Valuation of "Excess" Future Earnings.   Catlett and Olson[24] suggest six characteristics which can be used to distinguish goodwill from other assets in a business, as follows:

1. *The value of goodwill has no reliable and predictable relationship to costs which may have been incurred in its creation.* Some goodwill values may be created by expenditures which are absorbed as operating charges by the company; many favorable conditions and factors result without expenditures or efforts by a company.

2. *The intangible factors which may contribute to goodwill cannot be individually valued.* All of the various intangible factors which are favorable to a business as a whole contribute to the value of goodwill, but none of them, individually, is susceptible to the type of measurement that can be applied to a business's resources and property rights whose values exist apart from the business as a whole. Likewise, no valid bases exist for allocating costs to the intangible factors.

3. *Goodwill attaches only to a business as a whole.* Goodwill does not exist as a value apart from other assets. It is an inseparable part of a business or from a clearly delineated segment of a business.

4. *The value of goodwill may, and does, fluctuate suddenly and widely because of the innumerable factors which influence that value.* Factors affect both earning power and investor opinion about earning power. The value of goodwill does not have the general stability possessed by the value of most resources and property rights used in the production of profits.

5. *Goodwill is not utilized or consumed in the normal sense in the production of profits.* Rather, goodwill is the result of profits, or the expectation of them, and its value is a measure of the expectations.

6. *Goodwill appears to be an element of value which runs directly to the investor or owner in a business enterprise.* Only investors or owners establish value of a business taken as a whole and thereby of its goodwill.

[24] *ARS 10*, pp. 20–21.

Underlying these characteristics is the notion that goodwill exists whether or not it is recorded. Thus, it is proper to speak of recorded and unrecorded goodwill. While only purchased goodwill is recognized in the accounts, there may be many occassions which call for the calculation of total goodwill, recorded and unrecorded. For example, such a valuation is helpful in estimating a suitable sales price for a business as a going concern.

Conceptually, there appears to be considerable theoretical support and practical acceptance of the view that the goodwill of an entity is the present value of the "excess" future earnings (the superprofits) of the business. But the meaning of excess earnings is not clear. If it means the difference between the earnings of the business and the amount the earnings would have been had the business pursued its next best alternatives, excess earnings will normally always exist. If excess earnings refers to the excess earnings over those which would have been obtained by summing the individual earnings if assets were used as separate entities, the notion of goodwill as the result of the organization of resources is supported. The excess earnings are due to the organization. But this view of excess is not realistic, because many individual assets have no individual earning capacity except as an integral part of the entire business, which may carry the implication that substantially all earnings are excess and due to goodwill.

Although not precise, the general notion is that excess earnings means the earnings over and above those earned by similar businesses. The earnings of similar businesses may be and normally are in excess of the earnings which would accrue to the individual assets used independent of an organized business. By similar businesses is meant businesses in the same industry undergoing the same elements of risk and uncertainty. In measuring such excess earnings, adjustments would have to be made for the use of different accounting procedures and for different financial structures so that both earnings and risks are comparable among the similar businesses. In this sense, the excess earnings or superprofits which reflect the existence of goodwill are relative to earnings of other businesses. As a result, if the other businesses were to increase earnings, the company having goodwill might find its goodwill decreased in value because of the relative increase in the earnings of competitors in similar businesses even though the company's absolute earnings remain unchanged. Excess earnings would have decreased.

Since the price to be paid for goodwill is a payment for anticipated future excess earnings, there has to be a way to reduce these future excess or superprofits to their present value. The basic formula for the computation of such goodwill is:[25]

$$G = \left(\frac{D - rC}{j}\right)$$

where D = expected future perpetual annual dividend
$\quad r$ = constant annual rate of return typically earned in the industry perpetually
$\quad C$ = value of the capital of the business
$\quad j$ = perpetual annual rate of return to be earned on the goodwill

[25]Theoretically, this formula might be refined and expressed in present value terms as

$$G = \sum_{i=1}^{\infty} \frac{D_i - r_i C_i}{(1 + j_i)^i}$$

where D_i represents the annual dividend in period i
$\quad r_i$ represents the annual rate of return typically expected to be earned in the industry in period i
$\quad C_i$ represents the value of the capital of the business at the beginning of period i
$\quad j_i$ represents the annual rate of return to be earned on goodwill in period i

Thus, if a company pays an annual dividend of $60,000, has a capital of $500,000, wants to earn 20 percent a year on goodwill, and operates in an industry where the typical rate of return is 10 percent a year, the goodwill would be $50,000, computed as follows:

$$G = \left(\frac{D - rC}{j} \right) = \frac{60,000 - .10(500,000)}{.20} = \frac{10,000}{.2} = \$50,000$$

Practically, however, D, r, C, and j may fluctuate widely over the life of the business. The point is that D, r, C, and j can at best be only crudely estimated amounts. Furthermore, capital, C, may refer to the total tangible assets of the business valued at sales price, replacement cost, or on some other basis, or it may refer only to the common stockholders' equity. Thus, any calculation of the value of goodwill by the basic superprofit formula must be considered a rather rough estimate of goodwill.

Modifications of the basic formula, however, may provide a somewhat more realistic change of values for the goodwill of the business. For example, goodwill may be measured as the present value of the average of the high and low estimates of D, r, C, and j by years for various possible lives of the business. Such an approach for valuing goodwill as a range of values, whether or not supported by probability measures of each value, is more realistic as a measure of goodwill than such frequently used methods as multiplying excess earnings by an arbitrary number of years, typically three to five. But it is still a subjective estimate and appears to have rather limited support in law and business practice.

Purchase Price of Goodwill.   Restricting recorded goodwill to that which is purchased, however a purchase is defined, does not solve the problem of its valuation. This is particularly true when payment is made in noncash form. Thus, when goodwill is purchased by issuing shares of stock, the determination of the purchase price may be difficult. Also, the form in which payment is made may influence the purchase price. For example, income tax regulations may make one form of payment more desirable than another. This situation is no different from purchases of assets under different terms of payment; in general, the principles applicable for determining the acquisition cost price of any asset apply to goodwill. Catlett and Olson[26] point out that at times the purchase price "may be determined from the computations and records on which the purchase negotiations are based or from opinions of persons competent in making value determinations if the evidence from the negotiations is not clear."

Because goodwill is not purchased as a separate asset but as a part of a bundle purchase of assets and liabilities, its cost can seldom be determined in a direct manner. In any event, however, the starting point for determining the price or cost of purchased goodwill is the cost of the composite purchase of assets and liabilities of a going concern. If cash is paid, the cost of the assets in the composite purchase is equal to the cash paid plus any liabilities assumed. In determining the value of the liabilities assumed, it is customary to accept their book value as the appropriate amount. More accurately, however, the liabilities should be priced at their current value on the date of the acquisition. The current value of the liabilities might be above or below their book value because of changes, subsequent to the date the liabilities were incurred, in interest rates generally or because of a change in the credit rating of the borrowing company.

Where payment is in the form of noncash consideration, the cost of the acquisition is the fair value of the consideration given. By fair value, as used in this sense, is normally meant the sales price of the consideration given. Where such

[26]ARS 10, p. 76.

sales price is not readily determinable, the fair value of the consideration received may be used as the cost of the acquisition. In this situation, fair value refers to the purchase price of the consideration received. The assumption may be made that the sales price of the consideration given and the purchase price of the consideration received represent an equality. This concept of the quality of the value of the resources exchanged has led to the general principle of valuing acquisitions at the fair value of the consideration given or the fair value of the consideration received, whichever is more objectively determinable. APB Opinion No. 29 states:[27]

> . . . accounting for nonmonetary transactions should be based on the fair values of the assets (or services) involved. . . . Thus the cost of a nonmonetary asset acquired in exchange for another nonmonetary asset is the fair value of the asset surrendered to obtain it. . . . The fair value of the asset received should be used to measure the cost if it is more clearly evident than the fair value of the asset surrendered.

Since goodwill is purchased as part of a composite purchase of tangible and intangible assets for one lump sum, its cost must be determined by an allocation procedure, and the share of the total cost allocated to goodwill is frequently the residual amount. That is, a value is determined for the other assets, and any residual balance is treated as the cost of goodwill. This process has been used extensively in valuing consolidated goodwill. Because this procedure, in the case of consolidated goodwill, frequently results in a very large goodwill valuation, the concept of a pooling of interests was introduced into accounting procedures. It had the desirable effect of not placing a large valuation on consolidated goodwill relative to the other assets of the consolidated entity because no goodwill is recognized under the pooling procedure. On the other hand, the pooling procedure has the undesirable feature of implying that something has occurred which has not, since the evidence that Wyatt[28] and many others have collected is that most business combinations are in economic reality purchase transactions and not poolings of interest.

AMORTIZATION OF GOODWILL

Having established the initial purchase price as the basis for recognizing acquired goodwill, the accounting treatment of this cost has, in the past, varied from an immediate write-off to retained earnings to continuous retention of the goodwill as an asset. In between the two extremes there have been a variety of different amortization schemes. APB Opinion No. 17 (superseding *ARB No. 43*, Chapter 5, and APB Opinion No. 6, Paragraph 15), sets forth the AICPA position on amortization of goodwill.

In essence, APB Opinion No. 17 states that goodwill is to be considered to have a limited life.[29] The limit of that useful life is the period estimated to be benefited up to a maximum of forty (40) years. However, Accounting Principles Board Opinions were not applied retroactively. Thus Paragraph 33 of Opinion No. 17 specifies that only intangibles (goodwill) acquired after October 31, 1970, must be amortized. Goodwill acquired prior to that date need not be amortized unless it becomes reasonably certain that the asset has become worthless. Recent issues of *Accounting Trends and Techniques* report[30] that of companies amortizing goodwill, about 40 percent disclosed an amortization period of less than forty

---

[27]APB Opinion No. 29, par. 18.
[28]ARS 5, "A Critical Study of Accounting for Business Combinations," AICPA, New York, 1963.
[29]APB Opinion No. 17, "Intangible Assets," AICPA, New York, 1970, pars. 27–29.
[30]AICPA, *Accounting Trends & Techniques*, New York.

years, about 45 percent disclosed an amortization period of forty years, about 5 percent disclosed an amortization period of legal or estimated life, and the remainder did not disclose a time period.

Factors to be considered in determining the useful life of an intangible asset include:[31]

1. Legal or regulatory provisions.
2. Provisions whereby the asset may be renewed or extended.
3. Economic factors such as obsolescence, demand, or competition.
4. Any relationships of the intangible with an individual or group of employees may cause the useful life of the intangible to follow the service life of those personnel.
5. Expected actions of others in the market place.
6. Useful life may appear indefinite and benefits not readily determinable.
7. A given intangible (such as goodwill) may be a composite of many assets with varying useful lives which may create difficulty in establishing a single life estimate to be used.

APB Opinion No. 17, following the lead of *ARB No. 43,* provides that regular charges for the amortization of goodwill should be made to income. *ARB No. 43* provided[32] that if the amount of a single charge-off is so material that it might distort earnings for the year, the charge should be made to retained earnings. APB Opinion No. 9 amended this to say that such material charges arising from unusual events of the period should be reported as extraordinary charges to income of the period. APB Opinion No. 30 superseded this section of Opinion No. 9 and specifies[33] that "write-down or write-off of . . . deferred research and development costs, or other intangible assets [presumably including goodwill] should not be reported as extraordinary items."

APB Opinion No. 17 specifically disallows lump-sum write-offs of goodwill to retained earnings immediately after acquisition. Despite this prohibition, proposals for immediate charge-off have been made. They are supported basically by the difficulty of the measurement problem involved in amortization and the effort to maintain consistency with the procedures used in accounting for internally created goodwill. Chambers, however, has taken the position that the goodwill should be written off immediately because it is an asset of the owners and not an asset of the entity. He states:[34]

> To regard goodwill as an asset of a going concern is to confuse two entities—the constituents as persons and the firm as an instrument. If the constituents accept an offer for a going concern in excess of the current cash equivalent of its capital, the difference is simply a gain to them. It arises only when the firm ceases to be the same firm by becoming the instrument of a new group of constituents. The new constituents, having laid out a sum in excess of the current cash equivalent of the old firm's components, may regard the advantage acquired as an asset of the new firm. But this excess, though represented by a money payment, is no different from the amount by which the subjective valuation of any single asset exceeds the price paid for it; and no such excess is regarded as part of the current cash equivalent of an asset. That cash has been paid may be recognized in the record; but its effect is in no way to increase the adaptability of the firm, and the indicated treatment of it is to reduce the amount of the residual equity from the price paid to the current cash equivalent of the new firm's component assets and liabilities.

[31]APB Opinion No. 17, par. 27.
[32]*ARB No. 43,* chap. 5, par. 8.
[33]APB Opinion No. 30, par. 23.
[34]Raymond J. Chambers, *Accounting, Evaluation and Economic Behavior,* Prentice-Hall, Englewood Cliffs, N.J., 1966, p. 211.

The main argument for nonamortization and continuous reporting of the purchased goodwill apparently rests on the assumption that the superior earning power which caused the goodwill to come into being will be retained through normal managerial activities. Since these managerial actions will retain goodwill indefinitely, the argument goes, the purchased goodwill should not be amortized. A secondary argument supporting nonamortization is that without evidence that the purchased goodwill has been used up in some way or that its value has decreased, any arbitrary write-off of goodwill is unrealistic and may distort the income measurement.

The argument for systematic amortization is that the cost of the goodwill is an expense of the superior earnings purchased and should be amortized accordingly. Dyckman[35] explains this reasoning in the following terms:

> If goodwill is to be amortized, the amortization method might logically be related to the process employed in valuing the superior earnings. Since this process involves interest calculations, one of the interest methods . . . would be appropriate.

The AICPA position, through APB Opinion No. 17, calls for the application of straight-line amortization to the write-off of goodwill unless it is possible to demonstrate a more appropriate method. Disclosure of the method and period of amortization is required.

Additionally, APB Opinion No. 17 states:[36]

> Amortization of acquired goodwill and of other acquired intangible assets not deductible in computing income taxes payable does not create a timing difference, and allocation of income taxes is inappropriate.

The income tax regulations which allow no deduction for amortized goodwill in computing taxable income tend to encourage the classification of acquired goodwill as a cost of tangible assets where a depreciation expense can be taken as a deduction for income tax purposes. This seems to create inequities and inconsistencies in amortizing purchased goodwill.

In reaction to many measurement problems involved in determining the cost of goodwill acquired, particularly the goodwill created by advertising and other internal efforts, and in amortizing such cost in a realistic manner, Catlett and Olson propose that the cost of purchased consolidated goodwill be treated as a reduction of the stockholders' equity in the consolidated entity. They reason that the amount paid for consolidated goodwill really represents an advance payment to stockholders of anticipated earnings. That is, the payment for goodwill is in reality a distribution of anticipated future earnings and should, therefore, like any distribution of earnings, be treated as a reduction of stockholders' equity. One might question the validity of this argument on the ground that the payment made for any asset is in reality a payment for the future receipts which the asset will provide. Therefore, any purchase of shares from a shareholder represents a payment for anticipated future receipts, whether that asset is goodwill or a tangible asset of any type. But Catlett and Olson[37] support their conclusions forcefully as follows:

> If goodwill is accounted for as a reduction in stockholders' equity, the balance sheet would provide, with the limitation of the cost basis, information regarding values of the separable resources and property rights of the continuing business—an objective of the balance sheet. That information would not be confused, as it would be by injecting the

---

[35]Thomas R. Dyckman, *Long-Lived Assets,* Wadsworth Publishing Co., Belmont, Calif., 1967, p. 109.
[36]APB Opinion No. 17, par. 30.
[37]*ARS 10,* pp. 90–91.

particular goodwill value of a segment of the business at a point in time—a value which no longer exists except perhaps, as a part of the overall goodwill value of the business. Similarly, the record of earnings of the business, an important yardstick which investors use in assessing the value of the business as a whole, would not be affected by amortization of that very value.

Accounting for goodwill as a reduction in stockholders' equity is superior to alternative methods of accounting for goodwill in several respects. The deficiencies of the present "nonaccounting" for goodwill which accompany the pooling of interest method are eliminated since the value of the goodwill evidenced by the business combination would be recognized and accounted for. Further, the accounting accorded the goodwill would be disclosed.

It should be noted that the Catlett and Olson recommendation arose from their consideration of consolidated goodwill. If applied to partnership accounting, it apparently would require the use of the bonus procedure rather than the goodwill procedure for recording the admission or withdrawal of a partner.

REPORTING OF GOODWILL

Of the two broad categories of goodwill—recorded and unrecorded goodwill—there seems little accounting support for efforts to report or disclose unrecorded goodwill. Occasional footnote references to unrecorded goodwill may be found in annual reports, but the general accounting policy seems to be that unrecorded goodwill need not be reported.

As to recorded goodwill, there seems to be general accounting acceptance of the notion that goodwill is a special type of asset and should be separated from other assets. It is probably the most intangible of the recognized intangible assets. When presented on the balance sheet, it frequently appears as the last item in the list of assets of the reporting entity. Also, many firms present it only as a nominal value, typically $1, to call attention to its existence. But there is strong support for the view that recognized goodwill should be reported in some way. Catlett and Olson, for example, suggest:[38]

> The reporting of purchased goodwill as a reduction of stockholders' equity can be accomplished by either of two methods: (a) by an immediate direct write-off of goodwill to a stockholders' equity account, such as capital surplus or retained earnings, or (b) by reporting goodwill as a deduction from stockholders' equity in the face of the balance sheet. A direct write-off would avoid showing a goodwill amount in the financial statements (although amounts could be disclosed in notes), while the second method would continue to report the goodwill amount in the financial statements.

Concerning goodwill of an acquired company in a combination, APB Opinion No. 16[39] states, "An acquiring corporation should not record as a separate asset the goodwill previously recorded by an acquired company. . . ."

Recent issues of *Accounting Trends and Techniques*[40] indicated that, of the instances of recognized goodwill reported, approximately 1 percent wrote it down to a nominal value, typically $1; 49 percent were in the process of amortizing it; 47 percent still carried it at an unamortized value; and in 2 percent of the cases the accounting valuations was "not determinable." Presumably all of the cases where goodwill was still carried at an unamortized value were instances of goodwill acquired prior to November 1, 1970, since APB Opinion No. 17 exempts such goodwill from the need for amortization.[41]

---

[38]*Ibid.*, p. 92.
[39]APB Opinion No. 16, par. 88.
[40]*Accounting Trends & Techniques, op. cit.*
[41]APB Opinion No. 17, par. 33.

BIBLIOGRAPHY

Accounting Principles Board: "Business Combinations," Opinion No. 16, AICPA, New York, 1970.

————: "Intangible Assets," Opinion No. 17, AICPA, New York, 1970.

————: "Reporting the Results of Operations," Opinion No. 30, AICPA, New York, 1973.

American Institute of Certified Public Accountants: "Accounting for Goodwill," *Accounting Research Study 10*, AICPA, New York, 1968.

Chambers, Raymond J.: *Accounting, Evaluation and Economic Behavior*, Prentice-Hall, Englewood Cliffs, N.J., 1966.

Edey, H. C.: "Business Valuation, Goodwill and the Super-Profit Method," in W. T. Baxter and Sidney Davidson (eds.), *Studies in Accounting Theory*, Richard D. Irwin, Homewood, Ill., 1962.

Edwards, Edgar O., and Philip W. Bell: *The Theory and Measurement of Business Income*, University of California Press, Berkeley, Calif., 1961.

Preinreich, Gabriel A. D.: "The Law of Goodwill," *The Accounting Review*, vol. 11, December 1936.

Spacek, Leonard: "The Treatment of Goodwill in the Corporate Balance Sheet," *Journal of Accountancy*, vol. 117, February 1964.

Sterling, Robert R.: "Determination of Goodwill and Bonus on Admission of a Partner," *The Accounting Review*, vol. 37, October 1962.

Yang, J. M.: *Goodwill and Other Intangibles*, The Ronald Press Company, New York, 1927.

Chapter **22**

Other Intangibles

ALLAN R. DREBIN
Professor of Accounting and Information Systems, Northwestern
University

DEFINITION

Intangible assets are items which possess economic value but lack physical substance. Their value is often dependent upon other business factors and is subject to considerable uncertainty. In many instances such assets have value only in the context of a particular business, and therefore cannot be transferred to another organization. Because of the uncertainty surrounding the valuation of these items, they are frequently ignored by financial analysts and recognized at only a nominal amount in the accounting statements. Yet such assets could represent significant economic resources to a company.

For an asset to be classified by accountants as an intangible asset, it is necessary that it lack physical substance, but this is not a sufficient condition for placing an asset in this category. Items such as bank deposits, accounts receivable, and investment securities, which represent claims to wealth rather than physical properties, are all considered to be "tangible" assets by accountants.

Nor is the lack of certainty with respect to value a characteristic unique to intangibles. Physical, tangible assets such as land and equipment could have their economic values affected by many unpredictable factors such as the location of a highway or the invention of a new process.

Although the combination of both factors—lack of physical substance and uncertainty of value—does seem to distinguish intangible assets, they are usually defined by enumeration. Hatfield[1] defined them in this manner many years ago:

> Intangible assets are defined as meaning patents, copyrights, secret processes and formulas, goodwill, trademarks, trade brands, franchises and other like property. The phrase is not particularly appropriate and, except by enumeration, the separation between tangible and intangible assets is not easily made. Accounts receivable are considered tangible assets, although literally there is nothing tangible about them. Real estate is considered typically tangible, a franchise intangible. But there is no real difference between them as regards tangibility, materiality, or realness. . . . While the term intangible assets is without etymological significance, it is still of use as a collective term, in general embracing the items given in the definition just quoted.

The definition is as accurate today as when it was written.

Goodwill is discussed in detail in Chapter 21. Leaseholds, which are often considered in the intangibles category, are discussed in Chapter 25. This chapter will focus on the other items in the intangibles classification.

ASSET RECOGNITION

Purchase Versus Development.   Intangible resources may be purchased from others or developed internally by a company. Although purchased intangibles are generally recorded as assets, self-developed intangibles are not. The Accounting Principles Board concluded that "a company should record as assets the costs of intangible assets acquired from other enterprises or individuals."[2] On the other hand, the APB concluded that, "costs of developing, maintaining, or restoring intangible assets which are not specifically identifiable, have indeterminate lives or are inherent in a continuing business and related to an enterprise as a whole—such as goodwill—should be deducted from income when incurred."[3] The Financial Accounting Standards Board has continued to support this point of view. In one of its first pronouncements, concerning the treatment of research and development costs, the FASB stated: "All research and development costs encompassed

---

[1]Henry Rand Hatfield, *Accounting: Its Principles and Problems, 1,* D. Appleton and Company, New York, 1927, p. iii.

[2]Accounting Principles Board, Opinion No. 17, par. 24.

[3]*Ibid.*

by this statement shall be charged to expense when incurred."[4] Although the scope of that statement was limited to research and development expenditures, one may infer that the FASB would apply the same reasoning to other intangible costs and reach a similar conclusion.

With respect to purchased intangibles, the FASB has continued to support the inclusion of these items in the asset category. In the same pronouncement the FASB is careful to make this distinction: "The costs of intangibles that are purchased from others for use in research and development activities and that have alternative future uses (in research and development projects or otherwise) shall be capitalized and amortized as intangible assets in accordance with APB Opinion No. 17. . . . However, the costs of intangibles that are purchased from others for a particular research and development project and that have no alternative future uses (in other research and development projects or otherwise) and therefore no separate economic values are research and development costs at the time the costs are incurred."[5]

With regard to purchased intangibles, APB Opinion No. 17 stated:[6]

> Intangible assets recorded singly should be recorded at cost at date of acquisition. . . . Intangible assets acquired as part of a group of assets or as part of an acquired company should also be recorded at cost at date of acquisition.

Concerning valuation at the acquisition date, APB Opinion No. 17 continues:[7]

> Cost is measured by the amount of cash disbursed, the fair value of other assets distributed, the present value of amounts to be paid for liabilities incurred, or the fair value . . . for stock issued.

The argument for omitting self-developed intangibles from the asset classification was advanced by J. M. Yang many years ago:[8]

> While it is recognized that the validity of the book values of typical tangible assets, particularly specialized fixed assets, depends in considerable degree upon the presence of *earning power,* most of the tangible assets have some market value apart from their use in the business, whereas the intangibles have as a rule no economic significance except in terms of the going concern as a whole. Further, the tangible assets are in general more determinate in amount, stable in value, and realizable than the intangibles. These considerations make the general measurement and accounting recognition of intangibles, where not specifically purchased, impracticable.

Because purchased intangibles are included as assets, while nonpurchased intangibles usually are not, a double standard for asset recognition exists, which makes comparisons among firms very difficult. Suppose, for example, that Company A has developed a patent as a result of its own research efforts. The patent would not be shown as an asset in the accounting statements of Company A. However, if Company A were to sell the patent to Company B for $100,000 cash, Company B would recognize the patent initially at its cost to that company, $100,000. Even though the patent remains unchanged, its transfer from the original owner to a new owner for a well-defined consideration gives rise to the recognition of an asset whereas none had been recognized before.

Cost Deferral. Although valuable intangible resources developed in the course of business are not generally recognized as assets, costs of certain activities such as research and development had sometimes been capitalized and treated as assets.

[4]Financial Accounting Standards Board, Statement of Financial Accounting Standards No. 2—*Accounting for Research and Development Costs,* par. 12.
[5]*Ibid.,* par. 11.
[6]APB Opinion No. 17, pars. 25 and 26.
[7]*Ibid.,* par. 25.
[8]J. M. Yang, *Goodwill and Other Intangibles,* The Ronald Press Company, New York, 1927.

The distinction between the separate concepts of deferring the costs of activities whose benefits are expected in future periods, and of recognizing the existence of a valuable resource should be noted.

The cost deferral concept emphasizes income determination and is directly related to the accepted definition of accounting income. The determination of accounting income is based on the process of matching costs with the revenues to which they relate. When costs are incurred which are expected to benefit revenues of future periods, they may be deferred until the time when they may be "matched" with the related revenues to determine income. The asset classification of the balance sheet is thus viewed as an array of costs awaiting final disposition through periodic charges against revenues, rather than as an inventory of resources owned by a company.

The relationship between the costs of activities which may be classified as intangibles and the subsequent production of revenues is not clear-cut, however. With items such as merchandise, it may be possible to trace the accumulation of costs through to the ultimate production of revenues. But activities such as research and development merely provide an increased potential for earning revenue with no assurance that any favorable results will be obtained.

The deferring of costs, while not explicitly recognizing economic value, also implies the existence of future benefits which are the essence of asset value. Under the heading "Conversions," the American Accounting Association Committee to Prepare a Statement of Basic Accounting Theory concluded:[9]

> A conversion is a recombination of asset services reflecting the production of new utility. Expenditures and other costs devoted to such activities as research and development, personnel recruitment and training, and marketing campaigns often involve an element of future usefulness and are examples of conversions that would be recognized if quantifiable and verifiable. Present practice recognizes such costs as assets and hence as conversion of cash and services to new asset status only when a physical product or such a legal privilege as a patent results. When practice refuses to recognize the conversion to asset status by assigning a zero value to the asset it assigns all the expenditure to the expense category, thus presenting an expense that is equally unverifiable as deserving expense status. This result is somewhat curious in view of a popular emphasis upon the income statement but understandable in terms of the tendency to conservatism in asset valuation. Relevance demands that the best available techniques for allocating these expenditures to asset and expense categories should be utilized. Decision models used by management are becoming more explicit and should be availed of for this purpose. Studies that quantify the future benefits of advertising and of research expenditures are becoming more prevalent, and where applicable should be used.

Although deferral of research and development costs through capitalization as intangible assets had become an accepted practice, the FASB statement requiring all such costs to be charged to expense when incurred essentially eliminates this alternative in published financial statements. The FASB statement became effective for fiscal years beginning on or after January 1, 1975, but must also be applied retroactively through prior period adjustment whenever financial statements for periods before the effective date are presented.

In arriving at their conclusion, the FASB considered four alternative methods of accounting for research and development costs:[10]

    a. Charge all costs to expense when incurred.

    b. Capitalize all costs when incurred.

    c. Capitalize costs when incurred if specified conditions are fulfilled and charge all other costs to expense.

---

[9]Committee to Prepare a Statement of Basic Accounting Theory, *A Statement of Basic Accounting Theory*, American Accounting Association, Evanston, Ill., 1966, pp. 35–36.

[10]FASB, *op cit.*, appendix B.

d. Accumulate all costs in a special category until the existence of future benefits can be determined.

In selecting the first alternative, the FASB cited the uncertainty of future benefits, the lack of causal relationship between expenditures and benefits, the fact that future benefits cannot be measured objectively, and the feeling that allocation of these expenses to several accounting periods "is considered to serve no useful purpose."[11]

The FASB apparently did not consider a market value approach. Rather than carrying costs forward to be matched against revenues of appropriate periods, an attempt could be made to show the values of resources owned by a company, regardless of their source. Such values would provide relevant information on the company's financial position, and changes in market values could adequately reflect the economic progress of the company. In the case of purchased intangibles, cost may be regarded as evidence of market value at the time of acquisition. With developed intangibles, however, there is likely to be little or no relationship between cost and market value. Nevertheless, there has been very little support among practicing accountants for the concept of showing intangibles (or anything else except perhaps marketable securities) at their estimated market values. The generally accepted procedure is to record purchased intangibles initially at cost, whereas self-developed intangibles are not shown on the balance sheet at all.

Determination of Cost. If cost is to be used as the basis for recording intangible assets, the cost of these items must be determined. At first it might seem as if this were a simple matter—the cost of an item is the amount paid to acquire it, which should be readily determinable. In the case of intangibles, however, even purchased intangibles, there are several complexities which could arise.

In *Accounting Research Study No. 7,* Paul Grady states:[12]

> All expenditures incident to the acquisition of an intangible asset are part of its cost. In addition to the price paid to a seller, cost of an intangible may include government fees, attorney's fees and expenses, experiment and development costs, assignment costs (where royalty and license agreements have been assigned for a consideration) and other expenditures directly identifiable with their acquisition. For example, legal and other expenses of successfully defending against an interference suit in Patent Office proceedings are part of the cost of acquiring a patent.

A special problem arises in the case of intangibles acquired upon corporate formation in exchange for stock for which a market value is not readily determinable. Occasionally this situation has been used to deceive, through recording the intangible asset on the basis of par value of the stock, which may be much in excess of its market value.

In a landmark case, the Securities and Exchange Commission[13] ruled that par or stated value of stock given in exchange for intangibles cannot be used as the basis for evaluating the acquired asset. The case concerned Thomascolor, Incorporated, whose registration statement contained a balance sheet in which the following item was included:

> Patents and Patent Applications (representing the amounts of such assets as carried on the books of predecessor interests plus the excess of the stated value of common stock issued therefore over the net assets acquired as shown by the books of such predecessor interests)—(Note 2) $2,014,941.03

---

[11]*Ibid.*

[12]Paul Grady, "Inventory of Generally Accepted Accounting Principles for Business Enterprises," *Accounting Research Study No. 7,* AICPA, New York, 1966, p. 261.

[13]U.S. Securities and Exchange Commission, *Accounting Series No. 73,* Washington, D.C., 1952.

Note 2 read as follows:

The amount of $2,014,941.03 at which the item "Patents and Patent Applications" is carried in the above balance sheet represents the valuation of such patents and patent applications by the Directors and is based upon the par value of the 579,800 shares of Class A Stock of $5 par value less 81,377²⁷⁄₄₉ shares returned to treasury and on 10 cents per share for the 100,000 shares Class B issued therefor with adjustments for other assets acquired and liabilities assumed.

The SEC disallowed this approach, ruling as follows:[14]

The entering of the assets acquired by Thomascolor at an amount equal to the par or stated value of the stock issued for the purpose of acquiring them was essentially an arbitrary procedure. The Thomascolor shares had not been traded in and there was no standard by which their actual value could be judged. It was impossible to value the intangibles acquired, particularly in view of the long history of failure despite the expenditure of substantial sums. Obviously the amount ascribed to patents and patent applications was merely a balancing figure, substantially in excess of the total of the amounts of intangibles in the books of the predecessors, and had no relation to actual values. . . .

Respondents urge that the recording of the assets in an amount equal to the par and stated value of the stock issued for the purpose of acquiring them is an accepted and proper accounting practice where the amount of stock issued is not arbitrarily fixed, but is arrived at on some rational basis. They argue that there are in this case substantial "elements" or "indicia" of arm's-length bargaining sufficient to permit the acceptance of an amount equal to the par and stated value of the stock issued. Respondents' position is in effect that where stock is issued in a series of transactions, some of which are concededly not the result of arm's-length negotiation, a figure based on the aggregate par and stated value of the stock so issued can be sustained in its entirety if part of the transactions contain elements of arm's-length dealing. We cannot accept respondents' view.

Determination of Value.   Although cost is the generally accepted procedure for recording intangible assets, there are instances in which it is important to establish the economic value of such an item. For example, *ARB No. 43*, in considering the accounting treatment of intangibles, referred to "their write-down or write-off at some later time where there is a substantial and permanent decline in the value of such assets."[15] This notion was carried over into APB Opinion No. 17 (which superseded the intangibles chapter of *ARB No. 43*), which states: "Estimation of value and future benefits of an intangible asset may indicate that the unamortized cost should be reduced significantly by a deduction in determining net income."[16] This implies that the value of intangibles must be determined in order to permit a write-down, although it does not suggest the writing up of these assets when their values are found to be in excess of cost.

Except for recently acquired purchased intangibles, there is likely to be very little relationship between the amortized cost of an intangible asset and its economic value. An intangible resource has economic value if, and only if, it may be expected to produce revenues above the level which might ordinarily be expected without the presence of such asset or if it can be expected to reduce future outlays for expenses. A copyright, for example, may be expected to produce royalty revenues in future periods. A patent could increase revenues either directly through royalty payments from licensing or indirectly through increasing sales of a product, or it could reduce outlays by permitting the use of more efficient operating procedures.

As each intangible asset is of necessity unique and does not trade regularly in public markets, there will rarely be a realistic market value of an intangible. A

[14]*Ibid.*
[15]*Accounting Research Bulletin No. 43,* chap. 5 (1953).
[16]APB Opinion 17, par. 31.

recent offer may be regarded as evidence of a minimum market value, but where an active market does not exist, such a bid may not reflect the true worth of the asset.

An approximation of the economic value of an intangible may be found by estimating the present value of the future revenues or expense savings which are expected to be generated by the asset. This expected stream of income contributions can be discounted at an appropriate rate to reflect the time value of money, as well as the risk and uncertainty connected with this stream, to determine the present value.

Suppose, for example, that a patent is expected to produce royalty income over a 10-year period as follows:

Year	Royalty Income
1	$ 8,000
2	18,000
3	25,000
4	30,000
5	34,000
6	43,000
7	44,000
8	39,000
9	27,000
10	12,000

The royalty income of each year would be multiplied by the present value factor, $(1 + r)^{-n}$, where n is the number of years until the income will be received and r is the discount rate. These factors may be found in tables of present values. Assuming a discount rate of 15 percent to reflect the time value of money as well as the inherent risk in holding this asset, the present value of the stream of royalty income would be calculated as shown in Exhibit 1.

EXHIBIT 1

Year	Royalty income	$(1.15)^{-n}$	Present value
1	$ 8,000	.870	$ 6,960
2	18,000	.756	13,608
3	25,000	.658	16,450
4	30,000	.572	17,160
5	34,000	.497	16,898
6	43,000	.432	18,576
7	44,000	.376	16,544
8	39,000	.327	12,753
9	27,000	.284	7,668
10	12,000	.247	2,964
	Present value	. . . .	$129,581

In federal income tax cases, the courts have permitted a method of evaluating intangibles known as "Hoskold's formula." This formula, which assumes uniform annual receipts, is based on the present value of the receipts at a specified rate of interest (usually from 8 to 15 percent for intangibles), together with a sinking fund which accumulates at the rate of 4 percent. The present value factors for selected interest rates, based on this formula, are shown in Exhibit 2.

To illustrate the use of this formula, assume that a patent is expected to produce royalty income of $28,000 per year for a period of 10 years. The annual income is first multiplied by the number of years to obtain the total income ($28,000 × 10 = $280,000). The total income is then multiplied by the present value factor. At 15

EXHIBIT 2   Table Based on Hoskold's Formula
(Rate of 4% interest, compounded annually, allowed on sinking fund)

Yrs.	6%	7%	8%	9%	10%	12%	15%
1	0.943396	0.934579	0.925925	0.917431	0.909090	0.892857	0.869565
2	0.908766	0.892946	0.876891	0.861777	0.847176	0.819408	0.781010
3	0.876389	0.853937	0.832607	0.812317	0.792993	0.756976	0.708694
4	0.846052	0.818370	0.792418	0.768072	0.745178	0.703254	0.648525
5	0.817570	0.785469	0.755780	0.728260	0.702675	0.656540	0.597680
6	0.790781	0.754961	0.722245	0.692177	0.664641	0.615547	0.554148
7	0.765540	0.726638	0.691435	0.659519	0.630410	0.579284	0.516457
8	0.741717	0.700174	0.663032	0.629635	0.599440	0.546979	0.483507
9	0.719198	0.675487	0.636765	0.602251	0.571286	0.518017	0.454455
10	0.697880	0.652354	0.612404	0.577066	0.545581	0.491906	0.428649
11	0.677672	0.630699	0.589748	0.553820	0.522019	0.468244	0.405574
12	0.658489	0.610277	0.568624	0.532281	0.500344	0.446702	0.384818
13	0.640258	0.591066	0.548887	0.512330	0.480337	0.427009	0.366049
14	0.622911	0.572950	0.530401	0.493737	0.461815	0.408936	0.348995
15	0.606385	0.555828	0.513053	0.476390	0.444619	0.392292	0.333431
16	0.590625	0.539630	0.496741	0.460167	0.428610	0.376914	0.319170
17	0.575581	0.524283	0.481376	0.444963	0.413671	0.362663	0.306056
18	0.561205	0.509716	0.466880	0.430685	0.399699	0.349420	0.293955
19	0.547455	0.496371	0.453178	0.417253	0.386603	0.337082	0.282754
20	0.534292	0.482719	0.440211	0.404592	0.374302	0.325559	0.272358
21	0.521680	0.470171	0.427920	0.392637	0.362729	0.314474	0.262682
22	0.509587	0.458216	0.416255	0.381334	0.351818	0.304658	0.253654
23	0.497979	0.446805	0.405166	0.370630	0.341517		
24	0.486835	0.435903	0.394619	0.360479	0.331775		
25	0.476122	0.425477	0.384571	0.350840	0.322549		
26	0.465820	0.415496	0.374988	0.341675	0.313799		
27	0.455905	0.405933	0.365839	0.332951	0.305488		
28	0.446356	0.396767	0.357096	0.324637	0.297587		

percent, the present value factor for 10 years, including sinking fund earnings, is 0.428649. Thus the value of the patent would be $280,000 × 0.428649, or $120,021.72.

Because of the great uncertainty in determining an economic or market value for intangibles, they are often recorded at a nominal value such as $1. The use of nominal value serves to point out the existence of the intangible assets without attempting to establish any realistic value for them. If the details of the intangible assets are disclosed through footnotes or other means, readers of the statements may then draw their own conclusions regarding worth.

AMORTIZATION AND WRITE-OFF OF INTANGIBLES

In *ARB No. 43*, the AICPA classified intangible assets for accounting purposes into two categories:[17]

(a) Those having a term of existence limited by law, regulation or agreement or by their nature (such as patents, copyrights, leases, licenses, franchises for a fixed term and goodwill as to which there is evidence of limited duration);

[17]*ARB No. 43*, chap. 5, par. 2.

(b) Those having no such limited term of existence and as to which there is at the time of acquisition no indication of limited life (such as goodwill generally, going value, trade names, secret processes, subscription lists, perpetual franchises, and organization costs).

Although the cost of type (a) intangibles was to be amortized over the period benefited, type (b) intangibles were not amortized unless it became evident that their term of existence was indeed limited and they had, in effect, become type (a).

In Opinion No. 17, the APB reversed this position with regard to type (b) intangibles, ruling "that the value of intangible assets at any one date eventually disappears and that the recorded costs of intangible assets should be amortized by systematic charges to income over the periods estimated to be benefited."[18] Thus all intangible assets are regarded as having limited lives, and their costs must be amortized over some relevant period. In the opposite direction, Opinion No. 17 also prohibited the widely accepted practice of charging the costs of intangible assets to income in the year the costs are incurred.

Amortization Period.   It might be noted that the phrase "periods estimated to be benefited" as used in Opinion 17 raises many questions as to how these periods should be determined. By the nature of intangibles their terms of existence are subject to great uncertainty, yet the determination of this period is of critical importance in the amortization procedure.

The APB suggests that the period of amortization should be determined from a consideration of "pertinent factors." Among the factors that should be considered, they cite the following:[19]

a. Legal, regulatory, or contractual provisions may limit the maximum useful life.

b. Provisions for renewal or extension may alter a specified limit on useful life.

c. Effects of obsolescence, demand, competition, and other economic factors may reduce a useful life.

d. A useful life may parallel the service life expectancies of individuals or groups of employees.

e. Expected actions of competitors and others may restrict present competitive advantages.

f. An apparently unlimited useful life may in fact be indefinite and benefits cannot be reasonably projected.

g. An intangible asset may be a composite of many individual factors with varying effective lives.

Many intangibles have a maximum life prescribed by law. A patent, for example, is granted for a period of 17 years and may not be renewed. Copyrights are issued for a period of 28 years with the possibility of renewal for another 28-year period at expiration, giving a total of 56 years. From an economic standpoint, however, it is rare that an intangible asset would maintain its value during the entire period of its legal existence. For example, a patent may be made obsolete by a new development which supersedes it. A copyrighted work may not provide any revenues after the first year or two of its existence. For these reasons, the useful life of an intangible asset should be regarded as the *shorter* of the legal or economic life.

There is an upper limit. The APB states that, "The period of amortization should not, however, exceed forty years. Analysis at the time of acquisition may indicate that the indeterminate lives of some intangible assets are likely to exceed forty years and the cost of those assets should be amortized over the maximum period of forty years, not an arbitrary shorter period."[20]

The Accounting Principles Board as a matter of general policy did not have its

[18]APB Opinion No. 17, par. 27.
[19]*Ibid.,* par. 27.
[20]*Ibid.,* par. 29.

Opinions apply retroactively. Thus Opinion No. 17 applies only to intangibles acquired after its effective date, October 31, 1970. The Board was specific on this point, stating:[21]

> 34. The provisions of this Opinion should not be applied retroactively to intangible assets acquired before November 1, 1970, whether in business combination or otherwise.
> 35. The Board encourages the application on a prospective basis to all intangible assets held on October 31, 1970 of the provisions . . . of this Opinion which require amortization of all intangible assets. Unless the provisions of this Opinion are applied prospectively, the accounting for intangible assets held on October 30, 1970, should be in accordance with Chapter 5 of ARB No. 43. . . .

Many corporations amortize goodwill recognized after October 31, 1970, but not goodwill recognized earlier. For example, a recent financial statement of American Home Products Corporation shows the following asset on its balance sheet:

> Goodwill, trademarks, formulae, patents, etc. $85,361,000

An accompanying note on accounting policies reads as follows:

> Intangible assets at December 31, 1974 include $3,584,000 of goodwill relating to acquisitions initiated after October 31, 1970 and patent rights, which is being amortized. The balance of $81,777,000 is not being amortized since the company believes there has been no diminution in value of these assets.

Amortization Procedure.   Once the amortization period has been established, the cost of the intangible asset may be amortized over this period by any systematic method. The APB, however, concluded that, "the straight-line method of amortization—equal annual amounts—should be applied unless a company demonstrates that another systematic method is more appropriate."[22]

Unlike depreciation of tangible assets, the amortization of intangibles is usually recorded through a direct credit to the asset account rather than to a contra account. The financial statements should disclose the method and period of amortization. Separate disclosure of accumulated amortization would be helpful to analysts who are accustomed to dividing accumulated (straight-line) depreciation by depreciation charges for the year to estimate the average age of long-lived assets.

Write-down or Write-off.   *ARB No. 43* stated that "The cost of type (b) intangibles should be written off when it becomes reasonably evident that they have become worthless. Under such circumstances the amount at which they are carried on the books should be charged off in the income statement."[23]

This was superseded by APB Opinion No. 17, which states:[24]

> A company should evaluate the periods of amortization continually to determine whether later events and circumstances warrant revised estimates of useful lives. If estimates are changed, the unamortized cost should be allocated to the increased or reduced number of remaining periods in the revised useful life but not to exceed forty years after acquisition. Estimation of value and future benefits of an intangible asset may indicate that the unamortized cost should be reduced significantly by a deduction in determining net income. . . . However, a single loss year or even a few loss years together do not necessarily justify an extraordinary charge to income for all or a large part of the unamortized cost of intangible assets. The reason for an extraordinary deduction should be disclosed.

[21]*Ibid.*, paragraphs 34 and 35.
[22]*Ibid.*, par. 30.
[23]*ARB No. 43*, chap. 5, par. 8.
[24]APB Opinion No. 17, par. 31.

APB Opinion No. 17 does not prohibit a complete write-off of the unamortized cost of an intangible asset in a year subsequent to acquisition, provided that a reasonable basis for such action can be shown. It does, however, disallow the write-off of an intangible asset in the year of acquisition.

APB Opinion No. 17 permitted a special write-down or write-off of an intangible to be treated as an "extraordinary item" in the income statement if the amount involved was material. However, APB Opinion No. 30 tightened the criteria for determination of items to be treated as extraordinary, and specifically excluded extraordinary status for write-offs of intangibles. Paragraph 23 states:[25]

> Certain gains and losses should not be reported as extraordinary items because they are usual in nature or may be expected to recur as a consequence of customary and continuing business activities. Examples include:
> (a) Write-down or write-off of receivables, inventories, equipment leased to others, deferred research and development costs or *other intangible assets*. [Italics supplied. Note that FASB Statement No. 2 supersedes the treatment suggested for R&D costs. Since Statement No. 2 does not permit their being recognized as assets, there can be no problem of subsequent write-off.]

Income Tax Treatment.   The income tax treatment of intangibles seems to have affected the accounting treatment of these items. However, there is no requirement that the accounting treatment conform to the income tax treatment.

For federal income tax purposes, costs of activities such as advertising may be regarded as a current expense regardless of their future benefits. Intangible property can be depreciated for tax purposes if its use in business is of definitely limited duration. The federal income tax regulation No. 1.167 (a)-3 states:[26]

> If an intangible asset is known from experience or other factors to be of use in the business or in the production of income for only a limited period, the length of which can be estimated with reasonable accuracy, such an intangible asset may be the subject of a depreciation allowance. Examples are patents and copyrights. An intangible asset the useful life of which is not limited is not subject to the allowance for depreciation. No allowance will be permitted merely because in the unsupported opinion of the taxpayer, the intangible asset has a limited useful life.

Intangibles which have been held depreciable for tax purposes include patents, copyrights, leaseholds, licenses, and franchises. Items which have been held not to be depreciable because of the indefinite duration of their usefulness include goodwill, trade names, trademarks, brands, and formulas.

Because intangibles which are not depreciable for federal income tax purposes must nevertheless be amortized over a period of forty years or less in financial statements, holding such assets will result in taxable income exceeding reported income. This excess is treated as a permanent, rather than a timing difference, and does not require interperiod allocation of income taxes. (See Chapter 36.)

Intangibles are considered "capital assets" in the hands of a purchaser, but not when held by the inventor or developer. Thus the sale of a patent or copyright by a firm which has purchased the right would qualify for capital gain or loss treatment for income tax purposes. On the other hand, the gain on a sale of such a right by the inventor or author would be taxed as ordinary income.

SPECIFIC INTANGIBLES

Although the discussion above applies to most items that can be classified as intangible assets, there are some factors that pertain to the treatment of specific items. These factors are discussed below.

---

[25]Accounting Principles Board Opinion No. 30, par. 23, 1973 (Emphasis supplied).
[26]U.S. Internal Revenue Service, Federal Income Tax Regulations, §1.167 (a)-3.

Patents. A patent is a legal device giving the holder the exclusive right of using or controlling a particular invention. Patents are granted for a period of 17 years, but there are several factors which could cause the useful life to be much shorter than this.

Although the patent may allow the holder to exclude others from using the process, it does not assure any economic benefit. If the process is not useful, the patent may have little or no economic value. A patent can also be superseded by the development of another process which is more economical or otherwise advantageous. If the patent pertains to a product which does not gain consumer acceptance, the patent will similarly be short-lived. Finally, the issuance of the patent merely serves to indicate the approval of the invention by the U.S. Patent Office, but this grant could be withdrawn through litigation if contested. The cost of a patent should be amortized over the legal life or the economic life, whichever is shorter.

The cost of a patent is not limited to the price paid to the seller; it may also include government fees, attorneys' fees and expenses, and other costs associated with its acquisition. The successful defense of an interference suit should be capitalized as part of the patent cost, whereas the cost of unsuccessful legal suits should be charged to expense.

Because there may not be any connection between the cost of a patent and its value, the accumulated cost should be examined periodically to make sure that it does not exceed the current value. If a patent has lost its commercial value for any reason, its unamortized cost should be written off. Patents are not generally written up when it is found that their value exceeds their cost.

Copyrights. A copyright gives the holder certain rights to published material. In some instances a copyright does not entitle the holder to the exclusive use of a work, but merely to receive royalty payments from others for public performances.

A copyright is granted for a period of 28 years, and may be renewed for an additional 28-year period. In some cases of "classic" songs, books, etc., the work may be expected to have economic value during the entire 56-year period of legal protection. These cases are rare, however, and in most instances the commercial life of a copyright is relatively short.

Many of the same factors which are considered in determining patent costs affect the costs of copyrights as well.

Research and Development Costs. As previously discussed, FASB Statement No. 2 requires that all research and development costs be charged to expense when incurred.[27] The determination of what constitutes research and development costs may entail some judgment, however. In this regard, the FASB has offered some broad guidelines: Research and development is defined as follows:

a. Research is planned search or critical investigation aimed at discovery of new knowledge with the hope that such knowledge will be useful in developing a new product or service (hereinafter "product") or a new process or technique (hereinafter "process") or in bringing about a significant improvement to an existing product or process.

b. Development is the translation of research findings or other knowledge into a plan or design for a new product or process or for a significant improvement to an existing product or process whether intended for sale or use. It includes the conceptual formulation, design, and testing of product alternatives, construction of prototypes, and operation of pilot plants. It does not include routine or periodic alterations to existing products, production lines, manufacturing processes, and other ongoing operations even though those alterations may represent improvements and it does not include market research or market testing activities.

[27]FASB, Statement No. 2, pars. 8–11.

The following are examples of activities that typically would be included in research and development:

   a. Laboratory research aimed at discovery of new knowledge

   b. Searching for applications of new research findings or other knowledge

   c. Conceptual formulation and design of possible product or process alternatives

   d. Testing in search for or evaluation of product or process alternatives

   e. Modification of the formulation or design of a product or process

   f. Design, construction, and testing of preproduction prototypes and models

   g. Design of tools, jigs, molds, and dies involving new technology

   h. Design, construction, and operation of a pilot plant that is not of a scale economically feasible to the enterprise for commercial production

   i. Engineering activity required to advance the design of a product to the point that it meets specific functional and economic requirements and is ready for manufacture.

The following are examples of activities that typically would be excluded from research and development:

   a. Engineering follow-through in an early phase of commercial production

   b. Quality control during commercial production, including routine testing of products

   c. Trouble-shooting in connection with break-downs during commercial production

   d. Routine, ongoing efforts to refine, enrich, or otherwise improve upon the qualities of an existing product

   e. Adaptation of an existing capability to a particular requirement or customer's need as part of a continuing commercial activity.

   f. Seasonal or other periodic design changes to existing products

   g. Routine design of tools, jigs, molds, and dies

   h. Activity, including design and construction engineering, related to the construction, relocation, rearrangement, or start-up of facilities or equipment other than (1) pilot plants and (2) facilities or equipment whose sole use is for a particular research and development project

   i. Legal work in connection with patent applications or litigation, and the sale or licensing of patents.

Retroactive Application.　　FASB Statement No. 2 is effective for fiscal years beginning on or after January 1, 1975, but it also had a retroactive effect. All research and development costs recognized as assets previous to that date were also required to be charged to expense. The Statement provided:[28]

> The requirement . . . that research and development costs be charged to expense when incurred shall be applied retroactively by prior period adjustment.

Disclosure.　　FASB Statement No. 2 also requires disclosure of the total research and development costs charged to expense in each period for which an income statement is presented. An example of such presentation in the footnotes of the annual report along with the description of another type of intangible was provided in a recent annual report of International Telephone and Telegraph Corporation:

> Research and Development: Significant costs are incurred each year in connection with research and development programs that are expected to contribute substantial profits to the operations of future years. Because of uncertainties involved in measuring the future benefits and the related lives, the Corporation charges current income with all costs incurred during the period. This practice is in accord with the recent statement issued by the Financial Accounting Standards Board (FASB).

---

[28]*Ibid.,* par. 15.

Research and development expenditures, which in 1974 and 1973 amounted to $452,000,000 and $400,000,000 respectively, including $239,000,000 and $212,000,000 of costs expended pursuant to specific contracts with customers, include certain engineering and other development costs not included in the FASB definition of research and development.

Business Development Costs: The Corporation expends significant amounts each year in connection with the establishment of new plants, businesses and products. These costs, which represent amounts invested to bring new activities into normal operation, are included in Other Assets and are amortized against the related future income, generally over a three to five year period. The deferred costs are subject to immediate write-off in those instances where a profit potential is no longer probable.

At December 31, 1974 and 1973, deferred business development costs, including amounts related to divestible operations under consent decrees and after deducting applicable reserves, amounted to $65,837,000 and $47,827,000, respectively. Amounts amortized to income in 1974 and 1973 aggregated $17,902,000 and $17,466,000, respectively.

Trademarks and Trade Names.   A trademark is a designation used to identify a particular commercial product or service. Such marks can be registered to provide added legal protection, but common law confers ownership on the earliest continuous user for a class of products in a geographic area. A trade name or brand may similarly be used to designate the products of a particular company.

The economic value of a trademark or trade name stems from its ability to afford the user superior earning power. Thus, for similar products, customers may be willing to pay higher prices, or to purchase larger quantities at the same prices, for products with well-known trade names.

The value of a trade name is illustrated in an early Internal Revenue ruling as follows:[29]

> It is recognized that in numerous instances it has been the practice of distillers and wholesale liquor dealers to put out under well-known and popular brands only so much goods as could be marketed without affecting the established market price therefor and to sell other goods of the same identical manufacture, age, and character under other brands, or under no brand at all, at figures very much below those which the well-known brands commanded. In such cases the difference between the price at which whiskey was sold under a given brand name and also under another brand name, or under no brand, multiplied by the number of units sold during a given year gives an accurate determination of the amount of profit attributable to that brand during that year, and where this practice is continued for a long enough period to show that this amount was fairly constant and regular and might be expected to yield annually that average profit, by capitalizing this earning at the rate, say, of 20 percent, the value of the brand is fairly well established.

The economic benefits of trademarks and trade names are sometimes ascribed to goodwill. Whereas goodwill relates to the excess earning potential of the organization as a whole, a trademark or trade name can presumably be separately identified and possibly transferred to another organization while the original organization continues in existence.

If a trademark or trade name is purchased, its acquisition cost includes the purchase price plus any additional costs of registration, legal fees, etc. Often, however, valuable trademarks and trade names are developed through years of advertising and customer satisfaction. In such cases, the advertising costs are not included as a cost of the trademarks or trade names but are charged to expense as incurred. Although some future benefits may be obtained from advertising in the

[29]U.S. Bureau of Internal Revenue, Committee on Appeals and Review, Methods of Determining Value of Intangible Assets, Cumulative Bulletin No. 2, Washington, D.C., 1920, p. 31.

form of a valuable trade name, the relationship between expenditures for advertising and the value of the resultant asset is extremely difficult to determine.

Trademarks and trade names do not have definitely determinable useful lives, but it is possible for their economic potency to expire. If customer acceptance wanes or it takes increased expenditures for advertising to maintain brand loyalty, the trademarks and trade names of a product could have little or no value. In addition, the legal status of these rights may be lost through failure to continue their use, through the successful challenge by another user, or through the name becoming the generic term for the product. Thus the costs of trademarks and trade names are often amortized over relatively short periods.

For federal income tax purposes, a distinction is made between trademarks and trade names and "trademark and trade name expenditures." The term "trademark or trade name expenditure" is defined in the Internal Revenue Code as any expenditure which[30]

> (1) is directly connected with the acquisition, protection, expansion, registration (Federal, State, or foreign), or defense of a trademark or trade name;
> (2) is chargeable to capital account; and
> (3) is not part of the consideration paid for a trademark, trade name, or business.

Because trademarks and trade names are of indeterminate life, the direct consideration paid in acquiring such assets cannot be amortized. However, trademark and trade name expenditures are afforded special treatment in the Revenue Code. Such expenditures made after December 31, 1955, may, upon election of the taxpayer, be treated as an asset and amortized over a period of not less than 60 months.

Organization Costs. The costs of organizing a corporation are frequently included in intangible assets. These costs include legal fees and other costs of obtaining the corporate charter, raising initial capital, and promoting the enterprise. Some accountants argue that reasonably anticipated losses from operations during the first few years should be included in organization costs. This viewpoint is not generally accepted, however.

These costs may be regarded as having perpetual life, benefiting all the years of corporate existence. For federal income tax purposes, however, such costs of newly formed corporations may be amortized over a period of not less than 60 months.

Because these costs are directly related to the existence of the organization as a whole, the acquisition of these items as part of the purchase of another corporation would be classified as an element of goodwill.

Going-Concern Value. The value of an existing company as a going concern, over and above the market value of specifically identifiable assets, may be regarded as an intangible asset. This item, usually attributed to the excess earning potential of the company, is commonly referred to as "goodwill." The latter term has come to have a more restricted meaning, however, limited to the excess amount actually paid in purchasing another company, over and above the market value of its specifically identifiable assets. Therefore we will use the term "going-concern value" to distinguish this concept.

Going-concern value is not recognized in published financial statements (whereas goodwill actually purchased is recognized). The determination of going-concern value may be of importance in evaluating an enterprise from the standpoint of prospective purchase, sale, or merger, however.

The procedure for estimating the going-concern value involves five steps:

1. Placing a value on specifically identifiable assets and liabilities,
2. Attributing a normal return to these identifiable net assets,

[30]U.S. Congress, Internal Revenue Code of 1954, §177(b).

3. Estimating the amount of earnings to be secured in future years,

4. Calculating the amount of excess earnings, that is, the amount by which expected future earnings exceed the normal return on identifiable net assets, and

5. Capitalizing the excess earnings by determining their present value at a reasonable rate of return, considering the risk involved.

To illustrate this procedure, consider the following example. A company has identifiable assets (cash, buildings, land, patents, etc.) that have a total appraised value of $550,000. Liabilities total $250,000. The company is expected to earn $45,000 annually for the indefinite future, and a return of 10 percent on net assets is considered normal in this industry.

The net identifiable assets less liabilities are valued at $300,000. Thus a "normal" return of 10 percent would yield earnings of $30,000 per year. As the company is expected to earn $45,000 per year, the excess earnings are calculated to be $15,000 per year.

Capitalizing these excess earnings requires the use of judgment. In particular, the duration of the excess earnings and a reasonable rate of return to apply to these earnings must be assumed, but there is no "correct" assumption that would be universally accepted.

A naive approach would be to assume these earnings will continue forever, and the rate of return on going-concern value should be the same as that for identifiable assets. This results in the excess earnings of $15,000 being capitalized in perpetuity at 10 percent, giving them a value of $150,000 (= $15,000/.10).

A more realistic approach would be to assume that these earnings will continue for a limited time, say 10 years. Even if there is a reasonable expectation that these excess earnings will continue beyond that time, the risks become greater in distant future years. At the same time, we may wish to apply a higher rate of return to the excess earnings than to identifiable assets because of the increased risks involved. Suppose we choose 15 percent as a reasonable rate for this purpose.

The present value of an annuity of $1 per period for 10 periods at 15 percent is $5.0188. Therefore the present value of the $15,000 excess annual earnings would be $75,282 (= $15,000 × 5.0188). This is the amount that would be attributed to going concern value.

STATEMENT PRESENTATION

Intangible assets are generally shown on the balance sheet, separately described, in the noncurrent asset section. Many companies simply include them with "other assets," making no separate disclosure of these items. The nature and treatment of intangible items may be disclosed in the accounting policies section of the notes to financial statements. A sample financial statement disclosure follows.

The Dennison Manufacturing Co. reported:

Other Assets
Excess of cost of investment in subsidiaries
  over net assets acquired (Notes A and B) $3,258,000
Miscellaneous receivables, investments, etc. 3,331,000
                                                             $6,589,000

Note A, Accounting Policies, contains this reference to intangibles, however:

Amortization of Intangible Assets—The excess of cost of investments in subsidiaries over the net assets acquired is, in general, being amortized over a forty-year period. Patents, copyrights, trademarks, and other intangible assets are being amortized over their estimated lives.

Commercial Solvents Corporation shows the following item under assets:

Goodwill, patents and other intangibles $3,853,344

Note 1(e), entitled "Goodwill, patents and other intangibles," discloses the amount included as goodwill ($3,748,000) and then states: "Patents and other intangible assets are being amortized on the straight-line basis over 4 to 10 year periods." Although it is possible to calculate the amount included as "patents and other intangibles" ($105,344), this amount is not stated separately.

BIBLIOGRAPHY

Accounting Principles Board: "Intangible Assets," Opinion No. 17, AICPA, New York, 1970.

American Institute of Certified Public Accountants, Industry Accounting Guide: *Accounting for Motion Picture Films*, AICPA, New York, 1974.

Baloff, Nicholas, and John W. Kenelly: "Accounting Implications of Product and Process Start-ups," *Journal of Accounting Research*, Autumn 1967, pp. 131–43.

Drebin, Allan R.: "Accounting for Proprietary Research," *The Accounting Review*, July 1966, pp. 413–425.

Financial Accounting Standards Board: *Accounting for Research and Development and Similar Costs*, Discussion Memorandum, FASB, Stamford, Conn., 1973.

———: *Accounting for Research and Development Costs*, Statement of Financial Accounting Standards No. 2, FASB, Stamford, Conn., 1974.

Gellein, Oscar S., and Maurice S. Newman: "Accounting for Research and Development Expenditures," *Accounting Research Study No. 14*, AICPA, New York, 1973.

Johnson, Orace: "A Consequential Approach to Accounting for R&D," *Journal of Accounting Research*, Autumn 1967, pp. 164–172.

Madden, Donald L., Levis D. McCullers, and Relmond P. Van Daniker: "The Materiality of Research and Development Expenditures," *Journal of Accounting Research*, Autumn 1972, pp. 417–420.

Materne, D. W.: "Capitalizing Personnel-Retention Costs," *Management Accounting*, November 1973, pp. 27–28, 34.

National Association of Accountants: "Accounting for Research and Development Costs," *Research Report No. 29*, New York, 1955.

Orton, Bryce B., and Richard D. Bradish: "The Treatment and Disclosure of Research and Development Expenditures," *Management Accounting*, July 1969, pp. 31–34, 42.

Peles, Yoram: "Amortization of Advertising Expenditures in the Financial Statements," *Journal of Accounting Research*, Spring 1970, pp. 128–137.

Sanders, B. T.: "Examination of Contemporary Practices in Accounting for Intangible Assets," *The Accounting Review*, October 1959, pp. 625–626.

Yang, J. M.: *Goodwill and Other Intangibles*, The Ronald Press Company, New York, 1927.

Chapter **23**

Current Liabilities

ROBERT E. SEILER
Professor of Accounting, The University of Houston

THE CONCEPT OF LIABILITIES

The term "liability" generally implies a debt or legal obligation requiring satisfaction at some future date. Satisfaction is usually accomplished by payment of a sum of money, but it may also be effected by transfer of assets other than money or by performance of services. The liabilities of an accounting entity are thus the equities, claims, or interests of its creditors.

Kieso and Weygandt[1] state that although liabilities may be defined as required future disbursements of assets resulting from past transactions or events, a more definitive concept is that liabilities (1) arise from cash, goods, or services that have been received or events that have occurred, (2) are payable in assets or services in the future, and (3) can be measured or closely estimated and expressed in monetary terms.

Current Liabilities Defined. Liabilities payable within the next accounting cycle are segregated from those not payable until a more distant date in order to facilitate the analysis of the company's financial statements. Contemporary practice indicates that current liabilities include (1) all obligations for which payment will require the use of existing current assets or will create other current liabilities and (2) all other obligations which will probably be paid from current assets within one year. The Committee on Accounting Procedure of the AICPA[2] defines current liabilities as follows:

> The term current liabilities is used principally to designate obligations whose liquidation is reasonably expected to require the use of existing resources properly classifiable as current assets, or the creation of other current liabilities. As a balance sheet category, the classification is intended to include obligations for items which have entered into the operating cycle, such as payables incurred in the acquisition of materials and supplies to be used in the production of goods or in providing services to be offered for sale; collections received in advance of the delivery of goods or performance of services; and debts which arise from operations directly related to the operating cycle, such as accruals for wages, salaries, commissions, rentals, royalties, and income and other taxes. Other liabilities whose regular and ordinary liquidation is expected to occur within a relatively short period of time, usually twelve months, are also intended for inclusion, such as short-term debts arising from the acquisition of capital assets, serial maturities of long-term obligations, amounts required to be expended within one year under sinking fund provisions, and agency obligations arising from the collection or acceptance of cash or other assets for the account of third persons.

The twelve-month time period in the definition of a current liability is usually the most significant factor in the segregation of current and long-term liabilities, but the length of the company's operating cycle is overriding in some cases. When the operating cycle exceeds twelve months, the company's current liabilities

[1] Donald E. Kieso and Jerry J. Weygandt, *Intermediate Accounting,* John Wiley & Sons, New York, 1974, p. 394.

[2] Committee on Accounting Procedure, *Accounting Research Bulletin No. 43,* AICPA, New York, 1953, chap. 3A (footnotes of Bulletin omitted).

include those payable within the next cycle; however, a full year must be employed in case the cycle is less than one year.

The Securities and Exchange Commission has stated (Rule 3-15 of Regulation S-X) that items due and payable within one year shall, in general, be classified as current liabilities. However, SEC practice permits the exclusion of items such as customers' deposits and deferred income, provided that an appropriate explanation of the circumstances is made.

The specific amount payable or the specific identification of the payee need not be known before a liability may be classified as current. Payables of estimated amounts, such as those for taxes, and payables to unknown persons, such as those for guarantees or product warranties, should be listed as current if the time of payment appears reasonably certain to fall within the next operating cycle.

Nondebt Items Included in Current Liabilities.   The standard legal definition of a liability, i.e., that which one is under legal obligation to pay another, is not considered broad enough for accounting purposes, All legal liabilities would be considered liabilities for accounting purposes, but not all accounting liabilities are recognized as legal debts at the balance sheet date. Accounting liabilities include a number of credit balances which do not involve the debtor-creditor relationship, and for this reason the Accounting Principles Board, in Statement No. 4,[3] defines a liability in a balance sheet context as follows:

> Economic obligations of an enterprise that are recognized and measured in conformity with generally accepted accounting principles. Liabilities also include certain deferred credits that are not obligations but which are measured in conformity with generally accepted accounting principles.

The inclusion of the term "deferred credits" in the above definition broadens the concept of a liability to include such items as estimated cost of repairs under guaranties granted in compliance with company policy. Such credit balances arise from the double-entry effect of recording expenses relating to the current period. The inclusion of such nondebt items is consistent with the concept of a current liability requiring the disbursement of current resources, for these credit balances represent estimated outlays which will be required within the next accounting cycle, even though the requirement may not be based upon strict legal requirements.

Measurement of Current Liabilities.   The amount of a legal debt is the sum of money or the dollar value of the goods or services that must be paid to discharge the obligation. When the amount is payable in the future, however, the present value of the dollar amount payable is sometimes recognized as the proper expression of the liability. Sprouse and Moonitz[4] state this view as follows:

> To measure a liability is to determine the "weight" or the "burden" of the obligation on the balance sheet date. This "burden" is the lowest amount for which the obligation could be effectively discharged. If, for example, payment in cash now will discharge the liability, that amount of cash is the measure of the liability, even though in fact payment is delayed. If the creditor will not or cannot accept cash now in discharge of the liability, the appropriate amount is that sum, which, if invested now (e.g., in a sinking fund) will provide the sums needed at maturity, even though in fact no explicit sinking fund or other investment device is actually used.

Since current liabilities are normally payable within one year, the amount of the discount is not usually considered material in amount and is thus ignored in

---

[3]Accounting Principles Board Statement No. 4, AICPA, New York, 1970, par. 132.

[4]Robert T. Sprouse and Maurice Moonitz, "A Tentative Set of Broad Accounting Principles for Business Enterprises," *Accounting Research Study No. 3,* AICPA, New York, 1962, p. 39.

practice. Further, the necessity of arbitrarily selecting a rate of discount has tended to discourage the use of discounted values for current liabilities. The slight overstatement of liabilities that results from carrying current liabilities at maturity value is usually justified on grounds of expediency, conservatism, and immateriality. Short-term trade payables arising from transactions with suppliers in the normal course of operations are specifically exempt from the present value calculation by APB Opinion No. 21, but the opinion requires trade notes, which are described as non-interest-bearing, to be stated at present value amounts.[5]

Although the amount of a current liability is in most cases reasonably definite, there are instances in which the amount is not known precisely. The American Accounting Association[6] indicates that liabilities "are measured by cash received, by the established price of noncash assets or services received, or by estimates of a definitive character when the amount owing cannot be measured precisely." However, if reasonable estimates are not possible, the existense of the obligation should be disclosed by footnote, even though an amount cannot be assigned to it.

FINANCIAL STATEMENT PRESENTATION

Detail of Disclosure. Most of the detail concerning the company's liabilities need not be included in the reported financial statements. Although current liabilities must be recorded in the books of account in sufficient detail to facilitate their payment and ensure control over their incurrence, this same amount of detail would be unnecessarily cumbersome if included in the balance sheet. The detail which should be shown in the balance sheet depends upon its intended use, but broad categories are usually sufficient. Meigs, Johnson, Keller, and Mosich[7] state that for general reporting purposes the following eight classifications are recommended:
- Notes payable to banks
- Notes payable to trade creditors
- Accounts payable to trade creditors
- Current maturities of long-term debt
- Income taxes payable
- Other accrued liabilities
- Dividends payable
- Miscellaneous current liabilities.

Notes are segregated because of their legal status as negotiable instruments, and the amounts due trade creditors are segregated to distinguish these normally recurring liabilities from other types. Income taxes are segregated both because of their materiality and because the amounts are estimated. Advance receipts from customers are included in other current liabilities but should be separated if they are significant in amount. In addition to these eight classifications, debts owed to persons closely associated with the company constitute significant financial information and should be separately disclosed as payables to officers, stockholders, and employees.

As a general rule, any single material current liability that arises from an unusual source, is not certain in amount, is contingent upon some future event, has a prior claim on assets, or is to be paid from assets other than normal current assets should be separately reported and should be adequately described in a

[5]APB Opinion No. 21, AICPA, New York, 1971, par. 3a and 12.

[6]*Accounting Concepts and Standards Underlying Corporate Financial Statements and Preceding Statements and Supplements,* AAA, Columbus, Ohio, 1958, p. 16.

[7]Walter B. Meigs, A. N. Mosich, Charles E. Johnson, and Thomas F. Keller, *Intermediate Accounting,* 3rd ed., McGraw-Hill Book Company, New York, 1974, p. 273.

footnote or other parenthetical expression. The changing nature of a company's liabilities from one period to another thus makes absolute consistency and uniformity in classifications impossible.

Order of Presentation. The most frequent method of categorizing current liabilities is in accordance with the nature of the liability, such as accounts payable, notes payable, and taxes payable, with special items indicated by a descriptive title. These categories are sometimes placed in the balance sheet in order of maturity, with the earliest maturing item first, and sometimes in the order of their amounts, with the largest listed first. The nature of any security associated with the creditor's claim is rarely used as a basis for ordering the presentation, except in special Statements of Affairs prepared for liquidating companies or those in receivership.

A number of practical problems arise when liabilities are arranged in the order of maturity. The major problem occurs because the timing of payment is not uniform, such as in accounts payable where accounts with 30-day terms, 90-day terms, and even 6-month terms are included in the same category. Similarly, in the notes payable category there are notes with many different maturity dates. For this reason an arrangement based upon maturity is difficult to apply in practice. However, bank overdrafts are usually listed first among current liabilities in deference to their priority of maturity. A listing of current liabilities in the order of their amount adds little to the data being presented, especially since the amounts change from period to period and lead to inconsistencies in arrangement between accounting periods.

A uniform, generally accepted ordering of current liabilities does not exist for financial reporting. Although current assets are generally ordered in relation to their state of liquidity, this arrangement cannot be matched by a similar ordering of current liabilities.

Estimated Liabilities. An estimated liability exists when the amount payable cannot be ascertained with reasonable certainty on the balance sheet date. In such cases the amount must be estimated as accurately as possible, and the estimated amount is then used in the preparation of the balance sheet. Many liabilities cannot be known with certainty and must always be estimated because the exact amount may depend upon future events. Federal income tax liability, for example, depends upon the final assessment by the Director of Internal Revenue; liabilities for product guarantees depend upon the number of units of product which will need repair or replacement; and liabilities for tokens, tickets, and gift certificates outstanding depend upon the number submitted by customers for redemption.

Whenever possible, liabilities which are subject to reasonably accurate estimation should be reported in the main body of the balance sheet rather than by footnote. The amount should be estimated on the basis of all information available, and the account title should then indicate that the amount is estimated. Hendricksen[8] states:

> The distinction should be based on whether or not an expected value would be meaningful to readers of the financial reports as a representation of the approximate most probable (modal) value and the extent to which the expectations must be subjective. If an obligation has a 90 per cent chance of being $100,000 and a 10 per cent chance of being zero, the expected value would be $90,000 and this would be a meaningful representation of the liability, particularly if the probabilities are based on past experience. On the other hand if the obligation has a 90 per cent chance of being zero and a 10 per cent chance of being $100,000 the expected value would be $10,000 but this would not be as meaningful as a description of the probable amount to be paid. That is, if the

[8]Eldon S. Hendriksen, *Accounting Theory*, rev. ed., Richard D. Irwin, Homewood, Ill., 1970, p. 451.

most probable (modal) value of the obligation is positive, a liability exists and the amount should be estimated. If the obligation has a high probability of being zero, it should be classified as a contingent liability.

Offsets Against Assets. Generally accepted accounting practices do not permit the offset of an asset against a liability so that only the net amount appears in the statements. Such treatment is considered improper because it implies an irrevocable association between the two that seldom exists. The entire accounting framework is based upon a reflection of total properties employed in the operations of the company, matched on the opposite side of the balance sheet by the total equities of those properties. To offset one asset against a specific liability, even though the asset is pledged as security for that debt, would destroy the overall portrayal of properties and equities. Footnotes or parenthetical expressions are usually employed to reflect a specific relationship between an asset and a liability.

Two exceptions exist to the general rule prohibiting offsets. The first is when a legal right of offset exists and the creditor has a debt payable to the company as well as a receivable. Thus, a company may offset an overdraft in a bank account against its balance in another account at the same bank. Offset between two different banks, however, is not permissible.

The second exception to the general rule against offsets exists for a few government securities which represent an advance payment of taxes. Accounting Principles Board Opinion No. 10[9] describes the limited amount of offsetting permitted in this way:

1. It is a general principle of accounting that the offsetting of assets and liabilities in the balance sheet is improper except where a right of setoff exists. Accordingly, the offset of cash or other assets against the tax liability or other amounts owing to governmental bodies is not acceptable except in the circumstances described in paragraph 3 below.

2. Most securities now issued by governments are not by their terms designed specifically for the payment of taxes and, accordingly, should not be deducted from taxes payable on the balance sheet.

3. The only exception to this general principle occurs when it is clear that a purchase of securities (acceptable for the payment of taxes) is in substance an advance payment of taxes that will be payable in the relatively near future, so that in the special circumstances the purchase is tantamount to the prepayment of taxes. This occurs at times, for example, as an accommodation to a local government and in some instances when governments issue securities that are specifically designated as being acceptable for the payment of taxes of those governments.

An improper offset exists when accounts receivable contain individual accounts with credit balances which are not separated and shown as current liabilities. A credit balance in a receivable account represents a current liability, just as a debit balance in an account payable account represents a receivable.

Valuation accounts, such as those for accumulated depreciation and allowances for doubtful accounts, may not properly appear in the liabilities section of the balance sheet. These valuation accounts must be subtracted from their related asset accounts.[10] The general rule against offsets is not violated by subtraction of valuation accounts from assets, since the valuation account was established primarily to prevent direct credits to the asset itself and, as a contra account, is in reality a part of the asset account.

Debt to Be Refinanced. Sometimes debts which have maturity dates within the next accounting cycle are expected to be refinanced and consequently will not require an outlay of current assets. Commercial paper, construction loans, and the

[9]APB Opinion No. 10, AICPA, New York, 1966, par. 7.
[10]APB Opinion No. 12, AICPA, New York, 1967, par. 12.

maturing portion of long-term debt are examples of such items. SEC[11] requirements indicate that such items must be classified as a current liability unless the
following three criteria are met:

1. The borrower has a noncancelable binding agreement from a creditor to refinance
the paper or other short-term debt;
2. The refinancing would extend the maturity date beyond one year; and
3. The borrower's intention is to exercise this right.

Budgetary Allowances.   Credit balances in accounts established for budgetary
purposes during the accounting period should not be treated as liabilities on the
balance sheet. These budgetary allowances should be removed from the accounts
by transferring any balance to the account established when the original entry was
recorded. Repairs and maintenance, for example, are frequently budgeted in
fixed monthly amounts, with entries debiting Repair and Maintenance Expense
and crediting an account Allowance for Future Repair and Maintenance Costs.
During the year, as actual costs are incurred, the allowance is debited. Any over- or
underaccrual remaining at the end of the year must be closed to the Repair and
Maintenance Expense account prior to the preparation of financial statements.

Conversion of Foreign Currency.   When consolidated financial statements are
being prepared for two or more companies, one of which is a foreign company
with money amounts stated in foreign currency, the current liabilities should be
converted for consolidation purposes into dollars, using the rate of exchange in
effect at the balance sheet date. Since current liabilities may be discharged at the
balance sheet date by dollar payments computed at that rate, a realistic conversion
of current liabilities is effected.

DETERMINABLE LIABILITIES

There are three types of current liabilities: (1) those readily determinable, (2) those
contingent in amount, and (3) those which must be estimated. Most liabilities are
susceptible to precise measurement, and the amount and due date are readily
determinable. The amount of other liabilities may not be known exactly and must
be estimated, or their final existence may be contingent upon some event beyond
the control of the company. Determinable liabilities include such debts as trade
notes, dividends payable, and accrued property taxes. Estimated liabilities include
future payments under product guarantees and for the issue of trading stamps.
Contingent liabilities include those which depend upon the outcome of a law suit
or result from endorsements of notes.

Notes Payable.   Although trade notes payable may arise from the same sources
as trade accounts payable, they are evidenced by negotiable instruments and
therefore should be reported separately if material in amount. The maturity date
of these notes may extend from a few days to a year, and they may be either
interest-bearing or non-interest-bearing. It is normally customary to record trade
notes at their face value and to accrue interest on the interest-bearing notes, using
a separate interest payable account. If interest is included in the face value of the
note, making it for all practical purposes a non-interest-bearing note, the full face
value of the instrument, if it matures within a year, may be recorded in the notes
payable account without segregation of the interest portion. However, it is important that any interest included in the face value of the note be separately recorded
as interest expense and not as part of the cost of the goods or services acquired
when the note was given. Even though no interest rate was stated at the time the
note was issued, there nevertheless is implicit interest included in the face amount

[11]SEC Accounting Series Release No. 148, 1973.

of the note. This implicit interest would be removed from the cost of the asset or service acquired at the time of issuance of the note, by the use of an interest rate normal to the firm and industry.

Interest is sometimes subtracted from the face value of a note when funds are borrowed from a financial institution. This is normally called discounting the note, and the discount is the difference between the face value of the note payable and the proceeds from the loan. The discount is normally recorded in a debit account entitled Discount on Notes Payable and would be amortized to interest expense over the life of the note. Any balance in the discount account would be subtracted from the face value of the note payable on the balance sheet so that the liability is reflected at its present value.

Accounts Payable. Trade accounts payable are debts owed to trade creditors; they normally arise from the purchase of goods or services. Such debts exist in the form of open accounts and thus are usually distinguished from debts evidenced by promissory notes. Particular care must be exercised at the end of the fiscal period to ensure that all trade payables arising from the purchase of goods and services are recorded. A liability is generally considered to exist at the time title passes on the purchase of merchandise; if goods are received near the end of the period or if merchandise is shipped f.o.b. shipping point but an invoice has not arrived, a liability nevertheless exists and should appear in the statements.

Accounts payable to trade creditors may be recorded at the gross invoice price, excluding cash discounts, or they may be recorded net (less cash discounts). Showing the invoice at gross has been the more common practice, primarily because it is more expedient. If this method is followed and cash discounts are material in amount, the discounts available on unpaid accounts should be recorded at the end of the period and subtracted from the liability account. On the other hand, if the accounts payable to trade creditors are recorded at the net amount, any discounts not to be taken must be added back to the amount payable on the balance sheet date. Chapters 8 and 13 contain additional discussion of discounts.

Interest Payable. Interest payable is usually the result of an accrual and is recorded at the end of each accounting period except in unusual cases. Interest payable on trade notes, notes payable to banks, installment contracts, or other types of interest-bearing documents is usually reported as a single item; in the absence of significant legal differences in the nature or status of the interest, little is to be gained by segregating the various types of interest payable. Interest in default on bonds is an example of an item sufficiently important to warrant separate reporting. Interest payable on noncurrent liabilities, such as long-term notes payable, should be listed as a current liability since the interest is payable within the next operating cycle.

When a company has installment contracts payable, such as those incurred in the purchase of fixed assets, each installment includes a portion of principal and a portion of interest. If each installment that is payable within the next operating cycle is transferred from noncurrent to current liabilities, no distinction need be made between the portion of the current installment which is principal and the portion which is interest. Including both interest and principal in the same liability account is justified since the liability is paid at the same time and to the same person.

Wages and Salaries Payable. A liability for unpaid wages and salaries is created when employees are paid at fixed intervals and the balance sheet date does not coincide with a pay period. If the pay period ends on Friday, for example, but the accounting period ends on Wednesday, a current liability for the unpaid wages must appear in the balance sheet. The accrual should include unpaid wages and salaries of both office and factory employees, whether on an hourly, weekly, or monthly pay basis; it frequently also includes unpaid bonuses and commissions which are a part of employee compensation. However, commissions and bonuses may be reflected as separate liabilities if they are unusual in nature or significant in amount.

Unclaimed wages which have not been paid to employees because of failure to claim their earnings should be included in salaries and wages payable. If payroll checks which are long outstanding have been removed from the books and returned to cash, a liability exists for at least a period of several years, or until the statute of limitations removes the contingency. In some jurisdictions, such unclaimed amounts revert to the state under the applicable escheat law.

In most cases, wages and salaries payable appear in gross amount, and payroll taxes or other related withholdings are not segregated. A difficult problem is frequently encountered in the determination of the amount of wages and salaries payable on the balance sheet date. Calculation of the amount payable for a portion of a pay period can be a laborious process, especially when employees are paid on an hourly basis. An estimate of the liability can be accomplished by estimating the wage cost per day and projecting this daily cost for the number of days' unpaid wages. Unpaid commissions, fees, and similar types of employee compensation may also be estimated in the same way.

Employee Withholdings Payable.   Withholdings from employees' wages include old age and survivors' insurance, federal income taxes, and a host of miscellaneous deductions. Some of the deductions, such as those for hospitalization insurance, are frequently required by the employer, while others, such as union dues and savings bonds, are either optional or are required by contracts with labor unions. The liabilities for the withholdings are fequently recorded at the same time as the wage expense, as illustrated below:

Wage and Salary Expense	17,593.42	
Federal Income Tax Withholding		
Payable		1,952.11
Federal Old Age Benefits Payable		639.22
Union Dues Withholding Payable		156.00
Employee Savings Bond Withholding		
Payable		240.00
Group Hospitalization Withholding		
Payable		312.68
Wages and Salaries Payable to		
Employees		14,293.41

The company is acting as the employees' agent in withholding these sums, and the liability accounts are debited directly when monies are forwarded to the appropriate payee. Although separate accounts are used for the various withholdings, they need not be shown separately in the balance sheet.

Old Age and Survivors' Insurance Withholding.   Old age and survivors' benefits are authorized by the Federal Insurance Contributions Act and provide for the withholding of a percentage of the earnings of all covered employees. The employer matches the amount withheld from employees, and the two amounts are forwarded to the appropriate agency of the federal government. This deduction from employees' wages is often referred to as "the social security tax," although in reality the social security tax includes the state and federal unemployment compensation insurance paid by the employer.

Both the rate and base earnings upon which this tax is based have been changed frequently since the withholding was first authorized.

This withholding is sometimes called the OASI tax (Old Age and Survivors' Insurance), FOAB (Federal Old Age Benefits), or FICA (Federal Insurance

Contributions Act). The tax applies to employers of one or more persons, with certain limited exceptions. The amount withheld from employees, plus the matching amount paid by the employer, must be remitted regularly to an authorized bank. If the combined amount withheld from employees and assessed against the employer is more than $100 in any one month, the payment is made monthly, even though the reports are filed quarterly.

If an employee changes employers during the calendar year, the new employer does not consider any withholdings made by the previous employer in computing the wages subject to withholdings. Thus, the withholdings for that employee made by both employers may exceed the maximum. In such cases, the excess withheld from the employee is considered an advance payment on his federal income tax.

Income Taxes Withheld. Income tax withholdings from an employee's wages are determined by the number of his personal exemptions and the earnings for the period. The amounts withheld are payable to the governmental agency at the same time as the old age and survivors' insurance payments. The amount to be withheld in any given period is determined by formula or may be read from tables prepared and furnished by the government. These tables are constructed for varying combinations of earnings, pay-period intervals, and numbers of dependents.

Other Employee Withholdings. When withholdings are made from employees' pay for such things as union dues, hospitalization premiums, or savings bonds, the amounts are normally credited directly to liability accounts at the time withheld. A later remittance to the labor union or the insuring company, or the purchase and distribution of savings bonds to employees, relieves the company of its liability for the amounts withheld. The employer is acting as the employee's agent in making the withholdings, and the amounts are considered held in trust for the employee.

Unemployment Compensation Payable. In addition to the matching amounts which the employers must pay for FICA taxes, they are also subject to taxes for federal unemployment compensation insurance and state unemployment compensation insurance. Both types of unemployment compensation were made mandatory by the Federal Insurance Contributions Act.

State unemployment compensation tax is computed as a percentage of the employee's earnings, but the percentage is established by state regulatory bodies, even though the tax is required by federal law. The Federal Insurance Contributions Act made a state plan for unemployment compensation mandatory.

The frequency with which reports must be filed depends upon the regulations of the individual state, but reports are usually required on a quarterly basis. Quarterly returns must indicate the earnings of each employee, as well as the tax payable for that quarter. In some states employees must also contribute to the unemployment program through payroll withholdings.

The employer's contribution for the federal portion of the unemployment compensation is a fixed percentage, of a defined amount, earned by each employee during each calendar year with each employer. Payments are made annually to the federal government, and the annual report accompanying payment must be submitted no later than one month following the end of the calendar year. Unemployment benefits are paid to individuals only out of the various state unemployment funds; the federal unemployment contributions of employers are held to be used in case a state should have insufficient funds to cover its unemployed workers.

Property Taxes Payable. The liability for property taxes is normally based upon the assessed valuation of the properties as of a given date, using the currently approved tax rate. The date at which the assessed valuation is rendered usually differs from the balance sheet date. Accounting treatment has, in general, held that taxes accrue ratably over a tax year rather than occurring instantaneously as of the assessment date. *Accounting Research Bulletin No. 43* states:[12] "Generally the most acceptable basis of providing for property taxes is monthly accrual on the taxpayer's books during the fiscal period of the taxing authority for which the taxes are levied." However, the Committee indicates that consistency of application from year to year is the important consideration, and since special circumstances may suggest an alternative accrual period, selection of other accrual periods is acceptable.

The legal view is that taxes on real property are the liabilities of a given business as of the date on which the taxes become a property lien, usually the date of the assessment, Accountants, however, generally recognize that accrual on a straight-line basis provides a better measure of net income and financial position.

Sales and Excise Taxes Payable. Federal and state laws generally require businesses to act as agents for the government in the collection of sales and excise taxes. Generally, the sales taxes collected from customers are recorded separately at the time of collection, and the current sales tax liability represents taxes collected which have not yet been remitted to the appropriate governmental organization. Frequently, the collecting company is permitted to retain a small percentage of the collections to offset the clerical costs incurred in making and remitting the tax. The total collections from customers may not exactly equal the amount which must be remitted, especially if the remittance is computed as a percentage of total sales. The balance sheet should reflect only the amount payable to the governmental organization and should not include any portions to be retained by the company. Adjustment to the sales and excise tax liability accounts are frequently necessary on the balance sheet data to ensure that only the amount payable is included.

Profit Sharing Bonuses Payable. Many employment contracts provide for the payment of a bonus to officers or other employees, or for the distribution of a share of profits. The bonus is treated as an operating expense in the income statement, and any unpaid portion must be recorded as a current liability pending its payment. In some cases, the bonus calculation is based upon aftertax income, even though the bonus itself is an expense entering into the determination of taxable net income. To illustrate, suppose that a company subject to a 40 percent tax rate agrees to pay a bonus of 20 percent of aftertax net income, and the income before taxes or bonus is $100,000. The computation would require simultaneous equations, as follows:

$$\text{Bonus} = .20 \times (\$100,000 - \text{tax})$$
$$\text{Tax} = .40 \times (\$100,000 - \text{bonus})$$

Substituting the equation for tax into the original equation for the bonus produces the following single equation, which can be solved to determine the bonus:

$$\text{Bonus} = .20 \times [100,000 - .40(100,000 - \text{bonus})]$$
$$\text{Bonus} = .2 \ (60,000 + .4 \times \text{bonus})$$
$$\text{Bonus} = 12,000 + .08 \times \text{bonus}$$
$$.92 \times \text{bonus} = 12,000$$
$$\text{Bonus} = \$13,043$$

Dividends Payable. Dividends do not become legal liabilities until formally declared by the board of directors. Dividends to be paid in cash should be reported as liabilities whenever declared before the end of the balance sheet period, even though the date of record or the date of payment falls in the subsequent accounting period. The courts have held that after a dividend has been declared and made public information, it may not be revoked and has the same legal force as

[12]*ARB No. 43*, chap. 10A, par. 14.

any other unsecured debt. Unpaid dividends, if material in amount, should be shown separately on the balance sheet.

If there are dividends in arrears on cumulative preferred stock, the arrearages are not shown as liabilities on the balance sheet, even though the company has sufficient cash to pay the arrearage. However, a footnote should be used to reflect this information. Stock dividends should not be shown as liabilities.

A stock dividend does not require a payment or distribution of assets and represents nothing more than a transfer from the retained earnings account to the contributed capital account(s). Dividends payable in stock are properly shown with the capital stock in the owners' equity section of the balance sheet.

Current Portion of Long-Term Debt.   Current liabilities usually include that portion of a long-term debt which becomes payable within the next year. The maturing portion of a serial bond issue, for example, would be classified as a current liability under most conditions, even though the remainder of the bonds payable are classified as long-term debt. If payment is to be made on the maturing portion of the serial bond issue from cash in a special sinking fund shown as a current asset on the balance sheet, the bonds due to be retired must appear as a current liability. On the other hand, when an entire issue of bonds or other debt becomes payable within the twelve-month period, its inclusion in current liabilities implies that payment will be made with current assets. If payment is in fact to be made from a sinking fund which appears in another category of assets, the maturing issue should not be listed as a current liability if it is material in amount. When an entire issue of bonds payable is to be retired in the next year and assets for payment are held in a special sinking fund, neither the bonds payable nor the sinking fund should appear as a current liability or a current asset. Reflecting either or both of them as current items would inhibit the analysis of the company's working capital position.

Pensions and Retirement Plans.   Pension plans may be funded or unfunded, and the funding may be self-administered or trustee-administered, usually by an insurance company. When the pension or retirement plan is fully funded with an insurance company, the premiums which are payable annually represent the total cost to the company. In such cases, current liabilities must include all premiums payable within the next operating cycle which relate to employee services already performed, whether these amounts are for past service benefits or for current service benefits. If the past service portion of the pension agreement is to be paid to the insurance company over a stipulated period of time, such as ten years, only the current installment appears as a current liability.

Advances from Customers.   Monies received in advance from customers give rise to a liability for the future delivery of goods or services. Tuition fees received by a training institute and subscriptions received in advance by a magazine publisher represent this type of liability. The advances are originally recorded as liabilities and are then transferred from the liability account to the revenue account when the goods or services are delivered.

Advance receipts from customers for the performance of services or for future delivery of goods are current liabilities only if the performance or delivery is to be completed within the time period included in the definition of current liabilities. Advance collections on ticket sales would be considered current liabilities, while deposits received on a contract to be completed in two years would be a noncurrent liability.

Receipts from customers will become earned revenues only upon delivery of the goods and services, and thus these amounts contain an element of profit. In the absence of special circumstances, the profit should remain in the liability account, and no distinctions between the cost and profit elements should be undertaken until the revenues are earned. Liabilities payable in money and those payable in goods and services are not usually commingled on the balance sheet. Their separation permits a better interpretation of the current financial position of the company since the working capital drain required to discharge liabilities in goods and services is normally less than the full recorded liability.

Deposits received on containers are recorded in the same way as customer advances, that is, as current liabilities, if there is a reasonable expectation that the deposit will be refunded within the next accounting period. In some cases, customer deposits may not be listed as current liabilities because their return is not normally contemplated within the time period used to define current liabilities. Utility companies, for example, sometimes require a deposit to offset possible nonpayment of billings. Since there is no intent to refund the deposits to customers within the current operating cycle, these amounts may be more properly shown as a noncurrent liability.

Sometimes a separate liability category entitled "deferred credits," "deferred revenues," or "deferred liabilities" appears in the balance sheet, usually between current liabilities and owners' equity. These amounts usually arise either as a result of company policy in the recognition of revenue, such as on installment receivables, or because some doubt exists that income will ultimately be realized. The doctrine of conservatism underlies this practice. Welsch, Zlatovich, and White[13] describe four types of items found in this classification:

1. Revenues collected in advance, such as prepaid interest income, prepaid rental income, and advances received for services to be rendered. These items require that obligations, benefits, or services be rendered in the future before income is realized. Expenses may or may not be incurred in meeting the future obligation.

2. Credits arising through external transactions, such credits being difficult to classify otherwise. Examples of this type of item are: premium on bonds payable, unearned deposit on royalties, discount on reacquired securities, and deferred income on installment sales.

3. Credits arising through certain internal transactions. Examples of such credits are: deferred repairs, allowance for rearrangement costs, and equities of minority interests (on consolidated statements).

4. Credits arising from income tax allocation procedures (income taxes payable in future years).

The failure to identify each item clearly as a current liability, long-term debt, or owners' equity is a possible source of misinterpretation. Use of such a category should be avoided in order to enhance the analysis of the company's financial position. The term "unearned revenue" should also be avoided. Revenue is a measure of service rendered, and thus "unearned" revenue is a self-contradictory term.

ESTIMATED LIABILITIES

The term "estimated liability" describes legal obligations of uncertain amounts or which have uncertain due dates. If sufficiently objective data are available to make reasonably accurate estimates of the amount, then the debt should be reflected in the liability section of the balance sheet. If the probable maturity date, or time in which cash, goods, or services will be provided is less than one year, it must be classified as a current liability. Liabilities for product guarantees or for estimated federal income taxes would be current liabilities, even though the amounts are not absolutely determinable on the balance sheet date.

[13]Glenn A. Welsch, Charles T. Zlatkovich, and John Arch White, *Intermediate Accounting,* Richard D. Irwin, Homewood, Ill., 1972, p. 637.

Federal Income Taxes Payable.   Business units organized as proprietorships or partnerships are not taxable entities, and liabilities for federal income taxes normally do not appear on their financial statements. However, corporations are subject to the federal income tax, and the annual return with accompanying payment (the annual tax less the amounts already paid during the year) must be submitted on or before March 15 for the preceding calendar year, unless the company has approval to use a fiscal year ending on a day other than December 31. In such cases the return is due no more than 2½ months past the last day of the company's fiscal year.

Determination of the exact income tax liability is a complex task, and the taxable income usually differs from the corporation's reported pretax income. Differences are produced by income not subject to tax, expenses which are not deductible, and items taxed or deducted in one period but affecting reported income in another. The tax return contains a schedule which requires the reconciliation of reported net income with the taxable income appearing on the income tax return.

The income tax liability usually appears under the heading of "federal income taxes payable" or "estimated federal income taxes payable." It is an estimation because the final tax assessment is made by the federal government, and the submission of a tax return is required in order to furnish information which permits the Director of Internal Revenue to assess the tax. If the regulations are applied properly, the tax as computed by the corporation will be correct, but when errors or omissions occur, additional tax assessments are made or excess taxes paid are refunded.

In many cases, the tax liability cannot be determined precisely because of uncertainties in interpretation, the fact that certain areas are not covered by any established rule, or because the taxing authorities have not established clear boundaries and have allowed inconsistent borderline deductions. Thus, additional assessments or refunds are relatively common. Both the tax liability for the current year and any additional assessments for prior years are current liabilities, and the two taxes need not be separately reported in the body of the statement. However, footnotes which adequately explain the additional assessment may be required.

Deferred Income Taxes.   In those cases where the company's reported net income and its taxable net income differ, an interperiod allocation of income taxes may be necessary. A company engaged in long-term construction projects, for example, may measure its reported income on the basis of construction in progress but pay taxes only when its contracts are completed. Generally accepted accounting principles indicate that the tax expense appearing on the income statement should, in general, be computed by applying the current tax rates to the reported net income; consequently, a difference remains to be accounted for. In general, the classification of this credit in the balance sheet as either current or noncurrent may be determined (1) by the timing of its ultimate payment or (2) by the nature of the item producing the tax difference. Accounting Principles Board Opinion No. 11[14] takes the latter position for deferred taxes resulting from timing differences but employs the former for carry-forwards and carry-backs.

> Deferred charges and deferred credits relating to timing differences represent the cumulative recognition given to their tax effects and as such do not represent receivables or payables in the usual sense. They should be classified in two categories—one for the net current amount and another for the net noncurrent amount. This presentation is consistent with the customary distinction between current and noncurrent categories and also recognizes the close relationship among the various deferred tax accounts, all of which bear on the determination of income tax expense. The current portions of such deferred charges and credits should be those amounts which relate to assets and

---

[14]"Accounting for Income Taxes," Accounting Principles Board Opinion No. 11, AICPA, New York, 1969, par. 57–58.

liabilities classified as current. Thus, if installment receivables are a current asset, the deferred credits representing the tax effects of uncollected installment sales should be a current item; if an estimated provision for warranties is a current liability, the deferred charge representing the tax effect of such provision should be a current item.

Refunds of past taxes or offsets to future taxes arising from recognition of the tax effects of operating loss carrybacks or carryforwards should be classified either as current or noncurrent. The current portion should be determined by the extent to which realization is expected to occur during the current operating cycle.

Guarantee and Warranty Liabilities.   Guarantee and warranty liabilities are created when a company agrees to provide repair services or furnish parts to replace those found to be defective. Under these circumstances, a more accurate matching of costs and revenues is effected by an estimation of the future costs to be incurred as a result of current sales. Recording these future costs necessitates the recording of an estimated liability.

In some cases, the customer pays a special fee for future service or replacement guarantees covering a specified period of time. These fees must be accounted for in the same way as customer advances, i.e., recorded as a liability at the time received and considered as realized revenue over the period covered by the warranty contract. If the customer's payment is not intended to cover the full cost of servicing the unit over a specified contract period, the full amount should be recorded as a liability and not just the amount received, The balancing debit is a current expense.

In some cases, the expenses and costs incurred in providing services or replacement parts are debited in full to expense accounts, while the earned portion of fees received from customers is recorded in a separate revenue account, so that costs and revenues are not directly offset in the accounts. In other cases, the actual costs or expenses incurred are debited directly against the credits recorded at the time the customer's fees were received.

The contract with the customer sometimes contains a stipulation wherein the company agrees to perform a specified service at some designated time. For example, a company may agree to restore the surface of a property which is being mined at the termination of the mining contract, or to restore property to its original condition before returning it to a leasor. Such liabilities should be accumulated over the life of the contract by debits to current expense accounts and credits to an appropriate liability account. The liability would be considered current only if payment is contemplated or if costs are to be incurred during the next operating cycle.

Trading Stamps and Premiums.   A liability does not necessarily exist when a retailer gives customer trading stamps to be redeemed by an outside company. A retailer who pays a fixed price for the stamps transfers the obligation to the trading stamp company. The cost of trading stamps given to customers is simply a part of the retailer's operating expense. However, the trading stamp company will have a liability for the stamps issued to retailers.

Many companies offer their customers a variety of personal properties as premiums for the return of a specified number of wrappers, box tops, stamps. or certificates. The estimated costs of the premiums that will be given to customers in return for the wrappers or certificates during the next twelve months should be recorded as a current liability.

CONTINGENT LIABILITIES

A contingent liability is one that may materialize as a legal debt dependent upon the future occurrence of certain contingencies. Contingent liabilities arise from assigned accounts receivable, accommodation endorsements, purchase commitments, pending lawsuits, and discounted notes. Welsch, Zlatkovich, and White[15] define contingent liabilities as "potential liabilities arising from acts, events, or circumstances occurring before the date of the balance sheet or from conditions existing as of that date, but for which any legal indebtedness is contingent upon some future event or circumstance."

Two classes of items are sometimes described as contingent liabilities, differing in the degree of uncertainty about them. The first class is made up of items where there is a strong probability that a liability and loss will develop, such as may exist when funds are on deposit in a foreign bank where exchange is blocked. A loss is recorded in such cases by a debit to a loss account, with an offsetting credit to a liability or an asset. Most accountants consider any item in this class as an estimated liability, arguing that if it is sufficiently probable to warrant recording the loss and reflecting the liability in the body of the statement, it should no longer be defined as contingent.

The second class exists when the probability of loss is very remote but when disclosure is desirable. In such cases, a footnote or parenthetical expression is employed to provide disclosure but without the necessity of recording and recognizing the loss. The objective of reporting contingent liabilities is to disclose those contingencies which are sufficiently material in amount, that should they be realized, the financial position of the company would be adversely affected. Thus, although an infinite number of possible contingencies could occur, only the more material ones known to arise out of past operations need be disclosed. Adequate disclosure is possible in four different ways:

1. By parenthetical comment in the main body of the financial statement
2. By a footnote to the financial statement
3. By showing the contingency with other liabilities by extending the amount "short," so that it is not included in the dollar amount of payables
4. By an appropriation of retained earnings.

Only the last of these four methods entails an entry in the books of account, and because of the possibility of misinterpretation it is not used as frequently as the others.

Endorsements.   Contingent liabilities arise from accommodation endorsements or legal instruments and from assigning accounts receivable with *recourse*. The event upon which the contingency rests is the payment of the debt by the maker of the instrument or the customer, and should timely payment not be made, the contingent liability becomes a full legal liability. Footnotes are used for this contingency since amounts and probabilities of payment are difficult to determine.

Law Suits Pending.   This type of contingent liability is the result of unresolved legal action against the company. The outcome of legal action is usually difficult to predict, and may be contingent upon the findings of a court or the verdict of a jury. Even in those cases where the evidence may not be favorable to the defendant company, there is strong pressure not to include specific dollar liabilities in the financial statements since their use may unfavorably influence the position of the defendent company. For this reason footnotes are used almost exclusively for this type of contingent liability.

Purchase Commitments.   Purchase commitments for future delivery of materials or services are a normal part of the operation of a business, and the contingent liability thus created is not recognized in the accounts under normal conditions. The contingent asset to be received is presumed to offset the contingent liability for its payment, and thus no accounting entry or disclosure is deemed necessary. However, a different situation exists when a material decline in the market price of the goods or services ordered occurs, while the company is

[15]Welsch, Zlatkovich, and White, *op. cit.*, p. 644.

committed to pay the previously agreed amount. In such cases, a loss has occurred which should be recorded in the current period since it was in that period that the price decline occurred. The recording of such a loss necessitates the reflection in the accounts of the corresponding liability.

A distinction must be maintained between losses on purchase commitments which can be realistically measured and those contingent losses which might occur at some future date. The latter may be disclosed by means of a footnote or by establishment of a retained earnings appropriation. The former, however, should be recognized with a debit to a current loss account and a credit to a current liability if the receipt and payment of the goods or services is to be made within the next operating cycle. At the time of receipt of the goods or services, they are placed on the books at an amount equal to their current market value and not at the amount paid for them in accordance with the terms of the purchase commitment. The balancing debit is made to the liability account for the estimated loss.

BIBLIOGRAPHY

Accounting Principles Board: "Accounting for Income Taxes," Opinion No. 11, AICPA, New York, 1969.

————: "Interest on Receivables and Payables," Opinion No. 15, AICPA, New York, 1971.

————: "Omnibus Opinion—1966," Opinion No. 10, AICPA, New York, 1966.

————: "Omnibus Opinion—1967, Opinion No. 12, AICPA, New York, 1967.

————: Statement No. 4, "Basic Concepts and Accounting Principles Underlying Financial Statements of Business Enterprises," AICPA, New York, 1970.

American Accounting Association: *Accounting Concepts and Standards Underlying Corporate Financial Statements and Preceding Statements and Supplements,* AAA, Columbus, Ohio, 1958, p. 16.

American Institute of Certified Public Accountants, Committee on Accounting Procedure: *Accounting Research Bulletin No. 43,* 1953, chaps. 3A and 10A.

Hendriksen, Eldon S.: *Accounting Theory,* rev. ed., Richard D. Irwin, Homewood, Ill., 1970.

Kieso, Donald E., and Jerry J. Weygandt: *Intermediate Accounting,* John Wiley & Sons, New York, 1974.

Meigs, Walter B., A. N. Mosich, Charles E. Johnson, and Thomas F. Keller: *Intermediate Accounting,* 3rd ed., McGraw-Hill Book Company, New York, 1974,

SEC Accounting Series Release No. 148, 1973.

Sprouse, Robert T., and Maurice Moontiz: "A Tentative Set of Broad Accounting Principles for Business Enterprises," *Accounting Research Study No. 3,* AICPA, New York, 1962.

Welsch, Glenn A., Charles T. Zlatkovich, and John Arch White, *Intermediate Accounting,* Richard D. Irwin, Homewood, Ill., 1972.

Chapter **24**

Long-Term Liabilities

WILLIAM J. VATTER
Professor Emeritus of Business Administration, University of
California, Berkeley

THE NATURE OF LONG-TERM LIABILITIES

General Character of Long-Term Liabilities. Long-term liabilities are obligations with maturity dates more than one fiscal period past the report date—typically, long-term debt is payable after one year. Long-term liabilities are distinguished from current liabilities which are normally payable within a short period, usually not longer than a year from the report date. If an obligation is to be paid partly within the next fiscal period and partly at a later date, conventional practice separates the short-term and long-term elements; cross references will indicate that the two parts are related.

The time encompassed by long-term liabilities may be very long—corporate bonds may run for fifty years or more—but the concept of *liability* requires some determinable maturity date when the obligation is to be settled. Thus, long-term liabilities are distinguished from proprietary ownership or residual equities such as retained earnings.

Typically, liabilities arise from transactions and events which involve outside parties or conditions not within the control of owners or enterprise management; purely internal effects do not create liabilities. But sometimes the line which is drawn to separate liabilities from proprietorship may be a bit indefinite. Debt connotes liability; but some kinds of "income" bonds are scarcely to be distinguished from preferred stock, and convertible bonds are debt with a contingent feature of ownership shares. Dividends and property distributions may involve transfers from proprietary equity to current or long-term debt; reorganization may shift long-term debt to an interest in preferred or common stock. Nevertheless, even when an obligation does not involve specified amounts, or stated due dates, or strictly identifiable payees, the fact that an obligation has precedence over the claims of owners serves to establish the liability on at least an estimated basis. Some liabilities arise from equitable rather than legal considerations, because costs have been incurred; even though not precisely measureable they are estimated, as for employee pensions payable on retirement.

THE DISCOUNTING PROCESS

Importance of Compound Interest in This Area. The principal feature of accounting for long-term liabilities is that the long time periods involved make it imperative to recognize interest as a factor in the measurement of the amounts of obligations. A debt due in a few weeks or months does not typically raise much question about the time value of money, except where specific contractual payments are involved. Even then, the effect of interest on the accounting process is limited to short-term calculations, and reinvestment of proceeds is not specifically dealt with. But when an obligation extends over several years, the effect of interest is of some consequence; when interest payments are made semiannually on a long-term debt, the reinvestment situation requires that compound interest calculations be used.

Simple Interest Versus Compound Interest.   Simple interest differs from compound interest in the method of calculation. For one period, the accumulation of principal is computed:

$$P_2 = P_1(1 + i)$$

in which P_1 is the present amount of a principal sum, P_2 is the amount of that principal one period (year or part thereof) hence, and i is the rate of interest applicable to that period. Discounting, for the simple interest situation, is calculated:

$$P_1 = P_2(1 - i)$$

This computation is conventional and accepted. In a mathematical sense however, simple interest is biased; that is, the effect of interest is not the same when viewed looking forward as it is looking backward in time. It may be observed that if an accumulated sum $[P_2 = P_1(1 + i)]$ is discounted back to its present worth via "simple discount," the result is

$$[P_1(1 + i)](1 - i) = P_1(1 - i^2)$$

This is different from the figure started with. If $100 is accumulated at 6 percent for one period, the result is $106; 6 percent simple discount on $106 is $6.36; the present worth would be $100 $[1 - (.06)^2]$ or $100 − $0.36 = $99.64. This effect is not of great consequence in short-term interest calculations since most obligations are not both accumulated and discounted in the same calculation. But the bias thus introduced is serious if taken over several periods.

Compound interest calculations are not biased in this way because compound discount is the exact reverse of accumulation. Since division is the inverse of multiplication, the compound discount is calculated through *dividing* by the "conversion factor," $(1 + i)$. Thus a principal accumulates $P_2 = P_1(1 + i)$ and is discounted $P_2(1/1 + i)$. This procedure eliminates the effect of shifting principal amounts since

$$P_2 \left(\frac{1}{1 + i} \right) = P_1(1 + i) \left(\frac{1}{1 + i} \right) = P_1$$

Calculations which run over more than one period make even more difference between simple and compound interest. For accumulations under simple interest, accumulation for n periods is $P_n = P_1(1 + ni)$, and discounting is $P_1 = P_2(1 - ni)$. But under compound interest, the interest element is assumed to be reinvested at the given rate of growth, and accumulation becomes repetitive multiplication by the conversion factor: $P_n = P_1(1 + i)(1 + i) \cdots$ (n times). A simple way to write this is $P_n = P_1(1 + i)^n$, in which n is an exponent, that is, the number of times $(1 + i)$ is multiplied by itself to produce the effect of interest accumulation. $(1 + i)^n$ is referred to as the nth power of $(1 + i)$.

Discounting under compound interest is successive division by the conversion factor: $P_1 = P_n(1/1 + i)(1/1 + i) \cdots$ (n times), which may be written $P_1 = P_n(1 + i)^{-n}$, the negative exponent referring to the reciprocal of the corresponding positive power.

Interest Conversion Factors.   For convenience, we shall here use another notation for the factor $(1 + i)$—the conversion factor—in compound interest calculations. By using the symbol F to represent $(1 + i)$, we shall not only simplify the appearance of the compound interest mathematics, but we also emphasize the fact that the mathematical "operator" is not the rate of interest but the conversion factor $(1 + i) = F$, which is the effect of interest calculations for one period at the rate i. Since the processes of accumulation involve successive multiplications by $(1 + i)$, n such multiplications are represented by F^n, the exponent being used to indicate the power to which the conversion factor is raised by such repeated multiplications. Also, F^n may be used in discounting by employing the reciprocal, F^{-n}, instead of going through the more tedious (though equivalent) process of successive division.

These relationships are essential in the determination of amounts for long-term liabilities; an obligation of $100,000 due 20 periods hence at 6 percent per period actually represents only $31,180.50 [$=\$100,000 \times (1.06)^{-20}$] now. Any payment postponed to a future date has a present significance smaller than its nominal amount, because the funds may be invested in the interim.

Tables of Interest Factors. Since the computations of F^n and F^{-n} are time-consuming, tables of such factors are available. These cover various rates of interest and periods for both F^n and F^{-n} factors ($\frac{1}{12}$ to 50 percent rates, and 1 to 50 periods are not uncommon). Tables for the more commonly used rates are presented in the Appendix.

Annuities. Business transactions often require series of payments spaced evenly through time, for example, rentals or loan repayments. In the mathematics of finance, these are called "annuities"; the conventional "ordinary" annuity involves a periodic payment of x to be made at the end of each period (the payment interval) during the life of the contract (the term of the annuity). An installment note, for instance, might require the payment of $10,000 at the end of each year for a term of five years. With interest taken at 6 percent per year, the five payments would have discounted amounts or present worths, as follows:

$$
\begin{array}{lcr}
\$10,000 \times (1.06)^{-1} = & \$ & 9,433.96 \\
10,000 \times (1.06)^{-2} = & & 8,899.96 \\
10,000 \times (1.06)^{-3} = & & 8,396.19 \\
10,000 \times (1.06)^{-4} = & & 7,920.94 \\
10,000 \times (1.06)^{-5} = & & \underline{7,472.58} \\
& & \$42,123.63
\end{array}
$$

This computation may be abbreviated by the use of annuity tables. Since an annuity is a series of equal payments one conversion period apart, the present worth ("commuted value") of an annuity may be established.

$$xC_{\overline{n}|} = x(F^{-1} + F^{-2} + F^{-3} + \cdots + F^{-n})$$

Similarly, the total accumulated sum (future or terminal value or T) of an annuity is calculated:

$$xF_{\overline{n}|} = x(1 + F^1 + F^2 + \cdots + F^{n-1})$$

Tables may be constructed for annuity factors by merely adding the F^n factors for the given rate up to and including the specified number of periods.

Formulas for Annuities. To avoid the tedious additions that are required to state the $C_{\overline{n}|}$ and $F_{\overline{n}|}$ factors for annuities running for long terms (many periodic payments), there are formulas that can be used with any hand or desk calculator capable of exponentiation. These formulas are based on the fact that any specified annuity running over term n may be thought of as the difference between two perpetual series, one beginning at time t, the other (representing that part of the perpetual series that will *not* be received) starting at time $(t + n)$. The present worth of a perpetuity is that principal which will produce an income of x per period at rate i and still leave the principal undiminished at the end of the period. That is, taking the conversion factor $F = (1 + i)$, the commuted value of the perpetuity Z is

$$Z_0 = \frac{x}{F - 1} = \frac{x}{i}.$$

Then, $xC_{\overline{n}|} = x[Z_0 - Z_n(F^{-n})] = \frac{x}{i} - \frac{x}{i}(F^{-n}) = \frac{x(1 - F^{-n})}{i}$

To illustrate, the commuted annuity factor for 26 periods at 5¼ percent is $1 - (1.0525)^{-26}/.0525 = .735622/.0525 = 14.011$. The terminal annuity factor may be similarly established, but most simply it is

$$xT_{\overline{n}|} = x \left[\frac{1 - F^{-n}}{i} \right] F^n \quad \text{or} \quad x \left[\frac{F^n - 1}{i} \right]$$

In this case, the calculation is $2.782463/.0525 = 52.998$. There are tables for annuity factors, but the formulas avoid the need for them, if one is willing to do a little work with a calculator.

Interim Conversion Factors. Interest rates are sometimes expressed as nominal percentages per year, compounded for shorter intervals. Interest at 6 percent compounded or payable semiannually is not really the same as 6 percent per year, because the payment intervals are shorter. Interest being paid more frequently than once a year makes the effective rate somewhat higher. For example, 6 percent per year compounded semiannually does not represent a conversion factor of 1.06 per year, but 1.03 per half-year, and the accumulation effect over one year is $(1.03)(1.03)$, or 1.0609. Similarly, 6 percent per year compounded quarterly has an accumulation effect (conversion factor) of 1.06136 per year.

This increase in growth effect from more rapid compounding does not, however, grow proportionately to the shortening of the payment interval; "6 percent compounded monthly" represents a conversion factor of 1.06168 per year. Daily compounding produces a conversion effect of only 1.06183 per year. The limit to this increase of interest effect by faster conversion is, of course, instantaneous or "continuous compounding." For 6 percent per year, continuous compounding produces a conversion effect of 1.06184.

It is possible to compute interest over a longer period than the payment interval. This arises when payments are made, say, semiannually, but the interest rate is specified as 6 percent compounded annually. If such a series of payments is to be dealt with, the effective rate of interest must be expressed in terms of a conversion period that coincides with the payment interval. For example, if payments are to be made semiannually, when the rate of interest is specified at 6 percent per year with no shorter compounding period, the effect of interest must be stated in semiannual terms. A 6 percent per year effective rate is the result of compounding for two payment intervals of six months each, and the effect of interest per payment interval is

$$1.06 = (1 + x)^2 \qquad 1 + x = \sqrt{1.06} \qquad 1 + x = 1.02956$$

BORROWING AS A SOURCE OF FUNDS

Advantages of Borrowing. As was stated earlier, a good many long-term liabilities arise from financing transactions or borrowing. Business firms may borrow for various reasons. Small enterprises—especially proprietorships or partnerships—may have no other way to obtain funds for expansion; but even large companies find borrowing advantageous. Raising funds by borrowing does not affect the legal control of a company, as would the issue of additional stock. More important is the fact that interest on indebtedness is deductible for tax purposes, while dividends on common and preferred stock are not. Thus, a 10-percent bond issue will have a lower aftertax cost than a 7-percent preferred stock, as long as the marginal tax rate is more than 30 percent. At a 48-percent tax rate, the aftertax cost of the 10-percent bonds is 5.2 percent.

There is considerable disagreement among writers in corporate finance on whether the overall cost of capital can be reduced by including long-term debt in the firm's capital structure. One view, which is usually described as the traditional view, holds that there is an optimum mix of stock and bonds which will minimize the firm's cost of capital. This view holds that by issuing securities with differing degrees of risk, the firm can appeal to the preferences of different groups of investors, and, by the right combination, minimize its cost of capital. The other view holds that the cost of capital is independent of the financing instruments used. While debt may be issued at a lower rate than the presently prevailing cost for common stock, the effect of the issuance of debt is to increase the risk of the residual equity (common stock) and thus to increase its cost. The overall cost of capital made up of the lower-rate debt and the now higher-cost common stock will be unaffected.

Without regard to which of the two views described in the preceding paragraph is correct, many firms issue long-term debt instruments because they provide immediate lower cost of capital then the rate currently being earned on the common stock (perhaps relying on the view that the added risk introduced will be minimal). This is known as providing leverage by borrowing. For example, assume a firm that has only common stock outstanding is earning 12 percent on its stockholders equity of $10 million (earnings to common stockholders = $10,000,-000 × .12 = $1,200,000). If an opportunity to earn 12 percent on an additional investment of $2 million arises, what will be the effect on the earning rate on common stock if it is financed by debt at an 8-percent rate? Earnings before interest and taxes will increase by $240,000 (= $2,000,000 × .12). Interest on the $2 million debt will be $160,000. Assuming a 48-percent tax rate, this interest payment will reduce the tax liability by $76,800. Income to common stockholders will then be $1,356,800 [= $1,200,000 + $240,000 − ($160,000 − $76,800)], or a rate of return increased from 12 percent to over 13.5 percent. Of course risk is now greater as well.

Another possible advantage in borrowing is the effect of price-level increases. When dollars are borrowed at low price levels and repaid when prices are higher, the effect is a gain to the borrower. While this is not a certainty, prices generally have shown an upward trend; this makes debt attractive as a means of financing long-term growth. Of course, lenders, fearing this effect, have demanded higher interest rates to compensate them. As this is written, moreover, the shifts in price levels have precipitated some borrowing arrangements with variable interest rates, which by contract carry part of this advantage to the lenders—allowing the rate of interest to follow the price level or the rate on Treasury bills. Whether this will become a widespread practice is an interesting question.

Accounting for Notes.   The simplest case of long-term borrowing is the single-payment note. In the case of an equipment purchase, the purchase price may be settled by a single note for, say, $100,000, payable after three years "without interest." Although the note apparently is non-interest-bearing, the postponement of payment is certainly not free. The amount of the interest charge may frequently be established by the discount that could have been had for immediate payment. Suppose that the cash price were $75,000; the rate of discount may be found by observing that the present worth of the note is .75 of the face amount due three years hence. Entering a table of F^{-n}, the present-worth factors for three-year terms at various interest rates may be compared with the .75 specified. In the 10-percent rate column will be found the factor .75131, almost the same as the actual discount effect. The rate of interest is thus very close to 10 percent per year. The note should be recorded:

Equipment Cost 75,000
Long-Term Notes Payable ...   75,000

It is more common to record the note at the face amount with a contra-account for the discount of $25,000. However, this adds no real information; the obligation at the time of incurrence is that amount which would have settled the debt then, not three years afterward.

In accounting for this loan, interest would be computed at the 10-percent rate, even though no payment is required until the end of the three years. The first year's interest charge is $7,500, which would be charged as an expense and credited to Long-Term Notes Payable (or to the discount account, if one were used). The second-year interest charge is based upon the carrying value of $82,500 (original $75,000 plus unpaid interest of $7,500) and would be $8,250.

The third year's interest charge, based upon a carrying amount of $90,750, would be $9,075; this would bring the carrying amount to $99,825. The difference of $175 arises from the fact that the rate of interest was not exactly 10 percent per year. This difference (too small to be material) would simply increase the last year's interest charge to $9,250. The history of the obligation would thus be

Balance beginning of year	Interest added to debt	Balance end of year
$75,000	$7,500	$ 82,500
82,500	8,250	90,750
90,750	9,250	100,000

The accumulation could have been made on a straight time basis at $8,333.33 per year, and for practical purposes this would perhaps be satisfactory. But in such a case, the effective rate of interest in each year would be different (11.11, 10.00, and 9.09 percent) even though the three-year total of interest would be the same; this is because of the increase in the carrying amount for each year.

Installment Loans. The payment of an obligation may be handled in installments; the $100,000 equipment purchase may have been made payable in three equal payments "without interest." Such an arrangement combines interest and principal, but the effect of interest may be measured. At a cash price of $75,131, the rate of interest is considerably higher than 10 percent because the payments are due earlier than before. To see how high the rate is, we inquire what rate of interest will make $75,131 the present worth of three annual $33,333 payments. Using a $C_{\overline{n}}$ table, the three payments at 10 percent are worth $82,900; at 15 percent they commute to $76,107, and at 20 percent to $70,217. Evidently the correct rate of interest in this plan is between 15 and 20 percent; using a linear interpolation (approximation), the rate may be estimated at 15 percent plus 977/5,890 of the 5-percent difference in rates, which is about 15.8 percent.

Amortized Loans. Loans may be repaid according to an amortization schedule at some specified rate of interest, the payments to include interest at that rate, plus repayment of the principal over the term. This form of loan is common practice in residential real estate finance. The payments are computed by setting the initial principal as equal to an annuity of x for the given rate and time:

$$\$75,131 = x(C_{\overline{n}} \text{ at } i)$$

At 10 percent this becomes

$$\$75,131 = x(2.48685)$$
$$x = \$30,211$$

The way in which this payment serves to amortize the $75,131 principal may be seen in an amortization table, as shown in Exhibit 1.

EXHIBIT 1   Three-Year Amortization of $75,131 Loan at 10 Percent

Year	(a) Balance at beginning of year	(b) Interest on (a)	(c) Total (a) + (b)	(d) Payment made at end of year	(e) Balance forward (c) − (d)
1	$75,131	$7,513	$82,644	$30,211	$52,433
2	52,433	5,243	57,676	30,211	27,465
3	27,465	2,746	30,211	30,211	-0-

Bonds Payable.   Actually, a bond issue is an aggregation of many certificates of indebtedness formalized through legal procedures; it is often handled through a trust company, a marketing syndicate, or a group which sells those certificates in the investment market. The bonds are typically printed in denominations of thousands of dollars and are sold at whatever price the market will bear. The bond issue really arises from a contract called the bond or trust "indenture," executed by the corporation and a designated trustee. In the indenture various details are specified, such as the pledge of property or other protection for the loan, and the various rights and obligations of the corporation, as well as the dates, amounts of payment, and other details.

For accounting purposes, bonds are a specific kind of debt for which the accounting issues involved are more or less spelled out in the indenture. However, all bonds have certain features in common, which determine the major accounting procedures that are required.

Overall Nature of Bond Obligations.   A bond is a promise to pay (1) a principal sum at its maturity date, and (2) a series of interest payments which offset the accumulation of the principal. When a bond sells at its face value (principal amount to be repaid at the end of the term), the interest payments are exactly equal to the interest accumulations. An 8-percent, 20-year bond which is issued at par carries interest payments of 8 percent per year; however, traditionally bond interest is paid semiannually, which means that the effective rate is 8 percent compounded semiannually, or 4 percent each six months. The principal to be repaid is thus discounted for 40 periods at 4 percent (the F^{-n} factor is .20829) and the principal (say, $1 million face value) thus has a present worth of $208,290. The interest annuity consists of 40 payments of $40,000, payable semiannually. C_{40} at 4 percent is 19.79277, and the entire series of interest payments is thus worth $791,711. The sum of the present worth of principal repayment ($208,290) and the interest annuity ($791,711) is $1,000,001 less a rounding error of $1. This relationship is of significance in determining the price of a bond issue.

Kinds of Bonds.   There are various classes of bonds with different combinations of features, some of which are mentioned here. Some bonds have coupons attached to the major certificate, one for each interest payment. Such coupons are on their due dates presented for payment (through the banking system) to the trustee who has received the money to pay those amounts from the corporation. But other bonds are registered; that is, the trustee keeps a record of the bondholders' names and addresses and mails a check for the proper amount to each bondholder on the due date. Thus the trustee serves as a disbursing agent for the debtor corporation.

Nearly all bonds carry a specific rate of interest as part of the borrowing agreement. This is called the coupon rate since it is usually printed on the coupons, when these are used. The coupon rate, fixed in the indenture, is only roughly indicative of interest cost or yield on the issue, because bonds are sold in the open market where the price may or may not be the face or maturity amount.

Some bonds, however, have variable rates of return. Occasionally "income" bonds pay interest only if the company earns it, but in no event more than a specified rate. In this situation, it is not easy to distinguish income bonds and preferred stocks, both of which may be cumulative, with various other contingencies and arrangements.

Some bonds (an increasing number in recent years) are made convertible into common stock. Until so converted, however, these are treated as bond liabilities; conversion requires retirement of the bonds and replacement by shares of stock, as specified in the trust indenture.

The impression persists that bonds are "secured" obligations; that is, the payment of interest, principal, or both is guaranteed by the pledge of specific property. This is not without truth, but the various kinds and degrees of security cover a wide range; it would be difficult if not impossible for a balance sheet or even the footnotes thereto to cover all the details that could be involved. Seldom if ever is there any reference to specific properties pledged against bond issues within going-concern balance sheets. The reader is presumed to be aware of the need to establish the specific features of bonds by reference to financial manuals or other sources of information.

Mention should be made, however, of one specific kind of unsecured bond: debentures. Holders of debenture bonds simply rank as general creditors with other unsecured creditors. The risk involved in such securities varies with the financial strength of the debtor. Such issues are commonly protected by various requirements to limit dividends, to maintain working capital, or by other financial restrictions. Here, too, is good reason for the accountant to examine carefully the trust indenture.

ISSUANCE PROCEDURES FOR BONDS

Marketing Arrangements.   Bonds may be issued directly by the debtor corporation; this sometimes happens in the case of new, small, or closely held companies where the market for capital is so local and so restricted as to make direct sale the easiest course. But most bond issues are marketed through investment bankers, often operating as syndicates to combine effort and minimize risk of loss. "Underwriting" an issue (assuring the debtor corporation of a certain amount of funds from its sale) entails the risk of price fluctuations; often additional service and advice are entailed. But securities are thus "sold" at wholesale to investment bankers, who resell those securities to their customers. There are a number of legal procedures, filing of reports with the Securities and Exchange Commission or state corporations-control offices which are beyond the present scope of this chapter. No corporation should embark on any extensive financing campaign without competent advice on the legal and institutional pitfalls which can be involved.

Bond Authorization.   Bond issuance, like the issuance of other securities, has a legal basis. In the case of a corporation the issue of bonds is based upon action of the board of directors pursuant to stockholder authorization in some form. Bonds are sometimes authorized in an amount greater than the immediately expected issue. In such case, double-entry record may be made of this action:

Unissued 8% 20-Year Bonds 5,000,000
   8% 20-Year Bonds Authorized 5,000,000

This entry is really only a memorandum, as there is no actual transaction involving assets, liabilities, or shareholders' equity; the amounts are mere face values which may have little relevance to the actual issue price. If the bonds are then offered for subscription (as might be the case in a smaller corporation or under certain restrictions of the corporate charter or bylaws), suitable entries might record these in a fashion similar to that used for stock subscriptions:

Subscriptions Receivable, 8% 20-Year Bonds	2,082,000	
8% 20-Year Bonds Subscribed		2,082,000

This entry, unlike the preceding one, records a real claim for payment and an obligation to issue bonds at a stated price; but the bonds would probably not be issued unless paid for in full. When this occurs, collection of cash and issuance of bonds would be recorded:

Cash in Bank	2,082,000	
20-Year Bonds Subscribed	2,082,000	
Subscriptions Receivable, 8% 20-Year Bonds		2,082,000
Unissued 8% 20-Year Bonds		2,000,000
Premium on Bonds Payable		82,000

This entry assumes the authorization entry to have been made. If the authorization was not regarded as an accountable transaction (for reasons already hinted at) the credit (above) to Unissued 8% Bonds would have been made to the account 8% 20-Year Bonds Payable. It will be noted that, conventionally, the face amount of the bonds is separated from the premium or discount recognized in the subscription price. Determination and treatment of these premium or discount amounts are discussed in the following paragraphs.

Bond Prices.   Bonds, like other investment securities, are traded in markets where prices are established by competition between buyers and sellers. Bonds may be issued at any price, but the price reflects the market interpretation of the investment value of the promises contained in the bond and its indenture. It has been observed that a bond is a promise to pay some face or maturity value and a series of interest payments on specified future dates. The present worth of those payments, calculated at the current yield rate (which reflects the market appraisal of risk and desirability of the bond) is the price of the bond.

However, when bond prices are determined by bargaining rather than direct computation from given yield rates, the relationship between price and yield rate may be only approximate. The stated price of the bond issue recorded immediately above implies a yield rate of about 3.8 percent each six months (7.6 percent compounded semiannually), as shown in the computation:

Principal: $2,000,000(F^{-40}$ @ .038) = $2,000,000(.22496)	$ 449,920
"Interest" ($80,000 each six months for 20 years):	
$80,000(C_{40}$ @ .038) = $80,000(20.39578)	1,631,662
Computed price	$2,081,582

The price as computed is only a little less than the actual recorded one; this suggests that the yield rate of 3.8 percent each six months is only a little too high. The difference of $418 between the actual and the computed price is not of great consequence over 20 years on a $2,082,000 amount. Note that the $418 difference is viewed not as a result of decimal rounding but of the impossibility of computing and using the exact rate without the assistance of an electronic computer.

Nevertheless, it is the market (real, negotiated) rate of interest—or *yield*—that is the effective rate used in all bond valuations and pricing. The coupon or nominal rate, which determines merely how many dollars will be paid each six months, is not the effective rate, except in the rather uncommon case when the bond sells precisely at par in the market. This fact is here emphasized by the use of "interest" (in quotation marks) to designate coupon rates or the promised "interest" payments; interest (without quotes) means interest cost of the effective (market) rate established by the price of the bond.

Direct Calculation of Bond Price. Bond prices may be established for given maturities and coupon rates, as related to yields, by reference to "bond tables." A partial example is presented in the appendix of this handbook. There, it may be seen that a bond viewed from 20 years before its maturity, with a coupon rate of 8 percent (4 percent each six months) and a required yield of 3.8 percent (7.6 percent compounded semiannually), would sell at a price of 104.079 percent of par. This is almost precisely the same as was determined above; $2,081,582/ 2,000,000 = 104.0791.

Price Derived from Par and Yield. Another way to calculate the price of a bond is to compare it with one that would sell at par in the 7.6-percent market. Such a $1,000 bond would have to have 40 coupons of $38, payable each six months, to sell at par. The bond here under consideration carries $2 higher "interest" payments, and therefore sells at a premium, the amount of which is the present worth of an annuity of $2 for 40 periods at 3.8 percent. *$2 × 20.39578* would be *$41,* the premium for one $1,000 bond; the premium for the whole issue would be 2,000 times this, or $82,000, the same as indicated above.

Estimating Bond Yields or Prices. There is no easy way to calculate the effective yield precisely for any given bond, nor a simple way to find the exact price which would produce any specified yield. There are "bond" tables which show prices associated with given coupon rates and time to maturity. But these tables show prices in decimals, whereas market quotations are in eighths or thirty-seconds, and even the most detailed tables cover only certain specified terms—10 years, 10½, 11, 11½, etc. The usual way to calculate yields is by trial and error; approximations are used for most situations. One way to estimate the yield of a bond is to compare average investment with average income. For instance, a $1,000 bond with $40 coupons, offered at a price of $1,033 five years before maturity, might be the basis for the following yield estimates:

$$\frac{(\$40 - \$33/10)}{(\$1,033 + \$1,000)/2} = \frac{\$40 - \$3.30}{\$1,016.50}$$

$$= \frac{\$36.70}{\$1,016.50}$$

$$= .036104$$

The yield thus approximated by trial and error is 3.6104 per year, compounded semiannually. (As given in a bond table, such a bond at $1,033 would yield 7.2 percent compounded semiannually.) Such approximations are useful, but less than precise over long terms (over twenty years). The one just given here would tend to overstate true yield when prices are above par, and to understate them when they are below par.

Ancillary Issuance Costs. The issue prices for bonds are presumed to be net of all costs of issue. Legal fees, commissions, printing, and other costs of issue are deducted from the bond proceeds. This has the effect of amortizing such costs over the life of the issue as a part of the premium or discount involved. Meigs, Mosich, Johnson, and Keller[1] suggest that the ancillary issue costs may be capitalized as an asset and "amortized" over the life of the issue. This would not produce any substantial difference in total, but it would reduce the yield rate and the apparent interest cost.

[1]W. B. Meigs, A. N. Mosich, C. E. Johnson, and T. F. Keller, *Intermediate Accounting,* 3rd ed., McGraw-Hill Book Company, New York, 1974, p. 688.

Interim Interest. Bonds may be issued or acquired on dates different from those on which "interest" is payable. The complexities of this situation are usually resolved by accumulating the "interest" at the coupon rate for whatever period is necessary. Thus, an issue whose certificates were dated October 1 (interest dates April 1 and October 1) was actually sold and delivered on October 10; these bonds would have added to their price the accrued (simple) coupon interest. The issuer or seller would merely credit this extra amount to Interest Charges, thus partially offsetting the later payment of the regularly specified "interest." The inaccuracy thus introduced is seldom significant.

ACCOUNTING FOR OUTSTANDING BONDS

Interest Accruals. The accounting related to an outstanding bond issue involves not only the payments specified by the bond indenture, but also an appropriate method of matching interest charges with the fiscal period of the issuer. Since most bond issues involve the use of an intermediary trustee or disbursing agent, the entries for payments would be made when such funds are transferred to the trustee or interest disbursing agent as an "advance." This advance would be "expensed" when the report of final payment to bondholders was received. But when interest dates do not correspond to fiscal closing dates, an accrual entry must take up interest charges for reporting purposes. This requires not only a proration of cash "interest," but also that something be done about whatever premium or discount may have resulted from the issue.

Discount and Premium Amortization. Premium and/or discount are a part of the issue price of bonds, and they represent adjustments to "interest" cost. It has been observed that only a bond selling at par or face value has a yield rate equal to the coupon rate. If the bond sells at some other price, the difference (premium or discount) reflects the difference between the "interest" payments at the coupon rate and the effective yield rate.

Straight-Line Amortization. The simplest way to carry premium or discount into the periodic interest charge is to apply a straight-line (equal annual charge or credit) amortization of premium or discount. Thus, a 20-year 8-percent bond issue sold for $2,082,000 would require amortization of premium, $\frac{1}{40} \times \$82,000 = \$2,050$ each semiannum. Interest cost for each half year would be recorded:

Interest Charges	77,950	
Premium on Bonds Payable	2,050	
Interest Payable		80,000

If the bond had been sold at a discount, for example, at a price of $98.05, or $1,961,000 total, the first semiannual accrual entry would be

Interest Charges	80,975	
Discount on Bonds Payable ..		975
Interest Payable		80,000

In such a case, the difference between the issue price and par is spread over 40 periods, each six months. The carrying amount would thus increase to par (the redemption amount) at the maturity date.

Using straight-line amortization, the equal annual amounts charged to interest will not produce the same apparent percentage interest rate in each year. Amortization of premium causes the liability to decrease from year to year; an equal number of dollars charged each year for interest produces an increasing annual rate for successive years. Similarly, equal annual charges which include amortization of discount will appear as declining percentages of the increasing principal.

Accounting Principles Board Opinion No. 21 specifies that discount or premium should be "amortized as interest expense . . . over the life of the note [bond] in such a way as to result in a constant rate of interest when applied to the amount outstanding at the beginning of any given period." This would seem to rule out the straight-line amortization method, but the Opinion goes on to add, "However, other methods of amortization may be used if the results obtained are not materially different from those which would result from the 'interest' method." The "however" clause serves as a basis for continued acceptability of the straight-line method, although the interest (or more properly the "effective yield") method is preferred.

Interest or Effective Yield Amortization of Premium.   The interest or effective yield method results in an interest charge which is a constant percentage of the effective bond liability at the beginning of each period. The premium amortization is the excess of interest payable over this interest charge. For the 20-year, 8-percent bond sold for $2,082,000, the first six months' interest accrual would by this method be based on the yield rate (calculated above at 7.6 percent compounded semiannually);

Interest Charges	79,116	
Premium on Bonds Payable	884	
Interest Payable		80,000

The interest charge is 3.8 percent of $2,082,000; since the cash paid for this period is $884 more than the calculated interest cost, that amount is viewed as retirement of principal via the premium account. For the second six months, the carrying amount of the bonds would be $884 smaller or $2,081,116, and interest charges in the second period would then be 3.8 percent of this new carrying amount. The interest accrual for the second six-month period would require the following entry:

Interest Charges	79,082	
Premium on Bonds Payable	918	
Interest Payable		80,000

It will be observed that the premium amortization is a little larger in each successive period, but that the *ratio* of interest charges to the carrying amount (face and unamortized premium) remains constant at 3.8 percent. This scheme of amortization will write off the premium precisely over the term, but with somewhat different interest charges in the individual years than would be the case with the straight-line procedure.

Accumulation of Discount.   If the issue had been sold at a discount (8-percent coupons and 20-year maturity, but a price of $1,961,000), the market yield rate is 8.2 percent (4.1 percent per half-year). The first six months' interest cost would be 4.1 percent of $1,961,000, and the interest accrual entry would appear:

Interest Charges	80,401	
Discount on Bonds Payable ..		401
Interest Payable		80,000

For the second six-month period, the carrying amount of the liability would *increase* by $401 to $1,961,401, and the second six-month accrual entry would be

Interest Charges	80,417	
Discount on Bonds Payable ..		417
Interest Payable		80,000

Writing off the discount increases current charges to operations because the liability at maturity will be greater than the issue price. This excess (the discount) is a part of the interest cost, payable at maturity but chargeable to the periods during which the funds were used. Further, the amount of discount accumulation is not the same each year, but it is somewhat greater in each successive year as the liability grows toward its maturity value.

Interest Calculations, Interim Dates.   The bond year does not always coincide with the fiscal year of the company. This means that the amortizations as presented above must be realigned to fit the company reporting period. Suppose that the bond "interest" payment dates are April 1 and October 1, and the company reports cover the calendar year. Bonds issued on April 1 will, at December 31, have accrued nine months of interest. This would have included the entry given above for the first six months (ended September 30). The entry at December 31 would accrue one-half of the *second* six months' interest charges and amortization. The accrual entry at March 31 would take up the other half. This serves to meet the needs of financial statements without undue disturbance to the regular patterns of discount or premium amortization.

Changes in Market Rates After Issue.   Obviously, market prices change, and the current market yield rate on outstanding bonds changes with them. The question arises as to whether this has any effect upon the accounting for interest cost of that bond issue. If one accepts the proposition that reports and accounts should reflect current conditions and current prices, there would seem to be some reason to recognize changes in the cost of capital as they would appear by changes in actual bond prices and yields. But practice has not recognized this because the contract with the bondholders is not a currently alterable arrangement. A low price for a bond in the market does give opportunity for a company to reacquire its bonds at that price with some advantage, but this opportunity is not always of much significance because only a few bonds may be offered. More important, if the company has a profitable use for the borrowed capital, there is no point in paying it out. When bond prices rise sufficiently (and yields decline), there may be reason for the company's refunding the earlier issue; but that depends upon whether bondholders will give up their higher-than-current-market yield by selling their bonds. As long as the bonds are outstanding, conventional accounting statements do not reflect the changes in yield rates and bond prices; the yield rate in the interest expense calculations continues to be set by the initial issue price and the terms of the indenture. This is, of course, in accord with the principles of historical-cost based accounting.

RETIREMENT OF BONDS

Refunding of Debt

Providing the Cash for Repayment—Sinking Funds.   In some cases, and especially in quasi-public operations, it may be essential to make advance provisions for payment of the maturity amount when due. In order to be reasonably sure that such commitments will be met, borrowers may establish funds for the purpose to which systematic contributions will be made over the term of the borrowing contract. These funds, called "sinking funds," are invested to produce a desired return, and will accumulate the amount required to pay off the obligation at maturity. In some cases, sinking funds are provided to add security to an issue and thus make it easier to market.

The Trustee's Function in Sinking Fund Procedure.   The sinking fund is an example of a way in which an intermediary trustee can be useful. Obviously the funds are no protection to the bondholder unless removed from the direct control of the borrower. The trustee receives the sinking fund contribution, invests the available funds in appropriate ways, and uses the accumulated amount to pay off the bonds. In this situation, the intermediary acts for the benefit of the bondholders; his duties and activities are prescribed by the trust indenture, in which the trustee represents the bondholders as a group.

Contribution Amounts.   The periodic fund contributions are usually required by the indenture to be paid off at certain times and in specified amounts. Obviously a voluntary contribution made at merely convenient times would not be of much use in systematic debt retirement, nor would it afford much protection for bondholders. The amounts and payment dates are determined by calculation, which involves annuity tables. The terminal value of an annuity T_n is the total accumulation of the specific rents over n payment intervals with interest at some specified rate. There are also tables of $1/T_n$, the reciprocals of corresponding T_n factors. Such tables show the ratio of the periodic payment or rent to the principal repayable at maturity, on the express assumption that the entire accumulation will be invested at the specified rate of interest. A \$2 million maturity value may be accumulated over 40 interest periods by making semiannual contributions of \$26,525 if the fund can be invested to earn 6 percent compounded semiannually ($1/T_{40} @ .03 \times \$2,000,000 = \$2,000,000/75.4013 = \$26,525$). The rate expected to be earned in the fund does not bear any necessary relation to either the coupon or yield rate on the bond issue; it is merely what is expected to be earned by the fund as invested by the trustee. Obviously, the rate applicable to the fund may be (and usually is) less than the rate on the bond issue. This is a disadvantage to the borrower because the funds might (and probably would) earn more if used in the business for which they were borrowed. But like other costs, the difference in interest earnings on the fund and the borrowing rate may be worth incurring.

Relation of Borrower to Sinking Fund.   It may be worthwhile to stress that the borrower does not control the fund; it is really "bondholder's" money in the hands of the trustee. Yet the fund does serve to offset the borrower's obligations and is therefore an accountable item, even though it is not an asset to the borrower. The trustee will periodically report to the corporation the status of the fund, so that the proper accounting may be maintained for correct costs and financial position. He may also report to bondholders, but such reports are rare and of limited content. The borrower's payment to the trustee will be occasion for the entry:

Bond Sinking Fund	26,525	
Cash in Bank		26,525

When the trustee makes investments, there is no need to record these on the borrower's books, but income or loss will be reported periodically. Usually the trustee will report the position of the fund in detail as well as the related income and expense data each semiannum—certainly not less often than once a year. Typically these data will be received by the borrower in time for his own annual report; often, the reporting period coincides with that of the borrower.

Taking Up Fund Income and Expense.   The borrower seldom has reason to bring details of retirement fund transactions into his records. Usually, the only entry required on the books of the borrower is to take up the income (or loss) from the trustees' operations. This is

Bond Sinking Fund	xxx	
Bond Interest Charges	xxx	

By this entry, the sinking fund income merely reduces the interest charges on that bond issue. (Obviously, the accounting for several issues is kept separate.) If desired, the credit in the entry above might be made to Sinking Fund Income to preserve this detail; however, the net effect is not income to the borrower but only a reduction in his cost of borrowing. The fund belongs to the bondholders, and its assets and income merely offset the borrower's obligations and costs.

Income from sinking funds rarely necessitates allocation to fit the amounts into the borrower's fiscal period. Unless fluctuations from year to year are quite large, beginning and ending accruals would be alike, and would offset. Many trustees' reports are on a cash basis. If needed to prevent serious distortions, the trustee's reporting date could be synchronized with the corporate fiscal period.

Combining Interest and Retirement Fund Contributions.   If the trustee that handles the retirement fund is also the disbursing agent for the interest on the bonds, the payment for both purposes may be combined.

In the somewhat unusual case in which the fund is to be invested at the *coupon* rate of the bond issue, the combined payment for interest and retirement may be calculated from a table of $1/C_n$ factors for the applicable rate and term. But usually the fund is invested at a different rate, and the sinking fund contribution should be computed separately, as outlined above, and the amount required for interest *payments* added as a separate amount. This is applied to the case just described, a $2 million 8-percent bond to be retired by semiannual contributions to a sinking fund that is expected to earn 3 percent semiannually. The amount required for each semiannual payment to cover principal and interest would be $26,525, plus $80,000 for "interest," a total of $106,525.

Perhaps it is worth noting that a sinking fund invested at the coupon rate is mathematically equal to an amortized mortgage loan. Any compound interest calculation assumes that every dollar in the computation grows at exactly the same rate; that is, there is automatic reinvestment implicit in the accumulation of receipts and payments over time, unless the calculations specifically make it otherwise. If the rate of interest earned by the fund is equal to the coupon rate on the bonds and the bonds are to be retired at par, the sinking fund is mathematically no different from an amortized mortgage in which each payment combines interest and principal to retire the debt over the term.

Sinking Funds Invested in Bonds of the Same Issue.   The question may well be asked: Why is the sinking fund not used to acquire bonds of the issue it is supposed to retire? The answer is, of course, that this is indeed a good use of such funds, not only because it serves the intended purpose of the fund (to pay off bonds of that issue), but also because the rate of return may be higher than that of other investment opportunities for the trustee's investment.

But it must be recognized that investment in bonds of the same issue that the fund is supposed to pay off is really retirement of those bonds. In the absence of specific provisions to permit resale of those bonds, they must be regarded as effectively retired when they come into the hands of the trustee. Hence it is not acceptable to treat such bonds as outstanding and to show interest cost to the borrower (corresponding to income to the fund), when the bonds are actually held by the trustee, even though the trustee may consider them to be "live" investments of the fund.

When bonds of the issue are acquired by the trustee and reported to the corporation, the amount of bonds, the remaining unamortized premium or discount, and any premium, discount, or cost involved in the reacquisition by the trustee should be written off.

To illustrate, suppose that $2,000 face value of bonds (8-percent, 20-year $2 million issue, originally sold for $2,082,000) are acquired by the trustee seven months after the issue date. The bonds then have a carrying amount of $2,080 on a straight-line basis (original issue price $2,082, less seven months' amortization at $0.342 per month). Assuming that the trustee acquired these bonds at 103 (plus one month's accrued coupon "interest" at 8 percent per year), his cost was $2,073 ($2,060 + $13 "interest"). The trustee's report would (on a cash basis) show only the $2,073 payment. The borrower's books, however, would record:

Interest Charges	13	
Bonds Payable	2,000	
Premium on Bonds Payable	80	
Bond Sinking Fund		2,073
Gain on Retirement of Bonds		20

Thereafter, this $2,000 face value of bonds would be ignored in the borrower's records, even though the trustee would continue to be paid the cash "interest" and to report "income from investments" of this amount. The simplest treatment would of course be to cancel the bonds entirely, if necessary adjusting the sinking fund contribution to make up for the change in investment income. (The amount of this adjustment would of course be small, since the retirement amount is reduced by the reacquisition.) But most sinking fund indentures do not provide for this. Since the requirements of the indenture are satisfied only by payment of specified amounts, the cash transfers for interest will continue, with corresponding offsets of interest charges against sinking fund income. Any subsequent accruals or amortizations in the trustee's records and reports concerning these reacquired bonds would of course be ignored by the borrower in his own financial statements.

FASB Statement of Financial Accounting Standards No. 4 requires that the gain (or analogous loss) on bond retirement be shown as an extraordinary item net of tax effects, if the amount is material. If, however, the bond indenture *requires* periodic sinking fund retirements of the bonds, then the gain (or loss) is not extraordinary.

Financial Statement Presentation of Bonds Payable

Each Issue Separately Shown and Labeled.   The borrower will, of course identify and separate the accounting for each bond issue in the balance sheet or the notes thereto. For each issue, the general nature of the obligation should be revealed, as by caption, "6-percent 20-year second mortgage bonds" even though it may not be possible to indicate to just what property the second mortgage applies and what else may be involved in the bondholder's position. The caption must identify the issue, even though it cannot completely explain its provisions.

Authorization Amounts Disclosed.   The authorized amount of each issue should be given, especially where there are authorized but unissued bonds, and additional bonds may be issued upon management's decision to do so. Any part of the issue which matures at a date different from the rest of the issue should be segregated and reported separately, especially if the earlier maturity makes that portion of the bond a current liability.

Discounts or Premiums.   Discounts or premiums on issue should be amortized by an accepted method, and the balances subtracted from, or added to, the par or face amount of the liability. Bond discount formerly was frequently treated as an asset and bond premium as a liability separate from the par amount. Accounting Principles Board Opinion No. 21 ruled out such practice by holding that "The discount or premium . . . is not an asset or liability separable from the note [bond] which gives rise to it. Therefore the discount or premium should be reported in balance sheet as a direct deduction from or addition to the face amount of the note [bond]. It should not be classified as a deferred charge or deferred credit."

Other Offsets—Sinking Fund Balances.   Bond retirement funds or sinking funds should appear as deductions from the current amount of the outstanding debt, to reflect the net liability on the issue. It will be noted that this will serve to reduce the net liability by the amount of any reacquired bonds held alive by the trustee. Obviously any bonds treated as effectively retired would have been subtracted from the par, discount, or premium accounts by those entries. "Reserves" for sinking funds are misnomers; when there is appropriation of retained earnings it should be so labeled.

Treasury Bonds. Occasionally a borrowing company may acquire some of its own bonds which it may hold as "treasury" bonds. If such bonds cannot be resold under the terms of the bond indenture, they should be canceled with appropriate entries, to retire face, unamortized issue premium or discount, and any other costs or savings from reacquisition. If the bonds can be resold by the borrower, there is no objection to carrying them at cost, so long as that cost is not in excess of reasonably recoverable amounts. Any such excess is a loss from reacquisition of bonds. According to FASB Statement No. 4, material losses, net of tax effects, on acquisition of such treasury bonds are extraordinary. When such bonds are resold, their accounting status should be made the same as the other bonds of that issue as at that time, to avoid the need for separate premium or discount calculations related to probably immaterial amounts.

When treasury bonds do appear on the balance sheet, the amount should be subtracted from the bond liability which remains after deduction of sinking fund balances.

Serial Bonds. Sinking or bond retirement funds have the advantage of systematizing the repayment of bonds, but there are disadvantages. These arise from the fact that there is no assurance of obtaining a return on the sinking fund investment equal to the yield rate on the bonds, nor any certain way to retire a part of the issue before maturity. These disadvantages may be avoided by substituting an arrangement that calls for specific retirements on definite dates. Some of these arrangements are quite systematically arranged in patterns of serial maturities. That is, bonds of a given issue covered by a single indenture may have maturity dates of 5, 10, 15, and 20 years for example, one-fourth of the issue being due on each of the maturity dates, as specified on its face.

Such a serial bond issue is like any other issue, except that the several retirement dates complicate the computation of yield rates for the issue as a whole and thus make the accounting for discounts or premium a somewhat complex matter. This is not to say that there is no yield percentage that can be applied to the issue, for the average rate could indeed be computed. But this calculation would be a tedious one, and it is doubtful that such an "average" rate (for that is what it would be) really makes complete sense. A bond which matures early obviously has a yield different from one which matures later, for the length of term affects the yield substantially. There has been much written on this topic of the term structure of interest rates. Differences between two compared proposals may be *relatively* much larger or smaller than the absolute figures suggest. A 50-year term is 10 years longer, and 1¼ times as long as a 40-year term; but a 15-year term, 10 years longer than a 5-year term, is three times as long! To be precise in dealing with yields on serial bonds, we ought to compute a yield for each maturity block and account for each block's premiums or discounts separately; this is not easy, for example, when there are 20 blocks, with maturity dates two years apart.

The simplest way to handle discount or premium on a serial bond issue is to use the "bonds outstanding" method. This prorates the bond discount or premium so that each $1,000 unit bears the same dollar charge or credit per time period; the interest charges are thereby kept reasonably consistent. The method will be clear from the following example. Suppose that a $1 million 8-percent bond issue matures in amounts of $200,000 each year, beginning at the end of the fifth year after issue. There will be $1 million of bonds outstanding in the first five years, $800,000 during the sixth, $600,000 in the seventh, $400,000 in the eighth, and $200,000 in the ninth year, a total of $7 million "dollar years."

If the entire issue was sold for $1,014,000, the premium of $14,000 divided by the $7 million dollar year total gives a rate of premium amortization per dollar of bonds outstanding per year. The figure is 2/1,000 = .002. The premium amortization, cash interest, and total interest charges may be seen in the following schedule:

Year	Outstanding bonds.	Coupon "interest"	Premium amortized	Net interest cost
1	$1,000,000	$ 80,000	$ 2,000	$ 78,000
2	1,000,000	80,000	2,000	78,000
3	1,000,000	80,000	2,000	78,000
4	1,000,000	80,000	2,000	78,000
5	1,000,000	80,000	2,000	78,000
6	800,000	64,000	1,600	62,400
7	600,000	48,000	1,200	46,800
8	400,000	32,000	800	31,200
9	200,000	16,000	400	15,600
Totals	$7,000,000	$560,000	$14,000	$546,000

This apparently gives the same charge for each dollar of bonds outstanding per year and is a reasonable solution to the problem. But it is, after all, a "straight-line" solution of the problem, which does not show the true rate of interest in the individual years. The apparent rate of interest (7.8 percent) is a linear average rate but not the correct yield rate, because the correct yield rate should discount all the future payments to the issue price.

Single Yield Rate for the Entire Issue.   The basic problem in using the compound interest amortization with a single rate for the entire serial bond issue is to calculate the correct yield rate. This requires a trial-and-error approach. For example, the bonds-outstanding calculation just presented gives an apparent rate of 7.8 percent (3.9 percent semiannually). If this rate is applied to discount the payments involved, the present worth is approximately $1,010,545. The smaller premium suggests that the rate of 3.9 percent is slightly too high; trial of, say, 3.8 percent might indicate that the correct rate is between these, and the approximation could continue to any desired level of precision. Use of that rate would follow the compound interest yield procedure described earlier. Applying the yield rate to the carrying amount gives the initial charge for that period; the difference between the interest charge and the cash "interest" for that period is the amortization of premium or discount.

Separate Rates for Different Maturities.   This approach treats each block of bonds as a separate issue and establishes a yield rate for each block. The compound interest procedure will thus give appropriate charges and amortization amounts. This procedure is most useful when specific prices are established for each block of bonds—which is not uncommon. But if the entire issue is sold at a single price, there is no satisfactory way to prorate the discount or premium to separate blocks so as to establish a yield for each block.

REFUNDING

At Maturity.   At the maturity date, it may be desirable to continue borrowing, even though the old issue must be settled. Refunding is the process of setting up a new issue of bonds sufficiently large to retire the old issue; sometimes the new issue is larger, when growth requires additional capital and the market makes such additional borrowing advantageous. Refunding at maturity date is accounted for as a new issue of bonds, of which some or all of the proceeds are applied to payment of the predecessor obligation. This raises no particular problems since the two contracts are at least legally separable.

Before Maturity.   When market yield rates have fallen, it may be desirable to replace an outstanding obligation with one that can be marketed at a lower rate of yield. Many bond issues are made callable, to permit the borrower to refinance in this way; the bonds may, under the indenture, be redeemed before maturity at the borrower's option. To compensate the bondholder for what may be for him a disadvantageous repayment, a "call premium" is paid. Usually these vary with the remaining life of the bond. The call privilege raises questions as to the method of accounting for the call premium and other costs of the refunding, as well as the disposition of unamortized premium or discount on the old issue.

Call Premiums.   The call premium may be viewed as the extra cost of getting rid of the old issue, but it may also be considered as the cost of obtaining the lower rate or other advantages of the new issue. There is no really clear answer to this in most cases, and there has been a variety of practice regarding it in the past. Generally the amount is too large to warrant its absorption as mere interest cost of the period in which the call privilege is exercised. There are, conceivably, several ways to deal with the situation. One is to charge the call premium as a special item of the period of refunding. By this approach, no part of the call premium is charged against the new issue.

Alternatively, one might view the call premium as exclusively the cost of advantageous refunding, and the call premium may be subtracted from the proceeds of the new issue, thus being absorbed into the future interest charges via amortization of premium or discount. By this approach the call premium is not separately reported, except as ancillary information.

A third approach might be to amortize the call premium over the remaining life of the old issue, on the ground that the premium was paid to reduce interest in that interval of overlap.

Premium or Discount on the Retired Issue.   When a bond issue is retired before maturity, there is likely to be some amount of unamortized premium or discount. The unamortized balances must be dealt with. They present the same sort of problem as the disposition of the call premium and had been dealt with in the same variety of ways.

The problem was resolved by the Accounting Principles Board in Opinion No. 26, where it held that "a difference between the reacquisition price including call premiums, if any, and the net carrying amount of the extinguished debt should be recognized currently in income of the period of extinguishment as losses or gains and identified as a separate item." Subsequently, the Financial Accounting Standards Board, in Statement No. 4, determined that such gains or losses should be reported as extraordinary items on the income statement.

Establishing Discount or Premium on the New Issue.   When the old issue is paid off from proceeds of the new issue, there is not much question of what price was realized and how much discount or premium applies to the new issue. But when the new bonds are exchanged for the old ones, which are then canceled and retired (before maturity), it may not be easy to establish the premium or discount on the new issue.

If some of the refunding bonds are sold in the market, their price may be used to establish the premium or discount on the entire refunding. A market price of 102 suggests a premium of 2 percent on the whole new issue to be amortized over its term.

The Advisability of Refunding.   The obvious reason for refunding is financial saving. But this is not merely a matter of interest yields, discounts, and premiums. The decision to call and refund an issue of bonds involves future costs, rather than historical or even current prices; the choice of financing plans is a choice between alternatives, and it is the opportunity costs which are relevant to such decisions. However, Welsch, Zlatkovich, and White[2] suggest that a bond redemption formula

---

[2]G. A. Welsch, C. T. Zlatkovich, and J. A. White, *Intermediate Accounting,* 3rd ed., Richard D. Irwin, Homewood, Ill., 1972, p. 686.

may be useful in this situation. The formula, in terms of bond valuation measures, is

$$S = \left[M \times \frac{1}{(1 + i)^n} \right] + \left[I \times a_{\overline{n}|} \; i \right] - R$$

That is, the remaining payments on the bond issue—the discounted maturity amount M, plus the present worth of "interest" payments I (both commuted at the current cost of capital i) make up the current value of the bond obligations. When, because of lower market yield rates or other factors, this value becomes greater than the redemption price R (par and call premium), it is advantageous to refund.

To apply the formula, take a $1 million issue with coupon rate of 10 percent currently redeemable at 105, in a market with a yield rate of 8 percent (all rates compounded semiannually). This bond would be evaluated five years before maturity:

$$
\begin{aligned}
S &= \{\$1,000,000(1.04)^{-10} + \$50,000(a_{10} \; @ \; .04)\} - \$1,050,000 \\
&= (\$675,600 + \$405,500) - \$1,050,000 \\
&= \$1,081,100 - \$1,050,000 \\
&= \$31,100
\end{aligned}
$$

Refunding under these conditions is advisable, for the present worth of the excess cost is $31.10 for each $1,000 refunded. This, of course, assumes that all other things are equal. If the company has other alternatives, these must be considered in detail. This problem may be complicated when the periods of time covered by alternative commitments are different. To compare this refunding with a three-year term loan, we must know or assume what happens in the fourth and fifth years to be able to make any judgment as to relative merit. And the element of relative risk is a constantly evident factor that must be judged in each case.

ADDITIONAL RETIREMENT SITUATIONS

Purchase in the Market by the Borrower.   A borrower who has funds that are not needed for operations may well view the market quotations on outstanding bonds as an opportunity for savings. The decision to purchase bonds in this way is based on an analysis much like that just described in refunding. But the alternatives are somewhat different. The amount that would be required to pay off some existing debt would alternatively be invested in various ways.

The effective interest rate in such an analysis is not that of the bonds (either coupon or yield rate) because the bond purchase is not an investment but debt retirement. The effective interest rate in this situation is the *highest* comparable yield that could be had from investing elsewhere that amount needed to retire the bonds. Any lower yield is less desirable unless it is accompanied by lower risk or other offsetting features. But the investment term must be the same as the remaining life of the bonds.

Discounting the maturity amount and the "interest" payments at the "highest comparable yield" should produce a lower figure than the current market price of the bonds, if retirement is advantageous. This lower figure measures the cost of retiring the issue (the earning rate if invested elsewhere). If the cost of retiring the issue is less than the cost of continuing it, the bonds should be purchased and retired.

When bonds are reacquired, they are retired, even if not canceled. The par amount is carried as "treasury bonds," offset against outstanding face amounts on the balance sheet. Premiums and discounts arising from purchase, as well as those amounts remaining unamortized from the original issue, are preferably written off as gain or loss on bond retirement. If reissued, the bonds may, for practical reasons, be restated at the carrying value of the other bonds of that issue. This avoids the complication of tracing the discount or premium separately for the reissued bonds.

Purchase by Sinking Fund Trustee.   This has already been mentioned above. The essential point is that in the reports of the borrower, bonds held by a sinking fund trustee are treated as effectively retired, even though cash may still be transferred to the sinking fund to cover "interest" on the bonds so held, in keeping with fund calculations.

General Offers to Repurchase Bonds.   Sometimes in an effort to retire debt that is not callable, borrowers may make general public offers to purchase such securities. Any such purchases would be accounted for in the same way as detailed above; amounts in excess of or less than par, and any unamortized premium or discount, would appear as (extraordinary) gain or loss on retirement of bonds.

Conversion.   Some bonds carry the privilege of conversion into other securities, and this may serve as a means of retiring the debt. The conversion privilege is usually restricted to certain periods, and there is a specified conversion price or ratio, such as "at a price of $68 per common share" or in the ratio of "20 shares for each $1,000 principal amount (par) of bonds." All that is required to record such conversion is to transfer the book equity of the bonds (par plus or minus unamortized premium or discount) to appropriate stock equity accounts (see Chapters 28 and 29). But it should be stressed that the conversion should transfer the pro rata amount of all bond premiums or discounts and other costs that may be involved, against the credits to various paid-in capital accounts.

Some accountants would favor crediting the stock or paid-in capital accounts with the market value of the shares issued on conversion, showing the difference between this amount and the related bond equities retired as a gain or loss on conversion. This is in keeping with the view of market price as the opportunity cost of issuing shares to other parties or the amount that bondholders could realize by selling the shares immediately after conversion. However, it must also be recognized that convertible bonds are issued with full recognition of the possibility of conversion; the change in investment position is thus inherently assumed in the original issue. The weakness in using the market price of the stock issued on conversion is not only that the book value of the debt includes the expected value of the conversion privilege, but also that it results in a gain or loss to the corporation when only securities are exchanged. An advantage or disadvantage to other shareholders is not a gain or loss to the entity.

Reorganizations and Compositions.   Bonds are frequently involved in recapitalizations, reorganizations, and compositions in which securities may be exchanged to give priority or to rearrange the financial structure generally. Bonds may be exchanged for other bonds, or for preferred or common stock in various ways. Since such arrangements generally involve a scaling down of equities carried over to the new structure, the principal issue is to be sure that all the elements of exchanged, retired, or canceled obligations are written off along with the major equities involved. Since the details of this are generally spelled out in the negotiations, the accountant needs only to be sure that the negotiations do in fact cover all the necessary angles and that the resulting pattern of equities and interest will accomplish the desired results.

OTHER LONG-TERM LIABILITIES

The long-term liabilities that have been discussed in this chapter have their origin in borrowing transactions. Repayments of loans due after one year have been shown at their present worths using interest rates specified in the contracts or inferred from them. Liabilities arising from other transactions are subject to somewhat different treatment, as will appear in the following paragraphs.

Deferred Revenue Obligations.   When customers pay for goods or services in advance of delivery, these payments represent an obligation to complete the transaction, for revenue is not "earned" until then. This obligation may run for only a short period, and in such case is a current liability; but if the interval between the transfer of cash and delivery is longer than a year, the obligation is considered of long-term nature. An example is prepayment for magazine subscriptions. Receipts would be credited to a deferred revenue account, transferred to income as deliveries are made; at the end of each year the balance would be divided into short- and long-term maturities. Since the rate charged for long-term subscriptions is lower per issue, amortization on a straight-line basis would leave the liability at a kind of "present worth" which, though not explicitly determined, is implied in the contract.

Similar items arise from the receipt by fire and casualty insurance companies of premiums for three or five years in advance. Financial position for insurance companies is not judged in the same way as that for commercial and industrial ones, and the distinction between current and long-term liabilities is not maintained in their financial reports.

There may be other long-term liabilities in the form of advances on long-term construction contracts; these are really deferred revenue, typically shown at the amounts received—not discounted. Such items are specifically exempted from the need for discounting in Accounting Principles Board Opinion No. 21.

Product Warranties.   When a vendor company has agreed to make repairs or replacements of defective parts over a period of years, a liability is created for the estimated cost of making such repairs or replacements. Otherwise, the period of sale would not show part of the expense attributable to the revenues recognized in that period. Determination of such costs entails estimation, for their incidence is uncertain. Experience data provide a basis for such estimates; or laboratory testing will indicate likely failure rates for various parts and assemblies. Assume that over a five-year period for one such item these failure rates may be 1, 2, 2, 4, and 5 percent. The expected cost of making this replacement being $35 per unit, the current year's sale of 100,000 units implies costs to be incurred in the first year after sale of $35,000, and the other years should show $70,000, $70,000, $140,000, and $175,000, respectively. In the year of sale, the total estimated warranty expense of $490,000 is debited with a credit to Estimated Liability, Product Warranties. The outlays made during that year are charged against the Estimated Liability; if these are $32,000, the balance of $458,000 will appear as $73,000 current liability and $385,000 long-term liability.

This procedure serves to match costs against sales revenue unless the failure rates are incorrect. Adjustment may be made whenever the error becomes apparent. To be strictly logical, however, the liability should be shown discounted to present worth; the company has the use of the customers' money to cover these costs until they are incurred. And unless the expected costs of replacement are estimated in terms of the prices that will prevail when replacements occur, the liability is not precisely stated. In a period of rising prices these two errors may tend to offset each other.

Outstanding Tickets, Coupons, and Trading Stamps.   The obligation to honor tickets, coupons, or trading stamps is a liability unless limited by an expiration date. These obligations may involve refunds or the delivery of goods or services, and sometimes the period over which they extend may be long. Identifying the issue date of such obligations (by serial number, code markings, or otherwise) provides a basis for experience data to be collected, matching issues with redemptions over a time. Since some items may be entirely unredeemed, there may be no way to check the outstanding obligation, and/or to identify windfall income from unredeemed items. Reasonableness is the only test that can be applied. As in the case of product warranties, discounting and anticipated price changes are ignored.

Pension Liabilities. Obligations to provide some form of retirement income for superannuated employees or for those disabled by accidents constitute a class of long-term liabilities. Accounting for these will depend upon the way in which the situation is handled. A part of this group of obligations is covered by government agencies, and some firms have merely made specified contributions to a pension trust fund or to an insurance company to transfer the pension liability. In such cases, the accounting liability of the employer is merely the amount owed to the trust fund or the insurance company. But if, as has become increasingly the case, the company recognizes the entire liability in its accounting, the actuarially computed amount is the discounted net probable future payments to retired employees. There are a number of complex issues involved in accounting for pension costs, and they are discussed in Chapter 27.

Leases. Agreements to rent property for long periods may result in long-term liabilities for the lessee (reciprocal assets for the lessor), but the accounting procedures are complicated by different relationships between the parties to the contract as well as in the form and substance of the agreement. Situations in which long-term liabilities are recognized require the discounting of future payments by use of the interest rate specified or implied in the contract. A more complete discussion of lease liabilities is presented in Chapter 25.

Miscellaneous Other Debts. Whenever there exists a legal or equitable requirement to pay money or deliver services to outsiders at some determinable future time for benefits received currently, the liability should be recorded, even if the amount can only be estimated. For example, agreements to replace topsoil removed for strip mining or similar operations, to make improvements such as landscaping a real estate subdivision, or to restore leased property to its condition at the inception of the lease entail charges to expense and recognition of the liability thus recognized. The cost of future performance should be estimated and accumulated by systematic accrual over the term of the agreement to assign the future costs on the basis of benefits received.

Suppose that a development contract will require outlays estimated to be $15,000 at the end of two years, and also $25,000, $40,000, and $50,000 at the end of successive years, a total expenditure of $130,000. This cost might be assigned on the basis of annual sales in units in the five years, expected to be 8,000, 6,000, 7,000, 4,000, and 2,000 in order. The expense charges credited to a long-term liability account would then be $38,518, $28,889, $33,704, $19,259, and $9,630 in the successive years; the outlays when made would extinguish the liability at the end of the term, if the estimates were correct. The costs would have been recognized as expense in the years when benefits (as measured by sales) were received.

Although this treatment is conventionally accepted, it ignores the timing of events and payments; only a small part of the liability would be paid by the end of the third year, for example. This can be taken into account by compound interest methods to achieve a better allocation of costs with respect to timing and the interest cost.

The present worth of future outlays at 10 percent is $15,000(1.1)^{-2} + $25,000(1.1)^{-3} + $40,000(1.1)^{-4} + $50,000(1.1)^{-5}$. Using a table of F^{-n}, these reduce to $12,397 + $18,784 + $27,320 + $31,046; the total present worth is $89,547.

The benefit series would also be discounted: $8,000(1.1)^{-1} + 6,000(1.1)^{-2} + 7,000(1.1)^{-3} + 4,000(1.1)^{-4} + 2,000(1.1)^{-5}$, which would work out to $7,272 + 4,959 + 5,259 + 2,732 + 1,242$, a total of $21,464.

Dividing the present worth of future payments by the present worth of future benefits, we get $4.1718 as the unit relationship of cost to benefits. This unit cost applied to the sales volumes of individual years gives expense charges of $33,374, $25,031, $29,203, $16,687, and $2,344. This totals to only $112,639, because interest has not been computed on the difference between expense charges and payments in the individual years. This can be worked out in an amortization table:

Compound Interest and Cost Allocation

Year	(1) Beginning balance	(2) Interest at 10%	(3) Expense charge	(4) Actual payments
1	0	0	$ 33,374	0
2	$33,374	$ 3,337	25,031	$ 15,000
3	46,742	4,674	29,203	25,000
4	55,619	5,562	16,687	40,000
5	37,868	3,787	8,344	50,000
Totals	—	$17,360	$112,639	$130,000

Beginning balance (1) is the remainder of the preceding line, which is (1) + (2) + (3) − (4). These calculations assume that interest is charged at the end of each year; more refined computations assuming more and shorter periods would be somewhat more "accurate," but the net effect of this would not be substantial. The total of the "beginning balance" column is meaningless—an average computed from this total would not be correct unless based on an abstruse calculation which included compound interest effects.

Expense charges would then be the sums of interest and expense: $33,374, $28,368, $33,876, $22,249, and $12,131. This allocation is preferable to conventional procedure on logical grounds, but is not often followed in practice.

Contingent Liabilities.   Accounting Principles Board Statement No. 4 states in Paragraph 133:

> The *financial position* of an enterprise at a particular time comprises its assets, liabilities, and owners' equity and the relationship among them, plus those contingencies, commitments, and other financial matters that pertain to the enterprise at that time. . . .

In *Accounting Research Bulletin No. 50,* a contingency is defined as "an existing condition, situation or set of circumstances, involving a considerable degree of uncertainty, which may, through a related future event result in the acquisition or loss of an asset or the incurrence or avoidance of a liability, usually with the concurrence of a gain or a loss." Pending or threatened litigation, possible assessments of additional taxes, guarantees of indebtedness of others, and agreements to repurchase receivables that have been sold are examples of contingencies that may cause future losses.

It should be noted, however, that reasonably foreseeable outcomes do not create contingencies. Expected losses on short- or long-term receivables ought to be taken into account in measuring the revenues associated with the transactions creating them, and recorded in terms of the probabilities associated therewith. Risks associated with insurable properties or transactions ought to be covered by insurance, the premiums for which measure the probable losses. If not insured against, there is no way of predicting when, and if, such losses will occur. Properties cannot be in statistical jeopardy; no loss should be recognized until the feared event occurs.

There are also general risk contingencies which are not recognized in financial reports or even in supplementary notes thereto; wars, strikes, and catastrophes not ordinarily insured against are risks that have no more impact on one enterprise than on others in the same line of business, and no special considerations determine the amount or the probability of loss or obligation. Purchase orders outstanding generally fall into this class of liabilities; unless there are special reasons for potential loss, or the amounts are large enough to affect the situation, no special disclosure is required.

Whenever a potential loss or claim is material in amount or importance, depending upon some significant future factor, decision, or likely turn of events, that situation should be disclosed as an essential part of stating the financial position of the enterprise. Disclosure may be made by short entry (not carried into totals, but amounts shown within the balance sheet) or by footnote comments. Since most contingencies will be difficult to state in precise dollar amounts, footnote explanations will be needed. There is also the possibility of setting up appropriations of retained earnings; but Chapter 6 of *Accounting Research Bulletin No. 43* requires that the appropriation should be established only by charge to Retained Earnings, with a specific identification, in amounts determined by reasonable estimates of cost or losses. No costs or losses are to be charged to such an account, and no part of it should in any way be used to affect the determination of income for any year. The appropriation account should appear within the owners' equity classification on the balance sheet.

Obviously the recognition of contingent losses and contingent liabilities requires much judgment and acceptance of responsibility on the part of those responsible for presenting financial reports.

BIBLIOGRAPHY

Accounting Principles Board: "Early Extinguishment of Debt," Opinion No. 26, AICPA, New York, 1972.

————: "Interest on Receivables and Payables," Opinion No. 11, AICPA, New York, 1971.

Davidson, Sidney, James S. Schindler, and Roman L. Weil: *Fundamentals of Accounting,* 5th ed., Dryden Press, Hinsdale, Ill., 1975, chap. 15.

Financial Accounting Standards Board: "Basic Concepts and Accounting Principles Underlying Financial Statements of Business Enterprises," Statement of Financial Accounting Standards No. 4, AICPA, New York, 1970.

Kieso, Donald E., and Jerry J. Weygandt: *Intermediate Accounting,* John Wiley & Sons, New York, 1974, chap. 14.

Meigs, Walter B., A. N. Mosich, C. E. Johnson, and T. F. Keller: *Intermediate Accounting,* 3rd ed., McGraw-Hill Book Company, New York, 1974, chap. 18.

Simons, Harry: *Intermediate Accounting,* Comprehensive Volume, Southwestern Publishing, Cincinatti, Ohio, 1972, chap. 18.

Welsh, Glenn A., C. T. Zlatkovich, and J. A. White: *Intermediate Accounting,* 3rd ed., Richard D. Irwin, Homewood, Ill., 1972, chap. 17.

Chapter **25**

Leases

JOHN H. MYERS
Professor of Accounting, Indiana University

SIDNEY DAVIDSON
Arthur Young Professor of Accounting, University of Chicago

INTRODUCTION

The lease is a very old legal device. It was employed extensively centuries ago by the nobles and landed gentry to permit others to use parts of their real estate. The lease is still used extensively in connection with real estate—primarily in multiunit buildings in cities. In these traditional real estate leases, a primary reason for leasing has been that the property has not been available on any other basis. In recent years, some of this traditional leasing has declined as a result of new legal forms such as the condominium, which enables the user of a small amount of space to own a unit in a large building, and because of greater financial ability of the average consumer. However, leases are now more significant than ever since new uses of leasing have developed. Increasingly, personal property is being leased and financing is becoming a major element in the decision to lease.

Leasing of property has permitted, in many circumstances, use of property without balance sheet recognition of the property or the obligation to pay for it. This "off-balance-sheet financing" has become popular. Some companies have sold a major part of their property and leased it back. Others have induced financial institutions to build special-purpose property in return for a promise to lease this property for a long term of years. The spectacular size of some of the financing leases has been one of the factors leading to a reexamination of accounting theory on this subject in recent years. The American Institute of Certified Public Accountants has sponsored "Reporting of Leases in Financial Statements," *Accounting Research Study No. 4,* and the Accounting Principles Board (APB) has issued Opinions Nos. 5, 7, 27, and 31 on the subject of leases. The Securities and Exchange Commission (SEC) has issued its *Accounting Series Release No. 147.* As this book goes to press (Sept. 1976), the Financial Accounting Standards Board has issued a second exposure draft of a proposed Statement on leases that will supersede the APB Opinions. Citations in this chapter are to that exposure draft.

A lease is a contract by which a lessor conveys property to a lessee. An essential element of the conveyance is that the lessor conveys less than the total interest. Since the lease is a contract between two parties, they specify what its provisions shall be. Typical provisions are outlined briefly in the following tabulation from *ARS No. 4:*[1]

> *Duration.* The lease may run for any term, from a few moments to the entire expected economic life of the asset.
>
> *Alternatives at termination.* The option open to the lessee may range from none, through the right to renew or buy at nominal prices, to the right to purchase at the fair value.
>
> *Rental payments.* In many cases, rents are set to enable the lessor to recover the cost of asset plus a fair return over the life of the lease. The rents may be level, increasing, or decreasing. The rents may be predetermined or may vary with sales or some other factor, but usually a minimum amount is specified.
>
> *Duties of parties as to taxes, insurance, maintenance.* Either the lessee or the lessor may bear these obligations, or they may be divided between lessee and lessor.
>
> *Lessor's duties as to services (e.g., heat, elevator).* These duties may be numerous or nil.
>
> *Restrictions on lessee's activities.* The contract may restrict dividends and/or further leasing and debt.
>
> *Early termination.* The contract may grant the right to terminate on payment of a set scale of prices (prices often representing the lessor's unrecovered cost) plus a penalty.
>
> *Default.* The contract may state liquidated damages in terms such that the lessee is liable for all future payments at once and, when paid, the lessee is to receive title to property. Alternatively, the contract may state that the lessor is to sell and that lessor and lessee are to adjust any differences between the sale price and lessor's recovered cost.

[1]John H. Myers, "Reporting of Leases in Financial Statements," *Accounting Research Study No. 4,* AICPA, New York, 1962.

In any individual case, of course, any combination of provisions on these different points may be used. However, certain combinations of the various provisions are typical. Some common ones are as follows:

1. The term is for the entire expected useful life, and the rentals are set so that the lessor recovers cost of asset plus a fair return. Also, the lessee can buy the property at a nominal price at termination. Lessee must pay taxes, insurance, and maintenance. Lessee may terminate early by paying the discounted value of future rents, in exchange for which he will receive title to the property.

2. Same as (1) except that the lessee has no special rights on termination. (Since asset life presumably will have expired, these rights would usually have little value. However, subsequent economic changes may make them valuable.)

3. Same as (1) except that the life of the lease is shorter than the economic life of the assets (say, 50 percent) but the rent scale is accelerated to the point that lessor recovers full cost plus a fair return over the shorter life.

4. Same as (3) except that no termination rights are granted and the rent scale is lower than in (3). Provisions for early termination are probably absent.

5. Same as (4) but lessor pays taxes, insurance, and maintenance. Rent is higher than in (4) in order to cover lessor's extra costs.

6. Same as (5) except that the term is considerably shorter (say, 5 percent of the life of assets).

7. Same as (6) except that the lessor furnishes considerable services such as heat, elevator service, gas and oil for trucks, perhaps even drivers for the trucks.

These typical combinations thus range from some that approach the purchase of a current service through the traditional short-term lease to ones that seem to be purely financing devices. In addition, some of the lessors have borrowed heavily to finance the transaction, thus creating substantial leverage. These extremely different economic situations call for different accounting methods to portray the facts.

ACCOUNTING METHODS

The APB set forth two methods of accounting for leases in its Opinions on this subject. The "operating method" recognizes the payment and receipt of a lease rental, as rental expense for the lessee and as rental income for the lessor in the period in which the payment is due. The leased asset is viewed as remaining the property of the lessor. The "financing method" assumes that the lease is a method of financing an acquisition of property, and this method requires that the lessee set up the asset and liability with appropriate entries. They include entries for purchase and depreciation of the asset along with entries for setting up a liability and its eventual payment with interest. The financing method requires that the transaction be handled as a sale of property and an acquisition of a receivable with appropriate entries on the lessor's books. The FASB uses the term *capital lease* where the APB used the term *financing lease*. In this chapter, we use the terms interchangeably.

Complications arise because there are only two general methods of accounting for leases, the operating method and the financing method, yet there is a wide spectrum of lease contract situations. Some combinations of contract provisions clearly call for the use of the operating method. Other combinations clearly call for the use of the financing method. However, between these clear-cut situations there is a large gray area in which it is difficult to decide upon the appropriate accounting method.

Operating Method—Lessee.   The operating method is based on the theory that an obligation due to an outsider accrues day by day as the property is used. Payments are recorded by a charge to Rental Expense and a credit to Cash. Appropriate adjusting entries would be made if an accounting period ended between payment dates. This is the accounting method most commonly used in the past and is the one desired by lessees who wish to accomplish off-balance-sheet financing.

When the operating method is used, the lessee's periodic entries are straightforward. Each period the entry is

```
Rental Expense ........................... 50,000
    Cash ...............................          50,000
    To record annual rental under lease.
```

At the end of the lease term, the lessee may have the right to renew the lease at a prescribed or negotiated rental. If so, the entries will be the same as under the old lease with only the amounts changed. If, at the end of the lease term, the lessee has the right to purchase the assets and does so, then the entry is like that of any other purchase:

```
Property ................................................. XXX
    Cash ...............................................          XXX
    To record purchase of leased property at sum set forth in lease.
```

Maintenance, insurance, taxes, etc., if paid by the lessee, are handled in the normal way for any asset owned by the firm.

Operating Method—Lessor. When the lessor is accounting by the operating method, income from the lease is assumed to accrue on a regular basis. Entries will be made when cash is received, and appropriate accruals will be made if the accounting period ends between cash receipts dates. Also, since the lessor owns an asset with a finite economic life, entries for depreciation are necessary.

Entries for using the operating method on the books of the lessor are also straighforward. The entry for cash receipt and revenue recognition would be

```
Cash ................................... 50,000
    Rental Revenue ....................          50,000
    Annual rental income under lease.
```

The entry for depreciation would be the typical one:

```
Depreciation ................................. 5,000
    Accumulated Depreciation ................          5,000
    Depreciation of assets placed under lease.
```

The amount of the depreciation entry will be determined by the usual considerations of estimated useful life, salvage value, and depreciation method (straight-line, declining-balance, sum-of-the-years'-digits). When property has been leased, its economic service life to the lessor may terminate before the property is physically worn out or economically useless. This termination would occur if, by terms of the lease, the lessee had a right to buy the property, at a fixed price at a fixed date. The property's value to the lessor at that date could be no more than the fixed price which the lessee had the right to pay to acquire the property. These lease terms then, in effect, fix an upper limit to the value at the end of the specific period of time.

In addition to the entries for cash receipt and depreciation expense, the lessor must record any payment for insurance, maintenance, and taxes, if they are in fact paid by the lessor. By the terms of many leases, the lessee is to pay these expenses and in such case the entries should appear on the lessee's books, not on those of the lessor.

Financing Method—Lessee. In the following initial discussion of accounting for lessee and lessor, these assumptions are made:

1. The asset was purchased specifically for this lease for $223,255.
2. The lease is for five years, with annual payments of $50,000 at the beginning of each year, implying an annual interest rate of 6 percent.

3. The lessee may purchase the property for $1 at the end of the lease.
4. The estimated life of the property is five years.

Exhibit 1 shows the allocation of each $50,000 payment between interest and principal payment.

The first entries to record the signing of the lease, the acquisition of the property rights, and the assumption of the liability, followed by the first lease payment, are as follows:

```
Equipment Held under Lease  ....................   223,255
     Rental Obligations under Lease ..............           223,255
Acquisition of property under lease financing.

Rental Obligations under Lease  ..................    50,000
     Cash  ......................................            50,000
First payment under lease.
```

At the end of the first year, the entries, assuming use of straight-line depreciation, would be

```
Depreciation  ...............................................    44,651
     Accumulated Depreciation: Equipment Held Under Lease  ....           44,651
Straight-line depreciation for one year, no salvage value.

Interest Expense  ...........................................    10,395
     Interest Payable  ......................................           10,395
To record interest for first year.
```

When payment is made at the start of the second year, the entry is

```
Rental Obligations Under Lease .........    39,605
Interest Payable  ......................    10,395
     Cash  ...........................            50,000
Second payment under lease.
```

The subsequent entries for depreciation are for the same amount (since straight-line depreciation was assumed), and the subsequent entries for interest accrual and lease payments are for amounts determined from Exhibit 1. Upon expiration of the lease, the property will be fully depreciated and may be purchased for $1.

If the equipment is purchased at termination of the lease:

```
Equipment  ..........................    1
     Cash  ..........................            1
Purchase at expiration of lease.
```

The fully depreciated equipment would be written off:

```
Accumulated Depreciation: Equipment Held Under Lease  ......    223,225
     Equipment Held Under Lease  ........................           223,225
To write off equipment.
```

EXHIBIT 1   Amortization Schedule for Five Payments in Advance

	Interest (at 6%)	Reduction in principal value	Remaining principal value
Before 1st payment....................			$223,255
1st payment (at start of 1st year).........		$50,000	173,255
2d payment (interest on previous principal value @ 6%)........................	$10,395	39,605	133,650
3d payment..............................	8,019	41,981	91,669
4th payment..............................	5,500	44,500	47,169
5th payment..............................	2,831	47,169	0

If the assumption as to the life of the property were changed to ten years without changing the assumption as to the life of the lease, the annual payments, or the purchase amount, there would be several changes in the accounting entries. First, the annual depreciation entries would be for 10 percent instead of 20 percent of the initial value. Also, at the end of five years when the nominal purchase takes place, the account names for the asset and accumulated depreciation would be changed to show that the asset was now held outright instead of held under lease.

Other depreciation methods might have been used by the lessee, who might have chosen the sum-of-the-years'-digits or declining-balance method. The lessee might also choose to depreciate by a method designed so that the sum interest expense (declining each year) plus the depreciation would equal a constant amount. This is frequently described as the "sinking-fund" method of depreciation. Depreciation thus would increase each year, in contrast to the decreasing charges introduced by use of sum-of-the-years'-digits or declining-balance methods. The increase in depreciation would match the decrease in interest charges, so total expense would be the same each year. There is considerable doubt as to whether the sinking-fund method would be held to conform to generally accepted accounting principles.

If the property had been purchased by the lessor for a different amount or for a different purpose or had been manufactured by the lessor, there would be no change in the form of the entries on the lessee's books from those stated above, but as discussed later under "Determination of Capitalized Amount," a different value might have been determined.

Financing Method—Lessor.   The assumptions specified in the preceding section underlie the following entries. Although this illustration assumes that the same method is used by the lessor as by the lessee, there is no requirement that this be so. In fact, APB Opinions Nos. 5 and 7 prescribe different criteria for lessee and lessor. The FASB treatment uses the same list of criteria for both lessors and lessees, but adds an additional test for lessors before they can treat a lease under the financing method. [Lessors classify financial leases into two types: (1) sales-type leases by manufacturers of leased property; and (2) direct financing leases by leasing companies and other nonmanufacturers.] The entries for the lessor under a direct financing lease are as follows:

Equipment	223,255	
Cash		223,255
Purchase of equipment for lease.		
Contracts Receivable	223,255	
Equipment		223,255
Placing of equipment under lease.		
Cash	50,000	
Contracts Receivable		50,000
Collection of first lease rental.		
Interest Receivable	10,395	
Interest Income		10,395
To record interest for the first year.		
Cash	50,000	
Interest Receivable		10,395
Contracts Receivable		39,605
Collection of second lease rental.		

Entries for subsequent collections are like this last one, with amounts taken from the table given in the previous section. The only entry necessary at the expiration of the lease is the one to record transfer of title:

```
Cash  ........................   1
    Income  ................        1
Sale of residual rights.
```

Notice that the credit is to income in this case where the amount is nominal.

If there were a substantial payment, say $11,240, to be made at the expiration of the lease if the lessee wished to acquire the property, there would be a question at the date of signing of the lease as to whether the lessee would be likely to make the payment to acquire the property. If, at the inception of the lease, it was estimated that the property five years later would have no substantial value, use of the 6 percent rate and the entries shown above would be appropriate. If, contrary to these expectations, the lessee exercised the option at the end of five years, the entry at that time would be

```
Cash  ..............................................   11,240
    Income from Sale of Previously Leased Property ....        11,240
Sale of property with zero basis.
```

If the expectation at the date of signing the lease was that the lessee would exercise his or her option, a different interest rate is implicit in the transaction and the amount of the entries after the first two would be altered. The five annual $50,000 payments and the $11,240 payment at the end of the lease have a present value of $223,255 if discounted at an 8 percent rate. The amortization schedule under these circumstances would be as shown in Exhibit 2.

The entries for the first interest accrual and receipt of the second lease payment would be

```
Interest Receivable  ......................   13,860
    Interest Income  .....................        13,860
To record interest for the first year.

Cash  ...................................   50,000
    Interest Receivable  ..................        13,860
    Contracts Receivable  ................        36,140
Collection of second lease rental.
```

The entry at the end of the fifth year, assuming that the purchase option is exercised, would be

```
Cash  ...................................   11,240
    Interest Income  .....................        833
    Contracts Receivable  ................        10,407
Collection of purchase option.
```

EXHIBIT 2   Amortization Schedule for Five Payments in Advance with Purchase Option

	Interest (at 8%)	Reduction in principal value	Remaining principal value
Before 1st payment.....................			$223,255
1st payment (at start of 1st year).........		$50,000	173,255
2d payment (interest on previous principal value at 8 %).........................	$13,860	36,140	137,115
3d payment............................	10,970	39,030	98,085
4th payment...........................	7,847	42,153	55,932
5th payment...........................	4,475	45,525	10,407
Purchase option at end of 5th year........	833	10,407	0

If, contrary to expectation, the lessee does not elect to purchase the equipment at the end of the fifth year, the entry would be

```
Equipment .............................  10,407
     Contracts Receivable  ................         10,407
Recovery of equipment at end of lease.
```

The fact that the option was not exercised would indicate that the equipment may not be worth $10,407. If this indication is true, the equipment should be written down to a reasonable value.

In the above discussion about accounting for the lessor, it was assumed that the termination or residual value was nominal and the leased property would be retained by the lessee. If the lessor fully expects to receive the property back at the termination of the lease and to make some use of it at that time—perhaps to have a new lease to another lessee—the same principles will apply, but the entries will differ somewhat.

Assume the following facts:

1. The asset was purchased for $275,555 by the lessor.

2. The same five-year lease with $50,000 annual payments in advance is executed as above.

3. The lessee has no rights at termination other than to compete with others for purchase of the property.

4. The life of the property is more than five years and the estimated value at the end of five years is $70,000. Present value at 6 percent of the $70,000 asset received in five years is approximately $52,300.

The entry for the lessor at the execution of the lease might be

```
Equipment  ...................................  275,555
     Cash  .....................................         275,555
Purchase of equipment.

Contracts Receivable  ..........................  223,255
Residual Value of Equipment, Discounted .........   52,300
     Equipment ................................         275,555
Placement of equipment on lease with expected
     residual value of $70,000 discounted.

Cash .........................................   50,000
     Contracts Receivable  ......................          50,000
Collection of first lease rental at start of first year.
```

The entry at the end of the first year would be

```
Interest Receivable  ............................   10,395
Residual Value of Equipment, Discounted ...........    3,138
     Interest Income ...........................          13,533
To record interest income for first year.
```

The $13,533 is 6 percent of the unrecovered investment of $225,555 after receipt of the first lease payment.

A different situation exists where the lessor is a manufacturer, earning a profit both from manufacturing the equipment and from financing sales through lease contracts. If the criteria for a financing lease are met by the manufacturer, the lease is defined by the FASB as a sales-type lease. The entries assuming the same payment schedule as before and that the manufacturing cost of the equipment leased was $200,000 are illustrated in the next paragraph.

The entries at the execution of the lease would be:

```
Contracts Receivable  ...............................................  223,255
     Sales  .......................................................         223,255
Sale of property under lease contract to make five annual payments of $50,000.
```

```
Cost of Goods Sold  ................................................  200,000
    Finished Goods Inventory  .........................................        200,000
To record cost of goods sold for equipment sold on a sales-type lease.
```

Entries for the collection of cash and the recognition of interest income would be made as illustrated previously for direct financing leases.

The Financial Accounting Standards Board has considered the accounting for leveraged leases as part of its standard on leasing. Borrowing to buy property to lease is complicated by the fact that the cash inflow from the lease is likely to be arranged to occur substantially faster than the outflow for the debt service. In addition, the transaction frequently is worked out so that there are substantial tax deferrals. Occasionally, a transaction is worked out in which the lessor pays out more cash than is taken in. In present accounting, which does not consider imputed interest and present values, the transaction would appear to be a loss when in truth the timing of cash flows creates a substantial advantage to the lessor.

CHOICE OF ACCOUNTING METHODS

Choice by Lessee.   Opinion No. 5 of the APB was formerly controlling for the determination of accounting method by the lessee. It states that "The property and the related liability should be included as an asset and a liability in the balance sheet if the terms of the lease result in the creation of a material equity in the property."

Despite the increasing popularity of long-term leases as financing devices, few leases were held to "result in the creation of a material equity in the property." As a result the vast preponderance of long-term, noncancelable leases were treated as operating leases under the Opinion No. 5 rules.

The FASB Standard on leases supersedes APB Opinion No. 5 and substitutes for the former inflexible "creation of a material equity" test, a group of criteria. "If a lease meets *one* or more of the following four criteria, the lease shall be classified as a capital [financing] lease by the lessee. Otherwise it shall be classified as an operating lease."[2] The criteria are:

(a) The lease transfers ownership of the property to the lessee by the end of the lease term, as. . . .
(b) The lease contains a bargain purchase option, ...
(c) The lease term is equal to 75 percent or more of the estimated economic life of the leased property, ...
(d) The present value of the minimum lease payments . . . excluding that portion of the payments representing executory expenses such as insurance, maintenance, and taxes to be paid by the lessor, equals or exceeds 90 percent of the excess of the fair value of the leased property . . . over any related investment tax credit retained by the lessor

The salient terms in the criteria are described as follows:[3] *Bargain purchase option:* A provision allowing the lessee an option to purchase the leased property for a price that at the inception of the lease is expected to be substantially less than the fair value (exchange price) of the property at the date the option becomes exercisable.

---

[2]Emphasis supplied. As indicated earlier, only an exposure draft of a proposed Statement on leases is available as this book goes to press. Quotations are from the second exposure draft issued in July 1976. No paragraph numbers are cited since they are likely to change.
[3]The descriptions are paraphrases of the FASB language.

Lease term: The fixed noncancelable (or cancelable only upon the occurrence of some remote contingency) term of the lease plus all periods, if any, covered by bargain renewal options but not extending beyond the date a bargain purchase option becomes exercisable.

Estimated economic life of leased property: The estimated remaining period during which the property is expected to be usable for the general purpose for which it was designed without limitation by lease term.

Estimated residual value of leased property: The estimated fair value of the leased property at the end of the lease term.

Minimum lease payments: The payments that the lessee is obligated to make or can be required to make in connection with the leased property. Minimum lease payments would the following:

1. The minimum rental payments called for by the lease over the lease term.

2. Any lessee guarantee of the residual value at the expiration of the lease term, whether or not payment of the guarantee constitutes a purchase of the leased property. When the lessor has the right to require the lessee to purchase the property at termination of the lease for a certain or determinable amount, that amount would be considered a lessee guarantee. When the lessee agrees to make up any deficiency below a stated amount in the lessor's realization of the residual value, the guarantee to be included in the minimum lease payments shall be the stated amount, rather than an estimate of the deficiency to be made up.

3. Any payment that the lessee must make or can be required to make upon failure to renew or extend the lease at the expiration of the lease term, whether or not the payment would constitute a purchase of the leased property.

4. The payment called for by a bargain purchase option.

If a lease that does not contain a bargain purchase option contains two or more contractual obligations that represent alternatives, the one calling for the smaller total payment would be included in determining minimum lease payments unless the choice among the alternatives is to be made by the lessor, in which case the one calling for the greater total payment would be included. If the lease contains a bargain purchase option, only the minimum rental payments and the payment called for by the option would be the minimum lease payments.

Fair value of the leased property: The price for which the property could be sold. For example:

1. In a sales-type lease, the fair value of the leased property at the inception of the lease shall be the selling price that would have been obtained in a contemporaneous sale of the property by the lessor to an unrelated purchaser. Ordinarily, that price would be the normal selling price of the property. However, the determination of fair value shall be made in light of market conditions prevailing at the inception of the lease, which may indicate that the fair value of the property is less than the normal selling price and, in some instances, less than the cost of the property.

2. In a direct financing lease, the cost or carrying amount, if different, and the fair value of the property are the same at the inception of the lease. If the property was acquired for a particular lease, the fair value of the property at inception shall be considered to be its cost.

Choice by Lessor. APB Opinion No. 7 dealt with the choice of accounting methods by the lessor. The criteria which the Board set forth for the lessor were different from those set forth for the lessee, and the Board promised to give consideration to the question of different criteria. Despite lengthy study and consideration, the APB was unable to reconcile the difference in criteria for the lessee and the lessor before it went out of existence.

The FASB resolves the problem by stating that, from the point of view of the lessor, if a lease meets any of the criteria for capitalization by the lessee,

and in addition meets both of the following criteria it shall be classified as a sales-type lease or a direct financing lease, whichever is appropriate. . . . Otherwise, it shall be classified as an operating lease.

(a) Collectibility of the payments required from the lessee is reasonably predictable. . . .
(b) No important uncertainties surround the amount of unreimbursable costs yet to be incurred by the lessor under the lease. Important uncertainties might include commitments by the lessor to guarantee performance of the leased property in a manner more extensive than the typical product warranty or to effectively protect the lessee from obsolescence of the leased property. However, the necessity of estimating executory costs such as insurance, maintenance, and taxes to be paid by the lessor . . . shall not by itself constitute an important uncertainty as referred to herein.*

Leases Between Related Parties. Paragraph 4 of APB Opinion No. 10 required the consolidation of subsidiaries whose principal business activity was the leasing of property to the parent. That requirement is continued in the FASB pronouncement. The FASB explains that "The equity method is not adequate for fair presentation of those subsidiaries because their assets and liabilities are significant to the consolidated financial position of the enterprise."

Where consolidation is not required, the FASB directs that leases between related parties shall be classified in the same way as leases between unrelated parties. In the separate financial statements of the related parties, the reporting shall be the same as for similar leases between unrelated parties, modified as necessary in cases where it is clear that the terms of the transaction have been significantly affected by the fact that the lessee and lessor are related parties. The nature and extent of leasing transactions with related parties shall be disclosed.

FINANCIAL STATEMENT PRESENTATION

Presentation by Lessee.   A lease is an obligation, and the lessee must somehow tell users of its financial statements that the obligation exists. This is done directly on the balance sheet when the lease is handled by the financing method, but the financing method is appropriate only if one of the specified criteria is met. Because of the financial community's appraisal of debt, most lessees prefer to use the operating method of accounting for leases whenever possible. In cases where off-balance-sheet financing occurs through the use of the operating method, substantial additional information must be disclosed in the footnotes to the financial statements. Some of the same information must also be disclosed for capital leases.

The FASB pronouncement requires the following disclosures for operating leases having initial or remaining noncancelable lease terms of more than one year:

1. Future minimum rental payments required as of the date of the latest balance sheet presented, in the aggregate and for each of the five succeeding fiscal years.

2. The total of minimum rentals to be received in the future under noncancelable subleases as of the date of the latest balance sheet presented.

In addition, there must be disclosed, for all operating leases, the amount of rental expense for each period for which an income statement is presented, with separate amounts for minimum rentals, contingent rentals, and sublease rentals. Rental payments under leases with terms of a month or less that were not renewed need not be included.

*FASB Statement No. 13, Paragraph 8.

For capital leases, the FASB requires the disclosure of

1. The gross amount of assets recorded under capital leases as of the date of each balance sheet presented, in the aggregate and by major classes according to nature or function. The amount of accumulated amortization also shall be disclosed in total.

2. Future minimum lease payments as of the date of the latest balance sheet presented, in the aggregate and for each of the five succeeding fiscal years, with separate deductions from the total for the amount representing executory costs included in the minimum lease payments and for the amount of the imputed interest necessary to reduce the net minimum lease payments to present value. . . .

3. The total of minimum sublease rentals to be received in the future under noncancelable subleases as of the date of the latest balance sheet presented.

4. Total contingent rentals (rentals on which the amounts are dependent on some factor other than the passage of time) actually incurred for each period for which an income statement is presented.

The Securities and Exchange Commission requires disclosure of additional information for companies under its jurisdiction. Its requirements are set forth in *Accounting Series Release No. 147* and in Regulation S-X. It defines as a lease "any contractual arrangement which has the economic characteristics of a lease, such as a 'heat supply contract' for nuclear fuel" and its excludes "leases covering oil and gas production rights and mineral and timber rights." The Rule defines a financing lease as one which

during the noncancellable lease period either:
(i) covers 75 percent or more of the economic life of the property or
(ii) has terms which assure the lessor full recovery of the fair market value . . . of the property at inception of the lease plus a reasonable return. . . .

Disclosures as summarized below are required if gross rental expense exceeds 1 percent of the consolidated revenues:

(1) Total rental expense (excluding leases for a month or less which are not expected to be renewed). Contingent rentals shall be reported separately. Rentals on noncapitalized financing leases shall be shown separately for both categories.
(2) Minimum rental commitments under all noncancelable leases . . .
    (i)   for each of the five succeeding years
    (ii) for each of the next three five year periods
    (iii) the remainder as a single amount
(3) Additional disclosures
    (i)   basis for payments if dependent on factors other than time
    (ii)   existence and terms of renewal or purchase options, escalation clauses
    (iii) guarantees and obligations
    (iv) restrictions on dividends, further leasing, incurring of further debt
(4) For all noncapitalized financing leases:
    (i)   present value of minimum lease commitments. . . .
    (ii)   . . . interest rate, . . . for lease commitments in (i)
    (iii) present value of rentals to be received from existing noncancelable subleases in (i)
    (iv) impact upon net income . . . if all noncapitalized leases were capitalized, related assets amortized on a straight-line basis, and interest costs accrued on the basis of outstanding lease liability. . . . If the impact is less than three percent . . . that fact may be stated in lieu [of the above].

The following note from the 1975 annual report of Safeway Stores, Inc., illustrates the application of the SEC rule in a situation where certain financing leases are not capitalized.

MINIMUM RENTAL AMOUNTS (in thousands)

	Net all leases	Financing leases	Other leases	Rental income sublease	
				Financing leases	Other leases
1976	$128,976	$119,731	$16,036	$ 6,148	$643
1977	128,351	119,140	15,562	5,766	585
1978	126,881	117,587	15,175	5,401	480
1979	124,953	115,138	15,063	4,854	394
1980	122,050	111,299	15,352	4,354	247
1981–1985	535,532	479,092	71,785	14,581	764
1986–1990	390,091	331,339	63,360	4,256	352
1991–1995	210,898	157,543	54,938	1,318	265
After 1995	150,113	52.432	99,826	2,135	10

RENT EXPENSE AND LEASE COMMITMENT INFORMATION. Safeway and its subsidiaries occupy primarily leased premises, which were covered by 3,195 leases at year-end. Of these leases 2,580 are considered to be noncancelable, financing leases as defined by the Securities and Exchange Commission because the lease term covers at least 75% of the useful life of the property or the lease has provisions which, over the original term, assure the lessor full recovery of his investment in addition to a reasonable return on such investment. Also, 1,646 of the total leases can be cancelled by the Company by offer to purchase the properties at original cost less amortization, with purchase obligatory upon acceptance of the offer by the landlords. There were no significant amounts of property, other than real property described above, under lease during 1974 and 1975.

A summary of rental expense for such financing leases and other leases for 1975 and 1974 follows:

	(In Thousands)	
	1975	1974
Financing leases:		
Minimum rent	$120,094	$106,320
Rent based on sales	8,680	5,874
Less sublease rentals	(6,982)	(5,255)
	121,792	106,939
Other leases:		
Minimum rent	9,228	7,843
Rent based on sales	1,317	785
Less sublease rentals	(733)	(510)
	9,812	8,118
Total rent expense	$131,604	$115,057

Minimum rentals on all leases in effect at year-end and rental amounts included therein relating to financing leases, other leases and sublease rental income were approximately as shown in the following table for the periods indicated.

The present value of minimum lease commitments for financing leases was $951,810,-000 (after having deducted $33,462,000 for subleases) at year-end and $870,013,000 (after having deducted $17,360,000 for subleases) at the end of 1974. The ranges of rates used were from 3.00% to 9.25% in 1975 and 1974, and weighted average interest rates were approximately 6.8% in 1975 and 6.5% in 1974.

If, instead of recording rental expense, all financing leases were capitalized, related assets were amortized on a straight-line basis and interest costs were accrued on the basis of the outstanding present value, the impact on net income would be a reduction of $7,427,000 in 1975 and $6,579,000 in 1974. Included in this computation for 1975 was amortization of $57,264,000 and interest cost of $66,935,000; for 1974, amortization was $53,151,000 and interest cost was $59,207,000.

Allegheny Airlines, Inc., has a more complicated problem, which it presents in the following way in its 1975 report to stockholders.

At December 31, 1975, the Company was leasing 23 Douglas DC-9-31 aircraft; 21 for terms of 12 years, 1 for 9 years, and 1 under a short-term arrangement. The Company is also leasing 1 BAC 1-11 under a one year lease renewable until 1979. Several aircraft lease agreements contain certain financial restrictions, none of which are more restrictive than those contained in the Company's Restated Credit Agreement, as amended, or its other debt instruments.

The Company was also obligated under other leases for computer equipment, ground equipment, and ground facilities. The Company leases substantially all of its ground facilities including executive offices, overhaul and maintenance bases, and ticket and administrative offices throughout the system. The Company also utilizes for its flight operations public airports under lease arrangements with the municipalities or agencies owning or controlling such airports.

For purposes of the following disclosure, the Company has made a distinction between "financing" lease agreements and other lease arrangements. A "financing" lease is one in which the noncancellable lease period either covers 75% or more of the economic life of the property or has terms which assure the lessor, at the inception of the lease, full recovery of the fair market value of the property plus a reasonable return on investment.

Total rental expense for the two years ended December 31, 1975, was as follows:

	1975	1974
	(in thousands of dollars)	
Financing leases:		
Minimum rentals	$19,785	$18,564
Sublease rentals	(170)	(263)
	19,615	18,301
Other leases:		
Minimum rentals	8,414	9,219
Sublease rentals	(117)	(96)
	8,297	9,123
Net rentals	$27,912	$27,424

At December 31, 1975, minimum rental commitments under noncancellable leases (reduced by noncancellable sublease rentals) were as follows:

By Type of Property

Year Ended December 31	Flight Equipment	Facilities	Ground Equipment	Total
	(in thousands of dollars)			
1976	$11,087	$ 9,327	$3,798	$24,212
1977	11,053	5,790	3,298	20,141
1978	11,029	5,526	2,330	18,885
1979	10,798	5,430	1,997	18,225
1980	8,846	4,960	1,716	15,522
1981–1985	18,353	21,667	4,098	44,118
1986–1990	—	16,722	—	16,722
1991–1995	—	9,179	—	9,179
Remainder	—	8,469	—	8,469

By Type of Lease

	Financing	Other	Subleases	Total
	(in thousands of dollars)			
1976	$19,256	$5,228	$(272)	$24,212
1977	18,736	1,649	(244)	20,141
1978	17,772	1,342	(229)	18,885
1979	17,232	1,185	(192)	18,225
1980	14,965	640	(83)	15,522
1981–1985	43,363	1,057	(302)	44,118
1986–1990	16,695	314	(287)	16,722
1991–1995	9,179	267	(267)	9,179
Remainder	8,469	123	(123)	8,469

Substantially all leases included above provide that the Company also pay taxes, maintenance, insurance, and certain other operating expenses applicable to the leased property.

The present value, in the aggregate and by major categories of assets, of minimum lease commitments, applicable to noncapitalized "financing" leases and subleases at December 31, 1975 and 1974, were as follows:

	By Type of Property			
	Flight Equipment	Facilities	Ground Equipment	Total
	(in thousands of dollars)			
Present Value:				
Financing Leases:				
1975	$59,143	$39,850	$13,727	$112,720
1974	69,024	34,377	12,243	115,644
Financing Subleases:				
1975	(211)	(652)	(152)	(1,015)
1974	(261)	(1,129)	(180)	(1,570)
Interest Rates Used in Present Value Computation:				
Weighted Average:				
1975	5.5%	7.6%	7.2%	
1974	5.5%	7.0%	7.2%	
Range:				
1975	4.0–8.3%	5.3–12.5%	2.0–14.3%	
1974	4.0–8.3%	5.8–12.5%	5.0–14.3%	

If all the above "financing" leases and subleases were capitalized, the related property rights were amortized on a straight-line basis, and interest costs were accrued on the basis of the outstanding present value lease commitment, the increase (decrease) in expenses and the effect on net income (loss) would have been as follows:

	Year Ended December 31	
	1975	1974
	(in thousands of dollars)	
Rental Expense	$(19,600)	$(18,300)
Depreciation Expense	13,400	12,900
Interest Expense	7,700	7,100
Increase in Expense	$ 1,500	$ 1,700

Due to the operating loss in 1975 and the availability of operating loss carryforwards in 1974, the foregoing impact on net income (loss) is without tax benefit.

Allied Chemical Corporation in its 1975 annual report shows "capitalized lease obligations" in its balance sheet as a separate item just below "long-term debt." Many companies include capitalized lease obligations in their long-term debt and then, in a note to the statements, give details of the various debts. Inland Container Corporation in its 1975 annual report uses the following presentation of its long-term debt:

	1975	1974
7.90% promissory note, due 1976 to 1994	$30,000,000	$30,000,000
9.5% subordinated debentures, due 1976 to 1995	14,000,000	
Secured by land, buildings, or equipment—		
6% mortgage note payable, due 1976 to 1992	—	1,888,462
8.125% mortgage note payable, due 1976 to 1985	1,625,000	1,775,000

	1975	1974
Capitalized long-term lease obligations, 4.4%–9.0% due 1976 to 1991	5,368,374	5,293,926
6.25%–9% mortgage notes payable primarily Puerto Rico subsidiary, due 1976 to 1992	1,597,804	1,837,106
4.875%–10% unsecured notes to banks and insurance company, due 1976 to 1986	4,328,025	3,533,936
Other notes	26,600	31,920
	56,945,803	44,360,350
Less—Current portion	(3,411,483)	(1,185,416)
	$53,534,320	$43,174,934

In many cases the lease rentals capitalized arise in connection with acquisition of a plant from a municipal government unit which has issued industrial revenue bonds and pledged the lease rentals to servicing the debt. In such cases, instead of showing capitalized lease rentals, the company may show the industrial revenue bonds directly. American Air Filter Company, Inc., is an example. The following is part of one of the notes to its 1975 financial statements.

Long-term debt at October 31, consisted of:

	1975	1974
Long-term notes and mortgage notes payable:		
4% industrial revenue bonds maturing semiannually to May 1, 1986	$ 1,900,000	$ 2,060,000
5¾% to 6¼% industrial revenue bonds maturing annually to Sept. 1, 1993	2,550,000	2,675,000
Bank term loans with interest rates, adjusted periodically, of up to 115% of bank prime rate (U.S.) and 1½% over London Interbank Offered Deposit Rate (International), with principal amounts payable in installments to 1980	29,710,000	31,331,000
5% to 9% mortgage notes payable, due in installments to 2022	1,909,000	2,225,000
Total	$36,069,000	$38,291,000
6% convertible subordinated debentures, due March 1, 1990, with Sinking Fund requirements beginning in 1981	$12,040,000	$12,040,000

Property, plant and equipment with a net book value of $11,771,000 are pledged as collateral for industrial revenue bonds and mortgage notes payable.

Presentation by Lessor.   On the statements of lessors, the problem is one of showing the assets and the related revenue properly. If the lease is handled by the operating method, the asset will be among the property, plant, and equipment assets or in a separate section for assets held for lease. GATX (formerly General American Transportation Corporation) in its 1975 balance sheet divides its property, plant, and equipment into three parts: rolling stock; Great Lakes vessels; and manufacturing, repair, and terminal facilities. The first two of these represent items rented to others. On the income statement "gross income" is divided between that from services (including leasing) and manufacturing. Expenses, however, are not so divided. Although a number of companies separate assets as does General American Transportation, few separate the revenue.

The FASB requires the following disclosures with regard to operating leases in the reports of the lessor:

1. Cost of property on lease.
2. Minimum future rentals on noncancelable leases as of the date of the latest

balance sheet presented, in the aggregate and for each of the five succeeding years.

3. Total contingent rentals included in income for each period for which an income statement is presented.

In addition to the total cost of property on operating leases, cost by major property categories as of the date of latest balance sheet must be presented. The amount of accumulated depreciation shall also be disclosed by major property categories.

Greyhound Leasing & Financial Corporation is an example of a lessor using the financing method for recording leases. Its balance sheet shows, as the largest item, Equipment Leases and Other Contracts Receivable. From this figure the company subtracts Unearned Income and Allowance for Doubtful Accounts. Another item on the balance sheet is Estimated Residual Value of Equipment and Other Property on Finance Leases. Cost is given parenthetically. Note A to the 1975 financial statements summarizes the method of handling the leases as follows:

> . . . Substantially all equipment leases are finance leases whereby Greyhound Leasing is entitled to receive as rent an amount equal to or greater than the equipment cost over the non-cancellable lease term. Contracts receivable, unearned income and the residual value of equipment are recorded when lease contracts become effective. The unearned income (representing the difference between aggregate lease rentals or other payments and the cost of the related equipment, commissions and other direct expenses, less estimated residual value at the end of the lease terms) is generally taken into income on a declining bases over the life of the related lease. Substantially all selling and administrative expenses incident to consummating and recording leases are charged to income when incurred. No earned income to offset these expenses is recognized at the time the leases are recorded.

Greyhound Leasing also has substantial property leased and handled by the operating method.

In determining the financial statement amounts for lessors under the financing method, the FASB distinguishes between sales-type leases and direct financing leases. For sales-type leases the lessor would:

1. Record as gross investment in the lease the sum of the minimum lease payments (excluding executory expenses) and the estimated residual value.

2. Record the difference between the gross investment and its present value (computed at the rate of interest implicit in the lease) as unearned income to be recognized as earned over the life of the lease so as to produce an equal periodic rate of return on the net investment in the lease.

3. Record as the sales price the present value of the minimum lease payments (excluding executory expenses) and deduct from it as cost of sales the sum of the cost of the leased property and any initial direct costs of negotiating and closing the transaction, less the present value of the residual.

For direct financing leases, the lessor would:

1. Record as gross investment in the lease the sum of minimum lease payments (excluding executory expenses) and the estimated residual value.

2. Record the difference between the gross investment in the lease and the sum of the cost of the leased property and any initial direct costs of negotiating and closing the lease as unearned income to be amortized over the lease term so as to produce an equal periodic rate of return on the net investment in the lease.

DETERMINATION OF CAPITALIZED AMOUNT

When future lease rentals are to be capitalized, the question arises of how to determine the capitalized value. In at least three types of cases, the amount to be capitalized will be apparent from details of the leasing transaction. First, if property is bought by the lessor specifically for the actual lease contract, this purchase price is usually controlling. The lease transaction is primarily a financial one; this being the case, the lessor entered into the transaction for the interest rewards, and the present value of the future lease payments would be equal to his purchase price. The amount to be capitalized by the lessee would be the cost of the property. The interest rate implicit in the transaction could be derived from the cost and rental schedule. The lessee would rarely be ignorant of the purchase price paid by the lessor. Second, in the case of a sale-and-leaseback, the purchase price certainly is apparent to the lessee. Third, when property is purchased from an outsider, the lessee may have been a participant in the negotiations, but even if he was not, he is likely to know an approximate price from his alternative decision analysis.

In the cases where the capitalizable amount is not apparent from surrounding facts, it will be necessary to determine that amount by assumption of an interest factor and the application of the compound interest formula. This is (assuming that the first payment occurs at the end of the first period):

$$PV = R \; \frac{1 - (1 + i)^{-n}}{i}$$

where PV = the present value of an annuity—the amount to be capitalized
R = the periodic rent
n = the number of periods for which the rent is to be paid
i = the interest rate per period

The periodic rent and number of periods are specified in the lease contract, so that only the interest rate needs to be determined to arrive at the amount to capitalize. If the period for compounding the interest differs from the period for which rent is paid, the mathematics becomes somewhat more difficult. If such is the case, reference may be made to a book on compound interest mathematics. However, such refinement in the mathematics probably is not warrented considering the assumptions necessary to determine the rate of interest.

The method of determining the interest rate to use in the formula is not defined. Many different methods are advocated, and this lack of definition has led to the allegation that capitalizing lease rentals will introduce arbitrariness and subjectivity into accounting. However, the situation is not as bad as many of the critics of capitalization allege. In many practical situations, the present value is known from the negotiations, as pointed out above. In the remaining ones, there is some control through the logic of economics even though different reasoning leads to slightly different rates.

The FASB requires that where the implicit discount rate cannot be determined by the lessee from the terms of the lease, "the discount rate to be used in determining present value shall be the lessee's incremental borrowing rate."

SALE-AND-LEASEBACK

Occasionally, companies sell property and promptly lease it back. The terms of the leaseback are usually such that the transaction is equivalent to an outright borrowing. The lessee is to pay maintenance, insurance, and taxes. Rental payments are set to repay the buyer-lessor his purchase price plus interest. At termination, the lessee is entitled to residual rights for a nominal lump-sum payment or is entitled to continued occupancy for a minimal rental. The transaction should be handled by the financing method.[4]

[4]U.S. Securities and Exchange Commission, *Accounting Series Release No. 95,* December 1962.

In the current economic era of rising prices, it is likely that the sale price exceeded the seller's original cost less accumulated depreciation. Thus, there is a gain to be accounted for. It must not be taken into income in the year of sale-and-leaseback but must be matched against depreciation expense of the property acquired by lease over the life of the lease. The gain should not be considered as income in the year of the transaction for at least two reasons. One is that the gain did not really arise in an independent, arm's-length transaction. The price paid for the asset was determined in part by the seller's agreement to pay lease rentals. The level of lease rentals certainly influences the price even though the possible value if sold to an independent party had some influence on both the sale price and the rental level. In addition, this sale-leaseback transaction is a financing transaction, not a sale. The property stays in the seller-lessee's control. Without any change in operating characteristics or risks of the business, the seller-lessee can control when this sale-leaseback will take place. Within the limits of current value, he can also control the amount of the sale price. He thus controls the time and amount of the transaction.

The Accounting Principles Board covered these matters in its Opinion No. 5:[5]

> The Board is of the opinion that the sale and the leaseback usually cannot be accounted for as independent transactions. Neither the sale price nor the annual rental can be objectively evaluated independently of the other. Consequently, material gains or losses resulting from the sale of properties which are the subject of sale-and-leaseback transactions, together with the related tax effect, should be amortized over the life of the lease as an adjustment of the rental cost (or, if the leased property is capitalized, as an adjustment of depreciation).

The FASB concurred in this general view that all gains and losses on sale-leaseback transactions should be amortized over the life of the lease. (The one exception arises if the fair value of the property sold is less than its undepreciated cost, in which case the loss would be recognized immediately up to the amount of the difference between undepreciated cost and fair value.) The FASB also held that where the lease is a capital lease, as will usually be the case, the deferred profit shall be deducted in the balance sheet from the asset recorded under the capital lease.

Entries to record a sale-and-leaseback for $2,500,000 of a property with a book value of $2,000,000 might well be as follows:

Lessee			*Lessor*		
Accumulated			Property	2,500,000	
Depreciation	1,000,000		Cash		2,500,000
Cash	2,500,000		Purchase of property		
Deferred Gain .		500,000	in sale-leaseback.		
Property		3,000,000			
Sale of property in sale-					
leaseback.					
Property Rights			Rents Receivable	2,500,000	
under Lease	2,500,000		Property		2,500,000
Lease Obligation		2,500,000	Lease of property at		
Lease of property at			present value of future		
present value of rents			rentals.		
receivable for 20					
years with interest at					
8%.					

The entries for the first year of operations, assuming a 20-year lease and an 8 percent interest rate, would be

[5]APB Opinion No. 5, par. 21.

	Lessee			Lessor	

Lessee			*Lessor*		
Lease Obligation	54,631		Cash	254,631	
Interest Expense	200,000		Interest Income		200,000
Cash		254,631	Rents Receivable		54,631
First lease payment at			First lease payment at		
end of one year.			end of one year.		
Depreciation	100,000				
Deferred Gain	25,000				
Accumulated					
Depreciation (20-					
year straight-					
line)		125,000			

LEASEHOLD IMPROVEMENTS

Leasehold improvements are additions to the property made by the lessee. They become the property of the lessor when affixed to the property. If the leasehold improvement has a life longer than the current fiscal year, it is proper for the lessee to spread its cost over its useful life as is the case with any fixed asset. Useful life to the lessee cannot be longer than the remaining life of the lease unless the lessee has a right to renew the lease. If the lessee has the right to renew and is likely to do so, then the useful life of the improvement is limited by the renewal terms of the lease. If the lease expires before the physical usefulness is gone, the remaining usefulness belongs to the lessor. The lessee should record the cost of the improvement in an account bearing a title descriptive of the asset and containing terms to identify it as a leasehold improvement. The balance should be amortized regularly as if it were an owned asset being depreciated.

The lessor typically makes no entry for leasehold improvements. Lessees are not likely to make improvements which are substantially useful beyond the original terms of the guaranteed renewal terms of their leases. Therefore, there is little likelihood that the leasehold improvement will prove valuable to the lessor. If there is likely to be value, it is also likely that the lessee would try to get the lessor to share in the cost. To the extent that the lessor shares in the cost, then, of course, an asset would be recorded in the amount of lessor's cost.

DEFERRED TAXES

The Internal Revenue Service may from time to time use different criteria from those used by the taxpayer for judging whether a lease should be capitalized. Thus, some leases that are not capitalized on the books may be required to be treated as purchases for tax purposes, and vice versa. Differences in accounting for tax purposes and financial reporting purposes may give rise to tax deferrals. Tax deferrals arising from leasing activities should be treated as those arising from any other cause (see Chapter 36).

BIBLIOGRAPHY

Axelson, Kenneth S.: "Needed: A Generally Accepted Method for Measuring Lease Commitments," *Financial Executive,* July 1971, pp. 40–52.

Cary, William L.: "Corporate Financing Through the Sale and Leaseback of Property: Business and Tax Policy Considerations," *Harvard Law Review,* November 1948, pp. 1–41.

Defliese, Philip L.: *Should Accountants Capitalize Leases—The Economic Case Against It at Present,* Coopers & Lybrand, New York, 1973.

Hall, William D.: "Current Problems in Accounting for Leases," *Journal of Accountancy,* November 1967, pp. 35–42.

Hawkins, David M., and Mary M. Wehle: *Accounting for Leases,* Financial Executives Research Foundation, New York, 1973.

Huefner, Ronald J.: "A Debt Approach to Lease Accounting." *Financial Executive,* March 1970, pp. 30–36.
Myers, John H.: *Accounting Research Study No. 4,* "Reporting of Leases in Financial Statements," AICPA, New York, 1962.
Nelson, A. Tom: "Capitalizing Leases—The Effect on Financial Ratios," *Journal of Accountancy,* July 1963, pp. 49–58.
Shanno, David F., and Roman L. Weil: "The Separate Phases Method of Accounting for Leveraged Leases: Properties of the Allocating Rate and an Algorithm for Finding It," *Journal of Accounting Research,* Fall 14, 2 (Autumn 1976).
Wyatt, Arthur R.: "Accounting for Leveraged Leases," *Arthur Andersen Chronicle,* April 1974, pp. 39–49.
Zises, Alvin: "The Psuedo-Lease—Trap and Time Bomb," *Financial Executive,* August 1973, pp. 20–25.

Chapter **26**

Accounting for Labor

LAWRENCE L. VANCE
Professor of Business Administration, University of California, Berkeley

INTERNAL CONTROL CONSIDERATIONS FOR LABOR ACCOUNTING

Accounting for labor poses an important internal control problem for two reasons: (1) Accuracy, as well as promptness, is necessary to avoid morale problems with the workers; and (2) the large number of individual payroll checks and number of persons involved in the payments offers a tempting area for concealment of fraud. The usual need for reliable cost information for managerial use and sometimes for reporting to outsiders (as required by some government contracts, for example) is, of course, present here as well as elsewhere. Labor costs are often the basis for allocation of other costs to such objects of costing as lots of product or individual jobs or contracts. This fact makes accounting for labor all the more important.

Attention in designing internal control systems for labor should be given to adequacy of personnel as well as to organization and records, but the most crucial areas are likely to be in the division of labor or organizational arrangements which dictate who produces what data. This division of labor, which is designed in part to gain the advantage of specialization and the protection of the records by providing special custody of them, also minimizes the possibilities of fraud by restricting the span of control of any one person in the process. Division of labor at several points is recommended.

Hiring. Centrally controlled hiring, as is done by a permanent personnel department, is recommended. The alternative is hiring by individual supervisors or departments. The recommendation is not intended to exclude the immediate supervisor from the hiring process—he may make recommendations, conduct interviews, and make the final choice among eligibles—but the recommendation assures that the concern's personnel policies are carried out; it provides a central, official record of authorized rates of pay and other data; and it avoids the possibility of excessive nepotism or other favoritism.

Timekeeping. Timekeeping should be a separate special assignment, the function of which is to see that an accurate record of work done is made. Various devices are used in differing circumstances to carry out this function. Many concerns use attendance time cards to record the time in and time out of workers, the nature of the work done by each worker being known or else separately recorded. Exhibit 1 shows an attendance time card, designed for use with a time clock that records time in or out when the insertion of the card activates the printing device in the clock. In some cases, timekeepers make periodic checks on the presence of workers and perhaps on the recording of the job or work assignment they are working on. This may be a desirable procedure where workers are scattered over a wide area, as in a shipyard, and where their assignments may change fairly frequently. Exhibit 2 shows a time card designed to record time spent on sundry jobs. It may be kept by the individual worker, by an immediate supervisor, or a timekeeper. Often the recording of time and attendance can be done economically only by a foreman or supervisor; this is the case for crews out on construction sites, although large projects of this sort may support a separate timekeeper. In this situation, a job time report is commonly used; this lists the names and hours of the workers on the job, usually weekly. Where workers are continually on one assignment, as in an office, a weekly time card of the sort shown in Exhibit 3 may be used.

In most circumstances, it is desirable to see that timekeeping is as independent as possible from the other work of payroll preparation and payment and from the operating responsibilities. Persons with operating responsibilities are often not disposed by personal aptitude or training to keep the needed record well and they are distracted from it by the operating activity, which is likely to seem much more important to them. Performance of the timekeeping function by someone not in a

EXHIBIT 1   Attendance Time Card

NAME				NO.			
		WEEK ENDING					
DEDUCTIONS		RATE	HOURS	EARNINGS			
$ ____	REG. $ ____		____	$ ____			
F.I.C.A. $ ____	O.T. $ ____		____	$ ____			
INC. TAX $ ____				$ ____			
____ $ ____				$ ____			
____ $ ____	TOTAL HOURS ____			TOTAL EARNINGS $ ____			
MISC. ____ $ ____ (DESCRIBE BELOW)	$ ____		$ ____	TOTAL DEDUCTIONS $ ____			
				NET PAY $ ____			

R E G U L A R					E X T R A		
HRS.	IN	OUT	IN	OUT	IN	OUT	HRS.

PAY BASIS $ PER

Form C579   TIME CARD

EXHIBIT 2   Attendance Time Card

Mechanic's Name _____

Number _____ Date _____

JOB NO.	WORK DONE		ELAPSED TIME
		Stop	
		Start	
		Stop	
		Start	
		Stop	
		Start	
		Stop	
		Start	
		Stop	
		Start	
		Stop	
		Start	
		Stop	
		Start	
		Stop	
		Start	
		Stop	
		Start	
		Stop	
		Start	

— TIME CARD Form C578   PRINTED IN U.S.A.

EXHIBIT 3   Weekly Time Card

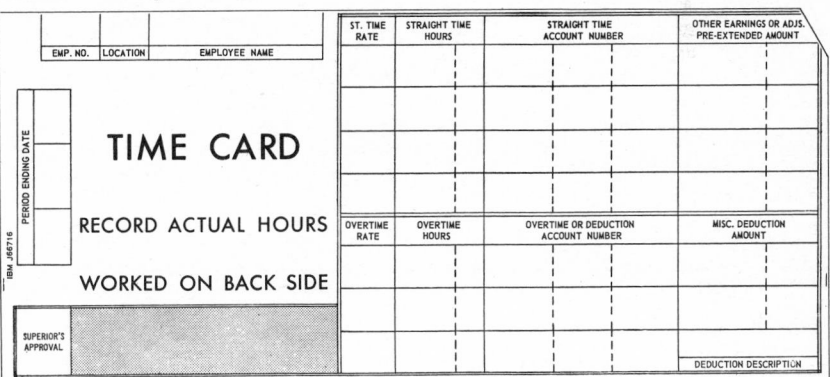

				ST. TIME RATE	STRAIGHT TIME HOURS	STRAIGHT TIME ACCOUNT NUMBER	OTHER EARNINGS OR ADJS. PRE-EXTENDED AMOUNT
EMP. NO.	LOCATION	EMPLOYEE NAME					
PERIOD ENDING DATE		**TIME CARD**					
		RECORD ACTUAL HOURS		OVERTIME RATE	OVERTIME HOURS	OVERTIME OR DEDUCTION ACCOUNT NUMBER	MISC. DEDUCTION AMOUNT
IBM J66716		WORKED ON BACK SIDE					
SUPERIOR'S APPROVAL							DEDUCTION DESCRIPTION

position to profit from an overstatement of the time worked is also needed to discourage efforts at fraudulent padding of the payroll.

Payroll Preparation. Calculation of the amounts due, listing and summarization of the payroll, and preparation of the checks should be done by persons who are not responsible for timekeeping. This is a clerical function conveniently separated from the timekeeping, at least in large organizations. It also permits a review of the time reported by persons not responsible for its reporting, so that a fraudulent or accidental overstatement of time can be noticed. Such overstatements are readily guarded against in computerized systems by including in the computer program for payroll a comparison of the time or amount with a predetermined limit. Predetermined limits are also printed on checks, for example, "This check not valid for more than $250.00."

Payroll Distribution. Actual delivery of the checks to the workers, or to the mails, should be made by a person or persons not involved in the timekeeping or payroll calculation, listing, and summarizing. This prevents anyone (other than the worker being paid) who has overstated time or the amount due, or who has inserted a fictitious name, from taking the resulting check and forging a signature on it and obtaining the cash. For this kind of control to be effective, the person distributing the checks must see that all check numbers in the series being distributed (prenumbered by the printer) are present or accounted for, and someone must have the responsibility of controlling the numbers issued. Separate distribution of the checks makes relatively easy the identification of a fictitious name when the checks are in hand and the distribution is made to the workers in person.

Use of Checks Rather than Currency. Payment by check permits all the safeguards provided by prenumbering and control of the checks, by the requirement of authorized signatures (weakened in very large payrolls by use of signature printing devices, which must be specially controlled), by the automatic provision of a receipt from the worker in the form of his endorsement, and by the fact that payroll robbery is almost completely discouraged. The alternative is payment in currency. If this is necessary (as when sometimes required by union contract), it should be controlled by a precount of the cash required, by the insertion of cash in an individual envelope for each worker, and by the obtaining of a written receipt from each worker as his envelope is delivered. Physical safeguards of the cash must be specially designed in this situation.

Where accounting is computerized, the payroll calculation, listing, and summarization will be a computer function. Internal control in this case involves separation of input preparation (i.e., timekeeping and other basic payroll data) from operation of the computer and control of its program, and separation, as noted above, of the distribution of checks. In advanced computer systems, workers can signal the computer from the work station so that it can record time and job worked on for each worker continually. In less complete systems, it may be possible to economize on use of records by recording time on punched cards which can be fed into the computer after the time recorded has been punched in. The cards may, of course, be prepunched with the worker's number, pay rate, standard deductions, and so on.

OBJECTIVES OF LABOR AND PAYROLL ACCOUNTING

Four objectives are important in accounting for labor, as follows:
1. Prompt and accurate computation (and payment) of worker compensation
2. Determination of payroll tax and other liabilities arising from labor
3. Computation and reporting of product and service costs arising from labor
4. Preparation of information useful in personnel management and labor relations activities.

Prompt and Accurate Computation and Payment of Worker Compensation. Summary Record of Payroll. Many of the considerations to be kept in mind in designing a system for prompt and accurate computation and payment of payroll have been covered above in the discussion of internal control for payrolls, including the provision for accurate time records and for the issuance of checks. Other records of significance in this process are a listing of the names, amounts, and check numbers, usually referred to as the "payroll," and the individual earnings

EXHIBIT 4

PAYROLL FOR WEEK FROM 19 TO 19 DATE PAID 19 NO.

* USE APPROPRIATE SYMBOLS TO DESIGNATE REASONS FOR EXEMPTION

PRINTED IN U.S.A. WEEKLY PAYROLL

	EM-PLOYEE NO. *	NAME	INC. TAX EX.	S	M	T	W	T	F	S	TOTAL TIME		REG. RATE	EARNINGS			*EXEMPT	PAYROLL DEDUCTIONS				PAID		
											DAYS OR HOURS	O. T. HRS.		REGULAR		TOTAL			F.I.C.A.	INCOME TAX WITHHELD		NET AMOUNT	CHECK NO.	
		AMOUNTS FORWARDED																						
1																								1
2																								2
3																								3
4																								4
5																								5
6																								6
7																								7
																								8
30																								
31																								
32																								32
33																								33
34																								34
35																								35
36																								36
37																								37
38																								38
39																								39
40																								40

EXHIBIT 5

COMPENSATION RECORD

NAME _____ SOC. SEC. NO. _____ PHONE _____

DEPT. OR PLACE _____ EMP. NO. _____

OF WORK _____

EXEMPT F.I.C.A. ☐ INC. TAX ☐ INCOME TAX STATUS _____

FROM _____

REASON _____

NAME	DATE	RATE			

FIXED EARNINGS / EARNINGS — FIXED DEDUCTIONS / DEDUCTIONS

NO. OF EXEMPTS — EFFECTIVE DATE — DATE OF EXEM. CERT.

PERIOD ENDING				NET PAY	CHECK NO.	CUMULATIVE EARNINGS

Period: 1, 2, 4, 5, 6, 7, 8, 9, 10, 11, 12, 13, 14

TOTAL / YEAR TO DATE

COO. FORM 3111

DATE EMPLOYED _____ DATE TERMINATED _____ REASON FOR TERMINATION _____

SPOUSE _____ PHONE _____ PERSON TO NOTIFY IN EMERGENCY _____

26-6

records. The payroll summarizes the compensation for a period—usually a week, a half-month, or a month—giving such details as may be considered useful for future reference. In addition to names, worker numbers, and numbers of checks issued, the payroll typically records the total and net pay, various kinds of deductions made from pay, such as social security tax, union dues, income tax withheld, savings or pension plan deductions, and so on; it may list other details, such as hours worked and the number of overtime as against regular time hours (significant where overtime premium is paid). In traditional records, these several details are listed in individual columns, and may be added to obtain summary statistics and summary totals for journal entries for the general accounts. In computerized systems, print outs are made with similar data for reference in case of inquiry or dispute and to serve as support for entries in the accounts and for audit. Exhibit 4 shows a typical payroll sheet of the traditional type.

In hand-kept systems, it is possible to economize on record keeping by writing two or three records at once by use of carbons or carbon substitutes. For example, the payroll check, individual worker's earnings record, and payroll sheet may all be written at once. This process is conveniently carried out by means of pegboard arrangements which facilitate positioning the forms and holding them in place as the writing is done.

Under federal law, a record of hours, earnings, and related data must be kept for each employee. This is known as an "individual earnings record." It is the means of proving compliance with federal law regarding hours, minimum wages, and so on, and is also useful in giving management a basis for reviewing the progress and status of an individual when promotions or wage increases are being considered. A typical form for this record is given here as Exhibit 5.

The law and good practice require that the employee be given a statement showing what deductions have been made from his pay. In simple hand-kept systems, this may be done with a form such as that shown in Exhibit 6. In machine systems, including computer systems, it is convenient to print the statements as a stub or a detachable lower section of the employee's check.

EXHIBIT 6

EMPLOYEE'S STATEMENT

Date Paid _____

Employee's Name _____

Employee's No. _____

Received From _____
(EMPLOYER)

Amount Earned $ _____

Hours Worked: _____ $ _____

Regular _____   DEDUCTIONS: _____ $ _____

Overtime _____   _____ $ _____

Total _____   F. I. C. A. @ _____ % $ _____

Income Tax _____ $ _____

_____ $ _____

_____ $ _____

Total Deductions $ _____

Net Amount Paid $ _____

Save This Statement for Your Records

BURROUGHS CORPORATION - TODD   DIV. - L HADLEY—   PRINTED IN U.S.A.   Form C514

Determination of Payroll Tax and Other Liabilities Arising from Labor. Under the social security system established through federal law, old age and disability insurance, together with Medicare and unemployment insurance, are financed through payroll taxes. Old age, disability, and Medicare are financed by taxes levied on both employer and employee and paid to the federal government. Rates or bases change from time to time in response to changes in price levels as required by law or as Congress adjusts the program. Unemployment insurance is financed in almost all states by taxes on the employer alone. The unemployment insurance program is administered by the state governments under standards established in federal legislation. (If a state should fail to carry on an acceptable program, the federal government would collect the tax in that state anyway; therefore, there is a powerful incentive for the states to maintain the program.) All these "social security" taxes are levied as a percentage of payroll. Some forms of employment are exempt, but most of the workers of the country are covered. Computation of the tax is usually possible by means of tables published by the tax authorities.

Most important in size among the remaining liabilities connected with payroll is the federal income tax withholding program. This is based on the income tax status of each wage earner, which must be declared by the wage earner on a form filed with the employer and called an Employee's Withholding Allowance Certificate (Form W-4 of the U.S. Treasury Department, Internal Revenue Service). Although accuracy in exemptions claimed is emphasized, the employee has the right to report fewer exemptions than he or she is entitled to, thereby effectively requesting a *higher* rate of withholding than the proper number of exemptions would produce. Employees who are in the higher income tax brackets may wish to do this in order to avoid having to make periodic payments directly to the Internal Revenue Service on the basis of an estimate of their tax liability for the year. Form W-4 is shown here as Exhibit 7. Some state and local taxing authorities also use a withholding system; records must be provided and computations of deductions made in conformity with the local requirements.

EXHIBIT 7

Form **W-4** (Rev. Dec. 1975) Department of the Treasury Internal Revenue Service	**Employee's Withholding Allowance Certificate** (This certificate is for income tax withholding purposes only; it will remain in effect until you change it.)	
Type or print your full name		Your social security number
Home address (Number and street or rural route)		Marital status ☐ Single ☐ Married
City or town, State and ZIP code		(If married but legally separated, or spouse is a nonresident alien, check the single block.)
1 Total number of allowances you are claiming		
2 Additional amount, if any, you want deducted from each pay (if your employer agrees)		$
I certify that to the best of my knowledge and belief, the number of withholding allowances claimed on this certificate does not exceed the number to which I am entitled.		
Signature ▶_____ Date ▶_____ , 19_____		
		16—83587-1

Other liabilities associated with payroll include a wide variety of deductions made by agreement with employees and, in many industries, additional payments to pension, health, and welfare funds. Union dues, savings plans (directed toward purchase of U.S. government bonds, stock of the employing company, or otherwise), and insurance plans are examples of additional deductions from workers' pay. Deductions are of course made in accordance with the agreement, and the amounts are ordinarily fixed per person or can be readily picked from simple tables covering the plan.

Amounts withheld from employees by law or by agreement give rise to liability accounts which substitute for the amount that would otherwise have been paid to the worker. Making the calculations, maintaining the records, and preparing summary statements (returns) to accompany the periodic payment of the amounts withheld to the designated authority or contractor involve substantial expense for the employer, but these functions do not directly increase the amount paid out for labor services as the taxes levied on payrolls and the additional welfare payments which are borne by the employer do. The accounting for liabilities connected with payrolls accordingly takes the following general form:

```
Wages Expense (or Labor Cost) ..............................  XXXX
      Vouchers Payable (amount immediately paid to workers)  ..........  XXXX
      Federal Income Tax Withheld  .................................  XXX
      State Income Tax Withheld  ...................................   XX
      Federal Old Age Tax Withheld  ................................   XX
      Union Dues Withheld  .........................................   XX
      Group Insurance Premium Withheld, etc ........................   XX
To record payroll per register

Vouchers Payable  .........................................  XXXX
      Cash  ........................................................  XXXX
To record payment to workers.

Federal Old Age Tax Expense  ..............................   XX
State Unemployment Tax Expense  ...........................   XX
Federal Unemployment Tax Expense  .........................   XX
Welfare Fund Contributions Expense  .......................   XX
      Federal Old Age Tax Payable  ................................        XX
      State Unemployment Tax Payable  .............................        XX
      Federal Unemployment Tax Payable  ...........................        XX
      Welfare Fund Contributions Payable  .........................        XX
To record employer's contributions to social security and welfare
   programs.
```

If desired, the liability accounts for the employees' and employer's contributions to the old age program may be combined, but when separated there is some benefit in the check their separate calculation and recording give on the accuracy of each one.

Payment of the withheld and accrued taxes and other obligations to the several recipients on the various due dates completes the cycle. Payments to tax authorities require a report on prescribed forms (tax returns) and other payments often require listings of individual names and amounts (union dues, insurance premiums, savings bonds, etc.). Exhibit 8 shows the face of the Employer's Quarterly Federal Tax Return form. (Note that amounts withheld exceeding $100 in one month must be deposited monthly with the Federal Reserve System.) Exhibit 9 shows the Annual Federal Unemployment Tax Return form. The accounting for the employer's tax and related contributions in terms of cost or expense is considered below where labor costs in general are discussed.

Computation and Reporting of Product and Service Costs Arising from Labor. Cost accounting in general is covered in other parts of this volume, but some considerations of special significance for labor are given in this chapter. These include:

1. Identification of labor cost with product or service
2. Labor in standard cost systems
3. Accrued payroll
4. Special problems in accounting for labor cost.

Identification of Labor Cost with Product or Service. Cost accounting systems are oriented in one of two basic directions, i.e., toward accumulation of costs by processes or by jobs. The two approaches may be combined in one plant for different portions of the work, and the basic nature of the orientation may be

EXHIBIT 8

Form **941**
(Rev. Jan. 1976)
Department of the Treasury
Internal Revenue Service

**Employer's Quarterly
Federal Tax Return**

SSA Use Only

Schedule A—Quarterly Report of Wages Taxable under the Federal Insurance Contributions Act—FOR SOCIAL SECURITY

List for each nonagricultural employee the WAGES taxable under the FICA which were paid during the quarter. If you pay an employee more than $15,300 in a calendar year, report only the first $15,300 of such wages. In the case of "Tip Income," see instructions on page 4. IF WAGES WERE NOT TAXABLE UNDER THE FICA, MAKE NO ENTRIES IN ITEMS 1 THROUGH 9 AND 14 THROUGH 18.

F □ 2 □ U □ E □
S □ 1 □ L □ T □
X □ 0 □ V □ A □

1. Total pages of this return including this page and any pages of Form 941a ▶	2. Total number of employees listed ▶	3. (First quarter only) Number of employees (except household) employed in the pay period including March 12th ▶		
4. EMPLOYEE'S SOCIAL SECURITY NUMBER	**5. NAME OF EMPLOYEE** (Please type or print)		**6. TAXABLE FICA WAGES** Paid to Employee in Quarter (Before deductions)	**7. TAXABLE TIPS REPORTED** (See page 4)
000 00 0000 ▼			▼ Dollars Cents	Dollars Cents

If you need more space for listing employees, use Schedule A continuation sheets, Form 941a.
Totals for this page—Wage total in column 6 and tip total in column 7 ⟶

8. TOTAL WAGES TAXABLE UNDER FICA PAID DURING QUARTER. $ _____   ◁

(Total of column 6 on this page and continuation sheets.) Enter here and in item 14 below.

9. TOTAL TAXABLE TIPS REPORTED UNDER FICA DURING QUARTER. $ _____   ◁

(Total of column 7 on this page and continuation sheets.) Enter here and in item 15 below. (If no tips reported, write "None.")

Employer's name, address, employer identification number, and calendar quarter.
(If not correct, please change)

⌐ Name (as distinguished from trade name)   Date quarter ended   ⌐
▶ Trade name, if any   Employer Identification No.
Address and ZIP code

.........Entries must be made both above and below this line; if address different from previous return, check here □.........

Name (as distinguished from trade name)   Date quarter ended
▶ Trade name, if any   Employer Identification No.
Address and ZIP code

	T		FP	
	FF		I	
	FD		TOT	

10. Total Wages And Tips Subject To Withholding Plus Other Compensation . . . . . ⟶		
11. Amount Of Income Tax Withheld From Wages, Tips, Annuities, etc. (See instructions) . . .		
12. Adjustment For Preceding Quarters Of Calendar Year		
13. Adjusted Total Of Income Tax Withheld . . . . ⟶		
14. Taxable FICA Wages Paid (Item 8) . . . $ .... multiplied by 11.7% = TAX		
15. Taxable Tips Reported (Item 9) . . . $ .... multiplied by 5.85% = TAX		
16. Total FICA Taxes (Item 14 plus item 15) . . . . ⟶		
17. Adjustment (See instructions) . . . . ⟶		
18. Adjusted Total Of FICA Taxes . . . . ⟶		
19. Total Taxes (Item 13 plus Item 18) . . . . ⟶		
20. TOTAL DEPOSITS FOR QUARTER (INCLUDING FINAL DEPOSIT MADE FOR QUARTER) AND OVERPAYMENT		
Note: If undeposited taxes at the end of the quarter are $200 or more, the full amount must be deposited with an authorized commercial bank or a Federal Reserve bank. This deposit must be entered in Schedule B and included in item 20.		
21. Undeposited Taxes Due (Item 19 Less Item 20—This Should Be Less Than $200). Pay To Internal Revenue Service And Enter Here ⟶ $		
22. If Item 20 Is More Than Item 19, Enter Excess Here ▶ $ And Check If You Want It □ Applied to Next Return, Or □ Refunded.		
23. If not liable for returns in the future write "FINAL" (See instructions) ▶ Date final wages paid ▶		

Under penalties of perjury, I declare that I have examined this return, including accompanying schedules and statements, and to the best of my knowledge and belief it is true, correct, and complete.

Date ....   Signature ....   Title (Owner, etc) ....

Form 941 (1-76)

EXHIBIT 9

Form **940** Department of the Treasury Internal Revenue Service		Employer's Annual Federal Unemployment Tax Return							19**75**
Name of State 1	State reporting number as shown on employer's State contribution returns 2	Taxable payroll (As defined in State act) 3	Experience rate period 4 From— / To—	Experi- ence rate 5	Contributions had rate been 2.7% (col. 3 × 2.7%) 6	Contributions pay- able at experience rate (col. 3 × col. 5) 7	Additional credit (col. 6 minus col. 7) 8	Contributions actually paid to State 9

(blank rows for entry)

| | | Totals ▶ | | | | | | |

10 Total tentative credit (Column 8 plus column 9). . . . .

11 Total remuneration (including exempt remuneration) PAID during the calendar year for services of employees

Exempt Remuneration	Approximate number of employees involved	Amount paid
12 Exempt remuneration. (Explain each exemption shown, attaching additional sheet if necessary):		
13 Remuneration in excess of $4,200. (Enter only the excess over the first $4,200 paid to individual employees exclusive of exempt amounts entered on line 12)		

14 Total exempt remuneration . . . .
15 Total taxable wages (line 11 less line 14) . . . .
16 Gross Federal tax (3.2% of line 15) . . . .
17 Enter 2.7% of the amount of wages shown on line 15 . . . .
18 Line 10 or line 17 whichever is smaller . . . .
19 Net Federal tax (line 16 less line 18) . . . .

Record of Federal Tax Deposits for Unemployment Tax (Form 508)

Quarter	Liability by period	Date of deposit	Amount of deposit
First			
Second			
Third			
Fourth			

20 Total Federal tax deposited . . . .

21 Balance due (line 19 less line 20—this should not exceed $100). Pay to "Internal Revenue Service" . . ▶

22 If no longer in business at end of year, write "**FINAL**" here ▶

Under penalties of perjury, I declare that I have examined this return, including accompanying schedules and statements, and to the best of my knowledge and belief it is true, correct, and complete, and that no part of any payment made to a State unemployment fund, which is claimed as a credit on line 18 above, was or is to be deducted from the remuneration of employees.

Date ▶   Signature ▶   Title (Owner, etc.) ▶

T	
FF	
FD	
FP	
i	
T	

(If incorrect
make any
necessary ▶
change.)

Name (as distinguished from trade name)

Trade name, if any

Address and ZIP code

Calendar Year
1975

Employer Identification No.

16—■—1

Form **940** (1975)

---

obscured by use of standard cost procedures. However, whether actual costs are being accumulated by processes or by jobs or have been calculated one way or the other to obtain a standard cost figure, one of the basic approaches will be involved. Work done and its cost must accordingly be identified in an actual cost system with a process (or department) or with a job or lot of product.

Identification with processes where production is organized around processes is simpler because most of the workers typically do not move from one process to another, and their cost can be identified simply by recording the name of the department or process in which they work on an attendance time card or report.

The job order situation is different in that jobs are often of short duration, so that time during a day must be separately recorded for each job a worker is on. This is done by use of a job time card or report, as illustrated in Exhibit 2 earlier in this chapter. In some cases, where workers are assigned over a considerable period of time to a particular job, such as a government contract or the construction of a ship, an attendance time card may serve the purposes of job order accounting. These remarks apply to workers who are in direct contact with the product or service; that is, they work in producing departments. Their labor is described as direct labor. Other workers are employed in facilitating, or service, departments and are classified as indirect labor. The latter may be identified with the service department in the same way as direct labor in a processing department is identified. Chapter 41 on production costs treats the problem of tracing costs from service departments to producing departments.

It is evident that subsidiary records, preferably tied to a general ledger, must be kept to accumulate information about the labor cost incurred in the several departments or on the several jobs. The Wages Expense or Labor Cost account used earlier in this chapter to indicate the general form of labor accounting is therefore a summary account only. To identify labor cost with the final product or service, it is necessary to accumulate the cost of operating the various processes (in an actual cost process system) until the process that finishes the product is reached, at which point the final division of total cost by units of product or service may be made to obtain a total unit cost. Similarly, costs invested in particular jobs must be accumulated to arrive at a final total cost for the job. Job cost sheets or accounts will be required for this purpose.

Labor in Standard Cost Systems. When standard costs are introduced, the unit cost figures are available in the standards, so the detailed accumulation of actual costs may be avoided. Standards, in total, and total labor cost actually incurred seldom come out precisely the same, and the variance must be analyzed for effective management action and disposed of in the accounts. For these purposes, a detailed record of actual costs will be helpful if it can economically be maintained along with the standard costs.

In establishing standard costs and in revising them, the concept of a learning curve is useful. This term refers to a chart in which the time (days, weeks, etc.) is plotted on the horizontal axis and the number of units of product per man (or per team, etc.) is plotted on the vertical axis. It is common experience that when a new product is introduced, a learning curve will at first rise steeply and then level out as the task is learned and becomes more or less routine. Preparation of such charts from records of labor time and output facilitate calculation of reliable standard costs by indicating when the labor time is stabilized. They may also be used to estimate costs more accurately where it is necessary to produce certain products at intervals, possibly with some new workers as well as old ones, since the old workers have to get back into the routine for the product and new workers have to learn the technique.

Accrued Payroll. Industrial wages are typically paid weekly, or sometimes biweekly. This means that payroll periods generally will not coincide with the calendar month, which is usually the basis for accounting statements. This problem may be solved in a cost accounting system that is integrated with the general ledger accounts by recording credits to an Accrued Payroll or similar summary account for labor on an accrued basis. The credits to this account are matched by debits to various cost categories. They are obtained by listing the earnings by jobs or departments (depending on the kind of cost work being done). The debits to Accrued Payroll would be made at the time of payment or vouchering of the payroll. The recording of labor costs and credits to payroll accruals would be made at convenient intervals, perhaps payroll dates, and always at the end of the month or other accounting period.

Special Problems in Accounting for Labor Cost. Two problems are the subject matter of this section: (1) Difference between the total time paid and the total time accounted for in jobs, and (2) accounting for labor payments not directly connected with a job, such as overtime premiums not related to a particular job or contract. In an actual job cost system, some provision for discrepancies between time reported as spent on jobs and total time in attendance and paid for must often be made. This arises where time is paid for on an attendance basis or on the basis of a standard day, but assignment of cost to jobs is made on the basis of separate job time cards or reports. The difference may be due to time waiting for jobs, to errors, or to simple idle time. In cases where time between jobs is likely to be insignificant, the time reported for jobs may be required to be equal to attendance times—workers being required to report the waiting time as spent on the next job. This is clearly misleading if waiting or idle time is significant. In the latter case, the difference between time paid for and time reported on jobs may be charged to an idle or waiting time account and treated as an element of overhead. The amount may be developed as a total, perhaps by departments, by simply taking the difference between cost of time reported for jobs and time paid for during a period. A similar extra payment arises when piecework rates do not cover minimum guaranteed pay, when bonuses are paid, and when minimum annual wages in excess of earned hours are paid. The same accounting can be used for these cases, but where more than one of these causes are present, the separate sources should be identified for managerial information.

Some labor payments cannot be clearly identified with particular jobs or contracts even when the work is performed in direct contact with the product or service activity. This occurs in the case of overtime premium paid not because the particular job required overtime work but because the total volume of work exceeded normal hours and overtime had to be done on one job or another to maintain reasonable deliveries. In this case also, the overtime premium may be accounted for separately as an element of departmental overhead. Note that only the premium is involved; the base rate is treated as any other direct labor cost. If the hourly rate is $2.50 and overtime is paid at 1½ times the base rate, the premium for an overtime hour is $1.25.

Data for Personnel Management.   Increasing attention is given by accountants to the behavioral aspects and effects of accounting procedures or policies. This field is as yet not well explored, but some aspects of it have long been in use and these, together with some cautions developed out of experience with traditional approaches, are the subject of this section.

Personnel departments have operated for many years and characteristically use certain forms of record and information about employees and about applicants for employment. The emphasis in such application forms as the one shown here as Exhibit 10 has been on obtaining as much information as possible to enable a manager to pick the most desirable candidate from management's viewpoint. In addition to the kinds of information listed in this exhibit, a variety of aptitude tests, personality inventories, and similar devices have been used in an effort to exclude individuals who might exhibit some undesirable trait on the job or cause a higher than desired turnover. Although a reasonable amount of information about an employee or prospective employee is undoubtedly a management necessity, the quest for information should be tempered by an awareness of some of the reactions to excessive zeal in this area that have appeared in recent years. For example, it has been widely contended that much of the prying into the personal history of an employee is an unreasonable invasion of privacy and that it has implications of police state methods. Where such information is exchanged between employers, a conspiracy to defeat a person may be alleged. It is contended that much of the information asked for is not really relevant to the question of the ability of the person to do the work, but is based on prejudice or outmoded moral attitudes. The question of whether or not a person has been divorced is often

EXHIBIT 10

26-14

APPLICATION FOR EMPLOYMENT

*NAME

ADDRESS _____ PHONE _____

POSITION APPLIED FOR _____

EMPLOYEE'S S. S. ACCT. NO. _____ DATE _____

SALARY EXPECTED $ _____

MALE ☐ FEMALE ☐   MARRIED ☐ SINGLE ☐   DIVORCED ☐ SEPARATED ☐   WIDOW(ER) ☐   DEPENDENTS: SPOUSE ☐ CHILDREN:____ PARENT(S) ☐ OTHERS ____

DATE OF BIRTH (MONTH) (DAY) (YEAR)   AGE ____   U. S. CITIZEN? YES ☐ NO ☐

FATHER'S FULL NAME _____

PREVIOUS EMPLOYMENT RECORD (LIST YOUR LAST POSITION FIRST)

FROM	TO	EMPLOYER	CITY AND STATE	NATURE OF WORK	BOND-ED?	SALARY RECEIVED STARTING	SALARY RECEIVED ENDING	PER	REASON FOR LEAVING

PHYSICAL RECORD

HEIGHT	WEIGHT	COLOR OF EYES	COLOR OF HAIR

CONDITION OF HEALTH _____

PHYSICAL DEFECTS _____

ARE YOU WILLING TO UNDERGO PHYSICAL EXAMINATION? ____

OTHER REFERENCES (LIST ONLY THOSE QUALIFIED TO GIVE IMPARTIAL AND EXACT INFORMATION)

NAME	ADDRESS	BUSINESS

EDUCATION

	YEARS
ELEMENTARY SCHOOL	
HIGH SCHOOL (NAME)	
UNIVERSITY (NAME)	

CORRESP. COURSE ☐ BUSINESS COLLEGE ☐

MAJORED IN _____

NIGHT SCHOOL ☐ NATURE OF PRESENT STUDIES _____

LANGUAGES SPOKEN _____

GENERAL

OWN OR BUYING HOME ☐ BOARD ☐ LIVE WITH SPOUSE ☐
RENT HOME ☐ LIVE WITH PARENTS ☐ RELATIVES ☐

OWN CAR ☐   LIABILITY INSURANCE $ ____   PROPERTY DAMAGE INSURANCE $ ____   LIFE INSURANCE $ ____   HEALTH ☐ ACCIDENT ☐

SERVICE, U. S. ARMED FORCES ____   DATE ENTERED SERVICE ____   DATE RELEASED FROM SERVICE ____   BRANCH OF SERVICE ____

RELATIONSHIP TO EMPLOYER ____   EMPLOYED HERE BEFORE? ____   CAN YOU BE BONDED? ____

SPECIFY TYPES OF WORK YOU CAN PERFORM OTHER THAN ABOVE _____

HUSBAND OR WIFE EMPLOYED? ____   NAME OF EMPLOYER ____   ADDRESS ____

IN CASE OF ACCIDENT NOTIFY: NAME _____

ADDRESS _____ PHONE _____

THE FOREGOING IS AN ACCURATE STATEMENT OF FACTS TO THE BEST OF MY KNOWLEDGE AND BELIEF

SIGNATURE OF APPLICANT _____

INTERVIEWER'S REPORT (APPLICANT WILL NOT WRITE BELOW)

INTERVIEWED BY ____   DATE ____   APPEARANCE ____   PERSONALITY ____

RECOMMENDATION _____

*MARRIED WOMEN GIVE HUSBAND'S LAST NAME, MAIDEN FIRST NAME AND MAIDEN LAST NAME

BURROUGHS CORPORATION TODD COMPANY DIV. Form C169

PRINTED IN U.S.A.

thought to be an unwarranted invasion of privacy. It is also widely contended that the standards of education and other achievement required are higher in many cases than is really necessary for the work involved in a particular position. All this may be viewed in the light of efforts to find work for minorities and for persons previously considered unemployable. An approach which emphasizes the possibility of placing a person in a job, rather than eliminating anyone who has a supposedly undesirable trait, may be more fruitful in solving social problems and thereby maintaining the health of a free enterprise system. In any event, the problems posed by the traditional approaches should be borne in mind and avoided by a careful review and deletion of requests for information that may raise problems.

The employee's earnings record, mentioned early in this chapter, which is required under federal laws regulating wages and hours and other conditions of employment, is useful in reviewing an employee's record for purposes of promotion or otherwise. Standard forms are available for maintaining an employment history of each employee; these give a more compact record than the individual earnings record (which lists each paycheck) and also provide for other information, such as description of jobs held. A file containing reports on work performance made by supervisors may be maintained, especially for employees in management positions. The confidential nature of such material must be carefully protected to avoid unnecessary damage to the employee and possible liability on the part of the employer. In general, it is suggested that the cultivation of a cooperative spirit, in which the employer tries to provide as much opportunity for development of the individual employee as possible, is likely to lead to more successful employee relations than the maintenance of a purely self-interested viewpoint on the part of management. The personnel records should reflect this policy.

Other measures, such as company newsletters which describe activities of the company and which give the employee a sense of community with the other personnel in the organization, can also be effective in building good employee morale. Such a newsletter offers means of communicating management policy to employees and may avoid misunderstandings derived from inadequate communication. This and further measures to improve working relationships lie outside the scope of accounting, but it is helpful for the accountant to understand that the information he demands or presents, if not obtained or presented so as to gain the cooperation rather than the resentment of other employees, may do more harm than good.

Chapter **27**

Pension Cost

ERNEST L. HICKS
Partner, Arthur Young & Company

RENÉ A. MILLER
Principal, Arthur Young & Company

INTRODUCTION

The private pension system in the United States has exhibited a pattern of growth that reflects both the expansion of the economy and the adoption of the social objective of providing a measure of economic security for persons retiring from employment. The development of private retirement plans has resulted in large part from the initiative of employers and labor leaders, but public agencies have both encouraged and regulated private plans through tax and labor laws, laws setting standards of fiduciary obligation for trustees, and laws requiring disclosure concerning various aspects of retirement and welfare plans.[1]

In 1974 the Congress enacted the Employee Retirement Income Security Act of 1974, "ERISA."[2] This revolutionary legislation will have far-reaching consequences for employers that operate in interstate commerce or that have tax-qualified pension plans. ERISA modified standards for eligibility, vesting, and funding; established standards of conduct for fiduciaries of employee benefit plans; set reporting and disclosure requirements for such plans; liberalized the treatment of plans covering self-employed individuals and shareholder employees of Subchapter S corporations; set limits on contributions and benefits; changed the tax treatment of lump sum distributions; allowed persons not covered by employer-sponsored retirement plans to create individual plans. This chapter takes into consideration the aspects of ERISA that affect an employer's accounting for the cost of a pension plan.

---

[1]The private pension system has not been alone in providing economic security. Public pension programs have also been developed over the years. Foremost is the federal program of old-age social insurance (Federal Old-Age, Survivors, and Disability Insurance) created by the Social Security Act of 1935. For many persons, benefits under this program are the primary source of retirement income. For others, benefits provided by employers under private retirement programs are the primary source.

[2]Subsections (b) and (c) of sec. 2 of ERISA state the policy of the Act: "(b) . . . to protect interstate commerce and the interests of participants in employee benefit plans and their beneficiaries, by requiring the disclosure and reporting . . . of financial and other information . . . by establishing standards of conduct, responsibility, and obligation for fiduciaries . . ., and by providing for appropriate remedies, sanctions, and ready access to the Federal courts; (c) . . . to protect interstate commerce, the Federal taxing power, and the interests of participants in private pension plans and their beneficiaries by improving the equitable character and the soundness of such plans by requiring them to vest the accrued benefits of employees with significant periods of service, to meet minimum standards of funding, and by requiring plan termination insurance."

ACCOUNTING PRINCIPLES

Since 1966, Opinion No. 8 of the Accounting Principles Board (APB)[3] has been the leading expression of the principles of accounting for pension plan costs. In 1974, the Financial Accounting Standards Board (FASB) issued an interpretation of Opinion No. 8 expressing the FASB's general conclusion that enactment of ERISA had not made it necessary to change Opinion No. 8. Nevertheless, in the Interpretation, the FASB announced its intention to put the subject of pension cost accounting on its agenda.[4]

For purposes of this discussion, private retirement programs are grouped into three categories: (1) deferred-compensation contracts with individual employees, (2) defined-contribution plans, and (3) defined-benefit plans. Most plans in the second and third categories are given effect through formal plans whose provisions are intended to meet the requirements of ERISA and the requirements for qualification imposed under the Internal Revenue Code. If the plan is qualified: (1) the employer's contributions are deductible for federal income tax purposes within specified limits; (2) earnings of trust funds established under the plan are not subject to federal income tax; and (3) employees are taxed only when they receive benefits.

Deferred-Compensation Contracts with Individual Employees. A deferred-compensation contract typically is a contract of employment with an individual executive; it requires the executive to perform specified duties during periods of active employment and establishes the total amount of compensation during that period. The contract provides that the executive also will receive periodic payments (the "deferred compensation") after retirement, either for life or for a specified number of years; it may also provide for payments to a beneficiary when the executive dies. The contract may also specify that after retirement, the executive (1) will not compete with the employer and (2) will act as a consultant when requested to do so by the employer. The right to receive the deferred payments may be contingent on fulfilling these and other conditions.

Accounting. In 1967, the Accounting Principles Board issued its Opinion No. 12[5] dealing with, among other matters, "deferred compensation contracts." Paragraph 6 of the Opinion provides that:

[3] Accounting Principles Board, "Accounting for the Cost of Pension Plans," Opinion No. 8, AICPA, New York, 1966. Until the APB issued Opinion No. 8, employers followed pension accounting principles set forth (although with less specificity) in *Accounting Research Bulletin (ARB) No. 36* (1948) and *No. 47* (1956) of the Committee on Accounting Procedure of AICPA. *ARB No. 36*, later incorporated in *ARB No. 43*, "Restatement and Revision of Accounting Research Bulletins" as Chapter 13(a), dealt mainly with past service cost, recommending allocation of such cost generally to "current and future periods." *ARB No. 47* added a preference for systematically accruing current and future service cost during the expected period of active service of covered employees, and accounting for past service cost over some reasonable period (not defined). *ARB No. 47* recognized an alternative method "for the present" and "as a minimum." Under the alternative method, financial statements were to "reflect accruals equal to the present worth, actuarially calculated, of pension commitments to employees to the extent that pension rights have vested in the employees, reduced, in the case of the balance sheet, by any accumulated trusteed funds or annuity contracts purchased."

[4] Financial Accounting Standards Board, "Accounting for the Cost of Pension Plans Subject to the Employee Retirement Income Security Act of 1974," Interpretation No. 3, 1974. The FASB has also added to its agenda the subject of accounting and reporting by employee benefit plans. The conclusions reached by the FASB on this subject may affect indirectly the conclusions reached with regard to the employer's accounting for the cost of a pension plan.

[5] Accounting Principles Board, "Omnibus Opinion—1967," Opinion No. 12, AICPA, New York, 1967.

> . . . deferred compensation contracts should be accounted for individually on an accrual basis. Such contracts customarily include certain requirements such as continued employment for a specified period and availability for consulting services and agreements not to compete after retirement, which, if not complied with, remove the employer's obligations for future payments. The estimated amounts to be paid under each contract should be accrued in a systematic and rational manner over the period of active employment from the time the contract is entered into, unless it is evident that future services expected to be received by the employer are commensurate with the payments or a portion of the payments to be made. If elements of both current and future services are present, only the portion applicable to the current services should be accrued.

In applying the paragraph quoted above, an appraisal must be made of the circumstances expected to prevail following the executive's retirement. In general, the excess of the cost of the future payments over the value of any services the executive is expected to perform following retirement should be recognized as an expense during the working lifetime. (See pages 25-9 to 25-10 with regard to deferred-compensation contracts with individual employees which, taken together, are equivalent to a pension plan.)

Defined-Contribution Plans. Defined-contribution plans provide retirement benefits for retired persons as members of groups, rather than as individual contracting parties. These plans comprise primarily deferred profit-sharing plans and money-purchase plans. Under plans of both types, an employee's benefits are the amounts that can be provided (often by purchase of an annuity) by the sums contributed for that employee.

Deferred Profit-Sharing Plans. The amount of an employer's contribution for a given period under a deferred profit-sharing plan is calculated under a formula specified in the plan; the total amount is in turn allocated among participants using another formula prescribed in the plan. Earnings of the trust fund, and in some instances amounts becoming available because of the withdrawal of other participants, are also so allocated.

Money-Purchase Plans. A money-purchase plan differs from a deferred profit-sharing plan primarily in the method of determining the employer's contributions. In a money-purchase plan, the contribution is ordinarily determined as a percentage of the compensation of participating employees.

Accounting. Defined-contribution plans do not ordinarily raise difficult accounting questions. The amount contributed *for* a reporting period (whether or not paid *in* the period) is the expense for the period.

Defined-Benefit Plans. This chapter is concerned primarily with defined-benefit plans. Such plans state the amount of the benefits, or the method of determining the benefits, to be received by employees after retirement. In some plans, the payment is the same for all retired employees (for example, $200 per month). In plans for hourly employees, the benefit is typically a specified amount per month (for example, $10 for each year of credited service). In plans for salaried employees, the benefit is more often related to compensation (for example, an annual pension equal to a specified percentage, such as 2 percent, of total earnings for the entire period of employment or a percentage, such as 30 percent, of the average earnings for a specified period, such as five years, immediately prior to retirement). In some instances, social security benefits reduce the benefits payable under the employer's pension plan.

The terms of a defined-benefit plan reflect the interaction of many factors. (This is also true of other types of retirement plans, but the impact on the accounting considerations is greater for defined-benefit plans.) Some plans are negotiated (resulting from collective bargaining); others are unilateral (established by an employer without negotiation). As to many aspects of a plan, the standards specified in ERISA are important considerations. Before ERISA became effective, a few plans were unfunded (periodic payments were made directly to retired employees on a pay-as-you-go basis); under ERISA, a plan must be funded (the employer sets funds aside for future pension benefits by making payments to a funding agency—in an insured plan to an insurance company, in a trust fund plan to a trustee). Some plans are contributory (the employees bear part of the cost of the stated benefits or voluntarily make payments in order to increase their benefits); others are noncontributory (the employer bears the entire cost). These differences, together with various eligibility requirements, specified retirement ages, disability options, and levels of benefits, contribute to an almost infinite variety of plans.

Accounting. The principles of accounting for the cost of a defined-benefit pension plan are the primary concern of this chapter.

ACTUARIAL TECHNIQUES

To understand the accounting principles for pension cost, one must know something of the techniques actuaries use in estimating pension cost and must be familiar with the specialized terminology. The paragraphs that follow are intended to draw the outlines, from a layman's viewpoint, of actuarial techniques;[6] certain of the specifics will be considered in more detail in later sections.

Actuarial Valuation. Basic to the fabric of pension costing is the process by which actuaries determine the amounts to be used in computing the periodic cost of a pension plan (other than a plan that uses insurance or annuity policies calling for payment of specified premiums). This process is referred to as an "actuarial valuation" of the plan. A valuation is made as of a specific date, which need not coincide with either the beginning or end of the period for which pension cost is being determined. Valuations are usually made annually, but some employers have them made at less frequent intervals. ERISA contemplates an actuarial valuation at least every three years unless required more frequently by regulations in particular cases.

In making valuations, actuaries ordinarily work with information furnished by the employer, for example, the sex, date of birth, employment date, and compensation of each employee covered by the plan. The calculations are made for a specific group—ordinarily, employees presently covered by the plan, former employees having vested rights, and retired employees receiving benefits. It is recognized that subsequent valuations can be expected to produce different results, even in the absence of changes in other factors, because the composition of the group will have changed.

The purpose of an actuarial valuation is to estimate the actuarial cost of benefits to be paid over varying periods of time in the future and, in some cases, the cost of payments for expenses of administering a plan or trust. The actuarial cost is expressed in terms of the present value, as of the date of the valuation, of the expected future benefit payments. The present value is the amount which, if invested at the date of the valuation at a stated rate of interest, would provide the benefits expected to become payable.[7]

[6]For a more comprehensive discussion of actuarial techniques, see Ernest L. Hicks, "Accounting for the Cost of Pension Plans," *Accounting Research Study No. 8,* AICPA, New York, 1965, appendix C.

[7]In pension plan valuations, actuaries combine (1) arithmetic probability factors (examples are factors for changes in compensation levels and for mortality) bearing on the amounts of benefits expected to become payable with (2) arithmetic factors representing the accretion of interest. To most actuaries, determining the present value of future pension benefits means applying factors of both types.

The resulting determinations are estimates, since in making a valuation actuaries must tentatively resolve a number of significant uncertainties concerning future events. In doing so, they use factors called "actuarial assumptions." Although these assumptions do not affect the actual (ultimate) cost of a plan, they have an important effect on present estimates of the cost.

Actuarial Cost Methods. The primary purpose of an actuarial valuation is to provide information to be used in establishing the amount the employer is to recognize as an expense or contribute to a fund (frequently identical amounts). The techniques used by actuaries in making the calculations are called "actuarial cost methods," or "funding methods."[8] Exhibit 1 shows the principal methods currently in use.[9]

EXHIBIT 1   Principal Actuarial Cost Methods

Method	Prior service cost	
	Separately assigned	Included in normal cost
Accrued benefit cost method		
Unit credit method.................................	x	
Projected benefit cost methods		
Entry age normal method............................	x	
Attained age normal method..........................	x	
Individual level premium method......................		x
Aggregate method....................................		x
Terminal funding method (provision for the total cost—ordinarily, the cost of a single-premium annuity—made at or near time of employee's retirement)		

An important aspect of an actuarial cost method is the manner in which it deals with prior service cost. Prior service cost is the cost assigned, for purposes of the actuarial calculations, to employees' service credits (credits for years of employment recognized in determining retirement benefits or eligibility to receive them) for years prior to the date of determination (ordinarily, the date of an actuarial valuation). It includes past service cost, the cost assigned to service credits for years before the inception of the plan. Increases or decreases in prior service cost which arise when a pension plan is amended and which are analogous to past service cost are referred to in this chapter as "prior service cost increments." The normal cost of a pension plan is the cost assigned, for purposes of the actuarial calculations, to service credits for years subsequent to the inception of a pension plan or subsequent to a particular valuation date.

The differences among methods in the treatment of prior service cost assume importance in pension cost determinations for both accounting and funding purposes. Moreover, such determinations are affected by the differences among

[8]"Actuarial cost method" is the newer name developed by the Committee on Pension and Profit-Sharing Terminology of the American Risk and Insurance Association. See Joseph J. Melone, "Actuarial Cost Methods—New Pension Terminology," *The Journal of Insurance,* September 1963. The expression "funding method," which continues in use, reflects the emphasis placed, before the issuance of APB Opinion No. 8, on the determination of amounts to be paid.

[9]Actuarial cost methods are discussed in greater detail in "Accounting for the Cost of Pension Plans," APB Opinion No. 8, AICPA, New York, 1966, appendix A, and in *ARS No. 8,* appendix C.

actuarial cost methods in the viewpoints they adopt in assigning pension cost to periods of time. The unit credit method deals only with the cost of benefits that have accrued (in the limited sense that the units of employee service on which the benefits are to be based have been rendered). Consequently, the past service cost under that method is the present value at the inception of the plan of pension benefits based on employee service to that time. The normal cost assigned to any year (before adjustment for actuarial gains) is an amount which represents the present value of the increase in employees' retirement benefits resulting from the additional year's service credits.

The other actuarial cost methods (except for the terminal funding method), looking forward, deal with the cost of employees' projected benefits. In so doing, they disregard the periods during which the related employee service credits were accumulated. Thus, under the entry age normal method, which is frequently used, the normal cost for a year is in theory an aggregation of amounts for each employee (or an amount based on a level percentage of total annual compensation) which, if placed at interest annually, would at the employees' retirement dates equal the then present values of their pensions. The prior service cost under this method is the amount of a theoretical fund so accumulated to the date of determination.

Actuarial Assumptions. In making actuarial determinations, actuaries must assign values to a number of significant uncertainties concerning future events. Although the ultimate cost of a pension plan is not affected by the actuarial assumptions selected, the effect on the cost for specific years can be material. The following brief review may help in understanding the uncertainties.

Interest (Return on Funds Invested). The interest assumption used in an actuarial valuation is an expression of the average rate of earnings expected on the funds invested or to be invested to provide for the future benefits. Investments may include equity securities as well as debt securities, together with investments in real estate or other assets.[10] Accordingly, earnings include dividends and rentals on real estate as well as interest. Realized and (under certain circumstances) unrealized gains or losses on fund investments are also considered by actuaries to be an element of investment return.

Expenses of Administration. In some instances, the expenses of administering a pension plan, for example, fees of attorneys, actuaries, and trustees, and the cost of keeping pension records are borne directly by the employer. In other cases, such expenses, or some of them, are paid by a trust or insurance company from funds contributed by the employer. In the latter cases, expenses to be incurred in the future must be considered in estimating the employer's pension cost.

Benefits. Several assumptions must be made as to the types and extent of the future benefits whose present value is used in expressing the cost of a pension plan. The principal such assumptions are discussed briefly in the following paragraphs.

Future Compensation Levels. Benefits under some pension plans depend in part on future compensation levels. For example, the annual retirement benefit may be a stated percentage, for each year of service, of the employee's average compensation for the final five or ten years of employment. Under plans of this type, provision is ordinarily made for normal increases arising from the progression of employees through the various earnings categories, based on the employer's experience. Provision is not specifically made, however, for general earnings-level increases, such as those which may result from inflation.

Cost of Living. In order to protect the purchasing power of retirement benefits, some plans provide that the benefits otherwise determined will be

---

[10]ERISA limits investments that may be held in a pension fund.

adjusted from time to time to reflect variations in a specific index, such as the Consumer Price Index of the U.S. Bureau of Labor Statistics. In estimating the cost of such a plan, actuaries make provision for expected changes in the cost-of-living index.

MORTALITY.   The length of time an employee (and a survivor under a joint and survivor annuity option) covered by a pension plan will live is a determining factor in the amount and timing of the benefit payments to be provided. If an employee dies before becoming eligible for pension benefits, no payments are made (although in some plans lump-sum or periodic benefits are paid to beneficiaries). The total amount of pension benefits for employees who reach retirement is determined in large part by how long they (and their survivors) live thereafter. Actuaries rely on mortality tables in estimating future pension payments. A high degree of judgment must be exercised in selecting and using mortality tables, since they are developed from a universe which may not have the same characteristics as the group to which the table is to be applied.

RETIREMENT AGE.   Most plans provide a normal retirement age, but many plans permit employees to work thereafter under certain conditions. Some plans provide for retirement in advance of the normal age in case of disability, and most plans permit early retirement at the employee's option under certain conditions. When there are such provisions, actuaries must estimate their effects on the amount and timing of the benefits which will ultimately be paid.

TURNOVER (WITHDRAWAL).   In many plans, an employee who leaves the employer for any reason other than retirement and before completing vesting requirements (see following paragraph) forfeits the right to receive benefits. In estimating the amount of future benefits, actuaries may make allowance for the effect of turnover (withdrawal).

VESTING.   An employee's right to receive a pension "vests" when it is no longer contingent upon the employee's remaining in the service of the employer. A pension plan covered by ERISA must provide vesting in accordance with standards set forth in the Act. Vesting is taken into consideration in estimating the effects of turnover.

Social Security Benefits.   For plans that provide that pensions otherwise payable are to be reduced by all or part of social security benefits, it is necessary to estimate future social security benefits. Ordinarily, this estimate is calculated as if the level in effect at the time the valuation is being made would continue.

OPINION NO. 8 OF THE APB

General Aspects.   Before discussing the accounting principles expressed in Opinion No. 8, it is useful to consider certain general aspects of that Opinion.

By its terms, Opinion No. 8 applies to financial statements that purport to present financial position and results of operations in conformity with generally accepted accounting principles. It applies to financial statements for interim periods as well as to statements for full fiscal years, and to unaudited financial statements as well as to those examined by independent public accountants.

In view of the complexity of the Opinion (reflecting the complexity of the subject matter) and of the number of directives it expresses, materiality is especially important in applying the Opinion's provisions. It is widely understood that official statements on matters of accounting principle are not intended to be applicable to immaterial matters; the customary note to that effect appears in Opinion No. 8. The materiality of matters entering into the determination of pension cost is ordinarily judged in terms of their effect on the financial statements, rather than their effect on periodic pension expense. The possible future effect of matters which are currently not material should also be considered in establishing pension accounting policies.

The following other overriding considerations should be borne in mind in applying the provisions of the Opinion:

Accounting Versus Funding. The Opinion is concerned with accounting for pension cost; determining the amounts to be funded is a financial matter not covered by the Opinion. Most companies choose, however, to have the accounting and the funding coincide.

Actuaries. The computation of pension cost for accounting purposes requires the use of actuarial techniques and judgments. The Opinion provides that pension cost should generally be determined from a study by an actuary, giving effect to the conclusions set forth in the Opinion.

Consistency. The Opinion contemplates that once the practices to be used in accounting for pension cost have been selected, the resulting method will be followed consistently.

Pension Plans Covered. Opinion No. 8 applies primarily to retirement plans of the defined-benefit type. It defines a pension plan (to which its provisions apply) as "an arrangement whereby a company undertakes to provide its retired employees with benefits that can be determined in advance from the provisions of a document or from the company's practices" (par. 8). Such an arrangement may be embodied in a written plan or may be implied from a well-defined, although perhaps unwritten, policy. The pension benefits contemplated by the definition are usually periodic (ordinarily monthly) pension payments. If death benefits and disability payments (applying after termination of employment) are provided under a pension plan, their cost would ordinarily be accounted for under the principles set forth in Opinion No. 8.

In some pension plans the employer's legal obligation is specifically limited to contributions made to the pension fund. The funding standards imposed by ERISA (discussed below) may alter the significance of such a limitation, which in any event does not affect the employer's accounting for the cost of the plan. Paragraph 16 of Opinion No. 8 states in part:

> . . . in the absence of convincing evidence that the company will reduce or discontinue the benefits called for in a pension plan, the cost of the plan should be accounted for on the assumption that the company will continue to provide such benefits. This assumption implies a long-term undertaking, the cost of which should be recognized annually whether or not funded. Therefore, accounting for pension cost should not be discretionary.

In addition to the definition of a pension plan quoted at the beginning of this section, Opinion No. 8 identifies the types of plan to which it applies (par. 8):

Defined-contribution plans, to the extent specified (see pages 27-20 to 27-21).

Deferred-compensation contracts with individual employees which, taken together, are equivalent to a pension plan.

Deferred profit-sharing plans which are in substance pension plans (for example, because they specify minimum benefits).

Unfunded, insured, or trust fund plans.

Plans whose cost is incurred outside the United States when the cost is included in financial statements intended to conform with generally accepted accounting principles in the United States and when the plans are "reasonably similar" to those contemplated by Opinion No. 8.

Opinion No. 8 identifies the following types of arrangements to which it does *not* apply:

Death and disability benefits provided under a separate arrangement.

A company's practice of paying retirement benefits to selected employees in amounts determined on a case-by-case basis at or after retirement.

Defined-contribution plans (except to the extent indicated above).

Deferred-compensation contracts with individual employees (except to the extent indicated above).

Deferred profit-sharing plans (except to the extent indicated above).

Deciding whether an arrangement is a pension plan covered by Opinion No. 8 is not difficult in most instances. On the other hand, some arrangements for providing retirement benefits require careful study. An example is supplied by requirements under the laws of some countries (such as countries in South America) regarding severance, retirement, death, and other benefits.

Companies with More than One Plan. Companies may have different pension plans for different groups of employees or for employees in different locations; occasionally, a basic plan and a supplemental plan cover the same group of employees. As to the accounting in these situations, Opinion No. 8 concludes (par. 37) that:

> A company that has more than one pension plan need not use the same actuarial cost method for each one; however, the accounting for each plan should conform to this Opinion. If a company has two or more plans covering substantial portions of the same employee classes and if the assets in any of the plans ultimately can be used in paying present or future benefits of another plan or plans, such plans may be treated as one plan for purposes of determining pension cost.

BASIC ACCOUNTING METHOD

The general outlook of Opinion No. 8 (not stated explicitly in the Opinion) is toward recognizing pension cost over a period between the dates employees are hired and the dates they are retired. In recognition of the existence of differences in viewpoint as to the composition of pension cost, Opinion No. 8 (par. 17) specifies that the annual provision for such cost (pension expense) is to be determined consistently and in a manner that brings the amount within prescribed minimum and maximum limits:

> ... the annual provision for pension cost should be based on an accounting method that uses an acceptable actuarial cost method ... and results in a provision between the minimum and maximum stated below. The accounting method and the actuarial cost method should be consistently applied from year to year.
>   a. *Minimum.* The annual provision for pension cost should not be less than the total of (1) normal cost, (2) an amount equivalent to interest on any unfunded prior service cost and (3) if indicated [under circumstances discussed later] ... a provision for vested benefits.
>   b. *Maximum.* The annual provision for pension cost should not be greater than the total of (1) normal cost, (2) 10 per cent of the past service cost (until fully amortized), (3) 10 percent of the amounts of any increases or decreases in prior service cost arising on amendments of the plan (until fully amortized) and (4) interest equivalents ... on the difference between provisions and amounts funded.

Exhibit 2 tabulates the components of the maximum and minimum provisions to facilitate comparison. As the tabulation shows, the essential differences between the minimum and maximum provisions are in the handling of past service cost and prior service cost increments (item 2) and vested benefits (item 3) (both discussed in greater detail in later sections).

The minimum/maximum structure under Opinion No. 8 provides wide flexibility in formulating an accounting procedure. The minimum/maximum structure, however, should not be interpreted as permitting either an annual choice of

EXHIBIT 2   Minimum and Maximum Costs of Pension Plan Components

Cost to be provided for	Extent of provision	
	Minimum	Maximum
1. Normal cost	Included in full	Included in full
2. Prior service cost (includes past service cost and prior service cost increments)	Interest on unfunded portion	10% of initial amounts (until fully amortized)
3. Vested benefits	Provision required under certain circumstances	Not applicable
4. Interest equivalents on any difference between accounting provisions and amounts funded	Included (or deducted) under certain circumstances in connection with item 3	Included (or deducted)

method or a choice in any year among various amounts of pension cost that happen to fall within the two limits. Consistency also contemplates continuity of actuarial cost method and of the procedure for dealing with prior service cost. A change in method, if material in effect, would require disclosure in a note to the employer's financial statements as a change in the application of an accounting principle.

ERISA established funding standards that will eliminate the significance, for most companies, of the upper and lower limits imposed by Opinion No. 8. (In view of the enactment of the ERISA standards, the FASB's study of pension cost accounting may lead it to modify at least that aspect of Opinion No. 8.) ERISA imposes upper and lower limits on pension plan contributions. The primary administrative vehicle for monitoring the minimum funding requirements of ERISA is the "funding standard account." In addition, there are a "full funding limitation" and an "alternative minimum funding standard account." The operation of these funding accounts is illustrated, in simplified form, in Exhibit 3.

COMPONENTS OF PENSION COST

The treatment, under Opinion No. 8, of the four components of pension cost—normal cost, prior service cost (past service cost and prior service cost increments), vested benefits, and interest—is discussed in greater detail below. This treatment is also compared with the treatment under ERISA, generally with the minimum funding standard account. Readers are cautioned to understand that interpretations of ERISA may change as regulations are issued and experience is gained.

Normal Cost. Both the minimum and maximum annual provisions under Opinion No. 8 include the normal cost of the plan. ERISA affords normal cost similar treatment. Normal cost is the cost assigned, for purposes of the actuarial calculations, to service credits for years subsequent to the date of a particular actuarial valuation.

Prior Service Cost. Past service cost and prior service cost increments also receive consideration under the minimum or maximum calculation. Past service cost is the pension cost assigned, for purposes of the actuarial calculations, to service credits for years prior to the inception of a pension plan. Prior service cost is the cost assigned to service credits for years prior to the date of a particular actuarial valuation; it includes past service cost. Increases or decreases in prior service cost which arise when a pension plan is amended and which are analogous

EXHIBIT 3   Funding Example Under ERISA[a]

This Exhibit illustrates the alternatives available under the Funding Standard Account and the Alternative Minimum Funding Standard Account. Though not intended to show all the complexities of the funding requirements, the chart traces a single plan through three consecutive plan years, including a change from the alternative funding standard to the basic funding standard.

Briefly stated, the operation of the Funding Standard Account develops a series of debits, as described on lines (1) through (5), and a series of credits, as described on lines (7) through (9), which are netted to determine the account balance. When a plan is funded at the minimum required level, the excess of credits over debits on line (11) will be zero. A positive balance in line (11) means that more funding has taken place than is essential to meet minimum standards; for a negative balance, the converse is true.

The plan year beginning January 1, 19X0, generates debits of $77,160 to the Funding Standard Account, and (under this standard) the employer must contribute at least this amount during the plan year to avoid a funding deficiency. However, the contribution required under the Alternative Minimum Funding Standard Account is smaller, and the employer can elect to comply with the funding standards by using the alternative method and making a contribution of only $75,000. The chart is based on the assumption that the employer makes that election and will now be required to maintain both funding standard accounts.

On January 1, 19X1, the plan is amended to provide increased benefits resulting in an increase in the Unfunded Past Service Liability as shown in item (C). In addition, the actuarial experience during 19X0 results in a loss of $250,000. These events have a significant impact on the employer's decision to use the alternative or the basic funding standard. Under the alternative standard the excess of the present value of accrued benefits over the market value of assets has increased to $312,300 on January 1, 19X1.

ILLUSTRATION OF THE MINIMUM FUNDING STANDARD

Basic Data		January 1, 19X0	January 1, 19X1	January 1, 19X2
(A)	Valuation Date	January 1, 19X0	January 1, 19X1	January 1, 19X2
(B)	Unfunded Past Service Liability	$422,800	$420,400*	$417,840*
(C)	Increased Unfunded due to Plan Amendment	—	150,000	148,260*
(D)	Experience Gain or (Loss) from Prior Years		(250,000)	15,000
Funding Standard Account				
DEBITS				
1.	Normal Cost for Year	$ 49,100	$ 59,800	$ 65,800
2.	Item (B) amortized over 40 years from 1/1/X0	28,060	28,060	28,060
3.	Item (C) amortized over 30 years from 1/1/X1	—	10,790	10,790
4.	Loss in Item (D) amortized over 15 years from 1/1/X1	—	24,980	24,980
5.	Excess of Debit Balance in Funding Standard Account over Debit Balance in Alternative Funding Standard Account Amortized over 5 years	—	520	520
6.	TOTAL DEBITS (1) + (2) + (3) + (4) + (5)	$ 77,160	$124,150	$130,150
CREDITS				
7.	Employer Contributions	$ 75,000†	$125,000	$130,000
8.	Gain in Item (D) amortized over 15 years from 1/1/X2	—	—	1,500
9.	Excess (with interest) of Debit Balance in Funding Standard Account over Debit Balance in Alternative Minimum Funding Standard Account	—	2,300	—
10.	TOTAL CREDITS (7) + (8) + (9)	$ 75,000	$127,300	$131,500
11.	Excess (Deficiency) of Credits over Debits (10) − (6)	($ 2,160)	$ 3,150	$ 1,350
12.	Credit (Debit) Balance beginning of year [line (13) from prior year with interest]	0	($ 2,300)**	$ 905**
13.	Credit (Debit) Balance	($ 2,160)	$ 850	$ 2,255

[a]Example developed by Dreher, Rogers & Associates, Inc., during October 1974, and reproduced with their permission.

*Unamortized Balance.

**Brought forward from prior year at 6½%.

†Based on Alternative Minimum Funding Standard Account.

to past service cost are referred to in this chapter as prior service cost increments. The Opinion No. 8 minimum provision for pension cost includes interest on any unfunded prior service cost but does not include amortization of the unfunded

Exhibit 3 *(continued)*

If the employer returns to the basic Funding Standard Account, any funding deficiency on the standard—developed while using the Alternative Funding Standard—must be amortized within 5 years of returning to the basic standard. The impact of this catch-up contribution is developed in lines (5) and (9) resulting in the necessary adjustments. In 19X1, the illustrative plan has the choice of continuing with the Alternative Funding Standard and paying $365,800 or returning to the basic Funding Standard and making a contribution of $124,150. In the illustration it is assumed that the employer returns to the basic Funding Standard.

The mechanics of calculation are essentially the same for the plan year beginning January 1, 19X2, except that 19X1 experience produces a gain which is to be amortized over the following 15 years. Whichever account — basic or alternative—is used to determine the minimum funding requirement, the amount so determined cannot exceed the Full Funding Limitation as displayed following the Alternative Minimum Funding Standard Account.

In comparing the statute's description of the Alternative Minimum Funding Standard with that discussed in the Conference Committee Report, there is some uncertainty as to how the amount of "accrued benefits" is to be calculated. The statute seems to refer to a liability for all accrued benefits whether or not vested. On the other hand, the Conference Committee Report says "liabilities are to be valued on the same basis as the Pension Benefit Guarantee Corporation would have computed them if the plan terminated." This seems not only to limit the benefits to be taken into account to the vested benefits, but also to further reduce the benefits by various limitations taken into account in arriving at the Benefit Guarantee Corporation's liability. Regulations will be required to clarify these and other points related to the alternative standard.

ILLUSTRATION OF THE ALTERNATIVE MINIMUM FUNDING STANDARD

Valuation Date

		January 1, 19X0	January 1, 19X1	January 1, 19X2
	DEBITS			
(1)	Normal Cost*	$ 43,200	$ 53,500	$ 59,900
	Excess of Present Value of Accrued Benefits over Market Value of Assets:			
	(a) Accrued Benefits	750,100	886,900	993,300
	(b) Assets	718,300	574,600	668,700
(2)	Excess	$ 31,800	$ 312,300	$ 324,600
(3)	Total Debits (1) + (2)	$ 75,000	$ 365,800	$ 384,500

FULL FUNDING LIMITATION

	January 1, 19X0	January 1, 19X1	January 1, 19X2
Entry Age Normal Accrued Liability	$1,141,100	$1,362,400	$1,453,000
Entry Age Normal Cost	49,100	59,800	65,800
Total	$1,190,200	$1,422,200	$1,518,800
Assets**	$ 700,000	$ 574,600	$ 668,700
Limitation	$ 490,200	$ 847,600	$ 850,100

*Lesser of Normal Cost under cost method used or Unit Credit Normal Cost.
**Lesser of Assets under Actuarial Valuation Method used or Market Value.

amount itself. Under ERISA, the minimum funding standard requires funding of unfunded prior service cost over 30 or 40 years, depending on the circumstances. The maximum provision under Opinion No. 8 includes 10 percent of the initial past service cost and of prior service cost increments (until fully amortized). This stipulation was in accord with the maximum rate at which, prior to the effective date of ERISA, contributions to a pension fund could be deducted for federal income tax purposes. Under ERISA (and for federal income tax purposes) the corresponding provision is now based on ten years rather than 10 percent. Thus, the maximum under Opinion No. 8 is less than the maximum now allowable for federal income tax purposes. For income tax purposes, however, this provision is subject to the effects of the other funding standard provisions.

When prior service cost is amortized for accounting purposes, the following provision of Opinion No. 8 (par. 23) applies:

> . . . in applying an actuarial cost method that separately assigns a portion of cost as past or prior service cost, any amortization of such portion should be based on a rational and systematic plan and generally should result in reasonably stable annual amounts. The equivalent of interest on the unfunded portion may be stated separately or it may be included in the amortization; however, the total amount charged against income in any one year should not exceed the maximum amount. . . .

Opinion No. 8 expresses a preference (par. 17) for an approach (described in par. 12) under which each year's expense includes an appropriate portion of past service cost and prior service cost increments. It is important to note that, except by coincidence, a pension cost provision determined under this approach ordinarily would not correspond with either the minimum or the maximum provision described in par. 17; rather, it would be between the minimum and maximum provisions.

If either the individual level premium method or the aggregate method is used, past service cost and prior service cost increments are not identified separately; the annual provision calculated under these methods consists entirely of normal cost. Consequently, the flexibility made available by the minimum/maximum structure is not present when these cost methods are used.

Both the individual level premium method and the aggregate method are characterized by declining annual charges to expense (assuming no change in the size of the employee group). Consequently, a method of accounting under which past service cost and prior service cost increments are amortized systematically in declining annual amounts would seem to be acceptable if the aggregate charge to expense is within the limits of the minimum/maximum structure.

Vested Benefits.   Vested benefits, as defined in the glossary of Opinion No. 8, are benefits that are not contingent on the employee's continuing in the service of the employer. In most plans, payment of the benefits will not begin until the employee reaches the normal retirement date; in some plans, payment of the benefits will begin when the employee retires or otherwise leaves the service of the employer (which may be before or after the normal retirement date).

Under Opinion No. 8, provision should be made for vested benefits under the minimum calculation when the following conditions apply (par. 17):

> A provision for vested benefits should be made if there is an excess of the actuarially computed value of vested benefits . . . over the total of (1) the pension fund and (2) any balance-sheet pension accruals, less (3) any balance-sheet pension prepayments or deferred charges, at the end of the year, and such excess is not at least 5 percent less than the comparable excess at the beginning of the year.

The method of computing the amount of the provision, if one is required, is specified in par. 17 of Opinion No. 8.

The intent of Opinion No. 8 is to require a provision for vested benefits only if expense charges comprising normal cost and interest on unfunded prior service cost will not make reasonable provision for such benefits. The use of a reduction factor of 5 percent is indicative of a 20-year period to provide for vested benefits.

Consideration need be given to vested benefits in the annual provision only if the actuarial cost method is one that determines prior service cost separately and if prior service cost is not being amortized or is being amortized over a period longer than 40 years. Consequently, a separate provision for vested benefits will not be required for employers that conform their accounting policy with the funding requirements of ERISA (funding standard for prior service cost not longer than 40 years).

Interest Equivalents.   The actuarial cost methods used in assigning the cost of a pension plan to periods of time assume that contributions by the employer (and in some instances by employees) will provide part of the money needed to pay benefits and that interest and other earnings on pension fund investments (referred to collectively as "interest") will provide the balance. If the employer's contributions exceed those assumed, the portion of the total cost to be met by interest is increased and the employer's future contributions are correspondingly reduced. If, on the other hand, the employer's contributions are less than those assumed, the interest which would otherwise have been earned on fund investments must eventually be contributed by the employer if the expectations of the procedure are to be fulfilled.

Accordingly, the Opinion requires that the annual provision for pension cost consider the effect of interest on any difference between pension cost provisions recorded for accounting purposes and the amounts funded. This is accomplished under the minimum/maximum structure as follows:

Minimum: Provision must be made for interest on any unfunded prior service cost or, if a provision for vested benefits is required, on the difference (under one of two alternative calculations) between accounting provisions and amounts funded.

Maximum: Provision for interest on unfunded past service cost and prior service cost increments is included in amounts provided for past service cost and prior service cost increments under the 10 percent limitation applicable to such costs, and must also be made on the difference between accounting provisions and amounts funded.

ACTUARIAL COST METHODS

Acceptable Methods. In discussing actuarial cost methods, Opinion No. 8 concludes (par. 24) that:

> Each of the actuarial cost methods described [in an appendix to the Opinion] . . . , except terminal funding, is considered acceptable when the actuarial assumptions are reasonable and when the method is applied in conformity with the other conclusions of this Opinion. The terminal funding method is not acceptable because it does not recognize pension cost prior to retirement of employees. For the same reason, the pay-as-you-go method (which is not an actuarial cost method) is not acceptable.

Actuarial cost methods other than those described in the appendix in the Opinion may be used. The acceptability of other methods would be determined from the guidelines expressed in Opinion No. 8.

Employees Included in Cost Calculations. In general, the pension cost for an employee is associated with his entire working lifetime. Accordingly, Opinion No. 8 provides (par. 36) that:

> . . . all employees who may reasonably be expected to receive benefits under a pension plan should be included in the cost calculations, giving appropriate recognition to anticipated turnover. As a practical matter, however, when the effect of exclusion is not material it is appropriate to omit certain employees from the calculations.

The Opinion accepted the then widely followed practice of omitting from pension cost calculations those employees likely to leave the company within a short time after employment, if the effect of their exclusion was not material. With some exceptions, ERISA requires that employees become eligible to participate in a plan when they have completed one year of service and have attained age 25. Consequently, it is anticipated that all eligible employees will now ordinarily be included in cost calculations.

ACTUARIAL GAINS AND LOSSES

As discussed earlier, actuaries must deal with several uncertainties in estimating the cost of a pension plan. These uncertainties relate to interest (return on funds invested), to expenses of administration, and to the amounts and timing of benefits to be paid. Actuaries use actuarial assumptions in tentatively resolving these uncertainties.

Opinion No. 8 does not deal with the selection of actuarial assumptions. Rather, it accepts the actuarial cost methods described (other than terminal funding) *when the actuarial assumptions are reasonable* (par. 24). This stipulation allows for the exercise of judgment in the selection of assumptions. The important consideration is the effect of the assumptions taken together, rather than the effect of any single assumption. Unless the assumptions, taken together, appear to be unreasonable, the requirements of Opinion No. 8 are probably being met. As an extreme example, if the sole consideration in selecting a set of assumptions had been an intention to develop the least possible provision for pension cost, the assumptions probably would be considered unreasonable. ERISA similarly requires that the actuarial assumptions be "reasonable" in the aggregate and take into account "the experience of the plan and reasonable expectations."

Regardless of the actuary's degree of skill, it is unlikely that actual events will coincide with each of the corresponding assumptions used. As a result, the actuarial assumptions may be changed from time to time as experience and judgment dictate. In addition, whether or not the assumptions as to events in the future are changed, it may be necessary to recognize in the calculations the effects of differences between actual prior experience and the assumptions used in the past. The effects on actuarially calculated pension cost of (1) changes in actuarial assumptions and (2) deviations between actual experience and the actuarial assumptions used are called "actuarial gains and losses." If the new assumptions are more optimistic or if experience has been favorable, the adjustments which result are actuarial gains; if the new assumptions are less optimistic or if experience has been unfavorable, the adjustments are actuarial losses. The net effect of the gains and losses determined in a particular valuation is ordinarily dealt with as a single amount.

General Rule for Treatment of Actuarial Gains and Losses.   In general, the Opinion requires (par. 30) that:

> ... actuarial gains and losses, including realized investment gains and losses, ... be given effect in the provision for pension cost in a consistent manner that reflects the long-range nature of pension cost.

Three methods of handling the gains or losses are considered to be acceptable:

1. Use a *spreading* method under which gains and losses are applied to current and future cost, either through the normal cost or through the past service cost (or prior service cost on amendment).

2. Use an *averaging* method under which an average of annual net gains and losses, developed from those that occurred in the past with consideration of those expected to occur in the future, is applied to the normal cost.

3. Apply net actuarial gains to *reduce prior service cost* in a manner that reduces the annual amount equivalent to interest on, or the annual amount of amortization of, such prior service cost, and does not reduce the period of amortization.

Spreading is not accomplished through the routine application of the unit credit method; a separate adjustment of the normal cost resulting from the routine application of that method is necessary for spreading or averaging. The Opinion considers a period of from 10 to 20 years to be reasonable for this purpose.

ERISA requires that actuarial gains and losses be amortized in applying the "minimum funding standard account." "Net experience gains and losses" are ordinarily to be amortized over 15 years (20 years in the case of a multi-employer plan) and "changes in actuarial assumptions used under the plan," are to be amortized over 30 years.

The essential consideration in selecting one of the three alternatives and consistently applying it from year to year should be to avoid significant fluctuations in the effect on annual cost. Spreading techniques such as those used for unrealized appreciation (depreciation) of pension fund assets (see below) might be used in accomplishing this objective.

An Exception to the General Rule.   An exception to the general rule that actuarial gains and losses are to be spread, averaged, or treated as reductions of prior service cost is provided in Opinion No. 8 (par. 31) under the following circumstances:

> Actuarial gains and losses should be recognized immediately if they arise from a single occurrence not directly related to the operation of the pension plan and not in the ordinary course of the employer's business. An example of such occurrences is a plant closing, in which case the actuarial gain or loss should be treated as an adjustment of the net gain or loss from that occurrence and not as an adjustment of pension cost for the year. Another example of such occurrences is a merger or acquisition accounted for as a purchase, in which case the actuarial gain or loss should be treated as an adjustment of the purchase price. However, if the transaction is accounted for as a pooling of interests, the actuarial gain or loss should generally be treated [under the general rule].

The "single-occurrence" gains or losses may give rise to balance sheet debits or credits. In funded plans, a gain may remain in the fund as if a prepayment; in unfunded plans, the debit or credit will affect previously accumulated unfunded liabilities.

This application of the exception to a merger or acquisition accounted for as a purchase was modified, in part, by Opinion No. 16 of the APB, which expressed the accounting principles for business combinations. When a combination is accounted for as a purchase (as distinguished from a pooling of interests) the cost of an acquired company is allocated, in the financial statements of the acquiring company, to the assets acquired and the liabilities assumed. An "accrual for pension cost" to be included in liabilities is described as follows (par. 88, footnote 13):

> An accrual for pension cost should be the greater of (1) accrued pension cost computed in conformity with the accounting policies of the acquiring corporation for one or more of its pension plans or (2) the excess, if any, of the actuarially computed value of vested benefits over the amount of the pension fund.

Until the Financial Accounting Standards Board interprets Opinion No. 8 or Opinion No. 16 or issues a Standard to supersede either, acquiring companies will continue to follow Opinion No. 16 in accounting for business combinations. They will continue to face uncertainty in applying par. 88 of Opinion No. 16 until the FASB reconciles footnote 13 of that paragraph with par. 18 of Opinion No. 8, dealing with the liability which should be shown in the balance sheet.

When a transaction is accounted for as a pooling of interests, a new basis of accountability does not arise; the constituent companies continue on a combined basis. If adjustments were made by the pooled companies to conform their pension plans, the resultant actuarial gain or loss would be handled, as for any continuing business, in accordance with the general rule.

Unrealized Appreciation or Depreciation.   The general rule for accounting for actuarial gains and losses, quoted earlier, specifically identified realized investment gains and losses as part of actuarial gains and losses. The Opinion deals separately with unrealized appreciation and depreciation as follows (par. 32):

> . . . unrealized appreciation and depreciation should be recognized in the determination oɪ ʲhe provision for pension cost on a rational and systematic basis that avoids giving undue weight to short-term market fluctuations. . . . Such recognition should be given either in the actuarial assumptions or as described [under the general rule] . . . for other actuarial gains and losses. Ordinarily appreciation and depreciation need not be recognized for debt securities expected to be held to maturity and redeemed at face value.

The Opinion provides alternatives in recognizing unrealized appreciation or depreciation. This element may either be recognized as an adjustment of the interest assumption or handled as an actuarial gain or loss. If unrealized appreciation is recognized by adjusting the interest factor, consideration should also be given to the possible effect of inflation on employee benefits (not usually an actuarial assumption).

The Opinion also provides flexibility in determining the amount of appreciation or depreciation to be recognized as an actuarial gain or loss. It gives examples of methods that may be used to avoid giving undue weight to short-term market fluctuations, but it does not prohibit the use of other methods. Certain of the available methods, some of which are mentioned in the Opinion, are illustrated in the following sections.

Moving Average.   Exhibit 4 illustrates the use of a moving average in recognizing pension fund market values.

EXHIBIT 4   Illustration of Moving Average Method for Recognizing Changes in Market Values of Pension Investments

	Pension fund at year-end		Ratio of market value to cost (%)	Fund value at year-end for calculating pension expense	
	At cost	At market value		Percentage of cost	Amount
Year 1 ...	$ 800,000	$1,000,000			
2 ...	1,000,000	1,300,000			
3 ...	1,200,000	1,600,000			
4 ...	1,400,000	2,000,000		134	$1,876,000
1 to 4 ...	$4,400,000	$5,900,000	134		
Year 5 ...	$1,600,000	$1,900,000		131	$2,096,000
2 to 5 ...	$5,200,000	$6,800,000	131		
Year 6 ...	$1,800,000	$2,600,000		135	$2,430,000
3 to 6 ...	$6,000,000	$8,100,000	135		

The procedure may be varied in numerous ways. For example:

1. A four- or five-year average may be used.

2. With an average for any number of years, quarterly amounts may be used instead of annual amounts.

3. With any method of computing the average, the fund value for calculating pension expense may be limited to a percentage (such as 80 percent) of the quoted market value.

Long-Range Rate of Appreciation.   Exhibit 5 illustrates a procedure which annually increases by a fixed or determinable percentage the value of equity securities for purposes of calculating pension expense. The percentage (3 percent is used in the example) is the expected long-term rate of growth. The procedure uses a separate account to accumulate the amount of appreciation which has been recognized. The sum of the cost of the equity securities and the appreciation account is not permitted to exceed a stated percentage (80 percent is used in the example) of the market value of the equity securities.

The procedure may be varied in numerous ways:

1. The addition to the appreciation account may be based on the average cost and appreciation account balances, rather than on the beginning balances.

2. The addition may be based on the beginning balances reduced for securities sold.

3. A percentage other than 3 percent may be used in calculating the addition.

4. The percentage used may be a variable rate, determined by deducting the effective rate of dividends received from a fixed rate (such as 7 percent).

EXHIBIT 5   Illustration of "Long-Range Rate of Appreciation" Method for Recognizing Changes in Market Values of Pension Investments

	Year 1	Year 2	Year 3
Cost of equity securities:			
Balance at beginning of year.................	$2,000,000	$2,200,000	$2,440,000
Purchases.................................	240,000	300,000	400,000
	$2,240,000	$2,500,000	$2,840,000
Sales.....................................	40,000	60,000	80,000
Balance at end of year......................	$2,200,000	$2,440,000	$2,760,000
Market value at end of year...................	$3,000,000	$3,200,000	$3,700,000
Appreciation account:			
Balance at beginning of year.................		$ 60,000	$ 120,000
Deduction for securities sold—based on ratio of cost of securities sold to beginning cost balance		1,600	3,900
		$ 58,400	$ 116,100
Addition—3 % of the sum of beginning cost and appreciation account balances, subject to the effect of the 80 % limitation................	60,000	61,600*	76,800
Balance at end of year......................	$ 60,000	$ 120,000	$ 192,900
Fund value for calculating pension expense—sum of year-end cost and appreciation account balances.....................................	$2,260,000	$2,560,000	$2,952,900

*The sum of the year-end cost and appreciation account balances was limited to $2,560,000 (80 % of $3,200,000).   Otherwise, this amount would have been $67,800.

5. The entire amount of any gain (loss) may be applied as a reduction of (increase in) the appreciation account. (In the example, the reduction for sales was on a pro rata basis.)

Percentage of Total Appreciation.   Exhibit 6 illustrates a method which recognizes each year a fixed percentage of the total appreciation. For this example it has been assumed that the percentage chosen is 10 percent and that the fund value for

EXHIBIT 6.   Illustration of "Percentage of Total Appreciation" Method for Recognizing Changes in Market Values of Pension Investments

	Pension fund at year-end		10 % of appreciation	Net appreciation recognized cumulatively	Fund value for calculating pension expense
	At cost	At market value			
Year 1......	$2,000,000	$2,700,000	$ 70,000	$ 70,000	$2,070,000
Year 2......	2,200,000	3,000,000	80,000	150,000	2,350,000
Year 3......	2,400,000	3,300,000	90,000	240,000	2,640,000
Year 4......	2,600,000	3,300,000	70,000	40,000	2,640,000*
Year 5......	2,800,000	3,800,000	100,000	140,000	2,940,000†
Year 6......	3,000,000	4,200,000	120,000	260,000	3,260,000

* Limited to 80 % of market value.
† Alternatively, the amount might be increased, subject to the 80 % limitation, to recognize appreciation foregone in Year 4 because of the limitation.

calculating pension expense is to be limited to 80 percent of the quoted market value.[11]

For most employers, the actuarial valuation that provides the basis for computing the amount of pension expense for a given fiscal year is made early in the year. When there is a significant change in circumstances, such as a sharp decline in the market values of pension fund investments, a question may arise as to whether computations based on information pertaining before the change took place are adequate for computing the year's pension expense or for determining the related disclosures.

Both the long-range view of pension cost under Opinion No. 8 and the practical considerations for actuaries support the use of pension cost computations based on information that is not fully current. Also, actuaries ordinarily use one of several techniques, some of which are described above, to moderate the effects of fluctuations in the market value of fund investments. If the techniques used give a reasonable result, it should not be necessary to update computations of annual cost made in accordance with the actuary's normal procedures.

There are two types of circumstance in which unrealized appreciation or depreciation need not be recognized: (1) appreciation or depreciation on debt securities expected to be held to maturity and redeemed at face value, and (2) appreciation or depreciation which will be applied in accordance with the provisions of the plan in determining variable retirement benefits. This latter exception is expressed in the Opinion (par. 33) as follows:

> Under variable annuity and similar plans the retirement benefits vary with changes in the value of a specified portfolio of equity investments. In these cases, investment gains or losses, whether realized or unrealized, should be recognized in computing pension cost only to the extent that they will not be applied in determining retirement benefits.

See page 27-25 for a discussion of the fund balance to be used in determining unfunded amounts to be disclosed.

OTHER ACCOUNTING CONSIDERATIONS

Defined-Contribution Plans. Defined-contribution plans were discussed earlier. Opinion No. 8 adds the following concerning such plans (pars. 38 and 39):

> Some defined-contribution plans state that contributions will be made in accordance with a specified formula and that benefit payments will be based on the amounts accumulated from such contributions. For such a plan the contribution applicable to a particular year should be the pension cost for that year.
>
> Some defined-contribution plans have defined benefits. In these circumstances, the plan requires careful analysis. When the substance of the plan is to provide the defined benefits, the annual pension cost should be determined in accordance with the conclusions of this Opinion applicable to defined-benefit plans.

These paragraphs require that careful consideration be given to the facts of the situation. If a plan specifies formula-based contributions (for example, a given amount per hour or per unit of production) to be made to a fund administered by a labor union or by representatives of a group of employers and of one or more labor unions, the contributions applicable to a particular year should be the pension cost for the year.

A plan that covers employees of a single company (or of a group of related

---

[11]In discussing actuarial gains and losses, Opinion No. 8 notes that some actuarial valuations recognize only a portion, "such as 75 percent," of the market value of a fund. This percentage was mentioned for illustrative purposes only. The percentage selected in any situation must be governed by the circumstances; 80 percent was assumed in this example.

companies) may specify both formula-based contributions and defined benefits. Initially, the benefits stated in such a plan are those which the contributions expected to be made by the employer can provide. Ordinarily, if the actuarial cost method used in relating benefits and contributions under a defined-contribution plan is acceptable for accounting purposes under the Opinion, it would be unlikely for indications to exist at the inception of the plan necessitating an accrual pattern differing from the payment pattern. If the defined contributions subsequently appear to be inadequate or excessive for the purpose of funding the stated benefits on the basis originally contemplated (for example, because of a change in the level of the employer's operations), either the contributions or the benefits, or both, may be adjusted in negotiations. Under such circumstances, or if the defined contributions differ from an accounting charge conforming with the criteria set out in the Opinion, determining an appropriate accounting accrual requires careful analysis based on the facts of each situation.

Insured Plans. As indicated earlier in discussing the applicability of Opinion No. 8, it applies to insured plans as well as to those funded by other means. This point is reemphasized in the Opinion as follows (par. 40):

> Insured plans are forms of funding arrangements and their use should not affect the accounting principles applicable to the determination of pension cost. . . . Pension cost under insured plans should be determined in conformity with the conclusions of this Opinion.

Types of Insured Plans. Insured plans are pension plans under which a life insurance company provides the funding instrument.

One class of insured plan uses contracts in which premiums and benefits are determined for each covered employee. Under one such arrangement, the insurance company issues an *individual policy or policies* for each employee, usually to a trustee. Another form of arrangement in this class is a *group annuity contract* issued to the employer. (Both individual and group contracts may provide death benefits in addition to retirement benefits.) Each of these types of arrangement specifies the premiums to be paid by the employer and the benefits to be paid to participants.

In the other class of insured arrangement, amounts contributed by the employer are not identified with specific employees until they retire. One such arrangement is called a *deposit administration contract* (or, more explicitly, a *deposit administration group annuity contract*). The insurance company keeps a separate account of the funds contributed by the employer and adds interest at an agreed rate, which is subject to change at intervals (typically five years). When an employee retires, the insurance company issues an annuity which will provide the benefits stipulated in the pension plan and transfers the single premium for the annuity from the employer's accumulated contributions. The premium rates for annuities are stated in the deposit administration contract. These rates, like the interest rates, are subject to change at intervals (again, typically five years). The insurance company usually makes charges for its expenses only through the annuity premiums. Periodic dividends based on experienced expenses, mortality, and investment earnings are credited to the employer.

A similar type of funding instrument is the *immediate participation guarantee contract,* which differs from a deposit administration contract principally in the treatment of expenses, mortality, and investment earnings. Expenses are charged directly to the employer's account, rather than through annuity premiums as they are under a deposit administration contract; mortality among retired employees affects the employer's cost at shorter intervals; annual investment earnings credits are based on the insurance company's experience, rather than on a guaranteed rate.

Cost Under Insured Plans. Inasmuch as the cost under an insured plan is normally developed by the insurance company, questions arise as to whether the pension cost has, in fact, been determined in conformity with the Opinion's conclusions. Accordingly, the following guidelines are given in the Opinion (pars. 40 and 41):

> Cost under individual policy plans is ordinarily determined by the individual level premium method, and cost under group deferred annuity contracts is ordinarily determined by the unit credit method. Cost under deposit administration contracts, which operate similarly to trust-fund plans, may be determined on any of several methods. Some elements of pension cost, such as the application of actuarial gains (dividends, termination credits, etc.), may at times cause differences between the amounts being paid to the insurance company and the cost being recognized for accounting purposes.
>
> Individual annuity or life insurance policies and group deferred annuity contracts are often used for plans covering small employee groups. Employers using one of these forms of funding exclusively do not ordinarily have ready access to actuarial advice in determining pension cost. Three factors to be considered in deciding whether the amount of net premiums paid is the appropriate charge to expense are dividends, termination credits and pension cost for employees not yet covered under the plan. Usually, the procedures adopted by insurance companies in arriving at the amount of dividends meet the requirements of Paragraph 30 [regarding the treatment of actuarial gains]; consequently, in the absence of wide year-to-year fluctuations such dividends should be recognized in the year credited. Termination credits should be spread or averaged in accordance with Paragraph 30. Unless the period from date of employment to date of coverage under the plan is so long as to have a material effect on pension cost, no provision need be made for employees expected to become covered under the plan. If such a provision is made, it need not necessarily be based on the application of an actuarial cost method.

The Opinion recognizes that employers using insured plans exclusively do not ordinarily have ready access to actuarial advice in determining pension cost. This may be particularly true of employers with individual annuity or life insurance policies and group deferred annuity contracts covering small employee groups. Consequently, attention must be given, as a minimum, to the factors mentioned in the Opinion. In particular, determining whether a provision is necessary for employees not yet covered will require careful consideration. One approach would be to use an estimate based on premiums that would be charged to cover currently those employees not yet covered, giving consideration to the composite likelihood that such employees will leave the company's employ before attaining coverage.

Effect of Funding.   Unless specified in the plan, it is necessary to choose the type of *funding instrument* (for example, a life insurance or annuity contract or a trust agreement) and a specific *funding agency* (for example, a specific life insurance company or a specific trust fund administered by a corporate or individual trustee). In some cases, two or more types of funding instrument (and, perhaps, two or more funding agencies) are used in combination.

When a life insurance company provides the funding instrument, the pension plan is known as an *insured plan.* Insured plans were discussed in the preceding section.

When the funding instrument is a *trust agreement* and the funding agency a *trust fund,* the pension plan is called a *trust fund plan.* Under this type of arrangement, the employer's payments are made to a trustee. The trustee invests the funds in accordance with the terms of the trust agreement and either pays retirement benefits from the accumulated funds or purchases annuities from such funds for employees who retire. The trustee may be a bank or trust company, or an individual or individuals. Depending upon the terms of the trust agreement, the trustee may have sole discretion in investing the trust funds or may be subject to the general direction of the employer in making investments. Ordinarily, the trustee accepts the instructions of the employer as to the identity of the beneficiaries who should receive payments under the plan and as to the amounts of the payments.

In discussing the effect of funding on the accounting for the cost of a pension plan, Opinion No. 8 points out that its provisions apply also to plans that are unfunded and draws accounting distinctions between unfunded and funded plans. Because ERISA requires funding for plans covering active employees, these distinctions may have only limited continuing significance.

A pension plan may become overfunded (that is, have fund assets in excess of the prior service cost assigned under the actuarial method in use for accounting purposes) as a result of *contributions;* in this event, under Opinion No. 8, provisions for pension expense should be reduced by amounts equivalent to interest on any excess of prior-year funding over accounting provisions (pars. 44, 43). If a pension plan becomes overfunded as a result of *actuarial gains,* the gains should be accounted for in accordance with the requirements of the Opinion for actuarial gains (pars. 44, 30). In most circumstances, an overfunded condition is relieved by cessation of contributions (but accounting provisions would ordinarily continue on a reduced basis). If a pension plan was overfunded on the effective date of the Opinion, the amount by which it was overfunded was to be treated as an actuarial gain realized on that date and was to be accounted for in accordance with the requirements of the Opinion for actuarial gains.

Income Taxes.   The need for interperiod income tax allocation is touched upon in the Opinion in par. 45:

> When pension cost is recognized for tax purposes in a period other than the one in which recognized for financial reporting, appropriate consideration should be given to allocation of income taxes among accounting periods.

In the absence of unusual circumstances, "appropriate consideration" would lead to allocation of income taxes. This is consistent with the requirement for comprehensive allocation expressed in APB Opinion No. 11, "Accounting for Income Taxes."

As a general rule, the federal income tax consequences of a pension plan depend on whether the plan is a *qualified* one, that is, whether it complies with certain requirements of the Internal Revenue Code and of the Internal Revenue Service. One practical effect of these requirements is that, on a cumulative basis, normal cost plus an amount equivalent to interest on any unfunded prior service cost must be funded. Funding of amounts in excess of the prescribed maximum (see page 27-13) is discretionary for income tax purposes. The minimum/maximum structure under Opinion No. 8 conforms in many respects with the corresponding limitation for income tax purposes; nevertheless, differences between tax and accounting charges may arise. For example, while Opinion No. 8 requires that actuarial gains be spread, averaged, or applied to reduce past service cost, tax regulation requires immediate recognition of such gains under certain circumstances. Further, some companies may have decided, as a consequence of the issuance of Opinion No. 8, to select for accounting purposes an actuarial cost method other than that applied for income tax purposes.

PRESENTATION IN FINANCIAL STATEMENTS

General Disclosures.   The importance of pension plans on financial position and results of operations led the Accounting Principles Board to the conclusion that the following disclosures should be made in financial statements or their notes (par. 46):

1. A statement that such plans exist, identifying or describing the employee groups covered.
2. A statement of the company's accounting and funding policies.
3. The provision for pension cost for the period.
4. The excess, if any, of the actuarially computed value of vested benefits over the total of the pension fund and any balance-sheet pension accruals, less any pension prepayments or deferred charges.
5. Nature and effect of significant matters affecting comparability for all periods presented, such as changes in accounting methods (actuarial cost method, amortization of past and prior service cost, treatment of actuarial gains and losses, etc.), changes in circumstances (actuarial assumptions, etc.), or adoption or amendment of a plan.

Opinion No. 8 includes an illustrative disclosure which reads, in part, as follows (par. 46):

> The company and its subsidiaries have several pension plans covering substantially all of their employees, including certain employees in foreign countries. The total pension expense for the year was $_____, which includes, as to certain of the plans, amortization of prior service cost over periods ranging from 25 to 40 years. The company's policy is to fund pension cost accrued. The actuarially computed value of vested benefits for all plans as of December 31, 19___, exceeded the total of the pension fund and balance-sheet accruals less pension prepayments and deferred charges by approximately $_____. A change during the year in the actuarial cost method used in computing pension cost had the effect of reducing net income for the year by approximately $_____.

If the employer's accounting policies conform with the requirements of the Opinion and if there have been no changes affecting comparability, the actuarial cost method being followed and the actuarial assumptions being used are not ordinarily identified.

The APB's Opinion No. 22 (April 1972) requires that a company's financial statements include a description of its significant accounting policies. The Opinion expresses a preference for the use of a separate "Summary of Significant Accounting Policies." Some or all of the information described above may be included in such a summary.

The following sections discuss certain aspects of the disclosure items listed above.

Actuarially Computed Value of Vested Benefits. The "actuarially computed value of vested benefits," as used in the Opinion, represents the present value, at the date of determination, of the sum of (1) the benefits expected to become payable to former employees who have retired or who have terminated service with vested rights, and (2) the benefits, based on service rendered before the date of determination, expected to become payable at future dates to present employees, taking into account the probable time that employees will retire, at the vesting percentages applicable at the date of determination.

The concept of vesting applies, for the most part, only to benefits that have accrued (in the limited sense that the employee service on which they are based has been rendered). This is the concept used under the accrued benefit cost method. If the actuarial cost method used in the basic pension cost calculations is a projected benefit method (for example, the entry age normal method), a separate actuarial calculation of the value of vested benefits may be necessary.

In determining the vested amount, there may also be instances when the accrued-benefit concept must be modified. The words "taking into account the probable time that employees will retire" usually mean normal retirement. It may be, however, that present employees, if they were to terminate their service at elective dates prior to their normal retirement dates, would receive benefits having a present value greater than that of the benefits they would receive if they worked until their normal retirement dates. In this event, the actuarially computed value of vested benefits should include the excess multiplied by the probability of termination before normal retirement.

An actuarial valuation as of a given fiscal closing date is seldom available when financial statements as of that date are being prepared. A footnote to Opinion No. 8 explains that the "actuarially computed value of vested benefits" will ordinarily be based on the actuarial valuation used for the year. The appropriate "as of" dates for the determination of the value of vested benefits and for other factors in the computation (the amount of the pension fund and any balance sheet pension accruals less pension prepayments or deferred charges) will depend on the circumstances; consistency is a primary consideration. Under one approach, the actuarially computed value of vested benefits would be as of the valuation date, and the amounts of the pension fund and net balance sheet accruals would be as of the end of the employer's fiscal year. If the amount of the pension fund is regularly reported only as of the valuation date, it should be satisfactory for the value of vested benefits and the pension fund to be as of that date; the net balance sheet accruals might then include the amount funded or accrued for the fiscal year, reduced by any portion funded before the valuation date. Under still another approach, all three amounts would be as of the valuation date. Only in very rare circumstances (such as when a material, extraordinary change in the level of vesting has taken place after the valuation date) would a valuation made within the employer's fiscal year be updated.

• TOTAL OF PENSION FUND. Opinion No. 8 does not specify whether the assets in a pension fund should be stated at cost, at market value, or at some other value in determining whether a provision for vested benefits is required. ERISA stipulates that ". . . the value of the plan's assets shall be determined on the basis of any reasonable actuarial method of valuation which takes into account fair market value and which is permitted under regulations prescribed by the Secretary of the Treasury." In developing the disclosures with regard to vested benefits, employers should weigh the significance of any decline since the actuarial valuation date in the market values of pension fund equity securities and of those debt securities not expected to be held to maturity. It is especially important to consider whether the basis of determining the fund value should be the same as the basis used in determining the amount of vested benefits.

• PORTION NOT YET CHARGED TO EXPENSE. Item 4 of the disclosure list calls for disclosure of the portion of the actuarially computed value of vested benefits not yet charged to expense, but does not call for disclosure of the unfunded or unaccrued prior service cost. The Securities and Exchange Commission's *Regulation S-X* continues to require disclosure of unfunded prior service cost in financial statements filed with the Commission.

Matters Affecting Comparability. Disclosure item 5 is concerned with the nature and effects of significant matters affecting comparability for all periods presented. Examples of the changes referred to in the Opinion include the following:

• ADOPTION OR AMENDMENT OF A PLAN. In the year of adoption or amendment of a plan, it is usually appropriate to give detailed disclosure of the nature of the new plan or of the amendments to an existing plan.

• CHANGES IN CIRCUMSTANCES. The usual change in "circumstances" for a pension plan leads to a change in an actuarial assumption. This type of change is in the same category as a change in the estimated useful life used to determine depreciation of an asset. Such a change affects comparability but not consistency. Disclosure of its nature and effect might be somewhat as follows: "A change during the year in certain of the actuarial assumptions used in computing pension cost had the effect of reducing net income for the year by approximately $_____."

• CHANGES IN ACCOUNTING METHODS. Included in this category of changes would be: (*a*) a change in actuarial cost method—for example, from the entry age normal method to the individual level premium method; (*b*) a change in the amortization period of past service cost and prior service cost increments—for example, from 20 to 30 years, or from a policy of not amortizing to a policy of amortizing; and (*c*) a change in the treatment of actuarial gains and losses—for example, from spreading over 10 years to spreading over 20 years, or from spreading to averaging. (Changes in accounting method affect both comparability and consistency, and would be mentioned in the auditors' report if the effects were material.) Opinion No. 20 also specifies general disclosures regarding the nature of and justification for an accounting change and its effect on earnings.[12]

The FASB's Interpretation No. 3 supplemented the disclosure requirements of Opinion No. 8. Under Interpretation No. 3, if it appears likely, before a plan becomes subject to the participation, vesting or funding requirements of ERISA, that compliance will have a significant effect on the amount of an employer's periodic provision for pension expense, periodic funding of pension costs or unfunded vested benefits, the facts and an estimate of the effect (or an explanation if it is not practicable to give an estimate) is to be disclosed.

Pension Amounts in the Balance Sheet.   On the subject of balance sheet presentation of pension cost, Opinion No. 8 concludes (par. 18) that:

> The difference between the amount which has been charged against income and the amount which has been paid should be shown in the balance sheet as accrued or prepaid pension cost. If the company has a legal obligation for pension cost in excess of amounts paid or accrued, the excess should be shown in the balance sheet as both a liability and a deferred charge. Except to the extent indicated in the preceding sentences . . . , unfunded prior service cost is not a liability which should be shown in the balance sheet.

If accounting charges for pension cost exceed payments, it may be desirable to avoid, as possibly misleading, the use of words such as "accrued" and "liability" in an employer's balance sheet. Instead, a descriptive expression such as "Provisions for pension cost in excess of payments" or "Pension cost charged to expense but not funded" may be preferable.

The expression "legal obligation" is not defined in Opinion No. 8 and is not a term of art in accounting. In applying the Opinion, the expression has generally been interpreted to mean the unfunded cost of vested pension benefits under plans (infrequently encountered) that do not include a provision requiring, specifically or in effect, that employees look only to the pension fund for benefits.

Almost all pension plans have provisions intended to limit the employer's liability. Most unilateral plans give the employer the right to terminate the plan at any time, whereas a negotiated plan is usually kept in force for a limited period, such as two to five years, by a separate agreement with employees. The inclusion in ERISA of funding requirements and provisions relating to guarantee of employee benefits have raised questions as to whether the Act created a legal obligation for unfunded pension cost.

In Interpretation No. 3, the FASB concluded that a legal obligation was not created, except in the following two respects:

(1) The amount currently required to be funded for a plan subject to ERISA should be recognized as a liability unless a waiver has been obtained from the Secretary of the Treasury to permit funding less than the required annual minimum amount.

(2) If there is convincing evidence that a pension plan will be terminated and

---

[12]Pursuant to the Securities and Exchange Commission's Accounting Series Release No. 177 (September 10, 1975), certain information regarding an accounting change must appear in the quarterly Form 10-Q.

the liability on termination (calculated in accordance with the requirements of ERISA) will exceed fund assets and related prior accruals, the excess liability must be accrued or, if the calculation is not practicable, the circumstances must be disclosed in a note to the financial statements.

Pension Benefit Guarantee Corporation.   The preceding reference to plan termination turns attention to the Pension Benefit Guarantee Corporation (PBGC), created by ERISA. This new Corporation is to pay "guaranteed benefits" (as defined in ERISA) to participants of a terminated plan if the assets of the plan are insufficient to fund such benefits. In order to obtain funds for this purpose, the PBGC will charge employers an annual premium (initially, equal to $1 per participant per year—$0.50 per participant for multi-employer plans). Presumably, employers will expense these premiums as incurred.

If the PBGC is required to pay benefits under a terminated plan, the employer becomes liable to the PBGC for the short-fall, but only to the extent of 30 percent of the employer's "net worth" (not defined in ERISA). A plan termination insurance program is to be established, pursuant to ERISA, to be financed by insurance premiums paid by employers. After premiums have been paid by an employer for five years, the PBGC will assume the employer's liability. Presumably, employers will expense the premiums for the insurance coverage as incurred.

CHANGES IN ACCOUNTING METHOD

When a change is made from one method of accounting for pension cost to another, a question arises as to whether recognition should be given to the difference between the cost provided under the superseded method and the cost that would have been incurred had the new method been used in the prior periods. On this point, Opinion No. 8 concluded (par. 47) that:

> ... pension cost provided under an acceptable method of accounting in prior periods should not be changed subsequently. Therefore, the effect on prior-year cost of a change in accounting method should be applied prospectively to the cost of the current year and future years, in a manner consistent with the conclusions of this Opinion, and not retroactively as an adjustment of retained earnings or otherwise.

Opinion No. 8 provided (par. 49) that the effect of any changes in accounting methods made as a result of the issuance of the Opinion should be applied prospectively.[13] Similarly, the FASB's Interpretation No. 3 (par. 3) concluded that

> ... any change in pension cost resulting from compliance with the Act [ERISA] shall enter into the determination of periodic provisions for pension expense *subsequent* to the date a plan becomes subject to the Act's participation, vesting and funding requirements.

If a pension plan is adopted or amended during a company's fiscal year, it is acceptable to account for the resultant pension cost or change therein only from the date of adoption or amendment. To require accrual retroactively to the beginning of the fiscal year would violate the proscription, expressed in par. 47 of the Opinion, against retroactive charges on adoption or amendment of a plan.

INFLUENCES ON ACCOUNTING AND REPORTING OTHER THAN OPINION NO. 8

Management's selection of an accounting method meeting the requirements of Opinion No. 8 and the reporting obligations imposed on private pension plans are influenced by factors not within the purview of this chapter.

---

[13]Par. 48 of Opinion No. 8 made provision for the treatment of any unamortized prior service cost and of any amount of overfunding existing at the effective date of the Opinion.

The federal income tax consequences of a pension plan are a major consideration in business planning. Significant advantages attach to a plan which is "qualified," that is, which complies with certain requirements of the Internal Revenue Code and of the Internal Revenue Service. These requirements are substantially the same as those of ERISA. While the amount of pension cost that is deductible for income tax purposes does not control for accounting purposes, many managements may wish to avoid significant book-tax differences (and the consequent need for the allocation of income taxes for accounting purposes) by structuring their method to comply with both the income tax/ERISA requirements and Opinion No. 8.

The Securities and Exchange Commission specifies, in Rule 3-16 (g) of its Regulation S-X, the requirements for disclosure of pension and retirement plans in financial statements required to be filed with the SEC under the various acts. Such disclosures must include:

1. A brief description of the essential provisions of any employee pension or retirement plan and of the accounting and funding policies related thereto . . . ;
2. The estimated cost of the plan for each period for which an income statement is presented . . . ;
3. The excess, if any, of the actuarially computed value of vested benefits over the total of the pension fund and any balance sheet pension accruals, less any pension prepayments or deferred charges . . . as of the most recent practicable date;
4. If a plan has not been fully funded or otherwise provided for, the estimated amount that would be necessary to fund or otherwise provide for the past service cost [called prior service cost in this chapter] of the plan . . . as of the date most recently determined;
5. A statement . . . of the nature and effect of significant matters affecting comparability of pension costs for any periods for which income statements are presented.

Disclosure of the unfunded prior service cost is a more inclusive requirement than the disclosure, specified in APB Opinion No. 8, of the excess of the actuarially computed value of vested benefits over the total of the pension fund and any net accruals or deferrals.

Regulation S-X also notes that "If the amount which would otherwise be required to be shown with respect to any item is not material, it need not be separately set forth in the manner prescribed." This exclusion is similar to that specified in Opinion No. 8.

Other regulatory agencies may exert an influence on the amount and timing of charges for pension cost. For example, the Cost Accounting Standards Board has prescribed requirements as to the composition and measurement of pension cost by contractors subject to the CASB's promulgated standards.[14]

The Accounting Principles Board, in Opinion No. 8, recognized "that accounting for pension cost is in a transitional stage, [and] that the range of practices would be significantly narrowed if pension cost were accounted for at the present time within limits. . . ." The range of accounting practices may well be further narrowed in the future, either as the result of statements of accounting policy issued by the Financial Accounting Standards Board in recognition of ERISA's requirements, or as public policy indicates additional regulatory controls over the private pension system.

In the interim, it can reasonably be said that the benefits of consistency in accounting for the cost of pension plans and the narrowing of the range of differences in accounting resulting from the issuance of Opinion No. 8 will provide a bench mark for those having responsibility for the establishment of future accounting practices.

[14]Cost Accounting Standard on Composition and Measurement of Pension Cost, Part 412, 40 *Federal Register* 43873.

BIBLIOGRAPHY

Commerce Clearing House: *Pension Reform Act of 1974—Law and Explanation,* Commerce Clearing House, New York, 1974.

Five Articles on Accounting for the Cost of Pension Plans, AICPA, New York, 1968.
This publication accumulates in one place the following items:

Phoenix, Julius W., Jr., and William D. Bosse: "Accounting for the Cost of Pension Plans—APB Opinion No. 8," *The Journal of Accountancy,* August 1967, pp. 27–37; "More Information on APB No. 8," *The Journal of Accountancy,* October 1967, pp. 31–40.

Hicks, Ernest L.: "Pension Cost and the Auditor," *The Journal of Accountancy,* September 1967, pp. 70- 73.

Dreher, William A.: "Alternatives Available under APB Opinion No. 8: An Actuary's View," *The Journal of Accountancy,* September 1967, pp. 37–51.

Sloat, Frederick P.: "What Should Be Included in the Actuarially Computed Value of Vested Benefits," *The Journal of Accountancy,* October 1967, p. 33.

———: "Actuarial Considerations Involved in Pension Cost Under APB Opinion 8," *The Journal of Accountancy,* December 1967, pp. 54–58.

Hicks, Ernest L.: "Accounting for the Cost of Pension Plans," *Accounting Research Study No. 8,* AICPA, New York, 1965.

Pomeranz, Felix, Gordon P. Ramsey, and Richard M. Steinberg: *Pensions, An Accounting and Management Guide,* The Ronald Press Company, New York, 1976, chap. 6.

Sloat, Frederick P.: "Accounting Recognition of Appreciation and Depreciation of Equities Held in Retirement Plan Funds," *The New York Certified Public Accountant,* January 1966, p. 35.

Chapter **28**

Contributed Capital

JOSEPH S. BURNS
Partner, Touche Ross & Co.

MARTIN S. GANS
Partner, Touche Ross & Co.

CONTRIBUTED CAPITAL

Accounting for the corporate form involves a recognition of the corporation's artificially unlimited life. The biography of this life is somewhat explained in the stockholders' equity section of a corporate balance sheet. Sources of capital, both contributed and earned, are described and measured to furnish users of the financial statements with, it is hoped, useful information for their decision making.

The stockholders' equity section of the balance sheet with its related footnotes is one of the few places in the financial statements in which the narrative information is perhaps more important than the reported numbers on the face of the statement. The knowledgeable investor understands that the value of an investment can be significantly altered by transactions which affect stockholders' equity and by legal changes in the relative rights, limitations, and privileges of various classes of owners. Information about such changes and transactions is disclosed in large part in footnotes or in a separate statement of changes in stockholders' equity. Accordingly, the investor who appreciates the value of this information must view the stockholders' equity section as much more than the amount needed to balance the left side and the right side of the balance sheet. The stockholders' equity section is, in fact, the initial reference point for a wealth of valuable information which will be found throughout the financial statements and related notes.

Corporations operated for profit have many sources for new or additional capital, but only two are relatively permanent—funds invested by stockholders and funds generated by the earning process which are retained for use in the business. Accounting for retained earnings does not typically involve the complex reporting and disclosure requirements of accounting for contributed capital. See Chapter 29.

Typically a balance sheet will include some or all of the following components of contributed capital:

Preferred and preference stocks

Common stock

Capital contributed in excess of par value (This title and "additional paid-in capital" are used interchangeably hereafter.)

Treasury stock.

A common misconception is that the amounts reported for contributed capital, together with the retained earnings, provide the user with some definitive measure of the market value of the company. In fact, the amounts reported as stockholders' equity are simply the residual effect of applying accounting principles based on historical costs to the company's assets, liabilities, and operations. The user must look beyond the reported amounts in the equity section of the balance sheet for information about past earnings experience, potential dilution of ownership, dividend expectations, and contingent interests.

Additional information, such as the relative seniority of the various classes of equity, liquidating preferences, information about conversion privileges, voting rights, options and warrants, etc., is usually not shown on the balance sheet, but is shown in a separate statement of stockholders' equity or in the footnotes.

This chapter does not attempt to cope with the specific requirements of accounting for contributed capital in regulated industries such as the transportation and insurance industries or public utilities. Also, accounting for business combinations is not discussed, but see Chapter 33.

Reporting Requirements and Legal Requirements. The statutory regulations under which an organization is incorporated may place various restraints on the capital structure of a corporation. Some of these restraints are matters of substance and should be disclosed in the financial statements. Others are matters of form and do not require disclosure. This has given rise to varying opinions by accountants as to the proper accounting and financial statement presentation of a firm's capital structure.

In general, accountants do not agree with those who suggest that financial statements should be limited merely to following legal requirements. Such requirements may differ from state to state, and because of amendments, the requirements may even vary from one time to another. Proper disclosure results whenever the financial statements reflect the underlying economic substance of the reported events. The proper accounting treatment of a transaction may be based upon objectives different from the legal requirements. The two sets of objectives may not result in the same form of reporting. For example, under California law, when outstanding shares of common stock are purchased from an officer or director and retired by a company, the transaction ordinarily must be recorded by reducing retained earnings for the amount paid in excess of par. Stock repurchases from shareholders who are neither officers nor directors are recorded by reducing additional paid-in capital for the amount paid in excess of par. From the accountant's point of view, stock repurchases should be reported identically, irrespective of the seller. In practice, however, many accountants have followed the legal requirements for recording and reporting such transactions.

COMMON STOCK

Attributes of Common Stock.   The common stockholders have a unique position in the structure of the corporation. They retain the residual interest in the economic resources of an enterprise after consideration of all other obligations. Common stockholders alone, among all of the investors and creditors of the firm, have no promise of a guaranteed return. Consequently, they stand to suffer the most from unsuccessful operations. Conversely, the common stockholders may gain the most from successful operations.

Typically a corporation has only one class of common stock. However, in some companies there may be two or more classes of common stock with each different class reflecting variations in voting rights, dividend prospects, or other special rights or preferences. In some cases, dividend preferences and voting restrictions may result in a common stock class which more closely resembles preferred stock than common stock.

Legal Factors and Requirements for Incorporation.   Most companies may choose the state for incorporation. For companies whose operations are national or regional, the state selected for incorporation may be chosen mainly because its statutes offer lenient registration and reporting requirements or tax advantages, or both. Other considerations for selecting a particular state include the flexibility of capital structures, prospects of liability attaching to managers and shareholders, requirements for shareholder meetings, definitions of legal capitalization, voting rights and privileges, and preemptive rights. There may be other factors which should be reviewed with benefit of legal advice by any company considering incorporation.

State law governs the procedural steps taken to incorporate. In most states, the Secretary of State's Office oversees the filing process.

The certificate (articles) of incorporation, once approved by the state, becomes a public document. The charter of the corporation, in effect, is prescribed by the corporation law of the state and the specific articles of incorporation. Typically state law requires the articles to include the name of the corporation, purpose of formation, address of its corporate and home office, information about the capital structure, a detailed description of each class of securities, and an indication of its planned life, if not perpetual. Changes to the articles often require shareholder approval. Ordinarily such changes meet no resistance from the state.

The affairs of the corporation are conducted according to bylaws or rules drawn by the incorporators. Bylaws are not a matter of public record. Bylaws may mirror the articles of incorporation but cannot extend corporate powers beyond those specified in the charter. Most bylaws deal with securities issuance, policy for transfer of share ownership, dividends, and meetings of shareholders and directors.

Registration and Transfer of Shares. Except for corporations with publicly traded or widely held securities, the maintenance of shareholder records is a relatively simple task. Stock certificates are recorded in a stock certificate book, and a stock transfer journal is maintained to record new issues, cancellations, and transfers.

As the shareholder list expands, the need for a more versatile system which can handle large numbers of transactions may develop. In addition, the major exchanges require controls which the typical corporation finds uneconomic to provide. Thus independent registrars and transfer agents, who specialize in providing services for transfers of stock, are usually used.

Negotiability of stock certificates is governed by the Uniform Stock Transfer Act and the Uniform Commercial Code. While most stock certificates currently in use are large printed or engraved documents, experimentation is underway to facilitate data processing with stock "cards" (of computer processing size) and also to eliminate certificates entirely through the use of automated stock ownership and transfer applications.

Par and No-Par Value Stock. The articles of incorporation establish the type of capital stock to be issued, whether it is par value stock or no-par value stock. Today, the distinction between par value and no-par value stock has little financial reporting significance. The original concept of par value was that it represented an investment pool which was to be maintained for the security of creditors. This investment pool has been defined as "legal," "statutory," or "stated" capital, and many states generally prohibit corporations from paying dividends out of such legal capital. The par value concept has become generally obsolete as creditors have adopted sophisticated techniques for evaluating the ability of the enterprise to meet its obligations on a timely basis. There are, however, some legal differences between par value and no-par value stocks. In most states, creditors can hold stockholders liable for the debts of the corporation only if the stock was initially issued for a consideration less than par value. Depending upon the state of incorporation, when certificates are issued in these circumstances, a creditor in liquidation proceedings may hold the stockholders liable for the differences between the consideration given for the stock and its par value. In order to avoid this problem, many companies issue no-par value stock which is not assessable. No-par value stock is legal in nearly all states. No-par stock will usually have a stated value, which represents simply an allocation of the selling price to the common stock designated by the corporation.

Changes in Par or Stated Values. State statutes control the ability of the corporation to change its capital from par value shares to no-par value shares, to reduce the par or stated values, or to change from no-par to par. Unless there is a change in the aggregate stated capital, entries are not required in the company's books. If stated capital in the aggregate is reduced, the difference should be credited to capital contributed in excess of par (or stated) value. Changes in par or stated value may also be used to increase stated capital as long as retained earnings or capital contributed in excess of par (or stated) value is available to transfer to the par or stated value account. Capital contributed in excess of par (or stated) value should be exhausted before any transfers are made from retained earnings.

Initial Stock Issuance. Stock may be issued through public offering or by private placement. Deciding which is preferable can be difficult. State and federal securities laws bear on the decision. Generally, a private placement involves relatively few purchasers, whereas a public sale involves the offering of securities to a large number of prospective purchasers, many of whom do not have detailed knowledge of the company's present financial position or its history. Most public offerings require significant attention to the applicable federal and state securities requirements. These include an in-depth narrative description of the registrant's business, management, plans, and prospects. Financial information both in statement and tabular form is required. In many cases the financial statements and certain other financial information must be certified by independent accountants. Frequently, financial information is provided for five years or more. Even though public offerings receive more publicity than private offerings, private placements comprise the majority of new issues.

Certain public sales of common stock are exempted from registration with the Securities and Exchange Commission. One form of exemption relates to offerings by banks and other federally regulated companies, such as public utilities, insurance, and transportation companies. Another type of exemption includes public offerings in which the shares are to be issued entirely within one state—an *intrastate offering*. Recognizing the significant expense involved in a public offering under the Securities Act of 1933 and the subsequent reporting requirements of a publicly held company, a company may consider the intrastate offering as a way to avoid registration with the SEC. The intrastate procedure is not as simple as it may seem. Strict compliance with the SEC's terms of exemption is essential. Efforts at such full compliance are difficult and often unsuccessful. As a result, the ensuing problems and costs often outweigh the advantages originally sought.

Accounting for the Issuance of Common Stock. When a company issues common stock for cash, an amount equal to the total proceeds is credited to the contributed capital accounts. If a company issues common stock with a par value, a portion of the proceeds equal to the total par value of the stock issued is credited to the "common stock" account, with the remainder being credited to "additional paid-in capital" (see subsequent sections of this chapter for a description of "additional paid-in capital"). Similarly, on the rare occasions when common stock is issued for cash at a price less than the total par value, the capital stock account is credited for the aggregate par value of the shares issued, and additional paid-in capital is reduced by the difference between the aggregate par value and the proceeds received. If this discount or difference exceeds the balance in the additional paid-in account, any remainder is debited to the retained earnings account. (Some companies are allowed, or required, by state law to set up a separate negative equity account, rather than reflect a reduction in retained earnings for stock issued at a discount. Customarily in the preparation of financial statements, such negative balances will be reclassified as a reduction of retained earnings.)

When no-par value common shares having a stated value are issued, the same accounting applies as for the issuance of par value shares; i.e., the aggregate stated value of the shares issued is credited to the common stock account with any premium or discount receiving similar treatment as that described for par value shares. When no-par value stock without a stated value is issued, it is customary to credit the full amount of the proceeds to the common stock account. (In some instances the board of directors may designate a certain portion of the proceeds of such an issue as being applicable to common stock. This is the same as assigning a stated value to the no-par value shares, and the accounting for these shares should be similar to that for "no-par value—stated value" shares.)

Subscription Shares. In some instances companies may issue shares for notes receivable at some future date. In similar transactions, companies may accept subscriptions from potential investors to purchase shares at some later date or on an installment basis. Even though no cash or stock certificates have been exchanged, the corporation's financial statements usually should reflect the transaction because the substance of the sale has occurred.

Initial accounting recognition of the subscription agreement requires a debit to stock subscriptions receivable and a credit to common (preferred) stock subscribed for the par or stated value of the subscribed shares. If the total consideration to be paid exceeds the par or stated value, the excess is credited directly to Capital Subscribed in Excess of Par Value. The actual proceeds may not be limited to cash. Services or property may be part or all of the consideration. (See section on "Noncash Share Transactions.") Upon collection, the appropriate asset account is debited, and Stock Subscriptions Receivable is credited for the fair market value of the consideration or the fair market value of the shares, whichever is the more readily determinable. If the amount debited to the asset account differs from the corresponding balance in the receivable account before collection, then the difference is debited or credited to Capital Contributed in Excess of Par Value.

When the conditions of the subscription agreement are satisfied, the balance of the subscription account is transferred to common (or preferred) stock, and the shares are issued. Depending upon statutory provisions, the certificates may be issued before the proceeds are collected in full. The terms of the agreement determine when the shares are delivered.

In the event that the subscriber ultimately defaults on the subscription obligation, various state laws may stipulate the procedures to be followed. Generally one of the following situations will result: the issuing corporation may (1) return all payments to the subscriber; (2) issue shares corresponding to the amount paid before default; (3) declare all partial payments to be forfeited by the subscriber and the proceeds of any subsequent issue of these shares to remain with the corporation; or (4) declare all partial payments to be forfeited by the subscriber and the subscribed shares to be sold on a "best efforts" basis, net of resale costs.

Where shares are subscribed in material amounts, it is usually appropriate to show common shares subscribed separately from common shares issued in the stockholders' equity section of the balance sheet. Depending upon the circumstances, the receivable may be included on the asset side of the balance sheet (classified as current or noncurrent according to its terms), or as a deduction from stockholders' equity accounts. The SEC has consistently maintained that receivables for capital stock subscriptions should not be shown as assets at a given balance sheet date unless the receivable has been subsequently collected prior to the date the financial statements are issued (and accordingly disclosed). When the receivable for subscribed shares is to be shown as a reduction from stockholders' equity, it is usually set forth as a separate item following all other stockholders' equity accounts.

Noncash Share Transactions. When common shares are issued for assets other than cash (such as properties, property rights, intangible assets, etc.) or for services, the valuation for the consideration for the journal entries becomes more judgmental. The general guideline (as set forth in Chapter 5 of *Accounting Research Bulletin No. 43*) is that the transaction should be valued based on either the value of the shares issued or the value of the goods or service received, whichever is more clearly evident. For a large publicly held corporation, the market price of the shares issued may provide the best indicator of the proceeds. In a smaller, more closely held corporation, the value of the assets acquired may be the best indicator. Even within these guidelines, prudent and conservative judgment must be exercised in determining the value of the proceeds. In most states, the board of directors is empowered to ascertain the value of consideration given in exchange for shares. Additionally, the SEC has adopted certain policies regarding the issuance of shares to promoters in exchange for services or the issuance of shares for nonmonetary assets with no readily determinable value. Specifically, the SEC may require that no value be assigned to such proceeds (other than to the extent of cash or other liquid assets included in the proceeds), since the ultimate value of such nonmonetary assets is directly related to the future and fortunes of the corporation itself.

A so-called implicit discount may arise when property or services are exchanged for stock, and the fair market value of the property and services is less than the par value of the shares issued. This situation is most likely to occur whenever the property or services have highly subjective market values. (See section on "Stockholder Donations.")

Stock Issuance Costs. There are usually some costs associated with the issuance of common stock. These include statutory filing fees, legal and accounting fees, and printing costs. In major public offerings these costs may be significant. Accounting practices for such costs have differed: some companies have followed a practice of cost deferment, whereas others more commonly deduct costs of issuance from the sales proceeds. The former treatment views the costs related to share offerings as intangible assets which should be recorded and subsequently amortized to earnings over a reasonable period. The latter practice maintains that such costs are not related to the major objectives of the corporation and consequently should not affect income. Rules of the SEC allow either method.

Conditional Securities (Contingent Issues). Conditional securities represent contractual obligations of the company which are potentially calls on the company's capital if some event occurs. Conditional securities have the potential of diluting the rights of shares currently outstanding. Included in this category of securities are stock subscription rights, stock warrants, convertible debt or other senior securities, and stock options.

Stock Subscription Rights. Stock subscription rights, like stock warrants and stock options which are discussed below, entitle the holder to purchase stock at a stated price, usually during a specified time period. Rights are normally issued to existing holders of the company's stock, and the stock purchase price is often less than the current market price of the stock. Outstanding rights are recorded on a memorandum basis only; no change in the stockholders' equity accounts is reflected as a result of their issuance. Information about the rights, including the purchase price and the expiration date, should be disclosed in the footnotes to the financial statements. Upon exercise of stock subscription rights, the company records the transaction in the same manner as for any other issuance of common stock for cash.

Warrants and Convertible Senior Securities. Warrants are similar to stock subscription rights except that warrants are often sold, separately or attached to other securities, to purchasers who are not stockholders. The stock purchase price specified by the warrant is often greater than the current market price of the stock, and the price specified by the warrant may change with the passage of time.

If detachable warrants are issued in conjunction with debt, the proceeds from the sale of the warrant-bearing security should be allocated between the debt and the warrant based upon the relative fair values of each at the time of issuance. The amount allocated to the warrants should be recorded as additional paid-in capital. However, if warrants are issued in conjunction with a borrowing agreement and are not detachable or if convertible debt is issued, the proceeds are not segregated for accounting purposes. None of the proceeds from the sale of convertible debt instruments are attributed to the conversion privilege. APB Opinion No. 14 discusses the underlying theory of this treatment in detail.

Warrants issued with preferred stock are seldom separately disclosed on the balance sheet. The proceeds from sales of this security are recorded as stockholders' equity, and any attempt to segregate further the amounts received would be difficult and would serve no purpose.

Stock Options. A corporation offers stock options to its employees to: (1) promote employee ownership and interest and (2) provide additional compensation to employees at a lower employee tax rate.

Stock options differ from other conditional securities in that they are usually granted only to company employees, frequently as part of a compensation plan, and are nontransferable. Stock options are accounted for in the same manner as warrants except where an element of compensation to the employee is reflected in the purchase price.

Accounting for stock options is covered extensively in the literature of the AICPA—in Chapter 13B of *ARB No. 43* and in APB Opinion No. 25. Generally stock option plans are categorized as compensatory or noncompensatory. Noncompensatory plans are defined as being limited to plans which are generally available to all employees and which permit exercise of options for a relatively limited period. Specific criteria for noncompensatory stock option plans are set forth in Paragraph 7 of APB Opinion No. 25.

All other stock option plans are defined as being compensatory—even though the issuance of stock options may not, in many circumstances, result in a charge to earnings for compensation.

Compensatory stock option plans can be viewed as being of two general types—traditional plans and complex plans. Traditional stock option plans are the "qualified" and "restricted" plans that have been commonly used by corporations for the last 25 or 30 years. The fundamental accounting for such plans is straightforward: to the extent that such plans involve a measurable amount of compensation, the compensation costs should be charged to earnings and credited to capital contributed in excess of par value. For traditional plans, compensation is measured at the date the option is granted. There is deemed to be compensation to the extent the market value of the securities exceeds the option price at the grant date. Many stock option plans (and the tax regulations to make these tax exempt to the recipient) require that the option price be not less than the market price at the grant date, and accordingly, such plans are viewed as being, in effect, noncompensatory and thus involve no charge to earnings.

Complex stock option plans are a more recent phenomenon. Such plans may tie the number of shares or the option price to employee performance or to the company's earnings performance. Complex plans may also provide the employee with alternative stock option packages. These plans may even involve "phantom" securities, i.e., future compensation rights that are tied to the corporation's common stock price but that do not require the actual issuance of common stock. The general rules regarding compensation are that earnings are charged for the difference between the "option price" and the fair value of the securities at the measurement date. The measurement date is defined as that date when both the number of shares and the option price are definitely known. In those instances where an element of compensation is determined to exist, such compensation should be charged to earnings over the active service period contemplated in the option plan.

APB Opinion No. 25 contains a description of the various kinds of traditional and complex stock option plans in existence and suggests accounting guidelines for treating the many variable aspects of such plans.

The pronouncements of the AICPA and the rules of the SEC provide for broad disclosures relative to contingent securities. Generally, there must be adequate disclosure to allow common shareholders to assess the effect a conversion or exercise of contingent securities might have on their equity rights. Customary disclosures include:

- Number of common shares reserved for issuance on conversion or exercise of contingent securities
- Brief description of the terms and conditions under which conditional securities may be converted or exercised
- Exercise or conversion prices
- Termination date
- Details of conversions or exercises during the period(s) being reported upon
- Contingent security agreements.

For publicly held companies, this list should be expanded to include the detailed reporting requirements of Rule 316(n) of Regulation S-X.

In addition to all of the above, APB Opinion No. 15 sets forth specific guidelines for considering contingent securities in the calculation of earnings per share. Reference should be made to Chapter 30.

Stock Dividends, Stock Splits, and Reverse Splits.   There are various reasons advocated for declaring stock dividends. Management may desire to permanently retain (or "capitalize") undistributed earnings for use in the firm. Such an action formally indicates to shareholders that the possibility of future cash dividends will be reduced to the extent of the capitalization. Management may issue a stock dividend rather than a cash dividend in order to conserve working capital. Additionally, it should be emphasized that there are no distributions of assets involved in a stock dividend. Moreover, since the stock is distributed on a pro rata basis, no stockholder's proportionate ownership is ever increased as a result of a stock dividend. A large stock split-up may reduce the fair market value of the shares and stimulate greater trading activity. The increased activity may result in a wider distribution of shares. When a stock split results in the issuance of fractional shares, management may distribute to the stockholder the cash equivalent of the fractional share. The fair market value of the shares at date of declaration becomes the basis for the determination. The resulting distribution reduces working capital to the extent of the cash distributed. Such cash distributions are generally not taxable to the recipient but are treated as a reduction in the cost basis of the stock.

The results of a common stock dividend and a stock split are the same. In both instances there is a proportional distribution of stock to existing stockholders. The assets of the company are unaffected, as are the proportionate interests of the stockholders. However, the two terms have distinct implications, and different accounting treatments apply.

A *stock dividend* is defined in *ARB No. 43* as a share distribution "prompted mainly by a desire to give the recipient shareholders some ostensibly separate evidence of a part of their respective interests in accumulated corporate earnings." A distribution of less than 20 or 25 percent of the number of shares previously outstanding would normally be considered a stock dividend. Since a stock dividend requires that a portion of retained earnings be capitalized, and thus made part of permanent capital, a problem arises as to the proper valuation of the shares issued in connection with the stock dividend. In this regard, *ARB No. 43* recommends that retained earnings be transferred to capital stock and capital surplus in an amount equal to the fair value of the shares issued.

A *stock split* is defined as a share distribution "prompted mainly by a desire to increase the number of outstanding shares for the purpose of affecting a reduction in their unit market price and, thereby, obtaining a wider distribution and improved marketability of the shares." A stock split does not call for a transfer of retained earnings into the permanent capital accounts. The company may choose to reduce the par value of outstanding stock in proportion to the amount of stock being issued as a result of the split. This treatment would leave the amounts attributed to the capital accounts unchanged. However, the outstanding shares would be correspondingly increased. Alternatively, the company may leave par values unchanged and reflect the stock split by transferring into the capital stock accounts the equivalent of the par value of the stock issued as a result of the split. This amount can be transferred out of the capital account or out of retained earnings. *ARB No. 43* indicates that whenever a stock split is accomplished by such a transfer it should be described in all corporate disclosures as a "stock split-up effected in the form of a dividend."

A *reverse stock split* is sometimes referred to as share consolidation. Reverse splits are used when earnings and stock prices are both low. The objective is to raise the price of the company's shares to a market value which is expected to be more attractive to potential investors. A reverse split is accomplished by increasing the par value or stated value of the company's stock and issuing new share certificates.

PREFERRED STOCK

Preferred stock is a class of corporate equity that is senior to common stock. Preferred stocks usually involve a promise of cash payments to the preferred shareholders in the form of periodic dividends of a specified amount. Some preferred stocks give the stockholders limited voting privileges, and in some cases the preferred stockholders are entitled to participate in dividends in excess of the specified minimum dividends (participating preferred). The preferred stockholders have a claim on the assets of the company subordinate to that of debt holders; however, preferred stockholders generally have preference over common stockholders in dividend rights and in liquidation.

It is not uncommon for preferred stockholders to have rights in liquidation which are greater than the par value of the preferred stock. Additionally, preferred shareholders may be entitled to receive unpaid dividends (cumulative preferred stock) before a dividend may be paid to common shareholders.

In some instances preferred stockholders will be guaranteed protection against dilution of their interests. Normally, the protective provisions ensure that no debt instrument or preferred stock with superior preferential rights will be issued without the consent of a specified majority of existing preferred stockholders, or that their collective consent is needed for certain major corporate actions such as sale of the business or reorganization.

As indicated, there can be many different types of preferred stock; there can also be more than one class of preferred. In order for users to understand the rights and privileges available to the preferred security holder, financial statements should contain disclosures about all of the important characteristics of each class: a brief description of dividend and voting rights, liquidation preferences (if different from par values), conversion privileges, and amounts of cumulative dividend arrearages. (See section on "Financial Statement Presentation.")

CAPITAL DONATIONS

Municipalities and governmental agencies may grant a corporation rights or property with the hope of attracting or promoting industrial development or employment. The grant is usually in the form of an outright donation or a donation contingent upon employment of a specified number of individuals or occupancy for a specific period of time.

Adherence to the cost principle suggests that no entry be made in the accounts since the corporation has not incurred cost. Proponents of this view maintain that it is undesirable for identifiable capital donations—plant sites, tax abatements, etc.—to be considered as benefits to the corporation for which there are not related costs. It is usually assumed that the donations would be ultimately realized through lower recorded costs in future accounting periods.

However, others argue that blind adherence to the cost principle in this instance fails to disclose properly the direct economic effect of all resources under corporate control. In this case the fair market value of the donated assets should be debited to the appropriate asset account and the corresponding credit should be made to an account such as Other Contributed Capital—Donated Plant Site. When the donor stipulates performance requirements, the assets should be described as contingent. Both methods have some theoretical merit, and it appears that current practice accepts either method.

Stockholder Donations.   Prior to the inception of no-par and low-par value stock, an apparent subterfuge to avoid violation of rules against issuance of stock below par involved donations of a substantial number of shares to the company. The company would then resell these shares, usually to raise working capital. (As donated shares had become treasury stock, they could then be sold at any price.)

If the donated shares were originally issued in a noncash transaction, the presumption of implicit discount may arise. *ARB No. 43* (Chap 1, Section A) states:

> If capital stock is issued nominally for the acquisition of property and it appears that at about the same time, and pursuant to a previous agreement or understanding, some portion of the stock so issued is donated to the corporation, it is not permissible to treat the par value of the stock nominally issued for the property as the cost of that property. If stock so donated is subsequently sold, it is not permissible to treat the proceeds as a credit to surplus of the corporation.

The appropriate accounting treatment for transactions of this nature is to adjust overvalued assets downward and simultaneously reduce stated capital by the par or stated value of the donated shares.

CAPITAL CONTRIBUTED IN EXCESS OF PAR VALUE (ADDITIONAL PAID-IN CAPITAL)

Capital contributed in excess of par value is the account for reflecting all amounts contributed to the corporation exclusive of those ascribed to common stock and preferred and preference stocks. Capital contributed in excess of par value is also often referred to as "additional paid-in capital" or, less preferably, as "capital surplus."

Capital contributed in excess of par value most frequently arises as paid-in capital which the company receives for stock sold in excess of its par value. Other transactions which affect capital contributed in excess of par value include donations of capital, transfers of retained earnings, capitalization of stock dividends, treasury stock transactions, and business combinations accounted for as poolings of interest.

REACQUIRED STOCK

Companies may acquire their own equity securities for a number of reasons and in a number of ways. In some circumstances reacquired stock is cancelled and retired. At other times the stock may be held for subsequent reissuance. There is a wide variety of accounting treatments which are available to record and to report on reacquired stock. The appropriate treatment depends upon the purpose and the specific nature of the transaction. The common thread running through each of these alternatives goes back to the earliest pronouncements of the AICPA: profit or loss should not be recognized by a company as a result of reacquiring its own shares.

Preferred Stock Retired. In order to maintain flexibility in its financing structure, a corporation will sometimes attach a "conversion privilege" or "call option," or both, to preferred shares. The privilege to convert preferred shares to common shares at a predetermined rate may appear to have advantages for both the shareholder and issuing corporation. The preferred shareholder is able to acquire common stockholder rights whenever those rights become economically desirable. On the other hand, the corporation may obtain a far wider distribution of its preferred stock or a better price for such stock by "sweetening" the issue with a favorable conversion ratio. (The conversion ratio determines the number of common shares that will be issued for each preferred share surrendered.) Upon conversion, the par or stated value of the preferred stock is debited and common stock is credited for the par or stated values of the common shares issued; any difference between the par or stated values of the preferred stock and the common stock is credited (or debited) to capital contributed in excess of par value. In those cases where the par value of the common shares issued is greater than the amount removed from the preferred stock accounts, capital contributed in excess of par value is debited for the difference. If the balance of capital contributed in excess of par value is exhausted, the remaining debit would be made to retained earnings. Retained earnings should never increase as a result of conversion.

The terms of the preferred stock may permit the issuer to "call" the preferred shares at a specific price, which normally exceeds the original issue price, or to require conversion of the preferred into common after a stated period. This option provides some flexibility to the corporation and the common shareholders, but at a cost. In the event that the terms of the preferred stock become burdensome to management's financial goals, the issue may be called (reacquired and cancelled). If the common shareholders feel that their interests are threatened by the preferences, they may force management to call the preferred shares by electing a majority of board members who are sympathetic to their views. Other things being equal, callable preferred stock should provide lower original issue proceeds than noncallable preferred stock.

In any event, when the preferred stock is called at a premium (a premium results whenever the call price exceeds the issue price), the par value and any other specific elements of contributed capital related to the issue should be removed from the accounts. The call premium should ordinarily be debited to retained earnings. If the issue is called at an amount less than the issuance price, the difference between the issuance price and the call price should be credited to capital contributed in excess of par value. This procedure reflects the accepted notion that a corporation should not credit retained earnings in transactions involving its own securities. Preferred shares reacquired through the exercise of the conversion or call option are usually retired.

Common Stock Reacquired. A company may acquire its own common stock for retirement or for later reissuance. If the stock is retired, the accounting to be followed is essentially the same as for preferred stock which is retired.

When a company reacquires its own stock with the intention of subsequent resale, the stock is referred to as *treasury stock*. State laws usually limit the amount of treasury shares either to amounts in excess of legal capital, i.e., capital contributed in excess of par value and retained earnings, or to unrestricted retained earnings. Also, most states require a temporary or permanent restriction of retained earnings to the extent of the cost of the shares acquired.

Treasury shares represent a reduction in total shareholders' equity, and should be shown as such. Some companies list treasury stock among the noncurrent assets when the shares are purchased for distribution under an employee stock option plan. With proper disclosure, APB Opinion No. 6 permits treasury stock to be shown as an asset under limited circumstances. Nevertheless, reporting treasury shares as an asset creates the paradoxical situation of a corporation owning part of itself. Also, treasury shares have no value under liquidation proceedings. Voting and dividend rights also do not attach to stock certificates held in the treasury. Commonly, treasury stock is recorded at cost of the reacquired shares and reported as a deduction from the stockholders' equity accounts (with parenthetical disclosure of the number of shares held in the treasury). This is called the *cost method*. But this practice is not universal. Some companies allocate the reduction in stockholders' equity resulting from the acquisition of treasury stock to both common stock, capital contributed in excess of par value, and retained earning accounts—thus treating the treasury stock as though it had been retired. This is called the *par value method*. The par value method requires specific identification of shares acquired and the entries made on original issue of these shares. Thus, it is not widely used. Accounting Series Release No. 146 of the SEC discusses the use of treasury stock to effect poolings of interest. Follow-on interpretations of this release restrict the methods by which treasury stock can be used to achieve poolings of interest accounting treatment.

Treasury stock transactions are often regulated by state laws and by stock exchange rules—which are by no means uniform. Unfortunately, these regulations also prevent uniform accounting treatment for treasury stock.

During periods of depressed stock prices, managers may be tempted to reacquire large blocks of outstanding shares. In some cases, the acquired blocks are so large that the remaining shareholders comprise a small minority of the previous stockholder group. Such a practice is sometimes referred to as "going private." The reacquisition is commonly accomplished by means of a cash and/or bond offer (where the fair market value of the cash/debt offer is greater than fair market value of the stock). With the number of stockholders and outstanding shares greatly reduced, management may obtain some relief from reporting requirements of the SEC and other governmental agencies. "Going private" is subject to increasing regulation by the SEC.

FINANCIAL STATEMENT PRESENTATION

We noted earlier in the chapter that the balance sheet amounts for contributed capital may not be as important to the investor as the various disclosures related to the contributed capital accounts. We further noted that the amount of disclosure relative to contributed capital accounts is voluminous, but varied.

Exhibit 1 illustrates the stockholders' equity section of a hypothetical balance sheet. (This example does not purport to reflect all kinds of contributed capital accounts or related disclosures that might exist in any particular situation.)

There are a number of comments to be made about the stockholders' equity section illustrated in Exhibit 1. The various stockholders' equity accounts have been included in the example in the order most frequently seen in present-day financial statements, beginning with the most senior equity securities, descending to common stock and other contributed capital accounts. Retained earnings customarily comes after the contributed capital accounts, and treasury stock is most commonly reflected (in a contra-account) as the final item in the stockholders' equity section. It will be noted that there is a broad range of disclosures in the example regarding the attributes of various equity securities. Although this is a common presentation, some companies prefer to include these disclosure details

EXHIBIT 1   Illustrative Balance Sheet Disclosure of Stockholders' Equity

	December 31	
Stockholders' Equity	19X1	19X2
6% cumulative preferred stock, par value $100, authorized 5,000 shares, issued and outstanding 3,000 and 2,000 shares	$300,000	$200,000
Convertible $3.50 preference stock, no par value, stated value $50, authorized, issued, and outstanding 1,200 shares at each year-end (involuntary liquidation preference $50,000)	60,000	60,000
Common stock, no par value, stated value $1, authorized 15,000 shares, issued 10,000 and 8,000 shares	10,000	8,000
Capital contributed in excess of par value ...	200,000	150,000
Retained earnings	250,000	190,000
Less treasury stock at cost (500 and 300 shares of common stock)	(40,000)	(25,000)
Total stockholders' equity	$780,000	$583,000

in footnotes rather than on the face of the balance sheet—a practice that is acceptable.

Note that the prescribed dividend rate for the senior securities (preferred and preference stocks) is stated—6 percent for the preferred stock and $3.50 for the preference stock. Also, the cumulative dividend privileges relative to the preferred stock are disclosed. With respect to all equity securities, the par or stated value is disclosed as well as the number of shares authorized, issued, and outstanding. There is disclosed for the convertible preference stock the amount the preference stockholders are to receive in case of involuntary liquidation. This disclosure is required because the liquidation preference in our example differs significantly from the stated value. Finally, note that with respect to the treasury stock, the carrying basis (cost) and the number of shares in the treasury are both disclosed.

There are a number of other disclosures regarding contributed capital accounts which are customarily included in the notes to the financial statements and not on the face of the balance sheet. With respect to senior securities, preferred, and preference stocks, there should be disclosed any rights of security holders to participate in earnings and dividends above the stated rate. Dividend arrearages should be clearly set forth in the financial statements. There should be complete disclosure of conversion privileges, including the conversion price, any restrictions on timing of conversion, a brief description of any antidilutive provisions, and disclosure of the number of common shares reserved for ultimate conversion. Where articles of incorporation or other corporate documents provide for the call of senior securities, disclosure of the call price and the timing of the call option should be made. Where there is provision for redemption of securities, the redemption price and timing limitations should be disclosed. Additionally, if there is a provision for a sinking fund, the amount of sinking fund requirement should be disclosed.

As noted earlier, there are a number of disclosure requirements for common stock options. Disclosure requirements in this area are set forth in Paragraph 15 of *ARB No. 43*, which states:

> In connection with financial statements, disclosure should be made as to the status of the option or plan at the end of the period of report, including the number of shares under option, the option price, and the number of shares as to which options were exercisable. As to options exercised during the period, disclosure should be made of the number of shares involved and the option price thereof.

Rule 3.16(n) of the SEC's Regulation S-X provides for certain additional disclosures, including:

- The years during which options were granted
- The years during which the options become or will become exercisable
- The aggregate fair values of shares under option at the balance sheet date, per share and in total, and the same information at the grant dates
- The number of shares becoming exercisable during each period, with information as to the option price and fair value thereof, per share and in total
- The fair value of options exercised during the year, per share and in total.

Other contingent securities (warrants, rights, and convertible debt) will customarily require disclosures similar to those required for stock options (other than the detailed disclosure requirements of Regulation S-X). The principal import of all these disclosures relating to contingent securities is to provide common shareholders with adequate information to assess the potential impact of all contingent calls upon their equity.

There should also be disclosed any other information about transactions, events, or conditions that might have an impact on the equity interest of the preferred and common shareholders. Examples of such additional disclosures might include the details of stock repurchase agreements or disclosure of common shares contingently issued or issuable in connection with a business combination.

QUASI-REORGANIZATIONS

A company which has experienced substantial losses may become insolvent and be unable to meet its obligations to creditors and investors. In these circumstances, under court supervision and the federal bankruptcy laws, a forced sale of remaining assets and a formal reorganization of the company may be required. However, a company may have sufficient net assets to remain solvent given some relief from debt service and preferred dividend requirements. It may desire to revalue its assets and liabilities and to "begin anew." Such a revaluation, with the accompanying elimination of any cumulative deficit, is termed a *quasi-reorganization.*

The AICPA and the SEC have specified those conditions under which a quasi-reorganization is acceptable and have set forth the related accounting requirements. These conditions and requirements are explained in detail in *ARB No. 43,* Chapter 7a, and SEC Accounting Series Release No. 25.

Briefly, the quasi-reorganization of a corporation involves the formal adoption of a plan to restate all of its assets and liabilities at current values and to charge the accumulated deficit (negative retained earnings) to the contributed capital accounts.

The current valuation of assets and liabilities should not be overly conservative. The revaluation process forms a new basis of accounting for the company; however, the tax basis of the assets and liabilities remains unchanged. This causes permanent differences between book and tax accounting expense. Future tax benefits may also result from net operating loss and investment tax credit carryforwards. APB Opinion No. 11 states that such benefits should be recognized as assets in a quasi-reorganization "only if realization is assured beyond a reasonable doubt." If realization is not assured at the quasi-reorganization date, yet the benefits are realized at some future date, the tax savings should be credited to capital contributed in excess of par value and not recorded as income.

After adjustments to the capital structure in a quasi-reorganization, the retained earnings account must be dated to indicate what amounts are accumulated from the date of reorganization. The SEC's Regulation S-X requires the dating of retained earnings to continue for ten years and disclosure of the amount of deficit eliminated for at least three years.

ACCOUNTING RESEARCH STUDY NO. 15

In 1973 the AICPA issued *Accounting Research Study No. 15*, entitled "Stockholders' Equity." This was the last research study published by the AICPA's Accounting Research Division before it went out of existence that year.

The Study attempts to analyze past and present accounting practices for stockholders' equity with recommendations for reporting improvements. Most importantly, the Study views stockholders' equity as a cohesive part of the balance sheet rather than a loose grouping of accounts and transactions.

The authors cannot predict how the FASB or the SEC will react to the issues raised in *ARS No. 15*. Regardless of how these groups ultimately react, the study has significant current value as a source of information on accounting for stockholders' equity.

BIBLIOGRAPHY

Accounting Principles Board: "Accounting for Convertible Debt and Debt Issued with Stock Purchase Warrants," APB Opinion No. 14, AICPA, New York, 1969.

————: "Accounting for Income Taxes," APB Opinion No. 11, AICPA, New York, 1967.

————: "Accounting for Stock Issued to Employees," APB Opinion No. 25, AICPA, New York, 1972.

————: "Earnings Per Share," APB Opinion No. 15, AICPA, New York, 1969.

American Institute of Certified Public Accountants, Committee on Accounting Procedure: *Accounting Research Bulletin No. 43*, AICPA, New York, 1953.

Kieso, Donald E., and Jerry J. Weygandt: *Intermediate Accounting*, John Wiley & Sons, New York, 1974, chaps. 15–16.

Melcher, Beatrice: "Stockholders' Equity," *Accounting Research Study No. 15*, AICPA, New York, 1973.

Welsch, Glenn A., Charles T. Zlatkovich, and John Arch White: *Intermediate Accounting*, Richard D. Irwin, Homewood, Ill., chaps. 19, 21, and 22.

Chapter **29**

Retained Earnings
and Dividends

OSCAR S. GELLEIN
Retired Partner, Haskins & Sells, and Member, Financial Accounting
Standards Board

J. MICHAEL COOK
Partner, Haskins & Sells

RETAINED EARNINGS—INTRODUCTION

Definition and Significance.   Retained earnings represents the accumulated net income of a corporation since its inception, reduced by distributions to shareholders, amounts transferred to paid-in capital accounts, and certain other charges and credits. If losses, dividend distributions, transfers, and other charges in the aggregate exceed income and other credits, the result is a deficit. Retained earnings may be subdivided or "appropriated" to indicate that a portion of the balance is not currently available for dividends. The lack of appropriation, however, does not indicate that all retained earnings are available, immediately or otherwise, for distribution to shareholders, since funds derived from earnings may have been reinvested in long-lived assets.

Terminology. *Accounting Terminology Bulletin No. 1,* issued by the Committee on Terminology of the American Institute of Certified Public Accountants in 1953, recommended terms that clearly indicate the source from which earned proprietary capital is derived, suggesting "retained income," "retained earnings," "accumulated earnings," or "earnings retained for use in the business." Terms consistent with this *Bulletin* were used in over 90 percent of the reports included in a survey of 2,650 annual reports for 1973 and 1974 contained in the National Automated Accounting Research System.

Distinction Between Retained Earnings and Other Capital Accounts. The report of the Study Group on the Objectives of Financial Statements[1] stated that the objective of the statement of financial position should be to provide information "useful for predicting, comparing, and evaluating enterprise earning power. This statement should provide information concerning enterprise transactions and other events that are part of incomplete earnings cycles." Another objective cited by Hendrikson[2] is "to provide information to stockholders, investors, creditors, and other interested groups regarding the efficiency and stewardship of management and regarding the historical and prospective economic interests of the groups holding specific equities and the groups (such as employees, customers, and the government) that have a general economic interest in the corporation."

The principal means used to accomplish these objectives in connection with stockholders' equity is classification by source. As Hendrikson[3] states:

> Classification of stockholders' equity by its source is generally considered to be the major classification objective in balance sheet presentation. This emphasis is not misplaced because a description of the sources of capital provides useful information regarding the historical development and the current position of the corporation. Corporate growth provided through internal sources of funds is relevant information when compared with a firm that has grown entirely through the sale of preferred and common stocks or through the sale of debentures.

Accounting Research Study No. 3[4] adds:

> A distinction between invested capital and retained earnings has relevance to stockholders. For example, when cash dividends are distributed, stockholders are entitled to assurance that they are based on current or past profits and do not constitute merely a return of some of the cash or other assets originally invested in the enterprise or of previous earnings converted into invested capital. The distinction between invested capital and retained earnings is also significant from the viewpoint of creditors. Invested capital constitutes a buffer against enterprise losses. These losses must exceed the amount of retained earnings and stockholders' invested capital before creditors' equities are impaired.

When transfers are made from retained earnings to contributed capital, however, the original classification by source is lost. As noted in *Accounting Research Study No. 15:*[5]

[1]*Report of the Study Group on the Objectives of Financial Statements,* AICPA, New York, 1973, p. 36.

[2]Eldon S. Hendriksen, *Accounting Theory,* rev. ed., Richard D. Irwin, Homewood, Ill., 1970, p. 508.

[3]*Ibid.,* p. 509.

[4]Robert T. Sprouse and Maurice Moonitz, *Accounting Research Study No. 3,* AICPA, New York, 1962, p. 42.

[5]Beatrice Melcher, *Accounting Research Study No. 15,* AICPA, New York, 1973, p. 93.

Transfers from retained earnings to capital stock or additional capital obviously lose their original designation. Thus, a general classification of capital surplus may include a conglomeration of items applicable to several classes of stock either presently or previously outstanding. A few corporations describe additional capital as "capital contributed and earnings capitalized in excess of stated value of common stock." That caption, of course, tells something—differing components of equity are combined in one amount—but its only value is to serve as a flag.

Accepted departures from a classification based on source are found in financial statements of banks. Banks periodically transfer amounts from retained earnings to permanent capital accounts in compliance with statutory requirements, to increase lending limits, or for other purposes. In addition, transfers are made to the reserve for loan losses in amounts equal to the excess of the loan loss provision deductible for tax purposes over the amount recognized under generally accepted accounting principles, less the related tax effect. Although this portion of the reserve is not available to absorb losses, it is not considered a part of stockholders' equity for reporting purposes.

A secondary objective of distinguishing between retained earnings and paid-in capital is to indicate the amount of equity potentially available for dividends. In most cases the amount available is limited to the balance of retained earnings, that is, the amount of retained earnings not previously reduced by dividends. Under laws of some states, amounts of contributed capital in excess of the par value of issued shares also are available for dividends. As a practical matter, the amount actually available for dividends, as discussed more fully later, may be affected by numerous factors, including the applicable laws of the state of incorporation, contractual commitments restricting the distribution of retained earnings, and financial policies of the corporation.

The need to distinguish between paid-in capital and retained earnings is recognized in *Accounting Research Bulletin (ARB) No. 43,* Chapter 1A:

> Capital surplus, however created, should not be used to relieve the income account of the current or future years of charges which would otherwise fall to be made thereagainst. [Exceptions cited are reorganizations and quasi-reorganizations.]
>
> Earned surplus of a subsidiary company created prior to acquisition does not form a part of the consolidated earned surplus of the parent company and subsidiaries; nor can any dividend declared out of such surplus properly be credited to the income account of the parent company.

In addition, Rule 5-02(39) of Regulation S-X requires that the balance sheet contain separate captions for paid-in capital, other additional capital, and retained earnings (classified between appropriated and unappropriated).

APPRAISAL CAPITAL

Accounting Principles Board (APB) Opinion No. 6, issued in 1965, reaffirmed the position taken by the Securities and Exchange Commission in its Accounting Series Release (ASR) No. 8, issued in 1938, that writing up property, plant, and equipment within a given entity based on appraised values is not in conformity with generally accepted accounting principles. Appreciation resulting from write-ups prior to the effective dates of these pronouncements should be separately classified within stockholders' equity.

TRANSACTIONS AFFECTING RETAINED EARNINGS

Although the primary component of a corporation's retained earnings is its net income as reported in periodic income statements, other transactions and events

may require increases or decreases in this account. These transactions and events will be considered under the following classifications:
- Prior period adjustments
- Dividends and stock splits
- Treasury stock transactions
- Redemption of preferred shares at a premium
- Subsidiary and investee transactions
- Recapitalizations and reorganizations
- Miscellaneous.

PRIOR PERIOD ADJUSTMENTS

Criteria of APB Opinion No. 9.   APB Opinion No. 9, issued in 1966, limits prior period adjustments to those that are material and that meet all of the following criteria:

- The adjustment can be specifically identified with and directly related to the business activities of particular prior periods.
- The adjustment is not attributable to economic events occurring subsequent to the date of the financial statements for the prior period.
- The adjustment depends primarily on determinations by persons other than management.
- The adjustment was not susceptible of reasonable estimation prior to such determination.

The Opinion states that such adjustments are rare in modern accounting and relate to "events or transactions which occurred in a prior period, the accounting effects of which could not be determined with reasonable assurance at that time, usually because of some major uncertainty then existing." The uncertainty usually would be disclosed in the prior period's financial statements and, in most cases, the auditors' opinion thereon would be expected to be appropriately qualified because of the uncertainty.

The Opinion cites the following examples of prior period adjustments:
- Material nonrecurring adjustments or settlement of income taxes
- Material nonrecurring adjustments resulting from renegotiation proceedings
- Settlements of significant amounts resulting from litigation or similar claims.

Specific examples of such adjustments are the following:

Material Nonrecurring Adjustments or Settlement of Income Taxes. Ashland Oil, Inc., 1973 annual report:

> During 1973 the Company substantially resolved federal income tax issues for the years 1961 through 1967 relating primarily to income from foreign crude oil transactions. The resulting income tax adjustment of $10,800,000 (including accrued interest, net of tax effect) for these years and for similar issues for the years 1968 and 1969 has been recorded as an adjustment applicable to the respective years to which the tax and interest applied (for years 1961 through 1967—$7,300,000; 1968—$1,300,000; 1969—$1,300,000; and interest only of $300,000 for each of the years 1970, 1971 and 1972).

Material Nonrecurring Adjustments Resulting from Renegotiation Proceedings. Norris Industries, Inc., 1972 annual report:

> Substantially all of the Company's military sales are subject to renegotiation under the Renegotiation Act of 1951. In September 1972, a settlement was concluded as to the year ended July 31, 1968, resulting in the Company recording a provision for refund amounting to $2,424,000. Retained earnings at July 31, 1968 and net income for the year then ended have been restated from the amounts previously reported in the amount of $1,124,000, after related income tax benefits of $1,300,000.

Settlement of Significant Amounts Resulting from Litigation or Similar Claim. Pfizer, Inc., 1973 annual report:

> In 1973, the Company has provided in its accounts a charge to retained earnings in the amount of $41,500,000, less estimated tax reduction of $21,500,000. These amounts apply and have been charged to specific years prior to 1967. Retained earnings at the beginning of 1972 and the appropriate accounts included in the Consolidated Statement of Financial Position at December 31, 1972 have been restated to include these charges. The $41,500,000 sum represents amounts which have been paid or which would be paid under agreements which have been made in settlements other than those in 1969 and 1971, together with an estimate of related expenses, and past expenses in connection with the litigation.

Special Changes in Accounting Principle. APB Opinion No. 20, issued in 1971, requires that most changes in accounting principle be reported by including the cumulative effect of the change in net income in the period of the change with no restatement of amounts previously reported. Prior period adjustment is limited to:

- A change from the LIFO method of inventory valuation to another method
- A change in the method of accounting for long-term construction contracts
- A change from the "full cost" method of accounting which is used in the extractive industries
- A change made when a company first issues its financial statements in connection with an initial public distribution of securities.

The 1973 annual report of The Rath Packing Company illustrates a change from the LIFO method:

> Effective with the beginning of the 1973 tax year, the basis of pricing pork product inventories was changed from last-in, first-out (LIFO) cost to approximate current market, less allowance for selling and distribution expenses, and the revised basis of pricing has been reflected retroactively in the accompanying financial statements. Approval for this change in accounting principle has been received from the Internal Revenue Service. The change was made to reduce the effect on earnings of cyclical fluctuations in supply and purchase cost of hogs, which effect had been significantly magnified by the use of the LIFO accounting method. In addition, the revised basis of pricing will make the Company's financial statements more comparable with those of other companies in the industry, most of whom no longer use the LIFO accounting method.
>
> The retroactive effect of this change in accounting principle is reflected in the financial statements by increases of $4,544,000 in inventories and retained earnings at September 30, 1972 and by an increase of $2,843,000 in retained earnings at the beginning of the 1972 fiscal year. This change also had the effect of increasing net earnings for the 1973 fiscal year by $2,862,000, or $2.40 per share, and of reducing net loss for the 1972 fiscal year by $1,701,000, or $1.43 per share.

Change in the Reporting Entity. A change resulting in financial statements which in effect are of a different reporting entity should be reported by restating the financial statements of all prior periods. APB Opinion No. 20 indicates that this type of change is limited mainly to:

- Presenting consolidated or combined statements in place of statements of individual companies
- Changing specific subsidiaries comprising the group of companies for which consolidated financial statements are presented
- Changing the companies included in combined financial statements
- Combining companies in a pooling of interests (for a more detailed discussion of this topic, refer to Chapter 33).

The 1973 annual report of Overhead Door Corporation discloses a change in the reporting entity resulting from a pooling of interests:

> On February 28, 1973, Overhead Door Corporation exchanged 330,000 shares of its Common Stock for the net assets of Childers Manufacturing Company (Childers). This

acquisition was accounted for as a pooling of interests, and the financial statements for 1972 have been restated to include Childers' accounts. A reconciliation of previously reported operations of Overhead Door Corporation with restated operations for 1972 is as follows:

	Overhead Door Corporation as reported	Childers Manufacturing Company	Overhead Door Corporation as restated
Net sales and other income	$79,403,000	$6,702,000	$86,105,000
Net income	4,837,000	698,000	5,535,000
Net income per Common Share	1.30	—	1.36

Separate operations and other changes in stockholders' equity of Childers Manufacturing Company for the two months ended February 28, 1973 are summarized as follows (unaudited):

Net sales and other income	$995,000
Net income	68,000
Proceeds from exercise of stock options	15,000

There were no significant transactions between Overhead Door Corporation and Childers prior to acquisition.

Previously reported retained earnings at January 1, 1972 has been increased by $999,000 to include retained earnings of Childers at that date.

Corrections of Errors.   According to APB Opinion No. 20, corrections of errors discovered after the issuance of prior period financial statements should be reported as prior period adjustments. Such errors "result from mathematical mistakes, mistakes in the application of accounting principles, or oversight or misuse of facts that existed at the time the financial statements were prepared." Errors should be distinguished from changes in accounting estimates which do not result in retroactive restatement. Changes in accounting estimate are the result of new information, subsequent developments, better insight, or improved judgment. Additionally, a change to an accounting principle which is generally accepted from one which was not is considered to be the correction of an error.

An example of a prior period restatement resulting from an accounting error is disclosed in the Financial Comments section of the 1972 annual report of LTV Corporation:

> In the course of an extensive operational audit by LTV of the vocational school operations of a subsidiary in 1972, it became apparent that accounting errors had been made in all periods since the acquisition of the school operations in 1969. The errors arose in calculating tuition income, primarily because of incorrect data reported from the field as to the rate and number of student drop-outs. The resulting required reductions in sales and results of operations for years prior to 1972 are as follows (in thousands except per share amounts):

Year	Sales	Results of operations	Per share
1969	$ 320	$ 167	$0.04
1970	3,173	1,650	0.39
1971	910	473	0.07
	$4,403	$2,290	

Prior year amounts in the Statement of Capital Surplus and Retained Earnings were correspondingly adjusted.

Adoption of Certain Authoritative Pronouncements. Authoritative pronouncements of accounting rule-making bodies, such as the Accounting Principles Board, the Financial Accounting Standards Board, and AICPA Committees formulating Accounting and Audit Guides, may require retroactive application by adjustment of prior period financial statements.

Examples of such changes are the following:

Change to Equity Method of Accounting (APB Opinion No. 18). Cabot Corporation, 1973 annual report:

> In 1973 the Company retroactively adopted the equity method of accounting for earnings of 20 percent to 50 percent-owned affiliated companies. The effect of the change in policy was to decrease 1972 net income by $207,000 ($0.04 per share) from that previously reported, and to increase equity in net assets of affiliates by $2,487,000 at September 30, 1971. Retained earnings at September 30, 1971, was also increased by $2,487,000 to reflect this change.

Change to Deferral Method of Income Recognition (AICPA Finance Company Audit Guide). Transamerica Financial Corporation, 1973 annual report:

> In accordance with the Finance Company Audit Guide of the American Institute of Certified Public Accountants the Company, effective January 1, 1973, adopted the policy of deferring extension fees and nonrefundable fees charged at the origination of certain loans and amortizing them over the lives of the related loans. In prior years such fees were taken into income when received. Beginning retained earnings has been reduced by the cumulative effect of this change, $1,300,000 (net of the related income tax benefit of $1,385,000). The effect of the new policy on net income was not material for 1973 or 1972.

Financial Statement Presentation of a Prior Period Adjustment. Financial statements for all prior periods presented should be restated, with appropriate footnote disclosure. The adjustment usually appears in the statement of retained earnings in the manner indicated in the following example:

	19X1	*19X0*
Balance at beginning of year, as previously reported	$647,000	$576,000
Add adjustment for the cumulative effect on prior years of changing from the LIFO to the FIFO method of inventory pricing (Note A)	28,000	24,000
Balance at beginning of year, as adjusted	$675,000	$600,000

A footnote to the financial statements for the year in which the adjustment is made should disclose the effects of the adjustment (both the gross amount and its effect on net income) for all prior periods presented. For the special changes in accounting principle, changes in the reporting entity, and corrections of errors discussed above, disclosure of the effect on income before extraordinary items and earnings per share is also required. In addition, disclosure of the nature of and justification for special changes in accounting principle is required. For poolings of interest, special disclosure rules apply (see Chapter 33). Financial statements for periods subsequent to the year in which the prior period adjustment is made need not repeat the required disclosures.

Adjustments Not Qualifying for Prior Period Treatment. Items not meeting the criteria of APB Opinion No. 9 for prior period adjustment should be included in the financial statements in the year of adjustment as extraordinary items, as separate components of income before extraordinary items, or as adjustments to existing financial statement components (see Chapter 12 for criteria for extraordinary items).

Under APB Opinion No. 20, changes in accounting principles, other than those special changes described above, are reported by including the cumulative effect (net of tax) on beginning retained earnings as a separate item immediately preceding net income of the period of the change. Notes to financial statements should disclose the nature of and justification for the change, including an explanation of why the new method is preferable. Required disclosures in the year of change include the effect of adopting the new accounting principle on income before extraordinary items, on net income, and on the related per-share amounts. Income before extraordinary items and net income must be computed on a pro forma basis and shown on the face of the income statement as if the newly adopted accounting principle had been applied during all periods presented; related per-share amounts should be shown on the face of the income statement or in the notes.

An example of this type of change is disclosed in Note 2 of the 1973 annual report of Lykes-Youngstown Corporation:

> Effective January 1, 1973, expenditures for relining and rehabilitation of blast furnaces were capitalized and will be depreciated over the estimated productive life of the respective furnace linings. Prior to 1973 such expenditures were charged to cost of products sold in the year in which the expenditures were incurred. This change in accounting principles was made to recognize that blast furnace relinings last for several years and should be charged to the operating costs of the period in which the related benefits are obtained, resulting in a more appropriate matching of revenues and costs. Had this change not been made, income before extraordinary item and cumulative effect of an accounting change would have been $4,286,000 ($.48 per share) less for the year ended December 31, 1973. The cumulative effect on prior years of this change, in the amount of $11,552,000 (after reduction for federal income taxes of $4,040,000) is included in net income for the year ended December 31, 1973. The proforma amounts shown on the consolidated statement of income have been computed assuming retroactive application of the newly adopted accounting principle. Proforma fully diluted earnings per share are not presented pursuant to the limitations imposed by the concept of anti-dilution.

The applicable section of the income statement in this report appears in Exhibit 1.

The effect of a change in accounting estimate is also excluded from prior period treatment under APB Opinion No. 20. Such changes should be accounted for in the period of change if the change affects that period only, or the period of the change and future periods if the change affects both. Financial statements of the current period should disclose the effects of income before extraordinary items, net income, and earnings per share.

DIVIDENDS—THEIR NATURE AND FORMS

A dividend represents a pro rata distribution by a corporation to a defined class of stockholders. When the term is used without qualification or other description, there is a general presumption that the distribution is one that reduces retained earnings and is not a return in whole or in part of contributed capital or capital arising from a source other than earnings. The form of distribution may be in corporate assets (or a claim against corporate assets), or with the use of the appropriate qualifying adjective it may be in stock of the corporation of the same or a different class. Cash is most commonly used to pay dividends since, in a pro rata distribution, it is easily divided among stockholders having varying degrees of equity interests.

The form of the distribution will determine whether the dividend will cause a reduction of working capital or other assets, an increase in liabilities, or the

EXHIBIT 1   Partial Income Statement

	Year Ended December 31	
	1973	1972
Income Before Extraordinary Item and Cumulative Effect of Accounting Change	24,856,000	17,580,000
Extraordinary item—gain on sale of investment, less income tax of $2,447,000 (Note 2)		8,018,000
Cumulative effect on prior years of an accounting change, less income tax effect of $4,040,000 (Note 2)	11,552,000	
Net Income for the Year	$36,408,000	$25,598,000
Net Income Attributable to Common Shares		
Net income for the year	$36,408,000	$25,598,000
Preferred dividend requirements	(13,686,000)	(13,692,000)
Income for common shares	$22,722,000	$11,906,000
Average number of common shares outstanding	8,985,000	8,973,000
Per common share:		
Primary:		
Income before extraordinary item and cumulative effect of accounting change	$ 1.24	$ .43
Extraordinary item		.90
Cumulative effect of accounting change	1.29	
Net income	$ 2.53	$ 1.33
Fully diluted:		
Income before extraordinary item and cumulative effect of accounting change	$ 1.26	$ .89
Extraordinary item		.41
Cumulative effect of accounting change	.59	
Net income	$ 1.85	$ 1.30
Proforma income amounts assuming the change in accounting method had been applied retroactively (Note 2):		
Income before extraordinary item	$24,856,000	$15,442,000
Net income	$24,856,000	$23,460,000
Per common share:		
Primary:		
Income before extraordinary item	$ 1.24	$ .20
Net income	$ 1.24	$ 1.09

issuance of additional shares, thereby increasing contributed capital, without any change in total shareholders' equity. The source of distribution may be retained earnings, hence a distribution of profits, or contributed capital, resulting in a return of shareholder investment.

Regardless of form or source, dividend distributions are not expenses of doing business and therefore do not enter into the determination of a corporation's net income. As noted in the Report of the Study Group on the Objectives of Financial Statements,[6] however, shareholders generally expect to receive a return on investment, which in most cases includes dividends. Therefore, from a financial standpoint, corporate management may well consider dividends to be an element in the overall cost of capital.

DIVIDEND POLICY

The major factors influencing a corporation's dividend policy include:
- Statutes defining sources for distribution
- Governmental regulations

---

[6]*Report of the Study Group on the Objectives of Financial Statements, op. cit.*, p. 19.

- Restrictive covenants in indentures and other contractual limitations
- Profitability and stability of profits
- Liquidity and resources available for distribution
- Rate of growth and plans for business expansion
- Access to and status of capital markets
- Tax considerations.

Apart from limitations imposed by these factors, however, the amount and manner of each dividend distribution is at the discretion of the board of directors.

SOURCES OF DIVIDENDS AND LEGALITY

The sources of dividends to be paid in cash or property are governed by the laws of each state; there is considerable diversity in these laws. Although it is beyond the scope of this chapter to analyze these laws, the following excerpt from Welsch, Zlatkovitch, and White[7] illustrates some of the more typical variations:

> There are at least two limitations which appear uniform, namely, that dividends may not be paid from legal capital (usually represented by the capital stock accounts), and that unappropriated retained earnings are available for dividends. Between these two limits there are numerous variations, depending upon the respective state statutes, some of which are:
>
> 1. All contributed capital, other than legal capital, is available for dividends.
> 2. Specified items of contributed capital, other than legal capital, are available for dividends.
> 3. Contributed capital, other than legal capital, is available for dividends on preferred stock but not on common stock.
> 4. Unrealized capital increment from revaluation of assets is not available for dividends.
> 5. Unrealized capital increment from revaluation of assets is available for stock dividends only.
> 6. Capital losses and deficits must be restored before payment of any dividends.
> 7. Dividends from retained earnings must not reduce such balance below the cost of treasury stock held.
>
> The accountant has a definite responsibility in circumstances where the propriety and legality of dividends is at issue to (a) insure that such matters are passed upon by an attorney and (b) ascertain that the financial statements fully disclose all known and material facts concerning such dividends.

A corporation which declares and pays dividends from sources other than retained earnings should disclose the attending circumstances in its financial statements.

CHARGING DIVIDENDS TO PERMANENT CAPITAL ACCOUNTS WHEN RETAINED EARNINGS EXIST

The charging of dividends to permanent capital when retained earnings exist is commented upon by Rappaport:[8]

> Where a company purports to segregate earned and capital surplus, the financial statements are perverted when dividends are charged to capital surplus while there is an earned surplus credit balance, and the showing of an earned surplus credit balance after the payment of dividends gives a false picture of corporate strength when the earned surplus credit remains only because the dividends have been charged to capital surplus.

[7]Glenn A. Welsch, Charles T. Zlatkovich, and John A. White, *Intermediate Accounting*, 3rd ed., Richard D. Irwin, Homewood, Ill., 1972, p. 814.

[8]Louis H. Rappaport, *SEC Accounting Practice and Procedure*, 3rd ed., The Ronald Press Company, New York, 1972, chap. 18, p. 32.

DIVIDENDS IN KIND

Although not a common practice, corporations occasionally distribute assets other than cash as dividends to stockholders. The 1974 edition of *Accounting Trends and Techniques*[9] indicates that in a study of 600 companies, only one of the 513 companies which made distributions to common stockholders paid dividends in kind. Similar studies in 1970–1976 confirm the relative infrequency of such distributions. Generally, such dividends are taxable to the recipient on the basis of the fair market value of the property on the date distributed, and the distributing corporation realizes no gain or loss for federal income tax purposes. The accounting treatment may differ, however, from the tax treatment. APB Opinion No. 29, issued in 1973, requires that nonreciprocal transfers to owners (a transfer of assets or services only in one direction, in this case from the corporation to its stockholders) "should be accounted for at fair value if the fair value of the asset distributed is objectively measurable and would be clearly realizable to the distributing entity in an outright sale at or near the time of distribution." Exempted from this pronouncement are "distributions to owners of an enterprise in a spin-off or other form of reorganization or liquidation [to be discussed in a subsequent section of this chapter] or in a plan that is in substance the rescission of a prior business combination" and a "pro rata distribution to owners of an enterprise of shares of a subsidiary or other investee company that has been or is being accounted for under the equity method." The recorded amounts of the assets distributed are used in accounting for such distributions, after giving effect to any impairment of value.

An example of a dividend in kind, paid in shares of stock of another company, is indicated in the 1973 annual report of Kansas City Southern Industries, Inc.:

> On November 16, 1973, the Board of Directors declared a dividend, payable in shares of Common stock of Mapco, Inc., equivalent to the value of approximately 50 cents per share, upon the outstanding Common stock of the Company to shareholders of record at close of business on November 28, 1973, with such rate determined by the closing market price of Mapco, Inc. Common stock on November 16, 1973. A nontaxable gain of $503,000, representing the excess of market value over cost, was recorded in the income statement as a result of this transaction.

A similar distribution is disclosed in the 1973 annual report of Wytex Corp.:

> Pursuant to a dividend declaration, the Corporation distributed 12,139 shares of Conroy, Inc. common stock to its common shareholders of record June 6, 1973, at the rate of one Conroy share for each ten shares of the Corporation's common stock held. The quoted market value of the Conroy shares of $61,810 was charged to retained earnings as a dividend in kind, and the excess ($28,897) of the quoted value over the cost of the shares was credited to income as a gain on security transactions.

If the fair value of the dividend in kind is not determinable within reasonable limits, the accounting should be based on the recorded amount of the assets distributed, and accordingly no gain or loss would be recognized. The Opinion also notes that fair value may not be determinable within reasonable limits when there are major uncertainties about the realizability of that amount. If a dividend in kind is paid, required disclosures include a statement concerning the nature of the transaction, the basis of accounting for the assets transferred, and any gains or losses recognized.

[9]George Dick and Richard Rikert, eds., *Accounting Trends and Techniques,* 28th ed., AICPA, New York, 1974, p. 327.

SCRIP DIVIDENDS

Although it is rarely done, a corporation may pay dividends in scrip, or promissory notes. The accounting for a scrip dividend is similar to that for a cash dividend, except that upon distribution the credit entry will be to a notes payable account instead of cash.

LIQUIDATING DIVIDENDS

A liquidating dividend is a special distribution from permanent capital accounts involving a partial return of shareholder investment, and occurring most frequently in industries with wasting assets. Simons[10] states that:

> Corporations owning wasting assets may regularly declare dividends that are in part a distribution of earnings and in part a distribution of the corporation's invested capital. Entries on the corporation books for such dividend declarations should reflect the decrease in the two capital elements. This information should be reported to stockholders so that they may recognize dividends as representing in part income and in part a return of investment.

As noted in *Accounting Research Study No. 7*,[11] liquidating dividends may also be paid to effect a partial or complete reduction of the capital of a corporation.

> Dividends paid with the express intent of reducing the capital of the corporation, and with a view toward partial or complete dissolution, are known as liquidating dividends or distributions of capital. Accounting for these dividends should follow the intent expressed in resolutions of the directors or stockholders. When a liquidating dividend has been declared and all the legal steps taken requisite to the reduction of the stock, but the payments to stockholders have not been made, the balance sheet should show the outstanding stock at its reduced amount and the liquidating dividend as a current liability, adequately described.

CONSTRUCTIVE DIVIDENDS

Under Section 301 of the Internal Revenue Code, informal distributions to shareholders without board approval are treated as dividends if made by a corporation "with respect to its stock" unless the distribution is in satisfaction of the shareholder's claim as a creditor. The difference between consideration exchanged and fair value in a transaction between a corporation and its shareholders may be similarly treated. Such informal distributions, "constructive dividends," include compensation considered excessive by the Internal Revenue Service, reimbursement of a shareholder's personal expenses, and payments to shareholders for rent, interest, and the purchase of assets in excess of the fair value of the consideration received by the corporation.

Although the corporation will not be allowed a tax deduction for a distribution treated as a constructive dividend, it may be appropriate to record the distribution as a charge to income (rather than as a dividend) for accounting purposes. For example, salaries or bonuses paid to shareholder-employees may be considered excessive by the Internal Revenue Service. These payments should be reflected as an expense if they are deemed to represent compensation, despite the contrary

[10]Harry Simons, *Intermediate Accounting*, 5th ed., South-Western Publishing Company, Cincinnati, 1972, p. 742.

[11]Paul Grady, *Accounting Research Study No. 7*, AICPA, New York, 1965, pp. 200–201.

position of the Internal Revenue Service, recognizing that generally there is no objective standard of measurement for the value of personal services.

The accounting treatment of transactions with shareholders in which the exchange price differs from fair value is not clearly defined. In some instances any difference between the exchange price and fair value, based on appraisals or amounts charged or paid to unrelated parties, is treated as a contribution to capital when the difference results in a credit to the corporation, or as a dividend distribution in the reverse situation. In other instances these transactions are recorded at the exchange prices and the transactions are disclosed in the notes to the financial statements. These differing treatments have not been resolved, although this question was the subject of a 1969 exposure draft of an APB Opinion. The Board at that time generally advocated full disclosure of such transactions without accounting recognition of fair values. The Opinion was never issued as a formal pronouncement.

Before recording a charge to retained earnings for a constructive dividend not issued to all shareholders in proportion to their respective stock ownership, the company should determine the legal implications of the transaction. A preferential distribution may be illegal in the state of incorporation, and as such may establish a claim against the recipients.

SIGNIFICANT DIVIDEND DATES

Date of Declaration. The formal announcement of the board of directors' intention to issue a cash, property, or scrip dividend creates a liability, which usually cannot be rescinded without stockholder consent (exceptions include fraudulent or illegal dividends—an attorney should be consulted if in doubt). The dividend liability should be recorded at the declaration date, even though the payment date may be sometime in the future.

Date of Record. This date is generally a few weeks after the date of declaration and is used to establish the list of stockholders entitled to receive the dividend. If shares are traded between the date of declaration and the date of payment, the holder on the date of record is entitled to receive the dividends. As a practical matter, however, listed stocks are usually traded "ex-dividend" on the fourth business day preceding the record date, so that the list of stockholders eligible for the dividend can be compiled on a timely basis.

Date of Payment. This date generally follows the date of record by a few weeks and marks the actual distribution of cash, property, or script.

STOCK DIVIDENDS AND STOCK SPLITS

Definitions. A stock dividend is defined in *ARB No. 43*, Chapter 7B, as

> . . . an issuance by a corporation of its own common shares to its common shareholders without consideration and under conditions indicating that such action is prompted mainly by a desire to give the recipient shareholders some ostensibly separate evidence of a part of their respective interests in accumulated corporate earnings without distribution of cash or other property which the board of directors deems necessary or desirable to retain in the business.

The *Bulletin* defines a stock split as

> . . . an issuance by a corporation of its own common shares to its own common shareholders without consideration and under conditions indicating that such action is prompted mainly by a desire to increase the number of outstanding shares for the purpose of effecting a reduction in their unit market price and, thereby, of obtaining wider distribution and improved marketability of the shares.

Thus, the basic distinction, for accounting purposes, between a stock dividend and a stock split is in the underlying intention of the corporation. If a part of retained earnings is to be permanently capitalized, the transaction should be accounted for as a stock dividend; if the distribution is intended to reduce the market price of outstanding shares, the transaction should be accounted for as a stock split. The stated intention of the transaction, however, must be consistent with its effect. *ARB No. 43* indicates that the intended effect of a stock dividend would ordinarily be accomplished when the additional shares issued did not exceed 20 to 25 percent of the number previously outstanding. A distribution in excess of such percentages would ordinarily constitute a stock split.

The New York Stock Exchange rules are somewhat more precise. Any share distribution of less than 25 percent is considered to be a stock dividend, whereas distributions of 25 percent or more are considered to be stock splits. The Exchange stipulates, however, that splits of 25 to 100 percent of the previously outstanding shares may require treatment as stock dividends when "in the opinion of the Exchange, such distributions assume the character of stock dividends through repetition under circumstances not consistent with the true intent and purpose of stock split-ups."

The SEC, in its Accounting Series Release No. 124, issued in 1972, adopted a policy similar to that of the New York Stock Exchange. Distributions of less than 25 percent of the shares outstanding, and those over 25 percent if "part of a program of recurring distributions designed to mislead shareholders," should be accounted for as stock dividends.

Accounting for a Stock Split.   Since there is no apparent intention to distribute accumulated earnings when a stock is split, no accounting entries are required if the par or stated value is proportionately reduced in relation to the amount of the stock split (for example, when a change from a $1 par value stock to a 50 cents par value stock is accompanied by an issuance of shares equal to 100 percent of the number of shares previously outstanding). In circumstances where the par or stated value is not changed, or the change is not in proportion to the amount of the stock split, transfers from paid-in capital or retained earnings are necessary. For example, the 1973 annual report of Texas Instruments Incorporated disclosed a two-for-one stock split in which the unchanged par value of the shares issued was charged to additional paid-in capital.

At times, a stock split is effected in the form of a dividend, and it is impossible to avoid the term "dividend," either in the announcement of the stock split or in disclosure of the transaction in the financial statements. In these situations, terminology such as "stock split effected in the form of a dividend" is desirable to make the substance of the transaction clear. For example, Bic Pen Corporation, in its 1973 annual report, disclosed a stock split effected in the form of a 100 percent stock dividend:

> On July 27, 1972, the Company declared a 2-for-1 share split in the form of a 100% share dividend of 3,240,000 shares, $1 par value, distributable on September 7, 1972. In connection therewith, $3,240,000 was transferred from retained earnings to common shares.

Accounting for a Stock Dividend.   In accounting for a stock dividend, an amount of retained earnings equivalent to the fair value of the additional shares issued is permanently capitalized. This usually results in capitalizing an amount in excess of the legal minimum requirements. The most reasonable measure of the fair value would seem to be the market value at or near the date of declaration of the dividend, and in practice this date is the most widely used. However, other dates are used on occasion, such as date of record or date of issuance, or some appropriate average price for a pertinent period. In recognition of the need to capitalize permanently the fair value of the stock issued in a stock dividend, the Committee on Accounting Procedure in *ARB No. 43* stated that:

> . . . the corporation should in the public interest account for the transaction by transferring from earned surplus to the category of permanent capitalization (represented by the capital stock and capital surplus accounts) an amount equal to the fair value of the additional shares issued. Unless this is done, the amount of earnings which the shareholder may believe to have been distributed to him will be left, except to the extent otherwise dictated by legal requirements, in earned surplus subject to possible further similar stock issuances or cash distributions.

The *Bulletin* also points out that the issuance of a small number of additional shares may have little or no apparent effect on the price of the stock.

The New York Stock Exchange has developed standards of disclosure which require that, in addition to the accounting requirements of the AICPA, the following information be disclosed in shareholder notices of stock dividends:

- The amount capitalized per share and the aggregate amount thereof
- The relation of the aggregate amount to current undistributed earnings
- The account or accounts to which the aggregate amount has been charged or credited
- The reason for issuing the stock dividend
- The fact that the sale of the dividend shares would reduce the shareholders' proportionate equity.

Accounting Series Release No. 124 states the position of the SEC on the issuance of stock dividends where there are insufficient retained earnings to cover the required transfer to permanent capital. Such transactions are considered as "characteristic of a manipulative scheme." The Release also cautions that if the accounting for the transaction is improper or the disclosure is inadequate, the SEC will deem the transaction to be misleading.

Exceptions.   For closely held companies, there is no need to capitalize retained earnings other than to meet legal requirements since misconceptions as to the nature of stock dividend distributions should not exist in these cases, given the shareholders' intimate knowledge of the issuing company.

Banks generally account for stock dividends by transferring the par value of the shares issued from their surplus account to capital stock. In many cases, an amount is also transferred from their undivided profits to surplus, but not usually in an amount equal to the fair values of the additional stock issued.[12]

Criticism of Current Accounting Practices.   Criticism of the current accounting practices for stock distributions generally centers on the distinction made between stock splits and stock dividends. Arguments against current practice can be summarized as follows (an expanded discussion is presented in *Accounting Research Study No. 15*[13]):

- The dividing line between stock splits and stock dividends of 20 to 25 percent of the currently outstanding stock is arbitrary and has no theoretically or empirically justifiable basis.
- There is no difference between a stock split and a stock dividend, in that the only change brought about is in the proportionate ownership of the corporation represented by one share of stock. The proportionate interest of each shareholder is the same before and after the distribution.
- The rationale for distinguishing a stock dividend from a stock split espoused by *ARB No. 43* is that "many recipients of stock dividends look upon them as distributions or corporate earnings and usually in an amount equivalent to the fair

---

[12]Committee on Bank Accounting and Auditing, *Audits of Banks,* AICPA, New York, 1969, p. 55.

[13]Melcher, *op. cit.,* pp. 213–220.

value of the additional shares received." Thus, while recognizing that in theory there is no effective difference between a stock dividend and a stock split, the ARB bases its conclusion on an assumption about stockholder reaction.

- The effect on retained earnings is misleading. Distribution of a small number of shares may reduce retained earnings more than the distribution of a large number of shares.

- Empirical studies[14] indicate that the stock market eventually discounts the effect of a stock dividend, thus invalidating the assertion in *ARB No. 43* that, in most cases, stock dividends "do not have any apparent effect on the share market price, and consequently, the market value of the shares previously held remains substantially unchanged."

Changes proposed which would overcome these objections include the accounting for stock dividends in the same manner as stock splits or the use of retained earnings appropriations to cover legal capital requirements if not satisfied through use of other paid-in capital. The accounting distinction currently in use, however, continues in effect.

Reverse Stock Splits.   A reverse stock split occurs if the result of the split is a contraction of the number of shares previously outstanding. Like a regular stock split, no accounting entries are required unless the par or stated value is not increased in proportion to the amount of the reverse split. If a reduction of the stated capital account is necessary, the entry would be to increase additional paid-in capital, rather than retained earnings.

An example of a reverse stock split is disclosed in the 1973 annual report of Bunker Ramo Corporation:

> The shareholders on April 24, 1973, approved a reclassification of common stock through a 1 for 3 reverse stock split on the issued, outstanding and reserved shares of the corporation's common stock. All shares and earnings per share amounts for 1972 have been adjusted to give effect to this reverse split.

Fractional Shares.   Stock dividends generally give rise to fractional share interests. For example, an investor holding 75 shares would, after declaration of a 2 percent stock dividend, be entitled to 1½ additional shares. Since only whole shares are usually issued, the fractional share interests are commonly settled by issuing scrip certificates or by payment in cash. If immediate cash payment is made, retained earnings are charged for the full share distribution, and the cash portion is accounted for as a cash dividend. Scrip certificates which do not carry rights associated with share ownership usually have limited life and may be traded. Often the issuing corporation designates a trustee to purchase and sell scrip certificates in its behalf, and to redeem them for full shares. When scrip is issued, a credit is made to a fractional share interest account, which is closed to capital stock as the scrip is redeemed for shares. Forfeited amounts may be transferred to capital surplus, if statutes so provide, or returned to retained earnings.

Stock Dividends or Stock Splits—Treasury Stock.   Practice varies as to whether any treasury shares participate in the distribution accompanying a stock dividend or stock split. Practice may be influenced by the planned use of the treasury shares. For example, if the treasury shares are intended for issuance in connection with employee stock options, the number of shares under option is usually adjusted for any stock dividends or splits, and the treasury shares accordingly may participate in the distribution. Unless there are reasons such as this for doing so, no useful purpose is served by allowing treasury shares to participate in the additional distribution, since they are essentially equivalent to authorized but unissued shares. The legal requirements of some states specifically prohibit considering treasury shares as outstanding when issuing stock dividends.

[14]*Ibid.*, p. 215.

Date of Recording a Stock Dividend.   Unlike a cash, property, or scrip dividend, a stock dividend does not represent a liability of the corporation at the date of declaration. Instead it represents a proposed realignment of the capital accounts, which is revocable until the dividend shares are distributed. For example, Physio-Control Corporation made the following disclosure in a 1973 8K filing with the SEC:

> At a meeting of the Board of Directors of the Company held January 26, 1973, a fifteen percent (15%) stock dividend was declared payable on March 1, 1973 to stockholders of record on February 15, 1973. At a subsequent meeting of the Board of Directors held February 22, 1973, the fifteen percent (15%) stock dividend was cancelled. The cancellation occurred because while under Delaware law the Company is permitted to capitalize only the par value of the dividend shares, SEC Accounting Series Release No. 124 requires the capitalization of the aggregate fair market value of the dividend shares. Application of the requirements of Delaware law would have required a transfer from surplus to capital of approximately $53,000, while the effect of the SEC Release No. 124 would have required a transfer of approximately $3,100,000 and would have resulted in a negative earned surplus.

Accounting literature does recommend that a stock dividend be recorded at the date of declaration, but it is also considered acceptable to defer the recording until the date of issuance, provided that disclosure of the declaration is made in financial statements. Although deferral of the recording could be justified on the grounds that stock dividends, unlike cash dividends, can be rescinded by the company's directors prior to issuance, the Securities and Exchange Commission prefers the recording of such dividends when declared, since such rescissions are rare. In a balance sheet presentation of a stock dividend payable, it is common to include it as a separate amount under common stock at the par or stated value of the shares to be issued, with the market value of the dividend having been charged to retained earnings and any excess of market value over par or stated value credited to paid-in capital.

Effect of Stock Dividend or Stock Split on Earnings per Share.   APB Opinion No. 15, issued in 1969, states that:

> If the number of common shares outstanding increases as a result of a stock dividend or stock split or decreases as a result of a reverse split, the computations [of earnings per share] should give retroactive recognition to an appropriate equivalent change in capital structure for all periods presented. If changes in common stock resulting from stock dividends or stock splits or reverse splits have been consummated after the close of the period but before completion of the financial report, the per share computations should be based on the new number of shares because the readers' primary interest is presumed to be related to the current capitalization. When per share computations reflect such changes in the number of shares after the close of the period, this fact should be disclosed.

DIVIDENDS ON PREFERRED STOCK

The accounting for cash dividends on preferred stock is similar to the accounting for cash dividends on common stock. The preferred stock may be cumulative or noncumulative. Cumulative preferred stock with a stipulated dividend rate is entitled to receive any arrearage of dividends previously passed plus the amount currently payable before any dividends are paid on common stock. An arrearage in preferred stock dividends is not a liability to be reflected in the balance sheet, since the liability for a dividend arises only as a result of the declaration of a dividend by the board of directors. The amount of dividend arrearage, both per share of preferred stock and in total, should be disclosed for each class of preferred shares.

DIVIDENDS OF COMPANIES WITH SPECIAL TAX STATUS

The dividends of certain companies are often based on the minimum amounts required to be paid to maintain a special tax status. For example, qualifying regulated investment companies and real estate investment trusts pay federal income tax only on undistributed income if dividends paid are at least 90 percent of their otherwise taxable income. An illustrative disclosure of the tax status and dividend policy of such companies is included in the 1973 annual report of the Adams Express Company:

> No provision has been made for Federal income taxes on net investment income, capital gain or net unrealized appreciation of investments since it is the policy of the Company to comply with the provisions available to investment companies as defined in applicable sections of the Internal Revenue Code and to make distributions of investment income and capital gains sufficient to relieve it from all, or substantially all, Federal income taxes.

"Small business corporations" as defined in Section 1371 of the Internal Revenue Code (Subchapter S corporations) may elect to have their income taxed directly to shareholders, which is similar to the tax treatment of a partnership. As a result, the dividend policy of many Subchapter S corporations is to provide the shareholders with sufficient cash for payment of taxes on their proportionate share of the corporation's taxable income. Other Subchapter S corporations may distribute all, or substantially all, of their income as dividends. The tax status and dividend policy of a Subchapter S corporation and any estimated dividend requirements not declared at the date of the financial statements should be disclosed.

TREASURY STOCK TRANSACTIONS

The acquisition of a corporation's own preferred or common shares, or rights, warrants, or options to purchase such shares may result in reductions of retained earnings in certain circumstances. This matter is dealt with extensively in Chapter 28 on "Contributed Capital."

REDEMPTION OF PREFERRED SHARES AT A PREMIUM

Accounting Series Release No. 45, issued by the SEC in 1943, requires that amounts paid preferred shareholders upon redemption in excess of amounts originally paid in on such shares should be charged to retained earnings, together with amounts paid for accumulated unpaid dividends. The charge to retained earnings may be viewed as a form of "dividend" to liquidate the interests of the shareholders whose stock is redeemed. If there are any other sources of capital in excess of par related to the shares retired, then a pro rata reduction of those paid-in capital accounts would generally be made before any excess is charged to retained earnings. Retirement at a price less than the issue price would be accounted for as a credit to paid-in capital, rather than retained earnings.

The timing of the charge to retained earnings is not specified in Release No. 45 or in other authoritative literature, and poses an interesting accounting problem. Three methods are possible:

- An immediate charge
- Nonrecognition of the charge until the preferred stock is redeemed
- A periodic charge over the term to redemption using an effective rate method.

An immediate charge is appropriate for nonconvertible preferred stock which requires redemption, since there is certainty of cash redemption, barring any future modification of the terms of the preferred stock issue. An example of this type is indicated in the 1972 annual report of First Security Corporation, in which a transfer of $10,019,067 was made from retained earnings to the preferred stock account in order to state preferred stock at liquidating preference value.

Nonrecognition of the charge until redemption is also appropriate, especially when redemption is not mandatory. An example of the disclosure appropriate in these circumstances is included in the 1973 annual report of Weyerhauser Company:

> In April 1969 the shareholders authorized 2 million preferred shares of which 1,500,920 shares subsequently were issued and designated $6.75 Convertible Cumulative Preferred Shares, Series A, without par value. Beginning July 20, 1972, these shares were callable and on September 25, 1972, all shares then outstanding were either redeemed at a price of $106.21875 per share, including an amount equal to accrued and unpaid dividends, or converted into common shares at a rate of one preferred share for 1.7544 pre-split common shares.

The cost to redeem or convert the Series A shares in excess of amounts paid in was shown as a deduction in the statement of consolidated retained earnings.

The third method, a periodic accumulation over the term to redemption, would be acceptable for most nonconvertible issues with mandatory redemption. This treatment is based on the theory that the excess of redemption value over the amount paid in upon issuance is the result of a lower than normal dividend rate, and as such, should be amortized as an adjustment, in effect, of the cash dividend, somewhat similar to the amortization of debt discount as an adjustment of interest expense. Accretion of the excess would result in a constant effective dividend rate through periodic charges to retained earnings. This practice is illustrated in the 1972 annual report of Colonial Commercial Corporation, in which a 6 percent cumulative redeemable preferred stock is stated at its present value to maturity, based on a imputed dividend rate of 9 percent:

> This stock provides for dividends to be paid at the rate of $.30 per share per annum and has a face redemption value of $5 per share (aggregate $500,000). The stock is redeemable $100,000 in 1982 and $200,000 in each of 1983 and 1984. The accompanying financial statements include such stock at its face redemption value less unamortized discount to reflect the present value of such obligation.

SUBSIDIARY AND INVESTEE TRANSACTIONS

Stock Dividends of Subsidiaries. Occasionally, a subsidiary will declare stock dividends or effect stock splits, thus permanently capitalizing a portion of the subsidiary's retained earnings. This raises the question of whether the transaction should be reflected in the consolidated financial statements. *ARB No. 51* states on this point that:

> This does not require a transfer to capital surplus on consolidation, inasmuch as the retained earnings in the consolidated financial statements should reflect the accumulated earnings of the consolidated group not distributed to the shareholders of, or capitalized by, the parent company.

It is appropriate, where material, to disclose the effect of such transactions on consolidated retained earnings available for dividends. For example, W. R. Grace & Co., in its 1973 annual report, noted that consolidated retained earnings include "approximately $17,000,000 transferred to capital stock accounts on the books of subsidiary companies." Texas Utilities Company also stated in its 1973 annual report that consolidated retained earnings at December 31, 1973, "includes $24,-329,000 representing the Company's equity in undistributed earnings since acquisition included in transfers by a subsidiary from earned surplus to stated value of common stock, which transfers have been eliminated in consolidation."

Retained Earnings of Subsidiary as Source of Parent's Dividend. As stated in *ARB No. 43*, the retained earnings of a subsidiary accumulated prior to acquisition do not constitute a part of consolidated retained earnings; and any dividends declared and paid to the parent should be treated as a return of capital by the parent. Earnings accumulated by the subsidiary subsequent to acquisition may not be available for payment to the parent because of certain legal or contractual commitments. Any such restrictions causing a material portion of consolidated retained earnings to be unavailable for dividends should be disclosed.

The availability of unremitted subsidiary retained earnings for distribution by a parent is a complicated legal question which should be resolved through consultation with an attorney. Of course, a parent can avoid this difficulty, and increase its own retained earnings, by having the subsidiary declare and pay a dividend from its unrestricted retained earnings.

Sale of Subsidiary Stock. The manner of distribution generally determines the appropriate accounting for a sale of subsidiary stock. As pointed out by Nemec:[15]

> When the offering takes the form of the subsidiary's direct sale of a number of unissued shares, the resulting change (usually an increase) in the parent's equity in the subsidiary's net assets is shown as additional contributed capital. However, if a portion of the parent's holdings in the subsidiary is sold in a secondary offering, the transaction is reported in the statement of earnings. A combination offering of unissued shares and shares owned by the parent may also be made, in which case the two segments are accounted for separately in the consolidated statements as additional contributed capital and earnings.

An interesting example of both types of distributions is disclosed in the 1973 annual report of National Distillers and Chemical Corporation:

> In September 1972, a subsidiary, Almaden Vineyards, Inc., sold to the public 1,562,-123 shares of its common stock, thereby reducing the Company's interest in Almaden from 100% to 84.36%. The offering price of the new shares issued was in excess of their net book value. The company's share of such excess after underwriting commissions and expenses [$23,087,000] has been credited to Common Stockholders' Equity paid-in capital. In December 1973, the Company completed an exchange of 1,046,932 shares of common stock of a subsidiary, Almaden Vineyards, Inc., for 2,013,329 shares of common stock of the Company. The exchange, which was announced in May 1973, resulted in a reduction of the Company's interest in Almaden from 84.36% to 73.89%. The excess (after deducting expenses of $1,538,000) of the market value on November 1, 1973 of the National common stock surrendered over National's carrying value of the Almaden stock delivered aggregated $25,868,000, and this amount was credited to income as an extraordinary gain in 1973. There is no Federal income tax to the Company with respect to this gain. The value of the National shares acquired, amounting to $32,968,000, has been charged to common stockholders' equity.

According to the *Accountants SEC Practice Manual*,[16] issuance of additional shares by the subsidiary is treated as a capital transaction in the consolidated financial statements because of an unwritten rule of the SEC and is based on the theory that equity financing by a subsidiary results in an infusion of paid-in capital and as such should not give rise to income in the consolidated financial statements, whereas a parent's sale of subsidiary stock results in a partial divestiture requiring gain or loss recognition. In addition, the latter transaction results in a direct cash flow to the parent, whereas the former does not.

[15]Marilyn J. Nemec, "Reporting in Consolidated Statements the Sale of a Subsidiary's Stock," *The CPA Journal*, March 1973, p. 214.

[16]Howard L. Kellogg and Morton Palaway, *Accountants SEC Practice Manual*, Commerce Clearing House, Chicago, 1971, p. 874.

In fact, APB Opinion No. 18, issued in 1971, required that parent companies in consolidation must recognize gain or loss on sales of stock in unconsolidated domestic subsidiaries and investees accounted for by the equity method. Although the Opinion deals solely with unconsolidated subsidiaries, presumably the same accounting treatment would be required for a consolidated subsidiary, since a basic tenet of the Opinion is that "a transaction of an investee of a capital nature that affects the investor's share of stockholders' equity of the investee should be accounted for as if the investee were a consolidated subsidiary."

A similar accounting treatment for subsidiary stock issuance is advanced by Copeland, Crumbley, and Wojdak.[17] They suggest recognizing both the reduction in equity in unremitted earnings resulting from dilution of the parent's proportionate interest, and the increase in paid-in capital related to the capital infusion into the subsidiary. This method was used by Presidential Realty Corporation, which disclosed the following transaction in its 1971 annual report:

> In July 1971, All-American Realty Company, Inc. (Amreco), a subsidiary, sold through a rights offering to Presidential's shareholders a 19.4% stock interest in and $1,500,000 of 11% subordinated sinking fund debentures of Amreco. During the two years ended October 31, 1971 the contribution by Amreco to Presidential's net income amounted to $556,437 and $467,540 respectively.

The accompanying Statement of Consolidation Paid-In Surplus and Retained Earnings disclosed a related increase in paid-in surplus of $201,661 and reduction of retained earnings of $380,222.

Subsidiary Purchase of Parent Company Stock or Its Own Stock.   The purchase of parent company stock by a subsidiary is treated in consolidated financial statements as though the parent had acquired its own stock. *ARB No. 51* states that "shares of the parent held by a subsidiary should not be treated as outstanding stock in the consolidated balance sheet." Meyer[18] also notes that "when a subsidiary owns stock of its parent . . . the cost of the subsidiary's investment would be an aggregate deduction from total consolidation net worth . . . [and] individual net worth accounts are reduced in what becomes a modified version of the constructive retirement approach to treasury stock." This approach is also supported by a committee of the American Accounting Association:[19]

> Shares of the controlling company's capital stock owned by a subsidiary before the date of acquisition of control should be treated in consolidation as treasury stock. Any subsequent acquisition or sale by a subsidiary should likewise be treated in the consolidation statements as though it had been the act of the controlling company.

A purchase by a subsidiary of its own stock is treated similarly, except that the usual procedure is to reduce stockholders' equity in consolidated financial statements only to the extent of the parent's equity in the cost of the subsidiary's treasury stock. Literature supports this approach (see Griffin, Williams, and Larson[20] for a detailed presentation of the entries required by the parent and eliminations in consolidation).

An example of treasury stock held by subsidiaries is shown in the 1973 annual report of Rapid-American Corporation, in which the caption "Preference stock in treasury at cost, equity in subsidiaries' cost of their treasury stock and subsidiary's

---

[17]Ronald Copeland, D. Larry Crumbley, and Joseph F. Wojdak, *Advanced Accounting*, Holt, Rinehart and Winston, New York, 1971, p. 139.

[18]Philip E. Meyer, "Some Accounting Ramifications of Treasury Stock," *The CPA Journal*, November 1973, p. 1019.

[19]American Accounting Association, Committee on Concepts and Standards, Supplementary Statement No. 7, "Consolidated Statements" *Accounting Review*, April 1955, p. 196.

[20]Charles H. Griffin, Thomas H. Williams, and Kermit D. Larson, *Advanced Accounting*, rev. ed., Richard D. Irwin, Homewood, Ill., 1971, pp. 485–487.

cost of investment in Rapid-American Corporation common stock (less par value) and warrants" is included as a deduction in the stockholders' equity section of the consolidated balance sheet.

Capital Transactions of Investees. APB Opinion No. 18 requires that "a transaction of an investee of a capital nature that affects the investor's share of stockholders' equity of the investee should be accounted for as if the investee were a consolidated subsidiary." Thus if an unconsolidated subsidiary or qualifying affiliate engages in any of the transactions discussed in this section, capital adjustments by the investor will be necessary.

RECAPITALIZATIONS AND REORGANIZATIONS

Increase in Par Value. A recapitalization which increases the par or stated value of shares may require capitalization of retained earnings. For example, assume that a corporation has the following equity accounts:

```
Capital stock, par value $10, 1,000 shares
   issued and outstanding  ............ $10,000
Additional paid-in capital arising from
   capital stock issuance  ..............   65,000
Retained earnings  ...................  150,000
```

If the corporation decides to increase the par value of its shares to $100, the following entry is made:

```
Capital stock, $10 par value  ..........   10,000
Additional paid-in capital  ............   65,000
Retained earnings  ...................   25,000
       Capital stock, $100 par value  .............  100,000
```

A reduction in par value would be treated in a similar manner, except that retained earnings cannot be increased. Thus, the entire reduction in par or stated value would be added to additional paid-in capital. A recapitalization that is intended to eliminate a deficit is a quasi-reorganization and is described in Chapter 28 on "Contributed Capital."

Conversion of Preferred Shares. The conversion of preferred shares to common shares would result in a charge to retained earnings if the total paid in for the shares being converted is less than the par or stated value of the shares into which they are converted. For example, assume the following data for a corporation:

```
Preferred stock, par value $10, issued 500,000
   shares, each share convertible into two shares of
   common stock  ............................ $5,000,000
Premium on preferred stock  ....................     500,000
Common stock, par value $8, authorized 2,000,000
   shares, issued 500,000 shares  .................   4,000,000
Retained eranings  ............................   3,000,000
Preferred dividends in arrears  .................  $.20/share
```

The entry to record the conversion of 200,000 shares of preferred stock into 400,000 shares of common stock would appear as follows:

```
Preferred stock (200,000 × $10)  ......... 2,000,000
Premium on preferred stock ($500,000 ×
   200,000/500,000)  ....................     200,000
Dividends on preferred stock ($20 ×
   200,000)  ............................      40,000
Retained earnings (balance of charge)  ....     960,000
       Common stock (400,000 × $8)  ...............  3,200,000
```

Divisive Reorganizations. Spin-offs, split-offs, and split-ups are collectively described as divisive reorganizations. In each case, a segment of the assets of an existing business entity is transferred to a separate entity. A *spin-off* occurs when shares in the segment are distributed to the original entity's shareholders without surrender of their shares. A *split-off* is similar to a spin-off, except that shares of the original entity are exchanged pro rata for shares of the new entity. A *split-up* occurs when all of the operations of the original entity are transferred to two or more new entities, and the original entity ceases to exist.[21]

APB Opinion No. 29, issued in 1973, states as follows:

> Accounting for the distribution of nonmonetary assets to owners of an enterprise in a spin-off or other form of reorganization or liquidation or in a plan that is in substance the rescission of a prior business combination should be based on the recorded amount (after reduction if appropriate for an indicated impairment of value) of the nonmonetary assets distributed. A pro rata distribution to owners of an enterprise of shares of a subsidiary or other investee company that has been or is being consolidated or that has been or is being accounted for under the equity method is to be considered to be equivalent to a spin-off.

Thus, the Opinion precludes gain recognition in accounting for a divisive reorganization. The Opinion is silent, however, on the effects of such a transaction on the retained earnings of the existing entity and whether or not any retained earnings should be carried forward to the new entity. Powell[22] discusses the subject of starting the new entity with retained earnings and sets forth the following conditions which may justify such accounting:

- The transferee corporation has acquired a sufficiently integrated segment of the corporation's net assets and personnel to form a going business, and has not merely acquired certain assets such as a plant building.
- There is reasonable evidence that the business acquired had contributed to the income of the transferor and that the circumstances and factors responsible for its profitable contribution can be expected to continue after separation.
- Substantially all of the assets and business then acquired had been previously held by the transferor.

The 1974 annual report of Pier 1. Imports, Inc. discloses a spin-off of its previously pooled retail fabric business into a new entity, Trinity Trade Corporation. The 1974 financial statements of Trinity Trade Corporation showed a beginning deficit and included the following note disclosure:

> Prior to March 31, 1973, the retail fabric companies of Saybrook, Fabric World and King's Fashion Fabrics, which companies were acquired by Pier 1. Imports, Inc. (Pier 1.) in fiscal years 1970, 1972 and 1973, respectively, and accounted for as poolings of interest in those years, operated as wholly-owned subsidiaries of Pier 1. As of that date, all the common stock of these subsidiaries was transferred by Pier 1. to Trinity Trade Corp. (Trinity), incorporated on March 30, 1973, in exchange for 539,649 shares of Trinity's common stock. The assets and liabilities were recorded on the books of Trinity at the carrying value recorded on the books of the predecessor companies. The excess of the carrying value transferred over the par value of the common stock is reflected as capital surplus [and accumulated deficit] in the accompanying consolidated balance sheet.

The accompanying consolidated balance sheet at March 31, 1973, sets forth the components of stockholders' equity as follows:

Common stock, $1 par value, 1,000,000
    shares authorized, 539,649 shares
    outstanding 539,649
Capital surplus 3,272,015
Accumulated deficit .... (913,010)

---

[21]Valdean C. Lembke, "Some Considerations in Accounting for Divisive Reorganizations," *The Accounting Review,* July 1970, p. 458.

[22]Weldon Powell, "Business Separations," *The Journal of Accountancy,* March 1957, p. 56.

In other situations, however, the financial statements of the new entity reflect no beginning retained earnings. Two such cases are the spin-off of newly formed Louisiana Pacific Corporation from Georgia Pacific Corporation in 1973 and the spin-off of newly formed Simlog Leasing Corporation from Simlog Corporation in 1971.

At present there are some variations in the accounting for such transactions by transferors. Although income statement presentation of the discontinued operation conforms with APB Opinion No. 30 (see Chapter 3), there is no general agreement on the manner of recording the diminution of stockholders' equity in the divisive reorganization. For example, the consolidated statement of stockholders' equity in the 1974 annual report of Pier 1. Imports showed the net cost of the assets spun off as a *dividend in kind* and made the following disclosure:

> During fiscal 1973 the Company formed Trinity Trade Corp. (Trinity) into which was merged its retail fabric business. Effective September 30, 1973, the Company distributed a dividend in the form of 100% of the common stock of Trinity Trade Corp. to the stockholders of the Company in order to effect a spin-off of its retail fabric operations. Accordingly, the Company's retail fabric business has been reflected as discontinued operations in the accompanying financial statements. The Company retained its wholesale fabric business, the operating results of which are included in the accompanying income statements as continuing operations.

An alternative treatment is disclosed in a 1972 proxy statement of Georgia-Pacific Corporation concerning the spin-off of Louisiana Pacific Corporation:

> At the date the proposed spin-off becomes effective, Georgia-Pacific will charge its earned surplus and its paid-in surplus a total of $150,000,000, representing the net book value of the assets of Louisiana-Pacific being distributed to Georgia-Pacific stockholders. The charge to earned surplus represents the portion of Georgia-Pacific's earned surplus considered applicable to the Louisiana-Pacific operations and will be computed based upon the ratio of the net book value of the assets before and after the spin-off.

The 1973 annual report shows a $122,500 reduction of additional paid-in capital and a $27,500 reduction of retained earnings.

Another approach is to charge consolidated retained earnings for that portion attributable to the operations spun off into the new entity. If the new entity carries forward an equal amount of beginning retained earnings, the original equity classification by source would not be affected by the divisive reorganization. If the operations spun off were originally acquired in a business combination accounted for as a purchase, however, the charge to consolidated retained earnings should not be for an amount greater than the new entity's earnings since acquisition (since earnings prior to acquisition are not included in consolidated retained earnings).

MISCELLANEOUS ENTRIES TO RETAINED EARNINGS

Change in Subsidiary or Pooled Company Reporting Period. An existing subsidiary or a newly pooled company may have a year-end that differs from that of the reporting entity. If it is decided to conform year-ends for reporting purposes, a direct entry to retained earnings is usually made in the year of the change for the net results of operations for the overlapping period. For example, the 1972 annual report of E. H. Crump Companies, Inc. disclosed:

> In September 1972, the Company acquired the outstanding stock of the following companies in exchange for 330,440 shares of its common stock in transactions accounted for as poolings of interest: Stone Insurance Agency, Incorporated; Fisher-Brown, Inc.; Insurance Underwriters, Inc. of Georgia; and Davant and Gordon, Inc. These companies are included in the 1971 financial statements based on their respective fiscal years most nearly corresponding to the Company's calendar year. The $130,842 difference

between the pooled companies' 1971 net income reported on a fiscal year basis and a calendar year basis has been credited to retained earnings and represents revenues of $376,661 less expenses and income taxes of $230,674 and $15,145, respectively. The 1972 financial statements include the accounts of all companies on a calendar year basis.

As an alternative, the operations of such companies may be included in the statement of operations for the period of the change and the immediately preceding reporting period, with the overlapping results eliminated by a direct charge to retained earnings. For example, the 1973 annual report of Nabisco, Inc., disclosed this treatment as follows:

> In October, 1973, Nabisco, Inc. acquired Associated for 867,230 shares of its common stock. The transaction has been accounted for as a pooling of interests. Associated's results of operations for its fiscal year ended May 31, 1973, which reflects net sales and net income of $66,285,000 and $4,137,000, respectively, have been combined with Nabisco's results of operations for 1972. After the acquisition by Nabisco, Associated changed to the calendar year basis for reporting. The consolidated results of operations for 1973 include Associated's net sales and net income of $71,651,000 and $3,835,000, respectively, for the year ended December 31, 1973. As a result of this presentation, Associated's net income of $1,645,000 for the five months ended May 31, 1973, which has been included in both years, has been deducted from retained earnings. For the nine months ended September 30, 1973, prior to its acquisition, Associated had net sales and net income of $54,267,000 and $2,594,000, respectively.

Redemption of Stock Purchase Warrants. The excess of amounts paid to acquire stock purchase warrants (not to exceed the fair value at date of redemption or repurchase) over amounts assigned to the warrants at issuance is charged to retained earnings. An illustration is disclosed in the 1973 annual report of Southland Financial Corporation:

> In 1973 the Company purchased the 85,000 warrants which had been issued in connection with the Las Colinas Development Notes, and the cost of $1,487,500 was charged to retained earnings.

Board Resolution to Capitalize Permanently a Portion of Retained Earnings. A corporation may, by board resolution, permanently capitalize a part or all of existing retained earnings, if the capitalization is not prohibited by law or contractual agreement. For example, the 1971 annual report of the Reynolds and Reynolds Company discloses such a transfer of $299,250 from retained earnings to paid-in capital.

RESTRICTIONS OF RETAINED EARNINGS

Types. As was noted under "Distinction Between Retained Earnings and Other Capital Accounts," the entire balance in retained earnings may not be "available" for dividends, because of certain legal or contractual commitments, or because of a need for funds for internal corporate purposes. Johnson and Gentry[23] classify these retained earnings restrictions into three basic categories:

Contracts:
 With creditors. For instance bond indentures, in addition to requiring the establishment of a sinking fund for the payment of the bonds, may place a limitation on the amount of dividends that may be paid; the purpose is to prevent the impairment of working capital that might result from cash deposits in the sinking fund and cash disbursements for dividends.

---

[23]Glenn L. Johnson and James A. Gentry, Jr., *Finney and Miller's Principles of Accounting, Intermediate,* 7th ed., Prentice-Hall, Englewood Cliffs, N.J., 1974, p. 532.

With preferred stockholders. Retirable preferred stock is sometimes issued; a restriction on dividend payments to common stockholders may be imposed to preserve funds to meet the stock-retirement commitment with the preferred stockholders.

Law:

The statutes of many states prescribe that dividend payments and disbursement for the acquisition of treasury shares must not impair the stated capital.

Voluntary action of directors:

To indicate that dividends will be limited in order to accumulate funds for plant expansion or other purposes.

To indicate the existence of a contingency that may result in a loss but contingency so problematical that a charge to current revenue would not be justified.

Disclosure in Financial Statements.   Any significant contractual or legal restriction should be disclosed. *Accounting Research Study No. 7*[24] states that:

> Restrictions may be indicated by footnote or parenthetical notation. Restrictions imposed by bond indentures, bank loan agreements, state laws, or charter provisions are examples of those which should be disclosed. The restriction may be based upon the retention of the balance of retained earnings as of a specified date, upon the corporation's ability to observe certain working capital requirements, or upon other considerations. When there is more than one type of restriction, disclosure of the amount of retained earnings, so restricted, may be based on the most restrictive covenants likely to be effective in the immediate future. In other words, restrictions seldom, if ever, pyramid in amount.

In addition, Accounting Series Release No. 35, issued by the SEC in 1942, interprets "generally accepted and sound accounting practice" as requiring disclosure of restrictions on retained earnings which limit its availability for dividend purposes. Examples of characteristic restrictions requiring disclosure include those imposed by:

- Treasury stock requirements
- Dividend arrearages on cumulative preferred stock
- An excess of involuntary liquidation preference over the par or stated value of preferred stock
- Restrictive provisions of a trust indenture or loan agreement
- Restrictive provisions of the corporation's articles of incorporation
- An order or requirement of a regulatory agency.

Rule 3-16(h) of Regulation S-X also requires disclosure of the most restrictive of such dividend restrictions, with an indication of its source, pertinent provisions, and the amount of retained earnings so restricted or free of such restrictions.

Disclosure may be made in the footnotes to the financial statements or by means of retained earnings appropriations. Although in certain instances, bond indentures and similar agreements require appropriations, footnote disclosure is currently the most common method in all but a few specialized and regulated industries (such as insurance, banking, and utilities).

Treasury Stock Requirements.   In some states legal restrictions on retained earnings available for dividends are imposed by statute, in that dividends issued after a treasury stock acquisition are limited to the excess of the balance of retained earnings over the cost of any treasury shares. The 1973 annual report of the Cornelius Company, for example, states that "retained earnings and capital surplus are restricted in the amount of $9,300,866 representing the cost of Common Stock in treasury."

Dividend Arrearages on Cumulative Preferred Stock.   Most agreements for the issuance of cumulative preferred stock require that no dividends may be paid to common stockholders as long as there are cumulative unpaid preferred stock

[24]Grady, *op. cit.*, p. 203.

dividends. Since such provisions restrict the amount of retained earnings available for distribution to common stockholders, the amount and nature of any material restriction should be disclosed.

Excess of Involuntary Liquidation Preference over Par or Stated Value of Preferred Stock. Preferred stocks requiring or permitting future redemption may require that a premium over par be paid in the event of redemption. If state law restricts retained earnings to the extent of this premium, the restriction should be disclosed.

Restrictive Indenture or Loan Agreement Provisions. It is necessary to disclose restrictions imposed by such agreements which limit cash dividend payments to specified amounts or limit the acquisition of treasury stock. Usually, however, there are no restrictions placed on the payment of stock dividends, since the purpose of these agreements is to protect creditors, who are not affected by the declaration of stock dividends.

A covenant frequently included in lending agreements requires the maintenance of a minimum amount of net working capital. The question arises whether a working capital covenant should be considered a restriction on retained earnings available for dividends. It could be argued that dividends could be paid from noncurrent assets or from funds obtained through the issuance of long-term debt; although such action would be unlikely, it would not be prevented by a covenant of this type. An answer to the question cannot be provided here since the determination depends on the nature of the particular working capital covenant, which is essentially a legal matter. Even if a working capital covenant of this type is not interpreted to be a retained earnings restriction, however, disclosure of the restricted net current assets may be necessary. An example of this type is the 1973 annual report of Braniff Airways, Inc.:

> The Civil Aeronautics Board order approving the reorganization referred to in Note 2 and certain loan agreements provide, among other things, for restrictions relating to the payment of cash dividends and for the maintenance of certain minimum working capital and asset coverage ratios. Under the most restrictive asset coverage ratio and minimum working capital requirement which have the effect of restricting the payment of cash dividends and under the most restrictive retained earnings provision, $54,531,-000, $68,650,000, and $55,762,000, respectively, of the Company's retained earnings was restricted at December 31, 1973.

Restrictive Provisions of the Corporation's Articles of Incorporation. An example of a restriction of this type is disclosed in the 1973 annual report of Kansas Power and Light Company:

> The Company's Articles of Incorporation provided certain restrictions on the payment of cash dividends on common stock. The restrictions at December 31, 1973 and 1972 were $4,357,950 and $4,385,510 respectively.

Order or Requirement of a Regulatory Agency. State law or certain regulatory agencies may also impose limitations on payment of dividends. The 1973 annual report of United States Trust Company of New York discloses that:

> The New York State Banking Law restricts the availability of surplus for the payment of dividends. At December 31, 1973, $9,750,000 of surplus was so restricted.

Restrictions on Consolidated Retained Earnings. As was discussed under "Subsidiary or Investee Transactions," consolidated retained earnings may not be totally available for dividends since unremitted subsidiary retained earnings may not legally be a source for distribution by the parent. Nevertheless, it is customary to disclose restrictions on components of consolidated retained earnings because the reader may interpret the balance to represent an amount available to the parent for distribution. Massey-Ferguson Limited, for example, in a footnote on dividend restrictions in its 1973 annual report disclosed that:

The long-term loan agreements of certain subsidiary companies contain restrictions on the payment of dividends. Under the most restrictive of these, approximately $93,000,000 of consolidated retained earnings is not available for the payment of dividends to shareholders of Massey-Ferguson Limited. Of the remaining unrestricted $200,000,000, approximately $120,000,000 represents the company's equity in the unrestricted portion of profits of various subsidiaries and associate companies outside North America which have not been remitted to Canada. Transfers of earnings from companies outside North America are generally subject to the approval of Exchange Control Authorities, but permission to pay dividends is normally obtainable.

Voluntary Restrictions. Dividend restrictions may be imposed by a resolution of the board of directors as a formal expression of financial policy and the administration of retained earnings. For example, Great Western United Corporation in its 1972 annual report disclosed that:

> In October 1971 the Company's Board of Directors discontinued the payment of cash dividends on the common stock. In February 1972 the Board of Directors discontinued the payment of cash dividends on the $3.00 convertible serial preferred stock and also established a special purpose reserve of surplus in order to conserve working capital. With the establishment of the reserve, there was no surplus legally available for the payment of dividends. Payment of dividends on the $1.88 cumulative preferred stock is mandatory if there is surplus available, while the payment of dividends on the $3.00 convertible serial preferred stock and the common stock is within the discretion of the Board of Directors.

Disclosure of a voluntary retained earnings restriction is rare. This type was not classified in a study of retained earnings restrictions disclosed by 431 companies included in the 1974 *Accounting Trends and Techniques* survey of 600 companies.[25]

APPROPRIATIONS OF RETAINED EARNINGS

Nature. Appropriations of retained earnings are the result of an action taken by a company's board of directors to transfer a specific amount of retained earnings to a separate account. Appropriations are common in regulated industries such as banking (a portion of the "Reserve for Loan Losses") and insurance ("Mandatory Securities Valuation Reserve") but are otherwise rarely used.

Although accounting literature states that retained earnings appropriations may also be used to disclose the possibility of future losses, this practice is almost nonexistent. In a 1973 Financial Executives Institute survey of 64 companies,[26] none indicated that an appropriation account was used for future losses, although 35 companies indicated one or more accounts were used for this purpose. All but three of the 35 companies accumulated the future loss reserve through periodic charges to income, and all 35 classified the future loss reserve outside the equity section of the balance sheet.

Use of the Term "Reserve." In 1948 the Committee on Accounting Terminology of the AICPA recommended that in accounting practice the term "reserve" be limited:

> . . . to indicate that an undivided or unidentified portion of the net assets, in a stated amount, is being held or retained for a special purpose, as in the case of a reserve (a) for betterment or plant extensions, or (b) for excess cost of replacement of property, or (c) for possible future inventory losses, or (d) for general contingencies. In this sense a reserve is frequently referred to as an appropriation of retained income.

The Committee expressed the opinion that this usage conforms most closely to the commonly accepted meaning of the term. Deductions from accounts receivable

[25]Dick and Rikert, *op. cit.,* p. 207.

[26]*FASB Discussion Memorandum—An Analysis of Issues Related to Accounting for Future Losses,* Financial Accounting Standards Board, Stamford, Conn., 1974, pp. 75–89.

and fixed assets to reflect estimated loss in collection and accrued depreciation are merely a reflection of the accounting process of cost allocation and income determination. The use of the term "reserve" to describe a liability adds little to a direct statement of the obligation, which itself indicates that a portion of the assets will be required for its discharge. When the exact amount of the obligation is uncertain, it would be better to use such terms as "estimated," as, for example, "estimated federal income taxes payable."

RIGHTS TO RETAINED EARNINGS IN LIQUIDATION AND DISSOLUTION

Preferred shareholders may be entitled to payments in liquidation prior to common stockholders. Frequently, for example, the preferred stock's liquidation preference is considerably greater than par value, and this preference may be greater in voluntary liquidation than in involuntary liquidation. If the preferred stock is cumulative, it may also be entitled to receive unpaid dividends prior to any distribution to common shareholders. Participating preferred stock is sometimes entitled to share with common stock in the distribution of any remaining assets.

The existence of more than one class of common stock may also create certain preferences in liquidation. For example, the 1973 annual report of Hamilton Brothers Petroleum Corporation disclosed:

> Each share of common stock is entitled to dividends in an amount equal to four times that declared on each share of Class "A" Stock in each year (noncumulative) until $1.00 per share has been declared for each share of common stock; thereafter, each share of each class participates equally in additional dividends declared. Also, distributions in liquidation are to be apportioned in a four-to-one ratio to each share of common stock and Class "A" Stock until $20 has been distributed to each share of Common Stock. Thereafter, each share of each class participates equally in further distributions. Each share of each class has one vote per share on all matters except as provided by law.

In the absence of preferred stock or two-class common stock, however, each common shareholder has the right to receive, in liquidation, his proportionate share of corporate assets remaining after all corporate liabilities have been satisfied.

RETAINED EARNINGS—FINANCIAL STATEMENT DISCLOSURE

APB Opinion No. 12, issued in 1967, requires that:

> When both financial position and results of operations are presented, disclosure of changes in the separate accounts comprising stockholders' equity (in addition to retained earnings) and of the changes in the number of shares of equity securities during at least the most recent annual fiscal period and any subsequent interim period presented is required to make the financial statements sufficiently informative. Disclosure of such changes may take the form of separate statements or may be made in the basic financial statements or notes thereto.

Regulation S-X requires the following information to be disclosed in SEC filings:

> Other stockholders' equity.—
> (a) Separate captions shall be shown for (1) paid-in additional capital, (2) other additional capital and (3) retained earnings (i) appropriated and (ii) unappropriated.
> (b) If undistributed earnings of unconsolidated subsidiaries and 50 percent or less owned persons are included, state the amount in each category parenthetically or in a note referred to herein.
> (c) For a period of at least 10 years, subsequent to the effective date of a quasi-reorganization, any description of retained earnings shall indicate the point in time from

which the new retained earnings dates and for a period of at least three years shall indicate the total amount of the deficit eliminated.

(d) A summary of each account under this caption setting forth the information prescribed in Rule 11-02 shall be given for each period for which an income statement or summary of operations is being filed.

Preferred shares.—

(1) If callable, the date or dates and the amount per share at which such shares are callable shall be stated. If convertible, the terms of conversion shall be stated briefly.

(2) Arrears in cumulative dividends per share and in total for each class of shares shall be stated.

(3) Aggregate preferences on involuntary liquidation, if other than the par or stated value, shall be shown parenthetically in the equity section of the balance sheet. When the excess involved is material there shall be shown (i) the difference between the aggregate preference on involuntary liquidation and the aggregate par or stated value; (ii) a statement that this difference, plus any arrears in dividends, exceeds the sum of the par or stated value of the junior capital shares and other stockholders' equity applicable to junior shares, if such is the case; and (iii) a statement as to the existence of any restrictions upon retained earnings growing out of the fact that upon involuntary liquidation the preference of the preferred shares exceeds its par or stated value.

Rule 11-02 referred to above further requires that a summary be given for each class of other stockholders' equity in the balance sheet, including:

1. Balance at beginning of period.—State separately the adjustments to the balance at the beginning of the first period of the report for items which were retroactively applied to periods prior to that period.

2. Net income or loss from income statement.

3. Other additions.—State separately any material amounts, indicating clearly the nature of the transactions out of which the items arose.

4. Dividends.—For each class of shares state the amount per share and in the aggregate.

(a) Cash.

(b) Other.—Specify.

5. Other deductions.—State separately any material amounts, indicating clearly the nature of the transactions out of which the items arose.

6. Balance at end of period.—The balance at the end of the most recent period shall agree with the related balance sheet caption.

PRESENTATION OF RETAINED EARNINGS CHANGES

Annual surveys since 1968 by the AICPA[27] indicate a trend toward presentation of retained earnings changes in a separate statement:

	Number of Companies					
Type of presentation	1973	1972	1971	1970	1969	1968
Separate statement of retained earnings changes	408	396	386	370	370	352
Combined statement of income and retained earnings changes	185	199	209	227	227	245
Changes shown in balance sheet	7	5	5	3	3	3
Total companies	600	600	600	600	600	600

[27]Dick and Rikert, *op. cit.*, p. 323, and Woolsey Carmalt (ed.), *Accounting Trends and Techniques*, 26th ed., AICPA, New York, 1972, p. 267.

If the only changes in retained earnings are net income and dividends, and there are no changes in other stockholders' equity accounts, a combined statement of income and retained earnings would be the most efficient manner of presentation. If, however, there are several transactions affecting retained earnings and other stockholders' equity accounts, a separate statement summarizing all such changes is generally presented.

BIBLIOGRAPHY

Accounting Principles Board: "Accounting Changes," APB Opinion No. 20, AICPA, New York, 1971.
———: "Accounting for Nonmonetary Transactions," APB Opinion No. 29, AICPA, New York, 1973.
———: "Earnings per Share," APB Opinion No. 15, AICPA, New York, 1969.
———: "Equity Method of Accounting for Investments in Common Stock," APB Opinion No. 18, AICPA, New York, 1971.
———: "Omnibus Opinion—1967," APB Opinion No. 12, AICPA, New York, 1967.
———: "Reporting the Results of Operations," APB Opinion No. 9, AICPA, New York, 1966.
———: "Reporting the Results of Operations," APB Opinion No. 30, AICPA, New York, 1973.
———: "Status of Accounting Research Bulletins," APB Opinion No. 6, AICPA, New York, 1965.
American Institute of Certified Public Accountants: "Objectives of Financial Statements," Report of the Study Group on the Objectives of Financial Statements, AIA, New York, 1973.
American Institute of Certified Public Accountants, Committee on Bank Accounting and Auditing: Audits of Banks, AIA, New York, 1969.
American Institute of Certified Public Accountants, Committee on Terminology: "Review and Resume," Bulletin No. 1, AIA, New York, 1953.
American Institute of Certified Public Accountants, Committee on Accounting Procedure: "Consolidated Financial Statements," Accounting Research Bulletin No. 51, AICPA, New York, 1959.
———: "Restatement and Revision of Accounting Research Bulletins," Accounting Research Bulletin No. 43, AICPA, New York, 1953.
Carmalt, Woolsey, ed.: Accounting Trends and Techniques, 26th ed., AICPA, New York, 1972.
Copeland, Ronald, D. Larry Crumbley, and Joseph F. Wojdak: Advanced Accounting, Holt, Rinehart and Winston, New York, 1971.
Dick, George, and Richard Rikert, eds.: Accounting Trends and Techniques, 28th ed., AICPA, New York, 1974.
Financial Accounting Standards Board: FASB Discussion Memorandum—An Analysis of Issues Related to Accounting for Future Losses, Stamford, Conn., 1974.
Grady, Paul: "Inventory of Generally Accepted Accounting Principles for Business Enterprises," Accounting Research Study No. 7, AICPA, New York, 1965.
Griffin, Charles H., Thomas H. Williams, and Kermit D. Larson: Advanced Accounting, rev. ed., Richard D. Irwin, Homewood, Ill., 1971.
Hendriksen, Eldon S.: Accounting Theory, rev. ed., Richard D. Irwin, Homewood, Ill., 1970.
Johnson, Glenn L., and James A. Gentry, Jr.: Finney and Miller's Principles of Accounting, Intermediate, 7th ed., Prentice-Hall, Englewood Cliffs, N.J., 1974.
Kellogg, Howard, and Morton Palaway, Accountants SEC Practice Manual, Commerce Clearing House, Chicago, 1971.
Lembke, Valdean C.: "Some Considerations in Accounting for Divisive Reorganizations," The Accounting Review, July 1970.
Melcher, Beatrice: "Stockholders' Equity," Accounting Research Study No. 15, AICPA, New York, 1973.
Meyer, Philip E.: "Some Accounting Ramifications of Treasury Stock," The CPA Journal, November 1973.
Nemec, Marilyn J.: "Reporting in Consolidated Statements the Sale of a Subsidiary's Stock." The CPA Journal, March 1973.
Powell, Weldon: "Business Separations," The Journal of Accountancy, March 1957.

Rappaport, Louis H.: *SEC Accounting Practice and Procedure,* 3rd ed., The Ronald Press Company, New York, 1972.

Simons, Harry: *Intermediate Accounting,* 5th ed., South-Western Publishing Company, Cincinnati, 1972.

Sprouse, Robert T., and Maurice Moonitz: "A Tentative Set of Broad Accounting Principles for Business Enterprises," *Accounting Research Study No. 3,* AICPA, New York, 1962.

Welsch, Glenn A., Charles T. Zlatkovich, and John A. White: *Intermediate Accounting,* 3rd ed., Richard D. Irwin, Homewood, Ill., 1972.

Chapter **30**

Earnings per Share

FRANK T. WESTON

INTRODUCTION

As indicated in Chapters 2 and 3, the format for reporting financial data by business corporations emphasizes three basic statements. One of these, the balance sheet or statement of financial condition, shows the financial position of the entity at a particular date. Another, the statement of income—either separately or combined with a statement of retained earnings—shows the results of operations of the entity for one or more periods. In recent years, primarily because of the interest of users of financial statements in comparing investment opportunities among various corporations, a technique has been developed which combines certain elements of these two basic financial statements into a single statistic—the earnings per share of common stock. As a result of the increasing investor interest in corporate securities, this statistic has become one of considerable importance not only to the investor, but also to the management of business corporations and to the independent public accountants whose reports accompany the financial statements of business entities.

PURPOSE AND LIMITATIONS OF THE EARNINGS PER SHARE STATISTIC

The purpose of the computation of the earnings per share statistic may be defined as the attribution of the earnings of an entity for a period to the various elements of its capitalization structure, based on their relative legal or economic relationships, preferences, and privileges. The computation is thus prepared from the information contained in two of the basic financial statements. In addition, the computation also reflects any significant changes which may have taken place in the capitalization structure during the period for which the earnings per share data are being presented.

Uses of Earnings per Share.   The earnings per share statistic is a handy tool to use in comparing the operating results of business entities, either the same entity over one or more periods of time, or two or more entities. For an entity with a simple capitalization structure, that is, common stock only, the earnings per share statistic reduces the two component variables, the capitalization of the entity and the net income for the period, into a single figure. The figure so computed may be compared with prior estimates of the earnings per share for the period and also with forecasts of earnings per share, similarly computed for future periods. When the earnings per share statistics for two or more periods for such an entity are compared, the effects of the two variables are combined so that a meaningful comparison can be made. Thus, if there is no change in the capitalization structure between the two periods, the statistic shows the relative changes in the net income of the entity. If there are changes in the capitalization structure during the periods, the per share data will effectively reflect the changes and produce a figure of net income per common share which is a meaningful measure of the results of the period in terms of the outstanding shares. Thus, the earnings per share computation is a valuable device for reducing complex accounting information to a simple statistic.

The resulting figure of earnings per share for an entity can be compared with dividends paid for one or more periods. This comparison gives meaningful information as to the proportion of net income which is paid to stockholders in the form of dividends and the proportion which is retained for corporate use.

A further use of the earnings per share statistic is in the evaluation of the shares outstanding. This is usually done by means of price-earnings ratios, which have been developed by analysts as a means of determining the value of a share of common stock based on the general conditions of the industry and the future prospects of the entity in particular.

Limitations of Earnings per Share. While the earnings per share statistic is a useful tool in the case of a corporation with a simple capital structure, it does have its drawbacks, even in such a case. For example, the simple statistic of earnings per share does not disclose significant changes in the nature of the business. Thus, if a company were to shift from manufacturing a product for sale to leasing the product to its customers, the net earnings per common share might not change between years but the nature of the business and the risks involved would have changed considerably. Similarly, while "extraordinary items" included in the net income for a period are separately reflected in the earnings per share statistics, any unusual items which might significantly affect the amount of net income for the period but which would not qualify for separate disclosure in the earnings per share data as extraordinary items (or as discontinued operations, as discussed in a later section) would not be separately disclosed by the simple earnings per share statistic. In similar vein, significant changes in operating ratios, such as the gross profit percentage or the relationship of administrative expenses to operating profit, would not be disclosed in the per-share statistic.

If all or a portion of the annual net income is retained for corporate use, the investment per share increases accordingly. Under these conditions, an increase in the amount of earnings per share from year to year may reflect merely the same (unchanged) rate of earnings on a greater investment, rather than an apparent improvement in performance levels, or a rate of growth greater than the real rate after adjustment for the increased investment.

Also, changes in the composition of the capitalization structure would not be disclosed by the earnings per share data. While the computations themselves would reflect such changes, the per-share statistic standing alone would not inform the reader as to the substance of the underlying changes, which might significantly affect the status of security holders.

Investors using the per-share statistic should also appreciate that there are various other shortcomings to the data in addition to those of a purely mechanical nature outlined above. For example, the per-share amount usually does not represent the amount available for dividends to the common stockholder. Neither does an increase in the amount of earnings per share from one period to the next indicate that a similar increase in dividends should be expected or is warranted. Furthermore, since the statistic reflects, as indicated above, a combination of financial data of great variety, all of which are themselves subject to estimates and uncertainties as to future developments, the resulting earnings per share statistic carries no more assurance as to future certainty than do the underlying earnings themselves. In addition, when a corporation has a complex capitalization, there is no assurance that an increase or decrease in the absolute amount of earnings in the future will necessarily result in a proportionate increase or decrease in the earnings per common share. Finally, the investor must appreciate that an increase in the amount of earnings per share will not necessarily result in a corresponding increase in the market value of the common stock. A great many other factors also influence that value.

Thus, while the earnings per share statistic has the appearance of being a simple, informative, all-inclusive tool for investment analysis and decision, its very simplicity may be deceptive. Accordingly, experienced investors rarely, if ever, use the statistic standing alone; they combine its use with a careful review of the basic financial statements—the balance sheet, the statement of income, and the statement of changes in financial position—in making a realistic evaluation of the financial accounting aspects of the investment opportunities involved.

The Problem of Complex Capitalization Structures. The above discussion as to the purpose and limitations of the earnings per share statistic has approached the subject in terms of a simple capitalization structure consisting only of common stock. When securities other than common stock are outstanding, for example when there are preferred shares or when convertible securities or options and warrants are outstanding, the computation becomes more complex. Some of the complexities involved are discussed below.

METHODS OF COMPUTATION

In view of the increasing interest in investments in corporate equity securities and the increasing use of the earnings per share statistic in making investment decisions, it is essential that computations of earnings per share be made on a consistent basis for all corporations. Accordingly, guidelines have been developed for the computation and reporting of such data. The authoritative source of such guidelines for the public accounting profession is Opinion No. 15 of the Accounting Principles Board of the American Institute of Certified Public Accountants, issued in 1969. The methods of computation, ranging from the simple situations to those involving very complex securities, have as their purpose a meaningful and consistent attribution of the earnings of the entity for a period to the various elements of its capitalization structure.

Common Stock Capitalization. When only common stock is outstanding, the computation of earnings per share is simply a matter of dividing the net income by the shares outstanding during the period. However, since the number of shares outstanding may fluctuate during the period—as the result of issuance of shares for cash or other considerations, or as the result of the acquisition of shares for the treasury or for retirement—an averaging technique should be used to reflect properly the portions of the year during which the shares were outstanding. Thus, if a corporation sold significant amounts of common stock halfway through the accounting period, these shares should be reflected in the computation of earnings per share only for the period during which they were outstanding. In this case, assuming no other issuances or retirements during the period, the number of shares to be reflected in the computation would be those outstanding at the beginning of the period, weighted for the entire period, plus those outstanding for half the period weighted for that period. Thus, if 1 million shares were outstanding at the beginning of the period and 400,000 shares were issued halfway through the period for cash, the number of shares to be used in computing earnings per share for the period would be 1.2 million shares. As indicated, the weighting is based on the respective time periods involved. A similar technique would be used in case significant amounts of common shares were acquired for the treasury or for retirement during the period. This weighting technique is also used when common shares are issued on conversion of other securities or upon the exercise of options and warrants.

In applying these techniques in simple capital structure situations, care must be exercised to reflect the substance of the changes in the capital structure and not merely the form. Accordingly, certain exceptions are required to the general rule that issuance or reductions in outstanding common shares are weighted based on the time of occurrence. Two relatively simple exceptions are the issuance of additional shares in stock splits or the reduction of outstanding shares through reverse stock splits, and the issuance of shares in stock dividend transactions. In these cases, there are no proceeds or other considerations involved; there is merely a change in the aggregate number of shares outstanding without any change in the aggregate amount of capitalization. Therefore, increases and decreases of this nature in the common shares outstanding are reflected for the entire period involved. This is seen to be logical in, for example, the case of a 2 for 1 stock split occurring at the middle of the accounting period. The capitalization structure at the end of the period consists of double the number of shares outstanding at the beginning of the period. However, investors reviewing financial data, including earnings per share statistics, should be given information expressed in terms of the present capitalization structure, and the income for the entire period should be related to the present structure, since nothing of economic significance has happened in terms of the aggregate amount of investment available to the corporation to generate earnings. Therefore, changes in the common stock outstanding as a result of this type of transaction are reflected for the entire period, without weighting. Earnings per share data for all prior periods presented should be similarly adjusted, retroactively.

Poolings of Interests.   Another exception to the use of time periods for weighting common shares outstanding exists in the treatment of shares issued during a period in a business combination accounted for as a pooling of interests. In this case, in accordance with the pooling-of-interests concept that the corporations are considered to have been retroactively combined for a number of periods, the common shares issued in the business combination are likewise considered to have been issued at the beginning of the earliest period being reported on. In determining the number of common shares to be included for the current and prior periods, appropriate recognition should be given not only to the exchange ratio involved in the business combination but also to any significant changes in the outstanding common or other shares of the acquired company whose securities are being exchanged for the common stock of the surviving company.

Reflecting the Effects of Subsequent Events.   As is true in the reporting of other significant financial information, it is customary to make additional disclosures affecting earnings per share data whenever subsequent events indicate that the information otherwise reported might possibly be subject to misinterpretation or might be inaccurate in terms of current conditions. For example, if significant conversions of securities into common stock occur after the close of the period but before completion of the financial report, it is customary to furnish supplementary disclosure of the earnings per share for the period expressed in terms of the revised capitalization structure, as if the conversions had occurred at the beginning of the period. Thus, while the historical earnings per share would be based on the capitalization during the period, the more meaningful information for investors using the financial data subsequent to the date of its issuance would be the earnings per share expressed in terms of the then-current capitalization structure.

On the other hand, when changes in common shares outstanding occur as a result of stock splits or reverse splits or stock dividends after the close of the period but before completion of the financial report, it is customary to restate the earnings per share data for all periods to reflect such changes. When the historical earnings per share are restated for such changes, the financial statements should contain appropriate disclosure.

Complex Capitalization Structure—Preferred Stock.   When securities other than common stock are outstanding, the computation and reporting of the earnings per share data become more complicated. If the additional security is a preferred stock, the computation of earnings per share of common stock reflects the deduction of the amount of earnings attributable to the senior security based on its contractual terms. Thus, if the preferred stock is cumulative, the dividend requirements for the period are deducted from net income in order to determine the balance of earnings attributable to the common shares. If the dividends on preferred stock are not cumulative, then only the amount declared during the period is deducted from net income. When the number of preferred shares outstanding during the period changes because of retirements, conversion, or issuances of additional preferred shares, appropriate recognition should be given to the claims of the preferred shareholders against the earnings in accordance with the provisions of the security.

Since the usual senior preferred stock has a claim on the earnings of the entity of a fixed amount, any attribution of earnings to such a security in excess of the amount to which it is entitled under its terms would be inappropriate. Accordingly, it is not considered proper to report earnings per share for senior preferred stock by dividing net income by the number of preferred shares outstanding. Since investors in such securities are often interested in the number of times or the extent to which the dividend requirements have been met, it is satisfactory to divide the net income by the total annual dividend requirements for such stock and express the result in terms of the number of times the dividend requirements are "covered." This statistic is quite different from earnings per share, and any disclosures of this type should therefore avoid use of the latter term and should be clearly expressed to avoid possible confusion.

Potential Dilution.   Many capitalization structures are more complex in that they contain securities other than common stock and senior preferred stock. Securities such as convertible preferred stock, convertible debt, options, and warrants are not unusual. Furthermore, agreements may exist for the issuance of additional shares of common stock based on the fulfillment of certain conditions in the future. While the common shares issuable under the terms of these securities and agreements are not outstanding at the present time, it is essential that the investor or potential investor be informed as to the potential impact which issuance of additional common shares under the terms of these securities would have on earnings per share. Any reduction in earnings per share which such issuances would cause is called "dilution."

A number of problems exist with respect to the computation and disclosure of the potential dilution which exists as a result of the existence of such securities and agreements. In order to have a meaningful base against which to measure the extent of the potential dilution, it is customary to compute the dilution in terms of the current level of earnings. This approach permits a comparison of the historical earnings per share for the current period with the potentially diluted earnings per share assuming conversion, exercise, or issuance of the additional securities involved for the same period. However, because of the number of variables involved, it would be a rare case in which the computed dilution—measured by the difference between the historical earnings per share and the potentially diluted earnings per share at the current earnings level—would in fact result at any other level of earnings. For this reason, the disclosure of potential dilution based on the current earnings level is sometimes criticized as being unrealistic. However, use of data based on the current earnings level does clearly disclose an absolute measure of potential dilution, expressed in close relationship to the current earnings per share—the statistic in which the investor currently has considerable interest.

Critics of the disclosure of dilution in these absolute terms claim that the level of net income would have to be considerably higher before the holders of convertible securities, options, etc., would exchange their securities for common shares; under these conditions, therefore, the earnings per share on a fully diluted basis would still be higher than the historical earnings per common share previously reported. However, this line of reasoning overlooks the fact that, had the convertible securities not been outstanding and had the common shares not been issued thereunder, the earnings per share would have increased proportionately with the increase in the earnings applicable to the common shares. Dilution would in fact result from the issuance of the shares.

Another method of disclosure of potential dilution has been suggested—the expression of the potential dilution in terms of a percentage of the historical or primary earnings per share. This method appears to have several disadvantages, however. In the first place, an expression of dilution as a percentage of the primary figure would probably be more confusing to the average investor than disclosure of a second per-share figure from which the absolute potential dilution could readily be computed. Furthermore, use of a percentage might imply that this same percentage of dilution would result at different earnings levels. As indicated above, this would seldom be true.

While the thrust of the disclosure of potential dilution is protection of the investor or the potential investor, questions are raised as to whether the effect of the issuance of additional shares should not be disclosed in the financial statements, regardless of whether the effect on earnings per share is dilutive or incremental. However, present practice concentrates on the potentially adverse effects of such contingencies and, due in large part to the position taken on this matter by regulatory agencies, incremental effects due to conversions and other potential issuances are seldom disclosed.

Convertible Preferred Stock. The method of computing the potential dilution varies, depending on the type of security involved. In the case of convertible preferred stock, an assumption is made that the shares were converted at the beginning of the period. In making the computation, therefore, the preferred dividend requirements on these preferred shares are disregarded. The equivalent common shares into which the preferred shares are convertible are added to the common shares outstanding for the period, and the total is divided into the amount of net income. If the resulting amount of earnings per share is less than the earnings per share computed on the historical basis, disclosure of the "fully diluted" or "if converted" amount is required.

Since, as indicated above, the thrust of the disclosure of potential dilution in earnings per share is to the future, the fact that the conversion ratio of the preferred stock into common stock might be at a level which would make conversion during the current period unlikely is not considered relevant.

Convertible Debt. In case the security involving the additional issuance of common stock is a convertible debt issue, a similar assumption of conversion at the beginning of the period is made. In this case, however, the interest expense on the debt, less any applicable income tax effect, is added to net income for the period. This adjusted amount is then divided by the sum of the average number of common shares outstanding and the number of common shares assumed to have been issued in conversion of the debt. If the resulting amount of earnings per share is less than that computed on the historical basis, disclosure of the fully diluted amount is required.

Options and Warrants. If the additional common shares which are contingently issuable relate to outstanding options or warrants, a somewhat similar computation of potential dilution is made. In this case, the options and warrants are assumed to have been exercised at the beginning of the period. Since, with these securities, the assumption of exercise generates assumed proceeds to the entity, some further assumption must be made as to the use to which the proceeds are put. A number of assumptions could be made—the acquisition of shares of the company for its treasury, the investment of the assumed proceeds in investment-grade securities, or the use of the proceeds to retire outstanding debt. The method which is currently required is that which assumes that the proceeds are used for the purchase of shares for the treasury.[1] Under this computation, the assumed proceeds are considered to have been used to purchase shares at the market price of the shares at the close of the period. Any excess of the number of shares assumed to be issued upon exercise over those assumed to have been so purchased is included in the number of shares considered to be outstanding for the entire period (or from date of issuance of the options or warrants if issued during the period) in the computation of fully diluted earnings per share. Because of the

---

[1]See Accounting Principles Board, "Earnings per Share," APB Opinion No. 15, AICPA, New York, 1969, par. 42 and 36.

method of computation, whenever the market price per share of the stock is less than the exercise price per share under the options and warrants, expressed in equivalent shares, the assumed purchase would result in the acquisition of more shares than would be issued. Since this effect would not be dilutive, disclosure is not made. Thus, under this method there is dilution only when the market price is greater than the exercise price; the amount of the computed dilution increases proportionately as the market price rises above the exercise price.

When the number of shares subject to options and warrants is substantial in relation to the common shares outstanding, the use of the "treasury stock method" described above is limited to the purchase of shares equal to 20 percent of the common shares outstanding at the end of the period.[2] This approach recognizes that it may be unrealistic to assume that a corporation could purchase a significant number of shares at the current market price. Accordingly, when the shares obtainable under options and warrants are in excess of 20 percent of the outstanding common shares at the end of the period, the proceeds from the assumed exercise of all the options and warrants are applied first to purchase up to 20 percent of the number of outstanding common shares, at the market price at the close of the period. Any excess of proceeds is then applied first to reduce any outstanding debt and then to invest in U.S. government securities or commercial paper. In the latter cases, net income is adjusted for the reduction of interest expense, less any income tax effect, or for the increase in investment income, less any income tax effect. The effects of these computations are aggregated and, if such effect is dilutive, it is reflected in the fully diluted computation. If the effect is not dilutive, it is not reflected in the fully diluted computation.

Other Contingent Issuances.   When the potential dilution relates to agreements to issue additional shares, similar pro forma computations are made giving effect to the assumed issuance of the shares. If the condition of issuance is an increased level of earnings, the possibility of dilution is computed by assuming an increase in earnings to the specified level and including in the outstanding common shares the number of shares issuable at that level. If the amount so computed is less than the historical earnings per share, disclosure of the dilution is required.

In some cases, the issuance of additional shares is dependent on the market value of the common stock at some future date. Computations of earnings per share data should be based on the number of shares issuable based on the market price at the close of the period. No further assumptions are warranted.

A number of other circumstances may exist in which additional shares may be issued or in which the number of shares to be issued may increase or decrease upon the nappening of certain events. Thus, securities may be convertible into common stock at increasing or decreasing rates, or the right of conversion may be postponed or terminated. The computations of potential dilution and the presentation of fully diluted earnings per share data under these circumstances generally reflect the most advantageous (from the point of view of the holder of the security) conversion ratio to be in effect during the succeeding ten years. The latter approach is based on the assumption that the average investor is not significantly influenced by conditions which may exist more than ten years in the future.

See "Antidilutive Effects" below for further problems in computing dilution.

COMMON STOCK EQUIVALENTS

Occasionally, a capitalization structure contains securities which are considered to be the substantial equivalent of common stock. These securities are designated as "common stock equivalents."

---

[2]*Ibid.*, par. 42 and 38.

The concept that a security other than common stock should be considered the equivalent of common stock for purposes of the computation of earnings per share developed as a result of the issuance of increasingly complex securities containing characteristics of both senior securities and common stock. As indicated previously, the computation of earnings per share data attributes the earnings of an entity for a period to the various elements of its capitalization structure, based on their relative legal or economic relationships, preferences, and privileges. In making this attribution, it is generally recognized that the substance, rather than the form, of the various elements of the capitalization structure should govern. Accordingly, it is often necessary, in the computation of earnings per share, to reflect certain securities, which are considered to be in substance the equivalent of common shares, as common shares. In evaluating the characteristics of a security which may indicate that it is a common stock equivalent, particular attention must be paid to those terms which give the holder of the security the right to become a common stockholder. Thus, the conversion privilege in a convertible preferred stock or a convertible debt, and the purchase option in the case of options and warrants, may indicate that the security involved is in fact the substantial equivalent of a common stock. The application of this concept to various types of security is discussed below.

Convertible Preferred Stock and Convertible Debt. Various methods have been suggested to determine whether a particular converible security is a common stock equivalent. These are generally based on a comparison of the estimated value of the "senior security" characteristics of the security—primarily its fixed yield in terms of interest or dividends—and the market value of the security. In the case of a security which is convertible into common stock, the market value of the security may be based to a significant extent on the option to convert into common stock. For example, if a convertible preferred stock of $100 par value carries a fixed dividend rate of 4 percent based on its par, it would have an investment value as a senior security of approximately $57, based on an assumed required yield of 7 percent and disregarding the conversion feature. If this stock were convertible into, say, two shares of common stock and if the common stock had a market value of approximately $50 per share, the convertible preferred stock might well have a market value of slightly more than $100 per share—approximately 180 percent of its investment value. The yield would be 4 percent on its market value. In such a situation, the question at issue is whether the convertible preferred stock derives such a substantial portion of its value from its common stock characteristics, as distinguished from its senior security characteristics, that it should be considered as a common stock equivalent in computing earnings per share.

If, in the above example, the market value of the common stock were to be $65 per share, then the market value of the convertible preferred stock would be approximately $135 to $140 per share—approximately 240 percent of its investment value. Under these conditions, it would be quite evident that the security was being traded on the basis of its convertibility into common stock and that the fixed dividend yield—2.9 percent on market value—was of considerably less importance. Since the marketplace evaluates the stock in terms of its common stock convertibility and thus looks in a very significant way to the right of the preferred stockholder to share in the value potential of the common stock, it appears logical that any attribution of earnings of the corporation to the various securities outstanding should also give recognition to this fact. Stated another way, if 1 million shares of common stock are outstanding, along with 200,000 shares of the convertible preferred stock described above, it is clear that the marketplace evaluates the common shares and the preferred shares as the equivalent of 1.4 million common shares. If this is so, then the earnings should be attributed to the aggregate equivalent shares. Under these conditions, to attribute all the earnings of the company to the 1 million shares of common stock would result in a material overstatement of the earnings per share and a disregard of the economic substance of the provisions of the preferred stock. This is the basis of the concept of common stock equivalents.

Time of Determination. In the application of the above concept, a question arises as to whether the determination of the nature of a convertible security and thus its treatment in the computation of earnings per share should be based on an evaluation of the security's characteristics at the time of its issuance and only then, or whether effect should be given to changes in the relative values of the characteristics at regular, subsequent intervals. Views differ as to which of these approaches results in more meaningful and useful earnings per share data for investors.

While there are arguments in support of each side of this particular question, the preponderant view presently requires the determination of the status of a convertible security as a common stock equivalent only at the time of issuance of the security.[3] In other words, subsequent market value changes do not affect the classification of the security as a common stock equivalent for the purpose of computing earnings per share.

In the view of many accountants, the determination of the status of a convertible security as a common stock equivalent only at the date of its issuance does not result in the most meaningful and useful presentation of the earnings per share statistic. For example, if the market value of the common stock involved were to increase substantially following issuance of a convertible security, it might well be that the marketplace would evaluate the convertible security as the substantial equivalent of common stock. Many convertible securities are designed for this purpose—that is, their nature changes as the underlying common stock increases or decreases in value. It is considered unrealistic to disregard these obvious economic factors in a computation which purports to attribute the earnings of a corporation to the elements of its capitalization structure based on a meaningful evaluation of their characteristics. Such a current attribution should, in the view of these accountants, be based on present circumstances, and not on those existing at the date of issuance, possibly years previously.

Method of Determination. As indicated above, the methods suggested to determine whether a particular convertible security is a common stock equivalent are generally based on a comparison of the estimated value of its senior security characteristics—its investment value—and its market value. In these determinations there are three variables—the cash yield in interest or dividends, the capitalization factor for the security (based on current conditions of the risk involved and the cost of money) which, when applied to the cash yield, determines the investment value, and the overall market value of the security. As shown in the examples above, the market value of the convertible security is often directly affected or based to a substantial degree on the value of the underlying common stock into which it is convertible.

Given the yield, the capitalization factor, and the overall market value of the security in question, a judgment must be made as to the point at which the common stock characteristics are reflected in the value of the security to such an extent that the security is the substantial equivalent of a common share for purposes of attributing earnings. (It is important to note that common stock equivalency is a notion closely related to economic and market factors related to investment in equity securities in a going concern. It is not based on, and may even be in conflict with, legal relationships or liquidation preferences.) Of the various methods proposed, one which received widespread use was expressed in terms of the relationship of the market value of the security to its investment value. Thus,

[3]*Ibid.,* par. 28.

whenever the market value of the convertible security was 200 percent or more of its investment value, the security was considered a common stock equivalent. In the example cited, when the market value of the common was $50 per share, the convertible preferred stock would not be considered a common stock equivalent since its market value was only 180 percent of its investment value. When the market value was $65 per share, the convertible preferred stock would be considered a common stock equivalent since its market value was in excess of 200 percent of its estimated investment value.

As is evident from the above, the determination of the point at which a convertible security should be considered a common stock equivalent is largely a matter of judgment and convention. If the determination were to be made on a continuing basis, it would doubtless be advisable to establish uniform limits for the initial qualification of a common stock equivalent and for the reversal of this classification. Such limits should be far enough apart so that there would not be a continual shifting of classification based on minor fluctuations in market values. Ranges of 150 to 200 percent for initial qualification and 100 percent for subsequent reversal have been proposed.

One of the disadvantages of the method outlined above is that it requires a determination of investment value for each convertible security. It is often difficult to determine the investment values of such securities since this requires an estimate of the risk and money cost factors, which vary from company to company and from year to year. For this reason, this method, while doubtless theoretically superior, has not been widely supported.

The accepted method at present for the determination of the status of a convertible security is based on the same general approach, but it utilizes the same capitalization factor for all companies at any particular time of issuance. This is done by using the current bank prime interest rate as a bench mark. Thus, this method compares the yield of a convertible security, expressed as a percentage of its market value at date of issuance, with the then-current bank prime interest rate. If the yield is less than 66⅔ percent of the bank prime interest rate, the convertible security is considered a common stock equivalent at the date of its issuance and forever thereafter.[4]

Using the examples given above and assuming that the bank prime interest rate at date of issuance was 7.5 percent, the convertible preferred stock with a market value of $104 would be a common stock equivalent, since its yield of 4 percent on its market value would be less than two-thirds of the bank prime interest rate of 7.5 percent, or 5 percent. Disregarding the difference between the 7 percent capitalization factor used above and the assumed 7.5 percent bank prime rate, it is clear that this method gives basically the same results as the investment value/market value method at the 150 percent level.

This method has the advantages of simplicity and of consistency of application among companies. However, it disregards risk differentials between companies. Accordingly, it does not effectively differentiate between the securities of a high-risk issuer and those of a low-risk issuer. It also assumes a direct correlation between the bank prime interest rate and yield rates on long-term borrowings and on preferred stocks, which is not necessarily realistic.

Options, Warrants, and Other Securities.   Securities other than convertible preferred stocks and convertible debt may also merit classification as common stock equivalents. The most common such securities are options and warrants to purchase common stock. Since these securities generally have no yield, their entire value is derived from the right to obtain common stock and they thus clearly are common stock equivalents in the marketplace. Certain problems arise, however, in

[4]*Ibid.,* par. 33.

determining the *number* of common shares to be reflected in the computation of historical earnings per share under these conditions. (This problem is different from that arising in the computation of potential dilution under outstanding options and warrants since the latter computation is a *pro forma* one which assumes the exercise of these securities at the beginning of the accounting period and permits some assumptions as to the *pro forma* use of proceeds for the period. See the section on "Potential Dilution—Options and Warrants" above.)

One method of determining the number of shares of common stock represented by outstanding options and warrants is based on the relationship of the value of the option or warrant to the market value of the common stock. Thus, if a company has 100,000 warrants outstanding enabling the holders to acquire 100,-000 shares of common stock at $40 per share, and if the market value of the common stock is $50 per share, the value of each warrant might be approximately $22. The percentage relationship of the market value of the warrant to the market value of the common stock—44 percent ($22 divided by $50)—would then be applied to the total shares obtainable by the warrant holders (100,000) to determine the number of equivalent common shares, 44,000, to be included in the denominator in the computation of historical earnings per share.

This method is similar in concept to the investment value/market value method of determining the common stock equivalent status of convertible securities described previously, since it is based on the evaluation of security characteristics in the current marketplace. Its primary disadvantage is that a value must be established for each option or warrant for purposes of the calculation. As compared to the methods described below, it has significant appeal since it does not require any adjustment of historical earnings or any assumed attribution of earnings on the assumed proceeds from exercise.

A number of other methods exist for the computation of historical earnings per share when options and warrants are considered to be common stock equivalents. Most of these are similar to those discussed under the potential dilution of options and warrants in an earlier section. Their principal weaknesses are that they require adjustments of historical earnings or unrealistic assumptions as to the use of proceeds, which are considered by many accountants to be unsatisfactory in the computation of historical earnings per share.

The method which is generally accepted at present is the treasury stock method.[5] When it is used for the computation of historical earnings per share, the proceeds of exercise are assumed to have been used to purchase common stock at the *average* market price during the period. (For the fully diluted computation, the market price at the close of the period is used if it is higher than the average price.) The limitation on the use of the treasury stock method when the shares obtainable under options and warrants exceed 20 percent of the outstanding common shares also applies in the historical computation. Under this method, there is no effect on historical earnings per share unless the exercise price of the option or warrant is less than the average market price of the common stock.

In addition to the securities discussed above, other complex securities may also qualify as common stock equivalents. Certain participating securities, two-class common stocks, and other securities which derive significant portions of their value from their common stock characteristics might require such treatment. In all these cases, it is necessary to evaluate the various preferences and privileges provided by the terms of the security and to reflect the substance of the situation in accordance with the overall concepts governing the computation of earnings per share.

Occasionally, special circumstances exist which require that earnings per share be computed using one of several complex methods. A relatively common exam-

[5]*Ibid.*, par. 36.

ple is the computation for real estate investment trusts when options or warrants are outstanding. In this case, the "two-class" method is used. This method first attributes to each type of outstanding security any distribution made to its holders; then the balance of undistributed income is allocated to all the common shares and common stock equivalents outstanding. The per-share distribution on the common stock is then added to the undistributed income per share to obtain the earnings per common share. Thus, consider a real estate investment trust with 1 million shares of common stock, with a market price of $30 per share, outstanding, as well as warrants to purchase 200,000 shares of common stock at $10 per share, and with earnings of $2,000,000, of which 90% or $1,800,000 was distributed to shareholders to qualify under the Internal Revenue Code and thus to avoid taxation. Its primary or basic earnings per share would be $1.98, computed by (1) dividing the distributed earnings ($1,800,000) by the number of common shares receiving the distribution (1,000,000) to obtain $1.80 per share, (2) dividing the undistributed earnings ($200,000) by the total number of common shares and common stock equivalents outstanding (1,133,333) to obtain $.18 per share, and (3) adding the amounts so computed. (The number of common stock equivalent shares is computed by using the treasury stock method described above. With a market price of $30 per share, the assumed proceeds from assumed exercise of the warrants ($2,000,000) are applied to acquire treasury shares (66,667 shares), with the balance (133,333) of the issued shares considered to be outstanding.) Use of the "two-class" method avoids attributing to one class of security (the warrants) earnings which have already been distributed to another class of security (the common stock). In this case, the fully diluted earnings per share would be $1.76—the earnings ($2,000,000) divided by the total number of common shares and common stock equivalents outstanding (1,133,333).

Antidilutive Effects. In the application of the concept of common stock equivalents, certain overriding limitations have also been applied. Thus, if the effect on earnings per share as otherwise computed of considering a security as a common stock equivalent resulted in an increased amount of earnings per share, that is, an antidilutive or incremental effect, the common stock equivalent would not be reflected in the computation of historical or primary earnings per share. This is consistent with the present approach to the computation and disclosure of potential dilution discussed in a preceding section. However, under this approach, a security which is deemed to be a common stock equivalent may enter into the computation of historical earnings per share in one period but not in another, due entirely to its effect on the computed amount.

An interesting computational problem arises when the capitalization structure contains a number of convertible securities whose effects on either primary or fully diluted earnings per share must be tested to determine whether they are individually dilutive or antidilutive. The problem is to determine the order in which the computations reflecting assumed conversion should be made. It is generally accepted that the amounts reported as primary and fully diluted earnings per share should reflect the *maximum* dilution or potential dilution and therefore should exclude any securities whose effect would be to increase per share amounts otherwise computed. The accepted method of determining the proper sequence for the computations is to rank the per-share effect of the conversion of each security in terms of one common share, and then to make successive cumulative computations, starting with the most dilutive issue, until all securities are included or until one security has an antidilutive or incremental effect on earnings per share. At that point, that security is excluded and the prior cumulative amount reflects the maximum dilution.[6]

[6]Davidson, Sidney, and Roman L. Weil, "A Short-Cut in Computing Earnings Per Share," *Journal of Accountancy,* December 1975, pp. 45–47.

Recognition of Common Stock Equivalents in the Financial Statements. The concept of common stock equivalents outlined above has been applied to date only in the computation of earnings per share. Questions arise as to whether, if certain securities are the substantial equivalent of common stock, the basic financial statements should not also give recognition to this and classify these securities along with common stock as an element of stockholders' equity. While a consistent application of the concept would seem to require such treatment, it is not as yet generally accepted. The major change in present practice required by the recognition of common stock equivalents in the basic financial statements would be the classification of convertible debt which is a common stock equivalent in association with stockholders' equity, either as a separate caption or as a clearly defined element. The corollary to this treatment would be the classification of the interest paid on such convertible debt as a distribution to holders of common stock equivalents, which would mean that it would not be deducted from net income but would be shown with other distributions in the statement of retained earnings. Such proposed classifications raise important questions of a legal as well as an accounting nature and may well create further problems from the point of view of regulatory agencies, including the income tax authorities.

DISCLOSURE OF EARNINGS PER SHARE DATA

As the interests of investors and others in financial statement presentations, and particularly in the reporting of earnings per share data, have increased, disclosure practices have developed to such an extent that there are certain generally accepted patterns of disclosure of data related to this type of information.

It is now generally accepted that the amount of earnings per share should be disclosed on the face of the statement of income.[7] In case there are any outstanding securities or agreements which could cause potential dilution, it is generally accepted that the fully diluted earnings per share should also be shown on the face of the statement of income.[8] It is further expected that there be adequate disclosure of the bases of the various computations involved, and a description of the terms and characteristics which cause certain securities to be considered common stock equivalents in these computations. Furthermore, the financial statements should contain a description of the pertinent preferences and privileges of the various securities outstanding, including such information as conversion rates, liquidation preferences, participation rights, and sinking fund requirements. In certain complicated cases, schedules or reconciliations of the data and methods used in the computations should be provided.

If a company has an investment in another company which is accounted for by consolidation or by use of the equity method of accounting and if the latter company has outstanding securities which are convertible or which are common stock equivalents, certain adjustments may be necessary in computing earnings per share data for the parent company.[9] If material, these adjustments should be disclosed.

If extraordinary items are present, earnings per share data with and without inclusion of the extraordinary items should be disclosed. Similarly, if the income statement segregates income from continuing operations from the results of discontinued operations, earnings per share data for income from continuing operations and for net income should be presented on the face of the income

---

[7]See Accounting Principles Board, "Earnings per Share," APB Opinion No. 15, AICPA, New York, 1969, par. 12.

[8]*Ibid.*, par. 15.

[9]*Ibid.*, par. 65–69.

statement.[10] If the income statement includes a caption and an amount for the cumulative effect of an accounting change, the per-share amount of the change should also be shown on the face of the statement of income.[11]

As explained above, certain supplementary per-share data should also be furnished if subsequent events tend to diminish the relevance of the historical data.

CONCLUSION

The increasing emphasis placed on the computation and presentation of earnings per share data is an indication of the dynamic nature of the accounting and reporting process. As a need appears for information derived from financial accounting data, disclosure is provided and related computational guidelines are developed, which become generally accepted. While some accountants believe that the criteria for the computation of earnings per share data are not matters of accounting principle, many other accountants feel that since these data are based on elements of the financial statements and since it is obviously essential that all corporations follow the same general guidelines in the computations, accounting principles should include guidelines for the preparation of this important business statistic.

While it is agreed that the earnings per share statistic does have value, it is essential that all users bear in mind that these data do have many limitations. The careful investor will become fully informed as to the limitations and shortcomings of the earnings per share statistic before he uses it in his investment decisions. Accountants, for their part, have a responsibility to make sure that all computations are made in accordance with the guidelines which are generally accepted in the business community. In this way, the earnings per share statistic will prove most meaningful and useful to all concerned.

BIBLIOGRAPHY

Accounting Principles Board: "Accounting Changes," APB Opinion No. 20, AICPA, New York, 1971.
———: "Computing Earnings Per Share," Unofficial Accounting Interpretations of APB Opinion No. 15, AICPA, New York, 1970.
———: "Earnings Per Share," APB Opinion No. 15, AICPA, New York, 1969.
———: "Reporting the Results of Operations," APB Opinion No. 30, AICPA, New York, 1973.
Davidson, Sidney, James S. Schindler, and Roman L. Weil: *Fundamentals of Accounting,* 5th ed., The Dryden Press, Hinsdale, Ill., 1975, Appendix 26.1.
Davidson, Sidney, and Roman L. Weil: "A Short-Cut in Computing Earnings Per Share," *Journal of Accountancy,* December 1975, pp. 45–47.
Kieso, Donald E., and Jerry J. Weygandt: *Intermediate Accounting,* John Wiley & Sons, New York, 1974, chap. 17.
Welsch, Glenn A., Charles T. Zlatkovich, and John Arch White: *Intermediate Accounting,* Richard D. Irwin, Homewood, Ill., 1972.

[10]See Accounting Principles Board, "Reporting the Results of Operations", APB Opinion No. 30, AICPA, New York, 1973, par. 9.

[11]See Accounting Principles Board, "Accounting Changes," APB Opinion No. 20, AICPA, New York, 1971, par. 20.

Chapter **31**

Partnership Accounting

R. GLEN BERRYMAN
Professor of Accounting, University of Minnesota

THE PARTNERSHIP FORM OF ORGANIZATION

Attributes.   A business or profession may be conducted as a sole proprietorship, general partnership, limited partnership, corporation, joint venture, syndicate, trust, or other form of organization. The owner or owners adopt a form based upon their evaluation of the relevant factors surrounding the firm's operations, such as risk of adverse legal action and federal and state income tax considerations. The majority of business firms in the United States are operated as sole proprietorships. Businesses frequently begin as sole proprietorships, then change to the partnership form when there are needs for additional capital and managers, and then, to the corporate form. The Uniform Partnership Act, or Uniform Limited Partnership Act, adopted in most states, covers the rights and obligation of partners and parties dealing with a partnership.

Accounting records must be maintained which reflect transactions between the partner and the business entity. A capital account, reflecting all transactions related to a partner's long-term contribution of funds, must be maintained. The current (drawing) account shows all transactions representing temporary changes in the partner's investment in the partnership, withdrawal of profits, buying from or selling to the business, etc. For example, a partner might withdraw certain products for personal use although they were owned by the partnership and were held for sale in the ordinary course of business. Such withdrawals would be charged to the partner's current account. Also, partners' shares of earnings are usually credited to their current accounts. Transfers between the current account and the capital account are made periodically as the partners make decisions on the amount of permanent capital needed. Occasionally, the capital and current accounts are merged into a single account. A loan account will be set up if a partner either borrows from or makes a loan to the partnership with the intent that repayment take place at a future date.

Section 6 of the Uniform Partnership Act defines a partnership as "an association of two or more persons to carry on as co-owners of a business for profit." Though a partnership is not recognized as a legal entity, it is clearly an entity for purposes of accounting. Assets, liabilities, and equities are treated as those of a separate and distinct business unit and should not be commingled with those belonging to the individual partners.

In the event of financial difficulties, a partnership may be petitioned into bankruptcy. Such petition may place only the partnership in bankruptcy or it may place the partnership along with one or more of its partners in bankruptcy. Partnership creditors have first claim to partnership assets in a bankruptcy proceeding. Creditors of individual partners in the partnership have first claim on the personal assets of the respective partners. In most jurisdictions, a partnership may hold title to real estate, may sue in the courts, and may be sued in its own name.

In a partnership, each person with an ownership interest has certain rights and responsibilities. These should be defined and set out explicitly by the contract of partnership, sometimes called the "articles of partnership." Essential provisions are reviewed in a later section.

In contrast to the sole proprietorship and partnership (general and limited), the corporation is a legal entity, as noted by Chief Justice Marshall of the U.S. Supreme Court in the following terms: "A corporation is an artificial being, invisible, intangible, and existing only in contemplation of law. Being the mere creature of law, it possesses only those properties which the charter of its creation confers upon it, either expressly or as incidental to its very existence."[1] Exhibit 1 summarizes the key differences between a partnership, a limited partnership, and a corporation.

[1]Dartmouth College v. Woodward, 4 Wheat. (U.S.)518(1819).

EXHIBIT 1   A Comparison of General Partnership, Limited Partnership, and Corporate Form of Organization

Aspect	General partnership	Limited partnership	Corporation
Creation	By contract between two or more parties.	By contract between two or more parties, under statutory enabling legislation, with recording of certificate in prescribed office.	Under statutory enabling legislation with charter granted by a governmental entity.
Legal status and activities	Not a legal entity; may carry out any legal activity agreed upon by the partners. Each partner has authority to bind the partnership when dealing with outsiders in the usual manner.	May carry out all activities that a partnership without limited partners may undertake, except as limited by its recorded certificate.	Is a legal entity and may carry out all activities authorized by its charter.
Life of organization	Ceases at death, withdrawal, or addition of a partner, or earlier by contractual provision. Business operation may continue by contractual arrangement.	Ceases at death, withdrawal, or addition of general partner, or earlier by contractual provision. Withdrawal or addition of limited partners need not terminate the partnership. When all limited partners cease to be such, partnership is terminated.	Perpetual, unless limited by charter.
Ownership share transferability	Only with consent of all other partners.	General partners interests may be changed only with consent of all partners. Limited partner interests may be assigned; assignees may become substituted limited partners with consent of all other partners or by action of assignor if certificate gives assignor such authority.	Freely transferable.
Management	Each partner is entitled to an equal voice unless the partnership agreement provides otherwise.	Only general partners have rights to manage.	Responsibility is vested in the board of directors.
Status of owners	Each partner is a principal and an agent of the other partners.	Each general partner is principal and agent of the other general partners. Limited partners do not serve as principal or agent for other partners.	Stockholder is neither principal nor agent, but has contractual rights only.
Liability of owners	Unlimited liability for debts of the partnership and torts of partners, unless limited by contract (subject to limitations).	Limited partners not liable to creditors unless they take part in control of the business. General partners have liability similar to that of partners in a general partnership.	Stockholder not liable for debts of corporation.
Additional owners	Creates new partnership. All current partners must consent.	Additional limited partners may be admitted upon filing amendment to original certificate, subject to rights of original partners.	Limited by charter and preemptive rights of current shareholders.

Alternative Forms. A *joint venture* is usually a temporary partnership organized by two or more parties for the purpose of carrying out a specific business plan. It is typically, though not necessarily, of short duration. A *syndicate* is an association of persons who combine to carry out a financial or industrial project such as the underwriting of a bond, stock, or other security issue. Although a syndicate is typically formed to carry out a single business operation, it may carry out a series of operations such as the purchase and development of a real estate tract. A joint venture, in contrast to a syndicate, usually contemplates a series of business operations. Each partner in a "regular" partnership is an agent of the partnership and has the authority to make binding commitments for the partnership. A member of a joint venture is not necessarily an agent of the other members of the venture and does not automatically have authority to bind the venture in contracts. In a partnership, the death of a partner dissolves the partnership, while in a joint venture the death of a venturer does not necessarily dissolve that venture.

Another form of business organization is that of *joint stock company.* This is quite similar to the regular partnership in that it is formed by a contract among the parties, is not a legal entity, and makes each member of the company assume unlimited liability with respect to obligations incurred by the company while he is a member thereof. It differs from a partnership in that its directors, elected by members of the company, are responsible for its business operations. The members are not agents of the company. The shares of the company are transferable without the consent of the other members, and the death of a member does not dissolve the company.

A special type of partnership is the limited partnership. This is composed of one or more general partners plus one or more limited partners. In a regular partnership, the organization is formed by contract among the partners. In a limited partnership, it is essential for the organization to be formed on the basis of a specific enabling statute. Further, the limited partners do not assume responsibility for debts of the partnership beyond the capital they have paid into the partnership or have agreed to pay in. A limited partnership agreement may contain specific provisions for the retirement of a limited partner or provision for him to assign one or more of his rights as a partner. Action in accordance with such provisions does not automatically terminate the partnership or dissolve it.

Each limited partnership must have at least one substantial general partner. Failure to do so could result in the limited partners being classified as general partners. To perfect the position of the limited partners (liability for partnership debts only to the extent of their actual or agreed upon capital contribution), the certificate stating the name and character of the business, location, names of general partners and of limited partners, etc., must be filed in the office of the public official designated in the enabling state statute. A limited partner may contribute cash or property but not services. The name of the limited partnership is not to contain the surname of a limited partner unless that surname is also the surname of a general partner.

A mining partnership, commonly regulated by specific state statute, is an association of two or more owners of mineral rights who organize for the purpose of obtaining a profit from extraction of the minerals. Generally mining partners have the right to sell their partnership interests, and the acquirees become members of the partnership. The partnership is not terminated by sale of a partner's interest or death. A member does not automatically become an agent of the partnership; usually one partner is named as manager and only such person has the authority to bind the partnership. All partners do have unlimited liability for partnership debts as do general partners in other partnerships.

Different classes of partners may be created by the contract or subsequent amendment thereto. A general partner incurs unlimited liability for the debts incurred in the course of partnership business. A general partner typically is active in the management of the business and known to the public as a principal and an agent of the organization. Limited partners are not liable for debts incurred by the firm beyond their contributed capital unless in addition to the exercise of their rights and powers as a limited partner, they take part in the management of the business. A silent partner has unlimited liability but takes no part in the conduct of regular partnership business. A secret partner has all the usual obligations and rights of a general partner but the participation in the contract partnership is not known by the public.

Ownership of Assets and Liability for Debts. Section 8, paragraph 3 of the Uniform Partnership Act states "Any estate in real property may be acquired in the partnership name. Title so acquired can be conveyed only in the partnership name." The above rule differs from the common-law rule which prevented effective passage of title to real estate if a partnership name was used. Real estate used by a partnership can be recorded in the name of one or more partners or a third party. In these cases, a trust relationship exists between the owner of record and the partnership, and the partnership is the equitable owner of the realty.

Equitable title to realty used by a partnership but recorded in a partner's name may be obscure. Questions to raise in determining equitable ownership to realty would include the following:

1. Has the income or the proceeds from the sale of the property been treated as partnership funds?

2. Have taxes and other associated expenses been paid by the partnership?

3. Has the property been improved with funds furnished by the partnership?

4. Has the property been recorded on the books and financial statements of the partnership?

As with realty, other assets of the partnership may be held by the partnership in its own name. This applies to inventories, receivables, bank account balances, securities, fixed assets other than realty, etc. The partnership would have the title to such items, and individual partners acting as agents of the partnership would have the right to convey them to third parties in the ordinary course of business. Further, a partner as agent of the partnership would have the power to encumber the property through a borrowing arrangement.

Prospective partners are usually concerned with their potential liability for debts of the partnership and debts incurred by other partners as agents of the partnership. The following provisions in the Uniform Partnership Act are related to such concerns:

Section 15 (Nature of Partner's Liability.) All partners are liable
a) Jointly and severally for everything chargeable to the partnership under sections 13 and 14. (Partnership Bound by Partner's Wrongful Act and by Partner's Breach of Trust.)
b) Jointly for all other debts and obligations of the partnership; but any partner may enter into a separate obligation to perform a partnership contract.
Section 17 (Liability of Incoming Partner.) A person admitted as a partner into an existing partnership is liable for all the obligations of the partnership arising before his admission as though he had been a partner when such obligations were incurred, except that this liability shall be satisfied only out of partnership property.
Section 36 (Effect of Dissolution on Partner's Existing Liability.)
(1) The dissolution of the partnership does not of itself discharge the existing liability of any partner.
(2) A partner is discharged from any existing liability upon dissolution of the partnership by an agreement to that effect between himself, the partnership creditor and the person or partnership continuing the business; . . .
(3) Where a person agrees to assume the existing obligations of a dissolved partnership, the partners whose obligations have been assumed shall be discharged from any liability

to any creditor of the partnership who, knowing of the agreement, consents to a material alteration in the nature or time of payment of such obligations.

(4) The individual property of a deceased partner shall be liable for all obligations of the partnership incurred while he was a partner but subject to the prior payment of his separate debts.

Section 40 (Rules for Distribution.)

(h) When partnership property and the individual properties of the partners are in possession of a court for distribution, partnership creditors shall have priority on partnership property and separate creditors on individual property, saving the rights of lien or secured creditors as heretofore.

(i) Where a partner has become bankrupt or his estate is insolvent the claims against his separate property shall rank in the following order:

I. Those owing to separate creditors,
II. Those owing to partnership creditors,
III. Those owing to partners by way of contribution.

A careful review of the language of the above sections discloses that the partner does not have unlimited liability with respect to all aspects of partnership business. Under Section 15, it is noted that the ordinary obligations of a partnership give rise only to a joint liability on the part of the partners. Under Section 17, a new partner does not assume personal responsibility for any debts contracted by a partnership prior to his or her becoming a member of that partnership. Under Section 36, a partner's personal liability to a specific creditor can be eliminated by a specific agreement between that person, the partner, and the partnership continuing a business. Further, Section 40 provides that the personal liability of partners for debts to the partnership does not come into play until the partnership's assets are in the hand of a court for distribution and the partnership property is found to be inadequate to satisfy the claims of creditors. In contrast to the joint liability that partners have for the debts incurred in the ordinary course of business by a partnership, the liabilities of partners for torts committed by a partner or an employee of the partnership are joint and several. A person not a member of a partnership might make a representation to another person that he or she was a member of the partnership or might permit a partner to represent that he or she was a member of the partnership. If another party relied upon such representation to his detriment, the nonpartner who was represented as a partner would be held liable as though he were a member of the partnership.

Life of the Organization. One of the alleged weaknesses of the partnership form of organization is its uncertain life. In those businesses in which long-term commitments are essential, some degree of certainty as to continuity of the organization is highly desirable. Under common law, a partnership is dissolved if one of the partners dies, withdraws from the partnership, or is legally incapacitated. However, Section 27 of the Uniform Partnership Act (Assignment of Partner's Interest) provides:

> (1) A conveyance by a partner of his interest in the partnership does not of itself dissolve the partnership, nor, as against the other partners in the absence of agreement, entitle the assignee, during the continuance of the partnership, to interfere in the management or administration of the partnership business or affairs. . . .

The assignment of a partner's interest does not give an assignee the right to partnership status, particularly those rights related to management of the business. Section 18 (g) provides "No person can become a member of a partnership without the consent of all the partners." An individual could become a partner only if accepted as such by all existing partners.

Although a partnership can be terminated by one partner, such right can be circumscribed substantially by an appropriate provision in the articles of partnership. Such a provision could indicate not only the partner's right to withdraw from the business but also a formula for determining the value of the partner's interest and responsibilities to the partnership, and the rate at which withdrawals can be made. Such a provision could help assure an orderly transition of the operation from one set of partners to another set and also minimize the risk of loss to outsiders when one partner retires from the partnership and is cashed out. Another provision might involve a requirement that all partners as of a certain date are required to maintain a certain minimum capital investment for a certain minimum period of time. Buy/sell arrangements are frequently helpful in providing for orderly transition from one set of partners to a subsequent set of partners.

Advantages and Disadvantages of the Partnership Form.   Advantages claimed for the partnership form of organization include the following:

1. Ease in Formation and Dissolution.   A simple contract between two or more people can give rise to a partnership. Dissolution can proceed with an oral or written statement by a partner to the other partners. The rights and responsibilities of each partner in the event of a dissolution will be governed by the initial contract and related amendments, or, where they are silent, by the Uniform Partnership Act in those jurisdictions in which it is in force. This contrasts with the corporation, in which a formal application for a charter from the state must be prepared and filed. When the corporation is dissolved its charter is surrendered to the state. A limited partnership must have a certificate prepared and filed, but this can be simpler than the preparation of incorporation papers.

2. Relative Flexibility in Partnership Actions.   Changes in the capital structure of a partnership can be achieved by mutual agreement among the partners, in contrast to the corporate situation where the issuance of new stock may involve an amendment to the charter, preemptive rights of shareholders, etc. Major changes in business operations would be the subject of an informal agreement or amendment to the initial partnership contract, whereas in the corporate situation a charter amendment might be required. Though most corporate charters are drawn in very general terms to permit maximum flexibility in conduct of corporate business, it is typically easier to change a partnership agreement.

3. Personal Character of the Organization.   Many persons feel that a partnership retains more of a personal character than does a corporation. Historically, professional groups such as attorneys and doctors, which have public service as their principal work, have employed the partnership form. More recently, however, many such groups have been organized as or been converted to professional corporations. Individuals practicing in the corporate form continue to have personal responsibility for their errors of omission or commission.

Disadvantages of the partnership form include the following:

1. Personal Liability of Partners.   Partners are personally responsible for all debts of a partnership, in contrast to the corporation situation in which the owner's possible liability is limited to the capital investment. A general partner may be called upon to contribute substantially more than the initial capital in the event of partnership financial difficulties.

2. Lack of Business Continuity.   Since the partnership is legally dissolved when a partner dies or withdraws, outside parties may feel less assurance in dealing with a partnership than with a corporation. On the other hand, it is possible, as noted above, for business continuity to be provided for if a partnership agreement has an appropriate "buy-out" arrangement.

3. Transference of Ownership.   No rights of a partner in a partnership can be sold or assigned unless the other partners concur in such sale or assignment. In particular, the right to participate in management cannot be assigned without concurrence of all other partners. This is in contrast to the corporation, where all ownership rights are transferred by a sale of corporate stock, and stock gives rights to manage only through its right to vote for members of the board of directors, to propose resolutions at annual meetings, etc.

4. *Difficulty in Raising Large Amounts of Capital.* No significant difference exists with respect to raising debt-type capital, since the individual shareholders of a closely held corporation and the partners in a partnership are both likely to be asked by the lender to guarantee a substantial loan. However, equity capital sources are likely to be more available to the corporation as a result of the ease of transferring interests and the absence of personal liability for such capital providers. Limited partnership interests can frequently be negotiated since such investors can avoid personal liability beyond their agreed-upon investment and can usually assign their interests freely.

Tax factors, both federal and state, must be considered before deciding whether the corporate or partnership form of organization is preferable. The taxes to be levied, including federal and state income taxes, franchise taxes, and property taxes, must be computed with respect to each form of organization. Both current and prospective tax levies should be considered in weighing this factor. Further, since the tax field is not static, tax changes may suggest a reevaluation of the decision to incorporate or to operate as a partnership.

A partnership must file an annual federal income tax return, which is an information return only, since the partnership itself pays no federal income tax. The distributive shares of partnership income are included in the personal tax returns of the partners. This is in contrast to the corporation, which is a taxable entity. However, under Internal Revenue Code Section 1371 *et seq.,* it is possible for certain corporations to elect to be treated as partnerships and have their distributive shares of income included in the personal tax returns of their shareholders. Strict limits exist as to which corporations are eligible for this tax status, a "tax-option" corporation. Requirements for this so-called "Subchapter S Corporation" include:

1. The corporation must have no more than one class of stock.

2. The corporation must have no more than ten shareholders.

3. The shareholders must all be individuals, except that an estate may be a shareholder.

4. The corporation's gross receipts from passive income, such as rents, royalties, dividends, interest, annuities, and gains from sales or exchanges of stock or securities, must not exceed 20 percent of gross corporate receipts.

The partnership form is frequently desirable when losses are anticipated, since such losses (ordinary and capital) can be passed through to the individual partners. Losses in excess of the cost of the partnership interest can be passed through if there are certain debts of the partnership outstanding at year end.

THE PARTNERSHIP FINANCIAL STATEMENTS

The basic classifications for partnership financial statements are the same as those employed for other forms of business organizations. However, certain particular subclassifications are commonly used by partnerships and some disclosures related to the partnership type of organization are necessary. Particular attention must be directed to transactions between the partner and the partnership to be sure that such transactions during the period and the position as of the end of the period have been adequately reflected. Footnote disclosures may be needed in order to reflect fully such transactions and to report any such commitments that have been made.

The owners' equity section of a partnership balance sheet will differ significantly from a corporate and from a sole proprietorship balance sheet. Partners' permanent capital accounts and the balance of their current (or drawing) accounts should be shown separately in order to indicate the extent of long-term commitment to the enterprise. The separation serves as a continuing reminder to the reader of the financials of the partners' basic commitment to the partnership in the terms of capital. In the event of dissolution, partners will be entitled to return of their loan and current account balances before any return of their capital accounts.

The current account balance shown separately in owners' equity represents the amount due to or from the partnership by the partner, and is the result of considering withdrawals by the partners, their distributive shares of profits, small short-term contributions or loans, and any amounts not subject to specific settlement plan. Significant partner loans to or from the business, subordinated to the rights of outside creditors, should not usually be included in the capital account but should be classified as assets or liabilities. Classification of such loans as current or long-term is dependent upon the reasonably anticipated settlement date.

With respect to the income statement, salaries paid to partners for personal services and interest on partners' capital account balances should be reflected as expenses of the period, unless otherwise provided in the articles of partnership. Further, a schedule showing the disposition of net income to the various partners should be included in the set of financial statements. In some instances, the income applicable to individual partners for tax return purposes will differ significantly from that determined in accordance with generally accepted accounting principles. In such case disclosure of the amount and nature of the discrepancy may be needed. Tax allocation is not required in partnership financial statements, since a partnership is not a taxable entity for income tax purposes.

Material items involving partners, such as rent paid to a partner, should be reflected specifically in the statements or footnotes. The objective of such disclosures is to assure readers that they will be informed fully of transactions that do not involve arm's-length dealings. Also, it is appropriate to offset a receivable from a partner against an amount due the partner if settlement is to be made on a net basis. The disclosures mentioned are consistent with those required by the Securi-

---

EXHIBIT 2

KECK AND UBL
Balance Sheet (Condensed)
December 31, 19x7
Assets

Current assets:			
Other current assets		$ 90,000	
Advance to Keck		16,000	$106,000
6% 6-year note, due June 30, 19x9, from Ubl			10,000
Property, plant and equipment (at cost less accumulated depreciation)			
Land (contributed by Keck)		$ 34,000	
Buildings and equipment	$65,000		
Less: accumulated depreciation	35,000	30,000	64,000
			$180,000

Equities

Current liabilities:		
Other current liabilities	$ 30,000	
Account payable—merchandise purchased from Keck	12,000	$ 42,000
Partners' equities:		
Permanent investment (capital account)	$110,000	
Undistributed profits (current account)	28,000	138,000
		$180,000

EXHIBIT 3

KECK AND UBL
Schedule of Changes in Partners' Equities
For Year Ended December 31, 19x7

	Keck	Ubl	Total
Permanent investment, Jan. 1, 19x7	$60,000	$40,000	$100,000
Additional cash investment per agreement of June 30, 19x7	—0—	10,000	10,000
Permanent investment, Dec. 31, 19x7	$60,000	$50,000	$110,000
Undistributed profits, Jan. 1, 19x7	$14,000	—0—	$ 14,000
Interest on permanent investment at 6%	3,600	2,700	6,300
Partners' salaries for 19x7	25,000	20,000	45,000
Share of net income for 19x7	40,000	40,000	80,000
	$82,600	$62,700	$145,300
Withdrawals: Salaries	$25,000	$20,000	$ 45,000
Other	40,000	32,300	72,300
	$65,000	$52,300	$117,300
Undistributed profits, Dec. 31, 19x7	$17,600	$10,400	$ 28,000

EXHIBIT 4

KECK AND UBL
Income Statement
Year Ended December 31, 19x7

Sales	$400,000
Cost of goods sold	250,000
Gross margin	$150,000
Operating expenses:	
Selling expense	$ 10,700
Administrative expense	8,000
Partners' salaries	45,000
Interest on partners' investment	6,300
	$ 70,000
Net income for 19x7	$ 80,000

Allocation of Income Statement Items to Partners

	Keck	Ubl	Total
Salary allowance	$25,000	$20,000	$ 45,000
Interest on partners' permanent investment	3,600	2,700	6,300
Net income for 19x7 (50% for Keck and 50% for Ubl)	40,000	40,000	80,000
Total allocation	$68,600	$62,700	$131,300

ties and Exchange Commission in connection with statements filed with that organization. Illustrative of SEC rules is the following disclosure requirement:[2]

> *Other current assets*—(a) State separately (1) total of current amounts, other than trade accounts subject to the usual trade terms, due from directors, officers, and principal holders of equity securities other than affiliates; (2) total of current amounts due from parents and subsidiaries; and (3) any other amounts in excess of ten percent of total current assets, indicating any such amount due from affiliates other than parents and subsidiaries.

[2]Securities and Exchange Commission, *Regulation S-X*, Rule 5-02 (7)(a). A similar rule with respect to disclosure of liabilities is Rule 5-02 (25).

The initial partnership financial statements should be included as a part of the partnership agreement. Such inclusion will establish the specific assets which the partnership is taking over from partners personally or from a predecessor partnership, the valuations of such assets, and the liabilities which the partnership is expected to assume.

Financial statements of limited partnerships are frequently prepared on a tax basis only, based on the assumption that the limited partners are investors primarily interested in the tax status of their investments. This approach has been taken in situations where "tax shelters" have been sold to the public. If a registration with the Securities and Exchange Commission is required, the presentation must be based on generally accepted accounting principles (GAAP).[3] Tax basis data may be presented in footnotes or supporting schedules, but they cannot supplant the GAAP basis presentations.

An illustrative set of partnership financial statements is shown as Exhibits 2, 3, and 4.

THE ARTICLES OF PARTNERSHIP

Essential Inclusions. Simons and Karrenbrock[4] suggest that the following matters be covered in the articles of partnership.

(1) The partnership name, the partners entering into the agreement, and the location of the business.

(2) The effective date of partnership formation and the duration of the contract.

(3) The character and the scope of the business and its location.

(4) The investments by each partner and the values assigned to such investments.

(5) The rights, powers, and duties of the partners, as well as any limitations upon the authority of partners.

(6) The books and accounts of the partnership and the fiscal year that is adopted.

(7) The profit-and-loss-sharing ratio, including any special provisions for the recognition of differences in investment and service contributions.

(8) Special interest charges and credits relating to investments by partners, and special compensation allowed for services rendered by partners.

(9) Partners' investments and withdrawals subsequent to formation and their treatment in the accounts.

(10) Life insurance on partners and treatment of insurance premiums, recoveries on policies, etc.

(11) Special procedures for settlement of a partner's interest upon his withdrawal or death.

(12) Methods for resolving disputes between partners.

Assignment of values to contributed assets, as noted in item (4) above, is of critical importance because gains or losses subsequent to dates of property contribution to the partnership will be distributed to the partners in accordance with their profit-sharing ratios. Gains or losses attributed to periods preceding contribution are applicable 100 percent to the contributing partner. Timing of contribution of cash and noncash assets should be specified as an aid in fixing values and setting the starting date for attributing revenues and expenses to the partnership.

The classes of partners, including any particular provisions with respect to limitations on liability, should be stated explicitly, as noted in item (5) above. Any rights of the partners to borrow money from the partnership and the rate of interest to be paid on such loans should be specified. The obligation of a partner to

[3]Securities and Exchange Commission, *Accounting Series Release No. 162*, September 27, 1974.

[4]Harry Simons and Wilbert E. Karrenbrock, *Advanced Accounting*, 4th ed., South-Western Publishing Company, Cincinnati, 1968, pp. 5–6.

loan money to the partnership, the rate of interest, and other terms of such transactions should be specified to minimize the chance of dispute.

Extreme care should be taken in drafting the articles to assure a common understanding as to the applicable principles of income determination, asset valuation, and measurement of liabilities. To minimize disputes as to accounting methods, the articles could specify the use of generally accepted principles of accounting. Further, where accounting alternatives exist, the articles could (1) list the methods selected or (2) specify the procedure for selecting methods or (3) use a combination. Adoption of new standards of accounting promulgated by the Financial Accounting Standards Board, and Releases of the Securities and Exchange Commission could also be specified. Elements such as when to recognize revenue and what year to expense employee bonuses should be considered. Particular care needs to be placed on when to recognize unusual items such as gains on disposal of fixed assets, losses that result from selling a segment of business, etc.

The rights of individual partners to perform certain management functions exclusively, minimum hours of work by partners, exclusive rights to serve as an agent of the partnership, etc., should be specified in the articles. Rights of partners in the event of dissolution should be specified. This would include but would not be limited to:

1. Statements as to responsibilities of the individual partners during a dissolution and liquidating process

2. Methods to be used in determining values of assets which are to be distributed to partners rather than sold

3. Plans for distributing cash prior to completion of all liquidation procedures

4. Provisions for partners to buy out other partners in the event of dispute or death of one of their number

5. Methods for calculating goodwill.

Interpretations When Articles of Partnership Are Silent. A carefully drawn article of partnership can serve as an effective guide to operating relationships and business objectives as well as state procedures for resolving disputes. However, no drafter of articles is likely to foresee all contingencies or avoid all ambiguities; hence guidance must on occasion be obtained by reference to the applicable statute, usually the Uniform Partnership Act.

The articles of partnership, unless they contravene one of the provisions of the statutes covering partnerships or are against public policy, determine the rights and duties of partners. Section 18 of the Uniform Partnership Act emphasizes the importance of the articles when it states: "The rights and duties of the partners in relationship to the partnership shall be determined, subject to any agreement between them, by the following rules. . . ."

Differences of opinion with respect to such rights and duties are handled in the same way under common law and the Uniform Partnership Act. The latter provides in Section 18 (h): "Any difference arising as to ordinary matters connected with the partnership business may be decided by a majority of the partners; but no act in contravention of any agreement between the partners may be done rightfully without the consent of all partners." A problem might exist as to what constitutes a majority of the partners if equal numbers voted on each side of an issue. No precise procedure exists in the law for resolving this; as a result, the partnership agreement should normally provide a specific device for settling such differences. As to actions in "contravention of any agreement between the partners," it is necessary to have unanimous agreement among the partners to effect such change. Depending upon inclusions in the initial articles of partnership, such actions might include the shifting of business objectives, closing out operations at a specified address, or disposition of a major segment of the partnership's business.

FORMATION OF PARTNERSHIPS

Initial Capital. Cash, property, personal services, business contracts, trademarks, etc., contributed by partners to a partnership at the outset constitute the initial capital of that partnership. The value of each contribution should be recognized as an asset. Difficulties in valuation of services, noncash assets, or noncash assets subject to debts, liens, or claims frequently exist. For example, a partner might contribute to the partnership the use of a piece of vacant property for a period of twenty-five years, with the provision that the partnership would be required to pay the property taxes, including special assessments on the property, during that period. The fair market value of the net rentals, discounted to the date of the transfer of the rights to use of the property, should be the measure of the contribution of that partner. Disagreements as to the discount rate, fair market value of rentals at the various dates, etc., should be resolved by mutual agreement of the parties prior to transfer of the assets.

The amount of the initial contributions of capital by the partners is expected to remain intact, subject only to losses which might decrease the amount or subsequent agreements among the partners which would require further contributions or a reallocation of balances among them.

On occasion, an existing going concern may be contributed to a partnership as one partner's share of the initial capital. In such an instance, it may be appropriate to recognize that the value of the business as a going concern is greater than the book value of the assets or the sum of their individual fair market values. The total going-concern value would be entered in the partner's capital account as the contribution. The difference between the going-concern value and the fair market value of the individual assets might be set up as goodwill (assuming that no specifically identifiable assets exist relative to such amounts) on the initial balance sheet of the partnership.

Partner's interests in capital may not be the same as their profit and loss ratios. Values assigned to partnership assets and liabilities at the onset of the business or at any time a contribution of noncash assets is made are extremely important. Subsequent changes in value become partnership gains and losses and are allocated in accordance with the profit and loss ratios specified in the partnership agreement. If no profit and loss ratios are specified, then the law presumes them to be equal. However, it is possible to have the partnership agreement specify that partners' capital accounts are to be adjusted later relative to gains and/or losses on dispositions of named contributed property. Thus, initial valuation must be fairly recorded or provision made for subsequent adjustments if equity and the original agreements among the partners are to be preserved. Equity as to income tax considerations requires the partners to recognize the implications associated with the fact that the tax basis of assets contributed to a partnership does not change at contribution date regardless of the fair market value of the property.

Some partners may wish to sell assets to "their" partnerships rather than contribute those items, because of such factors as income tax considerations and amounts of contributions by other partners. Such procedure is appropriate, but should be carefully documented to minimize the risk of subsequent controversy.

Changes in Asset Valuation. Assets held for extended periods of time may change greatly in value. So long as the membership of the partnership and the profit and loss ratios remain unchanged, there is no serious problem with respect to the time such incremental value is recognized. However, in many partnerships these factors do change. Prior to changing a profit and loss ratio or membership in the partnership, asset revaluation should be considered. Otherwise gains or losses may be allocated to parties not properly chargeable or creditable with such changes in value.

A new partner must consider not only the fair market value of the assets but also the potential liability for capital gains tax on any fair market value which exceeds the basis of that asset to the partnership. If asset values have declined below their book value, an incoming partner will be interested in the value of the loss which has not been deducted on tax returns of the other partners. The interest of existing partners in increases or decreases in fair market values in relation to the tax basis of the assets will be opposite to that of incoming partners. Adjustments to asset values, whenever changes in profit and loss ratios take place or when a partner is admitted or retired, should recognize the inherent benefit or cost associated with the difference between the fair market value and the tax basis of the assets held. To illustrate the above:

BLACKMAN AND DORRIS
Balance Sheet
December 31, 19x7

Common stock of Durango Corp. at cost	$300	Blackman, capital	$150
(market value is $1,000)		Dorris, capital	150
	$300		$300

Assume further that Ungerman is interested in becoming a member of the partnership by buying out Dorris's interest entirely and that Blackman is willing to accept Ungerman as a partner. The revaluing of the assets would involve recognition of the increment in market ($700) and the related capital gains tax effect ($175, assuming a 25 percent tax rate), or a net of $525. The journal entries for revaluation and the admission of Ungerman to partnership might be as follows:

```
1.  Revalue the asset:
    Common Stock of Durango Revaluation
      Increment  ...................... 700.00
        Deferred Federal Income Taxes—
          Unrealized Gains  ..............      175.00
        Blackman, Capital  ..............      262.50
        Dorris, Capital  ...............      262.50

2.  Transfer Dorris's interest to Ungerman:
    Dorris, Capital  .................... 412.50
      Ungerman, Capital  ..............      412.50
```

Since partnerships are not subject to federal income tax, nonrecognition of income tax effects related to valuation changes is acceptable. The onus for such knowledge is then placed on the individual partners. In the above illustration, the deferred tax account would then be omitted, the credits to the two capital accounts in the first entry would be $350 each, and the balance transferred to Ungerman would be $500, independent of the amount paid by Ungerman to Dorris.

Disposition of a Partner's Interest. There are three ways for a partner to dispose of a partnership interest: (1) sale to an outside party, (2) sale to other partner(s), and (3) retirement, with partnership assets being distributed, or the partnership issuing notes or equivalent payable to the partner. With (1) and (2), no change in partnership assets takes place. After revaluation, the capital, current, and loan accounts related to the retiring partner are transferred to the new and/or old partner(s). In order to assure equity between the new and/or old partners when relative profit and loss ratios change, revaluation of assets should take place just before the admission of the new partner. Since a new partnership results, it is appropriate for revaluation to take place, since relative profit and loss ratios are likely to change. An example of a sale to an outside party was given above.

The following example illustrates sale to other partners, with tax effects being disregarded.

DAVID, EDWARD & FRANKLIN
Balance Sheet
December 31, 19x7

Assets, at cost $45,000	David, capital $10,000
(market value of $60,000)	Edward, capital ... 15,000
	Franklin, capital ... 20,000
$45,000	$45,000

Edward is buying out David and paying $15,000 for David's interest. Profits and losses have been shared equally, and after the buy-out will be allocated 60 percent to Edward and 40 percent to Franklin. Note that in neither situation are profits and losses shared in the capital ratios.

1. Revalue the assets:
   Assets—Revaluation Increment ... 15,000
      David, Capital   5,000
      Edward, Capital   5,000
      Franklin, Capital   5,000

2. Transfer David's capital to Edward:
   David, Capital 15,000
      Edward, Capital   15,000

Failure to revalue the assets would result in Edward being credited with only $9,000 of the gain (60 percent) when the assets were sold, instead of $10,000 as noted above ($5,000 increment applicable to both David's and Edward's capital accounts).

The following example illustrates retirement of a partner. Assume the same initial balance sheet as above, the same undervaluation of assets, and that retiring partner David is to be paid in cash by the partnership.

1. Revalue the assets (same as 1 above)
2. Retire David from the partnership:
   David, Capital 15,000
      Cash   15,000

The revised balance sheet would report assets of $45,000, Edward's capital as $20,000, and Franklin's capital as $25,000.

A member of a partnership who retires may be paid more or less than the balance in his or her capital account, after recording the needed asset revaluations. Either a bonus method or goodwill method will have to be used for handling such transactions. To illustrate, assume the same partnership balance sheet shown above and the same asset revaluation. Assume further that David is to retire and receive $20,000 in assets from the partnership. If the bonus method is employed, a charge will be made against Edward's and Franklin's capital accounts. The difference between the assets to be distributed and the balance in David's capital account will be allocated in accordance with the Edward and Franklin profit and loss ratios, as noted below:

David, Capital 15,000
Edward, Capital 2,500
Franklin, Capital 2,500
   Assets   20,000

On the other hand, if the goodwill method is employed, recognizing goodwill to the extent that the remaining partners have purchased it, the following entry is needed:

David, Capital 15,000
Goodwill 5,000
   Assets   20,000

Goodwill might also be recognized to the full extent implied by the transaction. Then the journal entry would be as follows:

```
David, Capital  ..........  15,000
Goodwill  ................  15,000
        Edward, Capital  .....      5,000
        Franklin, Capital  ....      5,000
        Assets  .............     20,000
```

Or, David might receive only $10,000 from the partnership. This amount might be the result of poor bargaining power on the part of David, an overstatement of asset values, a bleak outlook as to future profits, or other reasons. If the bonus method is used, the journal entry to record David's withdrawal is as follows:

```
David, Capital  ..........  15,000
        Edward, Capital  .....      2,500
        Franklin, Capital  ....      2,500
        Assets  .............     10,000
```

If assets were overvalued, they should be written down to current market values. Use of the goodwill method would be inappropriate in this situation.

Admission of a New Partner. A party can become a partner only with the consent of all the existing partners. However, partners can assign their financial interests in a partnership to another party or parties without the consent of the other partners provided no prohibition on such action is stated in the partnership agreement. Such assignment will not permit the purchaser any rights to manage, but will permit sharing in the partnership profits and losses. If such assignment takes place, the partnership will only note on the assigning partner's accounts that his or her financial interests have been assigned.

A partnership interest can be acquired by either: (1) purchase of an interest from an existing partner or partners, or (2) contribution of assets. The sale of an existing interest to an outside party was illustrated above. When there is a purchase of an interest by contributing assets, the values assigned to assets contributed by the incoming partner are of utmost importance.

The credit to the incoming partner's capital account need not necessarily equal the market values of the items contributed. Goodwill may be recognized when a partner is admitted, with the amount allocated to the old or new partners or both. Also, a bonus may be charged and/or credited to the new and/or old partners.

The following sets of assumptions will serve to illustrate alternative accounting methods for recording admission of a partner. The balance sheet for Black and White is shown below:

BLACK AND WHITE
Balance Sheet
December 31, 19x7

```
Assets at cost  ...............  $40,000    Black, capital  ...  $24,000
    (market value of $20,000)              White, capital  ...   16,000
                                $40,000                         $40,000
```

Assume that profits and losses are shared equally and that Gray, the incoming partner, is to contribute assets with market value of $20,000 and receive a one-third interest in capital. No bonus or goodwill is implied, so Gray's entry to partnership is recorded as follows:

```
Assets  ...................................  20,000
    Gray, Capital  ..........................     20,000
```

An agreement to admit a new partner contributing assets to a partnership should state whether the bonus method or the goodwill method is to be employed to recognize differences arising from the relationship of his or her capital interest to the market value of the assets he or she contributes. If the bonus method is chosen, the bonus may be applicable to either the incoming partner or to the existing partners. The following formula approach is suggested to ascertain the accounting entries:

Let x = credit to the new partner's capital account
a = percentage of partnership equity applied to the incoming partner
b = contribution of the new partner
c = balance of existing partners' capital accounts

Then $$x = a(b + c)$$

Apply this to the illustration above, but assume that Gray is to receive a one-quarter interest in capital. Substituting in the equation, note that:

$$x = .25(20,000 + 40,000)$$
$$= \$15,000$$

The difference between Gray's contribution of $20,000 and the credit to Gray's capital account of $15,000 would be split equally between the existing partners since they share profits and losses equally. The entry to record the admission of Gray is as follows:

Assets	20,000	
Black, Capital		2,500
White, Capital		2,500
Gray, Capital		15,000

If the goodwill method was used, an additional unknown would be used, namely:

$$y = \text{total capitalization}$$

If goodwill is applicable to the existing partners, the formula employed would be expressed as

$$y = \frac{b}{a}$$

or if goodwill is applicable to the incoming partner,

$$y = \frac{c}{1 - a}$$

Apply this to the illustration above and capitalization may be determined as follows:

$$y = \frac{b}{a}$$

Substituting, $y = 20,000/.25$, or $80,000. Goodwill is $20,000 [= $80,000 − ($20,000 + $40,000)]. The entry to record Gray's admission is as follows:

Assets	20,000	
Goodwill	20,000	
Black, Capital		10,000
White, Capital		10,000
Gray, Capital		20,000

On the other hand, if goodwill is believed to be applicable to the incoming partner, the calculation would proceed as follows:

$$y = \frac{c}{1 - a}$$

Substituting, y = \$40,000/(1 − .25), or a \$53,333 total capitalization. Since the assets (\$20,000) contributed by the incoming partner, plus the assets of the existing partners (\$40,000), total \$60,000 and this is greater than the indicated capitalization of \$53,333, goodwill of the entering partner is nonexistent. This is obviously not feasible, so the preceding formula in which goodwill is allocated to existing partners must be used.

If the agreement allocates the incoming partner a one-half interest in capital for the \$20,000 investment, the second method could be employed. Total capitalization would be \$80,000, goodwill would be \$20,000, and the new partner's capital account would be credited with \$40,000.

Sometimes the credit to the new partner's capital account or total capitalization will be known and one or the other items mentioned will be unknown. Such a change in the list of knowns and unknowns does not change the formulas.

The goodwill and bonus methods will produce identical results as to partners' equity in the partnership if (1) the incoming partner's share of profits is equal to the initial ratio of the income partner's capital to total capital and (2) the existing partners continue to share profits in proportion to their original ratios. In the event that both the above conditions are not met continuously after admission of the new partner, the goodwill and bonus methods will give different results.

PARTNERSHIP NET INCOME

Determination of Periodic Net Income.   Periodic net income for a partnership is usually determined in the same manner as for other types of business organizations. Timing of revenue and expense recognition is particularly important for a partnership since profit and loss ratios may change from period to period and membership in the partnership may also change. The rules listed in Accounting Principles Board Opinion No. 9 of the American Institute of Certified Public Accountants apply to such determination.

Under APB No. 9, which would apply unless a partnership contractual provision specifies otherwise, virtually all items coming to light in the current year are recognized as applicable to this period's income. Exceptions, called "prior period adjustments," would have to meet the stringent tests specified at paragraph 23 therein, namely:

> ... material adjustments which (a) can be specifically identified with and directly related to the business activities of particular prior periods, and (b) are not attributable to economic events occurring subsequent to the date of the financial statements for the prior period, and (c) depend primarily on determinations by persons other than management and (d) were not susceptible of reasonable estimation prior to such determination. Such adjustments are rare in modern financial accounting.

Partnership contracts may contain special provisions with respect to timing, measurement, and allocation of income. Also, special methods for recording transactions between a partner and the partnership may be specified. If one of these conflicts with generally accepted accounting principles, the accountant reporting on the fairness of such statements must indicate the nature of the deviation and its effect.

In the interest of full disclosure, the following types of transactions between a partner and the partnership should be specifically identified and summarized in the financial statements or their related notes: (1) salary, (2) interest on capital investments, (3) interest on loans, (4) margins on sales, and (5) rentals. Revenue and expense attributes of such transactions are customarily treated as affecting income and are not considered as a division of profits. Where applicable, each category should be recognized because of its effect on income determination and the resultant portion of profits applicable to each partner. Each of the items should be reviewed critically to determine reasonableness. If an excessive or inadequate amount is noted, there may be a partial division of profits rather than it being entirely an expense or revenue item. If services are rendered or loans made, the salary or interest cost should be recognized as appropriate elements in determining profitability of the business.

Interest on capital might be calculated in any one of the following ways: (1) a percentage of the beginning, ending, or average capital investments; (2) a percentage of capital in excess of a specified dollar amount (with interest being charged any partner whose balance is below a specified minimum); and (3) a percentage of capital balances, in excess or deficiency, based upon the proportion required by the partnership agreement. This calculation can be troublesome if the term "capital" is not precisely defined. Distinction should be made in the partnership contract as to whether capital means initial capital contributed, the sum of all capital and current accounts outstanding at the beginning of the year, the average balance of the combined capital and current accounts, or some other definition.

Revenues, expenses, and losses should be recorded in partnership records, and partnership statements should be prepared on a basis that conforms to the practices typical in the industry in which the partnership operates. Revenue and expense items, whether they arise from transactions with partners or nonpartners, should be handled as though they were expenses or revenue of the partnership and not as distributions of profit.

Allocation of Net Income and Losses. The terms of the partnership contract are critical as to the allocation of profits among the partners. When the partnership contract is drafted, the fiscal year-end should be established and the bases for allocating all elements of profits, expenses, and losses stated clearly. Not only may the amount of income attributed to partners differ, but also the types of income and deductions may differ. An illustration of allocation of partnership net income was presented as part of Exhibit 4 earlier in this chapter.

If the partnership agreement is silent as to profit and loss allocations to partners, such will be allocated in equal amounts to each partner. Section 18 of the Uniform Partnership Act provides:

> The rights and duties of the partners in relation to the partnership shall be determined, subject to any agreement between them, by the following rules: a) Each partner shall . . . share equally in the profits and surplus remaining after all liabilities, including those to partners, are satisfied; and must contribute towards the losses, whether of capital or otherwise, sustained by the partnership according to his share in the profits.

Simons and Karrenbrock[5] suggest the following ways of allocating profits and losses:

(1) Equally.
(2) In an arbitrary ratio.
(3) In the ratio of partners' capitals.
(4) Interest to be allowed on partners' capitals, the balance to be divided on some arbitrary basis as agreed.
(5) Salaries or bonus to be allowed for partners' services, the balance to be divided on some arbitrary basis as agreed.
(6) Interest to be allowed on partners' capitals, salaries to be allowed for partners' services, the balance to be divided on some arbitrary basis as agreed.

[5]Ibid., p. 12.

Quite commonly the partnership agreement specifies that profits and losses be divided equally. Then, if there are three partners and income totals $120,000, the following closing journal entry allocating income would be made:

```
Income summary ........................... 120,000
    A, Current account .....................        40,000
    B, Current account .....................        40,000
    C, Current account .....................        40,000
```

If a loss of $120,000 had been incurred, the reverse of the above entry would have been made.

Arbitrary ratios are frequently employed for profit distributions. Such ratios normally recognize the anticipated relative contributions of the partners, including special knowledge of an individual partner, hours to be spent, experience, reputation, etc. Such a ratio might be expressed as 3 to 2 to 1 for a three-person partnership.

Different items of income are sometimes allocated on different bases and may be related to initial asset contributions or tax circumstances of individual partners. For example, a different distribution formula might be employed with respect to dividends and interest received on investments from that used to allocate operating margins realized from trading operations. Or, regularly recurring income items might be allocated in one manner but unusual gains and losses, such as those resulting from sale of a segment of a business, might be allocated in another manner. Obviously, great care needs to be taken in drafting the partnership contract so that ambiguities relative to income allocations are minimized.

Tax Considerations. Internal Revenue Code Section 702 specifies that the following items of partnership income must be set out separately:

(1) short-term capital gains and losses,
(2) long-term capital gains and losses,
(3) gains and losses from sales or exchanges of Section 1231 property (primarily fixed assets used in a business or profession),
(4) charitable contributions,
(5) dividends for which there is an exclusion or for which there is a deduction for dividends received by corporations,
(6) taxes paid or accrued to a foreign country and to U.S. possessions,
(7) other items of income, gain, loss, deduction, or credit, and
(8) taxable income or loss, exclusive of the above items.

Illustrative of the items contemplated under (7) above are intangible drilling and development costs in the extractive industries, additional first-year depreciation, amounts received on accounts previously written off as bad debts, contributions to a qualified pension plan or a profit-sharing plan, and soil and water conservation expenditures.

Generally, the Internal Revenue Service permits allocations of special items specified by the partnership agreement unless tax avoidance is the principal purpose for such provisions. For example, a partner might contribute a piece of machinery with a $5,000 basis but a fair market value of $10,000. Depreciation allowable to the partnership is limited to the $5,000 basis since the contribution was made to the partnership tax-free. Up to 100 percent of the depreciation provision could be allocated to noncontributing partners.

In deciding upon income allocation, consideration should be given to the individual partners' personal tax positions. It might be advantageous, for example, to allocate items subject to capital gains tax to relatively high tax bracket taxpayers and ordinary income items to relatively low tax bracket partners. Compensation for such difference could then be undertaken through the medium of adjusting the profit and loss ratios otherwise decided upon. Also, the partners' share of the partnership investment in new Section 38 property and used Section 38 property is needed for purposes of computing the investment credit applicable to each partner. Again, the partnership agreement might be used to advantage to specify the portions applicable to each partner.

The amount of partnership loss which an individual partner may include on his or her personal tax return is limited to the adjusted basis of his or her partnership interest as of the end of the partnership tax year in which the loss occurred, but before deducting the current year's loss. To minimize the chance of a loss not being available to a partner, it may be desirable for the partner before year-end to contribute assets to the partnership to the extent the loss exceeds his or her basis. Subsequent withdrawal, if agreed upon by all partners, would be possible after year-end. A partner allocated losses in excess of the basis of his or her partnership interest is generally entitled to deduct as a loss only the basis of the partnership interest. A partner who contributes assets to the partnership at a later date is entitled to the loss deduction in the year of the contribution.

TERMINATION OF PARTNERSHIP OPERATION

Dissolution, Termination, and Distribution.   The terms dissolution, termination, and distribution should be differentiated. *Dissolution* implies the ending of a specific partnership agreement but not necessarily the ending of the business. Dissolution, for example, takes place at the death of a partner. At that time the estate of the deceased partner becomes entitled to the value of the deceased partner's interest in the business. Thus, a transfer of the deceased partner's interest from the owners' equity category to the liability classification takes place.

Termination of the business involves termination of the business operations, including liquidation of the assets or their transfer to some of the partners and payment of all debts. *Distribution* involves transferring some or all of the assets to creditors and partners.

Termination of a partnership business may result from the same causes that terminate any other going concern, such as inability of a firm to compete effectively, desire of owners to get out of business, shortage of working capital, etc. Because of the unique character of a partnership, it is often possible for one partner to force termination of the business, if there is no provision in the articles of partnership to prevent it. If the partner requesting termination and the other partners cannot agree upon the amount he or she is to receive and when, then in the absence of a provision for resolution of such differences (e.g., by arbitration), a sale of the business as a going concern or liquidation of individual assets and payment of all liabilities will of necessity ensue. During liquidation, gains and losses should be allocated to the partners' current accounts in their profit and loss ratios unless another ratio is specified by the partnership agreement. The partnership agreement is the governing instrument, and it continues to govern the relationships among the partners until the partnership operation is completely terminated.

If certain assets are to be distributed to the partners, their values should be adjusted to market and the differences between carrying value and market should be recorded as gains and losses on liquidation. At distribution the current value of such assets should then be charged against the partners' current accounts. In this way, all partners share in gains or losses on all assets, whether they are distributed to the partners or sold to outsiders.

Various types of accounts between a partner and the partnership may exist, including capital, current, and loan accounts. The rights of partners to partnership funds are always subordinated to those of outside creditors. With respect to partners' claims against the partnership and the partnership claims against the partner, a right of offset exists. Thus, if the partnership owed a partner money on a loan but the partner owed the partnership a current account balance, the debit and credit balances would be offset and settlement in liquidation would be on the basis of a net amount.

Extreme care needs to be taken with respect to distribution of cash obtained in the liquidation proceedings. Distributions must first go to satisfy creditor claims. Creditors having priorities must be paid before other creditors, and secured creditors have first claim on proceeds from assets to which their lien applies. If not all creditor claims can be satisfied at a given time and a distribution is to be made, such distribution should be on a pro rata basis for that category of creditors whose claims cannot be paid in full. After outside creditors have been satisfied, distributions can be made to partners.

Section 40 (b) of the Uniform Partnership Act states the following rules for making payments in liquidation.

> The liabilities of the partnership shall rank in order of payment, as follows:
> I. Those owing to creditors other than partners,
> II. Those owing to partners other than for capital and profits,
> III. Those owing to partners in respect of capital,
> IV. Those owing to partners in respect of profits.

Section 40 (d) states:

> The partners shall contribute, as provided by section 18 (a), the amount necessary to satisfy the liabilities; but if any, but not all, of the partners are insolvent, or, not being subject to process, refuse to contribute, the other partners shall contribute their share of the liabilities, and, in the relative proportions in which they share the profits, the additional amount necessary to pay the liabilities.

Section 40 (i) provides:

> Where a partner has become bankrupt or his estate is insolvent the claims against his separate property shall rank in the following order:
> I. Those owing to separate creditors,
> II. Those owing to partnership creditors,
> III. Those owing to partners by way of contribution.

It is clear that the partnership creditors other than partners rank ahead of partners. Because of the right to offset, there is no doubt that the partner as a creditor ranks below all outside creditors. Further, it may be appropriate in some instances to make payment to partners with respect to their capital balances even though other partners have loan balances still outstanding. This condition may exist where the partner with the loan balance has a deficit in his capital account and the right of offset is applied.

Personal assets of a partner are applied first to payment of claims against him personally, as noted under Section 40 (i) above. To the extent that he is entitled to funds from the partnership at its liquidation, these are available for his personal creditors. If he has more than enough personal assets to pay his personal creditors, then the excess would be available for contribution to the partnership to pay otherwise unsatisfied partnership creditors or to settle claims of other partners whose capital accounts have credit balances. Creditors of the partnership must look first to partnership assets. If these prove insufficient to satisfy their claims, creditors may look to an individual partner's personal assets, but must recognize that their claims are subordinated to those of the partner's personal creditors.

Lump-Sum Distributions in Complete Liquidation.   When sale of assets and payments to all creditors in liquidation have been completed, all gains and losses will be known and should be distributed to the partners' accounts. If any partner's account has a deficit at that point in time, a determination will have to be made as

EXHIBIT 5

JASPER AND KRICTON
Partnership Liquidation Statement
Three Months Ended November 30, 19X1

Event or Position	Assets		Liabilities to others	Jasper			Kricton	
	Cash	Other		Loan	Current	Capital	Current	Capital
Profit and loss ratios........................						60 %		40 %
Account balances, Sept. 2, 19X1..............	$ 3,000	$97,000	$55,000	$15,000	$5,000	$10,000	($1,000)	$16,000
Realization on other assets and distribution of loss..	62,000	(97,000)				(21,000)		(14,000)
Payment of liabilities.......................	(55,000)		(55,000)					
Balances.................................	$10,000	—0—	—0—	$15,000	$5,000	($11,000)	($1,000)	$ 2,000
Apply right of offset........................				(6,000)	(5,000)	11,000	1,000	(1,000)
Pay partner's loan..........................	(9,000)			(9,000)				
Pay partner's capital account................	(1,000)							(1,000)

31-23

EXHIBIT 6

JASPER AND KRICTON
Partnership Liquidation Statement
Three Months Ended November 30, 19X1

Event or position	Assets		Liabilities to others	Jasper			Kricton	
	Cash	Other		Loan	Current	Capital	Current	Capital
Profit and loss ratios.............						60 %		40 %
Account balances, Sept. 2, 19X1.......	$ 3,000	$97,000	$55,000	$15,000	$5,000	$20,000	($1,000)	$6,000
Realization on other assets and distribution of loss..	62,000	(97,000)				(21,000)		(14,000)
Payment of liabilities........	(55,000)		(55,000)					
Balances.............	$10,000	–0–	–0–	$15,000	$5,000	($1,000)	($1,000)	($8,000)
Apply right of offset..........					(1,000)	1,000		
Pay partner's loan...........	(10,000)			(10,000)				
Balances*...........	–0–	–0–	–0–	$ 5,000	$4,000	–0–	($1,000)	($8,000)

* Represent rights of Jasper to contribution from Kricton. Rights are unenforceable since Kricton's personal assets are insufficient to pay personal creditors.

to whether contribution from that partner can be expected. If no contribution is possible, such deficit from the individual partner must be distributed to the remaining partners on the basis of their individual profit and loss ratios. Before any cash is distributed, not only must gains and losses incurred during liquidation be distributed to partners' capital accounts but also losses due to the inability of the partnership to obtain contribution to cover deficits in partners' capital accounts must be recognized.

The Statement of Partnership Liquidation shown in Exhibit 5 illustrates the process the accountant follows when losses do not produce net debit balances for any partner.

Exhibit 6 carries a partnership through a liquidation process in which it is assumed that one partner, Kricton, is personally insolvent and unable to make payment to the partnership for the debit balance in his capital account. The balances on the books would not be closed out since Jasper would continue to have a right against Kricton for contribution. If Kricton should acquire assets at a later date and assuming that he was not discharged from such obligations in a bankruptcy action, Jasper might attempt collection.

Installment Distributions.   In Exhibits 5 and 6, all the assets were realized before any distributions to partners took place. Frequently, partners will request that some distribution be made to them prior to complete realization of its assets and incurrence of all liquidating expenses. At such point in time, total losses are unlikely to be known. The person undertaking the liquidation process must be extremely careful not to make an improper distribution since he could be held personally liable for losses resulting from such improper distribution. Therefore, it is necessary that payments be made only to those partners who would have net credit balances remaining in their personal accounts after all possible losses have been distributed to those accounts. Such losses would include both losses on realization of assets and possible losses resulting from inability to gain a contribution from partners with net debit balances in their personal accounts.

Frequently, partners want a plan for distribution for cash or other assets

EXHIBIT 7

LUELLA AND MERTON
Calculation of Loss Which Prevents a Partner from Sharing in Cash Distributions

Event or position	Assets		Liabilities	Luella (combined)	Merton (combined)
	Cash	Other			
Profit and loss ratios......				60 %	40 %
Balances Oct. 1, 19X1.....	$3,000	$97,000	$55,000	$30,000	$15,000
Loss to eliminate Merton from sharing in cash distributions..............		(37,500)		(22,500)	(15,000)
Balance.................	$3,000	$59,500	$55,000	$ 7,500	—0—

Schedule for Cash Distributions during Liquidation

First $55,000.................................	$55,000	—0—	—0—
Next $7,500...................................	—0—	$7,500	—0—
All over $62,500..............................	—0—	60 %	40 %

EXHIBIT 8

31-26

LUELLA AND MERTON
Partnership Liquidation Statement
Two Months Ended November 30, 19X1

Event or position	Assets Cash	Assets Other	Liabilities to others	Loan	Luella Current	Luella Capital	Merton Current	Merton Capital
Profit and loss ratios..........						60%		40%
Account balances, Oct. 1, 19X1...	$ 3,000	$97,000	$55,000	$15,000	$5,000	$10,000	($1,000)	$16,000
Realization on other assets and distribution of loss..	57,000	(71,000)				(8,400)		(5,600)
Payment of liabilities..........	(55,000)		(55,000)					
Apply right of offset...........							1,000	(1,000)
Payment to partner*............	(5,000)			(5,000)				
Account balances, Nov. 1, 19X1	—0—	$26,000	—0—	$10,000	$5,000	$ 1,600	—0—	$ 9,400
Realization on other assets and distribution of gain.	30,000	(26,000)				2,400		1,600
Balances, Nov. 30, 19X1........	$30,000	—0—	—0—	$10,000	$5,000	$ 4,000	—0—	$11,000
Payments:								
Partner's loan................	$10,000			$10,000				
Partner's current account.....	5,000				$5,000			
Partners' capital accounts....	15,000					$ 4,000		$11,000
Total payments.............	$30,000			$10,000	$5,000	$ 4,000		$11,000

*Calculation of Installment Payment Appropriate
As of November 1, 19X1

	Loan	Luella Current	Luella Capital	Merton Current	Merton Capital
Balances as of Nov. 1, 19X1, but before payment to partners...........	$15,000	$5,000	$ 1,600	($1,000)	$10,400
Distribute possible loss on sale of remaining assets of $26,000..............			(15,600)		(10,400)
Balances..............................	$15,000	$5,000	($14,000)	($1,000)	—0—
Apply right of offset.................	(9,000)	(5,000)	14,000		
Balances..............................	$ 6,000	—0—	—0—	($1,000)	—0—
Distribute possible loss if Merton were to become personally insolvent.....	(1,000)			1,000	
Cash to be distributed..............	$ 5,000	—0—	—0—	—0—	—0—

prepared prior to liquidation. This will minimize the need for a calculation of proper payments to partners at various times during the liquidation process. Exhibit 7 illustrates an advance plan for cash distribution. Exhibit 8 presents a Partnership Liquidation Statement and a schedule showing the amount to distribute at a time prior to completion of the liquidation process. It is to be noted that in an installment liquidation procedure each distribution is to be made on the assumption that: (1) Partners with deficits will not be able to pay amounts owed to the partnership, and (2) no net recovery on remaining assets is possible.

INCORPORATING A BUSINESS OPERATED AS A PARTNERSHIP

The need to limit liability or make transfer of ownership interests easier may suggest converting from the partnership to the corporate form or organization. The corporation would then take title to the assets and assume the liabilities of the old partnership. The old partnership would be dissolved and the partners become stockholders of the new corporation. Prior to transference of title, the new corporation must obtain a charter from some state. A contract between the old partnership and the corporation should be executed covering the specific items to be transferred and the shares of stock to be issued therefor.

EXHIBIT 9

HOMER AND JETHRO
Balance Sheet
January 31, 19X2
Assets

Cash..		$ 6,000
Trade receivables.................................		10,000
Inventories..		20,000
Equipment..............................	$25,000	
Less: Accumulated depreciation.............	6,000	19,000
		$55,000

Equities

Trade payables....................................	$ 4,000
Bank loan...	15,000
Homer, capital (60% of profits)	16,000
Jethro, capital (40% of profits)	20,000
	$55,000

Entry 1—Revalue the assets

Goodwill.................................	5,000	
Inventory................................	4,000	
Accumulated Depreciation.................	6,000	
Store Equipment......................		5,000
Revaluation Account....................		10,000

Entry 2—Distribute revaluation

Revaluation Account.......................	10,000	
Homer, Capital.......................		6,000
Jethro, Capital.......................		4,000

Entry 3—Issue corporate stock to partners

Homer, Capital...........................	22,000	
Jethro, Capital...........................	24,000	
Capital Stock (460 shares, $100 par).......		46,000

EXHIBIT 10

HOMER AND JETHRO
Balance Sheet
January 31, 19X2
Assets

Cash..		$ 6,000
Trade receivables.............................		10,000
Inventories..................................		20,000
Equipment.................................	$25,000	
Less: Accumulated depreciation.............	6,000	19,000
		$55,000

Equities

Trade payables.................................	$ 4,000
Bank loan......................................	15,000
Homer, capital.................................	16,000
Jethro, capital.................................	20,000
	$55,000

Entry 1—Revalue the assets

Goodwill..................................	5,000	
Inventory.................................	4,000	
Accumulated Depreciation.................	6,000	
Store Equipment......................		5,000
Revaluation Account..................		10,000

Entry 2—Distribute revaluation

Revaluation Account......................	10,000	
Homer, Capital.........................		6,000
Jethro, Capital.........................		4,000

*Entry 3—Receipt of corporate stock
for net assets of the partnership*

Corporate Stock..........................	46,000	
Trade Payables...........................	4,000	
Bank Loan...............................	15,000	
Cash.................................		6,000
Trade Receivables......................		10,000
Inventories...........................		24,000
Equipment............................		20,000
Goodwill.............................		5,000

Entry 4—Distribute corporate stock to partners

Homer, Capital..........................	22,000	
Jethro, Capital...........................	24,000	
Corporate Stock.......................		46,000

Prior to transferring assets, they should be placed on the books at current value and the gain or loss on such revaluation calculated and allocated to the partners' accounts in their profit and loss ratios. Though profit and loss will be recorded on the books of the partnership, it is customary for incorporation of an existing partnership business to be carried out in a tax-free manner. The values shown on the corporate books following the transfer will not necessarily be the same as their tax basis.

One of the decisions facing a partnership to be incorporated is whether to retain its existing set of books or to open a new set of books covering activities of the successor corporation. If the existing partnership books are to be retained, the following procedures should be employed:

1. Determine the specific assets to be revalued and record such revaluation in the accounts.

2. Close net revaluation balances to the appropriate partners' accounts in their profit and loss ratio.

3. Close the partners' accounts and set up the appropriate capital stock and additional paid-in capital accounts.

An illustration of this procedure in a partnership where the partners share profits and losses in a 60-40 ratio is noted in Exhibit 9.

If the partnership books are to be closed out and a new set of corporate books opened, different procedures are needed, namely:

1. Revalue the partnership assets.

2. Record such revaluation in the partners' capital accounts in their profit and loss ratio.

3. Record the transfer of the assets and assumption of the liabilities by the corporation in return for its stock.

4. Record the transfer of the stock to the partners in full settlement of their partnership interest.

With respect to the corporate books, the usual entries applicable to incorporation include the recording of the assets acquired and issuance of stock therefor. Exhibit 10 indicates the entries to close the partnership books.

BIBLIOGRAPHY

Dixon, Hollis A., and Jennifer Fisher: "An Integrated System of Partnership Accounting for Financial and Tax Purposes," *Arizona Society of Certified Public Accountants Quarterly,* vol. 67, pp. 6–14, May 1967.

Griffin, Charles H., T. H. Williams, and Kermit D. Larson: *Advanced Accounting,* rev. ed., Richard D. Irwin, Homewood, Ill., 1971, chaps. 2–4.

Lentilholm, J. W.: "Determination of Goodwill and Bonus on Admission of a Partner," *The Accounting Review,* vol. 29, pp. 754–756, July 1964.

Meigs, Walter B., A. N. Mosich, and E. J. Larsen: *Modern Advanced Accounting,* McGraw-Hill Book Company, New York, 1975, chaps. 1–2.

Simons, Harry, and Wilbert E. Karrenbrock: *Advanced Accounting,* 4th ed., South-Western Publishing Company, Cincinnati, 1968, chaps. 1–4.

Chapter **32**

Adjustments for Changing Prices

CLYDE P. STICKNEY
Associate Professor of Accounting, University of North Carolina at
Chapel Hill

TYPES OF ADJUSTMENTS

Most accounting measurements are made in terms of the number of dollars (or other monetary unit) that were or will be expended for the object of measurement. This measure is commonly referred to as "historical cost." For example, if during 1973 a firm acquired a machine for $2,000 cash, the machine would be accounted for three years later, during 1976, as having a historical cost of $2,000, and the depreciation of the machine during the year 1976 would be based on that figure. Accounting based on historical cost provides no information about the effects of any price changes—either about changes in all prices affecting the general purchasing power of the dollar or about changes in the specific prices of individual assets being used. The effects of price changes are ultimately reflected in the measurement of income, but the effects are implicitly merged with all the other factors affecting the business enterprise.

Depending on the objectives to be served, there are several ways to deal explicitly with changing prices in accounting measurements and to report the effects so isolated.

Historical Amounts Adjusted for Changes in the General Price Level. Historical cost can be stated in terms either of the units of money or of the units of general purchasing power that were expended for the object of measurement. The

Financial Accounting Standards Board has proposed that the conventional financial statements expressed in units of money be adjusted for changes in the general purchasing power of the monetary unit and that certain information from the adjusted statements be disclosed.[1]

These adjustments introduce the need for measurements of general purchasing power, but the need for such measurements is neither new nor restricted to accounting. For some time, various agencies of the U.S. federal government have been publishing indexes that measure changes in general price levels. Similar indexes are published in other countries. To the extent that such indexes provide acceptable measures of general price-level changes, they can be used in accounting to measure historical costs in terms of units of general purchasing power. For example, during the three-year period, 1973 to 1976, the general price level in the United States increased about 30 percent, as indicated by the Consumer Price Index (CPI) prepared by the Bureau of Labor Statistics and by the Gross National Product Implicit Price Deflator (GNP Deflator) prepared by the Department of Commerce. The machine acquired in the previous example for $2,000 of 1973 purchasing power could be accounted for three years later as having a restated cost of $2,600 of 1976 purchasing power (= $2,000 × 1.30), and the depreciation of the machine during the year 1976 would be based on the latter figure.

It is possible to make the purchasing power measurements of historical cost and depreciation in terms of 1973 dollars ($2,000), or 1976 dollars ($2,600), or dollars of any other date. If, however, other accounting measurements are to be made in terms of purchasing power and reported together with those for the machine, it is crucial that a common measuring unit be used, especially if the arithmetic operations of addition and subtraction are involved. Since accounting information is intended to be used in making current decisions, it seems reasonable that accounting reports should be stated in terms of current dollars—the terms in which the decision maker is most likely to be thinking. The FASB has proposed that the financial statements be restated to the general purchasing power of the dollar as of the most recent balance sheet date.[2]

Current Prices of Specific Items.   The prices of specific items, such as the machine acquired during 1973, may change less or change more than the general price level or may even move in the opposite direction. The CPI reflects the average change in the retail prices of a "basket" of consumer goods; the GNP Deflator reflects the average change in prices of all goods and services produced in the economy. It is unreasonable to expect, therefore, that such indexes could provide meaningful measures of the changes in the price of any specific item. Accounting for the current prices of specific items is distinctly different from accounting for unadjusted historical cost (i.e., units of money) or accounting for historical cost adjusted for changes in the general price level (i.e., units of general purchasing power). To illustrate, assume that during the three-year period there had been no technological changes affecting the machine acquired during 1973, and that the current price for a new identical machine on December 31, 1976, was $2,500. In 1976, the machine could be accounted for on the basis of its replacement cost of $2,500, and the depreciation of the machine during the year 1976 would be based on that figure. Other possibilities for determining current value are discussed in some detail later in this chapter.

Current Prices of Specific Items and Adjustments for Changes in the General Price Level.   The separate effects of changes in the general price level and changes in specific prices may be accounted for. Perhaps this can be most vividly

---

[1]Financial Accounting Standards Board, "Financial Reporting in Units of General Purchasing Power," Proposed Statement of Financial Accounting Standards, Stamford, Conn., 1974, par. 31.

[2]*Ibid.*, par. 36.

illustrated by analyzing an investment in marketable securities. Assume that the 1973 acquisition in the example above was a block of listed common stock at a cost of $2,000, that the December 31, 1976, price for the stock was quoted at $2,700, and that the general price level increased 30 percent during the three-year interim.

At acquisition in 1973, the stock was worth $2,000. For the investor to be equally well off on December 31, 1976, in terms of general purchasing power, the stock must have a value of $2,600 (= $2,000 × 1.30); it is actually worth $2,700. There has been a "real" gain in economic resources held by the investor in the amount of $100 of December 31, 1976, general purchasing power—a holding gain of $100 measured in 1976 dollars. The other $600 is not a gain in an economic sense; rather, it is the additional number of dollars that must be held on December 31, 1976, merely to maintain the amount of general purchasing power invested during 1973.

HISTORICAL AMOUNTS ADJUSTED FOR CHANGES IN THE GENERAL PRICE LEVEL—OBJECTIVES

Money serves two purposes: a medium of exchange and a store of value. The value of money is determined by the amount of goods and services for which it can be exchanged. Different amounts of money must be exchanged for identical goods or services at different times; that is, the purchasing power of money changes. Sometime in the past, one dollar may have been exchangeable for one hour of a particular kind of labor; today, perhaps four dollars must be exchanged for one hour of the same kind of labor. Sometime in the past, one dollar may have been exchangeable for 10 pounds of aluminum ingot; today, perhaps one dollar is exchangeable for only 3 pounds of aluminum ingot. Changes in the prices of labor and aluminum are examples of changes in specific prices. Changes in the general price level are measured by changes in indexes based on aggregations of specific prices and thereby represent average changes in all, or large numbers, of specific prices.

The primary objective of adjusting historical amounts for changes in the general price level is to convert monetary units (for example, dollars) reflecting varying amounts of general purchasing power into a common measuring unit reflecting a uniform amount of general purchasing power for all measurements. This objective is analogous to translating measurements in foreign monetary units, perhaps Canadian dollars or Swiss francs, into their equivalent amounts in United States dollars in the process of consolidating the financial position and operations of foreign subsidiaries with the financial position and operations of the U.S. parent corporation.

Adjustments of historical amounts to reflect changes in the general price level are designed to improve accounting measurements in a number of ways that are described in the following sections.

To Make the Results of Arithmetic Operations Using Accounting Measurements More Meaningful. When dollars representing different amounts of general purchasing power are intermingled, the results of arithmetic operations may be difficult to interpret. For example, it may not be meaningful to report that the $10,000 cash on hand today, plus the $20,000 cost of inventory purchased one year ago, plus the $80,000 cost of land acquired twenty years ago, plus the $60,000 depreciated cost of equipment purchased during the last ten years, equals $170,000 of total assets. Although the total of 10,000 United States dollars, 20,000 Canadian dollars, 80,000 Swiss francs, and 60,000 Danish kroner is 170,000 monetary units, the sum has little economic significance because the monetary units are not equivalent. Likewise, the general purchasing power of one year's dollar is not equivalent to those of other years.

To Make Interperiod Comparisons More Meaningful. Interperiod comparisons made in monetary units representing different amounts of general purchasing power may be meaningless or misleading. A direct comparison of the sales of Shell Oil measured in Dutch guilders, of British Petroleum measured in British pounds, and of Exxon measured in United States dollars would be meaningless; the need for a common measuring unit is obvious. Similarly, in a ten-year comparative summary of the operations of a U.S. corporation, a 30-percent increase in dollars of sales reported during a period when the general price level increased 50 percent may be misleading.

To Improve the Meaning and Measurement of Income. The failure to account for the changing purchasing power of the dollar may distort the measurement of income. The Financial Accounting Standards Board has stated:[3]

> . . . investors and others often look to the income statement, or to ratios that are based in part on measures of income, for information about the ability of an enterprise to earn a return on its invested capital. In the conventional income statement, revenues are measured in dollars of current, or at least very recent, purchasing power, whereas certain significant expense items are measured in dollars of different purchasing power of earlier periods. Depreciation and cost of goods sold are two of the most commonly cited examples, although the problem arises whenever amounts in the income statement represent expenditures of dollars of different purchasing power. In periods of inflation, depreciation and cost of goods sold tend to be understated in terms of the purchasing power sacrificed to acquire depreciable assets and inventory. Further, information stated in terms of current general purchasing power may indicate that an enterprise's income tax and dividend payout rates are significantly different in terms of units of money and in units of general purchasing power.

To Provide Explicit Information About the Impact of Inflation Across Firms. Within a given country, inflation and deflation affect different firms differently. The effects depend on industry characteristics and management policies. In the absence of adjustments for changes in the general price level, the impact of changes in the general purchasing power of the dollar is necessarily submerged with all the other factors affecting the performance of the firm. Therefore, the user of accounting reports must either assume that all firms are affected similarly or make approximations of the impact of changing price levels on one firm versus another. The Financial Accounting Standards Board has stated:[4]

> Changes in the purchasing power of the dollar affect individual enterprises differently, depending on the amount of the change and the age and composition of the enterprise's assets and equities. For example, during periods of inflation, those who hold monetary assets (cash and receivables in fixed dollar amounts) suffer a loss in purchasing power represented by those monetary assets. On the other hand, in periods of inflation, debtors gain because their liabilities are able to be repaid in dollars having less purchasing power. In periods of deflation, the reverse is true. Conventional financial statements do not report the effects of inflation or deflation on individual enterprises.

GENERAL PRICE-LEVEL ADJUSTMENTS—THE ADJUSTMENT PROCEDURE

Data for Demonstration. The demonstration that follows is designed to illustrate the kinds of information uniquely provided by adjustments for changes in the general price level and to identify some of the most significant problems encountered in implementing such adjustments. These are the kinds of adjustments proposed by the Financial Accounting Standards Board's Exposure Draft.

[3]FASB, *op cit.*, par. 66.
[4]Financial Accounting Standards Board, "Reporting the Effects of General Price-Level Changes in Financial Statements," FASB Discussion Memorandum, Stamford, Conn., 1974, p. 8.

Other special problems are discussed after the demonstration. The basic information has been accumulated in the accounts of Demonstrator Corporation in terms of historical numbers of dollars. The comparative balance sheet (Exhibit 1) and intervening income statement (Exhibit 2) summarize the basic historical information.

In order to provide an element of realism to this illustration, the GNP Implicit Price Deflator for the period 1954 to 1973 has been used for years 1–20, respectively. This twenty-year period includes about ten years of gradual inflation (approximately 1.9 percent annual inflation from 1954 through 1963) and about ten years of more significant inflation (approximately 3.7 percent annual inflation from 1964 through 1973).

GNP Implicit Price Deflator (year 5 = 100)					
				Quarterly Average	
Yearly Average			Quarter	Year 19	Year 20
Year 1	89.6	Year 11	108.8		
Year 2	90.9	Year 12	110.9		
Year 3	94.0	Year 13	113.9		
Year 4	97.5	Year 14	117.6	1st	144.6	150.0
Year 5	100.0	Year 15	122.3	2nd	145.3	152.6
Year 6	101.6	Year 16	128.2	3rd	146.5	155.7
Year 7	103.3	Year 17	135.2	4th	148.0	158.9
Year 8	104.6	Year 18	141.4		
Year 9	105.8	Year 19	146.1		
Year 10	107.2	Year 20	154.3		

Adjustment Calculations. In order to restate the dollars of varying purchasing power reported in financial statements prepared on a historical basis into dollars of uniform purchasing power as of the date of the most recent balance sheet, a series of calculations must be made using an index that reflects changes in the dollar's purchasing power. Given an appropriate index, the historical amount and the date of the historical amount must be known. The historical amount is then multiplied by a fraction, the numerator of which is the index for the most recent balance sheet date and the denominator of which is the index for the date of the historical amount.

For example, the cost of an asset acquired for $10,000 during year 6 could be restated to an equivalent number of end-of-year-20 dollars as follows:

$$\frac{\text{Index at end of year 20}}{\text{Index at date of acquisition (during year 6)}} \times \$10,000$$
$$= \text{cost of asset in terms of end-of-year-20 dollars}$$

The FASB recommends that the GNP Implicit Price Deflator be used in restating the financial statements.[5] Inasmuch as daily GNP indexes are not available, the index to be used for end-of-year will be the index which measures the average of prices for the last quarter, the latest index available for the year.

Technically, the index at date of acquisition should be used for the denominator. As a practical matter, in the absence of truly rampant inflation during the year of acquisition, satisfactory results may be obtained by using the GNP index for the quarter in which the acquisition took place or even the average index for the year in which the transaction originated.

[5]FASB, *op cit.,* par. 35.

EXHIBIT 1

DEMONSTRATOR CORPORATION
Balance Sheet
Historical Dollar Basis (thousands omitted)

	December 31	
	Year 20	Year 19
Assets		
Current assets:		
Cash	$ 140	$ 120
Accounts receivable (net of allowance for		
uncollectibles)	400	380
Inventories (at first-in, first-out cost)	520	500
Prepayments	40	50
Total current assets	$1,100	$1,050
Investment in stock of United, Inc. (at cost)	160	160
Property, plant, and equipment:		
Land	$ 80	$ 80
Buildings (net of accumulated depreciation) ..	210	220
Equipment (net of accumulated depreciation) .	550	520
Total property, plant, and equipment (net) .	$ 840	$ 820
Total assets	$2,100	$2,030
Liabilities and Stockholders' Equity		
Current liabilities:		
Trade accounts payable	$ 160	$ 210
Other current liabilities	40	60
Total current liabilities	$ 200	$ 270
Advances on maintenance contracts	30	20
Sinking fund debentures (6%)	500	500
Deferred income taxes	20	10
Total liabilities	$ 750	$ 800
Stockholders' equity:		
Preferred stock (2,000 shares, 5%, $100 par		
value, $105 redemption value)	$ 200	$ 200
Common stock (50,000 shares, $1 par value) ..	50	50
Additional paid-in capital	400	400
Retained earnings	700	580
Total stockholders' equity	$1,350	$1,230
Total liabilities and stockholders' equity	$2,100	$2,030

Using the GNP index, the restatement calculation for the asset acquired during year 6 for $10,000 is

$$\frac{\text{Index for 4th quarter, year 20}}{\text{Index for year 6}} \times \$10,000 = \frac{\text{cost of asset in terms of}}{\text{end-of-year-20 dollars}}$$

$$158.9/101.6 \times \$10,000 = \$15,640$$

Monetary Versus Nonmonetary Accounts. In the process of restating historical amounts for changes in the general price level, it is essential to distinguish between (1) those accounts that are automatically stated in current dollars and therefore require no price-level adjustments, and (2) those accounts that require price-level adjustments in order to be stated in terms of current dollars. Cash, claims to a fixed amount of cash, and obligations to pay a fixed amount of cash are necessarily measured in current dollars, the number of which is not affected by changes in the general price level. In his pioneering work on the subject of price-level adjustments, Henry W. Sweeney labeled such items "money-value assets" and "money-value liabilities," describing the former as "like cash in the fact that they remain rigidly and irrevocably set at previously determined money amounts, irrespective

EXHIBIT 2

DEMONSTRATOR CORPORATION
Combined Statement of Income and Retained Earnings
For the Year Ended December 31, Year 20
Historical Dollar Basis (thousands omitted)

Revenues and gains:
Product sales	$2,578	
Earned on maintenance contracts	22	
Gain on sale of equipment	40	
Total revenues and gains		$2,640

Expenses:
Cost of goods sold	$1,980	
Selling, general, and administrative	276	
Depreciation	124	
Interest	30	
Income taxes	100	
Total expenses		2,510
Net income		$ 130
Dividends on preferred stock		10
Increase in retained earnings		$ 120
Retained earnings, January 1		580
Retained earnings, December 31		$ 700
Earnings per common share		$2.40

of how the value of the money in which they are measured changes."[6] Assets for which the values are not stringently set at fixed amounts he called "real-value assets."[7]

In the more recent discussions of price-level adjustments, the distinction is generally referred to in terms of "monetary" and "nonmonetary" items. For example, Ralph C. Jones states that "a balance sheet account is monetary if it consists of cash or if it represents a claim to an obligation to pay a fixed sum of money. All other balance sheet accounts are nonmonetary."[8]

The critical nature of this distinction in accounting for the impact of changing price levels is well stated by Raymond J. Chambers:[9]

> The importance of the distinction lies in the fact that monetary assets and non-monetary assets are subject to quite different risks. Holdings of monetary assets are subject to the risk of changes in the purchasing power of money. If, for whatever reasons, the general level of prices rises, the purchasing power of a unit of money tends to fall; a greater number of units is required to buy a given good. Clearly then, non-monetary assets are subject to the same influences, but in an opposite direction. If the price level is expected to rise, it is clearly preferable to hold goods and to incur fixed obligations than it is to hold monetary assets. This applies generally as well as to persons, for a rise in the level of prices implies a prospective rise in the rate of cash inflows to a firm, an effect which the holding of cash will not procure. Non-monetary assets are subject also, however, to the risks of changes in customers' preferences, in technology, and in the demands, therefore, both for producers' goods and their products. The expectations which gave rise to their purchase may be more or less than fully realized; what is realized, in fact, is only discovered when goods have been converted to

[6]Henry Sweeney, *Stabilized Accounting*, Harper & Brothers, New York, 1936, p. 16. Reissued by Holt, Rinehart and Winston, New York, 1964.

[7]*Ibid.*, p. 19.

[8]Ralph C. Jones, *Effects of Price Level Changes on Business Income, Capital, and Taxes*, AAA, New York, 1956, p. 9. The FASB proposal also uses the terms "monetary" and "nonmonetary" in distinguishing between these two kinds of items.

[9]Raymond J. Chambers, *Accounting, Evaluation and Economic Behavior*, Prentice-Hall, Englewood Cliffs, N.J., 1966, pp. 196–197.

monetary assets through the market. If one wishes, one may hedge against the risks of holding monetary assets by incurring obligations; the practice is eminently exemplified by firms whose assets are principally monetary assets.

As is demonstrated below, explicit measurements of the gains and losses from holding monetary assets and liabilities are the unique product of general price-level adjustments.

Comparative Statements. In preparing price-level-adjusted comparative financial statements (for example, comparative balance sheets and comparative income statements), the previous period's figures should be restated in terms of current dollars.[10] If adjusted statements have been prepared for the previous year, this restatement can be accomplished by multiplying each amount in the previous period's adjusted statements by the change in the index during the current period. For example, if adjusted statements had been prepared for Demonstrator at the end of year 19, all amounts in those statements would be measured in dollars whose purchasing power is reflected by the index for the last quarter of year 19, that is, 148.0. For comparative statements prepared at the end of year 20, each amount in the year 19 statements could then be multiplied by 158.9/148.0 so that all amounts—year 19 as well as year 20—would be stated in fourth-quarter, year-20 dollars. In making price-level adjustments for year 20 then, only year-20 transactions would need to be analyzed.

The following illustration assumes, however, that Demonstrator has not previously prepared price-level-adjusted statements. Accordingly, it is necessary to analyze the amounts in each account completely in order to determine the date of their origin. The first time adjustments are made to uniform dollars will inevitably involve greater effort than that required in subsequent years.

GENERAL PRICE-LEVEL ADJUSTMENTS—THE BALANCE SHEET

Cash. The amount of cash held by Demonstrator on December 31, year 20, is $140,000. Those dollars are necessarily 140,000 December 31, year 20, dollars. Cash is the quintessential of a monetary asset; no adjustment is necessary.

In constructing a comparative balance sheet, however, the number of year-19 dollars held at December 31, year 19, cannot be compared directly with the number of year-20 dollars held today. A year-19 dollar and a year-20 dollar represent different amounts of purchasing power. Accordingly, the number of dollars held on December 31, year 19, must be restated to an equivalent number of year-20 dollars as follows:

$$\frac{\text{Index at end of year 20}}{\text{Index at end of year 19}} \times \frac{\text{dollars of cash at}}{\text{end of year 19}} = \frac{\text{purchasing power held}}{\text{in cash at end of year 19}} \text{ measured in terms of end-of-year-20 dollars}$$

$$158.9/148.0 \times \$120,000 = \$128,838$$

This, of course, does not mean that $128,838 was held by Demonstrator at December 31, year 19; it means that the dollars held as cash by Demonstrator at that date are equivalent to $128,838 of December 31, year-20 purchasing power. Demonstrator's comparative cash position, measured in dollars of identical purchasing power was $140,000 at December 31, year 20, versus $128,838 at December 31, year 19.

Receivables. The adjustment procedures for receivables, because they are monetary assets, are the same as for cash. On the latest balance sheet date,

[10]FASB, *op. cit.*, par. 53.

Demonstrator had a claim against its customers for $400,000 (after deducting an allowance for amounts estimated to be uncollectible). That claim is stated in terms of December 31, year-20 dollars. Because receivables constitute a monetary asset, no adjustment is necessary.

For a comparative balance sheet, however, an adjustment is required to restate the accounts receivable balance at the end of year 19 to end-of-year-20 dollars.

$$158.9/148.0 \times \$380,000 = \$407,986$$

The $380,000 net accounts receivable held by Demonstrator at the end of year 19 had purchasing power equivalent to $407,986 year-20 dollars. Demonstrator's comparative accounts receivable position measured in dollars of identical purchasing power was $400,000 at December 31, year 20, versus $407,986 at December 31, year 19.

Inventories. Most inventories are measured in terms of historical acquisition cost—the number of dollars expended in the past in obtaining the quantities of inventories now on hand. If all measurements are to be made in terms of today's dollars, it is necessary to convert the historical cost of inventories into an equivalent number of today's dollars. To do so requires knowing the dates of acquisition and the historical cost, which for inventories presents a special problem.

If acquisition costs are specifically identified with items of inventory, as may be the case for an inventory of automobiles, expensive jewelry, or elegant furniture, the date of acquisition of each item and the number of dollars expended for each item provide the basic information required for the price level adjustment. The historical number of dollars is multiplied by a fraction, the numerator of which is the current index and the denominator of which is the index for the date of acquisition.

In the more common case, however, accumulation of specific identification information is impractical; a FIFO, LIFO, or average cost flow assumption is used. The price-level adjustment must be consistent with the assumption.

During year 20, Demonstrator purchased inventory having a cost of $2,000,000; the cost of inventory on hand increased $20,000 from a beginning inventory of $500,000 to an ending inventory of $520,000; the cost of goods sold was $1,980,-000. Some simplifying assumptions about the December 31 inventories are in order. Based on the FIFO assumption used by Demonstrator, the $520,000 inventory on hand on December 31, year 20, was the most recent $520,000 acquired.

If inventory acquisitions are made more or less continuously throughout the year, it is reasonable to assume that the $520,000 ending inventory, which is about one-fourth of the year's purchases, was acquired during the last quarter of year 20. Because all amounts in the adjusted statements are being stated in terms of fourth-quarter, year-20 dollars, no adjustment for inventories purchased during that quarter is necessary.

An adjustment for Demonstrator's December 31, year 19, inventory is necessary, however, if both inventory amounts are to be reported in dollars of the same purchasing power. The adjustment is made using the index (in the denominator) for the last quarter of year 19 of 148.0 on the assumption that the $500,000 December 31, year 19, inventory again represented about one quarter's purchases:

$$158.9/148.0 \times \$500,000 = \$536,824$$

Demonstrator's comparative inventory position measured in December 31, year 20, dollars was $520,000 at December 31, year 20, versus $536,824 at December 31, year 19.

This adjustment was based on the FIFO cost flow assumption and assumed that purchases were spread more or less evenly throughout the year. The adjustment procedure, however, can be adapted to other inventory methods (for example, LIFO) and to situations where purchases are concentrated in certain seasons. The essential data are the approximate date of acquisition applicable to the inventory on hand (which, in the case of LIFO, may be many years ago) and the price level index applicable to that period.

For example, the LIFO cost flow assumption requires records of layers of inventory that are distinguishable on the basis of dates of acquisition. The initial or bottom layer is created in the year LIFO is adopted and, if the physical quantity of inventory increases over time, other layers must be identifiable according to years during which incremental quantities were acquired. Price-level adjustments of LIFO inventories require that the historical dollar cost of each layer be adjusted by using the index applicable to the date of acquisition of that layer as the denominator in the adjustment fraction.

The general price-level restatement of inventories is more complicated when the lower-of-cost-or-market valuation basis is used. These adjustments are discussed later in the chapter.

Prepayments. Prepayments are nonmonetary assets. As such, they must be restated from the number of dollars expended in making the prepayment to an equivalent number of dollars of purchasing power as of the date of the balance sheet. For example, prepaid insurance, prepaid rent, and prepaid advertising are investments in future service potentials—protection against risk, provision of shelter, and enhancement of sales. None of these items is measured on the basis of the future receipt of a fixed number of dollars. Prepaying rent for a building or a machine is one way of investing in the future service potentials to be derived from the building or machine; outright purchase of the building or the machine is another way of accomplishing essentially the same thing. Prepaid property taxes constitute a nonmonetary asset representing the rights of use and occupancy and the benefits of whatever services may be supplied by the governmental unit that levied the tax. Usually no claim to cash exists; the asset is measured on the basis of a past cash outlay, not a future cash receipt. Inventories of miscellaneous supplies are sometimes also classified as prepayments. These supplies, nonmonetary assets, represent past expenditures for future services to be received from the supplies. It is not possible here to examine every item that might possibly be included in prepayments. Those examined may help clarify the grounds for assessing whether other items are nonmonetary items.

Demonstrator's prepayments for December 31, year 20, are comprised of two items: miscellaneous supplies that cost $30,000 and prepaid property taxes in the amount of $10,000. The amounts for December 31, year 19, were $35,000 and $15,000, respectively.

The supplies inventory is assumed to equal approximately one year's purchases, which are made fairly evenly throughout the year. It is impractical to identify individual items with dates of acquisition. Accordingly, the average index for the year is used for the denominator. In effect, this assumes that the beginning inventory of supplies has been used and that the ending inventory accumulated steadily throughout year 20.

$$\text{Year 20: } 158.9/154.3 \times \$30,000 = \$30,894$$
$$\text{Year 19: } 158.9/146.1 \times \$35,000 = \$38,066$$

If supplies are a significant item, then a cost flow assumption will be required and they can be restated using the adjustment procedure described previously for inventories.

Demonstrator's property taxes are paid during May of each year and amortized over 12 months commencing in June. Five-twelfths of each payment remains unamortized at year's end. Since payments are made during May, the index for the second quarter of each year is used in the denominator.

$$\text{Year 20: } 158.9/152.6 \times \$10,000 = \$10,413$$
$$\text{Year 19: } 158.9/145.3 \times \$15,000 = \$16,404$$

On an adjusted basis, total prepayments at the end of year 20 amounted to $41,307 (= $30,894 + $10,413) as compared to $54,470 (= $38,066 + $16,404) at the end of year 19.

Investments. Demonstrator Corporation accounts for its 15 percent investment in the common stock of United, Inc., at cost. The investment was made during year 14 when United, Inc., was organized. Although United's operations have proved to be profitable, no dividends have been declared.

The account "Investment in Common Stock" represents a nonmonetary asset measured on the basis of the amount of cash invested during year 14. Accordingly, the following price-level adjustment is required:

$$158.9/117.6 \times \$160,000 = \$216,190$$

Because there were no changes in the account during year 20, this amount applies to both December 31, year 20, and December 31, year 19, in the comparative balance sheet.

If Demonstrator owned at least a 20-percent interest in United, Inc., it would account for its investment on the basis of its equity in United's net assets. United's financial statements would also be adjusted for price-level changes, and Demonstrator would merely adjust the investment account to the amount of its equity in the adjusted net assets as of December 31, year 19, and to the amount of its equity in the adjusted net assets as of December 31, year 20. In the absence of dividends, the change in Demonstrator's equity in United's adjusted net assets during year 20 would be shown as an income item in Demonstrator's year-20 adjusted income statement.

It would not be possible for Demonstrator to adjust properly its equity in United's net assets unless United's financial statements were first adjusted for price-level changes. The initial investment of $160,000 could be adjusted as above, but annual changes in Demonstrator's equity in United's unadjusted net assets could not be adjusted properly merely by reference to Demonstrator accounts. Such changes would involve a mixture of dollars having a variety of purchasing powers. Adjusting each year's change on the basis of that year's index would not provide an accurate adjustment.

Property, Plant, and Equipment. Price-level adjustments for property, plant, and equipment are straightforward, but because large numbers of items and an equally large number of acquisition dates are likely to be involved, the initial adjustment process may be tedious. Fortunately, once the initial adjustment is made, subsequent year's adjustments are likely to be relatively simple.

Demonstrator purchased its land when the corporation was formed, in year 1. No other land acquisitions have been made and none of the original land has been sold. Accordingly, the following adjustment is applicable for both December 31, year 20, and December 31, year 19.

$$\text{Land: } 158.9/89.6 \times \$80,000 = \$141,875$$

Demonstrator's building was constructed during year 1 and occupied early in year 2, at which time payment of the $400,000 cost was made. The building is being depreciated on a straight-line basis over a 40-year period. The adjustments are as follows:

BUILDING AT DECEMBER 31, YEAR 19

Cost: 158.9/90.9 × $400,000 .... $699,230
Accumulated depreciation: 158.9/90.9 × $180,000 .. 314,653
    New book value $384,577

BUILDING AT DECEMBER 31, YEAR 20

Cost: (same as above) $699,230
Accumulated depreciation: 158.9/90.9 × $190,000 .. 332,134
    Net book value $367,096

Alternatively, the adjusted cost, $699,230, could be divided by the 40-year life to determine the amount of adjusted depreciation for year 20, $17,481. This amount, in turn, could be added to accumulated depreciation at December 31, year 19 ($314,653 + $17,481 = $332,134), or subtracted from the net book value at December 31, year 19 ($384,577 − $17,481 = $367,096). Care must be exercised in using these alternative approaches to be sure that the Buildings and Accumulated Depreciation accounts at the end of year 19 are restated to end-of-year-20 dollars.

The equipment held by Demonstrator on December 31, year 19, was comprised of items acquired over several years and at the historical costs indicated in Exhibit 3. By applying the appropriate adjustment factor to the historical amounts of cost and accumulated depreciation, restatements of those amounts in terms of December 31, year 20, dollars are obtained.

EXHIBIT 3   Equipment at December 31, Year 19

Year acquired	Stated in historical dollars		Adjustment factor	Restated in terms of Dec. 31, year 20, dollars	
	Cost	Accumulated depreciation		Cost	Accumulated depreciation
Year 9	$ 260,000	$136,500	158.9/105.8	$ 390,491	$205,008
Year 12	80,000	60,000	158.9/110.9	114,626	85,969
Year 14	470,000	258,500	158.9/117.6	635,059	349,283
Year 17	240,000	75,000	158.9/135.2	282,071	88,147
Totals	$1,050,000	$530,000		$1,422,247	$728,407
Net book value $520,000				$693,840	

During July, year 20, Demonstrator sold the equipment acquired during year 12 for $56,000 cash. The company follows the practice of taking a half-year's depreciation in the year of acquisition and a half-year's depreciation in the year of sale or other disposition. This equipment was being depreciated on a straight-line basis over a 10-year period; one-half year's depreciation during year 20 amounted to $4,000. Upon sale, therefore, the net book value of the equipment was $16,000 (cost $80,000 less accumulated depreciation $64,000) and the gain on the sale was $40,000 (all amounts in historical dollars).

Demonstrator acquired new highly specialized equipment during September, year 20, at a cost of $160,000. For reporting purposes, it decided to depreciate this equipment on a straight-line basis over a period of four years; one-half year's depreciation during year 20, the year of acquisition, amounted to $20,000.

Exhibit 4 shows these two transactions and the depreciation on other items of equipment in historical dollars. Again, by applying the appropriate adjustment factor to the historical amounts of cost and accumulated depreciation, restatements in terms of December 31, year 20, dollars are obtained.

EXHIBIT 4   Equipment at December 31, Year 20

	Stated in historical dollars			Restated in terms of Dec. 31, year 20, dollars	
Year acquired	Cost	Accumulated depreciation	Adjustment factor	Cost	Accumulated depreciation
Year 9	$ 260,000	$149,500	158.9/105.8	$ 390,491	$224,533
Year 14	470,000	305,500	158.9/117.6	635,059	412,789
Year 17	240,000	105,000	158.9/135.2	282,071	123,406
Year 20	160,000	20,000	158.9/155.7	163,288	20,411
Totals	$1,130,000	$580,000		$1,470,909	$781,139
Net book value $550,000				$689,770	

It should be noted that in future years only the second set of computations need be made. Next year, in a comparative balance sheet prepared for December 31, year 21, the net book value of equipment at December 31, year 20, as stated above in December 31, year 20, dollars can simply be adjusted by applying the fraction:

$$\frac{\text{Fourth quarter, year 21 index}}{\text{Fourth quarter, year 20 index}} \times \$689{,}770 = \begin{array}{l}\text{December 31, year} \\ \text{20, net book value} \\ \text{restated in terms of} \\ \text{December 31, year} \\ \text{21, dollars}\end{array}$$

Current Liabilities.   Trade accounts payable and other current liabilities (usually wages and salaries, utilities, and similar items representing services already received but for which payment has not been made) are monetary items directly measured on the basis of a fixed number of dollars required for their settlement. As such, they are automatically stated in terms of current dollars. No adjustments of the December 31, year 20, balances are necessary. As in the case of cash and receivables, for comparative purposes the year-19 balances must be restated in terms of current dollars:

Trade accounts payable: 158.9/148.0 × $210,000 = $225,466
Other current liabilities: 158.9/148.0 × $ 60,000 = $ 64,419

Advances on Maintenance Contracts.   In some businesses, payments from customers are received in advance of the earning process. The collection of three-year subscriptions by magazine publishers, the collection of insurance premiums by insurance companies at the outset of a period of coverage, and the advance collection of rentals by landlords are examples. Such advance collections represent obligations requiring future settlement in goods and services. Measurements are typically made on the basis of the historical amounts of cash received in the past rather than on the basis of the future outlay required for their settlement. Measured in this way, they represent nonmonetary liabilities which require price level adjustments.

Demonstrator sells two-year maintenance contracts on certain types of the equipment in which it deals, the sales being spread rather evenly throughout the year. About $2,000 of the December 31, year 19, advances on maintenance contracts balance of $20,000 arose from contracts sold during year 18. The adjustment is, therefore,

Sold during year 18: 158.9/141.4 × $ 2,000   . $ 2,248
Sold during year 19: 158.9/146.1 × $18,000   .   19,577
Total $21,825

Of the total advances on maintenance contracts at December 31, year 20, of $30,000, about $6,000 arose from year 19 sales and about $24,000 from year 20 sales. The adjustment is, therefore,

158.9/146.1 × $ 6,000 .... $ 6,526
158.9/154.3 × $24,000 .... <u>24,716</u>
Total .... <u>$31,242</u>

On an adjusted basis, total advances on maintenance contracts at the end of year 20 amounted to $31,242, as compared to $21,825 at the end of year 19.

Long-Term Debt. Demonstrator's 6-percent sinking fund debentures were issued at par during year 14 to provide additional working capital and funds for purchase of equipment. Sinking fund payments will commence in year 23; the debentures mature in year 33.

The obligation to make periodic interest payments and a principal repayment at maturity is measured in terms of specified numbers of dollars, regardless of changes in the purchasing power of the dollar; the obligation is a monetary item measured directly on the basis of the future amounts of cash to be expended in its settlement. The amount reported in the conventional balance sheet, $500,000, is the present value of those future payments discounted at the rate of 6 percent. No adjustment of the December 31, year 20, balance is required. For comparative purposes, the year 19 balance must be restated to end-of-year-20 dollars:

Year 19: 158.9/148.0 × $500,000 = $536,824

Deferred Income Taxes. The deferred income taxes account reported on the balance sheet of Demonstrator Corporation represents the accumulated number of dollars of tax savings that resulted from the use of accelerated depreciation on certain items of equipment for tax purposes rather than the straight-line depreciation method used for the same items in the financial statements. According to one view, the account represents a monetary liability measured directly on the basis of the number of dollars to be paid in the future when the depreciation allowable for tax purposes is less than the depreciation reported in the financial statements. This view is often described as the "liability" method of interperiod tax allocation. The measurement usually assumes that current tax rates will continue unchanged in the future. Viewed as a monetary liability, no adjustment of the December 31, year 20, balance would be required. For comparative purposes, the year-19 balance would be restated in terms of current dollars:

158.9/148.0 × $10,000 = $10,736

APB Opinion No. 11[11] adopts the so-called deferred method of interperiod tax allocation. Under this method, deferred income taxes are not considered to constitute a liability for income taxes to be paid in the future. Rather, interperiod tax allocation is treated as "a procedure whereby the tax effects of current timing differences are deferred currently and allocated to income tax expense of future periods when the timing differences reverse. . . . The tax effects of transactions which reduce taxes currently payable are treated as deferred credits." According to this view, deferred income taxes represent an "actual tax reduction in the current period" that should not be reflected in the current period's income but rather should be carried forward in the balance sheet as a deferred credit "until released to income when recorded depreciation exceeds tax depreciation." The method is said to emphasize "the income statement rather than the balance sheet,

[11]Accounting Principles Board, "Accounting for Income Taxes," Opinion No. 11, AICPA, New York, 1967, par. 35.

by removing from income the actual tax reduction realized in the current period by reason of tax depreciation exceeding book depreciation."[12]

Under the deferred method, the amount of deferred income taxes is measured on the basis of past tax reductions rather than on the basis of future cash outlays. Following this line of reasoning, the account must be adjusted to reflect the purchasing power saved in the past. In keeping with APB Opinion No. 11, this is the procedure adopted in the FASB proposal: deferred taxes are designated as nonmonetary.[13]

Demonstrator's deferred income taxes have accumulated during the past four years as indicated in Exhibit 5. The adjustment assumes that income taxes are paid and the savings accrue more or less continuously throughout the year. Viewed as a deferred credit, Demonstrator's deferred income taxes are restated to $21,531 as of December 31, year 20, as compared to $11,233 as of December 31, year 19.

EXHIBIT 5   Deferred Income Taxes

Year	Historical dollars	Adjustment factor	Restated in terms of Dec. 31, year 20, dollars
Year 17	$ 2,000	158.9/135.2	$ 2,351
Year 18	5,000	158.9/141.4	5,619
Year 19	3,000	158.9/146.1	3,263
Balance, Dec. 31, Year 19	$10,000		$11,233
Year 20	10,000	158.9/154.3	10,298
Balance, Dec. 31, Year 20	$20,000		$21,531

In this illustration for Demonstrator Corporation, it was assumed that, as of the end of year 20, there have been no reversals of prior years' timing differences. In a year in which a reversal does occur, the historical dollar amount charged to the deferred taxes account must be restated for cumulative inflation since the deferred tax provision was originally made.

As a liability, deferred income taxes would automatically reflect a current measure of the purchasing power represented by the number of dollars estimated to be payable in the future in the settlement of the liability; as a deferred credit, deferred income taxes must be adjusted to reflect a current measure of the purchasing power represented by the number of dollars of actual tax reduction experienced in the past.

In the adjustment process, the analysis of other items classified as deferred credits (and deferred debits) can be troublesome. The analysis may be more readily understood if such accounts are mentally reclassified. For example, unamortized discount on bonds payable is not an asset; it should be treated as a contra-account to its related liability. Similarly, if deferred income taxes are to be viewed as deferred credits representing past actual tax reductions whose recognition in the measurement of income has been postponed, perhaps permanently, the adjustment process may be more readily understood if deferred taxes are viewed as a component of common stockholders' equity, in the same way as retained earnings.

Stockholders' Equity.   Price-level adjustments of stockholders' equity accounts depend on the nature of the information those accounts are intended to convey. For the most part, distinctions are made between capital stock, additional paid-in capital, and retained earnings in historical-dollar financial statements. Admittedly,

---

[12]Paul Grady, "Tax Effect Accounting When Basic Federal Income Tax Rate Changes," *Journal of Accountancy,* April 1964, pp. 25–27.

[13]FASB, *op. cit.,* Appendix C.

however, the accounts do not necessarily reflect reliable legal distinctions; for example, the retained earnings account in a consolidated balance sheet has no legal significance because the consolidated enterprise has no legal existence as such.

Alternatively, stockholders' equity (1) could be treated as a single residual amount (the difference between total assets and total liabilities); (2) could consist of two accounts, the fixed amount of preferred stockholders' equity and the residual amount of common stockholders' equity; (3) could consist of accounts that distinguish between paid-in capital and retained earnings; or (4) could consist of some other combination of accounts. In the adjustment process, amounts that are fixed in terms of numbers of dollars (e.g., the liquidation value of preferred stockholders' equity) are monetary items that are automatically stated in current dollars; other amounts not so fixed are nonmonetary and must be adjusted.

Preferred Stockholders' Equity. Preferred stock may be either monetary or non-monetary, depending on the basis used in determining its amount. Preferred stock is usually stated in the conventional balance sheet at the aggregate par value of the number of preferred shares issued and outstanding, or, in the case of no-par shares, at the aggregated stated value of such shares. In this case, preferred stock is a nonmonetary item since the valuation reflects dollars of general purchasing power of the period in which the preferred stock was issued. Preferred stock is sometimes stated at the redemption price or liquidation value of the outstanding shares instead of the aggregate par or stated value. The preferred stock is treated as a monetary item in this case.

In the proposed Statement of Financial Accounting Standards, the Financial Accounting Standards Board stated:[14]

> Nonmonetary preferred stock shall be restated by multiplying its unit-of-money carrying amount by the ratio of the index of general purchasing power at the current balance sheet date to the index of general purchasing power at the date the nonmonetary preferred stock was issued. Preferred stock shall not be restated to an amount in excess of its fixed liquidation price; at such time as preferred stock has been restated to an amount equal to its fixed liquidation price, it shall be classified as a monetary item.

In times of rising prices, this means that preferred stock issued for prices near redemption value will almost always be classified as a monetary item.

Assume that the preferred stock of Demonstrator Corporation was issued during year 5 and has a redemption value of $105 per share. The aggregate par value of the outstanding preferred stock would be restated as follows:

$$158.9/100.0 \times \$200,000 = \$317,800$$

The general price-level-adjusted aggregate par value amount exceeds the redemption value of $210,000 (= 2,000 shares × $105). The preferred stock is therefore treated as a monetary item and shown on the end-of-year-20 balance sheet at $210,000. The December 31, year 19, amount must be restated for comparative purposes.

$$158.9/148.0 \times \$210,000 = \$225,466$$

Common Stockholders' Equity. As discussed above, the distinctions among the common stock account, the additional paid-in capital account, and the retained earnings account are primarily legal in nature; all are components of the common stockholders' equity. From an economic point of view, the common stockholders' equity is a single, inseparable, residual sum; in preparing price-level-adjusted financial statements, it is probably best to treat it as such. On this basis, common stockholders' equity is measured as the difference between (1) total adjusted assets

---

[14]FASB, *op. cit.*, par. 45.

and (2) total adjusted liabilities plus preferred stockholders' equity. In the case of Demonstrator Corporation:

$$\text{Year 20: } \$2,516,238 - (\$752,773 + \$210,000) = \$1,553,465$$
$$\text{Year 19: } \$2,564,600 - (\$859,767 + \$225,466) = \$1,479,367$$

For the first year in which general price-level-adjusted finincial statements are prepared, it is usually necessary to "plug," as shown above, to obtain the amount of the common stockholders' equity at the beginning and end of the period. In subsequent years, however, the common stockholders' equity at the end of the period can be independently determined by adding to the adjusted beginning common stockholders' equity the adjusted net income, adjusted increases in capital stock accounts, and other increases in the common stockholders' equity and subtracting adjusted dividends and other decreases in the common stockholders' equity during the period.

Demonstrator's comparative balance sheet prepared on a completely price-level-adjusted basis appears as Exhibit 6.

Should it be considered desirable to separate the amount of common stockholders' invested (paid-in) capital from retained earnings, the former may be adjusted for price-level changes and the latter treated as the residual amount. Such a division need not have any legal connotation. Any further breakdown of invested capital along legal lines into stated capital and additional paid-in capital components, however, is likely to be confusing. As financial information, the distinction has no meaning; as legal information, the amounts of stated capital and additional paid-in capital are fixed in terms of numbers of dollars. In other words, as legal information, they are monetary items not requiring price-level adjustments. Accordingly, the fixed legal amount of common stock and additional paid-in capital would create a purchasing power gain that would have to be included in retained earnings. This would imply that part of common stockholders' equity had a gain at the expense of another part—a nonsensical result.

GENERAL PRICE-LEVEL ADJUSTMENTS—THE INCOME STATEMENT

Revenues. Demonstrator's revenues were derived from sales and from the expiration of the two-year maintenance contracts which it sold. Product sales and sales of maintenance contracts were both spread evenly throughout the year. The Financial Accounting Standards Board's proposal suggests adjusting revenues and expenses spread evenly over the year using the ratio of the fourth-quarter price level to the year-average price level. Since the year-average price level approximates June 30 prices and the fourth-quarter price level centers on November 15 prices, the adjustment is effectively a four-and-one-half month adjustment rather than a six month one. To get a full half-year adjustment, some writers[15] have suggested an adjustment equal to one-half of the price change from the fourth quarter of the previous year to the fourth quarter of this year.

Following the Financial Accounting Standards Board's suggestion of a four-and-one-half month adjustment, the following adjustment is applicable to product sales:

$$158.9/154.3 \times \$2,578,000 = \$2,654,855$$

If sales were seasonal or if the price changes had not been reasonably uniform during the year, it would be preferable to use quarterly sales and quarterly

[15]Sidney Davidson and Roman L. Weil, "Inflation Accounting, What Will General Price Level Adjusted Income Statements Show?" *Financial Analysts Journal*, January/February, 1975, pp. 27–31 and 70–81; also September/October, pp. 42–54.

EXHIBIT 6

DEMONSTRATOR CORPORATION
Balance Sheet
Price-Level-Adjusted Basis
(All amounts stated in terms of December 31, Year 20, dollars)

	December 31	
	Year 20	Year 19
Assets		
Current assets:		
Cash	$ 140,000	$ 128,838
Accounts receivable (net of allowance for		
uncollectibles)	400,000	407,986
Inventories (at first-in, first-out cost)	520,000	536,824
Prepayments	41,307	54,470
Total current assets	$1,101,307	$1,128,118
Investment in stock of United, Inc. (at cost)...........	216,190	216,190
Property, plant, and equipment:		
Land	$ 141,875	$ 141,875
Buildings (net of accumulated depreciation)	367,096	384,577
Equipment (net of accumulated depreciation) ...	689,770	693,840
Total property, plant, and equipment (net) .	$1,198,741	$1,220,292
Total assets	$2,516,238	$2,564,600

Liabilities and Stockholders' Equity		
Current liabilities:		
Trade accounts payable	$ 160,000	$ 225,466
Other current liabilities	40,000	64,419
Total current liabilities	$ 200,000	$ 289,885
Advances on maintenance contracts	31,242	21,825
Sinking fund debentures (6%)	500,000	536,824
Deferred income taxes	21,531	11,233
Total liabilities	$ 752,773	$ 859,767
Stockholders' equity:		
Preferred stockholders' equity		
(2,000 shares, 5%, $100 par value, $105		
redemption value)	$ 210,000	$ 225,466
Common stockholders' equity		
(50,000 shares, $1 par value)	1,553,465	1,479,367
Total stockholders' equity	$1,763,465	$1,704,833
Total liabilities and stockholders' equity	$2,516,238	$2,564,600

indexes. In the case of Demonstrator for year 20, the difference would not justify the additional effort.

The revenues earned on maintenance contracts during year 20 were portions of the advance payments received upon the sale of such contracts, as is shown in Exhibit 7 (also see the adjustments of advances on maintenance contracts considered previously).

EXHIBIT 7   Revenues Earned on Maintenance Contracts

Earned in year 20 on contracts sold during	Historical dollars	Adjustment factor	Restated in terms of Dec. 31, year 20, dollars
Year 18	$ 2,000	158.9/141.4	$ 2,248
Year 19 ($18,000 − $6,000)	12,000	158.9/146.1	13,051
Year 20 ($32,000–$24,000)	8,000	158.9/154.3	8,238
Total	$22,000		$23,537

Cost of Goods Sold.   The cost of goods sold can be restated in terms of current dollars as follows, utilizing information shown in the inventories adjustment section above:

	Dec. 31, year 20, dollars
Beginning inventory 158.9/148.0 × $500,000	$ 536,824
Purchases 158.9/154.3 × $2,000,000	2,059,624
Goods available for sale	$2,596,448
Less ending inventory (Dec. 31, year 20)	520,000
Cost of goods sold	$2,076,448

Note that this calculation assumes that the purchases also were made evenly throughout the year. To the extent that this is not the case, quarterly purchases with adjustments based on quarterly indexes should be used.

Selling, General, and Administrative Expenses.   Demonstrator's selling, general, and administrative expenses must be adjusted as shown in Exhibit 8.

EXHIBIT 8   Selling, General, and Administrative Expenses

Historical dollars	Expiration of prepayments	Dec. 31, year 20, dollars
	Supplies:	
	Dec. 31, year 19, adjusted balance (based on assumption	
	that supplies inventory at end of year 20 is equivalent to	
$ 35,000	year 20's purchases) 158.9/146.1 × $35,000	$ 38,066
	Property taxes:	
15,000	Dec. 31, year 19, adjusted balance 158.9/145.3 × $15,000	16,404
14,000	Paid in May, year 20, 158.9/152.6 × $14,000	14,578
	Other operating expenses (assumed to be incurred about	
	evenly throughout the year):	
212,000	158.9/154.3 × $212,000	218,320
$276,000	Total	$287,368

Depreciation.   Demonstrator's adjusted depreciation expense can be calculated directly on the basis of the adjusted costs determined earlier for building and for equipment. The amounts of adjusted depreciation are determined by dividing the adjusted costs by estimated useful lives. (See Exhibit 9.)

EXHIBIT 9   Depreciation

Year acquired	Stated in historical dollars		Estimated useful life, years	Restated in terms of Dec. 31, year 20, dollars	
	Cost	Year 20 depreciation		Cost	Year 20 depreciation
Building:					
Year 2	$400,000	$ 10,000	40	$699,230	$ 17,481
Equipment:					
Year 9	260,000	13,000	20	390,491	19,525
Year 12	80,000	4,000	10*	114,626	5,732*
Year 14	470,000	47,000	10	635,059	63,506
Year 17	240,000	30,000	8	282,071	35,259
Year 20	160,000	20,000	4*	163,288	20,411*
		$124,000			$161,914

*One-half year's depreciation is taken in year of acquisition and one-half in year of disposal.

Interest Expense.   Interest accrues evenly throughout the year on the 6-percent sinking fund debentures. The following adjustment is required:

$$158.9/154.3 \times \$30,000 = \$30,894$$

Income Taxes.   The Income Tax Expense account is comprised of amounts accrued during the year ($90,000) plus the increase in deferred income taxes ($10,000) resulting from the use for tax purposes of accelerated depreciation for certain assets that are being depreciated on a straight-line basis for financial statement purposes. The income tax accruals were spread rather evenly throughout the year:

$$158.9/154.3 \times \$100,000 = \$102,981$$

Gain on Sale of Equipment.   As indicated earlier, during July, year 20, Demonstrator sold for $56,000 equipment that had a book value of $16,000. The equipment had been acquired in year 12 at a cost of $80,000; the accumulated depreciation at time of sale was $64,000. The historical gain amounted to $40,000. The proceeds of the sale, measured in terms of current dollars, were

$$158.9/155.7 \times \$56,000 = \$57,151$$

The book value of the equipment measured in terms of current dollars was

$$158.9/110.9 \times \$16,000 = \$22,925$$

Accordingly, the adjusted gain on sale of equipment was

$$\$57,151 - \$22,925 = \$34,226$$

Monetary Gains and Losses.   Measurement of the monetary gain or loss experienced by Demonstrator Corporation during year 20 as a result of the increase in the price level from 148.0 at the end of year 19 to 158.9 at the end of year 20 requires the identification of all transactions affecting monetary assets and monetary liabilities during the year. This is an important step. The resulting information is the unique product of general price-level adjustments. The effects of inflation (deflation) on the management of monetary working capital and management's policy governing capital structure are explicitly revealed.

This step also provides a check on the accuracy of the adjustment procedures. The reconciliation of the beginning and ending balances of common stockholders' equity provided by adjusted income including monetary gains and losses guarantees that the assumptions and analysis in the adjusted balance sheet are consistent with the assumptions and analysis in the income statement. In this analysis which follows, the calculation of the gain or loss on net monetary working capital and on long-term monetary debt are shown separately.

Gain or Loss on Net Monetary Working Capital.   Net monetary working capital refers to the excess of current monetary assets over current monetary liabilities. In the case of Demonstrator:

	December 31	
	Year 20	Year 19
Cash	$140,000	$120,000
Accounts receivable (net)	400,000	380,000
Total current monetary assets	$540,000	$500,000
Trade accounts payable	$160,000	$210,000
Other current liabilities	40,000	60,000
Total current monetary liabilities	$200,000	$270,000
Net monetary working capital	$340,000	$230,000

As indicated earlier, Demonstrator's sales and collections of accounts receivable are spread fairly evenly throughout the year. The same is true of its purchases and the incurrence of interest and operating expenses. A few lump-sum cash transactions, however, are inevitable. In the case of Demonstrator, three have been identified:

Second quarter:		
May—payment of property taxes		$ (24,000)
Third quarter:		
July—sale of equipment	$ 56,000	
September—purchase of equipment ..	(160,000)	(104,000)
Net isolated cash outlays		$(128,000)

Net monetary working capital increased by $110,000 (= $340,000 − $230,000) between the beginning and end of the year. Isolated net cash outlays during the year as determined above are $128,000. Therefore, the increase in net monetary working from all other transactions except the isolated cash outlays must have been $238,000 (= $110,000 + $128,000). The transactions affecting the net monetary working capital accounts during year 20 are summarized as follows:

Net monetary working capital, Dec. 31, Year 19 ...	$230,000
Plus increase in net monetary working capital during	
year 20 ignoring isolated outlays (plug)	238,000
Less isolated monetary outlays	(128,000)
Net monetary working capital Dec. 31, Year 20	$340,000

The gain or loss on net monetary working capital can be calculated in three parts: (1) the beginning balance, (2) the change during the period ignoring isolated cash transactions, and (3) the isolated cash transactions.

1. The monetary loss from "rolling forward" the beginning of the year balance in net monetary working capital accounts is $16,939, determined as follows:

$$(158.9/148.0 \times \$230,000) - \$230,000 = \$16,939$$

That is, $246,939 of end-of-year-20 purchasing power is required to obtain the equivalent of $230,000 of end-of-year-19 purchasing power. Because the beginning amount of net monetary working capital represents a fixed number of dollars, the increase in the price level during the year results in a loss in purchasing power.

2. In addition, ignoring the isolated cash transactions, the balance of net monetary working capital increased $238,000 during the year. If we assume that this increase took place steadily as sales, purchases, and accruals of expenses occurred throughout the year, a further loss in purchasing power is involved:

$$(158.9/154.3 \times \$238,000) - \$238,000 = \$7,095$$

3. The isolated cash transactions also must be taken into consideration. The isolated expenditure of $24,000 cash during the second quarter negated any subsequent loss in purchasing power on that amount. Similarly, the isolated net expenditure of $104,000 during the third quarter eliminated any subsequent loss in purchasing power on that amount.

$(158.9/152.6 \times \$ 24,000) - \$ 24,000$	$ 990
$(158.9/155.7 \times \$104,000) - \$104,000$	2,137
Negated purchasing power loss on isolated	
transactions	$3,127

In summary, then, the loss in purchasing power suffered as a result of holding net monetary working capital during year 20 is the net result of these three components.

Loss on Jan. 1 balance of net monetary working
    capital $16,939
Loss on increase in balance during year 7,095
    Subtotal $24,034
Negated loss on isolated transactions 3,127
    Year 20 loss on net monetary working capital ... $20,907

Other methods of calculating the loss on net monetary working capital can be used. For example, a detailed statement of sources and uses of monetary working capital for the period under consideration can be adjusted item by item. Exhibit 10 illustrates this method of calculating the loss on net current monetary assets. Using this method, those sources and uses that occurred continuously throughout the year are adjusted using the average index for the year; the isolated or lump-sum sources and uses are adjusted using the index applicable to the date on which such transactions occurred.

EXHIBIT 10

DEMONSTRATOR CORPORATION
Calculation of Monetary Gain or Loss on Net Current Monetary Items
For the Year Ended December 31, Year 20

	Historical dollars	Adjustment factor	Restated in terms of Dec. 31, year 20, dollars
Balance in net current monetary accounts, January 1	$ 230,000	158.9/148.0	$ 246,939
Increases in net current monetary accounts:			
Sales	$2,578,000	158.9/154.3	$2,654,855
Maintenance contracts sold	32,000	158.9/154.3	32,954
Sale of equipment	56,000	158.9/155.7	57,151
Total increases	$2,666,000		$2,744,960
Decreases in net current monetary accounts:			
Merchandise acquired	$2,000,000	158.9/154.3	$2,059,624
Supplies acquired	30,000	158.9/154.3	30,894
Property taxes paid	24,000	158.9/152.6	24,991
Selling, general and administrative costs incurred	212,000	158.9/154.3	218,320
Interest accrued	30,000	158.9/154.3	30,894
Income taxes paid	90,000	158.9/154.3	92,683
Dividend declared	10,000	158.9/154.3	10,298
Equipment acquired	160,000	158.9/155.7	163,288
Total decreases	$2,556,000		$2,630,992
Balance in net current monetary accounts, December 31	$ 340,000		$ 360,907
Monetary loss on net current monetary items ($361,182 − $340,000)			$ 20,907

Long-Term Debt. During periods of inflation, a firm that has long-term monetary debt outstanding recognizes a monetary gain. In effect, the debt is repayable in dollars having less purchasing power than the dollars borrowed in the past. Of course, during periods of deflation, outstanding long-term debt has the opposite effect. Demonstrator borrowed $500,000 upon the issuance of its sinking fund debentures during year 14, at which time the price-level index was 117.6. During the seven years this debt has been outstanding, Demonstrator has enjoyed a gain in purchasing power of $175,595 computed as follows:

$$(158.9/117.6 \times \$500,000) - \$500,000 = \$175,595$$

This is a gain in the sense that the company would have to repay $675,192 (= 158.9/117.6 × $500,000) current dollars to replace the amount of purchasing power borrowed in year 14, whereas the obligation calls for a settlement of only $500,000 current dollars.

Demonstrator's gain on outstanding long-term debt during year 20 was $36,-824.

$$(158.9/148.0 \times \$500,000) - \$500,000 = \$36,824$$

The long-term monetary debt may be merged with the calculation involving net monetary working capital, but in so doing a useful item of information is lost. The management of net monetary working capital tends to be distinctly different from the establishment of corporate policy governing the extent to which financing is by means of long-term debt and by means of stockholders' equity. Also, an important distinction is made in the general price-level-adjusted statement of changes in financial position between monetary gains and losses on net current monetary assets and on long-term debt. This distinction is discussed later in the chapter.

If deferred income taxes were accounted for by the liability method, a monetary gain would be recognized as in the case of long-term debt. The effect would be to recognize not only the postponement of income tax payments but also the advantage of paying those postponed taxes in the future with "cheaper" dollars. Under the deferred method, any monetary gain will be recognized only when the accumulated historical amount of deferred income taxes is reduced. The actual number of dollars paid in deferred taxes at that time will be less than the reduction in the adjusted Deferred Income Taxes account. The difference will be the related accumulated monetary gain during the entire deferral period. This being the case, the deferred method might well produce the anomaly of a monetary gain during a period of deflation.

Preferred Stock. If preferred stockholders' equity and common stockholders' equity are viewed together as total stockholders' equity, the existence of outstanding preferred stock does not call for any adjustments in measuring net income. On

EXHIBIT 11

DEMONSTRATOR CORPORATION
Income Statement
For the Year Ended December 31, Year 20

	Historical dollars	Restated in terms of Dec. 31, year 20, dollars
Revenues and gains:		
Product sales	$2,578,000	$2,654,855
Earned on maintenance contracts	22,000	23,537
Gain on sale of equipment	40,000	34,226
Monetary gain on long-term debt ...	-0-	36,824
Total revenues and gains	$2,640,000	$2,749,442
Expenses and losses:		
Cost of goods sold	$1,980,000	$2,076,448
Selling, general, and administrative ..	276,000	287,368
Depreciation	124,000	161,914
Interest	30,000	30,894
Income taxes	100,000	102,981
Monetary loss on net current monetary assets	-0-	20,907
Total expenses and losses	$2,510,000	$2,680,512
Net income	$ 130,000	$ 68,930
Preferred dividends	(10,000)	(10,298)
Monetary gain on preferred stock	-0-	15,466
Net income to common stockholders ...	$ 120,000	$ 74,098
Earnings per common share (based on 500,000 outstanding shares)	$2.40	$1.48

the other hand, in determining the net income attributable to the common stockholders' equity, as distinct from total stockholders' equity, the adjustments for outstanding preferred stock must be considered.

Demonstrator follows the practice of declaring and paying preferred dividends on a quarterly basis. Accordingly, the adjustment for the preferred stock dividend may be accomplished as follows:

$$158.9/154.3 \times \$10,000 = \$10,298$$

The preferred stockholders' equity in Demonstrator Corporation is fixed in terms of numbers of dollars. As inflation continues, that constant number of dollars represents less and less purchasing power, in a manner identical to outstanding long-term debt. In computing price-level-adjusted earnings per share of common stock, the common stockholders' monetary gain on outstanding preferred stock must also be taken into consideration. The gain on preferred stock accruing to Demonstrator's common stockholders' equity during year 20 was

$$(158.9/148.0 \times \$210,000) - \$210,000 = \$15,466$$

Adjusted Income Statement. Demonstrator's income statement, restated in terms of current (December 31, year 20) dollars, compared with the year-20 income statement prepared on a historical basis, appears as Exhibit 11.

GENERAL PRICE-LEVEL ADJUSTMENTS—THE STATEMENT OF CHANGES IN FINANCIAL POSITION

The Financial Accounting Standard Board's proposal does not require the preparation of a general price-level-adjusted statement of changes in financial position. There may be important differences, however, between the historical dollar amount and the general price-level-adjusted amount for several items in this statement, particularly in the amount of working capital provided by operations. The procedures for adjusting the statement of changes in financial position are described in the following sections. As is the case in preparing the statement of changes in financial position in historical dollars, the adjusted statement is most easily prepared after the restated balance sheet and income statement have been prepared. The historical-dollar statement of changes in financial position of Demonstrator Corporation is shown in the first column of Exhibit 12.

Working Capital Provided by Operations. The calculation of working capital provided by operations begins with the net income amount from the price-level-adjusted income statement. General price-level-adjusted net income for Demonstrator Corporation, as shown in Exhibit 11, is $68,930.

Several additions to and subtractions from net income are required to determine working capital provided by operations. The depreciation charge for the period is usually the most significant addback. For Demonstrator Corporation, the historical-dollar depreciation charge of $124,000 is restated to $161,914, as shown in Exhibit 9. Similarly, an addback to net income is required for the increase in deferred taxes during the period. The addback for Demonstrator Corporation of $10,298 is calculated as follows:

$$158.9/154.3 \times \$10,000 = \$10,298$$

This addback amount is also equal to the change in the price-level-adjusted deferred income taxes account for the period. Addbacks of this type would also be made for depletion, amortization of goodwill and other intangible assets, amortization of discount on noncurrent debt, and the minority interest in earnings if these items appear in the conventional income statement. The price-level-adjusted amounts for these addbacks can generally be determined from the price-level-adjusted income statement.

EXHIBIT 12

DEMONSTRATOR CORPORATION
Statement of Changes in Financial Position
For the Year Ended December 31, Year 20

	Historical dollars	Restated in terms of Dec. 31, year 20, dollars
Sources of working capital:		
Net income	$130,000	$ 68,930
Add:		
Depreciation expense	124,000	161,914
Increase in deferred income taxes	10,000	10,298
Increase in advances on maintenance		
contracts	10,000	9,417
Total	$274,000	$250,559
Subtract:		
Gain on sale of equipment	40,000	34,226
Monetary gain on long-term debt	-0-	36,824
Working capital provided by operations	$234,000	$179,509
Sale of equipment	56,000	57,151
Total sources of working capital	$290,000	$236,660
Uses of working capital:		
Preferred dividends	$ 10,000	$ 10,298
Purchase of equipment	160,000	163,288
Total uses of working capital	$170,000	$173,586
Increase in working capital	$120,000	$ 63,074

Analysis of Increases (Decreases) in Working Capital

Cash	$ 20,000	$ 11,162
Accounts receivable	20,000	(7,986)
Inventories	20,000	(16,824)
Prepayments	(10,000)	(13,163)
Trade accounts payable	50,000	65,466
Accrued expenses	20,000	24,419
Increase in working capital	$120,000	$ 63,074

An addback to net income is required for maintenance contract transactions by Demonstrator Corporation in calculating price-level-adjusted working capital provided by operations. The revenue recognized from maintenance contracts during year 20 arose partially from sales of maintenance contracts during years 18 and 19. Also, cash was received from the sale of maintenance contracts during year 20 which will not be recognized as revenue until year 21 or 22. The revenue recognized from maintenance contracts during year 20 on an accrual basis must therefore be converted to a working capital basis. An analysis of the Advances on Maintenance Contracts account, a noncurrent liability account, for year 20 appears below.

	Historical dollars	Restated in terms of Dec. 31, year 20, dollars
Balance, Jan. 1 (Exhibits 1 and 6) ...	$20,000	$21,825
Plus maintenance contracts sold during		
year 20 (Exhibit 10)	32,000	32,954
Less revenue recognized from		
maintenance contracts during year		
20 (Exhibit 7)	(22,000)	(23,537)
Balance, Dec. 31 (Exhibits 1 and 6) ..	$30,000	$31,242

The conversion of maintenance revenue to a working capital basis requires an addition to general price-level-adjusted net income of $9,417 (= $32,954 − $23,537). A similar procedure would be employed for intercorporate investments accounted for using the equity method. The restated equity in the affiliated corporation's earnings for the year would be subtracted and the restated dividends declared would be added to convert to a working capital basis. This conversion would likely require a net subtraction rather than a net addition since the amount of the equity in current earnings would probably exceed the amount of dividends declared.

Two subtractions from net income are required for Demonstrator Corporation to determine working capital provided by operations. The general price-level-adjusted gain on the sale of equipment of $34,226 must be subtracted. The proceeds from sales of noncurrent assets are usually classified as nonoperating sources of working capital rather than as operating sources. Another subtraction, which will appear in the general price-level-adjusted statement but not in the historical-dollar statement, is the monetary gain on long-term debt during periods of inflation. This monetary gain is included in net income but does not provide working capital. This long-term monetary gain must therefore be subtracted. The monetary gain on preferred stock does not have to be subtracted, since the gain produces an intrastockholders' equity adjustment and is not included in net income. A monetary loss on noncurrent monetary assets during periods of inflation would be an addback rather than a subtraction.

Exhibit 12, which shows the statement of changes in financial position of Demonstrator Corporation in historical dollars and as restated for general price-level changes, summarizes the adjustments to net income to derive working capital provided by operations discussed in this section. General price-level-adjusted working capital provided by operations is $179,509, as compared to $234,000 in historical dollars. The difference between these amounts is largely explained by the upward restatement of cost of goods sold and the monetary loss from rolling forward the beginning of the year amount of net monetary working capital.

Other Sources of Working Capital. The sale of equipment resulted in an increase in working capital of $56,000 in historical dollars. This amount is restated as follows:

$$158.9/155.7 \times \$56,000 = \$57,151$$

Similar adjustments must be made for working capital provided by issuing noncurrent debt and capital stock.

Other Uses of Working Capital. The working capital used for preferred stock dividends is restated as follows:

$$158.9/154.3 \times \$10,000 = \$10,298$$

The working capital used in acquiring equipment must also be restated.

$$158.9/155.7 \times \$160,000 = \$163,288$$

Similar adjustments would be made for working capital used in redeeming bonds and acquiring treasury stock.

Analysis of Changes in Working Capital Accounts. The change in each working capital account shown in the lower portion of Exhibit 12 is obtained directly from the general price-level-adjusted comparative balance sheet in Exhibit 6.

GENERAL PRICE-LEVEL ADJUSTMENTS—SPECIAL PROBLEMS

Manufactured Inventories. The demonstration assumed that all inventories were purchased. For manufacturing companies, the adjustment procedure is bound to be somewhat more complicated. It may be convenient to adjust manufacturing companies' inventories according to the three components as they would appear in a statement of cost of goods manufactured: materials, labor, and overhead.

The materials component can be adjusted in the manner described for Demonstrator Corporation's cost of goods sold. Adjustments of the labor component are simpler because there are no beginning and ending inventories of labor. If we assume that production is spread evenly throughout the year, labor cost can be adjusted using the average index for the year.

Adjustments of overhead costs are likely to be the most difficult, and they may also be the most significant. Many overhead costs involve current cash outlays (for example, utilities, indirect labor, general and administrative salaries). These overhead costs can generally be adjusted in the same manner as direct labor. Other overhead costs involve amortization of previous cash outlays (for example, depreciation of building and equipment). The adjustment of depreciation charges on buildings and equipment for a manufacturing firm is no different from the adjustment of depreciation expense described in the demonstration for a nonmanufacturing firm. Here, as in other cases, the crucial data are the date of expenditure and the price-level index applicable to that date.

Some inventory items may be stated at the standard cost of manufacturing the items. If the cost standards used in valuing the inventory reflect end-of-the-period prices, then the items are already stated in current dollars and no adjustment is required. If, however, the cost standards used are significantly out of date or if manufacturing cost variances are partially allocated to units in ending inventory, then the valuation of the units is probably closer to acquisition cost in historical dollars. In this case, price-level adjustments of the ending inventory are required.

Measurements Based on Current Market Prices. Monetary assets are not necessarily the only accounts that are automatically stated in current dollars and therefore require no restatement. Investments held by a mutual fund are typically stated at their market values on the date of the balance sheet. These investments are already stated in terms of current dollars and do not require restatement. On a comparative balance sheet, the investments at the beginning of the period, shown at beginning-of-the-period market prices, will have to be restated to the general price level at the end of the period. The gain or loss recognized from market price changes in historical dollars will not usually be the same as the price-level-adjusted gain or loss. The historical and price-level-adjusted gain or loss will only be the same if the weighted average change in market price for the portfolio of investments is equal to the change in the general price level.

Some inventory items may be stated at net realizable value (that is, the number of dollars expected to be received upon the sale of the inventories). For example, certain products in agricultural and natural resource industries are frequently measured at their net realizable values rather than their historical costs. Since these inventory items are already stated in terms of current prices, no price-level adjustment is necessary. If, instead, these items are stated at acquisition cost, a price-level restatement will be necessary. The need for price-level adjustments, therefore, is determined by the measurement procedure employed rather than by the inherent nature of the item itself.

Even though price-level adjustments are not required for assets measured at current market prices or net realizable values, it is important to distinguish such assets from monetary assets. Monetary assets represent claims to a fixed number of dollars; therefore holding them necessarily gives rise to measurable monetary gains (deflation) and losses (inflation). Whether gains or losses result from holding nonmonetary assets, however they may be measured, depends on the movement of the prices of those specific assets relative to changes in the general price level.

Cost or Market, Whichever Is Lower. The well-established accounting practice of writing down current assets whenever their historical costs are greater than current market value applies to accounts whose historical amounts have been adjusted for changes in the general price level. For example, *ARB No. 43*[16] states that "in the case of marketable securities where market value is less than cost by a substantial amount and it is evident that the decline in market value is not due to a mere temporary condition, the amount to be included as a current asset should not exceed the market value;" similarly, "Inventory pricing"[17] requires that a loss be recognized "whenever the utility of goods is impaired by damage, deterioration, obsolescence, changes in price levels, or other causes. The measurement of such losses is accomplished by applying the rule of pricing inventories at cost or market, whichever is lower."

These requirements apply whether the measurements of cost are made in terms of historical numbers of dollars or in terms of invested purchasing power stated in current dollars. For example, the Financial Accounting Standards Board has stated:[18]

> Those nonmonetary assets that are stated in unit-of-money financial statements at the lower of cost or market (for example, inventory and some investments) shall be stated, in terms of units of general purchasing power, at the lower of (a) the unit-of-money cost of the asset restated to units of current general purchasing power . . . or (b) market. If (a) is greater than (b), the restated cost shall be written down in the general purchasing power financial statements just as would be done in the unit-of-money financial statements. The amount of the write-down shall be included in determining general purchasing power net income in the same manner as it would be in determining unit-of-money net income.

The following example illustrates the application of the lower of cost or market rule:[19]

> . . . assume inventory that was purchased for $100 in 19X1 (general price level index = 100) has a market value of $90 at the end of 19X2 (index = 110). A $10 write-down to market would be reflected in the 19X2 unit-of-money income statement, and the inventory would be carried at $90 in the unit-of-money balance sheet. The cost of the inventory restated for changes in the general purchasing power of the dollar is $(X2)110 (= $100 × 110/100). Applying the lower-of-cost-or-market rule just as was done in the unit-of-money financial statements results in a $(X2)20 write-down to market in the 19X2 general purchasing power income statement (most likely as part of cost of goods sold), and the inventory would be carried at $(X2)90 in the general purchasing power balance sheet. The cost of an asset will sometimes be written down for purposes of reporting in units of general purchasing power even though no write-down was required for purposes of reporting in units of money. If the market value of the inventory at the end of 19X2 in the previous example had been $105 (rather than $90), there would have been no write-down in the unit-of-money financial statements. A write-down from the restated cost of $(X2)110 to market value of $(X2)105 would nonetheless be required in the general purchasing power financial statements.

If the price of an inventory item increases less rapidly than the general price level, then a write-down to market will be required in the general price-level-adjusted statements. The write-down will usually be reflected in higher cost of goods sold for the period. If the price of the inventory item increases more rapidly than the general price level, then the item will be reported at its restated acquisition cost in the price-level-adjusted statements. No write-up to the higher market

[16]American Institute of Certified Public Accountants, *Accounting Research Bulletin No. 43*, New York, 1953, chap. 3, par. 9.

[17]*Ibid.*, chap. 4, par. 8.

[18]FASB, *op. cit.*, par. 42.

[19]*Ibid.*

value is permitted. If the price of the inventory item increases at the same rate as the general price level, restated acquisition cost and market will be the same.

Price-level adjustments of historical amounts invested in items of property, plant, and equipment may also produce measurements that are clearly in excess of their current worth, in which case write-downs might seem to be in order. For example, assume that the land acquired by Demonstrator Corporation in year 1 is located in an area where land values have not increased substantially during the 20-year period the land has been held. Perhaps recent sales of similar land in the vicinity have been made at about $120,000. Although, in a balance sheet prepared on a historical basis, Demonstrator's land may be properly reported at a cost of $80,000, it would seem inappropriate to report Demonstrator's land at a price-level-adjusted cost of $141,875 in its December 31, year 20, adjusted balance sheet. The cost-or-market rule would set an upper limit of $120,000.

The application of the lower-of-cost-or-market rule to noncurrent assets such as property, plant, and equipment is an unsettled issue, even in historical dollar accounting. APB Statement No. 4 states:[20]

> In unusual circumstances, persuasive evidence may exist of impairment of the utility of productive facilities indicative of an inability to recover cost although the facilities have not become worthless. The amount at which those facilities are carried is sometimes reduced to recoverable cost and a loss recorded prior to disposition or expiration of the useful life of the facilities. . . . Noncurrent assets whose market prices have declined are *generally* retained in accounting records at their recorded amounts until they are disposed of or have become worthless [emphasis added].

The Financial Accounting Standards Board's statement that "the same accounting principles used in preparing unit-of-money financial statements shall be used in preparing financial information stated in units of general purchasing power"[21] would seem to preclude application of the lower-of-cost-or-market rule to property, plant, and equipment in general price-level-restated accounting reports in most cases.

The cost-or-market rule has long been criticized because of its conservatism; it requires that losses be recognized but does not permit the recognition of gains. Also, in practice, such inventory losses are frequently buried in the cost of goods sold rather than reported separately as a holding loss. The use of current prices of specific items, whether higher or lower than cost, together with adjustments for changes in the general price level, is designed to eliminate these criticisms of the lower-of-cost-or-market rule.

Estimated Liabilities.   Estimated liabilities arising from warranty, premium, and some pension plans are nonmonetary in that they represent obligations to provide goods or services whose prices may fluctuate. As with other nonmonetary items, these items must be restated to the general purchasing power of the dollar on the most recent balance sheet date.

In some cases, the historical-dollar amount of the estimated liability is already stated in current dollars and needs no restatement. For example, the amount shown for estimated warranty claims is often reassessed at the end of each period in light of changing material prices, wage rates, and rate of customers' claims. The end-of-the-period balance in the liability account is increased or decreased to reflect the estimated future costs of the warranty plan. Under these circumstances, the estimated liability would not need to be adjusted for price-level changes. As

---

[20]Accounting Principles Board, "Basic Concepts and Accounting Principles Underlying Financial Statements of Business Enterprises," Statement No. 4, AICPA, New York, October 1970, par. 183.

[21]FASB, *op. cit.,* par. 34.

was the case with inventory items stated at market prices, estimated liabilities stated at end-of-the-year prices are not monetary items. The estimated liability does not represent an obligation to pay a fixed number of dollars. The amount to be paid in the future depends upon changes in the prices of specific goods and services.

Consolidation of Foreign Subsidiaries.   Two possible methods exist for consolidating foreign subsidiaries in price-level-adjusted financial statements: (1) the accounts of foreign subsidiaries can be adjusted for general price-level changes using a price-level index for the foreign country and then the adjusted amounts can be translated into United States dollars (adjust-translate method); and (2) the accounts of foreign subsidiaries can be translated into United States dollars and then the translated amounts can be adjusted for general price-level changes using a price-level index for the United States (translate-adjust method). If exchange rates between the foreign currency and the United States dollar changed continuously and precisely to reflect changes in the relative general purchasing powers of the monetary unit of the two countries involved, then the adjust-translate method and the translate-adjust method would produce virtually identical results. Because exchange rates do not always change precisely to reflect changes in relative purchasing powers,[22] the two methods can produce different results. An example may serve to clarify the differences.

Assume that U.S. Domestic Company established a wholly owned Foreign Subsidiary on January 1, year 1, with an investment of $100,000. The investment was immediately converted into 500,000 units of local currency (LC), the exchange rate being $0.20 per LC, or 5LC to $1. Foreign Subsidiary immediately purchased land for LC800,000, paying LC300,000 in cash and signing a long-term mortgage note for LC500,000. During year 1, Foreign Subsidiary had no other transactions. The U.S. general price level increased 10 percent and the general price level in the foreign country increased 25 percent during year 1. At the end of year 1, however, the exchange rate remained unchanged at $0.20 per LC (LC5 to $1). Balance sheets under both methods are shown in Exhibit 13.

In preparing financial statements by the adjust-translate method, price-level-adjusted statements in terms of December 31, year 1, LC are first constructed using a general price-level index for that country. Those price-level-adjusted statements are then translated from foreign monetary units to dollars at the current exchange rate, in the example at the rate of $0.20 per LC (LC5 to $1). In preparing financial statements under the translate-adjust method, the historical amounts in the foreign subsidiary's accounts are first translated using appropriate exchange rates. In general, current exchange rates are used for monetary items and the exchange rates in effect at the historical dates are used for nonmonetary items. The resulting historical amounts stated in numbers of dollars are then adjusted for changes in the U.S. price level since those historical dates.

Each of the two methods has its advantages and disadvantages. The choice must depend on the primary informational objectives to be served. For example, in the adjust-translate balance sheet, land is reported at $200,000. That is the historical amount of foreign purchasing power that was invested in foreign land, translated into December 31, year 1, dollars based on the current exchange rate; it would take 200,000 December 31, year 1, dollars to duplicate the foreign purchasing power invested in land. In the translate-adjust balance sheet, land is reported at $176,-000. That is the historical amount of U.S. purchasing power that was invested in foreign land, measured in terms of December 31, year 1, dollars. The $176,000 understates the amount of foreign purchasing power invested in the land and the

[22]Robert Z. Aliber and Clyde P. Stickney, "Accounting Measures of Foreign Exchange Exposure: The Long and Short of It," *The Accounting Review*, January 1975, pp. 44–57.

EXHIBIT 13

FOREIGN SUBSIDIARY
Balance Sheet
December 31, Year 1

	Adjust-translate			Translate-adjust		
	Historical LC	Adjusted, dollars (25% inflation)	Translated, dollars ($0.20 per LC)	Historical LC	Translated, dollars ($0.20 per LC)	Adjusted, dollars (10% inflation)
Cash	200,000	200,000	$ 40,000	200,000	$ 40,000	$ 40,000
Land	800,000	1,000,000	200,000	800,000	160,000	176,000
	1,000,000	1,200,000	$240,000	1,000,000	$200,000	$216,000
Long-term debt	500,000	500,000	$100,000	500,000	$100,000	$100,000
Stockholders' equity	500,000	700,000	140,000	500,000	100,000	116,000
	1,000,000	1,200,000	$240,000	1,000,000	$200,000	$216,000

Statement of Income and Stockholders' Equity
For the Year Ended December 31, Year 1

	Adjust-translate		Translate-adjust		
Monetary loss on net monetary working capital (0.25 × LC200,000)	LC (50,000)	$ (10,000)	(0.10 × $40,000)		$ (4,000)
Monetary gain on long-term debt (0.25 × LC500,000)	125,000	25,000	(0.10 × $100,000)		10,000
Net income	LC 75,000	$ 15,000			$ 6,000
Stockholders' equity, Jan. 1—LC500,000 ...	LC625,000	125,000	LC500,000	$100,000	110,000
Stockholders' equity, Dec. 31 ...	LC700,000	$140,000			$116,000

$200,000 overstates the amount of U.S. purchasing power invested in the land. This phenomenon is the direct result of the failure of exchange rates to equate the purchasing power of the monetary units in question.

If the primary goal is the consistent reporting of historical amounts in terms of U.S. purchasing power, the translate-adjust procedure would seem preferable. On the other hand, if the primary purpose is to reflect the performance of foreign investments in the unique economic environment in which they operate, the adjust-translate procedure would be preferable. The Financial Accounting Standards Board appears to favor the translate-adjust method.[23]

> An objective of general purchasing power accounting is to express all amounts in a single unit of measure, namely, units of general purchasing power of a single currency such as the U.S. dollar. Accordingly, the Board has required that financial statements of foreign branches, subsidiaries, and other investees first be translated into U.S. dollars and then restated for changes in the dollar's general purchasing power. . . . The alternative, restatement for changes in the purchasing power of a foreign currency prior to translation, would result in an intermingling of units of the general purchasing power of the dollar and units of the general purchasing power of a foreign currency and would, therefore, be inconsistent with the objective stated above.

One further problem in consolidating foreign operations in general price-level-adjusted statements should be noted. In the illustration of the two procedures, the foreign cash and the long-term debt payable in foreign currency were treated as monetary items for purposes of both foreign currency translation and general price-level adjustment. Thus, the amounts reported for foreign cash and long-term debt on December 31, year 1, reflect the exchange rate and U.S. general price level on that date. Monetary gains and losses are recognized on the January 1, year 1, balances in long-term debt and cash, respectively, as a result of rolling forward the beginning-of-the-year amounts to the general price level at the end of the year. If the exchange rate had changed during the year, foreign exchange gains and losses would also have been recognized on the beginning-of-the-period amounts of these monetary items.

Treating foreign cash and long-term debt as monetary for purposes of translation is consistent with the stated objective of translation which "requires that foreign statements be translated in a way that the underlying local currency transactions are accounted for the same as though they had been foreign currency transactions of the enterprise originally measured and recorded in dollars rather than in foreign currency."[24] If cash and long-term debt had originally been recorded in dollars, they would be considered monetary items. Likewise, treating translated cash and long-term debt as monetary for purposes of general price-level adjustments is consistent with the objective of expressing all amounts in terms of a single unit of measurement, the general purchasing power of the dollar at the end of the period. The translated dollar amounts for cash and long-term debt before adjustment for general price-level changes reflect the purchasing power of the dollar at the beginning of year 1. These amounts must be rolled forward to the purchasing power at the end of the year and monetary gains and losses recognized for the period.

APB Statement No. 3 and the FASB proposal take the position that foreign currency and claims receivable or payable in foreign currency should be treated as nonmonetary items *for purposes of general price-level adjustments.* Monetary items have been defined as cash and claims to cash that are fixed in terms of numbers

---

[23]FASB, *op. cit.,* par. 80.

[24]Financial Accounting Standards Board, "Accounting for the Translation of Foreign Currency Transactions and Foreign Currency Financial Statements," Statement of Financial Accounting Standards No. 8, Stamford, Conn., 1975, par. 19.

of United States dollars regardless of changes in the general price level.[25] According to this definition, foreign cash, foreign receivables, and foreign payables are not monetary items because their amounts are not fixed in terms of United States dollars. The United States dollar equivalents of these items change as foreign exchange rates change, that is, as the specific prices of foreign monetary units change.

Consider the effect of treating the cash and long-term debt accounts of Foreign Subsidiary as monetary and as nonmonetary items. When these items are treated as monetary, they are stated on the balance sheet at the end of year 1 at their translated dollar amounts, $40,000 for cash and $100,000 for long-term debt. A net monetary gain of $6,000 is recognized for the year as a result of holding net monetary liabilities while the general price level increased 10 percent. When these items are treated as nonmonetary, their translated dollar amounts are adjusted for the 10-percent increase in the U.S. price level during the year. This adjustment merely converts the historical amounts from dollars of January 1, year 1, purchasing power, the date when the cash was received and long-term debt was issued, to an equivalent number of December 31, year 1, dollars.

One result of treating foreign cash, foreign receivables, and foreign liabilities as nonmonetary is that the dollar amounts at which these items are stated on the balance sheet may exceed the dollar equivalent of the foreign amounts involved at the end of the period. Thus, while the 200,000LC could be converted on December 31, year 1, into $40,000, treating cash as a nonmonetary item results in reporting it at $44,000 (= 200,000LC × $.20 × 1.10). It seems appropriate under these circumstances to adjust the cash account to its dollar equivalent of $40,000 at year-end and reflect the $4,000 difference as a loss in determining net income. A similar adjustment would be made to reduce the amount shown for long-term debt from $110,000 (= 500,000LC × $.20 × 1.10) to $100,000. The $10,000 difference would be reflected as a gain in determining net income. These adjustments are implicitly required by the FASB proposed statement. Since these items are explicitly designated as nonmonetary, these adjustments cannot represent monetary gains or losses. It is not clear, however, whether they represent foreign exchanges gains or losses or some other type of gain or loss.

Note that whether foreign cash, foreign receivables, and foreign liabilities are treated as monetary or as nonmonetary, net income for the period, after adjusting cash and long-term debt downward as described above, will be the same. If these items are treated as monetary, a monetary gain of $6,000 will be recognized. If these items are treated as nonmonetary, a gain of $6,000 will be recognized from writing down the restated amount of cash and long-term debt to an equivalent amount of end-of-year dollars. The only difference may be in the designation of the gains and losses (that is, monetary, foreign exchange, or something else).

GENERAL PRICE-LEVEL ADJUSTMENTS— CRITICISMS

Disagreements about the desirability of adjusting financial statements for general price-level changes have existed for many years. It is important that users of these statements understand just what they do and do not represent. The more important criticisms of general price-level accounting are discussed in the following sections.

The Change in the General Price Level Is an Inappropriate Threshold for Measuring Profitability. General price-level accounting has been criticized for implicitly using the change in the general price level as a threshold for measuring profitabil-

[25]FASB, *op. cit.,* par. 10.

ity for all firms. To illustrate the manner in which the change in the general price level is used as a threshold in measuring profitability, assume that a firm lends $100,000 to one of its key suppliers on January 1. The loan is to be repaid one year later with interest at 8 percent. The firm's return, or income, from the loan is measured by the difference between the interest revenue earned and the monetary loss recognized (assuming inflation) for the period. The calculation of the monetary loss is based on the change in the general price level for the year. A positive return will be reported in the general price-level-adjusted income statement only if the rate of interest charged (8 percent) exceeds the rate of general price inflation experienced.

Another example of how the change in the general price level serves as a threshold in measuring profitability relates to use of the lower-of-cost-or-market valuation basis for marketable securities and inventories. Assume that a firm purchases inventory items on September 1 of a particular year at a cost of $100,000. From September 1 to December 31, the purchase price of these items increases 4 percent while the general price level increases 6 percent. The general price-level-adjusted acquisition cost is $106,000 (= $100,000 × 1.06), while market is $104,000 (= $100,000 × 1.04). In the price-level-adjusted financial statements, the inventory would be written down by $2,000 and the "loss" reflected in net income for the period.

Critics of general price-level accounting argue that the change in the general price level is an inappropriate threshold for measuring profitability. With respect to nonmonetary items, it is suggested that the change in the general price level is an inappropriate standard for assessing decisions to invest in particular nonmonetary assets. For example, assume that a firm purchases and holds inventory in anticipation of increased acquisition costs or builds a capital-intensive plant in anticipation of increased labor costs. These investments are made in anticipation of changes in the prices of specific goods and services. Any economic advantage from these purchase decisions may be partially or completely offset in the restated earnings report when cost of goods sold and depreciation charges are restated upward for cumulative general price inflation since acquisition. The presumption of general price-level accounting is that there is no economic advantage if the prices of the specific goods and services do not rise as quickly as the general price level. This implies that firms always have the flexibility to invest in a broad range of consumer goods and services rather than acquiring inventory, plant, or equipment. Firms do not always have such wide flexibility.

Critics of general price-level accounting also argue that the change in the general price level is an inappropriate standard for assessing decisions to invest in monetary items. It is suggested that the general price index measures price changes for too wide a variety of goods and service. Of more importance to the firm is its ability to maintain purchasing power for the types of goods and services it normally purchases. A firm in the steel industry, for example, is not likely to be particularly concerned with maintaining the purchasing power of its net monetary assets for the wide range of consumer goods and services included in the GNP index. The steel company is more likely to be concerned with its ability to maintain purchasing power for the various raw materials and productive facilities used in manufacturing steel. Thus, the monetary gain or loss recognized in the general price-level-adjusted income statement may reflect a gain or loss in purchasing power for too broad a "basket" of goods and services.

The General Price Indices Are Not Sufficiently Reliable for Use in Accounting Reports. Criticisms have been directed at some of the procedures followed in preparing general price indexes, creating uncertainty about their reliability and accuracy.

One criticism is directed at the use of posted prices for some items rather than prices of actual transactions. Stigler and Kendahl[26] have documented several cases where posted prices were used despite significant differences from the prices of actual transactions.

A second criticism of the procedures is that the goods and services included in the "market basket" and the weights applied to aggregate individual price changes in the price index are not updated on a sufficiently timely basis.[27] As a result, it is questionable whether the GNP index measures changes in the prices of goods and services actually being purchased during a particular period and in the proportions suggested by the weights used in the index.

A third criticism of the price index compilation procedures is the treatment of quality changes. To measure pure price changes adequately, any portion of an actual price change attributable to quality changes in the good or service must first be identified. Triplett[28] and Barzel,[29] among others, have found significant bias in certain components of the GNP index as a result of failing to account adequately for quality changes.

Critics of general price-level accounting argue that these and other defects of the compilation procedures raise serious questions about the propriety of using the indexes to adjust historical-dollar financial statements. These critics counter the usual response that "all firms use the same indexes and any misstatement across firms will be equal" by suggesting that varying degrees of index accuracy through time do create differences across firms depending on the age and structure of their assets and equities.

The Benefits of Comprehensive Restatement Do Not Exceed the Costs. With respect to the benefits of general price-level-adjusted financial statements, several surveys of financial analysts and other statement users suggest that the statements contain little useful information.[30] Additionally, critics of general price-level accounting argue that the costs of designing and maintaining accounting systems for generating general price-level-adjusted data are not insignificant. Even more significant are the costs to be incurred in educating financial statement users about the meanings of the statements and the types of interpretations which should and should not be made from them.

Others, who feel that general price-level-adjusted statements may have some information value after an extensive educational effort, argue that there is sufficient information in the conventional statements for users to make their own desired adjustments for the effects of inflation. Several studies, for example, have shown that a high degree of association exists between the rate of return on stockholders' equity in historical dollars and as adjusted for general price

---

[26]George J. Stigler and James K. Kendahl, *The Behavior of Industrial Prices,* National Bureau of Economic Research, No. 90, General Series, 1970.

[27]For several examples, see Clyde P. Stickney and David O. Green, "No Price Level Adjusted Statements, Please (PLEAS)," *The CPA Journal,* January 1974, pp. 28–29.

[28]Jack E. Triplett, "Quality Bias in Price Indexes and New Methods of Measurement," in *Price Indexes and Quality Change,* Zvi Griliches (ed.), Harvard University Press, Cambridge, Mass., 1971, p. 198.

[29]Yoram Barzel, "Productivity and the Price of Medical Services," *Journal of Political Economy,* 77 (November–December 1969), pp. 1014–1027.

[30]Ralph W. Estes, "An Assessment of the Usefulness of Current Cost and Price-Level Information by Financial Statement Users," *Journal of Accounting Research,* Autum 1968, pp. 200–207; Thomas R. Dyckman, "Investment Analysis and General Price-Level Adjustments," *Studies in Accounting Research,* No. 1, American Accounting Association, Evanston, Ill., 1969; Don E. Garner, "The Need for Price-Level and Replacement Cost Data," *Journal of Accountancy,* September 1972, pp. 94–98.

changes.[31] Given the historical-dollar measure, the price-level-adjusted measure can be easily estimated. Others, such as Davidson and Weil,[32] have developed somewhat more elaborate procedures for estimating the impact of restatement on net income. Their procedure, which also relies on information from the historical-dollar financial statements, gives specific consideration to the inventory and depreciation methods used by a particular firm. Thus, it is possible to estimate various components of general price-level-adjusted net income, such as sales revenue, gross margin, and monetary gains and losses.

If estimation models such as those described above can be refined, then perhaps information from price-level-adjusted statements which is found to be useful can be obtained without requiring firms to make comprehensive restatements.

CURRENT PRICES OF SPECIFIC ITEMS*

Objectives. In recent years, the focus in financial reporting has shifted increasingly from providing historical reports on managements' stewardship to providing information that is helpful in making rational investment decisions. In keeping with this trend, many accountants have proposed that accounting measurements rely more heavily on measures of current prices of specific items. This is not a new idea, but the frequency of such proposals, the zeal of their advocates, and the widespread support the proposals have received, particularly among academicians, is a relatively recent development.

This enthusiasm has not been reflected in practice. Prior to the release of Accounting Principles Board Opinion 6 in October 1965, fixed assets were occasionally written up to appraisal values.[33] In its review of all *Accounting Research Bulletins,* however, the Accounting Principles Board[34] took the position that "property, plant, and equipment should not be written up by an entity to reflect appraisal, market or current values which are above cost to the entity."

Among the asserted advantages of the use of current prices of specific items are: (1) a more meaningful statement of financial position, (2) an improved measure of the results of primary, recurring operating activities, (3) the recognition of gains and losses resulting from holding assets during the periods when the specific prices of these assets change, and (4) the segregation of the results of ordinary operations from holding gains and losses.

AAA Committees' Analysis. The underlying considerations have been set forth by a Concepts and Standards Committee of the American Accounting Association in its consideration of accounting for long-lived assets:[35]

> *Basic Considerations.* 1. The allocation of investor capital within the economic system is heavily influenced by the cumulative effect of investor decisions. The firm's reported net income and financial position are among the primary quantitative measurements affecting these decisions. . . .

*See also Chapter 46.

[31]Russell J. Peterson, "Interindustry Estimation of General Price-Level Impact on Financial Information," *Accounting Review,* January 1973, pp. 34–43; John K. Simmons and Jack Gray, "An Investigation of Differing Accounting Frameworks on the Prediction of New Income," *Accounting Review,* October 1969, pp. 757–776.

[32]Davidson and Weil, *op. cit.*

[33]*ARB No. 43, op. cit.,* p. 73. The Securities and Exchange Commission, however, requires large publicly held industrial firms to disclose replacement cost data for inventories and plant; *Accounting Series Release No. 190,* March 1976. See Chapter 48 of this handbook.

[34]Accounting Principles Board, "Status of Accounting Research Bulletins," *Opinion No. 6,* AICPA, New York, 1965, p. 42.

[35]Committee on Concepts and Standards—Long-Lived Assets, "Accounting for Land, Buildings, and Equipment," *The Accounting Review,* vol. 39, July, 1964, pp. 693–694.

Specifically, the purpose of financial statements is to assist the investor in making his own qualitative judgments about a firm. Among the major attributes of financial statements which facilitate this process are the following:

a. *The measurement and reporting of current income should provide a basis for the prediction of future earnings.* To facilitate the predictive process, reported current income should include: (1) the result of ordinary operations, (2) catastrophic losses and discovery of assets, and (3) holding gains and losses.

Income from ordinary operations is measured by matching current revenues and current cost expirations including depreciation. Holding gains and losses relating to long-lived assets result from holding such assets during the periods of value change (other than value change resulting from depreciation). . . .

The three components of current income referred to above should be reported separately. Because these components result from different causes, they are likely to exhibit different patterns of behavior. As a consequence, separate reporting of these items makes the income statement a more effective basis for income prediction.

b. *The statement of financial position discloses asset composition and capital structure.* Such information is relevant to the appraisal of the firm's stability and the soundness of its financial policies. The statement of financial position also furnishes a measure of resources for which management is responsible and which it uses in the earning of income. In computations such as the calculation of rates of return, it is equally as important to have a currently relevant economic quantity for the denominator (usually some measure of resources employed) as for the numerator (usually some measure of current earnings).

At the same time, another American Accounting Association Committee on Concepts and Standards was arriving at essentially the same conclusions with respect to inventories.[36]

Accountants have long recognized holding losses as an essential part of proper inventory measurement. However, such losses have not been reported separately except in unusual cases where substantial losses have occurred. Price (holding) gains are rarely, if ever, reported explicitly. Neither FIFO nor LIFO spotlights price gains or losses. For example, when prices rise, FIFO buries price gains in the regular income figure; LIFO excludes the effects of price changes from the income statement:

		LIFO			FIFO
Sales, 500 @ $.20	....	$1,000			$1,000
Beginning inventory . 1,000 units @ $.10 = $100				$100	
Purchases .... 5,000 units @ $.15 = 750				750	
Available for sale	$850			$850	
Ending inventory ... 1,000 units @ $.10 = 100	750	1,000 @ $.15	150	700	
Gross margin	$ 250			$ 300	

The $50 price gain (which is attributable to the 1,000 units in ending inventory @ $.05) is ignored in the $250 LIFO gross margin figure and is submerged in the $300 FIFO gross margin figure.

In contrast, in this simplified case the use of replacement cost will spotlight price gains as follows:

Sales, 5,000 @ $.20	$1,000
Cost of goods sold—at current replacement cost, 5,000 units @ $.15 ...	750
Gross trading or transaction margin	$ 250
Price or holding gain, 1,000 units @ $.05	50
Gross trading margin plus price gain	$ 300
Inventory balance, 1,000 units @ $.15	$ 150

[36]Committee on Concepts and Standards—Inventory Measurement, "A Discussion of Various Approaches to Inventory Measurement," *The Accounting Review*, vol. 39, July 1964, pp. 705–706.

When meaningful measurement can be made, it seems evident that the segregation of price or holding gains or losses (from inventory planning and control decisions) and trading or transaction gains or losses (from exchange of goods and services at replacement price levels) will be more helpful than their usual combination into one gross margin measure.

Distinctions between trading and price facets of operations can be important in evaluating business performance and prospects. Managers must make decisions on inventory commitments, decisions on when and how much to buy and on how much to carry. Such decisions inevitably entail risks with respect to price changes. These decisions sooner or later affect reported net income; they also have an important bearing on financial position.

Inventory management decisions should be accounted for more clearly so that the user of the financial statements may readily focus on management's success or failure in dealing with the problem of inventory price changes. For example, it is not uncommon for speculative inventory build-ups to occur because managers believe a price cycle has neared bottom, or because managers fear an impending strike or other disruption of supply. If prices soar, the possession of a large inventory acquired at lower than current replacement prices may be of immense significance to present and prospective investors.

Of course, this significance also holds for the opposite case, where management guesses wrong. CPAs are on guard to see that management reports these price losses, these opportunity losses or declines in expectations. But reports of price gains are usually delayed until sale, and then they are submerged in an income figure that fails to isolate trading gains and price gains—gains that usually arise from different types of decisions. The ignoring or burying of price losses and gains hinders timely and accurate measurement of organizational performance.

Current Costs and Operating Income.   The use of current prices is based on a particular concept of income and a particular view of the way in which income measurements are used by investors. The AAA Committee on Long-Lived Assets explained this view as follows:[37]

> Income from ordinary operations should represent an amount, in current dollars, which, in the absence of catastrophic loss or discovery of assets, is available for distribution outside the firm without contraction of the level of its operating capacity; or, stated in another way, the amount which, by retention, is available for expansion of operating capacity. Measurement of this concept of income from ordinary operations can be accomplished only if the expiration of service potential is measured in terms of current cost. That is, in order to continue operations without contracting the level of operating capacity, exhausted services must be restored; the relevant cost of expired services is the current cost of restoration.
>
> For example, a firm may maintain some level of basic raw material inventory in order to continue operations at a given level. In the measurement of income from ordinary operations, the relevant expired cost when that material is utilized is the cost of replenishing the inventory. The number of dollars paid sometime in the past for the particular units of material used this period is not relevant.
>
> The identical concept applies to depreciation; that is, depreciation must be based on the current cost of restoring the service potential consumed during the period. The measurement problems are greater in the case of depreciation, however. The physical exhaustion of inventories is subject to actual count or weight; the expiration of the intangible services emanating from plant assets is subject only to rough, subjective evaluation. In addition, the determination of current cost may be more easily accomplished for inventories than for plant assets. Despite these measurement problems, the conceptual need for current-cost depreciation in the determination of income from ordinary operations cannot be denied.
>
> Income from ordinary operations is important to investors in making investment decisions. This amount, when compared with cash dividends, is relevant to an appraisal of the intent of the management to contract or expand the operating capacity of the

---

[37]Committee on Concepts and Standards—Long-Lived Assets, *op. cit.*, pp. 695–697.

firm. Secondly, it facilitates prediction of future income from ordinary operations, assuming that costs other than depreciation are also stated in current terms. Third, interfirm income comparability is improved by universal measurement of depreciation on the basis of current cost. Finally, insofar as depreciation represents a reduction in the stock of assets for which management is responsible, this reduction is more clearly indicated by current-cost depreciation on all assets than by depreciation based on unmodified historical cost.

The *total* net income of the period is the maximum amount which, in the absence of stockholder capital transactions during the period, could be distributed outside the firm without contraction of the amount of stockholder equity at the beginning of the period. This is in contrast with *operating* income, which was defined earlier in terms of maintaining operating capacity.

Where holding gains and losses are reported, it is presumed that evidence meeting the specified tests of objectivity and verifiability is available. Under these conditions, holding gains and losses should be treated as increases and decreases in the measurement of net income for the period during which the gain or loss occurs.

Holding gains and losses resulting from unanticipated changes in technology or demand are necessarily directly reflected as changes in the equity of the stockholders. A favorable change in market conditions for example, improves the position of the enterprise relative to other enterprises not subject to the change. However, such gains are not distributable without contraction of operating capacity and therefore do not enter into the measurement of income from ordinary operations. Similarly, such losses do not necessarily reduce operating capacity and therefore are not deducted in arriving at income from ordinary operations. Nevertheless, such value changes do represent changes in the equity of the stockholders and must be recognized in the overall measurement of total net income for the period during which such changes occur.

It should be understood that, over the life of the firm, the measurement of total net income based on current prices of specific items will be identical with that based on historical acquisition costs. The differences are solely a matter of timing and information—no mean considerations in view of the number of transactions occurring daily that involve an exchange of ownership and that are influenced significantly by accounting measurements. The use of current prices recognizes changes in value when the changes take place rather than only when the value changes happen to be realized in exchanges for liquid assets. In the process, the measurement of operating income is said to be improved and a more meaningful statement of financial position is said to be provided.

Concepts of Current Prices.   Several different kinds of current prices have been proposed: for example, the price at which an identical asset could currently be purchased, the price at which equivalent service potential could currently be purchased, and the price at which the asset could currently be sold outside the firm.

Current Price of Replacing an Identical Asset.   Imperial Tobacco Company of Canada has used current replacement costs in measuring fixed assets and depreciation in its published financial statements. Imperial Tobacco Company bases its current prices of fixed assets on cost of replacement in kind, even though it is recognized that many of the assets involved would never be exactly duplicated. According to one report:[38]

> The company did not use the current market price of an asset as replacement cost except when that asset was an exact duplicate of the asset owned by the company. Imperial officials believed that machinery and equipment currently available might well represent greater efficiency than did existing equipment and that acquisition of greater efficiency, as opposed to mere replacement, was a matter of investing new capital, not the preservation of existing capital. . . . The definition of replacement cost used by

[38]D. R. Ladd and J. F. Graham, *Imperial Tobacco Company of Canada, Limited,* ICH 8C1, Intercollegiate Case Clearing House, Boston, 1963.

Imperial was the amount of money required to exactly duplicate any particular asset without regard to the factor or factors which caused the change from the historical cost of the asset in question.

Edwards and Bell[39] also advocate the use of the current cost of identical assets:

> It must be remembered that it is not the current cost of equivalent services provided by the fixed asset over some time period which we wish to measure, but the current cost of using the particular fixed asset which the entrepreneur chose to adopt and is still using. It is that particular decision that the entrepreneur wishes to evaluate on the basis of accounting data. It may well be that he then may wish to compare these data with opportunity cost data relating to selling and/or replacing the fixed asset, but in order to make this decision about the future, he must have information about the actual present and past.

Current Price of Replacing Equivalent Service Potential.   The AAA Long-Lived Assets Committee favors the use of entry prices—specifically, the price at which equivalent service potentials could currently be purchased.[40]

> At the acquisition date of an asset, the value of its service potential is presumed to be at least as great as its purchase price. If this were not the case, the asset presumably would not have been purchased. In most cases, purchase price provides the only objective evidence of the value of the service potential embodied in the asset. . . .
> The current cost of obtaining the same or equivalent services should be the basis for valuation of assets subsequent to acquisition, as well as at the date of acquisition.

A distinction is sometimes made between reproduction cost and replacement cost. Reproduction cost refers to the cost of identical property, as advocated by Edwards and Bell and used by Imperial Tobacco Company; replacement cost refers to the cost of equivalent property as advocated by the Long-Lived Assets Committee. Paton and Paton[41] offer support for the latter in this way:

> It should be understood that the significant replacement cost is the cost of providing the existing capacity to produce in terms of the most up-to-date methods available. Thus it's largely a waste of time to estimate the cost of replacing an obsolete or semiobsolete plant-unit literally in kind; such an estimate will neither afford a basis for a sound appraisal of the property nor furnish a useful measure of current operating cost. The fact of interest is what it would cost to replace the capacity represented in the existing asset with a machine of modern design. To put the point in another way, cost of replacing in kind is a significant basis on which to measure the economic importance of property in use only in the case of standard, up-to-date facilities.

Current Price at Which Asset Could Be Sold.   Raymond J. Chambers[42] is probably the leading advocate of the use of exit prices, that is, the prices at which assets could currently be sold.

> At any *present* time all past prices are simply a matter of history. Only present prices have any bearing on the choice of an action. The price of a good ten years ago has no more relation to this question than the hypothetical price twenty years hence. As individual prices may change even over an interval when the general purchasing power of money does not, and as the general purchasing power of money may change even though some individual prices do not, no useful inference may be drawn from past prices which has a necessary bearing on present capacity to operate in a market. Every measurement of a financial property for the purpose of choosing a course of action—to buy, to hold, or to sell—is a measurement at a point of time, in the circumstances of the

[39]Edgar O. Edwards and Philip W. Bell, *The Theory and Measurement of Business Income,* University of California Press, Berkeley, 1961, p. 186.

[40]Committee on Concepts and Standards—Long-Lived Assets, *op. cit.,* pp. 694–695.

[41]William A. Paton and William A. Paton, Jr., *Asset Accounting,* The Macmillan Company, New York, 1952, p. 325.

[42]Chambers, *op. cit.,* pp. 91–92.

time, and in the units of currency at that time, even if the measurement process itself takes some time.

Excluding all past prices, there are two prices which could be used to measure the monetary equivalent of any nonmonetary good in possession, the buying price and the selling price. But the buying price, or replacement price, does not indicate capacity, on the basis of present holdings, to go into a market with cash for the purpose of adapting oneself to contemporary conditions, whereas the selling price does. We propose, therefore, that the single financial property which is uniformly relevant at a point of time for all possible future actions in markets is the market selling price or realizable price of any or all goods held. Realizable price may be described as *current cash equivalent*. What men wish to know, for the purpose of adaptation, is the numerosity of the money tokens which could be substituted for particular objects and for collections of objects if money is required beyond the amount which one already holds.

Selecting the Appropriate Current Price Concept.   Whether the current replacement cost or the current selling price of assets and equities is the appropriate current price concept depends on the uses made of financial statement information. Since the information needs of various users may differ, the relevant current price concept may also differ. Revsine offers support for this view as follows:[43]

> Observation suggests that the audience for financial reports is quite diverse. One characteristic of this diversity is that there are probably differences in the objectives of various categories of users. These differences in objectives imply there could be differences in the decision models used to achieve these disparate objectives. If the decision models vary among groups of users, then it is also possible that the information needed to satisfy the respective decision models varies among groups. That is, diversity in decision models implies (but does not necessarily guarantee) diversity in needed information. As a consequence of this potential diversity in information needs, accounting reports prepared under one measurement basis may be relevant for the information needs of one group and irrelevant to other groups.

Revsine[44] suggests that financial statements based on current replacement costs may be particularly relevant to users interested in predicting future operating flows of a firm and future distributable operating flows to investors in the firm. The current replacement cost of assets serves as an estimate of the future cash flows required in replacing assets' services used up during the period. These estimated future cash flows will affect the availability of resources for maintaining or increasing operating capacity and for making distributions to investors.

McKeown[45] indicates that financial statements based on current selling prices, or exit values, may be particularly useful in assessing the liquidity of a firm since exit-value statements measure assets at the net amount which could be realized from their disposal within a short time of the balance sheet date.

The Study Group on the Objectives of Financial Statements concluded that different valuation bases may be relevant *within* a particular set of financial statements.[46]

> The Study Group believes that the objectives of financial statements cannot be best served by the exclusive use of a single valuation basis. The objectives that prescribe statements of earnings and financial position are based on user's needs to predict,

[43]Lawrence Revsine, "Replacement Cost Accounting: A Theoretical Foundation," in *Objectives of Financial Statements,* Joe J. Cramer, Jr., and George H. Sorter (eds.), AICPA, New York, 1974, Vol. 2, p. 179.

[44]*Ibid.,* pp. 182–192.

[45]John C. McKeown, "Usefulness of Exit-Value Accounting Statements in Satisfying Accounting Objectives,"in *Objectives of Financial Statements, op. cit.,* Vol. 2, p. 162.

[46]Accounting Objectives Study Group, *Objectives of Financial Statements,* New York, AICPA, 1973, pp. 41–43.

compare, and evaluate earning power. To satisfy these information requirements, the Study Group concludes that different valuation bases are preferable for different assets and liabilities. That means that financial statements might contain data based on a combination of valuation bases. . . . Current replacement cost may be the best substitute for measuring the benefits of long-term assets held for use rather than sale. Current replacement cost may be particularly appropriate when significant price changes or technological developments have occurred since the assets were acquired. . . . Exit value may be an appropriate substitute for measuring the potential benefit or sacrifice of assets and liabilities expected to be sold or discharged in a relatively short time.

In selecting the appropriate valuation basis for financial statements, it is clear that the information needs of financial statement users must first be identified. This identification process is essentially an empirical one toward which much research effort needs to be directed.

Determining Current Prices.   One of the major criticisms leveled at proposals to use current prices in accounting is the difficulty of determining such prices for many kinds of items. A variety of possibilities has been suggested.

In the American Accounting Association's *A Statement of Basic Accounting Theory*,[47] it is argued that the techniques already utilized in accounting practice in the process of applying the lower-of-cost-or-market rule to inventories, where market is defined as current replacement cost, should be equally acceptable for determining replacement costs that are in excess of historical cost:

The current replacement cost of merchandise inventories can usually be secured from the supplier's current catalogue. . . . In manufacturing situations, market is deemed to be replacement cost based upon current prices for materials and labor and customary overhead costs.

The matter of determining current replacement costs of manufactured inventories also received the attention of the American Accounting Association's 1964 Inventory Committee:[48]

Although in most situations the determination of replacement cost can be accomplished with a high degree of objectivity, difficult problems may arise, particularly in manufacturing situations. In the case of a merchandising enterprise, the determination of replacement cost should be easier, because extensive reliance can be placed on recent invoice prices. Sometimes it will be necessary to obtain quotations from suppliers as of the inventory pricing date. These quotations should be compatible with the company's usual purchasing procedures for the particular item in regard to quantities, discount terms, and method of shipment. A similar situation should prevail in the case of the raw material inventory of a manufacturing concern.

Calculation of the replacement cost of the finished product or work in process inventory of a manufacturer will not be such a simple process. It will be necessary to determine the current (replacement) cost of each element of the total cost of the inventory units. In many cases the current cost of raw materials and labor should be determinable with tolerable precision by employing current wage rates and material costs multiplied by the actual (or standard) quantity of labor or material related to the partially or fully completed product. In the case of indirect manufacturing costs, adjustment of historical cost to current cost by the use of index numbers which give effect to changes in the price level of indirect costs factors may be the best available procedure.

As a practical matter, currently attainable standard costs of manufactured goods should suffice in many instances. In most other situations, the divergence of replacement cost from acquisition cost will largely be traceable to volatile prices for the raw material components rather than to significant changes in direct labor or factory overhead.

[47]American Accounting Association, *A Statement of Basic Accounting Theory*, Evanston, Ill., 1966, p. 74.
[48]Committee on Concepts and Standards—Inventory Measurement, *op. cit.*, p. 710.

In *A Statement of Basic Accounting Theory,* a number of possibilities are also suggested for determining the current replacement cost of equipment: (1) Where the same item, or a service equivalent is available, purchase price, new, on the current market, adjusted for depreciation; (2) acquisition price of items similar to those held in the current used market; (3) in the case where current market prices are available only for items reflecting technological improvements, current purchase price, new, with a downward adjustment to reflect obsolescence; (4) by applying specific price indexes for equipment of the broad classification within which equipment falls.

These suggestions and the other suggestions made in the *Statement* for particular kinds of assets (e.g., long-term investments, buildings, land, and various intangibles) are consistent with those of the earlier Long-Lived Assets Committee:[49]

> Where there is an established market for assets of like kind and condition, quoted prices provide the most objective evidence of current cost. Such prices may be readily available for land, buildings, and certain types of standard equipment. Where there is no established market for assets of like kind and condition, current cost may be estimated by reference to the purchase price of assets which provide equivalent service capacity. The purchase price of such substitute assets should be adjusted for differences in operating characteristics such as cost, capacity, and quality. In other cases, adjustment of historical cost by the use of specified price indexes may provide acceptable approximations of current cost. Appraisals are acceptable only if they are based on the above methods of estimating current cost. Whenever there is no objective method of determining the current cost of obtaining the same or equivalent services, depreciated acquisition cost should continue as the basis of valuation.

Based on its study of the index number problem, the staff of the Accounting Research Division of the AICPA concluded:[50]

> Changes in the prices of specific commodities can be reflected in financial reports by the use of appropriate price series for the individual accounts that appear in those reports. Fortunately, . . . a wealth of price data is collected and published by various agencies of the Federal Government. Some of these prices have been converted into indexes, others have not. The nonindexed price series are easily converted into indexes. . . . The subindexes of the Wholesale price Index would supply many of the needed indexes. The most troublesome area would be finding good indexes to adjust building values, due to the inadequacies in construction cost indexes currently compiled; however, the solution is in process.

Feasibility of Financial Statements Based on Current Prices. Part of the research undertaken by the Study Group on the Objectives of Financial Statements was an empirical test of the feasibility of preparing replacement cost and exit-value financial statements for an actual firm engaged in the production of electronic equipment.

Revsine summarizes the results of efforts to prepare the firm's financial statements on a replacement cost basis as follows:[51]

> Very few implementation problems were encountered during the course of the study. In those cases where data were initially absent, it was usually possible to reconstruct the missing information or to develop some surrogate approach. One might reasonably expect that even these occasional problems would diminish were market based measures widely adopted for reporting purposes.
> This study has indicated that the test company was already employing what is

---

[49]Committee on Concepts and Standards—Long-Lived Assets, *op. cit.,* p. 695.

[50]Staff of the Accounting Research Division, "Reporting the Financial Effects of Price-Level Changes," *Accounting Research Study No. 6,* AICPA, New York, 1963, pp. 113–114.

[51]Revsine, *op. cit.,* pp. 241–244.

essentially a replacement cost system for internal inventory accounting. This itself indicates the practicality of the replacement cost inventory procedures more forcefully than any academic study ever could.

With regard to fixed assets, the results were less equivocal but still essentially favorable. Market prices for 62 percent of the manufacturing equipment (as a percentage of original historical cost) were readily available. While the remaining portion of the equipment was valued by index adjustment, this was largely dictated by time constraints. It is possible that some portion of these assets could also have been valued directly.

Land was valued directly, although conservatively, by reference to a rejected offer that the test company had recently received. While cost considerations led to an index adjustment for the building, direct appraisal is a preferable, and obviously available, alternative in realistic circumstances.

On the basis of these results, it would appear defensible to conclude that the data necessary to prepare replacement cost financial statements were generally available. Thus, this case study did not disclose any obstacles which would impede the implementation of replacement cost reports. Whether this conclusion can be generalized to other situations is a subject for future research.

McKeown summarizes the results of efforts to prepare exit-value financial statements for the same electronic equipment manufacturer as follows:[52]

> Preparation of two exit-value balance sheets and an exit-value income statement for X Company demonstrated that in this case readily available market prices could be determined at very little cost for the land and building and most of the equipment. Market prices for the rest of the equipment (mainly metal furniture) were estimated again at nominal cost by use of general guidelines suggested by used furniture dealers. A more accurate estimate for these items might have been obtained by employing an appraiser. However, the cost of appraisal of these items woulld have been significant (five percent of appraised value) and would probably be incurred every three or five years if at all. This procedure of relatively infrequent appraisals should yield accurate estimates because, according to the used furniture dealers, the resale price is determined mainly by the type and quality of the asset rather than the age. Thus, barring major changes in the used asset market, an appraisal of a particular item (possibly adjusted by a specific price index) should be valid for several years.
>
> Measurements of items other than fixed assets were readily computed at nominal cost. The only way management would have had any effect on the exit-value figures reported would have been solicitation of special offers for particular assets. Although this activity could be called manipulation, the economic fact remains that management could realize the offered amount. Further, the effect of these offers could easily be segregated. Other than the solicitation of special offers, management cannot manipulate the exit-value figures because the measurements are taken from the markets rather than management estimates. This provides less opportunity for manipulation of profit figures than is available under conventional accounting procedures (alternative depreciation methods, sale of particular fixed assets to realize an available gain or loss, etc.).
>
> The conclusion must be reached that critics of exit value who base their opposition on lack of feasibility of implementation will find no evidence to support their position in this case. Preparation of exit-value statements for X Company was possible at a reasonable cost.

CURRENT PRICES OF SPECIFIC ITEMS AND ADJUSTMENTS FOR CHANGES IN THE GENERAL PRICE LEVEL

Objectives. By combining general price-level adjustments, as described in an earlier section of this chapter, with the use of current prices of specific items, as described in the immediately preceding section of this chapter, all of the asserted advantages of both can be obtained. The major impact of the use of general price-

[52]McKeown, *op. cit.*, p. 227.

level adjustments is the measurement of price-level gains on net monetary working capital and long-term debt. Indeed, it will be recalled that the measurement of price-level gains and losses is the unique product of price-level adjustments. The major impact of the use of current prices of specific items is the measurement of holding gains and losses on nonmonetary items, particularly inventory and fixed assets. The major incremental information supplied by combining general price-level adjustments with the use of current prices for specific items is the disaggregation of holding gains and losses into "real" and "fictional" components.

To illustrate the measurement of "real" and "fictional" holding gains and losses, assume that a quantity of raw material was acquired on January 1, year 1, for $10,000 cash. The same batch of raw material was sold on December 31, year 1, in the form of the company's finished product. A realiable index of the general price level increased 8 percent during the year, indicating that in terms of general purchasing power $10,800 was the December 31, year 1, equivalent of $10,000 on January 1, year 1. Owing to an increasing demand for the limited supply of raw material, however, it cost $12,500 to replace that quantity of raw material on December 31, year 1. Assuming that the finished product was sold at a price in excess of the current cost of production, operating income (sales revenues less cost of goods sold and other operating expenses) would implicitly include an $800 "fictional" profit (= $10,800 − $10,000) due to the 8 percent general price inflation and a $1,700 "real" profit (= $12,500 − $10,800) attributable to the increase in the raw material specific price in excess of the increase in the general price level. The reporting of the real and fictional components of holding gains and losses is the unique product of financial statements adjusted for changes in both the general price level and for changes in the prices of specific items.

The principal advantages of recognizing both general and specific price changes may be summarized as follows:

1. The balance sheet at the end of the period reports assets and liabilities, both monetary and nonmonetary, at their current prices at the end of the period.

2. The comparative balance sheet for the beginning of the period reports all assets and liabilities at their beginning-of-the-period prices but restated into dollars of end-of-the-period general purchasing power. The comparative balance sheets, therefore, reflect a common measuring unit.

3. The income statement separates the results of operating activities from holding activities. Operating income is the difference between revenues recognized and expenses reported. Expenses are measured in terms of the current prices of goods and services at the time of their sale or use. Both revenues and expenses are restated though into dollars of end-of-the-period general purchasing power. Changes in the prices of nonmonetary assets held until the end of the period (or to the time of sale if sold during the period) are recognized as holding gains and losses. These holding gains and losses are disaggregated into their "fictional" component (change in specific prices equal to the change in the general price level) and "real" components (change in specific prices greater or less than the change in the general price level). Net income also includes a general price-level gain or loss from holding monetary items during a period when the "specific price" of monetary items, (i.e., the general purchasing power of the dollar) changes.[53]

Special Problems. Several different concepts of "current price" have been advocated and a variety of ways of determining current prices have been suggested. These matters were discussed earlier in this chapter. The addition of general price-level adjustments does not affect those considerations.

[53]For a more comprehensive theoretical analysis of reporting the effects of general and specific price changes, see Robert R. Sterling, "Relevant Financial Reporting in an Age of Price Changes," *Journal of Accountancy*, February 1975, pp. 42–51.

Similarly, the problems of choosing an appropriate general price-level index and adopting an appropriate procedure for the consolidation of foreign subsidiaries must be faced with the use of current prices of specific items in the same way that they must be faced in making adjustments to historical amounts. These problems were also discussed earlier in this chapter.

Two other special problems discussed in connection with the adjustment of historical amounts for changes in the general price level—manufactured inventories and measurements based on net realizable value—are essentially unchanged by the use of current prices. But, the rule of cost or market, whichever is lower, has no counterpart when using current prices of specific items. In effect the rule is *always use market*, whether higher or lower.

Clearly, the critical problem in using current prices is their objective determination, whatever concept of current price is adopted and whether general price-level adjustments are made. Nothing further can be added to the earlier discussion until more experience with the use of current prices has accumulated.

A demonstration of the use of current prices of specific items and adjustments for changes in the general price level would combine the features of the illustrations presented previously in this chapter. A clear and detailed demonstration of this process appears on pages 81 to 95 of *A Statement of Basic Accounting Theory.*[54]

BIBLIOGRAPHY

American Institute of Certified Public Accountants: "Financial Statements Restated for General Price Level Changes," *Statement of the Accounting Principles Board No. 3,* AICPA, New York, June 1969.

Chambers, Raymond J.: *Accounting, Evaluation, and Economic Behavior,* Prentice-Hall, Englewood Cliffs, N.J., 1966.

Davidson, Sidney, Clyde P. Stickney, and Roman L. Weil: *Inflation Accounting,* McGraw-Hill Book Company, New York, 1976.

Edwards, Edgar O., and Philip W. Bell: *The Theory and Measurement of Business Income,* University of California Press, Berkeley, 1961.

Financial Accounting Standards Board: "Financial Reporting in Units of General Purchasing Power," *Proposed Statement of Financial Accounting Standards,* Stamford, Conn., 1974.

————: "Reporting the Effects of General Price-Level Changes in Financial Statements," *FASB Discussion Memorandum,* February 1974.

Staff of the Accounting Research Division: "Reporting the Financial Effects of Price-Level Changes," *Accounting Research Study No. 6,* AICPA, New York, 1963.

Sterling, Robert K.: "Relevant Financial Reporting in an Age of Price Changes," *Journal of Accountancy,* February 1974, pp. 42–51.

Study Group on the Objectives of Financial Statements: *Objectives of Financial Statements,* Vol. I and II, AICPA, New York, October 1973 and May 1974.

Sweeney, Henry W.: *Stabilized Accounting* (reissued), Holt Rinehart and Winston, New York, 1964.

[54]American Accounting Association, *op. cit.*

Chapter **33**

Mergers, Acquisitions, and Poolings of Interests

ARTHUR R. WYATT
Partner, Arthur Andersen & Co.

INTRODUCTION

Growth has been a way of life for American business virtually from the day business activity began in colonial times. Growth can be accomplished either from forces within the business unit or through combination with other business units. Combinations of one type or another have been effected ever since colonial times, including a few periods of relatively intensified activity around 1900 and again in the 1920s. In the period subsequent to World War II, however, growth by combination accelerated markedly, so that during the 1950s and 1960s business combinations increased at a rapid rate to become a common phenomenon on the American business scene.

Definition of Terms.   Various terms have been used to describe business combinations, and the passage of time has blunted the precise meaning once associated with many of the terms. A *merger* is a business combination in which two or more entities join together with one being fused into the other. A *consolidation* is a combination in which two or more entities join together and go forward under a new name or a new legal form. An *acquisition* (or a *purchase*) is a combination in which little or no effort is made to continue in existence the identity of the acquired company. An acquisition can take the form of a merger or of a consolidation. A *pooling of interests* is a combination in which two or more entities join together, "marry," or pool their interests and go forward as one entity (and in some respects as if they had always been one entity). A pooling of interests may also take the form of a merger or of a consolidation.

The terms identified above all have rather well-defined technical meanings, but over the years they have come to be used interchangeably to a considerable extent. The term *business combination* is used as the more broad generic term to describe a business transaction in which two or more entities join together. This term encompasses all those identified above and is used throughout this chapter except when the more specific technical meaning implicit in the other terms is intended.

The business combination event embraces numerous complexities requiring careful consideration prior to consummation; legal, taxation, financial, marketing, production, personnel, and other matters all require careful attention before final terms are agreed upon. Likewise, accounting for a combination requires advance consideration. Not uncommonly the accounting consequences of a combination will affect the terms of the combination. The accounting aspect of combinations is complicated by the fact that two generally accepted methods of accounting for business combinations exist in practice. These two methods may be equally applicable to some combinations, with the results flowing from the application of each producing quite different balance sheets upon consummation of the combination, quite different income statements in periods subsequent to the combination, and even quite different income statements on a retroactive basis for periods prior to the combination.

Historical Development.   Prior to the mid-1940s, most business combinations were accounted for as purchases. The acquiring company recorded the transaction at the fair value of the consideration it gave in the combination transaction. For many combinations the fair value of this consideration was easy to measure since it involved either cash or a combination of cash and notes payable over a relatively short period of time. If a lump-sum price were paid for the acquired company, a common situation, the amount paid was allocated among the several specific resources and property rights acquired. For some combinations a portion of the consideration was allocated to an intangible, goodwill. Generally, the goodwill value was recognized when the allocation of the purchase price to the several specific resources and property rights did not absorb all of the purchase price. Any excess of the purchase price over the fair values of the specific resources and property rights was charged to goodwill.

Combinations effected for common stock prior to the mid-1940s were accounted for in a similar manner. The fair value of the stock issued (generally based upon market values at the time of the transaction) became the measure of the consideration given. Goodwill might be recognized in combinations effected by stock, in a manner similar to that noted for cash acquisitions. However, at this time common stocks were selling at relatively low multiples of earnings, with the result that stock prices per share were relatively much closer to the fair values of the underlying specific resources and property rights than was true in the years following World War II.

Various changes in economic circumstances during the postwar period led business managements and their accountants to seek alternative methods to account for business combinations. Many began to challenge the continued applicability of the capitalization-amortization pattern of accounting for goodwill recommended by the bulletins of the American Institute of Certified Public Accountants (AICPA) and supported by the Securities and Exchange Commission (SEC). The amortization pattern adopted was often based on arbitrary assumptions and, of course, acted to lower reported net income below what would be reported in the absence of amortization. Further, the income tax laws did not permit goodwill amortization to be deductible in determining taxable income. Many found within these tax laws a practical basis for challenging the amortization through income of the cost of goodwill.

Tax Arrangements.   At the same time, other provisions of the Internal Revenue Code specified that certain types of business combinations could qualify as corporate reorganizations that would be "tax-free." Corporate reorganizations that so qualified were tax-free in the sense that the selling company (or its stockholders) did not generate any income or gain subject to tax in the reorganization (combination) transaction. In reality, the transaction was tax-deferred rather than tax-free, since the tax basis of the securities received by the seller in the reorganization transaction carried forward the same tax basis as was possessed by the securities or assets conveyed to the buying corporation. Any tax incurrence was delayed until such time as the securities newly received by the seller were sold or otherwise disposed of. While a number of technical considerations must be met for a combination to be tax-free, a characteristic of certain types of tax-free reorganizations is that the seller must receive all, or substantially all (i.e., no less than 80 percent) of his consideration in the form of voting stock. Thus, the tax law provided a stimulus for some business combinations to be effected by the use of voting securities rather than by cash or other assets.

Effect on Earnings per Share.   Other forces in the economy provided added impetus to the use of stock. For some companies desiring to grow externally cash was not readily available, and no other source of assets could be developed on a timely or economical basis. Use of unissued stock was the convenient substitute. At the same time came the recognition that the statistic of earnings per share (one measure by which the success of an enterprise was measured) might be improved by an acquisition for stock. Thus, a company whose earnings multiple was, say, 40 (stock price of $80 when earnings were $2 per share) could acquire a company whose multiple was, say, 10 and thereby produce an increase in earnings per share.

For example, assume the following:

	Company A	Company B
Reported earnings	$10,000,000	$2,000,000
Shares outstanding	5,000,000	250,000
Earnings per share	$2	$8
Market price per share (average)	$80	$80

If a combination were effected on a share-for-share basis, the resulting company would have (assuming other conditions remaining unchanged) earnings of $12 million and shares outstanding of 5.25 million. Thus, earnings per share would increase from $2 to $2.29. If the earnings multiple of 40 remained unchanged, the price of Company A stock would increase from $80 to over $91 per share. Company A could even offer Company B a premium, offering, say, two shares for one. Here the Company B shareholders would receive two shares of stock valued at $80 each for each $80 share of their Company B stock. Even here the resulting company earnings per share would increase from $2 to $2.19 (=$12,000,000/5,500,000) and an earnings multiple of 40 would produce a price per share of over $87. Results of this nature, of course, provided encouragement for others to attempt similar combinations.

American business prosperity in the period after World War II through much of the 1950s and 1960s led to increased earnings per share for American corporations and was accompanied by gradual inflation and by generally higher multiples attached by the investment community to corporate earnings. As an increasing portion of business combinations came to be effected by use of stock, the fair value of the shares exchanged by the acquiring company (generally as measured by the market price at or near the combination date) commonly exceeded the book value or the net assets of the acquired companies. Often the amount of the excess was substantial. Accountants had traditionally classified all or a portion of an excess arising in this manner as goodwill. The substantial amounts of goodwill thus generated in an accounting environment that supported amortization by charges to income, as noted above, caused many to challenge this aspect of accounting for goodwill. The result was to develop a new concept of accounting for those business combinations effected by means of voting stock. This concept is known as "pooling of interests" and its widespread acceptance has been fostered in part by the opportunity to bypass the recognition and subsequent accounting for goodwill at a time when the economic environment encouraged growth in business via the combination route.

The Basic Concepts.   Conceptually, business combinations came to be classified in two categories: purchases and poolings of interests. A purchase combination exists when one company clearly acquires or purchases the other so that the acquired company is absorbed, in a business sense if not legally, into the acquiring company. In a purchase combination the ownership and management interests of the acquired company either disappear or are clearly subordinated after the combination. Thus, a purchase combination is viewed much like any purchase. What was once owned by one party is now owned by another, and the former owners retain no particular financial or business interest in the property sold.

A pooling of interests, however, has a quite different concept. A pooling-of-interests combination exists when the various interests in the combination fuse their divergent parts into one enterprise. Neither is buying out the other. Rather, the interests are joining together, as in a marriage, to go forward as one united enterprise. The combination is viewed as one in which the interests of the various constituents continue in somewhat the same roles as existed prior to combination. All the former stockholders continue as stockholders, the former managements retain their managerial responsibilities, and all that really happens in a business sense is a change in legal designations of what formerly were separate corporations.

ACCOUNTING RESEARCH BULLETINS

Accounting Research Bulletin No. 40.   The Committee on Accounting Procedure of the AICPA issued *Accounting Research Bulletin No. 40* in 1950. In this bulletin the Committee indicated the nature of the accounting treatment for each type of combination and concluded that the accounting treatment would be presumed to rest upon the nature of the transaction, the attendant circumstances, and not upon legal distinctions. The attendant circumstances of a pooling of interests included a continuation in the surviving company of all or substantially all the equity interests in the combining companies. Likewise, continuity of management or of the power to control management was contemplated. The combining companies would normally be expected to be of relatively the same size and would be in business activities which were similar or complementary.

A purchase, on the other hand, would exist when the ownership interests after the combination were substantially altered, when management continuity was not effected, when the relative size of the constituents was disproportionate, and when the constituent companies had been engaged in dissimilar or noncomplementary activities. No one of the criteria was considered to be determinative, and the accountant was expected to review all the characteristics of the combination to determine its proper classification. One clear differentiation did exist, however, and that was that any substantial amount of cash in the transaction would be presumptive of a purchase combination.

The accounting differences contemplated by this bulletin can be summarized briefly: In a purchase the assets acquired are accounted for at their fair values at the date of acquisition, generally as measured by the cash paid or value of other assets paid or stock issued, while in a pooling of interests the assets of the combining companies are merged together at existing book values. Thus, in a pooling of interests the fair values of the considerations exchanged are not relevant; only book values have significance. No goodwill arises in a pooling of interests, as existing asset book values are carried forward, although certain adjustments are permitted to conform the accounting practices of the combining entities. In a purchase the purchase price is allocated among the various resources and property rights acquired, and to the extent that an excess exists after the allocation, an amount of goodwill is recognized in the transaction.

Accounting Research Bulletin No. 43.   The distinctions between purchases and poolings of interests as set forth in *ARB No. 40* were largely continued in *ARB No. 43* (as Chapter 7c), issued in 1953. *ARB No. 43* was primarily a restatement and revision of the preceding 42 bulletins, and since practice under *ARB No. 40* was not extensive prior to the preparation of *ARB No. 43,* no significant revision was made.

Accounting Research Bulletin No. 48.   The AICPA issued as *ARB No. 48* a more thoroughgoing revision of the guidelines for accounting for business combinations in 1957. To some extent this bulletin reflected changes in practice that had developed subsequent to the issuance of *ARB No. 40,* and to some extent it developed the pooling-of-interests concept more fully in areas not previously dealt with to any extent. The various attendant circumstances were again discussed. Thus, continuity of ownership interests, continuity of voting rights, continuity of operations, continuity of management, and similarity in size continued to be the criteria by which a business combination was to be evaluated for purposes of determining the appropriate accounting treatment.

ARB No. 48 did attempt to establish the extremes for the similarity of size criterion at about 90 to 95 percent for any single constituent. That is, the relative share interests subsequent to the combination were expected to be in a ratio of 19 to 1 or less if the combination were to qualify as a pooling of interests for accounting purposes. Any size disparity greater than 19 to 1 was to be indicative of a purchase combination. However, this size criterion proved to be ineffective over the years following issuance of *ARB No. 48,* so that for practical purposes similarity of size became virtually insignificant in evaluating business combinations.

ARB No. 48 recognized one aspect of the pooling concept which had evolved in practice—that the retained earnings of the constituents in a business combination should be pooled or merged together in accounting for the pooling of interests. Some hesitancy had existed to pool the retained earnings accounts in earlier applications of the pooling concept, possibly because of doubts as to legal consequences and because of an earlier AICPA position that a company could not increase its retained earnings by the acquisition of another company. As a pooling of interests came to be better understood as a business event quite different from an acquisition, a joining together of retained earnings accounts was not considered to fall under the earlier prohibition. Likewise, retained earnings came more and more to be viewed in an accounting sense as the aggregation of the reported earnings over a company's life, less amounts distributed as dividends or otherwise adjusted by transactions affecting the capital accounts. Legal status as to availability for dividend distribution assumed lesser significance.

Another extension of the pooling concept recognized in *ARB No. 48* concerned the use of pooling accounting when one of the constituents in the combination remained legally in existence as a subsidiary of another constituent. To some accountants this position appeared to be in clear violation of the pooling-of-interests concept. On the other hand, however, many combinations which otherwise would qualify for pooling accounting contained valid business reasons for continuing one entity as a subsidiary. If such a combination met the pooling criteria in other respects, the subsidiary status appeared insufficient in substance to warrant purchase accounting.

Finally, *ARB No. 48* clarified certain reporting aspects of business combinations. Under the pooling concept the constituents were viewed as if they had always been one business unit; for example, assets were carried forward at book values and retained earnings accounts were combined. Under this concept the operating results for the constituents in the year of combination would be presented on a combined basis from the start of the year, as if the companies had been pooled for the entire period. Under purchase accounting, on the other hand, operating results of the constituents would be combined only for the period following the effective date of the combination. Further, *ARB No. 48* recommended that presentations of historical data on operating results should be restated after a pooling to include the data of the pooled company for the prior periods. At times, combining the operating results for the entire year or presenting restated historical data might result in changes which would be immaterial, and if so the bulletin indicated that restatement would not be necessary.

ACCOUNTING PRINCIPLES BOARD OPINIONS

Accounting Principles Board Opinions Nos. 6 and 10. Opinions Nos. 6 and 10 of the Accounting Principles Board, issued in 1965 and 1967, respectively, contained sections to clarify the pooling concept. Thus, Opinion No. 6 strengthened the recommended positions of *ARB No. 48* as to reporting combined operating results of a combination after a pooling of interests from the start of the period of combination and as to the presentation of restated historical operating data. Under the Opinion the recommended reporting and restatement were to be followed in all poolings of interests unless the results thereof would be immaterial, in which case disclosure of the fact of immateriality would be necessary. Opinion No. 10 recognized a practice that had evolved of effecting business combinations that qualified as poolings of interests after the end of a fiscal year, with the inclusion of the pooled companies and their operating results as if the combination had been effected prior to the end of the fiscal year. Opinion No. 10 attempted to limit such "post-year-end poolings" to those effected within a reasonable period after the end of the year.

Accounting Principles Board Opinion No. 16. In 1970 the APB superseded all existing authoritative literature on accounting for business combinations by issuance of Opinion No. 16. Significant portions of that Opinion and its Interpretations are presented in the Appendix to this chapter. Opinion No. 16 continued to recognize the purchase and the pooling-of-interests methods, but it specified different criteria by which to determine the method appropriate for a given combination. One conclusion was that the two methods were not alternatives from which a selection could be made. Either the specified criteria existed, and the combination was to be accounted for as a pooling of interests, or one or more of the criteria was absent, and the combination was a purchase. In addition, a given business combination could no longer be accounted for partially as a purchase and partially as a pooling.

Certain of the previous criteria for distinguishing a purchase from a pooling were no longer viewed as necessary. Thus, the relative size of the combining companies was no longer considered relevant, a recognition that a "size test" had proved to be unworkable in practical application. Likewise, the concepts of continuity of management and continuity of ownership were no longer specified as necessary. These criteria were replaced by a more elaborate set of conditions that had to be present if the combination were to be viewed as a pooling of interests.

While the criteria to be met when a business combination is to be accounted for as a pooling of interests are set forth in detail in the Appendix, certain of the criteria merit additional comment. The combining companies must be autonomous (not a part of another entity) and independent of each other. The combination must be effected within one year after its initiation and can involve only the issuance of common stock in exchange for the common stock interest of other combining companies. No special voting or dividend-sharing arrangements are permitted. Each combining company must refrain from changing its equity interests or from acquiring its own shares for a period of two years prior to the combination, and no contingent share issuance arrangements to former stockholders of a combining company can exist at the date a combination is consummated. Finally, the combined corporation cannot agree to reacquire any stock issued, cannot enter into any financial arrangements for the benefit of former stockholders, and cannot intend or plan to dispose of a significant part of the assets of the combining companies until two years after the combination.

The principal aim of these criteria is to assure that the formerly separate stockholder groups "pool their interests" on a mutual risk-sharing basis in the combination. Certain of the criteria were also aimed at preventing, or precluding, various alleged abuses of the criteria for pooling under *ARB No. 48*. Despite the rather elaborate set of criteria, a substantial number of "interpretations" of Opinion No. 16 were found necessary in the first few years after its adoption. In addition, on several occasions the Securities and Exchange Commission issued Accounting Series Releases that, in effect, amended the criteria of Opinion No. 16. For example, *ASR No. 135* specified that certain stockholders ("affiliates") could not dispose of shares received in a pooling combination for a specified period following the combination, and *ASR No. 146A* established new standards for the reacquisition of shares (treasury stock) by a combining company in the two-year period prior to a combination and for a "reasonable" period following a combination.

Accounting Principles Board Opinion No. 17.   Coincident with the issuance of Opinion No. 16 the APB also issued Opinion No. 17, "Accounting for Intangibles." The principal conclusion of that Opinion, that the cost of intangibles (including goodwill) should be amortized by charges to income over a period not to exceed forty years, altered existing practice in accounting for goodwill. While the conclusions of Opinion No. 17 do not affect the determination of whether a business combination is a purchase or a pooling of interests, the conclusions often have a significant effect on the postcombination results of a business combination accounted for as a purchase.

ACCOUNTING FOR A BUSINESS COMBINATION

The distinctions between a purchase and a pooling of interests may by sharpened through the example in Exhibit 1. The example will focus on two accounting aspects of a business combination: the accounting for the combination transaction itself and the consequences of that accounting in fiscal periods subsequent to the combination.

Assumption One.   First, assume that the managements of A Company and B Company negotiate to consummate a combination in which A Company buys all the common stock of B Company for $16 million.

Since cash is the consideration, purchase accounting is appropriate; pooling accounting would not be acceptable. A Company gives up $16 million in cash and receives in return all the B Company stock, which entitles it to B Company's receivables, inventories, and plant and equipment (assuming B Company will use its cash to liquidate its current payables).

The initial accounting problem for A Company involves the allocation of the $16 million cash to the various assets acquired, assuming for the moment that B Company is to be dissolved. The book value of the assets acquired (also the book value of B Company's stock) is $10.8 million. Thus, the price paid exceeds the book value of the assets acquired by $5.2 million. The question is, what accounting disposition should be made of the $5.2 million?

A common answer to this question is to label the $5.2 million as goodwill. This answer is frequently merely an expedient one, since in concept goodwill is the

EXHIBIT 1   Financial and Operating Data for A Company and B Company

	A Company	B Company
Cash....................................	$ 28,800,000	$ 800,000
Receivables (net)........................	36,600,000	3,000,000
Finished goods, raw materials, etc..........	50,400,000	3,600,000
Plant and equipment....................	72,600,000	4,200,000
Other assets...........................	3,200,000	—
Goodwill..............................	1,600,000	—
	$193,200,000	$11,600,000
Current payables........................	$ 43,800,000	$ 800,000
Long-term liabilities....................	48,000,000	—
Common stock:		
A(6,000,000 shares at $10 par)...........	60,000,000	
B(60,000 shares)......................		6,000,000
Capital in excess of par.................	18,900,000	—
Retained earnings......................	22,500,000	4,800,000
	$193,200,000	$11,600,000
Sales..................................	$206,800,000	$12,600,000
Cost of sales...........................	136,000,000	7,100,000
Gross margin on sales..................	$ 70,800,000	$ 5,500,000
Other operating expenses.................	42,000,000	3,388,000
Income before taxes.................	$ 28,800,000	$ 2,112,000
Federal income tax (assume 50%)..........	14,400,000	1,056,000
Net income.......................	$ 14,400,000	$ 1,056,000
Earnings per share.....................	$2.40	$17.60
Market price range, past three months......	$28–$52	(1)

(1) Limited market.   Only sale in last three months between two existing stockholders for 200 shares at $340 per share.

appropriate label only if the amount involved represents the cost of acquiring excess earning power possessed by the acquired company. (See Chapter 21 for a more complete discussion on goodwill.) More commonly, one would expect all or part of the $5.2 million to be attributable to various of the specific resources or property rights possessed by B Company.

Thus, for example, B Company may have provided more than adequate allowances for uncollectible receivables, may have undervalued its inventories by establishing unneeded obsolescence or shrinkage reserves, may have written down its plant and equipment through depreciation entries at a more rapid rate than they were actually depreciating, or it may possess valuable secret processes or patent rights which have not been recorded.

The main principle is that careful study should be made of B Company to determine as closely as possible the fair values of the various resources and property rights it owned prior to the combination. In fact, such study would normally be an integral part of the negotiation process preliminary to reaching the final combination terms. Only the difference which remains after determining the fair values of the separable resources and property rights acquired in comparison to the purchase price should be labeled goodwill.

Assume that careful review of B Company's records, discussions with appropriate officials, and access to other sources of information revealed the following fair values for B Company's assets:

Receivables	$3,000,000
Inventories	4,800,000
Plant and Equipment	6,000,000
Patents	700,000

These values should be recorded for the acquisition, and since the sum of these values ($14.5 million) is $1.5 million less than the purchase price, goodwill of $1.5 million would also be recorded.

If B Company were to be dissolved as a separate company, the accounting entry for the acquisition would be as follows on the books of A Company:

Receivables	3,000,000	
Finished Goods, Raw Materials, etc.	4,800,000	
Plant and Equipment	6,000,000	
Patents	700,000	
Goodwill	1,500,000	
Cash		16,000,000

If B Company were to be operated as a subsidiary company and maintain its own accounting system, A Company would make the following entry for the combination:

Investment in B Company	16,000,000	
Cash		16,000,000

The values for the specific assets, as indicated in the preceding entry, would become embodied in A Company's financial statements at year-end through the process of preparing consolidated financial statements. The "Investment in B Company" would be replaced in the consolidated statements by the assets as shown in the first entry.

If the combination were effected by issuance of 320,000 shares of common stock having a fair value of $16 million and one or more of the criteria for a pooling of interests were not met, the combination would be accounted for as a purchase. The only change in the two entries above would be a credit to Common Stock for $3.2 million and a credit to Capital in Excess of Par for $12.8 million rather than a credit to Cash.

Assumption Two.   Now, assume that the negotiations between A Company and B Company lead to an agreement to combine in which A Company agrees to exchange 320,000 shares of its stock for all 60,000 shares of B Company stock outstanding. The A Company board of directors establishes $50 per share as the fair value of the common stock conveyed in the combination. Since common stock is the consideration involved here, and assuming that all the criteria specified in APB Opinion No. 16 are met, the combination will be accounted for as a pooling of interests.

The essence of the pooling concept is that the combination has produced nothing of real economic substance. As a corollary, pooling accounting leaves the relationships existing prior to combination basically undisturbed. Thus, the basis of accountability for the assets of both companies remains the book value of those assets at the time of combination. Minor adjustments are sometimes made for the assets of the pooled company (B Company in this case) in order to conform the accounting practices of the constituents. In general, however, the fair value of the shares issued to effect the combination is of no consequence to the accounting entries.

Under the pooling concept, and again assuming that B company retains its cash and current payables, the entry to account for the combination would be as follows if B Company were dissolved as a separate company:

Receivables	3,000,000	
Finished Goods, Raw Materials, etc	3,600,000	
Plant and Equipment	4,200,000	
Common Stock (320,000 shares at $10)		3,200,000
Capital in Excess of Par		2,800,000
Retained Earnings		4,800,000

All these values are those which appeared in B Company's books prior to combination, except for the credits to Common Stock and Capital in Excess of Par. Since par value per share of A Company common stock is $10, only $3.2 million can be credited to Common Stock even though $6 million appeared as common stock for B Company. The difference becomes additional paid-in capital. At times the par or stated value of the shares issued exceeds the related capital stock and paid-in capital of the pooled company. In such a situation, any paid-in capital in excess of par on the books of the other company could be used to absorb the excess, or the retained earnings of the pooled company could be reduced to permit recording of the appropriate amount of paid-in capital. Thus, under pooling accounting the book values of the several assets are carried forward, and the retained earnings of the pooled company is likewise carried forward except for any portion needed to achieve appropriate balances for the paid-in capital accounts.

If B Company were to be operated as a subsidiary company and thus maintain its own accounting system, A Company would make the following entry to record the combination:

Investment in B Company	10,800,000	
Common Stock		10,800,000

In the year-end accounting process of preparing consolidated financial statements, the various balances in B Company's asset accounts would replace "Investment in B Company," and the amounts as shown in the previous entry for Common Stock, Capital in Excess of Par, and Retained Earnings would replace the credit above to Common Stock. The end result in the consolidated statements would be identical to that resulting from the previous entry.

Summary of Accounting Alternatives. These illustrative assumptions, while simplified in nature, lead to the following observations:

1. A business combination effected for cash (or notes) is considered to be a purchase combination and is accounted for accordingly.

2. A business combination effected for stock is considered to be a pooling of interests, providing all criteria of APB Opinion No. 16 are met. If any one of the criteria is not met, the combination is considered to be a purchase, and the accounting would be based on the fair values exchanged.
3. For a purchase combination:
   a. The fair values of the resources and property rights acquired or the fair value of the consideration given, whichever is more clearly evident, provide the basis for future accountability.
   b. The retained earnings of the acquired company are not carried forward as such after the combination but become capitalized, in effect, in the combination entry.
4. For a pooling-of-interests combination:
   a. The book values of the resources and property rights of the pooled company provide the basis for future accountability.
   b. The retained earnings of the pooled company are carried forward in the combined entity, except to the extent necessary to effect adjustments to paid in capital.
5. No real accounting significance attaches to whether the purchased or pooled company (B Company, above) loses its legal existence or continues as a subsidiary company.

Postcombination Effects. Of greater significance than the distinctions in the accounting entries to give effect to the combination are the differences in the effects on financial presentations in subsequent periods resulting from these entries. Virtually all asset values (including goodwill) become charges against revenue in future income statements. This means that if B Company had not entered into a combination with A Company, its assets (except cash) of $10.8 million would have been charged against future revenues in some manner, either directly through depreciation charges or as cost of sales, or indirectly through collection of receivables and use of the proceeds of collection for operating expenses, inventory acquisitions, or plant asset additions or replacements.

If A Company acquires these assets in a purchase combination at a price of $16 million, its future revenues may be charged with $16 million for these same assets. If revenues are not affected by whether A Company or B Company owns and operates the assets, future net income of the two companies combined into a single, consolidated entity would be $5.2 million less over the same period than the sum of the net incomes of the two companies operating and reporting independently, disregarding any related income tax effects.

If, on the other hand, the combination of A Company and B Company is considered to be a pooling of interests and the assets of B Company are carried forward after the combination at $10.8 million, regardless of the fair values exchanged in the combination, the combined entity will report the same net income from the operation of these assets as B Company would have operating them separately, assuming no variation in revenues or changes in operating conditions, etc.

Exhibit 2 summarizes the postcombination effects on net income of the three assumed sets of facts presented above. In addition to the assumed fair values previously set forth, also assume that:

1. Inventory turns over rapidly in the combined entity, so that all the B Company inventory at the combination date was sold within the next operating period. Thus, the $1.2 million difference between book value and fair value of B Company inventory is charged to cost of sales in the period after combination.
2. Plant and equipment and patent costs are amortized over a ten-year period, with the amortization included in operating expenses.
3. Goodwill on the A Company balance sheet at combination date is not

**EXHIBIT 2   Operating Results of A Company and B Company (combined)
Year After Combination**

	Purchase for cash	Purchase for stock	Pooling for stock
Sales.....................	$219,400,000	$219,400,000	$219,400,000
Cost of sales..............	$144,300,000	$144,300,000	$143,100,000
Operating expenses.........	45,638,000	45,638,000	45,388,000
Goodwill amortization.......	300,000	300,000	—
Total...................	$190,238,000	$190,238,000	$188,488,000
Income before taxes.........	$ 29,162,000	$ 29,162,000	$ 30,912,000
Federal income tax..........	14,731,000	14,731,000	15,456,000
Net income................	$ 14,431,000	$ 14,431,000	$ 15,456,000
Shares outstanding..........	6,000,000	6,320,000	6,320,000
Earnings per share..........	$2.41	$2.28	$2.45

amortized. Goodwill arising in the combination is amortized over five years and is not deductible for income tax purposes.

4. The purchase combination involving an exchange of stock does not meet the requirements of a tax-free reorganization.

The first column reports what one might expect from a cash acquisition—an increase in earnings per share (from $2.40 for A Company prior to combination to $2.41 on a combined basis). However, the increase in this example is nominal and less than one might expect from a cash acquisition. The new values assigned to the assets of B Company acquired resulted in increased charges to income as compared with B Company's previous operating resultts. In fact, an increase in reported earnings does not always result from a cash acquisition, particularly when the purchase price indicates a wide disparity in the fair values of the acquired company's assets as compared to the book values of those assets.

Furthermore, the above example does not make provision for the cost of the $16 million in cash used to acquire B Company. Assuming an 8 percent interest rate, the cost would be $640,000 (after taxes), or 11 cents per share. Thus, earnings per share would actually fall to $2.30.

The second column indicates that if the purchase of B Company were effected in exchange for stock, earnings per share would decline to $2.28 from $2.40 prior to the combination, assuming the conditions cited in the example. The increase in net income was less than proportionate to the increase in the number of shares outstanding as a result of the combination. A similar observation to that made in reference to the data in the first column is appropriate to this assumption also; reported earnings are affected by the disparity between the fair values of the assets acquired and their book values.

The data in the third column indicate the results of the combination if stock were used and if the combination met all the criteria to be accounted for as a pooling of interests. The net income reported is substantially higher ($15,456,000 compared with $14,431,000) than under the two other assumptions. This result can be attributed to the fact that book values are brought forward for the assets of B Company in a pooling of interests, whereas current fair values are brought forward in a purchase. When the book values are lower than current values, lower charges to revenues, and thus a higher net income, will result. Similarly, no goodwill is recognized in the combination transaction, so that future income does not have to bear any charge for goodwill amortization. The result is that earnings per share of $2.45 can be projected for the combined business, as compared with $2.28 under a purchase for stock or $2.41 ($2.30 after adjustment for the cost of money) under a cash purchase.

The facts assumed in the illustration are admittedly oversimplified to highlight the main issues. On the other hand, the facts assumed are not unreasonable; certainly during periods of gradual inflation one would expect the fair values of the assets of a company being acquired or merged to be in excess of their book values. Under these conditions, and with increasing emphasis on earnings per share as a measure of enterprise success, the pooling-of-interests method of accounting became widely accepted. The terms and attendant circumstances of many business combinations were structured in such a way that pooling-of-interests accounting was appropriate.

The Negative Goodwill Situation. Under different circumstances, on the other hand, purchase accounting might be preferred for a combination effected by an exchange of stock. Even though Opinion No. 16 eliminated the option that previously existed as to choice of accounting method for a business combination, purchase accounting remains applicable to almost any business combination because of the relative ease with which one or more of the pooling criteria can be violated. Assume that in the above illustration the book value of B Company's net assets was $16 million and the agreed-upon purchase price was $10.8 million. Under pooling accounting A Company would be accountable for $16 million, the book value of assets acquired, even though the fair value of the consideration given was $5.2 million less than this. Apparently some factors exist so that the assets of B Company are overvalued, a circumstance which makes accounting for the book value undesirable after the combination since such book values would become charges to income in succeeding periods.

Under purchase accounting, on the other hand, the difference of $5.2 million, or the excess of book value over fair value of the consideration in the combination (sometimes denoted "negative goodwill" in accounting jargon) will be allocated to particular assets to state them at fair value or will be allocated to long-lived assets if an excess remains after fair values have been recognized. The reduction in the carrying amounts of the assets will reduce charges to income in future periods. Under these conditions accounting for the combination as a purchase would result in a higher earnings per share than would result from accounting for the combination as a pooling of interests.

Summary. A few generalizations on the accounting aspects of business combinations are appropriate, even though exceptions may be found as circumstances vary. Combinations effected for cash are considered to be purchases, so that the fair values of the assets acquired become the basis of accountability for those assets. Earnings per share after a combination effected for cash will frequently be higher than they were previously, although as the gap widens between the fair values and book values of assets subject to charge in future income statements, the increase in earnings per share diminishes and may become a decrease in some cases. In making comparisons between precombination and postcombination earnings, one should take care to consider the cost of the capital used to effect the combination.

Combinations effected for stock will merit classification as a pooling of interests when all of the criteria specified in Opinion No. 16 are met. If one or more of the specified criteria is not met, the combination will be accounted for as a purchase. Generally, if the fair value of the stock issued in the combination exceeds the book values of the assets of the company to be absorbed, efforts will be made to see that all of the specified criteria are met so that pooling-of-interests accounting can be used. The book values then become the basis of accounting for these assets. The earnings brought forward by the absorbed company will generally be higher in relation to the combined postcombination earnings than the shares issued in the combination are in relation to postcombination shares outstanding, thus increasing postcombination reported earnings per share. On the other hand, if the fair value of the stock issued in the combination is less than the book value of the assets of the company to be absorbed, purchase accounting will be desirable and efforts will be made to see that one or more of the specified criteria for pooling-of-interests accounting is not met. The fair value of the stock issued then becomes the basis of accounting for the assets, and the reduction in book values for the assets of the absorbed company will enhance reported earnings in future years as the assets are amortized.

PRACTICAL ASPECTS AND DEVELOPMENTS IN ACCOUNTING FOR BUSINESS COMBINATIONS

As business combination activity evolved and expanded in the 1960s, many new and innovative characteristics were utilized in combination transactions. These innovations involved the use of a variety of new and somewhat unique securities, the use of two or more different securities or assets in a given combination, and forms of combination arrangements that satisfied the pre-Opinion No. 16 criteria for use of pooling-of-interests accounting. Many of these innovations created dilemmas in an accounting sense and led accountants to modify or alter existing concepts and practices in order to give effect to the intent of the transactions. Many also were responsible for certain of the criteria included in Opinion No. 16 in an effort to eliminate what some viewed as "abuses" of the pooling concept. Several examples of these practical developments are considered in the following paragraphs.

Use of Convertible Securities. During the 1960s, convertible preferred stock was used increasingly to effect combinations, whereas previously this type of security was rarely used. Had such a security been used in earlier years it would have been strongly suggestive of a purchase transaction. As the pooling concept evolved, however, securities that were voting when issued and that were convertible into common shares gradually became encompassed within the concept. Convertible securities were particularly useful to companies which desired eventual equity financing but at a price higher than market price at the time of the combination. The convertible securities issued really became a deferred issuance of common stock at a price higher than existed for the common at the time the securities were issued.

The convertible preferred securities were attractive to many companies for several reasons. First, they enabled the shareholders of the selling company to receive dividends after the combination at least equal to those received prior to combination. Not uncommonly the shareholders of the selling company were receiving proportionately greater dividends at the time of combination than shareholders of the buying company. An issuance of common stock sufficient to provide the shareholders of the selling company with dividends at least equal to those previously received would mean that the buying company would either have to issue an excessive number of common shares or increase the dividend payout on all common shares. At times a significant increase would be necessary. The preferred shares permitted a higher dividend payment on those shares without also increasing the payment on the common shares. In addition, by making the preferred shares convertible into common at a conversion price higher than that at which the common was selling at the time of combination, the buying company could achieve the combination with the issuance of fewer shares of common than if the common were issued at the transaction date.

The criterion in Opinion No. 16 that specified that only common stock could be exchanged if the combination were to be a pooling of interests effectively reduced the use of convertible securities to effect a combination.

Use of Treasury Stock.   On the surface the use of treasury stock rather than previously unissued stock appears to be an insignificant difference in evaluating a combination for accounting purposes. In either case, shares of common stock are issued, and if other criteria are met pooling-of-interests accounting would appear to be appropriate. However, assume the following situation: A Company desires to acquire B Company and desires to pay cash to consummate the transaction; B Company shareholders prefer to receive common stock; in addition, A Company desires to follow pooling accounting in order to avoid the recognition of the excess of the current fair values of B Company's resources over their book values. A Company might decide to enter the marketplace to acquire approximately the number of shares of its own stock needed to effect the combination. While careful planning is necessary to prevent any upsetting effect on the market price of the stock, for larger companies whose shares are widely traded this generally poses no problem. After obtaining the shares (now treasury shares) A Company could consummate the combination within a few weeks by using these shares to effect the combination. The result is a combination effected for stock, but with no increase in total shares outstanding since the shares issued to bring about the combination had been acquired for that purpose. In substance, A Company effected the combination for cash, but since the form of the combination event involved stock, accountants argued that pooling accounting was appropriate. Opinion No. 16 (as supplemented by *Accounting Series Release No. 146A* of the Securities and Exchange Commission) created certain barriers to the use of pooling accounting when treasury shares have been acquired in the two years prior to initiation of the combination.

Part Purchase, Part Pooling.   Another unusual accounting result was achieved in combinations accounted for in part as a purchase and in part as a pooling. Assume A Company owns, say, a 35 percent interest in B Company which was acquired for cash several years ago. If all or substantially all of the remaining 65 percent interest in B Company is obtained by issuance of common stock, the resultant combination would likely have been considered a 35 percent purchase and a 65 percent pooling prior to issuance of Opinion No. 16. Thus, the goodwill associated with the 35 percent purchase would appear in the postcombination financial statement, while no goodwill would be associated with the 65 percent pooling. Retained earnings applicable to the 65 percent portion would be carried forward as retained earnings in the postcombination statements, while the retained earnings applicable to the 35 percent portion would be eliminated for statement presentation.

The part-purchase, part-pooling approach to accounting for a combination was somewhat inconsistent with the pooling concept of accounting for two merged companies as if they had always been one company. This approach is no longer permissible under Opinion No. 16.

Contingent Payments.   Combinations which involve contingent payments generally arise from a disagreement among the parties as to the appropriate values of the companies involved. For example, the sellers may demand a price for excess earning capacity that the buyers feel is unsupportable. As a compromise, the terms agreed upon might include a provision for a fixed number of shares, say, 200,000, with an additional provision for a contingent payment of up to 50,000 additional shares within the following five years. Generally, the operating results of the selling company during the five-year period will determine what portion of the additional 50,000 shares will be paid.

In some instances payment of the additional shares is contingent upon the market action of the buyer's stock in the forward period. For example, the buyers may argue that while the 200,000 shares are worth only $10 million at today's prices, these shares can be projected to be worth $20 million within five years because of the growth characteristics of the company which the market recognizes.

Compromise terms may include provision for up to 50,000 additional shares to be issued, depending upon the actual market performance of the buyer's stock.

With either of the above examples, prior to issuance of Opinion No. 16 a combination effected entirely for stock would have qualified for pooling accounting. Since the value of the consideration issued to bring about the combination is not significant to accounting for a pooling, the contingent aspect of part of the shares would have little effect on the accounting. The issuance of any of the contingent shares would result only in an entry increasing capital stock and reducing capital in excess of par of the buying company. The issuance of the contingent shares would not affect in any way the amounts recorded for the assets and properties taken over in the combination if it were accounted for as a pooling. On the other hand, under purchase accounting the fair value of the contingent shares issed would generally result in the recording of an additional amount of goodwill. Contingent payments, whether related to future earnings or future market prices, preclude pooling accounting under Opinion No. 16.

Continuity of Ownership.   One of the criteria by which proposed accounting for a business combination has been judged is the continuity of ownership. Thus, a combination effected by stock results in a continuing of ownership interests, whereas a combination effected for cash results in elimination of one group of the previous ownership interests. Pooling-of-interests accounting has been tied closely to the continuity of ownership interests. As the pooling concept evolved, however, the insistence on continuity of ownership interests gradually diminished, as exemplified by use of convertible securities and by the part-purchase, part-pooling approach.

Opinion No. 16 did not provide, among its criteria, for a continuity of ownership interests. However, early experience under Opinion No. 16 indicated that incoming shareholders often were "bailed out," or received cash, shortly after the combination. As a result, the Securities and Exchange Commission, in *Accounting Series Release No. 135,* requires certain shareholders (affiliates) receiving shares in a combination to retain them at least until operating results of the combined entity for thirty days have been reported. The intent of this limiting provision appears to be to retain continuity of interests as a criterion of pooling-of-interests accounting, at least for a brief period of time, for shares issued to affiliates.

Post-Year-End Poolings.   On occasion, pooling accounting prior to Opinion No. 16 resulted in a company incorporating the assets and earnings of a company into its financial statements for a period even though it had no financial interest in the company during that period. Assume that A Company has a fiscal year ending December 31, and assume further that it contemplates a combination with B Company. The combination may be consummated under a variety of conditions with varying effects on financial presenations.

Thus, A Company may purchase B Company for cash on October 1, in which case A Company will include the assets and liabilities of B Company in its balance sheet at December 31 and will include the operations and earnings of B Company from October 1 to December 31 in its income statement. If the combination took place on November 15, the result would be the same, except that the income statement would include the earnings of B Company only from November 15. If the combination took place in January or later in the following year, even though it was prior to the date the auditors of A Company completed their examination, the combination would not affect the A Company financial statements at December 31. Disclosure of the combination might be accomplished by footnote if it were material.

On the other hand, A Company may bring about its combination with B Company in such a manner that pooling-of-interests accounting is appropriate. Under the pooling concept the result was the same whether the combination was effected on October 1, November 15, in the following January, or at any other date prior to the date the auditors of A Company complete their examination of the December 31 financial statements. This result was to include the assets and liabilities of B Company in the balance sheet of the combined companies as of December 31 and to include the operations and earnings of B Company in the income statement of the combined companies for the entire year. Thus, under pooling accounting the earnings of B Company for a year could be reported in a combined income statement of A Company and B Company for that year even if the two companies did not effect the combination until after the end of the year being reported on. Opinion No. 16, however, concludes that the combination must be consummated prior to the end of the fiscal year for the operations of the two companies to be reported on a combined basis for that fiscal year. Post-year-end poolings no longer are permissible.

Restatement of Prior-Year Data. A somewhat related problem arises in the presentation of comparative financial data subsequent to a business combination. If the combination is accounted for as a purchase, no restatement is made for previously reported data. The operating results of the year of combination and the financial position after combination would be compared with the previously reported operating results and financial position for earlier years. Full disclosure would be made of the combination, and *pro forma* information would be presented as if the companies had been combined for the periods being reported upon.

If the combination is accounted for as a pooling of interests, however, the pooling concept indicates a need to restate the financial data reported for periods prior to the combination. Such restatement would be necessary to present the financial data for the prior years on the basis that the combined entities had always been one company. Comparisons made between data for the year of combination and those for earlier periods would then include information for all units currently a part of the combined entity. In practice, however, restatements of prior years' data have sometimes not been made, on the basis that the newly combined unit is immaterial to the total enterprise. Comparisons made between the current year's data and those for prior years will not be misleading in the absence of restatement because of the immaterial effect which restatement would have.

Standards of materiality, however, are not well defined. Gradually the AICPA, through Opinions No. 6 and 10 of the Accounting Principles Board, reenforced the policy of restatement of prior years' data if such data are presented in periods after a pooling-of-interests combination. The Securities and Exchange Commission has similarly supported such restatements. Under the pooling concept the usefulness of comparative data would appear to rest importantly on the restatement of the data for earlier years to encompass that of newly combined units.

SUMMARY

Growth through business combination has become an integral part of American economic development. Combinations have created a number of accounting problems related to: (1) accounting for the combination transaction, (2) accounting for operations subsequent to the combination, and (3) reporting the results of operations and financial position of the combined companies in a manner to permit comparisons with prior years. An overriding problem is related to the need to identify the characteristics of the combination so as to classify it appropriately for accounting purposes. Innovations in combination approaches and in types of securities used to effect the combination hindered clear identification in many cases. As a result, the APB issued Opinion No. 16 in an attempt to eliminate certain alleged abuses and to limit pooling accounting to combinations meeting all the specified criteria. Experience in applying Opinion No. 16 indicates, however, that some of the criteria are more arbitrary than sound. Numerous interpretations have been issued to guide practitioners, and the Financial Accounting Standards Board, the successor to the Accounting Principles Board, continues to assess the need for revised standards to account for business combinations.

BIBLIOGRAPHY

Alberts, William W., and Joel E. Segall (eds.): *The Corporate Merger,* The University of Chicago Press, Chicago, 1966.

Briloff, Abraham: "Dirty Poolings," *The Accounting Review,* July 1967.

Catlett, George R., and Norman O. Olson: "Accounting for Goodwill," *Accounting Research Study No. 10.* AICPA, New York, 1968.

Gunther, Samuel P.: "Lingering Pooling Problems," *CPA Journal,* June 1973.

———; "Poolings—Purchases—Goodwill: A Review of APB Opinions 16 and 17," *New York Certified Public Accountant,* January 1971.

Hagendorf, Stanley: *Tax Guide for Buying and Selling a Business,* Prentice-Hall, Englewood Cliffs, N.J., 1967.

Hennessey, J. H., Jrs: *Acquiring and Merging Businesses,* Prentice-Hall, Englewood Cliffs, N.J., 1966.

Lev, Baruch: "Microeconomic Consequences of Corporate Mergers," *Journal of Business* (University of Chicago), January 1972.

McCarthy, George D., and Robert E. Healy: *Valuing a Company: Practices and Procedures,* The Ronald Press Company, New York, 1971.

Morrison, P. C., and J. F. Morrison: "Business Acquisitions Illustrate Need for Greater Uniformity in Accounting Principles," *Financial Analysts Journal,* January 1967.

Mosich, A. N.: "Impact of Merger Accounting on Post-Merger Financial Reports," *Management Accounting,* December 1965.

Nurnberg, H., C. P. Stickney, and R. L. Weil: "Combining Stockholders' Equity Accounts Under Pooling of Interests Method," *The Accounting Review,* 50, 1 (January 1975), 179–183.

Sapienza, Samuel R.: "Business Combinations and Enterprise Valuation," *Journal of Accounting Research,* Spring 1964.

———: "Examination of AICPA Research Study No. 5—Standards for Pooling," *The Accounting Review,* July 1964.

Wright, R. F.: "Corporate Mergers, Acquisitions and Divestitures," *New York Certified Public Accountant,* January 1967.

Wyatt, Arthur R.: "A Critical Study of Accounting for Business Combinations," *Accounting Research Study No. 5,* AICPA, New York, 1963.

———: "Inequities in Accounting for Business Combinations," *Financial Executive,* December 1972.

Wyatt, Arthur R., and Donald E. Kieso: *Business Combinations: Planning and Action,* International Textbook Co., Scranton, Pa., 1969.

APPENDIX: AC SECTION 1091[1]
Accounting for Business Combinations

Effective to account for business combinations initiated after October 31, 1970, unless otherwise indicated

Applicability of Accounting Methods

.42 The Board finds merit in both the purchase and pooling-of-interests methods of accounting for business combinations and accepts neither method to the exclusion of the other. The arguments in favor of the purchase method of accounting are more persuasive if cash or other assets are distributed or liabilities are incurred to effect a combination, but arguments in favor of the pooling-of-interests method of accounting are more persuasive if

[1]AICPA, Professional Standards, Volume 3, published by Commerce Clearing House, 1976, footnotes omitted.

voting common stock is issued to effect a combination of common stock interests. Therefore, the Board concludes that some business combinations should be accounted for by the purchase method and other combinations should be accounted for by the pooling-of-interests method.

.43 The Board also concludes that the two methods are not alternatives in accounting for the same business combination. A single method should be applied to an entire combination; the practice now known as part-purchase, part-pooling is not acceptable. The acquisition after the effective date of this section of some or all of the stock held by minority stockholders of a subsidiary—whether acquired by the parent, the subsidiary itself, or another affiliate—should be accounted for by the purchase method rather than by the pooling-of-interests method.

.44 The Board believes that accounting for business combinations will be improved significantly by specifying the circumstances in which each method should be applied and the procedures which should be followed in applying each method. The distinctive conditions which require pooling-of-interests accounting are described in paragraphs .45 to .48, and combinations involving all of those conditions should be accounted for as described in paragraphs .50 to .65. All other business combinations should be treated as the acquisition of one company by another and accounted for by the purchase method as described in paragraphs .66 to .96.

Conditions for Pooling-of-Interests Method

.45 The pooling-of-interests method of accounting is intended to present as a single interest two or more common stockholder interests which were previously independent and the combined rights and risks represented by those interests. That method shows that stockholder groups neither withdraw nor invest assets but in effect exchange voting common stock in a ratio that determines their respective interests in the combined corporations. Some business combinations have those features. A business combination which meets *all* of the conditions specified and explained in paragraphs .46 to .48 should be accounted for by the pooling-of-interests method. The conditions are classified by (1) attributes of the combining companies, (2) manner of combining interests, and (3) absence of planned transactions.

.46 *Combining companies.* Certain attributes of combining companies indicate that independent ownership interests are combined in their entirety to continue previously separate operations. Combining virtually all of existing common stock interests avoids combining only selected assets, operations, or ownership interests, any of which is more akin to disposing of and acquiring interests than to sharing risks and rights. It also avoids combining interests that are already related by substantial intercorporate investments.

The two conditions in this paragraph define essential attributes of combining companies.

    a. Each of the combining companies is autonomous and has not been a subsidiary or division of another corporation within two years before the plan of combination is initiated.

A plan of combination is initiated on the earlier of (1) the date that the major terms of a plan, including the ratio of exchange of stock, are announced publicly or otherwise formally made known to the stockholders of any one of the combining companies or (2) the date that stockholders of a combining company are notified in writing of an exchange offer. Therefore, a plan of combination is often initiated even though consummation is subject to the approval of stockholders and others.

A new company incorporated within the preceeding two years meets this condition unless the company is successor to a part of a company or to a company that is otherwise not autonomous for this condition. A wholly owned subsidiary company which distributes voting common stock of its parent corporation to effect the combination is also considered an autonomous company provided the parent corporation would have met all conditions in paragraphs .46 to .48 had the parent corporation issued its stock directly to effect the combination.

Divestiture of assets to comply with an order of a governmental authority or judicial body results in an exception to the terms of this condition. Either a subsidiary divested under an order or a new company which acquires assets disposed of under an order is therefore autonomous for this condition.

    b. Each of the combining companies is independent of the other combining companies.

This condition means that at the dates the plan of combination is initiated and consummated the combining companies hold as intercorporate investments no more than 10 percent in total of the outstanding voting common stock of any combining company. For the percentage computation, intercorporate investments exclude voting common stock that is acquired after the date the plan of combination is initiated in exchange for the voting common stock issued to effect the combination. Investments of 10 percent or less are explained in paragraph .47-b.

.47 *Combining of interests.* The combining of existing voting common stock interests by the exchange of stock is the essence of a business combination accounted for by the pooling-of-interests method. The separate stockholder interests lose their identities and all share mutually in the combined risks and rights. Exchanges of common stock that alter relative voting rights, that result in preferential claims to distributions of profits or assets for some common stockholder groups, or that leave significant minority interests in combining companies are incompatible with the idea of mutual sharing. Similarly, acquisitions of common stock for assets or debt, reacquisitions of outstanding stock for the purpose of exchanging it in a business combination, and other transactions that reduce the common stock interests are contrary to the idea of combining existing stockholder interests. The seven conditions in this paragraph relate to the exchange to effect the combination.

a. The combination is effected in a single transaction or is completed in accordance with a specific plan within one year after the plan is initiated.

Altering the terms of exchange of stock constitutes initiation of a new plan of combination unless earlier exchanges of stock are adjusted to the new terms.

A business combination completed in more than one year from the date the plan is initiated meets this condition if the delay is beyond the control of the combining companies because proceedings of a governmental authority or litigation prevents completing the combination.

b. A corporation offers and issues only common stock with rights identical to those of the majority of its outstanding voting common stock in exchange for substantially all of the voting common stock interest of another company at the date the plan of combination is consummated.

The plan to issue voting common stock in exchange for voting common stock may include, within limits, provisions to distribute cash or other consideration for fractional shares, for shares held by dissenting stockholders, and the like but may not include a pro rata distribution of cash or other consideration.

Substantially all of the voting common stock means 90 percent or more for this condition. That is, after the date the plan of combination is initiated, one of the combining companies (issuing corporation) issues voting common stock in exchange for at least 90 percent of the voting common stock of another combining company that is outstanding at the date the combination is consummated. The number of shares exchanged therefore excludes those shares of the combining company (1) acquired before and held by the issuing corporation and its subsidiaries at the date the plan of combination is initiated, regardless of the form of consideration, (2) acquired by the issuing corporation and its subsidiaries after the date the plan of combination is initiated other than by issuing its own voting common stock, and (3) outstanding after the date the combination is consummated.

An investment in stock of the issuing corporation held by a combining company may prevent a combination from meeting this condition even though the investment of the combining company is not more than 10 percent of the outstanding stock of the issuing corporation (paragraph .46-b). An investment in stock of the issuing corporation by another combining company is the same in a mutual exchange as an investment by the issuing corporation in stock of the other combining company—the choice of issuing corporation is essentially a matter of convenience. An investment in stock of the issuing corporation must be expressed as an equivalent number of shares of the investor combining company because the measure of percent of shares exchanged is in terms of shares exchanged in the combination as follows:

The number of shares of voting common stock of the issuing corporation held by the investor combining company at the date the plan is initiated plus shares it acquired after that date are restated as an equivalent number of shares of voting common stock of the investor combining company based on the ratio of exchange of stock in the combination.

The equivalent number of shares is deducted from the number of shares of voting common stock of the investor combining company exchanged for voting common stock of the issuing corporation as part of the plan of combination.

The reduced number of shares is considered the number exchanged and is compared with

90 percent of the outstanding voting common stock of the investor combining company at the date the plan is consummated to determine whether the terms of condition .47-b are met.

Since the number of shares of voting common stock exchanged is reduced for an intercorporate investment in voting common stock of the issuing corporation, the terms of condition .47-b may not be met even though 90 percent or more of the outstanding common stock of a combining company is exchanged to effect a combination.

A combination of more than two companies is evaluated essentially the same as a combination of two companies. The percent of voting common stock exchanged is measured separately for each combining company, and condition .47-b is met if 90 percent or more of the voting common stock of each of the several combining companies is exchanged for voting common stock of the issuing corporation. The number of shares exchanged for stock of the issuing corporation includes only shares exchanged by stockholders other than the several combining companies themselves. Thus, inter-corporate investments in combining companies are included in the number of shares of stock outstanding but are excluded from the number of shares of stock exchanged to effect the combination.

A new corporation formed to issue its stock to effect the combination of two or more companies meets condition .47-b if (1) the number of shares of each company exchanged to effect the combination is not less than 90 percent of its voting common stock outstanding at the date the combination is consummated and (2) condition .47-b would have been met had any one of the combining companies issued its stock to effect the combination on essentially the same basis.

Condition .47-b relates to issuing common stock for the common stock interests in another company. Hence, a corporation issuing stock to effect the combination may assume the debt securities of the other company or may exchange substantially identical securities or voting common stock for other outstanding equity and debt securities of the other combining company. An issuing corporation may also distribute cash to holders of debt and equity securities that either are callable or redeemable and may retire those securities. However, the issuing corporation may exchange only voting common stock for outstanding equtiy and debt securities of the other combining company that have been issued in exchange for voting common stock of that company during a period beginning two years preceeding the date the combination is initiated.

A transfer of the net assets of a combining company to effect a business combination satisfies condition .47-b provided all net assets of the company at the date the plan is consummated are transferred in exchange for stock of the issuing corporation. However, the combining company may retain temporarily cash, receivables, or marketable securities to settle liabilities, contingencies, or items in dispute if the plan provides that the assets remaining after settlement are to be transferred to the corporation issuing the stock to effect the combination. Only voting common stock may be issued to effect the combination unless both voting common stock and other stock of the other combining company are outstanding at the date the plan is consummated. The combination may then be effected by issuing all voting common stock or by issuing voting common and other stock in the same proportions as the outstanding voting common and other stock of the other combining company. An investment in 10 percent or less of the outstanding voting common stock of a combining company held by another combining company requires special computations to evaluate condition .47-b. The computations and comparisons are in terms of the voting common stock of the issuing corporation and involve:

Stock issued for common stock interest. The total number of shares of voting common stock issued for all of the assets is divided between those applicable to outstanding voting common stock and those applicable to other outstanding stock, if any, of the combining company which transfers assets (transferor company).

Reduction for intercorporate investments. The number of issued shares of voting common stock applicable to the voting common stock interests of the transferor combining company is reduced by the sum of (1) the number of shares of voting common stock of the issuing corporation held by the transferor combining company at the date the plan of combination is initiated plus shares it acquired after that date and (2) the number of shares of voting common stock of the transferor combining company held by the issuing corporation at the date the plan of combination is initiated plus shares it acquired after that date. The shares of the transferor combining company are restated as the equivalent number of shares of voting common stock of the issuing corporation for this purpose. Restatement is based on the ratio of the number of shares of voting common stock of the transferor combining company which are outstanding at the date the plan is consummated to the number of issued shares of voting common stock applicable to the voting common stock interests.

Comparison with 90 percent. The reduced number of shares of stock issued is compared with 90 percent of the issued number of shares of voting common stock applicable to voting common stock interests to determine if the transfer of assets meets the terms of condition .47-b.

c. None of the combining companies changes the equity interest of the voting common stock in contemplation of effecting the combination either within two years before the plan of combination is initiated or between the dates the combination is initiated and consummated; changes in contemplation of effecting the combination may include distributions to stockholders and additional issuances, exchanges, and retirements of securities.

Distributions to stockholders which are no greater than normal dividends are not changes for this condition. Normality of dividends is determined in relation to earnings during the period and to the previous dividend policy and record. Dividend distributions on stock of a combining company that are equivalent to normal dividends on the stock to be issued in exchange in the combination are considered normal for this condition.

d. Each of the combining companies reacquires shares of voting common stock only for purposes other than business combinations, and no company reacquires more than a normal number of shares between the dates the plan of combination is initiated and consummated.

Treasury stock acquired for purposes other than business combinations includes shares for stock option and compensation plans and other recurring distributions provided a systematic pattern of reacquisitions is established at least two years before the plan of combination is initiated. A systematic pattern of reacquisitions may be established for less than two years if it coincides with the adoption of a new stock option or compensation plan. The normal number of shares of voting common stock reacquired is determined by the pattern of reacquisitions of stock before the plan of combination is initiated.

Acquisitions by other combining companies of voting common stock of the issuing corporation after the date the plan of combination is initiated are essentially the same as if the issuing corporation reacquired its own common stock.

e. The ratio of the interest of an individual common stockholder to those of other common stockholders in a combining company remains the same as a result of the exchange of stock to effect the combination.

This condition means that each individual common stockholder who exchanges his stock receives a voting common stock interest exactly in proportion to his relative voting common stock interest before the combination is effected. Thus no common stockholder is denied or surrenders his potential share of a voting common stock interest in a combined corporation.

f. The voting rights to which the common stock ownership interests in the resulting combined corporation are entitled are exercisable by the stockholders; the stockholders are neither deprived of nor restricted in exercising those rights for a period.

This condition is not met, for example, if shares of common stock issued to effect the combination are transferred to a voting trust.

g. The combination is resolved at the date the plan is consummated and no provisions of the plan relating to the issue of securities or other consideration are pending.

This condition means that (1) the combined corporation does not agree to contingently issue additional shares of stock or distribute other consideration at a later date to the former stockholders of a combining company or (2) the combined corporation does not issue or distribute to an escrow agent common stock or other consideration which is to be either transferred to common stockholders or returned to the corporation at the time the contingency is resolved.

An agreement may provide, however, that the number of shares of common stock issued to effect the combination may be revised for the later settlement of a contingency at a different amount than that recorded by a combining company.

.48 *Absence of planned transactions.* Some transactions after a combination is consummated are inconsistent with the combining of entire existing interests of common stockholders. Including those transactions in the negotiations and terms of the combination, either explicitly or by intent, counteracts the effect of combining stockholder interests. The three conditions in this paragraph relate to certain future transactions.

   a. The combined corporation does not agree directly or indirectly to retire or reacquire all or part of the common stock issued to effect the combination.

   b. The combined corporation does not enter into other financial arrangements for the benefit of the former stockholders of a combining company, such as a guaranty of loans secured by stock issued in the combination, which in effect negates the exchange of equity securities.

   c. The combined corporation does not intend or plan to dispose of a significant part of the assets of the combining companies within two years after the combination other than disposals in the ordinary course of business of the formerly separate companies and to eliminate duplicate facilities or excess capacity.

Subsidiary Corporation

  .49 Dissolution of a combining company is not a condition for applying the pooling of interests method of accounting for a business combination. One or more combining companies may be subsidiaries of the issuing corporation after the combination is consummated if the other conditions are met.

Chapter **34**

Consolidated Statements

LOUIS H. JORDAN
Professor of Accounting, Fordham University

INTERCORPORATE STOCK INVESTMENT

The right of a business corporation to hold shares of stock of other corporations is not an inherent or "natural" right. In the United States this privilege was first extended by New Jersey to all corporations subject to its jurisdiction. It was gradually extended by other states until today it is considered part of the normal complement of powers of incorporated units.

Acquisition of Shares. An investment in shares of stock may be acquired in any manner in which any other property may be acquired. The major types of consideration used in the acquisition of shares are cash, debt, and shares of capital stock.

Cash. The acquisition of shares for cash, or on short-term credit, involve few accounting problems at the date of purchase, whether Company A acquires shares of Company B upon initial issuance or subsequently in the market from shareholders of B. Cost of the investment is the amount of cash paid or the present cash equivalent of the amount promised to be paid in the future.

Debt. If, upon initial issuance, Company B agrees to accept bonds or other long-term debt of A in settlement of A's subscription, a valuation problem arises. In this case, the market value of the bonds becomes the proper measure of A's investment in B's shares, as well as the proper measure of A's debt. A valuation problem arises, also, if A acquires stock of B by the issuance of debt to B's shareholders. As a practical matter, this type of exchange is not likely to occur in the market through a broker because of the difficulty of establishing the terms of barter. In all cases in which assets are acquired for consideration other than cash, the nominal or face amount of the consideration employed must be carefully tested to determine whether it will serve as a measure of the cost of the asset acquired.

Exchange of Shares. Company A might acquire stock of Company B by the issuance of its own stock. This type of exchange occurs frequently by direct negotiation between A and the stockholders of B, usually through B's board of directors. For example, A offers to issue to the shareholders of B its own shares in exchange for the shares of B. The effect of this plan is to make shareholders of A out of former shareholders of B. The former shareholders of B still retain an indirect interest in B through A's ownership of shares of B. This type of arrangement, or some variant of it, is extensively employed in business combinations (see Chapter 33) and in the creation of the intercorporate relationships which call for consolidated financial statements.

Pooling. The exchange of common shares of A for common shares of B raises not only a valuation problem but also the question of the nature of the event itself. Is the exchange simply the agreement of two groups of shareholders to join together as co-owners in the combined activities of A and B? This interpretation of the exchange leads to the pooling-of-interests concept as developed in the preceding chapter. This concept suggests that there is no new basis of accountability for the net assets of B and that the proper valuation by A of its investment in B, and hence the consideration received by A for its shares exchanged, is the underlying book value of B's shares.

Purchase.   An alternative interpretation of the exchange of common shares of A for common shares of B is that A purchases the ownership interest in B. In settlement of the purchase price, A issues its own shares. This interpretation focuses attention on the negotiated purchase price between buyer and seller, evidence of which is found in the market value of shares issued by A and in the market value of the shares of B acquired. In a perfect market, the ratio of exchange would be expected to be such that the evidence from either direction would reflect the negotiated purchase price. The net assets of B are being revalued in the market. This new basis of accountability usually exceeds the book value of the underlying equity acquired.

Consolidated Statements.   Intercorporate relationships which result in consolidated financial statements are the main focus of this chapter. More specifically, purchase transactions involving the use of cash will serve as a basis for discussing intercorporate relationships and for working out the implications of consolidated financial statements. At appropriate points in the discussion the consequences of share exchanges interpreted as poolings will be considered.

Subsequent Valuation of Acquired Shares.   Assume that Company P purchases all the common shares of Company S on January 1, 19X0, for $700,000 cash. Assume, also, that the owners' equity of Company S on the same date is $650,000, subdivided as follows:

> Common Stock, 10,000 shares, $50 par value $500,000
> Retained Earnings 150,000
> $650,000

Assume further that Company S reports net income of $30,000 for 19X0 and declares a dividend of $1 per share on January 5, 19X1. P's accounting for S on its book depends on whether P uses the equity method or the cost method of accounting for investments.

Equity Method.   At the end of 19X0 P can determine the increase in its investment in S. If S's reported income is in accordance with generally accepted accounting principles, the increase in P's investment is sufficiently objective to warrant recognition. The following analysis is appropriate for Company P as of December 31, 19X0:

> (1)
> Investment in Common Stock of S 30,000
>   Revenue from Investment in S   30,000

The dividend declaration of January 5, 19X1, is interpreted as follows:

> (2)
> Dividends Receivable 10,000
>   Investment in Common Stock of S   10,000

If Company S reports a loss for 19X0 instead of a profit, the analysis in (1) would show a decrease in the investment account with a charge for the loss on the investment. The dividend in either case is correctly interpreted as a reduction in owners' equity of S and a reduction in the value of P's interest in that equity. It should be emphasized, however, that this interpretation presupposes that P's share of the increase or decrease in S's net assets from operations has already been recognized by P.

Investment at Cost.   If Company P maintains its investment in S using the cost method, the analysis will differ. On the cost basis, no recognition is given to P's interest in the reported income of S for 19X0. Instead, the dividend declaration on January 5, 19X1, would be analyzed as follows:

```
Dividends Receivable  ...................  10,000
    Dividend Revenue from S  ...........          10,000
```

Equity Method Versus Cost.   A summary of the two alternatives for Company P in accounting for its Investment in Company S account in its own ledger follows:

	Equity method	Cost basis
Jan. 1, 19X0		
Acquisition of 10,000 shares	$700,000	$700,000
Dec. 31, 19X0		
Share of B's earnings	30,000	
Jan. 5, 19X1		
Dividends	(10,000)	
Balances	$720,000	$700,000

The book value of S's common shares increased from $650,000 on January 1, 19X0, to $670,000 on January 5, 19X1, an increase of $20,000. Since P owns all of S's common stock, the entire increase is reported by P as shown by the equity method above. On the cost basis, P's investment in S is unchanged during the same period. Thus, the cost basis is unsatisfactory for reporting the complete history of an investment in shares of another company.

If Company P initially acquires only 8,000 (80 percent) of the common shares of Company S for $70 per share on January 1, 19X0, the analysis compares the initial investment of $560,000 with an underlying equity of $520,000 (= 80 percent of $650,000). Similarly, P's share of dividends and earnings is limited to 80 percent of the amount applicable to S's common shares as a class. Accordingly, the analyses of the changes in S's net assets in (1) and (2) above are modified to reflect P's share on only 80 percent.

A subsequent acquisition by P of the additional 2,000 shares of S's common stock (20 percent) on the market would involve no new problem. From the date of acquisition, the increased percentage of ownership would be employed to calculate P's share of changes in the book value of S's shares.

Stock Dividends.   The receipt by Company P of additional shares of stock as a dividend on its investment in Company S requires no revision of the total investment, but the increased number of shares should be noted by P. No revision is required because: (1) the stock dividend merely shifts amounts in subdivisions of S's net assets without changing the total; and (2) the relative rights of shareholders remain unchanged. The same conclusions apply to split-ups and to changes in the par value of common shares.

Controlling Interest.   The ownership of more than 50 percent of the voting stock of a corporation usually carries with it the power to elect a majority of the board of directors and, thus, to determine policy and control its operations. When one corporation controls another through stock ownership, the dominant company is referred to as the parent company, and the company under control as the subsidiary. In some cases, the ownership of a majority of the voting stock of a corporation may not constitute control. For example, a company with majority ownership may also be party to a voting trust agreement which shifts equal or superior power to others. Temporary ownership of voting stock, as in the case of an investment banker, usually does not involve the power to dictate operating policy. *Accounting Research Bulletin No. 51*[1] states:

> The usual condition for a controlling financial interest is ownership of a majority voting interest, and, therefore, as a general rule ownership by one company, directly or indirectly, of over fifty percent of the outstanding voting shares of another company is a condition pointing toward consolidation. However, there are exceptions to this general rule. For example, a subsidiary should not be consolidated where control is likely to be temporary, or where it does not rest with the majority owners (as, for instance, where the subsidiary is in legal reorganization or in bankruptcy).

Many companies dominate others through ownership of less than half the voting stock. In these cases, the ownership of voting shares of the subordinate corporation is widely diffused, except for the substantial block held by the dominant company. Such dominance is the consequence of apathy of the owners of a majority of the voting stock, or of their satisfaction with the policies of the major shareholder. For example, if Company A holds 40 percent of the voting shares of Company B but only one-third of the remaining 60 percent of the shares are voted at corporate elections, Company A is clearly able to control the selection of B's directors and to determine its policies. In addition, a controlling interest in a corporation may be derived from relationships other than stock ownership. For example, the terms of debt financing may transfer control to bondholders. Whether one company has a controlling interest in another is a matter for determination in each case.

Control through stock ownership, resulting in parent-subsidiary relationships, emphasizes two aspects of the problem of intercorporate investment: (1) the basis of maintaining the investment, and (2) criteria for consolidated financial statements. The superiority of the equity method over the cost basis is clearly evident in parent-subsidiary relationships. The parent company has detailed knowledge of the subsidiary's activities. There is no uncertainty regarding the relationship between the investment and the underlying equity owned. Accordingly, the investment account should reflect the portion of the proprietorship of the subsidiary actually owned.

Consolidated Statements.   Consolidated financial statements are in order if the activities of a subsidiary are functions which could be performed by the parent as part of its own operations. Many corporations establish or acquire controlling interests in subsidiaries which perform functions which in other corporations are performed by departments or divisions. Subsidiaries that perform the following functions, among others, for the benefit of the parent or other subsidiaries are integral parts of the business entity:

1. Manufacture parts, product lines, or supply utilities such as gas, water, electric power, or transportation.
2. Sell goods or services produced by affiliates.
3. Furnish technical and managerial services and advice.
4. Hold property, plant, or equipment for the benefit of affiliates.
5. Finance the sales of affiliates by handling installment contracts. (Many firms do not consolidate financing subsidiaries, but a strong logical case for consolidation can be made.)

Excluded from the area of consolidation under the concept of integrated operations are activities of controlled companies which could not be performed by the parent company. For example, a commercial bank whose stock is owned by a nonbanking company should not be consolidated with its parent. Under existing law, the nonbanking parent could not operate a commercial bank as a department.

[1]Committee on Accounting Procedure, *Accounting Research Bulletin No. 51,* AICPA, New York, 1959, par. 2.

Thus, consolidated financial statements are appropriate whenever the activities of two or more corporations are under central control through stock ownership of a parent company which could perform the same activities as part of its own operations. *ARB No. 51*[2] indicates the following standard:

> In deciding upon consolidation policy, the aim should be to make the financial presentation which is most meaningful in the circumstances. The reader should be given information which is suitable to his needs, but he should not be burdened with unnecessary detail. Thus, even though a group of companies is heterogeneous in character, it may be better to make a full consolidation than to present a large number of separate statements. On the other hand, separate statements or combined statements would be preferable for a subsidiary or group of subsidiaries if the presentation of financial information concerning the particular activities of such subsidiaries would be more informative to shareholders and creditors of the parent company than would the inclusion of such subsidiaries in the consolidation. For example, separate statements may be required for a subsidiary which is a bank or an insurance company and may be preferable for a finance company where the parent and the other subsidiaries are engaged in manufacturing operations.

Similarly, the financial effects of control of two or more business units, incorporated or not, by one person or family, might best be shown in combined statements prepared along the lines of consolidated financial statements. *ARB No. 51*[3] states:

> To justify the preparation of consolidated statements, the controlling financial interest should rest directly or indirectly in one of the companies included in the consolidation. There are circumstances, however, where combined financial statements (as distinguished from consolidated statements) of commonly controlled companies are likely to be more meaningful than their separate statements. For example, combined financial statements would be useful where one individual owns a controlling interest in several corporations which are related to their operations. Combined statements would also be used to present the financial position and the results of operations of a group of unconsolidated subsidiaries. They might also be used to combine the financial statements of companies under common management.

Unconsolidated Subsidiaries. If a subsidiary is not consolidated, the parent's investment in it appears both on the parent's separate and on its consolidated balance sheet, if there are other subsidiaries that are consolidated. The superiority of the equity basis in accounting for intercompany investments is developed above. In 1959, *ARB No. 51* expressed a preference for the equity basis in dealing with unconsolidated subsidiaries in consolidated statements, but it did not disapprove the cost basis that was more commonly used at that time. However, in Opinion No. 10 the Accounting Principles Board[4] took a stronger position, requiring the use of the equity method for domestic subsidiaries. This position was reaffirmed in Opinion No. 18, Paragraph 14, as follows:

> The Board reaffirms the conclusion that investors should account for investments in common stock of unconsolidated domestic subsidiaries by the equity method in consolidated financial statements, and the Board now extends this conclusion to investments in common stock of all unconsolidated subsidiaries (foreign as well as domestic) in consolidated financial statements. The equity method is not, however, a valid substitute for consolidation and should not be used to justify exclusion of a subsidiary when consolidation is otherwise appropriate. The Board also concludes that parent companies should account for investments in the common stock of subsidiaries by the equity method in parent-company financial statements prepared for issuance to stockholders as the financial statements of the primary reporting entity.

---

[2]*Ibid.*, par. 3.
[3]*Ibid.*, par. 22.
[4]Accounting Principles Board, "Omnibus Opinion—1966," Opinion No. 10, AICPA, New York, 1966, par. 3.

At the same time the Board deferred further consideration of the treatment of foreign subsidiaries in consolidated statements.

Significant information relative to unconsolidated subsidiaries must be disclosed. Opinion No. 18[5] requires:

> When investments in unconsolidated subsidiaries are, in the aggregate, material in relation to financial position or results of operations, summarized information as to assets, liabilities, and results of operations should be presented in the notes or separate statements should be presented for such subsidiaries, either individually or in groups, as appropriate.

NATURE AND PURPOSE OF CONSOLIDATED STATEMENTS

When a parent company establishes control over one or more subsidiaries, emphasis is shifted from the separate corporate units to the area of integrated operations of which the individual companies are parts. This area of activities under common control constitutes an economic and business entity, as *ARB No. 51*[6] states:

> The purpose of consolidated statements is to present, primarily for the benefit of the shareholders and creditors of the parent company, the results of operations and the financial position of a parent company and its subsidiaries essentially as if the group were a single company with one or more branches or divisions. There is a presumption that consolidated statements are more meaningful than separate statements and that they are usually necessary for a fair presentation when one of the companies in the group directly or indirectly has a controlling financial interest in the other companies.

Hendriksen[7] observes an inconsistency in the above statement by the Institute:

> This objective implies that we should look through the legal relationships of the corporations and view the enterprise as a single economic unit. But the emphasis on the interests of the shareholders and creditors of the parent company is inconsistent with this major objective.

Accounting Entity.   The business entity, consisting of parent and one or more subsidiary companies, is the accounting entity for which consolidated statements are prepared. Economic realities are given precedent over legal separateness, with parent and consolidated subsidiaries viewed as a single business unit.

The significance of the entity concept in preparing consolidated financial statements is emphasized by Moonitz:[8]

> The leading principle in the technique of preparing consolidated statements is the elimination of all evidences of intercompany relationships. This principle is universally acknowledged and, for the most part, adhered to in practice. The objective attained by elimination is the suppression of amounts and accounts reflecting transactions among the constituent units and the retention of only those data pertinent to the showing of the affiliation as an economic or business entity. In essence this requires a shift in viewpoint from that of a legal abstraction—the business corporation—to that of an accounting abstraction—the effective business unit. The shift must be made, and it must be complete.

Viewing a group of closely held affiliated companies as the entity, Moonitz developed a systematic structure for dealing with the problems posed by their

---

[5]Accounting Principles Board, "The Equity Method of Accounting for Investments in Common Stock," Opinion No. 18, AICPA, New York, 1971, par. 20-c.

[6]*ARB No. 51,* par. 1.

[7]Eldon S. Hendriksen, *Accounting Theory,* Richard D. Irwin, Homewood, Ill., 1970, p. 515.

[8]Maurice Moonitz, *The Entity Theory of Consolidated Statements,* The Foundation Press, Brooklyn, 1951, p. 84. The Moonitz volume is a classic in the literature on consolidation.

interrelationships. His conclusions regarding controversial issues in consolidation result from the rigorous application of the principle of elimination to the entity:

1. A parent company may maintain its investment in a subsidiary at equity, reflecting its share of changes in net assets of the subsidiary.

2. Separate statements of a subsidiary should distinguish between transactions with affiliates and those with outsiders so that minority interest and creditors may judge the results of affiliation on the subsidiary.

3. All intercompany markups in assets should be eliminated, with assets shown at cost (or other accepted basis) to the entity, regardless of the size of the minority interest.

4. If acquisition price is evidence of unrecorded intangibles, they should be reported in full, regardless of the size of the minority interest.

5. Intercompany long-term obligations should be treated as treasury bonds.

6. Mutual shareholdings should be treated as treasury shares.

7. Minority interest should be computed after consolidated adjustments.

The significant features of the entity theory developed by Moonitz are contained in an excellent statement by a Committee on Concepts and Standards of the American Accounting Association.[9]

In "The Entity Concept," the 1964 Concepts and Standards Research Study Committee of the American Association discusses the entity concept in the following terms:[10]

> In accounting the entity with which we are concerned may be defined as *an area of economic interest to a particular individual or group*. The boundaries of such an economic entity are identifiable (1) by determining the interested individual or group, and (2) by determining the nature of that individual's or that group's interest. An economic entity encompasses the activities, events, and utilization of resources (intangible, as well as tangible, nonquantifiable, as well as quantifiable) that affect the interest of the individual or group. Simply stated, the committee advocates a "user-oriented" approach in determining an entity: That is, accounting reports about entities are developed to meet the needs of particular individuals or groups.

Viewpoint of Controlling Interest. Consolidated financial statements are prepared for the benefit of management and stockholders of the parent company. As a consequence, they are prepared from the point of view of those shareholders who collectively exercise central control. From this viewpoint, owners of stock of a subsidiary not held by the parent are outsiders.

Consolidated statements do not replace completely the statements of each corporate constituent. Separate statements will continue to serve various interested groups. For example, minority interests and creditors of a specific affiliate are interested in the separate financial condition of that affiliate. For such groups, separate statements will continue to be supplied, as *ARB No. 51* suggests:[11]

> In some cases parent-company statements may be needed, in addition to consolidated statements, to indicate adequately the position of bondholders and other creditors or preferred stockholders of the parent. Consolidating statements, in which one column is used for the parent company and other columns for particular subsidiaries or groups of subsidiaries, often are an effective means of presenting the pertinent information.

Complete reporting consists of (1) consolidated statements of the integrated group, (2) statements of the parent company, and (3) statements of each subsidiary. However, the earlier view that consolidated statements were auxiliary in

---

[9]Committee on Concepts and Standards, "Consolidated Financial Statements," *The Accounting Review*, vol. 30, pp. 194–197, April 1955.

[10]AAA Committee Report, "The Entity Concept," *The Accounting Review*, vol. 40, pp. 358–376, April 1965.

[11]*ARB No. 51*, par. 24.

nature has given way to the current view that they are primary rather than secondary. Consequently, separate statements of the parent have gradually disappeared from annual reports to stockholders.

Basic Premises. It is clear from the above considerations that underlying consolidated financial statements are the following basic premises:

1. Parent and consolidated subsidiaries form an economic unit.

2. Consolidated statements are more meaningful than separate statements of the parent and are usually necessary for a fair presentation of the condition of the parent.

3. Generally accepted accounting principles are applicable to consolidated financial statements.

Two generally accepted accounting concepts should be emphasized because of their relevance to consolidated statements:

1. The importance of proper asset valuation

2. Consistency of application of accounting principles.

Limitations of Consolidated Statements. It is not suggested that consolidated statements have no weaknesses. However, we should keep in mind the objectives of consolidated statements. Obviously, they do not show details of the constituent units. Creditors of the separate subsidiaries look to separate financial statements for information relevant to their claims because the concept of the business corporation as a separate legal entity is generally followed by the courts. Nor can questions regarding the legality of dividend declarations by subsidiaries and by the parent be answered by consolidated statements.

Foster[12] considers the limitations of consolidated statements to be the following:

1. They are not substitutes for statements of individual companies.

2. Certain distortions may occur in presenting liabilities and ownership equities.

3. Tests of financial condition and earning power must be determined with care because differences exist in the same items among the various companies.

Foster recognizes, however, that consolidated statements serve a useful purpose. "Only by consolidation can the top management get a complete picture of the conservative or speculative tone of the entire capital sources structure." The absence of a consolidated income statement "can badly distort the picture of the earnings to the majority stockholders . . . to such an extent that some may be influenced to sell at a sacrifice below what they should be able to receive on the market."

Rules of the Securities and Exchange Commission. Article 4 of Regulation S-X contains the SEC's general rules for consolidated and combined statements in filings with it. The following points are adapted from those rules:

1. Consolidated statements must clearly exhibit the financial condition and results of operations of the registrant and its subsidiaries.

2. Consolidate only majority-owned subsidiaries.

3. Consolidate subsidiaries having different fiscal periods than parent only if

   a. The difference is not more than 93 days.

   b. The closing dates of the subsidiaries are expressly indicated.

   c. The necessity for the use of different dates is explained.

   d. Changes in fiscal periods of parent and subsidiaries are indicated and the treatment is described.

4. Disclose the effect of foreign exchange restrictions when foreign subsidiaries are consolidated.

5. Combined statements may be filed for groups of majority-owned subsidiaries not consolidated. If they are essential for proper presentation of the facts, they must be filed.

---

[12]Louis O. Foster, *Understanding Financial Statements and Corporate Annual Reports,* rev. ed., Chilton Book Company, Philadelphia, 1968, pp. 76–77.

6. Disclose the principle for inclusion and exclusion of subsidiaries. Changes from previous year must be indicated.
7. Reconcile investments as shown on parent's books with equity in net assets of subsidiaries. Show amount and disposition of any differences, both for consolidated and unconsolidated subsidiaries.
8. Reconcile the earnings of unconsolidated subsidiaries with dividends received from them.
9. Show separately minority interest in capital and in retained earnings. Show minority interest in consolidated income as a separate item in the income statement.
10. Eliminate intercompany transactions and items; otherwise, state the reasons for not eliminating them, and indicate how they are treated.
11. Special requirements apply to the following:
    a. Insurance companies
    b. Banks and bank holding companies
    c. Public utility holding companies
    d. Certain companies in promotional or development stage.

CONSOLIDATED BALANCE SHEET AT ACQUISITION

A consolidated balance sheet as of the date of purchase of a controlling interest by a parent company is a beginning balance sheet of a new business entity. It is a statement which reflects the financial position of an integrated group of two or more corporations under common control. Basically, such a balance sheet is prepared from data supplied by the balance sheets of the constituents. To consolidate the balance sheet of Company P and Company S, it is necessary to eliminate any duplication of data. For example, if Company P has an obligation to S, Company S has a claim on P. In a statement reporting the financial position of a single business unit of which P and S are subdivisions, these interdivisional relationships have no significance. When P pays S, cash moves from one subdivision to another, but it remains within the area of integrated operations and has no effect on the combined resources of P and S. Whether cash moves from one company to the other or remains in one bank account is a matter of indifference from the consolidated point of view.

In similar fashion, duplication exists between the investment account on the books of P and the related net asset accounts of S represented by that investment. We cannot include as assets both the investment and the resources behind that investment without double counting. On the books of P, the investment is in the nature of a control account, showing in the aggregate what is shown in detail on the books of S. In consolidation, we substitute for the aggregate the more detailed classifications of S. This substitution permits us to develop combined totals for each significant classification without double counting.

The elimination in consolidation of pairs of reciprocal accounts in no way constitutes, in itself, a correction or revision of the accounts of the individual companies. They are eliminated only in consolidated working papers, never from the accounts of the constituent companies. Their continued presence in the underlying accounts is necessary for separate statements and in order to reflect properly intercorporate relationships. They are eliminated in consolidation solely because the point of view shifts from each corporation as a separate entity to each corporation as a cell in a larger business unit.

This principle of eliminating reciprocal data underlies all procedures for the preparation of combined statements, whether of divisions or branches of a single company, or of two or more corporations. The application of this principle may be difficult in some cases. A problem may arise from a lack of consistency between the sets of records involved. For example, a pair of reciprocal accounts may be stated at different amounts as a result of incomplete or inaccurate recording by one or both of the companies. An essential preliminary step in preparing consolidated statements, therefore, is to complete the records of each company. All cases of disagreement between pairs of intercompany accounts should be reconciled and the records of the individual companies corrected or completed before the formal task of consolidation is undertaken.

The following cases indicate the basic problems encountered in preparing a consolidated balance sheet at date of acquisition. Assume the following data of Companies P and S on July 1, 19X0:

	Company P	Company S
Cash.............................	$200,000	$ 50,000
Other assets (details omitted)........	300,000	150,000
	$500,000	$200,000
Liabilities (details omitted)..........	$150,000	$ 80,000
Capital stock—P (2,000 shares)......	200,000	
Capital stock—S (1,000 shares)......		100,000
Retained earnings—P..............	150,000	
Retained earnings—S..............		20,000
	$500,000	$200,000

Case A: Investment (100 Percent) at Book Value. On July 1, 19X0, Company P purchases for cash 1,000 shares of Company S at $120 per share and records the transaction as follows:

(1)
Investment in S—P 120,000
    Cash 120,000

After the purchase, the composition of P's assets is as follows:

Cash .... $ 80,000
Other assets ....,........ 300,000
Investment in S 120,000 $500,000

The following eliminating entry, when applied to the data above, will remove the reciprocal data and facilitate the preparation of a consolidated balance sheet at July 1, 19X0:

(2)
Capital Stock—S 100,000
Retained Earnings—S 20,000
    Investment in S—P 120,000

The resulting consolidated balance sheet will report the following amounts:

Assets:
    Cash $130,000
    Other assets 450,000 $580,000
Liabilities 230,000
Net assets:
    Capital stock—P (2,000 shares) $200,000
    Retained earnings 150,000 $350,000

The consolidated data above conform to the position of the AICPA as expressed in *ARB No. 51:*[13] "The earned surplus or deficit of a purchased subsidiary at the

[13]*ARB No. 51,* par. 9.

date of acquisition by the parent should not be included in consolidated earned surplus."

Case B: Investment (100 Percent) in Excess of Book Value. If P pays $140 per share, we may make the following analysis:

Cost of 1,000 shares of S (100 percent)		$140,000
Equity acquired:		
Capital stock of S	$100,000	
Retained earnings of S	20,000	120,000
Excess of cost over equity acquired		$ 20,000

Any of the following possibilities or combinations of them may explain the reason P is willing to pay an amount in excess of book value for the shares of S:

a. Specific assets of S are understated.

b. Specific liabilities of S are overstated.

c. P sustains a loss on the purchase.

d. S has unrecorded intangibles.

e. P invests in intangibles arising from combined operations.

The understatement of specific assets *(a)* or overstatement of specific liabilities *(b)* would likely become known to P and to the former stockholders of S in negotiating the purchase price of S's stock. If either of these possibilities apply, appropriate adjustments should be made to the accounts of S before proceeding with the consolidation.

If P pays $140,000 for common stock of S worth only $120,000, P makes a poor bargain and sustains a loss *(c)*. This interpretation is not usually accepted as reasonable, since evidence on which to base such a conclusion lies in the future. Cost of an asset in a normal market transaction is generally accepted as a measure of worth at the date of acquisition. In the extremely rare case where evidence of a loss at acquisition is sufficiently strong, the investment should be reduced with a like reduction in the earnings of P.

If S has unrecorded intangibles *(d)*, we have a special case of understated assets *(a)*, which is sufficiently important to warrant separate attention. If, after determining the effect of the first four possibilities, we are left with the fact that P paid $140,000 for stock having a book value of $120,000, it must be concluded that the stock of S is worth $140,000. Company S must, therefore, possess goodwill or other intangibles not reflected in its accounts. The following adjustment, although rarely found in practice, is appropriate for S:

Goodwill—S	20,000	
Appraisal Increase—S		20,000

The goodwill of S is revealed in connection with the acquisition by P of the ownership interest in S. Goodwill of this type is not created by the price P pays, but rather P is willing to pay the price it does in part because of the prior existence of unrecorded values of S. P pays a price higher than book value because the recorded proprietorship of S is understated, because of the omission of goodwill from its records.

Still another possible explanation for the excess of cost over book value is that P makes an investment in benefits to be derived from integrated operations *(e)*. S as a separate unit may not be worth more than book value, but as a key part of integrated operations P is willing to pay more than book value. The intangible attaches not to S, but to P and S combined. If the evidence supports this interpretation, P's investment may be analyzed as follows:

Investment in S	120,000	
Investment in Intangibles	20,000	
Cash		140,000

ARB No. 51 describes the treatment of the excess as follows:[14]

> Where the cost to the parent of the investment in a purchased subsidiary exceeds the parent's equity in the subsidiary's net assets at the date of acquisition, as shown by the books of the subsidiary, the excess should be dealt with in the consolidated balance sheet according to its nature. In determining the difference, provision should be made for specific costs or losses which are expected to be incurred in the integration of the operations of the subsidiary with those of the parent, or otherwise as a result of the acquisition, if the amount thereof can be reasonably determined. To the extent that the difference is considered to be attributable to tangible assets and specific intangible assets, such as patents, it should be allocated to them. Any difference which cannot be so applied should be shown among the assets in the consolidated balance sheet under one or more appropriately descriptive captions. When the difference is allocated to depreciable or amortizable assets, depreciation and amortization policies should be such as to absorb the excess over the remaining life of related assets.

Accounting Principles Board Opinion No. 16 reaffirms this view by stating:[15]

> A portion of the total cost [of acquiring a company or group of assets] is then assigned to each individual asset acquired on the basis of its fair value. A difference between the sum of the assigned costs of the tangible and identifiable intangible assets acquired less liabilities assumed and the cost of the group is evidence of unspecified intangible values.

Ideally, goodwill as in *(d)* or other intangibles as in *(e)* should be shown in the records of the company involved and amortized in accordance with generally accepted accounting principles. If not reflected in the accounts of the appropriate company, goodwill or other intangibles must be developed as a reconciling amount in the consolidation process.

Assume that *(d)* above, unrecorded goodwill of S, explains why P pays $140,000 for the stock of S. The following sequence of entries applied to the initial data will give effect to (1) the investment by P, (2) the adjustment for S, and (3) the elimination of duplication to yield consolidated data:

(1)

Investment in S—P	140,000	
Cash		140,000

(2)

Goodwill—S	20,000	
Appraisal Increase—S		20,000

(3)

Capital Stock—S	100,000	
Retained Earnings—S	20,000	
Appraisal Increase—S	20,000	
Investment in S—P		140,000

The resulting consolidated balance sheet will report the following amounts:

Assets:		
Cash	$110,000	
Other Assets	450,000	
Goodwill	20,000	$580,000
Liabilities		230,000
Net assets:		
Capital stock—P (2,000 shares)	$200,000	
Retained earnings	150,000	$350,000

---

[14]*Ibid.*, par. 7.

[15]Accounting Principles Board, "Business Combinations," Opinion No. 16, AICPA, New York, 1970, par. 68.

Case C: Investment (100 Percent) at Less than Book Value.   If P pays $105 per share, or $105,000, for the stock of S, it acquires the proprietorship of S for $15,000 less than book value. Corresponding to the five alternatives for explaining paying more than book value are four alternatives for explaining why P is able to purchase for less:

f. Specific assets of S are overstated.

g. Specific liabilities of S are understated.

h. P enjoys a profit on the purchase.

i. General overvaluation of S.

The first three explanations are consistent with the corresponding three cases where cost exceeds book value, but with opposite adjustments. The fourth explanation, sometimes referred to as "negative goodwill," is somewhat similar, but opposite, to positive goodwill illustrated previously. *ARB No. 51* described the treatment of this situation as follows:[16]

> Where the cost to the parent is less than its equity in the net assets of the purchased subsidiary, as shown by the books of the subsidiary at the date of acquisition, the amount at which such net assets are carried in the consolidated statements should not exceed the parent's cost. Accordingly, to the extent that the difference is considered to be attributable to specific assets, it should be allocated to them, with corresponding adjustments of the depreciation or amortization. In unusual circumstances there may be a remaining difference which it would be acceptable to show in a credit account, which ordinarily would be taken into income in future periods on a reasonable and systematic basis. A procedure sometimes followed in the past was to credit capital surplus with the amount of the excess; such a procedure is not now considered acceptable.

Accounting Principles Board Opinion No. 16 took an even more stringent view of "negative goodwill." It says:[17]

> The total market or appraisal values of identifiable assets acquired less liabilities assumed in a few business combinations may exceed the cost of the acquired company. An excess over cost should be allocated to reduce proportionately the values assigned to noncurrent assets (except long-term investments in marketable securities) in determining their fair value. If the allocation reduces the noncurrent assets to zero value, the remainder of the excess over cost should be classified as a deferred credit and should be amortized systematically to income over the period estimated to be benefited but not in excess of forty years. The method and period of amortization should be disclosed.

Since there are likely to be few, if any, cases where an excess remains after writing noncurrent assets down to zero, explanation *(i)* usually turns out to be a special case of *(f).*

Most published consolidated balance sheets show no consolidated goodwill. This reflects two facts: (1) very many, probably most, consolidated subsidiaries are organized by the parent and there can be no goodwill at inception and (2) where an acquisition of a going business is made, an effort is made to have the sum of the valuations of tangible and specifically identifiable intangible assets less liabilities assumed equal acquisition cost.

Case D: Minority Interest.   If P purchases less than 100 percent of the stock of S, the purchase price may equal, exceed, or be less than book value as discussed in cases A, B, and C above. The present case considers the effect of an outside or minority interest with the purchase price in excess of book value. If P purchases only 800 shares of S (80 percent) at $140 per share, the following analysis is appropriate:

---

[16]*ARB No. 51*, par. 8.
[17]APB Opinion No. 16, par. 91.

```
Cost of 800 shares of S (80%) ................ $112,000
Equity acquired:
    Capital stock of S  .............. $80,000
    Retained earnings of S  .......... 16,000    96,000
Excess of cost over equity acquired ............ $ 16,000
```

Which of the possible explanations listed in case B above applies to the $16,000 difference? The difference may attach to P (as in *c*, or *e*) or to S (as in *a*, *b*, or *d*).

Investment in Intangibles.   Assume that P makes an investment in intangibles arising from combined operations (*e*). The entries below (1) record the investment; (2) eliminate duplication; and (3) set forth the minority interest in S. When applied to the initial data, they develop information for the consolidated balance sheet.

(1)

```
Investment in S (80%)—P ...............................    96,000
Investment in Intangibles—P ...........................    16,000
    Cash ............................................                112,000
```

(2)

```
Capital Stock—S ......................................    80,000
Retained Earnings—S ..................................    16,000
    Investment in S—P ...............................                96,000
```

(3)

```
Capital Stock—S ......................................    20,000
Retained Earnings—S ..................................     4,000
    Minority Interest in Capital Stock of S ...............          20,000
    Minority Interest in Retained Earnings of S ..........           4,000
```

COMPANY P
Consolidated Balance Sheet
July 1, 19X0

```
Assets:
    Cash ........................................... $138,000
    Other assets ...................................  450,000
    Investment in intangibles .....................   16,000  $604,000
Liabilities ....................................................  230,000
Net assets:
    Minority interest in S:
        Capital stock ......................... $ 20,000
        Retained earnings .....................    4,000  $ 24,000
    Controlling interest:
        Capital stock ......................... $200,000
        Retained earnings .....................  150,000   350,000  $374,000
```

"Minority interest" is the term usually applied to an outside capital stock interest. The term is not entirely satisfactory because it implies quantitative inferiority, which is not always the case. For example, the preferred stock of S, of which P owns none, may exceed its common stock in which P has a controlling interest.

Although minority interest is part of consolidated proprietorship, as shown in the balance sheet above, it appears among the liabilities in some published annual reports to shareholders. Many published balance sheets show minority interest in an indeterminate section, below total liabilities, but before the stockholders' equity section.

Unrecorded Goodwill in Full.   Assume that the reason P pays $112,000 for an interest in S having a book value of $96,000 is the existence on the part of S of unrecorded goodwill. Is $16,000 or some other amount the proper measure of the goodwill? The following analysis discloses one view of the problem:

Cost of 80% interest in S $112,000
Equivalent cost of 100% (112,000 ÷ 0.8) $140,000
Book value of S 120,000
Unrecorded goodwill of S .... $ 20,000

If this analysis is accepted, instead of entries 1 to 3 above, the following entries would (1) reflect the investment for P; (2) adjust S for goodwill in full; (3) eliminate duplication; and (4) set forth the minority interest:

(1)

Investment in S (80%)—P	112,000	
Cash		112,000

(2)

Goodwill—S	20,000	
Appraisal Increase—S		20,000

(3)

Capital Stock—S	80,000	
Retained Earnings—S	16,000	
Appraisal Increase—S	16,000	
Investment in S—P		112,000

(4)

Capital Stock—S	20,000	
Retained Earnings—S	4,000	
Appraisal Increase—S	4,000	
Minority Interest in S (total)		28,000

COMPANY P
Consolidated Balance Sheet
July 1, 19X0

Assets:
Cash		$138,000	
Other assets		450,000	
Goodwill		20,000	$608,000
Liabilities			230,000

Net assets:
Minority interest in S		$ 28,000	
Controlling interest:			
Capital stock	$200,000		
Retained earnings	150,000	350,000	$378,000

This view has considerable logical merit, but has not been accepted in practice. Goodwill is limited to the excess of purchase price over the fair market value of tangible and specifically identifiable intangible assets acquired less liabilities assumed.

Case E: Investment in Preferred Stock. In the special case where a parent purchases the same percentage interest in each class of stock of a subsidiary, no new problem is involved. The parent acquires an interest in total proprietorship, no matter how that proprietorship is allocated among classes of shareholders. In preparing a consolidated balance sheet, the parent's total investment in the subsidiary is compared with its share of total proprietorship. Any discrepancy between investment and book value is disposed of as discussed above.

Company P's interest in preferred stock of S will likely be a different percentage than its ownership of common stock of S. If the preferred is nonvoting and nonparticipating, the acquisition is interpreted as an effective redemption of the preferred securities and does not give rise to goodwill. Any discrepancy between cost and book value of the preferred is a gain or loss to the subsidiary.

If the preferred stock is participating, it has attributes of common stock and part of its market price is undoubtedly due to this feature. Therefore, the price paid in the market by P may serve as a measure of the value of the subsidiary and indicate unrecorded goodwill.

Case F: Exchange of Shares—Pooling.   A significant feature of each case above is that the shareholders of S disinvest in the activities of S when they transfer their shares to P for cash. If P acquires the shares of S by issuing its own shares, however, the stockholders of S have not disinvested completely in the activities of S. As stockholders of P they continue to hold a beneficial interest in S through P's ownership of S.[18]

Assume that P exchanges 700 of its own shares (having a market value of $200 each) for 1,000 shares of S (having a market value of $140 each). If this exchange is interpreted as a "pooling of interests" on the part of the shareholders of P and S, market values are ignored and the consideration P receives for the issuance of 700 shares is deemed to be the underlying book value of the stock of S. P's analysis is as follows:

```
Investment in S  .................. 120,000
     Capital Stock  ...............          70,000
     Additional Paid-in Capital  ....          30,000
     Retained Earnings  ...........          20,000
```

If S continues in existence as a legal entity and as a subsidiary of P, the following elimination prepares the accounts of P and S for consolidated statements:

```
Capital Stock—S  ................ 100,000
Retained Earnings—S  ............  20,000
     Investment in S—P  ..........          120,000
```

The resulting consolidated balance sheet reports the following:

```
Consolidated assets: Various  ................. $700,000
Consolidated liabilities: Various ...............   230,000
Consolidated net assets:
     Capital stock—P  .............. $270,000
     Additional paid-in capital  .......   30,000
     Retained earnings  .............  170,000
                                       $470,000
```

When a parent-subsidiary relationship is established by pooling of interests, there is no discrepancy between cost to the parent and book value of equity acquired to be reflected in the consolidated balance sheet. Nor are retained earnings of the subsidiary at acquisition eliminated in consolidation. The problems associated with poolings and other business combinations are dealt with extensively in Chapter 33.

Consolidated Policy.   In all cases where consolidated financial statements are prepared, it is desirable to indicate the consolidation policy being followed. This policy is typically stated in the form of a footnote to the financial statements.

Recent years have witnessed a significant trend toward the consolidation of more and more subsidiaries. The Accounting Principles Board adopted a firm policy requiring consolidation of certain types of subsidiaries. Opinion No. 18 says:[19]

> In APB Opinion No. 10, paragraph 4, the Board stated that the accounts of subsidiaries (regardless of when organized or acquired) whose principal business activity is

---

[18]The complexities that can arise here are dealt with in H. Nurnberg, C. P. Stickney, and R. L. Weil, "Combining Stockholders' Equity Accounts in Poolings of Interests," *The Accounting Review*, 50, 1 (January 1975), pp. 179–183.

[19]APB Opinion No. 18, par. 15.

leasing property or facilities to parent or other affiliated companies should be consolidated. The Board also concluded that the equity method is not adequate for fair presentation of those subsidiaries because their assets and liabilities are significant to the consolidated financial position of the enterprise. The Board reaffirms those conclusions.

Consolidation of foreign subsidiaries and those less than 100-percent owned has also increased, so that the broader consolidation (except for captive finance companies and any insurance companies or banks owned) is now the general rule.

CONSOLIDATED BALANCE SHEET AFTER ACQUISITION

In preceding sections, it was suggested that an investment in another corporation may be maintained either on the equity method or on a cost basis. If the equity method is used, the parent will reflect its share of all changes in the subsidiary since the date of acquisition. In such cases, the preparation of consolidated statements is simplified. If the investment is kept on a cost basis, however, various completion entries are needed to bring the investment up to date. Regardless of which method the parent uses, the same final results in consolidation are achieved.

Case A: Investment at Equity. Assume the following data for P and S on July 1, 19X2:

	Company P	Company S
Dividends receivable from S.........	$ 8,000	
Investment in S (80% at equity).....	136,000	
Other assets (details omitted)........	406,000	$250,000
	$550,000	$250,000
Dividends payable..................	$ 20,000	$ 10,000
Other liabilities (details omitted).....	150,000	90,000
Capital stock (par $100)............	200,000	100,000
Retained earnings..................	180,000	50,000
	$550,000	$250,000

P purchased 800 shares of S at $140 per share on July 1, 19X0, when the recorded proprietorship of S was $120,000.

To the extent not already performed, the following steps must be taken before preparing a consolidated balance sheet:

1. Reconcile cost of investment and underlying book value at date of acquisition.

2. Reflect parent's share of changes in net assets of the subsidiary since date of acquisition.

3. Eliminate the parent's investment in the subsidiary against the net assets of the subsidiary.

4. Reclassify minority interest.

5. Reconcile and eliminate other reciprocal accounts. Each of these steps except (2) has been discussed already, but additional comments are in order.

A comparison of the carrying value, $136,000, with the underlying equity in the net assets of S, $120,000 (80 percent of $150,000), reveals an excess of $16,000. Because P keeps its investment in A at equity, this discrepancy must have arisen at date of acquisition. This conclusion is substantiated by comparing cost of $112,000 with underlying equity at acquisition of $96,000 (80 percent of $120,000).

(1a)
Goodwill—S 16,000
   Investment in S   16,000

In addition, APB Opinion No. 17, Paragraph 29 requires the systematic amortization of goodwill over a period not in excess of forty years. Because the reported earnings of S for the two years since acquisition did not include amortization of goodwill the following analysis is appropriate:

(1b)
Retained Earnings—P   800
   Goodwill   800

Since becoming a subsidiary of P, S has earned net income of $40,000 and has declared dividends of $10,000, causing its retained earnings to increase from $20,000 to $50,000. Following the equity basis, P has recognized its share of these changes period by period. Specifically, P's accounts already show the effect of the following:

(2a)
Investment in S 32,000
   Revenue from Investment   32,000

(2b)
Dividends Receivable from S 8,000
   Investment in S   8,000

Elimination of the 80 percent investment against underlying equity requires no further discussion:

(3)
Capital Stock—S 80,000
Retained Earnings—S 40,000
   Investment in S—P   120,000

The minority interest of 20 percent is separately set forth:

(4)
Capital Stock—S 20,000
Retained Earnings—S 10,000
   Minority Interest in S   30,000

Other reciprocal items in this case are dividends declared by S but not yet paid. It will be observed that P has recorded properly its share of the dividends. For the consolidated balance sheet, this intercompany claim is submerged by the following elimination:

(5)
Dividends Payable—S 8,000
   Dividends Receivable—P   8,000

Information for a consolidated balance sheet of Company P at July 1, 19X2, may be formulated by applying entries 1a, 1b, 3, 4, and 5, above, to the data shown in the accounts of P and S. Entries 2a and 2b are not used because they have been recognized by P in its accounts.

The consolidated balance sheet contains the following data:

Total consolidated assets:
   Total assets of P (per books) $550,000
   Total assets of S (per books)   250,000
   Combined assets (per books) $800,000
   Add: Goodwill of S (entry 1)   15,200
   Deduct: Investment in S (entries 1a and 3).... (136,000)
         Dividends receivable (entry 5) ...... (8,000) $671,200

Total consolidated liabilities:
Total debts of P (per books) $170,000
Total debts of S (per books) 100,000
Combined debts (per books) $270,000
Deduct: Dividends payable (entry 5) .... (8,000)   262,000
Total consolidated net assets $409,200
Deduct: Minority interest in S (entry 4) 30,000
Controlling interest $379,200

Represented by:
Capital stock—P $200,000
Retained earnings 179,200 $379,200

Case B: Investment at Cost. If P maintains its investment at acquisition cost of $112,000, rather than at equity of $136,000, the accounts of P and S at July 1, 19X2, show the following:

	Company P	Company S
Dividends receivable from S.........	$ 8,000	
Investment in S (80% at cost).......	112,000	
Other assets (details omitted).......	406,000	$250,000
	$526,000	$250,000
Dividends payable..................	$ 20,000	$ 10,000
Other liabilities (details omitted).....	150,000	90,000
Capital stock (par $100)............	200,000	100,000
Retained earnings.................	156,000	50,000
	$526,000	$250,000

The five preliminary steps as discussed in case A, above, must be taken in order to prepare a consolidated balance sheet. The entries that apply directly to case B are reproduced here without repeating the discussion:

(1a)
Goodwill—S 16,000
    Investment in S   16,000

(1b)
Retained Earnings—P 800
    Goodwill   800

On the cost basis, P recognized its share of the dividends declared by S as follows:

(2a)
Dividends Receivable 8,000
    Revenue (Retained Earnings)   8,000

The effect of this dividend is already in P's retained earnings. If P had not recorded the dividend, it would be necessary to do so as part of the preliminary procedure. An additional entry is needed to recognize P's share of the earnings of S since date of acquisition that are retained by S (80 percent of $30,000):

(2b)
Investment in S—P 24,000
    Revenue from Investment (Retained
        Earnings)   24,000

The adjustment converts the investment account to the equity basis.

```
                      (3) and (4)
Capital Stock—S  ........................ 100,000
Retained Earnings—S  ....................  50,000
     Investment in S—P  .................            120,000
     Minority Interest in S  ................            30,000

                         (5)
Dividends Payable  ......................    8,000
     Dividends Receivable  ................             8,000
```

Entries 1a, 1b, 2b, 3 and 4, and 5 convert the data on the books of P and S to the same information as developed in case A above for a consolidated balance sheet at July 1, 19X2.

Various shortcuts may be taken in formulating adjusting and eliminating entries without adjusting the underlying accounts when only a consolidated balance sheet is desired. For example, entries 1a, 1b, 2b, 3, and 4 may be combined into a single entry:

```
Goodwill  ...............................   15,200
Capital Stock—S  ........................  100,000
Retained Earnings—S  ....................   50,000
     Investment in S—P  .................            112,000
     Retained Earnings—P  ...............             23,200
     Minority Interest in S  ................            30,000
```

This condensed analysis presupposes a thorough understanding of the several separate steps discussed above that are necessary to develop it.

Intercompany Markups in Assets. Assume that S sells 10,000 units of finished product to P at $12. If the cost to S is $10 each, S reports a gross profit of $20,000. Assume also that P sells all 10,000 units to outside customers at $15 and reports gross profit of $30,000. The business entity, consisting of P and S, has realized total profit of $50,000, since all units acquired from S have been sold by P. If there is a minority interest in S of 20 percent, it shares in the profits of S to the extent of $4,000. Controlling interest shares in profits on these units to the extent of $46,000, as follows:

```
Profit reported by P, 100%  ...............  $30,000
Profit reported by S, 80%  ................   16,000  $46,000
```

A similar analysis applies regardless of the distribution of the total profit of $50,000 between S and P. If P obtains the product at $9 per unit, S reports a loss of $10,000; P in turn reports profits of $60,000. Minority interest shares in the loss to S to the extent of $2,000, while the controlling interest increases by $52,000 ($60,000 less $8,000 loss). Because the controlling interest is being subsidized in this case, the minority interest will probably object to the pricing policy of S.[20] Since pricing policy is not within the scope of this discussion, we shall accept the allocation of realized profits agreed upon by the companies.

Markup in Inventories. If P has not sold all the units received from S, the question of the proper measure of inventories arises. Assume that P has on hand 3,000 units purchased from S for $36,000, but which cost S only $30,000. According to generally accepted accounting principles, cost is the primary basis for measuring inventories. "Cost" must be interpreted as referring to the accounting entity concerned; if consolidated statements are in order, the entity is P and S combined. The cost of the unsold items to this entity is the cost to S of $30,000. Consequently, the valuation on P's books is above cost to the entity and should be

---

[20]See Edward J. Smolinski, "The Adjunct Method in Consolidations," *Journal of Accounting Research,* vol. 1, 2 (1963), pp. 149–178, particularly pp. 159–164, for a clear statement of the latent legal power of the minority interest.

scaled down. This elimination of intercompany profit from inventories has the effect of deferring the intercompany profit until the period of sale outside the consolidated group.

It should be emphasized that elimination of intercompany markups in assets is a consequence of the cost basis of valuing assets. If it were generally accepted to state inventories at net realizable value, for example, profit would be taken up in the period of production or acquisition, and no elimination of intercompany markup would be required.

In the case under consideration, gross profit to S is eliminated from inventories held by P. This conforms to the usual practice of interpreting cost in the narrow sense to include manufactured cost but to exclude selling and administrative costs. However, if the subsidiary is the manufacturing unit in a vertically integrated group, its selling and administrative costs may be akin to factory overhead costs. In such cases, a different measure of profit might be used in reducing inventories to cost.

If the intercompany markup to be eliminated from P's inventories is $2 per unit, or $6,000, how will the elimination affect controlling and minority interests? Although the inventories are on the books of P, the profit from the intercompany markup is on the books of S. Consequently, the following adjustment is in order:

(1)

Retained Earnings—S	 6,000	
Inventories—P	....	6,000

Instead of writing down inventories directly, a contra-account such as Allowance for Intercompany Markup may be used. If P has an 80 percent interest in S and has already taken up its share of profits reported by S, the following reclassification is needed:

(2)

Retained Earnings—P	 4,800	
Investment in S—P	....	4,800

The effect of these entries is to reduce the minority interest by $1,200 (20 percent of $6,000) and the controlling interest by $4,800.

From the preceding analysis, the technical procedure to be followed in all cases involving the elimination of intercompany markups in assets may be derived:

1. Reduce the asset for the full amount of markup being deferred.
2. Reduce the earnings of the company reporting the profit in the first place.
3. Adjust the other accounts affected by the revised data in 2.

On the assumption that profit on sales to P is realized from the point of view of the minority interest, an alternative treatment restricts the elimination of intercompany markups to the interest of the parent. This alternative is deficient in two respects: (1) Consolidated statements are not prepared from the point of view of the minority shareholders, who should look to the separate statements of the subsidiary for information regarding their investment; and (2) the valuation of assets becomes a function of the size of the controlling and outside interests. This alternative is effectively barred by *ARB No. 51*, which requires eliminating the entire intercompany markup on assets remaining within the group.[21]

> The amount of intercompany profit or loss to be eliminated . . . is not affected by the existence of a minority interest. The complete elimination of the intercompany profit or loss is consistent with the underlying assumption that consolidated statements represent the financial and operating results of a single business enterprise. The elimination of the intercompany profit or loss may be allocated proportionately between the majority and minority interests.

[21]*ARB No. 51,* par. 14.

Another alternative, apparently widely used in practice, eliminates the entire intercompany markup against the controlling interest. This method is neither approved nor proscribed by *ARB No. 51*. It is acceptable as far as the valuation of assets is concerned, but it is defective in that the transition from accounting for separate companies to accounting for the group as a unit is incomplete. Obviously, the controlling interest absorbs the entire elimination of intercompany profit if no minority interest exists or if P sells to S.

Careful consideration must be given to cases involving the transfer of assets at a loss. If the loss has not been sustained, it should be deferred until realized by transfer outside the group or by use. If the transfer of inventories at a loss is occasioned by changed market conditions, the lower-of-cost-or-market rule may sanction the write-down below cost, and no deferral would be required.[22]

Markup in Fixed Assets. The same problems are encountered with fixed assets as with inventories. For example, an intercompany markup on land is deferred as long as the land remains within the group. In the case of depreciable assets, intercompany markups are deferred until realized through use or sale. Assume that P acquires for $100,000 equipment which cost Company S $70,000 to manufacture. With straight-line depreciation based on an estimated useful life of 10 years and no scrap value, P records depreciation of $10,000 each year. However, depreciation based on cost to the consolidated group is $7,000 each year. The intercompany profit is realized through use at the rate of $3,000 each year. At the end of the first year of use, the following elimination is in order for a consolidated balance sheet:

```
Retained Earnings—S  ............. 27,000
Allowance for Depreciation—P  ....   3,000
      Equipment—P  ..............         30,000
```

If any portion of P's depreciation charge is applicable to inventories in the hands of P or S at year-end, a further adjustment is needed to eliminate the intercompany element. It may become extremely difficult to trace all possible interrelationships of this sort, but it must be done if the amounts are significant.

Markup in Assets at Acquisition. The preceding discussion deals with intercompany profits arising after affiliation. Assume that, when P acquires control of S, assets in the hands of one were acquired from the other at a markup. Should the intercompany markup be eliminated?

One view accepts the prices at which assets move before acquisition of control as a proper basis of accountability and would make no elimination. This view seems reasonable, but it may lead to an inconsistency in valuation. For example, inventories at the date of acquisition are stated at cost including the intercompany markup, but similar ending inventories are stated at cost excluding intercompany markup.

An alternative view eliminates from assets markups at date of acquisition of control as well as markups arising later. This policy may be followed with little difficulty where the parent reports the profit. If the profit is on the books of the subsidiary, elimination will affect the book value of equity acquired by P.

Intercompany Bondholdings. If bonds of an affiliate are acquired directly from the issuing company, reciprocal accounts are created which will be eliminated in consolidation. For example, S issues at 90 bonds having a par value of $300,000, one-third of which are taken by P:

```
                        (1)
Cash ...........................  270,000
Discount on Bonds—S  ............   30,000
      Bonds Payable—S  ...........          300,000
```

[22]See Smolinski, *op. cit.,* for a complete discussion of the possible treatments.

(2)
Investment in S Bonds—P	90,000	
Cash		90,000

For a consolidated balance sheet at date of issue, the following elimination is proper:

(3)
Bonds Payable—S	100,000	
Investment in S Bonds—P		90,000
Discount on Bonds—S		10,000

If both companies amortize the discount at the same rate, the bond accounts on the books of P will equal one-third the amount on the books of S at the same date. Because no valid reason exists for different treatments of discount by P and S, divergent treatments can be brought into agreement for consolidated statements.

If the bonds of an affiliate are acquired from third parties, a discrepancy between book values is expected. Assume in the above case that S issued its bonds at 90 in the open market. Entry 1 above applies. Five years later, P acquires one-third of this issue for 93 and records the investment net:

(2a)
Investment in S Bonds—P	93,000	
Cash		93,000

If the bonds mature in ten years from issuance and S amortizes discount by the straight-line method, P has effectively retired for $93,000 bonds having a book value of $95,000. Thus, the entity has a gain of $2,000. Is this increase in consolidated net assets attributable to P or to S? In the absence of clear-cut evidence to the contrary, it seems reasonable to assume that the affiliate purchasing the bonds is merely acting as agent for the issuer and that any gain or loss is assignable to the issuing company. The following elimination prepares the accounts for consolidation:

(3a)
Bonds Payable—S	100,000	
Investment in S Bonds—P		93,000
Discount on Bonds—S		5,000
Retained Earnings—S		2,000

Stock Dividends. Additional common shares issued by a subsidiary as a dividend on existing common shares reclassifies a portion of retained earnings as stated capital. Because total book value of the common stock remains unchanged, an ordinary stock dividend does not affect the allocation of a subsidiary's net assets between controlling and minority interests. Nor does a stock dividend affect the allocation between controlling and minority interests of changes in book value.

Assume the following: (1) P acquired 90 percent of the common stock of S on July 1, 19X1; (2) S declared a 10 percent stock dividend on June 30, 19X6, and capitalized earnings at $150 per share; (3) data for S are as follows:

	7/1/X1	7/1/X6	Change
Common stock, par $100......	$100,000	$110,000	$10,000
Additional paid-in capital.....	—0—	5,000	5,000
Retained earnings...........	50,000	65,000	15,000
	$150,000	$180,000	$30,000

As indicated above, the common stock interest in S has increased $30,000 since P acquired a controlling interest. Of this amount, 90 percent, or $27,000, will be included in the retained earnings of the controlling interest in a consolidated balance sheet. If S declares no stock dividend, the same result emerges. In this event the retained earnings of S at July 1, 19X6, shows an increase of $30,000. The situation is described in *ARB No. 51* as follows:[23]

> Occasionally, subsidiary companies capitalize earned surplus arising since acquisition, by means of a stock dividend or otherwise. This does not require a transfer to capital surplus on consolidation, inasmuch as the retained earnings in the consolidated financial statements should reflect the accumulated earnings of the consolidated group not distributed to the shareholders of, or capitalized by, the parent company.

If during the five-year period S declares a series of stock dividends totaling 50 percent of the shares outstanding at July 1, 19X1, and capitalizes $150 a share, we have the following comparative data:

	7/1/X1	7/1/X6	Change
Common stock, par $100......	$100,000	$150,000	$50,000
Additional paid-in capital.....	—0—	25,000	25,000
Retained earnings............	50,000	5,000	(45,000)
	$150,000	$180,000	$30,000

Although the change in proprietorship is the same as before, P's share of S's earnings since acquisition of $27,000 is no longer matched by a balance in the Retained Earnings account of S. If the rule of law restricting cash dividends to earnings not previously capitalized applies to S, it is not possible for S to pay a cash dividend large enough to transfer $27,000 of assets to P. As a consequence, the cash dividends P may legally declare may likewise be restricted. Consolidated retained earnings might be reclassified to the extent of $22,500 ($27,000 less $4,500) to reflect the portion that has been capitalized by the stock dividend of S, or the situation might be explained in a footnote. This situation will arise whenever S reduces its retained earnings account by transfers to stated capital below the balance at the date P acquired control.

CONSOLIDATED INCOME STATEMENT

To avoid duplication of data, intercompany items are eliminated in the consolidated income statement as in the case of the consolidated balance sheet. Reciprocal items to be eliminated typically take the form of revenue-expense pairs; that is, a revenue account of one company is matched by an expense account of the other.

Revenue-Expense Pairs. These accounts arise from a wide variety of business transactions involving the sale of goods and services. Reciprocal accounts may arise, also, from intercompany loans or advances. For example, P borrows $500,-000 from S and gives a 6 percent note. P has $30,000 interest expense each year, and S has interest revenue of the same amount. From a combined point of view, these events have no effect on assets, liabilities, or owners' equity; they merely shift resources between S and P. In consolidation, all evidence of this relationship is eliminated. Specifically, the note payable of P is eliminated against the note

[23]*ARB No. 51,* par. 18.

receivable of S; interest revenue of S is eliminated against interest expense of P; and if interest has accrued, the interest payable of P is eliminated against the receivable of S.

In similar fashion, reciprocal accounts arising from intercompany services are eliminated. P may rent facilities from S, giving rise to rent revenue to S and to rent expense to P. P may furnish specialized services to S for a fee, creating revenue and expense accounts.

True revenue-expense pairs are eliminated without difficulty. The elimination is made for the sole purpose of avoiding inflated revenue and expense totals in the consolidated income statement. Because revenues and expenses are reduced by the same amount, the elimination does not affect the amount of consolidated income. Nor does the elimination affect the amount of income of any constituent unit or the allocation of income between controlling and minority interests.

Intercompany Sales with Asset Retained. Many intercompany transactions, especially those involving sales of tangible assets, cannot be eliminated as readily as the reciprocal accounts discussed above. This condition exists because the revenue of the vendor is matched in whole or in part by an asset of the purchaser rather than by an expense.

Equipment at Cost. Assume S sells equipment to P for $70,000, which is S's cost to manufacture. If P pays in full for the equipment, the accounts of the two companies at the end of the year of sale include the following:

	P	S
Equipment................	$70,000	
Sales to P.................		$(70,000)
Cost of sales to P.........		70,000

The intercompany sale is reflected by S in a revenue account (sales to P) and by P in an asset account (equipment). It would not be proper, however, to eliminate this pair because the equipment is still held by P. The following elimination is more appropriate:

Sales to P—S 70,000
    Cost of Sales to P—S   70,000

Equipment (less depreciation) is carried into the consolidated statements, but no revenue or expense from the transfer is included. Obviously, depreciation on the equipment will be recorded by P and will not be eliminated. No adjustments are needed in subsequent years; the records of P will reflect the history of the investment in the equipment. The cost of the equipment is shown at a smaller amount than if it had been acquired in an arm's-length transaction, but this is frequently the case with self-constructed assets.

Equipment at Markup. Assume that the equipment which cost S $70,000 to manufacture is sold to P for $100,000. If consolidated statements are prepared immediately after the sale, the following elimination removes the intercompany markup:

(1)
Sales to P—S 100,000
    Cost of Sales to P—S   70,000
    Equipment—P   30,000

Instead of a reduction in the equipment account directly, a suitable contra accoun may be used, such as Allowance for Intercompany Markup in Equipment. If 1 records depreciation of $10,000 during the period of the sale, an additional entry is needed to reduce depreciation to cost to the entity of $7,000:

(2)

Allowance for Depreciation—P 3,000
    Realized Gain on Intercompany Sales—S   3,000

In subsequent years S shows the intercompany markup of $30,000 in retained earnings. But $3,000 of the markup is considered realized during the first (and each subsequent) year. Consequently, at the end of the second year, P again having recorded depreciation of $10,000, the appropriate elimination is:

(3)

Allowance for Depreciation—P 6,000
Retained Earnings—S 27,000
    Equipment—P   30,000
    Realized Gain on Intercompany Sales—S   3,000

In entries 2 and 3, the realized gain on intercompany sales indicates the portion of S's deferred markup which is realized by S each year as a consequence of P's use of the equipment. From the entity view, the gain may be interpreted as a reduction in depreciation recorded by P. Consequently entries 2 and 3 may be recast:

(2a)

Allowance for Depreciation—P 3,000
    Depreciation Expense—P   3,000

(3a)

Allowance for Depreciation—P 6,000
Retained Earnings—S 27,000
    Equipment—P   30,000
    Depreciation Expense—P   3,000

Entries 2a and 3a are more commonly used, but they obscure the fact that income of S is increased each year as a result of realization of a portion of the intercompany markup. The following reclassification each year should be considered in determining S's contribution to consolidated income for purposes of determining minority interest:

Net Income—P 3,000
    Net Income—S   3,000

Inventory at Cost. If S sells its product at cost to P, who in turn sells to outsiders, the elimination is similar to that for equipment sold at cost:

(a)

Sales to P—S xx
    Cost of Sales to P—S   xx

Inventories in the possession of P and S at the end of the period enter the consolidated balance sheet at cost. Sales by P and S to outsiders enter the revenue and expense categories in determining consolidated income.

The elimination above is conceptually proper and may be employed with perpetual or periodic inventory procedures. In the latter case, however, elimination may take the following form:

(b)

Sales to P—S xx
    Purchases from S—P   xx

The effect of entry b on the consolidated income statement is identical to entry a.

Inventory at Markup. If inventories are transferred between affiliates at a markup, the intercompany sales are eliminated as above. Consideration must be given, also, to any intercompany markups in beginning and ending inventories.

Assume sales to P of 10,000 units at $12 that cost S $10 each. P sells 7,000 of these units to outsiders at $15, having on hand 3,000 units at the end of the year. Relevant accounts for the two companies show the following:

	P	S
Inventory (ending)...........	$ 36,000	
Sales to P.................		$(120,000)
Cost of sales to P...........		100,000
Sales to outsiders............	(105,000)	
Cost of sales to outsiders......	84,000	

An analysis of these accounts discloses the following:

	Cost to P	Cost to group	Intercompany markup
Intercompany sales......	$120,000	$100,000	$20,000
Ending inventory........	(36,000)	(30,000)	(6,000)
Cost of goods sold.......	$ 84,000	$ 70,000	$14,000

The following entry will prepare the data of P and S for consolidated statements:

(1)

Sales to P—S	120,000	
Cost of Sales to P—S		100,000
Inventory—P		6,000
Net Income—S		14,000

The above analysis divides the intercompany markup on S's sales to P of $20,000 into two components: (1) $14,000 realized by S as a consequence of P's sales to outsiders, and (2) $6,000 eliminated from P's inventory and, hence, deferred until sold to outsiders. The following sequences will accomplish the same result:

(1a)

Sales to P—S	120,000	
Cost of Sales to P—S		120,000

(1b)

Cost of Sales to P—S	6,000	
Inventory—P		6,000

With periodic inventory procedures, the following version is appropriate:

(1a)

Sales to P—S	120,000	
Purchases from S—P		120,000

(1b)

Ending Inventory (Cost of Sales)	6,000	
Inventory—P		6,000

Assume that during the following year S sells an additional 10,000 units to P and that P has a year-end inventory of 2,000 units purchased from S. Unit costs and prices are the same as in the preceding year. Relevant accounts for P and S show the following:

	P	S
Inventory (ending)...........	$ 24,000	
Sales to P..................		$(120,000)
Cost of sales to P..........		100,000
Sales to outsiders............	(165,000)	
Cost of sales to outsiders......	132,000	

An analysis of these intercompany transactions shows the following:

	Cost to P	Cost to group	Intercompany markup
Beginning inventory.....	$ 36,000	$ 30,000	$ 6,000
Intercompany sales......	120,000	100,000	20,000
Ending inventory........	(24,000)	(20,000)	(4,000)
Cost of goods sold	$132,000	$110,000	$22,000

The markup on beginning inventory (deferred from the previous year) is realized during the current year. Of the $20,000 markup recorded by S currently, $4,000 is still in P's inventories and should be deferred. Total intercompany markups realized by the entity during the year amount to $22,000. This amount is evidenced by the fact that cost of goods sold to outsiders by P of $132,000 had a cost to S of $110,000. The following entry reflects the analysis:

(2)

Retained Earnings—S	6,000	
Sales to P—S	120,000	
Cost of Sales to P		100,000
Inventory—P		4,000
Net Income—S		22,000

The above elimination may be divided into components as follows:

(2a)

Retained Earnings—S	6,000	
Cost of Sales to P—S or		
Beginning Inventory—P		6,000

(2b)

Sales to P—S	120,000	
Cost of Sales to P—S or		
Purchases from S—P		120,000

(2c)

Cost of Sales to P—S	4,000	
Inventory—P		4,000

The accounts of P and S are converted to data for consolidation by means of adjustments and eliminations as discussed above. If consolidated statements are prepared for P and S on a continuing basis from year to year, the analysis of markups in inventories at the end of one year applies to beginning inventories the following year. Hence, the analysis need not be repeated if the data are in the proper form. For example, entry 2a above has the same effect as 1b at the end of the first year and would not be used if the data we are working with already includes its effect.

To summarize the two-year period, we have the following after eliminating intercompany sales and markups in inventories:

	Year 1	Year 2
Consolidated sales........................	$105,000	$165,000
Consolidated cost of sales..............	70,000	110,000
Consolidated income....................	$ 35,000	$ 55,000
Source of consolidated income:		
Company S...........................	$ 14,000	$ 22,000
Company P...........................	21,000	33,000
Total (as above).......................	$ 35,000	$ 55,000

In connection with this summary, it should be observed that (1) the amount of income is restricted to sales to outsiders, and (2) the source of the income is consistent with transfer prices agreed upon by S and P.

The use of separate accounts by P and by S to record intercompany transactions facilitates the preparation of consolidated statements. Likewise, identification of consolidating adjusting and eliminating entries with the subsidiaries affected facilitates the determination of minority interest.

Allocation of Consolidated Income and Retained Earnings. Consolidated income is the profit from the combined activities of the units under centralized control. Intercompany relationships are eliminated as discussed above so that consolidated revenues and consolidated expenses represent transactions with individuals and firms outside the entity. If there is no minority interest, the entire consolidated income increases the controlling interest.

If there is a minority interest, care must be taken to assign to it the proper share of income of the subsidiary after taking into consideration consolidating adjustments. These adjustments, as discussed above, are for gains or losses not realized from the point of view of the entity or for gains or losses recognized in consolidation that are not reflected this period in the accounts of the affiliates.

Assume that P purchased 80 percent of the common stock of S in January, 19X1, for $80,000 when the total book value of the common stock of S was $100,000. P maintains its investment in S at cost. At the end of 19X2, the accounts of the two companies include the following data:

	P	S
Net assets evidenced by:		
Capital stock..................	$150,000	$100,000
Retained earnings:		
Balance 1/1/X2..............	50,000	20,000
Income 19X2................	24,000	10,000
Dividends 19X2..............	(10,000)	(5,000)
	$214,000	$125,000
Income 19X2:		
Sales.......................	$300,000	$200,000
Dividends from S..............	4,000	
Cost of sales..................	(200,000)	(150,000)
Other expenses................	(80,000)	(40,000)
	$ 24,000	$ 10,000

The inventory of P at 1/1/X2 contains intercompany markups of $5,000. During 19X2, one-half of S's sales were made to P, whose inventory at 12/31/X2 contains markups of $2,000 on purchases from S.

When both a consolidated balance sheet and a consolidated income statement are prepared, it is convenient to eliminate the intercompany stock relationship as of the beginning of the current year, leaving to the consolidated income statement the function of summarizing combined activities. If this procedure is followed, the investment account is adjusted to include P's share of the change in net assets of S determined on a consolidated basis to the beginning of the current year. The following consolidating adjustments and eliminations are based on this procedure:

(1)

Investment in S—P	12,000	
Retained Earnings 1/1/X2—P		12,000

80% of increase from $100,000 to $115,000; see 3 below.

(2)

Capital Stock—S	100,000	
Retained Earnings, 1/1/X2—S	15,000	
Investment in S—P		92,000
Minority Interest in Stock, 1/1/X2		20,000
Minority Interest in Earnings, 1/1/X2		3,000

(3)

Retained Earnings, 1/1/X2—S	5,000	
Cost of Sales—S		5,000

Markup in beginning inventory.

(4)

Sales—S	100,000	
Cost of Sales—S		100,000

(5)

Cost of Sales—S	2,000	
Inventory—P		2,000

Markup in ending inventory.

(6)

Dividends from S—P	4,000	
Dividends (declared)—S		4,000

The analysis above converts the data on the books of P and S to the following for inclusion in consolidated financial statements as of December 31, 19X2:

Consolidated income:

Sales	$400,000
Cost of sales	(247,000)
Other expenses	(120,000)
Consolidated income	$ 33,000
Minority interest (20% of $13,000)	2,600
Controlling interest	$ 30,400

	Controlling interest	Minority interest	Total
Consolidated retained earnings:			
Retained earnings, 1/1/X2	$ 62,000	$ 3,000	$65,000
Income (above)	30,400	2,600	33,000
Dividends	(10,000)	(1,000)	(11,000)
Balance, 12/31/X2	$ 82,400	$ 4,600	$87,000
Consolidated net assets evidenced by:			
Capital stock	$150,000	$20,000	
Retained earnings (above)	82,400	4,600	
Total	$232,400	$24,600	

Fiscal Period Problems. Special attention must be given to the determination and allocation of earnings when a subsidiary is purchased during the accounting period. Two problems are involved: (1) determining underlying book value of the subsidiary at date of acquisition and (2) determining consolidated results of operations for the period. Ideally, financial statements of the subsidiary are available as of the date of acquisition. In the absence of a formal closing, however, income of the subsidiary for the year may be allocated to estimate the status of the subsidiary at the date of acquisition. Alternative methods for dealing with the latter problem are spelled out in *ARB No. 51*:[24]

> When a subsidiary is purchased during the year, there are alternative ways of dealing with the results of its operations in the consolidated income statement. One method, which usually is preferable, especially where there are several dates of acquisition of blocks of shares, is to include the subsidiary in the consolidation as though it had been acquired at the beginning of the year, and to deduct at the bottom of the consolidated income statement the preacquisition earnings applicable to each block of stock. This method presents results which are more indicative of the current status of the group, and facilitates future comparison with subsequent years. Another method of prorating income is to include in the consolidated statement only the subsidiary's revenue and expenses subsequent to the date of acquisition.

Consolidation is facilitated when the fiscal periods of parent and subsidiaries are the same. If they are different at acquisition, the parent should require modification. In the absence of complete synchronization, consolidated statements may be prepared if the difference in fiscal periods is relatively short. *ARB No. 51* states:[25]

> A difference in fiscal periods of a parent and a subsidiary does not of itself justify the exclusion of the subsidiary from consolidation. It ordinarily is feasible for the subsidiary to prepare, for consolidation purposes, statements for a period which corresponds with or closely approaches the fiscal period of the parent. However, where the difference is not more than about three months, it usually is acceptable to use, for consolidation purposes, the subsidiary's statements for its fiscal period; when this is done, recognition should be given by disclosure or otherwise to the effect of intervening events which materially affect the financial position or results of operations.

Many corporations have the fiscal period of foreign subsidiaries end one month before the parent's fiscal period to facilitate speedy preparation of financial statements. Thus many corporations reporting on a calendar-year basis have their foreign subsidiaries end the year on November 30.

Allocation of Income Taxes. Income tax expense reported on the consolidated income statement should be based on the amount of consolidated income in accordance with generally accepted accounting principles for accrual and deferral of income taxes (Chapter 36). If consolidated income tax returns are filed, no special problem is encountered in the preparation of consolidated financial statements. In preparing separate statements for each constituent, however, consideration must also be given to income taxes. If each constituent is to reimburse the parent for its share of the tax on the group, allocation on some basis is necessary. The problem may become significant, if there is a substantial minority interest.

Neither the technical aspects of income taxation nor the theoretical issues of tax allocation are discussed here. However, some indication of the complexity of the problem may be obtained from the following situation involving a parent company and two of its subsidiaries:

[24]*Ibid.*, par. 11.
[25]*Ibid.*, par. 4.

	P	S-1	S-2	Consolidated
Income before taxes, 19X1....	$100	$60	$(200)	$(40)

Who receives the tax benefit for the loss of S-2 and how is it measured? Any allocation of income taxes should be equitable to all members of the group. Among the methods found in practice are the following: (1) Allocate to each unit the amount of tax it would pay if a separate return were filed; (2) allocate consolidated taxes in the ratio of the separate tax each would pay, if separate returns were filed, to the sum of all the separate taxes so computed; and (3) allocate consolidated taxes in proportion to the contribution of each member to taxable income. Section 1552 of the Internal Revenue Code of 1954 lists several methods of making the allocation in arriving at the earnings of each company. Rule 45(b)(6) of the SEC gives alternative methods available to companies subject to the Holding Company Act of 1935.

If separate income tax returns are filed by a parent and its subsidiaries, each pays the tax on its own taxable income. The parent's taxable income includes earnings of the subsidiaries only to the extent that they are transferred to the parent. The dividends so received by the parent are subject to a tax credit of 85 percent. Consolidated financial statements, however, should give effect to this tax at the time earnings are taken into consolidated income, rather than in the period dividend transfers are actually made. Obviously, this rule does not apply if it is unlikely that the earnings will ever be transferred in a taxable distribution. APB Opinion No. 23 explains this situation as follows:[26]

> The presumption that all undistributed earnings will be transferred to the parent company may be overcome, and no income taxes should be accrued by the parent company, if sufficient evidence shows that the subsidiary has invested or will invest the undistributed earnings indefinitely or that the earnings will be remitted in a tax-free liquidation.

If affiliates pay taxes on intercompany items which are eliminated in consolidation, such taxes are prepaid from a consolidated view. Such prepayments are allocated to the periods in which the intercompany profits are taken into consolidated income.

CHANGES IN DEGREE OF CONTROL

Changes in the degree of ownership may result from additional purchases from the minority interest, from sales to the minority interest, or from share transactions with the subsidiary. Such changes require careful attention in comparing cost of investment with equity acquired. Generally, if two or more purchases are made over a period of time, the cost of each block is compared with underlying book value applicable to that block. Illustrations which follow indicate the problem and the procedure.

Purchases from Outside Interests. Assume that P obtains control of S by a series of acquisitions at different dates, rather than by acquiring its entire controlling interest at a single date:

[26]Accounting Principles Board, "Accounting for Income Taxes—Special Areas," Opinion No. 23, AICPA, New York, 1972, par. 12. See also par. 7–14.

	7/1/X0	7/1/X1
Net assets of S (per books):		
Common stock (1,000 shares)........	$100,000	$100,000
Retained earnings.................	20,000	40,000
	$120,000	$140,000
P's investments in S:		
(1) 300 shares at $140 (30%)........	$ 42,000	
(2) 500 shares at $150 (50%)........		$ 75,000
Equity acquired...................	36,000	70,000
Excess of cost over book value......	$ 6,000	$ 5,000

If the excess of cost over book value is explained as an investment in goodwill by P, the following analysis is appropriate for P:

(1)

7/1/X0:

Investment in S 42,000
   Cash 42,000

(2)

6/30/X1:

Investment in S 6,000
   Gain on Investment in S ... 6,000
30% of $20,000 income.

(3)

7/1/X1:

Investment in S 75,000
   Cash 75,000

(4)

7/1/X1:

Goodwill 11,000
   Investment in S 11,000

Entry 4 reclassifies the investment in accordance with the interpretation and analysis given above. P now has an investment in S stated at $112,000 which is precisely equal to the underlying book value of S (80 percent of $140,000). These reciprocal amounts are eliminated in consolidation. P's investment in goodwill becomes part of consolidated assets, while the gain on its investment (entry 2) represents P's share of the increase in the retained earnings of S during the year and becomes part of the controlling interest.

The following entry eliminates the intercompany investment and reclassifies the minority interest, thus preparing the data for consolidated statements:

(5)

Common Stock—S 100,000
Retained Earnings—S 40,000
   Investment in S—P 112,000
   Minority Interest in S 28,000

ARB No. 51 illustrates some problems in this area as follows:[27]

When one company purchases two or more blocks of stock of another company at various dates and eventually obtains control of the other company, the date of acquisition (for the purpose of preparing consolidated statements) depends on the circum-

[27]*ARB No. 51,* par. 10.

stances. If two or more purchases are made over a period of time, the earned surplus of the subsidiary at acquisition should generally be determined on a step-by-step basis; however, if small purchases are made over a period of time and then a purchase is made which results in control, the date of the latest purchase, as a matter of convenience, may be considered as the date of acquisition. Thus there would generally be included in consolidated income for the year in which control is obtained the postacquisition income for that year, and in consolidated earned surplus the postacquisition income of prior years, attributable to each block previously acquired. For example, if a 45% interest was acquired on October 1, 1957, and a further 30% interest was acquired on April 1, 1958, it would be appropriate to include in consolidated income for the year ended December 31, 1958, 45% of the earnings of the subsidiary for the three months ended March 31, and 75% of the earnings for the nine months ended December 31, and to credit consolidated earned surplus in 1958 with 45% of the undistributed earnings of the subsidiary for the three months ended December 31, 1957.

Sale to Outside Interests. A change in degree of ownership affects the allocation of consolidated net assets between controlling and minority interests. Consolidated net assets increase by the amount outsiders pay the controlling interest for shares of the subsidiary. As a basis for considering a shift from controlling to minority interest, assume that P purchases all the stock of S for $140,000 on January 1, 19X1. The net assets of the two companies one year later at December 31, 19X1, with P maintaining the investment at equity, are as follows:

	P	S
Net assets represented by:		
Capital stock, par $100.........	$200,000	$100,000
Retained earnings:		
Balance, 1/1/X1.............	$ 70,000	$ 30,000
Income, 19X1...............	45,000	20,000
Dividends, 19X1.............	(10,000)	(5,000)
Balance...................	$105,000	$ 45,000
Total owners' equity...........	$305,000	$145,000

If the discrepancy between cost of $140,000 and the underlying equity of S at date of acquisition is due to unrecorded intangibles of S, the following entry will prepare the data for a consolidated balance sheet at December 31, 19X1:

Capital Stock—S	100,000	
Retained Earnings—S	45,000	
Goodwill—S	10,000	
Investment in S—P		155,000

With no minority interest, consolidated net assets at December 31, 19X1, is equal to the controlling interest composed of the following:

Capital stock—P	$200,000
Retained earnings	105,000
	$305,000

On January 1, 19X2, P sells 200 shares of S at $160, reducing its interest to 80 percent. The amount of gain or loss P reports on the sale depends on the basis of maintaining the Investment account. In this case, the gain is either $1,000 or $4,000, calculated as follows:

		Equity basis	Cost basis
1/1/X1	1,000 shares of S at $140.....	$140,000	$140,000
12/31/X1	Earnings of S..............	20,000	
	Dividends of S.............	(5,000)	
1/1/X2	Balance..................	$155,000	$140,000
One fifth of investment in S............		$ 31,000	$ 28,000
Sales price (200 at $160)...............		32,000	32,000
Gain.....................................		$ 1,000	$ 4,000

The total gain on the shares sold for the entire holding period is the same whether the cost or equity method is used. P reports income on the equity basis of $4,000 prior to sale and $1,000 upon sale; whereas, on the cost basis, P reports income of $1,000 for dividends prior to sale and $4,000 at the point of sale. The total profit is the same in either case.

The decrease in the controlling interest of S may be observed from the following analysis of the net assets of S (in thousands):

	Total	Controlling interest		Outside interest
		Acquisition	Subsequent	
Jan. 1, 19X1:				
Capital stock.................	$100	$100		
Retained earnings..............	30	30		
Recognition of goodwill............	10	10		
Total......................	$140	$140		
During 19X1:				
Income......................	$ 20		$20	
Dividends....................	(5)		(5)	
Dec. 31, 19X1....................	$155	$140	$15	
Jan. 1, 19X2:				
Shift of 20 % of P's interest.......	—0—	(28)	(3)	$31
Balance.......................	$155	$112	$12	$31

The analysis above aids in formulating consolidating entries. With the investment at equity and recognizing goodwill of S in full, the following entry is in order for consolidated statements on January 1, 19X2, after the creation of the minority interest:

Capital Stock—S	100,000	
Retained Earnings—S	45,000	
Goodwill—S	10,000	
Investment in S—P		124,000
Minority Interest in S		31,000

Consolidated net assets at January 1, 19X2, are equal to the following:

Minority interest in S	$ 31,000
Controlling interest:	
Capital stock	$200,000

Retained earnings:
    Balance, 12/31/X1 .... $105,000
    Profit on sale (equity basis)   1,000   106,000   306,000
Consolidated net assets $337,000

As a consequence of the shift in degree of ownership, consolidated net assets increase by $32,000, the amount received by P for the shares sold. Controlling interest increases by $1,000 as a consequence of substituting assets of $32,000 for an investment which has an adjusted value of $31,000. This increment is clearly disclosed by the equity method.

When goodwill of S is recognized in full, as above, a decrease in ownership does not change consolidated goodwill. If at acquisition P makes an investment in intangibles of $10,000 (excess of cost of $140,000 over equity acquired of $130,-000), the sale of 20 percent of its holdings decreases its investment in intangibles to $8,000. In such case, minority interest is $29,000 rather than $31,000.

When the parent decreases its holdings in a subsidiary, consolidated statements may be prepared as though the parent held the smaller number of shares since date of acquisition and maintained the investment at cost. For example, the following analysis is appropriate at January 1, 19X2, for the cost basis:

Capital Stock—S 100,000
Retained Earnings—S 45,000
Goodwill—S 10,000
    Investment in S—P 112,000
    Retained Earnings—P 12,000
    Minority Interest in S 31,000

Consolidated net assets at January 1, 19X2 are equal to:
Minority interest in S .... $ 31,000
Controlling interest:
    Capital stock $200,000
    Retained earnings:
        P (before sale) $90,000
        Profit on sale (cost) 4,000
        Share of S since acquisition 12,000   106,000   306,000
Consolidated net assets $337,000

Obviously, if P sells all its shares of S, the parent-subsidiary relationship is discontinued, and S is no longer consolidated. When this occurs, *ARB No. 51* states that the following procedure is proper:[28]

> Where the investment in a subsidiary is disposed of during the year, it may be preferable to omit the details of operations of the subsidiary from the consolidated income statement, and to show the equity of the parent in the earnings of the subsidiary prior to disposal as a separate item in the statement.

Changes in Shares of Subsidiary. If the subsidiary increases its shares of common stock, any shift in the degree of ownership must be carefully analyzed. Assume that P purchased 8,000 shares (80 percent) of S's common stock on January 1, 19X0, at $70 per share when S's net assets stood at $650,000. On January 1, 19X1, when its net assets are $660,000, S issues 10,000 additional shares of common stock at $60. Three cases will be distinguished:

Case I (Use of Rights). Rights to subscribe to the 10,000 shares are extended to all holders of common shares. If P exercises its rights, it will make an additional investment in S of $480,000. If the other rights are also exercised, P retains its 80 percent interest in S, holding 16,000 out of 20,000 shares. The parent's interest in the increase in the net assets of S is precisely equal to its additional investment.

[28]*Ibid.,* par. 12.

Case II (All to P).   No rights are issued, but the additional shares are acquired by P for $600,000. Company P now holds 18,000 shares, or 90 percent of Company S. Because P increases its investment by paying less than book value, P benefits at the expense of the other shareholders. The following tabulation shows this shift of interest:

Net assets of S	Total	Interest of Company P	Interest of others
Before issuance of additional shares (80% to P)...	$ 660,000	$ 528,000	$132,000
After issuance of additional shares (90% to P)...	1,260,000	1,134,000	126,000
Increase (decrease)............................	$ 600,000	$ 606,000	$ (6,000)
Investment................................	600,000	600,000	—0—
Shift without payment.......................	$ —0—	$ 6,000	$ (6,000)

Company P should adjust its Investment account for the gain of $6,000; the other shareholders have a loss of $6,000. This adjustment is due to a shift of interest between stockholders, not to the valuation procedures employed by P or by S.

Case III (All to Outsiders).   Company P does not subscribe to any of the new shares; all are acquired by other shareholders. P now holds only 8,000 out of 20,000 shares, or 40 percent. In this case, P has suffered a loss due to a shift of interest in book value and should reduce its investment in S accordingly:

P's interest before issuance of additional shares: 80% of $660,000 ..... $528,000
P's interest after issuance of additional shares: 40% of $1,260,000 504,000
Loss in book value .... $ 24,000

Care must be exercised to avoid burying in consolidated goodwill a loss in book value resulting from a shift in degree of ownership.

A shift of interest between groups of shareholders will always occur when rights are not extended to all shareholders of a class or when rights are extended to all but are not exercised by some. All conceivable cases fall within the limits of the three cases above, or may be solved by a similar analysis.

OTHER RELATIONSHIPS

In addition to the major issues and problems encountered in preparing consolidated statements discussed above, several special cases of application deserve attention. Foremost among these are intermediate holding companies, reciprocal shareholdings, and foreign subsidiaries.

Intermediate Holding Companies.   When a subsidiary acquires the controlling interest in another company, it becomes a parent or holding company. The top parent has an indirect interest in the new subsidiary. For example, if T owns 80 percent of P, which acquires 70 percent of S, T acquires an indirect interest in S of 80 percent of 70 percent, or 56 percent. Minority interests own 20 percent of P and 44 percent of S. The latter consists of a direct minority interest in S of 30 percent and an indirect minority interest through P of 14 percent of S (20 percent of 70 percent). These ratios are useful in allocating profits and losses of subsidiaries to controlling and minority interests without first consolidating P and S and then T and PS.

No new problem is presented when a subsidiary becomes a parent. The action of the subsidiary may be interpreted as if its parent had made the investment directly. The difference between the price paid by P and the underlying equity acquired must be explained in some fashion. If the tangible assets of S are revalued so the underlying equity acquired by P equals purchase price, there is no problem. In the absence of adjustments of specific assets and liabilities, an excess of cost over book value may be interpreted (1) as an investment in intangibles by P or (2) as evidence of unrecorded intangibles of S.

A new problem is created when a parent becomes a subsidiary. For example, T acquires control of P after P has a controlling interest in S. The problem exists because T is acquiring an interest in P and S together. It is likely that T will make an independent evaluation of each company being brought under control. Consequently, any difference between P's cost and underlying equity in S at date of acquisition may have to be revised.

Assume the following condensed data as of January 1, 19X1:

	T	P	S
Various assets.....................	$500,000	$120,000	$300,000
Investment in P (90% at cost)........	360,000		
Investment in S (80% at cost)........		220,000	
	$860,000	$340,000	$300,000
Capital stock......................	$500,000	$200,000	$200,000
Retained earnings..................	360,000	140,000	100,000
	$860,000	$340,000	$300,000

T has just acquired 90 percent of P. P acquired its interest in S when the equity of S was $250,000.

Solution I (Previous Price Ignored). T ignores the price paid by P for its investment in S and makes its own evaluation of P and S. In this case, T purchases a 90 percent direct interest in P, exclusive of P's interest in S, and a 72 percent indirect interest in S. The following analysis is appropriate:

Consolidated assets:
Various assets $920,000
Goodwill 36,000
                                                                                        $956,000

Consolidated net assets:
Minority interests:
  Capital stock—S (20%) $40,000
  Retained earnings—S .... 20,000 $ 60,000
  Capital stock—P (10%) $20,000
  Retained earnings—P 16,000   36,000 $ 96,000
Controlling interest:
  Capital stock—T $500,000
  Retained earnings 360,000 $860,000
Total net assets $956,000

Solution II (Previous Price Recognized). T recognizes intangibles evidenced by P's investment in S. This solution involves two elements of goodwill, as follows:

(1) Cost of P's investment in S $220,000
    Equity acquired: 80% of $250,000 200,000
    Excess of cost over equity .... $ 20,000

(2) Cost of T's investment in P $360,000
    Equity acquired: 90% of ($340,000 plus $40,000) 342,000
    Excess of cost over equity .... $ 18,000

The resulting consolidated balance sheet at January 1, 19X1 shows the following:

```
Consolidated assets:
  Various assets  ...............................................  $920,000
  Goodwill  ......................................................    38,000
                                                                   $958,000

Consolidated net assets:
  Minority interests:
    Capital stock—S (20%)  .........................  $40,000
    Retained earnings—S  ...........................   20,000  $ 60,000
    Capital stock—P (10%)  .........................  $20,000
    Retained earnings—P  ...........................   18,000    38,000  $ 98,000
  Controlling interest:
    Capital stock—T  ......................................  $500,000
    Retained earnings  ....................................   360,000   860,000
  Total net assets  .........................................................  $958,000
```

Reciprocal Shareholdings. Reciprocal shareholdings exist when two companies own voting shares of each other.[29] Such mutual relationships are created by the purchase on the market by a subsidiary of shares in the parent or by the issuance by a parent of additional shares to the subsidiary. In either event, the shares of P held by S are not outstanding in the hands of the public. Consequently, in a consolidated balance sheet such shares are eliminated in determining the controlling interest. The same effect is obtained if P acquires its own shares. The similarity between mutual shares and treasury shares is readily apparent. In some jurisdictions, the same restrictions applicable to a company's transactions in its own shares apply to transactions of its controlled affiliates.

The accounting problem created by mutual shares is the allocation of income and proprietorship between controlling and minority interests rather than determining total income and total proprietorship. Assume the following data at January 1, 19X1:

	P	S
Various assets.........................	$514,000	$ 95,000
Investment in S (80% at cost)...........	136,000	
Investment in P (10% at cost)..........		70,000
	$650,000	$165,000
Capital stock.........................	$500,000	$100,000
Retained earnings....................	150,000	65,000
	$650,000	$165,000

P acquired 80 percent of S when the total book value of S was $150,000. S has just acquired 10 percent of P. If the excess P pays over book value is interpreted as an investment in goodwill, the consolidated balance sheet immediately after the mutual relationship is established shows the following:

```
Consolidated assets:
  Various  ......................................  $609,000
  Investment in goodwill  ...........................   16,000
                                                     $625,000
```

[29]This problem is discussed at length in Roman L. Weil, "Reciprocal or Mutual Holdings: Allocating Earnings and Selecting the Accounting Method," *The Accounting Review*, vol. 48, 4 (October 1973), pp. 749–758.

```
Consolidated net assets:
  Minority interest in S (20%):
    Capital stock  ........................  $ 20,000
    Retained earnings  ...................    13,000  $ 33,000
  Controlling interest:
    Capital stock—P  ......................  $500,000
    Less: Shares held by S  ...................    50,000  $450,000
    Retained earnings  ......................  $162,000
    Less: Premium on shares held by S  ........    20,000   142,000
      Total controlling interest  .........................  $592,000
  Total net assets  ...................................  $625,000
```

In the case above, S pays $70,000 for a 10 percent interest in P which has a par value of $50,000 and an adjusted book value of $66,200. Because P has a controlling interest in S, it is unlikely that the price paid by S is evidence of the market's evaluation of unrecorded goodwill of P. Consequently, in the balance sheet the payment in excess of par is deducted from the retained earnings of the controlling interest. This is the same result that would be achieved if P acquired the shares instead of having S do so.

During 19X1, P operates at a profit of $20,000 exclusive of any earnings of S and S operates at a profit of $10,000 exclusive of any earnings of P.

The conventional treatment is based on the assumption that mutual shares are entitled to share in profits just as are outstanding shares. Simultaneous equations are needed to determine the "adjusted" profits of P and S to be used in determining controlling and minority interests:

Let

$$P = \text{adjusted income of P}$$
$$S = \text{adjusted income of S}$$

Then

$$(1)\ P = \$20,000 + .8S$$
$$(2)\ S = \$10,000 + .1P$$

Solving,

$$P = \$30,434 \quad S = \$13,043$$

The adjusted incomes are meaningless except as intermediate figures in the allocation of consolidated income. Note that the sum is greater than consolidated income of $30,000. The adjusted figures include duplications which must be removed:

```
Allocation:
  Minority interest: 20% of $13,043  ......  $ 2,609
  Controlling interest: 90% of $30,434  ....   27,391
  Consolidated income  ....................  $30,000
```

Following this method of allocating profits, the consolidated balance sheet at December 31, 19X1, ignoring the amortization of goodwill for simplicity, shows the following:

```
Consolidated assets:
  Various assets  ..........................................  $639,000
  Investment in goodwill  ..................................    16,000
                                                              $655,000

Consolidated net assets:
  Minority interest in S (20%):
    Capital stock  ....................................  $ 20,000
    Retained earnings:
      Balance, 1/1/X1  ....................  $ 13,000
      Income, 19X1  ......................     2,609    15,609  $ 35,609
```

Controlling interest:

Capital stock	$500,000	
Less: Shares held by S	50,000	$450,000

Retained earnings:

Balance, 1/1/X1	$162,000		
Income	27,391		
	$189,391		
Less: Premium on shares held by S ...	20,000	169,391	619,391
Total net assets			$655,000

ARB No. 51[30] states that "shares of the parent held by a subsidiary should not be treated as outstanding stock in a consolidated balance sheet," but it indicates nothing as to the allocation of income.

Simultaneous equations were used above to allocate changes in net assets, not total net assets. Mutual shares may be treated as treasury shares for a consolidated balance sheet at the date the mutual relationship is established. Simultaneous equations are not needed in those cases where there is no minority interest. For example, P owns 90 percent in each of two subsidiaries, with the subsidiaries owning 10 percent of each other. The entire consolidated income and consolidated net assets are assigned to the controlling interest; consequently, there is no need to calculate adjusted income of each subsidiary.

Simultaneous equations are used when mutual shareholdings are between two subsidiaries and there is a minority interest. For example, P owns 80 percent of two subsidiaries, who in turn own 10 percent of each other. There is a minority interest in each subsidiary of 10 percent. Because no shares of P are held intercompany, adjusted income of P is assigned to the controlling interest without dilution. Although a treasury stock interpretation may be given to the mutual relationship between the subsidiaries in preparing separate statements for the minority interests, the treasury stock feature is of little importance in this case for consolidated statements.

Foreign Subsidiaries. The accounts of subsidiaries kept in currencies other than that of the parent must be translated into a common monetary unit before they can be consolidated. The existence of foreign subsidiaries focuses attention on the consolidating policy of the parent company. Some companies follow a practice of consolidating only domestic affiliates, while others consolidate foreign subsidiaries as well. Economics or political instability or stringent restrictions on the movement of funds may make it advisable to exclude foreign subsidiaries from formal consolidation. In the absence of such conditions, however, foreign subsidiaries should be consolidated.

Attention must be given to accounting principles and conventions followed by the foreign subsidiary in maintaining its records. Ideally, accounting principles should be consistently applied between units of an integrated group as well as between time periods. But the standard here is no higher than for divisions of a single corporation, or for components of inventories, for example. Special attention must be given to terminology and to the classification of data.

By far the most difficult problem faced in consolidating foreign subsidiaries is determining a realistic policy for translating the monetary units in the face of fluctuating exchange rates. In many respects, the problem is similar to the problem of changes in the price level in the domestic currency. Both relate to fluctuations in the purchasing power of the monetary unit as evidenced by the ratio of the price of one commodity to another. These considerations led the Financial Accounting Standards Board to seek to coordinate the pronouncement on translation of foreign currencies with that on reporting in units of general purchasing power.

[30]*ARB No. 51*, par. 13.

The problem of foreign exchange transactions and translations are dealt with extensively in Chapter 35.

BIBLIOGRAPHY

AAA Committee Report: "The Entity Concept," *The Accounting Review*, vol. 40, pp. 358–367, April 1965.

Accounting Principles Board: "Accounting for Income Taxes—Special Areas," Opinion No. 23, AICPA, New York 1972.

———: "Business Combinations," Opinion No. 16, AICPA, New York, 1970.

———: "The Equity Method of Accounting for Investments in Common Stock," Opinion No. 18, AICPA, New York, 1971.

———: "Intangible Assets," Opinion No. 17, AICPA, New York, 1970.

American Institute of Certified Public Accountants, Committee on Accounting Procedure: *Accounting Research Bulletin No. 51*, AICPA, New York, 1959.

Foster, Louis O.: *Understanding Financial Statements and Corporate Annual Reports*, rev. ed., Chilton Book Company, Philadelphia, 1968.

Hendriksen, Eldon S.: *Accounting Theory*, Richard D. Irwin, Homewood, Ill., 1970.

Nurnberg, H., C. P. Stickney, and R. L. Weil: "Combining Stockholders' Equity Accounts in Poolings of Interests," *The Accounting Review*, 50, 1 (January 1975).

Smolinski, Edward J.: "The Adjunct Method in Consolidations," *Journal of Accounting Research*, 1, 2 (1963).

Weil, Roman L.: "Reciprocal of Mutual Holdings: Allocating Earnings and Selecting the Accounting Method," *The Accounting Review*, 48, 4 (October 1973).

Chapter **35**

Foreign Exchange Transactions and Translations

GEORGE C. WATT
Retired Partner, Price Waterhouse & Co.

BACKGROUND

When the authoritative committee of the American Institute of Certified Public Accountants issued early pronouncements on the translation of the financial statements of foreign entities in the middle 1930s, the word "fluctuation" frequently appeared, and indeed foreign currencies in relation to the U.S. dollar did both strengthen and weaken within a span of five years. Following World War II, however, most foreign currencies weakened in relation to the U.S. dollar, and accountants became accustomed to thinking of principles that would best accommodate this one-way change in exchange rates. It was not until 1970, and particularly 1971, that the U.S. dollar weakened in relation to many foreign currencies. The Accounting Principles Board issued an Exposu Draft in December 1971 which was intended to give guidance in dealing with this problem. An Accounting Research Study of the AICPA was in progress at the time, and it was concluded that the APB should await the publication of the Research Study before issuing a definitive Opinion. Later, it became apparent that the Financial Accounting Standards Board would supersede the APB. The issuance of *FAS No. 8* in October 1975 currently governs practice. The short, 37-paragraph Statement is supported by 205 paragraphs in four appendixes; the fifth appendix is a glossary. Those who wish to review various concepts, principles, and methods should refer to the FASB Discussion Memorandum on this subject of nearly 200 pages dated February 21, 1974. In March 1974, the FASB released a Financial Statement Model on Accounting for Foreign Currency Translation prepared by its research staff for illustrative purposes. Those wishing to study further the "cause and effect" of various methods in use prior to the issuance of *FAS No. 8* will find ample material for study in this 100-page Model in a 10 by 13-inch spiral binder.

In view of this current authoritative pronouncement, this chapter will deal largely with implementation matters and occasionally interject the view of the author. It is assumed that the definitive FASB Statement, *FAS No. 8,* is available to readers of this chapter.

FOREIGN ASSETS AND LIABILITIES
OF U.S. CORPORATIONS

Paragraph 3 of *FAS No. 8* describes the scope of this section as follows:

> *Foreign currency transactions*—an enterprise (a) buys or sells on credit goods or services whose prices are stated in *foreign currency,* (b) borrows or lends funds and the amounts payable or receivable are denominated in foreign currency, (c) is a party to an unperformed forward exchange contract, or (d) for other reasons, acquires assets or incurs liabilities denominated in foreign currency.

Footnote 2 of *FAS No. 8* admirably illustrates several complex transactions.

Time of Transaction Basis. The "time of transaction" basis for translation is founded on the premise that once the transaction is recorded, the nonmonetary assets (such as imported inventory) and nonmonetary liabilities (rare instances may arise), expenses and revenues arising in a foreign currency transaction are permanently fixed in terms of dollars at the exchange rate prevailing on the date the transaction takes place. Exchange rate fluctuations subsequent to the original transaction date cause exchange gains and losses, as shown in the table below.

U.S. IMPORTER—DUAL CURRENCY RECORD

	Local currency (credit)	U.S. dollars (credit)
June, 19X1: Purchase of inventory, exchange rate 10:1		
Inventory..		100
Payable, LC1,000...................................	(1,000)	(100)
January, 19X2: Settlement, exchange rate 11:1		
Payable, LC1,000...................................	1,000	100
Cash...		(91)
Gain on foreign exchange...........................		(9)

Note: At year-end 19X1, assume the rate of exchange was LC 11 to U.S. dollar. Importer should report the gain of $9 in 19X1 and not in the year of settlement, 19X2.

Such exchange gains and losses are generally considered to be "realized" immediately if the change in the exchange rate is ascribed a quality of permanence. However, conservatism and a reluctance to risk assessment of income taxes on gains on unsettled transactions frequently resulted in a deferral of net exchange gains on such transactions until settled, prior to *FAS No. 8*. Paragraphs 7, 16, and 17 of *FAS No. 8* require the application of the time of transaction method and consequently the recognition of an exchange gain or loss at each balance sheet date to reflect the current exchange rate for any unsettled receivable or payable denominated in a foreign currency.

Time of Settlement Basis. The "time of settlement" basis is founded on the premise that a transaction is not complete so long as the monetary asset or liability arising therein is unsettled. An importer or exporter using the time of settlement basis for translating foreign currency accounts into dollars can, within limits, adjust nonmonetary assets and nonmonetary liabilities, expenses, and revenues for changes (as a result of exchange rate fluctuations) in the amounts of unsettled foreign monetary assets and liabilities arising in the same transaction. In the illustration above, the accounts would be adjusted under the time of settlement basis for the unsettled transaction as follows:

	Local currency	U.S. dollars (credit)
June, 19X1:		
Inventory...		100
Payable, rate 10:1....................................	(1,000)	(100)
Close accounts for 19X1 with transaction not paid but rate weakened to 11:1		
Inventory...		(9)
Payable...		9

Note: If inventory had been sold by year-end, the credit would be taken to cost of goods sold.

This method is no longer acceptable.

View of Author. The requirement of *FAS No. 8* to apply the time of transaction method *to every situation* causes an unfortunate distortion of income, usually between adjacent periods, on the importation of unsold inventory where the payable in foreign currency is unsettled and the U.S. importer can raise the selling price to compensate for his additional cost of settlement following a strengthening of the foreign currency. The result is an unusual charge, say to the fourth quarter of 19X1, followed by an unusually high gross profit in the first quarter of 19X2 when the item is sold at an increased U.S. dollar selling price maintaining, from the merchant's point of view, a consistent U.S. dollar profit margin based on replacement cost and settlement of the foreign payable at a less favorable exchange rate. This method was demonstrated as distortive at Illustration One on page 7 of the FASB Discussion Memorandum even where the selling price was not raised. When selling price is raised, the distortion is even more clear, as Exhibit 1 shows. Those charged with explaining variations in the results of operations among periods should keep this situation in mind. This distortion is a high cost to pay for eliminating judgment required to determine that no loss really occurred— assuming that the market will withstand an increase in selling price.

Although Exhibit 1 shows a foreign currency strengthening, a similar situation relative to unsold inventory will arise when a foreign currency weakens. The distortion in this case could be avoided by not picking up the unrealized gain until the inventory is sold. In fact, competition may force a decrease in the selling price in the subsequent period, which should result in reporting a constant gross profit

EXHIBIT 1   Effect on Determination of Income of Importer

This example was adapted from page 7 of the February 21, 1974, FASB Discussion Memorandum, *Accounting for Foreign Currency Translation*. Assumption 4a was added to illustrate an increase in sales price.

Assumptions

1. Purchase of 100,000 widgets at FC 200,000 in 1969, 1970, 1971, and 1972.
2. Exchange rates:

Prior to December 31, 1971	FC 1 = $1.00
At December 31, 1971	FC 1 = $1.10
After December 31, 1971	FC 1 = $1.10

3. Each year's purchase is paid for and sold in the year following purchase.
4. Selling price $3.00 per widget. 4a. Selling price increased to $3.20 on January 1, 1972.
5. First-in, first-out method used.
6. The effect of the exchange rate change (i.e., the exchange adjustment) is recorded on December 31, 1971.

	4. Constant Sales Price		4a. Increased Sales Price	
	Two Transaction	One Transaction	Two Transaction	One Transaction
1970				
Sales	$300,000	$300,000	$300,000	$300,000
Cost of sales (and cost of inventory at December 31, 1969)	200,000	200,000	200,000	200,000
Gross profit	$100,000 (33%)	$100,000 (33%)	$100,000 (33%)	$100,000 (33%)
1971				
Sales	$300,000	$300,000	$300,000	$300,000
Cost of sales (and cost of inventory at December 31, 1970)	200,000	200,000	200,000	200,000
Gross profit	$100,000 (33%)	$100,000 (33%)	$100,000 (33%)	$100,000 (33%)
Exchange loss (from 1971 purchase)	20,000	—	20,000	—
Income	$ 80,000	$100,000	$ 80,000	$100,000
1972				
Sales	$300,000	$300,000	$320,000	$320,000
Cost of sales (and cost of inventory at December 31, 1971)	200,000	220,000	200,000	220,000
Gross profit	$100,000 (33%)	$ 80,000 (26%)	$120,000 (38%)	$100,000 (31%)
1973				
Sales	$300,000	$300,000	$320,000	$320,000
Cost of sales (and cost of inventory at December 31, 1972)	220,000	220,000	220,000	220,000
Gross profit	$ 80,000 (26%)	$ 80,000 (26%)	$100,000 (31%)	$100,000 (31%)

Comment—This illustration demonstrates that where the importer has an unsettled payable denominated in a foreign currency and corresponding unsold inventory, the two-transaction method causes severe variations between periods when exchange rates change.

in dollars. Further, if the obligation is settled prior to the sale of the inventory, the gain should be deferred to the period of the sale of the inventory to avoid distortion between periods. However, this is no longer acceptable.

The author's view, that only certain importer transactions required deferral of gains or losses, would have required a judgment as to the effect of the change in the exchange rate on the selling price of the unsold imported inventory which was not yet paid for. Paragraphs 114 and 115 of *FAS No. 8* show that the Board felt that such transactions could be hedged when the purchase was committed, but hedging has a cost and yet it may have no effect on the changes in the subsequent dollar selling prices that contribute to variations in gross profit of an importer. The "uniform" method has its drawbacks.

FOREIGN ASSETS AND LIABILITIES OF FOREIGN CORPORATIONS

The same problems are encountered by branches and subsidiaries of U.S. corporations as are encountered by U.S. corporations who are importers and exporters. Often, the "foreign" transaction is based on a contract to be settled in U.S. dollars, but settlement in any currency foreign to the foreign entity involves the same issue. Paragraphs 8 and 11 of *FAS No. 8* require application of the time of transaction method to such balances before the foreign entity financial statements are translated to U.S. dollars as a branch or as a subsidiary to be consolidated. This has the same disadvantage described under "View of Author" in the previous section, "Foreign Assets and Liabilities of U.S. Corporations," but it is agreed that the applications should be identical.

LOCAL CURRENCY FINANCIAL STATEMENTS

FAS No. 8 does not govern statutory financial statements of a foreign branch or foreign subsidiary of a U.S. parent company. While the time of transaction basis may be appropriate in hard currency countries, its strict application in countries experiencing constant inflation is not practical. Where price-level financial statements are prepared in such countries, some relief is afforded. The comments which follow show the dimension of the problem.

Where a foreign subsidiary purchases fixed assets or inventory that remains unsold, the same distortion described above for a U.S. importer could arise under the time of transaction method. In some countries large projects cannot be financed locally, as the capital market simply will not support large borrowings.

With the issuance of *FAS No. 8,* the comments under the following three captions are not acceptable under U.S. generally accepted accounting principles, and any application in local currency financial statements should be made only if the procedures are accepted in the country of the reporting company. Paragraph 8 of *FAS No. 8* does not govern foreign financial statements.

Purchase of Plant by Foreign Subsidiary.   Assume that a foreign corporation which is a subsidiary of a U.S. company arranged for extended credit terms to obtain U.S. steel to build a plant in the foreign country. The price of the steel was $100,000 delivered at the plant site. The steel was delivered early in the year when the exchange rate was LC10 = $1, so construction in progress was charged LC1,000,000 and a liability account was credited in dual currency records in the amounts of LC1,000,000 and $100,000. At the end of the year the plant was still under construction and the exchange rate had deteriorated to LC12 = $1. Using the time of settlement basis, especially since the plant had not commenced operations, it would be proper to charge construction in progress and credit the liability account in the amount of an additional LC200,000, thereby avoiding recognition of an exchange loss of that amount. (The same effect could be obtained by debiting a deferred charge account, which would then be amortized over the life of the plant.) Note that there is no need for a foreign branch or foreign subsidiary of a U.S. company to adjust the U.S. dollars first recorded, provided the test outlined in the next section is met.

Limitations on Adjustments.   The entry in local currency in the preceding example cannot be accepted even under the time of settlement basis if the result will be to increase the cost of the plant in local currency to an amount in excess of future economic value, that is, if the result will be to increase depreciation charges to a level that will preclude profitable operations in the foreign country in terms of local currency. It may be possible to apply the lower-of-cost-or-market rule in this case by restating plant costs incurred during the year using price-level restatement techniques, which are gaining acceptance in some foreign countries; the amount of exchange loss charged to construction in progress would be limited to the approximate amount by which the construction in progress account would have been increased by the price-level adjustment. Alternatively, it might be necessary to evaluate the reasonableness of the charge to construction in progress by studying budgets, forecasts, or other available data. Certainly the estimated local currency selling price of the product the new plant is expected to produce is the key to whether the additional LC200,000 may be charged to plant, or whether all or some portion should be charged off in local currency and then the $100,000 plant written down proportionately, or all the way to $83,333. Usually, however, local selling prices can be increased to absorb such additional charges. The U.S. dollar problem arises only in translation of branch and subsidiary financial statements—a subject treated later in this chapter.

If the liability were not discharged in subsequent years while the exchange rate continued to deteriorate, but the building was completed and operations were begun, continuing to charge the exchange losses to the asset account would result in steadily increasing annual depreciation charges in local currency, and the same test described in the previous paragraph would again be applied. Once a plant is complete and operating, however, there is a theory that subsequent exchange weakness is purely a financial charge against income resulting from unsettled foreign (maybe U.S.) contracts and such treasury function risks are period charges in local currency (often called the "speculation" theory). The longer the liability remains unsettled, the more there is a presumption that the speculation theory is more appropriate.

Purchase of Inventory by Foreign Subsidiary. If the item obtained under a contract for settlement in U.S. dollars had been an inventory item, the reasonableness of charging the exchange loss to inventory would depend on the estimated net realizable amount in local currency of the inventory being more than the restated cost, which includes the additional local currency charge. If the liability were not discharged in subsequent years while the exchange rate continued to deteriorate, but the inventory items were being sold, it would be illogical to charge all the exchange losses to the inventory account and it would be impossible to adjust the local currency cost of goods sold in prior years. In this case, a period charge to exchange loss in local currency is required. In translating foreign branch and foreign subsidiary financial statements—a subject treated later in this chapter—no dollars are assigned to the additional local currency charge to a nonmonetary asset account.

Dual Currency Records. Using the time of settlement basis, which is no longer permitted in the United States, it is necessary to maintain dual currency records for each unsettled foreign currency transaction (both the debits and the credits); there is no shortcut. Using the time of transaction basis, dual currency records need be maintained only for foreign currency *monetary* assets and liabilities.

BROAD PRINCIPLES OF TRANSLATION OF FOREIGN FINANCIAL STATEMENTS

Basic translation principles apply equally to consolidated and unconsolidated subsidiaries, to branches, to more limited types of foreign operations, and to unsettled transactions receivable or payable in foreign currency. The problems of the propriety of including foreign subsidiaries in consolidated financial statements and the reporting of an investment in and earnings of unconsolidated subsidiaries are discussed in general in Chapter 34.[1]

---

[1] Those interested in this subject may consult *Accounting Research Bulletin No. 43*, AICPA, New York, 1953, chap. 12, par. 8 and 9, and par. 14 of APB Opinion No. 18.

Official Literature. *FAS No. 8,* dated October 1975, establishes the generally accepted accounting principles in this area. Paragraphs 9 to 15 describe in general terms the method prescribed in the Statement. For all practical purposes it is applied today as the monetary/nonmonetary method. Paragraphs 16 and 17 prohibit the deferral of gains and losses that arise from the line-by-line application of the *FAS No. 8* method. In Paragraph 122 it is indicated that the Board "found the temporal method . . . the most useful in meeting the objective." Nevertheless, *FAS No. 8* does not use the term in its authoritative procedural paragraphs. Further, the Board did not use the terms monetary or nonmonetary, but the author continues to find them useful in describing broad characteristics of balance sheet accounts.

View of Author. The requirement of *FAS No. 8* to apply its method *to every situation* and to prohibit deferral of gains and losses regardless of "the expected economic effect of a rate change on business activities conducted in a currency other than dollars" (Paragraph 79E) causes large translation gains and losses expressed in U.S. dollars to be reported in the year of a change in the rate offset by amortization of nonmonetary items over a span of years. It can be said that the author's view of permissible deferrals in defined circumstances of translation differences arising under the temporal method is consistent with his view previously expressed relative to unsold inventory of an importer. Similarly, the FASB pronouncement is consistent in denying deferrals in both situations. Deferrals should have been permitted in net monetary liability situations when the temporal method produces (1) a *debit* U.S. dollar adjustment when a foreign currency *strengthens* in relation to the U.S. Dollar, and (2) a *credit* U.S. dollar adjustment when a foreign currency *weakens.* Those charged with explaining variations in the results of operations among periods should keep these situations in mind. The author's view is known as the "cover concept" and is described in Paragraphs 79E, 96–111, and 174 and 175 of Appendix D of *FAS No. 8.* In the usual situation both inventory and property, plant, and equipment are the assets associated with "cover." The Board rejected the "cover concept" for the reasons set forth in Paragraphs 176–180 and 194 because it invokes a judgment as to expected future earnings. Indeed it should. Further, the FASB said it is complex. Yes, but only by requiring judgment. Paragraph 96 describes the author's objectives accurately as follows: "That is, the translation method should . . . avoid producing an exchange loss if the economic effect of a rate change appears to be beneficial and . . . an exchange gain if the economic effect appears to be detrimental."

Definitions. Certain terms used extensively throughout the succeeding discussion are defined below. The section of this chapter relating to selection of exchange rates should be read in conjunction with the definitions of the principal exchange rates commonly applied in practice (closing free exchange rate, average free exchange rate for the month, historical exchange rate).

Appendix E of *FAS No. 8* is a glossary of terms. The terms temporal method and monetary/nonmonetary are not used in the Statement, but because of their common usage, those definitions are retained in the supplementary glossary which follows.

Average free exchange rate for the month—Arithmetical average of daily free exchange rates for a month. The rate for each day is usually the average of the high and low quotations for that day. In cases of extreme fluctuation weighted averages may be desirable (temporarily).

Average monthly free exchange rate—Arithmetical average of the rates quoted for the last day in each month for the period.

Black market rates—Exchange rates for buying or selling currency established by unauthorized dealers in foreign exchange, often in violation of governmental regulations, and almost invariably higher for purchasing a hard currency than the official or free rate for the same currency.

Blocked accounts—Bank accounts of nonresidents restricted by the monetary authorities of the country in which the accounts are located. Generally, the funds may be used within the country but cannot be exported or exchanged for other currencies.

Blocked currency—Currency completely restricted as to its exchange for dollars or other currencies except through special permission from the government imposing the restriction.

Composite rate—Rate expressing the relationship of translated units of one currency to units of another currency for the same item. In the United States, such rates are calculated by dividing the dollar balance of an account by its corresponding foreign currency balance.

Convertible currency—Currency which may be used without restriction, by both residents and nonresidents, for all trade and capital transactions and payments with any other country.

Current rate—Quoted exchange rate at the end of a period. It is usually called the year-end rate if the period ends at the close of a company's fiscal year and may be called the closing rate at the end of interim months. (Also closing free exchange rate.)

Devaluation—Governmental action lowering the value of the country's currency, either by reduction of its gold or silver backing or of its equivalent value in terms of other currencies.

Dividend rate—Exchange rate at which a company pays dividends to nonresident shareholders.

Dual currency records—Accounting records maintained simultaneously both in the local currency and in the foreign currency in which a specific transaction occurred. Normally, dual currency records need be maintained only for unsettled foreign currency accounts receivable and payable (and, of course, the parent's investment).

Free rates—Exchange rates at which local, U.S., Swiss, or other banks will buy or sell a currency.

Monetary assets and liabilities—An asset or liability which (1) *is* cash, (2) is a claim *collectible* in a fixed amount of cash, (3) is an obligation *payable* in a fixed amount of cash, or (4) is a valuation account for such an asset or liability. The fact that a monetary asset or liability is recorded at an estimated amount does not make it nonmonetary.

Multiple exchange rates—Several official exchange rates applicable to the same foreign currency. These various rates apply to specific transactions and are designed to encourage or discourage imports or exports of certain commodities and to conserve the country's supply of foreign currencies. The term may be applied to official and free rates for the same foreign currency.

Nonmonetary assets and liabilities—All assets and liabilities which are not monetary (the equity accounts are considered separately).

Official rate—Exchange rate at which the central bank or other monetary authority of a country will buy or sell its local currency.

Penalty rate—Official exchange rate applicable to particular transactions and designed to discourage such transactions. Such a rate is higher for purchasing dollars than the official rate for unregulated transactions.

Preference rate—Official exchange rate applicable to particular transactions and designed to encourage such transactions. Such a rate is lower for purchasing dollars than the official rate for unregulated transactions.

Prevailing rate—Exchange rate in effect at the time a specific transaction occurred, or, at which local currency was converted into a foreign currency. (Same as historical rate.)

Remittance rates—Exchange rates at which foreign funds are remitted or may be remitted to another country.

Repatriation—Requirement of a government for a foreign company that makes export sales and receives payment in dollars to use a stated percentage of the dollars received from these sales to purchase currency of that country. Sometimes the government sets a special penalty rate at which the currency must be purchased and/or sets the sales price for the sole purpose of computing the amount returnable regardless of the actual negotiated sales price.

Unrealized exchange gain or loss—Gain or loss arising in translation of financial statements because of the effects of exchange rate fluctuations between the local currency and the dollar on the local currency monetary items. When deferrals of translation adjustments are prohibited, as in *FAS No. 8*, the term has no application.

Year-end rate—Quoted exchange rate at the end of a company's fiscal year.

Conversion Versus Translation. It is important that the difference between conversion and translation be emphasized. *Conversion* is the actual exchange of currency of one country for that of another. A remittance of U.S. dollars to the United Kingdom is converted into sterling at the rate prevailing at the time of the remittance; there is no question as to what exchange rate is applicable.

Translation is the restatement of amounts in a given currency in terms of another currency by applying an exchange rate. The accounts of a foreign subsidiary or branch are restated in terms of U.S. dollars by applying "appropriate exchange rates." Foreign currency accounts on the books of importers and exporters are restated in terms of the dollar by applying "appropriate exchange rates." The determination of which exchange rates are "appropriate" is governed by *FAS No. 8*.

TRANSLATION OF ACCOUNTS OF FOREIGN BRANCHES AND SUBSIDIARIES

Selection of Exchange Rates. It should not be inferred that the official exchange rate is always inappropriate. For example, during the years 1950 through 1966, the free exchange rate for the pound sterling varied approximately plus or minus 1 percent from £1 = $2.80 (the official rate). At the end of any of those years it would have been appropriate to translate monetary assets and liabilities at £1 = $2.80 even if the free rate was £1 = $2.78 or £1 = $2.82. And for most companies it is probable that by the latter years of the period involved the use of historical rates for nonmonetary assets (possibly excepting fixed assets) and liabilities and the use of the average free exchange rate for revenues and expenses (possibly excepting depreciation) would have yielded results differing insignificantly from those obtained by simply translating such accounts at the official exchange rate. Similarly, there are circumstances where an average monthly free exchange rate (arithmetical average of the rates quoted for the last day in each month for the period) might well be used in place of the average free exchange rate for each month (arithmetical average of the rates quoted each day for a month) for the period. Paragraphs 13 and 29 of *FAS No. 8* sanction the "use of averages or reasonable approximations."

Theory of FAS No. 8 Method. Paragraphs 82 and 122 describe the "concept." Very briefly, Paragraph 82 states in part that "foreign statements prepared for purposes of combination, consolidation, or equity accounting should be prepared in conformity with U.S. generally accepted accounting principles, and translation should not change the measurement bases used in those foreign statements."

The following excerpts are from FASB Status Report No. 30, dated October 28, 1975, announcing the release of *FAS No. 8*, Foreign Currency Translation.

> The Statement requires a method that is similar to the monetary-nonmonetary method presently used in practice and the temporal method described in *Accounting*

Research Study No. 12. It requires that exchange gains and losses resulting from the translation process enter into the determination of income in the current period, and not be deferred.

Under the method adopted, cash, receivables, and payables are translated at the foreign exchange rate in effect at the balance sheet date. Other assets and liabilities are translated at the historical foreign exchange rate in effect when the assets were acquired or the liabilities were incurred, except that the exchange rate in effect at the balance sheet date is used to translate assets and liabilities that are accounted for on the basis of current prices, such as marketable securities carried at market, and estimated warranty obligations.

The final Statement also requires a method of deferral of gains or losses on a forward exchange contract when the contract is intended as a hedge of an identifiable foreign currency commitment.

Financial statements may not be adjusted for a rate change that occurs after the date of the financial statements, although disclosure of the rate change and its effects, if significant, may be necessary.

Mathematical Considerations.   In practice it is convenient to express rates as the number of local currency units to the dollar, such as LC160 = $1. On the other hand, the use of such rates (160–1) does not lead to an easy comparison with changed rates to obtain a difference. For example, if the rate changes from 160–1 to 200–1, the difference is not 40–1. On the other hand, a decimal, when multiplied by the local currency units, gives the same U.S. dollar amount as LC160 = $1 and the difference between two decimal rates may be applied directly to local currency units to obtain the dollar difference.

> LC 1,000,000 at   100–1 is $10,000
>   1,000,000 at   160–1 is   6,250
>   1,000,000 at   60–1 is 16,666 (error)
> LC 1,000,000 at .0100 is $10,000
>   1,000,000 at .00625 is   6,250
>   1,000,000 at .00375 is   3,750 (correct)

Therefore, the use of decimals facilitates the explanation of changes and the calculation of the difference. Decimal expressions of exchange rates should be carried to a minimum of three *significant* digits, for example, $0.00375.

If a Brazilian subsidiary exports goods to Belgium and invoices in terms of Belgian francs, the bank of designation is the key to deciding the appropriate cruzeiro/franc exchange rate for translating the receivable. If the francs are to be deposited in Belgium for the Brazilian company's account, the closing free exchange rate at which banks sell cruzeiros in Belgium is most appropriate. If the Belgian company is to remit a check for deposit in Brazil, the closing free exchange rate at which banks buy francs in Brazil is most appropriate.

For purposes of translation of a Brazilian subsidiary's financial statements, the rate at which the subsidiary can buy dollars (as they do in remitting dividends) is most appropriate. In practice, however, a quotation from a U.S. source of the rate at which banks buy cruzeiros in the United States is often used instead.

Dollar Transactions.   When transactions originate in terms of U.S. dollars, it is necessary to maintain dual currency records for the unsettled side of the transaction, that is, for the amount receivable or payable. However, on the other side of the entry, when nonmonetary assets and nonmonetary liabilities, equity account items (other than the parent's investment), revenues, and expenses originate in U.S. dollars, it is not necessary to maintain the identity of the U.S. dollar amounts in those local currency accounts. U.S. dollar transactions in those accounts should be translated into local currency amounts at the equivalent local currency rates prevailing at the time of the original entries and thereafter considered as local currency transactions. The subsequent translation of these amounts into U.S.

dollars, for financial statement purposes, should be made in accordance with the basic principles set forth throughout this chapter. However, some companies maintain a subnumber for each account in the chart of accounts to assist in supplemental analysis of costs, which is especially useful to management when exchange rates change.

TRANSLATION OF SPECIFIC ASSET AND LIABILITY ACCOUNTS

Appendix A of *FAS No. 8* gives specific guidance for the translation of certain accounts and enlarges on the application of the rule of cost or market, whichever is lower.

Amplification and enlargement of the Appendix A guidelines follow.

Marketable Securities and Investments. Whether investments are short-term (classifiable as marketable securities) or long-term (classifiable as investments) does not affect the recommended translation techniques. The comments which follow assume that it is the practice of the companies to carry investments at the lower of cost or market in local currency; when market values are lower than cost, an allowance for losses is provided in local currency reducing such costs to market.

Claims. Bonds, notes, and other claims representing fixed amounts collectible at maturity, and the related allowance for losses, if any, should be translated at the closing free exchange rate. If such claims were acquired at a premium or at a discount, the unamortized balance is also monetary, according to the *FAS No. 8* description for the issuer, and hence similar treatment is recommended for the holder.

Convertible bonds payable are monetary, according to an *FAS No. 8* table included in Appendix A, and hence similar treatment is recommended for the holder.

Equity Securities. Statement of Financial Accounting Standards No. 12 (December 1975), "Accounting for Certain Marketable Securities," requires that the cost-or-market test be based on the aggregate cost and aggregate market of marketable equity securities. Equity securities, such as common stocks, if carried at cost, should be translated at the historical exchange rates. However, even when there is no allowance for losses in local currency, an allowance for losses may be required in dollars to the extent that the current market value of a security translated into dollars at the closing free exchange rate is less than the historical cost of that equity security translated at the historical exchange rate. [That is, translate for memorandum purposes the market value of each security at the closing free exchange rate and subtract any foreign income tax (that would be based on a sale at the local currency market value) translated at the closing free exchange rate; to the extent that this translated dollar amount is less than the historical dollar cost, a dollar allowance for losses may be required in the balance sheet.] If a parent or a subsidiary has a significant equity investment in another company carried at cost, it may be appropriate to evaluate the need for an allowance for losses by reference to the value of the underlying equity determined by translating all items in the balance sheet of the other company without regard to the market price at which its stock is traded locally. If an unconsolidated foreign subsidiary or a significant investment is carried at equity, *FAS No. 8* translation procedures should be applied, although some shortcuts may be taken when the equity is not significant to the investor.

Inventories (Raw Materials, Work in Process, Finished Goods). Conceptually, inventories are nonmonetary assets and should be translated at historical exchange rates. An exception would be inventories of items such as precious metals or agricultural commodities stated at market value (net realizable amount); market value by definition is a current concept, and translation should be at the closing free exchange rate.

When exchange rates weaken during the period of inventory accumulation, local currency selling prices generally tend to increase enough to recover the equivalent dollar cost of the inventory to be sold and to provide sufficient funds to purchase (or manufacture) inventory replacements. This, of course, may not be true either in those cases where government price controls are in effect or in instances where local market conditions do not permit price increases.

As a practical matter, inventories may be translated at the closing free exchange rate at the end of each period when the free exchange rate is fairly stable and purchases (or manufacturing operations) are fairly consistent from month to month during the period of inventory accumulation. However, when the free exchange rate has fluctuated significantly during the period of inventory accumulation, inventories should be translated at the rates in effect during their periods of accumulation (that is, at the average free exchange rate for each month in which the inventories were deemed to have been accumulated) whether selling prices have or have not fluctuated with significant exchange rate changes.

If the inventory at the end of the period is 1,000,000 pesos, the following translation, based only on local currency control account entries and a FIFO flow assumption, usually gives a reasonable result:

Purchases	Pesos	Rate	Dollars
December	450,000	.200	$ 90,000
November	500,000	.215	107,500
October*	50,000	.230	11,500
	1,000,000		$209,000

* Total October purchases were 400,000 pesos.

If inventories are translated at historical exchange rates, even when there is no allowance for losses in local currency an allowance for losses may be required in dollars and a lower-of-cost-or-market test should be applied to the inventories *after translation* to assure that dollar equivalent inventories are not overstated. An appropriate measure of the market value of the inventories expressed in dollars is local currency selling price, less applicable selling expense, translated at the closing free exchange rate and subtract any foreign income tax (that would be based on a sale at the local currency market value) translated at the closing free exchange rate. Cost to complete will have to be estimated for raw materials and work in process. In the event this test discloses that estimated net dollar equivalent of realization at the close of an accounting period is less than gross dollar equivalent cost, a dollar allowance for losses is required in the balance sheet. An illustration of a market value test for finished goods follows:

Market value test	Pesos (credit)	Rate	Dollars (credit)
Inventory cost	10,000	1.00	10,000
Estimated:			
Selling price	(12,000)	.80	(9,600)
Selling expenses	500	.80	400
Income tax on P1,500			
profit at 40%	600	.80	480
Net realizable value	(10,900)		(8,720)
Allowance for loss	-x-		1,280

If a local currency allowance for losses has been translated, the amount thereof will usually not produce the necessary dollar adjustment. Application of the cost-or-market test will result in immediate recognition of the estimated loss that will actually occur when selling prices cannot be advanced sufficiently to offset the effect of a declining exchange rate. It should be noted that in the circumstance where a foreign subsidiary has provided a local currency allowance for losses on the total inventory (not item by item), the net local currency balance translated at a weaker free exchange rate will equal the net dollar translated amount obtained by more elaborate calculations.

When the monetary/nonmonetary translation method was used, experience with devaluation of the U.S. dollar and upward revaluation of the German mark in 1971 provided convincing evidence that in these circumstances inventory should usually be translated at the new current rate when local selling prices of the foreign component will be maintained (see Paragraph 12 of the December 20, 1971, APB Exposure Draft). However, this is prohibited by *FAS No. 8*.

Inventories (Stores or Supplies). Stores or supplies are conceptually the same as other inventories, but certain practical problems arise. Therefore, stores or supplies will be considered in three categories: major spare parts, run of mill materials and supplies, and commissary stores.

Translation at historical exchange rates is particularly important when there are valuable older items or parts that will eventually be transferred to fixed asset accounts. For exceptionally valuable individual items, dual currency records should be maintained. Other items of this type (whose turnover ratio presumably would be low) might be carried in a separate control account translated at monthly average rates as shown in Exhibit 2.

EXHIBIT 2   Separate Control Account, Translated at Monthly Average Rates

	P	Rate	$
Balance, June 30, 19X1............	1,662,049	2.50	$664,820
Purchases, July.................	203,282	4.80	42,350
	1,865,331	2.64	$707,170
Issues, July.....................	(110,289)	2.64	(41,776)
	1,755,042	2.64	$665,394
Purchases, August...............	303,971	4.80	63,327
	2,059,013	2.83	$728,721
Issues, August...................	(150,836)	2.83	(53,299)
	1,908,177	2.83	$675,422
Purchases, September............	205,958	5.00	41,192
	2,114,135	2.95	$716,614
Issues, September................	(121,263)	2.95	(41,106)
Balance, Sept. 30, 19X1..........	1,992,872	2.95	$675,508

Note: When the period-end rate (2.95) in the future approaches, say, 5% of the month-end rate (5.00), this dollar control may be abandoned and all transactions translated at the month-end rate.

Comment: This "moving average" prices issues at an average obtained after the current-month purchases have been considered, since this technique is recommended for control accounts only. There is, however, no objection to issues being priced at *beginning* of the month composite rate, if the month-end balances are relatively large in comparison with monthly issues.

Evaluation of the need for an allowance for losses is particularly difficult for such inventories and should usually be undertaken by those who will consume the supplies; under inflationary conditions the local currency costs of older items may appear very conservative, yet the historical dollar cost equivalent may be in excess of current replacement cost.

Run-of-the-mill materials and supplies should not require the maintenance of dual currency records. Items of this type (whose turnover ratio would presumably be reasonably high) might be carried in a separate control account translated at monthly average rates, using the technique illustrated in Exhibit 2.

Where a company as a matter of policy carries commissary stores for resale to employees on an essentially nonprofit basis, the closing free exchange rate should be used for translation purposes. Otherwise, a lack of profit in local currency becomes a dollar loss when the exchange rate has weakened at time of sale.

Property, Plant, and Equipment. Property, plant, and equipment should be translated into dollars at the free exchange rate at the time such assets were acquired and thereafter translated at historical exchange rates, at least in control accounts if not item by item. Depreciation should be based on the dollar equivalent of cost and should be computed using the same depreciation rates as are applied to local currency cost. The dollar equivalent of cost should be distributed over the same period as the local currency cost so that properties are fully depreciated simultaneously in both local currency and dollars. The effect of the foregoing procedures is not only to retain the historical dollar equivalent of properties and related accumulated depreciation, but also to ensure the use of such dollar amounts in the computation of dollar gain or loss resulting from the disposal of these assets.

When exchange rates fluctuate moderately during the year, a composite exchange rate may be computed for the year as a whole and retirements in subsequent years may then be translated at the single composite rate for their year of acquisition. When exchange rates fluctuate very infrequently or very moderately (for example, the dollar to pound sterling rate from 1949 to 1967), the official exchange rate or a supported rate can appropriately be used, with a new local currency fixed asset control account being opened each time a significant change in the rate is effected; subsequent retirements would be translated at the official or supported rate for their *period* of acquisition. (One set of control accounts would have served for about 18 years at £1 = $2.80 relative to the pound sterling.)

Revaluation Accounts. Some foreign countries allow companies to write up properties and compute depreciation allowances for tax purposes or price control purposes on the higher amount. The original dollar equivalent of these properties should be retained in the dollar financial statements. If a company maintains separate accounts for the revaluation write-up, accumulated depreciation on the appreciation, revaluation surplus, and depreciation charges based on the write-up, no problems will arise; such accounts are simply not translated into dollars. If separate revaluation accounts are not maintained, a composite exchange rate must be used that will yield the original dollar equivalent cost, depreciation thereon, etc.; this situation should normally be avoided because difficulties arise in recording sales and retirements from composite accounts.

Prepaid Expenses and Deferred Charges. Most prepaid expenses, such as insurance or rent, and deferred charges such as preoperating costs, are clearly nonmonetary assets which should be translated at historical exchange rates. However, each type of item included in these categories must be separately evaluated; if a prepaid or deferred amount is collectible and is expected to be collected, it is monetary and should be translated at the closing free exchange rate. In practice, the lack of materiality of prepaid and deferred amounts has frequently led to their being translated at the closing free exchange rate despite their theoretical nature. Unusual problems presented by deferred tax credits or debits are discussed below.

Deferred Tax Credits or Debits. APB Opinion No. 11 adopted the "deferred method" of interperiod income tax allocation and specifically rejected the "liability method." The basis of the deferred method is that a deferred tax credit arose because of a benefit received, or a deferred tax debit arose because of a cost incurred in advance of matching it with revenue. Therefore, either would be translatable at historical exchange rates.

However, deferred tax credits arise because there has been no cash disbursement for taxes but one is expected eventually. Whether credit balances are "deferred credits" (APB Opinion No. 11) or whether they are liabilities, if reversals of such tax differences ever take place, they will, in a company which continues to be profitable, give rise immediately to taxable income and to additional taxes payable at that time. For the purpose of translation, such credit balances should have been considered monetary liabilities and translated at the closing free exchange rate. The author's view is supported in a research study published by the Financial Executives Research Foundation in 1974, "An Appraisal of Interperiod Income Tax Allocation."

The author's view was not accepted by the FASB. *FAS No. 8* prescribes in Paragraph 50c that only "deferred taxes that relate to assets or liabilities translated at the current rate shall be translated at the current rate."

Deferred Income or Deferred Credits. These items are monetary only to the extent that their disposition is expected to result in a reduction of a monetary asset or an addition to a monetary liability, and they are in effect refundable deposits, as shown in a table in Appendix A of *FAS No. 8*. If advances from customers have to be refunded, they are monetary; if advances from customers are discharged by delivery of existing merchandise, they are nonmonetary; if advances from customers are discharged by delivery of merchandise yet to be purchased or manufactured, they are monetary (the related costs have not yet been incurred). In a given situation, it may be impracticable to trace out such advances on an order-by-order basis and a compromise position may be necessary.

When the benefits from the investment credit or similar grants are deferred, the deferral is a nonmonetary item. The grants arose through a reduction of a monetary liability (income taxes payable) or through addition to a monetary asset (cash or a receivable account) and will be disposed of by transfer to income in future periods. When it is reasonably anticipated that a portion of the deferral will be recaptured, such amount is monetary and should be translated at the current exchange rate.

As can be seen from the foregoing, many deferred income and deferred credit accounts are nonmonetary. However, each must be carefully evaluated.

Convertible Debt. An additional problem arises when debt is convertible into equity securities of the subsidiary. Conceptually, the debt should probably be a monetary item to the extent that it is expected to be paid but a nonmonetary liability to the extent that it is expected to be converted. *FAS No. 8*, Appendix A, coded this item as current rate (monetary) probably on the basis that its characteristic at issuance (debt) should remain constant until redeemed or converted.

Estimated Liabilities. Pension, severance pay, and similar types of reserves are monetary items translatable at the closing free exchange rate. A related situation arises in connection with pension liabilities because of the statement in Paragraph 18 of APB Opinion No. 8 that "if the company has a legal obligation for pension cost in excess of amounts paid or accrued, the excess should be shown in the balance sheet as both a liability and a deferred charge." This deferred charge is a valuation account, monetary and translatable at the closing free exchange rate; the "asset" is recorded only because it is considered necessary to disclose the liability on the face of the balance sheet. However, if a company has prepaid (deferred) pension cost because of advance funding, such amount is a nonmonetary asset (representing costs incurred) and should be translated at historical exchange rates.

TRANSLATION OF SPECIFIC EQUITY ACCOUNTS

FAS No. 8 has little to say about translation of the equity accounts.

Minority Interests. Although normally classified as a liability (because it is not part of the parent company shareholders' equity), the portion of equity attributable to the minority interests is really a combined equity account. After all other items in the financial statements of a foreign company have been translated into dollars, minority interests should be computed as the minority percentage of ownership of the dollar equivalent of earnings and of the dollar equivalent of net assets based on the historical cost of the subsidiary (not the parent), adjusted if necessary to comply with accounting principles generally accepted in the United States and before consolidating entries ascribing excess costs and goodwill. (This assumes no outstanding preferred stock; see next section.) It is not appropriate to translate minority interests at the current rate. There is no justification for a U.S. company to recognize a greater or lesser share of translated earnings than it is entitled to by its percentage of ownership of the company. If local currency minority interests were translated into dollars at the current rate, the U.S. company would recognize a greater equity than it is entitled to when exchange rates declined, and a smaller equity when the rates strengthened. *FAS No. 8,* Paragraph 43, supports the author's view.

Preferred Stock. Paragraph 44 of Appendix A of *FAS No. 8* now adequately deals with the translation of those preferred stocks that have many characteristics of debt.

Common Stock and Additional Paid-In Capital. The historical cost of an investment must be used to evaluate adequately results of operations in relation to funds invested. Accordingly, capital stock and additional paid-in capital should be translated at the rate prevailing when contributed by the parent company and others. If stock was purchased for U.S. dollars, the original dollar cost should be maintained; if purchased with local currency assets, the stock should be translated at the rate in effect when the stock was acquired. The foregoing assumes that the foreign subsidiary is a new operation. If a company acquires a foreign going concern, the same valuation problems arise as when a domestic going concern is acquired. Paragraph 40 deals with a pooling-of-interest and Paragraph 41 deals with a purchase transaction. Paragraph 41 does not warn that most purchases of a foreign company should be treated as a tax-free purchase, making the evaluation of individual assets acquired complex (see Paragraph 89 of APB Opinion No. 16).

Retained Earnings. Retained earnings in dollars resulting from translation represent annual earnings as translated for each of the years of accumulation, reduced by dividends paid.

Dividends Paid. Cash dividends to the parent company are normally translated at the remittance rate in effect when local currency is converted into dollars; payments to the minority interest, whether in local currency or some other currency, are translated at the same free exchange rate at the time of payment. The charge to retained earnings is grossed up for any taxes withheld, which should be translated at the free exchange rate at the time the dividends are paid.

Legal, General, and Contingency Reserves. Such reserves are usually mere appropriations of retained earnings arising from local law or custom. Frequently they are included in dollar equivalent consolidated retained earnings. However, such reserves usually constitute a restriction on the availability of retained earnings for dividend payments. The amount of such restriction can be calculated by use of the closing free exchange rate. Under generally accepted accounting principles, no exchange gain or loss arises from any translation adjustments to these reserves; there is merely a transfer between appropriated and unappropriated retained earnings. The appropriated retained earnings as translated is frequently used only to provide footnote information on dividend restrictions.

As a practical matter, the amount of local currency unappropriated retained earnings is the amount available for dividend declarations, and a memorandum translation of that amount at the closing free exchange rate provides the balance of unrestricted retained earnings (unrestricted by the reserve); any dollar equivalent retained earnings in excess of such unrestricted retained earnings could not be remitted and hence is in a measure restricted as far as dividends are concerned.

TRANSLATION OF SPECIFIC INCOME STATEMENT ACCOUNTS

Paragraph 13 of *FAS No. 8* governs the translation of revenue and expense accounts. The assumption is made that the financial statements are translated each month and that therefore (1) the beginning and ending dollar equivalent balance sheets are properly stated in accordance with the principles previously described, and (2) the average free exchange rate for the month is applicable to the translation of revenues and expenses arising in transactions occurring during the month. It is axiomatic that whenever an account is translated at historical exchange rates in the balance sheet, charges or credits to income statement accounts resulting from depreciation, amortization, or other transfer from such balance sheet accounts will also be at historical exchange rates. Otherwise a "delayed" foreign exchange gain or loss will appear in subsequent income statements and partially defeat the convention of applying historical exchange rates to certain balance sheet items. In a given situation, of course, the financial statements may be translated only quarterly, semiannually, or annually; an appropriate average free exchange rate for such period should then be applied to revenues and expenses arising in transactions occurring during that period, always remembering that ideally each such revenue or expense item would be translated at the free exchange rate on the day of the actual transaction. (For example, it may be desirable to calculate a *weighted* average free exchange rate for the period, or to apply the free exchange rate at the time of the actual transactions to specific unusual, material items.)

Sales. Sales should be translated at the average free exchange rate for the month. Transfers from nonmonetary liabilities (certain deferred income accounts) should be translated at the appropriate historical exchange rates.

Dividend Income. Cash dividends received on any local investments should be translated at the average free exchange rate for the month; income taxes on the dividends withheld at the source should be translated into dollars at the same exchange rate. The total amount of the dividend (including taxes withheld) should be shown as dividend income and the amount of the tax withheld should be classified as provision for income taxes.

Stock dividends may be reflected as revenue in local currency in accordance with requirements in some countries, but should not be translated into dollars under any circumstances. Any income taxes payable on stock dividends received should be translated at the average free exchange rate for the month and classified as provision for income taxes.

Interest Income. Translate interest income at the average free exchange rate for the month. (This is also true for transfers from an unearned finance charges account which appears in the balance sheet as a valuation account against accounts receivable and which consequently is a monetary account.) If interest income were collected in advance, the deferred interest income would be a nonmonetary liability and the transfer to interest income would be translated at the appropriate historical exchange rates.

Gain or Loss on Disposal of Properties. Any gain or loss resulting from disposals of properties should be based upon the historical dollar equivalent of cost of such assets and dollar equivalent of related accumulated depreciation, with local currency realization or net salvage value being translated into dollars at the average free exchange rate for the month in which the disposal occurs.

Gain or Loss on Disposal of Investments. If claim-type marketable securities and investments are disposed of for a local currency amount which differs from the amount shown on the books (net of allowance for losses, if any), the difference is a gain or loss to be translated at the average free exchange rate for the month. However, if the claims were receivable in another foreign currency which was devalued prior to disposal of the investments, the book value would be adjusted to the new exchange rate as of the date of disposal before computing dollar equivalent gain or loss in order to avoid mixing exchange gains and losses with gain or loss on disposal of investments.

Any gain or loss resulting from disposal of equity-type marketable securities and investments should be based upon historical dollar equivalent cost of such assets and any *dollar* provision for losses thereon, with local currency realization being translated into dollars at the average free exchange rate for the month in which the disposal occurs. It is not usual to consider any part of this gain or loss as attributable to exchange rate fluctuations (see *FAS No. 8*, Paragraph 169).

Costs and Expenses. Most current costs and expenses should be translated at the average free exchange rate for the month. Transfers from nonmonetary assets (such as beginning inventories, certain prepaid expenses and deferred charges, intangibles) should be translated at the appropriate historical exchange rates.

Depreciation, Depletion, and Amortization. Depreciation was discussed previously in regard to translation of property, plant, and equipment. The same basic principles apply to depletion of natural resources and amortization of leasehold improvements: They should be based on the U.S. dollar equivalent of cost and should be computed using the same depletion or amortization rates as are applied to local currency cost.

Provisions for Losses on Receivables and Investments. Provisions for losses on receivables and claim-type investments should be translated at the average free exchange rate for the month. Calculating provisions for losses on equity-type investments was discussed earlier in connection with the translation of marketable securities and investments—equity securities.

Provision for Income Taxes. Translate at the average free exchange rate for the month. There is a tendency to disregard whether such taxes are paid in installments during the year or after the year-end.

Provision for Deferred Income Taxes. As previously mentioned, *FAS No. 8* prescribes in Paragraph 50c that only "deferred taxes that relate to assets or liabilities translated at the current rate shall be translated at the current rate." Paragraph 50a prescribes the determination of deferred tax balances related to other assets and liabilities and determined by the gross change method—namely, at historical rates. Paragraph 50b prescribes the determination of deferred tax balances related to other assets and liabilities and determined by the net change method—namely, at the average rate of exchange for the period. Paragraphs 51 and 52 illustrate the determination by the net change method.

Exchange Gains and Losses. When the subsidiary has exchange gains or losses resulting from settled or unsettled transactions in foreign currencies (currencies other than the local currency and the dollar), such exchange gains or losses are realized according to Paragraph 8 of *FAS No. 8* and should be translated at the average free exchange rate for the month. If such realized exchange gains or losses of the subsidiary are not translated, they will effectively be shifted from the realized to the unrealized category that arises from the translation to "home" currency of the parent company.

To the consolidated entity, no exchange gain or loss on *dollar* monetary items results from fluctuations in the exchange rate between local currency and the dollar; therefore, if the subsidiary has recorded exchange gains or losses resulting from such fluctuations, the local currency amount thereof should not be translated. Foreign taxes payable (or the amount payable reduced by such fluctuations) are an element of consolidated tax expense, as admirably set out in Paragraph 18 of *FAS No. 8.*

Exchange gains and losses arising in translation because of the effects of exchange rate fluctuations between the local currency and the dollar on the local currency monetary items are unrealized. Paragraph 17 of *FAS No. 8* requires their immediate recognition in net income for the period in which the rate changes. Paragraph 20 states that the need for a provision for deferred taxes shall be determined in accordance with APB Opinion No. 23 relative to subsidiaries and APB Opinion No. 24 relative to investments in common stock accounted for by the equity method (other than subsidiaries and corporate joint ventures).

Minority Interest in Earnings. Dividends paid to outsiders holding preferred stock are a charge against consolidated net income and should be translated at the free exchange rate at time of payment. The minority (common stock) interest in earnings is the applicable percentage of the subsidiary's total dollar equivalent net income (after dollar equivalent preferred dividends have been paid to both outsiders and the parent company).

Prior Period Adjustments. A prior period adjustment would be translated in the current year at the rate in effect when it is recorded (average free exchange rate for the month). If the adjustment is reflected retroactively in prior years in accordance with APB Opinion No. 9, the effects are multiple. Assume a substantial assessment in 19X5 for income taxes applicable to 19X1 and 19X2. Income taxes payable and retained earnings at the end of each year since 19X1 will have to be adjusted; also minority interests (both the liability and the share of net income) in common stocks, if any. Income tax expense and net income for 19X1 and 19X2 will be altered.

On the theory that monetary liabilities should ideally be translated at the exchange rate to be in effect at the time they are discharged, the exchange rate in effect when the additional taxes are first assessed is objective evidence of the appropriate exchange rate and the prior period adjustments should be reflected in the prior periods in terms of such later exchange rate. This eliminates alterations to previously calculated unrealized exchange gains and losses and thereby simplifies the adjustment procedure considerably.

SPECIAL SITUATIONS

Exchange Controls. Exchange rates fluctuate in accordance with the supply of and demand for a foreign currency in a given market. Many countries, especially the so-called underdeveloped ones, have instituted exchange controls to help keep supply and demand in balance. The controls range from virtually automatic licensing procedures to outright prohibition of remittances abroad and compulsory repatriation of assets owned abroad. In between are a number of controls (e.g., multiple exchange rates) which cause unusual translation problems. At the lower extreme of control (e.g., virtually automatic licensing procedures), no significant translation problem normally arises. At the upper extreme of control (e.g., outright prohibition of all remittances abroad), it may be questionable whether any value whatsoever should be assigned to assets in or related to the country involved.

Appropriate translation procedures when exchange controls exist must be evaluated individually, based on the facts involved in each situation. Sometimes translation, as such, is not really at issue. For example, if significant foreign cash accounts are restricted as to conversion and if using these funds for local payments is impracticable, they should be shown as noncurrent assets and reduced to estimated realizable amount; alternatively, these restricted funds may be excluded from the financial statements and disclosed in the notes only. Similarly, if remittances are restricted and if receivables are not likely to be collected within one year, they should be classified as long-term receivables and shown separately, if material, and estimated losses on receivables not protected by forward exchange contracts or other hedging devices should be provided for currently to reduce the receivables to estimated realizable amount. Similar problems arise in evaluating other foreign assets under tight exchange control conditions.

Black Markets. When meaningful exchange controls exist, it is probable a black market also exists. Black market rates are established by unauthorized dealers in foreign exchange, often in violation of governmental regulations, and are almost invariably higher for purchasing a hard currency than the official or free rate for the same currency. Many of the transactions on the black market are speculative in nature. The volume of transactions at black market rates may be limited and most businesses do not normally obtain funds at these rates. Therefore, translation of unsettled accounts or financial statements of foreign subsidiaries at black market rates would normally be inappropriate. Nonetheless, one in possession of relevant economic information and aware of the political factors involved in a particular situation may obtain from black market rates a useful indication of the future free exchange rate.

Multiple Exchange Rates. Regulation of the economy of some countries is undertaken through the medium of multiple exchange rates. A country having a free rate of 10 to 1 may offer a "preference" for the importation of certain goods by allowing remittance at a favorable or preference rate of 9 to 1. Government agencies often control (hold down) the selling prices locally of the company in consideration for the "preference" offered (entitlement) on request for foreign exchange to remit to the supplier (often the parent company). On the importation of such inventory, unrealized gains and losses between fiscal years will result unless the accountant takes special precautions. As long as the inventory and the account payable to the foreign supplier of the inventory item purchased at a preference rate are in balance, no unrealized exchange gains and losses can occur. Exhibit 3 shows one method of preventing unrealized gains and losses from occurring when inventory and accounts payable balances are not exactly equal. This illustrates one translation technique required to prevent the *overstatement* of profit by $0.20 because of the treasury action of paying for importations in *advance* of sale.

The advantage of this technique is that it permits all sales and cost of sales figures to be translated at the free rate. This removes the requirement of specifically identifying the cost of those items which were purchased at a preferential rate. (Materials and supplies inventories may be handled similarly.)

Inventory Purchased at a Preference Rate. If the supplier is paid by the foreign subsidiary at a preferred rate of exchange in advance of the inventory being sold, special accounting techniques are required to prevent the erroneous overstatement of profit by rigid line-by-line translation procedures in the period of remittance to the supplier, only to be followed by an equally erroneous "paper" loss in the period when the inventory is sold. Although the unrealized exchange gain at time of payment may be blocked from income by several mechanical methods, the one illustrated in Exhibit 3 in which an account receivable (in home country currency only) is used, is the easiest to operate, does not distort internal management reports in U.S. dollars, and an account receivable balance corresponds with the entitlements to "preference" which the treasurer has available and unused. It is now prescribed by *FAS No. 8.*

This treatment is prescribed by *FAS No. 8,* Paragraph 228 and Footnote 12. The author's preference for classifying the "difference" as a deferred charge rather than an account receivable is no longer permitted.

EXHIBIT 3   Multiple Rates—Purchase of Inventory

Opening Balance Sheet	P	$	Note
Cash..................................	370	$ 5.0	A
	(60)	(.8)	C
	310	$ 4.2	
Inventory (three units of one item)......	180	2.4	B
Account receivable........................		.6	B
		(.2)	C
Total assets........................	490	$ 7.0	
Intercompany payable:			
Three units purchased...............	(180)	$(3.0)	B
Payment for one unit................	60	1.0	C
	(120)	$(2.0)	
Capital stock.........................	(370)	(5.0)	A
Total liability and capital stock........	(490)	$(7.0)	

Notes:
  A   Cash received for capital stock at 74/$—the free rate.
  B   Products imported at 60/$—the preferential rate. Liability is
      translated at the preferential rate, but the inventory is charged at
      the free rate, the dollar difference being carried as an account
      receivable. As a result, the inventory which cost $3.0 in the United
      States is carried at $2.4 in the foreign country.
  C   Payment of liability of $1 is made before inventory is sold.   Credit
      is made to deferred charges at this time.

Statement of Income	P	$
Sales—at the free rate..........................	(60)	$ (.8)
Cost of sales—at the free rate...................	60	.8
Net income................................	0	$ 0

Closing Balance Sheet		
Cash—Opening balance plus sale proceeds........	370	$ 5.0
Inventory—Opening balance less cost of sale......	120	1.6
Account receivable —(.6 − .2)....................		.4
Total assets.....................	490	$ 7.0
Intercompany payable.........................	(120)	$ (2)
Capital stock................................	(370)	(5)
Retained earnings...........................	0	0
Total liability and capital stock...............	(490)	$(7.0)

Inventory Purchased at a Penalty Rate.   Some countries tend to discourage importation of certain items by the application of a penalty rate. Thus, when the free
rate is 10 to 1, the foreign exchange board may require the payment of 11 to 1 in
connection with remittances abroad for classified luxury items. Again special
techniques are required. Unrealized exchange gain would result in this situation
from the sale locally (of the inventory item purchased at a penalty rate) in advance
of payment for the item to the foreign supplier. Entries opposite to those illus-

trated in Exhibit 3 are appropriate. There should be no hesitancy to translate the inventory item at more dollars than the original dollar cost in the United States since that is the purpose of the foreign government in discouraging such purchases. Of course, the inventory item should pass the cost-or-market test, using local selling price translated at the free rate to measure market as described previously under "Inventories (Raw Materials, Work in Process, Finished Goods)."

Fixed Assets Purchased at a Preference Rate. Large numbers may be involved in the acquisition of fixed assets at a preference rate where clearly the foreign government was encouraging the acquisition of fixed assets by offering the "preference." Unless special techniques are employed, the amount of the "preference" in the acquisition of the fixed assets may be taken into income (an unrealized gain) and the fixed assets remain translated at an unrealistically high number which will develop "heavy" translated depreciation in subsequent periods (or may even cause a translated loss). Clearly no realizable gain resulted from acquiring the plant, and the government's "preference" should be reflected in a lower translation of the original cost. An example of a technique to prevent the reporting of the unrealized exchange gain at time of payment for the fixed asset is shown in Exhibit 4.

EXHIBIT 4   Multiple Rates—Purchase of Equipment

Opening Balance Sheet	P	$	Note
Cash...........................	370	$ 5.0	A
	(180)	(2.4)	C
	190	$ 2.6	
Equipment......................	180	2.4	B
Account receivable..............		.6	B
		(.6)	C
		0	
	370	$ 5.0	
Payable to U.S. supplier.........	(180)	$(3.0)	B
	180	3.0	C
	0	0	
Capital stock..................	(370)	(5.0)	A
	(370)	$(5.0)	

Notes:
A Cash received for capital stock at 74/$—the free rate.
B Equipment purchased at preferential rate—60/$. Liability is translated at the preferential rate but the equipment is charged with the free rate, the dollar difference being carried as an account receivable. As a result, equipment costing $3.0 in the United States is carried at $2.4 in the local country.
C Payment of entire liability at preferential rate.

Profit is not made by purchasing equipment. Actually the foreign government is offering a subsidy (preference) to encourage the importation of the item. Therefore, the accountant should not be reluctant to translate the local currency used to acquire a tractor at $8,000 in the property accounts even when $10,000 was paid to the U.S. manufacturer. Conversely, if the foreign government wishes to restrict the importation of, say, automobiles, it may establish a penalty rate and the accountant should translate the excessive local currency used to acquire an automobile at $8,000 in the property accounts even when only $4,000 was paid to the

U.S. dealer. These results are understandable since current assets (used) are translated at the free (or dividend remittance) rate.

A second important advantage under this technique is that all charges to fixed assets may be translated at the free rate. Mechanization leads to such considerations being given heavy weight.

Repatriation of Export Sales Proceeds. Certain export sales by foreign companies to U.S. dollar customers (including affiliated companies) are permitted by the foreign country on the basis that a given percentage of the dollar revenue will be returned (repatriated) to the foreign country for the purpose of purchasing its foreign currency. Certain foreign countries set the sales price for the sole purpose of computing the percentage to be returned, regardless of the actual negotiated sales price by the foreign company. Certain foreign countries also regulate the exchange rate at which the U.S. dollars will be converted into local currency. In effect such regulations are a form of taxation when the rate is unfavorable, yet it is not appropriate to classify any such dollar differences ("penalties") as taxes. This will result in fewer equivalent sales dollars being reported when the fewer local currency units received are translated at the free rate than are actually collected from U.S. customers. It would be a more accurate indication of volume of sales if they were reported in the amounts collected from U.S. customers. This is especially apparent if an item is produced and sold in the United States by one of the consolidated companies and the same item is produced in a foreign country by an affiliated company and sold in the United States at the same price. This is prohibited now by Paragraph 228 of *FAS No. 8.*

Forward Exchange Contracts. There are a number of ways of hedging against foreign exchange fluctuations. If a company has sold pesos short 90 days and the peso is devalued during the 90-day period, the unrealized gain on the incomplete hedging transaction should be accrued and taken into income in the period in which the exchange rate changes (Paragraph 23 of *FAS No. 8*). Such accruals may result in timing differences in some taxing authorities. The author would have preferred to follow the policy of immediately recognizing future losses but deferring gains in excess of losses. This view was expressed by him in his comments appended to *Accounting Research Study No. 12* at page 99.

Paragraphs 24 and 27 of *FAS No. 8* require deferral of gains and losses relative to forward exchange contracts intended to hedge only identifiable foreign currency commitments.

Major Devaluation. A deteriorating value of a foreign currency is no proof of a deteriorating value of investments in the foreign country involved. At the end of 1960, the Brazilian cruzeiro's free exchange rate was approximately Cr200 = $1. By the end of 1965 it had deteriorated to approximately Cr2,200 = $1. It is not required that land bought for $100,000 (Cr20,000,000) in 1960 be translated at $9,091 in 1965. Of course, continued translation at $100,000 would be questionable unless the market value of the land had increased to Cr220,000,000.

On the other hand, in countries which maintain a constant rate for some 20 years or more and in which the local economy is not "inflation"-conscious, a sudden devaluation may well have occurred in circumstances where the recuperative power of nonmonetary assets is slight; extreme care should be exercised in applying the historical exchange rate to fixed assets in this situation, as required by Paragraph 12 of *FAS No. 8.* While Paragraphs 14 and 46 give ample warning on overstatement of inventory and application of a cost-or-market, whichever is lower, test in dollars, no mention is made of fixed assets—an area not well defined in authoritative pronouncements. APB Statement No. 4, Paragraph 183, at M-5C, deals with the matter, but APB Statements are advisory and do not establish requirements. Only Footnote 18 to Paragraph 46 refers to "an asset other than inventory" and therefore sounds a very obscure warning that on occasion the translation of fixed assets at historical exchange rates may result in cost of sales expressed in dollars in excess of estimated future revenue in dollars.

MINIMIZING FOREIGN EXCHANGE LOSSES

Minimizing losses from unfavorable fluctuations in exchange rates or from periodic devaluations of foreign currencies is one of the chief treasury functions of any company holding assets in the form of foreign currency or realizable in foreign currency. Effective protection against such losses is a matter of constant surveillance of economic conditions in each country in which such assets are held, anticipating developments, and using the available means of protection as soon as it appears that the danger of loss outweighs the cost of such protection.

The Problem.   The risk of foreign exchange loss is run not only by companies with bases of operations abroad, but also by any company with a receivable or payable to be collected or paid in a foreign currency. Foreign exchange problems vary from company to company, but all the companies presumably have the same objective: to maximize net income expressed in U.S. dollars. To meet this objective a decision must be made whether to hedge net assets held against a potential loss from foreign currency exchange fluctuations, and, if so, what means should be used to hedge against such a potential loss.

The "exposure" of the trader is limited to his foreign currency receivable or payable; the exposure of the company operating abroad is far more complex and involves the classification of assets and liabilities and measuring the relationship among classes.

Early Detection of Currency Weakness.   Any company with "exposed" foreign assets to protect should establish an "early warning system" to detect the signs of currency weakness before unfavorable fluctuations in exchange rates transform local currency profits into dollar losses. Companies with the best record in protecting against foreign exchange losses are those which have head-office-trained personnel assigned on a continuing basis to the task of monitoring economic developments abroad and attempting to forecast exchange rate trends for years in advance. Measures against foreign exchange losses are cheaper and easier to take when their need is anticipated. This function may well be a primary responsibility of local management, but periodic reports to head office are recommended as a precautionary measure.

These are some of the signs of currency weakness which the surveillance system must detect and evaluate:

1. *Inflation.* Spiraling prices are the surest indicator of currency weakness. While internal inflation is not always simultaneously reflected in a weakened exchange rate and even though governments can maintain an appearance of strength in their currencies, external devaluation tends strongly in the long run to parallel internal devaluation. Inflated real estate values may have particular significance because they may mean real estate is being used as a haven for a currency in trouble.

2. *Money in circulation.* An increase in money in circulation disproportionate to the trend in gross national product is an early warning of inflation.

3. *National budget.* Recurring deficits generally precede local inflation.

4. *Rising interest rates.* Borrowing in the local currency is the chief defense against losses from foreign exchange. Rising interest rates may be the result of such defensive borrowings (for remittance abroad, or for investment in tangible assets) motivated by lack of confidence in the local currency. Eventually the interest cost may become higher than the expected loss from devaluation.

5. *Balance of trade.* Devaluation of the local currency is one remedy applied by governments to cure a decline in exports and to discourage imports.

6. *Balance of payments.* A favorable balance of trade can be more than offset by outward capital movements. If the net balance of payments continues to be unfavorable over a period of time, the government may try to stem the tide by devaluing the local currency.

7. *Foreign exchange quotations.* Rising costs of dollars for future delivery indicate that sellers of dollars have less confidence in the local currency and are commanding higher premiums for parting with their dollars. The existence of a black market for dollars points to the possibility of an official devaluation, as holders of dollars refuse to sell them at existing unrealistic official rates.

While the early warning system monitors events abroad, calculations of exposure to foreign exchange losses must be made at intervals dependent upon the volatility of the currencies concerned. The more imminent the danger of loss, the more frequently should the exposure be calculated.

The seven matters discussed in the preceding paragraphs are relevant to an appraisal of the U.S. economy. When our domestic problems outrun those of a foreign country, we tend to say that the foreign currency will strengthen in relation to the U.S. dollar rather than saying that the U.S. dollar will weaken in relation to the foreign currency.

Measuring the "Exposure." Calculating the exposure at any given date is mainly a matter of segregating the assets and liabilities on the balance sheet in such a way as to bring to light the net amount of assets that are subject to a decrease in value in the event of currency deterioration. Cash and local currency receivables are the most exposed assets. Property and plant accounts are usually considered as not exposed, on the generally accepted assumption that their value will usually rise in proportion to the devaluation of the local currency. The same theory applies to inventories to some degree, depending on whether the inventories are subject to price controls. Inventories not subject to price controls can generally be treated for this purpose in the same way as are property and plant, that is, excluded from the calculation. On the other hand, inventories subject to price control might conservatively be handled in the same way as cash for an internal management report.

The preceding comments about inventories should be kept in mind when calculating exposure. A formula for that calculation follows:

Add:

    A. Current assets (excluding prepaid expenses)

    B. Investments to be recovered in fixed amounts of local currency

    C. Long-term receivables, net of any allowances.

Subtract:

    D. Inventories not subject to price controls

    E. U.S. dollar assets included in A, B, and C and not already eliminated through D

    F. Local currency liabilities (including reserves such as pension reserves).

The algebraic sum of these items equals net assets exposed to risk of loss through exchange fluctuations. Effect should be given in these calculations to protection already obtained through forward exchange contracts.

The net assets exposed, as calculated in local currency, should then be translated into U.S. dollars at the exchange rate prevailing at both the balance sheet date and at the exchange rate forecast for any date ahead. The resulting difference between the asset values at the two dates is the loss on foreign exchange forecast for the period between the two dates unless preventive action is taken. The costs of protection against the loss should be investigated and weighed against the anticipated loss.

The calculation of exposure is illustrated in Exhibit 5. The frequency of the

EXHIBIT 5   Local Currency Net Assets Exposed to Exchange Risk at End of Period

	Local currency
1. Total current assets (including prepaid expenses)......................	510,000
2. Add: Long-term receivables, less allowances...........................	48,700
3. Investments receivable in fixed local currency amounts............	79,500
4. Total (lines 1, 2, and 3)..	638,200
5. Less: "Dollar" assets in above amounts (lines 1, 2, and 3)...............	(65,800)
6. Inventory amounts not under price control.....................	(111,200)
7. Prepaid expenses...	(30,000)
8. Total (lines 5 through 7)......................................	(207,000)
9. Assets "exposed" (line 4 minus line 8)...............................	431,200
10. Total current liabilities...	(363,100)
11. Total long-term liabilities	(92,500)
12. Total (lines 10 and 11)..	(455,600)
13. Less: "Dollar" liabilities in above amounts (lines 10 and 11)............	174,900
14. Liabilities covered (line 12 minus line 13).......................	(280,700)
15. Net assets exposed to exchange risk (line 9 minus line 14)..............	150,500

	U.S. dollars
16. Net assets exposed to exchange risk expressed in dollars at period-end exchange rate (.2000)......................................	$30,100
17. Forecast change in exchange rate by next report (present .2000 minus forecast .1500 = change)..	.0500
18. Loss forecast if no action taken (line 15 times line 17)..................	$ 7,525
19. Loss since last report..	$ 2,000

Notes:

1. Local management should insert in the space at the foot of this exhibit their forecast and comments on the degree of confidence in the local currency and the treasury actions planned for the ensuing quarter (or year), if required, and amounts hedged, if any.

2. Intercompany receivables and payables should be excluded entirely from the foregoing calculation.

3. Effect should be given to protection already obtained through forward exchange contracts. Also, it may be advisable to adjust line 15 to reflect any anticipated change in the net monetary position before the exchange rate changes.

4. The estimated foreign tax benefit of additional local currency accruals in the future for settlement of dollar payables or the estimated taxes payable on gains from forward exchange contracts should be described.

Intercompany Accounts. It is important to note that intercompany receivables and payables should be excluded entirely for the exposure calculation. If a French subsidiary owes dollars to its U.S. parent, there is no exposure; there can be no exchange gain or loss on dollars in dollar financial statements. Carrying this situation one step forward: If a French subsidiary owes francs to its U.S. parent, there is also no exposure; a net gain or loss cannot arise when a company owes itself money, and consolidated statements presuppose the existence of a single reporting entity; furthermore, the U.S. parent is "long" the same number of francs that the French subsidiary is "short," which is a perfect hedge.

However, more should not be read into the preceding paragraph than is stated therein. The fact that a consolidated loss cannot result from intercompany accounts does not mean that protection from losses is not available from, for example, prompt payment by a foreign subsidiary of its dollar obligations. Although dollar payables do not reduce the exposure to losses on local currency assets, conversion of local currency assets into dollars does reduce exposure. In other words, payment of dollar obligations decreases local currency assets exposed and a reduction in net local currency exposed assets reduces risk.

The tax consequences in the different taxing authorities are another consideration in structuring the exposure to a change in the exchange rate. If a French subsidiary owes dollars rather than francs to its U.S. parent and the French franc weakens in relation to the U.S. dollar, the French subsidiary will have to charge income for the additional francs and a timing difference will arise until the account is settled. The tax consequence is in the French income tax in this case and will give rise to a tax benefit.

The foregoing comments about subsidiaries and intercompany accounts also apply to branches and intracompany accounts.

preparation of this report is dependent upon the stability of the local currency in relation to the U.S. dollar.

Means of Protection.   The means of minimizing foreign exchange losses when a foreign currency weakens and the guidelines to be followed when there is an exposure to such loss are enumerated below. Of course, not all of them are applicable or possible to follow in every case (when the foreign currency is expected to strengthen, an opposite course is usually indicated). The feasibility, cost, tax effects, and resulting benefits of each must be considered.

1. Convert local currency receivables into cash to the maximum extent through intensive collection efforts, reduction of credits terms, offering more generous discounts for prompt payment, and discounting the receivables through financial institutions.

2. Make maximum remittances abroad in the form of provisional dividends. Unremitted earnings increase net assets exposed.

3. Invoice export sales to harder currency countries in the currency of the buyer.

4. Pay U.S. dollar obligations to suppliers (including parent company or head office) promptly.

5. Maximize local payables through insistence on more generous credit terms from suppliers. Delay tax payments wherever possible.

6. Reduce the parent company or head office investment of hard currency and borrow locally for all purposes. The reasonableness of local interest rates (and their income tax effect) should be examined in the light of their relationship to the inflation or devaluation factor rather than to interest rates in other countries.

7. Purchase foreign exchange forward for hard currency obligations such as dividends, technical service fees, etc., that are known in advance.

8. Accumulate inventories (of types not subject to price controls). Arrange for payment in local currency, if possible; if not possible, purchase the hard currency forward.

9. Use currency or credit swaps in those instances where local financing cannot be arranged. (If hard currency financing cannot be avoided, it should be made in the form of loans rather than equity investment. Monetary authorities are more likely to provide hard currency for repaying a loan than for repatriating an equity investment.)

10. Convert local currency and remit in the form of hard currency as loans, advances on profits or royalties, deposits on purchases, etc., to the maximum extent possible. (Local tax effect might partially offset the protection from exchange loss.)

11. Invest unremittable funds in assets which are most likely to rise in value as the value of money deteriorates.

When a foreign currency tends to strengthen in relation to the U.S. dollar, the problem of a foreign exchange "loss" that results from the strict application of the *FAS No. 8* method in a net monetary liability financial position situation is frequently not one that warrants all the 11 steps enumerated above. In some situations this reported "loss" does not accord with the economic outlook as discussed previously under "Broad Principles of Translation of Foreign Financial Statements, View of Author."

Accounting conventions determine the amount reported as foreign exchange gain or loss in financial statements, and it is possible to arrange forward contracts with a view to minimizing "reported" foreign exchange losses. On the other hand, the author believes that some *FAS No. 8* "reported" losses should have been permitted to be deferred, and in these situations an expense incurred for forward exchange contracts to eliminate a "reported" exchange loss is not justifiable in view of the "expected future economic effects of a rate change"—for example, when the German mark strengthened in relation to the U.S. dollar in 1971–1973 and the subsidiary's product was manufactured primarily from materials of German origin and sold in the German marketplace.

FAS No. 8 has established rigid translation procedures to be applied uniformly in all situations. The accountant can compensate somewhat by analyzing cause and effect in a particular company circumstance and disclosing in textual explanations the resulting variations between periods which appear to be exaggerated. This analysis and quantification is required, if practicable, by Paragraph 33 of *FAS No. 8*.

DISCLOSURE REQUIREMENTS

Paragraphs 32–34 of *FAS No. 8* contain reasonable disclosure requirements and supersede *FAS No. 1*, which was complex by reason of alternative practices being acceptable in 1973 and 1974. Paragraph 107 of Appendix D of *FAS No. 8* indicates that the Board believes it may be difficult or impossible to disclose the effect of rate changes on sales and earnings because it may be difficult or impossible to quantify the economic effects of rate changes (for example, on selling prices, sales volume, and cost structures). The SEC adopted amendments to Guide 22 (Securities Act of 1933) and adopted Guide 1 (Securities Exchange Act of 1934) in 1974. These are identical Guides which require that all filings under the 1933 Act and filing on Forms 10 and 10-K under the 1934 Act must contain a section entitled "Management's Discussion and Analysis of the Summary of Earnings (or Summary of Operations)." The purpose of this section is to provide investors with management's analysis of the financial data in order to better enable the investors to compare periodic results of operations and to assess the source and probability of recurrence of earnings (losses). While there are authoritative pronouncements relative to "consistency" of accounting principles applied, Guide 22 and Guide 1 are the only pronouncements dealing with the broad subject of "comparability." Notwithstanding the FASB's comment in Appendix D, Paragraph 107, that it may be impossible to quantify the economic effects of rate changes, and Paragraph 224, that the disclosures urged by Paragraph 33 are not forecasts, the author believes that Paragraph 33 does in fact require forecasting such matters for the purpose of valuing assets in a closing balance sheet. Where a rate change has had a material effect on carrying values and results of operations relative to financial statements of a current period when two or more periods are presented, "textual analysis" of the effect of the rate change should be made in the footnotes to the financial statements. As previously mentioned, it is the author's view that the *FAS No. 8* method without mechanics for deferral of translation adjustments will develop large exchange gains and losses, some of which are unrealistic in the circumstances in the year reported and have a contra effect on subsequent years as nonmonetary assets are charged to income. The author recommends that the estimated effect on subsequent years also be disclosed.

HOME CURRENCY DEVALUATIONS

FAS No. 8 does not admit to special circumstances in the event of a home currency devaluation. A home currency devaluation should give rise to an increased translated amount for nonmonetary assets and a direct debit and credit to the parent company's investment and appraisal surplus accounts, respectively, to prevent an erosion of home currency (U.S. dollar) investment abroad. This possibility was analyzed at Paragraphs 74–78 of Part II, Chapter 4, of the FASB Discussion Memorandum, and the author's view was briefly set forth. *FAS No. 8*, the Standard itself, does not mention this situation, and the author remains hopeful that, given a recurrence of 1971–1973, the FASB will consider appropriate steps to prevent the reporting as income abroad of those amounts required to maintain capacity overseas. Perhaps familiarity with price-level accounting will tend to liberalize thought in this whole area.

TRANSLATION FOR TAX PURPOSES

The foregoing discussion applies to translation for financial statement purposes. The receipt of income from foreign branches, affiliates, and subsidiaries and the payment of foreign income taxes thereon raises numerous questions as to the proper method of translation into U.S. dollars. Basically, translation starts all over again from the local currency records for tax purposes. The brief comments that follow do no more than sketch the basic procedures under frequently encountered situations.

Direct Tax Credit. The general rule is that a cash basis taxpayer takes a credit for foreign taxes when paid and translates the taxes into dollars at the rate in effect at date of payment (see Revenue Ruling 73-491). This may well be at a rate different from that at which the taxable income is translated, because the foreign tax may be paid in a subsequent year. An accrual basis taxpayer, or a cash basis taxpayer who elects the accrual method of computing the foreign tax credit, credits foreign taxes for the year at the exchange rates prevailing when the tax installments were paid and unpaid installments at the year-end rate (see Revenue Rulings 73-491 and 73-506). A notification is required when such installments are paid and an adjustment is necessary. In the case of investment income, such as dividends, interest, and royalties, foreign income and the related foreign withholding tax should be translated at the same exchange rates, generally the rate in effect at the time of payment for both cash and accrual basis taxpayers. The general rule is subject to many exceptions.

Branch Profits and Taxes. Two methods are described in Revenue Rulings under the Internal Revenue Code for the translation of foreign branch assets and earnings into dollars. Revenue Rulings 75-105 through 107 clarified the application of these methods.

Net Worth Method. The net worth or balance sheet method requires assets other than fixed assets and long-term liabilities recorded on the books in foreign currency to be translated into dollars at the rate prevailing at the close of each taxable year. Fixed assets and long-term liabilities are translated at historical rates. Any increase (or decrease) in opening and closing net worth, when added to remittances during the year translated at the rate at the time of remittance (usually the dollars received are used), is the U.S. dollar measure of net profit (or loss). This is similar to the current-noncurrent method used pre-*FAS No. 8* by some companies relative to translating financial statements of foreign subsidiaries. This method reflects so-called unrealized gains and losses in income. The translation of long-term liabilities at historical rates tends to offset fixed assets also translated at historical rates, and the unrealized gains and losses are thereby minimized.

Profit and Loss Method. The other method, the profit and loss method, applies to a foreign branch which keeps a separate set of books and renders a financial report to the home office at the end of each year. In this situation, the profits of the branch are first computed in the foreign currency, and any remittances, expressed in local currency, made to the head office are deducted therefrom. To determine the dollar amount of net profit, the remittances are to be taken in at the exchange rate prevailing at the time of remittance (the dollars received) and the remaining profit is translated at average or year-end rates. The profit and loss method of computing net income is less common than the net worth method.

Obviously, this method does not pick up unrealized gains and losses on balance sheet items, and depreciation is not translated at historical exchange rates.

Branch Foreign Taxes Accrued.   Normally, the foreign tax accrued for foreign branch earnings will be translated at the year-end rate, except where an average rate is used under the profit and loss method. This is based on the theory that the foreign tax on unremitted earnings should be evaluated at the same rate as the unremitted earnings. However, in cases where the exchange rate fluctuates between the date of accrual (year-end) and a later date of payment of the tax, the Internal Revenue Service has ruled that the exchange rate at the time of payment of the tax must be used. This adjustment after a tax return has been filed may be left until the tax return is reviewed by the Internal Revenue Service, but a notification is required earlier in accordance with Section 905(c) of the Internal Revenue Code.

Deemed Paid Credit.   The receipt of dividend income from a foreign corporation is subject to U.S. income tax, but a "deemed paid credit" is allowed against the U.S. tax for foreign income taxes paid by a foreign corporation in which the U.S. shareholder owns at least 10 percent. The comments which follow are not a full treatment of the various circumstances that require different computations of the credit for foreign income taxes paid, but are limited to a few observations as to the translation of the foreign currency amounts involved.

Under the normal foreign tax credit computation, the deemed paid foreign tax credit is computed by translating the underlying foreign income taxes, the accumulated foreign earnings, and the dividend at the rate in effect when the dividend is received. In the exceptional case where the subsidiary, in substance, keeps its books in U.S. dollars, taxes may be translated at the rate in effect at time of payment of the taxes.

Earnings and profits of the foreign subsidiary are computed in accordance with U.S. tax concepts. If the U.S. shareholder chooses, he may use the more specific rules of tax accounting provided for shareholders having Subpart F income. These provide for the computation of earnings and profits in accordance with tax accounting principles, and provide for specific tax accounting elections to be made solely for U.S. tax purposes.

Exchange Gains and Losses on Net Current Assets.   When earnings and profits are computed for the purposes of determining Subpart F income, the former "minimum distributions" provisions (ending 1975) and the related foreign tax credit, and gains on sales or exchanges of stock in controlled foreign corporations under Section 1248, Income Tax Regulations Section 1.964-1, must be used. Under these regulations, the translation of earnings and profits of a foreign affiliate reflects fluctuations in exchange rates and the exchange loss (a dollar only amount) on net current assets is allowed as a deduction. This can have the effect of substantially reducing earnings and profits of a foreign subsidiary expressed in U.S. dollars and thus increasing the effective foreign tax rate with respect to dividends received from such a corporation. However, a gain on net current assets increases earnings and profits. Under the normal foreign tax credit computations, where Subpart F is not involved, the specific tax accounting rules which can be used seem to exclude the provisions which reflect exchange fluctuations.

Translation of Foreign Taxes.   Where Subpart F income is involved, "the earnings and profits and the dividend paid therefrom which produce the fraction to be used in computing the "deemed paid" foreign tax credit under section 902 of the Code must be translated into U.S. dollars at an average rate of exchange used in computing the earnings and profits [for the year the dividend is attributed to on a LIFO basis] under Section 1.964-1 of the regulations. However, the foreign taxes used in computing the foreign tax credit must be translated into U.S. dollars at the rate of exchange prevailing at the date the dividend was paid," according to Revenue Ruling 74-230, which concludes with an illustration that is just complex enough to make the intent of the wording clear. Some have questioned the equity of this recent ruling in situations where the exchange rate used to translate foreign taxes differs from the rate used to translate earnings and profits.

REPORTS TO THE U.S. TREASURY

On February 14, 1975, Title 31, Part 128, Subpart C of the Code of Federal Regulations was amended by adding Paragraphs 128.35 and 128.36. They require that nonbanking companies and nonprofit institutions file certain forms on positions in foreign currencies with the Federal Reserve Bank of New York, acting as the fiscal agent of the Department of the Treasury. The currencies specified were those of Belgium, Canada, the Netherlands, France, Germany, Italy, Japan, Switzerland, and the United Kingdom.

Foreign Currency Form FC-3/3a. Foreign Currency Form FC 3/3a is a monthly and/or quarterly report of assets, liabilities, and forward exchange positions in specified foreign currencies of firms located in the United States.

Companies Required to Report. All nonbanking business concerns and nonprofit institutions located in the United States should report their foreign exchange positions and the positions of their U.S. branches, partnerships, and subsidiaries. Reports should be made whether such nonbanking concerns are sole proprietorships, partnerships, corporations, or U.S. branches and subsidiaries of foreign nonbanking concerns. Reports are required from those firms (1) whose position in any of the specified foreign currencies at any month end is $1 million or more for any of the broad balance sheet categories such as liquid assets, short-term trade payables and other liabilities or (2) who have forward exchange contracts to receive or deliver at some future date any of the specified foreign currencies in the gross amount of $1 million or more at any month end.

Monthly reports on Form FC-3 are due one month after the last calendar day of the month reported. Quarterly reports on Form FC-3a are due 45 days after the last day of the calendar quarter reported.

Foreign Currency Form FC-4. Foreign Currency Form FC-4 is a quarterly consolidated report of assets, liabilities, and forward exchange positions in specified currencies of foreign branches and majority-owned foreign subsidiaries and partnerships of U.S. firms.

Companies Required to Report. All U.S. nonbanking business concerns and nonprofit institutions should report the foreign exchange positions for all their foreign branches and majority-owned foreign subsidiaries and partnerships. Reports should be made whether such nonbanking concerns are sole proprietorships, partnerships, corporations, or U.S. branches and subsidiaries of foreign nonbanking concerns (having foreign branches or majority-owned foreign subsidiaries and partnerships). Reports on Form FC-4 are required if the position in specified currencies of foreign branches, subsidiaries, or partnerships of a firm is $1 million or more at the end of the calendar quarter for any of the broad balance sheet or forward exchange contract categories previously described relative to Form FC-3/3a. Reports are due 45 days after the end of the calendar quarter reported.

BIBLIOGRAPHY

Financial Accounting Standards Board: Discussion Memorandum, *Accounting for Foreign Currency Translation,* Stamford, Conn., February 21, 1974.
———: Financial Statement Model on Accounting for Foreign Currency Translation, Stamford, Conn., March 1974.

————: *Statement of Financial Accounting Standards No. 8,* October 1975, Stamford, Conn., 1975.

Lorensen, Leonard: "Reporting Foreign Operations of U.S. Companies in U.S. Dollars," *Accounting Research Study No. 12,* AICPA, New York, 1972.

National Association of Accountants: "Management Accounting Problems in Foreign Operations," *Research Report No. 36,* New York, 1960.

Teck, Alan: "Control Your Exposure to Foreign Exchange," *Harvard Business Review,* January-February 1974.

————: "Using Computers for Foreign Exchange Tax Planning," *International Tax Journal,* Fall 1975.

Watt, George C.: "Unrealized Foreign Exchange Gains Arising from Funds Borrowed in Local Currency," *NAA Bulletin,* February, 1965, pp. 3–11.

Wheeler, J. E., and W. H. Galliart: *An Appraisal of Interperiod Income Tax Allocation,* Financial Executives Research Foundation, New York, 1974.

Chapter **36**

Accounting for Corporate Income Taxes

HOMER A. BLACK
Professor and Chairman of Accounting, Florida State University

This chapter deals with the major problems involved in measuring and reporting in financial statements the effects of corporate income taxes. It gives primary attention to the effects of the federal income tax, by far the most important American tax both in impact on the corporation and in complexity. The same principles apply to accounting for state and foreign taxes on corporate income.

CORPORATE TAXABLE INCOME VERSUS PRETAX ACCOUNTING INCOME

In the early days of the American corporate income tax, a simple cash basis was used in measuring taxable income. This was significantly modified in 1918. The principle developed then, and still in effect, is stated as follows in the 1954 *U.S. Internal Revenue Code,* par. 446:

> (a) General Rule.—Taxable income shall be computed under the method of accounting on the basis of which the taxpayer regularly computes his income in keeping his books.
> (b) Exceptions.—If no method of accounting has been regularly used by the taxpayer, or if the method used does not clearly reflect income, the computation of taxable income shall be made under such method as, in the opinion of the Secretary or his delegate, does clearly reflect income.

Although the quoted rule remains in effect nominally, through the years many important differences have developed between the amounts of the periodic *taxable income* and the *pretax accounting income* reported by corporations in their financial statements.

Differences in Objectives. The objectives of *income taxation* are quite different from the objectives of measuring and reporting *accounting income. Accounting's* purpose is to provide comparable, consistent information about the financial activities of entities. The *income tax* was originally intended primarily to obtain revenue for government operations from taxpayers according to their presumed ability to pay. More recently the income tax has also been used in attempts to control the price level, to promote fuller employment, to foster some business activities (such as exploration for natural resources), to inhibit others (such as gambling), and to stimulate capital investment. Other differences between pretax accounting income and taxable income may be attributed to inadequate understanding of accounting concepts by legislators; still others, by a desire for administratively enforceable standards. Given such diverse objectives, it is only natural that the methods of measuring taxable income and pretax accounting income should differ markedly. It is essential that one clearly recognize the differences between these two concepts of income.

Permanent Differences.   Individual differences between the items used in computing taxable income and those used in measuring pretax accounting income may be either permanent differences or timing differences. *Permanent differences* occur when revenue or expense amounts which are included in pretax accounting income are never reported in computing taxable income, or when income or deductions reported in computing taxable income are never included in financial statements. One such permanent difference relates to the interest revenue on municipal securities owned by a corporation. This interest is a component of accounting income but is excluded from taxable income.

Timing Differences.   Timing differences are differences between the periods in which transactions affect taxable income and the periods in which they enter into the determination of pretax accounting income.

Timing differences result from three major causes:

1. *Tax timing of income components.*   Revenues or expenses which are included in pretax accounting income of one year enter the taxable income calculation in an earlier or later year.

2. *Exclusions from pretax accounting income.*   Some items excluded in the calculation of pretax accounting income of a given period are included in retained earnings or other equity accounts, but enter the computation of taxable income in an earlier or later year.

3. *Operating loss carry-backs and carry-forwards.*   Operating losses for tax purposes may be carried to other years to compute the income tax payable.[1]

Tax timing differences arise from either mandatory or elective provisions of the income tax laws and regulations. There are four general types of situations which result in timing differences:

1. *Revenues or gains are included in taxable income after they are included in pretax accounting income.*   These differences usually result from the taxpayer's voluntary election. EXAMPLE: Use of the sales basis for recognizing income in the financial statements and the installment sales method of computing taxable income, thus reporting taxable income only when the accounts are collected.

2. *Expenses or losses are deducted in computing taxable income later than in computing pretax accounting income.*   These differences usually result from requirements and interpretations of the tax laws. EXAMPLE: Deduction of the estimated future costs of servicing products sold under warranty in the income statement, while waiting until the period in which the liability becomes specific and assets are consumed to deduct the cost in the tax return.

3. *Revenues or gains are included in taxable income before they enter pretax accounting income.*   These differences result from requirements and interpretations of the tax laws. EXAMPLE: Rent collected in advance is reported in taxable income in the period of collection but is included in pretax accounting income later when it is earned.

---

[1]Homer A. Black, "Interperiod Allocation of Corporate Income Taxes," *Accounting Research Study No. 9*, AICPA, New York, 1966, p. 2.

4. *Expenses or losses are deducted in computing taxable income before they are deducted in determining pretax accounting income.* Some of these differences result from voluntary election; others, from tax requirements and interpretations. EXAMPLE: Reporting accelerated depreciation in the tax return but straight-line depreciation in the financial statements.

Many American corporations are subject to one or more tax timing differences in reporting income, the tax effects of which are often of major significance. These *tax effects of timing differences* are the differentials in income taxes of a period which can be attributed to reporting income determinants in the financial statements of a period other than the one in which they affect taxable income.

The Problem.   In view of the many significant differences which frequently exist between a corporation's pretax accounting income and its taxable income of the same period, accountants have had to decide how to measure the income tax expense of a period and how to report the related balance sheet accounts. In making its decision the Accounting Principles Board considered the following three major views as to how to measure the income tax reflected in the financial statements of a period:

1. It is the tax which is computed on the current year's income tax return.

2. It is the potential income tax effect of all transactions which enter the pretax accounting income calculation of the period.

3. It is the tax computed on the current year's income tax return, except in "instances in which specific nonrecurring differences between taxable income and pretax accounting income would lead to a material misstatement of income tax expense and net income."[2] In such cases, income tax expense should be computed by adjusting the amount reported on the current tax return, if the amount of the adjustment can reasonably be expected to be paid as tax or to be recovered within a relatively short time.

THE NATURE OF THE CORPORATE INCOME TAX

Kohler[3] defines a *tax* as:

> . . . a charge levied by a governmental unit against the income or wealth of a person, natural or corporate, for the common benefit of all. The term does not include specific charges made against particular persons or property for current or permanent benefits and privileges accruing only to those paying such charges, such as licenses, permits, other privileges, and special assessments.

Accountants have voiced a variety of opinions as to the *nature* of the charge for the corporate income tax which appears in the financial statements. A basic question is whether the tax is (1) a *distribution* of accounting income or (2) a *determinant* to be used in calculating accounting income.

Is Income Tax a Distribution or a Determinant of Income?   Some accountants have held that income tax is by nature a distribution rather than a determinant of corporate income. Treating it as a distribution would greatly simplify accounting, especially for differences of tax timing, because presumably the amount of the distribution would equal the tax shown on the current year's tax return.

Kohler[4] defines a *distribution* as "any payment to stockholders or owners of cash, property, or shares, including any of the various forms of dividend; in noncorporate enterprise, a *withdrawal.*"

---

[2]Accounting Principles Board, "Accounting for Income Taxes," Opinion No. 11, AICPA, New York, 1967, par. 7.

[3]Eric L. Kohler, *A Dictionary for Accountants,* 5th ed., Prentice-Hall, Inc., Englewood Cliffs, N.J., 1975, p. 466.

[4]*Ibid.,* p. 182.

Dividends are unquestionably distributions, but income taxes do not qualify as a distribution of income under the foregoing definition in the same sense that dividends do, because:

1. Taxes are paid to the government, which is neither a stockholder nor an owner of the corporation.

2. Earning of taxable income is sufficient to establish a legal obligation to pay income taxes, but a legal liability to pay a dividend results only when the board of directors formally declares one.

3. Although earning of taxable income in the current year is the legal basis for assessing income taxes, the existence of either income for the current year or accumulated retained earnings may be sufficient legal basis for declaring a dividend.

4. Income tax is computed by a formula established in advance by an outside agency, while the amount of a common stock dividend is determined internally by the judgment of the board of directors. If there is taxable income, an income tax assessment necessarily follows. However, in deciding upon a proposed dividend declaration, the board of directors must consider its legality, feasibility, and desirability. Neither feasibility nor desirability from the corporation's point of view is a consideration in assessing the year's income tax.

It is sometimes argued that income taxes are a distribution of income rather than a determinant because their amount is based on taxable income; if there is no taxable income, there is no income tax. But the formula for computing the amount of a charge should not be confused with the proper classification of the charge in the financial statements. Some types of employee compensation are based on the existence and amount of income before considering the compensation; still, any resulting compensation is an expense to be deducted in computing corporate income.

The weight of current opinion indicates that the income tax charge is not a distribution of corporate income. It is an income determinant, but the question remains: What kind of determinant is it?

Nature of Income Tax in the Income Statement.   Among those who agree that income tax is an income determinant, there are many differences of opinion as to its nature for purposes of measuring and classifying the periodic charge against income. The principal views are that it is:

1. An expense to be matched by periods with pretax accounting income as the latter accrues;

2. An expense to be deducted from pretax accounting income in the period(s) when taxable revenue and tax deductions are reported in the tax return;

3. A unique type of charge, different from expenses.

Keller[5] reasons that the intent of income tax legislation is to subject all income, with certain specified exceptions, to the tax. Differences in the timing of tax payments on the income which is not excepted result from administrative feasibility or from economic, political, or social influences. It is the *earning of income* which results in the tax charge, he concludes. The periodic accrual in the financial statements should, therefore, reflect the income tax cost associated with income earned, regardless of when the related tax liability is paid.

In recent years there has been little support for reporting the tax computed in the tax return of a period, without modification, as the income tax expense of that period. There has been more support for recognizing this as the general rule, subject to some exceptions. For example:

> . . . there should be a general presumption that the income tax cost reported for a year should be the amount shown on the tax return; the only exceptions to this premise

[5]Thomas F. Keller, *Accounting for Corporate Income Taxes,* Bureau of Business Research, The University of Michigan Press, Ann Arbor, 1961, pp. 110–111.

justifying tax allocation are those instances where specific nonrecurring or sporadic differences between taxable income and financial income can be reasonably expected to result in an increase or decrease in actual tax payments in the foreseeable future.[6]

How to measure and classify the charge for income taxes is discussed further under the later sections "Three Concepts of Interperiod Income Tax Allocation," "Justification of the Three Concepts," and "Problems in Applying Interperiod Income Tax Allocation."

BACKGROUND OF INCOME TAX ALLOCATION

Basic Definitions and Purposes. As corporate tax rates have increased, it has become more important to associate the income tax effects of material extraordinary events and similar transactions with their results in the financial statements. This need has led to *intraperiod income tax allocation,* defined in APB Opinion No. 11 as:

> The process of apportioning income tax expense applicable to a given period between income before extraordinary items and extraordinary items, and of associating the income tax effects of adjustments of prior periods (or of the opening balance of retained earnings) and direct entries to other stockholders' equity accounts with these items.

APB Opinion No. 30 also requires intraperiod tax allocation in reporting the results of discontinued operations and gains and losses from disposal of a segment of the business.

The accounting method developed to deal with material timing differences between taxable income and pretax accounting income is called *interperiod income tax allocation.* It is the process of assigning to the income tax expense of a period the total income tax effects of the income components which accrue during that period. These components may be reflected in the income tax returns of the same period or an earlier or later period; thus, the related income tax may be paid in the same period as, before, or after the income component is used in measuring pretax accounting income.

Historical Background of Income Tax Allocation. Differences between pretax accounting income and taxable income have existed to some extent since the enactment in 1909 of a federal law taxing corporate income, which required essentially that income be taxed on the cash basis. The cash basis requirement was later rescinded for taxpayers who kept accounting records, but other important differences between taxable income and pretax accounting income have arisen. The importance of these differences was accentuated by the increase of corporate income tax rates to a sustained high level in the 1930s.

Major developments which have tended to cause taxable income to differ materially from pretax accounting income have been the tax loss carry-over provisions enacted in the late 1930s; the wave of corporate bond refundings about the same time, accompanied by different methods of reporting for tax and accounting purposes; the accelerated amortization privilege granted for emergency facilities in the 1940s and early 1950s; and the more recent tax provisions designed to stimulate capital investment by businesses. The tax stimuli to investment include various elective methods for postponing taxes, such as accelerated depreciation (permitted in the Revenue Act of 1954) and the liberalized depreciation guidelines (established in 1962), as well as the investment tax credit (first enacted in 1962).

Chronology of Official Pronouncements. The following is a brief historical out-

---

[6]Price Waterhouse & Co., *Is Generally Accepted Accounting for Income Taxes Possibly Misleading Investors?* New York, 1967.

line of the major publications of the American Institute of Certified Public Accounts and the Financial Accounting Standards Board relating to accounting for income taxes.

December 1942. *Accounting Research Bulletin No. 18*, "Unamortized Discount and Redemption Premium on Bonds Refunded (Supplement)," was the first official AICPA pronouncement on interperiod income tax allocation. It recommended (1) *intra*period allocation of income tax between income and retained earnings when the issuer charged retained earnings for the unamortized discount, issue cost, and redemption premium on bonds refunded; or (2) *inter*period allocation of income tax when the issuer elected to spread the unamortized balances over the remaining life of the old bond issue.

December 1944. *ARB No. 23*, "Accounting for Income Taxes," dealt with reporting income and excess-profits taxes where (1) material items used in computing taxable income are not reflected in the income statement and (2) material items included in the income statement are not reflected in taxable income.

November 1952. *ARB No. 42*, "Emergency Facilities—Depreciation, Amortization, and Income Taxes," advocated interperiod income tax allocation where amortization of emergency facilities for income tax purposes was more rapid than depreciation for financial statement purposes.

June 1953. *ARB No. 43*, "Restatement and Revision of Accounting Research Bulletins," combined in Chapter 10(b) the existing pronouncements on accounting for income taxes, with some modification of the method of reporting the effects of tax loss carry-overs.

October 1954. *ARB No. 44*, "Declining-Balance Depreciation," stated that ordinarily deferred income taxes need not be recognized when depreciation is deducted more rapidly in the tax return than in the income statement, unless it is reasonably certain that the reduction in taxes during the earlier years is merely a deferment of income taxes until a relatively few years later.

July 1958. *ARB No. 44 (Revised)*, "Declining-Balance Depreciation," reversed the position in *ARB No. 44* and required interperiod tax allocation as the general rule when accelerated tax depreciation was used for tax purposes and straight-line depreciation for book purposes. It stated that recognition of deferred taxes is needed to obtain an equitable matching of costs and revenues and to avoid income distortion, even when the payment of taxes is deferred for a relatively long time.

1966. *Accounting Research Study No. 9*, "Interperiod Allocation of Corporate Income Taxes," by Homer A. Black, was published to provide a vehicle for exposure of income tax matters before the Accounting Principles Board issued an opinion.

December 1967. Accounting Principles Board Opinion No. 11, "Accounting for Income Taxes," concluded that:

> . . . comprehensive interperiod tax allocation is an integral part of the determination of income tax expense. Therefore, income tax expense should include the tax effects of revenue and expense transactions included in the determination of pretax accounting income.

1972. "Accounting Interpretations of APB Opinion No. 11, Accounting for Income Taxes," was issued to clarify and illustrate some of the points discussed in the Opinion.

April 1972. APB Opinion No. 23, "Accounting for Income Taxes—Special Areas," dealt with the following areas as to which Opinion No. 11 deferred modifying the practices of accounting for income taxes:

Undistributed earnings of subsidiaries

Investments in corporate joint ventures

"Bad Debt Reserves" of Savings and Loan Associations

"Policyholders' Surplus" of Stock Life Insurance Companies

April 1972. APB Opinion No. 24, "Accounting for Income Taxes—Investments in Common Stock Accounted for by the Equity Method (Other than Subsidiaries and Corporate Joint Ventures)," outlined income tax accounting procedures for stock investments of less than 50 percent.

October 1972. APB Opinion No. 25, "Accounting for Stock Issued to Employees," dealt with Accounting for Income Tax Benefits in paragraphs 16–18.

March 1973. "Accounting Interpretation of APB Opinion No. 23" dealt with Disclosure of Untaxed Undistributed Earnings of Subsidiary.

May 1973. APB Opinion No. 28, "Interim Financial Reporting," dealt with Income Tax Provisions in paragraphs 19–20.

October 1975. Financial Accounting Standards Board *Statement of Financial Accounting Standards No. 9*, "Accounting for Income Taxes—Oil and Gas Producing Companies," amended the provisions of APB Opinions No. 11 and No. 23 with respect to those companies.

INTRAPERIOD INCOME TAX ALLOCATION

Intraperiod income tax allocation (defined earlier under "Background of Income Tax Allocation") reports separately the income tax effects of (1) income before extraordinary items, (2) extraordinary items, (3) gains and losses from disposal of a segment of the business, (4) prior period adjustments, and (5) direct entries in other stockholders' equity accounts. The Accounting Principles Board concluded that taxes should be allocated within the financial statements of a period in order to obtain an appropriate relationship between income tax expense and these five classes of items.

The income tax expense associated with income before extraordinary items is computed by determining the income tax effect of the revenue and expense transactions which enter into income before extraordinary items, excluding the tax consequences of items omitted from such income. The income tax attributable to an extraordinary item, a prior period adjustment, a gain or loss on disposal of a segment, or a direct entry in another stockholders' equity account is the difference between income taxes computed with and without including the transaction which created the difference between taxable income and pretax accounting income. The total income tax charge for a period may be divided into two or more charges, or into charges and credits, whose algebraic sum is the total income tax charge for the period.

Exhibit 1 shows how intraperiod tax allocation may be applied in condensed financial statements. The normal tax rate is 22 percent of taxable income, and the surtax is 26 percent of income in excess of $25,000.

THREE BASIC CONCEPTS OF INTERPERIOD TAX ALLOCATION

Three basic methods of accounting for the tax effects of timing differences developed in accounting practice between the issuance of *ARB No. 18* in 1942 and APB Opinion No. 11 in 1967. Many variations of the basic methods were used, with the result that a given type of tax timing difference was accounted for in many different ways by different corporations.

The Principles of Three Basic Allocation Concepts. *ARS No. 9* described the three basic interperiod tax allocation methods as follows:

Liability Concept. Under the "liability" concept, a liability for a postponed tax payment is considered to arise when (1) revenue or gain is recognized in pretax accounting income before it is taxed, or (2) an expense or loss is deducted for tax

EXHIBIT 1   Intraperiod Income Tax Allocation

X COMPANY
Income Statement
Year Ended December 31, 19X1

Income before income tax and extraordinary loss		$1,000,000
Deduct income tax on above		473,500
Income before extraordinary loss		526,500*
Extraordinary loss	$600,000	
Less applicable income tax reduction	288,000	
Extraordinary loss, net of tax effect		(312,000)*
Net income		214,500*

X COMPANY
Statement of Retained Earnings
Year Ended December 31, 19X1

Retained earnings at beginning of year:		
As previously reported		$9,000,000
Add prior period adjustment	$2,000,000	
Less applicable income tax	960,000*	
Prior period adjustment, net of tax effect		1,040,000
As restated		10,040,000
Add net income for 19X1		214,500
Retained earnings at end of year		$10,254,500

*Related per share amounts must be shown on face of income statement.

purposes before it is deducted in computing pretax accounting income. This concept also holds that an asset for prepaid taxes arises when (1) revenue or gain is taxed before it is reflected in pretax accounting income, or (2) an expense or loss is deducted from pretax accounting income before it is deducted for tax purposes.

The liability concept bases the income tax expense of a period on the period's pretax accounting income, excluding permanent differences between accounting and taxable income. The difference between the current year's income tax expense and the tax shown on the current tax return is either a *liability for taxes to be paid in the future* or an *asset for prepaid taxes.* Both are computed by using the tax rate expected to obtain in the future when the timing differences reverse.

Deferred Concept. The deferred concept treats the tax effects of timing differences as postponed charges or credits to the income tax expense of the future periods when the timing differences reverse. If (1) a revenue or gain enters the tax return before it accrues for pretax accounting income purposes, or if (2) an expense or loss is deducted earlier for accounting income than for tax purposes, the related tax effect is a *deferred charge.* It is to be added to income tax expense in the future year(s) when the timing difference reverses. On the other hand, if (1) an expense or loss is deducted for tax purposes before it accrues in measuring accounting income, or if (2) a revenue or gain enters accounting income before it is taxed, the related tax reduction is a *deferred credit.* It is to be deducted from income tax expense in the future when the timing difference reverses.

The deferred tax effect is computed by using the income tax rates of the period in which the timing difference originates.

Net of Tax Concept. This approach considers taxability and tax deductibility to be factors in the valuation of individual assets and liabilities. For example, a part of a depreciable asset's value stems from the deductibility of depreciation on the asset in future income tax returns. Taking depreciation for tax purposes thus reduces the value of the asset; deduction of accelerated depreciation hastens this value decline. Financial statements should therefore include a depreciation adjustment equal to the tax effect of taking different depreciation for tax and pretax accounting income purposes.

If the timing of a revenue or expense accrual for tax purposes differs from the accrual for accounting purposes, the net of tax concept requires that the tax effect of the difference be used to adjust the particular revenue or expense item, as well as the related asset or liability. This might be done by adjusting the revenue, expense, asset, or liability account directly, showing the account at a *net of tax* amount. Alternatively, assets and liabilities may be adjusted by using contra accounts.

Illustration of the Three Basic Concepts. Four hypothetical cases are used in Exhibits 2 through 5 to show the basic procedures for measuring, classifying, and reporting the tax effects of timing differences under the three basic concepts of interperiod income tax allocation. The cases are simplified to highlight the effects of the three concepts on the financial statements. The presentations follow the logic of the concepts rather than the many variations that might be found in accounting practice.

EXHIBIT 2   Case A—Revenue Is Accrued Before Being Taxed

Gross margin of $100 on installment accounts receivable of $200 is deferred for tax purposes at the end of Year 1. All related expenses are reported in tax returns and recorded in pretax accounting income in the same year. The accounts receivable are fully collected in Year 2 with no additional cost.

Tax Returns	Year 1	Year 2
Other revenues less expenses	$1,000	$1,000
Installment sales profit		$ 100
Taxable income	$1,000	1,100
Income tax payable	480	528

Income Statements

	Liability		Deferred		Net of Tax	
	Year 1	Year 2	Year 1	Year 2	Year 1	Year 2
Other revenues less expenses	$1,000	$1,000	$1,000	$1,000	$1,000	$1,000
Installment sales profit	100		100		52	48
Income before taxes	$1,100	$1,000	$1,100	$1,000	$1,052	$1,048
Income taxes	528	480			480	528
Payable for current year			480	$ 528		
Tax benefit deferred to future years			48			
Tax benefit in prior years deferred to current year				(48)		
			528	480		
Net Income	$ 572	$ 520	$ 572	$ 520	$ 572	$ 520

Balance Sheet Items, End of Year 1

	Method		
	Liability	Deferred	Net of Tax
Assets:			
Installment accounts receivable	$200	$200	$152
Liabilities:			
Federal income taxes payable	480	480	480
Federal income taxes payable in future years	48		
Deferred Credits:			
Reduction in federal income taxes			48

SOURCE: Homer A. Black, "Interperiod Allocation of Corporate Income Taxes," *Accounting Research Study No. 9*, AICPA, New York, 1966, p. 16.

EXHIBIT 3   Case B—Expense Is Accrued Before Being Deducted For Tax Purposes

Estimated costs of fulfilling warranty contracts for products sold are recorded in the accounts at $100 in Year 1 and paid in Year 2.

Tax Returns	Year 1	Year 2
Other revenues less expenses	$1,000	$1,000
Warranty costs		100
Taxable income	$1,000	$ 900
Income tax payable	480	432

Income Statements

	Method					
	Liability		Deferred		Net of Tax	
	Year 1	Year 2	Year 1	Year 2	Year 1	Year 2
Other revenues less expenses	$1,000	$1,000	$1,000	$1,000	$1,000	$1,000
Warranty expense	100		100		52	48
Income before taxes	$ 900	$1,000	$ 900	$1,000	$ 948	$ 952
Income taxes	432	480			480	432
Payable for current year			$ 480	$ 432		
Tax benefit for future years			(48)			
Tax benefit applicable to current year deferred in prior years				48		
			$ 432	$ 480		
Net Income	$ 468	$ 520	$ 468	$ 520	$ 468	$ 520

Balance Sheet Items, End of Year 1

	Method		
	Liability	Deferred	Net of Tax
Assets:			
Prepaid income taxes of future years	$ 48		
Deferred charge, income taxes		$ 48	
Liabilities:			
Federal income taxes payable	480	480	$480
Liabilities under warranties	100	100	52

Source: *Ibid.,* p. 17.

The assumed facts in all four cases are:

1. Annual revenues exceed expenses by $1,000 for both accounting and taxable income purposes, except for (a) items recognized in different years for accounting and tax purposes and (b) income tax expense.

2. The income tax rate is 48 percent each year.

Comparison of the results of the four cases shows:

1. Net income is the same under all three methods when no changes in tax rates are anticipated and no current costs which are recorded on a net of tax basis are components of assets. For example, if depreciation on a net of tax basis is included in inventory cost, differences in periodic income are likely to result.

2. Income before taxes is the same under the liability and deferred methods but different under the net of tax method.

3. Income tax expense is based on pretax accounting income under the liability and deferred methods. Income tax expense equals the income tax payable for the year under the net of tax method.

4. In the illustration, the tax effect is labeled differently in both the income statement and the balance sheet for all methods. However, in statement presenta-

EXHIBIT 4   Case C—Revenue Is Taxed Before Being Accrued

Rent of $100 is collected in Year 1 and earned in Year 2.

Tax Returns	*Year 1*	*Year 2*
Other revenues less expenses	$1,000	$1,000
Rent collected	100	
Taxable income	$1,100	$1,000
Income tax payable	528	480

Income Statements

	Liability		Deferred		Net of Tax	
	Year 1	*Year 2*	*Year 1*	*Year 2*	*Year 1*	*Year 2*
Other revenues less expenses	$1,000	$1,000	$1,000	$1,000	$1,000	$1,000
Rent revenue		100		100	48	52
Income before taxes	$1,000	$1,100	$1,000	$1,100	$1,048	$1,052
Income taxes	480	528			528	480
Payable for current year			$ 528	$ 480		
Tax benefit of future years			(48)			
Tax benefit applicable to current year deferred in prior years				48		
			$ 480	$ 528		
Net Income	$ 520	$ 572	$ 520	$ 572	$ 520	$ 572

Balance Sheet Items, End of Year 1

	Method		
	Liability	Deferred	Net of Tax
Assets:			
Prepaid income taxes of future years	$ 48		
Deferred charge, income taxes		$ 48	
Liabilities:			
Federal income taxes payable	528	528	$528
Rent collected in advance	100	100	52

SOURCE: *Ibid.*, p. 18.

tion deferred credits are sometimes classified as liabilities and deferred charges and prepaid taxes might be reported under a similar asset caption.

The Three Concepts Contrasted   The differences in the financial statement effects of the three basic interperiod allocation concepts are now summarized.

Effects on Income and Net Assets.   In the hypothetical cases illustrated, each year's net income is the same under all three methods. Net assets at any year's end are also the same under all methods in the illustrated cases. The income and net assets reported by the three concepts will not differ unless one or both of the following conditions exist:

1. The effective tax rate changes, or is expected to change, during the time span affected by the timing difference.

2. All or part of the tax effect of a timing difference is deferred to future periods as a factor in determining an asset's cost.

Effects on Financial Statement Presentation.   The income tax expense shown in the income statement is a single amount under the *liability concept*. It is computed by multiplying pretax accounting income (excluding permanent differences) by the relevant tax rates.

The *deferred concept* also computes income tax expense by multiplying pretax accounting income (excluding permanent differences) by the relevant rates. The rates used differ from those under the liability concept, as explained in the next section, if tax rates change. Income tax expense is composed of three elements:

1. An amount equal to the tax payable for the current year
2. The tax effect of timing differences which originate in the current year
3. Amortization of tax effects of timing differences deferred from earlier years which reverse in the current year.

Income tax expense under the *net of tax method* equals the income tax payable for the current year. It cannot necessarily be computed by multiplying pretax accounting income by specific income tax rates. The amounts of individual revenues and expenses, as well as pretax accounting income, differ from those under the other two methods by the amounts of timing differences which originate or reverse in the current year.

The tax effects of timing differences are shown as a liability for taxes payable in future years and as an asset for prepaid taxes when the *liability method* is used.

Under the *deferred method,* the balance sheet credit is sometimes classified as a

---

Exhibit 5   Case D—Expense Is Deducted for Tax Purposes Before Being Accrued

The cost of $600 for a machine with an estimated life of two years is depreciated on the straight-line basis in the accounts and the sum-of-the-years'-digits basis* in the tax returns. Depreciation is a period expense.

Tax Returns	Year 1	Year 2
Other revenues less expenses	$1,000	$1,000
Depreciation	400	200
Taxable income	$ 600	$ 800
Income tax payable	288	384

Income Statements

	Method					
	Liability		Deferred		Net of Tax	
	Year 1	Year 2	Year 1	Year 2	Year 1	Year 2
Other revenues less expenses	$1,000	$1,000	$1,000	$1,000	$1,000	$1,000
Depreciation	300	300	300	300	348	252
Income before taxes	$ 700	$ 700	$ 700	$ 700	$ 652	$ 748
Income taxes	336	336			288	384
Payable for current year			$ 288	$ 384		
Tax benefit deferred to future years			48			
Tax benefit in prior years deferred to current year				(48)		
			$ 336	$ 336		
Net Income	$ 364	$ 364	$ 364	$ 364	$ 364	$ 364

Balance Sheet Items, End of Year 1

	Method		
	Liability	Deferred	Net of Tax
Assets:			
Machinery, at cost	$600	$600	$600
Accumulated depreciation	300	300	348
Unexpired cost	$300	$300	$252
Liabilities:			
Federal income taxes payable	288	288	288
Federal income taxes payable in future years	48		
Deferred Credits:			
Reduction in federal income taxes		48	

*The sum-of-the-years'-digits basis is not applicable to assets with two-year lives; it is used only to illustrate the concepts.

Source: *Ibid.,* p. 19.

liability, a deferred credit, or in a section between liabilities and stockholders' equity. The deferred tax charge may have a caption like that of the prepaid tax resulting from the liability concept. By reference to balance sheet classifications alone, it may be difficult to determine whether the liability or the deferred concept is being used.

The *net of tax method* causes individual assets and liabilities to be less than under the liability and deferred methods (except for intercompany profit in consolidated statements). The difference is the cumulative future tax effect of timing differences. Net of tax balance sheet items may be described as "net of taxes," "less related tax effect," or "less deferred taxes." Alternatively, the tax effects of timing differences may be deducted separately from the related assets and liabilities.

Effects of Tax Rate Changes on the Three Methods.   When the tax rates applicable to tax timing differences change, or are expected to change, significant differences in the effects of the three methods may result. Such tax rate changes may result from:

1. Congressional action, or anticipated action, which will raise or lower the schedule of tax rates

2. Fluctuation of the taxable income of a company, causing a part of its income to be taxed at a higher or lower rate within the existing rate schedule.

When changes in the effective tax rates have occurred or are expected, the liability method results in different net income, net assets, and retained earnings from the other two methods. The following comparison of the methods is in terms of tax rate increases; differences of opposite sign would occur when tax rates decline.

The liability concept views the credit resulting from a postponement of taxable income as an *obligation* to be paid in the future. Accounting for the tax effect of timing differences is intended to show the total tax paid, or to be paid in the future, as a result of the income which accrues during the current period. In concept, the correct rate to use in measuring the liability on the timing difference is the *future tax rate* which will be in effect when the obligation matures. Where a different future rate can reasonably be anticipated, it is used in computing the liability on the tax timing difference. However, the best practical estimate of the future is often that the current rate will continue. This concept holds that the liability matures and is settled when the timing difference reverses, even if it is replaced by another deferred tax liability which originates then.

The *deferred concept* measures the balance sheet credit for deferred taxes at the rates in existence when the timing difference originates. This concept views the *tax avoided* in the current period as a *benefit*, to be deducted in computing tax expense of the future year when the timing difference reverses. The deferred credit's amount is not affected by tax rate changes which occur in years after the timing difference originates.

The *net of tax concept* assumes that *taxability* and *tax deductibility* are separable attributes in measuring asset and liability items affected directly by tax timing differences, and in measuring the related expenses and revenues. It holds that:[7]

> . . . The value of the asset is thus affected by the amount and time distribution of related tax payments expected over its life. In practice, however, the amortization of cost attributed to loss of tax deductibility is recorded at the rate in effect when the timing difference originates. Therefore, although in theory the method would result in the same net income as would the liability method if tax rates were predicted accurately, in practice the periodic net income is the same as that of the deferred method.

When tax rates change, or a change can be reasonably predicted, the liability method requires that the liability for future income tax be recomputed at the new

[7]Black, *op. cit.*, p. 23.

rate. The other two methods require no adjustment; the amounts originally deferred are returned to income in the periods of reversal. Under both the deferred and the net of tax methods, however, a procedure for amortizing the balance sheet accounts for timing differences must be adopted when tax rates change.

JUSTIFICATION OF THE THREE CONCEPTS

This section presents the chief arguments that have been advanced for and against each of the three concepts of interperiod tax allocation. It summarizes the position of the Accounting Principles Board with respect to the use of these concepts. All three concepts rely heavily on the matching of expenses and revenues, but they disagree as to how this matching should be accomplished and on the nature of the balance sheet accounts which result from interperiod income tax allocation.

The Liability Concept. The liability concept is based on the notion that accrual of income subject to tax in some period results in a corresponding accrual of income tax expense. The income tax expense of a period thus equals the total of income tax already paid and to be paid in the future, or tax paid less future reductions, on the period's pretax accounting income.

Moonitz summarized his position in favor of the liability concept as follows:[8]

> ... we have treated income taxes on an accrual basis, and have let the tax follow the income—if revenue subject to tax in some period is recognized in the records, the corresponding tax liability is also recognized; if expense is permitted as a tax deduction in some period, the related "benefit" is reflected in the records. ... The income tax, then, is not treated differently from the other items accounted for; instead, it has been treated consistently with them.

Liability concept proponents emphasize that the current reduction in taxes caused by timing differences is coupled with an increase in taxes in future periods. Hill, on the other hand, contends:[9]

> The so-called "liability" held to result from a current "under payment" of the period income tax does not fit the common definition of a creditor claim. This is not a matter of the degree of certainty surrounding the amount of the supposed debt. It is simply that no one owes anyone anything in the presently accepted sense of the word "liability." The amount shown under this caption represents, not what the firm *is* liable for, but what the firm *expects to be* liable for at some future time.

Price Waterhouse & Co. points to the absence of documentary evidence of a liability, stating:[10]

> Not a single source document can be unearthed to support the $930 million of excess charges against income [resulting from interperiod tax allocation]. The source documents behind income tax costs are tax returns and canceled checks. But the $930 million is over and above what these show. This is not true of the unchanging or increasing amount of accounts payable in the balance sheet. These can be backed up by an itemized list of vendor's invoices showing to whom, and when, each individual amount is payable; and, in short order, there will be canceled checks to complete the evidence.

The foregoing quotations opposing the liability concept stress the absence of a legal debtor-creditor relationship for postponed taxes, a relationship essential to the legal concept of liability. A liability recognized by interperiod tax allocation is

[8]Maurice Moonitz, "Income Taxes in Financial Statements," *The Accounting Review,* vol. 32, pp. 175–183, April 1957.
[9]Thomas M. Hill, "Some Arguments Against the Interperiod Allocation of Income Taxes," *The Accounting Review,* vol. 32, pp. 357–361, July 1957.
[10]Price Waterhouse & Co., *op. cit.,* p. 27.

clearly not a *legal* liability; but just as clearly, accounting is not limited to the narrow legal concept of a liability. Accountants recognize the need to go beyond existing legal obligations in recording liabilities. As Grady explains:[11]

> The "going concern" concept has been useful in broadening the scope of accounting beyond the limitations of liquidation value and of strictly construed legal rights and obligations. . . .
>
> . . . The case of estimated liabilities for guaranties, for collection costs, etc., comes to mind. In this area, accounting has shown a tendency to follow through on the going-concern concept, whereas the courts and the taxing authorities have usually insisted on the existence of a legally enforceable obligation before permitting recognition of the liability and the related expense. For accounting at its present stage of development, the existence of probable future outlays, arising from or related to past transactions, is sufficient in most cases to warrant the recognition of a liability; for legal purposes (including income taxation) a further condition is usually necessary; namely, the identification of a specific legal person to whom the obligation runs, and who has the right to sue for payment, if necessary.

The Deferred Method. Under the deferred concept, the income tax expense of a period is computed as the algebraic sum of:

1. A charge equal to tax payable currently
2. A credit equal to a tax addition, or a charge equal to a tax reduction, deferred to future periods
3. A charge for the amortization of additions, or a credit for the amortization of reductions, deferred from prior periods.

Hicks supports the deferred concept in the following terms:[12]

> . . . balance sheet items may properly represent amounts which have been temporarily diverted from the stream of a company's transactions and are being held for use in determining net income in a subsequent year. This is true of amounts carried forward for inventories, for fixed assets, for deferred research and development expenditures, for items of unearned income. It is also true for the balance sheet amounts, be they charges or credits, resulting from income tax allocation.
>
> . . . Nor . . . is tax allocation a process of recognizing currently a tax liability expected to be incurred, or a tax reduction expected to be achieved, in the future; instead, it is in most instances a process of deferring, to a future year or years, a current tax reduction or tax payment.

Proponents of the deferred method emphasize the matching of revenue and expense in determining periodic income; to them balance sheet accounts result mainly from the income measurement process. Under their interpretation a large group of assets represents incurred costs that have not yet been matched against revenue. The deferred charge for income tax is one of these; it need not represent a receivable from the government. Deferred credits represent benefits already received but not yet recognized in income.

In *Accounting Series Release No. 85* (1960) the Securities and Exchange Commission advanced the following arguments in support of the deferred method of accounting for the timing difference resulting from using accelerated depreciation in the tax returns. The Release stated:[13]

> . . . In a year in which costs are deducted for tax purposes in amounts greater than those used for financial statement purposes, then, unless corrected, there is a failure properly to match costs and revenues in the financial statements by the amount of the

---

[11]Paul Grady, "Inventory of Generally Accepted Accounting Principles for Business Enterprises," *Accounting Research Study No. 7*, AICPA, New York, 1965, pp. 28–30.

[12]Ernest L. Hicks, "Income Tax Allocation," *Financial Executive*, October 1963, pp. 47–49.

[13]U.S. Securities and Exchange Commission, "Statement of Administrative Policy Regarding Balance Sheet Treatment of Credit Equivalent to Reduction in Income Taxes," *Accounting Series Release No. 85*, February 1960.

tax effect of the cost differential. To correct the resultant distortion in periodic net income after taxes, it is therefore necessary to charge income in earlier years with an amount equal to the tax reduction and to return this amount to income in subsequent years when the amount charged for financial statement purposes exceeds the amount deducted for tax purposes.[3] . . .

Footnote 3: Since the deferral is made for the purpose of allocating to future periods the effect of income of the current tax reduction, it is not contemplated that the portion returned to income exactly offset the increased tax to be paid in future years. The amount of additional taxes payable in future years may vary from the reduction obtained earlier because of changes in the tax rates or because of failure to earn taxable income corresponding to the tax reduction previously taken.

In later releases (see *ASR No. 102*) and informal opinions, the SEC favored the deferred method, urging the reporting of property at cost less depreciation and not approving the net of tax approach.

Advocates of the deferred concept state that the tax benefit—the amount by which a current tax payment is reduced—must be deferred to future periods to reduce the charge to income tax expense when the timing difference reverses. The result is a novel kind of deferral. Accrual adjustments are required in periodic income measurement when the cash outlay or receipt follows the expense or revenue; deferral adjustments are needed when the cash outlay or receipt precedes the expense or revenue. Unlike other deferred items, the deferred tax is based on neither a past nor an expected future cash outlay or receipt. The deferred concept holds that a future period is benefited because of the absence of a cash payment for taxes in the current period. An amount *not paid* is thus shifted from the present to a future period in order to match expenses and revenues.

The matching which results from the deferred method is difficult to criticize if the view is accepted that the current income effects of tax timing differences are all that is to be accounted for—that future effects may be ignored. If the relationship between the current temporary tax reduction and the future tax payment is recognized, however, the deferred method does not always result in good matching. Mismatching will occur in the future periods of timing difference reversal if tax rates change. Proponents of the deferred concept argue that it is necessary to defer the current temporary tax reduction to offset the higher tax charge to income in the future when the timing difference is reversed. But if tax rates increase, the higher tax payment differs from the deferred credit intended to offset it. The income tax expense of the period of reversal bears the full effect of the rate change; the expense has no functional relationship to pretax accounting income. The effects of tax rate changes are thus spread over future years which should be unaffected by them.[14]

The deferred method is the only method recommended by the Accounting Principles Board in Opinion No. 11.

The Net of Tax Concept.   Although not an advocate of the net of tax concept, Powell gave this explanation of its rationale.[15]

. . . Tax deductibility gives value to an asset (or a service, for that matter). The fair value of an asset whose cost is not tax-deductible is less than the fair value of an otherwise identical asset whose cost is tax-deductible. Therefore, the using up of the deductibility should be recognized in matching costs and revenues for purposes of determining income. To be specific, when the same depreciation method is used for a given asset, for both book and tax-return purposes, there is appropriate matching of income taxes and revenue. When, as a result of using different methods, book depreciation is less than tax-return depreciation, allocation is necessary to charge against income, as a cost, that part

---

[14]Black, *op. cit.*, pp. 50–51.

[15]Weldon Powell, "Accounting Principles and Income-Tax Allocation," *New York Certified Public Accountant,* January 1959, pp. 27–28.

of the tax deductibility attaching to the asset, which has expired. What is the measure of the cost? The tax differential . . . the related tax deferral has balance-sheet standing because it is necessary to be considered in stating costs correctly in future periods.

A logical corollary of this proposition . . . is that the amounts equivalent to the tax differential should be carried through depreciation accounts, if a depreciable asset is affected. This makes a tax differential not a tax item at all, but simply a part of the measure of the cost of using an asset.

Explanations of the net of tax method usually emphasize that it is really a valuation method, not an income tax allocation method. The underlying assumption is that taxability and tax deductibility are factors in the valuation of assets and liabilities; in accounting practice the amount is measured by the tax effect. In evaluating the concept one must therefore (1) examine the underlying premise, that is, determine whether differences in timing involve income taxes or other expense and revenue items; and (2) determine whether the results accomplish their purpose.

Bierman and Dyckman propose a theoretical model which defines depreciation as the decline, measured ex ante, in the net present value of an asset over time. This decline is based on an analysis of two types of cash flows: the productive or cost-saving benefits, and those attributable to tax savings resulting from depreciation deductions. However, recognizing uncertainty, difficulty in tracing cash flows to specific assets, and reluctance to change the existing philosophy of depreciation, they recommend a compromise approach. The compromise results in periodic depreciation charges that differ from conventional patterns, together with a credit to a contra-asset account for the additional expense related to the more rapid deduction of depreciation for tax than for book purposes.[16]

The net of tax method probably results in acceptable matching if its nature is depreciation accounting, or other expense or revenue accounting, rather than income tax accounting, *and* if its procedure for amortizing the tax effects is systematic and rational.

On the other hand, if the net of tax method is a tax allocation method, it has two principal weaknesses:

1. It is subject to the same mismatching as the deferred method when rates change. Net income is normally the same under both methods.

2. The tax effects are scattered throughout the income statement and balance sheet as part of individual revenue, expense, asset, and liability items, possibly with improper and undisclosed offsetting. It may be difficult to determine the tax status of a company which uses this method.

Combination of Methods.   After analyzing the merits of the liability, deferred, and net of tax concepts, *ARS No. 9* recommends that a combination of methods be used. It holds that the proper accounting for income taxes should be based on the amount and timing of the cash payments for taxes which flow from the corporation to the government. If a cash payment for taxes occurs before the tax expense is deducted in computing accounting income, an asset arises. A liability results if tax expense is recognized in the accounting statements before the cash payment is made for taxes. The following four types of situations are analyzed:

1. *Revenues or Gains Taxed After Accrual.* (EXAMPLE: Installment sales method for tax but not for accounting purposes.) Income tax allocation here is a recognition of an expense and a liability. The revenue accrues currently; the related tax is payable in the future. The amount of the income tax expense and the liability is the payment expected to be made when the tax is assessed. Income tax expense on

---

[16]Harold Bierman, Jr., and Thomas R. Dyckman, "New Look at Deferred Taxes," *Financial Executive,* January 1974, p. 49.

this timing difference is charged to the period in which the revenue enters accounting income.

2. *Revenues or Gains Taxed Before Accrual.* (EXAMPLE: Rents and royalties collected before being earned.) Tax allocation here is a process of deferring and later amortizing the prepaid income tax. Although the revenue is unearned, the cash collection is taxed currently. The tax actually paid on revenue to be recognized in the future is the amount of the prepaid income taxes. It is charged to the periods when the related revenue is recognized in accounting income, without regard to later tax rate changes.

3. *Tax Deduction Before Expense Accrual.* (EXAMPLE: Accelerated depreciation for tax purposes only.) The deduction first reduces the amount of taxes paid; later the absence of a deduction increases taxes paid. This seesaw effect results in postponement of a tax payment. The accounting recommended follows that of Type 1: the accrual of an expense and a liability at estimated future effective tax rates.

4. *Expense Accrual Before Tax Deduction.* (EXAMPLE: Estimated expenses such as product warranties and pension costs, which are not tax deductible until specifically incurred.) Income tax is paid when an expense accrues for accounting purposes, but it cannot be reported as a tax deduction until the future. The result is a prepaid tax "asset." Its amount is computed by multiplying the expense or loss by the tax rate of the period in which it accrues (but is not deductible for tax purposes). The prepaid tax should be charged to income tax expense in those future periods when the expense becomes a tax deduction.

APB Opinion No. 11 Requirements. In Opinion No. 11, the Accounting Principles Board prescribed the use of the *deferred method exclusively* in interperiod income tax allocation "since it provides the most useful and practical approach to interperiod tax allocation and the presentation of income taxes in financial statements." The Board recommended use of one of the following procedures for applying the deferred method:

1. In computing their tax effects, timing differences may be considered *individually* or similar timing differences may be *grouped.* "Similar" timing differences are individual timing differences which arise from the same kinds of transactions. Thus, all timing differences related to depreciation are similar, but depreciation differences should not be combined with differences related to gross margin on installment sales.[17]

2. If similar transactions are *grouped,* the change in deferred taxes for a period for a group may be computed by either of the following two methods:

a. Under the *gross change method* the change is a combination of the amount of tax effects of timing differences which originate in the current period, measured at current rates, and the reversal of tax effects arising from timing differences which originated in prior periods, measured at the rates reflected in the accounts at the beginning of the period.

b. Under the *net change method* a single computation is made at current tax rates for the net cumulative effect of both originating and reversing differences which occur during a period, and which relate to a group of similar timing differences.

The Opinion "applies to financial statements which purport to present financial position and results of operations in conformity with generally accepted accounting principles." It does not apply to the following:

1. For businesses whose rate-making process is regulated, items which enter net income at a different time under rate-making regulations. Costs which are normally deducted currently, but are required to be deferred for rate purposes, may be deferred in the financial statements when it is clear that the costs will be recoverable out of future revenues.

[17]AICPA, "Accounting Interpretations of APB Opinion No. 11," New York, 1972, sec. 9.

2. Undistributed earnings of subsidiaries where income has been, or there is evidence that it will be, permanently invested by the subsidiaries, or where any distribution would probably be a tax-free liquidation (see later section, "Undistributed Earnings of Subsidiaries").

3. Intangible development costs in the oil and gas industry (see later section, "Oil and Gas Producing Companies").

4. "General reserves" of savings and loan associations (see later section, "Savings and Loan Associations").

5. "Policyholders' surplus" of stock life insurance companies (see later section, "Stock Life Insurance Companies").

6. Deposits in statutory reserve funds by United States steamship companies.

COMPREHENSIVE VERSUS LIMITED INTERPERIOD TAX ALLOCATION

In *ARS No. 9*, Black recommended that interperiod income tax allocation be applied comprehensively to all material timing differences between pretax accounting income and taxable income, including those which are expected to recur over relatively long periods of time. He advocated recording assets as well as liabilities which result from interperiod tax allocation.

The Accounting Principles Board, in Opinion No. 11, also favored comprehensive allocation, stating that " . . . comprehensive interperiod tax allocation is an integral part of the determination of income tax expense. Therefore, tax expense should include the tax effects of revenue and expense transactions included in the determination of pretax accounting income."

In dissenting from the majority position in APB Opinion No. 11, Biegler, Davidson, and Queenan favored determining income tax expense on the basis of partial allocation, arguing:

> . . . to the extent that comprehensive allocation deviates from accrual of income tax reasonably expected to be paid or recovered, it would result 1) in accounts carried as assets which have no demonstrable value and which are never expected to be realized, 2) in amounts carried as liabilities which are mere contingencies and 3) in corresponding charges or credits to income for contingent amounts.

Revolving Account Versus Indefinite Postponement Concept.   The advocates of *comprehensive interperiod tax allocation* trace the duration of the tax effects of a timing difference associated with each transaction from time of origin to time of reversal. This is known as the "revolving account" concept. Under this concept the reversal of the timing differences resulting from specific transactions should be accounted for, even if these differences are offset in the period of reversal by similar differences which originate in that period. The revolving account concept views the $480 tax timing difference which originated in Year 1 as maturing in Year 3, even if an equal or larger tax timing difference associated with accelerated tax depreciation originates in Year 3. The Year 3 differences are interpreted as distinguishable phases of separate timing differences, and are accounted for separately.

Under the opposing view, a timing difference which results from a given type of cause, such as accelerated tax depreciation, never reverses unless there is a decline in the cumulative amount of the timing difference, while, at the same time, the firm remains profitable. If there is no taxable income in the future, there will be no income taxes payable, no matter how large the reversal. This is known as the "indefinite postponement" concept. Under this concept the tax effect of a timing difference which results from accelerated tax depreciation is postponed indefinitely, provided total tax-deductible depreciation each year continues to equal or exceed total depreciation deducted in the income statement.

APB Opinion No. 11 explains the *partial allocation* position, which results from the interpretation that a tax timing difference may be postponed indefinitely, as follows:

> Under partial allocation the general presumption is that income tax expense of a period for financial accounting purposes should be the tax payable for the period. . . . When recurring differences between taxable income and pretax accounting income give rise to an indefinite postponement of an amount of tax payments or to continuing tax reductions, tax allocation is not required for these differences. . . . Amounts not reasonably expected to be payable to, or recoverable from, a government as taxes should not affect net income. . . . The application of tax allocation procedures to tax payments or recoveries which are postponed indefinitely involves contingencies which are at best remote and thus . . . may result in an overstatement or understatement of expenses with consequent effects on net income.

Those favoring partial tax allocation according to APB Opinion No. 11 believe that the only exceptions to the general presumption that income tax expense for a period should equal the income tax payable for the period

> . . . should be those instances in which sporadic nonrecurring differences between taxable income and pretax accounting income would lead to a material misstatement of income tax expense and net income. If such nonrecurring differences occur, income tax expense of a period for financial accounting purposes should be increased (or decreased) by income tax on differences between taxable income and pretax accounting income provided the amount of the increase (or decrease) can be reasonably expected to be paid as income tax (or recovered as a reduction of income taxes) within a relatively short period not exceeding, say, five years. An example would be an isolated installment sale of a productive facility in which the gross profit is reported for financial accounting purposes at the date of sale and for tax purposes when later collected. Thus, tax allocation is applicable only when the amounts are reasonably certain to affect the flow of resources used to pay taxes in the near future.

Advocates of the revolving account concept reason that deferred tax accruals resemble accounts payable, whose individual components turn over regularly even though the total account balance may grow. Adherents of indefinite postponement disagree, as stated in APB Opinion No. 11 (paragraph 28):

> For these other items, the turnover reflects actual, specific transactions—goods are received, liabilities are recorded and payments are subsequently made. For deferred tax accruals, on the other hand, no such transactions occur—the amounts are not owed to anyone; there is no specific date on which they become payable, if ever; and the amounts are at best vague estimates depending on future tax rates and many other uncertain factors. . . . accounting deals with actual events, and . . . those who would depart from the fact of the tax payment should show that the modification will increase the usefulness of the reports to management, investors or other users. To do this requires a demonstration that the current lower (or higher) tax payments will result in higher (or lower) cash outflows for taxes within a span of time that is of significant interest to readers of the financial statements.

Pointing out that income is earned by employing all of the entity's assets and that income tax is based on total entity income, Davidson[18] argued that efforts to link segments of the income tax with individual transactions are artificial. He maintained that there is a liability for future income taxes only if the income tax payable for some future period is increased because the tax was not paid currently. He stated that there is no liability for deferred taxes associated with accelerated tax depreciation if the tax rules for depreciation are expected to remain as liberal as

[18]Sidney Davidson, "Accelerated Depreciation and the Allocation of Income Taxes," *Accounting Review*, vol. 33, pp. 173–180, April 1958.

they are now, and if a policy of regular investment in assets subject to depreciation is maintained. He concluded:

> ... attention must be centered on the taxpaying entity, the firm as a whole. For a static or growing firm, current tax savings from this source will not adversely affect income tax charges of future years. In fact, the growing firm can look forward to an ever-increasing annual tax saving continuing year after year. Only a moribund firm with declining investment in capital assets is likely to be faced by a substantial deferred tax liability, and then only if its dying years are profitable ones.

In Opinion No. 11, the Accounting Principles Board majority rejected the partial allocation concept as stressing cash outlays, a departure from the accrual basis of accounting. Comprehensive allocation, they felt, "results in a more thorough and consistent association in the matching of revenues and expenses, one of the basic processes of income determination."

PROBLEMS IN APPLYING INTERPERIOD INCOME TAX ALLOCATION

Some of the major problems in applying interperiod income tax allocation are deciding what tax rates to use, whether future tax effects should be measured at their discounted present values, and how the accounts resulting from tax allocation should be presented in the financial statements.

Tax Rate to Be Used in Tax Allocation.   Under the deferred concept approved by APB Opinion No. 11, the tax rates of the period in which the timing difference originates are the relevant ones. In any given period the taxable income of a corporation may be subject to normal tax, surtax, and capital gains tax rates. The question thus arises as to which of these rates, or what combination of them, should be used in measuring the tax effect of a timing difference. The use of the differential rate associated with the particular timing difference is required by Opinion No. 11, which states:

> The tax effect of a timing difference should be measured by the differential between income taxes, computed with and without inclusion of the transaction creating the difference between taxable income and pretax accounting income.

The tax effects of long-term capital gains transactions should be measured by using the special rates which apply to long-term capital gains.

Discounting in Measuring Deferred Taxes.   The advantage of electing to postpone payment of taxes stems from the fact that a dollar in hand now is worth more than a dollar to be received at some future time. It follows that the present burden of a tax liability to be paid in the future is the future sum to be paid, minus discount at an appropriate rate for the waiting period. Under the liability concept of interperiod income tax allocation, some authorities hold that discount must be deducted in measuring the income tax expense and liability for postponed taxes.

In Opinion No. 10 the Accounting Principles Board stated that deferred taxes should not be accounted for on a discounted basis "pending further consideration of . . . the broader aspects of discounting as it is related to financial accounting in general." This statement was reaffirmed in Opinion No. 11. Opinion No. 21, which deals with the "broader aspects of discounting as it is related to financial accounting in general," contains a footnote which states that the Board concluded in Opinion No. 10 that deferred income taxes should not be accounted for on a discounted basis and that the conclusion of Opinion No. 10 is not modified by Opinion No. 21. The Board did not point out that in Opinion No. 10 the conclusion was tentative pending further study; in Opinion No. 21 which provided the further study and called for a general application of discounting, the Board implied that the conclusion in Opinion No. 10 was a firm and fully reasoned one.

The Board might, more appropriately, have said that under the deferred concept adopted in Opinion No. 11, discounting is properly ignored in measuring the deferral for income taxes. The amount of the deferred charge or deferred credit is the difference between the *current year's* taxes (1) including and (2) excluding the timing difference, and it is unrelated to the date of payment.

Bierman and Dyckman, in presenting a theoretical model treating the tax effects of more rapid tax-than-book depreciation as additional depreciation, use an aftertax, default-free interest rate for purposes of illustration. The result is to use the discounting process in measuring expense and the related contra-asset.[19]

Nurnberg recognizes that "unlike other liabilities, interest expense on deferred tax liabilities is an opportunity cost, not an incurred cost, hence represents a departure from generally accepted accounting principles." Nevertheless, he concludes that accounting for deferred tax liabilities on a discounted basis is more informative than not doing so, provided the interest expense related to them is disclosed separately.[20]

ACCOUNTING FOR TAX EFFECTS OF OPERATING LOSSES

The Internal Revenue Code provides that a "net operating loss" for a given year may be carried over to other years to reduce the taxable income in those years. Consequently, the total income tax for a series of years may be less than if a tax were levied for each year independently. The current carry-back period is three years and the carry-forward period, seven. An operating loss in Year 4 can therefore be carried successively, until exhausted, to Years 1, 2, 3, 5, 6, 7, 8, 9, 10, and 11, in that sequence. If the taxpayer prefers, carryforward *only* can be used: 5, 6, 7, 8, 9, 10, and 11.

Carrying back of losses to prior years for which taxes have been paid results in a refund of taxes. Loss carry-forwards have the potential of reducing tax payments in future profitable years. The deduction of a given year's losses in other tax periods results in a special kind of tax timing difference. In the periods to which the loss is applied, pretax accounting income will differ from taxable income, after deducting the operating loss carry-over.

Accounting for Tax Loss Carry-backs.   There is little disagreement as to how to account for tax loss carry-backs. Chapter 10B of *ARB No. 43* provided that the income tax refund resulting from a tax loss carry-back should be reflected in income of the loss year. APB Opinion No. 11 agrees that the tax effects of such carry-backs be included in the results of the loss year.

Accounting for Tax Loss Carry-forwards.   There are two major views of the causes of the value of loss carry-forwards and of their appropriate treatment in the income statement. Under one view the value of the loss carry-forward is created by the earnings which it offsets in the carry-forward period. The earnings of the carry-forward period should therefore benefit by the tax reduction, because they produced its value.

The opposing view is that the tax effects of an operating loss carry-forward are attributable to the year in which the loss occurred. The reduction of taxes in the later year is thus an adjustment of the previously reported net income or net loss of the loss year. According to Arthur Andersen & Co.,[21] "the inclusion in current-

[19]*Op. cit.,* pp. 44ff.
[20]Hugo Nurnberg, "Discounting Deferred Tax Liabilities," *The Accounting Review,* October 1972, p. 657.
[21]Arthur Andersen & Co., *Accounting for Income Taxes,* New York, 1961.

year income of a material tax benefit resulting from a prior-year loss will always result in 'misleading inferences'."

APB Opinion No. 11 set forth as the usual procedure that the tax benefits of loss carry-forwards not be recognized until realized, in whole or in part, in later years. These benefits would then be reported as extraordinary items in the income statement of the period of realization. As an exception to the usual procedure, the Board provided that " . . . in those rare cases in which realization of the tax benefits of loss carry*forwards* is assured beyond any reasonable doubt, the potential benefits should be associated with the periods of loss and should be recognized in the determination of results of operations for those periods."

A third method of accounting for loss carry-forward benefits would be to report them as a prior period adjustment in the year of realization.

Exhibit 6 shows how these three reporting methods affect net income in the loss year and the year of realization.

The following facts are assumed:

1. The income tax rate is 48 percent in both years.

2. An accounting net loss of $100,000 occurs in Year 1 and is carried forward and deducted in Year 2's tax return.

3. Pretax accounting income and taxable income before deducting the loss carry-forward are both $100,000 in Year 2.

Consistent with the assumption underlying income tax allocation—that the income tax should follow the income—Method A in Exhibit 6, which recognizes the loss benefit in the loss year, results in superior matching in both years.

Under the method recommended by APB Opinion No. 11 as the general rule (Method B), the benefit is included in Year 2 income when realized. Net income of Year 2 is therefore increased by the amount of the carry-forward realized, although income before extraordinary items is functionally related to operating

EXHIBIT 6   Possible Methods of Reporting Loss Carry-forward Benefits

		Tax loss benefit recognized	
			In realization year as
	In loss year (A)	Extraordinary item (B)	Prior period adjustment (C)
Year 1			
Operating loss before tax..............	($100,000)	($100,000)	($100,000)
Income tax reduction.................	48,000		
Net loss, Year 1...................	($ 52,000)	($100,000)	($100,000)
Year 2			
Operating income before tax...........	$100,000	$100,000	$100,000
Income tax expense.................	(48,000)	(48,000)	(48,000)
Income before extraordinary items......	$ 52,000	$ 52,000	$ 52,000
Extraordinary item: Reduction of Year 1 taxes........................		48,000	
Net income, Year 2................	$ 52,000	$100,000	$ 52,000
Beginning retained earnings...........			xxx,xxx
Add prior period adjustment: Reduction of Year 1 taxes...........			$ 48,000

income before tax. With respect to net income, the matching result is poor in both the loss year and the year of realization.

Under Method C, uncertainty prevented showing the benefit of the loss carry-forward as a reduction of the Year 1 net loss. When the benefit is realized in Year 2, however, it is not reflected in Year 2 income, but as an adjustment of the prior year's income. The result is better matching in the year of realization than the matching under the APB method.

Loss Carry-Forward Benefits as an Asset. The superior matching which results from using Method A, recognizing the tax loss benefit in the loss year, requires showing an asset for the tax benefit in the loss year's balance sheet. This is often a questionable procedure because the value of the loss carry-forward is subject to unusual uncertainties. Income prospects are always somewhat uncertain; this uncertainty is magnified when a corporation has operated at a loss. A business which incurs an operating loss greater than the taxable income of the three-year carry-back period cannot automatically assume that it will be profitable in future years. Profit expectations become even more dubious after a succession of loss years. New companies should not ordinarily anticipate a value for a tax loss carry-forward until they have established a dependable earnings history.

When certain stringent safeguards are met, however, it may be both appropriate and useful to report tax loss carry-forward benefits in the loss year. Hicks[22] suggested as a guide that tax benefits of carry-forward losses "be recorded in the year of loss, but only to the extent that earnings during the carry-forward period were expected, *beyond reasonable doubt in the light of the information at hand,* to be sufficient to permit realization of the benefits."

APB Opinion No. 11, which partially adopted the Hicks recommendation, states:

> Realization of the tax benefit of a loss carry*forward* would appear to be assured beyond any reasonable doubt when both of the following conditions exist: (a) the loss results from an identifiable, isolated and nonrecurring cause and the company either has been continuously profitable over a long period or has suffered occasional losses which were more than offset by taxable income in subsequent years, and (b) future taxable income is virtually certain to be large enough to offset the loss carry*forward* and will occur soon enough to provide realization during the carry*forward* period.

Examples of situations in which it may be appropriate to recognize an asset for a tax loss carry-forward benefit are:

1. A well-established company with a long history of increasing earnings, and with excellent future prospects, incurs a loss from an unprofitable venture into a new field.

2. An otherwise profitable company abandons an unprofitable product line, increasing the prospects of future profits.

3. Temporary large losses result from unusually high costs related to a strike settlement during the year, a disastrous crop failure, or temporary government restrictions on imports, exports, or production.

The asset and the income effect resulting from recognizing the loss carry-forward benefit in the loss year should, according to APB Opinion No. 11, be computed at the tax rates expected to be in effect when the tax loss benefit is realized. Any subsequent changes in tax rates should be accounted for in the period of change as an adjustment of the asset and of income tax expense.

Effects of Operating Losses on Interperiod Allocation. The effects of interperiod tax allocation must be considered when accounting for the tax benefits of operating loss carry-overs, both in the year of loss and the years to which the loss is

---

[22]Hicks, *op. cit.,* p. 50.

carried for tax purposes. Any of the following three situations may exist in combination with tax timing differences:

1. The entire loss is offset against past taxable income and the tax refund is recognized in the accounts currently.

2. A loss carry-forward remains after carrying back the loss and recognizing the refund; its probable future benefit is recognized currently.

3. Same as (2), except that the carry-forward benefit is not recognized currently.

In situations (1) and (2), the net operating loss does not change the accounting for assets and liabilities resulting from tax timing differences. Assets for carry-forward benefits are recorded because taxable income is expected during the carry-forward period.

Both interperiod tax allocation and recognition of loss carry-forward benefits depend upon the expectations of future taxable income. APB Opinion No. 11 recommends for situation (3):

> . . . In the usual case when the tax effect of a loss carry*forward* is not recognized in the loss period, adjustments of the existing net deferred tax credits may be necessary in that period or in subsequent periods. In this situation net deferred tax credits should be eliminated to the extent of the lower of (a) the tax effect of the loss carry*forward*, or (b) the amortization of the net deferred tax credits that would otherwise have occurred during the carry*forward* period. If the loss carry*forward* is realized in whole or in part in periods subsequent to the loss period, the amounts eliminated from the deferred tax credit accounts should be reinstated (at the then current tax rates) on a cumulative basis as, and to the extent that, the tax benefit of the loss carry*forward* is realized.

ACCOUNTING FOR INCOME TAXES IN SPECIAL AREAS

Undistributed Earnings of Subsidiaries. Before April 1972, accounting for interperiod tax allocation on undistributed earnings of subsidiaries was governed by Paragraph 16 of *ARB No. 51,* which provided:

1. Estimated income taxes should be provided for at the time the earnings are included in consolidated income, where it can reasonably be assumed that part or all of the undistributed earnings will be transferred to the parent in a taxable distribution.

2. It is not necessary to provide for income tax to the parent where (a) the income has been, or there is evidence that it will be, permanently invested by the subsidiary; (b) where the only likely distribution would be in the form of a tax-free liquidation; or (c) when the taxes are immaterial in amount.

Because this concept of accruing income taxes was applied inconsistently and disclosure was inadequate, APB Opinion No. 23 (April 1972) provided:

1. Including undistributed earnings of a subsidiary in the parent's pretax accounting income, either by consolidation or by the equity method, may result in (a) a timing difference, (b) a difference that may not reverse until an indefinite future period, or (c) a combination of both types of differences, depending on the parent's intent and actions.

2. It should be presumed that all undistributed earnings of a subsidiary will be transferred to the parent. Therefore, the undistributed subsidiary earnings included in consolidated or parent income should be accounted for as a *timing difference,* except to the extent that the criteria denoting indefinite reversal, stated in item 3, are met. Unless indefinite reversal is indicated, the income tax expense of the parent should include taxes that would have been withheld if the undistributed earnings had been remitted as dividends.

3. It is not necessary to provide for taxes on undistributed subsidiary earnings if sufficient evidence shows that the subsidiary has invested or will invest the undis-

tributed earnings indefinitely, or that the earnings will be remitted in a tax-free liquidation.

4. If circumstances change and it becomes apparent that the subsidiary will remit some or all of the undistributed earnings in the future but the parent has not recognized income taxes, the parent should accrue taxes attributable to the remittance as an expense of the current period. If it becomes evident that some or all of the undistributed earnings on which taxes have been accrued will not be remitted in the near future, the parent should adjust current income tax expense. Neither tax adjustment is an extraordinary item.

5. When income tax has not been accrued on undistributed subsidiary earnings, the following should be disclosed in notes to the financial statements:

a. A declaration of intent to reinvest undistributed subsidiary earnings, or a declaration that the undistributed earnings will be remitted as a tax-free liquidation, and

b. The cumulative amount of undistributed earnings on which the parent has not recognized income taxes.

The principles applicable to undistributed earnings of subsidiaries also apply to the tax effects of differences between taxable income and pretax accounting income attributable to earnings of *corporate joint ventures* that are essentially permanent, and that are accounted for on the equity basis.

Other Investments on Equity Basis. In April 1972, APB Opinion No. 24, "Accounting for Income Taxes—Investments in Common Stock Accounted for by the Equity Method (Other than Subsidiaries and Corporate Joint Ventures)," was issued. The Board concluded that the tax effects of timing differences associated with an investor's share of the earnings of investee companies are related to either (1) probable future distributions of dividends or (2) anticipated realization or disposal of the investment, and therefore are essentially *timing differences*. The Board believes that ability of an investor to exercise significant influence over an investee differs significantly from a parent's ability to control a subsidiary's investment policies, and that only *control* can justify the conclusion that undistributed earnings may be invested for indefinite periods.

The Board recommended accounting based on all facts and circumstances, as follows:

1. If evidence indicates that an investor's equity in undistributed earnings of an investee will be realized in the form of dividends, an investor should recognize income taxes attributable to the timing difference as if the equity in earnings of the investee that the investor included in income were remitted as a dividend during the period, recognizing available dividend-received deductions and foreign tax credits.

2. If evidence indicates that an investor's equity in undistributed earnings of an investee will be realized by ultimate disposition of the investment, an investor should accrue income taxes attributable to the timing difference at capital gains or other appropriate rates, recognizing all available deductions and credits.

Savings and Loan Associations. In APB Opinion No. 23, the Board concluded that a difference between taxable income and pretax accounting income attributable to a bad debt provision that is credited to a part of the general reserves and undivided profits of a savings and loan association may not reverse until indefinite future periods, or may never reverse. The association controls the events that lead to the tax consequence and must take specific action before the timing difference reverses. The following accounting treatment is recommended:

1. Associations should not provide income taxes on this difference.

2. If circumstances indicate that the association is likely to pay income taxes currently or in later years because of known or expected reductions in the bad debt reserve, income taxes on that reduction should be accrued as tax expense of the current period. The tax accrual is not an extraordinary item.

3. Notes to the financial statements should disclose:

a. The purposes for which the reserves are provided and the fact that income taxes may be payable if the reserves are used for other purposes.

b. The accumulated reserve amount for which income taxes have not been accrued.

Stock Life Insurance Companies.   The provisions of the Internal Revenue Code permit the exclusion from taxable income of a stock life insurance company of amounts determined under a formula, and the allocation of those amounts to policyholders' surplus until the surplus equals a specified maximum. The amounts excluded from taxable income and designated as policyholders' surplus are includible in taxable income of later years if the company elects (1) to distribute the policyholders' surplus to stockholders as dividends, (2) to transfer amounts from policyholders' surplus to shareholders' surplus designated for tax purposes as available for any business purpose, or (3) to take or fail to take certain other specific actions.

In APB Opinion No. 23 the Board concluded that a difference between taxable and pretax accounting income attributable to amounts designated as policyholders' surplus may not reverse until indefinite future periods, or may never reverse. The insurance company controls the events that create the tax consequences. The following accounting treatment is recommended:

1. No income taxes should be accrued on the difference between taxable and pretax accounting income attributable to amounts designated as policyholders' surplus.

2. If circumstances indicate that the insurance company is likely to pay taxes currently or later because of known or expected reductions in policyholders' surplus, income taxes on that reduction should be accrued as tax expense of the current period (not as an extraordinary item).

3. Notes to the financial statements should disclose:

a. The treatment of policyholders' surplus under the Internal Revenue Code and the fact that income taxes may be payable if the company takes certain specified actions (which are described);

b. Cumulative amount of policyholders' surplus for which income taxes have not been accrued.

Oil and Gas Producing Companies.   Intangible development costs in the oil and gas industry are often deducted in determining taxable income in the period in which the costs are incurred. Usually the costs are capitalized for financial accounting purposes and amortized over the productive life of the wells. There is a question as to whether the tax effects of the current tax deduction of these costs should be deferred and amortized over the productive life of the related wells. This and other similar types of items in the petroleum industry would be normal timing differences were it not for their interaction with percentage depletion for income tax purposes.

Some oil and gas producing companies have allocated income taxes with respect to these intangible drilling and development costs and other exploration and development costs which enter taxable income and pretax accounting income in different periods. Others have not allocated income taxes related to such costs, citing the fact that percentage depletion over the life of oil and gas properties is expected to exceed costs of that type that are capitalized and amortized in determining pretax accounting income.[23]

In *Statement of Financial Accounting Standards No. 9* (1975), the Financial Accounting Standards Board required (effective January 1, 1975) interperiod tax

---

[23]*Statement of Financial Accounting Standards No. 9,* "Accounting for Income Taxes—Oil and Gas Producing Companies," FASB, October 1975, pp. 1–2.

allocation for intangible drilling and development costs and other costs associated with exploration and development of oil and gas reserves that enter taxable income and pretax accounting income in different periods. An oil or gas producing company that had not previously allocated income taxes related to intangible drilling and development cost differences had to begin allocating taxes on the *difference* between: (1) IDC financial accounting/tax differences originating in the period and (2) the reversal of similar differences during the period.

In computing deferred income tax expense, an oil or gas producing company with an excess of estimated statutory depletion allowable as an income tax deduction in future years over the amount of cost depletion may elect to recognize interaction with percentage depletion. If this election is made, income taxes must be deferred on the amount by which originating timing differences exceed reversals during the period, except that the amount on which income taxes are deferred in that period is limited to the excess of cumulative IDC financial accounting/tax differences at the end of the period over the sum of (a) excess statutory depletion and (b) cumulative IDC financial accounting/tax differences with respect to which income taxes have been allocated.

Some companies allocated income taxes before January 1, 1975, in accordance with APB Opinion No. 11, with respect to IDC financial accounting/tax differences without recognizing interaction with percentage depletion. This will continue to be an acceptable method.

Companies that have not previously allocated income taxes, but begin to do so in accordance with *FASB Statement No. 9,* must disclose the amount of cumulative IDC financial account/tax differences at the end of the period as to which income taxes have not been allocated. Also, when it becomes probable that future reversals of IDC financial accounting/tax differences will exceed future originating differences of the same type, and that the excess income tax effect will be charged to income tax expense, the company must disclose that probability.

FINANCIAL STATEMENT REPORTING OF INTERPERIOD TAX ALLOCATION

Balance Sheet. Opinions of the Accounting Principles Board require separate balance sheet classification of the following elements:

1. Taxes estimated to be currently payable,
2. Net amount of current deferred charges and current deferred credits relating to timing differences,
3. Net amount of noncurrent deferred charges and credits relating to timing differences,
4. Refundable taxes arising from carry-backs of operating losses and investment credits,
5. Future tax benefits of carry-forwards of operating losses and similar items that have been recognized because realization is assured beyond a reasonable doubt, and
6. Deferred investment credits where the deferral method is used.[24]

Deferred charges resulting from interperiod tax allocation are not receivables under the APB interpretation, and deferred credits are not payables. The current portions are those which relate to assets and liabilities classified as current. For example, if installment accounts receivable are reported as a current asset, the deferred tax credit for the tax effects of uncollected installment receivables is a current item.

Balance sheet assets relating to loss carry-backs and carry-forwards are current

---

[24]"Accounting Interpretations of APB Opinion No. 11," *op. cit.,* sec. 21.

if realization is expected to occur during the next year or operating cycle; otherwise, they are noncurrent.

Exhibit 7 shows balance sheet excerpts reflecting how the following would appear under APB recommendations:

1. There are current installment accounts receivable of $300,000, on which there is a deferred tax credit of $72,000.

2. The current liability for estimated servicing costs under warranties is $100,-000; the related deferred charge for taxes is $48,000.

3. The deferred tax credit arising from using accelerated depreciation for tax purposes only is $144,000.

4. Rent collected in advance on a long-term lease is $100,000. The related deferred tax charge is $48,000.

5. A division was sold for $100,000 less than its book value.

EXHIBIT 7   Interperiod Tax Allocation in the Balance Sheet

X CORPORATION
Balance Sheet
December 31, Year 4

Current assets:

Installment accounts receivable.....................................	$300,000

Current liabilities:

Liability under warranties	100,000
Income tax payable (Note C)..	43,500
Net deferred credit for income taxes (current portion) (Note A)...........	24,000

Long-term liabilities:

Rent collected in advance on long-term lease..........................	100,000
Net deferred credit for income taxes (noncurrent portion) (Note B)........	96,000

Note A. The net deferred credit for income taxes (current portion) results from:

Deferred tax credit for gross profit not yet taxed on installment receivables.	$ 72,000
Less deferred tax charge for deductions not yet allowed for estimated warranty service costs...	48,000
Net deferred tax credit (current portion)	$ 24,000

Note B. The net deferred credit for income taxes (noncurrent portion) results from:

Deferred tax credit for cumulative excess of accelerated tax depreciation over straight-line depreciation per books.................................	$144,000
Less deferred tax charge for rent collected in advance...................	48,000
Net deferred tax credit (noncurrent portion).........................	$ 96,000

Note C. Income tax payable is computed as follows:

Income tax on income from operations..............................	$101,500
Add decrease in net current deferred tax credit.........................	6,000
Deduct increase in net noncurrent deferred tax credit...................	(16,000)
Income tax from operations payable currently........................	$ 91,500
Deduct tax reduction from loss on sale of plant Division X	(48,000)
Income tax currently payable.....................................	$ 43,500

Income Statement.   The Accounting Principles Board requires that the income statement disclose the following components of the period's income tax expense, with appropriate intraperiod allocation:

1. Taxes estimated to be payable,

2. Tax effects of timing differences,

3. Tax effects of investment credit, whether the deferral or the flow-through method is used, and

4. Tax effects of operating losses.[25]

[25]*Ibid.,* sec. 20.

These amounts may be presented as separate components of the income statement, or as combined amounts with the components disclosed parenthetically or in a note.

Exhibit 8 illustrates the presentation of these tax items in an income statement, reflecting the same transactions used for Exhibit 7.

When the tax benefit of an operating loss carry-forward is realized but has not been previously recognized, the tax benefit should be reported as an extraordinary item.

Tax effects of prior period adjustments and direct entries to other stockholders' equity accounts should be shown as adjustments of such items, with disclosure of the amounts of related tax effects.

EXHIBIT 8   Interperiod Tax Allocation in the Income Statement

X CORPORATION
Income Statement
For the Year Ended December 31, Year 4

Income from continuing operations before income tax		$225,000
Deduct income tax expense (Notes A, B, and C)		(101,500)
Income from continuing operations		123,500
Deduct loss on disposal of Division X	($100,000)	
Less applicable income tax reduction	48,000	(52,000)
Net income		71,500

Statement of Changes in Financial Position.   To the extent that net deferred tax charges and net deferred tax credits are current accounts, no special adjustment is needed in computing the funds (working capital) derived from operations. Changes in the net *noncurrent* deferred charges and credits for taxes must be considered, however, in computing funds (working capital) obtained from operations. The computation is as follows:

Funds (working capital) derived from operations:	
Income before extraordinary items	$123,500
Add charges not reducing working capital:	
Depreciation	100,000
Net increase in deferred tax credit (noncurrent portion; Note C)	16,000
Funds derived from operations	$239,500

The funds obtained from the sale of Division X would consist of the proceeds of sale plus the income tax reduction of $48,000 occasioned by the loss on sale of the division.

Other Disclosures.   APB Opinion No. 11 requires the following general disclosures:

   (a) Amounts of any operating loss carryforwards not recognized in the loss period, together with expiration dates (indicating separately amounts which, upon recognition, would be credited to deferred tax accounts);

   (b) Significant amounts of any other unused deductions or credits, together with expiration dates; and

   (c) Reasons for significant variations in the customary relationships between income tax expense and pretax accounting income, if they are not otherwise apparent from the financial statements or from the nature of the entity's business.

   ... the nature of significant differences between pretax accounting income and taxable income. ...

APB Opinions No. 2 and No. 4 require disclosure of the method adopted (deferral or flow-through) in accounting for investment credits and the amounts of unused carry-forwards, together with expiration dates.

SEC *Accounting Series Release No. 149* requires disclosure of items that caused deviations of income tax expense or a percentage of pretax financial statement income from the statutory tax rate and the components of timing differences. These disclosures are illustrated in Exhibit 9, a typical income tax footnote disclosure for a manufacturing company with a wholly owned nonconsolidated subsidiary.

INCOME TAXES IN INTERIM FINANCIAL STATEMENTS

APB Opinion No. 28, "Interim Financial Reporting," issued in 1973, prescribed accounting methods for computing income taxes in interim financial statements.

EXHIBIT 9   Illustrative Income Tax Footnote Disclosure Required by Accounting Series Release No. 149 for an International Manufacturing Company with a Wholly Owned but Unconsolidated Company Subsidiary

Note 5—Income tax expense for financial reporting was reduced by investment tax credits of $12.9 million in 19X1 and $9.9 million in 19X0. In addition, investment tax credit of $4.7 million has been deferred at the end of 19X1 by International Credit Company and remains to be amortized.

Income Taxes	Year ended Dec. 31, 19X1	Year ended Dec. 31, 19X0
Continuing operations:		
Currently payable:		
Federal	$45,918,000	$ 69,044,000
State	5,275,000	6,851,000
Non-U.S.	37,252,000	29,451,000
	88,445,000	105,346,000
Deferred:		
Federal	4,276,000	(39,693,000)
State	884,000	(4,175,000)
Non-U.S.	230,000	2,492,000
	5,390,000	(41,376,000)
Total income tax expense from continuing operations	93,835,000	63,970,000
Discontinued operations:		
Current payable	(48,615,000)	(37,974,000)
Deferred	38,376,000	(39,347,000)
Total income tax expense from discontinued operations	(10,239,000)	(77,321,000)
Total	$83,596,000	$(13,351,000)

Deferred tax expense results from timing differences in the recognition of revenue and expense for tax and financial statement purposes. The source of these differences for the years 19X1 and 19X0 and the tax effect of each follows:

Income Taxes Deferred	Year ended Dec. 31, 19X1	Year ended Dec. 31, 19X0
Excess of tax over book depreciation	$21,312,000	$ 26,530,000
Difference between financial and tax reporting on long-term contracts in process	13,232,000	(40,988,000)
Provisions for warranties	(29,154,000)	(26,918,000)
	5,390,000	(41,376,000)
Losses recorded in prior years on discontinued operations currently deductible for tax purposes	38,376,000	(39,347,000)
Total*	$43,766,000	$(80,723,000)

Deferred federal income taxes have not been provided on cumulative undistributed earnings of $275 million from certain subsidiaries which have been reinvested for an indefinite period.

The federal income tax returns of the Corporation and its wholly owned subsidiaries are settled through December 31, 19W5, and it is believed that adequate provisions for taxes have been made through December 31, 19X1.

The reconciliation between the federal statutory tax rate and the International effective consolidated tax rate for 19X1 and 19X0 is as follows:

Effective Consolidated Tax Rate	Year ended Dec. 31, 19X1		Year ended Dec. 31, 19X0	
	Amount	Effective rate	Amount	Effective rate
Tax expense if based on federal statutory tax rate applied to income before taxes of continuing operations	$131,957,000	48.0%	$ 98,961,000	48.0%
Increases (reductions) in taxes resulting from:				
Income of U.S. subsidiaries exempt from tax or subject to tax at reduced rates	(31,011,000)	(11.3)	(26,744,000)	(13,0)
Investment tax credit	(12,931,000)	(4.7)	(9,895,000)	(4.8)
State and local income taxes less reduction in federal income tax	3,203,000	1.1	1,392,000	.7
Miscellaneous items	2,617,000	1.0	256,000	.1
Total—continuing operations	93,835,000	34.1%	63,970,000	31.0%
Tax applicable to discontinued operations	(10,239,000)		(77,321,000)	
Income taxes (reduction)	$ 83,596,000		$(13,351,000)	

*Includes deferred taxes of $7,983,000 in 19X1 and $11,825,000 in 19X0 attributable to wholly owned subsidiaries reported under the equity method of accounting.

U.S. subsidiaries exempt from tax are U.S. prossessions companies, and subsidiaries subject to reduced income tax rates include a Domestic International Sales Corporation (DISC) and a Western Hemisphere Trade Corporation.

The Board recommended that at the end of each interim period the company make its best estimate of the effective tax rate expected to apply to the full fiscal year, and use that rate in providing for income taxes on a current year-to-date basis.

The effective tax rate should consider anticipated investment tax credits, foreign tax rates, percentage depletion, capital gains rates, and other available tax planning alternatives. No effect should be included for the tax related to significant unusual or extraordinary items that will be reported net of their tax effect.

The tax effects of losses that occur in the early part of a fiscal year (if carry-back is not possible) should be recognized only when realization is assured beyond a reasonable doubt. Existence of an established seasonal pattern of losses in early interim periods, offset by income in later interim periods, should constitute evidence that realization is assured beyond reasonable doubt, unless other evidence indicates that the seasonal pattern will not prevail.

In later interim periods the tax effects of losses incurred in early interim periods may be recognized if their realization (although at first uncertain) has become assured beyond a reasonable doubt. When tax effects of losses of early parts of a fiscal year are not recognized in that interim period, no provision for taxes should be made for income that accrues in later interim periods until the tax effects of the previous interim losses are utilized.

Publicly traded companies which report summarized financial information at interim dates must report, significant changes in estimates or provisions for income taxes.

THE INVESTMENT TAX CREDIT

General Provisions. In 1962 Congress enacted an investment tax credit for the purpose of stimulating capital investment and economic growth. The credit, which was used to reduce the income tax payable for a year, equaled a specified percentage of the cost of certain types of depreciable assets which were acquired and placed in service after 1961. The amount of the credit was subject to certain statutory limitations. Parts of the credit not utilized in one year could be carried over to the tax returns of other years. Under certain conditions, an investment credit that was allowed in one year might be recaptured in a later year.

Originally there was a corresponding reduction in the tax depreciation base of the assets on which the investment credit was allowed. This provision was removed retroactively in 1964. The credit was temporarily suspended on assets acquired during parts of 1966 and 1967. The investment tax credit was repealed in 1968, but reenacted in 1971, and increased in 1974.

Background of Accounting Treatment. Even while the original investment tax credit was being considered by Congress, the Accounting Principles Board was deliberating on the proper accounting treatment for the credit. The Board hoped to establish a uniform accounting method for the credit which would apply from its effective date, thereby forestalling the proliferation of methods that had been developed to account for income tax allocation. Accordingly, APB Opinion No. 2 was issued in December 1962, concluding that the allowable investment credit should be reflected in net income over the productive life of the property acquired, rather than in the year in which the property was placed in service.

A large *minority* of the APB favored deferring only the part of the investment tax credit equal to the increased future taxes that would result from reducing the tax depreciation basis of the property. They advocated allowing the remainder of the credit to "flow-through" to income in the year the investment credit was allowable for tax purposes.

The Securities and Exchange Commission announced in *ASR No. 96* that it would accept either the deferral method or the partial flow-through method, citing as justification the substantial diversity of opinion among responsible persons as to how to account for the credit.

A lively debate among accounting practitioners and educators followed. Many objected to Opinion No. 2 because they thought that the adoption of one method by the Board, to the exclusion of all others, would lead to undesirable rigidity in accounting.

The Revenue Act of 1964 repealed retroactively the provision which reduced the depreciable base of property by the amount of the investment credit.

APB Opinion No.4, issued in March 1964, stated:

> . . . the authority of Opinions of this Board rests upon their general acceptability. The Board, in the light of events and developments occurring since the issuance of Opinion No. 2, has determined that its conclusions as there expressed have not attained the degree of acceptability which it believes is necessary to make the Opinion effective.

The APB reiterated its majority's view that the preferable procedure was to take the investment credit into income over the life of the property acquired. However, the Board stated that under the circumstances, the "flow-through" method, treating the credit as a reduction of income taxes of the year the credit arises, was also acceptable.

Support for Alternative Accounting Methods. The APB argued in Opinion No. 2 that the nature of the investment credit must be established before deciding the appropriate accounting treatment. Its members unanimously agreed that the investment credit should influence the net income computation; they differed as to the period or periods in which income should be affected.

The Board examined the following views as to the nature of the investment credit:

1. *Subsidy by way of contribution to capital.* The Board concluded that this interpretation was the least supportable because it conflicted with the agreed-upon conclusion that the investment credit increases the income of some period.

2. *Tax reduction.*   This view is that the investment credit is a selective reduction of taxes of the year in which the credit arises, measured chiefly by the amount of new investment in qualified property. The Board felt that the investment credit is an administrative procedure which permits the taxpayer to retain cash equal to a tax otherwise payable, not a factor in computing taxes related to the income of a period.

3. *Cost reduction.*   The Board favored the cost reduction interpretation, giving particular weight to two points:

a. Earnings arise from using facilities, not from acquiring them.

b. The ultimate realization of the credit is contingent to some degree on future developments.

The Board stated that:

> Where the incidence of realization of income is uncertain, as in the present circumstances, we believe the record does not support the treatment of the investment credit as income at the earliest possible point of time. . . . spreading the income in some rational manner over a series of future accounting periods is more logical and supportable.

Often cited in support of the cost reduction theory is this excerpt from the House Ways and Means Committee report: "The investment credit will stimulate investment because—as a direct offset against the tax otherwise payable—it will reduce the cost of acquiring depreciable assets."

The cost reduction proponents argue that under the tax reduction (flow-through) theory earnings for a period will depend significantly on how much a business spends for property additions during the period rather than on how profitably it uses them.

Opponents of the cost reduction theory (flow-through advocates) contend that:

1. The practical effect of the legislation should govern the accounting treatment, rather than an effort to read the mind of Congress as it enacted the investment credit.

2. Property acquisitions and the tax credit result from two completely separate events, which differ in that:

a. The cash retained as a result of the credit may be used for purposes other than capital investment.

b. The credit depends on more than investment in property; it can be used only when the investor has significant taxable income.

c. The investment credit does not directly influence the price of property.

d. The tax liability, not the purchase liability, is reduced by the investment credit.

e. It is difficult to describe meaningfully in the balance sheet the concept of either deferred investment credit or property cost minus the investment credit.

3. Countering the argument that realization of the credit is uncertain, flow-through advocates assert that the results of these contingencies can be evaluated as readily as those of many other contingencies which are normally estimated in the accounting statements.

In dissenting to Opinion No. 4, Moonitz stated:

> . . . while it is conceivable that the tax reduction method may be right, or that cost reduction may be right, or that both are wrong and some other unspecified possibly right, the investment credit cannot be two different things at one and the same time. . . . The method preferred by the majority of the Board permits identical items bought from the same supplier at identical prices to be recorded at different "costs" depending upon the tax status of the purchaser and not upon the conditions prevailing in the transaction between buyer and seller. . . .

Financial Statement Reporting of the Investment Credit.   The financial statement reporting of the investment credit depends, of course, on whether the flow-through or cost reduction approach is used. If flow through is used, there will be no balance sheet reporting of the investment credit. On the income statement, the entire investment credit for the year is usually recorded as a reduction of current-year income tax expense, with the amount of the reduction shown parenthetically on the face of the income statement or in a footnote.

If the deferral (cost reduction) approach is followed, the customary balance sheet procedure is to show the deferral somewhere between liabilities and stockholders' equity, frequently combined with the deferred credit for federal income taxes. Subtractions of the deferred investment credit from the property account is rarely seen in published financial reports. In the income statement, the amortization of current and earlier years' investment credits is usually shown as a deduction from current year's income tax expense.

Under the statute, unused investment credits in one year may be carried back or forward to other years. If the carry-back provision is used, that amount is added to the amount of investment credits otherwise applicable to the year in which the property is placed in service. If the unused investment credit is carried forward, it is reflected only in the year in which it becomes a deduction from income tax expense. APB Opinion No. 2 provides that the investment credit carry-forward "would not appear as an asset. Material amounts of unused investment credits should be disclosed."

In late 1971 the APB issued an exposure draft of a proposed Opinion which would have prescribed the deferral method as the only allowable method of accounting for the investment tax credit. Although the SEC supported the proposed requirements, Congress negated the proposed opinion by the following language in the Revenue Bill of 1971:

> . . . no taxpayer shall be required to use, for purposes of financial reports subject to the jurisdiction of any federal agency or reports made to any federal agency, any particular method of accounting for the credit allowed by . . . section 38. . . .

In response, the Accounting Principles Board stated that it:

> . . . unanimously deplores Congressional involvement in establishing accounting principles for financial reports to investors, which largely have been the responsibility of the Securities and Exchange Commission and the accounting profession. The APB further deplores Congressional endorsement of alternative accounting methods, especially since there has been strong demand by Congressmen and others for the elimination of alternative methods which confuse investors.

INTERPERIOD TAX ALLOCATION IN REGULATED INDUSTRIES

In regulated utilities the accounting policies of interperiod income tax allocation and of deferring the tax effects of the investment credit are referred to as *normalization.* The opposing accounting policies of reflecting the tax effects of timing differences in current income, and of reporting the investment tax credit in current income, are called *flow-through.*

The choice of accounting methods by regulated businesses is especially significant, since the regulatory agency uses the accounting measurement of income as a factor in establishing the level of rates which the utility is permitted to charge its customers.

Using a simulation model, Brigham and Nantell concluded that normalization is preferable, stating:[26]

[26]Eugene F. Brigham and Timothy J. Nantell, "Normalization Versus Flow Through for Utility Companies Using Liberalized Tax Depreciation," *The Accounting Review,* July 1974, p. 446.

Flow through accounting is totally inconsistent with the traditional theory of rate-making, as it benefits one class of customers (current customers) at the expense of another class (future customers). Under flow through, sharp short-term rate cuts are made, but future customers must pay the piper through higher rates. Normalization, by contrast, involves establishing a deferred tax reserve, which is treated as "costless" capital, and all the firm's customers, both present and future, benefit from the existence of this "costless" capital. Thus, in our view, normalization is consistent with traditional public utility rate-making theory, but flow through is not.

BIBLIOGRAPHY

American Institute of Certified Public Accountants: "Accounting for the 'Investment Credit,'" APB Opinion No. 2, New York, 1962.
————: "Accounting for the 'Investment Credit,'" APB Opinion No. 4 (Amending No. 2), New York, 1964.
————: "Accounting for Income Taxes," APB Opinion No. 11, New York, 1967.
————: "Accounting for Income Taxes—Special Areas," APB Opinion No. 23, New York, 1972.
————: "Accounting for Income Taxes—Investments in Common Stock Accounted for by the Equity Method," APB Opinion No. 24, New York, 1972.
————: "Accounting Interpretations of APB Opinion No. 11," New York, 1972.
————: "Restatement and Revision of Accounting Research Bulletins," *Accounting Research Bulletin No. 43*, New York, 1953.
————: "Declining-Balance Depreciation," *Accounting Research Bulletin No. 44*, New York, 1954.
————: "Declining-Balance Depreciation," *Accounting Research Bulletin No. 44* (Revised), New York, 1958.
Bierman, Harold, Jr., and Thomas R. Dyckman: "New Look at Deferred Taxes," *Financial Executive*, January 1974.
Black, Homer A.: "Interperiod Allocation of Corporate Income Taxes," *Accounting Research Study No. 9*, AICPA, New York, 1966.
Davidson, Sidney: "Accelerated Depreciation and the Allocation of Income Taxes," *The Accounting Review*, vol. 33, pp. 173–180, April 1958.
Financial Accounting Standards Board: "Accounting for Income Taxes—Oil and Gas Producing Companies," *Statement of Financial Accounting Standards No. 9*, Stamford, Conn., 1975.
Hicks, Ernest L.: "Income Tax Allocation," *Financial Executive*, October 1963.
Keller, Thomas F.: *Accounting for Corporate Income Taxes*, Bureau of Business Research, The University of Michigan Press, Ann Arbor, 1961.
Nurnberg, Hugo: "Discounting Deferred Tax Liabilities," *The Accounting Review*, October 1972.
Price Waterhouse & Co.: *Is Generally Accepted Accounting for Income Taxes Possibly Misleading Investors?* New York, 1967.

Chapter **37**

Human Resource Accounting

R. LEE BRUMMET
Willard J. Graham Professor of Business Administration,
University of North Carolina at Chapel Hill

Within the most recent decade accountants, financial managers, personnel managers, and general managers have reflected a new and increasing interest in the subject of human resource accounting. Although still in an early period of development from the conceptual and procedural viewpoints and also in academic circles and in business practice, the subject of human resource accounting possesses general intuitive appeal and long-run potential.

DEFINITIONS OF HUMAN RESOURCE ACCOUNTING

In *Accounting: The Language of Business*,[1] Davidson et al. define human resource accounting as "a term used to describe a variety of proposals that seek to report and emphasize the importance of human resources—knowledgeable, trained, and loyal employees—in a company's earning process and total assets." Since the subject is still in its early stages of development, alternative definitions reflecting a range of breadth and coverage are available to provide freedom for exploration of many potentially useful aspects of the subject.

Human resource accounting is proposed by its advocates as a logical and significant extension of the scope of enterprise accounting. It is the process of measuring and reporting the human dynamics of an organization. It is the assessment of the condition of human resources within an organization and the measurement of the change in this condition through time. It is the process of providing information about individuals and groups of individuals within an organization to decision makers both inside and outside the organization.

In its more limited context, and more consistent with conventional accounting practice, human resource accounting involves the concept of human resources as assets, determines invested costs and related cost expirations, and in some instances estimates and provides surveillance over economic value of the human organization. Although some authors may conceive of human resources even more broadly than those within the organization and also include customers and other outside constituencies, assessment of the significance of these groups to an organization involves even greater measurement problems and is not included in the definition of human resource accounting treated in this chapter.

THE CONCEPT OF HUMAN CAPITAL

The concept of human capital which is basic to human resource accounting at the enterprise level is not of recent origin. Investment in human capital is considered in the writings of Adam Smith. As economists and other social scientists have sought to understand the nature and causal aspects of industrial growth, particularly within the past fifty years, the human factor has been given increasingly greater recognition. Significant researchers and authors on the concept of human capital include, among others, T. W. Schultz, Gary Becker, E. F. Dennison, and L. Thurow.

Studies have been made to assess the cause-and-effect relationships of relative investments in human capital and other forms of capital and rates of economic and social change in different countries of the world as well as to assess the impact of in- and outmigration of certain countries' human resources—the brain drain or gain. In some of these studies emphasis has been given to the role of education in the development of human capital and efforts to assess rates of return from various levels of education and other training inputs. For example, in 1971,

---

[1]Sidney Davidson, Clyde P. Stickney, James S. Schindler, and Roman L. Weil, *Accounting: The Language of Business*, 2nd ed., Thomas Horton and Daughters, Glen Ridge, N.J., 1975, p. 25.

Schultz dealt with the concept of human capital and estimated rates of return of 35 percent, 25 percent, and 15 percent for elementary school, for high school, and for college instruction, respectively. In another study Dennison compared growth rates in eight European countries with the United States, identified 23 contributing factors, and estimated that education accounted for 15 percent of the growth of income in the United States from 1950 to 1962.

These studies using the concept of human capital have clear relevance for policy makers in the public sector. On a national, or macro, level, human capital is becoming an operational concept, but its use at the enterprise level is very much in its infancy.

HUMAN RESOURCES AND ENTERPRISE ACCOUNTING—HISTORICAL DEVELOPMENT

The significance of human resources in organizations or at the enterprise level has been recognized in the literature of organization and management theory and practice throughout history, but the accounting process has been limited largely to financial and physical resources. Taylor and Glautier state that:[2]

> The reason why accountants have failed to recognize human capital as an asset may be explained in terms of the manner in which accounting developed historically. Accounting information originates essentially from the results of financial transactions . . . the only transaction which is recognizable [in the case of human resources] is the contractual obligation to make a periodic payment in return for periodic services under a wage agreement. Hence, wages and salaries are treated as current costs in the manner as rent payments for land leased by the firm, for neither is owned as assets.

In any event, it was not until the early 1960s that specific suggestions started to appear for inclusion of human resource representations in routine assessments of enterprise condition or within the structure of accounting systems of enterprises. During the past two decades emphasis on recruiting, training, employee motivation, and work environment, and on the use of employee attitude and perception surveys, attest to the increasing recognition of the role of human resources in organizational effectiveness. Substantial identifiable outlays in these areas may account, in part, for the increasing consideration of accountants' involvement in this new subject of human resource accounting.

In 1964, suggesting that human resources constitute the most significant operational asset of most organizations, Hermanson[3] argued that financial statements would be more complete and more useful to managers and investors if they included such resources. He proposed an "unpurchased goodwill method" for "valuing" human assets. This first approach involves the capitalization of the "excess of actual over normal income" to be shown as human assets. The second method utilizes an "average efficiency ratio" as a scalar to be applied to the calculated present value equivalent of future wage and salary payments to employees to determine an asset representation. Although these approaches are clearly vulnerable on both conceptual and practical grounds (to be discussed later in this chapter) and although Hermanson's work did not draw significant prompt response, his efforts are noteworthy as an early analysis of the potential for this new area of concern by accountants.

---

[2]P. J. Taylor and M. W. E. Glautier, "Accounting Information and Industrial Relations: Social Implications and Cost and Benefit Considerations," *Economic Research Papers,* University College of North Wales, Bangor, 1974, pp. 7–8.

[3]Roger H. Hermanson, *Accounting for Human Assets,* Michigan State University, Graduate School of Business Administration, Bureau of Business and Economic Research, Occasional Paper No. 14, East Lansing, Mich., 1964.

Hekimian and Jones, writing in the *Harvard Business Review* in 1967, emphasized the importance of human resources in the planning process and particularly in resource allocation decisions. They suggested an internal competitive bidding process by profit center or investment center managers to establish human resource "values" approaching an "opportunity cost." This work, although of apparently limited practical import, drew attention to the subject of human resource accounting and contributed to general receptivity for later efforts to operationalize certain human resource accounting methods.

Also in 1967, Likert published *The Human Organization: Its Management and Values*.[4] One chapter of this well-known work is devoted to "human asset accounting." Likert emphasizes the importance of the human element in organizations and the significant failure of accountants to deal with it as an asset. Calling attention to the magnitude of this omission in corporate balance sheets as indicated by large differences between market and book values of the owner equity in many corporations, he argues that managers make inappropriate decisions due to lack of information about the firm's human assets. Likert's work drew important attention to human resource accounting (he called it *human asset accounting*), particularly from personnel and behavioral experts. This basic work has been followed by other publications on human resources by Likert and his associates.

Although the works of Hermanson, Hekimian and Jones, and Likert prior to 1968 dealt with the concept of human assets or human resources and the need for balance sheet representation, they did not deal with ongoing assessment or an up-to-date monitoring of these resources, or an integration of human resource accounting within the framework of conventional accounting.

In 1968 and 1969, Brummet et al.,[5] in close association with Likert, published in several journals more specific suggestions at the enterprise level than had been included in previous publications.

In 1966, the R. G. Barry Corporation, a leisure footwear manufacturer with headquarters in Columbus, Ohio, began the development of a "human resource accounting system" involving the monitoring of human resource investments through capitalization and amortization of certain human resource costs. The Barry management was assisted in its efforts by researchers from the Institute for Social Research and the School of Business Administration of the University of Michigan in Ann Arbor, Michigan.[6] On January 1, 1968, this cost-based human resource accounting system was implemented to include 96 individuals making up the managerial personnel of the Corporation. The 1969 Annual Report of the R. G. Barry Corporation included amounts capitalized as human resources. This report drew attention from many business managers and from the business news media. Since 1969, the system has been refined and expanded to include a

[4]Rensis Likert, *The Human Organization: Its Management and Value*, McGraw-Hill Book Company, New York, 1967.

[5]R. Lee Brummet, William C. Pyle, and Eric G. Flamholtz, "Accounting for Human Resources," *Michigan Business Review*, March 1968; R. Lee Brummet, Eric G. Flamholtz, and William C. Pyle, "Human Resource Measurement—A Challenge for Accountants," *The Accounting Review*, April 1968; R. Lee Brummet, Eric G. Flamholtz, and William C. Pyle, "Human Resource Accounting: A Tool to Increase Managerial Effectiveness," *Management Accounting*, August 1969; R. Lee Brummet, William C. Pyle, and Eric G. Flamholtz, "Human Resource Accounting in Industry," *Personnel Administration*, July-August 1969; R. Lee Brummet, Eric G. Flamholtz, and William C. Pyle (eds.), *Human Resource Accounting: Development and Implementation in Industry*, Foundation for Research in Human Behavior, Ann Arbor, Mich., 1969.

[6]Editors' footnote: The materials in the sections "Techniques for Cost-Based Human Resource Accounting" and "R. G. Barry Corporation" are based upon William Pyle's research with the R. G. Barry Corporation. See Pyle, "Human Resource Accounting," *Financial Analyst Journal*, September–October 1970, pp. 69–78.

majority of the employees of the Corporation. Balance sheets have shown "net investments in human resources," and income statements have included an adjustment for the "net increase or decrease in human resource investments."

Since 1968, several American corporations and corporations based in Europe and Japan have experimented with many of the possible facets of human resource accounting using highly varied approaches. The list includes American Telephone and Telegraph, General Telephone and Electronics, Texas Instruments, General Motors, Westinghouse Electric, Emery Air Freight, Mobil Oil, A B Volvo of Sweden, Proctor and Gamble, and others.

The number of articles on human resource accounting appearing in accounting, personnel, and management literature has continued to grow since 1968.[7] They range widely, both in terms of the pros and cons of conceptual propriety and the potential favorable and unfavorable impacts of implementation of the concept.

Committees of the American Accounting Association, the Government Accountants' Association, and the American Institute of Certified Public Accountants have studied human resources accounting over the past few years, and some of them have reported on the state of the art as they perceive it and the potential for the future.[8] Seminars have been sponsored by the National Association of Accountants, certified public accounting firms, and management organizations in the United States, Canada, and European countries. These efforts attempted to expand the awareness of the subject and to be responsive to expressed interests of people from both private and public sector organizations. At least two book-length publications are now available on human resource accounting.[9]

As for other facets of accounting, the possibilities for human resource accounting may be dichotomized into historical cost-based approaches and replacement or value-based methods. While historical cost-based methods remain dominant in extant accounting, the current interest in value-based accounting provides a receptive setting for consideration of both of these aspects of human resource accounting. Cost-based human resource accounting or human resource cost accounting fits more naturally into long-standing conventional accounting practices. While this setting brings with it significant constraints and vulnerability, it provides a familiar back-drop for considering the commonalities of human resources and other resources and a basis for examining the fundamental aspects of the concept of human resource accounting.

[7]An excellent, selective, but reasonably complete bibliography on human resource accounting with background articles on human capital was prepared by Edmond Marques of the European Institute for Advanced Studies in Management in Brussels in late 1974. This bibliography covered works from the United States, Canada, and various countries in Europe and included 134 dated entries as follows:

Date of origin	Number of entries
Prior to 1968	12
1968	3
1969	9
1970	13
1971	16
1972	25
1973	25
1974	31

[8]American Accounting Association, "Report of Committee on Human Resource Accounting," *The Accounting Review*, Supplement to Vol. XLVIII, 1973, pp. 169–185; American Accounting Association, "Report of the Committee on Accounting for Human Resources," *The Accounting Review*, Supplement to Vol. XLIX, 1974, pp. 115–124.

[9]Eric Flamholtz, *Human Resource Accounting*, Dickenson Publishing Company, Encino, Calif., 1974; Edwin H. Caplan and Stephen Landekich, *Human Resource Accounting: Past, Present and Future*, National Association of Accountants, New York, 1974.

TECHNIQUES FOR COST-BASED HUMAN RESOURCE ACCOUNTING

Techniques for cost-based human resource accounting are analogous to those for accounting for plant or other physical resources. They involve (1) recording of investments in human resources through a capitalization process,[10] (2) recording of routine expirations of such capitalized items using an established amortization procedure, (3) recording of losses to recognize special expirations due to obsolescence of investments in certain skills or knowledge capabilities or the turnover of personnel, and (4) reporting or communicating to interested parties on the dynamics and condition of human resources in terms of investments therein.

Exhibit 1 shows the fundamental aspects and some of the classification possibili-

EXHIBIT 1   Generalized Model of a Cost-Based Human Resource Accounting System

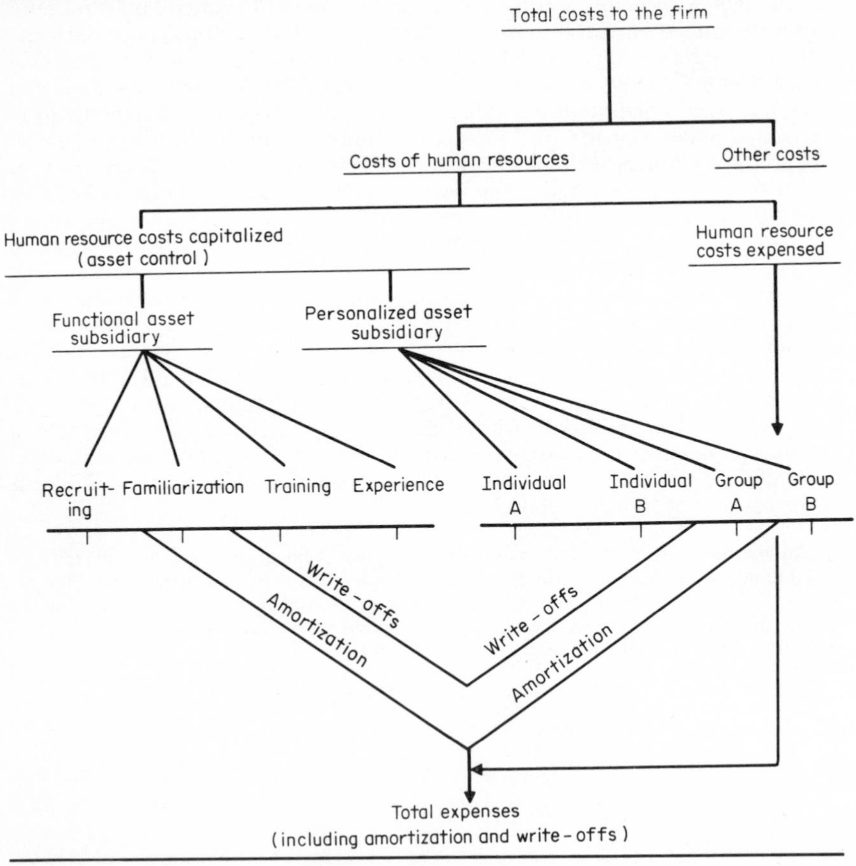

[10]It should be noted that, in this context, capitalization refers to the recording of human resources as assets in human resource form—a practice that is not usual in conventional accounting. It affects the original distinction between payments for current services (expenses) and investments from which future returns may be expected (assets). This distinction does not in any way affect the procedures for capitalizing the payment for current services into process or finished goods inventories. Under this system amortization of human resource investments in certain individuals would also be includable in these inventories.

ties for a cost-based human resource accounting system. Functional groupings of invested costs may be recognized such as the sample set shown for recruiting, familiarization, training, and experience building. A clear description of the content of each functional group should be developed. As an example, the R. G. Barry Corporation has included recruiting and experience building among the seven groups of costs considered and explains their content as follows:[11]

> Recruiting outlay costs—costs associated with locating and selecting new [management] personnel. This category includes search fees, advertising, interviewer or interviewee travel expenses, allocations of personnel and acquiring department time for internal screening, interviewing, testing, and evaluation expenses. Outlay costs for unsuccessful candidates are allocated to the cost of obtaining the candidate hired.
>
> Investment building experience costs—costs associated with investments in on-the-job training which occur after the initial familiarization period and which are expected to have value to the company beyond the current accounting period. Investment building experience is the development of a capability which would not reasonably be expected as a normal part of the person's job.

Another grouping of investments should be made by individuals for supervisory or managerial personnel and, as a practical expedient, for groups of individuals involved in relatively routine and similar job assignments. This individualized classification is necessary to trace cost effectiveness and to identify expirations that are conditioned by individual circumstances and behavior.

As depicted in Exhibit 1, a system of control and subsidiary accounts may be used to maintain investment balances by function, by individual and groups of individuals, departments or project teams.

Invested costs may be captured from basic documents such as invoices or expense vouchers or they may be identified as wage and salary payments made to those involved in personnel activities or portions of wage and salary payments made to individuals in whom investments are being made. Examples of this latter type of cost would include wages or salaries paid during periods devoted to training and a prescribed portion of the wage or salary payments made during the first days or weeks of employment before the employee is in a position to perform at a normal level anticipated for the position. This amount will depend upon the particular circumstances relative to the learning process for each given position.[12] The systems and procedures aspects of a cost-based human resource accounting system should be worked out as a joint effort between the personnel and accounting departments. Many of the basic documents that feed the system will originate in the personnel or human resource department.

Classifying human resource investments by nature of input and identifying them with individuals and groups of individuals make it possible to use cost standards. Clearing accounts may be established for the functional accounts such as recruiting, familiarization, training, and experience building. Each of these accounts may be charged with the actual costs incurred and relieved with a standard amount for each individual in whom the investment is made to generate cost control information. These standard amounts will differ depending on the position involved.

[11]R. L. Woodruff, Jr., "Human Resource Accounting," *The Canadian Chartered Accountant*, September 1970, pp. 157 and 158.
[12]An adaptation of the conventional learning curve may be used to determine the portion of wages to be capitalized during the early period of employment. As the employee's performance improves, a larger portion of the wage payment applies to performance and a smaller portion is an investment made in anticipation of further performance improvement until performance contributes in full in return for wage payments made.

Standard costs might, for example, be established as shown in Exhibit 2. Using standards such as these, all charges to asset accounts can be made at standard.

EXHIBIT 2   Standard Costs of Human Resource Investments

	Line employees	Foremen	Supervisors	Middle managers
Recruiting ...	$ 500	$ 800	$ 1,000	$2,000
Familiarization	1,000	1,200	15,000	2,000
Training	1,000	2,000	4,000	8,000

Having capitalized the costs of human resources that are expected to yield long-term benefits to the firm, a procedure must now be established to recognize their expiration. Human resource investments are of a highly varied nature with a large range of lengths of benefit periods. Further uncertainties of voluntary employment tenure, physical and mental health conditions of employees, and even mortality add to the complication of deciding upon appropriate amortization practices.

Expirations of human resource investments should be recognized in a pre-established and systematic manner by association with those periods during which the benefits of the investments are experienced by the entity.[13] As examples, costs of recruiting should be amortized over a period of time which is the best estimate of the remaining time that the individual will remain actively in the employ of the company. Training costs should be amortized over a period which is the best estimate of the time during which the benefit for such training will be enjoyed by the firm.[14] Special training to develop a skill which will be utilized for a short time period should be amortized rapidly. General executive training, on the other hand, may be amortized over the estimated remaining tenure of the recipient with the company. Amortization time periods should never extend beyond the date of the recipient's tenure with the organization.

Unlike physical resources, human resources are potentially self-activating or self-generating. This characteristic places a serious limitation on input cost-based accounting for human resources. However, within the constraints of such a cost-based system, this crudeness may be minimized by a continual reassessment of the amortization policy.

In addition to periodic reviews and updates of amortization practices, a periodic assessment of human resources and positions occupied should be made to identify (1) significant physical health changes in individuals that may justify write-offs or changes in amortization policy, (2) changes in job requirements or changes in positions held by certain individuals that may obsolete the unamortized portion of some human resource inputs and thus call for write-offs, (3) transfers of individuals among departments that may require a regrouping of asset balances for segment accounting, and (4) resignations or layoffs that should be recorded as losses in the amount of the unamortized balances. These periodic reviews should ordinarily be made by the personnel department with assistance from line managers and supervisors.

Procedures for a cost-based system will provide asset balances (book value figures) for unamortized inputs to human resources in the form of the various functions and various individuals and groups of individuals in the company's

---

[13]The choice of straight-line, accelerating, or decelerating rates should be based on similar justification as those used for choosing rates for physical assets and is not considered here.

[14]As a practical expedient it may be appropriate to amortize all human resource investments over a limited set of time periods, classifying the several investment groupings into the time period groupings.

employ. They will also provide expense figures for regular amortization, obsoleted inputs, health deteriorations, voluntary resignations, layoffs and other identified causes.

The two most well-known examples of cost-based human resource accounting in practice are the R. G. Barry Corporation (mentioned earlier) and Touche Ross & Co. of Canada.

R. G. Barry Corporation. The annual report for 1973 of the R. G. Barry Corporation included the following narrative and financial statements:

> Beginning in 1966, R. G. Barry began the development of an information system designed to provide data about human resources in dollar terms. This effort was undertaken because it is our belief that management is the process of planning, organizing and controlling a complex mix of resources to accomplish the objectives of the organization. Conventional accounting provides adequate information on the physical and financial resources of the business. Our interest was to develop an information system which would provide data on the condition of the human resources of the business in the language of other business information, namely dollars.
>
> Human resource accounting is an attempt to identify, quantify and report investments made in recruiting, acquiring, training, familiarizing and developing people. Outlay costs connected with these activities are accumulated and capitalized where they are

---

"The Total Concept"   R. G. Barry Corporation and Subsidiaries Pro-Forma (Conventional and Human Resource Accounting)

	1973 Conventional and human resource	1973 Conventional only
Balance Sheet		
Assets		
Total Current Assets	$18,311,713	$18,311,713
Net Property, Plant and Equipment	3,500,227	3,500,227
Excess of Purchase Price over Net Assets Acquired	1,285,829	1,285,829
Deferred Financing Costs	173,278	173,278
Net Investments in Human Resources	1,964,243	—
Prepaid Income Taxes and Other Assets	213,500	213,500
	$25,448,790	$23,484,547
Liabilities and Stockholders' Equity		
Total Current Liabilities	3,909,083	3,909,083
Long Term Debt, Excluding Current Installments	6,970,000	6,970,000
Deferred Compensation	143,150	143,150
Deferred Income Tax Based Upon Full Tax Deduction for Human Resource Costs	982,122	—
Stockholders' Equity:		
Capital Stock	1,902,347	1,902,347
Additional Capital in Excess of Par Value	5,676,549	5,676,549
Retained Earnings:		
Financial	4,883,418	4,883,418
Human Resources	982,121	—
	$25,448,790	$23,484,547
Statement of Income		
Net Sales	$43,161,564	$43,161,564
Cost of Sales	28,621,050	28,621,050
Gross Profit	14,540,514	14,540,514
Selling, General and Administrative Expenses	10,783,922	10,783,922
Operating Income	3,756,592	3,756,592
Interest Expense	598,846	598,846
Income Before Income Taxes	3,157,746	3,157,746
Net Increase in Human Resource Investment	184,293	—
Adjusted Income Before Income Taxes	3,342,039	3,157,746
Income Taxes	1,615,147	1,523,000
Net Income	$ 1,726,892	$ 1,634,746

expected to have value beyond the current accounting period. The basic outlays in connection with acquiring and integrating new people are amortized over their expected tenure with the company. Investments made for training or development are amortized over a much shorter period of time. Total write-off of an individual's account occurs upon his departure from the company.

During 1973, total investments in management and non-management resources exceeded total amortization and write-off by $184,293. The investment amount represents the outlay to bring people on board and orient them to the organization and their work; in addition, a major portion of the investment total reflects the development activities undertaken by people within the organization.

This past year saw a sizable number of people participating in development activities which will provide Barry with a strong corps of people for future growth.

In the 1972 Annual Report, the explanation of human resource accounting-related activities foretold of increased reliance on growth and development of internal human resources for staffing future positions. In 1973, openings were filled from our current ranks at a rate substantially higher than the past. As a result, economics of external recruiting and orientation were realized as well as providing advancement opportunities for current Associates. In 1974, efforts to systematically plan and evaluate formal and informal development activities will be increased. Furthermore, the financial accounting of development efforts will allow us to capture the dollar investments as well as provide a means to prepare cost-benefit analysis of comparable programs. Development activities will focus on providing available resources for forecasted positions, preparing back-up people to assume key positions, and to provide training for individuals that is responsive to their job and career interests.

As we have said in previous annual reports, the impetus for the development of an information system to account for human resources was provided by a perceived need for the information internally. As a result of pioneering activities of R. G. Barry in this area, many other companies are now beginning to apply HRA measurements. Some are using our approach, others are investigating alternative systems.

We are pleased that more and more companies recognize the need for this kind of information in order to improve the effectiveness of internal management decision-making processes.

It may be noted that the deferred federal income tax figure shown on the Barry Corporation balance sheet is exactly one-half of the net investment in human resources. This should be expected to be the incremental tax rate (48 percent in 1973) times the net investment in human resources. This amount could also be affected by amortization of human resources included in process or finished goods inventory.

Barry Corporation discontinued publication of formal HRA reports in 1974. The Corporation commented at that time that it continues to use the data internally.

Touche Ross & Co. of Canada.   The approach used by this firm of accountants and consultants is reported in an article by Michael O. Alexander[15] and summarized in a publication of the National Association of Accountants as follows:[16]

The CPA firm of Touche Ross & Co., Canada, has introduced human resource accounting as part of its management information system in the belief that a good human resource accounting system can provide information of vital importance for both short-term and long-term decision-making and performance measurement. In the

---

[15]Michael O. Alexander, "Investment in People," *Canadian Chartered Accountant*, July 1971.

[16]Edwin H. Caplan and Stephen Landekich, *Human Resource Accounting: Past, Present and Future*, National Association of Accountants, New York, 1974, pp. 68 and 69. [The authors prepared these observations based on: (1) a description of the firm's HRA effort by Michael O. Alexander (1971), a Partner of Touche Ross & Co., Chartered Accountants, and P. S. Ross and Partners, Management Consultants, who is responsible for directing the firm's Innovative Research Group, and (2) on information obtained in an interview with Gerald H. B. Ross, a member of the Innovative Research Group.]

initial stage, the focus was on using the already available information as input to the system. Thus, the information on investments in human assets has been based on historical costs.

Some of the efforts in the initial development phase have been directed to specific managerial problems. One such problem is the high turnover of personnel. The cost associated with the high turnover rate could not be readily ascertained from conventional accounting data. Another set of problems refers to relationship between performance measurements and costs involved in developing the firm's human resources.

It is normal practice in a public accounting firm to measure performance in terms of chargeable hours, i.e., the time spent on work in rendering service to the clients. This single measure does not allow for adequate recognition of the factors, such as investments in human resources, that are not directly related to chargeable hours.

In terms of short-run performance results, it is, therefore, clearly undesirable to have any potentially productive hours that cannot be charged to clients. Most of the training and development of human resources, however, will necessarily come at the expense of chargeable hours. This means that conventional accounting measures, in the absence of other evaluators of human performance, may actually encourage a manager to neglect investments in human resources. Yet, there can be little doubt that it is these very resources which determine the long-run survival and success of a public accounting firm. The Touche Ross system is designed to modify the firm's performance measurement by adding an additional dimension—changes in the condition of human assets.

The investment in each employee is calculated in terms of both out-of-pocket costs and opportunity costs (chargeable hours foregone). These data are used in developing reports which provide information such as: (a) comparison of the dollar value of planned versus actual hours of staff time devoted to investments in human resources and (b) changes in human resource account balances, including increases (due to investments for recruiting, orientation, formal training, etc.) and decreases (due to transfers, terminations and amortization). Under this system, each manager is explicitly responsible for human resource investments within his organization in the same way that he is responsible for planning and accomplishing a certain level of chargeable hours.

These examples and others can be cited as experiments with the application of conventional cost-based accounting to human resources. Yet they are not generally recognized for external reporting as a part of generally accepted accounting principles. Nor are they used for income tax purposes.

One significant exception should be noted in the case of professional sports teams. Large amounts paid as bonuses to athletes to join and perform for a professional team or a significant portion of the cost of a professional team franchise may be capitalized in accord with generally accepted accounting principles and Internal Revenue Service requirements and depreciated over the "useful service lives" of the athletes. This exception to the usual practice of not recognizing human resource assets can be explained only on grounds of materiality of identifiable amounts involved. Some organizations are more highly human resource intensive than others. Some make larger investments in people than do others. Some have a relatively smooth pattern of investments in people through time while others experience a very "lumpy" time pattern of investments. The professional sports team is an example of high human resource intensity with large initial outlays for personnel, and therein is found the basis for capitalization of their human resource investments.

Historically cost-based accounting for human resources has serious limitations just as it does for financial or physical resources. Ideally, as many accountants would argue, a balance sheet should reflect the economic significance of an organization's assets and claims thereon and income measurement should assess the changes of these economic phenomena for specific time periods. In this setting cost-based human resource accounting suits the purpose only to the extent that cost inputs are good representations of economic significance or "value." One can hardly claim any great validity of such a representation of human resources. Thus, although cost-based human resource accounting may be a reasonable forerunner to "value"-based human resource accounting and although some writers appear to assume it to be the main feature of the subject,[17] substantive exploitation of the potential of the area must include "fair value" accounting or the development of approaches or models for the measurement of economic value of human resources.

HUMAN RESOURCE VALUATION MODELS

Numerous authors have hypothesized models for use in calculating (estimating) the value of human resources of an organization. A few have made limited efforts at validation. These models involve some similarities, but they do vary somewhat in both concept and in choice of surrogates. The following paragraphs provide brief explanations and critiques of those proposed in the literature since the current interest in human resource accounting became apparent.

Hermanson's Unpurchased Goodwill Model.[18] Hermanson has suggested that the value of human resources of an organization may be assessed by capitalizing earnings in excess of normal earnings for the industry or group of companies of which the firm is a part. He calls the approach the unpurchased goodwill method. If, for example, the average return on "owned assets" in a particular industry over the past five years has been 12 percent and the firm at issue has enjoyed a 15 percent return on its "owned assets" of $6,000,000, then its unowned assets (human resources) are assumed to be valued at $1,500,000 since the profit $900,000 (= $6,000,000 × .15) is assumed to be 12 percent of total owned and unowned assets of $7,500,000.

This approach has limited merit since (1) it is historically based and thus of limited use as a predictor, (2) even if it were based on projected earnings rates it would be no better than the predicted earnings themselves, (3) it assumes human resources to be the total of all "unowned" assets, making no allowance for unowned assets other than human resources or for the various bases used for stating owned assets on the organization's books, and (4) it implicitly assumes a zero value for all human resources in competitive situations since a positive value requires *above average* earnings.

Hermanson's Adjusted Discounted Future Wages Model.[19] Hermanson has also suggested the discounting of future compensation with an adjustment using an "efficiency ratio" to determine the value of an individual. In his illustration, he uses a five-year period and applies an adjustment which is a calculated ratio of the average earnings rate on owned assets of the employing firm to the average rate on owned assets of all firms in the economy.

This method is obviously related to Hermanson's unpurchased goodwill model and shares some of the same limitations. In addition it may be criticized on the grounds that future compensation is as much a measure of the liability of the firm employing the individual as it is an asset. The concept, therefore, may relate to the human capital represented in individuals *employed by the firm*. It should be noted that both of Hermanson's models are suggested as possibilities for external reporting and not necessarily for management use.

Hekimian and Jones' Competitive Bidding Model.[20] These authors suggest a procedure by which profit center managers bid for the services of valuable

[17]In an article entitled "Human Capital: Asset or Liability?", *Financial Executive*, September 1975, pp. 37 and 38, Marvin Weiss states emphatically that "HRA [Human Resource Accounting] is basically the decision to capitalize rather than expense appropriate costs."

[18]Roger H. Hermanson, *op. cit.,* pp. 7–11.

[19]*Ibid.*

[20]James S. Hekimian and Curtis H. Jones, *op. cit.*

employees of their various divisions. The maximum bid price would be used as the "value" of the individual, since it would represent the estimated current equivalent of the optimum use of the individual's services among the profit centers.

This approach could establish some estimates of value for certain individuals and provide an investment base for the high bidder to encourage a performance to yield a reasonable return. It is, at best, only a very partial solution since it would apply to and only be manageable for a very small subset of the total human resources of an organization.

Lev and Schwartz's Present Value of Future Earnings Model.[21] These authors consider the use of the economic concept of human capital in financial statements and conclude from Irving Fisher's theory that "capital is thus defined as a source of income stream and its worth is the present value of future income discounted by a rate specific to the owner of the source. . . ." This leads them to suggest that the estimated human capital value of a person y years old is

$$E(V_y^*) = \sum_{t = y}^{T} P_y(t + 1) \sum_{i = y}^{t} \frac{I_i^*}{(1 + r)^{t - y}}$$

where $E(V_y^*)$ = expected value of the human capital value of a person y years old
$\quad\quad\; T$ = person's retirement age
$\quad\; P_y(t)$ = probability of the person dying (We note that if this concept is to be useful for a specific firm, then the term "dying" must include the possibility that the individual will leave the firm for any reason, such as resignation or retirement.)
$\quad\quad\; I_i^*$ = expected earnings of the person in period i
$\quad\quad\; r$ = discount rate specific to the person

This model provides a reasonable measure of human capital which could be useful for aggregation in macro statistics and in assessing the dynamics and mobility of such capital. While the authors indicate that capital values determined by use of this model will provide financial statement users with valuable information about changes in an organization's labor force, the model's use for practical decisions of managers of organizations or of potential investors in organizations is obscure or even nonexistent.

From the firm's viewpoint, the calculated amount is as much a liability as an asset and thus these equal amounts net out to zero in any case. Recognizing this distinction between the concepts of human capital *in* the firm and human capital *of* the firm, Morse has suggested two separate components of the subject to be human asset accounting and human capital accounting:[22]

> Human asset accounting is concerned with determining the value of human resources employed in an organization *to the organization*. Human capital accounting is concerned with determining the value of human resources employed in an organization *to the employees* of that organization.

Brummet, Flamholtz, and Pyle's Economic Value Model.[23] In an early work Brummet et al. suggested multiple measures of human resources including an economic value concept involving the forecasting of future earnings, the discounting of these forecasted future earnings, and the prorata association of this amount

[21] Baruch Lev and Aba Schwartz, "On the Use of the Economic Concept of Human Capital in Financial Statements," *The Accounting Review,* January 1971.

[22] Wayne J. Morse, "A Note on the Relationship Between Human Assets and Human Capital," *The Accounting Review,* July 1973, p. 593.

[23] R. Lee Brummet et al., "Human Resource Accounting . . . A Challenge for Accountants," *op. cit.,* pp. 222 and 223.

with all assets including human resources. This suggestion is similar to the Hermanson proposal but places human resources on a level with other resources in their contribution to earnings rather than relating only an excess of normal earnings, if any, to human assets.

Flamholtz's Stochastic Rewards Valuation Model.[24] This model visualizes the movement of individuals through different roles or positions in the organization as a stochastic process depending on prior roles or service states held by the individual in the system. To make the model operational and calculate an individual's expected realizable value to the organization requires the following steps: (1) Define the mutually exclusive set of "states" an individual may occupy in the system (organization), (2) determine the value of each state to the organization, (3) estimate a person's expected tenure in an organization, and (4) find the probability that a person will occupy each possible state at specified future times. A person's expected realizable value $E(RV)$ may now be expressed as[25]

$$ E(RV) = \sum_{t=1}^{n} \left[\sum_{i=1}^{m} \frac{R_i - P(R_i)}{(1 + r)^t} \right] $$

where R_i = value, R, to be derived by the organization in each possible service state, i

$P(R_i)$ = probability that a person will occupy state i
t = time
m = state of exit
r = appropriate discount rate

This model, with some variations, has been operationalized at Lester Witte & Company, CPAs in Chicago, and is reported as a case study in some detail in the book by Caplan and Landekich.[26]

This model has considerable merit since it will provide results that are responsive to perceived probabilities of tenure and promotability which are generally indicative of the time over which the organization will enjoy the services of the individual and the magnitude of these periodic services, respectively. On practical grounds, it has limitations because of the subjectivity of the probability estimates and the value of the service awards. It should also be noted that the model does not deal explicitly with the periodic cost of maintaining the individual in the organization to produce the service state rewards to the organization. In other words, the service state rewards need to be determined as a net excess of benefits to the organization over the maintenance costs of retention of the individual.

Net service rewards may be estimated using a variety of possible surrogates. Flamholtz has used replacement cost estimates defining this concept as the cost of replacing a person with another capable of rendering an equivalent set of services to the organization. He has conducted field studies in an effort to validate replacement cost and other surrogate measures of value.[27]

Jaggi and Lau[28] have proposed a variation of this model, applying it to homogeneous groups of employees and using a Markov chain representation of potential movement within the firm or exiting the firm before death or retirement based on

[24]Eric G. Flamholtz, "The Theory and Measurement of an Individual's Value to an Organization," Ph.D. dissertation, University of Michigan, 1969, and "A Model for Human Resource Valuation: A Stochastic Process with Service Rewards," *The Accounting Review*, April 1971, pp. 253–267.

[25]Eric G. Flamholtz, *Human Resource Accounting, op. cit.*, pp. 168 and 169.

[26]Edwin H. Caplan and Stephen Landekich, *op. cit.*, pp. 109–120.

[27]Eric G. Flamholtz, *Human Resource Accounting, op. cit.*, pp. 216–219.

[28]Bikki Jaggi and Hin-Shiang Lau, "Toward a Model for Human Resource Valuation," *The Accounting Review*, April 1974, pp. 321–329.

historical data. They claim, with some intuitive justification, that the procedure is likely to provide greater accuracy and reliability.

Also, Sadan and Auerbach[29] have drawn on the Flamholtz and the Lev and Schwartz models to suggest a stochastic model for valuation of human resources. They claim that the use of a general Markov transition matrix can be operationalized readily and that the use of their model will contribute to manpower analysis by study of the effects of alternative manpower plans, and that its application is generally consistent with recommended accounting principles.

Flamholtz's Determinants of an Individual's Value to a Formal Organization Model.[30]   On a conceptual and theoretical level, Flamholtz has tried to identify the key variables that determine an individual's value to an organization and the interrelationships of such variables. He recognizes that these determinants may lend themselves to monetary or nonmonetary indicators. Drawing to some extent on his earlier work and on a limited field test with a major international firm of certified public accountants, he has developed the model shown in Exhibit 3.

EXHIBIT 3   Revised Model of the Determinants of an Individual's Value to a Formal Organization

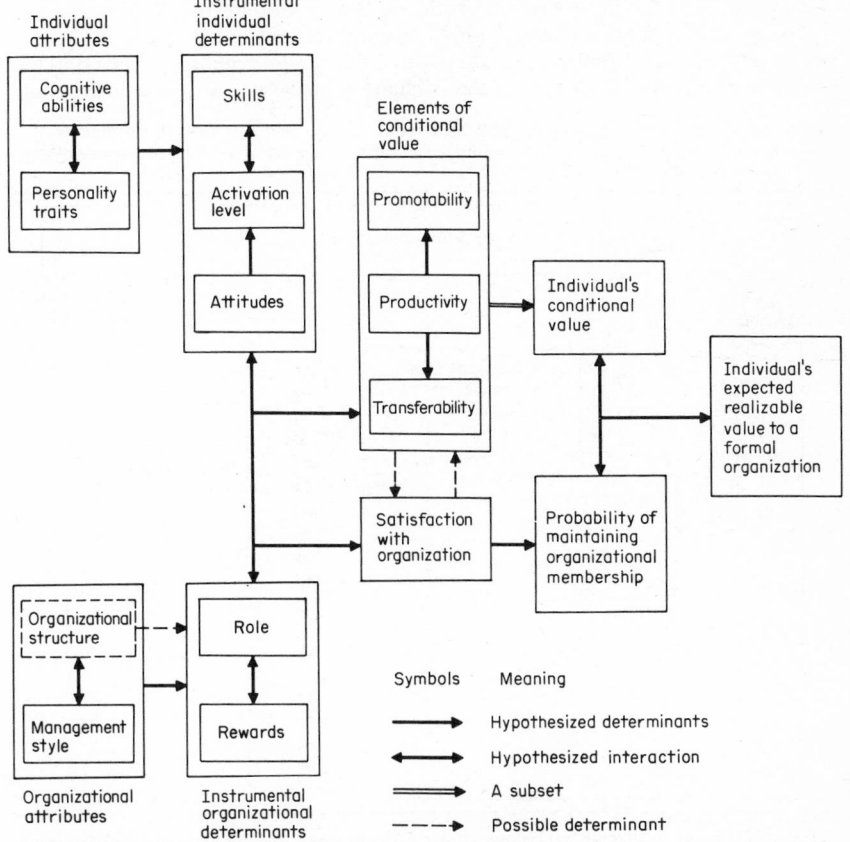

[29]Simcha Sadan and Len B. Auerbach, "A Stochastic Model for Human Resources Valuation," *California Management Review,* Summer 1974, pp. 24–31.

[30]Eric G. Flamholtz, "Toward a Theory of Human Resource Value in Formal Organization," *The Accounting Review,* October 1972, pp. 666–678.

Flamholtz suggests appropriately that this "model is suggested as a first step toward the development of a theory. . . ." It is conceptual, theoretical, and perhaps only impressionistic. Yet it is an interesting start that other researchers will amplify, revise, and perhaps implement.

The Likert Causal, Intervening, and End-Result Model.[31]   Most of the models suggested in the previous paragraphs have emphasized the assessment of individual values to a firm and have not dealt with the group or interactive process among people, so important to the success of many organizations. The work of Rensis Likert deals almost exclusively with this latter consideration.

Likert's model is based on measured relationships among three groups of variables that he refers to as causal, intervening, and end results. The terms imply the longitudinal cause-and-effect relationships which he has in many instances documented through his research. End-result measures are largely "hard measures" such as production, waste, sales, costs, profits, or other results amenable to measurement in the conventional accounting process. In Exhibit 4 below, he assumes managerial leadership as causal; organizational climate, peer leadership, group process, and subordinates' satisfaction as intervening; and total productive efficiency as the end result. The directions of the arrows indicate the causal relationship and the numerals represent coefficients of determination.

To the extent that one is able to establish significant relationships among causal, intervening, and end-result variables and to establish the time lags involved in the change response, it is possible to assess changes in these causal and intervening

EXHIBIT 4   Relationships among Human Organizational Dimensions and to Performance (Rensis Likert, "Human resource accounting: Building and assessing productive organizations," *Personnel*, May/June 1973, p. 12.)

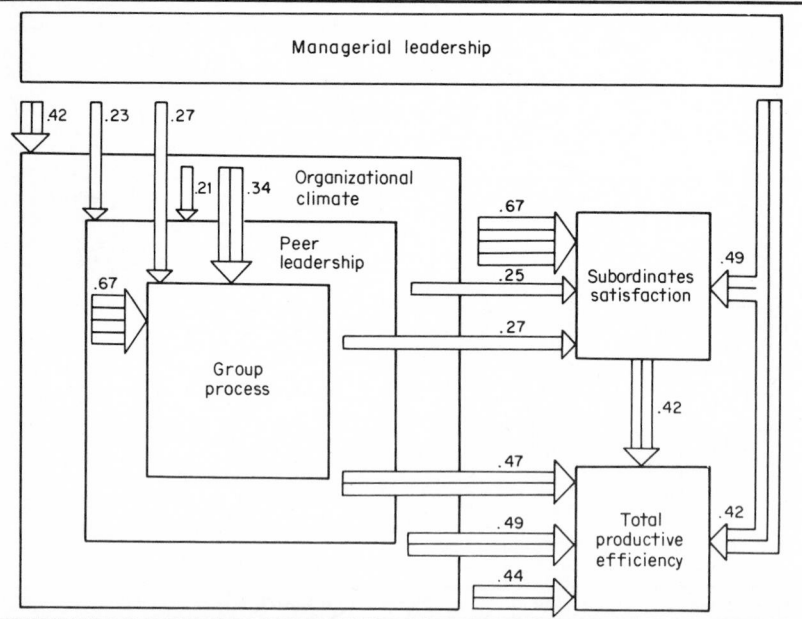

[31]Rensis Likert, *The Human Organization: Its Management and Value,* McGraw-Hill Book Company, New York, 1967; "Human Organizational Measurements: Key to Financial Success," *Michigan Business Review,* May 1971; with William C. Pyle, "A Human Organization Measurement Approach," *Financial Analysts Journal,* January–February 1971; and with David G. Bowers, "Improving the Accuracy of P/L Reports by Estimating the Change in Dollar Value of the Human Organization," *Michigan Business Review,* March 1973.

variables, predict the anticipated future impact on the "hard measured" future results, and discount this expectation to determine the change in value of the human organization. The magnitudes of the correlation measures are used to weight the causal and intervening measures in the determination of the anticipated change in results which influence the measure of human resource value.

Likert's model has been researched and at least partially validated in numerous organizations. It is, however, limited to assessment of change and does not assess existing value. It is limited to interactive conditions and does not deal with individual capabilities and the knowledge base embodied in the human resources. Its reliance on statistical analysis may be a practical hindrance and its implicit assumption of constancy through time of the degree of relevance of identified variables is a vulnerable area for concern.

Myers and Flowers' Five Dimensions Model.[32]   These authors propose a procedure for assessing the work force of an organization and estimating costs of various inputs to improve the effectiveness of the human organization. Dimensions of human assets are suggested to include knowledge, skills, health, availability, and attitudes. Assessments using checklists and subjective appraisal are suggested for measurement of the first four of these attributes, and perception surveys are used for an assessment of attitudes. The five dimensions are considered to be factorial rather than additive. The authors point out that "if one is lacking, the others are rendered correspondingly ineffective. Before deciding to improve one dimension, consideration must be given to the level of the others. . . . It may not be cost effective to improve the knowledge of an employee if his attitude is poor." Decisions should be based on cost effectiveness of each of the five dimensions.

Attitudes are suggested to be dominant. "Attitudes, including both personal values and job attitudes, constitute a readiness to respond to various life situations and, as such, give direction to knowledge, skills, health, and availability."

This way of looking at human dimensions may be useful for personnel-related decisions but may not be considered human resource accounting. However, Myers and Flowers go farther in suggesting the "dollarizing of attitudes" as follows:

Individual	Annual salary	Job grade	Tenure	Attitude weight	Attitude score	Weighted attitude score
1. John Doe	$14,000	28	5	5	1.05	5.25
2. Mary Brown	7,000	57	11	5	1.12	5.60
3. Harry Smith	9,000	12	22	7	1.21	8.47
4. Bill Jones	6,500	72	3	3	1.26	3.78
5. Jim Johnson	18,500	30	4	6	1.15	6.90
	$55,000			26		30.00

$$\text{Attitude index} = \frac{\text{weighted attitude score}}{\text{attitude weight}} = \frac{30.00}{26} = 1.15$$

Dollarized attitudes = attitude index × annual payroll = 1.15 × $55,000 = $63,250

Gain = $63,250 − $55,000 = $8,250

$$\text{Gain per person} = \frac{\$8,250}{5} = \$1,650$$

Attitude scores are determined using 1.0 as the breaking point between "turn-offs" and "turn-ons." These scores are then weighted based on positions and tenure to determine the "attitude index." "Dollarized attitudes" are determined by

[32]M. Scott Myers and Vincent S. Flowers, "A Framework for Measuring Human Assets," *California Management Review*, Summer 1974, pp. 5–16.

multiplying annual salaries by attitude scores for individuals or the attitude index for a group of individuals. The authors suggest that in this way attitude scores are connected into "financial returns on payroll investments expressed in terms of gain, break-even, or deficit." This conversion and implied concept of return on investment surely will not be satisfying to accountants, but the work of these authors is an interesting addition from the personnel field to the literature of human resource accounting.

Ogan's Discounted Certainty Equivalent Net Benefits Model.[33]   With only minor exceptions, the valuation models considered thus far emphasize human resource contributions to a firm ignoring the costs to the firm of retaining such resources. From the proprietary viewpoint of the organization this is inadequate. Ogan has proposed a model which includes explicit consideration of both the cost and benefit aspects of the value of human resources to an organization. His model, expressed in general terms, is

$$K_{kj} = \sum_{j=1}^{n} \sum_{k=t}^{L-t} \frac{1}{(1+r)^k} \tilde{V}_{qj}$$

where L = end of estimated useful life of the employee for the organization
    j = jth individual, $j = 1, 2, \ldots, n$
    r = a discount rate external to the organization (risk free)
    $\tilde{V}_{qj}$ = certainty-equivalent net benefits generated by human resources
    t = some time period from 1 to L which is a point in the useful life of employee to which the certainty-equivalent net benefits that occur after t are discounted
    K_{kj} = adjusted total net present values of human resources in a professional service organization
    $q = k + t$

The model is used to sum the discounted "certainty equivalent net benefits" with determinants as shown in Exhibit 5.

EXHIBIT 5

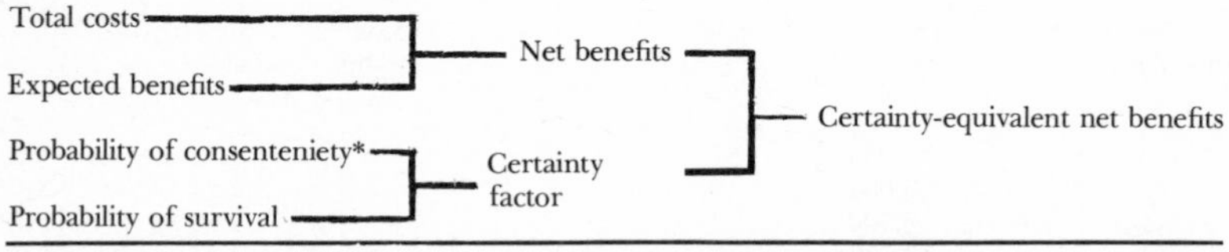

*Individual's consent to remain employed by the organization, i.e., the probability of not resigning.

This model has merit for use in organizations or groups of people whose contributions or "benefits" are readily determined or predictable, such as the case of salespeople, consultants, or other instances where revenues are based on billings for time spent with customers or clients. The model can be run at regular intervals to determine, and perhaps monitor, the changes in the value of human resources. For example, the material shown in Exhibit 6 reflects a possible analysis of causes of a change in the calculated results of applying the model at the beginning and at the end of a particular time interval.

The use of the model proposed by Ogan would present serious problems in many situations where "benefits" to the organization attributable to specific indi-

[33]Pekin Ogan, *A Human Resource Value Model and Its Operationalization in a CPA Firm*, doctoral dissertation, University of North Carolina, 1974.

EXHIBIT 6   Statement of Changes on Human Resource Value[a]

Human resource values were increased by:		
New employees	$300,500	
Increase in value of current employees	8,000	
Employees transferred in	175,000	
Total increases		$483,500
Human resource values were decreased by:		
Termination	$ 23,000	
Retirement	75,000	
Death	45,000	
Employees transferred out	38,000	
Decrease in value of current employees	52,500	
Total decreases		$233,500
Net increase or (decrease)		250,000
Add: previous HRV balance		500,000
Current human resource value		$750,000

[a]Pekin Ogan, *A Human Resource Value Model and Its Operationalization in a CPA Frim*, doctoral dissertation, University of North Carolina, 1974, p. 162.

viduals is difficult if not impossible to determine and quantify. Further, the model does not include any explicit recognition of the importance of interaction among individuals to group or organizational performance.

Brummet and Taylor's Human Resource Value Index Model.[34]   Suggesting that a knowledge of the dynamics of human resource values in an organization is more important than a knowledge of an estimate of value at a particular time, Brummet and Taylor propose the development of a human resource value index (HRVI). The initial value of an organization's human resources may be estimated and than "tracked" with successive calculations of this HRVI.

The HRVI is determined by applying an interactive multiplier (IM) to the summation of the products of individual performance ratios (IPRs) and corresponding measures of position contribution potential (PCPs). That is,

$$HRVI = IM[\Sigma(IPR \times PCP)]$$

Position analysis profiles are used to develop performance standards, which when related to personnel performance assessments will produce the individual performance ratios (IPRs)—the relation of current performance levels to standard or ideal performance levels. These measures are then weighted by the organization's perceived importance of respective positions. The Hay Plan or other recognized wage and salary assessment plans may be used to determine these weighting factors or the position contribution potentials (PCPs). Salary ranges established for each position may be used on the assumption that they reflect the relative significance of positions.

Summing the products of these two factors for each individual, the total is then multiplied by a measure of the interactive condition (IM). This measure may be determined using techniques proposed by Likert or others, scaling the results to show 1.0 as a neutral condition, less than 1.0 as detractive, and more than 1.0 as contributive.

This model for determination of a human resource value index may be used to assess human resources as currently allocated in an organization. It may lend itself to the application of optimization techniques to learn how personnel may be assigned better and thus the cost of the present allocation. Data generated by use

[34]From an unpublished work of R. Lee Brummet and Robert Taylor, "Human Resource Accounting—A Completed Model," University of North Carolina, Chapel Hill, N.C., 1974.

of the model may facilitate a marginal analysis of resource allocation to evaluate training and upgrading expenditures or the effectiveness of salary increases.

An appealing feature of this model is its explicit inclusion of both individual and group condition factors. While it is not based on the usual concept of value as the present worth of future contributions, and although it does not provide an output of the "value of the human organization," it has merit potentially as a useful operational tool for managers.

INTEGRATION OF COST-BASED AND VALUE-BASED HUMAN RESOURCE ACCOUNTING

A clear analogy may be drawn between the problem of cost-based and value-based data for human resources and similar data for other resources included in the conventional accounting model. Costs of recruiting, training, job enrichment, etc., may be identified in transactional form and recognized as investments. Dealing with such balances in an accounting system and representing in- and outflows may be visualized readily by accountants.

Valued-based data defies or at best strains the facility of the conventional accounting model as an ongoing dynamic construct for the entity. The model does not facilitate the recording of second-order variables such as attitude changes that are, by nature, nontransactional. Until a new conception of a much broader and more versatile accounting model is available, a fully exploitive calculus of human resources of an organization will not be possible.[35]

Assessment of human resources and human resource value dynamics of an organization may, within the constraints of the conventional accounting model, take the form of periodic human resource inventory adjustment with the attendant limitations of lack of timeliness and certainty with which cause-and-effect relationships may be inferred. Nevertheless, recognizing the conceptual relationship of estimated cost and value surrogates and conventional results measures may set the stage for further development.

Exhibit 7 portrays this relationship. Conventional accounting systems assess the end-result phenomena captured in the current period and relate them to incomplete measures of investments in earlier periods. By adding human resource investments dynamics information (a potential product of cost-based human resource accounting) and interspacing measures of human resource condition (a potential product of value-based human resource accounting), concepts of return on investment may be refined, and concepts of return on human resource building investments and return on human resource utilization may be introduced into management thinking and, in turn, impact on management decisions.

Exhibit 8 illustrates, in unrealistically simple form, the substance of such possibilities within the conventional accounting constraint.

It is at least interesting to note that during the first quarter of 19X0, a new investment of $95,000 was made while the estimated value of human resources increased $96,000 and book-value write-offs amounted to $60,000, accounting for the $61,000 increase of the excess of estimated value of human resources over their book values. By separating the representations that are cost-based and those that are value-based the reader is put on guard to make his own interpretations of each set of figures based on a knowledge of the measurement techniques that produced them.

[35]Trever Gambling has suggested the need for accountants to broaden their scope of concerns and develop metasystems to include second-order effects and eventually recognize the interactive nature of *real* systems. See Trevor Gambling, "A Systems Approach to Human Resource Accounting," *The Accounting Review,* July 1974, pp. 538–546.

EXHIBIT 7   Cost and Value Surrogates and End Results

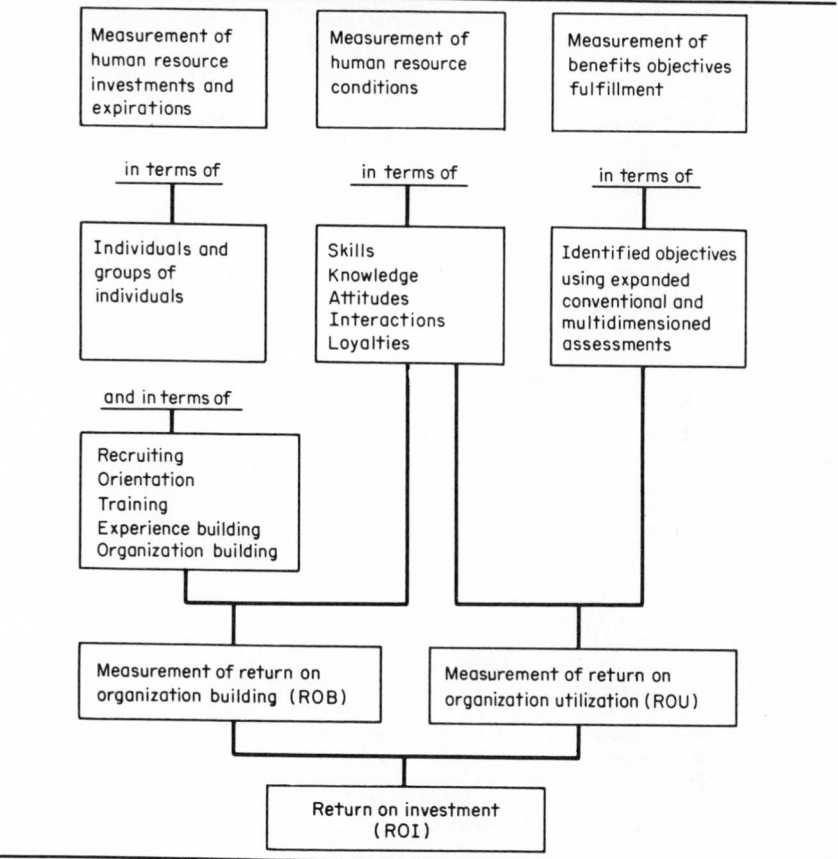

USE OF HUMAN RESOURCE ACCOUNTING
INFORMATION FOR MANAGEMENT DECISIONS

Management emphasis on profit maximization or profit targets makes the calculation of such profit a critical process. The failure of organizations to capitalize certain investments in human resources causes profit to be significantly understated in periods of rapid human resource building and significantly overstated in periods of human resource deterioration. In this way managers and indeed stockholders and the public are misled and perhaps caused to make counterproductive decisions. The dangers in this area are particularly great for segment performance reports using profit center accounting. A manager may use a management style which gets results measured by conventional accounting in the short run as highly contributive to profit even though employee attitudes are deteriorating and antagonisms are growing. The manager's actions may be detrimental to the organization even though profits appear very satisfactory. A fully implemented human resource accounting system would bring this situation to a reckoning so as to prevent the rewarding of poor performance and make possible the rewarding of good, more complete performance.

A significant aspect of performance measurement is the use of return on assets

EXHIBIT 8
_____

EXAMPLE COMPANY
Balance Sheet, January 1, 19X0

Current Assets		$ 700,000
Plant		1,300,000
Investment in Human Resources	$500,000	
Excess of Estimated Value over Cost of Human		
Resources	300,000	
Estimated Value of Human Organization		800,000
Total Assets		$2,800,000
Current Liabilities		$ 300,000
Capital Stock		1,000,000
Retained Earnings:		
Financial, Product, and Plant Resources	$700,000	
Human Resources—Cost	500,000	
Human Resources—Additional Value	300,000	1,500,000
Total Liabilities and Capital		$2,800,000

Income Statement for Quarter Ended March 31, 19X0

Sales			$2,000,000
Expenses:			
Depreciation of Plant		$ 82,000	
Human Resource Expenditures		715,000	
Other Expenses		913,000	1,710,000
			$ 290,000
Income Tax Charges (48%)			139,200
Income Before Recognizing Change in Estimated Value			
Value of Human Resources			$ 150,800
Additions to Human Resources		$ 95,000	
Less: Amortization	$45,000		
Write-offs	15,000	60,000	
Net Increase in Investment in Human Resources			35,000
Net Increase in Excess of Estimated Value of Human			
Resources over Cost			61,000
Income Including Change in Estimated			
Value of Human Resources			$ 246,800

Balance Sheet, March 31, 19X0

Current Assets		$ 832,800
Plant		1,318,000
Investment in Human Resources	$535,000	
Excess of Estimated Value of Human Resources	361,000	
Estimated Value of Human Organization		896,000
Total Assets		$3,046,800
Current Liabilities		$ 300,000
Capital Stock		1,000,000
Retained Earnings:		
Financial, Product, and Plant Resources	$850,800	
Human Resources—Cost	535,000	
Human Resources—Additional Value	361,000	1,746,800
Total Liabilities and Capital		$3,046,800

_____

or return on investment. Using human resource accounting this measure or performance index becomes

$$\frac{\text{Conventional profit or profit contribution} \pm \text{change in human resources}}{\text{Conventional assets or investment} + \text{human assets}}$$

Used as a critical measure, new decision areas are highlighted and different decisions may be made. An interesting possibility exists for intracompany "transfer pricing" of people. As individuals move from one segment to another, the asset bases of these calculations change so that responsibility heads are charged with or released from an incremental amount of profit expectation. This practice, if it could be implemented, could encourage more effective assignment and utilization of personnel.

The conventional practice of "expensing" all human resource expenditures has deterred managers from giving close scrutiny to these costs. Human resource accounting, when fully implemented, can give managers criteria for determining the optimum amount and mix of human resource expenditures. This must involve measures of return on investments in recruiting, training, experience building, and other personnel areas and the related trade-offs. It can encourage managers to extend well-known capital budgeting procedures to human resource investments and to develop postaudit techniques to provide experience data for the making of new decisions. The managerial incentives in this area are exactly analogous to those leading to expenditures for research and development.

One of the most usual concerns of personnel directors is employee turnover. Some organizations have made studies of cost of turnover to provide information for personnel decisions. Few, if any, have altered the information process to capture these costs on a regular continuing basis. Human resource accounting can assist by identifying unrecovered investments in exiting employees and by providing continuously updated cost information for those activities such as recruiting and training that are occasioned by personnel turnover. It can provide information that will assist in determining wage and salary and fringe benefit policy that may be appropriate to optimize the rate and nature of personnel turnover.

A final area to be mentioned, but by no means the only remaining possible area, is that of measuring effectiveness and efficiency of the personnel function or department of a company. Human resource accounting can help to bring under close surveillance the costs and results (benefits) of a personnel department. Cost and result standards may be set up for the several activities of the personnel department and actual performance measured in relation to them. As a result the personnel function may be given a more prominent position in the organization— a role which it may well deserve.

IMPACT OF HUMAN RESOURCE ACCOUNTING ON MANAGEMENT CONCEPTS AND BEHAVIOR

The significance of information availability and visibility in organizations and in society is well known. The conventional accounting model and the performance signals that it produces have come to impact upon, if not direct, management's efforts to accomplish its objectives, particularly in the primary area of profitability. Accordingly, the inclusion or exclusion within the accounting model of potential bits of information conditions the views of decision makers and affects the decision made.

The immediate impact, by conventional accounting, of human resource costs on reported profits may lead to decisions that are influenced by tax considerations or biases toward reporting larger or smaller profits for the period at hand. For example, a manager trying hard to minimize tax payments will look with greater favor on human resource investment that is expensed than on physical resource investment to get a short-run tax advantage, while a manager already conscious of the embarrassing aspects of a declining profit trend may favor physical resource investment over human resource investment so as to postpone the impact upon recorded profits. Human resource accounting could eliminate this unintended and unjustified bias.

It is argued often that managers will, by nature, emphasize the maintenance of assets that are represented regularly on the balance sheet as opposed to "off-balance-sheet" items. To the extent that this is true, human resource accounting may direct managers' attention and degree of emphasis to the personnel of the organization and encourage maintenance and upgrading programs and experiences for this resource that might otherwise fail to be given consideration.

It may be suggested further that human resource accounting is in itself a way of communicating to the people of an organization that their role is considered critical, and that managers are going to be evaluated, at least in part, on the basis of their contribution to the development of the human resources under their control. If this communication is effective it will most certainly affect decisions and behavior.

The assessment of human resource conditions through either cost-based or value-based data is likely to encourage managers to take a longer-run view of their decisions. The impact of human resource investments as well as other decisions and management styles are now represented as a human resource condition precedent to the ultimate productivity or effectiveness of the organization. Human resources become the first-order effect and conventional profit or cash flows become the second- or third-order results. Managers must now think through this process and become aware of the longitudinal linkages and the sequential decisions necessary for the organization to exploit fully its potential success. Although currently not in the lexicon of management concepts, human resource capital budgeting may become a highly contributive field for consideration. Techniques may be developed to justify the amount and the mix of periodic human resource investments.

Several authors have recognized the potential impact of human resource accounting in providing a new basis for management thought and action. Wright observes that:[36]

> A new way of thinking about the human resource is emerging. It is apparent that the reconceptualization of the only vital factor of production will have a profound impact on the way managers manage. The new set of concepts is coming as an outgrowth of the design of accounting systems adequate to measure the costs of human resources and to report manpower as a capital asset. Though of itself the revised accounting system will not improve the management of . . . [people], it will provide substantive evidence of . . . [their] value and, therefore, act to emphasize that . . . [each person] *is a unique entity requiring individualized consideration.*"

IMPLEMENTATION PROBLEMS

Problems of implementation of human resource accounting systems are both technical and conceptual. The technical problems of cost-based systems are not insurmountable. The input cost-tracing requirements are, for the most part, analogous to other cost-tracing problems with which accountants deal on a regular basis. Many of the cost expirations are readily identifiable as individuals leave the employ of the organization or as input costs are made obsolete by changed human resource needs of the company. Accountants need only be tolerant of some greater degrees of uncertainty in the prediction of useful lives of the organization's investments and develop models which will enable them to lessen such uncertainty. Such models may provide some highly useful decision inputs as well as serving needs of the accounting system.

The major problem for implementing a cost-based human resource accounting system may be one of cost justification since it is difficult, if not impossible, to cost

---

[36]Robert Wright, "Managing Man as a Capital Asset," *Personnel Journal,* April 1970, p. 290.

justify any human resource accounting effort without some experimentation based on faith and conviction—a condition not uncommon in organization decision making.

The technical problems of value-based human resource accounting are substantial. Recognizing this, accountants and business managers may be expected to innovate with great caution. Neither the typical general manager nor the trained accountant has the measurement expertise to implement a value-based system. The technical aspects of the measurement practices should come from the psychologist, the psychometrician, and the behavioralist. Accountants must explore these areas in order to perform as members of an interdisciplinary team to implement value-based human resource accounting.

At least as formidable as the technical problems are the conceptual hurdles that must be cleared before an organization can expect significant progress in implementing a human resource accounting system. Some aspects of these conceptual problems are as follows:

1. Cultural constraints and taboos may exist to cause concern for any association of dollar measures with people. Some may fear the implication of discrimination or dehumanization even though such accounting may be likely to cause managers to show much greater concern for the well-being of the organization's employees.

2. Accountants tend to insist on legal ownership as a prerequisite for an asset and to require substantial certainty of future benefits to be received to justify capitalization in any accounting system. Yet it may well be argued that an organization should account for and monitor those things which are most significant in the organization without regard for legal ownership or certainty of the value represented, and human resources meet such a criterion.

3. Accountants and others reflect a visibility or physical asset bias which causes them to insist on capitalization of the cost of obvious improvements of plant and equipment yet show reluctance to consider personnel development as an asset. Yet it may be argued that unless there is evidence that a decision to send a manager to a training program was a mistake, the associated costs to the firm should be capitalized and matched against future benefits even though the manager's physical appearance does not change to a noticeable degree.

4. The necessity for an interdisciplinary involvement—at least for value-based human resource accounting—may be a serious deterrent to implementation. This may gradually disappear as managers and accountants realize that the information specialist must work in close collaboration with, and be receptive to, new developments in fields other than their own. In this instance the accountant must cooperate particularly with those in the fields of psychology and social system measurement.

A committee of the American Accounting Association has suggested that the more important obstacles to acceptance of human resource accounting are the following:[37]

(a) Human resource accounting has to some managers seemed a hastily constructed discipline made up of "recycled parts" from other disciplines. . . . The result is not always pleasant and often the parts have not functioned satisfactorily in their original habitat. . . .

(b) The field of "human resource accounting" unfortunately has an exploitative connotation to some people. A *resource* is usually something that is used up; and *accounting* implies using a tool that will make this exploitation process as efficient as possible. . . .

[37]Report of the Committee on Accounting for Human Resources, *The Accounting Review,* Committee Reports Supplement, 1974, p. 122.

(c) It is difficult to change management's view of people from being an expense rather than a resource.

HUMAN RESOURCE ACCOUNTING—PUBLIC REPORTING AND ATTESTATION

As for most new developments in accounting, internal experimentation and refinement and codification should precede general use and disclosure in public reports. Published corporate reports over the past several years show some increased emphasis upon personnel or human resource information, but inclusion of dollar representations are very seldom reported. Some exceptions may be noted.

Electronic Data Systems has reported the capitalization and related amortization of certain training costs and with apparent approval of its external auditors.

Certain professional athletic organizations have capitalized player development costs and purchased player contracts and reported such amounts with related amortizations in their published reports.

In 1967, the Flying Tiger Line, Inc., included an item on its balance sheet for "training costs applicable to aircraft, being amortized." This treatment of "initial training and pre-operating costs" was a part of an unqualified opinion of the firm's external auditors. However, the company changed its practice in 1969 to "expense" such costs.

Abt and Associates, Inc., includes an asset representation in the amount of the present value equivalent of the salaries estimated to be paid in the future to its currently employed personnel on its "Social Balance Sheet." In this instance human resource accounting is a part of a suggested "Annual Report and Social Audit." The external auditors do not give an opinion on these data.

The R. G. Barry Corporation shows its cost-based human resource accounting data fully integrated into its balance sheet and income statement but supplementary to the "conventional only" data and with a very clear disclaimer of its external auditors. Gordon Zacks, the president of R. G. Barry, has indicated that while human resource accounting is not currently generally accepted practice, he expects it to become so in the future. The company stopped formal publication of human resource accounting data in 1974. R. L. Woodruff, Vice President for Human Resources and Management Services, has indicated that "we have discontinued publication of the HRA 'total concept' financial statement in our annual report to stockholders. As we stated originally, the purpose of Human Resource Accounting was to provide internal management with more complete information on resources managed, not for the investing community. Because of the interest in the topic, however, we did publish the HRA statements for several years in our annual report."[38]

The possibility of including human resource accounting in public reports brings with it the question of attestation by independent auditors. Cost inputs to human resources are readily subject to verification by the auditor and thus present no new problems. Cost expirations, on the other hand, if based on the theoretically sound assessment of future benefits remaining for the organization, present some problems for the accountant because of the limited state of the art for prediction of human behavior. Yet the accounting profession tolerates estimates related to the future in depreciation accounting and other areas that are perhaps as unpredictable in its conventional practice. The codification of standard practice for human resource cost expirations might justify acceptance by the independent auditor.

The attestation of value-based data for human resources in public reports

---

[38]R. G. Barry Corporation form letter, undated, by Robert L. Woodruff.

presents quite different and more substantial problems for accountants. At the time of this writing, the author knows of no value-based human resource quantitative data in published reports. However, with the rapidly growing interest in value-based accounting generally, with its partial dependence upon rapidly developing nonaccounting disciplines, the possibility for value-based human resource accounting at some time in the future should not be ignored.

Human resource information requirements of governmental agencies, such as the Office of Health, Education, and Welfare, the Equal Employment Opportunity Commission, and others, is increasing rapidly. Society, operating through such agencies, may soon consider this information to be as critical as the conventional financial information on Forms 10-K required by the Securities and Exchange Commission. Pressures for independent attestation to improve the credibility of such information may increase. As these changes are perceived, the accounting profession should and is likely to respond and develop some reasonable vehicles for serving in this capacity.

The Committee on Measurement of Corporate Social Performance of the American Institute of Certified Public Accountants has suggested that accountants may give some assurances short of attestation for social performance information by "(1) defining that assurance, (2) giving one's authority for it and (3) taking reasonable precautions that the audience for the report will not be such as to misunderstand and misuse it." It suggests the acronym "redsa" to refer to a "review to develop a suitable appraisal." This could potentially also be used in connection with human resource information.

Flamholtz suggests that[39]

> Human resource accounting will ... have an impact upon corporate financial reporting. In the future, corporations will report on their investments in human assets. At first, this information will be reported in the President's letter of corporate annual reports. The purpose will be to show management's attention to building human assets. Some companies may choose to include this information in a statement of intangibles, and some will include it in pro-forma financial statements. Ultimately, however, it will be included in conventional financial statements as a generally accepted accounting practice.

Notwithstanding the various possibilities and the instances of usage that have been noted, there appears to be little prospect for the inclusion of human resource accounting as an integral part of generally accepted accounting principles within the next several years.

HUMAN RESOURCE ACCOUNTING AND SOCIAL PERFORMANCE ACCOUNTING

Accountants and professionals in several other disciplines are reflecting increased interest in the field of social accounting or the measurement and reporting of social performance of organizations. Some common aspects of social accounting and human resource accounting have caused several authors to deal with the two subjects as nearly synonomous even though they are quite separate and have quite different objectives. Both areas deal with the study and assessment of people and they both rely, in part, on measurement techniques closely associated with the fields of psychology and sociology. There is a subset of social accounting which deals with the assessment of a company's impacts on its employees as perceived by its employees and society. Human resource accounting, on the other hand, deals with the employees' impacts on a company as perceived by the company. In this context this subset of social accounting and human resource accounting are alike

[39]Eric Flamholtz, *Human Resource Accounting, op. cit.*, p. 336.

to the extent that there is an intersection of individual, familial, and societal fulfillment and organizationally related performance. This intersection is clearly not void, but to assume it to be 100 percent is unjustified. Social accounting is likely to be adopted by managements because of a changed perception of the role of the business organization in our social structure. Human resource accounting will be adopted by businesses if managements and stockholders come to believe the information to be useful in fulfilling their purposes.

A FINAL NOTE TO ACCOUNTANTS

Human resource accounting is still in its infancy. Much more research and experimentation is necessary. Yet at this time it presents an inviting challenge to accountants. The profession may well consider the following:[40]

> The increasing interest in [human resource] accounting is likely to result in a dilemma for many accountants. On one hand, human resource accounting is a new and virtually unknown area for accountants. Moreover, this area deals with variables that are particularly difficult to measure and are beyond the range of what has been considered "accounting" in past. On the other hand it is clear that accountants have special skills which can be applied in the development of human resource accounting systems. The critical question is whether accountants will be willing to use these skills in a solution to human resource accounting problems or whether they will prefer to restrict themselves to the more conventional models with which they are familiar.

Performance of organizations may be viewed usefully as the success achieved in the acquisition, development, and utilization of resources. One of the most important, if not the most important, is the human component. Extant information systems in organizations and in society do not provide adequate information relevant to this human resource. Information systems and particularly accounting systems can and may in the future deal with the human resource to reflect its premier position as the most important asset of any organization.

BIBLIOGRAPHY

Alexander, Michael O.: "Investments in People," *The Canadian Chartered Accountant,* July 1971.

Brummet, R. Lee: "Accounting for Human Resources," *The Journal of Accountancy,* December 1970, pp. 62–66.

Brummet, R. Lee, William C. Pyle, and Eric G. Flamholtz: "Human Resource Accounting: A Tool to Increase Managerial Effectiveness," *Management Accounting,* August 1969, pp. 12–15.

————: "Human Resource Accounting in Industry," *Personnel Administration,* July/August 1969, pp. 34–46.

————: "Human Resource Measurement—A Challenge for Accountants," *The Accounting Review,* April 1968, pp. 217–224.

Caplan, Edwin H., and Stephen Landekich: *Human Resource Accounting: Past, Present, and Future,* National Association of Accountants, New York, 1974.

Elias, Nabil S.: *Elias' Experimental Study of the Effects of Human Asset Statements on the Investment Decision,* Research Summary 8-1, University of Minnesota.

Flamholtz, Eric G.: *Human Resource Accounting,* Dickenson, Encino, Calif.: 1974.

————: "A Model for Human Resource Valuation: A Stochastic Process with Service Rewards," *The Accounting Review,* April 1972, pp. 148–152.

————: "Towards a Theory of Human Resource Value in Formal Organization," *The Accounting Review,* October 1972, pp. 666–678.

Gambling, Trevor: *How to Put the Accounting into Human Resource Accounting,* University College of North Wales, Bangor, Gwynedd, occasional paper presented at the Human

---

[40]Edwin H. Caplan and Stephen Landekich, *op. cit.,* pp. 135 and 136.

Resource Accounting Seminar, European Institute for Advanced Studies in Management, Brussels, November 28–29, 1974.

Glautier, M. W. E.: *Human Resource Accounting: A Critique of Research Objectives for the Development of Human Resource Accounting Models,* University College of North Wales, Bangor, Gwynedd, occasional paper presented at the Human Resource Accounting Seminar, European Institute for Advanced Studies in Management, Brussels, November 28–29, 1974.

Hekimian, James, and Curtis H. Jones: "Put People on Your Balance Sheet," *Harvard Business Review,* January-February 1967, pp. 105–113.

Hermanson, Roger H.: *Accounting for Human Assets,* occasional paper No. 14, Bureau of Business and Economic Research, Michigan State University, East Lansing, Mich., 1964.

Hermanson, Roger H., et al.: "Human Resource Accounting," supplement to *The Accounting Review,* 1973, pp. 169–184.

Jaggi, Bikki, and Hon-Shiang Lau: "Toward a Model for Human Resource Valuation," *The Accounting Review,* XLIX, 2 (April 1974), pp. 321–329.

Kiker, B. F.: "The Historical Roots of the Concept of Human Capital," *Journal of Political Economy,* vol. 74, no. 5, 1966, pp. 481–499.

Lev, Baruch, and Aba Schwartz: "On the Use of the Economic Concept of Human Capital in Financial Statements," *The Accounting Review,* January 1971, pp. 103–112.

Likert, Rensis: *The Human Organization: Its Management and Value,* McGraw-Hill Book Company, New York, 1967.

Likert, Rensis, and William C. Pyle: "A Human Organizational Measurement Approach," *The Financial Analysts Journal,* January/February 1971, pp. 75–84.

Pyle, William C.: "Human Resource Accounting," *The Financial Analysts Journal,* September/October 1970, pp. 69–78.

———: *Human Resource Accounting, A Tool for Improving Managerial Decisions,* Doctoral dissertation, University of Michigan, 1971.

———: "Monitoring Human Resources 'On Line,'" *Michigan Business Review,* July 1970, pp. 19–32.

Saunders, D. A.: *Human Resource Accounting,* Ashridge Management College, Berkhamsted, Hertfordshire HP4 INS, occasional paper presented at the Human Resource Accounting Seminar, European Institute for Advanced Studies in Management, Brussels, November 28–29, 1974.

Schultz, T. W.: "Investment in Human Capital," *American Economic Review,* LI, March 1969, pp. 1–17.

Thurow, L.: *Investment in Human Capital,* Wadsworth Publishing Company, Belmont, Calif., 1970.

Woodruff, R. L., Jr.: "Human Resource Accounting," *The Canadian Chartered Accountant,* September 1970, pp. 156–161.

Wright, Robert G.: "Managing Man as a Capital Asset," *Personnel Journal,* April 1970, pp. 290–298.

Zacks, Gordon: *How We Rebuilt Our Company,* Barry Corporation, Columbus, Ohio.

———: "People Are Capital Investments at R. G. Barry Corporation," *Management Accounting,* November 1971.

———: "Report of the American Accounting Association Committee on Human Resource Accounting," *The Accounting Review,* supplement to vol. 49, 1974.

Chapter **38**

SEC Procedures and Regulations

PAUL M. FOSTER
Partner, Coopers & Lybrand

JOSEPH M. CONDER
Partner, Coopers & Lybrand

THE SEC AND THE LAWS IT ADMINISTERS

The Securities and Exchange Commission is an independent regulatory agency of the United States government. There are five Commissioners appointed by the President with the consent of the Senate. One Commissioner is designated as the Chairman by the President. The Commission has a bipartisan makeup since no more than three Commissioners may be members of the same political party.

The Commission is assisted by a professional staff organized into divisions and offices directly responsible to the Commission, as shown by the organization chart in Exhibit 1.

Regional office functions are generally limited to broker-dealer matters, suspected trading violations, and handling the abbreviated Regulation A filings for offerings not exceeding $500,000. All other functions of the Commission take place in Washington, D.C.

Accountants generally have more contact with the *Division of Corporation Finance* than with any other group. This Division handles the direct case work of reviewing registrant companies' filings of registration statements, proxy statements, and periodic reports. The Division is organized into a number of branches, each of which contains accountants, lawyers, security analysts, and examiners. Upon completion of its review of a filing, the Division customarily issues a "letter of comment" outlining deficiencies to be corrected or additional information to be furnished before reports are cleared or registrations become effective. Some comments tend to be trivial; others are quite significant and even precedent-setting. If the registrant or its accountants do not agree with the accounting positions expressed in the letter of comment, the SEC staff is open to discussion by telephone or in person to try to resolve the differences. The Chief Accountant of the Division has the authority to reverse the original determination.

In certain circumstances, the SEC staff may determine, at its discretion, not to conduct the customary review of registration statements described above, but instead to make a different, less complete review. One such type is the "cursory review," established in 1968 in response to an increase in the volume of filings. When the SEC staff makes a cursory review, it advises the registrant of that fact and that no comments, either written or oral, can be expected. The registrant is required to furnish to the SEC, as supplemental information, representation letters from its chief executive officer, independent accountants, and underwriter, stating that they are aware of the cursory review and of their statutory responsibilities. The SEC staff generally declares the registration effective upon receipt of those letters.

The Chief Accountant of the Commission, as distinguished from the Chief Accountant of the Division of Corporation Finance, operates at the policy level. He or she is the principal staff advisor to the Commission on all matters of accounting and auditing. More than anyone else in the agency, the Chief Accountant of the Commission determines how much influence the SEC has on accounting principles and auditing practice, both of which are discussed later.

Legislative Basis.   The accountant is most concerned with the following Acts: the Securities Act of 1933, the Securities Exchange Act of 1934, and the Investment Company Act of 1940.

The Securities Act of 1933.   This Act is concerned primarily with the distribution of securities rather than with trading in securities. The law provides for the registration of securities with the Commission before they may be sold to the public.

The 1933 Act is a *disclosure* statute designed to give the prospective investor an adequate basis for making investment decisions and to prevent misrepresentation or fraud in the sale of securities. These objectives are generally accomplished by

EXHIBIT 1 Organization Chart of the Securities and Exchange Commission

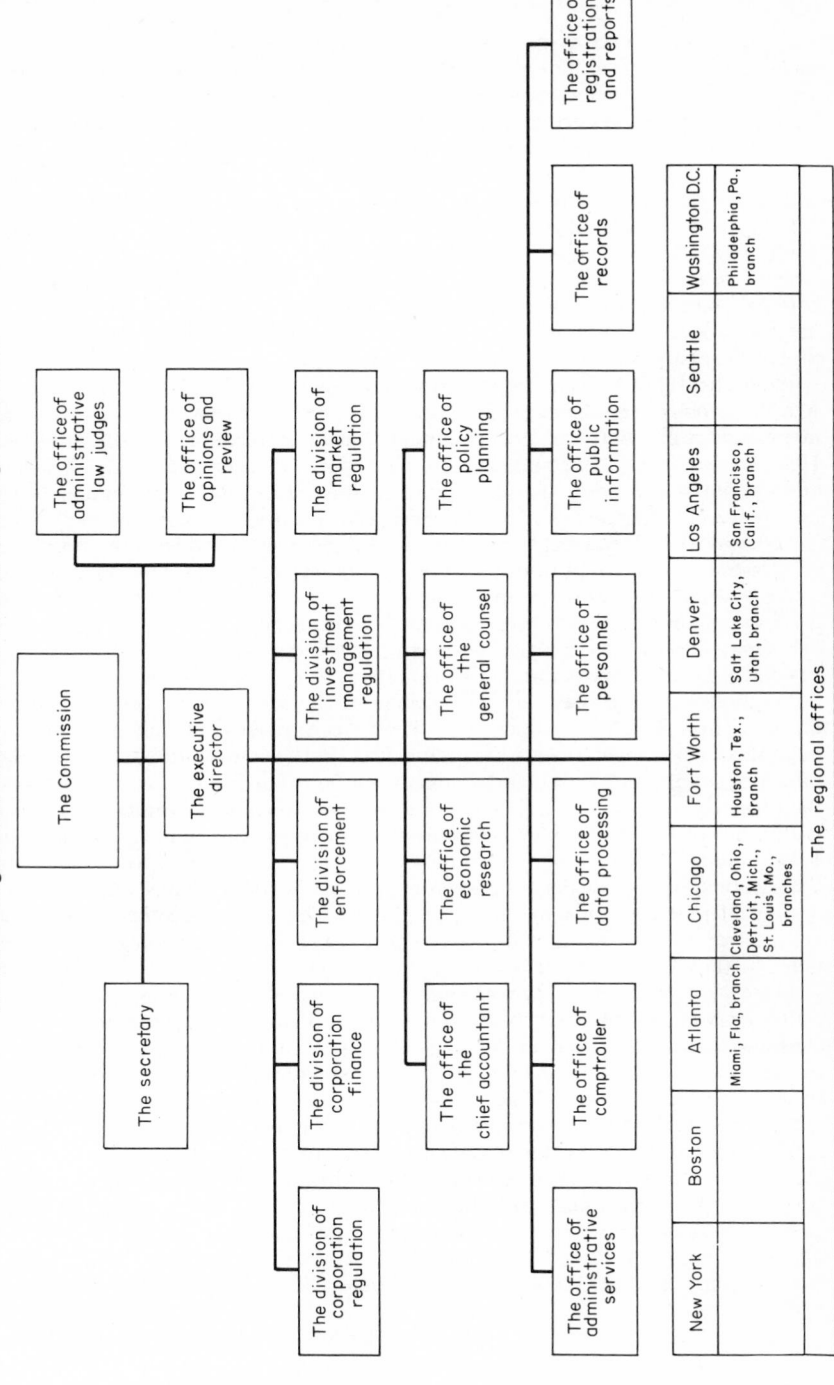

requiring disclosure of specified financial and other information regarding the issuer of securities.

Required disclosure is provided by means of a registration statement which includes a prospectus. The prospectus (which is Part I of the registration statement) must be furnished to the buyer of the registered security. Preliminary "red herring" prospectuses are frequently used to permit formation of underwriting syndicates and to provide information to interested parties in advance of the actual offering.

The preparation of a registration statement is a complicated, technical process. To the management of a first-time offeror, it can well be a traumatic, albeit frequently satisfying, experience.

The Securities Exchange Act of 1934.   The 1934 Act provides for registration of national securities exchanges, securities listed on exchanges, and broker-dealers. It is concerned primarily with the trading of securities which have been previously distributed.

While the 1934 Act calls for registration of securities not covered by the 1933 Act, its principal significance to registrants is the continuing reporting requirements it places upon them. Most companies having securities registered under the 1933 Act or the 1934 Act must file[1] annual reports, quarterly reports, and certain other reports relating to the occurrence of specified events. The annual report now requires essentially as much financial data as a registration statement.

The Investment Company Act of 1940.   This Act is concerned with the regulation of investment companies (mutual funds and other companies engaged primarily in the business of investing, reinvesting, or trading in securities). The Act classifies investment companies into the following two principal types:

- Open-ended (shares issued and repurchased daily)
- Closed-ended (fixed number of shares).

A substantial percentage of transactions in the securities markets is effected through investment companies. The 1940 Act provides for the regulation of investment companies concerning such matters as the composition of the board of directors, margin purchases, and management fees. The Act requires disclosure of the financial and investment policies of these companies and prohibits changes in the nature of the business or in the investment policies without approval of the stockholders. The Act also requires the Commission's advance approval of certain transactions, such as dealings between the company and affiliates and insiders.

A problem that has plagued many companies over the years is that of becoming an "inadvertent investment company." These are basically companies which at any point in time happen to have 40 percent of their noncash assets in investment securities. For purposes of the computation, all assets are taken at fair market value rather than at the amount shown on the company's books. The question of what constitutes "investment securities" has been litigated in recent years. The SEC staff still tends to adhere to some of its original interpretations, notwithstanding recent court cases interpreting the law to the contrary. Becoming involved in questions relating to "inadvertent investment companies" is expensive and time-consuming and, more important, an assertion or a ruling that a company does so qualify can result in substantial 1940 Act restraints on the kinds of transactions into which such a company may enter. It is, therefore, important for any company to discuss 1940 Act matters with counsel as soon as the first sign of a question on this topic appears.

Other Acts.   The SEC administers the Public Utility Holding Company Act of 1935, the Trust Indenture Act of 1939, and the Investment Advisers Act of 1940. The Commission also serves as advisor to federal courts in reorganization pro-

---

[1]For certain exceptions, see "Continuing Reporting Obligations" in this chapter.

ceedings under Chapter X of the National Bankruptcy Act and has certain limited duties under Section 851 of the Internal Revenue Code of 1954.

PUBLIC OFFERINGS—REGISTRATION WITH THE SEC

The preparation of a registration statement for filing under the Securities Act of 1933 is almost invariably a combined operation. Representatives of the management of the registering company, the underwriters, the independent public accountants, counsel for the company, counsel for the underwriters, and, occasionally, engineers or appraisers all have important roles in preparing the registration document. When the registration statement has been completed, an executed copy, together with conformed copies and exhibits, is taken or mailed to the principal office of the SEC in Washington, D.C., for "filing" with the Commission.

Processing of Registration Statement. The registration statement is processed in the Division of Corporation Finance, which reviews the document to see whether it contains untrue statements of material facts or omissions of material facts which make the statements that are made misleading—in short, whether there has been full and fair disclosure. In the processing, the registration statement will be reviewed by a group working individually and collectively under the supervision of an Assistant Director of the Division. The group usually includes a lawyer, an accountant, and a financial analyst; a copy of the registration statement is furnished to each of them. If necessary or desirable, they will consult with other experts (such as mining engineers or petroleum engineers) or with other departments of the government. The reviewers prepare memoranda of their findings.

The SEC's letter of comment, customarily sent upon completion of the review, sets forth in detail those matters that the staff feels require revision or expansion. Sometimes the letter requests supplemental information which upon receipt and review by the staff may produce additional comments. The SEC's comments are carefully considered by everyone concerned with the registration statement.

Matters having to do with financial statements and schedules and the summary of operations are usually delegated to the issuer's financial and accounting personnel and the certifying accountants in order that an agreement may be reached on what to do about the SEC's comments. In the majority of cases, the registration statement is amended in accordance with the letter of comment. However, if the comments relate to revision of the financial statements and the registrant desires to discuss or possibly rebut them, the SEC staff is usually available for telephone discussion or an appointment in Washington. In a good many cases, the comments may be modified or withdrawn, or supplemental information may satisfy them.

When there is agreement as to the changes to be made, the amendment is filed and the changes are examined by the staff. In some cases, a further letter of comment may be necessary.

When a registration statement is filed, usually there is a meeting of minds between the issuer and the underwriter as to the type of security to be sold. In almost all cases, however, the issuer and the underwriter do not agree as to the price at which the securities are to be offered to the public, the underwriter's discount or commission, or the net proceeds to the issuer. If the registration statement relates to preferred stock or bonds, there is usually no agreement at the time of the initial filing as to the precise terms, the interest rate, or the dividend rate, an assumed price being used for the purpose of filing. These matters usually are still undecided at the time of filing the amendment that cures the deficiencies, if any.

While the registration statement and the amendment curing the deficiencies are in process of preparation, negotiations are conducted leading to the final underwriting agreement. At the appropriate time, the underwriting agreement is completed and signed by authorized representatives of the issuer and the underwriter. At this time, another amendment to the registration statement is prepared, which fills in the blank spaces in previous SEC filings relating to such items as the interest rate, the dividend rate, the public offering prices, the underwriter's discount or commission, and the net proceeds to the company. This is called the "price amendment," and at the time of its filing the issuer and the underwriter customarily request acceleration (waiver of 20-day waiting period) so that the proposed offering to the public may be made promptly and the company may receive the proceeds.

Form S-1. *Form S-1* is the form most commonly used to register securities under the 1933 Act. A listing of the items of information required to be included in the form provides a good indication of the types and quantity of data required by the SEC in the registration process:

Part I. Information required in the prospectus:

Item 1.	Offering price information and distribution spread
Item 2.	Plan of distribution, names of underwriters and their participations, and nature of the underwriters' obligation
Item 3.	Use of proceeds to registrant
Item 4.	Sales of securities other than for cash
Item 5.	Capital structure
Item 6.	Summary of operations
Item 7.	State and date of incorporation and type of organization of the registrant
Item 8.	Parents of the registrant and basis of control
Item 9.	Description of the business and its development during the past five years
Item 10.	Description and location of principal plants, mines, and other physical properties
Item 11.	If organized within five years, names of and transactions with promoters
Item 12.	Pending legal proceedings other than routine litigation
Items 13, 14, 15.	Information as to capital stock, funded debt, or other securities being registered
Item 16.	Names of directors and executive officers and the principal occupations of the latter during the past five years
Item 17.	Remuneration paid by the affiliated group during latest fiscal year to (1) each director and each of the three highest paid officers of the registrant who received more than $30,000, and (2) all directors and officers as a group
Item 18.	Outstanding options to purchase securities from the registrant or subsidiaries
Item 19.	Principal holders of registrant's securities
Item 20.	Interest of directors, officers, and certain other persons in certain material transactions during last three years or in any proposed transaction
Item 21.	Financial statements

Part II. Information not required in the prospectus:

Item 22.	Arrangements limiting, restricting, or stabilizing the market for securities being offered
Item 23.	Expenses of the issue
Item 24.	Relationship with registrant of experts named in the registration statement (including accountants)
Item 25.	Sale of securities to special parties
Item 26.	Recent sales of unregistered securities
Item 27.	List of subsidiaries of the registrant
Item 28.	Franchises or concessions held by the registrant and subsidiaries
Item 29.	Indemnification arrangements for officers and directors
Item 30.	Accounting for proceeds from sale of capital stock being registered
Item 31.	List of financial statements and exhibits.

The *financial statements* called for in Item 21 are the traditional balance sheet, income statements (three years), statements of additional paid-in capital (three years), statements of retained earnings (three years), and statements of changes in financial position (three years). Financial statements of an interim period of the current fiscal year are also required if the prospectus is prepared other than at year-end. Financial statements for the three years are required to be certified, but interim statements may normally be presented on an unaudited basis. Consolidated statements are called for; separate statements of the parent company may also be required, depending on the application of certain rules (see discussion under "Annual Reporting" below).

Prescribed schedules must be furnished in support of balance sheets and income statements. The schedules provide additional information on such matters as plant additions and retirements; receivables from directors, officers, and employees; long-term debt; indebtedness to and from affiliates, and stock reserved for warrants or other rights. Income statements may be omitted from Item 21 if the required information is included in the summary of operations (Item 6).

Summary of Operations (Summary of Earnings). This is, without a doubt, the most important financial statement in most prospectuses. It gives the prospective investor a bird's-eye view of the company's operations, expressed in financial terms. The Summary is basically a five-year comparative income statement which permits the reader to look beyond the absolute earnings and earnings-per-share figures to their trend over the five-year period. In the case of prospectuses prepared other than at year-end, data must be included for the interim period of the current year and also the comparable interim period of the preceding year. In addition, quarterly data required to be included in a footnote to the Summary of Earnings of certain registrants (see "Quarterly Reporting" below) need to be shown for the two most recent years and subsequent interim quarters.

The SEC does not require the Summary in Form S-1 to be certified by independent public accountants. If, however, it is furnished in sufficient detail to satisfy the requirement for the three-year income statement called for and the latter statement is consequently omitted, the Summary has to be certified for a minimum of three years. In some cases the company may ask the accountant to extend his opinion to cover the first two years of the Summary also.

The instructions for the Summary of Operations provide that, whenever necessary, the registrant must furnish information or explanations of material significance to investors in appraising the results shown. Specifically, SEC Guides for Preparation and Filing of Registration Statements require a separate section entitled "Management's Discussion and Analysis of the Summary of Earnings" immediately following the Summary. Such a section should include a statement explaining (1) material changes from period to period in the amounts of revenue and expense items and (2) changes in accounting principles or practices or in the method of their application that have a material effect on net income as reported. The discussion should concentrate on the later years and interim periods covered by the Summary and must explain fluctuations in excess of specified percentages. Illustrative examples of subjects which might be covered in the discussion and analysis as set forth in the Guides are:

1. Material changes in product mix or in the relative profitability of lines of business;
2. Material changes in advertising, research, development, product introduction, or other discretionary costs;
3. The acquisition or disposition of a material asset other than in the ordinary course of business;
4. Material and unusual charges or gains, including credits or charges associated with discontinuance of operations;
5. Material changes in assumptions underlying deferred costs and the plan for amortization of such costs;

6. Material changes in assumed investment return and in actuarial assumptions used to calculate contributions to pension funds; and
7. The closing of a material facility or material interruption of business or completion of a material contract.

On occasion it is necessary to revise the earlier years' figures from those previously published in a Summary of Operations. These are some of the events that may call for revisions:

Acquisitions treated as poolings of interests. It is also necessary to include a reconciliation of sales and net income previously published with the revised amounts included in the current Summary.

Other changes in the reporting entity resulting from inclusion or exclusion of certain subsidiaries for the first time.

Discontinued operations. Amounts of sales, costs, and expenses are pulled out of the regular captions and merged into a one-line presentation described as "discontinued operations."

Changes in accounting principles. Actual revisions of earlier figures are required if the change is (a) from the LIFO inventory method to another method, (b) in method of accounting for long-term construction-type contracts, (c) to or from the "full cost" method of accounting for an extractive industry, or (d) mandated by a FASB pronouncement. For all other changes, the cumulative effect relating to earlier years is shown as a special item in the income statement of the year of change. The effect on each of the earlier years, however, must be shown on a pro forma basis on the face of the Summary.

Changes from an unacceptable accounting principle to an acceptable principle or other significant corrections of previously published statements.

The *interim period,* if any, since the end of the fiscal year (commonly called the "stub" period) takes on special significance because it normally represents the latest available information about the company's operations. Since these interim periods are not required to be audited, and generally are not, a special burden is placed upon company management, especially the chief financial officer, to make sure that the Summary presents fairly the net income and other data of the interim periods. The same responsibilities exist whether the information is in the form of full financial statements or merely capsule (i.e., paragraph) data. In either event, management is required to make an affirmative statement relating to fair presentation along the following lines:

The summary of earnings for the (periods) ended (date) and (date) has been prepared from the records of the Company without audit by independent public accountants, and, in the opinion of the Company, reflects all adjustments, consisting only of normal recurring accruals, necessary to present fairly the results shown for the (periods).

If there are any adjustments other than normal recurring accruals, management is required to submit a supplemental letter to the SEC describing in detail the nature and amount of adjustments entering into the determination of the amounts shown.

Management's responsibility for fair presentation of the interim periods is not lessened by the fact that their independent public accountants have performed review procedures with respect to the unaudited periods and have issued a "comfort letter" to the underwriters. Such letters generally state that they are ". . . solely for the information of, and assistance to, the underwriters in conducting and documenting their investigation of the affairs of the Company. . . ."

The "comfort letter" runs to material not covered by the auditors' opinion and involves "negative assurance" from the auditors that, as a result of limited, specified procedures, nothing has come to their attention that caused them to believe that specified matters do not meet a specified standard, i.e., that unaudited financial statements were not prepared in conformity with generally accepted accounting principles applied on a consistent basis. The "specified procedures" to be followed by the auditors are generally determined by the underwriters. The types of information usually covered by negative assurance are:

1. Unaudited financial statements included in the registration statement;
2. Subsequent changes in the company's capitalization, long-term debt, and certain other financial statement items;
3. Tables, statistics, and other designated financial information in the registration statement.

Other Forms. While Form S-1 is the usual vehicle for registration of the securities of a commercial or industrial company, at least on a first-time registration, there are a number of other forms which may or must be used under certain conditions.

Form S-2 may be used by commercial and industrial companies in the development stage. The principal criterion for judging the development stage is that the company has not had any substantial revenue from sales of products or services, or any substantial net income from any source, during the preceding five years. The form does not contemplate a summary of earnings but does require traditional financial statements to the extent that they are appropriate.

Form S-5 is used to register securities of open-ended management investment companies under the Investment Company Act of 1940. (Form S-4 is used for closed-ended funds.) Financial statements required include statements of assets and liabilities, operations, changes in net assets, realized gain or loss on investments, and unrealized appreciation or depreciation of investments.

Form S-7 is a short form for use by specified or defined mature, stable, profitable companies. The financial statement requirements are actually enlarged, however, since certain financial statements are required for five years rather than three.

Form S-8 may be used to register securities to be offered to employees pursuant to a stock purchase, savings, option, or similar plan. In addition to information about the company, the form requires considerable information about the plan, including its financial statements. There must be included a summary of operations of the company as well as its comparative financial statements. The latter requirement can usually be met by incorporating by reference the company's published annual report.

Form S-9 is used for registration of nonconvertible, fixed-interest debt securities by large utility and other companies. The number of items of information required in the prospectus is reduced to five. The financial statement requirements are substantially similar to those of Form S-7.

Form S-16, adopted in 1971 in the nature of an experiment, provides a simpler method of registration for companies entitled to use Form S-7. The basic technique is to incorporate by reference material filed under the 1934 Act for major portions of the normal disclosure requirement. The incorporated material consists of the latest annual report or the latest prospectus which contains certified financial statements for the latest fiscal year, all reports filed since the end of the fiscal year (Forms 8-K, 10-Q), and the definitive proxy statement for the latest annual meeting of stockholders and any subsequent special meeting. Management is required to describe any material adverse change in the registrant's affairs since the end of the latest fiscal year, and the company's auditors must consent to the use of their opinions contained in the material incorporated by reference.

Full disclosure of all the pertinent facts and figures which are needed by a prospective investor to make a judgment about the company's securities is the principal objective of preparing a registration statement for a public offering. Company management, their attorneys, their independent public accountants, the underwriters and their attorneys, while their interests and functions vary, should all strive for full disclosure.

CONTINUING REPORTING OBLIGATIONS

In addition to the special one-time filing requirement in connection with each *sale* of securities, the SEC requires the filing of annual, quarterly, and special event reports related to the *trading* of securities previously issued. Generally, such continuing reporting is required of:

1. Every issuer of a security listed on a national securities exchange under Section 12(b) of the Securities Exchange Act of 1934,

2. Unlisted issuers registered under Section 12(g) (generally companies with over 500 shareholders and total assets in excess of $1,000,000), and

3. Unlisted issuers who registered a security under the 1933 Act (required to file periodic reports for the fiscal year in which the registration statement became effective and for each subsequent year in which there are 300 or more security holders at the beginning of the year).

The principal annual report form is Form 10-K; the quarterly form is Form 10-Q, and the special event form is Form 8-K.

Form 10-K has grown considerably in significance during the 1970s. Its content has been expanded and its filing date accelerated by 30 days, from 120 days to 90 days after the close of the fiscal year.

Annual Reporting. *Annual reports on Form 10-K* are designed to provide the public with up-to-date "standardized" financial information (standardized in the sense of content and disclosure required). The SEC annual report is essentially an expansion of the stockholders' annual report to provide certain additional required information. The following items must be included in Form 10-K:

Part I

1. Description of business
2. Summary of operations
2A. Projections (proposed)
3. Properties
4. Parents and subsidiaries
5. Legal proceedings
6. Increases and decreases in outstanding securities
7. Approximate number of equity security holders
8. Executive officers
9. Indemnification of directors and officers
10. Financial statements and exhibits

Part II
(if not covered by a timely, definitive proxy statement)
11. Principal security holders and holdings of management
12. Directors
13. Remuneration of directors and officers
14. Options granted to management to purchase securities
15. Interest of management and others in certain transactions.

The Summary of Operations is identical to that previously described. The same financial statements are required as in registration statements except for the number of years covered. Form 10-K requires financial statements for two years, both of which must be certified. See Exhibit 2 for more detailed requirements of the various forms.

The financial statements which must be filed may be summarized as follows:

Financial statements of the registrant (may be omitted if certain conditions are met)

Consolidated financial statements

Financial statements of unconsolidated subsidiaries and 50 percent or less owned persons accounted for on the equity method

Financial statements of affiliates whose securities are pledged as collateral.

EXHIBIT 2   Number of Years to Be Reported on SEC Forms for Various Financial Statements

	Form 10-K and Form S-8	Form S-1	Form S-7 or Form S-9
Balance sheet, latest fiscal year-end(s)	2	1	1
Statement of income, latest fiscal years	2	3	5
Statement of retained earnings, latest fiscal years	2	3	5
Statement of changes in financial position, latest fiscal years	2	3	3[a]

[a] However, Interpretation 1 of APB Opinion No. 19 requires this statement for each period for which an income statement is furnished.

Many professional accountants and company executives believe there is little need for the separate financial statements of the parent company, or that such statements, read alone, may be misleading. The SEC continues to insist that they be filed, however, subject to the following exceptions. The registrant may file consolidated statements and omit its individual statements if it meets *either* of the following conditions:

(i) The registrant is primarily an operating company and all subsidiaries included in the consolidated financial statements being filed, in the aggregate, do not have minority equity interests and/or indebtedness to any person other than the registrant or its consolidated subsidiaries in amounts which together exceed 5 percent of the total assets as shown by the most recent year-end consolidated balance sheet. Indebtedness incurred in the ordinary course of business which is not overdue and which matures within one year from the date of its creation, whether evidenced by securities or not, and indebtedness of subsidiaries which is collateralized by the registrant by guarantee, pledge, assignment or otherwise are to be excluded for the purpose of this determination.

OR

(ii) The registrant's total assets, exclusive of investments in and advances to its consolidated subsidiaries, as would be shown by its most recent year-end balance sheet if it were filed, constitute 75 percent or more of the total assets as shown by the most recent year-end consolidated balance sheet; and the registrant's total sales and revenues, exclusive of interest and dividends received from or its equity in the income of the consolidated subsidiaries, as would be shown by its income statement, for the most recent fiscal year if it were filed, constitute 75 percent or more of the total sales and revenues shown by the most recent annual consolidated income statements.

The reason for omission of the parent company statements should be stated in the list of financial statements filed whenever such statements are omitted.

The financial statements of any one or more unconsolidated subsidiaries or 50 percent or less owned persons accounted for by the equity method may be omitted if, in the aggregate:

(a) Neither the registrant's and its other subsidiaries' investments in and advances to, nor their proportionate share of the total assets (after intercompany eliminations) of, such subsidiaries and other persons do not exceed 10 percent of the total assets as shown by the most recent consolidated balance sheet; (b) the total sales and revenues (after intercompany eliminations) of such subsidiaries or other persons, reduced to the percentages of equity interests held by the registrant and its subsidiaries in such subsidiaries and other persons, do not exceed 10 percent of the total sales and revenues as shown by the most recent annual consolidated income statement; and (c) the registrant's and its other subsidiaries' equity in the income before income taxes and extraordinary items of the subsidiaries and other persons does not exceed 10 percent of such income of the registrant and consolidated subsidiaries for the most recent fiscal year; provided that, if such income of the registrant and its consolidated subsidiaries for the last fiscal year is at least 10 percent lower than the average of such income for the last five fiscal years, such average income may be substituted in the determination.

Quarterly Reporting. *Quarterly reporting* has received considerable attention in recent years both inside and outside the SEC. In 1975, for example, in Securities Act Release No. 5611, the Commission instituted a requirement that annual reports of certain listed and other large registrants include in a footnote specified quarterly financial data for each of the four quarters of the current and preceding years. Information required includes net sales, gross profit, income before extraordinary items and cumulative effect of a change in accounting, net income, and per-share data, with an explanation of any changes resulting from year-end audit adjustments. The interim data must be reviewed by an independent accountant in accordance with established professional standards and procedures[2] for such a review. See discussion in Chapter 5.

Form 10-Q, the principal form used for quarterly reporting, previously required only summarized profit and loss information, summarized capitalization and stockholders' equity information, and information concerning sales of unregistered securities. The profit and loss information was for the current and preceding years and on a year-to-date basis—three months, six months, and nine months, respectively, in the three Forms 10-Q required between annual Forms 10-K. The capitalization and stockholders' equity information was as of the end of the latest quarter.

Securities Act Release No. 5611 significantly changed the financial information required to be included in Form 10-Q. The principal new requirements are these:

a. Presentation of condensed financial statements, without routine footnotes. This calls for balance sheet, income statement, and statement of changes in financial position for the current and preceding years.
   1. Income statement for quarter and year-to-date.
   2. Balance sheet as of end of quarter.
   3. Statement of changes in financial position for year-to-date.
   While Rules 3-08 and 3-16 of Regulation S-X (see below) and other requirements that call for detailed footnote disclosure and schedules do not apply, the Commission reminds that "disclosures must be adequate to make the information presented not misleading."

b. With respect to a material change in application of accounting principles, the required letter from the registrant's independent accountant must state whether or not the change is to an alternative principle which in the accountant's judgment is preferable under the circumstances. (Previously, the accountant merely had to state approval of the change, which implied that the accountant was satisfied that management believed the new principle to be preferable to the old.)

c. New requirement for a narrative analysis by management of the results of operations, explaining the reasons for material changes in the amounts of revenue and expense items between the most recent quarter and the quarter immediately preceding it, between the most recent quarter and the same quarter in the preceding year, and, if applicable, between the current year-to-

---

[2]See later section entitled "SEC Influence on Auditing Practice" for the definition of "established professional standards and procedures."

date and the same period in the preceding year. Explanations cover such items as unit sales volume, prices charged and paid, labor costs, and discretionary spending programs.

d. New instruction permitting registrant to furnish any additional information which management believes will be of significance to investors and requiring registrant to indicate whether a Form 8-K was filed during the quarter reporting either unusual charges or credits to income or a change of auditors.

e. New instruction encouraging, but not requiring, the review of Form 10-Q financial information by independent accountants. If the review is made in accordance with established professional standards and procedures for such a review, the registrant may state that the independent accountant has made the review. If such statement is made, the registrant must indicate whether all adjustments or additional disclosures proposed by the independent accountant have been reflected in the data presented and, if not, why not. In addition, a letter from the accountant confirming or otherwise commenting upon the registrant's representations may be included as an exhibit to Form 10-Q.

Special Reporting.   There are two *special reports* we discuss briefly—proxy statements and current reports (Form 8-K).

Proxy statements are used to transmit information to shareholders in the course of soliciting their proxy to vote their shares at a meeting of shareholders.

Certified financial statements generally must be included in the proxy statement if action is to be taken at the shareholders' meeting with respect to any of the following matters:

Authorization or issuance of securities other than for exchange

Modification or exchange of securities

Mergers, consolidations, acquisitions, sale of assets, liquidations, and similar matters.

While considerable flexibility is permitted, the financial statements required are essentially the same as those required for a registration statement except for the omission of supporting schedules and other items described below.

Technically, the proxy rules require that the consolidated financial statements included in a proxy statement be in conformity with the requirements of Form 10, the form for original registration under the 1934 Act. This form, in turn, requires three years' certified financial statements plus a five-year summary of operations. Parent company financial statements of the registrant are not generally required in a proxy statement. Financial statements of the company to be acquired, however, should be on both a consolidated basis and a parent company basis.

The reason for this distinction is that Item 15(a) of the proxy rules, which relates to the registrant, calls for financial statements of "the issuer and its subsidiaries." That phrase has been construed by the SEC staff to relate to consolidated financial statements only. The SEC is not, however, precluded from asking for parent company financial statements under the blanket authority given them by Item 15(c). Requirements relating to the company to be acquired are governed by Item 15(b), which calls for financial statements of "each person" as would currently be required on Form 10. Technically, therefore, this requires parent company financial statements of companies to be acquired, unless a proper reason for omission exists.

While the registrant's consolidated financial statements are required to be audited, the proxy rules specify that the financial statements of the company to be acquired shall be "certified if practicable." This bit of leniency enables registrants to proceed with acquisitions of companies that have never been audited, whereas a more stringent rule by the SEC might preclude such acquisitions.

Proxy statement requirements are less stringent also in the area of interim financial statements. In proxy statements relating to acquisitions, the SEC staff seeks to have the most recently available data included, but in most cases they are not stringent about applying a ninety-day policy. In fact, where no acquisition is involved and only the registrant's consolidated financial statements are included, the SEC in many cases does not require any interim financial data beyond the end of the company's last fiscal year. In some of those cases, a simple offer to furnish additional copies of previously mailed quarterly financial reports will suffice for the interim data.

The SEC staff is also somewhat lenient in permitting omission of financial statements of consolidated subsidiaries and 50 percent or less owned companies in proxy statements. This leniency is tempered by the degree of significance of the matter for which omission is requested in relation to the matter to be voted upon at the meeting. Requests for such omissions may be presented informally to the staff.

Other than the above differences, the SEC generally endeavors to apply the Form S-1 financial statement disclosure concepts to proxy statements. This is an administrative practice and is not set forth in the rules.

Where a pending or proposed business combination is reported in the proxy statement, it is necessary to include tabular comparative per-share data so that the reader may evaluate the earnings, dividends, and book value of each company individually and in relation to each other. There are generally two acceptable formats for these comparisons. One is to present the per-share data of each company on a historical basis followed by the pro forma per-share data after giving retroactive effect to the exchange. The reader may then apply the exchange ratio to information shown for a particular company to evaluate the transactions.

The other acceptable manner of presenting comparable per-share data is to present information of the *acquiring* company on a straight historical basis and information of the *company being acquired* on: (a) a straight historical basis, or (b) the basis of the total net income, dividends, or book value divided by the number of shares of the acquiring company being offered in exchange. This will permit a ready comparison of the two companies stated in terms of the same unit of measurement. It is more convenient in that the reader is spared the burden of adjusting figures in the exchange ratio in order to produce a proper comparison. Where the company being acquired is fairly large in relation to the acquiring company, pro forma combined per-share data are also appropriate. The pro forma data are, of course, also given in terms of the same unit of measurement, namely, shares of the acquiring company.

Forms 8-K (current reports) must be filed only when certain significant events occur. Following is the type of information that must be filed:

1. Changes in control of the registrant
2. Acquisition or disposition of a significant amount of assets other than in the ordinary course of business
3. Material legal proceedings
4. Changes in registered securities
5. Changes in collateral for registered securities
6. Material defaults on senior securities
7. Material increases in amounts of outstanding securities
8. Material decreases in amounts of outstanding securities
9. Granting or extension of options to purchase securities of the registrant or its subsidiaries
10. Extraordinary item charges and credits, other material charges and credits to income of an unusual nature, material provisions for loss, and restatements of capital share account
11. Submission of matters to a vote of security holders

12. Changes in registrant's certifying accountant
13. Other materially important events
14. Financial statements of acquired businesses reported in Item 2.

Of particular interest to independent accountants is Item 12, which apparently is designed to deter companies from changing auditors for the purpose of getting new ones who are more sympathetic to their views than the old ones. The instructions for Item 12 are presented in their entirety:

Item 12. Changes in Registrant's Certifying Accountant

If an independent accountant who was previously engaged as the principal accountant to audit the registrant's financial statements resigns (or indicates he declines to stand for re-election after the completion of the current audit) or is dismissed as the registrant's principal accountant, or another independent accountant is engaged as principal accountant, or if an independent accountant on whom the principal accountant expressed reliance in his report regarding a significant subsidiary resigns (or formally indicates he declines to stand for re-election after the completion of the current audit) or is dismissed or another independent accountant is engaged to audit that subsidiary:

(a) State the date of such resignation (or declination to stand for re-election), dismissal, or engagement.

(b) State whether in connection with the audits of the two most recent fiscal years and any subsequent interim period preceding such resignation, dismissal, or engagement, there were any disagreements with the former accountant on any matter of accounting principles or practices, financial statement disclosure, or auditing scope or procedure, which disagreements if not resolved to the satisfaction of the former accountant would have caused him to make reference in connection with his report to the subject matter of the disagreement(s); also, describe each such disagreement. The disagreements required to be reported in response to the preceding sentence include both those resolved to the former accountant's satisfaction and those not resolved to the former accountant's satisfaction. Disagreements contemplated by this rule are those which occur at the decision-making level; i.e., between personnel of the registrant responsible for presentation of its financial statements and personnel of the accounting firm responsible for rendering its report.

(c) State whether the principal accountant's report on the financial statements for any of the past two years contained an adverse opinion or a disclaimer of opinion or was qualified as to uncertainty, audit scope, or accounting principles; also describe the nature of each such adverse opinion, disclaimer of opinion, or qualification.

(d) The registrant shall request the former accountant to furnish the registrant with a letter addressed to the Commission stating whether he agrees with the statements made by the registrant in response to this item and, if not, stating the respects in which he does not agree. The registrant shall file a copy of the former accountant's letter as an exhibit with all copies of the Form 8-K required to be filed pursuant to General Instruction F.

SEC INFLUENCE ON ACCOUNTING PRINCIPLES

Although the SEC has the authority to prescribe the accounting principles to be followed in financial statements filed with it, the Commission has not, with certain exceptions, invoked its authority to dictate accounting principles to be followed by registrants. In Regulation S-X it has set forth its requirements as to the form and content of financial statements filed under the several laws administered by it. In its decisions and in the Accounting Series Releases it has stated its opinions concerning a limited number of accounting principles and practices. Under the Holding Company Act it has promulgated two uniform systems of accounts which are applicable to a small number of companies. Under the Investment Advisers Act it has specified the books, records, and other information which must be maintained by investment advisors subject to the Act. As to the large body of accounting principles underlying the preparation of financial statements, however, the SEC has for the most part been content to rely on generally accepted principles of accounting as they exist or evolve with the passage of time.

By and large, the job of developing and modernizing generally accepted accounting principles has gravitated to the accounting profession, particularly the American Institute of Certified Public Accountants and its Committee on Accounting Procedure and later the Accounting Principles Board. Since 1973, the leading organization with respect to accounting principles has been the Financial Accounting Standards Board.

In testifying before a Congressional subcommittee in 1964 on efforts to eliminate or reduce accounting alternatives, former SEC Chairman William L. Carey said that the Commission had encouraged the accounting profession to exercise leadership in accounting and auditing matters but, at the same time, had not hesitated to criticize and prod, to take exception to accounting presentations, and to discipline members of the profession when circumstances warranted. The policy of reliance on the profession for the enunciation of accounting principles, formalized and set forth in Accounting Series Release No. 150, adopted in 1973, reads as follows:

RELEASE No. 150, DECEMBER 20, 1973, 38 F.R. 1260
STATEMENT OF POLICY ON THE ESTABLISHMENT AND IMPROVEMENT OF ACCOUNTING
PRINCIPLES AND STANDARDS.

Various Acts of Congress administered by the Securities and Exchange Commission clearly state the authority of the Commission to prescribe the methods to be followed in the preparation of accounts and the form and content of financial statements to be filed under the Acts and the responsibility to assure that investors are furnished with information necessary for informed investment decisions. In meeting this statutory responsibility effectively, in recognition of the expertise, energy and resources of the accounting profession, and without abdicating its responsibilities, the Commission has historically looked to the standard-setting bodies designated by the profession to provide leadership in establishing and improving accounting principles. The determinations by these bodies have been regarded by the Commission, with minor exceptions, as being responsive to the needs of investors.

The body presently designated by the Council of the American Institute of Certified Public Accountants (AICPA) to establish accounting principles is the Financial Accounting Standards Board (FASB). This designation by the AICPA followed the issuance of a report in March 1972 recommending the formation of the FASB, after a study of the matter by a broadly based study group. The recommendations contained in that report were widely endorsed by industry, financial analysts, accounting educators, and practicing accountants. The Commission endorsed the establishment of the FASB in the belief that the Board would provide an institutional framework which will permit prompt and responsible actions flowing from research and consideration of varying viewpoints. The collective experience and expertise of the members of the FASB and the individuals and professional organizations supporting it are substantial. Equally important, the commitment of resources to the FASB is impressive evidence of the willingness and intention of the private sector to support the FASB in accomplishing its task. In view of these considerations, the Commission intends to continue its policy of looking to the private sector for leadership in establishing and improving accounting principles and standards through the FASB with the expectation that the body's conclusions will promote the interests of investors.

In Accounting Series Release No. 4 (1938) the Commission stated its policy that financial statements prepared in accordance with accounting practices for which there was no substantial authoritative support were presumed to be misleading and that footnote or other disclosure would not avoid this presumption. It also stated that, where there was a difference of opinion between the Commission and a registrant as to the proper accounting to be followed in a particular case, disclosure would be accepted in lieu of correction of the financial statements themselves only if substantial authoritative support existed for the accounting practices followed by the registrant and the position of the Commission had not been expressed in rules, regulations or other official releases. For purposes of this policy, principles, standards and practices promulgated by the FASB in its Statements ànd Interpretations[1] will be considered by the Commission as having substantial authoritative support, and those contrary to such FASB promulgations will be considered[2] to have no such support.

In the exercise of its statutory authority with respect to the form and content of filings under the Acts, the Commission has the responsibility to assure that investors are provided with adequate information. A significant portion of the necessary information is provided by a set of basic financial statements (including the notes thereto) which conform to generally accepted accounting principles. Information in addition to that included in financial statements conforming to generally accepted accounting principles is also necessary. Such additional disclosures are required to be made in various fashions, such as in financial statements and schedules reported on by independent public accountants or as textual statements required by items in the applicable forms and reports filed with the Commission. The Commission will continue to identify areas where investor information needs exist and will determine the appropriate methods of disclosure to meet these needs.

It must be recognized that in its administration of the Federal Securities Acts and in its review of filings under such Acts, the Commission staff will continue as it has in the past to take such action on a day-to-day basis as may be appropriate to resolve specific problems of accounting and reporting under the particular factual circumstances involved in filings and reports of individual registrants.

The Commission believes that the foregoing statement of policy provides a sound basis for the Commission and the FASB to make significant contributions to meeting the needs of the registrants and investors.

By the Commission.

George A. Fitzsimmons
Secretary

[1]Accounting Research Bulletins of the Committee on Accounting Procedure of the American Institute of Certified Public Accountants and effective opinions of the Accounting Principles Board of the Institute should be considered as continuing in force with the same degree of authority except to the extent altered, amended, supplemented, revoked or superseded by one or more Statements of Financial Accounting Standards issued by the FASB.

[2]It should be noted that Rule 203 of the Rules of Conduct of the Code of Ethics of the AICPA provides that it is necessary to depart from accounting principles promulgated by the body designated by the Council of the AICPA if, due to unusual circumstances, failure to do so would result in misleading financial statements. In such a case, the use of other principles may be accepted or required by the Commission.

The above statement of policy in no way alters the Commission's or the staff's intention to require such accounting or disclosures as may be necessary in their opinion to avoid misleading inferences in particular cases.

Accounting Series Releases.   Accounting Series Releases are used by the Commission or its Chief Accountant to publish views on various accounting principles and disclosure matters. (ASRs are also used to publicize disciplinary actions against accountants, which subject will be covered later.) Some of those in recent years which deal with accounting principles are:

ASR	Year	Subject
102	1965	Balance sheet classification of deferred income taxes arising from installment sales
118	1970	Accounting for investment securities by registered investment companies
130	1972	Pooling-of-interests accounting
134	1973	Accounting for catastrophe reserves
135	1973	Pooling-of-interests accounting
146	1973	Effect of treasury stock transactions on accounting for business combinations
146A	1974	Same
162	1974	Use of GAAP by limited partnerships
163	1974	Capitalization of interest by non-utility companies
185	1975	Use of GAAP by bank holding companies and banks

Accounting Disclosures. In keeping with the general thesis that the SEC's major responsibility revolves around full and adequate disclosure to investors, the SEC has frequently taken the lead in requiring certain accounting disclosures. A notable example is the newly required (ASR No. 190) disclosure of replacement cost data by certain large registrants. These companies must disclose what it would cost to replace their inventories and productive plant at current prices, as well as amounts of depreciation and cost of sales using replacement costs. They must also disclose how replacement costs are computed.

Occasionally, the SEC pointedly states that its accounting disclosure requirement is being promulgated because the Accounting Principles Board or the Financial Accounting Standards Board has failed to give sufficient attention to the matter. ASR Nos. 147, 148, and 149 (see below), issued in 1973, are examples of such a situation.

Principal among recent ASRs dealing with disclosure matters, in addition to ASR No. 190 just mentioned, are the following:

ASR	Year	Subject
113	1969	Disclosure problems relating to restricted securities held by investment companies
116	1970	Same
117	1970	Statements of source and application of funds
138	1973	Unusual charges and credits to income
142	1973	Reporting cash flow and other related data
147	1973	Improved disclosure of leases
148	1973	Disclosure of compensating balances and short-term borrowing arrangements
149	1973	Improved disclosure of income tax expense
151	1974	Disclosure of inventory profits reflected in income in periods of rising prices
164	1974	Defense and other long-term contract activities
166	1974	Disclosure of unusual risks and uncertainties in financial statements
169	1975	Disclosure problems relating to the adoption of the LIFO inventory method
177	1975	Quarterly reporting
194	1976	Disagreements with former accountants

Regulation S-X. Regulation S-X is the principal accounting regulation of the SEC in its administration of the Securities Act of 1933, the Securities Exchange Act of 1934, the Public Utility Holding Company Act of 1935, and the Investment Company Act of 1940. Promulgated originally in 1940, the regulation has undergone several general revisions since that date. A public accountant who becomes involved in certifying financial statements intended for filing under any of these Acts should have an up-to-date copy of Regulation S-X at hand. Similarly, no corporate financial officer should undertake registration or SEC reporting responsibilities without having ready access to Regulation S-X.

In addition to certain requirements as to independence and accountants' reports, Regulation S-X deals principally with the form and content of financial statements and supporting schedules, as distinguished from the accounting principles which are applied to business transactions in arriving at the dollar amounts to be presented. For guidance as to which financial statements are to be included in the various types of filings, one must generally look to the instructions applicable to the particular form involved.

The rules contained in Regulation S-X are much too voluminous to present in any detail in a general book of this character, but its order of contents is given here.

Subject	*Content*
Article 1 Application of Reg. S-X	States applicability and defines terms used in Regulation S-X.
Article 2 Qualifications and Reports of Accountants	Covers qualifications and independence of accountants and requirements for accountants' certificates.
Article 3 Rules of General Application	States general rules which should be considered in applying specific provisions of the regulation.
Article 4 Consolidated and Combined Financial Statements	States rules governing the presentation of consolidated and combined financial statements.
Article 5 Commercial and Industrial Companies	
Article 5A Commercial, Industrial, and Mining Companies in the Promotional, Exploratory, or Development Stage	States specific provisions applicable to the financial statements and supporting schedules of the indicated types of companies.
Article 6 Management Investment Companies	
Article 6A Unit Investment Trusts	
Article 6B Face-Amount Certificate Investment Companies	
Article 6C Employee Stock Purchase, Savings, and Similar Plans	
Article 7 Insurance Companies Other Than Life and Title Insurance Companies	
Article 7A Life Insurance Companies	
Article 8 Committees Issuing Certificates of Deposit	
Article 9 Bank Holding Companies and Banks	
Article 10 Natural Persons	
Article 11 Statements of Other Stockholders' Equity	Prescribes the content of statements of other stockholders' equity (paid-in additional capital and retained earnings).

Subject	*Content*
Article 11A Statement of Source and Application of Funds (Changes in Financial Position)	Prescribes the form and content of statements of changes in financial position.
Article 12 Form and Content of Schedules	States rules governing the form and content of supporting schedules to financial statements.

Staff Accounting Bulletins.   Staff Accounting Bulletins are informal statements by the Chief Accountant of internal accounting policies currently being followed by the SEC staff. These statements are now being issued to the public in an effort to expose, for the first time, general policies of the SEC with respect to questions of accounting. They are not identified as holdings in particular cases, although such holdings are the genesis of virtually all SEC policy. The Bulletins are not promulgated under the Administration Procedure Act and thus do not have the force and effect of law.

Ad Hoc Positions.   In addition to all the published positions taken by the SEC on accounting principles, there are reports of instances where the Commission has tended to dictate "proper accounting" by the administrative technique of refusing to clear a filing unless the accounting is changed. In many of these cases, it is not so much a matter of applying proper accounting as it is an effort to get to the "right answer." At issue in a particular case, for example, may be whether, in view of all the facts and circumstances, it is appropriate to treat a loan fee as income at the time of making the loan, or whether it should be spread over the life of the loan or, possibly, taken into income in proportion to principal payments received. There may not be a clearly enunciated accounting principle covering the situation, so it is left to the SEC staff and the registrant's representatives to hammer out a reasonable answer.

In this connection, it is important to call attention to the Commission's policy, expressed in ASR No. 4 and cited in ASR No. 150 quoted above, that disclosure will be accepted in lieu of correction if the registrant has substantial authoritative support and the Commission has not taken a public position on the point involved.

The Financial Accounting Standards Board, in prescribing accounting principles, has followed the philosophy of the Accounting Principles Board in seeking to reduce accounting alternatives. The efforts of the FASB thus far have taken the "cookbook approach," i.e., the adoption of detailed accounting procedures to be followed where a specified set of circumstances exists. One large accounting firm's reaction to this has been the recent filing of a petition asking the SEC to (1) revoke ASR No. 150, quoted above; (2) rescind their requirement, cited above in connection with Form 10-Q filings, that an auditor express an opinion as to whether a client's change in accounting principle is to an alternative that is preferable; and (3) define the term "substantial authoritative support" (originally used in ASR No. 4 and quoted above in ASR No. 150). This petition raises a basic regulatory question, and it will likely be vigorously contested by much of the accounting profession. If the petition is successful, the current objective of reducing alternatives would be superseded by independent accountants exercising professional judgment as to proper accounting in specific circumstances. The question of whether the FASB could adapt to this change in philosophy might then arise.

SEC INFLUENCE ON AUDITING PRACTICE

Over the years, the SEC has probably had as much influence on the way auditors practice their profession as their own professional organizations, their own quality review programs, and the courts. Most of the larger clients of the big accounting firms are registered with the SEC, and accounting firms are cautious not to run afoul of the SEC in a manner that might cause embarrassment or other adverse consequences to their clients.

Disciplining of Auditors.   The Commission can set the qualifications for accountants and can decide whether they are truly independent of the companies they are auditing. Under Rule 2(e) of its Rules of Practice (disciplinary rules for governing professionals), the Commission may deny, temporarily or permanently, the privilege of appearing or practicing before it to any person who is found by the Commission (1) not to possess the requisite qualifications to represent others, or (2) to be lacking in character or integrity or to have engaged in unethical or improper professional conduct, or (3) to have willfully violated, or willfully aided and abetted the violation of, any provision of the federal securities laws, or the rules and regulations thereunder. In addition to suspending accountants, other disciplinary actions taken by the Commission include censure requiring quality control reviews and programs and forbidding the taking of new clients who file or are contemplating filing with the Commission. There have been cases where the Commission has recommended criminal proceedings to the Department of Justice. Regardless of which type of action is taken by the Commission, the greatest harm to the accountants is likely to be the damage to their reputation.

Recent disciplinary actions by the SEC against accountants, as disclosed by publication in Accounting Series Releases, are the following:

ASR	Date	Problem; Action
153	2/25/74	Quality of auditing; censure, quality review program, peer review, nonacceptance of new SEC clients by one office of firm for 12 months, nonacceptance of any new real estate SEC clients by any office of firm for 12 months
157	7/8/74	Withholding of information from Commission; censure
167	12/24/74	Quality of auditing; peer review, adoption of specified audit procedures
173	7/2/75	Quality of auditing; peer review, adoption of specified audit procedures, study of specified method of accounting, nonacceptance of new SEC clients for 12 months, follow-up peer review for two succeeding years
174	7/2/75	Quality of auditing; censure
176	7/22/75	Quality of auditing; peer review
191	3/30/76	Quality of auditing; censure, peer review

Setting of Auditing Standards.   As in the case of accounting principles, the Commission prefers to let the accounting profession set its own auditing standards. Securities Act Release No. 5611 brings this point vividly home.

In connection with the requirement that annual financial statements of certain registrants include selected quarterly financial data in a footnote, the Commission, in Release No. 5611, states that this "necessarily will associate the independent public accountant with these data in some fashion" even though the footnote is labeled "unaudited." The Release amends Rule 2-02 of Regulation S-X by adding a new paragraph (e), as follows:

> If the financial statements covered by the accountant's report designate as "unaudited" the note required by Rule 3-16(t), it shall be presumed that appropriate professional standards and procedures with respect to the data in the note have been followed by the independent accountant who is associated with the unaudited footnote by virtue of reporting on the financial statements in which it is included.

In the same Release, the Commission also proposed to further amend Rule 2-02 by specifying review and reporting procedures to be followed by independent accountants with respect to the unaudited data, unless the Auditing Standards Executive Committee (AudSEC) of the American Institute of CPA's adopted a statement of standards and procedures that the Commission was satisfied would adequately protect the interests of investors. AudSEC subsequently issued Statement on Auditing Standards No. 10 establishing professional standards and procedures for limited reviews of interim financial information, which the SEC has accepted as the "appropriate professional standards and procedures" for an independent accountant's review of interim data included (1) in the "unaudited" footnote to audited financial statements pursuant to Regulation S-X, and (2) in Form 10-Q, when a client requests such a review. In a further statement on auditing standards, SAS No. 13, AudSEC set forth guidelines for reporting on limited reviews.

Liability of Accountants. Many accountants have been sued in recent years for a variety of reasons, and some have even been convicted of criminal offenses. In most cases, the accountant's professional service to a publicly owned company was involved. Readers who desire to gain additional information on this subject are directed to the following important cases:

Case	Citation
BarChris	Escott et al. v. BarChris Construction Corp. et al., 283 F. Supp. 643 (S.D., N.Y. 1968)
Continental Vending	U.S. v. Simon et al., 425 F.2d, 796 (2nd Cir. 1969)
Yale Express	Fisher et al. v. Kletz et al., 266 F. Supp. 181 (S.D., N.Y., 1968)
National Student Marketing	U.S. v. Natelli, Docket No. 75-10004

It is readily apparent that the accounting profession must take something of a defensive position in conducting its audits of public companies. Just as some football coaches claim that "the best defense is a good offense," accountants can best protect themselves by doing a professional audit, maintaining an independent attitude, and refraining from accepting clients that may represent obvious risk situations. In nearly every case where public accountants have been held liable, the accountants have performed at a level significantly lower than the public was entitled to expect in the particular circumstances.

BIBLIOGRAPHY

Defliese, Philip L., Kenneth P. Johnson, and Roderick K. Macleod: *Montgomery's Auditing,* 9th edition, The Ronald Press Company, New York, 1975.

Poloway, Morton, and Dane Charles: *Accountants' SEC Practice Manual,* Commerce Clearing House, Chicago, 1976.

Rappaport, Louis H.: *SEC Accounting: Practice and Procedure,* 3d ed., The Ronald Press Company, New York, 1972.

Skousen, K. Fred: *An Introduction to the SEC,* South-Western Publishing Co., 1976.

Chapter **39**

Cost Analysis*

GORDON SHILLINGLAW
Professor of Accounting, Columbia University

*Certain exhibits and explanations in this chapter have been adapted from Gordon Shillinglaw, *Cost Accounting: Analysis and Control,* 3rd ed., Richard D. Irwin, Homewood, Ill., 1972.

Cost is the amount of resources sacrificed to achieve a particular objective. These resources are usually measured in monetary terms. Cost analysis therefore can be defined as the estimation in monetary terms of the amounts of resources that have been or will be consumed to accomplish some objective. The objective may be the operation of a factory, the manufacture and sale of a particular product, or the provision of delivery service to one class of customers.

The primary purpose of cost analysis is to provide management with data for use in decision making. It may also be undertaken to provide data that will help explain management actions or decisions to other parties. The principles and methods outlined in this chapter are designed to suit the decision-making purpose. Departures from these principles and methods for other purposes will depend on the purpose of the analysis and the specific requirements of the user.

THE INCREMENTAL PRINCIPLE

Decisions always require comparisons of alternatives. Any choice between two alternatives must be based on real or perceived differences between them. These differences are referred to as *differentials* or *increments,* and the requirement that data for decisions should be estimates of increments is called the "incremental principle." Absolute figures are useful in decision making only to the extent that they can be converted into differential data.

Emphasis on Cash Flows. The analytical problem in decision making is to estimate the costs and benefits of each alternative that has been identified and then find the alternative for which the benefit/cost relationship best satisfies the decision rule that management has decided to apply. In most cases, the analyst tries to measure both costs and benefits in monetary terms. More specifically, the question is how the choice between any two alternatives is likely to affect the flow of cash into or out of the organization.

The focus on cash is fundamental. Resources received in nonliquid form are not convertible through ready sale into liquid form. For example, shares of stock in other companies, which must be held for at least several months before sale, ordinarily cannot be used conveniently to pay the company's debts, pay dividends, or buy new equipment. Only cash can be used for these purposes. For this reason, the monetary increment or incremental gain must be measured by the effect of the decision on the future net cash flow—the margin between receipts and outlays of cash.

Net cash flow is not the same as accounting net income. For example, suppose that a company has 100,000 plastic rings in inventory, originally purchased for use in a product that the company no longer manufactures. These rings originally cost 10 cents each. They have no current scrap value. A company engineer has just discovered that these rings can be used in another product which ordinarily incorporates rings of a cheaper quality, available at a price of 2 cents each. For income measurement, the use of the old, more expensive rings might be recorded by a transfer to expense of $100,000 \times \$0.10 = \$10,000$. For the decision, however, management should know that use of these rings would require no cash outlay at all. In cost analysis, whenever cash flow and income figures differ, the cash flow figure should be used.

Steps in Cash Flow Analysis. Assuming that the increments can be estimated with reasonable certainty, the basic approach to analysis is as follows:
1. Identify and describe the alternatives.
2. Decide which determinants of cash flow will be affected by the decision.
3. Estimate values for each of these determinants under each alternative.
4. Select the alternative with the most favorable (least unfavorable) cash flow.
5. List intangible factors that might reinforce or lead away from this choice.

If uncertainty is substantial and either the apparent probabilities of high and low errors are unequal or management's attitude toward gains and losses is asymmetric, then step 3 should be repeated for other possible outcomes. If possible, probabilities should be attached to each of these outcomes.

If the alternatives differ in the timing of the inflows and outflows of cash, the problem is an investment problem and the cash flows occurring at different points of time must be translated into their time-adjusted equivalents. This is typically accomplished by discounting the cash flows to find their present value at some common date (see Chapter 8). Once this has been done, steps 4 and 5 above can be performed on the time-adjusted data.

Incremental Cost. The cost estimates that are relevant to incremental analysis are estimates of differential or incremental cost. Incremental cost is the difference in total cash outlays that will result from selecting one alternative instead of another.

For example, a café proprietor is studying the profitability of reopening a billiard room in the rear of the café. The billiard tables have been unused for several years but are in usable condition. The monthly cost estimates are shown below:

Costs	Operate the billiard room	Do not operate the billiard room
Food and beverages sold	$4,500	$4,000
Salaries and wages	1,600	1,200
Supplies	150	100
Utilities and heat	60	50
Rent	500	500
Insurance	80	80
Miscellaneous	110	70
Total	$7,000	$6,000

The incremental cost in this case is $7,000 minus $6,000 or $1,000 a month.

The term "incremental cost" is often used in another sense, to refer to the elements of cost that will change as a result of the decision. For example, in this illustration the only costs affected by the decision are the costs of food and beverages, salaries and wages, supplies, utilities and heat, and miscellaneous resources consumed. The analysis can be simplified slightly in this case, significantly in others, by eliminating the unaffected items completely. The simplified comparison would be as follows:

Costs that will change	Operate the billiard room	Do not operate the billiard room
Food and beverages sold	$4,500	$4,000
Salaries and wages	1,600	1,200
Supplies	150	100
Utilities and heat	60	50
Miscellaneous	110	70
Total	$6,420	$5,420

Sunk Cost. Any cost element that is unaffected by management's choice between alternatives is a sunk cost. In the first table above, two of the elements were sunk:

Rent $500
Insurance 80

Reopening of the billiard room would leave these costs unchanged. Even though the accounting system might allocate some of these costs to the billiard room, such allocations do not represent incremental cash outlays and should be ignored.

Negative Increments. The cost differences in the preceding examples were additions to cost. Incremental cost may also be negative; that is, a management decision may reduce costs. This reduction may be referred to as a cost saving, but the analytical method is still incremental. For example, if the café proprietor is now operating the billiard room and wishes to know how much could be saved by closing it, the incremental cost should be measured by the amounts of cash outlays that will be made only if the billiard room remains open.

Future Cost. Resources that are to be used under one or more alternatives should be measured at their anticipated prices, not at prices that have been paid in the past. For example, a company purchased 50,000 pounds of a certain material last year at $0.50 a pound. The company uses this material as a raw material for several products. If 20,000 pounds are used to fill an order for a special product, the company will have to buy 20,000 pounds at the current price of $0.60 a pound to rebuild its inventories of this material to the desired level. In this case, the cash outlay required by the special order would be 20,000 pounds × $0.60 = $12,000. The historical cost figure of $0.50 a pound has no relevance because it does not measure the future cash outlay that acceptance of the order would entail.

Opportunity Cost. Replacement cost per unit is not always the relevant multiplier to use in incremental analysis. An earlier paragraph cited a case in which the incremental cash outlay from the use of a stock of plastic rings was zero. In this case, replacement cost was irrelevant because acceptance of the proposal would not obligate the company to replace the items used.

The general concept that applies to both of these situations is the concept of opportunity cost. For cash flow analysis, the cost of a nonmonetary asset already owned by the company should be measured by the amount of cash that must be sacrificed to make this asset available for its proposed use. This is its opportunity cost.

Measuring Opportunity Cost. One possible measure of opportunity cost is the asset's current liquidation value. This is applicable if the best alternative to the asset's proposed use is to sell it. A decision not to sell is equivalent from a cash flow viewpoint to a decision to buy.

Another measure of opportunity cost is replacement cost. This is applicable if use of the asset will require the company to buy a replacement unit for use elsewhere in the company.

A third possibility is the asset's present value in some alternative use. This present value figure is the relevant measure of opportunity cost if it is greater than the asset's current liquidation value and if the proposed diversion of the asset will not necessitate purchase of a replacement asset for the alternative use.

The opportunity cost concept applies to services as well as to tangible assets. For example, a proposal which will require a member of the sales staff to spend one day a week in the office should be charged with an amount equal to the value to the company of the sales that would be made if the day were spent calling on customers.

Separate Costs for Separate Purposes. It should be clear from these definitions that the magnitude of incremental cost and of incremental profit depends on the decision to be made and the alternatives being compared. For example, the plant manager's salary is a sunk cost if the problem is to decide whether to install additional materials handling equipment, but it is presumably an incremental cost if abandonment of the plant is in question, and it may be partly incremental if the question is whether to double the plant's capacity.

COST/VOLUME RELATIONSHIPS

The immediate objective of cost analysis is to identify the determinants of cost and to quantify their effects. One important cost determinant is operating volume, expressed as a rate per period of time (for example, hours per week, pounds per day).

Variable Costs.   Costs that change in response to small changes in volume are known as *variable* costs. Exhibit 1 shows two of the many possible patterns of cost variation. The straight line in Exhibit 1 represents a cost that changes in direct proportion to changes in volume, for example, a royalty charge computed at a constant amount per unit sold. In contrast, the curved line shows costs rising sharply at first, then more gradually as volume achieves normal operating levels, and then sharply again as operations began to approach capacity limits.

EXHIBIT 1 Variable Costs

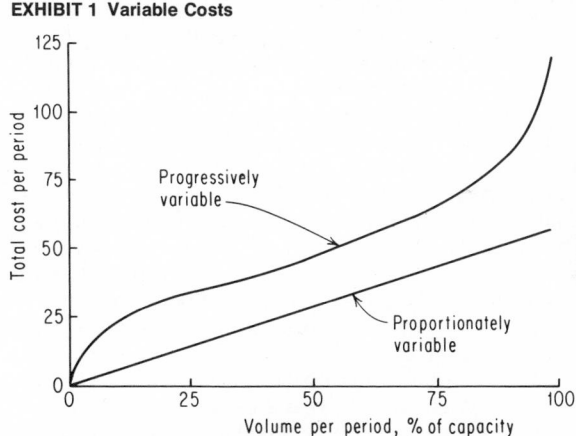

Volume per period, % of capacity

Marginal Cost.   The average variable cost per unit computed from the straight line in Exhibit 1 will be the same at all operating volumes. For a cost described by the curved line, however, average unit cost will vary, as shown in column 3 of Exhibit 2.

Of even more significance are the figures shown in column 4. These represent marginal cost, the added cost that results from the production of one additional unit of goods or services per period of time. In this case, marginal cost first decreases due to economies of larger production quantities, then levels off, and finally increases as diseconomies set in in the upper reaches of the output range.

Volume in this illustration has been measured in "units," with no indication of what kinds of units are referred to. The most obvious choice is the number of units of goods or services produced. This can be used for operations which produce only a single product or service, but when output is diverse something else must be found. The usual solution is to use some form of input measure, such as direct labor hours or pounds of material used. The best input unit to use is the one correlating most closely with cost variations, but a less accurate measure may be

EXHIBIT 2   Average Variable Cost and Marginal Cost

(1)	(2)	(3)	(4)
Weekly volume (000 units)	Weekly cost ($000)	Average variable cost (2) ÷ (1)	Marginal cost [(2) − line above in (2)]
1	$ 3.50	$3.50	$3.50
2	6.75	3.37	3.25
3	9.75	3.25	3.00
4	12.75	3.19	3.00
5	16.00	3.20	3.25
6	19.50	3.25	3.50
7	23.50	3.36	4.00
8	28.25	3.53	4.75

used if it can be made available more cheaply than the preferred measure. This question will be examined more fully in Chapter 41.

Fixed Costs. Costs that do not change as a necessary result of relatively small changes in volume are known as *fixed* costs. For analytical purposes it is useful to recognize two broad classes of fixed costs: capacity costs and programmed costs.

Capacity Costs. Many of the resources consumed in a period are consumed to provide or maintain the organization's capacity to produce or sell. These are known as *capacity* costs or *supportive* costs.

Capacity has three dimensions: physical capacity, provided by buildings, machinery, furniture, etc.; organizational capacity, provided by management, supervisory, and staff personnel; and financial capacity, provided by working captial and other financial resources. In all three senses, capacity can be changed only slowly. It takes time to conceive of the need for new facilities, arrange for financing, complete facilities construction or acquisition, provide the necessary staff and personnel, and put all of these resources to work. Capacity reductions also take time. This means that during any short period of time, the firm must operate with a relatively constant stock of productive resources, including organizational and financial resources.

As volume increases, average capacity cost per unit will decline. A cost that will amount to $2,000 a month, no matter what the operating volume, will average $1 a unit if volume is 2,000 units a month or $0.50 a unit at a volume of 4,000 units. The effect on average total cost will depend on the relative importance of capacity costs and the shape of the variable cost function. If variable costs tend to be proportional to volume, average total costs will decline almost indefinitely as output expands. If average variable costs increase with increases in volume, however, this increase will offset the decline in average capacity costs at some stage, and average total cost will begin to rise.

Capacity costs can be classified further into *standby* costs and *enabling* costs. Standby costs are those that will continue to be incurred if operations or facilities are shut down temporarily. Examples are depreciation, property taxes, and some executive salaries. Enabling costs are those that can be avoided by a temporary shutdown but must be incurred if operations are to take place. Some of these are likely to be constant over the entire output range; others are likely to vary in steps. For example, one departmental supervisor may be adequate for single-shift operation, but operation of a second shift will require a second supervisor.

Step-variable capacity costs would be classified by an economist as variable costs; executives and accountants classify them as fixed within the capacity range they support. Some accountants call these *semifixed* costs. If the steps are sufficiently small, however, for most analytical purposes they may be averaged out and treated as part of the variable costs.

Programmed Costs. Many discussions of fixed costs focus entirely on the relationships between volume and total or average capacity costs. Fixed costs also include a second category, however, fundamentally different from the first. These are costs designed neither to maintain current operating capacity nor to meet the demands placed on the system for the production and delivery of goods and services. Instead, they are established by autonomous management decisions to meet objectives other than the fulfillment of service demands.

Costs in this group are known by a variety of names, including programmed costs, discretionary costs, and managed costs. Some programmed costs are incurred to obtain and retain sales orders; the cost leads to volume rather than the other way around. Some are incurred to achieve other kinds of results unrelated to current operating volume—ideas for new products, for example. Still others yield services to management and can be justified only by management's perception of the value of these services—for example, financial reporting systems.

Programmed costs tend to be budgeted at specified levels for individual time periods. Once the budget is set, programmed cost per unit will be low if volume is high and high if volume is low. The size of the programmed cost budget, however, should be determined by estimates of the effectiveness of these costs in achieving the objectives desired by management. If increases in budgeted spending seem likely to increase volume by a larger percentage than the increase in spending, average cost will fall. If additional spending produces a less than proportional increase in volume, however, average cost will rise. This is illustrated in the following table:

Total programmed cost	Volume achieved	Average programmed cost
$10	50	$0.20
20	125	0.16
30	200	0.15
40	250	0.16
50	280	0.18
60	300	0.20
70	310	0.23

The concept of marginal cost has no meaning in connection with programmed costs. Marginal costs measure the effects of increasing volume: programmed costs do not change as a result of changes in volume and therefore cannot be marginal with respect to those changes.

Semivariable Costs. Some cost elements have both fixed and variable components. For example, some consumption of electric power is independent of operating volume, while another component is likely to vary directly with volume.

Fixed Costs and Sunk Costs. Knowledge of cost behavior is important in incremental analysis whenever two alternatives differ in the rate of utilization of existing facilities and organization. It should not be assumed, however, that fixed costs are always sunk costs or that variable costs are always incremental.

For example, property taxes are usually fixed costs. They will not be increased if the company is able to obtain additional volume to utilize plant capacity more fully. For a plant utilization decision, therefore, property taxes are not only fixed but also sunk costs. In the decision to expand the plant's operating capacity, however, these fixed costs are no longer entirely sunk because a larger plant will carry a greater assessed valuation and therefore greater property taxes.

Similarly, variable costs are not always incremental costs. For example, if the company is considering whether to rent or own its manufacturing plant, total variable manufacturing costs are unlikely to be affected by the choice. Therefore, they must be treated as sunk costs for the purpose of reaching this specific decision.

ANALYSIS OF JOINT COSTS

When the processing of a single input or set of inputs yields two or more products, these products are referred to as joint products. Gasoline and fuel oil are joint products.

The existence of joint products creates the phenomenon of joint costs—the costs of those input factors that are necessary for the manufacture and separation of all the joint products as a group. Costs incurred for the production of an individual joint product are known as separable costs or specific costs. Livestock, purchasing, and slaughtering costs are true joint costs of all the products that will eventually be marketed by a meatpacker, but tanning costs are specific costs of the tanned cowhides produced.

Joint Products as a Group.   For the group of joint products as a whole, the question is whether the total revenue to be derived from the sale of all joint products, less any processing and distribution costs necessary to place these products in marketable form, is adequate to cover the incremental costs of the joint inputs. For example, the decision to work a mine which produces ore containing gold, zinc, and lead must be based on consideration of the volumes produced and the market prices of all three metals.

A related problem is to determine the maximum price that the company can afford to pay for joint inputs of a given grade or specification. This will depend on the relative yield of each product to be derived from the joint input. For example, in buying raw materials that vary in quality, the price that can be paid will be higher on grades that yield a greater proportion of high-value products. The maximum purchase price is a function of the total value of all the joint products, less all the joint costs of processing or conversion.

Individual Joint Products.   Once it has been determined that joint production is profitable, the next question is how far to process each of the joint products. For example, should cowhides be tanned or should they be sold untanned? For this kind of decision, the question is whether the sale value of the product can be increased by more that the additional costs of separate processing. The cost of the steer no longer has any meaning for this decision. What is relevant is opportunity cost, in this case the amount that could be realized from the sale of the untanned hides. If hides can be sold untanned for 50 cents a pound, then 50 cents a pound is the opportunity cost of any hides that are retained for further processing. The relevant comparison is:

Market value of tanned hides		$0.60
Less: Market value of untanned hides	$0.50	
Incremental separate processing cost	0.08	0.58
Incremental processing profit		$0.02

Accounting Allocations of Joint Costs.   Most accounting systems allocate joint costs among the joint products in proportion to their relative values. The purpose of this allocation is to derive unit costs for use in costing inventories for external financial reporting. Unit costs derived in this way do not represent incremental cost, however, and should be totally ignored in managerial decision making.

APPLICATION OF COST DATA TO DECISIONS

Most of the cost data that are developed routinely by an accounting system are multipurpose data. They are used for such diverse purposes as financial reporting to shareholders, income tax calculations, departmental performance review, and managerial decision making. No one method of organizing the data can be perfect for all applications, and accounting data therefore often need to be modified to meet the needs of the decision maker. Examination of six different kinds of decision situations should indicate the problems encountered in adapting data bank figures:

1. Using idle capacity
2. Rationing scarce capacity
3. Pricing new products
4. Selecting customers
5. Replacing equipment
6. Selecting an order quantity.

Using Idle Capacity.   Most organizations always have some idle capacity in at least one major productive facility; most have idle capacity in all departments at least some of the time. Utilization of this idle capacity can be a source of increased profit.

Order Acceptance.   The simplest capacity-utilization decision arises when a potential customer offers to place a single order for a specified amount of goods or services. In this case the programmed fixed costs are all sunk and all that management needs to do is estimate the incremental costs of filling the order and the possible effects on future prices and future orders.

The only cost that is relevant to a decision to accept an order for a single additional unit of product is its marginal cost. The incremental cost of larger orders is the sum of the marginal costs of the incremental units. For example, if one more unit will cost $2.50 and a second additional unit will cost $2.60, the total incremental cost is $5.10.

The shape of the marginal cost curve is seldom known with much precision. Fortunately, the analyst is often able to assume that marginal cost is constant and equal to average variable cost for much of the output range. When this assumption is valid, the incremental cost of a small change in volume can be approximated by multiplying average variable cost by the amount of the change. When the increment in volume is greater, however, increments in capacity costs must be considered and incremental variable cost may be either greater or less than the average. Particular attention should be paid to such cost elements as overtime premiums, warehousing labor, delivery labor, and factory supervision.

The total effect of a large number of small orders will be similar to that of a single large order, although the effect on order handling costs and machine setup costs may be greater. If management is likely to be faced with the problem of accepting or rejecting a number of such orders, the relevant cost information consists of variable cost per unit, if this can safely be assumed to be constant, and the amount of the increase in fixed costs that can be expected to accompany volume increases of various magnitudes. Management must then decide whether the change in volume will cause an increase in fixed costs.

Estimates of incremental cost are usually stated as average cost per unit, and management may insist on a single unit cost estimate. In such cases, the accountant should obtain the best available estimate of the sensitivity of sales to price. If volume is highly sensitive, then the average cost should include estimates of changes in fixed costs as well as in the variable costs. If volume is relatively insensitive, then average variable cost is likely to be more relevant.

Program Expansion.   The firm may be able to affect the flow of customer orders by changing the scope or direction of its marketing programs. Decisions to increase marketing program costs to produce capacity-absorbing orders require examination of two variables that do not enter into simple order acceptance decisions; incremental program costs and marketing response functions.

Incremental program costs are relatively easy to estimate because they are usually specified in the proposal—hire an extra salesperson, spend more on advertising, etc. The difficult task is to estimate the response functions—that is, the effects of the incremental program costs on the volume of firm orders received. Historical data provide rough estimates of average responses but seldom reveal much about the incremental responses. Due to this uncertainty, estimators are often asked to provide optimistic and pessimistic forecasts as well as their primary predictions. These permit management to judge the sensitivity of results to errors of estimation and therefore the riskiness of the decisions. A further refinement is to require the submission of a rough probability estimate for each of several possible volumes, thereby permitting the construction of decision trees, payoff tables, and estimates of expected value.

For all of these cases, the estimated incremental profit is typically measured by deducting from incremental revenues the incremental costs of obtaining them (programmed costs) and the incremental costs of manufacturing and delivering the goods or services. The increments in manufacturing and delivery costs are estimated on the same bases as in the order acceptance decisions discussed above.

Rationing Scarce Capacity.   When capacity is scarce, management must choose between alternative uses of this capacity. In such cases, the costs of the scarce input ordinarily should be ignored. For example, if management must decide whether to sell a product in limited supply to one customer at a price of $2 or to another at a price of $2.20, the decision can be made without any factory cost data at all. Total manufacturing cost will be the same under either alternative.

Single Capacity Constraint.   A figure that is often used in capacity rationing decisions is the rate of variable profit per unit of capacity. For example, if production is limited by the amount of product that can be processed in the forming department, the profitability of each product might be computed in the following way:

$$\text{Profit per forming hour} = \frac{\text{price} - \text{average variable cost per unit}}{\text{forming hours required per unit}}$$

Forming department capacity could then be allocated first to the product with the highest profit ratio, and so on down the ladder until all capacity was utilized.

This solution can be attacked on both analytical and marketing grounds. From an analytical viewpoint, average variable cost may not be a good measure of the incremental cost of manufacturing and distributing individual products. Some products that use little forming department time may require large amounts of time in other departments. If product volume is big enough, some of the fixed costs of these other departments may be properly included in incremental cost.

The policy of granting complete priority to highest-margin products can also be criticized on marketing grounds. Sales of one product may be linked to sales of another; sales in the future may depend on the company's willingness and ability to fill orders now. In other words, the profit index may either over- or understate a product's true relative profitability.

Even so, the variable profit figures may be useful for marginal adaptations of the production and sales plan. A high variable profit (price minus average variable cost) means that the company can afford to spend more to make a sale. If variable profit is $5 for product X and $2.50 for product Y, the sales staff presumably should be instructed to work on product X whenever the likelihood of making a sale of X is better than half the likelihood of making a sale of Y.

Multiple Capacity Constraints.   The problem becomes even more complex if more than one capacity limitation is operative. For example, one product may have a relatively high profit per forming department hour but a low margin per finishing department hour. The gain from effective utilization of forming capacity may be more than offset by inefficiency or suboptimization in the use of finishing capacity.

To take a simple case, assume that the company has two products, each of which is processed in the same two production departments. The available data are as follows:

Product	Variable profit per unit	Machine-hours required per unit		Order backlog (units)
		Dept. X	Dept. Y	
A............	$10	4	2	1,000
B............	6	1	3	2,500

Capacity is 4,500 hours in department X and 7,500 hours in department Y.

Product A is the more profitable of the two, and one solution would be to produce the 1,000 units of product A, filling in with product B until one department's capacity was reached. Department X's capacity would be critical in this case, and the solution would be:

Product	Output (units)	Capacity utilized		Variable profit
		Dept. X	Dept. Y	
A...................	1,000	4,000	2,000	$10,000
B...................	500	500	1,500	3,000
Total..............		4,500	3,500	$13,000
Capacity available.....		4,500	7,500	
Idle capacity..... ...		0	4,000	

The existence of idle capacity in Department Y suggests that it might be profitable to shift some production from A to B, which uses department Y more intensively. If one unit of A were to be dropped, this would permit production of four units of B because it would release four hours of department X capacity. Four units of B contribute $24 of profit instead of $10, for a net gain of $14 for every unit of A that is dropped.

A second possible solution, therefore, would be to produce as much product B as department Y could handle. One unit of product B requires three hours in department Y and thus department Y's capacity would be completely absorbed by 2,500 units of product B and would contribute $15,000 in profit. This is better than the first solution, but this time some of department X's capacity would be idle:

| Product | Output (units) | Capacity utilized | | Variable profit |
		Dept X	Dept. Y	
A....................	0	0	0	0
B....................	2,500	2,500	7,500	$15,000
Total...............		2,500	7,500	$15,000
Capacity available.....		4,500	7,500	
Idle capacity..........		2,000	0	

Once again the opportunity cost analysis is revealing. If a unit of product B were to be withdrawn, this would release capacity in department Y to make 1 ½ units of product A. The gain would be $15 (= 1½ × $10); the loss would be $6. Thus a net gain of $9 would result from this shift.

The optimum solution obviously lies somewhere between these extremes. When department X is underutilized, it pays to substitute product A for product B. When department Y is underutilized, it pays to substitute product B for product A. This suggests that the optimum solution will be reached when both departments are fully utilized.

One way to reach this solution is to use the substitution ratio in department Y. By cutting back one unit of product B, capacity is released for 1½ units of product A. This substitution will keep department Y fully occupied and will use five hours of department X's idle capacity:

Added production of A: 1½ × 4 .... 6 hours
Less: Reduced production of B: 1 × 1 ... 1 hour
Net increase in use of Department X .... 5 hours

Because department X has an idle capacity of 2,000 hours, this means that both departments will be fully utilized if 400 units of B are subtracted from the second solution. This will release enough capacity to produce 600 units of A. The profit under this solution is

$$600 × \$10 + 2,100 × \$6 = \$18,600$$

which is $3,600 greater than the better of the two previous solutions. This could have been predicted because the benefit from substituting 1½ units of A for one unit of B was found to be $9, and we made 400 of these substitutions.

The feasibility of the solution can be checked by deriving the input requirements:

| Product | Units produced | Hours required | |
		Dept. X	Dept. Y
A.................	600	2,400	1,200
B.................	2,100	2,100	6,300
Total.............		4,500	7,500

The same solution can also be derived algebraically in this case. Full utilization of department X can be represented by the following equation:

$$4A + 1B = 4,500$$

The full utilization equation for department Y is

$$2A + 3B = 7,500$$

Two equations in two unknowns can be solved simultaneously to yield the values for A and B that we have already derived.

This is a special case of the kind of problem for which linear programming is ideally suited. Linear programming is a device which yields a solution to a resource allocation problem when an algebraic solution is unobtainable, that is, when the number of unknowns exceeds the number of equations. See Chapter 11.

Pricing New Products. Cost figures can enter into product pricing decisions in two ways: (1) in conjunction with price/volume estimates, to identify the most profitable sales volume; and (2) in conjunction with estimates of desired profit margins, to identify normal or target prices.

Profit/Volume Pricing. If satisfactory estimates of the price sensitivity of a product's sales can be obtained, a profit-maximizing price can be selected. In the following table, for example, where unit variable cost is $3.10 and fixed costs are $165,000, $6 is the profit-maximizing price:

(1) Price	(2) Units sold	(3) Sales (1) × (2)	(4) Cost	(5) Profit (3) − (4)
$5	100,000	$500,000	$475,000	$25,000
6	80,000	480,000	413,000	67,000
7	50,000	350,000	320,000	30,000

Costs for this kind of analysis should include any costs that will be affected by a change either in price or in volume. Factory materials cost, for example, will be affected by volume, while sales commissions will respond to changes in both prices and volume. Costs which are related to the product but unrelated to price or volume, such as some forms of advertising or market research, can be ignored. They enter into any evaluation of the desirability of introducing the product into the market, but are irrelevant to price/volume analysis.

Changes in marketing cost should be included in this kind of analysis only if they are related to product price. A marketing cost does not change because volume changes; instead, it may change in order to produce a volume change. Pricing analysis is not concerned, however, with choosing the optimum amount of marketing effort; only if price and marketing effort are interdependent should changes in marketing cost be introduced into the pricing analysis.

To put this another way, the costs and volume shown for each price should represent the estimated optimum amount of marketing effort at that price. If adding $50,000 to marketing effort would increase sales at a $5 price from 100,000 to 150,000 units, for example, this would be a better combination than the original estimate, as the following table shows:

	Revenues	Costs	Profit
Low effort (data from table above)............ ..	$500,000	$475,000	$25,000
High effort..................................	750,000	680,000	70,000

In other words, a $5 price appears to be more profitable than a $6 price because with effort, it will bring in a profit of $70,000 higher than the amount available at any other price.

Cost Formula Pricing.   Difficulties in estimating the price/volume relationship limit the direct application of profit/volume pricing. Another limiting factor in many cases is the dependence of sales in one period on price in previous periods. Price may be kept deliberately below the short-term optimum so as to achieve a greater penetration of the market and impede the entry and growth of competitors during the early stages of the product's life cycle.

In either of these circumstances, company price setters often rely heavily on cost-plus pricing formulas. The basic justification for the widespread use of such formulas is that they help the decision maker to predict either the competitor's costs or a competitive price. For example, if the firm has been operating for some time in a market in which markups over cost average 50 percent, it may be able to assume that the same relationship will hold on new products.

This kind of thinking is particularly valid in oligopolistic industries. Recognizing that price competition is likely to be self-defeating, the pricer may set a price that is expected not to attract competitors unduly and then focus competitive efforts on other factors such as delivery, credit terms, and so forth.

Formula pricing does not necessarily mean that market forces are ignored in pricing new products. Anyone who is at all familiar with department store operations, for example, knows that percentage markups over cost vary from department to department and often for different lines of merchandise within a given department. Most differences in markup reflect well-established customs in the trade which guide the pricer toward a competitive price. Furthermore, the customary markups change from time to time, and most department store buyers who make the pricing decisions are free to alter the markup if they see a reason to do so.

Cost-based pricing formulas in manufacturing firms are likely to be "full-cost" formulas, in which full cost is defined as estimated or standard manufacturing costs. Although formulas based on variable product cost can be constructed, they ignore differences in input requirements that may be very important. A product requiring a great amount of machine time but little labor time will pass through departments in which fixed overhead is relatively high. Products requiring only simple assembly operations ordinarily require far less fixed overhead. In the short run, the price of the first kind of product can be reduced substantially without creating an incremental loss; in the longer period, however, heavy overhead requirements may give it far more price protection than the simple assembled product. At least some of the fixed costs, in other words, are likely to be relevant to the pricing decision.

The development of factory unit cost estimates for use in formula pricing is described in detail in Chapters 41 and 42. Costs derived from such systems should be examined to make sure that they include only those costs reasonably attributable to the product. Exhibit 3, for example, shows a simple two-tier cost structure. Full product cost would include provisions for the categories of nonattributable costs described in the two blocks at the bottom of Exhibit 3. Since these are not attributable to individual products, they should be excluded from the pricing base. These costs must be covered by the margins on all products combined, but the contributions made by individual products need not be identical.

The amount of fixed cost included in product cost will depend on the operating volume over which the fixed costs are to be spread. High volume means low unit fixed cost, and vice versa. A good starting point is "designed capacity." For factory costs, this is the average operating level assumed by the designers when they were deciding how big a plant to build. It will typically be less than maximum physical

EXHIBIT 3   Relationship Between Service Department Cost and Product Cost

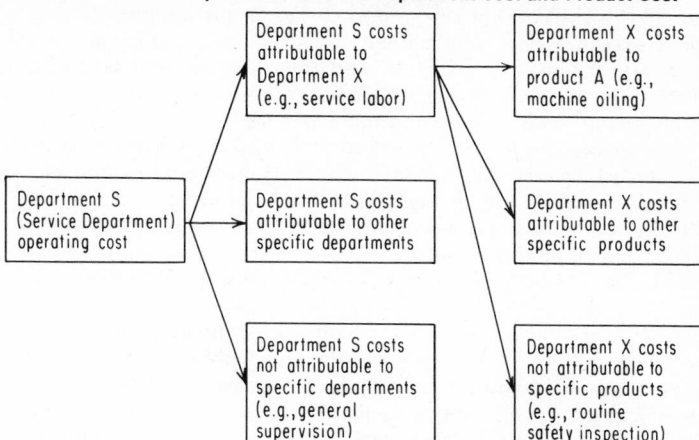

capacity and will depend to some extent on industry practice as to the number of shifts worked in a normal week.

This is not to imply that price and volume are totally independent of each other. Pricing formulas are used partly because price/volume relationships are unknown and partly to establish long-term targets. If setting price at the target level would preclude the attainment of normal volume or something close to it, the product's long-term survival prospects are dim and management should know this.

A refinement of cost-based formula pricing is return-on-investment pricing. This differs only in that the cost base includes an estimate of the required implicit interest on the amount of capital attributable to each individual product. The general approach is the same.

Full cost formulas seldom incorporate sophisticated estimates of selling and administrative costs. These costs, if included at all, enter the formulas through simple averages, such as overall percentages of manufacturing cost. These averages will be inadequate if selling and administrative costs are strongly affected by product characteristics. The price that will produce a normal return on investment at normal volume will vary with the amount of marketing effort required to achieve that volume. Most marketing costs are programmed costs, of course, unresponsive to changes in the rate of production or sales. Such costs do not enter into profit/volume pricing, but they have to be a factor in decisions to market the product in the first place or retain it on a continuing basis. A product that cannot cover the costs attributable to it cannot survive indefinitely.

Selecting Customers.   Customers and potential customers may be classified by location, by industry, by function (wholesaler vs. retailer), or by other characteristics. Knowledge of the cost of serving customers in a particular group may be the basis for deciding to charge them higher prices or perhaps not to sell to them at all.

Customer profitability analysis consists of four steps:

1. Classify the customers into groups.
2. Measure the product mix and volume for each group.
3. Estimate the manufacturing costs attributable to the products bought by each group.
4. Estimate the nonmanufacturing costs attributable to each group.

This process is described in detail in Chapter 43, but the third and fourth steps deserve special attention here.

Estimates of Manufacturing Costs.   The basic question in this kind of analysis is how much cost would be eliminated if a particular customer group were to be dropped. This is the concept referred to earlier as attributable cost.

Factory costs can seldom be attributed directly to specific customer groups. They must first be attributed to products, and these in turn can be identified with different customer groups. Most companies use standard factory cost to represent attributable factory costs. The assumption that standard cost is a good approximation to attributable cost should be examined carefully if fixed costs constitute a large portion of factory costs. Indivisible fixed costs that cannot be traced to specific products should not be attributed to those products. Furthermore, a fixed cost that can be traced to a particular product but is highly indivisible ordinarily should not be attributed to a customer group. Such a cost can be eliminated only by dropping the product entirely, not by cutting out some of the consumers of that product.

Estimates of Nonmanufacturing Costs.   Nonmanufacturing costs should be classified into two categories for customer profitability analysis. In the first category are the various kinds of programmed costs, such as marketing research and product research. Some of these can be traced directly to specific customer groups, such as the salaries and expenses of sales staff who call only on customers in a single group. Most of the others are not readily attributable to individual customer groups, however, and should be included in the analysis only insofar as meaningful measures of attributability can be developed. Average cost per sales call, for example, is likely to be a very poor measure of the cost of soliciting customer orders—only a special analysis of the effects of dropping a customer group can identify the attributable portion of these costs.

The second category of nonmanufacturing costs consists of the costs of organization support and order-filling activities. For broad support activities, such as the costs of corporate executive offices, cost attributability to customer groups is minimal. For others, the two-stage analysis diagrammed in Exhibit 4 is appropriate. The first stage is to identify the cost of performing the individual service functions such as invoice writing, payroll preparation, and customer delivery to calculate a cost per unit of functional service. The second stage is to estimate the number of units of functional service required by each customer group.

EXHIBIT 4   Assignment of Nonmanufacturing Costs to Revenue Segments

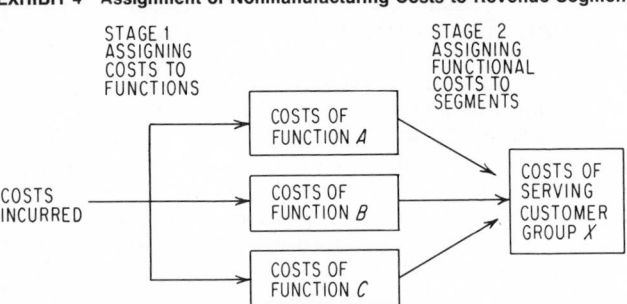

In the first stage, the company must identify the costs of performing individual functions and state these as unit costs—for example, cost per order or cost per payroll line. The unit cost divisor may be the number of service units produced (for example, number of paychecks) or a more abstract determinant of cost (for example, dollar value of items in storage). In either case, this divisor is referred to as the function's governing factor.

In the second stage, every functional cost that has a governing factor that depends on the number, size, or other dimension of customer orders should be identified. Other items should be excluded from the analysis. The cost of writing a customer invoice, for example, is clearly an order-related cost; the salary of the marketing vice-president just as clearly is not.

As an illustration, suppose that the problem is to investigate the cost of processing small orders. None of the nonmanufacturing costs can be traced directly to small orders; for example, all order clerks handle orders of all sizes; therefore all costs have to go through the two-stage analysis shown in Exhibit 4.

For example, suppose that functional cost analyses have revealed the following unit cost totals:

Governing factor	Unit cost
Number of orders	$1.00 per order
Value of orders	0.001 per dollar
Number of product units ordered	0.03 per unit
Number of order lines	0.01 per line

This table, of course, represents the summation of all of the functional cost elements governed by each of the factors listed; a full example would have to list each function separately.

The next step is to find out how many units of each of these governing factors are associated with orders of various sizes. Suppose that a sample of orders yields the following statistics:

Size class	Number of governing factor units			
	Orders	Order value	Product units	Order lines
$1–$99...........	50,000	$ 1,000,000	200,000	100,000
100–199.........	20,000	2,600,000	500,000	60,000
200–499.........	20,000	5,600,000	1,100,000	80,000
500 and up......	10,000	6,000,000	1,200,000	50,000
Total...........	100,000	$15,200,000	3,000,000	290,000

Because the question in this case is how much it costs to obtain and service an order, these statistics next should be restated as averages, as follows:

Size class	Average number of governing factor units per order			
	Orders	Order value	Product units	Order lines
$1–$99...........	1	$ 20	4	2.0
100–199.........	1	130	25	3.0
200–499.........	1	280	55	4.0
500 and up......	1	600	120	5.0
Average..........	1	$152	30	2.9

The final step is to multiply these statistics by the unit cost figures cited earlier. The end result is the unit cost of an order, as summarized below:

| Size class | Servicing costs attributed to | | | | Total cost per order |
	Each order	Value of the order	Number of units in the order	Number of order lines	
$1–$99........	$1.00	$0.02	$0.12	$0.02	$1.16
100–199......	1.00	0.13	0.75	0.03	1.91
200–499......	1.00	0.28	1.65	0.04	2.97
500 and up....	1.00	0.60	3.60	0.05	5.25
Average.......	$1.00	$0.152	$0.90	$0.029	$2.08

Replacing Equipment.   Equipment is ordinarily replaced to achieve one or more of three results:

1. Lower costs
2. Greater volume
3. Greater versatility.

If the motive is greater volume or greater versatility, incremental revenues will be important to the decision. In all cases, however, cost differences are likely to be substantial and should not be overlooked.

Equipment replacement decisions differ from the decisions discussed above in that costs must be estimated separately for two or more different time periods. The reason is that a cost saving or other cash inflow that will take place five years ahead is worth less to the company than an immediate saving. For example, Exhibit 5 shows the present value of the cost savings expected at the end of each year from two different machines. This present value represents the amount that these savings are worth to a company which expects after-tax earnings of 8 percent on its investment. (See interest tables in the Appendix.) Each machine has an expected life of five years, but the savings on machine B are expected to build up gradually as production volume increases, while machine A gets its maximum benefit immediately. The lifetime savings from the two machines are identical, but machine A has a higher present value because near money is worth more than distant money.

EXHIBIT 5   Present Value of Cost Savings

| Year | Machine A | | Machine B | |
	Cost saving	Present value at 8%	Cost saving	Present value at 8%
1	$100	$ 93	$ 35	$ 32
2	90	77	45	38
3	70	55	60	48
4	45	33	80	59
5	10	7	95	65
Total........	$315	$265	$315	$242

For example, the company will receive $65 more at the end of year 1 with machine A than with machine B. If this amount can be invested for four years at a rate of return of 8 percent, it will be worth more to the company than a similar benefit four years later.

The cost saving from replacement is the difference in cost in any year between the cost of operating the present machine and operating the replacement. These forecasts must be made for the number of periods prior to the date when the replacement machine, in its turn, will be replaced or retired.

Most equipment costs fall into the categories of setup labor, production labor, production materials, maintenance labor and materials, materials handling labor, employee fringe benefits, power, tooling and fixtures, insurance, and taxes. These elements must be estimated both for the existing machine and for the proposed replacement.

Three cautions need to be observed in replacement cost analysis. First, even though factory overhead or burden rates are often developed on a direct labor base, overhead cost savings cannot be determined by multiplying labor savings by the burden rate. Profitable replacement often requires the partial substitution of overhead costs for direct labor costs; that is, total savings will be less than direct labor savings rather than greater.

Second, annual depreciation on existing equipment is not "saved" if the machine is replaced. Depreciation charges, as ordinarily calculated, are allocations of original cost (or replacement cost, in some instances). As such they represent sunk costs. The real depreciation figure that is relevant to a replacement decision is the decline in the disposal value of the equipment that will take place in the future if it is not replaced.

Similarly, the current book value of the existing equipment is a sunk cost that need not be covered by the anticipated cash savings from the operation of the new machine. Only the present salvage value of the old machine is relevant. The incremental cash flows associated with the purchase and salvage values of machines in a replacement decision are thus as shown in the accompanying table:

	Alternative A: Keep old machine	Alternative B: Replace with new machine	Difference
At time of replacement	0	− cost of new machine + salvage of old machine now	− cost of new machine + salvage of old machine now
At end of estimated life of new machine	+ salvage of old machine at end of life	+ salvage of new machine at end of life	+ (salvage of new machine − salvage of old machine) at end of life

The third caution in this kind of analysis is that costs of floor space occupied should be computed on an incremental basis. In many cases, an increase in floor space requirements will lead to no increase in total occupancy costs; in such cases, the incremental cost is zero. Similarly, if the new machine occupies less space than the present machine, the actual cash saving may be zero. In each case, the question is whether total company space costs will increase or decrease. The present average cost per square foot of floor space is almost never a good basis on which to forecast this increment.

Selecting an Order Quantity. The decision as to how much merchandise or material to purchase in a single order requires cost estimates of a slightly different kind. The act of purchasing the goods leads to a one-time purchasing cost. In most cases, the salary of the purchasing agent himself should be treated as a sunk cost, irrelevant to the decision and therefore excluded from the analysis. Incremental purchasing costs consist of such items as telephone charges, clerical salaries, postage, and forms costs. Unless each purchase requires special activities such as the preparation and reproduction of diagrams, blueprints, etc., incremental purchasing costs are likely to be very low.

Of greater significance are inventory carrying costs—mainly the costs of storage space, insurance, spoilage, and interest. The greater the inventory, the greater the carrying costs per period. Most of these costs can be expected to vary proportionately with the size of the inventory. Care must be exercised to see that space costs are estimated on an incremental basis (see final paragraph under "Replacing Equipment" above).

One simple order-size formula utilizing this kind of data is as follows:

$$EOQ = \sqrt{\frac{2DP}{CR}}$$

in which EOQ = optimum number of units per purchase order
D = total number of units needed per year
P = ordering cost per purchase order
R = purchase price per unit
C = carrying cost per dollar of average inventory
CR = carrying cost per unit per year

As this formula indicates, the larger the annual requirements or the larger the order cost per order, the larger the order should be. Conversely, greater carrying costs call for smaller purchase lots because smaller and more frequent purchase lots reduce the average inventory quantity. See Chapter 11 for a more extended discussion.

METHODS OF ANALYSIS

Cost data for decision analyses often can be found in the company's records of past cost experience. Sometimes the best analytical technique is to apply trend factors to the historical cost figures. Cost relationships are likely to be more complex than this would imply, however, and more sophisticated techniques are frequently necessary. Some of these techniques build on data already in the cost files; others require the generation of new data. Five groups of techniques deserve a brief introduction:

1. Statistical regression analysis
2. Observation
3. Synthesis of work elements
4. Personal judgment
5. Time-pattern analysis.

Statistical Regression Analysis.   Statistical regression analysis is widely used to estimate the historical relationship between costs and volume. The result is typically stated in the form:

$$C = a + bV$$

where C = total cost per period
a = fixed costs per period
b = average variable cost per unit of volume
V = volume per period

The line of relationship sometimes can be estimated adequately by plotting a set of historical observations on a sheet of graph paper and drawing a line which seems to fit the observations best (as in Exhibit 6). In other cases, mathematical analysis becomes necessary, usually by the method of least squares. This consists of finding a line such that the sum of the squares of the vertical deviations from the line will be at a minimum.

EXHIBIT 6   Graphic Method for Analyzing Cost Variability

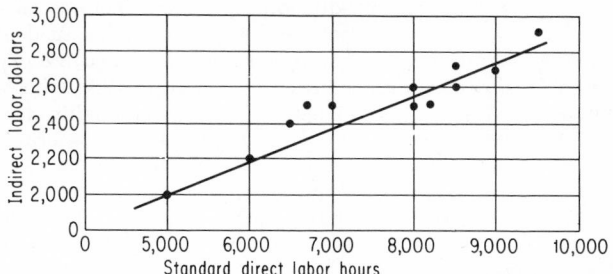

Regression analysis can also be applied to estimate the effects on cost of more than one variable. Analysis of this kind is known as multiple regression analysis, and leads to a formula in the form:

$$C = a + bV + cX$$

in which X stands for the value of some variable other than volume (for example, external temperature) and c represents the rate of variation of cost with variations in this other variable. See Chapter 10 for a more extended discussion.

Observation. When historical data are out of date or unreliable, or when volume is not the main variable in the decision, the analyst may be able to estimate costs on the basis of observations made specifically for that purpose. These observations are ordinarily made by industrial engineers and are of two types:

1. Observation of existing operations
2. Experimentation.

Observation of Existing Operations. The two most common kinds of observations are: (1) time studies or time-and-motion studies and (2) work sampling. Time-and-motion studies are widely used in manufacturing operations as part of methods improvement programs or in the establishment or revision of incentive wage rates. Work sampling is most commonly applied to clerical operations as part of methods improvement programs.

In a time study, engineers use a stopwatch to measure the amount of time required for specific operations. They then apply a leveling factor to adjust for the difference between the observed performance and what they judge to be normal performance. They then add a standard allowance for such factors as fatigue, rest time, and production interruptions.

In work sampling, in contrast, no attempt is made to time individual operations. Instead, the engineer accumulates a set of cross-section observations, each showing what the various employees were doing at a particular point in time. The total amount of time required for a given function is then estimated by multiplying the total time spent on all functions by the percentage indicated by the sample for this particular function.

Time studies are most useful when the individual task consumes a substantial amount of time and can be expected to be repeated many times. Work sampling is useful when a given task takes a relatively short time and the nature of the task is likely to change substantially from one period to the next.

Both methods assume that costs vary proportionately with volume. They might be used to identify cost-volume relationships, but only if fairly substantial methodological problems can be solved. Techniques analogous to time studies can be used to measure the consumption of materials and some additional cost elements other than labor; work sampling is used only to identify manpower requirements and utilization.

Experimentation.   Experimental production runs are sometimes made to provide the basis for time studies or time and motion studies. Aside from this, experimentation is seldom used for cost estimation, mainly because experimental data often cannot be obtained with reducing existing operating efficiency.

Experimentation is most practical when operations are highly divisible. This permits the company to change a small part of its operations without disrupting the entire system. It also permits the use of the unaffected operations as a control against which to measure the experimental results.

Synthesis of Work Elements.   A third main method of estimation is the synthesis of work elements. The prime example is the construction of cost estimates from commercially available tables of the amount of time required to perform basic physical motions, for example, Methods-Time Measurement systems (MTM).

The same approach underlies the construction of standard costs for a new product from the standard costs of an existing product. Labor and materials data for identical operations or parts can be transferred bodily for this purpose.

Personal Judgment.   In the end, all cost estimates are personal judgments of the future effects of present conditions. Even if the highly precise statistical regression technique is used, the indicated cost-volume relationship is likely to be rejected if it does not seem reasonable.

Personal judgment is also used, however, as a direct method of deriving cost estimates. First, the analyst can examine a standard list of accounts and estimate the amount of cost likely to be charged to each account under specified conditions. This is sometimes called the "inspection of accounts" method. Although highly unsophisticated, this approach should not be totally scorned. Most judgmental estimates are based on personal experience. The estimates of shrewd analysts may have a stronger factual foundation than the more sophisticated statistical regression analysis.

Personal judgment also enters into cost estimation in another guise, through the engineering estimate. Engineers will be asked to compute the cost of operating a machine which the company has never owned. By studying the machine and the performance characteristics specified by the manufacturer, the experienced engineer can draw on previous experience to derive a fairly accurate cost estimate.

The personal judgment method is undoubtedly the most widely used. It can also be called the method of historical analogy. The human mind stores data from the past and delivers them when they are needed. Even experimental methods generate data that are historical by the time they are accumulated. The advantage of the more sophisticated methods is that the process by which the data are converted into cost estimates is more visible, with assumptions, adjustments, and allowances specified as clearly as the analysis demands. Judgmental estimates are more difficult to document and to trace back to the underlying assumptions.

Time-Pattern Analysis.   All of these methods of analysis ignore the possibility that cost performance will change from period to period. One cause of such changes is that equipment often declines in efficiency as it gets older. This can be highly important for equipment replacement decisions. Data on cost-age patterns can be derived from equipment maintenance records, using a form of regression analysis.

Another cause of changes in cost performance is the so-called learning curve. Aircraft manufacturers during the 1939–1945 war discovered that unit cost declined as a function of the cumulative number of units produced, and that this decline could be predicted fairly accurately. These patterns were reflected in learning curves, showing the percentage decline in unit costs that could be expected from a given percentage increase in cumulative output. Thus an 80 percent learning curve was one in which doubling cumulative output would reduce cumulative unit cost by 20 percent. If the first 1,000 units cost a total of $10,000 to produce, or $10 a unit, the average cost of the first 2,000 units would be expected to be $8. To achieve this, of course, the cost of the second 1,000 units would have to be only $6,000, or $6 each.

Identification of the cost improvement pattern may be extremely useful in product pricing. In bidding on orders for custom products, for example, it can provide the basis for quantity discount schedules. In other situations, bidders who base bids on costs of the first units may find themselves priced out of the market.

COST-PROFIT DIAGRAMS

The results of a cost analysis are almost always shown in one or more summary tables of figures. The meaning of these data often can be made clearer, however, by presenting them in pictorial form. Two closely related devices used for this purpose are the profit-volume chart and the break-even diagram.

Profit-Volume Charts. Decisions are often highly sensitive to the estimates of sales or production volume. The profit-volume chart is one device for visualizing the anticipated impact on profit of variations in operating volume.

Exhibit 7 shows one kind of profit-volume diagram. In this case, the volume of sales is measured along the horizontal axis, and total costs and total revenues for each sales volume are represented by the vertical distances above the base line. The vertical distance between the total revenue and total cost lines represents the expected profit or loss at that volume (indicated by the shaded areas on the chart).

EXHIBIT 7   Profit-Volume Chart

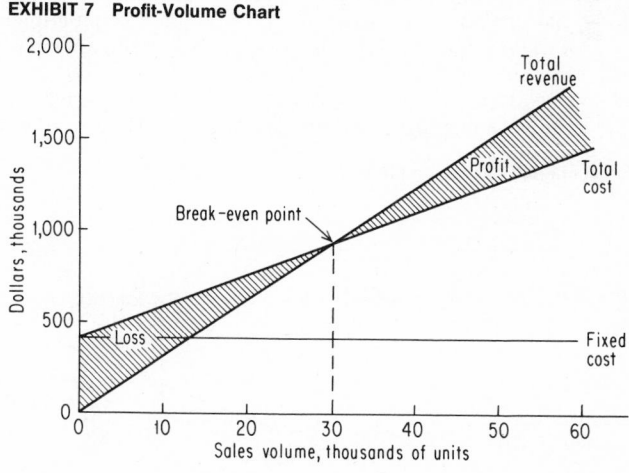

In this traditional form, the total cost line is depicted as a straight line extending from zero volume to the highest volume shown on the chart. As we have already seen, this is an oversimplification. Variable cost rates are computed for a limited portion of the total output range, covering perhaps that 30 to 40 percent of the total range within which the company expects to operate. Although the straight-line cost function is reasonably representative within this range, the profit spreads

EXHIBIT 8   Profit-Volume Chart

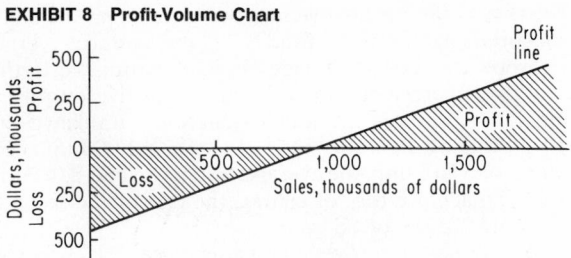

to the left and right of this range have little meaning and are introduced only to facilitate the explanation of the nature of fixed costs.

This same set of data is shown in a slightly different way in Exhibit 8. Separate lines for costs and revenues are eliminated by plotting the profits only. Volume is again measured along the horizontal axis, and profit or loss is represented by the vertical spread between the profit line and the zero-profit base line.

The profit-volume diagram can help the manager in decision making by showing the sensitivity of profit to variations in volume. It can also be used to illustrate the comparison between two alternative decisions. For example, Exhibit 9 shows the estimated effect on profit of a change in product selling prices. The broken line in this exhibit represents the profit obtainable at various levels of sales at prices that are 10 percent higher than current prices, represented by the solid line. This shows that although increased prices are expected to reduce physical sales volume, dollar profit is expected to increase.

Break-even Diagram.   Some profit-volume charts are referred to as break-even charts. In the diagram in Exhibit 7, for example, the break-even point is the volume at which the total revenue and total cost lines cross. Many managers find the break-even point useful as a partial measure of the risks involved in a particular course of action. A decision that will raise the break-even point is often presumed to be riskier than other decisions. This notion is often implemented by the calculation of the margin of safety, or the spread between anticipated volume and the break-even volume.

The break-even concept can also be applied in other ways. For example, Exhibit 10 shows the relative advantage and disadvantage of using a special-purpose

EXHIBIT 9   Effect of Price Change on Profit

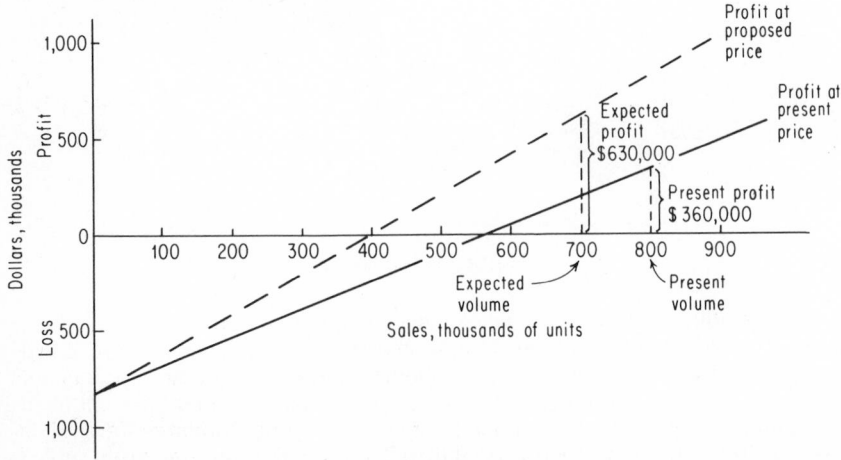

EXHIBIT 10   Guide to Production Scheduling

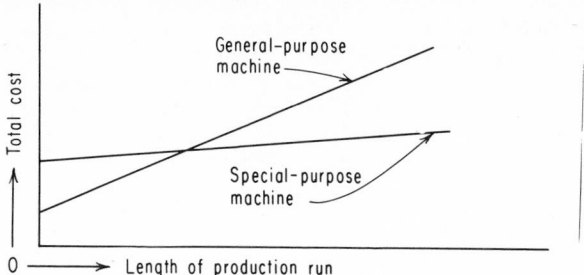

EXHIBIT 11   Cumulative Cash Position Resulting from Capital Expenditure Proposal

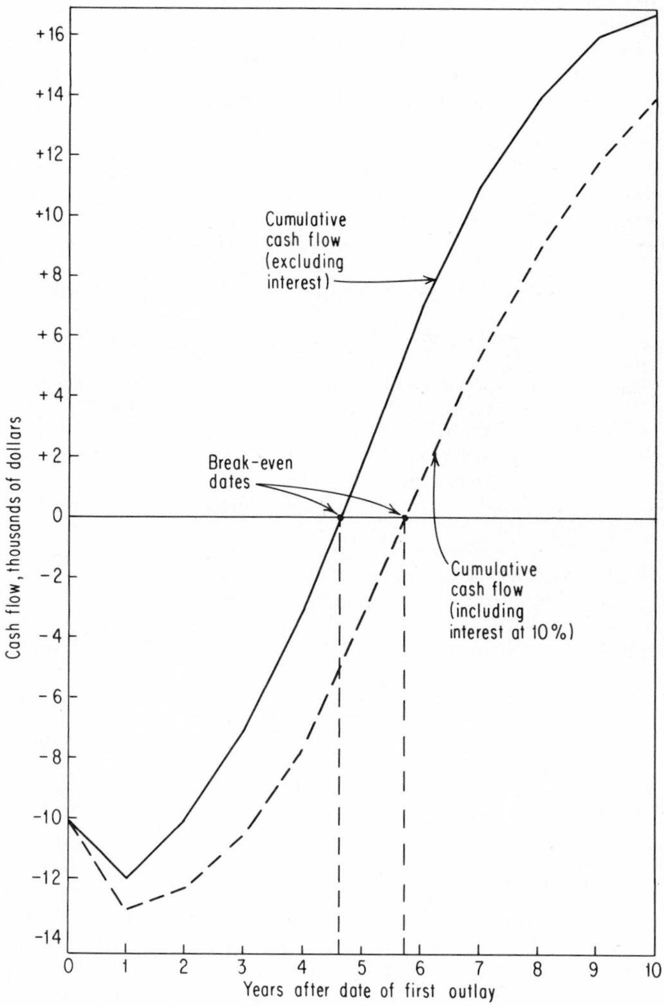

machine instead of a general-purpose machine. The special-purpose machine has a high setup cost and low running costs. The general-purpose machine has high running costs but a low setup cost. The diagram shows the planner which machine will be more economical for any given production run.

The diagram in Exhibit 11 is similar in shape to the others but provides an entirely different message. This shows the anticipated cumulative cash flows from a capital expenditure proposal. The solid line shows that the project will have returned the initial investment in full by shortly after the middle of the fifth year. The broken line shows that the initial outlay will be completely paid off before the end of the sixth year, even after allowing for interest at 10 percent on the amounts invested.

BIBLIOGRAPHY

American Institute of Certified Public Accountants: *Cost Analysis for Pricing and Distribution Policies,* New York, 1965.

Andress, Frank J.: "The Learning Curve as a Production Tool," *Harvard Business Review,* January-February 1954, pp. 87–97.

Beyer, Robert, and Donald J. Trawicki: *Profitability Accounting for Planning and Control,* 2nd ed., The Ronald Press Company , New York, 1972.

Dean, Joel: *Managerial Economics,* Prentice-Hall, Englewood Cliffs, N. J., 1951, especially chaps. 5 and 6.

DeCoster, Don T., Kasi V. Ramanathan, and Gary L. Sundem (eds.): *Accounting for Managerial Decision Making,* Melville Publishing Co., Los Angeles, 1974.

Dopuch, Nicholas, Jacob G. Birnberg, and Joel Demski: *Cost Accounting: Accounting Data for Management's Decisions,* 2nd ed., Harcourt Brace Jovanovich, New York, 1974.

Hartley, Ronald V.: "Decision Making with Joint Products," *Accounting Review,* October 1971, pp. 746–755.

———: "Some Extensions of Sensitivity Analysis," *Accounting Review,* April 1970, pp. 223–234.

Horngren, Charles T.: *Cost Accounting: A Managerial Emphasis,* 3rd ed., Prentice-Hall, Englewood Cliffs, N. J., 1972.

Johnson, Glenn L., and S. Stephen Simik, II: "Multiproduct C.V.P. Analysis Under Uncertainty," *Journal of Accounting Research,* Autumn 1971, pp. 278–286.

Johnston, John: *Statistical Cost Analysis,* McGraw-Hill Book Company, New York, 1960.

Levin, Richard I., and C. A. Kirkpatrick: *Quantitative Approaches to Management,* 2nd ed., McGraw-Hill Book Company, New York, 1971.

Manes, Rene: "A New Dimension to Break-Even Analysis," *Journal of Accounting Research,* Spring 1966, pp. 87–100.

Rappaport, Alfred (ed.): *Information for Decision Making, Quantitative and Behavioral Dimensions,* 2nd ed., Prentice-Hall, Englewood Cliffs, N. J., 1975.

Rappaport, Alfred: "Sensitivity Analysis in Decision Making," *Accounting Review,* July 1967, pp. 441–456.

Shillinglaw, Gordon: *Managerial Cost Accounting,* 4th ed., Richard D. Irwin, Homewood, Ill., 1977.

Solomons, David (ed.): *Studies in Cost Analysis,* 2nd ed., Richard D. Irwin, Homewood, Ill., 1968.

Weil, R. L., "Allocating Joint Costs," *American Economic Review,* December 1968, pp. 1342–1345.

Williams, Thomas H., and Charles H. Griffin (eds.): *Management Information: A Quantitative Accent,* Richard D. Irwin, Homewood, Ill., 1967.

Chapter **40**

Budgeting

WALTER R. BUNGE
Management Consultant

CONCEPT OF MANAGERIAL BUDGETING

The Central Idea of Budgetary Planning. The modern budget is a managerial tool incorporating organizational and financial planning, analysis of the behavior characteristics of costs, the setting of objectives, and evaluation of performance. It uses the language of accounting, and in a very real sense it gives added purpose to accounting by increasing its effectiveness in the day-to-day control of the operation of an enterprise. The budget expresses the responsibilities delegated to the various organizational subdivisions of a company. It spells out quantitatively what is expected of each member of management at every level, in terms of expected goals and the cost expected to be incurred to accomplish the tasks assigned, whether they be line or staff functions.

Furthermore, the budget summarizes and consolidates these factors of planned revenue and expense into a *pro forma* presentation of the consequent profit situation as expressed in an income statement and the financial condition resulting from these planned actions as shown in the balance sheet.

Accounting, on the other hand, supplies the data on actual performance, after the fact. Thus, when properly designed and integrated, the two systems in combination provide management with the means for planning and assigning specific operating objectives which are also performance criteria, and the means for subsequent measurement of actual operating results against those criteria.

The process of establishing the criteria in the form of a well-coordinated budget requires a planning discipline which is, in itself, of great benefit to an organization. The planning should be participated in by all levels of management and in all functions of the company. The budget is therefore also a means of bringing to light the potential problem areas, the debilitating impediments which lie at the level of line operations and which are likely to escape notice if all planning is done on a centralized basis by the specialists.

Long-Range Planning Sets the Direction. The budget is really the short-range plan. It is specific and establishes the exact route to be followed for a period usually lasting to the end of the subsequent year. This is a commitment of direction which in most cases can be reoriented and corrected if it proves to be wrong, only at the costly expenditure of both time and money. A long-range plan provides the necessary general direction for the long term, and is therefore an important preliminary essential.

The long-range plan need not be in detail but it should cover more ground than mere estimates of the rate of growth and desired profit levels. Sales projections should be broken down by the various products, models, lines, departments, or services to indicate those which are in a declining phase and are likely to be replaced and those which will need added promotion because they are just being established or are in trouble. Expected expansion into new territories, changed methods of distribution, changes in credit, purchasing facilities, financing—in fact, long-range plans for every phase of operations are requisite background for developing the more minute program for the coming year.

Specific Action Planning. Sometime around the middle of a fiscal year, the specific action plans for the coming year should be taking shape within each functional area of the company. The general marketing strategy and the resulting anticipated sales volume and mix are among the most important influences and are continually taken into account in the development of the budget of every department. The current sales estimate for the subsequent year is therefore obtained as part of the supporting material when work is begun on establishing the next year's budget.

With the expected general level of volume in mind, each department is required to develop specific operating plans for the coming year. As these plans take form there should be interchange of information between areas whose activities affect each other. Improvements in facilities and methods, product changes, inventory programs, major repair programs, growth, and other factors will all influence the emerging operating plans.

Operating Budgets. As these plans crystallize, it becomes necessary to express in writing the costs which they imply so that the emerging plans of the various areas may be carefully reviewed and coordinated. The cost estimates of every department, down to the lowest recognized organizational unit and expressed in detail by account classification, are the budget estimates or requests. When these are officially approved, they become the budgets. The individual departmental budgets, computed at operating levels appropriate to the sales volume forecast, are consolidated to form a tentative master budget for the company.

At this point, the operating plans of the entire company are reviewed in the perspective of their relation to and effect on each other, and it is determined if the results—if everyone can accomplish what he now plans—are satisfactory. This is an opportunity to weigh individual plans as they fit into the whole, to balance and adjust. Any proposed changes are discussed with affected areas before becoming final. This broad participation, agreement, and commitment goes far to assure that the objectives will be met if at all possible. It removes the restrictive feeling of operating under an arbitrary budget imposed on operating personnel by top management, often far removed from local conditions.

Budgetary Control. Control begins with operation in the budgeted period. Each member of management who is responsible for spending the company's money or obtaining revenue has definite objectives, and he has a budget which spells out in detail what his revenue contribution or operating cost is expected to be. This awareness of what is expected is the first essential of control.

At the end of each month (or other reporting period) a statement is issued to each department showing actual performance (actual income or actual expenses or both) compared to the agreed plans as expressed in the budget. Variances are shown, and these highlight the areas that require attention.

Relationship Between Accounting and Budgeting. The accounting system and the budget are built around the same organizational structure, and both are information systems concerned with the same operations and financial situations. Accounting reports quantify information on actual past events and conditions; the budget reflects what those values were expected to be, and what is expected in the future.

Accounting has three basic functions in a business. The first is the custodial or official record-keeping function. It supplies the data required for reports to stockholders, government, and other agencies such as the stock exchange. This is the summarization of the results of operations. The budget helps to organize and formalize the planning required for these operations, expresses objectives, and then becomes a means to measure the extent to which the plans have been achieved.

The second function of accounting is to assist management in evaluating individual performance and to provide departmental costs for later assignment to products or services. For this, accounting classifies and assembles expenses by departmental responsibility. In this function budgeting and accounting follow almost parallel paths. The budget expresses and quantifies delegated responsibility, and accounting supplies the corresponding accountability by reporting actual performance.

The third basic function of accounting is the determination of the end product cost, the cost of specific products or services, often segregated into standard costs and variances. The budget can assist in the establishment of standards, but it does not diminish the importance of or interfere with cost accounting, and it frequently simplifies analysis of variances. However, the budget does not primarily emphasize finished product costs or variances from planned costs at that late stage. Rather, it is concerned with the variances from planned costs as they happen, before the product has reached its final stages. It is also concerned with overhead costs—evasive items which are not pinpointed and controlled by types of expense in product cost accounting.

Definition of a Budget and Budgetary Control.   The following definitions[1] summarize the concept of budgeting:

> *Budget*   A coordinated financial program or plan of operations, segregated into responsibility areas, indicating amounts, expected to be required for specific purposes or received from specific sources, and approved by responsible management. The consolidation of all pertinent budgetary allowances. The term is applied to the combined plans of an entire enterprise, to any of its subdivisions, and to the specific detailed financial plan of a single area, function, project, or account.
>
> *Budgetary Control*   The exercise by line management of control over costs through continuous appraisal of actual expenditures, using as a guide the planned costs as expressed in the budget. This principle is also applied to the various types of income and to items that affect the balance sheet, such as receivables, inventories, cash, fixed assets, etc.

Types of Budgets.   There are two basic types of budgets, fixed and variable. A fixed budget is not subject to change as conditions vary; it is a set of specific, unvarying monetary allowances. A variable or flexible budget contains some elements that are fixed and others that fluctuate in accordance with normal requirements under differing conditions. It is expressed as a simple formula composed of two elements: a fixed monetary amount per accounting period (day, week, or month), and a variable amount expressed as an amount per unit of production or effort, or as a percentage of some measure of volume, such as direct labor or sales.

Fixed Budgets.   Fixed budgets set forth allowances for specific purposes, each having definite monetary limitations. The allowances are actually appropriations and the control may be exercised in terms of the finest account detail, or a certain amount of discretion may be permitted among the detail accounts within an expense category.

Governmental budgets are almost always fixed budgets. In industry, fixed budgets are appropriate for those departments whose work load does not have a direct current relationship to sales, production, or some other volume determinant related to the department's operations. The work of the departments is deter-

---

[1]Walter R. Bunge, *Managerial Budgeting for Profit Improvement,* McGraw-Hill Book Company, New York, 1968, p. 217.

mined by management decision rather than by sales volume. Most administrative, general marketing, and even manufacturing management departments are in this category. Fixed appropriations for specific projects or programs not necessarily completed in the fiscal period also become fixed budgets to the extent that they will be expended during the year. Examples are appropriations for capital expenditures, major repair projects, and specific advertising or promotional programs.

In some areas, production departments for example, the work load fluctuates significantly and the requirements for personal services, supplies, and materials vary materially with volume, though not necessarily in the same degree. In these cases a fixed budget is not practical since it does not serve as an accurate criterion for expenditures. Some companies solve this problem by rebudgeting whenever volume changes significantly or by establishing a series of fixed budgets set at incremental levels of work load. This is really a substitute for a variable budget, is cumbersome, and does not lend itself as readily to changes in product mix.

Variable Budgets.   Variable budgets were developed to reflect the actual behavior characteristics of costs and the relationships of revenue and expenses over a wide range of volume levels.

Variable budget allowances are developed from analyses of requirements over a broad span of operating levels. The allowances are checked for practicality and approved by management. The budget becomes an operating plan rather than a fixed set of appropriations. The composite of all of the individual fixed and variable budget allowances of a company, or a major unit, becomes a mathematical model of its operations. Given the sales input, the normal expenses and resulting profit are readily obtained. Thus the variable budget formula is applicable for control purposes at any reasonable volume level; in addition, it is highly useful for financial forecasting and profitability studies.

The Profit Plan.   The profit plan is the presentation in financial terms of the operating plans for the subsequent year. It consists of a *pro forma* income statement for the year and a balance sheet as of the end of that year, the capital expenditure budget, the cash budget, and such subsidiary schedules as may be desired.

If a variable budget is used, the income statement will be developed by applying the variable budget formula to the forecast sales to arrive at the various items of expense and determine the resulting profit. This is usually done for each month of the year, also showing quarterly results. The transactions thus developed then form the basis for both balance sheet and cash projections.

It is essential to distinguish between the profit plan, the budget, the forecasts, and the subsequent projections.

The *profit plan* is the financial expression of the operating program for the coming year as it is agreed to at the outset of that year. It is based on the most recent forecast of sales available at that time and the budget reflecting conditions which are assumed to exist during the year.

The *budget*, if it is a variable budget, is the formula indicating the costs of carrying out the operating program at any reasonable level of sales. If a fixed budget is used, the summary of the budget will be the profit plan income statement.

Forecasts of sales and of operating conditions will probably be updated from time to time during the year. These changes will not affect the original profit plan, which remains as the continuing base or standard from which the effect of changes in conditions are measured.

As the year progresses, new *projections* of operating results for the year are made as required. These revised projections are based on the actual results for the expired portion of the year, plus projections for the remaining months. The latter are based on the new forecasts of sales applied to the budget formula. This budgeted profit is then adjusted to provide for anticipated budget variances, which a study of the performance for the past months and any changed conditions indicate as being probable.

DESIGN AND PREPARATION OF AN OPERATING BUDGET TAILORED TO THE COMPANY

Sales Forecasting. Volume directly or indirectly affects all areas of a company. It is such a vital factor in the entire field of profit planning and budgeting that preparation of the sales forecast warrants first attention. In order to obtain views from differing vantage points and thus lessen the risk of overlooking important influencing factors, many companies have devised a system of utilizing the specialized information of several sources, each having a somewhat different approach. For example, independent forecasts may be obtained simultaneously by each of the following methods:

1. *By product line.* Developed by product line managers or specialists, these forecasts take into account the prospects of the industries or customer classes who buy the particular product or service. Current popularity trends of specific products, new developments and improvements in products, action of competitors, the economic climate of the industry, the fluctuating demands by types or sizes of customers, and similar factors are known best by this group of employees.

2. *By geographical territories.* If there is a field sales force, the supervisor of each territory should have a good feel for the local economic conditions and prospects. If trends are developing, if expansion or retraction is planned in a territory, if competition is active or weak, or if a new promotion or local emphasis is planned, the manager of the area involved has on-the-spot information which should be reflected in his forecast.

3. *By statistical calculation.* First the general economic conditions are forecast, with the gross national product segregated into its component sectors. Special attention is directed to those aspects of the economy which are especially pertinent to the industry as, for example, personal income, consumer spending patterns, government spending, and the price outlook. Industry projections are obtained or developed, and, where practicable, the company's share of the industry's projected market is estimated. Conditions expected for supplier and customer industries are also pertinent. Anticipated automobile production and housing starts (which affect appliance sales) are important parts of the steel industry studies. Spending for defense and major government projects, such as road building, school construction, and defense expenditures, all are considered where pertinent.

Some companies have found such statistics as births, family formations, number of telephones installed, and the percentage of the population in various age groups to have significant correlation to their own sales curves. Estimates of these will then be made and used at least as checkpoints for the sales forecast.

The factors mentioned are used extensively in manufacturing industries, and much of this data is applicable to mercantile and financial institutions as well. The money market, with its effect on interest rates and collections, affects most companies indirectly but it will directly influence gross revenues of financial institutions and, of course, the cost of lendable funds for banks.

When preliminary forecasts of sales are received from the several separate sources, they are studied by the marketing management. After discussions with those directly involved, a tentative forecast is developed and then reviewed with top management, bringing into the discussion the areas other than marketing to ensure feasibility and compatibility with the other functions, particularly manufacturing, purchasing, personnel, and finance. Finally an official sales forecast is set.

Continuing Sales Forecasts. Using the best possible forecast of sales (or other sources of revenue) not only contributes to the reliability of the annual profit plan and budget, it is essential also for interim revised profit projections and forecasts of cash flow. For this reason many companies do not rely solely on annual sales forecasts, but also update them periodically to reflect more recent developments. In this way a current forecast of revenue is always available for studies or projections, including the annual budget and profit plan preparation. The thorough and comprehensive process of sales forecasting described is done at least annually. The updating is often done quarterly, each new forecast adding another quarter, thus providing continually updated sales estimates for the succeeding five or six quarters (to obtain the full fiscal year ahead when required). The interim forecasts are often not as comprehensive as the annual ones, with the effort expended depending on each individual situation.

Expense Budgets Reflect Behavior Characteristics. A well-conceived budget has applicability far beyond the mere expression of the currently estimated revenue and expenses, and greater value than merely its use as a measure of the achievement of those determined objectives. It forms the very basis of profitability studies, make-or-buy decisions, and similar calculations. Knowledge of the microeconomics of the company, which is essential for both long- and short-range planning and forecasting, is unfolded through the process required for developing a good budget. It is important therefore that the budget accurately depict the actual behavior characteristics of the various expenses of the company at any reasonable volume and mix.

Only a variable budget will satisfy all these requirements, since a fixed budget does not reflect the behavior patterns of the various expenses and is therefore inadequate for either planning or control. (The budgets of some departments will, very probably, be fixed budgets for the reason that their expenses are set by management decision and are not expected to fluctuate within the budget period. The company as a whole will, however, be on a flexible budget basis.)

Budgets Follow Lines of Authority. The structure of the budget follows the organizational lines of authority of the company since it reflects the quantification of delegated responsibility. Departmental budgets are prepared for every unit of authority, down to the lowest section that has distinct operating accountability. Summaries are made for each higher level of authority.

Estimates of expense requirements are made for each expense account used in the company's accounting system, and all items for which accounting is made follow the procedures used in the accounting system. This applies to purchases, direct labor and materials, allocations, and all other aspects of accounting procedure. The accounting and budget systems must be parallel since plan and performance will be reported together.

Budgets Reflect Influences of Trends and Volume Load Levels. Budgets for those departments which are not affected by operating volume within the budget period, the fixed budgets, present no special problems. Their amounts represent management decisions; they do not flex automatically in response to volume changes. They should be broken down, however, into monthly or at least quarterly amounts in appropriate columns. This is to provide for seasonal peaks if they exist and also to alert management to trends. A gradual buildup of personnel, for example, will mean a substantially higher plateau of costs to carry over into the following year. This will not be nearly as apparent if annual figures only are shown or if average monthly figures are used for the budget.

Variable budgets present a different problem. One of the two factors of a variable budget allowance is the volume factor. This is the multiplier which determines the amount of variable budget allowance appropriate for the load level of the department each month. The multiplier or volume factor must be selected for each department. It may be direct labor hours or dollars, or it may be in terms of tons, gallons, or units produced. Often a volume factor is already in use for cost accounting purposes, and this is usually a satisfactory measure of the effort required.

Involvement of Department Heads.   It is essential that the head of each department participate in making the budget estimates for his department. When the original estimates are consolidated and reviewed, the department heads should be consulted if changes seem desirable. Even if drastic alterations are necessary, the department heads should be kept informed and the reasons explained. This gains acceptance, wins cooperation, provides better information, and goes far to ensure the success of the entire program.

The objectives and the technical aspects of managerial planning and control have reached the stage of general acceptance. Increasing attention is now being given to the psychological aspects—to creating the will to achieve, cooperatively, constructively, and as a team. This is good administration, effective leadership, and it is essential. The cornerstone is actual and recognized participation at all levels of management, in both planning and control.

Segregation of Fixed and Variable Expenses by Account.   To achieve a variable budget it is necessary to segregate fixed and variable expenses. Probably the first attempts to do this took the form of segregation of the chart of accounts, designating each expense account as either fixed or variable, and reporting the two groups separately in departmental statements. This method is still in use. While many of the expense accounts are neither entirely fixed nor entirely variable, they are classified according to whether they are predominantly one or the other.

This method does not result in a precise index of the behavior pattern of costs, but in balance and for the company as a whole, it has proved to be so much superior to a disregard of cost characteristics that the method has its adherents. At worst, it certainly alerts management to some of the economic principles involved and provides a rough estimate of the effect of volume on costs and profits.

A serious disadvantage of segregation of fixed and variable expenses by account classification is inherent in the difficulty of grouping the expense accounts logically for statement purposes. Reporting of expenses is generally most useful if expenses are reported by responsibility and, under these groupings, by the category or nature of the expense. This creates a dilemma if there are both fixed and variable expenses in one category, which must then be split. For example, all the labor under a foreman is not variable, and so labor must then be segregated into two sections, one for variable and one for fixed. Supplies and repairs present similar problems. This rather arbitrary separation of similar expenses can be confusing to operating personnel and it makes summarization more difficult.

The confusion inherent in segregation by account is particularly apparent in the account for shop salaries. These are usually classified as fixed, but what happens if another shift is added? Then the "fixed" expense of shop salaries becomes variable as foremen or clerks are added for the new shift.

These difficulties are magnified under a direct cost system, in which only variable expenses are currently charged to direct product cost and fixed expenses are considered time costs and separately accounted for. Yet direct costing is gaining in favor because it more accurately reflects the true economic effects of volume changes and materially helps in analyzing the reasons for variations in costs and profitability. The chief difficulty, however, is the obviously inaccurate information provided by the necessarily crude separation of the fixed and variable characteristics of cost.

Segregation of Fixed and Variable Expenses by Performance Analysis in the Budgeting Process. Establishing a budget by performance analysis includes the following steps of managerial analysis and planning:

1. A careful review of the most recent six to twelve months of operation as reported in the departmental cost or operating reports. Any abnormalities should be noted—any trends, peaks, or unusually high or low costs in any accounts. These should be discussed and the reasons determined.

2. The period should be "lived over," as though it would all happen again. In retrospect, the second time around and having benefited from the experience, what would now be required to produce the same output, accomplish the same objectives? This assumes no changes in wages or prices, only gains in efficiency, methods, or economies that may be effected because of experience. Each expense account is reviewed in this way.

3. Now expected changes are reviewed. Will there be any changes in facilities or methods? Anything new that will affect operating costs should be anticipated as far as possible. The first estimate for the next year's budget which is recorded on a budget establishment work sheet is the estimated amount required for each account, per month, based on the revised current year's costs (according to step 2), at the same average volume level as step 2 (not next year's volume), and adjusted for the effect of the anticipated changes. This column of figures represents the best available estimate of what it would cost next year to produce or accomplish the same output as in the current year, but also reflects new conditions and contemplated improvements in technique and efficiencies.

4. At this point, next year's anticipated volume is considered. It must be borne in mind, however, that the expected volume will not be spread evenly over the year. This is true even though no marked seasonal patterns may exist in the industry, since unexpected disruptions can occur, causing both slack and makeup periods, and volume might change even if it is not expected. Estimates of requirements for each expense account are then made for volumes preferably of one-quarter or one-third above and one-quarter or one-third below the current year's volume, which is represented by the first estimates. This provides carefully considered estimates of requirements over a wide range of volumes, almost surely covering the next year's volume. If it does not, adjustments can be made in the high- and low-volume estimates if necessary to provide for anticipated business, but the spread between the high and low estimate should be equally broad.

The broad spread of possible volume requires the department head to plan realistically for personnel requirements, possible change in shifts, capacities, and similar operating problems. In estimating the effect of volume, the monthly reports of past periods are reviewed to see what effect volume had on costs in those periods, but changing conditions must also be taken into account. This is the crucial analysis that will determine the true behavior characteristics of the expense accounts.

Computation of Fixed and Variable Elements in Costs. The behavior characteristics of any partially variable expense account are expressed in a two-part formula. (The formula for any entirely fixed or entirely variable expense account will, of course, have only one element.) It is important to recognize that the many expense accounts which are sometimes classed as semivariable do not lend themselves to segregation by fixed and variable individual items or charges. Their partially variable characteristic is inherent in their very nature. The formula is simply a mathematical expression of this characteristic. The two elements of the formula are only the means of arriving at the total cost at any given volume.[2]

[2]*Ibid.*, p. 52.

A formula which expresses the inherent tendency of a cost to vary consists of fixed and variable elements, but these are elements only. No attempt has been made to identify the parts or the elements of an expense account or the items which are charged therein which may be fixed and those which may be variable. Expenses are not of this nature. The formula is simply a mathematical concept, a way of expressing in a formula the behavior characteristics of a type of cost. It is a mathematical equivalent of a line on a chart; no separate accounts are kept and no distinction is made in the ledgers of the fixed and variable elements of the formula. Normal accounting is entirely adequate.

The computation of the formula for fixed and variable allowances is fairly simple. To illustrate, assume that the volume factor for a department is direct labor in dollars. (It could be direct labor hours, units produced, or any similar measure.) The account for indirect labor is budgeted as shown in Exhibit 1 for the

EXHIBIT 1   Illustration of Computation of Fixed and Variable Elements in Costs

Account: Indirect Labor   Volume factor: Direct Labor Dollars
Average direct labor per month in recent experience: $90,000
Cost estimates for Indirect Labor at three volume levels in proposed budget:

	Volume (in Direct Labor Dollars)	Budgeted Cost of Indirect Labor
At current average volume	$ 90,000	$16,200
At high volume	120,000	18,600
At low volume	60,000	13,800

Computation of Fixed and Variable Factors:
  Variable Cost (at extremes of range):

	Direct Labor	Indirect Labor
At high level	$120,000	$18,600
At low level	60,000	13,800
Additional direct labor of	$ 60,000	
Requires increased expense of		$ 4,800

Therefore the *variable* portion of this expense can be expressed as $\frac{\$4,800}{\$60,000}$, or 8% of direct labor

Fixed Cost:

	At High Volume	At Low Volume	At Current Volume
Direct labor	$120,000	$60,000	$90,000
Total budgeted cost	$ 18,600	$13,800	$16,200
Variable cost at 8% of direct labor	9,600	4,800	7,200
Fixed cost (total less variable)	$ 9,000	$ 9,000	$ 9,000

Complete formula for Indirect Labor:
  8% of direct labor plus $9,000 per month

three levels of operation. Except in rare cases,[3] the extremes of volume are used in the calculation. As production rises from $60,000 of direct labor to the $120,000 level, an increase of $60,000, the cost of indirect labor rises from $13,800 to $18,600, an increase of $4,800. This means that the $60,000 of increased production requires $4,800 of *additional* indirect labor, therefore that each $1 of additional direct labor requires 8 cents of additional indirect labor ($4,800 ÷ $60,000 = $0.08). Indirect labor therefore rises at the rate of 8 percent of the rise in direct labor. This is the *variable* portion of the indirect labor account.

The total indirect labor used at the level represented by $120,000 of direct labor has been set at $18,600. The variable portion is 8 percent of direct labor, hence

[3]See calculation of negative fixed allowance below.

$9,600 (8 percent of $120,000) at this level. Since the total indirect labor is $18,600 and the variable portion has been calculated to be $9,600, the remaining fixed portion is $9,000 ($18,600 − $9,600). At the low level of $60,000 of direct labor, the total indirect labor cost is $13,800 and the variable portion is 8 percent of $60,000, or $4,800; therefore the fixed portion is the remainder, or $9,000, the same as at the high level. At the current (recent average) level, direct labor is $90,000; the total indirect labor is $16,200; and the variable portion is 8 percent of $90,000, or $7,200; therefore the fixed portion is again $9,000. These calculations are shown in Exhibit 1.

A graphic illustration of the indirect labor expense account is shown on Exhibit 2. In practice, the calculations are made on a work sheet for each department. This is explained later in the text and illustrated in Exhibit 4.

EXHIBIT 2 Graphic Presentation of Behavior Characteristics of Indirect Labor

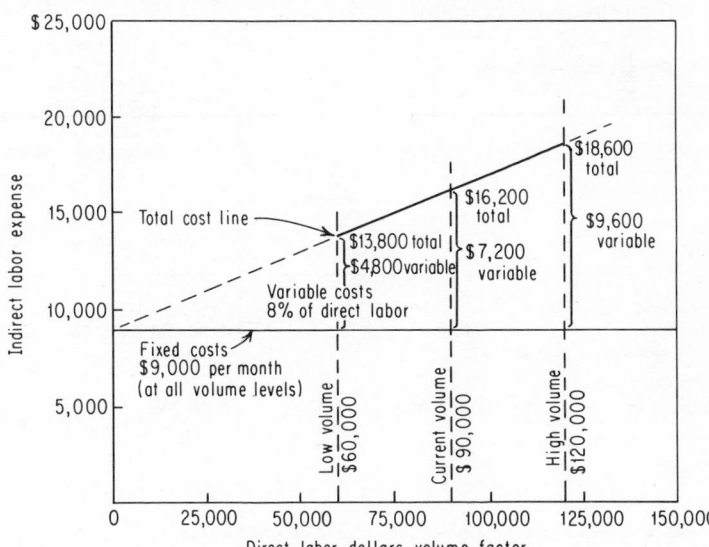

Cost formula for indirect labor: 8% of direct labor + $9,000 per month

Preparation of Variable Budgets. Variable budgets are more intricate than fixed ones, and usually they pertain to departments whose work is much more insulated from financial presentations than is the case within the fixed budget areas. They are also often the departments with the largest expenditures. For these reasons a greater amount of personal attention and direct help is given in the preparation of the annual budgets to departments in areas having predominantly variable budgets than to the administrative and other office-type departments.

Variable budgets can be profitably employed in mercantile, service, and even financial institutions, and occasionally in marketing and administrative service departments. Because of the greater number of applications in manufacturing areas, however, the principle will be illustrated here using a productive department in a factory as an example. A competent budget person who has the ability to communicate with manufacturing personnel, an understanding of the processes and problems involved, and the ability to draw out ideas and reconcile differences will meet with the foreman of the production department in his own area to assist him with his budget. Meeting in the manufacturing environment puts the foreman much more at ease and goes far to eliminate a feeling that arbitrary restrictions are being imposed. After all, financial management is going to manufacturing management to obtain its expert opinions, and this should be apparent. It is helpful to have the foreman's clerk or helper and also his superior present. They will add background data and contribute information on plans of related departments, as well as serve to outnumber the financial representatives in the meeting—a psychologically helpful device.

The budget person begins by outlining the general program, the expected economic conditions including company volume, and the general budgetary principles involved. He will then present the budget estimate work sheets, a copy of which should remain with the foreman. The budget estimate sheet will list the expense accounts used by the department, the average production in recent experience, the average monthly cost for the same period in each expense account, a space for notations, and columns for estimates of cost for the coming year. Such a work sheet is illustrated in Exhibit 3.

EXHIBIT 3   Budget Estimate Sheet
Department _____ Year _____

	Average monthly cost	Notes	Estimated cost at		
			Current volume	High volume	Low volume
Volume factor, dollars of direct labor...........	$ 90,000		$ 90,000	$120,000	$60,000
Number of shifts........	1½		1½	2	1
Expense accounts:					
Indirect labor...........	$ 17,043	New conveyor	$ 16,200	$ 18,600	$13,800
.					
.					
.					
.					
Repairs and maintenance.	2,536	Old machines put into use at high volume will need more repairs	2,500	3,200	2,000
.					
.					
.					
.					
Total departmental cost..	$142,250		$141,900	$181,000	$80,500

The budget person then discusses each expense account. The average cost for the output achieved in the experience period is shown on the work sheet. Were there any unusual items included in the experience figures? Scanning the monthly reports of the department will indicate unusual items. These may need explaining. Are similar items likely to occur again? Have improvements in methods changed requirements? What are the plans for next year? Will they affect this expense?

If the calendar could be turned back and the current year lived over again, under the same conditions and with the same volume of output, what would the foreman do the second time around? Could efficiency be improved and expenses reduced with the benefit of hindsight? The budget estimate for the current volume column is based on what would now be required, taking these things into account. Changed conditions are then considered, things like the effect of new methods or newly installed equipment. With these factors in mind, an estimate is made of the next year's monthly cost for this expense account at the current average volume, and the figure is entered in the current volume column.

The Estimate Sheet for Variable Budgets. Exhibit 3 shows the indirect labor expense account entered on the budget estimate sheet. The average cost per month at a volume level of $90,000 of direct labor was $17,043 during the current year. The monthly figures were higher during the first few months but a new conveyor was installed (see note), after which the cost gradually dropped. The best current estimate is that only $16,200 will be required next year under the changed conditions. This is entered in the current volume column.

As soon as the current level cost is settled, estimates are made for the high and low levels of volume. With volume one-third higher, additional indirect labor will be required and the second shift will be filled out (see "number of shifts" on Exhibit 3). Operating plans call for adding $2,400 of personnel at this level (less than a proportionate increase) and this is supported by experience figures. The cost at the high-volume level is therefore entered at $18,600 ($16,200 + $2,400) in the next column. If this is the rate of increase, it is agreed that when volume declines the decrease in expense will follow the same rate of decline. The low-volume requirements are therefore set at $13,800, and this figure is entered in the $60,000 volume level column. Estimates of each expense account are made similarly.

Sometimes, however, costs do not follow a straight line but produce a curved cost line. The entry of repairs and maintenance expense on Exhibit 3 illustrates this situation. It is estimated that an additional volume of $30,000 in direct labor will require $500 per month of maintenance expenses, and this is the indicated increase in cost between the low and current levels. At the high level, however, older machines are put into use and this entails some additional repair cost; also, repairs may be more costly because they may need to be done when machines are available at night or on weekends, entailing higher costs. Therefore the high level is estimated at $700 above the current level rather than the normal rise of $500 per month, resulting in the $3,200 estimate (Exhibit 3).

Checks for Reasonableness During Budget Estimating. One indication of the reasonableness of each expense estimate is its relation to past experience as shown both on the average monthly cost column of the budget estimate sheet and on the cost reports of the department, which are continually referred to during the budgeting process.

A simple check of the flexibility of the expense is also available at this point. Since the spread from the high-volume level to the low is set at one-third above and below the current level, respectively, the volume at the low level is just half that at high volume. (If the midpoint is considered as 1, the high is $1\frac{1}{3}$ and the low $\frac{2}{3}$.) This provides a quick check of cost patterns during the budgeting process. If the estimate at high level is double that at low, the expense is entirely variable. If the high allowance is less than double the low allowance, there will be a fixed element in the budget formula. If, however, the budget estimate at the high point is more than double that at low, an abnormal situation exists in which each added unit of production becomes more costly for this expense item. This is possible in some cases, such as overtime and night shift premiums.

When all expenses are entered, the columns are totaled. This provides a comparison of next year's estimated costs with the current costs at the same level of production (in the current volume column). The effect of volume on unit costs at all three levels can also be quickly calculated at this point. If the projections do not seem reasonable, this is the best time to discuss the situation with the foreman.

Computation of a Department's Fixed and Variable Budget Allowances. The principle of computing the fixed and variable elements of the budget allowance

EXHIBIT 4 Work Sheet for Computation of Budget Allowances
Department _____ Year _____

Column designation	Estimated cost at: Current volume A	High volume B	Low volume C	Variable cost (High—Low) Amount D	% of direct labor E	Variable cost at high volume F	Fixed cost G	Budgeted cost at current volume Variable H	Total I	Variance from current volume budget J	Adjusted fixed cost K
Volume factor, dollars of direct labor	$90,000	$120,000	$60,000	$60,000		$120,000		$90,000			
Expense accounts: Indirect labor................ Note: All expense accounts are listed. As an alternative, if detail subaccounts are used, they may be grouped and only expense account categories may be listed, with budget allowances computed for expense categories only. Example of adjustment to provide for irregular or curved cost patterns:	$16,200	$18,600	$13,800	$4,800	8%	$9,600	$9,000	$7,200	$16,200	—	$9,000
Repairs and maintenance......	2,500	3,200	2,000	1,200	2%	2,400	800	1,800	2,600	100+	750
Totals for department......	$141,900	$181,000	$80,500	$78,000	130%	$156,000	$25,000	$117,000	$142,000	$100+	$24,950
Explanation of entries and computations	Estimated cost at three volume levels, from Budget Estimate Sheet (Exhibit 3)			B − C (Change in cost as volume changes)	Variable allowances (Amounts in D divided by $60,000 volume factor)	Volume factor of $120,000 multiplied by allowances in E	B − F (Total cost at high volume less variable cost at high volume)	Variable allowances in E multiplied by $90,000 volume factor at current volume	H + G (Variable costs plus fixed costs)	I − A (Budgeted cost less estimated costs)	Final fixed allowance (usually G plus or minus ½ of J)

Preliminary computation of fixed and variable allowances

Test of allowances at current volume

Final fixed allowance

formula from the estimated expenditures at three levels of operating volume has been explained earlier on pages 40-9 to 40-11. The application of this principle to the expense accounts of a department is illustrated in Exhibit 4.

The figures from the three columns of estimates for the coming year are copied directly from the budget estimate sheet. The current, high, and low columns are adjacent in columns A, B, and C; their differences are entered into the next column, D. These are the cost increases for an increase in direct labor, which is shown at the top of the column. Therefore, dividing each cost increase by the increase in direct labor will produce the variable expense rate, which is entered in the next column, E. This is the variable budget allowance for each expense account.

Computation of the fixed allowance is next. This could be done at any level, but the high level is used here. The direct labor at high level is $120,000 and this is shown at the top of the column F. This is the volume factor, which is multiplied by the variable expense rate for each expense account in column E. The products are entered in column F, headed "variable cost at high volume." The variable cost is then subtracted from the total cost at high volume, which is in column B, and the difference is entered in the fixed cost column, G. This completes the preliminary computation.

To arrive at the fixed and variable allowances, the high- and low-volume figures were used. In order to test the computation and determine what allowances will result at the current volume level, the variable allowances in column E are applied to the current level volume factor of $90,000 in the next column, H. These variable allowances are added to the fixed allowances (which are the same for all volume levels) in column G, and the sums entered in the total current volume cost column, I. These total allowances are compared to the budget estimates in column A. Any differences, over or under, are entered in the variance column, J.

If the computations are correct, and if the expense follows a straight line, the figures in columns A and I will agree. Differences of a few dollars will result from rounding and can be disregarded. Larger differences (assuming correct computations) indicate a curved expense line.

Adjustment of Budget Allowances to Compensate for Moderately Curved Expense Patterns. The budget estimates for the repair and maintenance expense account illustrate a curved expense pattern. This is shown on Exhibit 4. Because of the somewhat irregular expense pattern, a difference of $100 appears in the variance column, J; the budgeted cost is greater than the cost estimate at the current volume level. Thus the allowance as computed would result in a budget equal to the cost estimate at the high and low levels, but would be $100 too high at the current level. A practical way to adjust the allowances is to reduce the fixed allowance if it is high or increase it if it is low at the current level, by one-half of the variance. In the illustration, the allowance is high by $100, so the fixed allowance of $800 is reduced by $50, making the adjusted fixed allowance $750 per month. The variable allowance of 2 percent of direct labor remains unchanged.

This adjustment to the calculated budget for repairs and maintenance expenses is shown graphically in Exhibit 5. The budget allowance as now adjusted will coincide with the expense curve of the budget estimate at levels of $75,000 and at $105,000 of direct labor. From these points the lines will gradually diverge, in one direction toward the high and low extremes, and in the opposite direction toward the center. As actual volume varies from month to month, the budget will never be far from the estimated expense curve, and cumulatively it will be quite close. This is therefore an entirely satisfactory compromise budget, not quite following anticipated expenditures, but not far away, with a tendency for the "overs" to offset the "unders." It is much more practical to use a uniform type of formula than to

EXHIBIT 5   Illustration of Adjustment of Fixed Budget Allowance to Compensate for Moderately Curved Expense Patterns (Repair and Maintenance Account on Exhibit 4)

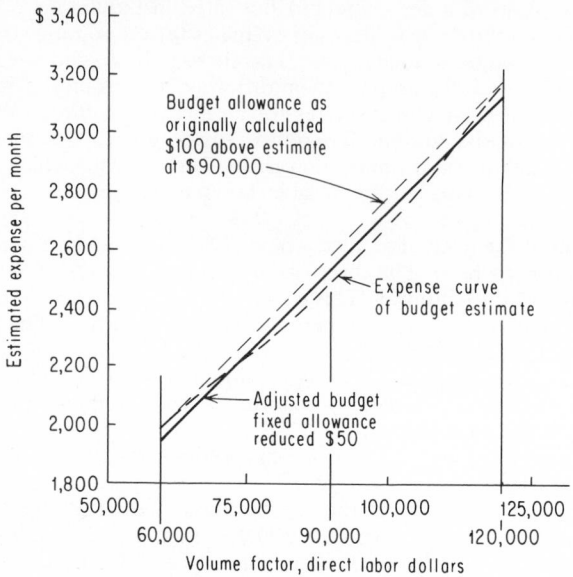

develop a special treatment to arrive at precise figures for what is, after all, only an estimate.

Treatment of Negative Fixed Budget Allowances.   There is one situation that merits special handling, however. Mention was previously made of the peculiarity in connection with overtime premium and shift premium which occurs if these expense items are isolated. In this case the budget estimate is likely to be zero at low volume and rise rather abruptly when volume rises to the pressure point, usually just beginning somewhere around the current level. In this case it is advisable to use the *current* and *high* level cost estimates and volume factors instead of the high and low points to compute the budget allowance formula. Since the expense at high volume is more than double that at the low volume, a negative fixed allowance will result when budget allowances are computed. This is normal; it simply expresses the slant of the expense line as volume increases. Since the actual expense curves from zero upward but never dips below zero, the budget allowance also should be set at zero until a positive total budget results from the budget calculation. During the year, the calculation of budget allowances (variable rate × volume factor − the negative fixed allowance) will result in a net negative figure at low volumes and a positive figure at high volumes. A zero budget allowance should be used whenever the computation results in a negative figure; the positive allowance is used when it appears. This expresses the curved nature of this expense.

Volume Factors for Service Departments.   When the maintenance and repair department is operated similar to a production department, having its own direct labor with burden applied thereon, no special problem arises in connection with the volume factor. The same base is used as is used for burden application, direct labor. A problem sometimes arises, however, in the case of a central tool room, an in-plant transportation department, or a similar service area serving several departments. In these cases the volume factor should be a measure of the combined work load of the departments serviced. This may be the total direct labor of the combined serviced departments, their total units of output (possibly weighted), or the total service used, such as truck hours for transportation.

Preparation of Fixed Budgets. Estimating operating costs for the succeeding year for those departments whose current expenses are not directly or measurably affected by volume factors, while less complicated, must be just as carefully done as the estimates of departments having variable budgets. One type of budget estimate sheet for fixed departmental budgets is illustrated in Exhibit 6.

The first three columns, A, B, and C, indicate the current annual costs of running the department. Expenses for the expired portion of the year are entered for each expense account in column A, taken directly from the monthly expense reports of the department. Departments of this type often have onetime or seasonal expenses, such as association memberships, conventions or major meetings, or annual publication or catalog costs. Some of these may have been included in column A and will not be repeated for the remainder of the year. Others may be scheduled to occur in the remaining months of the year. Also the number of personnel may have changed, or a change may be contemplated. For these reasons it is necessary to estimate separately the expenses for the remaining months of the year to arrive at the estimated cost for the current year. Estimated amounts for each expense account for the remaining months are entered in column B and the estimated totals for the year (column A plus column B) are entered in column C.

It is useful to have the approved budget for the current year also on the work sheet, and it is entered in the next column D. This helps to call attention to an unusual expenditure which was not anticipated and is not likely to recur. It also indicates areas of increasing costs which should either be reversed or taken into account for the next year.

The current expenditures under each expense account should be reviewed, just as were those of the production departments, to see if greater efficiencies or effectiveness could be achieved if it were possible to live the year over again. This is the starting point for estimating the next year's expenses. Changes in programs, systems, and approaches may be contemplated, and this is the time to get their cost effects on paper, in perspective with other costs and with other plans in other areas of the company. The expected annual expenses are separated into quarterly amounts to show trends and seasonal costs, and to assist in cash budgeting.

Sometimes special, large accounts are not included in departmental operating costs but are accounted for separately. Examples of such items are advertising, major promotions, and an annual convention of a large group of employees and customers. The same type of budget estimate can be used, with the same columns. The expense accounts used will follow the accounting treatment or departmental supporting detail.

It is quite possible that some sales sections or even service departments in administrative areas should be budgeted on a variable basis. Sales departments in which commissions are a significant item and data handling departments whose paper-work load is directly dependent on a volume factor such as sales or invoices handled are examples. These departments will follow the variable budget procedures, and their budget allowances will consist of the two-element formula instead of the single fixed factor.

Assembling and Testing the Operating Budgets. Assembly and testing of the budgets of all phases of operations are done with annual figures only. Use is made of the quarterly breakdowns of the fixed budgets later when cash flow and master budgets are prepared.

Budget allowances of the departments having variable budgets, as proposed in the budget estimate sheets and developed in the work sheets for computation of budget allowances, are used to compute budgeted operating costs for the coming year by applying the budget allowances to the forecast sales volume for the year.

EXHIBIT 6 Example of Budget Estimate Sheet (for a Department Having a Fixed Budget)

Department _____

Column designation	Current year's experience			Budget for current year	First quarter	Second quarter	Third quarter	Fourth quarter	Total year	Remarks
	Expense for ___ months of 19___	Estimated expense for remaining ___ months	Estimated cost for current year							
	A	B	C	D	E	F	G	H	I	
Number of employees, (end of periods)....										
Expense accounts:										
. . . . .										
Totals for department										

By this time, revisions of the sales estimates may have been made. The new sales forecasts should be reviewed and approved by the sales or marketing department, and by the chief executive officer of the division or the company. If any significant change in the level of in-process and finished goods inventories is contemplated during the coming year, this will need to be taken into account to arrive at the volume of production, which will be the basis for computing the work loads (volume factors) of the various production departments.

The forecast production for the year is the basis for determining each department's work load, expressed in terms of the respective volume factors. This will take into account the mix of the products involved, and will be done on the basis of experience or normal production scheduling. The departments are then listed on a work sheet providing columns for:

A. Department code and name
B. Volume factor (to achieve the year's production)
C. Variable budget allowance
D. Variable budget amount (extension of B × C)
E. Fixed allowance, annual amount (monthly fixed budget allowance × 12)
F. Budget for year (Variable allowance in column D + fixed allowance in E).

Testing for Reasonableness of Budgets.   During the process of preparing budget estimates of each department, the reasonableness of proposed budgets was tested by comparing estimates with experience figures on a monthly average basis. This was done by expense groupings, at the departmental totals, and by comparing burden rates or unit costs of current operations with those resulting from the budget estimates.

A further check is now possible. For this check, a work sheet is prepared comparing the costs for that portion of the current year which has been recorded (the expired portion of the year) and the costs for the same volumes and mix as budgeted for next year. This work sheet has the following columns:

A. Department code and name
B. Actual volume factors for expired portion of current year
C. Proposed variable budget allowances
D. Budgeted variable expense, next year's basis (items in column B × items in column C)
E. Budgeted monthly fixed allowances, next year's basis
F. Budgeted fixed allowances for period (column E × number of expired months in current year)
G. Budgeted total cost, next year's basis (column D + column F)
H. Actual expense, current year
I. Proposed budget over or under (−) current year's costs
J. Percentage of increase or decrease (−).

This work sheet will show the change in total cost from current experience to next year's estimated (and budgeted) costs. If several departments show unexplained variances, these can be analyzed individually in the same way, listing each expense account.

Budgets of departments in areas of the company having fixed budgets are already compared to current costs on the budget estimate work sheets (Exhibit 6).

These tests can be made as budget estimate sheets become available during the budgeting program. There may very well be valid reasons for budgets, particularly of individual departments, to vary appreciably from current experience, but the reasons should be known and agreed to. The percentage of increase or decrease in the total fixed expenses, variable expenses, and combined expenses at the current level and mix of production, which these tests reveal, is also useful economic information for profit planning.

PREPARATION OF *PRO FORMA* BUDGETED INCOME STATEMENT

When the budget estimates have been completed for each department and have been scrutinized for validity, a *pro forma* income statement can be prepared.

There are now available the forecast of sales and the budgeted expenses of every department of the company, from production to administrative and general expenses, all scaled to the forecast sales level. If direct materials and direct labor costs are not run through departmental accounts but are charged to inventory accounts as consumed, these will need to be estimated on the basis of the sales forecast. Other nondepartmental items such as sales allowances, inventory adjustments, and similar items are also projected at this time.

All the information normally required to prepare an income statement down through net operating income is now available on a budgeted basis. The budgeted income statement for the next year, at the forecast sales level, is then prepared in the same manner as if actual figures were used. Items of other income and expense and income taxes are tentatively estimated. These may need to be revised somewhat when the capital expenditure and cash budgets are completed.

The statement should be in detail (not a condensed version) and in the form to which the executives of the company are accustomed. If there are separate product lines or divisions, subsidiary statements and schedules of these are also produced. This follows the same procedure as is used in preparing statements of actual operations each month.

Determining the Composite Expense Formula for the Company or a Division. A formula expressing the composite behavior pattern of the cost of operating the company (and its divisions if applicable) is required to project the budgeted income statement at any reasonable level of activity, and for break-even studies. The commonly used volume factor for this purpose is net sales. The formula for total operating costs is the total dollars of fixed expenses plus a percentage of net sales. This is the composite of all the budgets, at the currently estimated sales mix and cost characteristics.

As a part of the preparation of the budgeted income statement (or statements) provision should be made to total separately the fixed and the variable expenses of each section. The fixed expense factor of the composite formula is the total of all fixed expenses in the statement. The variable factor is the percentage arrived at by dividing the total variable expenses by the net sales figure. This represents the profit-volume formula at the budgeted conditions of sales mix and cost behavior characteristics of the combined operations.

Budget Reviews and Adjustments. The tentative budget statements are now studied at length by the top financial executives, then discussed with the top executives of the other areas of the company, as appropriate and as indicated by the critical analyses. The projected results are not necessarily satisfactory at this point but they do reflect what would happen if every area of the company were to proceed in accordance with its current plans.

The statements, with their subsidiary schedules, are then reviewed by top management in consultation with the chief financial officer. Meetings are held with the executives heading the various functions to discuss each aspect, their respective goals, the general balance of activities, and the extent to which the budgets achieve the company's objectives.

Desired adjustments and revisions are discussed with management down the organizational lines of responsibility. Final revisions to the budgets are made in cooperation with those who are responsible for the sections affected and who made the original budget estimates. Some unpopular revisions may need to be made, but they are discussed with those affected, and their work sheets are noted.

Revisions are then made on the supporting budget work sheets and new revised statements are made. Revisions are not finally approved by top management until their effect on the balance sheet is determined.

PREPARATION OF *PRO FORMA* BALANCE SHEET

When the budgeted income statement has been tentatively approved (except for minor adjustments in the other income and expense area, etc.), a projected balance sheet as of the end of the budgeted year is prepared to show the effects of the budgeted transactions on the financial condition and to indicate cash requirements.

Since the year prior to the budgeted period is ordinarily not yet over, a projection of the balance sheet as of the beginning of the budgeted period (the end of the current year) must be made. This should not be too difficult because only a very short period will usually be remaining in the current year when the next year's budget is in its last stages of completion.

A work sheet for the forecast balance sheet is prepared with all the accounts in the trial balance listed in a description column at the left of the columnar sheet. The projected balance sheet as of the beginning of the budgeted year is then posted in the first two money columns as debits and credits. This constitutes the opening trial balance for the budgeted year.

The budgeted transactions of the year are summarized in the next two columns, also in debit and credit form. All the items of revenue and expenses budgeted for the year have been summarized in the budget preparation forms and reflected in the budgeted income statement. This is the basis for the entries of revenue and expense on the work sheet, and the accounting treatment follows that which is normally done in the company for actual instead of budgeted items.

Starting at the top of the income statement, Accounts Receivable is debited and Sales credited for sales. Cost of Goods Sold is debited and Inventory is credited appropriately. The expense accounts listed in the income statement are debited and Accounts Payable credited for all items except (1) payrolls, which are credited to Cash or Accrued Payrolls, and (2) accruals and provisions which have their own credit accounts. Any detail required, such as the separation of departmental expenses between payroll and other costs, is available from the budget summaries.

So far expenditures of production departments were represented only by implication, since the cost of goods sold came from inventory. Therefore Inventory is debited with the value of budgeted production. The corresponding credits are determined by the summary of the production budgets, and will include Cash (or Accrued Payroll) for payrolls, Allowance for Depreciation, other provision credits if any, and Accounts Payable for all purchases. Items carried in raw materials inventory or supply inventories can be treated as Accounts Payable credits, with the Inventory account adjusted later.

When all entries covering operating budgets have been made on the work sheet, the new balance of the profit and loss accounts can be extended to the next two columns on the work sheet, which were provided for the forecast profit and loss (the fifth and sixth money columns). These two columns will then reflect the budgeted income statement as currently projected.

Projection of Balance Sheet Items.   The balance sheet accounts, however, are still in a raw state and need adjustment. The Cash account is the residue account, all other transaction affecting it, so it is scrutinized last. Projected collections of accounts receivable are credited to that account and debited to Cash. Decisions must be made on the desired and probable level of inventories. The anticipated (scheduled) levels of such items as prepaid insurance and depreciation allowances must be determined. The capital expenditure budget for the year should also be entered on the work sheet, crediting Accounts Payable, or debt accounts if financing is contemplated.

When transactions affecting Accounts Payable are completed, the credit balance in this account is brought down to the budgeted year-end level by debiting it and crediting the Cash account.

When all these entries have been made on the work sheet, the Cash account will have many entries in it, each representing some type of transaction, such as payrolls, accounts payable payments, tax payments, and collections of accounts receivable. The balance indicates the net cash flow effect for the year, at this point. This will later be scheduled by months, but at this stage will indicate the net adjustment that may be desirable in debt or investment accounts. If funds are to be borrowed or repaid, the entry is made.

The balance sheet as at the end of the budgeted year can now be completed. This will show, in some detail, the effect of the next year's budget and financial plans on the financial condition of the company.[4]

The Cash Budget.   A cash budget shows in some detail the anticipated cash receipts by sources, and the anticipated expenditures listed by the way in which payments will be made. This is quite different from the net figures shown on a statement of source and application of funds. In a cash budget gross receipts and gross expenditures must be shown, and they must be listed by types of transactions or documents which underlie the cash payments and receipts. This is to facilitate comparison of actual transactions with the budget and to simplify analysis of variances. Cash transactions and balances should be shown for each month. Exhibit 7 illustrates the layout of a cash budget.

Almost everything required except the timing of the transactions has already been provided in the budget work sheets and summarized in the work sheet for the forecast balance sheet. All anticipated transactions must necessarily be reflected there, and those affecting cash have been isolated and appear as separate summary entries in the Cash account.

When the balance sheet was projected, expenses of the various types of departments, inventory levels, and other items requiring payments were recorded on an annual basis. A review of each of these will be necessary to determine probable monthly cash requirements.

To do this the summarized work sheet entries to the Cash account are analyzed to determine the probable timing of receipts and payments. The largest single item is likely to be accounts receivable collections. Given the timing and mix of the sales volume (from the sales forecast), the credit department or treasurer's office should be able to estimate the time of collections, taking into account the opening receivable balance. Other items of income, such as interest and dividends from investments, royalties, etc., can be estimated from experience if no better means is available. Major accounts payable payments will generally follow production and other departments' budgets, but judgment gained from experience will be needed in making the estimates of monthly disbursements. Consultations with departments directly involved in the expenditures are usually required for a realistic budget and will serve well later when performance is evaluated.

When listing cash disbursements, it is advisable to list major items separately. Thus if there are several major payrolls, paid at different times, separate listing will facilitate future analyses of variances (see Exhibit 7).

After anticipated cash transactions are entered for each category and each month, the resulting monthly cash balances are determined, month by month. This may indicate cash available for short-term investing or debt reduction or, on the other hand, borrowing may be considered. This would, of course, require

---

[4]For a complete illustration of this technique see Bunge, *op. cit.,* pp. 116–131.

EXHIBIT 7   Form of Cash Budget

	January	(Columns for each month and for the total year. Quarterly subtotals may be included.)
Estimated net sales billed (memo only).........		
Cash, beginning of period....................		
Cash receipts:		
Accounts receivable.......................		
Royalties and miscellaneous income..........		
Scrap, etc............................:.....		
Borrowings...............................		
Other....................................		
Total receipts..........................		
Cash available.............................		
Cash disbursements:		
Payroll:		
Hourly payroll.........................		
Salary payroll.........................		
Commissions...........................		
Accounts payable vouchers.................		
Sales or excise taxes......................		
Real estate & personal property taxes.........		
Federal income taxes......................		
State income taxes........................		
Retirement, major insurance, or other major lump payments.........................		
Social security and withheld taxes...........		
Interest..................................		
Capital expenditures.......................		
Repayment on borrowings..................		
Dividends................................		
Other....................................		
Total disbursements.....................		
Cash, end of period.........................		

corresponding adjustments in the cash budget listing of cash received and disbursed, and if ultimately approved, in the other budgeted statements, including the *pro forma* balance sheet and income statement.

Final Review of Budget. The entire budget is now ready for top management's final review. The material consists of a forecast of sales, in detail; a forecast statement of income, also in detail; summaries of departmental expenses by responsibility areas, supported by detailed departmental budgets; the capital expenditure budget, indicating the portion affecting the coming year; the cash budget; and the balance sheet at the beginning and end of the budgeted year. All of the schedules may show comparisons with the current year.

Again, if changes and adjustments are made, they should be discussed with those affected and agreement, or at least understanding of position, reached.

THE MASTER BUDGET AND PROFIT PLAN

When the year ahead has been planned in thorough detail, the functional subplans are all coordinated and balanced, and their parts, their summation, and their projected effects have been approved as official objectives, these become the documented budget formula. This is the profit plan.

It is true that the actual performance will almost certainly not be exactly as planned. It is also true that the budget itself, being flexible, will change with volume changes, and therefore will still set forth approved objectives even though they are quantitatively different from the original profit plan. Yet it is useful to define and express the objectives that were agreed upon at the beginning of the year. This provides a point from which to measure deviations, whatever their cause.

The review, analysis, evaluation, and projections required to compile all these data have provided a wealth of information about the operating characteristics of the company—its microeconomics—which should be available in a form convenient for use.

For these reasons a master budget is usually prepared in report form after the year's budget and profit plan are officially approved. A typical master budget book might contain the following material:

1. A brief narrative outlining the year ahead, the major programs, objectives, problems, and anticipated economic assumptions on which the profit plan was based. It may also touch on the longer-range plans and the way in which the budgeted year fits in with those objectives.

2. The budgeted income statement for the entire company, by quarters and for the year.

3. The projected balance sheet as at the start of the budgeted year, and at the end of each quarter.

4. The forecasted sales on which the statements were predicted. This will be detailed by division, product line, etc., and by quarters.

5. Income statements or statements of contribution by division, product line, or other appropriate segregation.

6. The cash budget for the year, by months, and by categories of receipts and disbursements.

7. If significant, a statement of inventory changes, by quarter, showing the approved inventory levels.

8. The capital expenditure budget, showing project expenditures made on open appropriations prior to the year; expenditures scheduled for the year, by quarters; and expenditures scheduled for subsequent years, by years. Items are often classified by purpose, such as expansion, major repair or replacement, safety, etc.

9. The expense budgets, usually shown in summary form. Budgets are summarized by type of expense as well as by major departmental breakdown, following organizational lines of responsibility. Variable budgets are summarized at forecast production volume levels and the summarized budget formulas are indicated.

10. Break-even information, shown both graphically and by formula. This should also include product line or division break-even data where applicable.

BUDGETARY CONTROL OF OPERATIONS

During the year budget reports are issued, usually monthly, to every unit for which a budget was established. Summaries are issued for every level of supervision. It is good practice to give to all levels of management, in addition to the reports covering their own expenses, both the summary and the detailed reports for the first level below them.

Departmental operating performance reports usually have the accounts listed down the center, with money columns to the left for the month and to the right for the year to date. Columns are provided for actual expenses, budget, and variance. There are many variations to suit local wishes; some companies use percentages of variance in addition; some omit the budget column; some omit the amount of variance, showing only actual, budget, and percentages.

The income statements for the entire company and for its subdivisions should also be prepared with budget comparisons. Here, too, the variable budget permits valid budget evaluations at any volume level. The balance sheet and cash budget as presented in the master budget should be compared with the actual results, and reasons and implications of the significant variances explained. Major variations in the balance sheet accounts may indicate unfavorable trends which could easily lead to dire results if not caught in time. The source of these unfavorable trends may not be in the balance sheet accounts but in the actions or performance of the operating areas, to which they should be traced.

Each member of management responsible for the operation of a department should be familiarized with the budget and then required to account for variances from his budget. This is done in several ways. Some companies hold meetings at each management level a few days after statements have been issued. This gives all department heads time to review their performance reports and prepare to discuss them with their superiors. Others require written reports on major variances setting forth the reason for the variance, what will be done to correct it, and an estimate of the final variance in the account by year-end.

Surveillance of Cash and Other Balance Sheet Accounts.   Ordinarily, the master budget or profit plan includes monthly projections of cash balances. Each month significant variances in cash should be analyzed to determine the reasons for the differences from planned balances. This is facilitated by the form of the cash budget as it appears in the master budget, which shows the anticipated totals for each major type of transaction (see Exhibit 7).

Variances in the regularly recurring operational transactions, such as collections on accounts receivable and payments for hourly and salary payrolls and accounts payable, may occur because of volume of activity, slow or fast collections, or the inclusion of a varying number of payrolls in a month. Periodic payments for taxes of different types may vary because of variations in activity, profit or sales fluctuations, or tax rate changes. Payments for the nonoperating items (interest, capital expenditures, borrowings) may be delayed or accelerated because of temporary changes in the respective projects or borrowings.

The implications of these variances in cash and their effect on future periods should be determined and plans reviewed accordingly. These controls will greatly improve cash planning.

Variances in the other balance sheet accounts not already explained by the analysis of cash are also well worth commenting upon, complete with implications, in the monthly budget reviews.

Budgeting Strategies.   Probably the most important single factor in the acceptance and success of a budget is the genuine participation of all the members of management who have responsibility for the operation of a section for which separate accounting is maintained. Respect and enthusiasm for budgeting, and for accountability in general, will soon be replaced by resentment if a budget is arbitrary or if it is imposed without discussion with the department meant to be controlled thereby. This discussion should be genuine; the budget should be a synthesis. It should be directed from the top, and general plans, limitations, and objectives should be spelled out from the top, but the working out of detailed operating requirements should proceed from the bottom up, with two-way communication between.

The budget should be attainable. Department heads will be encouraged to beat their budgets if the budgets are reasonable and the department heads receive credit for their accomplishments. But department heads will strongly resent being forced to struggle to live within an arbitrary or unreasonably tight budget. Such a budget is often arbitrarily cut below anticipated expenditures on the theory that all budgets tend to be exceeded somewhat, and holding allowances low may keep expenditures more nearly at actual requirements. Department heads sense and resent this ploy. When that happens the *esprit de corps* is lost and efficiency suffers.

Budgets, even fixed ones, should not be inviolate. If budgets are reasonably tightly set, if they are set at probable actual needs, some will be exceeded and some will have balances left. This is nothing but the law of averages. If a ruling is made, as it sometimes is, that expenditures over budgets will not be tolerated, two undesirable results will occur: budgets will be padded wherever possible, resulting in a larger overall budget, and some necessary expenditures will be tentatively avoided, possibly at great eventual cost. Budget variances should occur if a budget is realistic, but they should be explained and they will probably be offset elsewhere. A variance serves to highlight a situation that needs attention, and this is desirable.

Terms.   Much confusion exists over certain terms, with the result that understanding suffers. The following terms should be clear in the minds of all management dealing with budgets:

A *forecast* is simply an estimate of what will take place. A *sales forecast* is the best current estimate of the sales for the period covered.

A *variable budget* is not a forecast. It is a flexible operating plan plan or program, segregated into areas of responsibility, and indicating varying amounts deemed to be required under a range of possible conditions. It is really a formula expressing the behavior pattern of costs within a probable range of volume.

A *profit plan* is an expression (really a forecast) of what will happen if the sales forecast is exactly achieved and every budget is exactly met. It is an objective, or set of objectives—an operating plan for the coming year.

A *projection* is a new estimate of the year's results made during the budgeted year, based on information then available. For example, after six months of operation a new forecast of the year's profits is required. The first six months is actual, and these data will be used instead of either budget or profit plan. The profit for the remaining six months will be projected using the latest sales forecast and the budget formula. This may need some adjustment if experience for the first six months indicates a budget variance which is likely to continue, either at the same rate or at a modified rate. The total of the results of the first six months and the adjusted budgeted results for the last six months is the new projection of the year's results.

Budget Revisions.   This raises the point of whether a budget should be revised during the year if it is not being met. Most authorities agree that except in unusual circumstances, a budget should not be revised during the year. The reasons are several. The budget has drawn a line from which variations are measured and their implications studied. If the line constantly changes, it becomes more difficult to interpret the overall performance and make accurate projections. Also, if a significant change is made, say in wage rates, it becomes important to know the effect of the change. Because of the differing individual rates and the labor content in inventories, this is not readily apparent, except from an analysis of the change in the labor variances. This requires constant standards or unchanged budgets. Finally, those who would change budgets for justified negative variances would need also to reduce favorable variances to be consistent, and to avoid finally inflating the budget. This is difficult, and also discouraging. Department heads who achieve a budgetary savings want to receive credit for that effort, not have it taken away from them. The latter would lead to a practice of using up budget balances to avoid losing them.

THE USE OF BUDGETS IN LONG-RANGE PLANNING

Corporate long-range planning looks ahead for five or ten years in developing a plan for orderly growth. It involves the establishment of general direction, objectives related to size, degree of diversification, geographical coverage, etc. Much of this must be stated in broad and general terms, and the economic climate in which the company will function is very uncertain. Yet the plans and their effect must be expressed in money terms.

The cost behavior characteristics revealed by the budgetary process and spelled out in the budget cost formulas and break-even information in the master budget are very useful in determining the costs, profits, and the cash flow required in planning. When capacities of present facilities are no longer adequate, the addition of new facilities will add to fixed costs. Variable costs are likely to maintain the same ratios to sales, however, as long as current processes continue.

If changes in current products, processes, or operating conditions are planned, the cost formulas will need to be modified accordingly, but the proved base of current cost behavior patterns will be a convenient starting point for projecting costs.

Because of the uncertainties inherent in long-range forecasting, three forecasts are sometimes projected, one at an optimistic level, one at a pessimistic or extremely conservative level, and one at a balanced, in-between level.

Balance sheet information must also be developed. Working capital required can be estimated on the basis of the effect of added volume on inventory requirements, accounts receivable and payable, etc., using current policies as a base. Fixed assets will be affected by capital expenditures and retirements. In long-range planning, cash generated is usually projected on a cash flow basis, cash flow being defined as net income plus depreciation. Requirements for dividends and capital expenditures will then determine the amount of financing which may be needed.

BIBLIOGRAPHY

Bunge, Walter R.: *Managerial Budgeting for Profit Improvement,* McGraw-Hill Book Company, New York, 1968.

Heckert, J. Brooks, and James D. Wilson: *Business Budgeting and Control,* The Ronald Press Company, New York 1967.

Hill, Leland Halsey: *Upward in the Black; How to Manage a Business for Profit,* Prentice-Hall, Englewood Cliffs, N.J., 1966.

Jones, Reginald L., and H. George Trentin: *Budgeting: Key to Planning and Control,* rev. ed., AMA, New York, 1971.

Knight, W. D., and E. H. Weinwurm: *Managerial Budgeting,* The Macmillan Company, New York, 1964.

Stedry, Andrew D.: *Budget Control and Cost Behavior,* Prentice-Hall, Englewood Cliffs, N.J., 1960.

Vatter, William J.: *Operating Budgets,* Wadsworth Publishing Company, Belmont, Calif., 1969.

Welsch, Glenn A.: *Budgeting: Profit Planning and Control,* 4th ed., Prentice-Hall, Englewood Cliffs, N.J., 1976.

Chapter **41**

Production Costs

WILLIAM L. FERRARA
Professor of Accounting and Price Waterhouse Faculty Fellow, The
Pennsylvania State University

INTRODUCTION

Production has been defined as "The function of making or fabricating, as distinguished from distributing or financing. . . ."[1] Thus, one can define "production costs" as the costs of making or fabricating a product.

This definition of production costs can be deceptive in its simplicity, especially in today's market-oriented economy. The point here is that as production becomes more consumer-oriented in terms of various "extras" such as color choices (e.g., household appliances) or special packaging, the distinction between production and distribution costs becomes blurred. With this point in mind one can expect some differences of opinion on distinctions between production and distribution costs. These differences tend to disappear as one proceeds to a discussion of the purposes for which production costs are accumulated. The specific elements of cost to be considered come into rather clear focus as soon as the purpose for which they are to be used is specified.

BASIS FOR ACCUMULATION OF PRODUCTION COSTS

Recurring Needs Versus Nonrecurring Needs. Production costs are accumulated for a variety of purposes. A useful twofold classification of these purposes or needs is in terms of whether the accumulations are designed to fill "recurring" or "nonrecurring" needs. Recurring needs are those needs for cost accumulations which arise on almost a scheduled basis, e.g., the need for periodic responsibility accounting reports. Nonrecurring needs do not arise on a scheduled basis since they are essentially unique situations which cannot be anticipated, or cannot be expected to recur in the same form. A good illustration of a nonrecurring need would be cost data needed in evaluating a decision relative to entering a new market or producing a new product.

Recurring needs for data can be subclassified as (1) product cost measurements and (2) performance (responsibility) measurements. Product cost measurements are most often related to inventory valuation in external reporting. However, that is not the sole purpose of product costing since product costs can be especially useful in pricing decisions and product mix decisions. Cost accumulations for performance measurement are basically for control purposes in the sense that they are used to evaluate the performance of individuals and groups in terms of the costs they are able to influence.

It is difficult to classify nonrecurring needs for data. Each need represents a unique or one-time occurrence and the data has to be accumulated especially for the particular purpose at hand. Perhaps the best way to gain an appreciation of nonrecurring needs is to consider them to be the subject of special studies required to quantify the variables in particular decision situations; no rational accountant would attempt to provide data for one-time decisions via the regular recurring reports of an accounting system.

CLASSIFICATION OF PRODUCTION COSTS

Basic Classifications. Cost classifications are exceedingly numerous. Among the most prominent of these for purposes of analyzing production costs are the following:

Incremental Costs. The change in total costs that would be occasioned by adopting one alternative instead of another. Often referred to as "differential" or "avoidable" costs.

[1] Eric Kohler, *A Dictionary for Accountants,* 4th ed., Prentice-Hall, Englewood Cliffs, N.J., 1970, p. 344.

Nonincremental Costs. The costs that would not change by adopting one alternative instead of another. Often referred to as "sunk" or "unavoidable" costs.

Variable Costs. Costs which will vary in total with the number of units produced. A form of incremental cost in the sense that such costs will increase or decrease in total as production increases or decreases.

Fixed Costs. Costs which will not vary in total with the number of units produced within given volume ranges. Within a volume range of, say, 100,000 to 200,000 units, fixed costs will remain at $300,000, for example; to get to the range of 200,000 to 300,000 units, however, fixed costs will have to be increased by $20,000 in order to reflect the salary of an additional foreman. Thus, within a given volume range fixed costs may be considered nonincremental in relation to changes in volume, but fixed costs can be incremental when comparing cost differences between two volume ranges.

Managed Fixed Costs. Fixed costs which can be changed in a short period of time, e.g., one year or less. Service department costs such as production planning and inventory control are examples of these costs. Sometimes referred to as "discretionary" or "programmed" costs.

Committed Fixed Costs. Fixed costs which cannot be changed in a short period of time. These costs are primarily related to long-term investments in plant and equipment and salaries of key personnel.

Semivariable Costs. Costs which are partially variable and partially fixed. Often referred to as "semifixed" or "mixed" costs. Royalties on a patent for a manufacturing process might be a good example in that the royalty charge might be a fixed fee plus a charge per unit produced using the process. It is normally recommended that semivariable costs be separated into their fixed and variable components.

Direct Costs. Costs which can be traced to individual units of output or segments of the enterprise. Sometimes referred to as traceable, specific, or separable costs.

Indirect Costs. Costs which cannot be traced to individual units of output or segments of the enterprise. Sometimes referred to as nontraceable, common, general, or joint costs.

Direct Materials. Costs of materials which can be traced to individual units of output.

Direct Labor. Costs of labor which can be traced to individual units of output.

Factory Overhead. All production costs other than direct materials or direct labor. Sometimes referred to as burden, oncost, or factory expense.

Variable Factory Overhead. The variable portion of factory overhead. Considered a direct cost in terms of units of output since by its variable nature it can be traced reasonably well to individual units of output.

Fixed Factory Overhead. The fixed portion of factory overhead. Considered an indirect cost in terms of units of output since there are usually only arbitrary ways of assigning fixed costs to individual units of output.

Prime Costs. The sum of direct materials and direct labor.

Conversion Costs. The costs to convert direct materials into finished product; hence, the sum of direct labor and factory overhead.

Period Costs. Costs which are assigned to the expense of a period of time either directly (president's salary) or via an apportionment between asset and expense (inventory and cost of goods sold). In direct costing (discussed subsequently) period costs are considered the equivalent of fixed costs.

Product Costs. Costs which are assigned to individual units of product, either directly as are direct costs or by apportionment techniques as are indirect costs. In direct costing, product costs are considered the equivalent of variable costs.

Controllable Costs. Costs which are subject to the influence of a particular person or group in the enterprise. All costs at some point in time are subject to the influence of a particular person or group in an enterprise; in this sense all costs are controllable. The often used adjective, noncontrollable, really connotes controllable "by someone else."

Relation to Classes of Needs and the Accounting System.   The above classifications of costs are or can be exceedingly useful to the person who is interested in isolating the various classes of costs appropriate to the fulfillment of varying needs for cost data. In summary form, needs and classifications of cost can be related as shown below. The relationships are not purported to be airtight; they are simply intended to indicate general tendencies.

Nonrecurring needs:
   Incremental versus nonincremental costs
Recurring measures of product cost:
   Direct material, direct labor, variable factory overhead, and fixed factory overhead costs
Recurring measures of performance:
   Controllable, direct or traceable, fixed, and variable costs

Basic incremental cost concepts fit the nature of nonrecurring needs which require special studies to quantify the variables in particular decision situations. No other cost concepts could satisfy this need since the problem is essentially one of identifying those costs which will be altered by adopting one alternative instead of another.

Recurring measures of product costs would have to consider the variable costs of production (direct materials, direct labor, and variable factory overhead) since these costs have been identified as costs which can be traced to individual units of output. These variable costs of production are often called "direct" costs since they can be traced directly to individual units of output. The major argument in recent years concerning what constitutes product costs relates to fixed factory overhead costs. Since fixed costs are costs that do not vary with production within certain volume ranges, there is a conceptual problem in identifying fixed factory overhead with individual units of output.

Recurring measures of performance can be thought of in terms of measuring the performance of a man or a group as well as the performance of an activity. For the measurement of a man or group, the appropriate cost concept relates to controllability, whereas for the measurement of an activity the appropriate cost concept relates to the directness or traceability of costs to a segment of an enterprise. It would be well to remember that the definition of direct costs under performance measurement is based upon traceability to an enterprise segment whereas the definition of direct costs under product cost measurement is based upon traceability to an individual unit of output. It is usually advantageous to include the distinction between fixed and variable costs in measures of performance for activities as well as persons or groups.

In succeeding pages our attention will be devoted exclusively to the recurring needs for data accumulations as they relate to measuring product costs. Those interested in recurring needs for performance measurement data are referred to the chapters on budgeting and standard costs. Those interested in nonrecurring needs for data and further analysis of incremental concepts are referred to the chapter on cost analysis.

MEASURING PRODUCT COSTS

Purpose of Product Costing.   The basic purpose of product costing is the accumulation of cost per unit of output. These costs can be predetermined via standard or estimated cost systems or they can be actual costs. In this chapter only actual cost systems will be considered, with a modification designed to introduce predetermined overhead rates. Standard costs are the subject of Chapter 42.

Unit of output should be defined broadly so as to recognize different types of production and to recognize various classes of output. Two basic forms of production exist, namely, job order and process. Job order production, in its purest form, is used in those instances where production is on the basis of a specific order placed by a specific customer and such order usually involves special production characteristics. These special characteristics preclude the possibility of producing for inventory in the typical job shop. Process or continuous production is used in those instances where the product produced is basically a standard product which enables the producer to produce for inventory and not for each order after it comes in. It should be clear that job order and process production as described represent extremes and between these extremes there is an infinite variety of possibilities. Still, for our purposes the main factor to consider is the extent to which one might be able to produce for general consumer needs as opposed to the specific needs of a specific consumer.

In the case of job order production the basic unit of output is the job, whereas for process production the basic unit of output is the standard product. Depending on the circumstances of each case, recognition of significant units of measure might involve modifications within the context of the job and the standard product. For example, a job might include ten copies of a special type of equipment and one could refer to the cost per unit on that job. Similarly, one might prefer to deal with cost per 1,000 board feet in a lumber mill rather than cost per board foot, especially under conditions where prices are quoted and goods sold in terms of thousand board feet.

The costs per unit of output obtained by product costing can be and are used in:

1. External financial reporting—placing a dollar value on inventories and cost of goods sold in financial statements.

2. Internal financial reporting—analyses of product line profitability, evaluation of alternative pricing policies, and evaluation of the profitability of producing products in different plants.

Basic Entries in Product Costing.   As is shown in Exhibit 1, there are six basic journal entries in a production cost system.

Entries 1 and 2 simply reflect the dollar amounts of direct materials and direct labor, respectively, used in production during a particular period of time. Entries 3 and 4 are concerned with factory overhead. In entry 3 the actual factory overhead costs are recorded. Since factory overhead is generally traceable to production only on the basis of estimates, entry 4 reflects the estimated amount of factory overhead applied to production (thus, charged to work in process) during a particular period. The method of determining such estimates is considered in the next section.

Entry 5 reflects the completion of work in process which is transferred to finished goods inventory until it is sold. Entry 6 reflects the cost of goods sold by a transfer from the Finished Goods Inventory account to the Cost of Goods Sold account. In succeeding pages it will be shown that the major difference between job order and process cost accounting is the way in which the dollar amounts of these transfers are calculated.

Applying Factory Overhead.[2]   The amount of applied factory overhead is derived by multiplying a factory overhead rate and a measure of factory activity, e.g., $2 per direct labor hour times the number of direct labor hours worked. Both the overhead rate and the measure of activity are determined on the basis of a great deal of analysis.

Departmental Versus Factory-wide Rates.   Factory overhead rates can be deter-

---

[2]Much of the material in this section is adapted from I. Wayne Keller and William L. Ferrara, *Management Accounting for Profit Control,* 2nd ed., McGraw-Hill Book Company, New York, 1966, chap. 6.

EXHIBIT 1   Production Cost System—Process or Job Order—Basic Journal Entries

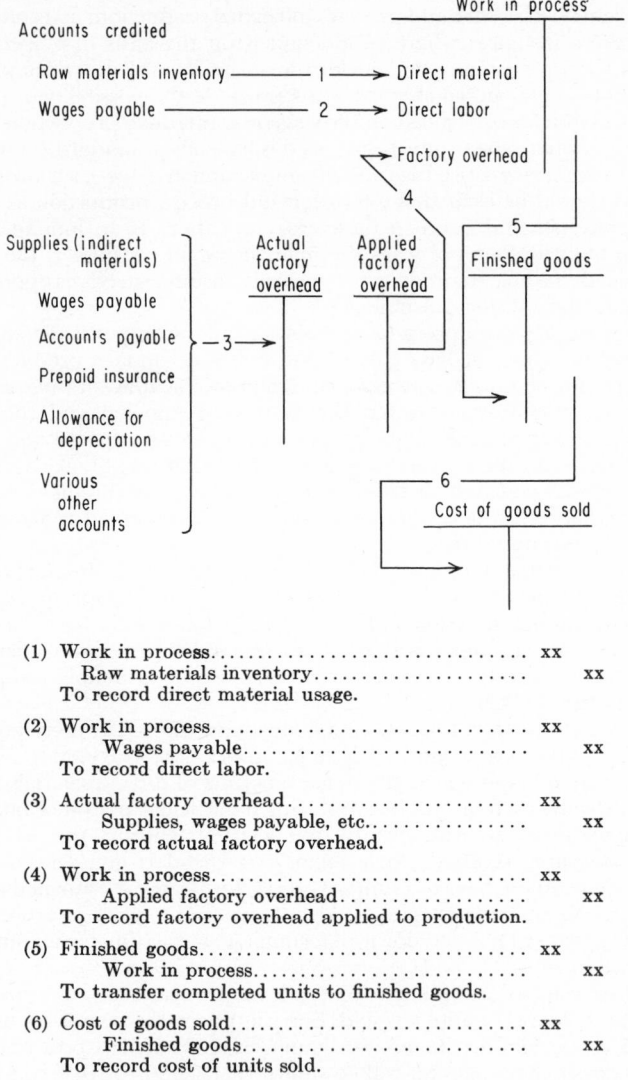

(1) Work in process.............................. xx
    Raw materials inventory.....................   xx
    To record direct material usage.

(2) Work in process.............................. xx
    Wages payable...........................   xx
    To record direct labor.

(3) Actual factory overhead....................... xx
    Supplies, wages payable, etc..............   xx
    To record actual factory overhead.

(4) Work in process.............................. xx
    Applied factory overhead..................   xx
    To record factory overhead applied to production.

(5) Finished goods............................... xx
    Work in process..........................   xx
    To transfer completed units to finished goods.

(6) Cost of goods sold............................ xx
    Finished goods...........................   xx
    To record cost of units sold.

mined for the factory as a whole or for each department within the factory. Overhead rates for the factory as a whole are used by some companies, but the utility of such rates is questionable. A factory represents a myriad of activities, which can hardly be summarized into one satisfactory overhead rate. This point is easily seen in a foundry consisting of four departments such as melting, molding, coremaking, and finishing. Each of these activities is essentially different, and furthermore an overhead rate for melting should probably be based upon pounds melted, whereas an overhead rate for the other departments should probably be based upon direct labor hours or perhaps even units produced (molds, cores, finished castings).

Determining Factory Overhead Rates. Factory overhead rates can be based upon advance estimates of costs or upon actual overhead costs after they are incurred. Overhead rates based upon advance estimates are called predetermined rates, whereas overhead rates based upon incurred costs are called actual rates. Whether the overhead rate is predetermined or actual, the method of determination is essentially unchanged and is as follows:

1. Distribute factory overhead to departments (service and production departments).

2. Distribute service department costs to production departments.

3. Divide the costs distributed to each production department by the measure of activity appropriate for each department.

Distributing Factory Overhead to Departments. Factory overhead is distributed to departments as completely as is possible. In some cases, such as salaries, indirect labor, supplies, and depreciation on equipment within each department, perfect accuracy is possible since these costs can be assigned directly to a specific department. In other cases, allocation bases are necessary since the costs cannot be assigned directly to a specific department. For example, rent or depreciation of a building is generally distributed to departments on the basis of square feet occupied by each department. Insurance and taxes on equipment are usually distributed on the basis of the book value of equipment in each department; electricity can be distributed on the basis of number of electric outlets, fixtures, or even the rated horsepower of equipment in each department. The major problem in distributing factory overhead costs to departments is to find a basis of distribution which is a satisfactory measure of the cost applicable to each department.

Exhibit 2 illustrates the calculation of departmental overhead rates. Note the basis of distribution used as well as the redistribution of service department costs to producing departments, which is explained below. Also note the calculation of separate factory overhead rates for each of the producing departments.

Distributing Service Department Costs to Producing Departments. After the factory overhead costs are distributed to each department, the next step is to distribute service department costs to producing departments. The reason for this type of distribution becomes evident when one recognizes that producing departments are the only departments through which the products being manufactured flow. If overhead rates are to be reasonable estimates of the amount of factory overhead applicable to units produced, such rates must include costs incurred for the producing departments as well as costs incurred within the producing department. Service departments (maintenance, material handling, personnel, etc.) exist only for the purpose of facilitating the operations of producing departments, and thus they are in reality costs of the producing departments. Service department costs are distributed to producing departments on the basis of service rendered.

In Exhibit 2 the service departments are power and material handling. Power costs, in this case, are distributed on the basis of an engineering survey of potential and actual power usage in each department. Material handling costs are distributed on the basis of the dollar value of materials and supplies requisitioned.[3]

Dividing Total Costs Distributed to Producing Departments by Appropriate Activity Measures. The third and final step in determining an overhead rate for each producing department is to divide the total factory overhead costs distributed to

---

[3]There are many intricacies involved in the distribution of service department costs. For a description of some of them see Keller and Ferrara, *op. cit.,* pp. 119–123; Gordon Shillinglaw, *Cost Accounting: Analysis and Control,* 3rd ed., Richard D. Irwin, Homewood, Ill., 1972, chap. 10; Sidney Davidson, James S. Schindler, and Roman L. Weil, *Fundamentals of Accounting,* 5th ed., The Dryden Press, Hinsdale, Ill., chap. 20, particularly Appendix 20.1; and Robert S. Kaplan, "Variable and Self-service Costs in Reciprocal Allocation Models," *The Accounting Review,* vol. 48, pp. 738–748, October 1973.

EXHIBIT 2 Calculation of Departmental Overhead Rates

Classification	Basis of distribution	Service departments		Producing departments			Total
		Power	Material handling	Stamping	Finishing	Assembly	
Salaries	Actual salaries per dept.	$ 5,000	$ 6,000	$ 6,000	$ 6,500	$ 5,400	$ 28,900
Indirect labor	Actual indirect labor per dept.	8,000	20,000	8,200	9,400	4,300	49,900
Supplies	Actual requisitions per dept.	1,200	2,100	680	1,200	1,500	6,680
Employee benefit programs	Total payroll per dept.	200	400	800	600	400	2,400
Payroll taxes	Total payroll per dept.	425	850	1,700	1,275	850	5,100
Property taxes—building	Square feet per dept.	250	250	500	500	500	2,000
Insurance—building	Square feet per dept.	50	50	100	100	100	400
Depreciation—building	Square feet per dept.	625	625	1,250	1,250	1,250	5,000
Property taxes—equipment	Book value of equipment	96	48	432	336	288	1,200
Insurance—equipment	Book value of equipment	12	6	54	42	36	150
Depreciation—equipment	Actual equipment in each dept.	4,000	2,500	27,000	24,000	16,000	73,500
Total overhead cost per dept.		$19,858	$32,829	$46,716	$45,203	$30,624	$175,230
Distribution of service department costs:							
Power	Engineering survey	(19,858)	1,986	5,958	5,957	5,957	
Subtotal			$34,815	$52,674	$51,160	$36,581	$175,230
Material handling	Materials & supplies requisitions		(34,815)	12,185	13,926	8,704	
Total overhead cost per producing dept.				$64,859	$65,086	$45,285	$175,230
Measure of activity (direct labor hours)				20,000	10,000	7,000	
Factory overhead rates per dept.:							
Total overhead per dept.				$3.24	$6.51	$6.47	
Measure of activity per dept.							

41-8

each producing department, including its share of service department costs, by the measure of activity appropriate for each producing department. In some cases an appropriate measure of activity is obvious, whereas in others it is more or less obscure. In such cases, judgment must be exercised. An obvious measure of activity for a department through which only one product flows would be units processed. However, most departments process more than one product or many sizes and varieties of the same product, and in such cases we must rely on more general measures of output. Two of these more general measures of output are machine-hours and direct labor hours. An application of machine-hours would be in an automated department, whereas an application of direct labor hours would be in a hand-assembly operation. A less obvious measure of activity might be direct labor hours in the finishing department of a foundry. In some cases less exact measures of activity are used since they are more easily obtained. For example, direct labor costs per department are frequently more easily obtainable than direct labor hours per department. Prime costs (direct material plus direct labor) are also easily obtainable and thus are used as a measure of activity in some cases. The main issue in selecting a measure of activity is finding a measure which is related to the incurring of factory overhead. The relationship should be functional in the mathematical sense; that is, there should be a significant degree of correlation between the measure of activity chosen and incurrence of factory overhead costs. An additional requirement of a measure of activity is that it should be economical to obtain and use.

Quantifying the Entry for Factory Overhead Applied.   When the factory overhead rates are established for each department, all that is necessary to determine the amount of applied factory overhead is to multiply the overhead rate for each department by the actual activity for each department and then total the applied amounts for each department. For example, the journal entry to apply factory overhead in a hypothetical situation would be:

Work in Process 154,000
    Applied Factory Overhead   154,000

The basis for the above entry would be the following type of calculations:

Department	Rate	Activity	Amount
I	$3.00 per direct labor hour	30,000 direct labor hours	$ 90,000
II	2.00 per machine-hour	19,500 machine-hours	39,000
III	2.50 per dollar of direct labor cost	$10,000 direct labor cost	25,000
			$154,000

Actual Versus Predetermined Factory Overhead Rates.   Rates for applying factory overhead can be determined on the basis of actual or estimated cost data. Rates based on actual cost data are called "actual" rates, whereas rates based on estimated cost data are called "predetermined" rates. Actual rates are generally calculated monthly or annually. In either case, the calculation of actual rates follows the procedure outlined in previous paragraphs.

Predetermined rates for factory overhead are calculated in the same procedural manner as actual rates. However, predetermined rates are generally set for a year in advance on the basis of estimated activity and estimated overhead costs. The first step in setting predetermined rates is estimating activity for the year, and the second step is estimating factory overhead costs for the estimated activity level.

The estimate of activity is a forecast of direct labor hours, machine-hours, direct labor cost, etc., for the coming year. On the basis of this forecast, an estimate of factory overhead will be made for each producing and service department. With these estimates made, an estimated or predetermined factory overhead rate can be established in the same manner as shown for actual rates in Exhibit 2. With the use of standard cost concepts, more refined methods of establishing predetermined rates are available.

A major problem in the use of actual rates is that all entries concerning applied factory overhead must be delayed until the rates are calculated. If actual rates are calculated annually (an extreme case), it would be impossible to prepare monthly financial statements, and furthermore difficulties would arise during the year in cases where a total manufacturing cost per unit or per job was needed in the determination of selling prices and pricing policies. Actual rates calculated on a monthly basis would reduce these problems somewhat, but most firms eliminate the problems involving the use of actual rates by using predetermined rates. Monthly and annual financial statements can be prepared more readily with predetermined rates, and furthermore predetermined rates are helpful in establishing and evaluating pricing policies.

Underapplied and Overapplied Factory Overhead.   A direct result of predetermined rates is the possibility of underapplied or overapplied factory overhead. In almost every instance, estimates and actual results differ, and thus there will almost always be a difference between actual and applied factory overhead when predetermined rates are used. If the applied overhead exceeds the actual overhead, the overhead is overapplied. If the applied overhead is less than actual overhead, the overhead is underapplied. The following T accounts illustrate cases of over- and underapplied factory overhead.

Overapplied Factory Overhead

Actual Factory Overhead	Applied Factory Overhead
468,000	495,000

The amount of overapplication in the above accounts is $27,000 (= $495,000 − $468,000).

Underapplied Factory Overhead

Actual Factory Overhead	Applied Factory Overhead
468,000	425,000

The amount of underapplication in the above accounts is $43,000.

Disposition of Under- and Overapplied Factory Overhead.   A major accounting problem is the disposition of overapplied or underapplied factory overhead. In monthly financial statements the under- or overapplied amounts are usually carried forward and shown in the balance sheet as deferred charges (underapplied) or deferred credits (overapplied). The theory behind this treatment is that there is an element of seasonality in the estimates, and the results of succeeding months may tend to offset differences between actual and applied amounts which occur early in the year. A perfect case in point is the bills for heating the plant, which occur only during the cold months of the year.

At the end of the fiscal year any difference between actual and applied overhead is generally disposed of by closing the difference to cost of goods sold. Thus underapplied factory overhead is added to cost of goods sold, and overapplied factory overhead is subtracted from cost of goods sold. In some cases the difference is divided between inventories (balance sheet) and cost of goods sold (income statement).

The theory behind closing overapplied and underapplied factory overhead to cost of goods sold is that there was an error in setting the predetermined rate, and therefore cost of goods sold is not properly calculated. Of course, if there was an error in the predetermined rate, neither work in process nor finished goods is properly stated. Thus it would seem proper to divide the overapplied or underapplied factory overhead between cost of goods sold and inventory (work in process and finished goods). An exact but costly and generally impractical method for handling this situation would be to revise the predetermined rates on the basis of information available at the end of the year and then correct previous entries for applied factory overhead on the basis of the revised rate.

A reasonable approximation to this entry can be made on the basis of total factory costs or direct labor costs in inventory and cost of sales. The direct labor cost basis would be appropriate when direct labor hours or dollars are used to apply factory overhead. For example, assume that the following direct labor costs are included in work in process, finished goods, and cost of goods sold at the end of a fiscal year:

Work in Process	$ 100,000
Finished Goods	300,000
Cost of Goods Sold	2,600,000

The proportion of direct labor costs in each category will determine how to dispose of the difference between actual and applied factory overhead—an underapplication of $43,000 as in the preceding example. The data can be shown in the following manner:

	Direct labor costs	Dollar value, %	Division of underapplied amount
Work in process	$ 100,000	3⅓	$ 1,433
Finished goods	300,000	10	4,300
Cost of goods sold	2,600,000	86⅔	37,267
	$3,000,000	100	$43,000

The entries resulting from the above calculations would be as follows:

Work in Process	1,433
Finished Goods	4,300
Cost of Goods Sold	37,267
Applied Factory Overhead	425,000
Actual Factory Overhead	468,000

Disposition of over- or underapplied factory overhead on the basis of total factory costs included in inventories and cost of goods sold would be handled in the same manner as shown for direct labor costs.

When the amount of under- or overapplied factory overhead allocable to inventories is not material, an argument can be made to close the entire amount to cost of goods sold. Such an argument, even though subjective in nature, is quite understandable.

Under standard costing when predetermined rates are based on standards rather than expectations of actual amounts, the possibility arises of underapplied factory overhead being partially or completely wasted resources. The possibility of overapplied factory overhead being a gain because of actual costs being less than standard also arises. Some authors hold that any predetermined rate is a form of standard, thus offering a conceptual justification for closing the difference between actual and applied factory overhead to cost of goods sold.

Multiple Overhead Rates. For some departments it may be desirable to have two or more overhead rates in order to arrive at more nearly accurate product costs. For example, in fabricating special parts from fiberboard blanks, there may be no constant relationship of labor costs to machine time. Some products may require relatively high man-hours and low machine-hours and vice versa. Where such conditions exist, an overhead rate might be determined per labor hour for those costs which relate to labor—supervision, employee benefits, payroll taxes, etc. Another rate would be determined for those costs which relate to machinery—maintenance, depreciation, property taxes, insurance, etc.

There can be no stated rule as to when more than one overhead rate should be used for an operation. Only judgment based on an intimate knowledge of products and production processes will determine when more than one rate is needed to secure reasonable product costs. The accounting entries are the same as when a single rate is used for an operation or department.

Fixed and Variable Overhead Rates.   In recent years, the most often recommended form of multiple overhead rate relates to the segregation of factory overhead into fixed and variable portions in each department. The result is a variable factory overhead rate and a fixed factory overhead rate for each producing department. This breakdown not only refines the application of factory overhead to units of product, it also facilitates the inclusion of an enterprise's cost structure in its regular recurring reports (see section on direct costing) and provides data needed for a variety of cost analyses.

Fixed and variable overhead rates are used in exactly the same way as one overhead rate per department is used. The determination of fixed and variable overhead rates can follow the basic procedure outlined above and illustrated in Exhibit 2 as long as the costs are separated into fixed and variable portions. However, some accountants may wish to make a change in the determination of these rates in order to recognize the significant difference between fixed and variable costs. The change relates to the nature of the measure of activity used to divide fixed factory overhead costs in order to determine the fixed factory overhead rate.

Measure of Activity for Fixed and Variable Overhead Rates.   Perhaps the best way to illustrate the issue of which measure of activity to use is by simple algebraic expressions. For example, fixed and variable overhead rates may be determined as follows:

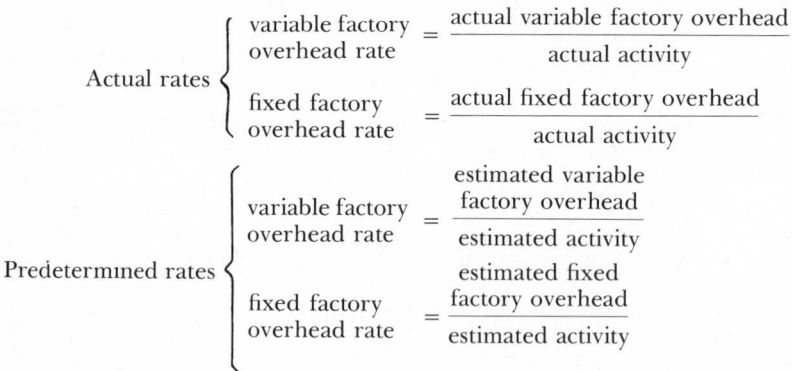

The computation of these overhead rates follows the procedure outlined in Exhibit 2, modified only by the separation of overhead into fixed and variable portions.

The change which may be recommended in the above calculations relates only to the fixed factory overhead rate. It is based upon the concept that fixed factory overhead represents the availability of capacity which may or may not be fully used. The fact that fixed factory overhead will remain the same total dollar amount within given volume (activity) ranges is indicative of this fact that fixed factory overhead represents the availability of capacity. In order to provide for a

EXHIBIT 3

Job Cost Sheet								No. 954		
Cusiomer		Frigidbox, Inc.								
Order Rec. 9/1/--			To be comp. 10/20/--				Comm. Code 576			
Quan. on order 30,000			Material #143				Print No. 763 -14 -091			
Blank Size 48" x 96"			(cut 2 pts. per blank)							

Item   Bottom insulating panel

Description   44" x 36"   Notched and drilled per print

Material		Labor			Applied Overhead					
							Variable		Fixed	
Date	Amt.	Date	Dept.	Amt.	Date	Dept.	Rate	Amt.	Rate	Amt.
9/6	10,086.40	9/6	420	11.00	9/6	420	50%	5.50	100%	11.00
		9/7	421	25.20	9/7	421	70%	17.64	110%	27.72
		9/9	422	28.40	9/9	422	100%	28.40	80%	22.72
Total	10,086.40	Total		64.60				51.54		61.44

Other Charges			Cost Summary		
Date	Reference	Amount			
9/4	Voucher 9-076	170.80	Material	10,086	40
			Labor	64	60
			Variable overhead	51	54
			Fixed overhead	61	44
Production Data			Other charges	170	80
Date	Spoiled Units	Good Units			
9/9	400	30,000	Total	10,434	78
			Cost per 1,000		
			Good units	347	83

measure of unutilized or idle capacity (the volume variance), a measure of activity other than actual or estimated activity is used in the denominator in determining the fixed factory overhead rate. Most often these rates are based on the use of a denominator referred to as "normal volume" which is usually a certain percentage (say, 80 percent) of the physical capability of facilities or an average of expected activity over a period of years. The measure of the volume variance is then the difference between the normal volume and the capacity actually used multiplied by the fixed factory overhead rate.

Job Order Cost Systems.   The main ingredient in a job order cost system is the job cost sheet as illustrated in Exhibit 3. All facets of a job from its inception to its completion are summarized on a job cost sheet. There is always space on the sheet to include data on materials, labor, and overhead costs. In addition there is usually space for fixed and variable overhead rates and for inclusion of "other charges," such as special nonreusable tools or dies required for the job that do not fit the normal material, labor, or overhead classifications but are still directly identifiable with a job.

In Exhibit 3 one can follow every facet of cost for job no. 954. Cost data are shown in detail and are also summarized. Production data for the job are also shown in order that a cost per unit on the job may be shown on the job cost sheet.

From the point of view of the double-entry framework of financial accounting, the job cost sheet is especially important for the following reasons:

1. Job cost sheets for incomplete jobs represent the work in process inventory.
2. Job cost sheets for completed jobs which are still on hand represent the finished goods inventory.
3. Job cost sheets for completed jobs which have been delivered represent cost of goods sold.
4. The dollar total of jobs completed during a period of time represents the basic data for an entry transferring dollar amounts from work in process to finished goods.
5. The dollar total of jobs delivered to customers during a period of time represents the basic data for an entry transferring dollar amounts from finished goods to cost of goods sold.

From the point of view of internal uses of accounting data, the job cost sheet can be useful in comparing job cost estimates with actual job cost data in order to isolate inefficiencies and improve estimating procedures. Determining sales prices and profitability per job is also closely related to estimated and actual costs per job.

Process Cost Systems. The basic feature of process costing is the accumulation of cost by processes (departments or subdepartments) rather than by jobs. A unit cost of production is calculated for each process and the total unit cost is the sum of the unit costs for each process through which a product must flow.

Such unit costs are derived by "simple" division as follows:

$$\frac{\text{Total costs of a process}}{\text{Units produced in a process}} = \text{unit cost of a process}$$

The total costs of a process are not difficult to accumulate since direct materials and direct labor are identifiable by process, and overhead applied (fixed and variable) is also identifiable by process since the overhead is applied on the basis of a measure of activity applicable to a process. The only source of difficulty in this simple division is the determination of "units produced in a process." This difficulty is really minor, once it is realized that the calculation of units produced is essentially and necessarily an average.

Calculating Average Units Produced (Equivalent Units). Units produced during a particular period of time must of necessity be an average since both at the beginning and end of a period there are partially completed inventories of work in process. The partial completion of work in process at the beginning and end of a period can also be expressed in terms of the fact that all units started during a period are rarely completed during that same period or that some units completed during a period were normally started during a preceding period.

In order to calculate the average units produced during a period of time, we must work with a combination of data pertaining to beginning work in process, ending work in process, units put into process, and units completed during a period. An illustration of how this averaging might work is as follows:

Basic Data for a period:

Beginning work in process:	5,000 units 20% complete
Ending work in process:	20,000 units 40% complete
Put in process:	150,000 units
Completed and transferred to finished goods:	135,000 units

Average Units Produced Calculation:

1. Based on completed portions of work in process (output method):

Transfers to finished goods	135,000
Completed portion of ending inventory, 20,000 × .4	8,000
Total possible units completed during a period	143,000
Less: Completed portion of beginning inventory, 5,000 × .2	1,000
Average units completed during a period	142,000

2. Based on incomplete portions of work in process (input method):

Units put into process	150,000
Incomplete portion of beginning inventory, 5,000 × .8	4,000
Total possible units completed during a period	154,000
Less: Incomplete portion of ending inventory, 20,000 × .6	12,000
Average units completed during a period	142,000

The two methods shown for calculating "average" units produced are usually referred to as methods for calculating "equivalent units" of production. This more common terminology will be used in succeeding sections. As shown, the calculation can proceed via either units of input or units of output. In both cases the idea is to determine first the "total possible units completed" and from this deduct the number of units not completed in order to obtain the equivalent units completed.

The earlier comment that "units produced in a process" in a particular period of time must be an average should now be more understandable. The partially complete beginning and ending inventories of work in process bring forth the averaging problem. In addition, one other facet of this averaging process should be emphasized; that is, the fact that in the usual calculation of equivalent units another averaging technique is used. This is the assumption that a beginning or ending work in process inventory is all at one stage of completion; e.g., 40 percent or 20 percent, as in the preceding illustration. Common sense forces us to realize that all work in process inventory is not at one stage of completion. A statement such as work in process inventory is 20 percent complete really means that, on the average, work in process is 20 percent complete. Not all items in a production line can be at the same stage of completion.

Equivalent Units for Each Cost Factor. In the preceding discussion it was assumed that all productive factors were at the same stage of completion in beginning and ending inventories. This, of course, is not necessarily true. Direct materials, for instance, can be added at the inception of processing, which means that the materials portion of work in process will be 100 percent complete and partial completion will then relate to the conversion costs (direct labor and factory overhead). In other situations there will be more than one type of direct material in a product, which means that cases can arise where one material is added 100 percent at the inception of processing; another can be added 100 percent at any other stage of processing; still another can be added uniformly during the entire processing operation; and finally another can be added uniformly during any particular phase of the processing operation.

Normally one assumes that direct labor and factory overhead are both added uniformly during the entire processing operation, but this need not be the most rational assumption in every case. For instance, in a highly mechanized operation, whatever labor there is might be added entirely at the beginning of an operation (process) when individual units are placed onto or into some type of mechanical equipment. Under these conditions, direct labor or portions of it could be treated as 100 percent complete from the inception of processing, while factory overhead could be treated as being added uniformly during processing. Such conditions are rare; in succeeding illustrations it will be assumed that direct labor and factory overhead are added uniformly during the entire processing operation and both will be considered simultaneously under the title "conversion costs."

Recognizing the fact that materials and conversion costs can be at different stages of processing, our preceding numerical illustration can be modified as follows, using the output method of calculating equivalent units. Note that a separate calculation (column) is used for materials and conversion costs. Also note that since, in this case, materials are always 100 percent complete, the equivalent units of materials completed are equal to units put into process. Under such conditions one could easily prefer to skip the materials column and deal only with the conversion cost column. The format, however, is especially useful in those situations where direct materials are added other than 100 percent at the beginning of processing.

Basic Data for a Period

Beginning work in process: .... 5,000 units
    Materials 100% complete
    Conversion costs 20% complete
Ending work in process: .... 20,000 units
    Materials 100% complete
    Conversion costs 40% complete
Put into process .... 150,000 units
Completed and transferred to finished goods: .... 135,000 units

	Materials	Conversion costs
Transfer to finished goods	135,000	135,000
Completed portion of ending inventory	20,000	8,000
Total possible units completed during a period	155,000	143,000
Less: Completed portion of beginning inventory	5,000	1,000
Equivalent units completed during a period	150,000	142,000

Process Cost Calculations in a Single-Process Operation. For illustrative purposes, let us assume that the immediately preceding data on equivalent units represents the production quantity data for a particular period of time, with additional data on costs as follows:

Beginning inventory costs:
    Materials .... $ 5,000
    Conversion 2,400
Costs incurred this period:
    Materials $165,000
    Conversion 326,600

The problem can now be stated in terms of "costs to be accounted for" and "costs accounted for" as follows:

Costs to Be Accounted for:

Beginning inventory:
    Materials: 5,000 units, 100% complete .... $ 5,000
    Conversion: 5,000 units, 20% complete ... 2,400
Costs incurred this period:
    Materials 165,000
    Conversion 326,600
        Total $499,000

Costs Accounted for:

Transfer to finished goods: 135,000 units ... $?
Ending inventory:
    Materials: 20,000 units, 100% complete ... $?
    Conversion: 20,000 units, 40% complete .. ?
        Total $499,000

Note that all costs must be accounted for, regardless of whether they are beginning inventory costs or the costs associated with productive factors added this period. Since by implicit assumption no units have been spoiled, all costs can be accounted for via the transfer to finished goods and the ending inventory. The specific mode of accounting for these costs proceeds by first calculating unit costs for the month and then using such unit costs to determine the ending inventory and transfer costs, as shown below using a FIFO assumption.

Unit Cost Calculations:

Materials cost:

$$\frac{\text{Costs incurred this period}}{\text{Equivalent units this period}} = \frac{\$165,000}{150,000} = \$1.10$$

Conversion cost:

$$\frac{\text{Costs incurred this period}}{\text{Equivalent units this period}} = \frac{\$326,000}{142,000} = \$2.30$$

$$\text{Total unit cost} = \$3.40$$

Transfer to Finished Goods: 135,000 Units

Beginning inventory: 5,000 units	
Materials: 100% complete	$ 5,000
Conversion: 20% complete	2,400
Costs necessary this period to complete: beginning inventory:	
80% × 5,000 units × unit conversion cost (2.30)	9,200
Remainder of transfer: 130,000 units @ total unit cost ($3.40) ..	442,000
Total	$458,600

Ending Inventory: 20,000 Units

Materials: 100% complete 20,000 @ $1.10	$ 22,000
Conversion: 40% complete 40% × 20,000 × $2.30	18,400
Total	$ 40,400

Costs Accounted for:

Transfer	$458,600
Ending inventory	40,400
Total	$499,000

Using "Average Cost" Rather Than "FIFO Cost." The preceding illustration assumed a FIFO inventory flow, as is evident in the calculation of the transfer to finished goods. A slight modification could simplify the calculation of the dollar amount of the transfer. The modification would involve an average of beginning inventory costs and current costs as shown below:

	Materials		Conversion	
	Equivalent units	Cost	Equivalent units	Cost
Beginning inventory	5,000	$ 5,000	1,000	$ 2,400
Current production	150,000	165,000	142,000	326,600
Totals	155,000	$170,000	143,000	$329,000
Average		$1.097*		$2.301*

*Rounding error adjusted.

With these average unit costs, the transfer and ending inventory would be calculated as follows. Note that the total "costs accounted for" is still equal to the previous total. The only change is an averaging process which makes the unit costs slightly (not significantly) different but greatly simplifies the calculation of the transfer. For this reason the averaging process is highly recommended, and it will be used in succeeding illustrations.

Transfer 135,000 units @ $3.398	$458,730
Ending inventory:	
Materials (20,000 × $1.097)	21,940
Conversion (8,000 × $2.301)	18,330*
	$499,000

*Rounding error adjusted.

An easier approach to calculating equivalent units in the "average" unit cost calculation, which obtains the same results, is available. It was not used above since the mode of calculation tends to obscure the fact that an average is being calculated. Note the same equivalent unit total as shown below:

	Materials	Conversion
Transfer to finished goods	135,000	135,000
Ending inventory (20,000 units):		
Materials—100% complete	20,000	
Conversion—40% complete		8,000
Equivalent units	155,000	143,000

Process Cost Calculations in a Multiprocess Operation. In a multiprocess operation, process cost calculations are essentially the same as in a single-process operation. However, since more data and facts are involved, it is usually necessary to prepare more orderly schedules of data in order to facilitate understanding by report recipients. Two basic schedules are recommended, namely, (1) Production Quantity and Cost Report and (2) Equivalent Unit and Unit Cost Report. These reports are illustrated below, as Exhibits 4 and 5. "Average cost" flow is assumed.

EXHIBIT 4   Production Quantity and Cost Report, February 19—

	Process I	Process II
Quantity to account for:		
Beginning inventory units.................	1,000	2,000
Units started (or transferred in) this period	12,000	10,000
Total............................	13,000	12,000
Quantity accounted for as follows:		
Units completed and transferred out	10,000	11,000
Ending inventory units....................	3,000	1,000
Units lost	0	0
Units spoiled.............................	0	0
Total............................	13,000	12,000
Costs to account for:		
Beginning inventory:		
Transfers in...........................	$ 0	$ 6,100
Direct materials	1,100	1,200
Conversion...........................	390	700
Costs added this month:		
Transfers in...........................	0	30,067
Direct materials......................	12,000	11,000
Conversion......................	21,600	10,000
Total............................	$35,090	$59,067
Costs accounted for as follows:		
Units completed and transferred out.........	$30,067*	$55,058*
Ending inventory:		
Transfers in (1000 × 2.614)...................	0	3,014
Direct materials (3000 × 1.008) (500 × 1.061)..	3,024	530
Conversion (1000 × 1.999) (500 × .930)........	1,999	465
Units lost......	0	0
Units spoiled...........................	0	0
Total............................	$35,090	$59,067

*Rounding error adjusted.

EXHIBIT 5   Equivalent Unit and Unit Cost Report, February 19—

	Process I		Process II		
	Material	Conversion	Transfers in	Material	Conversion
Equivalent units:					
Transfers out........	10,000	10,000	11,000	11,000	11,000
Ending inventory....	3,000	1,000(⅓)	1,000	500(½)	500(½)
Total............	13,000	11,000	12,000	11,500	11,500
Unit costs:					
Beginning inventory costs.............	$ 1,100	$ 390	$ 6,100	$ 1,200	$ 700
Current month costs..	12,000	21,600	30,067*	11,000	10,000
Total costs........	$13,100	$21,990	$36,167	$12,200	$10,700
Equivalent units.....	13,000	11,000	12,000	11,500	11,500
Unit cost..........	$ 1.008	$ 1.999	$ 3.014	$ 1.061	$ 0.930
Total unit cost.....		$3.007*			$5.005

*Rounding error, total unit cost = $3.0067, so 10,000 units transferred to Process II = $30,067.

A review of these reports should point out the following:

1. In a multiprocess industry, transfers from one process to another must be explicitly considered; they are actually a form of direct material added to a process.

2. Both physical units and dollars should be accounted for as illustrated in Exhibit 4.

3. Materials can be added 100 percent at the beginning in one process and in some other fashion in a subsequent process, e.g., uniformly during processing, as in this illustration.

4. Units lost (e.g., shrinkage) or spoiled can be introduced into the calculations if either or both arise.

It is possible to consider the fixed factory overhead portion of conversion costs as a separate factor in order to maintain a distinction in the accounts between variable and fixed costs. To accomplish this, all that is necessary is a separation of conversion costs into fixed and variable columns as shown in Exhibit 5. Such a separation would also be necessary for the fixed and variable portions of costs transferred into a process. In order to keep the illustration somewhat simplified, these factors were not included in this illustration. To include the separation of fixed and variable costs would not change the basic features of Exhibits 4 and 5; all that would be necessary is the addition of more columns and unit cost calculations in Exhibit 5.

Process Costs—Summary.   The preceding discussion should make it clear that the main difference between job order costing and process costing is the difference between keeping track of costs in terms of processes versus keeping track of costs in terms of jobs. Under process costing the individual process is the center of attention. The unit costs by cost category as well as the total unit cost for each process are necessary for external reporting purposes. Cost of goods sold and inventory values in external reports flow directly from such unit cost calculations. The same is true of the basic journal entries underlying the calculation of cost of goods sold and inventory values.

The internal management need for useful information is also facilitated by process costing. Performance measurement and control of processes are greatly facilitated by comparison of actual and expected unit costs. Determination of sales prices and product profitability is also related to such unit cost figures.

Treatment of Spoiled and Lost Units. The accounting treatment of spoiled or lost units under actual cost systems is conceptually easy to follow. All one has to do is decide upon the answer to one question: To what extent, if any, are the costs of spoiled or lost units to be borne by the good units produced?

This question has three possible answers:

1. Such costs *are not* to be borne by the good units produced; they are to be considered losses in the income statement for the period they are incurred.

2. Such costs *are* to be borne by the good units produced.

3. Such costs *are* to be borne by the good units produced but only to the extent of normal (expected) rates of spoiled or lost units; costs applicable to abnormal (unexpected) rates of spoiled or lost units are to be considered losses in the income statement for the period they are incurred.

Upon reflection, almost everyone would tend to accept the third answer given, since in any production setting (job order or process) some spoilage is to be expected and the costs of this expected spoilage should be built into the unit costs of good units produced since part of the costs necessary to obtain good units relate to incurring the expected spoilage costs. What is said here of spoilage also fits the case of lost units (e.g., normal versus abnormal shrinkage), although lost units would seem to relate more to process costing than to job order costing.

In order to see how each of the three possible answers to the above question might be quantified, the data relative to job no. 954 in Exhibit 3 is reproduced below:

```
Total cost ......................... $10,434.78
Good units produced ...............   30,000
Spoiled units .....................      400
Assumed normal spoilage—
  1% of good units (300 units)
```

Note the differences in the treatment of this data under each of the three answers to our basic question.

Answer 1—Spoilage Costs Are 100% Loss:

$$\text{Unit cost per 1,000} = \frac{\text{total costs}}{\text{good units} + \text{spoiled units}}$$
$$= \frac{10,434.78}{30.4} = \$343.25$$

$$\begin{aligned}
\text{Spoilage loss} &= \text{spoiled units} \times \text{unit cost} \\
&= \quad\; 0.4 \quad\;\; + \;343.25 = \$137.30 \\
\text{Job cost} &= \text{good units} \times \text{unit cost} \\
&= \quad\; 30 \quad\;\; \times \;343.25 = \$10,297.48* \\
\text{Total cost} &= \text{spoilage loss} + \text{job cost} \\
&= \quad 137.30 \quad + \;10,297.48 = \$10,434.78
\end{aligned}$$

Answer 2—Spoilage Costs Are 100% Job Costs:

$$\text{Unit cost per 1,000} = \frac{\text{total costs}}{\text{good units}} = \frac{10,434.78}{30} = \$347.83$$

$$\begin{aligned}
\text{Spoilage loss} &= \quad\; 0 \\
\text{Job cost} &= \text{good units} \times \text{unit cost} \\
&= \quad\; 30 \quad\; \times \;347.83 = \$10,434.78* \\
\text{Total cost} &= \text{spoilage loss} + \text{job cost} \\
&= \quad\;\; 0 \qquad\; + \;10,434.78 = \$10,434.78
\end{aligned}$$

Answer 3—Spoilage Costs Are Job Costs to Extent of Normal Spoilage:

$$\text{Unit cost per } 1{,}000 = \frac{\text{total costs}}{\text{good units} + \text{abnormal spoilage}} = \frac{10{,}434.78}{30.1} = \$346.67$$

Spoilage loss = abnormal spoilage × unit cost
.1 × 346.67 = $34.67

Job cost = good units × unit cost
30 × 346.67 − 10,400.11*

Total cost = spoilage loss + job cost
34.67 + 10,400.11 = $10,434.78

*Adjusted for rounding error.

As can be seen by analysis of the above figures, the approach to handling spoilage depends upon the calculation of unit costs. The extent to which spoilage costs are to be treated as a loss is directly related to the amount of spoiled units included in the unit cost calculation. Conversely, the extent to which spoilage costs are to be treated as a cost of good units is directly related to the amount of spoiled units excluded from the unit cost calculation.

Under process costing the approach to handling spoiled units is the same as that shown for job order costing. However, to be more precise in this case, one must refer to the extent that lost or spoiled units are included in the equivalent unit calculation, which ultimately is reflected in the unit cost calculation.

Several special problems arise in connection with spoilage calculations. The two most prominent of these are related to the following implicit assumptions in the previous analyses:

1. Spoilage is not detected or detectable until units are complete.
2. Spoiled units have no value.

When spoilage is detected before completion, spoiled or lost units must be measured in terms of equivalent spoiled units, if the units are partially complete as to any process. When spoiled units have a value (scrap value) such value must be considered somewhere in the accounts. Such scrap value could be treated as miscellaneous income, a reduction of spoilage losses, a reduction (credit to) of costs, or a reduction of both spoilage losses and costs. The reduction of both spoilage losses and costs is probably the most defensible method of handling scrap values. As for the method of allocating such scrap values between spoilage losses and costs, it is likely that most would find it acceptable to use the proportions of normal and abnormal spoilage to make the allocation. The final theoretical issue is which costs (e.g., direct material, direct labor, or factory overhead) should be reduced by the amount of scrap value of spoiled units assigned to costs? This issue may have no satisfactory or nonarbitrary answer within the framework of an actual cost system, even though factory overhead is the cost usually selected. A standard cost type of system under which standard rates of spoilage and standard or expected salvage values are both considered probably provides the only theoretically defensible method of handling this issue.

Joint and By-products. Joint products arise in those cases where *two or more distinct products inevitably emerge* from a single raw material. Examples of joint products are the various cuts of meat derived in the meat-packaging industry from a head of beef and the various grades of fuel oil and gasoline derived in the petroleum-refining industry from a barrel of crude oil.

In most instances, joint products are subclassified according to the economic value of each joint product. Joint products of lesser value are called by-products, whereas those of greater value retain the title joint product (sometimes prime or coproduct). Thus, the only real difference between by-products and joint products is in relative values. For example, in the meat-packing industry the various cuts of meat from one head of beef may be considered joint products, whereas the hides, fats, and intestines may be considered by-products. Another somewhat different example would be the classification of a single product into perfects (the joint product), seconds, and even thirds depending upon the nature and extent of defects or various quality grades as in food processing industries.

Basic Issue in By-product and Joint Product Costing. Since by-products and joint products are produced simultaneously, there arises the problem of determining how much cost is applicable to each product. In the meat-packing industry, one knows how much a head of beef costs, but difficulties arise when one tries to determine how much of that cost applies to the various cuts of meat as well as the hides, the fats, and the intestines. The same difficulties arise in petroleum refining, dairying, and many other industries where all one knows for sure is the cost of a barrel of crude oil or the cost per hundredweight paid to a dairy farmer for fresh milk. Thus the issue in by-product and joint product costing is the allocation of costs to the many products which can be derived from a basic raw material.

The issue is more readily identified when one considers the purpose of allocating costs to individual joint products. For the purpose of deciding whether or not to produce certain joint products in fixed or varying combinations, there is no need to allocate costs to joint products. The decision to make and sell various joint products depends solely upon the total revenue and the total unallocated costs necessary to process the various possible combinations of joint products.[4]

For what purpose, then, are costs to be allocated to joint products? The purpose is tied directly to inventory valuation. Current practice dictates the general rule that inventories must be valued at cost, which then necessitates the allocation of costs to joint products; without such an allocation, inventories of each individual variety of joint product could not be valued at cost.

Solving the Basic Issue. A truly satisfying solution to the inventory valuation problem via an allocation of costs to joint products is not available. The reason for this is that there is no nonarbitrary method of allocating costs to joint and by-products. If the reader does not think this is true, consider how much of the cost of 100 pounds of raw milk is applicable to each and every one of the many products which can be derived from 100 pounds of raw milk. One will soon come to the realization that the only objective knowledge obtainable is a knowledge of the cost of the raw milk and a knowledge of the types and quantities of products which can be derived from it.

The methods (arbitrary as they inherently are) which are used to allocate costs to joint products involve first the distinction between joint and by-products and second the allocation of costs to joint products on a sales value or physical quantity basis.

Valuation of By-products. Since by-products are considered to be of lesser value and ancillary to the main goals of producing and selling joint products, the joint products are the focal point of allocating costs. Thus, one of two approaches is adopted in the case of by-products:

1. No cost is allocated to the by-products and any sales revenue received from them is credited to miscellaneous income.

2. Cost is allocated to the by-products in an amount equal to their net sales value or their net value as a substitute material.

Case 1 above essentially refers to situations where the value of by-products is immaterial. In a sense by-products of immaterial value could be considered waste

---

[4]For an elaboration of this point see Keller and Ferrara, *op. cit.*, pp. 588–591, and R. L. Weil, "Allocating Joint Costs," *The American Economic Review*, vol. 68, pp. 1342–1345, December 1968.

or scrap. In case 2 the value of the by-products would be considered material even though their value is significantly less than the value of joint products.

Case 2 represents a situation where the accounts are "rigged" in order to produce either a "normal" profit or no profit on the sale or disposition of by-products. No profit seems reasonable if one follows the line of thinking that the joint products represent the main production and distribution goal, which means that by-products are an unavoidable side effect which should be neutralized. The zero profit approach to by-product valuation involves valuing the by-product at its sale or substitute value less estimated cost to dispose of the by-product via sale or via delivery to an internal using division.

The normal profit approach to by-product valuation attempts to recognize psychological (or behavioral) considerations which could be critical in terms of efficient and economical disposition of by-products. The psychological considerations come to the fore where the unit of a company which produces a by-product is not the unit of the company which uses or disposes of the by-product. To encourage use of the by-product as a substitute material, the using unit should be offered some incentive such as a charge for the by-product which is lower than the cost of the preferred material. To encourage the disposition of a by-product, the disposing unit should be offered some incentive such as a charge for the by-product which will enable them to make a profit on its disposition. The amount of normal profit to be recognized can only be set in an arbitrary fashion such as use of the firm's or unit's average actual or goal profit as a percentage of sales.

Valuation of Joint Products—General. The problem in allocating costs to the joint products is essentially a matter of reducing the total costs applicable to the sum of the joint and by-products by the value attributed to the by-products and then allocating this net cost to the joint products, using some variation of relative sales values or physical quantities. A simplified illustration of each of the two basic methods of allocating this net cost to joint products should make these basic approaches clear.

Valuation of Joint Products—Based on Physical Quantities. A basic raw material costs $100 per hundredweight. Cost of processing the raw material is $80, and the processing results in products X, Y, and Z in the quantities and values shown below:

Product	Weight, lb	Sales price per lb	Sales value
X	50	$3.00	$150.00
Y	30	5.00	150.00
Z	20	0.60	12.00
	100		$312.00

Products X and Y are the joint products while product Z is the by-product. Normal costs of disposing of product Z are $0.14 per unit and normal profit as a percentage of sales is 10 percent ($0.06 per unit). The value attributable to the 20 pounds of by-product Z is:

Net sales value of Z = sales value of Z − (disposal costs + normal profit)
8.00 = 12.00 − (2.80 + 1.20)

Total costs attributable to the joint products (X and Y) are the cost per hundredweight of raw material ($100) plus the processing costs ($80) minus the net sales value of Z ($8), or $100 + $80 − $8 = $172. It is this $172 that is allocable to the joint products X and Y. The physical quantity basis of allocating these costs simply states that each joint product should bear cost in proportion to its weight, which in this case means that each unit of X and Y will be assigned the same unit cost per pound as follows:

$$\text{Cost per lb of X or Y} = \frac{\text{joint cost attributable to X and Y}}{\text{weight of X and Y}}$$
$$= \frac{\$172}{80 \text{ lb}}$$
$$= \$2.15 \text{ per lb}$$

The cost of $2.15 per pound of either X or Y is what is used to derive inventory values and cost of goods sold data for products X and Y.

Valuation of Joint Products—Based on Sales Values.   The costs attributable to joint products X and Y are the same as above, i.e., $172. The method of allocating them is quite different since it is based on sales values so as to produce an equal gross profit percentage for each of the joint products. Basically the method involves expressing total costs applicable to joint products as a percentage of the sales value of joint products and then multiplying each product's selling price by this percentage in order to derive the product's unit cost. The calculations are as follows:

$$\text{Cost as a percentage of sales value} = \frac{\text{cost applicable to X and Y}}{\text{sales value of X and Y}}$$
$$= \frac{\$172}{\$300}$$
$$= 57.3\%$$
$$\text{Unit cost of X} = \text{selling price of X (57.3\%)}$$
$$= \$1.719$$
$$\text{Unit cost of Y} = \text{selling price of Y (57.3\%)}$$
$$= \$2.865$$

Physical Quantities Versus Sales Values.   A useful summarization of the above methods is as follows:

	Allocation based on physical quantity		Allocation based on sales value	
	X	Y	X	Y
Sales price	$3.00	$5.00	$3.00	$5.00
Allocated unit cost	2.15	2.15	1.71	2.87
Gross profit	$0.85	$2.85	$1.28	$2.13
Gross profit percentage	28.3%	57.0%	42.6%	42.6%

The basic philosophy of the physical quantity method is to produce unit costs which are equal, while the basic philosophy of the sales value method is to produce an equality of gross profit percentages. Either the sales value method shown above or variations of it[5] are considered preferable since they do not penalize any product's profit potential; i.e., the equality of gross margin percentage tends to

[5]One variation would be to have equal gross profit amounts per unit while another variation would be to utilize equal gross margin amounts or percentages after recognition of marketing costs specifically identifiable with each product.

provide equal motivation to sell each of the joint products.[6] This neutrality of profit potential is another instance where behavioral considerations play a significant role in accounting.

Valuation of Joint Products—Processing After Separation. If any of the joint products are processed after they are separated from one another, two problems arise when using the sales value method of allocating joint costs:

1. Which sales values are to be used—sales values at point of separation or sales values after further processing?

2. What is to be done if there is no sales value for a joint product at the point of separation?

Since the costs to be allocated to the joint products are the costs incurred before separation, it is usually considered appropriate to use sales values at the point of separation to allocate the joint costs. Thus in the preceding illustration, if product X could be sold at separation for $3 per pound or could be sold for $4 per pound after further processing at a cost of $0.76 per pound, the $3 per pound sale value at separation would be used to make the allocation of joint costs. Use of the $3 sale value would result in the same calculations shown earlier.

If no sales value exists at separation, the sale value after further processing is used. Thus, using the earlier illustrative data and the fact that product X has no sales value at separation but can be sold for $4 per pound after further processing at a cost of $0.76 per pound, the following calculations result:

Sales Value of Joint Products

Product	Weight, lb	Sales price per lb	Sale value
X	50	$4.00	$200.00
Y	30	5.00	150.00
Total			$350.00

Total Cost of Joint Products:

Costs to separation point less value assigned to
  by-product Z $172.00
Costs after separation: $0.76 per lb of X 38.00
    Total $210.00

Cost as a Percentage of Sales Value:

$$\frac{\text{Cost}}{\text{Sales value}} = \frac{210.00}{350.00} = 60.0\%$$

Unit Costs:

X = selling price × (60.0)
  =   4.00   × (60.0)
  =   2.40
Y = selling price × (60.0)
         5.00   × (60.0)
  =   3.00

These unit cost calculations represent allocations of the total costs before and after separation. They are designed to yield an equal gross profit margin (40.0 (= 1.00 − .60) percent) on the ultimate sale value of the joint products. In order to determine how much of the costs before separation pertain to each product, one need only deduct the unit costs after separation from the total unit costs already calculated, as shown below:

[6]Another feature favoring the sales value method is that the physical quantity method can yield unit costs greater than selling prices.

Product	Total unit cost	Unit cost after separation	Unit cost at separation
X	$2.40	$0.76	$1.64
Y	3.00	0	3.00

These calculations can be verified by multiplying unit costs at separation and quantities of each product at separation in order to see if the total costs to separation point ($172) are accounted for. Thus:

Product	Weight, lb	Unit cost at separation	Total costs to separation
X	50	1.64	$82.00
Y	30	3.00	90.00
			$172.00

DIRECT COSTING

The subject of direct costing has received much attention and discussion during the past few decades. One of the main problems in these discussions is that usually the discussants do not specify their definition of direct costing. In order to avoid this difficulty it would be appropriate to recall the words of Waldo W. Neikirk,[7] one of the early contributors to the direct costing literature:

> Direct costing should be defined as a segregation of manufacturing costs between those which are fixed and those which vary directly with volume. Only the prime costs plus variable factory overhead costs are used to value inventory and cost of sales. The remaining factory expenses are charged off currently to profit and loss. However, the point to be emphasized is that direct costing is primarily a segregation of expenses and only secondarily a method of inventory valuation.

The essentials of the above definition are three:
1. The segregation of costs refers only to manufacturing costs.
2. Only variable manufacturing costs are inventoried.
3. The inventory valuation aspects of direct costing are secondary.

Over time, certain features of Neikirk's definition have been modified. It is these modifications and the supposed secondary position of inventory valuation which are discussed below.

Cost Segregation and Direct Costing. Two essential modifications of the cost segregation features of Neikirk's definition have been adopted over the years. These are:

1. All costs are considered, i.e., manufacturing, marketing, and administration.
2. A segregation of all costs into fixed and variable categories as well as a segregation of fixed costs into those which are traceable to an enterprise segment as opposed to those which are common (joint) to more than one enterprise segment are also recommended.

The reasons for the adoption of these two modifications are to provide for the essentials of cost-volume-profit analysis and contribution reporting in the regular recurring profitability reports of enterprise segments.[8] An illustration of this for a product line is as follows:

[7]Waldo W. Neikirk, "How Direct Costing Can Work for Management," *NAA Bulletin,* p. 525, January 1951.
[8]For example, see Robert Beyer and Donald J. Trawicki, *Profitability Accounting,* 2nd ed., The Ronald Press Company, New York, 1972, chap. 2 and 7.

Product Line Contribution Statement

	Amount	%
Sales............................	$300,000	100
Variable costs:		
Production...................	$ 81,000	
Packaging...................	69,000	
Marketing...................	21,000	
Total variable..............	$171,000	57
Marginal contribution	$129,000	43
Traceable fixed costs:		
Production...................	$ 13,500	
Packaging...................	10,000	
Marketing...................	18,000	
Total traceable fixed.........	$ 41,500	14
Segment contribution............	$ 87,500	29

Cost-volume-profit analysis is built into the contribution statement by the segregation of costs but more importantly by the percentage column, which yields automatically the profit-volume (PV) ratio of 43 percent. This is the ratio which indicates the percentage of each sales dollar which is available to cover fixed costs and which contributes directly to profits after fixed costs are covered. It is also the percentage which is used to divide fixed costs in order to determine the break-even sales dollar volume. For instance, in this case, the break-even point relative to the fixed costs traceable to our product line is $41,500/.43, or $96,512.

The inclusion of two contribution figures in the above statement is necessitated by the fact that there is a desire to include all traceable costs in a segment report as well as a desire to include the PV ratio (marginal contribution percentage). The only way to provide for both is as shown above. In a certain sense, the justification for both is that the marginal contribution builds into the report useful short-run analytical data while the segment contribution leans toward providing useful long-run analytical data.

Exclusion of nontraceable or common fixed costs from the segment report is usually justified on the basis that the only way one might assign such costs to a segment is arbitrarily. An arbitrary assignment has no objective basis and as such it is quite difficult to support its inclusion in a segment report.[9]

Inventory Valuation and Direct Costing. The increased utility of enterprise segment profitability reports which include the direct costing philosophy cannot be denied. By way of comparison to this added utility, the inventory valuation issue does seem less important, although many would take exception to such a position.

The basics of the inventory valuation issue are theoretically related to the distinction between fixed and variable manufacturing costs. Definitions for each of these are as follows:

Fixed Costs. Costs which will not vary in total with the number of units produced, within given volume ranges.

Variable Costs. Costs which will vary in total with the number of units produced.

These definitions seem almost harmless from an inventory valuation standpoint until one makes a slight and reasonable change in the words used in the definitions:

[9]Exclusion of nontraceable costs from segment reports is not universally accepted. See Beyer and Trawicki, *op. cit.,* pp. 156–165.

Fixed Costs. Costs of getting ready to produce or the costs of providing the capacity necessary to produce.

Variable Costs. Costs of actually producing units. These are the costs which are incurred only when there is production.

Upon the preceding distinctions rests the basic argument for direct-costing inventory valuation. The fixed costs are not considered costs of production; they are considered costs of getting ready to produce. Furthermore, these fixed costs are considered to be costs of the period in which they are recognized since they are incurred for the purpose of providing ability to produce within a specific period of time. In essence, they are considered costs of time periods (period costs) and thus completely chargeable to the income statement of the period of time during which they were incurred.

On the other hand, variable costs are not related to time periods; they are related to products. Thus, the variable costs are often referred to as product costs as opposed to period costs (fixed costs). The variable costs are incurred only when actual production takes place, and a convincing case can be made for the view that only variable costs should be included in inventory since they are the only costs which are truly necessary to produce an inventory (assuming that the human and physical facilities provided by fixed costs are present).

From the above comments one can readily appreciate the fact that the direct-costing inventory valuation controversy revolves around the idea that the only costs which must be incurred to build up an inventory are the variable costs. The fixed costs will be incurred with or without the inventory buildup. The ultimate conclusion of this is that variable costs are the only costs to be considered in inventory values.

The alternative to the direct-costing inventory valuation concept is the so-called absorption-costing view, which embraces the idea that at least some fixed costs should be included in inventory valuation. The basis for the inclusion is related to the matching concept of accounting, which in essence involves suspending costs in the balance sheet until they can be matched against the revenue they produce. Absorption costers feel that no product as well as no inventory could be produced without the incurrence of fixed costs and as such fixed costs should be considered as part of the total costs to produce output. They further feel that if fixed costs are a part of the costs to produce output they should be included in inventory values. The real problem for the absorption costers is a determination of how to assign fixed manufacturing costs to individual units of output. On this point there is no unanimity of opinion.[10]

An important aspect of this inventory valuation problem is the position of the American Institute of Certified Public Accountants. In *Revision and Restatement of Accounting Research Bulletins (ARB No. 43)* the following comment appears,[11] "It should also be recognized that the exclusion of all overheads from inventory costs does not constitute an accepted accounting procedure." This comment was interpreted by some to include the possible acceptability of direct-costing inventory valuation since direct-costing inventory valuation includes some overhead (variable). In order to clarify this erroneous impression, Maurice Moonitz wrote a letter which appeared in the *NAA Bulletin* in 1961,[12] in which he tried to clarify the situation with the following words:

Although the committee did not express its opposition to the use of direct costing in

[10]For some added commentary and discussion on these issues see Keller and Ferrara, *op. cit.,* pp. 689–705, and chap. 16, "Inventories," in this handbook.

[11]*Accounting Research and Terminology Bulletins,* final ed., AICPA, New York, 1961, p. 29.

[12]"Direct Costing and Public Reporting," *NAA Bulletin,* October 1961, pp. 45–46. Moonitz was Director of Accounting Research of the AICPA at the time.

the external financial reports in so many words, there is no doubt that it did react unfavorably to such a procedure.

In my opinion, nothing in the accounting research bulletins issued by the Committee on Accounting Procedure can or should be used to support the use of direct costing in published financial statements.

Thus an authoritative pronouncement by the AICPA is in opposition to the direct-costing inventory valuation philosophy. However, Wilmer Wright, one of the most eloquent proponents of the direct costing philosophy, has pointed out two very interesting aspects of this argument:[13]

1. The Institute of Chartered Accountants in England and Wales has suggested in *Recommendation 22* that direct costing inventory valuation may be appropriate in any situation where levels of inventory fluctuate widely.

2. A survey by his firm indicated that of all U.S. companies using direct costing for internal management reporting, 40 percent were also using direct costing for their external reporting. Not one indicated a qualification in the certification by their certified public accountants. Each case had been appraised on the basis of consistency and materiality.

A more recent survey (1972) yields results similar to Wright's.[14] However, one may not be able to count on obtaining similar results in future surveys if some recent actions have impacts beyond their intended purposes. For example, in 1973 the Internal Revenue Service specifically identified direct costing as an unacceptable method of inventory valuation for tax purposes.[15]

Direct Costing—Illustrative Problem. To summarize the discussion of direct costing and to illustrate the differences between direct costing and absorption costing in income reporting, the following illustrative problem is presented.

Basic Data:

Sales	200,000 units	@ $15
Production	220,000 units	
Normal volume	220,000 units*	
Beginning inventory	none	
Ending inventory	20,000 units	
Direct materials	$240,000	
Direct labor	310,000	
Variable factory overhead	330,000	
Fixed factory overhead	440,000	
Variable selling & administrative costs	250,000	
Fixed selling & administrative costs	400,000	

Direct-Costing Income Statement:

Sales		$3,000,000
Variable costs:		
Manufacturing (200,000 units @ $4)	$800,000	
Selling & administrative	250,000	1,050,000
Marginal contribution		$1,950,000
Fixed costs:		
Manufacturing	$440,000	
Selling & administrative	400,000	840,000
Net income		$1,110,000
Direct-costing inventory value 20,000 units @ $4†		$ 80,000

---

[13]*Modern Accounting Theory,* Morton Backer, ed., Prentice-Hall, Englewood Cliffs, N.J., 1966, pp. 431–433.

[14]Stephen Landekich, "Cost Allocations to Inventory," *Management Accounting,* March 1973, pp. 51 and 72.

[15]Internal Revenue Service Regulation §1.471–11, September 1973.

Absorption Costing Income Statement:

Sales...	$3,000,000
Cost of goods sold (200,000 units @ $6).........................	1,200,000
Gross profit on sales..................................	1,800,000
Selling & administrative costs............................	650,000
Net income...	$1,150,000
Absorption costing inventory value 20,000 units @ $6‡.........	$ 120,000

---

* Normal volume and actual production are assumed to be equal, which eliminates the possibility of a volume variance.
† Variable manufacturing cost per unit
‡ Total manufacturing cost per unit.

As is evident from this illustration, there are two differences between a direct-costing and an absorption costing income statement:

1. Only the direct-costing income statement includes the segregation of costs into fixed and variable categories.

2. The difference in the net incomes reported ($40,000) is accounted for by the difference in the inventory values.

An often recommended approach to reconciling the direct-costing controversy is to prepare a statement which includes the fixed-variable segregation and also adjusts the final income figure to an absorption costing basis, as shown in the following statement.

Combined Direct Costing—Absorption Costing Income Statement:

Sales..		$3,000,000
Variable costs:		
Manufacturing......................	$800,000	
Selling & administration..............	250,000	1,050,000
Marginal contribution...........................		$1,950,000
Fixed costs:		
Manufacturing......................	$440,000	
Selling & administration..............	400,000	840,000
Net income before inventory adjustment...........		$1,110,000
Add: Fixed costs included in inventory		40,000
Net income......................................		$1,150,000

The final statement assumes the validity of Neikirk's earlier comment relative to the primary importance of segregating costs into fixed and variable components and the secondary importance of the inventory valuation issue.[16]

BIBLIOGRAPHY

Anton, Hector R., and Peter A. Firmin: *Contemporary Issues in Cost Accounting*, 2nd ed., Houghton Mifflin Company, Boston, 1972.

Beyer, Robert, and Donald J. Trawicki: *Profitability Accounting*, 2nd ed., The Ronald Press Company, New York, 1972.

Davidson, Sidney, James S. Schindler, and Roman L. Weil: *Fundamentals of Accounting*, 5th ed., The Dryden Press, Hinsdale, Ill., chap. 20.

[16]Walter B. McFarland has provided an interesting approach to including these basic ideas in an income statement for the firm as a whole. See *Concepts for Management Accounting*, NAA, New York, 1966, pp. 133–165.

Dopuch, Nicholas, Jacob G. Birnberg, and Joel Demski: *Cost Accounting*, 2nd ed., Harcourt Brace Jovanich, New York, 1974.

Horngren, Charles T.: *Cost Accounting: A Managerial Emphasis*, 3rd ed., Prentice-Hall, Englewood Cliffs, N.J., 1972.

Kaplan, Robert S.: "Variable and Self-Service Costs in Reciprocal Allocation Models," *The Accounting Review*, 48, pp. 738–748, October 1973.

Keller, I. Wayne, and William L. Ferrara: *Managerial Accounting for Profit Control*, 2nd ed., McGraw-Hill Book Company, New York, 1967.

McFarland, Walter B.: *Concepts for Management Accounting*, NAA, New York, 1966.

Matz, Adolf, and Othel J. Curry: *Cost Accounting*, 5th ed., South-Western Publishing Company, Cincinnati, 1972.

Moore, Carl L., and Robert K. Jaedicke: *Managerial Accounting*, 3rd ed., South-Western Publishing Company, Cincinnati, 1972.

Shillinglaw, Gordon: *Cost Accounting: Analysis and Control*, 3rd ed., Richard D. Irwin, Homewood, Ill., 1972.

Thomas, William E. (Ed.): *Readings in Cost Accounting, Budgeting, and Control*, 4th ed., South-Western Publishing Company, Cincinnati, Ohio, 1973.

Weil, R. L.: "Allocating Joint Costs," *The American Economic Review*, 68, pp. 1342–1345, December 1968.

Chapter **42**

Standard Costs

LAWRENCE J. BENNINGER
Professor of Accounting, University of Florida

INTRODUCTION

Standard costs came into prominence in the Great Depression of the 1930s as a means of reducing costs and increasing efficiency. They may be generally defined as objective, predetermined costs to be used as a basis of comparison with the actual costs. Standard costs may be thought of as an extension of the predetermined overhead rate idea used rather early in the development of overhead accounting. In a very real sense, just as predetermined overhead costs represent the substitution of estimated overhead for actual, standard manufacturing costs substitute a system of statistical representations for all of the actual costs. Standard costs are applicable to the operating costs of most businesses and governmental institutions.

Uses of Standard Costs. Standard costs were initially developed as a means of reducing or minimizing cost. As standard cost systems evolved, other objectives were sought in their utilization, for instance, as an aid to product pricing and convenience in accounting for inventories. Some of the more commonly stated uses of standard costs are contained in the following list.

Standard costs provide data useful:

1. For control over cost
2. In the costing of inventories
3. For ascertaining interim and annual profits
4. In planning and budgeting
5. In the study of alternatives
6. In the pricing of present or prospective products.

Standard costing, therefore, can aid management in achieving its objectives. Little wonder, then, that its popularity has continued unabated over the years. Because standard costing gives essentially a statistical representation of an organization's costs, its use and further development tie in nicely with increasing emphasis given to the computer and allied mathematical and statistical techniques.

Basic Terminology. The comparison of the actual and standard costs of an organization, especially by detailed operations, represents a basic objective of a standard cost system. Consequently, where possible, costs are activity-oriented; that is, costs are measured and related to specific operations and responsibility units of an organization. Because standard cost accounting for manufacturing represents the most highly developed area of standard costing, terminology discussions throughout most of this chapter will be expressed in terms of production problems. However, a section on standard marketing costs is included.

Standard Hour (Standard Labor Hour). Were the production facilities of a manufacturing organization devoted to the manufacture of a single product, all manufacturing costs, both on a standard and actual basis, could easily be established by unit of product. The objective of comparing actual with standard costs is more complex in a multiproduct firm. There, in order to compare the actual and standard costs of operations and cost centers, some unit to be used as a common denominator of production must be established. Because time is needed to effect all production, time allowed is a common way of expressing the achievement of diverse production. Standard time is expressed in terms of machine or labor time, depending upon which is the more suitable expression for a particular operation. A standard hour is defined, therefore, as that output which should be produced in a particular operation in one clock hour. Throughout the remainder of this chapter, for convenience, direct labor hours allowed will be employed to express standard production.

Operation. Although the word "operation" may be used in a general way simply to express activity, in standard cost accounting it has a technical connotation. An operation refers to the lowest practical subdivision of manufacturing activity. By "practical" is meant that significant costs are capable of being traced to the defined activity, and control efforts of management are aided by a comparison of actual and standard costs at this level. Examples of operations are the utilization of a drill press, a lathe, or a stamping machine, and the assembly of component parts prior to further processing.

Cost Center. Because the word "department" has been used ambiguously to refer to areas of analytical interest as well as to areas of responsibility of varying scope, the more restricted term "cost center" has come into favor in standard cost accounting. Cost center refers to an area of responsibility under the jurisdiction of an individual at the lowest level of management organization. A cost center, therefore, does not necessarily refer to a stipulated amount of space to be occupied or the accomplishment of some distinct and unified function. Space occupied by different cost centers may in fact vary widely, and operations under the command of a particular supervisor may be diverse and not capable of logical classification under some general heading. To determine the scope of a cost center, reference must be made to an organization chart wherein top management has decided (hopefully with the advice of lower levels of management) which specific operations shall be the responsibility of a particular supervisor.

Factory cost centers are subclassified into two types of centers. A production cost center may be defined as a cost center that gives rise to standard hours. A service cost center is defined as a center that expedites the work of production cost centers and that does not earn standard hours.

BASIC CONDITIONS ESSENTIAL TO THE OPERATION OF A STANDARD COST SYSTEM

Before discussing the operation of a standard cost system, some conditions essential to its successful operation must be mentioned. These basic conditions are:

1. Operations for which standard costs are derived are standardized.
2. A system of responsibility accounting is in effect.
3. Good budgeting is practiced.
4. A carefully conceived communication and reporting system is operational.
5. There exists a group of qualified personnel with continuing responsibility for the establishment and revision of standards.

Variations in these conditions may take place when weaknesses are counterbalanced by added strengths.

Standardization of Operations.   The first condition assumes an efficient plant layout permitting the efficient movement of production through the plant. It assumes that operations will be specialized and that, where possible, duplication of effort will be avoided. Standard operations will in turn call for the use of standard designs, materials, and supplies.

Responsibility Accounting.   Where standard costing is utilized for control purposes, as it commonly is, there must exist a defined delegation of responsibility. Specific operations will be placed under the jurisdiction of cost center supervisors. Overlapping of responsibility will be avoided. Cost center supervisors will report to stipulated managers who in turn will be responsible to another level of management. Accounts will accumulate costs so as to portray them by level of management.

Budgeting and Standard Costing.   Budgeting and standard costing have reciprocal relationships in that each depends upon the other for its effective operation. To achieve good standard costing, a comprehensive master budget is prepared periodically. Such a budget will provide data concerning normal volume and specific products to be produced and sold. It will provide information concerning prospective factor prices. Standard costing will, in turn, supply data concerning material and labor usage as well as variable cost rates of indirect costs that are essential in the preparation of the manufacturing budget.

Communication and Reporting System.   For the successful operation of a standard cost system, the existence of a well-developed communication and reporting system is essential. Management at all levels must take part in formulations affecting their areas of responsibility and reporting. A system of periodic reports must be developed which will portray and summarize favorable and unfavorable operations of cost centers and other areas of responsibility. Reports should be constructed so as to pinpoint problem areas and lead to the taking of corrective steps. Reports will bring out significant variances on an hourly, daily, weekly, or monthly basis, as warranted.

Standards Group or Committee.   The establishment of a standards group or committee is essential to the successful operation of a standard cost system. Standards cannot be constructed and then forgotten. Their successful use requires their constant scrutiny and periodic revision. Responsibility should be placed upon a standards group or committee to construct desired standards and to revise them periodically. Such a committee will include technical production staff as well as accounting personnel.

ACCOUNTING AND REPORTING FOR STANDARD COSTS

Standard Cost Accounts. Although actual costs may be kept in one set of accounts and standards maintained on a statistical basis, modern practice unites actual and standard costs in the same system of accounts to achieve maximum benefits from standard costing. A standard cost system will ultimately come to the point where it will show in one or more accounts:

Standard Cost Account	
Actual	Standard

The difference between the two sides of the account would be termed a "variance."

Flow of Costs. A more complete representation of accounts in a standard cost system stressing the flow of costs is shown in Exhibit 1.

EXHIBIT 1   Flow of Costs

Production Cost Center No. 100	
a. "actual"	c. standard
b. service cc	f. variance

Work in Process	
c. standard	d. standard

Production Cost Center No. 200	
a. "actual"	c. standard
b. service cc	f. variance

Finished Goods	
d. standard	e. standard

Production Cost Center No. 300	
a. "actual"	c. standard
b. service cc	f. variance

Cost of Goods Sold	
e. standard	
f. variance	

Service Cost Center	
a. "actual"	b. standard
	f. variance

All centers, both production and service, are charged initially with costs having to do with their own productive effort (see *a* in Exhibit 1). Some of these costs are charged to the center on an actual basis—direct and indirect labor cost, for example. The word "actual" is in quotation marks in Exhibit 1 to indicate that some costs represent actual consumption billed the center at a standard price, for example, the withdrawal of an actual quantity of materials carried in stores at a standard price. Similarly, those centers receiving services from service cost centers are charged on an actual consumption basis billed at a standard price (*b* in Exhibit 1). As production cost centers individually complete their processing efforts, the Work in Process Summary account is charged at standard, and the applicable production cost center account is credited (*c*). When finally a document indicates that a product has received all necessary processing and has arrived at finished stores, the Work in Process Summary account is credited at standard and the Finished Goods control account is similarly charged. A sale will result in a standard debit to the Cost of Goods Sold account and a standard credit to the Finished Goods account. The common practice of transferring at least some variances to the Cost of Goods Sold account is illustrated by entry *f*.

Coding and Identification of Costs. Charges to cost center accounts may be detailed by expense item and where possible identified with individual operations. Thus through proper coding, detailed cost information is available in a well-developed, responsibility-oriented standard cost system.[1] The following steps are illustrative. First, data concerning natural expense classifications are made available:

2.0 Direct labor cost
3.1 Indirect labor—W
3.2 Indirect labor—X
3.3 Indirect labor—Y
4.1 Indirect materials—W
4.2 Indirect materials—X
4.3 Indirect materials—Y
6.0 Depreciation
8.0 Property taxes
9.0 Direct material

Second, expenses classified as variable are identified by operations as well as cost centers. Thus the digit in the "10's" position in Operation No. 110 and No. 120 refers to a specific operation conducted by Cost Center No. 100. Direct labor cost of Operation No. 110 is shown as 112. Third, where expenses are not identifiable by operations, they are identified simply by cost center; for example, direct material used in Cost Center No. 100 is coded as 109.

Proper classification and identification of accounts through some type of coding system permit the preparation of a cost center performance report as illustrated in Exhibit 2.

EXHIBIT 2   Production Cost Center Report

Production cost center No. 100
Total standard hours _____

Expense No. Items	Fixed costs		Operation 110 Standard hours ____		Operation 120 Standard hours ____		Totals	
	Act.	Stan.	Act.	Stan.	Act.	Stan.	Act.	Stan.
2.0 Direct labor cost........			x	x	x	x	x	x
3.1 Indirect labor—W.......			x	x	x	x	x	x
3.2 Indirect labor—X.......	x	x	x	x	x	x	x	x
3.3 Indirect labor—Y........	x	x	x	x	x	x	x	x
4.1 Indirect mat.—W			x	x	x	x	x	x
4.2 Indirect mat.—X			x	x	x	x	x	x
4.3 Indirect mat.—Y	x	x	x	x	x	x	x	x
6.0 Depreciation............	x	x					x	x
8.0 Property taxes..........	x	x					x	x
9.0 Direct material..........							x	x
Totals...............	x	x	x	x	x	x	x	x
Total variances........		x		x		x		x
	x	x	x	x	x	x	x	x

Production Cost Center Report.   Exhibit 2 is a basic standard cost report which provides for a number of comparisons of actual and standard costs: (1) for all

[1]Such a system is presented by Stanley B. Henrici, *Standard Costs for Manufacturing,* 3rd ed., McGraw-Hill Book Company, New York, 1960.

items of expense if desired; (2) for variable expense items identified with operations; and (3) for fixed costs items for the cost center as a whole. Variances are computed by item of expense, for total fixed costs of the center, and for variable costs of individual operations. The production cost center report is used as a basis for determining the efficiency of supervisors and guiding supervisors towards analyses that will improve their performances. Instead of including all the expenses of a cost center it may show only the variable or, alternatively, the controllable costs of a cost center. A report similar to the production cost center report is prepared for service centers.

Standard Product Cost Card.   Exhibit 3 summarizes the standard costs of producing a single product. There will be as many of these as there are standard products. The standard product cost card is the underlying document for all standard cost analysis, and it provides a basis for charging the Work in Process Summary, Finished Goods, and Cost of Goods Sold accounts as well as relieving the production cost center accounts of standard costs.

EXHIBIT 3   Standard Product Cost Card

Name of product_____   Product code No._____   Standard lot size_____

Material costs	Material code No.	Quantity allowed	Standard price	Totals	Per unit
Operation No.___					
No.___	_____	_____	_____	_____	
No.___	_____	_____	_____	_____	
Total materials cost per unit......................................					$

Variable cost of operations	Standard hours allowed	Cost per standard hour	Totals		
Operation No.___					
No.___	_____	_____	_____		
No.___	_____	_____	_____		
Total variable cost of operations per unit............................			_____		

Fixed cost of cost centers	Standard hours allowed	Cost per standard hour	Totals		
Cost Center No.___					
Cost Center No.___	_____	_____	_____		
Total fixed cost of cost centers per unit............................			_____		
Total standard cost per unit of product............................					$

CONCEPTS OF STANDARD

There are a number of concepts of standard in general use, with as many shades of variation in their application as there are standard cost systems. A general summary of these are:
1. Past performance standards
2. Basic or bogey standards
3. Currently attainable standards
4. Ideal standards assuming use of present facilities
5. Expected actual standards indicating performance anticipated under conditions of control
6. Normal or long-run standards
7. Superstandards.

Past Performance Standards. These standards do not necessarily emphasize the recent past. Their intent is simply to codify in standard form the organization's experience as regards material, labor, and facility usage. The standard price component of standard cost may be past-oriented, but it is more likely to represent present factor prices with the standard usage component reflecting past experience.

A number of reasons can be presented to support the use of past performance standards such as the following:
1. It is convenient to construct them. All the data are at hand. If change is not rapid, these standards may in fact best represent the present state of efficiency of men and facilities.
2. The standards provide an encouragement for improvement since if past efficiency is bettered, this will be favorably reflected in performance reports of cost centers.

The most significant adverse criticism which may be made of this type of standard is that a standard cost is typically established to ferret out inefficiencies and to challenge improvement. Ways of doing things in the past may include a multitude of gross inefficiencies. Consequently, an apparent improvement may take place with little change in the underlying situation. People may be rewarded for performance which as a matter of fact remains quite unsatisfactory.

Basic or Bogey Standards. These tend to be much like past-oriented standards except that in theory their use is extended indefinitely. One interpretation of these is that base-period efficiencies and prices become a type of bench mark, a 100 percent index figure for the factor in question. Subsequent changes in performance are expressed, therefore, so as to present indexes of efficiency showing performance as it deviates from above and below 100 percent. Although this type of standard may be employed in the accounts, it is more likely to be utilized on a statistical basis outside of the accounts. Basic standards have the same advantages and disadvantages of past performance standards. Because they are intended for use over an extended period of time, however, they are likely to become out of date and therefore lose much of their utility for control purposes.

Currently Attainable Standards. These standards involve as careful and objective a study as is feasible of materials to be utilized and work methods. An attempt is made to express in standards what can be attained by individuals and groups working at high levels of efficiency. A commonly expressed policy with this type of standard is: When in doubt, increase the tightness of the standard. Proponents of currently attainable standards argue that their use provides an incentive, a challenge to performance improvement. However, this assumption needs testing. It may be that low-level performance standards will better challenge some people. Because currently attainable standards tend to be set on the high side, reflecting potentialities of better workers on their better days, their employment tends to give to numerous unfavorable variances, sizable in dollar amount. As a consequence, management may find it difficult to decide which "inefficiency" to investigate.

Ideal Standards Assuming Use of Present Facilities. This concept assumes that the standard will be established so as to reflect what could be accomplished under the most favorable conditions. Standard labor time, for example, may be arrived at after time and motion study and subsequent reeducation of the efforts of the most skilled members of a working force. Even before the current interest in behavioral psychology on the part of accountants, this type of standard had been decried as unrealistic and self-defeating. Obviously, its use would tend to give rise to substantial variances; instead of representing the exceptional to be investigated, variances would become common, and much of the control by comparison use of standard costing would be lost.

Expected Actual Standards Under Conditions of Control. This type of standard represents an effort to attempt to perceive what performance will be in the coming fiscal period utilizing present work force and facilities and assuming the normal operation of motivational devices and control efforts. Although present efficiencies play a large part in the construction of standards of this nature, wise use of expected actual standards also implies a constant questioning of work methods, product design, and types of raw materials used. Furthermore, consideration is given to learning-curve phenomena with extrapolations being made as to changes which may naturally be anticipated with increased production experience. Standards are, therefore, established so as to be representative of efficiencies and factor prices anticipated for the fiscal period. In essence what is wanted as a standard, assuming control is maintained, is the average efficiency for the period as will be expressed in the final actual cost of goods sold figure. Thus, if product A actually costs $1.50 per unit on an average, assuming no significant changes in conditions from those forecast, the standard should have been set at $1.50. Proponents argue that under this approach variances will tend to be small in amount and that when large variances appear, they will warrant investigation. Such variances, the argument runs, represent a deviation from the attainable cost as construed in the annual profit plan.

The chief objection to expected actual standards is that they do not "challenge" effort, they do not motivate. The fear is that their use will encourage a type of "standpatism." The answer to this charge lies partly in the anticipated alertness of the standards group or committee in making the annual revision of standards and in part to the fact that these standards represent a positive goal embodied in the annual budget. The modern professional manager is more likely to be motivated by his or her participation in realistic planning and goal seeking. Special incentives outside the standard cost system may be offered to simulate innovation.

Normal or Long-Run Standards. The inherent philosophy of normal standards is that they will epitomize the long run. When so used in connection with variable costs, they, like past standards and basic standards, tend to lose touch with current reality. Commonly, however, normal standards are utilized in connection with the denominator of the fixed overhead rate formula. (See discussion on "Concepts of Normal Overhead" below.

CONSTRUCTION OF STANDARDS

Direct Cost Price and Rate Standards. Adequate price standards are essential to the operation of a standard cost system. Those who advocate the use of dollar standards as opposed to those who favor the use of standards in physical terms only argue they want a monetary weighting to guide the analyst as to the significance of costs and variances. On the other hand, assuming the weighting of physical quantities with dollars, the analyst would like to avoid the confusion that results from comparing different quantities priced in terms of different prices per unit of measurement. Consequently, the standard cost accountant often states that price standards are used as a filter to arrive at differences in quantity usage from standard. The accountant likes to avoid the following situation:

January excess usage: 400 lb @ $5 per lb	$2,000
February excess usage: 500 lb @ $4 per lb	2,000
Change in efficiency	—0—

An objective of establishing price standards is therefore to make readily apparent changes in prices or rates as contrasted to changes in usage. The standard cost accountant would like to make a comparison of excess usage with the price factor remaining fixed, assuming the same grade and quality of materials are used. In the foregoing illustration, standard prices would be used as a filter in order to obtain more meaningful information concerning usage. Using standard prices, the foregoing would appear:

January excess usage: 400 lb @ $5 per lb	$2,000
February excess usage: 500 lb @ $5 per lb.	2,500
Unfavorable change in efficiency	$ 500

Material Price Standards. In establishing material price standards, reference is made to current invoices, list prices, seasonal variations in price, and purchase contracts. Where a good system of annual budgeting is in effect, material price standards may be constructed by reference to the purchase budget. To illustrate computation of a material price standard, assume that an organization planned a beginning inventory of a particular item of 1,000 pounds that was carried at a price of $0.35 per pound. Assume also the following planned purchases at net invoice price:

	Quantity	Cost
Opening inventory	1,000	$ 350
Purchases:		
January	10,000	3,820
February	10,000	3,820
March	10,000	3,820
April	15,000	6,015
May	15,000	6,015
June	15,000	6,015
July	12,000	5,040
August	12,000	5,040
September	12,000	5,040
October	8,000	3,450
November	8,000	3,450
December	9,000	3,963
Totals	137,000	$55,838

The average inventory price for the item for the period is therefore $0.408 per pound (= $55,838/137,000 lb). Material usages will be evaluated in terms of this price.

Price standards may be set equally as well by reference to prices embodied in long-term contracts. Where detailed budgets are not available and long-term contracts are not customary, reference must be made to less satisfactory data such as current prices adjusted for estimates of change.

Labor Rates. Standard labor rates may be arrived at by reference to labor budgets. Alternatively, rates may be computed by reference to union contracts or levels of rates in existence in the locality modified by anticipated adjustments. It would be desirable from a standard costing point of view that there be established a single rate for each task in an organization. This may, however, be impracticable because of rate differentials due to seniority or the fact of the existence of differential rates arising from the operation of a wage incentive plan. Despite these problems, a single rate can be obtained utilizing a weighted average approach similar to that employed with inventories. Where an operation is construed as embracing several individuals working at different rates, some standard composition of hours and applicable rates must be computed. For example, assume that an operational cycle normally calls for:

$$
\begin{array}{ll}
\text{10 labor hours @ \$4.00 per hour} & \ldots \text{\$40.00} \\
\text{8 labor hours @ \$4.20 per hour} & \ldots \text{33.60} \\
\underline{\text{4}}\text{ labor hours @ \$5.00 per hour} & \ldots \underline{\text{20.00}} \\
\underline{\underline{\text{22}}}\text{ labor hours} \quad \ldots\ldots\ldots\ldots\ldots\ldots & \underline{\underline{\text{\$93.60}}}
\end{array}
$$

The average labor rate comes to approximately $4.25 (= $93.60/22) per hour. Variances which will develop from the use of this composite rate will reflect, therefore, not only changes in individual employee rates but also changes in the proportion of numbers of hours worked by differently rated individuals in the group.

Direct Material Usage Standards. These may be established by means of a variety of methods, depending in part upon the philosophy of the standard setter, the problem at hand, extent of experience with usage, and time available for the process. The following are common approaches to the construction of material usage standards:

1. Engineering drawings, formulas, and computations
2. Weighing and measuring
3. Past experience
4. Test runs.

ENGINEERING DRAWINGS, FORMULAS, AND COMPUTATIONS. Under this approach, the product or part to be produced is first represented on paper by means of various drawings giving desired dimensions. To illustrate, a representation of a 6½-inch speaker enclosure is presented as well as a list of its component wood materials:

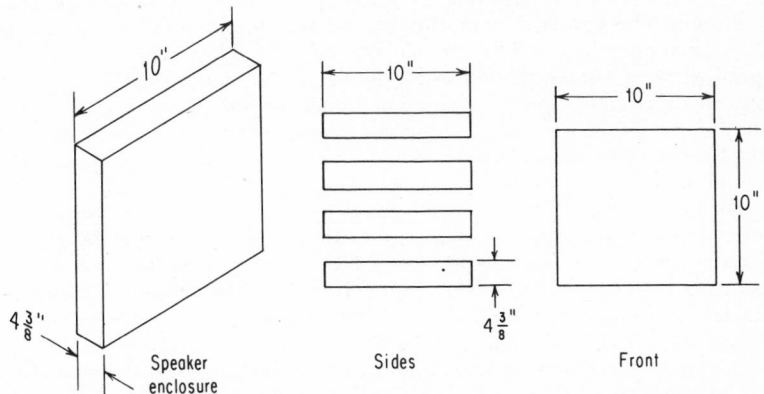

Speaker enclosure   Sides   Front

The speaker is to be made of oiled walnut hardwood paneling with a wood fabric grill covering. From the foregoing, component parts of the speakers are therefore:

4 grooved sides, 4⅜ by 10 inches oiled walnut paneling
1 10 by 10 inch walnut paneling facing with 6½-inch diameter circular cut
1 12 by 12 inch wood grill fabric.

The paneling may be purchased in 4 by 6 foot sheets at $1.96 per panel. Since 64 side pieces 4⅜ by 10 inches can be cut from a panel and this provides for the manufacture of 16 boxes, 63 panels will be required for the production of sides needed for 1,000 boxes (= 1,000/16). Similarly, 28 grill facings, 10 by 10 inches, can be cut from a 4 by 6 foot panel; therefore 36 panels (= 1,000/28) will be required for the manufacture of speaker enclosure facings. A total of 99 wood panels, 4 by 6 feet, are required, therefore, for the manufacture of 1,000 speaker enclosure units. Total cost of these is $194 (= 99 × $1.96), and the cost per box approximately $0.20. Alternatively, and perhaps more usefully, this cost may be expressed as: $0.03 per side (= $1.96/64) and $0.07 per facing (= $1.96/28).

It will be noted that unavoidable waste loss takes place because of the need to work with 4 by 6 foot panels. This is included in the direct material costs. Depending upon the experience of the company and its philosophy of standard costing, an additional allowance may be made for anticipated normal spoilage of panels occurring in the cutting process.

The wood fabric grill covering to be placed over the grill facing panel is purchased in bolts a yard wide. A square yard can be cut into nine pieces approximately 12 inches square. The cost per grill fabric covering is therefore $0.25 (= $2.25/9).

Standard direct material costs per speaker enclosure unit is summarized as follows:

> 4 oiled walnut side pieces of wood paneling, 4⅜ by 10 inches @ $0.03 .. $0.12
> 1 oiled walnut facing piece of wood paneling, 10 by 10 inches @ $0.07 .   .07
> 1 piece of woven wood grill fabric, 12 by 12 inches @ $0.25 25
>
> Total direct material cost per speaker $0.44

In addition to the use of the foregoing direct materials, indirect materials such as glue, small nails, and finishing oil stain will be required to obtain the finished product. Because it would be inconvenient to account for these on a per box basis, they are included among indirect material costs.

WEIGHING AND MEASURING.   This approach may be quite similar to the first illustrated, for standard weight may be based upon a model of the product under consideration. The standard amount of stainless steel utilized in the manufacture of a stipulated quantity of tableware may be determined by a process of weighing the product as it comes from molds. Similarly, the amount of a satisfactory quantity of white goose down contained in a standard-size pillow, 7½ inches high, may be ascertained by weighing out the desired quantity contained in a model.

PAST EXPERIENCE.   Actual usage of materials is indicated by the experience of an organization. This experience may be used in the establishment of material standards or the modification of standards determined by other means.

TEST RUNS.   Trial, experimental, or test runs provide a basis for the judgment of material usage under conditions of actual operations. Test runs may indicate, for example, that even with the best of supervision, a certain amount of spoilage is inevitable, and this may be allowed for in the standard.

Accounting for Spoilage.   Waste represents unavoidable material losses due to the fact that raw materials may not be utilized in full because of differences in the quality or dimensions of raw materials as contrasted to the quality or dimensions required for the manufacture of products. Spoilage, on the other hand, represents a destruction of a potential in raw materials. For example, in the speaker enclosure illustration, experience may indicate that five percent of the panels to be cut are lost as a result of a combination of inefficiency in the sawing operation and variations in the basic quality of the paneling used.

A spoilage allowance may be incorporated in the raw material usage standard or it may be separately stated as a portion of the factory overhead cost. For example, if it is estimated that as a matter of fact 104 rather than 99 panels are required in the production of 1,000 speaker enclosures, the cost of five additional panels $9.80 (= $1.96 × 5) may be incorporated in the cost per speaker enclosure. The 1,000 speakers may be assessed an additional raw materials charge of approximately 1 cent per unit (= $9.80/1,000) to cover the costs of the anticipated spoilage of five panels per 104 brought into the cutting operation. On the other hand, a separate factory overhead account for spoilage may be maintained to be charged for the actual material cost of spoilage and correspondingly credited for material spoilage at the rate of 1 cent per speaker enclosure produced.

Direct Labor Time.   Direct labor may be defined as that labor which has an obviously traceable relationship to the manufacture of a specific product. The creation of product is significantly and causally related to the efforts of this type of labor. A standard direct labor hour may not take place without the appearance of product. Thus, in the establishment of direct labor hours, a careful investigation is made of the interrelationship of labor effort and the production of product. Such a relationship may be ascertained by:

1. Motion and time study
2. Motion study and tables of motion times
3. Test runs
4. Past experience.

MOTION AND TIME STUDY.   This involves a careful investigation of the movements and efforts required by a worker to accomplish a designated task. After a determination of proper motions and subsequent education of the employee, an operation is time-studied. For example, to utilize a multispindle in the drilling of screw holes, a basic labor operation may be:

1. Pick up part and position it in the spacer.
2. Effect the drilling.
3. Move drilled part to designated container.

Each of these operations may in turn be subdivided into more detailed operations. For example, "Pick up part and position in spacer" may be detailed into:

1. Employee move from machine to part container.
2. Pick up part.
3. Move part to drill.
4. Position part prior to drilling.

MOTION STUDY AND TABLES OF MOTION TIMES.   An approach similar to motion and time study is to first review an operation with a view to ascertaining the proper motions. Once these are determined, resort may be made to standard motion time reference works. These indicate time allowed for each of a multitude of possible hand, arm, leg, etc., movements made in modern industry.

TEST RUNS.   Where feasible and when properly conducted, test runs provide exceptionally good information as to labor time required to accomplish stipulated operations. Under test runs, conditions of work and type of worker to be used as well as the operation itself are all carefully controlled. Labor times arrived at under these circumstances offer strong guidance concerning the standard labor time of an operation.

PAST EXPERIENCE.   This may be used as the sole basis for the establishment of labor time standards or it may supplement other methods employed. Study of past experience brings to the fore the problem of individual variations in efficiency, the effect of changes in quality of materials, interruptions, and normal delay time. Past experience used exclusively may perpetuate inefficiencies in time standards established. On the other hand, when used in conjunction with other approaches to standard time setting, it may inject a necessary realism into the content of the standard.

Machine Time. In many instances, direct labor time may not in fact come into existence in the conduct of an operation. Except for the pressing of buttons or levers and pulling of switches, production may be conducted without substantial labor effort. In such instances, there will still be costs that vary with activity: use of supplies, power, cost of setups, and machine attending. Consequently, time studies are undertaken to ascertain machine time allowances per unit of each of the products produced.

Dual Significance of Direct Labor Time and Machine-Hour Standards. As contrasted to material quantity standards, standards for direct labor and machine time have a dual significance. First, of course, undue usage or favorable usage of direct labor or machine time will be investigated for cause. Second, and equally significant, is the fact that in those standard cost systems where a precise distinction is made between fixed and variable costs, direct labor or machine time becomes a common denominator of output. Standard direct labor time and standard machine time obtained from reference to actual production represent the basis for the computation of variable standard cost. They may be referred to simply as standard hours or standard productive hours. Standard hours multiplied by standard prices and rates result in the standard cost amounts that will be compared with actual cost amounts on a number of levels.

Overhead Expense Standards. In addition to direct materials and direct labor cost, a host of other expenses are incurred in manufacturing operations, such as indirect materials, supplies, indirect labor, factory utilities, factory taxes, and factory depreciation. These are commonly summed up under the terms manufacturing overhead, factory overhead, or indirect manufacturing expenses. Because by their nature variable manufacturing overhead costs are activity-oriented and generally deemed more subject to supervisory control, rates for these are determined on an individual basis by operations of cost centers. Fixed factory overhead cost, on the other hand, includes costs that are not activity-oriented in the short run. They take place because of the general circumstances of having a plant in a position to produce (committed costs) or because management has budgeted a stipulated amount to be spent (programmed costs). Consequently, these costs have interest largely because of the convention of assigning them to products.

Variable Manufacturing Overhead Expense Standards. These expenses take place on a number of levels in a factory. For example, variable supplies expense may be incurred directly and specifically in connection with the operation of a specific machine utilized on a specific operation. On the other hand, there may be certain types of greases and oils which because of their common use by all operations of the center and the matter of economy of costing become difficult to relate to the individual operation. They are, consequently, standardized at the cost center level. Finally, there are some variable overhead expenses which as far as measurement is concerned are incurred some distance from both the operation and the cost center. Power cost represents a variable overhead item that may be charged the company via a single meter. To obtain adequate operational and product costs, each of these types of variable overhead expenses must be related to the standard hour of appropriate operations. Depending upon the nature of the manufacturing expense item, the following approaches may be employed:

1. Study of past experience with expense items that are variable in nature and the subsequent budgeting of adjusted amounts per standard hour

2. Correlation analysis of past experience with both the expense item and standard hours, using the method of least squares or the "high-low" method

3. Studies of indirect cost behavior during test runs
4. Simple estimates.

PAST EXPERIENCE APPROACH TO ESTABLISHMENT OF STANDARD VARIABLE RATES. Account data indicating past experience with variable overhead expenses may be arrayed and examined. Depending upon the subjective judgment of the supervisor and the standards committee, standards may be set on the basis of average experience or revised upward or downward.

CORRELATION ANALYSIS OF PAST EXPERIENCE. Use of least-squares analysis or the less valuable "high-low" method has the advantage of not only ascertaining a variable cost rate for an expense item but also of subdividing an expense into its fixed and variable components. Correlation analysis of experience will typically come up with the formula:

$$Y = a + bx$$

where Y represents the total cost, a the fixed portion of the cost, b the variable cost rate, and x standard hours.

In preparing a least-squares analysis of experience with an overhead expense item, it may be found that a is a zero quantity or is negligible in amount. The expense item is therefore classified as a wholly variable overhead cost. Furthermore, a rate for it is ascertained from the analysis. On the other hand, the reverse might be true with the variable rate zero or so insignificant in amount that the cost cannot be construed as anything but a fixed cost. Finally, a correlation analysis can show a mixed cost containing both fixed and variable elements. For example, least-squares analysis may indicate supplies cost as $200 + 0.10x$, signifying that the item has a monthly fixed portion of $200 and an element which varies with output at the rate of 10 cents per standard hour.

TEST RUNS. Where work conditions are carefully controlled, test runs provide information concerning current usage which may be more valuable than analysis by other means. In contrast to subjective studies or correlation analysis of past experience, test runs provide current information concerning data arising under conditions of careful supervision and control. Data from test runs may be used for subjective considerations or some form of correlation analysis and summarized in formula form as was indicated under correlation analysis.

SIMPLE ESTIMATES. The word "simple" is employed here as a contrast of this method with the preceding methodologies. A person with considerable industrial experience can, when required, take a pencil or calculator in hand and make a good educated guess concerning the amount of indirect expense to be incurred in connection with a stipulated amount of output. This approach should be used only when lack of data makes the use of other methods impossible. Care should be taken to see that these guesses do not provide for inbuilt or undesired inefficiency but will represent a degree of efficiency obtainable under the circumstances.

Variable Overhead Budget Standards. Studies such as the foregoing assist the analyst in setting variable overhead rates. When indirect labor cost is established at 10 cents per standard direct labor hour, there is an assumption that in fact only 10 cents will be spent per direct labor hour for indirect labor cost. Standard variable overhead rates, therefore, represent budgeted expenses per direct labor hour. Assuming operations are conducted efficiently from the point of view of time taken, differences between actual and standard variable overhead will be traceable to spending more dollars for variable overhead items per direct labor hour than was budgeted.

Overhead Efficiency Standards. These become established whenever a stated amount of time is established as allowed per unit of output. For example, the analyst in sets direct labor time standards, comes to the conclusion that 10 minutes is to be allowed per piece in the conduct of a particular operation, and thereby indicates a standard as to the efficiency of time utilization. When more time is taken on the operation than the allowed 10 minutes per piece, from the point of view of the standard this effort will have been spent fruitlessly. The overhead cost of extra effort can be ascertained by multiplying the extra time taken by the operation's variable overhead rate. Variances which arise because of greater or lesser use of time are termed "efficiency" (unfavorable or favorable) variances and will be discussed later in the chapter under the general heading of "Variance Analysis."

Fixed Manufacturing Overhead Standards.   Fixed manufacturing overhead items represent manufacturing costs that tend to remain constant in total amount per budget period despite changes in output. Fixed charges are obtained by reference to contractual obligations, local tax rates, depreciation rates, correlation analysis, and management decisions. The budget committee will estimate the amounts likely to be expended during the period for each class of fixed cost. Such a compilation is usually presented on a standard fixed cost summary as in Exhibit 4. That summary will usually indicate trivial variations in fixed cost totals at varying levels of activity, but they are customarily ignored in setting fixed overhead standards.

EXHIBIT 4   Standard Fixed Cost Summary

Production Cost Center No. 300

Expenses	Standard hours			
	6,000	7,000	8,000	9,000
Indirect labor..........................	$ 800	$ 800	$ 800	$ 800
Indirect materials and supplies..........	180	180	200	200
Utilities.............................	150	150	150	150
Factory taxes........................	100	100	100	100
Factory depreciation..................	400	400	400	400
Service center costs..................	250	250	250	250
Totals...........................	1,880	1,880	1,900	1,900

Normal hours.. 8,000
Normal fixed rate per standard hour.......................... $0.2375

To the absorption-minded accountant, fixed costs must be allocated to output. To set a fixed cost standard, total estimated fixed costs must be divided by some activity measure. This is usually normal or anticipated standard hours (see below). In the situation illustrated in Exhibit 4, normal activity for Cost Center No. 300 is construed to be 8,000 standard hours per month. The standard fixed overhead rate for the center is therefore $0.2375 per standard hour (= $1,900/8,000 hours).

CONCEPTS OF NORMAL OVERHEAD

From an actual cost standpoint perhaps the most "actual" overhead rate is computed by taking the fixed costs of a particular month and dividing them by some common denominator of output for that month. Assuming varying output over the several months of a fiscal year, such a procedure leads to as many as 12 different unit costs of fixed overhead per cost center per product in one year and raises questions about the usefulness of the calculations. Accountants have generally come to favor procedures which lead to fixed cost rates which remain constant at least during a year, and many accountants favor rates which remain basically unchanged—insofar as the effect of changing volumes are concerned—for a period of years.

Three procedures receive varying acceptance as "normal" fixed cost rates and will be discussed under the following headings:

1. Annual concept of normal
2. Average utilization concept
3. Practical capacity concept.

Annual Concept of Normal.   Under this approach, the budgeted fixed overhead cost for a fiscal year is divided by a common denominator of output for that year. When cost center fixed cost rates are employed, cost and output figures used are those of a particular cost center. The basic objective is to compute a fixed overhead rate for a cost center or other area which will apply all the annual fixed overhead cost of the area to its output for the period.

For convenience, the following amounts are used to illustrate various concepts of normal:

Annual fixed overhead costs	$31,500	$31,500	$31,500
Standard hours of output	50,000	70,000	90,000
Normal rates	$0.63	$0.45	$0.35

Under the annual concept of normal overhead, any one of the three columns might represent conditions in existence in a particular year. For example, if it is assumed that output for a year is anticipated to be 90,000 standard hours, then the fixed overhead rate for that year is $0.35 per standard hour. Although production may vary widely from month to month, inventory will be costed at a constant fixed cost rate. If the output and fixed cost turn out to be as forecasted, all fixed costs will be charged to product produced. Instead of showing fixed costs and volume on an annual basis, the data will more commonly be shown for a month with monthly average fixed costs in the numerator of the formula and monthly average output in the denominator: $2,625/7,500 = $0.35.

Average Utilization Concept.   Once the advantages of a constant monthly overhead rate for fixed costs are appreciated, the question arises, why allow the rate to fluctuate over each of several years? The columns of illustrative materials in the preceding section are indicative of what could conceivably take place using an annual rate for each of the three years: $0.63 for the first year, $0.45 for the second, and $0.35 for the third year. Normal utilization proponents say that the correct approach to the problem is to construct an average rate to be used over a number of years. They argue that plant and facilities were constructed so as to provide a stream of product over a period of years and that the fixed overhead costs resulting over those years should be shared equally by all the units of output achieved. Consequently, the numerator of the annual fixed cost rate formula represents average annual fixed costs and the denominator represents average annual output. As a practical matter, the numerator used is the anticipated actual fixed costs of a year.

The workings of the average utilization concept is illustrated in the following two T accounts for fixed factory overhead, one representing a year of low output (50,000 standard hours) and the other a year of high output (90,000 standard hours). Debits to each of these accounts show actual fixed factory overhead for a year; credits, applied fixed factory overhead. The average output through the years is assumed to be 70,000 standard hours and the appropriate rate $0.45 per hour.

Fixed Factory Overhead (50,000 standard hours)			Fixed Factory Overhead (90,000 standard hours)		
31,500		22,500		31,500	40,500
	Variance	9,000	Variance	9,000	

In the year of low output, fixed factory overhead cost occurs much as usual and amounts to $31,500. Multiplying the average utilization rate of $0.45 by standard hours earned of 50,000, a total of $22,500 of fixed factory overhead cost is applied to the production of the period. A capacity variance indicating $9,000 of underabsorbed fixed overhead cost arises. Subsequently, in a year of high output (90,000 standard hours), again $31,500 of fixed overhead cost is recognized. During this year the average utilization rate of $0.45 is multiplied now by 90,000 hours, resulting in the application of $40,500 of fixed factory overhead cost. The capacity variance shows overabsorbed fixed factory overhead cost of $9,000, which exactly balances underabsorbed fixed overhead cost taking place in the period of low output.

The foregoing data are, of course, simplified for purposes of illustration. The theory of the average utilization rate envisages a number of years for averaging. The idea is that some of the fixed costs incurred in a period of low output are a cost of having capacity available when needed in periods of high output, and that, by and large, underabsorbed fixed costs taking place in periods of low output will be balanced by overabsorbed fixed costs taking place in periods of high output. Although in theory the variance should be carried forward from year to year, the variance is commonly disposed of in the year of its occurrence, usually as a period charge.

Practical Capacity Concept. Under the practical capacity concept of normal, fixed overhead cost per standard hour is computed at close to the maximum potential level of output. Because some interruptions in work are recognized as unavoidable, especially as an organization produces near its ideal capacity level, the practical capacity exponent chooses as "practical" some level below the maximum. The fixed overhead cost per standard hour is obtained by dividing the annual fixed overhead cost by this volume. The resulting rate obtained is called the practical capacity rate.

In the normal rate illustration given above, $31,500 of fixed overhead cost was divided by 90,000 standard hours to obtain the $0.35 annual concept of normal rate. The 90,000 standard hours may also represent practical capacity to produce. In the theory of this approach, $0.35 is *the* fixed factory overhead cost per standard hour. Those who urge use of the practical capacity rate argue that the $0.45 average utilization rate is not cost but that it is inflated by a 10-cent *loss* due to the failure to utilize facilities. T accounts show the workings of this concept:

Factory Overhead (50,000 standard hours)			Factory Overhead (90,000 standard hours)		
31,500		17,500		31,500	31,500
	Variance	14,000			

In the first T account, only 50,000 standard hours were achieved. Under the theory of the approach, 40,000 standard hours were unemployed. The capacity variance of $14,000 representing underabsorbed fixed factory overhead cost is looked upon as an index of managerial inefficiency concerning the use of capacity. The variance is not construed as a product cost; it is considered a loss, and in theory is best shown as an administrative expense of the period. Note that in the second T account, 90,000 standard hours were achieved, and fixed factory overhead cost applied was equal to the amount of fixed factory overhead incurred.

Advantages and Disadvantages of Concepts of Normal. The strongest claim made for the use of the average utilization rate is that if estimates and forecast are correct, all the fixed overhead cost will have been assigned to product over a period of years at a constant rate. Secondarily, this unit cost will be the most representative cost for inventory accounting, profit determination, and managerial decision making (insofar as absorption costs are useful in these regards).

The practical capacity proponent argues that this approach is the most useful for purposes of cost control, that when capacity variances arise under the practical capacity approach, they indicate the cost of unused facilities. A strong stimulus is provided for greater use of capacity.

The outstanding disadvantage of the average utilization approach is that the capacity variance as initially constructed has no relevance as a cost control device. For example, what is the significance of a capacity variance taking place in Cost Center No. 400 during the third month of a year when operations are conducted as anticipated at 40 percent below capacity? Considerable supplementary information is necessary to make a judgment.

On the other hand, the weakness of the practical capacity approach is the strength of the average utilization method. Operation at practical capacity levels may not be possible due to depressed economic conditions. The unit cost constructed may have no practical meaning, especially as applies to current profit determination and managerial decision making. The constant presentation of capacity variances, which are often beyond the control of present management, may have an adverse effect upon control processes.

CONTROLLABLE COSTS

It is obvious that all costs are controllable by someone in an organization over the longer term. Not only this, but it is equally true that a cost uncontrollable at one level of an organization is controllable at some other level. The words "controllable" and "uncontrollable" have arisen as terminology tools of short-run interest employed in the area of responsibility reporting. Attention is directed at a level of responsibility, such as the cost center, and the question is raised, which costs chargeable to this area can be said to be under the control of the supervisor in charge, and which should be either not assigned to this supervisor or assigned elsewhere in the organization?

Definition.   Controllable costs are those costs subject to modification and change at a particular level of management; uncontrollable costs are those which are not. To illustrate, there is little question that power cost is a charge to cost of the operations of the heat-treat center of a spark-plug manufacturer. However, if the power is not metered to this center, its cost is not controllable by the heat-treat supervisor, and the supervisor cannot be held for its increase above some desirable amount. If responsibility is to be assigned for this particular cost, it must be charged to the factory superintendent and then only in a very general sort of way.

Effect on Accounts and Reports.   The subdivision of costs into controllable and uncontrollable need not be reflected in the accounts proper, nor will they affect computations of unit costs or rates. The impact of the classification will be felt primarily in the responsibility reports prepared for various levels of the management of an organization. For example, although all the fixed costs applicable to a production center will be incorporated in that center's normal rate and although all the variable costs of an operation will be incorporated in the operation's variable rate used for product costing, some of the center's fixed and some of the center's variable costs may not be brought to the performance report for the center. If allocated administrative costs included in the center's fixed cost rate are deemed uncontrollable, they need not be shown on the supervisor's performance report, and the same applies to depreciation expense. Similarly, if allocated power cost is not controllable by the supervisor, it is not displayed on the center's performance report. All these costs are, however, utilized in standard product costing rates.

Effect on Variance Analysis.   Use of the idea of controllable and uncontrollable costs will affect particularly those items included in the "budget variance," to be discussed later in "Variance Analysis." The words "controllable" and "uncontrollable" may be applied to capacity variances. Where operations are proceeding as anticipated, capacity variances arising under the average utilization concept are termed uncontrollable. Under the practical capacity concept, all such variances are thought of as controllable.

SERVICE CENTER ACCOUNTING

The "responsibility accounting" approach has been broadly extended to service center accounting in recent years. In its application, the service cost center is held responsible for the associated costs of producing a service, and the consuming cost center (either production cost center or other service cost center) is held responsible for its consumption.

Accounting for Service Center Costs.   To facilitate responsibility accounting, the costs of a service cost center are subdivided into fixed and variable. The service cost center is held responsible for monthly budgets of fixed cost. Differences between actual fixed and budgeted fixed costs are indicated in the performance report of the service cost center supervisor. In turn, budgeted amounts of these costs are assigned to other centers on an "ability to consume" basis.

For example, in accounting for a maintenance service center, monthly actual fixed costs of maintenance are compared with monthly budgeted fixed costs, and the supervisor asked to explain differences. In turn, budgeted monthly fixed costs are assigned to consuming cost centers on some agreed basis, for example the dollar value of machinery and equipment in those areas. The assignment of service cost center fixed costs to consuming centers is accomplished merely to expedite the assignment of total factory fixed costs to product.

Variable service cost center costs are standardized on a "unit of sale," basis, such as a repair hour, btu, or other quantitative representation of the output of a service center. Much as variable indirect costs are standardized for production cost centers, these costs will be standardized on a unit of sale basis for service cost centers. In turn, consumption by production cost centers will be standardized at a stipulated quantity of the service per standard hour of output. Monthly, the service cost center supervisor must explain differences between the actual variable cost of producing the service sold and its budgeted cost. Where service center cost is classified as a controllable cost of a production cost center, differences between the actual quantity purchased and the standard quantity allowed priced at budgeted unit of sale price must be explained by the service cost center supervisor.

Illustration of Standard Cost Accounting for Service Centers: Fixed Costs. Assume the operation of a maintenance service cost center. A tabulation of its monthly budgeted and actual fixed costs is shown in Exhibit 5.

EXHIBIT 5   Responsibility Accounting for Service Center: Fixed Costs

Expense item	Budgeted monthly expense	Actual expense	Budget variance
W	$1,800	$1,880	$ 80
X	120	150	30
Y	50	50	0
Z	80	70	(10) credit
Totals.......	$2,050	$2,150	$100

Monthly budgeted maintenance center fixed cost is assigned to production cost centers as follows:

Cost center No.	Survey percentage	Assigned expense*
Prod. No. 100............	10	$ 200
Prod. No. 200............	20	400
Other centers............	70	1,450
Totals...............	100	$2,050

* Amounts rounded.

Assume, for illustration, that maintenance fixed cost represents the only fixed costs of Production Cost Centers Nos. 100 and 200. Their normal rates are computed as follows:

PCC No.	Total maintenance fixed cost	Normal hours per month	Normal rate	Standard hours earned	Maintenance fixed cost to product	Capacity variance
100	$200	4,000	$0.05	3,000	$150	$50
200	400	1,000	0.40	1,200	480	80 credit

Allocated budgeted maintenance fixed costs and amounts applied as a result of the application of normal rates are displayed in T accounts given for each production cost center:

Production Cost Center No. 100		Production Cost Center No. 200	
$200	150		400	480
	(Variance 50)	(Variance 80)	

In an actual situation, capacity variances arising in production cost centers because of the fixed costs of maintenance would be merged with amounts resulting from the receipt of other fixed charges by production centers and their application to product by means of a comprehensive normal rate.

Illustration of Standard Cost Accounting for Service Centers: Variable Costs. As many jobs as possible accomplished by a maintenance service center will be standardized. Where special materials and supplies are utilized on a maintenance job, these as well as the number of clock hours allowed will be standardized by the job. The maintenance cost center will be permitted, therefore, to charge consuming cost centers for standard quantities of special materials and supplies as well as allowed clock hours priced at a budgeted rate per maintenance hour. Where possible, for each job undertaken by the maintenance department, there will be a job order sheet to indicate standard and actual quantities of materials and supplies consumed as well as standard and actual maintenance hours. Where jobs are not standardized, consuming cost centers will be charged for maintenance service at a budgeted rate per hour of service plus, if special materials and supplies are used, the cost of these.

A monthly performance report is prepared for the supervisor of the maintenance cost center to summarize his costs and to itemize variances. Such a report would include the fixed costs illustrated in Exhibit 5 as well as the variable costs displayed in Exhibit 6.

EXHIBIT 6   Responsibility Accounting for Service Department: Variable Costs

Maintenance Service Cost Center
Total standard hours of service 500

Expense items	Maintenance hour rates	Budgeted costs	Actual costs	Variances
Materials and supplies, A-1...........	.....	$ 50	$ 60	$ 10
Materials and supplies, A-2...........	.....	200	230	30
Materials and supplies, A-3...........	.....	100	80	(20) credit
Operating expense, B-1..............	$4.10	2,050	2,250	200
Operating expense, B-2..............	0.70	350	400	50
Operating expense, B-3..............	0.20	100	110	10
Totals........................	$5.00	$2,850	$3,130	$280

Excess usage and savings of materials and supplies on various jobs are indicated by the first three items listed on Exhibit 6. Net excess material and supply usage amounted to $20. Budgeted operating expenses given in Exhibit 6 were obtained by multiplying the 500 maintenance hours earned by the maintenance service center by the $5 maintenance hour rate. Budgeted operating costs (last 3 lines, Exhibit 6) were exceeded by $200, $50, and $10 for operating expense items B-1, B-2, and B-3. If these are classified as controllable, they are the responsibility of the maintenance cost center supervisor.

Maintenance hours sold by the Maintenance Service Cost Center were consumed in the following amounts by various cost centers:

Cost Center No.	Maintenance Hours Charged
Production No. 100	45
Production No. 200	50
Other centers	405
Total	500

In general, production cost centers are permitted to utilize a standard quantity of maintenance service time priced at a standard rate per hour. To this are added standard allowances for special maintenance materials and supplies priced at standard prices. Production Cost Center No. 100 does not ordinarily utilize special maintenance materials and is allowed therefore only maintenance time of .01 maintenance hours @ $5 an hour for each standard hour achieved. Its standard variable maintenance cost is therefore $0.05 per standard hour. During the month of January, the center purchased 45 maintenance hours and earned 3,000 standard hours. The results of its operations with regard to maintenance cost are summarized in the T account for the production center.

Production Cost Center No. 100

Maintenance cost 225	To work in process 150
	(Variance 75)

Because Production Cost Center No. 100 consumed 45 hours of maintenance service but was allowed only 30 (3,000 standard hours × .01 maintenance hour), it has a variance which results from the use of 15 more maintenance hours than is allowed for at standard. The $75 variance will appear on the January performance report of this center.

Production Cost Center No. 200 is allowed the following maintenance costs per standard hour:

Materials and supplies, A-1	....	$0.025
Maintenance hours, .04 × $5	......	.200
Total cost per standard hour	....	$0.225

During January, this center was charged for $40 cost of maintenance materials and supplies, A-1, and 50 hours of maintenance service. During this period Production Cost Center No. 200 earned 1,200 standard hours. The results of its operations with regard to maintenance cost are summarized below.

Production Cost Center No. 200			
Materials, A-1	40	To work in process	270
Maintenance hourly cost	250	(Variance 20)	

Production Cost Center No. 200 was allowed $30 for maintenance materials and supplies, A-1 (1,200 standard hours × $0.025) and $240 of hourly maintenance service (1,200 standard hours × $0.20). The center has a total variance of $20 resulting from $10 of excess materials consumption and from the fact that two maintenance hours in excess of standard were used: actual hours 50 − (1,200 standard hours × .04). The $20 variance will be shown on the monthly performance report of Cost Center No. 200.

A summary of the variances relating to both the fixed and variable costs of the maintenance service cost center and the efforts of the two production centers illustrated is shown in Exhibit 7.

EXHIBIT 7   Maintenance Service Center Variance Summary

Costs	Maintenance service center	Production center No. 100	Production center No. 200
Fixed cost variances:			
Budget..................	$100		
Capacity.................	....	$ 50	$(80) credit
Variable cost variances:			
Budget..................	280	75	20
Totals................	$380	$125	$(60) credit

In practice Exhibit 7 would need to be extended to include a number of other centers which consumed maintenance service and which in turn passed their costs on to production centers. In any event, the sum of amounts finally charged to work in process for maintenance center costs and all variances arising from actual-standard maintenance cost comparisons will equal the actual costs charged the maintenance department.

VARIANCE ANALYSIS

Variance analysis and subsequent procedures followed as a consequence of the analysis represent to many accountants the acme of the utilization of a standard cost system for purposes of control. A broader construction of the word "control" would include organizational changes and cost studies preceding the adoption of standard costing, the process integrating standard costing and budgeting, and the evolution of a sound accounting and reporting system. Nevertheless, variance analysis highlights the comparison process inherent in standard cost accounting and brings to the forefront active control and feedback considerations demanding the attention of the accountant and management.

General Significance of Variances. Depending upon the philosophy of the organization, three, or possibly four, constructions may be placed upon variances. They may, on the one hand, indicate (1) variations in efficiency; (2) changes in market prices from prices established primarily to facilitate usage analysis; and (3) differences between actual and standard costs indicating incorrectly established standards. Assuming one takes the point of view that cost differences resulting from above- or below-capacity performance are not necessarily a matter of efficiency but often a matter of the working out of some average, a fourth construction may be placed upon variances. (4) They may simply indicate a cost differential arising from anticipated fluctuations in activity from some given measurement called normal. Therefore, they will not be currently interpreted as cost changes requiring managerial attention.

Criteria for the Evaluation of Variances.[2]   When variances arise, they should be grouped where possible within one of the three or four classes presented in the preceding section. If a variance is unexplainable or obviously a matter of an incorrectly established standard, the assistance of the standards committee should be sought. Criteria are needed, however, to determine whether other types of variances require explanatory or corrective action by management. Some general guides are as follows:

1. The interpretation of standards as "statistical means" and the subsequent investigation of variances lying outside some predetermined control limits. The breadth of the control-limit band may be established partly on the basis of past experience and partly upon monetary values involved.

2. A weighing of potential benefits against the potential costs of the investigation. Subjective probabilities concerning the extent to which the process is in control may be employed.

3. The preparation of tables of anticipated efficiency and capacity variances to be compared with actual amounts of variances.

4. The expression of variances as a percentage of standard and their investigation when they exceed a given percentage or deviate a stated percentage from similar past percentages.

5. Guidance via a consideration of the dollar size of the variance with larger amounts calling for exploratory attention.[3]

This last approach has been criticized by writers who argue that a large variance may as a matter of fact be within acceptable control limits, that it is not largeness or smallness of amount which is critical but whether the variance amount lies within or without a normal universe of variation. Only when a variance, small or large, falls outside of stipulated limits will the process be deemed out of control, and the variance investigated.

Isolation of Variances.   Standard cost amounts and reports are designed so as to facilitate comparisons of actual and standard costs. Differences (variances) are displayed on a variety of bases: by element of expense, by element of expense per operation, and by total controllable expenses of operations and cost centers.

[2]See Nicholas Dopuch, Jacob G. Birnberg, and Joel Demski, *Cost Accounting,* 2nd ed., Harcourt Brace Jovanovich, New York, 1974. They present an unusually able discussion concerning "Assessing the Significance of Standard Cost Variances," chap. 12.

[3]See Gordon Shillinglaw, *Cost Accounting: Analysis and Control,* 3rd ed., Richard D. Irwin, Homewood, Ill., 1972, p. 352.

Alternatively or additionally, variances by elements of cost, such as direct materials, direct labor, and factory overhead may be subdivided into price, usage, and other factors. However constructed, variances will usually be presented routinely at the close of each month. When an operation or cost center is having problems of maintaining control, variances may also be computed by the week, day, or hour, as desired.

Decision Significance of Variances. Once it is determined that a standard needs revision (independent of whether cause for the change lies inside or outside the organization), the impact of the revised standard upon decision models employed by the organization requires consideration. For example, a change in material prices or quantities needed may have implications for the organization's inventory control model. Similarly, a change in any of the components of standard variable costs may affect the contribution margin of products manufactured enough to alter their optimum quantities as determined by the firm's output model. The sensitivity of the decision model to changes in variable manufacturing costs should be ascertained. "When feasible, the critical limits for the parameter values—for example, the contribution margins—could be determined in advance so that management would know whether observed variances are decision significant at the time they are observed."[4]

Conventional Variance Analysis, Direct Materials, and Direct Labor. Most writers on standard costing subdivide the direct materials and direct labor variances into price (rate) and usage factors. Formulas for the computation of these variances are as follows:

Material price variance = actual quantity purchased ×
(purchase)   (standard − actual unit price)
Material usage variance = standard unit price ×
                               (standard − actual quantity used)
Labor rate variance = actual hours taken ×
                           (standard − actual rate)
Labor usage variance = standard hourly rate ×
(efficiency)   (standard − actual hours taken)

To illustrate briefly, if 1,000 pounds of direct materials are purchased at $1.10 per pound and the standard unit price is $1 per pound, computation of the *material price variance* is 1,000 lb × ($1 − $1.10) = −$100. Since the actual price of this material is greater than standard price, the purchase gives rise to an unfavorable material price variance of $100.

Computation of the *material usage variance* is illustrated by $1 × (450 − 400) = $50, where $1 is the standard unit price of materials, 450 pounds is the standard material allowance, and 400 pounds is the actual material usage. Since actual usage of the material is less than that allowed for at standard, the variance of $50 is favorable.

Similar computations are made for the *direct labor rate variance* and the *direct labor usage variance* utilizing the formulas given above.

Conventional Factory Overhead Variance Analysis: Two-Variance Approach. Conventional factory overhead variance analysis depends upon the utilization of the concept of the flexible budget and a careful differentiation between fixed and variable costs. Either a formula or columnar approach may be taken to the flexible budget, with the stipulation that for absorption costing purposes some stated activity level be considered "normal."

A formula flexible budget for a cost center may be expressed algebraically as

$$y = a + bx$$

[4]Dopuch, Birnberg, and Demski, *op. cit.*, p. 494.

where y refers to the overhead cost of a specific cost center, a represents budgeted monthly fixed costs, b the cost center standard variable overhead rate, and x some unit of measurement denoting activity. Substituting monetary amounts and hours in the formula, the monthly budget for a cost center appears as $\$9,000 + \$0.80\,x$, where x represents direct labor hours. A normal fixed overhead rate for the center of \$1.80 is obtained by dividing budgeted monthly fixed costs of \$9,000 by normal monthly output which, for purposes of illustration, is assumed to be 5,000 direct labor hours. The total factory overhead rate for the cost center is, therefore, \$2.60 per direct labor hour (\$1.80 fixed rate + \$0.80 variable rate).

The formulas for calculating variances are

$$\text{Budget variance} = \text{flexible budget cost for standard activity achieved} - \text{actual overhead cost incurred}$$

$$\text{Capacity variance} = \text{standard fixed rate} \times (\text{normal volume} - \text{actual volume of output})$$

To illustrate computation of the foregoing variances, assume the following facts: The center worked 4,500 direct labor hours to produce items which at standard should have been achieved in 4,000 direct labor hours. Actual factory overhead costs of the center are \$12,700, consisting of \$9,200 fixed costs and \$3,500 variable costs. Factory overhead applied for the center of \$10,400 is computed by multiplying 4,000 standard hours earned by the total cost center factory overhead rate of \$2.60. The total factory overhead variance of \$2,300 is unfavorable (12,700 actual − \$10,400 applied).

Cost center flexible budget cost totals \$12,200 and consists of \$9,000 fixed and \$3,200 variable cost (\$0.80 × 4,000). Applying the formula given for the budget variance, the unfavorable budget variance is \$500 (flexible budget \$12,200 − actual overhead \$12,700). The budget variance can be divided into fixed and variable cost components. The fixed cost element is \$200 (\$9,200 − \$9,000) and the variable cost portion \$300 (3,500 − \$3,200).

Similarly, utilizing the capacity variance formula, the capacity variance is \$1,800 [= \$1.80 × (4,000 − 5,000)], where \$1.80 is the standard fixed cost rate, 5,000 the normal hours, and 4,000 the standard hours earned. The variance is "unfavorable" since output achieved was 1,000 direct labor hours below normal. Adding the unfavorable capacity variance of \$1,800 to the unfavorable flexible budget variance of \$500, the total unfavorable overhead variance of \$2,300 for the cost center is obtained.

Conventional Factory Overhead Variance Analysis: Three-Variance Approach. Under a three-variance approach, the budget variance computed under the two-variance approach is subdivided into expenditure and efficiency factors. Formulas for the three variances are

$$\text{Budget variance (expenditure)} = \text{flexible budget cost for actual activity} - \text{actual overhead cost incurred}$$

$$\text{Efficiency variance} = \text{standard variable overhead rate} \times (\text{standard activity} - \text{actual activity})$$

$$\text{Capacity variance} = \text{standard fixed overhead rate} \times (\text{normal volume} - \text{actual volume of output})$$

To illustrate the computation of these variances utilizing amounts given in the illustration of the two-variance approach, the flexible budget is now based upon actual activity of 4,500 direct labor hours rather than the 4,000 standard direct labor hours earned. The flexible overhead budget is, therefore, \$12,600 [\$9,000 fixed and \$3,600 variable (\$0.80 × 4,500)]. Actual factory overhead costs are

$12,700, and an unfavorable budget (expenditure) variance of $100 is, therefore, computed. This is an amalgam of a $200 unfavorable fixed cost budget variance and a $100 favorable variable cost budget variance [(4,500 × $0.40)− $3,500)].

The unfavorable factory overhead efficiency variance is $400 [= $0.80 × (4,000 − 4,500)]. Direct labor hours allowed for production accomplished totaled 4,000, while 4,500 direct labor hours were actually employed. What is assumed to be wasted time of 500 hours is evaluated at the standard variable overhead rate of $0.80 per direct labor hour.

As a consequence of the foregoing computations, the unfavorable budget variance of $500 obtained under the two-variance method of overhead variance analysis has been subdivided into a budget (expenditure) variance of $100 and an efficiency variance of $400, both variances unfavorable.

The capacity variance obtained under the three-variance method of overhead variance analysis is computed as was done under the two-variance method: $1,800 = [$1.80 × (5,000 − 4,000)]. The normal volume of 5,000 continues to refer to standard hours pertaining to good production. From it are subtracted standard hours allowed for actual production attained. Under- or overnormal hours of output are evaluated at the standard fixed overhead rate.

The variances computed under the three-variance approach when combined equal the total variance of $2,300 obtained by subtracting applied factory overhead of $10,400 from $12,700 actual factory overhead:

Budget variance (expenditure) .... $ 100
Efficiency variance   400
Capacity variance 1,800
                                    $2,300

Seasonality and Standard Cost Variances:[5] Expenditure. The accountant encounters some unique variance problems with regard to expenditure and volume changes emanating from seasonal operations. For example, the a portion of the flexible budget formula, $a + bx$ (discussed in the section on the two-variance approach) refers to the average budgeted fixed cost per month. Fixed overhead expenses for a particular month may, however, be greatly in excess of the average amount budgeted because of nonroutine expenditures incurred seasonally.

For the sake of simplicity in illustration, assume that a consists of $12,000— $11,500 monthly fixed costs of a routine nature, such as depreciation, indirect labor, and supervision, plus $500 for maintenance. Annual maintenance charges are budgeted at $6,000 and are all actually incurred in May. Obviously, if fixed expenses take place as planned, fixed overhead costs incurred during May will total $17,500 (= $11,500 + $6,000). Comparing this $17,500 with the formula budgeted fixed costs of $12,000 will result in the showing of a variance of $5,500. Similarly, were $11,500 of fixed expenses to take place during each of the other 11 months of the year as planned, favorable monthly variances of $500 would appear. Consequently, even though expenses are conforming to those planned, variances appear each month.

This problem may be solved by using a "balancing" acount. Each month the "normal" maintenance costs of $500 (= $6,000/12) are debited to the actual overhead account and credited to the balancing account. Maintenance costs are debited as incurred to the balancing account (while various asset and liability accounts are credited). Therefore, if seasonally planned maintenance expenditures are held to $6,000, no variance will arise in the balancing account. However, if maintenance cost is materially over or under the amount planned, a variance requiring scrutiny will appear. Because the overhead accounts proper are charged

[5]See Shillinglaw, *op cit.*, pp. 479–480, for an alternative treatment.

with $500 monthly for maintenance costs, they will agree with the amount contained in the flexible budget formula.

Volume Variances Due to Seasonality.   A second problem arises when planned operating activity fluctuates seasonally. A forecasted favorable or unfavorable variance may be counterbalanced in whole or in part by an unanticipated volume variance. A careful analysis is required to distinguish between these two and properly inform management.

For example, assume that the monthly flexible budget formula is $12,000 + $1.50x, where x is direct labor hours, and that normal volume is 6,000 standard direct labor hours per month. The fixed overhead rate is, therefore, $2 per direct labor hour (= $12,000/6,000 hours). Assume that during August 6,000 hours are worked when because of seasonal trends only 3,000 standard hours were budgeted. Although no variance caused by volume changes would be indicated by the account, the activity denominator of fixed overhead costs was based on the assumption that only 3,000 hours would be earned during August. Thus a volume variance of a seasonal nature of $6,000 (3,000 under normal hours multiplied by the fixed rate of $2.00) was expected. The following two T accounts indicate the problem:

Manufacturing Overhead

12,000	

Applied Manufacturing Overhead

	As planned 6,000
	Not planned 6,000

Although the two overhead accounts show no variances, the analyst wants to be able to identify the favorable volume variance resulting from 3,000 hours of unanticipated production. This information can then be directed to management attention. For the disposition of the unanticipated favorable volume variance, see "Disposition of Variances," below.

Mix and Yield Variances.[6]   Material usage variances may be subdivided into mix and yield variances in situations where several materials are entered together and processed to obtain a batch of product. For example, the standard mix of raw materials required to produce 1 pound of product K is as follows:

Material X, ¾ lb @ $1 per lb   = $0.75
Material Y, ½ lb @ 2 per lb   = 1.00
Standard cost per lb of product K = $1.75

If the raw materials used are purchased at prices other than the standard prices indicated, material price variances are constructed as is indicated earlier in this chapter.

To illustrate the computation of mix and yield variances, assume that the following batches of materials are processed to yield 95 pounds of product K:

Materials X, 70 lb @ $1 = $ 70
Materials Y, 55 lb @ 2 = 110
Totals   125 lb $180

The 95 pounds of product K have a standard cost of $166.25 (= 95 × $1.75). There is, therefore, a material usage variance of $13.75 (= $180.00 − $166.25).

Material Mix Variance.   As indicated, the cost of the actual mix of 125 pounds at standard prices is $180. Had the proper mix of materials been made, the average

[6]For an extended treatment of mix and yield variances, see Adolph Matz, Othel J. Curry, and George W. Frank, *Cost Accounting,* 5th ed., South-Western Publishing Company, Cincinnati, Ohio, 1972, pp. 513–517.

cost per pound of material would have been $1.40 (= $1.75 standard cost/1¼ lb of both materials); therefore, 125 pounds of standard mix should cost $175. Subtracting the $175 (standard mix cost of 125 pounds of materials) from the $180 (actual mix of 125 pounds at standard prices) results in an unfavorable mix variance of $5.

Material Yield Variance.   According to the standard mix formula, one pound of product K should result from the processing of 1¼ pounds of the standard raw material mix. Consequently, 100 pounds of product K should have been produced from a standard mixture of 125 pounds. In fact, only 95 pounds were produced. There is, therefore, a yield variance of $8.75 (5 lb @ $1.75).

In summary, from an input of 125 pounds of raw materials costing $180 at standard prices, there resulted good product of 95 pounds valued at standard cost at $166.25. The resulting material usage variance of $13,75 is subdivided into a mix variance of $5 and a yield variance of $8.75. Formulas summarizing mix and yield computational procedure are shown below:

Mix and yield formulas:

Mix variance = (actual quantity of materials used × average standard mix cost per pound) − (the total of actual quantities of materials employed × respective individual standard prices)

Yield variance = (standard yield from total materials employed − actual yield) × standard cost per unit of product

Utility of Variance Analysis.   The proper design and installation of a standard cost system can in itself have a salutary effect upon the operations of an organization because, in the process, materials and operations become standardized and administrative organization is placed upon a responsibility basis. Variance analysis represents the continuing and dynamic effort to assure attainment of results desired from the standard cost system. In essence, variance reporting represents a potential attention-directing force. Where standards are established on a realistic basis, deviations from them are incorporated in reports, and management is charged with the responsibility of investigating and explaining them and, if possible, correcting conditions which created them. This calls for the ability of self-criticism, cooperation, and knowledge of pertinent operations. The proper utilization of standards and variances lead to a favorable cycle of investigation, explanation, correction, and feedback of information helpful to the future conduct of operations.

Feedback Value of Variance Analysis.   Once a variance has been examined for cause and, where necessary, corrective action taken, the circumstances surrounding the variance must be digested by the organization's information system. A standard may need revision or the impact of unsatisfactory supervision needs to be remembered. Not only must steps be taken to assure that the problem will not become repetitive, but also that lessons learned from the experience will be incorporated in the education and activity of supervisors.

DISPOSITION OF VARIANCES

Once variances have been used for control, the accountant must then properly dispose of them in the accounts. Typically two problems are involved in variance disposition: (1) their handling during the year, and (2) their accounting at year-end.

Interim Accounting for Variances.   During the fiscal year, variances will be reported and analyzed as indicated in the preceding section. Where variances are not expected to balance out over the year, they should be charged monthly to the Income Summary account. Where, however, it is anticipated that efficiency and capacity variances will more or less balance out in the course of the year, they are best carried forward from month to month, their final balances to be considered at year-end.

Annual Disposition of Variances—Price and Efficiency Type. Where variances are carried forward from month to month, the disposition problem arises at the end of the year.

A naïve attempt at conversion of actual costs may be made by allocating these to Inventory and Cost of Goods Sold accounts. Any such attempt is doomed to failure. Variances computed by the month or the year do not relate themselves proportionately to standard costs shown in accounts. They relate to specific production accomplished at specific times. Such production is not ordinarily distributed among Inventory and Cost of Goods Sold accounts in proportion to standard cost balances contained therein. Nevertheless, where variance balances are considered significant, it is not an unusual practice to allocate them to Inventory and Cost of Goods Sold accounts following nice arithmetic procedures based upon the ratio of variance to standard cost.

The more common, and more defensible, method of disposing of variances of the price and efficiency type is to charge them either to the Cost of Goods Sold or the Income Summary account. Although this procedure is largely a matter of convenience, its practice is sometimes defended by the rationalization that variances are a cost of inefficiency and are therefore a proper expense. With regard to material price and labor rate variances, such a defense is not always logical since the variance in many cases is not a matter of managerial inefficiency, but of economic and social factors outside the control of management. Nevertheless, no more reasonable treatment is available, and the charge to expense is generally followed. If sufficiently material, presentation as a separate line on the income statement would be desirable.

Annual Disposition of Variances—Capacity Type. Where a normal rate has been established following the annual concept of normal, the resulting variances will receive one of the two treatments discussed in the preceding section. Use of the practical capacity concept of normal assumes that the capacity variance represents a "loss" rather than a cost, and therefore the variance should be shown in the income statement as a period cost. Where the average utilization concept of normal is employed, a case can be made for the deferral of the capacity variance to the next period. A debit capacity variance indicates that the annual fixed costs incurred with the hope of having facilities available in periods of above-normal output were not fully utilized this period. Similarly, a credit balance indicates the likelihood of a fixed cost of idleness in some later period but changeable to the output of this period of above-normal production. Despite these theoretical considerations, capacity variances resulting from the use of the average utilization concept are either allocated or handled as a period change as discussed in the preceding section.

STANDARD MARKETING COST ACCOUNTING

Objectives. Although a variety of objectives are sought in the use of marketing cost accounting and analysis, the major objective held in the employment of standard marketing costs is the evaluation and control of marketing activities. This objective may be subdivided into: (1) the problem of the overall direction and control of marketing efforts by major segments (ventures), and (2) the more limited and detailed control of costs incurred by responsibility units. Although these subdivisions will merge at some point, their delineation will prove helpful to this discussion.

Much of today's marketing cost analysis is accomplished on a statistical basis without the use of detailed ledger accounts. In practice, work-sheet classification and analysis may be more expeditiously employed.

Use of Functional Classifications. Insofar as a plan of accounts is concerned, account classifications may be established to show income and expense by major segments of a business. Products, channels of trade, markets, and districts are examples of segments. Many writers have recommended the use of intermediate functional-type classifications which would pick up marketing costs prior to their allocation to segments. Costs classified under the headings of storage, packing and shipping, transportation-out, advertising, sales promotion, and others provide management with useful information concerning the function as well as the costs of specific technical operations incidental to the conduct of the function. More important, however, many functional costs, such as storage, packing and shipping, and transportation-out, are more readily related to products sold by segments or to the segment operation itself than are individual items of unallocated marketing expense. Thus, one of the chief uses of standards in marketing cost accounting is as a means of cost allocation.

A second level in the use of standard functional costs is where the standards are employed to accomplish the objective of allocation but are also used for purposes of control over functions. Standard costs determined for packing and shipping operations may be utilized as a basis for the transfer of the cost of these to product or district classifications. On the other hand, they may also be utilized to construct a standard flexible budget to aid in the control of packing and shipping activities.

A third level of standardization of functional costs occurs where marketing costs may in fact be readily traced to segments without the use of standards, but standard costs aid in the control of the function. Although, for example, actual transportation-out costs may be easily traced to district classifications, comparison of actual and standard transportation cost aids in their control.

Bases for the Allocation of Marketing Costs. In the process of transferring marketing costs from functional classifications to those reflecting objects of managerial interest, bases of allocation are employed. A basis of allocation attempts to make an expense or cost category divisible over objects of managerial interest on some equitable or justifiable basis. Some common marketing cost categories and applicable bases of allocation are given in Exhibit 8.

EXHIBIT 8   Bases for the Allocation of Marketing Costs

Expense	*Basis of Allocation*
Advertising	Circulation or space utilized.
Bad debts expense	Balances of accounts receivable weighted by customer credit ratings.
Billing	Number of invoice lines or number of invoices.
Credits and collections	Balances of accounts receivable weighted by customer credit ratings. Number of sales invoices.
Delivery by company vehicles	Number of miles weighted by space occupied. Number of equivalent units. Number of miles weighted by poundage.
Order filling	Number of invoice lines.
Packing and shipping	Standard time required plus standard direct charges for special packing materials.
Sales order costs	Number of sales orders.
Salesmen's salaries	Direct or standard time allowed.
Storage	Space occupied weighted by average time in storage.
Transportation-out (outside carrier)	Mileage or ton-miles weighted by standard classification rate per standard shipper.

A schematic plan for the utilization of functional accounts in marketing cost accounting is presented in Exhibit 9.

EXHIBIT 9   Flow of Standard Marketing Costs

Marketing expenses	Functional accounts	Segment accounts
Marketing cost control	Storage	Domestic market
Actual | Actual	→ Actual | Standard	→ Standard
→	→	
	Other functions	Foreign market
	→ Actual | Standard	→ Standard
		→

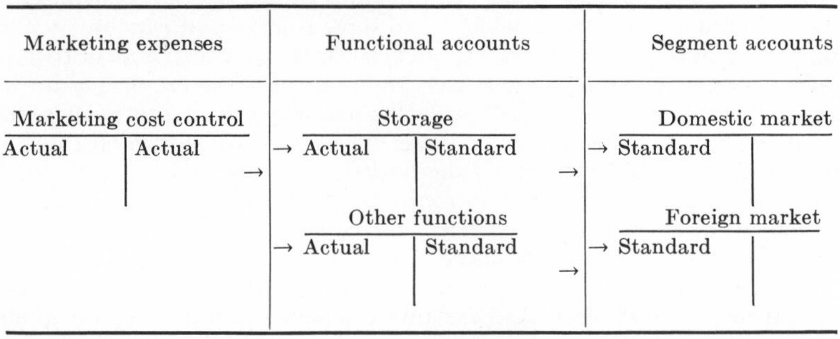

Segment Accounting. Costs assigned to segments may be of the nature of total costs, "direct costs," or a body of directly traceable costs which include both fixed and variable elements. Attempts are made at times to assign total marketing costs to a segment classification with a view to making an overall appraisal or to impress upon directing officers their responsibility for securing revenues which will cover more than the directly incurred cost of a segment. Because of the arbitrary nature of many of the cost assignments, such data must be employed with care.

Costs brought to segment classifications may be in the form of standard manufacturing costs, standard functional costs, and actual costs. For example, actual salespeople's expenses may be collected at the district level. Profit and loss appraisals of the district may be made, therefore, on the basis of mixed standard and actual costs.

Standard Flexible Budget Costs for Salespeople's Expenses. Control over actual costs included in a segment may be attempted by means of a standard flexible budget. Where, for example, a salesperson is provided with a car and is reimbursed for per diem expenses, a rather complicated budget may be utilized. Budgeted fixed costs per month may include the salespersons's basic salary as well as car-leasing costs. Lodging and meals may be standardized on a working day basis. Commissions and entertainment expense may be budgeted as a percentage of sales, and gasoline on the basis of the standard number of miles of travel. Standard flexible budgets are particularly useful in the control over marketing costs when utilization of such budgets assumes a policy wherein cost allowances are correlated with standard activity. Actual activity and accompanying cost allowances may, therefore, be evaluated in the light of this policy.

It should again be emphasized that although standard marketing costs are useful to the construction of flexible budgets for some marketing activities, the significance of marketing cost standards lies less in their utilization as target-type control data and much more as a means of providing information concerning the costs of marketing functions, products, segments, or other objects of managerial interest. Once these are known, a basis is provided for the overall direction and control of marketing activities.

UTILITY OF A STANDARD COST TABLEAU[7]

Calculating and keeping track of two variances each for direct materials, direct labor, and variable overhead, plus three for fixed overhead, can be done efficiently

[7]The material in this section is taken from S. Davidson, J. S. Schindler, and R. L. Weil, *Fundamentals of Accounting,* 5th ed., The Dryden Press, Hinsdale, Ill., pp. 701–708. These authors give credit to David O. Green of the University of Chicago for devising the tableau.

with a Standard Cost Tableau. The Standard Cost Tableau introduced in this section displays the uniformity of the variance calculations. To use the Standard Cost Tableau and to review the operation of a standard cost system, consider the following data for the Buffalo Manufacturing Company for the month of September.

The Buffalo Manufacturing Company produces a single product. The standard cost system data are as follows:

Standard direct labor cost per hour	$6 per hour
Standard materials costs per pound	$1.50 per pound
Standard quantity of materials per finished unit of product ...	3 pounds
Standard direct labor hours per finished unit of product	5 hours
Variable overhead rate applied per standard direct labor hour	$1.35 per hour
Budgeted fixed costs for September	$9,375
Budgeted capacity for September in units of finished product .	2,500 units

Overhead is applied to product on the basis of direct labor hours. The information on actual events for the month of September is as follows:

Raw materials purchased (10,000 lb @ $1.60 per lb	$16,000
Raw materials used in pounds	5,400 pounds
Direct labor costs incurred (11,000 hr @ $5.70 per hr)	$62,700
Variable overhead costs incurred	$14,300
Fixed overhead costs incurred	$ 9,525
Equivalent number of finished units produced in September .	2,000 units

The Standard Cost Tableau for the Buffalo Manufacturing Company's operations during the month of September is shown in Exhibit 10. The numbers in the top left-hand corner of each cell corresponds to the numbers in the paragraphs below, which show how costs and variances are calculated in the tableau. In general, actual costs are shown in column A. Column E shows the actual inputs to production at standard, or budgeted, costs. Column H shows the standard costs applied to product. Columns B, F, and G show the nine variances that will become period costs; F is used only for fixed overhead, the only cost component with a capacity or volume variance. Columns C and D are used only for the direct materials calculations. Recall that the materials price variance is computed for all units purchased, whereas the materials quantity variance is computed only for units of raw material used. Column C records raw materials received at standard prices and column D records raw materials used in production at standard prices. The order of the computations shown in Exhibit 10 could be somewhat different.

Materials

(1) Record in column A the actual purchase price for 10,000 pounds of raw materials bought for $16,000 or $1.60 per pound.

(2) Record in column C the raw materials received into inventory at standard costs. The entry is 10,000 pounds times $1.50 per pound.

(3) Calculated the raw materials price (or rate) variance for column B. 10,000 × ($1.60 − $1.50) = $1,00 (unfavorable). That variance could be determined as the difference between columns A and C, but the independent calculation is $10,000 pounds purchased × ($1.60 per pound paid − $1.50 per pound standard). In the Standard Cost Tableau all unfavorable variances are positive and marked (U). All favorable variances are negative and are marked (F). The journal entry that records the above tableau entries would be

Raw Materials Inventory	15,000	
Materials Price Variance (unfavorable)	1,000	
Miscellaneous Accounts Payable		16,000

(4) Record the issue of raw materials into the production process. During the month 5,400 pounds were used at a standard cost of $1.50 per pound. The

EXHIBIT 10 Buffalo Manufacturing Company

Standard Cost Tableau for the Month of September

$$A = H + B + F + G + [C - D]$$

Actual Costs = Costs Applied + Variances + [Net Change in Raw Materials Inventory at Standard Cost]

	A	B	C	D	E	F	G	H
			Raw materials inventories at standard cost					
	Actual cost incurred	Price and rate variances[a]	Purchased	Used	Actual input at standard prices (standard cost control)	Capacity variance[a] (at standard cost)	Quantity variances[a] (at standard cost)	Actual output at standard prices (standard cost applied)
1. Direct material	(1) 10,000 × $1.60 $16,000	(3) 10,000 × ($1.60 − $1.50) $1,000 (U)	(2) 10,000 × $1.50 $15,000	(4) 5,400 × $1.50 $8,100	(4) $1.50 × 5,400 $8,100		(6) $1.50 × [5,400 − (2,000 × 3)] −$900 (F)	(5) $1.50 × (2,000 × 3) $9,000
2. Direct labor	(7) 11,000 × $5.70 $62,700	(9) 11,000 × ($5.70 − $6.00) −$3,300 (F)			(8) $6.00 × 11,000 $66,000		(11) $6.00 × [11,000 − (2,000 × 5)] $6,000 (U)	(10) $6.00 × (2,000 × 5) $60,000
3. Variable overhead	(12) $1.30 = $14,300/11,000 $14,300	(14) 11,000 × ($1.30 − $1.35) −$550 (F)			(13) $1.35 × 11,000 $14,850		(16) $1.35 × (11,000 − 10,000) $1,350 (U)	(15) $1.35 × (2,000 × 5) $13,500
4. Fixed overhead	$9,525	(19) $9,525 − $9,375 $150 (U)			(18) Budgeted Fixed Costs $9,375/12,500 = $.75 $9,375	(21) $.75 × (12,500 − 11,000) $1,125 (U)	(22) $.75 × (11,000 − 10,000) $750 (U)	(20) $.75 × (2,000 × 5) $7,500
Column totals	$102,525	−$2,700 (F)	$15,000	$8,100	$98,325	$1,125 (U)	$7,200 (U)	$90,000

[a] For all variances: Positive numbers marked (U) are unfavorable. Negative numbers marked (F) are favorable.

amounts in columns D and E are always identical and equal the standard cost of raw materials used: $5,400 \times \$1.50 = \$8,100$.

(5) Calculate and record in column H the standard costs of raw materials applied in manufacturing the finished product. Two thousands units were produced and require, at standard, 3 pounds of material with standard cost $1.50 per pound: 2,000 units × 3 pounds × $1.50 per pound = $9,000.

(6) Calculate and record in column G the materials quantity (or usage) variance. That variance could be determined as the difference between the amounts in columns E and H, but the independent calculation is

(5,400 pounds used − 6,000 pounds standard) × $1.50 standard cost
$$= -\$900 \text{ (favorable)}$$

The journal entry that records tableau entries (4), (5), and (6) would be

Work in Process (standard usage at standard cost) 9,000
  Materials Quantity Variance (favorable)   900
  Raw Materials Inventory (actual usage at standard cost) ...   8,100

Direct Labor

(7) Record in column A the actual direct labor costs of $62,700.

(8) Record in column E the direct labor costs that would be charged at standard rates for actual direct labor usage:

$$11,000 \text{ hours} \times \$6 \text{ per hour standard} = \$66,000$$

(9) Calculate the labor rate (or price) variance. That variance could be determined as the difference between columns A and E, but the independent calculation is

11,000 hours used × ($5.70 rate paid − $6.00 standard rate)
$$= -\$3,300 \text{ (favorable)}$$

(10) Record in column H the standard direct labor costs applied in manufacturing the finished product. Two thousand units were produced and each requires, at the standard performance level, 5 hours with standard rate $6 per hour. Two thousand units × 5 hours × $6 per hour = $60,000 of direct labor costs applied at standard rates.

(11) Calculate and record in column G the direct labor quantity variance. That variance could be determined as the difference between the amounts in columns E and H, but the independent calculation is

(11,000 actual hours − 10,000 standard hours) × $6 per hour
$$= \$6,000 \text{ (unfavorable)}$$

The journal entries to record the direct labor information in tableau entries (7) through (11) would be

Work in Process (standard usage at standard cost) 60,000
Direct Labor Quantity Variance (unfavorable) 6,000
  Wages Payable (actual costs)   62,700
  Direct Labor Price Variance (favorable)   3,300

Variable Overhead. The data indicate that variable overhead is applied using direct labor hours as the activity base at a rate of $1.35 per standard direct labor hour charged to production. The actual variable overhead costs were $14,300 and 11,000 direct labor hours were actually used. Therefore the actual variable overhead cost per actual direct labor hour used is $14,300/11,000 = $1.30.

(12) Record in column A the actual variable overhead costs of $14,300.

(13) Record in column E the variable overhead costs that would be charged at standard rates for direct labor hours actually used:

$$11,00 \text{ hrs.} \times \$1.35 \text{ per hour} = \$14,850$$

(14) Calculate the variable overhead price variance. That variance could be determined as the difference between columns A and E, but the independent calculation is

$$11,000 \text{ direct labor hours used} \times (\$1.30 \text{ actual rate} - \$1.35 \text{ standard rate})$$
$$= -\$550 \text{ (favorable)}$$

(15) Record in column H the standard variable overhead costs applied in manufacturing the finished product. Two thousand units were produced and each requires, at the standard level of performance, 5 hours of direct labor each of which is charged with $1.35 of standard variable overhead costs:

$$2,000 \text{ units} \times 5 \text{ direct labor hours} \times \$1.35 \text{ standard charge per hour} = \$13,500$$

(16) Calculate and record in column G the variable overhead quantity variance. That variance could be determined as the difference between the amounts in columns E and H, but the independent calculation is

$$(11,000 \text{ actual direct labor hours} - 10,000 \text{ standard hours}) \times \$1.35 \text{ per hour}$$
$$= \$1,350 \text{ (unfavorable)}$$

The journal entries to record the variable overhead cost information in tableau entries (12) through (16) would be

Variable Overhead Control	14,300	
Miscellaneous Accounts Payable		14,300
To record variable overhead costs.		
Overhead Applied (at standard)	13,500	
Variable Overhead Quantity Variance (unfavorable)	1,350	
Variable Overhead Price Variance (favorable)		550
Variable Overhead Control		14,300
To apply variable overhead and to record variable overhead variances		

Fixed Overhead. The data indicate that the budgeted fixed costs for the month are $9,375 and that the activity base is direct labor hours. The capacity for September is given as 2,500 finished units. The fixed overhead variances could be calculated using finished units for the activity base, but since direct labor hours are specified as the activity base for overhead, we use direct labor hours as the activity base for fixed costs. Since 5 direct labor hours at standard are required for one unit of finished product, the capacity for September in direct labor hours is 5 × 2,500 = 12,500 direct labor hours. The fixed cost rate to be applied to product is, then, $9,375/12,500 = $.75 per hour. (If units of finished product were used as the activity base, the fixed costs would be applied to units of finished product at $9,375/2,500 = $3.75 per unit.)

(17) Record in column A the actual fixed overhead costs of $9,525.

(18) Record in column E the budgeted fixed overhead costs of $9,375. For fixed overhead costs, the "Actual Inputs at Standard Prices" (column heading for E) are the budgeted fixed costs for the period.

(19) Calculate the fixed overhead price variance as the difference between columns A and E. Ordinarily there is no independent calculation.

(20) Record in column H the standard fixed overhead costs applied to the product. The activity base is direct labor hours:

$$2,000 \text{ units of product} \times 5 \text{ hours per unit} \times \$.75 \text{ per direct labor hour} = \$7,500$$

(Alternatively, if the activity base is units of finished product, $2,000 \times \$3.75 = \$7,500$.)

(21) Calculate and record in column F the Fixed Overhead Capacity Variance. That variance must be calculated as follows:

(12,500 hours budgeted capacity $-$ 11,000 hours used) $\times$ \$.75 per hour
$$= \$1,125 \text{ (unfavorable)}$$

(22) Calculate and record in column G the fixed overhead quantity variance. That variance could be determined as column E minus columns F and H, but the independent calculation is

(11,000 actual hours $-$ 10,000 standard hours) $\times$ \$.75 per hour
$$= \$750 \text{ (unfavorable)}$$

The journal entries to record the fixed overhead cost information in tableau entries (17) through (22) would be

```
Fixed Overhead Control  ...................................  9,525
    Miscellaneous Accounts Payable  ........................          9,525
To record fixed overhead costs.

Overhead Applied (at standard)  ...........................  7,500
Fixed Overhead Price Variance (unfavorable)  ................    150
Fixed Overhead Quantity Variance (unfavorable)  ............    750
Fixed Overhead Capacity Variance (unfavorable)  ............  1,125
    Fixed Overhead Control  ..............................          9,525
To apply fixed overhead and to record fixed overhead variances.
```

The variances calculated using finished units as the activity base are different from those shown here. This should not be surprising, since 80 percent (2,000/ 2,500) of capacity was used in September if finished product is the activity base, while 88 percent (11,000/12,500) was used if direct labor hours is the capacity base. When the activity base is measured in units of *output,* rather than units of input, the fixed overhead quantity variance will always be zero because there is, by definition, no deviation between actual output and "standard output" for that actual output. The resulting variance analysis is sometimes called a "four-way" analysis of overhead variances because only four—two for variable and two for fixed overhead—variances are computed.

Tableau Relations.   The order in which columns E, F, G, and H are shown in the tableau derives from the order of appearance of the various measures of the activity base used in the multipliers for the fixed overhead calculations. The major time-saving device of the Standard Cost Tableau is the information in column E. The numbers shown there after the first row are not part of any standard-cost journal entry, but they are, nevertheless, used or usable for all of the variance calculations but one (capacity). Notice in the top portion of the tableau cells that there is a helpful pattern of repeating uses of the same number as a multiplier for the various multiplications that must be performed.

The following relations hold within the tableau.

For row 1 (direct materials):

$$A = B + C \qquad D = E \qquad E = G + H$$

For rows 2 and 3 (direct labor and variable overhead):

$$A = B + E \qquad E = G + H$$

For row 4 (fixed overhead):

$$A = B + E \qquad E = F + G + H$$

For all rows:

$$A = H + B + F + G + (C - D)$$

The last equation says that actual costs (A) equal the sum of standard costs applied (H), plus all variances $(B, F,$ and $G)$, plus the net charge in raw materials inventory $(C - D)$. Work in process is debited with the amounts in column H, while the variances from columns $B, F,$ and G are charges (if positive) or credits (if negative) to income for the period.

BIBLIOGRAPHY

Davidson, S., J. S. Schindler, and Roman L. Weil: *Fundamentals of Accounting,* 5th ed., The Dryden Press, Hinsdale, Ill., 1975.

Dopuch, Nicholas, Jacob G. Birnberg, and Joel Demski: *Cost Accounting: Accounting Data for Management's Decisions,* 2nd ed., Harcourt Brace Jovanovich, New York, 1974.

Henrici, Seanley B.: Standard Costs for Manufacturing, 3rd ed., McGraw-Hill Book Company, New York, 1960.

Horngren, Charles T.: *Cost Accounting: A Managerial Emphasis,* 3rd ed., Prentice-Hall, Englewood Cliffs, N.J., 1972.

Lu, F. S.: "Controlled Cost: An Operational Concept and Statistical Approach to Standard Costing," *The Accounting Review,* vol. 42, pp. 321–330, April 1967.

Matz, Adolph, Othel J. Curry, and George W. Frank: *Cost Accounting,* 5th ed., South-Western Publishing Company, Cincinnati, Ohio, 1972.

Shillinglaw, Gordon: *Cost Accounting; Analysis and Control,* 3rd ed., Richard D. Irwin, Homewood, Ill., 1972.

Chapter **43**

Distribution Costs

HERBERT F. TAGGART
Professor Emeritus of Accounting, The University of Michigan

DEFINITION AND CHARACTERISTICS OF DISTRIBUTION COSTS

Definition. Distribution costs (often called marketing costs) include all costs of stimulating and directing demand for goods and services and the costs of getting goods and services into the hands of consumers, including the costs involved in keeping records of sales and collections.

Business Functions and Their Costs. The functions of business, looked upon broadly, may be divided into two categories: production and distribution. Every business activity falls into one category or the other. However, two "handmaiden" functions are often distinguished because, looked at individually, they are niether production nor distribution. These are finance and general administration. These functions serve both production and distribution, and their costs are therefore production and distribution costs; but, in an enterprise which both produces and distributes, these ancillary functions serve the major functions jointly, and the division or allocation of their costs between the two basic functions involves the use of discretionary procedures to such an extent that the result may be of doubtful utility. However, certain activities often included under the head of "finance" or "general administration" are of such a character that they can be related in a logical and useful way to the two major functions.

Distribution. As noted, the principal functions of distribution are (1) those aimed at creating or stimulating demand and (2) those which follow the placing of orders by customers. The two main branches of distribution are accordingly epitomized as "order getting," and "order filling." The specifics, however, go well beyond a narrow interpretation of these terms. Order getting includes market research, advertising, sales promotion, personal selling, impersonal selling (such as mail-order selling), and in some cases technical services, such as application engineering and the like. Order filling includes the paper work involved in processing customers' orders, issuing shipping documents, passing on credit, inventory control, and customer accounting, as well as the physical operations of picking stock, packing shipments, loading cars or trucks, and similar items. It also includes collection routines and, in many cases, bad debts expense.

Distribution is the sole function of mercantile enterprises, such as wholesalers and retailers, so that all costs of such enterprises fall into the distribution area. To this statement there are, of course, some exceptions, such as coffee roasting by grocery wholesalers and the drapery and floor-covering workrooms of retailers. These partake of the nature of production, but they are commonly of relatively minor importance. It can be said in substance, therefore, that the costs of even the finance and general administrative functions of mercantile enterprises are distribution costs.

This broad description of the distributive process will be the foundation for consideration of distribution costs in this chapter. It does not follow, however, that in the typical business entity all these activities are carried on in organizational segments which are under the jurisdiction of distribution executives. Some functions essential to the distributive process are carried on in other branches of the enterprise, such as the factory. A complete study of distribution costs must take into account such activities.

Production.   The term "production" applies equally to goods and services, and the distribution functions for both are identical except that in the usual case services do not require physical handling and delivery. Production shares some service functions with distribution, an example being personnel. This fact gives rise to problems of cost allocation between production and distribution. In certain cases, given operations may qualify and be accounted for as production in one instance and as distribution in another. A good example is packing goods for shipment. If this operation is performed as a continuous part of the production process, it will ordinarily be accounted for as a cost of production. If, on the other hand, goods arrive at a certain state of completion, are placed in storage, and are packed for shipment only after orders are received, the packing function falls in the distribution area.

Finished goods storage is another function which falls somewhere between production and distribution. If the finished goods warehouse is under the supervision of factory executives, its operating costs may be included among factory costs. If, on the other hand, warehousing of finished goods is entirely divorced from the factory, the associated costs will probably be accounted for in the distribution category.

Finance.   Basically, finance involves providing the cash resources necessary for operating the entire business. The function includes planning financial policies, issuing and maintaining records of securities and loans negotiated, and cash planning and management. Most of these operations come under the aegis of the treasurer and/or the controller. In some companies finance also embraces the entire accounting establishment, including maintaining all accounts, financial data processing, credit and collections, and related activities. Some of these areas fall into the territory previously described as distribution, and for purposes of this chapter they will be so treated.

Administration.   Administration may be divided into two categories: specific and general. Each substantive business function has its own administrative personnel to see to it that it is carried on efficiently, economically, and in accordance with policy. In addition, the company as a whole requires administration, performed at the top by the board of directors, and under their guidance by the company officers. In practice, "administration" is also a catchall, where functions which may really belong elsewhere but for various reasons are not so assigned may find a home. Partly this may be due to the fact that some functions frequently included in administration jointly serve several or all other functions, just as "general administration" does. Such a function may be personnel, for example, which may have overall responsibility for setting employment standards and hiring policies, devising compensation plans, dealing with employee representatives, and allied activities for all parts of the organization. Any complete statement of the costs of a major function, such as distribution, must include an allowance for such costs.

There is a question whether the more general aspects of general administration and of finance should be allocated at all to the operating functions such as production and distribution. Such allocations are bound to be somewhat arbitrary, and for this reason they should always be regarded as being no better than reasonable approximations of the truth. However, if what is desired is a representation of the net income derived from the several segments of the business, such allocations must be made.

It would obviously be impossible to deal with all the cost analysis and control problems of every type of distributive activity in anything short of an encyclopedia. This chapter therefore confines itself to a consideration of those aspects of what is usually thought of as a "typical" manufacturer, wholesaler, and retailer, though recognizing that the description may not fit any specific member of any of these groups. The principles and procedures, however, are adaptable to the particular circumstances of any enterprise which performs the functions to which they relate.

Importance of Distribution Costs.   To belabor the fact that distribution costs are important and worth a great deal more attention than has sometimes been given them is hardly necessary. Exhibit 1 provides an unusually complete breakdown of distribution costs of the same line of products at three levels. A manufacturer of mechanical equipment, from its own records and other sources, prepared a tabulation from which the figures in Exhibit 1 are adapted. They illustrate the functional classification of distribution costs, an analytical device which is of basic importance in the study and evaluation of costs. They also demonstrate what appears to be a common pattern of distribution cost relationships, as far as such a pattern can be traced in published sources. The retailer's costs absorb a substantially greater portion of the consumer's dollar than do those of the wholesaler, and the distribution costs of the manufacturer, who relies heavily on the wholesale and retail channels, are apt to constitute a relatively small fraction of the total.

Prevalence of Joint or Common Costs.   One of the most significant characteristics of distribution costs is the frequency with which joint or common costs are

EXHIBIT 1   Analysis of Retail Price

	Total	Manufacturer	Distributor	Dealer
Manufacturing cost plus profit....	50.9%	50.9%	—	—
Distribution costs:				
Administrative...............	11.7%	1.3%	1.3%	9.1%
Selling.....................	9.7	.9	1.9	6.9
Advertising.................	7.7	3.3	1.5	2.9
Transportation & delivery......	6.0	1.9	0.8	3.3
Storage & handling...........	2.2	0.9	1.3	—
Order service................	0.3	0.1	0.2	—
Market research..............	0.1	0.1	—	—
Product planning.............	0.1	0.1	—	—
Product service..............	(1.3)	0.1	0.2	(1.6)
Occupancy...................	3.3	—	—	3.3
All other....................	4.3	—	—	4.3
Net before income taxes........	5.0	—	2.0	3.0
Total distribution cost.......	49.1%	8.7%	9.2%	31.2%
Retail price....................	100.0%	59.6%	9.2%	31.2%

encountered. Joint costs are those which are common to two or more segments of the business. The segments may be chronological or geographical or they may consist of customers, customer groups, orders, shipments, products, product lines, distribution functions, or any other significant object of scrutiny. Whenever the analyst attempts to determine the costs of relatively narrow segmental categories, such as individual customers or products, the great bulk of costs will be found to be joint or common, and their application to such segments requires the development of logical methods of allocation. This situation is somewhat in contrast to that often encountered in the study of manufacturing costs where direct labor and materials bulk large, and joint costs are in the main confined to overhead items.

Direct and Indirect Costs.   Costs which are not joint or common to more than one distribution segment are usually referred to as direct, while the joint or common costs are said to be indirect. These terms must be used with care, however, since directness and indirectness always involve a point of view which must constantly be kept in mind. Thus a cost which is direct when looked at in one way is indirect when regarded from a different standpoint. For example, selling cost which can be clearly identified with a particular customer is indirect when considered in relation to the several commodities which the customer buys. Varying degrees of indirectness must also be recognized. The selling cost just referred to is indirect with respect to the commodities by only one step or degree. Only one method of allocation or assignment is necessary to establish its relationship with the individual commodities. The salary of the president of the company, on the other hand, is only remotely related to any significant analytical segment, and, if it is to be allocated at all, must be dealt with in several successive stages.

Directness and indirectness relate also to time periods. The most obvious examples are costs which are chargeable to the operations of a given year, such as most labor service items, as opposed to costs which have to be allocated or assigned to time periods, such as depreciation. Such time allocations are occasionally matters of considerable significance.

Fixed and Variable Costs.   A concept related to the preceding discussion, but by no means identical in definition or effect, is the dichotomy between fixed and variable costs. Fixed costs are those costs which, for a given period of time, do not fluctuate with changes in the rate of business activity. Variable costs, on the other hand, do increase with increased activity and decrease as activity decreases, though not necessarily at the same rate.

Costs are fixed for a variety of reasons: because of contractual arrangements, as in the case of salaries; because they are imposed by outside authority, subject to no control within the business, as in the case of property taxes; because of accounting conventions, as in the case of depreciation; because of decisions by top management, as in the case of some advertising authorizations. The terms controllable or avoidable (for variable) and uncontrollable or unavoidable (for fixed) are sometimes used synonymously with the parenthetically indicated terms, but this usage is somewhat questionable. Management can, by taking proper thought and action, exercise a degree of control over the most fixed of costs, though usually the measures taken have their effects in the long run, and not immediately. Variable costs can, by their nature, be controlled more directly and immediately.

Distribution costs are sometimes spoken of and treated as if they were all fixed. This is particularly true when price policies are under consideration. The expression "selling and administrative overhead" is illustrative of this tendency, since administrative costs, being largely salaries and occupancy cost, do tend to be predominantly fixed. It is an error, however, to think of distribution costs as an essentially fixed category. Large segments are decidedly controllable because they vary with activity.

DISTRIBUTION COSTS IN THE ACCOUNTS AND IN FINANCIAL REPORTING

Distribution Cost Accounts. The first step in orderly examination of any subject is logical classification. Such classification results in grouping like phenomena and in distinguishing unlike data. It makes possible the drawing of logical conclusions and the taking of appropriate actions, if any action is indicated. In the accounting area these objectives are arrived at by two mechanisms, principally by making comparisons and by establishing responsibility. Proper account classifications promote these objectives by making possible the collection of basic data in a logical manner.

Natural Divisions and Functions. The most common and useful classifications of costs are in terms of natural divisions and functions. Natural divisions are sometimes called objects of expenditure. The term refers to what is bought, as contrasted with what is accomplished. Functions, on the other hand, represent what is accomplished—the distribution activities. Natural divisions include the items which the "person in the street" would probably list if he were asked to name the merchant's expenses—wages, rent, fuel, electricity, insurance, taxes, and so forth. Functions are the operations which the merchant carries on by means of the services derived from these expenditures—purchasing, selling, advertising, delivery, and the like. The functions correspond to the responsibilities for getting these tasks done according to plan. Each function utilizes personal services, supplies, and the other objects of expenditure.

The most acceptable system of cost classifications utilizes both of these concepts, since both are necessary for attaining the desired objectives. The functional breakdown is controlling, providing the major subheads of the chart of accounts, each function being supported by the natural expenses which it entails. Account classifications which answer to this description vary infinitely in scope and particularity, depending on the organization of the accounting entity and the purposes to be served.

Distribution Costs in Financial Reports. The usual published financial report contains almost no details of distribution costs. In many cases, in fact, distribution costs are lumped together with cost of goods sold and all other operating expenses in a single conglomerate figure. It is therefore a safe generalization to say that substantially no information about distribution costs can be obtained from the usual published reports except, of course, in the case of merchandising enterprises, where nearly all operating costs are of a distribution nature. Even here the detail shown is apt to be very sketchy. The reasons for this paucity of information are clear and reasonably convincing. The average stockholder would be little enlightened by a more detailed breakdown, and competition might be too much so. Cost facts, beyond the bare essentials, are among the most jealously guarded business secrets. One of the very real penalties of running afoul of the price-discrimination provisions of the Robinson-Patman Act is that, if the cost proviso is resorted to as a defense, the innermost details of the respondent's distribution activities must be exposed. This fact unquestionably has a bearing on the infrequency with which the cost defense has been invoked.

Problems of Timing. It is a safe assertion that the distribution costs which are in published statements, whether identifiable or not, are all in the income statement and constitute all such costs incurred during the period included in the report, regardless of their true relationship to the revenues of the period. Distribution costs, in other words, are seldom, if ever, capitalized or deferred to future periods. (This statement, of course, does not apply to distribution facilities, such as warehouses or sales offices, the costs of which are capitalized and depreciated as are other capital assets.)

This failure to defer distribution costs, even where they are clearly for the benefit of subsequent periods, constitutes, in some cases at least, an obvious disregard of the general rule that expenses should be matched with the revenues for whose benefit they are incurred. Examples of the incurrence of substantial and often accurately measurable distribution costs in one period which are obviously for the benefit of one or more subsequent periods are not unusual. They ordinarily relate to the creation or stimulation of demand. A new product is about to be introduced or a new sales territory entered. Preliminary advertising, promotional efforts by salespeople, signing up of dealers and distributors, establishment of sales offices, may entail heavy expenditures, with no return in the form of revenue during the period when they are incurred. In spite of an obvious failure of such costs to match current revenues, they are almost certain to be written off immediately. For this there are, of course, two reasons. One is "conservatism," the contention that such costs should not be deferred since there is no way of knowing that they will be productive or, if they are, what period of time they will benefit. The other reason is that such expenditures can be deducted for tax purposes, and there is an understandable reluctance to have the books out of step with the tax returns.

Schiff[1] points out that transportation of finished goods from plant to warehouse and the cost of storing them up to the time of shipment to customers should be added to inventory costs if the matching concept is to be faithfully followed. This is particularly true in businesses where production and sales cycles differ, especially if monthly reports are relied upon for judging executive performance.

Though the arguments for charging off such expenditures at once may be sufficiently compelling to condone this infraction of the matching rule, this treatment of such items is likely to present some problems in the analysis of distribution costs and the interpretation of their fluctuations from period to period. This is because the objective of a great many such analyses is to relate the costs to concurrent sales of commodities or services to specific classes of customers. If the immediate objective of the expenditure is not current sales, but rather to lay the foundation for future sales, whatever analysis is made must take this fact into account.

PURPOSES OF DISTRIBUTION COST ANALYSIS

Definition.   An authoritative definition of distribution cost analysis is as follows:[2]

> Distribution cost analysis is the assembling of the various items of distribution cost into meaningful classifications and their comparison in this form with alternative expenditures and with related sales volumes and gross margin. More specifically, it is a technique used by individual business concerns for the determination of the costs of performing specific marketing activities and of costs and profits for various segments of the business such as products or product groups, customer classes, or units of sale—and a study of these findings in the light of possible alternatives.

Purposes.   The principal ends to be served by distribution cost analysis may be summed up under two heads: cost control and assistance in consideration of pricing policies. The values of distribution cost analysis for these purposes are summarized in the following manner:[3]

---

[1]Michael Schiff, *Accounting and Control in Physical Distribution Management,* The National Council of Physical Distribution Management, Chicago, 1972, pp. 1–8.

[2]"The Values and Uses of Distribution Cost Analysis," a pamphlet published by the American Marketing Association, Chicago, 1957.

[3]*Ibid.*

Distribution cost analysis may be used by businessmen as an aid in determining profitable objectives for the business, in setting policies and procedures of operation, in determining the efficiency of their organization, and in measuring the profitability of operation in individual segments of the business.

More specifically, distribution costs analysis may be used:

1. To determine the kinds and amounts of expense incurred in each separate marketing activity such as outside selling, billing, warehousing, and delivery.

Availability of such cost data permits effective assignment of responsibility for cost performance to specific individuals supervising the activities. They make it possible also to trace the reasons for changes in cost over a period of time or variations in cost from budget, and the detailed record provides a basis for corrective action. They open the way to development of standard costs where standards are feasible.

2. To evaluate marketing methods, policies, and operating procedures.

Distribution cost analysis provides basic data for appraising the value of services (such as credit or delivery), methods of sale (by telephone, mail, or personal solicitation), and company performance of functions as opposed to use of outside organizations (for delivery, warehousing, and the like). It facilitates judgment as to when and where agents, distributors, or other middlemen will be more economical than direct sale.

3. To determine the marketing cost and profitability of the company's various products or customers.

Cost analysis permits calculation of these facts for individual products and customers or for such groups of them as product lines, brands, styles and sizes, classes of trade, sales territories, and the like. Such data are useful, too, in estimating costs and profits for proposed products or for changes in product or customer mix.

4. To determine the relationship between cost and order size—as a basis for diminishing losses on small orders and as a basis for quantity-discount schedules conforming to the Robinson-Patman Act.

Any general use of distribution cost analysis by businessmen for the appraisal of marketing structure, policy, and plans would have significant economic implications. The effect would be to increase the general level of marketing efficiency. Competition, in turn, may be expected to transfer much of the economy gained to the public through lower prices. Thus, widespread use of distribution cost analysis would be the equivalent of a general technological advance in industry. The reduction in unit costs and increase in efficiency from use of distribution cost analysis may be even greater than that attained as a result of the pioneer work in time and motion studies and cost accounting in the factory.

Cost Control. Cost control is a process which pervades all levels of a business enterprise and engages, or should engage, the attention and support of every member of the organization. From the top, members of the board of directors exercise cost control in making decisions with respect to capital investments, areas of operation, and other basic policies. At the bottom, clerks or laborers exercise cost control in the way they use their time and how they treat company property. In between, the burden of cost control falls on supervisory personnel at all levels. These are the people who are responsible for the efficiency and economy with which business functions are carried out. It is primarily for them that cost analyses are prepared. The cost analysis reports which they receive should therefore be aimed at two basic ends: to provide guidance in carrying out their cost-control responsibilities, and to measure their success or failure.

Mechanics of Cost Control. Cost control is basically a matter of people reacting intelligently to the circumstances in which they find themselves. In order to react intelligently, however, they must have a means of understanding and evaluating the circumstances. This is what the mechanics of cost control provides.

Sales Plans and Goals. Cost control of distribution operations (as contrasted with top-level decisions made by boards of directors and executive officers) starts with a sales plan or goal based on market research, a study of company history, and surveys of the market and of competition. All levels of the marketing organization should participate in preparing the sales plan, since everyone from the field salesperson to the vice-president in charge of sales can make a contribution to the task. The sales plan, like all operating plans and budgets, should not be imposed from above. It should instead be the joint effort of all concerned, so that when it is adopted all participants will feel that their contributions have been given adequate weight and for that reason will be encouraged to shoulder their share of the responsibility for its success.

Rakes[4] emphasizes this point in describing sales forecasting procedures in his company:

> For a long time, salesmen were not called upon to participate in developing the marketing plan. Planning normally stopped at the sales manager level. If the sales manager is very close to his market area, his forecasts can be most effective. However, if the party submitting the forecast is not committed to making it happen, then the subsequent production and sales plans will be of little value. It is of little benefit to have a sales manager committed to a sales plan if the salesmen in the field who are calling on accounts are not committed to the same plan. To correct this situation, we decided to have each individual salesman forecast his sales for each product, customer by customer. By comparing forecasts with actual results, a measure of performance can be established for each salesman which can be tied in to bonuses or incentive compensation plans.

In the case of the salesstaff, the sales plan will normally take the form of a quota each is expected to meet, and hopefully to exceed. Each salesperson's compensation and chances for retention and promotion will depend upon his or her success. The sales quota must be sufficiently detailed to provide each salesperson with guidelines for efficiently using time and placing sales efforts. It should be detailed as to products and product lines. It may be quantified in terms of physical units, dollars of sales, dollars of gross margin, or in other ways.

In the case of sales supervisors, such as district or regional sales managers, the sales plan will consist of a consolidation of the sales quotas of those under their supervision. Their compensation and hopes for economic betterment, too, will depend on how well the personnel under their guidance perform.

Other branches of the distribution organization are also affected by the sales plan (as, of course, is true of the production or procurement organization). For example, warehousing and physical handling must be available at the right times and in the right places. Even the clerical staff must be geared to handle the work load which the sales plan will generate.

Budgets.   Distribution cost budgets must be prepared in the light of the sales forecast, and vice versa. The two are interdependent, since the volume of sales is influenced by the amount of money which management is willing to commit to the distribution process, and the amount of expenditures is determined in significant measure by the volume of sales desired. Of course, there is a limit to the capability of added expenditures in any given situation to produce added revenues, and thus must be recognized by those charged with preparing both sales plans and budgets. Chapter 40 should be consulted for rules of budget preparation and administration.

Distribution Cost Standards.   As in the case of manufacturing, the development and use of cost standards is entirely feasible in certain areas of distribution. This is particularly the case in clerical activities and in warehouse functions. The procedures for developing standards in these areas do not differ from those in manufacturing. Time and motion studies provide the basic data.

In order getting, however, the cost standard concept is, generally speaking, inappropriate. Keller[5] points this out with respect to field selling. Much cost analysis revolves around the concepts of functions and units of functional service.

    [4]Harold W. Rakes, *Grass Roots Forecasting,* Management Accounting, Vol. LVI, No. 3, p. 33, September 1974.
    [5]I. Wayne Keller, "Relative Profit Margin Approach to Distribution Costing," *NACA Bulletin,* vol. 30, no. 13, March 1949.

This is all very well in a factory (or an office) where, says Keller, "all circumstances are conducive to accurate recording of measurable work, and substantially accurate unit costs are secured." In selling, says this author,

> . . . cost per call is frequently set forth as one of these unit costs to be established. But what is a call? If the salesman has called upon the Jones Company and found the purchasing agent was not in, was that a call? You might say no. Let us eliminate that and consider only productive calls. But, what is a productive call and who decides that it falls into that category? I do not believe the salesman will record many nonproductive calls, for his innate optimism will lead him to consider all contacts productive to a degree.

It must be agreed that the concept of cost standards does not fit the activities of the salesperson, the creative functions of the advertising copywriter, the consideration of a customer's credit problems, and many other distributive functions. As a matter of fact, trying to straitjacket such operations within the cost standard concept may well defeat its own purpose, since it may result in work badly done and in frustrated and unhappy personnel. Where work is sufficiently routine and repetitive, and under direct and close supervision, however, the use of cost standards is to be recommended.

Responsibility for Cost Control.   As indicated above, cost control is the responsibility of every member of a business organization. Particular onus must be borne by those in supervisory positions at all levels. This is sometimes difficult to achieve in the distribution area, especially in those branches which consider themselves to be creative and artistic rather than humdrum and routine. This attitude characterizes almost the entire area of demand creation and channeling. To secure the cooperation of the persons engaged in these activities requires no small skill in salesmanship on the part of those who are charged with making the cost control mechanics work.

No cost control system will activate itself or motivate those whose cooperation is required unless someone is put in charge of devising suitable reports, making sure that they get into the proper hands, and following up to determine whether necessary actions have been taken. Ordinarily the company controller or someone within his organization is charged with these duties. Regardless of how well this activity is organized and staffed, however, it will be a failure unless top management is wholeheartedly behind it.

Pricing Policy.   It is almost an economic truism that the individual costs of merchants or producers do not determine their selling prices. Even the monopolist has to consider the factor of demand, and other sellers cannot ignore competition. As Beyer[6] says, "cost is probably the least important of the considerations . . . in a businessman's setting of his product prices." This does not mean, however, that costs can or should be ignored in the establishment of production, selling, and pricing policies. And distribution costs are of the same importance, *ceteris paribus,* as are production or acquisition costs. The common practice of adding a percentage (usually of manufacturing cost) to cover selling and administrative expense is a wholly inadequate recognition of this fact.

According to Joel Dean,[7] costs have these valid uses in the establishment of selling prices:

1. To measure the effects of alternative prices upon profits.
2. To guess what people (customers, competitors, and potential competitors) will do in response to a proposed price.

[6]Robert Beyer and Donald J. Trawicki, *Profitability Accounting for Planning and Control,* 2nd ed., The Ronald Press Company, New York, 1972, p. 297.

[7]Joel Dean, "Cost Forecasting and Price Policy," *The Journal of Marketing,* vol. 13, no. 3, pp. 284–285, January 1949.

3. To justify a course of price action that has already been decided upon. . . . Examples include satisfying the government that the provisions of the Robinson-Patman Act have been met, justifying prices before a regulatory commission, and convincing customers that the price rise was "necessary."

To these should be added a fourth use, which is to assist in determining whether alternative specifications or methods of production or selling methods and policies might bring about a satisfactory profit objective when price is so fixed by custom or competition that the individual seller can do nothing about it. In this use, price becomes a determinant of cost, rather than the contrary. As Dean puts it, "frequently the relation of cost to price is, in practice, inverted. The practical problem is to tailor costs to fit a predetermined selling price."

Price Differentiation. Total costs, including manufacturing or procurement as well as distribution, are of importance in consideration of total prices. In thinking about differential prices to classes of customers or in the light of differing quantities or methods of sale, distribution costs are of major significance. The chief exception to this statement is found in custom industries, such as job printing, where the size of an order may have a substantial effect on unit manufacturing as well as distribution costs. Differentiating prices for this reason should not be confused with so-called marginal or incremental pricing, which is founded on the proposition that, in considering the acceptance of a particular order or of business from a particular customer, fixed or "sunk" costs may be ignored. This type of pricing has limited utility in special circumstances (for example, for government contracts or for exports), but it is not acceptable for pricing where the Robinson-Patman Act is involved or as a built-in feature of pricing policy generally.

Pricing Under the Robinson-Patman Act. The usefulness of distribution cost analysis in considering price differentials is by no means confined to the matter of compliance with the Robinson-Patman Act, though it is often assumed that this is the case. Manufacturers or merchants who wish to offer price inducements for greater volumes of purchases or larger sizes of orders may do this intelligently only if they have at least an approximate idea of the cost savings involved. Even where such differentials are dictated by competition, sellers should not be content to meet such competition blindly. One obvious aspect of such a situation is that by studying their cost differentials they may discover how to increase them.

The portion of the Robinson-Patman Act which deals with price differentiation is Section 2(a), which generally forbids discrimination in price "between different purchasers of commodities of like grade and quality," with some exceptions. One of the exceptions is the cost proviso which reads as follows:[8] "That nothing herein contained shall prevent differentials which make only due allowance for differences in the cost of manufacture, sale or delivery resulting from the differing methods or quantities in which such commodities are to such purchasers sold or delivered."

Although the cost proviso includes manufacturing costs among those which may be taken into account in justifying price differentials, they are considered almost exclusively in custom industries where production takes place only after receipt of customers' orders. In substantially all cases where goods are produced for stock, reliance must be placed on the analysis of distribution costs.

For a law which has been on the statute books since 1936, there are remarkably few reliable guidelines to assure compliance. This is particularly true with respect to the cost proviso. One thing is sure: reliance on the cost proviso after a complaint has been issued or a private suit under Sec. 4 of the Clayton Act has been started is difficult, expensive, and uncertain. The cost proviso has been described, with

[8]Sec. 2(a), 15 U.S.C. 13 (a).

much justice, as "illusory." It is nevertheless true that sellers who wish to be in compliance with the law are well advised to conduct studies of their distribution costs for this purpose. Such studies have at least two important advantages. They make a favorable impression on the Federal Trade Commission investigator, thus perhaps forestalling formal complaints, and they often uncover uneconomic aspects of the sellers' sales organization and methods which can be corrected.

Cost studies made for Robinson-Patman purposes involve analyses by commodities, customer groupings, order sizes, channels of trade, territories (sometimes, at least), and otherwise. These analyses are described hereafter under appropriate heads. The procedures suitable for managerial purposes do not necessarily differ from those needed for the cost defense, except that the latter must usually be more detailed and objective. Specific comments are reserved until later. Such "rules of the game" as are thoroughly established are detailed in Taggart's *Cost Justification.*[9]

Financial Reporting by Conglomerate or Diversified Companies. Another area in which distribution cost analysis may be of use is in reporting the results of operations of so-called conglomerate or diversified companies. To the extent that such companies choose or are required to publish figures showing the net results of operating in more than one industrial line, distribution costs common to two or more lines may have to be separated. It is to the advantage of everyone concerned that the methods used for such separations be as logical and defensible as possible.

MECHANICS AND PROCEDURES

Cost Comparisons. In its simplest form distribution cost analysis consists of time-period comparisons of parallel arrays of natural expense items, accompanied by some effort to appraise the changes from period to period. Thus this month is compared with last month, or with the same month last year and this year to date is compared with last year to date. Also the expenses are related to the factor which is presumed to cause or to justify the changes the comparison reveals. In most cases this factor will be sales, generally in dollars, but sometimes in physical units. The expenses which have remained unchanged per dollar of sales or per unit sold are assumed to have been properly controlled, whereas those whose rate has varied appreciably require further study. An attempt is made to ascertain the reason and perhaps fix the blame for costs whose rate has increased, and some effort should be made to seek the causes for decreased rates of expenditure and to encourage their continuance.

In small, uncomplicated enterprises, such as convenience groceries, this analytical procedure has much to recommend it. It is unsophisticated. It requires little more than a reasonably detailed chart of expense accounts and a healthy curiosity on the part of managers to know how well their efforts at expense control are working. It may lead them to attempt a simple form of budgeting, and their comparisons will then take on a new dimension: actual against budget.

As firms grow in size and complexity these measures become inadequate. To cite a simple example, when a convenience grocery takes on a line of fresh meats the relationship of expense levels to sales becomes more complex. In order to understand the forces at work and their effects, it is necessary to sort out the expenses so as to know which pertain to groceries and which to meats. Whatever analytical procedures are in use must then be applied separately to each branch of the business. Also the manager of the grocery department becomes responsible for his expenses and the manager of the meat department for his.

Further increases in size and complexity demand still more sophisticated cost

[9]Herbert F. Taggart, *Cost Justification,* Bureau of Business Research, The University of Michigan, Ann Arbor, 1959.

analyses and control measures. Operating functions become identified, and the functional breakdown of costs becomes essential to their study and control. Cost comparisons, whether by time periods or with budgets, are made by functions, so that the manager of the function may be informed and held responsible. Cost standards may be developed in certain areas, and comparisons are made between actual and standard costs. Deviations of actual from standard costs are analyzed to determine their causes and to ascertain appropriate actions. The establishment of branch stores or warehouses or sales offices adds a geographical aspect to the cost comparisons. Each such unit becomes a center to which all the cost comparison techniques may be applied, and in suitable cases the performance of each such decentralized operation may be compared with others in the same category.

Complete Functional Analysis. The logical conclusion to this evolution is arrived at when it is desired to know costs in terms of commodities sold or services performed, customers, channels of trade, order sizes, territories, and so forth. A comprehensive description of what is involved is found in the report of the Federal Trade Commission's Advisory Committee on Cost Justification.[10] Though this report was prepared with the cost proviso of the Robinson-Patman Act in mind, the analysis procedures are in sufficiently general terms so that they furnish guidance in all circumstances.

Relevant Costs. Since the sole purpose of distribution cost analysis is to enable management to arrive at intelligent decisions with respect to business problems, it is essential that the cost data on which management relies be relevant to these problems. That is, the costs which management is asked to take into account must have a logical relationship to the decisions which management must make. This makes it necessary to examine different costs for different purposes.

For the purpose of deciding whether certain actual or proposed differential pricing plans conform to the requirements of the Robinson-Patman Act, for example, all related costs, whether fixed or variable, are pertinent. In view of the interpretation of this law by the Federal Trade Commission and the courts, it is plainly impossible to arrive at a reliable conclusion on the basis of anything short of fully allocated costs.

On the other hand, many business decisions require that certain costs be ignored. These are the costs which would not be affected by the decision in question. The best examples are to be found in connection with decisions to increase or decrease production, to add a product to the line (or delete one from the line), to add or abandon a sales territory, to serve or refuse to serve specific customers or classes of customers. In all these cases the relevant costs are those which would be increased or decreased if the decision is made to take the action proposed. If a cost will be neither increased nor decreased by the decision, it may be ignored, and the decision makers' thinking should not be confused by putting before them tabulations containing irrelevant costs.

Generally speaking, the costs which may be ignored in such cases are the fixed, or relatively fixed costs, while the costs which must be taken into account are the variable costs. This is the principal reason for attempting to divide all costs between these two categories.

Accountants' opinions differ widely as to the degree to which attention should be concentrated on variable costs. Some would apparently be willing to exclude fixed costs entirely from the decision-making process. Others advocate full costing with equal vigor. Schiff and Mellman[11] report that, in the companies which they studied, "The net profit approach, where all costs and expenses are allocated to

[10]Reproduced in *ibid.,* pp. 551–572.
[11]Michael Schiff and Martin Mellman, *Financial Management of the Marketing Function,* Financial Executives Research Foundation, New York, 1962.

products is most frequently used. . . ." At the same time they found much use made of cost analyses which were not carried out so far.

Perhaps the best advice is that both variable and full costing have their merits and uses and each should be employed where it best meets the need. It should be kept in mind, of course, that neither of these devices is a matter of absolutes. Costs which would not vary with a small change in volume or over a short period of time may well show variation when larger changes or longer time periods are involved. A cost is neither fixed nor variable because of its name. The only way to tell how to classify it is by a realistic consideration of how it would actually react to the proposed change in circumstances.

COST ANALYSIS IN DISTRIBUTIVE ENTERPRISES

Every concern engaged in retail or wholesale selling of goods or services indulges to some degree in distribution cost analysis if it keeps books at all. The vast majority of such enterprises, being small, neither need nor employ sophisticated analyses. The methods they use are unlikely to go beyond simple cost comparisons, usually by time periods. They may go a step further if there are trade association or similar statistics available, and check to see whether they are doing as good a managerial job as their contemporaries. Larger retail and wholesale enterprises may carry on detailed studies of operating costs and results. Some of these are described below.

Retailing.   Cost analysis in the retail field has been promoted by the National Retail Merchants Association (NRMA) and other trade associations, by the U.S. Department of Commerce, by university bureaus of business research, and by manufacturers who provide accounting advice and assistance to their dealers.

NRMA Expense Accounting.   By far the best known and most carefully formulated scheme of accounting for costs at the retail level is that of the National Retail Merchants Association. The activities of this Association in this area began with the appointment of a committee in 1916. Its report recommended the creation and adoption of a common expense accounting language. As the committee remarked,[12] "The prime object is to establish a basis of understanding between the stores so that in conversing with one another, or comparing statistics of operation, the terms used and the meaning attached to them may be identical to all." The achievement of this objective made possible the publication by the Controllers' Congress of the Association of an annual compilation entitled "Merchandising and Operating Results of Departmentized Stores," and by Harvard University of the annual reports called "Operating Results of Department and Specialty Stores." (The latter publication was taken over by the NRMA in 1963.) Without the standardization of terminology and classification of accounts these reports would have been unfeasible, or at least much less intelligible and useful. The Association has also published many valuable studies of significant aspects of store operation and cost control.

NRMA Expense Accounting Manuals.   The National Retail Merchants Association has published a series of expense accounting manuals which have contained definitions of terms and instructions which enable participating stores to inform themselves about their own costs and to participate in the joint collection of expense statistics.

The system of expense accounting described in this manual is constructed around 20 natural expense categories and 23 "expense centers"—another name for functions. Each expense center is charged with the natural expenses which it

---

[12]Quoted in 1950 edition of the National Retail Dry Goods Association (NRDGA), *Standard Expense Accounting Manual,* New York, p. 9.

incurs. For example, the first expense center, management, is charged with payroll, taxes, supplies, services purchased, unclassified, traveling, insurance, professional services, and donations. This manual places a good deal of emphasis on the multistore organization. The 23 basic expense centers are designed to be those which are adequate for the branch store, and provision is made for "fanning out" these functions into a finer breakdown suitable for use by the main, or central, store which provides staff services and supervision for all units of the group. For small, unitary stores the manual also suggests keeping expense accounts only in terms of the natural divisions, if the complete dual classification of expenses is unduly complex. Thus flexibility is provided so that any store may adopt whatever version of the system may be best suited to its own needs.

Cost Allocations.   Two types of common cost allocations are provided for—among stores in a multistore group, and among selling departments within a given store. In both cases the manual recognizes the reluctance of some managements to allocate common costs and their preference for internal operating statements which carry cost analysis only far enough to ascertain contribution margins.

Production Unit Accounting.   An important feature of the manual for purposes of expense control is what is called "production unit accounting." This is based on the proposition that each expense center constitutes a "job of work" to be done, and that, for most centers the work accomplished can be measured in terms of work units, or "units of measure," as the manual calls them. Thus the work unit for the cash office is $100 of cash receipts handled, and for the sign shop is 100 square inches of signs made. By measuring these work units and watching unit costs, productivity and efficiency are promoted. The units of measure are also useful in making the cost allocations among and within stores.

Merchandise Management Accounting.   This method of measuring the relative profitability of individual items on the retail merchant's floor is also known as "item profitability analysis." It is an attempt to provide retail merchandise managers with cost and operating data in terms of the individual commodities for which decisions must be made. Such data, if reliably obtainable, should have much more meaning for decision making than overall departmental financial data, which lump all commodities together.

This method is based on a functional analysis of costs and a careful distinction between fixed and variable expenses. It results in a showing of the contribution made by each item studied toward meeting fixed costs and adding something to the profit pool. It is particularly applicable to big-ticket items such as major appliances and furniture. In its early stages it was promoted by an appliance manufacturer which wished to show that its appliances made greater contributions to fixed expenses and profits than competing brands.

An illustration used in an address before the National Retail Dry Goods Association gives some indication of what is involved. Variable expenses involved in handling a particular item are determined by conventional accounting techniques to be as follows:[13]

Receiving	$0.65	Delivery	$3.63
Warehousing	$1.45	Installation	$3.50
Selling	6.0%	Warranty	$2.10
Advertising	2.5%	Markdowns	4.0%
Carrying charges (credit)	(2.75%)	Other costs	1.17%
Credit expense	$2.00		

Given selling price and laid-down cost, the contribution of this item can readily be computed.

---

[13]Derived from an address by Robert I. Jones before the NRDGA annual conference, January 9, 1957.

It is clear that figures of this sort could be of immense assistance in determining policies with respect to stocking, pricing, and promotion of commodities, and in negotiations with suppliers, who can have great influence on a number of the cost categories and in particular on installation and warranty costs.

Wholesaling.   Distribution cost analyses required by the wholesaler differ neither in scope nor in kind from those suitable for the manufacturer. Retailer, wholesaler, and manufacturer are equally interested in analyses which aid in solving problems of cost control, and each of them has or may have the need to control the operations of branches which are geographically separated from the principal headquarters. Branch accounting is not given specific attention here, since the problems of branch accounting are largely mechanical rather than analytical. Branch accounting involves methods of assuring prompt and accurate communication, maintenance of uniformity in accounting procedures and policies, avoidance of the waste involved in decentralized functions which could be more economically handled at a central location, and similar matters. In the area of analysis, branch accounting involves merely the application at several locations of the same procedures which are used by the unitary enterprise.

With respect to segmented analysis, the retailer is interested primarily in product (merchandise) breakdowns, while wholesalers and manufacturers are equally concerned with customer and order-size analyses. The sections covering these subjects which follow are therefore equally applicable to wholesalers and manufacturers.

TERRITORIAL COST ANALYSIS

Perhaps the most common form of distribution cost analysis by manufacturers is analysis by territories. Part of the reason for the prevalence of such analyses is the fact that many territorial expenses are direct. All that is required to obtain the data on such costs is a chart of accounts which contains a territorial breakdown. More importantly, it is difficult to see how a satisfactory territorial sales organization can be established and maintained without knowledge of the costs involved.

A large company is apt to have more than one level of territory. At the lowest level is the district and at the intermediate level the region. The material which follows is couched in terms of sales districts, but, since sales regions are merely groups of sales districts, essentially the same procedures and considerations apply to regions as to districts. The region's costs are the summation of the costs of the districts of which it is composed, with regional management and functional services added. Regional management and functions (such as, for example, personnel selection and training) supplement and to some extent supplant the related home office activities.

Objectives.   The principal objectives of territorial cost analysis are described in *NACA Research Series No. 21* as follows:[14]

> 1. To determine profitability of each geographical unit in the company's marketing area. In this case, manufacturing costs and sales (or gross margin) must also be analyzed by territories.
> 2. To estimate the effect which a proposed change in territorial operations can be expected to have on profits.
> 3. To measure the effectiveness with which management in charge of an individual territory is doing its work.

---

[14]"The Assignment of Nonmanufacturing Costs to Territories and Other Segments," *NACA Bulletin*, vol. 33, no. 4, part 3. p. 528, December 1951. The NACA (National Association of Cost Accountants) changed its name to the NAA (National Association of Accountants), subsequent to the issue of this study.

Business Decisions Affected by Knowledge of Territorial Costs.   The prime purpose served by an analysis of territorial operating data is to determine whether the territorial executives are doing their jobs. Both revenue and cost data are necessary for this purpose, since territorial managers are charged with adhering to company policies with respect to pricing, product mix, and other matters which affect revenues and gross margins, as well as with the control of costs. Decisions with respect to keeping and rewarding territorial personnel are among the most important served by analysis of territorial operations.

Other managerial decisions which require a knowledge of territorial costs are as follows:

1. Changes in intensity of sales coverage. Involved are proposals to add to or subtract from the regular sales force; to utilize the services of special salespeople supplied by home or regional offices, and other methods of contacting larger or smaller numbers of customers or spending more (or less) time with each.

2. Changes in intensity of advertising and sales promotion. Decisions relating to the use of local advertising media are involved, as well as the use of displays, point-of-sale material, samples, demonstrators, and the like.

3. Changes in territorial boundaries. Should new territories be added, or old ones abandoned? Should a territory be split, or combined with all or part of another? Light on such questions is thrown by studies of territorial profitability and the effects on territorial operating costs and effectiveness of changes in population, types of industry, traffic conditions, and other factors which affect the mobility of salespeople and their ability to provide adequate coverage of the area.

4. Changes in methods of covering a territory. Customers may be contacted by telephone, by personal visitation, by mail, by local advertising. The relative costs of each form of solicitation are significant, and the proper choice of methods or combinations of methods is dependent to a major extent on cost analyses which demonstrate their economic effectiveness. Methods which are suitable for one territory are not necessarily suitable for another.

Direct Costs.   The direct costs of operating a sales territory are those which are generated within the territory and the amount of which is not determined by any sort of proration or allocation. Precisely what the direct costs are will depend on the functions performed by the territorial organization. They will invariably include direct selling costs, such as salespeople's compensation, travel, and customer entertainment. They will include also rent, utilities, supplies, and other operating costs of the district sales office, if there is one. Salespeople's equipment, such as samples, literature, price lists, order forms, and the like, are also direct costs, although some of these items are usually supplied by headquarters and may or may not be charged to the territory on a cost basis. Ideally they should be, but if they are not material in amount they may be included in sales administration overhead and allocated to territories along with other costs of the administrative function.

If the territory has its own warehouse facilities and delivery system, the costs of these functions, too, are direct territorial costs. In such a case the territorial manager becomes more than a sales manager and is responsible for substantially all company activities domiciled in the territory. He may well have, in this event, territorrial sales, warehousing, and delivery executives as his immediate subordinates. Another group of activities which may or may not take place within the territory embraces credit and collection, billing, customer accounting, and related clerical functions. Some if not all of these areas are likely to be centralized, however, in a large organization, and especially one which is equipped with a computer.

Readily Allocable Indirect Costs.   The costs of such functions as those mentioned in the preceding paragraph, to the extent that they are centralized and shared by two or more territories, can ordinarily be allocated to the respective territories on logical and acceptable bases. Such allocations require measuring the services received by each territory and attaching appropriate unit costs. The receiving and storage portion of warehousing cost, for example, may be charged to territories in terms of territorial sales volumes, measured in physical units if possible, or in dollars if uniformity of sales mix permits. The order picking and packing activities in the centralized warehouse may be assigned to territories on the basis of the number of orders shipped, providing each territory's orders are of approximately equal average size. If they are not, a detailed cost study of picking and packing will disclose the costs of handling various sizes of orders, and an equitable assignment to territories may then be made. It is to be noted, of course, that such a study of order processing costs is necessary for other distribution cost analyses, so that the territorial assignment is not its sole purpose.

Delivery, if by common carrier, should present few difficulties. If delivery is made by company truck fleet, however, and trips cross the boundaries of more than one territory, there will be some problems in an equitable cost assignment. Relative ton-miles or some other physical measurement of service received will probably achieve reasonable equity. Again, the cost of company-operated delivery functions must be analyzed for purposes of control, and the further analysis for allocation to territories may well be justified as a control measure.

The allocation of centralized credit, billing, customer accounting, and related costs to territories can usually be done by using as units of functional service the numbers of customers, orders, shipments, invoice lines, and other appropriate measures. In this area, however, the cost analyst should consider whether the increased accuracy attained by meticulous adherence to logical procedures is worth the time and effort. These costs may be of such relatively minor magnitude that merging them with other administrative items for allocation on a broad base may be satisfactory. It should not be forgotten, however, that a territory which has many small customers and correspondingly small orders requires much more of these services in proportion to sales volume than does the opposite type of territory.

The costs of certain types of regional or home office personnel may also be charged against territorial operations with a good deal of assurance. These are people who provide specialized assistance to all territories and perhaps perform technical supervisory functions. Examples are internal auditors, advertising and sales promotion specialists, product specialists, sales engineers, and the like. Also missionary salespeople, sales training specialists, and others of similar character can be treated the same way. Charges for their travel and a per diem for their services are the appropriate cost assignment method.

Remote Indirect Costs.   Many company-wide costs are not so easily assigned to territories. Such a cost may be national, and especially institutional, advertising. Probably the best basis for allocating such costs to territories is relative sales potential, measured by population or in some other suitable way. Territorial sales quotas or goals may also be used. Actual sales dollars is hardly a satisfactory basis. Such advertising is aimed at potential sales, and the territory which does not achieve its potential should not be rewarded by being charged a lower share of general advertising. Neither should the territory which exceeds its quota be penalized.

Home office sales administration obviously must be charged to territories if territorial net profits are to be ascertained. No single basis for such an allocation is ideal. Equal amounts to each territory are sometimes used for this purpose. Other measures are based on the numbers of people supervised, or their total compensation, or the total of direct territorial expenses. The ideal measure, of course, would be the burden on time and energy of the administrative organization imposed by each territory. At least two insurmountable obstacles prevent the use of this factor. One is the extreme difficulty, if not impossibility, of obtaining such a measure. Reliable time reports from such people as the general sales manager are hardly conceivable. Estimates of time spent by the same individuals will be strongly influenced by what happened yesterday. The other obstacle is the fact that the attention required by individual sales districts fluctuates widely from year to year. A territory where the sailing is smooth this year may have to break in a new salesperson next year, or may be threatened by exceptionally keen competition, or have a marked turnover in dealerships. Allocation of this type of cost should be on the basis of long-run considerations not influenced by short-term crises.

Market research falls into the same cost category with general sales administration. It seldom has a discernible connection with specific sales territories. Substantially all market research is forward-looking—devoted to the products or demand-influencing methods of next year or following years. This is a cost which might conceivably be capitalized or deferred and charged against the future periods which it benefits. Orthodox accounting, however, calls for charging it against the revenues of the year in which it is incurred. In any particular year the market research cost incurred and charged immediately to expense is in lieu of charges for earlier years' market research which might have been deferred and charged to this year. This treatment may be the only practical approach and thus makes good accounting sense. The only exception might be a year in which expenditures for this purpose were materially larger than normal. Allocation of this cost to territories may well be on the same basis as the allocation of general marketing administration.

Distribution's share of general company administration is even more remote from the territory. The only purpose served by its allocation is to arrive at a figure of net territorial profit, and the validity of such a figure would be questioned by many authorities. Any allocation method contains a considerable element of arbitrariness. Actual or potential sales or the total of previously assigned costs have approximately equal logical merit.

Territorial Operating Reports. The results of territorial operations need to be reported to the various levels of management. At the bottom are the territorial managers. Frequently they receive reports on only those items over which they have direct control: sales and direct territorial expenses. *NACA Research Series No. 21* quotes one company executive as follows:[15] "My personal preference is to stop with the 'territorial manager's margin.' Why bother him with items he can't control? In fact, why even show the figures if you do not want an argument on how expenses are distributed?"

And indeed if the territorial managers' performance is to be evaluated on the basis of some variety of contribution margin, and especially if their compensation is to be geared to this, there is much to be said for this point of view. On the other hand, some companies routinely charge their field locations with assessments for home office costs. Where this is a long-standing practice, it would be of questionable wisdom not to follow it also in territorial performance reports.

The exact items to be included in the computation of territorial contribution will differ according to company organization and the degree of the territory's autonomy. The figures on the reports should, of course, be accompanied by comparisons with quotas and budgets and with the same figures for other time periods, and perhaps with other territories.

Reports to higher levels of management may be on a net profit basis, or at least something closer to net profit than the territorial contribution. Precisely how such reports should be prepared depends to a great extent on what management wants

[15]*Ibid.,* p. 533.

or what it is used to. The accountant who prepares reports for these people can scarcely afford to ignore these factors. The purpose of such reports is largely to demonstrate whether or not each territory is carrying its full share of the load. If such reports are prepared, they should be accompanied by comparisons with planned or budgeted results. Decisions and conclusions should be based on the degree of success achieved by the territory in carrying out its assigned tasks, and not on absolute profit or loss results.

Robinson-Patman Aspects. It is not unusual for price-discrimination complaints to be limited to certain geographical areas. The areas chosen may not, of course, correspond precisely with the respondent's sales districts. Nevertheless, the existence of territorial cost data, prepared in the ordinary course of business, may be of great assistance to sellers who are attempting to defend their pricing policies. Generally speaking, if a price discrimination complaint is so geographically limited, costs of other areas are excluded from consideration.

Also, the company which wishes to avoid such a complaint by reviewing its costs and prices to see whether a clear case of cost justification could be made will ordinarily select a few representative sales districts in order to keep the scope of the study within reasonable bounds of time and expense. Such a study also is greatly expedited by the existence of a regular scheme of studying district operations for managerial purposes.

CUSTOMER COST ANALYSIS

Purposes. According to *NACA Research Series No. 21,*[16] the purposes of distribution cost analysis by customers are as follows:

(1) To determine how sales effort should be apportioned among different customers or classes of customers;

(2) To decide whether or not an individual account should continue to be solicited;

(3) To establish price differentials based upon differences in marketing costs incurred to serve various classes of customers; and

(4) To help to explain profit or loss shown on specific products or territories.

This study suggests that cost analysis by customers will ordinarily be done on the incremental basis. "The costs assigned to customers are those which will differ if one alternative is chosen rather than another." This statement reflects the fact that the bulk of the decisions which relate to customers are of the sort which is best served by this limited analysis. This is certainly the case where the analysis relates to individual customers, and also is true for the most part where customer groupings are involved.

If, however, the problem is that of price differentiation, full allocation of costs is essential. The incremental approach is inappropriate and inadequate if the legality of price differences is under consideration, and the adoption of a discount schedule or other scheme of price differences among customers without giving consideration to possible legal consequences is risky at best.

Analysis by Individual Customers. Complete cost analysis in terms of individual customers is rare. Such analyses on a comprehensive bases would be inordinately costly and unlikely to yield information which would be of much use in making the type of decisions which are commonly made with respect to individual customers. Considerations other than costs will ordinarily determine whether to drop or add a customer or whether to cultivate an existing customer more intensively or less so. The customers' potential, rather than their current performance, is the key question. If they could become profitable customers, sales effort is likely to be

[16]*Ibid.,* 33, p. 543.

spent on them, even though cost analysis might show that their business is now done at a loss.

The escapable costs of serving an individual customer are apt to be very small. Except for the cost of the merchandise itself, they will probably consist of whatever might be saved by discontinuing the salesperson's calls. And this is apt to be negligible unless the circumstances are unusual. If the customer's place of business lies along the salesperson's regular route, the only cost involved is that of his or her time while calling. Even with respect to that, the question must be asked as to what the salesperson would do with that time if he or she did not spend it in this way. If there exists no more profitable way of spending the time involved, the opportunity cost, at least, is nil.

Analysis by Customer Classes. The grouping or classification of customers for purposes of making managerial and pricing decisions is a matter of critical importance. Faulty classification can cost a great deal in unnecessary price concessions, in customer goodwill, and in competitive position. It can make cost justification of price differentials impossible and thus lead to a Federal Trade Commission cease-and-desist order or the loss of a treble damage suit.

Customers may be classified along many lines. One is geographical, according to sales districts or territories. Another type of customer classification depends on the function which the customer performs in the distributive process. Thus customers are designated as wholesalers, jobbers, distributors, retailers, industrial users, governmental units, and so forth. A very common classification is in accordance with volume of purchases over a period of time—usually a year, but sometimes a shorter period.

Classification of customers according to the sizes of orders they place is sometimes attempted, but this may not be a valid customer classification. In most lines of business any customer is likely to place orders of varying sizes, so that the only valid customer classification related to order sizes is in terms of the average size of orders placed. In such a classification it will usually be found that the larger customers (those who buy in larger volumes over a period) tend to place larger orders on the average, but this is not necessarily true—they may merely buy more often. In certain lines of business, such as perishable foods, for example, periodic volume and order sizes sometimes go hand in hand. A grocer may, for instance, take roughly the same amount of dairy products day after day. In such cases volume analysis and order-size analysis coincide. For the most part, though, cost analysis in terms of sizes of orders has an uncertain relationship to customers.

Cost Analysis by Distributive Channels. Where sellers deal with customers at various levels (wholesalers, retailers, consumers) a study of their costs of serving such groups will commonly show distinct differences. To a major extent this is likely to be due to using different selling methods or sales personnel for each customer category. Such practices make possible substantial identification of costs with each customer group (the direct costs of that group) and a correspondingly low amount of indirect costs which must be allocated. As a result, cost analysis by distributive channels is apt to be easier and more reliable than the analysis of customer groups in terms of size. Aside from this factor, however, cost analysis by channels differs not at all from that by size groups.

The business decisions which may be affected by channel analysis are much more apt to be of a managerial character than related to price. Price differentiation by channels is strongly influenced by competition and trade custom, and relative costs have only a remote bearing. Cost analysis is an aid to efficiency in cultivating each channel, however, and is useful in answering problems of method and intensity. It is of importance also in deciding whether to drop or add channels, and in this instance, at least, the incremental approach is the appropriate one.

Analysis by Volume Groups. The analysis of distribution costs in terms of customers grouped according to their annual (or other periodic) purchase volumes is commonly associated with differential pricing decisions. This is not at all surprising, in view of the fact that a high proportion of all differential pricing schemes are based on annual volumes, and most such analyses adopt the price-differentiating groupings as the framework of the analysis. Such analysis is, of course, essential to determining whether or not the pricing plan conforms to the requirements of the Robinson-Patman Act.

The usefulness of this type of analysis is not wholly confined to the pricing area, however. It throws light on why and to what extent small accounts are unprofitable, and on what to do about this situation. It may help to explain, as *NACA Research Series No. 21* says, why certain commodities and territories are exceptionally profitable or unprofitable.

Establishment of Volume Groups for Analytical Purposes. Uncritically to adopt for cost analysis purposes the volume groupings previously established solely for reasons of marketing strategy is to defeat the real purposes of the analysis. The analysis should reveal the strengths and weaknesses of the existing volume groups to the end that they may be defended as being the most suitable, or altered if it is found that they are not. Essential for this purpose is the adoption for analytical purposes of a finer breakdown than would be practical for use in a discount plan. Thus one company, in making such a study to aid in devising a new pricing system, categorized customers into 17 volume groups, nine of which spanned intervals of only $1,000. The plan finally adopted contained six customer classes, the narrowest being $3,000. With the aid of modern data-processing equipment a study of this sort presents no serious mechanical difficulties.

There is no royal road to perfection in the choice of volume groups. The groups selected to present the picture of cost-volume relationships will finally be chosen on the basis of judgment, in the light of both accounting and commercial realities. What competitors are doing (if the issue is one of price differences) is bound to have an important effect, though it must be borne in mind that under established policies of administering the Robinson-Patman Act competitors' price schedules cannot merely be copied. If the questions to be answered by the analysis relate to managerial rather than price decisions, the groupings chosen must be such as will throw light on the management problems.

Direct Costs: Selling. A major segment of distribution costs is direct selling, and a major portion of direct selling is directly chargeable to the business done with specific customers. The cost of the time which salespeople spend on customers' premises or in doing paper work or other service on behalf of specific customers is a direct cost of doing business with those customers. To measure this cost is not simple, however. It requires a knowledge of how the salespeople spend their time, which few employers possess and which many sales supervisors would say is impossible to get. It is a fact, however, that this kind of information has been obtained many times and that it is by no means as burdensome and unreliable as is sometimes claimed.

The best source of information about how salespeople spend their time is the salespeople themselves. Most salespeople make daily or weekly reports of their activities—the places they have been, the customers on whom they have called, the prospective customers solicited, and so forth. Rather seldom, however, are salespeople routinely asked to report time spent in these various activities, and this is the statistic necessary to compute the cost of putting the salesperson into the customer's premises. Nearly always, therefore, when customer costs are to be ascertained, the salesperson's reporting system must be expanded to include an analysis of his or her working time. Exhibit 2 is an example of a time reporting form devised by one company for this purpose. It is not presented as a model, but

EXHIBIT 2   Time Reporting Form

SALESMAN'S DAILY TIME REPORT

List all customers and prospects contacted this date. See instructions below.

A. Account name	B. Customer code number	C. Type of account		D. Customer class	Time spent			
		Cust- omer	Pros- pect		E. Travel		F. Sales	
					Hours	Tenths	Hours	Tenths

District _____ Date _____ Signature _____ Salesman's code no. ____

INSTRUCTIONS

One of these reports is to be completed each workday by each sales manager and salesman. Negative reports are required on days when no contacts are made. Reports for Saturdays, Sundays, and Holidays are required only if contacts with customers or prospects are made on those days. Instructions for each of the lettered columns are as follows:

A. The account name of each customer or prospect with whom or for whom time is spent is to be entered in this column.

B. The customer code number is to be entered here.

C. Please indicate with a check mark (√) in the appropriate column whether the account listed is a customer or a prospect. If an account has purchased within the past twelve months, classification should be as a customer.

D. Both customer and prospect accounts are also to be classified and coded on this report so as to distinguish between accounts in the following manner. Use Code Number 1 for accounts we franchise or endeavor to franchise. Use Code Number 2 for direct accounts or prospective accounts such as builders, mobile home manufacturers, government agencies,etc.

E. Time spent in travel from home or office to the first call each day and time spent traveling to subsequent calls will be recorded in this column on the same line on which the name of the account appears. Time spent in travel from home to office and from the place of business of the last customer or prospect called on during the day, to home or office, will not be recorded.

F. Time spent with or on behalf of each account is to be recorded in this column. Include all time spent with an account whether it be at his place of business or elsewhere, or time spent on the telephone with him. Also record any office time or other time that can be positively identified as having been spent on behalf of a particular account. Time spent in general office work, sales meetings, product training meetings, etc. will not be recorded.

FORWARD COMPLETED REPORTS TO YOUR DISTRICT OFFICE TO ARRIVE ON THE MONDAY FOLLOWING THE WEEK COVERED BY THE REPORTS.

merely to show the manner in which this company accumulated the desired information.

Another company, which employs the salespeople's reports for managerial purposes, provides them with punched cards which are so arranged that the salesperson can report in detail on a day's activities by merely making marks at the appropriate places on the cards.

Sampling Procedure.   In order to minimize the burden on both the salespeople and the clerical staff, something less than 100 percent reporting for a full year must ordinarily be used. The company which uses the punched-card procedure described above, for example, receives reports from approximately 20 percent of its sales force covering one assigned day per month throughout the year.

The usual procedure for special cost studies is to select both temporal and geographical samples in such a manner that a fair representation of the whole will be achieved. The sampling process for this purpose is not scientific, but judgmental. The time sample must be chosen in such a way as to minimize the effects of seasonality. It may be possible to do this by choosing a month (if one month is adequate) in which sales equal approximately one-twelfth of the annual total. It must be remembered, however, that seasonality of salespeople's activities and seasonality of sales may not coincide. The customer sample must include reasonably proportionate representation of customers of all sizes whose buying habits—as to product mix, order sizes, etc.—are also fairly representative of all customers. This end is usually achieved, or attempted, by assembling a group of sales districts whose sales statistics, percentagewise, in total, bear a close resemblance to the corresponding statistics for the entire sales area. Some geographic spread is usually thought to be desirable in this connection.

There is sometimes some doubt as to the reliability of time data obtained in this way. It is thought that salespeople may tend to report what they think will do them the most good rather than the actual truth. There is indeed some danger of this. It can be minimized, however, by three steps. The first is careful instruction of the salesperson in advance, with explanations of the purpose of the study, the need for accurate data, and a plea for cooperation. The second is assurance to the reporting salespeople that the data will not be used in any way to prejudice their advancement or compensation. In some cases the salespeople are given assurance that only financial people will see the individual reports and that they will not be made available to sales management. A typical assurance of this sort is as follows: "We want to emphasize that these reports are *in no way used to appraise your selling performance.* Each report is compiled with the others to establish a general pattern of effort devoted to individual products and activities. Your individual reports will not leave this unit." The third essential step is to put someone in charge of receiving and examining the reports who will take prompt steps to remedy defects or correct omissions.

One alternative to having salespeople do their own reporting is to send someone along with them to observe their operations. This procedure may well achieve superior accuracy in reporting what the salesperson actually does, but it is extremely costly and is likely to alter the salesperson's routines in such a way as to make the information of questionable value.

Where the salesperson is paid a straight commission it may be thought that time studies are unnecessary, since both customer and commodity costs can be ascertained by merely looking at the commissions earned. This is a false assumption. The salesperson's employer is buying his time and directing him how to spend it. The salesperson's instructions are intended to achieve the employer's objectives, such as thorough coverage of a district, and the salesperson is not, therefore, at liberty to maximize income by spending time only on the more fruitful accounts. The commission system is merely a method of computing the compensation for the salesperson's time, not an indication of the cost of obtaining a particular order or of doing business with any particular customer.

Direct Costs: Other. In addition to the cost of salespeople's time spent with or on behalf of customers, other costs may be directly identified with customer groups. Customer entertainment—meals, drinks, ball-game tickets, and the like—is a good example. Identification of these items is commonly required on salespeople's expense reports and they therefore present no problem. The cost of product samples given to customers may require special reporting or may be reported routinely. In many cases this is not a material item. Some companies keep adequate records of catalogs and literature supplied to customers, but frequently this is not done, and accounting for costs of these items as direct charges becomes difficult if not impossible. They are apt to be highly seasonal, and keeping track of them for a brief period would therefore be inadequate. In the absence of records, the existence of definite policies with respect to the distribution of such materials, together with evidence that the policies are adhered to, may serve the purpose.

Order processing and filling and delivery are also direct costs of serving customers, but there are likely to be difficulties in identification and measurement. In the case of order processing and filling, while it is obviously impossible to observe and report on these activities in the same way as can be done with salespeople, it is feasible to keep track of the numbers and sizes of orders received and shipments made over a representative period and to apply to them costs determined by means of time studies. The direct costs of deliveries by common carrier can be measured readily enough, but if delivery is by seller-owned or leased trucks, delivery costs must be allocated with some degree of indirectness.

Advertising and sales promotion usually include elements of both direct and indirect costs. Advertising allowances are direct customer costs and can be accounted for as such. Point-of-sale advertising materials are also inherently direct costs, but measuring the cost chargeable against a given customer or customer group may not be easy. Records of such materials are apt to be lacking. If definite policies as to the distribution of such materials exist and are adhered to, however, they may substitute for records. If sales promotion activities are carried on at customers' premises they may be reported on in the same way as salesmen's visits. Sales promotion campaigns are likely to be seasonal or sporadic, however, and therefore to present difficulties in sampling.

Readily Allocable Indirect Costs. The cost of delivery by company fleet is ordinarily allocable to customer volume groups with reasonable precision. Statistics on the number and sizes of deliveries are essential. Costs of getting the trucks to the customers' premises may be allocated on a stop basis, although the time of delivery personnel while at the delivery points will vary according to the size of the deliveries. Time studies of deliveries of various sizes will probably be necessary. If goods are physically homogeneous the measurement of delivery size is a simple matter. If they are not, however, some difficulty may be encountered. If all sizes of customers purchase approximately the same product mix even this problem can be solved. Distance of deliveries does not affect the calculations if customers of various sizes are evenly scattered geographically. If the study were one of individual customer costs, distance would, of course, have to be taken into account.

General advertising, particularly that directed toward the ultimate consumer, can be reasonably assigned to customer volume groups only on a dollar sales basis. This cost is usually omitted from Robinson-Patman studies because it produces no cost differentiation.

Customer accounting, credit, and collection may usually be treated on a transaction basis, though some of these activities—for example, the preparation and mailing of monthly statements—are more or less uniform per customer.

Field warehousing of goods may well be assigned to customer groups on the basis of dollar sales. This is true, however, only if the purchases of all groups are reasonably homogeneous. In some cases large orders are shipped from the factory and small orders from field locations. This condition requires a study of the utilization of field warehousing in order that the cost may be assigned only to those customers who get the benefit. Again a dollar sales basis may be appropriate.

Remote Indirect Costs. Supervisory and supporting costs in general follow the personnel or the costs of the functions supervised or supported. Precisely what is appropriate depends on organization and circumstances in each instance, but reasonable approaches are usually not hard to find. When incremental costing is involved most of these costs will not be allocated, since they tend to be unaffected by rather wide swings in total volume of business. A caveat is required with respect to sales supervisors, such as district and regional sales managers, and even top-ranking home office personnel. Direct customer contacts by these people are not unusual, and if there is an appreciable amount of such activity, it must be properly accounted for. Evidence of the time and cost involved is sometimes difficult to pinpoint, but an effort must be made to do so, since costs of such contacts run high per hour, and may make considerable difference in evaluating the business of the customers who are thus contacted. Such customers tend to be in the upper volume brackets. Customer contacts made by supervisory personnel in the course of routine trips in company with field salesmen need not be accounted for in this way. Such contacts are incidental to the supervisor's normal duties of observing the field force and instructing them in their duties.

Assignment of the cost of cultivating prospective customers to customer volume groups presents serious difficulties. The ideal, perhaps, would be to have reliable estimates of the demand potentials of the prospects called upon, and to assign the cost of calling on each one to the corresponding quantity bracket. Lacking such information, a possible allocation method is to consider the entire cost category as general sales promotional effort, and hence to use dollar sales as the allocation basis. This yields no cost differential among brackets, however, except for a desire to produce a figure of net profits, the cost might well be left out of the calculation.

The dollar sales method is presumably the best treatment of the cost of market research for purposes of customer analysis. This method of allocation assumes that, whatever the current research projects may be, their purpose is to maintain and improve the marketing structure as a whole, and their cost should be borne equally by each sales dollar.

Bad debts expense is seldom an item of any significance, and it makes little difference how it is allocated, if at all. If it is to be allocated, however, this should be done by taking a long-range view. Bad debts experience over a series of years (perhaps as many as five) should be taken into account. What is needed is data with respect to which classes of customers give rise to bad debts. If this is not ascertainable, allocation to customer classes on the basis of sales dollars may be the only feasible procedure.

Robinson-Patman Considerations.   For purposes of testing conformity of differential pricing systems with the Robinson-Patman Act, customer costing and classification are crucial. The customer classification of greatest significance is that in terms of volume, since differential pricing is very generally based on periodic volume. There are, however, many unanswered questions with respect to such grouping of customers. In the Chicago fluid milk case, the Supreme Court[17] called for "the use of classes for cost justification which are composed of members of such self-sameness as to make the averaging of the cost of dealing with the group a valid and reasonable indicium of the cost of dealing with any specific group member."

In similar vein the report of the Advisory Committee on Cost Justification had this to say about classification of customers and other business segments:[18]

> The privilege of classification is not a license to disregard sound business and accounting concepts. In order to become the basis for cost justification of price differentials, the classification should be logical and should reflect actual differences in the manner or cost of dealing. Great care should be taken in establishing price classes to make sure that all members of the class are enough alike to make the averaging of their costs a sound procedure. Customer groupings may properly be based not only on quantities sold but also according to the way customers place their orders: whether for immediate delivery or later shipment on a fixed schedule; in large or small orders; placed directly at the factory or through a sales branch; for on-peak or off-peak manufacture, etc. These trade factors may all be reflected in cost and as criteria for customer classification.   .

Some sellers have attempted to meet one challenge to volume classification by adopting a dual discount plan, one discount scale being based on the customer's entire purchases and justified by differences in selling costs, and the other scale being based on deliveries at each receiving point (where the customer takes deliveries at two or more locations) and justified by differences in order processing and filling and delivery costs. No such plan has been tested in any public proceeding before the Federal Trade Commission or the courts, but it has obvious merit, especially in sales to chains and other multiunit customers.

Customer classifications other than by volume are somewhat less vulnerable to attack. Territorial price differences, for example, may be clearly justified by differences in transportation cost alone, and injury to competition at the secondary level is rather unlikely. Classification by channels of trade may be shielded from the operation of the Robinson-Patman Act by lack of competitive effect. Such

[17]*U.S. v. Borden Co. et al.,* 370 U.S. 480.

[18]Report of the Advisory Committee on Cost Justification to the Federal Trade Commission. See note 10.

classification is not foolproof, however. Merely calling a customer a wholesaler, for example, does not make him one.

Excessively wide dispersion of costs within customer volume groups is difficult to prove under ordinary circumstances. A factual situation such as existed in the Standard Motor Products case[19] is unlikely to be repeated. There the respondent had accumulated time data for all sales personnel and all customers for an entire year, as well as data concerning the number and size of orders and shipments. From this unusually complete information a Commission employee was able to compute what he called individual customer costs. Call, order, and shipment data accumulated on a sampling basis could never be put to such a use. They may be entirely adequate to establish average costs for a customer class, but they prove nothing about individual customer costs beyond the limited time period included in the sample, and they are not ordinarily collected in such a way as to make even this information easy to compute. In the fluid milk case, the Supreme Court drew inferences of probable wide dispersion of costs from the characteristics of the dairy business which, in the Court's opinion, made the dairy companies' grouping procedures "like averaging one horse and one rabbit." Other sellers should heed this decision and avoid, as far as possible, customer classifications which are subject to such an attack.

ANALYSIS BY ORDER SIZE

The Small Order Problem. Substantially every business is plagued by the problem of what to do about orders which are too small to pay for the out-of-pocket costs of obtaining and filling them. Cost analysis helps to define the parameters of this problem, though it does not necessarily tell what to do about it.

Simple Analysis to Determine Break-Even Point. A relatively simple analysis will suffice to determine the point at which a sales transaction stops losing money out-of-pocket and starts to make a contribution toward common expenses and profits. Sevin describes one such study.[20] All distribution costs were classified in accordance with the factor by which it was assumed that they varied, with the following results:

1. Overhead and routine costs of handling an order $0.55
2. Overhead and routine costs of handling the shipping order and invoice ... 2.60
3. Cost of handling each item or line on the invoice 0.15
4. Financial cost per dollar of volume 0.08
5. Cost per salesperson's call 4.25

Thus, if a salesperson brought in an order for one item whose selling price was $1, the assignable costs would be the sum of the above items, or $7.63. If the gross margin on this sale is 28 percent, the loss would be $7.35. If the order came in by telephone, the loss would still be $3.10. The minimum profitable one-line order received without a salesperson's call would be about $17, or, if obtained by means of a salesperson's call, about $38.

Unfortunately, the description of the costs used in this study is too meager to be sure that only incremental costs were used. However, the company which made the study concluded that about 50 percent of its orders were handled at a loss. In considering the incremental costs of any such volume of orders as this, the incremental cost category must be defined much more broadly than would be the case if the addition or subtraction of only one order were under study. The

---

[19]*In re* Standard Motor Products, Inc., 68 FTC 1248 (1965).
[20]C. H. Sevin, *How Manufacturers Reduce Their Distribution Costs,* U.S. Department of Commerce, Economic Series No. 72, 1948.

elimination of 50 percent of all orders would certainly result in a substantial curtailment of clerical and order-handling staff, and, if orders are in large measure obtained by personal solicitation, the sales staff might also be decreased or, at the very least, put to more profitable employment.

Solutions to the Small Order Problem. Refusal of orders below the break-even point is not, of course, the only cure for the small order problem. Rejection of such orders entails the possibility of offending customers and the likelihood of decreasing the penetration of particular marketing areas. Both of these results distress the sales department, especially since large and profitable customers often place small orders for entirely legitimate reasons. Alternatives to rejection include measures to decrease the costs of handling small orders, persuasion of customers to order in larger quantities, and price differentiation.

Cost savings may be effected by decreasing or eliminating sales calls on customers whose orders are usually small and substituting mail or telephone solicitation. If the customer relationship is such that orders are received only at the time of a salesperson's visit, cutting the number of calls in half may result in doubling the size of orders. On the other hand, reducing or eliminating calls on such customers may mean losing them entirely. This result, of course, is the same as if small orders were rejected, but in many instances the loss of business would be more than offset by the gain in efficiency.

For manufacturers, a cost-saving alternative to accepting and filling small orders may be to refer the customers who usually place them to a wholesaler or jobber who is in a position to handle such orders more efficiently than is the manufac-

EXHIBIT 3   Functional Expenses and Bases of Allocation to Orders

Functional Costs	Bases of Allocation to Order-size Groups
1. Selling expense—direct: Costs of time spent calling on customers—except sales promotion calls	Time study by salesmen (for test period, salesmen record time of entering and leaving each store called on)
2. Selling expense—indirect: Travel time, time spent on nonproductive calls, miscellaneous working time, and travel expenses	Number of calls
3. Routing orders	Time study (number of orders routed and routing time)
4. Assembling orders and loading trucks	Time study (each order assembled separately)
5. Packing: Container forming, packing, container sealing, weighing, preparing bill of lading, stocking containers	Time study (packing one order completed—by one packer—before next order is started)
6. Truck delivery—direct: Cost of time spent in customers' stores	Time study (time clock on truck records time stopped at store and time deliveryman returns to truck)
7. Truck delivery—indirect: Travel time (total time worked less direct time)	Number of deliveries
8. Freight delivery	Direct (freight charged direct to order)
9. Billing (cutting orders, pricing, extending, and comparing orders and invoices)	Time study
10. Accounts receivable	Time study
11. Other office costs	Number of orders
12. Branch rent	Dollar sales
13. Branch supervision	Total direct time of above functions

SOURCE: Adapted from C. H. Sevin, *How Manufacturers Reduce Their Distribution Costs*, U.S. Department of Commerce, Economic Series No. 72, 1948.

turer. This entails paying the intermediary for his services, but it still may be cheaper than direct dealing with the customers in question.

Price Differentiation by Order Size.   The adoption of a plan of price differentiation based on sizes of orders is, of course, subject to scrutiny for possible violation of the Robinson-Patman Act, and should for that reason, as well as for management purposes, be preceded by a cost study.

Cost Functions and Bases of Allocation.   An excellent example of the type of cost study required for this purpose is provided by Sevin.[21] The cost functions utilized and the methods of applying them to the order size groups are shown in Exhibit 3.

Some explanation is necessary in order to clarify procedures. Salespeople reported their time at customers' premises on order blanks. Where no order was received, an order blank was prepared nevertheless and marked N.S. (no sale). Promotional calls were not reported on order blanks but were included in the salesperson's total working time, which was reported weekly on a separate reporting form. All working time, including travel and time worked at home or in the office, was reported on this form. All working time except customer contact (item 1) was assigned to item 2 and divided by the number of productive calls. Though the nature of the business is not disclosed, there are indications that sales calls were brief. The customers were retail stores, and it is probable that the commodities involved were relatively standard consumer's goods.

The other cost functions are reasonably well explained in Exhibit 3. It is to be noted that item 7 contains all truck operating costs. Item 6 is merely the cost of the time spent by the truck driver at customers' premises. Both sales personnel and truck drivers timed themselves. Time studies of internal operations, both clerical and handling, were presumably carried out by the time-study staff, following normal procedures to obtain adequate samples of orders of various sizes.

Results of Study.   Exhibit 4 shows the results of this study in terms of percentages of the dollar values of the several size groups. The 13 cost functions of Exhibit 3 are condensed into five groups. The fairly steady and consistent decrease in costs

EXHIBIT 4   Marketing Costs by Order-Size Groups (Percentage of Sales)

Order-size groups, all customer classifications combined	Warehouse assembling, packing, and routing	Office billing, accounts receivable	Delivery expenses	Selling expenses	Other branch expenses	Total marketing costs
$0.01–$3.75.......	3.11	2.72	5.33	9.40	0.96	21.52
$3.76–$6.25.......	2.10	1.64	3.28	5.62	0.96	13.60
$6.26–$8.75.......	1.56	1.15	2.44	3.89	0.96	10.00
$8.76–$11.25......	1.25	0.90	1.96	3.05	0.96	8.12
$11.26–$13.75.....	1.06	0.75	1.65	2.76	0.96	7.18
$13.76–$16.25.....	0.90	0.64	1.40	2.29	0.96	6.19
$16.26–$23.75.....	0.80	0.51	1.25	1.96	0.97	5.49
$23.76–$31.25.....	0.64	0.40	1.00	1.73	0.98	4.75
$31.26–$38.75.....	0.56	0.33	0.87	1.90	0.99	4.65
$38.76–$61.25.....	0.51	0.25	0.79	2.43	0.99	4.97
$61.26–$88.75.....	0.41	0.17	0.65	1.86	0.99	4.08
$88.76–$121.25....	0.38	0.13	0.59	2.17	1.00	4.27
$121.26–$168.75...	0.35	0.10	0.54	2.06	1.00	4.05
$168.76–$231.25...	0.36	0.08	0.57	2.29	0.99	4.29
$231.26 and over...	0.34	0.06	0.57	2.27	1.00	4.24

SOURCE: *Ibid.*, p. 62.

[21]*Ibid.*

per sales dollar as the orders get larger is evident. Selling expenses, however, reach their lowest level in the case of orders ranging from $23.76 to $31.25, and thereafter the tendency is slightly upward. This suggests that the salespeople tend to cultivate the accounts which supply these orders more intensively than the smaller accounts. There is no observable trend of costs in the case of "other branch expense." This is doubtless partially due to the allocation of branch rent on the basis of dollar sales. It may be remarked that this cost could have been analyzed in detail and assigned to the several operating functions, thus producing some cost differentiation.

Permissible Price Differences.   The order-size groupings in this study are somewhat unusual in appearance, but it must be assumed that they fit the circumstances and needs of the particular situation. The intervals spanned by the groups follow the usual pattern of both order-size and customer groupings in that they are relatively small at the lower end of the scale ($2.50 in Exhibit 4) and become larger as quantity or volume increases. Such an increase is necessary because cost differences tend to decrease as quantity or volume goes up. This effect is very noticeable in Exhibit 4. Despite the increase in quantity intervals, cost differences become insignificant after the $88.75 order-size level is reached, and it is evident that the last five groups should be sold at the same price, if cost difference is the criterion for price difference.

Assuming that the seller in this case wishes to adopt a pricing plan which could be defended under the Robinson-Patman Act, it is also obvious that the three groups ranging from $23.76 to $61.25 would have to be treated as one. The effective number of order-size groups would therefore be reduced to nine. Exhibit 5 shows these groups and the significant cost differences. Precisely what price differences should be adopted here depends on marketing considerations. The cost differences presumably set an upper limit and, to be on the safe side, some margin of safety should be allowed.

Relation of Order-Getting Costs to Order Sizes.   The relation between order-getting costs and the sizes of particular orders is not a simple one, though the studies of the small-order problem usually assume that it is. These costs are direct selling, advertising, and sales promotion.

EXHIBIT 5   Cost Differences by Order-Size Groups

Group No.	Size range	Total marketing costs, %	Cost differences, %
1	$0.01– 3.75	21.52	
			7.92
2	$3.76– 6.25	13.60	
			3.60
3	$6.26– 8.75	10.00	
			1.88
4	$8.76–11.25	8.12	
			0.94
5	$11.26–13.75	7.18	
			0.99
6	$13.76–16.25	6.19	
			0.70
7	$16.26–23.75	5.49	
			0.70
8	$23.76–61.25	4.79*	
			0.60
9	$61.26 and up	4.19*	

* These costs are approximated by simple averaging.

Selling Costs. In the study whose methods are described above, orders were apparently obtained only by sales calls. In a situation where this is the case, or substantially so, it is not unreasonable to charge the cost of the call directly to the order obtained. In a very large number of businesses, however, the relationship between sales calls and customers' orders is by no means so simple.

Some salespeople take no orders at all. Their work is exclusively that of promoting sales through providing information about products available, checking the buyer's inventory and his needs for the coming months, taking care of complaints, educating the buyer's personnel in the resale or use of the seller's products, and similar activities. Customers place their orders by mail or telephone.

A somewhat more common case is that in which the salesperson takes orders when on the customer's premises but these orders do not constitute all, or perhaps even a majority, of orders. A not uncommon situation is one in which the salesperson gets a large order for a season's needs, possibly providing for several shipping dates and quantities, and this principal order is later supplemented by fill-in orders sent by mail or telephone.

In all such cases a one-to-one ratio between calls and orders clearly does not exist, and the cost of direct selling must be applied to orders in some other way. For this purpose no universally satisfactory method can be recommended, because of the infinite variety of circumstances surrounding the transactions. Careful study will usually reveal a logical approach.

Advertising and Sales Promotion. It is a safe generalization that there is no logical relationship between these costs and orders as such. Advertising and sales promotion must be spread pro rata over sales units or sales dollars of the products to which they are related. This is obvious where these activities are directed at the ultimate consumer rather than the immediate customer, and hardly less obvious when confined to trade media. It is difficult to perceive how one dollar of revenue gets more benefit than another.

COST ANALYSIS BY COMMODITIES

Purposes. *NACA Research Series No. 20* lists the purposes of analysis of distribution costs by commodities as follows:[22]

1. To determine profitability of present products under conditions currently prevailing.
2. To aid in estimating the effects that proposed changes in products, methods of marketing, or selling emphasis will have on product costs and profits.
3. To provide cost information which management wishes to have when making decisions with respect to selling prices or acceptance of business at a given price.

To these purposes may well be added that of assisting in the preparation of operating budgets and their administration. Adequate analysis of costs by products will help to determine the effects on costs of increases or decreases in volume, as well as those of changes in products, methods, and emphasis. Also, when pricing policy is under consideration, budgeted costs may be more appropriate than actual costs.

Individual Commodities Versus Commodity Groups. The same research study concluded that the companies which carry on continuous or repetitive commodity costs analysis apply it to groups of commodities rather than to individual items. The reasons for this are apparent. It costs less to analyze costs by groups, and the results obtained are more reliable and meaningful. This is because the product

[22]"The Assignment of Nonmanufacturing Costs to Products," *NACA Bulletin,* vol. 32, no. 12, August 1951. See note 14.

groupings ordinarily follow organizational lines. Each product department may have its own sales force, its own advertising, its own warehousing. The costs of these functions thus become direct charges to the product groups, and no allocations are necessary. Studies of individual products, on the other hand, are likely to require allocations of substantially all marketing costs.

Furthermore, many of the management decisions which must be made with respect to products relate to a cohesive line of products rather than to individual items, and the costs pertaining to the line are the relevant costs. Studies of the costs related to individual products are likely to be occasional rather than periodic. One such occasion might be the threat or advent of a price discrimination complaint concerning a particular commodity rather than the line as a whole.

Methods of Commodity Grouping.   How commodities are classified and grouped for cost study purposes depends mainly on the questions to be answered. Grouping by organizational responsibility is clearly desirable in nearly all cases, but other classifications may also be useful. The organizational classification will usually result in grouping of products which are alike physically or by industry designation. Subgroupings by sizes, grades, and other characteristics may be useful. Packaged goods may be distinguished from the same items sold in bulk; goods sold under seller-owned brands from goods sold unbranded or under brands owned by buyers; goods sold for use by the buyer from those which the buyer resells to others. Distribution methods and costs may differ significantly along all these lines.

Direct Costs.   The amount and variety of costs which may be charged directly in commodity analysis depend primarily upon the degree and kind of product grouping which underlies the study. Product groups frequently have their own exclusive sales and promotional personnel, for example, whose entire compensation and expenses are a direct cost of the product group. Similarly, product groups may be the beneficiaries of exclusive advertising, and they may be served by exclusive warehouses.

If entire sales and promotional organizations are not devoted to the product groups under analysis, it is not at all unlikely that certain individuals may be product specialists and therefore directly chargeable. Some forms or elements of advertising may similarly be direct, even though entire advertising programs are not.

Outward transportation and delivery costs will probably be direct charges to product lines if warehousing of each line is separate. Where more than one product or product line involved in the study are warehoused together, however, storage and delivery will usually be common costs and will therefore have to be allocated.

Some portions of other expenses may also be identifiable with particular product groups. For example, certain market research projects may relate entirely to specific lines or products. Some caution should be exercised here, however, since market research is a long-run endeavor which goes in cycles, so that the product areas which are under study change from year to year. The benefits which a line of products is currently receiving are generally not from research projects being currently carried on, but from those of last year or the year before. Looked at in this light, market research becomes a very general cost which must be allocated to product lines not on the basis of the projects being carried on at any one time but rather with regard to the research program of a number of years. The purpose of the research program may well be to sustain and promote the enterprise as a whole rather than to benefit particular segments at a particular time. If this is the case, direct assignment is inappropriate, and some rather broad allocation base, such as sales dollars, may better reflect the true incidence of these costs.

The general rule with respect to the identification and application of direct costs is that this should be done to the greatest extent feasible where the cost elements are material. The best way to accomplish this is to provide adequate account classification so that such costs may be identified without question.

A special problem arises in the case of mixed accounts, containing both direct and indirect elements of cost. Such an account might be supplies, for example. If it is desired to ascertain the distribution costs associated with a particular product or product group, exclusive of all others, this account may be analyzed to discover any supply items directly related to the segment in question. This should be done only if the added accuracy to be thus achieved is worth the added time and trouble. If it is decided to make such an analysis, the account should also be searched for direct costs pertaining to the other products or product groups and these should be eliminated before the residue of indirect costs is allocated on whatever basis may be suitable. This process, known as "double screening," is essential to avoid excessive charges to the segment under study. It is to be noted that the same procedure is applicable in all cost analyses, whether by products or by customers.

Readily Allocable Indirect Costs.   Where salespeople sell more than one of the products or product groups under study to the same customers in the course of the same visits, their compensation must be allocated. The fact that they may be paid entirely on a commission basis does not avoid this necessity. The salesperson's time is what is being purchased, and if he spends time trying to sell a commodity, even unsuccessfully, some part of his compensation is attributable to that commodity, whatever the mode of computing the compensation.

Salespeople's time reports are generally the best indicator of how their time is spent with respect to commodities. The broader the commodity groupings, the more reliable the salespeople's reporting is likely to be. Companies with broad lines of products which attempt to get precise reports of time spent on each item have generally been disappointed.

A sometimes satisfactory substitute for time reports is found in estimates by the salespeople, especially if the reasonableness of such estimates is confirmed by their supervisors. *NACA Research Series No. 20* reports that one company used a variant of this procedure by asking salespeople, supervisors, and executives to rate the company's product lines on the basis of the relative effort required to sell them.[23]

> Successive samples of ratings . . . were taken until several hundred replies had been obtained. While individual rating sheets showed wide variations, when combined a quite consistent pattern was found. It was concluded that this was a reasonably good measure of the relative amounts of effort required to sell the various lines and that it accordingly should serve as a good basis for allocating salesmen's salaries and expenses to product lines.

Unfortunately the research study does not explain precisely how this was done. A possibility would seem to be to apply these ratings to the sales dollars of the several commodity classifications and to allocate in proportion to such weighted sales dollars.

In commodity analysis, salespeople's travel and other expenses and the costs of supervisory and supplementary selling functions, such as sales offices, should be assigned to product groups in proportion to the assignment of sales compensation. An exception to this rule should be made for any commodity specialists among the supervisory staff whose salaries and expenses are direct charges to the commodities under their charge.

Time studies are the key to the allocation of costs of picking and packing orders for products or product groups if these activities are carried on jointly for several or all lines. Costs of storage can usually be allocated on the basis of floor space occupied by each group or line. Seasonal variations may complicate such calculations, but an annual average can usually be worked out.

[23]*Ibid.,* p. 1572.

Most of the clerical costs of order processing, invoice preparation, customer accounting, inventory control, and so forth, can be allocated on a transaction basis. A count of the number of sales transactions in which each commodity or commodity group is involved may be made for a representative period of time and the results used to assign this group of costs for an entire year. In some highly mechanized accounting systems such counts are extremely easy; in others, special arrangements must be made. Time studies of these operations are ordinarily unnecessary since it is not an unreasonable assumption that a given clerical operation with respect to one commodity item requires the same amount of time as for another. If any of these operations are decentralized, so that they apply to only one commodity segment, the procedure must be modified accordingly.

Delivery costs incurred in common for more than one product group must be allocated. Common carrier charges can usually be prorated on a weight bases, with due allowance for the fact that some items may fall into a different freight classification than others. The distance factor does not enter into the cost allocations, since it may usually be assumed that all products are shipped the average distance, whatever that may be. The sample on which the study of delivery costs is based should be broad enough to neutralize the distance factor.

Costs of operating company truck fleets can usually be assigned to products on the basis of weight or bulk. In this case neither stops nor distance enter into the calculations, except that the sample must be large enough to be sure that the effects of these factors on total costs are adequately represented.

Remote Indirect Costs.   Institutional advertising is a good example of a cost which must be allocated on a more or less arbitrary basis. Such advertising mentions products, if at all, only in a very general terms, or as examples of the advantages of buying our brand instead of brand X. It must be spread over the entire line of commodities and services associated with the company name. Sales dollars, or perhaps gross margin dollars, is the most common basis. The use of gross margin dollars may be particularly appropriate where gross margins differ widely, some goods being carried mostly for the convenience of customers or to fill out a line, while profits depend on sales of the products with longer margins.

No advertising cost is applicable to products with which the company name and reputation are not associated. Such products may be the company's own unadvertised and unidentified brands or products made for sale under customers' brands. A potentially difficult situation arises where it is generally known that Company A manufactures goods for Company B under B's brand name. Should A's advertising be allocated to the B products? Generally speaking, the answer is in the negative unless A's fame and reputation far outshine those of B and B is in effect relying on A's advertising to sell the B brand goods. A negative answer is obvious, for example, if A is a small manufacturer and B is large and widely known for the quality and reliability of the goods it handles. In such a case, B's customer is certainly relying on B's reputation and is not motivated to buy from B because of A's advertising of its own line of branded goods.

In situations where timing of selling activities, even by way of estimates, is too difficult or expensive, relative sales dollars or gross margin dollars may be the best answer for commodity allocation. Which variety of dollars should be chosen depends to some extent on instructions to salesmen as to where and how to expend their efforts, how sales quotas are prepared, and what inducements are provided for maximizing either total sales volume or total gross margin. Particularly in the case of challenge in a Robinson-Patman proceeding, it is important that objective support be provided for the choice of either type of dollars or any other broad basis of allocation.

As in all cost analyses, general administrative costs, if allocated at all, will follow the costs of the personnel and activities administered. Such costs will not be allocated at all, of course, if what is wanted is commodity contribution margins since these costs are little affected by moderate changes in volume.

Robinson-Patman Considerations. Price discrimination complaints may relate to specific products or to product lines, and neither may fit the seller's regular pattern for commodity cost analysis. In such cases, a special analysis will be necessary, coupled, of course, with an analysis by customer or order-size classes, depending on which variety of price differentiation is in use. Another reason why a special study may be necessary is that allocation methods entirely satisfactory for management use may not meet the exacting standards insisted upon by the Federal Trade Commission or the courts. Estimates of major elements of cost, such as selling expense, must be bolstered by objective indications that they are not biased. It should be emphasized again, however, that the seller who has made careful cost analyses in the ordinary course of business stands a much better chance of convincing Commission investigators that a complaint should not be issued than does one who has not.

ORGANIZATION FOR DISTRIBUTION COST ANALYSIS

No kind of accounting gets done by itself. Someone has to plan it, be provided with the necessary help, and be given the requisite authority to see that it gets done. Distribution cost analysis is a neglected area in the vast majority of companies. The reasons lie in ignorance of its techniques, failure to appreciate its benefits, and an understandable reluctance to spend money where the return is deemed to be uncertain.

The following description of the functions of the distribution cost accountant is derived from the operating manual of a large industrial company. It not only portrays the responsibilities of this member of the financial staff but suggests the uses to which adequate information about distribution costs may be put.

BASIC RESPONSIBILITIES OF THE DISTRIBUTION COST ACCOUNTANT

   I Keep abreast of current practices, trends and developments in distribution cost accounting and other subjects relating to distribution costs—self development.
     a. Reading—cost accounting and marketing literature
     b. Attend conferences and seminars
     c. Contacts inside and outside company
     d. Contact with distribution operations through level of sale to ultimate customer.
  II Initiate the distribution cost accounting objectives, policies and plans of the department.
     a. Short-range and long-range plans—analysis and control of costs
     b. Knowledge of basic financial and marketing plans and objectives of department.
 III Prepare special analyses by commodities, channels of distribution, classes of customers, territories, size of orders, etc. to relate costs to results obtained for use by management in the guidance of marketing effort.
  IV Prepare analyses and estimates required for the establishment of prices, discount structures and promotional plans.
     a. Functional discounts
     b. Quantity discounts
     c. Special promotions
     d. Direct shipments
     e. Special accounts or orders.
   V Prepare special analyses of finished goods inventories for use in establishing the location and levels of inventories. This would include measuring the effect on profits, residual income, return on investment, etc.
  VI Assist in the development of standards (or indices) where applicable for control of distribution costs, measurement of efficiency of operations or effectiveness of expenditure, and direction of effort.
     a. Joint effort with marketing
     b. Isolate costs by responsibility
     c. Develop basis for measurement—unit of production.

    VII Provide assistance to managers in the preparation of budgets and appropriation requests.
        a. Interpretation of accounting requirements
        b. Comparisons with other similar operations
        c. Estimates of costs of distributing new products or expanding markets for present products, etc.
   VIII Prepare and transmit reports on distribution costs and analyses and interpretation of cost data to aid management in controlling costs.
        a. Responsibility and functional reporting
        b. Comparisons with standards
        c. Reports for special situations.
     IX Advise and counsel, upon request, independent wholesalers on distribution cost accounting matters.
        a. Analysis of operating data
        b. Yardsticks for measurement
        c. Exchange of key information.

BIBLIOGRAPHY

Beyer, Robert, and Donald J. Trawicki: *Profitability Accounting for Planning and Control,* 2nd ed., The Ronald Press Company, New York, 1972.

Crowningshield, Gerald R., and Kenneth A. Gorman: *Cost Accounting, Principles and Managerial Applications,* 3rd ed., Houghton Mifflin Company, Boston, 1974, chap. 18.

Dean, Joel: "Cost Forecasting and Price Policy," *The Journal of Marketing,* vol. 13, no. 3, pp. 279–288, January 1949.

Matz, Adolph, and Othel J. Curry: *Cost Accounting, Planning and Control,* 5th ed., South-Western Publishing Company, Cincinnati, Ohio, 1972, chap. 22.

NACA Research Series No. 20: *The Assignment of Nonmanufacturing Costs to Products,* August 1951.

NACA Research Series No. 21: *The Assignment of Nonmanufacturing Costs to Territories and Other Segments,* December 1951.

Schiff, Michael: *Accounting and Control in Physical Distribution Management,* The National Council of Physical Distribution Management, Chicago, 1972.

——— and Martin Mellman: *Financial Management of the Marketing Function,* Financial Executives Research Foundation, New York, 1962.

Shillinglaw, Gordon: *Cost Accounting: Analysis and Control,* 3rd ed., Richard D. Irwin, Homewood, Ill., 1972, chap. 13.

Taggart, Herbert F.: *Cost Justification,* Bureau of Business Research, The University of Michigan, Ann Arbor, 1959.

Chapter **44**

Divisional Reports

DAVID SOLOMONS
Arthur Young Professor of Accounting,
University of Pennsylvania

DIVISIONAL ORGANIZATION AND PERFORMANCE

Several factors in recent years have made the divisional form of organization increasingly popular. Mere growth has caused companies to look for some means of breaking their operations down into segments of more manageable size. More important still, perhaps, has been the trend toward diversification, both through mergers and acquisitions and also through the development of new products and new activities within existing companies. Though a corporation is more than the sum of its parts, any segmentation of a company's activities, whether by geographical area or by product groups, creates a need on the part of corporate management to know how each segment is performing. Something more detailed than the measurement of overall corporate performance is therefore required.

Even stockholders and creditors will be better informed about a company's activities, and therefore about its prospects, if they have access to information about its various activities separately. More will be said about this aspect of divisional reporting at the end of this chapter; but the main emphasis throughout this discussion will be on the needs of management rather than on the needs of those who, though they have a financial stake in a company, are not responsible for its day-to-day operations.

The Nature of Divisionalization and Its Advantages.   Unfortunately, the term "division" is used by different companies to mean different things. Functionally organized companies sometimes refer to their production divisions or their marketing divisions, while merchandising companies commonly split up their markets regionally by means of geographical divisions. These uses of the word "division" are not the meaning to be given to it here. In the present context, a division will refer to a segment of a business which, within limits (to be discussed later), controls both its manufacturing and marketing activities. It can therefore constitute a profit center and also, often, an investment center, and this has great significance for the choice of measure to be used in appraising the division's performance.

The essence of divisionalization is delegated profit responsibility. The task of divisional management is to use the division's resources profitably, and though limits are set by corporate management on what may be done with the resources, the divisional form of organization allows for greater freedom of action by divisional management precisely because a profit measure of performance is available. This means that detailed instructions about what the division is to do and how it is to proceed can be replaced by broader directives, capped by the general requirement that the division's activities shall result in a satisfactory profit.

Three advantages can be claimed for a divisional type of organization. First, decentralized decision making is likely to result in better decisions because the people who make them are closer to the scene of action and have a smaller area of responsibility to worry about. Second, greater efficiency results from the sense the divisional managers have that they are running "their" businesses. In motivating these managers, divisional profit plays an important part. Third, giving a person responsibility for running a division is perhaps the best way of providing preparation for a top management role at the corporate level. A divisional organization provides its own executive development.

The Nature of Divisional Performance.   The way in which divisional goals are specified obviously plays an important part in motivating divisional managers because it is by their success in attaining these goals that their performance must be judged. Goals that cannot be expressed in quantifiable terms are unlikely to be effective, precisely because success or failure in attaining them cannot be measured. However, to be quantifiable is a necessary but not a sufficient quality in a goal because ill-conceived goals may motivate divisional managers in the wrong direction. Some of the profitability ratios that are widely used in divisional reports are open to this criticism. This point will be taken up again shortly.

It is easy to defend the primary position accorded to profit (or some derivative of it) as a measure of performance in a divisional organization. In the first place, unless a company is profitable, it is unlikely to survive for very long, and if it does not survive, nothing else much matters. Second, profitability, better than any other single index of performance, reflects a great many other ingredients of performance, such as growth, market penetration, product leadership or productivity, all of which are bound to have an impact on a company's profit sooner or later. Thus, there is a comprehensive quality to profitability which other performance measures lack.

A good deal will have to be said to qualify the simple concept of profitability before it can be safely put to use for divisional reporting purposes. But first it is necessary to consider the responsibilities that corporate management delegates to divisional management since the degree of delegation affects the nature of the performance that needs to be measured.

Delegation of authority to divisions is never undiluted, for if it were, the divisionalized company would virtually have transformed itself into an investment trust. There are always corporate constraints on the management of a division as to how it runs the segment of the company's business entrusted to it, and these constraints inevitably affect the nature of the tasks by which management is to be judged. The extent of divisional autonomy varies from company to company, and so, therefore, must the precise meaning of "divisional performance." In one company, divisional management may have almost complete control over the setting of selling prices, subject only to an informal requirement to consult with, say, the corporate vice-president in charge of marketing before any of a few particularly sensitive prices are changed. At the other extreme, in another company, almost any change in prices or discounts or other conditions of sale may require corporate approval. It is obvious that divisional management has less genuine responsibility for the results of the division in the second case than in the first.

Variations in the extent of divisional independence are to be found in almost every area of managerial responsibility. In some companies, purchasing is totally decentralized; in others, all important purchases are made centrally; in yet others, certain divisions are given the responsibility for purchasing some bulk items for other divisions as well as for themselves. The extent to which research, advertising, personnel services, data processing, credit and collection, and other services are centralized or decentralized is equally subject to great variation. Thus, divisional performance hardly ever means precisely the same thing in any two companies, even though on the surface they appear to have quite similar organizations.

Managerial Performance and Enterprise Performance. What a company expects of its divisional managers is clouded somewhat by the fact of corporate interference with divisional autonomy. This suggests a need to distinguish between the performance of a division and the performance of its managers. The divisional managers can be held responsible for and can take credit for the division's results only to the extent that they *control* its activities. Managerial performance, then, means performance in this limited area. But corporate management is concerned with more than this when it tries to form judgments about the success and the prospects of the total divisional activity. For this purpose, everything relating to the division is relevant, whether it is the responsibility of divisional or of corporate management. Thus, the cost of research carried out in a corporate research laboratory on a divisional project, at the request of, or at least with the acquiescence of, the divisional management, is properly chargeable in determining the profits earned both by the division and by its managers. If the research were carried out on a project which the division had not agreed to, but which corporate management thought ought to be proceeded with and which might be of long-run benefit to the division, then it might be proper to charge the cost of the project to the division as an expense not controllable by its management.

A straightforward example of an expense clearly chargeable to a division but not controllable at divisional level is the divisional general manager's own salary. Corporate administrative expenses charged to divisions on some "equitable" basis may fall into the same category since divisions have no control over the level of such expenses and will usually have no more than a right to be consulted about the basis on which they are allocated to divisions.

If divisional performance is to be measured by profitability, then a distinction must be drawn between controllable profit, by which alone the division's manager should be judged, and divisional net profit, which will bring together all costs inflicted on the company and all revenues enjoyed by the company because of the division's existence. Such costs and revenues could conceivably make themselves felt quite outside the division's sphere of operations. The distinction between divisional profit and controllable profit (which is a part, but only a part, of divisional profit) makes it possible, in a single income statement, to report information by which both the division and its managers may be judged.

Performance Measurement and Management Motivation. Mention has already been made of the importance that attaches to the choice of measures of performance, in a decentralized business especially, because of the effect such measures may have on management motivation. It is clear, for instance, that if managers knew, or thought they knew, that they were to be judged *exclusively* by the share of the market that they could command, they would be likely to cut prices and increase sales promotion expenditures since this would be likely to lead to sales expansion, even though such expansion was unprofitable. Emphasis on a high rate of capital turnover could have the same effect. Conversely, if the criterion of performance were thought to be the rate of net profit to sales, then a manager might well prefer to run a business that showed a profit of $10,000 on $100,000 of sales, rather than $12,000 on $150,000 of sales, even though the company was $2,000 worse off, in terms of profit, as a result.

Probably no single measure of performance, used exclusively, is free from the danger that it may lead to misdirected effort on the part of management. Certainly accounting net income itself is not untainted. Its particular taint is of being shortsighted since it is widely recognized that, for a time, profit can be increased by "milking" the future. This can be done by reducing expenditures on research and development, on training, even on advertising in the short run, and by neglecting product quality and customer relations. Eventually, of course, profits will suffer, but by that time, if high *current* profits are promptly rewarded, the manager responsible will have been promoted.

To recognize this danger is to be on the way to avoiding it. One simple way of minimizing the risks of myopia when looking at profit statements for a division is to look at them together with budgets for the next year or two. A manager who is thus required to think of the future as well as the present is much less likely to forget that the way the division is run today will have repercussions well beyond the end of the current accounting period.

CRITERIA OF PROFIT MEASUREMENT FOR DIVISIONALIZED COMPANIES

All the problems of profit measurement that are found in a nondivisionalized company are present in the divisionalized company, but there are additional problems as well when profits are to be attributed to segments of a business that are not entirely unrelated to each other. Of course, in the case of the "pure" conglomerate, where the corporation is merely a shell to house a number of unrelated businesses, the difficulties of profit attribution are minimal; however, this case will not require much of our attention in the present context.

In selecting or in judging accounting procedures where the determination of the profitability of segments of a company is important, and not just of the company as a whole, two criteria must be met in addition to those which apply to all profit and loss accounting. They are the criteria of profit independence and profit covariability. The more closely integrated the affairs of the divisions become with each other, the more difficult it will be to satisfy these criteria, and only rarely, even where divisions are largely unrelated to each other, will it be possible to secure complete profit independence and covariability. With this word of warning, let us now examine these criteria more closely.

Profit Independence.   If divisional performance is to be judged in profit terms, a division's profit should so far as possible be independent of levels of performance achieved by other parts of the corporation. This is what we shall call the rule of profit independence, and there are probably few divisionalized companies that satisfy it completely.

A division will not be profit-independent where it is required to bear a proportion of the corporation's central administrative expenses. First, the level of expenditure on central administration will invariably have been outside the division's control, and usually the division will have had little say about how its share of these expenses was computed. Again, profit independence may be lost where transfers of products or services take place between divisions at actual cost and the buying division is not free to buy outside, because here also the effects of inefficiency or extravagance in one division can be passed on to another in the cost-based transfer price.

Profit independence does *not* mean that a division should be free to escape some part of the cost of its activities if these costs happen to arise within the company but outside the division. Indeed, we shall see that the rule of covariability, discussed next, requires that this does not happen. Profit independence requires only that these costs, external to the division but associated with and caused by its activities and therefore properly chargeable to it, should reflect the results of its activities alone. Thus interdivisional transfers priced at market price or at standard cost could be regarded as preserving profit independence, while transfer prices based on actual cost might not. But other considerations enter into transfer pricing also, as we shall see.

Profit Covariability.   The rule of profit covariability is so closely related to the rule of profit independence, though different from it, that it is difficult to discuss the two rules separately. The covariability rule requires that a division's reported profit should correspond as closely as possible to the contribution the division makes to the *corporate* results. This requirement may sound like a truism, but on closer examination it will become evident that there are several reasons why a division's contribution to corporate profitability may be different from the profit that is reported in its own profit and loss statement.

The clearest such reason is the existence of interdivisional conflict. For example, where two divisions are in direct competition for a particular sale, the profit which the successful division makes on the sale will, from the company's point of view, be partly or wholly offset by the unsuccessful division's abortive selling expenses. These will not appear as a deduction from the successful division's profit in its accounting statements, though they will result in a deduction from corporate profits in the company's consolidated statements.

The question whether interdivisional competition is good for the corporate health is a controversial one and there are not only differences of opinion among companies about it, but also changes of opinion from time to time within the same company. Obviously a distinction should be made between two different kinds of competition:

1. Two divisions sell substantially the same product, though perhaps in a slightly different price range and with some differences in quality. The divisions of General Motors or Ford are examples of this situation.

2. Two divisions sell different products which serve substantially the same purpose, for example, a glass bottle division and a can division of a container company.

There would seem to be a much stronger case for the second kind of interdivisional competition than the first. The differences in the techniques of production reinforce the argument that separate bottle and can divisions are more likely to seek out new uses for their products which are not directly competitive than if this were the responsibility of a single division. In the automobile example, on the other hand, the use of many common parts in competing lines weakens the case for the maintenance of separate divisions. Ultimately, judgment as to the desirability of competition between divisions, from the company's point of view, is likely to depend on the question of whether the company gets a bigger share of the market, however that may be defined—automobiles in one case above, containers in the other—by having the divisions compete with each other rather than by combining them. There is also the question of whether the additional cost of having two divisions rather than one is commensurate with any benefits that result from the separation of authority, but this question is likely to play a subordinate part in the decision whether to maintain the competing divisions as separate entities or to combine them.

A different kind of interdivisional conflict may arise in pricing transfers between divisions. An increase in the price charged by division A for products transferred to division B might add less to A's profit than it takes away from B's because the impact which this cost increase has on B's pricing policy might greatly reduce the market for its products. A's attempt to maximize its own profits at the expense of B would then have reduced the total corporate profit. This is a clear case of suboptimization, as this phenomenon is called. Suboptimization lies hidden behind many situations that confront divisionalized companies, and it will therefore occupy more of our attention later. The problem arises essentially because the whole is not equal to the sum of its parts in a segmented company. Conduct that is optimal for each part looked at separately is not necessarily optimal for the whole company; and to achieve the best result for the whole company may require one part of the company to follow a course of action that may appear to conflict with its own best interests.

Accounting Procedures and Covariability.   Loss of covariability may result from competition between divisions or from transactions between divisions. But it may also result from accounting procedures that make a division's reported profit react favorably to a decision taken within the division when the decision in fact causes the corporate profit to react negatively.

The treatment of depreciation may give rise to such a situation. A method of computing the depreciation charge on assets that does not reflect the true expiration of asset service values—by using the straight-line method, based on time, for example, instead of a service-unit method based on asset usage—may do so by failing to reflect in the division's operating statements the cost to the corporation of asset erosion. Accounting errors of this sort are, of course, ultimately self-correcting when assets are finally disposed of, but they may persist for a considerable time.

It is important to recognize the general category to which this case belongs.

Whenever a division of a company can escape a charge for a cost it inflicts on the company there is likely to be a loss of covariability leading to conduct by the division that may be unfavorable for the company. Where no attention is paid to the rate of return a division earns on its investment and where no charge is made to the division for the capital invested in it, the division has no incentive to economize in the use of capital. The company, not the division, bears the cost. The same is true of centrally provided services for which divisions are not charged. This is not an argument for making divisions bear a part of *all* corporate expenses, but only those which by their conduct they can cause to increase or decrease.

Covariability may be lost not only through a failure to charge for certain corporate expenses, but also through the choice of an unsuitable method of charging. The illustration that follows describes a situation in which both of the rules we have been discussing—the rules of profit independence and of covariability—are broken by an ill-chosen method of allocating central administrative expenses.

The results of a company, with its three divisions, for the first quarter of 19X1 are shown in Exhibit 1. All the costs can be directly allocated to divisions except the central administration expenses, and these, it has been decided, shall be apportioned between divisions in proportion to their sales.

EXHIBIT 1   Operating Statement, First Quarter, 19X1 (thousands omitted)

	Div. A	Div. B	Div. C	Company total
Net sales.....................	$1,000	$500	$500	$2,000
Cost of sales................	550	240	215	1,005
Division direct expenses........	150	60	85	295
	$ 700	$300	$300	$1,300
Divisional contributions........	$ 300	$200	$200	$ 700
Central administration expenses.......	200	100	100	400
Net profit before taxes........	$ 100	$100	$100	$ 300

A detailed examination of division A's business reveals that it falls fairly clearly into two classes, one of them showing a much lower margin of profit than the other. Of the division's total contribution of $300,000, $260,000 is produced by sales of $600,000, while the remaining sales of $400,000 contribute only $40,000 to the division's profit. The division would have replaced this part of its business with more profitable lines if it had been able to do so, but until these could be found, the division's management preferred to get a small contribution from the facilities devoted to the low-margin business rather than to leave them idle with no contribution at all—until it was realized that so long as corporate management maintained the present method of charging out central administrative expenses, the division could improve its apparent results by liquidating its low-margin business. The result for the company and for the division, if the division acts accordingly and everything else continues as before, *including the level of central administration expenses,* is shown in Exhibit 2. The company is $40,000 a quarter worse off than it was before, while division A is doing $10,000 a quarter better than it was before. Not only has the covariability rule been broken, but the rule of profit independence has also. The profits of divisions B and C have been reduced by $25,000 a quarter, after division A's action in getting rid of its low-margin sales, although they themselves have done nothing to worsen their performance.

Two Criteria or One?   Are the rules of profit independence and profit covaria-

EXHIBIT 2   Company Results After Division A Liquidates Its Low-Margin Business (thousands omitted)

	Div. A	Div. B	Div. C	Company total
Net sales............................	$600	$500	$500	$1,600
Cost of sales.........................	260	240	215	715
Division direct expenses................	80	60	85	225
	$340	$300	$300	$ 940
Divisional contributions................	$260	$200	$200	$ 660
Central administration expenses.........	150	125	125	400
Net profit before taxes...............	$110	$ 75	$ 75	$ 260

bility really two rules or one? Can a division inflict losses on the corporation (either directly or through one or more of its other segments) or bring gains to it without a breach of the independence rule? If it cannot, then the covariability rule would embrace the independence rule, and the two rules could be reduced to one.

As a matter of fact, every breach of the covariability rule does mean that some part of the company is having its profit independence infringed upon (if for this purpose we are prepared to regard the corporate head office as a profit center, and not just its divisions). But in each division looked at separately, there can be a loss of independence without a loss of covariability, and vice versa. Thus suppose a company has three divisions, A, B, and C. Division A has been buying some of its material from one of B's customers but decides to give its business to another supplier, and this causes B's customer to withdraw its business from B. The affairs of division C are quite separate from the other two. Then A's profit is independent of the rest of the company but not covariable with its contribution to corporate profitability (because it has inflicted losses on B that do not show up in its own profit statement); B's profit is not independent (having been affected by A's action in changing suppliers) but it is covariable; C's profit is both independent and covariable. The two rules are best kept separate.

THE TREATMENT OF COMMON COSTS

The treatment of costs that are incurred, generally at the corporate level, for the benefit of several or all of the company's divisions is one of the two critical areas that distinguish divisional profit statements from those of centralized nondiversified companies. (The other one, of course, is the transfer price problem.) "In the current controversy concerning the desirability and feasibility of financial reporting on some segment basis by diversified companies, the difficulty mentioned most often by corporate representatives is the problem of allocating common cost."[1] This is an area in which it is idle to look for right answers because they do not exist. Some methods of handling these costs are better than others in given situations, and there is probably room for more uniformity of method between companies than now exists. But while a consensus about the purposes of common cost allocation is within reach, unanimity about how to attain these purposes is a long way off.

The allocation of common costs serves, or is thought to serve, several different

[1]Robert K. Mautz and K. Fred Skousen, "Common Cost Allocation in Diversified Companies," *Financial Executive*, June 1968, p. 15.

purposes. The one that is most often mentioned by corporate executives, when they are called on to defend their allocation practices, relates to divisional pricing practices. It is necessary, they say, to ensure that divisions set their selling prices at a level that will cover not only their own costs but also the division's share of corporate costs and show a profit over and above both layers of cost. There are other reasons for cost allocation, but they are generally subordinate to the one just mentioned. It can be argued that unless common costs are allocated, divisional profitability cannot be accurately assessed; and that unless divisions are made to bear the cost of centrally provided services, rational decisions cannot be made about the size of central service departments and how much of their services each division is to get. The fact is that the case for common cost allocation is a mixture of good and bad logic. It calls for closer analysis, as does the nature of common costs themselves.

How Important Are Common Costs? Some quantitative assessment of the importance of common costs in measuring the profitability of the segments of diversified companies can be gained from the results of the Financial Executive Research Foundation's study of financial reporting by such companies.[2] In a sample of 255 large companies responding to a questionnaire based on 1966 data and excluding federal income tax from noninventoriable common costs, 25 percent of the companies reported common costs as representing 10 percent or more of sales (for 16 companies—6 percent—the figure was over 20 percent). For the whole group, the average percentage of noninventoriable common costs (excluding income tax) to sales was 7.83 percent, while the average percentage of net income to sales was only 6.29 percent. It is clear, therefore, that the treatment accorded these common costs could, in many of these companies, make a material difference to the relative profit performance of a company's divisions.

Classification of Common Costs. Since common costs are not all alike, a classification of them is necessary before a sound accounting treatment can be prescribed. At once, a broad dichotomy suggests itself between the functions of corporate administration and control on the one hand and the centralized provision of services such as data processing and accounting, product development, process improvement, training, and other personnel services on the other. These services are of a kind that divisions would have to pay for if they were independent businesses, and the quantity of service taken by a division can, to a considerable extent, be determined by decisions taken within the division itself. The same is not true of such corporate activities as the work of the board of directors and top management, internal audit, many treasury functions, some of the work of corporate counsel, and institutional advertising. Pure research of a long-run nature carried out in the corporate research laboratory also belongs in this group, if, as is often the case, it cannot be identified with any existing division.

Central Service Departments. Surprisingly, many companies do not distinguish between these quite different categories of common costs, and bring them together for allocation purposes.[3] This practice has nothing to commend it except simplicity. Indeed, to group all central services together in a single category, let alone combining them with corporate administration and control, is still too crude because in distinguishing between controllable and noncontrollable costs, some fall

[2]*Ibid.*

[3]The Conference Board (formerly the National Industrial Conference Board), "Allocating Corporate Expense," *Studies in Business Policy No. 108,* New York, 1963. It may be possible in the future to say more about actual business practice in these matters, now that the Cost Accounting Standards Board has started to publish statistics derived from aggregated disclosure statement responses. Unfortunately, from the *Board's Progress Reports to the Congress 1974 and 1975* it is not possible to obtain much useful information. The 1976 report is more promising.

on one side of the line and some on the other. Three different situations can be distinguished:

1. Divisions are free to take a service from a central service department, or to buy it from an outside source, or to do without the service altogether. Market research, management services, and computer services might fall into this group. Any charges a division accepts from a central service department in such circumstances are "controllable expenses" just as much as any other purchases it makes outside.

2. Divisions are not free to get the service from outside, but they are free to decide how much of a service they will take, and even to take none at all. Centralized purchases of materials are in this category. Where charges made for the central purchasing department's services are based on the volume of purchases taken by a division, the charge is in part controllable and in part not since the division can control the quantity of service it takes but not the price.

3. Divisions have no choice as to the source, quantity, or price of the service they will take. Some of the services of a personnel department, such as contract negotiation, are of this kind, and any charges made for these services are not controllable by the division. Other personnel services such as the provision of training courses are more like centralized purchasing, which was discussed above.

Attributes of a System of Charging for Central Services.   An ideal system of charging divisions for centrally provided services, if one could be established—we are not now talking about corporate administration and control—would achieve two desirable results. First, it would lead the operating departments, to the extent that they were able to regulate the amount of service that they took, to demand just the "right" amount of service, no more and no less. By the right amount is meant that amount of service which just equates the incremental value of the service to the operating division at the margin with the incremental cost of supplying it. Too high a charge per unit of service will make the division decline to take service it ought to have; too low a charge will lead to excessive demands for service. Of course, if the charge made for the service is a lump sum that does not vary with the amount of service taken, then the division will be foolish not to take as much as it can get, so long as increments of service have any value to it at all.

The right course for a division may be to take no service from a central service department but to buy it itself from an outside source. From a corporate point of view, this is the right course to take when the cost of buying the service outside is less than the incremental cost of providing it internally, given, of course, that the quality of the service, reliability of supply, and other nonprice factors are equally satisfactory. The ideal charging system we are seeking would provide divisions with the information they need to make such "make-or-buy" decisions rationally.

The second desirable result that an ideal charging system would secure would be to motivate the service department that is providing the service to operate as economically as possible. A charging system that enables the service department to pass on to the operating divisions, in the service charges it makes to them, any excess costs incurred through its own inefficiency or redundant manpower, is unlikely to do this.

The kind of charging system to which the foregoing discussion points would have two principal characteristics. First, it would use a two-part tariff, consisting of a fixed charge per quarter or per annum, plus a charge per unit of service taken. If divisions are to be given a choice of taking the service from the corporate service department or of buying it outside, under the two-part tariff arrangement they would have to commit themselves to one source or the other for, say, a year at a time. The unit-service charge would be relevant when the division was weighing the merits of an outside source of supply during the year, while it was still committed to the internal service department. The fixed charge would be relevant when it was considering a change for the following year.

The second characteristic of an ideal charging system would be that both parts of the two-part tariff would be based on standard costs rather than actual costs. This would bring home to the service department the impropriety of passing on to the divisions any costs occasioned by substandard performance.

Central Administrative Expenses. The considerations that bear on the treatment of service department costs have no relevance when we turn to corporate administrative expenses. Divisions cannot choose how much of top management's attention they will take up, and there are no make-or-buy decisions to be made. Quite different criteria as to the methods of allocation to be used apply, therefore. Indeed, the first question to be answered is whether such expenses need to be allocated at all.

A survey carried out by the Conference Board into the practices of 158 companies with regard to the allocation of corporate expenses, the results of which were published in 1963, showed that 53 percent of the companies surveyed allocated all corporate expenses to divisions, 36 percent allocated some expenses, and only 11 percent did not make any allocations.[4] But this last group understates the opposition to allocation somewhat, since of the 36 percent that allocated some expenses, about half made charges for central services only where some measure of the consumption of services could be found. If we classify these companies as nonallocators, we get a total of 29 percent of the 158 companies making no allocation of central administration expenses, against 53 percent that allocated all such expenses. The divided state of opinion on this issue is clear. The needs (or the supposed needs) of external reporting to stockholders by diversified companies may lead to an extension of these allocation practices in the future. The requirements of outside bodies such as the Cost Accounting Standards Board and the Federal Trade Commission raise yet other issues. But it is still legitimate to ask whether, for management's own purpose, anything is gained by the allocation of central administrative expenses.

The pricing argument for allocation has already been mentioned. From a short-run point of view, this argument is not too convincing. To the extent that prices are determined by competitive conditions in the market, they will be the same, whether corporate expenses are allocated to divisions or not. And to the extent that a division has the power to set or at least to influence its prices, expense allocations that are fixed in the short run ought not to affect these prices. It is enough if the division sets its prices so as to optimize its total contribution to central expenses and profit, because whatever prices do, this will also optimize the division's net profit after allocations. In the short run, therefore, the question of allocation seems to be irrelevant to the pricing issue.

In the short run, an allocation of central expenses can make an operation that is making a positive contribution to corporate profits look unprofitable. Although it is unlikely that many people will be misled when looking at the results of a whole division, if the practice is carried down to product lines within divisions, as it often is, the danger of eliminating contribution-making products may be considerably greater.

Whenever possible, a division should be charged with any cost it inflicts on the company, wherever these may "surface." To the extent that an increment of central expenses is attributable to a division, in the sense that central expenses would be smaller by that amount if the division were to close down, that increment is properly chargeable to the division. In the short run, it must be admitted, it is

[4]Conference Board, *loc. cit.*

not often feasible to quantify such amounts. However, if a longer view is taken of this problem, a more convincing argument for allocating some central expenses, at least, comes to light. It has often been noted that, looked at over a period of years, administrative expenses do not exhibit the invariability that they are commonly supposed to have in the short run, but in fact creep up more or less at the same pace as the volume of company activity expands. If, then, the avoidable costs of operating a division are defined not by reference to cost behavior only in the short run, nor with an eye merely to small changes in the level of activity, it becomes reasonable to allocate to divisions all but a hard core of corporate administrative expenses that would be eliminated only if the whole corporation were liquidated.

Bases of Allocation for Corporate Administrative Expenses.   A wide variety of allocation methods is found in practice. As to the bases of allocation most commonly used, two separate studies[5] show that about one-quarter of the companies interrogated favor the use of a single basis of allocation for all allocated expenses. Almost as many appear to favor two bases and almost another quarter favor three. Where a single basis is used, this may be sales, net income before charging allocated expenses or some other profit figure, divisional investment, or total direct expenses—and this does not exhaust the list. Another widely used single base is more complex—the so-called Massachusetts formula, used by several states in determining what proportion of a company's profit shall be subject to state corporate profits tax. When used for allocating corporate expenses to divisions, the formula gives equal weight to sales, assets employed, and number of personnel or payroll. Like any simple formula, it is arbitrary; but it probably comes as close as any single allocation basis can to measuring the relative administrative burden a division places on a corporate headquarters, and this is what the sought-for basis is supposed to reflect.

Though the use of different bases for different expenses is likely to reflect, better than any single basis, the long-run avoidable cost incurred at the corporate level in administering a division, it also creates more possibilities of dispute. Of course, any expenses incurred at corporate headquarters directly traceable to a division should be charged to it directly and should not be lumped in with other expenses for allocation on the chosen basis or bases.

What has been said about allocation of expenses to divisions applies equally to allocation within divisions to product lines or product groups, except that the proportion of directly traceable cost (other than the cost of goods sold) is probably lower. The danger of turning a contribution-earning product line into an apparent loser as a result of expense allocations that do not represent avoidable costs even of a long-run nature needs particularly to be guarded against. It must be noted, however, that for certain regulatory purposes, or for the purpose of setting prices in a noncompetitive situation where the price is to be based on cost, it may be necessary to resort to cost allocations which in other circumstances might be best avoided. The Cost Accounting Standards Board has issued Standard 403 on "Allocation of Home Office Expenses to Segments" and has other aspects of the allocation problem under consideration. The Federal Trade Commission's Line-of-Business Reporting project presents another situation in which allocations not required for management's own purposes may be necessary for other purposes. This project is referred to more fully below.

The allocation of income taxes to divisions raises different issues from those which are relevant to the treatment of expenses. Tax allocation is discussed separately later in this chapter.

---

[5]*Ibid.;* also Mautz and Skousen, *op. cit.*

THE RATE OF RETURN CRITERION

Few companies are content to judge divisional performance on the basis of the division's absolute profit since on this basis the bigger the division, the better its performance would generally appear to be. Relating profit to sales, and using that ratio as the criterion of performance, can lead to undesirable behavior on the part of management, as has already been explained, though it is a widely used criterion nevertheless. Undoubtedly, the measure of performance in most general use, either as the sole criterion or as "first among equals," is the rate of return on investment (ROI), that is, divisional net profit as a percentage of divisional investment. Both the numerator and denominator in the ROI computation admit of many variations, and we shall look at some of these shortly. But overriding these more detailed questions is the broader issue: Is ROI an appropriate criterion by which to judge the performance of a division, or its managers, or of both?

There is a good deal to be said on the positive side. ROI is capable of objective measurement, in spite of the considerable latitude made possible by the variations in method already referred to. It does make it possible to compare profitability for units of different size, to the extent that size is adequately represented by the amount of investment. And it does encourage a manager to economize in the use of capital because, other things equal, the less capital employed in a division, the higher the ROI. Thus, an incentive is provided for capital-economizing moves such as disposing of redundant assets or choosing a less capital-intensive rather than a more capital-intensive method of expansion.

The most serious objection to the ROI criterion of performance is precisely that it may provide too strong an incentive to economize capital and may discourage investment that ought to take place. A manager who is seeking to show the highest possible rate of return on investment will be reluctant to undertake any investment that will lower the present ROI. The higher the ROI is now, the more restrictive the attitude to expansion is likely to be—*even if additional capital is available quite cheaply.* From the stockholders' viewpoint, any investment of capital that will show a return in excess of its cost ought to be made. By setting a manager the goal of maintaining the highest possible rate of return on capital, or even of maintaining any rate in excess of the cost of capital, a conflict is created between the interests of the manager and the interests of the company's stockholders.

Before pursuing this point, it is necessary to distinguish between its backward-looking and forward-looking aspects. Performance measurement is obviously concerned with the past, decision making with the future. But one affects the other because the criteria by which managers are to be judged affect the decisions they will make. The decision affected here is not so much the specific decision to invest, which in a well-run company will be taken on the basis of a discounted cash flow calculation, but rather the decision of a divisional manager to *seek* a capital appropriation from the corporate treasury. The desire to preserve a high average rate of return for a division could cause its management to turn away from opportunities for profitable expansion. That is the danger of the ROI criterion which has to be guarded against.

Residual Income as an Alternative Criterion. If the objection to ROI just advanced is valid, it becomes important to find an alternative criterion that will still relate profitability to size but will not tend to inhibit expansion in the way ROI may do. Such a criterion is available in "residual income." Like ROI, residual income admits of many variants, but it may broadly be defined as the excess of net income over the cost of capital employed in earning it. It is not a ratio, like ROI, but an absolute number of dollars, and this is a distinct advantage in itself since it brings an added simplicity to the task of motivating management. To instruct managers to maximize the residual income of their divisions or to achieve some target level of residual income is surely simpler than instructing them to do something about the *rate* of return on capital. But more important, an instruction to maximize divisional residual income is an instruction to seek any expansion in the division that will earn more than the cost of the capital required for it. If this instruction is carried out, the division's results should be optimized.

The relationship between ROI and residual income may be brought out by a simple illustration (Exhibit 3).

EXHIBIT 3   Comparison of ROI and Residual Income

	Division A	Division B
Capital invested.....................	$1,000	$1,500
Net profit...........................	150	200
ROI.................................	15 %	13.3 %
Residual income when cost of capital is		
6 %.................................	$ 90	$ 110
8 %.................................	70	80
10 %.................................	50	50
12 %.................................	30	20
14%	10	(10)

Several points of interest emerge from Exhibit 3. First, judged by the ROI criterion, division A shows a better performance than B, and this relative performance is unaffected by the cost of capital. By the residual income criterion, it is not possible to say which division is performing better until the rate at which capital can be raised has been determined. If capital is relatively cheap, for example 6 percent, division A's capital costs $60, and its residual income (the excess of net profit over the cost of capital) is $90. Division B's capital costs $90, and its residual income is $110—a superior performance by this criterion. If the cost of capital goes higher, division B's superiority will diminish, and at rates over 10 percent B will be the inferior division. It is not surprising that a low cost of capital will favor the more highly capitalized division and a high cost of capital will penalize it. The break-even rate is 10 percent because this is the ratio of B's extra $50 profit (compared with A's) to its extra investment of $500.

It might be argued that, with half as much capital again at risk as division A, B must show at least half as much profit again as A to be able to claim a comparable performance. But this would be erroneous. The cost of capital already allows for the risks associated with investment, and residual income is what is left after these risks have been compensated for. To take account again of the heavier investment in B would therefore be double counting.

It is worth noting that, if the amount of capital invested in a division is taken as given, then the main advantage of residual income over ROI is lost because any course of action that increases residual income will also increase ROI. The value of residual income as a target figure to maximize is that it can be affected both by how *much* capital is used by the division and by how profitably it is used. If the amount of capital used cannot be varied at all by the divisional manager—not a very common state of affairs, it may be said, though there may be circumstances in which expansion is very difficult—then residual income has little to commend it over ROI.

Some Problems of Measurement.   It cannot be said of residual income that it is free of any of the problems of measurement that beset the calculation of ROI because just as the latter is based on a determination of divisional profit and divisional investment, so is the calculation of residual income. In addition, if residual income is to be used, the cost of capital has to be determined. The case for residual income clearly does not rest on computational simplicity as compared with ROI. It rests, as has already been made clear, on the superior motivational value of residual income.

Turning to the problems of measurement themselves, probably enough has been said about the measurement of divisional profit. The measurement of divisional investment remains to be considered. The problems are the same, whether the investment base is to be used in a calculation of ROI or of residual income. The principal problems are three in number. How is investment to be defined? How are assets to be valued? How are shared assets to be treated in computing the investment in any one division? It is because these questions do not admit of uniquely correct answers that calculations of divisional ROI or residual income lack precision. But though there are no "right" answers, there are answers that command fairly widespread acceptance.

Defining Investment.   In defining investment, we can look at the matter from the "sources" side or the "uses" side. From the sources side, distinctions can be drawn between equity investment, total stockholders' investment (including preferred stocks), total long-term investment (including bonds and mortgages), and total investment (including short-term notes and accounts payable). From the uses side, different distinctions are relevant, for example, between total assets and assets employed in the business (that is, excluding investments in other companies). There is also the question as to how redundant assets (for example, surplus machinery or idle cash balances) should be dealt with.

Each of these definitions is appropriate to a different purpose, and the immediate task is to choose the investment base most appropriate to the measurement of divisional performance in terms either of ROI or residual income. Since divisions do not generally have separate capital structures (unless they happen to be organized as subsidiary companies), the sources of capital (subject to one reservation to be mentioned shortly) are not relevant to the determination of a division's investment base. Since the main objective is to encourage the divisional manager to be as economical as possible in the use of capital, the definition of investment base selected should be designed to serve this purpose; the one that does this best is assets employed in the business (including redundant assets) minus accounts payable properly attributable to the division. Redundant assets are included in order to give the division an incentive to dispose of such assets by sale or transfer to another part of the company. Accounts payable are deducted to encourage the division to take full advantage of all the cheap credit it can get from suppliers. This is the one exception, referred to above, worth making to the general rule that the sources of capital are not relevant to the determination of a division's investment base, because it is usually the only financing decision the division can influence.

Valuation.   We have now defined a division's investment base in general terms, but to quantify it the assets that go into it have to be valued. There is a fundamental difficulty here that makes all the readily available bases of asset valuation (such as cost or cost less depreciation) unsatisfactory. The difficulty is that it is illogical to choose a value for an asset or complex of assets and use it to compute a rate of return by relating the asset's income or cash flow to the asset value. The value of an asset is *derived* from its expected cash flow by discounting the latter by an appropriate discount rate. But, of course, if we do this to get an investment base and calculate an ROI from it, we shall simply go round in a circle and finish up with an ROI equal to the discount rate used in the discounting operation, at least when the asset's expected cash flow and its actual cash flow coincide.

Some way of breaking out of this circle has to be found, and for practical purposes replacement cost is the best valuation basis to use. By replacement cost is meant the cost of replacing the asset in its current condition. Price-level changes between the time the asset was acquired and the valuation date are thus automatically taken into account, and so is any deterioration or obsolescence that the asset may have suffered during its working life. Replacement cost is thus superior to any valuation derived from historical acquisition cost, with or without a deduction for depreciation.

Though the above discussion of valuation has been couched in terms of fixed assets, it is just as applicable to current assets, and particularly to inventories. Other divisional assets, such as accounts receivable, present no particular problems of valuation, though there may be difficulty in identifying certain assets as belonging to a particular division. This is the next problem to be taken up.

The Treatment of Shared Assets.   Computing the ROI or residual income of a division is less straightforward than it is for a total company because it is not always easy to say to which division a particular asset or group of assets belongs. Some assets, such as manufacturing plants, may be shared by two or more divisions. Some assets, like research laboratories and administrative offices, are usually corporate assets, providing services for all divisions. Other assets, like accounts receivable, are theoretically attributable to divisions but may not easily be attributable in practice because they are pooled and handled on a corporate basis. The cash in the corporate treasury is also such an asset. If the sum of all the divisional investments is to be equal to the total corporate investment, then all of these assets must be allocated to divisions somehow.

The fact is that it is *not* necessary to allocate the whole of a company's assets to divisions before an ROI measure of performance can be used. Truly shared assets, like a shared plant, can indeed be allocated, on the basis of floor space, say, without undue arbitrariness. Accounts receivable, where collection and accounting are handled centrally, can be allocated to divisions approximately where it cannot be done precisely, on the basis of divisional sales weighted for differences in the average length of credit allowed by different divisions. Other corporate assets are probably best left unallocated. It makes no particular sense to allocate fractions of a corporate research laboratory or of the corporate head office building to each division; and though a case could be made for attributing portions of the corporate cash balance to divisions, there is too much room for argument about how this should be done to make it an attractive proposition. So long as these unallocated assets are treated consistently from year to year, they are best omitted from the divisional investment bases.

Controllable Investment.   The distinction drawn earlier between the performance of a division and the performance of its management required that a corresponding distinction be drawn between divisional net profit and controllable profit. But this is not enough if ROI or residual income is to be used to assess managerial performance, since controllable profit clearly needs to be related to controllable investment rather than to total investment, where such a distinction is practicable. Assets which are bought or constructed by decision of the division's managers fall into controllable investment; those which are used by the division but which were not acquired or cannot be discarded by decision of its managers constitute noncontrollable investment.

Divisional current assets will normally be part of controllable investment, though it is possible that a division may be required to carry reserve stocks against the wishes of its management, and these would then form part of its noncontrollable investment. Fixed assets are not so easy to classify because, being relatively long-lived, a large proportion of them will have been acquired before the division's present managers were appointed. Moreover, corporate approval always has to be obtained before any substantial investment in or disposal of fixed assets can be made. Thus, the degree of control over fixed investment is at best limited. Yet, since investment in or disposition of fixed assets of a division will rarely be made and such assets will rarely be discarded by corporate management unless the division's management requests it, this does constitute control of a kind over fixed assets. For this reason, it is recommended that fixed investment be treated as controllable except in special circumstances. One such circumstance may be encountered when a division has declared certain equipment redundant, but corporate approval for disposal has not been given because it is thought that a use for the equipment might be found elsewhere within the company. The best accounting treatment for such assets is to take them off the division's charge altogether, by transferring them to some corporate account. But even if this is not done, they should at least be excluded from the division's controllable investment.

A RECOMMENDED FORM OF DIVISIONAL PROFIT STATEMENT

Exhibit 4 is a form of divisional income statement that brings together many of the matters discussed above, so as to give not one but several different profit measures of divisional performance.

The statement distinguishes between the division's external and internal sales and, for the latter, between those made at market prices and those priced on some other basis, such as cost. The purpose of this distinction is to show to what extent the division is dependent on orders from other divisions for its business. It would be relatively simple to carry this distinction further if desired, so as to separate variable profits on external and internal sales. Dependence on other divisions is not so great where an outside market for transferred products exists since there is

EXHIBIT 4   Form of Divisional Income Statement Showing Distinction Between Controllable and Noncontrollable Items

Sales to outside customers		$xxx	
Transfers to other divisions priced at market value		xxx	
Transfers to other divisions at prices not based on market value		xxx	
			$xxx
Less:			
Variable cost of goods sold or transferred		$xxx	
Variable divisional expenses		xxx	
			xxx
Variable profit			$xxx
Less:			
Controllable divisional overhead		$xxx	
Depreciation on controllable fixed assets		xxx	
Property taxes and insurance on controllable fixed assets		xxx	xxx
Controllable operating profit			$xxx
Add/deduct:			
Nonoperating gains and losses			xxx
			$xxx
Less: Interest on controllable investment			xxx
Controllable residual income before taxes			$xxx
Less:			
Noncontrollable divisional expenses		$xxx	
Central administration expenses charged to division		xxx	
Interest on noncontrollable investment		xxx	xxx
Net residual income before taxes			$xxx
Less: Taxes on income			xxx
Net residual income after taxes			$xxx

a possibility of diverting them to that market. It is because of this difference in the degree of dependence that the model statement distinguishes between transfers priced at market prices and those priced on other bases.

The distinction between controllable and noncontrollable items is maintained in the statement, so far as it can be drawn in practice, to give the division's "controllable operating profit." After bringing in nonoperating gains and losses such as profits and losses on disposal of fixed assets or on foreign exchange, and deducting interest on controllable investment, the statement shows controllable residual income before taxes. The concept of residual income has already been discussed. Of course, where an ROI criterion rather than residual income is to be used, no charge for interest on divisional investment, whether controllable or noncontrollable, will be made.

If one measure of the performance of the division's management has to be selected, controllable residual income before taxes seems to be the strongest candidate. To judge the results of the division's business, as distinct from its management, applicable noncontrollable charges have to be deducted. Noncontrollable divisional expenses comprise items directly chargeable to the division but not controllable by its management, for example the divisional general manager's own salary. Central administration expenses charged to the division, which have already been discussed, will normally be apportionments, rather than direct charges.

Allocating Taxes to Divisions.   One question remains to be considered and that is the treatment of income taxes. Unless a division happens to be separately incorporated as a subsidiary company, its income taxes will not be assessed separately, and even where it is separately incorporated the parent corporation may choose to file a consolidated return. Where this is the case, or where the division is not separately incorporated, should income tax be allocated to divisions or left as a charge to be borne centrally by the corporation? Company practices vary, but where taxes are allocated, the allocation is usually made in a somewhat arbitrary manner.

For the purpose of evaluating the performance of a manager, it is before-tax profit that seems to be relevant since tax is not a controllable expense. But when the results of a division's business are to be evaluated, tax has a different significance. A division may be engaged in a business to which Congress has chosen to give favorable tax treatment. If the results of such a business are to be properly judged, therefore, it is the after-tax profits that are relevant. But this means something more than simply allocating the corporation's total tax bill among divisions in proportion to their profits, unless it so happens that by chance this does reflect their relative susceptibility to tax.

What is required is to allocate the total corporate tax burden between divisions so as to reflect as nearly as possible the tax which each division would pay if it were a separate entity. This treatment will put tax benefits as well as tax burdens where they belong. And if it is after-tax profits that are relevant in evaluating a business, then divisions making losses should, by the same token, get credit for the tax relief they bring to the corporation. To a degree, this goes beyond treating the loss-making division as if it were a separate entity because if it were, it would not be able to recover tax on its losses by offsetting these losses against the profits of other businesses. But the suggested treatment is consistent with the rule of (after-tax) profit covariability.

THE TRANSFER PRICE PROBLEM

If there is one problem which is peculiar to divisionalized companies, and which goes to the heart of the divisionalization concept, it is what is commonly called the *transfer price problem.* If divisions were entirely independent of each other except in the sense that they were answerable to the same corporate management and body of stockholders and had a common source of supply of capital, the problem would not exist. A valuable aspect of divisionalization would be missing, however, since presumably the corporation benefits from having divisions do business with each other rather than with suppliers and customers outside the corporate family. A complete absence of interdivisional transactions raises doubts about the rationality of having these divisions under one corporate roof.

What is the transfer price "problem"? It is that, ideally, a divisionalized company must always be seeking two conditions that may in certain circumstances prove to be simultaneously unobtainable. One of these conditions is a substantial degree of decentralization of decision making and freedom for divisional management to follow courses of action they think best for their divisions. The other condition is maximum attainment of the goals of the corporation as a whole, whether these be closely linked with long-run profitability or something else. The goal is to achieve divisional autonomy *without* suboptimization, that is, to maintain divisions' freedom of action without forcing the corporation to accept a profit or other desired goal lower than could be achieved if all its activities were directed from a centralized corporate management.

The nature of the transfer price problem depends on whether the material, component, or product being transferred between divisions can or cannot be bought and sold freely on an outside competitive market. Where such a market exists, theoretically, at least, there is no reason why both of the two conditions discussed above should not be secured simultaneously. But the prognosis is not nearly so good where there is no outside market for the transferred item, or where there is a market but the prices that rule in it are in part dependent on the activities of the two divisions themselves because they are large enough in relation to the total size of the market to influence what happens there. The absence of any market will usually be caused by the fact that a material or product is being transferred in a semiprocessed form (for example, an unrefined chemical) or is highly specialized to the needs of the transferee division.

Why Transfer Prices Are Not Neutral. A superficial consideration of transfer pricing might suggest that the manner in which prices are set between affiliates or the level at which they are set are of little importance to the corporation as a whole, so long as neither affiliate has outside stockholders; what comes out of one corporate pocket goes into another, however much money is involved. Such a simplistic view would be quite misguided, because it loses sight of the fact that, in a decentralized organization, managers are supposed to be free to react to internal prices in much the same way as to external prices. If a transfer price is higher than it need be and there is no outside market, the buying division may refuse to deal or may buy less than it would take at a lower price. By reacting in this way, it may be doing what is best in terms of its own profitability, but the actions of the two divisions together may not be best for the corporation. The "what comes out of one pocket goes into the other" argument would hold only if divisional behavior were unaffected by the price at which materials and products passed between divisions. Though situations do exist where some variation in price does not materially affect behavior, clearly this is not the normal state of affairs.

The ideal which a transfer pricing system must aim at is that it should lead divisions to achieve the same levels of production and sales, looking at their activities as a whole, as would be achieved by a fully integrated, centralized company. The fact of decentralization may cause these activities to be carried out with greater efficiency, but that is not the point at issue here. The nature and scale of the activities ought not to be changed simply because they are divided between two or more divisions. But they will probably be changed, if it costs a buying division more to increase its supply of a material, component, or product than it costs the total corporation to increase it. And this, unfortunately, is just the effect that an ill-considered transfer pricing system may have.

This point is easily illustrated. Suppose division A, which supplies material to a finishing division, B, charges for the material on a standard cost basis. Its fixed costs are $400 a day, and the variable costs of supplying the material are $1 a unit. Normal capacity is 200 units a day, and standard cost per unit is therefore computed at $400/200 for fixed cost plus $1 for variable cost, a standard cost of $3 a unit. This is what division B will have to pay for each unit it takes. B's own profit, ignoring any other activities it may have, will depend on how much of A's material it chooses to convert, and it will probably wish to expand the conversion activity so long as expansion adds to its own profit.

Now suppose that division A is operating below normal capacity and division B is also not working at capacity and could expand its activity beyond its present level but it would incur additional costs of its own of $1.50 a unit and it could add to its gross revenue $3.50 a unit for the additional units of product it could sell. If B has to pay A $3 a unit for the material it takes, it can hardly be expected to expand since it will lose $1 a unit on every unit it sells ($3.50 − $3 − $1.50). From the corporate point of view, however, B ought to take on the additional business because, looking at the two divisions together, the company would be $1 a unit better off for each unit that B can sell ($3.50 revenue minus incremental costs of $1 for A and $1.50 for B) until capacity for A is reached.

This illustration should make clear the nature of the danger that transfer pricing may present. Transfer prices based on a supplying division's *average* total costs (whether these are actual or standard costs) have the effect of transforming that division's fixed costs into a buying division's variable costs. This is why, when a company's activities are divided between divisions and the divisions are free to deal with each other at arm's length, the aggregate of the divisions' activities may not be the same and may not be so profitable for the company as under centralized direction.

Marginal Cost and Transfer Prices.   The transfer pricing rule this argument leads to is a "marginal cost" rule—that a supplying division should be prepared to supply other divisions at a price equal to its incremental cost so long as there is unutilized capacity. If its incremental cost is fairly constant over a considerable range of output, the rule as stated above defines the price sufficiently. If incremental cost is different at different levels of output, then the incremental cost that is relevant for transfer pricing purposes is the incremental cost at the output margin. For a division supplying two or more other divisions with material or components, its output margin will be determined by how much is taken by the other divisions in the aggregate, but this in turn will be determined by the transfer price they have to pay. The transfer price, then, has to be determined by comparing two schedules, one showing the varying quantities the consuming divisions will take at various prices, and the other the marginal cost of the supplying division at various levels of output. There will be one figure of marginal cost that will equate output with the amount the consuming divisions wish to take. This sets the marginal cost transfer price.

In spite of its theoretical attractiveness, marginal cost is seldom used as a basis for transfer pricing, for reasons to be discussed later. But it is in fact closely related to what is probably the most widely used basis, that is, market price. Where appropriate, market price has everything to commend it as a basis for transfer pricing, both on theoretical and practical grounds. But the circumstances in which it is appropriate and what "market price" means need to be spelled out.

The existence of an outside competitive market for a material or component which is the subject of interdivisional transfers provides an objective basis for pricing transfers that meets all the requirements of an ideal system. Within the broad general specification of such a system as was laid down earlier, three elements can be identified:

1. The level of transfer prices when based on market prices will be relatively free from argument. This eliminates one factor which is apt to become the subject of dispute when other bases of transfer prices are used.

2. As a correlative to the objectivity and independence of outside market prices, when used as transfer prices they tie in well with a system of divisional profit measurement of which profit independence is an important desideratum. Indeed, market price is the only basis of transfer pricing which does so at all well. This takes on added significance when it is desired to use ROI or residual income as a means to motivate divisional management, because without a divisional profit figure which is substantially independent of other divisions' activities, the effectiveness of such measures of performance is substantially reduced.

3. The use of competitive market prices as a basis for transfer prices implies the existence of an outside market and it also implies freedom for divisions to buy and sell in it. Whether they actually do so or not does not matter. But freedom of access to it provides a mechanism whereby each division can seek the maximum satisfaction of its own ends without any danger to the company of suboptimization. A supplying division whose incremental costs per unit are high in relation to the market price may be unable to supply as much as using divisions would like to take (at the market price) without injuring its own profit performance. Its costs may be so high that it is unwilling to supply anything at all. This will not hurt the using divisions if they can go to the market and make up any shortage of internal supply by outside purchases. Conversely, a low-cost supplying division may want to produce more than other divisions are willing to take at the market price. All it has to do is sell its surplus output on the market, after supplying its fellow divisions with what they are willing to buy. Subject to one refinement, to be mentioned shortly, transfers at market price with freedom for divisions to buy and sell outside protect both the company and its divisions from having their profitability sacrificed to divisional self-seeking on the one hand and corporate policy on the other.

Market Prices in Practice.   Access to markets is not free of cost. There are costs of obtaining information about prices, terms of trading, and availability of supply; there will usually be expenses associated with delivery and receipt of goods; and there will be risks of default on delivery and on payment. These costs are usually absent or minimal when affiliates do business with each other. Now suppose a buying division, faced with the choice of buying from another division or from an outside supplier at the same price, chooses to go outside, and the selling division has to dispose of its output on the outside market; then the company as a whole will probably incur expenses of resorting to the market (twice) that it would save if the transaction took place internally. To encourage divisions to deal with each other, with consequent economies to the company, it is usual to set market-based transfer prices at a level somewhat below the outside market price in recognition of these savings. The incentive this gives buying divisions to keep their business in the family removes a possible conflict between their own interests and the company's.

Unfortunately, in the real world, perfect markets are the exception rather than the rule, and only perfectly competitive market prices, when used as transfer prices, give all the advantages described above. For many kinds of basic raw materials, market imperfections may not be too serious, though even here there will usually be many different grades and specifications of what passes as the same material, and there will be conditions of sale implicit in a price, relating to such things as waiting time for delivery and payment terms. A price quoted for an isolated transaction may not hold for a series of transactions or a long-term contract. This is a particularly serious point that has often given rise to dispute between divisions when a buying division has produced an outside quotation as evidence in support of a claim that a transfer price charged by a supplying division was too high. In markets for manufactured components and finished products, the imperfections are probably worse since markets are likely to be narrower than for materials. Sometimes, however, the situation is not as bad as it looks because, although a component being priced may be unique or almost so, the process which produced it may be a common one and there may be many processors qualified to make it, so that truly competitive prices for the component are obtainable.

What, if any, is the connection between the rule, widely used in practice, of basing transfer prices on outside market prices, and the generalization put forward earlier that the cost to a division of increasing its supply of a transferred product should be the same as the cost to the company of doing so? This generalization pointed, it will be remembered, to an incremental or marginal cost rule of transfer pricing. What does this have to do with market price?

The answer is that resort to market prices is no more than a special case of the application of the marginal cost rule. Whether the selling division sells to another division, to the outside market, or to both, at the outside (competitive) price, rational behavior will lead it to sell just that amount which equates its marginal cost with the outside price. At this point, its own profit will be at a maximum. Thus, at the margin of its activities, marginal cost is brought into equality with market price. It is in this sense that the market price rule for transfer prices can be said to be a special case of the marginal cost rule where competitive markets exist.

Alternatives to Market Price.   Where the narrowness of a market is such that prices in it are not independent of the quantities a particular company's divisions buy or sell in it or where prices would not be unaffected if these divisions turned from dealing with each other to dealing through the market, then the conditions will not be present to give all the advantages of a market-based transfer price system. At the limit, of course, there may be no market at all. Some other basis of pricing transfers then has to be found.

Among the most commonly used alternatives to market price are actual average cost, with or without a percentage addition to give the supplying division a return on its capital; standard cost, with or without an allowance for return on capital; and negotiated prices.

Actual Average Cost.   Actual average cost will normally only be used where a standard cost system is not in operation. Transfer prices based on actual costs will fluctuate from month to month as costs change, if they are made to follow costs closely, though usually in practice they are not varied more frequently than once a quarter. Transfer prices will also be affected by changes in efficiency in the supplying division, so that gains and losses of efficiency are passed on to other divisions. This is objectionable because it is in conflict with the rule of profit independence. Another serious objection to actual average cost has already been discussed—that it converts a supplying division's fixed costs into a buying division's variable costs, with the consequent danger of suboptimization.

The addition to cost of an allowance to give the supplying division a return on investment only increases this danger in the short run because the additional cost to the buying division to cover this allowance does not reflect any additional cost to the company, since in the short run the capital invested in the supplying division is fixed. This is just one example of how a desire to maintain separate profit accountability by divisions—which, of course, is the reason for including a return on the supplying division's capital in the transfer prices it is allowed to charge—may create or exacerbate a conflict between divisional and corporate interests.

To compute the percentage addition to cost that is required to give a division a specified rate of return on its investment, all that is necessary is to know its average markup on sales and its average rate of turnover of investment. The relation between these quantities is given by:

$$\frac{P}{I} = \left(\frac{C}{S}\right) \left(\frac{S}{I}\right) \left(\frac{P}{C}\right)$$

where P = profit
I = investment
C = cost of goods sold
S = sales

Thus, if it is desired to give a division a return of 16 percent per annum on its investment, when average markup is 20 percent on sales (that is, cost is 80 percent of sales) and investment is turned over twice a year, then 10 percent must be added to the cost of transfers, as the following equation shows:

$$0.16 = 0.8 \times 2 \times \frac{P}{C}$$

$$\therefore \frac{P}{C} = 0.10$$

Standard Cost. · Much of what has just been said about transfer prices based on actual cost applies equally to the use of standard cost as a base for pricing. But of the two, standard cost is to be preferred. One advantage of standard cost is that it is less volatile, so that transfer prices can remain constant over longer periods. Another is that substandard efficiency and substandard capacity usage in the supplying division do not affect other divisions through increased transfer prices.

Negotiated Prices. When asked how they set transfer prices, many companies simply say that they are left to be negotiated between divisions. This will sometimes mean that a cost formula is worked out between the divisions, and sometimes that the price is determined in relation to the market price of a nearly equivalent product. Negotiation over a cost formula no doubt sometimes leads to a transfer price based on marginal cost, especially where the supplying division has considerable unused capacity. On the other hand, where the division is short of capacity and there are several competing uses for its products, both in other divisions which it supplies and on outside markets, none of the traditional methods of transfer pricing will be able to ensure that the company as a whole makes the best use of its resources.

Transfer Prices with Limited Capacity. Consider a division which supplies several other divisions with a basic material and which can also sell its product on an outside market. Suppose it does not have the capacity to meet all demands on it at current prices. If other producers of the same product are also short of capacity, or if there are no other producers of precisely the same product, the divisions that use the material may have to curtail their activities if, for its own good reasons, the supplying division chooses to sell its product to outsiders—perhaps because the rules of transfer pricing laid down for it would allow it a smaller profit on internal sales than on sales made outside. In any case, the supplying division will normally have no means of knowing how much profit the corporation is losing because other divisions are not getting all the material they need, even if the supplying division were disposed to put corporate interests before its own.

It is clear that in such a situation nothing less than a corporate solution will do if the outside market price cannot be altered. A divisional view is not enough. Someone above the divisional level must take all the relevant information—the demand function in the outside market for the product of the supplying division, the demand functions for the products of the using divisions, the costs of the using divisions, and the capacity of the supplying division—and must determine, by mathematical programming methods, what distribution of the product between the using divisions and the outside market will make the largest contribution to the company's earnings. This may not be the distribution the supplying division would choose if left to itself.

METHODS OF MAINTAINING COMPATIBILITY BETWEEN DIVISIONAL AUTONOMY AND CORPORATE PROFIT MAXIMIZATION

Probably enough has been said by now to show that a divisionalized company, unless its divisions are self-contained and need have no contacts with each other, is in constant danger of conflict between its two main aims, namely, to give freedom of decision making to its divisions, allowing them to be guided by a search for their own profit, and at the same time to ensure maximum profitability for the corporation as a whole. Almost the only situation in which these aims are quite unlikely to conflict at all is where competitive markets for transferred products exist outside the company, where divisions are allowed access to them, and where these market prices are used as transfer prices.

Where competitive markets are absent, the company is faced with a difficult choice between, on the one hand, full divisional autonomy coupled with profit responsibility and probably suboptimization to a greater or lesser degree, or, on the other hand, a partial withdrawal from decentralization, either through the enforcement of centralized decisions or insistence on a method of transfer pricing, such as marginal cost pricing, that is out of harmony with divisional profit responsibility.

When transfer prices are set equal to marginal cost, the supplying division will probably be left with some or all of its fixed costs uncovered, except to the extent that it makes profits on sales to outside customers. This loss can be provided for in the supplying division's budget; or it can be given a subsidy of like amount by corporate headquarters; or it can be allowed to charge out its fixed costs separately to the division it supplies, and also to add a charge for interest on its capital. But the basis on which this is done must not be the volume of production supplied interdivisionally; otherwise the system virtually reverts to an "average cost" system of charging, and the object of marginal cost pricing is defeated.

One way of trying to minimize conflict between a corporation and its divisions is to make the divisional general managers wear two hats, a divisional hat as divisional general manager and a corporate hat as a vice-president of the corporation. There is much to be said for this arrangement, if only because it makes communications between divisions easier and reduces friction or at least brings it out into the open so that corporate management can deal with it. How far this protects a manager from the feeling of being pulled in opposite directions will depend to a great extent on how genuinely the manager feels that evaluations will not be based on divisional earnings where these have been sacrificed in the interests of corporate profit maximization.

Another way of controlling the possible incompatibility of divisional and corporate interests is through the budgeting mechanism. Divisional performance is usually thought of as being judged against some optimum, either explicit or implicit, which has been set for it. But it can just as well be judged by reference to some other target figure determined, not by reference to what the division might achieve if left uncurbed to pursue its own ends, but by reference to a reduced goal set for it, taking into account the profit which it helps other segments of the company to earn by its contribution to their activities. This target, though lower in terms of the profit the division is expected to show, is not necessarily easier to attain. It simply formalizes the expected result of asking the division to take action conducive to corporate profitability rather than its own.

A special problem arises where a separately incorporated division has minority stockholders who have an interest in the division's earnings but not in the earnings of the parent corporation. In such a situation, fairness to these stockholders (and the law[6]) must take precedence over the suboptimization problem. It is unlikely, in any case, that transfers between this division and other divisions will represent a major source of its income because if they did, the minority stockholders would probably have been bought out. In the absence of a market price for the transferred products (always the preferred basis for transfer prices), standard cost plus an allowance for interest on the division's capital is the recommended basis, as the one least likely to give rise to disputes.

External Reporting of Segment Results.   The emphasis throughout this chapter has been on the managerial uses of divisional reports. Their use for reporting to stockholders has become increasingly important in recent years, for since 1969 in registration statements and since 1970 in SEC Form 10-K, and since 1974 in annual reports to stockholders companies subject to the Commission's jurisdiction have been required to disclose the revenues and income (before income taxes and extraordinary items) derived from each material "line of business" for each of its past five years. A line of business is material if during either of the most recent two years, it accounted for at least 10 percent of revenues or 10 percent of income or loss before income taxes and extraordinary items. If a company's revenue is $50 million or less, the applicable percentage is 15 percent. Where it is not practicable to state the contribution to income before income taxes and extraordinary items for any line of business, the contribution to the results of operations most closely approaching such income is to be disclosed.

It is noteworthy that the Commission has made no attempt to define a "line of business," but has taken the position that "management, because of its familiarity with company structure, is in the most informed position to separate the company into components on a reasonable basis for reporting purposes." It is likely that these components will normally correspond to the company's divisions. As to the limitation of disclosure to the 10 most important lines (or fewer, if the percentage test so results), there is difference of opinion as to whether this provides enough information about a company's operations. A survey of 270 financial analysts by the Financial Analysts Federation in 1972 found a substantial majority of them dissatisfied with the number of segments reported on by companies and the way the segments were defined. One example may serve to explain why. General Motors Corporation recognizes three segments within its huge business, automotive products, nonautomotive products, and defense and space products. Anyone interested in G.M.'s refrigerator business or its business in locomotives or air conditioning will not be well served by the segmented information the company provides.

The Financial Accounting Standards Board has been working for some time on the problem of segmental reporting. A definitive standard, requiring information on segments, is expected to be issued by the end of 1977. A discussion memorandum was issued in 1974 and an exposure draft was issued in 1975.

The two major problems of divisional profit reporting discussed at length in this chapter—the allocation of common costs and transfer pricing—both demand solution for external reporting, though the solutions chosen for this purpose need not be the same as those adopted for management's own reports.

---

[6]See Edward J. Smolinski, "The Adjunct Method in Consolidations," *Journal of Accounting Research*, vol. 1, no. 2, pp. 149–178, Autumn 1963.

For reporting to stockholders, many persons favor leaving common costs unallocated, so that the reporting segment's earnings are reported in the form of its "contribution" to the corporation's common costs and profit. This seems to be the only way of avoiding completely the charge of arbitrariness that can be brought against virtually any method of common cost allocation. But this will leave some companies showing substantial contributions that are liable to misinterpretation as being net profits. The alternative is to allow companies to select any method of allocation they think appropriate, on condition that they disclose fully the method used.

As for transfers between divisions, it seems best to eliminate these from external reports completely, leaving divisions (or other reporting segments) to report only sales and profits made in outside markets. This implies that divisions using materials or products made by other divisions shall bear the costs of making such items, including a share of fixed costs. The problem of accounting for transfers will be minimized if the reporting segment is large since many of the transfers that enter into management reports for smaller segments will become intrasegment rather than intersegment when several small segments are combined for reporting purposes.

The Federal Trade Commission's Line-of-Business Reporting Program. Section 6 of the Federal Trade Commission Act gives the Commission a mandate to gather and compile information about the conduct of business in the United States. At least since 1970, when the Commission adopted a staff recommendation on the subject, work has been going forward on the collection and analysis of line-of-business data reported by companies at the request of the Commission. The first year for which data was collected was 1973. Information was requested from 345 of the largest U.S. manufacturing companies. Of these, 228 complied with the request. The remaining companies contested the Commission's order in the courts. Meanwhile, the Commission went ahead with the program, and has considerably revised the forms on which information is now collected.

While recognizing that there is an incremental cost to U.S. industry of complying with this program, the Commission argues that the merger movement of the 1960s and the continuing trend toward diversification in industry has caused published corporate financial reports to be much less informative about what is going on in particular industries than was formerly the case, because companies are no longer in one industry but are in several. Thus information about profitability which a free enterprise system is supposed to need to function efficiently is no longer readily available. By collecting information about sales, cost of goods sold, and broad expense categories from the country's largest manufacturers classified into about 250 industry types, it is hoped to rectify this deficiency. A similar classification of assets employed by these companies is intended to reveal the relative profitability of employment of capital in different industries. The results will be published as industry aggregates, so as not to disclose information about individual companies.

The Commission has made no secret of the fact that it has a second reason for pressing forward with the program. It seeks to improve its capability of detecting where industry-wide infractions of the antitrust laws may have taken place. Where the financial results of one industry become merged with those of another as they do in the accounts of diversified companies, no clear picture of what is happening in a particular industry can be obtained.

The essential problem posed by the FTC project is whether the industrial omelet can be unscrambled. Those who say it cannot be done argue that the information which will be published by the Commission will at the best be useless and at the worst misleading. On the other side it is argued that the FTC will be able to provide for the public the kind of information (after aggregation) that industry already provides for itself. It may be several years before one side or the other of this argument is proved to be right.

BIBLIOGRAPHY

Abdel-Khalik, A. Rashad, and Edward J. Lusk: "Transfer Pricing—A Synthesis," *The Accounting Review*, vol. 49, no. 1, pp. 8–23, January 1974.

Backer, Morton, and Walter B. McFarland: *External Reporting for Segments of a Business*, National Association of Accountants, New York, 1968.

Conference Board, The (formerly the National Industrial Conference Board): "Allocating Corporate Expenses," *Studies in Business Policy No. 108*, New York, 1963.

———: "Interdivisional Transfer Pricing," *Studies in Business Policy No. 122*, New York, 1967.

Dearden, John: "Mirage of Profit Decentralization," *Harvard Business Review*, November/December 1962, pp. 140–154.

Hass, Jerome E.: "Transfer Pricing in a Decentralized Firm," *Management Science*, February 1968, pp. B-310–B-331.

Hirschleifer, Jack: "Economics of the Divisionalized Firm," *Journal of Business*, vol. 32, pp. 96–108, April 1957.

———: "On the Economics of Transfer Pricing," *Journal of Business*, vol. 31, pp. 172–184, July 1956.

Mautz, Robert K.: *Financial Reporting by Diversified Companies*, Financial Executives Institute, New York, 1968.

——— and K. Fred Skousen: "Common Cost Allocation in Diversified Companies," *Financial Executive*, June 1968, p. 15.

Rappaport, Alfred, Peter A. Firmin, and Eugene M. Lerner: *Segment Reporting for Managers and Investors*, National Association of Accountants, New York, 1972.

Rappaport, Alfred, Peter A. Firmin, and Stephen A. Zeff: *Public Reporting by Conglomerates*, Prentice-Hall, Englewood Cliffs, N.J., 1968.

Smolinski, Edward J.: "The Adjunct Method in Consolidations," *Journal of Accounting Research*, vol. 1, no. 2, pp. 149–178, Autumn 1963.

Solomons, David: *Divisional Performance: Measurement and Control*, Financial Executives Research Foundation, New York, 1965, and Richard D. Irwin, Homewood, Ill., 1968. This book contains an extensive bibliography relating to the subject matter of this chapter.

Tomkins, Cyril: "Another Look at Residual Income," *Journal of Business Finance and Accounting*, vol. 2, no. 1, pp. 39–53, Spring 1975.

———: *Financial Planning in Divisionalized Companies*, Haymarket Publishing, London, 1973.

Chapter **45**

Fund Accounting

ROBERT H. KUHN
Partner, Ernst & Ernst

STEPHEN R. HOLSTAD
Partner, Ernst & Ernst

CONCEPT OF FUND ACCOUNTING

Fund accounting principles are essentially identical for both governmental units and not-for-profit organizations. The principles are presented in this chapter in terms of governmental units.

Nature of Governmental Units. Governmental units are established and exist to provide a wide variety of services to the public. These units form an intricate, interwoven pattern of functional and geographical divisions in several tiers. They may exist to perform a single, relatively simple function, such as that of a local special district for mosquito abatement, or to provide a multiplicity of complex services, such as those of a large city. Each of these units is highly circumscribed by a complex pattern of statutory enactments, court decisions, and customs as to its sources of revenues and the purposes for which such revenues may be expended. Almost universally the available revenues are less than the aggregate cost of services being demanded by some portion of the public it serves.

These complexities and circumscriptions create a twofold need to subdivide the fiscal affairs of the governmental unit and provide separate sets of accounts in which to summarize the financial operations of each of its several distinct functions. First, such subdivisions help administrative officers comprehend the financial resources available to carry out each function and make it possible to summarize the financial operations of each function. Second, they provide the information which enables the administration to demonstrate its compliance with the multiplicity of legal requirements and other parameters of its financial actions. Each subdivision constitutes what is known as a "fund."

Fund Defined. A fund is a subdivision of the fiscal activities, assets, liabilities, revenues, and expenditures of the governmental unit, related to the conduct of a specific function or activity, or the attainment of a specific objective. It is a separate fiscal and accounting entity with a self-balancing set of accounts.

Similarities of Governmental Fund Accounting and Accounting for Commercial Enterprises. The basic concepts of governmental fund accounting in terms of a debit and credit double-entry system of accounts and periodic determination of financial position and results of operation conform closely with those followed in commercial accounting. The basic objective of commercial accounting, however, is to achieve an accurate matching of costs and revenues to permit periodic determination of net income in response to the profit motive. The absence of the profit motive eliminates from governmental accounting certain accounting principles and practices followed in commercial accounting. Some governmental units (using the absence of periodic measurement of net income as a rationale) depart significantly from an almost universally accepted principle of commercial accounting in that they follow the cash basis of accounting rather than the accrual basis. Cash basis accounting is sometimes appropriate in accounting for certain governmental transactions, such as those recorded in debt service funds. Best practice, and the recommendation of the National Committee on Governmental Accounting,[1] however, dictates that accrual accounting should be followed for all other material classes of revenues and expenditures.

Other concepts generally applied in commercial accounting are also pertinent to governmental fund accounting. Among these are the concepts of the going concern, the monetary expression of accounts based upon historical cost, the dependability of data through internal control, materiality, and the concept that timeliness in financial reporting requires estimates. It is also assumed, of course, that governmental accounting's primary aim is to present financial information accurately with full disclosure and objectivity. Terminology, format, and content of financial presentations for governmental units should conform to those followed in commercial accounting except as required to accommodate the unique features of governmental operations.

Differences Between Governmental Fund Accounting and Accounting for Commercial Enterprises. While there are many similarities between accounting and financial reporting of governmental units and of commercial enterprises, there are also some significant differences stemming from differing objectives. Commercial enterprises are operated to make a profit and hence put a great emphasis on proper periodic determination of net income. In order to produce revenue, commercial enterprises incur costs. This creates a cause-and-effect relationship between the two, leading to the significance of the determination of net income.

Governmental units exist to provide a service or group of services to the citizens they serve. Their financial operations consist of exercising their taxing powers and other means of raising revenues and of spending these resources to provide desired services. Usually, these services are ones which it is assumed can be provided most efficiently through governmental action or for which the citizens have felt a need which has not been met through private enterprise. The objective is to render maximum service at a minimum cost, particularly in those situations, as is often the case, when available income is insufficient to provide all services desired.

Such limitations of income have resulted in the development of budgetary planning in governmental units. Budgets were developed and almost universally used in government accounting long before they were generally used by commercial enterprises. In governmental accounting, a presentation of operating results without budgetary comparisons is generally considered to be something less than full disclosure. The AICPA, in its audit guide[2] for governmental units, states: "For financial reporting purposes, the statement of revenues and expenditures of the general fund and certain special revenue funds should include a comparison with a formal budget in order to be in conformity with generally accepted accounting principles." Operating statements, then, usually present a summary of revenues by major sources and expenditures by major function or object, showing at the foot the excess or deficit in revenues. The actual amounts of revenues and expenditures shown are also usually compared with the budget, line by line. The expendi-

---

[1]National Committee on Governmental Accounting, *Governmental Accounting, Auditing, and Financial Reporting,* Municipal Finance Officers of the United States and Canada, Chicago, 1968.

[2]American Institute of Certified Public Accountants, *Audits of State and Local Governmental Units,* New York, 1974.

tures are frequently departmentalized, which aids in fixing responsibility for conforming to planned usage of available resources as set forth by the adopted budget. The budget and the statement of revenues and expenditures may also be organized by "programs" following the concepts set forth in the section of this chapter headed "Program Budgeting."

Absence of the need for periodic determination of net income also has its effect on the balance sheet accounts. For example, inventories and their management, which are frequently a major factor in determination of net income of a commercial enterprise, are relatively unimportant in governmental units. Hence, one of the most complex areas of judgment in conventional enterprises, from both an operating and accounting sense, is not present.

Similarly, assigning the cost of assets with lives extending over several years to accounting periods through depreciation is not followed, except in utility-type operations. Because governmental general obligation credit does not rest upon financial condition (in a balance sheet sense) but upon the power to tax, valuation of assets is not significant. Instead the emphasis is placed upon a determination of resources which will be available for appropriation, that is, cash and items which will become cash within the budgetary cycle. The usual indexes of financial strength developed through ratio analysis of a balance sheet are unimportant. Consequently, balance sheets of governmental funds, except for utility funds, include only current assets and current liabilities.

Overriding all these causes for differences between commercial and governmental accounting is the need to be able to demonstrate that a complex structure of legal requirements and restrictions have been complied with. Indeed, these laws themselves not infrequently specify that certain accounting procedures must be followed. In any case, they must constantly be kept in mind in developing the accounting and reporting systems. For example, generally a government may not spend except in accordance with appropriations passed by its governing body. Budgetary comparisons indicate compliance by exhibiting the fact that expenditures, category by category, are not greater than the amount budgeted or appropriated. Similarly, segregation of resources for specified purposes into separate funds aids in demonstrating that they have been expended for those specified purposes and no others. The AICPA audit guide states: "However, this requirement for compliance to be expressed in the accounting system does not obviate generally accepted accounting principles for purposes of reporting financial position and results of operations. In financial reporting, in the event of conflict between legal provisions and generally accepted accounting principles, the latter should take precedence."[3]

BASIC PRINCIPLES

The National Committee on Governmental Accounting has developed the following 13 principles. These principles do not represent either a complete or a separate body of accounting principles, but, instead, are a part of the entire body of generally accepted accounting principles and deal specifically with governmental units. Each is accompanied by a short explanation.

1. Legal Compliance and Financial Operations

A governmental accounting system must make it possible: (a) to show that all applicable legal provisions have been complied with; and (b) to determine fairly and with full disclosure the financial position and results of financial operations of the constituent funds and self-balancing account groups of the governmental unit.

[3]*Ibid.*

The primary requirement of accounting for a governmental unit is to demonstrate that it has conducted its financial affairs in compliance with all the legal provisions imposed upon it. The sources of these provisions are, among others, state constitutions, statutes enacted by state legislatures, charters, ordinances, and resolutions of the unit's own governing body. Such provisions include restrictions on purposes for which the derived revenues may be expended, rate limits on taxes, etc. The most specific, and one of the most important enactments affecting financial operations, is the annual budget of the unit. Upon adoption by the governing body, the expenditures specified in the budget become appropriations which, generally, may not then be exceeded without specific authorization by action of the governing body. Frequently there may be restrictive limits on such actions by constitutional or statutory provisions.

To permit such determinations, the fund structure, the budgetary document, the chart of accounts, and related procedures must all be coordinated with one another. Accounting for actual revenues and expenditures must conform with the budget in terms of fund structure and chart of accounts to permit comparison of actual fiscal operations with the authorizations of the governing body.

It is essential that readily understood information be made available in sufficient detail to provide a comprehensive portrayal of the financial position of a governmental unit and of its operating results. The system should encompass the preparation of balance sheets, often on a monthly basis, and of periodic statements of revenues and expenditures. The degree of detail included in such statements may vary according to the class of reader for whom the statements are intended, ranging from condensed summaries for members of the public (but without limitation upon their right of access to additional detail if they desire it) to highly detailed statements of departmental revenues and expenditures for operating heads of departments.

2. Conflicts Between Accounting Principles and Legal Provisions

If there is a conflict between legal provisions and generally accepted accounting principles applicable to government units, legal provisions must take precedence. Insofar as possible, however, the governmental accounting system should make possible the full disclosure and fair presentation of financial position and operating results in accordance with generally accepted principles of accounting applicable to governmental units.

For a variety of reasons, there may be occasions when legal enactments include provisions with respect to accounting matters which conflict with generally accepted accounting principles. What may have been generally accepted at the time of enactment of a statutory or constitutional provision may later be recognized as having inherent flaws which cause it to be superseded by other principles. Sometimes legislators have been lacking in understanding or misinformed as to which principles are (or should be) generally accepted. Once enacted, statutory or, particularly, constitutional requirements are usually difficult to change.

The AICPA audit guide has suggested that "the following legal compliance accounting principle is appropriate:"

A governmental accounting system should incorporate such accounting information in its records as necessary to make it possible to both (a) show compliance with all applicable legal provisions and (b) present fairly the financial position and results of operations of the respective funds and financial position of the self-balancing account groups of the governmental unit in conformity with generally accepted accounting principles. Where these two objectives are in conflict, generally accepted accounting principles take precedence in financial reporting.

Where there is a need to report the compliance of financial transactions with legal requirements and it can be reported in supplemental schedules, this form should be used.[4]

3. The Budget and Budgetary Accounting

An annual budget should be adopted by every governmental unit, whether required by law or not, and the accounting systems should provide budgetary control over general governmental revenues and expenditures.

Because a governmental unit may have a limited ability to tax or to provide revenue by other means, and because it must use its ability to tax judiciously to maintain the economic well-being of its constituents, it is essential that it plan carefully what services it expects to provide, what the cost of those services will be, and the sources of revenues from which they will be financed. After adoption by the appropriate legislative body, such a plan constitutes a budget for the year's operation. See the section of this chapter headed "Budgeting Techniques."

In many cases, budgeting has been limited to an annual or current operating budget. While the current operating budget is most important and is recommended for adoption whether required by law or not, there is also a need to plan for a longer time span through long-term budgets. If planning is done on an annual basis only, a governmental unit may find itself compelled to resort to stopgap methods of financing, which may result in inequitable distributions of tax burdens or lead to inefficiencies in operation. If planning is extended beyond the current year for a period of four or five years, needs may be anticipated in time to permit more effective coordination of activities to inform the public of the necessity for additional revenues or curtailment of services well before they are asked to respond by authorizing increased tax rates or accepting curtailment. Another form of long-term budget which is useful (but no substitute for the one discussed above) is the "capital budget," which is also directed toward a determination of needed capital improvements and the means of financing them.

Having prepared and adopted a budget, the accounting system should be established in such a way as to provide budgetary control over revenues and expenditures. To do this effectively, the budget and the accounts must be prepared and maintained on a coordinated basis. The funds and programs maintained in the accounting records and the chart of accounts for each fund must correspond with the fund structure contemplated by the budget and with the line items of estimated revenues and appropriations. Similarly, the timing basis should correspond as between the budget and the accounts. It is recommended that both budgeting and accounting be done on an accrual basis as to major items of revenues and expenditures. Revenues "susceptible to accrual" (see AICPA audit guide) should be included in the period in which earned or for which they are levied. Expenditures (with the exception of accrued interest on general obligation bonds) should be included in the period in which liabilities for goods or services are incurred.

Estimated revenues and appropriations should be recorded in the accounts at the beginning of the fiscal year. This is accomplished by debiting the various estimated revenues accounts, crediting the appropriation accounts, and debiting (or crediting) "Fund Balance" for the deficiency (or excess) of revenues. Commitments in the form of purchase orders or contracts for services are recorded as encumbrances at the time they are approved. The recording entry is a debit to Encumbrances and a credit to the Reserve for Encumbrances. Thus the estimated amount of the expenditure is recorded and provides a means to prevent overexpenditure of appropriations through absence of control over committed amounts.

[4]Ibid.

When invoices are received, the encumbrance entry is reversed and the actual expenditure recorded by a debit to Expenditures and a credit to Vouchers Payable. At the end of the fiscal year any Encumbrance accounts which remain unfilled are closed, together with Appropriations and Expenditures, to Fund Balance. Note that the unfilled encumbrances are not reversed, thus leaving the Reserve for Encumbrances open to receive the charges for the related goods and services when ultimately received in the subsequent year. Similarly, Revenues and Estimated Revenues are closed to Fund Balance at year-end.

4. Fund Accounting

Governmental accounting systems should be organized and operated on a fund basis. A fund is defined as an independent fiscal and accounting entity with a self-balancing set of accounts recording cash and/or other resources together with all related liabilities, obligations, reserves, and equities which are segregated for the purpose of carrying on specific activities or attaining certain objectives in accordance with special regulations, restrictions, or limitations.

For reasons set forth earlier, it is necessary to segregate the accounting for various activities of governmental units into separate funds. Each fund must have its own self-balancing set of accounts within the accounting records, although there need not be a physical segregation of assets (such as bank accounts) unless required by law or by contractual terms. Each of these funds may have transactions within itself, with external parties, or with other funds of the same governmental unit. In the latter case, it is essential that the integrity of each of the funds be maintained, requiring that interfund receivable and payable accounts be provided, and that each interfund transaction be recorded as a complete debit and credit entry within each of the affected funds so that each fund remains in a balanced condition within itself. Funds may be established by constitutional or statutory provisions, charter, ordinances, or administrative decisions. They may exist to account either for specific sources of revenues or for specific activities.

5. Types of Funds

The following types of funds are recognized and should be used in accounting for governmental financial operations as indicated:

(1) The General Fund to account for all financial transactions not properly accounted for in another fund;

(2) Special Revenue Funds to account for the proceeds of specific revenue sources (other than special assessments) or to finance specified activities as required by law or administrative regulation;

(3) Debt Service Funds to account for the payment of interest and principal on long-term debt other than special assessment and revenue bonds;

(4) Capital Projects Funds to account for the receipt and disbursement of monies used for the acquisition of capital facilities other than those financed by special assessment and enterprise funds;

(5) Enterprise Funds to account for the financing of services to the general public where all or most of the costs involved are paid in the form of charges by users of such services;

(6) Trust and Agency Funds to account for assets held by a governmental unit as trustee or agent for individuals, private organizations, and other governmental units;

(7) Intragovernmental Service Funds to account for the financing of special activities and services performed by a designated organization unit within a governmental jurisdiction for other organization units within the same governmental jurisdiction;

(8) Special Assessment Funds to account for special assessments levied to finance public improvements or services deemed to benefit the properties against which the assessments are levied.

Most of these types of funds represent sources of revenues or activities which are more or less continuous and repetitive. They are generally controlled by annual or biennial budgets and should be accounted for on the basis of the fiscal year as the basic accounting period. However, Capital Projects Funds and Special Assessments Funds are used to finance and account for projects which may extend over several years. Accounting records and reports must exhibit the cumulative total cost of each such project together with sources and amounts of the capital to finance them. Because it is necessary to report progress periodically, such funds also require at least annual closings and reporting.

6. Number of Funds

Every governmental unit should establish and maintain those funds required by law and sound financial administration. Since numerous funds make for inflexibility, undue complexity, and unnecessary expense in both the accounting system and the overall financial administration, however, only the minimum number of funds consistent with legal and operating requirements should be established.

It is important that the number of funds utilized be kept at a minimum consistent with the need to establish legal compliance, sound administration, legal requirements, and operational needs. Few governmental units will find it necessary to establish funds within all eight of the categories enumerated under principle 5 above.

7. Fund Accounts

A complete self-balancing group of accounts should be established and maintained for each fund. This group should include all general ledger accounts and subsidiary records necessary to reflect compliance with legal provisions and to set forth the financial position and the results of financial operations of the fund. A clear distinction should be made between the accounts relating to current assets and liabilities and those relating to fixed assets and liabilities. With the exception of Intragovernmental Service Funds, Enterprise Funds, and certain Trust Funds, fixed assets should not be accounted for in the same fund with the current assets, but should be set up in a separate, self-balancing group of accounts called the General Fixed Asset Group of Accounts. Similarly, except in Special Assessment, Enterprise, and certain Trust Funds, long-term liabilities should not be carried with the current liabilities of any fund, but should be set up in a separate, self-balancing group of accounts known as the General Long-Term Debt Group of Accounts.

A chart of accounts must be provided for each of the funds so that it may display the fact that it has complied with legal provisions as well as make a fair presentation and full disclosure of (1) the results of operations for any given period and (2) its financial position at any given date.

The kinds of accounts which need to be provided may be divided into two primary groups, budgetary accounts and proprietary accounts. The budgetary accounts are those which portray the operation of the budget and the current status of such accounts as estimated revenues and appropriations. Proprietary accounts show the actual operations of the fund (through accounting for revenues and expenditures) as well as its financial condition (through the reporting of assets, liabilities, reserves, and fund balances). Usually the accounts for an individual fund include only current assets and current liabilities related to the operation of that particular fund so that the amount available for future appropriation can be determined at all times. Since the amount of resources of an operating fund that has already been expended, including that which has been expended for fixed assets, is not available for future appropriation, fixed assets and long-term debt (except for certain funds) are carried in separate groups of accounts.

The General Fixed Assets Group of Accounts consists of a self-balancing group of accounts but is not considered to be a fund. It is, rather, the residual reservoir of all the fixed assets of the governmental unit which are not employed in the operation of commercial-type activities or held in trust. The credit balance accounts in this group are established to show the sources of financing for the fixed assets.

Exceptions to the principle of segregating fixed asset accounts are necessary with respect to Intragovernmental Service Funds, Enterprise Funds, and certain Trust Funds. These exceptions are required by reasons relating to the purposes generally served by each of these funds. For example, in an Enterprise Fund the revenues of the fund are generally intended to cover all costs of providing the service for which the enterprise was established. It is necessary that depreciation be included among the costs to demonstrate that all costs have been covered and to avoid impairment of the fund's capital. In addition, the fixed assets of the Enterprise Fund may be pledged under bond ordinances related to their financing.

Similarly, the general bonded debt of the governmental unit should be accounted for in a separate, self-balancing group of accounts. Those obligations which are issued on the basis of the general credit and taxing powers of the governmental unit should be accounted for in this group of accounts. The related debit balance accounts are the Amount Available in Debt Service Funds and the Amount to be Provided for Payment of Bonds. Revenue bonds, on the other hand, are normally accounted for in the respective Enterprise Funds established for the operation of the facilities which they financed.

8. Valuation of Fixed Assets

The fixed asset accounts should be maintained on the basis of original cost, or the estimated cost if the original cost is not available, or, in the case of gifts, the appraised value at the time received.

"Original cost" is used in this context to mean the purchase price or construction cost of each asset, including the charges necessary to place it on location and ready for operation. It includes, therefore, costs of site preparation, transportation, professional fees, and any other charge directly attributable to the acquisition of the asset. Governmental units frequently receive properties by gift or by dedication from land developers and others. The fair market value of such assets at the date they are received (as determined by competent appraisers) should be recorded as their cost.

It is important that proper accounting control be established over all the assets of the governmental unit. In some cases in the past, there has existed a laxity in the recording of such assets on the part of governmental units. Where this situation exists, an inventory should be taken of all fixed assets owned and an estimate made of the original costs of such assets. These assets should then be recorded at estimated cost to establish accounting control.

9. Depreciation

Depreciation on general fixed assets should not be recorded in the general accounting records. Depreciation charges on such assets may be computed for unit cost purposes, provided such charges are recorded only in memorandum form and do not appear in the fund accounts.

Because of the similarities in the nature of the operations of governmental Enterprise Funds and the desire to make comparisons of such enterprises with privately owned enterprises, depreciation generally is recorded as an expense in these funds. There are a number of other activities carried on by governmental units in funds other than Enterprise Funds where it is desirable to know the costs of providing certain services or of accomplishing certain tasks. In any study to determine such costs, it is desirable to include a charge for depreciation of the assets used for such purposes over their estimated useful lives. It should be recorded only in memorandum form, however.

10. Basis of Accounting

The accrual basis of accounting is recommended for Enterprise, Trust, Capital Projects, Special Assessment, and Intragovernmental Service Funds. For the General, Special Revenue, and Debt Service Funds, the modified accrual basis of accounting is recommended. The modified accrual basis of accounting is defined as that method of accounting in which expenditures other than accrued interest on general long-term debt are recorded at the time liabilities are incurred and revenues are recorded when received in cash, except for material or available revenues which should be accrued to reflect properly the taxes levied and the revenues earned.

One of the primary concepts of accounting is that it will provide information which permits periodic reporting of significant data. The time at which a transaction is recorded therefore becomes important. The accrual basis is a superior method of accounting for transactions because it relates revenues and expenditures to the time period in which the revenues arise or the benefits of the expenditures are received. The principle quoted above recommends full accrual basis accounting for five of the types of funds which are set forth in principle 5, and the modified accrual basis for the remaining three types. The modified accrual basis is recommended for the latter funds because some of their revenue sources are difficult to estimate in advance and frequently come into existence only a short time before receipt. Examples of these sources of revenue include current income taxes, sales taxes, gross receipts taxes, and many miscellaneous sources of revenue. Revenue sources which give rise to legally enforceable claims and are readily subject to accurate estimates (such as property taxes, charges for current services, and grants or transfers from other governmental units) should be recorded on an accrual basis. Property taxes should be included as revenues not later than the time at which they are billed to the taxpayers. In some cases, they should be accrued at an earlier time (for example, when the local governmental unit acts upon a levy ordinance and a higher level of government takes over the process of billing and collecting the tax). Where property taxes are recorded on the accrual method, there should be provided an allowance for the estimated amount of uncollectible taxes. This Allowance for Uncollectible Taxes should be shown in the balance sheet as a deduction from Taxes Receivable.

Sometimes statutory or other legal provisions require that a cash basis budget be adopted for General and Special Revenue Funds. In such cases the accounting basis must follow the required basis of budgeting in order to demonstrate budgetary compliance.

An exception is made to the full accrual basis in the case of general debt interest costs which are recorded in Debt Service Funds. Principal and interest payments on bonds are known in advance. Tax levies are provided in the amounts required to meet these fixed obligations. Under these circumstances, it is felt that the accrual of interest would not serve a useful purpose.

11. Classification of Accounts

Governmental revenues should be classified by fund and source. Expenditures should be classified by fund, function, organization unit, activity, character, and principal classes of objects in accordance with standard recognized classification.

As used in this principle, the term "fund" means an accounting subdivision of the governmental unit, and the term "source" means the nature of the revenue item. Revenues may also be classified by subunits through which their collection was effected.

In accounting for expenditures, "fund" has the same meaning as that described above; "function" means the purpose for which a group of activities or programs are carried out, such as public safety, sanitation, or education. The "organizational unit" might be a department, bureau, or division of the governmental structure.

Each organizational unit will be charged with the responsibility for carrying out one or more activities or programs. "Character" of expenditures refers to differentiation of current expenses from capital outlays or debt redemptions. "Objects" refer to the article purchased or the services obtained, such as personal services, contractual services, and commodities.

All these elements should be reduced to writing in the form of a chart of accounts to be followed by the governmental unit in the preparation of its budget as well as in the maintenance of its accounting records for its actual expenditures. In preparing such a chart of accounts, greatest attention should be given to matching the functions, organization units, and activities with the actual organization structure of the governmental unit. Thus, responsibility for incurring expenditures can be directly related to those persons who are in a position to exercise control over them. This concept has sometimes been referred to as "responsibility accounting and budgeting."

12. Common Terminology and Classification

A common terminology and classification should be used consistently throughout the budget, the accounts, and the financial reports.

Unless accounts are kept and reported on the same basis that was contemplated at the time of adoption of the budget, the control aspects of the budgetary document will have been lost completely. In addition, no data will be developed to guide the preparation of the budget for the succeeding fiscal year.

13. Financial Reporting

Financial statements and reports showing the current conditions of budgetary and proprietary accounts should be prepared periodically to control financial operations. At the close of each fiscal year, a comprehensive annual financial report covering all funds and financial operations of the governmental unit should be prepared and published.

Fiscal control can be achieved only if actual financial results are compared to budgetary expectations and reported (to administrative officials and to legislative bodies) in a timely fashion, accurately and with full disclosure.

BUDGETARY TECHNIQUES

Program Budgeting. *Program budgeting* is a term used to refer to a budgetary technique which focuses on public services, or programs, in contrast to the traditional line-item, object of expenditure budgeting systems which have been followed by many state and local governments. Perhaps a more accurate term would be "output-oriented" budgeting. Some think that program budgeting applies only in budgetary planning; others view it as the framework for the entire financial management process.

Program budgeting can provide a means for governmental personnel in both the executive and legislative branches to develop more useful and meaningful financial information for planning, management, and control. Many governmental units have taken steps to introduce program budgeting and are requiring departments and agencies to develop program budgeting, not only for budgeting and controlling funds, but also for managing and evaluating departmental operations, including the development of performance standards for use in measuring accomplishments against defined goals and objectives. These budgetary techniques are being applied in varying degrees today by several different types of governmental entities such as federal agencies, states, regional planning organizations, counties, municipalities, school districts, and quasi-governmental entities. Changes are occurring in recognition of the need for increased information and budgetary sophistication, as well as in response to the emphasis on program planning, control, and accountability encouraged or required by the federal government in connection with federal grant and assistance programs.

In most cases, program budgeting is used to supplement, not replace, line-item budgeting and accounting procedures. In a relatively small number of instances, however, program budgeting techniques have replaced traditional methods of budgeting. The need for better internal information, the continuing growth of public expenditures, the greater demands by governmental officials and the public for more information and improved reporting, and the federal emphasis on program information all have contributed to the increased interest by state and local governments in program budgeting.

Types of Budgetary Techniques. There are various types of budgetary techniques followed by governments, which can be categorized as either input-oriented or output-oriented, depending on the specific focus on the budgetary process. Most budgets represent some combination of both input- and output-oriented processes, notwithstanding that the budget may be reviewed and adopted in a "traditional" line-item format.

On the other hand, where appropriations are made by broad program categories and subcategories, appropriations and allotments are established within these categories for financial control purposes. Conversely, even the most simple line-item budget may be partly based upon work measurement and other performance data, even though this may not be reflected in the budget document.

Traditional Budgeting. Most smaller governmental jurisdictions follow traditional input-oriented budgetary processes. The budget is planned and adopted in a line-item, object of expenditure (input) format by funds, departments, and agencies, subject to the limitations and constraints governing revenues and expenditures.

The traditional budgetary process focuses on the specific items or "objects" for which resources (inputs) are expended. In the traditional approach, budgetary planning (and budget format) is developed by organizational unit and subunits. Expenditures are shown by object class, e.g., salaries and wages, maintenance, etc. The focus in the budgetary process is usually on incremental *changes* in levels of expenditure for each object classification or line-item from the prior budget. This process reflects the concern over safeguarding public funds and control which has characterized budgeting and financial management in governments for generations.

Output-Oriented Budgeting. At the other end of the spectrum is the output-oriented or "program" budget in which the primary budgetary focus is on programs and services, and which has as its basic objective improving both the allocation and the planning and management of resources. A number of output-oriented budgeting (and financial management) systems have evolved over the years including performance budgeting, PPBS, program budgeting, zero-based budgeting, and management by objective. The scope and procedures of each of these systems may vary significantly, but they all are essentially output-oriented systems.

Evolution of Output-Oriented Budgeting Systems. The basic concepts of program budgeting date back to 1912 and the recommendations formulated by President Taft's Commission on Economy and Efficiency in its report, *The Need for a National Budget.* Little real progress in introducing program budgeting was made, however, at the state/local level until the advent of performance budgeting subsequent to World War II.

The Performance Budget. Impetus was given to performance budgeting following recommendations of the Hoover Commission in 1949 for improving financial management practices in the federal government. The primary focus in the performance budgetary process is on relating budgetary requirements to workload, and involves: establishing work units for measurable activities within departments, determining what budgetary resources will be required to accomplish the projected workload, and measuring and controlling budgetary performance in relation to these criteria.

The performance budget system provides useful management information which may be used in developing a more meaningful budget for measurable activities, and thus a better means for measuring and improving operational performance and productivity. But, with its focus on workload and productivity and the relationship of the budget to resources required to accomplish work output, performance budgeting does not provide an adequate framework for improving top management decision making regarding program needs and priorities or resource allocations.

Planning-Programming-Budgeting Systems (PPBS). PPBS, or Planning-Programming-Budgeting Systems, emerged from the federal government in the 1960s as a budgeting philosophy and approach which would overcome the deficiencies of the traditional and performance budgeting approaches. PPBS represents a "systematic" approach to budgetary planning, management and resource allocation in which:

1. Public service goals and objectives are established;

2. Programs and alternatives are identified through which these goals and objectives may be met and the costs thereof are determined on a multiyear basis;

3. Priorities are established among and between programs on a rational basis considering revenues available and other factors;

4. Extensive use is made of systems analysis techniques for "optimizing" the decision process;

5. Budgetary and management performance is evaluated on a continuing basis.

The basic concepts involved were defined in a report[5] to a U.S. Senate Subcommittee, as follows:

> PPBS focuses on the output of programs whereas traditional budgetary approaches tend more or less to emphasize expenditure inputs. It assesses as fully as possible the total costs and benefits—both current and future—of various alternatives. It endeavors to determine rate of return per program, as well as the rate of return that may have to be foregone when one program is chosen over another.
>
> PPBS is a refinement of existing procedures rather than a completely new budgetary approach. In PPBS attention is focused on programs—rather than on type of expenditure or organizational entities.

Under PPBS, the elements of planning, programming, and budgeting are systematically combined. Planning is usually accomplished by establishing objectives and evaluating alternative methods to achieve these objectives. Programming is the process of defining the programs required to attain necessary goals and objectives for each program, and of establishing the cost of carrying out programs, including all costs of personnel, facilities, equipment and other costs for the fiscal period, or more preferably, for the life of a program.

This approach requires the introduction of an appropriate program structure and program cost accounting, the development of information systems to provide required data and information, and modernization and expansion of the basic account classification and coding structure. Most important, it views decision making as the end product of systematic budgetary analysis at all levels, including the legislative branch. The emphasis placed on "cost/benefit" and other types of analysis in decision making has proven to be very difficult, if not impossible, to

[5]Subcommittee on Economy in Government of the Joint Economic Committee, Congress of the United States, 90th Congress. *The Planning-Programming-Budgeting System; Progress and Potentials.* U.S. Government Printing Office, Washington, D.C., 1967.

implement, considering the lack of information and resources available within many governmental units. PPBS has been subsequently abandoned by the federal government as a formal system. It is still used by some state and local governments, although there are few, if any, operational systems which fully meet basic PPBS concepts of an integrated budgetary system.

Zero-Based Budgeting.   "Zero-based" budgeting is representative of a number of specific output-oriented budgetary systems which have evolved in recent years. With zero-based budgeting, in theory, all programs compete from year to year on an equal basis. Appropriations in prior years for any expenditure class or program do not enter into the decision of the amount of appropriation for that class or program in the current year. Departments and agencies are required to review existing programs, to analyze and evaluate alternative ways of providing service, and to develop "decision packages" for use by management in better planning and allocation of resources.

As with any output-oriented budgeting system, zero-based budgeting requires: significant internal commitment of resources, introduction of program budgeting, expansion or integration, or both, of the account classification and coding structure.

Objectives of Program Budgeting.   The budget is a plan for financial operations setting forth an estimate of proposed expenditures for a given fiscal period, together with a proposed plan for revenues and other financing of these expenditures. When adopted, the budget provides the legal framework for financial management and control. From this perspective the budget, and the budgetary process, must be developed so as to provide the required "vehicle" for financial planning, management, and control on a continuing basis.

The objectives underlying program budgeting, therefore, are much broader than the development of a program structure. Program budgeting:

1. Requires the establishment of public service goals and objectives, and the development of multiyear programs through which these goals and objectives can be obtained;

2. Provides a more rational basis for allocating scarce resources among competing programs and for establishing priorities resulting in better matching of proposed expenditures with anticipated revenues;

3. Provides a basis for improving management performance, and for a better demonstration of the discharging of accountability requirements on a continuing basis;

4. Encourages and requires better planning at all levels in relation to the public services to be provided (the emphasis shifts from control over resources to planning how resources are to be used in providing services);

5. Provides a better basis for justifying and explaining the budget to council, the citizens, media, public interest groups, etc.

Framework for Improving Budgetary Control.   If the budget is to serve a broader purpose, the budgetary process should incorporate planning and management considerations. It may be necessary to:

1. Develop an appropriate *program structure;*

2. Substantially revise the agency's basic *classification of accounts* and develop a *unified transaction coding structure* which will enable all revenues and expenditures to be coded to identify properly all required characteristics of a transaction, such as revenue source, fund, organizational unit, object of expenditure, function, appropriation, etc.

3. Reexamine the *organizational structure* to define properly organization responsibilities and introduce *"responsibility accounting"* (this is the process of assigning each expenditure amount to the organizational unit or cost center which is

responsible for administering or controlling the expenditure of that particular resource);

4. Develop the *systems and procedures* to provide required information for control, planning, management, and performance evaluation purposes;

5. Provide proper *indoctrination and involvement of legislators and key members of the executive branch* in the basic concepts involved.

Program Structure.   Program budgeting requires the development of an appropriate program structure which groups and categorizes related programs or activities in an orderly hierarchical structure by department or agency. While some programs may "cross" departmental lines, the program structure should be developed within individual agencies. It is easier to assign responsibility for program activities and results under an existing organizational structure of a single department or agency. Some changes in organizational structure may be desirable to relate programs more closely to organizational units.

The program structure should be developed on a basis which corresponds as closely as possible with the existing organizational structure and lines of responsibility within each department or agency. In this way, specific responsibility can be assigned for programs, and personnel can be more easily held accountable for program results.

Depending on the sophistication of an agency's accounting and budgeting requirements and related financial management information needs, the program structure can be expanded as needed. It is important to evaluate carefully how the information will be used by program personnel and officials at each level to determine if the effort required to code, classify, summarize, and report additional, more detailed financial information justifies the additional expenditure of time and resources. It is also important that consideration be given to introducing the program accounting systems and procedures required to report actual expenditures and accomplishments by program as well as by line-item and object of expenditure.

The program structure and related program documentation should be developed for each department or agency in conformance with guidelines prepared by the agency's Central Budget Office. The Central Budget Office should provide necessary guidance and direction in developing the program structure, and in actually developing the budget on a program basis, by department and on an overall basis.

Revisions to the Classification of Accounts and Transaction Coding Structure.   An agency cannot usually convert to a program budget without accomplishing a number of related changes or improvements in the classification of accounts, as referred to above. The classification of accounts must be revised or expanded to provide required data and information classified and categorized on a logical basis for purposes of budgetary planning, review, and management. A proper classification also will provide department and agency management with a framework within which supplemental internal financial management systems, procedures, and controls can be developed. Most local governments have classifications of accounts covering all elements except the program structure. It may be possible to expand the present chart of accounts to accommodate program budgeting and accounting requirements.

Many agencies which have introduced program budgeting have not revised their entire budgeting and accounting system to the program basis and, therefore, only their budgets are planned and submitted on a program basis. Other agencies report their financial information on a modified program budgeting basis using traditional line-item reporting of detailed expenditures with additional summarization of expenditures by major program and subprogram. In addition, legal requirements often impose specific requirements or constraints which must be reflected in the chart of accounts.

Other Considerations in Improving the Budgetary Process.   The related need for introducing responsibility accounting and establishing the organizational framework necessary for improving planning and management may be an important corollary to introducing program budgeting. This may result in the need for modernization or change in the governmental unit's organizational structure, or that of its major departments or agencies.

Adequate systems and procedures must be developed and implemented, or revised, to provide the information needed for planning, management, and control. These systems and procedures should be developed within the overall budgeting and accounting framework, rather than as separate, parallel systems within the various departments. The need for proper introduction to, and training in, new budgetary concepts for legislators and all levels of management is so fundamental that it is often overlooked—and with disastrous results.

Benefits of Program Budgeting.   Budgeting is the primary means for planning and controlling expenditures, whether for public or private activities. A governmental unit cannot operate either efficiently or effectively without a sound budgeting system. In many respects, budgetary practices (and in particular, program budgeting techniques) in government are more advanced than those used in industry and business. A budget is required by law in many governmental units and agencies and, as this document provides the legal framework for operations, governments and agencies have been forced to undergo a more formal budgetary process than many organizations in the private sector.

The GAO publication, *Standards for Audits of Governmental Organizations, Programs, Activities & Functions,* issued by the Comptroller General of the United States in 1972, sets forth proposed audit standards in three areas: financial and compliance; economy and efficiency; and program results. To accomplish the objectives underlying these standards will require governments to introduce program budgeting. Without output-oriented budgeting, it will not be possible to determine, on a *continuing* basis, if government funds are handled properly and whether programs are being administered efficiently, effectively, and economically.

THE PROCESS OF FUND ACCOUNTING

The same principles of double-entry bookkeeping are applied in fund accounting for governmental units as are applied in commercial accounting. The accounting equation is stated as "assets = liabilities + fund balance." "Fund balance" is equivalent to the usual "net worth" or "owners' equity." Confusion sometimes results where an entry affects two or more funds. It must be remembered, in such cases, that the accounting equation applies to each individual fund and the entry must include equal debits and credits for *each* of the funds affected.

The use of budgetary accounts for financial control in fund accounting also introduces some added entries as compared with commercial accounting. Such entries and some others, more or less peculiar to governmental accounting, are explained and illustrated in the following paragraphs for each class of fund.

The General Fund.   The General Fund accounts for all revenues and expenditures which are not required to be accounted for in another fund. Because of the nature of their operations, most governmental units receive a wide variety of revenues and expend their assets to provide the basic services which the governmental unit was organized to provide. The largest part of their revenues and expenditures generally flow through the General Fund. Other names are sometimes used, such as "Corporate Fund," "Education Fund" in the case of a school district, or some other name related to the general activities of the governmental unit.

Budget Adoption.   Accounting for the General Fund must be closely aligned with the budgetary process. Generally a governmental unit has no authority to expend any of its funds unless a budget or an appropriation bill or ordinance has been passed. Although the degree of detail may vary, the budget is a comprehensive plan of the financial operations incorporating estimates of the available revenues and other resources, and of the proposed expenditures to carry out the program of services for the year. Many jurisdictions require that a comprehensive budget be adopted by the unit before it is empowered to levy several forms of taxes to support its activities. Sound financial management, as well as legal constraints, make it imperative that the budgetary information be recorded in the accounts to facilitate periodic reports comparing actual with budget. Therefore, the chart of accounts must correspond with the line items in the budget, although the degree of detail may differ.

At the beginning of the fiscal year the budget should be recorded in the accounts as follows:

Estimated Revenues 500,000
    Appropriations   480,000
    Fund Balance   20,000
To record adopted budget.

The credit to the Fund Balance account arises in this example from the excess of estimated revenues over planned expenditures; the converse situation would of course result in a debit. The details of this entry by specific revenue sources and expenditure accounts would be recorded in subsidiary ledgers, or substituted for the above entry where the detailed accounts are carried as part of the general ledger.

Recording Taxes and Other Revenues.   After adopting the budget, the governing body usually enacts a tax levy. In the case of property taxes, the tax levy is divided by the total assessed valuation of all property subject to the tax to produce a tax rate. (The rate may be limited by law). The tax rate is extended against the assessed valuation of the property of all individual property owners in a tax roll and a bill is sent to each owner. The tax levy is recorded as a receivable at the time it is passed, together with an allowance for uncollectible taxes in an appropriate amount, by the following entry:

Taxes Receivable—19XX Levy 300,000
    Estimated Uncollectible Taxes—19XX Levy ...   12,000
    Current Tax Revenue   288,000
To record current property tax levy for the year.

Tax collections are recorded as follows:

Cash 170,000
    Taxes Receivable—19XX Levy   170,000
To record current property tax collections.

Some taxes are not collected by their due date, become delinquent, and usually result in the imposition of penalties and interest. In due course, the delinquent taxes may be converted into tax liens by court order, further subjecting the property owner to payment of court costs. Entries may be required to record the change in status and the additional amounts collectible (subject to appropriate allowances for losses in collection) if the unit itself is directly involved in the tax collection process and entitled to such additional amounts. In some cases the unit (such as a school district) may not bill and collect its own tax levy, this function being performed by some other unit (such as the county government). Eventually (usually after three or five years) the losses through failure to collect are recognized by the following entry:

```
Estimated Uncollectible Taxes—19XX Levy   12,000
Fund Balance  .........................    3,000
     Taxes Receivable—19XX Levy  ......            15,000
To write off uncollectible taxes on 19XX
levy.
```

The amount by which the actual losses differed from the allowance is debited or credited to the Fund Balance account.

Other revenue accounts would be accounted for in a similar manner except that no accruals are made for some items of revenue, because they were not anticipated or because they are minor sources of revenue. The following entry records receipt of such an item which was not previously accrued:

```
Cash .................................  10,000
     Revenues  .........................            10,000
To record revenue received not previously
accrued.
```

Recording Encumbrances and Expenditures. As purchase orders are issued, amounts appropriated become obligated to pay for the items ordered. These obligations are termed "encumbrances." It is customary in governmental accounting to record encumbrances at the time of issuance of purchase orders in the amount of the estimated cost of the item. In small units encumbrances may be controlled through use of an unfilled purchase order file which is summarized periodically in the preparation of financial reports. Larger units record encumbrances in the accounts as follows:

```
Encumbrances  .........................  25,000
     Reserve for Encumbrances  ..........            25,000
To record estimated amount of purchase
orders issued.
```

Detailed entries should be made to the individual appropriation expenditure accounts affected, thereby reducing the amount available for future encumbrances or expenditure for that item.

Salary appropriations (and some others with similar characteristics) for full-time employees are frequently not encumbered prior to the recording of actual liabilities. Unlike appropriations for such items as supplies and equipment, salaries are usually established in advance and controlled through administrative and personnel practices (such as authorized staffing tables) which prevent overexpenditure.

When materials and services are received in fulfillment of purchase orders, the encumbrance matures into a liability for a fixed amount. Two entries are then required. The first reverses the encumbrance previously recorded:

```
Reserve for Encumbrances  ..............  25,000
     Encumbrances  .....................            25,000
To reverse encumbrances for materials and
services received.
```

The second entry records the actual liability:

```
Expenditures  ..........................  24,000
     Vouchers Payable  .................            24,000
To record vouchers issued for materials and
services received.
```

Materials may also be ordered for inventory and accounted for in the same manner as in commercial accounting. Their purchase would be recorded as a debit to Inventory of Supplies and a credit to Vouchers Payable at the time the material is received. At the time of issuance from inventory for usage, an entry charging Expenditures and crediting Inventory of Supplies would be recorded. Likewise, many other transactions of types similar to those encountered in commercial accounting may arise, such as billings for services rendered, investment of excess cash, and loans between funds. In recording interfund loans, it must be remembered that a complete debit and credit entry must be made in each of the two funds affected.

Closing the Accounts. At the end of the accounting period, appropriation accounts are closed by the following entry:

```
Appropriation ........................... 450,000
      Expenditures ........................     402,000
      Encumbrances .....................      42,000
      Fund Balance ......................       6,000
To close out 19XX appropriation,
expenditures, and encumbrances to fund
balance.
```

Note that the above entry closes a $42,000 debit balance of encumbrances. In a previous entry, the offsetting credit for the $42,000 was carried to the reserve for encumbrances, which is not closed out but continues to be carried in the records. In a subsequent year when the related materials have been received, the expenditures would be recorded as follows:

```
Expenditures—19XX .................... 40,000
      Vouchers Payable ...................      40,000
To record liability for material received in
19XY which had been ordered in 19XX at an
estimated cost of $42,000.
```

The following entry would be recorded to close out the reserve for encumbrances for the year 19XX:

```
Reserve for Encumbrances—19XX ......... 42,000
      Expenditures—19XX ................      40,000
      Sundry Expenditures—19XY .........       2,000
To close expenditures chargeable to prior
year's reserve for encumbrances.
```

Actual and estimated revenues would also be closed at the end of the fiscal year of 19XX by the following entry:

```
Revenues .............................. 512,000
      Estimated Revenues .................     500,000
      Fund Balance ......................      12,000
To close out 19XX actual and estimated
revenues.
```

Fixed Assets. With the exception of certain funds, a clear distinction should be made between the accounts relating to current assets and liabilities and those relating to fixed assets and liabilities. Therefore, while the General Fund may purchase fixed assets from its revenues, these assets, once acquired, are not carried in the accounts of the General Fund. At the time of their acquisition, the General Fund records their purchase as an expenditure. At the same time, or at the end of the fiscal period, these assets are recorded in a separate self-balancing group of accounts called the General Fixed Asset Group of Accounts (discussed subsequently).

The basic principles illustrated above in accounting for the General Fund apply also to the other funds, with the additional comments and exceptions noted in the following paragraphs.

Special Revenue Funds.   Special Revenue Funds are established to account for revenues derived from a specific revenue source limited to specific uses. The distinguishing characteristic of these funds is that their revenues are earmarked to finance particular activities or functions. Examples of such funds are those established to account for services (such as an airport, a transportation system, or parking facilities) or recreational facilities (such as golf courses and swimming pools). Special revenue funds may be administered by the same administrative and legislative officials as the other activities of the unit, or they may be administered by an independent or semi-independent board or commission. Special Revenue Funds may be distinguished from Enterprise Funds in that their function is usually financed mostly by tax revenues. If the activity is financed entirely or predominately by user charges, it should be classified as an Enterprise Fund.

The accounting principles illustrated above for the General Fund apply also to Special Revenue Funds. The details of their budgets and charts of accounts should follow that for the General Fund except where a recognized authority has provided standard classifications, such as those developed by the U.S. Office of Education for the public schools.

Debt Service Funds.   Debt Service Funds account for the payment of principal and interest on general obligation bonds. General obligation bonds are those for whose payment the full faith and credit of the issuing unit are pledged and are generally payable from taxes and other general revenues. The fund excludes debt payable from special assessments and debt issued for the benefit of a governmental enterprise from whose revenues it will be serviced. General obligation bonds are sometimes issued to finance enterprise facilities under terms which provide that revenues from the enterprise are to be used to pay the principal and interest on the bonds. If it is likely that the revenues of the enterprise will be inadequate to service the debt and will therefore need supplemental servicing by tax revenues, then such indebtedness should be recorded in the Debt Service Fund. If, on the other hand, the Enterprise Fund appears likely to have sufficient revenues to amortize the debt, then it should be accounted for through the Enterprise Fund.

Although debt service on general obligation bonds may be financed from other sources of revenue, most bonds are serviced from the proceeds of general property taxes. The authorization to issue such bonds may include simultaneously the levy required to service them for all the years that they will be outstanding. Whether or not this is done, all debt service requirements should be budgeted regularly as part of the annual budget. Each bond issue constitutes a separate obligation and generally has its own property tax levy to support it and its own legal restrictions and servicing requirements. Appropriate provision must be made to develop information with respect to the status of each issue and its related revenues. This may make it necessary to have a separate fund for each individual bond issue. Having numerous funds, however, unduly complicates the accounting process; therefore, the minimum possible number of Debt Service Funds should be established, combining into a single Debt Service Fund, for example, all those serviced by the general property tax.

Budgeted expenditures will consist of principal payments, interest payments, and payment of agents' fees which are to be paid out during the course of the fiscal year. No accrual is recorded for interest from the last interest payment date to the end of the fiscal year. In most instances, no provisions for financing such accruals can be made in the annual budget and the accrual of such interest would produce a deficit in the Fund Balance account even though the revenues being produced were sufficient to meet the debt service requirements. The following entries illustrate the accounting for a serial bond issue in the Debt Service Fund:

Estimated Revenues	100,000		
Appropriations		97,500	
Fund Balance		2,500	
To record budgeted debt service for the year.			
Taxes Receivable—19XX Levy	105,000		
Estimated Uncollectible Taxes—19XX Levy		4,500	
Revenue		100,500	
To record property tax levy for the year.			
Cash	95,000		
Taxes Receivable—19XX Levy		95,000	
To record collection of 19XX taxes.			
Expenditures	97,500		
Bonds Payable		94,000	
Interest Payable		3,500	
To record as expenditures principal and interest payments becoming due during the year.			
Bonds Payable	94,000		
Interest Payable	3,500		
Cash		97,500	
To record payment of principal and interest.			
Appropriations	97,500		
Revenue	100,500		
Expenditures		97,500	
Estimated Revenues		100,000	
Fund Balance		500	
To close revenue, expenditure, and appropriation accounts for the year.			

Capital Projects Funds. Capital Projects Funds account for the acquisition of capital facilities by a governmental unit, except those financed by Special Assessment and Enterprise Funds. The sources of these funds may be the proceeds of general bond issues, grants from agencies or other governmental units, accumulated tax revenues levied for such purposes, or transfers from other funds. Most often capital projects are budgeted and authorized on an individual basis and separate funds are set up for each project, although a series of related projects may be accounted for in one combined fund. If one bond issue is used to finance a series of related projects, then only one Capital Projects Fund would ordinarily need to be used. However, if each project is separately authorized and financed, it becomes necessary to show that the proceeds of each bond issue were spent only for the specific purposes authorized and therefore separate funds must be established. Capital Projects Funds ordinarily are established only to account for the construction of major permanent facilities having relatively long lives. They are not used for the acquisition of equipment, which is usually financed from current revenues or by short-term obligations.

Budgeting for capital projects differs somewhat from that of the General Fund in that a capital budget is adopted which consists of a plan of proposed capital outlays and the means of financing them. It may cover a single fiscal year. More frequently, it covers a period of four to six years in the future, although it is normally revised annually and extended for an additional year into the future. Each year that part of the capital budget pertaining to the current fiscal year is incorporated into the annual budget for the forthcoming year. When the annual budget is adopted, the capital projects contemplated become appropriations and constitute authority to make expenditures on the projects so authorized.

When the financing for a project is to be derived from the sale of a bond issue, the initial journal entry would be a debit to Cash for the proceeds of the issue and a credit to Revenues of the Capital Projects Fund for the par value of the bonds. The proceeds are revenue of the Capital Projects Fund because they increase the fund's assets without a corresponding increase in liabilities. The liability for the bonds issued is recorded in the General Long-Term Debt Group of Accounts.

The proceeds from the sale of a bond issue frequently include a premium and interest from the nominal date of issue to actual date of sale. The premium represents an adjustment of the interest rate and should be transferred to the Debt Service Fund, together with the interest from nominal date of issue to date of sale. In some jurisdictions, however, these additional proceeds may, by statute, be expended to finance the project. Proceeds of bond issues and other cash accumulated to finance a project may not need to be used for considerable periods of time. Under these circumstances, investments are frequently made and interest is earned until the cash is needed to pay for the construction costs. Generally, if permitted by statute, the interest earned is retained in the Capital Projects Fund and used along with other cash available to meet authorized project expenditures. Sometimes the interest earned is transferred to the appropriate Debt Service Fund to offset the interest costs of the bonds issued to finance the project.

The cost of completed projects should be recorded in the General Fixed Assets Group of Accounts. In other respects, the accounting entries to record construction and other acquisitions of capital assets follow those described for the General Fund.

Enterprise Funds. Enterprise Funds are established to account for self-supporting services carried on by governmental units. The most frequent examples of such enterprises are municipally owned public utilities providing water, gas, or electricity to citizens. Other examples include transit systems, port facilities, airports, hospitals, parking facilities, etc. Some of these activities may be partially supported by general tax revenues. In such instances, the principal source of revenues should determine whether the activity is to be accounted for as a Special Revenue Fund or as an Enterprise Fund. Once such a decision has been made with respect to a particular activity, however, it should be followed consistently because the accounting practices for the two categories of funds are different and will reflect different operating results.

The accounting for Enterprise Funds generally follows very closely the accounting principles and procedures that would be appropriate for a commercial enterprise engaged in the same activity. Frequently their operations are subject to the same budgetary procedures as those employed for the General Fund, except that expenditures should not be controlled by rigid appropriations. Expenditures will vary with the levels of demand for service, which in turn will produce corresponding levels of revenue.

Because the facilities of Enterprise Funds are so frequently financed by revenue bonds (which require a determination of the operating results of the related self-supporting enterprise) it is necessary to establish a separate fund for each such enterprise to ensure that the resources of one are not illegally or improperly utilized by another.

These enterprises frequently have segregations of assets within the respective fund which constitute restricted assets and are sometimes referred to as "funds" or "accounts," particularly in the language of revenue bond ordinances. For example, proceeds of bond issues are quite often required to be segregated in Construction Funds; money accumulating to retire bonds may be required to be segregated as a Sinking Fund; protective covenants included for the benefit of bondholders may require segregation into several other "funds" such as Debt Service, Depreciation, Reserve, and Contingency. The "funds" should be called "accounts" instead.

Enterprise Funds frequently provide services for other governmental departments (such as providing water for their use) and in turn receive services (such as administrative or clerical assistance) from them. All these interfund relationships make it important to adhere strictly to the concept of individual fund entities; services rendered by an Enterprise Fund to other funds, or vice versa, should not be disregarded or canceled out. A billing should be made for the services on the same basis as they would be handled with other users. This is quite often required in order to comply with the provisions of revenue bond ordinances and, in any case, it is desirable in order to permit valid comparisons of operating results between municipally owned enterprises and similar enterprises privately owned or owned by other municipalities.

In the accounting for Enterprise Funds, it is important that the accrual method of accounting be followed because it is desirable to determine operating results. A clear distinction must be made between operating revenues and items which are nonoperating income or contributions to the capital of the Enterprise Fund. Fixed assets frequently constitute a large percentage of the total assets and represent the primary source of the enterprise's earning power. They are recorded as part of the assets of the Enterprise Fund and periodic charges are made against the operating revenues for their depreciation.

Account classifications and terminology appropriate to the particular type of enterprise should be followed. For example, a municipal water utility should conform its chart of accounts to the chart of accounts followed by the regulatory authority having jurisdiction over water utilities in that state.

Intragovernmental Service Funds. Intragovernmental Service Funds provide specified services or commodities for other departments of the governmental unit which establishes them. Such funds have sometimes been referred to in the past as "working capital funds." Service Funds render services directly only to other departments of the governmental unit, which distinguishes them from Enterprise Funds and other funds which are established to render services directly to the general public. Common examples of such funds are purchasing and supply departments, central garage and motor pool, etc.

The capital to establish a Service Fund can come in the form of long-term advances or permanent contributions from other funds or from the proceeds of sale of general obligation bonds. As the Service Fund provides services to other departments, it is reimbursed by transfers from the budget appropriations of the departments served. The concept of the Intragovernmental Service Fund requires that it recover its complete costs of operation, including all administrative costs, without producing any significant amount of profit. The expenditures to be incurred through a Service Fund are ultimately reimbursed by other funds and become expenditures to them. Such expenditures must be covered by appropriations in the respective funds utilizing the services of the Service Fund. Budgetary control over the operations of the Service Fund is therefore exercised through the accounts of the fund being served and no separate appropriations are made for the Service Fund itself. In the interest of sound financial management, however, a plan of operation should be prepared for each Service Fund each fiscal year.

The accounting entries for a Service Fund follow closely the pattern of a comparable commercial enterprise. Its billing to the other departments would be recorded as a debit to an account entitled "Due from General Fund," for example, and a credit to an account entitled "Billings to Departments."

Trust and Agency Funds. Trust and Agency Funds are established to account for cash and other assets received by a governmental unit in the capacity of trustee, custodian, or agent except in those cases in which the source is related to operation of an Enterprise Fund. While a distinction can be made between a Trust Fund and an Agency Fund, in both cases the governmental unit operates under a fiduciary capacity and, for this reason, both types are considered under one heading. Trust

Funds may be further classified as being expendable or nonexpendable. Expendable Trust Funds are those in which both principal and income therefrom may be expended for the purposes designated in the documents of trust. A common example of an Expendable Trust Fund is that established for pension and retirement systems for employees of the governmental unit. Nonexpendable Trust Funds are those in which the principal or corpus must be preserved intact and only the income may be used for the designated purposes. For this reason, it is important to maintain the accounts of a Nonexpendable Trust Fund in such a way as to identify the amount of its corpus or principal and the accumulated but unspent income. A separate self-balancing set of accounts should be maintained for each Trust or Agency Fund. To demonstrate that the terms of the trust documents or the agency agreement (expressed or implied) have been complied with, separate financial statements of each such fund should also be prepared periodically.

Generally, budgets are not prepared with respect to Trust and Agency Funds, and budgetary accounts are not maintained. There are certain exceptions, such as a Retirement Fund which accounts for its own operating expenses in addition to the payment of retirement benefits, or a fund for other purposes partly supported by general tax revenues, in which budgets and budgetary accounts should be adopted.

The accounting for most Trust Funds and Agency Funds is relatively simple, consisting primarily of recording cash receipts and disbursements. Upon receipt, the Cash account is debited and the Fund Balance credited. An expenditure is recorded in the opposite manner. Appropriate subaccounts should be maintained in such Agency Funds as Performance Deposit Funds to permit identification of the various individuals for whom the deposits are being held. Many Agency Funds act only as conduits (such as those for employee benefit plan deductions and payroll tax deductions), and therefore many have no balances at the end of the year.

Nonexpendable Trust Funds. Accounting for Nonexpendable Trust Funds and for Employee Retirement Funds is more complex. As mentioned above, the accounts for a Nonexpendable Trust Fund must be established in such a manner as to demonstrate compliance with the terms of the trust instrument, including a careful determination of net income in accordance with the terms specified by the donor. In distinguishing between corpus and income, the same principles apply in the case of governmental Trust Funds as those outlined in Chapter 44 of this book concerning fiduciary accounting.

Employee Retirement Funds. Accounting for an Employee Retirement Fund should be designed to show the amount and source of its assets which have been set aside for retirement benefits, and its liabilities as determined by an actuarial evaluation. In other words, the accrual basis of accounting should be employed to provide full disclosure of financial position on both a current and long-term basis. Revenues earned but not received and payments due but not disbursed should be shown as current assets and current liabilities, respectively, on the balance sheet.

The most important aspect of accounting for a retirement system is the determination and recording of its actuarial requirements. Actuarial studies should be, but often are not, conducted by professional actuaries for all public retirement systems to determine the ultimate liability for the authorized allowances and benefits to be provided under the plan. Reserve accounts should be recorded on the books to demonstrate compliance with legal requirements. The actual assets held by the fund to provide for payment of employee benefits should be reported; in addition, the records and statements should show the amount of assets (based on an actuarial study) which should be in the fund to pay benefits to current employees as they become eligible for such payments. If such accounts are maintained, a credit balance in the Fund Balance account will indicate that the fund is solvent or fully funded. A debit balance will indicate that a deficit exists and financing must be provided in the future to permit the fund to meet its commitments on schedule.

The following journal entries will illustrate the accounting for a retirement system in which it is assumed that administrative expenses are being paid as a departmental function within the General Fund, and that it is the policy of the municipality to operate on an actuarial reserve basis. (Also see Chapter 27 on pension costs.)

Due from General Fund	7,936	
Employees' Contributions		3,968
City's Contributions		3,968
To record employee contributions through payroll withholding and matching contribution from city.		
Employees' Contributions	3,968	
City's Contributions	3,968	
Reserve for Employees' Contributions		3,968
Reserve for City's Contributions		3,968
To transfer revenues to reserve accounts.		
Cash	7,936	
Due from General Fund		7,936
To record collection of contributions due from General Fund.		
Reserve for Employees' Contributions	9,843	
Reserve for City's Contributions	9,843	
Reserve for Retired Employees' Pensions		19,686
To transfer actuarial liability for retiring employees.		
Reserve for Employees' Contributions	9,656	
Due to Estates of Deceased Employees		5,675
Due to Resigned Employees		3,981
To record liability for refunds due to deceased or retired employees.		
Due to Estates of Deceased Employees	5,675	
Due to Resigned Employees	3,981	
Cash		9,656
To record payment of refunds.		
Expenditures—Pensions	2,785	
Pensions Payable		2,785
To record pensions payable to retired employees.		
Pensions Payable	2,785	
Cash		2,785
To record payment of pensions to retired employees.		
Reserve for Retired Employees' Pensions	2,785	
Expenditures		2,785
To close out expenditures for the year.		
Interest Earned on Investments	9,863	
Reserve for Employees' Contributions		3,785
Reserve for City's Contributions		3,785
Reserve for Retired Employees' Pensions		2,293
To record distribution of interest from investments to reserve accounts as specified in retirement plan.		
Reserve for Retired Employees' Pensions	1,795	
Reserve for Actuarial Gains and Losses		1,795
To adjust reserve to actuarial determination of value at end of year.		
Fund Balance	2,793	
Actuarial Deficiency		2,793
To adjust actuarial deficiency at end of year as determined by study.		

In addition to the customary basic financial statements, an Employee Retirement Fund also requires a statement setting forth an analysis of changes in its actuarial and other reserves. Because of deficiencies in statutes or ordinances in some jurisdictions, the actuarial reserve basis of accounting for retirement systems may not be followed. In these cases, it is important that adequate disclosure be made in a note to the financial statements regarding the difference between the reserve requirements on a statutory basis and those on an actuarial basis.

Special Assessment Funds.   Special Assessment Funds are employed to account for the financing and construction of public improvements for the principal benefit of certain property owners. These improvements (such as paving of residential streets, curbs and gutters, and sidewalks) are paid for, either completely or in large part, by the owners of adjacent property. The limited area of benefit is the essential characteristic which distinguishes such improvements from those that benefit the entire community and are paid for out of general revenues or through general obligation bonds.

Each separate local improvement project must be accounted for through a separate fund, because the related special assessment bonds or warrants are payable only from the collections assessed against benefited property owners. The fact that some part of the total cost of the project may be deemed to represent a public benefit payable from the General Fund (or that the bonds carry an additional pledge of the full faith and credit of the municipality) does not alter the need to create a separate fund for each project.

Each Special Assessment Fund accounts for the expenditure of the proceeds of the sale of bonds in defraying construction costs of the designated improvement, and also accounts for the collection of the assessments levied against individual property owners.

Generally, the property owners have an option of paying the full assessment immediately or of paying in installments, together with interest, over a period of several years. If the assessment includes such an installment feature, the related bonds issued to finance the project are likewise payable in installments over a period of time equal to that given to the property owners. Each bond may be payable in installments or the entire issue may be callable serially by number. Accounting for the latter form is simpler because it obviates the need for maintaining a record of bonds payable by installment maturities.

Since the bonds issued to finance the project are a liability of the fund which accounts for the expenditure of their proceeds, each Special Assessment Fund must continue in existence until the bonds are fully retired. After completion of the construction financed by the fund, the accounting consists of recording collections on assessments receivable and the servicing of the outstanding bonds. Upon final retirement of the bonds, any balance which remains should be disposed of in accordance with applicable legal provisions.

Journal entries illustrating the operation of a Special Assessment Fund are as follows:

Special Assessments Receivable—Current	10,000	
Special Assessments Receivable—Deferred	90,000	
Due from General Fund	10,000	
Fund Balance		110,000
To record approved special assessments against property owners (payable in ten installments) and amount due from General Fund for public benefit.		
Cash	90,000	
Bonds Payable		90,000
To record proceeds from sale of special assessment bonds at par.		
Cash	19,500	
Special Assessments Receivable—Current		9,500
Due from General Fund		10,000
To record collections on special assessments and public benefit from General Fund.		

```
Special Assessments Receivable—Delinquent  ....................     500
    Special Assessments Receivable—Current  ...................              500
To record delinquencies in payment of assessments.

Expenditures  .............................................   105,000
    Contracts Payable  .......................................           105,000
To record construction cost under contract with Hard Rock
Construction Co.

Expenditures  .............................................     5,000
    Due to General Fund  ....................................             5,000
To record construction cost of work done by Street Department.

Contracts Payable  .........................................   105,000
Due to General Fund  .......................................     5,000
    Cash  ....................................................           110,000
To record payment of construction costs.

Interest Receivable  .......................................     4,612
    Interest Revenue  ........................................             4,612
To record interest receivable on deferred assessments.

Interest Expense  ..........................................     4,500
    Interest Payable  ........................................             4,500
To record interest payable on special assessment bonds.

Interest Revenue  ..........................................     4,612
    Interest Expense  ........................................             4,500
    Fund Balance  ...........................................               112
To close interest revenue and expense accounts to fund balance.

Fund Balance  ..............................................   109,000
    Expenditures  ...........................................           109,000
To close expenditures to fund balance.
```

In subsequent years, entries would be made to record current installments receivable on the assessments to property owners as follows:

```
Special Assessments Receivable—Current  ........................   10,000
    Special Assessments Receivable—Deferred  ...................          10,000
To record current installment receivable on special assessments.
```

Upon completion of the construction phase of the project, an entry would be
made in the General Fixed Assets Group of Accounts to record the cost of the
improvement as an asset, with an offsetting credit to the account "Investment in
General Fixed Assets—Special Assessments."

General Fixed Assets Group of Accounts. The General Fixed Assets Group of
Accounts is maintained to account for all the fixed assets of the governmental unit
which are not accounted for in an enterprise, intragovernmental service, or trust
fund. A fixed asset for this purpose should be defined as a tangible piece of
property having a life longer than one fiscal year. In addition, it is customary to
account for only those assets having a value in excess of some fixed minimum
amount, to avoid the necessity of maintaining detailed accounting and inventory
records on units of property so small that the time and expense involved in the
record keeping is not justified.

Most governmental units have a substantial investment in fixed assets which may
be, and usually are, in scattered locations. Sound administration and protection of
such assets can only be achieved through the establishment of appropriate
accounting records as well as periodic physical inventorying, particularly of movable equipment. Such procedures are essential to the fixing of responsibilities for
custody on the part of individual public officials. A financial report of a governmental unit without complete and accurate fixed asset information is deficient in
that it fails to disclose properly an important piece of financial information.

The asset account classifications maintained for the General Fixed Assets Group
of Accounts is similar to that maintained for a commercial enterprise. The

National Committee on Governmental Accounting recommends the following major classes for statement presentation: Land, Buildings, Improvements Other Than Buildings, Equipment, and Construction in Progress. Subdivisions of these accounts may be provided which are appropriate to the needs of the specific governmental unit.

So that the General Fixed Assets Group of Accounts may be self-balancing, credit balance accounts in the form of several "Investment Accounts" should be established to account for the resources from which the assets were acquired. The following account titles have been recommended:[6]

Investment in General Fixed Assets from:
Capital Projects Funds
  General Obligation Bonds
  Federal Grants
  State Grants
  Local Grants
General Fund Revenues
Special Revenue Fund Revenues
Special Assessments
Private Gifts

All entries in the General Fixed Assets Group of Accounts (except for property received by gift) are counterparts to entries recording expenditures in the various other funds. For property acquired through Capital Projects Funds, an entry is recorded here as "Construction Work in Progress" at the end of the fiscal year if the project has not been completed. When the project is completed in a subsequent fiscal period, the costs incurred are transferred from Construction Work in Progress to the specific Asset account concerned. For assets acquired by General or Special Revenue Funds, the entry may be made in the General Fixed Assets Group of Accounts either at the time of the expenditure or on an accumulated basis at the end of the accounting period or the fiscal year.

Procedures must be provided for reports to be made to the accounting office on disposition of an asset (through scrapping, abandonment, trade-in, or sale) so that proper adjustments may be made to remove the cost of the assets disposed of from the General Fixed Assets Group of Accounts.

General Long-Term Debt Group of Accounts. The General Long-Term Debt Group of Accounts is a separate self-balancing group of accounts in which is recorded all the unmatured, long-term indebtedness backed by the full faith and credit of the governmental unit. A revenue bond issued by an Enterprise Fund and payable only from its revenues is recorded in the Enterprise Fund. A general obligation bond which is issued for the benefit of a governmental enterprise, but which (as a matter of policy) is serviced by earnings of the enterprise, should be included in both the affected Enterprise Fund and the General Long-Term Debt Group of Accounts.

Another special case is that of a special assessment bond which carries a secondary pledge of the governmental unit's full faith and credit. In this case the direct liability should be included only in the Special Assessment Funds, but the contingent liability should be indicated by a footnote in the Statement of General Long-Term Debt.

At the time bonds are issued, an entry should be made in the General Long-Term Debt Group of Accounts recording the liability by a credit to the account Bonds Payable for the principal amount of the debt. The offsetting debit is to an account entitled "Amount to Be Provided for Payment of Bonds." After the entry to record the issuance of the bonds has been made, transactions are recorded in

[6]National Committee on Governmental Accounting, *op. cit.*

the General Long-Term Debt Group of Accounts which parallel those in the various Debt Service Funds. Increases in the Debt Service Fund balances available for payments on long-term debt are recognized in the General Long-Term Debt Group of Accounts by a debit to Amount Available in Debt Service Funds and a credit to an account entitled "Amount to Be Provided for Payment of Bonds." As bonds are retired through a Debt Service Fund, a simultaneous entry is made in the General Long-Term Debt Group of Accounts debiting Bonds Payable and crediting either Amount to Be Provided for Payment of Bonds or Amount Available in Debt Service Funds.

FINANCIAL REPORTING

Objectives of Financial Reporting.   Financial reports for governmental units must be prepared with the objective in mind of providing full disclosure on a timely basis of all material facts relating to their financial position and results of operation. As with any organization, financial statements of a governmental unit are used by different groups, each of which has its own particular needs. The financial statements are of interest to the following four groups: administrative or managerial personnel, governing bodies, investors, and the general public. Generally, no set of financial statements is developed solely for the use of one of these groups to the exclusion of the others. Consequently, the needs of each of the four groups must be kept in mind in designing and preparing financial statements and schedules. Different levels of summarization of the financial information may be used in order to accommodate the relative degree of need for detail of each of the four groups. Financial information may be presented first in the form of balance sheets, statements of revenue, statements of expenditures, etc. These in turn would be supplemented by footnotes and schedules setting forth the details of the various items appearing in the summary financial statements.

Financial reporting should be done both on an interim basis and on an annual basis. Interim financial reports should be prepared at least quarterly, but preferably monthly. To be of benefit to administrative officials and governing bodies, interim statements must be prepared within a few days after the completion of the accounting period. Annual financial reports should be prepared and published within a period of 60 to 90 days after the close of the fiscal year.

Interim Financial Reports.   Interim financial reports provide the financial data required by administrative officials to control current operations and to permit determination of compliance with legal and budgetary requirements. If prepared on a timely basis, they also permit the determination of changes in financial conditions and requirements because of the events which may have occurred subsequent to the time that the budget was prepared. If such information is available monthly, the existence of altered circumstances will be evident on a timely basis and will facilitate corrective action or the development of alternative courses.

The National Committee on Governmental Accounting recommends that all governmental units prepare interim financial reports including at least the following statements:

1. Statement of Actual and Estimated Revenue for the General, Special Revenue, and Debt Service Funds

2. Statement of Actual and Estimated Expenditures for the General and Special Revenue Funds

3. Comparative Statements of Revenue and Expense for Each Enterprise and Intragovernmental Service Fund

4. A Combined Statement of Cash Receipts and Disbursements and Ending Cash Balances for all funds

EXHIBIT 1

NAME OF GOVERNMENTAL UNIT
General Fund
Interim Statement of Actual and Estimated Revenue

Source of revenue	Total estimated for fiscal year 19X2	Month of October, 19X1			Six months ended Oct. 31, 19X1			
		Estimated	Actual	Actual over (under) estimate	Estimated	Actual	Actual over (under) estimate	Balance to be collected
Taxes:								
General property taxes—current........	$300,000	$50,000	$49,500	($500)	$290,000	$291,000	$1,000	$ 9,000
Penalties and interest on delinquent taxes—general property........	2,000	—	—		1,000	900	(100)	1,100
	$302,000	$50,000	$49,500	($500)	$291,000	$291,900	$ 900	$ 10,100
Licenses and permits: (et cetera)								
....								
Total revenue	$465,000	$60,000	$60,200	$200	$362,000	$361,000	($1,000)	$104,000

EXHIBIT 2

NAME OF GOVERNMENTAL UNIT
General Fund
Interim Statement of Actual and Estimated Expenditures

Function/Activity/Object	Total appropriated for fiscal year 19X2	Month of October, 19X1			Six months ended October 31, 19X1					
		Estimated	Actual	Actual (over) under estimate	Estimated	Actual	Actual (over) under estimate	Unexpended balance	Encumbrances	Unencumbered balance
General government:										
Legislative:										
Personal services........	$ 7,200	$ 600	$ 600	—	$ 3,600	$ 3,600	—	$ 3,600	—	$ 3,600
Supplies...............	1,000	100	110	($ 10)	500	450	$ 50	550	$ 100	450
Other services and charges...........	2,000	300	250	50	1,000	900	100	1,100	150	950
Capital outlays........	500	200	—	200	500	350	150	150	100	50
	$ 10,700	$ 1,200	$ 960	$240	$ 5,600	$ 5,300	$ 300	$ 5,400	$ 350	$ 5,050
Judicial:										
(Itemized by object)										
(et cetera)										
....	....	....	....	....	....	....	....	....	....	....
Total expenditures	$460,000	$41,800	$41,200	$600	$255,000	$248,000	$7,000	$212,000	$5,500	$206,500

5. A Forecast of Cash Position for all funds for the succeeding reporting period.

Exhibits 1 to 5 illustrate the format for each of these statements. Throughout the exhibits, it is assumed that the governmental unit's fiscal year begins on May 1.

Additional statements and supporting schedules should be supplied to supplement those illustrated in the exhibits as required for sound financial management of the governmental unit's affairs. Note that the first three of the exhibits are prepared for individual funds. The latter two show all funds in one statement, but it is important that each individual fund be shown separately and not netted out by consolidation into a single set of totals. Each fund is an independent financial entity and its cash transactions must be administered and evaluated separately without regard to those of other funds.

Annual Financial Reports. Annual financial reports should contain detailed financial statements and schedules for all funds and self-balancing groups of accounts in such manner as to disclose fully and present fairly the financial position and result of financial operations for the fiscal year. To provide an overview of the financial affairs of the governmental unit, the annual reports should contain four combined statements and three combined schedules, as follows:

1. Combined Balance Sheet—All Funds
2. Combined Statement of Revenue—Estimated and Actual, for the General and Special Revenue Funds

EXHIBIT 3

Water and Sewer Fund
Interim Statement of Revenue and Expense—Actual and Estimated

	Six months ended October 31, 19X1			Six months ended October 31, 19X0 actual	Increase (decrease) in actual
	Estimated	Actual	Actual over (under) estimated		
Operating revenues:					
Metered water sales............	$280,000	$283,500	$3,500	$275,600	$ 7,900
Bulk water sales...............	10,500	10,300	(200)	9,500	800
Sewer service charges...........	55,000	56,300	1,300	53,000	3,300
Other operating revenues........	3,000	2,700	(300)	2,900	(200)
Total operating revenues......	$348,500	$352,800	$4,300	$341,000	$11,800
Operating expenses except provision for depreciation (details shown in supplementary schedule)........	285,000	284,000	(1,000)	279,500	4,500
Net operating income before depreciation..............	$ 63,500	$ 68,800	$5,300	$ 61,500	$ 7,300
Provision for depreciation........	47,500	47,200	(300)	46,800	400
Net operating income	$ 16,000	$ 21,600	$5,600	$ 14,700	$ 6,900
Nonoperating income:					
Interest earnings..............	2,500	2,300	(200)	2,150	150
Rent—nonoperating property....	2,400	2,400	—	2,400	—
	$ 4,900	$ 4,700	($ 200)	$ 4,550	$ 150
	$ 20,900	$ 26,300	$5,400	$ 19,250	$ 7,050
Nonoperating expense:					
Interest—revenue bonds........	5,400	5,400	—	5,800	(400)
Fiscal agents' fees..............	300	250	(50)	300	(50)
	$ 5,700	$ 5,650	($ 50)	$ 6,100	($ 450)
Net income..................	$ 15,200	$ 20,650	$5,450	$ 13,150	$ 7,500

EXHIBIT 4

All Funds
Combined Statement of Cash Receipts and Disbursements
Six Months Ended October 31, 19X1

Fund	Balance May 1, 19X1	Receipts	Disburse-ments	Balance October 31, 19X1
General Fund..................	$ 66,700	$359,500	$248,000	$178,200
Special revenue funds:				
Airport.....................	16,800	70,200	68,300	18,700
Parks.......................	9,700	19,500	20,600	8,600
Motor fuel tax..............	27,300	15,600	22,700	20,200
Debt service funds:				
(et cetera)				
....	....	....	....	....
....	....	....	....	....
Total—all funds	$368,900	$895,600	$873,500	$390,000
Balances by depository— October 31, 19X1:				
Office cash funds............				$ 6,500
Bank A.....................				265,500
Bank B.....................				72,300
Bank C.....................				45,700
Total—all funds				$390,000

3. Combined Statement of General Governmental Expenditures Compared with Authorizations for the General and Special Revenue Funds
4. Combined Statement of Cash Receipts and Disbursements—All Funds
5. Combined Schedule of Delinquent Taxes Receivable by Funds
6. Combined Schedule of Bonds Payable by Funds
7. Combined Schedules of Investment by Funds

EXHIBIT 5

All Funds
Combined Forecast of Cash Position

Funds	Cash balance October 31, 19X1	Estimated receipts, November	Estimated disbursements, November	Estimated balance November 30, 19X1
General Fund.........	$178,200	$ 55,000	$ 53,500	$180,700
Special revenue funds:				
Airport.............	18,700	12,000	12,500	18,200
Parks...............	8,600	2,000	1,800	8,800
Motor fuel tax......	20,200	3,000	2,500	20,700
Debt service funds:				
(et cetera)				
....	....	....	....	....
....	....	....	....	....
Total—all funds	$390,000	$130,500	$134,500	$386,000

EXHIBIT 6

ANY CITY
Combined Balance Sheet—All Funds
April 30, 19X1

Assets and Other Debits	General fund	Special revenue funds	Debt service funds	Capital projects funds	Enterprise fund	Intragovernmental service fund	Trust and agency funds	Special assessments funds	General fixed assets	General long-term debt
Cash	$101,200	$ 55,300	$ 20,600	$275,400	$ 39,700	$10,800	$ 27,500	$137,100	—	$ —
Cash with fiscal agents	—	—	35,700	—	—	—	—	—	—	—
Investments and accrued interest	50,500	20,400	110,700	—	—	—	569,700	120,900	—	—
Taxes receivable—net	225,800	65,200	130,300	80,200	—	—	—	—	—	—
Accounts receivable—net	16,200	5,700	—	—	85,900	—	—	—	—	—
Special assessments receivable	—	—	—	—	—	—	—	416,700	—	—
Advances to Service Fund	50,000	—	—	—	—	—	—	—	—	—
Due from other funds	3,200	900	—	—	2,400	6,500	7,200	13,500	—	—
Inventories	2,300	700	—	—	17,300	—	—	—	—	—
Prepaid expenses	—	—	—	—	9,200	—	—	—	—	—
Restricted assets—Enterprise Fund:										
Cash	—	—	—	—	42,700	—	—	—	—	—
Investments and accrued interest	—	—	—	—	73,400	—	—	—	—	—
Land	—	—	—	—	70,800	10,500	—	—	$ 967,400	—
Buildings	—	—	—	—	160,700	30,200	—	—	450,500	—
Improvements other than buildings	—	—	—	—	352,300	7,800	—	—	905,700	—
Machinery and equipment	—	—	—	—	75,200	15,600	—	—	135,900	—
Construction work in progress	—	—	—	—	20,600	—	—	—	70,500	—
Amount available for retirement of serial bonds	—	—	—	—	—	—	—	—	—	$ 33,000
Amount to be provided for retirement of serial bonds	—	—	—	—	—	—	—	—	—	965,000
	$449,200	$148,200	$297,300	$355,600	$950,200	$81,400	$604,400	$688,200	$2,530,000	$998,000

ANY CITY
Combined Balance Sheet—All Funds
April 30, 19X1

	General fund	Special revenue funds	Debt service funds	Capital projects funds	Enterprise fund	Intragovernmental service fund	Trust and agency funds	Special assessments funds	General fixed assets	General long-term debt
Liabilities										
Vouchers payable	$100,300	$ 52,100	$ —	$ 49,800	$ 75,300	$ 6,000	$ 5,300	$ 22,700	—	—
Contracts payable	92,500	—	—	125,500	43,600	—	—	128,800	—	—
Due to other funds	22,900	2,300	—	—	6,700	1,800	—	—	—	—
Customer deposits	—	—	—	—	23,400	—	—	—	—	—
Advance from General Fund	—	—	—	—	—	50,000	—	—	—	—
Matured bonds and interest payable	—	—	264,300	—	—	—	—	—	—	—
General obligation serial bonds	—	—	—	—	—	—	—	—	—	$998,000
Revenue bonds	—	—	—	—	306,200	—	—	—	—	—
Special assessment bonds	—	—	—	—	—	—	—	490,000	—	—
	$215,700	$ 54,400	$264,300	$175,300	$455,200	$57,800	$ 5,300	$641,500	—	$998,000
Reserves and Fund Balances Retained Earnings										
Reserve for encumbrances	26,200	16,200	—	175,000	—	—	—	30,500	—	—
Reserve for inventory of supplies	2,300	700	—	—	—	—	—	—	—	—
Reserve for advance to Service Fund	50,000	—	—	—	—	—	—	—	—	—
Reserves for revenue bond restricted assets	—	—	—	—	116,100	—	—	—	—	—
Reserves—Employees Retirement System	—	—	—	—	—	—	326,400	—	—	—
Contribution from General Fund	—	—	—	—	100,000	20,000	—	—	—	—
Investment in fixed assets	—	—	—	—	—	—	—	—	$2,530,000	—
Fund balance	155,000	76,900	33,000	5,300	—	—	272,700	16,200	—	—
Retained earnings	—	—	—	—	278,900	3,600	—	—	—	—
	$449,200	$148,200	$297,300	$355,600	$950,200	$81,400	$604,400	$688,200	$2,530,000	$998,000

EXHIBIT 7

Combined Statement of Revenue—Estimated and Actual
General and Special Revenue Funds
Fiscal Year Ended April 30, 19X1

Source (Fund)	Estimated	Actual	Actual over (under) estimate
Taxes:			
(General)............................	$465,000	$452,600	($12,400)
(Special Revenue)......................	125,000	122,800	(2,200)
	$590,000	$575,400	($14,600)
Licenses and permits:			
(General)............................	63,000	64,700	1,700
(et cetera)			
....	....	....	....
....	....	....	....
Total revenue	$975,000	$952,400	($22,600)

Exhibits 6 to 9 illustrate several of the statements mentioned above. Each of the examples given for interim statements have their counterparts in the annual report and are not repeated here.

While a combined balance sheet may be prepared for a municipality as illustrated in Exhibit 6, no combined statement of operations should be prepared. To do so would involve the comparison of revenues and expenditures of the various funds when such comparisons are not valid because of the differences in the fiscal operations and accounting requirements of the various funds. The combined balance sheet is not analogous to a consolidated balance sheet prepared for a business enterprise; such a consolidation would not be appropriate because offsetting balances among funds are included in assets, liabilities, and reserves, and

EXHIBIT 8

Combined Schedule of Delinquent Taxes Receivable by Funds
April 30, 19X1

Delinquent taxes by year	Total	Funds		
		General	Special revenue	Debt service
Delinquent taxes:				
19X1................................	$15,900	$10,200	$3,100	$2,600
19X0................................	2,200	1,300	500	400
19W9	1,400	900	300	200
	$19,500	$12,400	$3,900	$3,200
Less allowance for uncollectible				
delinquent taxes...................	6,200	4,100	1,200	900
Net delinquent taxes receivable	$13,300	$ 8,300	$2,700	$2,300

EXHIBIT 9

Combined Statement of General Governmental Expenditures
Compared with Authorizations
General and Special Revenue Funds
Fiscal Year Ended April 30, 19X1

Function (Fund)	Reserve for encumbrances, 19X0	Expenditures, 19X0	Credit (charge) to fund balance	19X1 appropriations	19X1 expenditures	Encumbrances, April 30 19X1	19X1 unencumbered balance
General government:							
(General).............	$ 1,100	$ 900	$200	$ 63,000	$ 55,600	$ 3,200	$ 4,200
(Special Revenue)......	300	400	(100)	25,000	22,300	600	2.100
	$ 1,400	$ 1,300	$100	$ 88,000	$ 77,900	$ 3,800	$ 6,300
Public safety:							
(General).............	2,300	2,400	(100)	113,000	105,800	6,500	700
(Special Revenue)......	400	200	100	32,000	29,700	1,200	1,100
	$ 2,700	$ 2,600	—	$145,000	$135,500	$ 7,700	$ 1,800
(et cetera)							
....	....	....	....	....	....	....	....
....	....	....	....	....	....	....	....
Total general governmental expenditures	$16,500	$15,800	$700	$962,000	$920,600	$23,300	$18,100

because of the differences in the operating and accounting requirements among funds. It should be noted that there is no "total" column presenting the aggregate balances for each of the various classes of assets and liabilities of all the funds because inclusion of such figures could be misleading.

In addition to the combined statements listed above, statements for individual funds should be included following the combined statements and should consist of a Balance Sheet, a Statement of Changes in Fund Balance, and Statements of Revenues and of Expenditures (or an operating statement, as appropriate). In addition, appropriate schedules required for full disclosure of fund position and operation should be included as supplements to the primary financial statements for each fund.

BIBLIOGRAPHY

Caldwell, Kenneth S.: "Planning, Programming, and Budgetary Systems," in J. A. Cashin (ed.), *Handbook for Auditors*, chap. 52, McGraw-Hill Book Company, New York, 1971.

Caldwell, Kenneth S., and Robert C. Hacking: *Governmental Budgetary, Level I (Budgeting for Smaller Governmental Entities)*, Municipal Finance Officers Association, 1975.

Committee on Governmental Accounting and Auditing: *Audits of State and Local Governmental Units*, American Institute of Certified Public Accountants, New York, 1974.

Comptroller General of the United States: *Standards for Audit of Governmental Organizations, Programs, Activities & Functions*, U.S. General Accounting Office, Washington, D.C., 1972.

Hay, Leon E., and R. M. Mikesell: *Governmental Accounting*, 5th ed., Richard D. Irwin, Homewood, Ill., 1974.

Hovey, Harold A.: *The Planning-Programming-Budgeting: A Systems Approach to Government Decision Making*, Frederick A. Praeger, New York, 1968.

Kerrigan, Harry D.: *Fund Accounting*, McGraw-Hill Book Company, New York, 1969.

Leonard, Robert L.: "Accounting Needs of Local Government," *Journal of Accountancy*, November 1959, pp. 55–59.

Lyden, Freman J., and Ernest G. Miller: *Planning, Programming, Budgeting: A Systems Approach to Management,* Markham Publishing Co., Chicago, 1967.

National Committee on Governmental Accounting: *Governmental Accounting, Auditing, and Financial Reporting,* Municipal Finance Officers of the United States and Canada, Chicago, 1968.

Pinkelman, Franklin C.: "Michigan's Use of the Program Audit," *State Government,* Summer 1967.

State of Kentucky and Ernst & Ernst: *Financial Management Systems,* 1966.

State of Washington and Ernst & Ernst: *Planning-Programming-Budgetary Systems for State and Local Governments,* Olympia, Wash., 1968.

Subcommittee on Economy in Government of the Joint Economic Committee, Congress of the United States, 90th Congress. *The Planning-Programming-Budgeting System; Progress and Potentials.* U.S. Government Printing Office, Washington, D.C., 1967.

Tenner, Irving, and Edward S. Lynn: Municipal and Government Accounting, 4th ed., Prentice-Hall, Englewood Cliffs, N.J., 1960.

White, Robert H.: "Municipal Budgets," *Journal of Accountancy,* April 1960, pp. 55–61.

Chapter **46**

Replacement Cost/Current Value Accounting

DONALD R. BRINKMAN
President, Valuation Systems Corporation

REPLACEMENT COST DEFINITION

The definition of replacement cost in the Securities and Exchange Commission Staff Accounting Bulletin No. 7 interpreting the SEC's *Accounting Series Release No. 190* is:

> Replacement cost is the lowest amount that would have to be paid in the normal course of business to obtain a *new* asset of equivalent operating or productive capability. Replacement cost (new) is the total estimated current cost of replacing total productive capacity at the end of the year while depreciated replacement cost is the replacement cost (new) adjusted for the already expired service potential of such assets. [Emphasis supplied.]

Replacement cost should not be confused or interchanged with reproduction cost. Reproduction cost represents the reproducing of an asset in like kind using today's labor and material rates. The key difference between replacement cost and reproduction cost is the factor of technological change. Replacement cost takes changes in technology into consideration while reproduction cost does not (see the "Technological Factors," section of this chapter).

As defined by the staff interpretations of *ASR 190*, "Productive capacity is the measurement of a company's ability to produce and distribute. The productive capacity of a company can be measured by the number of units it can presently produce and distribute within a particular time frame. . . ." One significant clarification in applying the definition of replacement cost of productive capacity is that "The measurement is applied to 'what *is* in existence now' as opposed to attempting to measure hypothetical future operating capacity with various re-engineered alternatives." A good rule to follow in the measurement process is to ask the question *"what is?"* as opposed to *"what if?"* The next question to ask is: "What is the cost of equivalent capacity at the present time?"

REPLACEMENT COST BACKGROUND

Limperg's Theory. Professor Theodore Limperg, Jr., of the Amsterdam School of Economics, is credited with most fully developing the concept of replacement cost accounting. The Limperg theory is predicated on continuity of the firm, resulting in the necessity of maintaining capital. Therefore, assets used or sold will be replaced with other assets performing a similar function.

Limperg's theory strongly influenced the development of accounting in the

Netherlands after World War I. This development resulted in several major Dutch corporations developing replacement cost accounting systems. The most notable of these is Philips Industries, which has been practicing replacement cost accounting since about 1936. They have the most sophisticated replacement cost accounting system in the world.

Replacement Cost Developments in the United States. From the turn of the century, when "fair value" accounting principles were allowed by the U.S. Supreme Court (e.g., Smyth v. Ames[1]), the United States went through several accounting cycles before arriving at the present SEC replacement cost requirement.[2]

There were many problems with "unguided adjustments" to asset and equity accounts during the 1920s and 1930s. These "unguided adjustments" resulted in the AICPA, SEC, and New York Stock Exchange rejecting replacement cost/value adjustments and solidified their insistence on historical costs. This position was reinforced by the 1944 U.S. Supreme Court decision in the case of Federal Power Commission v. Hope Natural Gas Company.[3] In this case the Court sustained an FPC order using historical cost as the basis for accounting measurement.

During the post-World War II inflation, several corporations, including Chrysler, Du Pont, Hercules Powder, U.S. Steel, and Westinghouse, developed replacement cost depreciation methods. These were rejected by the SEC, AICPA, and the New York Stock Exchange. But this effort ultimately resulted in accelerated depreciation allowances as written into the 1954 Internal Revenue Code. With continued inflation came the need to change the historical-cost accounting model. This was evidenced by two famous cases: Speed v. Transamerica in 1956[4] and Gerstle v. Gamble Skogmo in 1967.[5] In both cases the courts required, under the special circumstances of each case, disclosures of current values since they were materially different from historical costs.

SEC DISCLOSURES REQUIRED FOR REPLACEMENT COST DATA

In *ASR No. 190,* issued in 1976, the SEC formally mandated disclosure of replacement cost data for•major U.S. corporations. The SEC mandate required replacement cost data for fiscal years ending on or after December 25, 1976.

The inclusions under the SEC rule are:

1. The current replacement cost of inventories at each fiscal year end
2. The replacement cost of goods sold at the times when the sales were made
3. The current cost of replacing (new) the productive capacity together with its depreciated replacement cost at each fiscal year end
4. The depreciation based on current replacement cost of productive capacity, using economic lives, and the straight-line method of depreciation.

Because of the imprecise nature of the disclosures required for replacement cost, the SEC has developed a "safe harbor rule." Provided that registrants use reasonable care, act in good faith, and disclose the methods used in preparing the replacement cost data, the safe harbor rule will provide them with some protection from the antifraud sections of the Securities Acts. The safe harbor rule is not available unless registrants disclose all information of which they are aware and which they believe necessary to prevent the data from being misleading.

[1]169 US 466 (1898).
[2]SEC, *Accounting Series Release No. 190,* 1976.
[3]320 U.S. 591 (1944).
[4]235 F.2d 369 (4rd Cir. 1956).
[5]298 F. Supp. 66 (E.D.N.Y. 1969).

REPLACEMENT COST MEASUREMENTS

The Accounting/Economic Link.   For assets, the historical-cost accounting system contains quantities and prices recorded at historical costs. At the time the purchases are made, the historical costs are equal to the current prices. After the purchases are made, prices change because of external economic forces and technological developments. Therefore, the key variables between historical costs and current costs are price movements and technological changes. If price movements are computed over time and technological change is measured, then the relationships between historical costs and replacement costs can be established.

Measurement Techniques.   The measurement technique which most directly measures the change in price over time is indexing. Indexing can provide a valid measurement of replacement cost provided that the index is adjusted for technological change. Other techniques which consider the recorded quantities (or equivalent function) at current prices and directly result in replacement costs are direct pricing, unit pricing, and functional pricing.

Indexing.   Indexing is one widely used technique to measure replacement cost, and it may be used both for inventories and for fixed assets. Indexing rolls forward a base cost, which may be an historical original cost or a recent replacement cost established by direct pricing.

The base cost is adjusted by the ratio of the current index of the index at the time the base cost was established. For example, assume that we have a machine with a historical original cost of $50,000 and a purchase date of May 1969. The current index for the machine is 2.1 and the May 1969 index is 1.3. The base cost ($50,000) is adjusted by the index ratio of 1.6 (= 2.1/1.3) to establish today's replacement cost at $80,000.

Measuring replacement cost by indexing lends itself well to a computerized approach. Because of large amounts of data and continuous change occurring throughout the economy, index series can develop into fairly sizable data bases. Index sources should, ideally, be obtained from publicly available areas and be government based. These tend to be the most supportable, are available on a frequent basis, and do not have unreasonable time lags between effective date and publication date. The following are considered to be generally available indexes:

- U.S. Bureau of Labor Statistics, Wholesale Price Index
- U.S. Bureau of Labor Statistics, International Wholesale Price Index
- U.S. Bureau of the Census, Census of Manufacturers Index
- U.S. Bureau of Reclamation, Construction Index
- New York Port Authority, Construction Index
- U.S. Department of Commerce, Composite Cost Index.

For indexing to reflect replacement cost properly, the base cost (historical original cost) must not be a *used* asset price, an asset modification, or a previously allocated purchase price from a business combination. In these cases indexing will not apply, and direct pricing will be more applicable.

Direct Pricing.   Direct pricing is the application of direct labor and material prices to an asset or group of assets. Specialized assets, or those requiring engineering modifications, are usually priced directly from engineering records or contract prices. Direct pricing requires data both internal and external to the firm. Internal data may include purchase orders, invoices, engineering estimates, and other internal sources of labor and material prices. External data may include supplier price lists, manufacturers' quotations, and published labor and material price books.

Unit Pricing.   Unit pricing may be generally subdivided into three types: estimated costing, job order costing, and process costing.

Estimated costing is used to identify (prior to actual construction, production, or acquisition) the expected cost of construction, production, or acquisition in terms of a predefined unit. The methods for determining estimated costs are as follows:

1. Record the costs of material over a specified period and develop the cost of the total construction, production, or acquisition. This can then be divided by a unit measure (pounds of cotton, square feet of building, etc.). Sampling of these results and a comparison with original cost estimates can aid in future unit cost projections.

2. Estimate direct labor by production rate or rate per hour.

3. Distribute administration and manufacturing overhead to various elements of construction/production.

Job order costing is compiled for a specific quantity of product, equipment, repair, or other service that moves through the production process as a continuously identifiable unit. Applicable material, direct labor, and a portion of overhead costs are charged to each job order. Material and labor costs are identified directly as they apply to a particular product or indirectly as they are charged to overhead. Manufacturing overhead is established by a standard overhead rate formula, which assigns a portion of costs which are identified as overhead to each quantity of product, equipment, repair, or service.

Process costing accumulates costs and production units period by period. At the end of each period, cost per unit of production is the average unit cost for that period. In process-type production, interim units of the production process are not discretely identifiable, but can be assigned a stage (or percentage) of completion. These units then represent effective (equivalent) production, defined as the quantity of complete units that would have been produced if all work performed had been applied only to those units begun and finished in a particular period. Basic problems associated with applying unit cost techniques involve the segregation of costs for unit allocation and the determination of proper overhead rates.

Functional Pricing. Functional pricing is generally used to determine the replacement cost for a processing function rather than for a specific static asset or asset group. Whereas the use of indexing requires a homogeneous group of assets, functional pricing can be applied to a heterogeneous group of assets. Functional pricing often combines indexing, direct pricing, and unit costing. Functional costing involves use of such information as:

1. Engineering studies
2. Recently built processes
3. Process plant designs
4. Major equipment suppliers
5. Manufacturers' quotations
6. Internal estimates for installation and/or modifications
7. Trade association studies.

Unit Pricing Versus Functional Pricing. Unit pricing is considered a static measurement unit (e.g., dollars per pound of beef, dollars per square foot of building). As an exmaple, to buy five pounds of hamburger for $4.00, the unit cost would be $0.80 per pound. Functional costing is a dynamic measurement. It measures the cost of the productive capacity based on the number of units that can be produced within a particular time period. For example, a meat packing plant with a replacement cost of $5 million has the capacity to process 500 head of cattle per day, resulting in the functional replacement cost of $10,000 per head of cattle per day.

Data Base Relationships. Conventional accounting records quantities and prices at historical costs at the time of acquisition. Over time, the prices change because of external economic forces. In order to measure replacement cost, we will define in the following paragraphs the types of quantity and historical price data required in the firm's internal data base, and the types of quantity and price data required in an external data base to measure replacement costs. The following paragraphs will encompass inventories and productive capacity subdivided between machinery and equipment and structures.

Inventories. For inventories, consideration must be given to raw materials, work in process, and finished goods. For raw materials, the firm's internal data should include quantities and historical costs. For work in process, the firm's internal data should include the type of costing that is performed (e.g., estimated costing, job order costing, or process costing). For finished goods, the firm's internal data should include quantities and unit costs.

The external data base should include raw material prices or an index of specific material prices. For work in process it should include an index of material prices and price indexes for the other elements of the costing formula. For finished goods it should include current prices.

Machinery and Equipment. For general-purpose machinery and equipment, the firm's internal data for groups should include quantities, historical original costs, and dates of acquisition. With the proper classification scheme (e.g., expanded standard Industrial Classification Codes, Census of Manufacturers Codes), these items can be coded and measured with specific price indices (e.g., Wholesale Price Index Components). For special-purpose machinery and equipment, the same treatment that applies to structures must be applied.

Structures. For structures, the firm's internal data should include quantities (sizes), construction type, and function type. A shortcut approach can be used if the structure is classified by construction type—framing type (e.g., steel, reinforced concrete) and type of function (e.g., office, warehouse, manufacturing). A cost per square foot to replace the structure or its function can then be determined. Generally, a building is used for more than one function (e.g., office and production). In these cases, each area used for a distinct function can be assigned a separate cost per square foot. The total replacement cost of the buildings is the sum of the individual area unit costs.

A building may also be measured for replacement cost by a functional systems estimate, in which the building is subdivided into functional components (e.g., foundation, roof, floors, interior walls, exterior walls). The dimensions for each component are obtained and an average replacement cost is assigned to each of the components according to the dimensions of the basic unit cost.

APPLICATION—AN EXAMPLE

Historical Cost Information. Our example firm (XYZ Company) is engaged in manufacturing toys. It produces three products: plastic trucks, bionic dolls, and garments for the bionic dolls. The XYZ Company is not large enough to be required to make replacement cost disclosures. We have kept the numbers small so that they will remain manageable in a brief illustration.

The fixed assets of the firm consist of office furniture, sewing machines, injection molding machines, lift trucks, air compressors, etc. The firm also has a special-purpose machine. This machine was purchased and modified by the firm to meet special manufacturing requirements of the firm. To measure replacement cost of the special-purpose machine requires consideration of technological change. The firm also leases three molding machines and owns some assets which are nonessential to the productive process.

The production and administrative areas of the firm are located in one building on five acres of land.

Major raw materials are plastic and rubber to make the toys and cotton cloth to make the garments. The plastic is obtained under a long-term contract, extending over the next three years at a price lower than current market price. The company also has some obsolete inventories.

Selling prices are reconsidered regularly. Standard costs of products are altered twice a year to reflect increases in labor and material costs.

The Balance Sheet and Income Statement based on historical cost are displayed in Exhibits 1 and 2. The existing fixed assets and inventories are shown in Exhibits 3 through 9. Summarized sales by months are displayed in Exhibit 10.

Preliminary Measurement Procedures. Replacement cost measurement methodology consists of two stages: preliminary measurement procedures and actual replacement cost measurements.

EXHIBIT 1

XYZ COMPANY
Balance Sheet
December 31, 1975

Assets

Current assets:			
Cash		$ 25,288	
Marketable securities at cost			
(market value $30,881)		29,925	
Notes receivable		7,213	
Accounts receivable		89,462	
Inventories		3,320,056	
Prepaid insurance		2,200	
Total current assets			$3,474,144
Noncurrent assets:			
Land		$ 188,972	
Building	$ 607,895		
Furniture and fixtures	14,017		
Machinery and equipment	741,696		
Leased assets	78,106		
Other assets	9,050		
	$1,450,764		
Accumulated depreciation	470,589	980,175	
Total noncurrent assets			1,169,147
Total assets			$4,643,291

Liabilities and Stockholders' Equity

Current liabilities:			
Bank loans		$ 50,000	
Accounts payable		68,790	
Wages payable and other			
accruals		49,800	
Estimated income taxes payable		42,250	
Total current liabilities			$ 210,840
Long-term liability:			
Long-term lease obligation			64,000
Total liabilities			$ 274,840
Stockholders' equity:			
Common stock, par value $3 per			
share, 800,000 shares			
authorized, 790,145 shares			
issued and outstanding		$2,370,435	
Retained earnings		1,998,016	
Total stockholders' equity			4,368,451
Total liabilities and			
stockholders' equity			$4,643,291

EXHIBIT 2

XYZ COMPANY
Income Statement
For the Year Ended December 31, 1975

Net sales		$4,256,503
Costs of goods sold		2,774,750
Gross margin		$1,481,753
Selling expenses:		
Sales salaries	$85,438	
Advertising	42,850	
Travel and entertainment	11,713	
Freight and delivery	5,775	
Consultant fees	9,700	$ 155,476
General and administrative expenses:		
Officers salaries	$95,625	
Office salaries	73,305	
Taxes	10,925	
Insurance	2,350	
Utilities	10,163	
Uncollected accounts expense	11,750	204,118
Total operating expenses		$ 359,594
Net operating income		$1,122,159
Other revenue and expenses:		
Interest and dividends earned	$ 7,750	
Rent revenue	24,250	
	$32,000	
Less interest expense	11,700	20,300
Net income before income taxes		$1,101,859
Estimated income taxes		288,704
Net income		$ 813,155
Retained earnings 12/31/74		1,184,861
Retained earnings 12/31/75		$1,998,016

The preliminary measurement procedures are designed to minimize the time and cost necessary to perform the actual replacement cost measurements. The importance of this step is dependent on the number of data elements involved. The larger the number of data elements the more time and cost will be expended in performing the actual replacement cost measurements. For the replacement cost measurements to be precise, each item would have to be valued at replacement cost as is done for historic cost. But this would require large amounts of time and substantial cost. Thus, the objective of the preliminary measurement procedures is to minimize the data problem by grouping and summarizing the data by accounts into smaller and more manageable proportions *without* sacrificing the accuracy of the replacement cost measurement results. Replacement cost measurements should result in material accuracy, not detailed precision.

1. Cost Analysis
    The purpose of the cost analysis is to determine the magnitude of costs in each fixed asset account and the number of items within the accounts.
    Implications of the Cost Analysis Table (Table 1):
    a. The furniture and fixtures are only 2 percent of the total fixed assets and can be treated as a group. The account (1100) may be indexed using a general Wholesale Price Index (WPI) for furniture and fixtures.
    b. Within the machinery and equipment account:
        (1) The sewing machines can be treated as a single unit and indexed

EXHIBIT 3

XYZ COMPANY
Account 1100
Furnitures and Fixtures

Quantity	Description	Cost	Acquis. date	Life	Annual deprec. expense	Accum. deprec. 12/31/75
35	Royal chairs 5155	$ 1,026	3/73	6	$ 171.00	$ 484.50
1	Double ped. desk	376	3/73	6	62.67	177.57
1	Side chair	94	3/73	6	15.67	44.40
1	Secretary desk	561	3/73	6	93.50	264.91
1	Double ped. desk	376	3/73	6	62.67	177.57
1	Arm tilter chair	146	3/73	6	24.33	68.94
80	Utility trays, fiber	114	2/73	6	19.00	55.42
60	Utility trays, green	1,136	3/74	6	189.33	347.11
5	Inspection table	250	3/73	6	41.67	118.07
10	Fiber truck	830	3/73	6	138.33	391.94
6	Packing rack	438	1/74	6	73.00	146.00
2	Recorder	1,286	1/74	6	214.33	428.66
3	Coat rack	264	1/74	6	44.00	88.00
35	Utility trays	559	3/73	6	93.17	263.98
50	Fiber utility trans.	798	3/73	6	133.00	376.83
3	Calculators	813	2/74	6	135.50	259.71
4	Desks	1,248	4/74	6	208.00	364.00
26	Stacking chairs	655	1/74	6	109.17	218.34
1	Carpets for offices	1,433	2/74	6	238.83	457.75
2	Exec. chairs	470	1/74	6	78.33	156.66
1	Selectric typewriter	874	4/74	6	145.67	254.92
6	Fire extinguishers	270	3/74	6	45.00	82.50
	TOTAL	$14,017			$2,336.17	$5,227.78

TABLE 1   Cost Analysis Table

Account	Description	Cost	% of total fixed asset costs
1100	Furniture and fixtures	$ 14,017	2
1200	Machinery and equipment		
	Sewing machines	$ 32,094	4
	Plastic machines	169,750	23
	Injection molding machines	318,678	42
	Unique machine	200,000	26
	Other	21,174	3
		741,696	98
		$755,713	100

EXHIBIT 4

XYZ COMPANY
Machinery and Equipment

Quantity	Description	Cost	Acquis. date	Life	Deprec. begin. date	Annual deprec. expense	Accum. deprec. 12/31/75
4	Sewing mach. 457GS	$ 2,892	1/73	10	6/73	$ 289.20	$ 747.10
1	Sewing Mach.	1,418	1/74	10	6/74	141.80	224.52
2	Sewing mach. 457G1	1,850	1/74	10	6/74	185.00	292.92
2	Sewing mach. 475G1	5,340	1/74	10	6/74	534.00	845.50
2	Sewing mach.	1,817	1/74	10	6/74	181.70	287.69
1	Sewing mach.	1,448	1/74	10	6/74	144.80	229.27
2	Sewing mach. 457G1	1,848	1/74	10	6/74	184.80	292.60
1	Sewing mach. BROTHER	539	1/73	10	6/73	53.00	136.92
2	Sewing mach. 457G135	1,915	1/73	10	6/73	191.50	494.71
1	Sewing mach.	322	1/73	10	6/73	32.20	83.18
2	Sewing mach. 457G135	1,915	6/73	10	1/74	191.50	383.00
1	Sewing mach. 457G135	1,122	6/74	10	1/74	112.20	224.40
1	Sewing mach. 457G135	1,072	6/73	10	1/74	107.20	214.40
1	Sewing mach. 457G135	1,206	6/74	10	1/75	120.60	120.60
1	Sewing mach. 167G1	2,695	6/73	10	1/74	269.50	539.00
1	Sewing mach. 167G101	1,632	6/74	10	1/75	163.20	163.20
3	Sewing mach. 291V3	855	6/74	10	1/75	85.50	85.50
5	Sewing mach. 291V3	1,426	6/74	10	1/75	142.60	142.60
1	Sewing mach. 291V3	285	6/74	10	1/75	28.50	28.50
2	Sewing mach. 291V3	602	6/74	10	1/75	60.20	60.20
1	Crown lift truck	3,746	1/74	10	6/74	374.60	593.12
1	Air compressor	1,131	1/74	10	6/74	113.10	179.08
1	Burroughs check writer	949	1/73	6	6/73	158.17	408.60
1	Plastic mach.	33,933	1/74	10	1/74	3,393.30	6,786.60
1	Injection mold. mach.	38,911	6/67	10	1/68	3,891.10	31,128.80
1	Injection mold. mach.	41,181	6/66	10	1/67	4,118.10	37,062.00
1	Injection mold. mach.	56,678	6/68	8	1/69	7,084.75	49,593.25
1	Injection mold. mach.	61,024	6/69	8	1/70	7,628.00	45,768.00
1	Injection mold. mach.	56,677	6/68	9	1/69	6,297.44	44,082.07
1	Injection mold. mach.	64,207	6/69	8	1/70	8,025.88	48,155.28
1	Plastic case printer	12,528	1/74	10	1/74	1,252.80	2,505.60
1	Water chiller	2,820	6/72	6	6/72	470.00	1,684.16
1	Plastic mach.	75,582	1/74	10	1/75	7,558.20	7,558.20
1	Plastic mach.	60,139	1/74	10	1/74	6,013.90	12,027.80
1	Unique mach.	200,000	1/66	15	1/66	13,333.33	133,333.32
	TOTAL	$741,696				$72,931.67	$426,461.69

EXHIBIT 5

XYZ COMPANY
Account 1300
Other Plant Assets

Quantity	Description	Cost	Acquis. date	Life	Annual deprec. expense	Accum. deprec. 12/31/75
4.68	Land in acres	$188,972	/73			
1	Building #1	607,895	/75	30	$20,263.17	$20,263.17
1	500-ton mold mach.	*	4/74	8		
1	500-ton mold mach.	78,106	4/74	8	9,763,20	16,272.03
1	500-ton mold mach.	*	4/74	8		
!	H.C. mach. (NE)†	2,000	1/74	10	200.00	400.00
2	H.C. mach. (NE)†	4,050	1/73	10	405.00	1,215.00
1	NE mach.†	1,500	1/74	10	150.00	300.00
1	NE mach.†	1,000	1/74	10	100.00	200.00
10	NE assets†	500	1/73	6	83.33	250.00
		$884,023			$30,964.70	$38,900.20

*Machine leased on an operating lease; not included among assets.
†These are not part of the productive process and will be valued at historic cost to comply with *ASR No. 190.* NE is an abbreviation for nonessential.

using composite life and age, since they constitute only 4 percent of the total fixed asset costs.
(2) The plastic machines will be direct priced since:
  (a) They represent 23 percent of total fixed asset costs.
  (b) There exists no general WPI index for plastic machines.
  (c) To compute composites for this group will cause inaccuracies in the replacement cost figures because of the large dollar amount involved.
(3) The injection molding machines will be direct priced because:
  (a) They represent 42 percent of total fixed asset costs.
  (b) Unique additions were made to the machines by the firm.
  (c) Using the composite life and age will give inaccurate results.
(4) The unique machine will be direct priced and adjustments made for technological changes.
(5) The other assets will be indexed using general WPI indices.
2. Detail Preliminary Measurement Procedures
  a. Furniture and fixtures—Account 1100
  Although the initial cost analysis shows this account to be insignificant in terms of dollars involved and could therefore be summarized as a single number with composite lives and ages and a general index applied, we have broken it into five distinct categories of assets in order to highlight the detailed preliminary measurement procedures that can be performed for obtaining increased accuracy. (See Exhibit 11.)
  An examination of the furniture and fixtures account yields the following results:

EXHIBIT 6

XYZ COMPANY
Account 2400
Raw Materials

Quantity	Description	Cost	Unit cost	Purchase date	Unit of measure	Standard cost at 12/31/75	Cost at 12/31/75
500,000	Polyethylene	$ 130,000	0.26	1/10/75	pound	0.27	$ 135,000
300,000	Polyethylene	78,000	0.26	1/01/75	pound	0.27	81,000
280,000	Rubber nitrite	162,400	0.58	1/15/75	pound	0.59	165,200
3,000	Cotton print cloth	1,290	0.43	1/07/75	yard	0.45	1,350
376,744	Cotton print cloth	162,000	0.43	1/31/75	yard	0.45	169,535
600,000	Polyethylene	162,000	0.27	2/02/75	pound	0.27	162,000
35,000	Cotton print cloth	15,750	0.45	2/02/75	yard	0.45	15,750
300,000	Rubber nitrite	177,000	0.59	2/02/75	pound	0.59	177,000
44,000	Cotton print cloth	19,800	0.45	2/15/75	yard	0.45	19,800
275,000	Rubber nitrite	162,250	0.59	2/31/75	pound	0.59	162,250
800,000	Polyethylene	224,000	0.28	3/01/75	pound	0.27	216,000
30,000	Cotton print cloth	13,800	0.46	3/01/75	yard	0.45	13,500
275,000	Rubber nitrite	162,250	0.59	3/01/75	pound	0.59	162,250
100,000	Polyethylene	28,000	0.28	3/15/75	pound	0.27	27,000
45,000	Cotton print cloth	22,050	0.49	3/31/75	yard	0.45	20,250
500,000	Polyethylene I.D.*	125,000	0.25	1/01/75	pound	0.25	125,000
200	Metal*	1,000	5.00	1/01/75	pound	5.00	1,000
		$1,646,590					$1,653,885

*Polyethylene I.D. and metal are obsolete inventories and will therefore be valued at net realizable value.

(1) Some assets should be categorized as machinery and equipment.
(2) The office furniture and fixtures will be grouped and measured with an index number.
(3) Calculators, typewriters, etc., will be grouped as a separate account and indexed.
(4) A separate index will be applied to the cafeteria equipment.
(5) A separate index will be applied to fire extinguishers.
The total depreciation expense and total accumulated depreciation amount for each group is the sum of actual expense and accumulated depreciation for each item within the group.
b. Machinery and equipment—Account 1200
(1) For purposes of indexing, sewing machines are grouped by vintage years. This results in four summarized entries for sewing machines by four different vintages as shown in the summary account for machinery and equipment (Exhibit 12). An alternative procedure is to summarize the four entries into one item with composite life and age, but this would naturally result in a greater variance of replacement costs.
(2) The plastic machines are not summarized since:

EXHIBIT 7

XYZ COMPANY
Account 2500
Work-in-Process

Quantity	Description	% completed	Effective quantity*	Standard cost	Cost
55,000	Plastic trucks— Model A	25	13,750	5.5820	$ 76,752.5
60,000	Plastic trucks— Model B	25	15,000	5.5820	83,730.0
32,000	Bionic dolls— large	25	8,000	5.7381	45,904.8
52,000	Bionic dolls— small	30	15,600	5.7381	89,514.4
20,000	Plastic trucks— Model A	50	10,000	5.5820	55,820.0
33,000	Bionic dolls	50	16,500	5.7381	94,678.7
73,920	Cut pieces— garment		73,920	1.5198	112,343.6
39,885	Pieces— garments	75	29,914	3.6915	110,426.6
22,500	Pieces— garments	80	18,000	3.6915	66,447.0
					$735,618.0

*Effective quantity is calculated by subtracting the percentage completed from 100 percent and applying this resultant percentage to the number of units put into production.

(a) They represent 23 percent of the total fixed asset costs.
(b) There exists no general WPI index for plastic machines.
(c) The composites will cause inaccuracies in the replacement cost calculations.

If there were additional machines of the same vintage and cost, they could be grouped into single items.

EXHIBIT 8

XYZ COMPANY
Account 2600
Finished Goods

Quantity	Description	Cost	Standard cost
20,000	Plastic trucks— Model A	$111,640	$5.5820
32,000	Plastic trucks— Model B	178,624	5.5820
57,000	Bionic dolls— large	327,072	5.7381
25,700	Bionic dolls— small	147,469	5.7381
44,900	Pieces— garments	165,748	3.6915
	Total	$930,553	

EXHIBIT 9

XYZ COMPANY
Account 3700
Cost of Goods Sold

Quantity	Description	Cost	Standard cost	Date
21,000	Plastic trucks— Model A	$ 122,472.0	5.8320	1/75
15,750	Plastic trucks— Model B	91,854.0	5.8320	1/75
19,800	Bionic dolls— large	118,564.4	5.9881	1/75
15,600	Bionic dolls— small	93,414.4	5.9881	1/75
12,000	Garments	47,298.0	3.9415	1/75
8,000	Plastic trucks— Model A	46,656.0	5.8320	2/75
5,000	Plastic trucks— Model B	29,160.0	5.8320	2/75
6,700	Bionic dolls— large	40,120.0	5.9881	2/75
3,000	Bionic dolls— small	17,964.3	5.9881	2/75
2,500	Garments	9,853.8	3.9415	2/75
6,000	Plastic trucks— Model A	34,992.0	5.8320	3/75
2,500	Bionic dolls— large	14,970.3	5.9881	3/75
3,400	Bionic dolls— small	20,359.5	5.9881	3/75
1,000	Garments	3,941.5	3.9415	3/75
4,400	Plastic trucks— Model B	25,660.8	5.8320	3/75
3,000	Plastic trucks— Model A	17,496.0	5.8320	4/75
3,700	Plastic trucks— Model B	21,578.4	5.8320	4/75
6,100	Bionic dolls— large	36,527.4	5.9881	4/75
2,300	Bionic dolls— small	13,772.6	5.9881	4/75
1,500	Garments	5,912.3	3.9415	4/75
600	Plastic trucks— Model A	3,619.2	6.0320	5/75
900	Plastic trucks— Model B	5,428.8	6.0320	5/75
1,000	Bionic dolls— large	6,188.1	6.1881	5/75
300	Bionic dolls— small	1,856.4	6.1881	5/75
2,000	Garments	8,383.0	4.1915	5/75
4,500	Plastic trucks— Model A	27,144.0	6.0320	6/75
7,100	Plastic trucks— Model B	42,827.2	6.0320	6/75

EXHIBIT 9 (Continued)

XYZ COMPANY
Account 3700 (cont.)

Quantity	Description	Cost	Standard cost	Date
2,000	Bionic dolls— large	12,376.2	6.1881	6/75
4,000	Bionic dolls— small	24,752.4	6.1881	6/75
1,700	Garments	7,040.6	4.1415	6/75
7,819	Plastic trucks— Model A	47,164.2	6.0320	7/75
8,700	Plastic trucks— Model B	52,478.4	6.0320	7/75
3,211	Bionic dolls— large	19,869.9	6.1881	7/75
1,233	Bionic dolls— small	7,629.9	6.1881	7/75
3,000	Garments	12,424.5	4.1415	7/75
2,200	Plastic trucks— Model A	13,270.4	6.0320	8/75
6,650	Plastic trucks— Model B	40,112.8	6.0320	8/75
5,520	Bionic dolls— large	34,158.3	6.1881	8/75
4,320	Bionic dolls— small	26,732.6	6.1881	8/75
5,678	Garments	23,515.4	4.1415	8/75
5,600	Plastic trucks— Model A	$34,339.2	6.1320	9/75
3,900	Plastic trucks— Model B	23,914.8	6.1320	9/75
6,500	Bionic dolls— large	40,872.7	6.2881	9/75
3,250	Bionic dolls— small	20,436.3	6.2881	9/75
7,210	Garments	30,581.2	4.2415	9/75
7,650	Plastic trucks— Model A	46,909.8	6.1320	10/75
8,800	Plastic trucks— Model B	53,961.6	6.1320	10/75
2,500	Bionic dolls— large	15,720.3	6.2881	10/75
1,970	Bionic dolls— small	12,387.6	6.2881	10/75
5,560	Garments	23,582.7	4.2415	10/75
8,860	Plastic trucks— Model A	54,329.5	6.1320	10/75
7,630	Plastic trucks— Model B	46,787.2	6.1320	10/75
5,960	Bionic dolls— large	37,477.1	6.2881	10/75
6,930	Bionic dolls— small	43,576.6	6.2881	10/75
7,120	Garments	30,199.5	4.2415	10/75

EXHIBIT 9 (Continued)

XYZ COMPANY
Account 3700 (cont.)

Quantity	Description	Cost	Standard cost	Date
9,000	Plastic trucks— Model A	55,188.0	6.1320	11/75
12,000	Plastic trucks— Model B	73,584.0	6.1320	11/75
14,000	Bionic dolls— large	88,033.4	6.2881	11/75
15,500	Bionic dolls— small	97,465.6	6.2881	11/75
10,000	Garments	42,415.0	4.2415	11/75
18,000	Plastic trucks— Model A	110,376.0	6.1320	12/75
24,000	Plastic trucks— Model B	147,168.0	6.1320	12/75
25,000	Bionic dolls— large	157,202.5	6.2881	12/75
29,000	Bionic dolls— small	182,354.9	6.2881	12/75
18,000	Garments	76,347.0	4.2415	12/75
	Total	$2,774,750.5		

EXHIBIT 10

XYZ COMPANY
Sales by Month—1975

Quantity	Description	Sales	Net whole- sale price	Date
21,000	Plastic trucks— Model A	$ 209,160	9.96	1/75
15,750	Plastic trucks— Model B	156,870	9.96	1/75
19,800	Bionic dolls— large	214,038	10.81	1/75
15,600	Bionic dolls— small	168,636	10.81	1/75
12,000	Garments	76,440	6.37	1/75
	Total	$ 825,144		
8,000	Plastic trucks— Model A	$ 79,680	9.96	2/75
5,000	Plastic trucks— Model B	49,800	9.96	2/75
6,700	Bionic dolls— large	72,427	10.81	2/75
3,000	Bionic dolls— small	32,430	10.81	2/75
2,500	Garments	15,925	6.37	2/75
	Total	$ 250,262		
6,000	Plastic trucks— Model A	$ 59,760	9.96	3/75

EXHIBIT 10 (Continued)

XYZ COMPANY
Sales by Month—1975

Quantity	Description	Sales	Net whole-sale price	Date
4,400	Plastic trucks— Model B	43,824	9.96	3/75
2,500	Bionic dolls— large	27,025	10.81	3/75
3,400	Bionic dolls— small	36,754	10.81	3/75
1,000	Garments	6,370	6.37	3/75
	Total	$ 173,733		
3,000	Plastic trucks— Model A	$ 29,880	9.96	4/75
3,700	Plastic trucks— Model B	36,852	9.96	4/75
6,100	Bionic dolls— large	65,941	10.81	4/75
2,300	Bionic dolls— small	24,863	10.81	4/75
1,500	Garments	9,555	6.37	4/75
	Total	$ 167,091		
600	Plastic trucks— Model A	$ 5,976	9.96	5/75
900	Plastic trucks— Model B	8,964	9.96	5/75
1,000	Bionic dolls— large	10,810	10.81	5/75
300	Bionic dolls— small	3,243	10.81	5/75
2,000	Garments	12,740	6.37	5/75
	Total	$ 41,733		
4,500	Plastic trucks— Model A	$ 44,820	9.96	6/75
1,076	Plastic trucks— Model B	10,716	9.96	6/75
2,000	Bionic dolls— large	21,620	10.81	6/75
4,000	Bionic dolls— small	43,240	10.81	6/75
1,700	Garments	10,829	6.37	6/75
	Total	$ 131,255		
7,819	Plastic trucks— Model A	$ 77,877	9.96	7/75
8,700	Plastic trucks— Model B	86,652	9.96	7/75
3,211	Bionic dolls— large	34,711	10.81	7/75
1,233	Bionic dolls— small	13,329	10.81	7/75
3,000	Garments	19,110	6.37	7/75
	Total	$ 231,679		
2,200	Plastic trucks— Model A	$ 22,462	10.21	8/75

EXHIBIT 10 (Continued)

XYZ COMPANY
Sales by Month—1975

Quantity	Description	Sales	Net whole-sale price	Date
6,650	Plastic trucks— Model B	67,896	10.21	8/75
5,520	Bionic dolls— large	61,051	11.06	8/75
4,320	Bionic dolls— small	47,779	11.06	8/75
5,678	Garments	37,588	6.62	8/75
	Total	$ 236,776		
5,600	Plastic trucks— Model A	$ 57,176	10.21	9/75
3,900	Plastic trucks— Model B	39,819	10.21	9/75
1,075	Bionic dolls— large	11,890	11.06	9/75
3,250	Bionic dolls— small	35,945	11.06	9/75
7,210	Garments	47,730	6.62	9/75
	Total	$ 192,560		
7,650	Plastic trucks— Model A	$ 78,107	10.21	10/75
8,800	Plastic trucks— Model B	89,848	10.21	10/75
2,500	Bionic dolls— large	27,650	11.06	10/75
1,970	Bionic dolls— small	21,788	11.06	10/75
5,560	Garments	36,807	6.62	10/75
	Total	$ 254,200		
9,000	Plastic trucks— Model A	$ 91,890	10.21	11/75
12,000	Plastic trucks— Model B	122,520	10.21	11/75
14,000	Bionic dolls— large	154,840	11.06	11/75
15,500	Bionic dolls— small	171,430	11.06	11/75
10,000	Garments	66,200	6.62	11/75
	Total	$ 606,880		
18,000	Plastic trucks— Model A	$ 183,780	10.21	12/75
24,000	Plastic trucks— Model B	245,040	10.21	12/75
25,000	Bionic dolls— large	276,500	11.06	12/75
29,000	Bionic dolls— small	320,740	11.06	12/75
18,000	Garments	119,160	6.63	12/75
	Total	$1,145,220		
	Grand total	$4,256,503		

EXHIBIT 11

XYZ COMPANY
Account 1100 (Summarized and Grouped)

Quantity	Description	Original cost	Annual deprec. expense	Accum. deprec. 12/31/75	Ref. Exhibit
76	Office furniture and fixtures	$ 6,649	$1,108	$2,379	3
225	Cafeteria equipment (utility trays)	2,607	434	1,195	3
21	Plant equipment	1,518	253	640	3
6	Office machines	2,973	496	931	3
6	Fire extinguishers	270	45	83	3
		$14,017	$2,336	$5,228	

(3) The injection molding machines are not summarized because grouping them across vintage years would cause inaccuracies in the replacement cost results.

(4) The unique machine will be direct priced.

(5) The other machinery and equipment items are grouped because of the low costs involved. The same index used for the general machinery and equipment group will be used in this case.

c. Other Assets—Account 1300 (Exhibit 13)

(1) Land is not valued at replacement cost. It is, however, included for balancing purposes.

EXHIBIT 12

XYZ COMPANY
Account 1200 (Summarized and Grouped)

Quantity	Description	Original cost	Annual deprec. expense	Accum. deprec. 12/31/75	Ref. Exhibit
8	Sewing machines	$ 5,659	$ 566	$ 1,462	4
13	Sewing machines	13,721	1,373	2,172	4
5	Sewing machines	6,804	680	1,361	4
14	Sewing machines	6,006	601	601	4
1	Plastic machine	33,933	5,393	6,787	4
1	Plastic machine	75,582	7,558	7,558	4
1	Plastic machine	60,139	6,014	12,028	4
1	Injection mold machine	56,678	7,085	49,593	4
1	Injection mold machine	61,024	7,628	45,768	4
1	Injection mold machine	56,677	6,297	44,082	4
1	Injection mold machine	64,207	8,026	48,155	4
1	Injection mold machine	41,181	4,118	37,062	4
1	Injection mold machine	38,911	3,891	31,129	4
1	Unique machine	200,000	13,333	133,333	4
5	Other machinery and equipment	21,174	2,369	5,371	4
		$741,696	$72,932	$426,462	

EXHIBIT 13

XYZ COMPANY
Account 1300 (Summarized and Grouped)

Quantity	Description	Original cost	Annual deprec. expense	Accum. deprec. 12/31/75	Ref. Exhibit
4.68 acres	Land	$188,972			
1	Building	607,895	$20,263	$20,263	5
1	500-ton molding machine*				
1	500-ton molding machine	78,106	9,763	16,272	5
1	500-ton molding machine*				
15	Nonessential machines	9,050	938	2,365	5
		$884,023	$30,964	$38,900	

*Machine acquired on an operating lease basis, not included in asset total.

(2) The building replacement cost is measured using the unit cost technique. The data for the building measurement is shown in Exhibit 14. The building is subdivided and classified into its subsystems and the dimension measures for the subsystems are collected using blueprints, engineering estimates, etc.

(3) There are three leased 500-ton molding machines. One lease is treated as a financing lease and the machine is shown among the firm's assets on the balance sheet. The other two leases are treated as operating leases, although one of them meets the criteria of the SEC *ASR No. 147* for a financing lease and must be treated as being capitalized for the purpose of replacement cost disclosure and of footnote disclosure on leases.

(4) The remaining assets consist of 15 nonessential machines which are treated as a single group. All of these will be valued at acquisition cost in the replacement cost measurements.

3. Inventories
   a. Raw Materials—Account 2400
   As shown in Exhibit 15, the account for raw materials is summarized into three main classes of raw materials, and two items which are obsolete are entered separately as exclusions. (These exclusions are the last two entries in Exhibit 15.) The raw material item polyethylene is being purchased under a long-term contract at $0.28 per pound from Vendor Company. The year-end price for this item is $0.30 per pound, but following SEC Staff Accounting Bulletin (SAB) No. 7 guidelines, the contract price is used to measure the replacement cost for this item.

   b. Work in Process—Account 2500
   Work in Process is summarized into three groups, and two average standard costs are associated with the categories. The constraints for grouping are as follows:
   (1) The different standard costs
   (2) Percentage completed
      The grouping method for a product with the same standard cost, but having different quantities at various stages of completion, is to average or weight the percent completed by the quantities to calculate an average percent completed. This calculation is used for the product groups with the same standard cost, but at various stages of completion.

EXHIBIT 14

XYZ COMPANY
Account 1300
Building Portion

System component	Unit of measure	Dimension	Unit cost	Total cost	Source
Site work	SITSF	408,000			Engr. dept.
Foundation	BLDSF	34,000			Engr. dept.
Floor	BLDSF	34,000			Engr. dept.
Interior columns	COLLF	192			Engr. dept.
Roof	RFSF	34,000			Engr. dept.
Exterior walls	WLSF	13,990			Engr. dept.
Exterior glazed openings	OPGSF	663			Engr. dept.
Interior walls	WLSF	8,429			Engr. dept.
Doors	DRSF	758			Engr. dept.
Specialty	BLDSF	34,000			Engr. dept.
Plumbing	FIXTR	42			Engr. dept.
Heating and ventilating	BLDSF	34,000			Engr. dept.
Electrical	BLDSF	34,000			Engr. dept.

Component	Description	Unit of measure
1. Site work	Measure total square feet of site. For parking areas determine the number of cars or the square feet of paved area. For sidewalks measure the square feet. For streets measure the square feet.	SITSF
2. Foundation	Measure the total building square feet. The measurement does not include basement walls or floors.	BLDGSF
3. Floor	Measure the total enclosed area. Include in the measurement all balconies, porches, and basements.	BLDGSF
4. Interior columns	Measure the columns in linear feet. Include the vertical interior columns and pilasters above the foundation. Do not include loadbearing walls or any load-bearing components of walls or structural members.	COLLF
5. Roof system	Measure total waterproofed roofed area.	RFSF
6. Exterior walls	Measure the total square feet of exterior walls including basement walls. Do not deduct for normal doors and windows. This measurement includes all structural members contained in the walls, including exterior finishes, insulation, core, and interior finishes.	EWSF
7. Exterior glazed openings	Measure in total square feet of the actual openings. This measurement includes frames, finishes, and type of glass or panels.	OPGSF
8. Interior walls	Measure in total wall square feet without deduction for normal doors.	IWSF
9. Doors	Measure total square feet of door openings including movable closures.	DRSF
10. Specialties	The inclusions are all the elements that make the building operative for its specific purpose.	BLDGSF
11. Plumbing	Count the number of normal fixtures. This does not include special fixtures for sprinkler systems, etc.	FIXT
12. Heating and ventilating	Measure total enclosed area. Where air conditioning is included, the tonnage of the air conditioning system is measured.	BLDGSF (tons)
13. Electrical	Measure the total enclosed area of the building.	BLDGSF

EXHIBIT 15

XYZ COMPANY
Account 2400 (Summarized and Grouped)

Quantity	Description	Cost	Standard cost	Ref. Exhibit
2,300,000	Polyethylene	$ 621,000	$0.27	6
1,130,000	Rubber nitrate	666,700	0.59	6
533,744	Cotton print cloth	240,185	0.45	6
500,000	Polyethylene I.D.	125,000	0.25	6
200	Metal	1,000	5.00	6
		$1,653,885		

For the plastic trucks, the average percent completed calculation is

$$\frac{(55,000 \times .25) + (60,000 \times .25) + (20,000 \times .50)}{135,000}$$

$$= \frac{38,750}{135,000} = .287 \text{ or } 28.7\%$$

For the bionic dolls, the average percent completed calculation is

$$\frac{(32,000 \times .25) + (52,000 \times .30) + (33,000 \times .50)}{117,000}$$

$$= \frac{40,100}{117,000} = .343 \text{ or } 34.3\%$$

Garments cannot easily be summarized in one group because of the differing labor components of the several items. The best approximation of the average percentage completed for garments with the same standard cost is

$$\frac{(39,885 \times .75) + (22,500 \times .80)}{62,385} = \frac{47,913.75}{62,385.00} = .768 \text{ or } 76.8\%$$

The summarized account for Work in Process is shown in Exhibit 16.
c. Finished Goods—Account 2600
The Finished Goods account is summarized into three main items as shown in Exhibit 17.

EXHIBIT 16

XYZ COMPANY
Account 2500—Work in Process (Summarized)

Quantity	Description	Cost	Standard cost	Average % completed	Ref. Exhibit
38,750	Plastic trucks	$216,302	$5.5820	28.7	7
40,100	Bionic dolls	230,098	5.7381	34.3	7
47,914	Garments	176,874	3.6915	76.8	7
73,920	Cut pieces of cloth	112,344	1.5198		
		$735,618			

EXHIBIT 17

XYZ COMPANY
Account 2600—Finished Goods (Summarized)

Quantity	Description	Cost	Standard cost	Ref. Exhibit
52,000	Plastic trucks	$290,264	$5.5820	8
82,700	Bionic dolls	474,541	5.7381	8
44,900	Garments	165,748	3.6915	8
		$930,553		

d. Cost of Goods Sold—Account 3700

LIFO accounting is used for inventories. Using LIFO, cost of goods sold closely approximates replacement cost of goods sold at time of sale. To reflect replacement cost more accurately, the depreciation component of the standard cost should be based on replacement costs for the fixed assets. After the replacement cost measurement is calculated for the fixed assets, the cost of goods sold is grouped by similar standard costs to update the depreciation components. The standard cost changed two times during the year. Therefore, for accuracy, all sales with similar standard costs are summarized by calendar quarters. Summarized cost of goods sold is shown in Exhibit 18.

EXHIBIT 18

XYZ COMPANY
Account 3700—Cost of Goods Sold (Summarized)

Quantity	Description	Cost	Standard cost	Date	Ref. Exhibit
66,850	Plastic trucks	$ 389,869	$5.8320	4/75	9
59,400	Bionic dolls	355,693	5.9881	4/75	9
17,000	Garments	67,006	3.9415	4/75	9
		$ 812,568			
38,469	Plastic trucks	$ 232,045	6.0320	8/75	9
21,584	Bionic dolls	133,564	6.1881	8/75	9
12,402	Garments	51,363	4.1415	8/75	9
		$ 416,972			
105,440	Plastic trucks	$ 646,558	6.1320	12/75	9
110,610	Bionic dolls	695,527	6.2881	12/75	9
47,890	Garments	203,125	4.2415	12/75	9
		$1,545,210			
		$2,774,750			

Replacement Cost Measurements

1. Replacement cost calculations

   a. Furniture and Fixtures—Account 1100 (Exhibit 11), replacement cost data shown in Exhibits 19 and 20.

   For each asset category within this account select the appropriate WPI index series. Index the historical original cost by vintage year to calculate replacement cost.

   b. Machinery and Equipment—Account 1200 (Exhibit 12), replacement cost data shown in Exhibits 21 and 22.

   (1) The sewing machines were indexed using the WPI index for sewing machines following the same procedure as followed for furniture and fixtures.

EXHIBIT 19

XYZ COMPANY
Account 1100—Furniture and Fixtures
Replacement Cost

Ref. Exhibit	Description	Index factor	Unit repl. cost	Gross repl. cost	Period repl. deprec.	Accum. repl. deprec.	Net repl. cost
11	Office furniture and fixtures	1.42		$ 9,442	$1,573	$3,378	$ 6,064
11	Cafeteria equipment (utility trays)	1.30		3,389	564	1,554	1,835
11	Plant equipment	1.43		2,171	362	915	1,256
11	Office machines	1.05		3,122	521	978	2,144
11	Fire extinguishers	1.21		327	54	100	227
				$18,451	$3,074	$6,925	$11,526

(2) The plastic machines were direct priced using current quantities and prices for materials and labor. The direct pricing results is a replacement cost of $182,000 for two of the machines and $179,000 for the third.

(3) The injection molding machines were direct priced resulting in a replacement cost of $87,900 for three of the machines, $110,000 for a fourth, and $64,900 for the fifth.

(4) Because of technological considerations, the replacement cost of the unique machine was measured using the functional pricing technique. The replacement cost of a functional equivalent of the unique asset was calculated using the procedure described in detail in the section on functional pricing (pp. 46-35 to 46-43). The gross replacement cost of a machine to replace the unique machine was $800,000, but because of its greater capacity and operating savings, the replacement cost new of a functional equivalent was calculated to be $475,425. Assuming that such a calculation was in accord with SEC requirements, that number would form the basis for replacement depreciation calculations. The XYZ Company uses the straight-line method of depreciation for its original cost records, so it would also use it for the replacement cost calculations. Even if the company had

EXHIBIT 20

XYZ COMPANY
Account 1100—Furniture and Fixtures
Replacement Cost

Description	Index factor	Original cost	Gross repl. cost	Period deprec. original cost	Period repl. deprec.	Accum. deprec. original cost	Accum. repl. deprec.
Office furniture and fixtures	1.42	$ 6,649	$ 9,442	$1,108	$1,573	$2,379	$3,378
Cafeteria equipment (utility trays)	1.30	2,607	3,389	434	564	1,195	1,554
Plant equipment	1.43	1,518	2,171	253	362	640	915
Office machines	1.05	2,973	3,122	496	521	931	978
Fire extinguishers	1.21	270	327	45	54	83	100
Total		$14,017	$18,451	$2,336	$3,074	$5,227	$6,925

EXHIBIT 21

XYZ COMPANY
Account 1200—Machinery and Equipment
Replacement Cost

Ref. Exhibit	Description	Index factor	Unit repl. cost	Gross repl. cost	Period repl. deprec.	Accum. repl. deprec.	Net repl. cost
12	Sewing machines	1.31		$ 7,413	$ 741	$ 1,915	$ 5,498
12	Sewing machines	1.23		16,877	1,689	2,672	14,205
12	Sewing machines	1.23		8,369	836	1,674	6,695
12	Sewing machines	1.15		6,907	691	691	6,216
12	Plastic machine		$182,000	182,000	18,186	36,378	145,622
12	Plastic machine		182,000	182,000	18,215	18,215	163,785
12	Plastic machine		179,000	179,000	17,922	35,843	143,157
12	Injection molding machine		87,900	87,900	10,982	76,869	11,031
12	Injection molding machine		87,900	87,900	10,984	65,906	21,994
12	Injection molding machine		87,900	87,900	9,760	68,327	19,573
12	Injection molding machine		87,900	87,900	10,996	65,972	21,928
12	Injection molding machine		64,900	64,900	6,506	58,558	6,342
12	Injection molding machine		110,000	110,000	11,012	88,095	21,905
12	Unique machine*		475,425	475,425	31,733	317,333	158,092
12	Plant equipment	1.43		30,279	3,388	7,681	22,598
				$1,614,770	$153,641	$846,129	$768,641

*The replacement cost depreciation figures in this schedule do not agree with the figures in the text owing to using only two decimal places in the calculation of the ratio.

used an accelerated depreciation method for its original cost records, *ASR No. 190* would still require the replacement cost calculation to be made using the straight-line method.

The results of the depreciation calculations are summarized in Table 2.

c. Other Assets—Account 1300 (Exhibit 13)

(1) The unit cost for the building components are obtained from construction cost estimating manuals and computer data banks. These unit costs are adjusted mathematically using multiple regression techniques based on their price movements to adjust for time and location (Exhibit 23). The unit cost multiplied by the dimension measures the total replacement cost of the system components. Adding the replacement costs of all the building components and of contractor's over-

EXHIBIT 22

XYZ COMPANY
Account 1200—Machinery and Equipment
Replacement Cost

Multiple	Unit repl. cost	Index factor	Original cost	Gross repl. cost	Period deprec.	Period repl. deprec.	Accum. deprec.	Accum. repl. deprec.
		1.31	$ 5,659	$ 7,413	$ 566	$ 741	$ 1,462	$ 1,915
		1.23	13,721	1,689	1,373	1,689	2,172	2,672
		1.23	6,804	8,369	680	836	1,361	1,674
		1.15	6,006	6,907	601	691	601	691
5.36	$182,000		33,933	182,000	3,393	18,186	6,787	36,378
2.41	182,000		75,582	182,000	7,558	18,215	7,558	18,215
2.98	179,000		60,139	179,000	6,014	17,922	12,028	35,843
1.55	87,900		56,677	87,900	7,085	10,982	49,593	76,869
1.44	87,900		61,024	87,900	7,628	10,984	45,768	65,906
1.55	87,900		56,678	87,900	6,297	9,760	44,082	68,327
1.37	87,900		64,207	87,900	8,026	10,996	48,155	65,972
1.58	64,900		41,181	64,900	4,118	6,506	37,062	58,558
2.83	110,000		38,911	110,000	3,891	11,012	31,129	88,095
2.38	475,425		200,000	475,425	13,333	31,733*	133,333	317,333*
		1.43	21,174	30,279	2,369	3,388	5,371	7,681
			$741,696		$72,932	$153,641	$426,462	$846,129

*The replacement cost depreciation figures in this schedule do not agree with the figures in the text owing to using only two decimal places in the calculation of the ratio.

head provides the replacement cost for the total building as shown in Exhibit 23.

(2) The leased machines are direct priced to a replacement cost of $122,500 each. Each of the machines is treated differently in the accounts. Machine #1 is capitalized on the books and is also so treated for replacement cost purposes. Machine #2 is accounted for in the formal records as being acquired on an operating lease, but since it meets the criteria of *ASR No. 147,* it is treated as a capitalized item in the replacement cost schedules. The third leased machine, #3, does not meet the *ASR No. 147* tests for treatment on a financing lease basis and is valued at historic cost in the replacement cost schedules.

In the cost calculations under replacement cost, depreciation on a replacement cost basis of machine #2 is included. The rental cost of that machine is included as an operating cost in the formal records, but is excluded in the replacement cost schedules. Depreciation of machine #1, but not its rental cost, is included in both the formal records and the replacement cost schedules. Rental cost, but not depreciation, of machine #3 is included in both sets of records.

(3) The other assets are nonessential to the productive process and are measured at historical cost. Replacement costs for other assets are shown in Exhibits 24 and 25.

TABLE 2   Summary of Depreciation Calculations

Historic cost	$200,000
Period depreciation (SL)	13,333
Accumulated depreciation (SL)	133,333
Net after depreciation	66,667
Gross replacement cost	$475,425
Period depreciation (SL)	31,695
Accumulated depreciation (SL)	316,950
Net replacement cost	158,475

EXHIBIT 23

XYZ COMPANY
Account 1301—Building Replacement Cost

System component	Unit of measure	Dimension	Unit cost	Total cost
Sitework	SITSF	408,000	0.36	$146,880
Foundation	BLDSF	34,000	0.42	14,280
Floor	BLDSF	34,000	1.18	40,120
Interior columns	COLLF	192	12.59	2,417
Exterior walls	WLSF	13,990	2.09	29,239
Exterior glazed opg.	OPGSF	663	5.32	3,527
Interior walls	WLSF	8,429	2.17	18,290
Doors	DRSF	758	4.00	3,032
Specialty	BLDSF	34,000	0.06	2,040
Plumbing	FIXTR	42	1,100.96	46,240
Heating and ventilation	BLDSF	34,000	0.65	22,100
Electrical	BLDSF	34,000	0.99	33,660
Roof	RFSF	34,000	5.12	174,080
Total direct cost				$535,905
Overhead (19%)*				101,822
Total replacement cost				$637,727
Original cost				$607,895

*Overhead percentage is derived from contractor's records as costs incurred for architectural fees, engineering fees, and other indirect costs.

    d. Inventories
       (1) Raw Materials—Account 2400 (Exhibit 15)
          Replacement costs for raw materials are measured by direct prices from current market quotes and long-term contract price for polyethylene. The replacement cost of raw materials inventory is shown in the upper portion of Exhibit 27.
       (2) Work in Process—Account 2500 (Exhibit 16)
          Finished Goods—Account 2600 (Exhibit 17) and Cost of Goods

EXHIBIT 24

XYZ COMPANY
Other Assets—Replacement Cost

Acct. no.	Ref. Exhibit	Description	Unit repl. cost	Gross repl. cost	Period repl. deprec.	Accum. repl. deprec.	Net repl. cost
1310	5	500-ton mold #1	$122,500	$122,500	$15,328	$25,547	$ 96,953
1310	5	Machine #2	122,500	122,500	15,328	25,547	96,953
1300	5	Other assets		9,050	938	2,365	6,685
1301	5	Building		637,727	21,258	21,258	616,469
1301	5	Exclusions 500-ton mold machine #3					
1320	5	Land					

EXHIBIT 25

XYZ COMPANY
Other Assets—Replacement Cost

Acct. no.	Unit repl. cost	Original cost	Gross repl. cost	Period deprec. original cost	Period repl. deprec.	Accum. deprec. original cost	Accum. repl. deprec.
1310	122,500 #1	$ 78,106	$122,500	$ 9,763	$15,328	$16,272	$25,547
	122,500 #2	78,106	122,500		15,328		25,547
1300		9,050	9,050	938	938	2,365	2,365
1301		607,895	638,470	20,263	21,276	20,263	21,276
	Total		$892,520	$30,964	$52,870	$38,900	$74,735
	Exclusions						
1301	Leased machine #3	78,106					
1320	Land	188,972					

EXHIBIT 26

XYZ COMPANY
Schedule of Standard Costs

	Opening inventory	To 4/30/75		To 8/31/75		To 12/31/75	
	Original cost	Original cost	Repl. cost	Original cost	Repl. cost	Original cost	Repl. cost
Plastic trucks	$5.5820	$5.8320	$6.8842	$6.0320	$7.1219	$6.1320	$7.2407
Bionic dolls	5.7381	5.9881	7.0696	6.1881	7.3073	6.2881	7.4261
Garments	3.6915	3.9415	4.6368	4.1415	4.8751	4.2415	4.9939
Cut pieces						1.5198	1.8064

Sold—Account 3700 (Exhibit 18) must be restated in replacement cost terms. The standard cost of each product must be recalculated taking into account the changed depreciation costs, the reduction in other manufacturing costs, and the replacement cost of raw materials. The XYZ Company has prepared a table of replacement standard costs for each of the three relevant dates. That table is shown in Exhibit 26. The replacement cost of work in process and finished goods inventories is shown in Exhibit 27. The replacement cost of goods sold is shown in Exhibit 28.

The Balance Sheet and Income Statement for XYZ Company on a replacement cost basis for fixed assets and inventories are displayed in Exhibits 29 and 30. The notes to those two statements are presented in Exhibit 31. Note that the holding gains, both realized and unrealized, do not enter into the income calculation but are credited directly to a special stockholders' equity account.

TECHNOLOGICAL FACTORS

There are three basic methods of accounting for technological change: use of an index series which adjusts for technological change (e.g., subsets of the Wholesale Price Index), use of indexes developed within the firm, and direct measurement.

Available Index Series. The Wholesale Price Index is a modified Laspeyres index composed of homogeneous aggregates of commodity prices representative of a class of prices known or assumed to move similarly. It is calculated as follows:

EXHIBIT 27

XYZ COMPANY
Raw Materials, Work in Process, Finished Goods
Replacement Cost

Acct. no.	Description	Quantity	Standard unit cost	Original cost	Repl. standard unit cost	Gross repl. cost	Net realizable value
2400	Polyethylene	2,300,000	$0.27	$ 621,000	$0.28	$ 644,000	
2400	Rubber nitrate	1,130,000	0.59	666,700	0.61	689,300	
2400	Cotton print cloth	533,744	0.45	240,185	0.49	261,535	
2400	Polyethylene I.D.*	500,000	0.25	125,000			$75,000
2400	Metal*	200	5.00	1,000			600
	Total			$1,653,885		$1,594,835	$75,600
2500	Plastic trucks	38,750	5.5820	$ 215,302	7.2407	$ 280,577	
2500	Bionic dolls	40,100	5.7381	230,098	7.4261	297,787	
2500	Garments	47,914	3.6915	176,874	4.9939	239,278	
2500	Cut pieces	73,920	1.5198	112,344	1.8064	133,529	
	Total			$ 735,618		$ 951,171	
2600	Plastic trucks	52,000	5.5820	$ 290,264	7.2407	376,516	
2600	Bionic dolls	82,700	5.7381	474,541	7.4261	614,138	
2600	Garments	44,900	3.6915	165,748	4.9939	224,226	
	Total			$ 930,553		$1,214,880	
	Grand total			$3,320,056		$3,760,886	$75,600

*Obsolete.

EXHIBIT 28

XYZ COMPANY
Account 3700
Replacement Cost of Goods Sold

Description	Quantity	Standard unit cost	Original cost	Repl. standard unit cost	Gross repl. cost	Date of sale
Plastic trucks	66,850	5.8320	$ 389,869	$6.8842	$ 460,209	4/75
Bionic dolls	59,400	5.9881	355,693	7.0696	419,934	4/75
Garments	17,000	3.9415	67,006	4.6368	78,826	4/75
Total			$ 812,568		$ 958,969	
Plastic trucks	38,469	6.0320	$ 232,045	7.1219	$ 273,972	8/75
Bionic dolls	21,584	6.1881	133,564	7.3073	157,721	8/75
Garments	12,399	4.1415	51,351	4.8751	60,446	8/75
Total			$ 416,960		$ 492,139	
Plastic trucks	105,442	6.1320	$ 646,570	7.2407	$ 763,474	12/75
Bionic dolls	110,610	6.2881	695,527	7.4261	821,401	12/75
Garments	47,890	4.2415	203,125	4.9939	239,158	12/75
Total			$1,545,222		$1,824,033	
Grand total			$2,774,750		$3,275,141	

The difference between the original cost and gross replacement cost represents the realized holding gain.

EXHIBIT 29

XYZ COMPANY
(Replacement Cost) Balance Sheet
December 31, 1975

Assets

Current assets:

Cash		$ 25,288	
Marketable securities at cost (market value $30,881)		29,925	
Notes receivable		7,213	
Accounts receivable		89,462	
Inventories		3,836,486	
Prepaid insurance		2,200	
Total current assets			$3,990,574

Noncurrent assets:

Land		$ 188,972	
Building	$ 637,727		
Furniture and fixtures	18,451		
Machinery and equipment	1,614,770		
Leased assets	245,000		
Other assets	9,050		
	$2,524,998		
Accumulated depreciation	927,771	1,597,227	
Total noncurrent assets			1,786,199
Total assets			$5,776,773

Liabilities and Stockholders' Equity

Current liabilities:

Bank loans		$ 50,000	
Accounts payable		68,790	
Wages payable and other accruals		49,800	
Estimated income taxes payable		42,250	
Total current liabilities			$ 210,840

Long-term liability:

Long-term lease obligation			128,000
Total liabilities			$ 338,840

Stockholders equity:

Common stock		$2,370,435	
Retained earnings		1,497,620	
Realized holding gains[11]		500,396	
Unrealized holding gains:			
On inventory[12]		516,430	
On plant assets[13]		553,052	
Total stockholders' equity			5,437,933
Total liabilities and stockholders' equity			$5,776,773

Symbolically:

$$I_n^L = 100 - \frac{\Sigma_i\, p_{ni}\, q_{0i}}{\Sigma_i\, p_{0i} q_{0i}}$$

where I_n^L = index number for year n (Laspeyres)

p_{ni} = price at year n of item i

p_{0i} = price at year zero (base year) of item i

q_{0i} = quantity at year zero (base year) of item i

Σ_i = sum over all items

EXHIBIT 30

XYZ COMPANY
(Replacement Cost) Income Statement
For the Year Ending December 31, 1975

Net sales			$4,256,503
Cost of goods sold:			
On historic cost basis		$2,774,750	
Adjustment to replacement cost basis[11]		500,396	
Replacement cost of goods sold			3,275,146
Gross margin			$ 981,357
Selling expenses:			
Sales salaries	$	85,438	
Advertising		42,850	
Travel and entertainment		11,713	
Freight and delivery		5,775	
Consultant fees		9,700	155,476
General and administrative expenses:			
Officers salaries	$	95,625	
Office salaries		73,305	
Taxes		10,925	
Insurance		2,350	
Utilities		10,163	
Uncollected accounts expense		11,750	204,118
Total operating expenses			$ 359,594
Net operating income			$ 621,763
Other revenue and expenses:			
Interest and dividends earned	$	7,750	
Rent revenue		24,250	
	$	32,000	
Less interest expense		11,700	20,300
Net income before income taxes			$ 601,463
Estimated income taxes			288,704
Net income			$ 312,759
Retained earnings, 12/31/74			1,184,861
Retained earnings, 12/31/75			$1,497,420

For example, consider two commodities, A and B, with the following prices and quantities purchased:

	Item A		Item B	
Year	Price	Quantity	Price	Quantity
1	$10.00	100	$10.00	100
2	11.00	95	10.50	105
3	12.10	90	14.05	110
4	13.30	85	11.60	115
5	14.70	80	12.20	120

The price of A increases by approximately 10 percent per year while the price of B increases by approximately 5 percent per year. The total quantity of A and B purchased remains constant at 200 per year, but more B and less A is purchased as the price of B declines *relative* to A.

The aggregate sum of the prices and quantities is shown in Exhibit 32.

The Laspeyres index series derived from these prices and quantities is as follows:

EXHIBIT 31   Notes to Financial Statements

1. The following accounts are stated at replacement cost:
   A. Plant Assets
   B. Inventories
   C. Cost of Goods Sold
2. The replacement cost of the following accounts were computed using WPI indices:
   A. Furniture and fixtures
   B. Sewing machines
3. The replacement cost of the building was computed on the basis of unit costs of the building components.
4. The replacement cost of the unique machine was computed after allowing for net effects of replacement on operating costs and depreciation.
5. One of the leased molding machines that qualifies as a financing lease under *ASR No. 147* and is presently expensed, was treated as a capitalized asset for the replacement cost calculations.
6. Assets not essential to the production process were valued at historical cost.
7. The standard costs for work in process and finished goods were updated to reflect depreciation on the replacement cost of fixed assets and the effects on operating costs. The updated standard costs used to value the two accounts are current standard costs as of 12/31/75.
8. The standard costs for cost of goods sold were updated at each point of sale to reflect the operating costs and depreciation on the replacement cost of fixed assets.
9. The depreciation expense for the period and accumulated depreciation was estimated on the basis of the average replacement cost of fixed assets using the straight-line method.
10. The raw material replacement cost was computed using:
   A. The long-term contract price for items being purchased under contract agreements in excess of two years.
   B. Current market prices as of 12/31/75.
11. Realized holding gains are measured by the difference between the replacement cost and historical cost of goods sold. They include realized holding gains on plant assets.
12. The unrealized holding gain on inventories is equal to the excess of replacement cost over historical cost of inventories at year end. Since this is the first year that replacement costs have been recognized, the ending balance and the increase during the year are the same. In subsequent years the increase in the balance will be the difference between the excess at the end of the year and the excess at the start of the year.
13. The unrealized holding gain on plant assets is equal to the excess of replacement cost over historical cost of net plant assets at year end, after allowing for the leased molding machine described in note 5. Also see the second sentence of note 12.

EXHIBIT 32   Data for Price Index Computations

Year	Total value of base year (0) quantities at current year (i) prices* $\Sigma_i\, p_{ni}q_{0i}$	Total value of current year (i) quantities at current year (i) prices† $\Sigma\, p_{ni}q_{ni}$	Total value of current year (i) quantities at base year prices‡ $\Sigma\, p_{0i}q_{ni}$
1	$2,000	$2,000	$2,000
2	2,150	2,148	2,000
3	2,315	2,305	2,000
4	2,490	2,465	2,000
5	2,690	2,640	2,000

*Numerator of Laspeyres index.
†Numerator of Paasche index.
‡Denominator of Paasche index. The equality of number in this column is an artifact of the example (caused by total purchases remaining constant at 200 units per year) and need not occur in general.

Year	Laspeyres index = $\dfrac{\text{total value of base year quantities at year } (i) \text{ prices}}{\$2{,}000}$
1	100.0
2	107.5
3	115.8
4	124.5
5	134.5

The total value weighted by the base year quantities is greater than the total value weighted by the actual yearly quantities, thus giving the Laspeyres index an upward bias when increased prices cause substitution of one commodity for another.

The use of the Wholesale Price Index where technological change has taken place may or may not properly measure the replacement value of an asset. Because the Wholesale Price Index is a Laspeyres index, it is weighted by base year quantities. The Wholesale Price Index will properly account for technological change:

Fully—When none of the constituent items has been obsoleted and when the changes which have occurred do not substantially change the actual quantities bought.

Partially—When an item has been obsoleted and its substitute has been "linked" into the Wholesale Price Index. Since the item has been obsoleted over a period of time, replacing the item with its substitute at a specific point in time does not account for the length of time it took for the substitute to replace the item.

Not at all—When the technological change that has occurred has caused a significant change in the proportion of the item's representation in the index. For example, technological change causing a large reduction in price and also causing an increase in the number purchased. Since the base year quantities are used in the index, only the decrease in price and not the increase in purchases has been accounted for.

Indexes Developed in the Firm.   The use of indexes developed in the firm can substitute for available index series where the available series do not adequately measure the effects of technological change. Where sufficient data to derive an index series exists, the internally developed indexes can adequately measure technological change by using a modified Paasche Index.

$$I_n^P = 100 \times \frac{\Sigma_i\, p_{ni} q_{ni}}{\Sigma_i\, p_{0i} q_{ni}}$$

where I_n^P = index number for year n (Paasche)
p_{ni} = price at year n of item i
p_{0i} = price at year zero (base year) of item i
q_{ni} = quantity at year n of item i
q_{0i} = quantity at year zero (base year) of item i
Σ_i = sum over all items

If we take the data previously used for the Laspeyres index series calculation and the summary in Exhibit 32, we derive the following Paasche index numbers:

Year	Paasche index = $\dfrac{\text{(total value of year } i \text{ quantities at year } i \text{ prices)}}{\text{(total value of year } i \text{ quantities at base year prices)}}$
1	100.0
2	107.4
3	115.3
4	123.3
5	132.0

The two index series are, then:

Year	Laspeyres (base year quantities)	Paasche (current year quantities)
1	100.0	100.0
2	107.5	107.4
3	115.8	115.3
4	124.5	123.3
5	134.5	132.0

Over the five-year period in the example, the price of A increased by about 10 percent each year while the price of B increased by about 5 percent each year. The Laspeyres index shows an average price increase of about 7.7 percent $(= \sqrt[4]{1.345} - 1)$, while the Paasche index shows an average price increase of about 7.2 percent $(= \sqrt[4]{1.32} - 1)$. The Paasche index reflects the substitution of B for A while the Laspeyres index does not.

The difference between the Laspeyres and Paasche indexes is the treatment of the current year quantities (q_n). The Paasche index recognizes changes in quantities purchased as well as the prices at which these quantities were purchased. Where technological change has occurred and relative prices have changed, more of the relatively lower-priced item will be sold (or purchased) and it is proper to recognize the changing quantity mix in constructing an index. The Laspeyres index ignores the effect of technological change upon prices when technological change affects the mix of commodities within the index. For this reason, we recommend the use of a Paasche index which is based on current quantities.

Direct Measurement. Direct measurement of technological change involves the same concepts and techniques used in capital budgeting. When technological change has occurred, a newer improved asset is available to replace the current asset. Because the newer asset is technologically improved, it is capable of being used at a lower cost.

The cost of a production process under a scheduled annual capacity is dependent upon many individual factors. These factors must be explicitly taken into account in formulating the replacement cost of a machine. The following factors are quantified in dollars to determine the operating costs of a machine and its probable replacement:

1. Rate of production
2. Set-up time
3. Set-up costs
4. Average cost of periodic maintenance
5. Average cost of replactment parts
6. Average time between breakdowns
7. Maximum length of production run
8. Average down time
9. Average waste and salvage
10. Average percentage of rework
11. Availability and cost of maintenance and service contracts
12. Ease of use and operator efficiency
13. Labor requirements

This list is not all-inclusive since all the costs depend on the production process. Any cost which is material should be included. Most of the data may be obtained from production schedules and budgets.

The operating costs for the current machines are derived from the actual costs as reflected in the plant records. The operating costs for the technologically improved replacement are estimated from engineering specifications and the manner in which the machine would actually be used. Engineers are required to make these estimates—that is, by reference to the actual physical processes involved in production.

The unit cost of production will be lower for a technologically improved asset. By applying this unit cost to the currently existing production process and determining the present value of this over the remaining useful life of the asset, we can calculate the replacement cost for the current asset.

FUNCTIONAL PRICING[6]

Functional pricing of productive capacity asks, first, what is the current productive capacity of existing assets in terms of some measure of output. For example, the telephone company might define its functional capacity in terms of calls completable per minute, a manufacturer of freight cars might define functional capacity in terms of cubic feet of freight cars producable per year, and a packing house might define functional capacity in terms of heads of cattle processable per month.

Functional pricing ignores the assets or group of assets currently used to produce a given output per unit of time and asks what is the lowest cost, including capital outlay and present value of future operating cost savings, at which an asset (or group of assets) can be acquired with the same or similar capacity. It takes into account differences in physical capacity, differences in operating costs, and differences in lives between the existing asset (or group of assets) and the replacement asset (or group of assets) in arriving at the economically equivalent price of existing capacity.

The most meaningful measure of replacement cost of productive capacity in an economic sense results from functional pricing of current productive capacity. The economic meaning of the functional price results from its considering more factors than the other methods. Because of its greater data requirements, functional pricing may not always be practicable to use. It cannot be used effectively when the asset(s) being evaluated provides more than one type of service. Functional pricing requires a single output measure.

Illustration.   We illustrate the application of functional pricing with the data shown in Exhibit 33. The first column of Exhibit 33 shows information about an existing asset for which replacement cost information is required. Each of the next five columns shows information about the asset that is most likely to be acquired as the replacement for the existing asset. Only one of these replacement assets is assumed to be available at any one time. The information required for functional pricing includes

- Remaining life of existing asset
- Periodic functional capacity of existing asset
- Periodic operating costs of existing asset
- Cost of replacement asset
- Remaining life of replacement asset
- Periodic functional capacity of replacement asset
- Periodic operating costs of replacement asset
- Discount rate per period to be used in present value computations.

In our examples, we assume a period of one year for both operating costs and functional capacity and a discount rate of 10 percent per year.

The most general, and most likely, situation that will be encountered in actual application of functional pricing is represented by case V, where the replacement assets differs from the existing asset in all important dimensions: life, operating

[6]This section was prepared by Roman L. Weil. It incorporates all pertinent information in the SEC Staff Accounting Bulletins through SAB No. 11, issued in August 1976.

EXHIBIT 33   **Illustrative Data for Demonstration of Functional Pricing**
Discount Rate Is 10 Percent per Year; Operating Costs and Production Occur at Year End

	Existing asset	Replacement asset				
		Case I	Case II	Case III	Case IV	Case V
Cost new	$15,000	$20,000	$20,000	$20,000	$20,000	$20,000
Original life	10 years	10 years	10 years	10 years	12 years	12 years
Remaining life	5 years	10 years	10 years	10 years	12 years	12 years
Annual functional capacity	700 units	700 units	1,000 units	700 units	700 units	1,000 units
Annual operating cost	$1,100	$1,100	$1,100	$1,000	$1,100	$1,000
Replacement cost of functional capacity in new condition	Y	$20,000	$20,000	$20,000	$20,000	$20,000
Replacement cost of functional capacity in current condition	X					
Accumulated depreciation based on replacement cost	$Y - X$					

costs, and functional capacity per year. We illustrate this most general case last, working up to it through a series of simpler cases.

The problem, in all cases, is the identification of the replacement cost of the existing asset in current condition, identified as X in the first column of Exhibit 33. The SEC, however, requires the disclosure of the replacement cost in new condition of the existing asset, Y, as well as the accumulated depreciation on the replacement cost of the existing asset, $Y - X$.

Case I.   The simplest case arises when the replacement asset is identical with the existing asset in all dimensions, except that the replacement asset is new and perhaps has a different acquisition cost. In this case, the replacement cost new of existing functional capacity is the same as the acquisition cost of the replacement asset, $20,000, and the replacement cost of existing capacity in current condition is the fraction of that equal to (remaining life/life new) $= 5/10 = .50$. The existing asset has replacement cost in current condition of $10,000 $(= .50 \times \$20,000)$.

Case II.   Here the replacement asset has a larger functional capacity than the existing asset. Two subcases should be distinguished here and later when functional capacity differs: the replacement asset is "divisible" or the replacement asset is "indivisible." In the illustration, the replacement asset has a functional capacity of 1,000 units per year while the existing asset has a functional capacity of only 700 units per year. The replacement asset is *divisible* if we can acquire a fraction of it (70 percent in the illustration) with all costs proportionately reduced or, which is the same thing, if we have ten of the existing assets which can be replaced with seven of the replacement assets. (In general, if the existing asset has functional capacity equal to Q percent of the replacement asset, then the replacement asset is divisible if Q replacement assets can replace 100 existing assets.)

First, assume divisibility. Then, the existing capacity can be replaced new for the replacement asset's cost multiplied by the fraction

$$\frac{\text{functional capacity of existing asset}}{\text{functional capacity of replacement asset}}$$

In the example, the existing asset has a functional capacity of 70 percent of the replacement asset, so that the replacement cost new, Y, of the existing asset is $14,000 (= .70 × $20,000). In its current condition, the existing asset has a replacement cost, X, of $7,000 (= .50 × $14,000).

If the replacement asset is indivisible, but still is the most cost/effective method of replacing existing capacity, then the multiplication by .70 should be omitted. The replacement cost of existing capacity in new condition is $20,000 and in existing condition is $10,000. The narrative discussion accompanying disclosure of these data should, in our opinion, explain that the replacement cost assumes acquisition of capacity 10/7 as large as existing capacity, but that this extra capacity would not be used for the foreseeable future. Readers of financial statements would probably be best served if they knew of the potential for expansion by the firm without the need for additional capital investment.

Case III.   In this case, the replacement asset has lower operating costs than the existing asset but has the same functional capacity. (In reality, with increasing labor and fuel costs, for example, relative to the costs of durable goods, it is likely that new assets will cost more than old ones, but will be more efficient in the use of fuel and labor.) To find X, the replacement cost of existing capacity in current condition, we shall examine the incremental cash flows from the replacement asset as compared to the existing asset. We ask at what price for existing capacity would the firm be economically indifferent between acquiring today the existing capacity with its implied future costs and acquiring today the replacement asset's capacity with its implied future costs. We answer this question by finding the equal annual cash outlay (annuity) that will acquire the services of the replacement asset. Assume all operating costs occur at year end, all production occurs at year end, and that the discount rate is 10 percent per year. (We assume flows occur at year end so that we can use the table for ordinary annuities at the end of this handbook, Appendix Table 4. Annuities in advance could be handled just as easily.)

The present value of an annuity in arrears of $1 for 10 periods discounted at 10 percent per period is $6.14457 (see Appendix Table 4). Thus the equal annual cash outlay to acquire the replacement asset which costs $20,000 is $3,254.91 (= $20,000/6.14457). The annual operating costs for the replacement asset are $1,000 per year, so the total annual outlay to acquire and use the replacement asset is $4,254.91 (= $3,254.91 + $1,000.00). The existing asset has only five years of life left, so we now compute the present value of the cost of acquiring the services of the replacement asset for five years. This amount is the present value of an annuity in arrears of $4,254.91 for five years. The present value of an annuity of $1 in arrears for five years discounted at 10 percent per year is $3.79079, so the annuity of $4,254.91 has a present value of $16,129.47 (= $4,254.91 × 3.79079). Thus, the present value of the total costs to acquire five years' functional capacity of the replacement asset is $16,129.47.

The existing functional capacity, already owned, costs $1,100 per year in operating costs or a present value of $4,169.87 (= $1,100 × 3.79079) for five years of operations. The difference between the present value of the replacement asset's cost stream and the existing asset's cost stream is $11,959.60 (= $16,129.47 − $4,169.87). Thus the firm can save a present value of $11,960 by using the existing asset rather than replacing it. Put another way, if the firm did not have either asset today and could acquire the replacement asset for $20,000 or could buy the existing asset secondhand, then it would prefer the existing asset if its cost were less than $11,960 and would prefer the replacement asset if the existing asset costs more than $11,960. Thus, in an economic sense, the replacement cost of the existing asset, X, must be $11,960.

This series of calculations can be done in perhaps a more readily understood fashion as follows:

Annual annuity to acquire replacement asset	$ 3,254.91
Annual operating costs to acquire functional output of replacement asset	1,000.00
Total equal annual costs to acquire functional capacity of replacement asset	$ 4,254.91
Less annual operating costs of existing assets	(1,100.00)
Incremental annual costs of acquiring replacement asset	$ 3,154.91
Present value of annuity of incremental annual costs for remaining life of existing asset (5 years): $3,154.91 × 3.79079	$11,959.60

To find Y, the replacement cost of the existing asset in new condition, we merely take the present value of annuity of incremental costs ($3,154.91) for acquiring the replacement asset for the life of the existing asset when new, 10 years in the example. The annuity factor for 10 percent and 10 years is 6.14457. Thus, the existing asset, were it to have 10 years of remaining life, would have a functional replacement cost new of $19,386 (= $3,154.91 × 6.14457). This amount is less than the cost of the replacement asset, $20,000, by $614, which is exactly equal to the present value of the cost savings of $100 per year implied by using the replacement asset rather than the existing asset. This is not surprising, because the only difference between the existing asset and the replacement asset is the operating cost savings of $100 per year. The existing asset must be less valuable to the firm by an amount equal to the present value of its operating cost in excess of the present value of the operating costs of the replacement asset.

The careful reader may wonder at this stage why the functional price of the existing asset in new condition (ten-year life) is $19,386, the asset has been used for half of its useful life when new (for 5 of the 10 years), and the new replacement cost of the existing asset is $11,960, which is *not* equal to half of $19,386. The pure functional pricing approach is based on economic calculations and discounting. It inherently requires a form of compound interest depreciation (see Chapters 8 and 20) if there is to be articulation between replacement costs new and net asset valuation when both are based on functional pricing. This problem is discussed below.

Case IV. Here the replacement asset is like the existing asset except that the replacement asset has a longer life, 12 years, than did the existing asset when new, 10 years. The methodology is the same as in case III, except that the annuity factor computing the present value of the acquisition cost of the replacement asset must be for 12, not for 10, periods. The calculation, parallel to that in case III, is:

Annual annuity to acquire replacement asset (present value factor for 12 periods at 10 percent is 6.81369; $20,000/6.81369 = $2,935.27)	$ 2,935.27
Annual operating costs to acquire functional output of replacement asset	1,100.00
Total equal annual costs to acquire functional capacity of replacement asset	$ 4,035.27
Less annual operating costs of existing asset	(1,100.00)
Incremental annual costs of acquiring replacement asset	$ 2,935.27
Present value of annuity of annual costs for remaining life of existing asset (5 years); $2,935.27 × 3.79079	$11,126.99
Present value of annuity of incremental annual costs for life of existing asset when new (10 years); Y = $2,935.27 × 6.14457	$18,035.97

The replacement cost of the functional capacity of the existing asset in current condition, X, is \$11,126.99 and in new condition (10-year life), Y, is \$18,035.97. (Note here, too, that net replacement cost of the 5-year-old asset is not one-half of replacement cost new, assuming a 10-year life.) The difference between the economic value of the replacement asset new (12-year life) and the economic value of the existing asset new (10-year life) is merely the present value new of the outlays of \$2,935.27 required in years 11 and 12 to obtain the services of the replacement asset's extra two years of productive life. That is, \$20,000 − \$18,036 = \$1,964 and \$1,964 = \$2,935 × $(1.10)^{-11}$ + \$2,935 × $(1.10)^{-12}$.

Case V, Divisible Replacement Asset. Finally, we have the case where the replacement asset differs from the existing asset in all important respects: functional capacity per period, operating costs, and estimated service life of the new asset. First, we treat the case of divisibility, where it is reasonable to assume that only 70 percent of the replacement asset need be acquired or where ten existing assets can be replaced with seven of the new. The computations are shown in Exhibit 34. The replacement cost of the functional capacity of the existing asset in current condition, X, is \$6,272.58; in new condition, Y, \$10,167.36. The difference between the cost of the replacement asset, \$20,000, and the value of the existing asset, if new, \$10,167.36, is caused by the interaction of the shorter life, higher operating costs, and smaller functional capacity of the existing asset. These factors operate to reduce the value of the existing asset as follows:

Divisible replacement asset with 12-year life, 1,000-unit functional capacity, and \$1,000 per year of operating costs	\$20,000.00
But existing asset has 30 percent smaller functional capacity; less 30 percent of \$20,000	(6,000.00)
But existing asset has only 10-year life when new, so we lose the outputs from years 11 and 12 of the replacement asset which have present value of costs of [\$2,754.69 × $(1.10)^{-11}$ + \$2,754.69 × $(1.10)^{-12}$]	(1,843.23)
But existing asset has operating cost disadvantage; present value of operating costs at 10 percent:	
Replacement asset at 70 percent size; \$700 per year for 12 years \$4,796.58	
Existing asset; \$1,100 per year for 10 years .... (6,759.02)	
Present value of operating cost disadvantage of existing asset	(1,989.44)
Economic value of existing asset in new condition with 10-year life	\$10,167.33

Aside from the rounding error, this is the same figure that is computed directly (and more understandably) in Exhibit 34.

REPLACEMENT COST DEPRECIATION. Assume that the replacement asset (case V) had the same characteristics at the beginning of the current year as it does at the end of the year. Then the replacement cost of the functional capacity of the existing asset in new condition would also be \$10,167 at the start of the current year. The SEC requires that replacement cost depreciation be computed on the average of beginning- and end-of-year replacement costs using straight line and the same service life as in the historical cost calculation. The replacement cost depreciation for the current year would be \$1,017 (= \$10,167/10) and the accumulated depreciation on a replacement cost basis would be \$5,084 (= \$10,167 × 5/10) and the net replacement value would be \$5,083 (= \$10,167 − \$5,084). We see from the computations that the economic value of the existing asset in its current condition is \$6,273. The SEC's method would show the net replacement cost as \$5,083 for the existing asset in current condition. The difference arises

EXHIBIT 34   Functional Pricing Illustrated Based on Data in Exhibit 33, Replacement Asset from Case V

	Replacement asset is divisible	Replacement asset is indivisible
Annual annuity to acquire replacement asset (present value factor for 12 periods at 10 percent is 6.81369; $20,000/6.81369 = $2,935.27)	$ 2,935.27	$ 2,935.27
Annual operating costs to produce functional output of replacement asset	1,000.00	1,000.00
Total equal annual costs to acquire replacement asset and to produce its functional capacity	$ 3,935.27	$ 3,935.27
Existing asset has functional capacity equal to 70 percent (= 700/1,000) of replacement asset	× 0.70	
Total equal annual costs to acquire functional capacity equal to that of existing asset in form of replacement asset	$ 2,754.69	
Less annual operating costs of existing asset	(1,100.00)	(1,100.00)
Incremental annual costs of acquiring replacement asset at current functional capacity	$ 1,654.69	$ 2,835.27
Present value of annuity of incremental annual costs for life of existing asset (5 years); $X = \$1,654.69 \times 3.79079$ (divisible); $X = \$2,835.27 \times 3.79079$ (indivisible)	$ 6,272.58	$10,747.91
Present value of annuity of incremental annual costs for life of existing asset when new (10 years); $Y = \$1,654.69 \times 6.14457$ (divisible); $Y = \$2,835.27 \times 6.14457$ (indivisible)	$10,167.36	$17,421.51

because the SEC requires the use of the straight-line depreciation method, while functional pricing, based on economics and present values, implicitly requires a form of compound interest depreciation.

To elaborate, consider the economic value of the existing asset if it had 6 years of life left. Then, it would have a present value equal to the present value of an annuity of $1,654.69 for 6 years. The present value of an annuity of $1 in arrears at 10 percent for 6 years is 4.35526; $1,654.69 × 4.35526 = $7,206.61. The decline in economic value during the current year is $934.03 (= $7,206.61 − $6,272.58 (and depreciation computed on the decline in economic values would be $934.03). Since depreciation in accounting is an allocation of costs to periods of benefit, we need not be overly concerned that the SEC disclosure will report a replacement cost depreciation figure that is different from the decline in value. What is troublesome, however, is that the *net* replacement value of a functionally priced asset is not its current economic value based on current differences between it and the replacement asset, but is based on hypothetical differences between the current replacement asset and the existing asset when new, some years ago.

In terms of the items in Exhibit 33, the SEC allows an economic calculation of Y, with X being derived from an assumption of straight-line depreciation. Better in our view would be an economic calculation of X and a net figure with a straight-line derivation of Y. (That is, if the net replacement cost in current condition is X and the asset has the fraction r/n of its depreciable life remaining, then the replacement cost new is $Y = X \times n/r$.) Then replacement cost depreciation for the year can be based on X, $6,273, and the remaining life of 5 years so that replacement cost depreciation would be reported as $1,255 (= $6,273/5). Best of all, the SEC would allow economic depreciation assumptions in derivations of replacement cost new and net, which would allow both X and Y as well as annual depreciation to be consistent with each other in an economic sense.

Case V, Indivisible Replacement Asset. If the replacement asset is not divisible, then the calculation would be just as in the first column of Exhibit 34, except that the multiplication by .70 would be omitted. This calculation is shown in the second column of Exhibit 34. The incremental annual costs of acquiring the replacement asset would be $2,835.27 (= $2,935.27 + $1,000.00 − $1,100.00). The present value of the existing asset in current condition (5-year life) would be $10,748 (= $2,835.27 × 3.79079) and in new condition (10-year life) would be $17,422 (= $2,835.27 × 6.14457).

SEC Disclosure of Replacement Costs with Functional Pricing. The Staff of the SEC has indicated that the economic calculations in present value terms is not required. For the purposes of this discussion assume the replacement asset is represented by case V in Exhibit 33. All that need be disclosed is the cost of the replacement asset, $20,000. The narrative accompanying the disclosure can, and should, mention the differences in operating costs and differences in functional capacity. Disclosure, including the narrative description of operating cost savings, will provide users with all the needed information so long as the asset being priced is the functional capacity of the firm as a whole. If functional pricing is used separately, for separate groups of assets, then proper aggregation in the narrative will be cumbersome. We discuss this next.

Aggregating Replacement Costs that Have Been Functionally Priced. Exhibit 35 gives data for this example. In that exhibit there are two existing assets each with replacements involving technological improvements. The first existing asset is identical with the one shown in Exhibit 33 and its replacement asset is represented by case V.

EXHIBIT 35   Illustrative Data for Demonstration of Aggregation Problem in Functional Pricing
Operating Costs and Production Occur at Year End; Discount Rate Is 10 Percent per Year

	Asset 1		Asset 2	
	Existing asset	Replacement asset	Existing asset	Replacement asset
Cost new	$15,000	$20,000	$12,000	$18,000
Original life	10 years	12 years	6 years	8 years
Remaining life	5 years	12 years	2 years	8 years
Annual functional capacity	700 units	1,000 units	50 units	80 units
Annual operating costs	$1,100	$1,000	$1,500	$1,200
Replacement cost of functional capacity of new condition	$10,167	$20,000	$5,918	$18,000
Replacement cost of functional capacity in current condition	$6,273	$20,000	$2,358	$18,000

The replacement cost of functional capacity of asset 2 is calculated in the same way as for asset 1 (Exhibit 34). In our opinion, the most useful disclosure is that the existing assets have a replacement cost of functional capacity in current condition of $8,631 (= $6,273 + $2,358) and that depreciation for the year based on those replacement costs, remaining lives, and straight-line depreciation would be $2,433 (= $6,273/5 + $2,358/2). As we understand the SEC SAB No. 11, all that need be disclosed in this case, assuming divisible replacement assets, would be the following. The replacement cost new of current productive capacity is $25,250 [= (.70 × $20,000) + (.625 × $18,000)], the accumulated depreciation on replacement costs is $14,500 [= (5/10 × .70 × $20,000) + (4/6 × .625 × $18,000)], and that operating savings of approximately $1,150 [= ($1,100 − .70 × 1,000) + ($1,500 − .625 × $1,200)] would result. Depreciation based on replacement costs would be $3,275 [= (.70 × $20,000/10) + (.625 × $18,000/6)]. Since the user cannot know for how many years the operating savings will persist (five years for asset 1 and two years for asset 2), the user is poorly placed to make the economic calculations from the disclosure. A possible solution would be to disclose operating cost savings by year for as many years as savings are anticipated, much like the disclosures under APB Opinion No. 31 for leases.

In disclosing replacement costs based on functional pricing when there has been presence of technological change since acquisition of existing assets, the accountant must realize that two offsetting forces are generally at work. Replacement assets cost more than existing assets but will be less costly to operate. (That is, as prices of labor, materials, and fuel rise relative to capital, the rational firm will substitute capital for labor, materials, and fuel in the production process.) As a result of replacement, whether actual or hypothetical, future depreciation charges will be larger than current depreciation charges but future operating costs will be less than current operating costs. (In general, the precise statement is that future operating costs will be in different proportion to future depreciation charges than current operating costs are to current depreciation charges. Whether future total costs are in total larger or smaller than current total costs is not important for this discussion.) It is important to be aware that technological change can be so rapid that the present value of the total costs of using replacement assets is less than the present value of the future costs of using existing assets. In that case, there have been holding *losses* on current assets that currently are not recognized in the conventional financial statements (although they should be, in my opinion). When there has been rapid enough technological change, distributable income based on replacement costs will be *larger* than that based on the historical costs and offsetting realized holding losses. The problem in the normal case is how to communicate the simultaneous facts of larger future depreciation and lower operating costs. There are essentially two alternatives:

1. Disclose depreciation based on the acquisition cost of replacement assets and future operating cost savings separately.

2. Disclose future depreciation assuming future operating costs are identical with current operating costs. The cost of the existing asset is reduced by the present value of the future cost savings in recognition of the partial obsolesence that has occurred.

Although these two methods of disclosure are economically identical, the disclosure is somewhat simpler if the second alternative is followed because only the numbers relating to plant and depreciation thereon need be disclosed. That is, we can disclose replacement cost of existing assets and the remaining life of those assets. Then we can compute replacement cost depreciation from net replacement cost of the existing asset in current condition and its remaining life. In the example of Exhibit 35, asset 1 would be shown to have a net replacement cost of $6,273 and depreciation based on five years remaining life of $1,255 (= $6273/5). The aggregation of replacement cost depreciation based on remaining lives by the accountant effectively does the required nonlinear combination of present value of future case operating savings that the user would have to do if alternative (1) is adopted. If alternative (1), above, were to be used, the narrative would become complicated unless results are not aggregated and the user would not be able to project operating savings beyond one year if results are aggregated.

Following alternative (2), we get replacement cost depreciation charges plus current operating costs that are the same as the total in alternative (1). There is no convenient format for disclosing the future stream of operating costs under alternative (1), but all important information is captured in the one depreciation figure under alternative (2).

Thus, we conclude that when functional pricing is used for more than one asset in replacement cost disclosures, users are likely to be best served if the present value of all operating savings are incorporated in computing replacement costs of existing assets in current condition assuming operating costs continue at the current level. The SEC does not, in general, allow alternative (2), but requires alternative (1); see SAB No. 11.

In this example, historical cost depreciation of existing assets 1 and 2 is $3,500 (= $15,000/10 + $12,000/6). Because of technological improvements, the present value of production costs with replacement assets is less than with existing assets in spite of the higher cost of replacement assets. Our suggestion—that replacement cost depreciation be based on replacement cost of existing assets in current condition assuming operating costs continue at current levels and remaining economic lives—gives a more readily interpretable number. In our example, we would report replacement cost depreciation of $2,433, which assumes that future operating costs are like current operating costs, whereas the disclosure suggested by the SEC would show replacement cost depreciation of $3,275 along with a narrative description of one year's operating savings that must, because of aggregation, be hard to incorporate into income statements projected beyond one year.

LIFE MEASUREMENT

Under generally accepted accounting principles (APB Opinions No. 9 and No. 20), remaining economic life of assets should be the same as remaining depreciable life. Under generally accepted accounting principles, estimates of depreciable lives are to be extended as new information becomes available indicating that lives of long-term assets will differ from those originally estimated. In principle, then, there can never be such a thing as a fully depreciated asset still in use. But, of course, many firms do have fully depreciated assets still in use. It has not, apparently, proven practicable to extend depreciable lives and, since auditors have approved the financial statements, it may be assumed that it has not made a material difference in the financial statements, at least for any one asset becoming fully depreciated. The SEC has indicated in Staff Accounting Bulletin No. 7 that the replacement cost disclosure is not the appropriate vehicle for correcting everything that is wrong with conventional accounting. According to Bulletin No. 7, if an asset is fully depreciated, but still in use, then its replacement cost new will be disclosed. Its accumulated depreciation will be the full replacement cost figure so that net replacement cost is zero and replacement cost depreciation is not increased because of fully depreciated assets. If the estimation of replacement costs is to be as useful to management as it can be, then management will want to recognize that fully depreciated assets still in use have future productive capacity and the net replacement cost of that productive capacity based on remaining economic life should be computed in full replacement cost financial statements.

Recorded Book Life Versus Economic Life. When economic remaining life and recorded remaining book life of an asset differ materially, it is necessary to measure the remaining economic life of the asset and adjust the book life to the economic life. The following sections provide life measurement techniques for machinery and equipment, buildings, and total plant.

Effect of Management Policy on Life. Determination of probable lives for machinery and equipment is dependent upon three component causes of depreciation: physical factors, functional obsolescence, and economic obsolescence. Management policy relative to repair and maintenance, disposition, and replacement also directly impacts the determination of useful service life.

Repair and maintenance policy seeks to maximize productivity of an asset by two principal means. First, preventive maintenance attempts to anticipate possible failure during crucial production runs by periodic replacement or repair of critical machine parts. Second, repair policy seeks to minimize downtime by maintaining stores of replacement parts or subassemblies; it also seeks to provide the necessary personnel to diagnose and correct machine failure with a minimum loss of productive capability.

Disposition policy involves the evaluation of technological change upon the methods of production. It seeks to balance the additional cost of newer, more efficient machinery and equipment against the advantage of retaining machinery even though it has a high degree of functional obsolescence.

Building Life Measurement. For buildings, estimates of depreciation are made by directly estimating the effective age of the component system. This is the actual age plus the reduction in estimated remaining life due to depreciation. For example, a 10-year-old functional system with a service life of 15 years would normally have a 5-year estimated remaining life. If, however, the physical and functional depreciation of the component system were such that the estimated remaining life were reduced to 2 years, then the estimated effective age would be $(5 - 2) + 10 = 13$ years.

The following standard service lives should be used as a starting point for estimating the effective age of a component system:

Functional system	Service life (years)
1. Site	20
2. Foundation	33⅓
3. Floor	20
4. Interior columns	33⅓
5. Roof	15
6. Exterior walls	20
7. Exterior glazed openings	15
8. Interior walls	10
9. Doors	15
10. Specialties	10
11. Plumbing	15
12. Heating, ventilating, and air conditioning	15
13. Electrical	15

FUNCTIONAL OBSOLESCENCE

Functional obsolescence is caused by deficiencies and/or excess in plant construction and design. Functional obsolescence is further classified as curable and/or incurable. For measurement purposes, the functional obsolescence must be considered separately. A summarization of the various types and the methodology for their measurement is the following:

Obsolescence Caused by Plant Design. The measurement of obsolescence caused by plant design can be obtained from discussions with plant engineering personnel. The objective is to determine the optimal design of the plant for its current utility. The considerations include the plant configuration on an overall basis as well as any interior design considerations. Additional insight into the obsolescence due to design factors can be obtained from the dimensions utilized in the historical data of previous construction projects for similar type facilities.

Obsolescence Caused by Construction. The other form of obsolescence is caused by actual construction materials used. An attempt to measure reproduction cost of all facilities will tend to require the consideration of functional obsolescence. In the valuation of new facilities and in considering replacement costs, the functional obsolescence washes out. Some consideration has to be made for structure specifics which relate to valid materials as opposed to excess contribution. Comparisons of unit costs from the historical data with unit costs based upon the description of the structure to be measured will give indication of excess construction costs.

Requirements for Measurement. Comparison of unit costs against historical costs will give indications of deficiency and/or excess in construction. Determination of optimal structure configuration and comparison of historical dimension relationships against actual dimension relationships will give indications of deficiency and/or excess in plant design.

BUILDING MEASUREMENT TECHNIQUE

Replacement costs for buildings and other construction are measured by the following techniques:

1. Identify and classify structures by their usage and framing type (e.g., light assembly plant steel frame (low-rise).
2. Collect local material prices and labor rates for construction unit price calculation.
3. Obtain dimensions and descriptions of structure components from plant drawings.
4. Verify drawings and visually inspect plant property.
5. Determine component unit costs based upon historical data.
6. Modify unit costs for particular structure based upon component description.
7. Determine replacement cost new utilizing modified unit costs and take-off quantities.
8. Identify renovations, additions, and improvements since original construction.
9. Identify present deficiencies and future repair requirements for structural components.
10. Review maintenance procedures and condition of structure.
11. Determine physical obsolescence.
12. Determine functional obsolescence due to construction material and techniques, and due to plant layout and design.

TOTAL PLANT LIFE MEASUREMENT

There are essentially five categories of measurement that play a crucial role in the profitability (hence, economic life) of a plant. These factors are

1. Physical factors
2. Cost factors
3. Revenue factors
4. External factors
5. Subjective factors

The major areas within these categories that should be measured in determining the economic life of a plant are outlined below.

1 Physical Factors Physical factors are determined from the operating costs and service lives of the buildings and machinery and equipment. The relevant considerations for life measurements at the asset level have been covered previously.

2 Cost Trends
a. Sanitation and air pollution
b. Building and machinery repair costs
c. Taxes
d. Steam, power, and refrigeration
e. Sewage
f. Energy—utility and demand
g. Labor—costs and availability

3 Revenue
a. Facility utilization
b. Unit performance
c. Past sales trends
d. Long-run market conditions
4 External
a. Population of marketing area
b. Employment and labor availability
c. Transportation facilities
d. Industrial growth—area and industry
5 Subjective
a. Property encumbrances
b. Lease commitments
c. Contractual commitments
d. Long-term contracts
e. Property leased out
f. Condemnation probability
g. Management planning decisions

Determination of economic life for a plant requires specific economic data for the operations and characteristics of the individual plant. However, in periods of rising costs and increased competition, the evaluation of economic life is an important factor in reporting the economics of operations.

CURRENT VALUE ACCOUNTING DEVELOPMENTS

Current value accounting is derived from the concept of measuring the changing values of assets and liabilities. We have discussed the replacement cost of inventories and fixed assets. In this section we will review the other facets of current value accounting.

Period-to-Period Value Changes. For the concept of period-to-period value changes, credit goes to John Hicks' view that "a man's income ... [and by inference of a business firm] is the maximum value which he can consume during a week and still expect to be as well off at the end of the week as he was at the begining."

In an enterprise, earnings are ultimately based on the changes in value of economic resources. Transactions have been the major criterion for value change recognition, but measurement by valuation should be regarded as the cornerstone of the accounting process. In other words, after all assets and liabilities are valued from period to period, the stockholders' equity should be calculated. A current value accounting model cannot and should not reflect the economic value of a total business but can present a more realistic expression of individual asset and liability values. It should assist investors in making their independent assessment of the value of a firm or of a share of its equity stock.

Value Bases. Replacement cost accounting is one technique of measurement within a framework of total current value accounting. Additional techniques used for valuation under current value accounting are:

- Present value, defined as the present value of expected future cash flows
- Net realizable value, defined as the value that could be obtained if the asset were disposed of at the present time.

When the SEC issued *ASR No. 190,* it also issued Staff Accounting Bulletin No. 7, which stated that SEC "will not object if these data (replacement cost) are supplemented by data setting forth the net realizable value and/or the 'economic value' of properties."

In addition to the nonmonetary assets (inventories and productive capacity) covered under *ASR No. 190,* current value accounting includes net monetary assets, land, natural resources, intangibles, and long-term debt.

OTHER ASSETS AND LIABILITIES

Net Monetary Assets. Net monetary assets are the cash and cash equivalents less all liabilities. Since long-term debt is treated separately in currently value accounting, it is excluded in the determination of net monetary assets. Under current value accounting, net monetary assets are measured by a purchasing power unit adjustment (using the GNP deflator) to reflect the monetary holding gain or loss from period to period. The average is based on net monetary assets held at the beginning and end of the year as reflected by the balance sheets of the previous and current fiscal years.

Land. Land values are determined through two methods. First, current price data (e.g., appraisals, recent sales of comparable land, tax assessment values, etc.) may be used. Second, yield rates on past land investments may be determined, taking into consideration the economic feasibility of replacing the land with another investment in comparable land, or the use to be made of the land, such as for rental.

Natural Resources. Valuation of natural resources involves the following:

1. Geological and engineering studies
2. Study of such operating data as extraction methods, quality grades, production costs, and recovery of capital investment
3. Determination of the amount and quality of reserves, additional development costs required to attain full production capability, and the primary yields and by-products obtainable from the reserves
4. Estimation of product selling prices.

Intangibles. Intangible assets are either amortizable or nonamortizable. Amortizable intangible assets are defined as those intangible assets having a determinable life, and acquired by purchase, rather than internal development. They consist of the following:

Patents
Patent applications
Franchises
License agreements
Royalty agreements
Employment contracts
Leasehold interests
Design rights
Technical libraries
Pending contracts
Water rights
Noncompetition agreements
Restrictive convenants
Technical assistance agreements
Computer software.

Since amortizable intangibles have a determinable life, they can usually be associated with a cash flow stream. Thus, they can generally be valued using the present value technique. The data available and the usefulness of the asset will determine whether the amortizable intangible should be valued using present value, replacement cost, or net realizable value.

Nonamortizable intangibles are defined as those intangible assets which generally do not have a determinable life. Nonamortizable intangibles which can be readily identified are

Trademarks and brand names
Technical "know-how"
Assembled organization and personnel
Market acceptance
Reputation
Established location
Secret processes and formulae
Distribution organization
Other elements of goodwill.

Some nonamortizable intangibles can be measured by replacement cost. Those nonamortizables which cannot be measured through a replacement cost can be measured only through a residual approach after valuation of the total enterprise. If a valuation of the entire enterprise could be made, the determinable assets (tangible and intangible) would be subtracted from the enterprise valuation and the remaining values would be considered attributable to the nonamortizable intangibles.

Long-Term Debt. Current value of long-term debt is measured by the present value technique. Future principal payments and future interest payments are discounted to present value utilizing the current money market rates for similar debt instruments.

BIBLIOGRAPHY

Alexander, Michael O.: *Accounting for Inflation: A Challenge for Business,* Maclean-Hunter Limited, Toronto, Canada, 1975.
——and Barrington J. Douglas: "A Feasible Method of Current Value Accounting," *CA Magazine,* September 1975.
Arthur Andersen & Co.: *Accounting Standards for Business Enterprises Throughout the World,* Chicago, 1974.
Backer, Morton: *Current Value Accounting,* Financial Executives Research Foundation, New York, 1973.
Bakker, Pieter: *Inflation and Profit Control,* Methuen Publications, Toronto, 1974.
Bedford, Norton M.: *Income Determination Theory: An Accounting Framework,* Addison-Wesley, Reading, Mass., 1965.
Bevington, Philip R.: *Data Reduction and Error Analysis for the Physical Sciences,* McGraw-Hill Book Company, New York, 1969.
Bowker, Albert H., and Gerald J. Lieberman: *Engineering Statistics,* Prentice Hall, Englewood Cliffs, N.J., 1972.
Brinkman, Donald R.: *A Quantitative Approach to Current Value Measurements,"* Valuation Systems Corporation, Rolling Meadows, Ill., 1975.
——and Paul H. Prentiss: "Replacement Cost and Current Value Measurement—How to Do It," *Financial Executive,* October 1975.
Burton, John C.: "Accounting That Allows for Inflation," *Business Week,* November 30, 1974.
Chambers, Raymond J.: *Accounting, Evaluation, and Economic Behavior,* Prentice Hall, Englewood Cliffs, N.J., 1966.
Davidson, Sidney, David Green, Jr., Charles T. Horngren, and George H. Sorter: *An Income Approach to Accounting Theory,* Prentice Hall, Englewood Cliffs, N.J., 1964.
Davidson, Sidney, James S. Schindler, Clyde P. Stickney, and Roman L. Weil: *Financial Accounting: An Introduction to Concepts, Methods, and Uses,* Dryden Press, Hinsdale, Ill., 1976.
Edwards, Edgar O., and Phillip W. Bell: *The Theory and Measurement of Business Income,* University of California Press, Berkeley, 1961.
Institute of Chartered Accountants in Australia and Australian Society of Accountants: *Preliminary Exposure Draft: A Method of "Current Value Accounting,"* Australian Accounting Research Foundation, Melbourne, June 1975.
Revsine, Lawrence: *Replacement Cost Accounting,* Prentice-Hall, Englewood Cliffs, N.J., 1973.

Rosen, L. S.: *Current Value Accounting and Price-Level Restatements,* Canadian Institute of Chartered Accountants, Toronto, 1972.

Ross, Howard: *Financial Statements—A Crusade for Current Values,* Pitman Publishing Corporation, New York, 1969.

Sandilands, F. E. P.: *Report of the Inflation Accounting Committee* (Sandilands Report), Her Majesty's Stationery Office, London, 1975.

Stigler, George, and James K. Kindall: *The Behavior of Industrial Prices,* National Bureau of Economic Research, New York, 1970.

Valuation Systems Corporation: *Replacement Cost Measurement: External Data Sources Reference Guide,* Valuation Systems Corporation, Rolling Meadows, Ill., 1976.

Vancil, Richard F., and Roman L. Weil: *Replacement Cost Accounting: Readings on Concepts, Uses, and Methods,* Thomas Horton & Daughters, Glen Ridge, N.J., 1976.

Chapter **47**

Fiduciary Accounting

SIDNEY I. SIMON
Professor of Economics, Rutgers University

DIFFERENCES FROM FINANCIAL ACCOUNTING*

A major difference between fiduciary accounting, used in estates and trusts, and financial accounting used by business firms, is in the basic approach to the recording process. The commercial enterprise centers its record keeping around the disclosure of changes in assets, liabilities, and owners' equity. The fiduciary, on the other hand, bases his accounting on only two factors—the assets he takes over and his accountability for them. Liabilities are not recorded by him until he pays them; this will reduce the assets for which he is accountable, just as will payment of legacies.

Separate Accounting for Principal and Income. Another important distinction from financial accounting is the necessity to account separately for the corpus or principal of the estate and for the income the estate may produce while it is held by the fiduciary. This is necessary because the latter must often pay taxes upon principal and income separately and because the deceased may have directed that the principal and income from his estate be distributed to different beneficiaries. Normally, the life tenant would be entitled to the income and the remainderman to the principal.

Principal. The principal of the estate is the property or group of assets which represent the estate or trust fund itself, while the income is the earnings on that principal during the period that the estate or trust is in the hands of the fiduciary. There may be receipts of principal, however, even after the fiduciary has taken over the original assets. These would include:

1. Assets of the deceased existing at his death but discovered after the fiduciary has filed his initial inventory.

2. Rent or interest accrued to the death of decedent or the beginning of the trust, although unpaid rent or bond coupons are not usually apportioned between principal and interest.

3. Stock dividends and proceeds from the sale of stock rights. Cash or property dividends declared but not yet paid at the date of death or the beginning of the trust are also considered principal.

4. Profits on the operation of a partnership or sole proprietorship earned prior to the decedent's death or beginning of the trust, and profits from the completion of the decedent's executory contracts.

5. Gains from the sale of fiduciary property for a price over that of its original inventory valuation or purchase price.

6. Insurance proceeds received for a loss which occurred prior to the beginning of the trust or estate and return of insurance premiums for policies in force before that date. Proceeds of insurance on losses which occur after the date of the commencement of the estate are considered principal only if they constitute a replacement of an estate asset.

Conversely, there may be disbursements of principal even after the fiduciary has taken over the original assets. Largely these would involve the payment of obligations incurred prior to the commencement of the estate or incident to its initiation and those which would mainly benefit the remainderman of the estate. These would include:

1. Debts of the deceased, including the expenses of his funeral and last illness, as well as any accrued interest thereon.

2. Legal fees, administration costs, and court costs in probating and defending the will and administering the trust estate, except those directly involved with the administration of income.

3. Federal estate taxes and state inheritance taxes (except where state law might

*A glossary of terms appears at the end of this chapter.

require recovery from legatees), income taxes of the decedent accrued prior to his death, and on gains from disposing of principal assets of the estate.

4. Brokerage fees for sales or purchases of estate assets.

5. Insurance premiums or real estate taxes accruing prior to the beginning of the estate or trust.

6. Permanent improvements to real estate which would not benefit solely the life tenant.

7. Losses due to wear and tear, theft, fire, or other casualty to the assets of the trust or estate.

8. Carrying charges on non-income-producing estate or trust assets.

Income.   Items which would involve credits to income include all receipts, other than those enumerated as principal, such as:

1. Rent, interest, royalties, and business profits accruing after the date of the beginning of the trust or death of the decedent, as well as cash dividends declared after that date.

2. Crops harvested or the natural increase of livestock owned by the estate.

Disbursements chargeable against income are those involving the collection of income:

1. The fiduciary's commissions and expenses for his collection, administration, and disbursement of income, including legal fees connected with matters pertaining to income.

2. All expenses connected with the care and maintenance of the trust property, as well as for ordinary repairs to it, except for depreciation and obsolescence.

3. Interest on mortgages and other encumbrances on the trust property during the life of the estate, and insurance premiums on the trust property, except those specifically protecting the interest of the remainderman.

4. Taxes assessed on income property, including income taxes on the income generated.

5. Losses of property caused by the negligence of the life tenant, or due to the theft or other casualty of purely income property.

6. Depletion or amortization of a wasting asset or leasehold, unless the testator or grantor of the trust has indicated that the life tenant is to receive the full value of the trust.

Accruals in Fiduciary Accounting.   Another major distinction between financial accounting and fiduciary accounting is in distinguishing between cash and accrual items. In financial accounting, one may use the cash or the accrual basis of record keeping as the method of matching expenses and revenue among fiscal periods; the use of the accrual basis is clearly dominant. Fiduciary accounting, on the other hand, generally uses the cash basis of record keeping, but it does recognize the significance of accruals in the distinction between principal and income at the time the estate or trust begins and again when it terminates. Incomes and expenses which have accrued at the death of the decedent or commencement of the trust are credited or charged to principal. Income and expenses which have accrued at the moment of termination of the trust or estate, or death of the life tenant, are considered as credits or charges to income. As with all accruals, the date of collection of the income or payment of the expense is thus not a controlling factor in the distinction between principal and income.

The state laws regarding the distinction between principal and income in the handling of accruals in fiduciary accounting are not always similar, so that one must consult the law of the state which affects the particular estate or trust. In general, however, the following are the usual rules with reference to the handling of various possible accrued items:

1. *Profits.*   With the exception of those for personal services, the fiduciary must complete all contracts entered into by the decedent and the profits thereon are

considered part of the principal. Similarly, partnership profits are considered as principal, although since a partnership usually terminates at the date of the partner's death, the question will not be important to the fiduciary since the firm's books will be closed at that date and all profits to that date will be principal. If, by specific directions of the articles of copartnership, the partnership business is continued for a specified time after a partner's death, such profits would usually then be considered as income, as is interest on a partner's capital after the date of his death.

2. *Dividends.* Cash or property dividends are usually considered as principal if they were declared before the decedent's death or beginning of the trust, regardless of when paid, and are income if declared after that date. Some states use the "ex-dividend" or record date for making the distinction. There is generally no difference from the above classification rules for extraordinary or irregular dividends, but liquidating dividends, as distinguished from earnings distributions, are always considered as principal of the estate. Stock rights and the proceeds from the sale of these rights are also generally considered as principal.

3. *Rent.* Any rent income or rent expense, accruing between the date of the commencement of the estate and the date of its termination, is usually considered as affecting income. That accrued before the date of the beginning of the estate, regardless of the date of payment, is principal. The same rules apply to the classification of royalties.

4. *Interest.* Similarly, interest income and expense accruing between the date of the death of the decedent or the beginning of the trust and the date of the termination of the estate or trust are generally considered as affecting income, while before such date they are principal. The rule usually differs, however, with reference to interest on savings bank deposits. In this case, the date the savings bank credits the interest to the depositor's account is the determinant; if it is credited after the commencement of the estate or trust, it is all considered income and does not accrue. Bond interest coupons collected, or receipts of interest, during the period of the fiduciary estate are considered as income, and no increase or deduction is generally made from the interest received for amortization of bond discount or premium.

5. *Taxes.* Property taxes which were assessed and became a lien on estate property prior to the date of the commencement of the fiduciary estate are chargeable to principal, regardless of when paid. Those becoming a lien after the beginning of the trust are income charges. Special assessments during the life of the estate or trust may be chargeable to principal or income or apportioned between them, depending upon whom the improvement will benefit.

6. *Crops and Livestock.* Crops harvested during the life of the estate are income, as are livestock born during the life tenancy. Costs of maintaining the land and livestock, as well as those of harvesting, are charged against income. When the testator has directed that a herd be unimpaired, livestock born during the tenancy and necessary to keep the herd intact are considered principal. If land is granted as a devise, crops growing at the time of the testator's death are part of the devise.

Repairs and Improvements. The accounting for repairs and improvements follows the usual rules of financial accounting. Additions, extraordinary repairs, and most betterments are chargeable against principal; ordinary repairs are income charges. In some instances, the part of the cost of a betterment which replaces wear and tear during the life of the estate may be considered an income charge, while that which improves or betters the property would be principal.

Depreciation or obsolescence of the estate assets is ordinarily not charged against income, but depletion of wasting assets is an income charge. The expressed wishes of the decedent or grantor of the trust are, however, considered. Thus, if he expressed the desire that the trust assets be preserved for the remainderman, then both depreciation and depletion are income charges. If, on the other hand, he desired the income beneficiary to receive that full income without deduction for asset declines in value, then both depreciation and depletion are charges against principal.

THE INVENTORY OF ASSETS

The first important duty of a fiduciary, executor, administrator, or trustee of an estate is to take over the estate assets and to prepare for the court a list or inventory of them, giving a full description of each item and assigning a value to it. Certain assets of the decedent may by law of the state be exempted from the estate, such as certain personal and household items and a limited amount of cash, but even these should ordinarily be inventoried in a separate schedule, as should real property passing directly to the decedent's heirs, so that all property left by the deceased is accounted for.

Among the items that should be included in the inventory are the following:

1. Cash in the decedent's possession, in his safety deposit box, or on deposit in checking or savings accounts or with savings and loan associations

2. Securities in the possession of the decedent or his broker or in his safety deposit box

3. Accrued interest on bonds and dividends declared on the stock listed above

4. The value of any interest in a business or partnership

5. Notes, accounts, or mortgages receivable, or receivable judgments, as well as advances to legatees or heirs, and the interest accrued thereon to the date of death of decedent

6. Jewelry and other valuables in the possession of the decedent or in his safety deposit box

7. Accrued rents or royalties receivable

8. Life insurance which names the estate as beneficiary

9. Real estate owned by the decedent, even though it may not be part of the estate but pass directly to his heirs or devises

10. Copyrights, patents, leases, or other valuable intangibles, as well as contract rights which do not involve personal services

11. Unpaid salaries, commissions, or fees.

The inventory does not include assets held by the decedent but belonging to others; however, assets he owned which were mortgaged or pledged are nevertheless listed at their full value without deduction for the amount of unpaid debt.

ACCOUNTING ENTRIES

Opening Entry. After completion of the inventory the fiduciary should use it as the basis, both as to items listed and the value given thereon, for the opening entry on his books of account. This entry would take the form:

```
Assets (detailed)  ...........................  xxx
    Estate Principal  .......................         xxx
To enter inventory property taken over by
fiduciary.
```

This entry differs from an opening entry in financial accounting in that liabilities are not recorded and the title of the accountability account is Estate Principal or Estate Corpus. Trustees may refer to it as Trust Principal.

Where the number of assets is very great, it may be advisable to debit an inventory control account for noncash assets, with the details given in a subsidiary ledger.

This opening accounting entry may be preceded by memorandum notations in narrative form giving important facts such as the date of death, the date of the reading of the will, the letters testamentary, the date of opening of the decedent's safety deposit box, etc., the names of appraisers, a note on court orders or other court actions, and other significant facts or events.

Transactions Which Increase Fiduciary Accountability. After the opening entry is made and posted, subsequent entries are made as further transactions or facts develop. Those which would increase the fiduciary's accountability include the following:

Discovery of Assets Subsequent to the Inventory. If additional assets are discovered after the initial inventory is filed with the court, they should be listed in an additional inventory, and recorded on the fiduciary's books as follows:

Assets (detailed) xxx
    Estate Assets Discovered xxx
To record assets in supplemental inventory.

The account, Estate Assets Discovered, is a temporary accountability account to aid the fiduciary in making his reports and will eventually be closed out to Estate Principal.

Gains on Disposable Assets. When estate assets are sold or otherwise disposed of, the asset account is credited with the value listed in the inventory, and Cash is of course debited with the amount realized. Another temporary accountability account, Gain on Realization, is credited with the gain on disposition (or Loss on Realization is debited with any loss on disposal).

Cash xxx
Loss on Realization xxx
    Y Co. Common Stock xxx
To record loss on sale.

The Gain on Realization or Loss on Realization accounts will also eventually be closed out to Estate Principal.

Receipts of Income. It is customary on the books of account to keep separate accounts for Principal—Cash (usually that which was taken over by the estate from decedent or grantor, or obtained by the collection of receivables or sale of estate assets) and Income—Cash (usually obtained from receipts of income during the period of the estate). While it is essential that estate cash be kept in a bank account separate from the fiduciary's own personal or business accounts, it is not necessary (although in large estates it is advisable) that principal cash and income cash be physically so separated in separate bank accounts. It is merely expedient to keep separate ledger accounts on the fiduciary's record books for each. This may be accomplished by having separate columns for each in the same cash receipts journal.

All the income received may be credited to a single income account, thus making an entry:

Cash—Income xxx
    Income xxx
To record receipts of
(details listed).

In larger estates, however, it is better to open separate income accounts such as Dividend Income, Interest Income, and other categories of income, and to credit the specific income account for the receipt.

Transactions Which Decrease Fiduciary Accountability. After taking his inventory, the fiduciary soon must proceed toward the payment of all claims against the estate. State laws usually require him to advertise for the filing of claims by published legal notices, and generally set a limit, often six months, within which creditors must file those claims. He then makes a report to the court of the claims that have been filed, and a determination is made of the solvency of the estate.

If the estate is solvent, no problem is presented, but if it appears that the assets of the estate will be insufficient to meet all its liabilities, then state statutes have generally set up an order of priority of payment of claims that must be followed.

Priority of Payments.   The order of priority of payment is usually as follows:
1. Funeral expenses
2. Expenses of the deceased's last illness
3. Allowances for support of the decedent's family
4. Expenses of administration of the estate.

Payment of Debts.   The fiduciary does not have to pay any other debts until he has determined the total liabilities which will be claimed against the estate. Should the estate assets be insufficient for all of them, payment under state law usually follows this order:

1. All debts entitled to preference under the laws of the United States and of the state
2. State and federal taxes for which the decedent was liable
3. Judgments and court awards against the deceased
4. Unsecured debts.

The entry for payment of the debts of the decedent would be

```
Debts of Decedent  ........................ xxx
      Cash—Principal  ......................        xxx
To record the payment of the following debts:
(details listed).
```

Similarly, expenses are not recorded until payment of them is made:

```
Funeral Expenses  ........................ xxx
      Cash—Principal  ......................        xxx
Payment of the following funeral expenses:
(details listed).
```

The Debts of Decedent and expense accounts are eventually closed out to the Estate Principal account.

Abatement of Legacies.   All debts must be paid before any legacies are paid or any heirs given their inheritance. If there are insufficient assets to pay the debts, bequeathed assets may be reduced or *abated* in proportion to their respective amounts. *Ademption* refers to the complete revocation of legacies where necessary. The assets of the estate are drawn upon to pay debts in the following order:

1. Personal assets not bequeathed
2. Personal assets bequeathed to residuary legatees
3. Personal assets bequeathed to general legatees, which legacies may be abated
4. Personal assets specifically bequeathed, which may also be abated
5. Real estate assets, but only after strict compliance with state law. If the will directs the sale of real estate to pay estate debts, this will be done before abatement of any legacies.

Payment of Legacies.   After payment of debts, and usually within one year of the death of the decedent, legacies are paid or distributed. Such payment or delivery is recorded:

```
Legacies Paid or Delivered  .................. xxx
      John Doe, Legatee  ....................        xxx
John Doe, Legatee  ........................ xxx
      Appropriate Asset  ....................      , xxx
Payment of legacy as follows:
(details listed).
```

When all legacies have been paid or distributed, the Legacies Paid or Delivered account will be closed out to the Estate Principal account. The account with each legatee is kept for informational purposes and becomes particularly important in certain special circumstances. Thus, when the fiduciary has paid the state inheritance tax for the legatee, his account is debited for the tax and Cash—Principal credited. If the legatee reimburses the estate for the amount of the tax, this entry would then be reversed. Interest earned on legacies, such as on specifically bequeathed securities, would also result in a debit to Cash—Principal and a credit to the legatee's account. Abatements can also properly be recorded by means of such individual legatee accounts.

Payment of Income Cash. Any expenses which are paid from income would result in a debit to an Expense—Income account (or a separate account for each such category of expense), and a credit to Cash—Income. If cash collected in the form of income is paid to income beneficiaries, the entries can be made:

```
Distributions to Income Beneficiaries  ........ xxx
     Income Beneficiary—Peter Doe .........        xxx
Income Beneficiary—Peter Doe  ............. xxx
     Cash—Income  ......................        xxx
Payment of income as follows:
(details listed).
```

The Distributions to Income Beneficiaries account will of course eventually be closed out to the Income Accountability account.

Accounting for Estate Taxes

Income Taxes. The fiduciary must file an income tax return for the decedent for the fraction of the year which preceded his death, and the tax on such income is a charge to Estate Principal. After the death of deceased, the estate, or trust when established, becomes a separate entity for tax purposes, and the fiduciary must file a separate return annually for it as long as it exists. Income taxes on the earnings of the estate or trust during its existence are charges against Estate Income.

Federal Estate Tax. The federal estate tax is based on the right of a person to give his assets to others upon his death (just as the federal gift tax is based on the similar right to transfer one's property before death) and is not affected by the relationship of the donor or deceased to the grantees or beneficiaries. It is based on the gross estate (all assets except real estate located outside the United States) less certain deductions for funeral and administration expenses, debts of the decedent, casualty losses during the administration of the estate, and various bequests for public, educational, religious, or charitable purposes. In addition, certain exemptions are allowed in arriving at the taxable value of the estate, which is based on its value at the time of death or earlier disposition of the property, or one year after the date of the death of the deceased, whichever may be the lower figure.

The entry for payment of the federal estate tax would be

```
Estate and Inheritance Taxes  ............... xxx
     Cash—Principal  ......................        xxx
Payment of federal estate taxes.
```

The Estate and Inheritance Taxes will eventually be closed out to the Estate Principal account.

State Inheritance Taxes. In addition to federal estate taxes, there are usually also inheritance taxes paid to the individual state. Inheritance taxes are generally based on the right to inherit or receive property, and the rate of tax usually increases the more the relationship of the beneficiary is removed from the deceased. Exemptions are also usually greater for heirs who are closer relatives of the decedent. It is customary for the fiduciary to pay the state inheritance tax for the legatee or beneficiary but to charge this against the amount due the ultimate recipient. He then either receives reimbursement from the legatee or reduces the amount of the legacy accordingly.

Subject to certain limits, the fiduciary may use state inheritance tax payments as a deduction from the gross estate for federal estate tax computation. Life insurance proceeds payable to the estate are part of the gross estate for estate tax purposes and of course part of the inheritance, for state inheritance tax purposes, of the heir or residual legatee to whom they eventually pass. The proceeds of policies payable to beneficiaries other than the estate are ordinarily not part of the gross estate for federal estate tax purposes, but for state inheritance tax purposes are generally considered part of the inheritance the beneficiary receives.

Entries for Operation of a Going Business. A fiduciary is occasionally called upon to continue the operation of a going business. Where the decedent was a member of a partnership, the fiduciary usually makes sure that the estate gets the appropriate share of the deceased in the liquidation of the partnership, in accordance with the provisions of the partnership agreement or the provisions of the will left by the decedent.

If, however, the deceased was the owner of an individual proprietorship business, it is possible the court may require its continuance for the period of the duration of the fiduciary's responsibility. The books of that business should then immediately be closed as of the date of the decedent's death, and an inventory made of its assets as well as a list of its liabilities. The assets of the business are then shown on the fiduciary's estate records, valued as appraised at the date of decedent's death, as assets of the estate, and all the liabilities of the business as estate debts, usually by means of controlling accounts on the estate records.

The business books are then reopened and all business transactions are recorded in the normal manner, including new liabilities. When the fiduciary relationship is ended, or periodically if this encompasses more than a year, the business records are again closed and the profit or loss for the period is ascertained. The fiduciary then records this change in the value of the business assets on the estate books by a debit or credit to the asset accounts and a corresponding credit to Gain on Realization or debit to Loss on Realization. The gain or loss will be closed out to Estate Principal, Estate Income, or income to a specific legatee in accordance with the terms of the will or document of trust.

Entries After the Final Accounting. After all debts, taxes, and legacies have been paid, or the life period of a trust or life tenancy has expired, the fiduciary renders a report called a "final accounting" to the court; this may sometimes even be followed by an amended or supplementary final accounting if new facts subsequently develop. After the final accounting has been made to the court, the fiduciary makes entries to close his books. By this time practically all his inventory asset accounts should have been already closed out by distribution or payment, which would have similarly reduced the Estate Principal or Estate Income accounts proportionately. He therefore now makes the various closing entries suggested at several places above, for instance:

Estate Principal	 xxx	
Administration Expenses	....	xxx
Funeral Expenses	....	xxx
Debts of Decedent	....	xxx
Loss on Realization of Assets	....	xxx
Legacies Distributed	....	xxx
Estate and Inheritance Taxes	....	xxx
Legal and Accounting Expenses	....	xxx
Fiduciary's Commissions	....	xxx

```
Assets Subsequently Discovered  ............ xxx
Gain on Realization  ........................ xxx
Gain on Distribution  ....................... xxx
        Estate Principal  ......................    xxx
Collections of Income  ..................... xxx
        Income  .............................    xxx
Income  ................................. xxx
        Expense—Income  .....................    xxx
        Distribution to Income Beneficiary  ......    xxx
```

This should ordinarily close out completely all the accounts on the fiduciary's books. If there should remain any assets which an executor, for instance, must deliver to a testamentary trustee, a further entry might be required to show a distribution as for example:

```
Estate Principal  ........................... xxx
Estate—Income  ........................... xxx
        J. Roberts, trustee  .....................    xxx
J. Roberts, trustee  ........................ xxx
        Cash—Principal  ....................    xxx
        U.S. Government 4's of 1998  ...........    xxx
        Cash—Income  .......................    xxx
```

THE FIDUCIARY'S BOOKS AND RECORDS

No particular accounting method for setting up the fiduciary's records is required by law. He needs a reliable, comprehensive set of books and accounts, however, to aid him in making his reports to the court and the tax authorities. It is important in this regard to note that the assets accounted for in the federal estate tax return are greater (because they include real estate, for instance) than those for which the fiduciary must account to the probate or other court.

The accounting period would depend upon the time set by the court for the various reports the fiduciary must make to it, but the books must be closed annually for income tax purposes.

While a single-entry system is possible, just about all fiduciary records are maintained today by means of a double-entry system. As noted above, however, the principal accounts involve only asset and proprietorship (accountability) accounts. Liability accounts are not kept, a liability only appearing as a deduction from accountability as the debt is paid. The accounts must be arranged to permit the required distinction between principal and income.

Journals. The fiduciary normally maintains three journals, a general journal, a cash receipts journal, and a cash disbursements journal. The setup for the general journal might be as follows:

General Journal

Date	Explanation	LF	Assets		Estate principal		Estate income		Sundry accounts		
			Dr	Cr	Dr	Cr	Dr	Cr	Account	Dr	Cr

The cash receipts journal might be designed in the following manner:

Cash Receipts Journal

Date	Explanation	LF	Cash—principal	Cash—income	Assets	Realization		In-come	Sundries	
						Loss	Gain			
			Dr	Dr	Cr	Dr	Cr	Cr	Account	Cr

In more involved or large estates, it might be well for the fiduciary to set up more columns. Thus, he might have separate columns for several different asset accounts with a sundry asset credit account, and separate columns to show individual items of income receipt, such as dividend income, interest income, etc.

A cash payments journal may be set up as shown on page 47-12.

Ledger Accounts. While systems have been devised for very simple estates which combine on the one multicolumn page a running journal and ledger, or which combine in one ledger account all the assets of the estate, it is generally advisable to keep a separate ledger page for each asset in the inventory and for each of the other accounts. In large, intricate estates, it also may be useful to segregate similar accounts into subsidiary ledgers with a controlling account in the general ledger. This is especially true, for instance, for the inventory of assets, or for the investments of the estate, or if the will has created several trusts and the fiduciary wishes to keep the details of each trust separated.

The form of the ledger account may follow the usual T-account form of financial accounting, or it may include three columns for debit, credit, and balance, or it may be designed to add many columns for explanations such as security numbers, dates of interest payment, maturity, etc.

FIDUCIARY'S ACCOUNTING REPORTS

The fiduciary is required, in addition to his income, estate, and inheritance tax returns, to make at least a final accounting to the court which has authorized and overseen his stewardship. Often he must make annual intermediary reports where settlement of the estate or the period of the life of the trust is prolonged, and occasionally he may be required to file an amended final report. The form of these reports varies with the requirements of the laws of different states but usually appears as a Charge and Discharge Statement, with separate sections for principal and income, supported by schedules for the different sections of each, as well as receipts and vouchers to prove the items listed. If all the assets of the estate have been paid out, distributed, or transferred by the executor or administrator to a trustee or residuary legatee, the charge and discharge items will be equal and the statement will balance out. If, on the other hand, assets still remain in the fiduciary's hands, then a third section of the report will be necessary to show by a schedule the assets for which the fiduciary is still accountable.

Charge and Discharge Statement. The Charge and Discharge Statement of a fiduciary is generally in report, rather than account form, and usually would be similar to that shown in Exhibit 1.

Commission of the Fiduciary. The compensation allowed to the fiduciary may

Cash Disbursements Journal

Date	Explanation	LF	Cash— principal Cr	Cash— income Cr	Funeral expenses Dr	Admin. expenses Dr	Debts of decedent Dr	Legacies distributed Dr	Estate & inheritance tax Dr	Sundry accounts	
										Account	Dr

EXHIBIT 1   Charge and Discharge Statement of Fiduciary

ESTATE OF JOHN DOE
Richard Roe, Executor
From Date to Date

First, As to Principal:
I charge myself with:

Assets as per inventory (schedule A)...............................	$xxx
Assets subsequently discovered (schedule B)..........................	xxx
Gain on realization of assets (schedule C)...........................	xxx

Total charges... $xxx

I credit myself with:

Funeral and administrative expenses (schedule D).....................	$xxx
Debts of decedent paid (schedule E).................................	xxx
Federal estate and state inheritance and income taxes (schedule F).......	xxx
Loss on realization of assets (schedule C)...........................	xxx
Legacies paid or delivered (schedule G).............................	xxx
Commissions, legal and accounting fees (schedule H)..................	xxx

Total credits... xxx

Balance of principal (schedule I)... $xxx

Second, As to Income:
I charge myself with:

Income received (schedule J)..................................... $xxx

Total charges... $xxx

I credit myself with:

Expenses chargeable to income (schedule K)......................... $xxx

Income taxes (schedule F)..	xxx
Distributions to income beneficiaries (schedule L).....................	xxx
Commissions, legal and accounting fees (schedule H)....................	xxx

Total credits... xxx

Balance of income (schedule M).. .... $xxx

Balance of principal and income .... $xxx

---

be set forth in the provisions of the will or trust instrument, or it may be set by the court pursuant to statutes of the state. It may be based upon the value of the estate or upon the amount that the fiduciary receives into his stewardship and the amounts he pays out. It is necessary in certain fiduciary relationships, such as in a trust, that commissions be computed and charged separately against income and against principal, as is true of all other expenses and fees of administering a trust.

Trust Fees and Expenses. In allocating the various fees and other expenses in the administration of a trust estate, the test is which party receives the benefit of the particular services—the life tenant or the ultimate remainderman. If assets of a decedent's estate are to be transferred to a trust, all the administrative expenses of the executor or administrator are charged to principal, as are the expenses of creating the trust. Once the trust comes into being, principal is charged with expenses related to the preservation of the trust assets, including those connected with changes in investments. Income, on the other hand, is charged with the expenses and fees relating to the collection of income, the operation of income property, and the disbursement of income. Careful allocation of such fees between principal and income is often a difficult matter requiring legal assistance.

CHARITABLE TRUSTS

Sometimes a will or grant sets up a charitable trust, which differs from a private trust in that it is usually established for an indefinite period of time, is administered by a board of trustees rather than a single trustee, and may have, instead of a definite named beneficiary selected by the grantor, a part of the public chosen as recipients by the trustees from time to time, such as research organizations, hospitals, schools, etc.

Charitable Trust Accounting.   The bookkeeping procedures for charitable trusts are in general similar to those for private trusts or for business organizations. Since these trusts are not supervised by a court, the only required reports are those demanded by the Internal Revenue Service, although many such trusts voluntarily make public annual reports of their operations. The distinction between principal and income receipts and disbursements, essential to all fiduciary records, is necessary for charitable trusts also. There are, however, some accounting differences from the estates previously discussed.

Since the charitable trust generally has an unlimited life, it may retain the principal assets or investments of the trust for a considerable period of time. Therefore, it usually carries such investments at cost and considers market value perhaps only parenthetically on its annual reports. In charitable trusts, bond discounts and premiums are generally amortized over the life of the obligation, whereas in the shorter term, private trust, such amoortizations are usually ignored. Office furniture and equipment used in administering the trust is often charged to income, and depreciation on trust assets is similarly an income charge.

Fund Accounting.   Trustees of charitable trusts often commit the trust to the payment of large sums of money to specific beneficiaries over long periods of time. They need to know periodically how much the trust is still committed to pay to the beneficiary. Therefore, they generally use a fund accounting system which shows the amounts appropriated and still to be paid, as well as the amounts already paid.

Thus, at the time the trustees decide how much to pay out for a particular year from income (although of course, appropriations may occasionally also be made out of principal), the entry would be made:

> Appropriations of Income xxx
>   Authorized Appropriations xxx
> Appropriations of income approved by the
> board of trustees for the ensuing fiscal
> year.

The Appropriations of Income account will of course eventually be closed out to the Trust—Income account. The Authorized Appropriations account will be closed out as grants are made to recipients.

When the board of trustees selects a particular organization for a grant of funds, it makes an award, and an entry is then made:

> Authorized Appropriations xxx
>   Grant Payable, Organization A xxx
> To record the award of $xxx to Organization A
> to support the following research, payment
> to be made as follows: (details)

When a payment is actually made on the grant, the entry is recorded:

> Grant Payable, Organization A xxx
>   Cash—Income xxx

If the grants in any one year are greater than the income of the period, or if the board of trustees decides to reduce the principal of the trust in making grants, the original debit, or part of the entry, or a subsequent entry could be made to Appropriations of Principal instead of from income.

Lapsed Appropriations and Grants.   If it should turn out that an appropriation or grant which has been made is never fully paid out for any reason, the original appropriation is reversed, as follows:

```
Grant Payable, Organization A  ..............  xxx
      Authorized Appropriations  .............        xxx
Authorized Appropriations  .................  xxx
      Lapsed Appropriations  ................        xxx
```

The Lapsed Appropriations account is closed out by a credit to Trust—Income.

Accounting for Special-Purpose Funds.   Sometimes a grant is made to a charitable trust or foundation to be used solely for a specific purpose. The entry to create a special fund set up to carry out that purpose would be

```
Assets (detailed)  ..........................  xxx
      XYZ Special Fund  .....................        xxx
      To record receipt of enumerated assets for XYZ
      Special Purpose.
```

If the assets were not donated separately but were to come from the general assets of the estate or private trust, the following entry might be substituted:

```
Trust—Principal  ..........................  xxx
      XYZ Special Fund  .....................        xxx
      To record the establishment of the XYZ Special
      Purpose Fund from trust assets.
```

Financial Reports.   The financial reports of a charitable trust, other than those which are part of Internal Revenue Service returns, usually take the form of an accounting for principal, roughly similar to a business firm's balance sheet, and a Statement of Income, Expense, and Appropriations which is somewhat similar to the income statement of a business firm. Of course, different types of statements may be used where more appropriate.

The principal section would show the various assets of the trust, valued at cost or fair market value at the date of receipt, with the Trust—Principal account and any unappropriated income corresponding to the capital and retained earnings of an ordinary business.

The income statement of the charitable trust would show as revenue all receipts of income as well as gifts which were not designated as additions to trust principal. Lapsed appropriations of prior years would also be considered as income. The charges to income in the statement would be for the administrative expenses of operating the trust, as well as the appropriations authorized against income during the period. The net figure would be unappropriated income for the period which (like net profit of a business) would be added to the total unappropriated income (like retained earnings) of the statement of principal (or balance sheet).

EQUITY RECEIVERSHIPS, TRUSTEES IN BANKRUPTCY, OR REORGANIZATION

Another type of fiduciary is appointed by a court to take over the affairs of a business which is in serious financial difficulties. An equity receiver may be appointed by a state court, or a trustee in a corporate reorganization may be appointed by a federal court, to administer the business in an attempt to bring it back on its feet and restore it, in healthier condition, to its original owners. A trustee in bankruptcy, on the other hand, is appointed by a federal court to wind up the affairs of the business and dissolve it. Where the business owns perishable assets, the federal court may also appoint temporarily a receiver in bankruptcy who takes over and immediately disposes of those assets, turning over the proceeds and remaining property to the trustee in bankruptcy when the latter is appointed. While each of these officials differs in some degree from the others, their accounting records and problems have a considerable degree of similarity.

Since each of these fiduciaries is appointed and his activities supervised by a court, he must make frequent reports to that court on his operations, so that accounting records must be kept. The form of the reports depends on the laws of the particular jurisdiction; it may be similar to the financial statements of any ordinary operating business, or it may take the form of a charge and discharge statement similar to those previously discussed. A report that is frequently prepared by these fiduciaries is the Statement of Affairs. While the law seldom actually requires the preparation of this statement (in fact, the Federal Bankruptcy Act calls for the debtor to file a questionnaire which has this same name but is different from the accounting statement under discussion), it is often drawn up because of its usefulness for a business in serious financial difficulties.

The Statement of Affairs. This financial statement has some similarity to the balance sheet because both are reports of the financial condition of a business at a given moment in time. The balance sheet shows the estimated value of the firm's assets on a going-concern basis, lists its liabilities, and arrives at its net worth. The Statement of Affairs assumes the liquidation of the firm and therefore lists its assets at their net realizable value, shows the liabilities in the order of their required preference in payment, and arrives at the estimated expected deficiency to creditors. The deficiency is usually explained by a schedule called the Deficiency Account, showing these predicted losses in detail. Frequently the Statement of Affairs is prepared to aid in deciding whether the firm actually is insolvent, should be liquidated or whether an attempt should be made to salvage it by continuing operations.

Presentation of Assets on the Statement. Rather than using the balance sheet classifications of current and fixed assets, the Statement of Affairs classifies assets as pledged with fully secured creditors (those which have been pledged and are expected to realize enough to pay off those claims fully), pledged with partially secured creditors (wherein are placed those assets which have been pledged but are not expected to realize sufficient money to pay off those creditors fully), and unpledged or free assets not related to any particular liability.

The asset side of the statement is usually set up with several columns. In addition, of course, to the name of the asset, there is usually a column to show its book value as now shown on the records of the firm, its appraised or estimated realizable value, and the estimated amount which will be available to unsecured creditors from the disposal of that asset.

It is possible for an asset to appear on the Statement of Affairs which might not have been on the balance sheet. Thus, for instance, an asset such as a patent may have already been written off but may nevertheless have a value that can be realized on liquidation. The book value column for such an item would list it at zero, but the other columns would show its realization value.

In displaying assets on such a statement, an asset which would appear as an individual single item on a balance sheet may be shown in more than one place on the Statement of Affairs. Thus, if the firm has pledged only part of the investment it owns, the pledged securities would be displayed under pledged assets, whereas the shares of the same investment which are not pledged would be placed under free assets.

Valuation reserves are, of course, deducted from the assets to which they relate, and any accrued interest should be added to the asset on which it is accrued. Where work in process inventory will require additional expenditures to make it salable, the additional costs to be incurred in completing it and the estimated realizable value of the completed asset should then be shown. Careful analysis must be made of prepaid expense assets to determine whether there will be any amount actually realized from them on dissolution.

Presentation of Liabilities on the Statement. Again, instead of using the balance sheet classifications of current and fixed liabilities, the Statement of Affairs classi-fies liabilities as preferred claims (those which by law have priority to the assets, such as administration expenses and certain wages and taxes), fully secured liabilities (where the pledged assets have a realization value sufficient fully to satisfy the claims), partially secured liabilities, unsecured liabilities, and contingent liabili-ties (such as discounted notes receivable which might become a liability eventually but which are not so at the moment).

In addition to the column for the names of the obligations, the liabilities side has columns for the book value of the liability and the amount unsecured. This arrangement means that pledged assets will be connected with the claims against which they were pledged by "contra" notations. Thus, for instance, land and building appraised to realize $100,000, upon which there is a mortgage of $60,-000, would be noted on the asset side with $100,000 in the Appraised Value column, but only $40,000 in the Estimated Amount Available to Unsecured Creditors column, with the notation "see contra" in the Accounts column. The mortgage of $60,000 will be shown in the Book Value column but will not be extended at all to the Amount Unsecured column, and the notation "deducted contra" will be made in the Accounts column.

The Deficiency to Unsecured Creditors.   The stockholders' equity accounts (or capital accounts) of the firm are shown in the book value column of the liabilities side but are not extended to the Amount Unsecured column. The total of the Amount Available to Unsecured Creditors (on the asset side) is then subtracted from the Amounts Unsecured column (on the liabilities side) to arrive at the Deficiency to Unsecured Creditors, which is then added to the Amount Available to Unsecured Creditors to bring the statement in balance.

It is customary to make up a schedule called Deficiency Account which proves or checks out the Deficiency to Unsecured Creditors arrived at on the Statement of Affairs. It will show the Estimated Losses on Realization of Assets on its left or debit side, and on its credit side will be displayed (1) Estimated Gains on Realiza-tion Assets, (2) Stockholders' Equity accounts, and (3) the Deficiency to Unsecured Creditors, which should bring the account into balance.

Illustration of a Statement of Affairs.   A typical form for a Statement of Affairs is illustrated in Exhibit 2, and a schedule for the Deficiency Account is shown in Exhibit 3.

Receivership and Trustee Accounting.   There are no specific requirements in law as to how the books and records of a fiduciary, given stewardship of a firm in financial difficulties, must be kept, nor indeed is it always necessary for him to open a new set of books. He may record his operations by continuing the books of the old firm. This is especially true of the trustee in bankruptcy who is charged with the task of liquidating the business.

Since, however, these fiduciaries are acting in a trust capacity and are answera-ble to a court for their activities, they usually find it expedient to maintain their own set of records, in addition to those of the business firm itself. Even the trustee in bankruptcy may wish to maintain a set of books of his own where it appears that the liquidation will be complicated and protracted. These additional fiduciary records are kept so that it can be clearly seen what the condition of the firm was when he took it over, and what are the results of his stewardship. While two sets of books would henceforth be maintained, those of the business firm and those of the fiduciary, it is not necessary that each transaction be accounted for by a simultane-ous entry in both. Rather, the day-to-day operations are recorded in the fiduciary's records and summarized from time to time on the records of the firm from the periodic reports of the fiduciary.

Opening the Fiduciary's Books.   The receiver opens his books by recording the assets which the court has ordered him to take over. While the trustee in bank-

EXHIBIT 2   Sample Corporation, Statement of Affairs

SAMPLE CORPORATION
Statement of Affairs
Date

Book value		Estimated realization value	Available to unsecured creditors
	Assets		
	Assets pledged with fully secured creditors:		
$150,000	Land & buildings..........................	$90,000	
(40,000)	Reserve for depreciation....................		
	Less: mortgage payable & accrued interest (contra)	60,500	$29,500
	Assets pledged with partially secured creditors:		
5,000	Government bonds.........................	$ 4,850	
	Accrued interest (deducted contra)............	150	
		$ 5,000	
	Unpledged assets:		
350	Cash....................................	$ 350	350
16,000	Accounts receivable.......................	9,000	9,000
(2,000)	Reserve for bad debts		
5,000	Raw materials inventory....................	3,500	3,500
6,000	Work in process inventory:		
	Value when completed $4,700		
	Less: Cost to complete 1,600	3,100	3,100
25,000	Finished goods inventory...................	12,000	12,000
35,000	Equipment...............................	10,000	10,000
1,200	Unexpired insurance.......................	0	0
0	Patents..................................	3,000	3,000
	Estimated amount available.................	....	$70,450
	Less: preferred creditors (contra)............	....	13,350
	Estimated available for unsecured creditors...	....	$57,100
	Estimated deficiency on unsecured liabilities (see Schedule)..........................	....	30,000
$201,550			$87,100
	Liabilities & Capital		
	Preferred creditors:		
$ 1,350	Accrued taxes............................	$ 1,350	
	Estimated liquidation costs..................	12,000	
	Total, deducted contra....................	$13,350	
	Fully secured creditors:		
60,000	Mortgage payable.........................	$60,000	
	Accrued interest..........................	500	
	Total, deducted contra....................	$60,500	
	Partially secured creditors:		
20,000	Notes payable............................	$20,000	
	Accrued interest..........................	100	
	Total..................................	$20,100	
	Less: security contra......................	5,000	$15,100
	Unsecured creditors:		
67,000	Accounts payable.........................	....	67,000
	Contingent liabilities:		
	Estimated liability on lawsuit................	....	5,000
	Capital:		
20,000	Capital stock		
33,200	Retained earnings		
$201,550	Total unsecured creditors..................	....	$87,100

EXHIBIT 3   Sample Corporation, Schedule of Estimated Deficiency on Unsecured Liabilities

SAMPLE CORPORATION
Schedule of Estimated Deficiency on Unsecured Liabilities
Date

Estimated losses on realization:

Land and buildings..		$20,000
Government bonds...		150
Accounts receivable..		5,000
Raw materials inventory......................................		1,500
Work in process inventory....................................		2,900
Finished goods inventory.....................................		13,000
Equipment..		25,000
Unexpired insurance..		1,200
		$68,750

Estimated gains on realization:

Patents..		3,000
Net loss on realization..................................		$65,750

Unrecorded expenses on liquidation:

Accrued interest on mortgage payable...............	$ 500	
Accrued interest on notes payable...................	100	
Estimated liquidation expenses.....................	12,000	
Estimated liability for lawsuit.....................	5,000	
	$17,600	

Unrecorded revenues on liquidation:

Accrued interest on government bonds...............	150	
Net expenses on liquidation.............................		17,450
Total estimated losses and costs on liquidation..................		$83,200

Less: Stockholders' equity:

Capital stock..	$20,000	
Retained earnings...	33,200	53,200
Estimated deficiency on unsecured liabilities...................		$30,000

ruptcy would record these at current appraised values, the trustee in reorganization, or the equity receiver who is given the responsibility of continuing the operation of the firm, generally records them at their book values, by debiting the individual assets at cost and crediting any valuation accounts as they appear on the firm's books. Liabilities existing prior to the commencement of the fiduciary relationship remain on the firm's books and are not entered on those of the fiduciary, so that distinction can easily be made between existing firm indebtedness and new debts incurred by the trustee or receiver. The net credit is made to an account called "X Company—In Receivership" or "Trustee's Equity." On the books of the company, the assets and valuation accounts are closed out to an account for the fiduciary himself. Thus, the entries might be made as follows:

Receiver's Books		*Firm's Books*	
Assets (detailed) xxx		J. Doe, Receiver xxx	
Accumulated Depreciation ..	xxx	Accumulated Depreciation xxx	
Allowance for Bad Debts	xxx	Allowance for Bad Debts xxx	
X Co.—In Receivership	xxx	Assets (detailed)	xxx

Payment of Prior Liabilities.   While the receiver does not take over on his records the existing debts of the business firm, he is ordered by the court to pay them. This requires an entry on the fiduciary's books to a temporary account, to aid in the later preparation of his report, and will require an entry on the firm's records too. Interest on this indebtedness will be similarly entered on both sets of records.

Receiver's Books

X Co.—Notes Payable—Old	 xxx	
X Co.—Accrued Interest Paid	... xxx	
X Co.—Interest Expense Paid	... xxx	
Cash		xxx

Firm's Books

Notes Payable	 xxx	
Accrued Interest Payable	 xxx	
Interest Expense	 xxx	
J. Doe, Receiver	....	xxx

The above three X Co. accounts on the receiver's records will eventually be closed out to the accountability account, X Co.—In Receivership.

Operation of the Business. Where the stewardship is one that requires the fiduciary to continue the business in operation rather than liquidate it, entries for the day-to-day operating transactions are then all made on the books of the receiver or trustee. They are not made on the records of the firm until taken up by a summary entry from a periodic report of the fiduciary. The account titles for these operating accounts should be similar to those used on the books of the firm to enable easy comparison between the operations of the receivership and those of the old management.

Receiver's Books		*Firm's Books*	
Purchases xxx		(No entry)	
Sundry Expenses xxx			
Cash	xxx		
Accounts Payable—New	xxx		
Cash xxx		(No entry)	
Accounts Receivable—New xxx			
Sales	xxx		
Sundry Incomes	xxx	(No entry)	
Sales xxx			
Sundry Incomes xxx			
Purchases	xxx		
Sundry Expenses	xxx		
Profit & Loss	xxx		
Profit & Loss xxx		J. Doe, Receiver xxx	
X Co.—In Receivership	xxx	Profit & Loss	xxx

Realization of Receivership or Trust Assets. Where, instead of a normal operating transaction, the fiduciary disposes of one of the firm's assets for which he is accountable, he must record this fact on his books with appropriate notation in a temporary account. No entry need be made in the firm's books at this time.

Receiver's Books		*Firm's Books*
Cash xxx		
Accumulated Depreciation xxx		(No entry)
Loss on Sale of Assets xxx		
Specific Asset	xxx	

Closing the Fiduciary's Books. Eventually, of course, the fiduciary relationship will be terminated. In the case of the trustee in bankruptcy, this would be when all the assets have been realized and distribution made to creditors. This should then close out all the fiduciary's accounts on his records, and by means of the data in his final report the firm's books are also closed out, all losses being charged against the capital accounts.

In the case of a trustee in reorganization or an equity receiver, the fiduciary relationship would end, by order of the court, when the reorganization has been effected or the firm restored to solvency. The fiduciary's final entry would then close out his asset and new existing liabilities accounts, temporary and permanent.

From the data in his report, the firm would take up these assets and liabilities on its books and close out the receiver's account. The entries might thus be as follows:

Receiver's Books		Firm's Books	
Accounts Payable New xxx		Cash xxx	
Accumulated Depreciation xxx		Accounts Receivable xxx	
Allowance for Bad Debts xxx		Assets (detailed) xxx	
X Co.—In Receivership xxx		Accounts Payable	xxx
Cash	xxx	Accumulated Depreciation ...	xxx
Accounts Receivable—New ..	xxx	Allowance for Bad Debts	xxx
Assets (detailed)	xxx	J. Doe, Receiver	xxx
Loss on Sale of Assets	xxx		
X Co.—Notes Payable—Old .	xxx		
X Co.—Accrued Int. Paid ...	xxx		
X Co.—Int. Expense Paid ...	xxx		
(No entry)		Profit & Loss xxx	
		Interest Expense	xxx
		Retained Earnings	xxx

Receiver's and Trustee's Reports. The fiduciary of a business in distress usually files his original inventory and statement of affairs with the court when he takes over his stewardship. In addition, he frequently submits periodic interim reports as he conducts the operations of or liquidates the business. He must also file a report when he terminates his fiduciary capacity. All these reports must follow the forms prescribed by the federal or state jurisdiction under whose authority he acted.

Charge and Discharge Statement. The final report may, as in the case of other fiduciaries, take the form of a Charge and Discharge Statement. The trustee or receiver would charge himself with: (1) the assets in the original inventory plus those subsequently discovered; (2) amounts realized on the sale of assets, and the gains on such realization (losses thereon will be among his credits); (3) liabilities incurred by the receiver; and (4) any income receipts, or the gross income items if he continues operations of the business. He would credit himself on the statement with (1) payments of debts and expenses given priority by law as preferred obligations; (2) the inventory value of assets disposed of, as well as any losses on such realization; (3) distributions to or payments of liabilities of the firm or those incurred by the receiver; and (4) expenses incurred by the receiver for the conduct of his administration or the operations of the business. This would leave as a balance, if any, the assets for which he is still accountable and returning to the owners of the firm.

Realization and Liquidation Statement. The final report of the fiduciary, and indeed his interim reports, may take the form of the traditional Realization and Liquidation Statement, sometimes called "Account," used in many jurisdictions. The statement is organized as a comprehensive ledger account and attempts to display on the one form all the financial facts of the trust or receivership. In the account or statement itself are summarized all the transactions relating to the assets and liabilities of the firm, as well as the revenues and expenses of administering the operation of the business or of its liquidation. This is usually accompanied by a schedule of cash receipts and disbursements and one or more schedules covering changes in stockholders' equity.

Such a statement would appear as shown in Exhibit 4.

The total of all the left-hand or debit items on the statement should of course equal that of all the items on the right-hand or credit side. The balance section should either be sufficiently detailed to indicate the various sources that make up the net gain or loss for the period, or there should be an accompanying schedule setting forth the details.

EXHIBIT 4   X Corporation, in Receivership

X CORPORATION, IN RECEIVERSHIP
John Doe, Receiver
for the Period from Date to Date

Assets

Assets to be realized:
  All assets (except cash) at inventory values at beginning of period
Assets acquired:
  New assets discovered or otherwise acquired

Assets realized:
  Proceeds from the disposition of assets during the period
Assets not realized:
  Book value at the end of the period of all assets (except cash) still retained

Liabilities

Liabilities liquidated:
  All obligations, old or new, paid during the period
Liabilities not liquidated:
  All unpaid obligations at the end of the period

Liabilities to be liquidated:
  All indebtednesses existing at the start of the period
Liabilities assumed:
  Obligations newly discovered or incurred during the period

Profit and Loss

Supplementary charges:
  Expenses of the administration and liquidation or operations of the business (but not including realization losses)

Supplementary credits:
  Revenues earned or accruing from the operations or during the period (not including realization gains)

Balance

Realization or operation gain:
  Realization gains, gains from liquidation of liabilities for less than book amounts, and operating profit

Realization or operation loss:
  Realization losses and operating loss

A cash account type schedule also would be attached to the report showing cash balance, receipts, and disbursements for the period. For a corporation, another schedule showing the opening balance and changes in capital stock, paid-in surplus, and retained earnings would also be included. The net gain or loss arrived at in the main statement would of course be added to or deducted from the retained earnings schedule balance.

As a final proof of the figures of the entire report, another schedule composed of significant balances might be appended. This would show on its asset side (1) the final cash balance from the cash account schedule, plus (2) the total of assets not realized from the credit side of the major statement. The total of these assets should equal the total of the liabilities and capital side, which would include (1) the total liabilities not liquidated from the debit side of the main statement, plus (2) the capital stock, (3) paid-in surplus, and (4) retained earnings or deficit (including the net gain or loss) balances for the period from the individual schedules.

There are, of course, other forms which the Statement of Realization and Liquidation can take. Sometimes, especially where the receiver or trustee continues the operation of the business, rather than liquidating it, the report is labeled a Statement of Realization, Liquidation, and Operations.

Illustration of Realization and Liquidation Statement.   To illustrate the form of this statement consider a firm with the following opening balance sheet.

Cash	$ 15	Liabilities	$140
Disposable assets	85	Capital stock	50
		Retained earnings (deficit)	(90)
	$100		$100

During the period the following transactions occur:
1. All assets are sold for $65.
2. Expenses of administration ($5) are paid in cash.
3. Creditors are paid $70.
4. Cash of $5 remains on hand.

The Statement of Realization and Liquidation would be as follows:

Assets

Assets at beginning (except cash):		Assets realized:	
Disposable assets............... $ 85		Disposable assets............... $ 65	
		Assets (except cash) on hand........ 0	

Liabilities

Liabilities paid off................. $ 70	Liabilities at beginning............. $140
Unpaid liabilities.................. 70	

Profit and Loss

Expenses of liquidation............ 5	
	$205

Balance

	Loss on liquidation:	
	On assets.................... 20	
	Expenses of liquidation....... 5	25
$230		$230

The closing balance sheet would be

Cash 5	Liabilities	$ 70	
	Capital stock	50	
	Retained earnings (deficit)	(115)	
$5		$ 5	

The schedule of capital would be

At beginning:
Capital stock .... $ 50		
Deficit .... (90)	$(40)	
Loss on liquidation	(25)	
Total capital now	$(65)	

The schedule of cash would be

At beginning	$15	
From sales of assets	65	
	80	
Expense paid .... $ 5		
Liabilities 70	75	
On hand at end	$ 5	

GLOSSARY OF TERMS

ABATEMENT: the proportionate reduction of legacies or devises to permit the payment of debts or expenses of the deceased or his estate.

ACCOUNTING: the procedure whereby a fiduciary reports to the court to demonstrate that he has faithfully carried out his duties with reference to the property entrusted to him.

ACT OF BANKRUPTCY: an act committed by a debtor, as designated by the bankruptcy law, which might give undue preference to certain of his creditors over others.

ADMINISTRATOR: a fiduciary appointed by the probate, surrogate's, or orphan's court to take over the assets of a decedent, pay the debts and expenses, and distribute his personal property in accordance with the laws of the state, in the situation where the decedent has not left a will.

ADMINISTRATOR-WITH-WILL-ATTACHED (CUM TESTAMENTO ANNEXO): the fiduciary who administers the estate of a deceased who left a will but either did not name an executor or the named executor does not so serve.

BANKRUPTCY: a federal court procedure through which an insolvent debtor's assets are taken over for the benefit of his creditors and the bankrupt is discharged from liability for his debts.

BENEFICIARY: the person for whose ultimate benefit the fiduciary manages property entrusted to him, considered to be the "equitable owner" of it.

BEQUEST: a legacy.

CESTUI QUE TRUST: beneficiary of a trust.

DECEDENT: a dead person.

DEMONSTRATIVE LEGACY: a bequest payable in cash from a specific fund.

DEVISEE: the beneficiary of a grant of real property, called a "devise," named in a will.

ESTATE: the decedent's interest in property at the time of his death. To a state court, estate refers only to the decedent's personal property. In bankruptcy, it refers to the bankrupt's interest in property at the time of initiation of the proceedings.

EXECUTOR: a fiduciary named in a decedent's will, and confirmed by the court, to carry out the provisions of the will in distributing his estate.

FIDUCIARY: one entrusted with the custody and management of property for the benefit of others.

GENERAL LEGACY: a gift of cash made in a will to a named beneficiary not payable out of a specified fund.

HEIRS: the beneficiaries or ultimate recipients of all property of a person who dies without leaving a will and whose property is disposed of in accordance with the state laws of descent for real property and state laws of distribution for personal property.

INTESTATE: a decedent who died without leaving a valid will.

LEGATEE: the beneficiary of a grant of personal property, called a "legacy," named in a will.

LIFE TENANT: one entitled to the use or income of property for the duration of his life.

PREFERENCE: any transfer of property by one who is insolvent toward payment for an existing unsecured debt.

PROBATE: the judicial action by which a will is confirmed, and the proceedings concerning the settlement of a testate's estate.

PROOF OF CLAIM: a signed written statement by a creditor setting forth the nature of a debt assertedly owed him by a bankrupt.

REMAINDERMAN: the person who receives the property or income of a life tenant upon the death of the life tenant.

RESIDUARY LEGACY: a bequest of all that is left of personal property of an estate after all debts, expenses, and other legacies have been paid.

SPECIFIC LEGACY: a bequest of a specific item of personal property other than cash to a named beneficiary.

TESTAMENTARY TRUST: a trust created by a will.

TESTATOR: one who makes a valid will or testament.

TRUSTEE: one who holds the legal title to real or personal property in trust for the benefit of another.

WILL: a document in proper legal form by which a person indicates his wishes for the disposition of his property at his death.

BIBLIOGRAPHY

Denhard, J. G., Jr.: *A Complete Guide to Estate Accounting and Taxes,* Prentice-Hall, Englewood Cliffs, N.J., 1964.

Grange, W. J., W. R. Staub, and E. G. Blackford: *Wills, Executors and Trustees,* rev. ed., The Ronald Press Company, New York, 1950.

Harris, H. I.: *Estates Practice Guide,* 2nd ed., Baker Voorhis and Co., New York, 1968 suppl.

Loring, A. P.: *Trustee's Handbook,* 6th ed., revised by J. F. Farr, Little, Brown and Company, Boston, 1962.

Oestreicher, J.: "Preparation of Fiduciary Accountings for Trusts and Estates," *The New York Certified Public Accountant,* October 1964, pp. 727–743.

Todd, K. R.: "Reporting Equities in Estate Accounting," *Journal of Accounting Research,* Autumn 1966, pp. 253–259.

Warren's *Heaton on Surrogate's Court,* 6th ed., Matthew Bender, New York, 1970 suppl.

Weinstein, E. A.: "Accountants' Examinations and Reports in Bankruptcy Proceedings," *The New York Certified Public Accountant,* January 1965, pp. 31–39.

Appendix

Compound Interest, Annuity, and Bond Tables

TABLE 1   Future Value of $1

$$F_n = P(1 + r)^n$$

r = interest rate; n = number of periods until valuation

Periods = n	¼%	½%	⅔%	¾%	1%	1½%	2%	3%
1	1.00250	1.00500	1.00667	1.00750	1.01000	1.01500	1.02000	1.03000
2	1.00501	1.01003	1.01338	1.01506	1.02010	1.03022	1.04040	1.06090
3	1.00752	1.01508	1.02013	1.02267	1.03030	1.04568	1.06121	1.09273
4	1.01004	1.02015	1.02693	1.03034	1.04060	1.06136	1.08243	1.12551
5	1.01256	1.02525	1.03378	1.03807	1.05101	1.07728	1.10408	1.15927
6	1.01509	1.03038	1.04067	1.04585	1.06152	1.09344	1.12616	1.19405
7	1.01763	1.03553	1.04761	1.05370	1.07214	1.10984	1.14869	1.22987
8	1.02018	1.04071	1.05459	1.06160	1.08286	1.12649	1.17166	1.26677
9	1.02273	1.04591	1.06163	1.06956	1.09369	1.14339	1.19509	1.30477
10	1.02528	1.05114	1.06870	1.07758	1.10462	1.16054	1.21899	1.34392
11	1.02785	1.05640	1.07583	1.08566	1.11567	1.17795	1.24337	1.38423
12	1.03042	1.06168	1.08300	1.09381	1.12683	1.19562	1.26824	1.42576
13	1.03299	1.06699	1.09022	1.10201	1.13809	1.21355	1.29361	1.46853
14	1.03557	1.07232	1.09749	1.11028	1.14947	1.23176	1.31948	1.51259
15	1.03816	1.07768	1.10480	1.11860	1.16097	1.25023	1.34587	1.55797
16	1.04076	1.08307	1.11217	1.12699	1.17258	1.26899	1.37279	1.60471
17	1.04336	1.08849	1.11958	1.13544	1.18430	1.28802	1.40024	1.65285
18	1.04597	1.09393	1.12705	1.14396	1.19615	1.30734	1.42825	1.70243
19	1.04858	1.09940	1.13456	1.15254	1.20811	1.32695	1.45681	1.75351
20	1.05121	1.10490	1.14213	1.16118	1.22019	1.34686	1.48595	1.80611
22	1.05647	1.11597	1.15740	1.17867	1.24472	1.38756	1.54598	1.91610
24	1.06176	1.12716	1.17289	1.19641	1.26973	1.42950	1.60844	2.03279
26	1.06707	1.13846	1.18858	1.21443	1.29526	1.47271	1.67342	2.15659
28	1.07241	1.14987	1.20448	1.23271	1.32129	1.51722	1.74102	2.28793
30	1.07778	1.16140	1.22059	1.25127	1.34785	1.56308	1.81136	2.42726
32	1.08318	1.17304	1.23692	1.27011	1.37494	1.61032	1.88454	2.57508
34	1.08860	1.18480	1.25347	1.28923	1.40258	1.65900	1.96068	2.73191
36	1.09405	1.19668	1.27024	1.30865	1.43077	1.70914	2.03989	2.89828
38	1.09953	1.20868	1.28723	1.32835	1.45953	1.76080	2.12230	3.07478
40	1.10503	1.22079	1.30445	1.34835	1.48886	1.81402	2.20804	3.26204
45	1.11892	1.25162	1.34852	1.39968	1.56481	1.95421	2.43785	3.78160
50	1.13297	1.28323	1.39407	1.45296	1.64463	2.10524	2.69159	4.38391
100	1.28362	1.64667	1.94343	2.11108	2.70481	4.43205	7.24465	19.21863

Periods = n	4%	5%	6%	7%	8%	10%	12%	20%
1	1.04000	1.05000	1.06000	1.07000	1.08000	1.10000	1.12000	1.20000
2	1.08160	1.10250	1.12360	1.14490	1.16640	1.21000	1.25440	1.44000
3	1.12486	1.15762	1.19102	1.22504	1.25971	1.33100	1.40493	1.72800
4	1.16986	1.21551	1.26248	1.31080	1.36049	1.46410	1.57352	2.07360
5	1.21665	1.27628	1.33823	1.40255	1.46933	1.61051	1.76234	2.48832
6	1.26532	1.34010	1.41852	1.50073	1.58687	1.77156	1.97382	2.98598
7	1.31593	1.40710	1.50363	1.60578	1.71382	1.94872	2.21068	3.58318
8	1.36857	1.47746	1.59385	1.71819	1.85093	2.14359	2.47596	4.29982
9	1.42331	1.55133	1.68948	1.83846	1.99900	2.35795	2.77308	5.15978
10	1.48024	1.62889	1.79085	1.96715	2.15892	2.59374	3.10585	6.19174
11	1.53945	1.71034	1.89830	2.10485	2.33164	2.85312	3.47855	7.43008
12	1.60103	1.79586	2.01220	2.25219	2.51817	3.13843	3.89598	8.91610
13	1.66507	1.88565	2.13293	2.40985	2.71962	3.45227	4.36349	10.69932
14	1.73168	1.97993	2.26090	2.57853	2.93719	3.79750	4.88711	12.83918
15	1.80094	2.07893	2.39656	2.75903	3.17217	4.17725	5.47357	15.40702
16	1.87298	2.18287	2.54035	2.95216	3.42594	4.59497	6.13039	18.48843
17	1.94790	2.29202	2.69277	3.15882	3.70002	5.05447	6.86604	22.18611
18	2.02582	2.40662	2.85434	3.37993	3.99602	5.55992	7.68997	26.62333
19	2.10685	2.52695	3.02560	3.61653	4.31570	6.11591	8.61276	31.94800
20	2.19112	2.65330	3.20714	3.86968	4.66096	6.72750	9.64629	38.33760
22	2.36992	2.92526	3.60354	4.43040	5.43654	8.14027	12.10031	55.20614
24	2.56330	3.22510	4.04893	5.07237	6.34118	9.84973	15.17863	79.49685
26	2.77247	3.55567	4.54938	5.80735	7.39635	11.91818	19.04007	114.4755
28	2.99870	3.92013	5.11169	6.64884	8.62711	14.42099	23.88387	164.8447
30	3.24340	4.32194	5.74349	7.61226	10.06266	17.44940	29.95992	237.3763
32	3.50806	4.76494	6.45339	8.71527	11.73708	21.11378	37.58173	341.8219
34	3.79432	5.25335	7.25103	9.97811	13.69013	25.54767	47.14252	492.2235
36	4.10393	5.79182	8.14725	11.42394	15.96817	30.91268	59.13557	708.8019
38	4.43881	6.38548	9.15425	13.07927	18.62528	37.40434	74.17966	1020.675
40	4.80102	7.03999	10.28572	14.97446	21.72452	45.25926	93.05097	1469.772
45	5.84118	8.98501	13.76461	21.00245	31.92045	72.89048	163.9876	3657.262
50	7.10668	11.46740	18.42015	29.45703	46.90161	117.3909	289.0022	9100.438
100	50.50495	131.5013	339.3021	867.7163	2199.761	13780.61	83522.27	828×10^5

TABLE 2   Present Value of $1

$$P = F_n(1 + r)^{-n}$$

r = discount rate; n = number of periods until payment

Periods = n	¼%	½%	⅔%	¾%	1%	1½%	2%	3%
1	0.99751	0.99502	0.99338	0.99256	.99010	.98522	.98039	.97087
2	0.99502	0.99007	0.98680	0.98517	.98030	.97066	.96117	.94260
3	0.99254	0.98515	0.98026	0.97783	.97059	.95632	.94232	.91514
4	0.99006	0.98025	0.97377	0.97055	.96098	.94218	.92385	.88849
5	0.98759	0.97537	0.96732	0.96333	.95147	.92826	.90573	.86261
6	0.98513	0.97052	0.96092	0.95616	.94205	.91454	.88797	.83748
7	0.98267	0.96569	0.95455	0.94904	.93272	.90103	.87056	.81309
8	0.98022	0.96089	0.94823	0.94198	.92348	.88771	.85349	.78941
9	0.97778	0.95610	0.94195	0.93496	.91434	.87459	.83676	.76642
10	0.97534	0.95135	0.93571	0.92800	.90529	.86167	.82035	.74409
11	0.97291	0.94661	0.92952	0.92109	.89632	.84893	.80426	.72242
12	0.97048	0.94191	0.92336	0.91424	.88745	.83639	.78849	.70138
13	0.96806	0.93722	0.91725	0.90743	.87866	.82403	.77303	.68095
14	0.96565	0.93256	0.91117	0.90068	.86996	.81185	.75788	.66112
15	0.96324	0.92792	0.90514	0.89397	.86135	.79985	.74301	.64186
16	0.96084	0.92330	0.89914	0.88732	.85282	.78803	.72845	.62317
17	0.95844	0.91871	0.89319	0.88071	.84438	.77639	.71416	.60502
18	0.95605	0.91414	0.88727	0.87416	.83602	.76491	.70016	.58739
19	0.95367	0.90959	0.88140	0.86765	.82774	.75361	.68643	.57029
20	0.95129	0.90506	0.87556	0.86119	.81954	.74247	.67297	.55368
22	0.94655	0.89608	0.86400	0.84842	.80340	.72069	.64684	.52189
24	0.94184	0.88719	0.85260	0.83583	.78757	.69954	.62172	.49193
26	0.93714	0.87838	0.84134	0.82343	.77205	.67902	.59758	.46369
28	0.93248	0.86966	0.83023	0.81122	.75684	.65910	.57437	.43708
30	0.92783	0.86103	0.81927	0.79919	.74192	.63976	.55207	.41199
32	0.92321	0.85248	0.80846	0.78733	.72730	.62099	.53063	.38834
34	0.91861	0.84402	0.79779	0.77565	.71297	.60277	.51003	.36604
36	0.91403	0.83564	0.78725	0.76415	.69892	.58509	.49022	.34503
38	0.90948	0.82735	0.77686	0.75281	.68515	.56792	.47119	.32523
40	0.90495	0.81914	0.76661	0.74165	.67165	.55126	.45289	.30656
45	0.89372	0.79896	0.74156	0.71445	.63905	.51171	.41020	.26444
50	0.88263	0.77929	0.71732	0.68825	.60804	.47500	.37153	.22811
100	0.77904	0.60729	0.51455	0.47369	.36971	.22563	.13803	.05203

Periods = n	4%	5%	6%	7%	8%	10%	12%	20%
1	.96154	.95238	.94340	.93458	.92593	.90909	.89286	.83333
2	.92456	.90703	.89000	.87344	.85734	.82645	.79719	.69444
3	.88900	.86384	.83962	.81630	.79383	.75131	.71178	.57870
4	.85480	.82270	.79209	.76290	.73503	.68301	.63552	.48225
5	.82193	.78353	.74726	.71299	.68058	.62092	.56743	.40188
6	.79031	.74622	.70496	.66634	.63017	.56447	.50663	.33490
7	.75992	.71068	.66506	.62275	.58349	.51316	.45235	.27908
8	.73069	.67684	.62741	.58201	.54027	.46651	.40388	.23257
9	.70259	.64461	.59190	.54393	.50025	.42410	.36061	.19381
10	.67556	.61391	.55839	.50835	.46319	.38554	.32197	.16151
11	.64958	.58468	.52679	.47509	.42888	.35049	.28748	.13459
12	.62460	.55684	.49697	.44401	.39711	.31863	.25668	.11216
13	.60057	.53032	.46884	.41496	.36770	.28966	.22917	.09346
14	.57748	.50507	.44230	.38782	.34046	.26333	.20462	.07789
15	.55526	.48102	.41727	.36245	.31524	.23939	.18270	.06491
16	.53391	.45811	.39365	.33873	.29189	.21763	.16312	.05409
17	.51337	.43630	.37136	.31657	.27027	.19784	.14564	.04507
18	.49363	.41552	.35034	.29586	.25025	.17986	.13004	.03756
19	.47464	.39573	.33051	.27651	.23171	.16351	.11611	.03130
20	.45639	.37689	.31180	.25842	.21455	.14864	.10367	.02608
22	.42196	.34185	.27751	.22571	.18394	.12285	.08264	.01811
24	.39012	.31007	.24698	.19715	.15770	.10153	.06588	.01258
26	.36069	.28124	.21981	.17220	.13520	.08391	.05252	.00874
28	.33348	.25509	.19563	.15040	.11591	.06934	.04187	.00607
30	.30832	.23138	.17411	.13137	.09938	.05731	.03338	.00421
32	.28506	.20987	.15496	.11474	.08520	.04736	.02661	.00293
34	.26355	.19035	.13791	.10022	.07305	.03914	.02121	.00203
36	.24367	.17266	.12274	.08754	.06262	.03235	.01691	.00141
38	.22529	.15661	.10924	.07646	.05369	.02673	.01348	.00098
40	.20829	.14205	.09722	.06678	.04603	.02209	.01075	.00068
45	.17120	.11130	.07265	.04761	.03133	.01372	.00610	.00027
50	.14071	.08720	.05429	.03395	.02132	.00852	.00346	.00011
100	.01980	.00760	.00295	.00115	.00045	.00007	.00001	.00000

TABLE 3   Future Value of Annuity of $1 in Arrears

$$F = \frac{(1 + r)^n - 1}{r}$$

r = interest rate; n = number of payments

No. of payments = n	¼%	½%	⅔%	¾%	1%	1½%	2%	3%
1	1.00000	1.00000	1.00000	1.00000	1.00000	1.00000	1.00000	1.00000
2	2.00250	2.00500	2.00667	2.00750	2.01000	2.01500	2.02000	2.03000
3	3.00751	3.01503	3.02004	3.02256	3.03010	3.04522	3.06040	3.09090
4	4.01503	4.03010	4.04018	4.04523	4.06040	4.09090	4.12161	4.18363
5	5.02506	5.05025	5.06711	5.07556	5.10101	5.15227	5.20404	5.30914
6	6.03763	6.07550	6.10089	6.11363	6.15202	6.22955	6.30812	6.46841
7	7.05272	7.10588	7.14157	7.15948	7.21354	7.32299	7.43428	7.66246
8	8.07035	8.14141	8.18918	8.21318	8.28567	8.43284	8.58297	8.89234
9	9.09053	9.18212	9.24377	9.27478	9.36853	9.55933	9.75463	10.15911
10	10.11325	10.22803	10.30540	10.34434	10.46221	10.70272	10.94972	11.46388
11	11.13854	11.27917	11.37410	11.42192	11.56683	11.86326	12.16872	12.80780
12	12.16638	12.33556	12.44993	12.50759	12.68250	13.04121	13.41209	14.19203
13	13.19680	13.39724	13.53293	13.60139	13.80933	14.23683	14.68033	15.61779
14	14.22979	14.46423	14.62315	14.70340	14.94742	15.45038	15.97394	17.08632
15	15.26537	15.53655	15.72063	15.81368	16.09690	16.68214	17.29342	18.59891
16	16.30353	16.61423	16.82544	16.93228	17.25786	17.93237	18.63929	20.15688
17	17.34429	17.69730	17.93761	18.05927	18.43044	19.20136	20.01207	21.76159
18	18.38765	18.78579	19.05719	19.19472	19.61475	20.48938	21.41231	23.41444
19	19.43362	19.87972	20.18424	20.33868	20.81090	21.79672	22.84056	25.11687
20	20.48220	20.97912	21.31880	21.49122	22.01900	23.12367	24.29737	26.87037
22	22.58724	23.19443	23.61066	23.82230	24.47159	25.83758	27.29898	30.53678
24	24.70282	25.43196	25.93319	26.18847	26.97346	28.63352	30.42186	34.42647
26	26.82899	27.69191	28.28678	28.59027	29.52563	31.51397	33.67091	38.55304
28	28.96580	29.97452	30.67187	31.02823	32.12910	34.48148	37.05121	42.93092
30	31.11331	32.28002	33.08885	33.50290	34.78489	37.53868	40.56808	47.57542
32	33.27157	34.60862	35.53818	36.01483	37.49407	40.68829	44.22703	52.50276
34	35.44064	36.96058	38.02026	38.56458	40.25770	43.93309	48.03380	57.73018
36	37.62056	39.33610	40.53556	41.15272	43.07688	47.27597	51.99437	63.27594
38	39.81140	41.73545	43.08450	43.77982	45.95272	50.71989	56.11494	69.15945
40	42.01320	44.15885	45.66754	46.44648	48.88637	54.26789	60.40198	75.40126
45	47.56606	50.32416	52.27734	53.29011	56.48107	63.61420	71.89271	92.71986
50	53.18868	56.64516	59.11042	60.39426	64.46318	73.68283	84.57940	112.7969
100	113.44996	129.33370	141.51445	148.14451	170.4814	228.8030	312.2323	607.2877

NOTE: To convert this table to values of an annuity in advance, take one more period and subtract 1.00000.

No. of payments = n	4%	5%	6%	7%	8%	10%	12%	20%
1	1.00000	1.00000	1.00000	1.00000	1.00000	1.00000	1.00000	1.00000
2	2.04000	2.05000	2.06000	2.07000	2.08000	2.10000	2.12000	2.20000
3	3.12160	3.15250	3.18360	3.21490	3.24640	3.31000	3.37440	3.64000
4	4.24646	4.31012	4.37462	4.43994	4.50611	4.64100	4.77933	5.36800
5	5.41632	5.52563	5.63709	5.75074	5.86660	6.10510	6.35285	7.44160
6	6.63298	6.80191	6.97532	7.15329	7.33593	7.71561	8.11519	9.92992
7	7.89829	8.14201	8.39384	8.65402	8.92280	9.48717	10.08901	12.91590
8	9.21423	9.54911	9.89747	10.25980	10.63663	11.43589	12.29969	16.49908
9	10.58280	11.02656	11.49132	11.97799	12.48756	13.57948	14.77566	20.79890
10	12.00611	12.57789	13.18079	13.81645	14.48656	15.93742	17.54874	25.95868
11	13.48635	14.20679	14.97164	15.78360	16.64549	18.53117	20.65458	32.15042
12	15.02581	15.91713	16.86994	17.88845	18.97713	21.38428	24.13313	39.58050
13	16.62684	17.71298	18.88214	20.14064	21.49530	24.52271	28.02911	48.49660
14	18.29191	19.59863	21.01507	22.55049	24.21492	27.97498	32.39260	59.19592
15	20.02359	21.57856	23.27597	25.12902	27.15211	31.77248	37.27971	72.03511
16	21.82453	23.65749	25.67253	27.88805	30.32428	35.94973	42.75328	87.44213
17	23.69751	25.84037	28.21288	30.84022	33.75023	40.54470	48.88367	105.9306
18	25.64541	28.13238	30.90565	33.99903	37.45024	45.59917	55.74971	128.1167
19	27.67123	30.53900	33.75999	37.37896	41.44626	51.15909	63.43968	154.7400
20	29.77808	33.06595	36.78559	40.99549	45.76196	57.27500	72.05244	186.6880
22	34.24797	38.50521	43.39229	49.00574	55.45676	71.40275	92.50258	271.0307
24	39.08260	44.50200	50.81558	58.17667	66.76476	88.49733	118.1552	392.4842
26	44.31174	51.11345	59.15638	68.67647	79.95442	109.1818	150.3339	567.3773
28	49.96758	58.40258	68.52811	80.69769	95.33883	134.2099	190.6989	819.2233
30	56.08494	66.43885	79.05819	94.46079	113.2832	164.4940	241.3327	1181.881
32	62.70147	75.29883	90.88978	110.2181	134.2135	201.1378	304.8477	1704.109
34	69.85791	85.06696	104.1838	128.2588	158.6267	245.4767	384.5210	2456.118
36	77.59831	95.83632	119.1209	148.9135	187.1022	299.1268	484.4631	3539.009
38	85.97034	107.7096	135.9042	172.5610	220.3159	364.0434	609.8305	5098.373
40	95.02552	120.7998	154.7620	199.6351	259.0565	442.5926	767.0914	7343.858
45	121.0294	159.7002	212.7435	285.7493	386.5056	718.9048	1358.230	18281.31
50	152.6671	209.3480	290.3359	406.5289	573.7702	1163.909	2400.018	45497.19
100	1237.624	2610.025	5638.368	12381.66	27484.52	137796.1	696010.5	414×10^6

TABLE 4   Present Value of an Annuity of $1 in Arrears

$$P_A = \frac{1 - (1 + r)^{-n}}{r}$$

r = discount rate; n = number of payments

No. of payments = n	¼%	½%	⅝%	¾%	1%	1½%	2%	3%
1	0.99751	0.99502	0.99338	0.99256	.99010	.98522	.98039	.97087
2	1.99252	1.98510	1.98018	1.97772	1.97040	1.95588	1.94156	1.91347
3	2.98506	2.97025	2.96044	2.95556	2.94099	2.91220	2.88388	2.82861
4	3.97512	3.95050	3.93421	3.92611	3.90197	3.85438	3.80773	3.71710
5	4.96272	4.92587	4.90154	4.88944	4.85343	4.78264	4.71346	4.57971
6	5.94785	5.89638	5.86245	5.84560	5.79548	5.69719	5.60143	5.41719
7	6.93052	6.86207	6.81700	6.79464	6.72819	6.59821	6.47199	6.23028
8	7.91074	7.82296	7.76524	7.73661	7.65168	7.48593	7.32548	7.01969
9	8.88852	8.77906	8.70719	8.67158	8.56602	8.36052	8.16224	7.78611
10	9.86386	9.73041	9.64290	9.59958	9.47130	9.22218	8.98259	8.53020
11	10.83677	10.67703	10.57242	10.52067	10.36763	10.07112	9.78685	9.25262
12	11.80725	11.61893	11.49578	11.43491	11.25508	10.90751	10.57534	9.95400
13	12.77532	12.55615	12.41303	12.34235	12.13374	11.73153	11.34837	10.63496
14	13.74096	13.48871	13.32420	13.24302	13.00370	12.54338	12.10625	11.29607
15	14.70420	14.41662	14.22934	14.13699	13.86505	13.34323	12.84926	11.93794
16	15.66504	15.33993	15.12848	15.02431	14.71787	14.13126	13.57771	12.56110
17	16.62348	16.25863	16.02167	15.90502	15.56225	14.90765	14.29187	13.16612
18	17.57953	17.17277	16.90894	16.77918	16.39827	15.67256	14.99203	13.75351
19	18.53320	18.08236	17.79034	17.64683	17.22601	16.42617	15.67846	14.32380
20	19.48449	18.98742	18.66590	18.50802	18.04555	17.16864	16.35143	14.87747
22	21.37995	20.78406	20.39967	20.21121	19.66038	18.62082	17.65805	15.93692
24	23.26598	22.56287	22.11054	21.88915	21.24339	20.03041	18.91393	16.93554
26	25.14261	24.32402	23.79883	23.54219	22.79520	21.39863	20.12104	17.87684
28	27.00989	26.06769	25.46484	25.17071	24.31644	22.72672	21.28127	18.76411
30	28.86787	27.79405	27.10885	26.77508	25.80771	24.01584	22.39646	19.60044
32	30.71660	29.50328	28.73116	28.35565	27.26959	25.26714	23.46333	20.38877
34	32.55611	31.19555	30.33205	29.91278	28.70267	26.48173	24.49859	21.13184
36	34.38647	32.87102	31.91181	31.44681	30.10751	27.66068	25.48884	21.83225
38	36.20770	34.52985	33.47071	32.95808	31.48466	28.80505	26.44064	22.49246
40	38.01986	36.17223	35.00903	34.44694	32.83469	29.91585	27.35548	23.11477
45	42.51088	40.20710	38.76658	38.07318	36.09451	32.55234	29.49016	24.51871
50	46.94617	44.14279	42.40134	41.56645	39.19612	34.99969	31.42361	25.72976
100	88.38248	78.54264	72.81686	70.17962	63.02888	51.62470	43.09835	31.59891

NOTE: To convert this table to values of an annuity in advance, take one less period and add 1.00000.

No. of payments = n	4%	5%	6%	7%	8%	10%	12%	20%
1	.96154	.95238	.94340	.93458	.92593	.90909	.89286	.83333
2	1.88609	1.85941	1.83339	1.80802	1.78326	1.73554	1.69005	1.52778
3	2.77509	2.72325	2.67301	2.62432	2.57710	2.48685	2.40183	2.10648
4	3.62990	3.54595	3.46511	3.38721	3.31213	3.16987	3.03735	2.58873
5	4.45182	4.32948	4.21236	4.10020	3.99271	3.79079	3.60478	2.99061
6	5.24214	5.07569	4.91732	4.76654	4.62288	4.35526	4.11141	3.32551
7	6.00205	5.78637	5.58238	5.38929	5.20637	4.86842	4.56376	3.60459
8	6.73274	6.46321	6.20979	5.97130	5.74664	5.33493	4.96764	3.83716
9	7.43533	7.10782	6.80169	6.51523	6.24689	5.75902	5.32825	4.03097
10	8.11090	7.72173	7.36009	7.02358	6.71008	6.14457	5.65022	4.19247
11	8.76048	8.30641	7.88687	7.49867	7.13896	6.49506	5.93770	4.32706
12	9.38507	8.86325	8.38384	7.94269	7.53608	6.81369	6.19437	4.43922
13	9.98565	9.39357	8.85268	8.35765	7.90378	7.10336	6.42355	4.53268
14	10.56312	9.89864	9.29498	8.74547	8.24424	7.36669	6.62817	4.61057
15	11.11839	10.37966	9.71225	9.10791	8.55948	7.60608	6.81086	4.67547
16	11.65230	10.83777	10.10590	9.44665	8.85137	7.82371	6.97399	4.72956
17	12.16567	11.27407	10.47726	9.76322	9.12164	8.02155	7.11963	4.77463
18	12.65930	11.68959	10.82760	10.05909	9.37189	8.20141	7.24967	4.81219
19	13.13394	12.08532	11.15812	10.33560	9.60360	8.36492	7.36578	4.84350
20	13.59033	12.46221	11.46992	10.59401	9.81815	8.51356	7.46944	4.86958
22	14.45112	13.16300	12.04158	11.06124	10.20074	8.77154	7.64465	4.90943
24	15.24696	13.79864	12.55036	11.46933	10.52876	8.98474	7.78432	4.93710
26	15.98277	14.37519	13.00317	11.82578	10.80998	9.16095	7.89566	4.95632
28	16.66306	14.89813	13.40616	12.13711	11.05108	9.30657	7.98442	4.96967
30	17.29203	15.37245	13.76483	12.40904	11.25778	9.42691	8.05518	4.97894
32	17.87355	15.80268	14.08404	12.64656	11.43500	9.52638	8.11159	4.98537
34	18.41120	16.19290	14.36814	12.85401	11.58693	9.60857	8.15656	4.98984
36	18.90828	16.54685	14.62099	13.03521	11.71719	9.67651	8.19241	4.99295
38	19.36786	16.86789	14.84602	13.19347	11.82887	9.73265	8.22099	4.99510
40	19.79277	17.15909	15.04630	13.33171	11.92461	9.77905	8.24378	4.99660
45	20.72004	17.77407	15.45583	13.60552	12.10840	9.86281	8.28252	4.99863
50	21.48218	18.25593	15.76186	13.80075	12.23348	9.91481	8.30450	4.99945
100	24.50500	19.84791	16.61755	14.26925	12.49432	9.99927	8.33323	5.00000

TABLE 5   Bond Values in Percent of Par: 6-Percent Semiannual Coupons
$$\text{Bond Value} = 6/r + (100 - 6/r)(1 + r/2)^{-2n}$$
$$r = \text{yield to maturity}; \; n = \text{years to maturity}$$

Market yield % per year compounded semiannually	Years to maturity							
	½	5	10	15	19½	20	30	40
3.0	101.478	113.833	125.753	136.024	144.047	144.874	159.071	169.611
3.5	101.228	111.376	120.941	128.982	135.118	135.743	146.205	153.600
4.0	100.980	108.983	116.351	122.396	126.903	127.355	134.761	139.745
4.5	100.734	106.650	111.973	116.234	119.337	119.645	124.562	127.712
5.0	100.488	104.376	107.795	110.465	112.365	112.551	115.454	117.226
5.1	100.439	103.928	106.982	109.356	111.037	111.202	113.752	115.293
5.2	100.390	103.483	106.177	108.262	109.731	109.874	112.087	113.411
5.3	100.341	103.040	105.380	107.181	108.445	108.568	110.458	111.578
5.4	100.292	102.599	104.590	106.115	107.180	107.283	108.864	109.792
5.5	100.243	102.160	103.807	105.062	105.935	106.019	107.306	108.053
5.6	100.195	101.724	103.031	104.023	104.710	104.776	105.780	106.359
5.7	100.146	101.289	102.263	102.998	103.504	103.553	104.288	104.707
5.8	100.097	100.857	101.502	101.986	102.317	102.349	102.828	103.098
5.9	100.049	100.428	100.747	100.986	101.149	101.165	101.399	101.529
6.0	100	100	100	100	100	100	100	100
6.1	99.9515	99.5746	99.2595	99.0262	98.8685	98.8535	98.6309	98.5088
6.2	99.9030	99.1513	98.5259	98.0650	97.7549	97.7254	97.2907	97.0546
6.3	99.8546	98.7302	97.7990	97.1161	96.6587	96.6153	95.9787	95.6364
6.4	99.8062	98.3112	97.0787	96.1793	95.5796	95.5229	94.6942	94.2529
6.5	99.7579	97.8944	96.3651	95.2545	94.5174	94.4478	93.4365	92.9031
6.6	99.7096	97.4797	95.6580	94.3414	93.4717	93.3899	92.2050	91.5860
6.7	99.6613	97.0670	94.9574	93.4400	92.4423	92.3486	90.9989	90.3007
6.8	99.6132	96.6565	94.2632	92.5501	91.4288	91.3238	89.8178	89.0461
6.9	99.5650	96.2480	93.5753	91.6714	90.4310	90.3152	88.6608	87.8213
7.0	99.5169	95.8417	92.8938	90.8039	89.4487	89.3224	87.5276	86.6255
7.5	99.2771	93.8404	89.5779	86.6281	84.7588	84.5868	82.1966	81.0519
8.0	99.0385	91.8891	86.4097	82.7080	80.4155	80.2072	77.3765	76.0846
8.5	98.8010	89.9864	83.3820	79.0262	76.3899	76.1534	73.0090	71.6412
9.0	98.5646	88.1309	80.4881	75.5666	72.6555	72.3976	69.0430	67.6520

TABLE 6   Bond Values in Percent of Par: 8-Percent Semiannual Coupons
Bond Value $= 8/r + (100 - 8/r) (1 + r/2)^{-2n}$
$r =$ yield to maturity; $n =$ years to maturity

Market yield % per year compounded semiannually	Years to maturity							
	½	5	10	15	19½	20	30	40
5.0	101.463	113.128	123.384	131.396	137.096	137.654	146.363	151.678
5.5	101.217	110.800	119.034	125.312	129.675	130.098	136.528	140.266
6.0	100.971	108.530	114.877	119.600	122.808	123.115	127.676	130.201
6.5	100.726	106.317	110.905	114.236	116.448	116.656	119.690	121.291
7.0	100.483	104.158	107.106	109.196	110.551	110.678	112.472	113.374
7.1	100.435	103.733	106.367	108.225	109.424	109.536	111.113	111.898
7.2	100.386	103.310	105.634	107.266	108.314	108.411	109.780	110.455
7.3	100.338	102.889	104.908	106.318	107.220	107.303	108.473	109.044
7.4	100.289	102.470	104.188	105.382	106.142	106.212	107.191	107.665
7.5	100.241	102.053	103.474	104.457	105.080	105.138	105.934	106.316
7.6	100.193	101.638	102.767	103.544	104.034	104.079	104.702	104.997
7.7	100.144	101.226	102.066	102.642	103.003	103.036	103.492	103.706
7.8	100.096	100.815	101.371	101.750	101.987	102.009	102.306	102.444
7.9	100.048	100.407	100.683	100.870	100.986	100.997	101.142	101.209
8.0	100	100	100	100	100	100	100	100
8.1	99.9519	99.5955	99.3235	99.1406	99.0279	99.0177	98.8794	98.8170
8.2	99.9039	99.1929	98.6529	98.2916	98.0699	98.0498	97.7798	97.6589
8.3	99.8560	98.7924	97.9882	97.4528	97.1257	97.0962	96.7006	96.5253
8.4	99.8081	98.3938	97.3294	96.6240	96.1951	96.1566	95.6414	95.4152
8.5	99.7602	97.9973	96.6764	95.8052	95.2780	95.2307	94.6018	94.3282
8.6	99.7124	97.6027	96.0291	94.9962	94.3739	94.3183	93.5812	93.2636
8.7	99.6646	97.2100	95.3875	94.1969	93.4829	93.4191	92.5792	92.2208
8.8	99.6169	96.8193	94.7514	93.4071	92.6045	92.5331	91.5955	91.1992
8.9	99.5692	96.4305	94.1210	92.6266	91.7387	91.6598	90.6295	90.1982
9.0	99.5215	96.0436	93.4960	91.8555	90.8851	90.7992	89.6810	89.2173
9.5	99.2840	94.1378	90.4520	88.1347	86.7949	86.6777	85.1858	84.5961
10.0	99.0476	92.2783	87.5378	84.6275	82.9830	82.8409	81.0707	80.4035
10.5	98.8123	90.4639	84.7472	81.3201	79.4271	79.2656	77.2956	76.5876
11.0	98.5782	88.6935	82.0744	78.1994	76.1070	75.9308	73.8252	73.1036

Index